31362

Current Biography Yearbook
1989

Current Biography Yearbook
1989

EDITOR
Charles Moritz

ASSOCIATE EDITORS
Judith Graham
Hilary Claggett
Robert Schuck
Irene C. Park

EDITORIAL ASSISTANT
Jill Kadetsky

THE H. W. WILSON COMPANY
NEW YORK

FIFTIETH ANNUAL CUMULATION—1989

PRINTED IN THE UNITED STATES OF AMERICA

International Standard Serial No. (0084-9499)

Library of Congress Catalog Card No. (40-27432)

PREFACE

The aim of *Current Biography Yearbook 1989,* like that of the preceding volumes in this series of annual dictionaries of contemporary biography, now in its fifth decade of publication, is to provide the reference librarian, the student, or any researcher with brief, objective, accurate, and well-documented biographical articles about living leaders in all fields of human accomplishment the world over. Whenever feasible, obituary notices appear for persons whose biographies have been published in *Current Biography,* and every attempt is made to pick up obituaries that have inadvertently been omitted in previous years.

Current Biography Yearbook 1989 carries on the policy of including new and updated biographical sketches that supersede or update earlier, outdated articles. Sketches have been made as accurate and objective as possible through careful researching by *Current Biography* writers in newspapers, magazines, authoritative reference books, and news releases of both government and private agencies. Immediately after they are published in the eleven monthly issues, articles are submitted to biographees to give them an opportunity to suggest corrections in time for publication of the *Current Biography Yearbook.* To take account of major changes in the careers of biographees, sketches have also been revised before they are included in the yearbook. With the exception of occasional interviews, the questionnaire filled out by the biographee remains the primary source of direct information.

Some persons who are not professional authors but who have written books are included under *Nonfiction* in addition to their vocational fields. The annual bestowal of Nobel Prizes has added articles to the volume. The pages immediately following contain *Explanations; Key to Reference Abbreviations; Key to Pronunciation;* and *Key to Abbreviations.* The indexes at the end of the volume are *Biographical References; Periodicals and Newspapers Consulted; Classification by Profession;* and *Cumulated Index—1981–1989. Current Biography Cumulated Index 1940–1985* cumulates and supersedes all previous indexes, and the reader will need to consult only that index in order to locate a name within that period of time.

For their assistance in preparing *Current Biography Yearbook 1989,* I should like to thank the associate editors.

Charles Moritz

Explanations

Authorities for biographees' full names, with some exceptions, are the bibliographical publications of The Wilson Company. When a biographee prefers a certain name form, that is indicated in the heading of the article: for example, Niemöller, (Friedrich Gustav Emil) Martin means that he is usually referred to as Martin Niemöller. When a professional name is used in the heading, as, for example, Anne Bancroft, the real name (in this case Annemarie Italiano) appears in the article itself.

The heading of each article includes the pronunciation of the name if it is unusual, date of birth (if obtainable), and occupation. The article is supplemented by a list of references to sources of biographical information, in two alphabets: (1) newspapers and periodicals and (2) books. (See the section *Biographical References*, found in the rear of this volume.)

Key to Reference Abbreviations

References to some newspapers and periodicals are listed in abbreviated form; for example, "Sat Eve Post 217:14 S 30 '44 por" means *Saturday Evening Post*, volume 217, page 14, September 30, 1944, with portrait. (For full names, see the section *Periodicals and Newspapers Consulted*, found in the rear of this volume.)

January—Ja	July—Jl	Journal—J
February—F	August—Ag	Magazine—Mag
March—Mr	September—S	Monthly—Mo
April—Ap	October—O	Portrait—por
May—My	November—N	Weekly—W
June—Je	December—D	Review—R

Key to Pronunciation

ā	āle	ō	ōld		*menu* (mə-nü); German ü, as in *grün*
â	câre	ô	ôrb		
a	add	o	odd		
ä	ärm	oi	oil		
		o͞o	o͞oze	ə	the schwa, an unstressed vowel representing the sound that is spelled
ē	ēve	o͝o	fo͝ot		a as in sofa
e	end	ou	out		e as in fitted
					i as in edible
g	go	*th*	*then*		o as in melon
		th	thin		u as in circus
ī	īce				
i	ill	ū	cūbe		
		û	ûrn; French eu, as in *jeu* (zhû), German ö, *oe*, as in *schön (shûn)*, *Goethe* (gû´te)	zh	azure
ᴋ	German *ch* as in *ich* (iᴋ)				
		u	tub	´	= main accent
ɴ	Not pronounced, but indicates the nasal tone of the preceding vowel, as in the French *bon* (bôɴ)	ü	Pronounced approximately as ē, with rounded lips: French u, as in	´´	= secondary accent

Key to Abbreviations

AAAA	Amateur Athletic Association of America	D.Pol.Sc.	Doctor of Political Science
AAU	Amateur Athletic Union	D.S.C.	Distinguished Service Cross
AAUP	American Association of University Professors	D.Sc.	Doctor of Science
A.B.	Arts, Bachelor of	D.S.M.	Distinguished Service Medal
ABA	American Bar Association	D.S.O.	Distinguished Service Order
ABC	American Broadcasting Company	EC	European Community
ACA	Americans for Constitutional Action	ECOSOC	Economic and Social Council (of the United Nations)
ACLU	American Civil Liberties Union	EDP	Electronic data processing
ADA	Americans for Democratic Action	EEOC	Equal Employment Opportunity Commission
ADP	Automatic data processing	EPA	Environmental Protection Agency
AEC	Atomic Energy Commission	ERA	Equal Rights Amendment
AFL	American Football League	E.R.A.	Earned run average
AFL-CIO	American Federation of Labor and Congress of Industrial Organizations		
AID	Agency for International Development	FAA	Federal Aviation Administration
		FAO	Food and Agriculture Organization (of the United Nations)
AIDS	Acquired immune deficiency syndrome	FBI	Federal Bureau of Investigation
		FCC	Federal Communications Commission
ALA	American Library Association	FDA	Food and Drug Administration
A.M.	Arts, Master of	FHA	Federal Housing Administration
AMA	American Medical Association	FPC	Federal Power Commission
AP	Associated Press	FTC	Federal Trade Commission
ASCAP	American Society of Composers, Authors and Publishers	GAO	General Accounting Office
ASEAN	Association of Southeast Asian Nations	GATT	General Agreement on Tariffs and Trade
		G.B.E.	Knight or Dame, Grand Cross Order of the British Empire
B.A.	Bachelor of Arts	G.C.B.	Knight or Dame, Grand Cross of the Bath
BBC	British Broadcasting Corporation	GOP	Grand Old Party (Republican)
B.D.	Bachelor of Divinity	GSA	General Services Administration
B.F.A.	Bachelor of Fine Arts		
B.L.S.	Bachelor of Library Science	HBO	Home Box Office
B.S.	Bachelor of Science	HHS	Department of Health and Human Services
CAA	Civil Aeronautics Administration	H.M.	His Majesty; Her Majesty
CAB	Civil Aeronautics Board	HUD	Department of Housing and Urban Development
C.B.	Companion of the Bath		
CBC	Canadian Broadcasting Corporation	ICBM	Intercontinental ballistic missile
C.B.E.	Commander of (the Order of) the British Empire	ICC	Interstate Commerce Commission
CBS	Columbia Broadcasting System	IGY	International Geophysical Year
C.E.	Civil Engineer	IMF	International Monetary Fund
CEA	Council of Economic Advisers	IRA	Irish Republican Army
CENTO	Central Treaty Organization	IRS	Internal Revenue Service
CIA	Central Intelligence Agency		
C.M.G.	Companion of (the Order of) St. Michael and St. George	J.D.	Doctor of Jurisprudence
CNN	Cable News Network	K.B.E.	Knight of (the Order of) the British Empire
CORE	Congress of Racial Equality	K.C.	King's Counsel
DAR	Daughters of the American Revolution	K.C.B.	Knight Commander of the Bath
D.C.L.	Doctor of Civil Law	KGB	Committee of State Security (Soviet secret police)
D.D.	Doctor of Divinity		
D.Eng.	Doctor of Engineering	L.H.D.	Doctor of Humane Letters
D.F.C.	Distinguished Flying Cross	Litt.D.	Doctor of Letters
D.J.	Doctor of Jurisprudence	LL.B.	Bachelor of Laws
D.Litt.	Doctor of Literature		
D.Mus.	Doctor of Music		

LL.D.	Doctor of Laws
M.A.	Master of Arts
M.B.A.	Master of Business Administration
M.B.E.	Member of (the Order of) the British Empire
MBS	Mutual Broadcasting System
M.C.E.	Master of Civil Engineering
M.D.	Doctor of Medicine
M.E.	Master of Engineering
METO	Middle East Treaty Organization
M.F.A.	Master of Fine Arts
MGM	Metro-Goldwyn-Mayer
M.Lit.	Master of Literature
M.L.S.	Master of Library Science
M.P.	Member of Parliament
M.Sc.	Master of Science
Msgr.	Monsignor, Monseigneur
MTV	Music Television
NAACP	National Association for the Advancement of Colored People
NAB	National Association of Broadcasters
NAM	National Association of Manufacturers
NASA	National Aeronautics and Space Administration
NATO	North Atlantic Treaty Organization
NBA	National Basketball Association
NBC	National Broadcasting Company
NCAA	National Collegiate Athletic Association
NEA	National Education Association
NFL	National Football League
NHL	National Hockey League
NIH	National Institutes of Health
NIMH	National Institute of Mental Health
NLRB	National Labor Relations Board
NOAA	National Oceanographic and Atmospheric Administration
NOW	National Organization for Women
NSA	National Security Agency
NSC	National Security Council
OAS	Organization of American States
O.B.E.	Officer of (the Order of) the British Empire
OECD	Organization for Economic Cooperation and Development
OMB	Office of Management and Budget
OPEC	Organization of Petroleum Exporting Countries
OSHA	Occupational Safety and Health Administration
PAC	Political action committee
PBS	Public Broadcasting Service
PEN	Poets, Playwrights, Editors, Essayists and Novelists (International Association)
Ph.B.	Bachelor of Philosophy
Ph.D.	Doctor of Philosophy
PLC	Public limited company

PLO	Palestine Liberation Organization
PTA	Parent-Teacher Association
Q.C.	Queen's Counsel
RAF	Royal Air Force
RBI	Run batted in
RCA	Radio Corporation of America
RKO	Radio-Keith-Orpheum
ROTC	Reserve Officers' Training Corps
SAC	Strategic Air Command
SALT	Strategic Arms Limitation Talks
SCAP	Supreme Command for the Allied Powers
SDI	Strategic Defense Initiative ("Star Wars")
SEATO	Southeast Asia Treaty Organization
SEC	Securities and Exchange Commission
SHAEF	Supreme Headquarters, Allied Expeditionary Force
SHAPE	Supreme Headquarters, Allied Powers Europe
S.J.	Society of Jesus (Jesuit)
S.J.D.	Doctor of Juridical Science
SLA	Special Libraries Association
S.T.B.	Bachelor of Sacred Theology
S.T.D.	Doctor of Sacred Theology
TVA	Tennessee Valley Authority
UAR	United Arab Republic
UK	United Kingdom
UN	United Nations
UNESCO	United Nations Educational, Scientific, and Cultural Organization
UNICEF	United Nations Children's Fund
UPI	United Press and International News Service
U.S.	United States
USFL	United States Football League
USIA	United States Information Agency
USO	United Service Organizations
USSR	Union of Soviet Socialist Republics
VA	Veterans Administration
VFW	Veterans of Foreign Wars
VISTA	Volunteers in Service to America
WHO	World Health Organization
YMCA	Young Men's Christian Association
YMHA	Young Men's Hebrew Association
YWCA	Young Women's Christian Association
YWHA	Young Women's Hebrew Association

Current Biography Yearbook
1989

Abé, Kobo
(ä´bä)

Mar. 7, 1924– Japanese writer. Address: 1-22-10 Wakaba Cho, Chofu City, Tokyo, Japan

The avant-garde author of thirteen novels, more than fifty short stories, and dozens of plays and radio and television dramas, Kobo Abé is considered a cosmopolitan rather than a strictly Japanese writer, and he is credited with introducing such Western concerns as alienation, existentialism, identity crises, rootlessness, depersonalization, and urban loneliness into Japanese literature. He alone among contemporary Japanese writers rejects his country's obsession with history and cultural tradition, so that his themes resonate not only among readers in Japan but in Eastern Europe, the Soviet Union, and the United States as well. He is considered, with some justification, to be a serious contender for the Nobel Prize.

Acknowledging no roots, Abé has defined himself as "a man without a hometown," for an allegiance to one's past and native place represents to him a fascistic type of cultural nationalism that he detests. Although he may very well be the first Japanese writer whose works interest Western audiences because of their universal appeal, some critics see in his writing a grappling with the corrosive effects of Westernization on Japanese society and culture. Among them is Michiko Kakutani of the *New York Times* (March 23, 1988), who believes that Abé's "distinctive vision of the contemporary world as a menacing, urban labyrinth in which people hunger for freedom but find themselves trapped in alienating rituals and roles" is one that "clearly reflects Japanese struggles with conformism, authority, and rapid industrialization."

Although many critics find Abé willfully obscure and deliberately difficult to read, he is, somewhat paradoxically, the best-selling Japanese novelist in the world, and a fifteen-volume set of his collected works sold more than 750,000 copies in seven years in Japan. "There's a hint of nihilism in my work," he has said. "My plays and novels tend to fly apart into a thousand pieces, and it's hard work to put the bits together again." Funny and fantastic, grotesque, surrealistic, and ironic, Abé's work has been compared to the dark and despairing novels of Kafka; the avant-garde plays of Beckett; the existentialist writings of Nietzsche, Heidegger, and Jaspers; and the cult entertainments of Monty Python and Godzilla. Abé himself has contended that Lewis Carroll is the author who has influenced him the most, along with Edgar Allan Poe.

Kobo Abé was born on March 7, 1924 in Tokyo, Japan, during a brief visit to that city by his parents, Asakichi and Yorimi Abé. His parents were from Hokkaido, the northernmost island of Japan, but were living in Mukden (now Shenyang), the largest city in Manchuria, where Asakichi Abé was a physician to the aggressively nationalistic Japanese community. Kobo Abé, whose given name was Kimifusa Abé, lived in Mukden from infancy to late adolescence. "This was frightening territory," he recalled for Henry Scott-Stokes during an interview for the *New York Times Magazine* (April 29, 1979). "You could travel for an hour or a day or three days by rail and always have the same view out of the window—a vast, flat plain—nothing like overcrowded Japan."

As a boy, Abé clowned for his friends and told them stories out of Edgar Allan Poe during their lunch hours in junior high school. He also collected insects, and in his writings insects are often used as horrendous metaphors. In 1931, when he entered grade school, Japan took control of Manchuria, renamed it Manchukuo, and installed a puppet government. As Abé became aware of the world around him, he was shocked by the way the Japanese treated the Chinese population. An admirer of the local Chinese culture, he began to rebel against the militaristic nationalism of the Japanese community and, when he was twenty, changed his first name to Kobo, the Chinese translation of Kimifusa.

When, in 1941, Abé returned to Tokyo to attend high school and begin his military training, Pearl Harbor was less than a year away. No matter how much he detested Japanese militarism, he longed to feel part of the war effort, to know that he belonged to his society. "I knew that if I could believe in fascism, then I could be happier," he told Alan Levy in an interview for the *New York Times Magazine* (November 17, 1974). "I tried hard, but I couldn't." Influenced by his father's wishes, in 1941 Abé entered Tokyo University Medical School, not because he really wanted to become a doctor, but because he could think of nothing else to do. Studying to be a gynecologist also kept Abé out of direct involvement in the war, and he was "overjoyed" in 1944 when the United States took the military offensive in the Pacific Theatre, and Japan's military defeat seemed certain.

After the war, Abé returned to Manchuria to be with his parents, but when his father died during a typhus epidemic he returned to his medical studies in Tokyo, supporting himself as a street vendor selling charcoal balls and bean curds. He also spent time with his mother, two sisters, and a brother who were trying to eke out a living on his grandparents' farm in Hokkaido. More interested in writing than in gynecology, he failed his medical exams but was given a face-saving passing grade when he promised the examiners that he would never practice medicine.

In 1947 Abé married an art student named Machi Yamada. The couple lived a rootless and bohemian life together, peddling rice cakes and seeking shelter with artist friends in abandoned shacks in bombed-out fields. Abé's first book, *The Road Sign at the End of the Road*, a confessional novel that he wrote as a student, was published in 1948. His reputation grew with his Kafkaesque short stories featuring Everyman characters whose identity is eroded under the watchful care of bureaucratic authority. Published in 1951, a novella called *The Crimes of S. Karma* won the Akutagawa Prize that year and established Abé as a professional author. *Hunger Union* (1954), *Animals Are Forwarding to Their Natives* (1957), *Eyes of Stone* (1960), and the plays *The Uniform* (1955) and *Here Is a Ghost* (1959) followed. They have not been translated into English.

Although Abé's deeply entrenched disdain for authority made him seem an unlikely candidate for membership in the rigidly hierarchical Communist party, he was nevertheless active in the party from 1950 to 1956, as an organizer of literary discussion groups for workers. He was also involved in Zengakuren, Japan's largest left-wing student movement which, in the 1950s, mounted militant demonstrations against nuclear weapons and American dominance. In 1956 he traveled to Eastern Europe on behalf of the party, during which he reported to his superiors in Tokyo that Hungary seemed to be on the brink of revolution. Although Abé did not formally resign from the party until 1962, he ceased party activity after the ruthless suppression of the Hungarian uprising. Nevertheless, the United States marked Abé as an intellectual with communist leanings and, in 1975, when Columbia University invited him to New York City to receive an honorary Doctor of Letters degree, the State Department imposed restrictions on his visit.

Through the years, Abé has continued to oppose rabid nationalism and militarism, but he no longer identifies himself with the Left and rarely takes stands on political issues, except through his fiction and his plays. "I believe that the state should interfere with people's lives to the absolute minimum necessary for government," he told Henry Scott-Stokes. "The great danger is that governments, nation-states, continue to get more powerful to the point where man's very existence is imperiled." Abé's popularity in the Soviet Union and Eastern bloc countries stems from the philosophical anarchism expressed in his writing because, although his metaphorical satire is often targeted at Japanese institutions, readers in Eastern Europe view it as a Kafkaesque criticism of their own experience under communism.

The success in American art cinemas of the film *The Woman in the Dunes* (1964)—an adaptation by Abé and Hiroshi Teshigahara of Abé's 1962 novel that won a special prize at the Cannes Film Festival—led to the book's publication in English, in 1964. *The Woman in the Dunes* deals with the ordeal of an insect collector who is kidnapped and forced to live with a woman in a sandpit, among constantly shifting sand dunes that threaten to engulf them. The novel focuses with relentless intensity on their daily struggle to prevent the blowing sands from annihilating their home. When the insect collector fails in his attempt to escape from the dunes, he accepts his fate and salvages some dignity out of his degradation. Writing in the *Saturday Review* (September 5, 1964), Earl Miner typified many readers who interpreted the novel as a metaphor for man's condition: "The sand is alive yet deadly, the hostile environment in which man must seek to establish his individuality, humanity, and civilization." In the *New York Times* (August 30, 1964), N. W. Ross noted that Abé "presents the most minute descriptions of the trivia of everyday existence in a sandpit with such compelling realism that these passages serve both to heighten the credibility of the bizarre plot and subtly increase the interior tensions of the novel."

In *The Face of Another* (1966), a scientist whose face is disfigured in a laboratory experiment constructs a mask and a new identity for himself only to discover that his new face develops a personality of its own and that the world is full of people hiding behind masks. Describing the theme of the novel as "the hell of being alive," Phyliss Grosskurth wrote in the *Boston Globe Magazine* (December 31, 1966) that "the freedom to reconstruct himself is almost unbearable. A face, [the scientist] realizes, is something one grows with, a daily reassurance in the mirror, a gatekeeper in communication with the outside world. . . . For Abé, the only true freedom is loneliness, a haven from the coagulating threat of man in the mass." In the essay "Moscow to New York," written in the mid-1960s, Abé wrote of *The Woman in the Dunes* and *The Face of Another*: "I have unintentionally explored the problem of loneliness. And as a practical conclusion, I feel that this loneliness is not at all pathological but the normal approach to human relations." What is necessary, he concluded, "is not a recovery from loneliness but rather a spirit that regards loneliness as to be expected and goes further, searching for an unknown, new path."

Abé completed his "1960s Trilogy" with *The Ruined Map* (1969), a philosophical thriller in which a private detective searching for a man in a huge metropolis himself becomes lost in an underworld urban labyrinth where corruption is indistinguishable from honesty and where, as Abé wrote, "even if you lose your way, you cannot go wrong." To find his quarry, the detective must merge his identity and imagine himself as the object of his search, so that he, the hunter, becomes the hunted. Summing up the theme of urban loneliness that *The Ruined Map* has in common with his previous two books, Abé once wrote in an explanatory note to his American publisher, Alfred A. Knopf: "Here in this city we have a huge, drifting vessel. Let us call it the SS *Labyrinth*. Somewhere there must be a bridge, an engine room. But where? No one knows. What remains? Certainty that we have lost our myths—the good full earth, the secure home—gone."

In 1970 Alfred A. Knopf published an English translation of Abé's 1959 novel *Inter Ice Age 4*. Another "philosophical thriller," in the words of Howard Hibbett, writing in the *Saturday Review* (September 26, 1970), it concerns a computer scientist who creates a program that gives him a sneak preview of what will be his fate and that of humanity—"the cruelty of the future," as Abé puts it. In that complex and abstract book, deficient in the everyday detail of human relationships, Abé's arid intellectualism vitiates the pleasures that a reader expects to derive from a novel. Unwilling to provide the reader with a clue, Abé wrote in a cryptic postscript to *Inter Ice Age 4* that the reader is free "to read into the novel either hope or despair."

In *The Box Man* (1974), Abé's next book, the protagonist cuts himself off from society by moving into a box, from which he observes life from behind a vinyl curtain that covers a cut-out window. Commenting in the *Saturday Review* (October 15, 1974), Bruce Allen decoded the novel as "a paradigm for the way modern man lives"—especially the isolation and alienation experienced by contemporary intellectuals. But the book reviewer Anatole Broyard, writing in the *New York Times* (December 31, 1974), charged Abé with reproducing "all of the worst features of Western 'experimental' fiction" and wondered why a novelist would create such a characterless character—one better suited for a sociological or philosophical tract. "The style is the man, we used to think, and now that Mr. Abé's man is anonymous, we get an anonymous style, sentences that could not have been written by a recognizable human being," Broyard complained.

Secret Rendezvous (1979) contained many of the surrealist literary devices and absurdist themes characteristic of Abé's previous novels, but its satire was aimed at more obvious targets, including modern medicine, sex therapists, and oppressive bureaucracies. A salesman's wife is abducted in an ambulance and taken to a bizarre underground hospital where nightmarish operations and erotic experiments take place, where doctors and patients change roles, and where the salesman, looking for his wife, loses his identity. Although Irving Malin, who reviewed the book for *Commonweal* (December 21, 1979), found *Secret Rendezvous* a philosophic challenge, D. J. Enright, in the *New York Review of Books* (September 27, 1979), wrote that much of it is "nightmarish," with "details that loom large and signify little; mounting complications; strongly gratuitous emotions; uncertainty about what is going on . . .; confusion of identity; time shifts; and a sense of drifting further and further away from whatever point there once was."

The Ark Sakura (1988), Abé's most recent novel, similarly mixes grotesquerie with realism. Its main character, a frenetic survivalist symbolically called "Mole," converts an underground quarry into an ark capable of surviving a nuclear holocaust and manned by a crew consisting of an insect dealer and other sleazy con artists. The ark is invaded by a gang of punks and a brigade of senior citizens in pursuit of nubile teenagers. The bizarre and violent events that those interlopers set off "are no doubt meant to galvanize Mr. Abé's dark view of modern society," Michiko Kakutani wrote in the *New York Times* (March 23, 1988), "but they're tired devices used to make obvious points—points made with considerably more imagination and force by the author's earlier books."

Until the early 1980s, Abé pursued a second career as a playwright and, beginning in 1973, as a writer, director, and producer in his own repertory theatre. His early scripts were conventional dramas. The best known, *Friends*, written in the 1960s, is about a lonely man who is plagued by a family of eight members who move in on him despite his protestations and gradually take over and ruin his life. In 1973 Seiji Tsutsumi, a friend from Abé's Zengakuren days who had abandoned radicalism to run his family's department stores, spent more than $1 million in building Abé his own 455-seat theatre on the ninth floor of the family-owned Parco Department Store in Tokyo's Shibuya district. As head of his own theatre, Abé began to experiment with more avant-garde productions, creating a typical Abé surreal juxtaposition—avant-garde theatre in the middle of a department store. Those productions, as witnessed by James Lardner of the *Washington Post* (May 9, 1979), were "a collage of opera, film, gymnastics, sculpture, ballooning, and wrestling." In his production of *The Little Elephant Is Dead*, which Abé took on tour of the United States in 1979, his actors wore costumes so huge that, when opened wide in "flying squirrel fashion," they served "as screens for the English dialogue to be projected on to." The production was one of 450 cultural events, titled Japan Today, that toured ten major American cities at a cost of $2 million. His play, Abé quipped, represented "Japan tomorrow." In the early 1980s Abé gave up the theatre, telling David Remnick of the *Washington Post* (January 20, 1986), "There is no country on earth less interested in theatre." What the Japanese liked in theatre, Abé said, was a form of ceremony, reminiscent of the cultural nationalism that he detests.

Abé's wife, Machi Yamada, who was the artistic director of Abé's now defunct theatre, is a successful artist in her own right. They have a daughter, Neri, and live in a seven-room house in Tokyo with a darkroom, lathe, and the latest in electronic gadgetry. For many years Abé wrote his works on scraps of paper, but he now uses a word processor and composes his music on a Moog synthesizer. His hobbies are photography, carving, and driving luxury cars: he has owned a Lancia, a Mercedes convertible, and a BMW.

Despite Abé's cosmopolitanism, he is fluent only in Japanese. Somewhat like his box man, he chooses to live a self-contained and semi-isolated life. He nevers opens his mail or answers the telephone, avoids appearances in the media, and rarely socializes with other writers and intellectuals. Gabriel García Márquez and the Irish writer Edna O'Brien are among his favorite authors, and the British playwright Harold Pinter and the French writer Alain Robbe-Grillet are among the few writers he considers his friends. Henry Scott-Stokes described Abé in 1979 as "a bushy-haired, black browed man of middle height with thick arms and a disarming smile. He has a broad face and wears heavy, black-framed eyeglasses." Writers who interview Abé often mention his distinctive laugh, which David Remnick observed is not "the sort of tittering giggle that one hears often in the streets of Tokyo. It is a belly laugh, a New York sort of laugh." It is perhaps symbolic of Abé's determined and artful internationalism.

References: Contemporary Authors new rev vol 24 (1988); International Who's Who, 1989–90; Kodansha Encyclopedia of Japan (1983); World Authors 1950–1970 (1975)

Adams, Alice

Aug. 14, 1926– Writer. Address: b. c/o Amanda Urban, International Creative Management, 40 W. 57th St., New York, N.Y. 10019; h. 2661 Clay St., San Francisco, Calif. 94115

The author of six novels and four short-story collections, Alice Adams is one of the most highly regarded chroniclers of interpersonal relationships in contemporary fiction. Her first collection of short stories, *Beautiful Girl*, elicited comparisons with the work of F. Scott Fitzgerald, Katherine Mansfield, and Flannery O'Connor, and her latest novel, *Second Chances*, is considered by many critics to be her strongest work to date. The typical Alice Adams heroine matures, over the course of a novel, from a young woman involved in a destructive love relationship to a well-rounded adult in midlife whose priorities have come to include work and friendship. Despite the length and ambitious scope of some of her novels, Miss Adams manages to create an impression of swiftness with her spare and elegant prose.

Many of Miss Adams's stories were originally published in literary periodicals, including the *New Yorker*, the *Atlantic*, *Grand Street*, the *Virginia Quarterly Review*, and the *Paris Review*. The recipient of a fiction grant from the National Endowment for the Arts in 1976 and a Guggenheim Fellowship in 1978, she has seen her work anthologized in *The Best American Short Stories, 1976* and in every annually published edition of *Prize Stories: The O. Henry Awards* from 1971 to 1989, with the sole exception of the 1983 collection. In 1982, in recognition of the twelfth consecutive ap-

pearance of her work in the O. Henry collection, Miss Adams won the O. Henry Special Award for Continuing Achievement, joining the company of Joyce Carol Oates and John Updike, the only previous winners of the award.

The only child of Agatha Erskine (Boyd) Adams and Nicholson Barney Adams, Alice Adams was born in Fredericksburg, Virginia on August 14, 1926. Shortly after their daughter's birth, the Adamses moved to a farmhouse in Chapel Hill, North

Carolina, where Alice spent her first sixteen years. Her childhood was materially comfortable but emotionally unsatisfying. She once described her family as "three difficult, isolated people." Her father, who taught Spanish at the University of North Carolina, disinherited her by leaving the family home to her stepmother, who put the house up for sale around 1958. "For a southern person, that's a very shaking experience," Miss Adams explained in a 1987 interview with Jean W. Ross for *Contemporary Authors*.

Of the two parents, Agatha Adams seems to have been the more influential in her daughter's decision to become a writer. "My mother," Alice Adams said during a 1980 interview for *Story Quarterly*, "wanted to be a writer and was a failed one. She was depressed, unhappy, and peripherally involved with the literary world." Agatha Adams read poetry to her daughter in the evenings, and before long Alice was writing her own poems. "I grew up in a semi-intellectual atmosphere and I was encouraged," she told Wayne Warga, as quoted in the *Los Angeles Times* (November 16, 1980). She hinted at the nature of that encouragement in a later interview, with Mervyn Rothstein for the *New York Times* (May 19, 1988): "Being a writer was considered a wonderful thing—by my mother, and really by everyone in town. My mother read all the time, so I thought, 'If I'm a writer, maybe she'll like me.'"

Having graduated from high school at the age of fifteen, Miss Adams was off to a head start—or so it seemed. "I was bright in school," she recalled to Nancy Faber for a *People* (April 3, 1978) magazine profile, "and ran into trouble because of that southern thing that women are supposed to be stupid." She found "that southern thing" just as viable in Cambridge, Massachusetts, where she attended Radcliffe College from 1942 to 1946, graduating at the age of nineteen. She was quoted in the *Dictionary of Literary Biography* as saying that a writing course in which she had enrolled "seemed fun. Except that the professor—a male teacher from Harvard [Kenneth Kempton]—said to me at the end of the course, 'Miss Adams, you're really an awfully nice girl. Why don't you get married and forget all this writing?'"

Less than a year after her graduation from Radcliffe, Miss Adams married Mark Linenthal Jr., a student at Harvard. During the interlude between her graduation in 1946 and her marriage, Miss Adams got a job at a New York publishing firm, but she was soon fired for, among other things, taking too much time off to visit Linenthal in Cambridge. The couple spent their first year together in Paris, where Linenthal studied at the Sorbonne, but even then their marriage was in trouble. "I loved Paris," Miss Adams recalled to Nancy Faber, "except I disliked him [her husband] so much."

Despite her misgivings, Miss Adams followed her husband to California in 1948. Their only child, Peter Adams Linenthal, was born in 1951. With her young son to care for, Miss Adams found little time to pursue her writing. In her interview with Jean

Ross, she described her late twenties and early thirties as the worst decade of her life. "I remember the fifties with sheer horror. . . . I was writing only in the most spasmodic, desperate way. . . . [Peter] was difficult then, I disliked my husband, and we didn't have any money, et cetera. And that was the fifties, when you were supposed to think all those things were quite wonderful." Because divorce was "very much not the thing to do" in the 1950s, Miss Adams underwent a period of psychoanalysis. "I was going to quite a stupid man who told me that I should stop writing and stay married," she told Jean Ross. Instead, Miss Adams divorced her husband in 1958 and published her first story, "Winter Rain," in *Charm* (July 1959).

Struggling to raise her son alone in San Francisco, Miss Adams held a variety of part-time clerical, secretarial, and bookkeeping jobs. "It was quite late when I felt I could make my living as a writer," she told Jean Ross. "I was well over forty." In the meantime, she indulged in a series of love affairs—in her words, to "make up for lost time"—and wrote short stories "as a sort of sideline." One of those affairs, with a man she has described as "a married, Catholic, fascist diplomat," became the subject of her first novel, *Careless Love*. "Finally I began to think of [the affair] as funny," she explained to Nancy Faber, "and that's when I wrote the book."

Prior to the book's publication by New American Library in 1966, Miss Adams announced, "This novel is an on-the-whole amused look at San Francisco, specifically at an enormous blonde divorcée . . . loosed in the city's social-sexual jungle." *Careless Love* "really bombed" in the United States but "did terribly well in England," the author was quoted as saying in the *Dictionary of Literary Biography*. "A lot of people were put off by the title," she explained, thinking it was just "one more sexy divorcée story." But the title was changed to *The Fall of Daisy Duke* (the title she preferred) for the book's British publication by Constable in 1967, which may have facilitated its reception in England as a humorous novel. One of the few Americans who shared the British view praised the author's "wry anatomizing" of Daisy Duke in an unsigned notice for the *New York Times Book Review* (May 22, 1966): "In a fetching first novel, . . . Miss Adams renders Daisy's ordeal faithfully—even to its stretches of boredom— and with considerable wit."

In the wake of *Careless Love*'s poor showing, Miss Adams began writing formulaic romances (few of which made their way into her three collections) for *Cosmopolitan*, *Redbook*, and *McCall's*. She did not break into the market for literary magazines until November 1969, when the *New Yorker* published "Gift of Grass," a story about a troubled teenager's effort to alleviate her stepfather's depression by giving him some marijuana. In 1971 "Gift of Grass" became her first story to be included in the O. Henry collection *Prize Stories*, where it was awarded third prize.

Throughout the 1970s Miss Adams's prizewinning short stories earned her increasing recognition. Interest in her work was heightened when *Families and Survivors*, her second novel, was published in 1975 by Alfred A. Knopf. (All of her subsequent books have been published by Knopf.) Spanning the three tumultuous decades between 1941 and 1971, *Families and Survivors* describes the changes experienced by Louisa Calloway, a Virginian who moves to San Francisco, gets married and divorced, and has a number of lovers before finding fulfillment in a second marriage and in a career as a painter. According to the author, as quoted in the *Dictionary of Literary Biography*, *Families and Survivors* is "a personal and—in a sense—social history. It is about what it was like for certain kinds of people—a rather limited kind—to survive the fifties. It makes a rather simplistic point, really, which is that the fifties were horrible and things got better in the sixties. And that, in general, second marriages beat first ones."

Reviews of *Families and Survivors* ran the gamut from scathing to enthusiastic. Writing in *Harvard Magazine* (February 1975), the novelist Anne Bernays faulted Miss Adams for her "intensely irritating habit of inserting herself into the narrative via parentheses that signal far more than we need—or want—to know." But the parenthetical foreshadowing incurred no objections from a reviewer for the *New Yorker* (February 10, 1975), who wrote, "In a lesser writer this illusion-shattering prophesying might be annoying, but Miss Adams's sense of timing is so acute and her eye for detail is so unvaryingly sensitive that it only enhances our pleasure in this excellent book." *Families and Survivors* was nominated for a National Book Critics Circle Award in 1975.

Alice Adams's next novel, *Listening to Billie* (1978), covers territory similar to that explored in *Families and Survivors*. It begins in the 1940s, with the heroine listening to the blues singer Billie Holiday in a New York club, follows her to San Francisco, and explores her painful but eventually triumphant emergence from a series of destructive relationships over a twenty-year period. For the heroine, independence is achieved by becoming a poet. In an interview with Patricia Holt for *Publishers Weekly* (January 16, 1978), Miss Adams said: "I was interested in writing about . . . the idea of women getting to work. . . . There has really been too much [written] about women and their endless problems with love and sex, and with the kind of addictive love affair that is so all-consuming it makes sex an excuse for delaying the things that matter, like getting down to work."

Reviews of *Listening to Billie* were mixed but generally favorable. Among Miss Adams's detractors was Jane Larkin Crain, who was troubled by the novel's "curious lifelessness." "Only rarely do any of the characters' reactions seem rooted in the scene at hand and not in a schematic sense of things fixed in the mind of the author . . . ," she observed in the *New York Times Book Review* (February 26, 1978). "A falsification of reality is under way here, a falsification that ostensibly hails and champions brave new turning points in the life of the contemporary woman, but which actually winds up minimizing and trivializing her." In her critique for *Ms.* (September 1980) magazine, Sheila Weller disagreed: "[Alice Adams has] created the fullness of a saga without any of a saga's lugubrious weight." And Anne Tyler, who reviewed the novel for *Quest* (March–April 1978), found the plot "as seductive as gossip" and the tone "quick, deft [and] precise." *Listening to Billie* was a Book-of-the-Month Club alternate selection.

The chorus of praise grew louder with the publication of Miss Adams's first collection of stories, *Beautiful Girl* (1979). Comprising sixteen stories written between 1959 and 1977, *Beautiful Girl* examines the multifaceted theme of loss and love. Susan Wood, who reviewed the book for the *Washington Post Book World* (January 21, 1979), was reminded of F. Scott Fitzgerald "in both style and subject matter." "Like Fitzgerald," she wrote, "[Alice Adams] has a fine satiric eye softened by a tenderness toward human desire and frailty." Especially well liked was a series of three stories about the Todds, a white southern family whose racism prevents them from sharing the grief of their black housekeeper, who has lost her lover. "Verlie I Say unto You," the first story of the trilogy, was singled out for praise by both Susan Wood and Katha Pollitt, who hailed Alice Adams as "a consummately pleasing writer" in her review for the *New York Times Book Review* (January 14, 1979). But she nonetheless complained that "too many of these stories are about a certain type of woman: She is married to someone prosperous . . . ; she has an independent income or a little part-time job, and no serious interests; she is romantic, prone to love at first sight, and she establishes her claim to sensitivity by rereading Jane Austen every summer. . . . I kept waiting for Miss Adams to flash an ironic smile toward these [characters]. . . . She never does."

Miss Adams's fourth novel, *Rich Rewards* (1980), is narrated in the first person by Daphne Matthiessen, an interior decorator who leaves an abusive lover in Boston and moves to San Francisco, where she eventually encounters an old flame, with whom she rekindles sufficient passion for a happy ending. Those who found themselves in sympathy with the heroine enjoyed the optimistic ending, but others found it unpersuasive. The author herself admitted that "you either have to like Daphne and go along with her or the book falls flat on its face," as she was quoted as saying in the *Dictionary of Literary Biography*. Reviews ranged from Anne Tyler's assertions, in the *New York Times Book Review* (September 14, 1980), that *Rich Rewards* was "a marvelously readable book" and that Daphne was "one of the most admirable female characters in recent fiction" to the disappointment expressed by Victoria Glendinning in the *Washington Post Book World* (October 12, 1980): "The banality of most of [Daphne's] insights about life and behavior do not merit the importance they seem to be given."

A more uniformly favorable critical reaction greeted the publication of Miss Adams's second short-story collection, *To See You Again* (1982). The general theme of the stories is change, as Benjamin DeMott observed in his review for the *New York Times Book Review* (April 11, 1982). "Alice Adams's heroes and heroines," DeMott wrote, "are ever on the lookout for means of trading current attachments, selves, environments, repressions for something fresher. . . . Miss Adams's manner is good-humoredly ironic and understated, and she's a deft social observer. (Her Las Vegas, sketched in one tale in this collection, is closer to the 'reality' than Hunter Thompson's.)" In his review for the *Washington Post Book World* (May 9, 1982), Stephen Goodwin concurred: "Adams casts a cold eye on romance, nostalgia, anything that smacks of sentiment. . . . Her stories are true and contemporary, a part of the history of our own times."

Nearly twice as long as any of her earlier books, Alice Adams's next novel, *Superior Women* (1984), traces the lives of five Radcliffe women from 1943 to 1983. Reviewers were sharply divided in their assessment of Miss Adams's achievement, some of them basing their judgment on their perception of her intentions. William L. Stull neatly summarized the dilemma in his essay about the author for the *Dictionary of Literary Biography*: "Was the book a serious, satiric novel of women's education, written in the tradition of Jane Austen's *Emma* and Mary McCarthy's *The Group*? Or was it lighter, spicier fare, a romance in the manner of June Singer's *The Debutantes* or Rona Jaffe's *Class Reunion*? Was it somehow both at once?" The unfavorable notices tended to come from those who believed *Superior Women* to be a lightweight entertainment, the positive ones from those who decided it was more satire than romance. One exception was Jonathan Yardley's review for the *Washington Post Book World* (September 2, 1984), in which he dismissed the novel as an "inert lump . . . in the . . . ongoing competition . . . to copy the formula that Mary McCarthy patented in *The Group*, . . . [containing] all the ingredients of the formula except interesting characters, interesting plot, and interesting prose." Several critics pointed out that Miss Adams was writing (and writing well) about the class system, the changing definitions of "superiority," and an exploration of the self through a "group portrait" of "several different young selves," as Lois Gould put it. The public apparently did not share the ambivalence of the critics, for *Superior Women*, in its paperback edition, became a bestseller.

With *Return Trips* (1985), her third collection of stories, Miss Adams delighted some readers and disappointed others, but most reviewers agreed with William Stull that *Return Trips* "shows a master writer at the height of her powers." In her appraisal for the *New York Times Book Review* (September 1, 1985), Beverly Lowry wrote, "Like a watercolorist whose every brush stroke must be perfect, this author's hand is lightning fast and brilliant." And Susan Schindehette, commenting in the *Saturday Review* (November–December 1985), called the stories examples "of sublime subtlety, of nuance and quiet perception—stories from a writer who is quite clearly an accomplished, absolute master of her craft."

Miss Adams's latest novel is *Second Chances* (1988), which focuses on the friendships among six men and women in their sixties who, originally from the East Coast, have relocated to a small town in northern California. Their concerns—relationships, sex, health, sickness, and death—allow Miss Adams to explore her trademark themes of friendship, love, separation, and loss and to write about aging in a nontraditional way. "I suppose when I myself began to think about turning sixty, I became interested in looking ahead," she said in an interview with Kim Heron for the *New York Times Book Review* (May 1, 1988). "I have the perception that people talk about old age in two ways. One is to focus on the horrors of it, . . . and the other is to romanticize it." *Second Chances* is about people's changing expectations of aging.

Commending the author for her "grasp of conditions of feeling that are special to the middle classes just now entering their sixties and seventies," Benjamin DeMott declared, in a review for the *New York Times Book Review* (May 1, 1988), that *Second Chances*, "a touching, subtle, truth-filled book," was the strongest work he had read by Miss Adams. Diane Cole, writing in the *Chicago Tribune* book section (May 1, 1988), called it "the richest and most satisfying novel that Adams . . . has produced." But Lindsay Duguid found fault with the book's "almost eerie absence of humor" and its "lack of tight guiding plot." "The effect of this intense survey punctuated with death and drama is to make one wonder why one is reading about the intimate details of strangers' lives," Duguid remarked in the *Times Literary Supplement* (July 29, 1988).

Aging has provided Miss Adams with more than a new subject to explore through fiction; it has, she feels, raised her critical standards and increased the difficulty of writing. "When you're younger," she said during the interview with Mervyn Rothstein, "you tend to be enthusiastic, and you let yourself get by with things that you wouldn't later on. It gets harder every time." But aging also has its benefits, among them a stronger sense of irony. "There's a need for irony," she told Rothstein. "If you took it all straight, with utter seriousness, you'd be severely depressed a great deal of the time."

After You've Gone, Miss Adams's latest short-story collection, appeared in the fall of 1989. Her fourteen stories orchestrate the theme of recovery from separation or loss, as experienced by the mostly upwardly mobile female characters. Echoing a sentiment often expressed by reviewers of her previous work, Ron Carlson praised her "facility as a writer" in his evaluation for the *New York Times Book Review* (October 8, 1989), but he added: "While I admire the cool surfaces of Alice Adams's stories, they leave me wanting more heat. In so much contemporary fiction, characters are leaping wildly from the frying pan into the fire, but in Ms. Adams's world they only get to remember the flames." A similar ambivalence was expressed by a reporter for *Publishers Weekly* (July 14, 1989): "All the stories are marked by Adams's ability to conjure up an entire landscape with a few details, by her delicate, unflinching exploration of women's emotional defenses and, less admirably, by a surfeit of cold and insensitive, controlling men with a tendency toward cruelty."

Tall and slender, with short blonde hair turning gray, Alice Adams has lived in San Francisco with Robert McNie, an interior designer, since 1964. Explaining their decision not to marry, Alice Adams said, during the interview with Nancy Faber,

"Marriage does seem to me primarily concerned with property. We are rather private people who feel our relationship is not the business of the state." Her son, Peter Adams Linenthal, is an artist. Miss Adams enjoys traveling and spends part of each winter in Mexico. She has taught at the University of California at Davis and at Berkeley, as well as at Stanford. She is a Democratic Socialist and a member of PEN.

References: N Y Times C p30 My 19 '88 por; People 9:48+ Ap 3 '78 por; Contemporary Authors new rev vol 26 (1989); Contemporary Literary Criticism vol 46 (1988); Dictionary of Literary Biography Yrbk 1986 (1987); Who's Who in America, 1988–89

Agassi, Andre

Apr. 29, 1970– Tennis player. Address: c/o Bill Shelton, International Management Group, One Erieview Plaza, Cleveland, Ohio 44114

Not since Jimmy Connors and John McEnroe dominated the tennis scene has an American player stirred fans the way Andre Agassi has managed to do. With an aggressive topspin forehand, which he hits when the ball is still on the rise, and an equally deadly return of serve, Agassi, at the age of eighteen, won six major tournaments in 1988 and reached the semifinals of both the French and United States Opens, rocketing from number ninety-one, in 1987, to number three in the world rankings. At the same time, he became the tennis world's newest heartthrob and exhibited a flair for

on-court dramatics, blowing kisses to the crowd, throwing pairs of his stonewashed denim shorts to spectators, and flicking his long, bleached blond hair. Agassi's earnings in 1988, including tournament wins and product endorsements, totaled over $2 million. But his detractors have continued to wonder if he has real staying power, since he won only two exhibition tournaments in the first ten months of 1989, though he again reached the semifinals of the United States Open, where he lost to Ivan Lendl. Ranked number six in the world in late 1989, Agassi has hired a conditioning coach to improve his stamina, and he has worked on varying his strategy away from a predominantly backcourt game. "I am blessed with a talent and I have an obligation to the Lord to make the most of it," he said in a 1988 interview.

Andre Agassi was born on April 29, 1970 in Las Vegas, Nevada, the youngest of the four children of Emmanuel ("Mike") Agassi, a showroom captain at Bally's Casino Resort, Las Vegas, and his wife, Betty, who works for the state of Nevada. An Armenian who boxed for Iran in the 1948 and 1952 Olympics, Mike Agassi became fascinated with the game of tennis at an early age, and he was determined that one of his children would become a tennis champion. After he moved to the United States in the mid-1950s and married, he decided to settle in Las Vegas, because of the suitability of its climate for playing tennis throughout the year. Mike Agassi taught all of his children how to play, but he cultivated Andre's development the most assiduously. When Andre was just an infant, his father tied a tennis ball over his crib to develop his eye coordination. When he could sit in a highchair, Mike Agassi taught him timing by taping a halved Ping-Pong paddle to his hand and tossing him a balloon that was partly filled with water. By the age of two, the boy was able to serve in a full court. At the age of four, he practiced with Jimmy Connors during an exhibition at a Las Vegas hotel, and the next year, he hit with Björn Borg. On the family's backyard cement court, with as many as eight ball machines spewing tennis balls at a variety of angles, Andre developed the basics of his game. "Don't just try to get it in," Mike Agassi advised his son, as quoted by Peter de Jonge in the *New York Times Magazine* (October 30, 1988). "Smack the ball. Crunch it. Hit it as hard as you can. We'll worry about keeping it in later." Before the age of twelve, Andre had hit with several other pros.

When Andre was thirteen years old, Mike Agassi, realizing that his son needed further coaching, sent the boy to the Nick Bollettieri Tennis Academy in Bradenton, Florida. "My father saw this story on Nick on *60 Minutes* where it showed him making these little kids cry and everything, and thought that was the place for me," Agassi jokingly told Peter de Jonge during an interview for the *New York Times Magazine* piece. Far from home, Agassi struggled with the pressures of winning and of living up to his father's expectations. A rambunctious teenager, he pulverized up to forty racquets a year, frosted the academy with shaving cream, and verbally abused his opponents. It was during that period, Agassi told the *Los Angeles Times* (April 2, 1989) reporter Brian Hewitt, that he began to experiment with beer and marijuana. Still, Bollettieri saw in the boy's rebelliousness a competitive spirit that only needed to be channeled in the right direction.

In spite of his only middling success as a competitor at the academy, Agassi, with the financial support of an endorsement contract from Nike, turned pro on May 1, 1986, two days after his sixteenth birthday. According to Peter de Jonge, the impetus came from a weariness of losing to players his own age rather than from his having outgrown the competition. Agassi's professional career got off to an auspicious start. In July he reached the finals of a tournament in Schenectady, New York, then upset Tim Mayotte, who was ranked number twelve in the world at the time, and Scott Davis at the Volvo International tournament in Stratton Mountain, Vermont. In the Volvo quarterfinals, Agassi played John McEnroe. On the first point of the match, Agassi sent McEnroe's blistering second serve booming back to him. McEnroe, who would ultimately win the match, was astounded. "That's the hardest anyone has ever returned my serve," he said, as quoted in the *New York Times* (April 8, 1988). In his first two tournaments, Agassi won $11,000.

Agassi's early winning streak was followed by a slump that lasted from mid-August 1986 to mid-April 1987, during which time he won only two matches. He was so discouraged after he lost in the first round of a tournament in Washington, D.C., in July that he seriously contemplated quitting the game. Heeding the counsel of the tour's minister, Fritz Glauss, who urged him not to quit, Agassi renewed his faith in Christianity. (He had attended the First Good Shepherd Lutheran School in Las Vegas as a child.) Christianity provided Agassi with "peace of mind and the understanding that it's no big deal if you get beat," he said, as quoted in *Sports Illustrated* (March 13, 1989).

Liberated by such insights, Agassi's game started to improve in the second half of 1987. In July, at Stratton Mountain, he advanced to the semifinals, where he lost to Ivan Lendl, the number-one player in the world, 6-2, 5-7, 6-3. In November Agassi captured his first title, beating Luiz Mattar, 7-6, 6-2, at the SuL American Open championships in Itaparica, Brazil. By the end of 1987, he had advanced to the quarterfinals of tournaments in Tokyo and Los Angeles and to the semifinals of a competition in Basle, Switzerland, and his ranking had improved from number ninety-one to twenty-five.

Given his erratic start, no one could have predicted the stunning success that awaited Agassi in 1988. He began his victory sweep in February by upending Sweden's Mikael Pernfors, 6-4, 6-4, 7-5, in the finals of the Volvo United States Indoor tournament in Memphis, Tennessee. At the Newsweek Champions Cup in Indian Wells, California a week later, he powered his way to the semifinals, where he was stopped by the West German Boris Becker, 4-6, 6-3, 7-5. On May 1 Agassi picked up the $38,000 first prize at the United States Clay Courts Championship on the Isle of Palms, South Carolina by defeating the American Jimmy Arias, 6-2, 6-2. A week later he defeated Slobodan Zivojinovic of Yugoslavia in the finals of the Eagle Tournament of Champions in Forest Hills, New York, 7-5, 7-6, 7-5, winning $127,600. Agassi prevailed with searing groundstroke winners and spectacular returns, including one shot that he made between his legs. He even managed to relieve some of the tension of the seesaw match by borrowing a fan's Panama hat to cover his face in embarrassment after missing a shot. "I've got to start coming in more," Agassi told George Usher of *New York Newsday* (May 9, 1988) after the match. "I'm getting more confidence in my volleys and serve, but I've got to get stronger physically."

Though he lost in the quarterfinals of the Italian Open in Rome in early May, Agassi resumed his winning streak at the French Open in Paris, taking on Mats Wilander, the tough-minded Swede, in the semifinals on June 3. After dropping the first three games of the match, Agassi reeled off six of the next seven games, capping the set with a topspin backhand lob that left Wilander gaping. Agassi dropped the next two sets but fought back to take the fourth before running out of steam in the fifth. Agassi drew laughter from the crowd and even from the usually intense Wilander when he borrowed a spectator's umbrella to shield himself from the rain while waiting for Wilander to serve. Wilander prevailed, 4-6, 6-2, 7-5, 5-7, 6-0, but Agassi had won the affection of spectators and his opponent's respect. "Right now, he has the really big forehand, but he needs to improve his net game and his serve," Wilander told John Feinstein of the *Washington Post* (June 4, 1988). "I think he's got a really good attitude, though. He doesn't seem to mind being famous. That's good. But he's not playing Wimbledon this year. I think he needs to be more than just a clay-court player."

Agassi skipped Wimbledon in early July to return home and rest, but he resumed his active schedule shortly after that. On July 17 he took the Mercedes Cup tournament in Stuttgart, West Germany, besting Andrés Gomez of Ecuador in the finals, 6-2, 6-2, to win the $49,500 first prize. In late July in Buenos Aires, he helped the United States Davis Cup team to qualify for the World Group by winning his two singles matches. The American Davis Cup team ended up defeating Argentina's squad, four matches to one. Agassi's brilliant play on the bronze dirt of Buenos Aires in windy conditions was marred, however, by an incident during his match against Martin Jaite. En route to a 6-2, 6-2, 6-1 demolition of his opponent, Agassi caught a weak second serve of Jaite's barehanded. The hotdog move gave Jaite the game and shocked observers. Agassi later apologized to Jaite and Argentina.

At Stratton Mountain, Agassi captured the Volvo International, defeating Paul Annacone of the United States, 6-2, 6-4, and winning $114,000. On August 21 he won the Mennen Cup tournament in Livingston, New Jersey, beating Jeff Tarango in the final, 6-2, 6-4. Perhaps more important, the victory boosted him to the number-four spot in the world rankings. At eighteen, he was the youngest player ever to hold that position. On August 28 Agassi won his fourth consecutive tournament, the Hamlet Challenge Cup in Jericho, New York, besting Yannick Noah of France in the finals, 6-3, 0-6, 6-4, and picking up $40,000 in prize money.

By the time Agassi arrived at the United States Open in late August, Americans were ready for a new hero. In the quarterfinals, Agassi met Jimmy Connors, the player he is most often compared to because of his aggressive baseline game, two-handed backhand, and flamboyant antics on the court. Agassi took control of the first set almost immediately, breaking Connors in the third game. When Connors, who had the crowd on his side, fought his way to a tiebreaker in the second set, Agassi used a combination of shots, including a topspin lob and a crosscourt forehand volley, to take the set. Agassi dominated the third set, winning the match, 6-2, 7-6, 6-1, to become the youngest male semifinalist in United States Open history. Before their match, Agassi had irritated Connors by predicting that he would win the contest in straight sets. "That was a mistake," Connors said, as quoted in *Sports Illustrated* (September 19, 1988), adding, "I enjoy playing guys who could be my children. Maybe he's one of them. I spent a lot of time in Vegas."

Agassi went into his semifinal match at the Open, against Ivan Lendl, with a 1988 match record of fifty-seven wins and seven losses, the best on the tour, and a twenty-three-match winning streak. He won the first set, 6-4, hitting the ball so hard that Lendl was repeatedly knocked off balance. But he ran out of steam and lost the next three sets, 6-2, 6-3, 6-4. "He's physically stronger," Agassi commented to Filip Bondy in an interview for the New York *Daily News* (September 11,

1988), about Lendl. "I need to get stronger, and to get more experience."

After the match, Lendl criticized Agassi for not trying, a charge that was echoed at a tournament in Los Angeles in September. There, in a semifinal match against McEnroe that Agassi won, 6-4, 0-6, 6-4, McEnroe accused him of tanking the second set—giving it away to conserve energy and start the next set fresh. In the finals of the Los Angeles tournament, Agassi lost to Mikael Pernfors, 6-2, 7-5. He blamed his defeat on a pinched nerve and "the long year." In an earlier quarterfinal match, Agassi had outraged Australia's Mark Woodforde by telling him to leave the umpire alone when Woodforde disputed a line call. "I think it's just a period where he's young," Woodforde told Brian Hewitt of the *Los Angeles Times* (April 2, 1989). "But I know that when he has lost recently, the person who has beaten him has been ecstatic. And it's like a score for everyone (on the tour)." But Agassi has his share of friends and admirers among the pros, including Wilander, Becker, Michael Chang, the teenage American star with whom Agassi has attended Bible classes, and Yannick Noah. "We're playing a sport," Noah told Ray McNulty of the *Florida Times Union* (September 14, 1988). "A lot of times, guys forget it's a game. . . . That's not how it should be. It should be fun and Andre is a fun player to play."

On October 11, 1988 Agassi defeated Stefan Edberg, 6-3, 6-4, in an exhibition match in Beijing, China. In December he played for the first time in the Nabisco Masters tournament at Madison Square Garden in New York City, which he entered with the world ranking of number three. Agassi lost to Lendl in a match that mirrored their semifinal encounter at the United States Open. Agassi broke Lendl's serve three times in the first set, which he won, 6-1, but Lendl won the last six points of a tiebreaker to win the second set, 7-6, and then closed out the match by breaking Agassi in the fifth game of the third set, taking it, 6-3. Tired from his efforts against Lendl, Agassi was ousted from the round-robin competition by Switzerland's Jakob Hlasek, 6-3, 6-2. In that match, Agassi made thirty-five unforced errors.

"Seeing Agassi play in person is a little bit like attending a Beatles concert during the 1960s," Brian Hewitt observed in his *Los Angeles Times* piece. Teenagers scream, girls present him with flowers, and older women climb onto their husbands' shoulders to get a better look at the young man with the amber eyes and the shaggy bleached mane. Fans send him 1,500 to 2,000 letters a week. The real proof of Agassi's popularity, however, is in his wallet. Sales of the acid-washed Nike shorts he wears have tripled since he first started wearing them at the Lipton tournament in March 1988. Nike's "Ace of Hearts" poster, in which Agassi is shown leaning on a sportscar against the neon backdrop of Las Vegas, had a first printing of 25,000 copies instead of the usual 5,000, and Agassi's agent, Bill Shelton, has said that he receives six to eight endorsement offers a day for Agassi's approval. When Agassi signed a contract on January 1, 1989 with Donnay racquets, which will net him an estimated $6 million over six years, orders for the racquet at a subsequent trade show doubled. Agassi will earn almost $2.5 million in 1989 alone for endorsing such products as Dupont's CoolMax tenniswear, Ebel watches, and Rayban sunglasses.

Agassi's appeal, however, was offset by mounting criticism during the first half of 1989. During the American Davis Cup team's 5-0 drubbing of the Paraguayan team in February in Fort Myers, Florida, he was criticized by the press for taunting his overmatched opponent, Hugo Chapacu, and for making faces at Paraguayan fans. In addition, Agassi had trouble adjusting to his new Donnay racquet. To date, the company has made over 100 different prototypes in an effort to come up with a racquet that works for the player. Also in February, at the Volvo United States Indoor tournament in Memphis, Tennessee, Agassi predicted that he would have a hard time repeating his 1988 success and then promptly lost to Johann Kriek, 6-7, 7-5, 6-3. At the Ebel United States Pro Indoor championship in Philadelphia later that month, Agassi lost to Tim Mayotte in the semifinals. Agassi further damaged his image when he canceled at the last minute a scheduled exhibition match in Toronto, Canada, against John McEnroe, pleading illness, although he was spotted the same day sunbathing in Florida.

March 1989 was another bad month for Agassi. During a match against McEnroe at the Buick WCT Finals in Dallas, he defaulted in the second set, saying that he had aggravated a pulled thigh muscle despite no visible limp. The crowd booed as he left the court, and McEnroe called the maneuver "bizarre, unbelievable, [and] immature," as quoted by the London *Observer* (March 26, 1989). At the Newsweek Champions Cup in Indian Wells, California, where he reached the quarterfinals, Agassi was criticized by the press for reverting to his old Prince racquet, disguising it by stenciling a Donnay logo on the strings. A few weeks later, at the Lipton International Players Championships in Key Biscayne, Florida, he suffered one of his most humiliating defeats, a 6-4, 7-5, 6-0 dunking by Carl-Uwe Steeb of West Germany, and then outraged some reporters when he said he did not know who his opponent was a week after the match.

Agassi responded to his critics with a newly realized humility. "I guess you could basically say that I got too big for my britches," he said, as quoted in the *New York Times* (May 5, 1989), as he struggled through the Eagle Tournament of Champions in Forest Hills, New York, where he lost to Lendl in the semifinals after defeating Aaron Krickstein, 6-1, 2-6, 6-3, and Jim Courier, 3-6, 6-3, 7-5. In March 1989 Agassi hired Pat Etcheberry, formerly a javelin thrower for Chile, as his conditioning and nutrition coach, with the goal of adding muscle to his five-foot-ten, 155-pound frame. Etcheberry joined an entourage that includes Nick Bollettieri, Agassi's coach, the agent Bill Shelton, and Agassi's brother, Phillip, who serves as his traveling com-

panion and adviser. John Parenti, a pastor from Las Vegas, recently joined the team, and Agassi's sister Rita, who is married to the former tennis great Pancho Gonzales, runs his fan club.

On April 9, 1989 the United States Davis Cup team ousted France, 5-0, in San Diego, with both Agassi and McEnroe defeating Yannick Noah and Henri Leconte. On May 14 Agassi won the finals of the Aldi Tournament in Ede, the Netherlands, coming from behind to beat Stefan Edberg, 4-6, 6-1, 6-2. Agassi played some of his best tennis at the Italian Open in May, winning, 6-3, 6-4, over Mexico's Leonardo Lavalle, and 6-3, 6-1 over Argentina's Guillermo Perez-Roldan. But a five-set (6-3, 4-6, 2-6, 7-6, 6-1) loss in the finals to Argentina's Alberto Mancini and a third-round loss (7-6, 4-6, 6-3, 6-2) to Jim Courier in the French Open led observers to question once again his ultimate potential, as did his decision to bypass Wimbledon, citing the need to "rest."

During the Davis Cup semifinals in Munich, West Germany in late July 1989, Agassi, ranked number six in the world and with a 7-0 Davis Cup singles record in 1989, lost to Boris Becker, 6-7, 6-7, 7-6, 6-3, 6-4, and then to Carl-Uwe Steeb, 4-6, 6-4, 6-4, 6-2, to give West Germany a 3-1 lead in the series. "Agassi is not a player who can come back when he's down," Steeb told Cindy Schmerler in an interview for the *New York Times* (July 24, 1989). "He's all over you when he's on top, but when he's losing, he's not going to come back." In an exhibition tournament in Tokyo on July 30, Agassi defeated Lendl, 7-6, 6-4, winning $220,000. A few weeks later, in the third round of the Volvo International Tennis Tournament at Stratton Mountain, Agassi was defeated by David Wheaton, 1-6, 7-6, 6-1. Later in the month, he lost to Goran Ivanisevic in the semifinals of the New Jersey Bell Yellow Pages Invitational in Princeton.

Coming into the United States Open, Agassi, who was seeded sixth, had a 1989 match record of twenty-eight wins and fourteen losses and earnings of $225,506. "There's no comparison between my confidence and motivation levels now and what they were at the start of the year," Agassi told Robin Finn of the *New York Times* (August 28, 1989). "Back in January, I was worried about living up to my number-three ranking. Now I just think about how I'm playing against my opponent. I feel stronger, and I feel I'm making progress." In a closely contested quarterfinal match against Jimmy Connors, who was visibly feeling the heat, Agassi managed to prevail in five sets, 6-1, 4-6, 0-6, 6-3, 6-4. He then lost to Lendl in the semifinals, 7-6, 6-1, 3-6, 6-1.

As quiet and thoughtful off the court as he is effervescent on it, Agassi live in Las Vegas with his family when he is not on tour. He reads the Bible almost daily, and he completed high school by taking correspondence courses. Agassi met his steady girlfriend, Amy Moss, who is a junior at Mississippi State University, in 1987, when she worked as a volunteer driver at a tournament.

References: Gentlemen's Q 59:416+ pors; N Y Newsday p88 My 9 '88 por; N Y Times C p5 Ag 28 '89 por; N Y Times Mag p42+ O 30 '88 pors; Newsweek 112:82 S 12 '88 por; Sports Illus 70:64+ Mr 13 '89 pors; World Tennis 36:19+ D '88 pors, 36:36+ Je '88 pors

Ailes, Roger E(ugene)

May 15, 1940– Communications consultant.
Address: Ailes Communications, Inc., 456 W. 43d St., New York, N.Y. 10036

Over the past two decades, Roger E. Ailes has emerged as one of the most sought-after media consultants to political candidates, usually Republican in persuasion. Known as a media wizard, Ailes operates from the premise that television has revolutionized politics, with image taking precedence over substance. His credo is "You are the message." "What I've learned firsthand, " he once said, "is that television has . . . changed the way we view each other. . . . You may think that's unfair, but that's the way it is." Ailes first reached national prominence when, in 1968, he orchestrated Richard M. Nixon's carefully packaged media appearances, for which Ailes was celebrated in Joe McGinniss's seminal book The Selling of the President (1969) as one of the first to practice the art of political image-making in the age of television. "This is the beginning of a whole new concept," he said, as reported in McGinniss's book. "This is it. This is the way they'll be elected forever more. The next guys up will have to be performers." In 1984 it was Ailes who coached President Ronald Reagan after his faltering perfor-

mance in the first debate against the Democratic presidential nominee, Walter F. Mondale, and Ailes was largely responsible for the president's more relaxed comportment and adept defusing of the issue of his age in the second debate. "My job is to present the best reality," Ailes noted on another occasion. "We ignore the bad points and present the good."

Ailes's reputation as a media wizard received further confirmation during Vice-President George Bush's successful bid for the presidency, in 1987 and 1988, during a race in which both candidates were criticized for mud-slinging in what has been termed "the nastiest presidential race in memory." As Bush's senior media adviser, Ailes helped his candidate to develop an effective speaking style, and he produced television commercials—often critical of Bush's opponents' records—which helped to reverse Republican senator Robert J. Dole's early lead in the primaries and Governor Michael S. Dukakis's edge in the general election. Ailes himself has admitted that he relishes combat. "Don't go look for a fight—but if you're hit, deck the bastard," he once said. Although he has been criticized for his abrasive manner and often negative campaign style, which has earned him the title "the dark prince of negative advertising," he is fiercely loyal to the candidates he has worked with. "I never want to lose," he has claimed. "I hate to lose. I'll give my life for a client."

Roger Eugene Ailes was born on May 15, 1940 in Warren, Ohio to Robert Eugene and Donna Marie (Cunningham) Ailes. His father worked as a maintenance foreman at the Packard Electric Plant in Warren and moonlighted as a house painter. Ailes's parents divorced when he was in his late teens. As a child, Ailes was often hospitalized for a chronic illness, and, as a result, he was picked on by neighborhood bullies. After one brutal beating when he was nine, his father taught him to fight and told him: "The worst thing that can happen to you is you can die. If you're not afraid of that, you don't have to be afraid of anything." Those words made an indelible impression on him. By the age of thirteen, Ailes had grown so fearless that he risked his life to rescue a pair of campers whose canoe had capsized. To help out with the family's nagging financial burdens, he peddled his mother's handmade embroidered handkerchiefs door-to-door, but his mother made him stop when he charged less to people for whom he felt sorry. "Even at age ten I was reading things in people's faces," he said in his book, You Are the Message: Secrets of the Master Communicators (1988).

Ailes worked his way through Ohio University in Athens, Ohio as a disc jockey and cohost of the Yawn Patrol, an early-morning show on the campus radio station. He was fascinated by every aspect of radio broadcasting, from opening up the station in the morning to writing his own scripts under the pressure of a deadline. After graduating with a bachelor's degree in fine arts in 1962, however, he turned down an offer from a radio station in Columbus, Ohio in order to accept a lower-paying job as a prop boy for KYW, the NBC-affiliated television station in Cleveland, where he worked on the set of a new talk show hosted by Mike Douglas. He soon was promoted to assistant director, with duties that included preparing cue cards and meeting celebrity guests at the airport. In 1965 he was promoted to producer of the *Mike Douglas Show*, partly because, the station president told him, he was creative and self-confident, but also because two years earlier he had had the courage to hit another producer who regularly harassed staff members. In the same year the show was moved to Philadelphia.

With Ailes as its producer and, during 1967–68, its executive producer, the *Mike Douglas Show* continued to grow in popularity. Under Ailes's supervision, the show's reach expanded from thirty-two cities to 180 markets, and it became the most widely viewed nationally syndicated show of its kind. Ailes won two Emmy Awards for the program, in 1967 and 1968. Although he drew high marks for his talents as a producer, his temper occasionally got the best of him. One time, he flew into a rage at an advertiser, picked the man up by the seat of his pants, and threw him off the station loading dock into a pile of snow.

Roger Ailes's career took off in another direction when the presidential hopeful Richard M. Nixon appeared on the show in 1967. Ailes had the opportunity to chat with Nixon in his office for an hour before airtime. At one point during their conversation, Nixon complained about having to resort to television gimmickry to get elected in the media age, to which Ailes replied: "It's *not* a gimmick. And if you believe that, you're going to lose again." Just days later, Nixon persuaded Ailes to give up his $60,000-a-year job with the *Mike Douglas Show* to become his media adviser. "I had it made . . . where I was," Ailes later told Lewis W. Wolfson of the *Washington Post* (February 13, 1972). "I took a hell of a gamble with my own career. I don't know anyone else around I would have done it for other than Nixon."

Roger Ailes's task during the 1968 campaign was to restrict Nixon's major media appearances to a carefully controlled series of media events. To that end, he created a series of one-hour television shows, aired live in ten cities, with the intention of presenting a less cold and aloof Nixon than the one who had confronted John F. Kennedy in the television debates held during the presidential campaign of 1960. The "Man in the Arena" shows that Ailes produced featured a row of panelists, picked by Ailes, and an audience, chosen by the local Republican committee, that cheered and converged on the stage at the end of the program. During each show, Nixon stood alone on a stark stage facing the panel of questioners—a tactic designed to enlist the sympathies of the television viewers. As Joe McGinniss noted in *The Selling of the President*, which revealed the inner workings of Nixon's media campaign in 1968, that tactic worked. Observing Nixon at the beginning of the first show, produced in Chicago, McGinniss said: "All the sub-liminal effects sank in. Nixon stood alone, ringed by forces which, if not hostile, were at least—to the viewer—unpredictable. . . . Richard Nixon was suddenly human: facing a new and dangerous situation, alone, armed only with his wits. In image terms, he had won before he began."

Ailes has emphasized that he recognized the limitations of television to transform someone's public persona completely. As he told *U.S. News & World Report* (February 8, 1988): "After 3,000 hours of television and working with everybody from Henny Youngman to Edward Teller, you have instincts. And the thing I knew about Nixon was that you were never going to make him warm and fuzzy, but he could handle that kind of tough situation." Ailes also created and produced the campaign's commercials, a one-hour campaign rally from Madison Square Garden in New York City, and a four-hour broadcast on the eve of the election. After Nixon's victory, Ailes was called upon from time to time to stage-manage various official events, such as Nixon's announcement of the withdrawal of troops from Vietnam and his nomination of Warren E. Burger as chief justice of the United States.

In 1969 Ailes went out on his own and founded Ailes Communications, a diversified television production and communications consulting company based in New York City. Financial assistance for the venture was provided by his brother Robert, who was a doctor. One of Ailes's first clients was the Republican National Committee, which hired him to provide media advice to Republican candidates who asked for his assistance. During the 1970 elections, a number of senatorial and gubernatorial candidates retained Ailes's services. As media adviser to Robert Taft Jr., who was challenging Governor James A. Rhodes for the Republican nomination for United States senator from Ohio, Ailes engaged in a bit of theatre that was widely credited with tipping that close race in Taft's favor. Less than a minute before the beginning of a crucial televised debate between the candidates, Ailes bounded onto the stage and handed Taft a folded piece of paper, saying in an audible voice, "Don't use this unless you have to." Rhodes was unaware that the paper read simply, "Kill!" and apparently believed that Taft had just been handed some damaging information that could be unleashed at any time during the evening. As a result, Rhodes was put off balance before the debate even started, and he never recovered. Taft ended up winning the election.

Adding a cultural medium to his accomplishments, in 1972 Ailes made his Broadway debut as a producer with *Mother Earth*, a rock musical consisting of sketches with ecological themes, which closed after only twelve performances. His second theatrical venture, as producer of Lanford Wilson's Off-Broadway play *The Hot l Baltimore*, which ran from 1973 to 1976, was much more successful. The production won four Obie Awards, including one for best new play Off-Broadway.

Meanwhile, Ailes returned to television as a producer and director of television specials, including *The Last Frontier* (1974), *Fellini: Wizards, Clowns and Honest Liars* (1977), and *Television and the Presidency* (1984), for which he won an Emmy Award. During 1975 and 1976, he served as executive vice-president of Television News, a short-lived syndicated news service funded by Joseph Coors, the brewing executive. Since 1978 he has worked as a consultant to CBS-TV in New York City. As executive director in 1981 of *Tomorrow Coast to Coast*, NBC-TV's late-night show starring Tom Snyder and Rona Barrett, Ailes supervised the first network interview to be held in thirteen years with Charles Manson, the convicted mass murderer, from the maximum-security prison for the criminally insane at Vacaville, California.

Ailes's reputation as a media magus suffered a setback in 1982, when two important clients were defeated in their bids for political office. Perhaps as a result of spreading himself too thin, Ailes allowed the staff of Senator Harrison H. Schmitt of New Mexico to produce two ads claiming that his Democratic challenger, Jeff Bingaman, was soft on crime. Quickly exposed as misleading, the ads generated a wave of sympathy for Bingaman, and Harrison Schmitt became the only incumbent Republican senator to be unseated in 1982. The other defeat occurred in the state of New York, where Republican gubernatorial candidate Lewis E. Lehrman, an Ailes client, spent six times more on his campaign than his opponent, Democrat Mario Cuomo, but narrowly lost the election. Ailes blamed the defeat partly on poor ad placement, which he did not control, and he vowed after that experience to supervise all media buys himself. He also hired Cuomo's media buyer, Catherine Farrell, and acquired a controlling interest in her media consulting firm, Farrell Media.

In 1984 Ailes was retained as a $12,000-a-month consultant to the "Tuesday Team," the people responsible for engineering President Ronald Reagan's reelection campaign. After the first televised presidential debate, on October 7, during which Reagan at times appeared confused and disoriented, Ailes was urgently pressed into service to direct the preparations for the second debate. Ailes determined that Reagan had been overly programmed with facts and figures before his first encounter with the Democratic nominee, Walter Mondale. For the second debate, held on October 21, Ailes advised that in response to every question, Reagan should relate it to one of his themes. Ailes also had Reagan undergo a "pepper drill," a standard Ailes technique, during which Ailes and some of the president's aides fired questions at him and gave him about ninety seconds to respond. To be effective, Ailes pointed out, Reagan needed to relax, to be himself, and, most important, to confront the age issue head on. "I felt pretty sure that if I could get him back to being *himself* again, he'd be okay," Ailes noted in his book. The media adviser was appalled to learn that no one had ever dis-

cussed the age issue with the seventy-three-year-old president or prepared a strategy to deal with it in the debates. As a result, Ailes sat down with Reagan and bluntly asked: "Mr. President, what are you going to do when they say you're too old for the job?" As Ailes related in his book, Reagan was silent for several moments, then responded with a joke that he had used before: "I want you to know that I will not make age an issue of this campaign. I am not going to exploit for political purposes my opponent's youth and inexperience." Ailes told Reagan to repeat that line and nothing else during the second debate, and he believes that line, which even drew an appreciative chuckle from Mondale, clinched the president's reelection.

The Reagan campaign, however, was not Ailes's only media coup that year. In the United States senatorial race in Kentucky, he produced devastating television spots for Republican Mitch McConnell, a county judge from Louisville, that depicted a look-alike of the Democratic incumbent Dee Huddleston running from a pack of bloodhounds through the Kentucky hill country while a voice-over denounced him for running from his record and missing floor votes. That ad campaign was credited with reversing McConnell's forty-four-point deficit in the polls and, ultimately, spurring his upset victory over Huddleston in a state where registered Democrats outnumbered Republicans four to one. Similarly, in the race for the United States Senate in Texas, Ailes's client, Phil Gramm, a Republican, turned the tide against his Democratic opponent, Lloyd Doggett, with a week-long ad campaign that criticized him for accepting a $500 contribution from a gay male strip joint in San Antonio. It was also in 1984 that Ailes's pugnacity erupted again. Confronted by two youths in leather jackets in the lobby of a Houston hotel late one evening, Ailes disabled one by breaking his wrist and hurled the other into the lobby fountain.

Ailes's reputation for hard-hitting aggressiveness was nowhere more evident than in his role as media consultant for Vice-President George Bush during his successful 1988 bid for the presidency, a role for which Ailes received reportedly a monthly fee of $25,000, plus commissions of approximately $3 million for the commercials he prepared. In the October 28, 1987 televised debate in Houston, Texas among Republican contenders, it was Ailes who coached Bush to repeatedly call Pierre ("Pete") S. du Pont 4th, one of the debate participants and the former governor of Delaware, "Pierre," instead of the more informal "Pete," to remind viewers of du Pont's patrician roots and to serve notice that he meant business as a presidential candidate. In January 1988, Ailes primed Bush during a limousine ride en route to his live confrontation with CBS News anchorman Dan Rather. It is widely believed that Ailes was behind Bush's decision to counter Rather's aggressive questioning about the vice-president's involvement in the Iran-Contra affair with the question: "How would you like it if I judged your career by those seven minutes when you walked off the set in New York?

Would you like that?" Although Ailes has neither confirmed nor denied his part in that counterattack, he has called the Bush-Rather shouting match "one of the great moments in television" and believes that it helped dispel Bush's so-called wimp factor, or charges that Bush lacked toughness.

Ailes's most critical contribution during the primaries came after Bush finished third in the Iowa caucuses on February 8, behind Senator Robert Dole of Kansas and Pat Robertson, the television evangelist. His strength sapped from a bout of walking pneumonia, Ailes nevertheless went three nights without sleep to put together a media campaign in New Hampshire, where the first primary election was held on February 16. A thirty-minute *Ask George Bush* television show, patterned after Nixon's "Man in the Arena" broadcasts some twenty years earlier, was broadcast. A televised endorsement from Senator Barry M. Goldwater of Arizona helped shore up conservative support. Most effective was the so-called Senator Straddle ad, which charged that Bush's principal opponent, Robert Dole, had reversed himself on such issues as tax increases, oil import fees, and arms control. The ad drew a blistering rebuke from Senator Dole, but it was widely credited with shifting the momentum to Bush, who won 38 percent of the total primary votes, compared to Dole's 28 percent. At the Republican National Convention, Ailes was among those recommending the selection of Senator Dan Quayle of Indiana, a former Ailes client, as Bush's running mate.

In addition to managing Bush's advertising campaign and overseeing an advertising budget of some $40 million, Ailes also helped the vice-president improve his speaking style and coached him for the debates. With his shrill speaking voice, distracting gestures, and often disjointed syntax that did not play well on the evening news, Bush posed special problems. To make him look and sound "presidential," Ailes advised Bush to slow his rate of speech in order to lower the pitch of his voice, to restrain his wild arm movements, and to stick to a prepared script, instead of adlibbing, to provide the media with "sound bites"—striking phrases and lines that the press could easily pick up on. The grooming paid off. Starting with the Republican National Convention, observers noticed that Bush seemed more his own person: he appeared more self-confident and relaxed enough to indulge occasionally in self-deprecating humor.

At the same time that Bush was showing a new confidence, Ailes was devising a series of television ads attacking the record of the Democratic presidential candidate, Governor Michael S. Dukakis of Massachusetts, and depicting him as a freewheeling liberal who was soft on crime, eager to raise taxes, and inexperienced in national security affairs. One ad, for instance, stated that the governor gave "weekend furloughs to first-degree murderers," adding that "many are still at large." Another commercial showed sludge and debris in Boston Harbor while a voice-over said that Dukakis had the opportunity to clean up Boston Harbor but "chose not to." Other ads depicted Bush as a gentle grandfather and "no-frills" businessman, in an effort to offset his image as an elitist. "Some people have a formula," Robert Squier, a Democratic consultant, told *Time* (August 22, 1988). "Ailes produces a spot to fit the situation." By August 19, 1988 a CBS News poll showed—for the first time—that Bush had an edge over Dukakis, 46 percent to 40 percent—a lead that he was to maintain until Election Day.

Lee Atwater, Bush's campaign manager, has said that Ailes "has two speeds. Attack and destroy." When Senator Edward M. Kennedy of Massachusetts asked, during the Democratic National Convention, "Where was George?" during the time that the Reagan administration was involved in the Iran-Contra affair, Ailes reportedly made up the acid reply that he was "home, dry, and in bed with his wife," alluding to Kennedy's involvement in the Chappaquiddick scandal. Bush softened that response to, "O.K., so I was home with Barbara—what's wrong with that?" That combative style is also evident in the way Ailes works with his clients. "He's very supportive in the beginning—he bolsters them, reinforces their egos," Robert Goodman, a Republican consultant, told *Newsweek* (September 26, 1988). "When he feels their confidence level is up, then he can be blunt to a fault. He'll say, 'You stink!'—and they listen." In spite of that style, the "intense and rough-hewn" Ailes was able to forge a close working relationship with the more modest, genteel Bush. As one friend of Bush's told *Newsweek* in the same article, the vice-president "doesn't take advice well—but he listens to Roger."

In his book, *You Are the Message*, Ailes revealed that, whether he is coaching political candidates or corporate executives, he never uses textbooks or a rigid set of rules. Instead, he relies heavily on videotape to demonstrate graphically what his clients are doing wrong and to monitor their improvement. For political candidates, he writes, the "like factor" cannot be underestimated, because people often vote based on whether they like one candidate better than another. "I call it the magic bullet," he says in his book, "because if your audience likes you, they'll forgive just about everything else you do wrong. If they don't like you, you can hit every rule right on target and it doesn't matter." Ailes made a conscious decision not to rely solely on political campaigns for his income. "I've kept active in other areas," he wrote in his book, "because I never wanted to be in a position where I had to take a campaign, for reasons of money. I think that's the wrong reason."

For his work on the Bush campaign, Roger Ailes was honored with a share of the top prize in the presidential television advertising category at the biannual awards dinner of the American Association of Political Consultants in January 1989. Later in the year, his services were hired by Rudolph Giuliani, the Republican nominee for mayor of New York City, and by Congressman Jim Courter, the GOP candidate for the governorship of New

Jersey. In both campaigns, Ailes tried to portray the Democratic opponents of the two candidates as weak on crime. Acknowledging the likableness of David Dinkins, Giuliani's opponent, Ailes brought into question Dinkins's personal finances and, in one commercial, accused Dinkins of giving campaign funds to a "convicted kidnapper." In the New Jersey governor's race, Ailes and Courter responded to charges from Congressman James J. Florio, the Democratic candidate, that Courter was "a polluter" by accusing Florio of "hiding his record on crime and drugs."

Because of his ample physique—he stands five feet, ten inches tall and weighs about 245 pounds—

and his blustery demeanor, Roger Ailes has been often called the Ernest Hemingway of political consultants. His balding head and whitening goatee make him look older than his actual age. Ailes's marriage to his first wife, Marge, ended in divorce. He married his second wife, Norma, in 1977. Ailes is a member of the Directors Guild of America, the American Federation of Television and Radio Artists, and the Radio-Television News Directors Association.

References: Newsweek 112:19+ S 26 '88 pors; Washington Post B p1+ Je 20 '88 pors; Who's Who in America, 1988–89

Almendros, Nestor

Oct. 30, 1930– Cinematographer; film director. Address: c/o Smith, Gosnell, & Nicholson, P.O. Box 1166, Pacific Palisades, Calif. 90272

For more than twenty years, beginning with his earliest collaborations with such French directors as François Truffaut, Eric Rohmer, and other leaders of the New Wave, Nestor Almendros, "a painter with light," has been a world-class cinematographer. His unique and unorthodox approach to movie photography, which is based on a rigorous study of period paintings and their effects of light, has resulted in such acclaimed films as Truffaut's *Wild Child* (1970) and Terrence Malick's *Days of Heaven* (1978). It has also brought him international recognition as a consummate artist as well as a masterly technician and manipulator of light. In

1976 Nestor Almendros received one of the highest honors that France can bestow when he was named a chevalier of the Ordre des Arts et des Lettres for his contributions to cinema.

Nestor Almendros was born in Barcelona, Spain on October 30, 1930 to Hermino and Maria (Cuyas) Almendros. His childhood was spent amid the tumult of the Spanish Civil War (1936–39). The boy's position was complicated by the fact that his was a Loyalist, anti-Franco family. His escape to the movies gave him a respite from the military and political upheavals around him. "Cinema was like a drug, a way out," he recalled in his 1980 autobiography, *A Man with a Camera*, "and American films were, of course, our staple diet." Almendros has called Frank Capra's 1937 utopian fantasy-adventure film *Lost Horizon* "the film that affected me most in those days."

Almendros became an avid filmgoer early in life, and as a boy he would often travel to the nearby suburb of Badalona to see a movie that had not yet opened in Barcelona. In addition to large-scale fantasy films like *Lost Horizon*, he developed an interest in more cinematically sophisticated and innovative movies such as Orson Welles's *Magnificent Ambersons* and John Ford's *Informer*. In *A Man with a Camera*, he credits the film critic Angel Zúñiga with shaping his sensibilities. "It was Zúñiga who opened my eyes to what cinema really was. His book *Una historia del cine* influenced me greatly, and I knew it almost by heart." "I liked *Lost Horizon*," Almendros told an interviewer from *Films & Filming* (June 1986), "the first Tarzan movies with Johnny Weissmuller, which were very visual. Then, a little later, the German expressionists like Murnau. When I was sixteen or seventeen I began to be a little sophomoric, as they say, and then I started liking silent movies which I saw in film libraries and so on."

Almendros's father immigrated to Cuba in 1940 and sent for the rest of his family to join him as soon as it was economically possible. Nestor moved to Havana in 1948, at the age of seventeen, and began studying philosophy and literature at the University of Havana, subjects that he chose more to please his family than himself, since cinema continued to be his supreme interest. Although Havana lacked film societies or film magazines, except for American fan publications, he found Cuba to be a paradise for film buffs, for he could see far more American films—and in English with Spanish subtitles rather than dubbed into Spanish—than were available in Spain, along with films from the Soviet Union, Germany, and France.

In 1948 Almendros organized Havana's first film society with a small band of enthusiasts, which included in its ranks such notables as the cinema scholar Carlos Clarens. Wanting to make movies of his own, Almendros was, by 1949, shooting with an 8-mm camera. Based on a work by Franz Kafka, his first film, entitled *Una confusión cotidiana* (*A Daily Confusion*), was made in collaboration with Tomás Gutiérrez Alea in 1949. Although it primarily served Almendros as an exercise in editing, *A Daily Confusion* was notable for the later success of those involved in its production. Apart from Almendros, they included Alea, who became one of Cuba's most celebrated film directors of the 1970s and 1980s, and Vicente Revuelta and Julio Matas, its two stars, who went on to distinguished careers in Cuban theatre.

Leaving Havana after the rise of the Fulgencio Batista dictatorship in 1952, Almendros went to New York City to study moviemaking at the Institute for Film Techniques, at City College, under Hans Richter, an experimental filmmaker who had been driven out of Europe by the Nazis. Despite Richter's inspired teaching, Almendros found the school's lack of resources a problem, and in 1956 he traveled to Italy to study at the Centro Sperimentale di Cinematografia in Rome. He found his experience there even less satisfying, however, because he had already learned much of what the school tried to teach him. The only exception was the art of lighting. "They taught us the commonplaces," Almendros recalled in *A Man with a Camera*. "In a gangster film the light 'had to' create sharp contrasts; in a mystery it 'had to' shine from below in order to cast long shadows; in a light comedy everything 'had to' be lit 'high key.'" But Almendros and his fellow students Luciano Tovoli, who was to become Michelangelo Antonioni's cinematographer, and Manuel Puig rejected those conventions. "It was at the Centro Sperimentale that I learned to question things, to say 'No!' and 'Why?'" he wrote in *A Man with a Camera*. It was also during this time that he began to develop his own solutions to lighting problems, rather than using those of other filmmakers, and first began to frame his own approach to cinematography.

Barred from the Italian film industry as a foreigner and unable to return to Batista's Cuba or Franco's Spain, Almendros took a job at Vassar College in Poughkeepsie, New York, where he taught Spanish and ran the audiovisual equipment in its language laboratory. He was soon shooting movies again, beginning with *58–59*, a short film that he made at Times Square in New York City during the New Year's Eve celebration of 1958, depicting the mounting frenzy of the crowd during the final ten minutes leading up to midnight. It was his first attempt to shoot a movie in "available light," a technique well known to still photographers but a novelty in pictures at the time. The film was well received in the New York experimental film community, and Almendros soon found himself in the company of such avant-garde cinematic figures as Jonas and Adolfas Mekas and Maya Deren, and he became a contributor to the iconoclastic journal *Film Culture*.

Following the fall of the Batista dictatorship in Cuba in 1959, Almendros returned to Havana, where he began working for the film production agency of the new Castro government as both a director and a cinematographer. During the next two years, he made movies glorifying the revolutionary new regime's advances in health care, agriculture, and education, which were often shot under primitive conditions in the Cuban countryside. Almendros credits the twenty documentaries he filmed during that period with helping him to overcome problems in lighting and to develop the techniques that he later refined into his unique photographic style. He soon wearied of the relentless output of blatant propaganda films demanded by the government, however, and began shooting a film of his own entitled *Gente en la playa* (*People at the Beach*), working on weekends in natural light. At first prevented by his superiors from editing the film, he was eventually able to finish it under a false title, but the incident spotlighted a rift with the Castro government that left Almendros's career stymied by 1961. He worked for a short time as a movie critic for the Cuban publication *Bohemia,* but he soon got into trouble because of his independent thinking. "I was fired from the film industry, fired as a film critic," he told Alan Hunter in *Films & Filming.* "What else could I do but leave? I was lucky to do that in 1962 because a few years later it would have cost me prison."

Almendros began his third exile in Paris, where he quickly felt an affinity with the New Wave cinema of François Truffaut, Eric Rohmer, and Jean-Luc Godard. He survived the next three years on the fringes of legality and poverty, without proper immigration papers or a work permit, by registering as a student in order to qualify for subsidized university housing and giving Spanish lessons on the side. By 1964 Almendros had grown tired of both his poverty and lack of film work. A chance encounter with the production of an anthology film entitled *Paris vu par . . .* (*Paris as Seen by . . .,* or *Six in Paris*) just as its cinematographer resigned afforded Almendros his first opportunity in three years to shoot a movie. After a one-day tryout, its producer, Barbet Schroeder, and its director, Eric Rohmer, hired him to finish the film. Trying to ease Almendros's financial situation, Rohmer got him a job as a director and cinematographer for French educational television. Almendros made twenty-five documentaries for television between 1964 and 1967.

In the mid-1960s Almendros worked on four short films, including Rohmer's *Nadja à Paris*

(*Nadja in Paris*, 1964) and *Une Etudiante d'aujourd'hui* (*A Student of Today*, 1965), but it was not until 1966 that he got the opportunity to do a full-length feature—Rohmer's *La Collectioneuse*, produced by Barbet Schroeder. That ninety-minute movie, quickly shot in color on a modest budget, gave Almendros his first opportunity to develop his ideas about shooting in natural light. *La Collectioneuse*, which he has since described as "a favorite" among his films, received a Silver Bear Award at the Berlin Film Festival.

Almendros broke into American films, after a fashion, with his second feature, *The Wild Racers* (1967), which was directed by Daniel Haller and produced by the low-budget filmmaker Roger Corman for American International Pictures. *More* (1968) assigned Almendros a much larger role than usual because its director, Barbet Schroeder, asked him to serve as its art director as well as cinematographer. The drama about young people destroying themselves with drugs gave Almendros an opportunity to achieve greater subtlety than had been apparent in his previous work. Vincent Canby of the *New York Times* (August 5, 1969) observed: "The camera never resorts to the sort of subjective nonsense we have come to expect in now obligatory LSD episodes in most movies. The camera simply sees everything in a purified way—objectively." *More*, which was screened at the Cannes Film Festival, scored a bigger hit in Europe than in the United States.

In 1969 Almendros was once again collaborating with Eric Rohmer, on the director's *Ma Nuit chez Maud* (*My Night at Maud's*), a subdued romantic drama shot in a low-key black-and-white that marked something of an international breakthrough for both men. In addition to being shown at the Cannes Film Festival, it received the Louis Delluc Prize and earned Oscar nominations in the United States for best foreign film and for Rohmer, as screenwriter. According to Almendros, writing in *A Man with a Camera*, it was his work in *My Night at Maud's* that first brought him to the attention of François Truffaut: "As most films are now generally in color, Truffaut thought I was one of the last to understand black-and-white techniques." Truffaut and Almendros collaborated, as director and cinematographer respectively, on *L'Enfant Sauvage* (*The Wild Child*, 1970), a semidocumentary account based on a true story about a boy, Victor of Aveyron, who had grown up alone in the woods of France in the late eighteenth century, and the efforts of a doctor, Jean Itard, to civilize him. Almendros's first attempt at achieving an archaic, period look in his work was acclaimed by the American Association of Cinema Critics, which awarded *The Wild Child* its first prize for its black-and-white cinematography.

In the midst of his burgeoning career as a cinematographer, Almendros found time to write, direct, and photograph *El Bastón* (1970), a short fiction film made in Barcelona, in the hope of reestablishing his directorial credentials. It was quickly obscured, however, by his work as cinema-

tographer on Rohmer's *Le Genou de Claire* (*Claire's Knee*) and Truffaut's *Domicile Conjugal* (*Bed and Board*), both made in 1970. In the next thirteen years, Almendros's work became closely associated with the films of Truffaut, for whom he photographed *Les Deux Anglaises et le Continent* (*Two English Girls*, 1971); *L'Histoire d'Adèle H.* (*The Story of Adele H.*, 1975); *L'Homme qui aimait les Femmes* (*The Man Who Loved Women*, 1977); *La Chambre verte* (*The Green Room*, 1977); *L'Amour en fuite* (*Love on the Run*, 1979); *Le Dernier Métro* (*The Last Metro*, 1980), which received the César Prize for photography from the French Academy of Film Arts and Techniques; and *Vivement Dimanche* (*Confidentially Yours*, 1983). All of those films made special use of Almendros's abilities, most notably *The Green Room*, a drama adapted from Henry James's "Altar of the Dead," about a man obsessed with lighting candles, in which Almendros embodied the story's stark, preelectric setting in vivid terms, and *Confidentially Yours*, which marked a return to black-and-white, in keeping with its detective story subject. "He was a very quiet man, [who] had a great difficulty communicating with people," Almendros recalled in *Films & Filming* of Truffaut, who died of a brain tumor in 1985, at the age of fifty-one. "So the first movie went very well but it was like there was a distance, and then, movie by movie, we got to be closer."

With Barbet Schroeder, he subsequently shot *La Vallée* (*The Valley*, 1971), a drama filmed on location in New Guinea, which was praised by Janet Maslin in the *New York Times* (May 17, 1981) for its cinematography: "Mr. Almendros's camera elegantly records many treks through the jungle and some mesmerizing encounters with Mapuga tribesmen." Three years later, again in conjunction with Schroeder, he photographed the documentary *Idi Amin Dada*, about the notorious dictator of Uganda. Filmed on portable equipment, *Idi Amin Dada* is regarded by Almendros as an historically vital document. "A little thing like the weight of a camera has an effect on the way a film was made," he explained in *Women's Wear Daily* (January 9, 1985). "*Idi Amin Dada* would not have been possible without hand-held cameras with direct sound. In the days of Hitler and Franco we can see only the faces, not the sound. The only direct sound we have of Churchill, Stalin, and Roosevelt is Fox Movietone records of their speeches. We have no record of their conversation. We have images of Hitler holding children. What was he saying?"

Almendros's other longtime screen association has been with Eric Rohmer, for whom he has photographed *L'Amour l'après-midi* (*Chloë in the Afternoon*, 1972); *Die Marquise von O.* (*The Marquise of O.*, 1975); *Perceval le Gallois* (*Perceval*, 1977); and *Pauline à la plage* (*Pauline at the Beach*, 1982), among other acclaimed films. Since the mid-1970s, however, his career has been increasingly associated with Hollywood. Beginning with such modest efforts as Monte Hellman's *Cockfighter* (1974), made for Roger Corman's New World Pictures, Almendros moved up quickly to the forefront of bankable cinematographers with Terrence Malick's *Days of Heaven* (1978), a haunting turn-of-the-century drama with the midwestern wheat harvest as its backdrop. *Days of Heaven* brought him his first Oscar. "Nestor Almendros's cinematography is at times so startling," a *Variety* (September 13, 1978) reviewer wrote, "you wish the projectionist would roll the film back a few feet so the footage could be enjoyed again." Joseph Gelmis of *Newsday* (September 17, 1978) hailed *Days of Heaven* as "a pictorial work of art . . . of intense visual beauty," while Philip French of the London *Observer* (June 3, 1979) called Almendros's photography "beautiful and innovative." And David Denby of *New York* (September 25, 1978) magazine opened his review by venturing his opinion that *Days of Heaven* was "one of the best-looking—no, beautiful—movies ever made."

Although Almendros continued filming in Europe, photographing Moshe Mizrahi's Oscar-winning 1977 drama *Madame Rosa*, starring Simone Signoret, in addition to his work for Rohmer and Truffaut, he became a far more familiar figure in Hollywood after the release of *Days of Heaven*. From the unpretentious comedy western *Goin' South* (1977), with Jack Nicholson, he moved on to *Kramer vs. Kramer* (1978), a domestic drama about divorce and child custody starring Dustin Hoffman and Meryl Streep and directed by Robert Benton. One of the most honored films of the decade, it won five Academy Awards, including those for best picture and best director. Almendros himself received Oscar nominations for *Kramer vs. Kramer* and for his next American film, Randal Kleiser's misbegotten 1980 remake of *The Blue Lagoon*, starring Brooke Shields.

Almendros's second film with Robert Benton, *Still of the Night* (1981), starring Meryl Streep and Roy Scheider, was a muddled failure despite his special effort to adapt the lighting and photography of classic film noir to its contemporary Hitchcockian setting. *Sophie's Choice* (1982), also starring Meryl Streep, this time under the direction of Alan J. Pakula, had a 1947 setting that Almendros approached in a different fashion. Sequences set in the pink house in which the film's Brooklyn scenes take place were deliberately played off of that pink, "a look like an old [Vincente] Minnelli movie, like *Meet Me in St. Louis*," according to Almendros in *Millimeter* (February 1983), while scenes set in the European concentration camps were bleached and desaturated.

In 1984 Almendros was employed once again by Robert Benton for *Places in the Heart*, a story of Texas farmers in the Great Depression that, like *Days of Heaven*, enabled him to achieve haunting effects with huge American vistas. In the same year, Almendros reemerged as a director, in collaboration with Orlando Jiménez Leal, with the release of *Improper Conduct*, a searing documentary about human rights abuses in Castro's Cuba during the 1960s and 1970s, based on interviews with former political prisoners. *Improper Conduct* was de-

scribed by a reviewer for *Newsday* (July 13, 1984) as "a harrowing story of totalitarian mentality run amok," and David Denby of *New York* (July 23, 1984) magazine called it "an eloquent and entertaining movie . . . [and] a major event in the moral education of the Left." Almendros followed it up in 1988 with another documentary, *Nobody Listened*, made in collaboration with Jorge Ulla, about the Castro government's repudiation of its original allies and supporters. Despite the fact that neither movie made money, Almendros justified their production during an interview for the *New York Times* (December 2, 1988). "I've had a successful career," he said. "I've made forty-seven movies and I've got several awards, and there's a moment when you owe something to society. I have access to camera and film, and I know how. The Cuban case is too scandalous not to talk about."

Almendros's recent films include *Heartburn* (1986), directed by Mike Nichols and starring Meryl Streep, and Martin Scorsese's segment of the 1989 omnibus film *New York Stories*, which also featured work by Francis Ford Coppola and Woody Allen. Among his recent tributes was a one-month retrospective of his major films, presented early in 1989 at the American Museum of the Moving Image in New York.

Looking like a Spanish grandee in one of El Greco's paintings, Almendros seems younger than his fifty-nine years, perhaps because of his thick, dark mustache. He is given to wearing elegant headgear, like Panama hats, to cover his thinning hair. He is fluent in English, though he retains a slight Spanish accent. As of 1985, when he was interviewed by Howard Kissel of *Newsday*, his pied-à-terre was an austerely furnished loft in New York City that commanded a view of the Empire State Building, though, like most cinematographers, he is a citizen of the world, ready to travel wherever his shooting locations may take him. Almendros is a member of the American Society of Cinematographers.

References: American Cinematographer 64:53+ Ap '83; Film Comment 23:18+ Jl–Ag '87; Films & Filming p22+ Je '86; Who's Who in America, 1988–89

Arens, Moshe

Dec. 7, 1925– Foreign minister of Israel.
Address: 49 Hagderot, Savyon, Israel

When the urbane and politic Moshe Arens assumed the post of Israel's defense minister in 1983 after his predecessor, the truculent war hero Ariel Sharon, was deposed for his part in Israel's controversial 1982 invasion of Lebanon, Israelis appeared to heave a collective sigh of relief. "The main advantage of Arens is that he is not Sharon," one Israeli journalist observed, echoing the sentiments of many of his compatriots, who perceived both men

Moshe Arens

Living in Manhattan's Washington Heights neighborhood, Arens attended George Washington High School with the future secretary of state Henry A. Kissinger. After his graduation, he enrolled at the Massachusetts Institute of Technology in 1943. Interrupting his education in 1944 to serve in the United States Army Corps of Engineers, he attained the rank of technical sergeant before his discharge in 1947. He had been active for several years in the Betar Zionist Youth Movement, a branch of the revisionist Zionist cause of Vladimir Jabotinsky, the right-wing Israeli ideologue who advocated establishing a greater Israel that would incorporate both banks of the Jordan River. Arens became its national commander in 1947, the year in which he graduated from the Massachusetts Institute of Technology with a B.S. degree in mechanical engineering.

When the 1948 Arab-Israeli war broke out, Arens defied his family's wishes by going to Israel to join the underground Irgun Zvai Leumi, then led by the right-wing firebrand Menahem Begin, who formed the hawkish Herut party that year on the foundation of Jabotinsky's principles. Arens served in Morocco and Algeria, as well as in Europe, where he helped to organize self-defense activities in Jewish communities. Arens has since somewhat testily defended his decision to fight for the independence of the Israeli state. "When people of a certain age ask me why I went to Israel in 1948, I reply, 'Why didn't you? . . . ,'" he told Bernard Weinraub of the *New York Times* (February 15, 1983). "In 1948 this was our last stand after the Holocaust; this was the chance that Jews had to show they would survive."

From 1948 to 1950 Arens worked with his American-born wife, the former Muriel F. Eisenberg, on Moshav Mevo-Betar, a border kibbutz run on Jabotinskyite principles. In 1951 the couple temporarily returned to the United States so that Arens could attend the California Institute of Technology, where he received a master's degree in aeronautical engineering in 1954. Afterward, Arens worked for the aircraft industry in New Jersey and, later, for the Curtiss-Wright Corporation's jet engine development program in California before returning to Israel in 1957.

From 1957 to 1962 Arens was an associate professor of aeronautical engineering at the Technion-Israel Institute of Technology in Haifa. In 1962 he became vice-president for engineering at the government-operated Israel Aircraft Industry, where he designed aircraft and missiles. Two years later he led a committee established to plan the adaptation of Ben-Gurion Airport to the supersonic jet era. Arens earned acclaim as the father of Israel's fighter aircraft program, directing the development of the Kfir fighter and the Lavi fighter, and in 1971 he was awarded the Israeli Defense Prize for his accomplishments. He also helped to found the Elron Company, the first high-technology firm in Israel, and served on its board of directors from 1962 until 1977.

as hawkish ideologues whose only apparent difference was in matters of style. Arens, a former Knesset member and aeronautical engineer who pioneered Israel's fighter aircraft program, soon proved himself a pragmatic conciliator, extending a tentative hand to moderate Arab leaders and helping to thaw relations between the United States and Israel.

Soon after he was named foreign minister in early 1989, Arens tried to prevent the United States from entering into a dialogue with Yasir Arafat's Palestine Liberation Organization. In the wake of the Palestinian uprising known as the *intifada,* observers expect Arens to have a difficult time persuading the Bush administration to capitulate on the Palestinian question. According to the Israeli political scientist Shlomo Avineri, however, "If there is someone who can present the case to the United States intelligently, it is he."

Moshe Arens was born on December 7, 1925 in Kovno, Lithuania and moved with his family to Riga, Latvia in 1927. His mother was a dentist, and his father was a businessman who made frequent trips to the United States to establish investments there. In 1939 Moshe fled the Nazi Holocaust by immigrating with his family to New York City. Although he remembers his parents as being "not particularly" Zionist, the horrors of the Nazis' "final solution" appalled him. "Riga probably had the highest percentage of Jews exterminated of any community in Europe, more than 95 percent," he told a reporter from the *Washington Post* (September 27, 1982). "So you can imagine that that made some impression on me." Unlike his brother Richard, who grew up to be an outspoken human rights activist, Moshe evolved into an avowed Zionist while he was still in his teens, resolving to go to what was to become Israel after World War II.

Arens was once described by Lucinda Franks in an article for the *New York Times Magazine* (March 25, 1984) as "a technocrat . . . who prefers to arrive at his decisions after many meetings and position papers." Although he disdained political machinations, Arens eventually gravitated toward public service. Active in the Herut party since he first immigrated to Israel, he served as chairman of the party's Tel Aviv branch and later headed its central committee. Elected to the eighth Knesset in 1974, he soon became a member of the Israeli parliament's Finance Committee, yet he declined an offer made the following year to become the chief scientist in the Defense Ministry.

After the victory, in 1977, of the Likud bloc, comprised of the Herut party and several minor right-wing parties, Arens was named chairman of the ninth Knesset's Defense and Foreign Relations Committee. A demanding taskmaster, he introduced management discipline into the work of the committee. During his second term, he voted against the Camp David peace agreement between Israel and Egypt, citing his conviction that Israel was ceding too much territory to Egypt. After the resignation, in 1980, of the defense minister, Ezer Weizman, Arens rejected Prime Minister Menahem Begin's proposal that he become defense minister. "I felt it would not be playing according to the rules," Arens explained in an interview for the *New York Times* (February 12, 1982). "Since I'd voted against the Camp David agreement, I felt that it would not be proper for me to get in the government and either be instrumental in carrying out policies I did not agree with, or, worse yet, trying to torpedo the government's policies."

Although he did not oppose the peace itself, Arens regretted the extent of Israel's concessions to Egypt, contending that Israel should have kept its two high-tech air bases in the Sinai and that the Jewish settlers in the Yamit region should have been permitted to stay there. Moreover, Arens felt that Egypt should have agreed to sell oil from the Alma oilfields to Israel at discounted prices, since Israel had discovered the site. "We should have tried for a better deal," he said during the *New York Times* interview.

Although he was reelected to the tenth Knesset in 1981, Arens did not serve out his full term, for in February 1982 Begin appointed him Israel's ambassador to the United States. Despite his neophyte status in diplomacy, his appointment was welcomed by Washington insiders, who considered him a plain-spoken advocate for the Israeli Right. Arens had already established himself as a hardliner whose opinions on Middle Eastern issues sometimes made even Begin appear moderate. As ambassador, Arens emerged as an articulate apologist for Israel's incursion into Lebanon in 1982, which he said was undertaken to protect northern Israel from repeated bombardments by the Palestine Liberation Organization and to induce the Syrians to withdraw from Lebanon.

Reportedly becoming more sensitive to American opinions on Israel's Middle Eastern policy, Arens privately encouraged the Likud government to be more open toward Reagan administration proposals, recommending at one point that Begin announce a temporary freeze on new settlements in the Israeli-occupied West Bank, a stratagem inspired by the United States. The massacre in September 1982 by Lebanese Christian Phalangists of several hundred Palestinian refugees in Beirut's Sabra and Shatila camps thrust Arens in the spotlight as Israel's spokesman for the policies of the increasingly controversial Likud government. The state-appointed Kahan Commission's attribution of indirect responsibility for the massacre to four top Israeli officials, including Defense Minister Ariel Sharon, led to a new direction in Arens's political career. The abrasive Sharon remained in the Begin cabinet as minister without portfolio, and Begin named Arens defense minister, a position second in importance only to the prime minister's post.

Political observers widely concurred that the personable Arens, though not expected to be any more lenient on key Middle Eastern issues than his predecessor, would prove far more dispassionate and realistic in his approach to defense policy. Arens assured a group of senior staff members that he was "an organization man" with "a broader and more objective perspective" than many of his compatriots who had taken part in the Lebanese war. The *Jerusalem Post* (February 15, 1983) pronounced him "a pragmatic hawk, who has demonstrated consistently over the past months that he is an independent thinker who is not afraid to change his views."

Unlike Sharon, Arens insisted that Israel maintain its strong ties to Washington, whose support he considered vital to the country's defense. As ambassador, he had often met with Capitol Hill leaders and persuaded Congress to approve $250 million in military aid that would allow Israel to proceed with plans to produce the second-generation Lavi fighter plane, which Arens felt was essential to establishing Israel's military independence. Arens had significantly improved flagging relations between Israelis and Americans, who welcomed his American accent, forthright style, and ability to negotiate without making biblical analogies or overt references to the Holocaust.

Arens took over the top defense post just as relations between the United States and Israel were nearing a critical impasse. When an American marine brandished a pistol in an effort to stop an Israeli tank in war-torn Beirut, Arens persuaded Secretary of Defense Caspar W. Weinberger to open a direct line of communication between American and Israeli troops in Lebanon. He also persuaded the Israeli foreign minister, Yitzhak Shamir, to resume the talks between Israel and the United States that had ceased under Sharon. Effecting a diplomatic coup, he released to the United States information gleaned from Israel's experiences in the Lebanese war. Although Arens maintained that his views on Israel's security requirements had not changed and that closer ties with the United States did not mean compromising Israel's commitment to keeping the occupied territories, the ice was clearly broken.

As the conflict in Lebanon intensified throughout early 1983, Arens stood his ground against domestic pressure for a partial troop pullback, voicing his concern that such a move might permanently partition Lebanon and declaring that Israel would sanction no total withdrawal until the Syrians and the Palestine Liberation Organization agreed to leave Lebanon. Although he continued to support the Likud bloc's controversial West Bank settlement policy and, following the murder of a Jewish student in Hebron in July 1983, authorized the dismissal of the West Bank city's Arab mayor, Arens nonetheless made overtures toward West Bank Arab leaders and reduced the use of force against the region's Palestinian residents.

As defense minister, Arens shored up a demoralized army, repaired Israeli relations with the Druse in Lebanon, and improved communication with opposition Labor leaders in Israel. In July he traveled to Washington with Foreign Minister Shamir to confer with Secretary of State George P. Shultz on the Lebanese confrontation, winning important concessions on increased military aid. In September 1983 Israel withdrew from Lebanon's Shuf Mountains to southern Lebanon, despite American fears of increased bloodshed and dissension among rival factions. That October, Begin stepped down as prime minister, and Yitzhak Shamir assumed the post, journeying to Washington once again with Arens to strengthen resumed American-Israeli relations.

Controversy arose in May 1984 over Arens's presence at the scene of the beating deaths of two captured Arab terrorists who had taken part in the hijacking of a bus the previous month and were later killed by Israeli security forces. The Israeli newspaper *Hadashot*, which defied government censorship to publish a report that revealed Arens had appointed a commission to investigate the suspicious deaths, was shut down for four days. The tabloid later published several previously censored photographs, one of which showed Arens standing with aides near the hijacked bus after directing a rescue attack by security officers. Another photo depicted an apparently unhurt hijacker being led away after his capture, even though Arens had previously asserted that the two captured hijackers died of wounds on the way to the hospital. The ministry report, which determined that both men had been killed before being taken from the site, also cleared Arens and Chief of Staff Moshe Levy of responsibility.

The parliamentary elections of July 1984 found Arens's Herut party and the Likud bloc running a close race with the Labor party. In the absence of a clear majority, a "National Unity" coalition government was formed, with Labor's Shimon Peres as prime minister and Likud's Yitzhak Shamir as foreign minister. Because of the stalemate, Peres and Shamir signed an agreement that they would switch jobs in October 1986. In his new post as minister without portfolio, Arens traveled to Washington in December 1985 on a confidential mission to discuss with Secretary of State Shultz the case of Jonathan Jay Pollard, a former United States Navy intelligence analyst who sold American military documents to the Israelis. Arens and other officials were later cleared of any direct knowledge of the operation.

At its March 1986 convention, the Herut party, bereft of the stability of Begin's leadership, was rocked by an internal power struggle that erupted into scuffling and name-calling. Herut leaders found themselves faced with a Labor party resolution calling on Prime Minister Peres not to honor the rotation agreement, but Peres eventually did turn the post over to Shamir, who subsequently gave Arens responsibility for Israeli-Arab affairs.

In September 1987 Arens resigned from the cabinet to protest its decision to abandon production of the Lavi fighter. As Shamir's closest ally, Arens was the subject of speculation that his resignation might reduce the likelihood that he would succeed Shamir as Likud leader. The November 1988 elections resulted in yet another stalemate that led to the formation a month later of a new Labor-Likud coalition government, headed by Yitzhak Shamir, that was determined to quell the yearlong Palestinian *intifada*.

Although the chairman of the Palestine Liberation Organization, Yasir Arafat, had at last recognized Israel's right to exist and renounced terrorism, thus inspiring the outgoing Reagan administration to agree to talks with leaders of the organization, the new National Unity coalition declined to drop Israel's longstanding refusal to negotiate with the PLO. In the wake of an attempted guerrilla attack on Israel the following February, Moshe Arens harshly criticized the United States and other Western nations. In March 1989 Arens met with Egypt's president, Hosni Mubarak, and Soviet negotiator Eduard A. Shevardnadze in Cairo. Arens rebuffed Shevardnadze's invitation to attend a UN-sponsored international peace conference that was to include representatives of the PLO, and the Soviet mediator refused to restore full diplomatic relations between Israel and Moscow.

In the following week, Arens castigated left-wing Knesset members who met with leaders of the dovish Peace Now movement and members of the PLO at a New York symposium. He traveled to Washington in April 1989 for a week-long round of talks intended to pave the way for Prime Minister Shamir to discuss a possible joint peace initiative in the Middle East, but the Bush administration demurred, asking instead that both Israel and the PLO take steps to ease tensions in the region. Members of the Senate Foreign Relations Committee informed Arens that, though official United States support for Israel remained strong, American public opinion on Israel's response to the *intifada* was eroding.

But Arens maintained that the only way to resolve the situation in the occupied territories was through negotiations among Israel, Jordan, and "truly representative" local Palestinians, rather than the Palestine Liberation Organization. Yet the proposal appeared destined for failure, since Arens's request for help from the United States was not sympathetically received. Speaking before the Conference of Presidents of Major American Jewish Organizations in New York in April, Arens appeared to relent to a degree, insisting that Israel was ready to negotiate with Palestinians in the West Bank and Gaza "even if some of them turn out to be PLO sympathizers."

Arens returned to Washington in May 1989 to promote the Shamir government's proposal allowing Palestinians in the occupied territories to hold elections offering limited self-rule during a five-year transitional period. He still firmly ruled out any possible role for the PLO, which he accused of trying to "scuttle" the election plan. On May 19 Arens urged the United States to promote Israel's initiative and to lead an international effort to raise $2 billion to fund housing, jobs, and education for Palestinians in refugee camps. His suggestion that President Bush join Shamir and Mubarak in a summit was received coolly by administration officials.

In October 1989 the Israeli Cabinet rejected Hosni Mubarak's offer to serve as host for direct talks between the Israelis and the Palestinians in Cairo. Arens said, as quoted in the *New York Times* (October 8, 1989), that accepting the invitation would have been "equivalent to proposing a meeting with a PLO delegation." A few weeks later, however, in a letter to Secretary of State James A. Baker 3d, Arens accepted "in principle" the United States's five-point proposal for an Israeli-Palestinian dialogue, although he had some "reservations" about certain points. Arens's reservations related to his desire for guarantees that the PLO would not be involved and that any discussions would be confined to "arrangements" for elections in the occupied West Bank and Gaza Strip. On November 2, 1989 the Israeli government announced its qualified endorsement of the American plan after Baker made what Joel Brinkley of the *New York Times* (November 3, 1989) described as "essentially minor modifications."

The slight, balding Arens wears wire-rimmed spectacles, which give him a diffident appearance that belies his firm adherence to matters of principle. Dubbed "Dr. Strangelove" by critics who consider his behavior enigmatic, he is an instinctive diplomat with a flair for building political alliances. As Eitan Haber of the conservative Israeli daily paper *Yedioth Aharanoth* has written, Arens "is a hawk in his views but wears silk gloves on his nails. He is so pleasant, dry, and boring, yet so human and fair, that it is difficult to fight him and it is hard to find someone who would say a bad word about him." Arens, who speaks rapid, barely accented English, has been described as urbane, cool, logical, reserved, and unemotional. He and

his wife, Muriel, have four grown children. As an American official and friend of Arens told a reporter from *Time* (January 2, 1989) magazine, "It will be tough to strike a deal with Arens. But if you have a deal, it sticks."

References: International Who's Who, 1989-90; International Year Book and Statesmen's Who's Who, 1989; Who's Who in Israel, 1985-86

Atwater, Lee

Feb. 27, 1951– Chairman of the Republican National Committee; political consultant. Address: Republican National Committee, 310 First St., S.E., Washington, D.C. 20003

The first professional political consultant to head either of the country's major political parties, Lee Atwater is the leader of a combative new breed of baby-boom Republicans who believe that their party has accepted minority status for too long, and who are determined to make the GOP the dominant political organization in the United States by the year 2000. Atwater orchestrated the successful presidential campaigns of Ronald Reagan in 1984 and of George Bush in 1988. It was the Bush campaign that established him as the recognized master of "negative" campaigning, the object of which is to achieve victory by attacking one's opponent on such "values" issues as crime, gun control, taxes, welfare reform, national defense, abortion, and school prayer.

According to Gerald M. Boyd of the *New York Times* (May 30, 1988), Lee Atwater "sees politics as a sort of nonlethal but still intense warfare." That bare-knuckle approach has made him extremely controversial, and the increasing popularity of his tactics among others in his profession has created concern in some quarters. "Lee Atwater did not invent the campaign consultancy business," Eric Alterman wrote in his profile of the Republican chairman for the *New York Times Magazine* (April 30, 1989), "but he may be the person most responsible for the way it's practiced today." By his own admission, Atwater takes little interest in the intricacies of government. "My job," he told David Remnick for an *Esquire* (December 1986) interview, "is the politics of politics. . . . The contest, the winning and losing thing is big for me. I can't stand to lose. . . . When I lose I get physically sick." But as Atwater also explained in his interview with Boyd, "I play to win. But I play by the rules. . . . Is it a matter of winning at all costs? No, that doesn't work because there is too much scrutiny. You have to follow a code, and if you don't you're going to get burned and your candidate is going to get burned."

Harvey Leroy Atwater was born on February 27, 1951 in Atlanta, Georgia, the older of the two sons of Harvey Dillard Atwater, an insurance claims adjuster, and Alma (Page) Atwater, a teacher. When Lee was five, his younger brother, Joe, died of burns suffered in a kitchen accident. Recalling his brother's death in the interview with David Remnick, Atwater said, "I think I learned pretty early that in the end, it's only you. To an extent, you're all alone." The Atwaters often moved during Lee's early childhood, before finally settling in Columbia, South Carolina when he was nine. An energetic and restless child, Lee Atwater was interested in wrestling and music. At A. C. Flora High School, he also distinguished himself as something of a prankster by publishing a scurrilous underground newspaper called *Big At's Comedy Ratings* and, as an eleventh grader, by delivering an oral book report on the Columbia telephone directory. "He said it jumped around too much from character to character without sustaining any of them," Robert C. Ellenburg, Atwater's English teacher, recalled to Eric Alterman. "He predicted it would have to be revised next year." Making his debut as a political consultant, Atwater organized his fellow student David Yon's tongue-in-cheek campaign for the office of student-body president. "I made up a whole lot of phony issues for him to run on," Atwater told David Remnick. Those spurious "issues" included free beer in the cafeteria, unlimited absences from class, and the abolition of grades lower than B's. Yon won, but the school principal called for another election.

By his senior year in high school, Atwater's interest in music had intensified. With a few classmates, he formed a white "soul" band called the Upsetter's Review, which performed all over South Carolina and which also sometimes played behind such nationally known acts as Percy Sledge and the Drifters. He begged his parents to allow him to continue playing with the band after high school, but they insisted that he attend college.

Largely because he had devoted so much of his time to playing music, Atwater's high school grades were so poor (even his mother, a Spanish teacher, gave him a D minus) that the only college that would accept him was nearby Newberry College, which did so only after Mrs. Atwater arranged a personal consultation with its admissions officer.

In the summer after his sophomore year at Newberry, Atwater, again at his mother's prompting, obtained an internship in the Washington office of South Carolina's longtime conservative Republican senator, J. Strom Thurmond. That experience, his first with national politics, had a profound effect upon him. According to David Remnick, Atwater studied Thurmond "the way hitters used to watch Ted Williams practice." "Boy did I learn from that man," Atwater told Remnick. Hooked on politics, Atwater immediately joined the College Republicans when he returned to school that fall. As he explained to Gerald M. Boyd, his decision to align himself with the GOP was motivated to some degree by the party's stance on individual freedom and partly by other considerations. "When I got into politics in South Carolina the establishment was all Democrats and I was anti-establishment," he told Boyd. "The young Democrats were all the guys running around in three-piece suits, smoking cigars, and cutting deals, so I said, 'Hell, I'm a Republican.'"

At the time that Atwater joined the South Carolina College Republicans, the state's largest schools, Clemson University and the University of South Carolina, controlled the organization, and smaller institutions such as Newberry had much less influence. Setting out to remedy that situation, Atwater asked the larger schools for a constitutional convention and, to his surprise, they agreed. Within a matter of months, the smaller colleges had taken control of the College Republicans, and Atwater had been elected state chairman, an office he used to establish Thurmond organizations at colleges throughout South Carolina. During his junior year at Newberry, Atwater managed his first campaign, helping William Edens to get elected mayor of Forest Acres, South Carolina. The following year, he was chosen as a delegate to the Republican National Convention in Miami.

By the time he received his B.A. degree in history from Newberry in 1973, Atwater had been appointed executive director of the College Republicans' national office in Washington, D.C. There, he first made the acquaintance of George Bush, who was then chairman of the Republican National Committee. The two men began meeting regularly, and Bush took such a personal interest in Atwater that on one occasion he lent the young man the use of his boat for a date with Sally Dunbar, who eventually became his wife. "Here was this guy, the chairman of the party, who took an interest in me and befriended me at a time when there was no obvious interest in it for him," Atwater told Gerald M. Boyd. "I became a big fan."

In 1974 Atwater returned to Columbia, South Carolina, where he established the political consulting firm Baker & Associates. (There was no one named Baker at the firm, and Atwater at first had no associates. He named the agency after a man named Baker whose portrait he had purchased at a garage sale.) His first year in the campaign consulting business was a rough one: he managed two campaigns (William Westmoreland for governor and Carroll Campbell for lieutenant governor) and lost both of them. "I was in over my head," Atwater, who at the time was just twenty-three years old, admitted in the interview with Boyd. "I felt I never wanted to get in that situation again, so I decided to learn from the bottom up."

For the next four years Atwater organized campaigns for local Republican office seekers in the South, racking up twenty-eight wins, before moving on, in 1978, to J. Strom Thurmond's campaign for reelection to the United States Senate. It was in that campaign that Atwater first used the "negative" campaign tactics for which he later gained notoriety. He learned that Thurmond's Democratic opponent, Charles Ravenel, had reportedly made a comment at a New York City fund-raiser about being embarrassed to be from South Carolina and expressing a desire to be the "third senator from New York." (Ravenel later denied ever making the remark.) Atwater immediately ran a commercial focusing on Ravenel's alleged comment, and the challenger's negative rating in the polls soon jumped from 12 percent to 43 percent. On election day, Thurmond was returned to office with 56 percent of the vote.

In the same year, Atwater managed Carroll Campbell's first congressional race. In the course of the campaign, a third-party candidate, allegedly at Atwater's urging, attacked the Democratic candidate, Max Heller, a Jew, for refusing to believe "that Jesus Christ has come yet," a remark that highlighted Heller's Jewishness in what is predominantly a Protestant state. Campbell won easily. Following the election, Atwater strongly denied any complicity in the attack, insisting it had occurred before he had become directly involved in Campbell's campaign.

In 1980 Lee Atwater was accused of employing "dirty tricks" tactics in a South Carolina congressional race between the Republican contender, Floyd Spence, and the Democrat, Tom Turnipseed. At a Turnipseed press briefing, a reporter who had allegedly been "planted" by Atwater rose and said that he understood that Turnipseed had formerly undergone psychiatric treatment and electroshock therapy. Turnipseed protested, but Atwater told reporters he would not respond to someone who, in his words, had once been "hooked up to jumper cables" (a comment for which he later apologized), and he insisted that he had not planted the reporter. Yet while Atwater has maintained his innocence in both the Turnipseed and Heller controversies, he has also said of his early days in South Carolina politics, "We had to use guerrilla tactics. Republicans in the South could not win elections by talking about issues. You had to make the case that the other guy, the other candidate, was a bad guy."

As manager of Ronald Reagan's 1980 South Carolina primary campaign, Atwater became embroiled in controversy once more. After learning that George Bush, also a contender for that year's Republican presidential nomination, had once supported gun-control legislation, Atwater hired Reid Buckley, the brother of the influential conservative editor and author William F. Buckley, to tape a radio commercial attacking Bush's position. But the voice on the commercial was identified only as "Mr. Buckley," leaving many listeners with the impression that William F. Buckley had branded George Bush a moderate who would attempt to limit their right to bear arms, a cherished prerogative in South Carolina. Bush was forced to go on the defensive, and Reagan won the primary in a landslide.

After the Republicans closed ranks, Atwater became the southern regional director for the Reagan-Bush ticket, which went on to carry every southern state except Georgia as part of a forty-four state landslide, and in 1980 he also managed six successful congressional campaigns. Following Reagan's inauguration, Atwater, at the age of twenty-nine, became special assistant to the president for political affairs. He remained in that post until 1984, when he was appointed director of the Reagan-Bush reelection campaign, steering the incumbents to an easy victory over the Democratic ticket of Walter F. Mondale and Geraldine A. Ferraro. Returning to the private sector, he then signed on as a partner with the Washington firm Black, Manafort & Stone, political consultants. In 1986 George Bush asked Atwater to serve as chairman of his political-action committee, the $5 million Fund for America's Future, which was used, in part, to get the "Bush-in-'88" campaign rolling. After laying the groundwork for that campaign, Atwater was asked, in February 1987, to become manager of the George Bush for President Committee.

The Bush campaign got off to a disappointing start, as the candidate finished third in the Iowa caucuses in January, trailing both Senator Robert J. Dole of Kansas and Pat Robertson, the religious broadcaster. Late polls showed Bush running behind Dole in February's New Hampshire primary, but the vice-president rebounded to win, went on to sweep the so-called Super Tuesday primaries in the South, and won the Republican nomination going away. The Bush-Dole battle was a heated one in which both candidates resorted to personal attacks on the other's character. At one point, Dole accused Atwater of being behind a series of disclosures about the personal finances of his wife, Elizabeth Hanford Dole, who had resigned from her position as secretary of transportation to work on her husband's campaign. Atwater responded by calling Dole "a typical schoolyard bully," adding, "He can dish it out but if someone hits him back, he starts whining." In addition, Atwater sent Dole a ten-page letter, in which he detailed negative campaign tactics that he said the senator had used against Bush.

In the general election campaign, Atwater masterminded the Republican strategy of depicting Governor Michael S. Dukakis of Massachusetts, the Democratic nominee, as being soft on national defense and crime. That strategy was highlighted by a controversial television spot featuring a convicted murderer named Willie Horton who, while on a weekend furlough from a Massachusetts state prison, committed a rape. In a speech to a group of Republican activists in early June, Atwater had reportedly said, "If I can make Willie Horton a household name, we'll win the election." Some observers detected racist overtones in the Republican attacks, since Horton is black and the woman he raped is white, but Atwater repeatedly insisted to reporters that the issue was crime, not race. And in the interview with Eric Alterman, he downplayed his role in the entire affair, saying he personally prohibited the use of any pictures of Horton in campaign ads and wrote to Bush campaign groups around the country, requesting that they stop all Horton-related television spots. "As a white southerner," Atwater told Alterman, "I have always known I had to go the extra mile to avoid being tagged a racist by liberal northerners. If anybody from the South says or does anything, it's racially motivated. I defy you to find any other campaign I have done where race has become the issue. . . . Race, politically, is a loser."

Atwater's key role in Bush's successful bid for the presidency established him as the most prominent political consultant in the United States. When, on November 17, 1988, Bush named him chairman of the Republican National Committee, succeeding Frank Fahrenkopf, who had announced his intention to resign when his term expired in January 1989, Lee Atwater became the first professional campaign consultant designated to lead either of the nation's major political parties. In commenting on Atwater's appointment, E. J. Dionne Jr. of the New York Times (November 18, 1988) wrote, "For Mr. Atwater, for whom politics is the love, and government simply the thing that happens after a campaign, this job is just right." Quickly establishing an agenda for the party, Atwater announced that the GOP would attempt to break the Democratic party's thirty-five-year hold on the House of Representatives by targeting, in each election year, twenty to thirty Democratic incumbents who appear to be most vulnerable and by recruiting highly qualified Republicans to oppose them. Atwater also pledged himself to continue the Republican effort, begun during Fahrenkopf's administration, to gain control of as many governorships and state legislatures as possible in order to block Democratic gerrymandering of congressional district lines following the 1990 census. (The GOP has received about 48 percent of the composite vote in recent races for the House of Representatives but controls only about 40 percent of the seats in that body.)

The most ambitious of Atwater's strategies involves the recruiting into the Republican camp of blacks and other minorities who have traditionally supported the Democratic party. In an Op-Ed article that appeared in the New York Times (February 26, 1989), Atwater wrote: "Making black voters welcome in the Republican party is my preeminent goal. . . . If our party is to step out of minority status it must be the party of all Americans. Anything short of that is unacceptable." He kicked off his effort to court black support even before officially taking over as GOP chairman on January 18, 1989. Three days earlier, on the anniversary of Martin Luther King Jr.'s birthday, he visited the Atlanta church where Dr. King had once preached, and he organized an all-star rhythm-and-blues revue to perform at one of George Bush's inaugural parties. The show featured several prominent black R&B performers, including Willie Dixon, Bo Diddley, and Sam Moore. (Atwater himself also sang and played the guitar.)

In February 1989 Atwater was appointed to the board of trustees of Howard University in Washington, D.C., one of the nation's most prestigious black colleges. The new GOP chief then endured two major setbacks in his campaign to entice blacks into the party, the first of which was the election of David Duke, a former grand wizard of the Ku Klux Klan, to the Louisiana state legislature as a Republican. Atwater not only quickly denounced Duke as a "charlatan" and had the Republican National Committee censure him, but he also taped a commercial for play on black radio stations, condemning him. A New York Times (February 22, 1989) editorial, however, after taking Atwater to task for his part in the Willie Horton television campaign, said he "inescapably" bore "some responsibility for making the Republicans so vulnerable to such racist infiltration." His problems were exacerbated when, on March 6, 1989, 200 Howard University students seized the school's main administration building to protest his appointment to the board of trustees. The students blamed Atwater for what they believed were racial innuendos in Bush's presidential campaign, especially the Willie Horton affair. A day later, Atwater reluctantly resigned from the board of Howard University.

Controversy continued to swirl around Lee Atwater in the summer of 1989. In early June, Mark Goodin, the communications director of the Republican National Committee, circulated a memo to some 200 GOP leaders entitled "Tom Foley: Out of the Liberal Closet." The memo compared the voting record of Foley, a Democrat from Washington, who had recently been elected Speaker of the House of Representatives, to that of Democratic congressman Barney Frank of Massachusetts, a staunch liberal and an acknowledged homosexual. The memo's title and the selection of Frank for comparison caused some Democrats to accuse the Republicans of implying that Foley too was homosexual. Summoned to the White House by President George Bush, Atwater denied any involvement in the preparation of the memo. He subsequently apologized to Foley, and he asked for and received Goodin's resignation. Although some Democrats called for Atwater's resignation in the wake of the Foley controversy, Bush remained loyal to his longtime friend, and Atwater's position was further strengthened when the Republican National Committee unanimously adopted a resolution supporting its chairman.

Atwater made headlines again in mid-June when he delivered a highly partisan address at the annual United States Conference of Mayors meeting, which, by tradition, is a nonpartisan gathering. During the speech, Atwater said the Republicans would make a determined effort to win the 1989 mayoral election in New York City and thereby establish a "political beachhead" in the nation's big cities.

In his *Esquire* profile, David Remnick described Lee Atwater as "wiry, sandy-haired, quick-eyed, and tight-mouthed, . . . a great mass of nerves and energy, a complex of tics and vibrations." Atwater and his wife, the former Sally Dunbar, whom he married on June 24, 1978, live with their two daughters, Sarah Lee and Ashley Page, in a small townhouse in downtown Washington. His two chief avocational interests are reading (both fiction and nonfiction) and rhythm-and-blues. The owner of six guitars, one of which was a gift from Ron

Wood of the Rolling Stones, Atwater also possesses an extensive collection of blues tapes. On visits to Columbia, South Carolina, he sometimes performs at Bullwinkle's, a local nightclub. The chairman typically puts in twelve- to fifteen-hour workdays, beginning with a meeting with his senior staff at 7:00 in the morning and usually ending with an evening speaking engagement or fund-raising appearance. Lee Atwater received an M.A. degree in journalism from the University of South Carolina in 1977, and he is in the midst of completing a doctoral dissertation on negative campaigning at the same institution. Although he usually eats only one meal a day, Atwater douses all of his food in hot pepper sauce, and he is part-owner of a barbecued-rib restaurant in the Washington suburb of Arlington, Virginia. His religious affiliation is Methodist.

References: Esquire 106:280+ D '86 pors; *N Y Times* A p11 My 30 '88 por, D p19 N 18 '88 por, p8 F 25 '89 por, D p23 F 26 '89; *N Y Times Mag* p31+ Ap 30 '89 pors; *Time* 133:27+ Mr 20 '89 pors; *U S News* 106:18+ Ja 23 '89 por; *Washington Post* B p6 Ap 22 '86 por

---

Augér, Arleen
(ō-zhā)

Sept. 13, 1939– Soprano. Address: b. c/o IMG Artists, 22 E. 71st St., New York, N.Y. 10021; h. 14 Townsend Ave., Hartsdale, N.Y. 10530

Since the late 1960s the soprano Arleen Augér has been renowned—and revered—throughout Europe for her opera, concert, and recital singing. With more than 140 releases to her credit, she is among the world's most recorded classical singers. Yet although she was born and reared in southern California, she was virtually unknown in the United States until the early 1980s. Her performances in concert halls in the United States have been greeted with delight. Describing Miss Augér's voice in an article for *Connoisseur* (January 1986) as a "ravishing, crystal-clear, lyric soprano," Barbara Jepson called the singer "a vocal chameleon" because "her voice changes tone and timbre frequently, mellifluous one moment, dark-hued and earthy the next."

Miss Augér's power springs also from her earnest desire to communicate closely with her audience, especially during song recitals. "Intimacy is the quality I seek," she told Daniel Webster in an interview for the *Philadelphia Inquirer* (February 18, 1988). "I have to make [the audience] realize that music is for *them*," she said. "A song is a very personal experience—or should be—and I try to make each one express something for each individual." In the opinion of at least one music critic, she achieved the intimacy she sought: "Hers

is the art of the microcosm, the details, the fine points. She sings the music as if she meant it, addressing the listeners as if she had something to say to them. That's what singing is all about," Melinda Bargreen wrote in the *Seattle Times* (October 31, 1984). Perhaps equally important to her success is the pleasure in performing she exudes. "This is a singer who loves to sing, and for all the right reasons," Bernard Holland noted in the *New York Times* (September 14, 1986).

Arleen Augér was born in Los Angeles on September 13, 1939 to Everett N. Augér, a French Canadian Protestant minister from Moose Jaw, Saskatchewan, and Doris (Moody) Augér, an American of British descent. Growing up in Long Beach, California, Miss Augér had little exposure to classical music and no voice training, although she took violin and piano lessons. She began singing at the age of fourteen in women's clubs and churches but grew up "vocally isolated," as she told Heidi Waleson in an interview for Ovation (March 1987). Miss Augér attended high school in Huntington Beach, and, after earning her B.A. degree in education from California State University at Long Beach in 1963, she taught music in Chicago, Denver, and Los Angeles for the following four years.

Not until she was in her mid-twenties did Miss Augér undertake voice lessons. In 1965 she began studying with Ralph Errolle, a former bel canto tenor, in Chicago. Two years later, she took a step that would permanently alter the course of her career. Prompted by the need to supplement her earnings as a first-grade teacher in Los Angeles, she entered the I. Victor Fuchs Competition, a music contest held in California. She won first prize, which included an audition with the Volksoper in Vienna, one of Austria's two principal opera companies.

Her audition, in which she sang one of Mozart's arias for the Queen of the Night in The Magic Flute, was so impressive that the Staatsoper invited her to audition the following day. In contrast to the complete absence of job offers that greeted her auditioning "for anyone who would listen" in the United States two months earlier, her audition with the Staatsoper, or Vienna State Opera, resulted immediately in a two-year contract. "The only role I knew at the time was the Queen of the Night," she told Joseph McLellan in an interview for the Washington Post (September 10, 1986). "But that was the role they needed immediately."

With little formal training and no stage experience, no repertoire, and virtually no knowledge of German, Arleen Augér launched her professional singing career. "I was absolutely a babe in the woods," she told Heidi Waleson in an interview for the New York Times (January 22, 1984). Recalling her first role with the Vienna State Opera during an interview with Marilyn Chase for the Wall Street Journal (August 16, 1984), Miss Augér said, "I . . . was coached by a Czech, so all my lines were in a Czech dialect. There was no rehearsal, and no time for stage directions. On performance night, I was pushed out onto the stage, and asked three performers where I was supposed to go. They pretended not to understand."

Miss Augér learned a dozen roles during her first two years with the Vienna Opera, and her repertoire with the company eventually included such parts as Olympia in Offenbach's Tales of Hoffmann, Najade in Richard Strauss's Ariadne auf Naxos, Constanze in Mozart's Abduction from the Seraglio, Micaela in Bizet's Carmen, and Gilda in Verdi's Rigoletto—"all those sickeningly nice girls," she once called them.

After at first expanding her repertoire, the soprano found her talent circumscribed by the rigid fach system, in which female singers were assigned roles only within a single narrow category. That restriction was made doubly irksome by the contrast between her voice and her size. "Even when I was starvingly thin," the statuesque soprano recalled during the interview with Barbara Jepson for Connoisseur, "I was tall for my category of voice. I had a light, lyric coloratura soprano and should have been singing soubrettes, but I was not the type to play those roles onstage. I'm more easily cast as a woman than a girl, and I always was that way. Then, too, many tenors come up to my shoulder."

Another disadvantage of performing with the Vienna State Opera was its volatile and intrigue-ridden atmosphere. During her seven years with the company, there were four directors. Furthermore, Miss Augér's schedule with the Vienna Opera was so demanding that her freedom to take advantage of outside opportunities was severely limited, though she did find time in 1969 to make a highly praised New York City Opera debut as the Queen of the Night. In 1970 she began to resist such constraints by branching out into art-song recitals. That year, Erik Werba, a noted Viennese piano accompanist, asked her to sing Hugo Wolf's difficult Italienisches Liederbuch in a series he hosted annually at the composer's summer home. She loved the music for its intimacy, and from 1970 on she has continued to give such recitals.

Miss Augér's dissatisfaction with the Vienna State Opera, coupled with her desire for independence and broader opportunities, prompted her to refuse a full-time contract. "My colleagues thought I was crazy," she has recalled during several interviews. "I would have had tenure." But she was willing to sacrifice a measure of security for artistic liberty. In 1974 she left the company for a university teaching position at the Hochschule für Musik und Darstellende Kunst in Frankfurt, Germany, where she taught until 1987. She also taught master classes at the International Summer Academy Mozarteum in Salzburg, Austria from 1974 to 1977. Teaching gave her the freedom to increase her concert and recital singing. Despite her full schedule, she did not relinquish opera entirely, and in 1975, for example, she made her La Scala debut in Milan, Italy in Ravel's L'enfant et les sortilèges.

In 1974, shortly after she relinquished her position with the Vienna State Opera, Miss Augér's talent was called upon in much the same last-minute fashion as her initiation into opera singing seven years earlier. Helmuth Rilling, a German conductor noted for his Bach interpretations, needed a last-minute replacement for a member of an ensemble he was taking to Japan to sing Bach's St. Matthew Passion and Haydn's Creation. He asked Arleen Augér to substitute. With no time to prepare in advance, she learned her role on the plane en route to Japan and rehearsed only once with the group in Osaka before going onstage. That experience began a long and productive relationship with

Rilling, with whom she recorded forty albums of Bach cantatas and other sacred music over a ten-year period.

Arleen Augér did not regret her decision to free herself from the Vienna State Opera, for performing in concerts was, she discovered, a joy. "I find that there is a personal contact with the audience that is often missing in opera, and this rapport helps my singing," she told Patrick J. Smith in an interview for *Musical America* (August 1984). She became a specialist in the music of Haydn, Handel, and Mozart, as well as Bach—a repertoire "not usually associated with that of an opera singer," as Smith noted in his article.

Despite her growing celebrity as one of the leading singers of baroque music in the world, Miss Augér seldom performed in her native United States, a lack of exposure that she attributes to managerial factors. Bookings in Europe were easily secured; but in the United States, according to Joseph McLellan's article for the *Washington Post*, she was neglected by her agent at Columbia Artists Management. "The breaking point came in 1978, when I made my Metropolitan Opera debut in *Fidelio* with Karl Böhm," Miss Augér told McLellan. "My agent at Columbia knew I was in New York and made no effort to contact me. Finally one day, out walking on the street, I saw my agent and recognized her, but she didn't recognize me. That was the end."

Reviewing Miss Augér's New York Metropolitan Opera debut for the *New York Times* (October 10, 1978), one critic wrote that she sang "buoyantly in elegant style and acted the part to perfection." That year Miss Augér also began singing for the summer Oregon Bach Festival. Blanche Moyse, a violinist and the director of the New England Bach Festival in Vermont, heard her sing in Oregon with Rilling in 1980 and began booking her for concerts at the New England Bach Festival the following season.

By 1984 Arleen Augér had toured the world ten times, had sung in more than forty music festivals in Europe, and had released more than 130 recordings. In January of that year she added to her list of accomplishments by giving her New York recital debut at Alice Tully Hall. Accompanied by the pianist Dalton Baldwin, she sang light German and French songs, including Mozart's "Das Veilchen," Schumann's "Aufträge," Debussy's "Mandoline," and Richard Strauss's "Hat gesagt, bleibt's nicht dabei." Peter G. Davis, in his review of her recital for *New York* (February 13, 1984) magazine, described her voice as "a luscious, smoothly rounded, cuddly tone that floats comfortably on the breath and negotiates every difficulty with the ease and purity of a finely tuned instrument." He added that her "special vocal gifts are complemented, enhanced, and further defined by her physical presence. Statuesque, titian-haired, and supremely self-confident, she strongly suggests that Teutonic feminine ideal embodied by all those archetypal heroines of romantic German opera: devoted, sensitive, modest, and vulnerable creatures who also exude a tantalizing aura, vague but unmistakable, of suppressed sensuality."

In the summer of 1984 Miss Augér returned to the Oregon Bach Festival, where her "echo" aria from the Christmas Oratorio was the "high point of the festival," according to Marilyn Chase of the *Wall Street Journal* (August 16, 1984). "Hers is a rounded, pliant, honeyed tone, so firmly grounded in mature technique and interpretation that she is able to soar above technique to the transcendent realms where exciting art begins."

Arleen Augér again drew raves in the summer of 1985, when she sang the title role in Handel's knotty *Alcina* with the Opera Stage company in London. She repeated the role in November 1986 for her Los Angeles opera debut with the Los Angeles Music Center Opera. Stephen Pettitt reviewed her performance for the (London) *Financial Times* (July 17, 1985): "In this role Arleen Augér shows commanding presence and a technique which is truly athletic. She decorates some of her *da capos* with real fire, deliberately testing the extent of her own compass." Martin Bernheimer, the music critic for the *Los Angeles Times*, wrote in his review of November 6, 1986: "In the virtually impossible title role, Arleen Augér looked appealingly devilish . . . and sang like an angel. We knew she would toss off the fioritura with nonchalant accuracy. We thought she would sing with sweetness and purity, with endless breath and expressive point, even with reasonable heft in the climactic outbursts. But we didn't know that she could be such a compelling, subtle, sensuous actress." For Angel Records, Arleen Augér also recorded *Alcina*, which had not been done for twenty years, delighting Robert Levine of the *Ovation* (November 1987) record review with her "spectacular pyrotechnics coupled with great attention to the text. The depth of feeling she exhibits . . . could move one to tears. This is a lush, silvery voice, fearless at both ends of the register, and rock-solid in between."

In January 1986, appearing with the redoubtable Dalton Baldwin as her accompanist in her first recital at the Ninety-second Street YMHA in New York City, Arleen Augér sang a program of lieder by Schubert, Wolf, and Mahler. "Her sustained high notes, her ornamental turns and above all her expressive shadings of pitch were the work of a vocal master. . . . But her real skills as a lieder singer, beyond the idiomatic excellence of her German, lie in her ability to point up psychological subtleties of text. She is a real Wagnerian in that regard," John Rockwell wrote in his review for the *New York Times* (January 25, 1986).

Arleen Augér's singing of Beethoven, Haydn, and Mozart that spring at Merkin Hall's On Original Instruments series of concerts sent the *New Yorker's* Andrew Porter, long an ardent fan, scurrying to the phone at intermission. "It was an evening of bliss without alloy . . . ," he wrote in his review of May 26, 1986. "Her tone had a beauty, freshness, and purity to dissolve listeners into an ecstasy of delight. Vocal sound of this quality is rare today, and the usual epithets of approval seem inadequate. Let me relate, to suggest my enthusiasm, that at the start of the intermission, after Miss Augér's Haydn group, I telephoned to friends within reach urging them to drop whatever they were doing and hasten to Merkin Hall (where there were just one or two seats still empty) to hear Miss Augér sing Mozart." Porter compared her singing to the young Lisa della Casa "at her most limpid" and the young Irmgard Seefried. "The directness of Miss Augér's singing, the beauty of her timbre, and the grace of her phrasing conspired to make this the finest lieder singing I have heard in years."

In July 1986 Arleen Augér sang before the largest audience of her life—300 million people—when she performed Mozart's *Exsultate, Jubilate* at the televised royal wedding of Prince Andrew and Sarah Ferguson in Westminster Abbey in London. It was a particular honor to be chosen as the first American to sing at a British royal wedding, especially when there were many fine English singers who could have been selected in her stead. Although thrilled to be invited to sing at the wedding, Miss Augér was dismayed to discover that television commentators had been talking during her performance. Heidi Waleson quoted her in the interview for *Ovation* as saying: "I felt like just another float in the Rose Bowl parade."

On rare occasions, critics have faulted Miss Augér for a lack of ease in high, forceful passages and for a "lack of hot-bloodedness." But even those imperfections have been attributed to her overall excellence. "Miss Augér's soprano technique and her musicality is so suffused with elegance . . . that shedding it seems impossible," Bernard Holland wrote for the *New York Times* (March 1, 1988) of her performance in a recital at Alice Tully Hall in the spring of 1988, which included an aria from Donizetti's *La Zingara*. "This is a voice with limits—it does not explode with vocal power nor can it overwhelm us with emotional ferocity. Yet Miss Augér prospers within her limitations—indeed, makes a virtue of them."

That elegance was also praised by Daniel Webster, the *Philadelphia Inquirer's* music critic, in his review of a Wayne (Pennsylvania) Concert Series recital in February 1988: "Augér's voice is brightly focused and almost perfectly placed. She gave the impression that each note had been thought out not only for its own weight, but for its place in the seamless musical line. Her control of placement and pitch enabled her to sing some notable soft high phrases with such clarity that they rang with the solidity of a more dramatic voice." The program was an amalgam of diverse eras and nationalities, with songs by Purcell, Mahler, Rossini, Handel, Mozart, Aaron Copland, and Lee Hoiby.

Such heterogeneity is typical of Arleen Augér, who had spent years resisting categorization as strictly a Bach and Mozart singer. "The more you can do, the more exciting the business is and the more you can keep your voice oiled. To have the widest variety of activity for the vocal cords as well as for the brain is certainly better for the overall

person. So I'm getting out of any boxes that anyone ever put me in," she said in the interview with Heidi Waleson for the *New York Times* profile. On a broader level, too, she insists on diversity. "I like to keep a mix of opera, concert, and recitals," Miss Augér said in the interview with Patrick J. Smith for *Musical America.*

One of Arleen Augér's reasons for turning her attention to the United States in 1984 was to broaden her opportunities. As she explained in an article she wrote for *Keynote* (August 1985), singers "are more readily 'typed" in Europe than in the United States. "Americans," she said, "have a desire to be as versatile as possible and to push back any barriers." At the end of her article she entreated her compatriots to recognize her versatility: "I sing Bach, Mozart, contemporary works, and everything in between. If it's for my voice, and my voice can do it well, I am happy to do it."

Although she still sings more frequently in Europe than in her native country, Miss Augér has acknowledged that her career possibilities have indeed increased since her American debut. "I've been fortunate that the major orchestras have opened themselves to me with other repertoire," she told Heidi Waleson for the *Ovation* interview. "Now, for the first time, I'm starting to have some choice in what I sing. Here in America, they are starting to say, 'We'd like to have Arleen Augér. What would she like to sing?'"

One consequence of Arleen Augér's expansion to recital and concert singing is that she has very little time to herself. "It does mean a lot of travel and wear and tear from airports and hotels, but that's the price you pay. When you come down to it, all you need is a place to put your alarm clock," she said, as quoted in the *London Evening Standard* (July 8, 1988). She does have a permanent home, in Hartsdale, New York, but spends little time there. The amount of traveling demanded of her also leaves little time to cultivate relationships. In an interview with the London *Daily Mail* (May 5, 1987), she said, "Naturally, I hope to have a relationship of value when I stop singing, but until then I choose to make my business my personal life as well. You get used to your own company when you're in a different town each night."

The five-foot, eight-inch soprano, "whose voluptuousness recalls that of ancient fertility goddesses," in the opinion of Barbara Jepson of *Connoisseur*, "is anything but a prima donna." Concurring with Barbara Jepson, Heidi Waleson described Miss Augér in *Ovation* as "formal, serious, private, a lioness in defense of her art, but frank, not above making a joke or discussing the vagaries of selecting a concert dress." Describing the impact on her self-image of her return to the United States, Arleen Augér told Heidi Waleson that it helped to develop her "as an artist and as a person." "My vision is much broader than before. I'm much stronger than before, much closer to being what I felt I was—something I would never have become if I'd stayed in the conservative confines of the European experience. I'm an accomplished vocal artist with a deep soul. I didn't recognize a lot of things about myself: how far I could go, what I had to offer. I feel more relaxed, confident of what I am. I'm a fatalist—I believe there are times for certain things. You must prepare for them, but you can't make them happen. I guess I was ready for all this."

In 1987 Arleen Augér received a Grammy nomination for best classical solo vocal recording for the *Villa-Lobos Bachianas Brasilieras* compact disc on the Delos label. In the following year she received another Grammy nomination in the same category for her *Love Songs* compact disc with Dalton Baldwin at the piano, on the same label. In November

1988 she won the Mumms Champagne-Ovation Magazine Classical Music Award for best solo vocal album for her recording of songs by Mozart, Wolf, and Strauss with Irwin Gage as her accompanist, on the CBS Masterworks label.

References: *Connoisseur* 216:34+ Ja '86 por; *Hi Fi/Mus Am* Ed 34:MA6+ Ag '84 pors; *Keynote* 9:31 Ag '85 por; *Maclean's* 99:8+ D 8 '86 por; *N Y Times* II p19+ Ja 22 '84 por; *Ovation* 8:20+ Mr '87 pors; *Philadelphia Inquirer* C p3 F 18 '88 por; *Wall St J* p22 Ag 16 '84; *Washington Post* B p7 S 10 '86 por; *International Who's Who, 1989–90; Who's Who in America, 1988–89*

Baker, Anita

1958– Singer. Address: c/o Elektra Records, 75 Rockefeller Plaza, New York, N.Y. 10019

The most accomplished new female vocalist of the 1980s may be Anita Baker, a five-foot-tall spitfire whose velvety contralto and three-octave range have made her pop music's most elegant performer of sexy ballads and mid-tempo love songs. "Always steeped in feeling," one reviewer rhapsodized, "her voice swings in tone back and forth from a smoky amber resonance to a breathy silver peal. That delivery lets her assume a unique stance as a vocalist: half jazzy torch singer, half soul sister." Miss Baker's combination of warm, gospel-inflected pop and cool jazz technique prompted the music critic Nelson George to coin an oxymoronic neologism for her distinctive style, which

he dubbed "retronuevo." Indeed, along with Luther Vandross, Whitney Houston, and Sade, Anita Baker is at the forefront of the trend that has been labeled the "quiet storm," a reaction against Eurythmics-style synth-pop and Prince-inspired technofunk that emphasizes uncluttered musical arrangements, acoustic instrumentation, expressive yet technically demanding vocalizations, and gorgeously well crafted love songs.

Anita Baker was born in Toledo, Ohio in 1958, but she grew up in Detroit, Michigan, the youngest member of a family of four girls. Although her mother, a single parent, operated a beauty shop in the ghettolike inner city, she managed to provide her daughters with the comforts of a middle-class upbringing and to instill in them a strong sense of the work ethic. As Rob Hoerburger noted in his *Rolling Stone* (November 20, 1986) profile of the singer, "If Anita and her sisters wanted to enjoy all the accessories of middle-class living—makeup and nice clothes and such—they had to work for them [by helping out in their mother's shop]."

The daughter of a traveling minister, Anita's mother made the church an important part of family life by taking her small brood to services, in which spontaneous gospel singing and fervent testimonials of faith were part of the ritual, and the congregation was composed of poor people and migrants from the South. "We belonged," Anita Baker told Rob Hoerburger, "to these storefront churches that weren't like the typical middle-class ones where everyone stuck to the program, where the choir would sing until it was time for the minister to come out and talk. In our churches, we followed the spirit a little more." In discussing that "easy country spontaneity" with Stephen Holden of the *New York Times* (September 3, 1986), Anita Baker said, "If someone in the back row wanted to moan the verse of a hymn while the minister came to the podium, it was okay."

Anita Baker fell in love with the idea of becoming a singer at the age of twelve. Since even in her adolescence her vocal timbre was low and silken, the great gospel singer Mahalia Jackson became her first musical idol. "Mahalia Jackson was the only singer who sounded remotely like me," she told John Barron of the *Chicago Tribune* (August 10, 1986). "I was talking in baritone back then." And in another interview, with Richard Harrington of the *Washington Post*, that took place a few days later, she said, "There was nobody else I could identify with except her, because her voice was heavy and kinda thick." For the next four years she sang nothing but gospel in church and, with a group of girlfriends, rhythm-and-blues and soul. But when she turned sixteen, she felt that she needed to "challenge [herself] musically," as she recalled in her discussion with Stephen Holden. "So I started paying more attention to jazz," she said. "Around the house, my mother played records by Sarah Vaughan, Nancy Wilson, Arthur Prysock, and Eddie Jefferson. I grew up singing along with that music without really knowing what it was." It was then, too, that Anita Baker began to appreciate Sarah Vaughan, the vocal artist she still reverently admires. "When I heard Sarah," she has recalled for Richard Harrington, "her voice was so thick, deep . . . and I'm going, 'Yeah!' She does more sitting on a stool than I do with all of my whatever. I'm amazed at what she does with just three pieces. There's a show, but it's not a *show*. I don't like to be introduced anymore. I just let the band start playing and I walk out—that's the way Sarah does it, and I like that. I got so much from her, in terms of just letting it fly, being loose."

It was also when she was sixteen that Anita Baker began to sing in Detroit bars. And although her mother prayed that her youngest daughter would not become addicted to big-city nightlife, she never tried to undermine Anita's aspirations. "[My sisters and I] were never forced to do anything creative or religious," Miss Baker has explained. "My family would expose things to us and if we took to it, fine." In 1978 she became the lead singer for Chapter Eight, a hard-core funk band that became popular on the Detroit disco-nightclub scene. Chapter Eight toured the country in a big Winnebago, playing dates on what Anita Baker has called the "chitlin circuit," and eventually signed a recording contract with Ariola Records, a struggling independent label in Los Angeles. Her group released an album in 1980 and a single, "I Just Want to Be Your Girl," which became a minor regional hit, but, as Rob Hoerburger pointed out in *Rolling Stone*, Chapter Eight's "screaming funk sound was too much for the postdisco audience." Ariola promptly dropped the band from its roster, apparently because executives at the now defunct company considered Anita Baker to be lacking in "star quality." "They said we didn't have what it takes," she told a reporter for *Newsweek* (January 19, 1987), "and since I was the one up front, that meant me. They told me I couldn't sing."

Returning to Detroit, Anita Baker found work waiting on tables in a bar. "I stopped singing," she said to Richard Harrington. "Professional people had told me, 'Don't waste any more of your time there.' So I didn't. . . . Coming out of inner-city Detroit, you think the practical thing, which is get a job like everybody else." It was her dulcet speaking voice that landed her a better job. Answering a want ad for a receptionist's job at a Detroit law firm, she was told by her prospective employers that they would "really like to have [her] voice over the phone." "I was real happy to see that I could do something else besides sing," Anita Baker recalled. "And my mother was happy—I was out of the clubs and the bars. I made $10,000 a year and had my own little apartment. It was very comfortable. Finally my mother could talk about me like all the other mothers talked about their daughters."

In 1982, however, Miss Baker received a call from Otis Smith, a former Ariola executive who had set up his own independent label, Beverly Glen. He asked the ex-vocalist for Chapter Eight to move to Los Angeles and record for his new company, but Anita Baker told him to "drop dead." "I had my Blue Cross card and my week's vacation," she explained to Richard Harrington. "Everybody else's daughter was working downtown in an office building; it was the thing to do." When Smith offered to match her $10,000-a-year salary, she again refused, but when he promised her a car and an apartment and said, "Anita, we don't want to just record you, we want to make you a star," she packed her bags and went to California.

In Los Angeles, Anita Baker began work on the album entitled *The Songstress*, which was released in 1983 by Beverly Glen as a radical departure from the synth-pop and technofunk styles that were at that time dominating the charts. "Otis was good at looking at the market and seeing what was absent and filling it," Miss Baker has remarked. "That was his forte. . . . Record executives would not touch a balladeer. But Otis was churning out the ballads, the love songs, and everybody was wondering, 'What's he doing? It's great!'" Although *The Songstress* remained on the rhythm-and-blues charts for over a year and spawned a single, "Angel," that made the rhythm-and-blues top ten, Miss Baker "never saw a dime in royalties," as she told Rob Hoerburger. She also began to wonder when they would do the next album. Although they had finished the tour and it was time for another album, Beverly Glen executives kept delaying it.

After about a year, Anita Baker started shopping around for a new record company. Two major labels courted her—Capitol/EMI and Elektra/Asylum—but Capitol backed off when Otis Smith threatened litigation against anyone who signed her to a contract. After a protracted court battle that Smith initiated, she was free to sign with Elektra, which granted her an unusual amount of freedom for a relative newcomer in the pop music business by allowing her to serve as executive producer of her first Elektra LP. "At one point during the sessions for *The Songstress*," she explained to Hoerburger, "Otis told me to sing a very high note. I told him I didn't think it belonged, that I didn't feel it, but he made me sing it anyway. I didn't want that to happen again." While searching for a producer to assist her, she was introduced to some of the biggest names in the West Coast recording industry, but as she told Stephen Holden, "I would leave the meetings with the choking sense of being patronized. I would be patted on the head and told not to worry and that everything would be taken care of. But that meant I wouldn't have anything to do with my own project, so I rebelled."

Eventually, Anita Baker chose the former guitarist for Chapter Eight, Michael J. Powell, as her producer. A more frustrating experience for her was gathering the material for her record, inasmuch as the most successful composers had already promised their best songs to established performers. She spent months going to Los Angeles publishing houses in her search for what she calls "fireside love songs with jazz overtones." But to her great disappointment, the publishers would assure her they had many of them, only to give her anything but that type of song in the long run. She finally recorded three songs that she had written herself, including "Been So Long" and "Watch Your Step," and five that had been composed by others. A self-described perfectionist, Miss Baker went $100,000 over budget, willingly paying for the extra recording costs out of her own pocket, since she was responsible for content, concept, engineer selection, musicians used, and the arrangements. She supervised all phases of the in-studio recording, even singing along with the musicians as they were laying down the basic tracks. She has acknowledged, "Sometimes the musicians don't want me there, but I'm there. There is a relationship between singer, musician and the song you just can't get when the singer is alone in an isolated room."

When Otis Smith's attempts to prevent its release failed, Rapture was brought out by Elektra in the late summer of 1986. It yielded two hit singles, "Sweet Love" and "You Bring Me Joy," and was enthusiastically received by critics. The reviewer for Rolling Stone commended Miss Baker for having produced a "modest album." "In these days of vocal extravaganzas," he wrote, "Rapture is an unexaggerated delight. It's also a difficult one to tackle. Baker's voice is a husky gurgle . . . and though she primarily sings well-crafted love songs, she doesn't take any shortcuts and won't allow her listeners any either. . . . [She is] an artist who's here for the long haul—an acquired but enduring taste." Stephen Holden announced in the New York Times that Rapture "established Miss Baker as one of the decade's two or three most promising pop-soul singers," though he felt that some of the album's numbers were too predictably arranged and that sometimes Rapture's "groove" got a "little too homogeneous." In the sping of 1987 Rapture captured two Grammy Awards for Miss Baker, and, although it had at first achieved only moderate sales, by the end of 1988 some five million copies of the album had been purchased.

While living in Los Angeles and working on Rapture, Anita Baker kept in touch with her gospel roots by singing from time to time at the Trinity Baptist Church. But as she has pointed out, she needs to have her "ears twisted around every now and then" by turning to the challenge of singing jazz. In the summer of 1986 she was asked to open for the pop singer Al Jarreau at the prestigious Montreux Jazz Festival in Switzerland, where she performed such standards as "God Bless the Child" and "Midnight Sun." "That's twenty years of jazz tradition," she commented, "and I was the only rookie there. Not to mention that it was my first performance out of the States. . . . The last person to touch ["Midnight Sun"] was Sarah Vaughan, and now I know why." Indeed, Anita Baker is embarrassed when critics compare her voice to Sarah Vaughan's, as they often do. "I belong on the charts, because I worked hard on [Rapture]," she explained to Rob Hoerburger. "But I'm not even close to Sarah Vaughan and Nancy [Wilson]. Maybe after twenty-five albums I might be, but now any comparison is an insult to them."

Nevertheless, Anita Baker's follow-up to Rapture, entitled Giving You the Best That I Got (1988), had a sultry jazz feeling that only served to invite more comparisons of her velvety delivery to that of Sarah Vaughan. "Every time I started to think about making the new record," she told Stephen Holden when he interviewed her for the New York Times (November 16, 1988), "Rapture kept staring me in the face, and so I kept procrastinating. For each song on Rapture, I wanted to find one that matched in style for the new album. . . . This album was about giving my audience more of what they had become accustomed to. It wouldn't have been good business for me to rush off and make a jazz album. But I know I've got to expand. My musicianship is limited, and the first thing on my list of things to do is to take some theory classes and learn more harmonies on the piano."

Racking up more than two million in sales in less than a month after its release, Giving You the Best That I Got became the fastest-selling pop album since the release in 1987 of Michael Jackson's Bad. Many reviewers, however, although they extravagantly praised Anita Baker's voice and her heartfelt interpretations of her material, were disappointed by the songs she had chosen to record. "It isn't street music, or dance music," Peter Watrous complained in the New York Times (November 20, 1988); "the sound of the acoustic piano is the album's signature. It has a veneer of sophistication . . . but the songs Ms. Baker has chosen rarely mention anything other than feelings. The album seems claustrophobic. . . . That leaves her voice to do the work, and for the most part, it does. Ms. Baker has an extraordinary voice, dotted with little scraps of her gospel past along with hints of singers from Patti LaBelle and Sarah Vaughan. . . . But her voice sounds like self-parody at times: she's putting so much technique into portraying lovestruck emotion that after a while her style takes over and starts calling attention to itself." And as the reviewer for People (November 28, 1988) put it, "That voice! Those songs! That was the reaction to . . . Rapture . . . the kind of record you could listen to over and over without dulling your appetite. . . . This time around, the reaction is: That voice! Those songs? Much of the material on Giving You the Best That

I Got seems a little too slick, and Baker isn't able to burrow down and inhabit the tunes as often as she did on Rapture."

The image that Anita Baker has cultivated in concert and in the videos that she has released to promote her singles is far from Janet Jackson's teen tramp, Whitney Houston's melodramatic yuppie, or Madonna's fashionable demimondaine. In her videos she usually appears in an elegantly simple setting while wearing full-length designer gowns and a light coating of makeup. "I don't ever want to need a costume," she has explained. "Look at what Sarah [Vaughan] does with just three pieces and a stool. That's my goal." In an article in the Village Voice (November 8, 1988), Carol Cooper confessed that one of her "initial reasons for liking" Anita Baker was that she is "anti-Whitney." "From her downy upper lip to her passionate writhing when performing, Baker was possessed rather than polished—a Sybil not a Muse." And in a Rolling Stone (October 23, 1988) review of her concert at New York City's Radio City Music Hall, David Fricke reported that she "has so much nervous energy to spare that she makes British chanteuse Sade seem like a cardboard cutout. . . . Baker couldn't

stand still for more than thirty seconds—twisting at the mike, plucking an invisible bass guitar à la Joe Cocker, rocking back and forth like a metronome with her eyes shut tight in tense concentration. Anita Baker didn't just sing about rapture, she embodied it."

Even when wearing high heels, the diminutive Anita Baker stands little more than five feet tall. In the London Observer (February 1, 1987), Anthony Denselow described her as a "bubbly and communicative woman with a great sense of humor," who had responded to a "year's dollop of stardom by wanting to return to the shopping malls, beaches, and junk foods of southern California." In the summer of 1987 she moved back from Los Angeles to the Detroit area to be near her family and her husband, Walter Bridgeforth, who works in marketing at IBM. She makes her home in a white colonial-style house that is situated on lakefront property in the affluent Detroit suburb of Grosse Pointe.

References: Chicago Tribune XIII p20 Ag 10 '86 por, XIII p6+ D 25 '88 por; Christian Sci Mon p25+ S 5 '86 por; Ebony 42:140+ O '87 pors; N Y Daily News p4 Jl 26 '87 pors; N Y Newsday II p17 Jl 26 '87 por

---

Barr, Roseanne

Nov. 3, 1952- Comedienne; actress. Address: c/o George Freeman, PMK, 8436 W. Third St., Suite 650, Los Angeles, Calif. 90048

One of a new generation of women who are changing television's outmoded depictions of the female sex, Roseanne Barr has turned her stand-up comedy routine into the role of a feisty, loud-mouthed, working-class mother on the ABC hit comedy series Roseanne and has been called "America's brightest new TV star." Roseanne made its debut in October 1988 and shot immediately into the top ten of the Nielsen ratings, where it has remained ever since. As Roseanne, Miss Barr juggles a job in a plastics factory and a disorganized household that consists of a husband and three children, using her cutting wit to cope with the hassles of everyday existence. "I want to do a show that reflects how people really live," she said recently. "Telling the truth at any point in time is really revolutionary." In March 1989 Roseanne won the People's Choice Award for favorite new television comedy series, and Miss Barr was named favorite female performer.

Roseanne Barr was born on November 3, 1952 in Salt Lake City, Utah. Her parents, Jerry and Helen Barr, sold blankets and crucifixes door to door to support the family, which included two other daughters and a son. As Helen Barr recalled to Gioia Diliberto in a conversation for People (April 28, 1986) magazine, "Life was not easy for Roseanne. It wasn't easy for me, either, because I'd nev-

er met anyone like her." When Roseanne was two years old, she ventured out into the street in front of her house, to keep cars from going too fast. Even after her mother spanked her, she did it again. "I was just a real weird woman from the day I was born," she told Jack Hicks of TV Guide (January 28, 1989). When she was three, she hit her head against a kitchen table leg, and one side of her face became paralyzed. In a panic, her mother called the rabbi, who said a prayer, but nothing happened. The next day, her mother called in the Mormon ministers, and that time the paralysis went away. Helen Barr took this as a sign from heaven that her daughter should be raised as a Mormon, and her husband, an atheist, did not object. "My whole life was a total dichotomy," Miss Barr told Susan Dworkin in an interview for Ms. (July–August 1987). "Because I had him for a father and her for a mother. My mother sent me to study Talmud at the Jewish school at the same time that she sent me to church to appreciate Jesus."

Another childhood experience that Miss Barr remembers is playing near some railroad tracks when she was eight and seeing a hobo jump off a train. As she recalled to Jack Hicks, she thought to herself, "When I get big, I'm gonna be a hobo," because "goin' on the road was always a fantasy." She wanted also to be a widow, she told Hicks, because the only happy women she knew in Salt Lake City were her two widowed grandmothers. Her penchant for comedy came, at least in part, from her father, whom she has described as a "comedy groupie" who collected the albums of Mort Sahl and Lenny Bruce. A regular viewer of The Ed Sullivan Show, Jerry Barr shouted "comedian!" whenever a comic appeared onstage, to alert his family to come in and watch. Miss Barr's family served as her first audience, cheering her on as she practiced skits after the Friday night Jewish Sabbath meal. All of the comics she watched on television influenced her style, she told Tom Shales for a Washington Post (March 7, 1987) profile. "I can feel Jack Benny in me, Totie Fields, Henny Youngman."

Religious disillusionment occurred at the age of fifteen, when Roseanne Barr read in a medical textbook that the temporary facial paralysis she had experienced at the age of three was a condition called Bell's palsy, which usually lasts for only forty-eight hours. Since her whole life up until then had been determined by her mother's interpretation of the Mormon "miracle," Miss Barr had a violent reaction to her discovery. The next day, she got drunk, smoked marijuana, and had sex. Then, she walked down the middle of a busy highway and purposely let a car hit her. She was knocked unconscious and dragged beneath the car. "When I finally came to, I was me," she told Jack Hicks. "Not the clone-Mormon princess everybody wanted me to be. That was when I welcomed myself and got on with it." Social workers, however, persuaded her to check into Utah State Hospital, a mental institution, where she stayed for eight months. That is one subject Miss Barr does not joke about. "I learned everything I need to know there. It made me everything I am," she told Joy Horowitz for the New York Times (October 16, 1988). "It's an incredible thing to have a group of insane people be your family for a year."

On her release from the hospital, Roseanne Barr went back to high school briefly, then dropped out. She went to work but felt stifled by the rigidly Mor-

mon milieu of Salt Lake City. One day, she picked up a women's liberation newsletter that had dropped on the sidewalk and experienced an emotional breakthrough. As she explained to Susan Dworkin: "I was seventeen years old. I went: 'My God, this is what it is! This is why everyone thinks you're nuts your whole life! Because you're an intelligent woman and you're in this town.'"

Miss Barr took her $300 in savings and got on a bus, eventually settling in Georgetown, Colorado, where she met Bill Pentland, the night clerk at a motel, and immediately fell in love with him. "He had the only bathtub in the area of our county," Miss Barr told Susan Dworkin. "So everyone went over there to have big dinners and take baths. He had comedy albums and his guitar and his art work. He's a great painter. . . . I was just so thrilled with him." Miss Barr and Bill Pentland moved into a house with six other people, "the biggest hippie commune on earth," with writers and artists from New York and Los Angeles, she recalled to Susan Dworkin. To support herself, she worked as a dishwasher.

In 1974 the couple got married and set up house in an eight-by-thirty-seven-foot trailer. Bill Pentland worked first as a garbage-truck driver, then as a mailman, while Roseanne Barr had three children ("I breed well in captivity," she used to joke onstage). For several years, she concentrated on being a housewife, although on the side she wrote poetry and satiric sketches that she stashed in Hefty bags. "If I'd had more money, I probably would still be home," she told Susan Dworkin. "Because I liked it. There was some kind of really cool feeling about organizing things and cleaning, cooking, caring for those people."

Family finances eventually forced Miss Barr to return to work. Having recently slimmed down from 200 to 105 pounds (Angry at her husband, she had decided to lose 100 pounds "just to spite him," she told Susan Dworkin), she sought a job as a cocktail waitress. Her first comedy routines were born at a bar in Denver, where she made cutting remarks at the male customers who made passes at her. The bar's patrons adored her and kept coming back for more. At the urging of her younger sister Geraldine, who had come to live with her, Miss Barr paid a visit to a Denver comedy club in August 1981. After sitting through the performances of several sexist male comedians, she took the stage herself to deliver a comic rebuttal to the offensive jokes she had just heard. When she got her first comedy-club job, she was promptly fired because the male club owner found her starkly stated working-woman's viewpoint offensive. In response, Miss Barr organized a women's comic showcase in Boulder and appeared in radical feminist clubs and "straight" comedy clubs, but her delivery failed to hit the mark with either type of audience.

She ended up appearing in punk clubs and motorcycle bars, where she zeroed in on the battle of the sexes. "I became Nemesis, the goddess of retribution," she told Tom Shales. "They didn't care for me so much, so I changed my act a little bit." Roseanne Barr gradually learned to soften her edges while she honed her own individual comic style and message. Still searching for her comic persona, she hit upon a new kind of comedy called "funny womanness." Discussing that idea with her husband and sisters, Miss Barr discovered, as she pointed out to Susan Dworkin: "The language is my life! Because I am a housewife! I'm not gonna go outside myself and say what I should be, I'm gonna say what is. . . . I suddenly knew I could do what Richard Pryor did for himself—get inside the stereotype and make it three-dimensional from within," Miss Barr continued. "And then I could call myself a domestic goddess. Then I could say: 'Hey, fellas, you've had it wrong all these years, we women are not the funny ones, we women are not the jokes. You are the jokes!'" Behind the jokes—about husbands who will not do dishes ("What's the matter—is Lemon Joy kryptonite to your species?"), about children who drive a mother crazy ("I do what it says on the aspirin bottle. Take two—and keep away from children")—lie Miss Barr's memories of the women she knew in her childhood, the women trapped in domesticity, the women in the state mental institution. She was determined to remember all the women she had ever known and not allow them, or herself, to be insulted anymore.

With her image solidified, Miss Barr took her act on the road, playing in clubs in Kansas, Arizona, Oklahoma, and Texas. At her younger sister's suggestion, in 1985 she auditioned at the Comedy Store in Los Angeles. When the owner, Mitzi Shore, hired her after a six-minute audition, Miss Barr decided to move to Los Angeles. Her husband, Bill, who had always been supportive of her efforts, quit his ten-year job with the Denver post office and moved the whole family to Hollywood. Pentland has admitted that, in the beginning, he was dubious about his wife's intentions of becoming a comedienne, but once he saw her perform, "[he] trusted her vision," he told Jack Hicks, though "it was a bit of a shock," since she used a lot of family material.

Roseanne Barr's routine at the Comedy Store was a hit. Within two weeks, the producer George Schlatter cast her in his television special Funny. Commenting on her talent, Schlatter told Jack Hicks, "The first time I saw Roseanne, I saw the person, the talent, that I did with Goldie Hawn and Lily Tomlin. She doesn't have their dimension, but she has that spark. She leaves you wanting more." Johnny Carson soon invited her to be a guest on the Tonight Show, on which she appeared three times. She also did her routine at Caesars Palace in Las Vegas and toured nationally with Julio Iglesias.

By that time, Roseanne Barr had fine-tuned her act. "Oh hi," she began, in an offhand way, as if surprised to see the audience. Her lines included: "Well, it's a thrill to be out of the house," and "So. I'm fat. I thought I'd point that out." Crunching Cheetos and delivering lines in her nasal voice, Miss Barr lampooned husbands who are unable to find their own socks—"They think the uterus is a tracking device"—and declared that she would do

housework once Sears came out with a riding vacuum cleaner, "like with a wet bar and stuff." On being a mother, she said, "I figure by the time my husband comes home at night, if those kids are still alive, I've done my job."

In 1986 Miss Barr appeared on an HBO special that starred Rodney Dangerfield, but her lines were "dumb and dirty," Tom Shales reported, and she regretted the performance. A year later, however, she had her own HBO special, The Roseanne Barr Show, which won Ace Awards (cable television's version of the Emmy) for best HBO special and best female in a comedy. One part of the show featured her stand-up routine; another depicted her in a family setting, interacting with a husband and kids—the precursor of what became, a year later, Roseanne.

After the disaster of the Rodney Dangerfield special, Roseanne Barr had decided that she would accept only those television offers that were true to her own life experiences and vision, as both a woman and a member of the working class. "I'm not gonna play a damn person who's making $500,000 a year and call that real American life," she told Tom Shales. "I see myself as sort of like Ralph Kramden. . . . I'm proud to be a working-class person. That's who I want to be and talk to and talk about. We're the backbone, we are. I just think it's a cool thing." Miss Barr got the chance to play that part when she was asked to star in a sitcom series developed by Matt Williams, a former writer for The Cosby Show. Williams's original concept was for a series about blue-collar working mothers, but, with The Cosby Show producers Marcy Carsey and Tom Werner, Williams decided to shift the focus to one working mother, with Roseanne Barr in the title role.

What Miss Barr had in mind for Roseanne was a realistic portrayal of a working-class family—one that showed the clutter, hassles, and arguments as well as the love. "I identify myself by my values as a woman, not as males perceive me," she told a reporter for Time (December 5, 1988) magazine. "It's a voice I feel I've never heard in the media, a voice that tells the truth and doesn't worry. It's like having coffee with your neighbor—the way you talk before the husbands come in." In some episodes, Roseanne comes home looking haggard after working eight hours in a plastics factory only to find the dishes still piled high in the sink, even though her husband, Dan (played by John Goodman), an independent construction contractor, has been home all day. The repartee between Roseanne and Dan, and between Roseanne and her three children, sustains the thin plot devices that focus on such everyday occurrences as a clogged sink or a child's problems at school. "Why are you so mean?" one child complains. "'Cause I hate kids and I'm not your real mom," Roseanne replies with a good-natured grin. "Now I know why some animals eat their young," she says on another occasion.

Since its debut in mid-October 1988, Roseanne has finished consistently in the Nielsen top ten. Critics hailed the show as the fall's most daring new sitcom and called it "the best thing since Cosby." Like *The Cosby Show*, *Roseanne* immediately struck a responsive chord with television audiences, and both shows grew out of stand-up comedy routines. In spite of Miss Barr's rudimentary acting ability—Ron Givens observed in *Newsweek* (October 31, 1988) that "there are other people standing around her, but you get the sense that Barr is acting near them rather than with them"—Cathleen Schine, writing in *Vogue* (November 1988), contended that Miss Barr brought "a strangely comfortable dignity" to her role, adding, "Her roaring nasal whine is, finally, the voice of reason." Roseanne Barr is now taking acting lessons from Roxanne Rogers.

One reviewer, Joyce Maynard of the *Chicago Tribune*, originally found the character Roseanne "obnoxious and insulting to the average American wife-mother and homemaker," but she revised her opinion after she was deluged by letters from viewers who disagreed. After watching the show again, she conceded in the *Chicago Tribune* (February 19, 1989), "On second thought what I was really seeing was just an imperfect woman (like the rest of us) who is a little more accepting of her imperfections than I am of mine." The second time around, Miss Maynard also noticed that Roseanne can make wisecracks at her family because of the understanding that "they love each other and enjoy each other's company." Harry F. Waters observed similarly in *Newsweek* (March 13, 1989) that Roseanne's "bark is simply her way of coping with overload."

From the start, Roseanne Barr identified strongly with her character and wrote many of her own lines. The adjustment from stand-up comic to television actress was not easy, especially when the producers required her to recite someone else's material. "I come from the place all stand-up comics come from, and then to say other people's words—it's weird," she told a reporter for *Newsweek* (October 31, 1988). She often clashed with Matt Williams and complained that he wanted to play down Roseanne's feminist perspective in favor of depicting a one-dimensional "sarcastic bitch." "At first, Matt Williams and I were doing two different shows. He thought he was writing 'Life and Everything,' with Roseanne Barr playing a role," Miss Barr explained to Jack Hicks for the *TV Guide* profile. "Haven't they seen my act? I'm not an *actress*—I'm *me*." She refused to say to her television husband, Dan, "I have no respect for you outside this bed," for example, pointing out to Jack Hicks, "I want a portrait of working folks with a little warmth and dignity, not buffoons. Bad grammar doesn't mean you're an idiot." Miss Barr also objected to the many eating scenes that the producers wanted, telling Hicks, "The other day, I was really fed up and said, 'Do you really want me 'n' John to sit here and stuff our faces until we *puke*?'"

Because of her disagreements with Williams, Miss Barr resorted to rewriting his scripts, with the help of her husband, Bill, who had been writing some of her material ever since they moved to Los Angeles. Tensions reached the breaking point in December 1988, when Miss Barr issued an ultimatum after completing the thirteenth episode: either she or Williams had to go. Rick Leed, Williams's agent, countered that Miss Barr was a woman who went "berserk" when she did not get her own way, but Miss Barr won out, and in January 1989 Williams left the show. As a result, Roseanne Barr gained creative control over the role she was playing, an unusual accomplishment for a newcomer to television. At the American Comedy Awards ceremony in May 1989, Roseanne Barr was named the funniest female performer in a leading role in a television series.

Roseanne Barr is five feet, four inches tall and weighs about 212 pounds. Her fifteen-year marriage to Bill Pentland, which produced three children, ended in divorce in July 1989, and she now shares living quarters with Tom Arnold, a comedian and comedy writer, whom she intends to marry after her divorce from Pentland becomes final in January 1990. Miss Barr makes more than $30,000 for each weekly segment of her situation comedy, and she owns 15 percent of the show. Her autobiography, *Roseanne: My Life as a Woman*, was published in September 1989. She is scheduled to make her film debut, costarring with Meryl Streep, in *She Devil*, an adaptation of the Fay Weldon novel *The Life and Loves of a She Devil*, in December 1989. Miss Barr takes her job as the television character Roseanne very seriously, sometimes putting in seventeen-hour days and, in spite of her new wealth, retains a strong sense of her working-class roots.

References: Ms 16:106+ Jl–Ag '87 pors; N Y Times II p1+ O 16 '88 pors; Newsweek 112:63 O 31 '88 por; People 25:105+ Ap 28 '86 pors; TV Guide 37:2+ Ja 28 '89 pors

Bass, Robert M(use)

Mar. 19, 1948– Financier. Address: Robert M. Bass Group, 201 Main St., Fort Worth, Texas 76102

In the past two years, Robert M. Bass has emerged as one of the most active investors in America, engineering a string of deals that has resulted in a personal fortune worth an estimated $1 billion and unremitting media attention, which he abhors. "I find it annoying to be singled out, for curiosity to be directed at me," he explained in a rare 1986 interview. In 1988 alone his Robert M. Bass Group was a partner in the $1.53 billion purchase of the Westin Hotel chain from the Allegis Corporation, selling the Plaza Hotel to Donald Trump for $410 million; headed the $702 million buyout of the Bell & Howell Company; made an unsuccessful hostile bid—worth $1.6 billion—for the Macmillan publishing company; and, in Bass's first megadeal, took

Robert M. Bass

over the bankrupt American Savings & Loan Association for $550 million in capital and $2 billion in government assistance. As one investor recently noted: "He's an exceptional investor. The one word you keep hearing about him is that he's very smart. I see him making well over a billion dollars in the next few years."

Robert Muse Bass was born on March 19, 1948 in Fort Worth, Texas, the third of the four sons of Perry Richardson Bass and his wife, the former Nancy Lee Muse. Perry Bass was president of Perry R. Bass Inc., an oil company in Fort Worth, participated in a number of civic-minded activities, such as the Boy Scouts of America, and served as the chairman of the Texas Parks and Wildlife Commission. Perry Bass inherited oil holdings from his uncle and business associate Sid Richardson, who died in 1959 and who also left $2.8 million to each of Perry Bass's four sons.

In spite of the Bass family wealth, Perry and Nancy Bass made sure that their sons' privileged background did not go to their heads, and they instilled in them the importance of hard work. "They were superior parents," Peter Schwartz, the founder of the Country Day School in Fort Worth, told a reporter for Business Week (October 3, 1988). "They wouldn't let those boys goof off." Sid Bass, the oldest son, was his parents' favorite, gregarious and smooth, whereas Robert Bass was known as the introvert.

Robert Bass attended the Phillips Andover Academy in Massachusetts, where he was a somewhat indifferent student. He eventually transferred to the less-pressured Governor Dummer Academy, also in Massachusetts, for his last two years of high school. There, he exhibited some artistic leanings and wrote for the academy's literary

magazine. He spent one year at the Wells Fargo Bank in Fort Worth before following his oldest brother, Sid, to Yale University (their father's alma mater), from which he graduated in 1971, and to Stanford University's Graduate School of Business, which awarded him an M.B.A. degree in 1974.

When Sid Bass graduated from Stanford with an M.B.A. degree in 1968, he took control of the family fortune—worth an estimated $50 million, mostly in oil assets—which was managed by Bass Brothers Enterprises, the company that Perry Bass had formed in 1960 for his four sons. With a classmate from Stanford, Richard Rainwater, Sid Bass aggressively invested the family funds, diversifying into stocks, bonds, and real estate, so that, by the early 1980s, Bass Brothers Enterprises had amassed a fortune worth between $4 billion and $6 billion.

In 1974 Robert Bass returned to Fort Worth and joined Bass Brothers Enterprises, where he took a back seat to his brother Sid and Rainwater and concentrated on real-estate deals. From the start, the Bass brothers exhibited an unerring knack for anticipating turnarounds and buyouts. Sid Bass liked to buy a stake in a company that he thought was undervalued, then pressure management to make changes. The Basses bought the Arvida Corporation, a real-estate firm in Florida, and sold it to the Walt Disney Company for $250 million worth of stock. They later bought additional Disney shares, realized an $850 million capital gain, and were instrumental in the resignation of the old management. The Robert M. Bass Group also bought a 10 percent interest in Alexander's, primarily because of its valuable real estate, and a 30 percent interest in Munsingwear.

In 1981 the Bass Brothers bought into, among other companies, Amfac (6.2 percent of the common stock), Blue Bell (6.8 percent of the common stock), and Western Airlines (8 percent of the cumulative preferred stock). At Robert Bass's instigation, Bass Brothers Enterprises and Bass Equity Enterprises bought a 4.5 percent interest in Marathon Oil for $148.2 million, in late October 1981. Marathon Oil was subsequently wooed as a takeover target by Mobil and United States Steel Corporation, and the Bass family earned a profit of $160 million on its by then 5.1 percent stake. After eighteen months of buying into Texaco, the Bass brothers sold their 10 percent stake for a profit of $400 million after Texaco's management asked them to leave the company.

By early 1984 the Bass Brothers Enterprises holdings in dozens of companies included hotels, real estate, venture capital, and manufacturing. Many of their deals involved plays on convertible securities. Acting as a white knight for Suburban Propane Gas Corporation, they netted about $5 million by selling to the National Distillers and Chemical Corporation. In their business dealings, all of the Bass brothers exhibited a characteristic penchant for privacy.

It was when Robert Bass participated in local politics in 1984—to fight the proposed extension of the interstate freeway because it would jeopardize the historic downtown section of Fort Worth—that he broke away from his brother's shadow and came into his own. Bass and his wife, Anne, whom he had married in 1970, joined I-CARE (Citizen Advocates for Responsible Expansion), and Bass helped fund architectural and environmental studies that pointed out weaknesses in the proposed construction. Breaking his characteristic reserve, Bass spoke at press conferences, took part in rallies, and hired lawyers from Washington, D.C. At one point, I-CARE placed a roadblock in front of the highway expansion. "Bob was persistent," one friend told William Meyers in an interview for *Institutional Investor* (August 1988). "He stuck with the protest like a mockingbird on a June bug. He just kept pecking and pecking away." Bass later continued his involvement in politics by serving as a member of the Texas Highway and Public Transportation Commission.

Wishing to strike out on his own in his business dealings as well, Robert Bass had started his own firm, the Robert M. Bass Group, in 1963 and had begun looking for his own deals. He quickly established a reputation as being more of a risktaker than his brother. "We're not clones," he explained in a 1987 interview. His first major deal involved an attempt to take the American Broadcasting Company private. Although that effort failed, his 4 percent stake in ABC translated into substantial profit when the network was bought by Capital Cities in 1985. With Interstate Properties, a Paramus, New Jersey–based real-estate investor, the Robert M. Bass Group bought a 21 percent stake in Alexander's, for $24.6 million. By November 1984 the two investment groups had secured seven seats on Alexander's seventeen-member board, and they attempted to turn the business around in spite of their scanty knowledge of retailing. After two years, Bass sold his shares to Donald Trump for a profit of $25 million.

In 1985 the Bass Brothers divided up their $2.75 billion in assets, and Robert Bass started making IRS filings separate from his brothers. That same year, the Robert M. Bass Group reported to the Securities and Exchange Commission that it owned an 8 percent interest in Taft Broadcasting, based in Cincinnati, Ohio. By August 1986 that interest had increased to 20 percent, amounting to an investment of $120 million. In May 1986 Taft invited four representatives from the Robert M. Bass Group to join its board of directors. Those nominated were John H. Scully, Richard C. Blum, David H. Lloyd, and William E. Obendorf.

In October 1986 Wometco Cable TV signed an agreement to sell its cable operations to a group that included the Robert M. Bass Group, the Taft Broadcasting Company, and executives from Wometco's cable operations for $625 million. Then, early in 1987, an investment group known as TFBA Limited Partnership offered to buy Taft for $824 million. TFBA included the Robert M. Bass Group, the American Financial Corporation, headed by Carl H. Lindner, and Dudley S. Taft, the vice-chairman of Taft Broadcasting. According to

the deal, Carl Lindner, the financier based in Cincinnati, would run the company and preside over Taft's restructuring, while Dudley Taft and Robert Bass would obtain parts of the business. Taft Broadcasting's three major divisions were its broadcast operation, an entertainment division (Hanna Barbera Productions), and a small amusement park unit. According to Dan Cook in *Business Week* (April 27, 1987), industry analysts were surprised by the arrangement, given the publicly known animosity between Taft and Bass, caused by Bass's removing Taft from his position as company president and designating him vice-chairman instead. Bass ended up with a debt-free television station in Columbus, Ohio and $157 million in cash, for a total of some $500 million.

From 1987 to 1988 Bass was involved in $3 billion worth of deals and investments, and a financial disclosure statement that he was required to file after he served on the State Highway and Public Transportation Commission indicated that he owned stock in twenty-four corporations, including Walt Disney, the Hospital Corporation of America, and American Medical International. The statement also listed forty-three partnerships, which were mostly in real estate; oil royalties from ten companies; land in three states and the District of Columbia; and notes receivable from sixty-six sources. Another major deal in 1987 involved a $702 million leveraged buyout of Bell & Howell, a publishing, career education, and information storage company in Skokie, Illinois. Bass and his investment partners originally paid $80 million for a 16.2 percent stock presence. They owned 90 percent of the company after the buyout.

When Allegis Corporation, the parent of United Airlines, announced in June 1987 that it intended to sell its Westin Hotel chain, one of the bidders it attracted was Robert Bass. Bass's aide Thomas J. Barrack Jr. enlisted the Aoki Corporation of Japan as an investment partner. When Bass entertained doubts about managing a hotel chain, Barrack persuaded him to let Aoki have sixty of the Westin hotels, keeping the Plaza Hotel in New York for himself. Barrack and Aoki priced the chain at $1.4 billion and agreed that Bass would have absolute control of the Plaza if their bid for the chain was accepted.

Although the twelve bidding finalists had until October 30 to make their formal bids, Bass and Aoki attempted to offer a preemptive bid, which was not accepted. When the stock market crashed on October 19, however, Barrack presented Allegis with the ultimatum that the Bass-Aoki offer of $1.3 billion would expire at the end of the business day. Allegis agreed to sell for $1.35 billion, in addition to the purchasers' assumption of $180 million in outstanding debt. Bass wanted to make sure he would be able to sell the Plaza, and Barrack had a preliminary meeting with Donald Trump—who talked to every bidder—before the Bass-Aoki bid was accepted. In March 1988 Trump agreed to buy the Plaza and a small apartment building next door for $410 million and to accept a management contract entitling Aoki to 2.25 percent of the hotel's gross revenues for two years. Bass contributed $250 million of the $1.53 billion asking price. His 71 percent stake in the Plaza turned into a profit of $50 million to $80 million when the hotel was sold.

In his first unfriendly takeover bid, in May 1988, Robert Bass made an unsolicited offer of $64 a share for Macmillan, the New York–based publishing and information services company, and announced that he was prepared to provide up to $250 million in financing for the transaction. The bid was prompted by Macmillan's plan to authorize a new class of preferred stock with super-voting rights, which would have devalued all common shareholders' stock. When Bass bought a 16.2 percent stake in Bell & Howell in 1987 and then a 7.5 percent stake in Macmillan, Macmillan bought an 8 percent stake in Bell & Howell in an attempt to keep Bass from taking over the company. Macmillan's board of directors also established a "poison pill" provision in August 1987 to deter hostile bids.

Responding to the initial Bass bid, Macmillan reorganized into two companies, Macmillan Publishing and Macmillan Information Company, and offered shareholders a package of cash and stock in the new companies. In June Bass raised his bid to $73 a share, or $2 billion, and proposed a restructuring plan similar to the one suggested by Macmillan but with a cash package that was worth $5.65 a share more. The Bass group would provide some $400 million and raise the rest through banks and subordinated debt.

In addition, the Robert M. Bass Group filed suit in the State of Delaware Chancery Court to keep Macmillan from restructuring the company, contending that Macmillan prevented the opportunity of accepting higher bids. Macmillan, in turn, sued the Bass group in the United States District Court in Manhattan, contending that Bass had violated securities laws in accumulating a 9 percent stake in the company. Macmillan rejected Bass's second offer, and the company was eventually bought by Robert Maxwell, the British media magnate. (The court concluded that Bass had filed suit legitimately to protect shareholder rights.)

The transaction that propelled Robert Bass into the media spotlight was his takeover of the bankrupt American Savings & Loan, a subsidiary of the Financial Corporation of America, based in Stockton, California, America's largest insolvent thrift bank and the second-largest, with assets of $30 billion and 186 branches. After eight months of intensive negotiations, led on the Bass side by David Bonderman, on September 3, 1988 the Federal Home Loan Bank Board (FHLBB) agreed to provide $2 billion in financial aid, including a $500 million note from the Federal Savings & Loan Insurance Corporation (FSLIC). Robert Bass agreed to buy the thrift for $550 million. The FHLBB originally signed an agreement to negotiate exclusively with the Robert M. Bass Group in April 1988. According to a reporter for Business Week (October 3, 1988), the government was particularly

eager to deal with Bass because of his financial expertise.

American Savings Bank was divided into the "good bank," holding $14 billion in deposits, $10 billion in good real-estate loans, and a $6 billion loan to the "bad bank," with $5 billion in bad real-estate loans and $14 billion in mortgage-backed securities, which will be liquidated. The FHLBB agreed to let Bass spend up to $1.5 billion of the good bank's money, through a third subsidiary, a merchant bank, capitalized with $50 million from the Bass group's investment, for leveraged buyouts, mergers, and acquisitions. Taking into account objections raised at a House Banking Committee hearing in early September, the Robert M. Bass Group withdrew the merchant bank voluntarily and made it a direct unit of American Savings & Loan, restricting its investment to $500 million. A fourth subsidiary, the American Real Estate Group, will sell real estate in the bad bank.

The government agreed to cover the losses of the bad bank, in exchange for 30 percent equity in the good bank and 75 percent of American Savings & Loan's tax benefits. Bass gained 70 percent ownership of the good thrift and $300 million in tax benefits, and he should make $400 to $500 million in profits over the next four years. Robert Bass thinks that the restructured company will make money by operating primarily as a traditional savings bank, taking deposits and making mortgages and other consumer loans. No matter what happens, Bass is expected to come out ahead. American Savings' $10 billion in bad real-estate assets are mostly covered by the $2 billion in assistance that the bank board has offered. Bass hired Mario Antoci, previously the president and chief operating officer of the parent company of Home Savings of America, as chairman and chief executive of American Savings & Loan.

Continuing his aggressive investment strategy, in December 1988 Bass bought 40 percent of the voting stock, worth $20 million to $40 million, in the St. Petersburg Times. Geraldine Fabrikant reported in the New York Times (February 1, 1989) that the Robert M. Bass Group owned 5.6 percent of Houghton Mifflin, the Boston-based textbook publisher. On April 3, the Bass group bought a 2 to 3 percent stake of the Tribune Company, a major newspaper and broadcast conglomerate.

The activity that has generated the most press recently is Bass's reported accumulation of 8 percent of Time Inc.'s stock, a move that began after the merger between Time and Warner Communications was announced on March 4, 1989. That purchase led to speculation that Bass might try to lead a takeover bid. J. Richard Munro, Time's chairman and chief executive officer, told Richard Gold of Variety (April 4, 1989), "I'm not at all concerned. I've had several conversations with Bass. He's not doing anything evil." In April 1989 an affiliate of the Robert M. Bass Group bought a 7.5 percent stake in the Vons Companies, the largest supermarket chain in southern California, for $37.7 million.

Robert Bass relies on a trusted cadre of advisers. His top aide is David Bonderman, a former Washington, D.C., attorney who aided Bass in his freeway fight. His other lieutenants include Barry Jackson, a real-estate specialist from Chicago; Thomas Barrack, a Los Angeles real-estate developer; Bernard J. Carl, a former vice-president of Salomon Brothers who has been called "one of the brainiest guys in finance today"; J. Taylor Crandall, formerly of the Bank of Boston; and three aides who formerly worked for Sid Bass and Rainwater—John H. Scully, a former Stanford classmate, and William E. Obendorf, who are both from San Francisco, and Peter T. Joseph, a leveraged-buyout specialist from New York. Joseph is the managing director of the Acadia Partners, a $1.6 billion fund organized by the Bass group that helped manage the Bell & Howell buyout.

Decisions are reached by consensus, although seven of the firm's ten principals live outside Fort Worth. Scully and Obendorf recommend investments, which are studied by one or two other partners who lead the negotiations, and Bonderman comes in to complete the deal. Deals come in through any of the partners and are assigned for investigation based on specialized expertise of the team. Bass stays involved throughout the process. In the fall of 1987 Robert Bass set up Castine Partners to handle investments in financial institutions and named Bernard Carl as its head. The Robert M. Bass Group operates out of the Bass family's Fort Worth office tower, designed by Paul Rudolph.

Outside of financial dealings, Robert Bass's main interest is historic preservation, and he is chairman of the National Trust for Historic Preservation, in Washington, D.C. He is also on the collectors' committee of the National Gallery of Art, and he has contributed toward the restoration of Blair House, a presidential guest house, and the Diplomatic Reception Rooms at the Department of State. Bass is a trustee of Rockefeller University. He has established a presence in Washington, buying three adjacent town houses—including the summer home of President Ulysses S. Grant—in Georgetown for $4 million in 1984. In June 1988 he bought a house for $1.8 million that abuts his property.

In addition, Bass is leasing 14,000 square feet of office space on Connecticut Avenue, leading some to speculate that he may have political aspirations. About the allure of Washington, D.C., to the Basses, one friend remarked to Barbara Gamarekian of the New York Times (September 15, 1988), "I think it is an interesting choice for Bob. It is a reflection of the man that they didn't go to New York." In the same article, William K. Reilly, the president of the Conservation Foundation, pointed out about Robert and Anne Bass: "They are very much a team. They both are extraordinarily earnest, serious people and I am endlessly surprised to discover that people who operate at the level that they do are interested in ideas. They don't talk in terms of wielding power and influence. They talk about making

a contribution." A registered Democrat, Bass donated $100,000 to each political party in 1988. He was recently named to the board of trustees of Stanford University.

Robert Bass, who is invariably described as boyish-looking, has blond hair and wears wire-rimmed glasses. He dresses in Savile Row suits and favors Hermès ties. Although Bass is known for his unassuming manner, his wife gave him a 1938 Bugatti convertible, worth $1 million, in 1986. Bass also drives a GM Suburban and a Volvo, and he was so impressed with the latter's engineering that he bought a local Volvo dealership. Possessing an offbeat sense of humor, Bass once taped a red cross on the back window of his Volvo before he drove an injured Bonderman to the hospital. The Basses have four children.

References: Bsns Month p13 N '88; Bsns W p96+ O 3 '88 pors; Forbes 141:92 F 22 '88 por; Fortune 118:64+ O 10 '88 por; Institutional Investor 22:47+ Ag '88 pors; N Y Times B p12 S 15 '88 por

Berri, Claude
(bâ rē′)

July 1, 1934– French filmmaker. Address: Renn Productions, 10 rue Lincoln, 75008 Paris, France

In the course of his twenty-five-year movie career, Claude Berri has become the "one-man band" of French cinema, but, according to the indefatigable producer, director, screenwriter, and former actor, none of his moves was premeditated. He once explained to an interviewer, "I became a writer because nobody would hire me as an actor; a producer because they didn't want to produce my films; and finally, a distributor because one day I got fed up with waiting for other people to do what I was perfectly capable of doing myself."

Berri's career as screenwriter and director has had its ups and downs: up in the 1960s, with such early autobiographical hits as *The Two of Us*, *Marry Me, Marry Me*, and *The Man with Connections*, then down in the 1970s, with a series of critical and commercial failures. Since the early 1980s Berri has been back on track with popular successes like *The School Master*, *Tchao Pantin*, and his most recent, record-breaking double hit, *Jean de Florette* and *Manon of the Spring*. As producer and distributor, he has been staking out commercial territory since the early 1970s with the films of Claude Zidi, Dino Risi, Bertrand Blier, Roman Polanski, Claude Sautet, Philippe De Broca, and, most recently, Jacques Demy. Meanwhile, he has also been involved in the production of art films, beginning with Eric Rohmer's *My Night at Maud's* and continuing with directors such as Maurice Pialat, Jacques Rivette, Luc Doillon, and Patrice Chéreau.

According to Berri, his commitments have always been the same: film as entertainment above all, respect for his audience, and absolute faith in the other directors he chooses to work with. On the occasion of his production company's twenty-fifth anniversary last August, Berri took a backward glance over his career and told an interviewer from *Premiere* magazine, "Twenty-five years to make a dozen films, produce or coproduce fifty, distribute *Apocalypse Now*, *Intervista*, *Yeleen*, etc., and make three children—it seems like yesterday!"

Claude Berri was born Claude Berel Langmann, the first of two children in a Jewish immigrant family from Eastern Europe. His parents, Hirsch and Beila (Bercu) Langmann, both worked as furriers in the Faubourg Poissonnière district of Paris. With the outbreak of World War II and the Nazi occupation, they were forced to go into hiding and placed their son in a non-Jewish family for safekeeping—an experience that later served as the basis for Berri's first feature, *The Two of Us*. With the end of the war, Claude rejoined his family and went back to school, but he was no student, and by the time he reached high school, he was regularly skipping classes. "I was literally allergic," he has recalled, "much more interested in pool, poker, ping-pong, and girls than in studying."

At the age of fifteen, after flunking his exams, Berri dropped out of school and went to work with his parents in the fur district, but he soon realized that this was no solution either. Inspired by a play he had seen, he began fantasizing about the theatre and enrolled in an acting class. In 1951 he got his first bit part in the movies and spent the next four years trying to pursue his acting career while continuing to work as a furrier. It was when he finally quit the fur district and started acting in the theatre that Claude Langmann became Claude Berri—via his middle name, Berel, and the suggestion of a civil servant who told him that an "i" at the end would sound more French.

Notwithstanding his talents, his ambitions, and his "exhilarating" memories of being onstage every night for more than three years, Berri came to realize that he simply did not look enough like a star to be one: his physique, he later acknowledged, did not "fit the going fashion . . . or any other, for that matter." The final blow came when, after he won a competition for budding young actors, its organizers were unable to find a theatre production to place him in. (He wound up playing opposite Brigitte Bardot in *La Vérité* for six days.) Unable to resign himself to what he saw as "the passive side of the actor's career"—waiting—Berri started to write his own scripts. He also collaborated with his father to produce a play that failed and, in 1960, persuaded his father to direct and act in two short films. "All of Paris came trooping to the house to see this Chaplin of the Faubourg Poissonnière," he recalled to Yonnick Flot in an interview for Flot's book *Les Producteurs* (1986), declaring that his father "had more talent for comedy than anyone I've ever met."

After writing the script for a television film (*Janine*, 1961) that was directed by his friend Maurice Pialat, Berri set out to make his own film, *The Chicken* (*Poulet*, 1963), which he based on a news item about a boy who tried to save his favorite chicken from the family soup pot by putting an egg in its nest every day. When money for the film was not forthcoming, he turned to two friends from his theatre days, Hélène Vager and Katarina Renn, and, with their financial backing, created his own production company, which he called Renn Productions. By Berri's own admission, he assumed his directorial role with so little technical know-how that the veteran cameraman Ghislain Cloquet was "pulling out his hair" when he saw Berri's ignorance.

In spite of those tentative beginnings, *The Chicken* made its way to the Venice Biennale, where it received an award for the best light entertainment film. Back in Paris, it also attracted the attention of the New Wave producer Georges de Beauregard, who invited Berri to contribute sketches to two showcase films, *Kisses* (*Les Baisers*, 1964) and *Luck and Love* (*La Chance et l'amour*, 1964). But Berri's real breakthrough came when *The Chicken* reached the United States and was awarded an Oscar for the best short film of 1966. "What did the Oscar do for me?" Berri asked a *Variety* reporter a few years later. "Everything." Following de Beauregard's showcases, which quickly passed into oblivion, Berri had prepared a full-length screenplay based on his own childhood experiences during the war, but even with the support of such established filmmakers as Louis Malle and Karel Reisz, he was unable to find a producer. Two months after he received the Oscar, he was able to start shooting, with adequate financing.

The Two of Us (*Le Vieil homme et l'enfant*, 1966) was, in Berri's words, "a story of love between an anti-Semite and a Jew," with the French superstar Michel Simon making his 140th screen appearance, in the role of the crotchety old grandfather who raves and rants about the Jews, the English, the Freemasons, and the Bolsheviks without ever realizing the true identity of the young boy named Claude (played by Alain Cohen, a nine-year-old recruit from a bar mitzvah class) that he is sheltering. When the film was completed, Berri was unable to find a distributor because of what was still considered its "sensitive" subject, but with help from Simone Signoret, François Truffaut, and others, he managed to get it into a chain of art houses, and, after Simon received the award for best actor at the Berlin Film Festival, it went into commercial distribution. Warmly praised by critics on both sides of the Atlantic, *The Two of Us* received its ultimate benediction from François Truffaut, who wrote: "For twenty years I have been waiting for the *real* film about the *real* France during the *real* Occupation—the film about the majority of the French, those who were neither collaborators nor resisters, those who did nothing either good or bad, those who survived, like characters in a Beckett play. . . . Now Claude Berri's first film . . . makes the long wait worth it."

The Two of Us had been coproduced with Renn Productions, and in the wake of that initial—and unexpected—success, Berri turned to financing the films of other directors as well. With Truffaut he coproduced Maurice Pialat's first feature, *Naked Childhood*, which was coscripted and edited by Berri's sister, Arlette Langmann, and at Truffaut's urging, he also coproduced Eric Rohmer's *My Night at Maud's*.

For his own films over the next few years, Berri continued to obey his semiautobiographical impulses. In *Marry Me, Marry Me* (*Mazel Tov, ou le mariage*, 1968), Claude the furrier's son (played by Berri himself) confronts his insecurities about marriage in the process of marrying the daughter of a rich Jewish diamond merchant from Antwerp; in *The Man with Connections* (*Le Pistonné*, 1970), Claude the aspiring actor (portrayed by Guy Bedros) winds up playing out the drama of the Algerian War as a draftee in Morocco; and in *Papa's Movies* (*Le Cinéma du Papa*, 1971), Claude the grateful son (Berri again) pays homage to his father, "the most important man" in his life. Although *Marry Me, Marry Me* encountered mixed reactions in France, it scored a critical and financial success in the United States, where Vincent Canby of the *New York Times*, among others, drew a comparison with Truffaut's autobiographical cycle, writing that Berri's Claude was "clearly a raffish, better-adjusted distant cousin to Truffaut's movie ego, Antoine." Although *The Man with Connections* did not enjoy a similar success in the United States and was dismissed by some French critics because of its unabashedly popular style, it drew a substantially better response from the French public, and a *Le Monde* critic found Guy Bedros to be Berri's "funniest and most perfect alter ego" to date. But *Papa's Movies* was a total flop in France and never even made it to American theatres.

For Claude Berri, who had been nurturing that film since the beginning of his directing career and who had worked on it with his father in its early stages, the failure of *Papa's Movies* was a traumatic blow. "I was humiliated," he told Yonnick Flot many years later, "I started to doubt myself." And in fact, it was at that point that he started to get seriously involved with the production and distribution of films. Since 1970, when he lost some 300,000 francs on a film he had produced as a favor to his brother-in-law, Berri had backed off from financing other directors' films, but now a chance encounter with the French filmmaker Claude Zidi got him going again. Zidi's *Les Fous du stade* (1972) was a far cry from the art films with which Berri had been involved, but it was also a tremendous financial success. As such, it pointed the way to his future role as a "commercial" producer and also guaranteed that he was able to continue producing such noncommercial directors as Jacques Rivette, Jean Eustache, and Luc Doillon. Just after the breakthrough with Zidi, when he was literally unable to find a Paris distributor for the next commercial film he was producing, Berri also teamed up with Christian Fechner and the brothers Jacques and Richard Pezet to create a major new distribution company, AMLF-Paris.

Within five years, Berri's production and distribution ventures allowed him to undertake the big international production that he was "dreaming of"—Roman Polanski's *Tess* (1979). In short order, the project became an incubus that left Berri with a cost overrun of twenty-five million francs as well as stress-induced diabetes, but by tapping AMLF's revenues from the distribution of *Apocalypse Now* he was able to bail out Renn Productions, see *Tess* through to a successful end, and get his blood-sugar level back to normal. For Polanski, that total dedication was proof not only of Berri's friendship, but also of his "unheard-of courage."

During that period of concentrated production and distribution activity in the 1970s, Berri also made four more films of his own—not as many as he wanted, he told Yonnick Flot, "and not as good" as he had hoped. *The Sex Shop* (*Le Sex-shop*, 1972), which he also wrote and starred in, was a domestic comedy about a husband who transforms his bookstore into a sex shop and takes to trying out the merchandise on his wife (Juliet Berto). According to Berri, the film was "more autobiographical than most of my films," but, he explained, "autobiographical in reverse . . . in terms of the couple, the relationship, and not the story of the sex shop or the orgies." While some American reviewers were mildly amused by that "discreetly indiscreet" (and X-rated) sex comedy, the French were largely outraged. "Berri's narcissism has reached unbearable proportions," Jean-Loup Passek complained in *Cinema 71*, contending that the film was "totally useless . . . nothing but a commercial operation."

With *The Male of the Century* (*Le Mâle du siècle*, 1975), Berri ventured yet another satirical look at male-female relations, now revolving around a jealous husband named Claude (played by Berri himself) who has a nervous breakdown when his wife (Juliet Berto) is taken hostage by an attractive bank robber. In France, more than one reviewer called into question Berri's heroic treatment of a supposed antihero, and even in the United States enthusiasm was noticeably on the wane. In the words of John Simon, the film combined the worst of the director's two earlier tendencies—"dreary autobiography and clean dirty jokes."

Less of a stir was created by Berri's next two films, *The First Time* (*La Première fois*, 1976) and *One Wild Moment* (*Un moment d'égarement*, 1977), but there was not a great deal of excitement either. The first was yet another autobiographical venture into which, as Berri admitted, he put all of the memories that he had not "slipped into" his earlier films. In his view, "the film had charm . . . but it didn't make me discover anything," and critics by and large shared his reaction. *One Wild Moment*, meanwhile, moved clearly out of the autobiographical mode with the two main characters named Pierre and Jacques and the action revolving around their teenage daughters, but, as one fairly sympathetic critic wrote, it was still "not the event of the year."

It was after *One Wild Moment* that Berri plunged into work on *Tess*, and, as he later explained, the eventual success of Polanski's film, which won three Oscars and one César (the French equivalent of the Academy Award), provided a kind of catharsis in his own directing career. As French critics were to note, with disdain or delight, depending on their orientation, Berri's post-*Tess* films were unabashedly mainstream, touching on issues of contemporary social interest, to be sure, but in a style that was above all entertaining—a good story with good actors. The first of those ventures, *I Love You* (*Je vous aime*, 1980), took up the question of male-female relationships from a woman's point of view through the story of a songwriter (Catherine Deneuve) and the string of lovers she has either left or is about to leave (Gérard Depardieu, Serge Gainsbourg, Jean-Louis Trintignant, Charles Marquand, and Alain Souchon). Although it was dismissed by French film connoisseurs as "a standard consumer item," the film was hailed by *Premiere* as Berri's best to date. "Packed with strong scenes, moments of suspense, bold strokes of inspiration," Marc Esposito wrote, "*I Love You* is also a great actors' film . . . , one of the most moving portraits of a woman that has been seen in the movies for a long time."

Even more of a popular success was *The School Master* (*Maître d'école*, 1981), inspired by an attack on public education called *Journal of an Educastrater* and starring the well-known stage performer Coluche, in the role of a substitute teacher who saves the faltering school system with his dedication and ingenuity. A number of French film critics were more exasperated than ever, accusing Berri of, among other things, sexism, racism, and beating the dead horse of public education, but

audiences were as charmed as Coluche's students, and, in Paris alone, more than 190,000 spectators flocked to see the film during the first week of its release, which Berri, as its distributor, had timed to coincide with school vacation.

Berri's collaboration with Coluche grew out of a long friendship, for the entertainer had actually made his first, albeit inconspicuous, film appearance in *The Man with Connections* a decade earlier. Convinced that Coluche had great acting potential, Berri had agreed to produce him in four films over thirty months, beginning with *The School Master* and including Jean Yanne's *One Forty-Five Before Jesus-Christ* (1982), Claude Zidi's *Banzaï* (1983), and Bertrand Blier's *My Best Friend's Girl* (1983). At the end of that period, during which Berri also produced Dino Risi's *Fantôme d'amour*, Claude Sautet's *Waiter!*, and Philippe De Broca's *L'Africain*, the two men came back together to make *Tchao Pantin* (1983), which was Berri's first "real fiction," Coluche's first dramatic role, and a smash hit for both of them. Adapted from a novel by Alain Page, who wrote the dialogue for Berri's scenario, *Tchao Pantin* was a sentimental action film about a down-and-out gas station attendant (Coluche) who befriends and later avenges a young Arab-Jewish dope dealer (Richard Anconina). Lavishly filmed in dim interiors and exteriors at a cost of nearly thirty million francs, the film tapped the mood of the French public with a mix of existential despair, local color, and the splendid performances of its two leading actors. It also garnered Césars for Coluche, Anconina, cameraman Bruno Nuytten, and the sound engineers, and when it was recycled on French television for the second time, the film broke all viewing records.

According to Berri, the success of *Tchao Pantin*, coming after his production coup with *Tess*, marked the end of his "period in the wilderness." On a more practical level, it also gave him the financial means to take on a project that he had been mulling over since the late 1970s: an adaptation of the writer-director Marcel Pagnol's 1963 Provençal saga, *The Water of the Hills*. After discovering the two-volume novel in a hotel bookstore in Morocco in 1979, he attempted for six years to persuade Pagnol's widow to relinquish the rights. Finally, in 1984, Berri began putting together what was to be the most expensive film ever made in France.

One of the lessons that Berri had learned from working with Roman Polanski on *Tess*, he later explained to *Premiere*, was the importance of finding first-rate collaborators. "A director—and here I'm speaking of myself—is above all an orchestra leader, someone who can pull together all the elements that go into making a film," he said. For his own superproduction, he turned to people he knew firsthand: Gérard Brach, his first coscenarist, for the adaptation of Pagnol's novel; Bruno Nuytten, for the cinematography; and his sister, Arlette Langmann, for the editing. Through sheer persistence he persuaded his friend Yves Montand to take on the key role of César Soubeyran in spite of the actor's initial reluctance to play what was essentially an aging villain. A promising character actor named Daniel Auteuil was cast in the role of Soubeyran's nephew, and Gérard Depardieu agreed to play the hapless newcomer, Jean de Florette, who becomes their victim.

After an unprecedented shooting period of nine months, in order to go through all the seasons, and another seven months of post-production, the first part of the four-hour film *Jean de Florette* opened in Paris in late August of 1986 to almost unanimous praise. It was followed three months later by an equally successful *Manon of the Spring* (*Manon des sources*). The two-film cycle attracted more than thirteen million French moviegoers, easily leading the year's box-office receipts in France, as it also did in Norway and Switzerland. Daniel Auteuil received a César for his performance, and Berri himself was awarded the Grand Prize of the French National Film Academy. Nor was the response any less favorable in the United States when the films arrived a year later. "You won't leave this one feeling deprived," David Ansen assured his *Newsweek* (November 9, 1987) readers about *Manon of the Spring*, speculating that "if there were filmmakers in the nineteenth century, this, you believe, is how they would have made movies: with larger-than-life characters, throbbing romantic music, embraces silhouetted against crystalline skies, and messengers from the past bringing shattering last-minute revelations."

With the financial success of *Jean de Florette* and *Manon of the Spring*, Berri became the largest independent producer in Europe, and the $70 million that the films grossed in France soon enabled him to launch five new productions for Renn's twenty-fifth anniversary year. (In 1986 a French conglomerate called the Chargers Group acquired a 50 percent interest in Renn, but Berri retains control over the company's activities.) He also began preparing a new film of his own which, he said, would go back to the personal scale of his early career, when he wrote, directed, and acted himself. In the new film, he told David Sterritt of the *Christian Science Monitor* (July 3, 1987): "It's a dream, it's true, and it's life. All my life I am making only one movie, and that movie *is* my life."

Pudgy, balding, and given to expressive gestures, Berri has little of the aura of the French *auteur*. He continues to take small parts in other directors' films, most recently in Maurice Pialat's award-winning *Under Satan's Sun* (*Sous le soleil de Satan*, 1987), but insists that he lacks the patience to return to real film acting. He now serves as founding president of the French Union of Producer-Directors. In recent years he has also had such a growing fascination with painting that he claims he sold the half-interest in Renn Productions in order to buy a particular canvas, and he has done a number of interviews with American artists, including Robert Rauschenberg, Roy Lichtenstein, David Salle, and Jasper Johns. In 1967 Claude Berri married the former Anne-Marie Rassam (Truffaut was their witness), by whom he has two sons, Julien and Thomas Langmann, born in

1968 and 1971, respectively. Now divorced, he also has a third son, Darius, who was born in 1985.

References: Christian Sci Mon p19+ Jl 3 '87 por; Le Monde p15 Ag 27 '88; N Y Times II p1 S 22 '68, II p11 Ja 18 '70 por, II p23+ D 7 '86, II p19+ Je 21 '87 por; Newsday (Weekend) p5 Je 26 '87 por; Premiere 2:104+ S '88 por; Flot, Yonnick. Les Producteurs (1986); Frodon, Jean-Michel and Loiseau, Claude. Jean de Florette: Le Folle aventure du film (1987); International Who's Who, 1989-90; Who's Who in France, 1986-87

Billington, James H(adley)

June 1, 1929– Librarian of Congress; historian. Address: Library of Congress, 101 Independence Ave., S.E., Washington, D.C. 20540

When James H. Billington, historian and authority on the Soviet Union, was nominated in the spring of 1987 as Librarian of Congress, Daniel J. Boorstin, retiring from that post, remarked that "it is a happy coincidence that this profound scholar of Russian culture should be nominated to head our national library when we are more than ever aware of our need for a deeper and more sympathetic understanding of the Russian past." It is a happy coincidence also that both the Library of Congress and the Woodrow Wilson International Center for Scholars at the Smithsonian Institution, which Billington directed from 1973 to 1987, share the goal, as he has pointed out, of encouraging "interaction between the world of affairs and the world of ideas."

In the course of a career devoted to humanistic scholarship Billington also taught history at Harvard and Princeton universities, contributed to popular magazines as well as learned journals, and wrote illuminating and provocative books on Russia and on revolutionary tradition. The comments in the *New York Times Book Review* of the political scientist Marshall Berman on *The Icon and the Axe* apply also to Billington's other books: "His writing at its best is both novelistic, bringing dozens of characters beautifully to life, and poetic, following images into their depths; and it shows how dedication to scholarship can nourish, rather than undermine, the powers of vision and imagination."

James Hadley Billington was born on June 1, 1929 in Bryn Mawr, Pennsylvania to Nelson and Jane (Coolbaugh) Billington. There were five Billingtons among the passengers on the *Mayflower*. When one of them, John Billington, became the first Pilgrim to be hanged, Governor William Bradford of Plymouth Colony declared the Billingtons to be "ye profanist family in all New England." Narrating the incident to Irvin Molotsky during an interview for the *New York Times* (April 18, 1987), James Billington admitted, "I'm not sure we're really related, but we've always kind of claimed it."

Because of the untimely death of his own father, Billington's father had to subordinate his apparently scholarly inclinations to earning a living early in life. He nevertheless transmitted to his son his love of reading. "My father didn't go to college but he filled our house with books that he bought at Leary's," he told Molotsky, referring to a well-known secondhand bookstore in Philadelphia. As a high school student during World War II, he was attracted to *War and Peace*, which at that time was arousing much interest, partly because of similarities between Russian resistance to Napoleon's army, as depicted in the novel, and to Hitler's forces. But unlike most Americans, Billington undertook to read Tolstoy's masterpiece in Russian. Over a period of years he succeeded, with the help of a tutor, a Russian émigré. "I felt I didn't just learn the language," Carla Hall quoted him in the *Washington Post* (April 18, 1987) as recalling. "I learned the culture and that's how I got interested in cultural history."

For his early formal education, Billington attended schools in the Philadelphia suburbs, graduating from Lower Merion High School in 1946. He was valedictorian of his class at Princeton University, which granted him a B.A. degree in 1950. His student years at Princeton, he evidently believes, influenced the eventual direction of his career. "I am in a sense a child of Princeton at the end of the Woodrow Wilson era where a sense of public service was part of one's life," he told Carla Hall. In 1953 he earned his doctorate from Oxford University, after three years of study under a Rhodes scholarship at Balliol College.

Billington entered the United States Army in 1953, as the war in Korea was reaching an end; by the time of his release from service three years later, he had attained the rank of first lieutenant. In 1957 he became an instructor in history at Harvard, where the following year he advanced to assistant professor. Also during the year 1958–59 at Harvard he was a fellow of the Russian Research Center, an appointment that makes clear the focus of his scholarship.

In 1958, moreover, Billington published a pioneering work, *Mikhailovsky and Russian Populism*, the first major biography to appear in English of the neglected but influential nineteenth-century Russian liberal journalist, social critic, propagandist of populism, and advocate of women's liberation. Specialists on Slavic studies generally welcomed the book as a contribution to an expanding consideration of political and social thinking in Russia before the Revolution. Arthur P. Mendel commended Billington in the *Political Science Quarterly* (December 1958) for giving his attention to a moderate radical (for Mikhailovsky disputed Marxism) and thus breaking with the prevailing tendency to concentrate on political extremism in Russian history. A shortcoming of the book, in Mendel's opinion, was "the rather confusing picture of Mikhailovsky that emerges."

A reviewer for the London *Times Literary Supplement* (April 25, 1958) had earlier pointed out, however, "If Mr. Billington's picture of [Mikhailovsky] sometimes seems dim and blurred, this is an accurate reflection of the man." The British scholar of Russian political and cultural affairs Robert Conquest, writing under the pseudonym J. E. M. Arden, commented in the *Spectator* (February 21, 1958) on the readability of Billington's combination of "scholarship and lucidity" and went on to suggest, "If you want to make an effort to understand the Russian background, and some of the whys and wherefores of the great groundswell of 'revisionism' which is once again flooding in to undermine the impressive sandcastles of orthodoxy, you could hardly do better than to start here."

While on the Harvard faculty, Billington was a Fulbright professor at the University of Helsinki in 1960–61 and a guest professor at the University of Leningrad in 1961. Moving to Princeton University in 1962, he taught history at his alma mater as associate professor for two years and then as professor from 1964 to 1974. On excursions from the Princeton campus, he returned to the Soviet Union in the posts of exchange research professor at the University of Moscow in 1964 and visiting research professor at the Institute of History of the Soviet Academy of Sciences in Moscow in 1966–67. Much of his work outside the classroom centered on his service from 1971 to 1973 as chairman of the Board of Foreign Scholarships, which directs international academic exchanges under the Fulbright-Hays Act. He remained a member of the board until 1976.

Among Billington's chief accomplishments during his tenure at Princeton was the completion in 1966 of his massive, encyclopedic *Icon and the Axe: An Interpretive History of Russian Culture*, an introduction to Russian intellectual life over

1,000 years and an exploration of the role of organized religion in its development. "I believe in highly interpretive scholarship—humanistic, synthetic, historical," Billington said in his conversation with Carla Hall of the *Washington Post*. "If you read about what people have aspired to, you are somehow better fortified for your own path." That is the attitude reflected in *The Icon and the Axe*, as a reviewer for the London *Times Literary Supplement* (December 29, 1966) indicated: "The book is indeed a carefully thought out and an essentially personal interpretation of Russia's cultural history; above all, it is a work of serious scholarship, so that even on those occasions when the author's conclusions invite discussions it will be found that they are based on a legitimate if novel interpretation of events."

Many of the comments on *The Icon and the Axe* in United States periodicals were also enthusiastic. More than a decade after its appearance, Marshall Berman praised Billington's history in the *New York Times Book Review* (September 14, 1980) as "probably the single finest American book on Russia and one of the most impressive achievements of American scholarship since the end of World War II." Calling attention to Billington's comprehensiveness, he noted, "He writes as vividly and knowledgeably about literature as about land tenure; he explores the relationship of spatial and architectural forms to political forms." Because of his familiarity with many languages, moreover, he was able to bring to light the enrichments to Russian culture from Polish, German, Italian, Jewish, English, French, and Dutch sources.

Scholarship of that caliber helped to qualify Billington eminently for his appointment in 1973 as director of the Woodrow Wilson International Center for Scholars. Created by Congress in 1968 as a "living memorial" to President Wilson, the independent, nonpolitical center promotes advanced study in the humanities and social sciences and is "a place where the world of ideas can interact, on neutral ground, with the practical world of public affairs," to quote Billington's observation on the center in the *Smithsonian* (August 1977). Since its founding the center has accepted some 1,200 scholars, or fellows, from around the world, selected in open international competition.

"We look for the scholar who seeks tentative answers to important questions, not those who provide definitive answers to trivial questions," Billington explained to Edward P. Morgan, who interviewed him for the *Smithsonian* article on the center. "We do no group or team research. Nor do we emphasize faddish 'relevance.'" Elsewhere, Billington has talked about the center's concern with providing space for "the idiosyncratic scholar," the researcher with "the probing mind" whose pursuit is the truth. But while stress is laid on individual study, the center does have specialized research programs that involve a number of scholars.

Dismayed by the decline in the United States in the study of the Russian language and culture, and by the consequent lack of preparedness to understand or deal with Soviet leaders in international affairs, in 1974 Billington spearheaded the establishment at the center of the Kennan Institute for Advanced Russian Studies, named after his friend, the Sovietologist George F. Kennan, who helped to set up the institute. Seven other programs have since been created at the center.

Also under Billington's direction, the *Wilson Quarterly* was launched at the center in 1976. "The news magazine of the world of ideas," as he characterized it, offers its 110,000 paid subscribers, many of them nonscholars, full-length articles on national and international social, political, and cultural matters; excerpts from specialized journals; book reviews; and other information about scholarly activities. The center's publications, furthermore, include books and research papers by its fellows and detailed guides for scholars to Washington's educational resources.

In 1980, while otherwise engaged with the sundry responsibilities of head of the Wilson Center, Billington published his third monumental work, *Fire in the Minds of Men: Origins of the Revolutionary Faith*, exploring a subject that had attracted him since he had witnessed the outbursts of dissent among many students and some teachers on college campuses during the 1960s. He took his title from Dostoevsky's novel *The Possessed*, in which, when a blaze erupts in a provincial town one night after an impassioned exchange of ideas at a gathering, an attendant cries out, "The fire is in the minds of men, not in the roofs of buildings." Concerned with "small groups and idiosyncratic individuals who created an incendiary legacy of ideas," Billington's story, as he explained in his introduction, "is not of revolutions, but of revolutionaries: the innovative creators of a new tradition" that developed during the 125-year period from the French Revolution to the Russian Revolution.

In what Billington has described as an "awesome chapter in the history of human aspiration," the protagonists are men and women of unyielding faith in the eventual emergence of a new and perfect order. The American specialist in Slavic studies Joseph Nathaniel Frank observed that the book treats "seriously the notion that political revolution is the secular religion of our time" and that it "is certain to cause furious controversy, and equally certain to become a classic." Reviewers did, indeed, disagree as to the merits and failings of Billington's work, his insights and blind spots, his interpretations, and his adequacy in following through on his theses. But his "staggering erudition," as one reviewer termed it, remained undoubted. "Billington dazzlingly invokes scholarship in French, German, Spanish, Italian, Russian, Czech, Croatian, and Polish, as he moves across Europe to South America, and very briefly to the United States," Peter Shaw wrote in *Commentary* (March 1981). Whatever reservations specialists might have regarding one or another aspect of *Fire in the Minds of Men*, they would likely agree unanimously with Shaw's assertion that "no discussion of revolution in the future can afford to neglect the massive documentation of violence and fanaticism which Billington has presented."

As director of the Wilson Center, Billington acquired the administrative experience and fundraising skills that, together with his excellence in scholarship, made him a likely candidate for the position of Librarian of Congress, in succession to Daniel J. Boorstin, who announced his resignation in the spring of 1987. President Ronald Reagan submitted Billington's nomination in April; the Senate confirmed it in July, and Billington was sworn in as the thirteenth Librarian of Congress on September 14, 1987. News of his appointment had been greeted warmly by the American Council of Learned Societies and other scholarly organizations. Like his predecessor, Billington is not a professional librarian; and while some library groups, such as the Special Library Association, supported him, the American Library Association informed the congressional committee of its preference for a professional librarian. It did not, however, testify against him.

The Library of Congress was established in 1800 to fill the research needs of the legislative branch of the government. As its services have expanded over the years to all divisions of the government and to the public throughout the nation, the responsibilities of the Librarian of Congress have accordingly increased. In its three buildings on Capitol Hill the library houses more than 200 million books, the largest collection in the world, as well as millions of maps and charts, manuscripts, photographs, prints, recordings, motion pictures, and videocassettes. It also maintains the Copyright Office, the American Folklife Center and the Center for the Book, and specialized facilities such as the Cataloguing Distribution Service, the National Library Service for the Blind and Physically Handicapped, and Research and Reference Services in Science and Technology.

In a speech at his swearing-in ceremony and in a press conference on that occasion, Billington proposed two directions in which the Library of Congress should move: "out more broadly and in more deeply." In moving out it would make its resources more widely available through increasing loans to local libraries, some of them in the form of circulating exhibitions, and through the use of "new technologies to share the substantive content and not merely the descriptive catalogue of the nation's library." But he argued that spreading material through new technological devices would be of little value unless the library were to play "a catalytic, if not a leadership, role in helping turn information into knowledge and distill it all into some wisdom. . . . It is the ranging, the discriminating, the challenging mind that will have to sort out and make some sense of all this profusion of publication and information that exists in our world and establish some priorities within it." During his press conference he also maintained, "Celebrating the life of the mind is something that a free people needs to do."

Returning to his theme in a symposium, "Knowledge and Power," sponsored by the Council of Scholars of the Library of Congress in mid-June 1988, Billington insisted: "Neither new money nor new programs alone will produce peaks of excellence or original ideas. They require time, freedom, access, and, above all, an inner moral impulse that can perhaps be cultivated more successfully if this Library and other Washington institutions nurture and celebrate intellectual—as they do artistic—creativity." One of the obligations of the Library of Congress, he said at that time, was to use its resources to address the problem of the decline of educational standards. He had earlier discussed the shortcomings of American schools, including universities, in the paper "Education and Culture: Beyond 'Lifestyles,'" presented in June 1984 at a conference titled "Virtue—Public and Private," sponsored by the Rockford Institute's Center on Religion & Society in New York. In his contributions to that conference and in his "conversation" for U.S. News & World Report (October 1, 1984), he deplored, among other weaknesses, the failure of teachers to transmit either traditional moral values, such as an understanding of the link between freedom and responsibility, or the basic historical facts and a core knowledge of the great works that make up their own cultural heritage.

Shortly after he took office as Librarian of Congress, Billington ordered a self-examination of the library that would, in his words, "create for the first time in the library's history an explicit set of institutional values by which we guide, measure, and judge our actions." The study, which was conducted by staff members and outside management consultants, found what Billington described as "an inertia of a large organization" caught between increasing demands and decreasing funds. To correct the problems, he and his team of advisers drew up a plan calling for the massive reorganization of the library's various divisions into two broad departments, Collection Services and Constituent Services, to reflect the library's newly identified seven values—service, quality, effectiveness, innovation, participation, staff recognition and development, and fairness.

Critics of the plan, including many of the library's employees, questioned the philosophy behind it, saying that the consultants had misunderstood "the culture of the library." Many also worried about possible layoffs and downgrading of responsibilities. Commenting on the staff "ferment," Billington told Jacqueline Trescott of the Washington Post (September 27, 1989): "What we are doing is trying to renovate both physically and in tangible human ways this marvelous resource at a time when we are entering the information age. . . . There are legitimate questions, and there are certainly legitimate debates. Considering the extensiveness of the change, the overall staff morale and even enthusiasm has been quite high." The reorganization plan took effect on October 2, 1989, over the objections of some staff members at almost every level.

Billington is a member of the editorial advisory board of *Foreign Affairs*. He formerly served as a member of the editorial advisory board of *Theology Today,* a director of the American Association for the Advancement of Slavic Studies, vice-chairman of the board of trustees of St. Albans School in Washington, and vice-chairman of the Atlantic Council's Working Group on the Successor Generation. He holds several honorary doctorates and is a member of the American Academy of Arts and Sciences and a Chevalier of the Order of Arts and Letters of France.

On June 22, 1957 James H. Billington married Marjorie Anne Brennan. Their children are Susan Harper, also a Rhodes scholar at Balliol; Anne Fischer; James Hadley; and Thomas Keator. When Billington was director of the Wilson Center, President Reagan consulted him on Soviet affairs, and, after he became Librarian of Congress, Nancy Reagan consulted him on her visit to Russia in the spring of 1988. He is considered a "hard-liner" on the Soviet Union, but declines to label himself. He also refuses to disclose his current political party preference. "I'm not a political person," he said in the *Washington Post* interview. "But I'm happy to confirm myself as a cultural conservative who believes in traditional values."

References: Chronicle of Higher Education 33:7+ Ap 23 '87 por; N Y Times p26 Ap 18 '87; Smithsonian 8:76+ Ag '77 por; Washington Post C p1+ Ap 18 '87 por; Contemporary Authors vol 117 (1986); Directory of American Scholars (1982); Who's Who in America, 1988–89

Boitano, Brian

Oct. 22, 1963– Figure skater. Address: c/o Leigh Steinberg, 2737 Dunleer Place, Los Angeles, Calif. 90064

A bright spot in an otherwise dismal showing by the American team at the 1988 Winter Olympic Games in Calgary, Alberta was the dazzling skating of Brian Boitano. One of only two American athletes to capture a gold medal at those games (the speed skater Bonnie Blair took the other), Boitano turned in a freestyle skating performance that seasoned observers ranked with the best they had ever seen to narrowly defeat the home-country favorite, Brian Orser, his longtime rival. His victory culminated a lifelong dream for Boitano, who began skating at the age of eight and who, unlike most top figure skaters, has had only one coach in his entire career—Linda Leaver. (By comparison, Peggy Fleming, the 1968 women's Olympic gold-medal winner, had ten coaches on the way to her Olympic triumph.) Miss Leaver is a suburban housewife, relatively unknown in the upper echelons of figure skating, who became a coach in order to help pay for her husband's college expenses.

In addition to his Olympic gold medal, Brian Boitano has won four United States national championships and two world titles. Ironically, it was his loss to Orser in the 1987 world championships that marked the turning point in Boitano's career. Following that defeat, he hired the skating choreographer Sandra Bezic, who revamped his style, adding to his natural athletic gifts more artistry and emotion. That changeover had much to do with his Olympic triumph.

Brian Boitano was born on October 22, 1963 in the central California city of Sunnyvale into an upper-middle-class Italian-American family. His father, Lew Boitano, was a banker, and his mother, Donna Boitano, was a housewife. The youngest by seven years of four children (he has a brother and two sisters), Brian Boitano was a solitary child who indulged in such private fantasy games as pretending he was invisible. His other, more outgoing childhood activities included playing baseball, a sport that his father had played at the semiprofessional level for the San Jose Bees, and rollerskating around the neighborhood. When he was eight, his parents took him to a performance of the Ice Follies in San Francisco, after which he pleaded with them to allow him to take ice-skating lessons. They sent him to Sunnyvale Ice Palace, a local rink, where he began his long collaboration with Linda Leaver, who had recognized his talent at one of his first group skating classes and had suggested that he begin taking private lessons with her. At his first lesson, Boitano mastered five single-revolution jumps, an astounding feat for a beginning skater.

"I thought he'd be great right away," Linda Leaver told E. M. Swift of *Sports Illustrated* (January 27, 1988). "Though Brian was only eight, I went home and told my husband that one day he'd be the world champion."

When, while still only eight years old, Boitano entered his first ice-skating competition, he captured first prize in the "pixie boys" division. "At ten he was doing things most twenty-year-olds weren't," Linda Leaver told David Levine of *Sport* (February 1988) magazine. By the age of twelve, he had collected seventeen regional medals, although that year he was nearly forced to give up skating because of a knee injury. Boitano captured the United States junior men's championship in 1978, placed eighth in the senior men's competition in the following year, moved up to fifth place in 1980, to fourth place in 1981 and 1982, and to second place in 1983 and 1984. Meanwhile, his reputation as an outstanding jumper was growing. At the United States championships in 1982, he became the first male skater to do a triple axel (three and one-half revolutions), and, at his first international competition, the 1983 world championships, Boitano landed each of the six different types of triple jumps (Lutz, Salchow, axel, flip, loop, and toe loop). Although he was the first man ever to do so in that event, he finished seventh. In spite of all the time he devoted to practicing and competing, he managed to become an honors student at Peterson High School in Sunnyvale.

In an attempt to scale even further athletic heights, Boitano began to work on a four-revolution, quadruple toe-loop jump. Administrators of the sport were finding it difficult to keep up with him. As Linda Leaver told David Levine: "Because he does some of his jumps so easily, Brian got a deduction once, in the national championships, because the judge thought he did a single [jump] instead of a double. Afterward the judge apologized. He said, 'It looked so easy. It just went right by me.'" Indeed, the tendency of judges to undervalue his jumping ability and his own discomfort with the political infighting of figure skating nearly led Boitano to give up the sport before the 1984 Winter Olympics in Sarajevo, Yugoslavia.

"They [the judges] want what they want and I want what I can give," Boitano explained to David Levine. "A lot of times they tried to mold me into something that they wanted to see, and I really resented that. A lot of politics fall into it, you know. If other guys skate well and they're politically over you, they're going to win even though you're better. . . . Judges would rag on me, you know. Just rag. 'He shouldn't skate to that music.' 'His hair is wrong.' 'He's fat.' 'If he doesn't change his costume he'll never win.' It was hard to wait it all out. I almost didn't. I kind of left my body; from '82 to '84 skating was a job for me and I didn't like it. The Olympic year, '84, was the hardest of my life. It was not fun."

Yet Boitano has conceded that the lack of aggressiveness that characterized his skating at the time also damaged his standing with the judges. "I was like a little technical robot when I was eighteen or nineteen," he recalled to E. M. Swift for *Sports Illustrated* (March 31, 1986). "I never missed [a jump]. And the reason I never missed was I never put any energy into my presentation. That's what people picked on me for: no presentation."

Boitano finished fifth at the Sarajevo games, while his fellow American Scott Hamilton captured the gold medal. Soon afterward, he placed sixth at the world championships. A year later, Boitano succeeded Hamilton, who by that time had turned professional, as United States champion. His four-minute final program, which included seven triple jumps and three double jumps, prompted Bob Ottum of *Sports Illustrated* (February 11, 1985) to marvel that "he seemingly spends more time in the air than on the ice." As Boitano put it, "Getting to this spot was like going over a tall mountain." Setting his sights on the world championship, he dropped his studies at De Anza Junior College in Cupertino, California and began training for six hours a day, six days a week. But he could do no better than third at the 1985 "worlds," as the international meet is popularly known, which were won by Aleksandr Fadeyev of the Soviet Union. In July 1985 Boitano was somewhat solaced by his capture of the men's free-skating competition at the National Sports Festival in Baton Rouge, Louisiana.

In February 1986 Brian Boitano overcame strained tendons in his ankles to take his second consecutive United States title. A month later, in Geneva, Switzerland, he staged a dramatic comeback to win his first world title. His technically perfect but relatively bland short program left him in fourth place as he entered the final event, the free-skating program that counts for 50 percent of the overall score. In it, he executed five perfect triple jumps and, in the words of E. M. Swift, "displayed the sort of fire and style that had been so flagrantly missing in his short program." Fortunately for Boitano, each of the three skaters he trailed, Aleksandr Fadeyev, Jozef Sabovcik of Czechoslovakia, and Brian Orser of Canada, skated poorly in the freestyle segment, and he captured the gold medal.

In easily winning his third consecutive United States title, Brian Boitano nearly became the first skater to perform a quadruple jump in competition. Although he made four complete revolutions, he landed slightly off balance and was forced to touch his right hand to the ice in order to maintain his equilibrium. His freestyle program also included the "Tano Triple," a self-devised jump in which he thrusts his left arm dramatically over his head while holding his right hand away from his body as he spins through the air. Boitano's performance earned him marks of 5.9 (out of a possible 6.0) from eight of the nine judges. At the 1987 world championships in Cincinnati, Ohio a month later, Boitano placed second to Brian Orser, who had been the runner-up in the 1984, 1985, and 1986 worlds, as well as in the 1984 Olympics. His attempt at a quadruple jump again failed, since he fell when landing. "I don't think winning or losing depended on that," he said afterward to Frank Litsky of the *New York Times* (March 14, 1987), adding, "Life goes on. I'll probably be a better skater for this happening."

Boitano did, in fact, become a better skater following his loss to Orser. The morning after the 1987 world championships ended, he realized that his preoccupation with perfect technique at the expense of expression and grace might cost him the gold medal at the 1988 Olympic Games. To help remedy the situation, he hired the celebrated skate choreographer Sandra Bezic, herself a five-time Canadian pairs champion. Discovering that Boitano was a technically overburdened skater who "was like a beautiful person wearing too much jewelry," she discarded his old moves and the pop music that he had been skating to, replacing them with classical routines and classical music. "What I didn't want to do was have Brian skate like a skater pretending to be a dancer," Sandra Bezic explained to Sally Jenkins of the *Washington Post* (February 12, 1988). "He didn't need flash and height. All he needed was line and clean technique. It was the 'less is more' concept." Linda Leaver was quoted as saying in the same article: "It takes a mature person to skate this way. He's just now learned to get into the music, to feel the emotion and skate from his heart. This was the last piece to come together."

The new short program that Sandra Bezic designed for Brian Boitano was performed to music from the ballet *Les Patineurs* (*The Skaters*), based on Meyerbeer's operas, which is about a young braggart who skates on a pond before a crowd of awed townspeople. At one point in his routine, Boitano flicks ice shavings off his skate blade and arrogantly tosses them over his shoulder. "It is a very cocky program, and I don't think I'm cocky," Boitano told Phil Hersh of the *Chicago Tribune* (February 18, 1988). "Sandra [Bezic] had a hard time making me arrogant." In his new long program, set to music from Abel Gance's film *Napoleon*, Boitano portrays a military character who, according to E. M. Swift, "battles and parades, dances and courts, broods and exults in victory." That routine features eight triple jumps. "He's always felt a little vulnerable on the ice," Sandra Bezic told Swift. "With these two programs, either as the military man or the arrogant boy, he can hide behind a character. It gives him a mask. That helps when you're putting your heart and soul on the ice."

In July 1987 Brian Boitano again unsuccessfully attempted the quadruple jump, this time at the United States Olympic Festival in Greensboro, North Carolina. Three months later, at the Skate Canada competition, he unveiled his new long program to a standing ovation at the Saddledome in Calgary, Alberta. But Brian Orser won the event, largely because of his superior performance in the compulsory figures segment, which involves laboriously tracing three variations of a figure eight on the ice and which counts for 30 percent of the total score. Boitano placed second. At the Novarat Trophy competition in Budapest in November 1987,

Boitano became the first skater ever to receive a score of 6.0 for a short program in a major international competition. In fact, he received four perfect scores in that segment and three more for his long program.

Brian Boitano skated to his fourth consecutive men's singles gold medal at the 1988 United States championships in Denver, Colorado, becoming the third man, after Scott Hamilton (1981–84) and Charlie Tickner (1977–80), to win four successive United States titles. He seized first place in the compulsory figures, and he made history with his short program by collecting perfect scores for composition and style from eight of the nine judges. Delays forced Boitano to begin his long program at 12:30 A.M., two and one-half hours after he was scheduled to skate, and he gave a less than spectacular performance, twice touching his hand to the ice at the end of a jump, but he was awarded what appeared to be excessively generous marks—nine 5.9s for technical merit and eight 5.9s and one 6.0 for composition and style—and won the event. "Everyone has a breaking point during the season, and I'm just glad that mine happened in Denver instead of Canada," Boitano told Dave Nightingale of the *Sporting News* (February 12, 1988), with regard to the Olympic Games in Calgary. "Now I can start to rebuild myself for the big show in February."

The much-anticipated "Battle of the Brians" at the Calgary games lived up to its billing, since Boitano and Orser each turned in outstanding performances in all three phases of the competition. In the compulsory figures segment, Aleksandr Fadeyev took first place, with Boitano finishing second and Orser third. Orser won the short program segment the next day; Boitano, skating a cautious but error-free program, finished second, and Fadeyev dropped all the way to ninth, effectively knocking himself out of contention for the gold medal. After the first two segments, Boitano emerged as the overall leader, with Orser a close second, setting up a showdown between the two skaters in the freestyle event. Usually accessible to the press, Boitano refused all media interviews, except for mandatory press conferences, in an attempt to limit distractions. At the drawing to determine the order in which the final six skaters would perform, Boitano got a break when he picked number one, his favorite position and one that would allow him to set the standard that Orser, skating third, would have to surpass.

Attired in a royal-blue military uniform and skating to the music from *Napoleon*, Brian Boitano, on February 20, 1988, gave one of the best freestyle skating performances in Olympic history. He flawlessly executed seven of eight triple jumps, slipping almost imperceptibly on the most difficult one, a three-and-one-half revolution triple axel. "He never missed a subtlety or a beat," E. M. Swift reported in *Sports Illustrated* (February 29, 1988). "And when, in a final flourish, he landed a double axel, then an Arabian, violently shaking his head and fists in conclusion, it was clear to everyone in the building that, well, this was the best that he could skate." Paul Wylie, one of his teammates, called Boitano's routine "the best performance I'd ever seen any skater skate." The judges concurred, granting Boitano five 5.9s and four 5.8s for technical skill and three 5.9s, five 5.8s, and one 5.7 for composition and style.

Unfortunately for Boitano, Orser was almost as good, and he had the additional advantage of skating in his home country before highly partisan spectators. But the Canadian's performance was damaged by two small mistakes: first, he made a minute stumble on a triple flip; then, near the end of his program, he decided to turn a triple axel into a double, thus leaving him with two fewer triple jumps than Boitano. Orser's technical merit scores included one 5.9 and eight 5.8s. For composition and style, he received one 6.0, five 5.9s, and three 5.8s. When the marks were totaled up, four judges had rated Orser the best, three had chosen Boitano, and two (from Denmark and Switzerland) had scored the skaters dead even, but the Danish and Swiss judges, reflecting Orser's two errors and Boitano's almost perfect execution, had both given the Canadian a 5.8 for technical merit and the American a 5.9 in the same category. That differential swung the two judges into Boitano's column and gave him the gold medal.

Writing in the *Sporting News* (February 29, 1988), Paul Attner hailed Brian Boitano's accomplishment as "one of the most memorable of these Games, if not in all of Olympic history." His performance was considered extraordinary mainly because it had come in Olympic competition, where, because of the excruciating pressure, even the very best skaters seldom, if ever, perform at peak levels. "Since I was fourteen, all I had heard was that everyone had won the Olympic gold and not skated their best," Boitano told Attner. "It was my dream since then to win the gold skating my best. And that's what I did."

In his final competition as an amateur, the 1988 world championships at Budapest, Boitano recaptured the world crown from Orser, who, as he had done in the Olympics a month earlier, placed second. His performance was highlighted by an outstanding short program, for which he was awarded a standing ovation. Shortly before Boitano skated his long program, Kurt Browning of Canada, who eventually finished sixth, became the first skater to complete a quadruple toe loop in competition. In attempting to duplicate Browning's feat, Boitano executed four complete revolutions, but he landed on both skates instead of just one.

Following the world championships, Brian Boitano embarked on a skating tour of Europe and the United States encompassing fifty cities. At its conclusion, he organized a group of advisers (which he jokingly refers to as "Team Boitano") to assist him in his business affairs. The group consists of the Los Angeles lawyer Leigh Steinberg, who serves as his agent, Linda Leaver, who functions as his personal manager, and his father, who advises him on financial matters. Unlike most previous skating gold medalists, Boitano decided not to join a traveling ice show, such as the Ice Capades or the Ice Follies, opting instead to devote his time to other projects. In December 1988, for example, he starred with Katarina Witt of East Germany, the winner of the women's figure skating gold medal at both the 1984 and 1988 Olympics, in a television special for ABC entitled *Brian Boitano: Canvas of Ice*. The skater became a teenage heartthrob following his Olympic triumph, and, in May 1988, a poster featuring him in tight jeans, an unbuttoned shirt, and a leather bomber jacket was released. In May and June 1989 Brian Boitano joined other champion figure skaters (including Brian Orser and Katarina Witt) in a thirty-city tour of the United States, the proceeds of which were donated to competitive amateur skating programs.

At five feet, eleven inches tall and 160 pounds, Brian Boitano is bigger than most male figure skaters. He has a handsome, angular face, with brown eyes and brown hair. Interviewers unfailingly describe him as extremely polite, affable, and modest. "He is informal, comfortable. Instantly likable," David Levine wrote. "With an outgoing manner and a musical, soft-edged voice he is a natural talker, quick to laugh and ready to dish some gossip (all discreetly off the record, of course)." Among the honors Boitano was accorded in 1988 were the Young Italian-American of the Year Award from the National Italian-American Foundation and the Victor Award for special contributions to sports. He was also nominated for ABC's Athlete of the Year Award. A connoisseur of fine cuisine who lists dining out as his favorite recreational activity, Brian Boitano plans to open an Italian restaurant called "Boitano's" in San Francisco, the city in which he now lives. He also intends to write an autobiography and to organize an annual "East-West Ice Show for Peace," which will feature top skaters from Japan, the Soviet Union, Europe, Australia, Canada, and the United States. Boitano devotes some of his leisure time to the Starlight Foundation, a charitable organization that grants wishes to terminally ill children.

References: Chicago Tribune D p1+ F 18 '88; People 29:29 F 15 '88 por; Sport 79:65+ F '88 pors; Sports Illus 68:105+ Ja 27 '88 pors, 68:20+ F 29 '88 pors; Washington Post E p9 F 12 '88 por

---

Bolkiah, Sir Muda Hassanal

July 15, 1946– Sultan of Brunei Darussalam. Address: h. Istana Darul Hana, Brunei; The Aviary, Osterley, England

The title "richest man in the world," according to *Fortune* magazine and the *Guinness Book of World Records*, belongs to Sir Muda Hassanal Bolkiah, the twenty-ninth sultan of Brunei, a tiny, petroleum-rich country on the northern coast of Borneo, in the South China Sea. Sir Muda's wealth,

Sir Muda Hassanal Bolkiah

which *Fortune* estimates at $25 billion, officially belongs to the country, but the sultan has exercised virtually absolute control over the economy and the government since Brunei won independence from Great Britain in 1984. Sir Muda's income from the production and export of oil and liquefied natural gas amounts to more than $2 billion a year, and the 250,000 citizens of the "Shellfare State," as Brunei is sometimes called, share in the bounty, averaging incomes of $22,000 a year. Since independence, the sultan has often made the headlines by acquiring hotels abroad, donating millions of dollars to worthy causes, and building the world's largest palace. In 1986 he tried to give $10 million in humanitarian aid to the Contras fighting in Nicaragua, through Elliott Abrams, the assistant secretary of state for inter-American affairs, who placed the funds in the wrong Swiss bank account. One journalist has described Sir Muda as "a pleasure-loving and taciturn man with a passion for polo, helicopters, and cars."

The oldest son of Sir Omar Ali Saiffudin, the twenty-eighth sultan of Brunei in a four-hundred-year-old family dynasty, Sir Muda Hassanal Bolkiah was born on July 15, 1946 in the capital city of Bandar Seri Begawan and grew up in the "modest Moorish-style" palace of his father on the outskirts of the city. Sir Omar was an ardent Anglophile. He built a memorial to Sir Winston Churchill, whom he once met; observed Queen Elizabeth II's official birthday as a national holiday; and gave Sir Muda the benefits of a British education. Sir Muda was taught first by private tutors (in English as well as in Malay, which is Brunei's official language) and then at the exclusive British-run Victoria Institute in Kuala Lumpur, Malaysia, which was another British colony. In 1966 Sir Muda was

sent to England with his brother to study at the Sandhurst Military Academy, the elite British military school.

Great Britain had been involved in Bruneian politics since the early seventeenth century. In 1888 the Bruneian royal family supported a treaty making their sultanate a British protectorate. In 1929 oil was discovered by the Shell Oil Company, although it was not until after World War II that Shell began to exploit it. In the late 1950s Great Britain urged the sultan to institute democratic reforms and make Brunei an independent country. Sir Omar resisted both demands. A treaty, signed in 1959, made Brunei an independent sultanate, with defense and foreign affairs left in the hands of Great Britain. In September 1959 Sir Omar promulgated Brunei's first written constitution, which provided for a chief minister who ran the government's administration, oversaw defense and foreign matters, and reported directly to the sultan, and for privy, legislative, and executive councils. In 1961 Sir Omar, who had ruled as sultan since 1950, named his oldest son the heir apparent and crown prince.

The constitution was suspended in December 1962, following an uprising against the sultanate by the Brunei People's party, backed by the North Borneo Liberation Army. The revolt was suppressed by 2,000 British Gurkhas (Nepalese tribal soldiers serving in the British army), who were transported to Brunei from Singapore. Some seventy-five rebels were killed and 1,000 were captured, a state of emergency was declared, and about fifty leaders of the left-wing, pro-independence Brunei People's party were imprisoned without trial. Embarrassed by the flagrant suppression of democratic rights, Great Britain threatened to deny Brunei further military protection unless concessions to democracy were made. Another blow to democracy occurred in July 1963, when the sultan decided not to join with Singapore, North Borneo, Malaya, and Sarawak in forming the Federation of Malaysia, objecting to the amount of oil revenues that Brunei would have to contribute to Malaysia's treasury. A more important reason for the sultan's backing out, according to some political observers, was the probability that the federation would insist on Brunei's adopting a more democratic form of government. (Indeed, Malaysia did not easily forget that rejection, and in 1977 sponsored a resolution in the United Nations demanding that free elections take place in Brunei.) Attempting to make some kind of gesture towards constitutional reform after a round of talks in London in 1964, Sir Omar created a legislative council, but only a few of the council's members were elected. The Bruneians appeared to be resigned to a combination of authoritarianism and dependence on Great Britain. In May 1967 the Brunei People's Independence Front party, the only surviving opposition party, lost fifteen of its twenty-five seats on the legislative council.

On October 4, 1967 Sir Omar abdicated the throne in favor of his son. Palace sources claimed that the fifty-one-year-old sultan stepped down in order to devote more time to spiritual matters, but many political observers believed that Sir Omar's retirement—and the ascension of an inexperienced young man to the throne—was a maneuver to ensure that Great Britain would continue to protect Brunei from domestic and foreign opposition and a way to avoid complying with Britain's call for a more representative government. One threat came from the Philippines, which enacted a law claiming that Sabah, an eastern neighbor of Brunei, was part of its domain. Without British protection, Bruneians feared, the Philippines might next extend its claim to Brunei. Sir Omar continued to wield considerable power behind the scenes, retaining the portfolio of minister of defense until 1979, when, after the death of his wife, he began to withdraw from public life.

Although he at first exercised little power, the young sultan enjoyed the perquisites of sovereignty that his father had bestowed on him. At his coronation ceremony on August 1, 1968, the twenty-two-year-old sultan was borne to the palace in a five-ton, 100-foot-long, gold-embossed carriage pulled by fifty-nine men. His gold crown was studded with diamonds, and among his many gifts was a $22,000 Lamborghini sports car, presented to him by his subjects. Throughout the 1970s the sultan maintained a reputation as a jet-setting playboy with a fondness for shopping sprees, fast cars, gambling in private casinos, and frequent visits to nightclubs in London and Paris. Among his mentors during that period was the American-educated Saudi Arabian arms dealer and businessman Adnan Khashoggi, who was known for assiduously cultivating the friendship of the world's most powerful statesmen. According to the sultan's unauthorized biographer, James Bartholomew, in an article for the *Manchester Guardian Weekly* (May 7, 1989), "The young sultan, shy and inexperienced in the way of the world, was influenced in a way which may have not been ideal."

Early in 1970 Sir Muda increased the powers of the sultanate by suspending the constitution and making the legislative council into a wholly appointive body. Negotiations with Great Britain continued throughout most of the 1970s, with the young sultan perceived as a figurehead for his father's decisions. In 1971 Sir Muda agreed with Great Britain that the sultan would be responsible for Brunei's internal affairs while Britain would handle its external affairs. On June 30, 1978, after twelve days of discussions between Sir Muda and the British minister of state, Lord Goronwy-Robert, Great Britain and Brunei agreed that Brunei would achieve full independence at the end of 1983. The Treaty of Friendship and Cooperation was signed on January 7, 1979, after the sultan received assurances from Indonesia and Malaysia that they would respect Brunei's independence, that they would support Brunei's membership in the Association of Southeast Asian Nations, and that they would not allow the sultan's adversaries to establish guerrilla bases in either country. As part of the treaty, Great Britain agreed to make a Gurkha battalion stationed in Hong Kong available, if necessary, to protect Brunei's oil fields, in exchange for the right to use unpopulated areas of Brunei as a training ground for jungle warfare. Shortly afterwards, Brunei became a member of the Organization of Islamic Conference.

On January 1, 1984 a ninety-minute ceremony marked Brunei's official independence from Great Britain. A more elaborate celebration took place on February 23, 1984 in the capital's new $50 million stadium. Foreign dignitaries from seventy different countries attended, including Ferdinand E. Marcos of the Philippines, President Suharto of Indonesia, and Prince Charles of Great Britain. Brunei's name officially became Brunei Darussalam, which means "Brunei, Abode of Peace." Upon independence, Sir Muda added the office of prime minister to his responsibilities and announced that his cabinet would primarily consist of members of the royal family. The council of ministers, privy council, chief minister, and state secretary were abolished. In February 1984 the thirty-three-member legislative council was dissolved as well. "We prefer expertise in government to being ruled by laborers and taxidrivers," Abdul Aziz, the chief minister, explained, as quoted in the *New York Times* (January 2, 1984), adding that top officials in the government learned about citizens' concerns through regular dialogues with the people. In the early 1980s the sultan himself visited village elders to find out about local problems, but he quickly lost interest in that endeavor. On the eve of independence, the government announced that it would release three of the remaining twenty political prisoners jailed after the 1962 rebellion. Brunei became a member of the Association of Southeast Asian Nations on January 7, 1984, and the 159th member of the United Nations in September 1984. In his maiden speech at the United Nations, Sir Muda expressed his loyalty to the West but asked that the Palestine Liberation Organization be recognized.

With the retirement of his father from public life, the sultan added his father's portfolio of minister of defense to his responsibilities. In 1986 he was listed as head of the Royal Brunei Police, the Public Service Commission, the Religious Affairs Department, the Petroleum Unit, the Anticorruption Bureau, the Brunei Investment Agency, the Economic Development Board, the Economic Planning Unit, customs, state stores, computers and statistics, immigration, labor, prisons, weights and measures, and the fire brigade. With one brother serving as finance minister and another as foreign minister, Brunei is run, in the words of James Bartholomew, "as a family business."

Like his father before him, the sultan has resisted all attempts at democratic reform. In 1985 a group of businessmen formed the National Democratic Party of Brunei (BNDP), calling for nationwide elections and the resignation of the sultan. Sir Muda responded by forbidding government employees, who make up 40 percent of the work force, to join the party. Leaders of the BNDP charged that the civil service is unaccountable to the public and works "to please only the sultan." In January 1988 the sultan declared the BNDP illegal and imprisoned two of its leaders. The state of emergency, declared in 1962, remains in effect, and it was only in 1989 that the last of the rebels imprisoned after the 1962 uprising were released from jail.

In the area of defense, Great Britain and Brunei amended their earlier agreement concerning the Gurkhas so that Great Britain now agreed to keep a battalion of Gurkhas in Brunei, under the leadership of the British ministry of defense. The battalion's maintenance costs would be paid by the sultan. In addition, Brunei's own troops were to remain under British command for five years. When the British refused to give the sultan control of the Gurkha battalion, Sir Muda moved Brunei's investment portfolio of $4.56 billion from Britain's Crown Agents to the newly established Brunei Investment Agency, which Morgan Guaranty Trust of New York and Citibank helped to set up. Sir Muda has also transferred $2 billion from an Asian bank to one in Switzerland, and he has widened his investments into Hong Kong and China.

Brunei's wealth stems from royalties on oil and liquefied natural gas, resulting in foreign reserves of $25 billion and an annual income that is conservatively estimated at $2 billion. Because the Seria oilfield, Brunei's first drilling site, has largely been depleted, most of the oil is now extracted from offshore oilfields and produced by Brunei Shell Petroleum and Brunei Shell Marketing. The liquefied gas is produced by Brunei LNG and transported in refrigerated tankers to Tokyo. The Bruneian government owns more than 50 percent of the shares in the Brunei Shell Petroleum Company, and it also owns shares in Brunei LNG. Thanks to its natural resources, Brunei boasts the highest standard of living in Southeast Asia. The average per capita income is $22,000, and most homes have electricity and a television set. Low-interest and interest-free loans for cars, houses, and television sets are available to everyone, and gasoline is subsidized. The government provides allowances for pilgrimages to Mecca, and there is no income tax. In addition, education and health care are free, and the government offers some subsidized housing.

According to Shell petroleum experts, Brunei has enough oil and natural gas reserves to last well into the next century. Nevertheless, in 1986 Sir Muda announced the fifth Five-Year National Development Plan, emphasizing the diversification of the local economy into such areas as scientific technology (especially the use of silica for the microchip and optics industries), agriculture, finance, industry, and manpower training. The sultan has also stressed the importance of raising the literacy level among Malays and providing them with technical education to reduce Brunei's dependence on foreign labor.

Recently, the sultan has expressed impatience with the rate at which diversification is proceeding, resulting from the difficulty in convincing Brunei-

ans that they could someday be facing an economic crisis. Undertaking some diversifying of his own, Sir Muda has made a number of real-estate investments overseas. Among his holdings are the Dorchester Hotel in London, which he bought for $50 million in January 1985, the Beverly Hills Hotel in Los Angeles, which he purchased in October 1987 for $185 million, and the Hyatt Hotel in Singapore. It is commonly believed that the sultan provided the financial backing for Mohamed al-Fayed, an Egyptian businessman and former associate of Adnan Khashoggi, when al-Fayed bought Harrod's, the exclusive department store in London, for $650 million. The sultan owns a number of other buildings in London, including a mansion near Kensington Palace and a forty-seven-acre estate in the Southall district of London, which contains, according to Bartholomew, the largest private garden in London outside of Buckingham Palace.

The security of Brunei is, to the sultan, indistinguishable from the sanctity of his throne, and it is towards this end that he cultivates Western leaders and public opinion. During his visit to New York City in September 1984 to speak at the United Nations General Assembly, Sir Muda presented Edward I. Koch, New York's mayor, with a $500,000 check to be used to provide meals to the elderly through the Citymeals-on-Wheels program. Sir Muda donated another $1 million to the United Nations Children's Fund.

At the suggestion of Mohamed Al-Fayed, who had, in turn, been prompted by the ABC News correspondent Pierre Salinger, the sultan donated $50,000 to establish the Ritz Paris Hemingway Award for the best novel in English translation. Al-Fayed had bought the Ritz, which was the American novelist Ernest Hemingway's favorite hotel in Paris, in 1979 and, with Salinger's help, wanted to publicize its connection with Hemingway. The sultan happened to be in Paris when preliminary discussions were underway, and Al-Fayed arranged a meeting with Salinger. The sultan's motive in providing the prize money most likely sprang from his desire to create a positive image in the West. He has also indicated an interest in supporting education in general. In addition, $100,000 was given to five groups and universities with programs in American literature and in improving the environment.

Another gift led to a different type of notoriety when Sir Muda inadvertently became linked to the Iran-Contra scandal. In 1986 the sultan had given $10 million to Elliott Abrams, the assistant secretary of state for inter-American affairs—money that the sultan was told would be used for humanitarian aid to the Contras in Nicaragua. The $10 million was supposed to be deposited in a Crédit Suisse account controlled by Lieutenant Colonel Oliver North, a member of the National Security Council. But North inadvertently gave Abrams the wrong account number, and the money was deposited instead in the account of a Swiss businessman, who later returned the $10 million to the sultan, along with $253,000 in interest.

Social problems in Brunei revolve around religious and ethnic issues. Brunei has 50,000 Chinese, who control the local business economy, but only a fifth of them are Bruneian citizens. There is also an ongoing conflict between Western secular values and religious orthodoxy. Malays who have been educated in the West do not relish being told where they can eat and what they can drink. And they will inevitably want a voice in the government. According to a reporter for the *Economist* (December 24, 1983), "It is not clear that the secretive, imperious sultan is aware of these problems or knows what to do about them." Although Bruneians are Sunni, rather than Shi'ite, Moslems, they have been influenced by the Islamic fundamentalism that has swept the Moslem world. As the self-proclaimed leader of Bruneian Moslems, the sultan has been a strong force for moderation. Barbara Crossette reported in the *New York Times* (February 1, 1986) that the sultan won a showdown with zealots in his own Religious Affairs Department in late December 1985, after the fundamentalists turned the once-joyous parade celebrating the prophet Mohammed's birthday into an austere demonstration in which women were segregated from men. The sultan boycotted the event and later denounced its organizers on the state-run television network. When the female television newsreaders, who were Moslem, shed their *chadors* at around the same time, their gesture signaled that the sultan had won a victory over the religious zealots.

Money is no object where the armed services are concerned. In 1988 the Royal Brunei Malay Regiment comprised 3,380 men, and its military equipment included Scorpion tanks, armored personnel carriers, and missile-firing attack craft armed with French-made Exocet guided missiles. Helicopters and speedboats are used to guard the borders from illegal immigrants attracted to Brunei because of its high standard of living. The sultan is fond of military exercises, and his regiment has been known to use the Exocet missiles, costing £100,000 each, for target practice.

One of the manifestations of the sultan's wealth is the Royal Brunei Polo Club, which was finished in 1980, four years after Sir Muda developed a passion for the game. Its facilities include a two-story, gold-domed clubhouse capable of accommodating 100 guests, three playing fields, a squash court, and a skeet-shooting range. Sir Muda's 138 horses, imported from Argentina along with their grooms, are worth more than $10,000 each. Fodder is flown in from Australia on a monthly basis.

The pièce de résistance of Brunei in terms of opulence, however, is the sultan's 1,788-room palace, the largest in the world. (The Vatican is the second-largest residential palace, with 1,400 rooms; London's Buckingham Palace has only 614.) Built on a man-made 100-foot hill overlooking Bandar Seri Begawan and surrounded by 300 acres of landscaped gardens, the gold-domed palace covers more than fifty acres. Its public banquet hall can accommodate 4,000 people, and the throne room can hold 2,000. The total cost of the palace, which was completed in 1984, has been estimated at between $250 and $400 million. Enrique Zobel, the president of the Ayala Corporation, the largest construction firm in the Philippines, helped Sir Muda lay out plans for the palace after the two met playing polo.

Sir Muda's family quarters contains 900 rooms for his extended family, which includes his three brothers and their wives and children. On the palace grounds are the sultan's own miniature mosque, a heliport (the sultan flies his own helicopters), a personal recreation center with squash, badminton, and tennis courts, a swimming pool, a practice polo field, and an underground garage for 800 cars. In addition to his Lamborghini, Sir Muda owns more than 100 cars, including a Rolls-Royce, which is the official car of the royal family, a gold-upholstered Land Rover, and an Aston-Martin. He also owns a Boeing 727, purchased in 1985 for $19 million from his friend Khashoggi. Sir Muda has since built a second palace, which boasts five swimming pools, including one which is Olympic size.

In public, the trim and mustached sultan maintains a military bearing whether wearing conservative custom-tailored Western suits or the ornamental uniform of the Bruneian royalty, complete with frills, epaulets, and a chest of medals. In 1965, when he was nineteen, Sir Muda married his cousin, Princess Saleha, "a sweet, bedimpled, soulful-eyed lass of sixteen," according to the official court biographer. With Rajah Isteri Anak Saleha, as she is now called, Sir Muda has one son and five daughters. In the late 1970s the sultan began a relationship with Marian Bell, an air hostess with Brunei's small nationalized airline. Half-Bruneian and one-quarter Japanese and British, Marian Bell, unlike the sultan's first wife, is thoroughly Westernized. Under Koranic law, a man is allowed four wives. In 1981 Marian Bell became the sultan's second wife, with the title Pengiran Isteri Hajjah Mariam. She has borne him one son. The sultan's full-titled name runs to a paragraph in length, but his subjects prefer to call him "H. H."—short for "His Highness."

References: *Economist* 289:40 D 24 '83; *Manchester Guardian W* p22+ My 7 '89 por; *Nat Geog Mag* 145:207+ F '74; *N Y Times* p14 O 15 '70, p10 F 18 '81, p9 Ja 2 '84, p2 F 1 '86 por; *Parade* p8 Jl 7 '85 por; *Washington Post* F p7 O 24 '68; *International Who's Who*, 1989–90

Boren, David L(yle)

Apr. 21, 1941– United States Senator from Oklahoma. Address: 453 Russell Senate Office Bldg., Washington, D.C. 20510

As a young and relatively unknown state legislator, David L. Boren rode a simple but highly effective campaign gimmick to the Oklahoma governorship. Now his state's senior United States senator, Boren is the most popular Oklahoma politician in recent memory and a major force in Congress. (The 1988 edition of *The Almanac of American Politics* identified Boren as one of the Senate's five most powerful members). A self-styled "maverick conservative," Boren is a staunch proponent of fiscal caution and the deregulation of private industry. Yet although he was among the small but important group of conservative Democrats who joined with Republicans to advance the domestic and foreign-policy agenda of President Ronald Reagan in Congress, he engaged from time to time in protracted struggles with the White House, most notably to obtain debt relief for hard-pressed farmers in 1985. As chairman of the Senate's Select Committee on Intelligence since January 1987, Boren angered the Reagan administration by holding up ratification of the Intermediate Nuclear Forces (INF) Treaty until he received assurances that the nation's surveillance satellites would be modernized. Despite his record of staunch support for the oil and gas industries, which are vital to Oklahoma's economy and have contributed heavily to his Senate campaigns, Boren has developed a reputation as an opponent of special interests for his long, though largely unsuccessful, effort to reduce the influence of political action committees, or PACs.

David Lyle Boren was born on April 21, 1941 in Washington, D.C., to Lyle H. Boren and Christine (McKown) Boren. His father was elected as a Democratic congressman from Oklahoma in 1936, when he was just twenty-seven years old. An opponent of President Franklin D. Roosevelt's New Deal program, Lyle Boren served for five terms, leaving office in 1947. David Boren's political initiation began at an early age: when he was just eleven, he worked as a page for Senator Robert S. Kerr of Oklahoma at the 1952 Democratic National Convention in Chicago.

Boren attended public grade schools in Seminole, Oklahoma, and in 1959 he graduated from Bethesda–Chevy Chase High School in Maryland. After entering Yale, he worked intermittently in Washington, D.C., as assistant to the director of liaison at the Office of Civil and Defense Mobilization from 1960 to 1962 and as a propaganda analyst for Soviet affairs at the United States Information Agency from 1962 to 1963. Boren graduated summa cum laude from Yale with a B.A. degree in history in 1963. Oxford University, which he attended as a Rhodes scholar, granted him an M.A. degree in government in 1965. While in England, Boren also served on the Speakers Bureau of the United States embassy in London, delivering speeches in more than sixty countries. After returning to the United States, Boren enrolled at the University of Oklahoma's College of Law, which in 1968 awarded him the Bledsoe Memorial Prize as that year's outstanding law school graduate.

Meanwhile, in 1966, David Boren was elected to represent Seminole County in the Oklahoma House of Representatives. He was reelected three times, running without opposition each time. During his eight years at the statehouse, he acquired a reputation as a reformer who pressed for measures that would require legislators to disclose their campaign finances and to make their voting records public. His crusade so discomfited the Democratic leadership that they removed him from two of the most coveted committees, rules and appropriations, although he rose to the chairmanship of the Elections Committee. In addition to discharging his duties in the legislature, Boren practiced law in Seminole and Wewoka, Oklahoma from 1968 to 1974, served as an officer in the Oklahoma Army National Guard, and taught political science at Oklahoma Baptist University in Shawnee, first as an assistant professor and, from 1969 to 1974, as a full professor and chairman of the social sciences division.

Shortly after he announced his intention to challenge incumbent David Hall for the Oklahoma Democratic gubernatorial nomination in 1974, Boren's own poll showed him to be the choice of less than 2 percent of the state's Democrats, but, with Hall under federal investigation for allegedly accepting kickbacks from architects and building contractors, the time appeared to be ripe for a reformist candidate like Boren. To attract media attention, the candidate reluctantly agreed to a suggestion from his cousin, James Boren (a political satirist whose book *When in Doubt, Mumble* was a bestseller), to carry a broom on the campaign trail as a symbol of his commitment to restoring clean government. "We were walking from town to town," David Boren explained to Douglas B. Feaver of the *Washington Post* (November 10, 1974), "and James wanted us to carry the broom to 'sweep out the old guard.' I didn't like the idea. I said I'd try it only for a week, but it got us tons of publicity and people started carrying brooms around." Soon, members of "Boren Broom Brigades" began appearing at every stop, waving their wooden-handled straw brooms as the candidate spoke. Capitalizing on the fad, the Boren campaign began passing out brooms of their own, the "clean sweep model," which, coincidentally, was manufactured in Lindsay, Oklahoma, the "broomcorn capital of the world."

In the Democratic gubernatorial primary election, the United States congressman Clem Rogers McSpadden received 38 percent of the vote, Boren 36 percent, and Hall a mere 27 percent. Because none of the three candidates received a majority, the two top vote-getters, Boren and McSpadden, were forced into a runoff. Refusing to court organized labor, ranchers, and other voting blocs whose support is usually considered imperative to success in Oklahoma politics, Boren defeated McSpadden by 54 to 46 percent, and he went on to win the general election handily over the Republican nominee, the state senator James Inhofe, by 64 to 36 percent, the third-largest victory margin in a gubernatorial election in the history of Oklahoma. At thirty-three, Boren became the youngest governor in the nation.

While serving in the Oklahoma legislature, David Boren had made a detailed study of the innovative program introduced by Governor Jimmy Carter of Georgia in order to reorganize and streamline the state government, and he began corresponding with Carter about those innovations. After taking office as governor of Oklahoma, Boren immediately called for reductions in state spending and set an example by cutting the size of his own staff, by selling the governor's airplane, by refusing to accept a $7,500 salary increase, and by persuading other state officials who had been given pay raises to reject them. The new governor also took steps to insure that appropriations bills for government agencies included provisions that specified the maximum number of employees the agency could have. "There's no more important issue than holding the line on government spending," Boren told one interviewer. He also instituted measures that compelled welfare recipients to register for work and stepped up prosecution of fathers who abandoned their families.

Governor Boren's administration also saw the enactment of legislation calling for campaign financing disclosure, stronger open-meeting laws for public bodies, and more competitive bidding on state contracts. Boren instituted several new educational programs, including the Oklahoma Foundation for Excellence, which honors outstanding public school teachers and high school seniors, and the Scholar-Leadership Enrichment Program, which offers Oklahoma college students the opportunity to attend seminars with leading international scholars. So conciliatory were his dealings with the legislature that he was dubbed the "scrambled eggs governor" because of his practice of inviting lawmakers who held opposing views to have breakfast with him, in the hope that such meetings would produce a consensus.

David Boren was the first governor to endorse Jimmy Carter in his bid for the Democratic presidential nomination in 1976, mainly because he believed Carter was committed to the deregulation of the oil and natural gas industries, the lifeblood of Oklahoma's economy. Drafting position papers on energy for the Carter campaign, he wrote about 90 percent of a letter promising deregulation of the price paid for newly discovered gas that, under Carter's signature, was sent to the governors of two other oil- and gas-producing states, Dolph Briscoe of Texas and Edwin Edwards of Louisiana. Carter was elected president, but he refused to live up to his campaign promise to propose deregulation of gas prices. In his indignation, Boren lashed out at the chief executive in 1978, repeatedly castigating him for his "breach of commitment" and sometimes even calling his energy policy "insane."

Although he was occasionally criticized for being overly responsive to the demands and needs of the oil and gas industries, Boren was nonetheless a popular governor. His chances for reelection to the governorship in 1978 appeared to be excellent, but he decided to run instead for the United States Senate seat vacated by the Republican Dewey F. Bartlett, who was retiring. During the primary campaign, another candidate accused Boren of being a homosexual, a charge that he adroitly deflected by swearing on his family Bible that he was unimpeachably heterosexual. He finished first in the seven-candidate Democratic primary, garnering 46 percent of the vote, but, since he failed to win a majority, he was forced into a runoff with Ed Edmondson, who had finished in second place. Boren handily defeated Edmondson, and in the general election he had an even easier time, besting the Republican Robert B. Kamm by 67 to 33 percent. In 1984 Boren took 90 percent of the vote in the primary and 76 percent in the general election, carrying every one of Oklahoma's seventy-seven counties in both races. His victory margin in the general election, in which he defeated Republican William E. Crozier, was the largest of any United States Senate candidate in Oklahoma's history.

In his first year on Capitol Hill, largely at the urging of the Democratic senator Russell B. Long of Louisiana, David Boren landed a seat on the influential Finance Committee, an assignment that enabled him to play a key role in shaping the Gramm-Rudman-Hollings deficit reduction package of 1985 and to protect the interests of the oil and gas industries. He was one of the small group of conservative Senate Democrats on whom President Ronald Reagan could usually count for support, even when some moderate Republicans strayed from the fold. During consideration of the 1981 budget bill, for example, Boren played a crucial role in defeating an attempt by Senator John H. Chafee, a Republican from Rhode Island, to restore about a million dollars worth of spending on domestic programs that Reagan wanted cut. In return, the administration included two of Boren's ideas in its tax reduction bill of the same year: decreasing the oil windfall profits tax and eliminating the inheritance tax for spouses.

On other domestic issues, Boren, as befitted a conservative, favored a constitutional amendment requiring a balanced federal budget, prayer in the public schools, and weakening gun control laws. In 1987 he was one of only two Senate Democrats (Ernest F. Hollings of South Carolina being the other) to vote to confirm Reagan's nomination of Robert H. Bork to the United States Supreme Court. Equally conservative on foreign-policy matters, Boren endorsed the administration's campaign to arm the Contra rebels fighting the Marxist-led Sandinista regime in Nicaragua. He also supported production of the MX missile and of chemical weapons, and he was the lone holdout in a 99-1 Senate vote calling on the administration to curtail the escort by American ships of neutral oil tankers in the Persian Gulf during the war between Iran and Iraq.

In 1985, however, Boren opposed the Reagan administration with a vengeance over the issue of debt relief for farmers. As a member of the Senate Agriculture Committee, he helped to focus national attention on the plight of family farmers, many of whom were encountering severe financial difficulties as a result of high interest rates, declining land values, a strong dollar, which hurt foreign sales, and competition from large commercial growers in agribusinesses. Despite his ingrained distaste for such stonewalling tactics, Boren led Democratic farm state senators in a filibuster of Reagan's nomination of Edwin Meese for the post of attorney general, the purpose of which was to put pressure on Senate Republican leaders and the administration to act on farm credit aid. Although the administration denounced the ploy as "blackmail," it eventually agreed to the Democratic request that existing loan programs be made easier to use. At that point, Boren called off the filibuster. Later in 1985 Boren cosponsored, with the Republican senator Rudy Boschwitz of Minnesota, a bill designed to wean farmers from the present price support system with a form of direct government aid until they could adjust to an exclusively free-market economy, but the measure failed to pass.

With the Democratic takeover of the Senate in the 1986 elections, David Boren became chairman of the Select Committee on Intelligence, a post that became available when the four senior Democrats on the panel resigned in order to take over other committees. His first major responsibility as chairman was to head the preliminary investigation into the Iran-Contra scandal. In late January 1987 the Intelligence Committee issued a report detailing its initial findings, following three weeks of hearings. Partly because two key figures in the scandal, Lieutenant Colonel Oliver L. North and Rear Admiral John M. Poindexter, refused to testify, citing their Fifth Amendment right not to incriminate themselves, the report listed fourteen major "unresolved issues." The report's chief finding was that President Reagan was apparently unaware that profits from arms sales to Iran were being used to fund the Nicaraguan Contras, but the report also concluded that the driving force behind the arms sales was not, as Reagan had steadfastly maintained, the desire to improve relations with Iran's "moderate" element, but rather to secure the release of American hostages held in Lebanon.

In December 1986 David Boren had become one of the eleven senators named to the special committee investigating the Iran-Contra scandal. During the committee's public hearings, which began on May 5, 1987, Boren expressed his anger at officials of the Reagan administration for making what he believed were deliberately misleading statements to Congress about the affair. In a heated exchange with the retired air force major general Richard V. Secord, Boren, after listening to the officer's claims of patriotism, challenged him to prove his loyalty by granting the committee access to pertinent bank records.

After President Reagan and Soviet leader Mikhail Gorbachev signed the Intermediate Nuclear Forces Treaty, eliminating medium- and shorter-range nuclear missiles, in December 1987, Boren held closed-door Intelligence Committee hearings on the compliance provisions of the agreement. Three months later the panel issued a report to the Senate Foreign Relations Committee pointing out that United States electronic and satellite surveillance systems were barely adequate enough to verify Soviet compliance with the treaty. The report went on to express "grave concerns" about the American capability of verifying Soviet compliance with a treaty then being negotiated by the two superpowers to eliminate long-range nuclear weapons. Later in March, Boren spoke with Reagan and advised him to petition Congress for additional funding to finance the improvement of the surveillance system. When, in April 1988, Boren learned that the administration had not, to that point, requested that money, he threatened a filibuster to delay Senate ratification of the treaty until it did so. The Senate ultimately approved the pact on the condition that the surveillance systems would be upgraded, but in April 1989, the administration of President George Bush, citing budget constraints, made it clear that it did not intend to proceed with the modernization, prompting Boren to threaten cuts elsewhere in the intelligence budget in order to provide the money.

One of the few members of Congress who does not accept contributions from political action committees, Boren, in 1985, introduced legislation designed to limit the growing influence of those fundraising organizations. Senator Boren's bill limited the total amount that House candidates could accept from PACs to $100,000. Senate candidates, meanwhile, could accept between $175,000 and $750,000, depending on the population of their state. In addition, the plan lowered the maximum amount each PAC could donate to a single candidate from $5,000 to $3,000 and increased the ceiling on individual contributions from $1,000 to $1,500. Pointing to the fact that PAC contributions to congressional candidates had increased from $12.5 million in 1974 to $113 million ten years later, Boren told Julia Malone of the *Christian Science Monitor* (December 3, 1985): "I feel very strongly that our political process ought to be one of grass-roots democracy. How in the world can we be surprised that Congress has such a hard time acting in the national interest when more and more of its campaign funds are coming from special-interest groups?" Boren's anti-PAC bill passed the Senate by a vote of 69-30 in August 1986, but it died in the House.

Senator Boren's critics have charged that his decision to refuse PAC money does not represent a great sacrifice on his part, since the independent oil producers and royalty holders so vital to Oklahoma's economy generally sidestep PACs and contribute to candidates directly. Those critics further point out that, in his 1984 reelection campaign, Boren received 25 percent of his contributions from executives and employees in just two industries: energy and financial services. Boren counters by noting that energy, agriculture, real estate, and financial services are the only major industries in Oklahoma, and that, unlike candidates who accept PAC money, he receives almost all of his contributions from in-state sources. In May 1989 Boren dismissed President Bush's proposal to eliminate PAC contributions altogether, noting that it failed to close loopholes that would permit special interests to pay a candidate's media expenses and otherwise disguise their contributions.

Unlike many of his fellow senators, David Boren is not highly telegenic. His entry in the congressional directory *Politics in America* (1988) describes him as a "pale and pudgy" man who "does not look on first glance to be a powerbroker or even a politician." Indeed, political cartoonists in Oklahoma once drew him as the Pillsbury Doughboy. Nonetheless, David Boren is regarded as one of the Senate's most affable members, and he is said to be universally well liked by his colleagues and their staffs. Cautious and hardworking, Boren is also a gifted speaker, equally at home in quoting Rousseau before an audience of intellectuals or in delivering an old-fashioned stemwinder on the campaign trail.

David Boren and the former Janna Lou Little were married on September 7, 1968. That union, which ended in divorce, produced two children: Carrie Christine and David Daniel. Since December 1977 David Boren has been married to Molly Wanda Shi, a former Oklahoma state judge. When not in Washington, the Borens reside in Seminole, Oklahoma. David Boren is a member of Yale University's governing board of trustees and of the Oklahoma Hall of Fame. His religious affiliation is Methodist.

References: N Y Times A p6 S 21 '86 pors; Wall St J A p1+ F 7 '78; Washington Post A p8 N 10 '74 por, A p25 N 21 '86 por; Almanac of American Politics, 1988; Politics in America (1988); Who's Who in America, 1989–90; Who's Who in American Politics, 1987–88

Boskin, Michael J(ay)

Sept. 23, 1945– Economist; United States government official. Address: Rm. 418, Old Executive Office Bldg., 17th St. and Pennsylvania Ave., N.W., Washington, D.C. 20500

Michael J. Boskin, the chairman of the Council of Economic Advisers in the administration of President George Bush, emerged as a leading economic adviser and consultant to the White House, several government agencies, and a number of congressional committees in the early 1980s, offering his expertise primarily in the areas of public finance and Social Security. A highly respected professor of economics at Stanford University, Boskin has written extensively on tax theory and policy, public debt, government spending, and retirement patterns and behavior, among other topics. In his most recent book, *Reagan and the Economy: The Successes, Failures, and Unfinished Agenda* (1987), he contended that Ronald Reagan's economic program had largely succeeded in dispelling the notion that the federal government could solve every economic problem. Professing that he is not an ideologue, Boskin recently told one interviewer, "I am eclectic, but I have a lot of strong principles." During the 1988 presidential campaign, Bush frequently consulted Boskin on matters of economic policy, and Boskin is responsible for the Bush campaign's "flexible-freeze" plan to balance the federal budget by allowing spending for most programs to grow only enough to keep pace with inflation and by offsetting any potential spending increase with a corresponding decrease somewhere else.

Michael Jay Boskin was born on September 23, 1945 in New York City, the second of the two sons of Irving and Jean (Kimmel) Boskin. When he was six years old, Boskin moved with his family to Los Angeles, where his father continued his work as a self-employed construction contractor and his mother took a job as a public accountant. Boskin's middle-class family values influenced his later development as an economist. His father, who had dropped out of college during the Great Depression, firmly believed in the value of saving for a rainy day. "As an academic economist I am known for espousing the importance of savings accounts," Boskin told a reporter for the San Jose Mercury News (April 24, 1988). While the family lived modestly in rented apartments, Boskin nonetheless grew up thinking that upward economic mobility was possible.

In the mid-1960s Boskin attended the University of California at Berkeley, where he majored in economics. His senior thesis, which examined the issues of taxation and the incentive to work among low-income families in Oakland, California, won him the economics department's highest citation as its top undergraduate. The study was subsequently published in the National Tax Journal. Awarded the Chancellor's Cup as the year's outstanding graduate, Boskin received his B.A. degree, with highest honors, in 1967. Remaining at the university for graduate work, he earned his M.A. degree in 1968 and his Ph.D degree in 1971, both in economics. His dissertation on the effects of income maintenance programs on the size of the labor force earned him the first National Tax Association Outstanding Doctoral Dissertation Award. During his college years, Boskin shared the liberal views of many of his classmates, but, as he explained to the reporter for the San Jose Mercury News, "I was never very far to the left. I was deeply concerned about the Vietnam War. We were never going to win it, and there were a variety of moral issues: how to deal with the fact that both sides were committing atrocities. It was the times. I was not a strong Kennedy-McGovern Democrat."

Boskin began his teaching career as an assistant professor at Stanford University in 1971, becoming a full professor in 1978, after spending the previous year as a visiting professor at Harvard University. Boskin was "busy and popular" at Stanford, where he devoted sixteen-hour days to research, writing, and teaching graduate and undergraduate courses, including "Econ One," which is Stanford's most popular course. In 1986 Boskin founded and assumed the directorship of the Center for Economic Policy Research at Stanford. The center is a business-funded think tank where scholars and students examine issues of economic interest. In addition to his academic work, Boskin served as an adviser and consultant to numerous organizations and government agencies, including the United States Treasury, the Department of Health, Education, and Welfare, the Joint Economic Committee of the Congress, the Advisory Council on Social Security, the Department of Labor, the Department of Defense, and the Northern Cheyenne Indian Tribal Council and Research Project.

During his years on the faculty of Stanford University, Boskin frequently published articles in professional and scholarly journals, wrote two books, and edited several more, among them The Crisis in Social Security; Problems and Prospects (1977), to which he also contributed a few chapters outlining his views on Social Security. In the introduction to that book, he argued that, while the Social Security program had accomplished certain goals, it was nonetheless in serious trouble, primarily due to changes in the economy since Social Security's enactment in the 1930s. He listed the long-term funding crisis, the presence of adverse incentives, and the program's built-in inequities as the most pressing problems. Among the changes in the economy that precipitated those problems were the growth in real per capita income, the increased role of government, the presence of more married women in the labor force, earlier retirement, the increase in life expectancy, and the decline in the birth rate. Because of the demographic changes in the population, the ratio of retirees collecting benefits to workers paying taxes will increase, Boskin predicted, crippling Social Security's long-term ability to provide benefits under the pay-as-you-go system, in which the taxes currently being paid by workers are transferred directly to retired beneficiaries. The term "adverse incentives" refers to individuals being discouraged from saving while they are, at the same time, encouraged to retire early so that they can collect Social Security benefits.

In Boskin's view, the root of the problem lies in the inequities built into the Social Security program, since the system provides benefits equally to the poor and non-poor. Boskin suggested that Social Security be restructured in two ways. First, there should be a provision for the intergenerational transfer of funds. Unlike the current system, where the funds come from earmarked taxes, funds should be routed through the government's general revenue and delivered to those who are found to be needy. Second, all individuals should be required to purchase retirement insurance that would guarantee at least poverty-level income during retirement. Boskin further suggested the establishment of a Social Security trust fund to finance the annuity (insurance) component of the plan. During the 1976 presidential primaries, Ronald Reagan relied on Boskin's research to attack the Social Security system, although Boskin took exception to the way Reagan used his research.

Boskin first came to national attention when he was profiled, along with several other young scholars, in a *Newsweek* (June 26, 1978) article entitled "The New Economists." These "new economists" called into question the government's previous methods for managing the economy, in light of the recessions of the 1970s, and reevaluated the Keynesian model of an activist government that "fine tunes" the economy by manipulating an inflation-unemployment tradeoff. They were dubious about the possibility of Keynesian precision and cautious about government intervention. Boskin, for example, disputed the idea that saving is static, believing that the tax system discouraged savings and investment. Easing the taxes on the interest in savings accounts, he argued, would encourage people to save and invest. "Even Keynesians agree that investment rates are too low," Boskin said, as quoted in the *Newsweek* article, "but they mechanically continue to look at what they conceive to be insufficient final demand as the cause of it."

In 1981 Boskin declined President Reagan's offer of a seat on the Council of Economic Advisers, because he was just settling into a new marriage. Four years later, he again refused an appointment in the Reagan administration—this time, as the Treasury Department's chief economist—for personal reasons. Remaining at Stanford, he continued his analysis of government spending and the American economy. In 1982 he coedited, with Aaron Wildavsky, *The Federal Budget: Economics and Politics*, in which he examined what he considered to be the appropriate role for the government in managing the economy. Predictably, Boskin displayed a preference for less government intervention, focusing on the potential problems of government attempts at the redistribution of wealth. Some programs intended to equalize the share of income between the poor and the non-poor actually work in reverse, Boskin claimed, redistributing money from the poor to the non-poor. As an example, he cited the minimum-wage program.

In Boskin's first independent book, *Too Many Promises: The Uncertain Future of Social Security* (1986), he again recommended that Social Security be separated into a transfer program based on need and an annuity program financed from payroll taxes. Boskin's arguments here had a greater urgency, for he predicted a crisis of "unprecedented proportion" unless the "inequitable, inefficient, and insolvent" social program was amended immediately. Contending that the tax increases of 1977 and 1983 had begun to erode public confidence in the Social Security system and that they were, in any case, inappropriate solutions to the problem, he offered his two-tiered approach as a "cost-conscious and target-effective" alternative. "Politically, of course, Boskin's proposal is very much an unbaked cake," Stephen Chapman observed in his review of *Too Many Promises* for *Fortune* (August 6, 1986). "Boskin's ideas should help Americans see the case for revolution."

The following year Boskin published his second book, *Reagan and the Economy: The Successes, Failures, and Unfinished Agenda*. Among the Reagan economic program's successes, Boskin counted the reduction of inflation at a lower cost than expected, the focus on the deterrents to high marginal tax rates, some slowing in nondefense spending, and the easing of government regulations and controls. He hailed as the most important Reagan-era contribution the idea that the government could not solve all economic problems. "The once-popular notion that the government, especially the federal government, is the proper answer to *all* of society's economic problems has been dealt a serious blow," Boskin maintained. "New spending programs will have to pass tougher tests for years to come, and that means less automatic budget growth in the future. Even if nothing else is done, the repudiation of bad policies will stand as a major accomplishment."

Boskin also addressed the problem of the huge surplus, amounting to more than $70 billion a year, that is expected to accumulate in the old age, survivors, and disability-benefits side of the Social Security program by the mid-1990s, while Medicare runs deficits. "I hope we will have the political courage to save the surplus rather than squander it," he told a reporter for *Fortune* (March 30, 1987). "When all the bids are in, Mr. Michael Boskin's new book is bound to stand as one of perhaps two or three indispensable studies," a reviewer for the *Economist* (January 16, 1988) commented. "Because he [Boskin] points willingly to errors in the blueprint, and to mistakes in implementing it that were the administration's fault, not that of Congress, his support for the basic goals of Reaganomics carries weight."

Although he was sympathetic to the aims of the Reagan economic program, in his book Boskin contended that the policies were oversimplified and that they did not necessarily complement one another. He was especially critical of the Reagan plan's overly optimistic projections, and he blamed the administration for the increase in the federal budget deficit and for the decline in savings. "I favor a tax increase as a last resort, if spending cannot be reduced," he wrote. "It is also important that the increase be on consumption, not on investment." In conclusion, Boskin noted that economic policy was less pressing an issue "than it was in 1980 because of the substantial improvements that have occurred since that time." As Peter T. Kilborn observed in the *New York Times* (June 5, 1988), Boskin delivered his criticism "gently, which perhaps explains how . . . [he] maintained close ties to the administration over the years without making obvious enemies."

At least partly because of his ties to the administration, it was widely rumored in the fall of 1987 that Boskin was being considered as a replacement for Beryl Sprinkel, a Chicago banker who had expressed a desire to resign from the chairmanship of the Council of Economic Advisers to return to private life. When the stock market crashed on October 19, 1987, however, Sprinkel remained as chairman to minimize any further disruption in the administration.

By the summer of 1988 Boskin had become a key adviser in George Bush's presidential campaign. He was well prepared for the role, having served as a consultant to several congressional committees and as the economic adviser to the White House chief of staff Howard Baker during his tenure as Senate majority leader. He had also helped Ronald Reagan prepare for his nationally televised debates with Jimmy Carter in the closing months of the 1980 presidential contest. Commenting on his role in the Bush campaign, Boskin said, as quoted in the San Jose Mercury News profile: "I explain the landscape. I might say that X is better than Y for specific reasons and give my own opinion, but I always try to be careful not to screen out alternative points of view." Among other things, he prepared position papers and reviewed proposals that were made by other economists. Boskin supported Bush's proposition to cut capital-gains taxes to 15 percent from 28 percent, a position in line with his belief in supply-side incentives, and he favored tax credits for research and development. He did not, however, wholeheartedly embrace Bush's stance of no new taxes. "A modest tax increase is O.K. if it's needed to sweeten the pot for a modest spending cut," he said, as quoted in Business Week (June 20, 1988). "But only as a last resort—and only as long as it is a tax on consumption."

Boskin also proposed that Bush adopt a "flexible-freeze" progam for balancing the budget by 1993 without a tax increase. Under the plan, the growth of government spending would be maintained at the rate of inflation, by offsetting any increases in spending in such areas as education, drug enforcement, and AIDS research with decreases in other areas. Bush staffers did not specify which programs would be cut, saying only that the list did not include Social Security. Criticism of Boskin's flexible-freeze plan focused on his assumption that Congress would accept nondefense spending cuts, which some observers thought was doubtful. The flexible-freeze plan was also criticized by Lawrence H. Summers, a professor of economics at Harvard and a former student of Boskin's. Summers, the top economic adviser to Michael S. Dukakis, the Democratic candidate, argued that the imposed spending cuts would most adversely affect the poor.

Other economic measures that Boskin advocated included the restoration of an investment tax credit, and he believed that the unemployment rate could fall to 5 or 5.5 percent without adding to inflation. He indicated that he would support increased government spending and temporarily drop the flexible freeze if a recession developed. "When the economy is in a serious recession," he explained to Peter T. Kilborn in the interview for the New York Times profile, "as in 1974–75 or in 1981–82, there is some opportunity for a government spending increase to get the economy moving a little bit." Finally, Boskin hoped to eliminate

"entitlements for the rich," which include agricultural subsidies to millionaire farmers and cost-of-living adjustments in Social Security payments to the very wealthy.

On December 6, 1988 President-elect Bush named Boskin chairman of the Council of Economic Advisers, a role that chiefly involves explaining the administration's economic policy to the public. At his confirmation hearings on January 26, 1989, Boskin said that he supported the Reagan administration's economic forecast of 3.2 percent growth for 1989, but he added that it was not to be construed as an official estimate of the Bush administration. He further indicated that the Reagan administration's projection of 6.3 percent average interest on three-month Treasury bills in 1989 was "not unreasonable," and he anticipated that short-term rates would "fall substantially" in the coming year. In his view, Boskin told the senators, the best way to increase the savings rate in the United States would be to cut the national deficit, and he proposed restoring tax deductions to IRA investors when the government "can afford to deal with the risk of losing some revenues." Boskin's nomination was unanimously approved by the Senate on February 2, 1989.

Many economists predicted that Boskin might succeed in restoring to the Council of Economic Advisers some of the prominence it lost during the Reagan administration, after Martin Feldstein, then the council's chairman, went public with his concerns about the budget deficit. Unlike the three men who served as chairman of the council under President Reagan, Boskin meets regularly with the president on a one-to-one basis, and he sends Bush a briefing memo almost every night. Since he joined the Bush campaign in 1988, Boskin has made it clear that any differences he has with Bush would be kept private. "I do not think it is the role of the adviser to go public about a disagreement with a decision the president makes," he told Peter T. Kilborn of the New York Times (December 7, 1988). "It's the president who got elected, not me."

Reflecting his intention to participate personally in the formation of economic policy, President Bush set up an economic policy apparatus within the White House. Boskin and Roger B. Porter, the assistant to the president for economic and domestic policy, who head the apparatus, contributed more to Bush's proposals to reduce the capital-gains tax and limit the increase in the minimum wage than did members of Bush's cabinet. Boskin is also a member of the Economic Policy Council, whose members include Vice-President Dan Quayle, Porter, Secretary of the Treasury Nicholas F. Brady (who chairs the council in Bush's absence), Richard G. Darman, the budget director, and various cabinet members involved in forming economic policy. Moreover, he is a regular at the Tuesday morning "Breakfast with Brady" sessions that are also attended by Darman and Secretary of Commerce Robert A. Mosbacher, and he sits on the Domestic Policy Council, which is headed by the attorney general, when that council deals with economic issues. "Boskin has done a great job," White House Chief of Staff John Sununu said, as quoted in the *Wall Street Journal* (August 3, 1989). "And not just on the academics of economic theory. He's been right there, involved in the details of policy."

On the subject of foreign trade, Boskin has proven to be an outspoken critic of employing retaliatory measures against unfair trading practices. "We must keep up the notion of free and liberal trade— we have to keep the goal in mind," he explained, as quoted by Hobart Rowen in the *Washington Post* (March 5, 1989). "The surest way to stumble into a global recession is through a trade war." On May 25, 1989 Bush publicly named Japan, Brazil, and India as unfair trading partners, against the advice of Boskin, Darman, and Treasury Secretary Baker, among others. Boskin believes that tariffs and quotas lead to higher prices on traded products, fuel inflation, and ultimately result in lower real income. According to Peter Kilborn, writing in the *New York Times* (May 22, 1989), Boskin and Darman advocated a policy of less government intervention to enable the dollar to fluctuate more widely, although the Bush administration denied that report.

Described in the *San Jose Mercury News* as a man "with a Brooks Brothers cut but street-smart," Michael J. Boskin is known for his pleasant manner. Modest by nature, he confines his boasting to pointing out that he has taught several well-known tennis players in his classes at Stanford. An avid tennis player himself, Boskin worked out with the varsity team when he was at Stanford, and he often plays with Lawrence Summers when they run into each other at conventions and seminars. Boskin also enjoys skiing. He and his second wife, the former Chris Dornin, director of publishing services for Hearst Magazines in New York, whom he wed on October 20, 1981, live with their cat, Norton, in Washington, D.C. An earlier marriage ended in divorce. Boskin has received a number of honors and awards, including the Abramson Award for Outstanding Research from the National Association of Business Economists in 1987 and Stanford University's Distinguished Teaching Award in 1988.

References: Bsns W p104+ Je 20 '88 por; N Y Times III p1+ Je 5 '88 pors, B p14 D 7 '88; Newsweek 91:59+ Je 26 '78 por; Time 133:48 Ja 30 '89 por; Washington Post A p14 D 7 '88 por; Who's Who in America, 1988–89

Brodkey, Harold (Roy)

1930– Writer. Address: b. c/o Janklow & Nesbit Associates, 598 Madison Ave., New York, N.Y. 10022; h. 255 W. 88th St., New York, N.Y. 10024

Harold Brodkey has been acclaimed as an American counterpart of Marcel Proust, and his writing has been compared to that of William Faulkner, Walt Whitman, William Wordsworth, and Ralph Waldo Emerson. The critic Harold Bloom, Sterling Professor of Humanities at Yale, has called him "an original" whose fiction "deals you a tremendous blow, a tremendous wound." Susan Sontag has said that she reads every word that Brodkey writes, and to Cynthia Ozick he is "a true artist." His reputation is based on two collections of short stories that were published thirty years apart: *First Love and Other Sorrows* (1958) and *Stories in an Almost Classical Mode* (1988). Comprising twenty-seven of Brodkey's thirty-six published stories, the books reveal a talented storyteller's development into a writer who takes enormous risks with structure and language in order to illuminate the darker side of the self with brutal honesty.

Brodkey has enhanced his reputation—and fueled skeptical literary gossip—by promising, but thus far failing to deliver, a Proustian novel to be entitled "Party of Animals." In progress since 1959, the autobiographical novel follows its protagonist, Wiley Silenowicz, from infancy through childhood, college, and adulthood. Those who have plowed through the thousands of pages of manuscript are extremely enthusiastic. The novelist Gor-

© Jerry Bauer

don Lish, who is an editor at Alfred A. Knopf, which published *Stories in an Almost Classical Mode*, told David Remnick of the *Washington Post* (February 19, 1986) that "one could take virtually any section of [\"Party of Animals\"] . . . and have a book that would surpass almost anything you and I have ever read. . . . Brodkey is trying to say everything he possibly can summon about the exchange that obtains in a family; everything that can register on the mind and heart is in his text." The critic Denis Donoghue has called it "a work of genius."

"Party of Animals" has been included in and withdrawn from publishers' catalogues since the 1970s, for Brodkey's continual need to revise the manuscript and his acute anxiety about its reception have delayed publication time and again. In his interview with David Remnick, Brodkey compared the release of the novel to giving away a daughter in marriage: "You don't really want to do it, it's so painful. And I'm afraid to publish the book for fear it will change the world around me too much; for fear that it won't change anything at all. . . . What's lacking is the authority and the will to say, 'This is what I've written.'" And in an interview with Dinitia Smith for *New York* (September 19, 1988) magazine he said, "I associate being recognized with being dead. I write like someone who intends to be posthumously discovered."

Harold Roy Brodkey was born Aaron Roy Weintraub to Russian-Jewish immigrants in Staunton, Illinois in 1930. His father, Max Weintraub, was an illiterate junk man and semi-pro fighter who once told Brodkey he had shot and killed a Ku Klux Klansman in order to protect a black boxer from a lynch mob. Ceil Weintraub, his mother, died when Brodkey was twenty-three months old. Her death made it impossible for him to separate himself psychologically from her, as he testified to Remnick: "If she had lived there would have been certain moments to declare independence. I never had that."

After Ceil Weintraub's death, Brodkey stopped walking, talking, and eating. He was left in the care of his father and a registered nurse, both of whom drank. At the age of two he was adopted by his father's second cousin, Doris Brodkey, and her husband, Joseph Brodkey. The name Brodkey is a corruption of the Russian name Bezborodko, according to an article by Frank Kermode for the *New York Times Book Review* (September 18, 1988). Harold Brodkey's natural father had neglected him, and may have beaten him, as evidenced by Mrs. Brodkey's reaction to her first encounter with the boy. "Doris Brodkey said she had never seen any sight so disgusting as when they went to get me," Brodkey told Dinitia Smith. In his autobiographical story, "Largely an Oral History of My Mother," the narrator's adoptive mother describes a parallel incident this way: "You were covered with sores, bruises—I threw up . . . I couldn't bear to touch you."

According to Brodkey, it took two years for his adoptive mother and a nurse to restore him to health, and throughout his childhood in University City, Missouri he remained psychologically unstable. The Brodkeys were a middle-class, nonobservant Jewish family, in contrast to Ceil Weintraub, who spoke Yiddish and prayed in Hebrew. (Hearing either of those languages still grieves Brodkey unbearably.) Joseph Brodkey owned, at various times, several farms and a small department store.

Describing his adoptive family to Dinitia Smith, Brodkey said, "There was a tremendous amount of affection, even at bad times. But always the sense it was earned, not genetically mine."

The Brodkeys' affection was not enough to stave off a series of breakdowns suffered by the boy whenever he was reminded too forcefully of his natural mother. The first occurred when he was in the first grade. His natural father took him back from the Brodkeys after an IQ test suggested that Brodkey was a genius. Upset by the way his father reminded him of his mother, he began vomiting violently, and Max Weintraub returned him to the Brodkeys immediately, confining subsequent contacts with his son to brief visits. By the age of eight the number of similar experiences had become sufficient to make Brodkey want to become a writer. "Enough had happened," he told Dinitia Smith. "This had to have some meaning. I didn't know any other way to find meaning except by writing things down."

But not all of his problems were psychological. When Harold Brodkey was nine, his adoptive father suffered a stroke or a heart attack and remained an invalid until he died five years later. When he was thirteen, Doris Brodkey developed cancer. He told Dinitia Smith that he owed his survival to kind neighbors. One neighborhood friend remembered him as being "tall and shy," and as "just brilliant, with almost a photographic memory." Despite his feelings of isolation, stemming from his reputation for extraordinary intelligence, his family's catastrophic illnesses, and his Jewishness, Brodkey managed to fit in at University City High School. In an interview with David Streitfeld for the *Washington Post Book World* (August 14, 1988), he recalled, "As far as the categories went in high school, I was sort of in with the normals. It was a great triumph." He edited the school newspaper, served on the student council, and graduated at the head of his class in only three years.

In 1947 Brodkey entered Harvard as a pre-med student, intending to earn enough money eventually to support his adoptive mother. Meanwhile, he worked in a shoe store to pay for his education and even managed to send some money back home. He performed so well in his courses that he was offered a scholarship, but when it became clear that his mother was not going to live, he drifted away from science. In his interview with David Streitfeld, he said of that period, "I fought to get my grades down far enough so there would be no chance to be a service to humanity." He turned his attention to writing, which he pursued despite the "advice" of a Harvard dean. Brodkey quoted the dean, in his interview with David Remnick, as saying, "A Jew can't be a good writer in English. That's a waste of your time."

After graduating from Harvard, Brodkey eloped with a Radcliffe graduate, Joanna Brown, in 1952. They went west, where Brodkey taught for a year. In 1953 they returned to New York, where Brodkey worked first as a page at NBC's studios and then as a researcher. In that year their only child, Ann Emily, was born. In 1954 Brodkey's stories began to appear in the *New Yorker*. Two years later, after having been promoted to the personnel department at NBC, Brodkey was offered a position in the sales division. In his interview with Dinitia Smith, he explained that his prospective bosses feared exposure in one of Brodkey's *New Yorker* stories, so he was "shunted off to the creative end," where he wrote two television screenplays.

In 1958 nine of Brodkey's semiautobiographical stories about childhood, adolescence, romance, and innocence were published by Dial Press under the title *First Love and Other Sorrows*. The book is distinguished not so much by its subject matter and formal qualities, which were considered to be typical of *New Yorker* stories of the 1950s, but for Brodkey's clarity of language and vision. Writing in the *New York Times* (January 12, 1958), William Goyen praised his "uncommon perception of the secret glow within the trivialities of our poor human majesty." William Peden agreed in *Saturday Review* (January 25, 1958): "Mr. Brodkey writes well, in a clear, uncomplicated, unaffected prose. He sees well, too; more important, he thinks about what he sees and understands its meanings and implications."

The strength of Brodkey's early fiction earned him a fellowship from the American Academy of Rome, also known as the Prix de Rome, in 1959. But Brodkey felt that his stories were fraudulent. "I was consciously lying when I wrote them," he told Remnick. "I was a happy man and I didn't want to screw it up. They were meant to be friendly and make a certain amount of money." He repeated this to Dinitia Smith, adding that he deliberately held back for fear of what writing with complete honesty would do to him, especially since he had a daughter. He provided further explanation in an article by Howard Kissel for *Women's Wear Daily* (August 14, 1984). "About twenty years ago," Brodkey was quoted as saying, "I realized if I weren't truthful I'd start writing like other people. . . . [W]hen I wrote those first stories I was happy. I thought everybody knew that happiness was laid over a structure of terror and pain and could be taken away from you at any minute. When I found people didn't understand the substructure, I knew I had to change the way I wrote."

One person who apparently did not understand that "substructure" was Brodkey's first wife, the former Joanna Brown. Kissel quoted Brodkey as saying, "My . . . wife threatened to divorce me unless I learned to lie. We used to go backstage at Off-Off Broadway productions and I would tell friends that the play was awful, which shocked her." Brodkey has told interviewers that the marriage was happy, but that Brodkey's happiness restrained him from being totally honest—both in his writing and in social situations. They were divorced in 1960.

There followed a period that Brodkey has described as "part Byronic, part E.T." He became acquainted with such celebrities as Marilyn Monroe and Richard Avedon, among others, and supported himself by publishing an occasional story, teaching at the college level, and socializing. "I am an incredibly good dinner guest," he told Remnick. "For years I used to be able to eat out every night for free with the best food and the best-looking women. I'm a good talker. I'm a charming guy."

During the 1960s and 1970s Brodkey spent many solitary hours lying on a couch in an effort to recapture the essence of childhood memories, such as "the physical qualities of light at certain moments," as he revealed in the interview with Remnick. "I found out that Proust had lied," he said. "You don't taste a madeleine cookie and everything comes flooding back." His intense introspection transformed his writing. "In the 1950s," Brodkey told Remnick, "I wrote in a way in which the lives I wrote about made a certain Freudian and sociological sense, but they don't. American lives are completely insane! . . . That's what I write about." Brodkey's prose became denser and richer. His stories of that period are structured through imagery and association as much as by plot, and are composed of labyrinthine sentences of suffocating intensity.

The best known of Brodkey's later stories is "Innocence," which was originally published in the *American Review* in 1973 and is one of the eighteen stories collected in *Stories in an Almost Classical Mode* (1988). A thirty-one-page tour de force chronicling Wiley Silenowicz's moment-by-moment sensations and thoughts as he labors to bring his girlfriend to orgasm, "Innocence" was no less controversial in 1988 than it had been in 1973. James Wolcott wrote in *Vanity Fair* (September 1988) that the story is even more misogynous than Norman Mailer's "The Time of Her Time," which he accused Brodkey of imitating. But the *New York Times* critic Anatole Broyard, reviewing an anthology of *American Review* stories, was impressed. "The author shows us . . . what an incredible complex of emotions, history, misconceptions, fears, hopes, defenses, risks, threats, promises, and God knows what else, all go into a single act of love," Broyard wrote.

Two of the pieces in *Stories in an Almost Classical Mode* won first place, respectively, in the 1975 and 1976 O. Henry Awards: "Story in an Almost Classical Mode," an excruciating account of a woman named Doris Brodkey dying of cancer, and "His Son, in His Arms, in Light, Aloft," an evocation of Wiley's adoration of his father. Other significant stories first published in the 1970s include "Largely an Oral History of My Mother," which is dominated by a mother's turbulent talk, and "Verona: A Young Woman Speaks," a young woman's richly metaphorical account of her travels with her parents as a child.

In 1985 the Jewish Publication Society of America published *Women and Angels*, a limited edition of three Brodkey stories, "Ceil," "Lila," and "Angel," which are also included in his latest collection. Although the book was not widely reviewed, many critics praised the stories, particularly "Angel," an account of an apparition in Harvard Yard. "'Angel' converted me to Brodkey's work," Harold Bloom was quoted as saying in Remnick's *Washington Post* article. "It's written in what used to be called the sublime style. It has overwhelming eloquence. Brodkey contaminates his reader with a spiritual anguish." Two published reviews also praised "Angel" but otherwise were extremely negative. Leon Wieseltier wrote in his appraisal for the *New Republic* (May 20, 1985) that "Ceil" and "Lila" "are not especially impressive, except to establish Brodkey as an unpleasant man immensely alive." D. J. Enright, writing for the *New York Review of Books* (November 6, 1986), went even further, declaring that the two stories were "more boring than nasty" and that much of the book "reads like an extended obituary produced by a team of more than usually fanciful computers."

Infuriated by those reviews, Brodkey responded in a letter to the editor of the *New York Review of Books*, in which he attacked both Wieseltier and Enright. He asserted that he had been misquoted, and he objected to being called an "unpleasant man." "I know of no other occasion in the last few decades . . . ," he wrote, "in which such a remark . . . has been applied to a living writer."

That literary tempest did not deter Brodkey from publishing *Stories in an Almost Classical Mode* in 1988. A large and demanding book about 600 pages long, it met with an erratic response. Reviewers tended to be sharply divided about the quality of Brodkey's prose. *Publishers Weekly* wrote that the book was "freighted with a magnificence of language" but *Kirkus Reviews* called it an "endless kvetch." Other readers, such as Michiko Kakutani, who reviewed the book for the *New York Times* (September 14, 1988), admired some of the stories, particularly the earlier ones, but felt that Brodkey needed an editor to curb his excesses.

In contrast, Frank Kermode wrote in his review for the *New York Times Book Review* (September 18, 1988): "Mr. Brodkey wishes to be and is a poet, never counterfeit, though not always current coin." Perhaps the most positive review was written by William McPherson for the *Washington Post Book World* (September 18, 1988): "Writing at this level of intensity, of seriousness, of risk: that is the work of a master. . . . If the anticipated novel never appears, or if it appears and fails, it will be a noble failure, not a failure of courage. Brodkey has already won that battle. He has published a heroic book. I believe it is a great one."

Since several of the stories were rumored to be parts of Brodkey's novel-in-progress, "Party of Animals," the unpublished novel received almost as much attention as did the stories themselves. According to Dinitia Smith, Brodkey first signed a contract for the manuscript in 1964 with Random House. Over the next several years, his style of writing grew more ambitious, and the novel became increasingly difficult to edit in accordance with the author's intentions. In 1970 Brodkey sold the manuscript for about $35,000 to Farrar, Straus

& Giroux, where it was edited, at different times, by Robert Giroux and Roger Straus. In 1976 the *New York Times* announced the imminent publication of the then 2,000-page novel, but it did not occur. In 1979 the manuscript was bought by Alfred A. Knopf, whose payment included $75,000 that went directly to Farrar, Straus & Giroux, according to Dinitia Smith.

During the ensuing decade, Brodkey has declared, at intervals, that the novel was almost ready for publication, but he has also demonstrated great reluctance to abstain from revising the work. Harold Bloom told Dinitia Smith that "there is in [Brodkey] what Freud characterizes as 'the need to fail.' There is an intense psychic suicide going on. The question is whether the creative and personal psychology will sabotage him or will allow him to properly organize and bring forth his work."

In addition to the Prix de Rome and the two O. Henry prizes, Brodkey has won fellowships from the National Endowment for the Arts and the John Simon Guggenheim Memorial Foundation. One of his stories, "Sentimental Education," inspired the movie *First Love* (1977), and the movie rights to another story reportedly have been purchased. He wrote the introduction to *Avedon: Photographs, 1974–1977* (1978) and has been photographed at least twice by Richard Avedon. In the late 1970s Brodkey taught literature and writing at Cornell University, and he has taught at City College, New York. His essays, stories, and poems have been published in *American Review*, *Antaeus*, *Partisan Review*, *Esquire*, and the *New Yorker*, among other periodicals. Since 1955 he has been closely associated with the *New Yorker*, where he is currently a staff writer.

Harold Brodkey's "face is elegantly long," in the words of David Remnick, "as if it grew up between two city buildings. His beard and hair are graying; his eyes are the clearest of windows—alternately searing, frightened, warm, delighted." Standing six feet, two inches tall, Brodkey keeps fit by working out regularly at a local gym. "After the gym," he told Dinitia Smith, "I feel depressed. I feel I've thrown my life away and should have been a gym instructor or an editor." To counter his depression, he listens to Bach, Mozart, Mahler, or Schubert. He assuages his fear of death by watching television, a form of treatment suggested by a friend, the novelist Don DeLillo. In 1980 Brodkey married the novelist Ellen Schwamm, with whom he lives in a six-room apartment on Manhattan's Upper West Side. Brodkey's daughter, Ann Emily, whom he calls "Tami," "Temi," or "Tammi" (according to the vagaries of reporters' renderings), is reportedly the only woman he trusts to edit his stories. He has one granddaughter, Elena, named after his second wife.

References: N Y Times Bk R p3+ S 18 '88 por; *New York* 21:54+ S 19 '88 pors; *People* 31:56+ Ja 9 '89 pors; *Vanity Fair* 51:45+ S '88 por; *Washington Post* B p1 F 19 '86 por; *Washington Post Book World* 18:15 Ag 14 '88 por, 18:38 S 18 '88 por; *Contemporary Authors* vol 111 (1984)

Brookner, Anita

July 16, 1928– British writer; art historian.
Address: 68 Elm Park Gardens, London SW10 9PB, England

Each year since 1981, when *A Start in Life* appeared, Anita Brookner has completed another short novel, including the 1984 Booker-McConnell Prize-winning *Hotel du Lac*, to gain and secure her place in the front ranks of contemporary English fiction writers. Little dramatic action invades her novels of bourgeois manners and morals because the turmoil and tension remain within her characters, often lonely, intellectual, fastidiously groomed women whose proper behavior veils rather than reveals their feelings and whose moral code foredooms their amorous and domestic expectations. The questions that her novels ask—*is* honesty the best policy in the pursuit of romantic love; *does* the tortoise win the race—are in themselves not new or unsettling, but her way of asking them *is*, as she holds readers spellbound by an elegant style that has been extolled for its subtle and ironic wit, its easy flow, its sharpness, and its luminosity. Internationally recognized as an authority on eighteenth-century French painting, Dr. Brookner wrote *Jacques-Louis David* (1981) and books on other artists and on art criticism, and for more than twenty years she lectured in art history at London's Courtauld Institute of Art.

A self-described "sort of Jewish exile," Anita Brookner was born in London, England on July 16, 1928, the only child of Newson and Maude (Schiska) Brookner. Her maternal grandfather was a native of Poland, as was her father, who had brought a flourishing family business with him to England from the Continent. Although she grew up in London and had a privileged public school education, she felt somewhat like an outsider in England. "I have never learned the custom of the country," she told Sheila Hale during an interview for the *Saturday Review* (May-June 1985). "We were aliens. Jews. Tribal. . . . I loved my parents painfully, but they were hopeless as guides."

Apparently in an attempt, however, to help his daughter overcome a sense of alienation, her father directed her to the novels of Charles Dickens when she was seven years old. It was from Dickens that she began to acquire her familiarity with the perennial myth of English fiction—that the good and decent person wins in the end against the bad person, a notion that her own novels were repeatedly to dispute. Her mother, who had given up a career as a singer upon marrying, helped to teach her daughter the disparity between expectation and actuality. "She wanted me to be another kind of person altogether," Anita Brookner was quoted in the *Saturday Review* as saying. "I should have . . . been more popular, socially more graceful, one of those small, coy, kittenish women who get their way. If my novels contain a certain amount of grief it is to do with my not being what I would wish to be." In another conversation, with John Haffenden for *Novelists in Interview* (1985), she said that she has inherited from her parents "a very great residual sadness."

Anita Brookner attended James Allen's Girls' School and then studied history at Kings College of the University of London for her B.A. degree. Listening to lectures at the National Gallery, which she liked to visit during her undergraduate years, she came to realize that a more congenial subject for her was art history. She accordingly enrolled at the Courtauld Institute of Art and earned a Ph.D. degree. Her doctoral dissertation, much of which she wrote during a three-year period of study in Paris, examined the literary sources of some of the genre pictures of the pre-Revolutionary French painter Jean-Baptiste Greuze.

From 1959 to 1964 Miss Brookner was a visiting lecturer in art history at the University of Reading in Berkshire. She left that post to join the staff of the Courtauld Institute as a lecturer at the appointment of its director, Anthony Blunt. Although that eminent art historian was later revealed to be an important figure in the spy scandal that also involved Guy Burgess, in Miss Brookner's memory he remains a friend and "an excellent teacher." She moved up at the Courtauld in 1977 to the post of reader in the history of art with the rank of professor. In 1967-68 she was also the first woman to hold the position of Slade Professor at Cambridge University. She has, in addition, been a fellow of New Hall, Cambridge. According to a profile of Anita Brookner in the London *Observer* (August 7, 1988), she is remembered as a "spectacular" lecturer and a popular and "exhilarating" teacher by former students, one of whom is quoted as saying, "She would sum up what you said and make it sound brilliant."

A personal faith in rationalism had attracted Anita Brookner to the French Enlightenment and led to her decision to concentrate on painting in France from about the middle of the eighteenth century to the middle of the nineteenth century, from neoclassicism to romanticism, in the decades of the Encyclopedists and the turbulent Revolutionary and Napoleonic eras. The period is of great interest to her, she explained in a *Publishers Weekly* (September 6, 1985) interview, "because it's to do with modes of behavior as much as ways of seeing things." She began her published studies in 1968 with *Watteau*, an introduction to the French baroque painter whose delicate, unrealistic scenes with their costumed figures point to the theatre as a principal inspiration.

The Genius of the Future: Studies in French Art Criticism: Diderot, Stendhal, Baudelaire, Zola, The Brothers Goncourt, Huysmans (1971) derives from the Slade lectures that Anita Brookner gave at Cambridge in 1967–68. In her untrodden approach to art criticism she looks at the views on art of six men of letters who were not art critics in the sense that term is now understood and points out the connection between those views and their personalities and the achievements for which they are acclaimed.

Like *The Genius of the Future*, Miss Brookner's biographical-critical studies *Greuze: The Rise and Fall of an Eighteenth Century Phenomenon*, published in 1972 in Great Britain and in the United States in 1974, which grew out of her doctoral thesis, and *Jacques-Louis David* (1981; 1987), on which she spent ten years, pay close attention to links between life and work, to historical background, and the cultural climate of the times. A lecture she gave at the Royal Academy, published as *Jacques-Louis David: A Personal Interpretation* (1974), had foreshadowed her scholarly monograph, the first to appear in English, on the French neoclassical artist who vigorously participated in the Revolution and later served as Napoleon's official painter and who, as Dr. Brookner noted in her preface, "subsumed into his remarkable life many of the fundamental preoccupations of the eighteenth century in terms of thought, belief, and behavior."

"Staggering" is the term that one reviewer of Anita Brookner's book on Greuze applied to the comprehensiveness of her knowledge of eighteenth-century France. The breadth of her sympathies and conviction of her feelings are no less impressive. Free of pedantry, her "exquisitely scholarly" writing, as it has been characterized, carries its brimming freight with grace, energy, and spontaneity. When John Haffenden asked her about a connection between her work as an art historian and as a novelist, she replied that she saw no connection: "It's a sort of schizophrenic activity." But the style of her books in art history, which a reviewer for the London *Times Literary Supplement* described as "sharp, elegant, and often witty," forms an undoubted link with her fiction. Her reference in the *Saturday Review* interview, moreover, to her art history books as "steps in the painful process of self-realization" suggests another link with her novels, which may well be a continuation of that process.

When she began her first novel, during a long summer vacation in 1980, Anita Brookner saw her effort as "a little exercise in self-analysis." Her heroine in *A Start in Life* (1981), published in the United States as *The Debut* (1981), is an introspective, strait-laced student of literature, Ruth Weiss, who strives for self-fulfillment away from the London household of her parents with its oppressive reminders of their European past. Lacking the confidence to see herself as an attractive, lovable woman, she nevertheless believes that by decent, unselfish behavior she will reap the rewards of romance promised in fiction. While in Paris working on her dissertation on Balzac, she becomes attracted to a middle-aged, married professor at the Sorbonne—a relationship that increases the doubts arising in her mind over the moral code of literature. A summons to return home to care for her ailing parents ends her burgeoning affair and leaves her with a drab and lonely middle age. The novel is a triumph of style over potential mawkishness. Fay Weldon, the British novelist and dramatist, praised it as "an exquisite bloom in the late flowering of English literature, elegant, bittersweet in its connotations, catching the breath with a sense of the marvellous and unexpected. And very, very funny."

As she pondered what went wrong, Dr. Weiss would keep thinking of the virtuous but hapless title character of Balzac's *Eugénie Grandet*. In Anita Brookner's second novel, *Providence* (Great Britain, 1982; United States, 1984), Kitty Maule, who teaches romantic literature at a London university, cannot avoid seeing parallels between the themes of Benjamin Constant's novel *Adolphe* and her own preoccupation with romantic love and with moral conduct. Kitty is a poised, well-groomed, and intelligent woman whose French upbringing by her immigrant grandparents has made her feel like an alien in her native England. Although she is given to much scrutinizing and circumspection, her desire to be more characteristically English encourages her falling heedlessly in love with Maurice, a handsome and charming history professor at the university and a member of the upper class. His indifference to or insensitivity to or exploitation of her feelings brings repeated disappointment. In a final heartbreaking disillusionment she apparently arrives at some awareness that she is the victim not only of his deception but of her own self-deception, or clouded vision.

Again "casting a moral puzzle," as she does in all her novels, in *Look at Me* (1983), Anita Brookner puts the innocent at the mercy of the sophisticated in the persons of Frances Hinton, a solitary young woman who narrates the story, and a dazzlingly glamorous couple, Nick and Alix Fraser. Like most of Miss Brookner's heroines, Frances is well-off, but from choice she works in a research medical library as curator of prints and photographs of works of art depicting disease. To fill her evenings, she

BROOKNER

writes stories based on events of the day at the office. Her loneliness and need for attention, combined with her passivity and her good manners, make it easy for the unconscionable Frasers to take her up as a sort of plaything for just so long as she remains amusing to them and compliant. When they summarily eject her from their charmed circle, she is saved from devastation because a barrier between herself and the truth, as she believes, has been let down, and she proceeds to write a novel—but as a substitute, it would seem, for living.

Not all reviewers accepted Frances's ordeal of melancholy, which too often seemed self-induced. Miss Brookner herself told John Haffenden, "*Look at Me* is a very depressed and debilitated novel, and it's one I regret." But in her review for the *New York Times* (July 4, 1983), Michiko Kakutani commented: "It is a horror story about monsters and their victims told in exceptionally elegant prose. It is a great pleasure to read, especially when one considers that Frances, in becoming a writer, may end up the biggest monster of them all."

Edith Hope, the heroine of *Hotel du Lac* (1984), is also a writer. Under "the more thrusting name" of Vanessa Wilde, she writes popular, old-fashioned novels that exemplify the myth of the tortoise and the hare: at the finish it is the meek and patient woman rather than her assertive and wily rival who wins the heart of the hero. Edith knows, however, that life contradicts the myth. Her friends have banished her from London to the genteel Hotel du Lac in Switzerland to recover from an "unfortunate lapse"—jilting her bridegroom on their wedding day, as it turns out. Recognizing herself as a "domestic animal," she longs for a home, but the man she loves deeply is married and will not leave his wife and children. The question that she feels compelled to answer during her "recuperation" is, "What behavior most becomes a woman?" It is a question set in the particular context that Miss Brookner acknowledged in the *Publishers Weekly* interview to be the subject of her fiction: "How to achieve love, how to be worthy of love, how to conduct love."

Although some literary critics, both British and American, shared the impatience that Walter Clemons expressed in his comments on *Hotel du Lac* for *Newsweek* (February 25, 1985): "It's airless," Anita Brookner's fourth novel became a transatlantic bestseller and the surprise and controversial winner of the 1984 Booker-McConnell Prize from the National Book League, Great Britain's most lucrative and prestigious literary award. The selection accorded with Julian Jebb's appraisal in the *Spectator* (September 26, 1984): "It is hard to convey the great qualities of this novel. Clearly it owes much to the classical French romances of the nineteenth century. But where else in modern fiction can we find the extraordinary blend of wit, seriousness and an unassuming attitude to philosophy enshrined in a perfectly told short novel?" He chided his fellow reviewers for their failure to recognize "a book which will be read with pleasure a hundred years from now."

By focusing in *Family and Friends* (1983) on a whole family over a period of years, rather than on a single individual, Anita Brookner expands her narrative scope considerably. The widowed matriarch Sofka and her two sons and two daughters comprise the well-to-do Dorn family, Europeans who moved to England between the wars. Her device of a series of group photographs to introduce members of the family and record changes with the passage of time enables Miss Brookner to compress her family chronicle into a short novel. Although two of the children leave home, one to end up at an Italian resort and the other at poolside in Hollywood, the Dorns occupy a closed world of rules and regulations that both unite and separate families—still a world in which the hare wins.

Unlike the unchosen and unclaimed women of Miss Brookner's earliest novels, Blanche Vernon of *A Misalliance* (1986), (American title, *The Misalliance*, 1986) has known the happiness of marriage for twenty years. Then her husband, Bertie, leaves her for a young, manipulative computer expert, a kittenish woman nicknamed "Mousie." In an effort "to keep panic at bay," Blanche engages in voluntary hospital service, between frequent visits to the National Gallery. At the hospital she is drawn to an exceedingly solemn three-year-old girl who does not speak, as if rejecting the world around her. Blanche offers her help to the child's fun-loving, exploitative stepmother, Sally Beamish, thereby fostering a relationship that she comes to realize is potentially damaging. Other insights follow that, together with incidents of chance, spare *A Misalliance* from the bitter and hopeless ending of some of its predecessors.

As the events of *A Friend from England* (1987; 1988) are narrated from the cynical perspective of Rachel Kennedy, its title character, Anita Brookner's familiar themes of innocence versus sophistication, of romantic love, domesticity, and filial duty take on a new, ironic twist. A liberated woman, Rachel is the part owner of a bookshop who prides herself on being in control. What this heroine is keeping at bay is an excess of emotion, so that even her occasional sexual indulgence is discreet, passionless, and uncomplicated. With the intention of obliging a contentedly married elderly couple, whose comfortable home she often visits, she undertakes to dissuade their daughter, Heather, younger and less worldly and sensible than she is, from an unsuitable marriage, to put an end to an "amorous commotion." But when she seeks out the errant Heather in Venice for a showdown, she is forced to face her own self-delusion and distorted perception.

The members of two generations of two families fill the extended narrative frame of *Latecomers* (1988; 1989), whose time scale also exceeds that of Anita Brookner's usual novel. Hartmann and Fibich, prosperous business partners and the heads of families, have been friends since boyhood, when as orphaned refugees from Nazi Germany they met in an English public school. As with so many of Miss Brookner's men and women of foreign background, they find it difficult to feel at home in England. But despite their lost childhood and delayed start in life, through their relationships with each other and with their wives and children, they are coming to an end of their prolonged search for a sense of belonging and peace of mind.

"Wit and (to a lesser extent) passion are both in evidence in *Latecomers*, the funniest and most mannered of [Anita Brookner's] books thus far," John Melmouth observed in the *Guardian* (September 4, 1988). Whether expressive of her finesse in sly irony or of her "merciless comic gift," as one reviewer called it, her sense of humor is one of her finest resources. "The wit I owe to the eighteenth century," she explained to Haffenden, "where the master of the put-down, of reductive wisdom, is Voltaire."

Another distinctive element of Anita Brookner's style is a verbal precision that some critics attribute to her training in art appreciation. Nothing revelatory of personality or state of mind or social status escapes her notice—the weight of a bracelet on a swollen wrist, the chipped spout of a teapot, a hand-stitched pleat, two flies in the kitchen, a polished or unpolished surface, and an abundance of colors. "Like Henry James, Anita Brookner deals in ambivalence and ambiguities, the mysteries of the human heart," Merle Rubin wrote in the *Christian Science Monitor* (March 1, 1985), "but unlike James, she never writes a sentence merely to increase the reader's sense of 'mysteriousness.' Her prose is swift, transparent, unflinching, her plotting ingenious but never contrived."

Anita Brookner recently left her position at the Courtauld Institute and plans to spend more time writing. Meeting her when she was still a teacher, Sheila Hale described her in the *Saturday Review* as "a slim woman, . . . far more carefully and elegantly dressed than most academics one encounters, with fine, wide eyes, a full sensuous mouth, and impeccably cut and polished auburn hair." Other interviewers have been impressed by her pleasing manners and "low, beautifully modulated" voice. For the past twenty-five years she has been living in a small, unpretentious flat off Fulham Road in London. Her ideal home, if she had married, would have had to have been large enough for her as a mother to raise six children— her own dream destroyed by reality.

References: Christian Sci Mon B p3 Mr 1 '85 por; *Guardian* p22 S 4 '85 por; *London Observer* Ag 7 '88 por; *Pub W* 228:67+ S 6 '85 por; *Sat R* 11:35+ My-Je '85 por; *Contemporary Authors* vol 120 (1987); *Contemporary Literary Criticism* vol 34 (1984); *Contemporary Novelists* (1986); Haffenden, John. *Novelists in Interview* (1985); *Who's Who*, 1989; *World Authors 1975–1980* (1985)

Brown, Ron(ald Harmon)

Aug. 1, 1941– Chairman of the Democratic National Committee; lawyer. Address: 430 S. Capitol St., S.E., Washington, D.C. 20003

When Ron Brown was elected by acclamation to the chairmanship of the Democratic National Committee on February 10, 1989, he became the first black leader of either major American political party. For Brown, the achievement was but the latest in a long series of "firsts" that included becoming the first black member of a social fraternity at Middlebury College, the first black chief counsel to a standing Senate committee (the Judiciary), and the first black partner at the 140-member lobbying-law firm of Patton, Boggs & Blow in Washington, D.C.

Brown made his political debut as district leader of the Democratic party in Mount Vernon, New York in 1971, when he was working for the National Urban League. From 1979 to 1981 he was a high-ranking aide to Senator Edward M. Kennedy, Democrat of Massachusetts. In 1981 he joined Patton, Boggs & Blow, where he remains a partner. In the meantime, he served as deputy chairman of the Democratic National Committee from 1982 to 1985 and as Jesse Jackson's convention manager in the summer of 1988. After Governor Michael S. Dukakis of Massachusetts won the Democratic

nomination in Atlanta, Brown served that fall as an adviser to the governor's ultimately unsuccessful campaign.

The party's third failure in a row to win a presidential election prompted Brown to argue that, if the Democrats continue to shrink from staking out strong positions on crime and national defense, the Republicans will continue to win national elections by portraying Democratic candidates as soft on those issues. In accepting the chairmanship of the Democratic National Committee, Brown warned, "If we don't define ourselves, our opponents surely will." He elaborated on that theme in a speech to the National Press Club five days later: "We as Democrats have to be a lot tougher. We have to say flat out: There is no one tougher than Democrats when it comes to protecting our children from drugs, when it comes to protecting our cities against crime, and when it comes to protecting our nation against aggression and terrorism."

Ronald Harmon Brown was born on August 1, 1941 in Washington, D.C., to William Brown and Gloria Brown-Carter, both graduates of Howard University. He grew up in New York's Harlem, at the Hotel Theresa on 125th Street, of which his father was the manager. Although he was an only child, he did not lack companions, for the hotel was located opposite the famous Apollo Theatre and was a mecca for black and white entertainers, professionals, sports stars, and politicians. Richard M. Nixon had a campaign photograph taken there with the eleven-year-old Brown in 1952. In an interview with Walter Isaacson of *Time* (January 30, 1989) magazine, Brown joked, "I immediately decided [after meeting Nixon] that I wanted to become a Democrat."

Brown spent all of his childhood and adolescence in Harlem, but the excellent schools that he attended were scattered throughout the city. He was the only black student at Hunter College elementary school on the Upper East Side, and his prep schools were the Rhodes School and the Walden School, both on New York's West Side. He also attended White Plains High School for a time. In 1958 he enrolled at Middlebury College in Vermont, where his membership in Sigma Phi Epsilon was the first instance of any fraternity at Middlebury accepting a black member. The action resulted in a revoked charter for the fraternity from its national association, to which the college responded by barring any fraternity with a racial exclusion clause from campus. Eventually, all such clauses were repealed by Middlebury College's fraternities.

Having served in the ROTC to help finance his education, Brown joined the United States Army after graduating with a B.A. degree in political science from Middlebury College in 1962. After training for a few months at Fort Eustis, Virginia, he was sent to West Germany to supervise logistics at an army base, where he was put in charge of a staff of sixty German civilians. Promoted to the rank of captain, he went to Korea as commandant of a school that trained Korean soldiers to work with American soldiers. "I learned to be comfortable taking command," Brown told Isaacson during the interview for *Time*.

On his return from Korea to the United States in 1966, Brown was hired by the National Urban League to do welfare casework on Manhattan's Lower East Side and to run a job-training program in the Bronx. A social worker by day, he studied at St. John's University School of Law in the evenings. He continued to work for the Urban League after obtaining his J.D. degree in 1970.

In 1971 Brown was elected district leader of the Democratic party in Mount Vernon, Westchester County, New York, where he helped to heal a split between the liberal and moderate factions of the party. David Ford, who was the Mount Vernon party chairman at the time, recalled for a New York *Daily News* (February 12, 1989) interview with Adam Nagourney that Brown "had a knack that he could sit down with anybody and reason with them." More important than that post to Brown's political career was his move, in 1973, to Washington, D.C., where he became a spokesman for the Urban League. Within five years Brown had progressed to the position of vice-president for Washington operations, the second-highest rank in that organization.

"Coming to Washington," Brown said in an interview with Thomas B. Edsall for the *Washington Post* (February 11, 1989), "was a way for me to establish my own identity, my own base, my own group of contacts and relationships, putting me into a spokesman role at a . . . time when the Urban League was a very important organization." Brown's prominence attracted the attention of Senator Edward M. Kennedy, who asked him in 1979 to be deputy manager of his presidential campaign. Brown readily accepted. "One of the reasons I was anxious to leave the Urban League," he told Edsall, "was [that] I was tired of being limited by a small pond. . . . You know, I was an expert on all things black."

Brown's first foray into national politics was well rewarded. Although Kennedy's victory in the 1980 California primary did not translate into a national victory, Brown's management of the California campaign earned him two top jobs: that of chief counsel to the Senate Judiciary Committee, of which Kennedy was the chairman, in 1980, and that of general counsel and staff director for Kennedy in 1981. That year Brown also served briefly as chief counsel to the Democratic National Committee before becoming its deputy chairman in 1982. Under the chairmanship of Charles T. Manatt of California, Brown increased the participation of public officials at national conventions and brokered a compromise that provided a larger role for low-income voters in the party without bankrupting the treasury of the Democratic National Committee.

When his term as deputy chairman expired in 1985, Brown devoted himself completely for the following three years to his work with Patton, Boggs & Blow. In 1981 he had been offered a partnership at a six-figure salary by its senior partner Thomas Hale Boggs, whom he had met at a party given by Senator Kennedy. A first-rate corporate lobbyist, Brown has numbered among his clients the former Haitian regime of Jean-Claude ("Baby Doc") Duvalier, American Express, Toshiba, and Sony. Clifford Alexander, a Washington lawyer and basketball partner of Brown's, has said of him: "He makes his opinions clear in a way that seems logical and fair, and he never boxes people into a corner. His approach is designed to get the job done."

In 1988 Brown was presented with a challenging opportunity to apply his finesse to a potentially explosive situation: the Democratic National Convention in Atlanta, where he was serving as Jesse Jackson's top strategist. According to Walter Isaacson, Brown took on the job of convention manager reluctantly, after being persuaded by party leaders who felt that he would be a "unifying influence" on the Jackson and Dukakis factions, and, by all accounts, he was. In an interview for the New York Daily News (February 12, 1989), Michael S. Dukakis described Ron Brown as "someone who reaches out to people," and Jesse Jackson praised what he called his "urban skills" in an interview for the New York Times (February 11, 1989). "Lobbyists learn coalition very early," Jackson observed. Donna Brazile, Dukakis's ranking black aide, characterized Brown for the Daily News interviewer as a "smooth operator" and as "the glue that kept those two together."

Nearly five months after the Democratic convention, Paul G. Kirk Jr. announced that he would not seek a second four-year term as chairman of the Democratic National Committee. In the ensuing scramble to elect a successor, Brown's work for Jackson proved to be an odd combination of asset and liability. Although the job had given him the national exposure that he needed to boost his candidacy, it also linked him in the public mind with Jackson's fiery style and radical message. The suggestion that Ron Brown is an ideologue was refuted time and again by acquaintances during his campaign. Joe Klein of New York (January 30, 1989) magazine quoted one unnamed Democrat as saying: "Brown is a careerist, not an ideologue. . . . He knows the nuts and bolts. He's smart; he talks well. He's a pol—in fact, I think the real reason why he went to work for Jesse was to advance his career."

Despite the fear on the part of some southern and western Democrats that the election of Ron Brown would increase Jackson's influence in the party and thereby send "the wrong message" to disaffected conservative white voters, Brown ran a masterful campaign on the theme of a unified party. He picked up enough endorsements to induce his four opponents—three former congressmen and one state party chairman—to withdraw from the race in the final week of January. Among those who endorsed Brown were Senator Kennedy, the former governor of Arizona, Bruce E. Babbitt, the New Jersey senator Bill Bradley, the AFL-CIO, and Governor Mario M. Cuomo of New York. Cuomo, who was Brown's instructor in legal writing at St. John's University, praised his former student's "intelligence, judgment, and ability to articulate."

On February 10, 1989 Ron Brown was elected by acclamation to chair the Democratic National Committee in a victory that was due in no small measure to his ability to distance himself from Jesse Jackson during the campaign. He failed to mention his contribution to the convention in an outline of his qualifications that he circulated among the 404 members of the Democratic National Committee, and he carefully bypassed the issue of race. So did many—but not all—of his detractors in the South and the West, who took pains to point out that "race is not the issue" and that they objected primarily to Brown's connections with Kennedy and organized labor—the same objections that they had raised four years earlier to the candidacy of Paul G. Kirk Jr., who is white. Having sidestepped the race issue during the campaign, Brown at last acknowledged it in his acceptance speech. "Let me speak frankly. I did not run on the basis of race, but I will not run away from it. I am proud of who I am and I am proud of this party, for we are truly America's last best hope to bridge the divisions of race, region, religion, and ethnicity." He promised the committee that "the story of my chairmanship will not be about race. It will be about the races we win in the next four years."

Setting ambitious goals for his tenure at the helm of a party that has captured the White House only once during the last six elections, Brown intends to increase the number of registered Democrats by five million, to gain control of at least five more state legislatures, to increase the number of Democratic state legislators by 600, and to see a Democratic victory in the presidential election of 1992. The Democratic party is not in as sorry a state as it might appear from recent elections. Paul G. Kirk Jr. rid the party of its debt, its special-interest group caucuses, and its midterm issue-oriented conferences that tended to facilitate factional squabbling at the expense of party cohesion. Democrats have done consistently well in congressional and gubernatorial elections, and Brown plans to keep that momentum going.

To regain the votes of conservative white Democrats without alienating black voters, who voted nine to one for the Democratic candidate in the last two presidential elections, Brown intends to reassure both groups that their concerns are best addressed by the Democratic party. His strategy is to maintain the Democrats' traditional commitment to civil rights and social justice and to adopt stronger positions on defense and crime. Some party members expressed the view that a tougher stance on crime would not be enough to reassure white voters who saw Brown's election as evidence that the party was beholden to blacks and saddled with liberal causes. But others commented that Brown, as a black person, would have more latitude in his efforts to reclaim the white vote precisely because Jackson supporters would be unable to charge him with racism. "If anyone can neutralize the Jesse Jackson factor . . . it is Brown," Stephen Hess, a political expert at the Brookings Institution, has said. The paradox was also noted by Robert S.

Strauss, the Democratic National Committee chairman from 1972 to 1977, who told the *New York Times* (January 26, 1989), "My personal view is [that] he has the opportunity, on a smaller scale, to be like Nixon to China or Reagan to Russia."

The danger in pursuing the white conservative vote, according to yet another viewpoint expressed during Brown's campaign, lies less in not succeeding than in taking the black vote for granted, but that danger seems to have been alleviated for Brown by the announced determination of his Republican counterpart, Lee Atwater, to break the loyalty of black Americans to the Democratic party. Brown has not ignored the challenge, but he remains confident. "I think Lee Atwater is going to discover that our voters don't fool so easily," Brown told the *New York Times* (February 11, 1989). According to Joe Klein of *New York* magazine, Atwater has admitted privately that he does not relish the prospect of facing Brown on the talk-show circuit.

In keeping with Brown's goal of helping to "craft a message that reaches out to voters who deserted us in the last several election cycles," the newly elected chairman said that the "road map to the presidency" the party needs to chart "includes the South and the West." He toured three states in the South shortly after taking office to reassure those who feared he would steer the party to the left in deference to Jackson. In his acceptance speech, Brown said, "I accept this responsibility beholden to no individual, afraid of no faction, and pledged to no institution except the Democratic party and its members." He demonstrated his independence by campaigning for the white Democratic nominee, Richard M. Daley, in Chicago's mayoral election of April 4, 1989, while Jackson supported Timothy Evans, a black alderman who ran as an independent.

Another issue that is perceived as a test of Brown's independence from Jackson is the possibility of a Jackson bid for the presidency in 1992. Brown has declared his neutrality in the election, following a tradition begun by his predecessor. But he has an opportunity to affect the outcome of the election by reversing or upholding recently adopted rules changes in the way delegates are allocated to Democratic candidates—rules changes that were demanded by Jackson at the Atlanta convention. The new rules banned winner-take-all primaries by mandating a closer relationship between a candidate's share of delegates and his or her share of the popular vote. Another change reduced the number of "superdelegates," defined by *Congressional Quarterly* as "party and elected officials who are guaranteed uncommitted delegate slots regardless of their state's primary or caucus vote." Pundits expected the new rules to lengthen the nomination process by making it more difficult to assemble a majority of delegates. Thus, the argument ran, a Jackson candidacy in 1992 would be more viable, since in 1988 the gap between Jackson's and Dukakis's delegate shares was greater than the distance between their shares of the popu-

lar vote. The Democratic National Committee restored automatic delegate status to its members on September 28, 1989, at its first meeting under Brown's chairmanship. Another change in the party's charter approved by the committee was in the chairman's term of office; previously lasting from convention to convention, the new term would be sandwiched between elections.

Ron Brown's "impish smile and baby face," in the words of Walter Isaacson, hardly make him look "like an agent of historic change. He has an outsize mustache, a quick wit, and an ability to energize any room he enters. . . . He sports Hermès silk ties accented with a silver collar pin, well-tailored suits, and monogrammed shirts with French cuffs." In his spare time he enjoys playing basketball, tennis, and going skiing. He married Alma Arrington, now a public-affairs director for a radio station in Washington, around 1963. They live in a four-bedroom town house near Rock Creek Park in Washington. The couple have two children: Michael Arrington, a law student at the University of Delaware, and Tracey Lyn, who graduated from Boston College in 1989.

Brown has been honored with the American Jurisprudence Award for Outstanding Achievement in Jurisprudence and the Award for Outstanding Scholastic Achievement in Poverty Law. He is a trustee of Middlebury College and serves on the boards of the United Negro College Fund, the University of the District of Columbia, and the Community Foundation of Greater Washington. In 1980 he was a Fellow of the Institute of Politics at the John F. Kennedy School of Government at Harvard University.

References: Ebony 44:36+ My '89 pors; Gentlemen's Q 59:142+ Jl '89 pors; N Y Daily News p53 F 12 '89; N Y Times p1+ F 11 '89 pors; Time 133:56+ Ja 30 '89 por; Washington Post A p1+ F 11 '89 pors; Who's Who among Black Americans, 1988; Who's Who in American Politics, 1989–90

Browne, Jackson

Oct. 9, 1948(?)– Singer; songwriter; musician; producer. Address: c/o Creative Artists Agency, 1888 Century Park East, Los Angeles, Calif. 90067

Once called the "quintessential lyricist of the 1970s," the singer-songwriter Jackson Browne made his name by composing and performing such classic songs as "Take It Easy," "These Days," "Rock Me on the Water," and "The Pretender," which were often covered by other artists, including Joe Cocker, Joni Mitchell, Gregg Allman, and the Eagles. In many of those early songs, which helped define what became known as the southern California sound, Browne plaintively addressed

Jackson Browne

me to play Dixieland like I would in a band. So I used to sit around . . . and he would play me records and I would cop the licks," Browne later told Josh Mills in an interview for the New York *Sunday News* (October 5, 1975).

As a teenager, Browne shunned popular music, listening instead to Mississippi John Hurt and Dave Van Ronk. A major influence was Bob Dylan, whose music helped Browne to develop as a lyricist. "He showed me what could be done with a simple tune if the lyrics were right," Browne told Josh Mills. He further explained that he was convinced that folk music would outlast rock-'n'-roll. "But it's that old doo-ron-ron that's had the longest-lasting effect on me as a musician and a songwriter," he added.

At the age of seventeen, Jackson Browne began writing songs like "These Days" and "Colors of the Sun," which eventually appeared on an album by Tom Rush, and he played briefly with the Illegitimate Jug Band, before the group achieved fame as the Nitty Gritty Dirt Band. After graduating from high school, Browne made what he later called "the classic pilgrimage" to New York City, where he spent a year playing his songs in Greenwich Village coffeehouses, such as Max's Kansas City. At Andy Warhol's East Village club, the Dom, he played backup for the German-born singer Nico. Meanwhile, performers, among them Nico, Steve Noonan, the Byrds, and the Nitty Gritty Dirt Band, included his songs on their albums, and Browne started to attract a folk-rock following.

Leaving the "absolutely strange" Warhol entourage in 1968, Browne returned to Los Angeles, where he discovered that his songwriting reputation had preceded him. The folk-rock veteran David Crosby called Browne one of the ten best songwriters of the day, declaring in a 1970 *Rolling Stone* interview, "The cat just sings rings around most people, and he's got songs that'll make your hair stand on end." In 1969 Browne opened at Hollywood's Troubadour Club for the newly discovered singer Linda Ronstadt. Gradually, Browne's opening-act sets began to draw critical notice. The reviewer Mike Jahn, writing in the *New York Times* (December 25, 1970) about Browne's first appearance in New York, at the Fillmore East, observed: "He plays an engaging flat-pick style guitar, and sings in a dusty voice most immediately reminiscent of Eric Anderson. . . . Mr. Browne is certainly worthwhile as a songwriter. . . . It seems obvious that Jackson Browne has a promising career ahead of him."

his own personal concerns, although he did not intend to write songs strictly as autobiography. "I want people to think about themselves, about their own lives and situations, when they hear these songs, not about me breaking up with my wife or something," Browne once said. By the mid-1970s, Browne was heavily involved in political causes, supporting the antinuclear movement by performing in rallies and organizing, in 1979, Musicians United for Safe Energy (MUSE).

Since making his first album, *Jackson Browne*, in 1972, Browne has recorded eight other discs. In 1980, with the release of *Hold Out*, critics noticed that Browne's music had become more rock-oriented, a trend that became more pronounced in *Lawyers in Love* (1983). After that album, Browne's recordings reflected his increased political consciousness. Almost all of the songs on *Lives in the Balance* (1986) deal with American involvement in Central America, and his latest LP, *World in Motion* (1989), handles such issues as apartheid and the arms race. "There's only so much information you can get out in a song," Browne said in a recent interview, "but a song is an emotional thing. And if it leads people to get information, then it's a powerful tool."

Born in Heidelberg, West Germany on October 9, 1948 (1950, according to some sources), Jackson Browne moved with his family to East Los Angeles, California when he was three. Browne came close to being a delinquent there, but he moved at the age of twelve to Highland Park, in affluent Orange County, just south of Los Angeles. Although he yearned to play the piano, his father, Clyde Browne, who was a teacher, was a Dixieland jazz fan and insisted that Jackson learn to play the trumpet when he was about eight. "My dad wanted

When the booking agent and manager David Geffen started Asylum Records in 1971 as a relaxed environment in which to record the "laid-back" Los Angeles sound, Jackson Browne was one of the first artists to sign on. Browne's debut album, *Jackson Browne*, released early in 1972, featured ten original songs and a backup group (later known as the Section) of a dozen session musicians, including Russ Kunkel on drums, Leland Sklar on bass, and Craig Doerge on piano. David Crosby contributed his resonant harmonies, and

Sneaky Pete Kleinow, of the newly disbanded Flying Burrito Brothers, played the pedal steel guitar. The catchy conga drum and uptempo beat of "Doctor My Eyes" took that song to number eight on the pop charts by March, and the soulfulness of "Rock Me on the Water" also scored a hit. In the same year, the Eagles achieved their first hit single with "Take It Easy," which Browne cowrote with Glenn Frey of the Eagles.

Performing first solo and then with David Lindley (formerly of Kaleidoscope) on violin, slide guitar, and harmonica, Jackson Browne appeared at the Bitter End and then at Carnegie Hall in New York, with Joni Mitchell in 1972. Critics appreciated the tender simplicity of his heartfelt music, with one reviewer for *Variety* (February 16, 1972) calling him "one of the best of today's crop of young performers." Alex Ward admitted in the *Washington Post* (September 7, 1972), "Not so long ago I was convinced that hearing just one more folkie-turned-soft-rocker would drive me right around the bend, but Jackson Browne makes it a downright pleasure to swallow that assumption." And Janet Maslin wrote about his songwriting in *New Times* (November 30, 1973): "No one else wrote quite so carefully, or so well. And no one else had anything like his gift for singling out universally affecting subject matter, then writing about it in such a private way."

Browne's next two albums, *For Everyman* (1973) and *Late for the Sky* (1974), continued in his characteristically introspective vein, with the exception of the rollicking, good-natured "Red Neck Friend." "It was my literary period: long-form, rambling songs in iambic pentameter with that run-on philosophical attitude," Browne later told Steve Pond. "I was wistful, searching bleary-eyed for God in the crowds." In 1975 *Late for the Sky* became Browne's first gold album, and his two earlier records followed suit soon afterwards. Personal and societal concerns once again defined Browne's lyrics. "No one ever talks about their feelings . . . without dressing them in dreams and laughter/I guess it's just too painful otherwise," Browne wrote in the song "The Late Show." *For Everyman* featured piano performances by Joni Mitchell and Little Feat's Bill Payne and harmony by Bonnie Raitt, the folk-blues singer and slide guitarist who still occasionally plays gigs with Browne. David Lindley and the Section remained Browne's staple accompaniment.

On tour with Lindley during the 1970s, Browne played to sold-out crowds, though several critics complained about his stage presentation. "If only Jackson Browne had a sense of humor, or could flash a smile, or something," Robert Martin bemoaned in a concert review for the Toronto *Globe and Mail.* "I admire Browne's compassion but prefer a little more steel in a songwriter," Martin continued. "It is unfortunate because he possesses almost every element required for genius except spunk." Poor sound control was also cited by some critics, including John Rockwell of the *New York Times* (October 18, 1976), who complained that

Jackson Browne's "not particularly distinctive baritone" was buried in "general electronic murk." But Browne took all the criticism in stride as a necessary part of maturing as a performer. "Earlier on," he told Jan DeKnock for the *Chicago Tribune* (September 4, 1983), "I got a lot of critical praise—that long, indulgent, long-winded kind. It sort of embarrassed me that I hadn't gotten more attacks, you know, like most of my friends, or that there were really fine artists who weren't being written about at all."

The Pretender (1976), which contained the hit single "Here Come Those Tears Again" and the title cut, became Browne's first platinum album. Produced by Jon Landau, the coproducer of Bruce Springsteen's *Born to Run,* the album had a newly polished pop sound. The songs on the album deal with the responsibilities of parenthood and with the despair stemming from the suicide of his first wife during the album's production. Writing in *Rolling Stone* (January 27, 1977), Dave Marsh called the song "The Pretender," in which Browne echoes the yuppie sentiment "I'm going to be a happy idiot/And struggle for the legal tender," a "breakthrough" for Browne. Describing himself "as someone who's always had reservations about admiring" him, Marsh observed, "I find that Jackson Browne touches me most deeply when he's most specific, least cosmic." Another reviewer, Larry Rohter, commenting on *The Pretender* in the *Washington Post* (November 24, 1976), remarked: "What's most disappointing is the blandness that pervades Browne's singing on all but a few songs here. For a songwriter who invests his lyrics with so emotional a content, Browne is a terribly deadpan, detached singer."

A documentary-style portrayal of the realities of life on the road, *Running on Empty* (1978) sold more than four million copies and generated hit singles of the title track and a cover of Maurice Williams's "Stay." The live album comprised previously unrecorded songs that were captured on a bus traveling down a New Jersey highway, in a room in the Hollywood Inn in Edwardsville, Illinois, and in various rehearsal rooms. "I wanted to make the kind of music that is experienced between people, not the kind that's conceived by one person and sung to a bunch of other people," Browne explained to Paul Nelson in an interview for *Rolling Stone* (March 9, 1978). *Running on Empty* impressed critics as "both authentic and artistically pleasing," as Carl Arrington described it in the *New York Post* (January 13, 1978).

In 1975 Browne's increasing social awareness translated into benefit concerts for American Indian projects in California and Santa Fe, New Mexico, and for Tom Hayden, the liberal candidate for the California state senate. In the wake of the Three Mile Island nuclear plant accident in 1979, Browne performed at a rally in San Francisco protesting the start of construction on the Diablo Canyon, California nuclear plant. Bonnie Raitt, Joan Baez, and Ralph Nader also made appearances. In 1979 Browne was an organizing member of Musicians United for Safe Energy, a nonprofit organization formed to promote and fund the antinuclear cause through performances. He helped to plan a number of "No Nukes" benefit concerts, which featured Browne, Bruce Springsteen, and other socially conscious artists, and provided financial support for the documentary film *No Nukes* (1980). In 1981 Browne was arrested for trespassing after he joined others in forming a human blockade to protest the Diablo Canyon nuclear power plant.

MUSE's opening event was a five-night music marathon at Madison Square Garden in September 1979, with performances by Browne, Bonnie Raitt, Bruce Springsteen, and others, culminating in the largest antinuclear rally (nearly 200,000 people) in United States history, at New York's Battery Park City landfill. At the first concert, Browne performed three new songs, including "Disco Apocalypse." As Robert Palmer reported in the *New York Times* (September 21, 1979), "His set was sparked by the excellent guitar and fiddle playing of David Lindley, and by a top-flight rhythm section." Browne also worked as a piano sideman on several songs sung by Bonnie Raitt. *Rolling Stone* included Browne in its 1980 "Heavy Hundred"—"the movers and shakers of the music industry"—for his work as a member of MUSE's board of directors. In 1985 he took part in the production of *Sun City*, an antiapartheid album featuring some thirty artists and organized by Steve Van Zandt, a former E Street Band member.

It was on *Hold Out* (1980) that Browne's music began to catch up with his lyrics, according to some reviewers. Crispin Cioe, for one, writing in *High Fidelity* (October 1980), felt that the album was Browne's best work to that date. He was accompanied on the recording by, in Cioe's words, an "absolutely first-rate band" whose "beautiful use of space and contrast provides both singer and songs with dramatic support and drive that have often been missing." But Kit Rachlis, reviewing the album for *Rolling Stone* (September 4, 1980), missed the old Jackson Browne and his acoustic guitar. "What we have is a song cycle with scarcely a single tune that has the moral imagination, pop grace or writerly precision of Browne's best material." What was missing from *Hold Out*, Rachlis further contended, was "humor, humility, detail, lightness of touch." The song "Disco Apocalypse"—"an affectionate nod to disco," in Browne's words—was at first greeted with skepticism by his fans, who were unprepared for its throbbing beat and flashing colored light show. But by October 1980, during a concert at the University of Michigan, in Ann Arbor, a packed audience proved to be more receptive to the song. The album also contains the hit single "Boulevard" and closes with the optimistic eight-minute anthem "Hold On Hold Out." *Hold Out*, which Browne coproduced, eventually reached number one on *Billboard*'s album chart.

At the peak of his popularity, in 1980, Browne and a nine-piece backup band embarked on a fifty-nine-city tour and appeared in concerts in Japan, Australia, and New Zealand in November and De-

cember. When David Lindley left before production began on Browne's next album to form his own band, his departure marked a new phase in Browne's musicianship, for Browne was, for the first time, forced to concentrate on arrangement, a task he had previously delegated to Lindley. "My work with David was characterized by a lack of arrangement," Browne explained to Jan DeKnock during the *Chicago Tribune* interview. "It really was based on what happened by his accompanying me. On the albums . . . everything is just sort of him playing along and people sort of taking the arrangements from what he happened to do. At the time, it might have even changed the next month when we got on the road. . . . I've worked really hard in the last three years to fashion a band out of the people I was already playing with and to reorder that and to restructure it and to have that influence my writing *before* making a record, *before* coming out on tour."

Lawyers in Love (1983), again coproduced by Browne, represented his slickest album to date, with the title song and "Tender Is the Night" becoming hit singles. Its jacket cover shows a bespectacled Browne in a three-piece suit, standing through the sun roof of a Mercedes-Benz that he is paddling through flood waters. That absurdist scene is emblematic of the often sardonic tone of the album's lyrics. In the title song, for example, against a backdrop of "ooh-sha-la-la," Browne sings, "I hear the USSR will be open soon/As vacationland for lawyers in love." In "Cut Away," Browne plaintively sings about the breakup of his marriage to the former fashion model Lynne Sweeney: "Somebody cut away this desperate heart/Cut it away before it tears my whole life apart." "Say It Isn't True" is an antiwar statement that Browne described to Jay Cocks of *Time* (September 12, 1983) magazine as being "sincere to the point of being embarrassing. It's me not caring if anybody thinks I'm corny."

"From a performer often deemed an archetype for the confessional singer-songwriter, this eerie, panoramic broadside promised a major shift in perspective," Sam Sutherland observed, in assessing the harder-edged rock emphasis of "Lawyers in Love" for *High Fidelity* (November 1983). "While reviving the element of social commentary that had appeared in varying degrees on past albums, the song reflected a new, mordant sense of humor." Christopher Connelly was another reviewer who applauded the tougher new sound of Browne's music as a "widening of perspective that allows Browne to escape, once and for all, the L.A. albatross that has hung around his neck for the last eleven years." Nevertheless, Browne's earlier, more laid-back style of music continued to be much in demand at his concerts.

Robert Palmer of the *New York Times* (July 13, 1983) pointed out that "*Lawyers in Love* is the first Jackson Browne album with music as tough and punchy as its best lyrics." Browne explained to Palmer that, instead of recording in a fancy studio, he and his musicians used a room in downtown Los

Angeles, playing as long as was needed to reach the versions of the songs that worked. "I know the first time I had a band, I wanted the emphasis on strict arrangements, in order to showcase the songs," Browne explained to Palmer. "But the musicians just wanted to dig in and *play* after a certain point, and so did I. So if you think there's a new intensity in the music, well, you're right, but a lot of it just comes from the musicians wanting to play more, having something of their own to say."

Browne's most overtly political album to date, *Lives in the Balance* (1986), is an indictment of American involvement in Central America. Browne, who had visited Nicaragua several times, had helped to produce some of the recordings by its Nueva Canción (New Song) artists. With the Statue of Liberty on its cover, the album opens with "For America": "The thing I wonder about the dads and moms/Who send their sons to Vietnams/Will they really think their way of life/Has been protected when the next war comes?" Five of the disc's eight songs deal with Central America, with "Black and White" and "In the Shape of a Heart" representing "the only vestiges of his folksy Mr. Lonelyhearts past," in the words of David Hiltbrand, writing for *People* (April 7, 1986). Although sales were far from brisk, *Lives in the Balance* was praised by critics for the honesty of its concerns and for its accomplished performances by Browne and his backup band, as well as by the saxophonist Clarence Clemons, from Bruce Springsteen's band. "With synthesizers, hard-edged guitar, and horn, Browne has beefed up his accompaniments to fit his agitated mood, and to escape association with this decade's lightweight rock contingent," a critic for *Audio* (July 1986) observed. Another critic, Jimmy Guterman of *Rolling Stone* (April 10, 1986), commented that Browne's ability to link the personal to the political "breathes life into these songs and prevents them from becoming too didactic." A reviewer for *Time* (March 10, 1986) called the song "Lawless Avenues," a saga of life in a southern California barrio, the album's centerpiece. "It is a truly spectacular song, fired by a heart that is still romantic and forged by a political spirit that will accept no alibis," the critic wrote. Browne made a video of the title track, on his own, and urged programmers to play the single "Lives in the Balance" and the video to help raise the political awareness of listeners.

In 1988 Jackson Browne went on a fifteen-city tour benefiting the Christic Institute, a nonprofit law firm that handles legal cases involving social justice and human rights. He became associated with it in 1986 when some of its members, who admired *Lives in the Balance*, approached him. One frequently performed song during that tour was a revised version of "Cocaine," which indicted the CIA for its alleged role in aggravating America's drug crisis by trading guns for drugs with the Contras in Nicaragua. *World in Motion* (1989) is another politically motivated album, addressing such issues as poverty, apartheid in South Africa, Central America, and the arms race. The album attract-

ed widely divergent reviews. Geoffrey Hines, assessing it for the *Washington Post* (June 25, 1989), bluntly asserted: "There's not a fresh, memorable melody on the disc, and every rhythm is stiff and uninviting. . . . The lyrics not only preach to the already converted but contain enough bland generalizations to glaze the eyes of the truest believers." On the other hand, Stephen Holden of the *New York Times* (June 9, 1989) considered *World in Motion* "at once the best-sounding and most politically pointed album of his career." For the album, Browne put together a new band, led by his coproducer, Scott Thurston, who played the keyboards. For "When the Stone Begins to Turn," a tribute to Nelson Mandela, Browne was joined by the Third World musical artists Sly & Robbie, Salif Keita, and Aswad.

Jackson Browne has produced albums for several friends involved in the Los Angeles music scene, most notably Warren Zevon and David Lindley, and he has taught a grade-school-level songwriting course. Browne continues to collaborate with Lindley, and he toured in 1989 with the latter's reggae-bluegrass–folk-rock group, El Rayo-X, as part of a "World in Motion" concert tour.

Jackson Browne's longish brown hair, wide, amiable smile, and slight build contribute to his boyish appearance. Although his perfectionism has slowed his album production schedules, the finished product is always of high quality. Browne and his first wife, Phyllis Major Browne, had one son, Ethan, who is now fifteen or sixteen years old and who began touring with his father at the age of three. Another son, Ryan, who is seven, lives in Australia with his mother, Lynne Sweeney Browne, who was married to Browne from 1981 to 1984.

References: Chicago Tribune XII p12 S 4 '83 pors; Hi Fi 30:109+ O '80 por; N Y Newsday p50 Mr 20 '75; N Y Sunday News III p8 O 5 '75 por; N Y Times p38 D 25 '70; New Times p66+ N 30 '73 pors; Rolling Stone p51+ Mr 9 '78 pors, p30+ Ag 7 '80 pors, p32+ S 15 '83 pors, p63+ Ap 10 '86 por, p157+ N 5-D 10 '87 por; Time 122:59 S 12 '83 por; Who's Who in America, 1988–89

Bunshaft, Gordon

May 9, 1909– Architect. Address: c/o Skidmore, Owings & Merrill, 220 E. 42d St., New York, N.Y. 10017

During his long tenure as chief design partner at the New York offices of Skidmore, Owings & Merrill, the architect Gordon Bunshaft launched a new era in skyscraper design and defined the quintessential contemporary office building for the American landscape—a clean-lined glass and steel structure whose tight skin, elegant yet monumental form, and emphasis on volume as opposed to mass

Gordon Bunshaft   Richard Derk/NYT Pictures

led to a new vision of what an urban landscape ought to look like. Bunshaft is one of the most influential of those architects who have taken the principles of Le Corbusier and Mies van der Rohe onto American terrain. Along with Mies van der Rohe and Philip Johnson's Seagram Building (1958), Bunshaft's canonical Lever House (1952) elegantly summed up the principles of the International Style and packaged them in clean, technically "pure" form that could also, on a more pragmatic plane, sell an elegant yet powerful corporate image to the public. Still considered Bunshaft's finest accomplishment and the prototypical modern office space, the Lever House wedded the ideals of a largely European International Style to an American corporate sensibility that placed a premium on elegance of presentation, richness of materials, and a straightforward monumentality that did not preclude attention to detail.

With their streamlined efficiency and delicate minimalization of surface details, Bunshaft's buildings themselves became symbolic, perfectly designed mechanisms suggesting logic, efficiency, and even technological progress itself. "I believe in disciplined architecture, in logical, rational buildings that make sense," Bunshaft noted in an interview recorded in *New York Newsday* (May 26, 1988). According to Bunshaft, the purpose of a building is not to create art but to get built. Most of his buildings have been commissioned by large corporations and clients who, in Bunshaft's words, "care about making . . . a good building. When you've got a client who cares about more than just making a buck—you know they're all finally realizing that good architecture makes money."

Gordon Bunshaft was born in Buffalo, New York on May 9, 1909, the son of David and Yetta Bunshaft, who were Russian-Jewish immigrants. The direction of his career was determined for him at the age of seven, when a family physician who had admired his drawings of houses suggested that he become an architect. Bunshaft received his B.A. degree in architecture from the Massachusetts Institute of Technology in 1933 and his master's degree from the same institution two years later. With funds from the Rotch Traveling Fellowship, he then traveled through North Africa and Europe. When his money ran out, he returned to the United States, where he worked for Edward Durell Stone as well as for the celebrated industrial designer Raymond Loewy. In 1936 Bunshaft landed a job with Louis Skidmore, of Skidmore and Owings, a Chicago-based architecture firm that had recently established offices in New York. When he was hired, Bunshaft was told by Skidmore to "think about design," not about clients. After designing a number of what he has described as "awful things" for the 1939 World's Fair, Bunshaft served in the United States Army Corps of Engineers from 1942 to 1946. He returned to Skidmore, Owings & Merrill in 1946, was named a partner shortly after that, and remained with the firm as its chief design partner until his retirement in 1979.

The Lever House was Bunshaft's first major project at Skidmore, Owings & Merrill, the "first real building [he] ever did"—and a seminal work that ushered in the era of the sleek, prototypical American skyscraper and spurred a commercial building boom in midtown Manhattan. Although conceived along Miesian lines, the Lever House added a number of features that were new to commercial office spaces. "I wanted to lighten things up in order to make Lever House less massive. I was looking for a new fresh approach," Bunshaft has said, in explaining his objective. Using the block between Fifty-second and Fifty-third Streets as his starting point, Bunshaft positioned two stainless steel and glass slabs, one laid horizontally on columns over an open plaza, the other balanced vertically. The building's small scale of twenty-one stories and glass skin that did not reveal its heavier, underlying structural supports contributed to its liberating effect on the streetscape and allowed the Lever House to break away from the tightly wedged limestone masonry of the Park Avenue apartment houses that surrounded it.

Since the building was designed to fill less than one-third of the "zoning envelope," it opened up an overhead space in which both air and light could circulate freely over Park Avenue. At ground level, Bunshaft further liberated the space by supporting the horizontal slab on a series of stainless steel columns, creating a walk-through plaza accessible at street level. With its wrap-around skin of heat-resistant green glass, blue-green spandrels, and slender vertical mullions, the building did not seem anchored to its site but appeared to float off it. In the twenty-five years since its completion, a number of critics, while still finding the building to be an "impressive, handsome object," have faulted it for its failure to integrate itself within Park Avenue's carefully defined sense of space and scale. Paul Goldberger, for example, writing in his book *On the Rise. Architecture and Design in a Postmodern Age* (1983), commented that although "the break with a straight row of limestone-fronted buildings seemed liberating . . . when it was done in 1952, it is now seen to represent a fundamentally anti-urban attitude." And Christopher Woodward, in his introduction to his book *Skidmore, Owings & Merrill* (1970), noted that the "directional office slab on a pad of service functions has had disastrous worldwide imitators." After a lengthy battle in 1982, the Lever House was classified as an official New York City landmark in March 1983.

During the mid- and late 1950s, Bunshaft finetuned the Lever House's glass and steel idiom for adaptation in a number of important commercial buildings in the New York metropolitan area. Chief among them are the Manufacturers Hanover Trust Building at Fifth Avenue and Forty-third Street (1954), the Connecticut General Life Insurance Building (1957), the Olivetti Building at Park Avenue and Fifty-ninth Street (1960), and the Chase Manhattan Building at One Chase Plaza (1961). Like the Lever House, the Manufacturers Hanover Trust project was also a building with a message. Bunshaft's design for a transparent glass and steel bank openly proclaimed that banks were no longer granite safe-deposit boxes for cash reserves, but open trading centers where credit is sold on the free marketplace. The design called for a bank structurally transparent to passersby on the street. Using only a thin sheet of glass to separate the sidewalk from the bank's interior, Bunshaft brought the mezzanine service operations, an escalator to the second floor, and a full-size safe fully within the public's view. In his *Concise History of Modern Architecture* (1979), Leland M. Roth praised the building for being "hospitable and engaging . . . , a transparent lure, an advertisement," though response in the intervening years had been somewhat less charitable to the building's formal design. Paul Goldberger, for one, writing in *The City Observed* (1979), commented that "it is best as a stage set; as a . . . Miesian statement it comes off as second-rate and ordinary."

Bunshaft's early work culminated in two buildings, one commissioned by PepsiCo in 1960 (later renamed the Olivetti Building), the other by the Marine Midland Bank in 1961. The eleven-story Olivetti Building is an elegant aluminum and glass box that floats above the sidewalk on piers. Relatively small in scale, the building is meticulously scaled to its site and reflects a craftsmanlike attention to questions of material and finish. Critical response to the building was overwhelmingly positive. Ada Louise Huxtable, reviewing the building in the *New York Times* (May 3, 1981), called it one of the city's "few modern landmarks . . . , designed with the precise and beautiful refinement of an expensive Swiss watch," and Paul Goldberger, in *The City Observed*, remarked that the building was "one of the few instances of modern architecture in New York succeeding at

what it set out to do—create an elegant, refined, and civilized environment that would enrich the city at large."

No less impressive in its contribution to the New York scene was the Marine Midland Building (1967) at 140 Broadway, which is generally considered to be the most refined building of Bunshaft's early American phase and the culmination of principles implicit in the Lever House. Designed not as a corporate headquarters but as a commercial building with rentable office spaces, the understated structure is sheathed in a bronze-tinted glass curtain wall framed by matte-black anodized aluminum that runs nearly flush with it. To accommodate its small site, the building was given a trapezoidal shape to conform with the shape of the block. The resulting building was a forceful yet not overbearing presence on Wall Street, powerful in its use of potentially harsh technological materials, yet discreet in its muted surface projections (no detail protrudes more than half an inch) and in its own shape that gently complies with the pull of its site. Additional details, including delicate three-inch mullions, restrained glazing bars, and cladding joints, combine to create, according to Paul Goldberger, a "soft building . . . that willingly molds itself to what is around it rather than defying its context."

In the early 1960s Bunshaft created two prize-winning designs for distinguished cultural institutions outside New York City. One was for the Beinecke Rare Book and Manuscript Library at Yale University; the other was an addition designed for the Albright-Knox Art Gallery, in Buffalo, New York. Both buildings were completed in 1963. Planned to house a spacious auditorium and a large collection of modern art, the Knox addition, by remaining faithful to the classical lines of the original museum, keeps a low profile and harmonizes beautifully with it. With its boxlike structure and waffled surface sited on a raised plaza of white granite, the Beinecke Rare Book and Manuscript Library provides a striking contrast with Bunshaft's addition for the Albright-Knox Art Gallery. Its six-story stacks house rare books behind glass, and its steel trusses covered by granite supply a frame for the translucent marble squares that compose the exterior of the building. So taken was Lady Bird Johnson with Bunshaft's achievement at Yale— appropriately described as a "cathedral for books"—that she commissioned him to undertake the planning of the Lyndon Baines Johnson Library.

Beginning with the mid-1960s, Bunshaft started moving away from the delicate glass and steel esthetic of the Lever House and Olivetti Building towards heavier, sculptural, and more monumental forms. Chief among those structures are the Lyndon Baines Johnson Library and Sid Richardson Hall at the University of Texas, Austin, finished in 1971, the W. R. Grace Building in New York City, completed in 1973, and the Hirshhorn Museum and Sculpture Garden, completed for the Smithsonian Institution in Washington, D.C., in 1974. Designed to contain documents from Johnson's entire political career, the Johnson Library was defined with two 200-foot walls faced with travertine and classically organized around a central podium whose massive staircase leads to five floors of glassed-in bookstacks containing presidential papers in red leather boxes. The top story contains study rooms, curators' offices, and rooms for research facilities. The library is situated on a wooded site in Austin, Texas. Most reviewers were awed by the building's monumentality. Ada Louise Huxtable of the *New York Times* compared a descent into the building to "entering an Egyptian tomb," and Arthur Drexler, in his introduction to *Skidmore, Owings & Merrill, 1963–1973* (1974), commented that the "place is different from other places; people have come here, because, in addition to wanting amusement, there is something important in the air. . . . This building can . . . be experienced *in vacuo* as the idea of monumentality, a monument in search of a hero, single-minded, undismayed, as unlikely in its time as the appearance of Brahms among the Wagnerites. . . . It is a monument equal to a man Americans will remember for a long time. It is architecture in service of emotion."

Considerably more controversial than the Lyndon Baines Johnson Library was Bunshaft's design for the Hirshhorn Museum, which called for a massive, doughnut-shaped art museum, 231 feet in diameter, that critics compared to a gun turret or a "fortress" for art. In order to ensure the visual continuity of the Mall's central lawn, the building was raised on four massive support columns. Windows were eliminated, and the entire structure was canted slightly off center, with the result that the building is largely non-interactive with either the Mall or the nearby cluster of Smithsonian buildings. The success of the design was much contested. William Marlin, writing in the *Christian Science Monitor* (October 4, 1974), remarked that it "creates a kind of tumult on the Mall, muscling its rotund self into view." In his review of the Hirshhorn Museum for the *New York Times* (October 8, 1974), Paul Goldberger, while noting the functional elegance with which one might tour the collections, entered a demurrer when he wrote, "Such a fortress is indeed an odd sort of structure in which to house art, and while the choice of such pompous monumentality may well have been made in good faith, it nonetheless calls into question the judgment of the architect and his clients."

In the late 1970s Bunshaft created two of his most monumental works, both located outside New York City: the 5.2-million-square-foot Haj Terminal at the King Abdul Aziz International Airport and the National Commercial Bank in Jeddah, Saudi Arabia. The Jeddah Tower, which Bunshaft considers to be his finest accomplishment, is a triangular-shaped building in which all outer window banks have been removed in order to shut out the harsh sunlight and abrasive wind of the desert. Into the enormous twenty-seven-story, 400-foot building, Bunshaft carved out three triangular

wells that provide recessed window views of the Red Sea and allow sunlight to reflect into the building's central core. The increasing monumentality of Bunshaft's work left critics divided. Paul Goldberger, for example, faulted him for striving more and more towards "a kind of monumentality that exists for its own sake," whereas Arthur Drexler argued that such monumentality was an experience that most architects are unwilling to grant. "There is a kind of malnutrition, or vitamin deficiency, attributable to the modern utilitarian style," Drexler wrote. "We are perishing of undernourishment, but cannot bring ourselves to recognize the ailment. Those architects who do, and who try to offer a more balanced diet, find themselves accused of offering cake while the populace lacks bread."

The bestowal of the Pritzker Award on Gordon Bunshaft in 1988 fueled further debate not only over the nature of the award process itself, but also over the continuing relevance of Bunshaft's work and the values implicit in modern and postmodern architecture. Paul Goldberger noted in the *New York Times* (May 22, 1988) Bunshaft's essential indifference "to a whole set of values that have become important in the last generation—values that are something more than changing fashion. They are summarized by the idea that buildings should be more than pieces of abstract sculpture; rather, they should be seen as having something to do with the physical and cultural makeup of the place in which they are built. Mr. Bunshaft [has tended], in spite of rhetoric about social needs, to design buildings that are pure objects first, cultural presences second." But Kurt Anderson, writing in *Time* (May 30, 1988), remarked that the pendulum was swinging back from more recent postmodern work— what Bunshaft terms "fashion architecture" —towards a modern architecture conceived along Corbusian and Miesian lines. As Bunshaft himself has pointed out: "Young architects are turning away from postmodernism, and I think they're going to turn toward precision even more than modernism did. It'll make Lever House look like a sentimental old lady."

Gordon Bunshaft, an avowed perfectionist, was once described by David Jacobs in a *New York Times Magazine* (July 23, 1972) article as seeming "a little incongruous" in the corporate headquarters of Skidmore, Owings & Merrill: "He is (despite a recent weight loss of some twenty-odd pounds) rather portly; he walks slowly, wears a crew cut, generously cut dark suits with suspenders and dark ties, and is usually biting down on one of his several black sandblast pipes. . . . He is economical with his words, which he spits out in a thick, raspy voice." Like his wife, the former Nina Elizabeth Wayler, whom he married on December 2, 1943, he is an avid collector of art, especially the work of Miró, Dubuffet, and Léger, as well as both Oriental and African sculpture. Their art collection is divided between their home in Manhattan and a house in East Hampton overlooking Georgica Pond. In addition to the Pritzker, Bunshaft has received many other awards, including the Brunner Award of the American Academy and Institute of Arts and Letters (1955), the Honor Award of the American Institute of Architects (1958), the Medal of Honor of the New York chapter of the American Institute of Architects (1961), the Chancellor's Medal of the University of Buffalo (1969), and the Gold Medal of the American Academy and Institute of Arts and Letters (1984). He is an academician of the National Academy of Design, a Fellow of the American In-stitute of Architects, and a member of the Ameri-can Academy and Institute of Arts and Letters, as well as an honorary member of the Fine Arts Acad-emy of Buffalo. From 1963 to 1972 he served on the President's Commission on Fine Arts.

References: International Who's Who, 1989-90; Menges, Axel. The Architecture of Skidmore, Owings & Merrill, 1963-1973 (1974); Who's Who in America, 1988-89; Woodward, Christopher. Skidmore, Owings & Merrill (1970)

Bush, Barbara (Pierce)

June 8, 1925- Wife of the President of the United States. Address: The White House, 1600 Pennsylvania Ave., Washington, D.C. 20500

Barbara Bush, considered a consummate political wife during her husband's eight-year tenure as vice-president of the United States under Ronald Reagan, may well be the best-prepared first lady to have assumed the ceremonial post in modern times. Ever since her marriage to George Bush for-ty-four years ago, Barbara Bush has devoted her energies to home, family, campaigning for her hus-band, and volunteering for a host of charities and carefully chosen, noncontroversial causes. Her five children (a sixth died of leukemia in child-hood) credit her with having raised a close-knit, well-adjusted family despite the frequent upheav-als associated with their father's peripatetic career. George Bush's ambitions led him from the navy to the oil fields of Texas through a dizzying progres-sion of elected positions and political appoint-ments, occasioning twenty-eight moves in seventeen cities before the Bushes moved into the White House in January 1989.

Her husband's first run for the presidency of the United States, in 1980, afforded Mrs. Bush an op-portunity to focus national attention on one of her pet concerns: the problem of illiteracy. Although Mrs. Bush had to settle for being the wife of the vice-president in 1981, the only change in her plans to work toward the eradication of illiteracy con-cerned the unwritten prohibition against upstaging either the first lady, the president, or the vice-president. As "second lady" she quietly promoted her philosophy of voluntarism at more than 530 lit-eracy events, partially offsetting the effects of Rea-gan's budget cuts in social programs without appearing to disagree with administration policy. One of her first acts as first lady was the establish-ment, in March 1989, of the Barbara Bush Founda-tion for Family Literacy, a privately funded nonprofit organization that emphasizes the role of the family in overcoming the literacy problems of both children and parents. Mrs. Bush's high level of personal involvement in literacy efforts demon-strates her intention to serve her cause not only as a symbolic figurehead, but to lead by example as well. Her forthright, down-to-earth approach to public life and her cheerful acceptance of the natu-ral effects of aging have endeared her to Republi-cans and Democrats alike, making her arguably the most popular first lady in recent memory.

Barbara Pierce Bush was born on June 8, 1925 in a New York City hospital to Pauline (Robinson) Pierce and Marvin Pierce, who lived in Rye, New York, an affluent suburb of New York City. One of Barbara's great-great-great-uncles was Franklin Pierce, the Democratic president of the United States from 1853 to 1857, who went down in history as the only elected president whose party did not renominate him for a second term. One year after Barbara's birth, her father was promoted to vice-president of the McCall publishing company, which published McCall's and Redbook maga-zines and McCall's pattern catalogues. By 1946 he was president of the company. Pauline Pierce, the daughter of an Ohio Supreme Court justice, was a prominent civic booster who enjoyed gardening, violin playing, and antique collecting. According to Donnie Radcliffe's biography of the first lady,

Simply Barbara Bush (1989), Barbara referred to Pauline Pierce as "a very good mother" with whom she nevertheless "did not have a great relationship." Mrs. Bush is quoted as saying of her mother: "She was not perfect, but I always think the world was more beautiful because my mother was there. She taught us all a lot of good lessons."

Chief among the lessons taught in the Pierce household—which included Barbara's older sister, Martha, her older brother, Jim, and her younger brother, Scott—was the tradition of noblesse oblige. A corollary was recalled by Mrs. Bush for *People* (November 21, 1988) magazine: "We were brought up to look after people's feelings." Also inculcated during her childhood was Mrs. Bush's lifelong love of reading. In an interview with Eden Ross Lipson for the *New York Times Book Review* (May 21, 1989), she recalled, "I think of my dad sitting in his chair by the fireplace and my mother on the couch reading, and after we children could read everyone was curled up with something."

Barbara attended the public Milton School through the sixth grade, the private Rye Country Day School for the following four years, and the private Ashley Hall boarding school, in Charleston, South Carolina, for her final two years of high school. A classmate of Barbara's has described Ashley Hall as a place where "being bad meant taking off your hat and gloves when you got out of sight of the school." During her Christmas break in 1941, the sixteen-year-old Barbara attended a dance at the Round Hill Country Club in Greenwich, Connecticut, not far from her home in Rye. Five foot eight and slender, with reddish-brown hair, Barbara caught the eye of George Herbert Walker Bush, a senior at Phillips Academy in Andover, Massachusetts and a resident of Greenwich. George Bush, she recalls frequently, was the handsomest boy she'd ever seen. They sat out a waltz together and, before long, they fell in love.

George Bush enlisted in the navy after graduating from high school in 1942 and spent the following year—Barbara's senior year—training to be a pilot. In September 1943 George was assigned to a torpedo squadron, in which he piloted a Grumman Avenger he had nicknamed "Barbara," and Barbara enrolled at the prestigious Smith College for women, where she captained the freshman soccer team. Meanwhile, the young couple had been exchanging letters since their return to school after their first meeting. "I didn't like to study very much," Mrs. Bush recalled, as quoted by Donnie Radcliffe. "The truth is, I just wasn't interested. I was just interested in George." She dropped out of Smith at the beginning of her sophomore year, around the same time that George's plane was shot down over Chichi Jima in the Pacific. He was awarded the Distinguished Flying Cross after being rescued by an American submarine, and his squadron was rotated home for Christmas leave in 1944. George and Barbara were married on January 6, 1945 at the First Presbyterian Church in Rye. "I married the first man I ever kissed," Mrs. Bush is widely quoted as saying, and she has called her marriage "the biggest turning point" in her life.

The Bushes spent the remaining months of the war in Michigan, Maine, and Virginia, where George trained new pilots until his release from active duty in September 1945. That fall he enrolled at Yale University, from which he graduated three years later. Mrs. Bush gave birth to their first child, George Walker Bush, on July 6, 1946 in New Haven, Connecticut. Asked whether she has any regrets about her decision to leave college after only one year in order to marry and raise a family, Mrs. Bush nearly always says she has none. But in an interview with Michael Kilian for the *Chicago Tribune* (November 30, 1986), she explained that, had she wanted to attend nearby Connecticut College while her husband went to Yale (which did not admit women until 1969), she could have done so. "But the truth is," she said, "I just didn't want to do it. Now I'm sorry I don't have that in my background."

Prior to the birth of her first child, Mrs. Bush had worked at the Yale Co-op for a year. She also got involved in the United Negro College Fund, whose Yale campus branch was headed by her husband. Aside from these activities, her only job experience had been working in a nuts-and-bolts factory in Port Chester, New York during the summer of 1942. She has said that she might have wanted to become a nurse, and she and George briefly considered farming. But Mrs. Bush chose to follow the advice of her husband early in their marriage, which she recalls as the commonly voiced but rarely fulfilled promise "Stick with me and I'll show you the world." In the interview with Michael Kilian, she explained: "I've been brought up in a family where if your husband wanted to do something, you'd do it, gladly. I still think there's nothing really wrong with that. I would say the same if a wife wanted to do something very badly. Her husband should do the same."

Since George Bush wanted to establish himself in the oil industry upon graduating from Yale in 1948, the first stop on the Bushes' lifelong odyssey was Odessa, Texas, where they lived for less than a year while Bush worked for the oil conglomerate Dresser Industries as an equipment clerk earning $300 a month. In 1949 he was promoted to a sales position and transferred to California, where the family lived in five cities—Huntington Park, Bakersfield, Whittier, Ventura, and Compton—in the space of one year. In 1950 the Bushes moved to Midland, Texas, where Bush established first an oil-and-gas dealership, then a petroleum corporation. He cofounded and became president of a subsidiary of that corporation in 1954; when the company became independent in 1959, the family, which by then included four boys—George Jr., John Ellis ("Jeb"), Neil, and Marvin—moved to Houston. A daughter, Dorothy, was born shortly thereafter. The Bushes lived in Houston until 1966, when, after an unsuccessful run for senator in 1964, George Bush was elected to the United States House of Representatives for the Seventh Congressional District.

A self-avowed "nester" who had expected to settle down and raise a family in the bosom of the Bush enclave in New England, Mrs. Bush was initially reluctant to set out for Texas with her two-year-old son in 1948. But all doubts soon vanished as she came to realize that her husband's sense of independence required that they move away from their families. "I think we'd have probably not grown up as quickly [if the move to Odessa had not occurred]," she once told Donnie Radcliffe. "I think it was very good for our marriage. When you are a couple all grown up, nobody's son or daughter, nobody's shadow, you are you."

Had leaving home been confined to a move, the break with the past would have been less traumatic for Mrs. Bush than it soon turned out to be. Her mother died in a freak automobile accident in October 1949, in which Marvin Pierce lost control of the car while trying to prevent a cup of coffee on the seat of the car next to his wife from spilling and possibly scalding her. Two months later Mrs. Bush gave birth to her second child, naming her Pauline Robinson Bush after the baby's grandmother; they called her Robin. Shortly after their second son, Jeb, was born in February 1953, Robin was diagnosed with leukemia and given three weeks to live if the disease were not treated. The Bushes took her to Memorial Hospital in New York City, where the Sloan-Kettering Foundation was engaged in leukemia research. There, Robin lingered for seven months before succumbing to the disease, in October 1953. The loss of their daughter was devastating to both parents, who relied on each other, on friends, on family members, and on their faith to work through their grief. As Mrs. Bush tells it, she was the strong one during the long period of illness, during which she rarely left Robin's side; but after Robin's death, it was George who held his wife together when she found it difficult not to withdraw from friends and family. Her now famous hair is said to have turned white in her early thirties as a result of the ordeal.

Mrs. Bush became deeply involved in charitable work after Robin's death, volunteering for everything from the Leukemia Society of America to the March of Dimes. Her days in Texas during the 1950s and 1960s were similar to those of many an American housewife upon whom neither economic necessity nor professional ambition made it incumbent to work for pay outside the home. "This was a period, for me, of long days and short years," she said in a speech at American University in 1985; "of diapers, runny noses, earaches, more Little League games than you could believe possible, tonsils, and those unscheduled races to the hospital emergency room, Sunday School and church, of hours of urging homework, or short chubby arms around your neck and sticky kisses; and experiencing bumpy moments—not many, but a few—of feeling that I'd never, ever be able to have fun again; and coping with the feeling that George Bush, in his excitement of starting a small company and traveling around the world, was having a lot of fun."

The Bushes lived in Washington, D.C., from 1967 to 1971 while George Bush served two terms in the House, and Barbara Bush wrote an issue-oriented monthly newspaper column for her husband's constituents in Houston. In 1966 Bush had sold his interest in his oil company for a reported (but unconfirmed) $1.1 million. In Washington Mrs. Bush kept up a busy schedule of volunteering, entertaining, and holding things together on the home front. In the interview for *People* magazine, her son Jeb recalled: "Dad was the chief executive officer, but Mother was the chief operating officer. We all reported to her. She did a good job of keeping the family intact."

The 1970s were as eventful for the Bushes personally as they were for the nation politically, and they were just as full of high points and low points. The decade began with an abortive run for the United States Senate by George Bush, who had the active support of President Richard M. Nixon. Partly as compensation for having risked and lost a safe seat in the House, Nixon appointed Bush ambassador to the United Nations. He assumed the post in March 1971, when he and Mrs. Bush moved into Waldorf Towers in New York City. Mrs. Bush plunged wholeheartedly into entertaining the ambassador's many guests, who were often invited on the spur of the moment. She also volunteered her time at the Memorial Sloan-Kettering Cancer Center, where she tried to cheer patients as a way of honoring the memory of her daughter.

In early 1973 Mrs. Bush learned that her husband had been asked to accept the chairmanship of the Republican National Committee. According to the interview with Michael Kilian, Mrs. Bush advised her husband: "Accept the national committee chairmanship only over my dead body. . . . You're a statesman, stay out of that." But he took the job, and the Bushes moved back to Washington, where George Bush presided over the Republican party during its nadir: the Watergate crisis. In October 1974 President Gerald R. Ford sent Bush to the People's Republic of China to head the United States Liaison Office in Beijing. "Watergate was a terrible experience," said Mrs. Bush in 1984, as quoted by Donnie Radcliffe, "so to go off to China and learn a whole new culture was beautiful. I loved the people. I loved the whole feeling." What she loved most of all, she has said frequently, was having her husband all to herself; her almost-grown children stayed behind in the United States. In China Barbara and George bicycled around the capital, studied Chinese, and learned Tai Chi.

From January to November 1976, George Bush served as director of the Central Intelligence Agency. The return to Washington produced an emotional letdown for Mrs. Bush, the immediate cause of which was her husband's inability to share the details of his highly confidential job. Moreover, she felt demoralized by the feminist movement. She elaborated on this "difficult time" at a press conference in March 1989, saying, "Suddenly women's lib had made me feel that my life had been wasted." But she soon overcame her feelings of inadequacy by immersing herself in volunteer work at a hospice, assembling a slide show on China, and giving lectures on her experiences there. She donated the money she earned to St. Martin's Episcopal Church in Houston, to which the Bushes returned in 1977 after Bush left the CIA.

Mrs. Bush and her husband spent the summer of 1978 at Walker's Point, the Bush family home in Kennebunkport, Maine. While George was assessing his prospects for a run for the presidency in 1980, Barbara searched for ways to give her philosophy of voluntarism a politically appropriate focus. In an interview with Edward Klein for the Sunday supplement *Parade* (May 21, 1989) magazine, she said: "Both George and I were brought up to feel that we were very lucky, and we ought to give back to society. And knowing that George was going to run for national office, I spent a whole summer thinking about what would help the most people possible. And it suddenly occurred to me that every single thing I worry about—things like teenage pregnancies, the breakup of families, drugs, AIDS, the homeless—everything would be better if more people could read, write, and understand." Among the advantages of waging a literacy campaign over other, more controversial causes was its familiarity to her; she had worked hard to help her son Neil overcome his dyslexia years earlier. Among Mrs. Bush's contributions to the fight against illiteracy during her husband's vice-presidency was authorship of *C. Fred's Story: A Dog's Life*, published by Doubleday in 1984. She donated her share of the profits to two national literacy organizations.

Barbara Bush emerged during the campaigns of 1980, 1984, and 1988 as a dynamic speaker noted for her warmth and lack of artifice, her candid demeanor, and her fierce loyalty to her husband. Generally adept at avoiding controversy by keeping a tight lid on any policy disagreements she may have with her husband, Mrs. Bush's few missteps were all the more conspicuous because of their infrequency. In 1984 she referred to Geraldine A. Ferraro, the Democratic candidate for vice-president, as a "$4 million—I can't say it, but it rhymes with 'rich.'" Hours later she called Ms. Ferraro to apologize, saying that she had thought the comment was off the record. In early 1989 Mrs. Bush created a flap when she voiced her opinion that semiautomatic rifles should be illegal at a time when the president's official position did not favor gun control. His subsequent approval of a temporary ban on imports of assault weapons led to speculation regarding the first lady's influence on the president's decisions. Mrs. Bush not only denied having any significant influence, but also reiterated her intention (first declared when her husband was elected to Congress in 1966) not to comment on controversial political issues. "I don't fool around with his office, and he doesn't fool around with my household," she is fond of saying.

Despite Mrs. Bush's protestations to the contrary, she is widely believed to have influenced her husband's 1988 campaign by advising him to tone down his harsh criticism of his Democratic opponent, Governor Michael S. Dukakis of Massachusetts. But the main reason she was ultimately judged to be a valuable campaign asset was her skill at diffusing the impact of potentially negative factors—her widely remarked matronly appearance and unsubstantiated rumors of her husband's infidelity—with a disarming combination of candor and self-deprecatory humor.

Barbara Bush's appearance and style have generated the same level of speculation about trend-setting that is accorded customarily to all first ladies, despite her avowed lack of interest in fashion. Reporting evidence of trends influenced by Mrs. Bush in an article for *USA Today* (April 21, 1989), Elizabeth Sporkin cited increased sales of the first lady's trademark three- to five-strand faux pearls, "Barbara blue" garments in the royal blue she favors, and large-size, colorful print dresses with matching jackets, but she concluded, "She isn't inspiring people to imitate her, but to be happy with themselves." The truth of that observation is attested to by the 35,000 pieces of fan mail received by the first lady during her husband's first hundred days in office.

The recipient of several awards and honorary degrees, Barbara Bush is most proud of having successfully raised five children, all of whom are married and have children of their own. Although she is being treated for a thyroid condition known as Graves's disease, Mrs. Bush has slowed her pace only slightly. Her preferred daily exercise includes jogging, tennis, swimming, riding an exercise bike, and walking her English springer spaniel, Millie, whose puppies made headlines in March 1989. Reading and gardening are two of Mrs. Bush's favorite activities; she also enjoys needlepoint and spending time with her eleven grandchildren. When asked by a reporter in 1989 about the legacy she would like to leave behind, Mrs. Bush answered, "I hope people will say, 'She cared; she worked hard for lots of causes.'"

References: Chicago Tribune V p1+ Ag 14 '88 pors; London Observer p13 Ja 22 '89; Newsweek 113:32+ Ja 16 '89 pors; People 14:22+ Ag 4 '80 pors, 30:55+ N 21 '88 pors; Time 133:22+ Ja 23 '89 pors; Washington Post F p1+ Je 5 '88 pors; Radcliffe, Donnie. Simply Barbara Bush (1989); Who's Who in America, 1988–89; Who's Who in the East, 1989–90; Who's Who of American Women, 1989–90

Campeau, Robert (Joseph)

Aug. 3, 1924– Canadian entrepreneur. Address: c/o Federated/Allied Stores, 1114 Ave. of the Americas, New York, N.Y. 10036

In less than two years in the late 1980s, the Canadian real-estate developer Robert Campeau, who loves to take risks, became the most powerful man

Robert Campeau

in the North American retailing industry. His leveraged takeovers—first of Allied Stores, which owns Jordan Marsh and Stern's, and then of Federated Department Stores, whose assets include Bloomingdale's and Abraham & Straus in New York City—have generated much controversy in the business media. Often described as a volatile, flamboyant, and driven man, Campeau is also a brilliant businessman who, in the words of one New York business analyst, "breaks any kind of mold that people in the industry and financial analysts are used to in all respects." Writing in the Toronto *Globe and Mail Report on Business Magazine* (March 1987), Arthur Johnson put it differently when he observed that Campeau's life story "resembles nothing so much as a Horatio Alger homily reset in the Great White North."

Robert Joseph Campeau was born on August 3, 1924 in the mining town of Sudbury, Ontario, the son of Joseph Campeau, a French-Canadian auto mechanic and former blacksmith who lost almost everything in the Great Depression, and his wife, Lucie. Of the fourteen children in the family, only seven—four boys and three girls—survived infancy. In a candid interview with Phil Patton for the *New York Times Magazine* (July 17, 1988), Campeau recalled the abject poverty of his youth, spent in a town so bleak that it was nicknamed "Sludgebury." "When I was growing up, I thought any house with indoor plumbing was a palace, and I hated the people who lived there," he said. Forced to leave school at the age of fourteen to go to work, Campeau used the baptismal record of a dead brother, two years his elder, to persuade officials at the International Nickel Company (Inco) that he was old enough to work full-time at a three-dollar-per-day job as an apprentice machinist.

Displaying an aptitude for carpentry and things mechanical, Campeau worked extra shifts and completed his four-year training program in just two years. By 1940 Canada was involved in World War II, and skilled manpower was in demand. Determined to get ahead, Campeau left Inco at the age of sixteen for a job with Canadian International Paper, as the manager of a pulp and paper mill in Ottawa, Ontario. Intending to put down roots, he bought a lot in the city in 1949 and, in his spare time, began building a home for his wife, Clauda, and their six-year-old daughter, but before the family could move in, a contractor offered to buy the dwelling. Campeau sold it to him, and the $3,000 profit he realized on the deal represented six months' salary for him. Convinced that there was a fortune to be made by building houses in the booming postwar economy, Campeau invested in some farmland, on which he built a fifty-house subdivision.

"I saw subcontractors making a lot of money even though most of them were inefficient," Campeau told Joanne Philpott in an interview for the Toronto *Globe and Mail* (August 3, 1984). By avoiding the same mistakes, he did so well that the Campeau Construction Company, incorporated in 1953, became the largest and most successful home builder in Ottawa, constructing as many as 1,000 new houses a year. In the early 1960s the company began shifting its operations into commercial developments, an astute business move because in 1968 Campeau's friend Pierre Trudeau, a fellow francophone, was elected prime minister of Canada, and any time the Liberal government's ministers needed office space for an expanding bureaucracy, they looked to Campeau. For example, when his company completed the first phase of Place de Ville, a massive office-hotel complex not far from Parliament Hill, the government rented 58 percent of the 558,000 square feet of office space.

In spite of his business successes in Ottawa, all was not well with Robert Campeau. An ambitious lakefront hotel-condominium development that he built in downtown Toronto in 1968 was years ahead of its time, but it proved to be a costly failure. Making matters worse was the disarray in Campeau's personal life. Following the birth of their daughter, Rachelle, Campeau's wife had discovered that she was unable to bear any more children, and, although the couple adopted two boys, Jacques and Daniel, they began to drift apart. But it was only after the couple divorced in 1969 that Clauda Campeau discovered that her husband had been keeping a mistress —German-born Ilse Luebbert, who had in 1963 given birth to Campeau's son, Robert Jr., and, two years later, to a daughter, Giselle. Campeau and Ilse Luebbert were eventually married, and in 1973 another son, Jean Paul, was born.

Campeau's business reverses and his turbulent home life took such a toll on him that in 1969 he was hit with the first of several severe bouts of depression. Campeau's brother Ovila, a semiretired clergyman, told Phil Patton that at the time Campeau seemed "really mixed up." After selling his business to Paul Desmarais, another Sudbury native, Campeau retreated to Florida in 1971 for a few months of soul searching. There, he went to work doing what he has always enjoyed most—building a house, an activity that proved to be therapeutic. Rejuvenated, Campeau returned to Ottawa where, backed by a $38 million bank loan, he bought his company back from Desmarais in 1972. He then embarked on another major building program, mainly in Montreal and Ottawa.

It was also around that time that Campeau decided to diversify his business interests. In 1973 he lost out to the Hudson Bay Company in a fierce takeover battle for a development company called Markborough Properties Limited, and the federal agency that regulates commercial broadcasting in Canada blocked his efforts to buy Bushnell Communications, a chain of radio and television stations. Rebuffed, Campeau turned once more to meeting the Liberal government's burgeoning demand for new office space in Ottawa, but he faced a battle every step of the way there, too, since he and Charlotte Whitton, Ottawa's conservative mayor, continued their long-running feud over construction bylaws. And members of Parliament in the ranks of the opposition Conservative party were outraged by what they regarded as the "cozy" relationship between Campeau and the Liberal government.

The Opposition's cries of protest became even more vociferous when, in 1976, Campeau signed a contract with the government for a $142 million office complex in Hull, Quebec, just across the Ottawa River from the national capital. Local residents dubbed the development—officially known as Les Terrasses de la Chaudière—as Place Campeau, and Tory members of Parliament were even less kind. "It's scandalous," one said, "a mire of crap." What especially irked Opposition members of Parliament, apart from inflated building costs, was a clause in the deal that called for the government not only to rent all of the space in Les Terrasses, but to buy it eventually, and the whole process was agreed to without the usual tenders being called. Bridling at charges of favoritism, Campeau produced his own set of numbers and argued that his building had actually saved money for the government. "It's not Ottawa that made it for me. I made it for Ottawa," Campeau said. "An entrepreneur makes his own opportunities."

Making his own entrepreneurial opportunities, in 1980 Campeau tried to take over Royal Trust Company, one of Canada's most powerful financial institutions. When he visited Kenneth White, the president of Royal Trustco, at his country estate and broached the idea, his host was outraged. "I guess I didn't expect him to hand his company to us on a silver platter, but I certainly didn't expect him to be so hostile, so emotional," Campeau has recalled.

Insiders on Bay Street (the Canadian equivalent of Wall Street) noted that White had pitched the battle, as one analyst put it, into a kind of financial "holy war, pitting the sacred trust of widows and orphans against a development mogul." While Kenneth White was offended that a relatively small company like Campeau's, with assets of just $866 million, would try to buy the $7 billion Royal Trustco, he apparently had a darker, more subtle objection to the takeover bid. As Peter C. Newman, the editor of Debrett's Illustrated Guide to the Canadian Establishment (1983), pointed out, "The upper-crusty Royal Trustco [was] a plum repository of WASP fortunes and defiance," and the self-appointed powerbrokers of Canada's business elite viewed Campeau, a francophone, as an outsider. White himself epitomized those prejudices when he said that Robert Campeau was "an unsuitable owner" for Royal Trustco.

The ensuing five-week battle for the company was a bitter one, and in the end Campeau's takeover bid failed. Backed by Richard Thomson, the head of the powerful Toronto-Dominion Bank, White marshaled a group of friendly businessmen, who bought up 55 percent of Royal Trustco's stock. As Campeau once explained, "The friends in the club got together and bought up the shares to keep me out." Apparently agreeing, the Ontario Securities Commission punished White and several company directors by temporarily banning them from dealing in Royal Trustco stock, although no criminal charges resulted from a 1981 investigation into the affair.

In one sense, at least, Campeau lost the battle but won the war. In March 1981 he netted more than $3 million profit by selling his Royal Trustco stock to the Reichmann family, which soon teamed up with the Bronfmans from Montreal to take over the trust company. Nevertheless, his financial victory was a hollow one for Campeau. His disappointment, when combined with the news of his first wife's death and an unpleasant falling out with his oldest son, Jacques, sent him into another severe bout of depression. As he had done in 1969, Campeau took some time off. He spent several months traveling with his wife in Europe, where he underwent a massage-type therapy called Rolfing. When the Montreal psychiatrist Alan M. Mann was appointed to the Campeau Company board of directors a short time later, speculation about Campeau's mental stability was rife in the Toronto financial community, and neither he nor Mann was willing to comment on their relationship. Campeau now attributes his depression to an allergic reaction to anesthesia administered during surgery for a hiatal hernia.

Such is Campeau's resiliency that he recovered from his illness and plunged back into his work with renewed enthusiasm and a fresh sense of direction. In March 1982 he announced that he was shelving plans for major real-estate developments in Dallas and Houston and was selling undeveloped properties in anticipation of other major undertakings in the United States. In January 1983 Campeau made a couple of other important decisions. He announced that, after thirty years, his company was leaving the residential housing business to concentrate on commercial real-estate development, and he moved both his home and his corporate headquarters from Ottawa to Toronto, the financial hub of Canada. As if to announce to the world that Robert Campeau had finally "arrived," he built a $5 million Normandy-style chateau in the city's most exclusive neighborhood.

In 1984 Campeau began construction of a sixty-eight-story Scotia Plaza bank building, a few blocks from the four black towers of the Toronto-Dominion Bank complex in downtown Toronto. Unfortunately for Campeau, when his staff was assembling the land for the Scotia Plaza development, someone overlooked a Toronto-Dominion lease on an office in a building slated for demolition. His old nemesis, Richard Thomson, was not about to do Campeau any favors, and the matter was settled only when Campeau agreed to buy out the lease at a cost of $24 million.

Some observers believed that though the Royal Trustco setback provided Campeau with an incentive for turning his attentions southward, it was his quarrel with Thomson over the Toronto-Dominion lease that was the factor that spurred him to action, perhaps because he wanted to make a point to Canadian outsiders. Campeau had a much simpler explanation. "If you make a lot of money in Canada you're frowned upon," he said. "[The country] is too far to the left for my liking." Campeau also criticized his old friend Pierre Trudeau for leaving the country in "an economic mess," with a soaring national debt. Nate Lawrie, the business columnist of the *Toronto Star* (November 7, 1986), pointed out that the main reason for that huge debt was the government spending from which Campeau had benefited so handsomely.

Although Campeau's big move into the United States in the fall of 1986 had long been anticipated, most observers were stunned by its thrust and magnitude. On September 4, 1986 Campeau set the financial world buzzing when he offered fifty-eight dollars each for up to 64 percent of the shares of Allied Stores Corporation, the third-largest retail chain in the United States, with assets that included such well-known stores as Brooks Brothers and Bonwit Teller. Allied's board of directors was at first incredulous and then fearful as it became apparent that he had the financial muscle to succeed in his plans.

The takeover battle was a difficult one that Campeau appeared to be losing, particularly after the appearance on the scene of a white knight bidder: the Ohio shopping-mall mogul Edward J. De-Bartolo. In the end, Campeau won out with a daring move that Wall Streeters call a "street sweep." On October 24, 1986 he withdrew his original offer for Allied, and when share prices tumbled, he stepped in and bought 48 percent of Allied's stock from a Los Angeles broker who had assembled it on his behalf. That holding, the largest single block of shares ever traded in American corporate history up to that point, when added to the shares he already owned, gave Campeau control-

ling interest in the company. Allied's management tried unsuccessfully in the courts to block the purchase, but on October 29 Campeau was given the final go-ahead that he needed. Conceding defeat, Edward DeBartolo withdrew his offer for Allied in return for a $116.3 million payoff and an option on Allied stock. The chairman of Allied Stores, Thomas Macioce, said, "We got our shareholders the best price possible."

Despite the high cost of his victory, Campeau was delighted, since the Allied takeover instantly established him as one of the major players in the North American retailing industry. It also gave him the gratification of defying Richard Thomson of the Toronto-Dominion Bank, who had been one of the backers of DeBartolo's competing bid. Some analysts speculated that Campeau's success might ultimately be his undoing, given the crushing debt load he had assumed in the takeover. One estimate put that figure at $8.5 billion. It soon became clear, however, that Campeau had come up with a workable solution to his cash squeeze. Taking a hands-on approach to management, he trimmed Allied's work force by two-thirds and pruned $70 million annually from the corporation's overhead. Next, he floated a $1.1 billion, high-interest bond issue that enabled him to pay down his short-term debt to First Boston Corporation and the New York banks that had bankrolled him. He also began selling some of Allied's less desirable assets. By August 1987 he had sold sixteen of Allied's twenty-four retail divisions for a total of $1.1 billion, which he used to retire more of his debt.

Although some investors, always alert to a good thing, pushed Campeau Corporation stock up to more than $27 from a 1987 low of $9.75, financial analysts were still uneasy about the company's long-term prospects. Many pointed to Allied's ongoing losses—$285 million in the first nine months of 1987—and to Campeau's unacceptably high debt-to-equity ratio as serious cause for concern, and some speculated that he had as little as $1 per share backing for each $22.50 of debt. Because it was a very thin line that he was walking, the slightest rise in interest rates or a dip in retail sales could have proven disastrous for him.

Even though the hallmark of Campeau's unorthodox entrepreneurial style has always been his audacity, few people were ready for his next move. On January 25, 1988 he launched a bid for a hostile takeover of the retailing giant Federated Department Stores, among whose chief assets was the trendy New York shopping emporium known as Bloomingdale's. Speculation on Wall Street was that Campeau had a partner in his scheme, but documents filed with the Securities and Exchange Commission showed that initially, at least, such was not the case. That situation soon changed, as the fight with Federated's hostile board heated up, and R. H. Macy & Company, the department store chain, entered the fray as a second bidder.

The struggle for Federated was virtually a replay of the Allied takeover, and again Campeau prevailed at the eleventh hour. Taking personal command of his own strategy, he deftly out-manuevered the opposition in the market as well as in the courts to pull off what Steve Coll of the *Washington Post* (April 6, 1988) described as "the biggest non-oil takeover ever." The deal was consummated when Campeau met personally with Macy's chairman, Ed Finklestein, at his New York town house. Finklestein agreed to withdraw Macy's bid in return for Campeau's promise to sell the department store part of Federated's assets and cover its $74 million in legal bills.

Campeau's initial offer had been $47 per share, but when the Federated board finally approved the sale on April 1, 1988, it did so at a price of $73.50 for each of 88.5 million outstanding shares. Campeau told reporters that the total cost of the deal was $8.8 billion—or a staggering $10.9 billion if assumed Federated debts were included in the calculations. Although Campeau termed the purchase of Federated Stores "a helluva deal," he had to admit, "We certainly didn't steal it."

Campeau raised some of the purchase price by selling Allied's prestigious Brooks Brothers stores to Marks & Spencer of Great Britain for $770 million, and through loans from the Reichmann family and his erstwhile rival Edward DeBartolo. In fact, Campeau and DeBartolo subsequently announced plans to join forces to build as many as 100 new shopping malls by the year 2000, all of them anchored by department stores in Campeau's Federated/Allied retailing empire, including Bloomingdale's, which Campeau hopes to convert into a national chain.

The move was only part of an aggressive expansion program that Campeau had planned. Again following the same strategy he had adopted two years earlier, he tried to service his short-term debt as quickly as possible by streamlining Federated's operations, by selling off $5.2 billion in unwanted assets, and through a $1.55 billion bond issue. Investors were wary, however, in view of Campeau's huge debts, management problems, and uncertainty about the health of the lagging retail sales that were reflected in a $219 million operating loss by Federated in the first quarter of 1988. One analyst noted: "The perception is that since the takeover [he] has run into difficulties. His cash flow is very poor, and he has a lot of debt to pay." Compounding Campeau's problems were rumors fueled by a front-page article in the *Wall Street Journal* in December 1988 that claimed he would soon be forced to sell some of his desirable assets in order to pay his debts.

In typical fashion, Campeau fought back against his critics when, in early January 1989, he placed a series of advertisements in major newspapers across North America. Headed "Nothing Succeeds Like Success," the ads argued that it was difficult to judge just how well Campeau was doing since he had done so much in 1988. "We can make a profit and we can have money for expansion, too," Campeau assured Isadore Barmash of the *New York Times* (January 14, 1989). But the stock market did not reflect Campeau's optimism. Campeau

Corporation stock had fallen to a twelve-month low of $14.13 by early January 1989, and investors and Wall Street analysts alike adopted a wait-and-see attitude on Campeau's long-term ability to balance a crushing debt against uneven cash flows. Meanwhile, back in Toronto, the media was watching as a complex legal battle between Campeau and his son Jacques over the voting rights to two million shares of Campeau Corporation made its way through the courts.

Throughout 1989, Campeau continued to sell some of his assets, including the Ann Taylor, I. Magnin, and Filene's department-store chains, to raise money to meet his astronomical interest payments, which were reported to be about $1 billion a year. On September 8, he announced that Bloomingdale's was on the auction block as part of a major restructuring effort. A few days later, he was forced to step down as head of the Campeau Corporation's retail operations and to give increased control to Olympia & York, a Canadian developer owned by the Reichmann family, in exchange for an emergency loan of $250 million. Under the terms of their agreement, Campeau retained his title as chairman but agreed to share responsibility for managing the corporation with at least four representatives of lenders and investors. In an interview with Isadore Barmash, the business correspondent of the *New York Times* (September 20, 1989), Campeau said, "I am delighted that we have decided to bring Olympia & York more prominently into the picture, and the loan will bring about the needed liquidity and enable us to preserve our company." He told Barmash that in the future he intended to concentrate his attention on real estate, where "my background shows that I have always had a conservative approach to financing."

A trim, silver-haired, but boyish-looking man with a taste for opulence and a fondness for diamond cufflinks, extravagant dinner parties, and European suits, Campeau has been described by Phil Patton, writing in the *New York Times Magazine*, as "a man who craves the spotlight." Charles Davies of the *Financial Post* (December 21, 1974) once described him as a distant person, fidgety, and inclined to clipped responses in casual conversation. A restless man who prides himself on the fact that he seldom sleeps more than five hours per night, he sometimes telephones associates in the middle of the night to discuss business. Although plagued with a chronically bad back, Campeau is a fitness buff who begins each morning with a long swim in his Olympic-size indoor pool. On the rare moments when he is not working, he relaxes on moose-hunting trips or on ski slopes. He is a devout Roman Catholic.

References: Fortune 115:102 Ja 5 '87 por, 118:70+ Ag 15 '88 por; N Y Times Mag p16+ Jl 17 '88 pors; N Y Times Biographical Service 19:408 Ap '88 por; Toronto Globe and Mail Report on Business mag p22+ Mr '87 pors, p36+ Jl '89 pors; Who's Who in America, 1988–89

Caroline, Princess of Monaco

Jan. 23, 1957– Princess of Monaco. Address: Palais de Monaco, Monte Carlo, Principality of Monaco

Long proclaimed the most beautiful princess in Europe, Caroline of Monaco is the firstborn child of Prince Rainier 3d, who has ruled Monaco since 1949, and the late Princess Grace, who died from injuries suffered in an automobile accident in 1982. Since neither Prince Rainier nor Caroline's brother, Prince Albert (who is heir to the throne), is married, the role of "first lady" of Monaco—if not the title, which she rejects—has devolved on Princess Caroline.

By all accounts, Princess Caroline has discharged her royal duties with what one reporter has described as "verve, intensity, and dedication." The thirty-two-year-old princess devotes her considerable energies to a number of charitable organizations in an effort to carry on the work her mother had performed. Fluent in five languages, the well-traveled princess is active on behalf of the arts and supports programs that benefit emotionally disturbed adolescents and the disabled. She is also a devoted mother of two boys and one girl, all of whom are under the age of six.

Born on January 23, 1957, Caroline Louise Marguerite de Grimaldi grew up in a glare of publicity that had begun even before her birth. Her parents' heavily publicized wedding, in 1956, was widely perceived as the culmination of a fairy-tale romance between a prince and a beautiful Hollywood actress. Caroline's father, Rainier Louis Maxence Bertrand Grimaldi, is descended from the ancient Genoese Grimaldi family, which has ruled Monaco since the year 1297. Her mother, the former Grace Patricia Kelly, was a much-loved actress of German and Irish parentage who grew up in Philadelphia and starred in eleven films between 1951 and her marriage in 1956.

Monaco is a tiny principality on the Mediterranean coast, nine miles east of Nice, France and a thirty-minute drive from the French-Italian border. Comprising about 481.85 acres, the country is little more than half the size of Central Park in New York City. Princess Grace's vigorous promotion of Monaco's cultural life and of its charitable institutions considerably benefited Monaco's thriving economy, which depends largely on tourism. Other sources of revenue are the financial services sector, corporate and indirect taxes, light industry, and the sale of tobacco and postage stamps. Gambling provides only 4 percent of the country's income. Monaco has 30,000 inhabitants, 5,000 of whom are Monegasque citizens not subject to taxes on income or property. The birth of Rainier's first child was eagerly awaited by the populace, who would be informed of the heir's gender by cannon shots—a twenty-one-gun salute for a girl, 101 for a boy. The news of Caroline's birth was signaled by the appropriate number of cannon shots and the pealing of bells, and her parents received 7,000 congratulatory letters on the day after her birth.

Baby Caroline's photo graced the cover of the March 25, 1957 issue of *Life* magazine, which also featured a six-page photo essay celebrating her birth. For the following four years, until the White House was taken over by the Kennedys, Princess Caroline received more media attention than any other child in the world. Despite her parents' desire to provide as normal a childhood as possible for their three children—Caroline, Albert Alexandre Louis Pierre (born on March 14, 1958), and Stephanie Marie Elisabeth (born on February 1, 1965)—their royal status, with its attendant risks and rewards, made that type of upbringing all but impossible. "I grew up in a special atmosphere," Princess Caroline told Diane de Dubovay in an interview for *McCall's* (September 1986) magazine, "which meant that I did spend an awful lot of time alone as a child. I didn't go to school until I was eight—I had a tutor. . . . I was the most horrible child. I never wanted to sit on anybody's lap, including my mother's. She was a very frustrated young mother when she had me. I was always squirming out of people's arms."

The perception of Caroline as a "horrible child" was apparently not shared by her teachers at Les Dames de St.-Maur, a Roman Catholic convent school not far from the palace, which Caroline attended from the age of eight until she reached the age of fourteen; nor was it shared by her teachers at St. Mary's Convent, a Roman Catholic boarding school in Ascot, England, from which she graduated in 1973 at sixteen. At both schools she was known as Caroline Grimaldi rather than by any title of royalty. Her teachers invariably phrase their recollections of Caroline in such terms as "brilliant, extroverted, and terribly curious," remembering their young charge as having been both practical and sophisticated and at ease in any situation.

Caroline's well-rounded upbringing was no accident. She inherited both her father's love of animals and athletics and her mother's interest in the arts. Caroline took ballet lessons at Marika Besobrasova's School of Dance in Monte Carlo and became accomplished at playing the piano and the flute. She excelled at every sport she undertook, including skiing, water skiing, swimming, horseback riding, and tennis. In her less strenuous leisure hours, she visited the zoo and played with a lion cub that had been given to her by its trainer. She spent her summers with her Kelly cousins in Ocean City, New Jersey, or at camp in the Pocono Mountains in Pennsylvania, reflecting Princess Grace's insistence that her children take pride in their American heritage. Caroline grew up speaking French and English and later added Italian, Spanish, and German.

Caroline's graduation from St. Mary's in 1973 provided her with the English equivalent of a high school diploma, but she needed to pass the *baccalauréat* (the French equivalent of a high school diploma) in order to attend her father's alma mater, l'Ecole Libre des Sciences Politiques in Paris, which had become the Institut d'Etudes Politiques in 1945. At sixteen she attended a boarding school near Paris, Dupanloup (of the Congregation les Dames de Saint Maur) to study for her French exams. Princess Grace moved into the Grimaldis' apartment on Avenue Foch with Caroline and Stephanie in an effort to shield her daughter from unwanted publicity. Caroline passed her "bac," with honors, in June 1974 and enrolled the following fall in the Institut, where she studied economics, finance, international relations, and constitutional law. Caroline left the Institut after only one year of study.

The level of media attention accorded Caroline's social life escalated dramatically after she was featured on the cover of *Time* (January 27, 1975) in honor of her eighteenth birthday. Gossipmongers extolled her beauty and vivacity but took a dim view of her makeup, heavy smoking, and décolleté dresses. Self-appointed matchmakers working for the tabloid press invented romances between the princess and Prince Charles (whom she denied ever having met), Prince Henri of Luxembourg, and Henri Giscard d'Estaing, the son of the French president, and any man whose momentary physical proximity to Caroline enabled the photographers to capture them together. Such fabrications reportedly strained the relationship between Grace and Caroline, both of whom downplayed any tensions there may have been. For instance, Grace was quoted by Sarah Bradford as saying: "We have our differences over clothes and boyfriends. But all mothers and all adolescents are like that, aren't they? Caroline wants to fly with her own wings, live for herself. It's natural and normal. In one sense she is more mature than I was at her age. . . . But in another sense she is more vulnerable." Caroline was equally respect-

ful of her mother, as quoted by *Good Housekeeping* (August 1976): "My mother is beautiful, but she is rather reserved. She is a marvelous housewife, full of self-control, always impeccable down to the smallest detail. I sometimes find it difficult to do the things Mother expects of me." When asked by the UPI reporter whether her plans for the future included acting, Caroline said: "I have no screen ambitions whatsoever. There is no competition. We all get along with each other. I don't want to compete in Mother's field. We're so different. She was shy. I'm not. My ambition is to keep on being a student for a while. There is so much to learn, isn't there?"

Home in Monaco for the summer after her year at the Institut, Caroline was persuaded by her parents that continuing her education at Princeton University in New Jersey, far removed from the attractions of a cosmopolitan social life, would allow her to concentrate on her studies. She was accepted by Princeton that fall and agreed to enroll but changed her mind, choosing instead to attend the Sorbonne in Paris, where she began seeing Philippe Junot, a business consultant for international investment banks whose background is upper-middle-class. His father was a deputy mayor of Paris who had once headed the Paris branch of Westinghouse Electric.

In the summer of 1977 Rainier invited Caroline and Junot to accompany him on a trip to the Galapagos Islands, and on August 25 the palace announced Caroline's betrothal to Junot. The royal blessing was given on the condition that Caroline complete her studies at the Sorbonne before the wedding. In June 1978 she received her *licence*, the French equivalent of a bachelor's degree, in philosophy, with academic credits in psychology. The princess and Junot were married in a twenty-minute civil ceremony on June 28, followed by a more elaborate Roman Catholic service on June 29 that was attended by more than 300 persons, including the Begum Aga, the Aga Khan, Princess Salima, the former King Umberto of Italy, Prince Bertil and Princess Lilianne of Sweden, Cary Grant, Frank Sinatra, Ava Gardner, David Niven, and Gregory Peck.

Princess Grace harbored doubts about the union's prospects for viability until the very eve of the wedding. In an interview for *Newsweek* (June 26, 1978) the previous week, Grace had said: "I think Caroline is still a bit young to be making such an important choice in her life. . . . Being Catholic, we consider marriage a very, very serious commitment and think it should be well thought out. What really matters is that she marry a man of character, decency, and substance." In the same interview, Caroline was quoted as anticipating her marriage with nothing but optimism.

After Princess Caroline became Mme. Junot, Rainier presented his daughter with a villa, the Clos St.-Pierre, which was a mere three-minute walk from the palace. But her primary residence was an apartment she shared with her husband on Avenue de Breteuil in Paris's seventh arrondissement. Long before the Junots' first anniversary, Princess Grace's misgivings about her son-in-law's ability to be a proper husband were vindicated. Ostensibly in Montreal on business, Junot was photographed dancing with a former girlfriend at the trendy Studio 54 in New York City, and shortly after that Caroline was seen in a nightclub with Robertino Rossellini, the son of the Swedish actress Ingrid Bergman and the Italian filmmaker Roberto Rossellini. Contrary to the commonly held assumption that Rossellini was a former boyfriend of Caroline's, the two were actually close friends who had known each other since childhood.

Junot's repeated infidelities dragged the ill-fated marriage through the tabloid scandal sheets of supermarket checkout counters until Caroline could stand the public humiliation and private disillusionment no longer. On August 9, 1980 a palace communiqué announced that a separation was in effect and that divorce was imminent. Caroline was granted a civil divorce on October 9, 1980, but her repeated entreaties to the Vatican for an annulment have gone unanswered to this day.

Caroline's resiliency, which would soon become evident in the wake of her mother's death, was demonstrated less than one year after her divorce in an interview with Princess Ira von Furstenberg for her book *Young at Any Age* (1981). In an excerpt that appeared in the *Chicago Tribune* (September 21, 1981), Caroline indicated that the divorce had not dissuaded her from the belief that she could yet find fulfillment in marriage and motherhood. After the two princesses discussed Caroline's beauty regimen, Caroline said, "If, however, one talks about beauty on a deeper level, I think the most important place to be beautiful is in the soul. The essential thing is to try to change, because I know only too well that there is a great deal that I have yet to learn. I think it would be beautiful to find peace, to be able to listen to one's inner self without outside influence. Beauty is also happiness, for which there is no prescription or explanation. At the moment I think happiness depends on the miracle of creation and nature. And for a woman, happiness is undoubtedly the joy of giving birth."

But before Caroline could experience that joy, she was subjected to overwhelming grief—her own and that of her family—following the death of her mother on September 14, 1982. Princess Grace had been driving along a winding mountain road, with Princess Stephanie in the passenger seat, from Roc Agel (the family farm) to the palace the previous morning, when she lost control of the vehicle. Princess Grace was removed from the vehicle after it plunged 110 feet down the mountainside. She slipped further and further into a coma until she died from a massive cerebral hemorrhage the following day. Stephanie suffered a vertebral fracture that narrowly missed paralyzing her. During the long period of mourning that followed, Caroline took care of her father and supervised the palace staff, earning praise for her fortitude from all quarters.

Caroline had already begun to take on some of the functions befitting her position before her mother's death. She served, for example, as president of the Monegasque national committee for the International Year of the Child in 1979, and two years later she founded a telephone hotline for troubled adolescents. In December 1982 she was named president of three organizations her mother had presided over: the Monaco Garden Club, the organizing committee for the International Festival of the Arts of Monte Carlo, and the Monagesque Princess Grace Foundation for young artistic talent. The following year she added the honorary presidency of the Monaco Girl Guides to her roster, and in 1985 she established La Compagnie des Ballets de Monte Carlo, thereby fulfilling one of her mother's dreams. The thoughts expressed by the French film actor Alain Delon in an open letter to Princess Caroline, which was published in *Paris Match*, were not held by him alone: "It is difficult to do the job of being a queen, as it is difficult to be a star. And, Madame, you are both. . . . Madame, the principality is very lucky to once again have a great lady."

Five foot eight in height and about 120 pounds in weight, with luxurious chestnut hair and deep blue eyes, Princess Caroline is strikingly beautiful. "Spontaneous, droll, and intelligent," in the words of Pepita Dupont, Caroline "has real presence and a magnetism that leaves almost no one indifferent to her." On December 29, 1983 she married Stefano Casiraghi, an Italian-born millionaire and entrepreneur who is three years her junior. They have three children: Andrea Albert Pierre (born on June 8, 1984), Charlotte Marie Pomeline (born on August 3, 1986), and Pierre Rainier Stefano (born on September 5, 1987).

References: *Chicago Tribune* VII p22+ Ap 20 '88 por; *Good H* 181:71+ Ag '75 pors; *Ladies Home J* 98:6+ Ja '81, 99:20+ S '82 por; *McCall's* 113:168+ S '86 por; *Newsday* A p4+ Je 13 '78 pors; *Newsweek* 91:66+ Je 26 '78 pors; Bradford, Sarah. *Princess Grace* (1984); Englund, Steven. *Grace of Monaco* (1984); Spada, James. *Grace: The Secret Lives of a Princess* (1987)

Cavazos, Lauro F(red, Jr.)

Jan. 4, 1927– United States Secretary of Education. Address: Dept. of Education, 400 Maryland Ave., S.W., Washington, D.C. 20202

When, on September 20, 1988, Lauro F. Cavazos was sworn in as the United States secretary of education, he became the first Hispanic-American cabinet officer in the country's history. His appointment by President Ronald Reagan was controversial at the time because it seemed designed to bolster the presidential campaign of George Bush among members of the increasingly influen-

Lauro F. Cavazos

tial Hispanic community, especially in Texas, at a time when the Republican candidate was trailing in the polls. Indeed, Cavazos was facetiously referred to as Bush's first cabinet appointment.

As head of the department that as a presidential candidate Ronald Reagan had once vowed to abolish, Cavazos has set a markedly different tone from that of his combative predecessor, William J. Bennett, who was outspoken in his hostility to the American education establishment and disdainful of "progressive" or experimental teaching methods. Cavazos promised to meet regularly with officials of the National Education Association and other professional groups and, unlike Bennett, to support limited bilingual instruction for the children of immigrant parents. He has set as his top priorities a reduction in the high school dropout rate, particularly among minorities, greater teacher accountability, and higher scholastic standards. His overarching goal, he has said, is to "reawaken in every child in this country the thirst, the cry, the hunger for education and have that be reinforced by parents, by teachers, by administrators at every level."

Taking heart from Bush's campaign pledge to become "the education president," Cavazos has promised to resist any further cuts in his department and has criticized as shortsighted those who are eager to balance the budget at the expense of educational programs. "We've heard a lot about budget and trade deficits," he has said. "We've got one that's equally dangerous—the education deficit."

Lauro Fred Cavazos Jr. was born on January 4, 1927 on the sprawling 800,000-acre King Ranch in southern Texas, the oldest son of Lauro Fred and Tomasa (Quintanilla) Cavazos. His paternal ances-

tors had settled in the area before Texas gained its independence from Mexico. Known locally as Don Lauro, his father was for forty-three years a foreman in the Santa Gertrudis cattle division of the King Ranch. A hard-driving ranch hand who as a young man took part in the last major gunfight against Mexican bandits in Texas, he exerted a profound influence on his five children. One of them, Joe Cavazos, who is now manager of a Sears store in Bossier City, Louisiana, described the household atmosphere to Jim Nesbitt of the Dallas *Times Herald* (August 11, 1988). "I think about Dad and the importance he put on education," he said. "That's the reason Larry [Lauro] is so successful. Larry lives education. I can remember Dad saying all the time, 'Get an education, get an education.' Larry took it to heart." So did the other Cavazos children. One brother, Richard Cavazos, became the first Hispanic-American general in the United States Army, and another, Robert Cavazos, was an all-American running back for Texas Tech University and is now a ranch owner in Corpus Christi, Texas. His only sister, Sarita Cavazos Ochoa, is a schoolteacher in Laredo, Texas.

Growing up in a bilingual household, Lauro Cavazos spoke English to his father and Spanish to his mother. He attended the first and second grades in a cramped one-room schoolhouse erected on the King Ranch for the children of its Mexican laborers. His teacher, one of his aunts, partitioned the room with a curtain to create two makeshift classes whenever possible, but the inadequacy of the school, which was not much bigger than Cavazos's current Washington office, angered his father, who in 1935 persuaded reluctant officials in nearby Kingsville to admit his children to an all-Anglo school. As the first Mexican-Americans ever enrolled there, Lauro and his siblings faced hostility from many of the other students. The family later moved from the ranch to a home in Kingsville.

On his graduation from high school in 1945, Cavazos enlisted in the United States Army, serving in the infantry during the final days of World War II. Discharged the following year, he planned to become a commercial fisherman, but his father persuaded him to enroll at Texas A & I University in Kingsville instead. He later transferred to Texas Technological College (now Texas Tech University) in Lubbock, where he earned a degree in zoology in 1949. During the next two years, he served as a teaching assistant there while he completed requirements for his master's degree in zoological cytology. He subsequently served as a research assistant at Iowa State University, in Ames, where he earned his doctorate in physiology in 1954.

Cavazos joined the faculty of the Medical College of Virginia in 1954 as an instructor of anatomy. He was promoted to assistant professor in 1956 and to associate professor four years later. Throughout his ten years on the Charlottesville campus, he also served on the editorial board of the *Medical College of Virginia Quarterly*. In 1964 Cavazos resigned to become a professor and chairman of the anatomy department at Tufts University School of Medicine in Medford, Massachusetts, but by that time he had begun looking beyond the classroom to administration. "My aspiration was always to reach the pinnacle of my profession, and be a full professor of anatomy," he told Martin Tolchin of the New York Times (October 20, 1988). "But as a professor, I found myself wondering why they did some things the way they did them."

Over the next sixteen years, Cavazos rose steadily through the administrative ranks, earning promotions to associate dean of the medical school in 1972, acting dean in 1973, and dean in 1975. Meanwhile, he also served on the editorial boards of the Anatomical Record and the Tufts Health Science Review, the scientific staff of the New England Medical Center Hospital in Boston, and the fellows program advisory committee of the National Board of Medical Examiners.

Although Cavazos was content at Tufts, he was unable to refuse an offer in 1980 to become president of his alma mater, Texas Tech University, and its medical school, the Health Science Center. Concurrently, he was named professor of biological science at the university and professor of anatomy at the medical school. The first alumnus ever named president of the Lubbock institution, Cavazos took understandable pride in overseeing the education of 24,000 students. At the time of his appointment, Texas Tech was the largest school in the nation to be headed by an Hispanic-American. He had barely settled into his office, however, when he received word that President-elect Ronald Reagan was considering him for the post of education secretary. Although flattered, Cavazos withdrew from the running in order to advance his agenda at Texas Tech.

Mindful of the important role that education had played in the success of his own family, Cavazos worked tirelessly to boost minority enrollment at Texas Tech. He visited high schools around the state to recruit promising black and Hispanic seniors, and several times a year he spoke before Hispanic groups in an effort to persuade parents to keep their children in school. During his tenure, Hispanic enrollment at Texas Tech nearly doubled, to 6.3 percent of the student body, and black enrollment jumped by a third, to 2.4 percent. Although the numbers were impressive, Cavazos had hoped for more.

As president of a state-supported university at a time when the Texas economy was reeling from the falling price of oil, Cavazos was forced to defend his budget before an austerity-minded legislature in Austin. When, largely through his efforts, state lawmakers rejected proposals to cut funds for the school, part of the reason may have been that Cavazos brought with him a reputation for efficiency and careful cost management. During his tenure, Texas Tech pared administrative costs to $179 per student, the lowest of any major university in the state and little more than half the average statewide. In recognition of his accomplishments, Cavazos was named Hispanic Educator of the Year

by the Texas chapter of the League of United Latin American Citizens in 1983, and in the next year he was given the Outstanding Leadership Award in the field of education by President Ronald Reagan.

Not everyone, however, praised Cavazos's administrative style, especially his tendency to act unilaterally without consulting those most affected by his decisions. In 1983, for example, the university, in a decision that Cavazos supported, dismissed Professor John Reichert, a highly regarded authority on energy who developed the first solar-powered, steam-driven electric turbine. Some members of the faculty wanted to discuss the reasons for the dismissal, but Cavazos simply refused to see them. Similarly, in 1984, Cavazos, in collaboration with certain university regents but without consulting faculty representatives, proposed revision of the university's tenure policy to require the 800-member faculty to undergo performance evaluation every five years. "It was the autocratic way he handled things," the law professor Dan Benson complained to Jim Nesbitt in the Dallas Times Herald piece. "He wanted his way. The faculty got the feeling they couldn't get to see the president and that he wouldn't listen to them. And that scared everybody." The faculty responded in October 1984 with a formal vote of no-confidence in President Cavazos. According to the Washington Post (August 11, 1988), the American Association of University Professors, in reviewing the matter, criticized Cavazos for having "had a profound effect upon faculty morale . . . to the detriment of the institution's well-being." Moreover, John Darling, Cavazos's chief assistant at Texas Tech, later resigned, citing differences over management style. The tenure affair seemed to create in Cavazos a renewed sensitivity, making him more approachable and more willing to listen to grievances. The tenure proposal was adopted, with some modifications, in 1986.

During his years at Texas Tech, Cavazos also served on the editorial board of the Journal of Medical Education, the Texas governor's task force on higher education, and his council on higher education management effectiveness. He was also a member of the biomedical library review committee of the National Institutes of Health's National Library of Medicine and of the selection panel for the National Aeronautic and Space Administration's journalist-in-space project. During 1984–85 he was chairman of the education committee of the Texas Science and Technology Council.

In May 1988 Cavazos announced that he was stepping down from his post at Texas Tech, effective July 1989, in order to take a sabbatical and eventually return to the classroom. Three months later, however, he learned that he once again was under consideration for the post of education secretary, this time to succeed the controversial William J. Bennett. Although at first glance he seemed an unlikely candidate, because he was a registered Democrat and had publicly criticized cutbacks in federal student-loan programs, he appeared to fit the Reagan administration's election-year criteria for the post. Although the White House denied that politics played any role in his selection, circumstantial evidence to the contrary was overwhelming. Made on the eve of the Republican National Convention and soon after George Bush had promised to name the first Hispanic cabinet member, the appointment appeared designed to invigorate the then flagging Bush campaign, especially in Texas, where the Democrats had taken on renewed strength with the recent vice-presidential nomination of Senator Lloyd M. Bentsen. Any doubts about the political nature of the appointment were dispelled when it was learned that only Hispanics were being considered for the post. Cavazos was chosen over Modesto ("Mitch") Maidique, the president of Florida International University, and Linda Chavez, a former White House aide. Alicia Sandoval, a spokesperson for the National Education Association, dismissed the appointment as "just a ploy to help get Bush elected and carry Texas . . . , a classic case of tokenism." But politics aside, all agreed that Cavazos was eminently qualified to fill the post.

At his confirmation hearing before Senator Edward M. Kennedy's Labor and Human Resources Committee, Cavazos was careful to praise his predecessor and the Reagan administration's education policy generally, but it was clear from the outset that he did not shrink from the government's role in education and placed a high value on the cabinet post that Attorney General Edwin Meese once dismissed as a "bureaucratic joke." "I frankly consider the Department of Education the most important and serious effort that we can do," Cavazos testified. "I pledge I will work very, very hard for the strongest Department of Education." Referring to the alarming report, "A Nation at Risk," that had been issued by the commission created by Reagan's first secretary of education, Terrel H. Bell, declared: "Secretary Bell issued the warning, Secretary Bennett took up the challenge and offered solutions. And I'm here to ensure that educational reform proceeds and that educational excellence once again returns to America." He further pledged to work closely with the NEA and the rest of the education establishment, which Bennett had once referred to collectively as "The Blob," and to defend the education budget against any further erosion, since under the Reagan administration the federal portion of all education spending had fallen from 9 percent to 6 percent. He also distanced himself from Bennett's policy in reaffirming his commitment to bilingual education, provided that it is limited to no more than a few years and leads to the ultimate goal of mainstreaming all students into English language classes.

On September 20, 1988 Cavazos was unanimously confirmed by the Senate and sworn in only a few hours later. On his first full day on the job, he held the department's first bilingual news conference, responding to questions from representatives of the Spanish language media, first in Spanish, then in English. Although he emphasized that competence in English was the goal of all educators, he may have drawn on his own experience as a Mexican-American in an all-Anglo school when he called for greater sensitivity to the needs of immigrant families. "You are dealing with a young child," he reminded reporters, "with a person who arrives at school the first day and doesn't understand what's going on, scared to death— scared to death if you can speak English, but it's double when you can't speak English." In one of his first acts as secretary, Cavazos invited the leaders of fifty major educational organizations to a get-acquainted session, at which he reassured them of his commitment to cooperation, not confrontation, and asked them for suggestions on how best to raise the standards of professionalism.

In his interview with Martin Tolchin, Cavazos spoke candidly about his concern that education is taken too lightly in the United States. "We hear so much about positioning America to compete," he said. "How can we achieve what we want to achieve if our citizens are not educated to their fullest potential?" He called for a renewed commitment to excellence in education, led by the federal government in partnership with teachers, schools, and state and local governments. In a speech at Arizona State University's College of Education on November 3, 1988, he outlined his program for improved education. Calling for more funds for educational programs and for a stepped-up recruitment of minority teachers, he encouraged innovation in teaching methods and urged greater emphasis on such basics as mathematics, science, geography, history, and English. He proposed the imposition of strict minimum academic standards and careful monitoring of student progress.

Cavazos also has called for greater teacher accountability and authority in running schools and freedom of choice for parents in choosing a public school for their children. He has often decried the alarming high school dropout rate, especially among Hispanics, blaming those ominous statistics not only on the economy, teen pregnancy, and drug and alcohol dependency, but also on the devaluation of education in American society, particularly among Hispanics.

On November 21, 1988 Cavazos was renamed to the cabinet by President-elect Bush, whose campaign rhetoric had promised to exalt the importance of the Department of Education and its mission. Vowing to become known as the "education president," Bush called for more federal spending despite the budget deficit, and for rewards for outstanding schools and teachers. In January 1989, however, Cavazos warned that, because of the federal deficit, the education budget may remain virtually unchanged. Although some financial incentives for improvement might be provided to teachers and schools, he said, primary attention will be focused on ferreting out model schools and spotlighting their success as role models for others to follow. Nevertheless, he has remained hopeful that one day all students can be persuaded to complete high school. "It is our expectation," he declared, "that the term 'dropout' will become obsolete."

On May 3, 1989 Secretary Cavazos released to the public the government's annual assessment of the state of education in the United States. Commenting on the report's conclusion that educational progress had been "stagnant" in spite of increased spending, he told reporters: "We are standing still. The problem is that it's been this way for three years in a row. We cannot be satisfied with mediocrity, and so it's time to turn things around." Since, in his view, money alone was not the answer, he suggested more homework, more parental involvement, and greater emphasis by the schools on boosting graduation rates.

Critics, among them Andrew Griffin, the executive officer of the Georgia Association of Educators, have charged that Cavazos is, in Griffin's words, "all talk, no action." "He keeps telling us that the problems are disgraceful, but he doesn't come up with any solutions," Jeanne Allen, an education policy analyst for the conservative Heritage Foundation, complained, as quoted in Time (May 29, 1989). Part of the problem, in the opinion of some observers, was what one called the "lackluster leadership" of George Bush.

At a conference on education attended by President Bush, Secretary Cavazos and other cabinet members, and the nation's governors held at the University of Virginia in September 1989, Bush endorsed the establishment of national educational goals and the standards to measure progress toward achieving them. Cavazos suggested, for example, setting goals for reducing the dropout rate, especially among minority students, and for increasing the number of students who continue their education beyond high school. As a first step toward that end, he awarded a $58.5 million grant to the Educational Testing Service to provide state-by-state breakdowns of student performance. "For the first time," Cavazos explained, as quoted in the New York Times (September 27, 1989), "representative students will be tested across the states, giving governors, state legislators, and education officials specific information about student performance in their own states as well as in comparison to others."

Lauro Cavazos had been described as a man who is more inclined to seek consensus than confrontation, but also as a strong-willed and at times autocratic leader. "If he gets pushed too far," a former colleague at Tufts has warned, "watch out." He has written dozens of articles on physiology, most of them based on research in his primary area of interest, the male reproductive system, and he has also contributed to scientific textbooks, including two about human dissection. He cuts gem stones for a hobby and has been active in the Boy Scouts and the United Way Campaign in Texas. Since December 28, 1954 he has been married to the former Peggy Ann Murdock, an operating-room nurse at Lubbock General Hospital. Of their ten grown children, seven are Texas Tech graduates, including a doctor, an architect, a teacher, and two airline pilots.

References: N Y Times A p20 Ag 11 '88 por, B p8 O 20 '88 por; Nat R 41:11+ Mr 24 '89; Time 132:80 D 5 '88 por, 133:76 My 29 '89 por; American Men and Women of Science (1986); Mexican-American Biographies, 1988; Who's Who in American Politics, 1989-90; Who's Who in the South and Southwest, 1986-87

Chapman, Tracy

1964- Singer; songwriter. Address: c/o Elektra/Asylum Records, 75 Rockefeller Plaza, New York, N.Y. 10019

When Tracy Chapman won in three categories at the 1989 Grammy Awards ceremony, including those of best new artist and best female pop vocal performance, her status as rock music's newest and youngest superstar was certified. Just two years earlier Miss Chapman was an obscure singer with a small but devoted following on the folk circuit in Cambridge, Massachusetts. Serious, shy, and decidedly unglamorous, it seemed obvious that she would never appear with Madonna or Don Johnson in a high-concept television commercial for Pepsi-Cola, but after the release of her stunning, multiplatinum debut recording, Tracy Chapman, she was soon sharing stages throughout the world with the likes of Bruce Springsteen and Sting. Although Tracy Chapman's quietly powerful songs have affinities with the folk movement of the civil rights era and the singer-songwriter phenomenon of the 1970s, her dramatic musical narratives expressing political outrage and her ballads and tender love songs have a contemporary sound and feel. "Folk music is full of literary songwriters, and the pop mainstream is full of soulful performers," one critic observed, "but Chapman is one of the few who can combine both characteristics and thus break out of the folkie ghetto."

Tracy Chapman was born in Cleveland, Ohio in 1964. After her parents divorced when she was four, her mother took custody of the two children, Tracy and her older sister, Aneta. Because her mother refused to ask for alimony payments from her ex-husband, her family received welfare checks from time to time, and she had to take a succession of ill-salaried jobs. Through her mother's struggle to provide for her family as a single parent living in the predominantly black working-class section of a Rust Belt industrial city, Tracy soon became aware of the constraints imposed on poor people, especially when those social forces are arrayed against black women—"these forces in society," as she observed, "making things more difficult than they ought to be." "There wasn't much to work with," Tracy Chapman recalled in an interview with Steve Pond for Rolling Stone (September 22, 1988). "We always had food to eat and a place to stay, but it was a fairly bare-bones kind of thing. As a child, I always had a sense of social conditions and political situations. I think it had to do with the fact that my mother was always discussing things with my sister and me—also because I read a lot. A lot of people in similar situations just have a sense that they're poor or disenfranchised, but they don't really think about what's created the situation or what factors don't allow them to control their lives." During her 1988 concert tour, Tracy Chapman informed many of her audiences that she had not been "awfully happy" growing up in Cleveland. The schools she attended were integrated, but, as she told Mark Cooper of the Guardian (March 26, 1988), the neighborhoods the students came from were mostly segregated ones. "It was an odd situation," she explained, "because you'd make friendships with people but it wouldn't go beyond the schooltime. There were a lot of really terrible things that happened."

Because her mother had been an amateur guitarist and both she and Tracy's sister, Aneta, had lovely voices, the Chapman household did not lack for music. Despite occasional bouts with poverty, there was always a record player in the home, acquainting Tracy with the wide range of styles and artists that her mother and sister liked. Although her personal favorites now number artists like U2, Aretha Franklin, Al Green, Miriam Makeba, and Bob Dylan, when she was growing up, as she told Steve Pond, she "heard Neil Diamond and [gospel singers like] Shirley Caesar and Mahalia Jackson [as well as] Gladys Knight and the Pips, Barbra Streisand, Cher, the Bee Gees, [and] the Four Tops." Her sister even listened to Journey at some point. In the first grade, she acquired her first musical instrument, a ukelele, and by the age of eight she had begun to play the organ, on which she also composed her own songs. "They were pretty terrible songs," she admitted when she spoke to Anthony De Curtis for a Rolling Stone (June 30, 1988)

profile, "about whatever eight-year-olds write about. You know, the sky. . . ." A few years later, Tracy began taking clarinet lessons. She also acquired the instrument that was her heart's desire, a guitar, albeit a cheap one with strings about "an inch off the fret board," as she told John Milward of the Chicago Tribune (August 14, 1988). By the age of fourteen she had composed "Cleveland '78," her first social commentary song.

According to Anthony De Curtis, Tracy Chapman's "political awareness deepened when, through a minority-placement program called A Better Chance, she enrolled at the Wooster School, a small, progressive private school in Danbury, Connecticut." "A lot of the people who were teaching us were just a few years out of college, and they were [politically] aware," Miss Chapman has recalled. "During my first year there was all this talk about the reinstatement of the draft, and people were really focused on that and the whole question of nuclear weapons. So I started to deal with some larger political issues, outside of where I had come from, what I had grown up seeing."

A born athlete, Tracy Chapman played on the girls' basketball, softball, and soccer teams at Wooster. More important, for the first time she heard contemporary folk-rock singer-songwriters like Joni Mitchell, Neil Young, Bob Dylan, and Jackson Browne. A "strong B, B-plus student," according to one of Wooster's deans, she also continued to write songs and to perform occasionally at her Episcopalian prep school's coffeehouse. The Reverend Robert Tate, who was then the school chaplain and who is thanked by Miss Chapman in the liner notes of her first album, took up a collection among students and teachers to purchase her a new guitar, a Fender that Tracy picked out in New York. As the head of the music department during Tracy's senior year told Steve Pond, Miss Chapman "didn't hang around the music building much." He remembers "seeing her playing her guitar and sitting on the white fence outside her dorm building or taking advantage of the acoustics in the small, high-ceilinged chapel." As Sid Rowell, the dean of students at Wooster, said to Anthony De Curtis, "We knew she would make it somehow, someday. The only question was when, because she wasn't the kind of kid who was going to compromise. She was going to have success on her terms." "She seemed to have a real good sense of herself musically," explained David Douglas, the current head of the music department, "and that's unusual for a high school-age kid. Her influences showed—and perhaps still do—but she had a clear sense of who she was."

In her senior year Tracy Chapman was accepted at five colleges, all of which offered her financial aid, and in the fall of 1982 she enrolled at Tufts University in Medford, Massachusetts, just outside Boston. She had planned to fulfill her lifelong ambition of becoming a veterinarian, but when she found the biology curriculum boring she changed her major to cultural anthropology, with an emphasis on West African cultures and ethnomusicology.

"I wanted to study something that really interested me . . . ," she told De Curtis, "something where I felt I was really learning something that would give some meaning to my life." At Tufts, she continued to write songs and perform, making the rounds of the Cambridge folk-club circuit and playing on the street in Harvard Square. When she spoke to the *Guardian*'s Mark Cooper, Tracy Chapman recalled that she became a street musician one summer when her job mowing lawns at the university grew unbearable. "It's worse than playing in a club," she said, "because there's so many distractions. You can feel rejected if people don't stop so you kind of insulate yourself. It's legal to street-perform in Cambridge but I refused to use any kind of amplification; a lot of people do and it's not fair because they drown each other out. So I just used to find spaces on the street that gave me a little acoustic support—like doorways. And people would have to come closer than they normally would."

At that time Miss Chapman also acquired a helpful admirer—Brian Koppelman, a fellow Tufts student, whose father, Charles Koppelman, is a managing partner of SBK, one of the world's largest music-publishing companies. Koppelman *fils* first heard her when he was booking speakers and performers for a campus rally calling for divestment from South Africa. "Somebody told me that there was a good protest singer I should try and get," Koppelman explained to Steve Pond. "So I went to see her, and lo and behold, there was Tracy Chapman, exactly like she is now, performing for 100 people." Koppelman told Tracy: "I never do this, because I try to be my own person, but I really think my father could help you." "And," he recalled for Pond, "she didn't really seem interested. Tracy genuinely was not interested in money." Nevertheless, Charles Koppelman heard her and promptly offered her a contract, which she took six months to sign, partly because she wanted to complete the requirement for her bachelor's degree before making a professional commitment to music.

But one of the reasons that Tracy Chapman may have been chary of signing contracts for a career in the entertainment business was that she failed to see how she might fit into the current musical scene. Although compelling and even spectacular in its own quiet way, her eclectic, folk-oriented music seemed unlikely to make much of an impact on black audiences fond of rap, Rick James, Prince—or even Anita Baker—on George Michael–besotted teenagers, or on trendy white kids who dote on the Replacements and Guns 'n' Roses. "I have to say that I never thought I would get a contract with a major record label," she admitted to De Curtis. "All the time since I was a kid listening to records and the radio, I didn't think there was any indication that record people would find the kind of music that I did marketable. Especially when I was singing songs like 'Talkin' 'bout a Revolution' during the 1970s—you know, fit right in with the disco era. I didn't see a place for me there."

Charles Koppelman arranged an audition with Bob Krasnow of Elektra Records. "He wanted to bring her in in person," Krasnow recalled when he spoke to Pond, "and there's nothing more uncomfortable than auditioning someone face to face. Can you imagine if you don't like them? So I have a hard and fast rule: I don't care who it is, I don't talk to them in person. But Charles was insistent, and I was seduced by the songs he played me." When he heard Tracy Chapman, Krasnow turned to Koppelman and exclaimed, "Hey, this is it!" Wanting to preserve the integrity of Miss Chapman's uncluttered and tough-minded music, Krasnow hired as her producer David Kershenbaum, a veteran studio professional known for his work with sophisticated artists like Joe Jackson, Joan Baez, and Graham Parker. The challenge that Kershenbaum and Tracy Chapman faced was one of weaving a backup group of musicians—an electric guitarist and bassist, a drummer, and a keyboard player—into a seamless musical garment for songs that were tailored to the simple requirements of a voice and an acoustic guitar. "My producer . . . and I discussed what kind of instrumentation we should use, and what kind of role arrangements should play in the songs," Tracy Chapman explained to Peter Watrous of the *New York Times* (May 15, 1988). "I wasn't concerned with pop radio, what it wants. I worked with the musicians on the record and tried to realize the ideas I'd had about adding things to the songs that would simply make it sound better, to highlight the way it works. . . . It could have turned into what you hear on pop radio. We were very conscious of that happening." As Kershenbaum told the *Chicago Tribune*'s David Silverman, "The biggest concern was keeping the instruments out."

Released on about the first of April 1988, by late summer *Tracy Chapman* had astonished the entire music business, for that folk-oriented offering by a young black woman making no concessions to the demands of pop radio had attained the number-one spot on *Billboard*'s pop albums chart and its first single, "Fast Car," had reached sixth place on the pop singles list. The disc succeeded on the strength of each of its eleven tracks. The opening cut, "Talkin' 'bout a Revolution," which Miss Chapman had written when she was a teenager, dealt with such unfashionable subjects as the recipients of welfare state and Salvation Army handouts and vowed that someday the "poor people gonna rise up and take what's theirs." Another pointed expression of Tracy Chapman's misgivings about the political status quo was the song "Why," which asked questions like, "Why are the missiles called peacekeepers/When they're aimed to kill/Why is a woman still not safe/When she's in her home?" On "Across the Lines" the assault of a black girl in a small town provokes a tragic race riot. In the final verse Tracy Chapman demonstrates her insight into mass psychology when she reports that the victim ultimately is faulted by the town: "Lots of people hurt and angry/She's the one to blame." The reggae-inflected "She's Got Her Ticket" is about a woman determined to free herself from a destructive relationship, and on the ironic "Mountains o' Things" she sketches a poor woman's debilitating fantasy of being rich enough to be an acquisitive Material Girl. In addition to those songs, which one critic described as "tales of power and menace," *Tracy Chapman* also featured the gorgeously crafted love songs "If Not Now . . . ," "For You," and the exquisitely tender "Baby, Can I Hold You."

Most critics, however, felt that the disc's most exceptional cuts were "Fast Car," the psychologically probing "For My Lover," and the compelling ballad "Behind the Wall." With an ambitious narrative structure reminiscent of one of Bruce Springsteen's social realist numbers, "Fast Car" is written from the point of view of a young poor woman "whose dreams," Richard Harrington wrote in the *Washington Post* (April 24, 1988), "are constantly deferred, first when she quits school and takes a menial job to support her alcoholic father and later when her boyfriend mistakes having that fast car for having a sense of direction." As the song builds to its emotional crescendo, Miss Chapman tries to sustain her aspirations for a better future, singing: "Maybe together we can get somewhere/ . . . You and I both get jobs/And finally see what it means to be living/ . . . We'll move out of the shelter/Buy a big house and live in the suburbs." By the song's conclusion, her dreams have been wrecked on the shoals of hard reality: "I got a job that pays all our bills/You stay out drinking . . . /See more of your friends than you do of your kids/ . . . I ain't going nowhere/So take your fast car and keep on driving/ . . . Is it fast enough so you can fly away?"

Described by one writer as an "edgy love song," "For My Lover" is about the pathology of obsessive love, and once again Tracy Chapman displays her gift for subtle psychological insight: "Two weeks in a Virginia jail/For my lover for my lover/And everybody thinks/That I'm the fool/But they don't get/Any love from you/ . . . Everyday I'm psychoanalyzed/ . . . They dope me up and I tell them lies/For my lover. . . . " Performed without accompaniment by Miss Chapman, "Behind the Wall" is a tour de force of stark beauty, grappling with the subjects of domestic violence and the abuse of women. She sings: "Last night I heard the screaming/Loud voices behind the wall/Another sleepless night for me/It won't do no good to call/The police/Always come late/If they come at all/ . . . Last night I heard the screaming/Then a silence that chilled my soul/I prayed that I was dreaming/When I saw the ambulance in the road/And the policeman said/'I'm here to keep the peace/Will the crowd disperse/I think we all could use some sleep.'" In the *New York Times* (November 30, 1988), Jon Pareles described the way in which the dramatic effect of her music was augmented by Miss Chapman's songwriting technique: "She often writes verses that are modal or (like many blues melodies) pentatonic, which create a sense of unsettled tonality, then resolves

them in a major-key chorus. . . . Her songs create drama as her voice fills the spaces in her guitar parts with warmth and quiet passion."

Tracy Chapman was showered with critical praise. In *Rolling Stone* (June 2, 1988), Steve Pond wrote that she had the potential to develop musically as a "forthright woman with a feel for modern urban music and the guts to force herself into the pop mainstream. . . . Her sound is not wholly new, but at its best it feels that way, because modern pop—as opposed to folk, a genre far too restrictive for Chapman—rarely accommodates women who sing with this much open political anger." A reviewer for the *Village Voice* praised Tracy Chapman for her unique stance in an industry in which women are judged as much by how they look in miniskirts as by how well they craft their songs. "One group shamefully underrepresented in record bins," the *Voice* critic asserted, "is college-educated, upwardly mobile, politicized black women, neither buppies nor B-girls, but with street sense and tempered careerism. Meanwhile the music biz sees women as sexual mannequins defined by their fishnets."

Some critics, however, obscured Tracy Chapman's originality by constantly invoking her superficial ties to such folksingers of the early 1960s as Joan Baez and to such singer-songwriters of the 1970s as Joni Mitchell and Joan Armatrading. But as Miss Chapman insisted, the African-American contributions to the roots of modern folk music are often overlooked, and that is the part of the folk tradition in which her music is rooted. And whereas singer-songwriters of the past tended to dwell, self-indulgently sometimes, on introspections written in the first-person singular, Miss Chapman has trained her gaze unflinchingly on the outside world, where individual pain is charged with political meaning. Also, like Bruce Springsteen's, her musical narratives encompass a world of vividly realized yet fictitious characters who exist outside of the bounds of her personal experience.

As Tracy Chapman told Wayne Robins of *New York Newsday* (May 3, 1988): "In both occasions [the 1960s and the 1970s], what [songwriters] were doing was simply communicating to people. There are two places to go for inspiration, inside or outside. I tend to think some combination of those two things tends to have more universal appeal." And she told Steve Pond that the stereotyped image of female folksingers as fragile and vulnerable was created "because they actually had a lot more control than other women in the music scene." "They wrote their own songs," she said, "they played them, they performed by themselves—there you have a picture of a very independent person, and trying to make them seem emotional and fragile and all puts a softer edge on it. As if there was something wrong with being independent."

Propelled by critical acclaim and sales of several million copies of her album, Tracy Chapman's rise to prominence was dizzyingly rapid. In June 1988, in an appearance at England's huge Wembley Stadium for the Nelson Mandela Birthday

Tribute, she mesmerized the teeming throng and an international television audience that numbered in the millions while performing with no accompaniment other than her own acoustic guitar-playing. And in the fall of 1988 she was a featured performer for the celebrated Human Rights Now! tour, which was organized by the British rock stars Sting and Peter Gabriel on behalf of Amnesty International, the humanitarian organization that exposes and seeks to redress abuses of human rights throughout the world. Planned as a consciousness-raising event more than a fund-raising one, the Human Rights Now! tour traveled to some fifteen nations, including Hungary, Zimbabwe, Japan, Argentina, and Brazil, and was headlined by Bruce Springsteen, Sting, Peter Gabriel, the Senegalese artist Youssou N'Dour—and Tracy Chapman. "It's as I planned it," she joked when she talked to Steve Pond, "[small] club dates to stadiums."

The acclaim for Miss Chapman was paralleled in 1988 by the emergence of a host of talented female musicians, among them Toni Childs, Suzanne Vega, Michelle Shocked, Natalie Merchant, and Sinead O'Connor. Those artists possessed distinct musical personalities, were strikingly intelligent songwriters as well as vocalists, and had more in common with older artists like Chrissie Hynde and Rickie Lee Jones than with MTV sirens like Madonna and Cyndi Lauper. Miss Chapman's lyrical concerns also reflected the current trend in rock music for songs that deal with the stark facts of life in the anxiety-ridden 1980s: AIDS, apartheid, drugs and violence, urban racial tension, and the imperiled environment. Those somber subjects have been powerfully addressed by such established older artists as Lou Reed, John Mellencamp, and Jackson Browne, but, as the producer David Kershenbaum observed, "Within the record industry, people were wondering if there was room for good music anymore. Then in walks Tracy Chapman and turns everything around." A few critics, however, nagged that the power of her message is attenuated by the fact that her audience consists largely of middle- and upper-income liberals, that she is, in the words of one writer, an "after-dinner conscience-comforter." When asked by Steve Pond how she felt about her yuppie audience, Tracy Chapman replied, "I don't know that they're yuppies. I know they can afford to pay a ticket price and buy the record, and that might put them in some particular economic status. But for me it's just really important to know that people are listening . . . [although some fans may not] care about any of the songs that have political content to them."

Tracy Chapman's second album, Crossroads, was released by Elektra in the fall of 1989. Many of the songs dealt with the theme of an individual's determination to maintain his or her dignity in the face of adversity and social oppression, and they were buoyed by the authority of Miss Chapman's voice, which has "more ingrained moral fiber than [that of] any folk singer since [Bob] Dylan in his prime," as Stephen Holden declared in the New York Times (October 1, 1989). However, critics agreed that the songs on Crossroads lacked the compelling narrative structure of earlier numbers like "Fast Car" and "Behind the Wall." As Mike Joyce noted in the Washington Post (October 4, 1989), "Where Chapman's first album was filled with . . . songs that drew you in as their narratives unfolded, Crossroads is basically a collection of moralistic musings and admonitions set to similarly spare arrangements, once again devised by producer David Kershenbaum." And in his New York Times review of Crossroads, Stephen Holden wrote that "the songs make clear political statements, [but] one doesn't have the same feeling of a specific character speaking that one had in 'Fast Car' and other songs on the first album."

Just as she eschews gimmicks in the recording studio, Tracy Chapman resorts to no stage theatrics in concert performances, winning over audiences simply through the power of her voice, which is a rich contralto, her melodies, which are memorable for their elegant simplicity, and her restrained, yet evocative, guitar-playing. Because she is, as Joan Baez has observed, "painfully shy," Tracy Chapman has only recently begun to banter with audiences and talk between numbers about her music. She dresses for the stage as she does in everyday life, in jeans, sneakers, and tank-top shirts. Although she has vocalized on stage with artists the stature of Bruce Springsteen and Sting before tens of thousands of rapt fans, she avoids the limelight and is intimately known only by her closest friends from the past and her family. "I'm just a very cautious person," she has explained, "and not very gregarious." She makes her home in a modest apartment in Boston, which she shares with an old friend and Candy, her pet dachshund.

References: Chicago Tribune V p12 Ja 19 '89 por; N Y Times C p15 Ap 6 '88 por, II p1+ My 21 '89 pors; Rolling Stone p15+ O 20 '88 pors; Washington Post C p7 Ap 20 '88, A p1+ S 14 '88 pors

Cheney, Richard B(ruce)

Jan. 30, 1941– United States Secretary of Defense. Address: Dept. of Defense, The Pentagon, Washington, D.C. 20301

After his first choice to head the Department of Defense, John Tower, was rejected by the United States Senate on March 9, 1989, President George Bush immediately nominated Richard B. Cheney, a staunchly conservative but pragmatic member of the United States House of Representatives, to the post, fully aware that Cheney, one of the most popular and highly respected members of Congress, would encounter little Senate opposition. A consummate Washington insider who has spent virtually his entire career in the federal government,

Richard B. Cheney

Cheney joined the staff of President Richard Nixon at the age of twenty-eight, and, by the time he was thirty-four, he had become chief of staff to President Gerald R. Ford. Within ten years of his election, in 1978, to the first of six terms as his home state of Wyoming's at-large congressman, he had advanced through the ranks to become Republican whip, his party's second-ranking post in the House. During his first few months as secretary of defense, Cheney has attempted to implement Bush administration directives calling for reductions in the defense budget and opposing the initiation of talks with the Soviet Union on reducing short-range nuclear missiles in Europe.

Born on January 30, 1941 in Lincoln, Nebraska, Richard Bruce Cheney is the son of Richard Herbert Cheney, a soil-conservation agent with the United States Department of Agriculture, and Marjorie Lauraine (Dickey) Cheney. In his early childhood, he moved with his parents to Casper, Wyoming, where his chief interests were hunting, fishing, and playing football and baseball. At Natrona County High School, Dick Cheney, as he prefers to be known, was cocaptain of the football team and, in his senior year, class president.

Following his graduation from high school in 1959, Cheney attended Yale University on a scholarship, but he dropped out after just three semesters. "I wasn't a serious student," he told Jeanette Smyth of the Washington Post (April 4, 1976). "I never buckled down." Returning to the West, Cheney spent the next two years working on power lines in Colorado, Arizona, and Wyoming. In 1963 he resumed his education, at the University of Wyoming. While he was an undergraduate there, he submitted an essay to the National Center for Education in Politics at New York University that one

official at the center has since described as "by far the best among fifty papers, almost of dissertation quality." In his senior year of college, Cheney obtained an internship in the Wyoming state legislature, a responsibility that required a 100-mile-a-day commute between the campus in Laramie and the capitol in Cheyenne.

The University of Wyoming awarded Dick Cheney a B.A. degree in political science in 1965 and an M.A. degree in the same discipline a year later. Selected for an internship by the National Center for Education in Politics, Cheney then moved to Madison, Wisconsin to work on the staff of Governor Warren Knowles. While he was living in Madison, Cheney also began work toward a Ph.D. degree at the University of Wisconsin, but in 1968 he left the program without completing his dissertation in order to accept an American Political Science Association congressional fellowship on the staff of Congressman William Steiger. Steiger, a Wisconsin Republican, later called Cheney "one of the brightest, most perceptive, most sensitive people I've ever had the chance to work with."

In 1969 Steiger temporarily loaned Cheney to the staff of Donald Rumsfeld, a former congressman who had recently become the director of the Office of Economic Opportunity in the new administration of President Richard Nixon. Impressed by the young man, Rumsfeld appointed him to the position of special assistant. When Rumsfeld became a White House counselor in 1970, he asked Cheney to be his deputy, and, when he took on the additional job of director of the Cost of Living Council a year later, he named Cheney assistant director for operations. The two men parted company in February 1973, after Nixon appointed Rumsfeld ambassador to NATO, and Cheney chose not to accompany him to Brussels, deciding instead to accept a vice-presidency at Bradley, Woods and Company, a Washington-based investment firm that advises private industry on legislative issues. When Gerald Ford succeeded to the presidency following Nixon's resignation, in August 1974, he appointed Rumsfeld head of his transition team. Rumsfeld immediately recruited Cheney to serve as his deputy. A month later, Ford named Rumsfeld assistant to the president, and Cheney, deputy assistant.

In all but title, Rumsfeld was White House chief of staff, and Cheney was his alter ego. According to Paul Healy of the New York Daily News (July 3, 1975), Rumsfeld and Cheney, who checked with one another continually throughout the day, were "as intuitive to one another as some identical twins." Often called upon to appease journalists and bureaucrats put off by Rumsfeld's abrasive manner, Cheney also regularly substituted for Rumsfeld at senior staff meetings and in briefings with the president. "Dick speaks for me—or the president . . . ," Rumsfeld told Healy. "Dick has natural good judgment and instincts. There's a nice tempo in his manner, he's very easy for people to get along with."

On November 5, 1975 Cheney succeeded Rumsfeld, who had been named secretary of defense, as Ford's chief of staff. Determined to keep a low profile, Cheney refused Ford's offer to upgrade the chief of staff position to cabinet-level status and continued to commute daily from his suburban home to the White House in a ten-year-old Volkswagen rather than in a chauffeured government car. Working an average of fifteen hours a day, he supervised a White House staff of almost 500, arranged the president's schedule, approved appointments to top-level federal jobs, oversaw the flow of memos to and from the president, and frequently consulted with him.

After Gerald Ford lost the 1976 presidential election to Jimmy Carter, the Democratic candidate, Cheney returned to Casper, Wyoming, where he worked briefly in banking before deciding to seek election in 1978 as his sparsely populated state's one member of the United States House of Representatives. During the Republican primary campaign, Cheney survived a mild heart attack and an attempt by one of his opponents, Ed Witzenburger, the popular state treasurer, to portray him as a carpetbagger and won his party's nomination by 7,705 votes. In the general election, Cheney easily defeated the Democratic nominee, Bill Bagley, winning 59 percent of the vote. He was subsequently returned to office by large margins in the elections of 1980, 1982, 1984, 1986, and 1988.

Cheney found serving in the House more to his liking than working on the president's staff. "The White House staff jobs give you a broader opportunity to influence a variety of events, but you're ultimately a hired gun," he told Martin Tolchin of the New York Times (April 6, 1982). "When you serve in the House, you may cast only one of 435 votes, but it's your decision to make." Early in his second term, Cheney scored a stunning victory over Congresswoman Marjorie S. Holt of Maryland, a five-term veteran, to become head of the Republican Policy Committee, the fourth-ranking GOP post in the House.

With a few exceptions, Cheney strongly supported the domestic and foreign-policy programs of President Ronald Reagan, consistently receiving high approval ratings from such conservative organizations as the American Conservative Union and Americans for Constitutional Action. He was an especially staunch advocate of Reagan administration efforts to strengthen defense. Although he favored the Soviet-American treaty banning medium-range nuclear missiles, he approved funding for the development of the multibillion-dollar Strategic Defense Initiative, popularly known as "Star Wars," the deployment of the MX missile, and the production of new chemical weapons. A supporter of continued military aid to the Nicaraguan Contras and to the insurgents in Afghanistan and Angola, he voted against a proposal requiring the president to notify Congress within forty-eight hours of the start of any secret intelligence operation, an outgrowth of the Iran-Contra scandal. The nay vote was consistent with Cheney's belief that the president's ability to implement foreign policy had been hampered by repeated congressional attempts to impose restrictions on the White House.

Cheney's record on domestic issues was equally conservative. In 1986, for example, he sided with the House's so-called conservative coalition of Republicans and southern Democrats on every one of the fifty votes on which the two groups joined forces. Among other things, he opposed busing to achieve racial desegregation in public schools, the Equal Rights Amendment, and abortion and supported prayer in the public schools and a Constitutional amendment requiring a balanced federal budget. Cheney's only major difference with President Reagan on domestic policy was his opposition to the administration's effort to cut corporate and capital-gains taxes.

With regard to issues of immediate relevance to his constituents, Cheney, as a member of the House Committee on Interior and Insular Affairs, resisted efforts by fellow committee members to raise the fees charged to ranchers for the right to graze livestock on public lands. In the debate over the development of wilderness areas, he took a middle course. Initially supportive of Interior Secretary James Watt's efforts to open up such areas to oil and gas leasing, he changed his position in 1982, after learning about several pending leases for land in northwestern Wyoming, near Yellowstone National Park. Cheney subsequently introduced legislation that banned oil and gas leasing in Wyoming wilderness areas and added more than 650,000 wilderness acres to the state.

On June 4, 1987 Dick Cheney became chairman of the Republican Conference, the third-ranking post in the House Republican hierarchy. A month earlier he had been named vice-chairman of the House committee investigating the Iran-Contra scandal. Following three months of hearings, Cheney delivered, on August 4, his closing statement. Although he conceded that the Reagan administration had made mistakes, he contended that there were "some mitigating factors . . . which, while they don't justify administration mistakes, go a long way to helping explain and make them understandable." Based on his examination of the facts, Cheney concluded: "There is no evidence that the president had any knowledge of the diversion of profits from the arms sale to the Nicaraguan democratic resistance. . . . There is also no evidence of any effort by the president or his senior advisers to cover up these events." Cheney advanced to the number-two Republican position in the House, with his election, on December 5, 1988, as party whip.

On March 9, 1989 the Senate, in a vote of fifty-three to forty-seven, rejected President George Bush's first choice for secretary of defense, former Texas senator John G. Tower. The following day Bush nominated Dick Cheney, a man with no previous defense-related experience, to head the department. Questioned by reporters about his health, Cheney, who had suffered three mild heart attacks and had had a coronary bypass in August 1988, said that his cardiologist had assured him that there was no medical reason why he could not fulfill the duties of the office. The nominee deftly deflected queries about his lack of direct experience in defense matters, pointing out that, as President Ford's chief of staff, he had attended all meetings of the National Security Council and that he was currently the senior Republican on the Budget Subcommittee of the House Intelligence Committee. Hailed by congressional leaders from both parties, Cheney sailed through his confirmation hearing, and, on March 17, 1989, he was unanimously approved by the Senate.

His swift confirmation by the Senate notwithstanding, Dick Cheney was expected to encounter some resentment at the Pentagon because he had not served in the military during the Vietnam War, although he was of draft age (he had first held a student deferment, then an exemption as a husband and father), and because he had supported the widespread use of lie detectors in the Defense Department. Moving quickly to assert his authority over the nation's defense establishment, on March 24 he publicly reprimanded General Larry D. Welch, the Air Force chief of staff, for discussing with members of Congress the various options for the deployment of MX and Midgetman missiles. "I think it's inappropriate for a uniformed officer to be in a position where he's, in fact, negotiating an arrangement," said Cheney, who was criticized by some of Welch's fellow officers for not first talking over the matter with the general. Cheney underlined his intention to hold the reins of power tightly by allowing only two or three subordinates to advise him on key personnel decisions, by making those decisions in strict secrecy, and by appointing only individuals with whom he was already acquainted. He further asserted his authority by naming David S. Addington, one of his most trusted congressional aides, his special assistant, a post that had been eliminated in the Reagan administration.

Only a few weeks after assuming office, Dick Cheney was faced with the unpleasant task of trimming $10 billion from the defense budget for fiscal year 1990—a chore necessitated by Bush's decision to reject the defense budget he had inherited from Ronald Reagan, which called for annual defense increases of 2 percent above inflation for the next five years. To meet the Bush target of zero percent real growth for 1990, in April 1989 Cheney outlined to the House Armed Services Committee the "very, very painful" cuts that he said represented "a fundamental shift in direction." His most controversial proposal was to halt the planned production, at a projected cost of $22.6 billion, of the Marine Corps' new V22 Osprey aircraft, a combination helicopter and plane. In addition, Cheney proposed rejecting the navy's request for $1.3 billion to modernize its F14 Tomcat fighter. His other cost-cutting recommendations included canceling or suspending production of two army helicopter models, an attack submarine, and the F15 fighter; slowing the development of the Air Force's B2 "Stealth" bomber; re-

tiring the aircraft carrier USS *Coral Sea* and a number of smaller ships; and cutting the active-duty personnel roster of the four services by 17,200.

On other key issues, Cheney confirmed to the Armed Services Committee the administration's decision, announced on April 21, to begin producing the new Midgetman missile and to move the fifty existing MX missiles from the silos where they had been housed to railroad cars. Cheney had previously advised Bush to scrap the $1.3 billion Midgetman program, believing it to be too costly. In keeping with the Bush administration's plan to place less emphasis on the Strategic Defense Initiative, Cheney whittled the program's budget from the $5.6 billion proposed by President Reagan to $4.6 billion, with projected spending over the next five years slashed from the $40 billion Reagan had envisioned to $33 billion. Cheney told the committee that the Pentagon would instead stress the research and development of the antimissile "brilliant pebbles" concept, in which thousands of interceptor rockets would orbit in space, ready to be activated in the event of an enemy missile attack. This plan is said to be less expensive and to require less advanced technology than the other space-based antimissile defense systems under development.

Overall, Cheney's five-year plan called for $64 billion in spending cuts, but the General Accounting Office, in a report released on May 9, 1989, estimated that defense spending over the five years would still exceed incoming revenue by at least $100 billion. In its report the GAO maintained that the shortfall stemmed partly from the administration's unrealistically low estimates of future inflation rates and overly optimistic predictions of annual economic growth. The controversial report, which had been commissioned by Congressman Andy Ireland of Florida, a member of the House Armed Services Committee, after Cheney had rejected his argument that the defense budget cuts were inadequate, was widely expected to intensify the debate between Congress and the administration over defense spending. On May 10 the Pentagon released a letter that Cheney had sent to Ireland, defending the spending plan.

The deployment of short-range nuclear missiles in Europe came to the forefront at a mid-April meeting of North Atlantic Treaty Organization defense ministers. On April 19, 1989 the United States delegation, led by Cheney, reached an agreement with West Germany to defer a decision on deploying upgraded short-range nuclear missiles on German soil until after the German national elections in December 1990. Five days later, following his return to Washington, Cheney rejected a request from two West German cabinet members to open negotiations with the Soviet Union on the reduction of short-range nuclear weapons in Europe, describing such negotiations as a "dangerous trap" in light of the overwhelming Soviet superiority in conventional weapons on that continent. "One of the Kremlin's primary goals remains the denuclearization of Europe," Cheney told reporters.

"Given this goal, and the perilous circumstances that could follow in its train if it's achieved, the alliance must maintain the will to resist the call." At a NATO summit in late May, Western leaders agreed to begin discussions with the Soviets on a partial reduction of short-range missiles, but only after the two sides have reached an accord to cut conventional forces.

Dick Cheney became involved in a mild controversy when he predicted, during a television interview broadcast on April 29, that the economic and political reforms undertaken by Soviet president Mikhail Gorbachev would eventually prove unsuccessful and that Gorbachev would then be replaced by a leader with a more anti-Western outlook. "I would guess that he would ultimately fail," Cheney said of Gorbachev. "That is to say, that he will not be able to reform the Soviet economy to turn it into an efficient modern society and that when that happens he's likely to be replaced by somebody who will be far more hostile than he's been in terms of his attitude toward the West." Cheney's comments angered President Bush, who has publicly applauded Gorbachev's efforts on numerous occasions since taking office. Cheney later conceded, as quoted in the *Washington Post* (May 4, 1989), that "perhaps" he had spoken "with more candor than was warranted" in predicting Gorbachev's downfall, but he denied that the issue had put him at odds with Bush.

The House passed its defense authorization bill for fiscal year 1990 on July 27, 1989. Subsequently blasted by Cheney, the bill generally favored conventional weapons systems over strategic arms programs. The Senate's defense authorization package, passed on August 2, favored strategic weapons to a greater degree, but it also provided substantial funding for the upgrading of conventional arms. In September a House-Senate conference committee began the laborious process of resolving the differences between the two bills, and, after prolonged deliberations, it released its compromise proposal on November 2. That plan authorized $3.57 billion for the Strategic Defense Initiative (the House had approved $3.1 billion, the Senate, $4.5 billion); $1 billion for the F14 Tomcat fighter (the House had suggested $857 million, the Senate, nothing); $255 million (for research only) for the V22 Osprey aircraft (the House had approved the same amount, the Senate, $508 million); and $1.1 billion for the Midgetman and MX missile programs (the House had approved $600 million for research only, the Senate, $1.2 billion). The proposal would require approval from both the House and the Senate before it would become law.

A stocky man with rugged features and thinning brown hair, Dick Cheney has a relaxed, easygoing manner. He often wears cowboy boots with his business suits. An avid outdoorsman and sports enthusiast, he enjoys camping, hiking, horseback riding, fishing, playing tennis, jogging, bicycling, and skiing. He was once a heavy cigarette smoker, but he gave up the habit following his first heart attack. Cheney and his wife, the former Lynne Anne Vin-

cent, have been married since August 29, 1964 and have two daughters, Elizabeth and Mary. The author of two novels, Mrs. Cheney formerly taught English at George Washington University. She is currently chairwoman of the National Endowment for the Humanities. Dick and Lynne Cheney are the authors of *Kings of the Hill* (1983), an account of eight speakers of the House of Representatives and their impact on American history. The Cheneys reside in the Washington suburb of McLean, Virginia. Dick Cheney's religious affiliation is Methodist.

References: *Chicago Tribune* A p8 Mr 12 '89; *N Y Daily News* p64 Jl 3 '75 por; *N Y Times* A p20 N 5 '75 por, A p10 Mr 11 '89, A p34 Mr 12 '89 por; *People* 19:82+ Je 27 '83 pors; *Washington Post* A p3 N 6 '75 por, G p1+ Ap 4 '76 pors, A p9 Mr 11 '89 por; *Almanac of American Politics, 1988*; *Who's Who in America, 1988–89*

Chung, Connie

Aug. 20, 1946– Broadcast journalist. Address: c/o CBS Inc., 51 W. 52d St., New York, N.Y. 10019

When Connie Chung left the National Broadcasting Company to accept a lucrative contract from the Columbia Broadcasting System in the spring of 1989, she was returning to the network where she had spent her formative years as a television journalist. She first joined CBS as a general assignment reporter in 1971, gaining a reputation for tenacity in her tireless coverage of George S. McGovern's presidential campaign, the Watergate scandal, and the vice-presidency of Nelson A. Rockefeller. After working as an anchorperson for KNXT, the CBS affiliate in Los Angeles, from 1976 to 1983, Miss Chung defected to NBC to anchor *NBC News at Sunrise* and the Saturday edition of the *NBC Nightly News*. By 1988 she had cowritten and hosted a number of documentaries, including *Life in the Fat Lane, Scared Sexless*, and *Stressed to Kill*, and had become one of the most visible newswomen on the network. Her duties at CBS include anchoring *Saturday Night with Connie Chung* and substituting for Dan Rather at the helm of the *CBS Evening News*.

Constance Yu-hwa Chung was born on August 20, 1946 in Washington, D.C., the tenth and youngest child of William Ling and Margaret (Ma) Chung. Five of the Chungs' first nine children died in their native China during World War II, when medical care was often unobtainable for civilians. William Ling Chung, a diplomat in Chiang Kaishek's government, moved his wife and four surviving daughters from Shanghai to Washington at the height of the Japanese bombing of China in 1944, and the family remained in America after Mao Zedong's victory in the Chinese Revolution of 1949. The only member of her family who was born in the United States, Connie Chung grew up in the Maryland suburbs of Washington, D.C. A quiet child who felt somewhat intimidated by her older sisters, she was nevertheless extroverted enough to appear in high school plays and variety shows and take an active role in student government. "You can't grow up in Washington, D.C., and not be extremely aware of news and what's going on on Capitol Hill," Miss Chung told Daniel Paisner in an interview for his book *The Imperfect Mirror* (1989). "It's part of local news, in addition to being network news. You can't grow up like I did without developing an interest for how this country works."

Between her junior and senior years at the University of Maryland, which she had entered in 1965 as a biology major, Connie Chung worked as a summer intern to Seymour Halpern, a Republican congressman from New York. She so enjoyed writing speeches and press releases for him that on her return to school, in September, she switched her major to journalism and obtained a part-time job as a copy clerk with WTTG, a Metromedia-owned television station in the capital. On her graduation from college in 1969, she became a news department secretary at WTTG, advancing to newswriter after she persuaded a teller from a local bank to replace her as secretary.

Connie Chung went on to become assignment editor and then on-the-air reporter at WTTG, covering everything from antiwar demonstrations to congressional activity on Capitol Hill, murders, and airplane disasters. "It was quite a shock for a girl from a sheltered Chinese home," she said about some of her grimmer assignments, "but I'd plow through and get there anyway." Then, in 1971, just as the Federal Communications Commission began pressuring the networks to hire more minorities and women, she applied for a job at CBS's Washington bureau. As Miss Chung wryly

remarked to Daniel Paisner, "They had only one woman at CBS News at the time, and I think they wanted to hire more. So they hired me, they hired Leslie Stahl, they hired Michelle Clark [a black reporter who died in a plane crash in 1972], and they hired Sylvia Chase. . . . In other words, a Chinese woman, a black woman, a nice Jewish girl, and a blond *shiksa* [the Yiddish term for a gentile woman]. And so they took care of years of discrimination."

During her early years at CBS, Connie Chung was known as a dogged and energetic reporter who was willing to tackle any assignment, though she recalls having to "push [her]self to be aggressive and callous." In an interview for *New York* (August 8, 1983) magazine, Dan Rather said that she "really wanted to be good. In those days, you couldn't be around her five seconds and not know that she was willing to do anything. . . . I mean, she was literally the first person off the bench to tug at [CBS Washington bureau chief William] Small's sleeve and say, 'Send me in coach.' That was very impressive." When she was assigned to cover George McGovern's presidential campaign in late 1971, Connie Chung often arrived at the senator's house at five in the morning for fear of missing him. According to Dan Rather, she was "right at [McGovern's] elbow every possible second. As a result, Connie became a one-woman encyclopedia of George McGovern."

In 1972 Connie Chung accompanied Richard Nixon on trips to the Middle East and the Soviet Union, and, though she did not cover the president's historic trip to Beijing in February of that year, she used her Chinese language ability to prepare stories on Chinese diplomats and Ping-Pong players. During the Watergate hearings in 1973 and 1974, Miss Chung was hard at the heels of several key figures in the scandal, including John Dean, John N. Mitchell, Richard G. Kleindienst, John D. Ehrlichman, and H. R. ("Bob") Haldeman. "I had a running date with Haldeman," she told a New York *Daily News* (December 2, 1984) reporter. Each morning, she stood in front of Haldeman's house, microphone in hand, and shouted questions at him when he came outside to pick up his copy of the *Washington Post* from the stoop. "One Sunday, I'd staked him out at church. To my surprise, he answered a question. 'Just this once. You asked so nicely,' he said." Connie Chung felt that the tumultuous Watergate years were "a great time to be in Washington," and she was equally enthusiastic about her next assignment—covering the vice-presidency of Nelson A. Rockefeller. "That was a great beat because he would toe the line only part of the time," she told Charles Kaiser in an interview for *Vanity Fair* (November 1988). "If you gave him a tough question, he would give a tough answer back. It was the best time for me as a reporter."

In 1976 Connie Chung moved to Los Angeles to become news anchor on KNXT (now KCBS), the local CBS television station. With Miss Chung doing telecasts three times a day, KNXT news went from third to second place in the ratings, and her salary skyrocketed—from about $27,000 a year when she left Washington to an estimated $600,000 by 1983, a figure that made her the highest-paid local news anchor in the country. In an era when local news was dominated by the lighthearted banter and persiflage known as "happy talk," Connie Chung's warm but straightforward manner and delivery won her a loyal following and a host of honors, including an award for best television reporting from the Los Angeles Press Club in 1977 and local Emmys in 1978 and 1980. She also hosted Terra, Our World, a Peabody Award–winning documentary on the environment, for the Public Broadcasting Service.

After spending seven years as a local newscaster, Connie Chung was eager to return to reporting national politics, especially as the 1984 presidential race approached. "I could see 1984 tap-dancing its way into my heart and not being able to really grasp it," she said during her New York interview. Therefore, when she was asked to anchor NBC News at Sunrise (formerly called Early Today), a half-hour nationally televised lead-in to the Today show, she seized the opportunity as if it were "a bird falling out of the sky." The new job, which also included serving as a political correspondent for the NBC Nightly News program, anchoring the network's Saturday evening news, and doing three prime-time, ninety-second newscasts a week, required her to take a hefty pay cut (most reports indicated that her salary dropped $200,000 yearly) and to make another bicoastal move, this time to New York City.

Connie Chung's arrival at NBC coincided with a decline in the ratings for Today, which had fallen behind ABC's Good Morning, America and was running neck and neck with the CBS Morning News, its rivals in the 7:00-to-9:00 A.M. weekday time slot. Network spokespersons expressed hope that NBC News at Sunrise, slated to run Monday through Friday from 6:30 to 7:00 A.M., would garner a larger lead-in audience for Today. Despite an enormous publicity buildup, however, NBC News at Sunrise failed to distinguish itself in its initial outing, on August 1, 1983. Newsweek (August 15, 1983) characterized it as "essentially a headline service" that was "hardly designed to get maximum yield out of Chung's seasoned interviewing skills, much less her quick, flip wit," and a reviewer for Variety (August 3, 1983) compared the program to "an all-news radio station." Nonetheless, viewers responded well to Connie Chung's on-camera confidence and allure, and the show's ratings began to improve. Her status as a rising network star was reaffirmed when, in November 1983, she made the first of many appearances on the Today show as a substitute for anchorwoman Jane Pauley.

Although she has denied that she is a workaholic, Connie Chung maintained a grueling schedule during her early years at NBC. Mondays through Fridays, she woke up at 3:00 A.M. and worked eighteen-hour days, sleeping for three hours at night and three hours in the afternoon.

Saturdays she devoted to writing and anchoring the NBC Nightly News. Her schedule became even more frenetic in the summer of 1985, when she was named chief correspondent for American Almanac, a monthly series that represented NBC's fourteenth attempt to create a successful prime-time news magazine. The program, which was anchored by Roger Mudd, made its debut on August 6 and aired sporadically for several months, amid announcements that it would eventually be granted a weekly slot. But the ratings for American Almanac were dramatically poor (in its November installment, it finished sixty-sixth in the ranking of sixty-eight network series), prompting NBC to shelve the show in February 1986.

A revamped version of American Almanac, entitled 1986, was launched as a weekly series on June 10, 1986, with Roger Mudd and Connie Chung as its coanchors. Miss Chung was given anchor status on the news magazine under the terms of a new three-year contract, which also called for her to fill in occasionally for Tom Brokaw on the weeknight edition of NBC Nightly News. In March she had relinquished her anchor duties on NBC News at Sunrise, leaving her free to develop stories for the nightly news and for 1986. In its first outing, 1986 failed to impress the New York Times television critic John Corry, who maintained that the program had considerable gloss (a thumping soundtrack, eye-catching opening graphics) but little substance. A segment about the lack of safety devices in light pickup trucks, reported by Connie Chung, elicited praise from Kay Gardella of the New York Daily News (June 10, 1986), but the show failed to attract an audience, and it was canceled in December.

From 1987 to 1989 Connie Chung divided her time between filing stories for the NBC Nightly News and cowriting and presiding over several prime-time documentaries. For Life in the Fat Lane (June 3, 1987), a one-hour program that a Variety (June 17, 1987) reviewer called "an interesting, sometimes amusing account of the heavies in our society," she interviewed overweight celebrities, among them the Los Angeles Dodgers' manager, Tommy Lasorda, the actress-singer Nell Carter, and the actor Dom DeLuise. Miss Chung explored fad diets and other reducing techniques of questionable worth, and, in a segment on eating disorders, the actress Jane Fonda talked to her about her experiences with bulimia and anorexia nervosa.

Connie Chung visited China for the first time in the fall of 1987, when, as part of an NBC news team that broadcast five programs live from Beijing and other cities, she interviewed several of her relatives, including her father's first cousin, who is an architect, and two of her first cousins—one, a university professor; the other, an accountant. "I was pretty anxious about it," she told Michael Ryan when he interviewed her for the New York Daily News (May 29, 1988). "I didn't want to go in with cameras rolling and reunite myself with these people. But I decided to try it, and it was the most rewarding experience I've ever had. They had a story to tell, and, through their experience, they told the history of modern China—how the war affected this family, how the Cultural Revolution affected that family. I went to my grandparents' graves . . . and I cried a lot with my relatives. I think it was meaningful to the viewers, because it was my family. My life has been much more defined by my roots since that experience."

The NBC documentary *Scared Sexless* (December 30, 1987), an examination of how acquired immune deficiency syndrome has affected sexual mores, was the highest-rated NBC news special since 1977, despite its generally negative reviews. The telecast, which made its points with the aid of clips from popular television shows and rock videos, opened with Connie Chung, standing in front of a four-poster bed, announcing, "The pendulum has swung. Fear of death could be the cold shower on casual sex." She talked about sexual awareness and changing social attitudes with Goldie Hawn, Alan Alda, Marcus Allen, and other celebrities, asking them personal questions that one television critic termed "irrelevant to the point of absurdity." Perhaps the most scathing review came from Tom Shales, the television critic of the *Washington Post*, who, although an admirer of Connie Chung's past work, wrote that *Scared Sexless* was "as tawdry as [Geraldo] Rivera at his gaudiest, an hour of flashing lights, rock tunes, and gags . . . crossing the documentary form with the *Hollywood Squares*." As a *coup de grâce*, Shales added, "Chung sullies her good name in the process. It will be hard to take her seriously for a while." Connie Chung called the review "devastating to read" but conceded, "Frankly, I thought he had some good points."

Tom Shales also took a dim view of *Stressed to Kill* (April 25, 1988), a report on the physical and mental toll that stress takes on the body. "Oh good," Shales's review began. "Here comes Connie Funn with another of her prime-time popumentaries." Conversely, John Corry of the *New York Times* (April 25, 1988) found the program to be "an interesting hour" that provided "useful information." Everyday pressures, Connie Chung pointed out on the air, can cause bodily harm, such as ulcers, backaches, headaches, and heart attacks. A former telephone company employee told Miss Chung how her job—calming irate callers and then selling them new telephone services—led to crippling stress; the actor Martin Sheen maintained that the heart attack he suffered while filming *Apocalypse Now* was stress-induced; and Robert C. McFarlane, the former national security adviser, revealed that stress was a major factor in his decision to attempt suicide during the early days of the Iran-Contra scandal.

In July 1988 Connie Chung narrated *Guns, Guns, Guns*, a hard-hitting NBC news report that focused on the easy accessibility of handguns in the United States and took an unflinching look at crimes committed with firearms in four parts of the country—California, Illinois, Texas, and Florida—over a period of just two days. In a lighter vein, the documentary *Everybody's Doing It* (July 12, 1988)

explored the subject of aging, with commentary from the comedian Bill Cosby, septuagenarian actors Hume Cronyn and Jessica Tandy, and Betty White, one of the stars of the television comedy series *The Golden Girls*. Although *Everybody's Doing It* also touched on the grimmer aspects of growing old, such as age discrimination, poverty among the elderly, and abuse of older people, Connie Chung strove to maintain an upbeat tone during the hour-long program.

The 1988 presidential election brought Connie Chung back into the political arena—first as an exit-poll analyst in important primary elections, then as a floor correspondent during the national nominating conventions. At the Democratic convention in Atlanta in July, she scored a journalistic coup by snaring the first interview with Jesse Jackson, and she was the first newsperson to talk to John F. Kennedy Jr. as he came off the podium following his speech introducing Senator Edward M. Kennedy.

Connie Chung's announcement, in March 1989, that she would rejoin CBS after her NBC contract expired in May ended months of speculation among television insiders. Her agreement with CBS, which is reportedly worth close to $1.5 million a year, called for her to anchor a revamped *West 57th*, CBS's least-successful prime-time news entry, and the *CBS Sunday Night News* and to be one of the principal substitute anchors for Dan Rather on the *CBS Evening News*. "It was a very, very tough decision," she said of her choice not to remain with NBC. "It was a question of two seemingly perfect offers, with one seemingly slightly more perfect than the other."

Saturday Night with Connie Chung, the successor to *West 57th*, made its debut on CBS on September 23, 1989. To the dismay of many critics, the hour-long show's format included re-creations, with professional actors, of actual news events. The premiere, for example, featured James Earl Jones as the Reverend Vernon Johns, the fiery minister who preceded the Reverend Dr. Martin Luther King Jr. in the civil rights movement. Following the staged sequences, Connie Chung moderated a discussion among several prominent civil rights activists. Defending the program's use of dramatization in an interview for *New York Newsday* (September 22, 1989), Miss Chung told Ben Kubasik: "We had only one photograph of Johns. There is no film of him, no recordings, no transcripts of his sermons. We went to other preachers who had heard Johns preach to reconstruct what he said and how he said it. The only way to bring Johns alive was by dramatization."

In their reviews of the first broadcast of *Saturday Night with Connie Chung*, the majority of television critics lambasted CBS News for, as a reviewer for *Variety* (October 4, 1989) put it, "sanctioning the bastardization of the news magazine format." Tom Shales, writing in the *Washington Post* (September 25, 1989), called the new show "a sleek news-entertainment hybrid." The craftsmanship was, in his view, "impressively high, the highest of any prime-time news hour on any network." As for Connie Chung, he found her to be "a solid, as well as highly telegenic," host. "It wasn't journalism," Shales concluded, "but it was good TV." Subsequent programs included interviews with the actor Marlon Brando and the country singer K. D. Lang and a "recapitulation," to use Walter Goodman's word, of the terrorist bombing of Pan Am flight 103 over Lockerbie, Scotland in December 1988.

Dark-eyed, with her black hair falling in soft waves to her shoulders, Connie Chung is five feet, three-and-one-half inches tall. According to her friends, she has a playful sense of humor, a robust laugh, and a talent for witty impersonations. On

December 2, 1984 she married Maury Povich, the host of Fox television's *Current Affair*. They live in a six-room apartment on Manhattan's West Side and spend their weekends in an 1840 manor house in New Jersey.

References: Harper's Bazaar 118:218+ O '85 por; N Y Daily News people p3 D 2 '84 por; N Y Daily News mag p24+ My 29 '88 por; New York 16:30+ Ag 8 '83 por; Newsweek 102:77 Ag 15 '83 por; People 19:34+ Je 13 '83 por, 23:150+ Je 10 '85 pors, 31:116+ Ap 10 '89 pors; Savvy 7:26+ F '86 pors, 9:46+ Ap '88 por; TV Guide p24+ Ap 19 '75 por; Vanity Fair 51:165+ N '88 pors; Paisner, Daniel. The Imperfect Mirror (1989); Who's Who in America, 1988-89

Claiborne, Liz

Mar. 31, 1929– Fashion designer. Address: Liz Claiborne, Inc., 1441 Broadway, New York, N.Y. 10018

Officially known as Elisabeth Claiborne Ortenberg, Liz Claiborne is the founder, president, chief executive officer, and chairwoman of Liz Claiborne, Inc., a billion-dollar corporation with innovative management that provides quality career clothes with uncommon style at moderate prices. After a twenty-five-year career as a designer for other Seventh Avenue firms, Liz Claiborne founded a small company with her husband, Arthur Ortenberg, and her partners, Leonard Boxer and Jerome Chazen, in 1976, and she soon commandeered the hearts and pocketbooks of working

women with her affordable, casual, mix-and-match sportswear separates. Tagged as the "reluctant revolutionary" of American fashion by *Fortune* (January 5, 1987) magazine and as "the great pathfinder" by a competitor, Bernard Chaus, Liz Claiborne was the bellwether for other American designers to serve the new market needs of the rapidly expanding women's work force. In the series "Women Who Have Changed the World," published in *Working Woman* in 1988, the piece on Miss Claiborne was titled "The Wizard of the Working Woman's Wardrobe." By many accounts, she outfits more women than any other American designer.

Liz Claiborne is a fashion translator or interpreter of current appealing trends, whose styling can be classic or adventurous, with a dramatic or lighthearted flair. "I get much more of a kick out of seeing women on the street wearing my clothes . . . than on the cover of a fashion magazine," she once said. "I could do something outrageous, but what would be the point if nobody wore it? I try to be fresh but bring my customers along slowly. I have to give them something new, some incentive to buy, but I don't want to shock them." On the one hand, Miss Claiborne views herself as her down-to-earth client, "the Liz lady"—an average American woman, "a working woman like myself," as she has put it. On the other, she is one of only three women (Katharine Graham and Marion O. Sandler are the others) to appear on the list of 800 powerful business people compiled by *Forbes* magazine.

Elisabeth Claiborne was born in Brussels, Belgium on March 31, 1929 to American parents from New Orleans, Omer Villère and Louise Carol (Fenner) Claiborne. She is a direct descendant of William C. C. Claiborne, who was the governor of Louisiana during the War of 1812. Miss Claiborne, who spoke French before learning English, spent her childhood in Brussels, until the imminent invasion of Belgium by the Nazis impelled the family to return to New Orleans in 1939. She recalls having been "dragged around to museums and cathedrals" in Europe by her "very old-fashioned" father, a banker at Morgan Guaranty Trust Company, from whom she acquired a love of painting and the aesthetic principle that "the look of things is as important as their function." From her mother, "a wonderful homemaker," she learned how to sew at an early age. During an interview with Nina Hyde for the *Washington Post* (December 8, 1985), Miss Claiborne recalled the strict rules for personal appearance that her parents, who kept her in pigtails, laid down: "You were . . . told, very clearly, what you wear and what you don't wear, what colors look well on you. You may disagree with what they thought, but they made those decisions."

Since her father did not think it essential for her to acquire a formal education, Liz Claiborne never graduated from high school. Instead, she returned to Europe to study fine arts, especially French impressionist painting, at art schools in Brussels, Belgium, in 1947, and in Nice, France, in 1948, because her father wanted her to become an artist. She had long realized that she would never become a painter, but, as she told Nina Hyde, she "went along." "I'm glad I had that training," Miss Claiborne added, "because it taught me to see; it taught me color, proportion, and many other things that I don't think I would have learned in design school. I then crammed and took pattern-making courses at night. . . . When you like to draw and love to sew—well, what else do you do but become a designer?"

Her Roman Catholic family was "dead-set" against her working in fashion, Liz Claiborne told Adam Smith for an *Esquire* (January 1986) feature article. "It was—well, too New York, too rough." On her own initiative, she entered a national design contest sponsored by *Harper's Bazaar* and won with her sketch of a woman's high-collared coat with a "military feeling." Living with an aunt in New York City, she applied for work in the Seventh Avenue garment district and, at the age of twenty-one, became "a sketcher, model, and pick-up-pins girl."

Liz Claiborne's art training was her admission ticket, because her first employer, Tina Lesser, one of the few sportswear designers at the time, could not draw. As a symbol of independence from her parents, Miss Claiborne had cropped her waist-length hair, only to learn that she had been hired as a model as well as a design assistant, and she was obliged to wear a bun at the back of her head. In the *Washington Post* profile, Miss Claiborne described Tina Lesser as "always a person with so much imagination and so unconventional in the clothing business. She had very definite ideas about how you constructed clothes and ruled with an iron fist, but she recognized talent and was fun to work with." In the same year, 1950, that she started her fashion career, Liz Claiborne married Ben Schultz, a designer for Time-Life Books. When her only child, Alexander G. Schultz, was born, the career-oriented Liz Claiborne became one of the comparatively rare working mothers in the 1950s.

Seeking diversified career experience, Liz Claiborne moved on to Ben Rieg, who designed tailored clothes, and then became Omar Kiam's assistant at his Seventh Avenue house. Her next stint—two years at the Junior Rite Company—was followed by one at the Rhea Manufacturing Company of Milwaukee, where she met the design executive Arthur Ortenberg. After complicated divorces from their first spouses, the two were married on July 5, 1957, when Liz Claiborne was in the midst of a five-year association (from 1955 to 1960) with the New York City firm of Dan Keller. Despite her own avowed preference for wearing pants, during the 1950s Miss Claiborne became known as a top designer of dresses.

In 1960 Liz Claiborne began her fifteen years of employment as chief designer for Youth Guild, the junior dress division of Jonathan Logan, meanwhile marking time because of her family responsibilities. "I had to be the Rock of Gibraltar," she told Michele Morris during the interview for *Working Woman*. "Art was the one who was always experimenting and changing jobs. He had his own company and then that went out of business, and he'd try this and that." Yet she was restless because she recognized from her own experience that there was a gap in the market for moderately priced career clothes, but she was unable to persuade the Youth Guild management that mix-and-match coordinated sportswear for the newly emerging women's work force was an opportunity whose time had come. She waited until her son and two stepchildren had finished college before she left Youth Guild, in December 1975.

Her own name first appeared on a label when Liz Claiborne, Inc., was launched on January 19, 1976, financed by $50,000 in personal savings and $200,000 from family, friends, and business associates. Liz Claiborne became the head designer and president of the sportswear company; her husband, an expert in textiles and business administration, served as secretary and treasurer; and a third partner, Leonard Boxer, contributed the production expertise. A year later, another friend, Jerome Chazen, was named vice-president in charge of marketing. From the first, the firm was inundated with orders, and the company was in the black by September 1976. Sales that first year passed the $2 million mark.

Liz Claiborne showed some thirty-five pieces in her first group of clothes, for the fall of 1976. Her casual camel plus color pants, knickers, pleated skirts, tattersall shirts, cowlneck sweaters, ponchos, shirt jackets, and hunting jackets—all components to be worn in a variety of combinations—made an outdoorsy sportswoman statement. She was justifiably proud of her realistic pricing, which asked thirty-six dollars for sweaters, forty-five dollars for pants, and eighty dollars for jackets. While scrutinizing the style and quality of a new design, she would put herself in the customer's place and ask herself, "How much would I pay for this?"

Her bestsellers in 1977 were a velour peasant blouse and a crêpe de chine version a season later. Although her original plan was to make 4,000 of the latter, she filled a demand for 15,000. Her velour sweatshirt paired with satin pants in pale pink or green represented her concept of relaxed dressing for evening. She made women confident about accepting culottes, a compromise between the skirt and traditional pants, as a refreshing variation in dressing for daytime. For spring 1978 she designed full skirts, loose tunics, and vests, mainly in rust and plum, as her interpretation of the layering then in fashion—combinations appropriate for both the office and leisure time. In 1978 sales soared to $23 million.

Describing the attire of working women when she founded her company, Liz Claiborne pointed out in an interview with Elsa Klensch for *Vogue* (August 1986): "They bought 'work clothes' . . . and casual weekend clothes. There didn't seem to be much in between. For work the business suit was queen." That was the skirted suit with tailored shirt and floppy bow tie, an adaptation of John T. Molloy's preferred men's "dress-for-success" executive suit. But since, as she maintained, "every working woman wasn't ending up in the boardroom or aspiring to that," her original concept was "to dress the women who didn't have to wear suits—the teachers, the doctors, the women working in southern California or Florida, the women in the fashion industry itself." Her influence liberated the desk set from their stiff navy, gray, or black suit uniforms, and she came to be called "the working woman's best friend."

In 1980 Liz Claiborne became the first woman in the fashion industry to be named Entrepreneurial Woman of the Year, and in June 1981 her firm went public, selling its stock for nineteen dollars per share and raising $6.1 million in that unusual move for a company in the volatile garment industry. The price jumped to thirty-one dollars in the first six months and split, two for one, in 1983, leading Merrill Lynch to designate its rapid acceptance by investors as "a case history for success." Even during the recession of the early 1980s, Liz Claiborne, Inc., prospered while other clothing companies were languishing.

In addition to maintaining a skilled management team, Liz Claiborne planned several seasons in advance and heeded the input, consisting of requests and complaints, from both consumers and retailers. Working in conjunction with store buyers, sometimes even escorting a line from sketches to completed garments, she coordinated delivery patterns to meet their needs. She added two lines yearly to the traditional four, generating a continuous flow of fresh merchandise that increased inventory turnover. A staff of traveling fashion consultants explained current collections to salespeople and helped them set up store displays with "Liz" maps. To keep her abreast of trends, Miss Claiborne's marketing department analyzed figures produced by a computerized system, unique to her company, known as System Updated Retail Feedback, which provided weekly reports on which styles, colors, and sizes were sold in a cross-section of stores.

Diversification spurred on the company's already phenomenal growth. The first adjunct to Liz Claiborne, Inc.'s two basic lines—active sportswear and a slightly dressier collection—was petite sportswear, in 1981, for small-boned women under five feet four. A dress division was launched in 1982, followed by a unit for shoes in 1983. One of the firm's few disappointments was the girls' line, begun in 1984 and phased out in 1987, which had been aimed at the age group of five to twelve. In 1985 Liz Claiborne, Inc., bought the Kaiser-Roth Corporation, the company it had licensed to produce accessories, including handbags, scarves, gloves, belts, and hats. That year a new "Lizwear" label featuring jeans was established and, bowing to demand, the firm introduced a collection of men's sportswear simply titled "Claiborne."

Another gamble that paid off was a perfume called "Liz Claiborne," a venture that began jointly with Avon Products but was ended by an out-of-court litigation settlement in 1988. Nine million samples were distributed during the first promotion, in 1986, even though Miss Claiborne dispensed with standard gift-with-purchase selling techniques and minimized advertising. Sex, the factor most often exploited for vending fragrances, was not emphasized. "I'd rather appeal to a woman's idealistic version of herself," Miss Claiborne explained. "She's active, whatever her age. It's the same feeling we try to give in the clothes." The spirited scent, designed to be worn at work or in the evenings, was attributed to Liz Claiborne's own instinctive preferences rather than to market research, as was the choice of her logo triangle shapes and red, yellow, and blue color schemes for the packaging.

Liz Claiborne, Inc., reached the half-billion-dollar summit in wholesale sales in 1985 (a 42.2 percent gain over 1984 and almost five times as much as the $116,831,000 recorded in 1981). When retail sales hit $1.2 billion in 1986, the fashion concern broke into the *Fortune* 500 list of the largest industrial companies in the United States. Ranked number 437, it was not only one of the youngest enterprises to scale that height, but also the first one started by a woman. Small wonder that at their annual meeting in May 1986, Liz Claiborne received a standing ovation from her stockholders. In 1987 the president and founder was elected to the additional posts of chairman of the board and chief executive officer. *Fortune* placed the firm at number two on its roster of "America's Most Admired Corporations," *Sales and Marketing Management* (June 1987) gave it the highest score in the apparel division of its Best Sales Force Survey, and *Business Month* (December 1987) declared it a runner-up in its "Five Best-Managed Companies of 1987." After its net earnings dipped for the first time in its history during the apparel business slump of mid-1987 to 1988, the fashion powerhouse descended to fifth place among "America's Most Admired Corporations."

Liz Claiborne, Inc., which already controls an estimated one-third of the $2 billion market for better women's sportswear, sells through some 3,500 retailers. Its first strategy to combat its losses was to set up more Liz Claiborne boutiques, which carry the full panoply of merchandise at department stores—the store-within-a-store concept pioneered by Ralph Lauren. It also moved into retailing itself, opening the first of a chain of stores named First Issue, in Manhasset, Long Island in February 1988. Designed by a separate team, the casual sportswear and accessories with the First Issue label are priced just below the Liz Claiborne label, in the $40 to $100 range, with new merchandise every two weeks. The First Issue stores were designed to compete with The Limited, The Gap, and Banana Republic. In 1989 prototype or "presentational stores" featuring the Liz Claiborne label are scheduled to open nationwide. Instead of competing with retail accounts, the stores will comprise part of the formalization of the company's "Project Consumer," demonstrating to retailers how to present the merchandise more effectively and how to enhance service to their customers. The company is also planning to add divisions for casual knit sportswear and for big and tall women.

In February 1989 Miss Claiborne and her husband, who own 5.6 million shares of company stock worth almost $100 million, announced that they would retire from active management in June 1989 to pursue "environmental, social, and other personal interests" but would remain board members. In the Vogue interview, Liz Claiborne had said that their young management team "could carry on very well without [her]" and that her husband's ambition was "to perpetuate this company into the next millennium." The fourth original partner, Jerome Chazin, is slated to become chairman of Liz Claiborne, Inc.

No one individual will inherit Miss Claiborne's mantle. Her creative spirit has been continuously nurtured in an extensive staff of talented designers and design assistants. The design process begins when the designers, who work within the firm's price structure and the technical capability of contracted manufacturers as well as within the guidelines of Liz Claiborne's aesthetics, present their initial ideas, called "wish lists," to the division head. They are aware of Miss Claiborne's preference for cleanly sculptured silhouettes and a tangy dash of color in apparel. As their editor, Liz Claiborne possesses final veto power, and she will often add something to a design. After quantities are designated, the fabric is designed by the textile-design department, a pattern is made, and a production sample is adapted for mass production. According to one of her vice-presidents, Miss Claiborne is "still the heart and soul of design at the company."

Liz Claiborne's sense of style and vibrant personality can be felt throughout the company's headquarters in midtown Manhattan. The plants she loves bedeck the corridors, and the walls are painted white as an enhancement for viewing fabric colors. "There is a gee-gosh cheerfulness about the place, a touch of Judy Garland and Mickey Rooney," Lisa Belkin wrote in a profile of Miss Claiborne that appeared in the New York Times (May 14, 1986). "At the weekly 'lines-in-process' meeting, Miss Claiborne sits at the head of the table and rings a delicate glass bell when discussions get too rambunctious." "She isn't tough enough," Jay Margolis has said. "If you show her two designs, she'll say one is very nice and the other is O.K. Well, 'O.K.' means she hates it but she doesn't want to hurt any feelings." The 3,400 employees in the company telephone directory are entered alphabetically by their first names. An industry analyst has observed, "The company is an amalgamation of a mom-and-pop shop and a sophisticated manufacturing company."

The recipient of many honors, the unassuming Liz Claiborne has been a guest lecturer at the Fashion Institute of Technology and Parsons School of Design, and she is a member of the board of directors of the Council of American Fashion Designers. In the opinion of Los Angeles Times writer Timothy Hawkins, Miss Claiborne has "a kind of Katharine Hepburn quality about her—a smart, straightforward manner, and an angular attractiveness that doesn't translate in photographs." The personal trademarks of the trim, five-foot-seven-inch designer, who has a deep, throaty drawl, are her closely trimmed black hair, huge round eyeglasses, and wide, winning grin. Her staff applauds when she appears in a dress instead of the pants she finds more comfortable.

Arthur Ortenberg insists that he and his wife are "just like ordinary people, only richer." In addition to their rented apartment in Manhattan's fashionable East Fifties, the couple owns a ranch in Montana, a retreat on St. Bart's, and an unpretentious oceanfront house and guest cottage in the village of Saltaire on Fire Island, where they are successfully preventing overdevelopment. Among other things, they created a bird sanctuary, dedicated wetlands, and supported restoration of the 1857 Fire Island lighthouse. Their personal foundation benefits the Wilderness Society, the Greater Yellowstone Coalition, wildlife preservation, and the Nature series on PBS. An enthusiastic runner and swimmer, Miss Claiborne also enjoys photography.

References: Bsns W p64+ Ja 16 '89 pors; Chicago Tribune V p1+ Mr 2 '89 por; Esquire 105:78+ Ja '86; Fortune 115:36+ Ja 5 '87 por; Los Angeles Times IV p7 Ag 27 '76, V p15+ S 12 '86 por; Ms 15:48+ N '86 por; N Y Times III p7 Jl 6 '80 por, IV p3 S 17 '84, III p1+ My 4 '86, D p1 F 27 '89 por; N Y Times Mag p56+ Mr 24 '85; Nations Bsns 75:46+ Ag '87; Newsday In Fashion p2+ Ap 13 '86 por; Vogue 176:304+ Ag '86; W p82+ O 6-13 '86 pors; Wall Street J A p12+ F 28 '89; Washington Post K p1+ D 8 '85; Women's Wear Daily p58+ Ag 4 '86 pors; Working Woman 13:74+ Je '88 pors; Contemporary Newsmakers, 1986; Who's Who in America, 1988-89; Who's Who of American Women, 1989-90

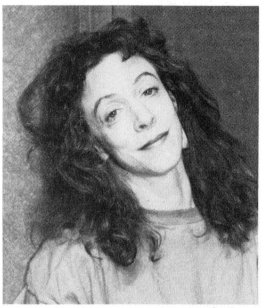

© 1987 Martha Swope

Clarke, Martha

June 3, 1944– Choreographer; dancer. Address: Crowsnest, c/o Sheldon Soffer Management, Inc., 130 W. 56th St., New York, N.Y. 10019

By her own description a "thief of style," Martha Clarke is the creator of plotless, dreamlike works that are perhaps best described by the term "moving paintings" and are often directly inspired by the works of famous painters: Bosch in *The Garden of Earthly Delights* (1984), Klimt and Schiele in *Vienna: Lusthaus* (1986), and Tiepolo and Grandville in *Miracolo d'Amore* (1988). Elegantly minimalist in concept, her surrealistic pieces reveal a visual imagination that willingly sacrifices narrative logic to create a unified mood through a succession of nonliteral images and dramatic vignettes that melt, merge, and overlap in a fluid and almost cinematic way.

In collaboration with the composer Richard Peaslee, the set designer Robert Israel, the lighting designer Paul Gallo, and a semiregular company of performers from professional ballet or modern-dance backgrounds, Miss Clarke, who began her career as a dancer in the late 1960s and achieved her first success as a member of the gymnastic dance company Pilobolus, has transformed her visual-arts sources and her own life history into an idiosyncratic hybrid of dance, drama, mime, and opera. Her controversial creations defy conventional categorization, but their signature is unmistakable. As the dance critic Amanda Smith has observed, "Always, at [the] heart, there is movement, the slow gestures and small moments that reveal the inner life, its anguishes and joys."

Named after the legendary dancer and choreographer Martha Graham, Martha Clarke was born in Baltimore, Maryland on June 3, 1944. Her father was a songwriter turned lawyer; her mother, an amateur chamber musician and, in her words, "professional bon vivant." Reared in the suburb of Pikesville, Miss Clarke, who has described her family's lifestyle during her childhood as "Gatsbyesque without the money," attended progressive private schools. She began taking dancing lessons at the age of six, but it was not until she was in her early teens and a student at the exclusive Perry-Mansfield School of Theatre and Dance in Steamboat Springs, Colorado that she became passionately interested in dance, after Helen Tamiris, the pioneering modern-dance choreographer, cast her as a child in *Dance for Walt Whitman*.

Encouraged by her teachers at the school, Miss Clarke spent several summers at the Connecticut College School of Dance's celebrated summer sessions, where her instructors included such well-known dancers as José Limón, Alvin Ailey, and Charles Weidman, as well as Louis Horst, Martha Graham's longtime musical director, who became an important influence on Miss Clarke's career and contributed to her decision to skip her senior year in high school and enroll in the two-year dance program at the Juilliard School in New York City. At Juilliard she concentrated on Graham technique, but she was drawn to the affecting dance-dramas of Anthony Tudor, whose balletic explorations of the human psyche had, in her view, "such . . . internal logic." Miss Clarke has called *The Garden of Villandry*, a dance about a woman torn between two men that she later co-choreographed, a "valentine to Tudor."

On leaving Juilliard, Martha Clarke joined Anna Sokolow's modern-dance company. "I didn't have the turnout for Tudor, or the extensions, and, since that wasn't important for Sokolow, that became my *choix*," she explained to Amanda Smith in an interview for a *Dancemagazine* (April 1986) profile. "What is missing from dance education, I got from Anna Sokolow—movement generated from a very strong emotional context that is extremely specific." She later credited Miss Sokolow's emotional expressionism as being "at the root of everything" she has done.

Not long after she began her professional career as a dancer, Miss Clarke married the sculptor Philip Grausman, left Anna Sokolow's company, and moved with her husband to Rome, Italy, where she gave birth to a son, David. On returning to the United States, she and her family settled in rural Connecticut. After a five-year hiatus she "stumbled back into movement," as she put it, when her husband took up a position as artist in residence at Dartmouth College, the home base of the fledgling Pilobolus Dance Theatre, then comprised of four Dartmouth undergraduates. Miss Clarke began working evenings with Alison Chase, the troupe's teacher, and the two women eventually joined the previously all-male group. "[Pilobolus] was very male-oriented," she told Amanda Smith. "It was gymnastic. It was goofball male humor. By bringing women in, there was the possibility of romance and gentleness and delicacy."

In her *New Yorker* (December 19, 1977) review of Pilobolus's successful engagement at the St. James Theatre on Broadway in the fall of 1977, Arlene Croce referred to the "distinct, and distinctly different, styles" of the company's two women and suggested that "it was their individual qualities of style, and not just their sex, that changed the troupe and made it complete." Moses Pendleton, one of the group's founders, described that change in terms of *Monkshood's Farewell*, a collaborative work drawn from medieval imagery that the group created in 1974. "Until *Monkshood's*, we tended to put things together from an abstract point of view, even though the works had always had a basic theatricality," he explained, as quoted in Robert Coe's *Dance in America* (1984). "But this was the first time that we began to organize the material with a dramatic logic."

Miss Croce found the imagery in *Monkshood's Farewell* to be suggestive of Breugel. Other pieces in Pilobolus's repertoire, including *Untitled*, which was created in 1975 and was perhaps the group's most popular early work, reminded her of Edward Lear. In *Untitled*, which the dance critic Deborah Jowitt has described as a *"fin-de-siècle* Freudian nightmare," Alison Chase and Martha Clarke appeared as nine-foot-tall Victorian women, whose long, voluminous skirts conceal two naked men. Both *Monkshood's Farewell* and *Untitled* were featured in a *Dance in America* segment devoted to the Pilobolus Dance Theatre that was first broadcast on PBS on May 4, 1977.

"To keep [her] sanity" during her association with Pilobolus, Miss Clarke created six solos. "Each of these was really a kind of private tutelage into my own psyche, an instructional for me about finding my own voice and keeping it alive," she explained to Amanda Smith. "In a collaborative process, you don't have the chance to go on that kind of journey." Commenting on some of those pieces in a review of a Pilobolus performance written for the *Village Voice* (August 22, 1977), Deborah Jowitt contended: "There's something not entirely Pilobolese about Martha Clarke; she's a naturalized citizen who retains a faint foreign accent. *Pagliaccio* is the second solo she's made about the vulnerability of the performer on stage, about the pathos of disguises. In most Pilobolus dances, the performers choose a way of holding themselves or moving and stick with it; Clarke seems more interested in changing, in revealing thought processes and motivations."

Recalling her seven years with Pilobolus for Amanda Smith, Martha Clarke described the "enormous amount of competition" among the group's members: "It was truly a company born out of the ashes of discontent and anger and clashing. However, the work that we did during the Reign of Terror was really quite wonderful, so strife is perhaps as good a creative soil as peace." But as she explained to Chip Brown in a later interview for the *Washington Post* (September 3, 1986), she grew increasingly frustrated. "The success of the company meant that our lives were booked three years in advance," she said, "After a while, collaboration became stale. I was ready to do work that focused on my own vision."

After leaving Pilobolus in 1979, Miss Clarke joined forces with Félix Blaska, a French dancer and choreographer whom she had met on tour in Paris, and Robby Barnett, a founding member of Pilobolus, to form the collaborative company Crowsnest. At the invitation of Charles Reinhart, the director of the American Dance Festival, the group made its debut at the festival in Durham, North Carolina in July 1979. In her review for the *New York Times* (July 18, 1979), Anna Kisselgoff applauded Crowsnest's performance as "a refreshing detour from the recently beaten formalist path in modern dance." She singled out for special praise Miss Clarke's dramatic solos, *Fallen Angel*, in which the choreographer, clad in an evening gown and wearing a black bird mask, danced to a Gregorian chant, and *Nachturn*, a parody of Romantic ballet set to piano music by Mendelssohn. In *Nachturn*, Miss Clarke, as a grotesque, barebreasted ballerina swathed in yards of white tulle, hobbled and leapt pathetically across the stage. Miss Kisselgoff also appreciated Martha Clarke's "great pictorial sense" and her "tendency toward making pictures come alive," as in her *La Marquise de Solana*, an exploration of the relationship between an aristocratic woman and her lowborn lover that was inspired by a Goya painting.

That transitional period in Martha Clarke's life, which saw the disintegration of her marriage as well as the beginning of Crowsnest, was the subject of Joyce Chopra's documentary film *Martha Clarke, Light and Dark: A Dancer's Journey*, which was broadcast by the New York City station WNET on May 25, 1981 and by the PBS network on June 22, 1981. The local broadcast coincided with Crowsnest's first New York season, at the New York Shakespeare Festival's Newman Theater. In her review of that engagement for *Dancemagazine* (December 1981), Julinda Lewis paid tribute to the way Miss Clarke's powerful presence seemed "to dominate every piece," even a group work such as *Haiku*, a series of haunting vignettes that perhaps best demonstrated the company's strengths. "Throughout *Haiku* the three dancers work as elements of a single unit . . . ," she observed. "Nevertheless, it is without a doubt Clarke's peculiar and penetrating imagination—and only that—that makes Crowsnest a stimulating experience."

Martha Clarke's transformation from dancer to performance artist and director began in 1974, when she was hired to choreograph a production at the Long Wharf Theatre in New Haven, Connecticut. There, she met the actress Linda Hunt, whom she was later to call her "artistic soulmate" and "bridge to the theatre." The two women collaborated on *Portraits*, a show that consisted of Miss Hunt's dramatic monologues and Miss Clarke's dance solos, in 1977, and on *A Metamorphosis in Miniature*, an adaptation with music of Kafka's *Metamorphosis*, in 1982. After seeing a performance of *A Metamorphosis in Miniature* at the tiny Cubiculo in New York City, Richard Gilman pronounced it "the best thing [he'd] seen on the stage for a year or longer." "They've fashioned something wonderfully true in its own way, whose fidelity to the original story is a matter of tone and vision rather than of detailed transposition . . . ," he wrote in his assessment for the *Nation* (February 27, 1982). "The result isn't Kafka's *Metamorphosis* on stage but a worthy, smaller dramatic equivalent." Produced by the Music-Theatre Group/Lenox Arts Center and directed by Miss Clarke, *A Metamorphosis in Miniature* won an Obie Award as the best new American play of the 1981–82 season.

Two years later, when Lyn Austin, the producer and director of the Music-Theatre Group/Lenox Arts Center, was looking for ideas for a new theatre piece, Miss Clarke suggested a work based on the surreal religious allegories of Hieronymus Bosch, the fifteenth-century Flemish painter known for his iconographic inventiveness. The result was *The Garden of Earthly Delights*, a series of sketches tracing human progress from the Garden of Eden to an apocalyptic hell derived largely from Bosch's disquieting panoramic triptych of the same name. A phantasmagoria of soaring angels, demons somersaulting slowly in midair, and coarse Flemish peasants, the piece for seven dancers and three musicians, who join in the on-stage action, marked the first of Miss Clarke's collaborations with the composer Richard Peaslee and Paul Gallo, a lighting designer. Although she is the first to admit that the work was a collaborative effort that also included the costume designer Jane Greenwood, the fantasy writer Peter Beagle, an authority on Bosch who served as a consultant, and the performers, Miss Clarke insisted upon grounding the piece in dance. "My thinking is that of a choreographer," she explained to Alan M. Kriegsman in an interview for the *Washington Post* (January 31, 1988). "And the movement is all generated by emotion—never out of pure design considerations, or kinetics, or the music."

The Garden of Earthly Delights opened Off Off Broadway at St. Clement's Church in November 1984 to a chorus of raves from the critics, among them Clive Barnes, the veteran dance and drama critic of the *New York Post*. "No attempt has been made to equal Bosch's colors or the fantastication of his inventions . . . ," Barnes wrote in his review of November 21, 1984. "There are no machines or monsters, nothing really of Bosch's Freudian fairy-tale jungle. No, the earthly delights here are presented with a touching simplicity, the kind of simplicity that sparks the imagination. It is almost as unforgettably haunting as the paintings themselves—no one would wish to say more or could fairly say less."

In creating *The Garden of Earthly Delights*, Miss Clarke had been drawn to the epic and encyclopedic possibilities of Bosch's paintings, which, in her view, "are an absolute rainbow of life—joy, humor, pain, beauty, cruelty, tenderness.

Everything." Reviewers, however, were struck by her translation of the painter's gargantuan vision into a necessarily diminished imaginative world. In his *New York Times* (June 21, 1987) review of a revival of the piece at the Minetta Lane Theatre, John Russell, the art critic and historian, noted how "Bosch's imagination is curbed, fileted, rebuilt in miniature" but "is not lost. Nor is it betrayed. What Ms. Clarke has done is to work from feeling, and from her own personal magic, rather than as a copyist or exegete." Productions of *The Garden of Earthly Delights* have since been staged in several other cities in the United States, including Los Angeles and Washington, D.C., and abroad, most notably in Madrid, where several of Bosch's works hang in the Museo del Prado.

Following their stunning success with *The Garden of Earthly Delights*, Lyn Austin asked Martha Clarke and Richard Peaslee to create a theatre piece about Hiroshima. Stymied by the task, the two decided to focus instead on the world of *fin-de-siècle* Vienna because of what Miss Clarke called its "complex possibilities." "It was the end of the old world, the period that Empire would fall, and twentieth-century art, philosophy and psychology were born in that time," she explained to Leslie Bennetts of the *New York Times* (April 23, 1986). But, she continued, the resulting work was also "about my life, and that of the other people [including Paul Gallo, the designer Robert Israel, and the playwright Charles Mee Jr.] who worked on it—how our lives can be thought of in terms of opposites. Love and anguish, creation and destruction, health and neurosis, the pleasure-pain principle"—Freud's Eros and Thanatos instead of Bosch's heaven and hell. "I really see [the two works]," she said in a later interview (*Newsday*, June 22, 1986), "as being in some way an interpretation of the same material, but in different clothing."

Vienna: Lusthaus—the title refers to a sixteenth-century pleasure pavilion—opened at St. Clement's Church in the spring of 1986 and transferred a few weeks later to the Public Theater. Like *The Garden of Earthly Delights*, it was inspired by works of art, in this case an exhibition of turn-of-the-century Viennese art and culture called "Dream and Reality" that Miss Clarke saw in Venice. Combining dance, music, words, and light, she re-created the sights, sounds, and shifting moods of the period in a succession of breathtaking, dream-like tableaux that become increasingly nightmarish as the world slides toward war.

The most controversial new work of the theatrical season, *Vienna: Lusthaus* quickly sold out most of its performances and generated a spirited debate between theatre people, who mostly admired it, and dance enthusiasts, who tended to dislike it. In their largely favorable reviews, drama critics compared the work to the imagist theatrical experiments of Robert Wilson, Ping Chong, the Mabou Mines troupe, Tadeusz Kantor, and Peter Brook. Frank Rich, who commented on *Vienna: Lusthaus* for the *New York Times* (April 21, 1986), was among its most enthusiastic champions. In her effort to evoke the character and atmosphere of a civilization on the verge of collapse, he wrote, Miss Clarke "has succeeded beyond one's wildest dreams—perhaps because she has tapped into everyone's wildest dreams. . . . The piece hits us at a preintellectual level, because [she] has distilled both the beauty and the ominous chaos of a vanished Vienna into a shape that seems completely contiguous with the modern world it has bequeathed to us." Although he acknowledged her debt to such painters as Gustav Klimt, Rich viewed her "overall canvas" as "an original creation occupying its own distinctive esthetic territory." *Vienna: Lusthaus* earned Martha Clarke her second Obie, for playwriting.

Following hard on the heels of *Vienna: Lusthaus, The Hunger Artist,* Miss Clarke's next collaborative effort, failed to arouse the excitement of its predecessor. An ambitious attempt to link the personal and literary worlds of Franz Kafka, *The Hunger Artist* opened at St. Clement's Church in February 1987 as a work in progress, but unlike Miss Clarke's earlier works, it never reopened as a completed piece. Dismissed as "a sort of performance-art Masterpiece Theatre" by Moira Hodgson, the drama critic of the *Nation* (April 4, 1984), it was Martha Clarke's first attempt to include singing and perhaps the last to include a spoken text ("Text and I are not happy bedfellows," she later told one interviewer).

Returning to the more familiar ground of movement and imagery, Miss Clarke tried, with *Miracolo d'Amore,* to create a "new form," a "combination of dance and opera and theatre." Her subject, she told one reporter, was "love—which means it can be about anything." To explore the varieties and vicissitudes of erotic love, she drew on such disparate sources as Tiepolo's Punchinello drawings, the female-flower figures of the nineteenth-century French caricaturist Grandville, Italo Calvino's Italian folk tales, and Darwin's *The Expression of the Emotions in Man and Animals.* More dependent on music than her earlier works, *Miracolo* was set to a Monteverdian score by Richard Peaslee and included among its cast members a countertenor.

Heralded in a long *Village Voice* article reverently entitled "Miracolo d'Martha" and in a front-page feature in the Sunday *New York Times* arts and leisure section, *Miracolo d'Amore* had its world premiere in the spring of 1988 at the Spoleto Festival U.S.A. in Charlestown, North Carolina, where it caused something of a minor scandal because of its use of full-frontal nudity. When the piece opened at the Public Theater in New York City several weeks later, reviewers were struck mainly by what they perceived as the secondhand quality of its emotion. Although he had nothing but praise for its technically impeccable staging, Frank Rich thought the work had "only scenic, not intellectual depth." "At no point . . . does *Miracolo* cohere and expand to take on a nightmarish life of its own, as *Vienna: Lusthaus* did . . . ," Rich observed in his *New York Times* review of June 30,

1988. "If anything, *Miracolo* seems to contract and evaporate as it goes along, as though Ms. Clarke were giving us a predigested formula gleaned from her past successes rather than imagining anew."

In creating her works, Miss Clarke usually follows a method that Ross Wetzsteon, writing in the *Village Voice* (June 21, 1988), called "collaborative improvisation in the service of auteur autobiography." Miss Clarke herself described the particulars of her approach to Wetzsteon as she began work on *Miracolo* in October 1987: "I have no idea where it's going to end. It's like collecting shells on the shore. Over the next several months I'll just gather together all these random visual oddities and in March or April I'll start trying to put them all together. Hack and slash, sew and knit. My pieces never come together until the last tenth. It's a *frightening* way to work, but the piece has to find its own logic." Over the years, Miss Clarke has been aided in her creative explorations by grants from the Guggenheim and Rockefeller foundations and from the National Endowment for the Arts. She recently received a fellowship to study film directing at Robert Redford's Sundance workshop for independent American filmmakers.

A slight woman with a lithe dancer's body, Martha Clarke has brown hair, large, expressive eyes, and an angular, mobile face that reminded the dance historian John Gruen of the young Martha Graham. Since her divorce from Philip Grausman, she has divided her time between an antique-filled nineteenth-century farmhouse in rural Connecticut that used to belong to Arshile Gorky and an apartment in New York City's Greenwich Village that was once the home of Marcel Duchamp. Her Manhattan apartment is conveniently near the large rehearsal spaces she needs for her work. Her dog, Betsy, frequently accompanies her to rehearsals.

References: Dance Mag 60:70+ Ap '86 pors; N Y Newsday II p15 F 22 '87 por; People 26:105+ S 1 '86 pors; Village Voice p29+ Je 21 '88 por; Washington Post D p1+ S 3 '86 pors, F p1+ Ja 31 '88 por

---

Condon, Richard

Mar. 18, 1915– Writer. Address: c/o Harold Matson, 276 Fifth Ave., New York, N.Y. 10001

Although Richard Condon decided to begin a writing career relatively late in life, at the age of forty-two, he has proved to be "original, prolific, and profitable, possibly in that order," according to one critic. Over the past three decades, Condon has written a series of satirical novels, usually drawing from the American political landscape, that are meticulously researched and that offer a conspiratorial view of the world, where the rich and powerful manipulate others for their own ends. "Every

Richard Condon

book I've ever written has been about abuse of power," he once said. "I feel very strongly about that. I'd like people to know how deeply their politicians are wronging them."

Condon's first two novels—The Oldest Confession (1958), concerning theft in the art world, and The Manchurian Candidate (1959), which remains his most popular work, telling the story of an American soldier in Korea who is captured by the Chinese and brainwashed to kill at their bidding—immediately established his reputation as a master of satire and suspense. The latter novel, Newsweek reported, "touched a nerve that made America jump." "I like to take a fact and mythologize it," Condon has explained. "If there is one thing I know I have, it is the ability to make things believable that are baroque, grotesque. . . . The tool I often use is humor." Most recently, Condon has been acclaimed for his trilogy of novels dealing with a Mafia family: Prizzi's Honor (1982), Prizzi's Family (1986), and Prizzi's Glory (1988), with Prizzi's Honor becoming the fourth Condon novel to be adapted to the screen. Although critics have praised Condon's talent for description and comic dialogue, the author harbors no illusions about his literary accomplishments. "The novel was not meant to be art but to exist as entertainment," he has stated. "I am a public entertainer who sees as his first duty the need to entertain himself."

Richard Thomas Condon was born in the Washington Heights section of Manhattan on March 18, 1915, the elder son of Richard Aloysius and Martha (Pickering) Condon. His father was an estate lawyer and aide to Governor Alfred E. Smith of New York, and his mother was a secretary in his father's law firm. Condon grew up in the Belleclair Apart-

ments in a comfortably middle-class neighborhood on Edgecombe Avenue. A nervous and sensitive child with a pronounced stammer, he typically fled from unpleasant circumstances. At thirteen, he abandoned Catholicism after a priest dragged him out of church by his ear for eavesdropping while an elderly penitent revealed her sins in the confessional. In high school, he dropped algebra because the teacher mimicked his speech defect every time she called on him. Condon recalls his father as a cold, distant figure. "My father was a shouter," he told Tom Buckley for a New York Times Magazine (September 2, 1979) profile. "When he shouted, I stammered." Speech therapy at Presbyterian Hospital's Neurological Institute improved the boy's diction somewhat, but he was unable to answer a telephone until he was nineteen.

Condon attended P.S. 169 and Junior High 115 before enrolling at De Witt Clinton High School, an all-boys school in the Bronx, where he was a champion backstroker. He graduated in 1934 with such poor grades that college was out of the question. Instead, he worked briefly as an elevator operator at the Roosevelt Hotel in New York, as a night reception clerk at a hotel in Bermuda (from which he was eventually deported for getting into a brawl with a pair of musicians over a girl), and as a waiter on the President Garfield, a round-the-world cruise ship. He was then hired for ten dollars a week by the Consolidated Lithographing Company in Brooklyn to write package inserts, the instructional or promotional slips of paper often found in the boxes of products.

He broke into legitimate print with the sale to Esquire magazine for seventy-five dollars of an article on the various Mickey Finn cocktails. That led to a job as an assistant copywriter at Kelly, Nason and Roosevelt, a midtown Manhattan advertising agency, where he received a salary of forty dollars a week. There, he wrote copy for such products as electric shavers and hearing aids, as well as an ad in the form of a short story that appeared in Collier's magazine. With that experience under his belt, he was then assigned to write for the agency an article entitled "Mid-Summer Skiing in Chile," which ran in Town & Country.

More important to Condon's future career, he wrote the words to an alphabet book designed by one of the agency's art directors. Through a connection of Condon's wife, the art director and Condon were able to approach Hal Horne, an executive at Walt Disney Productions, about turning the book into a movie. Horne did not show much enthusiasm for that idea, but he did ask Condon if he was interested in becoming the Disney company's eastern publicity director, since Horne had just fired the previous occupant of that position.

Condon accepted the job, which paid seventy-five dollars a week. Five months later he was promoted to national publicity director, with a weekly salary of $110. Operating out of Disney headquarters in New York, he managed the publicity campaigns for many new Disney features that have since become classics, including *Snow White and the Seven Dwarfs* (1938), *Fantasia* (1940), *Pinocchio* (1940), and *Dumbo* (1941). For *Pinocchio* he secured seventy-seven magazine covers and 117 magazine layouts. Condon's career nearly ended during his second year with Disney, when he arranged a publicity tie-in with National Pork Week for "The Practical Pig," a short cartoon sequel to *The Three Little Pigs*. His idea was to have display cards of the Disney characters featured in butcher shops across the United States during the week of the cartoon's premiere. Walt Disney was appalled at the prospect, comparing it to promoting movie stars in funeral parlors, and berated Condon for his insensitivity.

From 1942 to 1957 Condon held positions at Twentieth Century–Fox, Paramount Pictures, and United Artists. Between 1950 and 1952, he operated as an independent publicist out of an office in Manhattan, and in that post he was retained at one time or another by virtually all of the major movie producers, including Cecil B. DeMille, Samuel Goldwyn, Howard Hughes, and Darryl F. Zanuck. He also represented the Motion Picture Producers Association, the American Veterans' Committee, and the National Association for the Advancement of Colored People.

During 1951-52, with José Ferrer, Condon produced the plays *Twentieth Century* and *Stalag 17* on Broadway. The following year, he wrote a Broadway play of his own, *Men of Distinction*, starring Robert Preston, which closed after four performances. As United Artists' advertising and publicity director in Britain and Europe in the mid-1950s, Condon lived in London and Paris before moving to Madrid to direct publicity for Stanley Kramer's *Pride and the Passion* (1957), starring Cary Grant and Sophia Loren. The movie flopped, leaving Condon with a bleeding ulcer. An equally stressful experience touting *A King and Four Queens* (1956), starring Clark Gable, reaggravated the ulcer, prompting his wife to encourage him to quit the profession.

After screening nearly 10,000 films during his career as a publicist, Condon believed he had picked up the mechanics of storytelling and decided to try his hand at writing a novel. As he told Jean W. Ross for *Contemporary Authors* (1988), "I learned beginning, middle and ending for scenes—and, come to think of it, beginning, middle, and ending for sentences—and characters and exits and entrances. That was unconsciously washing over me for twenty-two years." As a result, he resigned from United Artists, receiving six months' severance pay, and returned to New York to work on *The Oldest Confession* (1958), the story of a businessman turned art thief who employs business tactics to steal masterpieces. The idea for the book came from a phenomenon that Condon had observed during the filming of *The Pride and the Passion* at El Escorial outside Madrid. Strong lighting used during part of the shooting revealed, above the sight line in the vestry, paintings by such masters as Goya, Velásquez, and El Greco, which

Condon speculated would not be seen again for another century.

An enthusiastic Richard Blakesley wrote in the *Chicago Tribune* (May 25, 1958): "If ever a first novel rated a spot high on the bestseller list, *The Oldest Confession* is it. It has all the ingredients: color, sustained action and suspense, intrigue, a large helping of sex, humor, intelligent dialogue, and that rarest element of all in these bear market days for fiction—readability." Paperback and movie rights were promptly sold, and *The Oldest Confession* was turned into an unsuccessful movie entitled *The Happy Thieves* in 1962, starring Rita Hayworth and Rex Harrison. Condon admitted in a 1975 interview that his first novel was his favorite.

It was his second novel, *The Manchurian Candidate* (1959), however, that propelled Condon to the front ranks of American authors. Written in just five months, the thriller tells the story of an American prisoner of war who returns from Korea brainwashed by his Chinese captors and ends up killing his stepfather, a demagogic politician modeled after Senator Joseph R. McCarthy, who is a pawn of the Communists. As Condon explained to Tom Buckley for the *New York Times Magazine* profile, "I wrote it fast, I had to. There were grocery bills and rent and school tuition to pay, but never mind that. The important thing was that I started living when I started working for myself."

Although critics found fault with Condon's convoluted plots and his tendency to moralize, they almost universally praised his ability to entertain. The critic for *Time* (July 6, 1959), for example, wrote about *The Manchurian Candidate*: "The book carries a superstructure of plot that would capsize Hawaii, and badly insufficient philosophical ballast. Yet Condon distributes his sour, malicious humor with such vigor and impartiality that the novel is certain to be read and enjoyed." Whitney Balliett expressed similar sentiments in his review for the *New Yorker* (May 30, 1959): "Richard Condon's first two novels are brilliant, highly individualistic, and hopelessly unfashionable demonstrations of how to write stylishly, tell fascinating stories, assemble plots that suggest the peerless mazes of Wilkie Collins, be very funny, make acute social observations, and ram home digestible morals." Movie rights to Condon's second novel were bought by the director John Frankenheimer and George Axelrod, the screenwriter, in 1959. Released in 1962, the film *The Manchurian Candidate*, starring Frank Sinatra, Laurence Harvey, and Angela Lansbury, was critically acclaimed.

In 1959 Condon moved to Mexico City, where he wrote his third novel, *Some Angry Angel* (1960), about a clawing gossip columnist. Some reviewers were put off by Condon's shrill tone. As Orville Prescott noted in the *New York Times* (March 25, 1960), "It is full of rage, action and words; but no true emotion comes through, nor any well-realized individuals. How could they, with Mr. Condon always shouting at the top of his voice, upstaging his own characters, interrupting his own story with irrelevant scraps of doggerel?" On the other hand, Quentin Reynolds, a self-described "charter member of the Richard Condon cult," wrote in the *New York Times Book Review* (March 20, 1960) that "*Some Angry Angel* is one of the most extraordinary books of the year."

Moving to Paris for a year, Condon completed *A Talent for Loving* (1961), a spoof of the Old West that received lukewarm reviews. In 1961 he settled in Switzerland, his home for the next decade. During that period, he produced *An Infinity of Mirrors* (1964), *The Two-Headed Reader* (1966), *Any God Will Do* (1966), *The Ecstasy Business* (1967), *Mile High* (1969), and *The Vertical Smile* (1971). *An Infinity of Mirrors*, concerning the repercussions of a marriage between a German officer and a French Jewess during the Nazi era, seemed to attract the most favorable notices. Tom Buckley, in his *New York Times Magazine* piece, called it Condon's finest work to date, and a reviewer for *Life* (September 18, 1964) remarked, "As usual, Condon's coupling of truth and inconsequence, fact and folderol, makes for erudite entertainment. And entertainment is Condon's creed."

Following the publication of *An Infinity of Mirrors*, Condon appeared to enter an irreversible slump, as he produced a number of novels that were criticized for being weighed down in trivial facts and scarcely credible situations. Christopher Lehmann-Haupt commented in the *New York Times* (May 24, 1974): "I gave up bothering with Richard Condon's books about five novels ago when in *Any God Will Do* he led me all the way through his snobbish hero's search for royal forebears, only to reveal at the end that said hero was actually the offspring of dwarfs." And a reviewer for the *Christian Century* noted that *The Ecstasy Business*, "like Condon's fourth novel, *A Talent for Loving* . . . , is an immoral waste of Condon's talent."

Mile High was singled out for exceptionally harsh criticism. John Barkham, for instance, writing in the *New York Post* (August 28, 1969), disliked having the action, which takes place during the Prohibition era in the first half of the book, switch abruptly to the 1950s in the second half. Barkham called the first half, in which the protagonist, an Irish financier, runs a bootlegging operation with the help of the Mafia, "vintage Condon—electric and menacing." But referring to the second half, Barkham added, "The element of improbability inherent in much of his fiction, which the reader willingly accepts in a good novel, here becomes so absurd that long before the end I found myself refusing to suspend disbelief anymore." *Mile High* was significant, however, in that it marked Condon's first association with Joyce Engelson, an editor at Dial. They developed such a productive working relationship that when Miss Engelson followed Richard Marek to G. P. Putnam's Sons, where he established his own imprint, Condon changed publishers so that he could continue to work with her.

In 1971 Condon purchased Rossenarra House, a Georgian mansion designed by James Hoban (whose most famous commission was the White House) in 1824, on twelve acres in the village of Kilmoganny, County Kilkenny, Ireland. Condon and his wife refurbished the house and lived there for the next nine years, an experience he humorously chronicled in a piece of nonfiction, *And Then We Moved to Rossenarra, or, The Art of Emigrating* (1973).

Following two less than warmly received works, *Arigato* (1972) and *The Star Spangled Crunch* (1974), Condon scored his biggest critical success since *The Manchurian Candidate* with his eleventh novel, *Winter Kills* (1974). Events in that novel closely resembled the assassination of President John F. Kennedy. Nick Thirkield, the half-brother of President Tim Kegan, who was assassinated in Philadelphia in 1960, overhears fourteen years later the deathbed confession of a man who claims to have been involved in the murder, leading Thirkield to reopen the case. Leo Braudy, writing in the *New York Times Book Review* (May 26, 1974), accused Condon of "virtuoso shoddiness" in his most recent novels but maintained that *Winter Kills* "puts Condon once again into the first rank of American novelists." Christopher Lehmann-Haupt, in his review for the *New York Times* (May 24, 1974), unequivocally averred that *Winter Kills* "is the best book Mr. Condon has written since *The Manchurian Candidate*." Commenting on Condon's paranoid frame of reference, Lehmann-Haupt wrote, "It may not be true that America is run by a small, conspiring oligarchy. It may not be true that things happen in the White House at the whim of movie stars and labor leaders, of courtesans and generals. But the possibilities are no longer inconceivable. At the very least, Mr. Condon gratifies our paranoia."

In what is arguably his most bizarre novel, *Money Is Love* (1975), a joint commission of angels from heaven and hell is formed to study human morality, using a recently deceased insurance salesman as the guinea pig. In his critique of that book for *Newsweek* (June 9, 1975), Arthur Cooper observed, "All this gives Condon an opportunity to create one of his surreal universes that reflect reality like a funhouse mirror." If Condon was shortsighted about the believability of that fantasy, he exhibited uncanny foresight in the handling of his business affairs. Sensing the potential of the videocassette industry, Condon included in his book contracts in the early 1970s a royalty provision for "video disks," as they were then called.

In 1979 a film version of *Winter Kills* was released to generally appreciative notices, but despite the favorable critical reaction, the film ran for only three weeks. (It was briefly re-released in 1982 and 1983.) The movie's strange disappearance seemed to justify Condon's paranoid view of the world, especially after the murder of one of the film's producers within days of its premiere. John F. Baker reported in *Publishers Weekly* (June 24, 1983): "Condon hints darkly that his theme, that a presidential assassination is in the interests of many of the world's most powerful people, may be behind the movie's strangely checkered career to date." In recent years the movie *Winter Kills*, like *The Manchurian Candidate*, has become something of a cult classic.

Condon's final batch of novels written in Ireland—*The Whisper of the Axe* (1976), *The Abandoned Woman* (1977), *Bandicoot* (1978), *Death of a Politician* (1978), and *The Entwining* (1980)—received tepid reviews at best and seemed to confirm the opinion of critics that Condon had "lost his punch." As one reviewer for *Publishers Weekly* (July 25, 1980) wrote about *The Entwining*: "Caught in a no-man's land between serious thriller and political satire, this book, like Condon's earlier *Death of a Politician*, fails to work as either."

In 1980 Condon sold Rossenarra House and, returning to the United States, settled in Dallas, Texas to be near his younger daughter and his grandchildren, thus ending more than two decades of self-imposed exile that had been punctuated by only brief visits to his homeland. That move appeared to resuscitate Condon's creativity, and he scored a hit with his next novel, *Prizzi's Honor* (1982), the story of the Prizzi family (whose name he cribbed from a map of Sicily), a group of comically ruthless mobsters who operate out of Brooklyn. Underboss Charley Partanna, the family's enforcer, falls in love with Irene Walker, a tax consultant who moonlights as a hired killer. Partanna finds out that Irene was the wife of a man he killed for swindling the Prizzis of $720,000 and that Irene now has a contract to kill him. Critics generally praised the novel as being more suspenseful than Mario Puzo's *The Godfather*, considered the classic of the Mafia genre. "Richard Condon is not Mario Puzo; suspense, not the family saga, is his forte," Robert Asahina noted in the *New York Times Book Review* (April 18, 1982). "And he winds the mainspring of the plot so tight that the surprise ending will knock your reading glasses off. Yet *Prizzi's Honor* is also a sendup of the prevailing sentimental picture of the underworld. . . . Mr. Condon's wicked sense of humor keeps the dealings and double-dealings in proper perspective."

Prizzi's Honor became a successful movie, directed by John Huston and starring Jack Nicholson and Kathleen Turner. Condon wrote the initial drafts of the screenplay, but Janet Roach completed the project when Condon underwent surgery for an aneurysm of the abdominal aorta. The film, released in 1985, was nominated for several Academy Awards, and the screenplay won awards from the Writers Guild of America and the British Academy of Film and Television Sciences.

Condon's nineteenth novel, *A Trembling upon Rome* (1983), continued the author's preoccupation with the abuse of power. This time, he looked at the Catholic church in the fifteenth century. As John Jay Osborn Jr. observed in the *New York Times Book Review* (September 4, 1983), "To Mr. Condon, everyone in the fifteenth century was in on some racket. . . . The best scam of all, Mr. Condon suggests, was run by the Catholic church."

Once again drawing inspiration from his ninety-four-volume reference collection on organized crime, Condon wrote *Prizzi's Family* (1986), setting that prequel to *Prizzi's Honor* in Brooklyn in 1969. Charley Partanna is caught between the sexy Mardell La Tour, a WASP socialite impersonating a floozie to help a friend research a college sociology paper, and Maerose Prizzi, who needs Charley to help her become the first female boss of the Prizzi mob. Julie Salamon, writing in the *Wall Street Journal* (October 1, 1986), called the book "a good read," adding, "Mr. Condon's puckish descriptive powers continue to be uniquely hilarious." She cited as an example Condon's depiction of Vincent Prizzi as a man who had "a face like a clenched fist. . . . He had gout, high blood pressure, ulcers, and psoriasis because he was a resenter."

In *Prizzi's Glory* (1988), Richard Condon rounded out his trilogy on the Prizzi family with a story recounting the Prizzis' attempt to gain the ultimate in respectability by capturing the White House in 1992. When the Don of the Prizzi family decides that his son should run for president, Charley Partanna steps in as the new head of the Prizzi financial empire after a total makeover, with a new name and a new appearance. He finally marries Maerose Prizzi, after a nineteen-year courtship. "Part of Condon's considerable craft lies in his ability to make absolute dastards absolutely charming," Ross Thomas wrote in his favorable review for the *Washington Post* (September 11, 1988). "His gift for dialogue is such that he can make his characters say remarkably terrible things using the most remarkably banal words. Best of all is his ability to tell a story so skillfully that you find yourself almost hoping that the Prizzis will make it to the White House after all."

Condon's writing habits are as organized as his tightly woven plots. Throughout his career, he typically has worked seven hours a day, seven days a week, with an average of five ten-day vacations a year. He has said that he reads about a dozen books of nonfiction a week, scouring them for unusual facts and liberally marking their pages with a yellow highlighter pen. "I read all kinds of factual books, and I remember the esoterica," he told Phillip Corwin for the *National Observer* (August 16, 1975). "They stick in my mind like glue." While writing he has admitted to getting so caught up in a story that he will slap his leg in laughter over a particular snatch of dialogue. To cure infrequent bouts of writer's block, he relies on solitaire.

Richard Condon stands six feet tall, weighs about 190 pounds, and has blue eyes and a ruddy complexion. He wears heavy rimmed glasses, prompting one interviewer to remark that he resembles a district supervisor for a utility company more than a novelist. Others have described him as affable, mild-mannered, and witty. In 1972 he suffered a heart attack, and he continues to be afflicted with high blood pressure and gout. Condon keeps fit on an exercise bike and shoots pool in his office during breaks from his word processor. His office also features a needlepoint that reads, "Condon's Law—When you don't know the whole truth, the worst you can imagine is bound to be close." Condon married Evelyn Rose Hunt, a former John Robert Powers model, on January 14, 1938. They have two grown daughters, Deborah and Wendy. With the latter he co-authored a cookbook, *The Mexican Stove* (1972). Condon has written some seven dozen articles on food and travel, which have appeared in various publications, including *Gourmet*.

References: N Y Times Mag p17+ S 2 '79; Condon, Richard. And Then We Moved to Rossenarra (1973); Contemporary Authors Autobiography Series vol 1 (1984); Contemporary Authors new rev vol 23 (1988); Who's Who in America, 1988–89

Corigliano, John (Paul)

Feb. 16, 1938– Composer. Address: b. c/o Michael Mace Associates, 315 West 57th St., New York, N.Y. 10019; h. 365 West End Ave., New York, N.Y. 10024

John Corigliano, who came of age in an era when composers were writing music that only other composers could fully appreciate—music that bewildered and alienated audiences—seems something of an anomaly, a composer who strives to hurdle the barriers between listeners and music. "I think and work my butt off for a year of my life," he has said, "to give an audience thirty minutes of comprehensibility." A throwback, he has written

fashionable tonal music that is emotional and highly accessible. Rather than cultivate a signature style, Corigliano has drawn from wide-ranging periods, places, and genres, shaping each composition to the unique constellation of circumstances that generate it: the commissioner, the occasion, and the characteristics of the musicians who perform it. The resulting fusion of often eclectic variables strikes some critics as charming but shallow, others as inspired. Aaron Copland, who, along with Leonard Bernstein, was a formative influence on Corigliano's work, has called the composer "the real thing—one of the most talented composers on the scene today." An outspoken zealot, Corigliano has campaigned tirelessly for contemporary music to be given hearings. Perhaps the best indicator of his success is that his own compositions have entered the active repertoire of major orchestras.

John Paul Corigliano was born on February 16, 1938 in New York City to John Corigliano Sr., the concertmaster of the New York Philharmonic from 1943 to 1966, and Rose (Buzen) Corigliano, a prominent piano teacher. Because his parents lived together only intermittently, John shuttled between his father's home in Manhattan and his mother's place in Brooklyn. "Johnny was torn between loyalties to his mother and his father," Corigliano's mother told Bernard Holland in an interview published in the *New York Times Magazine* (January 31, 1982). "He was a sad little boy."

Although as a youngster John Corigliano revered Walt Disney and planned to become a cartoonist when he grew up, he reveled in the sound of his father's practicing with the New York Philharmonic and listened with fascination to the repertoire of his mother's piano students. If he never mastered any single instrument, he did teach himself to be proficient at many. He refused further piano instruction after his first lesson with his mother ended in a quarrel, but he could improvise fluently on the piano when he was only six years old. "He learned a Chopin prelude by ear, and if you called out a composer—Bach or Beethoven—he could improvise in that style," his mother told Bernard Holland. Within a few years, he could harmonize or transpose virtually any piece of music he heard.

In high school, Corigliano began studying clarinet with Stanley Drucker of the New York Philharmonic, but, after two classes, his instrument was stolen, and he never resumed the lessons. In fact, when he entered his teens, he rejected classical music entirely in favor of pop, which was more acceptable to his peers at Midwood High School in Brooklyn. Although he took part in school performances, impressing teachers with his transposing and harmonizing facility, he failed to take any satisfaction from his accomplishments. One of his favorite teachers, Bella Tillis, described Corigliano to Bernard Holland as a "wonderful student" but one who "came to school every morning geared for disaster, thinking he'd flunk everything." Despite—or perhaps because of—his lack of confidence, he tried out every instrument in the orchestra, including the double bass, which, according to Bella Tillis, he picked up in a matter of minutes.

When he was in his early teens, Corigliano's interest in classical music was revived after a discussion with his father about the William Walton Violin Concerto prompted him to analyze the score. A high-fidelity phonograph given to him by his mother when he was fifteen indirectly led him toward composing. "It was a new toy," he told Bernard Holland, "and I bought a few records—like *Pictures at an Exhibition*—just for the sound. On one of them was the gunfight scene from Copland's *Billy the Kid*. I fell in love with the 7/4 time, the irregular rhythms, the flatted fifths in the harmony, the spacey sounds. I began imitating them on the piano and going to the library to get more Copland records. That's how I learned orchestration—listening to records with the score."

Alert to the precarious nature of such a career, Corigliano's father tried to discourage his interest in composing. "He had seen how contemporary composers were treated by orchestras," Corigliano has recalled. "'They get no rehearsal time,' he told me. 'Players mistreat them. Audiences don't want to hear their music.'" When Corigliano enrolled at Columbia University in 1955 with the intention of majoring in music, his father threatened to withhold his support. But he could not be dissuaded. As he explained in an interview with Daniel Cariaga for the *Los Angeles Times* (February 8, 1979), "I became a composer . . . because I didn't want to be a performer, but I did want to be involved in music." While studying with the composers Otto Luening, at Columbia, and Vittorio Giannini, at the Manhattan School of Music, he became obsessed with composition. A friend, the librettist William M. Hoffman, described to Bernard Holland Corigliano's tiny apartment on 104th Street: "John had a chair, a bed, and a Wurlitzer electric piano with earphones—he wasn't allowed to make any noise. No matter what hour you came to see him, he was there working with those earphones on." But Corigliano's obvious commitment failed to mollify his father. According to the composer's mother, when he graduated cum laude from Columbia in 1959, "his father was so sullen it was a funeral rather than a celebration." Assuaging his father's disapproval and measuring up to his success created both anguish and motivation. "I have spent my life trying to take the 'Jr.' off my name," Corigliano said during the Bernard Holland interview.

After his graduation, Corigliano held a number of broadcasting jobs: programmer for WQXR, the classical music station of the *New York Times*; music director for WBAI-FM; assistant to Leonard Bernstein in the preparation of CBS-TV's *New York Philharmonic Young People's Concerts*; producer for Columbia Masterworks classical recordings; and composer of orchestration for pop albums. In his spare time he composed, and recognition came quickly. In December 1961 at Carnegie Hall, the National Association for American Composers and Conductors presented the premiere of "Fern Hill," the first of a trilogy of settings for poems by Dylan Thomas, using voice, strings, harp, and piano.

It was the Pulitzer Prize-winning composer Charles Wuorinen who encouraged Corigliano to enter scores in competition. One of his early compositions, Violin and Piano Sonata, written in 1963 for his father, who had tossed it into a drawer, refusing to look at it, was awarded first prize at the Spoleto Festival Chamber Music Competition in 1964 by a unanimous jury that included Walter Piston, Samuel Barber, and Gian-Carlo Menotti. The four-movement sonata received its New York premiere in February 1966 at Carnegie Hall, with Ralph Votapek at the piano and John Corigliano Sr., who had finally relented, on the violin.

The San Antonio Symphony (of which the senior Corigliano was then concertmaster) commissioned the young composer to write a concerto for piano and orchestra for the inaugural concert of the 1968 World's Fair, in San Antonio, Texas. The four-movement and conservatively tonal concerto blended nineteenth-century romanticism with twentieth-century severity in a work that Harold C. Schonberg, reviewing its world premiere for the *New York Times* (April 9, 1968), pronounced "interesting" but "too derivative." In January 1977, when Malcolm Frager and the Kansas City Philharmonic gave the concerto its New York premiere at Carnegie Hall, Donal Henahan, in his critique for the *New York Times* (January 26, 1977), categorized the work as a "traditional virtuoso's vehicle of the sort that any fancier of the works of Rachmaninoff or Prokofiev would find entirely congenial." In 1971 the recording, on the Mercury label, won the Esther Award for Best Contemporary Recording.

Mercury Records also sponsored one of Corigliano's most controversial ventures when it commissioned the composer and the writer-producer David Hess to update Bizet's *Carmen*. His intent, Corigliano explained to Paul Hume of the *Washington Post* (September 9, 1970), was "to strip away about twelve layers of paint and makeup and show people what these characters were really like." *The Naked Carmen*, performed by such oddly assorted musicians as the Universal Military Bubblegum Band and the Detroit Symphony under Paul Paray, combined such disparate elements as classical orchestration, rock, Dixieland, folk, Spanish guitar, tap-dance music, and excerpts from newscasts featuring Vice-President Spiro Agnew. A reviewer for *Time* (August 17, 1970) magazine described it as a "rock extravaganza in which Bizet's score is emotionally stripped, musically raped, and symbolically incinerated in a simulated atomic blast of electronic caterwauling." David Sterritt of the *Christian Science Monitor* (March 24, 1971), on the other hand, found it "rather vague" but "consistently tasteful." He observed that it "emerges as one of those very rare cases when a classic work has been rendered less vulgar in its 'now-generation' incarnation."

If *The Naked Carmen* exemplified Corigliano's penchant for eclecticism, his Concerto for Oboe and Orchestra, a commission by the New York State Council of the Arts that he completed in 1975, established his reputation for accessibility. One observer recalled: "Even at the afternoon performances, in that sea of blue hair, people screamed. It was the feeling of an event, of 'Wow, what was that?'" Donal Henahan, reviewing for the *New York Times* (November 10, 1975) the world premiere of the five-movement, twenty-six-minute oboe concerto, performed by the American Symphony Orchestra with soloist Bert Lucarelli in Carnegie Hall, was surprised that Corigliano could create such an "absorbing work" out of "banalities" like the scales used in preconcert oboe warmups. He found it an "impressive work that the world's better oboe players will want to add to their repertories."

Corigliano's Etude Fantasy for Piano, written in 1976 and introduced by the pianist James Tocco at the Kennedy Center in Washington, D.C., was another crowd-pleaser. When, in March 1977, Tocco gave the one-movement, seventeen-minute work its New York premiere in Alice Tully Hall, the *New York Times* (March 18, 1977) critic Harold C. Schonberg hailed the étude as a "virtuoso piece of extreme difficulty, using virtually every weapon in the arsenal [including] a lengthy opening for the left hand alone that makes the Ravel Concerto for the Left Hand seem like child's play." Schonberg called Corigliano a "fine technician who knows the resources of the piano inside out" and commended him for composing a "stunning and idiomatic set of hurdles that only a pianist with an enormous technique would dare take on."

The Concerto for Clarinet and Orchestra, commissioned by the New York Philharmonic and given its premiere in December 1977 by the New York Philharmonic, with Leonard Bernstein conducting and Stanley Drucker as soloist, confirmed Corigliano's stature as composer, and audiences at all five performances gave it standing ovations. The three-movement, half-hour work used all of the musicians in the orchestra, provided nearly every one of them with a solo, and kept the percussion section busy. The first movement was characterized by soft, rapid chromatic runs; the second, an elegy for his father, who had died in 1975, by slow row tonalities; the third, an antiphonal toccata, quoted Giovanni Gabrieli's *Sonata Pian' e Forte* and was played by musicians stationed throughout the hall. The concerto immediately entered the repertoire and, a decade after its introduction, continued to captivate listeners. A capacity audience in San Francisco heard it played by the Chicago Symphony, under Sir Georg Solti with Larry Combs as soloist, and accorded it a standing, shouting ovation. The most demanding of American critics have showered it with superlatives.

The maverick film director Ken Russell was so impressed by the Concerto for Clarinet and Orchestra when he heard it performed by the Los Angeles Philharmonic under Zubin Mehta that he hired Corigliano to write the score for his 1981 movie *Altered States*. Its soundtrack was nominated for Academy and Grammy Awards and was recorded by RCA Victor Records. John Rockwell of the *New York Times* (December 27, 1981) rated it "the year's most lively film soundtrack album," adding, "Corigliano happily throws in orchestral coloristic devices of every sort . . . along with all manner of chilling electronic effects, and produces as compelling and extroverted a piece of music-drama as any heard this year." The composer later transformed the score into a fifteen-minute concert suite, *Three Hallucinations for Orchestra*, which was given its premiere on January 21, 1982 by Christopher Keene and the Syracuse Symphony.

Corigliano followed up his film success with a popular programmatic work, *Pied Piper Fantasy* (Concerto for Flute and Orchestra), which was given its world premiere in February 1982 by the Los Angeles Philharmonic, with the celebrated flutist James Galway, who had commissioned it. Five years later it was recorded for RCA Victor by Galway and the Eastman Philharmonia, under David Effron. The seven-movement, forty-minute retelling of the children's folktale was an audience-pleasing and highly theatrical mix of lyricism, dissonance, virtuoso passages, onomatopoetic elements, a German chorale-manqué, and children playing flutes, tin whistles, and drums. Corigliano's *Pied Piper Fantasy* led to another soundtrack commission—the film score for Hugh Hudson's *Revolution* (1985). The movie was panned, but the score was awarded the first Antony Asquith Award for outstanding achievement in film music by the British Film Institute in September 1986.

In *Fantasia on an Ostinato* for piano, composed in 1985 and based on a theme from the second movement of Beethoven's Seventh Symphony, Corigliano merged contemporary musical ideas with classical references in an engaging mélange. He told Nadine Thomas of the Lancaster, Pennsylvania *Intelligencer Journal* (January 1, 1988): "I attempted to combine the attractive aspects of minimalism with convincing structure and emotional expression. My method was to parallel the binary form of the Beethoven Seventh Symphony ostinato by dividing the Fantasia into two parts. . . . It isn't alienating because Beethoven is in it and yet it allows the music to be re-seen in another way." The fourteen-minute work, commissioned and given its world premiere by the New York Philharmonic under Zubin Mehta, was termed a "kind of thesaurus of contemporary styles" by Donal Henahan in the *New York Times* (September 19, 1986). "If any scholar of a future century should happen to unearth this piece," Henahan said, "the musical story of the last half-century might be deduced from it." Despite such eclecticism and the absence of an individual style, Corigliano's skill in writing for large orchestra appealed to the ear even when the music remained in "neutral," which, Henahan grumbled, was most of the time. In the last two minutes, however, when the Beethoven motif broke out, the "piece [took] on an affectingly elegiac air and the whole nineteenth century [came] flooding back," the critic reported.

In April 1987, after nearly seven years of work, Corigliano completed his full-length opera *A Figaro for Antonia*. A sequel to Mozart's *Marriage of Figaro*, with lyrics by William M. Hoffman, it is based on the third play in Beaumarchais's Figaro trilogy. The two-act opera buffa was commissioned by the Metropolitan Opera for $150,000 in honor of the Met's 1983 centenary and is scheduled for its world premiere on December 19, 1991. Corigliano confronted the commission characteristically, with the intention of creating a work that would be accessible to contemporary Americans. "When people realize opera is musical theatre, and they don't have to think it's an archaic form that was meant for a different continent, that's what really makes it for American opera," he told a reporter for *U.S. News & World Report* (April 5, 1982).

In September 1987 the Meet the Composer program appointed Corigliano the Chicago Symphony Orchestra's first composer in residence. His two-year residency augured well for introducing new music to the public. A few months into his assignment, when the Chicago Symphony received a major endowment for awarding annual commissions to young American composers, Corigliano was named to direct the project, one of the first of its kind in the United States. No more appropriate position could have been designed for Corigliano, who has often complained that "90 percent of music performed today is standard concert repertory written by dead people."

In addition to composing, Corigliano has taught composition at the Manhattan School of Music and holds the chair of Distinguished Professor of Music at Lehman College of the City University of New York. In his classes, he instructs students in such mundane concerns as the marketing of music, and he himself oversees every aspect of his own compositions, including financing, editing, program notes, jacket design, and promotion. He even drops in on record stores to ensure that his work is stocked. In writing music, he uses such visual and verbal aids as diagrams, colored charts, and typed scenarios of movements, mood, structure, and instrumentation, which he carries around until he is ready to write the actual notes. Composition is so stressful for Corigliano that he only begins when he has a commission, a deadline, and an assignment. "I'm always alone trying to figure out answers for things I don't have the answers to," he said in an interview for *M* (September 1984) magazine. "I become tense and depressed; then I find the answer and I'm happy. But there's always the next barrier just ahead. It's hard as hell." Indicative of his dark outlook is the shell sculpture that sits on one of the two pianos in his New York City Upper West Side apartment: three vultures roosting in a tree. Corigliano calls it "The Three Critics."

In his *New York Times Magazine* article, Bernard Holland described Corigliano as "almost spastic in his intensity." When combined with pre-performance anxiety, that intensity not infrequently results in violent gastric episodes. But even when he is away from the pressures of the concert

hall, his sensitivity to noise, particularly low frequencies, is a torment. After a neighbor turned up his quadraphonic speakers in the middle of the night, Corigliano found another apartment for him and paid his moving expenses, and, when the two little girls in the apartment above took to jumping out of bed at 7:30 in the morning, he bought wall-to-wall carpeting with thick padding for their room. Youthful in appearance for his age, Corigliano favors flannel shirts and faded blue jeans. His apartment in New York is filled with Oriental rugs, limited-edition prints, original art, antiques, and unusual collectibles. For relaxation, he stays in his country house in Carmel, New York.

References: Chicago Tribune XIII p12+ F 14 '88 por; Los Angeles Times IV p1+ F 8 '79 por; N Y Times II p19+ Ap 27 '80; N Y Times Mag p24+ Ja 31 '82 por; Who's Who in America, 1988–89

Darman, Richard G(ordon)

May 10, 1943– Director of the Office of Management and Budget. Address: b. Old Executive Office Bldg., 17th St. and Pennsylvania Ave., N.W., Washington, D.C. 20503; h. 1137 Crest Lane, McLean, Va. 22101

"Darmanesque," an adjective of recent coinage on Capitol Hill, is used to describe a complex legislative strategy designed to neutralize adversaries of a bill and thus enhance its chances for passage. The eponym of the word is the new director of the Office of Management and Budget, Richard G. Darman, who already has marshaled his considerable abilities on behalf of President George Bush in devising a proposed federal budget, which, though widely criticized for being too vague, at least avoided being condemned as "dead on arrival," as President Ronald Reagan's budgets typically were. A brilliant tactician renowned for his mastery of the complex budget process, Darman perfected his skills in the Reagan administration as deputy White House chief of staff and later as deputy secretary of the Treasury.

Although Darman played a key role in shaping the Reagan Revolution, from the 1981 budget and tax cuts to the sweeping tax reform act of 1986, his devotion to Reagan-style conservatism has always been suspect by the hard-line Right. Inspired to enter public service by the example of President John F. Kennedy, he became a protégé of the moderate Republicans Elliot L. Richardson and James A. Baker. A self-styled "policy junkie" and "chronic, multiple contingency planner," he seems to enjoy what for many in Washington is an agonizingly tedious process of negotiation among competing interests. He is, above all, pragmatic. "I am a long-term idealist and a short-term realist," Darman once said. "I really like to look at what works and what's feasible."

Richard Gordon Darman was born in Charlotte, North Carolina on May 10, 1943, the oldest of the four children of a wealthy textile manufacturer. He was raised in Woonsocket, Rhode Island, the site of some of the family's mills, and in Wellesley Hills, Massachusetts, an affluent suburb of Boston. At Rivers Country Day School, a preparatory school for boys in Weston, Massachusetts, near Boston, Darman was both a brilliant student and a versatile athlete. He received a nearly perfect score on his scholastic aptitude tests, captained the football, wrestling, and lacrosse teams, served as vice-president of the student council, and edited the school literary journal.

Then, as now, Richard Darman seemed to have an endless capacity for hard work. One summer, he worked two consecutive shifts in one of the family's textile mills in western Massachusetts, sorting freshly shorn wool for eighty hours a week and living on food from a vending machine. In 1960 he entered Harvard University, where, during freshman orientation week, he was stirred by a welcoming address by the dean of faculty, McGeorge Bundy. "I can still remember almost exactly what Bundy had to say," he told Robert Sam Anson for an article in Life (February 1985). "It was about the specialness of our freshman class and how we had a special obligation to make use of whatever talents we might have for some larger good. I suppose it was the conventional Harvard socializing message. But when you are seventeen, and the man who gives it to you goes to Washington three months later to become the national security adviser, and a lot of Harvard professors start following him, and the president himself has gone to your school, and you sit behind him at a football game as I did, well, it all has to have an effect on you." To broaden his horizons, Darman bicycled through the Italian Riviera and Morocco before graduating cum laude

with a B.A. degree from Harvard in 1964. He obtained an M.B.A. degree at the Harvard Business School in 1967.

In 1970 Darman joined the administration of President Richard M. Nixon as deputy assistant secretary of health, education, and welfare. His memos of policy analysis were soon noticed by Secretary Elliot L. Richardson, who promoted him to special assistant and chief troubleshooter. "There was an incisive clarity, a pungency in the way he said things that caught my attention," Richardson later recalled. When, in January 1973, Richardson was appointed secretary of defense, he took Darman along with him, and, four months later, Darman followed Richardson to the Justice Department when Richardson was hastily appointed attorney general, succeeding Richard G. Kleindienst, who had been implicated in the Watergate scandal. As special assistant, Darman was a member of the strategy team that engineered the ouster of Vice-President Spiro T. Agnew. Although Darman was instrumental in arranging the plea bargain by means of which Agnew pleaded no contest to income tax evasion and agreed to resign from office, he had little time to reflect on his victory.

Less than two weeks later, Richard Darman fell victim to the so-called Saturday Night Massacre, in which Attorney General Richardson and some members of his senior staff resigned rather than obey Nixon's order to fire Archibald Cox, the special prosecutor appointed by Richardson to investigate the Watergate scandal. Darman, who had always prided himself on planning for every contingency, was stunned and embittered. "For us to get out of our own office—the office of the attorney general!—we had to be searched by FBI agents who supposedly worked for the attorney general," he later said of the episode, as quoted in the New York Times (February 16, 1986). "So weird, leaving government for doing what you think is right, like some political prisoner. . . . It seemed so totally un-American, like a parody of a police state."

Having served in three cabinet departments in as many years, Darman joined the Woodrow Wilson International Center for Scholars in Washington in 1974 and in the following year became a director of ICF, a Washington-based consulting firm. In 1976 he reentered government service as assistant secretary of commerce for policy, in which post he took part in the law of the sea negotiations and caught the attention of Under Secretary James A. Baker. With the defeat of President Gerald R. Ford by Jimmy Carter in 1976, Darman resumed consulting work at ICF and lectured on public policy at Harvard's Kennedy School of Government.

In 1980 Darman coached Ronald Reagan for his debate with President Jimmy Carter and, following the Republican victory that year, became executive director of Reagan's transition team. When James A. Baker, Darman's boss at the Commerce Department during the Ford administration, was appointed White House chief of staff, he promptly named Darman as his principal deputy, with the title of assistant to the White House staff. According to his job description, which as transition director he drafted himself, Darman was responsible for managing the White House flow of paperwork and for advising Baker on selected issues. He did much more than that, however. Over the next four years, he emerged as the administration's principal legislative strategist, sitting in on cabinet and National Security Council meetings, preparing the president for summits and other important meetings, and even supervising the drafting of the president's speeches. Because his unseen hand influenced every important White House initiative, he became known as Reagan's "Mr. Inside." Often he put in thirteen- or fourteen-hour days, which he began and ended by preparing the president's morning and evening reading. He created and directed a White House legislative study group to plot the course of the Reagan agenda and to devise complicated strategies for overcoming congressional opposition.

Throughout the long and at times fragile negotiations with congressional leaders to enact the Reagan budget and tax cuts in 1981, Darman remained the authority to whom others in the executive branch turned for briefings on where matters stood. Even Budget Director David A. Stockman, renowned on Capitol Hill for his command of the intricacies of the federal budget, often stopped by Darman's office for advice. "I continued to learn from him that I didn't have as many answers as I thought," Stockman wrote of Darman in his book The Triumph of Politics (1986), "that I had built an edifice of doctrine, but not a theory of governance." In 1982, with the federal deficit increasing at least in part because of the previous year's tax cuts, Darman joined others in persuading the president to restore some of the lost revenue with a tax hike. Darman's stance renewed fears among some hard-line conservatives who all along had doubted that he genuinely espoused the Reagan philosophy.

Meanwhile, Darman played a key role in overcoming the partisan bickering that threatened to undermine attempts to bail out the beleaguered Social Security system. It was Darman who suggested the formation of a bipartisan commission to determine how best to ensure the solvency of the retirement system through the lifetimes of the baby boomers. Based on its findings, Congress enacted a bailout plan in 1983. Extending his influence to foreign affairs, Darman helped to plan the controversial sale of arms to Saudi Arabia in 1982 and took part in deliberations leading up to the dispatch of United States marines to Lebanon—which he opposed. He was a member of the American delegation at the annual summit meetings of the industrialized countries.

Despite his obvious talents for organization and contingency planning, Darman was not a universally popular figure among members of the White House staff. Although White House Counselor Edwin Meese conceded that Darman was "the nerve center" of the Reagan administration, he locked horns with him on more than one occasion and once denounced him as a troublemaker. And Secretary of State Alexander Haig was unnerved by Darman's tactics and even suspected him of leaking information damaging to him. In his book Speaking Out (1988), Larry Speakes, the White House press spokesman, blamed Darman for refusing him access to plans for the 1983 Grenada invasion, thus making it appear that Speakes had lied to the press when he denied that any unusual activity was underway. The national security adviser, William P. Clark, so resented Darman's encroachment on foreign affairs that he began routing memos directly to the president, bypassing Darman's office, and he once changed the cipher locks on the National Security Council's offices without giving Darman the new combination.

But others in the Reagan administration esteemed Darman. The White House aide David Gergen, for example, valued his dedication and breadth of knowledge. "He is completely devoted to public service and building institutions," Gergen was quoted in the Washington Post (January 11, 1985) as saying, "and in leaving the office of the presidency stronger than it was four years ago. Because of his service in the previous Republican administrations, he brought an institutional memory to the White House. He knew how it and other institutions are supposed to work and their weaknesses and as a result could anticipate a lot of troubles and problems."

During the 1984 election campaign, Darman was again recruited to groom Reagan for the presidential debates, this time by playing the role of the Democratic nominee, Walter F. Mondale, in practice sessions. At the beginning of Reagan's second term, the White House chief of staff, James A. Baker, and the secretary of the Treasury, Donald T. Regan, switched jobs, and Darman became deputy secretary of the Treasury. The Baker-Darman team, as the department came to be known on Capitol Hill, dominated the administration's economic agenda throughout the term. Darman was at Baker's elbow during the pivotal meeting of economic ministers of the Group of Five (the five major Western industrialized nations) that was held at New York's Plaza Hotel on September 22, 1985. It was Darman who drafted the critical passage of the joint communiqué that signaled for the first time that the five governments were prepared to join forces in halting the rise in the value of the United States dollar.

Darman's primary goal for the second term was a major revision of the tax code. For two years he lobbied Capitol Hill, building coalitions, allaying concerns, and always trying to focus debate on the popular issue of tax reform. His strategy, which he called a "binary choice," was to persuade members of Congress at critical stages to vote up or down on tax reform. "These guys are pretty representative," Darman explained to Peter T. Kilborn of the New York Times (October 26, 1986), "and 80 percent of the population doesn't like the status quo and wants reform. So any time you can force a binary choice, politicians are very hard-pressed not to choose tax reform." The strategy worked, at least in part, because, in slashing individual tax rates as well as deductions beneficial only to the affluent, Darman won over not only blue-collar workers but also those whom he called the "Rinso blues," middle-income white-collar workers who could not seem to get ahead and who resented the current tax structure as unfair.

Perhaps Darman's most crucial contribution during the two-year effort came in April 1986, when Republican Bob Packwood of Oregon, the chairman of the Senate Finance Committee, scuttled the bill because it had become bogged down with special-interest amendments. Darman helped to fashion a substitute measure that shifted the tax burden from individuals to corporations, prompting some Republicans to complain that the new bill would stifle growth. As the measure neared completion the following month, Darman canceled plans to accompany Reagan and Baker to the economic summit in Tokyo in order to stand ready to address lawmakers' last-minute concerns. Although Darman ultimately won passage of the most sweeping tax overhaul since World War II, he bruised some egos along the way, most notably that of the House Ways and Means Committee chairman, Daniel D. Rostenkowski.

Throughout the Reagan era, Darman was content to remain in the background, influencing policy and prodding Congress into action. A rare exception was a speech that he delivered to American and Japanese executives at the Japan Society in New York on November 7, 1986. In remarks that received broad media coverage, he lashed out at corporate America for a lack of energy and innovation in penetrating foreign markets. He dubbed much of big business a "corpocracy," which, like government bureaucracy, is "bloated, risk-averse, inefficient, and unimaginative." He ridiculed the typical executive for spending more time on his golf game than on research and development. Although Darman did not bother to clear the speech with the White House, he did get advance approval from Secretary Baker.

In April 1987 Darman announced that he was resigning in order to become a managing director at the investment banking firm of Shearson Lehman Brothers. Although Darman cited family considerations, many believed that he left because the Democrats had won back the Senate, and little economic initiative could be expected from a lame-duck president. He took time off from his Wall Street duties, however, to confer regularly with Baker about George Bush's presidential campaign, and he reprised his role as the Democratic opponent in preparing Bush for his debates with Governor Michael S. Dukakis. Darman's relations with Vice-President Bush reportedly had been cool, but the two men warmed to each other during their mock debates.

On November 21, 1988 President-elect Bush appointed Darman director of the Office of Management and Budget, which, since its inception as successor to the Budget Bureau in 1970, has grown into a vigorous policy arm of the president, responsible for setting budget priorities and currently maintaining a staff of about 525 and operating on a $40 million budget of its own. In accepting the post, Darman, who was on the record as advocating an increase in certain taxes in order to lower the federal budget deficit, went out of his way to assure the administration and the public that he could live with Bush's oft-repeated campaign pledge of no new taxes. "I have read extremely clearly the vice-president's lips on this subject," Darman said, a reference to Bush's now famous statement during his nominating speech at the 1988 Republican National Convention that he would tell those who pressed him to raise taxes to "read my lips—no new taxes."

Pressed at his confirmation hearing before the Senate Government Affairs Committee, Darman went further in ruling out a hike in gasoline taxes or any other tax that fair-minded people might construe as falling within Bush's campaign pledge. "If it looks like a tax to most Americans," he stated, "then it's a tax" and it would not be raised. During his testimony, Darman urged Congress to convert to a two-year budget process, instead of the current one year, in order to avoid lengthy annual negotiations. He also expressed concern about the ultimate cost of bailing out the nation's troubled savings and loan institutions and the cleanup of certain nuclear weapons plants.

One of his first acts as budget director was to pay a courtesy call on his old nemesis, Congressman Daniel D. Rostenkowski, at which the two men reportedly agreed to forget their past differences and start afresh. Darman immediately set about fashioning the first Bush budget for fiscal year 1990. What he came up with conformed to Bush's campaign pledges, including increasing funding for education and childcare, freezing the defense budget to the inflation rate, and, on the basis of unspecified cuts elsewhere, projecting a reduction in the deficit to below $100 billion, safely within the legal limits prescribed by the Gramm-Rudman-Hollings Act. The unspecified cuts were to be the subject of negotiation between the president and congressional leaders, according to the Darman plan. Critics charged that Darman was trying to get Congress to share the blame for any unpalatable spending cuts while reserving for Bush all credit for increases in education and other programs popular with the public.

During both the confirmation process and the consultation on the budget, some in Congress noted a mellowing in Darman's typically brusque manner. "It's a kinder, gentler Darman," Republican congressman Denny Smith of Oregon joked. Democrats saw in Darman someone they could work with. "Dick is not someone I would call doctrinaire or an ideologue," Congressman Leon E. Panetta, the incoming chairman of the House Budget Committee, noted. "I think his appointment sends a good signal to Capitol Hill that there's an interest in trying to work out an approach on deficit reduction."

Budget negotiations between the administration and congressional leaders concluded in April 1989. The announced agreement would trim the deficit by about $28 billion through a combination of one-time spending cuts and increased revenue to be generated, perhaps, through a change in the capital-gains tax rate. The negotiators vowed to work toward a long-term agreement for fiscal year 1991 in the fall of 1989, but prospects for such an agreement were dampened by a dispute between the White House and congressional Democrats over whether the capital-gains tax rate should be cut—a conflict that, in the opinion of most observers, would delay substantive action on reducing the deficit until after the 1990 congressional elections.

In his first speech as budget director, delivered before the National Press Club in Washington, D.C., on July 20, 1989, Darman attacked the federal government and the American people for their excessive self-indulgence and lack of concern for the future. He said that both the government and the people are afflicted with "now-now-ism," defining that as "a shorthand label for our collective short-sightedness, our obsession with the here and now, our reluctance to adequately address the future." Approved in advance by the White House, his speech was widely quoted.

Richard G. Darman stands five feet, nine inches tall and weighs about 180 pounds. He has been described as thin-skinned, abrasive, and impatient with lesser minds (he used to interrupt President Reagan in mid-sentence to correct his mistakes), but also witty and at times charming and affable—perhaps never more so than when he played Santa Claus at the 1981 White House Christmas party. Darman delights friends with his impersonations of former presidents and other political dignitaries. He eschews the Washington social whirl for the comfort of his richly furnished home in McLean, Virginia, which he shares with his wife, the former Kathleen Emmet, a cultural historian and author, whom he married on September 1, 1967, and their two sons, William and Jonathan. His hobby, he has said, is thinking. "I tend to deny the notion that work and pleasure should be distinguished," Darman once remarked. He carefully catalogues and cross-references his collection of books and articles, writes his own speeches, and cuts his own hair.

References: Bsns W p100+ Mr 13 '89 pors; Life 8:19+ F '85 pors; N Y Times III p6 F 3 '85; Washington Post B p1+ O 21 '81 pors; Who's Who in America, 1988–89; Who's Who in American Politics, 1989–90

Davidovich, Bella

(dä-vē-dō´vich)

July 16, 1928- Pianist. Address: c/o Columbia Artists Management, 165 W. 57th St., New York, N.Y. 10019; Agnes Bruneau Associates, 155 W. 68th St. #1010, New York, N.Y. 10023; Juilliard School, Lincoln Center Plaza, New York, N.Y. 10023

When Bella Davidovich emigrated from the Soviet Union to the United States in 1978, her native country lost a pianist who had earned the title Deserving Artist of the Soviet Union—second only to that of National Artist—by winning the quinquennial International Chopin Competition in Warsaw in 1949. Specializing in nineteenth-century composers and the Romantic repertoire, Davidovich performed in concerts and recitals throughout the Soviet Union and Eastern Europe in the two decades that followed and, later, in the Netherlands, Italy, England, and France. For twenty-eight consecutive seasons she performed as soloist with the Leningrad Philharmonic, the leading Russian symphonic orchestra, and for the sixteen years before her emigration she taught on the faculty of the Moscow Conservatory.

Bella Davidovich's arrival in New York City was unheralded, since she was virtually unknown in the United States as a result of government restrictions on concertizing in the West. Contributing to her anonymity was the absence of a long and high-ly publicized struggle with government officials over her emigration, permission for which was granted only six months after she applied. Davidovich's obscurity did not last long, however. On the strength of her reputation among the few Americans who had heard her play in Europe, she acquired a manager and a recording contract soon after her arrival in the United States. She made her debut at Carnegie Hall in October 1979, joined the faculty of the Juilliard School of Music in New York City in 1982, and became an American citizen in 1984.

Since then, Bella Davidovich has performed with the world's leading conductors, including Christoph von Dohnanyi, Charles Dutoit, Raymond Leppard, Neville Marriner, Riccardo Muti, Eugene Ormandy, and Klaus Tennstedt. Performing about 100 concerts a year, Davidovich has toured Israel, Japan, and European and Scandinavian countries. Her discography includes recordings of works by Chopin, Scriabin, Prokofiev, Rachmaninoff, and Saint-Saëns, all for Philips; the complete works for violin and piano by Ravel and the Grieg sonatas, on the Orfeo label; and the three Brahms piano sonatas, for Novalis. In the opinion of Thor Eckert Jr., writing in the *Christian Science Monitor* (December 11, 1980), "She truly represents the finest of *any* pianistic tradition, let alone the Russian."

Bella Davidovich was born into a Russian-Jewish family on July 16, 1928 in Baku, the capital of the Azerbaidzhan Soviet Socialist Republic and a port city on the Caspian Sea. Her parents and her younger sister, Alla, played musical instruments, and her maternal grandfather, Itzhak, was concertmaster of the Baku opera orchestra. Her mother, Lyusya, was a pianist who worked as an opera accompanist, and her father, Mikhail, was a surgeon who also worked in opera. Bella began playing the piano at the age of three, picking out the Chopin Waltz in B Minor by ear. It soon became clear that she possessed perfect pitch, and she began to take formal lessons when she was six. She became an excellent sight-reader with the encouragement of her mother, who brought home opera scores for Bella to read and play.

Throughout her childhood, Bella was often taken to opera and ballet performances in Baku, as well as to concerts by symphony orchestras in the nearby Caucasus Mountains in the summers. The operatic composers whose music she came to know during her childhood included Rimsky-Korsakov, Borodin, Verdi, Gounod, Puccini, and Wagner. That early exposure resulted in a lasting affection for opera, as she told Arthur Satz in an interview for *Musical America* (February 1983), which, like all her interviews with English-speaking journalists, was conducted with the assistance of an interpreter. "The thought of opera," she said, "always makes me smile, warms my heart. I love it. In my piano performances I try to evoke sounds from the instrument which are closest to the human voice. I always start with that in mind."

Bella Davidovich began performing publicly in Baku, playing Beethoven's First Piano Concerto when she was nine, the Schumann concerto at eleven, and the Grieg at thirteen. Encouraged, but not pressured, she proceeded at her own pace. "No one ever thought in terms of my having a 'career,'" she told Allan Kozinn in an interview for the *New York Times* (October 7, 1979). "My parents just noted an ability for music and decided to teach me and see what happened."

A year before the outbreak of World War II, Davidovich was sent to Moscow to study with Konstantin Igumnov, who had studied with Louis Pabst, a pupil of Liszt's. "He taught me everything I know about how to make a piano sing," she told Dean Elder, a consulting editor of *Clavier* (July–August 1983). "He explained that one should caress and not push the keys." Her tutelage under Igumnov was interrupted by her evacuation to the safety of Baku during the war. In 1946 she entered the Moscow Conservatory, where she resumed her studies with Igumnov until his death in 1948.

Yakov Flier, a pupil of Igumnov's, became her mentor at the conservatory. In her interview with Allan Kozinn, Davidovich explained how Flier's methods differed from those of most teachers, who, she said, "nearly always begin with new students by trying to break down what they had learned before and imposing their own will. What was particularly important about Flier . . . was that he never destroyed, he never acted like a dictator: he just directed. He would give advice, but he would never insist on things being done his way."

The 1949 Chopin Competition in Warsaw launched Bella Davidovich's concert career. At twenty-one, she was the youngest of the seven pianists representing the Soviet Union in the international contest. For her performance of the F-Minor Ballade, she shared first prize with Halina Czerny-Stefánska. The next year, she was engaged as a soloist with the Leningrad Philharmonic, and she toured widely with the orchestra for the following twenty-eight seasons, learning a new concerto each year. Averaging seventy concerts a year in the Soviet Union alone, she concertized in Eastern European countries as well.

Davidovich's repertoire grew to include Scarlatti, Mozart, Debussy, Prokofiev, and a handful of contemporary composers like Rodion Shchedrin, Dmitri Kabalevsky, and Kara Karaiev, but Chopin has remained one of her favorite composers. As she told Allan Kozinn: "It's hard to say why I was so drawn to the Chopin waltzes . . . at age four—it's too long ago. But I found his music particularly attractive. As I matured, I came to see Chopin as a very *truthful* composer. His works are informed by the greatest depth of human feeling, the greatest variety of moods. And because the goal he sets for the performer is the communication of all this, it is always a pleasure to return to his music."

Concentrating on classical and romantic composers, Davidovich gave solo recitals, in addition to her concertizing, and made seventeen recordings for Melodiya, the leading Russian label. She also performed in duets with her husband, the violinist Julian Sitkovetsky, until his death in 1958 from lung cancer at the age of thirty-two, after only eight years of marriage. Davidovich discussed her husband with David Dubal for his book *Reflections from the Keyboard* (1984): "He was not just a husband, he was a great friend. We talked the same language. And each of us knew who the other was, what the other stood for. When my son Dmitri was born, and he didn't sleep well at nights, we would both jump to his bed to pick him up. But my husband would say, 'I will do it. You save your hands.'"

Dmitri Sitkovetsky, Bella Davidovich's only child, was born in 1954. Like his father, he became a violinist and was soon playing duets with his mother. The careers of both mother and son were even more constrained by the state concert bureau, Goskontsert, than those of their non-Jewish colleagues. For instance, although Davidovich's stature as an artist and as a teacher at the Moscow Conservatory made her a natural choice to serve as jurist for music-contest preliminaries, she was not allowed to accept invitations to serve on international juries. "Jews are considered a lower echelon," she observed in an interview with Michael Walsh for *Time* (July 8, 1985) magazine. "I received my title Deserving Artist (earned in 1949) five years after friends who had won no competitions. In my career, everything, like playing in the West and teaching, happened with delays."

In 1967 Bella Davidovich was finally permitted to perform in the West. The place was Amsterdam, where she performed to enthusiastic audiences for the following twelve years. Her American debut was planned for October 1968, but was abruptly canceled when Czechoslovakia's ill-fated Prague "spring" ended with the Russian invasion. In 1971 she was allowed to tour Italy, where her pianism later so impressed Jacques Leiser that he became her manager in 1978.

Davidovich might have continued performing primarily in Eastern bloc countries if her son had not decided to emigrate in May 1977, in order to enroll at the Juilliard School on a full scholarship to study violin with Ivan Galamian. According to *People* (February 2, 1987) magazine, Dmitri Sitkovetsky wanted his mother to leave the country too, but she had to stay behind to care for her mother and her sister, seeing her son only during her limited Western tours through the remainder of 1977. Until her son's emigration caused her to fall out of favor with Soviet authorities, Davidovich had been "as highly regarded as Emil Gilels and Sviatoslav Richter," according to Allan Kozinn. But her European commitments for 1978 were canceled by Goskontsert, forcing her to choose between emigration and the prospect of never seeing her son again. "My son is my life," she told Michael Walsh. "I couldn't live without seeing him."

With her career more severely circumscribed than ever, Bella Davidovich applied in April 1978 for herself, her mother, and her sister to emigrate, and, after waiting the customary six months, all three of them were granted permission. Strict Soviet emigration laws required them to relinquish most of their possessions, including personal memorabilia. "Once I applied," the pianist recounted during an interview with Leslie Rubinstein for *Stagebill* (April 1987), "I had to quit my job at Moscow Conservatory after sixteen years, I had to

make arrangements for my Bechstein, our Guarnerius, the collection of silver, records, music, books, photos, even the Chopin Competition award, I had to leave them all behind. I was in the Soviet Union fifty years. It was painful and I was all alone, but I had my music, which gave me the courage when my husband died." When word leaked out that she would be leaving the country, her fans bought up the existing inventory of her records, anticipating that they would not be reissued.

Settling in the emigré community of Kew Gardens, Queens, in New York City in October 1978, Davidovich had to overcome a degree of obscurity unknown to her at any time during the previous thirty years. When she practiced the piano in her apartment, neighbors complained that she played too loudly. "Now they will ask ahead when I am going to be playing and stay home to listen," she told Lon Tuck in an interview for the *Washington Post* (April 19, 1982). The uncertainty inherent in starting over in a new country did not bother her. "I didn't think about it," she told Lon Tuck. "I decided I would just play. And the rest would happen as it happened."

Bella Davidovich's triumphant American debut, at Carnegie Hall in October 1979, vindicated her lack of trepidation. Her recital, which included the twenty-four Chopin Preludes and Schumann's "Carnaval," played to a standing-room-only crowd in the first sold-out Carnegie Hall debut since Sviatoslav Richter's in 1960, and the program was recorded live by Philips engineers. Thor Eckert Jr., writing in the *Christian Science Monitor* (December 11, 1980), called her Chopin appealing in its "gentle persuasion and its eloquently insightful, unfussy style." Charles Michener, in his review for *Newsweek* (October 22, 1979), wrote: "Davidovich went straight to the very human hearts of both works, exposing each rise and fall of Chopin's feverish moods with a kind of fiercely tender finesse and stage-directing the arrivals and departures of Schumann's musical who's who with exquisite panache. . . . Davidovich clearly belongs to that rarest breed of pianist, one who combines the most refined sense of shading and proportion with an emotional commitment to the composer—and the public."

In November 1979 Bella Davidovich made her West Coast debut, at Royce Hall on the campus of the University of California at Los Angeles. Playing Mozart's Sonata in A, she failed to distinguish herself. But as she moved into Beethoven's Sonata in E-flat, op. 31, no. 3, "suddenly little lightning flashes began to attract attention. From there on . . . there was no doubt that one was in the presence of a first-rate pianist, one of extraordinary technical skill and persuasive musical address," Albert Goldberg wrote in the *Los Angeles Times* (November 13, 1979). "Technique and temperament flared excitingly in Prokofiev's one-movement Sonata no. 3 in A Minor. . . . [Her Chopin Preludes were] at once subtle and straightforward, ultra-romantic but classically restrained, emotional but not sentimental, limpid in tonal values, daring in bravura, communicated with ardor, intensity and aristocratic elegance."

In 1980 Davidovich gave her first New York orchestral concerts. When, in early February, she played Chopin's F-Minor Concerto with the Brooklyn Philharmonia under Lukas Foss, although her fingerwork, dynamics, and rubato were flawless, according to a reviewer for the New York *Daily News* (February 4, 1980), he felt she lacked "real gut feeling." Playing Beethoven's First Piano Concerto with the Los Angeles Chamber Orchestra under Gerard Schwarz at Carnegie Hall later that month, she displayed "exquisite finish, a singing line, and graceful phrasing," in the opinion of Harold C. Schonberg, writing in the *New York Times* (February 28, 1980). In August 1980 Davidovich played Mozart's G-Major Concerto in the Mostly Mozart series at Avery Fisher Hall in New York City, prompting Speight Jenkins, writing for the *New York Post* (August 23, 1980), to rank her among those pianists who use phrasing to "communicate so directly that they seem to be speaking through their instruments." However, Joseph Horowitz, in a review for the *New York Times* (August 24, 1980), took her to task for "her habit . . . of beginning a phrase more loudly than she ends it."

Such contradictory reviews typify American responses to Bella Davidovich. Although a high opinion of her technical prowess and good taste is universally shared, some listeners come away from a performance thrilled by her passion, while others are disappointed by what they perceive as her pedantry. After hearing her play a traditional program of Haydn, Schumann, Mendelssohn, and Chopin in a recital at Avery Fisher Hall in November 1980, Speight Jenkins described Davidovich in the *New York Post* (November 17, 1980) as "a passionate and expressive pianist [who made] each composition a personal, extraordinarily musical statement [and in Haydn's F-Major Sonata] consistently made music, shaping each phrase to suit the piece and the mood." But Peter G. Davis, reviewing the same recital for the *New York Times* (November 17, 1980), found the Haydn sonata "clean and precise but without much expressive personality." Nonetheless, Davis credited her for the "sheer lucidity and total refinement of her work, not to mention its avoidance of mannerism [which] gave her performance a strong underpinning of musical logic that more volatile interpretations tend to lack." Davidovich challenges assertions that her playing is devoid of expression. Acknowledging her faithfulness to the score in the interview with Dean Elder of *Clavier*, she said: "I see the same notes that another pianist would see, but I might see a certain harmony or polyphony and try to bring it out, or emphasize different voices, too. . . . It's very much a state of mind, my own fantasy."

In April 1982 Bella Davidovich made her orchestral debut at the Kennedy Center in Washington, D.C., with the Philadelphia Orchestra under Eugene Ormandy. Playing Rachmaninoff's First Piano Concerto, she enraptured Joanne Sheehy Hoover, who extolled the performance in the *Washington Post* (April 20, 1982): "The unrelenting juxtaposition of this fiery attack with the intrinsic lyricism of her style sparked a tension that kept the performance on a quivering edge of excitement. . . . The concerto's unfolding was seamless in its silken beauty."

Having successfully launched her American performing career, Davidovich accepted the offer of a teaching post at Juilliard in 1982. Her pedagogical methods are thorough, according to her own description. "My approach is a well-rounded one, everything together. I demonstrate at the keyboard, as well as explain," she told Arthur Satz.

In July 1983 Bella Davidovich and her son performed together in New York City, for the first time, in a pre-concert recital in the Mostly Mozart Festival at Avery Fisher Hall. Playing Mendelssohn's F-Major Sonata and Brahms's Scherzo in C Minor (from F.A.E. Sonata), the Russian pianist and her violinist son displayed "completely attuned teamwork," in the opinion of Bill Zakariasen of the New York *Daily News* (July 20, 1983). In the concert itself, Davidovich delivered what Zakariasen considered to be a "scintillating" performance of Mendelssohn's First Piano Concerto, making the difficult piece sound "outrageously easy." The critic Tim Page, writing in the *New York Times* (July 20, 1983), also applauded Davidovich for her "whirlwind, supercharged performance of great brilliance," and added, "Miss Davidovich has an extraordinary technique; she didn't miss a note. If her interpretation seemed overemphatic at times, it boasted a visceral power that brought the house down."

It was Bella Davidovich's emphatic precision, her "very 'rightness,'" that Bernard Holland found "dull" in her recording of Chopin's Concerto no. 2 in F Minor, op. 21, with the London Symphony Orchestra under Neville Marriner. In his review for the *New York Times* (July 29, 1984), Holland wrote, "Miss Davidovich's stolid regularity of accent cuts Chopin's patterns into solid little segments, making them like even rivulets in a tideless calm. Her playing at any given moment is pristine, even lovely, but one has the sense of a marvelous pianistic machine designed to go nowhere."

Davidovich's control drew praise from Donal Henahan, in the *New York Times* (March 20, 1986), when he heard her play Mendelssohn's Sonata in F with Dmitri Sitkovetsky at his Carnegie Hall debut, in March 1986. Calling her delivery "fiery but precise," Henahan wrote, "Her intention was to be an equal partner in the enterprise. Drawing an uncommonly rich and varied tone from the piano, partly owing to generous use of pedal but also because of her ability to play at any dynamic level without brittleness or ugly crash, she took the lead boldly whenever the music so required. She also knew how to retire to the background when the violin's turn came around without fading out entirely." Together, Sitkovetsky and Davidovich performed with "impeccable musicianship and stylistic elegance," in Henahan's opinion. In December 1988 mother and son became the first Soviet emigrés to perform in the Soviet Union at the invitation of Goskontsert. Of the three concerts that Davidovich played in Moscow, two were dedicated to the memory of her late husband, and the third was a benefit to aid the survivors of the earthquake in Armenia on December 7, 1988.

At five foot one, Bella Davidovich has a slight figure, fiery red hair, and a youthful demeanor. Her face is heart-shaped, her nose aquiline. In describing her profile in an article for *High Fidelity* (October 1979), Joseph Horowitz thought she looked "startlingly like Chopin." Since her hands are remarkably small for so versatile a pianist, she has to work out special positions on the keyboard to facilitate her playing. At home in her apartment on Manhattan's West Side, Davidovich enjoys listening to vocal recordings and reading Russian books proscribed in the Soviet Union. Her English remains halting, partly because she has little time to study the language, and partly because she hob-

nobs with Russian-speaking friends wherever she plays. When she is not on tour, her mother and her sister often cook for her in their Queens apartment. Her son, who is married to Susan Roberts, an American soprano, lives in London. On September 4, 1989 Davidovich became a grandmother for the first time. Her granddaugther, Julia Sitkovetsky, was named after Davidovich's late husband, Julian.

References: Christian Sci Mon p18 D 11 '80 por; Clavier 22:12+ Jl–Ag '83 pors; Hi Fi 29:72+ O '79 por; Los Angeles Times IV p1+ D 12 '79 por; Mus Am 33:6+ F '83 pors; N Y Times II p18+ O 7 '79 por, C p16 Mr 27 '81 por, p21+ Mr 16 '86 por; Newsweek 94:96 O 22 '79 pors; People 27:107+ F 2 '87 pors; Time 126:91 Jl 8 '85 por; Washington Post B p1+ Ap 19 '82 pors; Women's Wear Daily I p48 S 19 '79 por; Dubal, David. Reflections from the Keyboard: The World of the Concert Pianist (1984); International Who's Who, 1989–90; Who's Who in America, 1988–89

Davis, Martin S.

Feb. 5, 1927– Corporation executive. Address: Paramount Communications Inc., 15 Columbus Circle, New York, N.Y. 10023-7780

Since becoming chairman and chief executive officer of Gulf+Western in 1983, Martin S. Davis has transformed the giant conglomerate of disparate businesses into a streamlined media and entertainment power. After announcing the company's plan to sell its highly profitable financial-services arm

in April 1989, Davis renamed the company Paramount Communications in June to reflect its emphasis on media. He also led a dramatic, though ultimately unsuccessful, attempt to buy Time Inc., following the announcement of a planned friendly merger between Time and Warner Communications. One financial analyst recently described Davis as "the quintessential manager in corporate America. I don't think that anyone else has been able to divest half of their operating businesses and still show earnings growth at a 30 percent annual rate over a period of time. That puts him in a league by himself."

The son of a real-estate broker who was a Polish immigrant, Martin S. Davis was born on February 5, 1927 and grew up in the Bronx, New York City. At the age of sixteen, he dropped out of school and joined the United States Army, but he was discharged after it was discovered that he was underage. Davis reenlisted when he was eighteen and served until 1946. After he earned his high school degree, he took some college courses at the City College of New York and New York University.

By responding to a help-wanted ad, Davis secured his first job in the entertainment industry in 1947, as an office boy at Samuel Goldwyn Productions in New York City. He started out clipping newspapers in the publicity department and was soon introduced to the art of negotiation by the studio president, James Mulvey. "He'd call me into his office and say, 'This is how you do a deal,'" Davis explained to Monci Jo Williams in an interview for *Fortune* (December 21, 1987). "Then he'd send me out to do my own, and yell at me when I blew it."

In 1955 Davis left Goldwyn for the financially troubled Allied Artists Pictures Corporation. Three years later he joined Paramount Pictures Corporation, then an ailing publicly owned studio, as sales and marketing director. He was promoted to vice-president of its subsidiary, Paramount Film Distribution Corporation, in 1962. When two dissident shareholders tried to take over the studio in 1965, Davis, whose job included investor relations, was put in charge of the defense, and he enlisted enough support to prevent a takeover. Largely because of his adroit handling of that situation, Davis was elected vice-president of Paramount Pictures Corporation, the parent company, in April 1966. At the same time, he was named executive assistant to George Weltner, Paramount's sixty-four-year-old president, adding weight to the widely held belief that the thirty-nine-year-old Davis was being groomed to succeed Weltner.

In an interview with the film critic Vincent Canby for the New York Times (April 29, 1966), Davis listed as his priorities the revitalizing of theatrical and television film production and the establishment of a youthful chain of command. Davis dismissed reports that Charles Bluhdorn, the head of Gulf+Western, who had joined Paramount's board earlier in April, might try to take over Paramount. But six months later, Davis was instrumental in arranging the merger, in which Bluhdorn, as a white knight, bought Paramount for about $130 million, in October 1966.

Following that purchase, Bluhdorn named Davis Paramount's chief operating officer. Davis was elected a company director later that year. In November 1966 he was elected an executive vice-president and named to Paramount's executive committee, and in 1967 he was elected a director of Gulf+Western. In 1969 Davis moved to the corporate staff as senior vice-president, and he became Bluhdorn's right-hand man. Davis developed a reputation as a behind-the-scenes strongman, prompting Bluhdorn to present him with a photograph of Mount Rushmore, with Davis's face positioned over Theodore Roosevelt's.

During the 1970s Davis defended the company and its chief executive during a lengthy investigation by the Securities and Exchange Commission, which charged that Gulf+Western had violated securities laws by risking millions of dollars of assets on unauthorized commodities trading and by using the pension fund to buy securities. A suit was also brought against Bluhdorn, charging him with improperly receiving personal loans from banks financing the company and keeping a disproportionate share of profits from sugar trading that rightfully belonged to the Dominican Republic. The basis of the suits was the testimony of Gulf+Western's former general counsel, who had been dismissed from the company after having been convicted of embezzling two law firms that represented Gulf+Western. In the course of the six-year investigation, Davis fired several attorneys when he did not like their handling of the case. Eventually, the suit was dismissed and the charges against Bluhdorn were dropped.

In February 1983 Bluhdorn died of a heart attack at the age of fifty-six, and, after a seven-and-a-half-hour board of directors meeting, Davis was elected to succeed him as vice-chairman and chief executive officer. David N. Judelson, the president of Gulf+Western and a close associate of Bluhdorn's for decades, resigned shortly afterwards. Under Bluhdorn, Gulf+Western had become "the quintessential conglomerate," in the words of one reporter, encompassing a variety of products and interests ranging from sugar plantations, financial services, apparel, bedding, and auto bumpers to jet engine fan blades, sports interests (including Madison Square Garden, the New York Knickerbockers basketball team, and the New York Rangers hockey franchise), and moviemaking, with assets at the time of his death worth almost $12 billion. Bluhdorn's knack for acquiring undervalued properties was satirized in Mel Brooks's film Silent Movie (1976), in which Gulf+Western was referred to as "Engulf and Devour." Bluhdorn also devoted substantial attention to a $900 million investment portfolio, made up of stocks in such companies as General Tire & Rubber, Brunswick Corporation, Mohasco, and Amfac.

Almost immediately, Davis exhibited a dramatically different style from Bluhdorn. In fact, Davis had openly disagreed with Bluhdorn's seemingly indiscriminate acquisition policy, and he had tried to dissuade him from his course. Within eighteen days of Bluhdorn's death, Gulf+Western completed the sale of Consolidated Cigar Corporation for $120 million. In March David Pauly of Newsweek (March 14, 1983) reported that the Wall Street financial community expected Davis to lend stability and a more traditional management style to the company, with the ultimate goal of concentrating on consumer, leisure, and service businesses, including Paramount Pictures, the Associates First Capital Corporation, and Kayser-Roth apparel. By April 1983 he had consolidated Gulf+Western's seven divisions into three, with hand-chosen executives heading each division, who met as an informal "operating board" on a monthly basis. "I think the company's too big, too diverse to operate with one president," Davis told a reporter for Business Week (April 4, 1983). "We now have three presidents as opposed to one." Barry Diller, the chairman of Paramount, became head of the $1.4 billion leisure-time operations, James I. Spiegel, formerly the president of Kayser-Roth, was picked to oversee the consumer and industrial products group, and Reece A. Overcash, the chairman of Associates First Capital, was chosen to run the financial-services division.

By December 1984 Martin Davis had substantially streamlined the company, selling Bluhdorn's $900 million investment portfolio and forty-six companies, including its Natural Resources division in Nashville, the Roosevelt Raceway, Arlington Park race track in Illinois, and E. W. Bliss. He also sold the sugar operations in Florida and the Dominican Republic for $200 million and the site of the old Madison Square Garden for $100 million. Jeffrey A. Trachtenberg of Forbes (December 3, 1984) magazine reported that Davis had sold off $1.5 billion of assets since Bluhdorn's death, reducing the $2.1 billion in debt that was Bluhdorn's legacy. In addition, Davis eliminated 100 jobs at corporate headquarters. "Everyone thinks of me as the great dismantler, but I'm not liquidating the company," Davis told Trachtenberg. In fact, Davis steered Gulf+Western on a $1 billion expansion course, buying mostly publishing operations, including Cebco, a science-book publisher, and 73 percent of Esquire, a publisher of textbooks and maker of educational films. (Gulf+Western had long owned the other 27 percent of Esquire.) In addition, Gulf+Western acquired NierBanc Corporation of Denver, the credit-card assets of Shoppers Charge Card Services in Indianapolis, Kayser Leasing of Madison, Wisconsin, Calvin Klein underwear, and Pandora Industries.

In September 1984 Barry Diller, who headed Gulf+Western's entertainment and communications group, made a surprise announcement that he was leaving to become head of the Twentieth Century–Fox Film Company. As reported in the *Wall Street Journal* (June 10, 1985), Diller said he had not received the power and autonomy he had been promised, whereas Davis claimed that Diller had spent too much of his time on Paramount, ignoring his other duties. He also thought that Diller and Paramount's president, Michael Eisner, were getting disproportionate shares of the executive bonus pool. The coup de grace came when Davis demanded that Diller fire Eisner. Diller resisted and then quit, after he was not offered a new contract. Davis announced that Diller was being replaced by Frank Mancuso, who had been on the Paramount staff for twenty years. Unwilling to work for someone he regarded as a former subordinate, Eisner left to become chief executive of Walt Disney Productions. The two resignations did nothing to enhance Davis's reputation as a manager, since both Diller and Eisner were highly regarded in the film industry. Their departure precipitated a flight from Paramount's middle-management ranks. Davis later admitted in a *New York Times* (February 23, 1986) article that he might have made a mistake in not trying harder to keep Eisner as the number-two executive reporting to Frank Mancuso.

In 1985 Davis bought Prentice-Hall for $700 million in cash, three times the company's book value and eighteen times its earnings. The acquisition of a leading publisher of college textbooks and business information, which was merged with Gulf+Western's Simon & Schuster, gave Davis the nation's largest book publisher and served as a springboard into the profitable areas of college book publishing and professional information services. In June 1985 Davis agreed to sell Gulf+Western's $2.7 billion-a-year consumer and industrial products group to the Wickes Companies for $1 billion in cash and the assumption of $90 million in debt. As Laura Landro reported in the *Wall Street Journal* (June 10, 1985), the sale halved the size of Gulf+Western and transformed the company "from a volatile giant with assets of $5 billion in a hodgepodge of low-growth, low-margin businesses" into a "streamlined company with en-

tertainment and communications assets of $3.7 billion and financial-services assets of $7 billion." Davis himself commented to Laura Landro, "We'll be a stronger, leaner, more growth-oriented company, with a solid base for expansion, both internally and through acquisitions."

In November 1986 the press reported that Gulf+Western had raised its profit margin from 7.8 percent of sales in 1983 to 14.6 percent and its return on equity from 7.6 percent to 12.3 percent. In addition, Davis instituted a stock-repurchasing plan, buying back more than eighteen million of Gulf+Western's eighty million outstanding shares by the end of 1986. "Under Davis, the company might be called 'Disgorge and Divest,'" a reporter wryly observed in *USA Today* (June 8, 1986), updating the company's previous derisive title of "Engulf and Devour." By December 1987 Gulf+Western had sold off companies worth $4 billion in revenues and eliminated 200 corporate-office employees. However, Gulf+Western increased the value of all the operations it divested before they were sold. For example, the assets of Associates First Capital were built from $5.8 billion in 1982 to $14 billion in 1989.

Although Paramount experienced a rough year in 1985 with the box-office failures of films that had been inherited from Eisner and Diller, it quickly regained its footing under the aegis of Frank Mancuso. In 1986 and, again, in 1987 Paramount led the industry at the box office, and hits such as *Coming to America* and *Crocodile Dundee II* in 1988 and *Indiana Jones and the Last Crusade* in 1989 ensured that the studio remained a Wall Street favorite. Paramount was distinguished especially by its ability to reap the most in revenues from its established properties, such as *Beverly Hills Cop* (1984) and *Raiders of the Lost Ark* (1981), and was among the most aggressive studios in pushing into new markets, such as first-run programming for local television stations. For instance, Paramount created new episodes of *Friday the 13th: The Series* and of *Star Trek*, which started as a network television series and was turned into a series of films, and sold the new shows directly to local stations.

Monci Jo Williams, writing in *Fortune* (December 21, 1987), noted that after four years under Davis, all three core divisions of Gulf+Western were thriving, with Paramount earning the first distinction of being Hollywood's leading film studio for two years in a row. For the twelve months ending July 31, 1987 Gulf+Western earned $330 million on revenues of $2.5 billion, with a return on equity of 16 percent. At the end of fiscal year 1982, its revenues had been $5.3 billion, and its return on equity stood at 7.7 percent.

In April 1989 Davis announced that the company planned to sell Associates First Capital Corporation, the highly profitable financial-services company that Bluhdorn had acquired in 1969 and the only unit in the Gulf+Western stable that was not related to entertainment or publishing, to the Ford Motor Company for $3.35 billion. In

1988 Associates generated 46 percent of Gulf+Western's total operating income of $748 million. Davis told John Holusha of the New York Times (July 29, 1989): "The sale of Associates is the final step in our strategic development into a pure entertainment company, with operations solely in the entertainment and publishing fields. It is our intention to aggressively build these core businesses and accelerate our growth worldwide." Reporting in Variety (April 12-18, 1989), Richard Gold cited insiders who speculated that the proceeds could be used to buy independent television stations, another movie studio or publishing house, a record company, or perhaps a network if the legal restraints on syndication were lifted in 1990.

After the Associates sale, in October 1989, Paramount's assets consisted of Paramount Pictures, Paramount Television, Simon & Schuster/Prentice Hall, Pocket Books, Silver Burdett & Ginn (a textbook publisher), Famous Players theatre chain, Madison Square Garden, the New York Knicks, the New York Rangers, the publisher Famous Music, 50 percent of the Cinamerica theatre chain, and 50 percent of the USA Network. In September 1989 Paramount reached an agreement, subject to FCC approval, to acquire 79 percent of TVX Broadcast Group, which comprises six television stations, four of which are in the top-ten markets. In fiscal 1988, before the sale of the Associates, Paramount's entertainment division accounted for 37 percent of the company's revenues and 31 percent of its operating profits; publishing accounted for 23 percent of both revenues and operating profits. Some observers thought that Davis might be scaling down the company in order to sell it, though Gulf+Western officially denied any intention of putting the company up for sale.

In corroboration of that stance, in June 1989, a day after Gulf+Western was renamed Paramount Communications to emphasize its media orientation, Davis made an unsolicited bid of $10.7 billion, or $175 a share, for Time, with Davis telling a meeting of securities analysts, as reported by Geraldine Fabrikant in the New York Times (June 7, 1989), "Time is a once-in-a-lifetime opportunity." His bid came just three weeks before shareholders of Time and Warner Communications were to vote on the proposed merging of the two companies.

Richard Munro, the chairman of Time, responded by sending Davis an irate letter, claiming that Davis had promised not to launch a hostile bid for Time. "You've changed the name of your corporation, but not its character," the letter read in part. "It's still 'Engulf and Devour.' . . . I'm disappointed that I can't rely on you as a man of your word. Live and learn." Apparently, Davis had previously discussed merging with Time on a few occasions since 1986, but his approaches had been rebuffed and Munro had indicated that he did not want to enter the motion picture industry. "I said we would not do anything hostile and would respect Time's decision to remain independent," Davis told John Greenwald for Time (June 19, 1989) magazine, further claiming that Time's proposed merger with Warner was tantamount to Time putting itself on the auction block, because Warner shareholders would end up owning 60 percent of the other company. In response, Time asserted that the proposed arrangement with Warner did not constitute a sale of the company, but simply an exchange of stock.

Following Paramount's bid, stocks of all three companies fluctuated wildly amid a flurry of rumors, including one speculation that foreign media magnates, such as Rupert Murdoch, might make a bid as well. There were even indications that Paramount might end up a takeover target, prompting Davis to comment to Bill Saporito of Fortune (July 3, 1989) magazine: "We do not have an entrenchment policy. If the proper offer was to be received by this company, which brings out the full value, we would very definitely consider it." On June 23, just twenty-four hours before Time was legally required to respond to Davis's $175-a-share bid, Davis announced that he was willing to go even higher. Thirty minutes after the New York Stock Exchange closed, Davis announced that Paramount would offer $200 a share, a total of over $12 billion, on the condition that Time end its merger deal with Warner. Analysts interpreted the new offer as a signal to Time that Time's stockholders were willing to sell. Davis's two-page letter to Munro read in part, as reported in the New York Times (June 24, 1989), "We hope that your board and management will now discontinue your efforts to preclude stockholder choice and give Time's shareholders an opportunity to consider our efforts." After a late-night meeting, the directors of Time and Warner converted the original stock swap into a $14 billion leveraged takeover of Warner by Time that did not require stockholder approval.

Paramount brought suit in Delaware Chancery Court to block Time's efforts to prevent shareholders from voting on Paramount's bid. The case turned on the question, when is a company up for sale? If Time became fair game on March 4, when it announced its original merger proposal with Warner, then the company might be forced to hold an auction and make a deal with the highest bidder. Time claimed that such a decision would set a dangerous precedent of compelling business to respond to arbitragers' short-term interests, and the company initiated a suit in federal district court in Manhattan, charging that Paramount's bid was fraudulent because Davis could not raise the $14 billion to buy Time without selling some of Time's assets. Davis vehemently denied that Paramount would sell off part of Time to reduce the debt. "We have the ability and the credibility to manage this debt," Davis told Geraldine Fabrikant for the New York Times (April 10, 1989). "Also, it will not last forever. We will bring it down in time." Paramount countersued, claiming that Time had not disclosed certain facts to its shareholders, such as the provision for Steven Ross, Warner's chairman, to receive $180 million under a long-term contract (Ross would serve as co–chief executive of the merged corporation for five years).

On July 14, 1989 Chancellor William T. Allen of the Delaware Chancery Court upheld Time, denying Paramount's attempt to block Time's proposal. The ruling was upheld by the Delaware Supreme Court on July 24 and had a number of far-reaching implications for future takeover cases. It established that, in the event of a hostile takeover attempt, a company's directors and managers have the power to make major policy changes, even if stockholders support another plan of action. Before the decision, a number of companies were worried that if Paramount won, in the future any company announcing a merger would be putting itself up for sale. The court's ruling gave a green light to friendly stock mergers.

The Time-Warner merger somewhat damaged Davis's image on Wall Street and in Hollywood as an astute and seemingly invincible corporate executive. According to Geraldine Fabrikant of the *New York Times* (July 26, 1989), Davis intended to expand the company, and McGraw-Hill and the Tribune company were mentioned as possible targets. Industry observers continued to speculate, and in early August Paramount's stock fluctuated amid unfounded rumors that Chris-Craft and Cablevision were preparing to bid for Paramount. In *Variety* (August 16, 1989), Richard Gold reported that Paramount's $3.35 billion in cash from the sale of Associates, combined with its failure to acquire Time, placed Paramount in a buy-or-be-bought situation.

Designated one of America's ten toughest bosses in 1984 by *Fortune* magazine, the well-groomed Davis has said that he prefers decisive action from his executives to memos and written reports. "If I'm considered a tough manager, I think it is accurate," Davis told Geraldine Fabrikant in an interview for the *New York Times* (February 23, 1986). "I won't object. I am demanding. I want team players. I want results." It has been reported that Davis has a quirky sense of humor, indulging in affectionate needling and pranks. An amateur photographer, he has strolled through headquarters taking pictures of the employees. He works in a wood-paneled office on the forty-second floor of Paramount's headquarters in New York City, with a magnificent view of Central Park.

Since 1971 Davis has raised nearly $34 million for the Multiple Sclerosis Society through a fundraiser called the Dinner of Champions, which he founded with the sportscaster Frank Gifford. He is chairman of the New York chapter and also serves on the national board. Davis is on the board of trustees of the Economics Club of New York, Fordham University, the Committee for Economic Development, Carnegie Hall, and New York University Medical Center. He is also the cochairman of the corporate steering committee of the Barbara Bush Foundation for Family Literacy. He periodically visits Hollywood and is described as a private person. He lives in Westport, Connecticut with his second wife, Luella. Davis enjoys horseback riding, swimming, skiing, and tinkering with old cars. He has a son, Philip. Another son, Martin Jr., is deceased.

References: *Bsns W* p80+ Ap 4 '83 por; *Forbes* 134:39+ D 3 '84 por; *Fortune* 116:105+ D 21 '87 por; *N Y Times* III p1+ F 23 '86 por, III p1+ Je 11 '89 por; *Wall St J* p1+ Je 10 '85; *Who's Who in America, 1988–89*

Dearie, Blossom

*Apr. 28, 1926– Singer; pianist; songwriter.
Address: c/o The Ballroom, 253 W. 28th St.,
New York, N.Y. 10001*

One of the last of the great supper-club singers, Blossom Dearie remains something of a cult star whose small but devoted following, centered mainly in New York and London, includes such celebrities as Marlon Brando, Vanessa Redgrave, and Raymond Burr. Miss Dearie's fans admire her for her tasteful renditions of ballads by, among others, Johnny Mercer, Michel Legrand, and Rodgers and Hart; her understated voice and ready wit; and her intransigent insistence that talking, smoking, and, frequently, the serving of food and drink be tabu during her performances. Her much-discussed vocal style has been described by Stephen Holden of the *New York Times* (September 9, 1982) as a "wispy, little-girlish soprano with a vibrato as rapid and fluttery as the beating of a hummingbird's wings." While conceding that, by traditional criteria, Blossom Dearie does not qualify as a great vocalist, Holden nonetheless has noted that "her exquisite conversational phrasing gives her material the aura and rhythm of short stories. . . . Everything that voice does expresses a singularly eccentric view of the world." "I think there is a hunger for romance in this loud, vulgar, violent world," Miss Dearie once told Annalyn Swan for a *Newsweek* profile. "People need someone like me."

Blossom Dearie was born on April 28, 1926 in East Durham, New York, a small town in the Catskill Mountains, about twenty miles from Albany. Her father, a bartender and hotel manager, was of Scottish and Irish ancestry; her mother, who was born in Oslo, Norway, immigrated to the United States as a small girl. Her parents had four sons between them from previous marriages. She was given her unusual first name after a neighbor brought some peach blossoms to her house on the day she was born. Recalling her early years for Charles Michener of *Newsweek* (May 27, 1974), Miss Dearie said that she had a "very provincial childhood, and we were all crazy about each other." Her first contact with music came at the age of two, when she began to sit on her mother's lap at the piano and pick out melodies. By the time she was three she had made up her mind to become a musician.

When she was five years old, Blossom Dearie began taking piano lessons. At the age of ten, while living with one of her stepbrothers in Washington, D.C., she studied under an instructor who, having introduced her to the works of Bach and Chopin, encouraged her to set her sights on entering the Peabody Conservatory in Baltimore, but when she returned to East Durham, she stopped studying classical music. When, as a teenager, she played in her high school's dance band and started to listen to jazz for the first time, she knew that jazz was what she really wanted to play. Her early jazz idols included Art Tatum, Duke Ellington, Count Basie, Teddy Wilson, and the singer Martha Tilton, who performed with the Benny Goodman orchestra.

After graduating from high school in the mid-1940s, Blossom Dearie moved to New York City to pursue a career in music. Renting living space "with a bunch of girl singers" in a midtown Manhattan hotel, she began performing with the Blue Flames, a vocal group within Woody Herman's famous big band. Later, she joined the Blue Reys, a similar vocal ensemble in the Alvino Rey band. She also "hung out" in the Manhattan apartment of the pianist and composer Gil Evans, where she met such jazz luminaries as Charlie ("Bird") Parker, Dizzy Gillespie, Miles Davis, and Gerry Mulligan. After leaving the Woody Herman and Alvino Rey orchestras, Miss Dearie performed in various New York nightspots, including the Chantilly Club in Greenwich Village, and she also performed for a time during intermissions at a West Fifty-second Street strip club.

In 1952, while working at the Chantilly Club, Blossom Dearie met Nicole Barclay, one of the owners of Barclay Records, who suggested that she go to Paris, where interest in American jazz artists was then running especially high. Once installed in the French capital, she formed an eight-member vocal group called the Blue Stars. "There were four boys and four girls," she informed Whitney Balliett during an interview for the *New Yorker* (May 26, 1973). "The boys played instruments and sang, and

the girls just sang." She soon discovered that her interaction with the other members of the group was strained not only by the language barrier but also by the vagaries and quirks of the mercurial French temperament. Although her fellow Blue Stars at first questioned her vocal concept for the group, they gradually acquiesced, especially after hearing their first recordings, one of which, a French version of "Lullaby of Birdland," became a hit in both France and the United States. While in Paris, Miss Dearie also studied French at the Berlitz School, played at the Mars nightclub, and met and became friends with the British singer and songwriter Annie Ross, with whom she later performed in London. More important, she met the American jazz record producer and impresario Norman Granz, who signed her to record for Verve Records, and she eventually recorded six solo albums for that label.

The success of "Lullaby of Birdland" led to several appearances on French television for the Blue Stars and brought them an invitation to perform in the United States—an invitation that the group was forced to turn down when several of its members were unable to obtain passports. After Blossom Dearie decided to leave the Blue Stars and return to the United States alone, the group dissolved, but later re-formed, first as the Swingle Sisters and later as the Double Six of Paris.

Blossom Dearie resumed her solo career upon returning to New York City in 1956, convinced that although she could start a vocal group there, she preferred to be what she has called "an individual personality." She made occasional appearances on NBC's *Tonight Show*, then hosted by Jack Paar, and performed at New York's Versailles nightclub and the Village Vanguard, playing opposite Miles Davis, with whom she became close friends. Reviewing her Verve album *My Gentleman Friend*, released in 1961, a critic for the *New York Times* (April 23, 1961) called her "a polished and sensitive performer, [and] a delightful pianist as well as singer."

Beginning in 1966, Blossom Dearie performed for one month each summer at Ronnie Scott's, a popular jazz club in London. "The English people took me in immediately," she explained to Charles Michener during the *Newsweek* interview. "I think it's because they still appreciate subtlety." Writing in the British publication *Melody Maker* (July 16, 1966), Max Jones observed that Miss Dearie had become known both as a singer's singer and a songwriter's singer, one of those artists who, as he put it, are "not usually acclaimed by the public at large, [but] whose craftsmanship or special subtlety endears them to their fellow professionals." "Her musicianship, humor and unfailing beat are qualities which help to make her a musician's singer," he went on to say. "But the most important of her assets is her power to bring a personal interpretation to a song while showing the utmost respect for a composer's intentions."

Although she composes the music for some of the songs she performs, Blossom Dearie has never professed a desire to write lyrics, because, as she has explained, she has "friends who do it so much better." One of those friends was the great lyricist Johnny Mercer, who wrote such songs as "I'm Shadowing You" and "My New Celebrity Is You" for her. The latter song was the last one that Mercer wrote before his death in 1976. "I miss [Mercer] very much, not only personally, but professionally," Miss Dearie said during an interview on the National Public Radio program *Piano Jazz*, shortly after the songwriter's death. "I haven't heard any funny songs lately," she added. "No one around now can write words and no one has a sense of humor. There's one exception, Dave Frishberg." Frishberg, the satirical songwriter, who also sings and plays piano, wrote the lyrics for one of Blossom Dearie's signature songs, "I'm Hip," and the words and music for two other numbers that Blossom Dearie frequently performs in her act: "Peel Me a Grape" and "My Attorney Bernie."

Despite the inclusion of outstanding songs in her repertoire, Blossom Dearie had decided by the early 1970s that her sophisticated music was being slighted by the marketing departments of the record companies to which she had been under contract. Rather than continue her uphill battle for acceptance with those companies, she started her own record label, Daffodil Records, in 1974, at about the same time that several other artists, including George Shearing, Marian McPartland, and Tony Bennett, were also starting their own labels. "The music business has turned into one gigantic cash register," Miss Dearie complained to the jazz critic Leonard Feather of the *Los Angeles Times* in an article reprinted in *Newsday* (July 31, 1977). "That's why it was logical for me to follow the trend, among people who have a specialized following, to start an independent company." One of Miss Dearie's stepbrothers, Walter Birchett, who is president of Daffodil Records, runs the business from his home in East Durham, New York, while Blossom Dearie serves as its marketing director and handles the bookkeeping. At the conclusion of live performances, she often stands by the door of a club and sells albums and cassettes to customers as they leave.

When *Blossom Dearie Sings*, her first album on the Daffodil label, was released in early 1974, the critic Rex Reed lauded the album in an appraisal that appeared in *Stereo Review* (March 1974). "Blossom Dearie is one of the all-time great singers and composers of popular music," Reed observed, "and this is one of her most agreeable albums. I'm not in a very elated state about today's music, but this record has filled me with delight, enthusiasm, and ecstasy. It is simply flawless." Blossom Dearie's next album, a two-record set released in 1977 and entitled *My New Celebrity Is You*, after the Johnny Mercer song, featured sixteen numbers, eight of which she had composed herself. Leonard Feather wrote that most of the songs were "hip, witty, and occasionally poignant," but John S. Wilson of the *New York Times* (June 2, 1977) contended that the eight Dearie compositions proved "to be an

overload" since they included some of the least interesting, though the lack of interest came less from her music than from her lyrics.

During the same year in which she established Daffodil Records, Miss Dearie performed at Carnegie Hall in New York with the veteran blues singer Joe Williams and the jazz vocalist Anita O'Day in a program called "The Jazz Singers." In March of 1975 she made her debut in Los Angeles, in performances at the Mark Taper Forum. In reviewing one of her Los Angeles appearances, a critic for *Variety* (March 12, 1975) cited her unique singing voice: "Dearie's sweetness is without sugar and she brings to the stage a melodic sound that is very easy to take for granted."

Back in New York, Blossom Dearie continued to perform at various clubs, and though several of those venues proved congenial for her intimate style, she became increasingly interested in controlling the atmosphere at her shows. At Michael's Pub in Manhattan, for example, where she and Dave Frishberg performed together for three weeks in the summer of 1981, she had a clause added to her contract that prohibited the serving of food during her performance. "The help in clubs is the enemy," Miss Dearie explained to John S. Wilson of the *New York Times* (August 7, 1981). "They're running around shouting orders, crashing plates. They want the taped music between sets louder so that they can get revved up and sell more drinks." When, in December 1981, she performed at the Horn of Plenty in New York's Greenwich Village, Rex Reed reported to the readers of the *New York Daily News* (December 23, 1981) that Miss Dearie was "more subtle, more sublime, and more delectable than ever."

Since 1983 Blossom Dearie has performed four nights a week for six months a year at the Ballroom, a nightclub in Manhattan's Chelsea district, from 6:30 until 8:00, Wednesday through Saturday. Writing in the *New York Daily News* (October 4, 1983), Patricia O'Haire commented that those early evening shows provided "pause and refreshment to those in need of same after a long day's journey through work." In 1985 Miss Dearie became the first recipient of the Mabel Mercer Foundation Award, consisting of a cash prize of $1,500, which is presented annually to an outstanding cabaret or supper-club performer.

Blossom Dearie leads a rather modest life, owing, in part, to her music's lack of mass appeal. "No, I don't make any money," she admitted to Scott Sublett during an interview for *Insight* (June 2, 1986). "I would like to have an apartment in London and one in Paris and a house on the Coast." Instead, she has just one apartment, and that merely a Greenwich Village studio. She rises at six each morning and begins her day either by swimming or by writing music. By restricting her performances to four days a week, she is able to spend the other three days attending to the business of Daffodil Records.

While living in Paris in 1955, Blossom Dearie married the Belgian saxophonist and flutist Bobby

Jaspar, but they later separated. Jaspar died in 1963, following heart surgery. Although she never remarried, Miss Dearie has said that she would like to. Interested in matters of health, she is especially enthusiastic about the virtues of Vitamin E. To relax, she attends the theatre and dines out with friends. When her colleagues are performing in New York, she likes to catch their early shows, but on most nights, she retires following the 11:00 P.M. television newscast.

Blossom Dearie is five feet three inches tall. In his profile of her for the *New Yorker*, Whitney Balliett described the singer in the following manner: "She stands pole-straight, and is short and country-girl solid. Her broad face, with its small, well-shaped eyes, wide mouth, and generous, direct nose, has a figurehead strength. Her hands and feet are small and delicate. Angelic honey-blond hair falls well below her shoulders. When she is listening, she gives continuous, receptive, almost audible nods. There is no waste in her laughter, which is

frequent and quick—a single, merry, high, descending triplet." A longtime friend of Miss Dearie's said of her in the same article, "She is absolutely pure. . . . She has this innocence that would take her across a battlefield unscathed." Yet her almost fragile persona, which seems tinged with equal amounts of humor and sadness, can be deceptive. She can quickly cut to the heart of a matter in the course of a conversation, and though affable, she is not one to mince words, often replying with a mere "yes" or "no." Once, while Blossom Dearie was performing at a party, a guest, unhappy with the singer's song selection, approached her and asked, "Can't you play something we can dance to?" Without missing a beat, Miss Dearie answered, "How well do you dance?"

References: Melody Maker 41:8 Jl 16 '66 por; New Yorker 49:46+ My 26 '73 por; Newsday II p3 Jl 31 '77 por; Newsweek 83:76+ My 27 '74 por; Cleghorn, Charles E. Biographical Dictionary of Jazz (1982)

DeLillo, Don

Nov. 20, 1936– Writer. Address: c/o Viking Penguin Inc., 40 W. 23d St., New York, N.Y. 10010

For twenty years, in his disturbing but often witty novels, Don DeLillo has been anatomizing the games we play in the face of death and cultural disintegration. Often relying on ideas, metaphors, and patterns of association to shape his best work—*End Zone*, *Ratner's Star*, *White Noise*, and

Libra—DeLillo writes in a precise, musical language that, although it has earned him the respect of critics and writers, has kept him a writer's writer, at least until recently. That relative obscurity may be due to the fact that his work is sometimes seen as abstract and depressing—he admires and is often linked to arcane writers such as William Gaddis and Thomas Pynchon—but it may also be the result of his consistent refusal to appear on talk shows, give readings, or indulge in any of the other contemporary arts of self-promotion. The critical attention paid to *White Noise* and *Libra*, however, has brought him a larger audience. Considered by many critics to be DeLillo's best novel, *Libra* is a sophisticated meditation on the assassination of John F. Kennedy and may represent the most successful attempt by a postmodern American writer to confront contemporary history.

Don DeLillo was born in New York City on November 20, 1936 and grew up in the borough of the Bronx. Little biographical information about his background is available, although he did tell Thomas LeClair in an interview published in *Contemporary Literature* (Winter 1982) that "being raised a Catholic was interesting because the ritual had elements of art to it and it prompted feelings that art sometimes draws out of us. . . . Sometimes it was awesome, sometimes it was funny. High funeral masses were a little of both and they're among my warmest childhood memories." He has also informed recent interviewers that he disliked college when he attended Fordham University from 1954 to 1958 and studied history, philosophy, and theology. He contends that the Jesuits taught him to be a "failed ascetic" and describes himself as having tried to emulate Stephen Dedalus, although "the setting [at Fordham] wasn't quite right." The allusions to James Joyce are perhaps significant, since most of DeLillo's books seem written with Joycean rigor and detachment, a quality that has led critics to characterize his narrative voice as one from "another planet."

Besides Joyce, DeLillo was also drawn to the "comic anarchy" of Ezra Pound, Gertrude Stein, and other modernists. "Although I didn't necessarily want to write like them," he said in his interview with Thomas LeClair, "to someone who's twenty . . . that kind of work suggests freedom and possibility." He also became interested in avant-garde film, especially the movies of Jean-Luc Godard, which had a greater impact on his early work than anything he read.

After graduating from Fordham, in 1958, DeLillo eventually landed a job at Ogilvy and Mather, a leading New York advertising agency. He worked there from 1961 until 1964, and in 1966 he began his first novel, Americana, setting out, like most ambitious first novelists, to capture "huge blocks of experience." Living on only $2,000 a year in an unheated Manhattan apartment, he often had to interrupt work on Americana to take temporary jobs, with the result that the novel took four years to complete. In spite of his privations and frustrations, however, he looks back upon that period of apprenticeship with nostalgia, perhaps because, when halfway through work on the novel, he began to view himself as a serious and committed writer. His only published work up to that time had been a story that appeared in Epoch.

Americana (1971) is a picaresque novel about a young television executive who quits his job and travels around the United States in an attempt to impose a pattern on his chaotic life by recording everything with a movie camera. Distinctive for its cinematic descriptions of barren landscapes and empty lives as well as for its flashy, self-reflexive language, the novel encountered a generally favorable reception when it was published. In his New York Times (May 6, 1971) review, Christopher Lehmann-Haupt called the plot overfamiliar but found that the writing "soars and dips." Although Thomas Edwards, reviewing it in the New York Times Book Review (May 30, 1971), thought the book too obviously ambitious, he admired its "savagely funny portrait of middle-class anomie." One of the most encouraging pronouncements came from Joyce Carol Oates, who called Americana "one of the most compelling and sophisticated first novels that I have ever read."

In discussing the writing of his next novel, End Zone (1972), DeLillo told LeClair, "I felt I was doing something easier and looser. I was working closer to my instincts." More compact and original than Americana, End Zone is narrated by Gary Harkness, a football star who comes to Logos College in western Texas after having been kicked out of four major football schools. As the team of misfits struggles through its scrimmages and games, the language of football comes to parody the jargon of nuclear war—Gary's other obsession, which, like football, is seen as a way to control experience. His obsession with control leads to setbacks on and off

the field, and at the end of the novel Gary withdraws to a hospital with a mysterious brain fever. Yet End Zone is far from grim. What Thomas Edwards had written about Americana also applies to DeLillo's second novel: "To see a . . . serious imagination discover and possess a potent metaphor . . . is finally exciting and life-serving." End Zone also confirmed his earlier impression that "this richly inventive new talent looks like a major one." Walter Clemons, a book reviewer for Newsweek, has recommended End Zone as the best DeLillo novel for readers to start with.

Great Jones Street (1973) takes up where End Zone leaves off. Bucky Wunderlick, a rock star whose lyrics have degenerated from politics and self-exploration to mere babbling, has withdrawn to a tacky apartment in lower Manhattan. In establishing Bucky's almost catatonic point of view, DeLillo satirizes the American counterculture, the media, and corporate greed. For all its technical skill, inventiveness, evocative description, and flashes of humor, however, this "game at the far edge" lacks the charm of End Zone, and whereas most critics conceded that it extended DeLillo's range, they also considered it an "in-between book," or an obviously transitional novel.

Having explored the metaphors of advertising, sports, and rock music, DeLillo next addressed the field of science. In Ratner's Star (1976), which he has said he intended as a work of "naked structure," he combined mathematical theory with elements of children's literature. The book is divided into two sections to correspond with Lewis Carroll's Alice's Adventures in Wonderland and Through the Looking Glass and What Alice Found There to create a science fiction novel that is also what LeClair calls "a conceptual monster, a totalizing work like . . . Pynchon's Gravity's Rainbow or Barth's Letters."

In attempting to review Ratner's Star in the Atlantic (August 1976), Amanda Heller admitted that there was "no way to describe . . . [this] cheerfully apocalyptic novel" about a fourteen-year-old genius and Nobel laureate, Billy Twillig, who is summoned to a space research center to decode a message from a distant planet. There, he encounters a collection of zany characters whose bizarre speech and behavior create a funny, if unnerving, picture of science run amok. Amanda Heller asked her Atlantic readers to imagine "Alice in Wonderland set at the Princeton Institute for Advanced Study."

The abstraction, density, and recondite language of Ratner's Star frustrated some critics. In his Newsweek (June 7, 1976) review, Peter Prescott complained that it was an overlong imitation of Thomas Pynchon, and reviewers for Time and the New Yorker disliked DeLillo's cartoon characters. Among the critics who nevertheless found the novel to be elegant and funny were J. D. O'Hara of the Washington Post Book World (June 13, 1976), who praised DeLillo for combining serious mathematical ideas with wacky humor, and George Stade, who, in the New York Times Book Review (June

20, 1976), called it an example of Menippean satire—a form in which characters are reduced to the ideas for which they stand. Stade placed DeLillo in the tradition of Swift and Melville.

According to the literary critic Michael Oriard, *Ratner's Star* concluded a quartet of novels about a quest for an ultimate meaning that remains elusive. Although many of DeLillo's earlier themes of paranoia and anomie recur in his fifth novel, *Players* (1977), that search for meaning has been reduced to the characters' quest for excitement. Lyle and Pammy Wynant are quintessential married yuppies, bored with their jobs and each other. To escape their ennui, Pammy goes off to Maine with a homosexual couple—one of whom becomes her lover and commits suicide—while Lyle, a stockbroker, becomes involved with terrorists and urban guerrillas.

In his enthusiastic review of *Players* in the *New York Times* (August 11, 1977), John Leonard celebrated its "wit, intelligence, and [incantatory] language." Other critics admired the brilliantly rendered, banal dialogue so listlessly exchanged between Pammy and Lyle and the novel's prologue, in which the characters, not yet introduced, watch and applaud a movie about hippie terrorists. In praising *Players* in the *New York Times Book Review* (September 4, 1977), the novelist and critic Diane Johnson noted DeLillo's lack of commercial success, attributing it to his habit of saying "deeply shocking things about America that people would rather not face."

DeLillo's next two books, *Running Dog* (1978) and the pseudonymous *Amazons* (1980), represent his partial retreat from what Diane Johnson has characterized as high, if shocking, moral satire. *Running Dog*, a parody of a thriller, involves a race to obtain a supposedly pornographic film of Adolf Hitler's last orgy at the end of the war, which turns out to consist of scenes of Hitler doing Charlie Chaplin imitations for the amusement of the children of Joseph Paul Goebbels. *Amazons*, published under the pseudonym of Cleo Birdwell, is a factitious sports memoir about Ms. Birdwell's career as the first female hockey player in the National Hockey League. While both books are obviously less ambitious than DeLillo's earlier novels, reviewers saw them as fast-paced, if sordid, and extremely funny.

Funded in part by a Guggenheim Fellowship in 1979, DeLillo spent three years in Greece, the Middle East, and India. Having been taught by his travels "how to see and hear all over again," he incorporated much of what he saw and heard in *The Names* (1982), an ambitious novel about Americans abroad. James Axton, its protagonist, works in Athens as a risk analyst for a firm that insures corporations against terrorism. Estranged from his wife and son, Axton feels cut off from himself and, in his self-alienation, becomes obsessed with a cult dedicated to murdering people in an almost random pattern based on their initials. His obsession gradually leads to the discovery that he has unwittingly been working for the CIA—

which functions here, as in other DeLillo novels, as a sort of supercult.

Writing in the *New York Times Book Review* (October 10, 1982), Michael Wood felt that the digressive structure of *The Names* blurred DeLillo's insights, and Robert Towers found in his *New Republic* (November 22, 1982) review that the "total impact [was not] equal to the brilliance of its parts," but both critics were impressed by the novel's intelligence, agility, and evocative atmosphere. Appraising it for the *New York Review of Books* (December 16, 1982), Josh Rubins saw DeLillo as having given up his fantastical satire and "flyaway characters" for a solid, almost Jamesian, narrator-hero and a direct approach to the problem of the contemporary corruption of American culture.

Since, on returning to the United States, DeLillo moved to the quiet suburb of Bronxville, New York, it is not surprising that his next novel, *White Noise* (1985), is permeated with the ambiance of suburbia. Its narrator is Jack Gladney, a professor of Hitler studies at a small college, who is happily married to Babette, a teacher of posture classes to the elderly and a reader of tabloids to the blind. Their several children from past marriages comment like a Greek chorus on the book's main event—a toxic gas leak. "All plots lead to death," Gladney says, and the gas leak becomes a "Toxic Event." Terrified of outliving Jack, Babette has an affair with a researcher in order to get hold of experimental pills that allegedly suppress the fear of death. Although the pills fail to work, Gladney becomes obsessed with the drug, and he desperately seeks to obtain it.

For all its almost surreal stylization, the description of the Gladney family is lovingly rendered. Because of that departure, perhaps, the book received considerable attention from the media. In his *Washington Post Book World* (January 13, 1985) review, Jonathan Yardley dismissed it as a collection of tired political ideas, saying, "Until [DeLillo] has something to say that comes from the heart rather than the evening news, his novels will fall far short of his talents." But most critics were enthusiastic. In spite of his reservations—namely, that DeLillo was having too much fun writing the novel for readers to take the Gladneys' fear of death seriously— Thomas Disch admired *White Noise* in his *Nation* (February 2, 1985) review for its wit and dialogue. In his assessment for the *Village Voice* (April 30, 1985), Albert Mobilio seemed to be answering Yardley's objections when he wrote, "Critics who have argued his work is . . . overly intellectual should take notice: DeLillo's dark vision . . . strikes at both head and heart." And in her evaluation for the *New York Times Book Review* (January 13, 1985), Jayne Anne Phillips remarked, "The voice guiding us through *White Noise* is one of the most ironic, intelligent, grimly funny voices yet to comment on life in present-day America." Few were surprised when *White Noise* won the 1985 American Book Award for Fiction.

After writing an article on the assassination of John F. Kennedy for *Rolling Stone* magazine in

1983, DeLillo bought a used copy of the twenty-six-volume Warren Commission Report and spent three years reconstructing the events that led up to Kennedy's death. Since he felt particularly drawn to Lee Harvey Oswald—DeLillo discovered they had briefly lived in the same Bronx neighborhood in the mid-1950s—Oswald's sad, painful story makes up most of his latest novel, *Libra* (1988).

Libra is also shaped by various real and imaginary conspiracies: the United States government wants to invade Cuba; CIA agents want their revenge against Kennedy for his failure to give full support to the Bay of Pigs invasion; and Cubans want to thwart Kennedy's plans to achieve détente with Castro. In addition, DeLillo created a CIA officer, Nicholas Branch, who is writing the CIA's secret history of the assassination. Branch's efforts to understand what happened link him to the author and afford DeLillo the opportunity to explore the nature of history and our changing perception of it.

Because of its subject matter and DeLillo's growing reputation, *Libra* was widely reviewed. In *Time* (August 1, 1988) magazine, Paul Gray criticized the book for advancing yet another dubious conspiracy theory (that the CIA planned to shoot at Kennedy and miss in order to galvanize public sentiment against Cuba): "There is a simpler possibility that *Libra* . . . skirts: a frustrated, angry man looked out a window, watched the President ride by, and shot him dead." And stepping up his earlier attacks on DeLillo's fiction, Jonathan Yardley of the *Washington Post Book World* (July 3, 1988) called *Libra* "fanciful journalism" and argued that DeLillo's doctrinaire left-wing politics kept his characters from coming to life. In his most acerbic comment, Yardley found DeLillo's technique of putting thoughts into the minds of living people to be "beneath contempt."

Few critics agreed with those acidulous judgments. For one thing, in an epilogue DeLillo makes clear that *Libra* is a work of imagination, not an historical document. For another, as Terrence Rafferty pointed out in a review in the *New Yorker* (July 3, 1988), *Libra* is not so much *for* "conspiracy buffs" as *about* them. In fact, much of the novel's power is generated by the tension between aesthetically pleasing explanations and the brute facts of Lee Harvey Oswald's world and the assassination. DeLillo "might have written this novel to exorcise his own tendency toward paranoid mysticism," Rafferty observed, going on to note that *Libra* ends with Oswald's mother standing by her son's grave "howling with animal confusion, an intimation of the more terrifying world" outside the world of conspiracies. Thus, Rafferty maintained that *Libra* is DeLillo's best novel not only "because it goes right to the source—to Dallas in November, 1963, the primal scene of American paranoia," but also because DeLillo's portrayal of Oswald's life, in language that is as "weirdly eroticized as prisoners' poetry," transcends that paranoia.

Other reviewers were equally impressed. Christopher Lehmann-Haupt of the *New York Times* (July 18, 1988) attributed the power of *Libra* to the seamlessness with which DeLillo bound the facts together with "every rumor, shadowy figure and crackpot theory." The novelist Anne Tyler, writing in the *New York Times Book Review* (July 24, 1988), admired the way DeLillo makes the reader less interested in "the . . . events of the assassination than in the pitiable and stumbling spirit underlying them." And John Leonard, who reviewed *Libra* in the *Nation* (September 19, 1988), linked DeLillo to Joseph Conrad, Franz Kafka, and T. S. Eliot, in underscoring his opinion that "Oswald, of course, is the Underground Man." *Libra* was nominated for the National Book Award and the National Book Critics Circle Award, and in September 1989 it received the first annual International Fiction Prize.

In addition to his novels, DeLillo has written several short stories and two plays, *The Engineer of Moonlight*, about a mathematician, and *The Day Room*, which takes place in a hospital. *The Day Room* was first performed in Cambridge, Massachusetts at the American Repertory Theatre in 1986 and then had runs at the Manhattan Theatre Club in New York City and at the Cooperative Stage in Chicago. Shortly before its New York opening, DeLillo told Mervyn Rothstein in an interview for the *New York Times* (December 20, 1987): "I think theatre is really mysterious and alluring for someone who has written a novel, and it seemed natural to me beginning a play that theatre itself would be one of the subjects I was interested in. And I began to sense a connection, almost a metaphysical connection, between the craft of acting and the fear we all have of dying. It seemed to me that actors are a kind of model for the ways in which we hide from the knowledge we inevitably possess of our final extinction. There's a sense in which actors teach us how to hide. There's something about the necessary shift in identity which actors make in the ordinary course of their work that seems almost a guide to concealing what we know about ourselves."

The interviews to which DeLillo agreed in conjunction with the publication of *Libra* reveal him to be an articulate and gracious man of high seriousness who is more comfortable talking about his work than about himself. Several interviewers noted his tendency to speak softly and slowly, carefully weighing each word. DeLillo is of medium height and has salt-and-pepper hair and brown eyes. While avoiding most of the literary world and the promotional circuit, he remains friends with other innovative writers, among them William Gass and William Gaddis. He continues to live in Bronxville with his wife, Barbara, a banking executive and harpsichordist. In 1984 DeLillo received the American Academy and Institute of Arts and Letters Award in Literature.

References: N Y Times Bk R p26 O 10 '82 por; Pub W 234:55+ Jl 1 '88 por; Contemporary Authors vols 81–84 (1979); Contemporary Novelists (1982); Dictionary of Literary Biography vol 6 (1980); World Authors 1975–1980 (1985)

Delors, Jacques (Lucien Jean)

July 20, 1925– President of the European
Commission. Address: b. Commission of the
European Communities, 200 rue de la Loi, 1049
Brussels, Belgium; h. 11 France, 19 boulevard de
Bercy, 75012 Paris, France

When Jacques Delors became president of the European Commission, the executive body of the European Community (EC), in 1985, he set out
immediately to revive a Europe plagued by inflation and stagnant growth as an economic power rivaling the United States and Japan. "It's a question
of survival or decline," he has said. What he proposed, with the Act of European Unity, was a plan
to integrate the twelve EC member countries into
a single market by 1992, allowing for the free circulation of goods, services, and people. Political unity
will become possible after economic unity is
achieved, Delors believes, and he pursues that goal
"like a chess player," advancing "one piece at a
time," one reporter has observed, "but beneath a
cool and even shy exterior lurks a passionate
visionary."

Jacques Lucien Jean Delors was born in Paris,
France on July 20, 1925 to Louis Delors, a low-level
bank employee, and Jeanne (Rigal) Delors. He was
raised as a Roman Catholic in a rough anticlerical
neighborhood. Since he came from a working-class
family, Delors did not attend the elite schools from
which French leaders are usually drawn. "I think
my first sense of social injustice came when I saw
my pals quitting school and going straight to the
factories," Delors told Scott Sullivan of Newsweek
(February 6, 1989). According to the Britannica
Yearbook 1985, Delors graduated from the University of Paris with a degree in economics before

starting to work at the Banque de France in 1945.
Scott Sullivan, however, in his Newsweek piece,
reported that Delors's father persuaded him to start
a career without attending a university, and he later took courses at night to obtain his degree. In any
case, from 1945 to 1962 he served as an executive
officer and department head at the Banque de
France, and, from 1950 to 1962, he was attached to
the staff of the director-general of the bank's securities department.

In 1950 Delors became an economic adviser to
the Confédération Française des Travailleurs
Chrétiens (Christian Trade Union Confederation),
continuing in that post after the union was renamed the Confédération Française Démocratique
du Travail (Democratic Trade Union Confederation) in 1964. He was involved in trade union work
at the same time that he advanced in his banking
career.

During the 1960s Delors taught economics at the
prestigious L'Ecole Nationale d'Administration.
From June 1959 until January 1962 he served in the
planning and investment section of the Economic
and Social Council, a 200-member advisory body
that the French government consults before drafting economic or social planning legislation. From
1962 to 1969 Delors headed the social-affairs division of the Commissariat Général du Plan (General
Planning Commission), a high-level civil service
post. In that position, he tried to reduce friction between French employers and their unions. It was
while working for that commission that Delors succeeded in expanding legislation in 1966 to provide
income for employees in training. In 1968 that legislation was amended to enable employees in
training to receive compensation equal to the
amount of their regular income. And in 1971 those
two laws were consolidated into a package stipu-
lating that no administrative body has a monopoly
in providing continous education, so that decisions
are made as close as possible to the level of the individual.

Until the student and labor protests in May 1968,
with their demands for a radical restructuring of
French society, and the resignation of Charles de
Gaulle as president on April 28, 1969, Delors had
refused direct political action, rejecting, by his own
account, seven or eight offers to join ministerial
cabinets under the presidency of Charles de
Gaulle. "But after the events of 1968," Delors told
Madeleine Gobeil in an interview for Le Maclean
(October 1974), "I though that since our society was
alarmed about itself and unsettled, it might be possible to push through a few progressive ideas." In
April 1969 Delors became secretary-general of the
interdepartmental Committee on Vocational
Training and Social Advancement, and, in June
1969, he assumed the duties of chief adviser on social and cultural affairs to Jacques Chaban-
Delmas, who had been appointed prime minister
by the newly elected president, Georges Pompidou.

Some of the progressive ideas that Delors had
developed were incorporated into six leaflets con-

taining an outline for a *nouvelle société* (new society) that Delors presented to Chaban-Delmas in June 1969. The proposed program included a partnership between government and labor unions, a wage policy, increased professional training, continuous education, and decentralization of the state. From August 1971 until July 1972 Delors served as chargé de mission for economic, financial, and social affairs to the prime minister, who introduced a series of measures aimed at democratizing France's rigidly bureaucratized and hierarchical economic and social structures. When Chaban-Delmas was forced to resign in July 1972 because of Gaullist party members' unhappiness with his overly liberal leanings and a scandal involving tax evasion, Delors also left government.

Returning to academia, Delors taught business management as an associate professor at the University of Paris-Dauphine, from 1973 to 1979, and in 1974 he resumed his teaching at L'Ecole Nationale d'Administration, where he remained until 1976. In January 1973 he became a member of the General Council of the Banque de France. Of greater significance was his founding, in February 1974, of the "Club Echanges et Projets," an informal association, or think tank, of some 200 intellectuals from all walks of life, including government officials, teachers, union activists, and corporation executives, who reconsider the role of the state in France and attempt to reduce inequalities among the French. To maintain their independence, Echanges et Projets members pay dues amounting to 10 percent of their annual income tax. They comprise three factions: left-democrats; the younger left-activists; and the group to which Delors himself belongs—the heirs to Charles Fourier and Pierre Joseph Proudhon, representing the libertarian trend in French socialism.

Many of the ideas that Delors and his colleagues explored during the 1970s would become policy goals in the 1980s, as Delors moved into positions of power in the French government and the European Community. For example, Delors and his associates popularized the idea that workers should be protected against the obsolescence of their professional skills just as they are protected from illness. The Echange et Projets association also studied the effects of industrial growth on French society. "In reaction to this society that is afraid to stop and therefore produces more and more until it reaches the level of futility, we must become inventors of frugality and simplicity," Delors told Madeleine Gobeil.

In December 1974 Delors formally joined the French Socialist party and moved inevitably into positions of leadership, though local party members at first subjected him to a grilling that he found humiliating. Delors won them over after he produced a series of insightful position papers. From 1976 to 1979 he served as the party's national coordinator for international economic relations, and in April 1979 he was elected to the party's central committee. The following June Delors was elected, on the Socialist list headed by François Mitterrand,

to the European Parliament, the legislative body of the European Economic Community. In September he was appointed chairman of the parliament's Committee on Economic and Monetary Affairs, a position he held until May 1981.

In that month Socialist party leader François Mitterrand became the first left-wing candidate to be elected president of France in twenty-three years. His platform for government-funded economic expansion included the nationalization of private banks and the five major industrial sectors, wage hikes, and increased social benefits for low-income workers. Mitterrand's election took place during an international economic crisis affecting the United States and other Western capitalist countries, including France, which suffered from stagnant growth and high inflation. In 1981 unemployment stood at 7.4 percent, compared to 2.8 percent in 1974. Ronald Reagan, who was inaugurated president of the United States four months before Mitterrand's election, advocated a supply-side approach to cutting inflation by deregulating the economy. Mitterrand proposed an opposite tack: government controls and investment and the stimulation of consumer demand.

Appointed minister of economics and finance in the cabinet of Prime Minister Pierre Mauroy, Delors was viewed as one of the more moderate members of the Socialist government, and he reassured his compatriots that there would be "no leap to collectivism" and that the Socialists hoped to negotiate changes rather than impose them. Nevertheless, Delors worked hard to promote the party's program. When France's largest private bank tried to sell its assets to a Swiss subsidiary in order to avoid nationalization, Delors accused its chairman of "unpatriotic behavior" and, after the bank was nationalized, forced him out of office. Determined to increase revenues by strict tax enforcement, Delors criticized the rich for turning tax evasion "into a noble art."

In 1982 Delors advocated a pause in the pace of Mitterrand's reforms, but Prime Minister Mauroy insisted on staying on course. By 1983 high inflation, a growing trade deficit, and a mounting international debt provided strong evidence that Mitterrand's economic program was not working. While one faction in the government argued for protectionist trade policies, a withdrawal from the European Monetary System, and stepped-up nationalization, Delors advocated a program of pro-Europeanization, free trade, and diminished state intervention that won Mitterrand's support. In March 1983 Mitterrand's cabinet resigned, and, when it was reorganized, Delors was in a position of increased power, as minister of the economy, finance, and budget, with responsibility for charting a new economic course. He introduced a program of economic austerity, or "austerity with a human face," as the Socialists called it, which included restrictions on wage increases to 5 percent and a limit on travel allowances abroad to $275 a year. His goal was to break the link between price and wage increases.

Mitterrand's inability to formulate a coherent economic policy stemmed from an identity crisis within Socialist ranks. The Socialist emphasis on collectivism clashed with a growing desire among the French for less state intervention. The economic failures of French socialism could be attributed to stale ideas, a decline in trade union membership, a fifteen-year decrease in industrial jobs, and a rising standard of living. "The wind is not with us," Delors told John Vinocur of the *New York Times* (December 26, 1984), "either in terms of ideas or if you're just looking at the raw facts. Intellectually, we're at the bottom of the curve. We've got to discover a new frontier."

Meanwhile, in international economic affairs, Delors gained heightened stature in his dealings with France's trading partners, reaching an agreement with West Germany to devalue the franc by 2.5 percent at the same time that the mark's value increased by 5.5 percent, after threatening that France would defect from the European Monetary System unless West Germany agreed to revalue the mark. Delors took the lead in criticizing the United States, arguing that the strength of the dollar hindered the economic recovery of Western European economies.

At the same time that his influence was rising within the French cabinet, Delors was elected mayor of Clichy, a working-class suburb of Paris. As mayor, Delors helped persuade twenty-five companies to relocate there. With an election victory in his first run for office and his new prominence in the cabinet, Delors set his sights on becoming prime minister of France. Though he was highly regarded in business circles, he was distrusted by radicals within the Socialist party, and, on July 17, 1984, Mitterrand named Laurent Fabius prime minister, with the directive to "represent no political party." Mitterrand then proposed Delors for the presidency of the executive commission of the European Community, an appointment that was approved by the leaders of the other Common Market countries.

Assuming office in January 1985 as head of the Brussels-based European Commission, Delors took charge of a secretariat consisting of fourteen other commissioners, from the ten member nations, over whom Delors had no political leverage because of each nation's power of veto. "It's a suicide post," one official told Peter Norman of the *Wall Street Journal* (July 26, 1984). "We've seen them come with high reputations before, and leave battered." The routine work of the EC president involved negotiating trade agreements between the Common Market and other trading powers. Delors also faced the immediate challenge of resolving an EC budget deficit and dealing with the proposed entry of Spain and Portugal into the Common Market.

In April 1985 Delors made his first trip to Washington, D.C., to ease misunderstandings between the United States and the European Community. In Delors's view, the Reagan administration's demand that Europe adjust to American laissez-faire policies threatened the European economy. "It is

impossible to import to Europe what I call the new American [economic] model," he told Steve J. Dryden in an interview for the *Washington Post* (April 21, 1985). "We are in a different position, with different traditions." Delors emphasized that Europe would not follow the American model of free-market deregulation but would keep its mixed economy with "rational" government controls and job-creating initiatives as a balance to private investment.

Jacques Delors was convinced that Europe had to create a strong economic union—"a market without borders"—in order to compete in the international marketplace. "Europe can turn into a museum visited by U.S. and Japanese tourists, who like our cuisine and culture, while the aristocrats talk about the old Europe. Or we can be an economic power," he told a reporter for *Fortune* (January 2, 1989). To that end, collaborating with Lord Cockfield, Delors produced the white paper of June 1985, *Implementing the Internal Market*, listing the 300 measures that the member governments of the Common Market would have to take in order to integrate their economies. The white paper envisioned a barrier-free community in which the 320 million EC members could enroll in the university of their choice, buy an insurance policy, or open a bank account in any country. Other measures would make product standards and professional qualifications uniform and standardize customs documents. A number of problems, however, had to be resolved first, including creating a common European currency and a central bank, removing disparities in taxes, abolishing frontier duties and customs, and institutionalizing workers' rights.

The idea of abolishing intra-European trade barriers appealed to multinational corporations as well as to conservative leaders like Great Britain's Margaret Thatcher, and in December 1985 the white paper was incorporated into the Act of European Unity—a revision of the Treaty of Rome—with 1992 designated as the deadline for the reforms to be implemented. In a break with the practice of requiring that all commission decisions be unanimous, the Act of European Unity sanctioned decisions by a majority of the twelve member nations. Delors's success in advancing the idea of European unity built on the momentum of the Ariane Satellite Launcher, a cooperative European space program; the Airbus, a joint European venture that enabled the European commercial aircraft industry to compete with that of the United States; and the "Chunnel," a tunnel under the English Channel, linking Great Britain and France, that is scheduled to be completed in 1993.

The Act of European Unity was ratified in May 1987, but many stumbling blocks remained before it could be fully implemented. At an emergency summit meeting in Brussels in February 1988, Delors threatened to resign if an agreement was not reached on the issues of farm reform, EC funding, and aid to poorer member countries. When Prime Minister Margaret Thatcher and the other EC leaders agreed on those issues, Delors said that the accords marked the "happiest day of [his] life."

An integrated Europe moved another step closer to reality in February 1988, when the twelve members of the European Community agreed to reduce their system of agricultural subsidies. In June the EC finance ministers ended restrictions on the flow of capital within the twelve nations. Later in the month, at a summit meeting of the leaders of the EC countries in Hanover, West Germany, Delors was selected for a second four-year term as president, beginning in January 1989 and running through 1992. In April 1989 he issued a report that outlined a three-stage plan for a unified monetary system and a European central bank. The first stage, which involves deregulation of the capital market, is scheduled for implementation by July 1990.

Margaret Thatcher was the most outspoken opponent of Delors's vision, showing her displeasure by not reappointing Lord Cockfield, who designed most of the 1992 program, to a second term on the European Commission. Although she favored the free-market orientation of the internal market, she denounced efforts by Delors to frame European unity in a political context. Mrs. Thatcher maintained that her country could not completely abolish frontier controls because of the threat of crime, illegal immigrants, and terrorists. Delors responded: "That which unites us is more important than that which divides us."

When Delors predicted in the summer of 1988 that, within ten years, the EC would make 80 percent of the economic and social decisions for its member nations, Mrs. Thatcher criticized Delors during a BBC radio interview, calling his ideas "absurd" and vowing that a unified Europe would "never come in my lifetime, and I hope never at all." Defending her own free-market policies in Great Britain, she insisted, "We have not successfully rolled back the frontiers of the state in Britain only to see them reimposed at a European level, with a European superstate exercising a new dominance from Brussels." Although Delors frankly admitted that his program for 1992 was designed to win over conservative business interests first, he was also determined to gain support from the unions. In an interview with a reporter for the French newspaper Libération (August 29, 1988), he explained that if he had made labor issues a top priority when he first became head of the EC, he would have "provoked a war of religions, and Europe would still be in total stagnation."

In September 1988 Delors unveiled a social program that, among other proposals, advocated uniform workplace health and safety standards, the right to lifelong job training, and the right to be covered by a collective agreement. Another proposal, modeled after worker-management relations in West Germany, suggested that workers take part in managerial decisions. "The reinvigoration of Europe is colliding with the weakness of the union movement," Delors told James Markham of the New York Times (September 25, 1988). "I am making a modest effort to contribute to a renewal of trade unionism." Although Mrs. Thatcher called those proposals "utopian" and "airy-fairy," Delors argued that worker delocalization from economic restructuring was inevitable, but that the 1992 target date would at least give workers an opportunity to anticipate the problems, plan a response, and win concessions.

Although an "anti-1992" backlash is likely, and many Europeans anticipate that the larger countries, including Mitterrand's France and Mrs. Thatcher's Great Britain, will become more zealous in guarding their national sovereignty, there is a widespread belief that the plan will gradually be implemented. According to Delors, there can be no turning back to a fractured, defensive, and economically weak Europe. Progress towards European unity is inevitable, he has insisted. In early 1989 the initiatives lost some momentum when Great Britain and France objected to unifying value-added tax rates in the European Community. Prime Minister Rocard of France suggested that the lowering of France's indirect taxes could "pauperize" the state.

"A short, neat figure with a mellifluous voice," according to James Markham, Delors speaks with "fervent intensity." His only language, besides French, is broken English. He is described by a colleague as "a very emotional man, capable of great gloom when things are going wrong and elation when they are going right." He often works fourteen-hour days, and he inspires loyalty from those who work under him. When he resigned from Mitterrand's government, "hundreds of secretaries and fonctionnaires hung from the windows of the Finance Ministry and applauded as he walked by," a reporter for Business Week (December 31, 1984) observed. Margaret Thatcher excepted, he gets along well with the conservative leaders in the European Community. "It is more important in this job to rally and convince than to shine," he told Markham, in a conversation for the New York Times (July 28, 1988). "If you become charismatic, you bother the governments."

Delors and his wife, the former Marie Lephaille, whom he wed in 1948, have one daughter, Martine. Their son, Jean-Paul, died several years ago of cancer. When not working, Delors enjoys movies, jazz, soccer, and the annual Tour de France. He crams a half hour of exercise into every morning, despite his heavy workload and frequent travel. Delors is the author of three books: Les Indicateurs Sociaux (1971), Changer (1975), and En sortir ou pas (1985), written with Philippe Alexandre. He has an honorary law degree from the University of Glasgow and is a chevalier in the Legion d'honneur.

References: Bsns W p55 D 31 '84; Christian Sci Mon p7 Ap 11 '83; France p28+ Spring '87; Le Maclean p30+ O '74 por; N Y Times p4 Jl 28 '88; Newsweek 113:32+ F 6 '89 pors; Wall St J p34 Ja 19 '84, A p10 Je 14 '89; International Who's Who, 1989-90

Diddley, Bo

Dec. 30, 1928– Musician; singer; songwriter.
Address: c/o Talent Consultants International
Ltd., 200 W. 57th St., New York, N.Y. 10019

One of the most influential artists in the history of American popular music is the legendary blues guitarist Bo Diddley, whose 1955 debut recording established the so-called Bo Diddley beat. Over the succeeding three decades, most of the major figures in rock-'n'-roll, including the Rolling Stones, the Who, and Bruce Springsteen, have either recorded Diddley's songs or written songs of their own based on that beat. Bo Diddley was the first guitarist to punctuate his performances with undulating body motions and the first to wield his guitar in a suggestive way—two techniques later aped by other artists. The composer of such instantly recognizable rock standards as "Who Do You Love," "I'm a Man," and "Mona," Diddley was inducted into the Rock-'n'-Roll Hall of Fame in 1987.

Bo Diddley was born Ellas Bates McDaniel on December 30, 1928 in Magnolia, Mississippi. When his father died shortly afterwards, his sixteen-year-old mother took her son to live in the nearby town of McComb, but, because she was unable to support him there, she left him in the care of her cousin, Gussie McDaniel. Accounts vary as to how the guitarist acquired his nickname. According to some sources, since he was a rambunctious child, he was nicknamed "bow diddley," black slang, meaning a mischievous, or "bully," boy. Other sources say the sobriquet refers to a type of homemade, single-string guitar called a "diddley bow," which is played by many novice Mississippi bluesmen. Diddley himself has said that he acquired the nickname in his youth, during his brief venture into

boxing. Bo Diddley sounded to him like a fighter's name. Gussie McDaniel moved with Bo to Chicago around 1933, as part of a massive black exodus from the Mississippi Delta region, and the youngster grew up on the city's largely black South Side, surrounded by the transplanted culture of his former home.

The McDaniels attended the Ebenezer Baptist Church, where, at age five, Bo Diddley began taking violin lessons from its musical director, O. W. Frederick. He later played in the church orchestra with such proficiency that Gussie McDaniel hoped that her adopted son would pursue a career as a concert violinist, a hope that became sidetracked after he began visiting a "sanctified," or Pentecostal, church near his home. Listening outside the door or standing on a box by a window, he was carried away by the uninhibited service taking place within. "The Baptist church was all stately and calm," he later recalled to the writer Michael Lydon, "but at the sanctified church, everyone was really rockin'." The deafening, pulsating music he heard there inspired him to adopt that beat for his own music.

Diddley first became interested in the guitar at the age of ten, but he continued his violin studies even after his half-sister gave him his first guitar, when he was thirteen. "I played the violin till I was fifteen," he told Bill Braunstein in an interview for the *Chicago Tribune Magazine* (January 6, 1980). "I'll tell you what put the brakes on me. I looked around and didn't see too many black violinists. That's when I grabbed the guitar, 'cause I seen plenty of black guitarists." Among the strong early influences on Bo Diddley were the legendary blues artists Muddy Waters and John Lee Hooker.

Bo Diddley dropped out of Foster Vocational High in Chicago at the age of fifteen. He began playing the guitar on street corners for nickels and dimes and later joined a group called the Langley Avenue Jive Cats, which played at parties, contests, and clubs. By day, he held various jobs, including those of construction worker, truck driver, and boxcar unloader. For a time he was also a light heavyweight boxer, but he gave it up at the age of nineteen because, as he puts it, he "kept getting whupped." His first club engagement, performed under his given name, came in 1951 at Chicago's 708 Club, and he worked at other South Side blues clubs throughout the early 1950s. By 1954 he had assembled a band that included Jerome Green on maracas, Otis Spann on piano, and Billy Boy Arnold on harmonica.

Anxious to increase his earnings and make a name for himself, Diddley, in late 1954, cut a demonstration record of two songs he had written. Although up to that point he had usually played blues in the restrained style of his idol, Muddy Waters, Diddley based his first recording on the exultant, frenetic music that he had heard in the Pentecostal church as a child. In early 1955 he played "Uncle John," one of the cuts from the demonstration recording, for Phil and Leonard Chess of the now defunct Chess Records Company in Chicago, which was in its day one of the nation's most prominent blues labels. The two men were sufficiently impressed to sign him to a contract. A week later, the number was recut under the name "Bo Diddley" and released that spring on the Chess subsidiary label Checker, with another Diddley composition, "I'm a Man," on the flipside. Fortunately for Diddley, white, middle-class teenagers were beginning to show their first collective interest in rhythm-and-blues. With its crunching, gyrating guitar sound, played to an hypnotic, off-center 4/4 beat that became known as the Bo Diddley beat, the single "Bo Diddley" rose to number two on the rhythm-and-blues chart and introduced a new star. "It was all really an accident," Diddley recounted to Braunstein. "I made the record, then went back to work. I didn't even think nothing of it. People would come up to me and say, 'You made a record?' and I would say, 'Yeah, big deal.' Then all of a sudden, boom, it started getting played, and that was it."

The success of his first single established Bo Diddley as one of early rock-'n'-roll's most influential performers. His second single, "Diddley Daddy," reached number eleven on the rhythm-and-blues chart, and his other early records, including "Pretty Thing," "I'm Sorry," and "Crackin'," also sold well. More important, several prominent rock artists of the era quickly picked up on the Bo Diddley beat—often described as resembling the "shave and a haircut, two bits" sound that one might make by bearing down on a car horn or by knocking on a door—and tailored it for their own songs. Among the Bo Diddley beat's earliest converts were the Everly Brothers and the ill-fated rock legend Buddy Holly. The latter recorded his own version of "Bo Diddley" and introduced its beat into a song called "Not Fade Away," which was recorded in 1964 by the Rolling Stones and has been a favorite of countless bands for many years. Other songs that have incorporated the Bo Diddley beat include Johnny Otis's 1957 hit "Willie and the Hand Jive" (recorded in the 1970s by Eric Clapton); "Hey Gyp" (Donovan); "Circle Sky" (the Monkees); "Magic Bus" (the Who); "She's the One" (Bruce Springsteen); and "Lover's Walk" (Elvis Costello).

In 1955 Diddley received his first national television exposure when he appeared on the CBS variety show *Toast of the Town*, hosted by Ed Sullivan. In the same year, he performed for the first time at New York's Carnegie Hall, and, over the next several years, he toured extensively, often as part of shows staged by the disc jockey and impresario Alan Freed. Elvis Presley made it a point to see Diddley at the Apollo Theatre in Harlem whenever his own travels brought him to New York, and he reportedly learned some of the pelvic gyrations for which he later became famous from watching Diddley. Diddley also became known to concertgoers for his array of custom-built guitars, which featured irregularly shaped (usually square or rectangular) bodies, often covered with such materials as fur or leather. Made exclusively for him by the Gretsch Company of Cincinnati, Ohio,

those distinctive guitars adorned the cover of his first album, *Bo Diddley* (1958), and each succeeding album for the next ten years.

When "Say Man," a number built around a series of good-natured insults exchanged between Diddley and Jerome Green, was released as a single in 1959, it became Diddley's first and only top-twenty pop hit and climbed to number three on the rhythm-and-blues chart. The period from 1959 to 1963 saw a softening of musical taste, as most of the harder rhythm-and-blues performers from rock's first wave faded away, but Bo Diddley remained popular. Faithful to his basic sound, he recorded nine albums during that period: *Go Bo Diddley* (1959); *Have Guitar Will Travel* (1959); *Bo Diddley in the Spotlight* (1960); *Bo Diddley Is a Gunslinger* (1960); *Bo Diddley Is a Lover* (1961); *Bo Diddley Is a Twister* (1962); *Bo Diddley & Company* (1962); *Surfin' with Bo Diddley* (1963); and *Bo Diddley's Beach Party* (1963). He scored another hit single in 1962 with "You Can't Judge a Book by Its Cover," written by Willie Dixon.

During the early 1960s, London was a hotbed of musical activity, much of it centered around American rhythm-and-blues. By 1962 young British musicians had begun to form bands built on the music of such rhythm-and-blues artists as Muddy Waters, Chester ("Howlin' Wolf") Burnett, "Little" Walter Jacobs, and Bo Diddley. One of those bands was the Rolling Stones, who included the Bo Diddley tunes "Diddley Daddy," "Cops and Robbers," and "Road Runner" on their first demonstration recording, cut in 1962. The Rolling Stones also recorded Diddley's "Mona" for their 1964 debut album, and they later used the Bo Diddley beat in many of their songs. Among the other British groups of that period who recorded Bo Diddley songs were the Animals, the Yardbirds, the Kinks, and the Moody Blues. When the British rock "invasion" of 1964 and 1965 brought that music to the United States, the writing credit "E. McDaniel" became familiar to millions of American listeners too young to remember the original hit "Bo Diddley." Over the next several years, many American groups recorded Bo Diddley songs, including "Who Do You Love," the most popular Diddley composition among American performers, which was recorded by the Doors, Tom Rush, and Quicksilver Messenger Service.

At the request of President John F. Kennedy, Bo Diddley performed in a private show at the White House in 1962. The following year, he toured Great Britain with the Rolling Stones, the Everly Brothers, and Little Richard. In the mid-1960s he released a collection of his greatest hits and, with Chuck Berry, recorded the extraordinary instrumental album *Two Great Guitars*. After that, however, his recording career faltered, which seemed somewhat ironical given his music's popularity among fellow artists. By 1967 he was also less in demand as a concert performer, finding himself rejected both by black audiences, who considered him an anachronism, and by white listeners, who were more attuned to the then popular "psychedelic" sound. By the early 1970s, Diddley had regained some of his drawing power, and, in 1971, he toured the United States with the renowned rock group Creedence Clearwater Revival. Reviewing a performance in Forest Hills, New York during that tour, Mike Jahn of the *New York Times* (July 19, 1971) observed of Diddley: "Old rock stars tend to repeat, often dully, their original sound. But this man has grown a great deal, and created a powerful blues rock of great imagination." In 1972 Diddley appeared at the prestigious Montreux Jazz Festival in Montreux, Switzerland, and in both 1973 and 1974 he performed at the Monterey Jazz Festival in Monterey, California.

Bo Diddley has appeared in two rock documentaries. In *The Big T.N.T. Show* (1966) he performed with, among others, Ray Charles, Joan Baez, and Ike and Tina Turner. *Let the Good Times Roll* (1973) concluded with Diddley and Chuck Berry enlivening the proceedings with their interpretation of the classic rock number "Johnny B. Goode." In early 1979 Diddley toured the United States with the internationally known British punk band the Clash. He made his first music video in 1983, in a joint venture with George Thorogood. In the same year he had a cameo role in the hit film comedy *Trading Places*, starring Eddie Murphy and Dan Aykroyd. On July 13, 1985 he was one of many artists to perform at the "Live Aid" benefit concert in Philadelphia, singing "Who Do You Love" with Thorogood before 90,000 people and a worldwide television audience numbering in the billions.

In 1985 Bo Diddley marked his thirtieth anniversary as a recording artist with a concert in Irvine, California. His backup band for the event, which was taped for presentation on Home Box Office, the pay-cable television network, included such rock notables as Ron Wood, Mick Fleetwood, and Carl Wilson. Five months after his return from a two-week European tour in August 1986, Diddley was inducted into the Rock-'n'-Roll Hall of Fame at a special ceremony at the Waldorf-Astoria in New York that ended with an all-star jam session featuring Bo Diddley, Bruce Springsteen, Chuck Berry, Smokey Robinson, Keith Richards, and John Fogerty. After making a seven-nation tour of Europe the following spring, he was back in the studio in July 1987 to record a new version of "Who Do You Love" for the movie *La Bamba* (1987).

Named after *Bo Diddley Is a Gunslinger*, one of Diddley's hit recordings of 1960, the first phase of the Gunslingers tour, on which the bluesman collaborated with the Rolling Stones guitarist Ron Wood, began in November 1987 in cities in the eastern and central United States and ended at the Ritz nightclub in New York, where it was taped for an MTV concert special entitled "Live at the Ritz—The Gunslingers Tour." In reviewing an earlier concert at the Ritz, a rock-'n'-roll venue in the East Village, the critic Jon Pareles of the *New York Times* (November 28, 1987) had written of Bo Diddley: "Now his delivery is even heartier [than in the 1950s] and his lead-guitar work never wastes a rough-cut phrase." In March 1988 Diddley and Wood took their Gunslingers tour to Japan for three weeks and then returned to the United States, where they performed in sold-out shows at the Fillmore West in San Francisco and the Palace in Los Angeles. After taking a three-month break, the Gunslingers tour resumed at the Hammersmith Odeon in London on June 28, 1988 and later moved on to five countries in Europe. On January 21, 1989 Diddley was a featured performer, along with Willie Dixon, Sam Moore, Joe Cocker, Ron Wood, and other stars, in "Celebration for Young Americans" at the Washington Convention Center, as part of the gala celebrating the inauguration of President George Bush.

A heavyset, imposing man, Bo Diddley is noted for his trademark horn-rimmed glasses and black Stetson hat. Beginning around 1970, he lived for several years on a ranch in Las Lunas, New Mexico, where in 1974 and 1975 he served as a part-time deputy sheriff. He sold the ranch in 1978 and now lives with his third wife, Kay, on a seventy-two-acre ranch just outside the small town of Hawthorne, Florida. Married since 1960, the couple has two grown daughters, Terri Lynn and Tammi. Diddley also has two children from his first marriage, to Ethel Mae Smith, which ended in divorce.

In early 1989 MCA Records announced plans to release "Bo Diddley: The Chess Box," a double-album compilation of thirty-six Diddley songs, in 1990, and the company has also begun to rerelease his original albums. Diddley still owns all of the one-of-a-kind guitars that helped to make him famous. His instruments are now manufactured by THC Guitars of Nashville, Tennessee, and by an Australian company, Kinman.

References: Chicago Tribune mag p18+ Ja 6 '80 pors; N Y Times C p28 Mr 20 '81 por, C p6 Ag 13 '82 por; Washington Post D p1+ F 16 '79 pors; Colman, Stuart. They Kept on Rockin' (1982); Harris, Sheldon. Blues Who's Who (1980); Tobler, John. Guitar Heroes (1978)

Dixon, Willie

July 1, 1915– Musician; songwriter; record producer. Address: c/o The Cameron Organisation, Inc., 2700 E. Cahuenga Blvd., Suite 4206, Los Angeles, Calif. 90068

With over 300 blues songs to his credit, Willie Dixon has been described as "one of the most quietly influential forces in the shaping of contemporary pop-rock-blues." Although his songs were originally covered in the 1950s by such legendary bluesmen as Muddy Waters and Howlin' Wolf, they did not gain a wide following until such Dixon classics as "Little Red Rooster," "Hoochie Coochie Man," "The Seventh Son," "I Just Want to Make Love to You," and "Bring It on Home" were discovered by

Willie Dixon

the Rolling Stones, Led Zeppelin, the Grateful Dead, and the Yardbirds, among other rock groups, who took to the rough edge and lurching rhythms of his music and to his lyrics, which are replete with sexual metaphors, slang, and humor.

In the 1940s Dixon played the bass fiddle with such groups as the Five Breezes and the Big Three Trio. In the 1950s and 1960s he worked as composer, producer, backup bass musician, and arranger for the Chicago-based Chess Records. But as rock-'n'-roll gained in popularity, Dixon started performing onstage again, both in the United States and abroad, often with the Chicago All-Stars, a group he formed in 1969. In 1988 MCA Records released *Willie Dixon: The Chess Box*, a collection of thirty-six of his best-known and some of his rarest recordings, and in 1989 he won a Grammy Award in the best traditional blues recording category for his album *Hidden Charms*. Dixon devotes an increasing amount of time to his Blues Heaven Foundation, which he established to ensure that the blues are not forgotten. "A lot of young blacks feel the blues are degrading because it was slave music," he said recently. "But blues are the most important music there is. The blues are the roots of all American music."

Born on July 1, 1915 in Vicksburg, Mississippi, Willie James Dixon was one of the fourteen children of Charlie and Daisy (McKenzie) Dixon. Raised on a farm, Dixon picked up from his mother the habit of rhyming everything he said. (Daisy Dixon later published several thin volumes of religious poems.) His first musical influence was a band featuring the blues pianist Little Brother Montgomery, which he followed through the streets of Vicksburg on the days he played hooky from elementary school.

While he was still in school, Dixon began writing poems and songs, including his first commercial success, "The Signifying Monkey," which was inspired by a cartoon that a classmate drew. Dixon had pamphlets of the poem printed and sold them for a nickel apiece. After working on a farm and at other odd jobs around Vicksburg as a child, Dixon lived in Chicago from 1926 to 1929. He held several jobs there and traveled by rail to New York City and back before returning to Vicksburg at the age of fourteen. According to his biographer, Don Snowden, Dixon also served two sentences on Mississippi prison farms, where he was introduced to the deepest form of the blues.

It was when Dixon became a singer of spirituals that he began working formally in music. He joined the Union Jubilee Singers, a Vicksburg-based gospel quartet organized by a local carpenter named Theo Phelps, in the early 1930s. With Phelps's training, Dixon learned to sing harmony, and the group—with Dixon singing bass—attracted a local following and was featured regularly on the Vicksburg radio station WQBC. By that time, Dixon was already a prolific songwriter, selling his tunes for ten to twenty dollars each to local country-and-western groups. Many were adaptations of love poems that he had been writing since his school days. "I used to write a lot of love poems you know," he recalled to Tam Fiofori for a *Melody Maker* (June 26, 1971) profile. "I wrote a lot of these songs, man. . . . I had bags of them, and I just thought nothing of them." Dixon had no formal publishing arrangement and no means of collecting money for any performances of his songs, since at the time, the only performing rights organization was ASCAP, the American Society of Composers, Authors, and Publishers, which favored more traditional popular songs over country-and-western music.

Indeed, Dixon left Mississippi for Chicago in 1936 to pursue a boxing career. He won the novice division of the Illinois State Golden Gloves Heavyweight Championship in 1937, under the name James Dixon, and served as a sparring partner for heavyweight boxing champion Joe Louis. His boxing career ended when he picked a fight with his manager after finding out that he was being cheated.

Fate intervened in the person of Leonard ("Baby Doo") Caston, a musician who spent a lot of time at the gym where Dixon trained. "Baby Doo Caston . . . used to sit around the gymnasium playing the guitar and he'd sing a lot," Dixon told Tam Fiofori. "And so he told me: 'Dixon, if I could get you to go out just to sing bass with me, we could make money.'" Dixon, who had continued to sing occasionally with various vocal groups, agreed, and the two began to work local clubs. Dixon sang bass until Caston built him his first instrument, a single-string washtub bass. In 1939 Dixon and Caston organized the Five Breezes, a group that made the rounds of taverns, playing improvised instruments. They were hired by Jim Martin, who ran a club on Chicago's West Side and bought Dixon his first bass fiddle. The Five Breezes were engaged for a two-year residency at Martin's club, and Dixon made his recording debut with the group in November 1940, when they cut eight sides for Bluebird Records.

In late 1941 the Five Breezes broke up, partly as a result of Dixon's arrest for refusing induction into the armed forces. "I told them I was a conscientious objector, and wasn't gonna fight for anybody," he told Snowden. After a year of legal wrangling, Dixon was freed. He later organized a group called the Four Jumps of Jive, which recorded four songs for the Chicago-based Mercury label in 1945. By the end of that year, however, Dixon was again teamed with Caston in a group called the Big Three Trio, which also featured the guitarist Bernardo Dennis.

The Big Three Trio, with Ollie Crawford replacing Bernardo Dennis the next year, worked local clubs in the Chicago area from 1946 to 1952 and developed a following based on their mix of harmony vocals and traditional blues. The group often jammed with other local blues musicians and occasionally played club dates in the Midwest and the Rocky Mountain region. The trio cut its first record, a version of Dixon's "Signifying Monkey" (also called "You Call Yourself the Jungle King, But You Ain't a Doggone Thing"), for the Bullet label in Memphis, Tennessee in 1946. The record sold 40,000 copies, comparable to 500,000 copies in the late 1980s. Moving to Columbia Records later in the year, the group re-recorded "Signifying Monkey" as the B-side of their rendition of "Wee Wee Baby, You Sure Look Good to Me," written by Joe Turner and Pete Johnson. In 1947 Dixon recorded with Memphis Slim and His House Rockers on the Chicago-based Miracle label.

It was during this period that Dixon met Leonard and Phil Chess, two Polish immigrants who ran El Mocambo, a club where Dixon occasionally played. They saw that Dixon was an experienced session musician with a good ear for talent and arrangements: he had served as backup for a number of Chicago blues artists for the Bluebird and Okeh labels. In 1947 the Chess brothers started a blues label called Aristocrat, and in 1950 they renamed the company Chess Records, which became the focal point for recordings by Chicago's blues stars. In 1948 Dixon produced his first session for Aristocrat, directing the recording of the blues singer Robert Nighthawk's single "Little Black Angel."

Dixon worked for Chess when he could, since most of his time was devoted to playing with the Big Three Trio. After the group broke up in 1951 because of Caston's marital problems, Dixon worked full-time for Chess. From 1951 to 1954 he was one of the label's busiest producers, session musicians, and talent scouts. He also continued to record music as a vocalist and musician. Champion Jack Dupree's "Walkin' the Blues," with Fred Below on the drums, was one tune that made it to the charts. Dixon also continued to write songs, although he had difficulty persuading artists to record them, until the Mississippi-born bluesman Muddy Waters agreed to record, in January 1954,

Dixon's "Hoochie Coochie Man," a song steeped in male sexuality and southern mysticism. At that session, which Dixon produced, Dixon played bass while Waters played the guitar and sang the song's swaggering lyrics, which begin: "A gypsy woman told my mama, before I was born / You got a boy child coming, / He gonna be a son of a gun / He gonna make pretty women jump and shout / And the world will want to know, what it's all about / Now I'm here." The combination of the two bluesmen proved to be a winning formula, and the song sold over 75,000 copies.

From then on, Dixon spent more time supervising sessions and playing bass on other artists' recordings of his own songs, including "Seventh Son," by Willie Mabon; "When the Lights Go Out," by Jimmy Witherspoon; "Mellow Down Easy," by Little Walter and His Jukes; and "Evil," by Howlin' Wolf. Chess Records capitalized on the Dixon-Waters combination, releasing "I Just Want to Make Love to You" and "I'm Ready" in 1954, with the former becoming one of Muddy Waters's most famous songs. In January 1955 the harmonica player Little Walter Jacobs recorded one of Dixon's biggest hits, "My Babe," which became Dixon's first song to reach number one on the rhythm-and-blues charts. Dixon's reputation as Chess's most successful blues composer was established, although he often had to use reverse psychology to persuade an artist to record his music. "A lot of times if I picked a song, the guy didn't want the song for himself," Dixon explained to his biographer, Don Snowden. "You'd have to use backwards psychology. I'd say this is a song for Muddy Waters if I wanted Howlin' Wolf to do it because they seemed to have a little thing going between them. I had been trying to give Little Walter 'My Babe' because of his style of doing things, but he fought it for two long years. I wasn't going to give it to anybody but him."

In spite of his success as a songwriter in the years from 1954 to 1957, Dixon was overshadowed at Chess by the rock-'n'-roll artists Chuck Berry and Bo Diddley. Dixon played bass on Chuck Berry's first Chess session, in May 1955, which produced the label's (and Berry's) first rock-'n'-roll hit, "Maybelline." Dixon was a virtual fixture at Berry's sessions through the early 1960s, playing bass—often with his own two sidemen, drummer Fred Below and pianist Lafayette Leake—on such Berry hits as "Roll over Beethoven" and "Sweet Little Sixteen." For Bo Diddley, Dixon managed many of that artist's recording sessions and provided him with two of his most popular songs, "Pretty Thing" (1955) and "You Can't Judge a Book by Its Cover" (1962).

From 1957 until 1959 Dixon worked as producer, arranger, and songwriter for the new, rival Cobra label, providing Otis Rush with a hit in "I Can't Quit You Baby" and supervising recording sessions for such figures as Magic Sam and Buddy Guy. When Cobra encountered financial problems, however, he returned to Chess in 1959, where he produced Howlin' Wolf's recordings of Dixon's

"Spoonful" and "Back Door Man" (both in 1960) and "I Ain't Superstitious" and "Little Red Rooster" (both in 1961), with Dixon embellishing on his stop-time technique by adding "lurching, herky-jerky rhythms" to "Back Door Man" and "I Ain't Superstitious," as Don Snowden explained. Other songs that Dixon wrote and produced in the early 1960s—his boom years as a songwriter—included "You Know My Love" (1960), by Otis Rush, and Muddy Waters's "You Need Love" and "You Shook Me" (both in 1962). He also wrote "Bring It on Home" (1963) for Sonny Boy Williamson, "Built for Comfort" (1963) for Howlin' Wolf, with horns taking the place of the harmonica, and "Wang Dang Doodle" (1965) for Koko Taylor.

Meanwhile, the Chicago blues were catching on in the rest of the United States and in England. A large white American audience discovered the music, thanks to events such as Muddy Waters's appearance at the 1960 Newport Folk Festival. Dixon and other blues greats, among them Big Bill Broonzy, Muddy Waters, Howlin' Wolf, and Memphis Slim, toured England as living legends in the late 1950s and early 1960s, and, in the wake of their performances and recordings, a new generation of musicians was introduced to such Dixon classics as "Hoochie Coochie Man," "My Babe," "Spoonful," and "I Just Want to Make Love to You." As a result, Dixon's songs became part of rock's standard repertoire.

The downhome raunchy lyrics of Dixon's "Little Red Rooster," for instance, had particular appeal to the Rolling Stones, who recorded the song at Chess in November 1963 and saw it climb to the top of the British singles charts in late 1964. A 1963 recording of the same song by the rhythm-and-blues singer Sam Cooke reached number seven on *Billboard*'s R&B charts and number eleven on its "Hot 100" pop charts. The Doors' rendition of "Back Door Man" on their 1967 debut album became a concert standard, as did "Spoonful," which was recorded by Cream.

Not all of the rock adaptations of Dixon's work were credited to him, a situation that twice resulted in legal action. In the early 1970s ARC Music sued the heavy-metal band Led Zeppelin, claiming that the songs "Bring It on Home" and "The Lemon Song," from the album *Led Zeppelin II*, were adapted from songs by Dixon and Howlin' Wolf. That case was settled out of court in 1972, as was another suit filed against the group by Dixon in 1985. The second suit claimed that "Whole Lotta Love," from *Led Zeppelin II*, was taken from his "You Need Love."

Rock's preeminence rejuvenated Dixon's career as a singer and recording artist, although it signaled the end of his backup work, since the harsher sound of rock required an electric bass. Dixon appeared with the Elmore James Broomdusters in Chicago during 1955 and toured Florida, Texas, and Mississippi with Otis Rush in a series of one-night engagements during 1956 and 1957. It was with Memphis Slim, however, that Dixon got the greatest exposure. The two appeared at Chicago's

Gate of Horn club at various times in 1959 and 1960, played concerts together in England and on the European continent in 1960, and appeared on NBC's *Today Show* in the same year. They also recorded together on the Bluesville label in 1959 and on the Verve/Folkways label in 1960.

Dixon toured Europe and America regularly throughout the 1960s, both with Memphis Slim and as part of the package shows Rhythm & Blues USA in 1962 and the Folk Blues Festival in 1963 and 1964. As part of the latter, he appeared on the British Granada television special *I Hear the Blues* (1963). He was also featured in the Canadian Broadcasting Corporation's *Festival Presents the Blues* (1966). In 1964 he became musical director for the Chicago-based Spivey label, and he recorded there in 1964 and 1969. Chess Records started to decline in the late 1960s, and Dixon severed his ties with the company after Leonard Chess died, in 1969. In 1968 he formed the Chicago Blues All-Stars, whose members, in addition to Dixon on bass and vocals, originally included Lafayette Leake at the piano, Shakey Horton on harmonica, Clifton James on drums, and Lee Jackson on guitar.

Dixon's first official studio album, *I Am the Blues*, released by Columbia in 1970, contained nine of his hits and prompted Don Heckman of the *New York Times* (April 5, 1970) to note that "Dixon's vocal skills are not exactly the equal of his songwriting abilities." He toured the United States, Canada, and Europe in the first half of the 1970s and played a series of concerts in Australia and New Zealand with the All-Stars in 1974. Cast in the role of an elder statesman of the blues, Dixon earned praise from critics for his habit of presenting running monologues during a set. "He plays . . . a standup wood bass," Jack Batten wrote in the Toronto *Globe and Mail* (July 15, 1970), describing a performance at the Colonial in Toronto, Canada, "and he sings with a surprisingly high-pitched, keening voice. He also talks a great deal, unlike most other blues men, and on his first set Monday night . . . , he offered a rambling patter between songs that worked into a kind of minor history of the blues." In the 1970s Dixon's film appearances included the British *Chicago Blues* (1970), *Out of the Blacks into the Blues* (1972), and the PBS-TV *Soundstage* (1974).

The amputation of his right leg (due to diabetes) in 1977 barely slowed Dixon down, as Basco Eszeki reported in *Living Blues* (Summer 1979) about a July 5, 1979 performance at Chicago's First National Plaza: "Willie's enthusiasm was evident from the way he moved about the stage like a benevolent bear, wearing a wide smile, leading the audience in clapping with the beat, and waving [the band members] on to play a few more bars of particularly hot solos."

During the 1970s, Dixon began legal action that culminated in a settlement in 1977 that gave him a greater share of songwriting royalties and allowed him to reclaim the copyrights on his songs—some 250 in number—from ARC Music. Dixon's 1978 album *What Happened to My Blues* (Ovation), made up of such numbers as "Pretty Baby" and "Uh Huh My Baby," earned him a Grammy nomination. He released the album *Mighty Earthquake and Hurricane* (Pausa) in the early 1980s. His 1986 album *Backstage Access—Live at Montreux* (Pausa) received another Grammy nomination and led to his appearance on the 1987 Grammy Awards telecast. He has also appeared with Eric Clapton and the 1980s rock-'n'-roll band Los Lobos. In 1981 he toured with Muddy Waters on the East Coast, their only appearances on stage together, culminating in four sold-out shows at the Roxy in Los Angeles.

In 1988 MCA Records, which owns the Chess catalogue, released a thirty-six-song collection entitled *Willie Dixon: The Chess Box*, a compilation of the most famous as well as some of the rarest recordings of his songs. The first production run of the three-LP-double-compact disc set sold out immediately. The collection includes one of the Big Three Trio's last recordings together, of Dixon's "Violent Love" (1951), as well as the previously unreleased Dixon recordings of "Crazy for My Baby" (1953), "Walkin' the Blues" (1955), and "29 Ways" (1956), with the pianist Lafayette Leake and Ollie Crawford on the backup, and "Pain in My Heart" (1951), with Crawford, Leake, the drummer Fred Below, and the saxophonist Harold Ashby.

Also in 1988 Capitol Records issued a new Dixon album, *Hidden Charms*, and Prestige/Bluesville reissued *Willie's Blues*, Dixon's first album as a bandleader, which was originally released in 1959. Dixon's 1963 number "Built for Comfort" received a fresh rendition in 1988 by the country-rock singer Dianne Davidson. His songs have also been covered in recent years by artists as diverse as the country singer John Anderson and the new-wave group the Violent Femmes. A new Dixon song, "Don't You Tell Me Nothing," performed by the composer himself, was featured in the score of Martin Scorsese's film *The Color of Money*. Koko Taylor's version of "Evil" appeared in the film *Adventures in Babysitting*, and Hoyt Axton's rendition of "Built for Comfort" in *Heart Like a Wheel*. The director Taylor Hackford asked Dixon to produce a new version of the Bo Diddley classic "Who Do You Love" for the 1987 film *La Bamba*. Dixon's life story was presented in an installment of the public-television series *Were You There?*, and, with "Baby Doo" Caston, he appeared in *I Am the Blues*, a concert-interview feature that has been aired regularly on cable television.

In 1982, in an effort to preserve the living memory of the blues, Dixon established the Blues Heaven Foundation. That organization has donated instruments from the Yamaha Music Corporation to high schools in Chicago and in Dixon's hometown of Vicksburg. Blues Heaven provides educational and legal assistance to blues artists, helps established performers and songwriters secure their rightful royalties, and documents and preserves blues performances. In 1988 the foundation created a $2,000 scholarship in honor of Muddy Waters, who died in 1983, for Chicago-area college students. Dixon talks regularly to student groups,

emphasizing the importance of the blues to American culture. His autobiography, "The Willie Dixon Story," written with Don Snowden, is scheduled for publication by Quartet Books in 1989.

Dixon began 1989, his seventy-fourth year, on a high note as a featured star of the "Celebration for Young Americans," the January 21 rhythm-and-blues show held at the Washington Convention Center in Washington, D.C., to celebrate the inauguration of President George Bush. Greg Tate of the *Village Voice* (February 7, 1989) wrote of that performance: "Willie Dixon, the Duke Ellington of Chicago blues, magisterially took the stage with Koko Taylor, propped up on a cane, dragging one leg behind him. . . . When the music got Dixon going he forgot he needed a cane, and bopped around the stage as spry as a spring chicken."

Described by one interviewer as "big, merry-faced, and sort of shy," Dixon still lives in Chicago for part of the year. He and his second wife, Marie, also maintain a home in Glendale, in southern California. Dixon reportedly has fourteen children, and his son Freddie Dixon is a bass player who has performed with the Chicago All-Stars. Dixon continues to write songs. "The biggest of my songs haven't come out of the drawer yet," he told a reporter for the *Pittsburgh Press*. "I write songs about every day or every other day. I just look at the various parts of life and the songs are there."

References: *Billboard* 79:21+ Je 24 '67; *Melody Maker* 46:21 Je 26 '71, 46:14 Jl 3 '71; Harris, S. *Blues Who's Who* (1979); Snowden, Don. *Willie Dixon: The Chess Box* album notes (1988); *Who's Who in America*, 1988–89

Dodd, Christopher J(ohn)

May 27, 1944– United States Senator from Connecticut. Address: 324 Hart Senate Office Bldg., Washington, D.C. 20510; h. East Haddam, Conn. 06423

Since 1980, when he bucked the conservative tide that accompanied the landslide of Ronald Reagan to become, at thirty-six years old, the youngest United States senator ever elected from Connecticut, Christopher J. Dodd has emerged as the Democratic party's principal strategist and spokesman for Central American affairs. He consistently opposed Reagan's efforts to arm the Contra rebels in Nicaragua, and in 1981 he handed the administration its first defeat in a foreign-policy dispute with Congress by engineering passage of a bill that tied military aid to El Salvador with that nation's progress on human rights. With the Democratic takeover of the Senate in 1986, he became chairman of the Western Hemisphere Affairs Subcommittee of the Senate Foreign Relations Committee, using it as the forum through which he has urged both the Reagan and Bush administrations to seek

Christopher J. Dodd

a peaceful and comprehensive solution to the social, political, and economic problems of Central America. In the area of domestic issues, Dodd has focused his energies on matters affecting children. He has deliberately avoided scattering his efforts across a broad range of issues, preferring instead to cultivate a reputation as an authority in select fields. "The most effective members of Congress," he has said, "are the ones who really try and focus in on a few issues. You can be a far better contributor institutionally if you limit yourself, develop some expertise."

Christopher John Dodd was born in Willimantic, Connecticut on May 27, 1944, the fifth of the six children of Thomas Joseph and Grace (Murphy) Dodd. His father, a Democrat from Connecticut, served in the United States House of Representatives from 1953 to 1957 and in the Senate from 1959 to 1971. He was censured in 1967 for converting campaign contributions to his personal use and died four years later.

Christopher Dodd was born with a caul, a legendary harbinger of good fortune that prompted the attending physician to speculate in the presence of Grace Dodd that her infant might grow up to be president. "What's the matter with Roosevelt?" Mrs. Dodd is said to have replied. One of Christopher Dodd's earliest memories is that of listening to his father retail the horrors of the Holocaust, which he had learned of in grisly detail as executive trial counsel to the chief prosecutor at the Nuremberg trials of Nazi war criminals. "Christy," as he was called as a child, spent his early years in West Hartford, Connecticut, growing up in a rambling white house on Concord Street amid the comings and goings of political advisers and spirited discussions of current affairs. He got his

first taste of campaigning at the age of eight by passing out leaflets for his father's first race for Congress.

When his father entered the United States Senate in 1959, the family moved to the Georgetown section of Washington, D.C. Dodd attended Georgetown Preparatory School, a Jesuit academy in nearby Rockville, Maryland, where he earned the nickname "Frosty" for his reputed ability to "snow," or glibly deceive, others. Following his graduation in 1962, he enrolled as an English literature major at Providence College, his father's alma mater, in Providence, Rhode Island, where he was an unexceptional student. "I had a wonderful time," he recalled of his days on the Roman Catholic campus for Elisabeth Bumiller of the Washington Post (July 13, 1983). "I studied, but I wasn't a bookworm. I mean, I didn't take it seriously." Because his father was one of the Senate's most ardent supporters of President Lyndon B. Johnson's policy in Vietnam, he helped to organize a prowar rally at the Rhode Island state capitol in 1965. During the second semester of his senior year, the muckraking columnists Drew Pearson and Jack Anderson ran a series of articles charging that Senator Thomas J. Dodd had used $116,000 in campaign contributions to pay personal bills, including his son's air transportation between Washington and Providence. When the growing scandal moved Providence College officials to withdraw their invitation for Senator Dodd to deliver the commencement address that year, Christopher Dodd was so furious that he skipped his graduation ceremonies and never returned to the campus until 1983, and then only because the college president agreed to say a few kind words about his late father.

As a Peace Corps volunteer from 1966 to 1968, Dodd was assigned to Monción, a village in the northwestern mountains of the Dominican Republic. Living alone in a cold-water tin-roof house, he served as a rural community developer for eleven villages encompassing 20,000 people. During his brief time there, he opened a school, a youth club, and a maternity hospital and launched a family planning program. Confronted as he was by grinding poverty, social injustice, and anti-Americanism for the first time in his life, Dodd began to have doubts about his father's simplistic worldview, which blamed much of the region's social unrest on communist agitation. "Growing up in a fairly affluent, sheltered environment, going to a Jesuit boarding school and a Catholic college, I never even saw blacks or Hispanics," he explained to Robert Friedman for Esquire (August 1983). "Then all of a sudden, living in this different society on a day-to-day basis—it was, I say this without any hesitation, the best experience of my life. It's affected everything I've done since."

One day in June 1967 Dodd picked up a Spanish-language newspaper carrying a photo of his father on its front page and learned that two days earlier Thomas J. Dodd had been censured by the Senate by a vote of ninety-two to five. Stunned by the news and feeling somewhat guilty for not having been at his father's side during the painful ordeal, he believed, and continues to believe, that his father was the victim of changing standards of official conduct and treacherous staff members who leaked incriminating documents to the columnists Pearson and Anderson. He has never forgotten the handful of senators who publicly defended his father.

At the end of his stint with the Peace Corps, Dodd hitchhiked his way across thousands of miles in Latin America before returning home on Christmas Eve in 1968. The following spring, he enlisted in the National Guard and underwent basic training at Fort Dix, New Jersey. He worked briefly as a part-time reporter for the *Northern Virginia Sun* in Arlington, Virginia, and in 1970 he campaigned for his father in his foredoomed bid to retain his Senate seat. That fall he entered the University of Louisville Law School, and, following his graduation in 1972 and his admission to the Connecticut bar the following year, he joined a law firm in New London, Connecticut.

Although Dodd had assured the firm's partners that he had no political plans, he was persuaded in 1974 by Al Goodin, one of his father's campaign aides, to run for the open House seat from Connecticut's Second Congressional District, comprising the largely rural eastern third of the state. Having won his party's nomination over two other major contenders, Dodd rolled over his Republican challenger, Samuel B. Hellier, with 60 percent of the vote, thanks in part to the GOP's troubles in the wake of the Watergate scandal. During his three terms in the House, Dodd seemed content to build his seniority quietly as the second-youngest member ever to serve on the influential Rules Committee. Because the function of the Rules Committee is to set the course of legislation through the House, a decision that can make or break a bill, Dodd avoided what he regarded as a potential conflict of interest by refusing to sponsor legislation that he later would have to consider on the rules panel. Unabashedly liberal despite the conservative tendency of his district, he championed human rights around the globe, pressed for assistance to the poor in meeting the soaring costs of fuel, and promoted the Peace Corps. He also intervened to help settle two strikes at the Electric Boat Company in Groton, the largest employer in his district.

With the announced retirement of Democratic senator Abraham A. Ribicoff of Connecticut in 1980, Dodd struck a deal with Democratic congressman Tobey Moffett of Connecticut's Sixth Congressional District, in which Moffett agreed not to challenge Dodd for the Democratic senatorial nomination and Dodd pledged to support Moffett in a bid to unseat Republican senator Lowell P. Weicker Jr. two years later. (Moffett upheld his end of the bargain, but Dodd, the Moffett forces later charged, offered only tepid support in 1982.) Nominated by acclamation at the state party convention in July 1980, Dodd paid homage to his father in his acceptance speech but denied that he was running for the Senate simply to vindicate Thomas Dodd.

In the general election campaign against Republican James L. Buckley, who had served a term as senator from New York, Dodd scored heavily with voters by contrasting his service in the state with Buckley's sudden interest in Connecticut affairs. Buckley, in turn, tried to tie Dodd to the unpopular Carter administration by making pointed references to failed "Carter-Dodd" policies. Buckley condemned Dodd's liberal voting record and even went so far as to suggest that, if the hawkish senator Thomas J. Dodd were still alive, he would vote against his own son. Such tactics failed to impress voters, however, and as Dodd pulled out to a substantial lead in the polls he began to devote more and more of his time to campaigning for Carter's reelection. Although Carter lost Connecticut decisively and the Republicans took control of the Senate for the first time in a generation, Dodd coasted to a 56 to 43 percent victory. In 1986 he was reelected with 65 percent of the vote, a record for a Connecticut Senate race, over former state representative Roger W. Eddy.

It was an emotional moment in the Senate as Dodd, wearing his father's watch fob and in possession of his father's chair on the floor, took the oath of office precisely one decade after the elder Dodd had left in disgrace. Democratic senator Russell B. Long of Louisiana, one of the few to speak out against the censure, offered to introduce a resolution exonerating him. "Russell," the younger Dodd said, "you don't have to. Every time I walk in there, it's a resolution."

Unwilling this time to play the role of a docile backbencher as he had in the House, Dodd became a high-profile player during his first months in the Senate and was named by his colleagues as one of the three most effective freshman senators, in a *U.S News & World Report* survey. Assigned to the Foreign Relations Committee, he closely questioned Ernest Lefever at his confirmation hearing to become assistant secretary of state in the new Reagan administration. Bearing down on a potential conflict of interest involving Lefever's association with the Nestlé Corporation, Dodd elicited damaging testimony that led to the committee's rejection of the nomination and Lefever's eventual withdrawal. In the same year he steered through the Republican-controlled Senate the first foreign-policy rebuff of the Reagan administration. Over the vigorous objections of Secretary of State Alexander M. Haig, Dodd won overwhelming committee approval for a certification bill that threatened to cut off military aid to El Salvador unless that country continued making progress on human rights and economic and political reform. Although Dodd resisted liberal pressure to mandate a cutoff of funds if El Salvador failed to cooperate for fear of losing Republican support, the bill required the president to certify whether El Salvador was taking steps to comply with internationally recognized human rights standards, to exert civilian control over the military, to press forward with land reform, and to hold free elections.

But when President Reagan certified in 1982 that El Salvador was in compliance with those restrictions, Dodd denounced the administration for overlooking evidence of an increase in government-inspired violence and torture and for making little progress in economic reforms, and he went on to oppose, with mixed success, substantial military assistance to that country. Dodd also was among the first to call for an end to arms shipments to the Contra rebels fighting to overthrow the Marxist-led Sandinista regime in Nicaragua. Throughout the Reagan terms, Dodd appeared frequently on television news interview shows as a counterweight to administration spokespersons on Central American affairs.

In April 1983, in recognition of his growing role as the party's primary authority on the troubled region, the Democratic leadership in Congress selected Dodd to deliver a ten-minute televised response to President Reagan's plea for more military assistance for El Salvador. In a controversial address, Dodd condemned the administration for seeking a military solution to poverty and social injustice and raised the specter of another Vietnam. "Instead of trying to do something about the factors which breed revolution," Dodd charged, "this administration has turned to massive military buildups at a cost of hundreds of millions of dollars. Its policy is ever-increasing military assistance, endless military training, even hiring our own paramilitary guerrillas. This is a formula for failure. And it is a proven prescription for picking a loser. The American people know that we have been down this road before—and that it only leads to a dark tunnel of endless intervention."

Dodd pointed out that the administration was asking for $140,000 per Sandinista guerrilla at the same time, he charged, that the Salvadoran oligarchy was stashing a fortune in Swiss bank accounts and government death squads were slaughtering tens of thousands of civilians, including American nuns and labor advisers. He depicted in graphic detail how Salvadoran security forces, using American weapons, had murdered suspected opposition members: "gangland style—the victim on bended knee, thumbs wired behind the back, a bullet through the brain." He went on to urge the administration to foster a negotiated settlement between Nicaragua and El Salvador.

Although reaction to the speech split largely along party lines, even some Democrats, most notably Senator Lloyd Bentsen of Texas and House Majority Leader Jim Wright of Texas, criticized its strident tone. Nevertheless, Dodd continued to press for a negotiated settlement and eventually came to oppose even humanitarian aid for the Contras. In 1984 Dodd's views formed the basis of the Central American plank of the Democratic party's platform.

Following the Democratic takeover of the Senate in the 1986 elections, Dodd assumed the chairmanship of the Foreign Relations Subcommittee on Western Hemisphere Affairs from the ultraconservative Jesse A. Helms of North Carolina. Dodd's practice of traveling frequently to Central America to meet with government leaders drew the ire of Secretary of State George P. Shultz, who denounced lawmakers, without naming Dodd directly, for trying to run their "own foreign policy." In 1987 Dodd was named chairman of the Central American Negotiations Observer Group, a bipartisan panel of senators created to monitor peace talks among Guatemala, El Salvador, Honduras, Nicaragua, and Costa Rica. That was the first time in memory that Congress had ever monitored international discussions in which the United States was not a direct participant.

Although Dodd has made his reputation in foreign policy, he also has emerged in recent years as a champion of children. While the Democrats were in the minority during the first six years of the Reagan administration, Dodd grew so frustrated trying to persuade the majority on the Labor and Human Resources Committee to hold hearings on a variety of issues affecting children that he, together with Republican Arlen Specter of Pennsylvania, founded the Children's Caucus, which held rump hearings on child abuse, the problems of latch-key children, and the alarming high school dropout rate. Following the Democratic takeover in 1986, Dodd assumed the chairmanship of the Subcommittee on Children, Families, Drugs, and Alcoholism. With Republican Orrin G. Hatch of Utah, he cosponsored the Act for Better Child Care, providing tax credits for day care and children's health insurance, which passed the Senate in June 1989 but faced an uncertain future in the House.

Politically, Dodd has demonstrated a willingness to buck the establishment. He supported Senator Edward M. Kennedy's challenge to the renomination of President Jimmy Carter in 1980 and was the first senator to endorse Gary Hart for president in 1984. Dodd's voting record has consistently won high marks from liberal rating groups. He opposed the Reagan defense buildup (except for the development of the Trident submarine, which is built in his district) and the broad tax cuts of the 1980s and, despite his Roman Catholic faith, has supported a woman's right to choose abortion. He broke Democratic ranks, however, to support the nomination of former senator John G. Tower to be secretary of defense. Many observers believed that he did so because Tower was among the handful of senators to oppose the censure of his father.

Christopher J. Dodd has been described as gregarious, brash, ambitious, and possessed of a childlike curiosity. His distinguished bearing belies a puckish sense of humor. In 1978, for example, he ended a long day of political meetings in Memphis by launching a food fight at an all-night Dunkin Donuts shop. He is an effective orator but less impressive in small groups. "Give me a room with 1,500 people," he has said. "I'm terrible with small talk." He speaks Spanish fluently. He married Susan Mooney, a speechwriter for his father, in August 1970. Since their divorce in 1982, he has been romantically linked with various women, including, briefly, Bianca Jagger, the former wife of rock star Mick Jagger. He lives in a converted nineteenth-century schoolhouse overlooking the Connecticut River in East Haddam, Connecticut.

References: Esquire 100:64+ Ag '83 por; Washington Post D p1+ Jl 13 '83 pors; Almanac of American Politics, 1988; Politics in America (1988); Who's Who in American Politics, 1989-90

Eastwood, Clint

May 31, 1930– Actor; film producer and director. Address: Malpaso Productions, Warner Brothers Studio, 4000 Warner Blvd., Burbank, Calif. 91522

Note: This biography supersedes the article that appeared in Current Biography in 1971.

Clint Eastwood's status as the world's top box-office attraction has not been accompanied—until recently—by critical acceptance. His on-screen image as a monosyllabic tough guy once prompted a reviewer to assign him to the Mount Rushmore school of acting. But Eastwood understands that the action hero is a man of few words and gestures. "Maybe being an introvert gives me, by sheer accident, a certain screen presence, a mystique," he once explained. "If I threw it all out for them to see, they might not be as interested." That interest has translated into over $1.5 billion that Eastwood's films, including the fourteen he has directed, have grossed. Since the death of John Wayne, he has almost singlehandedly kept the western alive as a commercially viable genre, and no movie cop is more famous than his Dirty Harry: when President Ronald Reagan vowed in 1985 to veto any tax hike,

he challenged Congress to "go ahead and make my day," quoting a line from the fourth Dirty Harry movie, Sudden Impact (1983).

With the introduction of a more conservative political mood in the early 1980s, film critics in the United States and abroad have reassessed Eastwood as a movie director and actor, finding "self-parodying subtlety" and "hidden depths" in his more personal films, in which he plays characters against type, such as a troubled detective in Tightrope (1984) and a dreamer running a tatty Wild West show in Bronco Billy (1980). In his most popular film, Every Which Way But Loose (1978), he shared the spotlight with an orangutan. Most recently, Eastwood has won acclaim for his direction of Bird (1988), a portrait of the legendary jazz musician Charlie Parker, which was featured at the New York Film Festival and the Metropolitan Museum of Art before its commercial run began. Taking on a new role, Eastwood spent two years as the much-publicized mayor of Carmel, California, from 1986 to 1988.

Clinton Eastwood Jr. was born in San Francisco, California on May 31, 1930, the older child of Clinton and Ruth Eastwood. (He has a younger sister, Jeanne.) During the Great Depression, his father had difficulty finding and keeping jobs. As a result, the family moved from one northern California town to another, with a one-wheel trailer in tow. Clint Eastwood attended some eight different grammar schools during what he has described as an introverted childhood.

When Eastwood was a teenager, his father landed an executive job with the Container Corporation of America, in Oakland, California. Clint took up competitive swimming at the various schools he attended, and he played basketball for Oakland Technical High School. His biggest interest, however, was jazz, and at the age of fifteen he played the piano for free meals at a club in Oakland. After graduating from high school in 1948, he worked as a lumberjack and a forest firefighter in Oregon and as a steelworker in Seattle, determined, in his words, "never to be dependent on anyone else."

Drafted into the army in 1951, during the Korean War, Eastwood never saw combat. En route to Korea, his plane ditched into the Pacific, forcing him to swim a couple of miles to shore. Pending an inquiry that was never held, he was made a swimming instructor at Fort Ord in California, where he met several actors, including Martin Milner and David Janssen, who encouraged him to try his luck in show business. Discharged in 1953, he enrolled in business administration at Los Angeles City College under the G.I. Bill but also began making the rounds of the studios and eventually landed a seventy-five-dollar-a-week contract at Universal Studios.

After eighteen months of playing bit parts in films such as the Francis the Talking Mule series and Revenge of the Creature (1955), Eastwood was dropped by the studio and wound up digging swimming pools in Beverly Hills to make ends meet. He was thinking about returning to college when, while talking to a friend in the cafeteria of the CBS television studios, he was spotted by a producer and tested for the cowboy role of Rowdy Yates in *Rawhide,* a series about cattle drives on the Great Plains that ran from 1959 to 1966.

Those apprentice years brought Eastwood national recognition and established his basic acting style, he told Tim Cahill in an interview for *Newsday* (July 7, 1985). "I became known for the way I act now. I played characters that were not terribly talkative. Economical characters." Eastwood also explained to Cahill that the *Rawhide* series was a valuable training ground. "All of a sudden, everything you ever studied about being an actor you could put into play every day."

But one thing the series failed to provide was career growth, and in 1964, during a four-month break in the *Rawhide* production schedule, Eastwood went to Spain to star for $15,000 in a "spaghetti western" directed by the Italian director Sergio Leone. The plot for that movie, cribbed from Akira Kurosawa's film *Yojimbo,* a samurai story resembling a western, called for Eastwood's character to manipulate, for profit, two families warring against each other in the same town. As the Man With No Name, Eastwood departed from his good-guy *Rawhide* image to become a western hero without the usual heroic attributes. "I was tired of playing the nice clean-cut cowboy in *Rawhide,*" he explained to Arthur Knight in a *Playboy* (February 1974) interview. Although Eastwood's character originally had more lines, the actor persuaded Leone to pare down the script. As he told Tim Cahill, "The script was very expository. . . . It was an outrageous story, and I thought there should be much more mystery to the person."

A Fistful of Dollars (1964) established Eastwood as an international superstar, and the film earned some $7 million in Europe, $4 million in Italy alone. Eastwood returned to Spain during the following two years to complete two sequels: *For A Few Dollars More* (1965), which also starred Lee Van Cleef, and *The Good, the Bad, and the Ugly* (1966), featuring Van Cleef and Eli Wallach. For the latter movie, Eastwood's salary had increased to $250,000, plus a percentage. In another Italian venture, Eastwood appeared in a segment of *The Witches* (1967) entitled "A Night Like Any Other," opposite Silvana Mangano.

Eastwood's overseas acclaim did not carry over to the United States until 1967, when the spaghetti western trilogy was finally released there. After fulfilling his commitment to the waning *Rawhide* series, in which he played the leading role in the last two seasons, Eastwood found himself approached by European distributors who were eager for him to star in an American film. As a result, Eastwood formed his own production company, Malpaso Productions, in 1968 and signed on to make a western for $40,000, plus 25 percent of the profits.

In the resulting *Hang 'Em High* (1968), Eastwood starred as a man who survives his own hanging and seeks revenge on the nine men responsible. Similar to the preceding spaghetti westerns, *Hang 'Em High* featured a new kind of hero—one who drew his gun first. Eastwood later confided, "I do everything that John Wayne would never do. I play the hero but I can shoot a guy in the back." United Artists recouped its investment in ten weeks, and *Hang 'Em High* remains one of its biggest-grossing films.

With *Coogan's Bluff* (1968), Eastwood began a fruitful partnership with the director Don Siegel. In that film, Eastwood took the part of an Arizona lawman who tracks a criminal in New York City, and his performance prompted Vincent Canby to remark in the *New York Times* (October 3, 1968), "Eastwood doesn't act in motion pictures; he is framed in them." *Where Eagles Dare* (1969), a World War II action story, and *Paint Your Wagon,* (1969), a Lerner and Loewe musical in which he sang two numbers, proved unpopular with critics and the general public. Another Don Siegel film, *Two Mules for Sister Sara* (1970), was followed by *Kelly's Heroes* (1970), a World War II story. In *The Beguiled* (1971), Eastwood played a different kind of role—a wounded Union soldier who is victimized by the sex-starved residents of a Confederate girls' boarding school during the Civil War. Although that movie was a commercial failure, Siegel considers it his best work.

By 1969 Eastwood was the world's top box-office draw. Not content with just that distinction, he assumed the role of director as well as that of leading actor in *Play Misty for Me* (1971), the story of a radio disc jockey hounded by a psychopath (Jessica Walter). The film received a lukewarm reception from Eastwood fans, who objected to this departure from his tough-guy roles, but it established his credentials as a director and has since achieved cult status on college campuses.

With *Dirty Harry* (1971), under the direction of Siegel, Clint Eastwood took on a new macho persona as police inspector Harry Callahan. Impatient with the incompetence of bureaucrats, Dirty Harry takes the law into his own hands, using violence to restore order. In *Dirty Harry,* Eastwood disposes of a homicidal maniac who has been on the loose because of the negligence of Harry's ineffectual superiors. The role was vintage Eastwood: a hard-nosed, cynical loner who's willing to bend—or break—the law to protect the weak.

Although Dirty Harry found instant rapport with a public fed up with inner-city crime, Eastwood's critics denounced the actor as a dangerous reactionary, or even a fascist. In the first Dirty Harry sequel, *Magnum Force* (1973), directed by Ted Post, Eastwood responded to his detractors by having Harry defend the system against a vigilante-style squad of police officers. "I hate the goddamn system," Harry says in the sequel. "But until someone comes along with some changes that make sense, I'll stick with it."

The popularity of the Dirty Harry movies at the box office was not matched by accolades from the critics. David Sterritt, for example, writing in the *Christian Science Monitor* (January 15, 1972), described Eastwood's performance in *Dirty Harry* as "flatly uninspired," and Pauline Kael, who remains perhaps the actor's most vociferously negative critic, said outright in the *New Yorker* (January 14, 1974): "Clint Eastwood isn't offensive; he isn't an actor, so one could hardly call him a bad actor. He'd have to *do* something before we could consider him bad at it."

In spite of such negative reviews, Eastwood has consistently appeared in Quigley Publications' annual list of the ten top box-office stars since 1968, and in 1972 he rose to the top of that list, surpassing even megastar John Wayne. It was also in 1972 that Eastwood returned to the western genre, portraying, in *Joe Kidd*, a gunfighter who takes up the cause of oppressed Mexican peasants. In *High Plains Drifter* (1973), he played a ghost who returns from the grave to take revenge on a town that harbored his killers. Eastwood ventured into comedy with *Thunderbolt and Lightfoot* (1974), a story about a Montana bank heist that also starred Jeff Bridges and George Kennedy. Jay Cocks, writing for *Time* (June 10, 1974), was pleasantly surprised to discover a less-wooden performance: "Eastwood unwinds a little from his customary characterization of a terse, razor-eyed stranger, breaking through to a kind of boyish affability." In another action film, *The Eiger Sanction* (1975), which Eastwood directed, he did his own stunt work, which included mountain climbing in Switzerland.

With his next few films, Eastwood established a pattern that he continues to follow—alternating movies geared to a mass audience with more personal films. *The Outlaw Josey Wales* (1976), for instance, which Eastwood directed and starred in, depicted a more vulnerable Eastwood. Against the background of the American Civil War, Eastwood played a Missouri farmer driven to violence by Union marauders who massacre his wife and children. Chief Dan George played his Indian sidekick. It was during the filming of that movie that Eastwood reportedly became involved with Sondra Locke, who played his romantic interest in the film, and who continues to maintain that role in real life. Writing in *Newsweek* (September 13, 1976), Jack Kroll observed that Eastwood's directing exhibited "some primeval stirrings of style and humor."

Dirty Harry returned to the screen once again in *The Enforcer* (1976), with Tyne Daly as his police partner. In *The Gauntlet* (1977), which he also directed, Eastwood played a detective in Phoenix, Arizona who tries to bring a prostitute (Sondra Locke) from Las Vegas to Phoenix to testify at a mob trial. "It is a movie without a single thought in its head, but its action sequences are so ferociously staged that it's impossible not to pay attention most of the time," Vincent Canby wrote in the *New York Times* (December 22, 1977).

In *Every Which Way But Loose* (1978), Eastwood poked fun at his macho image, playing a California trucker who makes ends meet by fighting local toughs. He is accompanied in his adventures by his sidekicks Ma, a foul-mouthed old lady

played by Ruth Gordon, and Clyde, an orangutan won in a bet. His love interest is a singer (Sondra Locke). Although reviews were poor—"This picture could be a litmus-paper test indicating to what low level public taste and gullibility have sunk," Archer Winsten wrote in the *New York Post* (December 20, 1978)—*Every Which Way But Loose* proved to be Eastwood's biggest hit to that date, grossing $87 million by mid-1982. The sequel, *Any Which Way You Can* (1981), featuring the same characters, again dismayed the critics but appealed to audiences.

After starring in Don Siegel's drama *Escape from Alcatraz* (1979), Eastwood made what is often considered one of his best movies, *Bronco Billy* (1980). Billy, played by Eastwood, is a former New Jersey shoe salesman who now owns a failing Wild West show, in which he performs as trick rider and sharpshooter. A fugitive heiress (Sondra Locke) signs up with the show, and she and Billy, overcoming initial hostility, fall in love. A throwback to the screwball comedies of the 1930s, *Bronco Billy*, which Eastwood directed, embodied his outlook on life. "If I ever had a message to get across, you'll find it in *Bronco Billy*," he once said. At one point in the film, for instance, one of the show's performers says to the heiress: "You can be anything you want, all you have to do is go out and become it." Eastwood's directing was singled out for praise by reviewers. Tom Allen, for example, avowed in the *Village Voice* (June 16, 1980): "No other American filmmaker has so convincingly conveyed a sense of his beliefs and an affection for a lifestyle as Eastwood does in *Bronco Billy*. . . . Now, it's time to take him seriously not just as a populist phenomenon, but as one of the most honest, influential personal filmmakers in the world today."

After *Firefox* (1982), about an American flyer assigned to steal a technologically advanced Soviet aircraft, Eastwood took on another more vulnerable role in *Honkytonk Man* (1982), in which he played a washed-up country singer who travels to Nashville during the Depression years with his fourteen-year-old nephew (played by Eastwood's son, Kyle) to audition with the Grand Ole Opry before dying of tuberculosis. The film was coolly received by critics. "Ultimately the movie depends on his ability to play a kind of country-and-western Camille," Gary Arnold wrote in the *Washington Post* (December 18, 1982), "and this tearjerking challenge proves beyond his range and a viewer's credulity." *Honkytonk Man* was the first Eastwood film to lose money, but he has no regrets. As he told Norman Mailer for a *Parade* (October 23, 1983) profile, "I just figure sometimes you have to do some things that you want to do and be selfish about it."

Dirty Harry appeared onscreen for the fourth time in *Sudden Impact* (1983), which Eastwood also directed. Harry becomes involved with a woman (Sondra Locke) who is seeking revenge on the men who brutally raped her and her younger sister ten years earlier. Assigned to arrest the woman, Harry eventually lets her go free, realizing that her method of vengeance is no worse than his as a cop. The film became Eastwood's biggest-grossing picture to date, making some $120 million. It was in *Sudden Impact* that Harry issued his now famous taunt to a gun-wielding opponent: "Make my day." Vincent Canby's appraisal of the film in the *New York Times* (December 9, 1983) summed up most reviewers' opinions: "The screenplay is ridiculous, and Mr. Eastwood's direction of it primitive." Notices were more positive for Eastwood's next effort, Richard Benjamin's *City Heat* (1984), a Prohibition-era gangster movie spoof in which the actor teamed with Burt Reynolds. Kathleen Carroll, writing in the New York *Daily News*, called the two a "casting director's dream of an acting team" who provide "instant audience gratification."

Critics were forced to sit up and take notice of a more complex acting performance in Eastwood's next film, *Tightrope* (1984), in which he played Wes Block, a troubled detective investigating the murders of several prostitutes. Block is a single parent with two daughters (one of whom was played by Eastwood's daughter, Alison), and he eventually falls for a rape counselor (Genevieve Bujold). Gene Siskel, writing in the *Chicago Tribune* (August 17, 1984), called Eastwood's characterization of Block "one of his finest screen performances," and David Denby of *New York* (August 27, 1984) magazine went so far as to say: "I've resisted Clint Eastwood for years, but it's time to stop making jokes. More and more, he's beginning to look like the last serious man in Hollywood."

Critics did not take too kindly to Eastwood's film *Pale Rider* (1985)—his first western in nine years—because of its outright plagiarism of the 1953 classic western *Shane*. Eastwood starred in and directed the film. He also directed and starred in *Heartbreak Ridge* (1986), the story of an aging marine sergeant who has the chance to lead his squadron into combat one last time, in Grenada. Vincent Canby of the *New York Times* (December 5, 1986) found Eastwood's performance "one of the richest he's ever given." Although the United States Marine Corps originally cooperated with Eastwood's endeavor (some of the film was shot at Camp Pendleton), it withdrew its support after the film was finished because of its violence and profanity. Eastwood resumed the role of Dirty Harry for the fifth time in *The Dead Pool* (1988).

On April 8, 1986 Clint Eastwood assumed a new role when he was elected mayor of Carmel, California, a job paying $200 a month. "I only took this job because it's in the community where I live," Eastwood told one reporter. The actual impetus stemmed from his frustration over his efforts to tear down an abandoned building next to the Hog's Breath Inn, a restaurant he partly owns in Carmel, in order to erect a two-story office and commercial building in its place. Eastwood spent a record $25,000 on his campaign ($750 had been the previous high), and he won by a "landslide," taking 2,166 votes to incumbent mayor Charlotte Townsend's

799 votes. Some of his achievements during his two-year term included the appointment of new members to the planning commission and the purchase of a twenty-two-acre ranch in Carmel for $5 million in order to protect the land from developers. Eastwood declined to run for reelection in 1988, citing his desire to spend more time with his children, as well as the adverse effect on Carmel of the huge amount of publicity his mayoralty had attracted.

Clint Eastwood's latest movie venture, *Bird* (1988), which is only the second movie he has directed but not starred in (the other was *Breezy*, made in 1973), succeeded in enhancing his status as a filmmaker. In his exploration of the world of jazz saxophonist Charlie Parker, commonly known as "Bird," Eastwood included rare, previously unreleased tapes of Parker's music (procured from Parker's wife, Chan) to depict a live performance convincingly. Critics cited for special praise Eastwood's evocation of Manhattan in the 1950s and the performances of Forest Whitaker as Parker and Diane Venora as Chan. Richard Schickel of *Time* (October 3, 1988) was so impressed that he stated that *Bird*, "with its passionate craft . . . , proclaims that Eastwood is a major American director." The reviewer for the *Chicago Tribune* (October 14, 1988) seconded that opinion, writing that the "dramatic authority and structural sophistication of *Bird* have startled many viewers into the realization that Clint Eastwood is an extremely accomplished filmmaker." At the Cannes Film Festival, *Bird* won a prize for outstanding technical achievement, and Forest Whitaker won the award for best actor. The movie was shown at the New York Film Festival and at the Metropolitan Museum of Art in New York in 1988. At the Golden Globe Awards ceremony in January 1989, Eastwood took the prize for best director for his work on *Bird*.

An interest in music has been evident in other films as well. Eastwood collaborated on the composing of the theme music for several of his motion pictures, including *Tightrope* and *Pale Rider*, played a bluesy piano on the soundtrack album of *City Heat*, and sang the song "Barroom Buddies" with Merle Haggard in *Bronco Billy*. In 1980 he formed Warner/Viva Records with the producer "Snuff" Garrett.

Eastwood's reputation for minimalism in his acting also applies to his directing, as he consistently produces films on time and under budget. He works quickly, often printing the first take of a shot. "I think a director ought to know what he wants before he sees it," Eastwood told Gene Siskel of the *Chicago Tribune* (June 9, 1985). "I'm not one of these guys who tries twenty different shots. That's not directing; that's guessing." He is highly organized and relies on a loyal and supportive veteran crew. Where other stars of his magnitude, such as Warren Beatty and Robert Redford, might complete a film every couple of years, Eastwood, in one seventeen-month period, made *Sudden Impact*, *Tightrope*, *City Heat*, and *Pale Rider*. Yet he confessed to Paul A. Witteman of *People* (January 10, 1983): "In the old days I always felt I had to do more. Now it's time to make some comments with my work that I'm interested in making."

The Museum of Modern Art in New York confirmed Eastwood's new respectability in 1980 when it ran a retrospective of his films. In 1985 Eastwood toured Europe, stopping first in Paris, where he was honored with a retrospective at the prestigious Cinémathèque and decorated as a chevalier of the Ordre des Arts et des Lettres. Another retrospective was held at the Filmmuseum in Munich, and, in London, Eastwood gave a lecture on film to the British Film Institute, at the invitation of the *Guardian*. On November 10, 1985 Eastwood attended a dinner at the White House in honor of the Prince and Princess of Wales, and on September 17, 1987 he welcomed Pope John Paul II at the Monterey, California airport.

Standing six feet, four inches tall and weighing 190 pounds, Clint Eastwood has receding, graying blond hair. To stay in shape, he runs a mile on the beach every morning and works out in an exercise room at home in the afternoon. He takes large doses of vitamins and believes in a low-fat diet, although he is fond of beer. His life style is unpretentious, and he is more often than not seen driving his pickup truck rather than the white Mercedes that he also owns.

Eastwood was married to Maggie Johnson, a swimsuit designer and model, on December 19, 1953, and they have two children. Their son, Kyle, is a film student at the University of Southern California; their daughter, Alison, lives with her mother. The couple was divorced sometime in the mid-1980s, and Maggie Johnson received a $25 million divorce settlement. The fan-shaped redwood-and-glass house Eastwood built on twelve oceanfront acres now belongs to his ex-wife. He lives nearby in a small stone house. Eastwood also maintains a home in the Los Angeles suburb of Sherman Oaks, near the offices of Malpaso Productions on the Warner studio lot, and a 2,000-acre ranch in northern California that was once owned by Bing Crosby.

References: N Y Daily News mag p6+ Ag 12 '84 pors; N Y Times Mag p16+ F 24 '85 pors; Newsweek 106:48+ Jl 22 '85 pors; Parade p4+ O 23 '83 pors; Playboy 21:57+ F '74 pors; Guérif, François. Clint Eastwood (1986); Who's Who in America, 1988–89

Erdrich, Louise

July 6, 1954- Writer. Address: b. c/o Michael Dorris, 307 Bartlett, Dartmouth College, Hanover, N.H. 03755; h. P.O. Box 70, Cornish Flat, N.H. 03746

At a time when many young novelists are chronicling the malaise of urban upper-middle-class life or focusing on personal crises, Louise Erdrich is plumbing the rich history and folklore of her Native American heritage—she is part Chippewa Indian—to create a mythical world that critics have compared to William Faulkner's Yoknapatawpha County. Her three critically acclaimed and best-selling novels, *Love Medicine* (1984), *The Beet Queen* (1986), and *Tracks* (1988), which are part of a projected tetralogy, trace three generations of Chippewa Indians in North Dakota, in the years from 1912 to 1984. Narrated from shifting points of view, Miss Erdrich's novels are populated, in the words of one critic, with a "cast of characters, at once ordinary and strange, like eccentric folk-art figures," who are depicted with a humor and pathos that give them universal appeal. "My characters choose me and once they do it's like standing in a field and hearing echoes," Louise Erdrich has said. "All I can do is trace their passage."

The lyrical quality of Louise Erdrich's prose, which is evident in her novels and short stories, prompted Gail Godwin to call the author "a sorceress with language," and one critic has observed that "[Miss] Erdrich's language has a bizarre but always perfect pitch, capable of conveying profound

and complicated emotions, startling in their purity." Her book of poetry, *Jacklight* (1984), was critically well received, and Miss Erdrich is one of only three poets under the age of thirty-five who are included in the *Norton Anthology of Poetry*. Miss Erdrich collaborates closely on all of her work with her husband, Michael Dorris, who is also part Indian and head of the Native American

Studies department at Dartmouth College. As Michael Curtis, the editor of the *Atlantic* who has published several of Louise Erdrich's short stories, has commented: "Some couples work together and help each other, but none of them insist to such lengths and in such a firm way on their mutuality."

Karen Louise Erdrich was born on July 6, 1954 in Little Falls, Minnesota. Her father, Ralph Louis, was of German descent; her mother, the former Rita Joanne Gourneau, is a Chippewa Indian. The oldest of seven children, Louise Erdrich grew up in the small town of Wahpeton, North Dakota, near the Minnesota border. Both of her parents worked for the Bureau of Indian Affairs boarding school in Wahpeton, her father as a teacher. Louise Erdrich's maternal grandfather was the tribal chairman of the Turtle Mountain Reservation, and his wife was part French-American and part Chippewa. The combined influence of Roman Catholicism and the traditional Chippewa religion resulted in a "Gothic-Catholic childhood," Miss Erdrich told Miriam Berkley for a *Publishers Weekly* (August 15, 1986) profile. "It was a small-town life—lots of kids living on a teacher's salary, and we were quite a chaotic, pretty typical family."

Although Louise Erdrich attended the Bureau of Indian Affairs boarding school, she never really thought about her Native American heritage. "I think that's the way a lot of people who are of mixed descent regard their lives—you're just a combination of different backgrounds," she told Miriam Berkley. In high school, Louise was a cheerleader for the wrestling team, and her teenage rebelliousness took the form of "dressing funny and listening to Joan Baez and keeping journals and reading poems and trying to be a little different," she told Dan Cryer for *Newsday* (November 30, 1986). During those years, she started thinking of herself as a writer. "My father used to give me a nickel for every story I wrote, and my mother wove strips of construction paper together and stapled them into book covers," she explained to *Contemporary Authors*. "So at an early age, I felt myself to be a published author earning substantial royalties. Mine were wonderful parents; they got me excited about reading and writing in a lasting way."

Louise Erdrich enrolled at Dartmouth College in 1972 as part of its first coeducational class. That experience helped her to begin to come to terms with the importance of her Native American heritage. Although Dartmouth was founded in 1769 under a charter that stressed the education of Native Americans, by 1972 it had graduated only twelve. That year, the college hired Michael Dorris, Louise Erdrich's future husband-collaborator, to teach anthropology and to chair the newly created Native American Studies Department. Like Miss Erdrich, Dorris is of mixed descent; his father is a member of the Modoc tribe. Miss Erdrich, who majored in creative writing, did not take a course from Dorris until her junior year. Even then, she recalled for Miriam Berkley, although the course material "was really saying something to [her]," it took years of ex-

periencing life firsthand before she really understood what she had learned in class.

Originally considering an academic career, Miss Erdrich changed her mind after she won a number of prizes for poetry and fiction during her undergraduate years and decided to become a writer. During her senior year, *Ms.* magazine published one of her poems. Harboring the romantic notion that a writer needed a wealth of experiences to draw upon, she worked at a variety of jobs both during and immediately after college. Among other things, she waited on tables in such places as Wahpeton, Boston, and Syracuse; worked on a construction site in North Dakota and in a mental institution in Vermont; edited the *Circle*, an Indian Council newspaper in Boston; and worked as a lifeguard. After graduating in 1976, she returned to North Dakota as a "poet in the schools," a job that, as she told Dan Cryer, took her "to some of the seediest hotels in the state."

In 1978 Miss Erdrich entered a nine-month masters program in creative writing at Johns Hopkins University. Her thesis included many poems later published in her collection of poems entitled *Jacklight* as well as material that later became the first chapter of her novel *Tracks*. On receiving her M.A. degree in 1979, she returned to Dartmouth as a writer in residence. She also worked on a textbook for children, *Imagination*, which was published in 1980. During her time away from Dartmouth, she had stayed in touch with Dorris and renewed her friendship with him after he attended one of her readings there. "She knocked me out with this absolutely dynamite poetry," Dorris told Mervyn Rothstein of the *New York Times* (October 13, 1986). Shortly thereafter, Dorris went off to New Zealand to do field research. He and Miss Erdrich started a correspondence and began to send each other samples of their poems and stories. In the meantime, in 1980 and 1981 respectively, Miss Erdrich attended the MacDowell and Yaddo writers colonies. When Dorris returned to the United States in 1980, he and Miss Erdrich began collaborating on short fictional pieces for magazines. They were married in October 1981.

The collaboration that started with letter-writing led to joint efforts on short stories, including a number of domestic tales written under the name Milou North that were published by the British magazine *Woman*. (Milou is a combination of the first syllable of each of their first names, and North refers to their general geographic location.) Another short story, "The World's Greatest Fisherman," which the couple submitted to the 1982 Nelson Algren fiction competition, won that contest's first prize of $5,000. Encouraged, the pair expanded the story into a full-length novel. The resulting *Love Medicine* (1984), which chronicles the relationships between two Chippewa tribe families in North Dakota in the years from 1934 to 1984, brought Louise Erdrich instant critical acclaim.

Each of the fourteen chapters in *Love Medicine* is a self-contained short story, narrated by one of seven characters, yet each chapter contains references to events and people mentioned elsewhere in the book. Critics singled out for special praise the lyrical prose with which she narrated her stories of love, poverty, courage, and tragedy. Magic is an important theme, and the title *Love Medicine* refers to Chippewa folk medicine and a belief in love potions. One story involves the love triangle between Nector Kashpaw, his wife, Marie, and Lulu Lamartine, whom Nector still desires even when he becomes a resident of a nursing home. After his grandson Lipsha catches Lulu and Nector "wooing" in the laundry room, he puts a love potion in Nector's sandwich. Nector ends up choking to death on the potion, and Lipsha feels a guilty responsibility for what happened. Commenting on that tale, Carol Hunter, writing in *World Literature Today* (Summer 1985), noted that Louise Erdrich's "sense of humor and skill with language make *Love Medicine* a dynamic novel."

Commenting on the lyricism of Louise Erdrich's prose, Marco Portales observed in the *New York Times Book Review* (December 23, 1984), "Miss Erdrich can bring an element of poetic stylishness to descriptions of ordinary events such as digging up dandelions: 'Outside the sun was hot and heavy as a hand on my back. I felt it flow down my arms, out of my fingers, arrowing through the ends of the fork into the earth.'" Robert Towers, however, writing in the *New York Review of Books* (April 11, 1985), found that Miss Erdrich's poetic prose overromanticized the novel, especially in sections that deal with serious subjects. "At times the language becomes overwrought to the point of hysteria or else so ecstatic that the reader may feel almost coerced into accepting a romanticized version of a situation—a version that the hard facts belie."

A critic for the *Kirkus Reviews* (August 15, 1984) noted that "despite flaws and excesses, this is a notable, impressive book of first fiction: the unique evocation of a culture in severe social ruin, yet still aglow with the privilege and power of access to the spirit-world." And Harriet Gilbert, writing in the *New Statesman* (February 8, 1985), praised Miss Erdrich's adept fusing of the comic and the serious: "*Love Medicine* . . . is a tragedy made ingestible by its author's humor, tenderness, perceptiveness and restraint." Several of the stories that appear in the novel were originally published in magazines such as the *Atlantic, Kenyon Review, Ms.,* and *North American Review.*

Gene Lyons, writing in *Newsweek* (February 11, 1985), lamented Miss Erdrich's "inexperience as a storyteller" and complained: "No central action unifies the narrative, and the voices all sound pretty much the same—making it difficult to recall sometimes who's talking and what they're talking about." Robert Towers concurred with that assessment, finding *Love Medicine* to be "a hard book to penetrate." He further noted, "The episodes, most of them dramatic monologues, are loosely strung together and the relationships of the various narrators and characters are so confusing that one must constantly flip back to earlier sections in an effort to get one's bearings."

Although Louise Erdrich is given credit for the authorship of *Love Medicine,* she has freely acknowledged Dorris's contribution to the novel, and she dedicated the book to him "because he is so much a part of it." (She subsequently dedicated two other novels to Dorris as well.) As she explained to Geoffrey Stokes of the *Village Voice* (September 9, 1986), in describing their unique collaboration: "You know, a person said, 'This doesn't work,' and the other person would storm away and throw the manuscript down and be furious for a while. But then we always, literally always, took the other person's suggestion ultimately." Dorris further explained to Dan Cryer: "We spent a year and a half thinking about these people day and night. We would take walks and imagine scenarios." In addition to being a national bestseller, *Love Medicine* received the 1984 National Book Critics Circle Award, the Virginia McCormick Scully Prize for best book of 1984, the Sue Kaufman Prize, the *Los Angeles Times* Award for best novel, and the best first fiction award from the American Academy and Institute of Arts and Letters.

Also in 1984, forty-four of Louise Erdrich's poems were published under the title *Jacklight,* which met with favorable reviews. Michael Loudon, for example, wrote in *World Literature Today* (Winter 1986): "I felt early in the reading the same narrative force, precise images, and complex characters that eventually found full expression in her celebrated novel *Love Medicine,* but the poems are far from mere exercises on the way to a novel. They are first-rate poems: the language again and again sings to its own vision."

The second novel in Louise Erdrich's projected tetralogy, *The Beet Queen* (1986), is set in the same region of North Dakota as its predecessor and covers the same period of time. As does *Love Medicine,* it contains bizarre and original characters, although here they are non-Indian or part Indian. The story begins with an episode of abandonment, when Adelaide Adare flies off with the airplane stuntman Great Omar from a fairgrounds, leaving her children, Mary and Karl, to fend for themselves by jumping on a freight train headed for Argus, North Dakota, where their aunt and uncle have a butcher shop. Mary grows up there, but Karl ends up at an orphanage and returns to Argus only intermittently over the years. On one visit he has an affair with Celestine James, a mixed-blood Chippewa who is Mary's best friend and who has a daughter, Dot, by him. Karl also has a homosexual affair with Wallace Pfef, a local businessman, who never gets over it. Dot becomes the Beet Queen of the novel's title. Like its predecessor, *The Beet Queen* consists of chapters narrated by different characters, and each chapter is titled after the name of its narrator. Overall, the novel was well received. Robert Bly wrote in his review for the *New York Times* (August 31, 1986): "This is a rare second novel, one that makes it seem as if the first, impressive as it was, promised too little, not too much." And Dorothy Wickenden noted in the *New Republic* (October 6, 1985): "What she brings to *The Beet Queen*, as she did to *Love Medicine*, is a prose of ringing clarity and lyricism, and a shrewd vision of the pathos and comedy that characterize provincial lives."

In comparing the novel with *Love Medicine* in the *Chicago Tribune* (August 31, 1986), John Blades discovered that *The Beet Queen* was "much lighter in tone, with episodes of domestic comedy and outright farce." Louise Erdrich explained to Blades that she shifted purposefully into a lighter mood in her second novel: "I'm so glad it's obvious. It's very much what I want people to notice in the book. This may sound wacky, but I really believe that to get a reader to respond deeply to something that's very difficult or sad or tragic, you have to have the opposite quality in the book, too. Maybe it's just as simple as saying that you have to have comic relief." In the same interview, Miss Erdrich acknowledged the influence of William Faulkner's "outrageous folk humor" on her own writing. She also noted that, like Faulkner's creation of the mythical Yoknapatawpha County, she has sought to create a "little postage stamp of native soil." "I haven't drawn any maps," she added, "but I do think it's a certain place that's being imagined more and more completely."

Several critics complained that Louise Erdrich created cartoons instead of real people in *The Beet Queen*. Dorothy Wickenden, for instance, was of the opinion that the author "relies too heavily on caricature," and she found the narrative to be "punctuated by a series of extraordinary scenes rather than sustained by an evolving plot and characters that grow and change." Michiko Kakutani of the *New York Times* (August 20, 1986), along with several other critics, called the novel's conclusion, in which the main characters end up assembled at the Argus beet festival, contrived. "It's unfortunate that *The Beet Queen* ends the way it does, for it's a conclusion that diminishes the impact of what is otherwise a remarkable and luminous novel."

Michael Dorris published his first novel, *A Yellow Raft in Blue Water*, in 1987, which, as with Louise Erdrich's novels, involved a joint collaboration. Louise Erdrich also collaborated on Dorris's next book, *The Broken Cord* (1989), which is a study of the effect of alcoholism among pregnant Native American women on their children. Fetal alcohol syndrome (FAS), as the condition is called, can lead to physical and behavioral abnormalities. The couple spent a year in Montana so that Dorris could conduct research there and on the Pine Ridge and Rosebud Indian reservations in South Dakota. In addition to its destructive effect on Native Americans, there is another more personal reason for Michael Dorris's interest in FAS: his oldest adopted child, Abel, suffers from severe learning disabilities and seizures caused by the syndrome. Dorris plans to use part of the "largess" that he received from Harper & Row to write the book to establish a fund for school systems and community health organizations to encourage experiments dealing with FAS. In addition, Dorris

and Louise Erdrich have proposed legislation requiring that warning labels about the dangers of alcohol to pregnant women be placed on liquor bottles.

Tracks (1988), Louise Erdrich's third novel in the projected tetralogy, is set in the years 1912 to 1924 and concerns the Chippewa families portrayed in *Love Medicine* at a time when they are being decimated by starvation, plagues, and the inexorable encroachment of the white man. As the narrator Nanapush says after sickness has diminished his people, "Our tribe unraveled like a coarse rope, frayed at either end as the old and new among us were taken." The novel's two alternating narrators are Nanapush, a Chippewa elder whom Katherine Dieckmann in the *Voice Literary Supplement* (October 1988) called Miss Erdrich's "most purely 'Indian' character," and Pauline Puyat, a young woman who is prone to religious fanaticism. Pauline's wearing her shoes on the wrong feet—as a form of mortification of the flesh—prompts Nanapush to remark, "God is turning this woman into a duck." *Tracks* traces the origins of the characters from the earlier novels, and its narrative centers on Fleur Pillager, a wild young woman with magical powers, and Eli Kashpaw. The romance that develops between Fleur and Eli is the result in part of the desirability of a woman who can beat a man at cards. Pauline is so jealous of Fleur's relationship with Eli that she vicariously seduces him through the sensuous Sophie Morrissey, using a love potion.

Critics appeared to be less impressed with *Tracks* than with Louise Erdrich's two previous novels. "No obvious dialectical tension exists between Nanapush and Pauline," Katherine Dieckmann noted in her review. "They're merely counterpoints, and their relationship is symptomatic of the overall lack of grand orchestration and perspectival interplay that made [Louise] Erdrich's first two novels polyphonic masterpieces." And Jeane Strouse, writing in the *New York Times Book Review* (October 2, 1988), found *Tracks* more self-conscious than Miss Erdrich's earlier works. "This novel feels a bit more didactic and wrought . . . , good and evil play out their parts somewhat too schematically, and the politics that previously came alive through the characters themselves sometimes seem imposed with a heavier hand."

E. Z. Sheppard, writing in *Time* (September 12, 1988) magazine, found the prose more affected than in the other two novels: "Despite its confident lyricism and clear passions, *Tracks* bears the marks of the academic writers' workshop." Sheppard also complained that the novel lacked coherence. "Plot is subordinated to episodic tours de force," he wrote. "In small doses, the graphic descriptions are impressive, but they can also be so relentless as to make the author sound like the thinking reader's Jean Auel." Calling *Tracks* a "Native American Gothic," Robert Towers took Miss Erdrich to task in his evaluation for the *New York Review of Books* (November 10, 1988) for allowing "the tragedy of the Indians to be overwhelmed by the sheer volume of sensational detail."

More-positive notices came from a reviewer for *Publishers Weekly* (July 22, 1988), who said: "This is a stunning story about people caught in the grip of passion and in the inexorable flow of history." And a critic for the *New Yorker* (November 21, 1988) called *Tracks* Louise Erdrich's "third, and finest, novel to date," further avowing that "the author captures the passions, fears, myths and doom of a living people, and she does so with an ease that leaves the reader breathless."

Most recently, Louise Erdrich and Michael Dorris have been collaborating on a novel that is tentatively titled "The Crown of Columbus," for which they received $1.5 million from Harper & Row, based on a five-page outline. Scheduled for publication in 1992, the novel concerns the discovery by a scholar at Dartmouth, named Vivian Twostar, of what appear to be the diaries of Christopher Columbus and her subsequent finding that he was not the man she thought he was. Dorris has explained to Charles Trueheart for a *Washington Post* (October 19, 1988) interview that the novel is revisionist history. "[Vivian Twostar] has a very stereotypic view of the inevitability of European and Indian contact. . . . And when she goes back and discovers that it could have been different but for a few chance happenings, she and Columbus almost form a relationship—but not in a hokey kind of way."

The unusually close working relationship that the couple maintains—virtually every work bears the imprint of both—prompted Louise Erdrich to explain to Miriam Berkley: "Some people don't believe it's possible to collaborate that closely, although we both have solitude and private anguish as well. You develop this very personal relationship with your work, and it seems fragile; you're afraid to destroy it. But I trust Michael enough so that we can talk about it. And every time I've been afraid to open it up, it has always been better for the work." In the interview with Charles Trueheart, Miss Erdrich described her husband, who acts also as her agent, as "a spiritual guide, a therapist, someone who allows you to go down to where you just exist and where you are in contact with those very powerful feelings that you had in your childhood." Each scene that Miss Erdrich writes goes through six or seven drafts.

Louise Erdrich's short stories have appeared in a number of publications, including the *New Yorker*, *New England Review*, *Kenyon Review*, *Chicago*, *Atlantic*, and *American Indian Quarterly*. The stories "Scales" and "Snares" are anthologized in *The Best American Short Stories* of 1983 and 1988, respectively, and "Saint Marie" and "Fleur" appear in *Prize Stories: The O. Henry Awards* in 1985 and 1987, in that order. "Scales" and "Saint Marie" became chapters of *Love Medicine*. Miss Erdrich has also received two National Magazine Fiction Awards for her short stories, in 1983 and 1987, and the Pushcart Prize in 1983. Since 1985 she

has served on the executive board of PEN, the international writers' organization, and she is a member of the Authors Guild. Louise Erdrich served as a judge in the Nelson Algren short-story contest in 1987.

Louise Erdrich has been described as tall and slim, with a high-cheekboned face and brown hair and eyes. She lives in a red-framed eighteenth-century farmhouse in Cornish, New Hampshire, thirty miles from Dartmouth, with her husband and their five children, three of whom were originally adopted by Dorris as a single parent. She returns often to North Dakota for visits with family and friends.

References: Christian Sci Mon p16+ Mr 2 '89 por; N Y Newsday p18+ N 30 '86 pors; Pub W 30:58+ Ag 15 '86 por; Washington Post B p1+ O 19 '88 pors; Contemporary Authors vol 114 (1985); Contemporary Literary Criticism Yearbook: 1985; International Authors and Writers Who's Who, 1986; Who's Who in America, 1988–89

Eschenbach, Christoph

Feb. 20, 1940– German pianist; conductor. Address: c/o Columbia Artists Management, Inc., 165 W. 57th St., New York, N.Y. 10019; Houston Symphony Orchestra, Jesse H. Jones Hall, 615 Louisiana St., Houston, Texas 77002

Orphaned and traumatized by World War II as a child, Christoph Eschenbach found solace and escape in music. His piano career was launched by his winning the arduous Clara Haskil competition, which gave him a reputation as a specialist in Mozart, Beethoven, and Schumann, though his taste was and remains far more broad-ranging. Eschenbach's intuitive musicianship and dazzling technique helped him become the first postwar German pianist to achieve an international career. Over the years he has appeared as a soloist with virtually every major orchestra in the world, and he has made more than a score of recordings. His individualistic and unpredictable performances fused intellectuality with emotionalism and evoked both enthusiasm and disapproval from critics. In 1971, at the height of his brilliant piano career, he began a gradual shift into conducting, often performing at first as both piano soloist and conductor simultaneously. After holding several guest conductorships with European orchestras, he took over as musical director of the Houston Symphony Orchestra in September 1988.

Christoph Eschenbach was born Christoph Ringman in what is now Wroclaw, Poland on February 20, 1940. His mother, a pianist, died in giving birth to him, and his father, a professor of musicology, was killed in combat when Christoph was four. The orphaned child was taken in by his grandmother. When the Soviet army invaded Germany in 1944, the two, suffering from hunger and illness, fled to Czechoslovakia and then to Poland. After the death of his grandmother in the winter of 1945–46, Christoph was taken to a refugee camp in East Germany, where he nearly died of typhus and starvation. Fortunately, a cousin of his mother's, a woman whose surname was Eschenbach, had begun a search for him. Although the camp was under quarantine when she reached it, she eventually obtained his release and took him home with her to Mecklenburg, in northern East Germany.

The Eschenbachs, who had no children of their own, adopted Christoph. Herr Eschenbach was a violinist; his wife taught piano and voice. The sounds of her lessons drifted into the upstairs bedroom, where the child lay convalescing. "That music actually seemed to nurture me back to health," he has recalled. He asked his new mother to teach him piano, but not until he was eight was he strong enough to undertake lessons. "My new mother was very careful in developing my early studies on the piano," Christoph Eschenbach told John Gruen in an interview for the New York Times (February 3, 1974). "I was never forced to practice. But I practiced anyway. I actually liked it. She was wonderful with children." In addition to piano, he learned the entire lieder and oratorio repertoire from his adoptive mother, and he played chamber music with his new parents and their musical friends. "My parents were clever enough not to make me a so-called prodigy. They did not show me around. They more wanted me to develop slowly," he recalled to an interviewer from the Houston Chronicle (September 4, 1988).

Nevertheless, it became evident after Christoph Eschenbach had taken two years of lessons that he was highly gifted. At the recommendation of Eugen Jochum, the German conductor and Bruckner spe-

cialist, his mother took him to Hamburg to study with Eliza Hansen, a protégée of both Artur Schnabel and Edwin Fischer, whose traditions she imparted to Christoph over the seven years that he was her pupil. He has declared himself in interviews to be a sort of pianistic grandson—or grandstudent—of Schnabel and Fischer. From Eliza Hansen he learned how to breathe through a phrase and how to produce a singing line. Although he studied violin and conducting in addition to piano, he discovered that the demands of that regimen were straining his physical and emotional resources. "Suddenly, it all became too much for me," Eschenbach told Gruen. "I decided to concentrate on the piano. It was, after all, my first love."

By the age of eleven, Eschenbach had begun collecting honors. In 1951 and again in 1952, he took first prize in the Steinway Young Pianists' Competition. In 1959, following four years of study in Cologne with Hans-Otto Schmidt-Neuhaus at the State Conservatory of Music, he won the Deutscher Hochschulen Competition in Stuttgart. Returning to Hamburg for further study with Eliza Hansen in 1959, he graduated from the Hamburg Academy of Music with highest honors and, three years later, won the Munich International Competition. He achieved his greatest competitive distinction in 1965, when he became the first winner of the grueling Clara Haskil Concours, an international competition in Lucerne, Switzerland whose repertoire requirements and jury standards were so exacting that no musician had met them since the contest was founded in 1963. The prize included a recording contract with Deutsche Grammophon and led to recitals and concerts with major orchestras throughout the United States and Europe.

Critical response to those early engagements was encouraging. In November 1966 Eschenbach's London recital debut at Festival Hall, with a program of Schumann, Beethoven, and Schubert, was praised by Noel Goodwin of London's Daily Express (November 21, 1966) for its "lively and sympathetic imagination as well as expert technique." His North American debut, at Montreal's Expo '67, brought him critical acclaim. He played four conservative works: Bach's Second Partita in C Minor, Mozart's Variations on the Theme "Ah, vous dirai-je, Maman," K. 265, Beethoven's Sonata no. 31, op. 110, in A-flat, and Brahms's F-Minor Sonata, op. 5. In the opinion of Francean Campbell of the Montreal Star (October 10, 1967), Eschenbach deserved to be heard "from one side of the continent to the other."

His United States debut, in January 1969, as a soloist with George Szell and the Cleveland Orchestra, prompted similar enthusiasm. "Nobody has the right to play Mozart the way Christoph Eschenbach did . . . unless he has lived with the music for about fifty years," wrote the Cleveland Plain Dealer (January 17, 1969) reviewer Robert Finn, who commended Eschenbach's "rhythmically supple playing . . . , penetrating musical understanding . . . , and long-arching lyric lines" in Mozart's Piano Concerto in F Major, K. 459. When Eschenbach played the same work for his Carnegie Hall debut four weeks later, Raymond Ericson of the *New York Times* (February 18, 1969) found Eschenbach's "crackling" style "just right for the sharp Mozartian wit" and noted the "loving, careful collaboration" among Szell, the orchestra, and soloist. Eschenbach's relationship with Szell continued offstage as well. "We had wonderful sessions together. . . . We worked like pupil and teacher, until he died in 1970," Eschenbach told John Gruen. "We had endless conversations, and endless two-piano sessions. Szell was a brilliant pianist. I studied all the Beethoven concertos with him. It was an unbelievable experience."

In March 1969 Christoph Eschenbach made his New York recital debut at Hunter College. Reviewing the event for the *New York Times* (March 24, 1969), Allen Hughes approved of Eschenbach's "pinging, bell-like tone" but was exasperated by what he perceived as the pianist's fussy and unpoetic interpretation of Schubert's Sonata in A (op. posth.). Alan M. Kriegsman of the *Washington Post* (February 16, 1970) leveled similar criticism at Eschenbach following a February 1970 recital of Berg, Schumann, and Schubert at the Lisner Auditorium in Washington, D.C. Kriegsman wrote that, despite the pianist's technical and analytical strengths, his performance was "not the substance of passion, but a dispassionately manufactured semblance. . . . The performer seemed to be imposing emotion instead of discovering it." But when Eschenbach played a Schumann program with the Cleveland Orchestra under Rafael Kubelik at Carnegie Hall a year later, Harold C. Schonberg of the *New York Times* (February 24, 1971) was struck by Eschenbach's "youthful fervor." "This was constantly exciting, individualistic playing, backed by a very strong technique, full of reckless daring," Schonberg wrote.

Eschenbach's recordings on Deutsche Grammophon were drawing applause as well. "This young man seems to have come early to an understanding of Mozart that few musicians ever acquire," Allen Hughes observed in a *New York Times* (November 5, 1967) review of Eschenbach's recording of Mozart's Variations on the Theme "Ah, vous dirai-je, Maman." On his recording of Beethoven's Concerto no. 1 in C, op. 15 for Piano and Orchestra with the Berlin Philharmonic under Herbert von Karajan, Eschenbach played "as if his piano were strung with spinal cords," according to a reviewer for *Time* (February 16, 1968) magazine. "What a revelation [Beethoven's "Hammerklavier" Sonata] is in the hands of Eschenbach!" Howard Klein of the *New York Times* (June 13, 1971) observed of a later recording. "This is the best 'Hammerklavier' on record." Eschenbach's recording of Hans Werner Henze's 1968 Piano Concerto no. 2 with the London Philharmonic Orchestra under the composer's direction won compliments for its clarity and verve. Henze wrote the concerto for Eschenbach, who

gave it its world premiere in Europe in 1968 and its American premiere in Chicago in 1969.

In 1971, despite his established keyboard success, Eschenbach began a gradual shift into conducting, ascending methodically through the Central European orchestras. "I have always wanted to be a conductor," he told Harlow Robinson of the *New York Times* (July 26, 1981). "The piano actually interfered. I had to establish a piano career because I won some competitions . . . and concerts came from all over. I like playing—I still like it. But my aim from childhood was to be a conductor." Eschenbach, who observed conductors throughout his piano career, studied conducting with George Szell and, to a lesser degree, with Herbert von Karajan. In an interview with Carl Cunningham for *Musical America* (March 1989), Eschenbach said: "One of the main things Szell taught was phrasing. He not only wanted listeners in the first two rows to hear the music clearly, but also listeners in the thirtieth row of the fifth tier. One almost had to exaggerate to accomplish that. In a sense, Karajan is at the other end of the musical spectrum. With Karajan, everything is melody and color, and the bridging of lines." The influences of the two conductors were to reveal themselves in Eschenbach's powerful thrust and textural detail.

Eschenbach made his American conducting debut with the San Francisco Symphony in 1975. At first he often undertook a taxing double role as both soloist and conductor, often to the detriment of his conducting. In the view of some critics who witnessed his performance at the Mostly Mozart Festival in New York in 1976, his inexperience on the podium betrayed itself in inconsistency, slipshod work with the baton, and lack of subtlety; his playing, on the other hand, was "clear, forthright, and unmannered," according to Robert Kimball, who reviewed the performance for the *New York Post* (August 10, 1976). A week later, the chief music critic for the same newspaper, Speight Jenkins, reported that Eschenbach "confidently steered a safe course between the Scylla of cool, technical, and bloodless playing and the Charybdis of gushing emotionalism."

In a benefit concert given at Avery Fisher Hall in New York in the spring of 1978 for victims of Nazi persecution, Eschenbach joined a fellow pianist, Justus Frantz, in a performance of Mozart's Concerto for Two Pianos in E-flat, K. 365. On that occasion, made even more poignant by its associations with Eschenbach's own childhood experiences during World War II, his conducting seemed controlled but "sometimes a little ungiving" to John Rockwell of the *New York Times* (May 2, 1978). But the critic went on to concede that "the two men interacted and answered each other with a lovely empathy." That July, Eschenbach appeared again at Avery Fisher Hall, this time during the Mostly Mozart Festival, playing and conducting two Mozart concertos, no. 21 in C, K. 467, and no. 27 in B-flat, K. 595. By altering the rhythms of some phrasings and producing some poorly timed instrumental entrances, he generated a "feeling of uncertainty," according to Donal Henahan of the *New York Times* (July 26, 1978), "the effect being that of listening to a genteel lady trying to disguise a slight hiccup."

Such mixed reviews did not discourage Eschenbach from persevering in his new vocation. By 1979 he had built up a solid classical repertoire that included all nine of Beethoven's symphonies, all four of Brahms's, seven or eight of Mozart's, several of Haydn's, four of Schubert's, Tchaikovsky's Fourth, Fifth, and Sixth, and major symphonic works by Stravinsky and Bartók. And regular conducting assignments continued to come his way. He was chief conductor of the Staatsphilharmonic Rheinland-Pfalz, in West Germany, in 1979, principal guest conductor of the London Philharmonic in 1981, first principal guest conductor of the Tonhalle Orchestra, in Zurich, Switzerland, in 1981, and chief conductor there in 1982.

Again to mixed reviews, Eschenbach made his New York Philharmonic conducting debut in February 1980, substituting for Bernard Haitink in presiding over a program that consisted of Bernd Alois Zimmerman's *Photoptosis*, Haydn's Symphony no. 104 in D, and Tchaikovsky's Symphony no. 6 (*Pathétique*) in B Minor. Though lacking in subtlety in the opinion of some critics, Eschenbach compensated with his driving energy, bold orchestral colors, and audacious dynamic contrasts. Eschenbach's "fiery" conducting, however, depended on "drive, energy, and vigor" rather than on subtle details, complained Raymond Ericson of the *New York Times* (May 25, 1980), who found it "effective enough" but "wearing" when Eschenbach led Beethoven's Piano Concerto no. 2 in B-flat, op. 19 from the piano for the New York Philharmonic Beethoven Festival in May 1980.

Eschenbach's conducting career gained momentum as critics, who had been skeptical at first, were won over as he gradually gained expertise. Leading the Vienna Symphony Orchestra without a score in Johann Strauss's overture to *Die Fledermaus*, Arnold Schönberg's *Verklärte Nacht*, and Mahler's First Symphony at Carnegie Hall in October 1982, Eschenbach tended to conduct without much variation in his hand movements, but the concert, dedicated to Glenn Gould, who had died earlier that day, was performed with freshness and feeling. In the Schönberg especially, the strings, "goaded by Eschenbach's sweeping, yet tender, conception, reached a truly transfigured level of emotion," Bill Zakariasen observed in the New York *Daily News* (October 6, 1982).

Although little noted at the time, a turning point occurred in December 1983, when Eschenbach made his Houston, Texas debut as a guest conductor. The bond between Houston and Eschenbach forged at that event was reinforced with a second guest engagement in October 1985 and strengthened even more in November 1985, when Eschenbach flew from Europe to New York to conduct the orchestra after Sergiu Commissiona fell ill and could not lead a scheduled Carnegie Hall concert.

Eschenbach prepared two piano concertos with soloist Emanuel Ax and, in a single two-hour rehearsal, revived the Bruckner Sixth Symphony, which he had conducted in Houston the previous month. The concert came off well, but more important, it nourished the growing mutual affection and respect between conductor and orchestra. Then, in an extraordinary feat in July 1987, Eschenbach rehearsed and performed three different programs in five days for Houston's first Mostly Mozart festival, playing Mozart's keyboard chamber music, conducting Mozart's orchestral music, and conducting and performing as soloist in three Mozart piano concertos. Carl Cunningham reported in the *Houston Post* (July 18, 1987) that Eschenbach "had the orchestra honed to an absolute brilliant sheen, [challenging it] to within an inch of [its] technical abilities."

When, in September 1988, Eschenbach became musical director of the Houston Symphony Orchestra, his presence was immediately felt, reinvigorating and raising the morale of the debt-plagued, depressed orchestra. In keeping with his commitment to present contemporary music along with standard works, his first program consisted of John Adams's *Short Ride in a Fast Machine*, Beethoven's Piano Concerto no. 5 (*Emperor*), and Brahms's First Symphony. He conducted the intense Beethoven and Brahms with his usual power and energy, and his musicians responded enthusiastically to his leadership.

A month later Eschenbach made his Houston Grand Opera debut, conducting Mozart's *The Marriage of Figaro*. The *Houston Post*'s Carl Cunningham (October 23, 1988) called it a "spellbinding" performance, a "gorgeous, joyous, touching tribute to the Salzburg master's genius . . . brought to life by the genius of Houston Symphony music director Christoph Eschenbach [who] illuminated all the fascinating nooks and crannies of Mozart's wondrous musical score." "His authority with the orchestra and the singers was complete. *Figaro* was in the palm of his hand," Ann Holmes noted in the *Houston Chronicle* (October 23, 1988). "Intensely focused and persnickety . . . he galvanized with energy and crackling expressiveness." Writing in the March 1989 issue of *Musical America*, Carl Cunningham predicted that Eschenbach will be the greatest conductor that Houston has ever had. "He is a fully mature musician, but he also has the youth and energy that were fading from the lives of his predecessors Stokowski and Barbirolli during their tenures," Cunningham observed. "He also seems to have the patience, the iron discipline, and an awareness of the practical realities."

Although Eschenbach still enjoys performing from the piano bench, he has become totally comfortable at the podium. "Conducting is in a way a wider range of musical experience," he told Harlow Robinson. "There are many more possibilities in coloring and shading. But the main point is that you deal with people, and not with an instrument. . . . You have to be a psychologist and a diplomat and a challenger and a stimulant—you have to do everything to move people, to motivate people. This is the aspect I find most interesting."

A stylish dresser, Christoph Eschenbach is of medium height, trim and intense-looking, with a moody cast to his brown eyes. Since his all-consuming interest is music, he has little time for anything else. In his rare free moments, he plays chamber music for the viola and socializes with other musicians, particularly the German pianist Justus Frantz. Although he has little time for what he calls "ordinary frivolities," he finds his vocation more than fulfilling. "Sometimes when I hear music," he told Harlow Robinson, "it carries me away, so I am almost paralyzed by it."

References: Mus Am 109:22+ Mr '89 por; N Y Times D p17+ F 3 '74 por, D p21+ Jl 26 '81 por; Who's Who in America, 1988–89

Mark Jury

Exley, Frederick

Mar. 28, 1929– Writer. Address: c/o International Creative Management, 40 W. 57th St., New York, N.Y. 10019

With the publication in 1988 of *Last Notes from Home*, the final part of his autobiographical trilogy that also includes *A Fan's Notes* (1968) and *Pages from a Cold Island* (1975), Frederick Exley consolidated his position as an unusual yet formidable voice in contemporary American fiction. Exley's novels are based on his own pain-racked life, which encompasses two failed marriages, three stays in mental institutions, and numerous sexual escapades under the influence of alcohol. "My

problem is always one of reining in reality, not of hyperbole," Exley said in a 1988 interview. Although his novels are highly readable, they have garnered more critical praise than popular success. But it seems likely that the extraordinary persona that Exley has created, the character Frederick Exley, who drifts through life on a sea of pain, frustration, rage, and compassion, searching for an ideal that he knows cannot be attained, will be increasingly recognized as one of the more memorable characters in modern fiction.

Frederick Exley was born in Watertown, New York on March 28, 1929, the son of Earl Exley, a telephone lineman, and Charlotte (Merkley) Exley. His siblings included a twin, Frances, an older brother, Bill, and a younger sister, Constance. Exley grew up in awe of his father, who was a local sports hero. One traumatic experience that Exley took as proof that he could not measure up to his father occurred when, at the age of thirteen, he played in the last quarter of a basketball game against his father, who managed to make three baskets in less than two minutes. Frederick Exley subsequently played football and basketball at Watertown High School.

Following his graduation from high school, Exley attended Hobart College, in Geneva, New York, where he was a predental student, and then transferred to the University of Southern California, from which he graduated in 1953 with a B.A. degree in English. Over the next fifteen years, Exley drifted through a number of jobs. Employed by the public relations department of the New York Central Railroad in Chicago, he was promoted to managing editor of its house organ, but he soon quit because he disliked the deviousness of public relations. He also taught high school in a rural part of New York and worked on his writing.

In 1968 Exley's first autobiographical novel, *A Fan's Notes*, was published by Harper & Row, after fourteen publishers had rejected it. Although the book is based on his life and its principal character is named Frederick Exley, it is subtitled "A Fictional Memoir." In a prefatory note Exley explained that the story resembled "that long malaise, my life," but that many of the characters and events were fictional and that he adhered only loosely to the pattern of his past life. He therefore asked to be judged "as a writer of fantasy." In an interview with Martha MacGregor of the *New York Post* (October 5, 1968), Exley explained that one or two key people who are featured in the book failed to sign releases. "I had to build a kind of disguise around them," he said. "But the major part was done straight."

Whatever the objective "truth" might be, *A Fan's Notes* supplies a wealth of material about Exley's early life. He does not, for example, portray himself as the most industrious of students. "I recall the shiver-inducing snap and crack of new texts opened for the first time on the eve of final examinations," he wrote, and he indicated that he was relatively unimpressed by his own literary talents. In college he wrote only one story that he felt possessed any merit, though in his memoir he disparaged even that effort. He also made it clear that he disliked teaching high school: "I found that by the Thanksgiving holiday the majority of my students despised me, I loathed them, and we moved warily about each other snarling like antic cats." He reemphasized that aversion in his interview with Martha MacGregor: "You take just as much abuse for $8,000 teaching school as you do for double the money in public relations."

But far more than a collection of anecdotes, *A Fan's Notes* is a tormented novel about the frustrations of a man who fails to attain his ideal and who subsequently lurches through life as a drunk and a perpetual loser with only a tenuous hold on his sanity. In one incident Exley is sent to jail in Miami—for an offense that is not explained—after the judge tells him he is a "fatuous lunatic." During another period, after his first marriage has fallen apart, he sinks into apathy, spending whole days lying on his mother's couch eating Oreo cookies and watching soap operas on television. Diagnosed as a paranoid schizophrenic, he ends up confined to a mental asylum on three separate occasions. Mike McGrady, writing in New York *Newsday* (July 19, 1969), called *A Fan's Notes* "an agonizing personal look at a man cracking under a variety of pressures." And yet the novel's Exley, in spite of everything that seems about to crush him, always possesses enough anger, insight, intelligence, humor, and sheer will to survive, to see him through. There is an uncompromising honesty in his outlook, and the narrative pulses with a robust energy.

In *A Fan's Notes* Exley strives for success and fame, ideals that were instilled in him by his father. "I suffered myself the singular notion that fame was an heirloom passed on from my father," the character Exley says. "Like him, I wanted to have my name one day called back and bantered about in consecrated whispers." After his father died of cancer at the age of forty, Exley transferred his hero worship onto Frank Gifford, the New York Giants football star, who was a football hero at USC while Exley was a student there. As Exley descends into his own private nightmare, Gifford becomes his alter ego, and Exley's enthusiastic support of the New York Giants brings him to life as nothing else can. "Each time I heard the roar of the crowd, it roared in my ears as much for me as him; that roar was not only a promise of my fame, it was its unequivocal assurance," Exley says. On the causes of his discontent, the character Exley explains: "I fought because I understood, and could not bear to understand, that it was my destiny— unlike that of my father, whose fate it was to hear the roar of the crowd—to sit in the stands with most men and acclaim others. It was my fate, my destiny, my end, to be a fan."

A Fan's Notes received excellent reviews, although most of them appeared some four months after the book's publication. Christopher Lehmann-Haupt of the *New York Times* (December 23, 1968) called it a "singularly moving, entertaining, funny book," and Mike McGrady, writing in

New York *Newsday* (July 19, 1969), commented, "Sometimes I am of the opinion that it is the best novel written in the English language since *The Great Gatsby*." After the book's publication in England in 1970, Derek Mahon described it in the *Listener* (January 29, 1970) as a "work of depth and seriousness—a moving, richly humorous record of humiliation and perseverance." Stanley Reynolds, who reviewed the book for the *New Statesman* (January 30, 1970), was one of the few dissenting voices. "The effect here is rather like getting buttonholed by a drunk in a bar who grips you by both lapels, breathing whisky and polysyllables into your face, and never uses two words where he can possibly find ten that'll do," Reynolds carped.

Exley's novel was nominated for a National Book Award, and it won the William Faulkner Foundation Award as the year's most notable first novel as well as the Richard and Hinda Rosenthal Foundation Award from the National Institute of Arts and Letters. The latter award is given to works of high literary merit that have failed to achieve commercial success. In spite of the critical acclaim, only 8,600 copies of *A Fan's Notes* were sold. Exley was to comment on the effect that the book's failure to sell had on him in his next book, *Pages from a Cold Island* (1975): "I'd made little money; my lifestyle of lugging my own soiled sweatshirts and skivvies to the laundromat and lunching on cheeseburgers and draft beer had altered not a whit." Since that time, however, *A Fan's Notes* has appeared in eight separate soft-cover editions and has become a cult classic among college students. A film version, starring Jerry Orbach, was made by Warner Brothers, but it was never put into general release. Exley thought that was just as well, since in his opinion the movie did not follow the book at all. For the rights to the film, Exley received a paltry $35,000.

Fortified by a $50,000 advance from his publisher and a $10,000 Rockefeller Foundation Award, Exley set to work on *Pages from a Cold Island*, the second volume in his projected trilogy. Shortly thereafter he was invited to teach for a semester at the University of Iowa Writer's Workshop. If Exley's characteristically self-deprecating persona in *Pages from a Cold Island* is to be believed, he felt ill-prepared for the task: "The truth was, I had so little to give the student and really had no understanding of what either he or I was doing there." Another detail that the reader learns about Exley's stay in Iowa City is his affair with a college student he refers to as April. ("Ex," as he is sometimes called, tends to have sex, which he describes in earthy and uninhibited language, frequently on his mind.)

Pages from a Cold Island is described as a work of nonfiction. The island of the title is Singer Island, at Riviera Beach in Florida; the adjective "cold" refers to Exley's own state of mind. Struggling to complete his book and in a state of deep depression and malaise, he has retreated to the island, where he cultivates friendships with others who have made aimlessness into a lifestyle. At one point his depression reaches its nadir, and the book records his second brush with suicide. After telephoning his friend, the poet and novelist James Dickey, he steps into the shower and holds a pistol to his head. But "whether I stood there five minutes or five hours I can't say." Eventually, Exley decided against the act, and he was able to rationalize why he decided not to end his life: "Suicide presupposes that something is being eliminated. . . . But what precisely was being eliminated in my case? Certainly not a man. Whatever I was eliminating was so inconsequential as to make the gesture one of trifling and contemptible ease and I began to think how much more felicitous the act would be if I sobered up, as best I could healed my mind and body, then erased some bone and tissue that at least conspired to resemble the human. Only then, I thought, might the gesture take on a certain flair or style."

Shortly after that incident, Exley reads an article by Gloria Steinem and concludes that discovering the source of her ability to care can help him get his book back on track. The interview he arranges with her is one of the comic highlights of the book. However, it is not Ms. Steinem, but the writer Edmund Wilson, another autobiographical writer with a strong attachment to upstate New York, who becomes the redeeming presence in the book. Exley credits Wilson with saving his life by showing him what literature really is. He traces Wilson's last days (he died in 1972), visits his upstate New York home, interviews his daughter Rosalind Baker Wilson and his secretary, Mary Pcolar, and reflects on his career. Wilson is presented as the literary achiever who lived a meaningful life, against whom Exley's own failings can be measured.

Reviews of *Pages from a Cold Island* were mixed. Ronald De Feo, writing in the *National Review* (September 12, 1975), compared the book unfavorably with *A Fan's Notes*: "By comparison, *Pages from a Cold Island* is slack, gossipy, and often petty. The troubled, defeated, comic narrator of the earlier book has grown coarse and loud." De Feo added that, in the book, Exley criticized Norman Mailer for posing and posturing, but he failed to notice the same faults in himself. Alfred Kazin, in his critique for the *New York Times Book Review* (April 20, 1975), was scathing in his comments. Pointing out that Exley prided himself on the total honesty of his work, Kazin wrote, "Exley cares for nothing but storytelling, has evidently read nothing but novels, and wouldn't recognize the unvarnished non-smart truth if it hit him." Jonathan Yardley, in his review for the *New Republic* (May 31, 1975), disagreed: "[Exley] matters, I think, because beneath the sad surface of a life seemingly given over to too much booze and too much random sex and too much aimlessness, there is a true writer, an artist unseduced by fad and fashion, pressing on to the fulfillment of his vision." And Richard P. Brickner, commenting in the *New Leader* (May 26, 1975), also took a favorable view of *Pages from a Cold Island:* "Unruly, brimming

over with more than enough love, self-abasement, envy, Exley is nonetheless admirable. He has the courage of his obsessions."

Like *A Fan's Notes*, *Pages from a Cold Island* did not sell well, and it was quickly remaindered. Exley later commented that using Edmund Wilson so prominently in the book had been a mistake, at least as far as creating a commercial success was concerned. "I mean, how many insurance men have ever read Edmund Wilson?" he asked Joseph P. Kahn during a *Washington Post* (January 26, 1987) interview. Still, Exley considers *Pages from a Cold Island* to be better than his first effort. "I think it's much more tightly constructed," he explained, as quoted in *Authors in the News* (1976). "I can still feel comfortable with a couple of things from *Pages*." Determined to complete the trilogy that he had set out to write, Exley told Christopher Zenowich in an interview for the *Chicago Tribune* (August 29, 1988): "What's the point of going half or two-thirds of the way? To risk a great happiness, you have to risk a great sorrow. Otherwise you go down the drain of illusion."

Last Notes from Home was finally published in 1988, twenty years after the first novel of the trilogy had appeared. Unlike the two earlier books, *Last Notes from Home* is described as a novel, and in it Exley claimed that he has "never written a single sentence about Frederick Exley except as he exists as a created character." In the book Exley travels to Hawaii to visit his older brother, William, a retired army officer who is dying of cancer. On the journey he meets a ravishing flight attendant named Robin Glenn and a drunken Irishman, Jimmy O'Twoomey, who keeps him captive on Lanai and hopes to bully him into finishing his novel and marrying Robin. As in the previous novels, there is an abundance of drinking, sex, and wild, self-destructive behavior, and Exley freely offers his opinions on everything from the My Lai massacre to the women's movement.

Reviews of *Last Notes from Home* were not uniformly enthusiastic. Christopher Lehmann-Haupt of the *New York Times* (September 22, 1988), for example, noted a falling-off from the standards of Exley's earlier novels, in terms of style, narrative technique, characterization, and tone. "The courageous woundedness of *A Fan's Notes* has turned to raucous boasting," Lemann-Haupt remarked, adding, "He equates his own failings with those of America, and draws too-easy analogies between his home base of Watertown, New York, and the world." In spite of those flaws, Lehmann-Haupt concluded that Exley's "music of angry contempt and self-loathing, for all its obscene sentimentality, still holds its quavering melody." In the *Chicago Tribune* (September 18, 1988), Jerold Pace wrote that, although much of it is excellent, "there are times when the book misses totally. Perhaps parody was the intent, but a great deal of it reads like warmed-over Philip Roth." Paul Gray, in his assessment for *Time* (October 24, 1988), observed: "Exley again demonstrates his skill at hallucinatory free association. The point of the exercise may be lost on those who expect stories to make sense." But Gray hoped that Exley would write a fourth novel.

Commenting on the entire trilogy in the *New York Review of Books* (January 19, 1989), Thomas R. Edwards thought that only *A Fan's Notes* could be considered a clear success, and he described *Last Notes from Home* as "a sad, baffled book, hard not to take as evidence of a talent in dissolution from rather ordinary causes." Edwards did praise the book's humor, however, and noted that the Exley character remained interesting, hiding a "thoughtful, literary, sensitive inside" behind a macho façade. Edwards concluded: "He is, I suppose, just a recalcitrant, unaccommodated man, wanting more than there is or ever was to be had. It's good to hear from him again."

Frederick Exley is five feet ten inches tall. In a profile for *People* (November 14, 1988), Jane Howard described him as "a lonesome, if not precisely monkish, romantic. . . . And though his face, devilishly handsome on the twenty-year-old book jacket of *A Fan's Notes*, is now puffy and gray-bearded, he still has mischief in his eyes and a rare, true laugh." Exley was married to Francena Fritz from 1967 to 1970 and to Nancy Glenn from 1970 to 1974. He has one daughter from each of his marriages: Pamela Rae and Alexandra, respectively. Exley lives in a three-room condominium near Alexandria Bay, New York, on one of the St. Lawrence River's Thousand Islands, only twenty-three miles north of Watertown, where he was born. He told Jane Howard that the islands are "as close as you'll get to paradise unless you spend a lot of time on your knees." His social life, he wrote in a article for *Esquire* (March 1986), "is circumscribed within the length of a football field."

Several members of his family live nearby, and Exley has a wide circle of friends, including the novelists William Styron and William Gaddis and the sports announcer Frank Gifford. "Fred loves having a surround," his friend Mary Cantwell told Jane Howard. "Wherever he is, he finds quasi-families who treat him as their child." Exley is known to consume large quantities of alcohol, but he never drinks when he is writing. Among his favorite authors are Nathaniel Hawthorne, Robert Penn Warren, John Cheever, and Vladimir Nabokov. In 1974 he received a silver medal from *Playboy* magazine for his article "St. Gloria and the Troll."

References: Chicago Tribune V p3 Ag 29 '88 por; Newsday W p3+ Jl 19 '69; People 30:163+ N 14 '88 pors; Washington Post B p1+ Ja 26 '87 pors; Authors in the News vol 2 (1976); Contemporary Authors vols 81–84 (1979); Contemporary Literary Criticism vols 6 (1976) and 11 (1979); Dictionary of Literary Biography Yearbook, 1981

Fang Lizhi
(fäng lē zhûr)

Feb. 12, 1936– Chinese astrophysicist; human rights advocate. Address: c/o United States Embassy, Beijing, People's Republic of China

One of China's most brilliant scientists, the astrophysicist Fang Lizhi is also the nation's most worrisome dissident. To the Communist party's four cardinal principles—socialism, people's democratic dictatorship, party leadership, and Marxist-Leninist-Maoist thought—Fang has opposed his own quartet of principles—science, democracy, creativity, and independence. Originally criticizing Maoism in the 1950s for constraining scientific thought, Fang grew increasingly disenchanted with socialism itself, in his belief that China's attempts at modernization can only take place in the context of a democracy. "Although one cannot say that every sentence of Marxism-Leninism is wrong," Fang commented in a 1988 interview, "one must admit that its basics are incorrect." Fang's outspokenness resulted in his being purged from the party in 1957 and 1987, but it made him a hero among Chinese students and intellectuals. When student-led prodemocracy protests erupted in 1989 on an unprecedented scale, leading to a restructuring of power in the Communist party, Fang was careful to steer clear of the protests, but the party blamed

the unrest on him. Fearing for his life, in early June, Fang took refuge in the American embassy in Beijing.

Fang's research into the structure of the universe has resulted in over 170 published papers and an international reputation, with his career reaching its peak in 1985, when he was appointed a vice-president of Keda, or the University of Science and Technology, in Anhui province. He was stripped of that post, however, following student protests at the end of 1986 and in early 1987, and he was reassigned to the Beijing Observatory. He won an appointment to the Institute for Advanced Studies in Princeton, New Jersey in 1986 and has been offered positions at Cambridge and other universities outside of China. "It's true that I could publish more scientific papers if I worked abroad," he said in a 1989 interview, "but the democracies have many astrophysicists, and China not so many. I love China, and even though I'm not so strong a nationalist, I want to stay where I can both have an impact on science and help to import democracy. Anyway, my friends tell me I should stay here and worry the leaders."

Fang Lizhi was born into a railroad clerk's family in Beijing, China on February 12, 1936. His parents were Cheng Pu and Peiji (Shi) Fang. Enrolling at Beijing University in 1952, where he soon established himself as a brilliant student of theoretical physics, Fang as the gadfly of the Chinese educational and political system emerged publicly three years later, at the founding meeting of the Beijing University Communist Youth League. "When it came time for our branch secretary to speak," Fang told Orville Schell in an interview for an *Atlantic* (May 1988) profile, "he let me express my opinion, since I had the loudest voice. I said that this kind of meeting was completely meaningless. I asked what kind of people we were turning out when what we should have been doing was training people to think independently. . . . After I spoke, the meeting fell into complete disorder. The next day the party committee secretary, who was the top person in charge of ideological work for students at Beijing University, spoke all day. He said that although independent thinking was, of course, all well and good, students should settle down and study."

Fang's concept of education coincided sufficiently with the official one to earn him straight A's at Beida, from which he graduated in 1956, and to win him an assignment that year to the Chinese Academy of Sciences' Institute of Modern Physics Research. At the institute Fang worked on nuclear reactor theory, but he again made his mark as a social critic in 1956, after Mao Zedong announced his intention to let "a hundred flowers bloom" by inviting intellectuals to speak their minds. Fang promptly wrote a paper calling for the reform of the Chinese educational system. "I couldn't stand it," Fang recalled to Ann Scott Tyson in an interview for the *Christian Science Monitor* (November 18, 1988). "Marxism dominated everything, including physics. But what Marx and Engels wrote about physics had become obsolete long before!"

As a result of his paper, Fang fell victim to Mao's 1957 Anti-Rightist Campaign, during which thousands of intellectuals were shipped off to labor camps. Fang was not imprisoned, but he was publicly rebuked by the party, and, when he refused to retract his statements and writings, he was expelled. Because of his considerable gifts as a scientist, however, Fang was not dismissed from his post at the Institute of Modern Physics Research, and he was later tapped to help organize a new physics department at Kexue Jishu Daxue (University of Science and Technology), or Keda, in Beijing. At Keda, Fang carried on his research in solid-state and laser physics and taught quantum mechanics and electromagnetics. He was appointed a lecturer in 1963, but in 1966 he was a victim of the purge of Chinese intellectuals that was a part of Mao's Cultural Revolution, and he was incarcerated in a *niupeng*, or "cow shed"—a form of solitary confinement that the Red Guards often used for intellectuals of the "stinking ninth category" (Maoists had divided Chinese society into nine categories). Released after a year, Fang was sent to a communal farm in Anhui province to be "reeducated." During the Cultural Revolution (1966-76), scientists were under orders to rid themselves of Western thought and to devise theories in the image of Mao's social maxims. In Anhui province Fang was cut off from almost all scientific literature and stimulation, except for his personal copy of the Soviet physicist Lev Landau's *Classical Theory of Fields*. "For six months I did nothing but read this book over and over again," Fang recalled to Orville Schell. "It was this curious happenstance alone that caused me to switch fields from solid-state physics to cosmology." During his years in exile, Fang's faith in Maoism was irreparably shaken.

In 1969 Fang was sent to Hefei, the capital of Anhui province, to teach astrophysics at the new Hefei branch of Keda. Fang continued his research of that subject, but his politically tenuous situation forced him to publish the results under a pseudonym. He did not find himself again in political favor until 1978, at the beginning of the post-Mao era of Deng Xiaoping, China's new supreme leader, when his party membership was restored and he was given tenure at Keda. In November 1978 he was allowed to leave China for the first time to attend a symposium in Munich on relativistic astrophysics. In April and May 1979 he traveled to Italy for a lecture tour, and in June he presented papers on general relativity and on the evolution of quasistellar objects (quasars) at a conference celebrating the 100th anniversary of the birth of Albert Einstein. In December 1979 Fang left China for a six-month research fellowship at the Institute of Astronomy at Cambridge University in England.

Over the next seven years, Fang wrote or collaborated on a steady stream of articles, using his own name. In the 1980s he explored such topics as the origin of the observed level of entropy, or structural randomness, in the universe; the role of invisible "dark matter" in the formation of large-scale structure in the universe; and the evidence that galaxies and quasars cluster in such a way as to make the universe a three-dimensional network of luminous superclusters separated by nonluminous "holes."

In a 1983 paper, "Is the Periodicity in the Distribution of Quasar Redshifts Evidence for the Universe Being Multiply Connected?," Fang and a coauthor, Humitako Sato, a Japanese astrophysicist, applied ideas from the branch of mathematics known as topology to data on quasars and suggested solutions to certain puzzles about the spectacularly energetic quasars and their relation to galaxies and evolution. That paper won the United States International Gravity Foundation Prize in 1985, the same year that Fang's scientific career within China reached its peak with his appointment as vice-president of Keda. Because of his popularity with students, Fang had been elected director of Keda's fundamental-physics department in 1980, and he had been nominated several times for the vice-presidency, but the Communist party had previously rejected him out of distrust of his political views.

By 1986 Fang had published some 130 scientific papers, and from March to July of that year, he was in residence at the Institute for Advanced Study in Princeton, New Jersey. Fang's prolific scientific output did not interfere with his political activities. In fact, his travels abroad, made possible by Deng's open-door policy, combined with his study of philosophy and politics, broadened his perspective on Chinese socialism and the role of Chinese intellectuals. In an interview for the Guangming Ribao newspaper that was translated into English and reprinted in the Beijing Review (December 15, 1986), Fang told the journalist Dai Qing, "If you have an opportunity to attend an international physics conference, you will discover that, although physics is discussed in the conference hall, outside when you are drinking coffee, for example, the final topic you discuss will often be focused on the unreasonable aspects of the West and the East." One example of the unreasonable in Chinese scientific thinking occurred in 1986 when Fang wrote the introduction to a translated essay on quantum cosmology by the theoretical cosmologist Stephen Hawking. One retired Chinese Politburo member, Hu Qiaomu, said that the introduction could not be published because it was not Marxist. "Cosmology is still concerned with the problem of whether the universe is finite or infinite," Fang explained to Edward A. Gargan during an interview for the New York Times (February 11, 1988). "That question is not solved for us. In Marxism, they already have solved this question. In a letter, Engels said that the universe must be infinite. So for Marxists, it is."

Rather than submit to such overrulings of science and thought, Fang insisted in his interview with Dai that "scientists must express their feelings about all aspects of society, especially when unreasonable, wrong, or evil things emerge." For Fang one of the unreasonable things was clearly socialism in China. In the course of the interview, Fang voiced an opinion he had first begun to express in 1977: that Marxism in China had outlived its usefulness.

Encouraged by a Chinese Ministry of Education report in 1985 on "The Reform of China's Educational Structure," Fang set to work with the president of the University of Science and Technology, his physics colleague Guan Weiyan, to make their university a model of educational reform. Fang and Guan drew up and put into action a plan for decentralizing power at Keda by turning decisions on such matters as research funding, the conferring of degrees, and faculty promotions over to special committees or to the relevant academic department and by allowing faculty and staff members to sit in on administrative meetings. They also sought to guarantee the right of free speech on their campus. As Fang explained to Dai: "The emergence and development of new theories necessitate creating an atmosphere of democracy and freedom in the university. In the university environment, there should be nothing that can only be upheld and that allows no questioning of why it must be upheld." To bolster further the circulation of ideas and to widen perspectives, Fang and Guan established foreign-exchange programs with the United States, Japan, France, Italy, and Great Britain. By the end of 1986, over 900 Chinese students and faculty had traveled, lectured, and studied abroad, and 200 foreign scholars had visited Keda.

The reforms at Keda drew praise from the People's Daily, the Communist party's official newspaper, and even convinced Fang that educational reform should take precedence over his scientific work. "I am determined to create intellectual and academic freedom—this will be my top priority," he told Orville Schell for the Atlantic interview. He embarked on a one-man crusade, giving speeches at Keda and at other universities that called for the removal of all restrictions on expression and thought in China. In a November 4, 1985 speech in Beida, Fang declared: "There is a social malaise in our country today, and the primary reason for it is the poor example set by party members. Unethical behavior by party leaders is especially to blame. . . . Many of us who have been to foreign countries to study or work agree that we can perform much more efficiently and productively abroad than in China. . . . Some of us dare not speak out. But if we all spoke out, there would be nothing to be afraid of."

At the end of 1986 Fang's challenge that everyone speak out was met to a degree with which even he was not comfortable. On December 5 students at his university took to the streets to demand the right to nominate student candidates to the local legislature. That helped to spark demonstrations involving tens of thousands of students at more than nineteen university campuses, culminating in protests in Beijing on January 1, 1987. Although Fang, whom the protesters hailed for his advocacy of freedom, defended the students' right to march as a right guaranteed under China's constitution, he expressed disapproval of the marches themselves. One result of the protests was Fang's nomination and election to the local people's congress in Hefei, in December 1986. Fang and Guan Weiyan, the university's president, were held responsible for the student disturbances by the local and national Communist party officials, and they were removed from their posts at the university and reassigned as research fellows at the Beijing Observatory and the Institute of Physics, respectively. As a result, Fang had to give up his seat in the local people's congress, although his wife, Li Shuxian, won a seat in Haidian, a Beijing district.

On January 19, 1987 Xu Leyi, an Anhui deputy party secretary, announced on television that Fang had been expelled from the Communist party and declared, "Over the last few years, Fang Lizhi, taking advantage of his position and reputation, made speeches both inside and outside the country to spread many extremely erroneous views in favor of bourgeois liberalization. Fang was one of the instigators of the student unrest over the past weeks that has had grave consequences." The day after his dismissal, Fang was denounced by Deng Xiaoping himself during a meeting with Noboru Takeshita, then the secretary-general of the Japanese Liberal-Democratic party.

Fang's dismissal served only to increase his prominence among Chinese intellectuals and students, and the foreign press began referring to him as China's Andrei Sakharov. In January 1987 Fang received hundreds of sympathetic letters, and, in February, he received a second batch of supportive mail that he noticed was more sophisticated politically. The shift in tone was the result of the party's sending to all party members ninety-one pages of Fang's speeches and interviews, which the party wanted its members to analyze and criticize in study meetings. The unintended result was that many party members found themselves sympathetic to the views that Fang expressed. Because Fang felt that the party would not risk further galvanizing his supporters by imprisoning him, he continued to speak out, although his movements, his ability to travel outside China, and his contact with students and reporters were restricted and his phone was bugged. However, he continued to teach, to attend scientific meetings, and to meet privately with friends. In Beijing, he lived in a five-room apartment that was considered luxurious by Chinese standards. During a trip to Australia in August 1987, he caused renewed rancor among party officials when he mentioned in a lecture that posters on Beijing campuses accused the children of well-known Chinese leaders of earning small fortunes illegally and salting the money away in foreign bank accounts. Deng Xiaoping responded by threatening to sue Fang, but he did not follow through on his threat. In February 1988 Fang was promoted to the second rank of professorship from the fourth rank, and the party allowed him to give a short interview to the New York Times (February 11, 1988), in which he dismissed the promotion as propaganda.

Continuing to speak his mind, Fang survived what one journalist has called "the twilight zone of tolerance" for dissent in China. "What else can I do? I must speak out," he said, as quoted in the Christian Science Monitor (November 18, 1988). "I have responsibility." Fang was never jailed but

several scheduled trips abroad—including a journey, scheduled for December 1988, to the United States for six months of research—were abruptly canceled. Fang and his wife, Li Shuxian, a physicist and fellow dissident, regularly held gatherings of like-minded intellectuals and students known as the Make a Friend Club, which in January 1989 called for the release of certain prominent political prisoners, privatization of industry, increased educational funding, a Chinese-Taiwanese peace treaty, and the deletion of the phrase "class struggle" from the Chinese constitution. On January 6, 1989 Fang wrote an open letter to Deng requesting amnesty for political prisoners, as part of the fortieth anniversary of the People's Republic.

The extent of the antipathy that Fang's beliefs aroused in Deng and his colleagues was dramatically illustrated in February 1989, when Fang and his wife were invited to attend a February 26 banquet at the Great Wall Sheraton Hotel in Beijing, hosted by the newly elected president of the United States, George Bush, during his first state visit to China. Fang and his wife drove to the affair with Perry Link, an American professor of Chinese literature, and his wife, who had also been invited. On the way, however, their car was pulled over by police on the pretext of a traffic violation. The couples decided to walk to the hotel, where they were told that they were not on the guest list. They then took a cab to the American embassy, but their cab was also pulled over for a traffic violation, and their subsequent efforts to board buses headed for the embassy were also thwarted. Trailed by police cars and policemen on foot, the two couples walked for an hour and a half to the home of the American ambassador, but they discovered that he was not in. David Horley, a Canadian diplomat, happened to notice them and invited them into his apartment, where they contacted American authorities and reporters. Fang ended up in the White House press briefing room at the Shangri-La Hotel, where he outlined the couples' frightening odyssey.

Open dissatisfaction with the Chinese government reached a breaking point in April 1989, when 3,000 students went on a hunger strike in Beijing's Tiananmen Square to protest corruption and nepotism in the government and to demand democracy. By May 4 the square was flooded with sympathizers, whose number eventually reached a reported million or more. Fang steered clear of the Tiananmen Square demonstrations. "I didn't want the government to be able to say this was just a Fang Lizhi movement," he said, as quoted in the Washington Post (August 4, 1989). Fang also noted that he was followed everywhere by security officers during the Tiananmen protests. The protests touched off a behind-the-scenes power struggle between hard-line leaders of the Communist party and more moderate officials, who had begun to organize after the April 15 death of Hu Yaobang, a moderate who had been purged in 1987 for dealing too leniently with the 1986 student demonstrations. In late May 1989 Deng and other hard-liners within the Politburo won the power struggle, ousted the party's most prominent moderate, Zhao Ziyang, and ordered troops into Beijing. At 2:00 A.M. on June 4, troops attacked the protesters in Tiananmen. "An estimated 5,000 citizens died in only a few hours," Howard G. Chua-Eoan reported in *Time* (June 19, 1989) magazine.

Between June 4 and June 8 prodemocracy figures such as Fang, accused of having "incited and organized this counterrevolutionary insurrection," were ordered to turn themselves in for "lenient treatment." Instead, Fang and Li Shuxian took refuge in the American embassy on June 5. In granting them refuge, American authorities ignored one of their own rules against granting asylum to nationals of the country in which an embassy is located and argued that Fang and Li Shuxian were in "personal danger." The Chinese government responded by issuing warrants for the arrest of Fang and Li for treasonous "counterrevolutionary" activities punishable by life imprisonment or death. The Chinese foreign embassy protested to the United States government that granting asylum to Fang had violated international law and interfered in Chinese internal affairs.

Fang and Li's presence at the embassy became an "irritant" in Sino-American relations that the United States attempted to resolve in June 1989 by suggesting that Fang and Li be allowed to immigrate to a third country, but nothing came of that initiative. The United States was restrained in its criticism of Deng and his colleagues, and Fang and Li declined interview requests in the interest of preserving the calm.

Fang Lizhi wears black horn-rimmed glasses and has been described as a rolypoly, cherub-cheeked "happy warrior," whose high spirits burst forth regularly in a deep infectious laugh. Fang and Li Shuxian met while both were studying at Beijing University in the 1950s. They were married in 1961 and have two sons. Their present asylum in the American embassy has been described as "temporary" by United States officials, but it has been noted that one instance of such temporary asylum—that of the Roman Catholic cardinal Jozsef Mindszenty in the United States embassy in Budapest—lasted for fifteen years. Fang won the National Award for Science and Technology in 1978, the Chinese Academy of Sciences Award in 1982, and the New York Academy of Sciences Award in 1988. In October 1989 he was named the recipient of that year's Robert F. Kennedy Memorial Human Rights Award.

References: Atlan p35+ My '88 pors; N Y Times IV p2 Ja 25 '87 pors; N Y Times Mag p27+ Ap 16 '89 pors; New Yorker 65:66+ Jl 3 '89; Science p417+ Ap 28 '89 pors; International Who's Who, 1989-90

Foley, Thomas S(tephen)

Mar. 6, 1929– United States Representative from Washington; Speaker of the United States House of Representatives. Address: b. Office of the Speaker, Room H-204, The Capitol, Washington, D.C. 20515; h. 704 W. Sixth Ave., Apt. 608, Spokane, Wash. 99204

On June 6, 1989 Democratic congressman Thomas S. Foley of Washington became the forty-ninth Speaker of the House of Representatives, succeeding Jim Wright of Texas, who had resigned amid charges of financial impropriety from the House Ethics Committee. Universally respected and well-liked for his affable, conciliatory manner, Foley has set out to restore public confidence in the House and reestablish comity among its members in the wake of the bitterly divisive, highly partisan wrangle over the alleged misconduct of his predecessor. During the twenty-five years that he has represented Washington's Fifth Congressional District, which covers the largely rural easternmost portion of the state, but which also includes Spokane, its second-largest city, Foley has developed a reputation as a fair, scrupulously honest legislator with a keen sense of compromise and an ability to gain the trust of colleagues on both sides of the political aisle. On assuming the speakership, Foley set as his top legislative priorities an increase in the

minimum wage, a revised clean-air bill, campaign finance reform, parental leave and childcare measures, and a resolution of the savings and loan industry crisis. He has also pledged to attempt to reform House ethics rules based on the recommendations of a bipartisan ethics task force.

Thomas Stephen Foley was born in Spokane, Washington on March 6, 1929, the only son of Ralph E. and Helen Marie (Higgins) Foley. His father, whom he has frequently called the dominant influence in his life, was Spokane County prosecutor during the 1930s and went on to serve as a superior-court judge for thirty-five years, the longest tenure of any judge in the state's history. Although Thomas Foley was raised in the prosperous, largely Republican South Hill section of Spokane, he developed a strong early loyalty to the Democratic party, thanks mainly to the influence of his parents. "I grew up believing that Franklin Roosevelt saved the country, that the Democratic party stood for a sense of social justice and opportunity," Foley told Ross Anderson of the *Seattle Times* (April 22, 1984). The Foleys' political orientation did not endear them to their neighbors, who, as Thomas Foley explained to Karen Dorn-Steele of the Spokane *Spokesman-Review* (April 2, 1989), "treated the Democratic allegiance of [the] family as one might treat a strange religion." "I learned at an early age that most of my friends were Republicans, but I had a fierce determination to defend the Democratic cause," he said.

A bookish teenager, Thomas Foley was, paradoxically, an indifferent student at Gonzaga High School in Spokane, and he once flunked algebra. Nicknamed "the senator" by his classmates, he overcame a pronounced lisp to become a state debating champion. During summer vacations, he worked in a local Kaiser Aluminum plant, where he acquired an enduring sensitivity to blue-collar concerns. Foley's self-described "checkered academic career" continued after he entered Gonzaga University in Spokane in 1947. During his junior year there, he was warned by the dean to improve his grade-point average or leave the university. Foley promptly transferred to the University of Washington in Seattle, where he buckled down sufficiently to earn a B.A. degree in 1951. Having long before decided that he wanted to follow in his father's footsteps, Foley then enrolled at the University of Washington's law school, but, after hearing an assistant dean describe the law as a "business" on his first day of class, he left the law school and registered instead at the university's Graduate School of Far Eastern and Russian Studies, with a view toward teaching history in college or joining the diplomatic corps. Two years later, however, he reentered the law school, which granted him an LL.B. degree in 1957.

After practicing law briefly in Spokane in partnership with his cousin Hank Higgins, Foley became, in 1958, the deputy prosecutor of Spokane County. Two years later, he was named assistant state attorney general. In 1961 he was hired by Senator Henry M. Jackson of Washington, a friend of his father's, as a special counsel on the Senate Interior and Insular Affairs Committee. Impressed by Foley and believing that Walt Horan, the Republican who had represented Washington's Fifth Congressional District since 1942, was vulnerable, Jackson encouraged his aide to oppose Horan in the 1964 election. Foley mulled over the idea for months, finally deciding to declare his candidacy only minutes before the filing deadline. As the only Democrat to register for Horan's seat, Foley won his party's nomination by default. Most political observers gave him little chance of defeating Horan in the general election, however, given the incumbent's twenty-two years of congressional experience and the Fifth Congressional District's solid Republican majority.

As was to become his custom, Foley ran an unusually genteel campaign, refusing to attack Horan and even praising him at times. The young lawyer impressed voters in the predominantly rural district with his knowledge of agricultural problems and his stand on other major issues. With fundraising help from the state's two Democratic senators, Jackson and Warren G. Magnuson, and the support of organized labor, Foley gradually gained ground on the incumbent. On election day he narrowly upset Horan, largely on the strength of Democratic president Lyndon B. Johnson's landslide victory. In a touching personal gesture that has come to be a Foley trademark, he held a reception in Horan's honor after the election.

In 1966 Foley beat back a fairly strong challenge from a new Republican candidate, Dorothy Powers, a popular columnist with the *Spokesman-Review*, and won reelection with 57 percent of the vote. Foley's popularity with his constituents reached its peak in the 1972 election, when he captured 81 percent of the votes cast in defeating Clarice Privette. The congressman's margins of victory steadily declined in the next four elections, however, and he came close to losing his seat in 1978 and again in 1980. In both of those elections, Foley's Republican opponents attempted to portray him as an ultraliberal whose positions were out of touch with those of his conservative district. The 1978 contest was a three-way battle, in which Foley received just 48 percent of the vote in besting the Republican nominee, Duane Alton, and Mel Tonasket, an independent candidate. In 1980 Foley stressed those issues on which he held conservative stands, such as his support for a tax cut, to stave off a determined challenge from John Sonneland, a conservative Republican, in a year in which the Republicans used Ronald Reagan's long coattails to gain control of the United States Senate and pick up thirty-three seats in the House. Sonneland challenged Foley again in 1982, but in that contest he took only 36 percent of the vote. Foley has been returned to office by increasingly impressive margins ever since.

One of seventy-one Democratic freshmen elected to the House in Lyndon Johnson's 1964 landslide, Thomas Foley supported all of that administration's landmark Great Society programs, but he grew to oppose expanding American involvement in the Vietnam War. As a member of the House Agriculture Committee, he helped draft the Meat Inspection Act of 1967, which provided the states with federal funds for imposing stricter standards on the packing industry. Foley was also a member of the Interior Committee, where he fought efforts to divert water from the Northwest to California and Arizona. The congressman has said that the most difficult vote of his career was his decision to oppose an anticrime bill enacted by the House in 1968 in response to the assassinations of the Reverend Martin Luther King Jr. and Senator Robert F. Kennedy and widespread rioting in the primarily black inner cities. One of only a handful of members to vote against the bill, Foley was particularly disturbed by its provision granting broad wiretapping authority to all levels of government.

While Foley has established a generally liberal voting record during his years in Congress, he has, perhaps because of the overwhelmingly conservative nature of his constituency, stopped short of joining the extreme left wing of the Democratic party. His approval ratings from Americans for Democratic Action, the liberal interest group, have fluctuated wildly, from a high of 86 percent in 1974 to a low of 30 percent in 1978. Still, the congressman's approval ratings from such conservative groups as Americans for Constitutional Action and the American Conservative Union have consistently been below 30 percent.

Although he is Roman Catholic and his district boasts a large Roman Catholic population, Foley has, throughout his congressional career, sided with the pro-choice side in the abortion controversy. He has also risked alienating conservative voters by supporting the Equal Rights Amendment and by opposing capital punishment, prayer in the public schools, a constitutional amendment requiring a balanced federal budget, and military aid to the Nicaraguan Contras. On defense issues, Congressman Foley has voted, among other things, to cancel production of the MX missile, and he has come out in favor of a nuclear freeze. Foley's most striking concession to his district's marked conservatism has been his consistent opposition to gun control. Asked to explain his position on this issue, Foley once replied, in an exaggerated western drawl, "I'm from the West, where 'Drop yer guns' is fightin' words." While the congressman has expressed dismay at the zealousness of some gun control opponents, he believes that a law requiring national registration of handguns would be impossible to enforce.

Foley began to emerge as a national figure in 1974, when he won his first leadership post, succeeding John Culver of Iowa as chairman of the Democratic Study Group, an organization of moderate and liberal House Democrats. In that capacity, he led the fight to open committee hearings to the public and to weaken the authority of powerful committee chairmen. He was aided in his efforts by the seventy-five new Democratic congressmen, many of them young and liberal, elected in 1974. Upon their arrival in Washington, D.C., these young Turks eagerly joined the move to wrest committee chairmanships from the old guard. One of their first targets was W. R. Poage of Texas, the conservative, seventy-five-year-old Democratic chairman of the Agriculture Committee. Foley was the second-ranking Democrat on the committee, but he refused to become involved in the effort to oust Poage and even nominated him for reelection with a stirring speech. "He had the grace to strongly defend Poage when it was apparent he would be beneficiary" of Poage's removal, Don Bonker, a former congressman from Washington State, told Jacqueline Trescott of the Washington Post (June 1, 1989). "It was an extraordinary moment in House history." Poage was so touched by the gesture that, after he was defeated by just three votes, he nominated Foley for the chairmanship of the committee. Once elected, Foley, in turn, named Poage vice-chairman. Then only forty-five years old, Foley was the youngest chairman of a major congressional committee in decades. He was also the first westerner to chair the Agriculture Committee.

Befitting his distaste for self-promotion, Foley refused to hold a press conference following his election as chairman of the Agriculture Committee, preferring instead to talk to reporters individually in his office. Unlike Poage, Foley attempted to accommodate Republican members of the committee, and he consulted regularly with the ranking Republican, William C. Wampler of Virginia. He also altered the focus of the committee from farm production to nutrition and consumer issues. "Agricultural legislation should be for consumers, as much as for farmers and ranchers," Foley said in an interview with Peter C. Stuart of the Christian Science Monitor (January 28, 1975) shortly after assuming the chairmanship. During his six years as head of the Agriculture Committee, Foley painstakingly forged coalitions between farm-state members protective of government price supports and big-city liberals who wanted to expand the food-stamp and school lunch programs. A controversial 1977 farm bill, in particular, demonstrated Foley's considerable skill at consensus-building. The Senate had passed a $14 billion bill setting farm subsidies and food-stamp benefits for the next four years, which President Jimmy Carter had vowed to veto as too expensive. To avoid a confrontation with the president, Foley put together a less expensive package, shepherded it through the committee, the House, and the House-Senate conference, and personally persuaded President Carter to sign it into law. "In agriculture, the members followed Tom Foley," Democratic congressman Lee Hamilton of Indiana observed, as quoted in a New Yorker (April 10, 1989) profile of Foley. "And the leadership quickly began looking to him for guidance."

In 1976 Foley defeated Congresswoman Shirley Chisholm of New York for the position of chairperson of the Democratic Caucus, the organization that selects the party's leadership in the House and formulates its rules and floor strategy, but he was not active in the post. Ironically, the 1980 Reagan landslide that almost cost Foley his seat was responsible for his next step up the leadership ladder, for both John Brademas, the House majority whip, and Al Ullman, the chairman of the powerful Ways and Means Committee, lost their bids for reelection. Speaker Thomas P. ("Tip") O'Neill offered Dan Rostenkowski of Illinois, the deputy chief whip, the option of either succeeding Brademas as majority whip or taking over as chairman of the Ways and Means Committee. When Rostenkowski chose the latter position, O'Neill named Foley majority whip, the third-ranking Democratic post in the House.

Although Foley seemed temperamentally ill-suited for the whip's post, which traditionally calls for a stern, often decidedly partisan hand, he managed to succeed on his own terms, trading on his reputation for fairness and integrity to persuade members to support the party agenda. Foley gained national attention in August 1982, when he was tapped to deliver the Democrats' televised response to President Reagan's call for public support of a compromise tax hike to curb the budget deficit. Foley's cool, reasoned speech urging fellow Democrats to face "economic reality" and support the president's initiative won favorable notices nationwide.

Foley subsequently emerged as a key figure on foreign-policy and budget matters. Perhaps his most significant contribution to managing the federal budget was his role in salvaging the Gramm-Rudman-Hollings deficit-reduction law in 1985. Recognizing that House Democrats were prepared to reject the version of that bill passed by the Republican-controlled Senate, Foley put together an alternative that divided funding cuts equally between domestic programs—except for Social Security—and defense. The compromise package eventually won the support of all but two of Foley's Democratic colleagues.

When Speaker O'Neill retired at the end of the 1986 congressional session, Jim Wright of Texas, the majority leader, was elected his successor, Thomas Foley moved up to the post of majority leader, and Tony Coelho of California became Democratic whip. All three formally assumed their new positions in January 1987. As majority leader, Foley served on the Permanent Select Committee on Intelligence, the Committee on the Budget, and the Select Committee to Investigate Covert Arms Transactions with Iran. Sandwiched between Wright and Coelho, both of whom were aggressively partisan, Foley provided the Democratic leadership with a much-needed stabilizing influence. Although some welcomed his voice of reason, others grew impatient with his cautious approach. "When you talk to Tom," Congressman Rostenkowski told Hays Gorey of Time (June 5, 1989) magazine, "you start biting your fingernails and you don't stop until you're up to your elbows. What he does is good, but sometimes getting there is frustrating." Despite such criticism, Foley has become enormously popular on Capitol Hill. In a poll of House and Senate aides, he was voted "the most respected member of Congress" in 1988 and again in 1989. Indeed, Foley is held in such high esteem by members of both parties that he was among

those Michael S. Dukakis, the Democratic presidential candidate, considered for his running mate in the 1988 campaign, but the congressman withdrew his name before Dukakis made his final decision.

On April 17, 1989 the House Ethics Committee released a report accusing Speaker Jim Wright of violating House rules in sixty-nine specific instances. The charges led Wright to announce, on May 31, that he would resign the speakership, effective upon the election of a successor. Six days later, the House, as expected, elected Foley Speaker, choosing him over Robert Michel of Illinois, the House Republican leader, in a straight party-line vote of 251 to 164. In his initial address as Speaker, Foley called for an end to the bitter partisan feud that had resulted in the resignations of Jim Wright and Tony Coelho, who had resigned in late May amid questions about alleged financial improprieties. "I am a proud Democrat," Foley declared, "but I appeal specifically to our friends on the Republican side that we should come together and put away bitterness and division and hostility."

On the same day that Thomas Foley took over as Speaker, Mark Goodin, the communications director of the Republican National Committee, circulated a scurrilous memorandum entitled "Tom Foley: Out of the Liberal Closet," which compared Foley's generally liberal voting record with that of Congressman Barney Frank, one of the House's most liberal members and an acknowledged homosexual. Outraged Democrats complained that the comparison was intended to call into question Foley's sexual orientation. Although President George Bush and other Republican leaders denounced the memo and Goodin was forced to resign, Foley nonetheless felt compelled to deny—at first privately, in a meeting with top congressional Democrats, and later publicly, in an interview on the Cable News Network—that he is gay. "I am, of course, not a homosexual, been married for twenty-one years," he told the CNN interviewer. "Lee Atwater [the Republican National Committee chairman] . . . called me up last night and apologized effusively for any such inference, repudiated it, and totally rejected it. So I think the issue is closed."

Thomas S. Foley is an imposing man, six feet, four inches tall, with wavy silver hair and blue eyes. Although the Speaker currently weighs about 250 pounds, his weight has fluctuated so dramatically during his years in Congress that he keeps three sizes of suits on hand. A self-described "Type B" personality, Foley takes neither himself nor his career too seriously, and he has confessed that he lacks the inner drive necessary to run for the presidency. Foley is a gifted raconteur who, in the words of Hays Gorey, "can regale a gaggle of beer guzzlers with a slightly off-color tale, then quote Rousseau, Burke, and Hobbes in a symposium of scholars at the Library of Congress." A committed "indoorsman," he delights in telling self-deprecatory anecdotes about his awkward attempts at outdoor activities. He sometimes goes on early-morning bicycle rides through the streets of northwestern Washington, D.C., but otherwise he disdains exercise. His chief avocational interest is classical music, particularly the works of Bach and Mozart. An audiophile, he has furnished his office with the latest in high-tech sound equipment.

On December 19, 1968 Foley married the former Heather Strachan, a lawyer whom he met when both worked on Senator Jackson's staff. Mrs. Foley joined her husband's staff as an unpaid administrative assistant following their marriage, and she is now his closest adviser. The Foley's sixteen-year-old Belgian sheep dog, Alice, accompanies them to work each day and is frequently seen at

Thomas Foley's heels as he makes his rounds of the Capitol. Thomas and Heather Foley live in a rented apartment in the fashionable Kalorama section of Washington, D.C. They also own an apartment in Spokane.

References: N Y Times D p20 Ag 18 '82 por, A p1+ Je 2 '89 pors, A p1+ Je 7 '89 por, B p11 Je 8 '89 por; New Yorker 65:48+ Ap 10 '89 por; Time 133:36 Je 5 '89 por; USA Today A p8 Je 6 '89 por; U S News 106:38+ Je 5 '89 por; Wall St J A p1+ Je 1 '89; Washington Post C p1+ Je 1 '89 por; Almanac of American Politics, 1988; Politics in America (1988); Who's Who in America, 1988–89

Forsyth, Bill

July 29, 1947– Scottish filmmaker. Address: b. c/o Directors Guild of America, 7950 Sunset Blvd., Hollywood, Calif. 90046; h. 20 Winton Drive, Glasgow G12, Scotland

Often referred to as a one-man Scottish film industry, Bill Forsyth has directed and scripted six feature films during the past decade, the first four of which were filmed in his native Scotland. Unlike many British filmmakers, he was not eager to work in Hollywood. In an interview with William Green for the (London) Telegraph Sunday Magazine (December 6, 1987), Forsyth explained: "I don't want to be a big commercial director—I don't have that much ambition. Popular films in the U.S.A. are based on a principle of manipulating the viewer, which is the opposite of everything I am trying to

do." Forsyth revealed the working principle behind all his films in an interview with David Friedman for New York Newsday (October 11, 1989): "I try to undermine all cinematic conventions when I work. I'm not very violent, but I do feel like a subversive. At every opportunity I ask myself, 'What can I do to make this not what it seems to be?'"

Although most of Forsyth's work has been praised for its charm, whimsicality, and gentle, bittersweet comedy, his films have not been commercially successful beyond "the limited sophisticated audience that you find in New York and other large cities," as he acknowledged in an interview with Stuart Rosenthal for the New York Times (September 18, 1988). Forsyth is best known for Gregory's Girl, for which he won a British Academy of Film and Television Arts Award for best screenplay after the film's release in 1981, and for Local Hero, which earned him a New York Film Critics Circle Award for best screenplay in 1983. His reputation as a director of light comedy notwithstanding, each of his films has a somber element that demonstrates his view that "comedy and darkness inhabit the same space." He elaborated on that concept in an interview with Erica Abeel for the New York Times (November 22, 1987): "Laughter in a movie to me is just a way of revealing the darknesses of the situations that the characters are in, a mechanism of coping with despair."

The director's world-view may have evolved out of his early memories of growing up with his two older sisters in a working-class Glaswegian neighborhood near the Clyde River in Scotland. He was born William David Forsyth on July 29, 1947 to William Forsyth, a former shipyard worker who had become a grocery warehouse manager, and Martha Forsyth, who worked in a grocery store. In the early 1950s the Forsyths' home was razed in a city-wide slum-clearance project, and the family was relocated to a western suburb of Glasgow. His parents conducted their lives with somberness, according to the New York Times article by Erica Abeel, who quoted Forsyth as saying, "I think it's a much more real way to conduct your life" because more of one's life is spent in apprehension and fear than in happiness.

As a student at the Knightswood secondary school in Glasgow, Forsyth was, he has recalled, "shy and introverted" and "always a bit dreamy." He liked his English classes, but he was generally uninvolved in school activities. According to one interviewer, he watched war movies and westerns once or twice a month, but another interviewer maintained that he did not go to the movies as a child or as a teenager. At any rate, he had no plans to become a filmmaker, even after attending a school-sponsored screening of Jacques Tati's *Monsieur Hulot's Holiday*, which he enjoyed tremendously. Forsyth's visual gags have since been compared to those of Tati, the late French comic genius.

On graduating from the Knightswood School, Forsyth and his friends planned to work for a year so that they could earn enough money for a trip to Greece. With that goal in mind, Forsyth answered a newspaper ad that read: "Lad required for film company." He accepted the five-pound-a-week trainee position with that one-man industrial film company over a higher-paying job in the insurance business solely because he did not have to report to work until 9:30 in the morning. After one year of assisting his employer in everything from writing to filming to editing, Forsyth became "quite attached to the idea of making films," as he has put it. Consequently, when his boss died one year after Forsyth was hired, Forsyth found similar work with a larger industrial film company in Glasgow.

From 1967 to 1968 Forsyth worked as an assistant film editor at the BBC in London. "I was twenty," he told Nan Robertson, who interviewed him for the *New York Times* (February 12, 1984), "and it was automatic to fly the nest for a more stimulating world. . . . I was back home within a year. I couldn't make it in London—it was no place to be poor. It quite shocks me, when I think upon it, how short a time I could survive in London."

For the following three years Forsyth was a freelance film editor based in Glasgow. After a program of his own experimental, structuralist short films made it to the Edinburgh Festival in 1970, he and two partners formed Tree Films, which was established to produce industrial films and documentaries sponsored by quasi-autonomous national governmental organizations (quangos), such as the Highlands and Islands Development Board.

Shortly after launching his production company, Forsyth was admitted into the inaugural class of Great Britain's first nationally recognized film school, which opened in Beaconsfield, near London, in 1971. He hoped that the National Film School would provide him with the opportunity to free his creative impulses from the imperatives of earning a living, but after half a year he dropped out "for one or two personal reasons," as he explained to Lawrence Van Gelder in an interview for the *New York Times* (May 23, 1982). "I had started to put a home together in Glasgow. I was homebuilding—emotionally." Ten years later the school awarded him a diploma that certified that he had "completed the course term between 1971 and 1981."

Back in Glasgow, Forsyth and his partners in Tree Films continued making industrial and documentary films for six years, while they dreamed of making feature films instead. "We used to imagine that we would make a film about steam engines and Dino De Laurentiis would see it one day on cable TV and offer us a feature film," he recalled to Brian Donlon in an interview for *Celebrity* (November 17, 1984). In the meantime, "the company had become quite moribund. . . . It's very hard work, you know," he told Van Gelder, "trying to make things like marine engines interesting."

When the company was dissolved by mutual consent in 1977, Forsyth struck out on his own, having decided "in a desperate act" that he "might as well make a feature movie," as he told Van Gelder. But despite his considerable experience in the film industry, which included *The Legend of Los Tayos*, a film he made for television in 1977, and *The Odd Man*, a documentary about writers in Scotland, Forsyth had never directed professional actors. He therefore believed that "the best thing and cheapest way" to make his first feature was to work with young actors who were amateurs.

Forsyth began spending his Friday evenings at the Glasgow Youth Theatre, which had been created to prevent delinquency among the unemployed teenagers in the neighborhood. He already harbored an idea for a script inspired by the "beat" writer Jack Kerouac's *Maggie Cassidy*, a novel of awakening adolescence that was published in 1959. Forsyth finished the script of *Gregory's Girl* in one year with the cooperation of the teenage actors themselves, who talked to the director at length about their concerns at school and at home. *Gregory's Girl* was not produced immediately, however, because of a lack of funds, for despite its amateur cast, its budget would come to $400,000, and Forsyth's proposals for financial backing were rejected by everyone he approached.

Undaunted, Forsyth was determined to finance *Gregory's Girl*. He quickly conceived another film that not only could be produced more cheaply, but also could provide a showcase for his talent. In three weeks he wrote the script of *That Sinking Feeling*, which portrays jobless youths who, in his words, "are spending their lives killing time. They live in a world which has reared them for labor and offers them nothing but idleness." To relieve their boredom, the youths plan to steal ninety-three stainless-steel sinks from a warehouse. The film was shot in 16-mm in three weeks in April 1979. Aside from the $3,000 that paid for the film stock and a remaining budget of $7,000, Forsyth "didn't use money," as he explained to Van Gelder during the *New York Times* interview. "I just put a co-op thing together with a lot of colleagues in the film business in Glasgow and a lot of the kids, so there were about fifty people in Glasgow who owned shares in the film," Forsyth recalled.

Although *That Sinking Feeling* had been made by, about, and for Glaswegians, it closed within a week of its opening in a Glasgow theatre. And though it was well received at the 1979 Edinburgh and London film festivals and was then shown for seventy-five weeks at the same Glasgow theatre, it was not released in England until 1981. American audiences had to wait until 1984 to see it, when it was blown up into 35-mm film and billed as *Bill Forsyth's That Sinking Feeling*, after the success of his second and third films had made him a bankable director.

In addition to delighting audiences with Forsyth's "irresistible blend of sweetness, silliness, and social conscience," to quote one reviewer, *That Sinking Feeling* eventually helped to finance the postponed production of *Gregory's Girl*. In the opinion of another reviewer, *That Sinking Feeling* made up in "whimsical dialogue, deadpan humor, high spirits, and ingenuity" what it lacked in "budget and polish." That view apparently was shared by Davina Belling and Clive Parsons, two independent producers who, after seeing the movie, helped Forsyth to obtain funds for *Gregory's Girl* from a Scottish television station, the British Film Institute, and private sources.

The first "exported" Scottish feature film to be produced entirely by Scots, *Gregory's Girl* was filmed on location in Cumbernauld, a government-sponsored "new town" located about halfway between Glasgow and Edinburgh, in the summer of 1980. Finished in time for the November 1980 Edinburgh Festival, it was released in Great Britain and the United States in 1981, and in Canada in 1983. Featuring many of the actors who appeared in *That Sinking Feeling*, *Gregory's Girl* proved as popular among moviegoers as it was among critics. Its story of teenage awkwardness centers on the attempts of an abstracted, gauche, and spindling sixteen-year-old to cope with his unrequited love for Dorothy, his school's star soccer player. Forsyth's handling of adolescence evoked a comparison to François Truffaut's *Small Change* from Vincent Canby, the film critic for the *New York Times*, and audiences responded enthusiastically to the director's favorite comic devices, such as running gags, non sequiturs, and witty dialogue. In the widely shared opinion of one reviewer, "*Gregory's Girl* explodes stereotypes, strips language clean, [and] redeems a degenerate genre with affection, tenderness, exuberant good humor, and endless surprises."

The idea for Forsyth's third film, *Local Hero*, was suggested to him by David Puttnam, the British producer of *Chariots of Fire*, which won the latter an American Academy Award in the same year that *Gregory's Girl* earned Forsyth a British Academy Award. Impressed by Forsyth's first film, Puttnam approached the director in 1981 with an idea for a script based on a newspaper account of the sale of a private Scottish island to an American oil company. Forsyth agreed to the $5.5 million project after he happened to visit some islands affected by Scotland's oil boom, in the course of filming a television adaptation of George Mackay Brown's short story *Andrina* for BBC-Scotland. In 1981 he began writing the script for *Local Hero*, the working titles of which were originally "The Gloaming" or "Oil Galore."

"It's a combination of *Apocalypse Now* and *Brigadoon*," Forsyth said of *Local Hero* when he began filming it in 1982. Joseph Gelmis, who interviewed the writer-director for *Newsday* (February 13, 1983), explained that Forsyth's script about an American oil company acquisitions man who is charged with the responsibility of transforming a Scottish coastal village into an oil refinery site resembles *Brigadoon* because the American and his boss (Burt Lancaster) become so enchanted with the place that they are unable to destroy its slow pace and special quality of life with their plan. And *Local Hero* is reminiscent of *Apocalypse Now* in the sense that both are "cautionary tale[s] about American imperialism," in Gelmis's words.

Released in 1983 to critical acclaim, *Local Hero* has since been touted by some reviewers as the best of Forsyth's six films. In addition to earning Forsyth a New York Film Critics Circle Award, *Local Hero* paved the way for the release of *That Sinking Feeling* in the United States in 1984. A commonly held view of *Local Hero* was expressed by Joseph Gelmis in his review for *Newsday* (February 17, 1983), in which he maintained that the film "is a tongue-in-cheek ecological tall tale, an immensely likable culture shock comedy. . . . A film of sensibility, its humor is gentle, subtle, slyly subversive, rather than strident and righteous."

Forsyth's fourth film, *Comfort and Joy*, was also inspired by a newspaper account—in that instance, of the blowing up of an ice cream vendor's truck for parking in another vendor's spot in Birmingham, England in 1980. According to Matt Wolf of the Associated Press, "Forsyth said . . . he was intrigued by the potential for violence in such a seemingly banal endeavor as the sale of ice cream." (After the film was made, six people died in a similar incident in Glasgow in April 1984, according to an article in the *New York Post* [October 9, 1984].)

Taking its ironic title from the Christmas carol "God Rest Ye Merry, Gentlemen," *Comfort and Joy* is about a Glasgow disc jockey who is abruptly abandoned by his girlfriend at Christmastime, and who decides to do a documentary on the local ice cream wars rather than his usually chirpy radio show in an effort to find some purpose to his life. Many viewers interpreted the film as a comedy about depression, including Forsyth himself when he was writing it, but when he completed filming, he decided it was not, after all, a comedy. Instead, it is a sad and ironic examination of the identity crises of adolescence, which Forsyth has described as a "kind of permanent terminal state." "There's no such thing as adulthood," he has said.

Comfort and Joy had its premiere in Los Angeles in the spring of 1984 before an invited audience that included Princess Anne. It was screened at the Cannes Film Festival on May 17, 1984 and was released commercially in the fall of that year. When some British film critics expressed their disappointment with *Comfort and Joy*, Forsyth asserted at a press conference that "there is something in the English sense of humor that lacks a strong ironic context." Earlier he had told Lawrence Van Gelder that Scottish humor is "a kind of mordant sense of humor, the humor of the gallows. . . . It's probably a kind of inferiority complex, being attached to England and stuff like that."

Although Forsyth believes that one reason for the film's relative success in America is that "Scottish humor has more in common with American humor—New York humor, to be exact," some Americans did not share Forsyth's indifference to plot, drama, and linear narrative in favor of character exploration. "Stories don't happen *to* characters, they grow *out* of characters," Forsyth insisted to David Sterritt of the *Christian Science Monitor* (February 16, 1984). While most American critics found something to like in the movie, especially the exploration of the relationship between the disc jockey and his girlfriend, many were disappointed with its dénouement.

Three years passed between the premiere of *Comfort and Joy* and the release of Forsyth's fifth film, *Housekeeping*. He adapted the screenplay from Marilynne Robinson's best-selling novel of the same name, which he had read while in New York to receive his award for *Local Hero* during the winter of 1983–84. The novel struck him so forcefully that he "became covetous" of its scenes, which he then "began to feel the need to own . . . in a movie," as he explained in the interview with Erica Abeel. "You're exposed to emotional information, poetical insights, thoughts—things are coming at you on different levels. When I read it, I felt this is how movies should be."

Set in the fictional town of Fingerbone, which is modeled on Marilynne Robinson's birthplace in Sandpoint, Idaho, *Housekeeping* concerns two orphaned teenage sisters who respond in opposite ways to their itinerant aunt, Sylvie, who arrives to be their guardian. Filming took Forsyth to British Columbia, Canada, but he lived in New York for two years during the making of the film because Diane Keaton, who had agreed to play Sylvie, was in New York. It was because of her that Cannon had agreed to finance the film, but, five weeks before filming began, Diane Keaton dropped out of the project.

David Puttnam, the producer of *Local Hero* who had become chairman of Columbia Pictures in 1986, not only took over the production of *Housekeeping*, but also found a replacement for Diane Keaton in Christine Lahti, a highly respected character actress. "Christine Lahti deserves a codirector credit for her work" with the actresses who played the two young girls, Forsyth told Green, "and she got much closer to the character of Sylvie than Keaton, who is a more mannered actress, would have done." British critics tended to fulfill Forsyth's prophecy of how the [English] public would react. "They're going to misunderstand it," he predicted to William Green. "They'll think it whimsical, or charming, and people will say that Sylvie . . . is eccentric and freespirited. They will see their idea of a Bill Forsyth film."

The tendency, on the part of some critics, to mistake Forsyth's low-key humor for heartwarming charm rather than the darker coloration that he sets out to impart to otherwise conventional comedies was again in evidence in the reviews of *Breaking In*, his sixth and most recent film. Released in October 1989 and scripted by John Sayles, *Breaking In* stars Burt Reynolds as an aging safecracker who teams up with a disaffected teenager in a series of heists. In the interview with David Friedman, Forsyth discussed the sense of anticipation he felt at the prospect of directing *Breaking In*, the first time he was to direct a film written by someone else. "I loved the idea of doing a film that undermines the 'buddy movie' convention," he said. "In most films, the main characters connect. In this one, I tried my hardest to make sure they wouldn't." But Hal Hinson, in reviewing the film for the *Washington Post* (October 13, 1989), nevertheless found "a father-son element to the pairing" of the career criminal and the teenager. "The movie . . . is filled with precious, perishable delights," Hinson wrote. "It's just possible that [Forsyth is] a master. But something in you pulls back from the highest praise. No great artist works entirely in beige." Hinson's conclusion reflected both the success and the limitations of Forsyth's attempt, as he told Friedman, "to give the film a bleak and dreary mood. I wanted people to realize there are darker implications to being a criminal. That it's a difficult, and very lonely, way to make a living."

Although Forsyth is a self-described homebody, the variously diverging accounts in the press of his family life suggest a measure of reticence on that subject. According to Sue Summers, who interviewed him for the *Independent* (November 21, 1987), Forsyth's partner, Adrienne Atkinson, gave birth to the couple's second child, Sam, during their two years in New York. No other source mentions a child older than Sam, but Erica Abeel noted in her November 1987 article for the *New York Times* that there were two children: Sam, then two and a half years old, and Doone, then four months old. William Green omitted any mention of Doone in his article for the *Telegraph Sunday Magazine*, noting only that "Forsyth is now [December 1987] back in Glasgow, with his wife and the son born to them in New York." Green, the only reporter to refer to Forsyth as being married, does not connect the term "wife" with Adrienne Atkinson by name, identifying her only as the production designer of *Housekeeping* and as one of Forsyth's "old and trusted colleagues from his previous films."

Bill Forsyth's "flowing black hair and long, grey-tipped beard" give him the appearance of a Scottish sage, in the opinion of Sue Summers. Other journalists have echoed her characterization of Forsyth as "an unassuming, relaxed man with the kind of gentle humor which surfaces in his movies." Another interviewer noted his "doleful eyes" and "aggressively casual dress." "What I am doing now," he told William Green, "is more or less exactly what I dreamed of doing fifteen years ago. . . . And I'm still wearing the same clothes."

References: Celebrity p14 N 17 '84 por; (London) Independent p18 N 21 '87 por; N Y Times II p21+ My 23 '82 por, p19 F 12 '84 por, II p23+ N 22 '87; (London) Telegraph Sunday mag p16+ D 6 '87 por; Film Directors (1987); International Who's Who, 1989–90; Wakeman, John. World Film Directors, 1945–1985 (1988)

Freilicher, Jane

Nov. 29, 1924– Artist. Address: b. c/o Fischbach Gallery, 24 W. 57th St., New York, N.Y. 10019

"Nature observed with a twist" is the definition that the art critic Eleanor Munro has given to the realist landscape and still-life paintings of Jane Freilicher. A member of the so-called second generation of the New York School, Freilicher has managed to blend abstract expressionism and realism, invention and observed fact, the radical and the traditional, into a fluid, lyrical style of her own. The accessibility of her work is deceptive, however, for behind the easy visual appeal of her light-drenched paintings of Long Island meadows and marshes, tranquil and unpeopled cityscapes, and quiet studio interiors lurks a serious debate on the nature of reality. As the painter herself has observed: "When I start painting, it's with this rush of feeling—an emotional reaction to something I find beautiful . . . which provides the . . . impetus to paint. Then, as the process of painting evolves, other things enter into it—a discovery of what it is I think I'm seeing." Although the repertoire of Freilicher's subject matter is confined to her own studios and their immediate surroundings, her responses make the simplest detail or most conventional composition an event. As the poet-critic John Ashbery has put it, the excitement in her canvases comes from "slight disparities in the sybilline replies uttered by a fixed set of referents."

Daring to be a figurative, realist painter, Freilicher has remained undeflected by the highly touted postmodern movements that have succeeded one another during her three-decade-long career. "To strain after innovation," she has contended, "to worry about being on 'the cutting edge' . . . reflects concern for a place in history or for one's career rather than for the authenticity of one's painting." Although she has always been esteemed by a small circle of her peers, it was only recently, with the revival of interest in realism, that she began to gain much wider popularity. Certainly, she has been selling better than ever before; in 1986, for example, some of her large landscapes fetched prices between $50,000 and $75,000. Younger artists of the 1980s have been much influenced by her work.

Jane Freilicher was born in Brooklyn, New York on November 29, 1924, the daughter of Martin and Bertha Niederhoffer. Her father was a linguist who worked as a court interpreter; her mother was very musical. From early childhood on, Jane Freilicher had liked to draw and paint, and as she recalled to one interviewer, she remembers "feeling exaltation over bits of nature available" in her native borough: "A bouquet of flowers. On Brighton Beach, picking up stones. . . . Without feeling that I had a specialized talent, I thought I might do something in art, not for fame or achievement, but out of a romantic inclination to do beautiful things. A free-floating feeling that something was creative in me." She also recalled, however, being disturbed by her first exposure to modern art when, in her early teens, her older brother dragged her to a Picasso exhibition at the Museum of Modern Art.

At the age of seventeen, right after she graduated from high school, she eloped with Jack Freilicher, a jazz musician, but their marriage was annulled. In 1944, through her ex-husband, Jane Freilicher met Larry Rivers, who had not yet abandoned playing the saxophone professionally for painting, and the painter Nell Blaine and her circle of artists and musicians. It was then that Jane Freilicher first became interested in art as a career and began to frequent museums and galleries. Exhibitions of Matisse, Bonnard, and Vuillard at the Museum of Modern Art significantly influenced the development of her style. She enrolled at Brooklyn College, majoring in art, and received her B.A. degree in 1947. Persuaded by Nell Blaine, she and Rivers enrolled in the Hans Hofmann School of Fine Arts in New York and Provincetown, Massachusetts. In 1948 she obtained an M.A. degree in art education from Teachers College, Columbia University, where she had taken a course from the renowned art historian Meyer Schapiro.

In 1952 Jane Freilicher held her first solo show, at the Tibor de Nagy Gallery in New York, where she continued showing until 1970. She and Larry Rivers introduced the gallery's director, John Myers, to the other artists and writers who formed the core of the 1950s art scene, including the poets John Ashbery, Kenneth Koch, the late Frank O'Hara, and James Schuyler, who were very much a part of the New York School and who remained her close friends. Ted Berrigan's article "Painter to the New York Poets" in *ARTnews* (November 1965) discussed their special relationship. Her portrait of O'Hara, a quick, sketchy (but exact) standing figure painted in 1951, seems a visual equivalent of her response to those writers' lack of pomposity and heavy symbolism.

Among other friendships Jane Freilicher established in those years was one with the critic-painter Fairfield Porter, who in 1952 reviewed her first exhibitions for *ARTnews*. Of the bright, loosely painted, largely expressionist canvases she was then doing, Porter wrote that, though her articulation of figures was "impossible and awkward," he found it a small fault when weighed against her thoughtful rendition of a firsthand experience of nature. Visits to Porter's home in the Hamptons, out on the South Fork of Long Island, induced Jane Freilicher and her second husband, Joseph Hazan, who is also a painter, to buy a summer home of their own nearby.

Although she had experimented with abstraction during her year of study with Hans Hofmann, Jane Freilicher remained committed to figurative art. "I had to have something to refer to besides myself," she has commented. "I felt that otherwise my paintings would be thin." In any case, rather than express what she knows, she paints to discover her feelings. Hofmann, the influential precursor of abstract expressionism, was not dogmatic in his teaching. He always kept an historical perspective on style, and his student had no difficulty accommodating such abstract expressionist techniques as vigorous, rapid brushwork and the use of color in place of line in the rendering of recognizable images. That can be discerned in paintings from the beginning of Jane Freilicher's career, such as *Early New York Evening* (1954), with its loosely brushed vase of irises making a visual counterpoint to the city smokestacks seen through the window, or *Still Life with Calendulas* (1955), with its Matisse-like blending of the patterns and colors of flowers, throw rugs, and curtains.

Jane Freilicher has gone on painting still lifes much in the same mode: her arrangements almost invariably include a vase of flowers, observed in juxtaposition with the scene beyond the studio window. Thus, in *Jade Plant* (1979) the brilliant green leaves make a marked contrast to the snowy white cloth underneath, while the plant itself is set off against the city buildings seen through the window. Occasionally she has also turned her attention to the human form, especially in the 1960s when she painted a series of female nudes, including *Nude on a Green Blanket* (1966). Painted flat and dispassionately, the bodies seem another form of still life, and despite their emphasis on creamy flesh tones those works are, as Gerrit Henry noted in *ARTnews* (January 1985), sensuous but not sen-

sual. *Backgammon* (1975), with two girls engrossed in their game outdoors, is in fact a landscape with figures that have become components of the meadow scenery.

Her views out over green salt marshes, ponds, and dunes and her ability to capture the peculiar milky quality of eastern Long Island light (which reminded Willem de Kooning, another neighbor, so much of his native Holland) remain Jane Freilicher's hallmarks. And yet she emphatically declared to Amei Wallach, who interviewed her for *Newsday* (September 14, 1986), that she is not strictly speaking a landscape painter: "If the landscape weren't here and I were locked in a room, I'd paint something else. If I were a landscape painter, I'd probably go to the Alps. Although it's beautiful here, it's undramatic. . . . This interplay between sky and land. It seems to me a challenge to maintain the horizontal format, to breathe enough loving care in it to make it come alive." As Wallach interpreted those statements, Jane Freilicher can be considered essentially a still-life painter who composes landscapes as if they were still lifes. Since the outdoor world is seen, from a distance, usually separated by a window, and the artist is not *in* it, her paintings set up a dialogue between inside and outside, and they are charged with a certain wistfulness and anxiety about time and change.

As the *New York Times* critic Michael Brenson has pointed out, the flowers that appear in almost all her works, setting up a tension between country wildflowers or city structures outside the studio, are *cut* flowers whose life is therefore brief. Dealing more directly with the issue of mutability, *The Changing Scene* (1981) makes a rueful commentary on the increasing threat to Long Island's open spaces. Wearing glasses, brushes in hand, the painter stands peering out her window at a bulldozer plowing up a field. The threat alluded to may be a double one: overdevelopment of the land, or the "reconstruction" of it through the eyes of the artist, assisted by glasses, and the very act of painting it. Despite her contention that recording certain places and times was never her priority, Jane Freilicher has come to feel that her work may eventually document a vanished era on Long Island. In any event, she feels that, though her landscapes refer to real things, they "have their own objective life as paintings, not as imitations of other things." As the *New York Times* senior art critic John Russell summed it up, in Jane Freilicher's, as in any landscape paintings worth looking at, "what finally matters is the distinctive workings of the artist's mind."

By the late 1950s, Jane Freilicher's palette had lightened, the more intense tones of abstract expressionism perhaps affected by her exposure to Long Island atmosphere. The raw, direct application of paint remained expressionist, however, as in *The Mallow Gatherers* (1958), where the shapes of the flowers are simply indicated by strokes of color. That brushy quality has been only slightly modifed over the years since the late 1960s. More recently, she has applied pigment thickly or thinly, wielded her brush loosely or tightly, or sometimes both ways on the same canvas. By 1970, according to Kenneth Koch's essay on his friend in *Columbia* (February 1987), a new quality of light had begun to assert itself in her work, a glow emanating from the canvas rather than merely illustrating scenery or objects. A notable example is *Flowers and Strawberries* (1980), in which the light from the sky outside washes across the broad color shapes of table, vase, and fruit bowl. Making light in a painting is a mystery, Jane Freilicher has conceded; all one can say is that "without it a painting is dead, it doesn't breathe."

Over the years Jane Freilicher's canvases have become larger and her compositions more complex. *Studio Interior* (1982), with its still-life arrangement of artist's utensils and, on an easel nearby, a slightly dissimilar painting of the assemblage, seems to question whether the actual painting or the painting represented in it is more true to reality. Asymmetrical, even illogical, arrangements of objects, skewings and blurrings of pictorial space have emphasized her theme of contrasts: between interior and exterior, openness and closure, still life and landscape. In *Flowers and Mirror before a Landscape* (1983), a vase of flowers on a table by a window extends the studio space into the fields outside; a mirror leaning against the window reflects another corner of the studio and its view outside. One's gaze is simultaneously pulled inside and forced outside. In *Outside World* (1985), with a wall telephone and a radio next to a window that affords a wide view of the outdoors, it is difficult to tell whether the exterior impinges on the interior or vice versa.

There is visual wit, too, in the late-1980s *Soap Opera*, where the screen of a small television set on the floor of the city studio glows but is blank: an invisible program and an equally invisible viewer. According to Michael Brenson, that sort of visual irony is what makes Jane Freilicher important for young narrative realists like Eric Fischl. Setting compositional challenges for herself, she proceeds empirically. She has acknowledged that "every inch of a painting is a decision" the moment that she paints it. Sometimes she will do a preliminary sketch on the canvas in charcoal or pastel, which is eliminated as she works out the painting. "I'm not very facile. . . . I really struggle with my paintings," she has explained. "They look rather simple, and people often think I just knock them off—and then they try to imitate them . . . but actually I have to push very hard to get what I accomplish."

Toward the mid-1980s a new, rather poignant romanticism could be detected in Jane Freilicher's paintings, such as *Cadmium Yellow Sunset* (1984), the vivid disc of the sun seen between trees as it sinks into a sky of deep blue and pink. Two years later she returned to a more characteristic manner, as in *Pines and Field in September*, in which John Russell found echoes of Claude Lorrain and J. M. W. Turner in the way the trees frame the landscape and draw the viewer into the deep recesses of its space.

Besides her easel paintings—usually in oil on canvas—Jane Freilicher has designed sets for little-theatre productions in New York and has done a number of book illustrations, beginning in 1953, when she contributed to Ashbery's *Turandot and Other Poems*, and in 1984 she was commissioned to do a lithograph for his *Self-Portrait in a Convex Mirror*. In 1975 she designed the cover for *The Art of Kenneth Koch*, and in 1980 she did one for *Homage to Frank O'Hara*. In 1965 the *Paris Review* published a portfolio of her drawings. Commissioned by the United States Department of the Interior to contribute to the bicentennial traveling exhibition "America 1976," Freilicher turned down its offer to send her anywhere in the country to do a landscape and chose instead to do a painting of the scenery she knows and loves best, outside her Water Mill home. When she was asked some years later if there had been any private, deeper meaning in her election of that familiar subject matter, she denied interest in symbolism, although she admitted that "landscape painting . . . is probably a metaphor for some kind of physical sensation in your body. . . . And maybe presenting it through the studio window even has some Freudian significance in that the pleasure of painting . . . has something to do with the permission to be a voyeur."

Although Jane Freilicher is not too fond of teaching, she has served as a visiting critic and lecturer at art schools throughout the country. Formal recognition of her achievements includes the Hallmark International Art Award, 1960; a fellowship from the American Association of University Women, 1974, and a grant from the National Endowment for the Humanities, 1976; membership in the National Academy of Design, 1982, and their gold medal in 1987; and election to the American Academy and Institute of Arts and Letters in 1989.

Currently represented by the Fischbach Gallery in New York, Jane Freilicher had the first of her several one-woman shows there in 1975. She has also had solo exhibitions at the Wadsworth Athenaeum, 1976, and at the Kansas City (Missouri) Art Institute, 1983. In 1986–87 a retrospective exhibition of her work from 1954 to 1986, which was organized by the Currier Gallery of Art in Manchester, New Hampshire, traveled to the Parrish Museum in Southampton, Long Island, then to the Contemporary Arts Museum, Houston, and the Marion Koogler McNay Art Museum, San Antonio. Accompanying the show was a generously illustrated monograph, *Jane Freilicher Paintings*, edited by the curator, Robert Doty, and with essays by Ashbery and others.

Jane Freilicher has been represented in a large number of group exhibitions, especially shows devoted to American realism. The list includes the 1955 and 1972 Whitney Museum of American Art, New York, annuals; "Recent Landscapes by Nine Americans," at the 1965 Spoleto Festival; "Thirty Years of American Printmaking," at the Brooklyn Museum in 1976 and the museum's 1984 print biennial; "Contemporary American Realism since

1960," a touring show organized by the Pennsylvania Academy of the Fine Arts, Philadelphia, in 1981; "American Still Life 1945–83," at the Contemporary Arts Museum, Houston, in 1983; "American Women Artists, Part One: Pioneers," at the Sidney Janis Gallery, New York, in 1984; and "American Realism: Twentieth-Century Drawings and Watercolors," a 1985–87 traveling show originating at the San Francisco Museum of Modern Art.

The list of private and corporate collectors of the artist's works is an impressive one. As for public collections, Jane Freilicher's work can be found in the Metropolitan Museum of Art, the Museum of Modern Art, the Whitney Museum, and the Brooklyn Museum, all in New York; the Corcoran Gallery and the Hirshhorn Museum and Sculpture Garden, in Washington, D.C.; the Guild Hall and the Parrish Art Museum, both on Long Island; and the Rose Art Museum of Brandeis University, near Boston.

Jane Freilicher is a trim and handsome woman who avoids pretension and extravagance in her private life. Her typical garb is a wraparound skirt, simple white blouse, and sandals; she wears her wavy brown hair in a short, informal cut. Her friends and fellow artists admire her lively wit and range of general knowledge. In 1957 she remarried (though she retained her first husband's surname), and she and Joseph Hazan have one daughter, Elizabeth. She divides her year between their house in Water Mill, where her second-floor studio provides an airy perch over the surrounding countryside, and a duplex apartment on lower Fifth Avenue. There, her glassed-in studio provides stunning views over Manhattan. It is from there that she painted, for example, a nostalgic picture of Jefferson Market (1985; oil on panel), a Greenwich Village landmark that is now a branch of the New York Public Library. She is spurred on by the belief that she is "relearning to paint with each new canvas. Always a new beginning, even if the subject matter remains much the same."

References: ARTnews 84:78+ Ja '85 por; Doty, Robert, ed. Jane Freilicher Paintings (1986); Who's Who in America, 1988–89; Who's Who in American Art, 1989–90

Friedan, Betty

(frē-dan´)

Feb. 4, 1921– Writer; feminist leader; educator. Address: b. One Lincoln Plaza, #40K, New York, N.Y. 10023; h. 31 W. 93d St., New York, N.Y. 10025

NOTE: This biography supersedes the article that appeared in *Current Biography* in 1970.

Betty Friedan has been called "the senior stateswoman of feminism" for her active support of women's rights during the past twenty-six years. When she published *The Feminine Mystique* in 1963, she had no inkling that the book would trigger a nationwide women's movement whose consequences continue to affect the lives of Americans. Surveying the changes in traditional sex roles that have occurred since the book was published, she wrote in the *New York Times Magazine* (February 27, 1983): "I am still awed by the revolution that book helped spark. . . . Even now, women—and men—stop me on the street to reminisce about where they were when they read it."

The book represented the first attempt to debunk the myth that women's fulfillment consisted entirely in their roles as wife, mother, and consumer. Betty Friedan exposed the myth—which she named the feminine mystique—as a guilt-inducing, growth-stunting denial of women's aspirations, abilities, and identity. In 1966 she cofounded the National Organization for Women (NOW) and became its first president.

As the number of people joining the struggle for women's equality proliferated in the 1960s and early 1970s, so did ideological differences within the feminist community. Betty Friedan always exhorted the women's movement to remain in the mainstream. Her unpopular insistence that men are allies, as well as her refusal to reject the family, elicited scorn from younger, more radical feminists. But to mainstream feminists, such as Judy Mann of the *Washington Post* (July 15, 1981), Betty Friedan has been "the preeminent philosopher of the modern women's movement, and [her] vision . . . is the strength of the movement."

Betty Friedan, who was born Betty Naomi Goldstein on February 4, 1921 in Peoria, Illinois, was the first of Harry and Miriam (Horwitz) Goldstein's three children. Her father, an immigrant Jew, worked his way up from street-corner button salesman to owner of a jewelry store. The Goldsteins became comfortable enough to be able to hire both a maid and a housekeeper, but her father never managed to earn enough money to satisfy the frustrated ambitions of her mother, who had been forced to quit her job as editor of the women's page of a Peoria newspaper when she married.

Her mother's unfathomable discontent was Betty Friedan's earliest encounter with the shortcomings of the feminine mystique, but she did not recognize it as one of the preconditions for her feminism until years later. Another contributing factor was the anti-Semitism she experienced growing up in Peoria. Despite her family's relative affluence, she found that those of her faith were barred from the high school sororities and the country club —experiences that sensitized her to social inequities.

Exclusion from the social life of the local elite did not prevent her from joining their ranks on an intellectual basis. She became valedictorian of her class and started a literary magazine in high school, successfully repeating the venture at Smith College for women in Northampton, Massachusetts, where she edited the college newspaper and studied under the noted Gestalt psychologist Kurt Koffka. She has called her college experience "a great, marvelous thing . . . , an unfolding of the mind."

Betty Friedan graduated summa cum laude from Smith with a B.A. degree in psychology in 1942 and spent the following year studying psychology on a research fellowship at the University of California at Berkeley. She turned down a second fellowship when she found herself being pressured to choose between further study and her boyfriend, whom she also left behind in favor of a job with a labor news service in New York City. She lived with Smith and Vassar alumnae in a Greenwich Village apartment for the duration of World War II, but the ménage broke up gradually as her friends married returning veterans or were dislodged from their jobs by the influx of men into the booming postwar economy. Betty Friedan was among those who lost their jobs in that manner, but she managed to find another reporting job before marrying Carl Friedan, a producer of summer theatre in New Jersey (who later became an advertising executive), in June 1947.

Mrs. Friedan took a maternity leave when she gave birth to her first child around 1949, after which she returned to work, but when she requested another maternity leave five years later, she was promptly fired, and a man was hired to replace her. "My own conscious feminism," she wrote in her third book, The Second Stage (1981), "began in later outrage at that mistaken either/or choice that the feminine mystique imposed on my generation."

At the time, however, she felt relief mingled with outrage. "I had begun to feel so guilty working," she testified in her semi-autobiographical book It Changed My Life (1976), "and I really wasn't getting anywhere in that job. I was more than ready to embrace the feminine mystique." In 1957 she moved with her family to an eleven-room Victorian house on the Hudson River in Rockland County, New York, where she soon discovered that family life in the suburbs did not square with the idyllic picture she had been led to expect. Ironically, Mrs. Friedan's articles for women's magazines, written during her years as a self-proclaimed housewife, contributed to the widespread myth of "happy female domesticity," as Marilyn French later reported in an article for Esquire (December 1983): "Her editors would cut references to her subjects' careers. . . . The reality of women's lives—physical, intellectual, emotional, was censored; what appeared was a fantasy."

Bored with writing articles that presented the domestic aspects of women's lives as their entire universe, Mrs. Friedan spent nearly one year in 1957 doing an extensive survey of her college classmates fifteen years after graduation. "I seized on the chance," she recalled in The Feminine Mystique, "thinking that I could disprove the growing belief that education made women 'masculine,' hampered their sexual fulfillment, caused unnecessary conflicts and frustrations. I discovered that the critics were half-right; education was dangerous and frustrating, but only when women did not use it." Documenting her discovery and using her training as a psychologist, she publicized her findings in The Feminine Mystique (1963).

The book was an instant success. Betty Friedan was deluged with letters. One woman wrote: "You set up a challenge to me. . . . So long as I can think of obtaining further education, . . . the future seems exhilarating. . . . Otherwise, death pangs grip at my very being and a depression sets in that nearly drowns me." Another wrote: "I am grateful because you dispelled some of the loneliness I have felt in a lifetime struggle for knowledge and achievement."

But not everyone's reaction to The Feminine Mystique was positive. Mrs. Friedan was amazed that the book elicited much more hostility from women than from men. Many women, she explained in It Changed My Life, "were violently outraged at the charge that American women have been seduced back into the doll's house, living through their husbands and children instead of finding individual identity. . . . I was cursed, pitied, told to 'get psychiatric help,' . . . and accused of being 'more of a threat to the United States than the Russians.'" She was no longer invited to dinner parties, and her children were ejected from their carpools. Mrs. Friedan and her family moved back to New York City in 1964. "I couldn't stand being a freak alone in the suburbs any longer," she later recalled.

Mrs. Friedan's activism took off as a result of her newly attained status as a best-selling author. She was interviewed on television talk shows, booked for speaking engagements, and, in 1964, asked to edit an entire issue of *Ladies' Home Journal*. From 1965 to 1970 she taught the writing of nonfiction at New York University and at the New School for Social Research. Meanwhile, she interviewed women all over the country in search of material for a second book that would describe the new patterns of women's lives.

Instead of finding women who were meeting the demands of marriage, motherhood, and career in new, readily discernible patterns, Mrs. Friedan encountered "only women with problems." Abandoning plans for the book, which was never completed, she decided that only political action could effect the social changes that she believed were necessary for women's liberation. The changes she envisioned entailed not only new legislation, such as the Equal Rights Amendment to the Constitution and the legalization of abortion, but also enforcement of existing laws, such as the ban on sex discrimination in employment, embodied in Title VII of the Civil Rights Act of 1964.

Title VII would at first have outlawed discrimination based only on race, color, religion, or national origin. The ban on sex discrimination was added as a delaying tactic, and it was still being treated as a joke one year later by those charged with enforcing it. Mrs. Friedan responded by attending a meeting of state commissioners on the status of women in Washington, D.C., in June 1965, and, when she discovered that the group was powerless even to enact a resolution expressing outrage, she and several others formed NOW.

NOW set up task forces devoted to single issues according to the interests and abilities of the members of its local chapters in order to facilitate broad-based participation and minimize bureaucratic impediments to swift action. Although the organizational structure succeeded in involving whole communities in local causes, it failed in its concomitant goal: to inhibit political infighting by directing women's anger against discriminatory laws and practices rather than against each other. Power struggles and ideological division within NOW emerged with the influx of younger, more radical feminists whose primary issues were often lesbianism, the myth of vaginal orgasm, and class warfare against men. By 1970 their influence had become so strong that Betty Friedan declined to seek reelection as president of NOW that year.

Mrs. Friedan believed that undue emphasis on sexual issues discredited the movement by alienating the majority of women, who identified neither with lesbianism nor with the wholesale rejection of men, children, and the family. She expounded her position in an interview for *Social Policy* (November 1970): "Sexual politics is highly dangerous and diversionary, and may even provide good soil for fascist, demagogic appeals based on hatred. . . . If we define our movement in antilove, antichild terms, we are not going to have the power of the women and the help of increasing numbers of men who can identify their liberation with women's liberation."

By contrast, when the women's movement was defined in terms of a straightforward demand for equal rights with men, large numbers of men and women supported the movement. When Mrs. Friedan called for a national women's strike for equality on August 26, 1970, the fiftieth anniversary of women's suffrage, she envisioned a day of work stoppages, parades, and marches. The strike proved to be the largest turnout for women's rights in the United States in fifty years, exceeding her wildest dreams.

Betty Friedan had in 1968 cofounded the National Conference for Repeal of Abortion Laws, which changed its name to the National Abortion Rights Action League (NARAL) in 1973, following the Supreme Court decision in *Roe v. Wade* establishing a woman's right to a safe and legal abortion. In 1971 she joined forces with Shirley Chisholm, Gloria Steinem, and Bella Abzug to found the National Women's Political Caucus (NWPC) to encourage women to run for office. But during the 1972 elections it became clear that the NWPC was merely organizing women, in her words, "into yet another passive bloc of votes to be used by female bosses, and delivered for the purposes of the same old male political machines." Disillusioned, she temporarily dropped out of politics and turned to writing, traveling, lecturing, and teaching, which she pursued throughout the 1970s and 1980s.

From 1973 to 1976 Mrs. Friedan studied psychology, sociology, and women's history. She tried to create an economic think tank for women, but failed to obtain funding, and organized and directed the First Women's Bank and Trust Company in New York City. In 1975 she and twelve other veterans of NOW, alarmed by its vote to move "out of the mainstream, into the revolution," formed another group to reorient its membership to mainstream issues. Variously reported as calling itself "Womensurge," "Womansurge," or "Womanswar," the group was never heard from again, for mainstream issues, despite their alleged appeal to the majority, were not in vogue among the "radical chic" women who seemed to have taken over the movement.

A case in point was the failure of the Equal Rights Amendment to be ratified by the necessary thirty-eight states after it was passed by Congress in 1972. Despite tireless campaigning by Betty Friedan and others and the unprecedented extension of the original seven-year deadline for ratification for three more years, only thirty-five states had ratified the ERA when its final deadline expired on June 30, 1982. Two weeks later it was reintroduced into Congress, only to be narrowly defeated by the House in November 1983.

Although NOW blamed the ERA's failure on the rise of conservatives and on corporate funding of ERA opponents, Betty Friedan blamed NOW to some degree: "The sexual politics that distorted the sense of priorities of the women's movement during the 1970s made it easy for the so-called Moral Majority to lump ERA with homosexual rights and abortion into one explosive package of licentious, family-threatening sex," she has said.

For nearly two decades Mrs. Friedan has been warning feminists of the dangers of abandoning the issue of the family to such archconservatives as Phyllis Schlafly and Marabel Morgan. The defeat of the ERA was one such danger. Another, according to Mrs. Friedan, is that of underutilizing the strength of the women's movement by alienating the very people whose support is vital to its further progress: men and young women.

In *The Second Stage* (1981), Mrs. Friedan outlined the issues that feminists should address during the next phase of the women's movement: flexible work schedules, parental leave, child care, and new housing arrangements. The restructuring of work and home will be accomplished, according to Mrs. Friedan, only when men believe feminist solutions are in everyone's interest. Women can help men appreciate the benefits of restructuring, she argued, only if feminists "confront anew their own needs for love and comfort and caring support" by reclaiming the family as the "new feminist frontier."

The Second Stage touched a raw nerve in the feminist community when it was excerpted in the *New York Times Magazine*. One unnamed letter writer, as quoted by Mary Walton in an article for the *Chicago Tribune Magazine* (October 25, 1981), charged that Mrs. Friedan "would destroy feminism in order to save it and beat the Moral Majority by joining it." Another responded: "Women who are the victims of rape, violence, and unpaid domestic labor will take little consolation from idealistic notions of co-parenting and corporate flexitime." Conservatives gleefully called the book a recantation, and Mrs. Friedan found herself being introduced as a "repentant feminist" to a group of Italian women in 1982.

She staunchly defended her position in an interview with Carolyn Faulder for the *Guardian* (June 16, 1982). "Anybody who reads the book will see that in no way am I advocating a return to the old obsolete image of the family or of the subservient woman. I'm dealing with the reality of today's evolving family." Erica Jong agreed in her review for the *Saturday Review* (October 1981): "[Mrs. Friedan's] understanding of the doubleness of things, her refusal to be conned by slogans, her insistence on psychological truth rather than political polemicizing, her insistence on seeing the feminist movement in historical perspective, her refusal . . . to throw out the baby with the bathwater, make the reading of this book a supremely optimistic experience. For those of us seeking a new direction for feminism, it is here."

Where that new direction might lead was indicated by Mrs. Friedan's reasons for opposing NOW's position on a maternity leave case, *California Federal Savings and Loan Assn. v. Guerra*, in 1986. The bank was challenging a law that mandated disability leave for women for pregnancy and childbirth and subsequent reinstatement to their jobs. NOW argued that such benefits should be extended to all workers and that the law favored women over men unfairly. Mrs. Friedan's argument was consistent with the majority opinion of the Supreme Court, which upheld the law in January 1987: The opinion stated that the law "allows women, as well as men, to have families without losing their jobs." Mrs. Friedan was quoted in *Time* (August 18, 1986) as saying, "There has to be a concept of equality that takes into account that women are the ones who have the babies. . . . Why should the law treat us like male clones?"

Mrs. Friedan's efforts to affirm both equality and differences between the sexes have not been limited to speaking out on court cases and writing books. She took part in the three International Women's Conferences sponsored by the United Nations and held in, respectively, Mexico City (1975), Copenhagen (1980), and Nairobi (1985). Her world travels included visits with Simone de Beauvoir, Indira Gandhi, Jihan Sadat, the Empress Farah Pahlevi of Iran, and Pope Paul VI. In national politics she played a key role in persuading the Democratic party to reserve 50 percent of delegate spots for women in 1976 and thereafter, and she was one of the delegates to the Democratic National Convention in San Francisco who nominated Walter Mondale and Geraldine Ferraro for the 1984 presidential ticket.

In 1988 Mrs. Friedan served as a distinguished visiting professor at the University of Southern California's journalism school and at its Institute for the Study of Women and Men. In 1989 she taught a course called "Women, Men, and the Media" at USC; she is also affiliated with USC's Andrus Gerontology Center. Since 1982 she has been researching and writing a fourth book, to be published by Summit Books under the title "The Fountain of Age," in which she intends to shatter the mystique of aging. Geriatricians and gerontologists, she observed in her introduction to the twentieth anniversary edition of *The Feminine Mystique* (1983), "talk about the aged with the same patronizing, 'compassionate,' denial of their personhood that [was] heard when the experts talked about women twenty years ago." Nevertheless optimistic, she views the changes wrought by the women's movement as solid and enduring.

Betty Friedan has been described as tiny and plump, with a tendency to gesticulate during her gravelly-voiced disquisitions. Shortly after her divorce in 1969, she started a "weekend commune" of friends who gathered for weekends and holidays for about ten years. She currently maintains three homes: a fortieth-floor, two-bedroom apartment filled with Victorian furniture, modern art, and books on Manhattan's West Side, an apartment in Los Angeles, and a 200-year-old cottage in Sag Harbor, Long Island.

Mrs. Friedan has three grown children—Daniel, a theoretical physicist; Jonathan, an engineer; and Emily, a public-health pediatrician—and two grandchildren. She has often declared that her children have been among the basic satisfactions of her life. She also enjoys jogging, reading mysteries and science fiction, and cooking exotic soups.

References: *Chicago Tribune mag* p12+ O 25 '81 pors, XVIII p3+ D 14 '86 por; *Christian Sci Mon* p15 D 10 '81 por, p1+ Ja 11 '88 por; *Guardian* p8 Je 16 '82 por; *Life* p96+ F '88 pors; *N Y Times* B p10 O 19 '81 por; *N Y Times Mag* p13+ Jl 5 '81, p35+ F 27 '83 por, p26+ N 3 '85; *People* 16:147+ N 16 '81 pors; *Washington Post* B p1+ O 19 '83 por; *Contemporary Authors* vols 65-68 (1977); *Contemporary Authors new rev* vol 18 (1986); *International Who's Who, 1989-90; Who's Who in America, 1988-89; Who's Who of American Women, 1989-90*

Fuller, Charles

Mar. 5, 1939– Writer. Address: c/o Esther Sherman, William Morris Agency, 1350 Ave. of the Americas, New York, N.Y. 10019

"It's very important for me as a black writer to change how Western civilization—which includes black people—perceives black people," the American playwright Charles Fuller told an interviewer in 1986. "That's at the heart of what I do." Fuller's attack on the prejudices that trap his complex black characters in a world hostile to their aspirations usually takes the form of an investigation of murder and betrayal, often in an historical or military setting—a technique that allows him to explore troubling questions about racism and the way it corrupts blacks and whites. As Fuller told David Savran for his book *In Their Own Words: Contemporary American Playwrights* (1988): "Even the worst man has something in him that is admired and loved by somebody else. If you understand that, you can't in a play describe characters as, for

example, the racist police commissioner or the black-power black. . . . When you try to overturn stereotypes, it's easy to be foolish enough to believe the same things about white people that white people have for so long believed about blacks. The work has to become more complex." According to the *New York Times* drama critic Frank Rich, "Mr. Fuller demands that his black characters find the courage to break out of their suicidal, fratricidal cycle—just as he demands that whites end the injustices that have locked his black characters into the nightmare." *A Soldier's Play* (1981), Fuller's most successful drama, won a Pulitzer Prize in 1982 and in 1984 was made into the critically acclaimed film *A Soldier's Story*.

The oldest of the three children and the only son of Charles Henry Fuller Sr., a printer, and Lillian (Anderson) Fuller, Charles Henry Fuller Jr. was born in Philadelphia, Pennsylvania on March 5, 1939. During his childhood, his parents took in some twenty foster children, two of whom they eventually adopted. Fuller's earliest years were spent in a Philadelphia housing project. Later, after his father established his own printing business, the family moved into a home in a racially mixed neighborhood in North Philadelphia. Devout Roman Catholics, Fuller's parents sent their children to integrated parochial schools. They also discussed social issues with them as a matter of routine. Fuller gained an early respect for the printed word by proofreading galleys for his father, who became one of the first blacks admitted to a local printers union. When he was about thirteen, Fuller saw his first play, at Philadelphia's Walnut Street Theatre. Although the play, which starred Molly Picon and Menasha Skulnik, was performed entirely in Yiddish, Fuller was enthralled. "It was live theatre and I felt myself responding to it," Fuller recalled to Herbert Mitgang during an interview for the *New York Times* (January 11, 1982).

In high school, Fuller and his close friend Larry Neal (who later became a poet, playwright, and critic) began reading voraciously in the local public library, sharing an interest in the few black writers then being published and in the works of Franz Kafka, André Malraux, James Joyce, and William Butler Yeats. "Everything about us, all the prejudices, all those things that people had retained in the mythological madness of racism, was in the books," Fuller told Jacqueline Trescott of the *Washington Post* (October 26, 1983). "It occurred to us: suppose you could change all these libraries, suppose you could make a dent in the preponderance of antiblack material. Wouldn't that be a wonderful thing to do?" With that goal in mind, Fuller and Neal began writing their own poetry, short stories, and essays.

Following his graduation from high school in 1956, Fuller entered Villanova University in nearby Villanova, Pennsylvania. Although he was also interested at that time in astronomy, music, and law, he decided to major in English, in the hope of becoming a professional writer. Since, in the 1950s, the literary world was still largely closed to blacks,

Fuller, while a sophomore at Villanova, was advised by one of his professors to abandon his literary aspirations, and, when he submitted stories to the student literary magazine, its editors were patronizing. In 1959 Fuller dropped out of Villanova and joined the United States Army. Stationed at bases in Virginia, Japan, and South Korea, he spent the next three years working in military laboratories, checking the quality of petroleum. The work left him with a lot of leisure time to read and write, and his years in the service, together with the stories his father had told him about working for the navy during World War II, provided Fuller with material he later used in his plays.

On his discharge from the service in 1962, Fuller returned to Philadelphia, where he worked as a loan-collection officer for a bank, as a counselor for minority students at Temple University, and as a housing inspector in Ludlow, one of the most impoverished neighborhoods in the city. In his spare time, he attended night classes at LaSalle College and continued to write short stories that largely consisted of dialogue. In the mid-1960s he began writing sketches for a local theatre company that eventually became known as the Afro-American Theatre of Philadelphia. "A group of us got together and decided to start a theatre," Fuller explained to David Savran. "At that time I wasn't really writing plays, but skits connected to community issues. I was interested in how you save your community—blacks and Puerto Ricans were living side by side and going to war every day. We did the skits in a church and I then began to write little playlets." One such playlet involved the theft of a television set from a group of blacks and Puerto Ricans who were too busy bickering with one another to notice what was going on around them. In another, Fuller's troupe staged a shootout on a neighborhood street. When crowds formed, they chased the "murderer" down the street and into the theatre (a church), where the play began. "We staged the shooting to get people into the theatre," Fuller explained to Jonathan Mandell of New York Newsday (December 12, 1988). "The play was about young people not killing one another."

During the late 1960s, the Afro-American Theatre staged other short pieces by Fuller, including The Sunflowers (1968), a group of six interrelated one-act plays, and The Rise (1968), a four-act drama about the black nationalist Marcus Garvey. The company's work attracted the attention of the management of the McCarter Theatre in nearby Princeton, New Jersey, which, in 1968, commissioned Fuller to write The Village: A Party, a two-act drama about a utopian community of five interracial couples and the problems that result when its leader, a black man, falls in love with a black woman, in violation of the community's rules. Before the play's debut, Arthur Lithgow, the director of the McCarter Theatre, brought the entire company, including Fuller, to Princeton for additional training. When The Village: A Party opened at the McCarter in November 1968, Dan Sullivan wrote in the New York Times (November 13, 1968): "Mr.

Fuller has written a not-too-fanciful fantasy about racial integration that somberly concludes that it will not at present solve anybody's racial problems. . . . The play's originality and urgency are unquestionable and so is the talent of the playwright."

Retitled The Perfect Party, the play moved to the Off-Broadway Tambellini's Gate Theatre in New York on March 20, 1969 and ran until April 6. In reviewing that production for the New York Times (March 21, 1969), Lawrence Van Gelder noted, "Mr. Fuller's smooth, natural dialogue and deft characterizations . . . keep The Perfect Party at a high level of interest until it falls victim to a quick, weak ending." Other reviews of the play were largely negative, and Fuller himself later admitted to Herbert Mitgang that The Perfect Party "was one of the world's worst interracial plays." Whatever its limitations, its production provided Fuller, who was still attending LaSalle College at the time, with a surge of confidence and professional experience that proved to be of crucial importance in his career. "I remember walking out on stage on opening night—to the applause of my family and friends, of course—and realizing I would never go back to school again," he told Helen Dudar during an interview for the New York Times (December 18, 1988). "I was a playwright, and that's what I was going to do."

With that objective in mind, Fuller moved to New York City in 1969. There, he wrote two plays for the New Federal Theatre at the Henry Street Settlement: In My Many Names and Days (1972), a collection of six one-act pieces about a black family, and The Candidate (1974), which deals with a black politician running for the office of mayor of an unnamed northern city. While in Princeton, Fuller had made the acquaintance of Douglas Turner Ward, the head of New York's Negro Ensemble Company, which was also staging a play at the McCarter, and Ward immediately recognized Fuller's promise as a playwright. On June 4, 1974 the Negro Ensemble Company staged Fuller's two-act play In the Deepest Part of Sleep at St. Mark's Playhouse, marking the beginning of a close association between Fuller and the Negro Ensemble Company that was to last for fifteen years. Set in Philadelphia in 1956, In the Deepest Part of Sleep is a sexually charged study of a mentally disturbed woman, her live-in nurse, her seventeen-year-old son, and the boy's stepfather, who is having an affair with the nurse. It met with mixed reviews.

In his 1982 interview with Herbert Mitgang, Fuller said that after In the Deepest Part of Sleep was produced, he decided that he wanted to do something bigger and beyond himself, "something historical that would stand outside normal black theatre." The result was The Brownsville Raid (1976), a dramatization of a 1906 incident in which President Theodore Roosevelt dishonorably discharged without a trial all 167 members of a regiment of black soldiers stationed in Brownsville, Texas because they were accused of staging a shooting spree on the town that resulted in the death of one man. After researching the affair extensively, John D. Weaver concluded in his book *The Brownsville Raid* (1970) that white residents of the town, resenting the stationing of black soldiers there, probably carried out the shootings and then planted evidence to make it appear that the soldiers were the perpetrators. Strongly supporting Weaver's theory, Fuller's play, which opened at the Theatre de Lys on December 5, 1976, focuses on the black sergeant major Mingo Saunders, a twenty-five-year veteran whose trust in the army is totally destroyed. Fuller also explored the relationship between Roosevelt and Booker T. Washington, the black educator and author, who had agreed to instruct the editors of the black newspapers he controlled to downplay the incident. "That was the larger story," Fuller told Paul D. Colford of *Newsday* (April 23, 1982), "since at the time no one would believe that the president or anyone else would care what black people thought." Sixty-six years later, by which time all but one of the soldiers had died, the army cleared the entire regiment of wrongdoing.

Reviews for *The Brownsville Raid*, which ran for 112 performances at the Off-Broadway Theatre de Lys, were generally favorable. Writing in the *New York Times* (December 6, 1976), Clive Barnes called it a "taut and most compelling drama," which is "never for a moment weighted down with history." And in her *New Yorker* (December 20, 1976) review, Edith Oliver, one of Fuller's most confirmed admirers, said, "At first, as [the soldiers] go about their military routines, they seem almost anonymous, but so skillfully has Mr. Fuller delineated them that at the end, when each soldier is stripped of his rifle and insignia, . . . we know all of them pretty well."

Fuller's next play, *Zooman and the Sign* (1980), was inspired by the community work he had done in the 1960s in Philadelphia. "One day," he told a reporter for the *New York Post* (April 13, 1982), "I went around to see about getting lawyers for this kid who had just killed another kid. The boy was just as calm as could be. So that's where *Zooman* came from." With a decaying Philadelphia neighborhood as its setting, the play details the attempt of a married couple to find the murderer of their twelve-year-old daughter, who was killed while playing jacks on the porch, and the frustration they feel when their neighbors—some of them witnesses to the killing—refuse to help. Outraged, the father hangs a sign on the porch that reads: "The killers of our daughter Jinny are free on the streets because our neighbors will not identify them." The sign attracts media attention and leads to several confrontations between the father and the neighbors. Interspersed with the family scenes are appearances by the psychotic murderer—the Zooman of the title—who delivers monologues that are at once funny, frightening, and pathetic. Characteristically, *Zooman and the Sign* has no comforting denouement, for, in his interview with Savran, Fuller revealed that he opposes the practice of giving his plays tidy endings. "Television re-

solves the most extraordinary problems in two hours," Fuller said. "Movies do it. I just don't believe in that. I think stories have gray endings. We don't simply close the door and step into a new life."

When *Zooman and the Sign* had its premiere at the Off-Broadway Theatre Four on December 7, 1980, it got mixed reviews and closed after just thirty-three performances. Although John Beaufort of the *Christian Science Monitor* (December 10, 1980) called it "a dense and complex play whose geniune concerns are matched by its deep discernments," other critics were less enthusiastic. Clive Barnes of the *New York Post* (December 8, 1980) found *Zooman and the Sign* to be "an evening of interesting but underdeveloped theatre," and Allan Wallach of *Newsday* (December 8, 1980) wrote, "We can feel the playwright's earnestness, but Fuller has let the message overwhelm the play." In spite of such lukewarm notices, *Zooman and the Sign* was, in 1981, granted two Obie Awards for excellence in Off-Broadway theatre: Charles Fuller was honored for excellence in playwriting, and Giancarlo Esposito, who portrayed Zooman, received an Obie for his performance. *Zooman and the Sign* also earned Fuller an Audelco Award for best playwright.

After his friend Larry Neal died suddenly of a heart attack in January 1981, Fuller decided to write a play in his memory. The result, *A Soldier's Play*, was inspired by Fuller's late-night bull sessions with Neal about race, politics, and literature, his own army experiences, and his father's anecdotes about working for the navy during World War II. Loosely modeled on Herman Melville's *Billy Budd*, *A Soldier's Play* centers on the investigation of the murder of a black technical sergeant named Vernon Waters at the fictitious army post of Fort Neal, Louisiana in 1944. It appears at first that Waters had been murdered by the Ku Klux Klan. Then, a black army lawyer, Captain Richard Davenport (a character based on Larry Neal), who has been sent to investigate, begins questioning Waters's men and fellow officers. Their testimony leads to a series of flashbacks that reveal Waters's disturbed personality. Obsessed with gaining the approval of his white superiors, whom he despises, Waters takes out his resentment on any black soldier whose behavior might justify racist perceptions. He treats his men with such cruelty—going so far as to hound one soldier to death—that it begins to seem likely that one of them committed the murder.

Fuller wrote *A Soldier's Play* in just four months, and the Negro Ensemble Company's production opened to a chorus of praise at Theatre Four on November 20, 1981. Frank Rich of the *New York Times* (November 27, 1981) was especially enthusiastic: "This is, in every way, a mature and accomplished work—from its inspired opening up of a conventional theatrical form to its skillful portraiture of a dozen characters to its remarkable breadth of social and historical vision." And writing in *Newsweek* (December 21, 1981),

Jack Kroll called *A Soldier's Play* "a work of great resonance and integrity, bound to be one of the best American plays of this season." On April 12, 1982 Charles Fuller became the second black playwright to be awarded the Pulitzer Prize for drama (Charles Gordone, author of *No Place to Be Somebody* [1970], was the first). *A Soldier's Play* also garnered the Audelco and Theatre Club awards for best play, the Outer Circle Critics Award for best Off-Broadway play, and the New York Drama Critics Award for best American play. It played to packed houses for 481 performances.

Featuring many of the actors from the original stage production, a film version of *A Soldier's Play*, retitled *A Soldier's Story*, under Norman Jewison's direction, was released in 1984. Fuller and Jewison made a controversial decision to change the original ending, in which Captain Davenport tells a white captain that he will have to get used to black officers. The film concludes with several platoons of black soldiers marching enthusiastically off to war, as Davenport, acting as narrator, informs the audience that none of the major black characters came back alive. The film gained mostly favorable notices, though some critics faulted the ending for being too sentimental. In her review for the *New Yorker* (November 26, 1984), Pauline Kael recommended that "the people who complain 'They don't make movies the way they used to' . . . take a look at this one." *A Soldier's Story* fared well at the box office and was nominated for Academy Awards for best picture and best screenplay.

Charles Fuller's latest work, *We*, a series of five plays about black history, had its genesis in the early 1980s. Increasingly upset by his repeated viewings of D. W. Griffith's silent film classic *The Birth of a Nation*, which depicts blacks of the Civil War and Reconstruction period in a far from flattering way, Fuller said he wondered what would happen if he were to write his own *Birth of a Nation*. Over the next several years, he read some 120 books on the Civil War to familiarize himself with the era, with the intention of writing a series of dramas about the history of black Americans from the Emancipation Proclamation of 1863 ("the point at which all my myths and stereotypes about black people begin," according to Fuller) until the turn of the century. *Sally*, the first play in the series, had its premiere on July 30, 1988 at the National Black Arts Festival in Atlanta, Georgia and moved to Theatre Four on November 9, 1988. The second, *Prince*, opened at Theatre Four on December 3, 1988.

The title character of *Sally*, which is set in Beaufort, South Carolina during the winter of 1862–63, is a recently widowed, newly freed slave. Unsure of how to handle her freedom, she becomes romantically involved with Prince, a sergeant in the Union Army's first all-black regiment. The play also deals with the resentment of Prince's men at being paid three dollars less per month than their white counterparts. *Prince* is about a group of former slaves working on a Virginia farm in 1864 and the anger they feel over not being paid for their la-bor. When one of them protests, he is jailed. Critics generally considered *Prince* to be the better of the two plays, but reviews for both were mixed. John Simon of *New York* (January 9, 1989) magazine found that Fuller "comes on like a rank tyro," and Edith Oliver of the *New Yorker* (January 9, 1989) expressed her disappointment in "nonvintage Fuller." But John Beaufort of the *Christian Science Monitor* (December 22, 1988) commented, "Candor marks the series of vignettes, dialogues, and brief interludes of action—all brought to riveting theatrical life under Douglas Turner Ward's direction."

Among Charles Fuller's other works are *Sparrow in Flight*, a two-act musical based on the life of the black actress Ethel Waters, which was staged by New York's AMAS Repertory Theatre in 1978, and a number of scripts for television, including *Roots, Resistance, and Renaissance*, a twelve-part series telecast by WHYY in Philadelphia in 1967; an adaption of the Ernest J. Gaines short story *The Sky Is Gray* (PBS, 1980); and an adaptation of the Gaines novel *A Gathering of Old Men* (CBS, 1987). Fuller has been awarded fellowships by the Rockefeller Foundation (1975), the National Endowment for the Arts (1976), and the Guggenheim Foundation (1977–78). His other honors include the Creative Artist Public Service Award (1974) and the Hazellitt Award of the Pennsylvania State Council on the Arts (1984).

Since August 4, 1962 Charles Fuller has been married to the former Miriam Nesbitt, a nurse and teacher whom he met while a student at Villanova University. They have two sons, Charles 3d and David. After living in New York for several years, the Fullers moved back to Philadelphia. Interviewers invariably describe Fuller as genial and soft-spoken. According to Helen Dudar, "he radiates calm and easy cheer. . . . He is a tall, dark-skinned man with a few white threads in a close-cropped beard, surprisingly small hands, and a modest paunch." The playwright has recently been trying to give up cigarette smoking, a habit he acquired as a teenager after seeing a photograph of the late English writer Aldous Huxley with a cigarette in his hand and thinking that the portrait represented what a writer should really look like. A propagandist in the cause of education, Fuller once purchased space on twenty billboards in Philadelphia, on which he had the following message painted: "Young People: Stay Free; Take Pride in Yourselves; GRADUATE!!" To relax, he shoots pool.

References: *Ebony* 38:116+ Mr '83 pors; *N Y Newsday* II p4+ D 12 '88 pors; *N Y Times* C p12+ Ja 11 '82 pors, B p5+ D 18 '88 pors; *People* 17:85+ Je 28 '82 pors; *Washington Post* B p1+ O 26 '83 pors; *Contemporary Authors* vol 112 (1985); *Contemporary Literary Criticism* vol 25 (1983); *Dictionary of Literary Biography* vol 38 (1985); *Who's Who in America*, 1988–89

Garwin, Richard L(awrence)

Apr. 19, 1928– Physicist. Address: IBM Corporation, Research Division, Thomas J. Watson Research Center, P.O. Box 218, Yorktown Heights, N.Y. 10598

For over three decades the physicist Richard Garwin has played an important behind-the-scenes role in shaping American defense policy. Once described by his mentor, the Nobel laureate Enrico Fermi, as the "only true genius I have ever met," Garwin has earned his influence by virtue of his technical brilliance. Since 1951, when at the age of twenty-two he helped build the hydrogen bomb, Garwin has contributed to the design of dozens of weapons systems and served as a technical adviser to four presidents. In 1952 he began a long-term association with IBM's Thomas J. Watson Research Center, where he has conducted groundbreaking research in experimental physics and computer design. He is best known, however, for his role as a defense consultant. He is a member of the scientific advisory group to the Joint Strategic Target Planning Staff, which helps determine a priority list of Soviet and satellite targets, and he has served as a high-level consultant on both strategic arms limitations treaties.

While a firm believer in a strong national defense, Garwin is also a staunch proponent of arms control. He has frequently criticized the weapons systems promoted by the White House and the Pentagon—including the B-1 bomber, the MX missile, and, most recently, the space-based Strategic Defense Initiative, popularly known as Star Wars—as leading the nation toward bankruptcy and an increased threat of nuclear war. His blunt style has alienated many in the Pentagon, but his

admirers see him as a lone voice of reason within the defense establishment. As the Star Wars controversy has intensified, Garwin has spent increasingly more time outside the laboratory carrying his message to the public. "A lot of people can do physics," he said in a 1984 interview. "I really like it, there is nothing better than going to work in the morning and coming home late, working in the laboratory, having fun. . . . However, the world seems to fall to pieces while people do that. Somebody has to come and take care of the world."

Of Polish and Hungarian descent, Richard Lawrence Garwin was born on April 19, 1928 to Robert and Leona S. Garwin in Cleveland, Ohio. His father was an electrical engineer and inventor who taught high school science. Despite the Great Depression, the family lived comfortably. At an early age, Garwin showed an extraordinary technical ability and intelligence. Family legend has it that he was repairing a neighbor's home appliances at the age of five. "My father cautioned me not to take apart machines that were *working*," he has recalled.

After attending public schools in Cleveland, Garwin sailed through the Case School of Applied Science, now Case Western Reserve University, where he earned a B.S. degree in 1947. He went on to the University of Chicago to study physics with Enrico Fermi, the Nobel Prize winner who engineered the first controlled atomic chain reaction. Garwin earned his doctorate in a record two years and scored the highest grade on Ph.D. exams in the University of Chicago's history. The admiration between Fermi and his student was mutual. Garwin recalls his mentor as a "rare combination of a theoretical and experimental physicist. He is certainly the person who is closest to me in spirit."

Garwin first became interested in defense issues after the USSR exploded its first fission bomb, in 1949. That event made Garwin nervous, and, while at the University of Chicago, he wrote a paper outlining ways to find out the Soviets' nuclear secrets. In 1950 Fermi helped Garwin obtain a summer job at the prestigious Los Alamos laboratory in New Mexico, where scientists were hard at work designing the hydrogen bomb. Within weeks, he developed a theory of nuclear fratricide, which held that atomic bombs could destroy each other during an attack. Although the basic plans for the H-bomb were drawn up by two Europeans, Edward Teller and Stanislaw Ulam, during his second summer at Los Alamos, Garwin transformed those crude plans into, in Teller's words, "something approximating a blueprint." He also invented the initiator for the bomb—"the match for the nuclear bonfire," as he has described it. Garwin's design was used in the bomb prototype tested successfully in November 1952 and, later, in the first H-bombs actually deployed for defense purposes.

Reflecting back on his key role in the H-bomb's creation, Garwin has insisted that it "was not the most important thing in the world or even in my life at the time." Asked if he felt any guilt about his invention, Garwin told John Tirman in an interview for an Esquire (October 1984) profile, "I think it would be a better world if the hydrogen bomb had never existed. But I knew the bombs would be used for deterrence."

In 1952 Garwin left the University of Chicago for IBM's Thomas J. Watson Laboratory, then affiliated with Columbia University, where he would have more freedom to work. In his early years there, Garwin specialized in low-temperature physics, superconductivity, and the properties of liquid and solid helium. In 1957 he and two Columbia colleagues, using materials found in the laboratory over a weekend, devised a famous experiment that proved that the weak force of the atomic nucleus causes subatomic particles to violate the law of parity, or mirror image symmetry. In 1961 came a second groundbreaking experiment that measured the magnetic moment of the heavy electron and proved that the theoretically derived standards for quantum electrodynamics were accurate to one part in a billion.

At IBM, Garwin developed a reputation for being able to put together sophisticated experiments from haphazard pieces of equipment in his laboratory. In the early 1970s he became embroiled in controversy with Joseph Weber, a physicist at the University of Maryland who claimed to have detected gravity waves—a force posited by Einstein's theory of relativity but never detected. According to a colleague, Garwin decided to "step in and take charge of the matter." In six months he built a smaller and less expensive antenna that was ten times more sensitive than Weber's and, a month later, announced that he had been unable to detect a gravity wave. In 1975 he publicly denounced Weber at a scientific conference in Boston for not revealing that a computer programming error may have produced the evidence of gravity waves. A parallel experiment conducted by J. Anthony Tyson at Bell Laboratories has confirmed Garwin's findings.

Meanwhile, Garwin continued to work on defense issues, spending his summers at Los Alamos until 1966. From 1966 to 1969 he served as a consultant to the Pentagon as a member of the Defense Science Board. One enterprise that he undertook was called Project Lamplight, which was designed to reinforce American air defenses against Soviet bombers. But Garwin began to think that missiles would pose more of a threat, and he later worked on the design of military satellites, radar, and ballistic and cruise missiles. He also took on the role of technical adviser to the United States government on larger defense issues. During the Korean War, it was widely speculated that the reason he made a visit to Korea at the request of President Dwight D. Eisenhower was to study the feasibility of using nuclear weapons there, but government officials claimed he was exploring potential military research areas for a new laboratory being established by the University of Chicago. In 1962 President John F. Kennedy appointed him a member of the President's Scientific Advisory Committee (PSAC), a post he held until 1965. In 1966

Garwin joined JASON, an elite, highly secretive group of scientists who undertake technical assignments for the Defense Department.

Garwin sat on the President's Scientific Advisory Committee in the Richard M. Nixon administration, from 1969 to 1972, but he soon ran afoul of the White House with his outspoken criticism of the "light" antiballistic missile system that had been approved by Secretary of Defense Robert S. McNamara in September 1967. Garwin believed the system could be easily circumvented by cheap penetration devices, an opinion supported by the Federation of American Scientists. He then proceeded to get in even more trouble by criticizing the proposed Supersonic Transport plane, or SST. In 1970 the Nixon administration decided to seek government funding to develop the plane for commercial use. Garwin was appointed head of a panel charged with analyzing designs submitted by Boeing and General Electric. "We spent about half the month at Boeing, hearing from G.E., the airlines, the intelligence agencies, and so on. We concluded that there's not a chance in the world that this will be a productive, safe, environmentally acceptable aircraft," he explained to John Tirman.

The White House, however, refused to release the report, and when it came time for Congress to vote on funding for the plane, Garwin was called on to testify, in May 1970, to the Joint Economic Committee of Congress. "There was a lot of skulduggery in the program," Garwin recalled to Eliot Marshall, as quoted in Science (May 1981). "I looked at the government testimony and decided it was really dishonest and misleading. Really just awful. The government was concealing information and giving false information. So I said, 'Yes, I'll testify, but you can't ask me about the report.'" Garwin told the congressional committee that in his opinion the SST would be too expensive and unacceptably noisy: it would create a sonic boom equivalent to fifty jumbo supersonic jets taking off at once. Congress vetoed the project.

Garwin's advice was sound. The SST proved to be an expensive disaster for the English and French governments, which did back it. But President Nixon did not appreciate what he saw as Garwin's disloyalty. When he reorganized his administration after the 1972 election, he abolished the PSAC. That was "the beginning of the end of independent science advice in the White House," John Tirman, the senior editor of the Union of Concerned Scientists, wrote in his Esquire article. And Garwin told Eliot Marshall, "The fact that PSAC has never been reconstituted is an indication that the government really believes more in expediency and secrecy than in understanding the best thing to do."

Nevertheless, Garwin was not deterred from his role as a "conscientious dissenter" to misguided policy choices. His next targets were the B-1 bomber and the MX missile system. In both cases, he argued that much simpler and more reliable weapons could do the same job at a lower price. Instead of developing the B-1 bomber, which requires a special tanker and is extremely expensive to operate, he proposed equipping widebodied commercial jets with cruise missiles. As he explained to a reporter for *U.S. News & World Report* (April 26, 1976), the direct operating cost of 120 cruise-missile carriers would be $920 million a year by 1985, while a force of 200 B-1 bombers would cost $1.56 billion.

In place of the MX system, which called for a complex underground system of mobile missiles, Garwin advocated the small submarine undersea mobile (SUM) system. In the process of making his arguments to White House, Pentagon, and State Department officials, Garwin alienated many of them. When they disagreed with him he was likely to treat them like "misguided graduate students," according to one observer. (His friends say he gets into trouble because he knows more about how *things* work than how institutions operate.)

Garwin's latest crusade is against President Ronald Reagan's Strategic Defense Initiative (SDI) concept of an antiballistic missile "astrodome," which would use x-ray and chemical lasers, particle accelerators, and rail guns to destroy Soviet missiles after they were launched. Garwin finds the technology exciting but, in his view, "the problem is, it won't work and it's dangerous to try it." "For any defense to be viable, it must be perfect—and we just can't achieve that," Garwin told David Van Biema for *People* (August 27, 1984). "If a fraction of the Soviets' 10,000 strategic nuclear warheads got through, the U.S. would be destroyed." In the first place, he has argued, missiles are extremely hard to track after their booster rockets drop off, and the Soviets will quickly find ways to circumvent the laser devices. As Garwin explained in the same *People* article, "The technologies to destroy these defenses are already in existence and won't cost the Soviets a tenth as much." In addition, he argues, the SDI research probably violates the 1972 Antiballistic Missile Treaty, one of the cornerstones of current arms control. Why take that chance, spend over a trillion dollars and twenty years on research, and end up with a system that most likely will not work, Garwin asks.

Garwin's views are shared by many members of JASON and other independent scientists. Reagan's science adviser, George A. Keyworth, and his staff accused them all of acting out of a sense of guilt over their role in building the nuclear bomb, a charge that Garwin dismisses as nonsensical. "I don't know of anybody who is more of a hydrogen bomb builder than I am, and I don't have any guilt feelings," he said in the *Esquire* interview. "I think that Keyworth and his staff really have no evidence that the opposition to the Star Wars initiative is due to guilt. I can't imagine why he said this. So they try to discredit people on the other side, they said we don't know about these things. Well, I *do* know." Garwin characterized the Reagan administration as the worst-informed on defense issues he had ever seen. "His cronies are all the way up. They put ideological purity over competence," he said in that same article. In an interview with John

Noble Wilford for the *New York Times* (November 16, 1983), he further stated that "it's just awfully hard to do anything because the president is so disconnected from any real workers in arms control, and this administration has so few of these workers left."

Frustrated by the president's attitude, Garwin took his message to Congress in numerous rounds of testimony against appropriations for the Star Wars scheme. When Congress also appeared to be caught in a bureaucratic stalemate on the issue, he began to go public with his criticisms. Accepting the Wright Prize for interdisciplinary scientific achievement in 1983, he delivered his message bluntly: "In my writings and congressional testimony, I've shown how time after time our national security choices have been misdirected by false argument, concealed assumptions, and hidden agendas, and how some of the best options have been ruthlessly suppressed. We have all so far paid for that with our wealth and our well-being. If we don't restore integrity to our government, we may well pay for it with our lives."

What Garwin does support is arms control. He accepts the necessity for nuclear weapons; without the deterrence to war between the major powers provided by the threat of their use, he believes, the world would be an even more dangerous place, where nations might act recklessly with impunity. "The only thing nuclear weapons are good for and have ever been good for is massive destruction and by that threat deterring nuclear attack," he told Tom Buckley in a profile for *Quest* (March 1981). But nuclear arms should be thought of in retaliatory rather than first-strike terms: "If you slap me, I'll clobber you," he has said. The United States could reduce its arsenal by a factor of ten, he has argued, and still have enough power to destroy the Soviet Union completely.

In a March 1988 article that appeared in the *Bulletin of the Atomic Scientists*, Garwin proposed an outline for radical weapons cuts, with the goal of reducing the number of weapons held by the United States and the USSR to 1,000 each, by 1997. He wrote that the 1972 Antiballistic Missile Treaty had to be "respected and strengthened" and that "there must be a ban on antisatellite tests and deployment and on space weapons." He also said that a verification program for the "destruction of remaining nuclear weapons and delivery vehicles must be formulated and followed." In addition, a "stringent antiproliferation regime" and a ban on nuclear tests would be needed to ensure that other countries did not acquire nuclear weapons.

While Garwin feels that the limits set by the 1979 Strategic Arms Limitations Treaty (SALT II), negotiated by President Jimmy Carter and Soviet Premier Leonid Brezhnev, are too high, he supports the treaty, which created a ceiling for the number of missiles, bombers, and warheads that each side could stockpile. Conservatives have objected to arms control in general and SALT II in particular because they believe that the Soviet Union will inevitably cheat and that the United States must retain a numerical and technological edge over it. Garwin believes that the Soviets are genuinely committed to reducing the level of nuclear arms and that maintaining a powerful nuclear deterrence is enough to keep them in line.

Garwin's plea for arms control reflects his deep-seated belief that the United States must learn to live "securely with the knowledge of its mortality." A limited nuclear war is an impossibility, Garwin has stated. He now believes that there is a 50 percent chance of a nuclear war before the end of the century, and he has grown pessimistic about the American government's ability to avert that disaster.

Because of his views on nuclear deterrence, Garwin is no more beloved by the antinuclear movement than he is by conservatives. During the Vietnam War, he was frequently attacked by antiwar activists, especially after he was sent to Vietnam in 1968 on a secret mission that many speculated had to do with assessing the role nuclear weapons could play in that war. Garwin denied the charges, telling Tom Buckley, "We went over to study the operation of a system of sensors that had been installed in the border area but did not work very well." Garwin only got as far as Thailand, however, because of the Tet Offensive.

Garwin's home base remains the IBM research center, which moved from Columbia University to Yorktown Heights, New York, in 1970, in part because of disruptions caused by Vietnam War protesters. The center is known for having one of the best technical staffs in the country. Garwin served as director of applied research at IBM from 1965 to 1966 and as director of the laboratory from 1966 to 1967. Since 1967 he has worked there as an IBM Fellow. He divides his time among the equivalent of four full-time jobs: as a Fellow at the lab, a defense consultant, an arms control advocate, and a faculty member at Cornell and Columbia universities and at the Kennedy School of Government at Harvard. A tireless worker who rarely eats lunch or takes vacations, Garwin holds some thirty patents on inventions as varied as a gaze control computer, which requires no manual operation, and a mussel cleaner. He helped develop a computer technique known as the FFT, or Fast Fourier Technique, which increases the efficiency of certain analytical tasks by a factor of 1,000, and he adapted laser optics for use in office copying machines.

A small man with a quiet voice, Garwin gives the impression of being colorless until he smiles and begins to talk about the things that matter to him. John Tirman described him as "a small, round man, with sturdy, workman-like hands and friendly brown eyes squinting from behind aviator-style glasses." Garwin loves gadgets and still has the aptitude for fixing household appliances that he first displayed as a child.

Garwin married his high school sweetheart, Lois Levy, in 1947, and the couple have three "superachiever" children: Jeffrey, the director of clinical research for McNeil Consumer Products; Tom, the American coordinator of the nuclear his-

tory program at the University of Maryland; and Laura, the physical-sciences editor of the prestigious British science magazine *Nature.* "I'm rather family oriented," he said in the *Esquire* interview. "Ever since I was twenty or so, I've felt that one has primary responsibility to one's immediate family as the basis of society." Only recently did he and his wife, Lois, completely furnish their home in Scarsdale, New York, because Garwin thinks it is a waste of time to accumulate possessions. Garwin maintains that scientists have a duty to lend their expertise to government programs—even if they disagree with government policy—and he plans to continue his tireless campaign until some semblance of reason returns to American defense policy.

References: Esquire p110+ 0 '84 por; Quest p17+ Mr '81 por; Science 212:763+ My 15 '81 por; International Who's Who, 1989-90

Gingrich, Newt(on Leroy)

June 17, 1943– United States Representative from Georgia. Address: b. 2438 Rayburn Office Bldg., Washington, D.C. 20515; h. Ascot Glen, Apt. #11J, 221 Upper Riverdale Rd., S.E., Jonesboro, Ga. 30236

No one in Washington, D.C., has profited more directly from America's heightened sensitivity to ethical standards in government than Newt Gingrich of Georgia, the newly elected minority whip in the House of Representatives—although that sensitivity may be his own undoing, as Gingrich faces a possible investigation into a questionable book contract. Few took Gingrich seriously when, in 1987, he launched a one-man crusade against the Democratic Speaker of the House, Jim Wright, charging that he was "the least ethical person to serve as Speaker in the House in the twentieth century." But as the House Ethics Committee turned up evidence corroborating Wright's alleged misconduct, Gingrich gained new respectability among House Republicans frustrated with their longstanding minority status. "The policy of going along to get along has been singularly unproductive in forcing to the floor issues that are important to the president and the American people," Gingrich once remarked, in defense of the guerrilla-style tactics that he and his conservative Republican colleagues habitually employed against the Democratic majority. But whether he is prepared to modulate his combative style to function effectively in the sensitive whip's post remains to be seen. "This is a very unpredictable period," Democratic congressman Leon Panetta of California told Robin Toner for the New York Times (March 24, 1989). "And Gingrich's election adds to that unpredictability because no one is sure if he'll be a statesman or operate as he has in the past."

Newton Leroy Gingrich was born in Harrisburg, Pennsylvania on June 17, 1943 to Kathleen (Daugherty) McPherson. He was adopted when he was about three by his mother's second husband, Robert Bruce Gingrich, a career army officer. As a result, Gingrich attended army base schools in Kansas and, during his father's tours of duty abroad, in France and West Germany. He abandoned an early ambition to become a paleontologist after he and his family visited a friend of Robert Gingrich's, a World War II veteran who lived near the World War I battlefield of Verdun, in France. Enthralled by the old soldier's story of how he survived the Bataan death march and sobered by his daytime visits to Verdun, Gingrich returned to high school in Stuttgart, West Germany to write a 180-page paper on the balance of global power, telling people that one day he would run for Congress and save Western civilization from destruction. "If you decide in your freshman year in high school," Gingrich told Lois Romano in an interview for the Washington Post (January 3, 1985), "that your job is to spend your lifetime trying to change the future of your people, you're probably fairly weird. I think I was pretty weird as a kid."

At the age of sixteen, Gingrich transferred to Newton D. Baker High School in Columbus, Georgia, where he, like many of his classmates, developed a crush on the pretty, twenty-three-year-old math teacher Jacqueline Battley. But unlike his classmates, Gingrich boasted that he was going to do something about it. On graduating in 1961, Gingrich enrolled at Emory University in Atlanta, where Miss Battley had taken a teaching position. He promptly showed up at her door unannounced and asked for a date. They were married on June 19, 1962.

After graduating from Emory in 1965, Gingrich received a master's degree from Tulane University

in 1968 and a Ph.D. degree in modern European history in 1971. His behavior at Tulane appeared to belie his future conservatism and hawkish foreign-policy views. He accepted student deferments rather than face the draft during the Vietnam War, experimented with marijuana, led a campus demonstration defending the school paper's right to print a nude photograph of a faculty member, and campaigned for Governor Nelson A. Rockefeller of New York for president in 1968 because of the governor's support of civil rights.

In 1970, while completing his doctorate at Tulane, Gingrich joined the faculty of West Georgia College in Carrollton, Georgia. After just one year as a history professor, he unsuccessfully applied for the chairmanship of the department. Although Gingrich's cocky style and brusque manner were resented by some faculty members, his lively classes were popular with students. After hours he invited favorite students to his house for extended bull sessions and organized an environmental-studies program. By 1974, however, he had grown restless in the classroom and began informing friends that one day he would become Speaker of the House. That year he ventured into politics, challenging the Democratic congressman John J. Flynt Jr. of Georgia's Sixth Congressional District and coming within 2,800 votes of upsetting him. Encouraged, Gingrich tried again in 1976, and again he narrowly lost to Flynt, who was aided by the coattails of the former Georgia governor Jimmy Carter, the Democratic nominee for president that year. Part of Gingrich's impressive showings in those two elections could be attributed to his use of modern campaign techniques, such as professional polling and a paid campaign staff, and to the support of environmentalists. When Flynt retired in 1978, Gingrich ran on a platform of lower taxes and opposition to the Panama Canal Treaty. He defeated Virginia Shapard, a Democratic state senator, by 7,600 votes. In subsequent years, Gingrich has been reelected handily from that rural and suburban district whose largest employer is Atlanta's Hartsfield International Airport.

As a freshman congressman, Gingrich emerged as the leader of a small group of young Republicans who were unwilling to play the traditional role of docile backbenchers. Gingrich criticized the GOP old guard for failing to stand up to the Democratic majority, and he vowed to win back the House from the Democrats before the end of the 1980s. "My friends and I are trying to figure out strategically what we have to do in this country in the next ten years to build a majority," Gingrich told David S. Broder in an interview for Broder's book Changing of the Guard: Power and Leadership in America (1988). During his first congressional term, Gingrich concentrated on building a Republican challenge to the Democrats on the issue of the government's budget, emphasizing the importance of tax cuts and spending restraints. "I am a Republican," Gingrich told Broder, "but I think the greatest failure of the last twenty years has been the Republican party, not the Democratic party. . . . I think in order for this civilization to survive, at least as a free society, we've got to have a more rigorous and cohesive sense of an alternative party."

According to Gingrich, neither political party has a workable vision. The Democrats continue to embrace the "liberal welfare state" first introduced by President Franklin D. Roosevelt, while the Republicans rely on an antigovernment stance that was first set forth by President Herbert Hoover. "There's a big gap in the middle for positive, dynamic conservatism," Gingrich explained to Steven V. Roberts of the New York Times (August 11, 1983). In February 1983 Gingrich began meeting on a regular basis with other young conservative congressmen, a group that Gingrich dubbed the Conservative Opportunity Society. As one member, Vin Weber of Minnesota, told Sidney Blumenthal, as quoted in the New Republic (September 3, 1984), "We were not close friends. We observed in each other a more confrontational style towards the Democrats."

One tactic the group employed was to force votes on such controversial issues as school prayer and trade with Communist countries. After the House proceedings began to be televised live over the Cable-Satellite Public Affairs Network (C-SPAN) in 1980, Gingrich and his followers tried another tactic—taking advantage of the "special orders" period, the time set aside after floor business was concluded to allow members to read material into the record, usually before an empty chamber. The predominantly junior Republicans who made use of special orders stated that their goal was to publicize their conservative agenda, but Gingrich and his colleagues employed the time to attack the opposition in front of some 250,000 C-SPAN viewers, often including President Ronald Reagan, on issues such as school prayer and abortion.

Tensions between the two parties reached the breaking point on May 8, 1984, when Gingrich and Congressman Robert S. Walker of Pennsylvania read from a report by the Republican Study Committee that criticized foreign-policy statements made by about fifty Democrats over the past fifteen years. With the camera focused on Gingrich, who paused periodically as if to give his targets a chance to respond, it appeared that the Democrats had nothing to say in their defense. On May 10, Speaker of the House Thomas ("Tip") P. O'Neill Jr. retaliated by ordering the cameras to pan the empty chamber during special orders, a move that was criticized by House Republicans. O'Neill felt obliged to defend his action and, on May 14, lambasted Gingrich for his histrionics. "You deliberately stood in that well before an empty House and challenged these people when you knew they would not be there," O'Neill thundered. "It is the lowest thing that I have ever seen in my thirty-two years in Congress." (O'Neill's use of the word "lowest" was ruled out of order and stricken from the record for lack of comity.) Gingrich was ecstatic over the publicity that O'Neill's reaction engen-

dered. "The minute Tip O'Neill attacked me, he and I got ninety seconds at the close of all three network news shows," Gingrich told a group of conservative activists, as reported by David Osborne in Mother Jones (November 1984).

House Republicans had mixed feelings about their newest media star. Some welcomed a fresh, bold combatant who could nettle the Democratic leadership, but others winced as he denounced O'Neill as a "thug" or as "an arrogant, overbearing boss." "I'm not sure," Republican congressman Mickey Edwards of Oklahoma told Lois Romano of the Washington Post (January 3, 1985), "how many people like to see someone up there ranting and raving and waving their arms and pointing their finger at another member of the House. His is a style of stridency, not ideology." Moreover, Gingrich had always been something of a loose cannon, directing his fire at anyone who veered from the truth as he saw it. He once denounced Robert J. Dole, the Republican chairman of the Senate Finance Committee, as "the tax collector for the welfare state," and he called David Stockman, the director of the Office of Management and Budget in the early years of the Reagan administration, "the greatest obstacle to a successful revolution from the liberal welfare state to an opportunity society." A strong supporter of the Reagan-era tax cuts, he condemned the $98 billion tax bill of 1982 as "the dumbest decision of the Reagan administration" and labeled all of official Washington "a large, open conspiracy to take away the money and freedom of the citizens of this country." He even went so far as to call President Reagan's 1985 rapprochement with Soviet leader Mikhail Gorbachev potentially "the most dangerous summit for the West since Adolf Hitler met with [British prime minister Neville] Chamberlain in 1938 at Munich."

The foundation of Gingrich's philosophy is laid out in his book Window of Opportunity: A Blueprint for the Future (1984), on which he collaborated with his second wife, Marianne, and David Drake, a science fiction writer. In that book, Gingrich, the cofounder and chairman of the Congressional Space Caucus, argued that space exploration can solve the world's most pressing problems. "If we will make an intensive effort to develop space," he wrote, "we will create millions of jobs on earth while creating thousands of jobs in space, while at the same time ensuring a solid balance of payments in foreign trade by producing goods and services others want but cannot produce for themselves." He suggested constructing a permanently manned space station from which the earth's environment could be monitored and where high-technology products could be efficiently manufactured, and he called for a millennium project to fire the nation's imagination—much as President John F. Kennedy did with his call for a moon landing by the end of the 1960s. Gingrich proposed the opening of a lunar research base on January 1, 2000, which he expected to lead to permanent moon colonies accommodating as many as 2,500 people by the middle of the next century.

At the August 1984 Republican National Convention in Dallas, Texas, Gingrich and his supporters succeeded in introducing a platform more conservative than the one proposed by President Ronald Reagan, including a commitment not to raise taxes, an antiabortion stance, and the inclusion of the phrase "conservative opportunity society." Gingrich consistently supported the Reagan administration's defense buildup and its campaign to aid the Contra rebels in their struggle against the Marxist-led Sandinista government in Nicaragua. However, he joined Democrats in supporting the creation of a national holiday in honor of the Reverend Martin Luther King Jr., and in 1984 he surprised observers by leading thirty-five like-minded conservatives in support of economic sanctions against the government of South Africa, despite the threat of a presidential veto.

Indeed, Gingrich believes that the incorporation of some of the Democratic party's programs into the Republican agenda is in his party's best interests. For instance, he has favored job training classes and childcare centers for people looking for jobs, tax credits for families who purchase home computers, and government bonuses to encourage poor children to learn to read. In 1985 he proposed an amendment requiring states to enroll 75 percent of eligible food-stamp recipients in three-year work programs, and he has suggested changing the Social Security system into a mandatory program based on individual retirement accounts. After the 1984 election he became the chairman of the Investigations and Oversight Subcommittee of the House Public Works and Transportation Committee.

In 1985 Gingrich's friends began talking of a "new Newt," one who, now that he had succeeded in getting the nation's attention, wanted to be taken more seriously. Never adept at interpersonal relations, he made a genuine effort to cultivate friendships in the House. "I will be somewhat less confrontational, and somewhat less abrasive in the future because I am no longer the person I once was," Gingrich told Lois Romano. "And it will take two to five years for my reputation to catch up and in some ways it never will. There are scars I have made in the last two or three years that will be with me through the rest of my career." Gingrich was chastened in part by an unflattering article that appeared in Mother Jones magazine in November 1984, in which he was portrayed as treating his first wife insensitively during their divorce in 1981, at a time when she was suffering from cancer. According to that article, Gingrich visited his wife in the hospital only to discuss the divorce settlement and had to be forced by court order to pay her adequate alimony and support for their two daughters, Linda and Jacqueline. Congressman Tony Coelho, a Democrat from California, sent a copy of that article to every Democrat in the House.

By 1987, however, Gingrich was back in rare form, this time launching broadsides against the most powerful Democrat in Washington, House Speaker Jim Wright of Texas, who had once called Gingrich a "professional pest." For months Gingrich stood virtually alone in calling for an investigation into some of Wright's financial dealings, including a book contract for Reflections of a Public Man, a collection of his speeches and essays, which was not sold through normal distribution channels but which enabled Wright to collect large royalties (55 percent) on bulk sales to his supporters and other interested parties. That arrangement circumvented House limits on outside income, since royalties are exempt. Not until May 1988, after the nonpartisan citizens' lobby organization Common Caused joined in the call for an investigation into Wright's book deal and his efforts to help savings and loan institutions, was Gingrich able to enlist the support of his fellow Republicans, with the notable exception of Minority Leader Robert H. Michel of Illinois, in formally requesting that the House Committee on Standards of Official Conduct take up the matter. "People warned me off from this," Gingrich told Peter Osterlund of the Christian Science Monitor (May 31, 1989), in recalling the early days of his campaign against Wright. "They said I'd be asking for political trouble. But I didn't come here to pleasantly rise on an escalator of self-serving compromises."

In March 1989, as the House Ethics Committee proceeded with its probe of Wright, the Senate defeated President George Bush's nomination of former senator John G. Tower of Texas to be his secretary of defense. On the same day that Bush named Congressman Richard B. Cheney of Wyoming, the House minority whip, to fill the cabinet post, Gingrich began phoning House members seeking their pledges of support for his taking over the whip's job. Minority Leader Michel quickly enlisted Edward R. Madigan, a moderate from Illinois, to run against Gingrich, but the Georgian managed to win over such younger moderates as Olympia J. Snowe of Maine and Claudine Schneider of Rhode Island, who responded positively to Gingrich's vision of winning back the House from the Democrats by 1992. "It's a commentary that the party wants to reach out and be aggressive," Gingrich explained to Jeffrey H. Birnbaum of the Wall Street Journal (March 23, 1989), after he was narrowly elected to the post by a vote of eighty-seven to eighty-five on March 22, 1989. Many political observers felt that Gingrich's election reflected Republicans' frustration with their thirty-four-year minority status. "We don't want a leadership that is going to fade into the woodwork," Vin Weber told Birnbaum.

Democratic reaction to Gingrich's election was mixed, with many expressing a distrust of Gingrich. "Newt has consistently attacked Democrats," Tony Coelho, then the majority whip, told Robin Toner in an interview for the New York Times (March 23, 1989). "Now, he's going to be asking for our votes. The question is, can he resolve himself to this new role? All of us, most especially the Bush administration, will be waiting for his answer." Other Democrats were more positive, believing that Gingrich's election would enable House Democrats to rally around almost any Republican stand more easily. Still others pointed out that Gingrich's election might prove detrimental to George Bush's agenda, since bipartisan support would be difficult to forge with Gingrich in the position of minority whip.

Only a month after his election to the post of minority whip, Gingrich found himself the subject of a House Ethics Committee probe, stemming from questionable book deals of his own. In a ten-count complaint filed with the House Ethics Committee on April 11, Democratic congressman Bill Alexander of Arkansas charged that Gingrich had violated House rules on outside gifts and income by benefiting from two partnerships that helped to finance and promote the two books Gingrich had written—a novel, which was never finished, and *Window of Opportunity*. According to Jeffrey H. Birnbaum of the *Wall Street Journal* (March 24, 1989), about a dozen people contributed $1,000 to the first book, which was never completed because of Gingrich's election to the House of Representatives in 1978.

For his second book, Gingrich established the COS Limited Partnership. Of the twenty-two limited partners, twenty-one invested $5,000 each and, after the book lost money, received tax benefits for their contributions. Gingrich's second wife, Marianne, was paid $11,500 in her capacity as general partner. In a news conference on April 25, Gingrich rejected any comparison between his arrangement and that of Wright's, maintaining that the money he received did not represent a political gift. "We wrote a real book, working with a real publisher, distributed to real bookstores, and sold to real people for a realistic standard royalty," Gingrich said, as reported by Janet Hook in *Congressional Quarterly* (April 29, 1989). Gingrich and his wife received royalties of 4 percent each. On the question of helping one investor, James Richards, an executive of the Southwire Company, a major employer in Gingrich's district, to obtain federal funds, Gingrich said that helping constituents negotiate with the government was his duty as a congressman. On Gingrich's election to the position of minority whip, Speaker of the House Jim Wright gave him a copy of his book, *Reflections of a Public Man*, inscribed in part: "For Newt, who likes books, too. Congratulations." In mid-April the House Ethics Committee released a report that accused Wright of violating House rules in at least sixty-nine specific instances, and on May 31, 1989 Wright announced his resignation from the House.

Gingrich became the subject of a second ethics probe when, in late July 1989, the *Atlanta Business Chronicle* reported that, in his 1986 and 1988 reelection campaigns, the congressman had taken two staff members off the payroll in order for them to work on his campaign and then returned them to the payroll after the election with significant, though temporary, increases in salary. Federal law and House rules prohibit rewarding staff members for campaign work. In addition, House rules bar granting temporary, year-end raises that can be construed as bonuses, although that prohibition is ignored by many members.

In defending his actions, Gingrich said the staff members in question had taken leaves of absence and had been paid by his reelection committee, and he noted that members of Congress commonly grant temporary salary increases to their assistants at the end of the year because those monies are lost to the office if not used by that time. On October 20, 1989 the Chicago law firm retained by the House Ethics Committee to investigate Gingrich's book deals recommended that the panel not conduct a formal investigation into the matter, although it acknowledged that a few "loose ends" remained that might be investigated by the committee.

As part of his efforts to increase the Republican ranks, Gingrich backed, with Congressman Thomas Foley of Washington, the Democratic majority leader, the National Voter Registration Act of 1989. The bill, which was approved in early May 1989 by the House Administration Committee, would enable voters to register by mail and would include voter registration forms as part of the applications for drivers' licenses. Gingrich is the ranking minority member of the House Administration Committee. He cofounded the bipartisan Military Reform Caucus, and in 1987 he became the ranking Republican on the Aviation Subcommittee.

Newt Gingrich is an intense, hyperactive figure with a cherubic face framed by a thick mass of graying hair. In his daily battle against a spare-tire waistline, he leaves his modest Capitol Hill apartment at dawn for a hike along the Mall. Gingrich is a Baptist deacon. In August 1981 he married Marianne Ginther, whom he had met the previous year. He is a member of the American Association for the Advancement of Science, the World Futurist Society, and the Georgia Conservancy.

References: *Washington Post* B p1 Ja 3 '85 pors; *Almanac of American Politics, 1988*; Broder, David S. *Changing of the Guard: Power and Leadership in America* (1988); *Politics in America* (1988); *Who's Who in American Politics, 1989–90*

Graf, Steffi

June 14, 1969– West German tennis player. Address: c/o Deutscher Sportbund, Otto Fleck Schneise, 12-D 6000 Frankfurt-am-Main, 71 West Germany

In 1988 a West German teenager with a ferocious forehand and an iron will joined the tennis world's most elite group when she took the titles in the Australian, French, and United States Opens and at Wimbledon to become a Grand Slam champion. Only the fifth person—the other four being Don Budge, Maureen Connolly, Margaret Court Smith,

Steffi Graf

and Rod Laver—to sweep the four events in a calendar year (Martina Navratilova won the four titles in succession, but not in the same year), Steffi Graf capped what many aficionados of the game believe to be the finest year ever in tennis by winning a gold medal at the 1988 Olympics, thus becoming the first player to capture the "Golden Slam," as her business managers called it. Moreover, she won her four Slam crowns on four different surfaces: rubberized Rebound Ace hardcourt in Australia, slow red clay in France, fast grass in England, and hard DecoTurf II in the United States. The other Grand Slam champions played all but the French Open tournament on grass.

Winless on the women's professional tour until 1986, Steffi Graf has been virtually unbeatable since, as she vaulted in the computer rankings from twenty-second at the end of 1984 to number one in mid-1987. Since taking her first Grand Slam title at the French Open in 1986, she has lost only nine matches to three players—four to Martina Navratilova, three to Gabriela Sabatini, one to Pam Shriver, and one to Arantxa Sanchez-Vicario. In addition to her intimidating topspin forehand, which is widely considered to be the best in the history of women's tennis, Graf possesses an explosive serve, a devastating slice backhand, and consistently strong ground strokes, and because of her astonishing speed, her court coverage is unparalleled. Combining athleticism and sheer physical power with a no-nonsense on-court demeanor reminiscent of Bjōrn Borg and with what Arthur Ashe calls "snap," she simply overwhelms her hapless opponents. "I think she can do pretty much anything," Martina Navratilova said recently.

The older of the two children of Peter and Heidi Graf, Stephanie Maria Graf was born in Mann-

heim, West Germany on June 14, 1969. She has a younger brother, Michael. Both parents were accomplished semiprofessional tennis players, and by the time she was four years old, Steffi, as she has always been called, was batting balls against the living-room wall of her home with a sawed-off racket. Recognizing his daughter's extraordinary eye-hand coordination and power of concentration, Peter Graf encouraged the child by rewarding consecutive hits with a lollipop or a small toy. "We broke a lot of lamps," Heidi Graf told John Jeansonne in an interview for *New York Newsday* (May 21, 1987). "Many. Then we moved everything downstairs into a playroom." There, using a string stretched between two chairs as a net, Steffi learned the rudiments of tennis, with twenty-five consecutive hits earning her an ice cream sundae. Within a few years, the girl had progressed sufficiently to continue her training outdoors on a real tennis court.

By the late 1970s, Peter Graf realized that his daughter possessed more than average athletic ability. To oversee her development as a tennis player, he gave up his partnership in a Mannheim automobile dealership and his work with a local insurance agency and moved with his family to Brühl, near Heidelberg, where he opened a tennis school. Under her father's tutelage, Steffi Graf improved so rapidly that she was soon practicing regularly at a nearby tennis club frequented by several up-and-coming young players, including Boris Becker. When she was twelve years old, Graf won her age-group competition at the European championships and reached the final of the West German youth championship, playing against eighteen-year-olds. The following year, she captured the West German eighteen-and-under title and generally played well enough to earn the twelfth spot in her country's adult rankings. She was equally impressive on the international junior circuit. After seeing her play in the junior tournament at Wimbledon in 1982, no less an authority than Billie Jean King confidently predicted that Graf would one day win the Grand Slam because of her quickness, strength, and seemingly infallible tennis instincts.

Having dominated her age group for several years, Steffi Graf turned pro at the age of thirteen. Within weeks of joining the international women's tour, she became the second-youngest player to be given a computer ranking—number 124—by the Women's International Tennis Association (WITA). But shortly thereafter, her promising professional career suffered a temporary setback when she tore the tendons in the thumb of her right hand—her racket hand—while playing in the Australian Open. After taking several months off to recuperate, Graf rejoined the tour. Quickly regaining her form, she reached the quarterfinals at Wimbledon and, a few weeks later, won a gold medal at the 1984 Olympic Games in Los Angeles, where tennis was a demonstration sport. By the year's end, she had advanced her computer ranking more than 100 places, to the twenty-second spot.

Although she failed to win a single major tournament in 1985, Steffi Graf nonetheless saw her computer ranking inch steadily upward as she gave a good accounting of herself in the Grand Slam events. She survived to the rounds of sixteen at the French Open and at Wimbledon, and at the United States Open she upset the more experienced Pam Shriver, 7-6, 6-7, 7-6, to earn a berth in the semifinals, where she succumbed to Martina Navratilova in straight sets. At her father's insistence, Graf took three months off following the United States Open to rest and to hone her skills. When she returned to tournament play in February 1986, she brought with her a formidable topspin backhand that helped propel her to the runner-up spot in back-to-back tourneys in Florida and in the Virginia Slims Masters contest in New York City and to number three in the world rankings.

Steffi Graf's loss—to Martina Navratilova in straight sets—in the final of the Masters tournament was to be her last for some time. A few weeks later, she embarked on a twenty-four-match winning streak that included victories over such top-ranked players as Chris Evert, Claudia Kohde-Kilsch, Gabriela Sabatini, and Martina Navratilova, and earned her four consecutive titles. Her stunning come-from-behind defeats of Evert and Navratilova, in straight sets, snapped the long winning streaks of both women. The win over Navratilova, on a slow clay surface at the West German Open in Berlin, was especially sweet, for, in the second set, she overcame a 3-1 deficit and reeled off five straight games. During this period Graf also racked up two doubles titles, pairing with Gabriela Sabatini in a tournament in Indianapolis, Indiana and with Helena Sukova in the West German Open.

Steffi Graf rode her winning streak into the early rounds of the French Open, easily dismissing her opponents even though she was battling the flu. In the quarterfinals, however, she wilted after losing match point in the second set and dropped the match to Hana Mandlikova, 2-6, 7-6, 6-1. A persistent flu virus and a broken toe on her right foot, suffered during a Federation Cup bout, kept Graf on the sidelines for most of the summer, but by late August she was fit and ready to face the competition at the United States Open in Flushing Meadows, New York. Seeded third, she breezed her way to the semifinals, where she came up against Martina Navratilova. Playing to the German girl's comparatively weak backhand, Navratilova jumped to a 6-1, 4-2 lead, but Graf gamely fought back to 5-4, at one stretch running off seven consecutive points, and eventually took the second set in a tiebreaker. The third and deciding set was also determined by a tiebreaker, this one won by Navratilova after Graf netted a backhand.

Martina Navratilova also ended Steffi Graf's hopes for a championship at the Virginia Slims Masters tournament at Madison Square Garden in New York City in November 1986, where she defeated her young challenger in the final, 7-6, 6-3, 6-2. After the match, a dejected Steffi Graf told reporters that she was going home "to rest" and "to work on my serve, my backhand, my net game." Her disappointing defeats in the major contests aside, Graf had compiled an impressive record in 1986, having taken the championship in eight of the fourteen tournaments she had entered and come in second in three more. In recognition of her achievements, she was named West Germany's Sportswoman of the Year.

True to her word, Steffi Graf took several months off the circuit in the winter of 1986-87 to concentrate on improving her game. Her strict training regimen, devised by her father, who acts as her coach and manager, and Pavel Slozil, the former Davis Cup player for Czechoslovakia who is her hitting coach and practice partner, included running, weightlifting, and jumping rope with weights on her ankles as well as several hours a day on the tennis court. According to most reports, she relishes her daily three-to-four-hour sessions with Slozil and often trains so hard her father has to restrain her. "My father makes sure I do not play too much," she told Peter Alfano in an interview for the *New York Times* (September 11, 1988). "It's tough keeping my hands off a racket."

Peter Graf, who regularly travels with his daughter and attends all her matches, has a reputation in tennis circles for being an autocratic taskmaster. Most often described in the press as "domineering," he is said to be abrasive with tour officials and reporters, and he has occasionally been chastised (and his daughter penalized) for illegal coaching from the sidelines. "I have to be careful with Steffi . . . ," he explained to Douglas S. Looney for a *Sports Illustrated* (March 16, 1987) profile of his daughter. "Steffi works much harder than the other girls because she wants to. I have never pushed her. That is why she is so good. How long we play has always depended on how long she wants to play."

Returning to the women's tour in February 1987, Steffi Graf lost only twenty games in taking five matches on her way to the final of a Virginia Slims tourney in Boca Raton, Florida, where she trounced Helena Sukova, 6-2, 6-3. Her victory moved her into second place in the computer rankings, behind Martina Navratilova. As if to validate her new position, in her next tournament—the Lipton Players International Championships in Key Biscayne, Florida—Graf, playing nearly flawless tennis, whipped Navratilova in the semifinals, 6-3, 6-2, then routed Chris Evert in the final, 6-1, 6-2. The matches took fifty-seven and fifty-eight minutes, respectively.

Over the next two months, Steffi Graf racked up consecutive victories in the Family Circle Cup, the WITA Championships, the Italian Open, where she rebounded after a disastrous start to beat Gabriela Sabatini, 7-5, 4-6, 6-0, and the Ladies German Championships. On the strength of her six straight titles and her number-two world ranking, she was seeded second in the French Open in late May. Of her first five opponents, only Helen Kelesi, who took her to a first-set tiebreaker in the fourth round, gave her much competition. But in her semifinal match, Graf was extended to three sets by Gabriela Sabatini, and in the final, against the wily Martina Navratilova, she needed to call on all her reserves of strength and speed to withstand the relentless pounding to her backhand. She finally took the contest, 6-4, 4-6, 8-6, and her first Grand Slam crown after Navratilova double-faulted two match points. She was the youngest women's singles champion in French Open history to that date.

Unlike the majority of her fellow competitors, Steffi Graf decided to bypass the traditional Wimbledon tune-up in Eastbourne, England to get in some extra practice. Although virtually a novice on grass courts, not having played on one for two years, Graf was seeded second at Wimbledon, thanks to her 39-0 match record for the year. In the first round, she unveiled her vastly improved serve in a 6-0, 6-2 blowout of Adriana Villagran. Gaining confidence with each successive round, she overpowered Pam Shriver in the semifinals, 6-0, 6-2, in just fifty-one minutes. Steffi Graf's opponent in the final was Martina Navratilova, who was playing for her eighth Wimbledon championship. Relying on experience and guile, Navratilova, a left-hander, used a slashing slice serve to keep the ball away from the right-handed Graf's powerful forehand. Never able to wrest control of the match, Graf fell in straight sets, 7-5, 6-3, to give Navratilova her sixth consecutive Wimbledon singles title.

In Federation Cup competition in August 1987, Steffi Graf whipped Chris Evert, 6-2, 6-1, and with teammate Claudia Kohde-Kilsch staged a comeback from a 1-6 first-set deficit to take the deciding doubles match from Evert and her partner, Pam Shriver, and give West Germany its first Federation Cup title. A few weeks later, she defeated Chris Evert again, in a Virginia Slims contest in Los Angeles and, as a result, seized the number-one ranking, which had belonged to Martina Navratilova for five years. Navratilova, however, conceded nothing, and, in the final of the United States Open, she made her case for the top spot by prevailing over Graf, 7-6, 6-1. To defeat her young challenger, Navratilova deliberately played to the girl's weaknesses—her erratic backhand and her timid net game. She rushed the net sixty-one times, forcing uncharacteristic errors from her increasingly befuddled opponent. Even Graf's usually reliable forehand deserted her, as she made twenty-one unforced forehand errors.

Steffi Graf rebounded from her defeat at the United States Open with a dazzling display of shot-making at the Virginia Slims Masters tournament in November, the traditional end-of-season contest for the game's top players. After making short work of her early-round opponents, she got off to an unusually slow start in the final, against Gabriela Sabatini, but she eventually shrugged off the loss of the first set to wear down her adversary, 4-6, 6-4, 6-0, 6-4, in the best-of-five match. The Masters title capped a remarkable year, in which Graf lost only two of seventy-two matches in winning eleven of

the thirteen tournaments she entered. Her winnings for the year were $1,063,785.

Steffi Graf carried her winning ways over into 1988 with an impressive showing at the Australian Open in Melbourne in January, losing just twenty-two games on her way to the final against Chris Evert. She won the first set of the championship match handily, 6-1, and led, 5-1, in the second before Evert fought back to force a tiebreaker, which Graf eventually won, 7-3. Chris Evert once again fell victim to Steffi Graf in the final of the Lipton International Players Championships in Florida in March 1988, taken by Graf in straight sets, 6-4, 6-4. The victory evened Graf's career record against Evert at six wins apiece, with the German girl capturing the last six. That same month, however, Graf was twice defeated in Virginia Slims tournaments by Gabriela Sabatini, who shrewdly drove her heavy topspin ground strokes deep into Graf's backhand corner.

Steffi Graf got her own back two months later at the French Open, where she bested Gabriela Sabatini in the semifinals, 6-3, 7-6. In the final, she rolled over Natalia Zvereva, the seventeen-year-old Soviet contestant, 6-0, 6-0, in thirty-two minutes. It was the first whitewash in a Grand Slam championship in seventy-seven years. In a speech to the crowd at Roland Garros Stadium after accepting her second Grand Slam trophy of the year, Graf (who had lost only twenty games in the tournament, nine of them to Sabatini) apologized to the crowd for the ease and quickness of her victory.

To prepare for an expected joust with Martina Navratilova at Wimbledon, Steffi Graf again passed up the tune-up events to practice with a male left-hander, who drilled serves to her backhand for several hours every day. The strenuous workouts paid off, as she thrashed her first seven Wimbledon opponents in easy matches, none of them lasting longer than fifty-nine minutes. As anticipated, her opponent in the final was Martina Navratilova, who was vying for a record ninth Wimbledon singles title. Visibly nervous, Graf made several unforced errors in dropping the first set, 5-7. Down 0-2 in the second set, she rallied to break Navratilova's serve and take control of the match. In winning twelve of the last thirteen games, she broke her opponent's serve seven times in a row and rang up fifty of the seventy-two points, many of them on crosscourt backhand and down-the-line service returns. Her 5-7, 6-2, 6-1 victory gave Graf her twenty-first consecutive Grand Slam singles match and her third Grand Slam crown in seven months. To make her triumph complete, Steffi Graf and her partner, Gabriela Sabatini, captured their first Grand Slam title as a team by beating Natalia Zvereva and Larisa Savchenko, 6-3, 1-6, 12-10, in the women's doubles championship.

Over the next two months, Steffi Graf solidified her hold on the number-one world ranking by dominating her challengers in a succession of Virginia Slim events. Her continued success sparked speculation in the press about her chances of becoming the first Grand Slam winner in eighteen years by capturing the United States Open title. Despite the distraction of being in the media spotlight, Graf cruised through the early rounds, losing only eleven games in successive wins over Elizabeth Minter, Manon Bollegraf, Nathalie Herreman, Patty Fendick, and Katerina Maleeva. Her first test was expected to come from Chris Evert (Martina Navratilova had been upset by Zina Garrison in the quarterfinals), whom she was scheduled to face in the semifinals, but Evert was forced to default the match because of acute gastroenteritis.

Instead, the test came from Gabriela Sabatini in the final. Thrown off her game by the swirling winds at the National Tennis Center and by Sabatini's looping topspin shots, which repeatedly pinned her behind the baseline, Graf nonetheless managed to break her opponent's serve twice in the first set to go up, 6-3. But, much to the delight of the crowd, Sabatini quickly recovered, as Steffi Graf, uncharacteristically rattled, committed a string of unforced errors in dropping the second set, 3-6. In the third set, however, Graf overpowered her admittedly winded opponent to take the set, 6-1, the Open title, and the Grand Slam on a wicked backhand passing shot down the line. Tossing her racket into the air, she rushed into the stands to embrace her father, other family members, and Pavel Slozil. After the victory ceremony, in which she was awarded a gold bracelet with four diamonds, for the four Grand Slam titles, in addition to the United States Open cash prize of $275,000, Steffi Graf said, as quoted in the *Washington Post* (September 11, 1988), that it had been a "relief" to win the Grand Slam: "Now, there's nothing else that people can tell me I have to do. . . . It's been a tough two weeks. It wasn't easy for me. Everybody telling me all the time that I would win unless I broke a leg."

Just a few days later, Steffi Graf was in Seoul, South Korea to take part in the 1988 Olympic Summer Games, where tennis was, for the first time, a medal sport. Her weariness visible, she struggled in the early rounds, but played one of the best matches of her career against the American Zina Garrison in the semifinals, losing only twenty-three points in her 6-2, 6-0 victory. In the gold-medal round against Gabriela Sabatini, she hit her ground strokes with even more authority than usual to win relatively easily, 6-3, 6-3. Her 1988 match-winning streak was halted at forty-six in the semifinals of the Virginia Slims Masters tournament in November by Pam Shriver, who withstood Graf's determined rally in the second set to win, 6-3, 7-6.

Two months later, Steffi Graf won the Australian Open without losing a set to collect her fifth consecutive Grand Slam title. Only in the final, against Helena Sukova, did she drop more than five games in a match. Indeed, she was to win forty-four sets in a row in 1989 before falling behind, 4-6, to Chris Evert in a Virginia Slims tournament in mid-March. Quickly recovering her form, Graf went on to win the match and the tournament. Her thirty-one-match winning streak came to an end in

the final of the Bausch & Lomb Championship on April 16, when she made sixty unforced errors in yielding to Gabriela Sabatini, 6-3, 7-6. The following month she avenged that defeat by trouncing Sabatini, 6-3, 6-1, in just seventy-eight minutes in the final of the West German Open.

Shooting for a record sixth consecutive Grand Slam crown, Steffi Graf encountered few obstacles on her way to the final of the French Open. In the title contest on June 10, 1989, however, she came up against a determined and inspired Arantxa Sanchez-Vicario. Sanchez-Vicario had not won a set in her three previous bouts with Graf, but in the final, she played brilliantly, battling back from 3-5 in the third set to capture the French Open, 7-6, 3-6, 7-5. "She was making some unbelievable shots, so close to the lines," Graf said of her seventeen-year-old opponent in a post-match press conference. "I was not the one who was putting pressure on . . . today."

When the two players met again, in the Wimbledon quarterfinals, Steffi Graf had the upper hand, turning back Sanchez-Vicario, 7-5, 6-1. After dismissing Chris Evert, 6-2, 6-1, in the semifinals, Graf again faced Navratilova for the title. Although Navratilova was the first player to wrest a set from Graf in the tournament, the defending champion coolly reasserted her authority to take her second straight Wimbledon trophy, 6-2, 6-7, 6-1. The two women met again two months later, in the final of the United States Open. Seemingly growing stronger with each set, Graf turned her game up as her older opponent faltered, eventually prevailing, 3-6, 7-5, 6-1.

Long-legged and slim, Steffi Graf stands five feet nine inches tall and weighs about 130 pounds. She has blue eyes, shoulder-length blond hair, unusually long arms, and hands large enough to hold two tennis balls while serving. According to her father, who perhaps knows her best, she has no particular hobbies, although she does enjoy reading (she is especially fond of the novels of Stephen King), shopping, going to movies, and listening to rock music. Until recently, she took the most pleasure in her occasional visits to her home in Brühl, where she helped prepare meals for her family and played with her dogs—Enzo and Max, both German shepherds, and Ben, a boxer. But because her enormous popularity (surveys show she has a higher recognition factor among West Germans than Chancellor Helmut Kohl) makes it impossible for her to live a normal life in her native land, she now spends most of her free time at her condominium in Florida. In addition to her million-dollar-plus annual winnings, Steffi Graf has endorsement arrangements with adidas shoes and tennis wear, Dunlop rackets, and Opel automobiles, among other products, that are reported by *Advertising Age* to be worth in excess of $3 million a year.

References: Chicago Tribune II p3 Jl 4 '88 por, IV p8 Ag 30 '88 por; N Y Newsday p151 Ag 29 '86 por; Sport 78:14+ My 21 '87 pors; N Y Times C p6 Mr 17 '86, C p1+ Ag 29 '88 por, VIII p9 S

11 '88; Scala p20+ S-O '87 pors; Sporting N p46
Je 20 '88 por; Sports Illus 66:34+ Mr 16 '87 pors,
70:78+ Je 26 '89; Time 129:58+ Je 29 '87 por;
Washington Post L p1+ S 6 '87 por, D p10+ Ag 28
'88 pors; International Who's Who, 1989-90

Graves, Michael

July 9, 1934- Architect; designer; university
professor. Address: 341 Nassau St., Princeton,
N.J. 08540

Regardful of the semiological aspects of architecture, perceiving a building as a means of communication, Michael Graves argues that the stripped-
down, abstract forms of modernism serve
primarily as a metaphor of the machine. They ignore nature and mankind, the human figure and
human aspirations, or, to use his phrase, "society's
pattern of rituals," which have historically been
part of architecture's representation. For more than
twenty-five years Graves has been developing his
architectural practice in Princeton, New Jersey,
while teaching at Princeton University, where he
is now Schirmer Professor of Architecture. During
that time his endeavor has been to restore to architecture its traditional figurative language, not by a
quoting or echoing of past images, but by a rephras-
ing of symbolic and structural elements—columns,
doorways, keystones—in a daring simultaneous involvement of cultural allusion, color, scale, and
juxtaposition that blends classical and modern
forms. Graves is both an influential theorist and a
diversified and prolific designer whose architectural drawings are exquisite works of art and
whose other achievements range from an addition

to New York's Whitney Museum of American Art,
perhaps his most prestigious and controversial
commission, to a fashionable, best-selling teakettle.

Michael Graves was born in Indianapolis, Indiana on July 9, 1934, the second son of Thomas
Browning Graves, a dealer in livestock, and Erma
Sanderson (Lowe) Graves. In childhood he showed
an apparently inborn proclivity for drawing and
painting, to which he also turned, he has recalled,
to escape from having to play the violin. But wary
of a career for their son in the fine arts, his conservative, practical parents urged him to consider architecture or engineering. He took his B.S. degree
in architecture at the University of Cincinnati in
1958.

Under the cooperative program at that university, Graves had helped to pay for his training in architecture by alternating two months of classes
with two months of nonacademic work. "By the
time I got to graduate school at Harvard," he said
in an interview for the New York Daily News (October 27, 1985), "I knew all the pragmatic stuff my
contemporaries were just learning." In 1959 he
earned his master's degree in architecture, and in
1960, as winner of the Prix de Rome and the Arnold W. Brunner Fellowship, he began a two-year
residency at the American Academy in Rome.

The paintings and buildings, especially those of
the Renaissance and post-Renaissance, that
Graves saw in Italy, his contact there with other
students and artists, and his conversations with art
historians and classical scholars—all contributed
immensely to the eventual shift in his concern from
architecture as an abstraction to architecture in relation to humanity. On his return from Rome in
1962, Graves became a lecturer in architecture at
Princeton. He advanced to assistant professor the
following year, to associate professor in 1967, and
to professor in 1972. Having found that his teaching
helps him to learn more about architecture, he has
frequently lectured at universities besides Princeton, as visiting professor at the University of Texas
at Austin, the University of Houston, the New
School for Social Research in New York City, the
University of California at Los Angeles, and the
University of North Carolina in Charlotte.

During his early academic years, Graves was associated with a group of other lively young architects and teachers called the Conference of
Architects for the Study of the Environment
(CASE), who met informally to discuss architectural education and urban problems and to comment
on each other's projects. He and Peter Eisenman,
another member of the group, worked for a time on
the design of a city extending from New York to
Philadelphia. In an interview with Barbaralee Diamonstein for American Architecture Now II
(1985), Eisenman related: "When Bob Geddes came
to Princeton as dean in 1967, he walked into the
basement of the architecture school, where Michael and I had a setup of eight or ten people working
on huge models. It was wild! There was a real underground in that school. There was something going on at the teaching level, but it was also that the
heat was there. We were lucky."

Their work on that imaginary metropolis, "New Jersey Corridor Study," led to the inclusion of Graves and Eisenman in the "Forty Under Forty" exhibition at the Architectural League of New York in 1966 and "The New City: Architecture and Urban Renewal" exhibition at the Museum of Modern Art in New York in 1967. A few years later, Graves and Eisenman joined three other architects, Richard Meier, John Hejduk, and Charles Gwathmey, to make up the New York Five, as Paul Goldberger, the architecture critic of the *New York Times*, named the group. In fulfillment of their objective to collaborate on a book to show their work—that is, their realized buildings—in 1972 they published *Five Architects*, which brought them an invitation to take part in the Milan Triennale the following year.

Highly provocative, *Five Architects* became a focus of spirited critical discussion within the profession over the nature and function of architecture. Summing up the general point of view of the five architects, whose work was notably dissimilar in many aspects, Goldberger pointed out in the *New York Times* (November 26, 1973) that they "rejected the notion of architecture as a social tool, rejected prefabrication, rejected the fads of computer design, megastructures and other bits of super technology, and instead have concentrated their efforts on what is perhaps the most traditional—and elevated—architectural problem of all: the making of form."

By the time of the publication of *Five Architects*, the buildings of Graves that had been completed or were nearing completion included the Union County Nature and Science Museum in Mountainside, New Jersey, the Hanselmann House in Fort Wayne, Indiana, and the Benacerraf House addition in Princeton. Aside from touches of color alluding to nature, the exteriors of the houses were white, which accounts in part for the New York Five's being sometimes referred to as "The Whites." But Graves has said that color has been important to him from the beginning, that his clients chose to leave the outsides of the houses uncolored, and that the insides did have color, such as the mural that he painted for the Hanselmann House. As cubism-inspired geometric explorations of light and shade and of solids and voids, much of Graves's early work manifests the influence of the Swiss architect Le Corbusier and documents the contribution of Graves—and of the New York Five—to the revival in the 1960s of some elements of the International Style.

The making of pure form, however, was not Graves's only concern. In an interview with Michael McTwigan for *American Artist* (December 1981), he explained that he had intended his buildings to register a "mythic and ritual structure of society" and acknowledged that he had not achieved his objective, that even other architects did not "read" in his buildings what he himself read: "My earlier work was overly abstract, even though I was trying to express thematic interests figuratively. But their abstraction was still greater than their relationship to nature or to mankind." His search for a way to make the thematic structure of his architecture more "readable" underlies the drawings, murals, sketches, models, and photographs displayed in his exhibition at the Max Protetch Gallery in New York City in the spring of 1979.

Applauding the exhibition as a "record of the development of the most extraordinary and provocative kind of architectural talent," Ada Louise Huxtable called attention in the *New York Times* (May 27, 1979) to "the most delicately assured and beautiful drawings to be seen in or out of the field of architectural design." Graves's work, she found, was particularly distinguished by its interaction of painting and architecture: "This is, in effect, a hybrid art, pushing new frontiers." Mrs. Huxtable further credited Graves with "slowly, painstakingly, and lovingly inventing a different language of form and meaning."

Somewhat similarly, in his essay for Graves's book *Buildings and Projects: 1966–1981* (1982), Vincent Scully, the architectural historian, wrote that "Graves seeks to create a new, or alternative, classical vocabulary." The architect himself, however, has made clear in interviews that his intention has not been to use a new or different or private language of architecture, but to "reestablish" its own language, a "common language" whose "general meanings are understood." What is novel, ingenious, and personal is Graves's articulation of the language. For his vocabulary he drew liberally from Mediterranean architecture, the classic architecture of Egypt, Greece, Rome, Italy, and France: pyramids, columns, pilasters, pergolas, keystones, vaults, all of which he mixed with elements of modern idioms, such as constructivism, futurism, and, especially, cubism.

Certain classical motifs enrich Graves's anthropocentric architecture both by their historical and literary allusions and by their suggestion of the human form. The base of a column, for instance, may correspond to a man's foot, its shaft to his trunk, and its capital to his head. Doors, windows, walls, floors, ceilings have a symbolic as well as a functional value. As he explained in his essay on figurative architecture in *Buildings and Projects: 1966–1981*: "All architecture before the Modern movement sought to elaborate on the themes of man and landscape. Understanding the building involves both association with natural phenomena (for example, the ground is like the floor) and anthropomorphic allusions (for example, a column is like a man). . . . Even today, the same metaphors are required for access to our own myths and rituals within the building narrative."

One way that Graves has elaborated on the theme of nature, or landscape, as in his Snyderman House in Fort Wayne, Indiana (1972–77), is through color coding that points to the function and significance of a structural element. The base of a building, or a ground plane anywhere in the building, is likely to be brown or terra cotta or dark green, whereas the color of the ceiling suggests the sky.

But Graves's use of color is not simplistic. "He compounds his work with multiple images and multiple meanings for each," C. Ray Smith observed in *Contemporary Architects*. "Blue on the floor, in the Claghorn kitchen, means the reflection of the sky through the window—and the shadow of a muntin should tell us so."

Of the many designs in Graves's 1979 Protech Gallery exhibition, the one attracting most attention was that for the Fargo-Moorhead Cultural Center Bridge, which was to span the Red River between North Dakota and Minnesota. The pink and yellow Kasota stone bridge would house an art museum above its roadways for cars and pedestrians and would link a concert hall and radio-television station on the Fargo side with a history museum on the Moorhead side. William Marlin of the *Christian Science Monitor* (April 27, 1979) described Graves's design as "a jubilantly composed interpretation of the area's sodbusting heritage and natural beauty." And yet it echoes what one critic called "almost Art Deco zaniness" and evokes, aside from Florence's Ponte Vecchio itself, the work of Claude-Nicolas Ledoux and Étienne-Louis Boullée, the late-eighteenth-century French visionary architects.

Even though political controversy and funding problems prevented construction of the bridge, the excitement that Graves's design aroused may well have given him some advantage in the competition in 1980 for the Portland Building in Oregon. The merits of his $22.4 million, fifteen-story structure included its fresh, innovative style, its energy efficiency, and its low cost of under fifty-two dollars a square foot. With its many small windows and its ornamental façade of garlands and of a huge keystone atop giant pilasters, Graves's design generated stormy debate. (Provisions in the original plan for a miniature village on the roof were eventually eliminated.) Among the Portland Building's champions was the architect Philip Johnson, who headed the competition jury. Its detractors included Pietro Belluschi, a Portland architect and the former dean of the School of Architecture and Planning at the Massachusetts Institute of Technology, who described the structure as an "oversize, beribboned Christmas package" inappropriate to Portland. Wolf Von Eckhardt, the architecture critic of *Time*, labeled it "Pop surrealism." But at the convention of the American Institute of Architects in New Orleans in 1983, the Portland Building won a National Honor Award for Graves.

The Portland Building, which opened in 1982, was Graves's first large-scale design carried to completion. During the next few years, he boldly restated his rejection of the austere steel-and-glass boxes of modernism with his pink, cream, and blue San Juan Capistrano Regional Library, designed in the required Californian Spanish missionary style, and his ambitious Humana Building, the headquarters in Louisville, Kentucky of the private health-care company. That eagerly awaited skyscraper, eye-catching and inviting with its base and tower of pink granite and arcade of red granite, delighted such admirers of Graves as Goldberger, who reassured readers of the *New York Times* (June 10, 1985) that despite "the awkwardness of its overall shape . . . Humana is a remarkable achievement—in every way Mr. Graves's finest building, a tower that proves his ability not only to work at large scale, but to create interior and exterior details as well wrought as those of any architect now practicing."

While the three major commissions were spreading his celebrity nationally, Graves was seeking to expand and diversify the production of his office in Princeton through scores of designs that enabled him to test and carry through his inventive ideas on a smaller scale. His residential works of the late 1970s include the Plocek House in Warren, New Jersey and additions to several houses, as well as plans for a vacation house in Aspen, Colorado and a beach house in Loveladies, New Jersey. Among his designs for commercial enterprises were furniture showrooms in New York, Chicago, Houston, and Los Angeles commissioned by Sunar, for which he also, from 1980 to 1982, designed furniture and textiles. In his comments on the award-winning showrooms in *Art in America* (September 1980), Martin Filler remarked that they "all began with more or less anonymous space in speculative commercial buildings, transformed by Graves into minor miracles of suggestive design. Using cheap materials and surface color and decoration, they show what talent can do even when pitted against the limitations of low budget and ungrateful existing spaces."

When, in the early 1980s, Graves was chosen to design the $37.5 million expansion of the Whitney Museum of American Art in Manhattan, he called his new commission "an incredible challenge." The challenge came, in fact, not only from the enormous difficulty of his task, but also from the outburst of protest that followed the announcement of his plan in May 1985. Built in 1966, the unadorned, dark-gray granite Whitney Museum is the creation of Marcel Breuer, one of the founding giants of Modernism. "I tried to make the Breuer friendly by picking up the rhythms of his whole composition and incorporating the original building into a larger whole," Graves said of his design, as quoted in the New York *Daily News* (October 27, 1985). He proposed constructing a counterbalancing pink building alongside the existing building and a "hinge," or cylindrical structure, to join the two buildings; a rectangular, five-story setback penthouse would surmount all three structures.

At the convention of the New York chapter of the American Institute of Architects in June 1985, the architect Abraham W. Geller charged that the Breuer building would be "literally crushed" if Graves's design were carried out. More than 600 prominent architects, artists, and civic leaders signed the petition of the Ad Hoc Committee to Save the Whitney in opposition to Graves's plan. Within the profession Graves had equally eminent supporters, including Philip Johnson and Vincent Scully, but in March 1987, in response to pressure from civic and neighborhood groups, Whitney officials unveiled Graves's revised, smaller, toned-down expansion plan. Partly because of the reduced size of the top structure, the Breuer building seemed less "crushed." "The design of the revision, however, remains in Mr. Graves's characteristic style," Douglas C. McGill wrote in the *New York Times* (March 11, 1987), "a postmodern amalgam of abstract forms that recalls architecture ranging from pyramids and palazzos to New York brownstones."

A third, revised plan for the Whitney Museum expansion was made public on December 20, 1988. Simpler and more abstract than his two earlier submissions, Graves's third proposal called for the construction of two structures: a large, boxy building along Madison Avenue whose main feature would be a monumental, three-story grid of gray and red granite and a second structure across the top to link the old and new wings. In Paul Goldberger's view, Graves's third plan was "ultimately as Gravesian as the two designs that preceded it" but "considerably more deferential to the Breuer building." "Mr. Graves is still speaking his own words," Goldberger explained in his appraisal for the *New York Times* (January 8, 1989). "The most important difference between the new design and its predecessors is that this time, Mr. Graves appears to be saying those words in Marcel Breuer's language."

Although the Whitney extension was, as Graves put it, "the most important commission of the decade," he continued to occupy himself with a variety of other undertakings. An exhibition at the Max Protetch Gallery in the winter of 1985 of his drawings and models for eighteen projects showed that he was also at work on plans for an alumni center at the University of West Virginia; a Napa Valley, California winery; an office building in Cambridge, Massachusetts; a health club in Tokyo; and a Diane von Fürstenberg boutique in Manhattan.

Another of Graves's recent commissions involved a $375 million hotel and convention complex, on which construction began in January 1988, for the vast Walt Disney World Epcot Center in Lake Buena Vista, Florida. One of the two blue-green and coral hotels is crowned by a pair of fifty-five-foot dolphins and the other, by a pair of forty-seven-foot swans. Exterior patterns of banana leaves and waves, a cascading waterfall, and a pool and lagoon also help to create a wonderland that rivals Disney's fantasies. Graves felt that the classical symbols of water, the dolphin, and the swan would be more appropriate to a convention hotel than Mickey Mouse or any other cartoon character and yet would have "the kind of warmth that the whole Disney experience gives."

In addition to buildings, showrooms, furniture, and textiles, the output of Graves's practice includes renovation of a Manhattan carriage house and fashionable apartments, exhibition booths and displays, rugs, costumes, murals, posters, magazine covers, and a tea service produced by Alessi in Milan. By 1988 more than 100,000 of his $115 "birdie" teakettles had been sold. He has also designed for Alessi a matching sugar bowl and creamer, a pepper mill, salt and pepper shakers, demitasse cups, and a bar cart.

Michael Graves is a fellow of the American Institute of Architects and of the Society for the Arts, Religion and Contemporary Culture and a trustee of the American Academy in Rome and of the Institute for Architecture and Urban Studies. Among his tributes are the Arnold W. Brunner Memorial Prize in Architecture of the American Academy and Institute of Arts and Letters (1980), the Henry Hering Memorial Award (1987), several National Honor Awards of the American Institute of Architects (AIA), twenty-five AIA awards from the New Jersey Society of Architects, many design awards from *Progressive Architecture* magazine, and the Designer of the Year Award for 1980 from *Interiors* magazine.

Somewhat ironically, in view of the European and classical strains in his style, Graves, along with some sixty assistants and other staff members, works in a colonial house (or two joined houses) in Princeton. As Paul Goldberger has observed, Graves "is calm and almost professorial in manner, with relatively little of the flamboyance of his architecture." He has been twice married and divorced. By his first marriage, to a painter, he has a daughter, Sarah Browing, and a son, Adam Daimhim. He is also the father of two stepdaughters, Anne Ashby Gilbert and Elizabeth Eastman Gilbert, the children of his second wife, a dancer. Since 1974 Graves has been gradually renovating and converting his own home, a brick and stucco warehouse, which, in his words, has the "feeling of a Tuscan farmhouse." It was built by craftsmen brought from Italy in the 1920s to work on construction on the Princeton campus. The university's policy against commissioning work from faculty members has deprived its campus of a building by the teacher who has set a confident and humanistic change of course for architecture throughout the country.

References: *Am Artist* 45:8+ D '81 por; *Art in America* 68:99+ S '80; *Esquire* 108:102 N '87 por; *N Y Daily News* (People) p3 O 27 '85 por; *N Y Times* II p25+ My 27 '78; *N Y Times Mag* p42 O 10 '82; *New Yorker* 61:58+ F 17 '86; *People* 17:87+ F '88 por; *Sat R* 9:40+ Mr '82 por; *Wall St J* p25 Ap 3 '81 por; *Contemporary Architects* (1987); Diamonstein, Barbaralee. *American Architecture Now* (1980); Graves, Michael. *Buildings and Projects: 1966–1981* (1982); *Who's Who in America, 1988–89*; *Who's Who in American Art* (1984)

Gray, C(layland) Boyden

Feb. 6, 1943– Counselor to the president; government official. Address: b. The White House, Washington, D.C., 20500; h. 1524 30th St., N.W., Washington, D.C. 20007

In his first personnel decision after being elected president of the United States in November 1988, George Bush announced the appointment of C. Boyden Gray to the office of counselor to the president, the assistant who is responsible for providing legal advice to the president and the White House staff as well as for overseeing compliance with the rules of ethics imposed on senior officials in the executive branch. In his first few months in office, Gray has, perhaps unwittingly, turned the traditionally low-profile position into a source of front-page news and has himself become a controversial figure. While serving as the chief policeman of ethics in an administration pledged not to tolerate even the slightest appearance of a conflict of interest, Gray stayed on as a director of a family-owned communications empire until news accounts prompted him to resign from its board and place his vast holdings into a blind trust.

In a public feud that is rare so early in the life of a new administration, Gray seemed to go out of his way to antagonize Secretary of State James A. Baker 3d, questioning his compliance with ethics rules and criticizing his widely heralded agreement with Congress on aid to the Contra rebels. Gray also came under fire for his role in the ill-fated nomination of former senator John G. Tower as defense secretary. Despite his shaky start, Gray's position seems secure, for he, like his nemesis Secretary Baker, is one of a small group of Bush intimates, dubbed the Untouchables, with whom the president has developed a comfortable working relationship. Gray, whose social background is similar to that of the president, served for eight years as counsel and deputy chief of staff to then Vice-President Bush. Gray's supporters, and even some of his critics, believe that his early problems arose from his political naïveté. "Boyden is maybe not wily and ingratiating," observed Lloyd Cutler, the White House counsel under President Jimmy Carter and Gray's mentor at a Washington law firm, "but I think that's one of his strengths. . . . He's the very essence of integrity."

Clayland Boyden Gray was born in Winston-Salem, North Carolina on February 6, 1943, the third of the four sons of Gordon and Jane Henderson Boyden (Craige) Gray. His brothers are Gordon Jr., Burton Craige, and Bernard. His father was secretary of the army under President Harry S. Truman and national security adviser to President Dwight D. Eisenhower; he also served as president of the University of North Carolina. His paternal grandfather, Bowman Gray, was president of the R. J. Reynolds Tobacco Company. Despite the wealth that surrounded him, C. Boyden Gray led a rather sad childhood, since he saw little of his busy father, and his mother died when he was ten years old. (With his father's remarriage, in 1956, he acquired a stepmother, the former Nancy Maguire Beebe.) After his mother's death, he was sent away to a boarding school, St. Mark's in Southboro, Massachusetts, where he never seemed to fit in. "Being a southerner at St. Mark's, I felt like the odd man out," he told Charles Babington of the Raleigh, North Carolina *News and Observer* (December 12, 1988). "You get a sense of what it means to be excluded." His favorite childhood memories are of living in the president's mansion on the campus of the University of North Carolina in Chapel Hill, where he had free run of the school's basketball and tennis courts.

At Harvard University during the early 1960s, Gray felt out of place, as a conservative southern Democrat, among his liberal classmates. Although he managed to be elected to the socially exclusive Porcellian club and worked on the Harvard *Crimson*, the college newspaper, he spent much of his time alone in study. He graduated magna cum laude with a B.A. degree in history in 1964. After serving in the United States Marine Corps, he took his father's advice and enrolled at the University of North Carolina law school, where, ironically, he also felt somewhat out of place after so much time in the North. He was editor in chief of the *University of North Carolina Law Review* and graduated first in his class in 1968. J. Dickson Phillips, then the dean of the North Carolina law school and later a federal appellate judge, saw enormous potential in Gray's assiduousness and scholarship. "He's one of the great young people that we've produced in this state in my lifetime," Phillips once said during an interview.

Gray's impressive academic record won him a coveted position as law clerk for Chief Justice Earl Warren. Although he found the work stimulating, even exciting, at times, he now looks back on his year at the Supreme Court as one of lost opportunity. It was at about that time, in 1969, that his father decided to sell the two Winston-Salem daily newspapers, the *Journal* and the *Twin City Sentinel*, which had been in the family for more than thirty years, to Media General. A frustrated journalist at heart, Gray has come to regret that he did not try to dissuade his father from making the sale. "The notion of deciding that I would give up the life in the middle of this great year, this honor [of clerking for the chief justice], to go back to North Carolina," he explained to Jon Healey of the *Winston-Salem Journal* (January 8, 1989), "I just couldn't focus on it. So I let it go."

Later that year Gray joined the prestigious law firm of Wilmer, Cutler and Pickering in Washington, D.C., where he became a protégé of one of its partners, Lloyd N. Cutler. For the next twelve years, Gray represented corporate clients before the federal government, with most of his caseload involving antitrust litigation and, to a lesser extent, regulatory law. He helped to plot lobbying strategy for clients and opposed legislation requiring lobbyists to disclose their activities more fully. Among the clients he brought to the firm was the Business Roundtable, made up of 200 top corporate executives who lobby for a probusiness environment. In 1976, having earned a reputation as an attorney who was careful about detail and adept at anticipating and forestalling problems, Gray was made a partner in the firm. In the following year he abandoned the political party of his father and registered as a Republican.

Following the election of Ronald Reagan as president in 1980, Admiral Daniel J. Murphy, the chief of staff for Vice-President elect George Bush, asked Deanne C. Siemer, the Defense Department's general counsel, to recommend someone for the post of counsel and deputy chief of the vice-president's staff. Siemer, who had worked at Wilmer, Cutler and Pickering, recommended Gray as a candidate who fulfilled Murphy's criteria of being "politically presentable, intelligent, and fun to do business with." At the job interview with Bush, Gray learned of old family connections with the vice-president elect, including the fact that their fathers had been golfing partners. The two achieved an instant rapport, and Gray agreed to join Bush's staff for what he thought might be a two-year stint. To avoid a conflict of interest between his public position and his personal fortune, Gray drafted a memorandum on his first day on the job announcing that he would not take part in any decisions affecting the communications, tobacco, oil and gas, or computer industries.

Gray's most significant and time-consuming contribution as the vice-president's counsel was his work on the Presidential Task Force on Regulatory Relief, which Reagan had created in 1981 to redeem his campaign promise to help business cut through bureaucratic red tape. Although Bush was nominally the director of the task force, Gray oversaw its day-to-day operation. From early 1981,

when he drafted the executive order creating the panel, to August 1983, when he conducted the presentation of its final report, Gray, working discreetly in the background, facilitated the review of nearly 7,000 government regulations governing trade, energy, agriculture, automobiles, prescription drugs, banking, and the environment. The panel recommended the elimination of 25 percent of them at an estimated annual savings of $15 billion. One set of regulations that was spared was that protecting the rights of the handicapped. Remembering the indignity he endured as an outsider at boarding school, Gray prevailed upon the panel to retain laws ensuring public access for the disabled.

Not everyone welcomed the work of the task force. Its critics charged that the elimination of certain regulations, particularly those affecting the inspection and enforcement powers of the Occupational Safety and Health Administration and the Food and Drug Administration, endangered the public. "I think [Gray] is a fine example of the fox guarding the chicken coop," Joan Claybrook, the president of the consumer group Public Citizen, said. "He worked in private practice representing the auto and many other industries, and, for the past two and a half years, he has played a major role in deciding which regulations will survive, or be scrapped."

When, in 1987, Gray was appointed to a Reagan administration working group that studied ways to develop non-fossil fuels, he donated his oil and gas holdings to Harvard University in order to avoid a conflict of interest. As a member of that group, Gray developed an enduring interest in alternative sources of energy, becoming such a tireless proponent of ethanol as a substitute for gasoline that, during the presidential campaign of 1988, Bush staff members often complained that he took up long periods of time at crucial planning sessions to discuss the merits of such fuels. Another pet project that Gray pushed during the heat of the campaign was the rights of the handicapped, which he worked into Bush's acceptance speech at the Republican convention. "Boyden was very sensitive politically on the disabled matter," the campaign director, Lee Atwater, said, "and he helped a lot of us see the light on that. My observation is that it wasn't just politics with him. He had a sincere belief and conviction, and he pursued it with feeling."

The day after his election to the presidency, George Bush named Gray legal counsel for the transition team and, subsequently, White House counsel. During the transition, the former campaign aide Craig Fuller tried to limit Gray's prospective clout in the White House, but he was himself frozen out of the administration in the infighting that ensued. As counselor to the president, Gray is the chief ethics officer of the White House, responsible for monitoring compliance with the president's edict that senior officials avoid even the appearance of a conflict of interest.

Ironically, although Gray had scrupulously detached himself from matters affecting his personal fortune while on the vice-president's staff and had begun to sell off or otherwise dispose of many of his holdings, including a block of RJR Nabisco stock, some of his activities did not seem to meet the Bush administration's more stringent conflict-of-interest rules. Critics pointed out that, from 1981 to 1988, Gray served as chairman of Summit Communications Group, the Atlanta-based radio and cable television conglomerate that his father had founded, earning hundreds of thousands of dollars in fees. Reagan administration guidelines decreed that the outside income of White House employees could be no greater than 15 percent of their government salary, but, because the rules did not extend to the vice-president's staff, Gray was technically exempt. Now that he was Bush's chief ethics officer, however, such technicalities did not provide much of a defense from those who questioned the administration's genuine commitment to avoiding the imputation of a conflict of interest.

Moreover, Gray had often failed to file timely financial disclosure forms, and he did not report $87,000 in deferred income from Summit, despite a 1982 Justice Department ruling that all income must be reported in the year in which it is earned, regardless of when it is actually received. While such details were being mulled over in the press, Gray insisted that he had always acted in good faith, explaining that he was unaware of the Reagan administration policy and the deferred-income ruling.

Although Gray no longer accepted fees for his work at Summit, he vowed to retain his seat on the board and dismissed suggestions that he put his holdings, which included a multimillion-dollar interest in Media General Corporation, into a blind trust. On February 6, 1989, however, Gray, acting on the advice of the leaders of Bush's Commission on Federal Ethics, reluctantly agreed to resign from Summit and create a blind trust for his holdings, which were valued in excess of $10 million.

Meanwhile, Gray was busy vetting White House statements for legal problems and sifting through the Federal Bureau of Investigation background checks on prospective appointments. President Bush relied on his narrow legal assessment of the qualifications of secretary of defense-designate John G. Tower, and he thus did not anticipate the firestorm of criticism over Tower's alleged drinking, womanizing, and private dealings with defense contractors that ultimately doomed the nomination.

Perhaps to divert attention from the controversy over his own financial activities, Gray leaked to the press that he had been trying to persuade Secretary of State James A. Baker to sell his stock in the holding company of the Chemical Bank of New York, whose outstanding loans to Third World countries could be directly affected by Baker's decisions. Reportedly furious at the disclosure, Baker disposed of the stock, but the widening public rift between two of Bush's closest advisers alarmed many in the new administration.

Just as the furor over the bank stock began to fade, Gray picked another fight with Baker, this time over the secretary's agreement with Congress to provide nonlethal aid to the Contra rebels opposed to the Marxist-led Sandinista regime in Nicaragua. Gray, who was never consulted about the pact and learned about it in the press, objected to a side letter attached to the agreement, in which President Bush agreed to cut off all aid at the end of November 1989 unless he received approval from four Democratic-controlled committees in Congress. In remarks that appeared in the New York Times on Easter Sunday, Gray asserted that the so-called gentlemen's agreement eroded presidential authority in foreign affairs and was tantamount to a congressional veto, which had been ruled unconstitutional by the Supreme Court in 1983.

Baker and the White House dismissed Gray's objections and at times ridiculed his concern. "I want to announce," the White House press secretary Marlin Fitzwater scoffed, "that Boyden Gray concurs in the constitutionality of the Easter Egg Roll." Although some observers saw the incident as another installment of the Gray-Baker feud or as yet another example of Gray's political naïveté, others believed that Gray acted out of genuine concern. "He has an academic interest in the whole subject of legislative vetoes," an unnamed administration official was quoted as saying in the Washington Post (March 31, 1989), "and part of his job is to protect Bush's position. This could set a precedent for the future, and he was doing his job by questioning it."

Despite the controversy over Gray's personal finances, the running feud with Baker, and charges that he bungled the Tower nomination, Bush has given no outward indication that his counsel's job is in jeopardy. Along with Baker, Secretary of the Treasury Nicholas F. Brady, and Secretary of Commerce Robert A. Mosbacher, Gray remains one of the "Untouchables" on whom the president relies for sound advice. Bush has "developed a confidence and trust level with Boyden that's not going to be shaken," the Republican party chairman, Lee Atwater, recently remarked.

C. Boyden Gray is a Lincolnesque figure who stands six feet, six inches tall and whose bushy eyebrows guard rather melancholy eyes. Invariably rumpled in appearance, he lopes around in a permanent slouch, at times with holes in his shirt and shoes. He has been described as aloof, distracted, serious-minded, and a workaholic, but his friends, who call him "CB," find him a witty and gifted raconteur. In 1987 he purchased for $4 million a stucco mansion built in 1852 by the shipping magnate Robert Dodge in the Georgetown section of Washington, D.C., but soon after that he separated from his wife, the former Carol Elizabeth Taylor, and he never occupied the home. They have one daughter. Still touting the benefits of alternate energy sources, he drives an ethanol-powered Chevrolet Citation. His sedentary recreation is bridge; his active one is tennis.

References: *Washington Post* D p1 Mr 31 '89 pors; *Winston-Salem (N.C.) Journal* Ja 8 '89; *Who's Who in America, 1988–89*

Greenspan, Alan

Mar. 6, 1926– Economist; United States government official. Address: Board of Governors, Federal Reserve System, 20th St. & Constitution Ave., N.W., Washington, D.C. 20551

NOTE: This biography supersedes the article that appeared in *Current Biography* in 1974.

As chairman of the seven-member board of governors of the Federal Reserve System, Alan Greenspan holds what has been called the second-most-important post in the United States government, after the presidency. The controller of the nation's money supply, the "Fed," as it is commonly known, is also responsible for harnessing economic growth while guarding against inflation, and for keeping the dollar sound. The system, which regulates about 7,000 member banks and oversees twelve regional Federal Reserve banks located throughout the United States, employs 25,000 people and has an annual budget of $1 billion. Nominated by President Ronald Reagan to head the central bank on June 2, 1987, Greenspan easily won Senate confirmation and took office on August 11 of that year. The chairman is a moderate Republican, who, like his predecessor, the Democrat Paul A. Volcker, views the fight against inflation as the Fed's principal duty and, also like him, believes that inflation can best be contained by limiting the growth of the money supply. A staunch proponent of deregula-

tion, Greenspan opposes all forms of government intervention in the economy, but beyond that subscribes to no rigid economic ideology. "He's not a Keynesian. He's not a supply-sider," Robert Kavesh, a friend of Greenspan's who is an economics professor at New York University, told Martin Mittelstaedt of the Toronto *Globe and Mail* (August 1, 1987). "I'd call him an eclectic economist, but with a very conservative bent."

Alan Greenspan was born in New York City on March 6, 1926, the only child of Herbert Greenspan, a stockbroker, and Rose (Goldsmith) Greenspan. His parents divorced when Alan was a child, and he was raised by his mother in the Washington Heights section of Manhattan. Endowed with a precocious fondness for numbers, he could, by the age of five, do large calculations in his head and reproduce the batting averages of major league baseball players. Following his graduation from Manhattan's George Washington High School, he studied music at the Juilliard School in New York before going on the road for a year as a tenor saxophone and clarinet player with the Henry Jerome band. Returning home, Greenspan enrolled at New York University and, in 1948, earned a B.S. degree, summa cum laude, in economics. After receiving his M.A. degree in economics from NYU in 1950, Greenspan began working toward a doctorate at Columbia University, where he studied under and became a close friend of the noted economist Arthur F. Burns, who would go on to serve as chairman of the Federal Reserve Board from 1970 to 1978. Greenspan left Columbia in 1953, without earning a doctorate, but he ultimately received his Ph.D. degree from NYU in 1977.

Soon after leaving Columbia, Greenspan joined forces with William Townsend to form the New York economic consulting firm of Townsend-Greenspan. A bond trader who had been active in the consulting business since the 1930s, Townsend served as its president until his death in 1958, when Greenspan, who had been vice-president, became its president and principal owner. Small but influential under Greenspan's leadership, the firm provided research, forecasts, and other services, without, unlike other consulting firms, aggressively seeking new clients. When Greenspan dissolved the firm in 1987, following his appointment as head of the Federal Reserve Board, Townsend-Greenspan had a staff of about twenty-five and approximately ninety clients, most of them major industrial and financial institutions. Between 1953 and 1955, Greenspan was an economics instructor at New York University.

In 1952 Alan Greenspan met the Russian-born best-selling novelist and social philosopher Ayn Rand, whose philosophy of "Objectivism" was to have a profound influence on him. Objectivism exalts laissez-faire capitalism and promotes "rational selfishness," in the belief that society functions most efficiently when people actively pursue their own self-interests, to the exclusion of the interests of society as a whole. Greenspan remained a close friend of Miss Rand's until her death in 1982.

"When I met Ayn Rand, I was a free enterpriser in the Adam Smith sense—impressed with the theoretical structure and efficiency of markets," Greenspan told Soma Golden of the New York Times in 1974. "What she did—through long discussions and lots of arguments into the night—was to make me think why capitalism is not only efficient and practical, but also moral." In the July 1966 issue of The Objectivist, a monthly journal published by Ayn Rand's disciples, to which Greenspan often contributed, the economist denounced "the welfare state" as "nothing more than a mechanism by which governments confiscate the wealth of the productive members of a society."

Greenspan did not become actively involved in politics until 1967, when, at Ayn Rand's urging, he accepted Richard M. Nixon's offer to serve as an adviser during his 1968 presidential campaign, with the title of director of domestic policy research. Following Nixon's victory, he became the president-elect's representative to the Bureau of the Budget during the period of transition between administrations, and he also served during the transition as Nixon's chairman for the Task Force on Foreign Trade Policy. Declining offers to become a full-time member of the Nixon administration, he returned to his New York consulting firm following Nixon's inauguration, in January 1969. He continued to advise Nixon informally and accepted assignments on the administration's Task Force on Economic Growth (1969), Commission on an All-Volunteer Armed Force (1969-70), and Commission on Financial Structure and Regulation (1970-71). In addition, he served on the Secretary of Commerce's Advisory Board (1971-72), the Security and Exchange Commission's Central Market System Committee (1972), and the Office of Management and Budget's Gross National Product Review Committee (1974).

Early in 1974 Nixon, who had been reelected in 1972, offered Greenspan the post of chairman of the Council of Economic Advisers. At first Greenspan declined the offer, but his resistance softened over the next several months, as the administration proved unable to find a suitable replacement for Herbert G. Stein, who was scheduled to resign in late summer. Finally, in July, Greenspan accepted the job. "I changed my mind," he explained to Soma Golden in a New York Times (July 24, 1974) article, "because some people in Washington destroyed my absolute conviction that I could do nothing to make things better." In particular, it was reported that Arthur F. Burns, then chairman of the Federal Reserve Board, told his former student that it was his patriotic duty to combat the inflation that was threatening capitalism. Greenspan won Senate confirmation on August 21 and took office on September 1.

As chairman of the CEA, Greenspan urged Gerald R. Ford, who had become president following Nixon's resignation on August 8, 1974, to make the curbing of inflation the nation's chief economic priority. Greenspan believed that a low rate of inflation was essential to creating the kind of confidence that would generate economic expansion and higher employment. When Greenspan took office the inflation rate was 11 percent, but by the time he left, in January 1977, following Ford's defeat by Jimmy Carter in the 1976 election, inflation had fallen to 6.5 percent. Ironically, however, Greenspan may have contributed to Ford's loss of the White House. In 1975 he had advised the president to cut taxes, a move that helped to pull the nation out of a severe recession, but when the economic spurt engendered by the tax cuts slackened in 1976, Greenspan, believing that the economy would soon right itself, recommended that Ford not take further action. Although the economy did rebound by the end of the year, Ford's inaction during the slowdown led some Americans to question his leadership capabilities and, in the opinion of some observers, may have contributed heavily to his defeat.

Apart from his success in reducing inflation, Greenspan's tenure as chairman of the Council of Economic Advisers was most notable for a statement he made at a government meeting shortly after he took office. "Everyone was hurt by inflation," Greenspan said. "If you want to examine percentagewise who was hurt most . . . , it was Wall Street brokers." Greenspan was attempting to make the point that, proportionately, stockbrokers had lost more income because of inflation than the poor, but most observers felt his comment showed a lack of sensitivity. Greenspan later recanted, saying, "Obviously, the poor are suffering more."

Following Carter's election to the presidency, Greenspan returned to Townsend-Greenspan. At the Republican National Convention in 1980, he was among those who urged Ronald Reagan to select Gerald Ford as his vice-presidential running mate, a possibility that Reagan eventually rejected. Nonetheless, he supported the Republican ticket of Reagan and George Bush and later praised the drastic budget reductions undertaken by Reagan in the early months of his first term. "The administration," he remarked in July 1981, "has done a job that any of us with experience in Washington would have said had only one chance in 100 of succeeding."

Between 1981 and 1983, Greenspan served as chairman of the National Commission on Social Security Reform, a fifteen-member body charged with recommending changes to save the Social Security system, which was approaching bankruptcy. The committee suggested cutting future benefits, raising payroll taxes, and delaying cost-of-living increases for retired workers. Its recommendations, which were largely adopted by Congress, ensured the solvency of the system for the next twenty-five years.

Greenspan involved himself in a number of other activities during the early and mid-1980s, including appearances on the lecture circuit. He served on the boards of several corporations, including Alcoa, Automatic Data Processing, Capital Cities/ABC, General Foods, J. P. Morgan & Company, Morgan Guaranty Trust Company of

New York, Mobil, and the Pittston Company. In 1985 he helped to promote sales of the Apple IIc computer by appearing in ads on television and in magazines. In the previous year, he and two partners had formed Greenspan O'Neil Associates, a money-management firm, but the venture failed to attract a sufficient number of clients, and it closed in early 1987.

Paul A. Volcker's unexpected announcement that he was resigning as chairman of the Federal Reserve Board when his term expired on June 1, 1987 left Ronald Reagan in something of a quandary. Appointed by Jimmy Carter in 1979 and reappointed by Reagan in 1983, Volcker had won such enormous respect from the business and financial communities for his success in dealing with inflation during his two terms that Reagan had hoped that he would stay on for a third term. Failing that, Reagan at first intended to name a supply-side economist to the position, but the Iran-Contra scandal and a plunging dollar had so weakened the president that he had to heed the demands of the market and the advice of his moderate advisers, Secretary of the Treasury James A. Baker and Chief of Staff Howard H. Baker, as well as of Volcker, that he appoint a nonideologue who would carry on the anti-inflation crusade. Given that scenario, Greenspan was the obvious choice, and Reagan offered him the post on June 2. News of Volcker's departure caused the dollar to plummet in world markets, but foreign and domestic investors quickly regained confidence with word of Greenspan's appointment.

Greenspan, who has said that he took only "milliseconds" to accept the nomination, appeared before the Senate Banking, Housing, and Urban Affairs Committee for confirmation hearings on July 21, 1987. During three-and-a-half hours of testimony, Greenspan told the committee that he thought the Federal Reserve Board's primary job was "achieving steady, maximum growth . . . [without] letting the inflation genie out of the bottle." He said that Volcker's policies had been "essentially on target," adding that he would try to "follow [in his predecessor's] footsteps." Greenspan also indicated that, in his opinion, a recession was not on the horizon, that the Third World debt situation was improving, and that any increase in the federal budget deficit would be "a very dangerous signal." He voiced his disapproval of the raising of taxes to reduce the deficit and predicted that a major decline in the trade deficit was imminent. In a lengthy exchange with Senator Donald W. Riegle of Michigan, Greenspan said he would be able to resist political pressure from the Reagan administration not to pursue a tight-money policy. "If the Senate confirms me, I will take an oath of office. And I take that oath seriously. It's just not credible to me that I would be advocating actions other than those I thought relevant to the situation." Greenspan added that, if his actions turned out to be incorrect, it "would not be on the basis of politics rather than economics."

On July 28, 1987 the Senate Banking, Housing, and Urban Affairs Committee voted unanimously to approve Greenspan's nomination. Its chairman, Senator William Proxmire of Wisconsin, who credited Greenspan with having "excellent personal qualities," told the press: "He is intelligent. He is respected by the business community that knows him and his work. He is an extraordinarily civil and decent man." After being unable to find a suitable buyer for Townsend-Greenspan by the July 31 deadline for putting all of his assets in a blind trust, Greenspan closed the firm. On August 3, the entire Senate confirmed his nomination by a vote of ninety-one to two, and, eight days later, Greenspan was sworn into office by Vice-President George Bush at a ceremony in the East Room of the White House.

On September 4, 1987, just twenty-four days into his term, Greenspan surprised many observers by announcing that he was raising the federal discount rate—the interest that the Federal Reserve charges its member banks—from 5.5 to 6 percent. That increase, the first since April 1984, reflected Greenspan's concern with what he viewed as the portents of inflation. The growing federal trade deficit, which reached an all-time high of $16.5 billion in July, was not only weakening the dollar but also threatening to drive up domestic prices on imported goods. In another ominous trend, the low unemployment rate, coupled with a decline in excess production capacity, increased the chances for a new round of inflation. Greenspan viewed his action on the discount rate as a small dose of anti-inflation medicine that would obviate the need for a larger dose at a later date. Some observers also interpreted Greenspan's move as an effort to emerge from the shadow of Volcker and show his independence. In the words of David Jones, the chief economist at New York's Aubrey G. Lanston & Company, as quoted in U.S. News & World Report (September 21, 1987), "Greenspan wanted to make it clear that he wasn't a wimp, that he was in control and that he would have a strong backbone in fighting inflation." At the same time, the rise in the discount rate was not so severe as to constitute a radical change in policy. As Mickey Levy, the chief economist for Fidelity Bank of Philadelphia, remarked in Fortune (October 26, 1987), "It was a shot across the bow, not a signal that the Fed was tightening further."

The new Fed chairman faced his first major crisis on October 19, 1987, the so-called Black Monday, when the Dow Jones Industrial Average fell by an all-time high of 508 points. Responding to the crisis, Greenspan, who several weeks earlier had alerted his staff to prepare for such an event, reversed his tight-money policy and moved to assure the stock market that the Fed would provide it with needed liquidity and would also aid any major financial institution that faced problems in funding its operation. Greenspan's masterly handling of the repercussions of the crash drew praise from the Wall Street Journal, among other publications.

After the stock market began to rally, Greenspan reverted to his more conservative approach. In several appearances that he made before congressional committees and in other forums, he argued that, although the economy was strong and the threat of inflation was weakening, the situation was "not without risks." Testifying before a House Banking, Housing, and Urban Affairs subcommittee in July 1988, Greenspan warned, "As a nation, we are still living well beyond our means, we consume much more of the world's goods and services each year than we produce. Our current account deficit indicates how much more deeply in debt to the rest of the world we are sliding each year." Greenspan does not believe, however, that allowing the dollar to slide further, relative to other currencies, will help the nation's economic problems by relieving the trade deficit. Even if the dollar were to tumble, he has contended, the nation lacks the additional productive capacity necessary to expand exports.

Greenspan's prescription for the nation's economic maladies focuses on reducing the huge federal budget deficit. "The importance of credible deficit reduction cannot be overemphasized," Greenspan told the National Council of Savings Institutions in December 1987. In light of the relatively low rate of savings in the United States, Greenspan has urged Congress to work not simply toward balancing the budget, but toward creating a budget surplus. He argues, however, that a general tax increase is inadvisable because "there are upside limits to the share of income that can be taxed." Likewise, he believes that defense spending, which is now approaching what he calls "maintenance levels," cannot be cut. Greenspan believes, therefore, that Social Security and other entitlement programs, which, when combined, make up almost half of federal expenditures, are the most feasible targets for trimming. He has also advocated a fifteen-cent-a-gallon gasoline tax.

In March 1988 Greenspan told the Senate Banking, Housing, and Urban Affairs Committee that he and other officials of the Fed had received a letter in January from Michael Darby, the chief economist on the staff of James Baker, then the secretary of the treasury, urging them to loosen the money supply in order to stave off a recession. Darby's action, which was seen by most observers as a political move intended to prevent an economic downturn that might have jeopardized George Bush's presidential hopes, was later repudiated by Baker. Greenspan complained to the White House about the interference and insisted to the Banking Committee that outside pressure would not sway the Fed. Indeed, in August 1988, after the monthly employment report showed payrolls, overtime, and earnings all on the increase, the Fed raised the discount rate to 6.5 percent.

Greenspan has differed from Volcker primarily on banking issues. More willing than his predecessor to pursue deregulation of the banking industry, he has contended that, because of technological advances, banks no longer have sole access to information that once gave them an advantage over

other institutions in making loans. But at the same time that those institutions have been usurping their traditional role as financial intermediaries, banks, in Greenspan's words, have been "frozen within a regulatory structure fashioned some fifty years ago." Accordingly, Greenspan has supported repeal of the Glass-Steagall Act of 1933, which prohibits commercial banks from underwriting securities, although he believes that, in order for banks to take advantage of such a repeal, the government must not extend its traditional safety features, such as the Federal Deposit Insurance Corporation, to banks that practice securities underwriting. He argues that depositors would be adequately protected if new laws forbade banking and securities firms from owning each other, but allowed a parent holding company to own both.

Greenspan also has relied more heavily on technical analyses of the economy than did Volcker. "He is always coming up with insights into the economy he has picked up from some set of numbers," Frank Morris, the president of the Federal Reserve Bank of Boston, told David R. Francis of the *Christian Science Monitor* (August 9, 1988). In addition, Greenspan, at least until the stock market crash, was less reluctant than Volcker to discuss Fed policy in public, although he realizes that the world financial community scrutinizes every word spoken by the Fed chairman in an attempt to detect hints of a possible change in monetary policy. Greenspan has thus learned to take great care in making pronouncements, saying that he "learned to mumble with great incoherence" during his first year in office. "If I seem unduly clear to you," he has told visitors, "you must have misunderstood what I said."

Greenspan's leadership style emphasizes collegiality and consensus. Highly approachable, he actively encourages input from other Fed officials, and his openness, symbolized by such gestures as the Fourth of July party that he threw in 1988 for all Fed staff members, has improved morale at the central bank. Greenspan has also established a good working relationship with the other Federal Reserve governors, whom he has allowed to speak out on Fed policy to a much greater degree than did Volcker.

On February 24, 1989 the Fed, "in the light of inflationary pressures in the economy," raised the discount rate to 7 percent, but beginning in June 1989, it shifted its focus away from fighting inflation and toward avoiding a recession. The Fed lowered interest rates once in June and twice in July, reversing a policy it had subscribed to since March 1988 of raising interest rates to combat inflation. In his semiannual report to Congress, delivered on July 20, 1989, Greenspan predicted a significant slowdown in economic growth, an apparent acknowledgment that the economy's seven-year expansion was drawing to a close. Viewing recession as a greater threat to the economy than inflation, Greenspan said that the Fed's monetary policy would play a key role in preventing a major economic downturn.

Brown-eyed and black-haired, Alan Greenspan stands six feet tall and weighs 180 pounds. The chairman dresses in custom-made shirts and conservatively cut suits and wears horn-rimmed glasses. To relax, he plays tennis and golf and avidly watches the games of the New York Mets baseball team. He enjoys listening to baroque music, especially that of Handel and Vivaldi, and he still plays the clarinet on occasion. His favorite authors include Tom Clancy and Eric Ambler. In addition to his technical wizardry, Greenspan, unlike many economists, is able to discuss larger political and social issues with confident ease. Although he is reputed to have a dry wit, he rarely makes public use of it. Frequently described as soft-spoken and shy, he nonetheless mingles comfortably in the high-powered social circles of Manhattan's Upper East Side and Washington's Georgetown. Greenspan was married to the artist Joan Mitchell, who introduced him to Ayn Rand, but their one-year union was annulled in 1953. A bachelor since then, Greenspan has kept company with a number of prominent women, including the broadcast journalist Barbara Walters. He is often accompanied at social gatherings by Andrea Mitchell, a reporter for NBC News.

References: Bsns W p29 Je 15 '87 por; Fortune 116:34+ Jl 6 '87 por; N Y Times D p1+ Je 3 '87 por; Time 129:50+ Je 15 '87 pors; Toronto Globe and Mail D p1+ Ag 1 '87 por; USA Today B p1+ Ag 11 '88 por; Who's Who in America, 1988–89

Griffith Joyner, Florence

Dec. 21, 1959– Former sprinter. Address: c/o Gordon Baskin and Associates, 11444 W. Olympic Blvd., 10th Floor, Los Angeles, Calif. 90064

Before the United States Olympic Trials in July 1988, Florence Griffith Joyner was better known for her fashion flair than for her feats in track. That all changed in the space of forty-eight hours when she shattered the previous world record of 10.76 seconds in the 100-meter dash four times (although the first time was discounted because of the wind) with, respectively, a 10.60, 10.49, 10.71, and 10.61. At the same time that she earned the unofficial title of the world's fastest woman, "FloJo," as she has come to be called, brought unprecedented glamour to women's track with her striking makeup, shoulder-length wavy hair, and the one-legged leotards, bikini briefs, and see-through bodysuits that she chose to compete in. "Looking good is almost as important as running well," she once said. "It's part of feeling good about myself."

At the 1988 Summer Olympics in Seoul, South Korea, in September, Griffith Joyner confirmed her star status by winning three gold medals in the 100- and 200- meter races and the 400-meter relay and a silver medal in the 1600-meter relay. She broke the 200-meter world record of 21.71 twice, with a 21.56 in the semis and a 21.34 in the finals. Inundated by offers for product endorsements, publishing ventures, and movie and television projects that were to earn her an estimated $4 million in 1989, Florence Griffith Joyner announced in February 1989 that she was retiring from track to concentrate on an acting and writing career.

Delorez Florence Griffith was born on December 21, 1959, the seventh of the eleven children of Robert and Florence Griffith. Her father, an electronics technician, and her mother, a seamstress, divorced when Florence was four. At that time Mrs. Griffith and her children moved from the Mohave Desert in southern California to the Jordan Downs housing project in the Watts section of Los Angeles, where some of the worst inner-city riots occurred in the aftermath of the assassination of the Reverend Martin Luther King Jr. in 1968. Nevertheless, Florence Griffith Joyner had "a very happy childhood," as she recalled to Pete Axthelm in an interview for Newsweek (August 1, 1988). "There were never days when we didn't have food. There were days when we had oatmeal for breakfast, lunch and dinner. But my mother always figured it out." To avoid confusion with her mother, young Florence was nicknamed "Dee Dee," a name that her friends and family continue to call her.

At the age of seven, Dee Dee began running track, partly because the sport enabled her to excel at something in which only one other sibling participated. When she visited her father in the Mohave

Desert, chasing jack rabbits helped improve her speed. In elementary and junior high school, Dee Dee competed in the 50- and 70-meter dashes with the Sugar Ray Robinson Youth Foundation, a program for underprivileged youngsters. "I would always win," she told Phil Hersh of the *Chicago Tribune* (July 22, 1988). When she was fourteen, Dee Dee won the annual Jesse Owens National Youth Games and was awarded an all-expenses-paid trip to a meet in San Francisco. The following year she won again. After that victory Jesse Owens congratulated her personally but told her that she could not attend the sectional competition in Texas because she had won the year before. "I had never been out of California, and I wanted to go," she recalled to Phil Hersh. "I started crying and said, 'I don't like that man, I don't like that man.' I found out later who Jesse Owens was."

At an early age, Dee Dee exhibited a desire to forge her own style. "I always wanted a gun set for Christmas, which no other girls wanted, or something in a color no one had," she explained to Phil Hersh. "It wasn't for attention—just something about me." As her mother told Pete Axthelm, "All the children were special, but Dee Dee was something else." In high school she kept a pet boa constrictor named Brandy. "When she shed, I saved *all* of her skin and painted it different colors," she recalled to Kenny Moore, who interviewed her for a *Sports Illustrated* (September 14, 1988) profile. She also pursued more conventionally feminine interests, such as crocheting and knitting, which she learned from her mother, and styling hair and fingernails, which she picked up from her grandmother, who was a beautician.

The Griffiths adhered to a strict family routine that included no television during the week and lights out at 10:00 P.M. Often quiet and self-contained, Dee Dee chronicled her thoughts in a diary and wrote poetry. Every Wednesday night the family held "powwows" during which they used the Bible to discuss what they had done wrong during the week. Because of Dee Dee's independent nature, Mrs. Griffith had to warn the others to lock the door on those nights so that she would not be able to escape. In spite of her rebelliousness, Griffith Joyner valued her disciplined upbringing. "Everybody in the family survived," she told Pete Axthelm. "Nobody does drugs, nobody got shot at. I used to say it was because we were afraid of Mama's voice. We didn't know how poor we were. We were rich as a family."

In 1978 Florence Griffith Joyner graduated from Jordan High School in Los Angeles, where she had set school records in sprinting and the long jump. In 1979 she enrolled at California State University at Northridge, where she intended to major in business, but a lack of funds forced her to drop out after her freshman year and take a job as a bank teller. Bob Kersee, the assistant track coach at California State, sought her out and helped her apply for financial aid. Kersee determined that Griffith Joyner should specialize in the 200-meter race because she was not fast enough coming out of the starting blocks. Kersee was a technical perfectionist, whereas Griffith Joyner relied on natural ability and practice to win. As she explained to John Jeansonne for *New York Newsday* (July 24, 1988): "Bobby's a very technical coach, and sometimes it went in one ear and out the other. I used to get so frustrated with my block starts that I'd actually cry."

In 1980 Kersee accepted an assistant coaching position at UCLA, and Florence Griffith Joyner, apparently with some reluctance, decided to follow him there. "I had a 3.25 in business [at Cal-State Northridge], but UCLA didn't even offer my major," she told Kenny Moore. "I had to switch to psychology. But my running was starting up, and I knew that Bobby was the best coach for me. So—it kind of hurts to say this—I chose athletics over academics." The move proved beneficial to her track career, as she competed against the top American runners. In the trials determining which athletes would represent the United States in the 1980 Summer Olympics (which the United States ultimately boycotted because of the Soviet invasion of Afghanistan), Griffith Joyner narrowly missed becoming a part of the Olympic team, coming in fourth behind, among others, Valerie Brisco, her old rival from her high school days. But in 1982 Griffith Joyner became NCAA champion in the 200 meters, with a time of 22.39 seconds. Even in college, her distinctive fashion flair was evident in her long fingernails painted in rainbow colors. As she recalled to Kenny Moore, one teammate was prompted to remark: "'We all *know* you're different. Why do you have to *show* it?' That went in one ear and out the other."

After winning the 400 meters in the NCAA championships in 1983 and placing second in the NCAA 200 that year, Griffith Joyner continued to train with Kersee and his World Class Track Club, although she no longer was a student at UCLA. In the 1984 Olympics in Los Angeles, sporting six-and-a-half-inch nails painted red, white, and blue, she won the silver medal in the 200 with a time of 22.04 seconds—almost a quarter of a second behind Valerie Brisco's 21.81. It has been suggested that Griffith Joyner was emotionally affected by her loss to her longtime rival and disappointed that she would not receive the same kind of media exposure. As a result, she became a customer service representative for the Union Bank company in Los Angeles and worked at night braiding women's hair. Those sedentary jobs caused her to gain weight, and by 1986 she was in semiretirement. She also ended her engagement to Greg Foster, a star hurdler. In 1986 her 200-meter time was one second slower than it had been in 1985. Kersee claimed that she was sixty pounds overweight in 1986, informing Phil Hersh that she "was so wide" he could not tell whether she was "coming or going." Griffith Joyner countered that she had gained about fifteen pounds.

In any case, in 1987 Griffith Joyner asked Kersee to help her train for the 1988 Olympic trials. Kersee was willing to help, but he told her that she would have to adhere to a rigorous regimen calling for her to work out harder. The training included postmidnight workouts to accommodate her schedule as a beautician and, on race days, a diet of amino acids, vitamins, and water. "I had to take inventory," she explained to Phil Hersh of the *Chicago Tribune* (July 18, 1988). "It was time to run better or move on." She received moral support in her efforts from her new boyfriend, Al Joyner, the triple jumper who won the 1984 Olympic gold medal and the brother of her World Class Track Club teammate Jackie Joyner-Kersee. Al Joyner and Florence Griffith were married in October 1987 in Las Vegas.

With the help of Kersee and Joyner, Florence Griffith Joyner worked herself down to 130 pounds and improved her speed, winning the silver medal in the 200 meters at the World Championship Games in Rome in the summer of 1987. She also ran the third leg of the 400-meter relay, helping the United States team to win a gold medal. The only record she broke in Rome was in the fashion department. As Phil Hersh reported in the *Chicago Tribune* (July 22, 1988), "Griffith Joyner defied heat, humidity and convention by running in a hooded, silver bodysuit that must have been designed for the Olympic speed-skating team from Pluto."

It was her anger over placing second in the 200 meters in Rome that motivated Griffith Joyner to improve her speed. "When you've been secondbest for so long, you can either accept it, or try to become the best," she told Craig A. Masback during an interview for *Ms.* (October 1988). "I made the decision to try and be the best in 1988." Ben Johnson's world-record-breaking 9.83-second race against Carl Lewis in the men's 100 in Rome provided Griffith Joyner with the technical knowhow to surpass her competitors. Kersee gave her a videotape of that race and stressed that it was Johnson's hair-trigger start from the blocks that gave him his edge over other runners. Johnson also told Griffith Joyner about his extensive weightlifting program. "If you want to run like a man, you have to train like a man, and weights are the main factor," she explained to Kenny Moore for *Sports Illustrated* (October 10, 1988).

When Griffith Joyner returned from Rome in September 1987, Kersee put her on a regimen of daily track workouts and weight-training sessions four times a week that included leg curls on a hamstring-leg extension machine to strengthen her gluteal and hamstring muscles and partial squats with 320-pound weights on her shoulders. She also ran 3.7 miles a day. Her job as a customer service representative at Union Bank allowed her to work out during lunch hour, and, after earning extra money styling clients' hair and fingernails, she often returned to the track at UCLA to practice, sometimes until after midnight, and she watched Johnson's videotape every day. "There were times when I wouldn't sleep for forty-eight hours because of everything I was trying to do," she recalled to Craig A. Masback, but by the end of the year, she had attained the number-one ranking in the 200 meters.

To give her more time to train, she left her bank job to work part-time in employee relations for Anheuser-Busch.

Looking ahead to the United States Olympic Trials in July 1988, Kersee and Griffith Joyner envisaged her excelling in the 200, and her training was geared to the longer races. "I knew that I'd be running the 200," she told Dave Nightingale of the *Sporting News* (July 25, 1988). "I thought I might do better in the 400. And I was even giving some consideration to running the 800." She added the 100 to her list after the Michelob Invitational in San Diego on June 25, 1988, when she ran a 10.89 in the 100-meter race. That time—her personal best up to that point—prompted her to tell Kersee, "I'm ready to break the record." Two weeks before the Olympic trials, Kersee and Griffith Joyner added speed work and practice starts to her regular workouts.

The United States Olympic track and field trials opened on July 16, 1988 at the Indiana University–Purdue University track stadium in Indianapolis. In the first 100-meter preliminary heat, Florence Griffith Joyner, wearing a lime green one-legged racing suit, clocked a 10.60, breaking the four-year-old world record of 10.76 held by Evelyn Ashford. Meet officials ruled, however, that the tailwind of 3.2 meters per second invalidated the time, since the maximum allowable wind was two meters per second. In the second round of 100-meter trials, Griffith Joyner, clad in a purple one-legged racing suit and white bikini bottom with purple squiggles, proved that her first time had been no fluke, clocking an astounding 10.49 seconds that shattered the world record by more than a quarter of a second. (In the seventy-five years that the International Amateur Athletic Federation has codified world records, the most time sliced off a previous record in the women's 100 was a tenth of a second.) The question of wind again became an issue because, on a day when the stadium flags flapped crisply, the wind gauge for the 100 registered 0.0, whereas the gauge for the triple jump read 4.3. Timing experts explained that the angle of the wind could make such a reading possible and legal. Kersee's reaction to Griffith Joyner's performance was one of astonishment. "No one could envision a 10.49 for a woman in the 100," he told Phil Hersh of the *Chicago Tribune* (July 17, 1988). "I'm still shocked about it, because I hadn't told her to run fast yet." And Griffith Joyner herself reacted with disbelief. "I couldn't believe it was 10.49," she related to Bryan Burwell of the *New York Daily News* (July 17, 1988). "I felt I could do 10.59, but 10.49? No way." Kersee predicted to Phil Hersh that Griffith Joyner would "come back tomorrow and win the 100 and then win the 200 and break the world record there."

On Sunday, July 17, Griffith Joyner, in a black bodysuit with yellow stripes on the side, ran against three-time Olympian Evelyn Ashford, among others, in the semifinal heat. Kersee had instructed his protégée to run under Ashford's 10.76. "I wanted her to run 10.71 or 10.72 in the semis and 10.50-something in the final," he explained, as quoted in the *Chicago Tribune* (July 18, 1988). Griffith Joyner won the semis in 10.70, beating Ashford by five feet. In the finals two hours later, wearing a one-legged blue leotard and a white bikini, she made even better time, clocking a 10.61 to defeat Evelyn Ashford by ten feet. In four races over two days, Griffith Joyner ran the four fastest 100 meters in women's track history, with three of the times unaided by the wind. Later in the week, she set an American record in the quarterfinals of the 200 meters, with a time of 21.77. (The world record of 21.71 was held jointly by Heike Drechsler and Marita Koch, both of East Germany.) She subsequently took the 200-meter semifinals in 21.90 and, wearing a white fishnet bodysuit, captured first place in the final, with a time of 21.82 seconds.

Although Kersee insisted that strength and endurance accounted for her phenomenal performance in the Olympic trials, Florence Griffith Joyner herself attributed her success to the discovery that a runner could attain greater speed by trying less hard. "For a long time I thought that being relaxed meant you were running slow, but it's the contrary," she told a reporter for *People* (August 29, 1988). "When you're trying to go fast, you're fighting against your body instead of letting go." She has also maintained that she was a late bloomer. "When it comes to track, I'm a slow learner," she told Pete Axthelm for *Newsweek*. "Some people can advance in four years. It's taken me twenty." And to John Jeansonne of *New York Newsday*, she explained, "It takes experience—time—to get strength, technique, to learn to concentrate on what you have to do, to be able to go to that line, confident that nobody else in that race can run with you."

Florence Griffith Joyner made as much of a sensation with her eye-catching outfits during the trials as she did with her running times. As Christine Brennan commented in her article for the *Washington Post* (July 22, 1988): "She is a Maybelline advertisement waiting to happen. And she knows it." On Saturday, her one-inch nails were painted orange with stripes on the tips, and on Sunday, they were fuchsia. Griffith Joyner explained to Elizabeth Sporkin of *USA Today* (September 7, 1988) that she put together bikini briefs and one-legged leotards because most of the uniforms she had to wear were uncomfortable. "I like high-cut legs and low-cut tops that give me more movement," she said. The only precedent for Griffith Joyner's individuality was Evelyn Ashford's wearing a full-length bodysuit during the 1984 Olympics.

Only a few weeks after the Olympic trials, Griffith Joyner fired Kersee and replaced him with her husband, explaining that she needed full-time attention, which Kersee was unable to offer because he coached six other athletes. She also claimed that he charged 18.5 percent of her earnings and that she owed her 10.49 time more to Al Joyner. "When Bobby was overwhelmed with his responsibilities to other athletes, Al was there to film me, advise me on my form, and encourage me to keep going," she

told Craig A. Masback. She also intimated to Pete Axthelm of *Newsweek* (September 19, 1988) that she had gone into semiretirement in 1986 because Kersee was charging her too much and that Kersee had tried to keep his wife, Jackie Joyner-Kersee, and Al Joyner apart. Furthermore, she called Kersee's track club a cult and alleged that one of its members, Valerie Brisco, was childishly dependent on Kersee and his wife. Kersee denied the charges.

Meanwhile, Florence Griffith Joyner had become a media sensation, appearing on the covers of *Newsweek*, *Sports Illustrated*, *Life*, *Ebony*, *Jet*, *Ms.*, the German magazines *Stern* and *Sports International*, three Japanese magazines, and *Paris Match*, which termed her "la tigresse noire," or the black tigress. In August Griffith Joyner ran in two races in Europe: the 100 in Malmö, Sweden and the 100 in Gateshead, England. Such was her acclaim following the trials that she was able to command $25,000 in appearance money per race, compared to a previous figure of about $1,500. To handle her burgeoning financial arrangements, she hired Gordon Baskin, who also handles Edwin Moses, as her business manager. "We probably had 200 calls in three days from all over the world," Baskin told Frank Litsky of the *New York Times* (August 4, 1988), from film producers, television, modeling agencies, fashion magazines, and other periodicals, including *Good Housekeeping*, *Ms.*, and *People*. Her performance in the Olympic trials moved her into the highest earnings bracket for track and field athletes, joining such stars as Ben Johnson, who earned $20,000 to $35,000 a meet, Edwin Moses ($30,000), and Carl Lewis ($25,000).

In September 1988, at the Summer Olympics in Seoul, South Korea, Griffith Joyner continued to rewrite the record books. In the 100 meters, she set an Olympic record in the trials, with a 10.62, and another Olympic record in the finals, where her 10.54—the second-fastest time ever—earned her the gold medal. Competing in the 200 meters four days later, she broke the world record twice—in the semifinals, with a 21.56, and in the finals, with a gold-medal-winning time of 21.34 seconds. (The previous world record of 21.71 had been set by Marita Koch of East Germany nine years earlier.) In those two events, Griffith Joyner added a radiant smile to her already dazzling reputation. As Pete Axthelm reported in *Newsweek* (October 10, 1988) about the 200-meter finals, Griffith Joyner, wearing one red and one blue sneaker and a white belt, could have gone faster, but she "slowed down slightly while well ahead to flash that million-dollar smile at the cameras." She exhibited the same reaction in the finals of the 100, recalling for Dick Patrick of *USA Today* (September 28, 1988): "It hit me right there at fifty. I thought, 'I have the race. I've finally got the gold.' I was so excited I couldn't do anything but smile."

In the 400-meter relay on October 1, Griffith Joyner won her third gold medal, running the third leg of the race. Two days before the 1600-meter relay, the United States coaches Terry Crawford and

Fred Thompson decided to include Griffith Joyner as the anchor runner in the event. Although the United States came in second, behind the Soviet Union, in that event, which took place just forty minutes after the 400-meter relay, Griffith Joyner ran a respectable 48.1, just behind Olga Bryzgina, who anchored the Soviet team. Griffith Joyner later told Kenny Moore in the interview for *Sports Illustrated* (October 10, 1988) that she valued the silver medal she received for that relay more than her golds: "I felt that the silver was the special one, because of the team's trust in giving me the chance. That silver is gold to me." With her four medals—three gold and a silver—Florence Griffith Joyner surpassed Wilma Rudolph's record of three gold medals, set in 1960, and narrowly missed tying the record of Fanny Blankers-Koen of Holland, who won four gold medals in women's track and field in the 1948 Olympics.

The one ominous note in Griffith Joyner's otherwise stellar performance was the rumor of possible steroid use, which gained momentum after the news broke, on September 27, that several athletes, including the 100-meter champion Ben Johnson, had been expelled from the Olympic Games for testing positive for anabolic steroids. Joaquim Cruz, the Brazilian 800-meter silver medalist, told television reporters from Brazil, as reported by Tom Weir in *USA Today* (September 30, 1988): "In 1984, you could see an extremely feminine person, but today [Griffith Joyner] looks more like a man than a woman." He further speculated, as reported by Brian Burwell in the New York *Daily News* (September 30, 1988), that she and Jackie Joyner-Kersee "must be doing something that isn't normal to get all those muscles." Cruz later claimed that he had been misquoted. Griffith Joyner, for her part, denied that she had ever taken drugs. "I was very hurt that someone would say something like that about me and about Jackie," she told Dave Rosner for *New York Newsday* (September 30, 1988). "It hurt me, but it didn't bother me. I know that I'm a champion. I am antidrugs. . . . Chasing all those records and giving the young kids coming up something to chase, that's what the sport is all about."

Immediately following the Olympics, Griffith Joyner expressed an interest in running the 400 in the 1992 Olympics in Barcelona, Spain, but she has since concentrated on commercial enterprises unrelated to sports. Among other things, she has appeared on the Arsenio Hall, David Letterman, and Larry King television talk shows, in an episode of the NBC sitcom *227*, and in *The Bob Hope Christmas Show with the All-American Champs*, and she has talked to the producer Norman Lear about hosting a children's television program. Following up on her lifelong interest in writing, she made plans to publish the ten children's books she has written about a boy named Barry Bam-Bam, as well as a romantic novel and the story of her life as an athlete since the 1984 Olympics.

Florence Griffith Joyner has received so many business offers that advertising executives have given her the nickname "Cash Flo." Her business deals include product endorsements for two major American soft drink companies and Japanese sports apparel and cosmetics firms, and she has done commercials for several Japanese products, including Mizuno running shoes. She has also made arrangements to promote Agfa film, Sally Hansen nail products, Proxy athletic footwear, and Toshiba America copiers. Griffith Joyner is also under contract with IBM to give a dozen motivational speeches to employees. In the spring of 1989 LJN Toys introduced a FloJo doll, for which she has designed about a dozen outfits to be sold separately.

On February 25, 1989, in a short tearful statement, Florence Griffith Joyner announced that she was retiring from track to devote more time to her writing and acting, although she will continue to serve as her husband's coach. The day before, she told Phil Hersh of the *Chicago Tribune* (February 25, 1989): "It's a matter of priorities. With all I want to do—designing, writing, acting, modeling—I realized there would be no time to train." Her retirement led to remarks from several athletes, including Ben Johnson's coach, Charlie Francis, and Darrell Robinson, an American sprinter, that Griffith Joyner wanted to avoid the mandatory spot drug testing that will be required of all athletes for the first time, starting in 1989. She has repeatedly and vehemently denied the allegations.

Florence Griffith Joyner is tall and soft-spoken. She reads the Bible every day, says a prayer before every meal, and calls her mother at least twice a day. She maintains her positive outlook by reading Norman Vincent Peale's best-selling inspirational book *You Can If You Think You Can*, and she often listens to a tape filled with positive messages before falling asleep. She and her husband live in a townhouse in Newport Beach, California, with a view of the city's lagoon. In 1988 Griffith Joyner was named French sportswoman of the year and athlete of the year by Tass, the Soviet press agency. In 1989 she received the United States Olympic Committee Award, the Golden Camera Award in Berlin, and the Harvard Foundation Award for outstanding contributions to society. She also won the 1988 Jesse Owens Award as the year's outstanding track and field athlete and the 1988 Sullivan Award as the top American amateur athlete.

References: Chicago Tribune V p1+ Jl 22 '88 pors; *Ms* 17:34+ O '88 pors; *N Y Daily News* p6+ S 11 '88; *N Y Newsday Sports* p16+ Jl 24 '88 pors, II p3 S 7 '88, p149 S 30 '88 por; *N Y Times* B p9 Ag 4 '88 por, A p15 S 30 '88 pors; *Newsweek* 112:55+ S 19 '88 pors, 112:58+ O 10 '88; *People* 30:60+ Ag 29 '88 pors; *Sporting N* p51 Jl 25 '88 por; *Sports Illus* 69:158+ S 14 '88 pors, 69:45+ O 10 '88 pors, 70:50+ Ap 10 '89 pors; *Washington Post* F p1 Jl 22 '88 pors, D p1+ S 30 '88 pors; *USA Today* D p1+ S 7 '88 por

Guisewite, Cathy (Lee)

(gĭs-wīt)

Sept. 5, 1950– Cartoonist. Address: c/o Universal Press Syndicate, 4900 Main St., Kansas City, Mo. 64112

One of only a handful of successful female cartoonists, Cathy Guisewite is the creator of the immensely popular *Cathy* comic strip, which first appeared in November 1976 and is now syndicated in some 500 newspapers. Although *Cathy* was originally created as a vehicle to depict Miss Guisewite's own personal experiences as she grappled with being a single career woman, when the cartoonist sent some samples to Universal Press Syndicate, executives there immediately recognized its universal appeal. Cathy struggles with personal relationships, career, mother, and a weight problem in what appears to be a state of "perpetual befuddlement." But her vulnerability and neuroses, which Miss Guisewite has a knack for humorously exposing, hit home to millions of readers. "I've heard from a lot of women that *Cathy* is a better role model because she bumbles and still tries to go on," she has said. "She's happy because she's a very optimistic character, [believing] that even when she's in the pits, things will get better."

Cathy Lee Guisewite was born on September 5, 1950 in Dayton, Ohio, the middle daughter of William Lee and Anne (Duly) Guisewite. Cathy and her sisters grew up in the small town of Midland, Michigan. Their father owned an advertising agency and put himself through college working as a stand-up comic. Cathy's mother worked in advertising before her marriage and taught grade school later on, but she regarded raising her children as a rewarding and challenging career in itself. Miss

Guisewite recalled to Mary James in *Woman's Day* (July 13, 1982): "I resented my mom for not being the kind of mother who sat home baking all day. . . . She took us to art museums and foreign films, and I hated everything she dragged us to." Anne Guisewite saved Cathy's childhood drawings and sent her first story, which she wrote at the age of six, to a magazine (the rejection slip remains one of the cartoonist's favorite keepsakes). "Most mothers tape their children's work to the refrigerator door," Miss Guisewite has joked. "Mine would send them off to the Museum of Modern Art." Cathy and her sisters were encouraged to produce their own greeting cards, and they illustrated miniature books as gifts.

During her undergraduate years at the University of Michigan, where she majored in English, Cathy Guisewite exhibited her flair for humor when she created "A College Girl's Mother's Guide to Survival" as a gift for one Mother's Day. Anne Guisewite mailed her daughter's guide to Tom Wilson, then a vice-president at the American Greetings Corporation, but in spite of his enthusiasm, it was never published. Miss Guisewite also took courses in creative writing in college, but since it did not occur to her to have any formal art training, after receiving her B.A. degree in 1972, she followed family tradition and joined the Campbell-Ewald advertising agency in Detroit, Michigan as a copywriter. A year later, she moved on to Norman Prady, Ltd. After writing radio commercials and magazine and newspaper ads for such products as brakes and shock absorbers, she began writing in 1974 for the prestigious W. B. Doner & Company in its Southfield, Michigan headquarters. Specializing in retail accounts, she became, in 1976, the firm's first female vice-president, acting as "head of a group of writers and artists," she has explained. One former colleague from Doner told *Advertising Age* (October 17, 1985) that Miss Guisewite was "incredibly prolific." "She could sit down and turn out ten scripts in a day, and they'd all be good. She was also one of the most loved persons the agency ever had." Commenting on her experience there for the same *Advertising Age* article, Miss Guisewite described Doner as "a thrilling place to work, because creativity was encouraged even on the mediocre accounts. It's where I trained my brain to write with a sense of humor."

Although Cathy Guisewite was successful at work, her personal life was, in her words, "a total disaster." "As I became more involved with my work, my love life started to fall apart," she told Janice Harayda for *Glamour* (July 1978) magazine. "I would try to meet men and nothing would happen, or I'd meet men I just didn't want to go out with at all. As a result, I started spending a lot of evenings at home writing about my feelings in my diary—something my mother had encouraged me to do when I was younger." She began supplementing her writing with stick-figure drawings, which she sent to her parents instead of letters to assure them she was coping. One series of sketches, for example, which became one of her first comic strips, depicted herself as anxiously eating everything in sight while waiting for the telephone to ring. She packs away three bagels, two bowls of fudge ripple ice cream, thirty-seven Oreos, and a Twinkie. "So what?" Miss Guisewite had Cathy say. "He'll never call me again." When the phone rings, she adds: "At least not after he sees me tonight." "When I saw myself in a drawing," Miss Guisewite told Janice Harayda for the *Glamour* profile, "I began to see the humor in situations that wouldn't otherwise have seemed funny."

Sensing the possibilities for a comic strip, Cathy Guisewite's mother researched comic-strip syndicates in the public library and solicited the advice of Tom Wilson, who had become the creator of *Ziggy*. Universal Press Syndicate, which handles *Ziggy* and *Doonesbury*, two of Anne Guisewite's favorite comics, headed the list of syndicates she gave to her daughter to contact. Apprehensive that her mother would submit the rough strips unless she herself took action, Cathy Guisewite dispatched eighteen samples to Universal. Within an hour and a half of opening the package, according to Margaret Mironowicz of the Toronto *Globe and Mail* (December 15, 1977), the syndicate executives unanimously decided to offer Miss Guisewite a contract. "Given the sentiments of the day, we thought there would be room for a strip that deals with young women," Lee Salem, the managing editor of Universal Press Syndicate, told Margaret Mironowicz. In spite of the rudimentary drawings, Salem recognized the cartoon's potential. "We felt that Cathy the character was real. That's what struck us about her work. It deals with what it's like to be young, single, and working today. We were struck by the honesty of her [Miss Guisewite's] sentiments."

The first *Cathy* strip appeared on November 22, 1976 in about sixty newspapers, but Miss Guisewite did not muster up enough courage to quit the security and routine of Doner until some nine months later. At first she resisted Universal's suggestion that she name the character after herself and bought a book of baby names for inspiration. "Not only did the character resemble me a little physically, but what I was writing about was quite personal," she explained to Cork Millner for a *Seventeen* (May 1983) interview. "I didn't want friends calling me up the next day, saying, 'Idiot. Why did you say that about yourself?'" But Miss Guisewite discovered that no other name worked. "She *had* to be 'Cathy,' to be, well, *me*," she told Cork Millner. "She's so close to how I think. Using the same name can be a little embarrassing at times, but it helps me to keep her true to life."

Guided by instruction books on how to draw cartoons and helped by the syndicate with "the little things—like connecting the heads to the bodies," Cathy Guisewite taught herself to draw acceptable cartoon figures. "I felt that I already had a natural knack for showing emotion and character in my drawings," she recalled for the *Seventeen* profile. "If a comic figure felt sheepish or wishy-

washy, the lines I drew would be wiggly; if the person was mad, the lines would be straight and hard. If a character was happy, the lines became soft and pleasant. If you try to 'feel' what you're drawing, it will work its way out to your hand." Although her art has mostly evolved through trial and error, Miss Guisewite admitted in an interview for *Contemporary Authors*: "I do look at other cartoonists' work and always have." For example, she studied *Beetle Bailey* strips to learn how to draw scenes involving flurries of activity and commotion. For her characters' facial expressions, she has said she was most inspired by Charles Schulz, the creator of the *Peanuts* comic strip, because "he's wonderful at capturing great expressions with very few lines." As Miss Guisewite's artistry has developed over the years, Cathy has changed in appearance. She was originally somewhat weakly defined, with shaky lines and sparse strands of hair, and she always wore pants and a long-sleeved shirt with a heart in the middle. Today, she still has no nose and no profile, but she is better defined, and she wears an assortment of outfits.

Cathy's appeal extends to "everyone whose life revolves around food, love, mother, career . . . the four basic guilt groups," Miss Guisewite once said. Different facets of her personality are brought out in her interactions with different characters in the comic strip. In her first collection of cartoon strips, *The Cathy Chronicles*, published by Sheed, Andrews & McMeel in 1978, Miss Guisewite prefaced the collection by introducing Cathy as four different personas. According to Andrea, who is, in Miss Guisewite's words, "an uncompromising feminist and Cathy's best friend," Cathy is "Woman"; according to Irving, "an uncompromising chauvinist pig and Cathy's boyfriend," Cathy is "My Lady"; Emerson, "an unsuccessful suitor," refers to Cathy as "My Girl"; and Cathy's Mom calls her "My Baby."

The Cathy Chronicles was republished as two paperback volumes by Bantam Books in 1981, entitled *What's a Nice Single Girl Doing with a Double Bed?!* and *I Think I'm Having a Relationship with a Blueberry Pie!* Cathy is a junior executive, the first woman at the company to be in charge of product testing, but she is sexually harassed by her boss, Mr. Pinkley, in one series of strips. Andrea drags her to her Women-of-Today Club, to assertiveness-training classes, and to a transcendental meditation session, where Cathy wants to select her own mantra—"Irving . . . Irving . . . Irving." In their "no strings, no ties, you do what you want, I do what I want" brand of "together relationship of the 1970s," Irving also wants her to do his laundry, wash his car, pick up his six-pack of beer, and watch football on her television set. When Andrea demands: "What do you and Irving have in common?" Cathy at first responds bleakly, "Nothing," then later adds adoringly, "He's everything to me," naming just one of "millions of things"—"Both of us like him." At another point, Cathy insightfully admits: "Sometimes you just have to break down and admit you need someone else! It's boring to be invincible all by yourself."

The strip has appealed most strongly to women in the eighteen to thirty-four age range. "I think the comic is based on my life" typifies the comments from female readers. Such "Cathy" statements as "Deep down, I think I really *like* to be pushed around," however, have been criticized by feminists who do not want to see another vulnerable woman ("a character built on human weakness," in Miss Guisewite's words) popularized. Editor Lee Salem had anticipated that the strip would offend both ardent feminists and "die-hard traditionalists." "Cathy is in the middle," he has explained. "And we think there are more women like Cathy than there are the others. . . . She's not wishy-washy. . . . She has strong feelings but doesn't always act on those." In the *Globe and Mail* interview, Miss Guisewite acknowledged that her strip was "a lot more irritating in the beginning . . . mainly because I had Cathy in a position where she lost a lot more than she won." Cathy began to develop, however, as her creator changed, becoming more assertive in her attitudes and relationships. Miss Guisewite, who has called herself a feminist, told Cork Millner for the *Seventeen* profile: "I don't write about the big picture and the emerging new woman. What Cathy is doing is floundering in the middle of two ideals or concepts: traditionalism and feminism."

Cathy incarnates everywoman as she shops for the sine qua nons of the 1980s: the microwave, home computer, and VCR; leaves her car for repairs with misgivings; succumbs powerlessly to the pitch of a real-estate broker; agonizes over selecting an IRA and the intricacies of the 1986 Tax Reform Act; sizes up ill-fated relationships in a nutshell: "We both want the other person to change"; and makes such incisive observations as: "Suddenly, the only way to become an individual is to join a group" and, when trying to understand Emerson's devotion, "How come the right words always come out of the wrong mouth?" Another time, she laments: "The only time I ever feel truly desirable is when the closest human being is ten miles away." Cathy often relives Miss Guisewite's personal experiences, such as the trauma of her high school class reunion, "but it took three years to have a sense of humor about it," Miss Guisewite told David Astor for an *Editor & Publisher* (June 25, 1983) article. "If I meet someone, she might meet someone. If I'm traveling a lot, I tend to send Cathy on a business trip." She also has confessed that she has left a boyfriend in the middle of an argument to jot down the details, although she insists, "I would never illustrate last week's date in the comic strip." As for her parents, she has admitted that she quotes them "about anything."

Central to the strip is the mostly supportive, although sometimes antagonistic, mother-daughter relationship, based, at least in part, on Cathy Guisewite's own relationship with her mother, which she has described as "a real combination of love and devotion and just total anxiety." In one classic mother-daughter exchange in the strip, the two compare clippings on marriage versus being single. Mom wins when she reads: "Single women have more cellulite." Cathy asks, "Where'd you get that?" Mom replies, "I made it up." The real Cathy encouraged her mother to write down some of her advice so that, she explained to Claudia Lapin for a *Savvy* (January 1988) profile, she can "seek her advice and reject it without having to be in the same room." (In the strip, Mom once fretted, "Sometimes I feel like a set of encyclopedias that no one ever opens.") Published by Andrews, McMeel & Parker in 1987, *Motherly Advice from Cathy's Mom, With Illustrations by My Beautiful and Talented Daughter* is a conversational compendium of tips on housekeeping chores as well as on health, appearance, economizing, and travel.

Trends that are treated in *Cathy* include the hit television show *thirtysomething* and medical "miracles," such as hair restorer for men and Retin-A, the wrinkle-remover for women. When asked by the *Contemporary Authors* interviewer what subjects are acceptable and what topics are off-limits, Miss Guisewite replied: "I'm not inclined to do anything that risqué, partly because I want my own mother always to be able to read the strip. Just like my life, I like to keep certain things sort of vague in the strip, about the specifics, for instance, of her relationships with the people she goes out with. I think people can interpret what's going on however they'd like."

In the 1987 collection of *Cathy* entitled *A Hand to Hold, an Opinion to Reject*, Cathy invites Irving to live with her. "I've never lived with anybody," Miss Guisewite remarked in a *Los Angeles Times* (May 7, 1987) interview, "but I'm interested in trying it out in the strip." (Irving, panic-stricken, runs off and eventually resurfaces with a moussed hairstyle and jungle safari-guide outfit.) Although Miss Guisewite is willing to explore live-in arrangements in her comic strip, her character will probably never marry. "I know how abandoned I feel when one of my friends gets married," she explained to Lynn Emmerman of the *Chicago Tribune* (May 10, 1987). "I won't let Cathy do that to her readers." Irving is "an accumulation of experiences with many men," Miss Guisewite told Janice Harayda in the interview for *Glamour*. "[Cathy's] relationship with Irving represents a real pull between a woman's intellectual and emotional self." She also commented in the same *Glamour* profile: "Cathy probably has my basic personality, but Andrea is a kind of alter ego . . . , the little voice that's always telling me to do things differently."

The topic of politics proved off-limits for *Cathy* when Miss Guisewite added a political tone to her strip during the final two weeks of the 1988 presidential election campaign. In one strip, Andrea urges women to vote, and, in another, she recommends Democratic candidate Michael Dukakis because of his support for a national day care plan, equal pay for women, and job-protected maternity leave. The editors of some twenty papers pulled the most pointed strips—"a partisan diatribe," according to one editor—or moved them to the Op-Ed pages. According to Miss Guisewite, her intent was "just to get people talking about women's issues in relationship to the candidates."

Cathy's first television special, a project that took four years to materialize, was aired on CBS in May 1987, with Miss Guisewite's father supplying the voice for the character Dad. According to Miss Guisewite's succinct plot description, "Cathy is up for Employee of the Year Award, Irving's out of town, and she's basically groveling for a date." The show won an Emmy Award for best prime-time animated program. A second television special, *Cathy's Last Resort*, was aired in November 1988.

Each year, the daily *Cathy* strips are gathered into a collection published by Andrews & McMeel, a Universal Press Syndicate company. Those compilations include: *What Do You Mean, I Still Don't Have Equal Rights?* (1980); *Another Saturday Night of Wild and Reckless Abandon* (1982); *A Mouthful of Breath Mints and No One to Kiss* (1983); *Men Should Come with Instruction Booklets* (1984); *Wake Me Up When I'm a Size 5* (1985); *Thin Thighs in Thirty Years* (1986); *Why Do the Right Words Always Come Out of the Wrong Mouth?* (1988); and *My Granddaughter Has Fleas* (1989). A collection of Sunday strips, *Climb Every Mountain, Bounce Every Check*, was published in 1983. Editions of selected cartoons by Ballantine Books are: *Sorry I'm Late. My Hair Won't Start*, *The Salesclerk Made Me Buy It*, *Stressed for Success*, and *My Cologne Backfired* (all published in 1986); *I'll Pay $5,000 for a Swimsuit That Fits Me!*, *Two Pies, One Fork*, and *It Must Be Something in the Ink* (all published in 1987); and *It's More Than a Pregnancy, It's a Religion* (1988).

"The strip is how I work out my anxieties," Miss Guisewite has remarked. "The most important thing is to write from the heart, not guess what could be sold." Leaving Detroit in late 1980, Miss Guisewite traveled up and down the West Coast for several months before settling in Santa Barbara, California, which reminded her of the peaceful town of her childhood. By 1984, however, feeling that she "needed anxiety in order to keep producing," she moved to Los Angeles, where "even a trip to the drugstore produces anxiety." Miss Guisewite now lives, according to Beth Ann Krier of the *Los Angeles Times* (May 7, 1987), in a "spacious, modern, and rather luxurious home-studio" in the semireclusive Hollywood Hills with Trolley, her ten-year-old collie-shepherd. When Miss Guisewite started out, creating the strip consumed all of her working hours, but today, she needs only about two hours for the daily strips and five for the Sunday comics. The writing of dialogue always comes first, and she has likened writing a four-frame strip to creating a ten-second commercial. "I write best when I'm depressed," she has said, "and I can only write the strip if nobody else is around." She likes to listen to music when working. For feedback and advice, Miss Guisewite relies on her younger sister, Mickey, who works as an advertising copywriter. "She has, I think, a great sense of comedy, and she's also

very blunt with me," she told Claudia Lapin. "She's almost always right. I've come to trust her opinion."

Miss Guisewite sends Universal Press Syndicate a four-week batch of strips at a time, and once a batch is finished, she calls the syndicate and reads the copy. When an idea for *Cathy* hits her, she immediately records it. "Any time I have any flickering of an idea, I write it down, so I have have piles of scraps of little pieces of paper around that are not jokes but beginnings of thoughts on things." Aided by a part-time secretary and a graphics designer, Miss Guisewite spends her afternoons designing and writing copy for a number of *Cathy* novelty products, which are marketed by Universal Licensing Corporation. Aimed at the adult woman, these items range from greeting cards and stationery to alarm clocks, cookie jars, and beach towels. She also contributes a monthly strip to *Glamour* magazine's "Viewpoint" page. Her income is reported to be in the six figures.

Cathy Guisewite is a self-confessed workaholic. "There's nothing else I like to do a lot, so this is what I do if I have time," she has said. "If I find I have a spare Saturday, I love to go to the office and work on things." That singular dedication has precluded any long-lasting romantic attachments. As she told *Glamour* (August 1982), her work "has made relationships very hard, because it isn't that the man reacts to my success so much as he reacts to the fact that I always put designing a trinket box or drawing a comic strip ahead of going out with him." On another occasion, she explained to Dan Sperling for *USA Today* (October 30, 1986) that she relished her single status: "I like being single. It's given me a huge amount of freedom to really go for it in my career. I think that I have avoided relationships that threaten that."

For relaxation, Cathy Guisewite enjoys shopping for bargains, playing tennis, skiing, and watching movies. Her favorite comic strips are *Doonesbury*, *Bloom County*, *Peanuts*, and *Calvin and Hobbes*. Her speaking engagements and promotions give her the opportunity to interview people and find out their reactions to *Cathy*. "Why aren't you fat?" is the question most often posed to her. Ironically, Miss Guisewite (who once said: "When I read about a woman who has it totally together, my reaction is to go home and eat a carton of Cool Whip") has to apologize for having reached her ideal weight of 105 pounds on her five-foot-two-inch frame. The size-five cartoonist has the same streaming, long brown hair parted in the center and brown eyes as her alter ego. Her voice has been described as low and scratchy, "with a hint of stifled laughter, and a midwestern twang around the edges." One interviewer noted that, when talking, she tends to illustrate points by giving examples from her comic strip.

In 1982 Miss Guisewite was the recipient of the Outstanding Communicator of the Year Award from the Los Angeles Advertising Women, and she was included in a San Mateo, California museum cartoon exhibit as one of the "ten influential twentieth-century cartoon artists," because she "depicts realistically yet humorously the trials of trying to survive as a 'Woman of the 1980s.'" In a *World Almanac and Book of Facts* poll by editors at daily newspapers across the United States, Miss Guisewite was selected as one of "America's Twenty-Five Most Influential Women" in 1984 and in 1986. In 1985 her colleagues in the National Cartoonists Society honored her with a nomination for a Reuben Award. Writing *Cathy,* Miss Guisewite has said, has taught her one of the great lessons of life: "Anything is possible if you listen to your mother."

References: *Chicago Tribune* V p3 My 10 '87 por; *Ed & Pub* 116:37+ Je 25 '83 por; *Human Behavior* 8:68+ Ja '79 por; *Interview* 14:72 Jl '84 por; *Los Angeles Times* (Advertising Supplement) p3+ My 3 '87; *Savvy* 9:50+ Ja '88 por; *Seventeen* 42:42+ My '83 por; *USA Today* D p4 O 30 '86 por; *Washington Post* D p1+ F 2 '79 por; *Woman's Day* p96 Jl 13 '82 por; *Contemporary Authors* vol 113 (1985); *Encyclopedia of Twentieth Century Journalists* (1986); *International Authors and Writers Who's Who* (1986); *Who's Who in America,* 1988–89

Hall, Arsenio

Feb. 12, 1955 (?)– Comedian; actor. Address: c/o The Arsenio Hall Show, Paramount Domestic Television, 5555 Melrose Ave., Los Angeles, Calif. 90038

Arsenio Hall is the stand-up comedian who first came to national prominence in 1987, during his thirteen-week stint as one of the interim hosts of the Fox network's now defunct late-night talk program, *The Late Show,* which was originally presided over by Joan Rivers. Hall parlayed that success into a two-year multimillion-dollar contract with Paramount Pictures, and, in June 1988, his first film, the comedy *Coming to America,* was released. Although panned by critics, *Coming to America,* in which Hall played second banana to Eddie Murphy, grossed nearly $128 million. Hall's good fortune continued with the announcement in August 1988 by Paramount Domestic Television

that he would host a new syndicated late-night talk show, beginning in January 1989.

Carried by approximately 170 stations nationwide, *The Arsenio Hall Show* collected unexpectedly high ratings in its first few months on the air. Like NBC's *Late Night with David Letterman,* the Hall show is geared toward baby boomers alienated by the contrived formality and schmaltz of Johnny Carson's *Tonight Show.* Hall believes that the talk shows that have unsuccessfully challenged Carson have failed because, in his words, "they tried to out-Johnny Johnny. I'm not going after Johnny's crowd. I'm going after Johnny's crowd's kids."

Arsenio Hall was born on February 12, in about 1955, in Cleveland, Ohio, the only child of Fred Hall, a Baptist preacher, and his wife, Annie. His overwhelming desire to escape from the ghetto in which he grew up was given its impetus by an incident that occurred when he was five. While he was in the bathroom, a rat ran across his foot, terrifying him. "I decided right then," Hall told Gerri Hirshey of *Vanity Fair* (July 1988), "that my big goal was to live in a house with no rats and roaches someday. Me and my mother. That's all I wanted." When he was nine, his parents divorced, and he was raised from that point onward by his mother, his grandmother, and his godmother. After the divorce Arsenio continued to see his father, whose work commitments limited the amount of time he could spend with his son. Although Hall has said that he derived his sense of humor principally from his mother, he credits the many hours he spent watching his father preach with giving him the ability to "work the crowd" that later proved indispensable in his career as a stand-up comedian.

At the age of seven, Hall began doing magic tricks. "Most kids had a paper route and mowed lawns to make a little money, but I was allergic to grass, so I did magic," he has recalled. "My father would do weddings, and I would do magic at the reception." He also performed at birthday parties and talent shows. Having few friends, he spent most of his time practicing his magic, listening to and imitating the dance steps of such musical groups as the Temptations and the Miracles, and listening to late-night radio talk shows. He also became a regular viewer of the televised *Tonight*

Show, starring Johnny Carson. "All-night radio and Johnny Carson were my friends," Hall told Barry Michael Cooper in an interview for the Village Voice (May 23, 1989). "They were always there with people, having conversations, discussing stuff. I kept Johnny on till my mother saw the blue light under the door and made me turn him off." It was at the age of twelve, he has said, that he decided he "wanted to do what Johnny Carson does."

During his teenage years Arsenio Hall played the drums in his high school marching band and orchestra and in his own group. Something of a class clown, he entertained his fellow students because, as he has put it, "at home there was no one to laugh at me, there was no one to play with me." His decision to become a stand-up comedian materialized when , during his senior year, the co-median-actor Franklyn Ajaye came to his school to promote the film Car Wash. Following his graduation from high school, Hall enrolled at Ohio University in Athens, Ohio, but in 1975 he transferred to Kent State University, where he became involved in theatre arts, worked as a disc jockey at the campus radio station, WKSR, and continued to perform magic. He received a B.A. degree in general speech from Kent State in December 1977.

After working briefly in advertising, Hall moved to Rosemont, Illinois, a Chicago suburb, to join his mother, who had taken a job there. One night, he wandered into a Rosemont nightclub called the Comedy Cottage, which showcases young comics. Impressed by the comedians he saw performing there, Hall decided that he would come back and do a routine of his own. He signed up to go on eight times, but each time fled in panic when the master of ceremonies introduced him. Finally, on his ninth try, he made it to the stage. He was so well received that he was soon working regular ten-dollar-a-night gigs at the club. "I used to write down my act in notebooks," Hall explained to Barry Michael Cooper. "I thought I was pretty good back then, but looking back through those notebooks today, I was terrible." His big break came on Christmas night in 1979, when he emceed a show featuring the singer Nancy Wilson. Impressed by the young comic, she financed his move to Los Angeles, where opportunities for aspiring comedians are much more plentiful than they are in Chicago. In addition to performing regularly in Los Angeles nightclubs, Hall appeared on telethons and benefit shows, and he auditioned for cartoon voice-over work. Then, on Nancy Wilson's recommendation, he became the opening act for the legendary soul singer Aretha Franklin. He then began opening for such stars as Neil Sedaka, Lynda Carter, Wayne Newton, Tina Turner, Tom Jones, and Patti LaBelle.

Although he eventually became a frequent guest on the Tonight Show, Arsenio Hall at first failed to impress the show's talent scout, Jim McCawley, who found his act "too barbed" for Johnny Carson's middle-of-the-road audience, but Hall did obtain bookings on the Merv Griffin Show and other programs. In 1983 ABC-TV selected him to co-host a summer replacement series, The Half-Hour Com-

edy Hour. More television engagements followed for Hall, including regular appearances on Thicke of the Night, the ill-fated late-night talk and variety show hosted by Alan Thicke, that eventually led Thicke to hire Hall as his co-host. Following Thicke of the Night's cancellation in July 1984, Hall became co-host of Paramount Television's music-variety show Solid Gold, and he finally got on the Tonight Show when Joan Rivers, who was sitting in for Carson, booked him as a guest. Hall also made guest appearances on Late Night with David Letterman.

In September 1986 Joan Rivers began hosting a late-night talk show called The Late Show on the fledgling Fox network. The program received respectable ratings in its first several weeks on the air, but its numbers soon plummeted, and in May 1987 Fox fired Miss Rivers and announced that The Late Show would be replaced at the end of the year by The Wilton North Report. Until then, a series of guest hosts would preside over the show. Hall, who had made several guest appearances on the program, was at first rejected for guest hosting duties, but the network later reconsidered and offered him the chance to serve as host for the show during the final months of its run. Uncertain as to whether the country was ready for a black talk-show host and advised by his manager to reject the offer, Hall hesitated at first. In spite of his doubts, he took the job, and his first show was telecast on August 17, 1987.

Aware that he had nothing to lose, Hall departed drastically from the standard talk-show fare by turning The Late Show into a sort of hip Hollywood party. "Joan was trying to take her audience from the Carson show," Hall told John Milward of the Chicago Tribune (June 26, 1988). "I figured I'd make a show for people who just didn't relate to the kind of show he's doing," a formula he would later adopt again on The Arsenio Hall Show. Sporting a diamond earring and often attired in leather clothing, Hall began each show by announcing, "We be havin' a ball!" before he embarked on his highly irreverent monologues. His guest list included personal friends such as Eddie Murphy and the actor-filmmakers Spike Lee and Robert Townsend as well as rock bands rarely seen on television. Unpredictability became the show's trademark. On one show, Hall even played a game of one-on-one basketball with the actor Elliott Gould. During his thirteen-week tenure as host, The Late Show received ratings slightly higher than those drawn by Joan Rivers. His numbers were especially strong among black viewers, and he became a favorite of hip young whites as well. When the show left the air in November 1987, Fox was deluged with letters from viewers demanding its return. The network offered Hall a $2 million contract to stay, but he rejected that deal to sign a two-year movie-television pact with Paramount worth almost $3 million.

Arsenio Hall had made his film debut in a cameo appearance in Amazon Women on the Moon (1987), a collection of unrelated vignettes that spoofed, among other things, science fiction movies and television situation comedies. It was generally lambasted by the critics. *Coming to America* (1988) was Hall's first substantial screen role. Directed by John Landis (who also directed the segment of *Amazon Women on the Moon* in which Hall appeared), *Coming to America* starred Hall's crony Eddie Murphy as a pampered prince from a fictitious African country who goes to New York and disguises himself as an impoverished student in the hope of meeting a woman who will love him for who he is rather than for his wealth. Hall played Semmi, Murphy's sidekick and friend, a role that paralleled the real-life relationship between the two men.

In *Coming to America*, Murphy's Prince Akeem is idealistic and noble, whereas Hall's Semmi is cynical and opportunistic. Semmi grumbles about having to live in a tenement rather than at the Waldorf-Astoria, impersonates the prince in order to impress a pretty girl, and secretly furnishes the slum flat that he and the prince share with a hot tub, a stereo system, and a VCR. In addition to their main roles, Hall and Murphy each played several minor characters, although they were barely recognizable in their heavy makeup. One of Hall's characters was an unattractive woman who attempts to pick up the prince in a singles bar. Another was an elderly barber who is forever arguing about sports and other subjects with a similar character played by Murphy. A third Hall characterization, that of a charismatic preacher, was, he said, based largely on his father.

Coming to America opened on June 29, 1988, and by the end of its run it had grossed almost $128 million, one of the highest totals in Hollywood history. But critical reaction to the film was mostly unfavorable, with Murphy, Landis, and the screenwriters David Sheffield and Barry Blaustein all taking a share of the blame. Writing in the *Washington Post* (June 27, 1988), Hal Hinson attacked *Coming to America* for failing to "live up to even the meagerest of expectations," and Richard Schickel of *Time* (July 4, 1988) magazine called Hall and Murphy's secondary characterizations "energetic and expert" but "never truly funny." A critic for *Variety* (June 29, 1988), however, felt that those characterizations were so "artfully" done that it was "sometimes hard to tell which one of them is playing whom." He added that "the contrast, unfortunately, only underscores how empty the central players are." As the sidekick of the enormously popular Eddie Murphy, Arsenio Hall, in the words of Mike McGrady of *New York Newsday* (June 29, 1988), "made the most of what is basically a talent showcase."

In August 1988, with *Coming to America* still attracting large crowds to the box office, Paramount Domestic Television announced that, beginning in early January 1989, it would produce a new one-hour late-night syndicated talk show to be hosted by Arsenio Hall. The show would originate from the Paramount studios, two blocks from Sunset Boulevard, in the heart of Hollywood. When approached by Paramount about hosting a talk show, Hall hesitated, still unconvinced, in spite of his successful stint on *The Late Show*, that a black late-night host would be able to attract a large audience on a consistent basis. But he changed his mind during an appearance on the *Tonight Show* to promote *Coming to America*. "I sat there watching Carson do his show," he explained to Alan Mirabella of the New York *Daily News* (December 30, 1988), "and realized how much I missed it, how for the rest of my life I'd dream of being Johnny. Right then, I decided I had to do another show." Hall accepted Paramount's offer, but only on the condition that he also be allowed to serve as the show's executive producer, a responsibility that would give him creative control.

In discussing his new show with Andy Meisler of the *New York Times* (January 1, 1989), Hall promised that the guest list would "reflect the black-white breakdown in America. It's not fifty-fifty. Blacks make up a certain percentage, and they'll make up that percentage on my show. When you look at my show, it will be like looking outside your window. You'll see women, men, black, white, whatever." (Hall's five-member band includes two women; his producer and his director are also women.) Although Hall avowedly intends to aim his show at younger viewers—"the MTV crowd," as he calls them—who do not watch Carson, he is quick to downplay suggestions that he hopes to dethrone the acknowledged king of late-night television. "Johnny's a legend," Hall told one interviewer. "He's like Mike Tyson. No one will beat him."

Sold by Paramount on a syndicated basis to both independent and network-affiliated stations, *The Arsenio Hall Show* competes against the *Tonight Show*, CBS's new *The Pat Sajak Show* (which also was launched in early January 1989), ABC's *Nightline* news program, syndicated reruns, local news shows, and *Late Night with David Letterman*, which follows the *Tonight Show* on most NBC stations. In August 1988 the Hall show scored a major coup when the CBS affiliates in three key cities—Atlanta, Detroit, and Cleveland—announced that they intended to carry it rather than the Sajak show. By launching time, *The Arsenio Hall Show* had been picked up by 135 stations, and, within eight months of its debut, it was being seen on about 170 stations, taking in 95 percent of the nation's television markets.

When *The Arsenio Hall Show* began on January 3, 1989, Hall deviated from the usual talk-show routine by sitting in a large cushioned chair (rather than behind a desk), with his guests seated to his right on a matching couch. After delivering an opening monologue and exchanging some friendly banter with his bandleader, Michael Wolff, Hall introduced his lineup of guests: the actresses Brooke Shields and Nancy Kulp, the actor Leslie Nielsen, and the singer Luther Vandross. His first few shows received mixed reviews. Although John J. O'Connor of the *New York Times* (January 11, 1989) speculated that, "with a touch more discipline," the Hall show "could turn out to be the freshest and hippest development the talk-show format has seen in decades," Tom Shales of the *Washington Post* (January 12, 1989) excoriated the program as "a punishing orgy of overkill," with a studio audience that is "loud and shrill" and "applauds everything but the exit signs." "Hall's show books the stupidest guests available, and the studio audience cheers them as heroes," Shales complained. Assessing Hall's first half-year of shows, Rick Kogan of the *Chicago Tribune* (June 29, 1989) lavished praise on the host. "At one moment he can sound like a graduate of Choate, at the next like some street corner hustler," Kogan observed. "It is that chameleonlike quality, embellished by his stylishness and street smarts, that will make Arsenio Hall the late-night king of this century's final decade."

In its initial week on the air, *The Arsenio Hall Show* notched a 4.2 rating and a 14 percent share of all sets actually in use during its time period, both well above expectations. During the closely watched ratings "sweeps" period in February, Hall received a 4.0 rating, better than Sajak's 3.3, but trailing Carson's 5.6. Hall's ratings during the February sweeps period were especially strong among viewers in the eighteen-to-thirty-four and eighteen-to-forty-nine age groups, his target audience. During the May sweeps period, Hall placed second in the late-night talk-show derby, ahead of Sajak and Letterman but still behind Carson. The show continued to draw strong ratings during the summer of 1989. In the July sweeps period, for example, it collected a nightly average of 2.9 million viewers in the coveted eighteen-to-thirty-four age group, to Carson's 2.4 million, although Carson's overall ratings for the month were still higher. Hall's success continued when, on May 23, 1989, he was named funniest supporting actor in a motion picture at the third annual American Comedy Awards, for his work in *Coming to America*. Two months later, *The Arsenio Hall Show* was nominated for three Emmy Awards.

Arsenio Hall is six feet tall and has a lean, athletic build. He wears his hair in a closely cropped, modified box-cut style and sports a mustache. The most notable trademarks of his appearance are the jeweled stud he wears in his left earlobe and his custom-made double-breasted suits. Hall lives in a condominium in West Hollywood and drives a black 1988 Ford Mustang. For relaxation, he spends time with Eddie Murphy or with the actor-comedian Richard Pryor, who is also a close friend. Hall likes to play basketball, a sport that he took up as a chubby teenager in order to help him lose weight and become more attractive to girls. A rabid fan, he often works basketball jokes into his routines and has had NBA stars such as Magic Johnson and Kareem Abdul-Jabbar as guests on his show.

Like Eddie Murphy, Arsenio Hall strongly disapproves of the use of illegal drugs, and a series of television commercials in which he discusses the horrors of drug addiction with young addicts is currently appearing on the MTV and VH-1 music-

video cable networks and on independent stations. Hall has said that, although he hopes to get married someday and start a family, his first priority for the time being is his career. "Because of my upbringing, it's important for me to do it right, to make sure it lasts, to make sure it works," he told Aldore Collier of *Jet* (April 10, 1989). "Right now, I don't think I'm prepared to give it 100 percent." Hall believes that the stresses of modern living have made the therapy of laughter more important than ever before. "We live in a world where we shot the pope," he told Collier. "It's an ugly world and laughter is very, very important. So, I take what I do very seriously." *Harlem Nights*, Hall's second picture for Paramount, in which he again appears in tandem with Eddie Murphy, was scheduled to be released in November 1989.

References: *Chicago Tribune* V p3 Jl 12 '88 pors, XI p3+ Ja 1 '89 pors; *N Y Daily News* p75 D 30 '88 por; *N Y Times* II p29+ Ja 1 '89 pors; *N Y Times Mag* p28+ O 1 '89 pors; *Newsweek* 113:68+ Ap 10 '89 pors; *Vanity Fair* 51:58+ Jl '88 pors; *Village Voice* p27+ My 23 '89 pors; *Wall St J* p1+ S 29 '89; *Washington Post* II p1+ Jl 10 '89 pors

Hanks, Tom

July 9, 1956– Actor. Address: c/o William Morris Agency, 1350 Ave. of the Americas, New York, N.Y. 10019

A classically trained stage actor with an enviable flair for light comedy, Tom Hanks has built his film career around his knack for portraying "average guys in an extraordinary situation," as he once put it. He has played such "average guys" with re-sounding success in a series of box-office hits, ranging from *Splash* in 1984 to *Big*, for which he received an Academy Award nomination as best actor of 1988. In his profile of the actor for *Connoisseur* magazine in 1986, Robert Goldberg attributed Hanks's appeal to his "eminently likable" on-screen persona and to his gift for seeming to be "on best-friends terms with his audience"—traits that Goldberg associated with the "old-fashioned" movie stars of the 1940s and 1950s, particularly Cary Grant and James Stewart. While he is flattered by such comparisons, Hanks himself has said simply, as quoted in a recent *Rolling Stone* interview, "I guess I come off in movies as a guy who you wouldn't mind hanging around with."

The third of four children, Tom Hanks was born on July 9, 1956 in Concord, California. When his parents divorced about five years later, he and his older siblings, Larry and Sandra, went to live with their father, Amos; his younger brother, Jim, remained with his mother. Both parents subsequently remarried—the mother three times, the father twice—and Tom grew up in an extended family group that included several step-brothers and step-sisters as well as numerous other relatives. Throughout the 1960s Amos Hanks, a chef, moved from one job to another, repeatedly uprooting his children and step-children. "By the time I was ten, I had lived pretty much in every kind of configuration, from big houses in the country to tiny apartments in big metropolitan areas," Tom Hanks told Lisa Birnbach in an interview for a New York *Daily News* (November 8, 1987) Sunday magazine profile. "I think I moved every six months when I was a kid. But I had a solid core of my older brother, my sister, and my dad."

By his own count, Hanks attended at least five different grammar schools during his childhood, and he was, perhaps as a result, "horribly, painfully, terribly shy," as he admitted to Bill Zehme for a *Rolling Stone* (June 30, 1988) cover story. Yet at the same time, he continued, "I was the guy who'd yell out funny captions during filmstrips. But I didn't get into trouble. I was always a real good kid and pretty responsible." Finally settling in Oakland, California, Hanks continued his education at Skyline High School, where he found an outlet for his "nervous energy," as he put it, in student theatrical productions. In retrospect, he told Bruce Buschel, who interviewed him for *Gentlemen's Quarterly* (January 1988), his nomadic boyhood seemed "the perfect upbringing" for an actor: "A lot of temporariness, never giving a second thought to leaving a place, traveling light, viewing simple pleasures as best. I do not have deep roots. I was drawn to acting in part because of the lifestyle. I throw everything in the back of a car and drive somewhere for six months."

Following his graduation from high school in 1974, Hanks enrolled at Chabot College, a junior college in nearby Hayward, California. In his second year there, he signed up for a course in which students read and then attended performances of such plays as Brecht's *Good Woman of Szechwan*, Albee's *Tiny Alice*, and O'Neill's *Iceman Cometh*. As he explained to Robert Goldberg in a conversation for *Connoisseur* (September 1986), the "big turning point" for him was *The Iceman Cometh*. "I literally could not wait to finish that play," he said. "I read the last page curled up on the front steps of my house. Then I went to see it at the Berkeley Repertory Theatre—150 seats, three-quarter staging. You were right on top of the stage, transported back to the Lower East Side of New York. This was the most magical thing that had ever happened to me. . . . I came out of the theatre enthralled with what those people had done that night. Four hours of concentration. I had never seen that anywhere else. . . . And I wanted to do something in the theatre, something as immediate and personal as that."

With that in mind, in 1976 Hanks transferred to California State University in Sacramento, which had a thriving theatre program. Although he took some acting classes, he was at first more interested in stage production and stage management than in performing. After having worked backstage on several campus productions as a set builder, lighting technician, and stage manager, however, he auditioned for and won a role in guest director Vincent Dowling's staging of Chekhov's *Cherry Orchard*. Taken by Hanks's enthusiasm and by his intuitive understanding of his character, Dowling, then the artistic director of the Great Lakes Shakespeare Festival in Lakewood, Ohio, recruited the young actor in 1977 for the festival's annual summer season.

Over the next three summers, Hanks honed his craft under Dowling's exacting direction, playing, by his own account, "mostly . . . small roles" in a score of productions. Among his more important roles were Grumio in *The Taming of the Shrew*, Cassio in *Othello*, and Proteus in *The Two Gentlemen of Verona*, for which he earned the Cleveland Critics Circle Award as best actor of the year in 1978. Hanks also worked on the company's lighting and set design crews. "It was like learning to play the violin on a Stradivarius," he recalled, in describing his three seasons with the Great Lakes Shakespeare Festival to Robert Goldberg. "This wasn't just singing, dancing. . . . This was the Bard. It automatically gave me a professional attitude. You had to be disciplined. You had to do your homework." During the winter months, Hanks was the associate technical director at a community theatre in Sacramento, where he "learned the trade of building shows."

After his third season with the Great Lakes Shakespeare Festival, Hanks decided to try his luck in New York City. There, he appeared in several Riverside Shakespeare Company productions, perhaps most notably its staging of Machiavelli's *Mandrake*, and doggedly made the rounds of the casting agents' offices. He auditioned for countless roles in theatre, television, and motion pictures before landing a small part in the 1980 slasher film

He Knows You're Alone. Finally, he was spotted by an ABC talent scout, who invited him to Los Angeles to try out for roles in several new network projects, including the pilot for the proposed series *Bosom Buddies,* a situation comedy about two philandering advertising copywriters who don female apparel in order to live in a low-rent hotel for women.

Bosom Buddies, which made its debut in November 1980, did reasonably well in the ratings, at least partly because it followed the popular *Mork and Mindy,* but it failed to impress the critics, many of whom dismissed it as "a one-joke series," to quote Kay Gardella. Hanks, however, received generally good notices for his "appealing" portrayal of Kip Wilson, and, following the show's cancellation in 1982, he found fairly steady employment as a supporting player in various episodes of the series *Taxi, Happy Days, The Love Boat,* and *Family Ties,* and as one of the stars of *Rona Jaffe's "Mazes and Monsters,"* a made-for-television movie about a fantasy game gone wrong that was first telecast by CBS on December 28, 1982.

Shortly after that, Ron Howard, who remembered Hanks from his guest spot in *Happy Days,* in which Howard had costarred, asked the actor to test for a role in the upcoming film *Splash,* which Howard was directing. Hanks initially read for the secondary part of the libidinous Freddie, which eventually went to John Candy, but Howard sensed that Hanks's boy-next-door charm was more suited to the central character, Allen Bauer, the addled produce manager who falls in love with a mermaid. Released early in 1984, the romantic fantasy was one of the year's surprise hits, grossing more than $60 million at the box office. The reviews for *Splash* were overwhelmingly favorable, but Hanks was largely overlooked by the critics, many of whom seemed to be as smitten with the beguiling mermaid, played by newcomer Daryl Hannah, as the lovesick Allen was. Among the handful who recognized Hanks's special talents were David Denby and David Ansen, who reviewed the film for the March 12, 1984 issues of *New York* magazine and *Newsweek,* respectively. Denby applauded the actor as "an expert comic" who was also able to "command the emotional center of his scenes." To David Ansen, Tom Hanks seemed "disappointingly bland at first glance," but the reviewer soon began to "pick up sly comic edges" in the actor's performance that reminded him of the routines of Johnny Carson or David Letterman—"all-American boys with mischief inside."

Later in 1984 Hanks appeared as Rick Gassko, the iconoclastic hero of the raucous, R-rated sex comedy *Bachelor Party,* a role he chose because, as he put it, the character was "intrinsically funny, not just goofy." For most reviewers, his energetic, smart-alecky performance was the main (some said only) reason to see the film. Hanks's next effort, the spy spoof *The Man with One Red Shoe* (1985), in which he took the part of an eccentric concert violinist who is mistaken for a secret agent, fared no better with the critics. In their estimation little more than a pale imitation of the 1972 French hit *The Tall Blond Man with One Black Shoe,* the film dropped out of sight within weeks of its release, and Hanks himself has since described it as "an absolute dog."

Hanks regained a measure of critical favor with *Volunteers* (1985), a comedy about a self-centered young playboy who, unable to pay his gambling debts, flees to Thailand as a Peace Corps volunteer. A few critics, perhaps most notably Walter Goodman of the *New York Times* and *Newsweek*'s David Ansen, credited the actor's droll impersonation of the snooty Lawrence Bourne 3d with giving the film its "seductively sardonic spirit," as Ansen put it in his review of August 26, 1985. "Bourne's character requires both the outsider smirk of a Bill Murray and the debonair inside moves of a Cary Grant," Ansen explained, "and Hanks has both." Other reviewers, however, among them the highly regarded Gene Siskel, writing in the *Chicago Tribune* (August 20, 1985), felt that Hanks's "foolish" decision to play Bourne with "a wildly inconsistent, imitation–Cary Grant voice" only aggravated the actor's "routine smugness." Further comparisons to Grant were inevitable following the release of *The Money Pit* (1986), a remake of the 1948 domestic-comedy classic *Mr. Blandings Builds His Dream House,* starring Grant and Myrna Loy. Savaged by the critics as a "miserable ripoff," to use Gene Siskel's description, of the earlier film, *The Money Pit* nonetheless took in more than $30 million, a tribute to Hanks's increasing stature as a box-office attraction.

Eager to test himself in a more substantial role, Hanks chose for his next venture *Nothing in Common* (1986), a comedy-drama about a glib, high-powered young advertising executive whose fast-track world is turned upside down when he is forced to come to terms with his parents' unexpected divorce. The richest, most fully developed character the actor had played to that date, David Basner metamorphoses over the course of the film from the quintessential self-centered yuppie into a sensitive, caring son. That Hanks was more than equal to the challenge is evident from the glowing notices accorded his portrayal by the majority of critics, even those who otherwise faulted the film for its "sentimentalities" and heavy-handed "TV-style seriousness." "The picture has both somber and ebullient moods, cut together without much modulation," David Denby observed in his review of *Nothing in Common* for *New York* (July 28, 1986), "and only Tom Hanks's virtuoso performance holds the pieces in place. . . . His David Basner is an advertising whiz who's also great with the ladies and funnier than Henny Youngman; but Hanks is not a gloater, not crappy and nasty like Bill Murray at his worst nor punkish and cheap like Chevy Chase. Those guys are comics; Hanks is a light-comedy romantic *actor.*"

By all accounts, Hanks's next two film credits—an American pilot in the forgettable wartime romance *Every Time We Say Goodbye* (1986) and

Pep Streebek, the wisecracking sidekick of Dan Aykroyd's Sergeant Friday in *Dragnet* (1987), an updated spoof of the popular television crime series of the 1950s—added little luster to his reputation. His breakthrough to full-fledged stardom came with the release, in the summer of 1988, of *Big*, a "body-switching" fantasy about a thirteen-year-old boy—Josh Baskin—who is magically transformed overnight into a thirty-five-year-old man, albeit one with an adolescent's mentality and sensibility. To prepare for the role, Hanks carefully observed the behavior of David Moscow, the teen-age actor who was to play Josh as a boy, and drew on his own childhood memories. "The hardest part—and also the appeal—of the role was to strip myself of all the adult layers," he told a reporter for *Time* (June 6, 1986) magazine. "It was to regain the kid's sense of play. I dug up memories—or scars—of myself in junior high school."

Hanks's appealing portrayal of a boy lost in an adult world earned him virtually unanimous raves from the critics, among them Janet Maslin of the *New York Times*. "Wide-eyed, excited, and wonderfully guileless, Mr. Hanks is an absolute delight . . . ," she wrote in her review of June 8, 1988. "*Big* features believable young teenage mannerisms from the two real boys in the cast, and this only makes Mr. Hanks's funny, flawless impression that much more adorable. For any other full-grown actors who try their hands at fidgeting, squirming, throwing water balloons, and wolfing down food in a huge variety of comically disgusting ways, this really is the performance to beat."

Just four months later, motion picture audiences saw a darker side of Tom Hanks in his impersonation of a self-destructive stand-up comic in *Punchline*. As Steven Gold, he is cocky, aggressive, driven, and, in his words, "incredibly unlikable and selfish." In preparation for the part, Hanks performed his own stand-up routine, which he had written with the help of a friend, the comedian Randy Fechter, in comedy clubs in Los Angeles and New York City. Eventually, he came to understand Steven's compulsion. "He was god of his universe as long as he had a microphone in his hand," the actor explained to Aljean Harmetz in an interview for the *New York Times* (September 25, 1988). "It's heady stuff to play, taking a room of 400 people wherever you want them. That feeling of unshared, uncompromised power corrupts." Hanks's disciplined approach to characterization, which he developed during his years with the Great Lakes Shakespeare Festival, also included creating a history for Steven, whom he saw as "an unloved child."

Punchline opened at theatres across the country in September 1988 to mixed reviews, some critics complaining that Sally Field was miscast as Lilah Krytsick, the New Jersey housewife who aspires to a career as a stand-up comic, and that the tentative relationship between Lilah and Steven was unconvincing at best. Hanks, however, received nothing but praise for his corrosive portrayal of Steven Gold. "The brilliance of Hanks's performance is its

transparency," David Ansen observed in his *Newsweek* (September 26, 1988) cover story about the actor. "You feel for Steven because Hanks understands him so completely and allows us to peer inside this brilliant s.o.b.'s stunted soul. You never catch him *wallowing* in the part. Steven may grandstand, but Hanks doesn't. His acting has wit, velocity, relaxation, and the extraordinary physical dexterity he demonstrated in *Big*. This guy may give you the creeps, but he holds you spellbound." Reflecting on his roles in the two films, which were shot back to back, Hanks told David Ansen, "I think that both of those are as complete a characterization as I've ever been able to do and as far away from myself as anything that I've done. *Big* was probably the purest, the least fake performance, but I think *Punchline* has the greatest stakes of anything I've done and, therefore, has more of my emotion in it."

Having starred in ten major motion pictures in just four years, an exhausted Hanks took several months off in 1988 before returning to the screen in The 'Burbs (1989), Joe Dante's black comedy about middle-class suburban xenophobia. Cast as the sole skeptic among several longtime neighbors who decide to take matters into their own hands when a new—and decidedly odd—family moves into their cul-de-sac, Hanks overcame the deficiencies of the "one-note" script to deliver what David Ansen, writing in *Newsweek* (March 6, 1989), hailed as "yet another deft and seemingly effortless comic performance."

In his next outing, *Turner and Hooch* (1989), a comedy about an uptight, small-town investigator (Turner) and a dog (Hooch) who is the only witness to a murder, Hanks held his own against the scene-stealing canine, "the Charles Laughton of four-legged thespians," as David Ansen put it in his review of the film for *Newsweek* (August 14, 1989). For Ansen, as for the majority of his colleagues, Hanks's "faultlessly funny" performance was the best part of what was otherwise "expertly executed dreck." Despite generally unfavorable notices, *Turner and Hooch* was the top box-office attraction at movie theatres around the country during its first few weeks of release in the summer of 1989.

Tom Hanks, who has described himself as "kind of goofy-looking," has curly brown hair, hazel eyes, and an impish, crooked smile. Distrusting what he has called "the American Hype Machine," he closely guards his privacy and in interviews steadfastly refuses to discuss his private life. He is, he told David Lida of *Women's Wear Daily* (August 4, 1986), "basically an average guy." "I have no hobbies," he continued. "I don't have one of those ranches in Alberta that I disappear to for months. When I'm not working, I wake up, drink some coffee, read the papers, and get on the phone and see what's going on." He also attends baseball games whenever possible, and he is a devoted fan of the Cleveland Indians. Hanks lives in Brentwood, California with his wife, the actress Rita Wilson, his costar in *Volunteers* whom he married on April 30, 1988. He has a son and a daughter from an earlier marriage to the actress and producer Samantha Lewes, which ended in divorce.

References: Connoisseur 216:62+ S '86 por; Esquire 107:49+ Mr '87 pors; Films & Filming p21+ Ap '89 pors; Gentlemen's Q 58:137+ Ja '88 pors; N Y Daily News mag p9+ Jl 21 '85 pors; N Y Newsday II p3+ Je 28 '87 pors; N Y Times C p15 Jl 6 '88 pors; Newsweek 112:56+ S 26 '88 pors; Rolling Stone p43+ S 25 '86 por, p38+ Je 30 '88 pors; Time 131:79 Je 6 '88 por; Contemporary Theatre, Film, and Television (1986)

Harris, Barbara (Clementine)

1930- Prelate of the Episcopal church in the United States. Address: Episcopal Diocese of Massachusetts, 138 Tremont St., Boston, Mass. 02111

Consecrated suffragan bishop of the 98,000-member Episcopal diocese of Massachusetts in February 1989, Barbara Harris thus became the first female bishop in the history of the Episcopal church in the United States and the worldwide Anglican communion of which it is a part. That radical departure from the 2,000-year "Catholic" tradition of apostolic succession sent schismatic shock waves throughout not only Anglicanism but, more comprehensively, the ecumenical movement that had been making progress toward a "reconciliation of ministries" in the universal church, especially among Roman Catholics, Eastern Orthodox, and Anglicans, to all of whom the validity of sacramental orders is the sine qua non of the continuation of the ministry begun when St. Peter, the first bishop,

under mandate from Jesus Christ, laid ordaining hands on his fellow apostles.

Rt. Rev. Barbara Harris is an African-American from Philadelphia who was a community relations executive with the Sun Oil Company before her ordination as a priest in 1980. In the controversy over her elevation to the episcopate, the gender issue important to traditionalists and ecumenicists was all but eclipsed by questions about her educational and pastoral credentials and by the opposition of conservative Episcopalians to what they considered her "left-wing" and "stridently" expressed views on social, political, and internal church matters, ranging from civil and women's rights and American policy in Central America to the ordination of homosexuals. For her part, Bishop Harris's elevation to the episcopate was a move "into the mainstream of those who seek God's justice, of those who seek God's peace, of those who seek God's brotherhood and sisterhood." As suffragan, or assistant, to Bishop David E. Johnson of the diocese of Massachusetts, she has been keeping a low polemical profile while concentrating on her sacramental and pastoral duties, most of which have thus far been in marginalized communities, especially prison populations. She remains undeterred by the death threats and obscene phone calls she has received since her consecration.

A third-generation Episcopalian, Barbara Clementine Harris was born to working-class parents in Philadelphia, Pennsylvania in 1930. Her mother, Beatrice Harris, was a church organist. Her father was a steelworker. The second of three children, she grew up with her brother and sister in the Germantown section of Philadelphia, where the whole family participated in the affairs of St. Barnabas parish. After graduating from the local girls' high school, she joined Joseph V. Baker Associates, a black-owned public relations firm specializing in relations between corporate clients and the African-American community. At the beginning of her career she studied at and graduated from the Charles Morris Price School of Advertising and Journalism in Philadelphia.

In 1958 Miss Harris became the president of Joseph V. Baker Associates, a position she held for ten years until she joined the Sun Oil Company's community relations department, of which she became manager in 1973. She spent much of her time away from business in the 1960s in the civil rights cause, participating in National Association for the Advancement of Colored People picket lines and selective patronage projects, in church-sponsored voter-registration drives in Mississippi, and in such demonstrations as Martin Luther King Jr.'s historic 1965 "freedom march" from Selma to Montgomery, Alabama. In the late 1960s she discovered the Church of the Advocate, an Episcopalian parish in North Philadelphia described by Paul Washington, then its rector, as "the cradle where the black movement in Philadelphia was born." She devoted herself zealously to the parish's work, which ranged from feeding the poor to hosting a Black Panthers conference that attracted thousands to

Philadelphia. As quoted by Peter Steinfels in a "Woman in the News" profile in the New York Times (September 26, 1988), Rev. Paul Washington observed that she "always had a strong sense of justice and compassion for the poor" and that she was "brilliant" in her ecclesiastical as well as her business dealings.

Among the twenty-eight autonomous national churches in the Anglican communion (total membership 70 million), only five have priests who are women: New Zealand, Canada, Brazil, Hong Kong–Macao, and the United States. The first American women, eleven of them, were ordained "irregularly," in defiance of the Episcopal policy of the time, by three bishops in the Church of the Advocate in Philadelphia on July 29, 1974. As the crucifer, or crucifix bearer, Miss Harris led the procession at that ceremony.

Deciding that she herself had a priestly vocation, Barbara Harris embarked on a novel course of theological and pastoral training while continuing to work for the Sun Oil Company. "I developed with the help of a mentor the first alternative program for [seminary] education in the diocese of Pennsylvania," she later recounted to an interviewer. "I was able to put together the same number of credits as any seminarian by taking work where I could, at nights, on weekends and vacations. I took the same general ordination examinations as any seminarian, passed them with flying colors." According to James L. Franklin in Christian Century (December 21–28, 1988), her formal academic training consisted of attendance at the Metropolitan Collegiate Center in Philadelphia in 1976 and the taking of several courses at Villanova University between 1977 and 1979. In addition, she spent three months in informal residence at the Episcopal Divinity School in Cambridge, Massachusetts just before her ordination. A biographical release from the diocese of Massachusetts received by Current Biography in April 1989 adds, without giving dates, that she studied "urban theology" in Sheffield, England and graduated from the Pennsylvania Foundation for Pastoral Counseling.

Barbara Harris received the diaconate in September 1979. In October 1980 she was ordained a priest by Bishop Lyman Ogilby of the diocese of Pennsylvania, who described her as a "very energetic, deeply committed Christian" and a "good communicator." Having left her last position (senior consultant) with the Sun Oil Company, Rev. Barbara Harris devoted herself full-time to her priestly duties, the earliest of which included assignment to St. Augustine of Hippo parish in Norristown, Pennsylvania and a four-year chaplaincy in the Philadelphia County prison system. Later she was assigned to the Church of the Advocate, where she became interim rector in March 1988.

While impressing her immediate superiors, peers, and parishioners with her parochial work, the Reverend Barbara Harris gained her wider reputation for polemicism through the printed word, beginning in 1984, when she left her prison chaplaincy to become the executive director of the Episcopal Church Publishing Company, headquartered in Ambler, Pennsylvania. For the Witness, an ecumenical journal of social concern published, without church imprimatur, by the Episcopal Church Publishing Company, Barbara Harris wrote a column called "A Luta Continua," Portuguese for "the struggle continues," the slogan of the anti-Portuguese Angolan rebels. In the breezily written column she expressed her "womanist" (a word she prefers to "feminist") views; vented her outrage against the injustices suffered by such peoples as American homosexuals and underclass blacks, the oppressed majority in South Africa, and those who were, in her view, the victims of American foreign policy elsewhere in the world; advocated prison reform; and criticized Episcopal church teachings and practices that she considered inimical to social, political, and economic justice.

Although many Episcopalians would remain opposed to the ordination of women, the issue was settled in principle in 1976, when the General Convention of the church, capitulating to the fact of repeated and ongoing unauthorized such ordinations, ruled that women could be included in all orders of the clergy—deacon, priest, and bishop. The episcopate aspect eluded public attention for ten years, during which the feminist force within the church gathered its strength and bided its time. That force was ready to show its full strength in 1987, when it won the signatures of the majority of American bishops on a report favorable to the consecration of women as bishops. In their minority report, the dissenting bishops warned that such a step could mean a breach with most of the Anglican communion, including, most ominously, the mother church, the Church of England. Heeding that warning, the backers of Barbara Harris for bishop in the diocese of Massachusetts, in communication with Archbishop Robert Runcie, the primate of England, waited one more year, until the conclusion of the 1988 Lambeth Conference, the conclave of Anglican bishops from around the world held in Canterbury, England every ten years. At the summer 1988 conference the Anglican bishops voted, 423 to 28, with 19 abstentions, to ask each Anglican province to "respect the decisions and attitudes of other provinces in the ordination and consecration of women to the episcopate, without such respect necessarily indicating acceptance of the principles involved."

The Lambeth resolution gave the green light to the open candidacy of Barbara Harris for suffragan bishop in the diocese of Massachusetts. When the voting for suffragan began in the Cathedral Church of St. Paul in Boston on September 24, 1988, there were six candidates, including a white woman and a black man. Over the course of several ballots, the field narrowed down to two: Barbara Harris and the Reverend Mr. Marshall Hunt, a Massachusetts favorite son. On the final ballot Rev. Barbara Harris bested Hunt by a vote of 145 to 108 among the clergy and 131 to 115 among the lay delegates.

When David E. Johnson, Boston's senior bishop, in keeping with protocol, asked the assembly to acclaim the choice of the Reverend Barbara Harris, the generally enthusiastic vocal response was marred by scattered shouts of "No!"

Over a period of four months Barbara Harris's election was ratified by a majority of the 118 bishops heading Episcopal dioceses, with the approval of their diocesan standing committees. During that period "Dear Colleague" letters and other memoranda regarding the Harris matter, much of it acrimonious, were circulated throughout the church. The lobbying against the consecration of Rev. Barbara Harris included, at its lowest level, innuendoes about her character, personal history, and lifestyle.

The ad hominem attacks dovetailed with excoriations of her "vitriolic . . . , abrasive, and confrontational" espousal of a theology and politics that some of her right-wing critics viewed as "pro-Marxist," "proterrorist," and heretical. Rev. John R. Throop, the executive director of Episcopalians United for Revelation, Renewal, and Reformation, characterized Rev. Barbara Harris as "rigid and narrow and closed to dialogue" and said, "By her past actions and pronouncements, Barbara Harris promises to be a regular source of division in the church." The Reverend Jerome F. Politzer, president of the conservative Prayer Book Society, charged that her election was the fraud-marked work of a "left-wing cabal," a "radical junta now destroying the church."

Aimed higher, and more on target, were questions about Barbara Harris's lack of a seminary or theological school degree and of ten years' experience as a priest, customary prerequisites for the episcopate. But gender was the essential issue, rooted in biblical precedent and church tradition and troubling to anyone taking apostolic succession seriously. The Reverend J. F. Titus Oates of All Saints Church in the Ashmont section of Boston was quoted by Lawrence J. Goodrich of the *Christian Science Monitor* (February 10, 1989): "I would oppose making [even] Mother Teresa a bishop. If we believe that Jesus Christ was God in flesh, then all that he said or did is to be taken note of. He never sent out a woman, even his mother, the highest creature ever born, as an apostle."

Father Oates is a member of the Episcopal traditionalist group called the Evangelical Catholic Mission (ECM), which issued a letter declaring, "The final crisis of the Episcopal church is now upon us. The Episcopal church is in rebellion against . . . the God-given order of the church." The letter called for a traditionalist synod to be held in Fort Worth, Texas in June 1989 "to consider how we shall be the church within the Episcopal church" in the face of "the institution's present disintegration." According to Father Oates, fifteen of the 120 Episcopal bishops nationwide signed the ECM declaration. One of those who signed, Bishop Edward McBurney of Quincy, Illinois, did so at the cost of an honorary degree from his alma mater, the Berkeley Divinity School at Yale University.

Between 1963 and 1988 the Episcopalian church in the United States declined in membership from 3.4 million to 2.5 million. That decline was roughly commensurate with the magnitude of defections from mainstream churches generally, in the direction of fundamentalist and Pentecostal denominations. With the ordination of women to the Episcopal priesthood, there began a new, relatively minor movement of traditionalist faithful *within* the mainstream, from Episcopalianism to Eastern Orthodoxy and Roman Catholicism. "There is always the possibility of people leaving the Episcopal church over this particular event [the consecration of Barbara Harris as bishop]," the Most Reverend Edmond Browning, the Episcopal church's presiding bishop, told Lawrence J. Goodrich of the *Christian Science Monitor*. "I am using every possible means to try to avoid that happening. I have tried to be in conversation with the ECM leadership to try to find ways to respect our diversity on this issue."

In the Anglican communion the consternation was worse. In response to schismatic rumblings from such groups as the Church Union and the Association for the Apostolic Ministry, Archbishop Runcie, the primate of the Church of England, declared: "For the moment, it is not for individuals to make declarations about whether they are in or out of communion with the Episcopal church." "The problem is," Bishop Mark Dyer explained, as quoted by Marjorie Hyer in the *Washington Post* (September 28, 1988), "when a woman bishop ordains a man a priest, for 50 percent of the Anglican communion that man is not recognized as a priest." Dyer, the bishop of Bethlehem, Pennsylvania, a Harris supporter, was the only American on the Anglican Commission on Communion and Women in the episcopate set up by Runcie to address the problem of possible inter-province conflicts. On November 25, 1988 the commission issued its recommendations: that the head of a national church be consulted on any invitation to one of his bishops to take part in the consecration of a woman as bishop, and that the invited bishop accept or reject the invitation in accordance with his national church's policy.

Ten to 15 percent of the parishes in the diocese of Massachusetts opposed the consecration of Rev. Barbara Harris. When the ratification of her election was announced on January 24, 1989, Rev. Andrew Mead, rector of the Church of the Advent in the diocese, told a reporter that he would neither recognize her consecration nor allow her to conduct religious services in his parish. "We're supposed to be part of the Catholic church," Mead explained. "This just ensures the drift of the Episcopal church to Protestantism." Roman Catholic archbishop John H. Whealon of Hartford, Connecticut, the cochairman of a group exploring Anglican–Roman Catholic unity, was saddened at what he considered "a major step back." The Reverend Robert G. Stephanopoulos, dean of the Greek Orthodox Cathedral of the Holy Trinity in New York City, voiced a similar sentiment but added that the problem really began earlier, with the ordination of women as deacons and priests. New York Lutheran bishop William Lazareth thought that Barbara Harris's consecration as bishop would test Anglicanism's historic role as a "bridge ministry" between Protestantism and Roman Catholicism.

Surrounded by sixty-one bishops (none from the Church of England) and joyously acclaimed by an audience of more than 7,000, Barbara Harris was consecrated a bishop in Hynes Veterans Memorial Stadium in Boston on February 11, 1989. The three-and-one-half-hour ceremony was both solemn and spectacular, an event worthy of an ecclesiastical Cecil B. de Mille. The only jarring moment came well before the "laying on of hands," when the Most Reverend Edmond Browning, the chief consecrator, in keeping with protocol, invited any dissenters to speak. Two objectors went to the microphone. Rev. John Jamieson, representing the Prayer Book Society, calling the ceremony "a sacrilegious imposture," declared that all consecrations, ordinations, and absolutions administered by Rev. Barbara Harris would be "null and void." Rev. James Hopkinson Cupit of the New York diocese's Church of the Resurrection expressed his dismay at a consecration which "will be an intractable impediment to the realization of that visible unity of the church" sought by the ecumenical movement.

Before her consecration, Bishop Harris told a press conference that she did "not intend to be an international Anglican gadfly, moving around to promote ordinations of women," although she would "be as supportive as possible." She also said that, although the Episcopal church has not been "as inclusive of gay and lesbian people as it might have been," she felt "bound to work within the structures of the church." In an interview with Monica Furlong at the time of her consecration, she elaborated on the homosexual issue: "I think it [the church] must simply be honest and either stop ordaining gays or stop passing the resolutions [saying it will not ordain them]. As it is, it forces Christians to lie about who and what they are. . . . Now I have promised to uphold the doctrines and discipline of the church and I will conform to what that discipline is at this time, but these are concerns I shan't lose. In the case of a priest who gets AIDS, rather than simply have him disappear and be replaced, I would hope to sit down with him and his congregation and encourage them to work through the alienation process together."

Bishop David E. Johnson, the senior Boston prelate, agreed, at least initially, not to send Barbara Harris into any parish that would find her presence "painful," on condition that representative members of such a parish meet with him and his new suffragan. Much of Bishop Harris's pastoral work was to be in prisons, hospitals, and local communities. "I'd like to do something that breaks down the we/they approach, especially in prisons," she told Monica Furlong. After spending seven months in the diocese of Massachusetts, Bishop Harris was welcomed by the 182 members of the House of Bishops, which unanimously adopted a statement reaffirming the ordination of women as priests and bishops. The statement, adopted in a spirit of reconciliation in Philadelphia on September 28, 1989, also counseled church leaders against insensitivity toward those unable to recognize the authority of ordained women.

Rt. Rev. Barbara Harris, as she can be addressed now that she is a bishop, has been described in the press as a "diminutive," "slight," "determined" woman, "stately at the altar" and "powerful in the pulpit." To the British ears of Monica Furlong, her gravelly voice and Philadelphia accent "sounded awfully like Katharine Hepburn." Asked by Miss Furlong how she thought she might approach her new duties differently than "the bishops we are used to," Bishop Harris replied: "I am a nurturing person. I don't feel that reserve about my person that many clerics do. I am exuberant, more outgoing, more hugging. My natural tendency is to embrace people, particularly the young and the old. I think if you have power it is important to use it with compassion. A matron in the prison service once taught me a lot about how to use power with compassion." The bishop represents the Episcopal church on the board of the Prisoner Visitation and Support Committee, a ministry in federal and military correctional institutions. She has an honorary degree in theology (1981) from Hobart and William Colleges. Married in 1962 and divorced three years later, the bishop has no children.

References: Chicago Tribune I p5 D 4 '88 por; Christian Century 105:1175+ D 21–28 '88; Christian Sci Mon p8 F 10 '89 por; Ebony 44:40+ My '89 pors; Guardian p36 F 16 '89 por, p8 Mr 10 '89 por; Manchester Guardian W p36 F 16 '89 por; N Y Times A p12 S 26 '88 por, p7 N 26 '88, A p12 Ja 25 '89 por, A p21 Ja 26 '89, p1+ F 12 '89 por, A p16 F 13 '89 por; Newsweek 113:58+ F 13 '89 por; Washington Post A p1+ S 25 '88 por, A p8 S 28 '88 por, A p3 D 4 '88 por

Harrison, George

Feb. 25, 1943– Musician; singer; songwriter; film producer. Address: c/o Warner Bros. Records, 3300 Warner Blvd., Burbank, Calif. 91510

NOTE: This biography supersedes the article that appeared in Current Biography in 1966.

Ever since England's mop-haired musical foursome known as the Beatles emerged on the American scene in 1964, George Harrison has been recognized as one of the world's top rock-'n'-roll musicians. As lead guitarist for the group and as a solo performer in his own right, Harrison has influenced the tastes of millions of listeners throughout the world. Through his early experiments with twelve-string guitars, he also helped to inspire, in-

George Harrison

directly, the development of "folk-rock" and the so-called California sound of the mid-1960s, and his performances on the sitar introduced multitudes of Westerners to that Indian instrument. Harrison's philanthropic work in the early 1970s, notably his role in organizing the concert for Bangladesh, stands out among rock music's most positive manifestations, and he has also made his mark as a film producer.

George Harrison was born on February 25, 1943 in Arnold Grove, a lower-middle-class area of Liverpool, England, one of the four children (three boys and a girl) of Harold and Louise Harrison. His father, a former steward with the White Star Line, became a bus conductor soon after his marriage. The youngest in a closely knit family, George Harrison was a quiet, introspective, and fiercely independent child, who, according to Philip Norman in his definitive Beatles biography *Shout!* (1981), even resented being brought to school by his mother as a toddler. He attended Dovedale Primary School before entering Liverpool Institute in 1954. His academic record was undistinguished, but he was greatly interested in sports, particularly cricket, soccer, and swimming. He also enjoyed listening to his father's record collection, which featured such American country singers as Jimmie Rodgers, and, as he has recalled, it was on those recordings that he first heard the guitar.

George Harrison became conscious of rock-'n'-roll during late 1955 as the new, controversial American music made its way across the Atlantic. His fascination with the guitar began in 1956, when he heard Lonnie Donegan's hit recording of "Rock Island Line." Soon after, he persuaded his mother to give him three pounds to purchase a guitar from a boy at school. He soon displayed an all-

consuming desire to learn the guitar and, with encouragment from his mother, began mastering some basic chords.

Early in 1956 Harrison's family had moved into a public housing project in Liverpool's Speke district. While riding a bus to school, Harrison made the acquaintance of Paul McCartney, a fellow student who was slightly older. Drawn together by their common love of guitars, the two boys spent hours together at the Harrison home playing and practicing. By the end of the year, George showed enough confidence in his skill to acquire a much better guitar, with thirty pounds borrowed from his mother.

Among Harrison's early guitar idols were the Americans Carl Perkins, Duane Eddy, Chet Atkins, Buddy Holly, and Eddie Cochran. He was also inspired by the Spanish guitar virtuoso Andrés Segovia. Harrison's proficiency developed in slow, painstaking fashion over several years into a deeply studied but precise and dexterous approach, akin to the classical guitar technique. When he was fourteen, he was introduced by McCartney to the Quarry Men, a local rock group that had been founded the previous year by John Lennon.

Allowed to sit in if one of the members failed to appear, Harrison was eventually eased into the Quarry Men—later renamed Johnny and the Moondogs—as its membership changed and its sound evolved into a leaner, tougher brand of music. The drummer left the group in 1958, and for most of that year the band was comprised only of the trio of Lennon, McCartney, and Harrison. By then Harrison was playing his first electric guitar, a Hofner Futurama, but since neither he nor Lennon could afford an amplifier, the band had to be content with whatever sound system was available to them.

During the early part of 1958, Harrison played with the Les Stuart Quartet while Lennon and McCartney occasionally performed as a duo called the Nurk Twins. The three were back together in August for a series of shows in West Derby with the drummer Ken Browne, who quit at the end of the season, and in 1959 they added the bass guitarist Stuart Sutcliffe, an art student friend of Lennon's, to the band. It was this fledgling quartet that came to the attention of Alan Williams, a Liverpool manager who offered them his services.

Among other stints, the Silver Beatles—as the group was then known—served as backup to the rock star Johnny Gentle on a two-week tour of Scotland in May 1960. A series of home recordings made of the group's rehearsals during that spring and unofficially released in the 1980s under the title *The Quarrymen at Home* reveals the degree to which Harrison's playing had developed. Although heavily derivative of Carl Perkins and other Memphis-based players, it showed a level of articulation and concentration seldom heard in British rock music of the period. On such songs as the Lennon-McCartney original "One after 909" and John Lennon's "I'll Always Be in Love with You," Harrison's style displayed an authentic soulfulness. Those tapes also include Harrison's earliest known recording as a lead vocalist, on the Carl Perkins song "Matchbox."

In the summer of 1960, the group, by then called simply the Beatles, expanded to a quintet with the addition of drummer Pete Best and obtained its first long-term booking, at the Indra Club in Hamburg, West Germany. During that extended engagement, the Beatles' sound tightened and toughened as they played sets lasting as long as eight hours a night amid the raucous, decadent setting of the city's red-light district. By September they had moved out of the tiny Indra Club into the much larger Kaiserkeller. Increasingly in demand, the Beatles seemed to have a promising future in Hamburg, but their stay was cut short when the authorities discovered that Harrison, who was only seventeen at the time, was below the legal minimum age for employment and that he and Lennon had no work permits.

The Beatles returned to Liverpool in December 1960, and in the following month they were booked into the Cavern, the city's leading jazz venue. The group became one of the club's most promising new rock-'n'-roll acts, and in April 1961 the band also obtained a return engagement in Hamburg, where the group was chosen by the West German orchestra leader and producer Bert Kaempfert to back the Liverpool rock-'n'-roller Tony Sheridan in a recording session. The Beatles' first formal recording session was held in early May 1961, and among the dozen or so tracks the group cut were two original numbers, including "Cry for a Shadow," a guitar instrumental written by John Lennon and George Harrison and featuring Harrison in a twangy guitar solo.

During a return engagement at the Cavern in the summer of 1961, the Beatles came to the attention of Brian Epstein, the owner of the North End Music Stores who was to serve as the band's personal manager until his death in 1967. At Epstein's urging, the group's members polished their appearance, and through his efforts they obtained, in July 1962, a recording contract with Parlophone Records, part of the prestigious EMI Group. Soon after, in August 1962, Pete Best was replaced as the group's drummer by Ringo Starr. Two months later the Beatles released as their first single two Lennon-McCartney originals—"Love Me Do" and "P.S. I Love You." Their second single, another Lennon-McCartney original, entitled "Please Please Me," was released in January 1963 and soon reached the top of the British charts in *Melody Maker* magazine. Thus began the Beatles' domination of British—and, later, American—rock, which lasted for the remainder of the decade.

Soon the Beatles were celebrated on an almost daily basis in the British press, which took instantly to the group's informal, irreverent attitude toward its success. After a tour of Sweden, in October, the Beatles appeared on November 4, 1963 in a Royal Command Performance at the Prince of Wales Theatre in London before an audience that included Elizabeth, the Queen Mother, and Princess Margaret.

Sometime during that flurry of activity, in late 1962 or early 1963, George Harrison became the first Beatle to travel to the United States, when he visited his sister, Louise, who was married to an American and living in St. Louis, Missouri. On February 7, 1964, amid a hastily mounted publicity campaign by Capitol Records, EMI's American label, the four Beatles arrived at Kennedy Airport in New York, where they were greeted by several hundred screaming teenagers. The following day they made their performing debut on national television, on CBS-TV's *Ed Sullivan Show*. Within weeks their records were occupying the top five spots on the American singles charts and the top two positions on the album charts, thus surpassing the group's British success. Harrison and his fellow Beatles won formal recognition for their contributions to Great Britain's economic well-being in June 1965, when Queen Elizabeth II made each of them a member of the Most Excellent Order of the British Empire.

The years from 1964 through 1966 were a mixed blessing for Harrison. He shared in the financial rewards amassed from the group's records sales, which, for albums as well as singles, routinely ran into the millions on several continents. But where Lennon and McCartney were recognized as the group's leaders and Ringo Starr, as its resident clown, Harrison was known to fans as the "quiet Beatle," because of his low-key demeanor.

One drawback of the Beatles' growing popularity was the shrieking frenzy of their fans, which at times made it impossible to hear the music. Harrison found his painstakingly acquired virtuosity lost in the vast halls required to accommodate the throngs of Beatles devotees. Unable to hear their own playing amid the screams, the Beatles quickly lost the edge they had spent years honing as a concert band. "At first, when we went on the road as a famous group, it was good fun," Harrison recalled in an interview in *Globe* (September 1969) magazine. "But we soon found out that we had to play our records to promote them. We could only sing our hits and none of the old rock things we'd loved doing in Liverpool and Hamburg." By 1966 the Beatles' concerts, although more profitable than ever, were frequently characterized by out-of-tune instruments, off-key singing, and missed cues.

The group's records during that period had similar drawbacks for Harrison. One of the hallmarks of the early Liverpool sound was the prominence given the rhythm guitars—featuring the loud, ringing chords that were in effect a signature of the Beatles and similar groups. For Harrison, it meant that his instrument was pushed deeper into the mix of the Beatles' songs than the term "lead" guitar would imply. For example, on songs such as "Long Tall Sally" and "Boys," Harrison's flashiest playing was literally buried beneath the rest of the band.

Despite those difficulties, however, Harrison managed to grow as a musician, songwriter, and performer. He sang lead on the Lennon-McCartney original "Do You Want to Know a Secret" on the Beatles' debut album, *Please Please*

Me, and he made his songwriting debut on their second LP, released in England under the title *With the Beatles* in 1963 and in the United States as *Meet the Beatles* in 1964, with a song entitled "Don't Bother Me." It was written as an exercise to see if he "*could* write a song," as Harrison noted in his book *I, Me, Mine* (1981). The song was featured in the Beatles' first full-length movie, a spoof of Beatlemania entitled *A Hard Day's Night,* which was filmed in the spring of 1964. It was Harrison's rendition of the title song, on a twelve-string Rickenbacker guitar not previously associated with rock-'n'-roll, that inspired the singer and guitarist Roger McGuinn to establish his rock group, the Byrds, which helped to pioneer the folk-rock sound. Meanwhile, Harrison's romance with Patricia ("Patti") Anne Boyd, a young actress who had had a small part in *A Hard Day's Night,* culminated in marriage on January 21, 1966.

Harrison again demonstrated his talent as a songwriter on the soundtrack album of the Beatles movie *Help,* released in August 1965, with "I Need You," a clever love song that was one of the brighter moments in the score. While working on the film he had become interested in the sitar, a Hindustani instrument similar to the lute that offered him a palette richer than any he had found with the guitar. He used the instrument in a recording of the John Lennon song "Norwegian Wood," a cut on the *Rubber Soul* album, which was issued in 1965 and which also featured the most successful of Harrison's early compositions, "If I Needed Someone." The last-named song was the first of Harrison's compositions to be featured in the Beatles' concerts during their 1966 American and Asian tours, and it was later recorded by the Hollies, a Manchester-based rock group.

The album *Revolver,* released in 1966, included three Harrison songs, among them the opening track, "Taxman," a satirical treatment of the British tax laws that were then taking a tremendous amount of the Beatles' hard-won earnings. It was considered the Beatles' first political song, with digs at Labour and Conservative policies alike. "Love You To," from the same album, was Harrison's first full-blown composition for sitar. An exquisitely arranged song embellished with two other instruments, the tamboura and the tabla, it sounded unlike anything the Beatles had recorded before.

"Love You To" and the sitar-based compositions that followed, "Within You, Without You," "Blue Jay Way," and "The Inner Light," put Harrison in a spotlight of his own for the first time in his career. Long eclipsed by the sheer productivity of John Lennon and Paul McCartney, he had found a voice all his own and a loyal and devoted audience among the world's Beatles fans. Soon, other bands, among them the Rolling Stones, began to use the sitar. By 1967, a boom had begun in sales of sitars, books on Eastern philosophies, and records by the Indian sitarist Ravi Shankar, principally among college students newly introduced to the music by Harrison.

In late 1966, following the end of the Beatles as a touring band, Harrison visited India with his wife and studied with Shankar for two months. Journeying to Kashmir, the Harrisons sought out students and holy men, and by the time they returned to England they were steeped in Eastern philosophy. The new learning was soon reflected in Harrison's songwriting, and his lyrics took on a more serious, didactic tone, beginning with "Within You, Without You" on the *Sergeant Pepper's Lonely Hearts Club Band* album, which was released in June 1967. Later that summer, Harrison and his wife persuaded the other Beatles to attend a lecture being given in London by the Maharishi Mahesh Yogi, a leading exponent of transcendental meditation and the founder of the Spiritual Regeneration movement. The members of the band subsequently became full-fledged adherents of the Maharishi's movement. Ringo Starr, Paul McCartney, and John Lennon eventually left in disillusionment, but Harrison has remained a devoted believer.

In early 1968 Harrison returned to playing the guitar in earnest, having realized that he had started too late in life to become a great sitarist. With the encouragement of such superstar guitarists as Jimi Hendrix and Eric Clapton, he returned to Western-style rock music with enthusiasm. On the two-record set *The Beatles* (commonly known as "The White Album"), which was released in November 1968, Harrison emerged with his own transmutations of riffs originated by Chuck Berry and Jimi Hendrix. His song "While My Guitar Gently Weeps," one of four that he wrote for the album, encompassed Harrison's heartfelt spirituality as well as his love of American blues. The song's celebrated lead guitar part, played by Eric Clapton, was the first of their many collaborative efforts. Harrison's songwriting blossomed into a multitude of styles, idioms, and directions through the remainder of the Beatles' history and beyond. His "Here Comes the Sun," from the *Abbey Road* album, is considered by some to be virtually an anthem to the optimism of the late 1960s, and it still brings crowds to their feet. "Something," from the same album, was Harrison's commercial breakthrough, the first of his songs to appear on a Beatles single and a number popular enough to be recorded by dozens of other artists.

Amid the extended breakup of the Beatles, which proceeded in various disputes running from mid-1969 through the spring of 1970, Harrison began working on a variety of outside projects. He collaborated with Eric Clapton on the song "Badge," performed with John Lennon's Plastic Ono Band, and served as a record producer for artists signed by the group's Apple label, notably the organist and singer Billy Preston.

Harrison's magnum opus, the triple album *All Things Must Pass,* which was released in November 1970, encompassed everything that characterized him as a musician, composer, and religious devotee. Comprised of songs he had been saving up for four years, it included spiritual anthems such as "My Sweet Lord" and "Isn't It a Pity"; love songs on which he collaborated with Bob Dylan, including "I'd Have You Anytime" as well as Dylan's own "If Not for You"; cautionary advice like "Beware of Darkness"; and stirring accounts of Harrison's own religious devotion, such as "Awaiting on You All." The album also contained two impromptu blues jams. Featuring such guests as Eric Clapton, Ringo Starr, and guitarist Dave Mason, *All Things Must Pass* also benefited from its dense, massive "wall of sound" production, a trademark of coproducer Phil Spector, which prompted some observers to describe the record as having near-Wagnerian sonic dimensions. *All Things Must Pass* entered *Billboard*'s charts at number five in the third week of December 1970, climbed to number one two weeks later, and held that spot for six more weeks, remaining on the charts until September 1971. It also generated such hit singles as "My Sweet Lord" and "What Is Life."

In the wake of *All Things Must Pass*, Harrison's celebrity rivaled that of John Lennon and Paul McCartney, and he found himself the beneficiary of much public goodwill. His music's message of spiritual regeneration was a positive one, and his continued work as a musician's musician, willing to play guitar with other stars, including John Lennon on *Imagine*, made him seem refreshingly humble amid the clashing egos of his former colleagues.

Harrison's popularity reached its peak in the early 1970s, following two widely acclaimed benefit concerts that he had organized to raise money to help feed the starving population of Bangladesh. Held at Madison Square Garden in New York City in August 1971, the concerts also featured Bob Dylan, Eric Clapton, Ringo Starr, Leon Russell, Billy Preston, and Ravi Shankar, who had first proposed the idea. The two benefits were followed in early 1972 by a live triple-album entitled *The Concert for Bangla Desh* and a concert motion picture of the same name. The event established George Harrison as rock-'n'-roll's leading philanthropist.

Living in the Material World, Harrison's long-awaited follow-up to *All Things Must Pass*, was released, along with an accompanying single, "Give Me Love (Give Me Peace on Earth)," in May 1973. Two days after their release, both were certified as gold records—signifying a million dollars in sales each—and both reached number one on their respective charts in June of that year. Harrison's next album, *Dark Horse* (1974), was also the first release on his own new Dark Horse record label. But neither it nor *Extra Texture* (1975) sold nearly as well as their predecessors, and Harrison's 1974 concert tour of the United States met with mixed response. His album *33 1/3* (1976) fared somewhat better, with a hit single entitled "You."

By the end of the decade, however, Harrison, like many artists of the 1960s, was affected by the rapidly changing public taste. His 1981 single "All Those Years Ago," written in the wake of John Lennon's murder late the previous year by a deranged fan, was a number-one hit, but his 1982 album,

Gone Troppo, was not a success. The mid-1970s were also a trying time for Harrison personally. In 1976 he lost a longstanding lawsuit filed against him by the copyright owner of the Chiffons' hit "He's So Fine," accusing Harrison of plagiarizing its melody and chorus in the composition of "My Sweet Lord." In 1977 Harrison and his wife, Patti, divorced after eleven years of marriage. The following year, he married Olivia Arias, whom he had met in Los Angeles in 1974.

Even as his musical fortunes flagged, however, Harrison found success in the field of motion picture production. In 1979 he set up HandMade Films to help a friend, the Monty Python alumnus Eric Idle, produce the English comedy group's religious satire *Life of Brian*. Although widely criticized by religious groups, especially in the United States, the movie was a major success. The company's other projects include the 1981 fantasy hit *Time Bandits*, directed by another Python alumnus, Terry Gilliam; *Privates on Parade* (1984), with John Cleese, also a veteran of the Python group; *Mona Lisa* (1986), an underworld drama starring Bob Hoskins; and *Withnail and I* (1987), about two unemployed young actors. Meanwhile, Harrison continued to make occasional guest appearances in musical programs, including one with his mentor, Carl Perkins, in a 1986 television special entitled *Blue Suede Shoes*. He also played in some benefit concerts, most notably the 1986 Prince's Trust Benefit.

In November 1987, following a five-year absence from the recording studio, Harrison reemerged with *Cloud Nine*, his most successful album since *All Things Must Pass*. Produced by Jeff Lynne, it embraced the lighter sides of Harrison's musical influences. In addition to "When We Was Fab," both a tribute to and satire of the dense psychedelic sound pioneered by the Beatles, the album contained several upbeat pop numbers, including "This Is Love," "That's What It Takes," and "Fish in the Sand." The song that sparked the album's rise on the *Billboard* charts, however, was "Got My Mind Set on You," an obscure song from the early 1960s written by Rudy Clark that Harrison had heard on his first visit to the United States. His revival of it on *Cloud Nine* was characterized by a lean, taut arrangement featuring crisp, emphatic guitars, a muscular saxophone break, and an ebullient vocal by the former "quiet Beatle." Both the song, which reached number one on the charts, and the accompanying music video were praised by audiences for showing a lighthearted side of Harrison that had only been glimpsed previously.

The following year Harrison joined Jeff Lynne, Tom Petty, Bob Dylan, and Roy Orbison on the best-selling album *Traveling Wilburys, Vol. 1*. Among Harrison's contributions to the album were the songs "Handle with Care" and "End of the Line," which one reviewer described as "buoyant enough" to serve as "the national cheerer-upper." "There's no effort to achieve the intensity of Dylan at his darkest, the transcendence of the Beatles at their brightest, or even the energy of Petty at his toughest," David Gates wrote in his review of the album for *Newsweek* (November 28, 1988). "But the Wilburys have managed to hit upon a versatile, almost neutral style—not too bluesy, not too pop-pish—to frame five first-rate voices and ten first-rate songs." All in all, he concluded, *Traveling Wilburys* "has turned out to be one of the year's best records." Harrison's most recent release is *Best of Dark Horse 1976-1989*, which includes fifteen cuts from his five solo albums on the Dark Horse label, among them the hit singles "Crackerbox Palace," "Blow Away," and "All Those Years Ago," and two new numbers, "Poor Little Girl" and "Cockamamie Business."

George Harrison, who has thick brown hair that is slightly graying, a thin beard and mustache, and a lean, slender figure, has been moving gracefully into middle-age. A prolific gardener, he enjoys planting the grounds of Friar Park, the huge estate he has owned since 1969, dominated by an enor-

mous mansion buit by the nineteenth-century ec-centric Sir Francis Crisp. He reserves as much time as he can for his wife, Olivia, and their son, Dhani, and he speaks with pleasure—as an aging rock-'n'-roller—of the boy's discovery of the popular music of the 1950s after seeing the movie *Teen Wolf*.

References: Film Comment 24:22+ My-Je '88 por; Harpers 267:42+ D '83; McCall's 115:32+ Ap '88 pors; Newsweek 76:85+ S 7 '70 por, 110:92 O 26 '87 por; People 15:40+ F 23 '81 por, 25:32+ Mr 24 '86 pors, 28:62+ O 19 '87 pors; Pulse p60+ D '87; Rolling Stone p36+ O 22 '87 por, p47+ N 5-D 10 '87 por; Brown, Peter, and Gaines, Steven. Love You Make; An Insider's Story of the Beatles (1983); Davies, Hunter. The Beatles (1968); Harrison, George. I Me Mine (1980); International Who's Who, 1989-90; Norman, Philip. Shout! The Beatles in Their Generation (1981); Who's Who in America, 1988-89

Hayes, Robert M(ichael)

Nov. 12, 1952– Lawyer; social activist. Address: b. O'Melveny & Myers, 153 E. 53d St., New York, N.Y. 10022; h. 533 E. 87th St., New York, N.Y. 10128

Through class-action lawsuits, Robert M. Hayes, for seven years the counsel for the National Coalition for the Homeless, forced government officials and the general public to address the mounting problems of the homeless, a group numbering three to four million in 1988, according to Coalition

estimates. Hayes began his crusade in the late 1970s, when he started to talk to the homeless on his way to work and discovered that they preferred the streets to the shelters provided by New York City. In 1980 Hayes won his first lawsuit on behalf of the homeless, which established the right to shelter for homeless men. In 1982 he gave up a promising career with a prestigious Wall Street law firm to work full-time for the National Coalition for the Homeless, which he founded in 1980. Focusing on the problems of New York City, whose homeless population increased to between 60,000 and 80,000 in 1988, Hayes filed a dozen lawsuits establishing the right to shelter for women, children, and families, the right to vote, and expanded services for different segments of the homeless population, including veterans, AIDS patients, and the mentally ill.

"I think it's fair to say that nothing interested the city less in 1979 than increasing services to the homeless," Hayes commented in a 1982 interview. "So, in the process, I learned a very important lesson: public bureaucracies do not respond to need. . . . They respond to pressure." Meanwhile, Hayes stepped up his efforts to press for more-permanent solutions to the homeless problem. "It is no exaggeration to say that there is a three-word solution to homelessness: housing, housing, housing," Hayes emphasized. Urban renewal has forced the poor onto the streets, Hayes and other social advocates have contended, while the federal government has cut its housing budget from $31 billion in 1981 to $7.3 billion in 1987. Hayes established a Washington, D.C., office in 1985 to work with Congress on legislation dealing with the homeless. That office helped draft and lobby on behalf of the Stewart B. McKinney Homeless Assistance Act, passed in 1987, and it helped write the Permanent Housing for Homeless Americans Act, which was introduced in Congress in January 1989.

Robert Michael Hayes was born in Brooklyn, New York on November 12, 1952, but he grew up in the Long Island suburb of Valley Stream, where his family moved shortly after his birth. His father, a businessman, died when he was twelve. His mother, a substitute teacher, raised the family in a traditional, middle-class Roman Catholic manner. Although she "would bridle at being described as a feminist," Hayes has said, his mother supported his social activism and kept the books for the National Coalition for the Homeless in its early days.

At Georgetown University in Washington, D.C., Hayes majored in English and wrote news and sports stories for the *Hoya*, the student newspaper, eventually becoming the paper's editor in chief. He also worked on the staff of *Georgetown Today*, the university's public relations magazine, and as an assistant editor of *Passenger Transport*, a trade paper published by the American Public Transit Association.

After graduating, cum laude, from Georgetown in 1973, Hayes took a job as an investigative reporter for the weekly *Long Island Catholic Newspaper*. After a sympathetically written article on the gay rights movement almost got him fired, he concentrated on issues that the church's hierarchy was concerned about, such as mental health and social service policy. It was through investigating those issues that Hayes became acquainted with New York State's policy of deinstitutionalization, or the discharge of mental patients from psychiatric institutions, regardless of whether they had a home or family. That policy was to have major repercussions on the problem of homelessness.

In 1975 Hayes entered New York University School of Law and began working part-time for New York City Councilman Carter Burden, who was then chairman of the council's Health Committee and for whom Hayes drafted advocacy papers on health insurance and nursing-home scandals. He also spent a semester as a volunteer legal aide for an antipoverty agency on New York City's slum-ridden Lower East Side, handling welfare and housing complaints. Hayes earned academic distinction at NYU, where he was a finalist in the law school's moot-court competition and an editor of the NYU *Law Review*. In 1976 he became a summer associate at Sullivan & Cromwell, the prestigious Wall Street law firm, which retained such blue-chip clients as Exxon, General Electric, and General Foods. Hayes made such a good impression researching antitrust and securities cases that the firm asked him back, and, after graduating in the top 5 percent of his class and passing the bar exam in 1977, he became a full-time associate, specializing in antitrust and securities litigation.

It was as a lawyer with Sullivan & Cromwell in the late 1970s that Hayes first became aware of the growing number of homeless men sleeping in doorways and panhandling for money. On his way to the subway from his apartment in New York City's Chelsea district, he passed the same homeless men every day. When cold weather set in, he wondered why they remained in the street and how they survived. "I shared the common myth about them," he told a reporter for *Time* (February 2, 1982) magazine. "I assumed that they lived on the street by choice." His curiosity aroused, Hayes visited the city-owned men's shelter and nearby flophouses on the Bowery in Lower Manhattan. "It was shocking," he told a reporter for the *American Bar Association Journal* (April 1984). "There were 250 men sleeping practically one on top of the other in one large room." The men slept on urine-stained cots separated by chicken wire, and there was no attempt to segregate the criminal and mentally deranged from the rest of the population. When all the beds were taken, the men were bused to an abandoned women's prison in the Catskill Mountains. So bad were the conditions in those shelters, Hayes told the reporter for *Time*, that many men "found life on the streets less degrading and safer than staying in those places."

Hayes's initial curiosity turned into indignation, and in early 1979 he approached one of Sullivan & Cromwell's partners, Roy Steyer, about doing some pro bono work on behalf of the homeless. Banking on the premise that his Sullivan & Cromwell connection would help him influence city officials, Hayes initially planned to lobby for more beds and for more-humane shelters. As he told Steven Brill during an interview for *Esquire* (December 1984), he hoped that "by talking to city officials about what was going on, they would be moved to do something." Hayes found out subsequently that city officials were willing to listen to him, but they were not prepared to act on his admonitions. In fact, Hayes told Steven Brill, one official said that shelter conditions were deliberately kept "forbidding" to "encourage these people to make other arrangements for themselves."

That remark unleashed the full force of Hayes's outrage. "It was then that I got angry," Hayes told Brill. "And when lawyers get angry, they can only think of one thing"—a lawsuit. Hayes found a clause in New York State's constitution stating that "the aid, care and support of the needy are public concerns and shall be provided by the state . . . as the legislature may from time to time determine." Basing his legal argument on that provision, the New York City municipal code, and the Equal Protection Clause of the United States Constitution, Hayes decided to file a class-action suit demanding that the city provide clean and safe shelter for every person who requests it. Sullivan & Cromwell allowed Hayes to research the case on the firm's time and provided him with another associate and a paralegal to help prepare the case. "It was really the last resort," Hayes recalled to the reporter for *Time*. "The homeless had no friends in government, formed no constituency. Someone had to help."

In preparing the lawsuit, Hayes drew on research conducted by Kim Hopper and Ellen Baxter, who had interviewed hundreds of homeless men for the Community Service Society of New York. He also recruited one of the homeless, Robert Callahan, to back up their evidence. Callahan, an alcoholic fifty-three-year-old World War II veteran, had lost his job, then his apartment, and was turned down for welfare assistance because he did not have a legal residence. Hayes filed *Callahan v. (Governor Hugh L.) Carey and (Mayor Edward I.) Koch* in the New York State Supreme Court in October 1979. (That case marked the first time that Hayes had ever acted as lead lawyer.) On December 5, 1979 the New York State Supreme Court Justice Andrew Tyler issued a preliminary injunction in favor of the plaintiffs, ordering the city to provide shelter to all who requested it. "We were shocked to get the injunction," Wendy Addiss, the associate who worked with Hayes on the case, told Steven Brill. "It was an incredible landmark win."

The city responded by opening additional shelters, which Hayes contended were no better than the old ones, and he was forced to return to court a number of times to force the city and the state to provide adequate food, shelter, and health care. In August 1980, before a final decision on the suit was reached, city and state officials signed a consent decree agreeing to the conditions under which the homeless would be sheltered. Six weeks later—and many times thereafter—Hayes was back in court to make sure the defendants held up their end of the agreement. (The final decision was handed down in January 1981.) By the winter of 1984 the city provided some 6,000 beds for the homeless, representing three times the number available in 1979, but Hayes still contended that conditions in the shelters were far from adequate. Callahan, meanwhile, was found dead in the street, as a result of natural causes, according to authorities.

In the summer of 1980, as the New York City police prepared to clean up Madison Square Garden and Penn Station in preparation for the Democratic National Convention, Hayes established the National Coalition for the Homeless. He and other social activists persuaded a church to open up for the homeless, who were forced to vacate the convention site, and he invited the media to document the event. "We ended up on the *Today* show, and when people called the show and asked where they could send contributions, we had to have an organization, so we formed the coalition," Hayes told Steven Brill. Hayes gave himself the title of counsel to the coalition. "I think it's good for me to present myself as a lawyer," he explained to Brill. "It makes me seem more responsible, more mainstream." With that identity, Hayes was able to secure funding from Exxon, the Morgan Guaranty Trust Company, and other blue-chip corporations. "How could we not fund this Sullivan & Cromwell lawyer who was taking care of the most untaken-care-of people in society," one executive queried Brill. "He was irresistible."

By his own account, Hayes began living a double life, working at Sullivan & Cromwell, which catered to the elite, during the day and touring flophouses to consult with his homeless clients at night. "You see the affluent people and utter poverty of others," Hayes told Robin Herman of the *New York Times* (August 30, 1981). "It requires a lot of long walks at night to try to understand." Meanwhile, Hayes's lawsuit gave him national prominence, and homeless advocates in different cities, including Chicago, Columbus, and Portland, Maine, began asking him for advice about helping the homeless in their areas. In February 1982 Hayes resigned from Sullivan & Cromwell to organize and work full-time for the National Coalition for the Homeless. In choosing to devote his career to that cause, Hayes accepted a 50 percent cut in his $40,000-a-year salary and moved from a luxurious office overlooking New York Harbor to a dingy space looking out on an airshaft. He also gave up the chance to become a full partner at Sullivan & Cromwell, a position that would have assured him an income of over $300,000 a year. "I realized what I wanted to do in life, so I did it," Hayes told Brill.

At the time that Hayes began aiding the homeless in earnest, in the early 1980s, the public was becoming increasingly aware of the dispossessed as a group, as their numbers began to escalate, from the tens of thousands to some three or four million in 1988, according to National Coalition for the Homeless estimates, and as their demographics changed from predominantly male to include women, children, and entire families. Among the causes for that increase were the 1982 recession, repercussions from neighborhood gentrification and urban renewal, the loss of manufacturing jobs, and overcrowding in mental hospitals leading to the release of patients. But the chief culprit, according to Hayes and other homeless advocates, was the lack of affordable housing. "Ever since 1947 the federal government has been committed to low-income housing, but the Reagan administration has abdicated from that commitment by budgeting far less than previous administrations for the construction of new public housing units," Hayes pointed out to George M. Anderson in an interview for *America* (December 24, 1983). "There are 600,000 people on the waiting list in New York, so it's almost worthless to apply. . . . But public housing is, by and large, an idea that works."

As full-time counsel to the National Coalition for the Homeless, Hayes lobbied politicians and provided publicity, fund-raising, and legal advice to the Coalition's local chapters. From a budget of $75,000 in 1982, the nonprofit coalition grew by 1989 into a $1.2 million operation, with corporations and private foundations providing about half of its funding and government subsidies supplying the rest. A Washington, D.C., office was established in November 1985 to work more closely with Congress on legislation concerning the homeless.

The principal target of Hayes's advocacy, however, remained New York City, against which he brought more than a dozen lawsuits, using the pro bono services of some of the city's top law firms. He established a separate New York Coalition for the Homeless to operate such social services as soup kitchens, lunch programs for families living in welfare hotels, and a summer camp for homeless children. The New York coalition also continued to press the city for more beds and better shelter conditions through lawsuits.

In addition to expanding the right to shelter on demand to women and children, Hayes's legal efforts have won for the homeless the right to vote, better conditions for boarder babies (infants who remain in hospitals until they are placed in a foster home), social services for older children who are leaving foster care, counseling and day-care services for homeless families, and "medically appropriate housing" for sufferers of AIDS. The New York coalition has sued the city and state several times over the discharge of mental patients without offering them a placement in a community residence. The situation in New York City has been exacerbated by the demolition of single room occupancy hotels (SROs), where many of the poor live, and their conversion into expensive condominiums and office space. In an Op-Ed article that appeared in the New York Times (November 27, 1986), Hayes criticized the "generous city tax breaks" offered to developers and the ease with which poor people could be evicted from the SROs into the street. Since 1971, Hayes estimated, 100,000 SRO apartments had been demolished due to the pressures of real-estate development. "The social fallout can be measured in the one-third of the homeless in shelters who list a SRO as their last address," Hayes wrote. Properly maintained and operated, Hayes continued, SRO hotels could offer a supportive environment.

In November 1987 Hayes acknowledged that New York City had become "clearly more responsible" in dealing with the homeless, due to "public insistence." One day in November, as Josh Barbanel reported in the New York Times (November 23, 1987), the city housed 8,513 single men in fourteen shelters and six lodging houses, 1,235 single women in eleven shelters, and 17,626 parents and children in thirty-five shelters and fifty-eight hotels. The city's budget for dealing with the homeless was $543 million in 1987—more than the city of Buffalo's entire municipal budget—and up from $362 million in 1986.

Now that the city had an elaborate shelter system in place, Hayes told Barbanel, it was time to shift the focus to more permanent solutions. Hayes was especially critical of the city's practice of pouring money into short-term shelters at the expense of upgrading and preserving abandoned tenement apartments and building new low-income housing. An interim plan, developed by the New York coalition with the archdiocese of New York and the Community Service Society, called for a hotel preservation law, which would establish a hotel housing commission. That commission would identify hotels that could be acquired and leased to nonprofit groups "who would operate them as caring, affordable residences," Hayes suggested in his New York Times Op-Ed piece. In situations where hotel owners were intent on converting their properties, the commission could allocate city funds to build permanent replacement apartments for the dispossessed tenants. Instead of the large barracks-style shelters, Hayes advocated small community-based shelters to allow homeless people to remain in their neighborhoods and specialized shelters to provide social services for families with children, veterans, drug addicts, the mentally ill, and the elderly.

In spite of his establishment credentials, Hayes worked as an outsider in his pursuit of reform. "You have to do enough preaching for people to care," he explained to Suzanne Daley of the New York Times (October 2, 1987). Then "you have to get something concrete"—a legislative victory or a court order. Finally, "you have to keep at it. If they miss a deadline, you sue." Those aggressive tactics, as well as his impatience with the public bureaucracy, made Hayes a controversial figure. Representatives of social service agencies accused him of being publicity-hungry and disdainful of their own work on behalf of the homeless. And New York City officials said that he underestimated their efforts. In 1984 Brendan Sexton, the director of the Mayor's Office of Operations, charged that Hayes was firing "preemptive legal strikes" at the Koch administration. "His effect on our decisions has become almost null because we assume he will sue us no matter what we do," Sexton told the reporter for the American Bar Association Journal. But State Supreme Court Justice Richard Wallach told the same reporter that "persistence and devotion are what prevailed against endless excuses from the bureaucracy." Hayes criticized Cardinal O'Connor for not addressing the problem of homeless pregnant women, attacked the Red Cross about the conditions of its shelters, and organized a picket line outside the home of George Clark, the chairman of the New York State Republican party, after Clark complained that homeless shelters would lead to drunks wandering the streets. The picket signs read "Homeless kids don't drink beer."

To Mayor Koch's charge that he and other homeless advocates were "urban guerrillas" trying "to bring down the whole system," Hayes and Kim Hopper responded, in a letter to the New York Times (February 13, 1988), that the policies that Koch was then taking credit for were first promoted by groups like theirs, such as low-cost drop-in centers offering food and clinical attention; shelters designed to meet the special needs of sub-populations of the homeless, such as the mentally ill, veterans, and the elderly; and the conversion of some of the city's vacant housing stock into low-rent apartments.

In 1986 the National Coalition for the Homeless initiated the Homeless Person's Survival Act, which was introduced by Senator Albert Gore Jr. Although the bill was not enacted, several of its measures became part of subsequent legislation. The Washington, D.C., staff of the coalition helped draft and push through Congress the Stewart B. McKinney Homeless Assistance Act, which Congress passed in July 1987, authorizing more than $1 billion for emergency and transitional shelters, permanent housing for the elderly, and increased health care, education, and job training. The actual amount Congress eventually allotted was $700 million over a two-year period, but Hayes and other advocates still called the bill a breakthrough. The coalition sued the Reagan administration several times to adhere to the provisions of the act. In December 1987 Congress passed a housing bill authorizing the Department of Housing and Urban Development to offer subsidies to an additional 152,000 families and to renovate 10,000 public housing apartments. It was the first such piece of legislation since 1981.

During the presidential campaign of 1988, the National Coalition for the Homeless asked the presidential candidates to support a three-point plan calling for the restoration of federal housing budgets to pre-Reagan levels, a federal guarantee of decent emergency shelters, and an executive order to enforce programs to aid the homeless. President George Bush appeared to have heard and acted on that message. In February 1989 Hayes accompanied Jack F. Kemp, the newly appointed secretary of housing and urban development, on a tour to visit the homeless in Baltimore and Philadelphia. "I'm looking at Jack Kemp as my client," Hayes told Sara Rimer for the *New York Times* (February 26, 1989). "My job is to make him the best possible advocate with the president, with Congress, with the Office of Management and Budget." He added: "Kemp said he was committed to preserving that housing stock. He said he didn't know how, but that it had to be done."

Over the years Hayes has expressed uneasiness at being the spokesman for a group of "totally disenfranchised people." "They can rightly challenge my legitimacy in that regard, but I try to visit shelters and talk with the homeless about their needs as often as I can," he told the reporter for the *American Bar Association Journal.* He made a point of visiting the shelters once a week. "Seeing homeless people fuels anger, and anger fuels our work," he explained to Suzanne Daley. His efforts have not gone unrewarded. In 1985 he received a MacArthur Foundation Fellowship, an unrestricted five-year grant of $172,000 to carry out the work of his choosing. According to Hayes, the grant money was used mostly to pay his salary. Hayes has also sold the movie rights to his life story, and he plans to funnel the $50,000 he received for that project into the homeless cause.

To the surprise of most observers, on October 1, 1989 Hayes left the Coalition for the Homeless to join the New York City branch of the Los Angeles–based law firm O'Melveny & Myers. "This may sound arrogant or stupid, but I felt I was too young to be a symbol, that I should have a few more years of substance," he explained to David Margolick of the *New York Times* (September 8, 1989). "I love to create lawsuits, but I'd like to spend more time litigating them. It's embarrassing to say this . . . , but I like being a lawyer." At his new firm, Hayes is a "special counsel," and he is expected to spend about a quarter of his time on public interest cases, including those involving the homeless.

Among the honors Hayes has won are the Outstanding Young Lawyer Award from the New York State Bar Association (1984), the Martin Luther King Jr. Humanitarian Award from the Black Christian Caucus (1985), and, in 1987, the New York Urban League Building Brick Award, the Distinguished Citizen Award from the State University of New York, and the Common Cause Public Service Achievement Award. He has also been the recipient of honorary degrees from Georgetown University, Fordham University, the New School for Social Research, and the University of Pennsylvania Law School.

Described by Steven Brill as "a cheerful but intense" wiry six-footer, Hayes has reddish-brown hair, a scraggly red beard, and wears wire-rimmed glasses that enhance his youthful and scholarly appearance. Brill also depicted Hayes as refreshingly "un-self-righteous" and "unsaintly" in his attitude towards his work and zealously guarded about his private life. He is the unmarried father of an adopted five-year-old daughter and lives in an apartment on New York's Upper East Side. "I live decently and hypocritically . . . ," Hayes told Brill. "I eat more than I need to, while some people starve. But what I think I have accomplished is that I've taken the work away from being exclusively for the saints and the Mother Teresa types and shown that it is something average people can care about and do something about."

References: American Bar Association Journal 70:39+ Ap '84 por; N Y Times E p7 D 12 '82, p25 N 27 '86, B p1 O 2 '87 por, A p1 N 23 '87, IV p4 F 26 '89; Nation 246:846 Je 18 '88; Progressive 46:20 D '82

Hendricks, Barbara

Nov. 20, 1948– Operatic soprano. Address: c/o Opera et Concert, 19 rue Vignon, 75008 Paris, France; Columbia Artists Management, Inc., 165 W. 57th St., New York, N.Y. 10019

For more than fifteen years—ever since she first emerged on the European operatic stage and in the American recital hall—Barbara Hendricks has been regarded as one of the most impressive lyric sopranos of her generation. No less an authority than Herbert von Karajan has compared her to the late Maria Callas in "passion and interpretive possibility," and critics have been virtually unqualified in their praise of her elegance, refinement, and style, especially in French art songs and German lieder. The American-born singer has been adopted by France as one of that country's favorite artists, and she has captivated legions of admirers of her quiet, understated art and personal magnetism across the four continents where her career has carried her.

Barbara Hendricks

Because she believes in "getting down to essentials" both in her musical life and in her profound commitment to social activism, Barbara Hendricks dedicates much of her professional career to concert and recital work and her leisure to Amnesty International and the UN High Commission for Refugees. "I am an anarchist in the sense that I want to tear down the frontiers that we put up to protect ourselves both personally and politically," she once said during an interview.

Barbara Hendricks was born in the small town of Stephens, Arkansas on November 20, 1948—in her grandmother's house, which was about the size of a coffee table, as she recalled in an interview with Barrymore Laurence Scherer for Opera News (August 1988). The daughter of a Methodist minister and an elementary-school teacher, she spent her childhood in many different places, since her father's ministry took the family from town to town throughout the southern border states. "Lots of tiny towns," she told Scherer. "Later, we were in Memphis and Chattanooga, until we finally ended up in Little Rock, where my parents still are."

Her first and only exposure to music came from the church and school choirs with which she sang. "We had no concert hall, no opera. There wasn't even a music station on the radio," she told Scherer. "I always sang in church and school choirs, so my first taste had to be there—Bach cantatas and motets. While I can't say there was a particular moment when I attended a concert, heard a piece and was overwhelmed, music was always around, and I just sang for the pleasure of it." Her education, however, was steered more toward academic subjects such as science and mathematics, both by her teachers and her own inclinations. "I was one of those people who really liked calculus,"

she recalled in an interview with Lon Tuck for the Washington Post (November 11, 1983).

In the fall of 1965 Miss Hendricks entered the University of Nebraska at Lincoln as a combined chemistry and mathematics major. "They'd given me aptitude tests [in high school] and said, 'This girl is good for math,'" she explained to Scherer. "The chairman of the department showed interest in me, and I liked the subjects, so who was I to complain?" In her genuine love of the physical sciences, she still has a lingering fascination for such subjects as quantum mechanics, telling Scherer, "A lot of people might think I'm crazy, but it was fantastic to see Bohr's theory being derived right in front of me."

By her junior year, however, Barbara Hendricks had already begun singing again, whenever the opportunity presented itself. "It was what I called my banquet repertory," she recalled for Lon Tuck, "and my highlights were things like 'Love Is Where You Find It.'" The turning point came when a member of her church choir asked if she could sing at a small annual community gathering in Lincoln. "I was reluctant because it was the night before a physics exam," she told Lon Tuck. "But finally I agreed, if I could go reasonably early in the evening. Well, one of the persons there was a prominent local lawyer named Richard Smith. He apparently liked my singing and he was a trustee of the Aspen Institute of Humanistic Studies and the summer music festival and school. He asked me if I would be interested in attending that summer." Faced with the choice of either studying at the Aspen Music Festival or learning about complex ion substitution during the summer of 1968, she opted for Aspen.

The direction of her life became clear during that summer in Aspen, for she found herself exposed to music and musicians in a way that she had never experienced before, and at a depth that made her painfully aware of her own lack of formal training. That newly discovered shortcoming was mitigated, however, by her introduction to the celebrated mezzo-soprano and specialist in the French song repertoire, Jennie Tourel, as her teacher at Aspen. "I had never heard of her," Hendricks candidly admitted in an interview with Heidi Waleson for the New York Times (October 26, 1986), but she soon found in Jennie Tourel a source of confidence, strength, and inspiration that made it possible for her to make up for the lost years. "I showed up that first day," she remembers, "and it was clear to Miss Tourel that I was not well prepared for the lesson. She let me know that I would have to do better, but she did it in a very nice way. So for nine weeks I studied with her. And at the end she said that she wanted me to come to New York and study with her at Juilliard."

Aware that nineteen was an advanced age at which to start vocal training, Miss Hendricks nevertheless accepted that invitation, but not without first seeking her father's counsel. Although he seemed astonished, he gave his approval. She submitted her application forms with assistance from Jennie Tourel, who attended her audition and accepted her. Barbara Hendricks completed her final year at the University of Nebraska with a blessing from some unexpected quarters, when the music-loving head of the chemistry department waived a requirement because he knew she was headed for Juilliard. During her final academic year, 1968–69, she decided to enter the Metropolitan Opera auditions. Since she knew relatively little about opera, Miss Hendricks learned some arias, including *Madame Butterfly*'s "Un bel dí" and the waltz from *La Rondine* (though she knew no Italian), from a long-playing recording by Leontyne Price. She won the Nebraska auditions but was eliminated at the regionals in Minneapolis. Nevertheless, the fact that she had gotten that far gave her some encouragement.

When Barbara Hendricks arrived at Penn Station in August 1969 she was a musical neophyte, with gaps in her learning that occasionally proved awkward at Juilliard for all concerned, especially since she was attending the school on a full scholarship. "I must have been as much a shock to them as they were to me," she has recalled. "I remember we all had to take at least one instrumental course in the first year, and mine was the piano. And I went in on the first day, and the teacher asked me to play a G-major chord and I said, 'I'm sorry, but I just don't know what that is,' and it was true. I could tell you about quantum theory, but I didn't know about that."

Barbara Hendricks found that situation daunting at first, and the backgrounds and abilities of her fellow students seemed even more intimidating. For one thing, she knew little or nothing about solfège (voice training in which the scales are sung to the sol fa syllables). And she, who had learned to read music in choirs, where most of the rehearsing was done by rote, found herself surrounded by people who had started their musical studies when they were children, people who not only had at their command an intimate knowledge of the titans of music but also an easy familiarity with recordings of their masterworks.

Encouraged by Jennie Tourel's assurances that her voice would permit her to succeed at Juilliard and launch a successful career, she persevered. She settled into her studies after that difficult beginning, helped by what she has called her "normal upbringing" and realistic attitude. "[I knew] that if it wasn't going to happen, I could do other things to make my contribution—medicine was one, and I was also interested in law," she pointed out to Scherer. She applied herself to the areas she was most anxious to learn: harmony, theory, and the study of languages.

In addition to serving as a guiding force behind her work at Juilliard, Jennie Tourel provided Barbara Hendricks with her first opportunity to travel to Europe, where the French soprano conducted master classes every summer. Although Miss Hendricks was also selected to take part in a celebrated series of master classes at Juilliard that were conducted by the legendary soprano Maria Callas, she found those sessions less productive than they

might otherwise have been, owing to the singer's sheer renown. Because of the glare of publicity surrounding the classes and the constant presence of an audience that included such musical luminaries as Sir Rudolf Bing and Elisabeth Schwarzkopf, the actual learning experience, she discovered, was limited.

It was a far different Barbara Hendricks who began entering and winning competitions after studying for some two years at Juilliard. She won the Geneva International Competition in 1971 and followed that in 1972 with first prize in the International Concours de Paris and the Third Biennial Voice Competition of the Kosciuszko Foundation. In 1972 she received a grant from the Sullivan Foundation, and early in 1973 she was one of fourteen recipients of the National Opera Institute's youth singer grants of $5,000.

In February of 1973 Barbara Hendricks performed in the Metropolitan Opera's revival, as part of its "Opera at the Forum" project, of the Virgil Thomson–Gertrude Stein opera *Four Saints in Three Acts* at Lincoln Center's Forum Theatre. In the course of praising the "superb" musical aspects of the overall low-budget production, Michael Feingold of the *Village Voice* (March 3, 1973) gave Miss Hendricks a "special award, for her ability to combine high F's with back bends."

Unfortunately, Miss Hendricks's joy over her early successes was overshadowed by Jennie Tourel's death, on November 23, 1973. "We came together at a time, the last five years of her life, which I sincerely believe she lived for me," she recalled of her teacher in the *New York Times* (October 26, 1986). "We had a strong relationship based on mutual respect and love. I had to go through a difficult struggle, searching for someone to replace her, someone who could say, 'Never mind, this is what's important.' I finally found that person in myself, and when I met my husband, he also gave me that support." She was doing a concert tour of Europe in 1973 when she met young Martin Engstrom, a Swedish-born businessman who was just starting a career in music management, during one of her appearances in Stockholm. The two struck up a friendship, and he became her European manager. At Engstrom's request, she came to Paris for a series of auditions in January of 1977, and they became engaged after his forty-eight-hour courtship. In April of that year, following their marriage, she moved to Paris.

Her more auspicious performances during the 1970s included an appearance at the Glyndebourne Festival, on May 23, 1974, in the title role of Pietro Francesco Cavalli's *La Calisto*, an Italian baroque opera. Writing in the British publication *Opera* (Autumn 1974), Arthur Jacobs faulted her vocal technique, which struck him as being "unfinished and patchy," but he had unreserved praise for her overall portrayal for its "charm" and "virginal innocence so appropriate to the youthful nymph." She scored her first professional American triumph in the Opera Orchestra of New York's concert version of Donizetti's *La Favorita* at Carnegie Hall, which starred Alfredo Kraus and Shirley Verrett, on February 26, 1975. "As [Leonora's] attendant, Inez," Robert Jacobson wrote in *Opera News* (April 19, 1975)," lyric soprano Barbara Hendricks astonished with her luminous high voice and quicksilver technique."

During the summer of 1975 Miss Hendricks sang the role of Clara in a landmark complete recording of the George Gershwin folk opera *Porgy and Bess*, with the Cleveland Orchestra under Lorin Maazel, for London Records. Her staged opera debut took place the following year at the San Francisco Opera, as Drusilla in Monteverdi's *L'Incoronazione di Poppea*, and she appeared later that same year as Amor in Gluck's *Orfeo ed Euridice* with the Netherlands Opera at the 1976 Holland Festival.

During 1975 and 1976 Barbara Hendricks appeared with the Los Angeles Philharmonic and the Philadelphia and Chicago Symphony orchestras. It was as a result of a concert with the Chicagoans, under the conductor Sir Georg Solti, that she was selected to appear in the world premiere of David del Tredici's *Final Alice* in 1976. Commissioned in connection with the American Bicentennial, that hourlong adaptation of Lewis Carroll's *Alice's Adventures in Wonderland* became a celebrated success that she later performed with a half-dozen major American orchestras, including the New York Philharmonic under Erich Leinsdorf at Avery Fisher Hall at Lincoln Center on March 24, 1977. Eighteen months later, in October of 1978, she performed the ingratiating work again, with the Philadelphia Orchestra under Eugene Ormandy at Carnegie Hall, and also took part in the recording of *Final Alice* by Solti and the Chicago Symphony for London Records.

Assisted by the pianist Lawrence Skrobacs and the clarinet virtuoso Richard Stoltzman, Barbara Hendricks made her recital debut at New York's Town Hall on November 14, 1976. The program, which was appropriately dedicated to the memory of Jennie Tourel, featured Schubert's "Der Hirt auf dem Felsen," five poems set by Fauré, Haydn's cantata "Arianna a Naxos," Seiber's *Drei Morgenstern Lieder*, Debussy's *Cinq Poèmes de Baudelaire*, and five songs by Richard Strauss. In reviewing the concert for the *New York Times* (November 15, 1976), Donal Henahan ranked Miss Hendricks "among the few . . . with the intelligence, the schooling, and the vocal finesse to step forward and make a success as recitalists."

Although her success now seemed assured in the United States, she decided to move to Paris in 1977, despite the efforts of friends to dissuade her. Her reply was, "They have orchestras over there, don't they?" She experienced no hiatus in her career, since leading European conductors with whom she had sung were delighted to have her more accessible, and her operatic career, in particular, took off in the years that followed. On December 14, 1978, Miss Hendricks made an auspicious debut with the Berlin Opera as Susanna in a new production of Mozart's *Marriage of Figaro*, con-

ducted by Daniel Barenboim. She later sang the role, which has since become one of her specialties, in Berlin, under Karl Böhm, and at the Aix-en-Provence Festival in France, with Neville Marriner on the podium. She played her first Gilda in Verdi's *Rigoletto* at the 1980 Orange Festival in France, and the following year she made her debut as Pamina in Mozart's *Magic Flute*, also at the Orange Festival.

By the end of the decade Barbara Hendricks was established as a recitalist throughout Europe, making many appearances on the Continent and in the Soviet Union and, less frequently, touring the United States and Japan. She soon found herself in the good graces of many of the world's most celebrated conductors, among them Leonard Bernstein, Carlo Maria Giulini, Claudio Abbado, James Levine, and, most notably, Herbert von Karajan, with whom she developed a close, long-term professional relationship. In addition to touring with both the Vienna and Berlin Philharmonic orchestras, of which Karajan was then music director, Hendricks performed such roles as the First Flower Maiden in Wagner's *Parsifal*, under Karajan at the Salzburg Festival, Donna Elvira in Mozart's *Don Giovanni*, and Liù in Puccini's *Turandot*. "Karajan is a magician," she has said of him. "Before we worked together, I expected him to be authoritarian, but musically I never had to concede anything to him."

Barbara Hendricks's only miscalculation during that period was her decision to turn down the role of the opera singer in the film *Diva* (1982), a French thriller that went on to become a major international hit. "If I had been totally unknown, I would have grabbed it," she explained to one interviewer. "But that was four years ago, and European audiences were familiar with me, and Americans knew my recordings. I thought it might be too confusing." Her screen debut had to wait until the fall of 1988, when she appeared as Mimi in Luigi Comencini's updated film version of Puccini's *La Bohème*, which was conducted by her one-time Juilliard classmate James Conlon.

Although Barbara Hendricks appeared in the United States regularly during the early 1980s, most of her exposure there was as a recitalist. Her few operatic appearances—limited by her own choice to no more than five engagements a year— were with the Boston and Santa Fe Opera companies, where she played Nanetta in Verdi's *Falstaff* and the title role in Janáček's *Cunning Little Vixen*, respectively. She restricts the number of opera performances that she gives each year because she places such a premium on rehearsal time. "I don't come up with instant characterizations or throw in meaningless gestures just to show I'm acting," she told Scherer during her *Opera News* interview. "Rehearsing an opera, it must be awful for the director to watch me, because I do nothing at the beginning but stand with my hands at my side and go where I'm told. Götz Friedrich directed [my first Susanna], and he was very hard on me at the first rehearsal, because he was not used to working that way. I said, 'You're not going to get Susanna out of me today. I hope to approach it in time, but not today.' Toward the dress rehearsal, he realized what I was trying to do, and he later thanked me." When Miss Hendricks made her long-awaited debut at New York's Metropolitian Opera, as Sophie in *Der Rosenkavalier* on October 30, 1986, Donal Henahan, writing in the *New York Times* (November 1, 1986), singled out her voice for its "stratospheric brilliance" and a "purity that came through clearly in the great final trio."

Despite the continuing demand for her work on the operatic stage, Barbara Hendricks has restricted her work even further in recent years to a small number of recitals and concerts, because of her desire to be with her family, pointing out to one interviewer, "It is simply much easier to take a concert in Munich, which is an hour away, than to come here." In addition to the *Turandot* and a Mozart Mass in C, with Herbert von Karajan on Deutsche Grammophon, she sang Susanna in a Philips recording of *The Marriage of Figaro* in 1985, with Neville Marriner and the Academy of St. Martin-in-the-Fields. She began appearing as a recitalist on EMI Records in the early 1980s. Among her most successful discs are a collection of *Negro Spirituals* (1983) accompanied by Dmitri Alexeev, *Mozart Opera and Concert Arias* (1984) with Jeffrey Tate and the English Chamber Orchestra, Villa Lobos's *Bachianas Brasileiras* (1986) with the Royal Philharmonic Orchestra, *Schubert Lieder* (1986) with Radu Lupu, and *Mozart Sacred Arias* (1988) with Marriner and the Academy. She has also recorded Handel's *Xerxes* for the CBS label and *Solomon* for Philips, Carl Orff's *Carmina Burana* for Victor, and Brahms's *German Requiem* for Deutsche Grammophon.

In Europe she remains one of the most visible of performers, with regular recital tours that may take her to Munich, Tel Aviv, and Strasbourg, and then back to Paris, Lyons, and Zurich. Her adoption of France as her second homeland has been repaid in kind by its people and government. During 1986, in addition to winning a French Grammy award, she was made a commandeur of the Ordre des Arts et des Lettres by the French government, and her appearance as guest host on the television show *Grand Echiquier* brought that popular three-hour interview and variety program the highest ratings in its history. In 1987 she was made Goodwill Ambassador to the UN High Commission for Refugees.

Although she continues to limit her operatic appearances ("I can't live on a steady diet of opera," she told a *New York Times* interviewer on the eve of her Met debut; "it drives me nuts"), Miss Hendricks is satisfied with her Mozart roles and has found room in her repertoire for such French operatic roles as Mélisande, Juliette, and Leila in *Les Pêcheurs de Perles*, as well as parts in less familiar operas, such as Lalo's *Le Roi d'Ys* and Chabrier's *Le Roi Malgré Lui*. Among the operatic roles that she would like to undertake in the future are Violetta in *La Traviata*, the Countess in *Capriccio*, and the Marschallin in *Der Rosenkavalier*.

Barbara Hendricks is a tall, attractive woman whose appearance prompted Barrymore Laurence Scherer to open his *Opera News* article with the flat statement: "Given her looks, she might have become a model." She and her husband, Martin Engstrom, have two children: a seven-year-old son, Sebastian, and a four-year-old daughter, Jennie, who is named in honor of her mother's beloved mentor. They live in Switzerland, where Engstrom keeps in constant touch with his Paris business by telex. In her rare leisure moments, Barbara Hendricks, an avid gourmet, enjoys cooking as a respite from her music and social activism.

References: N Y Times II p21+ O 26 '86 pors; Opera N 53:8+ Ag '88 pors; Ovation 10:31+ Ap '89 por; Washington Post C p1+ N 11 '83 por; International Who's Who, 1989-90; Who's Who in America, 1988-89

Hershey, Barbara

Feb. 5, 1948– Actress. Address: c/o Creative Artists Agency, 1888 Century Park East, Los Angeles, Calif. 90067

The roller-coaster career of the actress Barbara Hershey reached its peak in 1988, when, for her performance as a crusading South African journalist in the film *A World Apart*, she received an unprecedented second consecutive award for best actress at the prestigious Cannes Film Festival. (Miss Hershey had won the prize in 1987 for her portrayal of a Louisiana bayou woman in *Shy People*.) The back-to-back honors represented a remarkable comeback for an actress who, as recently as the early 1980s, had been reduced to accepting work in made-for-television movies. The critically acclaimed film *The Stunt Man*, in which she, appropriately enough, portrayed an actress, set Miss Hershey's career back on course in 1980, and she subsequently appeared in a string of successful films, including *The Right Stuff*, *The Natural*, *Hannah and Her Sisters*, and *Hoosiers*. Barbara Hershey's natural sensuality and her intuitive understanding of the subtleties of characterization are considered her greatest professional assets. "She's very unusual as an actress in that she's a leading-lady type who's a character actress underneath," Richard Rush, her director in *The Stunt Man*, once observed, as quoted by Ron Rosenbaum in a profile of Miss Hershey for *American Film* (May 1986). "It gives her that chameleonlike quality of being able to embody whatever fantasies are projected on her. She's really the ideal dream girl."

Barbara Hershey was born Barbara Herzstein on February 5, 1948 in Los Angeles, California, the youngest, by nine years, of the three children of Arnold Herzstein and his wife. Her father, a Jew from New York City's Lower East Side, was a handicapper and columnist for the *Daily Racing Form*; her mother, who was of Irish descent and a Presbyterian, was originally from Arkansas. Reared in a middle-class section of Hollywood, Barbara Herzstein became interested in acting at an early age and, by her own account, never aspired to any other profession. "It was all I ever, ever wanted to do since I can remember," she told Mike Downey in an interview for a *Gentlemen's Quarterly* (November 1987) profile. "I'd go home from the movies and act out the characters. I lived in a fantasy world. Whenever anyone asked, 'What do you want to do?' I would say, 'I'm an actress.' I didn't say I wanted to *be* an actress. So I always felt very blessed. . . . It was a comfort to know that sort of passion so young." Indeed her interest in acting was so intense that her family nicknamed her "Sarah Bernhardt," after the legendary French actress.

At Hollywood High School, Barbara Herzstein was a diligent student and a member of the pom-pom squad and the drama club. A shy teenager, she had few friends and dated infrequently, choosing to devote most of her time and energy to playing leading roles in student theatrical productions, among them Lady Macbeth and Martha in Edward Albee's *Who's Afraid of Virginia Woolf?* Recognizing her gift, Miss Herzstein's drama teacher recommended her to a Hollywood talent agent when she was just seventeen years old. The agent changed his young client's surname to Hershey and lined up guest spots for her on such television series as *Gidget* and *The Farmer's Daughter*. In 1966, shortly after she graduated from high school, having completed the requirements in only two and a half years, Miss Hershey landed the part of Kathy on the ABC-TV drama series *The Monroes*. The story of a pioneer family, *The Monroes* failed to attract an audience and was canceled after one season.

By this time, Barbara Hershey's parents had moved to the nearby city of Fullerton, where they opened a children's clothing store. Miss Hershey remained in Hollywood to pursue her fledgling career. Over the next two years, she appeared in episodes of a number of television series, including *The Invaders*, *Daniel Boone*, *High Chaparral*, and the dramatic anthologies *CBS Playhouse* and the *Bob Hope Chrysler Theater*. In 1968 Miss Hershey made her film debut as the daughter Stacey in the family comedy *With Six You Get Egg Roll*, starring Brian Keith and Doris Day. A year later, after playing a bit part in the western *Heaven with a Gun* (1968), she essayed her first starring role—the flirtatious, foulmouthed Sandy in *Last Summer*, Frank Perry's film adaptation of Evan Hunter's novel of the same name. The story of bored upper-middle-class teenagers who, while vacationing at the seashore with their families, corrupt a vulnerable girl, *Last Summer* created considerable public controversy for its explicit rape scene. According to Vincent Canby, who reviewed the film for the *New York Times* (June 11, 1969), "The best thing about the movie . . . are the performances that Perry has gotten from his new players, who manage to seem variously awkward and strident, dense and dumb, and sometimes very innocent, without ever being self-conscious about it."

With a critically acclaimed movie under her belt by the age of twenty-one, Barbara Hershey looked forward to a promising future as a film actress, but her reaction to a seemingly trivial incident during the location shooting of *Last Summer* had a profound (and largely negative) effect on her career. As she explained to an interviewer for the *New York Times* in 1973: "[There was a scene] where I had to throw the bird up in the air, trying to make it fly. The trained bird was very special. I felt her spirit. But we had to reshoot the scene over and over. I knew she was exhausted, and I told Frank Perry that I couldn't throw her again; and he told me on the last throw she had broken her neck. At that moment I felt her soul enter me. I didn't tell anybody for a long time. I just realized, finally, that the only honest, moral thing would be to change my name." Accordingly, Barbara Hershey became Barbara Seagull.

The name change (which turned out to be temporary) signaled the beginning of what has since become known as Barbara Hershey's "hippie phase." Late in 1969 the actress moved into a rustic log cabin in the Hollywood Hills with the actor David Carradine, whom she had met on the set of *Heaven with a Gun*. Her well-publicized unconventional lifestyle, which included, for a time, taking peyote—"It's been good for me, helped me to see things truthfully," she told a reporter for *Look* (November 3, 1970)—caused the Hollywood establishment to brand Miss Hershey a "flake." Her "flaky" image was reinforced in 1973, when she bore Carradine a son out of wedlock and gave him the rather offbeat name of Free. In recent years the actress has expressed great reluctance to discuss this period of her life, but, in a conversation with

Ron Rosenbaum for his *American Film* profile, she explained: "I was just doing what thousands of other young Americans were doing. . . . It's a little tiny part of my life that got for some reason put under a microscope. But it became dangerous then, because I never wanted to be a personality; I always wanted just to be an actress. I never wanted to tell other people how to live. I was just living my life."

Although she continued to work regularly in films throughout the early 1970s, Miss Hershey encountered increasing difficulty in securing roles worthy of her talent. Her screen credits for that period include a starring role in James Bridges's *Baby Maker* (1970), about a carefree young woman who agrees, for a fee, to bear a baby for a childless couple, and the part of the wife of a southern bigot in *The Liberation of L. B. Jones* (1970), the last film by the noted director William Wyler. *The Pursuit of Happiness* (1971), under Robert Mulligan's direction, featured Miss Hershey as the girlfriend of a rebellious young man who is imprisoned for accidentally killing a jaywalker with his car. She filled a similar role in Paul Williams's *Dealing: or The Berkeley-to-Boston Forty-Brick Lost-Bag Blues* (1972), in which she appeared as the girlfriend of a Harvard law student who makes extra money by transporting marijuana between Boston and Berkeley, California. After pointing out the film's faults in his review for the *New York Times* (February 26, 1972), Vincent Canby nonetheless conceded that "it treats its characters with such deadpanned comic affection that I found it appealing."

Perhaps the most notable of Miss Hershey's credits during the early 1970s was *Boxcar Bertha* (1972), Martin Scorsese's first studio film, in which she played the title character, a Depression-era drifter who falls in love with a labor agitator, portrayed by David Carradine. In his *American Film* profile of the actress, Ron Rosenbaum termed Miss Hershey's performance in *Boxcar Bertha* "amazing," adding, "She radiates a kind of incandescent sensuality." By the mid-1970s, however, many casting directors had begun to shy away from Miss Hershey. The few roles she snared were in such forgettable motion pictures as *The Crazy World of Julius Vrooder* (1974), *Diamonds* (1975), and *The Last Hard Men* (1976). In search of work, she also ventured into made-for-television movies, appearing in, among others, *Flood* (1976), *Sunshine Christmas* (1977), and *A Man Called Intrepid* (1979).

Barbara Hershey's career rebounded in 1978, when the director Richard Rush, ignoring the wishes of his financial backers, selected the actress to play Nina Franklin, the female lead in his unconventional action comedy *The Stunt Man*. "He cast me when no one else would," Miss Hershey told Jeff Silverman of the *Chicago Tribune* (March 22, 1987). "He fought for me when no one else wanted me. I'll be forever grateful for that." Released in 1980, Rush's fast-paced and wickedly comic satire about filmmaking starred Steve Railsback as Cameron, a Vietnam veteran on the run from the police who accidentally wanders onto a movie set, Peter O'Toole as the egomaniacal director who hires Cameron to replace a stunt man killed while attempting to perform a particularly risky stunt, and Miss Hershey as the leading lady with whom Cameron falls in love. "It may be the most original American movie of the year," David Ansen wrote in *Newsweek* (September 1, 1980). "It's funny, fast, literate, and audacious." Among *The Stunt Man's* many other admirers were Jay Scott of the Toronto *Globe and Mail*, the syndicated film critic Rex Reed, and the *New Yorker's* Pauline Kael, who described the film as "a virtuoso piece of moviemaking." The few reviewers who commented on Miss Hershey's performance did so negatively. Nevertheless, *The Stunt Man* was the first of her films to win general critical acclaim since *Last Summer*. More important, the film marked her transition from "ingénue" roles to women's roles, as she has pointed out to several interviewers.

In *Take This Job and Shove It* (1981), about a corporate executive who returns to his hometown to oversee the modernization of a brewery that his company has recently purchased, Miss Hershey appeared as the executive's former girlfriend, with whom he rekindles a romance. She had a more substantial part in *The Entity* (1983), an offbeat horror film in which she portrayed a single mother who is repeatedly beaten and sexually assaulted by an invisible force. Both of these films received mixed, though mostly unfavorable, notices.

With the release, in October 1983, of *The Right Stuff*, however, Barbara Hershey's career entered a new phase. One of the year's top box-office attractions, it was the first in a series of major motion pictures which, collectively, helped establish Miss Hershey as one of the country's most accomplished young actresses. Based on Tom Wolfe's 1979 bestseller, *The Right Stuff* chronicles the early days of the American space program. In the supporting role of Glennis Yeager, the independent, free-spirited wife of test pilot Chuck Yeager, played by Sam Shepard, she turned in a memorable portrayal that was described by one reviewer as "bewitching." She was equally unforgettable in *The Natural* (1984), Barry Levinson's film adaptation of Bernard Malamud's allegorical novel about the rise and fall of a gifted baseball player. Cast as Harriet Bird, the mysterious seductress who lures the young athlete Roy Hobbs (Robert Redford) to her hotel room, then inexplicably shoots him and leaps out the window to her death, leaving Hobbs physically and psychically wounded, Miss Hershey brought "a hint of deviltry to the small, key role," as Pauline Kael observed in the *New Yorker* (May 28, 1984). "She looks dangerously chic in her twenties clothes, and her veneered face says, Boy, do I have a surprise for you."

Barbara Hershey was surrounded by an all-star cast in Woody Allen's Chekhovian comedy-drama *Hannah and Her Sisters* (1986), in which she took the part of Lee, the youngest and prettiest of a trio of neurotic, emotionally dependent sisters. Over the course of the film, Lee, feeling increasingly trapped by her relationship with an eccentric middle-aged painter, willfully embarks on an adulterous romance with her brother-in-law, portrayed by Michael Caine. Allen explained his selection of Miss Hershey for the role to Ron Rosenbaum: "I wanted somebody that, the minute you saw her, the audience could feel without any convincing and dialogue that a guy could lose his heart over her, and I think she has that quality. . . . She's got a built-in attractive quality that immediately makes the character come to life. It's an earthy sensuality." The critics agreed with Allen's assessment of Miss Hershey's appeal. In her *New Yorker* (February 24, 1986) review, Pauline Kael asserted: "Barbara Hershey has a luscious presence here. She has a sexual vibrancy about her, and she fits her role—it's easy to believe that her brother-in-law would become obsessed with her." Gene Siskel, writing in the *Chicago Tribune* (February 7, 1986), concurred, adding that Miss Hershey "never has been better."

In her next film, *Hoosiers* (1986), David Anspaugh's tale of an Indiana high school basketball team's quest for the state championship in 1951, she convincingly portrayed a spinsterish teacher who initially dislikes but eventually warms to the school's unorthodox new coach, played by Gene Hackman. To prepare for the role, she told Myra Forsberg of the *New York Times* (March 29, 1987), "I tried to find the parts of me that were in her—she's very angry and she's very repressed and she's very unhappy. She never took the chance to leave the town and evolve . . . , and because of that she lives vicariously through her students."

The female lead in *Tin Men* (1987), Barry Levinson's comedy, set in the 1960s, about two aluminum-siding salesmen (Danny DeVito and Richard Dreyfuss) locked in a battle of wills, Barbara Hershey gave a highly praised performance as Nora, DeVito's unhappy wife. Vincent Canby, in his critique for the *New York Times* (July 17, 1988), called Nora the film's "humane, comic conscience. Without her no-nonsense presence," he continued, "Mr. Levinson's male-chauvinist jokes would turn unbearably sour. Something in Miss Hershey's personality *allows* those jokes to be funny. She gives the impression of being ahead of them, not impervious to insult and betrayal, but so indomitable that it would take bigger men than either Mr. DeVito or Richard Dreyfuss to defeat her."

Although neither of Miss Hershey's next two films was a major hit at the box office, the critical reaction to *Shy People* (1987) and *A World Apart* (1988) established the actress as a major star. *Shy People*, directed by Andrei Konchalovsky, starred Miss Hershey as Ruth Sullivan, an impoverished, illiterate Louisiana bayou woman struggling to raise her four sons by herself. For her touching performance, Miss Hershey received the award for best actress at the 1987 Cannes Film Festival. "[Barbara] Hershey's Ruth Sullivan is a complete performance based not only on good acting but the telling fine detail of a style of hair, a manner of

walking, a dress sense, and even false teeth," Allan Hunter observed in *Films & Filming* (July 1987). "Her energy and skill bring a complex woman to life and merited the best-actress prize."

Barbara Hershey's work in Chris Menges's stunning *A World Apart*, about one woman's personal struggle against apartheid in South Africa, brought her the most enthusiastic reviews of her career to date, as well as her second consecutive best-actress Award at Cannes. (Miss Hershey actually shared the award with two of her costars, Jodhi May, who played her daughter, and Linda Mvusi, who took the part of her black housekeeper.) As Diana Roth, a journalist and antiapartheid activist whose devotion to the cause threatens to destroy her relationship with her eldest daughter, Barbara Hershey, in the words of Stanley Kauffmann of the *New Republic* (July 18–25, 1988), accomplished "what is widely held to be impossible for a film actor, untrained in any formal way and confined to what's available in most film and TV scripts: she has become technically adept and, more astonishing, she has greatly deepened." James Lardner, commenting in the *Nation* (June 18, 1988), also praised Miss Hershey for giving "a great performance," and Mike McGrady of *New York Newsday* (June 17, 1988) applauded the actress for playing the difficult role "with restraint and with great dignity."

By most accounts, Miss Hershey's two most recent film efforts, *The Last Temptation of Christ* and *Beaches*, both of which were released in 1988, contributed little to the advancement of her career. *The Last Temptation of Christ*, based on the controversial novel of the same name by the Greek writer Nikos Kazantzakis, had its genesis in 1972 when, during the shooting of *Boxcar Bertha*, Barbara Hershey suggested to Martin Scorsese that he consider adapting the book for the screen. Scorsese liked the idea, but he was unable to persuade a motion picture studio to take on the project until 1987. Predictably, the film provoked an uproar among religious fundamentalists, who were particularly offended by a scene in which Christ (Willem Dafoe) dreams that he is making love to Mary Magdalene (Miss Hershey).

Directed by Garry Marshall, *Beaches* paired Barbara Hershey and Bette Midler in a sentimental drama about the long-lasting friendship between two women of vastly different backgrounds, one of whom develops a terminal illness. While impressed, for the most part, with the performances of the two actresses, critics uniformly faulted the film for its predictable plotline. Cast as the well-bred, affluent lawyer Hillary Whitney Essex, Barbara Hershey, according to Lynn Darling of *New York Newsday* (December 21, 1988), "does what she can within the narrow confines of her regal, repressed doomed character."

Barbara Hershey possesses the kind of sunny, all-American good looks most often associated with her home state of California. Of medium height, she has brown hair and brown eyes and what has frequently been described as a dazzling smile. Her live-in relationship with David Carradine ended in 1975. Since then, Miss Hershey has had custody of their son, who changed his name from Free to Tom when he was nine years old. The actress divides her time between a home in Santa Monica, California and a 300-year-old stone farmhouse in Connecticut. Her favorite leisure activities include gardening, drawing, cooking, and playing the flute and the piano. Describing her approach to acting, Miss Hershey has said: "You don't want to give everything away. What you hold back is as important as what you present. That makes it intriguing. Acting is a veil. It cloaks, and it reveals."

References: Am Film 11:20+ My '86 pors, 13:55+ D '87 pors; Chicago Tribune XIII p6+ Mr 22 '87 pors, XIII p4+ Ja 8 '89 pors; Esquire 98:178+ S '82 pors; Gentlemen's Q 57:284+ N '87 pors; Moviegoer 5:8+ O '86 pors; N Y Times II p17+ Mr 29 '87 por; Vogue 177:483+ Mr '87 por; Contemporary Theatre, Film, and Television (1986); Who's Who in America, 1988–89

© Dimitri Kasterine

Holroyd, Michael

Aug. 27, 1935– British writer. Address: c/o A. P. Watt Ltd., 20 John St., London WC1N 2DL, England

One of Great Britain's foremost biographers, Michael Holroyd established his reputation in 1968 with a monumental two-volume life of Lytton Strachey, the iconoclastic and irreverent biographer, essayist, and member of the Bloomsbury Group. His much-praised two-volume biography of the equally flamboyant Welsh painter Augustus John followed in 1974 and 1975. Since then, Holroyd has been working on an authorized three-volume biography of George Bernard Shaw, the first two installments of which were published to considerable critical acclaim in 1988 and 1989, respectively. His books have revived interest in his subjects' lives and careers, the late-Victorian and Edwardian periods in which they lived, and in the art of biography itself.

A self-described novelist manqué, Holroyd has an empathic appreciation of the underdog. "If I light on an unjustly neglected writer," he told an interviewer for the Guardian (March 2, 1971), "he becomes doubly good in my eyes." One such relatively ignored writer, Hugh Kingsmill, became the subject of Holroyd's first critical biography, in 1964. He has manifested his quest for justice not only in his desire to resurrect the reputations of the dead, but also in his concern for the rights of the living. The biographer has championed the rights of writers in his collection of essays, Unreceived Opinions, and as an active member of such professional organizations as English PEN, of which he was president from 1985 to 1988.

Michael de Courcy Fraser Holroyd was born in London, England on August 27, 1935, the only child of Ulla (Hall) Holroyd, who was Swedish, and Basil Holroyd, an Anglo-Irish businessman. After his parents divorced in 1943, they embarked on several other marriages. "One stepparent was Hungarian, another French," Holroyd told David Plante in an interview for the New York Times Magazine (September 11, 1988). "I was all over the place. The closest I got to a proper English life was when I stayed with my [paternal] grandparents in Maidenhead Thicket in the Berkshire countryside." To compensate for the lack of adventure afforded by "a regime of seventy- and eighty-year-olds," Holroyd spent much of his childhood reading.

Like his father before him, Holroyd attended Eton College, the historic public school near Windsor. His father insisted that he study math, physics, astronomy, botany, and chemistry in preparation for a lucrative career, and the case for entering a well-paying profession seemed strengthened when the family's investment in Indian tea plantations was wiped out during a Chinese invasion of India. But Holroyd hated that scientific curriculum and, on graduating from Eton in 1953, refused to go on to a university. His practical-minded father thought there must be some use for such stubbornness and arranged for him to be articled to a law firm, where he worked as an unsalaried apprentice for two years in possible preparation for a legal career.

In 1956 Holroyd enlisted in the army as a member of the Royal Fusiliers. While he was on a three-week leave, his orders to embark for Egypt during the Suez crisis were sent to the wrong address, and he was completely unaware that anything was amiss until he happened to see a newsreel of his regiment's departure. His habit of writing short stories and poems, which shielded him from even a minimal awareness of international news, nearly earned him a court-martial. By the time he left the National Service, in 1958, he had decided to become a writer.

Finding that no one in Maidenhead was interested in his literary services, Holroyd went to London with £100 given to him by his grandmother. "At first, being unembarrassed by money," he recalled in an essay for *Harper's* (October 1976), "I could find only intermittent quarters. . . . I put up in the Mayfair attic of a [friend's] house . . . wrapped up on cold nights in brown paper: something between a tramp and an undelivered parcel." For a while he wrote stories and verse, "the influence of which," he wrote in *Harper's*, "veered drastically between Wordsworth and T. S. Eliot." Finally he was commissioned by the *Twentieth Century* magazine to review an anthology of Oxford and Cambridge writing, for which he was paid one pound.

On a chance visit that he made to the Maidenhead public library in 1958 or 1959, Holroyd discovered that his serendipity proved more useful than all his literary striving in London. In coming across the works of Hugh Kingsmill, a neglected novelist, biographer, and literary critic who lived from 1889 to 1949, Holroyd found encouragement for his own ambitions. He wrote in his autobiographical essay for *World Authors 1970–1975*, "Under his influence, I stepped from my own life into other people's, where there appeared to be more going on." He also expressed his indebtedness to Kingsmill in an interview with Lindsay Miller for the *New York Post* (November 21, 1975). "He was the first author who made me think that I was not a minority of one in the world," Holroyd said.

Inspired by Kingsmill's perseverance in the face of neglect, Holroyd decided to write a biography about him. After putting the finishing touches on the manuscript in 1961, he submitted it to sixteen publishers who, though impressed, were skeptical about its sales potential, given the obscurity of both the biographer and biographee. But after the novelist William Gerhardie called it "the best book never published" in an article for the *Spectator*, Martin Secker published *Hugh Kingsmill: A Critical Biography* at his own expense in 1964. Holroyd was paid an advance on royalties of twenty-five pounds, which looked to him "more like a retreat than an advance."

Despite Holroyd's contention that *Hugh Kingsmill* is not a good biography, many critics, including Malcolm Muggeridge, admired its maturity and insight into its subject. As it turned out, Holroyd's research on Hugh Kingsmill led him directly to his next biography, his two-volume study of Lytton Strachey. Because Kingsmill had been unjustifiably accused of imitating the mandarin style of the iconoclastic biographer Lytton Stra-

chey, Holroyd began reading all the material ever published by Strachey, with the intention of refuting the charge. Discovering that no one had yet written a comprehensive critical appraisal of Strachey's work or a biography of him, Holroyd secured a fifty-pound advance from William Heinemann, Ltd., the well-known British publisher, and spent a year in writing a reappraisal of Strachey's career. In the process, he met the psychoanalyst James Strachey, the writer's brother and literary executor, who granted him access to some 30,000 of Strachey's letters and diaries.

That enormous cache of previously unpublished material changed Holroyd's original concept of the book, and with the help of a Eugene F. Saxton Memorial Fellowship (1963) and a Bollingen Foundation Fellowship (1965) he worked on it for six more years. "I began it as a young person," he told an interviewer for the *New Yorker* (May 25, 1968), "and ended it as a senile old man." Deciding not to treat Strachey in isolation, but to create a collective portrait of the Bloomsbury Group as well, Holroyd interviewed over 100 persons, including such celebrated survivors as Bertrand Russell, E. M. Forster, and Leonard Woolf. He ultimately accumulated so much material that his apartment, in his words, "looked like a defunct post office."

Eventually *Lytton Strachey: A Critical Biography* ran to 1,229 pages and appeared in two volumes. The first, *The Unknown Years, 1880–1910* (1967), discussed Strachey's family, his unhappy school days, and the exhilaration he felt at Cambridge, where he met many of the intellectuals who later became the core of the Bloomsbury Group. The second volume, *The Years of Achievement, 1910–1932* (1968), focused on Strachey's early failures, his relationships with Virginia Woolf and the painter Dora Carrington, and the fame (or notoriety) that followed publication of his *Eminent Victorians* (1918), in which he demythologized (some would say dismantled) the hitherto sacrosanct reputations of Cardinal Manning, General Gordon, Florence Nightingale, and Thomas Arnold. A revised edition of *Lytton Strachey* appeared in 1971. *Lytton Strachey* was highly praised by the majority of critics, many of whom agreed with the predictions of a *Times Literary Supplement* (February 29, 1968) reviewer that "Mr. Holroyd's two volumes form a portrait of an epoch in literature which will not be superseded. Clearcut, comprehensive, highly colored, and convincing, it will be recognized by contemporary readers and by those who come after as a splendid piece of work."

The first volume was, however, castigated by Strachey's friend Leonard Woolf in a review for the *New Statesman* (October 6, 1967). After characterizing Holroyd as "heavy-handed and heavy-minded," Woolf charged him with a failure to understand people, especially Lytton Strachey. Responding to Woolf's attack with characteristic graciousness, Holroyd told Martha MacGregor in an interview for the *New York Post* (April 27, 1968): "I think at first he disapproved of an outsider doing the book. Also, treating things with a certain candor as I did may have come as rather a shock." During the New Yorker interview, Holroyd defended his treatment of the thorny problem of Strachey's sexuality. "The homosexual thing went on for years in his case and in that of the others," he said. "It imperiled their lives. To put it down as trivial would have gone against my purpose—to give a complete picture." When that picture was rounded out by the publication of the second volume, a mollified Woolf called it "a considerable achievement," and in another review for the New Statesman (February 23, 1968) he praised Holroyd for "bringing Lytton to life."

If Lytton Strachey came to life in the pages of Holroyd's biography, a contributing factor may have been the fact that he had become an almost oppressively living presence to his biographer during the course of his research. As Holroyd explained in his essay for Harper's: "When I was deep in Lytton Strachey's life, what he called his 'black period,' with all its details of faulty digestion and late-Victorian neurasthenia, I began to feel infected by several out-of-date diseases. If symptoms like these were posthumously contagious, then my next subject, I had resolved, should be someone of amazing virility and euphoria."

He found the perfect candidate in Augustus John, a tall and strikingly handsome painter, drinker, and womanizer who lived a long and stereotypically bohemian life until his death in 1961. Augustus John was first published in two volumes, The Years of Innocence (1974) and The Years of Experience (1975), and appeared in a combined edition in 1976. In Augustus John, Holroyd examined John's days as an art student, his battles with his father, and the celebrity he achieved in the art world. He also dealt with John's hyperactive sexuality, drunkenness, irresponsibility, and belief in the legend of his own life—a belief that led him to end as a pathetic parody of himself in the last decades of his existence.

Augustus John received reviews that were sometimes puzzlingly contradictory. One critic observed, for example, that Holroyd seemed to have a masterly grasp of "art politics," but another felt that he misunderstood the history of British art. According to one reviewer, Holroyd handled John's life story "with consummate skill and unfailing sympathy," while another complained that the biographer was "out of sympathy" with his subject. Unqualified praise came from the art critic Hilton Kramer, who, writing in the New York Times Book Review (August 2, 1976), called Augustus John "extremely dramatic and extremely poignant, touched throughout by the humor that was an integral part of his extravagant appetite for life." That opinion was shared by most reviewers, many of whom were also admirers of Holroyd's evocation of the Victorian scene, lively sense of character, and satirical wit.

Each of Michael Holroyd's biographies has grown out of the book that preceded it. Just as Hugh Kingsmill led to Lytton Strachey because Kingsmill

was considered an imitator of the latter, Lytton Strachey led to Augustus John because the two men had been friends. John's widow, Dorelia John, assisted Holroyd with his research on both her husband and Strachey. Among the celebrities whose portraits were painted by Augustus John was George Bernard Shaw, who became what Holroyd has called his "next biographical victim."

There was an exception in Shaw's case: his biography was the first that Holroyd was asked to write. In 1973 he was approached by the residuary legatees of Shaw's estate: the British Museum, the National Gallery of Ireland, and the Royal Academy of Dramatic Art. The most recent biographies of Shaw had been published in 1956, the centenary of Shaw's birth, and a mere six years after his death. In many cases the biographers had known Shaw and had received his cooperation. The residuary legatees hoped that a new biography would increase Shaw's popularity before the copyright begins to lapse on his works in the 1990s.

Looking back on his reaction to being selected by the Shaw Estate in an interview with Eleanor Bron for the Listener (September 8, 1988), Holroyd said: "It was a great honor, but it was also a great terror. Shaw seemed so different from myself. Yet that was one of the reasons that I had become a biographer, to explore different lives." At first he found it difficult to keep "in step" with Shaw, but he overcame that obstacle by spending two years in the Dublin neighborhood where Shaw lived his first twenty years. Research on his Shavian project eventually took Holroyd to the Soviet Union, the United States, Germany, Sweden, Italy, and New Zealand.

Another intimidating factor was the sheer bulk of Shaw's oeuvre: fifty-five plays, five novels, volumes of music, drama, and social criticism, and approximately 250,000 letters. "Shaw, with his shorthand and with his secretaries," Holroyd explained in the Listener interview, "could write more words in a day than I could read in a day; and since he continued writing into his mid-nineties, you can see that this was rather an alarming calculation."

The first volume of Bernard Shaw was published in 1988 under the title The Search for Love, 1856–1898. Shaw was brought up in a ménage-à-trois household with his father, mother, and his mother's singing teacher. The Search for Love takes Shaw up to his marriage, at the age of forty-one, to Charlotte Payne-Townshend. Volume two, The Pursuit of Power, was published in 1989, and volume three, "The Lure of Fantasy," is expected to be released in 1991. A single volume of notes and sources will be published subsequently, as well as a condensed one-volume biography and a commentary on Shaw's plays. In 1987 Holroyd was paid an advance of £625,000 by the publishing house of Chatto and Windus for the entire project—the highest advance ever paid by a British publisher, either for a work of nonfiction, according to the Guardian (October 11, 1987), or for a work of biography, according to Publishers Weekly (October 14, 1988).

Critical praise from influential quarters for volume one of *Bernard Shaw* was as dazzling as Holroyd's record-breaking advance on royalties. The novelist Anthony Burgess wrote in the *Atlantic* (October 1988): "On the strength of this first volume it seems possible to predict that after the second and third, Michael Holroyd will have completed one of the three great literary biographies of the century, the other two being the late Richard Ellmann's lives of James Joyce and Oscar Wilde." George Painter, the biographer of Marcel Proust, called Holroyd "a major biographer . . . at the summit of his powers, maturity, wit, ease, insight, truth, and sheer reader enjoyability." Leon Edel, the definitive biographer of Henry James, predicted that if Holroyd "keeps up the pace, the wit, the vivacity, and the unraveling of the Shavian paradoxes—and why shouldn't he?—he will give us a masterly biography."

With his second volume of *Bernard Shaw*, subtitled *The Pursuit of Power, 1898-1918*, Holroyd proved himself worthy of the high expectations he aroused with the first installment—at least in the opinion of Nicholas Rudall, who reviewed it for the *Chicago Tribune* (September 10, 1989). Rudall wrote that, in analyzing the plays and political activities of Shaw's middle years, "Holroyd has now given us a richer, fuller picture of Shaw. The format of his first volume was so right that its continuation means that we can view Shaw through the prism of his life, his thought, and his art. And Holroyd does it with such grace and eloquence—with such style. A marvelous book." But Michiko Kakutani of the *New York Times* (September 15, 1989) felt that the volume lacked "the psychological drama of its predecessor," although she conceded that "Mr. Holroyd does an admirable job of giving us a lucid picture of Shaw in his maturity." Writing for the *New York Times Book Review* (September 16, 1989), Margot Peters contended that Shaw "does not really step live from the page," adding that "despite the biographer's real grasp of Shaw's ambiguities, the dynamics of his life are submerged." She was nonetheless persuaded by Holroyd's thesis that, in her words, "Shaw was an emotionally and sexually starved man whose forceful pronouncements masked estrangement, frustration, and pessimism."

Michael Holroyd has written and spoken engagingly about his craft. In an article for the London *Times* (September 14, 1974), he compared the biographer's life to that of an actor. The biographer, he pointed out, "must read, learn lines, metaphorically put on the clothes and become his subject—know what it is like to think, feel, move about the room like him." In an interview with Michele Field for *Publishers Weekly* (October 14, 1988), he explained that the fun of writing a biography is "like the fun of traveling or learning a new language. You come back with something gained." In his autobiographical essay for *World Authors* he wrote: "My aim has been to recreate worlds into which readers may enter, where they may experience feelings and thoughts, some of which may remain

with them after the book is closed. . . . I search for truth through the individual (not through groups), and try to give a literary pattern to the relationship between myself and my subject. I attempt to combine scholarship with storytelling, factual accuracy with narrative power."

The biographer has published one novel, *A Dog's Life* (1969), which he described during the *New Yorker* interview as "a study in limitations" of old people, such as the grandparents who raised him and gave him the idea for the story. "Old people are entirely indifferent to the outside world," he said. Although some reviewers relished his black humor, one found the book "a vacant exercise in misanthropy." Because libel problems prevented the book from being published in England, it was published only in the United States. "My fiction was too documentary," he has explained.

Holroyd has edited several books, including *The Best of Hugh Kingsmill* (1971; 1979), *Lytton Strachey by Himself: A Self-Portrait* (1971), *The Genius of Shaw* (1979), *The Shorter Strachey* (with Paul Levy, 1980), William Gerhardie's *God's Fifth Column: A Biography of the Age, 1890-1940* (with Robert Skidelsky, 1981), *Essays by Divers Hands*, Volume XLII (1982), and *Peter Harvest: The Private Diary of David Peterley* (1985). He has also written several radio and television scripts.

The impulse behind much of Holroyd's work has been his attempt to be an "unofficial trade unionist" for writers, a continuing concern that has led to his involvement in many writers' causes and organizations. He has campaigned for a public program to pay writers "royalties" each time their books are borrowed from libraries, and he supported the founding of the feminist publishing house Virago in 1973. Before becoming president of English PEN in 1985, he was chairman of the Society of Authors from 1973 to 1974 and of the National Book League, or Book Trust, from 1976 to 1978, and he served as vice-chairman of the Arts Council Literature Panel from 1982 to 1983. He was a fellow of the Royal Society of Literature in 1968 and a member of its council from 1977 to 1987. In 1988 he was made a Commander of the Order of the British Empire. In addition to the fellowships that enabled him to write *Lytton Strachey*, he received a Winston Churchill Fellowship in 1971. For *Lytton Strachey* he was granted the *Yorkshire Post* Book of the Year Award.

The six-foot, one-inch tall, 175-pound biographer has often been mistaken for the English actor Albert Finney. Holroyd describes his hair as "mouse" brown and his eyes as "blue (on good days)." Michele Field described him in *Publishers Weekly* as possessing "Richard Burton's craggy charm" underneath his "frayed cardigans and comfortable slouch." Since 1982 he has been married to the novelist Margaret Drabble, who is also the editor of the fifth edition of the *Oxford Companion to English Literature*. The fact that they live happily fifteen minutes apart in London—he in Ladbroke Grove, she in Hampstead—has evoked inquisitive comments from reporters. Holroyd once quipped, "If we weren't married people would say we were living together. But since we are married, they say we live apart." When asked what he enjoys besides his work, Holroyd has enumerated the following: playing squash occasionally, watching people dance, listening to stories, being polite, siestas, music, and avoiding tame animals.

References: Guardian p8 Mr 2 '71 por, p27 S 16 '88; Harper's 253:80+ O '76 por; Listener p4+ S 8 '88 por; Manchester Guardian W p20 O 11 '87 por; N Y Post p3 N 21 '75 por; N Y Times Mag p42+ S 11 '88; New Yorker 44:27+ My 25 '68; Pub W 234:45+ O 14 '88; Contemporary Authors new rev vol 18 (1986); International Who's Who, 1989-90; Who's Who, 1989; World Authors 1970-1975

Holtz, Lou

Jan. 6, 1937– Football coach. Address: c/o Athletics Department, Notre Dame University, South Bend, Ind. 46556

Although the position of head coach at Notre Dame is the most attention-getting coaching job in America, Lou Holtz likes to describe himself in unflattering terms: "I am five feet ten inches tall, weigh 152 pounds, speak with a lisp, and appear to be afflicted with a combination of beriberi and scurvy. I wasn't a great athlete. I'm not very impressive, I'm not very smart, I'm not very intelligent." But in just three years after taking over at Notre Dame, the school whose past and present gridiron glory justifies the claim that it is the home of "America's

team," Holtz took the Fightin' Irish to the national championship in 1988. Notwithstanding his penchant for self-deprecation, Holtz is, along with Michigan's Bo Schembechler and Penn State's Joe Paterno, one of the coaches who might someday be regarded as equals of such immortals from the collegiate past as Knute Rockne, Bear Bryant, Frank Leahy, Woody Hayes, and Ara Parseghian.

Probably the only coach in college football who has traded quips with Johnny Carson on the *Tonight Show*, Holtz is equally popular on the corporate lecture circuit, where he spices his high-priced speeches on motivational techniques with his trademark jokes and whimsical banter. He is also a skilled amateur magician, though the prestidigitation for which he is most renowned owes nothing to feats of optical illusion. He has a gift for taking over foundering football teams and turning them almost instantly into winners. Having worked his miracles at William and Mary, North Carolina State, and the University of Minnesota, Holtz took over at Notre Dame after his predecessor, coach Gerry Faust, compiled a five-year record of frustration, during which the team won thirty of fifty-six games and tied one. Faust's would have been a fair record at most colleges but not at Notre Dame, where Holtz quickly turned into reality the school's dream of "waking up the echoes" from the fabled Irish past.

Lou Holtz was born Louis Leo Holtz on January 6, 1937 on the West Virginia side of the Ohio River, in the small, northern panhandle town of Follansbee. When Lou's father was called away to military service during World War II, his family moved to the nearby town of East Liverpool, Ohio, where he attended Roman Catholic schools. It was in the third grade that Lou had his loyalty to the Fightin' Irish drummed into him by the nuns of St. Aloysius School, where students marched to the strains of the Notre Dame fight song. "I swear this is true," Holtz told Michael Wilbon of the Washington Post (September 12, 1986). "We had a jukebox there that played only one record—the Notre Dame fight song. They played the thing at recess, at lunch, at dismissal. And you'd better look straight ahead."

When Lou Holtz was six years old, his sixteen-year-old uncle, Lou Tychonievich, took the boy under his wing and became his mentor. In an interview with Ed Sherman for the *Chicago Tribune* (December 25, 1988), Holtz asserted that his uncle Ty was "the most influential guy in [his] life." He not only imparted his lively sense of humor to his nephew but also served as his first football coach, when Lou was still in elementary school. "He always had you laughing," Holtz told Sherman. "We used to call him sunshine." Holtz loved football from the time he was old enough to play, but because of his slight stature—he weighed barely 100 pounds as a high school sophomore—he was forced to become a student of the game in order to excel. His uncle Ty told Ed Sherman that Lou would "take the playbook and study every position. If I needed a receiver, he'd yell out, 'I'm a receiver.' If I needed a running back, he'd say, 'I'm a running back.'"

In an interview with Lawrence Linderman of *Sport* (November 1979) magazine, Holtz recalled that he was first encouraged to become a football coach when he was a junior in high school. "My high school coach told my parents that I ought to go away to college and become a coach, which really intrigued my folks because no one from either side of the family had ever been to college." But Holtz had no intention of ever leaving the Ohio River Valley, since his sole ambition was, as he told Linderman, "to have a job in the steel mill in Midlands, Pennsylvania, buy a car, have a girl by my side and five dollars in my pocket." Nevertheless, Holtz has always insisted that his workaholic dedication to coaching derives from a pervasive fear of failure that has dogged him since his high school days. As a teenager he displayed no special prowess in athletics and, since he graduated with a ranking of 234th in a class of 278, showed little intellectual promise. Consequently, he was popular neither with girls nor with the crowd of athletic "cool guys" who drove flashy cars.

To please his parents and to prove to himself that he could "do the work," Holtz enrolled at Kent State University but went home the summer after his freshman year and took a job in a steel mill. "I decided not to return to college," he said when he spoke to Lawrence Linderman, "but, after laboring in the open hearth for a few weeks, I went right back to [Kent State] and played football." A linebacker, Holtz never started for the Kent State Golden Flashes, and, when asked how someone with a physique as slight as his played such a physically punishing position as linebacker, Holtz replied, "Poorly." His football-playing career ended after his junior year, when he injured his right knee during a game of basketball. After that he served as coach of the freshman football team and as a scout.

Discovering that he liked coaching, Holtz graduated from Kent State in 1959 with a B.A. degree in history and then enrolled at the University of Iowa, where he coached the freshman football team while working for his M.A. degree in arts and education. From 1961 through 1963, he served as an assistant at the College of William and Mary (as coach of the offensive backs), before moving on to the University of Connecticut, where he coached the defensive backs in 1964 and 1965. His next two stints as an assistant enabled him to serve apprenticeships with two of college football's most famous head coaches: Paul Dietzel at the University of South Carolina and Woody Hayes at Ohio State University. He coached the defensive backs for Dietzel's Gamecocks in 1966 and 1967 and for Hayes's Buckeyes in 1968, the year in which Ohio State won the national championship with a New Year's Day drubbing of Southern California in the Rose Bowl. "I had to make every stop," Holtz said, "because I wasn't very big and I hadn't been a good athlete. I was an assistant for a while at . . . Connecticut, which is located in Storrs. . . . It used to be named Store, but they built another one. Boy, I've really lived in a lot of metropolitan areas."

In 1969 Holtz became a head coach at William and Mary, a small but academically prestigious college in the historical town of Williamsburg, Virginia with no tradition of gridiron success. Even against weak Southern Conference foes like the Citadel, Furman, Virginia Military Institute, and Richmond, the Indians were perennial losers. As Holtz likes to quip, the problem with the football program was "too many Marys and not enough Williams." In 1969, Holtz's first season, the Indians won only three of ten games, but in the following year they won five of twelve. Among the team's defeats was a 40-12 loss to fifteenth-ranked Toledo in the Tangerine Bowl, which was the first postseason bowl appearance in the history of the school. After the 1971 season, when the Indians posted a record of five wins and six losses, Holtz accepted the head coaching position at North Carolina State.

A member of the Atlantic Coast Conference, which, although one of the nation's premier basketball leagues, seldom fields nationally ranked football teams, with the exception of Clemson, the North Carolina State Wolfpack had won a total of merely nine games over the three-year period preceding Holtz's arrival. In 1972, his first season, Holtz reversed the Wolfpack's losing ways, posting a final record of eight wins, three losses, and a tie. After a 49-13 shellacking of West Virginia in the Peach Bowl, North Carolina State finished seventeenth in the Associated Press's final ranking of the top twenty teams. In 1973 the Wolfpack won nine of twelve games, including a 31-18 victory over Kansas in the Liberty Bowl, and finished at number sixteen in the final Associated Press rankings, but the 1974 team was to be the best that Holtz fielded in his four seasons at North Carolina State. The Wolfpack opened with six straight victories but were upset on two consecutive Saturdays by Atlantic Coast Conference foes, Maryland and the University of North Carolina, before rebounding to win their last three regular-season games, including an astonishing defeat of powerful Penn State. Facing a strong University of Houston team in the postseason Bluebonnet Bowl, the Wolfpack had to settle for a 31-31 tie, but they finished the season as the country's eleventh-ranked team in the Associated Press poll and as the ninth-rated team in the United Press poll. In 1975 Holtz's team began the season with the ranking of number thirteen, but the Wolfpack players were knocked out of the top twenty for the first time during Holtz's tenure when West Virginia defeated North Carolina State, 13-10, in the Peach Bowl.

Having taken the once-dismal Wolfpack to four consecutive appearances in postseason bowl games, Holtz was now considered a "miracle worker" with a genius for taking football programs that were mired in futility and turning them into winners. In early 1976 the New York Jets made him their head coach, charging him with the task of returning them to the championship form that they had not flashed since winning their first and only Super Bowl in January 1969. Holtz and his players suffered through the 1977 season, however, as the

Jets lost eleven of fourteen games, and New York sportswriters ridiculed the head coach as a "bucolic bungler who tried to infuse the Jets with rah-rah [collegiate] spirit that never had a chance to take root," as Lawrence Linderman observed in *Sport* magazine. Holtz admitted that it was he who was at fault rather than the Jets' players or management, and that he had failed "to make a total commitment to coaching professional football." "It was," he recalled, "almost a case of thinking, 'Well, if it doesn't work out or if I don't like it, I can always go back to college football.'" He also conceded that he "didn't know an awful lot about pro football." "I had always had an option quarterback-type offense," he told Linderman. "I thought that perhaps we might be able to run certain phases of the option with the Jets, but we couldn't. I just did a very poor job, even though I was only there eleven months."

When Holtz returned to collegiate ranks in 1978 it was as head coach of the Razorbacks at the University of Arkansas, one of the nation's traditional gridiron powers and a member of the formidable Southwest Conference. He was hired by one of the most popular and respected coaches in college football, Frank Broyles, who had stepped down as coach of the Razorbacks to become the school's athletic director. Although pro football is too sophisticated for the option quarterback-type offense that Holtz favors, Broyles lured him to Arkansas because, in his opinion, the two best option coaches in college football are Lou Holtz and Bobby Bowden, the coach at Florida State University. On the execution of the intricate option play, the quarterback tries to confound the defense either by keeping the ball himself for an off-tackle run or by quickly pitching the ball to a running back, who trails along a few yards behind the quarterback, for an end run. The key to the success of the option is the ability of the quarterback to "read" the reactions of defensive backs and linebackers while at the same time making snap decisions based on the defenders' responses. But because Holtz is chary of one-dimensional offensive attacks, he has mastered the "veer" formation, which enables his teams to pass as well as run the ball. Accordingly, a Holtz-assembled offense can be adequately maintained only by a quarterback who is both mobile and capable of passing with some accuracy. Regarded as one of football's foremost quarterback coaches, Holtz has molded such players as Dave Buckey at North Carolina State, Ron Calcagni at Arkansas, Ricky Foggie at Minnesota, and Tony Rice at Notre Dame into star quarterbacks.

Acknowledged to be one of the strictest disciplinarians in college football, Holtz has a reputation for holding players to high, no-nonsense standards of personal comportment that dates from his first season as coach at the University of Arkansas. During the regular eleven-game season, his Razorbacks lost just once, to their undefeated conference archrival, the University of Texas Longhorns. Consequently, Arkansas was invited to play Oklahoma, the once-beaten champions of the Big Eight Con-

ference, in the Orange Bowl on New Year's Day. A few days before the game, however, Holtz suspended for disciplinary reasons three players— two star running backs and a wide receiver—who had collectively accounted for almost 80 percent of the Razorback touchdowns in 1978. As Geoffrey Norman reported in *Sport* (October 1987) magazine, "The players were black, and for a time the other blacks on the team threatened to walk out in support of them. Arkansas went from mere underdog to hopeless underdog." But Holtz is one of the great motivators in modern sports. An unsung sophomore running back named Roland Sayles stepped forward, scoring four touchdowns and rushing for more than 200 yards, as Arkansas crushed the heavily favored Sooners by a score of 31-6 to end the season as the nation's second-ranked team behind the national champion, Notre Dame.

Over the course of the subsequent six seasons, Holtz compiled an overall record at Arkansas of sixty wins against only twenty-one losses and two ties, but, after his 1983 team lost five of eleven games, Broyles was on the verge of terminating his coach's contract when Holtz resigned to become head coach at the University of Minnesota. Although Broyles cited professional "burnout" as the reason for Holtz's departure, it was a television campaign commercial in which the Arkansas coach endorsed Jesse Helms from North Carolina for reelection to the United States Senate that sealed Holtz's fate. An ultraconservative politically, Helms was a leading opponent of the movement to make the late Dr. Martin Luther King Jr.'s birthday a national holiday, leading Arkansas fans to fear that Holtz's association with Helms might hurt the Razorbacks in their recruitment of black athletes. Holtz, for his part, contended that endorsing Helms was more an act of friendship than a declaration of political belief. He explained that Helms had befriended him during his tenure as coach at North Carolina State. An Arkansas journalist discussed the problems that Holtz encountered at the Fayetteville campus with *Sport* magazine's Geoffrey Norman. "Lou was a good coach," he said. "But he didn't care anything about the state. He was going around making motivational speeches for companies. Not just around the country but all over the world. He used to say that Fayetteville wasn't the end of the world but you could see it from there. . . . And he hated to recruit. He couldn't stand the rejection and some of those kids are going to reject you. Lou liked to think he could take any thirty and whip you. He started losing players out of Arkansas, and that had never happened before."

"We will get the heart and soul of our football team from the state of Minnesota," Holt quipped when he became the custodian of the Golden Gophers' football fortunes. "However, we'll have to go elsewhere for the arms and legs." Minnesota had not been a contender for the Big Ten championship since the early 1960s, but once again Holtz worked his program-building magic. Although the Gophers lost seven of their eleven games in 1984, in the following season they posted a winning record of six and five and were invited to postseason play in the Independence Bowl. In addition to earning the respect of its Big Ten opponents, Minnesota regained the loyalty of its alumni and student body, and the school's athletic facilities were upgraded. Although Holtz had signed a lifetime coaching contract with the University of Minnesota, he insisted on including an escape clause that would allow him to go without penalty to Notre Dame as the head coach of the storied Fightin' Irish. And at the end of the 1985 season, when the Irish were handed their first losing season in more than two decades by the Miami Hurricanes, who humiliated Notre Dame by a score of 58-7 on national television, Holtz replaced Gerry Faust as the head coach at South Bend, Indiana.

"What Faust had failed to do," wrote Skip Myslenski in the *Chicago Tribune* (November 28, 1985), "was win consistently at a school where nearly all of the twenty-three previous coaches had. The identification of football with the University of Notre Dame du Lac is so complete that the mosaic of Christ preaching on the exterior of the school library is called 'Touchdown Jesus.'" "I didn't come here to be a legend," Holtz remarked when he arrived at South Bend. "I just want to be a football coach. Preferably, a winning football coach." To turn the Notre Dame program around, Holtz played the role of hard-guy disciplinarian. Players were expected to arrive at team meetings on time, sit up straight in their chairs, and listen attentively when the coaches spoke. He also put his players through grueling physical fitness workouts, deceptively called "quickness and agility drills," that began at 6:15 in the morning. Almost all of the players were required to be able to bench-press 400 pounds, and they were drilled incessantly on the fundamentals like blocking and tackling. In recruiting, Holtz went after bigger and stronger offensive and defensive linemen as well as fleet receivers and defensive backs to give the Irish greater speed than they had possessed during Faust's five-year reign. In an interview with Gordon S. White Jr. of the *New York Times* (October 23, 1988), one of Holtz's players, Frank Stams, remarked, "We needed discipline. Maybe we didn't know it then but we know it now. We weren't really working together. . . . The right hand didn't know what the left hand was doing. Players didn't seem to think it was that important. There was no emotion toward other players as there is now. The team concept suffered."

In 1986 the Notre Dame schedule was acknowledged to be one of the most difficult in the country, since it included opponents like Michigan, Alabama, Penn State, and Southern California. Although Holtz's team lost six games while winning five—only the ninth time that Notre Dame had posted a losing record since the school fielded its first football team, in 1887—they were trounced on just one occasion, by Alabama. Their wide receiver and kick returner, Tim Brown, was awarded the coveted Heisman Trophy, and most observers

agreed that the Irish were the best team in the country with a losing record. In 1987 Notre Dame confronted another merciless schedule, but that time the Irish won eight of their first nine games and went on to finish the season with eight wins, three losses, and an end-of-season top-ten ranking. On New Year's Day Holtz's team squared off against Texas A&M in the Cotton Bowl. It was Notre Dame's first appearance in a major New Year's Day bowl game since 1981, but A&M prevailed by a score of 35-10.

At the outset of the 1988 season Holtz believed his young team would prove good enough to end the season by playing in yet another major bowl game, but he felt that Notre Dame was a year away from contending for the national title. (The national college football championship is a mythical one because it is decided by postseason polls rather than by a playoff system.) But the Irish eked out a narrow victory over formidable Michigan in their season opener, and, when they faced the defending national champions, the University of Miami, in a showdown at South Bend in mid-October, both the Hurricanes and the Irish were undefeated. In one of the most exciting contests of recent years, Notre Dame pulled out a 31-30 win to avenge the drubbing that Miami had administered in 1985. A few weeks later, Notre Dame occupied the nation's number-one ranking, and their archrival, the Trojans of the University of Southern California, was ranked second when the two teams met in a season-ending confrontation in Los Angeles. Once again Holtz displayed his mastery of motivational ploys when, shortly before the game, he suspended two of his key players on offense for coming chronically late to team functions. Nevertheless, the Irish completed their first undefeated season since 1973 when the defense shackled Southern California's all-American quarterback Rodney Peete, and Notre Dame notched a 27-13 victory to earn the number-one ranking in the polls.

Lou Holtz earned his first undefeated season with a team without superstars. The efficient, workmanlike offense was powered by a horde of talented running backs and by quarterback Tony Rice, a gifted option runner with a better than average arm. The team's real strength, though, was its defense, a gang of brutal intimidators who were led by defensive end Frank Stams and the linebackers Wes Pritchett and Michael Stonebreaker. On January 2, 1989 the Irish played for the national championship in the Fiesta Bowl against the only other undefeated team in the country, the Mountaineers of West Virginia University, whose explosive offense had averaged almost forty-three points per game and was usually detonated by their sensational young quarterback, Major Harris, an elusive scrambler who also had a lethally accurate cannon arm. However, the Notre Dame defense defused the Mountaineer offense, and Harris was outgunned by Rice, who passed for over 200 yards and ran for almost 100 more, as the Irish won their first national championship in eleven years with a 34-21 victory. Holtz commented that, up until then, he had thought that national championships happened only to "movie stars" rather than "average guys" such as he. The credit for success, he said, belonged to the team and its work ethic: "If there was one thing about this years's team that was really great, it was that our football team, from Day One, said, 'Hey, tell us what we have to do.'"

Unlike some of the schools that function as "football factories," Notre Dame is special because it refuses to compromise its ethical and academic standards in the quest for success in sports. Notre Dame athletes serve as full-time students in an academically competitive environment, and they are also expected to refrain from behavior that might embarrass the school. Consequently, in the months following their Fiesta Bowl championship, Notre Dame suspended several of Holtz's returning starters, some because of classroom problems, others for disciplinary reasons. Nevertheless, the Irish opened the 1989 season by mounting a strong defense of their national championship. After nine games Holtz's squad was undefeated, having beaten three teams ranked in the top ten, and Tony Rice was a leading contender for the coveted Heisman Trophy.

Notre Dame's gleaming image was, however, tarnished somewhat when a pregame brawl erupted between Irish players and players for the University of Southern California on October 21, 1989, an exciting contest that Notre Dame went on to win. A similar melee had been touched off by some Irish players before the start of the Miami game at South Bend in 1988. In addition, the Irish had been criticized for unsportsmanlike conduct when their defensive team incurred six personal fouls in the waning moments of the Fiesta Bowl, when the outcome of the game was settled. In the wake of the Southern Cal incident, Holtz apologized for his team, vowed to put an end to such fighting, and promised to resign as head coach if his team were to take part in another ugly brawl.

In an interview with the *New York Times's* Gordon S. White Jr., George Kelly, an administrator at Notre Dame, talked about the reasons for Holtz's success. "I worked under three great [coaches]: Bob Devaney at Nebraska and Ara Parseghian and Lou Holtz here. There were three things they had in common. First, they never took anything for granted. Second, they were excellent teachers who could have had chairs at any university. And third, they were really superbly organized people. Also, a good coach has to be a salesman to get and keep the attention of kids. The trouble is some coaches are fast-sell, used-car salesmen. Devaney, Parseghian and Holtz were Cadillac salesmen." Holtz himself told White that he "had never known a successful coach who wasn't organized." "But you know," Holtz said, "I don't consider myself a well-organized person. Sure, I guess I'm the tough disciplinarian everybody thinks I am. But organization is just doing all those little things."

As Gordon S. White Jr. observed, "Holtz appears disorganized and as nervous as a cat when he rapidly paces the sideline during games, kneels to pick up and chew grass for few seconds, and returns to high-speed pacing." But as George Kelly explained, "Lou's that way. It's his lifestyle. It's his speed. He always lives over the speed limit and he just hasn't been caught. I have a tendency to believe that that is when he's at his best. He does not go on the field of practice and plan things when he is walking out there. He has everything detailed long before a practice."

Douglas S. Looney noted in *Sports Illustrated* (April 21, 1986) that Holtz's sly sense of humor, his garrulity, and his boyish charm make him "a combination snake-oil salesman, evangelist [for his teams], and hard-nosed business executive." "That means," Looney wrote, "he is constantly talking out of both sides of his mouth. At one moment he is saying that last year's pass rush was so bad that the opposition either 'completed the pass or the quarter ended.' In the next breath he is saying of his players that 'If you can't hug 'em, pat 'em, and brag about 'em, you don't want 'em on the team. Well, I can do that with all of mine.'" With his slender frame and the thatch of straw-colored hair that falls over his forehead, Holtz has been said to resemble the little Dutch boy who plugged the dike with his finger. He and his wife, the former Beth Marcus, have two daughters, Luanne and Elizabeth, and two sons, Skip (who attended Notre Dame on a football scholarship) and Kevin Richard.

References: Chicago Tribune IV p1+ D 1 '85 pors; N Y Times V p9 S 9 '84 pors, C p1+ D 9 '85 por; Newsday p14+ S 14 '86 pors; Sport 8:25+ O '86; Washington Post D p1+ S 12 '86

Howar, Barbara

Sept. 27, 1934– Broadcast journalist; writer. Address: c/o Scarborough House, P.O. Box 459, Chelsea, Mich. 48118

"Objectivity bores me. I do not believe in it," Barbara Howar remarked in her autobiography, *Laughing All the Way.* Indeed, ever since she came to national prominence in the mid-1960s, Ms. Howar has given free rein to her candor and quick wit. One of the best-known hostesses in Washington, D.C., during the presidency of Lyndon B. Johnson, she parlayed her caustic sense of humor and her insider's knowledge of Washington society into a career as a writer and television interviewer. After co-hosting the Metromedia talk show *Panorama,* Ms. Howar appeared on the prime-time news program *Who's Who* and served as a permanent panelist on *We Interrupt This Week,* public television's first quiz show, and for half a decade she was a roving reporter on *Entertainment Tonight,* one of the most popular non-network programs on television. *Laughing All the Way* and Ms. Howar's novel, *Making Ends*

Barbara Howar

Meet, were bestsellers, and she has been a regular contributor to the *Washington Post*, *New York* magazine, and other publications.

A sixth-generation southerner, Barbara Dearing Howar was born on September 27, 1934 in Raleigh, North Carolina to Charles Oscar and Mary Elizabeth (O'Connell) Dearing. She and her two sisters—one older and one younger than she—were reared by a succession of black nannies. "I loved each of these women," she wrote in *Laughing All the Way* (1973), "surrogates for my absent parents, and a great part of whatever sense of morality I have came, I think, from what they had time to impart." As a schoolgirl during the early years of World War II, Barbara Howar played combat games and paraded around in a WAC uniform to demonstrate her enthusiastic support of the Allies. The day a photograph of her saluting a convoy bound for Fort Bragg was published in the Raleigh *Times* "was one of [her] proudest moments," she recalled in her autobiography, "and probably the beginning of a deep and abiding love of personal recognition."

Her thirst for the limelight, tendency toward nonconformity, and rebellious nature put Barbara Howar on a collision course with the teachers and administrators at the series of Catholic schools she attended. "I passionately hated Catholic school," she noted in her autobiography, "and suffered the nuns' and priests' ministrations to my soul with little grace. So, I might add, did they. Our mutual disregard for each other was our one thing in common. But for twelve years we lasted it out, each doing God's will grudgingly." During those years, Ms. Howar rarely missed a chance to demonstrate what she called her "blatant heathenism." In the seventh grade, for example, she edited an under-

ground newspaper called the *Epar News*, which took its name from the word "rape" spelled backward; changed benediction chants, turning, for instance, "Ora pro Nobis" into "ole rotten donuts"; put a painted turtle on the baptismal font; and stuffed an alley cat into the choir organ.

Because she had refused to take her education seriously, Barbara Howar was unable to pass a college entrance examination. As an alternative, she was sent to the Holton-Arms School, a finishing school in Washington, D.C., a city that she viewed "with an enthusiasm other small-town girls reserve for Hollywood or New York." During her months there, she attended Dwight D. Eisenhower's first inaugural ball, at the Mayflower Hotel, with Alabama congressman Frank Boykin, her roommate's uncle, and on several occasions traveled in school limousines to tea at the White House. As time went on she "developed a fascination for politics and politicians that proximity would not dull," as she put it.

After returning to North Carolina for her debut into society, Barbara Howar took a job with the Raleigh *Times*, as an assistant to Mark Ethridge Jr., a young liberal whose views were anathema to much of the southern establishment. Working in an otherwise all-male newsroom, she corrected copy and wrote stories and did layouts for the society pages. She also fetched coffee for her colleagues and, for a few weeks in 1954, "dealt with the irate telephone callers who objected loudly but anonymously" to the paper's editorial endorsement of the Supreme Court's decision in *Brown v. Board of Education of Topeka*, which barred racial segregation in public schools.

By 1957 Barbara Howar felt that she was ready "to conquer Washington," a conviction that she later labeled "a wild fantasy" based on "a vague but cosmetically encouraged resemblance to Grace Kelly and six years of elocution lessons at Miss Bootsie MacDonald's School of Tap and Toe." After a *Washington Post* editor refused to hire her, flatly declaring that he had "no places for women with experience, much less you kids who can't do anything," Ms. Howar prevailed upon Frank Boykin, who found her a patronage job as a secretary with the House Committee on Interstate and Foreign Commerce. The lone woman on the committee staff, she ran the mimeograph machine, hand-delivered bills and committee notices to congressmen, and took dictation by committing entire paragraphs to memory and typing the material later. In her spare time, she began her climb up the Washington social ladder, attending countless parties, flying on private planes to the Kentucky Derby, and snaring tickets for the opening nights of new Broadway musicals.

In 1958, her interest in the committee job waning, Barbara Howar decided "to do the only thing [she] had not tried: marriage." As she explained in her autobiography, "All I had to do was choose a man from among the available crowd who was going places, and move on to something new and more fulfilling." The man she selected, Edmund

Howar, was the son of one of Washington's most prominent builders and, in her words, "America's richest resident Arab." After the two were married in a civil ceremony, they settled into a large home in Georgetown and became regulars on the Washington party circuit. During the presidency of John F. Kennedy, Barbara Howar wrote, "it was fun merely to watch everyone dashing about frenetically shopping where Jackie did; ordering from Ethel's seamstress those sleeveless little garbardine dresses in the right shade of pink at just the right height above the knees." It was not until Lyndon Johnson became president, however, that Ms. Howar took center stage in Washington society. "I had not been sufficiently immersed in Kennedy life to be considered the Johnsons' enemy, and the Johnsons were low on untapped talent," she observed in *Laughing All the Way*. "Their quest for new faces, combined with my growing ambition, made us a natural combination: they had needs and I could be had."

Barbara Howar began her association with President Johnson as a "Lady for Lyndon" at the 1964 Democratic National Convention in Atlantic City, New Jersey. The following October, she served as Mrs. Johnson's hairdresser on the "Lady Bird Special" campaign train, and after the election she helped organize the inaugural balls. As a fashion adviser and confidante to the Johnson daughters, Lynda and Luci, in 1965 and 1966, Ms. Howar was a frequent guest at the White House, and she was singled out by the media as one of the Johnson camp's brightest lights—an intelligent, attractive woman who could be relied on for an irreverent quote. (When asked, for example, if she had professional experience in fashion, she replied, "No, just a great deal of experience in spending money.")

After Luci Johnson became engaged to Patrick Nugent early in 1966, Barbara Howar helped Luci shop for her trousseau, and in March of that year she and her husband chaperoned the president's daughter and her fiancé on a trip to New York. The Johnson girls, according to Ms. Howar, "needed a companion to steer them through public places, someone to shop with them, to chaperone their parties, go to movies, restaurants, discotheques. It became understood that I would accompany them anywhere at any time at any expense."

In the spring of 1966, Barbara Howar abruptly lost favor with the Johnsons—a fact that became evident when the White House canceled the lavish engagement party that she was planning for Luci Johnson and Patrick Nugent. Washington insiders speculated that the break was precipitated by Johnson's fear of a scandal should the public learn of Ms. Howar's love affairs with a United States senator and a White House aide. (The latter liaison ended dramatically when private detectives—hired by Edmund Howar—stormed the pair's Caribbean hideaway.) A brief reconciliation with her husband proved unsuccessful, and by 1967 Barbara Howar was newly divorced, receiving only a modest child-support stipend, and desperately looking for

sources of income to support herself and her two small children, Bader Elizabeth and Edmund Dearing. "There were no ads in the classified sections of the paper seeking ex-debutantes experienced at dishing up tea," she lamented at the time, as recalled in her autobiography. "Freedom was one thing; survival would be another."

A need for money, coupled with a long-suppressed desire to become a writer, prompted Barbara Howar to sign a contract with the *Ladies' Home Journal* for "a tell-all story about Lyndon Johnson and how he ate his peas mashed up in a bowl, Chinese-rice style." Her candid account of her two years in the Johnson orbit, a 7,500-word article titled "Why L. B. J. Dropped Me," was published in the April 1968 issue, which hit the newsstands one week before President Johnson announced, on March 31, that he would not seek reelection. Later in 1968 Ms. Howar signed on with Metromedia's Washington affiliate, Channel 5, to deliver thrice-weekly three-minute commentaries on life in Washington. Although she was well acquainted with the social scene in the capital, she required a crash course in politics. (When she covered the 1968 Republican National Convention, she failed to recognize Spiro T. Agnew, the governor of Maryland and the party's eventual choice for vice-president.) "Hours went into my commentary," she recounted in *Laughing All the Way*. "I wrote and rewrote; scores of tape recordings screeched back my twangy voice until, six months later, I could almost stand the sight and sound of myself on camera. . . . Doggedly, I went on camera three times a week, airing my opinions on anything from abortion to renegade priests to [Supreme Court Justice] Abe Fortas."

Barbara Howar's stint as a commentator ended when, as she put it, she "described George Wallace as the 'bigots' guru' and Wallace supporters were enraged." Shorty thereafter, in November 1968, Ms. Howar became a regular on *Panorama*, a live, weekday, Washington-based talk show that also starred Maury Povich and John Willis. Although she still considered herself a "recycled socialite with a newly aroused public conscience," her wit and vivacity proved to be popular with the *Panorama* audience. At first, Ms. Howar was delegated "all the frivolous interviews that producers consider women's work," but before long she was regularly sparring with the show's guests, including the author Jim Bishop, who had made what she considered to be derogatory remarks about Senator Robert F. Kennedy; Sheilah Graham, the Hollywood gossip columnist; the Reverend Carl McIntire, a firebrand radio evangelist; the promoters of the Miss America Pageant; the ultraconservative multimillionaire H. L. Hunt; and, in her words, "the better part of the entire United States Congress."

As her position with Metromedia became more secure, Barbara Howar was given other plum assignments, such as anchoring the network's East Coast coverage of Richard Nixon's inaugural ball in 1969, and she regained much of the social status that she had enjoyed in the mid-1960s. In a *New York Times Magazine* (March 8, 1970) article about the Washington social scene, Thomas Meehan called her "the leading unmarried woman" in the capital, a trendsetter whose "comings and goings are endlessly chronicled in the city's several society columns." Ms. Howar's association with *Panorama* ended early in 1971, after Metromedia executives refused to give her a raise. (Her salary was less than half that of her male colleagues.) Ben Bradlee, the editor of the *Washington Post*, immediately hired her to write a weekly column for the paper's style section. Her articles on fashion, entertaining, and Washington personalities also appeared in such national magazines as *Vogue*, *Esquire*, and the *Ladies' Home Journal*.

To supplement her income, Ms. Howar went on the lecture circuit, an endeavor that she despised and soon abandoned. She did not fare much better with *Joyce and Barbara: For Adults Only*, a syndicated interview show that she co-hosted with Joyce Susskind. The program, which was produced by Mrs. Susskind's husband, David, was touted as the first attempt to present female interviewers in "thirty minutes of adult conversation" with people in the news. Television critics, however, found little to praise in *Joyce and Barbara* during its brief life (only seventeen programs were videotaped), although Stephanie Harrington, in a review for the *New York Times* (June 13, 1971), wrote that Barbara Howar "is quick and clever and often very funny, and if she would only bone up on her subjects she might do very well on her own as an interviewer."

In the spring of 1973 Stein and Day published *Laughing All the Way*, Barbara Howar's lively, candid autobiography. Within weeks, it was a bestseller. Reviewers were impressed by her dry sense of humor, the clarity of her writing, and her insightful comments on the Washington personalities of the 1960s and 1970s. In addition to a frank account of her two-year association with the Johnson family, the book offered readers backstage glimpses of Dr. Henry A. Kissinger, Ms. Howar's frequent escort before his marriage to Nancy Maginnes, in 1974; Alice Roosevelt Longworth, the doyenne of Washington society; Katharine Graham, the publisher of the *Washington Post*; Joan Kennedy, the wife of Senator Edward M. Kennedy; Robert Kennedy's widow, Ethel; and Martha Mitchell, the outspoken wife of Richard Nixon's attorney general. Ms. Howar also wrote affectingly of her southern childhood, her close relationship with her mother, whose death in 1971 left her devastated, and her struggle to survive financially and emotionally after the disintegration of her marriage.

The publication of *Laughing All the Way* coincided with the release of Willie Morris's *Last of the Southern Girls*, a novel widely believed to be based on the life of Barbara Howar. Ms. Howar, who was linked romantically with Morris at the time, conceded that there were some similarities between her experiences and those of Morris's protagonist, Carol Hollywell, but, as she told a reporter for *Time* magazine: "He has his heroine involved with a congressman. Honey, I've never taken up with a congressman in my life. I'm such a snob, I've never gone below the Senate." Barbara Howar's novel, *Making Ends Meet*, which was published by Random House in 1976, focused on a person very much like herself: Lilly Shawcross, an abrasively witty, forty-year-old woman who is divorced, has two children, and works as a film critic for a Washington, D.C., television station. The book—which reaped a paperback advance of $800,000, reportedly a record for a first novel—showed Ms. Howar to be a first-rate storyteller. Erica Jong, commenting on *Making Ends Meet* for the *New York Times Book Review* (April 25, 1976), called the work "touching and clearly relevant to the lives of many women. Lilly Shawcross is afflicted with the modern female dilemma: her intellect is liberated, her emotions are another matter." Other reviewers gave the book high marks for its readability as well as its honesty.

In July 1976 Barbara Howar covered the social side of the celebrity-studded Democratic National Convention for *New York* magazine. Six months later she joined Dan Rather and Charles Kuralt as a regular on *Who's Who*, a prime-time CBS news magazine series that John J. O'Connor, the *New York Times*'s resident television critic, called "a class act, more akin to the glossy magazine than to the cheaply sensational tabloid." Nonetheless, relegated to a time slot opposite the then flourishing ABC sitcoms *Happy Days* and *Laverne and Shirley*, *Who's Who* was unable to find an audience, and it was canceled in June 1977.

Over the next few years, Barbara Howar continued to divide her time between print and broadcast journalism. In July 1978 the *New York Times* printed her irreverent paean to New York City, a town where "by law, women must express opinions, and I have never been made to wait the requisite twenty-four hours to hear what is being whispered behind my back." During the 1978–79 television season, Ms. Howar was a semi-regular on *We Interrupt This Week*, a sophisticated spoof of quiz shows, in which panelists tried to answer esoteric questions about the week's news. The program, a product of public television, had a sizable loyal following, but it was nonetheless axed in March 1979, after its funding was cut.

Three years later Barbara Howar landed a job as field reporter for *Entertainment Tonight*, a nationally syndicated blend of show-business news, gossip, and celebrity interviews that was then seen by an estimated 18.5 million viewers each night. She remained with the program for five years, often crisscrossing the globe on assignment. In one weekend, she jetted from Nashville, Tennessee, where she had been covering the fifteenth anniversary of the television show *Hee Haw*, to Monte Carlo for an interview with Prince Rainier.

In February 1987, after five years on the job, Ms. Howar left *Entertainment Tonight*. "It seemed like a good time to leave and start a new challenge," she explained, as quoted in the *New York Post* (February 3, 1987). On October 24, 1988 she narrated *Unauthorized Biography: Jane Fonda,* the first of a syndicated, prime-time series of celebrity profiles. She followed up, on March 8, 1989, with a sharply critical two-hour profile of Richard Nixon that John Leonard, no admirer of the former president, called an "icon-bashing, slash-and-burn" exposé. "Howar never lets up," Leonard observed in his television column in *New York* (March 15, 1989). "She waves her contempt like a pennant on a yacht." *Unauthorized Biography: The Royals,* a gossipy look at the British royal family, was similarly denounced by reviewers when it aired on June 7, 1989. The society columnist James Revson, commenting on the program in *New York Newsday* (June 6, 1989), saved his sharpest barbs for Ms. Howar: "The one big surprise is that Barbara Howar is the host of the program. There's something quite odd about Howar, the original Washington power climber, chatting away about royal deficiencies and dirt. It doesn't work."

Tall and slim, with a finely chiseled face and shoulder-length blonde hair, Barbara Howar is a striking woman. In her leisure hours, she enjoys cooking informal dinners for a small group of friends. "I don't cook by recipes, and, while it appears to be more evidence of my unwillingness to obey orders, I find it more fun to fool around with ingredients than to play culinary chemist with the fruits of somebody else's imagination," she told a reporter for the *Salt Lake Tribune* some years ago. "Cooking is an art form, not a scientific exercise, and I can never resist making up the rules as I cook." Ms. Howar makes her home in Washington, D.C.

References: Esquire 80:52+ Ag '73; *N Y Daily News* p64 D 3 '76 por; *N Y Post* p37 My 1 '73 por; *N Y Times Mag* p30+ Mr 8 '70 por; *National Observer* p23 Je 30 '73; *Newsweek* 77:93 Ap 12 '71 por; *Washington Post* K p1+ My 13 '73 por; *Women's Wear Daily* p14 Ap 23 '73 por; *Contemporary Authors* vols 89–92 (1983)

G. Paul Burnett/NYT Pictures

Hwang, David Henry

[wong]

Aug. 11, 1957– Playwright. Address: c/o William Craver, Writers and Artists Agency, 70 W. 36th St., New York, N.Y. 10018

"The fusion between East and West has already come to exist someplace in me," David Henry Hwang said in an interview for *U.S. News & World Report* (March 28, 1988). "I simply have to find it." The middle ground where East meets West has

been fertile soil for the prolific young Asian-American playwright, for, with few exceptions, the tension between the two conflicting cultures has dominated his work. Skillfully combining the conventions of the well-made play with the exotic theatricality of Oriental stagecraft, Hwang has explored what he has called "the mystery of our identity" in a remarkable series of plays, beginning in 1981 with *F.O.B.*, a compassionate look at social prejudice that he wrote while he was still an undergraduate, and culminating in 1988 with the Tony Award–winning *M. Butterfly,* an intriguing metaphor for the bewildering complexity of East-West relations.

The oldest of the three children of Henry and Dorothy Hwang, David Henry Hwang was born on August 11, 1957 in Los Angeles, California. His father, who had immigrated to the United States from Shanghai in the late 1940s, was president of a bank in Los Angeles's Chinatown; his mother, who had also been born in China but had been reared in the Philippines, was a pianist and music teacher. With his two sisters, Margery and Grace, David Hwang grew up in what he has since described as "relatively privileged financial circumstances" in San Gabriel, an affluent Los Angeles suburb. The privileges, in Hwang's case, included education at the Harvard School, an elite college prep academy in nearby North Hollywood, where he excelled in debate, and music lessons. (He is, by his own account, "a pretty decent violinist.")

"I knew I was Chinese," he told Jeremy Gerard in an interview for a *New York Times Magazine* (March 13, 1988) profile, "but growing up it never occurred to me that that had any particular implication or that it should differentiate me in any way. I thought it was a minor detail, like having red hair.

I never got a lot in school to contradict that. My parents brought us up with a rather nice sense of self." That "sense of self" was fortified at family gatherings, where Hwang's maternal grandmother told "talk-stories," as he has called them, about his ancestors' lives. Hoping to preserve the memories of those forebears, Hwang wrote, in his words, "sort of a novel" based on his grandmother's tales when he was just twelve years old and distributed copies to his relatives.

On his graduation from the Harvard School in 1975, Hwang enrolled at Stanford University with the intention of pursuing a law degree, but he soon discovered that his interest and talent lay elsewhere. Switching his major to English literature, he compiled an excellent academic record that eventually earned him membership in Phi Beta Kappa. While at Stanford, Hwang regularly attended performances at the Magic Theatre in San Francisco, where Sam Shepard was then the playwright in residence. Inspired by Shepard's independent vision, he asked his creative-writing teacher, John L'Heureux, to give him a tutorial in playwriting. "It just seemed to me to be the most magical form, the most social to some degree," he explained to Allan Wallach of Newsday (September 21, 1981). "I knew that I wanted to write things to create worlds, and then see the worlds right in front of me." In the summer of 1978 Hwang attended the first Padua Hills Playwrights Festival, a six-week workshop for aspiring young playwrights held in Claremont, California. It was there, under the guidance of Sam Shepard and other playwrights, that he began to work on F.O.B., an examination of the contrasting attitudes of American-born Chinese and recent immigrants—known as F.O.B.'s, for "fresh off the boat"—as revealed in the conflict between a brash young newcomer and his Chinese-American cousins.

Writing on weekends and between classes, Hwang soon completed a first draft of F.O.B. and, in March 1979, he directed its first performance, by students in his Stanford University dormitory. Encouraged by his professors, he submitted the text to the National Playwrights Conference at the O'Neill Theatre Center in Waterford, Connecticut—a prestigious annual workshop that has launched scores of new plays. In the spring of 1979 the conference accepted the work for production during its upcoming summer session. Within days of receiving his A.B. degree, with distinction in English, Hwang set out for Waterford, where he saw his play staged by professionals before a sympathetic and helpful audience of theatre critics and fellow playwrights. "The biggest thing I learned was how to filter criticism," he told Eric Pace of the New York Times (July 12, 1981). "I came out with the realization that I had written this play which knowledgeable and experienced people seemed to find enjoyable, and so I had to trust the instincts that created it in the first place."

Returning to California, Hwang taught creative writing at Menlo-Atherton High School in Menlo Park and, in his off hours, continued to write.

Meanwhile, Joseph Papp, the artistic director of the New York Shakespeare Festival, who had been searching for new plays by Asian-American authors, decided to mount a full-scale production of F.O.B. at the company's Public Theater in New York City. "F.O.B. reminded me of the 'greenhorns,' the Jews who came from Eastern Europe . . . ," Papp told Jeremy Gerard, in explaining his choice. "The principle of someone coming from the old country who didn't know how to behave himself was very much part of my own tradition." Papp was especially impressed by the way Hwang had used both Occidental and Oriental theatrical techniques to interweave the naturalistic details of contemporary American life with the psychological and emotional underpinnings of the characters' shared ethnic heritage.

Directed by Mako, the artistic director of the East West Players, a Los Angeles–based troupe that specializes in works dealing with the Asian-American experience, and starring John Lone, a Chinese actor trained in the stylized technique of the Beijing Opera, F.O.B. opened at the Public Theater's Martinson Hall on June 8, 1980 to generally favorable notices. Even those critics who found the work to be "overwritten" and, at times, "unwieldy" admired Hwang's compassion, wit, and resourcefulness. "Hwang hits home far more often that he misses . . . ," Frank Rich wrote in his review for the New York Times (June 10, 1980). "If West and East don't precisely meet in F.O.B., they certainly fight each other to a fascinating standoff." Although it ran for only forty-two performances, F.O.B. won an Obie Award as best play of the 1980–81 Off-Broadway season.

In the fall of 1980, while he was taking courses in playwriting at the Yale School of Drama, Hwang was commissioned by the Henry Street Settlement to write a new play for its forthcoming ethnic heritage series. Intrigued by the challenge of writing an historical play, Hwang chose as his subject the Chinese immigrants who had helped to build the transcontinental railroad in the mid-nineteenth century. Determined to dispel the commonly accepted image of the Chinese laborers as servile "little coolies," as he put it, he centered The Dance and the Railroad on a particular historical incident—a strike in 1867 that, in his view, showed them to be "strong and hardy and rebellious men." But because he also wanted his play to be more than a polemic, he decided to focus on the relationship between two idled workers, whose names he took from and personalities he shaped around the actors assigned to the roles: John Lone, who played the idealistic, self-controlled veteran worker, and Tzi Ma, who took the part of the naïvely optimistic young newcomer. To pass the time during the strike, the two practice the exacting, balletic movements of Chinese opera, dreaming of their eventual return to their homeland and to careers in the Chinese theatre.

After playing for a few weeks at the Henry Street Settlement's Federal Theater in the spring of 1981, The Dance and the Railroad transferred to the Public Theater, where it settled in for a long run. Considered by the majority of New York critics to be a tighter, more accomplished work than *F.O.B.*, the play was praised for its sensitively realized characterizations, dramatic insights, and hypnotic choreography, which was created by John Lone. As more than one reviewer pointed out, much of the action was humorous, but Frank Rich, commenting in the *New York Times* (March 21, 1981), detected "an underlying sadness" that rose "shatteringly to the surface in the play's final section, in which Ma and Lone improvise their own Chinese opera about their harrowing sea journey to America and their subsequent adventures in the ostensible promised land. By the end of that often funny burlesque," Rich concluded, "the two characters have subtly traded positions until finally we wonder if the wise Lone might not be the real slave, the real fool, the man who has lost the illusions of both his worlds." Nominated for a Drama Desk Award, *The Dance and the Railroad* was filmed for broadcast on television by ABC Arts Cable Productions.

The Dance and the Railroad was still running when Hwang's third effort, the contemporary comedy *Family Devotions*, opened at the Public Theater on October 18, 1981. Described by Hwang as "a Kaufman and Hart-type farce," *Family Devotions* revolves around a confrontation between members of a well-to-do, obsessively materialistic Chinese-American family, which resembles the playwright's in its history, attitudes, and Protestant fundamentalism, and a revered elderly uncle from China, who forces them to reexamine their values and their "connection to the past," as Hwang put it. For some reviewers, including Clive Barnes and John Simon, who had so admired *The Dance and the Railroad*, Hwang's ambitious, broadly satiric new work was a disappointment—a "situation comedy gone macabre," in Barnes's opinion; a "sort of Chinese *I Love Lucy*," in Simon's. For others, among them Frank Rich and the *New Yorker*'s Edith Oliver, *Family Devotions* was not only the author's "funniest" play to date, but also, as Miss Oliver noted in her review of November 2, 1981, his "most complex and fascinating," compounded as it was of "emotion and convictions, irony and humor, shrewdly observed characters and . . . mystery."

Temporarily putting aside his preoccupation with what he has called "the idea of being a minority in America," Hwang addressed the more universal "idea of relationships" in *Sound and Beauty*, a twin bill comprised of the thematically related one-act plays *The Sound of a Voice* and *The House of Sleeping Beauties*, which was presented at the Public Theater in October 1983. Set in a remote area of seventeenth-century Japan, *The Sound of a Voice* featured John Lone, who also directed the production, as a samurai who falls under the spell of the beguiling witch he has been sent to kill. Its contemporary companion piece, *The House of Sleeping Beauties*, a variation on a novella by the Nobel Prize–winning Japanese writer Yasunari

Kawabata, describes the poignant friendship that develops between an aging novelist and the madam of a bizarre Tokyo brothel, where the young women are kept in a state of drug-induced insensibility. In a program note, Hwang explained that he had created the last-named fantasy "to explore the relationship between Kawabata's suicide (the writer gassed himself in 1972) and his novella."

Sound and Beauty was greeted with qualified praise from the critics, most of them agreeing that *The Sound of a Voice* was the stronger of the two plays, at least partly because it benefited from the commanding performance of John Lone, as the warrior. Frank Rich, an admitted admirer of Hwang's customary "vibrant, freewheeling style," was among those who found the playwright's experiment with the "ascetic aesthetic mode," as Rich put it, intrusive. "We're keenly conscious of his efforts to duplicate the mode of Japanese literature and theatre," he wrote in his appraisal for the *New York Times* (November 7, 1983). "The spare visual and verbal brushstrokes are so artfully applied that effects intended as simple and delicate can come across as synthetic and laborious." The paucity of detail also troubled Michael Feingold of the *Village Voice* and John Simon of *New York* magazine, who reviewed the plays for their respective publications on November 21, 1983. "His mosaic seems to lack a few crucial, passionate tesserae," Simon observed, "and his ear sometimes fails him . . . [but] with *The Sound of a Voice*, the young playwright comes significantly closer to perfect pitch."

As Hwang explained to Jeremy Gerard, he was unprepared for the celebrity accorded him for having had four plays produced in New York in three years and, more important, unprepared for his newly acquired role of Asian-American spokesperson. "On the one hand, it was flattering," he said. "But on the other hand, growing up as a person of color, you're always ambivalent to a certain degree about your own ethnicity. You think it's great, but there is necessarily a certain amount of self-hatred, or confusion at least, which results from the fact that there's a role model in this society which is basically a Caucasian man, and you don't measure up to that. What was happening to me was that that quality about which I was ambivalent was being thrust into the forefront. . . . It was no longer that I was a playwright per se, but that I was an Asian-American playwright, and my Asian-Americanness became the quality which defined me to the public."

A long fallow period ensued, during which Hwang traveled in Asia, Europe, and Canada. While visiting Canada, he began work on *Rich Relations*, which he has described as "another attempt to write a spiritual farce . . . about [his] family"—except in this instance the family is Caucasian American. When the play, about a real-estate tycoon and his prodigal son, opened Off Broadway at the Second Stage in April 1986, it was roundly panned by the New York critics as little more than a tired and clumsy rehash of the playwright's earlier themes. Moreover, the characterization, which up until then had been one of Hwang's strong points, was considered to be unusually weak, with the sketchily drawn central figures serving "mainly as pawns in a kneejerk authorial morality play," to quote Frank Rich's *New York Times* (April 22, 1986) review. But like most of his colleagues, Rich regarded the comedy as "an aberration that a talented writer had to get out of his system."

Viewing his first failure as a liberating experience, Hwang decided to try his hand at writing for film and television. Over the next few years, he wrote the script for *My American Son*, a drama about the Iran-Contra scandal, for Home Box Office, the pay-cable service, and adapted Heinrich Harrer's book *Seven Years in Tibet* for the screen. Hwang is also the coauthor, with Frederick Kimbal, of *Mixed Emotions*, a television drama about an interracial marriage that was commissioned in 1985 by WCVB-TV in Boston as part of its yearlong campaign against racial prejudice.

Hwang returned to the stage in 1988 with the imaginative and provocative *M. Butterfly*. The inspiration for the play was a *New York Times* dispatch from Paris, published nearly two years earlier, about a peculiar case of espionage involving Bernard Boursicot, a French diplomat formerly stationed in Beijing. Following a lengthy trial that titillated all of France, Boursicot was convicted of passing intelligence information to his mistress of twenty years, who was in reality a male Chinese agent masquerading as an actress with the Beijing Opera. Fascinated by the diplomat's seemingly willful self-deception, Hwang decided to use the story as the basis for a play in which he could pull together his concerns about "racism, sexism, and imperialism."

Viewing the curious tale as a skewed variation on Puccini's *Madama Butterfly*, Hwang fashioned a complex and multilayered play of sexual and cultural role reversal in which the Frenchman, who at the beginning identifies with Puccini's Pinkerton, gradually assumes the role of the submissive Butterfly. After a four-week tryout in Washington, D.C., John Dexter's visually stunning production of *M. Butterfly* (the title is deliberately ambiguous) opened on Broadway at the Eugene O'Neill Theatre on March 20, 1988 to mixed reviews. Although virtually every critic admired the sumptuous staging and the incisive portrayals of John Lithgow, as the French diplomat, and B. D. Wong, as the Chinese agent-actress, some confessed that they had found the story improbable at best and Hwang's interpretation of it "shallow," "naïve," and "simplistic."

"The more Hwang tries to pin down his ideas—like those metaphoric butterflies he pointedly describes—the more they wiggle and die . . . ," Linda Winer observed in her opening-night review for *New York Newsday*. "Rather than dig into the intensely personal trauma of this freaky case, Hwang goes for a broader indictment of imperialism as an extension of the insecure but insatiable Western male ego." Frank Rich, John Simon, and John Gross were among the reviewers similarly troubled by the playwright's "overtly explicit bouts of thesis mongering," to use Rich's description. "It would have been better . . . ," John Gross observed in his evaluation of *M. Butterfly* for the *New York Times* (April 10, 1988), if Hwang "hadn't been tempted to pile on the ideas. . . . As it is, they clutter up the foreground of the play and seriously coarsen its texture. But luckily, despite these handicaps, the central action survives: bitter, affecting, and finally driven on by an anguish that even approaches—just a little—the passion of *Madama Butterfly*."

In addition to the 1988 Tony Award as best play of the year, *M. Butterfly* won Tonys for John Dexter's direction and B. D. Wong's electrifying performance. It also took the Drama Desk and Outer Critics Circle best-play honors and earned Hwang the John Gassner Award as the season's outstanding new playwright. A British production, starring Anthony Hopkins, opened to mixed reviews in London in April 1989 but nonetheless broke box-office records at the Shaftsbury Theatre in the first week of its run. *M. Butterfly* has also been staged in Buenos Aires and in Hamburg, and productions are scheduled in Paris, Oslo, Rome, Madrid, Tel Aviv, Sydney, Auckland, and New Delhi, among other cities.

Hwang examined the idea of the outsider from another perspective in *1000 Airplanes on the Roof*, a collaboration with the composer Philip Glass and Jerome Sirlin, the visionary stage designer, that has been described by its creators as "a science fiction music drama." Specifically designed as a small-scale touring piece, the multimedia work is essentially a ninety-minute monologue in which a character identified only as M recounts the story of his abduction by extraterrestrials and tries to come to terms with his alternately terrifying and revelatory memories of the encounter. When the work was first performed in Vienna in July 1988 as part of the Danube Festival of Lower Austria, one critic described it as being "part Freud, part Kafka, and part Steven Spielberg." Reviewers of its American premiere, at the American Music Theater Festival in Philadelphia two months later, ranked Glass's haunting score among "the most dramatic and moving" of his recent efforts. As for Hwang's text, it was judged "rich" and "gripping," even though, as Allan Kozinn pointed out in his *New York Times* (September 24, 1988) review, "we never know whether [the narrator] is to be believed or considered psychotic."

In June 1988 the American Playwrights Project, a joint venture of Jujamcyn Theatres and three independent theatrical producers, commissioned Hwang and five other American playwrights—Christopher Durang, David Rabe, Wendy Wasserstein, Marsha Norman, and Terrence McNally—to write new plays for the commercial theatre. Later in the same year, Hwang was commissioned by the Metropolitan Opera to write the libretto for Philip Glass's new opera "The Voyage," tentatively scheduled to have its premiere at the Met in October 1992, in commemoration of the 500th anniversary of Columbus's discovery of America. Hwang's other projects include adapting *M. Butterfly* for the screen, creating what he has described as "a Victorian rock musical" about Oscar Wilde, and collaborating with Philip Glass on a stage adaptation of André Malraux's novel *Man's Fate*.

In addition to the honors listed above, Hwang is the recipient of two awards from *Drama-Logue* magazine and the Golden Eagle from the Council on International Nontheatrical Events. Over the past few years, he has won playwriting fellowships from the Guggenheim and Rockefeller foundations and from the National Endowment for the Arts. A

slender, compact man with a cheerful, easygoing manner, David Henry Hwang is admittedly obsessed by his work and has few hobbies. By his own account, his only "vice" is his fondness for clothing by the Asian designer Issey Miyake. Hwang lives in a triplex in Manhattan. His marriage to the former Ophelia Chong, a Chinese-Canadian artist, broke up during the extended rehearsals for *M. Butterfly*.

References: N Y Times II p4 Jl 12 '81; N Y Times Mag p44+ Mr 13 '88 pors; Newsday II p17 S 27 '81 por; People 21:88 Ja 9 '84 por; Time 134:62+ Ag 14 '89 por; U S News 104:52+ Mr 28 '88 por

---

Hyde, Henry J(ohn)

Apr. 18, 1924– United States Representative from Illinois; lawyer. Address: 2104 Rayburn House Office Bldg., Washington, D.C. 20515; 50 E. Oak St., Addison, Ill. 60101

Henry J. Hyde was first elected to the United States House of Representatives in 1974 as one of a handful of Republican freshmen to win office in the face of the public revulsion against the Watergate scandal. Since then, he has emerged as an articulate spokesman for his party's dominant conservative forces and the most conspicuous, and arguably the most passionate, opponent of abortion in Congress. He is perhaps best known for the Hyde amendments, a series of riders to annual appropriations bills that since 1976 have restricted public funding of abortions for poor women. A Roman

Catholic champion of the national antiabortion movement, Hyde has never wavered in his conviction that human life begins at conception, and he therefore condemns all abortion, even in cases involving rape or incest, as murder. His ultimate goal remains a constitutional amendment outlawing abortion except as an inevitable consequence of saving the life of the mother.

As a senior minority member of the Foreign Affairs Committee and ranking Republican on the Intelligence Committee, Hyde was a forceful advocate of United States military assistance to the Contra rebels in their unsuccessful struggle to topple the Marxist-led Sandinista regime in Nicaragua. During the nationally televised Iran-Contra hearings in 1987, he was perhaps the most eloquent defender of President Ronald Reagan's Central American policy and the covert activities of the National Security Council aide Lieutenant Colonel Oliver L. North.

Henry John Hyde was born in Chicago, Illinois on April 18, 1924 to Henry Clay Hyde, a coin collector for the local telephone company, and Monica (Kelly) Hyde. He attended a Roman Catholic parochial elementary school and graduated from Saint George High School in nearby Evanston in 1942. Having received a basketball scholarship, he entered Georgetown University, in Washington, D.C., on whose team he played in the National Collegiate Athletic Association Eastern championship game in 1943. The following year Hyde dropped out of college to be commissioned an ensign in the United States Navy. Serving with the Seventh Fleet in the South Pacific, he took part in the invasion of the Philippines. After his discharge, as a lieutenant, junior grade, in August 1946, he resumed his studies at Georgetown University, where he obtained a B.S. degree in the following year. In 1949 Hyde received a law degree from the Loyola University School of Law in Chicago. He was admitted to the Illinois bar on January 9, 1950. Hyde remained on active reserve until he retired with the rank of commander in 1968, having served as officer in charge of the United States naval intelligence reserve unit in Chicago.

Having been reared in a solidly Democratic home, Hyde voted for the Democratic candidate, Harry S. Truman, in the presidential election of 1948, but he had already become disenchanted with what he perceived as the leftward drift of the party. "I was raised a Democrat by my family," he explained to Richard Mackenzie for an article in the *Washington Times* supplement *Insight* (August 31, 1987), "but I became concerned during the war about the far Left and the inordinate influence it was having with the Roosevelt administration, especially [with] Eleanor, then with the direction the Democratic party was going in postwar Europe." In 1952 he campaigned in Chicago for Dwight D. Eisenhower for president, and six years later he formally reregistered as a Republican. After practicing law in the Chicago area for about a decade, Hyde entered politics as a precinct captain at a time when Republicans in the city were struggling with little success against the well-oiled political machine run by Mayor Richard J. Daley. He later compared the plight of Republicans in Daley's Chicago with that of blacks in the South before the passage of the Voting Rights Act.

In 1962 Hyde agreed to be the sacrificial Republican candidate to challenge Roman Pucinski, the entrenched Democratic incumbent of the Eleventh Congressional District in northwestern Chicago. Four years later Hyde was elected to the first of four successive terms in the Illinois state house of representatives, where, as a staunch conservative, he supported the death penalty and more stringent antidrug legislation and opposed the Equal Rights Amendment for women. In spite of his controversial stands, he was named the "best freshman representative" by an association of Illinois political reporters. During 1971 and 1972 he served as majority leader and, in his last term, ran unsuccessfully for the post of speaker. Although Hyde was gratified by his discovery during his years in Springfield that he had a knack for legislative work, he wearied of the political infighting and considered returning to the private practice of law.

Acting on the advice of friends, Hyde instead decided to enter the race for the seat of retiring Republican congressman Harold R. Collier in 1974. Although he was familiar with only part of the Sixth Congressional District of Illinois, then comprising Chicago's western and northwestern suburbs and including Chicago O'Hare Airport, Hyde topped a six-man primary field with 49 percent of the vote. Because the district had long been a conservative Republican bastion, Hyde in normal times could be expected to coast over his Democratic opposition, but, in 1974, in the first congressional elections held since the resignation of President Richard M. Nixon after the Watergate scandal, the GOP was understandably nervous about its open seats. Moreover, the Democratic candidate, Edward Hanrahan, was popular in the conservative district because, as Cook County state's attorney, he had authorized a widely publicized, though highly controversial, raid on the radical Black Panthers organization in 1971. Hyde nevertheless managed to defeat Hanrahan by 53 to 47 percent, and he has been reelected handily ever since. Following the 1980 census, the Sixth District was redrawn to encompass Chicago's westernmost suburbs, including Wheaton.

Quickly emerging as a rising star of the party, Hyde was elected chairman of the seventeen-member freshman Republican class in Congress that year. He also won coveted appointments to the Judiciary and Banking and Currency committees, and, by the end of his first term, he had gained national attention as the acknowledged leader of the antiabortion forces in the House. In June 1976 Hyde, together with Republican Robert E. Bauman of Maryland, set out to determine how members of the House of Representatives felt about abortion in the wake of the Supreme Court's decision, in 1973, that set forth a woman's right to end an unwanted pregnancy under certain circumstances. With little expectation of victory, Hyde hastily drafted in longhand an amendment to the fiscal 1977 appropriations bill for the departments of labor and health, education, and welfare barring federal funding of elective abortions under the Medicaid program.

To Hyde's astonishment, the rider passed and became law on October 1, 1976. Although it was struck down as unconstitutional three weeks later by Judge John F. Dooling Jr. of the federal court in Brooklyn, New York, and a subsequent version was negated in 1978 by Judge John F. Grady of the United States District Court in Chicago, the Supreme Court in June 1980 upheld by the barest majority the right of federal or state governments to refuse to finance abortions, thus vindicating the basic principle behind the Hyde Amendment.

By attaching similar riders to annual appropriations bills ever since, Hyde has succeeded in reducing the number of federally funded abortions each year from hundreds of thousands to a few thousand. The only excuse for abortion that Hyde will condone is to save the life of the mother, since, under such circumstances, he does not consider such a procedure an abortion but a necessary treatment of a disease threatening the mother. Following the Supreme Court's *Webster* decision in July 1989, which allowed states more latitude than at any time since 1973 to restrict abortion rights, the Hyde Amendment was seriously challenged by Congress for the first time. In October legislation was passed that allowed federal funding of abortions in cases of rape or incest, but President Bush vetoed the bill, vindicating Hyde's strict antiabortion position.

Despite criticism that he is insensitive to the suffering of the victims of sexual assault, Hyde is unshakable in his defense of the unborn. "The killing of an innocent human life," he argued in an interview with *U.S. News & World Report* (May 4, 1981), "is not an equal trade-off for the emotional and physical damage from the crime of rape or incest. The fetus has committed no crime. Killing the unborn child would be an admission that there are values superior to human life, and I don't recognize any value superior to human life."

Hyde's unflagging zeal springs from his firm conviction that human life begins at the moment of conception. Although his position echoes that of the Roman Catholic church, he bristles at suggestions that his commitment is rooted in blind faith. "The hell with religion," he was quoted as saying in *People* (August 22, 1977) magazine. "Let's talk medical facts. That fertilized egg may be an appendage to a woman's body, but it is a different being. It's human life, not a bad tooth to be pulled out. If you leave it alone it will be an old man or old lady someday."

Heartened by the tide of conservatism that attended the election of Ronald Reagan as president and the Republican takeover of the Senate in 1980, Hyde tried to codify his notion of what constitutes life in legislation that he introduced in cosponsorship with the Republican senator Jesse Helms of North Carolina in 1981. The Helms-Hyde bill declared simply that "actual life begins from conception," a pronouncement that would have enabled states to outlaw abortion as a form of homicide. Although pro-choice groups predictably opposed the measure, antiabortion forces also criticized Hyde for settling for legislation that is subject to judicial review, instead of pressing for a constitutional amendment to ban abortion. Although Hyde has consistently supported such an amendment as the most certain way to reverse the Supreme Court's 1973 ruling, he has conceded that his objective is nearly impossible in the face of public opinion polls that show a majority of Americans support legal abortion. The Helms-Hyde bill died in committee, partly because of uncertainty over its effect on the legality of such popular contraceptives as the birth control pill and intrauterine devices, which act after conception.

During the 1984 presidential election campaign, in which abortion became a major issue, Hyde engaged Mario Cuomo, the Democratic governor of New York, in an indirect debate over the role of Roman Catholic public officials on the abortion question. In separate appearances at the University of Notre Dame, the two men epitomized the deep division in the church over whether abortion was an issue of public or private morality. Cuomo argued that Roman Catholic public officials should not attempt to foist their religious objections on the majority of Americans who favor legal abortion. In his well-received rebuttal on September 24, in which he rejected the notion that religious values have no place in political debate, Hyde called on Roman Catholic politicians to ignore the public opinion polls and join in saving the more than one million fetuses legally aborted each year. "The duty of one who regards abortion as wrong," he declared, "is not to bemoan the absence of consensus against abortion but to help lead the effort to achieve one." He went on to encourage the federal funding of adoptive services and other alternatives to abortion and called for an end to the present welfare system, which, he charged, fosters illegitimate births.

Sensitive to criticism by pro-choice forces that the right-to-life movement has been so consumed by the rights of the unborn that it has neglected the welfare of the born, Hyde has in recent years promoted better health care for pregnant women and the taking of steps to reduce infant mortality. In February 1989 he joined Democratic congresswoman Barbara Boxer of California, a pro-choice advocate, in cosponsoring legislation that would make it a crime to arrange the birth of a child through a surrogate mother. The Boxer-Hyde measure would not impose penalties on the surrogate mother or the prospective parents but would rather penalize the baby brokers, whom Hyde has compared to slave merchants. "By reducing childbearing to an occupation," Hyde has said, "surrogacy arrangements attack the essential human dignity of every person."

Hyde also joined liberals in voting to extend the Voting Rights Act for another twenty-five years, but only after undergoing a conversion of sorts during hearings on the bill before the Civil and Constitutional Rights Subcommittee of the House Judiciary Committee in 1981. A longtime opponent of the 1965 civil rights legislation requiring southern states with a record of racial discrimination to obtain federal clearance before altering their election laws, Hyde conceded that the law had been effective but objected to its extension on the grounds that it continued to punish the South long after blacks had secured the right to vote without harassment. "What this law does," Hyde declared in an acrid exchange with civil rights leaders testifying in favor of the extension, "is to label a handful of states as racist. Yes, it's worked. Yes, it's been a good law. Yes, there was a rational basis for it. But sovereign states of this country, after the experience of the civil rights movement and all, chafe at being labeled racist." But after hearing compelling testimony of continued efforts to thwart black registration, Hyde relented. "You're being dishonest if you don't change your mind after hearing the facts," Hyde told Steven V. Roberts of the *New York Times* (July 19, 1981). "I was wrong, and now I want to be right."

As a member of the Western Hemisphere Affairs Subcommittee of the House Foreign Affairs Committee, Hyde consistently supported the Reagan administration's Central American policy of arming the Contra rebels in their struggle to overthrow the Marxist-led Sandinista regime in Nicaragua. He also served on the so-called Iran-Contra committee created to investigate the Reagan administration's trade of arms for hostages with Iran and the diversion of some of the profits from that trade to the Contras. Hyde emerged as a principal defender of the administration and of Lieutenant Colonel Oliver L. North, the central figure in the scandal. "You are a dangerous person," he told North during the nationally televised hearings on July 13, 1987. "And the reason you are is you personify the old morality—loyalty, fidelity, honor, and, worst of all, obedience. . . . But remember, everybody remembers Billy Mitchell and nobody remembers who his prosecutors were." Hyde later denounced the panel's majority report, which blamed the Reagan administration exclusively for the fiasco, as "a bitterly political document." He believed that the conflicting Central American policies of the White House and Congress were "a recipe for gridlock" that well-intentioned individuals in the White House had sought to circumvent.

As the ranking Republican on the House Permanent Select Committee on Intelligence, Hyde has criticized Democrats on the panel for selectively leaking classified information for partisan advantage and questioned whether Congress was able to oversee the operations of the intelligence community responsibly. He blamed what he called "the calculated, politically motivated leaking of highly sensitive information" for the distrust that had arisen between Congress and the Central Intelligence Agency. In 1984 he recommended the creation of a joint intelligence committee to end the feuding between the House and Senate panels and to reduce the number of staff members with access to classified documents, a recommendation that eventually was incorporated into the majority report of the Iran-Contra committee.

During the race for the post of Republican whip in March 1989, Hyde came under pressure from some Republicans to run as a compromise choice between Newt Gingrich of Georgia and Edward Madigan of Illinois. Hyde's partisan, yet congenial, style seemed to fit neatly between the combative nature of Gingrich and the traditionally passive resistance to the majority that Madigan represented. But Hyde refused to challenge Madigan, who is an old friend and colleague. Not even a last-minute draft to stave off a narrow Gingrich victory could persuade him to run.

In the debate over the proposed bailout of the nation's troubled savings and loan institutions in 1989, Hyde sought to dilute a central portion of the bill favored by President George Bush. Aided by lobbying by the United States League of Savings Institutions, Hyde sponsored an amendment that would have applied to those savings banks that had taken over failed competitors under federal regulatory supervision. The amendment would have required an administrative hearing before a regulatory body on whether due process required an extension of time to meet the increased capital requirements. The practice of converting on paper the excess of liabilities over assets into goodwill and using that intangible asset to help the surviving institution to meet the capital requirements imposed by federal regulators became commonplace during the 1980s and was a major incentive for healthy savings and loan associations to purchase failed ones. But President Bush, who was committed to ending the practice, threatened to veto the bill if it included the Hyde Amendment, which then was killed by a margin of more than three to one.

The silver-haired and portly Henry J. Hyde stands six feet, three inches tall and weighs about 260 pounds. Esteemed by his colleagues for his ready wit, he is a forceful speaker, skilled debater, and gifted raconteur. Since November 8, 1947 he has been married to the former Jeanne Simpson of Arlington, Virginia, whom he met at a basketball game and who worked to help put him through law school. They have four children: Henry Jr., Robert, Laura, and Anthony. Hyde enjoys reading biographies, watching television, and smoking quality cigars, even if they come from Marxist Cuba.

References: Almanac of American Politics, 1988; Politics in America (1988); Who's Who in America, 1988-89; Who's Who in American Politics, 1989-90

Jahn, Helmut
(yän hel'mōōt)

Jan. 4, 1940- Architect. Address: Murphy/Jahn, 33 E. Wacker Dr., Chicago, Ill. 60601

In two American cities with what would seem to be maximum skyscraper density, the German-born architect Helmut Jahn has managed within the last eight years to inject a significant and flamboyant presence. As his office buildings have taken their places on the skylines of Chicago and, later, New York City, "Jahn-watching"—described by the Chicago Tribune architecture critic Paul Gapp in 1983 as the "newest architectural pastime"—has spread to the East. Jahn's flair for drama and color has also had such an impact in other midwestern cities, in Europe, and as far afield as Johannesburg and Durban, that John Zukowsky, the curator of architecture at the Art Institute of Chicago, has described his influence on world architecture as "staggering." In 1987 *Fortune* magazine rated him one of America's top seven contemporary architects, and the French art dealer and writer Ante Glibota acclaimed him as simply "the unchallenged master of American architecture today." Jahn has his detractors, however, who accuse him of conceiving of buildings as high-tech "objects" that incorporate too many gimmicky details and are not appropriately integrated into their surroundings.

Like so many of his contemporaries, Jahn has made a break with the pervasive influence of Mies van der Rohe, another German-born architect transplanted to Chicago, where he served as director of the Illinois Institute of Technology. Yet Jahn concedes that all of his work takes Mies as a point of departure, and for his attempts to reconcile modernist and postmodernist tendencies, he has been termed a "neomodernist" or "romantic modernist." As he has described them, his buildings are "neither abstract nor technological in nature. They are based neither on the past nor are they imitations. . . . Their strength lies in the tensions and transformations between the old and the new, nature and technology, abstraction and meaning." Thus, there is no one Jahn "look," and it is impossible to trace a clear progression of ideas from his earliest construction to his latest designs. It is possible, though, to summarize his concepts in terms of their reaction from the Miesian square-cornered, stark ("less is more") glass façade. Jahn's 1980 Xerox Centre in Chicago, a rounded building of forty-two stories, has been hailed as the first to "break the box." From that achievement, Jahn has gone on to design a number of octagonal, or, as he has called them, "omnidirectional" buildings, and his roof silhouettes represent a radical departure from Mies's flat surfaces. Jahn's may have gable, hip, or slanted shapes, or they may terminate in slender shafts. His façades are characteristically enlivened by mixes of reflective and textured glass, gridworks of mullions, and division into bays of different colored glass; they may be accented by horizontal bands or vertical strips of metal or of granite. Patterning may also be provided by beveling or by setbacks. A feature of many of Jahn's interiors are soaring, skylit atriums that, according to Paul Gapp, have "revived the art of civic monumentality."

Helmut Jahn was born in the farming village of Allersberg, near Nuremberg, Bavaria, on January 4, 1940, the oldest son of Wilhelm Anton, a schoolteacher, and Karolina (Wirth) Jahn. The family then moved to Zirndorf, where he was rated only a fair—even lazy—student. But from an early age he drew constantly, encouraged by his father, and one of his favorite forms of play was devising construction projects, for which he commandeered materials from neighborhood building sites. In 1965 Jahn received a diploma in engineering and architecture from the Technische Hochschule in Munich, where he was trained by teachers who had been students of Mies. He was then associated for a year with P. C. von Seidlein in Munich. Coming to the United States in 1966 as an exchange student, he did a year of graduate work at the Illinois Institute of Technology. In 1967 he caught the attention of one of Mies's associates, Eugene Summers, who helped further the young German student's career. Summers took him on as his assistant at the long established Chicago firm of C. F. Murphy Associates, a studio committed to Mies's International Style. Advancing rapidly from answering phones and making drawings to producing design sketches, Jahn had, by 1973, become a vice-president and director of planning and design. In 1981 the name of the firm was changed to Murphy/Jahn, with Jahn as one of its principals. He took over as president in 1982 and became chief executive officer the following year. As of 1987-88 Murphy/Jahn (with offices in New York and Frankfurt as well as Chicago) employed eighty architects, with more than half its business consisting of commercial and office construction. Projects in its home state of Illinois still account for most of the firm's work.

Jahn's energy and productivity are epitomized by the way he continually generates ideas, capturing them in lightning-fast realizations. Colleagues remark on the fact that he draws ceaselessly, for even while on the move he is never without his leather-bound sketch pad and favorite Mont Blanc pens, and instead of giving a client a single sketch for a project he will prepare several alternative plans. But "drawing well," he has remarked, "is only one ingredient in a profession in which you can never quite complete your education." Another facet of Jahn's career is teaching. He was a member of the design studio faculty at the Chicago campus of University of Illinois in the spring of 1981, served as Elliot Noyes Professor of Architectural Design at Harvard in the fall of that year, and taught as Davenport Visiting Professor of Architectural Design at Yale in 1983.

Helmut Jahn's rise to prominence began with his Kemper Arena (1974), a multipurpose oval structure in Kansas City, Missouri that won the American Institute of Architects (AIA) National Honors Award and a Chicago Chapter Award in 1975. Two years later came his St. Mary's Athletic Facility, a gymnasium with a glass façade boldly enlivened by red structural columns that show through from the interior. This building, on the Notre Dame University campus, won AIA national, state, and chapter prizes; and in 1980 St. Mary's College honored Jahn (who is a Roman Catholic) with an honorary Doctor of Fine Arts degree. Besides the Xerox Centre, at least two other of his designs at the beginning of the 1980s rank with his most acclaimed buildings: the Argonne Program Support Facility (1981), an addition to the Argonne National Laboratory, near Chicago, which is considered a model of energy-conserving engineering and which, appropriate to its function of nuclear energy research, symbolizes the sun in its overall design; and the addition to the Chicago Board of Trade Building (1982). For such achievements Jahn was given the Arnold W. Brunner Memorial Prize in Architecture by the

American Academy and Institute of Arts and Letters in 1982.

A unique exception to Jahn's urban-commercial architecture is a country house that he designed for a lakeside site at Eagle River, Wisconsin in 1980. A perfect cube, perched on concrete columns that raise it to treetop height, it both contrasts with its natural surroundings and complements them. Its exterior colors of green, red, and white are appropriate for all seasons, and its interior is in soft natural oak. The irregular fenestration pattern provides sweeping views.

Jahn's twenty-three-story hip-roof addition to the Chicago Board of Trade is an example of his characteristically elegant solutions to problems of design and engineering. On the one hand, he had to allow for the key feature of the new structure: a three-story trading hall that, in order to provide unobstructed views of the overhead stock quotation boards, has no supporting columns but instead relies on powerful trusses to redistribute and carry the weight down through the steel building frame. On the other hand, the design had to complement the forty-five-story limestone-sheathed parent building, which is considered a distinguished example of Art Deco architecture—a style for which Jahn has a particular affinity. The architect accomplished that by repeating throughout the interior the scalloped ornamentation of the lobby of the older structure and by using limestone to clad sections of the walls of the new glass building.

On the south side, Jahn's building makes its own statement with a façade of silver and black glass, the panes separated by mullions that form a dense grid across the surface. Where the old and new buildings face one another there is a twelve-story atrium, the south wall of which is dramatized by elevators that glide up and down in exposed shafts—an architectural metaphor for the mercurial volatility of the tenants' occupation. In many of his works Jahn's concern for the use to which they will be put results in a design that symbolizes the activity within. Although it is considered by many to be one of Jahn's finest structures, the Board of Trade addition has been criticized for its effect of insubstantiality ("a disturbing look of impermanence, of stageset theatricality") and for the clumsy handling of the limestone columns around the main entrance.

If that design was, in Paul Gapp's final estimation, "provocative," the State of Illinois Center (1985) became, in his words, "the most esthetically controversial office building ever constructed in Chicago." Although the governor of Illinois proclaimed it "the first office building of the year 2000" and it received one of Jahn's many AIA Chicago Chapter Awards, it is also, less reverently, referred to as "Starship Chicago." The futuristic complex of government office and retail space, in the middle of the Loop, eludes conventional architectural classification. It is a squat polygon, one side of which slopes inward in a seventeen-story curve. Behind the curved façade a circular atrium rises the full height to a cylindrical skylight roof, sliced at an angle and looking, to quote Paul Goldberger, the *New York Times* architecture critic, "as if it were about to revolve." The glass skin of the building is arranged in three setback tiers, each a different shade of blue, progressively darker from top to bottom; colored metal panels divide the façade vertically. Inside the atrium, salmon-pink terraces define the office floors, which are open to view. Hanging staircases, glass elevator shafts, and a lacelike network of exposed trusses further add to the feeling of openness and energetic movement, in accord with the architect's desire to create a structural symbol of open government.

According to Paul Goldberger, such features make the State of Illinois Center "hyperactive" and "not a little vulgar." He nevertheless conceded that the building has succeeded in becoming a genuine public place, filled with tourists, office workers, and passersby who are attracted by its visual presence and make use of its shops and restaurants. Unfortunately for the office workers, it was soon discovered that the summer sun beating on the huge expanse of glass caused a blinding glare on computer screens and created a heat buildup for which the original air-conditioning system was inadequate. In this respect, it is one of the few Jahn buildings that is not, so to speak, user-friendly.

Much attention has also been given to Jahn's Northwestern Atrium Center (1987), a forty-story multipurpose building that provides a new entrance to the heavily used Chicago & Northwestern commuter-line terminal as well as to floors of office space above. With its rounded setbacks at the base and top of the north and south walls, the colored façade appears to cascade down, at the same time recalling the Art Moderne style of the 1930s. Much of the interior detailing, in fact, repeats the high-tech slick ambience of that period. Another deliberate historical reference is made in the concentric arches of the main entrance, which echo Louis Sullivan's design for the Transportation Building at Chicago's World's Columbian Exposition of 1893. Jahn has also managed to recall old-time train sheds with thickets of exposed steel trusses and the light and spaciousness of the glass-enclosed atrium that forms the station concourse. The building has earned Paul Goldberger's praise for its genuine commitment to public needs and its provision of clear lines of access for rush-hour crowds of commuters.

The same concern (Jahn himself speaks of an architecture that is "more communicative and user-oriented") is behind his United Airlines terminal at O'Hare International Airport (1988). Not a skyscraper this time, it too won him an AIA award for a "visually exciting and elegant" building affording generous, naturally lighted spaces and solving the problem of passenger flow by means of a passageway that is "a celebration of movement."

In recent years, Jahn's work has gone up in many places other than Chicago. Philadelphia's skyline, for example, has been dramatically dominated since 1987 by his Liberty Place Tower, at sixty-three stories the tallest building in the city, rising even above the landmark statue of William Penn atop the city hall. It is in New York City, however, that most of Jahn's work has been concentrated since 1986. Working in the city has reinforced his concept of "infill," or integration of buildings within an architectural context. The grid layout of the streets and their existing buildings led him to "a tighter building, with more classical, less abstract shapes," he has said. Thus, Park Avenue Tower, a glass and granite office edifice in midtown, completed in 1986, tapers in an obelisk shape. IBM, its principal tenant, wanted a design that would befit its corporate image. Illuminated at night, the building takes on a futuristic glow, but its overall configuration is a bow to tradition. An office tower being completed just to the north of the Chrysler Building was conceived as a freestanding column, recalling the work of the Viennese architect Adolf Loos. Complete with base and flaring capital, its roof deliberately contrasts with the Chrysler Building spire. In the same way, the City Spire, a seventy-story combination of office and apartment spaces going up behind the City Center auditorium, will differ radically from the distinctive style of its older neighbor. Above the latter's Moorish-style tiled dome, Jahn's tower will rise in tiers to a conical finial sheathed in green copper.

Although Jahn contends that sheer building height is no longer a symbol of achievement in New York, there is, nevertheless, the contradictory case of one of his most spectacular commissions. In 1986 he was enlisted by Donald Trump to draw up plans for the developer's highly controversial Television City, to be erected on 100 acres of land along the Hudson River from Fifty-ninth to Seventy-second streets. His design called for six apartment houses, each over seventy stories high, flanking what was to have been the world's tallest building (150 stories, one-third of a mile high), housing offices and television studios. With its parks and shops, the complex was to be a city within a city, and Trump had declared he "wanted the ultimate in architecture . . . and, therefore, the ultimate architect." The developer ultimately rejected Jahn's plans, after a community board objected to the potential saturation of an already overcrowded area. A neighborhood redevelopment plan that has fared better and will be realized in the near future is Jahn's Livingston Plaza, a rejuvenation scheme for a downtown Brooklyn commercial site.

Helmut Jahn has completed three buildings in South Africa, notably 11 Diagonal Street, a high-rise office complex in Johannesburg (1983). Here, the glass skin of the tower glitters in the brilliant light in shades of silver, blue, and black and is faceted in a manner that makes a visual allusion to the diamonds marketed by the firm that commissioned the structure. His native country will soon have its first Jahn buildings, including the tallest building on the Continent, the Messe Frankfurt (Frankfurt Fair) convention center; a Hyatt hotel in Munich; and office buildings in Mannheim and West Berlin. Among other of his European projects now in the works are Amsterdam Towers, an office building in Rotterdam, and the Hôtel Paris Nord II.

Any appreciation of Jahn's enormous inventiveness must take into account the proposals he has submitted for competitions, but that have not been realized. They include such plans as those for Conference City in Abu Dhabi (1976), the Pahlavi National Library in Teheran (1978), based on traditional Persian bazaar design, and a sports complex in Naples (1987). He has also drawn up innovative designs for Southwest Center in Houston (1982), intended to be one of the tallest towers in the world; the San Diego Convention Center (1984), which would complement its waterfront siting with suggestions of ships' cranes and rigging and an open plan radically different from the usual boxed-in design of such spaces; and South Ferry Terminal. In accord with the architect's statement "I work in a certain image and adapt it," this last-named, proposed structure for Battery Park in New York manages to suggest both a lighthouse and the Eiffel Tower, with arches inspired by the latter at the base straddling subway stations and ferry slips.

A substantial number of gallery and museum exhibitions have documented the progress of Jahn's ideas from sketch to finished structure. He was, for example, represented in "The Presence of the Past," the American entry at the 1980 Venice Biennale, and in "Chicago and New York, More than a Century of Architectural Interaction," which was organized by the Chicago Art Institute and toured the country in 1984. Some of Jahn's sketches and models are included in the permanent collection of the Deutsches Architekturmuseum, which opened in 1984 in Frankfurt. In 1987 the privately operated Paris Art Center, under the aegis of Ante Glibota, put on the largest exhibition of Jahn's work ever assembled. Comprising drawings, 2,585 sketches, models, and over 200 photographs, the show was scheduled to travel to Zagreb, Barcelona, Rome, Seoul, and Frankfurt. Concurrently, Glibota published a monumental monograph on the architect. Entitled Helmut Jahn, it includes essays by Glibota and by Jahn himself and an extensive pictorial biography of the architect.

In 1970 Helmut Jahn married the former Deborah Ann Lampe. They have a son, Evan, born in 1978. In person, "the Baron of High Tech," as he is sometimes called, is as colorful and modish as his architecture. Lean and angular, romantically handsome, with longish dark blond hair parted in the middle, Jahn favors elegant, Italian gray silk suits and dashing hats. (A feature story in Gentlemen's Quarterly in 1985 commented that he "dresses like he designs: to kill.") At home in Chicago, he jogs regularly, goes sailing, plays tennis, and drives a red Porsche at high speeds; on his frequent travels, he skis or scuba dives whenever possible. Meanwhile, he customarily puts in sixteen-hour workdays. Despite a reputation for egotism and competitiveness, he has averred: "If you ask the people who work with me, they'd probably say I work by myself, and tell them what to do. . . . If you ask me, I think I work in a team. . . . I know what we are doing wouldn't be possible if there wasn't a group of people who work with me and make a lot of contributions."

References: *Contemporary Architects* (1987); Glibota, Ante. *Helmut Jahn* (1987); Miller, Nory. *Helmut Jahn* (1986); *Who's Who in America*, 1988–89

Janowitz, Tama

Apr. 12, 1957– Writer. Address: b. c/o Crown Publishers, Inc., 225 Park Avenue South, New York, N.Y. 10003; h. 92 Horatio St., #5E, New York, N.Y. 10014

With the publication, in 1986, of her first short-story collection, *Slaves of New York*, about the hipsters who inhabit the trendy art world of Manhattan's SoHo, Tama Janowitz became an overnight literary sensation, thanks as much to her self-impelled publicity campaign as to the merits of the book itself. That campaign included a star turn on the first "literary video" on MTV and the distribution of excerpts from *Slaves of New York* to the patrons of some of Manhattan's most exclusive restaurants. Although *Slaves of New York* met with stiff resistance from some critics and a later work, the novel *A Cannibal in Manhattan* (1987), encountered even less enthusiasm, both books became bestsellers, elevating Tama Janowitz to the pop-celebrity status befitting a protégée of Andy Warhol's. Miss Janowitz, a leading member of the so-called literary brat pack, has modestly said that her talent lies in "sort of being funny about the social conditions and mores of the time we live in," and she is, by her own admission, not a highly polished writer. "What interests me about writing," she has said, "is the raw energy, putting life and emotion onto the page. The poetry of language, to me, comes not from beautiful descriptions and pretty clichés but from the raw guts of life." One discerning critic has called her metaphors "emetic."

Of Hungarian and Polish ancestry, Tama Janowitz was born in San Francisco, California on April 12, 1957, the older of the two children of Julian Frederick Janowitz, a psychiatrist, and Phyllis (Winer) Janowitz, a poet who is now an assistant professor of English and poet in residence at Cornell University. Tama Janowitz has a younger brother, David. When she was five, the family moved to Amherst, Massachusetts, where her father had accepted a position as head of the mental health department at the University of Massachusetts. Her parents divorced when she was ten, and she and her brother were raised from that point onward by their mother, who supported them with her poetry grants. Over the next several years, the family moved frequently, settling in Israel for a time before returning to Massachusetts and living, successively, in Amherst, Newton, and Lexington.

Following her graduation from Lexington High School in 1973, a year ahead of her class, Tama Janowitz enrolled at Barnard College in New York City. Majoring in creative writing, she received several important awards during her undergraduate years, including a scholarship to the Breadloaf Writers Conference in Vermont in 1975, the Elizabeth Janeway Fiction Prize in 1976 and 1977, and the Amy Loveman Prize for Poetry in 1977. She was also honored with a guest editorship at *Mademoiselle* magazine, a brief distinction that ended in disaster. "Unfortunately," Miss Janowitz told Dinah Prince in a conversation for *New York* (July 14, 1986) magazine, "they sent me on a fashion shoot and they asked me to iron a blouse and I put the iron down on the sleeve and the whole sleeve just melted and I burst into tears." She also worked during her college years as a model for the Vidal Sassoon line of hair-care products. After receiving her B.A. degree from Barnard in 1977, she became an assistant art director at the Boston advertising agency Kenyon and Eckhardt. Perhaps because she was unable, in her words, "to draw, do layout, paste-up, mechanicals, or hold a T-square," she was laid off after six months. "I decided," she told Dinah Prince, "I wasn't cut out for a nine-to-five job."

In 1978 Miss Janowitz won a graduate fellowship to the writing program at Hollins College in Roanoke, Virginia. She took her M.A. degree a year later. While she was studying at Hollins, the *Paris Review* agreed to publish a portion of a novel she had written there under the pseudonym Tom A. Janowitz, a name she adopted because the narrator is a young man. The novel, *American Dad*, was eventually published under her real name by G. P. Putnam's Sons in 1981, and it brought her some critical praise. A thinly disguised autobiography, *American Dad* focuses on Earl Przepasniak, the son of a narcissistic father who is a psychiatrist and a mother who is an eccentric poet. The father, according to a *Kirkus Reviews* (February 15, 1981) forecast, is "every outlandish cultural aberration of the 1960s rolled into one: ecologist, mushroom hunter, house builder, philanderer, druggie, protohippie, eccentrically generous, totally self-absorbed," and the mother, according to Janice E. Davis of the Toronto *Globe and Mail* (May 30, 1981), is "an agoraphobic poet who confides most of the intimate details of her married life to her young son because she hasn't anyone else to talk to." She is accidentally killed by a falling postage meter during a fight with her husband, who is put into prison. While out on furlough, he maims himself with a chainsaw and his son steps in to care for him. Writing in the *New Republic* (June 6, 1981), Gordon Epps observed of the father that "there is not a false note in the presentation of this engaging villain," adding that "Janowitz has a sharp eye for the things of this world . . . and her sensuous writing enlivens the book." But he also felt that *American Dad* becomes "thin gruel" when Tama Janowitz focuses on the son's later escapades in Europe. "Earl's adventures are mostly filler, marring what is otherwise one of the most impressive first novels I've read in a long time," Epps remarked. The *Kirkus Reviews* critic agreed: "When the live wires like dad Robert and mom Mavis are onstage, this book has a headlong, juicy appeal; when they're not, it's drably standard." In spite of its generally favorable notices, *American Dad* sold fewer than 1,000 copies.

In 1980 Tama Janowitz entered the Yale School of Drama, where, over the next year, she wrote two plays, neither of which has been published. In 1981 and 1982 she was writer in residence at the Fine Arts Work Center in Provincetown, Massachusetts. Having received a grant of $12,500 from the National Endowment for the Arts, Tama Janowitz then moved into an apartment on the Upper West Side of Manhattan, where she completed work on a second novel, *A Cannibal in Manhattan*. Although Putnam, along with eighteen other publishing houses, rejected it, she wrote a third novel, *Memoirs of a Megalomaniac*, which also failed to find a publisher. When her fourth and fifth novels met a similar fate, she decided to try her hand at short-story writing, basing her material on the art crowd of lower Manhattan, of whose existence she became aware by accident. Seeking to make new acquaintances and too shy to speak to strangers in bars, she stumbled across an art gallery opening in SoHo and found it an easy place to meet new friends. As she explained to Cheryl Lavin of the *Chicago Tribune* (December 11, 1986): "There'd be 300 people and they'd spill out on the street and someone would give you a cheap glass of white wine and then the next thing you know someone would say, 'Well, what do you think of the painting?' So the art scene was the one scene I could walk into. You'd just go in and join the crowd. So I went."

Soon, Tama Janowitz was an habitué of the SoHo scene, frequenting its galleries, restaurants, and parties. "She became a human video camera," Dinah Prince reported, "picking up snatches of conversations, zeroing in on the odd hat or a new item on a chic menu. Each night, before climbing into bed, she would try to decipher her scrawls from a notebook, cocktail napkin, or matchbook." Two weeks of note taking provided her with enough material for her first story and, over the following months, she began submitting stories to magazines, some of which bought her work. In December 1984 her career got a major boost when the *New Yorker* published her "Slaves in New York," a short story about an emotionally and financially insecure young jewelry designer named Eleanor who shares a Manhattan apartment with an artist, Stash, mainly because she cannot afford a place of her own. Encouraged, Miss Janowitz then wrote three more stories for the *New Yorker* about the same duo.

In the summer of 1985, Tama Janowitz signed a contract with Crown Publishers for a book of short stories, which was published the following June under the title *Slaves of New York*. Discussing the title with Elizabeth Kastor of the *Washington Post* (August 30, 1986), Miss Janowitz explained: "When I say slaves of New York, I mean people come here as slaves to something. They're a slave to their sister's apartment. They're a slave to ambition—they want a job in publishing at the best salary. Or they don't fit in their hometown and they're a slave to that. Everyone in this country who was a misfit in their hometown comes to New York." The story "Modern Saint #271" tells of a young woman from a well-to-do Jewish family who, after a falling-out with her father, becomes a prostitute. "Case History #4: Fred" concerns a man who takes women he meets on the street on shopping sprees at Tiffany's. Eight of the twenty-two stories, including the republished "Slaves in New York," center on Eleanor and Stash, who are modeled on Miss Janowitz and a former boyfriend. Eleanor designs jewelry from bones, teeth, rhinestones, and pieces of silver, and Stash paints allegorical scenes featuring Chilly Willy, Bullwinkle, and other cartoon characters.

The failure of *American Dad* and her inability to get her succeeding novels published fueled Tama Janowitz's determination to make *Slaves of New York* a success. In November 1985, seven months before its publication date, she met the photographer Patrick McMullan and began making the rounds of trendy nightspots with him. Her name began to turn up in local gossip columns, and photos of her, shot by McMullan, started to appear in such magazines as *Details* and *New York Talk*, which cover lower Manhattan.

In April 1986 Tama Janowitz shifted her publicity campaign into high gear. Wearing banners inscribed with the words "Slaves of New York," she and a couple of friends walked around Manhattan, handing out excerpts from the book to people on the streets and in restaurants. In midsummer she starred in the first "literary video," a four-minute film that ran on MTV, the cable television music-video channel, that showed her walking through New York's meat-packing district in an evening gown, eating at a restaurant with her close friend

Andy Warhol, and discussing the "raw energy" of her fiction. "This is the first time in the history of Western civilization that a book has been sold on MTV," Cheryl Lavin wrote. "The first time since Johann Gutenberg invented the printing press that an author has been peddled like a rock star." In her interview with Elizabeth Kastor, Tama Janowitz admitted to a certain embarrassment about her flamboyant promotional activities on behalf of *Slaves of New York*. "It's so awful to be promoting yourself," she said. "On the other hand, who cares? I'm sure it will be useful in a story, twisted around or something."

Tama Janowitz's publicity campaign paid such rich dividends that *Slaves of New York* became the first short-story collection to hit the bestseller lists since Philip Roth's *Goodbye, Columbus* made the grade in 1959. In mid-August 1986 it appeared on the *New York Times* list of bestsellers for the first time, eventually peaking at number fifteen, and it made the bestseller list in every other major city in the United States. Critical response to *Slaves of New York* was mixed. Hermione Lee, writing in the London *Observer* (January 18, 1987), commented, "The city as cannibal jungle is a device as old as New York, but Janowitz makes it new again with her intoxicated relish for emetic metaphors," and Emma Tennant, in her review for the *Guardian* (January 23, 1987), hailed Miss Janowitz as "one of the most talented young writers" in America. "Janowitz's gift," Miss Tennant concluded, "has been compared to Dorothy Parker's. Yet, in dealing with . . . uneasy, imponderable relationships, Janowitz has more depth." Ken Kalfus of *Newsday* (July 13, 1986) wrote that Tama Janowitz, like Jane Austen, "intends to leave a record of contemporary manners," a viewpoint with which Victoria Radin of the *New Statesman* (February 27, 1987) agreed. "The book," she observed, "could easily serve as a document of the mores of the New York art scene in the late 1980s."

The most common criticism leveled at *Slaves of New York* was that its characters were paper-thin. Carol Anshaw of the *Village Voice* (August 5, 1986), for example, regarded them as "permanent transients in a dress-up and play-act milieu full of style without the slightest pretense of substance." Similarly, in her *Washington Post* review, Elizabeth Alexander speculated, "If Janowitz used her powers to create characters who were less trendy, less self-absorbed, less ephemeral—in short, characters with a little depth and heart—the results could be well worth the effort of this talented, detail minded writer." Miss Janowitz's linguistic inadequacies also came under attack from several critics, among them Raymond Sullivan of the *Wall Street Journal* (July 22, 1986), who noted, "Fiction is carried on through language, and Ms. Janowitz is not in control of the only one she's got." In his review for *Time* (June 30, 1986) magazine, R. Z. Sheppard characterized her language as "grating and imprecise." Yet another common criticism was the ambiguity of many of the stories. "We're never certain," Thomas DePietro complained in the

Hudson Review (Autumn 1986), "whether these often disposable tales are a symptom or a parody of the junk culture Janowitz chronicles so well." And Raymond Sokolov of the *Wall Street Journal* (July 22, 1986) found Tama Janowitz's prose "so restlessly indistinct that you never know how to take it."

The popular success of *Slaves of New York* brought Tama Janowitz the kind of instant celebrity status immortalized by her mentor, Andy Warhol. She was featured on the cover of *New York* magazine and made guest appearances on the television shows *Late Night with David Letterman*, *Today*, and *Good Morning, America*. Beginning in June 1987, she appeared in a series of magazine ads for Amaretto liqueur and Rose's Lime Juice. Defending her decision to appear in the lucrative ads, Tama Janowitz told Elizabeth Kaye of *Esquire* (November 1988): "It sounded fun. I mean, if a serious writer is supposed to be somebody who sits at home with little glasses, I mean forget it, I'll put on a tutu and go out to a nightclub. I mean, why can't I be a serious writer and still do the other stuff?" *Slaves of New York* also made Tama Janowitz a certified member of the so-called literary brat pack, a group of successful young writers whose yuppified works celebrate the lives of affluent young urbanites. In addition to Tama Janowitz, the coterie includes Jay McInerney, Bret Easton Ellis, David Leavitt, and Jill Eisenstadt. Although each has become known for unabashed self-promotion, Tama Janowitz, to quote R. Z. Sheppard, "represents the state of the artifice." According to Nikki Finke, in her article about the brat pack writers for the *Los Angeles Times* (June 22, 1987), "Janowitz, especially, has been criticized for becoming a multimedia celebrity with Madison Avenue–like sophistication and diligence," marketing herself "like a brand of toothpaste." "I would do any publicity that came my way," Miss Janowitz told Nikki Finke. "I just see it as a chance to sell the book."

Tama Janowitz's follow-up to *Slaves of New York* was a reworked version of her second, previously unpublished novel, *A Cannibal in Manhattan*. Released in September 1987, it has to do with a wealthy railroad heiress named Maria Fishburn who, while working as a Peace Corps volunteer on the fictional South Pacific island of New Burnt Norton, asks a cannibal, Mgungu Yabba Mgungu, to return with her to New York and become her husband. He accepts, and the rest of the novel details his assorted misadventures in Manhattan. Much like *Slaves of New York*, *A Cannibal in Manhattan* received a few positive notices, but it was panned by most reviewers. "There are some outrageously funny passages in this book," Margot Mifflin conceded in the *Chicago Tribune* (September 13, 1987), describing Mgungu as "an irresistibly idiosyncratic character who exposes New York as a jungle as hostile and unjust as any natural outback." Perhaps the most favorable review came from Isabel Raphael, who wrote in the London *Times* (February 25, 1988): "The misadventures of Mgungu are very funny. . . . Ms. Janowitz keeps the joke alive even when she moves into the sordid and the macabre. A writer with such vivid powers of imagination and observation and such a light hand with bathos . . . is a real find." Among those critics who savaged *A Cannibal in Manhattan* was Jonathan Yardley of the *Washington Post Book World* (September 25, 1987). "*A Cannibal in Manhattan* is utterly devoid of originality, energy, thematic purpose, charm—you name it, *A Cannibal in Manhattan* hasn't got it," Yardley wrote. "That it should give pleasure to anyone is quite beyond imagination." Equally harsh was Francine Prose, who assessed the novel for the *New York Times Book Review* (October 4, 1987): "Narrated by a cartoon, populated by cartoons, the book has no emotional center, no depth; little engages or moves us. . . .[Ms.] Janowitz is a much better writer than this." And Victoria Radin of the *New Statesman* (March 4, 1988) damned it with the observation that "*Cannibal* is a private joke that should have stayed in the closet." Its hostile reviews notwithstanding, *A Cannibal in Manhattan*, which Tama Janowitz also promoted with an MTV video, became a bestseller.

A film version of *Slaves of New York* was released in March 1989. With a screenplay by Tama Janowitz (who also had a small acting role), directed by James Ivory, and starring Bernadette Peters, the movie incorporated several stories from the book, concentrating on the Eleanor-Stash segments. The adaptation was both a commercial and critical failure, prompting Richard Schickel of *Time* (March 20, 1989) to quip: "They should have filmed Tama Janowitz's publicity campaign. It was a lot more entertaining, and possibly more sociologically edifying, than *Slaves of New York*." In the verdict of David Denby of *New York* (March 27, 1989) magazine, the screenplay "has no voice and no center. . . . The whole movie has a flustered, fluttering inconsequence." In his review for the *New Republic* (April 10, 1989), Stanley Kauffmann also faulted the script: "The film's limpness is due in large degree to the screenplay: it wants to be conventionally shaped, which the stories are not. If Janowitz had concentrated her screenplay on exploring lives, as her stories do, . . . the texture might have been more rewarding."

Profiles in the media on Tama Janowitz invariably include detailed descriptions of her exotic appearance. "With her intense, mascara-drenched green eyes, wild masses of long dark hair, and ivory-white skin, she seems to be a kind of chic tart with a wallflower complex," Dinah Prince wrote in her profile of Miss Janowitz for *New York* magazine. But Josephine Fairley of the London *Times* (January 16, 1987) saw her as "tiny, shy, and pretty in an Eastern European way, constantly fidgeting with a mane of black hair which looks like it hasn't had a comb through it since junior high school." Her wardrobe consists almost entirely of black clothes. Miss Janowitz lives in a studio apartment in Manhattan's West Village with her two Yorkshire terriers, Lulu and Beep-beep.

Tama Janowitz received an M.F.A. degree from Columbia University in 1985. For one year, beginning in September 1986, she was an Alfred Hodder Fellow in the Humanities at Princeton University. She received a second grant from the National Endowment for the Arts in 1986 and has been honored with awards from the CCLM/General Electric Foundation (1984) and the Ludwig Vogelstein Foundation (1985).

References: Chicago Tribune V p1+ D 11 '86 pors; Esquire 110:170+ N '88 pors; Guardian p36 Mr 10 '89 por; New York 19:36+ Jl 14 '86 pors; San Francisco Examiner-Chronicle E p1+ Je 28 '87 pors; Washington Post C p1+ Ag 30 '86 por; Contemporary Authors vol 106 (1982); Contemporary Literary Criticism vol 43 (1987)

Johnson, F(rederick) Ross

Dec. 13, 1931– Business executive. Address: 4385 Whitewater Creek Rd., N.W., Atlanta, Ga. 30327

As chief executive officer of the RJR Nabisco Company, Canadian-born F. Ross Johnson attracted international attention in the fall of 1988 when he attempted a leveraged buyout (LBO) of the nineteenth-largest corporation in the United States and the manufacturer of such household-name products as Oreo cookies, Ritz crackers, and Winston cigarettes. Johnson's initiative touched off a wild five-week bidding war between a management group he headed and a similar team led by Henry R. Kravis of the Wall Street investment banking firm of Kohlberg, Kravis, Roberts and Company. The Kravis-led group ultimately won control of

RJR Nabisco by paying an astounding $24.88 billion, almost double the previous record price for a buyout. Since LBOs are financed largely through loans, the interest payments on which are tax-deductible, the American taxpayer eventually underwrites the transaction. That factor, in conjunction with mounting concern about the potentially calamitous effects of such large-scale borrowing on the American economy, led many congressional and business leaders to call for restrictions on leveraged buyouts following the Johnson-Kravis duel.

Johnson's failed bid to take over RJR Nabisco represented his first significant setback in a long and distinguished business career. At forty, he became president of the Canadian subsidiary of Standard Brands Limited, an international food products firm, and, at forty-four, he was named chief executive of the company. Five years later, Standard Brands merged with Nabisco, the packaged-foods conglomerate, and, within three years, Johnson had become CEO. He performed a similar feat following Nabisco's purchase by R. J. Reynolds, the tobacco manufacturer, in 1985, this time being named chief executive only a year and a half after the merger. Known for his risktaking, unpredictable management style, Johnson dispenses with market research and generally makes important decisions based on gut feelings. "To Ross, everything is dynamic. Plans exist mostly as things to depart from," James Westcott, a Toronto management consultant and longtime friend, has said. Johnson has a reputation for being abrupt with associates and for demanding unquestioned loyalty from them, but in return he sees to it that they receive salaries substantially higher than those paid by competing companies.

Frederick Ross Johnson was born on December 13, 1931 in Winnipeg, Manitoba, Canada, the only child of Frederick Hamilton and Caroline (Green) Johnson. His father was a business executive who rose to be head of the Canadian division of the Schlage lock company. A born entrepreneur, Ross Johnson was only seven when he won a bicycle for his success in selling *Liberty* magazine subscriptions door to door. As a child, he sold candy when the circus came to town and rented out his large collection of comic books to friends. "I always wanted to go into business," he recalled to Joanne Philpott of the Toronto *Globe and Mail* (March 28, 1985). "I always had a job—paper routes, part-time at Eaton's [department store], that sort of thing, all through school." Although not an outstanding student ("No teacher ever accused me of being overly bright," he told Joanne Philpott), Johnson was always highly competitive and aggressive, according to friends. After graduating from Gordon Bell High School, he attended the University of Manitoba, in his hometown, where he played on the basketball team and was president of his fraternity. He graduated in 1952 with a Bachelor of Commerce degree.

Johnson began his career as an accountant with Canadian General Electric (CGE) in Toronto. "The day after I arrived . . . , they transferred me to Montreal," he recalled for Joanne Philpott. "I had to borrow twenty dollars from the company to get there. I was that broke." He later switched to the company's marketing department because, as he has quipped, "that's where all the good parties were." After being transferred back to Toronto, Johnson progressed quickly through the ranks to become head of CGE's lamp division and took classes at night at the University of Toronto, which awarded him an M.B.A. degree in 1956.

From 1962 to 1964 Johnson taught part-time at the University of Toronto. He was promoted to the position of director of marketing at CGE, before leaving the company in 1965 to become vice-president of merchandising with the T. Eaton Company, in Vancouver. A year later he switched jobs again, becoming executive vice-president and chief operating officer of General Steel Works, a small company that manufactured appliances. As Larry Black of the Toronto *Globe and Mail Report on Business Magazine* (January 1989) has noted, Johnson, by that point in his career, "had established a pattern. He moved on when the challenge of the job dimmed, or when his way to the top was blocked." True to form, he left General Steel Works in 1971 to accept a position in Montreal as president and CEO of the Canadian division of Standard Brands Limited, the multinational food products firm.

Within a few months of joining Standard Brands, Johnson made the acquaintance of several influential Montreal businessmen, including Paul Desmarais, the chairman of Power Corporation, and Brian Mulroney, who, thirteen years later, was to become prime minister of Canada. His rise through the Standard Brands' hierarchy was as predictably swift as it was steady. In 1973 the parent company in New York asked him to become a vice-president and head of the international division. He was named president and chief operating officer in 1975, and, a year later, following a boardroom struggle, he was appointed to succeed Henry Weigl as chief executive officer and chairman of the board. At forty-four years of age, Johnson was the youngest person in company history to hold those posts.

Shortly after taking on his new responsibilities, Johnson was faced with a major crisis. In early 1976 the price of sugar fell from sixty-one cents to thirteen cents per pound on international markets, and Standard Brands, which depended heavily on sales of high-fructose sweeteners, was hit so hard that its share earnings dropped overnight by almost 50 percent, to $2.40. "The boy wonder arrives and we go down to nothing," Johnson recalled to Bill Saporito of *Fortune* (July 18, 1988). "If earnings had dropped to $2.35, I would have been gone." Profits settled at $2.42, and his job was saved, but Johnson had learned a valuable lesson: in the sweetener business he was at the mercy of forces beyond his control. Since one of the hallmarks of his freewheeling, aggressive management style has been a desire to conduct business on his own terms, he sold Standard Brands' sweetener operation as soon as sugar prices stabilized. "You look at each situation and figure out where you stand," Johnson told Larry Black. "If you can't be dominant, then you get out."

In 1981 Johnson guided Standard Brands through a successful merger with Nabisco, the multinational packaged-foods company. By 1985, the resulting conglomerate—known as Nabisco Brands—employed over 70,000 people in fifty-five countries, boasted worldwide annual sales of more than $6 billion, and virtually monopolized some segments of the confections market. Johnson's dynamic young Standard Brands management team infused Nabisco with fresh ideas and enthusiasm. In his *Fortune* article, Bill Saporito joked, "When Johnson and company descended on Nabisco, it was as if Hell's Angels merged with the Rotary Club. . . . As one observer described it, all the Standard Branders seemed to be divorced guys who wore loafers, while the Nabisco crew were family types in lace-up shoes and suits." The success of Nabisco Brands could be attributed to the complementary nature of the Standard Brands and Nabisco product lines, as well as to their organizational and marketing strengths: Nabisco was firmly established in Europe and Japan, while Standard Brands had made significant inroads in the burgeoning Latin American consumer market and in South Africa. Another key element in the success of the union was the harmonious working relationship that developed between Ross Johnson and Nabisco head Robert Schaeberle. Despite some differences in management philosophy and a nine-year age disparity (Schaeberle is older), the two men worked well together.

When Schaeberle took early retirement in June 1984, Johnson, who had been president and chief operating officer of Nabisco Brands, became its chief executive officer. The new CEO masterminded a Nabisco victory over its rival Procter & Gamble in what industry analysts dubbed "the Great Cookie War," a battle for supremacy in the lucrative packaged-cookie market. Then, in June 1985, he steered the company through a $4.9 billion friendly takeover by R. J. Reynolds Industries, the giant tobacco processor, that resulted in a new company named RJR Nabisco, Inc. According to Bill Saporito, Wall Street hailed the union as "a perfect fit—each [company] sold consumer packaged goods, but had no overlapping products." Nabisco's brands included Oreo cookies, Ritz crackers, and Planters nuts; Reynolds' brands included Winston and Salem cigarettes, Smirnoff vodka, and Hawaiian Punch.

Only a few months after the merger, Johnson made a bid for the CEO's job, held by J. Tylee Wilson, by approaching the company's board of directors and asking them to choose between the two men. The board selected Johnson and, in August 1986, Wilson, although only fifty-five, announced his retirement. For the second time in five years, Johnson had seen his company bought out by a larger firm, only to emerge in both instances as the CEO of the new operation. (By contrast, most CEOs

lose their jobs entirely following a takeover.) "You have to compromise in your life," Johnson told Larry Black. "But I think if you have the ability to run something, you should run it." Johnson insisted to Scott Ticer during an interview for *Business Week* (April 17, 1987) that his assumption of the company's top job was "no palace coup," but, as one RJR Nabisco executive also told Ticer, "Ross is a locomotive, and Wilson just got out of his way."

Before stepping down, Wilson had sold off all of RJR Nabisco's shipping and oil operations, and Johnson continued that policy of returning the company to its core businesses of packaged foods and tobacco, selling the entire liquor division, and, in 1986, negotiating the $840 million sale of Kentucky Fried Chicken to PepsiCo Inc. All told, RJR Nabisco sold about thirty of its approximately fifty businesses in the first three years after the merger, and proceeds from the sales were used to buy back $1.6 billion in preferred stock and twenty-five million common shares. The net effect was a reduction of RJR Nabisco's debt and an increase in return-on-equity to a healthy 20 percent. In other significant actions, Johnson cut the corporate staff by two-thirds, to about 300 employees and, just two weeks after settling into the CEO's chair, announced that he was moving the company from Winston-Salem, North Carolina, where it had been headquartered for more than 100 years, to Atlanta, Georgia. "Winston-Salem is a wonderful place to live, but it is not a place for a head office," Johnson later explained.

In the midst of that extensive corporate reorganization, Ross Johnson somehow found time to help out his old friend, Canadian prime minister Brian Mulroney, who had run into difficulty in negotiating a free-trade agreement with the administration of President Ronald Reagan—an agreement that Johnson publicly supported in a speech before the Toronto Board of Trade. After American and Canadian negotiators got bogged down in details, he spearheaded the formation of the American Coalition for Trade Expansion with Canada, which became one of the largest single-issue business lobbies ever to operate on Capitol Hill. Spurred on by the coalition and by other groups, Congress overwhelmingly approved the historic free-trade agreement in the summer of 1988.

Meanwhile, on Wall Street, speculation was growing that Johnson had streamlined RJR Nabisco in order to create a war chest that could be used to make a major corporate acquisition, possibly of a food company, such as Kraft or Sara Lee. That speculation proved inaccurate, however, when, on October 19, 1988, Johnson announced to RJR Nabisco's board members that he and seven other managers intended to privatize the company through a $17.6 billion leveraged buyout. Johnson told the board that the company was performing well, but that its stock price was stagnant because of mounting public concern about the dangers of cigarette smoking. He proposed borrowing $15 billion (about 90 percent) of the money, a common practice in such buyouts, which have become increasingly common in recent years. Proponents of leveraged buyouts argue that they bring windfall profits to shareholders and encourage companies to be efficient so that they can pay off their debt. Critics of LBOs point out, however, that jobs are usually lost when the new owners sell off parts of the company or trim the payroll in an attempt to reduce expenses. They also note that, when the new owners eventually resell the company, they take in profits far more substantial than those made by the old shareholders at the time of the original sale.

The RJR Nabisco board reacted with shock to Johnson's proposal. His cause was further weakened when it became known that his offer of $17.6 billion, or about $75 per share, while exceeding the stock's $55-per-share market value, was still well below the real value of the company's assets, in the judgment of industry analysts and other potential buyers. Although Johnson later maintained that the bid had been dictated by his bankers, some observers suspected that Johnson assumed that the board, which he had always pampered with generous salaries and offers of special consulting contracts, would go along with what amounted to a "lowball" bid.

The board was still studying Johnson's offer when, four days later, Kohlberg, Kravis, Roberts and Company, a powerful Wall Street investment firm that specializes in leveraged buyouts, tendered a bid of $20.4 billion, or $90 per share, for RJR Nabisco. The effect of the bid was profound. "It made KKR look like saviors," James Sterngold of the New York Times (December 5, 1988) quoted an insider as saying. A few days later, the two sides met to consider the possibility of making a joint bid, but those discussions broke down. On November 3, the Johnson team, which had obtained the backing of the Wall Street brokerage firms of Shearson Lehman Hutton and Salomon Brothers, increased its bid to $20.9 billion, or $92 a share, but it was undermined once more when the board was shown studies indicating that if RJR Nabisco's divisions were sold individually, the company would be worth much more than $90 a share. Sensing that the entire matter deserved a great deal more deliberation, the board formed a five-member committee to entertain bids for the company.

The board's disenchantment with Johnson grew still stronger after a story in the November 5 issue of the New York Times revealed the details of a financial arrangement between Johnson, a select handful of his top executives, and Shearson that called for Johnson and his team to receive a package of incentives potentially worth in excess of $100 million each, should their bid be accepted. In addition, the group would own as much as 20 percent of the stock in the company and would have a virtual veto over decisions made by the board. That disclosure was a public relations bombshell that prompted a storm of criticism from the media and raised some fundamental questions about the ethics of management LBOs. Writing in Business Week (November 21, 1988), Judith H. Dobrzynski said the deal provided "a startling example of the

conflict of interest a chief executive faces when he participates in a buyout on both the buy side, trying to get the best terms for himself, and the sell side, representing the shareholders."

Johnson tried to respond to the charges in a letter to the committee chairman, Charles Hugel, but in arguing that it was not unusual in a management LBO for the buyout group to get up to 20 percent of the company's stock, Johnson failed to note that this particular bid was worth twenty to twenty-five times the average buyout. A 20 percent cut was therefore potentially worth billions of dollars. In an interview with Randy Whitestone of USA Today (November 28, 1988), Johnson said that the management group was required to put up $20 million of its own money to finance its share of the deal, and he contended that he had intended to split his profit with 15,000 RJR Nabisco employees. Even so, the damage to Johnson's cause had been done. As Henry Kravis, writing in Fortune (January 2, 1989), put it, "Ross Johnson turned out to be the best thing we had going for us because of all the adverse publicity he was collecting."

On November 18, the deadline for bids set by the committee, KKR offered $94 a share, and the management group bid $100. The committee then extended the bidding deadline to November 29 in order to allow a third group, headed by the First Boston Corporation, to submit a proposal, but when the deadline arrived, that group was unable to demonstrate that it could finance its bid; KKR offered $106 a share, and the management group, $101. The board began negotiating a final merger agreement with KKR on the evening of November 29. But the following morning, the management group submitted a new offer of $108 a share, which it upped later in the day to $112 a share, or $25.42 billion. Matching the $108-a-share offer, KKR then submitted a final bid of $109, or $24.88 billion, and gave the board thirty minutes to reach a decision. Slightly more than half an hour later, the board informed Henry Kravis that it had accepted his group's offer.

The KKR takeover of RJR Nabisco was easily the largest LBO in corporate history—almost twice as large as the biggest previous deal, Chevron's $13.3 billion takeover of Gulf in 1984. The board was believed to have selected the KKR team, even though it submitted a lower bid, for several reasons. KKR's proposal was seen as being more favorable to stockholders and employees and as involving a better debt-to-equity ratio; it also meant that KKR would have to sell off fewer businesses in order to repay its loan.

Following the sale, speculation arose on Wall Street that Johnson's group would file suit in an attempt to block the KKR takeover, but such suspicions proved groundless. Johnson also dismissed suggestions that, in turning down his group's bid, the board had rejected him personally. "I am convinced their [KKR's] bid was better than our bid," Johnson wrote in Fortune (January 2, 1989). "I know darn well that's how the board voted, because I know those board members too well." Kohlberg, Kravis, Roberts and Company assumed control of RJR Nabisco in early February 1989, at which time Johnson resigned as chief executive. The combined value of Johnson's generous severance package and the profits derived from the sale of his RJR Nabisco stock was estimated to be at least $30 million. Later in 1989, F. Ross Johnson and John Martin, a former RJR Nabisco vice-president who was a member of the management team, formed RJM Group, a firm that offers business advice to executives, directors, politicians, and athletes.

A large, imposing man, the bespectacled Ross Johnson is often described as gregarious and outgoing. According to Kevin Maney of USA Today (October 21, 1988), he "offers a quick smile and earthy language to anyone he meets." Johnson revels in the lavish lifestyle made possible by his financial coups. He owns homes in New York, Atlanta, and Florida, and he has been known to tip waiters fifty dollars for efficient service. In addition to Brian

Mulroney, with whom he has maintained a close friendship, Johnson numbers among his cronies such well-known figures as Bob Hope, Gerald R. Ford, Jack Nicklaus, Ben Crenshaw, Frank Gifford, and Bobby Orr. He has appeared in print ads for the fashion designer Oleg Cassini, another friend. A confirmed cigarette smoker, he enjoys cigars as well. He is an avid golfer, skiier, and tennis player. His second wife is the former Laurie Anne Graumann. From his first marriage, which ended in divorce, Johnson has two grown sons, Bruce and Neil. Still a Canadian citizen, Ross Johnson was named an officer of the Order of Canada in 1987.

References: Bsns W p175+ My 23 '88 por; Fortune 118:32+ Jl 18 '88 pors, 119:69+ Ja 2 '89 pors; N Y Times IV p13 O 21 '88 por; Time 132:76+ N 28 '88 por, 132:66+ D 5 '88 pors, 132:56+ D 12 pors; Toronto Globe and Mail II p3 O 22 '88 por; USA Today II p9 O 21 '88 por; Canadian Who's Who, 1988; Who's Who in America, 1988–89

Joseph, Stephen (Carl)

Nov. 25, 1937– Physician; New York City Commissioner of Health. Address: New York City Dept. of Health, 125 Worth St., New York, N.Y. 10013

BULLETIN: Dr. Stephen C. Joseph resigned as New York City health commissioner, effective December 31, 1989.

As an activist who thrives on challenges, the New York City health commissioner Dr. Stephen Joseph seems ideally suited for what is widely regarded as the most demanding public-health position in the United States. The pediatrician, who is an expert on international child health issues, brings to his work over two decades of public-health experience in settings as diverse as Nepal, Cameroon, Newfoundland, and Wyoming. Joseph was appointed to his post by Mayor Edward I. Koch in March 1986 largely to undertake a more aggressive campaign against New York City's number-one health problem, the AIDS epidemic.

Believing that AIDS, or acquired immune deficiency syndrome, is not merely a disease, but a "social phenomenon" that will have a far-reaching impact on the city and its residents, Joseph has launched an all-out attack on the epidemic. His measures have included the expansion of testing for the AIDS virus, the endorsement of hard-hitting, explicit ads intended to promote "safe sex," the free distribution of condoms at city clinics and hospitals, the introduction of an experimental program to supply drug addicts with clean needles, and the proposal of tougher enforcement of laws prohibiting prostitution. The health commissioner's tactics have offended some conservatives, who believe his approach encourages what they view as immoral activity, but, at the same time, AIDS activists have accused Joseph of not doing enough to provide adequate care for victims of the deadly disease. Yet in the midst of these and other controversies, Joseph insists that he relishes his position as chief health official of the nation's largest city. "Every professional wants to play in Yankee Stadium," he has said, "and in public health, this is Yankee Stadium."

Stephen Carl Joseph was born on November 25, 1937 in the Greenpoint section of Brooklyn, New York, the son of Max and Evelyn (Stern) Joseph. The family moved to the Bronx during Stephen's childhood, and he was raised in that borough. In 1955 he left New York City to attend Harvard University, which granted him a B.A. degree, cum laude, in biology. Joseph then attended Yale University Medical School, from which he received his M.D. degree in 1963. After completing his internship (in pediatrics) at Children's Hospital of Boston, Joseph received a commission from the United States Public Health Service in 1964 and went to Nepal as a Peace Corps physician, an experience that signaled the beginning of his lifelong interest in international public health. Joseph returned to the United States in 1966 and completed his residency at Children's Hospital a year later. In 1968 he received a master's degree in public health from Johns Hopkins University. The young doctor then became a special assistant to the assistant secretary for health and scientific affairs at the Department of Health, Education and Welfare, where he remained until 1969, when he was named director of comprehensive health services at the Office of Economic Opportunity. He also served, from 1969 to 1971, as an attending physician at the Children's Hospital of the District of Columbia.

In 1971 Joseph became a regional public-health physician for the Agency for International Development in Yaoundé, Cameroon, in central Africa. There, he worked with the University Center for the Health Sciences (UCHS), a nontraditional medical school designed to meet the needs of Cameroon's sparse, largely rural population. Developed in the late 1960s, UCHS, as Joseph explained in a 1977 paper for the medical journal *Pediatrics,* was established as an alternative to the Western model of educating physicians in medical schools linked to urban teaching hospitals. That model having been found to be inappropriate for developing African nations, whose populations are too small to support such hospitals, UCHS emphasized instead "team-based" medical care in which doctors, nurses, and technicians are trained together so that each person is capable of providing primary care. Joseph's work in Africa convinced him that the Cameroon model might also be appropriate in lightly populated, rural areas of the United States. In 1973 and 1974, while serving as a special consultant to the president of the University of Wyoming, Joseph drew up plans for a "statewide educational system for health professionals" that would replace the teaching hospital as the major training ground for physicians. Returning to Harvard in 1974, Joseph served as the director of the Office of International Health Programs at the Harvard School of Public Health and a faculty fellow in the Harvard Institute for International Development. He also lectured on child health at the school and served as an attending physician at Children's Hospital of Boston, where he had done his internship and residency.

From Harvard, Joseph went on to become deputy assistant administrator, in 1978, and, later, acting administrator of human resources development in the Bureau of Development Support at the Agency for International Development, and by 1981 he was its highest-ranking health professional. But later in the year he resigned in protest when the adminis-

tration of President Ronald Reagan voted against a proposal before the World Health Organization to forbid promotion of infant formula in developing countries, making the United States the only nation to vote against the proposal. Many public-health experts believe that the use in the Third World of infant formulas, which mothers often prepare incorrectly and under unsanitary conditions, has led to increased infant mortality rates and that the availability of those formulas also discourages breast-feeding, which is considered healthier for infants. Not surprisingly, the infant-food industry has disputed claims that its product contributes to greater infant mortality and has fought attempts to restrict its markets in developing nations. Joseph later explained his decision to resign to Crystal Nix of the *New York Times* (March 12, 1986): "The position [of the Reagan administration] was immoral as well as professionally unacceptable. After trying to change the position within the government, I felt I had no choice but to resign."

After leaving the federal government, Joseph became chief of pediatrics for the Grenfell Regional Health Services in northern Newfoundland, Canada. The only pediatrician in an area that contained about 17,000 children, many of whom could be reached only by airplane, boat, or snowmobile, Joseph worked long, hard hours. "I was up out of bed and down to the delivery room three, maybe four nights a week, and up all night with sick kids. And that's hard at forty-five," he explained to Don Singleton of the New York *Daily News* (June 7, 1987). Still, as an avid naturalist, Joseph found that the outdoor activities available in the wilds of Newfoundland helped to make up for his demanding schedule. In 1983 he returned to Washington, D.C., this time as special coordinator for child health and survival for UNICEF, a post that drew upon his extensive experience in international child health.

In February 1986, after Joseph returned from an international conference on child health in Kenya, Mayor Koch offered him the position of health commissioner of New York City, succeeding David J. Sencer, who had resigned in January. Joseph immediately accepted, and the new health commissioner, who officially took over the $90,000-a-year job on May 5, 1986, inherited a staff of some 4,000 workers and an annual budget of $170 million. When he took office, New York City was in the midst of the AIDS epidemic, the worst public-health crisis to hit the metropolis in the twentieth century. AIDS is a fatal illness that cripples the body's immune system, leaving the victim susceptible to cancer, pneumonia, and other diseases. Because of its large populations of homosexual men and intravenous drug users, the two groups most at risk, New York City has been hit especially hard by the epidemic, so much so that about one-quarter of all AIDS cases in the United States to date have been reported there.

Neither of Joseph's immediate predecessors at the health department, David Sencer and Reinaldo Ferrer, had been sufficiently aggressive in tackling the AIDS problem, causing the Koch administration to be assailed for its timid response to the crisis. By hiring Joseph, a man with a more activist temperament, the mayor hoped to mobilize the city for an all-out campaign against the terminal disease. At his first news conference, on March 11, 1986, Joseph called the health commissionership of New York City "the ultimate challenge." He outlined an ambitious agenda that included reducing the city's child-mortality rate, improving access to health services for the homeless, and removing environmental health hazards, but he insisted that AIDS was the chief health problem in the city. In later interviews, the health commissioner went so far as to label AIDS New York's single biggest problem, health or otherwise. During a *New York Times* (January 17, 1987) interview, he predicted that AIDS would change everything about the city, including its demography and its political and economic life. In another *New York Times* (May 17, 1988) story, he estimated the number of New Yorkers infected with the AIDS virus to be about 400,000. The same story reported that, by 1991, the city would have recorded 43,000 diagnosed cases of AIDS and 31,000 deaths from the disease.

Quickly setting to work to arouse public concern about the AIDS epidemic, Joseph first took steps to increase voluntary testing for the AIDS antibody in order to identify infected individuals before they spread the virus further, and, within a few months of his appointment, the number of AIDS cases discovered by the health department's AIDS surveillance unit had doubled. Using the media to preach "an aggressive gospel of prevention," he pointed out that, although science had not yet found a cure for the deadly disease, it had provided the knowledge to prevent its spread. To promote "safe sex," he wrote to the city's pharmacists and asked them to bring condoms out from behind the counter. The health department announced that it would distribute a million free condoms in municipal clinics and hospitals.

Joseph's most aggressive and controversial tactic in battling the AIDS epidemic to date has been a series of explicit radio, television, and newspaper advertisements aimed at raising concern among heterosexuals about the danger of the disease. Developed *pro bono publico* by the celebrated advertising firm of Saatchi & Saatchi Compton and released in May 1987, the ads featured such admonitions as "Don't Go Out Without Your Rubbers" and "Don't Die of Embarrassment." One of the television ads showed an elegantly dressed woman placing a condom in her purse before going out for the evening. The Catholic archdiocese of New York attacked the ads as "an implicit endorsement of sexual promiscuity" and New York City councilman Noach Dear labeled them "disgusting." Each of New York's four major daily newspapers rejected the ads; three television stations agreed to carry a few of the less explicit ones, and the New York City Transit Authority placed some of the ads in its subway cars.

The largely negative reaction to the ad campaign pleased Joseph. "I was delighted to see the controversy," he told David Firestone of New York *Newsday* (June 1, 1987). "The more controversy we have, the more we negotiate as a society what we want to do, and that's useful. And also, the more attention it gets the ads, which is exactly what we want. So I hope we'll have plenty more conflict about it." The commissioner said the ads were not meant to be deliberately offensive, but rather aimed at getting a point across. "The Department of Health is not the guardian of public morality. We are the guardian of public health," he remarked in an interview with Jane Gross of the *New York Times* (May 11, 1987). In the interview with David Firestone, Joseph also stated his belief that abstinence, advocated by many as the most viable way of fighting AIDS, was unrealistic for most people. "To place our faith in that as an adequate preventive of the spread of this virus would be like the militiamen at Lexington unloading their rifles and saying to the British, 'Don't come any further. Please go home.' It's not an adequate defense."

Later in 1987 Joseph sparked still more controversy when he suggested that the city give clean needles to intravenous drug users. About half of New York City's 200,000 intravenous drug users are believed to be infected with the AIDS virus, which is spread through the sharing of contaminated needles. Joseph's predecessor, David Sencer, first proposed supplying addicts with free needles in 1985, but Mayor Koch, after consulting law-enforcement officials, vetoed the idea. In light of that earlier rejection, Joseph proposed giving free needles to a small test group of addicts to determine if infection would be sufficiently reduced to justify implementing the program on a larger scale. Koch agreed to the plan, but the state health commissioner, David Axelrod, whose approval is required, did not. After long negotiations between the city and state health departments, however, Axelrod relented and permitted a pilot study that went into effect in the fall of 1988.

In another attempt to intensify awareness about AIDS among heterosexuals, Joseph recommended to the New York State Health Council in October 1987 that vaginal intercourse be placed on the list of activities prohibited in commercial sex establishments, such as houses of prostitution and massage parlors. Joseph said that "there's absolutely no question" that AIDS is transmissible through heterosexual intercourse if one of the partners is infected with the virus. In a related action, he called for mandatory AIDS testing for prostitutes, some 20 to 60 percent of whom are believed to be intravenous drug users. He also recommended a general crackdown on prostitution. In addition, the health commissioner suggested that doctors adopt a "duty to warn" exception to the time-honored code of patient confidentiality, arguing that the sex and needle-sharing partners of AIDS victims have the right to be made aware that they are at grave risk of being infected.

JOSEPH

In May 1987 Mayor Koch's Interagency Task Force on AIDS, which was headed by Joseph and staffed by top officials from several city agencies, issued a five-year plan aimed at combating the disease. Its report recommended that the epidemic be slowed through education and wider availability of testing, that adequate care be provided for those already infected, and that research be promoted on a cure for AIDS. Those recommendations came in the wake of a report by David Axelrod estimating that, by 1991, the cost of providing hospital care for AIDS patients in New York City would be $1 billion. Joseph himself has estimated that the overall cost of AIDS to the city will be $2 billion by 1991.

As the costs of the epidemic have escalated, Joseph has looked to the state and federal governments for assistance, but with only mixed results. AIDS activists have charged the city with not doing enough to provide services for victims, but, as Joseph points out, his power to expand services is limited, since it is the state health department that controls the hospital industry. "He's thrust into a position of responsibility without having the power to carry it out," Douglas Dornan, the executive director of the AIDS Resource Center, explained, as quoted by Bruce Lambert in the *New York Times* (August 30, 1988). Joseph agrees with that assessment. "There's a lot of leverage and authority I don't have," he admitted to Lambert. "At times it's frustrating, but it should never be used as an excuse to hide behind and not do the very best you can." In May 1988 the Interagency Task Force on AIDS issued a report stating that the city's ability to deal with the epidemic was nearing the breaking point and that greater state and federal assistance would be needed.

Controversy besieged Joseph again in July 1988, when, drawing on new epidemiological evidence, he reduced the official estimate of the number of AIDS-infected New Yorkers by half, from 400,000 to 200,000. AIDS activists, who had not been consulted before the announcement, exploded with rage, accusing the health commissioner of "cooking the numbers" and attempting to undercut their efforts to get more assistance for the victims of AIDS. Members of ACT-UP, an organization that advocates the rights of AIDS victims, held a sit-in at the health department at which twelve people were arrested. Several days later, ACT-UP members interrupted Joseph as he held a meeting in his office, occupied it, and engaged in a shoving match with the commissioner. The demonstration resulted in eleven arrests. On both occasions, Joseph refused to speak to the protesters, making clear that, despite his sympathy with their cause, he would not "have the department held hostage to a shouting mob." Offering to meet with three ACT-UP members at a future date, provided other members of the organization did not demonstrate during the meeting, Joseph pointed out that since researchers have raised their estimates of the percentage of people infected with the AIDS virus who will go on to develop the disease, the lowered estimate of infected individuals would not justify any cutback in ser-

vices. Saying he was "saddened" by the controversy, Joseph dismissed suggestions from AIDS activists that he step down. "You roll with the punches," he told Bruce Lambert. "It'll be a long time before I resign."

Speaking in Montreal at the Fifth International Conference on AIDS, in June 1989, Joseph recommended that New York City step up its attack on the disease by expanding testing and requiring doctors to report confidentially the names of those who test positive to city health authorities, who would then contact the sex and needle-sharing drug partners of the infected person. (All fifty states now require that doctors report diagnosed AIDS cases, but only twelve require the reporting of those individuals who merely harbor the virus.) Joseph's recommendations were strongly opposed by many AIDS organizations and health experts on the grounds that they would discourage members of high-risk groups from seeking testing for fear of discrimination and invasion of privacy if the result should be positive.

Although the AIDS epidemic has consumed about three-fourths of Joseph's time since he became health commissioner, he has managed to address other public-health issues. An ex-smoker, he strongly supported New York City's new anti-smoking regulations, effective in the spring of 1988, that prohibit or restrict smoking in public areas and places of employment. Joseph has also taken steps to have all children in New York City immunized against measles. In addition, he has called attention to the dangers of beach contamination by medical debris, a problem that plagued New York City and other areas on the East Coast during the summer of 1988. "I do believe this period of the 1980s will be remembered as the time the planet struck back," he commented to Bruce Lambert. "The planet is telling us we can't treat it this way anymore."

Dr. Joseph's flair for quotable remarks, his activist temperament, and his firm belief that public health is a "communication science" have made him the most visible and, in the opinion of many, the most effective health commissioner that New York City has had in many years. Dr. Harvey Feinberg, the dean of the Harvard School of Public Health, has said, "He has taken on what many consider the toughest public-health job in America, has done a highly creditable job, and is clearly a leading figure on AIDS policy." In the opinion of Bruce C. Vladeck, the president of the United Hospital Fund, a New York City foundation, "He's the most effective health commissioner this city has had in a generation. Steve has real skills as a communicator, articulator, and advocate."

Keeping to a grueling schedule, Joseph leaves his apartment on the Upper West Side of Manhattan at 7:30 A.M. and does not return until between 6:30 and 7:30 P.M., and three or four nights a week he gives lectures or makes television appearances. The telegenic health commissioner sports a salt-and-pepper beard. In his spare time, Joseph enjoys taking part in outdoor activities with his wife, Elizabeth Preble, who is the director of a family-planning project funded by the Agency for International Development. "For me, relaxation is basically outdoor stuff—wilderness travel, canoeing, backpacking, skiing," Joseph told Don Singleton for the *Daily News* article. Joseph has two daughters, Denise Ellen and Tara Anne, from an earlier marriage. He is a fellow of the American Academy of Pediatrics and a member of the American Medical Association, the American Public Health Association, and Alpha Omega Alpha, the

medical honorary society. He has published many papers and editorials on public health in such journals as *Pediatrics, Public Health Reports,* and the *American Journal of Diseases of Children.*

References: N Y Daily News p4+ Je 7 '87; N Y Newsday II p4+ Je 1 '87 por; N Y Times B p3 Mr 12 '86, B p1+ Ag 30 '88 por; New Yorker 62:38+ Ap 21 '86; Biographical Directory of the American Academy of Pediatrics, 1980; Who's Who in Government, 1972-73

Just, Ward

Sept. 5, 1935– Writer. Address: b. c/o Houghton Mifflin Co., 52 Vanderbilt Ave., New York, N.Y. 10017; h. 36 Avenue Junot, Paris, France

"The milieu I knew as a reporter is the milieu I write about—the world of journalists, politicians, diplomats, and soldiers," Ward Just once said of the subjects of his short stories and novels. Before devoting himself to fiction in 1970, he had been employed in journalism, mainly by *Newsweek* and the *Washington Post,* for over a decade. Many of the locales of his stories and eight novels, from *A Soldier of the Revolution* (1970) to *Jack Gance* (1989), are places where he lived and covered the news—Vietnam, Washington, Chicago and environs, Latin America, several European countries, and elsewhere. Similarly, the Vietnam War and the workings of American politics, among his major concerns as a journalist, are two of his perennial themes in fiction that finds loyalty and betrayal,

patriotism, duty, love, and truth and falsehood in impassioned and often tragic human relationships. Just's style combines a newsman's spare, energetic manner with Jamesian qualities of rumination and ambiguity. "The book is vintage Just," Abigail McCarthy wrote of *In the City of Fear* (1982) in the book review section of the *Chicago Tribune* (October 24, 1982). "Here are the sentences laden with meaning yet to be revealed, the conversations fraught with dark surmise, and ordinary events weighted with extraordinary significance."

Ward Swift Just's midwestern origin is conspicuous among the autobiographical overtones that permeate his fiction. He was born on September 5, 1935 in Michigan City, Indiana to Franklin Ward and Elizabeth (Swift) Just. His father, like his grandfather earlier, was the publisher of the *Waukegan News-Sun* in Waukegan, Illinois, some forty miles north of Chicago. The family had owned the paper since the late nineteenth century and continued to do so until 1983, when Ward Just, who was chairman of the company controlling the paper, his sister, and three family members sold their stock. Growing up in Waukegan and, later, in nearby Lake Forest, Just attended the Lake Forest Academy from 1949 to 1951. Then, after two years at the Cranbrook School in Michigan, he enrolled, in 1953, at Trinity College in Hartford, Connecticut.

In 1957, on leaving college, Just began his career in journalism as a reporter with the *Waukegan News-Sun.* For about a year, in 1959, he worked in the Chicago bureau of *Newsweek* before being assigned to that magazine's Washington bureau, at that time headed by Ben Bradlee. Just has recalled that he arrived in Washington a few months before the inauguration, in 1961, of President John F. Kennedy. What he has called "a magical time" in the nation's capital inspired many eager newcomers like Just, whose perception of historical change was deeply affected by the Kennedy assassination and its aftermath. In 1962 Just began working for the *Reporter* magazine, but he left the following year to become a *Newsweek* correspondent in London. When Ben Bradlee took over the position of managing editor of the *Washington Post* in 1965, he found a place for Just on his paper.

At Christmas in 1965 Just flew to Saigon to report on the war in Vietnam as a correspondent for the

Washington Post, which often ran his stories on the front page. The photographer Wally McNamee, at that time also with the *Post,* was recently quoted in the *Washingtonian* (September 1988): "My strongest memory of Ward is that he was a guy who really went to where the war was. I mean, he was fearless." On June 8, 1966, while traveling with a reconnaissance patrol of the 101st Airborne Brigade north of Pleiku in the Central Highlands, Just was wounded, especially in his back, by shrapnel from a grenade during an encounter with North Vietnam forces. Following a period of recuperation, part of the time in Washington, he returned to the battleground for a second tour.

When he finally left Saigon in May 1967, Just took a leave of absence from the *Washington Post* to stop over in Ireland for some months and write his first book, *To What End: Report from Vietnam* (1968). "The Vietnam thing is the rock bottom fundamental of my adult life, I guess," he said years later during an interview with Jack Fuller for the *Chicago Tribune* (October 24, 1982). "I find it so profoundly sad, such an appalling waste. . . . I keep trying to find something that will redeem it in some way, and I can't." *To What End,* which has been called "an impressionistic record," reflects Just's depression over the conflict and his despair over the elusiveness of its meaning. The reviewer for *Time* (June 12, 1968) magazine described it as "an almost apolitical and unusually successful attempt to convey a sense of Vietnam's violent confusion" and as "a detached and determinedly accurate assessment."

Back in the United States by the end of 1967, Just was assigned to cover for the *Washington Post* the presidential campaigns of Eugene J. McCarthy and Richard Nixon, among other major political events of 1968. He then joined his paper's editorial board but found writing editorials to be unfulfilling. "I felt silly commenting on news instead of digging it out," he told Herbert R. Lottman, who interviewed him for *Publishers Weekly* (March 13, 1987). Increasingly restive, in 1969 he took another leave of absence from the *Post* to go up to Vermont for the summer and write fiction, a literary endeavor that had been tempting him for many years.

A Soldier of the Revolution (1970), Just's first novel, is set in an unnamed Latin American country and is apparently based in part on his coverage for *Newsweek* of the revolt of the pro-Juan Bosch forces in Santo Domingo in the spring of 1965. His hero, a former monk who works for a nongovernmental organization in Latin America, becomes the captive of a group of revolutionary guerrillas in whose cause he finds he believes. "It doesn't hold together intellectually. But I loved doing it," Just said of his book, as Howard Means quoted him in the *Washingtonian* (September 1988). "It wasn't a success, except to me on my terms, but my fate in a sense was sealed." He left the *Washington Post* in 1970.

Before turning wholeheartedly to fiction, however, Just made a study of American soldiers in the Vietnam era that appeared in late 1970 as a two-

part piece in the *Atlantic* and in book form under the title *Military Men.* For his "fast-paced but episodic account of the 'new' American army," as the book was described in the *Virginia Quarterly Review* (Summer 1971), Just had interviewed men at army bases, West Point, and the Pentagon. Although *Military Men* clearly shows Just's empathy for soldiers, at least one reviewer considered it "antimilitary." But, as was pointed out in the *Virginia Quarterly Review,* "the author draws no general conclusions, but the men who train, fight, drink, love, gripe and mark time through these pages do. The picture they paint is one of an army in deep trouble over discipline, race relations, the intrusion of changing civilian values, and, above all, an unpopular war."

Later, from 1971 to 1973, Just contributed to the *Atlantic* nine short stories that he then assembled in *The Congressman Who Loved Flaubert and Other Washington Stories* (1973). The author's prefatory note to the collection helps to explain what he was seeking in writing fiction: "Journalism is useful, but truth wears many masks and in Washington facts sometimes tend to mislead. All the facts tend to mislead absolutely." That was a conclusion Just had reached while working on the editorial page. Talking with Michael Kernan for a 1973 *Washington Post* profile, he reiterated, "Facts don't lead you very far, facts don't lead you to the truth, they just lead to more facts."

Among the writers who have influenced him, Just has named F. Scott Fitzgerald first. But reviewers of *The Congressman Who Loved Flaubert* called attention to a similarity in tone to the early short stories of Ernest Hemingway, after whom Bradlee had nicknamed Just "Ernie" because of other resemblances between the two. Regarding content, however, Just owes nothing to Hemingway in establishing himself with his first collection of stories as a writer of authenticity, perception, and subtlety about Washington politics. The fascination with the political process revealed here remained with him throughout his career, and the key role of compromise in that process, which is stressed in Just's most recent novel, appears in one of his earliest pieces of fiction, the title story of *The Congressman Who Loved Flaubert:* "A man with ideology was wise to leave it before reaching a position of influence, because by then he'd mastered the art of compromise, which had nothing to do with dogma or public acts of conscience. It had to do with simple effectiveness, the tact and strength with which a man dealt with legislation, inside committees, behind closed doors. That was where the work got done, and the credit passed around."

The Washington ambience that Just understood so well, however, was not for him conducive to writing fiction. Moving to a rural home in Warren, Vermont, he wrote a novel of the American involvement in the war in Indochina, *Stringer* (1974), whose title character is an expert in espionage. Although attached to the American army in Vietnam as a civilian intelligence technician, he operates as an independent loner, by rules of his own, in an adventurous and dangerous mission. But the reader, who may enjoy the suspense of Just's story, becomes baffled by the state of mind into which Stringer falls—what seems a harrowing entanglement of surrealism, existentialism, and madness. Some reviewers hailed *Stringer* as the best of the Vietnam War novels to that date. The critic for *Time* (July 8, 1974) suggested that "this tough novel about an American guerilla-warfare expert who cracks up in an Asian jungle may be a parable of the American Vietnam disaster."

Away from Washington, Just re-created that city of power and intrigue in *Nicholson at Large* (1975), an ambiguous novel about ambiguity, among other themes. Like Just himself, the title character is a newsman who rejoiced in Washington during the promising years of Kennedy's Camelot administration and has witnessed the subsequent disappointments. Nicholson possesses a rare ability: looking at the black-and-white figuration that must be perceived as either a vase or two profiles confronting each other, he is able to see both images simultaneously. His "redoubtable talent" for handling the true as well as the false within a single person or event distinguishes his reporting and may raise the question of whether he can recognize the difference between the two. That question enters into his reappraisal of his work and private life when, in a career crisis, he contemplates exchanging journalism for a job as spokesman for the secretary of state.

Also in Vermont, Just reworked a novel that had occupied him intermittently over many years, *A Family Trust* (1978). And, since the book required him to draw on recollections of his first home, the Midwest, it may be noted that in Vermont he spent some time reading Marcel Proust's *Remembrance of Things Past*. *A Family Trust* chronicles the lives of three generations of the Rising family, whose patriarch, Amos, dominates the fictional small Republican city of Dement, Illinois through his influential newspaper. By a family trust regarding the management and sale of the paper, he seeks to retain control over the town beyond his death. It falls eventually to his beautiful, intelligent, and free-spirited granddaughter to decide the fate of the paper.

Family ties, especially between father and son, coping with change, and political maneuvering are among the recurrent themes of his fiction that Just handles with singular energy and eloquence in *A Family Trust*. "I have called *A Family Trust* old-fashioned," Doris Grumbach wrote in the *Saturday Review* (April 15, 1978). "It is, not only in form and in character but also in its defense of the old American virtues—decency, honesty, smallness, independence, faithfulness to family, trust in friends, and patriotism for town and country."

The prairie town Dement is the early home also of Tom Lewis, who becomes a Washington politician in the title fictional piece of Just's collection of two novellas and four short stories, *Honor, Power, Riches, Fame, and the Love of Women* (1979). Freud had once pointed out that by means of his imagination the artist wins the rewards that at first existed only in his imagination: "honor, power, and the love of women." Lewis sees imagination as having that role in politics as well as art. The protagonists of Just's stories are often men and women encountering stress in love relationships. For instance, both Lewis and the truce negotiator of the second novella, "Cease-fire," engage in extramarital affairs that contribute to a dangerous "collision between one's public and private selves." Various references to Henry James in the stories are in accord with Jonathan Yardley's observation in the *New York Times Book Review* (September 9, 1979) that Just "writes in a leisurely, reflective manner that is faintly reminiscent of James." In *Honor, Power, Riches, Fame, and the Love of Women* Yardley found some of Just's best work to date.

Perhaps the most ambitious and powerful of Just's novels, *In the City of Fear* (1982) is an unsettling portrayal of Washington during the Vietnam War. When he tries to explain what he sees as the direction and outcome of that war, an army officer on the battlefront has to use the word "kaleidoscope." In dramatizing the disintegrating effects of the unwinnable war on agonized Washingtonians—refracted purposes, scattered ideals, dissolved dreams—Just employs shifts and merges in time, scene, conversation, and narrative within narrative that themselves occasionally produce kaleidoscopic confusion. But most reviewers thought the cryptic allusions and puzzling style of *In the City of Fear* well worth the reader's efforts.

Once again Just grappled with the nightmare of the Vietnam War in *The American Blues* (1984), narrated by a journalist trying to heal the psychic wounds of his wartime experience and to break out of the writer's block that prevents him from finishing his book about Vietnam. Then, in a striking change of scene, Just turned to Africa and Europe for *The American Ambassador* (1987), whose hero, a foreign service officer, has notably not served in Indochina. The moral predicament that Just poses for the ambassador in his suspenseful story centers on a clash between his loyalty to his country and to his son, a terrorist whose hatred for the United States drives him to resolve to kill its representative, his father. The title *The American Ambassador* may be intended as a tribute to Henry James, who had a strong influence on the oblique, enigmatic way of unfolding the narrative in *In the City of Fear* and who comes again to mind in the conflict between the values of dissimilar cultures in *The American Ambassador*.

A less violent estrangement develops between father and son in *Jack Gance* (1989) and thrives in part on differences in attitude toward compromise, the son having learned an early, painful lesson from his father's decision to go to prison for tax evasion rather than concede to government demands. One of the three protagonists of *In the City of Fear*, Piatt Warden, is a pseudoliberal senator of whom Just may well have been thinking when he said in the *Washingtonian* interview that in that novel he was "trying to work out a theory that

Washington demands a certain amount of compromise. . . . You bargain away your soul bit by bit." In *Jack Gance*, again, the adaptable, pragmatic, complacent senator from Illinois, who owes much to compromise in his rise in Chicago and then in national politics, gives a lecture to a group of young visitors to Washington, in which he sums up what he has learned about the political process: "The essence of public life was compromise. That was what made the government go, gave it its very existence. It was exquisite, the give-and-take making a beautiful balance." To him, Washington was "a great city, always giving more than it received. It gave and gave and gave and gave and expected nothing in return except loyalty."

Ward Just's reporting from Vietnam earned him the Overseas Press Club Award in 1967. He also won the Washington Newspaper Guild Award in 1966 and 1967 and the National Magazine Award for nonfiction in 1970 and for fiction in 1980. His stories have been selected several times for the annual *Best American Short Stories*, and he was the recipient in 1985 and 1986 of the O. Henry Award. Just's most recent novel, *Jack Gance*, won him the 1989 Heartland Prize, given annually to midwestern writers or to those authors whose books feature

"distinguished writing about the places and people of middle America."

While at Phillips Academy in Andover, Massachusetts from 1982 to 1984 as writer in residence, Just wrote *The American Ambassador*, whose many varied settings include Martha's Vineyard, off Cape Cod, Just's summer home in recent years. He wrote *Jack Gance* in Paris, in the bohemian quarter of Montmartre, where he now lives with his third wife, the former Sarah Catchpole, a radio reporter. By his first marriage, to Jean Ramsay, which began on January 30, 1957, he is the father of two daughters, Jennifer Ramsay and Julia Barnett. He was divorced ten years later, and on October 20, 1967 he married Anne Burling. His son by that marriage, which also ended in divorce, is Ian Ward Just.

References: Chicago Tribune VII p3 O 24 '82 por, V p1+ Ja 25 '89 por; Esquire 102:49+ Jl '84 por; N Y Times Bk R p1+ Mr 15 '87 por; Pub W 231:67+ Mr 13 '87 por; Washington Post B p1+ Jl 20 '73 pors, B p1 S 16 '75 pors; Washingtonian p1+ S '88 por; Contemporary Authors 1st rev vols 25–28 (1979); Who's Who in America, 1988–89

Kasten, Robert W(alter), Jr.

June 19, 1942– United States Senator from Wisconsin. Address: 110 Hart Senate Office Bldg., Washington, D.C. 20510

Robert W. Kasten Jr., the senior senator from Wisconsin, is a conservative Republican who drew national attention from the media in 1983 for his bold stroke in aborting a scheduled plan requiring banks and other institutions to withhold income taxes from interest and dividend payments. In winning that battle he defied the leadership of his own party, turned aside a personal appeal from President Ronald Reagan, and in the process earned a reputation back home as something of a maverick. Since that time, Kasten has emerged as a knowledgeable, though low-keyed, member of the Budget, Appropriations, Commerce, and Small Business committees, but he has never been able to recapture the limelight. Although thought to be vulnerable politically because of a financial scandal that ended with the imprisonment of his business associate, he was reelected by a narrow margin in 1986.

Robert Walter Kasten Jr. was born in Milwaukee, Wisconsin on June 19, 1942 to Robert Walter and Mary (Ogden) Kasten. Since his father owned a shoe-manufacturing company, Kasten grew up in comfortable circumstances that enabled him to attend the Country Day School in Milwaukee and Choate preparatory school in Wallingford, Connecticut. He was captain of the lacrosse team and president of his social fraternity at the University

of Arizona, in Tucson, where he earned a B.A. degree in 1964. Two years later, after obtaining a master's degree in finance from the Columbia University Graduate School of Business, he was hired by Genesco, a footwear manufacturer in Nashville, Tennessee, as a managing coordinator and assistant to the vice-president. While working there, he joined the Wisconsin Air National Guard, where he rose to the rank of first lieutenant with the 128th Refueling Group by the time of his discharge in 1972.

In 1968 Robert Kasten left Genesco to become director and vice-president of the Gilbert Shoe Manufacturing Company in Thiensville, Wisconsin, where he settled into what he thought would be a long career in business. "I never planned on running for office," he told Alan Bursuk of the *Milwaukee Journal* (September 22, 1985). "I frankly thought I would spend my life being a small- or medium-sized businessman." But his experience at the Gilbert plant convinced him that, unless government regulation was restrained, the entrepreneurial spirit of the small businessman would be jeopardized. After losing his first bid for the Wisconsin state legislature, in 1970, he came back two years later to win a seat in the state senate. During his single term there, he was chairman of the Joint Survey Committee on Tax Exemptions and a member of the Joint Finance Committee. For his strong record on the environment, he was named Wisconsin conservation legislator for 1973 by the National Wildlife Federation.

In the 1974 Republican primary for Wisconsin's Ninth Congressional District, a Republican stronghold comprising Milwaukee's northern and western suburbs, Kasten upset the incumbent, Glenn R. Davis, a twenty-year veteran who had been a staunch defender of President Richard M. Nixon during the Watergate scandal, taking 57 percent of the ballots to Davis's 43 percent. He went on to defeat Lynn S. Adelman, the Democratic candidate, in the general election by a slightly smaller margin. Resigning from the Gilbert Shoe Company, Kasten took his seat in the House, where over the course of two terms he established the most conservative record in the Wisconsin delegation.

Appointed to the Government Operations Committee, Kasten consistently opposed what he regarded as excessive federal regulations, though on environmental issues he often joined the liberal bloc. As a member of the original House Intelligence Committee, he also sided with Democrats in criticizing certain covert activities of the Central Intelligence Agency and in citing Secretary of State Henry A. Kissinger for contempt after he refused to produce certain classified documents. Kasten later grew critical of the intelligence panel itself and opposed making it a standing committee. The Wisconsin Republican was best known in the House as the author of the so-called Kasten plan, an efficient scheme for organizing precincts during congressional campaigns.

In 1978 Kasten relinquished his House seat to run for governor of Wisconsin. Perhaps because he won the official endorsement of the Republican party and therefore was the clear favorite to win the GOP primary, he immediately began planning for the general election. His overconfidence cost him the primary, in which he was narrowly upset by a political newcomer, Lee Sherman Dreyfus, the chancellor of the University of Wisconsin.

Stunned by his first defeat, Kasten joined Milwaukee developer Oliver Plunkett in four real-estate partnerships, a business arrangement that eventually was to prove even more humiliating. As a general partner, he was not expected to take part in the day-to-day operations of the funds but was responsible for bringing in new investors, for which he was entitled to 1.1 percent of the funds' profits as well as a portion of front-end fees imposed on new investors. In 1982 the state securities commissioner charged Plunkett with real-estate fraud in connection with the funds, which by that time had cost investors tens of millions of dollars, and named Kasten and other general partners in a civil suit for securities-law violations.

The commissioner's investigation revealed that the Plunkett operation had engaged in illegal loans, employed unlicensed salesmen, and failed to register securities properly—crimes for which Plunkett and his accountant later went to prison. Most of the other general partners filed for bankruptcy, leaving Kasten and only one other partner responsible for the debts of the Plunkett enterprise. To avoid bankruptcy himself and to satisfy the funds' creditors, Kasten liquidated his personal assets, including valuable Milwaukee rental properties, and borrowed from his family. Although he managed to remain solvent, he watched his net worth dwindle from hundreds of thousands of dollars in 1981 to just $3,000, exclusive of his congressional pension, in 1986.

Fortunately for Kasten's political career, the Plunkett scandal did not break until after he was safely elected to the United States Senate in one of the most stunning upsets of the 1980 elections. On the heels of his defeat for governor, Kasten entered the race to unseat Senator Gaylord Nelson, who had held statewide office continuously for the previous thirty-two years. But Nelson, a Democrat, was also one of the Senate's most liberal members, and Kasten benefited greatly from the conservative mood attending the election of Ronald Reagan. Running on a platform of less government and lower taxes, Kasten edged aside Nelson, by a margin of 50 percent to 48 percent, to become part of the large Reagan class of senators that gave the Republicans control of the upper chamber for the first time in nearly thirty years.

Despite his experience in the House, Kasten encountered some difficulty in acclimating himself to the Senate. With the Republicans in the majority, he suddenly found himself chairman of the Appropriations Subcommittee on Foreign Operations even though he had no experience in Senate procedure. "It's this whole first-year process," he explained to Frank A. Aukofer, a Washington bureau reporter for the *Milwaukee Journal* (October 9, 1988). "The bells would go off and I wasn't even sure how to vote. . . . Then all of a sudden it's two and a half years later, and you make the decision to run for reelection, and you go right from learning the job to setting up the financial organization, then you spend time campaigning."

By 1983 Kasten felt enough at home in the Senate to stand up to the leadership of his own party in a bitter floor battle over an extension of the income tax withholding laws. Over Kasten's objections, the Senate had attached to the 1982 tax bill an amendment requiring banks and other institutions to withhold taxes from interest and dividend payments to individuals beginning in July 1983. The new law was designed to raise additional revenue primarily by capturing taxes due from the minority who chronically fail to report such income. Kasten and others argued that tax cheats could be snared more easily by requiring the Internal Revenue Service to cross-check information forms against individual income tax returns more assiduously by computer. Aided by a massive advertising and lobbying campaign by the American Bankers Association, Kasten rounded up enough pledges of support to repeal the measure in March 1983, but he was stopped cold by the Republican leadership. Senator Robert J. Dole of Kansas, the chairman of the Finance Committee, and Majority Leader Howard Baker of Tennessee teamed up to thwart Kasten's effort to attach the repeal measure to a popular bill extending unemployment compensation. Dole denounced Kasten as a tool of the banking industry and scolded him for holding up relief to the jobless during the worst American recession since the 1930s. "Let the unemployed wait until the bankers have four or five days on the Senate floor," Dole declared sarcastically. Not even a personal call from President Reagan, who vowed to veto any bill repealing the withholding provision, would budge the freshman senator. For his part, Kasten viewed the issue not as relief for bankers but as a proconsumer bill consistent with his pledge to restrain government interference in the marketplace. "There are too many regulators, too many regulations, too much of a regulatory process," Kasten argued in defense of his cause in an interview with David Shribman of the New York Times (April 12, 1983). "If economic life were a football or baseball game the government ought to be the umpire or the referee in a game of competition and risk taking. But the government has become the other team. Now, when we should be encouraging savings and investment, we find ourselves with new regulations on withholding for savings and investment."

With unemployment funds about to run out, Kasten agreed to drop his amendment in exchange for a pledge from Senator Baker that the repeal measure would be called up for a floor vote the following month. By the time that deadline arrived, it had become clear that Kasten had mustered enough votes not only to pass the bill but also to override a presidential veto. At the end of a day-long meeting, Kasten, Dole, and White House representatives reached a face-saving compromise that effectively killed the withholding plan without a straight up or down vote.

To date, the floor fight over withholding has represented the high-water mark in Kasten's career, and, although he has occasionally generated some interest in a few scattered issues, his achievements have been comparatively modest. Since 1982 he has tried to gain support for a comprehensive product liability law restricting the recent surge in damage claims awarded by juries for defective merchandise. With the support of manufacturers, wholesalers, retailers, and insurers, he introduced legislation to standardize liability law in all fifty states. He was rebuffed, however, amid a flurry of lobbying by lawyers and consumer groups who warned that the public's right to just compensation was threatened by provisions in the bill limiting the grounds for suit. He then sponsored several stripped-down versions of the bill, but they died either in committee or on the floor. Taking a different tack in 1986, he won passage of legislation enabling municipalities, schools, hospitals, and other suit-prone enterprises to pool their resources to purchase large group insurance policies or to insure themselves.

Most recently, in mid-1989, Kasten cosponsored legislation in the Senate to set capital-gains tax rates ranging from 7.5 to 14 percent for individuals and reaching a top of 17 percent for corporations. Restoring the differential, he argued, would promote the growth of small companies. "Without a capital-gains differential," he argued, as quoted in Nation's Business (July 1989), "investors aren't going to take a chance on smaller, riskier companies with a lot of growth potential when they can make safer, dividend-paying investments in larger corporations."

As chairman of the Appropriations Subcommittee on Foreign Operations, Kasten oversaw foreign-aid distribution and cooperated with the Reagan administration in providing more military and less economic assistance to friendly foreign governments. In 1983 he drafted the law that requires the State Department to compile an annual report comparing the voting records of foreign governments in the United Nations General Assembly with that of the United States. He has urged that, armed with that tabulation, the United States reward its friends in the United Nations with more generous aid and slash assistance to those countries that consistently vote against Washington. In 1986 he pointed out that such ostensibly friendly countries as Egypt, Mexico, Saudi Arabia, the Philippines, and El Salvador all voted against the United States more than two-thirds of the time. In an Op-Ed piece, entitled "Friends Owe Us Their Votes," in the New York Times (May 23, 1986), Kasten pressed the Reagan administration to "find ways of turning up the heat on nations that either depend on our defense umbrella, enjoy special trade advantages with the United States, or successfully lobby for our aid dollars." Similarly, he has urged that the United States insist that recipients of American aid cooperate on world environmental problems. Kasten won high marks for persuading the World Bank to rescind a loan to Brazil for the construction of a highway that threatened the already endangered Amazon rain forest.

While Kasten was chairman of the platform subcommittee on economic policy at the Republican

National Convention in 1984, he kept his firm stand against raising taxes. In the national debate leading up to the sweeping tax reform act of 1986, Kasten joined Republican congressman Jack Kemp of New York in proposing a single tax rate of 24 percent regardless of income and the elimination of virtually all deductions. Although the Kemp-Kasten bill did not prevail, it provided an impetus for the compromise that streamlined and blunted the progressive nature of the tax code. Kasten was quick to defend the measure against charges that it was skewed in favor of the affluent. "Tax reform wasn't for the rich," he commented during the *Milwaukee Journal* interview. "Tax reform was an effort to help the people who are trying to become rich."

As the 1986 elections approached, Democrats targeted Kasten's seat, since they perceived it as being ripe for turnover. Running in an off year without the benefit of President Reagan's coattails and bedeviled by ethical questions, Kasten seemed an unlikely candidate to become the first Republican senator to be reelected in Wisconsin in thirty years. As if the Plunkett scandal and the humiliation of near bankruptcy were not enough, Kasten was forced to explain why he had been three years or more late in filing his 1977 federal and state income tax returns. (He at first denied failing to file returns on time but later blamed the oversight on a member of his staff.) His arrest for drunk driving in Washington in 1985 added to his woes.

Trying to capitalize on the tribulations of his opponent was the Democratic candidate, Ed Garvey, Wisconsin's deputy attorney general, better known as the head of the National Football League Players Association, who had led the players in their first regular season strike in 1982. In what was arguably the dirtiest campaign of the year, Kasten and Garvey traded low blows right up to election day. Casting himself as a progressive, Garvey condemned Kasten as antilabor, anticonsumer, obsessed with military hardware, indifferent to ethical concerns, and likely to drink on the job. He even hired a private detective to dig up more dirt on Kasten, a scheme that backfired when it was revealed that the detective had posed as a newsman to gain access to sources of information. Kasten castigated Garvey for what he charged were Watergate tactics and went on to raise questions about Garvey's involvement in what he claimed was the mysterious disappearance of football players' funds while Garvey was association president. Stung by the latter charge, Garvey filed a $2 million libel suit but dropped it after Kasten issued what amounted to an apology. In the end, Kasten managed to hang on to his seat, defeating Garvey by four percentage points, 51 percent to 47 percent.

With the retirement of Senator William Proxmire in 1988, Kasten became Wisconsin's senior senator, and he is currently the ranking Republican on the Appropriations Subcommittee on Foreign Operations and the Commerce Subcommittee on Surface Transportation. Just how long he will remain in the Senate, however, is open to question.

He has called for a twelve-year limit on congressional service: six two-year terms for representatives and two six-year terms for senators. "We need turnover here," he told David Shribman in the 1983 *New York Times* interview. "We shouldn't become a town and an institution of political people. We need educators, businessmen, lawyers, and doctors, people from all different trades, coming here to serve. . . . If we don't change the Senate rules, you find yourself in a Catch-22. If you stay here you're able to make a difference and have the kind of influence that can help your state. I like this, but I would hope I wouldn't do this for the rest of my life."

Robert W. Kasten Jr. was married on January 4, 1986 to the former Eva Jean Nimmons. Friends have noticed that family life seems to have tempered his drive and ambition. Mornings he used to spend swimming laps in the Capitol pool he now devotes to playing with his daughter, Nora. Quiet and unassuming, he frequently goes unnoticed in public and typically introduces himself simply as "Bob Kasten" with no reference to his office. He enjoys skiing, playing tennis, hunting wildfowl, and reading historical fiction and self-improvement books. He likes to slip out at night to visit the monuments in Washington for a period of quiet reflection.

References: Milwaukee Journal S 22 '85; N Y Times A p15 Ap 12 '83 por; Almanac of American Politics, 1988; Politics in America (1988); Who's Who in America, 1988-89; Who's Who in American Politics, 1989-90

Keegan, John

1934– Military historian; educator; journalist. Address: c/o Jonathan Cape, Ltd., 32 Bedford Sq., London WCIB 3EL, England

The military historian and journalist John Keegan produced the first of his classic studies of warfare—*The Face of Battle*—at a time when he had "not been in a battle; nor near one, nor heard one from afar, nor seen the aftermath," as he stressed at the beginning of the book. Yet, in *The Face of Battle* and in such subsequent books as *The Mask of Command* and *The Price of Admiralty*, Keegan demonstrated an unsurpassed ability to depict the atmosphere of battlefield "killing zones," the experiences of ordinary soldiers, and the wartime distortions of social mores in minute detail. He succeeded, in part, because of his exhaustive research, which included numerous interviews with former combatants and repeated visits to battlefields in Europe and the United States. But by general consensus, the most important factors were his virtuoso powers of description and his acute analytical insights. As Gwynne Dyer observed in the London *Times Literary Supplement* (February

John Keegan

5-11, 1988), Keegan is "unique" among military historians "in his willingness to pursue his conclusions"—that war, ever more horrific, is in the process of abolishing itself and that heroism should be discredited—"wherever they may lead."

John Desmond Patrick Keegan was born in London, England in 1934. The central experience of his childhood was World War II, yet, as he recalled in his book Six Armies in Normandy; From D-Day to the Liberation of Paris, June 6th–August 25th, 1944 (1982), he "had a good war . . . , the good war not of a near-warrior at the safe end of one of the sunnier theatres of operations, but of a small boy whisked from London at the first wail of the sirens to a green and remote corner of the west of England and kept there until the echo of the last shot fired was drowned in the sighs of the world's relief in August 1945." The "green and remote corner" was the town of Taunton, in Somerset, where Keegan's father, an inspector of schools, supervised the wartime education of south London students who, with their teachers, he had been responsible for evacuating to the countryside.

Although gasoline was rationed throughout the war, Keegan's father, who had been designated "an essential user," retained his car and, as Keegan wrote in Six Armies in Normandy, "set off each morning, exactly as he had done days without number in London before the war, to call on headmasters and headmistresses, monitor standards of reading among eight-year-olds . . . and in general uphold the austere but uplifting ideal of standard and compulsory education for all." During his private-school holidays, which overlapped the terms of the state schools, Keegan often accompanied his father on his rounds. "Thus I began my discovery of the secret world of the English

countryside . . . ," he wrote. "As I grew a little and learnt to bicycle, these expeditions became my own." The events that he witnessed on his expeditions—particularly the massing of American troops in preparation for the Normandy invasion in 1944—combined with constant talk about the war and countless wartime precautions, such as the removal of rural signposts, which might have guided invaders, made an indelible impression on the boy. Keegan's growing interest in military affairs was encouraged by his father, a World War I veteran.

After the end of the war, the Keegan family returned to London. Shortly thereafter, John Keegan was stricken with tuberculosis. His private war with the disease was to last nine years, from his thirteenth year to his twenty-second. He spent five of those years in the hospital. It was, as Lewis Chester remarked in his profile of Keegan for the London Observer (September 22, 1985), "an interminable lesson in patience and sympathy with those on the edge." For most of that time, Keegan was a patient in the orthopedic wing of St. Thomas's Hospital, near Byfleet, Surrey. There, under the tutelage of a group of visiting teachers, he blossomed into a scholar proficient in French, Latin, and Greek. When he was finally strong enough to attend a school full-time, Keegan enrolled at Oxford University's Balliol College, where he majored in history. Left lame by his illness, he was forced to give up his dream of becoming a soldier. "I was certainly one of those who feel the applicability of Dr. Johnson's observation 'Every man thinks meanly of himself for not having been a soldier,'" he told Chester.

Following his graduation from Oxford, Keegan obtained a grant to travel to the United States to study the Civil War "in the actual places where it was fought," as he explained to Herbert Mitgang in an interview for the New York Times (December 1, 1987). "I set off by car down U.S. 1, got to Washington, and then on to the battlefields and sites. . . . In three or four months, I managed to do most of the Civil War." On his return to England, Keegan spent two years writing political reports for the United States embassy in London. Then, in 1959, he secured a teaching position in the war studies department at the Royal Military Academy, in Sandhurst. "I really got into life by being kept out of it for so long," he told Chester. "I couldn't be a soldier though I was absolutely fascinated by soldiers. I couldn't live in an empire, but I was fascinated by the military element in our imperial life. So I deliberately put myself in the position to experience these things vicariously. The irony was, of course, that most of the old world was gone. You could say I'm a writer in the pure sense—fed on myths and dreams."

At Sandhurst Keegan was surrounded by men who had actually been in battles, men for whom "'world historical events' were . . . the stuff of gossip, often light-hearted, sometimes rueful or caustic, always matter-of-fact," as he told an interviewer for Newsweek (April 3, 1989). In this atmosphere Keegan's lack of battle experience grew, in his words, into "something of the dimensions of a Guilty Secret." As he explained in *The Face of Battle* (1976), in his lectures he therefore generally avoided making close tactical analyses of battles, concentrating instead on "such subjects as strategic theory, national defense policy, economic mobilization, military sociology and the like—subjects which, vital though they are to an understanding of modern war, nevertheless skate what, for a young man training to be a professional soldier, is the central question: what is it like to be in a battle?"

It was in an attempt to answer that question that Keegan wrote *The Face of Battle*, in which he described in graphic detail three epic battles: Agincourt (1415), Waterloo (1815), and the Somme (1916). As he pointed out in the book's opening pages, most military historians, when analyzing a particular battle, took the commanding general's perspective—an approach that, in his view, "too often dissolves into sycophancy or hero-worship." Keegan instead chose as his focus the viewpoint and battlefield experiences of the common soldier. Indeed he so vividly depicted the sights and sounds and smells and, above all, the terror of battle in three eras that John Hackett, writing in the London *Times Literary Supplement* (July 30, 1976), remarked, "Those who have been in battle will find much in the evidence presented here, and in a good deal of the author's commentary, to illuminate their own experience."

Although there were some atrocities at Agincourt, Keegan concluded that the hand-to-hand fighting of fifteenth-century combat required "a sort of empathy with one's adversary, lending the ability to anticipate his actions." Modern warfare, on the other hand, had become so impersonal that "almost all the soldiers of the First World War and many of the Second, even from the victor armies, testify to . . . their sense of littleness, almost of nothingness. . . . The dimensions of the battlefield, completely depopulated of civilians and extending far beyond the boundaries of the individual's perception, the events supervening upon it—endless artillery bombardments, sudden and shatteringly powerful aerial bombings reduced [each combatant's] subjective role . . . to that of a mere victim" and minimized his ability to see opposing soldiers as human and, when disarmed, worthy of mercy. In the end, the eminent British historian J. H. Plumb commented in the *New York Times Book Review* (November 7, 1976), *The Face of Battle* taught "as much about the nature of man as of battle." A bestseller when it was first published, the book, with a new introduction by the author and additional illustrations, was reissued by Viking in 1989 under the title *The Illustrated Face of Battle: A Study of Agincourt, Waterloo, and the Somme.*

In his preface to *Six Armies in Normandy*, Keegan noted that his depiction of the plight of individuals and small groups in *The Face of Battle* led him to recognize "the peculiar nature of the larger body to which both belong, the Army itself." While he acknowledged that armies "closely resemble each other," he contended that each was also "a mirror of its own society and its values." "It seemed to me worth finding some episode through which the varying status of national armies might be exemplified," he continued. "And in the Normandy campaign of 1944 I believe that I had stumbled upon it." In *Six Armies in Normandy*, Keegan chronicled a battle fought by each of his six armies during the Normandy campaign: the American airborne assault that set the stage for D-day, the Canadian landing at Juno Beach, the opening of the River Odon corridor by the Scottish army, the English surge near Caen, the counterassault by the Germans at Mortain, and the closing of the Falaise gap by a Polish armored division. He concluded his book with the liberation of Paris by the Free French in August 1944.

Keegan won praise from reviewers for his ability to depict simultaneously the development of grand operational strategies and the "minutiae of what it was like to be behind that hedgerow or in that tank," as the critic for the *Economist* (May 1, 1982) put it. In the opinion of Drew Middleton, the *New York Times*'s longtime military correspondent, *Six Armies in Normandy* was "the best book written" on its subject. "Here is a coherent, lucid view of a vastly complex operation, brilliantly written by a military historian who has a fine eye for the telling detail that can bring alive a battle or a staff conference . . . ," Middleton wrote in his evaluation for the *New York Times Book Review* (August 15, 1982). "Mr. Keegan has the ability to choose precisely those descriptions he has gathered from survivors of the campaign that will let us see the battles."

Keegan had his own firsthand look at battle in 1984, when the London *Daily Telegraph* sent him to Beirut, Lebanon to cover the escalating civil war. The assignment in the war-torn city taught him "how physically disgusting battlefields are," Keegan told the *Newsweek* interviewer. "It was like being in a municipal garbage dump." It also taught him "what it feels like to be frightened." Keegan nonetheless accepted an offer to become the *Daily Telegraph*'s defense and military correspondent in 1986. Of his decision to give up his senior lectureship at Sandhurst in favor of a journalistic career, he told Herbert Mitgang, "I thought to myself, if I don't do it now, I'll be an academic all my life." At the *Telegraph*, he continued, "I discovered to my satisfaction that I could write quickly. I write three or four times a week, usually including one big piece." Keegan also accepted a position as a contributing editor of the weekly American newsmagazine *U.S. News & World Report.* Perhaps his most notable contribution to date was "Hitler's Grab for World Power," a special report that was published in the August 28–September 4, 1989 issue, on the fiftieth anniversary of the beginning of World War II.

Despite the pressure of journalistic deadlines, Keegan continued to find the time for other projects. In 1986 he published two books: *Zones of Conflict; An Atlas of Future Wars*, in which he and his coauthor, Andrew Wheatcroft, examined twenty-eight political hot spots where wars had recently been fought (the Falkland Islands), were still raging (Iran-Iraq), or were likely to erupt (North and South Korea), and *Soldiers; A History of Men in Battle*, a companion to the BBC-TV series of the same name that Keegan co-scripted. *Soldiers*, which he wrote in collaboration with John Gau and Richard Holmes, a former colleague at Sandhurst, surveyed land warfare from ancient to modern times, each chapter featuring a different kind of fighting force, such as infantry, cavalry, artillery, and armored divisions, as well as guerrilla and terrorist groups. In his appraisal for the *New York Times Book Review* (March 23, 1986), Edward N. Luttwak groused about the book's "Anglocentric perspective" and the authors' "reduction of soldiering to battle, without the routine that is its essence," but on the whole he found it to be "well-written" and "free of inaccuracies." When the thirteen-part television series made its debut in the United States on PBS in 1987, it was widely praised for its intelligence and imagination.

In *The Mask of Command* (1987), Keegan turned his attention to the personalities and personae of military leaders. Focusing on the fact that military commanders achieve success by making the possibility of death less reprehensible for their soldiers than disobedience of their orders, Keegan described and analyzed the leadership styles—the "masks of command"—of Alexander the Great, the Duke of Wellington, Ulysses S. Grant, and Adolf Hitler. A general, Keegan wrote, "may be many things besides the commander of an army. . . . He may be king or priest: Alexander the Great was both. . . . He may command by surrogate authority of a monarch, as Wellington did, or by endorsement of a democratic assembly, which gave Grant his powers. . . . He may be demagogue-turned-tyrant, and yet sustain his military authority, as Hitler did until five minutes past midnight."

Each of these men, Keegan argued, succeeded by exploiting forms of "the theatrical impulse," which "in no exceptional human being . . . [is] stronger than in the man who must carry forward others to the risk of their lives. What they know of him must be what they require. What they should not know of him must be concealed at all cost. The leader of men in warfare can show himself to his followers only through a mask, a mask that he must make for himself, but a mask made in such form as will mark him to men of his time and place as the leader they want and need." Thus, in an age steeped in the glories of warfare, as celebrated in the *Iliad*, Alexander became the military leader par excellence by making—and surviving—grand heroic displays at the head of his troops.

Wellington's mask, as Keegan described it, was that of a gentlemanly, imperturbable, purposefully antiheroic administrator of wars. Nonetheless, at Waterloo, while overseeing the progress of the battle, he showed himself to the troops on the front lines, where he might easily have been killed, time and again. Grant is shown as being analytical, taci-

turn, and utterly antitheatrical, exposing himself to danger at the front only when he felt it absolutely necessary. "Unlike Wellington, and even more unlike Alexander," Keegan wrote, "he felt no need to share the risks of the individual soldier. . . . War, he might have explained, had become too important *not* to be left to the general."

Keegan characterized Hitler as a remote, "false-heroic" commander. In his speeches, Hitler portrayed himself as sharing his soldiers' sufferings, but he normally sequestered himself in isolated command posts far from the fronts. Usurping the authority of his senior officers and military strategists, he directed his forces with antiquated strategies derived from his experiences as a soldier in World War I and attempted to negate the effects of the resulting military reverses with propaganda trumpeting his own heroism. "Shameless though Hitler's manipulation of the heroic value system was," Keegan observed, "its effectiveness was borne out by results. The German army of 1945, unlike that of 1918, fought unquestioningly to the end."

In his conclusion to *The Mask of Command*, Keegan contended that those most likely to survive a world war in the nuclear age were the political leaders responsible for starting it, largely because they would be secluded throughout the conflict in protected command centers. Therefore, he reasoned, "mankind, if it is to survive, must choose its leaders by the test of their intellectuality; and, contrarily, leadership must justify itself by its detachment, moderation, and power of analysis"—not by heroism or the rhetoric of heroism. Keegan "is an astute theorist," Jim Miller wrote in his review of the book for *Newsweek* (December 14, 1987). "But for those put off by abstract generalizations, his narrative verve and eye for the telling detail will prove satisfaction enough." In his review for the *New Republic* (November 30, 1987), however, Edward N. Luttwak complained that Keegan had "abjured systematic analysis" in *The Mask of Command*, although he conceded that Keegan "writes like an angel."

In his most recent book, *The Price of Admiralty: The Evolution of Naval Warfare* (1989), Keegan traced the evolution of naval military operations from the Battle of Trafalgar in the age of wooden, men-of-war sailing ships to the clash of steam-driven, ironclad dreadnoughts at Jutland to the World War II conflicts between aircraft carriers at the Battle of Midway and between Allied convoys and German submarines in the North Atlantic. In his description of the Battle of Trafalgar, Keegan effectively contrasted the exigencies of land warfare with those of war on the high seas: "The gun power of [English vice admiral Horatio Viscount] Nelson's Trafalgar fleet exceeded that of Napoleon's Waterloo army six times. . . . Six times as many guns, of much heavier calibre, could be transported daily by Nelson's fleet as by Napoleon's army." Nelson himself is described as being an exemplary wearer of the mask of command, combining an air of modesty with a mastery of ship and fleet management, an "actor's gift for attracting attention," the "devotion of subordinate officers," and a tactical sense that was "revolutionary." As Keegan pointed out, it was Nelson's exceptional skill as a tactician, along with Britain's centuries-long tradition of maritime excellence—epitomized by Nelson's "astonishingly efficient" flagship, the HMS Victory—that brought triumph at Trafalgar.

In the age of the dreadnoughts, the British maritime industry continued to produce excellent ships, but there were no Nelsons to command them. By contrast, in the battle between American and Japanese aircraft carriers at Midway in 1942, Keegan identified another extraordinary leader: Admiral Chester Nimitz, the commander in chief of the United States Pacific Fleet. Nimitz's order to counterattack "without regard for losses" the Japanese task force preparing to take Midway was, for Keegan, "one of the few truly crucial 'moments of decision' which can be isolated in the whole course of warfare." Such a "war-decisive" victory eluded Admiral Karl Dönitz, who orchestrated the German submarine "wolf pack" assaults on Allied ships from the safety of his headquarters in Germany. In Keegan's opinion, Dönitz was excessively brutal and ruthless. His "attack on sight" policy cost the Allies 30,000 men and sent 28,000 of his own submariners to their deaths. "The Hitler navy of which Dönitz was the chief architect," Keegan wrote, "had forsworn every principle of the sea's fellowship," adopting instead "a code of 'hardness' justified by an appeal to national survival."

In his review of The Price of Admiralty for the London Observer (January 8, 1989), William Golding protested that Dönitz's "code of hardness" was "only one example of how the rules of warfare as more or less agreed-upon in the eighteenth century and elaborated by idealists in the nineteenth and twentieth centuries were eroded by the time of the Second World War," but he nonetheless conceded that Keegan's book had "interested and sometimes fascinated" him. For most critics, the strength of the book, like that of Keegan's earlier works, was, in Christopher Lehmann-Haupt's words, "its power to impart both the big and little pictures of war." Above all, Lehmann-Haupt concluded in his review for the New York Times (April 6, 1989), The Price of Admiralty "is an essentially humanistic book" able to "lend a human dimension to the most abstract of military calculations."

Among Keegan's other credits are two editions of Who's Who in Military History; From 1453 to the Present (1976 and 1987), written with Andrew Wheatcroft, and The Nature of War (1981), which he wrote in collaboration with Joseph Darracott. He is also the editor or coeditor of several military reference works, including two editions of World Armies, published in 1979 and 1983, the Rand McNally Encyclopedia of World War II (1977), Who's Who in World War II (1978), and The Times Atlas of the Second World War (1989). His panoramic account of that conflict, The Second World War, is scheduled to be published by Viking in January 1990. In his Newsweek profile of Keegan, Jim

Miller described the historian as "soft-spoken and thoughtful . . . , the soul of British civility." A devout Roman Catholic, Keegan told Lewis Chester that, in light of the psychological cost that warfare extracts from victors as well as vanquished, "God is not mocked" by the carnage of war. "I do believe in another world," he said, "and that we're living a dream in a sense." Keegan and his wife, Susanne, have four children: Lucy, Thomas, Rose, and Matthew.

References: London Observer p10 S 22 '85 por; Newsweek 113:72 Ap 3 '89; Writers Directory (1988–90)

Kelly, Patrick

Sept. 24, 1954(?)– Fashion designer. Address: Patrick Kelly Paris, 6 rue du Parc Royal, 75003 Paris, France; Patrick Kelly Paris, A Division of Warnaco, 485 Seventh Ave., New York, N.Y. 10018

"People have to make happy clothes; there's just too much sadness in the world," Patrick Kelly, the fun-loving American fashion designer who lives in Paris, has said. When Kelly unveiled his first women's ready-to-wear collection in 1985, he was hailed as the new King of Cling. His tight, black tube minidresses were decorated with everything from bright, colorful, mismatched buttons and bows to miniature black baby-doll pins and other whimsical items, such as watermelons and bandannas. "I design differently because I am Patrick Kelly, and Patrick Kelly is black, is from Mississippi," he told Nina Hyde during an interview for a profile in the *Washington Post* (November 9, 1986).

The creator also of more subdued attire with "offbeat elegance" and of made-to-order, one-of-a-kind garments, Kelly was unanimously elected to be among the forty-four couturiers at the pinnacle of the fashion industry only three years after he made his splashy debut. In 1988 he became the first and only American designer to join the Chambre Syndicale du Prêt-à-Porter des Couturiers et des Créateurs de Mode, whose membership includes Mme Alix Grès, Yves Saint Laurent, Karl Lagerfeld, Sonia Rykiel, and Emanuel Ungaro.

"The kind of women who wear my clothes are those who're not afraid to show off their bodies," Kelly told Carol Mongo in a conversation for *Essence* (November 1986) magazine. "Other designers try to improve on what's there or cover everything up, but with my clothes, I'm saying whether you're fat or skinny, have big hips or no hips at all, you're beautiful just the way you are." Kelly's clients have included Jane Seymour, the Princess of Wales, Isabella Rossellini, Paloma Picasso, Gloria Steinem, Grace Jones, Farrah Fawcett, and Goldie Hawn.

Patrick Kelly was born in Vicksburg, Mississippi on September 24, in about 1954. He adamantly refuses to divulge his age. "I don't remember how old I am," he has insisted. "People will put you in a category if they know your age. So I've forgotten." He declines also to reveal the number of siblings he has, telling Bonnie Johnson of *People* (June 15, 1987), for example, only that he has "lots." She reported, however, that after his father's death in 1969, "Patrick and his two brothers were raised in a house full of ladies." Kelly was reared on a corn, pecan, and squash farm, where he worked in the fields with his grandfather. In an interview with Charles Whitaker for *Ebony* (February 1988), Kelly sought to dispel the Horatio Alger myth that is evoked by his rural Mississippi background: "I'm not some poor little black kid who struggled from nothing and then goes to Paris and makes it. I had a comfortable, happy childhood."

Kelly's father, Danie Kelly, was at various times a fishmonger, an insurance agent, and a cabdriver. His mother, Letha Kelly, who holds a master's degree, is a retired home-economics teacher, an artist, and a dollmaker. She wanted Patrick to become a doctor; other lines of work considered appropriate for the boy were farming, teaching, firefighting, mail delivery, and astronautics. Patrick's early interest in fashion design was discouraged. In the interview with Bonnie Johnson, Letha Kelly recalled her response to her son's ambitions: "I told him, 'Michelangelo was dead and gone before he was famous.'" In the same interview, Kelly explained, "In Mississippi you had to be a boy. A boy sewing a dress? Oooo-EEEE!"

It was Patrick's grandmother, Ethel Rainey, who was responsible for introducing him to the world of fashion and inspiring him with her own sense of style. A caterer, cook, and cleaning woman, Ethel Rainey used to bring home copies of *Vogue* and *Harper's Bazaar* from her employers' homes. Leafing through the pages of the magazines one day when he was about six, Patrick was struck by the complete absence of black models. "I told my grandmother that it was a shame," he recalled in the interview with Nina Hyde. "And she said, 'Well, maybe no one has time to design clothes for black women.' And I said, 'Okay, I'll make clothes for black women and they can be in *Vogue*.'"

Having taught himself to sew with the help of an aunt who was a seamstress and having learned the basics of sketching from his mother, Kelly was creating prom dresses for the girls in his neighborhood before he entered high school. His sense of style was inspired by the women he saw around him. "There weren't any fashion shows there, but there was fashion," he told Bonnie Johnson. "At the black Baptist church on Sunday, the ladies are just as fierce as the ladies at Yves Saint Laurent haute couture shows." He described his grandmother in an interview with Ben Brantley for *Vanity Fair* (March 1988) as "the most chic of all the people I ever worshiped or wanted to be around. More than any Garbo, than any Dietrich. . . . She was the chicest thing . . . down to her white uniform, with her . . . lace apron that looked like a tutu." He also credits his grandmother with having inspired his current enthusiasm for decorating with buttons. "I was forever ripping buttons off my shirt," he told Nina Hyde, "and she was always replacing them. One day I said I can't go to school with every button different. So, to distract from the different buttons she started putting buttons everywhere."

Before graduating from Vicksburg Senior High School in 1972, Kelly had already begun working in the fashion business by designing department-store windows and supplying sketches for the stores' newspaper ads. After graduation he attended Jackson State University for eighteen months on a scholarship, studying art history and black history, and aspiring to become a history professor. In an interview with Margot Hornblower for *Time* (April 3, 1989) magazine, he recalled a period of militancy at what was then an all-black school. His best friend committed suicide by hanging himself in jail. "I remember singing 'Burn, baby, burn' and knowing what it meant," he told Margot Hornblower. His heroes were Martin Luther King Jr. and Malcolm X. "Those two men made a big impression on me," he told Trish Donnally for *American Way* (June 1, 1988), "because they were trying to fight for equality and human rights, and that's a good reason to love somebody."

Kelly dropped out of Jackson State after one of his teachers assured him he would "never amount to anything," according to Michael Thomas, a cousin of his who was quoted by Margot Hornblower. Assessing his college experience in the interview with Nina Hyde, Kelly said: "[Jackson State] was a forest to me. Unless you have a lot of money and pay for a good education, you suffer. I suffered from it. Now my big thing is to educate myself. I take classes. I take from everybody around me. It took me [until] my age now [in 1986] to realize that you have to be humble to learn."

In 1974 Kelly moved to Atlanta, Georgia, reportedly to escape "Mississippi-style" racism as well as to resume his pursuit of a designing career. For a while he lived on the streets, sleeping in restaurants and all-night bars. "Whores [and] drag queens would give me their money to hold for them. People liked me," he told Margot Hornblower. He earned a living by collecting and sorting used clothing for the veteran's organization AMVETS; teaching at the Barbizon School of Modeling; and decorating the windows of Yves Saint Laurent's Rive Gauche boutique, a job he was given after a period of doing it without pay. He also sold stained glass that he had retrieved from houses that were undergoing demolition. He eventually opened his own antique-clothing boutique (on the premises of a beauty salon) with recycled AMVETS clothes—beaded gowns, Chanel suits, fur-trimmed items—as well as his own designs. He soon opened a second shop and was asked to stage fashion shows.

Kelly asked for the services of Pat Cleveland, the highly successful runway model, for one of his fashion shows, and her acceptance marked the beginning of a lasting friendship. At her urging, Kelly left Atlanta for New York City, where he attended the Parsons School of Design for eighteen months, designing clothes for black models, students, and the disco crowd at Studio 54 to raise money for tuition. Despite his having acquired a cult following for his intricately knotted T-shirts worn by dancers at Studio 54, Kelly was unable to establish himself as a designer on Seventh Avenue. Of those he approached, only Louis Dell'Olio and Donna Karan, partners at Anne Klein, received him warmly. "Every place else the door was slammed," he told Nina Hyde. "I don't know what it is to be white so I can only think that part of the rejection was because I was black." Running out of patience as well as tuition money, Kelly was set back further when he was evicted from his East Harlem apartment for nonpayment of rent. On the day of his eviction he fortuitously ran into Pat Cleveland, who advised him to pursue his designing career in Paris. That night a one-way plane ticket to Paris was delivered anonymously to Kelly, and he used it. He explained his reasons for leaving New York City to Carol Mongo for Essence (September 1985): "It's difficult getting discovered in America. I was one of thousands trying to make it in an enormous, impersonal industry; and with so much attention given to European designers, I felt I'd have a better chance of making it in Paris."

Most accounts date Kelly's arrival in Paris in 1979; a few cite 1980; others, 1981. All sources agree, however, that he landed a job his first night in town, when he attended a party with his friend Toukie Smith, the model. Kelly described the job offer in an interview with Pamela Johnson for Essence (May 1989): "They said, 'You want to be a designer?' I said yes. They said, 'Can you sew?' I said yes. They said, 'Do you know Paris?' I said yes. 'Do you know where to buy fabric here?' Yes. 'Do you have a sewing machine?' Yes. 'Do you have

people to help you sew?' Yes, yes, yes. I didn't have shit, honey. But I found out."

Kelly's first job, which he held until 1982, was that of costume designer for the dancers at Le Palace, a venue described by one journalist as "a Las Vegas-style nightclub and discothèque." For six months he lived and worked in a hotel room, sewing at night to avoid blowing the fuses at the hotel. He was assisted in his chores by models and singers who, having been captivated by the Kelly designs on display at Le Palace, often worked for little more than room and board in the hotel room. Between costume assignments he hawked coats of his own design on the sidewalk of le boulevard Saint-Germain, because, as he once explained, "Coats were the only thing people would try on outside in winter." He eventually moved his business to a flea market at Porte de Clignancourt. To help make ends meet, he sometimes catered home-cooked dinners of fried chicken and corn bread.

Whether Kelly was "officially 'discovered' by designer Paco Rabanne," as Carol Mongo reported, or was set on the path to success following an invitation to design the sportswear line of Giuliana (Roberta) di Camerino of Venice, it was not until 1985 that his hard work and ingenuity finally paid off. His transformation of a bolt of black cotton jersey tube cloth that he had found at a flea market into dresses—simple, unseamed, unhemmed, skintight cylinders with circles cutout for the arms, festooned with inexpensive, colorful bottons—came to the attention of Françoise Chassagnac, the owner of the trend-setting Victoire boutiques. She not only bought Kelly's dresses (the first time that she had purchased from an American designer), but allotted him showroom space, gave him a workshop, and provided the capital for his first ready-to-wear collection, which was unveiled in the spring of 1985. Bonnie Johnson quoted Chassagnac as saying: "Patrick was charismatic, and his dresses were elegant, colorful, funny, and unpretentious. I was bowled over." She introduced Kelly to Nicole Crassat, a fashion editor of the French edition of Elle. When the magazine devoted six full-color pages to Kelly's entire spring-summer collection in its February 1985 issue, the publicity elicited a deluge of orders for the clingy black dresses.

Commenting on his phenomenal success in the 1985 interview with Carol Mongo, Patrick Kelly credited the cultural milieu of Paris. "I find that people are more responsive here," he said. "They figure that if you made it all the way across the ocean and are willing to put up with all the obstacles, then you must be something special." One year later he told her, "I'm one who believes that if you work hard for what you want, remain open to learning, and trust in God, you'll be a success." An alternative explanation was provided by the couturier Christian Lacroix, who was quoted by Bonnie Johnson as saying: "The French function according to love at first sight. If they fall in love with you, they accept you. And Patrick is very lovable. Everybody loves him." Elsewhere Lacroix was quoted as saying, "Kelly's clothes are Parisian in spirit."

Kelly's cachet—fun designs that were less expensive than other French apparel—was easily exported to the United States, where Bergdorf Goodman was the first retailer to feature Kelly's eye-popping cutout knits. His success enabled him to found Patrick Kelly Paris with Björn Amelan, a photographers' agent. The new business was supported by Amelan's agent fees and Kelly's growing number of freelance contracts, including a 1986 deal with Benetton to design all its sportswear except sweaters. By 1987 Kelly had seventeen freelance designing assignments in addition to his own semiannual collections, which were shown at the Grand Hôtel in Paris. His styles for spring 1987 included the characteristic tube minidresses with bodices strewn with buttons or with miniature black baby dolls; full-skirted chambray dresses with small red bandannas suspended from tiny hearts sewn on at the hips; stretchy snakeskin prints overspread with shiny transparent sequins; and skinny knee-length dresses shirred from the hips to the hemline. For the fall of 1987 Kelly demonstrated "a solid sense of what is 'in' in Paris," according to Bonnie Johnson: "miniskirts, hourglass silhouettes, tailored plaid suits with flared jackets and ruffles for evening."

Despite the apparent success of Patrick Kelly Paris, the enterprise needed a strong financial backer to stave off bankruptcy. In the spring of 1987, Gloria Steinem, who had interviewed Kelly for NBC's *Today* show, introduced him to Linda J. Wachner, the president and chief executive officer of Warnaco, a $600 million New York–based apparel manufacturer. (Geoffrey Beene sportswear, Chaps by Ralph Lauren, Christian Dior, Hathaway shirts, and Warner and Olga lingerie are some of the divisions of the conglomerate.) When Kelly sold the worldwide rights to his women's ready-to-wear to Warnaco on June 30, 1987, his worldwide wholesale volume was $795,000 a year; by 1989 the figure would skyrocket to $7 million, with 60 percent of sales in the United States and distribution points in West Germany, Belgium, Great Britain, Italy, Japan, Australia, and France. As of 1988 his clothes were sold in 146 stores in the United States. Although the affiliation with Warnaco afforded Kelly more credibility and scope, it also raised concerns that the prices of his creations, which presently retail at $250 to $1,700 on the average, may escalate.

With the security provided by Warnaco, the designer established the first Patrick Kelly boutique, which fronts his studio in the Le Marais quarter of Paris. To celebrate its opening he conjured up a sixty-five-piece couture collection in a reeling three weeks, becoming the first American designer ever to show a couture collection—made-to-order, one-of-a-kind creations—in Paris, on July 29, 1987. In addition to more conventional, inconspicuous styles, the collection included such "antic ideas" as dunce-cap hats, a coat with buttons blanketing the lining, and a scarf of feathers. His 1988 spring and fall collections, unveiled the traditional six months in advance, were spirited, lighthearted, and novel: watermelon-shaped hats, earrings, pins, and bra cups of raffia; a slinky skirt of aqua sequins mated with a top of mere seashells (one covering each breast) and string; teddy bear prints accessorized with stuffed teddy bears; and dresses decorated with billiard balls, red plastic hearts, or oversized pearls.

Kelly's election to the Chambre Syndicale on June 13, 1988, which was sponsored by Pierre Bergé, the chairman of Yves Saint Laurent and the president of the Chambre, and Sonia Rykiel, enabled him to show at the Louvre. His first show there, in October 1988, featured a spoof of the Louvre's most celebrated resident, the *Mona Lisa*. Kelly called his décolleté leopard print gowns "Jungle Lisa Loves Tarzan" and affixed the label "Moona Lisa" to silver-star-studded dresses worn with Plexiglas-bubble headgear. Appearing for the first time in that spring 1989 collection as print designs as well as decorative accessories were dice, musical notes, crystals, pinwheels, and gardenias. In his fall 1989 collection he introduced bright red plastic lips on bodices in place of buttons, dangling charm-bracelet hearts, gumball-colored buttons on a bright plaid suit, saddle blankets as scarves and turbans, and the coupling of lace with tweed. The only major designer to salute the French bicentennial, he created a black knit shift featuring the outline of the Eiffel Tower in rhinestones.

Following the lead of Giorgio Armani, Valentino, and Gianfranco Ferré, Kelly planned to launch a less costly line named Patrick Kelly Loves You for 1990, but, because of his convalescence from an unspecified illness, the October 1989 showing of his spring 1990 collection was canceled, and his ready-to-wear line was "suspended." In the works that summer were negotiations for Kelly sunglasses, jewelry, perfume, furs, scarves, lingerie, stockings, and menswear. A film based on Kelly's life, to be produced by Michael Douglas, was under discussion. With his collection of about 6,000 black dolls, some of which he sells in his boutique, Kelly plans to open a doll museum. As Ben Brantley reported, the dolls "range from Aunt Jemimas and Hottentots to black Barbies and wiry jazz musicians, an army of stereotypes, positive and negative, enlisted for their owner." Kelly explained: "The offensive ones are to remind you that you have to fight to be free and happy. The happy ones are just to bring you joy." Because Kelly's Paris logo, a cartoonlike representation of a grinning black doll's face, is considered racist by some Americans, Warnaco did not ship to its American stores a recent line of shopping bags and buttons circulating in Europe that feature the symbol. The three-inch black baby-doll pins, which are worn proudly in Paris, have also proved controversial in the United States. "You know why some people are hung up with them? It's because they can't deal with themselves," Kelly told Pamela Johnson. "Recently somebody black told me they were harassed about wearing the black baby-doll pin. . . . [But] when Bette Davis gave David Letterman one on TV, then everybody wanted one. It was like, 'Oh, this is the right thing to do.'"

The pins, 800 of which he gives away each month, cram the pockets of Patrick Kelly's huge (size 56) blue denim overalls. Actually svelte and muscular, the tall, bearded, and ponytailed designer wears the overalls everywhere (topped with an Yves Saint Laurent tuxedo jacket on formal occasions) along with a bicycle racer's cap that bears the inscription "PARIS" on the upturned brim. The childlike persona that some perceive in Kelly "overlooks the very deliberate sophistication with which he presents his down-home image," according to Ben Brantley. "A certifiable fashion character" who rides a skateboard through the streets of Paris, Kelly is "as approachable as your next-door neighbor," wrote the *Los Angeles Times's* Betty Goodwin, in a profile subtitled "Maverick and Mastermind" (April 7, 1989). He

imports Aunt Jemima pancake mix, hominy grits, and corn bread from the United States, is compiling a cookbook of family recipes, and dreams of buying a farm in Mississippi. A zealous coupon shopper, he also rummages through flea markets in search of black dolls, black memorabilia, cobalt blue glass, and Bette Davis souvenirs. But Kelly already possesses that which is most important to him, as this statement quoted by Trish Donnally reveals: "The biggest diamond you can own is to be black, or to be Chinese, or to be white. To be whatever you are should be the biggest pride you have."

References: *American Way* p66+ Je 1 '88 por; *Ebony* 43:52+ F '88 pors; *Essence* 19:92+ My '89 pors; *People* 27:111+ Je 15 '87 pors; *Vanity Fair* 51:152+ Mr '88 pors; *Washington Post* G p1+ N 9 '86 pors; *Women's Wear Daily* p4+ Ja 15 '88 por

---

Kienholz, Edward

Oct. 23, 1927– Artist. Address: c/o L.A. Louver, Inc. 55 N. Venice Blvd., Venice, Calif. 90291

For over thirty years Edward Kienholz has used his sculpture to comment on the moral decline of contemporary life, most notably in his environmental tableaux—three-dimensional assemblages that invite the viewer's participation. "No one can walk *past* a tableau; he has to walk *into* it," Kienholz once explained, as quoted in *Time* (April 8, 1966) magazine. "And if one person ends up being better, then I'm completely vindicated." Whether recreating in squalid detail quintessentially American locales, among them a bar in Los Angeles (The

Beanery), a cell in a mental institution (*The State Hospital*), and a Las Vegas brothel (*Roxy's*), or dealing with such controversial social issues as desegregation (*Shine on Shine*) and teenage sex (*Backseat Dodge—'38*), Kienholz, who shares the credit for his work with his wife, Nancy Reddin Kienholz, finds man's current predicament "both ludicrous and tragic," in the words of one critic. "I think part of the reason why so many people began working in assemblage has to do with sensing and fearing rapid change," Kienholz said in a 1967 interview. "No sooner do you make peace with society than it changes again. I think the artists are trying to hold onto things."

Edward Kienholz was born on October 23, 1927 in Fairfield, Washington, the son of Lawrence and Ella (Eaton) Kienholz. Growing up on a wheat farm in Fairfield, a town of some 365 people near the Washington-Idaho border, Edward Kienholz assumed that he would become a farmer like his father. As a result, he was trained in carpentry, engineering, plumbing, and mechanics—all useful skills on a farm. While attending the local high school, he played the French horn in the band, sang in the choir, and earned letters in basketball, baseball, and football. At some point during this period, he began painting in oil and watercolor.

After his graduation from high school, Kienholz enrolled at Eastern Washington College of Education, but he left after a semester and a half. Over the next few years, he took classes at a number of other colleges, "wherever [he] could get a scholarship, and left whenever it ran out," he told a reporter for *Newsweek* (December 20, 1965). To support himself, he undertook an assortment of jobs, ranging from selling vacuum cleaners to working as an orderly in a sanitarium to opening a restaurant, which he called the Black Boris. In 1953 Kienholz drove to Los Angeles with some of his paintings stashed in the back of his ancient station wagon, a bowl of goldfish on the front seat, and an increasingly painful toothache. "I found a dentist who traded me a tooth extraction for a painting, and I thought to myself, 'This is utopia,'" he recalled to Douglas M. Davis in an interview for the *National Observer* (January 23, 1967). He immediately set up house in a shack, surviving on what he could hunt in the surrounding hills.

Although Kienholz began his artistic career as a painter, he turned to constructions in 1952 or 1953, during a stay in Las Vegas. "They got bigger and bigger," he told Davis. "I think I was after a kind of texture you can't get in painting." Kienholz made mostly wooden reliefs until 1956, when, in his words, his pieces "started to become three-dimensional." The new works were made from pieces of leftover wood that had been nailed or glued to a panel, then painted with a broom. Kienholz got into the habit of completing five or six reliefs a week, for two or three weeks at a time. Among those reliefs were *Triptych* and *George Warshington in Drag* (1957), the latter featuring various objects collected in junkyards. According to the critic Maurice Tuchman, who wrote an essay for the catalogue that accompanied a Kienholz retrospective at the Los Angeles County Museum of Art in 1966, the wooden fragments functioned as a kind of "armature, like a preparatory drawing on canvas, but they also served as a vessel into which paint could be poured and then smeared." Painting with a broom, Kienholz told Davis, was "more direct and exciting, more prone to accident." "I like accident," he explained. "Any painting, after all, can stop in any one of a million places." The act of pouring paint offered him a way, as he described it, of "getting into" the work, "swimming around in it, like in a bathtub." Kienholz viewed the "broom paintings" as exercises in "ugliness," believing that, if he "could make something really ugly," it would help him to "understand beauty."

By 1956 the wooden reliefs had become so large that they could no longer be mounted on a wall but had to be left standing on the floor. In *The Little Rock Incident* (1958), his first work named after a sociopolitical event, Kienholz attached the head of a deer to the relief painting and, a year later, in *The Medicine Show* (1959), he hinged certain sections of the construction, thus inviting the viewer to become involved in the experience. Critics praised both works for their fusion of strong psychological content and social realism. Another important work from this period is *God-Tracking Station* (1959), which he created in response to the Soviet Union's launching of the world's first artificial satellite. Kienholz's penchant for giving his works humorous titles, such as *The Psycho-Vendetta Case* (1960), allowed him "to be able to laugh at the piece and thereby be shed of it," as he explained to K. G. Pontus Hulten in a conversation for *Art in America* (June 1971).

Kienholz's first freestanding construction, *John Doe* (1959), which the artist fashioned from a male department-store mannequin that he had cut in half, was described by one reviewer as "the exquisite corpse of the great American masculine ideal." Other works helped establish Kienholz's reputa-

tion as a social critic. *Psycho-Vendetta,* for instance, refers to the execution of Caryl Chessman, the convicted kidnapper whose case attracted worldwide attention in the 1950s as a result of the four bestsellers he wrote on death row. *History as a Planter,* with its yellowed wartime news clippings and oven doors that, when closed, form a swastika, emphasizes the whitewash that time puts on evil.

After *Psycho-Vendetta,* Kienholz worked on a series of wooden boxes containing the torsos of mannequins that had been cut in half, covered with canvas, and painted. Late in 1961 he developed a series of wall-mounted assemblages constructed of tin and other materials. In *Blind Ignus* Kienholz combined tin with antlers and an American eagle; in *Queen for a Day* he mixed pieces of steel wool, paper, and a deer skull, prompting Tuchman to remark in his essay, "These extraordinary fusions of materials provoke some of the most sensuous tactile experiences in Kienholz's work."

The public first had the opportunity to see Kienholz's work in 1955, when the sculptor mounted a one-man show at the Cafe Galleria, a coffee shop in Los Angeles. The following year, Kienholz opened the Now Gallery in the back of a movie theatre. When his landlord went bankrupt six months later, he teamed up with Walter Hopps, who later became a curator at the Museum of Modern Art, to open, in 1957, the Ferus Gallery. The sculptor had another one-man show at the Syndell Studios in 1956, followed by a three-man show at the Ferus Gallery in 1958, and two-man shows there in 1959, 1960, and 1962 and at the Pasadena Art Museum in 1961.

In 1961 Kienholz completed the first of his nearly life-size tableaux, *Roxy's,* which was inspired by a notorious bordello in Las Vegas. A re-creation of the bordello as it was in 1943, the meticulously detailed tableau features a number of stained and disfigured mannequin-prostitutes; a bureau, its opened drawers filled with personal letters; an imposing madam, whose head is a rhinoceros skull, watching over the entrance; and even the scent of cheap perfume and disinfectant. The project began as a single figure, Zoe, but Kienholz later added others, including *Miss Cherry Delight, Fifi, A Lost Angel*—a figure with the face of an infant, the torso of a girl with a clock for a stomach, and the legs of a woman—and *Five Dollar Billy,* a truncated mannequin resting on a sewing-machine table who gyrates her hips when a viewer pumps the treadle. As Philip Leider observed in the *New York Times* (April 3, 1966): "Where the drift of modern sculpture is toward the creation of immediately legible single units . . . to be read in a single configuration, Kienholz has emphasized the access to detail that assemblage so freely permits. Where sculpture reduces, Kienholz catalogues. His pieces cannot conceivably be read as a single unit . . . but must be scanned as one scans a page of text, word for word, detail for detail." *Roxy's* was first exhibited at the Ferus Gallery in Los Angeles in 1961.

From 1961 to 1965 Kienholz created some of his finest works, and, by all accounts, his most savage indictments of contemporary American culture. They included *The Illegal Operation* (1962), *Backseat Dodge—'38* (1964), *The Wait* (1964-65), and the piece that is generally considered to be his masterpiece—*The Beanery* (1965), an almost life-size "reproduction" of a bar in Santa Monica, California. Kienholz furnished these works with materials from contemporary life in order to confront "the stuff, whether you think it's good or bad, that makes up life." While other assemblagists, such as Kurt Schwitters, set out to release some unsought beauty in the detritus of contemporary civilization, Kienholz accentuated the dilapidated, often coating over his work with an epoxy glaze or glass fiber to give the decay a sense of permanence. As Tuchman noted in his essay, Kienholz "makes no attempt to transform his material into precious stuff. He accepts the qualities of age and usage . . . but he changes one essential characteristic: to junk, the symbol of imminent death, Kienholz lends permanence." Commenting on *The Beanery*, Kienholz told Douglas M. Davis: "When I've finished something that complicated, I like to glaze everything with epoxy or paint it with glass fiber. That not only makes the piece tougher but draws all the pieces together, new and old, into one time."

In *The Wait* (1964-65), Kienholz depicted the dreary life of an old woman who lives in the memories of her past. The skeletal woman, whose head is a deer skull encased in a jar, sits in her living room surrounded by her favorite possessions, among them a stuffed cat, a live bird in a cage, a sewing basket, and a photograph album. Likening Kienholz to a preacher "inwardly tormented by the complex compatibilities of love and hate," Henry Hopkins maintained in *Art in America* (October 1965) that "not since Ivan Albright's *Into the World There Came a Soul Called Ida* has an American artist had the capacity or the inclination to strip man so naked and expose him so to public view."

Backseat Dodge—'38 (1964) depicts a young couple—the male figure made out of chicken wire and the female constructed out of plaster—passionately kissing on the backseat of a Dodge, from which the front half has been removed. "With my *Dodge*, the romantic nonsense is gone," Kienholz told a reporter for *Time* (April 8, 1966). Commenting on the piece for *ARTnews* (February 1965), John Coplans observed, "Kienholz has little in common with other artists working in assemblage; he makes no attempt to make an art object," adding that, in his view, the artist not only continued "to violate all standards of aesthetic propriety, but also to project a stream of art that is a blunt affront to the public."

The Beanery (1965) took nearly six months to complete and required the full range of Kienholz's skills—as an electrician, a carpenter, a plaster modeler, a chemist, and a sculptor. Conceived in 1958 but not executed until 1964, the massive assemblage, which is twenty-two feet long, seven and a half feet tall, and six feet wide, is laden with temporal references. For example, the customers' faces are clocks set at 10:10 (because the clock hands then resemble eyebrows), and, outside the bar, a newspaper-vending machine holds a supply of papers bearing the headline "Children Kill Children in Vietnam Riots." As Kienholz told one reporter, *The Beanery* "symbolizes going from real time—the August 28 headline—to surrealist time inside the bar where people waste time, lose time, escape time, ignore time." Inside the "bar" are seventeen figures—two of them store mannequins, the rest constructed from plaster casts. They include two Bekins moving men, a matron in a mink coat, a businessman in a gray flannel suit sipping a martini, and a muscular truckdriver in a T-shirt. To create an appropriately dingy atmosphere, Kienholz dimmed the lights, sprayed the surface with a compound concocted to smell like a combination of bacon grease, stale beer, and disinfectant, and played a tape of recorded noise from the real Beanery (a saloon in Los Angeles)—both background chatter and pop music, apparently blaring from a beat-up jukebox advertising such tunes as "It's Delightful, It's Delovely, It's deKooning," "I Enjoy Being a Goy" by the New Bible Bangers, and "Racing to Our Doom" by the Hell's Angels Choral Group. Over the entire construction, he poured polyester resin. "It drips, it adds texture, it transforms isolated individuals into interrelated people. It is the final gesture," Kienholz explained, as quoted in *Newsweek* (December 20, 1965).

When *The Beanery* was included in a Kienholz retrospective at the Los Angeles County Museum of Art in 1966, it was branded "pornography" and "revolting" by the County Board of Supervisors, which attempted to close the exhibition before its official opening. The museum compromised by promoting the show as being for "adults only." Critics, however, reacted favorably. The reviewer for *Life* (January 14, 1966) magazine called it the "most extraordinary three-dimensional art object made in the last twenty years," while *Newsweek*'s art critic (December 20, 1965) described it as a "quietly terrifying commentary on man—his frustration and dehumanization."

During the 1960s Kienholz also painted 110 watercolors, on each of which he hand-stamped a monetary or barter value. To acquire a work, the prospective buyer simply had to give Kienholz what was stenciled on the canvas, whether it was "$10,000," "a Rudi Gernreich Original," or "a '68 Eldorado." "I think art collecting is a glorified autograph hobby," Kienholz told Grace Glueck of the *New York Times* (April 6, 1969). "All I'm doing is creating a situation where human greed comes out." At the same time, however, Kienholz continued to treat morally sensitive issues in a way that, in the words of the critic Susan Larsen in *Artforum* (January 1982), "forced a culture to confront itself in a series of unforgiving, deeply felt tableaux." He explored the controversial subjects of integration in *It Takes Two to Integrate, Cha Cha Cha* (1961), abortion in *The Illegal Operation* (1962), war in *The Portable War Memorial* (1969), and mental illness in *The State Hospital*, in which the figure of a naked man, his head a lighted fish bowl, lies chained to his bunk. Kienholz's work involves "death and pain and sex and insanity and other things most people prefer to forget about," Paul Richard observed in an article for the *Washington Post* (November 18, 1967). Perhaps because of the nature of his subject matter, Kienholz gained wider acceptance in Europe than in the United States, although a 1970 traveling show brought him greater recognition in New York.

Two events in the 1970s strongly influenced the future direction of Kienholz's art. The first was his marriage to the photographer Nancy Reddin, whom he met in 1972 and married soon afterwards. Since 1973 the couple has collaborated on projects, but it was not until 1979 that Kienholz acknowledged their works as joint ventures. As he told Alan G. Artner for the *Chicago Tribune* (September 1, 1985): "She and I worked together since 1973, but in my maleness and general stupidity it took me till 1979 to recognize that she was doing as many and as important aspects as I. In a 1979 catalogue I just wrote a little addendum to acknowledge that it was *our* work. It wasn't mine. It was ours." The second major event was the Kienholzes' move, in 1973, from Los Angeles. Since then, they have divided their time equally between Hope, Idaho, where they own the Faith and Charity in Hope Gallery, and West Berlin, Germany.

The work that precipitated the couple's move to West Berlin was *The Art Show* (1963–77), a piece that is considerably lighter in tone than Edward Kienholz's earlier efforts. Kienholz had spent a year in West Berlin on a fellowship in 1973, where he began work on *The Art Show*, and he and his wife ended up remaining in the city for four years. The tableau features nineteen life-size plaster figures in various poses gazing at paintings in an art exhibit. Kienholz installed air conditioning vents and recordings of art reviews in the figures, so that each figure spouts criticism along with hot air. "An art show, if you think about it, is really an artificial social event," Kienholz explained to Alan G. Artner. "Instead of starting with something real, with blood and guts and genuine emotion, like some old guy starving to death in a hotel, you're starting with something that's essentially froth, social froth. Using that as the starting point, you may certainly interpret that different tone and not be far from correct. However, I like *The Art Show*, even if it may not turn out to be important."

Kienholz's increasing collaboration with his wife led to the creation of works that were slightly smaller in scale, more introspective, and less politically strident. "People also say I'm softer, not as biting hard, which perhaps is true," Kienholz told Alan G. Artner. "I'm certainly a hell of a lot happier as a human being. When I was young I was ready to smash anybody's head who didn't agree with me." With the "White Easel" series, Kienholz attempted to resolve the problem of finding the "right space" in his new studio in Hope, Idaho, by making part of the studio—a four-by-four-foot raw wood studio easel—the centerpiece of a tableau.

As Susan C. Larsen observed in *Artforum* (January 1982), individual works in the series focused the viewer's attention on "finely crafted images" partially hidden behind the distorting lenses of automobile windows or television screens mounted on white easels. In *White Easel with Face*, for example, the image of a magnified human face, seen through an automobile window, turns out to be a rubberized mask lying flat on the easel. Even in those more abstract works, Miss Larsen noted that Kienholz's "instincts for the visceral and the terrifying remain intact."

The "Spokane" series, undertaken between 1979 and 1983, includes *Sollie 17* (1979–80), *Night Clerk at the Young Hotel*, *The Pedicord Apts*, and *The Jesus Corner*. Closer in feeling to Kienholz's early tableaux, these pieces examine various aspects of life in a dilapidated section of Spokane, Washington. *Sollie 17*, for instance, depicts three different moments in the life of an old man who lives alone in a skid row hotel: he is shown reading a book, sitting on his bed, and looking in his mirror. "The sense of desolation and solitude is complete," Robert Silberman wrote in *Art in America* (March 1986). For Susan Larsen, *Sollie 17* was "as comprehensive and complete as Kienholz's earlier work," but it lacked "the rage and biting satire of his youth." As Silberman, for one, has pointed out, the "Spokane" series relies on "specificity of detail" rather than on shock tactics for its effect.

By contrast, Kienholz's *The Rhinestone Beaver Peepshow Triptych* (1980) and *Bout Round Eleven* (1982) are more abstract. In the former, a woman, naked except for her boots, sits on a ladder next to a slot machine, waiting for the next customer to insert the coin that will buy her services. Her face is a photograph of a beaver's head. Holding a mirror in one hand, she reaches out with the other toward a disembodied male arm that is holding a dead rat—a gesture that suggested to Robert Silberman "a profane version of the giving of life to Adam on the Sistine ceiling." In Silberman's view, Kienholz had, in this instance, used a "combination of elements so blatantly unsavory and preposterous that he loses the tension between realism and artificiality." In *Bout Round Eleven*, the photograph of a woman's face peers from behind a barred window whereas the female figure itself has a framed mask for a face. The woman's husband sits in front of a television set from which a dog's head erupts—a detail that is, in Silberman's words, "pure Kienholz: a powerful image symbolizing (perhaps) the horror underlying the couple's relationship."

As Robert Pincus pointed out in his review of a Kienholz exhibition titled "The Red, White, and Blue Series" for *Art in America* (May 1988), in the mid- to late 1970s the Kienholzes concentrated on German cultural themes, returning to American subject matter in 1980. Comprising works predominantly dating from 1987, "The Red, White, and Blue Series" included paintings, wall-mounted assemblages, life-size tableaux, and *The Caddy Court*, an outdoor sculpture made up of a 1966

Dodge van positioned between the two halves of a severed 1978 Cadillac. The van's doors, when closed, feature a photograph of the Supreme Court building; when the doors are open, the spectator finds shelves of law books, as well as several figures dressed in judicial robes and with animal skulls for heads. "Above and beyond its political overtones," Pincus remarked, "The Caddy Court is another of the Kienholzes' many meditations on the transience and impermanence of human life." Another piece in the show was inspired by the Iran-Contra hearings. The Politician with Contradictum Affixed Also features a rhinoceros skull with Attorney General Edwin Meese's testimony pouring from its mouth on a long strip of paper. The rhino's horn is painted in the argyle pattern of a jester's cap and has a bell on its tip. The most affecting work in the exhibition, in Pincus's view, was Shine on Shine (1987), a commentary on the status of blacks in American society. Its single male figure, a plaster cast of Abraham Lincoln with a photograph of Mount Rushmore for a head, sits on a shoeshine stand. A pair of disembodied hands shines the figure's shoes. "Together, these elements provide a powerful image of oppression," Pincus wrote. "If in conventional narratives of American history Lincoln is presented as a liberator of blacks, here he's depicted as the leader who set in motion the very forms of unjust authority that life after slavery has offered blacks in America."

The Kienholzes' most recent exhibition, which opened the new Louver Gallery on Prince Street in Manhattan in the fall of 1989, included yet another provocative work of social commentary, Claude Nigger Claude. Describing the piece in her review for New York (November 6, 1989) magazine, Kay Larson noted the impact of "its biting rage: A black man, operating an elevator that resembles a prison, confronts his Doppelgänger in whiteface. As usual, the artist implicates the audience: Why does the fellow in the suit look odd, while the man in the elevator cage seems right for his role?" In other works she found "a fresh sense of the fantastic that both lightens and enlivens the earnestness. A wild pig with its forefeet stuck in coffee cups gets the title Faux Pas. . . . [And in] People Holding Bound Ducks . . . , people who would fly . . . grasp birds immobilized with string and drenched in resin." Labeling the latter piece "truly Kienholzian in its wit and somber elegance," she wrote that it, too, implicates the viewer—this time "in some dread Faustian conspiracy that has annihilated the moral imagination of Western culture."

Edward Kienholz has been described in World Artists as a "burly, thick-set, gregarious man with a short beard." He lives with his wife and their two children, Noah and Jenny. An earlier marriage ended in divorce. Kienholz's work has been exhibited in various museums and galleries in the United States and at the Hayward Gallery in London, the Art Museum Ateneum in Helsinki, Stockholm's Moderna Museum, the Städtische Kunsthalle in Düsseldorf, the Galleria Bocchi in Milan, and the Nationalgalerie in Berlin. Some of his pieces are in the permanent collections of the Whitney Museum of American Art in New York City, the Museum of Modern Art in Tokyo, the Centre National d'Art Contemporain in Paris, and the Stedelijk Museum in Amsterdam, among others.

References: Art in America 74:138+ Mr '86; Chicago Tribune XIII p16+ S 1 '85; Guardian p10 My 27 '71; National Observer p18 S 23 '67; Dictionary of Contemporary Artists (1988); Who's Who in America, 1988–89; World Artists 1950–1980 (1984)

NYT Pictures

Kravis, Henry R.

Jan. 6, 1944– Investment banker. Address: Kohlberg, Kravis, Roberts and Company, 9 W. 57th St., New York, N.Y. 10019

As senior partner at the investment firm of Kohlberg, Kravis, Roberts and Company (KKR), succeeding Jerome Kohlberg Jr., who resigned in a heated policy dispute in 1987, Henry R. Kravis has altered the character of the firm that pioneered the contemporary practice of the leveraged buyout. In the process, he has served notice to corporate America that sheer size is no longer a deterrent to those who are determined to take over undervalued or inefficiently run companies. On November 30, 1988, at the end of an intense, often bitter five-week bidding war for RJR Nabisco, a Kravis-led group purchased the tobacco and food giant for a whopping $25 billion, almost doubling the previous record price for a buyout. With that transaction, Kravis sent a signal that the firm had broken out of its traditional passive role as a white knight, rescuing targeted companies from unwanted suitors, and was prepared to aggressively pursue vulnerable companies itself.

Since its founding in 1976, KKR has spent more than $60 billion to acquire some three dozen companies, earning for its limited partners, mostly pension fund managers and other institutional investors, annual rates of return far exceeding those of conventional investments. Although the size and number of the businesses that KKR controls change with each acquisition and spinoff, the revenues generated by companies operating under the indirect control of the firm at any given time would place it among the top conglomerates on the Fortune 500. Because Kravis and other takeover artists typically finance their deals with enormous amounts of debt, critics have warned that the highly leveraged financial structure of the corporations affected by the buyout binge of the 1980s may come crashing down at the next recession with dire consequences, not only for the investment bankers themselves but also for the economy at large. Congress is expected to consider legislation limiting the tax advantages of corporate debt or other measures designed to tame the takeover frenzy. In the meantime, however, Kravis remains the premier player in Wall Street's riskiest game. KKR is "to the leveraged buyout business," a director at the investment firm Lazard Frères and Company observed, "what Kleenex is to the tissue business."

Henry R. Kravis was born in Tulsa, Oklahoma on January 6, 1944. His father, Raymond F. Kravis, was a petroleum engineer and the owner of a geological survey business, who in the late 1940s held southwestern oil interests in partnership with Joseph P. Kennedy. Kravis attended Eaglebrook, a prep school in Deerfield, Massachusetts, where he played football and forged a lasting friendship with Michael Douglas, the actor and film producer. At Claremont Men's College, in Claremont, California, he majored in economics and, during his junior year, captained the golf team.

Through a friend of his father's, Kravis obtained a summer job at a Bear Stearns brokerage house, and after earning an M.B.A. degree from Columbia University, in 1969, he officially joined the Bear Stearns staff, where he was joined by his first cousin George R. Roberts. Together they worked for Jerome Kohlberg Jr., a corporate finance manager who pioneered the technique of what was then called "bootstrap" acquisition—the ferreting out of a small company or part of a large company whose true value was unrecognized in the marketplace and financing with minimal equity a management-led effort to purchase it. Fascinated by the relatively simple procedure that had seemed to escape the attention of competing houses, Kohlberg pressed Bear Stearns for more funds to expand his bootstrap operation. When Bear Stearns balked, Kohlberg resigned, taking Kravis and Roberts with him, and in 1976 established his own investment banking firm.

During its first six years of operation, Kohlberg, Kravis, Roberts was enormously successful at creating and managing limited partnerships for the purpose of acquiring, streamlining, and selling off undervalued companies. With three leveraged buyout funds totaling more than half a billion dollars, KKR took twenty companies private, earning for its limited partners a 36 percent average annual rate of return and an average of $50 million a year for itself. Among the firms that KKR acquired during that period were A. J. Industries, an automobile brake manufacturer, purchased for $23 million in 1977; Houdaille Industries, a maker of machine tools, for $335 million in 1979 (the first leveraged buyout of a major firm listed on the New York Stock Exchange); and the packager Lily-Tulip, for $151 million in 1981. (Five years later Lily-Tulip was sold to Fort Howard Paper.) KKR's most costly mistake during that early period was the acquisition of American Forest Products from Bendix Corporation for $425 million in 1981. After years of trying fruitlessly to reshape the company, KKR sold it at a loss to Georgia-Pacific.

In a typical leveraged buyout, KKR puts up about 10 percent of the purchase price in cash from its fund and finances the rest through "junk bonds"—high-yielding, low-quality commercial paper underwritten most often by Drexel Burnham Lambert. KKR immediately imposes a severe austerity program on the acquired company, usually including significant layoffs, and uses the increased cash flow to service the swollen debt. Over the course of several years, it sells off portions of the company to retire the debt and recoup its investment. What is left very often is a lean core business that KKR either spins off to management or another firm or returns to the marketplace through a public offering, all at virtually pure profit. Of that profit, KKR, as the fund's general partner, takes its "carry," typically 20 percent, and the remainder is distributed to the limited partners, a wide array of institutional investors that have included banks, insurance companies, state and corporate pension fund managers, and even the Salvation Army. But that is only one way in which KKR profits from a leveraged buyout. Like any other creator of a mutual fund, KKR commands a management fee, usually 1.5 percent of the fund's value, regardless of its performance. Moreover, because KKR provides brokerage service in buying and selling assets, it also pockets transaction fees.

In 1984 KKR undertook the first billion-dollar leveraged buyout with the acquisition of Wometco Enterprises, an entertainment and bottling company. KKR accelerated the pace of the takeover game in that year by introducing the public tender offer as the means by which it acquired the food distributor Malone and Hyde, and it paid $465 million for Amstar, a major sugar refiner, which in 1986 fetched nearly $700 million from a Merrill Lynch investment group. Meanwhile, KKR jumped into the bidding war for Gulf Oil, serving as a white knight welcomed by its management as an alternative to the hostile takeover threatened by the veteran corporate raider T. Boone Pickens. Although KKR offered more than $12 billion for the Pittsburgh-based oil company, it eventually lost out to a superior bid from Chevron Corporation.

After acquiring Storer Communications and Union Texas Petroleum for about $2 billion each in 1985, KKR took on Beatrice Companies, the food giant, for $8.2 billion. In 1984 KKR had entered into an agreement with Donald P. Kelly, the president of Esmark, the processor of Swift meats and other food products, to take that company private, but James L. Dutt, the chairman of Beatrice, moved in quickly with a higher offer. Then, in August 1985, Dutt was ousted by disgruntled outside directors amid confusion over the direction of the company, and, sensing that Beatrice was now in play, arbitragers started bidding up the price of the stock. Kravis interrupted an African safari to confer with his partners about making a bid for the company. Joining forces with Donald P. Kelly again, KKR ignored the expressed desire of Beatrice's management to remain independent and set about fashioning a deal they could not refuse. Thus, although KKR did not launch a blatantly hostile takeover of Beatrice, it clearly was not a white knight either. Instead, it offered a generous package of "golden parachutes," or severance pay of millions of dollars, for each of Beatrice's senior executives, including $6.4 million for Chairman William W. Granger Jr., for his four months of service following James Dutt's ouster. That, together with the purchase price of $6.2 billion and the promise to assume another $2 billion of the company's debt, won over the board in April 1986. Such an aggressive, yet ostensibly friendly, acquisition has come to be called a "bearhug."

Establishing BCI Holdings, KKR installed Donald P. Kelly as its president to oversee the acquisition, management, and liquidation of Beatrice. It wasted little time in slashing expenses, beginning with the elimination of the company's $80 million sponsorship of an auto racing team led by Mario Andretti. "The woman in the stands," Kravis explained wryly, "doesn't go out and buy a Playtex brassiere because she sees this car going around that says 'Beatrice' on it." As expected, KKR found willing buyers for the disparate parts of the conglomerate. In July 1986 it spun off Avis car rental to a management-led group for $225 million and $1 billion of assumed debt, and four months later it sold its regional Coke bottling plants back to Coca-Cola for another $1 billion. In December KKR unloaded the dairy products division to Borden for $315 million and spun off to management-led groups the Playtex line for $1.25 billion and 20 percent of the new company's stock, the Webcraft printing operation for $223 million, and Americold warehouses for $480 million. In July 1987 the consumer products division, which included such household names as Samsonite luggage, Culligan water softeners, and Stiffel lamps, was distributed to BCI shareholders in the form of a new company, E-II Holdings, so named by Donald P. Kelly to represent the resurrection of Esmark. With that transaction, which contributed another $1.5 billion, KKR and its investors had recouped nearly their entire investment. The remaining core business, the Wesson and Swift food groups, thus represented virtually pure profit and promised to return to investors close to seven times their initial investment. Although the stock market crash of October 19, 1987 greatly depressed the market for the remaining businesses and made their liquidation less certain, KKR nevertheless profited handsomely in the Beatrice deal, earning $45 million in management fees alone and many times that in transaction fees and profits.

Meanwhile, the Beatrice takeover had exacerbated tensions within KKR itself. In 1984, while the senior partner, Jerome Kohlberg Jr., was convalescing from brain surgery, Kravis and Roberts began assuming more authority. Although a unanimous vote of the partners was still required to launch an acquisition, Kohlberg increasingly found himself at odds with the junior partners who were eager to become more aggressive players in the mergers-and-acquisitions game. Proud of his unsullied reputation as a friend of management, Kohlberg wanted his firm to remain a pure white knight, aloof from the trench warfare of the growing horde of corporate raiders. He vetoed so many of his partners' suggestions that he became known in the office as "Doctor No." The three had no trouble agreeing to rescue Safeway, the large food retailer, from the predatory Haft brothers in July 1986, but the Beatrice deal that year sharpened the differences between Kohlberg, who had wanted no part of it, and Kravis and Roberts, who had reportedly longed to undertake their first hostile takeover. Although they compromised with the bearhug strategy, they went on to quarrel over procedure in a leveraged buyout of Owens-Illinois, the glass manufacturer, on behalf of its management over the bitter opposition of outside directors in February 1987. Less than two months after the Owens-Illinois deal, in what reportedly was an emotional parting, Kohlberg resigned from active participation in the company. With assistance from three junior partners—Paul E. Raether, Michael W. Michaelson, and Roberts's brother-in-law Robert I. MacDonnell—Kohlberg, Kravis, Roberts and Company embarked on a more aggressive course.

During the summer of 1987, KKR flexed its newly acquired muscle by amassing an unprecedented $5.6 billion leveraged-buyout fund, enough cash to parley into a $50 billion acquisition at typical debt-to-equity ratios. Somewhat chastened but undaunted by the stock market crash on "Black Monday," October 19, 1987, Kravis saw in the wreckage an opportunity for selective buying. "We got lucky, fat, and happy over the last few years," he admitted almost wistfully during an interview for the New York Times (January 4, 1988). "Now we're going to go back to the old days when we turned to banks for financing and held our positions for five or seven years." Early in 1988 the firm waded into the complex struggle over Texaco, which, having just settled a costly civil suit with the Pennzoil Company, was now trying to fend off corporate raider Carl C. Icahn. KKR took its first "toe hold" position in

Texaco, a 5 percent stake, which was welcomed, publicly at least, by both Icahn and Texaco management. In March 1988 KKR purchased the Stop and Shop chain of convenience stores for $1.2 billion and, three months later, bought the Duracell battery division of Kraft for $1.8 billion.

Meanwhile, Kravis was stalking his biggest prey so far—RJR Nabisco, the nineteenth-largest corporation in the United States and the manufacturer of such familiar products as Camel, Winston, and Salem cigarettes, Wheat Thins and Ritz crackers, Oreo and Fig Newton cookies, Del Monte vegetables, Planters Peanuts, and LifeSavers. Since Kravis and RJR chairman F. Ross Johnson had explored the possibility of launching a leveraged buyout of the food and tobacco giant, Kravis felt betrayed when, on October 20, 1988, Johnson and Peter A. Cohen, the chairman of the Shearson Lehman Hutton brokerage firm, announced an opening bid of $17 billion to take the company private. Four days later KKR joined in with an offer of more than $20 billion. Twice in the next two weeks the two sides met to try to forestall a bidding war. Each conference reportedly broke down in an atmosphere of acrimony.

Although KKR's war chest seemed ample enough to command financial backing to bid considerably higher, the deal was so colossal that both sides found it necessary to go overseas for additional sources of funds. Moreover, KKR's leading junk-bond underwriter, Michael R. Milken, and his firm, Drexel Burnham Lambert, were operating under the threat of federal indictment for alleged market manipulation, forcing KKR to seek a back-up group of underwriters. Kravis also had to be concerned that, unlike Shearson, which could reach into the capacious pockets of its parent company, American Express, KKR was out in the lending markets with nothing but its own full faith and credit.

On November 18 KKR raised its bid to $21.3 billion, which the Shearson-management group topped by $1.4 billion. At that point, Kravis lulled the opposition into thinking that he was about to withdraw from competition, going so far as to take a skiing vacation over the Thanksgiving holiday while his small staff quietly continued to crunch numbers in New York. With final bids set for November 29, the Shearson-management group barely nudged its offer to $22.9 billion, whereas KKR unexpectedly pledged $24 billion. Although Cohen and Johnson frantically increased their bid to $25.42 billion, the committee created to auction the company accepted KKR's final counteroffer of $24.88 billion on November 30, because it was structured with a more favorable debt-to-equity ratio and passed more profit through to shareholders. KKR's statement of intentions also promised fewer layoffs and more generous severance and moving allowances for dislocated employees than that of the management-led group.

Having undertaken the largest corporate buyout in American history, Kravis immediately set out to mend fences with the defeated management group. At the same time, he reassured consumers that their favorite products would be unaffected by the turnover. "Oreos will still be in children's lunch boxes," he told anxious parents. One of his first acts was to install J. Paul Sticht, a former RJR chairman popular with the work force, as the company's interim chief executive. (Sticht was succeeded as chairman and chief executive officer in April 1989 by Louis V. Gerstner, the former president of the American Express Company.) Under the terms of a formal agreement accepted by the Federal Trade Commission on February 3, 1989, KKR was given one year to sell certain Beatrice or RJR Nabisco units in packaged nuts, ketchup, and Oriental foods to avoid restricting competition in those areas.

With the successful blitz against RJR Nabisco, KKR demonstrated that few American companies were invulnerable to a takeover. "There is no magic number anymore," Professor James Scott of the Columbia Business School warned, as quoted in Time (November 7, 1988). "There is no safety in size." Indeed, with more than fifty competing leveraged buyout funds totaling some $250 billion now in place and theoretically capable of commanding ten times that amount in junk-bond financing, the prospect of bigger and bigger companies falling victim to the leveraged buyout frenzy has prompted calls for reform from Federal Reserve Board Chairman Alan Greenspan, Securities and Exchange Commission Chairman David S. Ruder, and many members of Congress. Meanwhile, Henry Kravis, the undisputed king of the leveraged buyout, sees little reason to change a system that has made him one of the wealthiest men in America.

By late 1989, however, there were some signs of trouble at KKR. Two of the firms—SCI Television, a collection of six network television stations, and Seaman Furniture—KKR helped acquire were unable to make scheduled payments on their debt, and, according to a report in the New York Times (August 17, 1989), "at least two other companies" in KKR's stable, Beatrice and the Florida construction company Jim Walter, "look as if they will disappoint investors." More troubling in the eyes of some industry analysts was the lawsuit filed in New York State Supreme Court on August 29, 1989 by Jerome Kohlberg, charging that his partners had breached his severance contract and "sharply cut back his stake in several companies they had acquired together through the firm." According to published reports, the companies cited in Kohlberg's complaint were Marley, Pacific Realty, M & T, and an offshoot of Houdaille called IDEX. The suit also implied that "other investors may also have been deprived of their rewards," as a reporter for Time (September 11, 1989) magazine put it. Responding to the suit, a spokesman for Kravis and Roberts said, as quoted by the New York Times (August 30, 1989): "We are saddened that Mr. Kohlberg felt it necessary to sue his partners and Kohlberg, Kravis, Roberts. We believe he is wrong both as to the facts and his interpretation of the agreement between us, and we fully expect to prevail in court."

Henry R. Kravis is a dapper, trim figure who stands five feet, eight inches tall. While he has been described as charming, polished, and urbane, he has also been characterized as impatient, aggressive, and hard-edged. His longtime friend Michael Douglas is said to have copied some of his mannerisms for his role as Gordon Gekko in Oliver Stone's film *Wall Street*. Besides skiing, Kravis enjoys hunting, fishing, horseback riding, and motorcycling. An avid art collector, he has adorned the walls of his homes and office with the works of Sargent, Monet, Renoir, and Pissarro. He serves on the boards of the New York City Ballet, Mount Sinai Medical Center, the Central Park Conservancy, the Spence School, and public television station WNET.

In 1987 Kravis donated $10 million to the Metropolitan Museum of Art for the construction of the Henry R. Kravis wing, which is scheduled for completion in 1990. The five-story addition will house the permanent collection of European sculpture and decorative arts as well as temporary exhibitions. In 1988 he donated another $10 million to Mount Sinai for the construction of the Kravis Women's and Children Center. An early supporter of George Bush, he donated $100,000 to Bush's presidential campaign and, as the candidate's New York cochairman, raised many times that amount. After divorcing his first wife, with whom he has three teenage children, Kravis began seeing Carolyne Roehm, a dress designer. Since their marriage in November 1985, the Kravises have become familiar figures on the New York social celebrity circuit. They share a $5.5 million duplex apartment in Manhattan, a pre–Revolutionary War stone farmhouse in Sharon, Connecticut, a ski house in Vail, Colorado, and a home on Long Island.

References: Fortune 118:52+ Jl 4 '88 pors, 119:34+ Ja '89 por; Newsweek 112:76+ N 7 '88; Washington Post A p1+ D 4 '88 por

Krens, Thomas

(krenz)

1946- Museum administrator. Address: b. The Solomon R. Guggenheim Museum, 1071 Fifth Ave., New York, N.Y. 10128; h. 11 W. 30th Street, New York, N.Y. 10001

Since the worlds of art and big business are now increasingly interlocked, it struck many of his colleagues as exactly right that Thomas Krens, who is both an art historian and a management expert, was appointed, effective July 1, 1988, director of the Solomon R. Guggenheim Foundation. That appointment made him director of both the Solomon R. Guggenheim Museum in New York City and the Peggy Guggenheim Collection in Venice, Italy. Although some observers professed not to have heard of Krens, the heads of other American art museums recognized the former director of the Williams College Museum of Art, in Williamstown, Massachusetts, as a powerhouse who represents the kind of manager those institutions now require—someone with "high-tech skills, entrepreneurial know-how and global ambitions," as a writer for the New York Times (May 29, 1988) put it.

Krens was the immediate personal choice of his predecessor, Thomas M. Messer, who retired after twenty-seven years at the helm of the Guggenheim Museum. As Messer declared in an interview, although "a passionate relationship with the art of one's time is preconditional more than anything else" for efficient directorship of the museum, that asset "can no longer be isolated from other things." Those "other things" are amply represented in the career of a man who "alternates easily between the language of business and the idiom of art."

Concurrent with taking up his new duties, Krens was appointed an adjunct professor of art history at Williams College, his alma mater, where he continues to give a course in twentieth-century art. He plans also to continue to serve as head of the planning board of the proposed Massachusetts Museum of Contemporary Art. That mammoth and controversial project, which he has spearheaded since 1985, involves the conversion of an abandoned factory site in the Berkshire Mountains town of North Adams into what is to be the world's largest museum of later twentieth-century art and the second-largest museum in the United States, after New York's Metropolitan Museum of Art.

Thomas Krens was born in Brooklyn, New York in 1946. Of the few other details of his personal life that he chooses to reveal, it is known that he was raised in Rochester, New York, where he attended high school and entertained some hope of capitalizing on his height by making his mark as a basketball player. A broken kneecap thwarted that ambition. He went on to Williams College, from which he received a B.A. degree, with honors, in political economy in 1969. During his undergraduate years, he took several studio art classes. After graduation, Krens traveled in Europe, and for a time he worked in Geneva, Switzerland as an apprentice to a master printmaker. On his return home, instead of becoming a stockbroker or businessman, as he had originally planned, he enrolled in a graduate studio art program at the State University of New York in Albany, receiving his M.F.A. degree in printmaking in 1971. Appointed to the studio faculty at Williams College, he served as an assistant professor there from 1972 to 1980. Between 1972 and 1974, he worked as an architectural draftsman at the dig at Knidos, Turkey that was organized by the archaeologist Iris Love, and from 1976 to 1980, he directed the artist-in-residence program at Williams.

In 1977 Krens was appointed assistant professor of the history of contemporary art in the graduate division of the college. He served in that position until 1980, when he became director of the Williams College Museum of Art. Even then managing to combine teaching with his executive duties, Krens gave a seminar in 1987 on "The Postmodern in Practice: Art, Architecture, and Design," which he taught with Heinrich Klotz, the director of the Deutsches Architektur Museum in Frankfurt, West Germany, and to which he invited such renowned architects as Robert Venturi and Frank Gehry as lecturers.

As head of the Williams College Art Museum, Krens presided over a six-year, $8 million expansion program that doubled the size of its physical plant. He has said that he welcomed the challenges presented, confident that he had "a historian's and an artist's acuity to the issue that needed to be addressed." On the other hand, he also noted, "I was an economist before I was anything else," and, realizing the need to become "fluent in tactics and strategy," he enrolled at Yale University's School of Management, where he earned a master's degree in 1984. Part of that fluency involved his recognition of the role of computer technology in executive problem-solving. He now sees computers "as pencils" and, by self-admission, employs software "aesthetically and acrobatically." Predicting that those museums that "digest technology first will probably do better," he intends to use computer applications to "help the Guggenheim into the twenty-first century . . . toward the end of maximizing the availability, presentation and exposure of art to a wider public."

During the eight years of his tenure as director of the Williams College Art Museum, Krens established his reputation as an aggressive, innovative administrator ("the Clint Eastwood of the museum directors' world," according to his good friend and fellow Williams College alumnus Robert T. Buck, the head of the Brooklyn Museum). He transformed a relatively modest campus institution into one of the country's first-rank college collections, with a fine curatorial staff and an outstanding program of exhibitions. Among the latter that Krens planned and organized were those devoted to the prints of the assemblage artist Jim Dine (1977) and the abstract expressionist painter Helen Frankenthaler (1980) and the drawings of the minimalist sculptor Robert Morris (1982). Catalogues of the Dine and Frankenthaler shows, with texts by Krens, were published by Harper & Row concurrently with the exhibitions.

Other major Williams College Art Museum shows initiated by Krens were "Political Painting: American and European Contemporary Paintings" (1983), "The Modern Art of the Print: Selections from the Collection of Lois and Michael Torf" (1984), "America in Transition: Realist Painting from the Twenties to the Forties" (1985), and "The Restoration of Thomas Hart Benton: The 'America Today' Murals" (1985). The last grew out of Krens's involvement as a trustee, from 1983 to 1985, of the Williamstown Regional Art Conservation Laboratory.

Krens has indicated that he did not consciously set out to head a museum, but that as his career began to develop he found that he "was engaged by it enormously" and that he took "great pleasure and pride in it." He also found it to be "fun." Steps along the way to the Guggenheim Museum have included several consultancies to which Krens was invited and for which he found time outside his Williams College responsibilities. Asked by Robert T. Buck to act as strategic planning consultant for the Brooklyn Museum, he worked from 1983 to 1986 on financial surveys for its forthcoming building expansion. In 1985–86 he acted as a consultant to the Art and Architecture Thesaurus for the Getty Art History Information Project, based in Bennington, Vermont. In 1986 he became a consultant to the Norman Rockwell Museum in Stockbridge, Massachusetts and to the Guggenheim Museum, and he continues to serve on the Advisory Committee of the Museum Design Project, a collaborative effort of the National Endowment for the Arts and the American Federation of Arts.

That is hardly a record to justify the dismissive reference to Krens as "a farm-team player," made by the art critic Grace Glueck in an article for the New York Times (May 29, 1988). In point of fact, Krens is one of the so-called Williams mafia, graduates of the college who, in recent years, have been appointed to command posts in major American museums: Robert T. Buck; James Wood, the director of the Art Institute of Chicago; John Lane, who heads the San Francisco Museum of Modern Art; and Kirk Varnedoe, the director of the department of painting and sculpture at the Museum of Modern Art in New York.

For the past four years Krens has been involved with the ambitious redevelopment scheme he envisaged for the sprawling, abandoned factory complex in North Adams, near Williamstown, that was left vacant when Sprague Technologies moved away. The site had attracted his attention and stimulated his imagination because of what he saw as its potential as a museum complex eminently suited for the display of the mammoth sculptures and paintings of the 1960s and 1970s. With 450,000 square feet, or almost 60 percent of the site, devoted to exhibition space, the rest of the tract could be developed into ancillary facilities. Krens also envisioned holding a triennial international art exhibition at the site, something akin in scope and importance to the Kassel Documenta, in West Germany.

The story of the progression of the Massachusetts Museum of Contemporary Art from idea to actual planning is a paradigm of the new involvement of government and corporate interests in the creation and display of works of art, and the continuing heated debate over the propriety of the entire venture raises questions about the shape museums may take in the next century. In the July 1988 "Art and Money" issue of Art in America, the freelance critic Ken Johnson's "Showcase in Arcadia" analyzes the ramifications of Krens's curatorial philosophy. According to Krens, the chief problem of museums today, especially in large cities, is lack of space. Ninety-seven percent of the Guggenheim's holdings, for example, now remain in storage for that reason. Because so many ultra-large works of the last twenty years remain unknown due to the lack of display space, there are those who contend that, once these works eventually emerge, the whole history of contemporary art will have to be rewritten.

At the same time, Krens endorses the idea of in-depth museum coverage. He would limit the number of artists included in the Massachusetts Museum of Contemporary Art to about fifty, each to be represented by thirty to forty works, so that, in his words, "you can see historical narratives, you can see developments." There are also plans for commissioning site-specific works. Perhaps one of the huge, cavernous buildings could be devoted to a series of paintings by the German figurative artist Anselm Kiefer, or one gallery given over to a previously unseen minimalist sculpture by Donald Judd: a 147-foot-long row of steel cubes. Special exhibitions would be limited to only one a year, but that would be a "must-see" show, aggressively "marketed." "I know marketing is a negative buzz word for art historians," Krens has acknowledged, "but I see it as part of a communicative function."

Some have questioned Krens's emphasis on space and size as criteria for the selection of art works. Others have debated his optimism that despite North Adams's relative proximity to Boston and New York, viewers will make return visits and that the Massachusetts Museum of Contemporary Art's collections will attract and sustain local interest. Krens's vision seems to have anticipated such doubts and suggested solutions. For example, by conducting negotiations with Penn Central, direct rail service from New York might be restored, and with the remaining part of the mill complex redesigned for commercial use, a deluxe hotel, restaurants, and shops for tourists could be provided, along with office space and a convention center. Some of the nineteenth-century brick buildings might be made over into condominiums for a colony of artists in residence. If such ideas have been decried as the commercialization of art, residents of the blue-collar town on the verge of depression welcome the new venture, which is expected to generate hundreds of new jobs and pump some $21 million a year into the local economy.

The prospect that the museum will be started with objects on long-term loan from private sources is also regarded as a dubious arrangement. At least five works from the London-based collection of the advertising magnate Charles Saatchi, some seventy from the New York art dealers Michael and Ileana Sonnabend, and 150 massive pieces owned by Count Giuseppe Panza di Biumo have been promised to the Massachusetts Museum of Contemporary Art. Panza, a Milanese industrialist whose holdings are considered by one curator to be "absolutely the most important collection of advanced American art," has agreed to lend his objects for six years, with an option to buy. The museum would also designate one building to house a significant group of contemporary architectural drawings and models lent by the Deutsches Architektur Museum. Critics of the plan, however, have contended that works of art increase in monetary value by being displayed in a museum and, once back in the owner's hands, can be sold advantageously. Krens has reassured those who reason along those lines that the museum will eventually establish a regular acquisitions policy, building up a permanent collection by purchases or gifts.

After intensive lobbying by Krens, John Barrett 3d, the mayor of North Adams, and other political leaders and with the enthusiastic support of Governor Michael S. Dukakis, an appropriations bill providing $35 million in state bonds was approved by the Massachusetts state legislature in March 1988. Of that sum, $1.75 million was allocated for a feasibility study and analyses of the project's environmental impact. Architects engaged to do preliminary planning in conjunction with those studies are the firm of Skidmore, Owings & Merrill, Frank Gehry and Robert Venturi, and Bruner/Cott & Associates. The museum is scheduled to open in March 1992.

While skeptics may wonder, those who know Thomas Krens are confident he can manage all his jobs and still maintain the proper priorities. For example, Arthur Levitt Jr., the head of the American Stock Exchange, has described him as "terribly focused. . . . He conceives of ideas most people would think are impossible—and then he carries them out." Krens himself has given assurance that his "primary responsibility will be the Guggenheim, no question. And I'll do . . . [Massachusetts Museum of Contemporary Art] . . . with one of the most extraordinary support staffs around. . . . I really delegate authority. I trust people." Soon facing him in New York will be the formidable task of seeing the landmark Frank Lloyd Wright museum building through the controversial expansion that will provide additional office and exhibition space in a new wing designed by Gwathmey Siegel. After the major show "Refigured Painting: The German Image, 1960–88" (for whose catalogue Krens contributed the keynote essay) closed in April 1989, Krens oversaw the installation of a smaller exhibition from the Guggenheim's permanent collection, the first in a series of such shows scheduled to run until mid-1990, when the museum is to be closed for restoration and construction.

Reopening of the museum is scheduled for November 1991, with a much-anticipated exhibition of Russian avant-garde art from 1910 to 1930, an international collaborative venture that will be the largest of its kind ever shown in the United States. As for Krens's exhibition plans in general, his aim is to mount "critically definitive and historically necessary" shows of what he terms the "high practitioners." Special exhibitions at the Guggenheim will be limited to perhaps five a year, as opposed to its former ten or fifteen. "By raising the quality of exhibition programming," Krens has explained, "the double advantage for me is that it satisfies me from a curatorial perspective, but also has the advantage of being the best strategic move from an operating perspective, lessening the squeeze on the budget." To his way of thinking, better shows attract audiences that will contribute financial support. He also sees his new museum's "potential as . . . a museum of twentieth-century art with an international focus, not limited to Europe but extending to South America and Asia as well."

The jury may still be out on whether, as Ken Johnson has reported, Krens is "a Barr (referring to the legendary Museum of Modern Art curator Alfred Barr) or a Barnum," but he is to many "the wave of the future personified," and Thomas Messer has spoken of his successor as "an extraordinary young man of great equanimity, of tact, of force." Krens has been known to stay up all night compiling computer-generated graphics and flowcharts and to observe ninety-hour work weeks. On a recent four-day trip abroad, involving stops in eight cities in three countries to meet with museum directors, Krens folded his six-foot five-inch frame into a plane seat and immediately whipped out his laptop computer and portable printer and fell to working continuously. He lives in a Manhattan residence he has maintained for twelve years. His favorite costume is blue jeans and running shoes, and he has often sported (even to dinner parties) a Yale baseball cap. Traveling from the home he shared with his mother in Williamstown, he often whizzed across campus on a BMW-900 motorcycle. As for his academic career, Krens has confided that, as he gets older, keeping in touch with ideas and students is increasingly important to him: "I

find it's a kind of refreshment for having to deal with all this other kind of stuff, like raising money."

References: Art in America 76:94+ Jl '88 por; J of Art 1:13 D '88 por; N Y Observer p1+ F 22 '88 por; N Y Times Mag p32+ Mr 5 '89 por; Who's Who in America, 1988–89; Who's Who in American Art (1986)

Krone, Julie

July 24, 1963– Jockey. Address: c/o Monmouth Park Racetrack, Oceanport Ave., Oceanport, N.J. 07757

In the twenty-one years that women have been racing thoroughbred horses, none has enjoyed more success than Julie Krone. When she rode her 1,205th winner, in March 1988, Miss Krone passed Patricia Cooksey to become the top female rider in history, and, by June 1989, she had won more than 1,600 races. The first woman to capture a riding championship at a major track and the first to compete in the prestigious Breeders' Cup races, Miss Krone, whose 1988 victory total of 363 made her the fourth-leading jockey in the nation, is now ranked by horse racing experts among the sport's best riders, male or female. Julie Krone, who has often told interviewers that racing is "in [her] bones," began riding at the age of two and is the daughter of a champion horsewoman. The horse owners and trainers whose mounts she rides unanimously cite her subtle ability to communicate with her horse during a race, spurring the animal on to peak performance. She has the knack of making her horse relax and knows when to be aggressive and when to hold back. "Not only does she have incredible drive," Peter Shannon Jr., one of the owners for whom Miss Krone races, has said, "but she thinks like a horse. She's actually in rhythm with the horse." Similarly, Paul Moran of *New York Newsday* (December 17, 1987) has observed that Julie Krone "rides with daring and verve that often seems to be reflected in the performances of the horses beneath her. They seem to respond, whatever the circumstances, to her daring, her willingness to take chances, and her determined, strong finishing style. She rides every horse to the wire—through the wire."

Julieann Louise Krone was born on July 24, 1963 in Benton Harbor, Michigan and grew up on a ten-acre farm in the nearby town of Eau Claire. Her father, Don Krone, taught art and photography at Lake Michigan College, in Benton Harbor, and at Benton Harbor High School; her mother, Judi Krone, a former Michigan state equestrian champion, bred and showed Arabian horses, taught riding, and was a 4-H leader. Julie has a brother, Donnie, who is three years her senior. "I was always going to be a jockey, and a *great* one, too," Julie Krone has said, and she was riding on the backs of the family horses before she could even walk. Judi Krone, who rode frequently while she was pregnant with Julie, placed her daughter atop a horse for the first time when she was only two. The horse proceeded to trot off; when it stopped galloping, Julie picked up the reins and tugged them, and the horse trotted back to the child's mother.

By the age of three, Julie Krone was making half-mile solo trips on her horse. Later, she began racing her pony around the family farm, jumping fences with the reins in her mouth and riding while standing up. "I was a wild kid," she admitted to J. E. Vader in an interview for *Ms.* (June 1988) magazine. "I got bit, I got stepped on, I got kicked in the head. I got dumped five miles from home; the pony ran back and I had to walk." She won blue ribbons at horse shows for her skill at dressage, the art of training a horse in obedience and precision of movement, and she won the twenty-one-and-under division at the Berrien County Youth Fair horse show when she was just five years old.

At the age of fifteen, Julie Krone nearly left home to join a circus, after astounding its owner with the tricks she could perform on a horse, but she backed out at the last minute. In 1979, during her spring vacation, she and her mother, now divorced, visited the famous Churchill Downs racetrack in Louisville, Kentucky, the site of the annual Kentucky Derby, where they met the trainer Clarence Picou, who agreed to give Julie a summer job walking and grooming horses as well as a place to stay. Since Julie Krone had not yet reached her sixteenth birthday and was therefore ineligible to work in Kentucky, her mother changed the date on her daughter's birth certificate to April 24, 1963. After returning to Michigan in the late summer, Julie Krone raced at fairground tracks, in what was her first professional riding experience. In December 1979 she dropped out of high school to move to

Tampa, Florida, where she intended to live with her grandparents while riding at Tampa Bay Downs racetrack, but the first time she went there, the guards refused her admission. Undeterred, she climbed over the fence, where she was seen by a woman who, thinking that Julie was lost, took her to see Jerry Pace, one of the track's trainers. Impressed by her chutzpah, Pace put her on a horse, and, just five weeks later, on only her eleventh mount, Julie Krone won her first race, atop a gelding named Lord Farckle.

In her first forty-eight races at Tampa Bay Downs, Miss Krone placed first nine times, second four times, and third ten times. There, she met Julie Snellings, a former jockey whose career had ended when she was paralyzed in an accident at Delaware Park racetrack in 1977 and who was working as a secretary in the stewards' office at Tampa Bay Downs. Miss Snellings not only gave Julie Krone valuable tips on her riding form but also introduced her to influential horse owners and arranged for her brother-in-law to be her trainer. She also persuaded her former agent, Chick Lang, to take the newcomer on as a client and bring her to Baltimore, where he lived, so that she could race at Pimlico, the home of the Preakness Stakes. Julie Krone lived with Lang and his family while racing at Pimlico and at two other Maryland tracks, Laurel and Bowie. Still only seventeen, away from parental restraints, and making large sums of money, she perhaps not surprisingly made some mistakes, the biggest of which was being discovered in possession of marijuana during a race at Bowie, an offense that resulted in her being suspended from racing for two months. "When you're that young and you're caught doing something wrong, it's devastating," she told J. E. Vader. "I was very depressed."

Following her suspension, Julie Krone went to great lengths to change the way she was perceived by the public and to cultivate what she now refers to as her "apple-pie image." As she explained to Gina Maranto of *Sports Illustrated* (August 24, 1987), "In this game, you can't be unattractive to anybody for any reason." Notwithstanding that effort, she encountered some difficulty in getting mounts following her return, and her problems greatly worsened several months later, when she was thrown from her horse during a race at Laurel, breaking her back. Convinced that she would never ride again, Miss Krone spent the next two months in bed. Finally, four months after the accident, she returned to the track, but she failed to win any of her first eighty races. She recalled that losing period to Gina Maranto: "One day on the backstretch I yelled, 'I quit! I quit! I quit! I can't stand it!'"

Her luck changed when she became the regular apprentice jockey for Bud Delp, one of the country's top trainers. In the fall and winter of 1981, she rode more than 100 winners for Delp at Pimlico and at Delaware Park, and by 1982, when she moved to the track in Atlantic City, she was bringing in some $1 million annually in purses for the horse owners and earning between $80,000 and $90,000 per year herself. The move to Atlantic City also brought her a change in agents. Since his father was general manager at Pimlico, Chick Lang was committed to staying at that track. When Julie Krone informed Lang that she intended to try her luck in Atlantic City, he asked his friend Larry ("Snake") Cooper to become her new agent, and the two of them have been together ever since. Miss Krone won more races than any other jockey at Atlantic City in 1982, thus becoming the first woman to win a racing title at a major track, and she captured a second Atlantic City championship in 1983.

Women have been racing thoroughbreds professionally since 1968, and today about 25 percent of the nation's 3,400 licensed jockeys are female. Yet, in his early years as Julie Krone's agent, Larry Cooper often ran into difficulty when he tried to secure mounts for her, because many owners and trainers were convinced that women riders lacked the necessary physical strength. "At the beginning, I got: 'Owner doesn't want to ride a girl, not strong enough,'" Cooper explained to J. E. Vader. "It's a lot tougher as a girl because if you do something wrong they blow it out of proportion." But Julie Krone has never believed that her sex would stand in the way of her success. "I guess I don't think it's that big a deal that I'm a woman competing against men," she told Neil Milbert of the *Chicago Tribune* (December 15, 1988). "Who cares about that? Times have changed." She has also said that sexist insults from fans are best silenced by winning races. "I only hear 'Go home, have babies, and do the dishes' after I've lost," she told another interviewer. "I know they'll be cheering for me when I come out the next day and win."

After leaving Atlantic City, Julie Krone began racing at three other New Jersey tracks: the Meadowlands, in East Rutherford; Monmouth Park, in Oceanport; and Garden State Park, in Cherry Hill. In July 1986 her carefully cultivated public image was impaired by her fight with a fellow jockey, Miguel Rujano. The incident began during the stretch drive of a race at Monmouth Park when Rujano, believing Miss Krone was crowding him, slashed her across the face with his whip. After the race ended, Miss Krone punched Rujano in the nose. He then threw her into the swimming pool next to the jockeys' room and held her underwater for several seconds, but she escaped and hit him with a lawn chair, ending the fracas. Both jockeys were fined $100, and Rujano was suspended for five days. In discussing the incident with Gina Maranto, the steward Richard Lawrenson said, "The guys try to intimidate women jockeys, but Julie let them know that she's not going to tolerate foolishness." For her part, Miss Krone has expressed mixed feelings about the incident. While she has admitted to a certain degree of remorse, she also has said, "Hey, this is a rough game, and you can't let yourself be a victim out on the track."

Meanwhile, Julie Krone continued her winning ways. Her 1986 earnings total of $2.3 million was the highest recorded by a woman rider that year. On August 19, 1987 she rode six winners at Monmouth Park, equaling that track's single-day record, and, two months later, she tied the Meadowlands' one-day mark by riding five horses to victory. Her yearly totals of 130 wins at Monmouth Park and 124 wins at the Meadowlands were the most of any jockey at those two tracks.

In December 1987 Julie Krone began racing at Aqueduct racetrack, one of the world's best, in the New York City borough of Queens. On December 13, 1987, the opening day of the Aqueduct winter meeting, she entered the record books once again by becoming the first woman to ride four winners in one day at a New York track. "Until Krone, the best of woman jockeys had little impact at a meaningful level of competition," Paul Moran wrote in *New York Newsday* (December 17, 1987). "She, however, has demonstrated she will have impact anywhere she rides, that she is an athlete who must be compared not to other female riders, but in the context of her performance against men." Julie Krone's 1987 total of 324 wins placed her sixth among the nation's jockeys, and she scored $4.5 million in purses to become, for the second consecutive year, the leading female money winner.

In February 1988 Julie Krone became involved in another incident with a male rider when, during a race at Garden State Park, the jockey Armando Marquez yanked the reins out of her hands as she was passing him in the stretch run. After slipping momentarily, she miraculously regained her balance and avoided falling from her mount. Although Marquez won the race, he was immediately disqualified and suspended for six months, and Miss Krone, who had finished second, was declared the winner. Discussing the incident with Bill Finley of the New York *Daily News* (February 22, 1988), she admitted that she had contemplated taking retaliatory action against Marquez, but thought better of it. "I remembered I was seriously reprimanded before when I fought with Miguel Rujano, and was told not to take the law into my own hands," she explained.

Julie Krone's career peaked on March 6, 1988, when she became the leading female jockey in history by riding her 1,205th winner, at Aqueduct. In celebration, her fellow jockeys doused her with champagne. By the conclusion of the winter meeting at Aqueduct, Miss Krone had ridden sixty-eight winners, though her success at that track was marred by an accident on April 24, 1988, when she fell from her horse and a hoof landed on her shoulder. Severely bruised over much of her body, she was barely able to move for three days. That accident could not have come at a more inopportune time for her, since it denied her a chance to race in the upcoming Triple Crown events.

Recovering from her injuries within a month, Julie Krone resumed her career at Belmont Park in Elmont, New York, but she had little success there, riding only two winners in fifty races and becoming involved in yet another accident, this one a three-horse affair, on May 30, 1988. Although she suffered only a slight concussion, the two other jockeys required hospitalization. Hoping to improve her luck, she returned to Monmouth Park, where she won five races at the opener on June 3, 1988. Her disappointment at leaving the New York tracks was evident in her comments to Bill Finley. "You don't want to bite the hand that feeds you," she told him, "but once you've had that feeling of being in New York, where there's such quality horses and such quality people, it stays in your veins."

In the summer of 1988, Julie Krone won the $250,000 Cornhusker Handicap at Ak-Sar-Ben racetrack in Omaha, Nebraska, atop Palace March, and, in what was regarded as the most stunning upset in a major race that year, she rode Gaily Gaily, a seventy-five-to-one shot, to victory in the Flower Bowl Handicap at Belmont Park. She picked up a $30,000 purse on October 2, 1988, when she defeated her idol, Willie Shoemaker, in a match race at Canterbury Downs in Shakopee, Minnesota. Shoemaker, the most successful jockey in history, presented her with his goggles before the race.

What Julie Krone regards as the most significant accomplishment of her career to date was her participation, in November 1988, in the annual Breeders' Cup races at Churchill Downs. The first woman ever to take part in that event, she guided Darby Shuffle to a second-place finish in the $1 million Juvenile Fillies race and then rode Forty Niner to fourth place in the cup's grand event, the $3 million Classic. At the end of 1988, Julie Krone claimed riding titles at Monmouth Park and the Meadowlands for the second consecutive year. Her 363 victories made her the fourth-leading rider in the nation, while her $7.7 million in winnings was ninth overall and, for the third consecutive year, ranked her as first among women jockeys.

Further success greeted Julie Krone in 1989. She was the second-leading rider at the 1988–89 Aqueduct winter meet and the third-leading jockey at the track's 1989 spring meet, during which she competed against such outstanding male riders as Angel Cordero Jr., José Santos, and Chris Antley. At Monmouth Park, she rode twenty-nine winners in the first twelve days of the summer meet. What Miss Krone has called one of "the best days of [her] life" came on July 23, 1989 at Arlington Park racetrack in suburban Chicago, where she claimed $16,500 by besting Jorge Velasquez in a match race and then took first place in the $87,500 Modesty Stakes. On September 10, 1989 Miss Krone rode two long shots to victory at Pimlico's "Maryland Million" show. She won the main event, the $200,000 Budweiser Maryland Classic, aboard Master Speaker, a seven-to-one shot, and then took Countus In to victory at thirty-five-to-one in the $150,000 First National Bank of Maryland Ladies event.

Following the Glassboro Handicap at the Meadowlands on September 23, 1989, Julie Krone and the jockey Joe Bravo engaged in a fistfight, after she accused Bravo of repeatedly interfering with her mount during the race. The track's stewards suspended her for fifteen days and fined her $1,500, while Bravo was suspended for five days and fined $500. The stewards explained that her role as the "aggressor" in the altercation justified her sterner punishment.

Julie Krone typically rises at 5:00 in the morning, arrives at the track by 6:30, and works the horses until about 10:00, when she goes home for a short nap. She returns to the track at noon to prepare for the day's races, which begin at 1:30 and end between 5:00 and 5:30. If she rides in evening races, her day may include as many as eighteen matches. She keeps to that demanding schedule six days a week, twelve months a year, and takes no vacations. "She's got more energy than anyone I've ever met," Larry Cooper has said. "She loves what she's doing and she never quits."

Blonde-haired Julie Krone is four feet, ten-and-one-half inches tall and weighs around 100 pounds. Her high-pitched, squeaky voice has been compared to that of a cartoon character on a Saturday morning children's television show. She dates Jerry Casciano, a commercial photographer. Her yearly income is estimated to be about $800,000, not including revenue from personal appearances and endorsements. Among the signs of her solvency are a two-bedroom condominium in Cherry Hill, New Jersey, a two-bedroom house in Atlantic Beach, New York, and a red Porsche 924S. She has made guest appearances on *Late Night with David Letterman* and the *Tonight Show*. For relaxation she reads, goes skiing, lifts weights, and practices aerobics. Her extroverted temperament reflects her riding style. "Her personality is so strong, she makes you hate her and love her at the same time," the jockey Diane Nelson has observed. "She's constantly going ninety miles per hour. If she's sad, it only lasts for a short period of time or she doesn't show it at all." Julie Krone described her love of horses to Neal Karlen in an interview for *New York Newsday* (December 11, 1988): "Shakespeare says, 'There's no secret so close as between a horse and a rider,' and it's true. You just look in their eyes. The horses with a lot of talent always seem like they're looking into the way beyond. They always have the look of eagles in their eyes. It's very romantic."

References: Ms 16:28+ Je '88 pors; New York 21:47+ Je 13 '88 pors; Newsweek 110:61 D 28 '87 por; People 29:111+ My 2 '88 pors; Sporting N p10 O 17 '88 por, p46 Mr 13 '89 pors; Sports Illus 67:62+ Ag 24 '87 pors, 70:84+ My 22 '89 pors

Lapham, Lewis H(enry)

Jan. 8, 1935– Editor; writer. Address: Harper's Magazine, 666 Broadway, New York, N.Y. 10012

Harper's magazine, America's oldest monthly magazine and one of its most highly esteemed, owes its survival through the 1980s in considerable part to its editor, Lewis Henry Lapham, whose persistence and ingenuity helped it to withstand the threats to general-interest "thought" periodicals that have been engendered by the media revolution of recent decades. Largely because of the format he devised in 1983, *Harper's* has been able to attract readers habituated to the pace of the varied and quick-changing images of television and yet retain much of its traditional intellectual and literary character as a "theatre of ideas," to use Lapham's phrase. Journalists have described the new *Harper's* as "witty," "stingy," and "perky" and have likened it to a gadfly in its hitting out at social ills. Pretension, complacency toward the status quo, greed, abuse of privilege and power, and worship of money are among the triggers of Lapham's moral indignation and the targets of his acerbic, but sometimes risible, irony as the editor of *Harper's* and as the author of *Fortune's Child* (1980), a collection of his magazine essays, *Money and Class in America* (1988), and "Imperial Masquerade," an examination of the political and cultural world of the Reagan years that is scheduled to be published in December 1989.

"I come from a background that was not big rich, but it was certainly affluent," Lewis Henry Lapham said in a *Publishers Weekly* interview. He was born in San Francisco, California on January 8, 1935, the older of the two sons of Lewis Abbot Lapham, a banker, and Jane (Foster) Lapham. His

brother is Anthony Abbot Lapham. A wealthy industrialist and a gentleman of accomplishments, his great-grandfather helped to found the Texas Oil Company and was said to read classical Greek and play the organ and cello. His grandfather, Roger Dearborn Lapham, served as mayor of San Francisco from 1943 to 1949. "The Lapham family enjoyed the advantages of social eminence in a city that cared about little else," Lapham wrote in *Money and Class in America*. In boyhood he often rode with his grandfather in official San Francisco limousines on ceremonial and other occasions. "I came to imagine," he has recalled, "that I was born to ride in triumph and that others, apparently less fortunate and more numerous, were born to stand smiling in the streets and wave their hats."

Possibly because of his own experience of the distinction between those who can afford to ride and those who have to walk, Lapham later borrowed from Roman usage the term "equestrian class" to refer to Americans of wealth and social status. In his portrayals of life in the United States the contrast between equestrian and pedestrian is a recurrent image. Lapham's formal education reinforced his sense of the well-off as a class of persons who took privilege as their due. His private school in San Francisco, for instance, "nurtured social rather than intellectual pretensions."

Similar values, Lapham found, prevailed on the East Coast—at his prep school, Hotchkiss, in Lakeville, Connecticut, from which he graduated in 1952, and at Yale University, where he received his B.A. degree in 1956. "Neither at the Hotchkiss School nor at Yale University," Lapham wrote in *Money and Class in America*, "did I come across many people who placed their trust in anything other than the authority of wealth." In the affluent post–World War II era of his student years, Lapham believes, Hotchkiss and Yale were not unique but, rather, representative in meeting the requirements of children of the prosperous middle class for whom "an education was a necessary ornament, something one couldn't afford to be without (like tennis clothes or dancing lessons)," to quote his contention in *Fortune's Child*.

For Lapham, nevertheless, attendance at Yale was not incompatible with academic interests. Upon his graduation, he studied history at Cambridge University in England for a year. Then, giving up his intention of becoming a historian, he returned to his hometown in 1957 as a reporter on the *San Francisco Examiner*, a Hearst newspaper. Within three years he moved to a reporting job on the now defunct *New York Herald Tribune*. In the spring of 1962, he was honored as co-winner, along with Pete Hamill of the *New York Post*, of the second annual Mike Berger Award of the Columbia University Graduate School of Journalism. The two stories for which he won the award concerned a Canadian student who falsified academic credentials from Columbia and a Bronx mechanic whose gun battle with the police terrified the neighborhood.

Soon afterward, having found "conventional reporting too confining," according to *Time* (January 23, 1976), Lapham left the *Herald Tribune* but remained in New York City in the post of editor of *USA-1*, a little-known and short-lived magazine. Six months later, in 1963, he became a contributing writer for the *Saturday Evening Post*, with which he retained an association until the late 1960s, when he began writing for *Life* magazine.

Among other national periodicals for which Lapham wrote was *Harper's* magazine. Founded in 1850, *Harper's* had acquired its reputation for excellence by publishing the Lincoln-Douglas debates, reporting on the Civil War, and offering its readers the fiction of Dickens, Thackeray, Melville, Mark Twain, and Stephen Crane, as well as illustrations by Winslow Homer, Frederic Remington, and other artists. Later writers whose work appeared in *Harper's* included Kipling, Conan Doyle, Willa Cather, and Sherwood Anderson and, more recently, Norman Mailer, David Halberstam, and Annie Dillard. Along with the prestigious *Atlantic Monthly*, *Harper's* ranked at the top among "thought" magazines in reflecting America's social and cultural scene for "an audience that had the time to read and take seriously the works of the literary and political imagination," as Lapham once said of its kind of readership in an essay in *Harper's* (September 1980).

When Lapham became a contract writer for *Harper's* in 1970, its editor was Willie Morris, whose liberal, aggressive policies had made the magazine one of the most provocative and controversial in the country. Because of a cost-cutting dispute with the publishers of *Harper's*, Morris quit in March 1971. The departure of most of the editorial staff in his support opened Lapham's way to the post of managing editorship, making him second in command under the new editor, Robert Shnayerson. Some four years later, Lapham took the title of editor and, upon Shnayerson's resignation in January 1976, moved up to the controlling slot.

The monthly essay, then called "The Easy Chair," that Lapham as editor wrote for *Harper's* and his general selection of articles often seemed to have a neoconservative slant. "Now the magazine once known for its cheerful progressivism appears to have taken a tendentious turn to the right," a writer for *Time* (January 23, 1978) observed. But never an ideologue, Lapham often balanced an attack on a particular subject with a defending article in another issue. In disregard of charges of inconsistency and negativism, he stirred up confrontation and debate so that a topic could be examined from all sides. "I tried to open the magazine to as many points of view as I could," he once explained, as quoted in the *New York Times* (June 18, 1980). "I assumed I was writing and editing for consenting adults who could come to their own conclusions."

Under Lapham's editorship, as it had under Morris's and Shnayerson's, *Harper's* lost money. Like the *Saturday Review*, the *Atlantic*, and other general-interest magazines offering a miscellany,

Harper's could not stop the defection of many of its readers to special-interest magazines, for sports, pets, hobbies, or whatever. When, in the late 1970s, its annual deficit surpassed $1 million, the Minneapolis Star and Tribune Company, its owner since 1965, began to search for a buyer. But failing to agree on terms with any of some sixty-five prospective purchasers, including a group organized by Lapham himself, on June 17, 1980 the Minneapolis Star and Tribune announced that *Harper's* August issue would be its last. Then, in an eleventh-hour rescue in early July, the John D. and Catherine T. MacArthur Foundation acquired the magazine under a partnership agreement with the Atlantic Richfield Foundation that set up a nonprofit Harper's Magazine Foundation to manage continued publication.

In an essay, "Intimations of Mortality," in the September 1980 issue of *Harper's*, Lapham, who remained as editor of the revived magazine, wrote about the widespread feelings of shock and deprivation with which the public had responded to word of *Harper's* imminent collapse. The outcry confirmed his belief that the nation needed and wanted a magazine offering an open expression of divergent views in exercise of "the capacity to see things whole." In August of the following year, he abruptly left *Harper's*, in part because he "couldn't work out an agreement with the board [of the Harper's Foundation] about what direction the magazine was going to go in," as his account of the matter was quoted in the *Washington Post* (July 13, 1983). Michael Kinsley replaced him in the editorship in September 1981.

By the time of his return to *Harper's* in July 1983, Lapham was ready to try out, with the support of its publisher, John R. ("Rick") MacArthur, a bold formula to restructure the magazine in an effort to distinguish it from the *Atlantic* and to increase circulation and advertising revenues. Instead of filling the magazine with lengthy articles, literary articles, and stories, he proposed to use each month only a few pieces of original reporting, criticism, fiction, poetry, and/or drama and devote the rest of the issue to an assortment of features, including his own essay, "Notebook." Perhaps the most catchy feature is "Harper's Index," a compilation of statistics drawn from a wide range of sources. Some of the items are of national significance, such as the amount of money budgeted for Star Wars during a single year; others are snatches of trivia, such as what percentage of Icelanders admit to a belief in elves. A "Readings" section comprises reprints of usually brief or excerpted essays, letters, interviews, stories, poems, and speeches. Another Lapham innovation, called "Annotation," subjects a text—a White House news release, a funeral contract, a PBS program schedule—to authorial critical comment. Most issues have an edited symposium titled "Forum," and an acrostic page and puzzle page are regular features of the new *Harper's*.

"The world today is a television cult, it's a telephone culture," Lapham has pointed out, as reported in the Toronto *Globe and Mail* (December 13, 1984), in accounting for the radical transformation of *Harper's* into a quick-reading magazine that has been called "a *Reader's Digest* for intellectuals" and "a highbrow *Reader's Digest.*" But in its provocative, sophisticated wit and its satirical edge, it bears no resemblance to *Reader's Digest.* Some of the changes in *Harper's* may have derived from television, but as Jennifer Hunter observed in the Toronto *Globe and Mail,* *Harper's* "is no superficial purveyor of information: what Mr. Lapham has tried to emulate is the brevity and immediacy of television, but not its mindlessness." By 1986 the magazine, which is not required to make a profit, was approaching the financial well-being of matching its income with its expenses.

Lapham's own earlier writing exemplifies the kind of journalistic achievement that he had largely to forgo in revamping *Harper's*: articles, or essays, of sufficient length to permit perspective and opinion and exploration of the circumstantial details of an event. *Fortune's Child: A Portrait of the United States as Spendthrift Heir* (1980) is a collection of some thirty revised pieces that he had written during the period from 1965 to 1979 for the *Saturday Evening Post, Life,* and *Harper's.* Topically diversified, the essays examine, for example, the weakness of the jury system in the notorious Candace Mossler and Melvin Lane Powers murder case, the negativism of Hollywood movies, the decline of American fiction, the loss of hundreds of thousands of dollars on the 1965 Broadway musical flop *Kelly,* and the insipidity of the Maharishi Mahesh Yogi with the Beatles on the banks of the Ganges. Lapham also takes iconoclastic swings at John F. Kennedy, Nelson A. Rockefeller, Jimmy Carter, and many others. But the essays are thematically unified in their bearing on the author's depiction and indictment of America as a spoiled rich kid squandering his World II legacy, the wealth that inundated the country after 1945.

An also severe upbraiding of the expanding equestrian class, Lapham's second book, *Money and Class in America. Notes and Observations on Our Civil Religion* (1988), illuminates "an odd paradox": "Never in the history of the world have so many people been so rich; never in the history of the world have so many of those same people felt themselves so poor," to quote from the preamble. In an interview for *Publishers Weekly* (February 5, 1988), Lapham said of his book, "It is an exorcism, a necessary working-out of my own attitudes toward money." His "speculative essay," as he has characterized *Money and Class in America,* deplores the nationwide spiritual, cultural, and political impoverishment that has followed from the upgrading of money from a commodity to a sacrament through an obsession that supplants all other systems of value with monetary wealth.

Some reviewers of *Money and Class in America* found fault with Lapham for overgeneralization, a complaint that had also been made against *Fortune's Child,* and for supporting his assertions with anecdote rather than documentation. The ob-

jection of several to his doom-and-gloom tone seemed like an echo of the charge that pessimism had infected his editing of the old *Harper's.* He has tended to shrug off such criticism with the observations that "the negative is the first half of the positive" and that "the major is implicit in the minor." For many readers, Lapham's wit and urbanity mitigate the grimness of his reflections. Praising him as "a lapidary craftsman, one who obviously polishes and rewrites until his prose shines," Louise Sweeney went on to point out in the *Christian Science Monitor* (May 26, 1981): "There is no marshmallow cream in Lapham's writing. He is instead something of a swashbuckler with words, who uses the glinting sword of his writing style to batter society's enemies as he sees them." In his comments for *Business Week* (February 22, 1988) on *Money and Class in America,* Daniel Moskowitz found Lapham to be "a wonderful writer, a connoisseur of the perfect word."

Style, together with earnestness of moral concern and sharp insight into the temper of our times, engaged also the readers of Lapham's syndicated column, which appeared in the *Baltimore Sun,* among other newspapers, until 1987. Those qualities have continued to captivate the audiences of his lectures at many universities throughout the country and of his remarks for CBS Radio's "Spectrum" and distinguished his tenure as host and executive editor of the twenty-six-week public television series *Bookmark,* a roundtable discussion among writers, editors, and critics that began in January 1989.

In October 1989 Lapham introduced on public television *America's Century,* a six-part series tracing the sudden rise and eventual slow decline of American power in the twentieth century. To Walter Goodman, who reviewed the series for the *New York Times* (October 23, 1989), *America's Century* "is never less than intelligent, yet it rarely enthralls. The history is familiar, as are many of the pictures, which are subordinate to Mr. Lapham's words." As for Lapham himself, he "makes a wry and restrained host, an agreeable respite from television's burbling and relentlessly upbeat personalities. And it is good to have the words spoken by the person who wrote them." Lapham was the editor, moreover, of *High Technology and Human Freedom* (1985), a compilation of papers, two of his authorship, presented in December 1983 at the Smithsonian Institution–sponsored symposium on the problem, as the title suggests, posed by George Orwell's *1984.* He serves as a trustee of the New School for Social Research and the Louis B. Mayer Foundation and is a member of the Council on Foreign Relations.

On August 10, 1972 Lewis H. Lapham married Joan Brooke Reeves. Their children are Lewis Andrew, Elizabeth Delphina, and Winston Peale. Lapham, a tall, trim man, "looks like a thoroughbred," according to Louise Sweeney, who interviewed him in 1981 for the *Christian Science Monitor.* "The most extraordinary feature in his even-featured, attractive face is his eyes," she noted. "They are the grayish-green of sage, what one friend calls 'those heavy-lidded eyes' that suggest the reporter who's seen it all. But the expression is lively, amused." The society-watcher Stephen Birmingham, who is accustomed to seeing Lapham in Newport and Palm Beach, believes that, unlike Truman Capote, he will not be ostracized for his scornful treatment of the upper crust. "He is firmly a part of the world of which he writes," Birmingham argued in Fortune (February 29, 1988). "These people know him, they have always known him, they accept him, and they will always accept him because he is one of them."

References: Christian Sci Mon C p2+ My 26 '81, p1+ Jl 16 '85 por; Fortune 117:121+ F 29 '88 por; Pub W 217:12+ Je 11 '80 por, 233:75+ F 5 '88 por; Time 111:84 Ja 23 '78 por; Toronto Globe and Mail p1+ D 13 '84 por; Celebrity Register (1986); Contemporary Authors vols 77–80 (1979); Who's Who in America, 1988–89

Lasorda, Tommy

Sept. 22, 1927– Baseball manager. Address: Los Angeles Dodgers, 1000 Elysian Park Ave., Los Angeles, Calif. 90012

If anyone were to cut Tommy Lasorda, the garrulous and combative manager of baseball's 1988 world champion Los Angeles Dodgers, he would "bleed Dodger blue"—a metaphorical slogan of his that exemplifies his combination of sincerity and instinctive showmanship. Lasorda joined the Dodger organization forty years ago as a minor-league pitcher, which he remained, except for two brief tries in the majors, until 1960. After working devotedly in the Dodger system for sixteen years as a scout, a farm-team manager, and the third-base coach in Los Angeles, he became manager of the Dodgers in time to guide the team to the National League pennant in 1977. Since then, the Dodgers have won five divisional titles, three additional pennants, and two World Series, the most recent in 1988.

Especially in 1988, the Dodgers' success was achieved against odds that probably would have been insurmountable without Lasorda's charged personality, his knowledge of the game, and his grasp of motivational and competitive psychology. Naturally good-natured and gregarious, he has an informal rapport with his players that contributes to team cohesiveness and camaraderie without undermining his authority, which he asserts in clubhouse tirades as fearsome as his dugout vituperation against umpires and opposing teams. His enthusiasm, optimism, and intensity in competition are contagious, and his aggressiveness often forces the opposition into defensive mistakes. As Jerry Sullivan observed in New York Newsday (October 2, 1988), Lasorda has come through more than a decade of success as a major-league manager a basically unchanged and simple man: "He remains baseball's bowlegged moveable feast, an American original . . . willingly present[ing] himself in caricature—as the engaging, eternally grateful baseball man performing the only job to which he's ever aspired." Through the 1989 season, in which the club finished fourth, fourteen games behind the league-leading San Francisco Giants, the Dodgers under Lasorda have won a total of 1,097 games and lost a total of 955. His .535 winning percentage is third-best among active major-league managers, behind only those of Sparky Anderson of Detroit and Whitey Herzog of St. Louis.

Thomas Charles Lasorda was born in Norristown, Pennsylvania on September 22, 1927, the second of the five children, all boys, of Sabatino and Carmella Lasorda, working-class immigrants from Italy. Sabatino Lasorda, who came from Abruzzi in central Italy, was a truck driver at the Bethlehem Steel quarry in Norristown who considered himself to be "the luckiest man alive" for living, working, and raising a family "in the greatest country on earth." A jovial man, he entertained family and friends with his singing, concertina playing, and storytelling. At the same time, he was a harsh disciplinarian who regularly administered spankings, most often not as punishments but as warnings to his sons—a curious practice from which Tommy Lasorda derived his own disciplinary philosophy in managing: "You anticipate mistakes; get your teaching done before they happen, rather than criticizing after the fact." In a profile in

New Times (October 14, 1977), Eric Lax quoted Lasorda regarding the similarity between familial and team discipline: "I kissed my father, Sam, every time I saw him until the day he died. His five sons would have gone through fire for him. But if we got out of line, the roof fell in. It's no different with a squad of twenty-five. Caring makes it all happen—it builds confidence and teamwork and gets those runs across the plate."

All four of Tommy Lasorda's brothers went into the restaurant business, in Exton, Pennsylvania, but Tommy himself aspired only to a career in baseball. In childhood, before his blood became, as he says, "Dodger blue," his dream was to play in Yankee Stadium. By his own, oft-repeated account, he was only a third-string pitcher on the Norristown High School baseball team. Undaunted by that lowly status, he tried out successfully with the Philadelphia Phillies in his senior year (1944–45) and dropped out of high school before graduation to sign a minor-league contract with the Phillies. The Lasorda the Phillies recruited was a smallish, chunky left-hander with a good right hook, a fair curve, a mediocre fastball, a propensity for fisticuffs, and a will to succeed that maximized his modest talent. Technically, he was in the Philadelphia farm system for four years (1945 through 1948), but two of those years (1946–47) were spent in military service. His win-loss record was 12-24.

Drafted into the Dodger farm system at his own request, Lasorda pitched 7-7 with the Class A Greenville (South Carolina) Spinners in 1949. The following year the Dodgers moved him up to their AAA farm club in Montreal, Canada. "From the day I signed with Montreal," he said years later, "I'd known the Dodger organization was for me." He was determined not only to devote himself to that organization, but to move up to its top, the mother club, which was in Brooklyn, New York until it moved to Los Angeles in 1958.

In his nine years with Montreal, Lasorda won 107 games and lost only fifty-seven. During those years he made two brief, unsuccessful forays into the major leagues. In one, pitching his single start for the Brooklyn Dodgers, he tied a National League record with three wild pitches in one inning against St. Louis on May 5, 1955. In the other, with Kansas City of the American League, he went 0-4 in 1956. According to Lasorda's career record as published by the Dodgers in 1988, he went 3-6 with Denver and 7-10 with Los Angeles before returning to Montreal in 1958. The sportswriter Roger Kahn knew Lasorda in the 1950s as a pitcher who was "variously eager, uproarious, agitated, combative, and even somewhat somber, but always charged with extraordinary vitality." In a profile in *Playboy* (April 1982), Kahn wrote: "There was no fake cool to Lasorda. You had to root for him. He had drive and intelligence, but he lacked what his forebears called *fortuna*—roughly, good luck."

Following a 2-5 pitching performance with Montreal in 1960, Lasorda became a scout for the Dodgers. His first managerial assignment for the Dodger organization was Pocatello, Idaho, where his team finished second in its league in 1965. He won Pioneer League pennants in each of his three years (1966–68) as manager of the Ogden (Utah) Dodgers. As a Triple-A manager (1969–72), he won two pennants (with Spokane in 1970 and Albuquerque in 1972), and he was voted Minor League Manager of the Year in 1970. In the winters he managed teams in the Dominican Republic, Puerto Rico, and elsewhere in the Caribbean. He also coached instructional ball in Arizona. His totals as manager in the Dodger farm system were 478 wins and 367 losses.

Lasorda's bellicosity reached its peak during his minor-league managerial career, when he habitually wreaked havoc in locker rooms, screamed a blue streak of invective from the dugout, and was ejected from one out of every five games. "I had a small man's complex, I guess you'd call it, when I was a player and started as a manager, and I got into so many fights," he told Eric Lax for *New Times*. "I think I've matured, though. I've realized that those things only tend to aggravate you. In managing you can do so much to help other people. . . . The two goals I had were to develop ballplayers for the Dodgers and outstanding young men for their families." Fifty-seven of his players moved up to the majors; eighteen would be on the Dodger roster at spring training in 1977.

Called up to Los Angeles in 1973, Lasorda served as the Dodgers' peppery third-base coach through 1976. During those years he turned down managerial offers from four other major-league teams, because he wanted to remain true to the Dodgers and was hoping, almost against hope, to succeed Walter Alston as manager in Los Angeles. Alston, a quiet, stoic, aloof mentor, the antithesis of Lasorda, had been managing the Dodgers since 1954, four years before they left Brooklyn. Under him, the team had won seven pennants and four world championships, but in 1976 it finished a distant second to the Cincinnati Reds for the second straight year in the National League West.

When Alston retired in September 1976, the club president, Peter O'Malley, named Lasorda to succeed him. "As a result," Larry Keith reported in *Sports Illustrated* (March 14, 1977), "when the Dodgers opened spring training last week, the scene in Vero Beach, Florida was quite different from what it had been for two decades. The man in charge was moving here, hurrying there, shouting orders, giving directions, laughing, talking a mile a minute, cajoling, and praising."

Lasorda's friend Frank Sinatra sang the national anthem on opening day at Dodger Stadium in 1977. With a 98-64 record, the Dodgers ran away with the National League West title that season, finishing ten games ahead of the Cincinnati Reds. They defeated the Philadelphia Phillies in the National League championship series but lost to the New York Yankees in the World Series. United Press International named Lasorda the National League Manager of the Year. Attendance in Dodger Stadium shot up to 2,955,087 in 1977, and over the following five years it rose to 3,608,881, a National League record.

After a nip-and-tuck race with the Cincinnati Reds and the San Francisco Giants in 1978, the Dodgers again won the title in the National League's western division and the league pennant and again lost to the Yankees in the World Series. Lasorda managed the National League All-Stars that year. The Dodgers dropped to third place in the West in 1979 and second in 1980. In the first half of the strike-bifurcated 1981 season they led the West, and in the postseason miniseries they vanquished the second-half leaders, the Houston Astros. They went on to win the league championship series, against the Expos, 3-2, and the World Series against the Yankees, 4-2. The Associated Press selected Lasorda the 1981 National League Manager of the Year.

The Dodgers finished second in the National League's western division in 1982. The following year they won the division title but not the league pennant. The Baseball Writers Association of America, in its first such vote, elected Lasorda the National League Manager of the Year for 1983. Hobbled by injuries, the Dodgers finished fourth in the West in 1984. In 1985 they won easily in the West but lost the league championship series to the St. Louis Cardinals. The decisive point in that loss was the decision not to walk the powerful St. Louis batter Jack Clark, who proceeded to hit a three-run homer off of Dodger reliever Tom Niedenfuer. Lasorda wept publicly and, in his words, "moped around for a day or two." There were extenuating reasons for pitching to Clark, but Lasorda's ability as a tactician was questioned in a storm of criticism by fans and sportswriters.

Los Angeles went into a prolonged slump, tallying a record of 73-89 in 1986 and identical figures in 1987. Attendance at Dodger home games suffered a drop of 467,184. Addressing the crisis, Los Angeles general manager Fred Claire (who had replaced Al Campanis, fired after making televised remarks interpreted as racist) did some astute trading and buying of players. The most valuable of his acquisitions was the intense, slugging outfielder Kirk Gibson, obtained from Detroit. Claire and Lasorda hoped that Gibson's winning attitude, combined with his talent, would spark the Dodgers, and their optimism was not disappointed.

Confounding the odds-makers, the Dodgers finished first in the National League West in 1988, with a 94-66 record, and Dodger pitchers contributed mightily to the achievement. Orel Hershiser had a 23-8 record and a late-season streak of fifty-nine consecutive scoreless innings, and Los Angeles relief pitchers set a club record of forty-nine saves. The leading reliever was Jay Howell, who saved twenty-one games. In the 1988 National League championship series the Dodgers defeated the New York Mets, to whom they had lost ten of eleven games in the regular season. The final series game was a shutout by Orel Hershiser.

Still the underdogs, the Dodgers moved on to face the Oakland Athletics in the World Series in mid-October 1988. Despite a plague of injuries, they beat the A's four games (two of them Hershiser's) to one. One of the injured was Kirk Gibson, who, despite his condition, pinch-hit a home run that decided the first game and set the tone for those that followed. In a poll of National League players conducted before the series, Lasorda received the most votes for league Manager of the Year, and following the series the Baseball Writers Association of America elected him National League Manager of the Year for the second time.

Lasorda has often referred to the success of the Dodgers in 1988 as a miracle, saving fans the price of "a trip to Lourdes." But the real miracle is Lasorda himself, a genuine old-fashioned rah-rah manager, almost an anachronism in the slick, commercialized world of contemporary professional sports, able to communicate with, and motivate, highly paid players like the father or big brother in a family. Closer to his players and fraternizing with them more than most managers, Lasorda imbues them with his own positive attitude, his intense will to win, and his devotion to the Dodgers. Although some of his screaming may seem generalized, he relates to them for the most part personally, one on one, goading the successful to even greater performances, consoling and encouraging the failures, talking moody players out of their funks, and restoring confidence in has-beens. He will resort to almost any motivational trick that will work, including uplifting "true" sports anecdotes that he fabricates. Whatever he does, he "makes everybody feel better for having him around," as Steve Garvey, the former Dodger star, has attested.

Aside from his success on the field, Lasorda's most important creation is bonhomie in the clubhouse. Even in an earnest pep talk, he cannot resist jesting. One of his favorite instructional stories is about a dog that fouls its master's carpet. For thirty consecutive days the master rubs the dog's nose in the excrement and puts the dog out the window. On the thirty-first day the dog rubs his own nose in the mess and jumps out the window. "See," Lasorda tells his players. "With proper training, the dog learned what it was supposed to do."

In the heat of competition Lasorda is fierce and profane, and he often seems to be acting the buffoon. Outside the heat and beneath the clowning, he is a clean-tongued (in private life), good-natured hugger, back-patter, and inveterate teller of stories, jokes, and parables. Unpretentious, loquacious, democratic, and sensitive to other people's feelings, he answers any phone he is near in the Dodger offices and talks baseball with callers without pressing his identity. He is friendly toward fans who approach him for autographs, and if they are Mexican-American he chats with them in Spanish, which he learned in his minor-league days in the Caribbean. His cavernous office is adorned with pictures not only of the Sacred Heart, Frank Sinatra, and Don Rickles (the comedian, a big Dodger fan), but also of the wives and children of his players. Having a phenomenal memory (of matters in and out of baseball), he knows all the wives and children by name.

For years Tommy Lasorda, who is five feet nine inches tall, weighed about 210 pounds. According to published reports, he quit smoking cigarettes and began eschewing hard liquor a few years ago. The reports do not make clear whether he still chews tobacco, goes out for a beer with his players, or drinks wine with his meals. Lasorda's meals— not to mention the frequent between-meal snacks—were legendary. His players vied with tall stories about the food they had seen him consume: dozens of clams, oysters, shrimp, or other appetizers followed by steak, chicken parmigiana, and mammoth portions of pasta fagioli. He offered cold cuts to the players, reporters, and others who visited him in his office, and he often talked to and joked with his guests while he dug into a mound of linguine.

When Lasorda reported to spring training in 1989 weighing 218 pounds, Hershiser and Gibson challenged him to lose thirty pounds by the All-Star break in July, promising to donate $20,000 and $10,000, respectively, to charity if he could take the weight off and keep it off through the remainder of the season. "At first, he told us that no one needed to tell him anything, that he was a fine piece of machinery," Hershiser recalled to reporters, as quoted in the Chicago Tribune (June 7, 1989), "and we told him that he didn't have the discipline and dedication to lose weight anyway. We said he was a fine one to talk, all that preaching he did to us. So when we called him on his own words, he accepted." With the help of the liquid supplement Ultra Slim-Fast, whose benefits he touts in television commercials, Lasorda lost nearly forty pounds by mid-August. He has donated his earnings from the commercials to St. Bernard's Convent, which is operated by the Sisters of Mercy.

Tommy Lasorda and the former Joanne Miller, who were married in 1950, have two grown children, Laura and Tom Jr. The Lasordas live modestly in a tract house in Fullerton, California, twenty-five miles south of Los Angeles. Lasorda, who has no hobbies or handyman abilities, spends much of his time at home watching television or walking the family dog. When driving his blue Thunderbird, he keeps the car radio tuned to big-band and "golden oldies" stations and sings along with the recorded voices of such "good friends" as Frank Sinatra, Vic Damone, and Frankie Avalon. Away from home, he is busy even during the off-season, appearing on television sports shows and commercials, giving scores of speeches on the lecture and banquet circuits (sometimes gratis, for worthy groups), and making other public appearances, at, for example, store openings and mobile-home shows. Lasorda owns Tommy Lasorda's Ribs and Pasta Restaurant in Marina del Rey, California, and he is an investor in Lasorda Foods, an Atlanta, Georgia–based company recently formed to make and market a frozen spaghetti sauce he created.

Ecumenically religious, Lasorda prays to "the Great Dodger in the sky," goes to a Roman Catholic Mass on Sunday, and invites ministers of other religious persuasions to conduct occasional prayer sessions in the Dodger clubhouse. "There are four things in life I've never regretted," Lasorda told Ron Fimrite for Sports Illustrated (January 30, 1984). "I've never regretted my love for God or my love for my family. I've never regretted living in the greatest country in the world. And I've never regretted one of my thirty-five years with the Dodgers."

References: N Y Daily News p53 My 24 '85; N Y Times C p3 Mr 20 '78 por; New Times 9:55+ O 14 '77 pors; Newsweek 112:78 O 24 '88; People 30:163+ D 19 '88; Sport 64:76+ Ap '77 por; Sporting N p9+ My 6 '78 por; Sports Illus 60:64+ Ja 30 '84 pors; Washington Post F p1+ O 14 '78 por, C p1 O 12 '88; Who's Who in America, 1988–89

Lean, David

Mar. 25, 1908– British filmmaker. Address: c/o Columbia Pictures, 711 Fifth Ave., New York, N.Y. 10022

NOTE: This biography supersedes the article that appeared in Current Biography in 1953.

For nearly half a century, ever since he first stepped behind a camera to co-direct the World War II film In Which We Serve, Sir David Lean has been dazzling international audiences with movies that demonstrate his mastery of both the smallest cinematic nuance and an overpowering epic scale. Lean established a unique command of the language of film, setting a new standard for its use in such memorable movies as *Brief Encounter*, *The Bridge on the River Kwai*, *Lawrence of Arabia*, *Doctor Zhivago*, and *A Passage to India*. Along with his colleague and contemporary Michael Powell and such celebrated masters of the past as Carol Reed and Alfred Hitchcock, he is among that handful of venerated British filmmakers who continue to attract new generations of moviegoers to their work from all over the world. In 1953 he was made a commander of the British Empire, and he was knighted in 1984.

David Lean was born in Croydon, south of London, England, on March 25, 1908, the younger of the two sons of Francis William le Blount Lean, a chartered accountant in a London firm, and Helena Annie (Tangye) Lean. Since both of his parents were devout Quakers who regarded motion pictures as sinful, while Lean lived at home he was denied the privilege of attending movies and had to content himself with listening enviously to friends who told of films they had seen. It was only after he was sent to the Leighton Park School, a Quaker institution in Reading, that he was able to go to the movies. "I became absolutely *dotty* about the movies," he told Jonathan Yardley for the *Washington Post* (February 2, 1989), "and I used to spend all my money going into the nine-penny seats, which were really quite nice, and I kept it a secret."

After compiling an undistinguished academic record, Lean left school to become an apprentice at his father's accounting firm. "By the time I was nineteen," he recalled for Hollis Alpert in an interview for the *New York Times Magazine* (May 23, 1965), "I was spending all my spare time at the movies, and was mad about photography. An aunt suggested to my mother that I ought to try film work." He went to Gaumont Studios the following day and was hired for a month's unpaid probation, during which he worked primarily as a "tea boy," the British equivalent of a "gofer." During his first year, he worked his way up from the humble job of clapper boy to the post of third assistant director. "There were no unions," he recalled in an interview for *Newsday* (December 19, 1970), "and I had the chance of going around doing all sorts of jobs, from making tea, turning the camera, going into the editing department, being an assistant director, and at one time even being wardrobe mistress."

Lean's most avid interest, however, was in the cutting room, where the editing and assembly of movies takes place. In 1929 he was given permission to observe the editing and synchronization procedure on Gaumont's first sound film, *The Night Porter*, and he quickly became adept at the new process of editing sound film. Recognizing his facility, in 1930 his superiors put him in charge of editing their Gaumont Sound News newsreels, for which he also wrote and recorded the narration. In the early 1930s he left Gaumont to work for British Movietone News, but he found himself back in feature films by the middle of the decade.

During the mid-1930s, Lean made his name as an editor by working on what were called "quota quickies," low-budget pictures shot in England but financed by American studios under a government-mandated quota. "I became a kind of film doctor," he has said of that period, "in which they would give me films which were very hard to cut or had been cut by somebody else, not too successfully perhaps, and I would put them together." He rejected his first offers to direct because they came mostly from producers of quota pictures. Instead, Lean became the highest-paid and most sought-after editor in British film, solidifying his standing in 1935 with work on his first major motion picture, Herbert Wilcox's *Escape Me Never*. Directed by Paul Czinner and starring Elisabeth Bergner, it was nominated for one Oscar and later remade in Hollywood. He then edited the Czinner-Bergner features *As You Like It* (1936), which starred a young Laurence Olivier, and *Dreaming Lips* (1937). In 1937 he was hired by the producer Gabriel Pascal to edit his landmark screen adaptation of George Bernard Shaw's *Pygmalion*, co-directed by Anthony Asquith and Leslie Howard, who was also its star. It became one of the most popular and honored British films of the decade.

Lean got his first chance to work behind the camera—and his first opportunity to work on a picture from the outset of production—on Pascal's 1940–41 production of Shaw's *Major Barbara*. His duties as assistant director as well as editor included the shooting of screen tests and very likely involved a major contribution to the directing of the film itself. Immediately after finishing *Major Barbara*, Lean was hired by the filmmaking team of Michael Powell and Emeric Pressburger to edit two thrillers, *49th Parallel* and *One of Our Aircraft Is Missing*. International box-office hits, the two films received a combined total of six Oscar nominations in 1942. So great was their success that the motion picture tycoon J. Arthur Rank set up a group of independent production units within his own company. Among them was Two Cities, under the producer Filippo Del Giudice, one of whose first projects was a film dedicated to the British Royal Navy, which was to be scripted and directed by Noel Coward, who would also star.

In Which We Serve was one of the most honored British films of World War II. In addition to being an editor's tour de force, with its exquisitely handled dissolves, flashbacks, sound edits, and jump cuts, it offered its directors a once-in-a-lifetime cast, including John Mills, Bernard Miles, and Celia Johnson, and riveting action scenes. Lean's handling of the battle sequences and his assistance on the script so impressed Coward that he gave the young man permission to direct any of his plays for the screen.

In 1944 Lean formed within the Rank Organisation an independent production company called Cineguild, in partnership with Ronald Neame, who had been the cinematographer of *Major Barbara* and *One of Our Aircraft Is Missing*, and Anthony Havelock-Allan, who had been an associate producer of *In Which We Serve*. Their first production—and Lean's solo directorial debut—was the 1944 domestic drama *This Happy Breed*, adapted from Coward's play. It was quickly followed by Coward's sophisticated fantasy-comedy *Blithe Spirit* (1945), which received an Oscar for its special photographic effects. Based on a Noel Coward one-act play, Lean's third film, *Brief Encounter* (1945), transformed a story of a furtive and unrealized love affair between a suburban housewife (Celia Johnson) and a married physician (Trevor Howard) into one of the most successful romantic movies of its generation, though most of it was played out against the unpromising setting of a dark and grimy railroad station. *Brief Encounter* brought Lean his first Oscar nomination as best director.

Lean's next film, *Great Expectations* (1946), starring John Mills, Valerie Hobson, and Alec Guinness, began his brief but felicitous association with the works of Charles Dickens. As masterly as the novel on which it was based, especially in its unforgettable opening sequence with Pip and the convict, Magwitch, in the churchyard, *Great Expectations* received three Academy Award nominations in 1947, including Lean's second best-director nomination. His 1948 adaptation of *Oliver Twist*, with Alec Guinness, Robert Newton, Kay Walsh, and John Howard Davies, may be an even more accomplished example of filmmaking, but it was deprived of Hollywood honors because of a three-year delay in its American opening, the result of its purportedly anti-Semitic characterization of Fagin. The film was finally released in America in 1951 with eleven minutes excised, and it was not until 1982 that a complete 35-mm version became generally available in the United States.

Following two more movies, *The Passionate Friends* (1948) and *Madeleine* (1949), both of which starred Lean's second wife, Ann Todd, the Cineguild partnership dissolved. In 1950 Lean accepted an offer from the movie magnate Sir Alexander Korda to join London Films. His first film for London, *The Sound Barrier* (1952), released in the United States as *Breaking the Sound Barrier*, was an extraordinary contemporary drama based on the development of supersonic aircraft. Both Lean's direction and Ralph Richardson's performance received British Academy Awards in 1953, and the script, which the playwright Terence Rattigan based on Lean's own scenario, was tendered an Oscar nomination.

In 1953 Lean made *Hobson's Choice*, a Victorian domestic drama about a tyrannical bootmaker who finally gets his comeuppance from his daughter and son-in-law that starred Charles Laughton, John Mills, and Brenda de Banzie. A hit with critics and public alike, *Hobson's Choice* has been described by Karol Kulik, in her 1975 book *Alexander Korda: The Man Who Could Work Miracles*, as "the warmest and most charming of Korda's postwar comedies."

By 1955 London Films had succumbed to the hard times afflicting the entire British film industry and was serving as a source of financing and story material for other filmmakers. Lean's next film, *Summertime* (1955), which was released in Britain under the title *Summer Madness*, was an international coproduction of London Films and the producer Ilya Lopert. Shot in Venice with an international cast that included Katharine Hepburn, Rossano Brazzi, and André Morell, it was the first of Lean's pictures to be filmed on location. A stylish and visually ravishing expansion of Arthur Laurents's Broadway play *The Sign of the Cuckoo*, about an American spinster who briefly finds romance while on vacation in Venice, the film earned both David Lean and Katharine Hepburn Academy Award nominations.

A year after completing *Summertime*, Lean was in the United States on holiday when his agent informed him that the producer Sam Spiegel had acquired the rights to Pierre Boulle's novel *The Bridge on the River Kwai*, which London Films had previously owned. Lean and Spiegel agreed on their approach to the story's central character, the inscrutable Colonel Nicholson, and tapped Alec Guinness for the role. At the insistence of Columbia Pictures executives, who financed *The Bridge on the River Kwai* but questioned the mass appeal of a film about British prisoners of war in a jungle, a role was written in for William Holden, as a cynical, two-fisted American. Filmed in Ceylon and completed in just under a year, *The Bridge on the River Kwai* went on to win six of the seven Oscars for which it was nominated, including best director for Lean, best actor for Guinness, and best picture. *The Bridge on the River Kwai* cost a then astronomical $3 million, and the film eventually made many times that amount, setting a new standard for moviemaking and film financing. One of the most important beneficiaries of the change was David Lean himself, who was elevated to the ranks of the world's top filmmakers.

Five years elapsed before Lean's next movie, *Lawrence of Arabia*, was released. The story of the enigmatic World War I hero T. E. Lawrence was based on his autobiography *The Seven Pillars of Wisdom*, which the Korda organization had previously owned and tried to film on half a dozen occasions before Spiegel acquired it in the late 1950s. For his screenplay, Lean turned to the playwright Robert Bolt, whose work led to a twenty-year association between the two. The score was composed by Maurice Jarre, with whom Lean has worked on every picture since. After considering Alec Guinness, Marlon Brando, and Albert Finney for the title role, Lean and Spiegel settled upon a little-known actor named Peter O'Toole. They also chose an unknown Egyptian actor named Omar Sharif for the supporting role of Sherif Ali.

Lawrence of Arabia was three years in production, with the actual shooting taking place over a period of nineteen months. Lean reportedly spent ten months in the Jordanian desert before being pulled—prematurely, according to some accounts—by Spiegel, who ordered the director to finish his work in Spain. When *Lawrence of*

Arabia opened in December of 1962, it scored an immediate success with critics and moviegoers, who were overwhelmed by its unusual mix of intimacy and epic scale. Although it was stretched across a vast Super-Panavision screen, amid huge vistas of desert and armies in combat, it managed to focus upon the subtlest nuances of complex characterization, shuttling between the infinitely large and the infinitely small. *Lawrence of Arabia* remained in release for over a year in its first run and earned seven Academy Award nominations, with Lean winning best-director and best-picture Oscars for the second time. The film also made stars of O'Toole and Sharif and earned Academy Awards for Jarre and cinematographer Frederick A. Young. The combined $50 million earned by *Lawrence of Arabia* and *The Bridge on the River Kwai* established Lean as one of the few completely bankable, big-budget "box-office" directors of the 1960s. When compared with such multimillion-dollar debacles as Joseph Mankiewicz's *Cleopatra*, his achievement seemed all the more impressive.

Doctor Zhivago (1965) marked something of a parting of the ways between David Lean and the critics, who had generally indulged in superlatives about his films ever since *In Which We Serve*. Bosley Crowther of the *New York Times* (December 23, 1965), for one, while praising the epic for its richly graphic storytelling, described its focus on the relationship between Zhivago (Omar Sharif) and Lara (Julie Christie) as "not enough for the crux of this film," which was "painfully slow going." *Doctor Zhivago* opened to unspectacular box-office receipts as audiences struggled with its heroic story, set against the background of the Russian Revolution, its inordinate length, and its difficult-to-pronounce title. But MGM, which financed the film for producer Carlo Ponti, played a pivotal role in its eventual success. "Today people can't believe it got the most terrible reviews," Lean explained to Stephen M. Silverman in an interview for the *New York Post* (December 12, 1984). "If it wasn't for [MGM president] Bob O'Brien, who put another $1 million into advertising and said: 'David, I'm going to hold on to the picture, I think we've got something good here,' who knows what would have happened?"

Doctor Zhivago's box office built gradually over the early months of 1966 and topped $100 million in its first two years of release. By the 1980s that figure had doubled to $200 million, making it the biggest financial success of Lean's career. As a result, although MGM executives were concerned when the director's next picture, *Ryan's Daughter* (1970), ran over budget, they covered its eventual $13 million cost. Despite negative reviews, mostly concerning its almost four hours of running time for what seemed like a slender story of a pastoral romance between an Irish girl and a British soldier, the movie recouped its production cost and made a profit over the next two years. *Ryan's Daughter* contained elements of the old and new in Lean's output: it was produced by his old Cineguild partner Anthony Havelock-Allan, and it featured John Mills, with whom Lean had not worked since *Hobson's Choice*, in an Oscar-winning supporting role. But *Ryan's Daughter* also included two youthful cast members, Sarah Miles (the wife of the screenwriter, Robert Bolt) and Christopher Jones, in scenes of passionate lovemaking, in keeping with the changing tastes of the era.

The critical hostility with which *Ryan's Daughter* was greeted took its toll, however, and it proved to be Lean's last picture for fourteen years. "After *Ryan's Daughter*," he admitted in *Time* (December 31, 1984) magazine, "I had such terrible notices that I really lost heart." He spent the next decade in search of subjects that were not only acceptable to him but also viable in a movie industry that seemed to be more interested in such gimmicks as killer sharks, flying saucers, special effects, and mindless violence than in plot, characterization, and meticulous attention to detail. In the winter of 1973 he received the Directors Guild of America's D. W. Griffith Award, the organization's highest honor, in a presentation by the legendary director-producer George Stevens. Despite that recognition, it was ten years before Lean got another assignment. His plans in the early 1980s for a revisionist story of the HMS *Bounty* and its famed mutiny, based on a screenplay by Robert Bolt, fell apart amid a long and acrimonious dispute with producer Dino de Laurentiis. And his long-cherished hope of creating a film based on the life of Gandhi was dashed when actor-director Richard Attenborough, who made his screen debut in Lean's *In Which We Serve*, made *Gandhi* (1981).

In 1983, while Lean was considering an offer to direct the film *Out of Africa*, the producers John Brabourne and Richard Goodwin asked him if he would direct a screen adaptation of E. M. Forster's classic novel *A Passage to India*. As it turned out, he had wanted to film the book ever since he saw a stage version by Santha Rama Rau in London in the early 1960s. Lean accepted and picked up his career right where he left off. Released in 1984, *A Passage to India* received rapturous critical notices. With a cast that included Judy Davis, Sir Alec Guinness, and Dame Peggy Ashcroft, the movie cut across generational lines to become a theatrical and home-video hit, and it was nominated for eight Oscars, including Lean's seventh for best director and best picture. It also brought Peggy Ashcroft her first Academy Award in her half-century career. Since Lean himself adapted the screenplay, from Forster's novel and Santha Rama Rau's play, and edited the film, it represented a personal triumph.

In the wake of *A Passage to India*, Sir David Lean was once again regarded as one of the world's top directors. The renewed attention paid to his career included a nationally telecast interview with Dick Cavett, entitled "A Conversation with David Lean," broadcast on the PBS network in March of 1985. The public's fascination with his films also rose phenomenally during the 1980s, largely because of the boom in home video. In 1986 Columbia Pictures and the film archivist Robert A. Harris undertook the restoration of *Lawrence of Arabia*, which had been severely edited in its many reissues, to its original length. Recut and reedited and in a superlative print enhanced by Dolby stereo sound, the restored *Lawrence of Arabia* opened in a first run at New York's mammoth Ziegfeld Theatre in February 1989, where it enjoyed a land-office business. By March 1989 it had opened in twenty-two additional cities. Meanwhile, Lean began work on his latest project, a screen adaptation of Joseph Conrad's novel *Nostromo* financed by European producer Serge Silberman and Warner Brothers, which was tentatively scheduled to begin shooting late in 1989.

David Lean is a tall, slender, distinguished-looking man with white hair and angular features. At eighty-one he is far more fit than his age would indicate, particularly when working on a movie. "He became younger and more dynamic," Maurice Jarre recalled of the director's return to work on *A Passage to India*. He spends much of his time today as a traveler, in hotels and on location, but he keeps a residence that he shares with Sandra Cook, a former art dealer, in a newly fashionable section of London's East End. He has been married four times: to the actress Kay Walsh, who starred in *In Which We Serve*, *This Happy Breed*, and *Oliver Twist*, from 1940 until 1949; to the actress Ann Todd, who starred in *One Woman's Story* and *The Sound Barrier*, from 1949 through 1957; to Leila Matkar, from 1960 until 1978; and to Sandra Hotz, from 1981 through 1985. He has one son, from his first marriage.

References: N Y Post p47+ D 12 '84, p55 Ja 14 '85, p17+ Ja 15 '85, p25 Ja 17 '85; N Y Times Mag p32+ My 23 '65 por; Newsday p25 D 19 '70; Time 126:58+ D 31 '84; Washington Post B p1+ F 3 '89 pors; Silverman, Stephen M. David Lean (1989); Who's Who in America, 1987–88; Who's Who, 1988

Lederman, Leon M(ax)

July 15, 1922– Physicist; educator. Address: c/o Department of Physics, University of Chicago, Chicago, Ill. 60637

In 1988 Leon M. Lederman shared the Nobel Prize in physics for his role in detecting the muon neutrino, a subatomic particle so elusive that it is, as he once wrote, "just barely a fact." The detection of the muon neutrino, in an experiment carried out in collaboration with two colleagues at Columbia University, Melvin Schwartz and Jack Steinberger, ushered in an era of spectacular advances in research in particle physics. Lederman's additional contributions to the cause include the discovery of such key pieces of the subatomic puzzle as the upsilon particle and the "bottom" quark. He has also been a driving force in the creation and perfection of the machines of modern physics, having served as director of Columbia University's Nevis Laboratories from 1960 to 1979 and as director of the Fermi National Accelerator Laboratory, or Fermilab, from 1979 to 1989, during which time its 2 trillion electron volt Tevatron accelerator was completed. Associated with Columbia University as a student and faculty member for more than three decades, Dr. Lederman was the Eugene Higgins Professor of Physics there from 1973 until he assumed the directorship of Fermilab. He is currently a professor of physics at the University of Chicago.

Leon Max Lederman was born in New York City on July 15, 1922, the son of Morris Lederman and Minna (Rosenberg) Lederman, Russian-Jewish immigrants who owned and operated a laundry. Reared in the borough of the Bronx, he "got an excellent education in New York's public schools," as he told one interviewer, but he credits his brother Paul as perhaps the major influence on his early education. "[Paul] was always tinkering with things at home . . . ," Lederman explained to Malcolm W. Browne in an interview for a *Discover* (October 1981) profile, and he "imparted a lifelong fascination for the kind of mechanical relationships that are part of science. Paul never even finished high school, but I count him as one of my best teachers."

Following his high school graduation, Lederman entered City College of New York, where he majored in chemistry. He received his B.S. degree from City College in 1943 and spent the next two years serving as a lieutenant in the United States Army Signal Corps. Discharged from military service at the end of World War II, Lederman decided to take advantage of the GI Bill to continue his education. Having enjoyed his undergraduate physics courses more than his chemistry courses, he enrolled in the graduate physics program at Columbia University. He earned his master's degree there in 1948 and his Ph.D. degree in 1951.

Remaining at the university as a research associate at Nevis Laboratories, the physics department's center for experimental research in high-energy physics, Lederman was, in his words, "handed the finest equipment to do the work I most wanted to do." The "equipment" at Nevis included a particle accelerator capable of boosting particles to energies of several hundred million electron volts. Lederman also had access to the 33 billion electron volt Cosmotron accelerator at Brookhaven National Laboratory on Long Island, where he discovered, in 1956, a new particle—the long-lived, neutral K-meson, which was to play an important role in some aspects of theoretical physics.

The following year Lederman, working with Richard L. Garwin and Marcel Weinrich, performed a key experiment that, together with a previous one conducted by a team of physicists under the direction of C. S. Wu, confirmed the then controversial theory that the principle of "left-right symmetry," or "parity," could be violated in certain physical processes. The possibility that parity could be violated arose after scientists noticed an irregular pattern of disintegration in two otherwise identical unstable particles known as "tau" and "theta": the "tau" particle decayed into three pions while the "theta" decayed into only two. As Robert P. Crease and Charles C. Mann pointed out in their book The Second Creation: Makers of the Revolution in Twentieth-Century Physics (1986), the difference in tau and theta decay "left physicists in a terrible bind." "On the one hand," they wrote, "describing two different particles with almost identical physical properties required a theory so complicated that nothing remotely like it had ever been seen in nature. On the other, asserting that tau and theta were the same thing meant that this particle could blithely decay as it pleased into products of even and odd total parity—in short, that parity was not conserved in its decay."

The theoretical physicists T. D. Lee and C. N. Yang published a paper on the question of parity conservation in weak interactions, in which they asserted that parity was preserved in the process that produced tau and theta but violated in the process by which they decayed. Lee and Yang suggested an experiment to determine whether the so-called weak force responsible for tau and theta and other decay indeed destroyed parity. According to the account in The Second Coming, over a meal at a restaurant near Columbia University on January 4, 1957, Lee, Lederman, Garwin, and "half the Columbia physics faculty" discussed the possibility of using a beam of muon particles, which decay in the grip of the weak force, to test Lee and Yang's theoretical calculations. If the nonconservation of parity was a general feature of weak interactions, the

electrons created when the muons decayed would ignore the lack of directional preference required by parity and "emerge more in one direction than another." A few days later, Lederman's experiment on muon decay at the Nevis synchrocyclotron dramatically established such asymmetry, and on January 8 Lederman telephoned Lee with the news that "parity is dead."

In the wake of the death of parity, theoretical physicists turned their attention to filling in the gaps in their understanding of weak interactions. They were especially puzzled by the peculiarly identical properties of the electron and a particle almost 200 times heavier, the muon, and by the fact that interactions involving either an electron or a muon always also involved a neutrino. A particularly pressing question was whether the neutrino that appeared in electron interactions was the same as the one that appeared in muon interactions. Finding an answer to this question became urgent in the late 1950s, in connection with a certain weak reaction—the decay of a muon into an electron and a photon—that in theory should have occurred but in reality never did. The absence of the reaction, which theoretically should have proceeded via an intermediate step that involved the mutual annihilation of a neutrino and an antineutrino, indicated that it was "damped" by some unknown physical reality. Contributing to the mystery was the fact that, above a certain energy level, theory predicted many more weak interactions than were known to occur. Those presumably were also damped.

"To our experimental group at Columbia," Lederman wrote in an article for Scientific American (March 1963), the puzzle of the missing muon decay reaction "was converted to a crisis by the further point emphasized to us by Lee. . . . Any mechanism that would serve to damp the weak-interaction rate at high energies would stimulate the very reaction that no one had been able to observe." Physicists eventually realized, Lederman went on to explain, that one way to "resolve the paradox" of the muon decay was to assume that the neutrino associated with the muon and that associated with the electron "are of different species." What was needed at this point, he said, was a "decisive experiment" to determine whether the neutrinos were of different species.

In 1960—the year Lederman assumed the directorship of Nevis Laboratories—he and two colleagues, Melvin Schwartz and Jack Steinberger, decided to test the neutrinos that arose with muons to see if they indeed differed from electron neutrinos. Calculating that Brookhaven's powerful new accelerator "might possibly provide high-energy neutrinos in the quantity needed to carry out a search for the second neutrino [the muon neutrino] and to observe the rates of weak interactions at high energies," as Lederman put in his Scientific American piece, the three physicists began their experiment at the Brookhaven National Laboratory in September 1961 and worked on it intermittently until June 1962.

Their experiment involved accelerating a beam of protons to 15 billion electron volts in the Brookhaven accelerator, then smashing the protons head-on into a beryllium barrier. The impact knocked loose beryllium protons and neutrons and created other particles, including pions, out of pure energy. The pions, in accordance with the goal of the experiment, decayed into muon particles and high-energy neutrinos. A steel wall then filtered out the other particles, leaving only a beam of neutrinos, which passed through the shield into a ten-ton "spark chamber," a particle-detecting device that Lederman's group had built to induce and detect neutrino interactions. The interactions between entering neutrinos and aluminum plates in the spark chamber generated electrically charged particles that left detectable trails of sparks in the chamber. When Lederman and his colleagues analyzed the fifty-one "events" thus counted over the course of the eight-month experiment, they discovered that the events had indeed been caused by the anticipated "second neutrino," which left muons as its calling card in the spark chamber. If the muons had been of only one type, Lederman explained in the Scientific American article, they would have produced "equal numbers of electrons and negative muons," but if "there were two kinds of neutrinos, the kind generated in our experiment should be unable to produce electrons and we should observe only muons."

The muon neutrino "fitted neatly" with the parity-destroying data that Lederman had collected in 1957, as Barbara Yuncker pointed out in a profile of the physicist for the New York Post (February 10, 1966). But the discovery had even wider repercussions. In Lederman's words, it "turned out to be extremely useful as a tool in studying and elucidating the properties of [other] particles." According to Malcolm W. Browne, in his assessment of the three physicists' landmark work for the New York Times (October 20, 1988), the muon neutrino "was the first experimental evidence that a different category of matter could exist along with the better-known kind. In time, theorists used this and other evidence to develop the 'standard model' theory" of atomic structure.

A major part of Lederman's scientific research in the 1960s and 1970s centered on the exploration of the inner structure of hadrons, a class of particles that includes protons and pions. The impetus for much of that work came from a theory first put forward in 1964 and since elaborated and established as definitive with the help of Lederman's experiments. In its original version, Lederman recalled in Scientific American (October 1978), the theory held that "the hadrons were all ensembles of only three elementary entities named quarks." The problem with quarks was that they were never seen in isolation because they were confined within particles such as protons by the most powerful of all forces, the "strong force." A quark could only become directly detectable if it were knocked out of the proton. Because of the nature of strong interactions, however, the energy required to blast

quarks loose is so great that it ends up creating new hadrons before it can break open the existing ones.

In a 1965 experiment Lederman and a group of colleagues sought to overcome that obstacle by tapping a kind of free energy source within atomic nuclei—the "Fermi motion" of their protons and neutrons—to knock quarks into the open. Using the 30 billion electron volt (GeV) synchrotron at Brookhaven, Lederman and his associates bombarded a metal target with a beam of high-energy protons. They hoped that the energy of the protons they fired would combine on collision with that of the "Fermi motion" of fast-moving protons and neutrons in the target, and the impact would jar quarks loose. In their analysis of the resulting debris, they found no lone quarks, but they did discover a never-before-detected entity: antideuteron, the antimatter version of deuteron, the nucleus of a deuterium, or heavy hydrogen, atom. It was the first complex antimatter particle ever observed, and it provided evidence that antimatter obeys the strong force just as ordinary matter does.

Continuing his investigation of the structure of matter, in 1967 Lederman and a team at Brookhaven used the facility's accelerator to bombard "uranium nuclei consisting of neutrons and protons, collectively known as nucleons (N)," with "energetic protons (p)." "We wanted," he explained in Scientific American (October 1978), "to know what happened when a pair of oppositely charged leptons (1+ and 1-) emerged, a reaction that can be written $p + N \rightarrow 1- + 1+ + $ anything. 'Anything' means we had no interest in the other particles produced." Lederman and his colleagues treated the lepton pairs they generated as the offspring of an invisible parent—a "virtual photon." By measuring the energy of the lepton pairs and the angle at which they diverged from each other, Lederman's team was able to calculate the vital statistics—the mass, energy, and momentum—of their virtual parents. The creation of these virtual photons in the proton-nucleon collisions in turn provided clues to the hidden structure of protons and nucleons.

In tabulating the mass of the virtual photons, Lederman expected a steady decrease in the number of the particles as their mass increased. Although he and his colleagues anticipated a smooth progression up the mass scale, they hoped to find a "cluster" at a certain mass, indicating, in Lederman's words, that "the lepton pairs emanated not from some virtual entity but from some real particle." As he explained it in his Scientific American article, "On the basis of Werner Heisenberg's uncertainty principle [concerning the velocity and position of particles] we could then estimate the size of whatever material within the colliding nucleons had served as the source of the new particle." He and his colleagues did detect an intriguing cluster in the masses of the virtual particles produced in their experiment, but the Brookhaven apparatus, like a microscope that reaches the limit of its magnifying power, was not powerful enough to give a clear picture of what became known in an excited physics community as the "Lederman shoulder."

In the early 1970s Lederman, hoping to solve the mystery of the "shoulder" and its implications for the "three quark" model of hadron structure, led a team of physicists in conducting an, in his word, "improved" version of the Brookhaven experiment on the more powerful accelerator at Fermilab, in Batavia, Illinois. But before Lederman's new team could begin collecting data, one of his former students, Samuel C. C. Ting, using the new particle detectors at Brookhaven, resolved the issue when he discovered a new particle, which he called the J. (The particle was discovered independently by Stanford University's Burton Richter, who dubbed it the psi.) "Lederman's shoulder" had been a badly smeared picture of the J/psi. The new particle caused what is known by physicists as the "November revolution" because it was found to consist of a brand new, fourth quark—"charm"—bound to its antiparticle.

After the November revolution, Lederman shifted the focus of his investigations from the 3 GeV energy level, at which the J/psi existed, to the unexplored area above 5 GeV. "This time we could monitor the distorting effects of our apparatus by examining how it altered the J/psi resonance, which we could not have done in 1968," Lederman wrote in *Scientific American*. In 1976 a member of Lederman's team, John Yoh, noticed a "small number of events" near 9.5 GeV and optimistically placed a bottle of champagne labled "9.5" in the group refrigerator. A number of technical difficulties, however, stood in the way of confirming or denying the importance of the 9.5 cluster. As Lederman explained it, the problem was that "the events of the greatest interest were also the rarest ones" and were as likely to be tricks of the apparatus as they were to be evidence of new particles to which the lepton pairs—muons—under analysis could be traced.

Lederman and his colleagues fine-tuned their apparatus until, in 1977, they were able to observe an unprecedented number of high-energy muon pairs and thus to obtain increasing evidence for the existence of a cluster near 10 GeV. As data continued to accumulate, Lederman concluded that "the resonance represented something real: a new particle." The particle, with a mass of 9.4 GeV and excited states at 10 GeV and 10.4 GeV, was named the upsilon. Easily the heaviest particle ever detected, it was expected to be short-lived, for it had "an enormous number of lower mass states into which it could decay," with "each state [contributing] to a shorter lifetime."

Since the particle, in fact, had a long lifetime, "the known laws of physics" had to be adjusted to account for its failure to disintegrate into lighter hadrons. Lederman and his fellow physicists finally decided that the upsilon was made from a new fundamental particle—an unexpected, massive fifth quark bound to its antiquark. Since the upsilon did not contain any of the four known quarks, it could not decay into more familiar particles. The new quark was dubbed "bottom" and, in the whimsical tradition of quark nomenclature, its interaction

with its antiquark was called "bottomonium." In the form of the upsilon, the bottom quark presented physicists with "an embarrassment of riches," as Lederman put it, not least of which was a "laboratory" for investigating the "inscrutable" strong force.

In 1979, two years after the discovery of the upsilon, Lederman was named director of the Fermi National Accelerator Laboratory, where the particle had been found. There, he smoothly shifted gears from experimentalist to administrator, lobbyist, recruiter, and fund-raiser. "I'm constantly shuttling to Washington to cajole federal and congressional officials into keeping budget cuts to a minimum," he told an interviewer in 1981. During his tenure at Fermilab, he managed to obtain the funds needed to upgrade the facility's equipment so that its scientists can probe ever more deeply into the secrets of matter.

One of the goals of physicists since Lederman's discovery of the bottom quark has been to detect bottom's expected opposite number, the "top" quark. Part of the drive to make the Fermilab accelerator more powerful has been the race to flush the top quark into the open. Once found and measured, it will allow scientists to complete what they call the "standard model" of the nature of the universe. To that end, the superconducting Tevatron accelerator, which is capable of colliding counterrotating proton–anti-proton beams at an unprecedented energy of 2 trillion electron volts, was constructed at Fermilab. With the machine at full power, Lederman announced to the press in 1988, "we think we will soon have the top quark in the bag." Other Fermilab projects Lederman has guided to completion include a new computing center and a neutron therapy facility, where cancer patients are regularly treated. He was also the force behind the formation of Fermilab's astrophysics group and its industrial affiliates organization, which encourages the transfer of technology from the laboratory to private industry.

At a press conference following the announcement, on October 19, 1988, that he had received the Nobel Prize, Lederman told reporters: "There's something spooky about the Nobel—it has its own special aura because of earlier winners, like Einstein and Enrico Fermi, whom we venerate. . . . But, to me, the most encouraging aspect of an award such as this is that, hopefully, young people will hear about this and be inspired to carry on this most basic type of research." In an effort to combat what he has called the "frightening" level of science illiteracy in the United States, Lederman initiated at Fermilab fifteen educational programs, including a popular Saturday morning physics class, for teachers and high school students. He was also instrumental in the establishment of the Illinois Science and Math Academy, a free public boarding school for gifted youngsters, in Aurora, Illinois. Lederman himself turned down an offer of another five-year term as director of Fermilab to return to teaching, at the University of Chicago, in March 1989. One of his aims is to teach a course on modern physics for non-science majors.

Leon Lederman has a son, Jesse, and two daughters, Rena and Heidi, from his first marriage, to Florence Gordon, a childhood sweetheart whom he wed in 1945. His second wife, Ellen Carr, is a photography instructor. The puckish, gray-haired Lederman has few hobbies, although he recently began taking piano lessons, and he admits to being a driven man. As he explained to Malcolm W. Browne for the *Discover* profile: "Part of being a scientist is compulsive dedication, the insistence on working without rest until you get what you're after. . . . The best discoveries always seem to be made in the small hours of the morning, when most people are asleep, when there are no disturbances and the mind becomes contemplative. You're out in a lonely portacamp [a prefabricated laboratory shack] somewhere, looking at the numbers on reams of paper spewing out of a computer. You look and look, and suddenly you see some numbers that aren't like the rest—a spike in the data. You apply some statistical tests and look for errors, but no matter what you do, the spike's still there. It's real. You've found something. There's just no feeling like it in the world."

References: *Chicago Tribune* p1+ O 20 '88 pors, mag p10+ N 6 '88 pors; *Discover* 2:45+ O '81 pors; *N Y Post* p35 F 10 '66 por; *N Y Times* B p13 O 20 '88 por; *People* 12:48+ Jl 23 '79 pors; *International Who's Who, 1989-90; Who's Who in America, 1988-89*

Lee, Ming Cho

Oct. 3, 1930- Theatrical designer. Address: b. School of Drama, Yale University, 205 Park St., New Haven, Conn. 06520; h. 12 E. 87th St., New York, N.Y. 10128

By general consensus the dean of American set designers, Ming Cho Lee has become over the course of his thirty-year career so influential a force in the theatre that insiders refer to his many followers as the "Ming Cho dynasty." The Chinese-born Lee, who became a naturalized American citizen shortly after immigrating to the United States in 1949, is credited with inventing the spare, sculptural unit set that revolutionized theatrical design in the 1960s. An unusually prolific and extraordinarily ingenious artist, he has designed the sets for more than 200 productions in the United States and abroad, including sixty operas, thirty Shakespearean dramas, and twenty ballets. The awesome, towering wall of stone and ice that he created for the play *K2* earned him a Tony Award for the outstanding scenic design of the 1982-83 Broadway season.

Ming Cho Lee was born in Shanghai, China on October 3, 1930, the only child of Tsufa F. Lee, a Yale graduate who worked as a representative for an international insurance company, and his wife, the former Ing Tang. When Lee was six years old, his parents divorced. The boy remained in the custody of his father and, for many years, saw his mother only on weekends. On those weekend visits, his mother frequently took him to see Western films, operas, and plays. During the Japanese occupation of Shanghai in World War II, the theatre became an even more important outlet for the somewhat withdrawn adolescent. "[The occupation] meant we had no more American movies," Lee recalled in a talk with Richard L. Coe of the *Washington Post* (May 25, 1975), "and, of course, we Chinese didn't patronize Japanese films. . . . That meant much live theatre. All sorts of styles, traditional and contemporary." The flourishing Shanghai opera was a particular favorite of the young boy. To complement her son's cultural education, Mrs. Lee also arranged for him to study ink drawing and landscape painting with the watercolorist Chang Kwo-Nyen.

Following the Communist takeover in 1949, the Lee family fled to the British colony of Hong Kong, where Ming Cho Lee completed his high school education. Lee had intended to continue his studies at the University of Hong Kong, but, because his knowledge of English was limited, he failed the matriculation exam. Instead, acting on the advice of his father, he enrolled at Occidental College in Los Angeles as an art major. "I knew I would have trouble with English and composition," he explained to Faubion Bowers in an interview for an *Opera News* (March 26, 1988) profile, "so I signed up for art to even out my grades. But then

I found out that I was really wrong for the art scene at the time. . . . Being Chinese, I had great difficulty with abstraction. In Chinese painting, there was always a subject. Words, a poem or calligraphy and visual imageries were not mutually exclusive. It was impossible for me to stare at a blank piece of canvas and have the teacher say, 'Just create!' Besides, in my heart I already had decided to go into theatre."

Switching his major to speech, Lee turned his creative energy to designing sets for campus theatrical productions. His first scenic designs were for a student production of Robert McEnroe's whimsical comedy The Silver Whistle, staged at Occidental College in December 1951. After receiving his B.A. degree from Occidental in 1953, he continued his training as a graduate student in theatre arts at the University of California at Los Angeles. While there, he became one of the first students ever to create the sets for a major university production when he was selected as the set designer for The Pearl, a ballet based on the story by John Steinbeck.

Impressed by Lee's student portfolio, Eddie Kook, a respected designer of stage lighting equipment who occasionally lectured at Occidental, recommended the young man to Jo Mielziner, then Broadway's premier scenic designer. Hired as an apprentice in 1954, Lee worked with Mielziner for nearly five years, eventually rising to the post of assistant designer. During that time, he assisted Mielziner in designing the sets for many Broadway productions, including the hits Silk Stockings and Cat on a Hot Tin Roof. Within weeks of his passing the examination for membership in United Scenic Artists, the theatrical craft union, in 1955, Lee designed his first professional show—a revival of the musical comedy Guys and Dolls—for the Grist Mill Playhouse in Andover, New Jersey.

Lee made his New York debut three years later, as the set and lighting designer for Herbert Berghof's staging of The Infernal Machine, Jean Cocteau's retelling of the Oedipus legend. The production, which opened at the Phoenix Theatre on February 3, 1958, received only lukewarm reviews, but Lee was singled out by several critics for having created a striking stage set that seemed "to echo the play's moral decay." Later in the same year, he designed the American costumes for the Metropolitan Opera's production of Madama Butterfly and the sets for several Off-Broadway shows, including a highly praised revival of Arthur Miller's Crucible.

After leaving Mielziner's studio in 1958, Lee worked briefly for the set designers George Jenkins, Rouben Ter-Arutunian, and Boris Aronson before striking out on his own. During his first few years as a freelancer, he spent most of his time designing sets for opera productions at the Peabody Institute of Music in Baltimore, Maryland, where his credits included The Turk in Italy, The Old Maid and the Thief, Werther, Amahl and the Night Visitors, and The Pearl Fishers, in which he first used vertical poles and pipe constructions to define space. Lee also designed several operas for New York's Empire State Music Festival, most notably the first full-scale American staging of Janáček's Katya Kabanova, the Baltimore Opera Company, and the Opera Company of Boston, for whom he devised an economical touring production—"all bamboo, no cherry trees," as he put it—of Madama Butterfly.

In 1961 Lee was named art director and designer in residence of the San Francisco Opera. He remained in the post for only one season, but his sets, which often warranted special mention from the critics, remained in use for many years. Reviewers were particularly taken by his designs for the company's new production of Lucia di Lammermoor. Working in collaboration with Leni Bauer-Ecsy, he created for Lucia a "strangely overpowering series of sets" that, in Alan Rich's view, "revitalized the opera beyond all expectation." Largely because of the expressionistic sets, "a great pall of gloom and menace hung over the whole work . . . ," Rich wrote in his New York Times (September 17, 1961) review. "This listener suddenly found himself aware of the work as a dramatic conception, and for this [the designers] deserve considerable praise."

Returning to New York City, Lee began, in 1962, what was to become an eleven-year association with the New York Shakespeare Festival's annual, free summer presentations at the Delacorte Theatre, an outdoor amphitheatre in Central Park that had been specifically designed for Shakespearean productions. For the Delacorte's inaugural production—The Merchant of Venice—in June 1962, he designed an airy, open set that took advantage of the theatre's natural environment as well as its sweeping thrust stage. In devising his set, Lee also had to consider the needs of The Tempest and King Lear, which were to follow The Merchant of Venice in the New York Shakespeare Festival's summer repertory program, and come up with a "visual statement," as he put it, appropriate to all three plays. His solution was a multilevel unit set of ramps and platforms that could easily be transformed into a flexible multiscene arrangement by adding portable elements. In The Merchant of Venice, for instance, Lee used freestanding tapestry panels to suggest the sumptuous interior of Portia's house.

Over the next ten years, Lee mounted more than a score of Shakespeare's plays for the New York Shakespeare Festival's annual summer seasons in Central Park. Because of the Festival's chronic budget problems, he came to rely heavily on adaptable unit sets, usually constructed of pipe scaffolding and raw-wood planks. His distinctive, minimalist approach to design, born of necessity, was eventually adopted by dozens of other designers, giving rise to a new, almost sculptural style of American set design in the late 1960s. The massive, simulated stone portals he created for the Festival's production of Sophocles' Electra, in the summer of 1964, earned him the Joseph Maharam Award for outstanding theatrical design. He won the Maharam Award again four years later for his fantastical, three-story setting for Jakov Lind's absurdist comedy *Ergo*, which the Festival mounted at its newly opened Public Theater in March 1968. He also designed the sets for many of the company's Off-Broadway productions, including the innovative pop-rock musical *Hair* and *Invitation to a Beheading*, the stage adaptation of Vladimir Nabokov's Kafkaesque novel, for which he received a Drama Desk Award, and for its Off-Broadway stagings of Ntozake Shange's long-running "choreopoem" *For Colored Girls Who Have Considered Suicide/When the Rainbow is Enuf*.

During his tenure as principal designer for the New York Shakespeare Festival, Lee drew up the plans for an Elizabethan-style, multilevel mobile stage that could be set up and struck in just a few hours, so that the company could take its open-air productions to parks and playgrounds throughout the five boroughs of New York City. He also redesigned the Delacorte Theatre, changing its basic shape from a fan to a horseshoe to bring the audience closer to the action, improve the sound quality, and allow more fluid staging. His other theatre-design credits include the Florence Sutro Anspacher Theatre, which has a thrust stage, and the 300-seat Estelle R. Newman Theatre, a more traditional, proscenium playhouse, in the New York Shakespeare Festival's Public Theater complex, and the Garage Theatre at the Harlem School of the Arts. Lee also served as a design consultant for the Performing Arts Center at the State University of New York at Purchase, for the acoustical shell and proscenium arch at the Cincinnati (Ohio) Music Hall, and for the Patricia Corbett Pavilion at the University of Cincinnati's School of Music.

While he was working for the New York Shakespeare Festival, Lee simultaneously served as principal designer for the Juilliard Opera Theatre and the American Opera Center of the Juilliard School of Music. In that post he created the sets for productions of *Gianni Schicchi*, *The Magic Flute*, *The Trial of Lucullus*, *The Rake's Progress*, and a number of other works. In addition, he began receiving commissions from such prestigious companies as the Metropolitan Opera and the New York City Opera. Drawing on his experience with the New York Shakespeare Festival, he designed, in 1965, a sturdy and efficient unit set for the Metropolitan Opera National Company's touring production of *Madama Butterfly* that was as remarkable for its taste and authenticity as for its economy.

The following year Lee was commissioned to design the sets for the North American premiere of Alberto Ginastera's *Don Rodrigo*, during the New York City Opera's first season in the New York State Theater at Lincoln Center. Admittedly somewhat daunted by the theatre's imposing size ("You just cannot design a minimal production there," he told one interviewer), Lee nevertheless managed to come up with "economical yet telling" sets, in the words of one critic, that virtually changed the direction of American operatic set design. Taking his cue from Ginastera's avant-garde score, he suspended sculptural pieces on gold pipes on either side of a central platform and used sections of white stone wall, against a gold mosaic backdrop, for certain scenes. As Faubion Bowers observed in the *Opera News* profile, "Singers were no longer acting in front of two-dimensional, nineteenth-century painted scenery; instead they were contained within a theatrical, sculptural environment, a locale within a framework." A critical and popular success, *Don Rodrigo* set the style for future New York City Opera productions and, eventually, for the productions of opera companies across the country.

Over the next two decades, Lee designed more than a dozen works for the New York City Opera, including the rarely performed modern opera *Susannah*, the New York premiere of Ginastera's *Bomarzo*, and the complete Donizetti Tudor trilogy. He won special commendation for giving "the look and feel of Handel's day," as one critic put it, to the company's faithful staging, in eighteenth-century style, of the composer's large-scale baroque operas *Giulio Cesare* and *Ariodante*. Frank Gannon, who reviewed *Ariodante* for the *Wall Street Journal* (September 17, 1971), was especially taken by Lee's "exquisitely conceived and realized" settings, particularly the "misty Fragonard ruins in his final triumphal painted ceiling."

As he has explained in several interviews, Lee often finds the key to the inner spirit of a play or opera in period designs, paintings, or other works of art. For example, Russian religious art inspired his conception of a basic unit structure, comprising countless brooding icons, for *Boris Godunov*, with which he made his Metropolitan Opera debut in 1974. Some critics, most notably Alan Rich, who reviewed the production for the *New York Times* (January 13, 1975), complained that Lee's semi-realistic sets were "cluttered beyond belief or good sense . . . with what looks like the plunder of every museum from Leningrad to Vladivostok." Most of them, however, agreed with David Sterritt of the *Christian Science Monitor* (December 23, 1974) that Lee's sets, "as breathtakingly lush as any in memory," both complemented and defined the opera's plot "with appropriate touches of sheer beauty and Slavic soulfulness."

Lee has since designed the Metropolitan Opera's productions of *I Puritani* and *Lohengrin*, in 1976, and, more recently, its stark, hard-edged *Khovanshchina*, in 1985, for which he created a monumental, onion-domed St. Basil's Cathedral and, for the spectacular immolation scene in the last act, a two-tiered wooden hermitage. Among his other opera credits are productions for the Opera Society of Washington, the Dallas Opera, the Hamburg Staatsoper, and the Teatro Colón in Buenos Aires. Lee has also designed the scenery for many ballets, most notably *The Witch of Endor*, for the Martha Graham Company; *The Lady of the House of Sleep*, for the Alvin Ailey Dance Theatre; the introspective *Night Wings* and the all-male *Olympics*, for the Joffrey Ballet; *Whispers of Darkness*, for the National Ballet of Canada; and, for the Royal Winnipeg Ballet, *Inquest of the Sun*.

By his own admission, Lee "can't resist" designing ballets. "Dance demands the purest kind of designing because you're dealing with the abstract essence of a dramatic statement, which I express either in sculpture or painting," he explained, as quoted in the *New York Times* (March 23, 1975). "There are no hours of dealing with props or cigarettes or where the ice box should go, as you must with a play. Next to dance, I enjoy designing opera and Shakespeare, which also take design away from the literal situation. I'm very bad on props. I don't like shopping around for them. That's why my Broadway career has never been very strong."

Lee's Broadway career began inauspiciously with the ill-fated *Moon Besieged,* a play about the American abolitionist John Brown that closed on December 5, 1962 after only one performance. Over the next eight years, he designed ten Broadway (or Broadway-bound) shows. None was a hit, four closed after one performance, and one folded during out-of-town tryouts. Lee himself, however, invariably received good notices. For many critics, among them Clive Barnes, Lee's atmospheric sets were "the most distinctive aspect" of *Here's Where I Belong,* a musical version of John Steinbeck's novel *East of Eden.* But as Barnes pointed out in his *New York Times* (March 4, 1968) review of the short-lived production, "No one ever walked out of a theatre humming the scenery."

Barnes continued to sing Lee's praises in his appraisals of the musicals *La Strada* and *Billy,* both of which closed in one night. Virtually every New York reviewer joined him in applauding Lee's stunningly realized shipboard setting for *Billy,* which was based on Herman Melville's novel *Billy Budd.* "The success of the occasion," Brendan Gill wrote in his otherwise scathing review for the *New Yorker* (March 2, 1969), "was the sets, by Ming Cho Lee—the deck, fo'c'sle, and captain's quarters of an eighteenth-century man-of-war, with a great mast and its accompanying cat's cradle of ratlines leaping heavenward, and, during a battle scene, authentic-looking cannon firing away at an invisible enemy."

Of the handful of Broadway shows Lee designed in the 1970s and early 1980s, only *The Shadow Box,* Michael Cristofer's Pulitzer Prize-winning play about three terminally ill patients spending their final days at a secluded hospice, was a certified hit. For *The Shadow Box* he devised an ingenious and attractive multipurpose set—a bungalow, flanked by trees, whose realistically appointed kitchen, living room, and porch could represent either a single dwelling or three separate cottages. As more than one critic has pointed out, Lee's style has evolved over the years from the minimalist designs he favored in the 1960s to his more naturalistic settings of the 1980s. The growing tendency toward realism was perhaps most evident in his scenic design for *K2,* Patrick Meyers's compelling drama about two mountain climbers, one of them seriously injured, marooned on an icy ledge near the summit of the world's second-highest mountain.

Following his customary practice, Lee began work on *K2* by making preliminary sketches and several scale models of the ice-encrusted cliff. He constructed the actual set—so massive that it filled the stage of the Brooks Atkinson Theatre and soared out of sight above the proscenium arch—by mounting sections of Styrofoam onto a plywood framework. To give his construction a translucent, slippery-looking surface, he stretched sheets of white tissue paper, painted with acrylic, over the Styrofoam base. Because of the fragile nature of the materials used in the set and the rough treatment it received (the script calls for one character to scale the cliff face repeatedly), the mountain was painstakingly repaired after every performance by the stage crew.

"When the curtain rises on this forbidding, sculptured face in the first glow of morning," Douglas Watt reported in his opening night review for the New York *Daily News* (March 31, 1983), "it is as if the play's star had just stepped out from the wings." Watt's colleagues agreed, most of them devoting as much—or more—attention to the set as to the play. As the *New York Times*'s Frank Rich observed, Lee's mountain was "so overpowering that the play itself may be a third through before you even begin to start listening to the two characters." Such reaction deeply disturbed Lee, who replied, as quoted in *Newsweek* (April 11, 1983): "I don't want my set to overpower this play, which has a lot of deeply felt things to say. I don't go to the theatre for sets. I want a human and emotional experience along with the visual." In addition to the Tony, *K2* earned Lee the Outer Critics Circle Award, the Drama Desk Award, and his third Joseph Maharam Award.

Long troubled by the "profit orientation" of American commercial theatre, which, in his view, stifles creativity and experimentation, Lee often accepts commissions from nonprofit regional theatres and small, experimental companies because they are more likely to stage new or controversial works. His most recent credits include *The Dog Lady* and *The Cuban Swimmer,* a twin bill at the Intar Hispanic American Theater in New York City, a revised version of Marsha Norman's *Traveler in the Dark,* at the Mark Taper Forum in Los Angeles, and Pam Gems's *Camille,* at the Long Wharf Theater in New Haven, Connecticut.

A member of the faculty at the Yale University School of Drama since 1969, Lee currently teaches scenic design three days a week and serves as cochairman of the drama department. He also acts as the design adviser to the Yale Repertory Theatre and supervises the creation and construction of the sets for all student theatrical productions. Increasingly alarmed by what he sees as the decline in quality of the students in the school's drama program over the years, Lee recently applied for a Guggenheim Fellowship to investigate the state of pre-professional training in the arts in the United States. "If young people shy away from the arts," he told Faubion Bowers, "the country will disappear in terms of its essence."

An affable man known for his infectious enthusiasm, Ming Cho Lee stands five feet nine and one-half inches tall and has graying black hair. In his rare leisure time, he attends the opera—his "special passion"—or listens to opera recordings. Lee shares a cluttered Upper East Side apartment, which doubles as his studio, with his wife, the former Elizabeth Rapport, whom he married on March 21, 1958. They have three sons: Richard, a composer and the librarian for the New York Chamber Symphony; Christopher, a carpenter for the Metropolitan Opera; and David, an independent filmmaker. Lee's long list of awards includes the Mayor's Award of Honor for Arts and Culture from the City of New York, the Arena Stage Company's Peter Zeisler Award, and a Qingyum, or "Blue Cloud," from the China Institute of America for "his total work in drama, dance, and opera."

References: N Y Post p29 Ja 27 '75 por; N Y Times II p19+ S 24 '67; Newsweek 71:105 Ap 22 '68 por; Opera N 52:14+ Mr 26 '88 por; Biographical Encyclopedia & Who's Who of the American Theatre (1966); Contemporary Designers (1984); Contemporary Theatre, Film, and Television (1986); Notable Names in American Theatre (1976); Who's Who in America, 1988–89; Who's Who in Opera (1976)

Lee, Spike

Mar. 20, 1957– Filmmaker; actor. Address: Forty Acres and a Mule Filmworks, 124 De Kalb Ave., Brooklyn, N.Y. 11217

Thanks to the overwhelming success of his independent debut film, *She's Gotta Have It*, and the popularity of his next two movies, *School Daze* and *Do the Right Thing*, Brooklyn's Spike Lee has emerged as the first notable black filmmaker to appear on the American scene in many years. A graduate of Morehouse College and New York University's film school, Lee has won acclaim for his accurate and unstereotyped depictions of the black middle class. Believing that he has a mission "to put the vast richness of black culture on film," Spike Lee has criticized attempts by white directors (most notably, Steven Spielberg in his *Color Purple*) to portray black life, since he contends that only black directors are capable of accurately depicting the black experience. "Movies are the most powerful medium in the world and we just can't sit back and let other people define our existence, especially when they're putting lies out there on the screen," he told Rita Kempley during an interview for the *Washington Post* (October 22, 1986). In spite of Hollywood's traditional skepticism about the commercial viability of black films, except for the "blaxsploitation" genre, Lee's work has generated approval from many movie industry insiders, among them David Picker, the former president of Columbia Pictures, who has called Lee "one of the most original young filmmakers in the world."

Spike Lee was born Shelton Jackson Lee on March 20, 1957 in Atlanta, Georgia, the oldest of the five children of Bill Lee, an acclaimed jazz bassist and composer, and Jacquelyn (Shelton) Lee, a teacher of art and black literature. He has three brothers and one sister. His mother, who died in 1977, nicknamed him "Spike" while he was still a toddler, and the sobriquet stuck. "I guess she thought I was a tough baby," Lee explained to Benilde Little of *People* (October 13, 1986) magazine. Lee's great-grandfather, William James Edwards, who graduated from the Tuskegee Institute in Tuskegee, Alabama, was an author and educator and a disciple of Booker T. Washington. The filmmaker's father and grandfather both obtained degrees from Morehouse College in Atlanta, and his mother and grandmother attended Morehouse's sister school, Spelman College. Following Spike's birth, the Lee family moved to Chicago, where they lived briefly before migrating, in 1959, to New York City and settling in the predominantly black Fort Greene section of Brooklyn. After achieving prominence as a jazz bassist in the early 1960s, Bill Lee saw his career take a downturn because he found it difficult to adapt to the increasingly popular electric bass. As a result, throughout most of Spike Lee's childhood, the family lived mainly on the money his mother earned from her teaching position at St. Anne's High School in the Brooklyn Heights section of Brooklyn.

Although he remembers having had an early interest in the movies, Spike Lee, as he explained to Nelson George during an interview conducted for a journal that he kept during the production of the film *She's Gotta Have It*, was "not the classic case where [he] saw one film and decided right then that [he] wanted to be a filmmaker." Rather, movies were just one part of a rich cultural upbringing that also included trips to plays, galleries, and museums in the company of his mother. His father, meanwhile, sometimes brought Spike along to his performances at the Blue Note and other Manhattan jazz clubs. Lee took guitar and piano lessons as a child, but unlike his brothers, David, Cinque, and Chris, and his sister, Joie, he never mastered a musical instrument. After graduating from John Dewey High School in Brooklyn, a progressive school with a more flexible curriculum than other New York secondary schools, in 1975, Lee, like his father and grandfather before him, decided to attend Morehouse College.

Lee's years at Morehouse had a profound and lasting influence upon him, which, years later, he would try to express in his film *School Daze*. In attempting to describe the effect that Morehouse, an institution with a largely black student body and faculty, had on him, he explained in the interview with Nelson George that it was "like Richard Pryor talked about in his concert film of his experience going to Africa, and the wonderful feeling he had being in a place where everybody is black. . . . Black professors, black doctors; it's a great experience in Atlanta." Majoring in mass communications, Lee immersed himself in such extracurricular activities as writing for the school newspaper, working as a disc jockey at a local jazz radio station, and, in his senior year, directing Morehouse's lavish coronation pageant on homecoming weekend. It was also while attending Morehouse that Lee first took an interest in making films. In his sophomore year, he started, in his words, "to dib and dab in super-8 filmmaking," and in the summer between his sophomore and junior years, he bought his first super-8 camera. Among the products of Lee's first cinematic experiments were *Black College: The Talented Tenth*, for which he wrote the script and which he described to Nelson George as "a corny love story at a black campus," and *Last Hustle in Brooklyn*, a film that juxtaposed footage of the 1977 New York City blackout with images of disco dancers.

After graduating from Morehouse in 1979, Lee obtained a summer internship at the Columbia Pictures studio in Burbank, California. He returned to New York that fall to begin work toward a master's degree in filmmaking at New York University's prestigious Institute of Film and Television, Tisch School of the Arts. He chose NYU, he later explained, partly because he simply "wanted to come home" but also because he believed the friends and connections he had made in his hometown would prove invaluable when he began making professional films. Lee's first year at NYU turned out to be a troubled one. One of only a handful of

blacks in the film school, he became the center of a controversy after submitting a ten-minute film entitled *The Answer*, which told the story of a young black screenwriter assigned to do a remake of D. W. Griffith's silent film classic *The Birth of a Nation*. A pointed critique of the racism displayed in Griffith's film, *The Answer* was not warmly received by Lee's instructors. Although the official pronouncement from the faculty was that he had not yet mastered "film grammar," Lee suspected that the dissatisfaction stemmed from his less than respectful treatment of the "father of cinema." Narrowly avoiding dismissal from the film school, Lee, in his second year of study, was awarded a teaching assistantship, under the terms of which he received full tuition in exchange for working in the school's equipment room. The position was of enormous benefit to the young filmmaker, since it enabled him to transfer the tuition money given him by his grandmother, Zimmie Shelton, to the production of films. Lee's second year at NYU marked the beginning of his long and fruitful collaboration with the cinematographer Ernest Dickerson, another black film student at the school. It was Dickerson who photographed Lee's second-year film, *Sarah*, the story of a Harlem family on Thanksgiving day.

In their final year at NYU, Dickerson and Lee collaborated on Lee's master's thesis film project, *Joe's Bed-Stuy Barbershop: We Cut Heads*. Produced, written, and directed by Spike Lee, filmed by Ernest Dickerson, and featuring an original jazz score by Bill Lee, *Joe's Bed-Stuy Barbershop* brought Lee his first serious artistic recognition. The hourlong color film offers a realistic, wryly humorous look at ghetto life in relating the story of a barber in Brooklyn's Bedford-Stuyvesant neighborhood whose shop serves as a front for the neighborhood numbers racket. *Joe's Bed-Stuy Barbershop* received a student Academy Award from the Academy of Motion Picture Arts and Sciences, became the first student production to be selected for Lincoln Center's prestigious "New Directors/New Films" series, and was aired to general critical acclaim on public television's *Independent Focus* series. It went on to be shown at film festivals in San Francisco, Los Angeles, Atlanta, and Locarno, Switzerland. "Eschewing the sex and violence clichés of blaxploitation gangster films," a critic for *Variety* (March 30, 1983) wrote, "Lee delivers a friendly portrait of black folkways." The predominantly favorable review went on to cite the film's "convincing street language and wit."

New York University awarded Lee a master's degree in filmmaking in 1982, and, because of the success of *Joe's Bed-Stuy Barbershop*, he was signed by the ICM and William Morris talent agencies. The young filmmaker expressed disappointment but not surprise when those firms failed to come up with any offers of employment, a development that, as he explained to Larry Rohter for the *New York Times* (August 10, 1986), "cemented in my mind what I always thought all along: that I would have to go out and do it alone, not rely on anyone else." While supporting himself on the $200-a-week salary he earned for cleaning and shipping film at a movie distribution house, Lee began a determined effort to produce his own films.

His first attempt at independent filmmaking was to be a film entitled "Messenger," a drama about a New York City bike messenger. It was in preproduction for eight weeks in the summer of 1984 before a dispute between Lee and the Screen Actors Guild killed the project because the union felt that Lee's script was "too commercial" to qualify for a waiver that would allow nonunion actors to appear in it. Such waivers are often granted to low-budget, independent films, and Lee believed that the Screen Actors Guild's refusal to award him one was "a definite case of racism." After assembling a cast and crew and spending some $40,000 on "Messenger," Lee was left with four days in which to recast the film with union actors, but his efforts failed, and the project had to be terminated. Undaunted, he immediately began working on the script of his next film.

Following the fiasco of "Messenger," Lee's new priority became, as he put it, "to come up with a script that could be done for as little money as possible, yet still be commercial." "I needed to do a movie that would have very few characters, and needed next to no location work, sets, or costumes," he explained during an interview with Simon Banner of the London Sunday Times (March 8, 1987). The script Lee wrote to fill that seemingly impossible bill was entitled She's Gotta Have It. Shot in twelve days in the summer of 1985, mostly in a small Brooklyn apartment and in nearby Washington Park, the film was produced on a miniscule budget (by Hollywood standards) of $175,000. She's Gotta Have It is a comedy about a young, attractive, and independent-minded black woman who simultaneously juggles three lovers with widely divergent personalities.

Although Lee had always been intrigued by the double standard that winks at promiscuity for men while condemning similar behavior by women, his primary motive for producing the film was to fill what he believes to be a vacuum in contemporary American cinema. "When was the last time you saw a black couple make love on the screen or kiss?" he asked Rita Kempley. "We wanted to . . . make an intelligent film that showed black people loving each other and black people falling out of love," he further explained to Nelson George. Lee's fierce determination to express that vision was evidenced by the obstacles he overcame during the production of She's Gotta Have It. When the American Film Institute refused to allow him to transfer the $20,000 grant they had awarded him for the production of "Messenger" to She's Gotta Have It, Lee was left to begin filming with only an $18,000 grant from the New York State Council on the Arts, so that he was forced to finance the film while it was in production. Following each day's shooting, Lee and the film's production supervisor, Monty Ross, contacted as many of their acquaintances as possible, asking them to send any money

they could spare. "We . . . never knew where the next nickel was going to come from," Lee told Simon Banner, "so we wrote to or called everybody we knew in the world, asking them to send money, even if it was just fifty dollars. Each day while we were shooting, someone would go back to my house to see if any checks had come and then rush them to the bank, and we'd just hope they'd clear in time." At one point, the film processing laboratory threatened to auction off the negative for She's Gotta Have It unless Lee could come up with the $2,000 he owed by five o'clock that afternoon. Lee contacted a friend, who agreed to pay the entire amount.

Spike Lee's zeal did not go unrewarded. She's Gotta Have It was a phenomenal success, becoming the first movie by an independent black filmmaker to receive major international distribution since Melvin Van Peebles's Sweet Sweetback's Baadasss Song in 1971. The film opened to a standing ovation at the San Francisco Film Festival, a demonstration that caused several film companies to compete for distribution rights, with Island Pictures eventually winning out. She's Gotta Have It next went to the Cannes Film Festival, where it was awarded the prize for best new film.

Officially opening in the United States on August 8, 1986 at New York's Cinema Studio, the film received largely favorable notices. In his review for the New York Times (August 8, 1986), D. J. R. Bruckner criticized She's Gotta Have It for being "technically messy" but conceded that it possessed "a touch of the classic." David Edelstein of the Village Voice (August 12, 1986) hailed it as "an almost unprecedented work—an all-black comedy of manners" and concluded his review with the simple prediction: "Attention will be paid." Among the most applauded aspects of the movie was, surprisingly, Lee's acting, so much so that, although he had no previous acting experience, his portrayal of the rapping, streetwise Mars Blackmon, one of the leading character's three suitors, led several critics to accuse him of stealing his own show. Reviewers also lauded Bill Lee's jazz score, Ernest Dickerson's cinematography, and a brief appearance by Spike's sister, Joie, as the former roommate of the main character.

She's Gotta Have It ultimately grossed over $7 million, including $1.8 million in its first three weeks, but the film's success did not surprise Lee, who had sensed that it would be a hit. "The whole point is that you can take an unknown, all-black cast and put them in a story that comes from a black experience, and all kinds of people will come to see it if it's a good film," he told Nina Darnton of the New York Times (November 14, 1986). "I wish Hollywood would get that message."

The popularity of She's Gotta Have It prompted Island Pictures to budget $4 million for Lee's next picture, School Daze, a musical set at a fictional black college in the South and based on the director's own experiences at Morehouse. In January 1987, however, after School Daze was well into preproduction, Island, fearful that the film would go over budget, backed out of the project. Lee began calling other studios immediately and within two days worked out a $6 million deal with Columbia Pictures. Lee, who had written the screenplay for *School Daze* under the title "Homecoming" shortly after graduating from film school, predicted before the film's release that it would generate controversy because of its depiction of the seldom-discussed conflict between light-skinned and dark-skinned blacks. "What I tried to do with this film is point out what I feel are all the superficial and petty differences that keep black people apart," Lee told John Minson of the *Guardian* (July 21, 1988). "These differences I feel are based on color, skin complexion, class. I think black people are the most un-unified people on earth—particularly black Americans." His alma mater, Morehouse College, where Lee had elected to film *School Daze*, asked him to leave after three weeks of shooting. "They said the film was a negative portrayal of black colleges and black people," Lee told Don Palmer of *Newsday* (September 23, 1987). "They gave me an ultimatum: Unless I let them read the script, they would not let us shoot on their campus. So we left." He completed filming *School Daze* at the graduate school of nearby Atlanta University. After the movie was completed, the United Negro College Fund, also in response to its controversial subject matter, canceled plans for a benefit premiere.

While many reviewers cheered *School Daze* for its fresh portrayal of the black college experience, others criticized the movie for what they perceived as its underdeveloped themes and took Lee to task for overambitiously attempting to stage a musical despite his lack of experience with that genre. In her review for the *New York Times* (February 28, 1988), Janet Maslin noted that the film's "satirical tone seems to come and go" and further complained that *School Daze* "includes lengthy, elaborate musical numbers that are well beyond the range of Mr. Lee's technical abilities." Writing in the *Village Voice* (March 22, 1988), Vernon Reid noted that "*School Daze* captures the rhythm, language, and spark of young black adulthood," but he added that, "as social commentary, the results are mixed." In spite of the controversy and the mixed reviews, Lee, who also had a small part in the movie, playing an eager fraternity pledge named "Half-Pint," staunchly defended *School Daze*. He told Rick Kogan of the *Chicago Tribune* (February 25, 1988): "I love this film. It's much better than *She's Gotta Have It*. The film *is* my four years at Morehouse. But I'm not trying to pick on black colleges. I used black colleges as a microcosm of black society." And he explained to an interviewer for *Ebony* (February 1988): "This film is about *our* existence, about being black in white America, and to me there is nothing more important than that."

A popular success, *School Daze* reached *Variety's* weekly list of the top ten money-making films in March 1988. The movie's climactic dance scene also spawned a new dance craze, "da butt," which became a vogue in black dance clubs. The song that accompanied the dance scene, also called "Da Butt," was a hit record, reaching number one on *Billboard* magazine's "Hot Black Singles" chart.

Spike Lee decided to switch film companies after *School Daze*, feeling that Columbia had failed to promote that film adequately and trying to avoid a personality conflict with the studio's new president, Dawn Steel. He took the script for his next film, *Do the Right Thing*, to Paramount Pictures, which agreed to finance the project at a cost of $6.5 million, but, when Paramount executives informed Lee that they would not release it unless he changed its controversial ending, he switched film companies again, this time taking *Do the Right Thing* to Universal Pictures, which released it in June 1989.

Do the Right Thing is a comedy-drama that deals with tensions between blacks and Italian-Americans during one swelteringly hot summer day in New York City. Lee produced, wrote, directed, and performed in *Do the Right Thing*, as Mookie, a pizza delivery man at an Italian-American pizzeria located in the predominantly black and Hispanic Bedford-Stuyvesant section of Brooklyn. The film became controversial principally because of its explosive climax, in which angry blacks burn the pizzeria to the ground after a white police officer kills a black youth.

Spike Lee developed the idea for the film after reading news accounts of an incident that occurred in the Howard Beach section of Queens, New York in 1986, in which a black man was killed by a car while fleeing a group of whites carrying baseball bats. The most talked about movie at the Cannes Film Festival, in May 1989, *Do the Right Thing* eventually became the subject of countless newspaper and magazine articles and television talk shows. (The *Village Voice* featured eight stories on the film in one of its issues, and *Newsweek* ran two reviews, one pro and one con.) Although critics charged that Lee was irresponsibly suggesting that blacks should resort to violence as a means of correcting injustices, Lee disputed that contention. "It wasn't made to incite riots but to provoke discussion about racism, something people do not want to talk about," he told one interviewer.

In his review of *Do the Right Thing* for the *New York Times* (June 30, 1989), Vincent Canby observed: "In all of the earnest, solemn, humorless discussions about the social and political implications of [the film], an essential fact tends to be overlooked: it is one terrific movie."

Because he likes to keep busy between major films, Spike Lee has accepted work on a variety of short projects, including directing music videos for such artists as Anita Baker, Miles Davis, and Branford Marsalis. One of his short films, featuring Marsalis and the actress Diahanne Abbott as a struggling couple with a young child, was broadcast on NBC's *Saturday Night Live* program in December 1986. In April 1988 Lee produced and directed a thirty-second television commercial on behalf of the presidential campaign of the Reverend Jesse Jackson. Filmed in Harlem and in subur-

LeMOND

ban Tarrytown, New York, the spot focused on Jackson's antidrug crusade.

The bespectacled Spike Lee stands five feet, six inches tall, weighs 125 pounds, and sports a mustache and a short beard. Observers frequently note Lee's fierce determination, unshakable self-confidence, and unflagging energy. A rabid sports fan, he is an especially ardent follower of the New York Knickerbockers basketball team and has said that one of the chief benefits of his success has been the opportunity to meet star athletes and get choice seats at major sports events. True to his middle-class roots, Spike Lee is determined not to let fame and fortune alter his lifestyle. He continues to live in a sparsely furnished apartment in the Fort Greene section of Brooklyn, and his production company, Forty Acres and a Mule Filmworks, operates out of a converted firehouse in the same borough. Lee owns neither a car nor a driver's license, relying instead on his bike and the New York City subways for his transportation needs. The film-maker has appeared with basketball star Michael Jordan in ads for Nike basketball shoes, portraying his Mars Blackmon character from *She's Gotta Have It*. Summing up his philosophy, Lee told Fred Brathwaite for *Interview* (March 1987), "I'm doing this because I want to make films and love film-making, and it's not to have ten million women dangling on my arm . . . or to make tons of money. That's really not the primary goal." In April 1989 Spike Lee announced the establishment of an annual fellowship for minority film students studying at NYU's Tisch School of the Arts.

References: Ebony 42:42+ Ja '87 pors; Film Comment 22:46+ S–O '86 pors; Guardian p23 Jl 21 '88 por; N Y Daily News mag p17+ Ag 10 '86 pors; N Y Times Mag p26+ Ag 9 '87 pors; People 26:67+ 0 13 '86 pors; Washington Post C p1+ 0 22 '86 pors

LeMond, Greg

June 26, 1961– Cyclist. Address: c/o LeMond Enterprises, 235 Hillcrest, Reno, Nev. 89509

In the summer of 1989 Greg LeMond rode to a dramatic eight-second victory in the world's most difficult and glamorous bicycle race, the Tour de France. In so doing he overcame far more than the 2,000-mile course and his 197 opponents. The victory capped his comeback from a baroque series of mishaps, illnesses, and injuries—including a broken wrist, an appendectomy, and shotgun wounds that left him near death. His slow return to form after his misfortunes, which began in 1987, had led many observers to conclude that he was finished as a cyclist, but their doubts just gave him "more incentive to prove them wrong," he told one interviewer. As LeMond battled for the lead in the 1989 Tour de France, a rival team's manager declared that the American cyclist was "incredible" for having come back to "a level 99 percent of these guys never reach." LeMond first arrived indisputably at that level in 1986, when he survived a "fratricidal" war with his mentor and teammate, the French cycling idol Bernard Hinault, to become the first American ever to win the Tour de France.

Gregory James LeMond was born in Los Angeles, California on June 26, 1961, one of the three children of Bertha and Robert LeMond. When he was seven years old, he moved with his family to Lake Tahoe, California, then, two years later, to Washoe County, in northwestern Nevada, where his father started a real-estate business. LeMond began cycling during the summer of 1975. "My dad bought himself a racing bike to get back into shape . . . ," he told Bob Ottum in an interview for a *Sports Illustrated* (September 3, 1984) profile. "I already had a Raleigh ten-speed I'd bought with my lawnmowing money, and we started riding together three or four times a week for an hour each time. That was fine, but next thing I knew, he had me riding sixty miles of the trip to Yosemite National Park. Listen: I was so tired I wanted to cry." At the time, LeMond was more interested in free-style skiing and viewed bicycle riding simply as a form of off-season training for the slopes. But in the winter of 1975–76 there was little snow, and LeMond continued to cycle.

Increasingly intrigued by bicycle racing, LeMond joined the Reno (Nevada) Wheelmen, a local cycling club, and in February 1976 he easily placed second in a twenty-five-mile race organized by the club. The following month, he won back-to-back intermediate events, for twelve-to-fifteen years-olds, in California. After winning eleven races in his age group during his first few months of competition, LeMond petitioned for and received permission to enter the division for sixteen-to-nineteen-year-olds. By the end of the year, he had taken the state junior championship and finished fourth in the junior nationals.

At about that time, LeMond dropped out of high school in order to devote himself to cycling. (He eventually earned his diploma by taking correspondence courses.) His dedication paid off with a victory in the junior nationals in 1977 and a bronze medal in the junior world championship team trials in 1978. In 1979, at the junior world championship meet in Buenos Aires, Argentina, Kenny De Marteleire, a young Belgian entrant, introduced LeMond to the more unpleasant realities of world competition by attempting to force him off the road during the final sprint. LeMond nonetheless hung on to finish the race and, when De Marteleire was disqualified, claim the gold medal. Having already won a silver in the individual pursuit and a bronze in the team time trial, LeMond became the first rider ever to win three medals in one world meet.

In April 1980 LeMond traveled to Europe with the United States national cycling team for a series of pre-Olympic tune-up races. He immediately distinguished himself with a victory in the grueling, 346-mile Circuit de la Sarthe bike race, one of the few European pro-am events. The win was the first for an American, professional or amateur, in a major stage race. LeMond next rode in the Ruban Granitier Breton, a five-day stage race in Brittany. On hand to watch him was Cyrille Guimard, the director of the Renault-Elf-Gitane professional cycling team. On the last day of the race, LeMond, who was then riding fifth overall, had a flat tire just as he made his move. He called for the team car, which follows the racers for quick repairs, but the French driver, who had been loaned to the American team, was, in LeMond's words, "loafing along way too far back." By the time the car arrived, LeMond had already lost several precious minutes. Enraged, he hefted his bicycle and flung it against the car.

Recognizing the drive and, in his word, "character" behind LeMond's outburst, Guimard offered the young American a spot on his Renault team for the 1981 season. LeMond, who had already received offers from two other professional teams, had been preserving his amateur status so that he could take part in the 1980 Olympics. When he was denied that opportunity by the United States boycott of the Summer Games in Moscow in protest of the Soviet invasion of Afghanistan, LeMond decided to turn pro and signed a contract with Renault. As he explained to Samuel Abt in a conversation for a *New York Times Magazine* (August 11, 1986) profile, during his first two or three years on the European professional circuit, he "always felt pretty tired in races." "I was confident," he told Abt, "but so many things go into making a rider succeed. A guy can have the physical qualities, but does he have the mental toughness to survive."

LeMond's physical qualities are more than adequate. His lung capacity, for instance, has been calculated to be one and a half times that of the average young man of his age. The unusual lung capacity helps set LeMond apart in the high-altitude stretches that are part of some of the great European races. Moreover, his wiry, five-foot-ten-inch, 158-pound frame strikes a balance between the speed required in the time trials of the long races and the muscle power needed for torturous climbs up steep mountain roads. In his first year in Europe, LeMond won five races and, more important, took fourth place in the prestigious, week-long Dauphiné Libéré in France, but his major victory of 1981 was the Coors Classic, held in the mountains of Colorado, in which he bested Sergei Souk-horouchenkov, the man he would have had to beat in Moscow for the Olympic gold medal.

Schooled in racing tactics by the captain of the Renault team, Bernard Hinault, a brilliant and occasionally ruthless strategist whose desire to win was so strong that he preferred breaking his opponents to merely defeating them, LeMond progressed rapidly. In his second year on the European circuit, he exploded out of the pack in a dramatic last-minute sprint to capture the silver medal in the 170-mile world championship race in Goodwood, England and, later, took the top prize in the twelve-day, 837-mile Tour de l'Avenir by a record-setting ten-minute margin. In 1983 his strong performances in the mountainous stretches earned him first place in the Dauphiné Libéré stage race and fourth place in the Tour of Switzerland and established him as a legitimate contender in cycling's world championship.

The 1983 world championship race, held in Altenrhein, Switzerland, was "a bear," according to LeMond. The 170-mile course was made up of laps, each of which included a vertiginous, 600-foot climb followed by two miles of steady climbing at a 10 percent gradient. "Each time up," LeMond told Ottum, "my lungs were on fire. And coming down, I mean, totally flat out, my eyes would water with the speed—tears streaming back along my temples and probably flying off like, you know, driving a car in the rain. But racing's like that: You're zooming forty and fifty miles an hour downhill and you're trying to see *everything*, straining to peek around the corners when there's no way to see what's ahead. . . . Some of the guys prefer to lead coming off the tops of mountains; they want to see their own line through the turns. Not me. I try to pop in there in a second or third spot and then I watch them. If they crash, I can slow down in time. . . . If they lose me on the downhill, I'll kill them on the uphill." LeMond's gold medal-winning rollercoaster ride around the course lasted, officially, for seven hours, one minute, and twenty-one seconds—a dazzling one minute and eleven seconds less than that of the runner-up. A series of in-the-money finishes in other races in 1983 earned LeMond the Super Prestige Pernod Trophy as that year's all-around cycling leader.

By this time LeMond had an impressive number of wins to his credit, but he had yet to ride in the most prestigious and difficult race of all, the Tour de France. Impressed by his protégé's extraordinary progress, Guimard approved LeMond's debut in the Tour de France in 1984—a year earlier than had been planned. The twenty-four-day, 2,600-mile race has been compared by LeMond to "running a marathon a day for three weeks." Aside from the danger of potentially fatal crashes on the seventy-mile-per-hour descents, the tour has built into it the possibility of physical or psychological exhaustion. LeMond came down with bronchitis shortly after the start of the 1984 Tour de France, and for the first two weeks he was well back of the lead pack, about fifteen minutes behind the leader. But when the group reached the French Alps, LeMond, a strong climber, shot ahead of his faltering competitors and held on to finish the Tour in third place. He was the first non-European competitor ever to finish in the top three.

In 1985 LeMond signed a four-year, $1.4 million contract with La Vie Claire, a new cycling team owned and managed by the entrepreneur Bernard Tapie and captained by the irascible and charismatic Hinault. An almost mythical figure in France, Hinault, who had won the Tour de France four times, had publicly selected LeMond as his heir apparent, but in 1985 LeMond and his La Vie Claire teammates were asked to forget personal ambitions and help Hinault win his record-tying fifth Tour de France. Teammates can help their designated leader's cause by controlling the pace of the race for him, by fending off attackers, and by allowing him to "draft"—to be pulled along in their slipstreams—until he can make his breakaway sprint for the finish line. During the 1985 Tour, LeMond dutifully followed his orders to help Hinault and, in the process, sacrificed a clear chance at victory. His second-place finish was nonetheless historic, for it was the best showing ever for an American. At the end of the race, a grateful Hinault declared: "If I am in the Tour de France next year, I shall only compete to help one of my teammates. . . . I will *make* Greg LeMond win."

When the 1986 Tour de France began on July 4 in Paris, it soon became apparent that Hinault did not intend to fulfill his promise to help LeMond win the race in any conventional fashion, if he indeed intended to fulfill it at all. That year's course took the riders from Paris in a great counterclockwise circle through Normandy, Brittany, the Pyrenees, and the Alps. As the race progressed, LeMond rode increasingly with the knowledge that the crowds lining the route were pulling for Hinault to win what would be an unprecedented sixth championship. On the first day in the Pyreness, at the Marie-Blanque pass, Hinault suddenly broke away, leaving LeMond behind to ward off his pursuers. By the end of the day, Hinault had established a five-minute-twenty-five-second lead over LeMond, who had dropped to third place in the overall standings. Stung by what he saw as Hinault's betrayal, LeMond told reporters, as quoted in *Sports Illustrated* (August 4, 1986), "I realize now that everything he said was designed to take the pressure off him." "It put him in a no-lose situation," LeMond explained, since a sixth victory would seal Hinault's immortality as a cyclist and a loss to LeMond would be interpreted as an act of selfless generosity. To make matters worse, the sympathies of La Vie Claire's sports director, Maurice Le Guilloux, and of many of LeMond's teammates were clearly with Hinault.

On the next day, Hinault "attacked" once more, breaking away alone on what was perhaps the most difficult stage of the tour. He quickly built up a three-minute lead in the stage, but in the last climb of the day—a steep 1,160 meters up to Superbagnères—his endurance broke down in the eighty-degree heat, and LeMond, aided by another American rider, swept past, cutting away all but forty-six seconds of the Frenchman's lead. Two days later Hinault made another breakaway. According to one La Vie Claire teammate, Hinault was trying to "crush Greg, to put him away," but LeMond went after Hinault, caught him, and warned that continued all-out competition between them would eventually end in losses for both of them.

The psychological warfare was so wearing that at one point LeMond considered quitting the race, but he hung on to take over the prized yellow jersey as the overall leader of the Tour after surging ahead on a dangerous downhill in the Alps toward the end of the seventeenth stage. During the next stage, LeMond and Hinault, their differences apparently reconciled, broke away from the pack and worked together to fend off a determined challenge from Switzerland's Urs Zimmermann. "For eighty miles, there were just the two of them, taking turns breaking the headwind, laboring up mountains, swooping downhill at nearly seventy m.p.h.," B. J. Phillips wrote in his account of the race for *Time* (August 11, 1986). "Like birds in flight, they whirred through the turns, locked back wheel to front wheel, fast and free." As they approached the finish line of the stage, LeMond, who still held a two-minute-forty-seven-second overall lead, slowed down so that Hinault could cross the line first.

Despite the public display of camaraderie, Hinault attacked again during the twentieth stage of the race. He made up some time when LeMond tumbled and lost thirty seconds, but it was not enough. Although he had won the stage by twenty-five seconds, he remained two minutes and eighteen seconds behind LeMond in the overall standing. Realizing he was unlikely to recover, he finally conceded the 1986 Tour de France to his American teammate. LeMond, who had desperately wanted to win the stage—the final time trial of the meet—to prove that, in his words, he had "the panache necessary to win the Tour de France," was not appeased by Hinault's publicly made speech of concession. "I just wish he had said at the start it's each one for himself," LeMond told reporters, as quoted in the *New York Times* (July 28, 1986). "He never said that and so I rode one kind of race. If he had said it's every man for himself, I would have ridden a different race."

The physical and psychological battle with Hinault told on LeMond during the remaining three stages of the race. He worried about the hundreds of thousands of fans who lined the route, many of them chanting Hinault's name. "I'm scared someone's going to push me over or poison my food," he admitted to one reporter. His fears were unfounded, however, and on July 27 he rolled into Paris for the final six laps up and down the Champs Elysées and claimed his victory. His total elapsed time of 110 hours thirty-five minutes and nineteen seconds was three minutes ten seconds faster than that of Bernard Hinault, who took second place. When asked about his tactics in the race, Hinault explained, as quoted in *Sports Illustrated* (August 4, 1986): "People think I wasn't too nice to Greg, and he may think so, too. But I pushed him to go to his very limit. He knows now to which point he can go, and this will help him in the future." Because of the peculiar nature of his mentor's final exam, LeMond was unable to enjoy his victory fully. "I have tapes of the race," he told an interviewer months later, "but I've never looked at them. I don't want to see it happen again."

As he prepared to defend his title in 1987, LeMond broke his wrist in a pileup in a European race. He was about to rejoin the tour when, on April 20, he was accidentally shot by his brother-in-law during a turkey-hunting expedition on a farm outside Sacramento, California. More than sixty buckshot pellets struck LeMond, breaking two ribs and piercing his intestines, liver, kidney, diaphragm, and heart lining. Near death, he was carried by police helicopter to the Sacramento trauma center of the University of California, Davis Medical Center, where surgeons removed all but about thirty of the pellets, most of which are lodged harmlessly in LeMond's back and legs. His recovery was slow and painful. "I'd pace the bedroom and just cry and cry because it hurt to much," he told Samuel Abt. "The shooting covered such a large part of my body and I had such a long incision that I didn't have any energy until five weeks after I got home."

Eventually, LeMond began to regain his strength, and in July, three months after the accident, he embarked on an intensive training program to get back into racing shape. Within weeks, however, he was felled again, this time by an emergency appendectomy. When he returned to racing in September, he found he "couldn't sprint." "I'd reach anaerobic, I'd go very quickly into oxygen debt," he told Abt. LeMond also found that he had lost some of his psychological edge. He was being regularly "dropped," or left behind, in races, he admitted to Abt, and on one occasion he had to be physically pushed up some hills by a teammate. LeMond was finally beginning to return to form when he was sidelined by an infection in his right shin, the result of a fall in a race in Belgium in mid-1988.

As the 1989 cycling season got underway, LeMond once again began the slow work of rebuilding his endurance. Having missed two consecutive Tour de France meets, his goal was a good showing in the 1989 race, scheduled to begin on July 1, but he rode poorly in several one-day races in the spring and struggled in the mountain stages of the Tour of Italy in June, finishing thirty-ninth overall, although he did take second place in the final time trial. While he was in Italy, he was treated for a severe iron deficiency, which affects the supply of oxygen to working muscles.

Given the difficulty of the course, which wound for 2,000 miles from Luxembourg counterclockwise around France, with four especially difficult stages in the Alps, and his poor placings in the spring meets, LeMond, racing for the Belgium-based ADR team, was not among the favorites to win the 1989 Tour de France. By the end of the first stage, however, he had already settled into fourth place. Five days later he won a forty-five-mile time trial and with it, the leader's yellow jersey. Five seconds behind him was two-time Tour winner Laurent Fignon. Fignon caught LeMond in the Pyrenees during the eleventh stage of the race, but, during another time trial a few days later, LeMond pulled ahead of Fignon, by forty seconds. He widened his lead by three seconds in the eighteenth stage, then lost it again during the nineteenth stage, as he attempted dizzying alpine climbs in opressively hot weather.

On the following day, Figon increased his lead to fifty seconds on what he called his "lucky mountain," L'Alpe d'Huez, where he had taken the yellow jersey in his Tour de France victories in 1983 and 1984. Undaunted, LeMond attacked and won the next stage, but Fignon finished right behind him and maintained his fifty-second overall lead. Having declared a truce, Fignon, LeMond, and the other leaders rode the seventy-nine-mile penultimate stage of the Tour in what Samuel Abt described as a "party" atmosphere. At the end of the day, LeMond remained fifty seconds behind, but he insisted that victory was still possible in the final, fifteen-mile time trial that would bring the Tour de France to its finish on the Champs Elysées.

For the final dash to Paris, the 138 riders who, out of the original group of 198, had made it to the last stage of the race, were started singly, two minutes apart and in reverse order of their position in the standings. When LeMond's turn came, he "went all out," as he put it. "I didn't think," he told reporters, "I just rode." Despite blustery wind conditions, LeMond completed the stage in twenty-six minutes, fifty-seven seconds, at an average speed of thirty-four miles per hour—the fastest ever for a Tour de France time trial. While waiting for Fignon to finish, he said later, as quoted in *USA Today* (July 24, 1989), "I was thinking, 'The last thing I wanted to do was race twenty-one days and 2,000 miles and lose the Tour de France by one or two seconds.'" It was Fignon, however, who finished seconds too late, in a time of twenty-seven minutes fifty-five seconds. LeMond's eight-second margin of victory was the narrowest in the history of the Tour de France. A few weeks later, he certified his status as the world's premier cyclist by winning the world championship road race in the midst of a downpour in Chambéry, France with a time of six hours, forty minutes, and fifty-nine seconds. LeMond is one of only five men (the others are Eddy Merckx, Stephen Roche, Louison Bobet, and Bernard Hinault) to win the Tour de France and the world professional title in the same year.

A blond, blue-eyed "Huck Finn with steel thighs," according to Bob Ottum, Greg LeMond keeps fit in the offseason by jogging, lifting weights, and skiing cross-country. He and his wife, the former Kathy Morris, whom he married in 1980, have two children, Geoffrey James and Scott. The Le-Monds spend the European cycling season at their home in Kortrijk, Belgium and the offseason at their lakeside retreat in Wayzata, Minnesota. LeMond is the author of Greg LeMond's Complete Book of Bicycling (1988), which he wrote in collaboration with Kent Gordis. In September 1989, following an international bidding war triggered by his comeback victory in the Tour de France, he signed a three-year, $5.5 million contract to race with the Z team, which is based in France.

References: Chicago Tribune IV p1+ Je 28 '87 pors; N Y Times p1+ Jl 24 '89 por; N Y Times Mag p40+ Je 5 '88 pors; People 22:64+ Jl 23 '84 pors, 26:34+ Ag 11 '86 pors; Sports Illus 61:52+ S 3 '84 pors, 65:12+ Ag 4 '86 pors, 71:12+ Jl 31 '89 pors; Time 128:56+ Ag 11 '86 pors

Levi-Montalcini, Rita

(lä´ vē-môn-täl-chē´ nē)

Apr. 22, 1909– Neurobiologist; research scientist. Address: Istituto di Biologia Cellulare, Via G. Romagnosi, Rome 00196, Italy

In October 1986, Dr. Rita Levi-Montalcini, the research scientist and neurobiologist, became only the fourth woman ever to be awarded the Nobel Prize for physiology or medicine, for her groundbreaking discovery in the early 1950s of the Nerve Growth Factor, a protein that is instrumental in the growth and differentiation of cells in the nervous system. Dr. Levi-Montalcini received the prize jointly with her colleague, the biochemist Stanley Cohen, who worked with her at Washington University in St. Louis, Missouri in the 1950s. Recently, with the availability of more sophisticated scientific tools, such as genetic engineering, the work of Dr. Levi-Montalcini and Dr. Cohen has taken on increased significance, as researchers explore how the Nerve Growth Factor can help them understand such disorders as cancers, birth defects, and Alzheimer's disease.

Dr. Rita Levi-Montalcini overcame considerable adversity to attain her present stature. She grew up in Italy during a period when few women pursued careers and elected to study medicine over the objections of her father. After receiving her medical degree from the University of Turin in 1936, being a Jew, she was forced into hiding, living in the Turin countryside and then in Florence, where she conducted experiments on chicken embryos in her homemade laboratory. In 1947 Dr. Levi-Montalcini moved to the United States to work with Dr. Viktor Hamburger in the zoology department at Washington University and ended up staying thirty years. In 1977 she returned to Rome to head the Laboratory of Cell Biology of the National Council of Research.

Rita Levi-Montalcini was born in Turin, Italy on April 22, 1909, the same day as her nonidentical twin sister, Paola, to Adamo Levi, an engineer and factory manager, and Adele Montalcini. The twins had a brother, Gino, who was seven years older, and a sister, Anna, who was five years older. Describing her upper-middle-class family life in her autobiography *In Praise of Imperfection: My Life and Work* (1988), Dr. Levi-Montalcini wrote that she was brought up in an environment "brimming with affection and never troubled by disagreement between my mother and father." Her parents, however, were a study in contrasts. While her mother was a woman of serenity and sweetness, Dr. Levi-Montalcini characterized her father as a dynamic, hot-tempered man who was the undisputed master of the household. "In spite of the fact that we only saw him at lunch and dinner and that he was often away . . . it was he who controlled our lives, even in small details," she wrote in her autobiography.

Adamo Levi's authoritarian ways and Victorian-era views of the subordinate role intended for women inspired awe and fear in his young daughter. Even as a little girl, she was reluctant to kiss him, attributing her hesitation to his bristling mustache. Although Dr. Levi-Montalcini harbored a more visible affection for her mother than for her father, "it was he rather than she who had a decisive influence on the course of my life," she wrote in her autobiography, "both by transmitting to me a part of his genes and eliciting my admiration for his tenacity, energy, and ingenuity." Their failure to communicate was "a cause of pain to him no less than to me," she wrote. Young Rita felt that her father, who called her his "shrinking violet," was disappointed in her timid nature. "I was apparently a very mild, submissive child," Dr. Levi-Montalcini told Frederika Randall during an interview for Vogue (March 1987). "But I was very strong inside; you might say there was a strong resentment in me."

Another attribute that she inherited from her father was "a secular, Spinozan conception of life," Dr. Levi-Montalcini wrote in her autobiography. The family was Jewish but not observant. As she recalled to Frederika Randall, when she was three years old, her father, who rejected the notion of strictly adhering to religious dogma, "taught [her] to repeat the sentence 'sono una libera pensatrice'—I am a free thinker." That sometimes put her father at odds with some of the family's more observant relatives, particularly on her mother's side. An ardent secularist, Adamo Levi also rejected the notion of observing any of the rituals of Roman Catholicism, the majority religion in Italy.

In school Rita Levi-Montalcini was serious and hardworking, and showed, she wrote, like her two sisters, "an outstanding aptitude for study." Nonetheless, she received only the limited education typically given to daughters of the upper-middle classes at that time, which culminated in several years at a girls' high school. It was generally expected that, although boys would go to a university and then take up a profession, girls would become wives and mothers. Following her graduation from high school, Rita had a very clear idea of what she did not want to do with her life. "My experience in childhood and adolescence of the subordinate role played by the female in a society run entirely by men had convinced me that I was not cut out to be a wife," she wrote in her memoirs. "Babies did not attract me, and I was altogether without the maternal sense so highly developed in small and adolescent girls." But she did not have an alternative plan. She was not artistic like her twin sister, shied away from establishing friendships with either boys or girls, and felt that she did not possess discernible talent in any area.

A turning point in Dr. Levi-Montalcini's life occurred when she was around twenty, when her former governess Giovanna was diagnosed as having cancer. The news shocked the younger woman, and she resolved to resume her studies and become a doctor. After her governess's death, she sounded out her father about her plans. "I began in a roundabout way," Dr. Levi-Montalcini recounted in her autobiography, "telling him that, since I had no vocation for married life or for having babies, I would like to go back to studying." Her father expressed strong doubts, citing the unsuitability of the profession for a woman, but he eventually approved her plan, though only reluctantly.

Rita Levi-Montalcini and her cousin Eugenia began a program of remedial studies, engaging one teacher for Latin and Greek and another for mathematics. They decided to tackle philosophy, literature, and history on their own. Passing her qualifying exams easily, at the head of the list of candidates, Rita Levi-Montalcini entered the Turin School of Medicine in the fall of 1930. One of her second-year teachers was Dr. Giuseppe Levi, a widely renowned professor of human anatomy and of histology—the study of the minute cellular structures of plant and animal tissues. Despite his reputation as a tough taskmaster and his imposing, if not intimidating, classroom manner, Dr. Levi became (and would remain, until his death in 1965) Dr. Levi-Montalcini's friend, mentor, sometime critic, and, ultimately, second father figure. Indeed, in her autobiography she likens Levi, whom she calls "the Master," to her father, noting that both were imperious, quick to anger, and intolerant of failure in themselves or others. Adamo Levi died, prematurely, in August 1932, when Dr. Levi-Montalcini was twenty-three. In her autobiography, she wrote that "over all these years, my veneration for him has continued to grow."

Studying under Dr. Levi, Rita Levi-Montalcini did her first work with nervous-system cells, which would become her lifelong area of expertise. Upon graduating from medical school in the summer of 1936, she decided to specialize in neurology, and she worked for a time as Levi's assistant. But Fascist government decrees in 1938 barred Jews from all university positions and forbade them to practice medicine. As a result, she was dismissed from her academic position at the Institute of Anatomy, and from the Neurology Clinic. In March 1939, following Dr. Levi's example, Dr. Levi-Montalcini left Italy for Belgium, undertaking neurological research at the Neurologic Institute of Brussels. Upon her return to Turin in December 1939, she practiced clandestinely as a doctor among the city's poor, but she gave it up a few months later because of the difficulty of getting prescriptions filled through Aryan doctors.

At the suggestion of a former Turin classmate, Dr. Levi-Montalcini set up a primitive laboratory in her bedroom in the apartment she shared with her mother and other family members and resumed the kind of research she had undertaken in Brussels. Operating under a microscope on chicken embryos, obtained from ordinary eggs, she analyzed the way in which the removal of peripheral limb tissues still lacking nerves affects the differentiation and development of motor cells in the spinal cord and of sensory cells in the ganglia at the rear of the spinal cord. Dr. Levi-Montalcini was aided in her research by Dr. Levi, who returned from Belgium in 1941, after hiding from the Nazis for a year. Dr. Levi-Montalcini and her family moved to a farmhouse outside Turin in the fall of 1942 to escape the Allied bombardment of the city, and she continued her experiments there, discovering that nervous-system cells in the first stages of differentiation move "toward distant locations along rigidly programmed routes." "Now the nervous system appeared to me in a different light from its description in textbooks of neuroanatomy, where its structure is described as rigid and unchangeable," she wrote. Dr. Levi-Montalcini used chicken embryos for her research because the nervous system of a chicken's brain is identical to the basic unit of the nervous system of all vertebrates.

In July 1943 Mussolini resigned as head of Italy's government, and it appeared that the long Fascist nightmare was over, but in September German troops occupied the portions of Italy not yet in Allied hands, including Turin. Realizing that their lives were in danger, Dr. Levi-Montalcini and her family resolved to flee. They made an abortive attempt to cross into Switzerland and, when that effort failed, elected to head south, hoping to cross American or British lines. A chance meeting on board a southbound train with one of Dr. Levi-Montalcini's former classmates, who was dressed in a Fascist uniform, impelled them to get off at the next stop—the city of Florence, which was still in German hands. Armed with false identity documents and fabricated names, they found lodging fairly quickly, after first assuring their prospective landlady that they were not Jews. Much later, they learned that she had seen through their ruse almost from the beginning, but, being anti-Fascist herself, chose to give them refuge anyway. Dr. Levi-Montalcini considered resuming her research at the local university's neurological institute, using her assumed name, but the facility's director, alarmed at the prospect, flatly refused. Instead, Dr. Levi-Montalcini and her sister turned to manufacturing false identity cards for friends who came to Florence, until British troops liberated the city in September 1944.

From September 1944 until May 1945, Dr. Levi-Montalcini worked for the Allied health service, ministering to war refugees in central Italy. Working in the midst of a typhoid epidemic, "my personal safety—my health—was more at risk than when we were hiding from the Nazis," she recalled to Roberto Suro of the New York Times (October 14, 1986). When the war ended, Dr. Levi made her an offer of her old job as a research assistant, and she returned to the University of Turin. Doubting the usefulness of the type of neurobiological research that she had been doing and the adequacy of her own scientific training, she began studying biology in greater depth.

In the summer of 1946, an article by Dr. Levi-Montalcini and Dr. Levi summarizing their wartime neuroembryology experiments in her homemade laboratory came to the attention of Dr. Viktor Hamburger, the chairman of the zoology department at Washington University in St. Louis, Missouri. Ironically, those experiments had been prompted by similar studies done earlier by Dr. Hamburger, which Dr. Levi-Montalcini had read about and had attempted to duplicate. Her conclusions, however, were completely different. Intrigued by her findings, Dr. Hamburger invited Dr. Levi-Montalcini to spend a semester at Washington University to conduct further research, and she sailed to the United States in September 1946.

Dr. Levi-Montalcini liked her new surroundings so much that what she had envisioned as a visit of six to nine months turned into a thirty-year stay. She worked as a research associate from 1947 to 1951, as an associate professor of zoology from 1951 to 1958, and as a full professor from 1958 to 1977, when she retired from the faculty as professor emeritus. She became a United States citizen in 1956 and continues to hold dual American and Italian citizenships. During her years at Washington University, Dr. Levi-Montalcini made frequent trips home to Italy to see relatives and friends, and she often consulted with old classmates from Turin University who, like her, came to the United States to do research, including Renato Dulbecco and Salvador E. Luria, both of whom, like Dr. Levi-Montalcini, ultimately won the Nobel Prize for physiology or medicine.

When she began her research at Washington University, Dr. Levi-Montalcini had little inkling that she would soon make the discovery that would eventually bring her science's most prestigious prize. At first she continued to be plagued by the same doubts about the usefulness and the future of her research that she had felt in Europe—doubts she would entertain until she achieved a breakthrough late in 1947. One day, as she sat before her microscope, staring at silver-salt-impregnated chicken-embryo sections, she saw the cells seem to take on a life that she had not noticed before, and she witnessed their behavior processes in an altogether new light. In her autobiography, she likened the dynamic action taking place under her microscope to that which takes place on a battlefield, with groups of cells advancing, retreating, and being killed off and cleared away. "It struck me that the discovery of great migratory and degenerative processes affecting nerve cell populations at the early stages of their development might offer a tenuous yet valid path to follow into the fascinating and uncharted labyrinth of the nervous system," Dr. Levi-Montalcini wrote in her autobiography. She shared her revelation with Dr. Hamburger, who became equally excited. She wrote of that experience: "Though in the years that followed, I was to taste the joy of discoveries of far greater import, the revelations of that day stayed permanently inscribed in my memory as marking not only the end of the long period of doubt and lack of faith in my research, but also the sealing of a lifelong alliance between me and the nervous system."

In January 1950 Dr. Hamburger received a letter from a former student, Elmer Bueker, who outlined experiments he had made by grafting mouse tumors onto chicken embryos. Bueker discovered that nerve fibers had infiltrated the tumor cellular mass after eight days of incubation, and he concluded that the tumor provided more favorable conditions for the fibers' growth. Deciding to repeat Bueker's experiments, Dr. Levi and Dr. Levi-Montalcini grafted cancer tumors taken from mice onto chicken embryos, and then watched as bundles of nerve fibers began to grow not only in the tumoral masses, but also in the noninnervated organs of the embryo, apparently in response to the release by the tumors of some kind of chemical, which would later come to be known as the Nerve Growth Factor (NGF). A series of extraembryonic graftings of tumors in which the same results were achieved confirmed Dr. Levi-Montalcini's hypothesis that the tumoral agent, which she then referred to as "the nerve-growth promoting agent," possessed a property capable of stimulating the development of receptive nerve cells and fibers that was transmitted in a way that was characteristic of a humoral substance. Dr. Levi-Montalcini presented the results of her findings at a symposium at the New York Academy of Sciences, in a conference entitled "The Chicken Embryo in Biological Research."

To determine the chemical nature of the factor, Dr. Levi-Montalcini decided to run some experiments at the in-vitro-culture unit at the Institute of Biophysics in Rio de Janeiro, Brazil, which had been set up by an assistant of Dr. Levi's, Hertha Meyer. Convinced that tumors transplanted into embryos would stimulate fiber growth, Dr. Levi-Montalcini examined cultures showing halo-shaped outgrowths of fibers around sensory and sympathetic ganglia grown near the transplanted tumors. In subsequent experiments, in which she cultured the ganglia for two or three days instead of twenty-four hours, she also noticed that the fibers' orientation was toward the neoplastic tissue, which she took as evidence of a neurotropic—or directional—effect.

Returning to Washington University from Brazil, Dr. Levi-Montalcini worked on a new series of in-vitro experiments with Dr. Stanley Cohen, a biochemist who was invited by Dr. Hamburger to join their team. They were able to extract NGF in greater quantities from snake venom and mouse salivary glands, and they identified the factor as a protein molecule. Those NGF experiments, conducted between 1953 and 1959, formed the basis for Cohen's subsequent discovery of a second growth factor, known as Epidermal Growth Factor, or EGF.

In the spring of 1961, with the support of Dr. Hamburger, Dr. Levi-Montalcini returned to Rome to establish a research laboratory there. She was motivated partly by a desire to spend more time with her mother, sister, and other relatives, and partly by the strong interest that her research work had aroused in the Italian scientific community. She began to spend half the year in St. Louis and half in Rome, where, starting in 1969, she oversaw the growth of the Laboratory of Cell Biology, which was attached to the quasi-governmental Council of National Research (CNR). She found that being an administrator created a whole new set of problems, including fighting with uncooperative bureaucrats. She was also frustrated by what she called "a total lack of interest" by the parent CNR in neurobiology. Nonetheless, she served as director of the cell biology laboratory from 1969 to 1979, when she reached the mandatory retirement age. She remains with the laboratory as a guest researcher.

Back in the United States, where she continued to teach and to conduct research at Washington University, Dr. Levi-Montalcini was accorded a rare honor: in 1968 she was elected to the prestigious National Academy of Sciences, in recognition of her research involving the Nerve Growth Factor. She was only the tenth woman elected to the academy since its founding in 1863. On September 22, 1986 Dr. Levi-Montalcini and her former collaborator at Washington University, Dr. Stanley Cohen, were named among six recipients of the Albert Lasker Medical Research Awards, given annually by the Albert and Mary Lasker Foundation. Each winner received $15,000 and a statuette of the winged victory of Samothrace. The Lasker Award frequently turns out to be a harbinger of the Nobel Prize, which is awarded several weeks later.

Indeed, on October 13, 1986 Sweden's Karolinska Institute for Medicine announced that Dr. Rita Levi-Montalcini and Dr. Stanley Cohen were the joint recipients of the 1986 Nobel Prize in physiology or medicine—the highest award the scientific community bestows in the medical field. They received jointly a cash award of two million Swedish kronor, or about $290,000. In announcing the award, the institute's Nobel Assembly said that the discovery of NGF in 1954 "opened new fields of widespread importance to basic science" and held out the prospect of shedding light on many disorders, such as cancers, the delayed healing of wounds, and senile dementia, including Alzheimer's disease.

One member of the research group at the Laboratory of Cell Biology, Vincenzo Bocchini, perfected a method for purifying NGF from mouse salivary glands, and for identifying it in a contaminant-free molecule. That enabled two scientists at Washington University to determine the amino acid sequence of the protein molecule in 1971. Twelve years later American scientists identified the DNA coding of the molecule and its originating gene, enabling reseachers to manufacture human NGF synthetically.

Dr. Rita Levi-Montalcini is a short, slender woman with gray-green eyes and silver-gray hair. She shares a quiet, book-lined apartment, not far from Rome University, with her twin sister, Paola, a painter of some renown. She has never married, fulfilling the prediction that she made nearly sixty years ago to her father that a domestic life of marriage and children was not for her.

In June 1987 Dr. Levi-Montalcini was one of two dozen prominent scientists who were honored in a special ceremony in the Rose Garden of the White House, where each received the National Medal of Science, the highest American scientific award. She is a member of the Harvey Society; the American Academy of Arts and Sciences; the American National Academy of Sciences; the Belgian Royal Academy of Medicine; the National Academy of Sciences of Italy; the European Academy of Sciences, Arts, and Letters; and the Academy of Arts and Sciences of Florence. Dr. Levi-Montalcini was the first woman member of the Pontifical Academy of Sciences in Rome.

References: Omni 10:70+ Mr '88 por; Time 128:66+ O 27 '86 por; Vogue 177:480+ Mr '87 por; American Men and Women of Science (1976); International Who's Who, 1989-90; Wasson, Tyler (ed.). Nobel Prize Winners: An H. W. Wilson Biographical Dictionary (1987); Who's Who in the World, 1989-90

Lewis, Flora

1923 (?)- Journalist. Address: b. New York Times, 229 W. 43d St., New York, N.Y. 10036; 3 rue Scribe, 75009 Paris, France

Over the course of a globe-trotting, forty-seven-year career, the New York Times foreign correspondent Flora Lewis has earned a reputation as one of the media's most astute observers of the international scene. Among just a handful of women who have risen to the top of what is still a male-dominated profession, Miss Lewis has, since 1980, written an influential, though nonideological, bi-weekly foreign-affairs column for the Times that has placed her in the forefront of the nation's opinion makers. She is also the author of four books on foreign affairs. John Garabedian of the New York Post once described Flora Lewis in the following manner: "She's at home anywhere in the world—in London, Paris, Bonn, Rome, Warsaw, and Prague. She's aggressive, she has more courage than many men, but is very much the woman—slender, feminine, a sculptured face, blue eyes, chic."

Flora Lewis was born in about 1923 in Los Angeles, California, the daughter of Benjamin Lewis, a prominent attorney, and Pauline (Kallin) Lewis. A gifted student, she received her high school diploma at the age of fifteen and, just three years later, was awarded a B.A. degree, summa cum laude, from the University of California at Los Angeles. She worked briefly as a cub reporter for the Los Angeles Times before moving to New York City to attend Columbia University's Graduate School of Journalism. After obtaining a master's degree in 1942, Miss Lewis was hired by the New York bureau of the Associated Press. She was soon transferred to Washington, D.C., to cover the navy and state departments, and in 1945 she was transferred again, this time to the AP's London bureau. On August 17, 1945, in London, Flora Lewis married Sydney Gruson, a New York Times foreign correspondent whom she had met while a student at Columbia University. The ceremony was performed on their lunch hour.

When the New York Times transferred Sydney Gruson to Poland in 1946, Miss Lewis resigned from the AP to go with him. For the next ten years, she worked as a freelance writer and contract reporter for a variety of American, British, and French newspapers and magazines, including the London Observer, France-soir, Financial Times, Time, and the New York Times Magazine. "I worked for everybody," she later said of that frenetic period, during which her assignments took her throughout Europe as well as to Israel and Mexico.

Returning to New York City in 1955, Flora Lewis worked as an editor for the McGraw-Hill publishing company during a one-year leave of absence from journalism. In the following year she became the first woman foreign correspondent ever to work for the Washington Post, at first covering Eastern Europe and later heading its bureaus in Bonn, West Germany and in London. In 1965 the Washington Post made her the first chief of its newly established New York City bureau.

By the end of 1966, the grind of daily newspaper reporting had begun to take its toll on Flora Lewis. She announced that she was leaving the *Washington Post* in January 1967 to begin writing a syndicated foreign-affairs column called "Today Abroad" that would appear three times a week in the New York metropolitan area newspaper *Newsday* (for which Sydney Gruson served as associate publisher in 1968–69), the *New York Post*, and in several overseas newspapers. Writing the column kept Miss Lewis in the media spotlight and on the move, as she traveled to Vietnam five times in five years, to the Middle East in 1967 to cover the Six-Day War, and to the 1968 political conventions in Chicago and Miami. Her Vietnam dispatches downplayed battlefield drama and emphasized military strategy. "By the time I got to Vietnam, I found the battlefield stories no longer very interesting," she explained to Julia Edwards, the author of the book *Women of the World: The Great Foreign Correspondents* (1988). "I was tired of reading about bullets that whoosh and marines screaming in anguish, and I didn't want to write it yet again." In February 1969 Miss Lewis lost one of her major outlets when the *New York Post* dropped her column following an editorial shake-up.

In July 1972 Flora Lewis returned to daily journalism as chief of the *New York Times's* Paris bureau, one of the newspaper's most coveted assignments. Several male reporters at the *Times,* believing the job should have gone to a man, expressed anger at her appointment. John Hess, one of the *Times's* senior Paris reporters, requested a transfer to the home office following the announcement, and an embittered male editor said of her, as quoted in *Newsday* (June 8, 1972), "She's a hell of a newspaperman." Her original assignment was to cover France only, but, as she explained in a May 1980 interview with *Esquire* magazine, "Somehow over the years, it's gotten bigger and bigger. I've gone as far as Tokyo, Havana, Cape Town. . . . In the last couple of years, I've been traveling probably two-thirds of the time."

In 1976, while continuing to serve as the Paris bureau chief of the *New York Times,* Miss Lewis received the additional title of European diplomatic correspondent. Four years later, she relinquished both positions to begin writing the biweekly foreign-affairs column for the *New York Times* that she continues to write today. Only the third writer to undertake the *Times's* foreign-affairs column, she succeeded two Pulitzer Prize winners: Anne O'Hare McCormick, who was responsible for the column from 1937 to 1954, and C. L. Sulzberger, who wrote it from 1954 to 1977. The position had been vacant for three years before Miss Lewis's appointment. It soon became apparent that the column provided the ideal forum for her manifold intellectual interests. "I'm simply not the kind of person who would enjoy being a specialist in one subject," she told the *Esquire* interviewer. In an article entitled "The Quantum Mechanics of Politics," which she wrote for the

New York Times Magazine (November 6, 1983), she revealed that, unlike most political columnists, her beliefs lean neither to the left nor to the right. "I'm a rock-ribbed, hard-nosed, knee-jerk, bleeding-heart moderate," she wrote. "I'm pretty sure people who have all the answers are wrong, at least most of the time."

Although nonideological, Flora Lewis has never shied away from taking strong positions in her columns and articles. In February 1982, for example, she wrote an article for the *New York Times's* Arts and Leisure section that sharply criticized the well-known Greek film director Constantin Costa-Gavras for what she perceived as the anti-American sentiments expressed in his film *Missing,* which starred Jack Lemmon and Sissy Spacek. *Missing* strongly implied that the United States government was involved in the 1973 military coup in Chile and might also have played a role in the death of Charles Horman, a young left-wing American journalist who disappeared while covering the coup and was later found murdered. In a lengthy appraisal of *Missing,* Miss Lewis stated her opinion that the film raised "serious ethical, moral and political as well as artistic questions." She censured Costa-Gavras for presenting the story entirely from the point of view of Horman's father (played by Lemmon), who traveled to Chile to search for his son, and she questioned his technique of presenting as fact events about which the truth has never been fully known. Basing her argument on investigations by the *New York Times* reporter Seymour Hersh that uncovered no evidence of involvement by the American government in either Horman's murder or the coup, she also pointed to testimony by former Central Intelligence Agency directors Richard M. Helms and William E. Colby that the government did not orchestrate the overthrow in Chile. "The definition of truth has always been difficult," Miss Lewis observed, "but he [Costa-Gavras] doesn't concede the distortion of art. In that way, he winds up distorting fact without even noticing."

Many liberals took exception to Flora Lewis's comments about *Missing.* Alexander Cockburn of the *Village Voice* (February 10–16, 1982) disapproved of the stance she had taken, and the New York freelance writer Andrew Kopkind issued an angry rebuttal in the *Nation* (April 17, 1982). "At bare bone, the structure of Lewis's case against intervention in the coup looks wobbly," Kopkind wrote, pointing out that Helms and Colby "are hardly fair witnesses."

In the early 1980s Flora Lewis drew the ire of some conservatives for castigating the foreign policy of President Ronald Reagan in her columns, in which she had attacked the extensive military buildup initiated by Reagan in the early months of his first term, saying it had exacerbated tension between the United States and the Soviet Union. She also criticized Reagan's Central American policy, accusing his administration of "gross mismanagement" in that region, particularly with regard to Nicaragua.

Flora Lewis is the author of four books, three of which were published between 1958 and 1967. Her first book, *Case History of Hope: The Story of Poland's Peaceful Revolutions* (1958), which detailed the relaxation of Soviet control over Poland in the four years following the death of Joseph Stalin in 1953, encountered generally favorable reviews. Writing in *Library Journal* (October 15, 1958), R. F. Delaney praised Miss Lewis's *Case History of Hope* as "extremely well written and brilliantly interpreted," and Christine Hotchkiss of the *New York Herald Tribune* (October 26, 1958) acclaimed it as "an unbiased, intensely interesting record of one of the great stories of our time." Miss Lewis's next book, *Red Pawn: The Story of Noel Field* (1965), recounts the puzzling life of the double agent Noel Field, a former State Department official who disappeared behind the Iron Curtain in 1949 and was followed within the next year by his wife, brother, and foster daughter. There, the four were arrested as spies and held until 1954. Reviews were mostly complimentary, with Tom Ross, for example, of the *Washington Post* (January 16, 1965) noting that *Red Pawn* functioned both as a spy thriller and as "a subtle intellectual history of a prototype figure of the age." The historian Arthur Schlesinger Jr., writing in the *New York Review of Books* (February 11, 1965), faulted Flora Lewis's interpretations and methodology, but he admired her investigative abilities and "the skill with which she has woven so many threads into a convincing general narrative."

In *One of Our H-Bombs Is Missing* (1967), Miss Lewis dealt with the collision, in 1966, of two American military planes—a B-52 bomber and a tanker—above Palomares, Spain and the resulting search for one of the B-52's bombs, which was discovered three months later. The book got mixed notices. Although in reviewing it for *Library Journal* (March 15, 1967), Allan Gibbons termed it "interesting and well-written" and "a clear and detailed analysis of a major event in recent history," other critics were less kind. In the weekly *America* (May 25, 1967), H. L. Rofinot found that Miss Lewis had not dramatized her story enough, adding that she "extended what could have been a superb magazine article into a mediocre book." And Anthony Bevan observed in the *New York Times Book Review* (April 23, 1967): "Miss Lewis reports her version in brittle journalese, and as if she were far away on the sidelines relying on secondhand news and gossip which she, apparently, does not always understand."

Flora Lewis's most recent book, *Europe: A Tapestry of Nations* (1987), is a country-by-country study of twenty-seven European nations, with information on the history, geography, government, and economy of each, along with brief portraits of their representative inhabitants. Reviewers had their reservations about *Europe: A Tapestry of Nations*. Although the British author Anthony Sampson, writing in the *New York Times* (December 14, 1987), complained that the book was overgeneralized and disjointed, he refused to place the blame for those faults entirely on Flora Lewis. "If this book, compendious and well-informed as it is, never quite achieves a shape and unity, that is probably the fault of the Continent, not the author," Sampson wrote in her defense. David P. Calleo of the *Washington Post* (October 25, 1987) seconded Sampson's opinion by noting that the book is "disjointed and uneven—not, of course, unlike Europe itself." Nevertheless, Calleo appreciated the vigor and precision of Miss Lewis's writing in a book that he discovered to be "full of interesting observations and information."

Flora Lewis has received many journalism awards during her long career. She has been honored four times by the Overseas Press Club: in 1957 for best magazine foreign-affairs reporting for her articles for the *New York Times Magazine*; in 1963 and 1977 for best daily newspaper or wire service interpretation of foreign affairs; and in 1979 for best analysis of foreign affairs in Western Europe. Each award was presented for work performed during the preceding year. Miss Lewis has also received the Edward Weintal Award "for distinguished reporting on American foreign policy and diplomacy" (1978); the French government's Cross of the Chevalier of the Legion of Honor, one of that country's highest peacetime awards (1981); the Matrix Award for Newspapers from New York Women in Communications (1985); the National Press Club's annual Fourth Estate Award for "a lifetime of contributions to American journalism" (1985); and the Elmer Holmes Bobst Award in Arts and Letters from New York University (1987). In addition, she has been awarded honorary degrees from many universities and colleges, including Mt. Holyoke, Bucknell, Marymount Manhattan, Columbia, Colgate, Dartmouth, and Princeton, the last-named of which cited her in 1981 for displaying "equanimity, precision, resourcefulness and courage" in stories that "have combined to shape a model of statesmanlike journalism."

Flora Lewis continues to make her home in Paris, a city that has enchanted her since her first visit on a bicycling tour as a schoolgirl. She lives in a comfortable, art-filled apartment on the banks of the river Seine, close to the Louvre museum, and walks to her office most mornings, something she considers "the greatest luxury" of her life. "I always discover something I didn't notice before," she told an interviewer for *France* (Fall 1986) magazine. "No matter even if it's the same old route to the office, you always see something new that is lovely. This is a city you never find boring." Because she dislikes waking up early, she rarely schedules early morning appointments. Although she says she no longer finds her work glamorous, her curiosity about life and people remains unabated. She concedes that she loves returning to Paris after making journeys to other places but has expressed a desire to move back to the United States eventually. "When I first came [to Europe], I was intending to stay not more than four years," she told the *Esquire* interviewer. "Now I've reached the point where I'll stay until there's truly something else I want to do. But I do feel that itch to get back home. I've spent almost my entire adult life abroad, and I find that in some ways I've become something of a foreigner myself."

As foreign correspondents for rival newspapers, Flora Lewis and Sydney Gruson competed with one another for stories for many years. They were divorced in 1973. They have two daughters, Kerry, born in Ireland, and Sheila, born in Israel, and a son, Lindsey, born in Mexico. Flora Lewis spent much of her career balancing the demands of her profession with those of marriage and motherhood, a situation that demanded constant compromise. "I'm perfectly willing to cook the dinner," she as-

sured a *Newsweek* interviewer in 1963, "but not on a day when there's a big political story breaking." Before the birth of her daughter Kerry, she delayed going to the hospital until the last possible minute in order to keep an appointment to interview a Polish political leader. And just before the birth of Sheila, she conducted the last interview ever held with Ali Razmara, then the Iranian prime minister.

References: Esquire 93:87+ My '80 por; N Y Post B p10 F 8 '67 por; *Newsweek* 61:91 Ap 22 '63 pors; *Contemporary Authors* vol 119 (1987); Edwards, Julia. *Women of the World: The Great Foreign Correspondents* (1988); *Who's Who in America,* 1988–89

Lucci, Susan
(lōō´ chē)

Dec. 23, 1946 (?)– Actress. Address: c/o All My Children, 101 W. 67th St., New York, N.Y. 10023

Arguably the best-known character in the history of televised American soap opera is Erica Kane of ABC's *All My Children,* who has been portrayed by Susan Lucci since the series made its debut in 1970. The archetypal "bitch goddess" and the woman that viewers "love to hate," Erica has, for the past nineteen years, wreaked havoc on the fictional town of Pine Valley, New York, going through five husbands and dozens of lovers (including one of her fathers-in-law) while hopping between careers ranging from a high-fashion model to a cosmetics company executive. As the first soap opera performer to star in prime-time made-for-

television movies as well as the first to appear on the cover of a major women's magazine (*Redbook*), Susan Lucci, in the opinion of Connie Passalacqua, who profiled her for *New York Newsday* (June 25, 1989), has broken "innumerable taboos associated with being a lowly soap actress," becoming in the process "daytime's unofficial standard-bearer to the entertainment world."

Jason Bonderoff, the editor of *Daytime TV* magazine, has said that Miss Lucci is "a transcendent personality as far as daytime goes," adding, "No one has ever come along who has the magic and charisma she creates." Yet despite those accolades and the overwhelming popularity of *All My Children* (an estimated eleven million people watch the show each weekday, on average), which is, in the opinion of a majority of critics, the best-written and best-acted soap opera, Susan Lucci has never been honored with an Emmy Award for her work, though she has been nominated ten times.

Susan Lucci was born on December 23 in Scarsdale, New York, a Westchester County suburb of New York City, and grew up in Garden City, Long Island. She was probably born in 1946, though some sources give her year of birth as 1948, 1949, or 1950. Her parents are Victor Lucci, a construction contractor of Italian descent, and Jeanette Lucci, a nurse of Swedish ancestry. Susan and her brother, Jim, who is six years her senior, were raised in comfortable upper-middle-class surroundings. "Since I was two and a half and would watch [soaps on] TV, I knew I didn't want to *watch* it, I wanted to *do* it," Miss Lucci told Gwen Kinkead in an interview for *Savvy Woman* (April 1989). During her childhood, *The Guiding Light* was her favorite soap opera, and the Italian-born actresses Claudia Cardinale and Sophia Loren became her first idols. Miss Lucci has said that the dark hair and eyes she inherited from her Italian father caused her to feel like something of an outsider during her childhood. "I was the only kid with dark features," she explained to Mike Hughes during an interview for the Lansing, Michigan *State Journal* (January 19, 1986). "I didn't have the blonde hair and blue eyes that everyone else had."

To cure her of her shyness, her mother once locked her out of the house in order to force her to play with the other children in the neighborhood.

Susan Lucci began to break out of her shell at the age of eleven, when she made her debut as "a Cinderella type" in a Girl Scout play and "felt totally at home onstage." She then took lessons in ice skating, horseback riding, painting, and piano. After attending a private Roman Catholic school for eight years, she enrolled at Garden City High School, where she was an honors student, a cheerleader, and a member of the newspaper staff. She played the female lead in student productions, including The King and I, traveled to Norway as an exchange student, and performed volunteer work for a local hospital. In her senior year, she placed second in a statewide "oral interpretation" contest, which was sponsored by the Forensic League.

When, after graduating from high school, Susan Lucci informed her parents that she intended to move to New York City and pursue an acting career instead of going on to college, they were less than pleased. "My . . . mother just threw her body in front of the door, saying, 'You are not leaving this house!'" she has recalled. Unable to break down her parents' resistance, she agreed to enroll in the highly regarded theatre program at Marymount College, a Roman Catholic school for women, whose main campus is located in Tarrytown, New York, about twenty-five miles north of New York City. During her years there, Miss Lucci appeared in such theatre department productions as Royal Gambit, Blithe Spirit, and The Chalk Garden. She also performed in experimental "theatre in the round" and in a local production of The Fantasticks. Just before graduating from Marymount, she made it to the semifinals of the New York State Miss Universe Beauty Pageant, but she had to withdraw from the contest so that she could take her final exams. After Marymount College granted Susan Lucci her B.A. degree in 1968, her father assumed that she would become a drama teacher, but she surprised him with the disclosure that she had not taken any education classes during her four years at Marymount and intended to follow through on her dream of becoming a professional actress. Victor Lucci relented, and Miss Lucci's first job was that of a "color girl" for CBS, an assignment that required her to report to the Ed Sullivan Theatre in New York each day and sit on a stool in front of a camera as a new lighting system for color television was developed.

While still employed at CBS, Susan Lucci received, from New York's Michael Hartig Agency, a reply to an unsolicited portfolio that she had submitted. After signing with the agency on a freelance basis, she attended auditions for soap operas, movies, commercials, regional theatre, and Broadway understudy jobs, but with so little success that she managed only to land bit parts in a few soap operas and in the films Goodbye, Columbus (1969) and Me, Natalie (1969). "Casting directors told me I should forget about television because I was dark," Susan Lucci recalled during an interview for Redbook (November 1987). "They said I might have a chance if I had blue eyes." Larry Masser, the Michael Hartig Agency representative who worked with Miss Lucci, told Ross Drake of TV Guide (June 5, 1971) that he "fell in love with Susan the minute she walked into [his] office," but he added, "The trouble is, she's a chic, fine lady. And they don't want girls in her age range for that sort of role. She's just a little too classy." Her luck seemed to improve when she was cast as the female lead in a low-budget film entitled Daddy, You Kill Me, in which she played the suicidal daughter of a prostitute, but the film was never released.

In late 1969 Larry Masser told Susan Lucci about a casting call for a new ABC soap opera, to be entitled All My Children. The "brainchild" of scriptwriter Agnes Nixon, whose long list of daytime drama credits included creating One Life to Live and serving as head writer for The Guiding Light and Another World, the series would revolve around four high school students: Phil Brent, Chuck Tyler, Tara Martin, and Erica Kane. Although Susan Lucci passed a preliminary audition for the role of Tara, Doris Quinlan, the show's original executive producer, thought she was better suited to portray Erica. "I certainly couldn't cast her as a young, innocent, sweet little Irish girl," Miss Quinlan explained to Barbara and Scott Siegel for their book Susan Lucci: The Woman behind Erica Kane (1986). "That's not what comes out. She's much more sophisticated. . . . She was perfect to play Erica, and that's how we cast her."

In her interview with Gwen Kinkead, Susan Lucci said that she identified with the Erica character immediately. "I was quite a lot like Erica back then," she told Kinkead. "I was . . . very self-centered, haughty, and arrogant." In discussing the early concept of Erica with Trustman Senger of the Washington Post (February 10, 1986), Miss Lucci described her as "the kind of girl who wouldn't go to study hall. She'd get the pass and go to the girls' room and change her hair-do." All My Children made its debut on January 5, 1970, and, in what would become a highly characteristic remark, Susan Lucci's Erica ended the first episode by telling Chuck (Jack Stauffer), "I'll bet you two Jefferson Airplane albums I can break up Phil and Tara before Christmas."

All My Children is set in the fictional community of Pine Valley, New York, supposedly about an hour's drive from New York City. In addition to Susan Lucci and Jack Stauffer, the show's other original players included Karen Lynn Gorney, as Tara Martin, and Richard Hatch, as Phil Brent. In its first few months on the air, All My Children also featured Rosemary Prinz, in the role of Amy Tyler, an antiwar and environmental activist who marries into a wealthy, conservative family. The Tyler character allowed ABC, in its early press releases, to call All My Children the first soap opera "to deal with current controversial political and social issues." In reviewing the new soap opera, the television critic Marvin Kitman of New York Newsday

(January 7, 1970) commented, "Even though I haven't the slightest idea what is going on in *All My Children*, I can't wait for tomorrow's installment to find out what ABC calls the problem and how to deal with it."

Unlike most soap operas, *All My Children* geared itself toward young viewers, and it became especially popular on college campuses. As Robert LaGuardia observed in his book *Soap World* (1983), "What college students saw in *All My Children* was a different way of looking at themselves: as members of caring families, as young people involved in old-fashioned, long-term romantic dilemmas, rather than as figures in the kaleidoscope of modern-day campus life." In August 1974 *All My Children*, for the first time, became the top-rated daytime drama. A love triangle between Tara, Chuck, and Phil dominated the show for the first eight years of its run, while Erica, the town troublemaker and Jezebel, moved through a series of marriages, affairs, and careers and had the first abortion in the annals of American soap opera.

In 1978 Susan Lucci received her first Daytime Emmy Award nomination as the best leading actress in a daytime drama. By that time, the other members of *All My Children's* original quartet of leading actors had left the series, but Susan Lucci, for several reasons, chose to continue doing the show. Miss Lucci had married Helmut Huber in 1969, and in 1975 she gave birth to the first of the couple's two children. Since soap opera actors work long, but relatively stable, hours (Susan Lucci works four twelve-hour days per week), remaining with *All My Children* allowed her to spend considerable time with her family and to stay in New York. "There's no question in my mind that my family comes first," she told Joanna Torrey of *Health* (October 1986) magazine. "I was offered a nighttime series, which meant moving to California and working five or six days a week. I decided to stay in New York where I can see more of my children." The generous compensation given her by ABC also enticed her to remain. In 1982 she signed a contract believed to be worth about $500,000, and she now reportedly earns $1 million a year, more than any other daytime star.

Critics have noted that much of the popularity of the Erica Kane character stems from the fact that, although she is an unregenerate vixen, she has a unique vulnerability that ingratiates her with the audience—an intriguing paradox that they attribute to Susan Lucci's skill as an actress. "Susan's been able to tread a fine line, that love-to-hate quality," Jason Bonderoff has explained. "You feel for Erica at the same time you want to rip her neck. To be able to play that is rare." In the opinion of *Soap Opera Digest's* Meredith Berlin, as quoted by Gwen Kinkead, "Susan Lucci has made Erica. That character is larger than life, and I don't know any actress in the world who has a better hold on her character than Lucci." The "campish" humor that Miss Lucci injects into her portrayal of Erica has also been widely praised for adding to the humani-

ty of the character. "Susan's a wonderful comedienne," Portia Nelson, one of her *All My Children* costars, told Barbara and Scott Siegel. "[She's] created a fascinating megalomaniac. Anybody else you'd want to kick in the teeth, but she manages to do something with such an innocent flair that it's always funny." And according to Connie Passalacqua, Susan Lucci's Erica is "the only soap character who both truly reflects her audience and at the same time winks in parody to it."

Various reasons have been advanced as to why Susan Lucci, despite ten nominations (in 1978 and in each year from 1981 through 1989), has never received the Daytime Emmy Award for best actress. Nominees for a Daytime Emmy submit videotapes containing what they believe to be their three best scenes from the preceding year to a "blue-ribbon panel" of stage, movie, and nighttime-television actors. The members of the panel meet in a hotel room several weeks before the awards ceremony, watch the videotapes, and select the winners. Some observers believe that jealousy over Susan Lucci's popularity and her monetary success have contributed to her failure to win an Emmy. Others have conjectured that, since Erica is a relatively unemotional character, the judges may mistakenly conclude that Miss Lucci's acting talents are limited. "As opposed to other soap actresses who tear apart the scenery, Susan plays Erica very lightly," the syndicated soap opera columnist Nancy M. Reichardt told Connie Passalacqua. "She takes Erica seriously, but she also plays her from a step back. Unfortunately, there are people in the industry who misconstrue that into thinking that Susan Lucci can't act." Similarly, the veteran actress Ruth Warrick, who portrays Phoebe Wallingford on *All My Children*, told a reporter for *People* (July 21, 1986) magazine: "Most of the winners have had very emotional scenes—they're crying, they're heartbroken—they're victims. That's the kind of scene that wins prizes. Erica has always been on top, and if something ever did upset her, she was over it in a minute."

The contract that she signed with ABC in 1984 allowed Susan Lucci to take time off from *All My Children* to do made-for-television movies, and, in May of that year, she costarred with Robert Urich in *Invitation to Hell*, playing Jessica Jones, the director of a country club who is actually the devil incarnate. The critic Kay Gardella of the New York *Daily News* (May 24, 1984) called *Invitation to Hell* "a well-acted, intriguing, but predictable film." Of Miss Lucci's performance, Miss Gardella wrote, "This is her first prime-time TV film and she's good in it—good and evil!" Although it was scheduled against such popular weekly series as CBS's *Magnum P.I.* and NBC's *Family Ties* and *Cheers*, *Invitation to Hell* easily won the ratings contest for its time slot. Susan Lucci's second film, *Mafia Princess*, which aired on NBC in January 1986, was based on the published memoirs of Antoinette Giancana, the daughter of the late Chicago crime boss Sam Giancana, who was portrayed in the movie by Tony Curtis. While conceding that the film was "sentimental and often clichéd," the critic Richard F. Shepard of the New York Times (January 18, 1986) credited it with evoking in the viewer "a concern about the principals, who are so well characterized by the actors who interpret them," adding that Susan Lucci portrayed Antoinette "skillfully." The usually exigent Tom Shales of the Washington Post (January 18, 1986) was less impressed. Labeling the film "ludicrous and pointless," he complained that it featured "the kind of enticingly ferocious overacting dear to the hearts of bad-movie lovers everywhere." Susan Lucci, in his opinion, "throttles the role of [Giancana's] daughter." Despite the mixed reviews, Mafia Princess, like Invitation to Hell, was a huge success in the ratings.

Later in 1986 Susan Lucci had a minor role in NBC's Anastasia: The Story of Anna, a four-hour miniseries about Anna Anderson, who, from the 1920s until her death in 1984, claimed to be the sole surviving daughter of Nicholas Romanov, the last czar of Russia, even though the entire Romanov family is believed to have been executed during the Bolshevik Revolution of 1917. Miss Lucci was cast as Princess Darya, a distant cousin of the Romanov family who befriends Anna (Amy Irving) when she comes to America to plead her case. The movie's cast also included such veteran actors as Rex Harrison, Claire Bloom, Olivia De Havilland, and Omar Sharif. Susan Lucci's minor role received little critical attention, though Tom Shales of the Washington Post (December 6, 1986) complimented the actress for doing "a credible job."

Susan Lucci's next venture into made-for-television films was the 1987 NBC drama Haunted by Her Past, in which she appeared as Karen Beckett, an upper-middle-class woman who, while vacationing at a restored colonial inn with her husband (John James), becomes possessed by the spirit of a 200-year-old murderess. Kay Gardella of the New York Daily News (October 5, 1987) lambasted Haunted by Her Past as "an outrageously bad film, which boils down to three hours of watching Susan Lucci . . . in narcissistic hair-brushing scenes." Reviewing the film more charitably in the Denver Rocky Mountain News (October 2, 1987), Bart Mills admitted that Haunted by Her Past was not without its faults, but he noted that Susan Lucci "is a professional to her fingertips, and she treats it all with the utmost earnestness."

In her most recent television movie, Lady Mobster, which aired on ABC in October 1988, Susan Lucci portrayed a corporation lawyer who marries into a mob family and then becomes its head. Jeff Jarvis of People (October 17, 1988), who termed Lady Mobster "the ideal Susan Lucci movie," gave the film a "B" rating, but a critic for Variety (November 2, 1988) panned it, observing of Miss Lucci's character, "It's doubtful anyone will be taken in by her."

Susan Lucci made her theatrical film debut with a cameo appearance in the 1982 comedy Young Doctors in Love, portraying an Erica Kane–like character who makes a pitch for a young physician.

In 1983 she appeared Off-Broadway in a one-night revival by the New Amsterdam Theater Company of the Kurt Weill musical One Touch of Venus at Town Hall. Miss Lucci was one of the ten ABC soap opera stars to perform on the 1983 MCA album Love in the Afternoon, singing Gershwin's "Someone to Watch over Me."

A stunning brown-eyed brunette with "flawless" olive-colored skin, Susan Lucci is five feet, two inches tall and reportedly wears the same size-four dress that she wore when All My Children went on the air nineteen years ago. Although she has been known to lose her temper occasionally (she once threw a container of yogurt at the director Henry Kaplan, and, at the Daytime Emmy Awards banquets in 1982 and 1983, she openly expressed her anger after failing to win), Susan Lucci is not considered a prima donna. "In a business filled with backstabbing and bitches, Susan is probably the only actress I've never heard a bad backstage story about," Nancy M. Reichardt told Connie Passalacqua. "She's a total professional." Miss Lucci is married to Helmut Huber, an Austrian-born businessman who also manages her career. They are parents of a daughter, Liza, and a son, Andreas, and reside in a fourteen-room, Georgian colonial house in an exclusive section of Garden City, Long Island. They also own a fourteen-room beachhouse in the Hamptons, on the south shore of Long Island. When not working, Susan Lucci enjoys traveling, skiing, and playing tennis. She has done television commercials for Diet Dr. Pepper soda and Revlon's Scoundrel perfume. Among the honors she has received are the 1980 Harvard University Award for best actress of the year and the 1988 Soap Opera Digest Editor's Award for "outstanding contribution" to daytime television drama.

References: Parade p18 Ja 15 '89 por; People 10:51+ Ag 7 '78 pors, 18:165+ D 13 '82 pors, 26:39+ Jl 21 '86 pors; TV Guide 19:27+ Je 5 '71 por, 31:20+ Ap 9 '83 por; Washington Post B p1+ F 10 '86 pors; Who's Who in America, 1988–89

Lujan, Manuel, Jr.

(loo´ hän)

May 12, 1928– United States Secretary of the Interior. Address: Office of the Secretary, United States Department of the Interior, 18th and C Sts. N.W., Washington, D.C. 20240

In February 1989, after twenty years as the only Hispanic Republican in the United States House of Representatives, Manuel Lujan Jr. joined the cabinet of President George Bush as secretary of the interior. The Department of the Interior administers, through the Bureau of Land Management, the National Park Service, and other agencies, approximately 470 million acres in the United States,

Manuel Lujan Jr.

including Alaska—more than one-fifth of the nation's 2.2 billion acres. Ever since concern for protecting the environment became politically viable with the passage of the Wilderness Act twenty-five years ago, the secretary of the interior has been charged with balancing environmental protection with development of the nation's natural resources. Manuel Lujan Jr. insists that both goals can be met, but his record in Congress reveals an attitude that strongly favors development over conservation.

As the ranking minority member of the House Interior and Insular Affairs Committee from 1981 to 1985, Lujan tended to back the administration of President Ronald Reagan, whose controversial first-term secretary of the interior, James G. Watt, pursued staunchly prodevelopment policies. Watt's successors, William P. Clark and Donald P. Hodel, continued to emphasize resource exploitation during the remaining years of Reagan's presidency. While environmentalists saw Lujan as an improvement over his predecessors, they were nonetheless disappointed by his selection. The League of Conservation Voters gave Lujan a 23 percent favorable rating, and the United States Chamber of Commerce reported that his votes were congenial to business interests 80 percent of the time. But unlike Watt, who was considered an uncompromising ideologue, Lujan has been described by friend and foe alike as a consensus builder and a good listener.

Manuel Lujan Jr. was born in San Ildefonso, a village on the Rio Grande northwest of Santa Fe, New Mexico, on May 12, 1928, the eighth of the eleven children of Manuel and Lorenzita (Romero) Lujan. Two of his siblings died in infancy. His brother Edward became the state chairman of the

Republican party in New Mexico. His father operated a flourishing insurance agency, served three terms as the Republican mayor of Santa Fe, and ran unsuccessfully for Congress in 1944 and for governor in 1948. Lujan attended Our Lady of Guadalupe elementary and junior high school and St. Michael's High School in San Ildefonso. In 1946 he enrolled as a business administration student at St. Mary's College in San Francisco, but at the end of his freshman year he transferred to the College of Santa Fe, from which he received a B.A. degree in 1950. In 1948 he joined his father's insurance agency in Santa Fe, where he worked for the following twenty years. Following an unsuccessful run for the New Mexico state senate in 1964, Lujan moved from the state capital to Albuquerque, where he expanded the family business.

In 1968, after serving for a time as vice-chairman of the state Republican party, Lujan topped a crowded Republican primary field with 35 percent of the vote to win the right to challenge five-term Democratic congressman Thomas G. Morris in New Mexico's First Congressional District, then comprising the northeastern third of the state, including its main population centers of Santa Fe and Albuquerque. (This was the first election in which New Mexico's two congressmen were elected by district instead of at large.) Campaigning on a pledge to work for a balanced federal budget and appealing to the ethnic pride of the region's traditionally Democratic Hispanic voters, Lujan upset Morris to become the state's first Hispanic congressman as well as the first Hispanic Republican in the House of Representatives. National party officials, seeing a chance to woo Hispanics away from their Democratic loyalties, trotted him out during televised coverage of the 1972 Republican National Convention in Miami Beach, Florida and, periodically thereafter, showcased him at party functions as the party's senior Hispanic member. Aside from such appearances, Lujan maintained a low profile during his two decades on Capitol Hill.

Throughout the 1970s Lujan was reelected to Congress by such overwhelming majorities that he became lax about campaigning. He nearly lost his seat in 1980 when, without benefit of a campaign manager, he ignored a challenge from Bill Richardson, a former state Democratic party leader who had recently settled in the district for his first try at elective office. "I assumed nobody would pay any attention to someone who'd just moved here a year before," Lujan later explained to a reporter from the Albuquerque *Tribune* (January 4, 1988). But Richardson hammered away at Lujan for missing key floor votes and for favoring business at the expense of consumers, winning strong support in the outlying counties, which was barely offset by Lujan's majority in Albuquerque.

Heartened by a narrow 51 to 49 percent loss, the Democrats geared up to unseat Lujan in 1982. The Democratic campaign was inadvertently aided by a 1982 Better Government Association report that raised ethical questions about Manuel Lujan Insurance Agencies, the firm founded by his father and operated by his brother Edward. According to *Politics in America*, the report charged that Lujan's insurance agency "had collected about $1 million in profits through a virtual monopoly over the issuance of Small Business Administration (SBA)-guaranteed bonds in New Mexico." As reported by *Newsweek* (January 9, 1989), some of the loans "later defaulted, at a cost to taxpayers of more than $5 million." Lujan maintained part ownership in the firm throughout his years in Congress. In 1982 he owned 45 percent, according to the *Newsweek* report, which also stated that he "still voted regularly for SBA bond appropriations." Although Lujan was never the subject of a formal investigation, allegations of conflict of interest cropped up periodically during subsequent reelection campaigns. Lujan was quoted by *Newsweek* as saying, "I now own 10 percent and I have not had anything to do with the agency for twenty years except for ownership." He has since sold his interest in the agency to his brother.

Despite the scandal, Lujan's 1982 campaign recovered, largely as a result of redistricting after the 1980 census awarded New Mexico a third congressional seat. The popular Richardson, instead of challenging Lujan again, ran (successfully) in the newly created Third District, which encompassed most of the outlying counties of the old First District, which in turn was left with Greater Albuquerque, Lujan's stronghold, and a few desert counties to the east. Even so, Lujan's opponent in the First District, the state treasurer Jan A. Hartke, ran an impressive campaign on a strong environmental platform, drawing more votes in Albuquerque than did Richardson two years earlier. But with so many of the outlying counties stripped away, Lujan managed to hang on to his seat by a margin of 52 to 48 percent, and his tenure was never again seriously threatened.

During his two decades in Congress, Lujan established a reputation as a quiet conservative whose primary concern was constituent service. "He took care of personal details," Jerry Apodaca, the former governor of New Mexico and a close friend, observed, as quoted by the *Washington Post* (May 15, 1989). "We used to kid him that he was the best caseworker we had in New Mexico. It's one of his greatest strengths." From 1969 to 1989 Lujan served on the House Interior and Insular Affairs Committee, where he was the ranking Republican during Reagan's first term. Despite party differences with the committee's Democratic chairman, Morris K. Udall of Arizona, Lujan established a cordial working relationship with Udall—a bit too cordial for some in the Reagan administration who expected Lujan to fight for their conservative agenda. Although Lujan lent passive support to most of the administration's initiatives, he balked at leading a frontal assault against Udall and at times openly resented Watt's tactics. In 1981, for example, Lujan learned from newspaper accounts that Watt had agreed to open 700 acres of New Mexico's El Capitán Wilderness to oil and gas exploration. Furious that he had not been consulted about

a matter of intense interest in his district and deluged by mail from angry constituents, Lujan belatedly introduced legislation to delay the project.

Such exemplary constituent service notwithstanding, Lujan received poor marks for his record on environmental issues. He cosponsored legislation designed to permit the development of oil and gas properties in the ecologically sensitive Arctic National Wildlife Refuge and voted to cut federal subsidies for water projects and energy conservation funds and to continue the sale of federal mining claims at bargain rates of $2.50 an acre, although he reversed himself on the latter issue in February 1989. He was ever skeptical of plans to thwart development projects in order to protect various endangered species, and he was a staunch supporter of the nuclear power industry, which consumes much of New Mexico's uranium production. There were a few exceptions to this pattern. In 1987, for example, he joined a 401 to 26 bipartisan majority in voting to override President Reagan's veto of a clean-water bill; he also voted against extending the deadline for major cities, including Albuquerque, to clean up their air or risk losing federal funds.

In 1985 Reagan considered—and rejected—Lujan for the post of secretary of the interior for the third time in five years. That year Lujan gave up his ranking status (but not his membership) on the Interior Committee to become the ranking Republican on the Science, Space, and Technology Committee, on which he served from 1977 to 1989. Although he had long supported the American space program, he sharply criticized the National Aeronautics and Space Administration in the wake of the fatal explosion of the space shuttle *Challenger* in January 1986. He charged that NASA was covering up defects that might have led to the disaster, condemned the presidential commission appointed by President Reagan to investigate the explosion for its unwillingness to affix blame, and criticized his own committee for failing to oversee NASA operations effectively. As a member of a presidential commission to consider long-term space policy goals, Lujan concurred in the commission's 1986 report, which called for the establishment of permanent bases on the moon and Mars within the next fifty years and the eventual commercial mining of their surfaces.

In 1986 Lujan suffered a heart attack and underwent a five-hour triple bypass operation. Thus, when he abruptly announced, on January 4, 1988, that he was retiring at the end of his tenth term in Congress, observers attributed his decision to poor health. Lujan denied that, saying, "The basic reason is that I see so many of my colleagues stay too long. After twenty years, it's time to come home." President-elect Bush persuaded him to postpone his retirement, naming him secretary of the interior on December 22, 1988.

In Lujan, Bush found a perfect compromise choice to satisfy both the party's moderates, who were promoting former senator Daniel J. Evans of Washington, and its conservatives, who were touting Governor Garrey Carruthers of New Mexico, a Watt disciple. The choice of Lujan was weighted heavily toward appeasing the conservatives. According to Cass Peterson of the *Washington Post* (May 15, 1989), "The appointment of a noted environmentalist, Conservation Foundation president William K. Reilly, as head of the Environmental Protection Agency left conservatives howling for a counterbalance at Interior." Moderate Republicans, in turn, seemed relieved that Bush had chosen a man less dogmatic than Reagan's appointees had been. "He's a pragmatic guy who operates in the world of the possible," commented Democratic congressman Bruce F. Vento of Minnesota, who served with Lujan on the Interior Committee, as quoted by the *New York Times* (December 23, 1988). "He is a known quantity to the members of Congress, and they will feel comfortable with him. No one would say he is an ideologue in the mold of Jim Watt."

In his acceptance speech on December 22, 1988, Lujan likened his prospective position to "that of landlord over the largest ownership of property" in the nation and emphasized his commitment "to the preservation of this heritage." He added, "If one little piece of our public trust is desecrated, we all suffer from it." A few months later, however, in a meeting with conservationists, he referred (jokingly, he insisted) to the 270 million acres administered by the Bureau of Land Management as "a place with a lot of grass for cows" and indicated that he supported opening national parks to livestock grazing.

Environmentalists greeted Lujan's appointment with resigned despondency. "We feel like we've gotten a lump of coal for Christmas," said Geoff Webb, the conservation director of Friends of the Earth, as quoted by the *New York Times* (December 23, 1988). Some were optimistic that Lujan's reputation for accessibility would render him amenable to persuasion, but others expected his policies to remain unaffected by his disposition. "He keeps the door open, he listens, and then he votes against you," James Maddy, the executive director of the League of Conservation Voters, complained, as quoted in the *Washington Post* (December 22, 1988).

At his confirmation hearing before the Senate Energy and Natural Resources Committee in January 1989, Lujan pledged to maintain a dialogue with environmentalists but made no specific commitments. He was confirmed unanimously by the full Senate on February 2. At a press conference following his swearing-in ceremony the following day, Lujan urged going forward with plans to open the Arctic National Wildlife Refuge to oil exploration but conceded that some acutely sensitive areas of the refuge might be exempted. He also encouraged the sale of oil leases off the California coast but placed the national park and wilderness systems off-limits to mining operations.

In March Lujan's sense of balance was tested on an issue that often found him at odds with environmentalists during his years in Congress—the lengths to which private industry should be required to go to refrain from further endangering a threatened species. At issue was the spotted owl, under review for possible classification as an endangered species, and the disruption to its habitat in the Northwest by the timber industry. Environmentalists argued that a vast tract should be set aside to ensure the survival of the species, while the timber industry warned that thousands of jobs could be lost in Washington and Oregon if the region were closed off to logging operations. Lujan did not hide his disdain for the environmentalists' position. "In looking at endangered species," he was quoted as saying in the *Oil and Gas Journal* (March 20, 1989), "the law says you cannot take into consideration economic disruption. That bothers me. Maybe we should change the law. . . . There ought to be some mechanism where you can take both things into consideration. Even if [the spotted owl] is an endangered species it probably doesn't need 3,000 acres per pair of owls. They probably can exist in a smaller area."

In April 1989 Lujan again angered environmentalists by deciding to renew a long-term water contract in California's Central Valley before its effect on the environment could be determined. The Environmental Protection Agency had invoked the National Environmental Policy Act in requesting that Lujan delay his decision until an impact study could be completed. When Lujan refused, the matter was automatically referred to the Council on Environmental Quality, which mediates such disputes between federal agencies. Without waiting for its ruling, Lujan ordered the renewal of the contract guaranteeing water delivery to the Orange Cove Irrigation District for the next forty years. It was the first time that a government agency had ever preempted a decision by the Council on Environmental Quality. Because this was the first of hundreds of long-term water contracts expected to come up for renewal, the EPA feared that Lujan's decision might set a dangerous precedent. Democratic senator Bill Bradley of New Jersey, as quoted in the *New York Times* (April 12, 1989), denounced the precipitate action as a "blatant power play by the secretary of the interior to prevent an impartial review."

Policy decisions, however, were not the only source of criticism directed at Lujan. Longtime Washington observers have noted that he often seems unprepared and ill-informed about important issues and that he has thus far failed to lay out any concrete departmental goals. According to a report in the *Arizona Republic* (March 5, 1989), he reads little and occasionally confuses facts in public. "He assimilates his knowledge from people," Joe Monahan, Lujan's former press aide, said, as quoted in the *Arizona Republic* article. "Some would consider that shallow, but that's how he operates." A particularly conspicuous gaffe was Lujan's assertion, in an interview with a reporter from the *Washington Post* (May 15, 1989), that Alaska should have priority over the federal government in regulating oil development off its shores because, he said, "they have the most to lose," but when asked if California, which has been trying to block federal attempts to increase offshore drilling activity, should have the same right, he offered no response except to joke sheepishly, "Well, I walked into that one, didn't I?" Lujan also has been slow to appoint his own team at Interior and, critics charge, has looked for direction from a stable of Reagan-era holdovers.

Reports that Lujan wields little clout within the administration were bolstered in the wake of America's worst oil spill in March 1989, when the *Exxon Valdez* dumped 260,000 barrels, or eleven million gallons, of oil in Prince William Sound off Alaska. As President Bush weighed the government's options, he dispatched to the scene Secretary of Transportation Samuel K. Skinner, William K. Reilly, the EPA administrator, and Admiral Paul A. Yost Jr., the commandant of the Coast Guard. Lujan remained in Washington, restricted to a subordinate role in shaping the government's response to the disaster. Although the oil spill did not shake Lujan's commitment to development in the region, he warned oil industry executives that, unless they responded quickly and responsibly to clean up the

mess, it could sour the public on offshore oil exploration in much the same way that the 1979 accident at Three Mile Island crippled the nuclear power industry.

Manuel Lujan Jr. has been described as affable, easygoing, and unpretentious. One of the achievements of which he is proudest was his creation of the Endowment for Excellence in Education in 1984. The fund, which within four years had grown to more than $250,000, annually provides a scholarship to one student from each high school in New Mexico's First Congressional District. Lujan has been married to the former Jean Kay Couchman since 1948. They have four children—Terra Kay Everett, James Manuel (Jay), Barbara Frae, and Robert Jeffrey (Jeff). In his spare time, Lujan enjoys woodworking, reading the novels of James Michener, and playing a weekly game of small-stakes poker. The Lujans maintain homes in Washington, D.C., and Albuquerque.

References: N Y Times A p25 D 23 '88 por; Mexican-American Biographies (1988); Politics in America (1988); Who's Who in America, 1988–89; Who's Who in American Politics, 1989–90

Lunden, Joan

Sept. 19, 1950– Broadcast journalist. Address: ABC-TV, Good Morning America, 1965 Broadway, New York, N.Y. 10023

When Joan Lunden joined WABC's *Eyewitness News* team in 1975, she had been in broadcast journalism for less than two years. An attractive woman with a comfortable on-air manner and a pleasant personality, she survived a barrage of brickbats hurled by television critics and even by her colleagues, some of whom complained that her rapid rise was based more on appearance than on journalistic expertise, and eventually flourished, as co-host of *Good Morning America*, ABC's weekday wakeup program. Over the past decade, her three very public pregnancies and the success of her award-winning cable television program, *Mother's Day*, have helped her to transcend labels like "Ms. Plastic" and, in the words of the humorist Erma Bombeck, have made her "a prototype for women of the eighties who want it all without sacrificing integrity and the importance of family." "People at home feel at ease with me," Miss Lunden has said, in explaining her appeal to Ryan Murphy for a *Saturday Evening Post* (September 1988) profile. "I'm a cousin to them, or a buddy, or a person at work. . . . If viewers feel they have something in common with you—the same dirty diapers and joys and sorrows and concerns—then all of a sudden there's a closeness. I really think that's happened with me. I'm living proof that people care about family."

Joan Lunden was born Joan Elise Blunden on September 19, 1950 in Fair Oaks, California, the younger of the two children of Erle Murray Blunden, a physician, and his wife, the former Gladyce Lorraine Somervill. (She changed her surname to Lunden in 1975, at the request of her superiors at WABC.) After her father, an avid amateur pilot, was killed in the crash of his private plane in January 1964, Joan and her brother, Jeffrey, were reared by their mother, an energetic and enthusiastic woman who worked as a real-estate agent in order to support the family. "She was made of 'strong stuff,' as they used to say . . . ," Joan Lunden said of her mother in her autobiography *Good Morning, I'm Joan Lunden* (1986), which she wrote with Ardy Friedberg. "As far back as I can remember she has tried to instill high aspirations, to get me to dream, to expand my horizons, and especially to go to college and be a success." Encouraged by her mother, Joan, an excellent student, took correspondence courses from the University of California at Berkeley while she was still in high school. Despite a heavy academic schedule, she found the time to participate in local beauty contests, take piano and dance lessons, and act as a majorette for the school's marching band.

Following her graduation from high school at the age of sixteen, Miss Lunden took a summer job as an assistant in an X-ray laboratory. She had intended to become a doctor, but three months "in close contact with blood and pain," as she described it in her autobiography, put an end to that ambition. Instead of beginning her premed studies in the fall of 1967, as she had planned, Miss Lunden signed up for the World Campus Afloat program, a shipboard school administered by Chapman College in Orange, California that combines an academic curriculum and world travel. During a four-month term aboard the SS *Ryndam,* she studied psychology and visited more than a dozen countries, including Spain, Morocco, South Africa, Kenya, Uganda, India, Thailand, and Japan. The sights she saw, Miss Lunden recalled in her autobiography, "were sobering, majestic, and enlightening." "Until that time I had never been confronted with many of the harsh realities of life . . . ," she wrote. "The contrasts of wealth and poverty, sickness and health, black and white and brown skins had a tremendous impact on my thinking from that point on."

Miss Lunden has referred to the years between 1968 and 1972 as her "flaky period." Having become interested in the peoples and cultures of the world during her travels, she enrolled at the Universidad de las Américas, then in Mexico City, in 1968 as an anthropology major, but she soon switched her academic focus to art and drama. To earn spending money, she worked part-time as a fashion model and, as her fluency in Spanish increased, as an actress in local television commercials. A chance encounter with a public-relations agent in 1970 led to a bit part as a saloon hostess in the offbeat Western film *Macho Callahan.* "I was probably on the screen a total of a minute and a half and didn't say a word," Miss Lunden has recalled, "but it was a lot of fun and my first real bite of show business."

On her return to the United States in 1972, Joan Lunden enrolled at American River Junior College in Sacramento, where she eventually earned an associate of arts degree. She also took a sixty-day modeling course and, on its completion, opened her own charm and modeling school. Although her enterprise was reasonably successful, she continued to look for career opportunities that, in her view, "seemed to have potential for the future." In 1973 a salesman for KCRA-TV, the NBC affiliate station in Sacramento, hired Miss Lunden to do some hand modeling in a few commercials the station was producing. Impressed by her unusual educational background, good looks, and travel experience, the salesman referred the young woman to Paul Thompson, then the station's news director. Thompson, too, was impressed. As he told Ryan Murphy, "When she walked through the door, I saw that she'd be good for television. She was attractive, yes, but she was also very bright. She didn't have any experience but was very interested in starting a TV career. So I hired her."

Miss Lunden joined the staff of KCRA in October 1973 as an apprentice to Harry Geise, the station's weatherman. After working behind the scenes for about two months, she made her first on-camera appearance as a last-minute substitute for the ailing Geise. Admittedly nervous, she talked so rapidly that she finished delivering the five-minute weather summary in less than two minutes. Not knowing how to fill the remaining time, she repeated the entire forecast. In spite of her embarrassing debut, Geise asked Miss Lunden to do the noon weather spot twice a week. Her duties at the station were soon expanded to include weekly—and then daily—consumer reports. When she accepted the new assignment, Miss Lunden's knowledge of consumer affairs was slight, but she quickly educated herself in the subject by taking consumer classes at a local college, talking to consumer advocates, and collecting enough articles and documents to fill two filing cabinets. Within six months of her arrival, Joan Lunden was coanchoring KCRA's daily noon newscast, and shortly thereafter she became the first woman to anchor the station's 6:00 P.M. news program. During her tenure at KCRA, she also occasionally hosted the station's special programs.

In 1975 Miss Lunden's tenacity and willingness to work long hours helped her land a job as a reporter for WABC-TV's *Eyewitness News* in New York City. She has described her first few months at the station as a "baptism by fire," in which she had to cover many of the unsavory and late-breaking stories that are the lot of the rookie reporters—assignments, Miss Lunden has put it, that usually involved "dead bodies, devastation, fire and smoke, prostitutes, and demonstrators." She also had to contend with the hostility of her newsroom colleagues, who made an issue of her inexperience as a street reporter and dubbed her "Barbie," after the plastic, albeit stylish and perfectly coiffed, children's toy.

In deference to her new employers, Joan Lunden changed her surname because station management worried that the New York television critics would have a field day with a name that sounded like "blunder." "As it turned out," she wrote later, "they had one anyway." Although Miss Lunden herself has acknowledged that she was hired at least partly because the ethnically diverse *Eyewitness News* team was "missing the blond, WASP category in their ethnic mix" that would appeal to more affluent suburban viewers, she was nonetheless both stung and energized by the barbs of television critics and her coworkers. "When I started out, I was a sitting duck," she told Ryan Murphy. "They just made mincemeat out of me. For the two years I was in Sacramento, barely a week would go by that I wasn't destroyed in print by one of the critics. Now, I grant you, I was not good. I was just starting. I made tons of mistakes. So some of the criticism was deserved. But some of it wasn't fair. And when I came to New York it was the same thing, the same bows and arrows. And it was only by staying on, and doing the job, and hanging in there that I finally got to the point where it stopped."

Miss Lunden's association with *Good Morning America* began in 1976, when she was hired to deliver weekly reports on new products of interest to consumers, such as "donut-type" spare tires, joggers' wastebaskets, and transistor radios that float. The informative and often entertaining spots caught the eye of the network vice-president in charge of the show, and when Nancy Dussault, who had shared hosting duties on *Good Morning America* with David Hartman since its premiere on November 3, 1975, announced that she would leave the program in April 1977, Joan Lunden was interviewed as a possible successor, but the coveted position went to Sandy Hill. Undaunted, Miss Lunden continued to polish her skills as a reporter, and by 1977 she was anchoring the Sunday evening *Eyewitness News* telecasts. The next year she was offered a small part in the film *Kramer vs. Kramer*, as the attorney who represents Dustin Hoffman's character in a child-custody case, but she declined the role. She also turned down opportunities to host the game show *Pass the Buck* and to star in Norman Lear's proposed situation comedy "Coast to Coast."

Between 1977 and 1980, Joan Lunden's role on *Good Morning America* gradually expanded. When Sandy Hill was on vacation or on assignment, Miss Lunden often did the "People in the News" segments and the commercials. Late in 1977 she took center stage on the program for the first time when both David Hartman and Sandy Hill developed laryngitis. From then on, she appeared frequently as a substitute co-host. Miss Lunden became a regular feature reporter on *Good Morning America* in February 1980, and six months later she succeeded Sandy Hill as the program's co-host. Like her two female predecessors, however, Miss Lunden was given the title reporter-interviewer; she was not officially designated co-host until her contract was renewed in August 1986.

Before beginning her new assignment, Miss Lunden, who had married Michael Krauss, a television producer, on September 10, 1978, created something of a stir in the industry by having a childcare clause written into her contract, which allowed her to set up a nursery adjacent to her office so that she could breast-feed her newborn daughter during working hours. With characteristic resourcefulness and ingenuity, she parlayed her pregnancy, childbirth, and experiences as a new parent into dozens of features for *Good Morning America*, including interviews with obstetricians, pediatricians, and other childcare professionals, looks at products for infants and new parents, and demonstrations of exercises designed especially for expectant mothers. At the same time, however, Miss Lunden was struggling to carve a niche for herself on a program that, from its inception, had been dominated by David Hartman. "I'd look at the rundown of stories and see that I was doing Dog Hero of the Month," she told Jane Hall in a conversation for a *People* (August 18, 1986) magazine profile. "If I asked to do a piece on, say, deficit financing, the producers would say, 'David already knows all about it.' Sometimes it really got me down."

As she explained in her autobiography, Joan Lunden eventually came out from behind Hartman's shadow by heeding the advice of Barbara Walters, the first woman television journalist to command both a high salary and equal billing with her male colleagues. "Whether it's money or stories you've been shorted on," Miss Walters told her, "you do yourself a disservice to get angry about what you don't get. Hone and polish each little bit you've been given until you make it a gem." Accordingly, during 1981 and 1982 Miss Lunden pursued the feature and human-interest stories she was invariably assigned with her patented combination of drive and affability. Among other things, she traveled to London to cover the wedding of Prince Charles and Lady Diana Spencer; to Knoxville, Tennessee, to report on the 1982 World's Fair; to Boston for Patriots' Day and the Boston Marathon; to Philadelphia for "Century IV," the city's tricentennial celebration; to New Orleans for the Mardi Gras; and to the Chicago Cubs' spring-training camp, where she suited up for batting practice. By 1983 she had gained enough stature as a reporter to tackle "hard news" stories, including interviews with such prominent public figures as Henry A. Kissinger, the former secretary of state, and Vice-President George Bush. In addition, she was one of only three American journalists to interview Prince Charles during his 1983 visit to the United States.

In February 1987, six months after Miss Lunden was officially named co-host of *Good Morning America*, David Hartman, who had reportedly been unable to come to terms with Capital Cities, which had recently assumed control of ABC, left the show. He was succeeded by Charles Gibson, an experienced network correspondent with a folksy, easygoing manner. The new arrangement made Joan Lunden the senior member of the *Good Morning America* team and gave her the preeminence that she had not enjoyed in the past. Ironically, she still had to contend with management's perception that she was best suited for "cooking pieces and the dumb stuff," but she had gained enough leverage to demand and receive plum assignments. For instance, even when Gibson was in Europe on assignment the producers tapped him to interview Henry Kissinger, who was in *Good Morning America*'s New York studio with Miss Lunden. "I put my foot down and got the interview," Miss Lunden told Jan Herman of the New York *Daily News* (August 31, 1987), "but I shouldn't have to fight for that." More recently, she has filed stories from Sweden, Ireland, and the Caribbean, but she passed up the chance to interview the actor Timothy Dalton, "the new James Bond," who was then on location in Tangier shooting the 1987 film *The Living Daylights*, because she feared the possibility of a terrorist attack and, as a parent, she felt she could not "afford to risk [her] life."

Throughout her tenure on *Good Morning America*, Joan Lunden has pursued a variety of other projects, most of them focusing on parenting. *Mother's Day*, a half-hour television show starring Miss Lunden and developed by her husband, Michael Krauss, debuted on the Lifetime cable network to warm reviews and enthusiastic viewer response in February 1984. Described by Krauss as "a sharing of information and a celebration of motherhood," the program features celebrity interviews, advice from experts on child rearing, product demonstrations, short cartoons, a "mamalogue," in which Miss Lunden discusses experiences she has had with her own children, and "Mothers, Note," useful bits of advice flashed on the television screen, such as "Check your first-aid kit for expiration date."

In 1986 Miss Lunden added *Mothers' Minutes*—a series of informational spots, broadcast on weekday afternoons by ABC, offering solutions to uncommon child-rearing problems—to her increasingly crowded schedule. She has also hosted several special programs for the network, including *Walt Disney's Happy Easter Parade* and *Our Kids and the Best of Everything*, on which she shared the spotlight with Alan Thicke. Her daily, syndicated talk show, *Everyday with Joan Lunden*, on which she discusses a mix of topics with her guests, made its debut in September 1989 on some 120 television stations around the country. In addition, Miss Lunden is featured in the 1986 instructional video *Your Newborn Baby: Everything You Need to Know*, which gives advice on a wide range of topics, including how to interview prospective pediatricians, how to choose the proper equipment for the care of an infant, and how to breast-feed. "There is so much crammed into this hour-long program," Bonnie Johnson wrote in a review for *People* (March 17, 1986), "that Lunden is forced to speak at an awesome clip. She handles it with amazing grace." Miss Lunden writes the syndicated column "Parent's Notes," and she is the coauthor, with her husband, of the books *Joan Lunden's Mothers' Minutes* (1986) and *Your Newborn Baby*, which was designed to complement her parenting video.

Joan Lunden has shoulder-length, curly blonde hair, light brown eyes, and a warm, friendly smile.

She and Michael Krauss live in a large, California-style house in Westchester County, north of New York City, with their three daughters, Jamie Beryl, Lindsay Leigh, and Sarah Emily. Miss Lunden's weekdays begin at 3:45 A.M., when she gets up and begins preparing for the day's broadcast. A chauffeured limousine picks her up at 4:30, and forty-five minutes later she arrives at the *Good Morning America* studio on Manhattan's West Side. On her way home from work, she often stops at a fitness center for an hour of aerobics and weight training before picking up her two older children at school.

Miss Lunden is the spokesperson for the American Lung Association's campaign to enlighten women about the dangers of smoking during pregnancy, and she often gives speeches, which she writes herself, on motherhood and related topics. Her long list of honors includes the Spirit of Achievement Award from Yeshiva University's Albert Einstein College of Medicine and awards from the National Women's Political Caucus, Baylor University, the Council of United Cerebral Palsy Auxiliaries, and the New Jersey Division on Civil Rights. In 1982 she was named Outstanding Mother of the Year by the National Mother's Day Committee.

References: *Chicago Tribune* VI p3 S 27 '87 por; *Ladies Home J* 104:62+ Ap '87 pors; *Parade* p22 Ag 28 '88 por; *People* 14:57+ N 3 '80 pors, 26:7+ Ag 18 '86 pors; *Sat Eve Post* 260:58+ S '88 pors; *TV Guide* 37:12+ S 2 '89 pors; *USA Weekend* p6 Ag 1-3 '86 por; *Washington Post* C p1+ Ag 19 '86 pors; *Who's Who in America, 1988-89*

LuPone, Patti

Apr. 21, 1949- Actress; singer. Address: c/o The Gersh Agency, 130 W. 42d St., Suite 1804, New York, N.Y. 10036

The contemporary American musical theatre contains no name brighter than that of Patti LuPone, star of two of the most successful musicals of the past decade, *Evita* and *Anything Goes*. Yet, as evidence of the parlous state of the American musical, neither of those productions is by a living American composer or lyricist, and despite the 1980 Tony Award she won for her performance in *Evita*, Miss LuPone was forced to go to England in 1985 to revive her sagging career. There, for her performances in the musicals *The Cradle Will Rock* and *Les Misérables*, she was hailed as the "first lady of the stage" by the London *Times*. She also became the first American to receive a Laurence Olivier Award, the British equivalent of the Tony Award, for her work in *Les Misérables*. After a post-*Evita* series of what she called "raging, crying parts," the role of the brash, sexy Reno Sweeney in Cole Porter's *Anything Goes* was a welcome change for her.

Patti LuPone

Not just a singing actress, Patti LuPone had an elite theatrical education at the Juilliard School's drama division. She then won high praise for her work in a series of classic and contemporary plays staged by the late John Houseman's Acting Company and appeared in five dramas by David Mamet. Miss LuPone hopes to sing someday at the Apollo Theatre in Harlem and at the Metropolitian Opera and to perform Greek tragedies in Greece.

Patti LuPone was born on April 21, 1949 in the village of Northport on New York's Long Island, the youngest of the three children and the only daughter of Orlando Joseph LuPone, a school administrator, and Angela Louise ("Patti") LuPone, an administrator at the C. W. Post College graduate library. She is the great-grandniece of the legendary Italian soprano Adelina Patti, whose name she bears. Her parents separated when she was twelve and later were divorced.

After the separation, Patti and her twin brothers, Robert, now an actor, and William, now a high school librarian, lived with their mother. All three LuPone children were exposed to the performing arts at an early age. Angela LuPone was an opera buff and an amateur pianist, and Orlando LuPone, while serving as principal of Ocean Avenue elementary school in Northport, introduced an extra-curricular program that included dancing. "I was enrolled at four," Patti LuPone recalled during an interview with Linda Winer for New York Newsday (October 18, 1987). "I did a tap number, looked down at the audience and said, 'Hey! They're all smiling at me! I can do whatever I want!' I was hooked . . . and never turned back." At Northport High School, she sang in the concert choir and madrigal group, played tuba in the marching band and cello in the school orchestra,

and appeared in school theatrical productions, including South Pacific. She also took private voice and piano lessons, studied dance and drama, and, with her brothers, developed a dance act called the LuPone Trio, which competed in contests and appeared at benefits all over Long Island. "She just had more energy than she knew what to do with and she just wanted to be in every puddle," Esther Scott, Miss LuPone's music teacher, has said. "Her voice had tremendous quality. She also had a very creative mind." Patti LuPone's entry in the 1967 Northport High School yearbook read as follows: "Most musical, most dramatic, class clown, the most well-known person in school, extremely talented, exuberant, outgoing, nuts, peppy, uninhibited. Will long be remembered."

Following her high school graduation, Miss LuPone, hoping to pursue a career in opera, auditioned for admission to the Juilliard School at Lincoln Center, but she failed the tryout. Then, on the advice of her brother Robert, then a Juilliard dance student, she auditioned for a spot in the school's newly created drama department, headed by the distinguished actor and director John Houseman, and was admitted. Of the thirty-six students enrolled in the first class in 1968, only fourteen graduated on schedule four years later, having survived Houseman's grueling regimen of thirteen-hour days (including six hours of pre-rehearsal warmups), with only one day off a week. "It was rougher at Juilliard than it has ever been on the outside world," Patti LuPone has said. Although he later called her "as devoted and assiduous a student as one could wish for," Houseman had little patience with the rambunctiousness of the young actress during her student days, and he once placed her on probation for her antics with the rebuke, "You do more acting in the corridors than in the classroom!"

Convinced that the drama department's first graduating class (whose members also included Kevin Kline) was uniquely talented, Houseman, together with his collaborator, Michel Saint-Denis, organized the group into a professional repertory troupe called the Juilliard Acting Company (a name that was later changed to the City Center Acting Company and, still later, to simply the Acting Company). Over the next three years, the company toured the United States for forty-eight weeks a year, performing both classical and contemporary plays. Supported largely by federal and state grants, as well as by private funding, the group presented workshops, classes, and a repertoire of eighteen plays in more than fifty cities in twenty-two states, often climbing off the company bus to play a one-night stand, then leaving immediately afterward for their next performance.

Patti LuPone made her Off-Broadway debut at the Good Shepherd-Faith Church, near Lincoln Center, on September 28, 1972, as Lady Teazle in the City Center Acting Company's production of Sheridan's School for Scandal. Reviewing the play for the New York Times (September 29, 1972), Clive Barnes credited LuPone's Lady Teazle with being "unusually sweet and vulnerable." And T. E. Kalem, in his review for *Time* (October 9, 1972) magazine, wrote that Miss LuPone "brings a peppery pique and sweet contrition" to the role. Commenting on her performance as Lizzie in James Saunders's *Next Time I'll Sing to You*, which opened at the Good Shepherd–Faith Church a month later, Mel Gussow of the *New York Times* (October 26, 1972) called Miss LuPone "a comic actress with enormous personal flair." She also played Kathleen in Brendan Behan's *Hostage*, Natasha in Maxim Gorky's *Lower Depths*, and Bianca in the Jacobean tragedy *Women Beware Women* before the company left on a cross-country tour, returning to New York in December 1973 to make their Broadway debut in Chekhov's *Three Sisters* at the Billy Rose Theatre. Miss LuPone's performance as Irina drew praise from Clive Barnes in the *New York Times*, and Allan Wallach of *Newsday* (December 20, 1973) wrote that she "captures the radiance of a young girl that is transformed by boredom and fatigue." Miss LuPone also appeared around that time as Lucky Lockit in John Gay's *Beggar's Opera*, as Hyacinthe in Molière's *Scapin*, and, once again, as Lizzie in *Next Time I'll Sing to You*.

The Juilliard troupe made its next New York appearance in the fall of 1975, performing a stage adaptation of the Eudora Welty novella *The Robber Bridegroom* at the Harkness Theatre, in which Patti LuPone played the adventurous daughter of a Mississippi plantation owner and Kevin Kline portrayed an amorous thief. Although the play ran for only two weeks, Miss LuPone earned a Tony Award nomination for her performance. (Her brother Robert was also nominated for a Tony that year for his portrayal of Zach in *A Chorus Line*.) As the streetwalker Kitty Duval in William Saroyan's *Time of Your Life* (a role that she later reprised for public television), Patti LuPone won enthusiastic notices, although critics unanimously panned the production itself. She also appeared again as Irina in *The Three Sisters*, as Raina in George Bernard Shaw's *Arms and the Man*, and as Prince Edward in Christopher Marlowe's *Edward II*, all at the Harkness Theatre.

In May 1976 Patti LuPone left the Acting Company to appear in *The Baker's Wife*, a musical produced by David Merrick that closed after six months on the road without reaching Broadway. In 1977 she traveled to Chicago to play the part of Ruth in the world premiere of David Mamet's two-character play *The Woods*, a drama about an urban couple grappling with the problems of communication and commitment during a vacation at an isolated, rural cabin. Writing in the *New York Times* (November 30, 1977), Richard Eder observed that Patti LuPone "makes Ruth totally alive, totally responsive. At the play's opening, even before she speaks, her suddenly widening eyes are a recital of all the sensations that crowd in upon her."

Musical roles dominated Patti LuPone's career in 1978. In March she appeared in David Mamet's *Water Engine* at the Plymouth Theatre on Broad-

way, providing a two-number singing interlude "in the manner of a hard-bitten 1930s band singer," according to Allan Wallach of *Newsday* (March 7, 1978). She was a cynical call girl in *Working*, a Broadway musical based on Studs Terkel's book of the same name that ran for twenty-five performances at the Forty-sixth Street Theatre in May and June. In October she was a schoolteacher turned pop-singer in the Hartford Stage Company's production of *Catchpenny Twist*, a musical set against the political turmoil of Northern Ireland.

In the same year Patti LuPone made her film debut with a small part in *King of the Gypsies*, a story of three generations of New York gypsies starring Eric Roberts and Judd Hirsch. After completing work on *1941*, Steven Spielberg's 1979 comedy about life in Los Angeles in the days immediately following the Japanese attack on Pearl Harbor, Miss Lupone flew back to New York to audition for the lead in the musical *Evita*, which was being brought to the United States after a successful run in London. She sang two songs from the Andrew Lloyd Webber score, "Rainbow High" and "Don't Cry for Me, Argentina," hoping only that the director, Harold Prince, would remember her for future roles, but her interpretation of "Don't Cry for Me, Argentina" actually brought tears to the eyes of several listeners, who had already heard the song performed that day by many other applicants. On the strength of her audition, she was chosen over some 200 other aspirants, among them Ann-Margret, Meryl Streep, and Raquel Welch, to play the coveted role of Eva Duarte Perón, the wife of the Argentinian dictator Juan Perón, who, during her husband's authoritarian rule, was revered almost as a saint by many of the country's downtrodden before dying of cancer at the age of thirty-three.

Evita began its American run on May 9, 1979 at the Dorothy Chandler Pavilion in Los Angeles, playing there for nine weeks before moving to the Orpheum Theatre in San Francisco, where it played for seven weeks and became the highest-grossing play in that city's history. A few West Coast critics were less than impressed by Patti LuPone's performance, and rumors circulated that Prince was considering replacing her before *Evita* reached New York. Although Prince publicly backed Miss LuPone and assured her that he was not shopping around for a new Eva Perón, she admitted that the rumors damaged her confidence. Nonetheless, according to Viola Hegyl Swisher, writing in *After Dark* (September 1979), Argentinians who saw the play in Los Angeles and were old enough to remember Eva Perón found Patti LuPone's impersonation more than credible. One of them told her following a performance, "That's Evita all right. . . . I swear to God, you've got her to a T."

On September 25, 1979 *Evita* opened at New York's Broadway Theatre. Two weeks before the opening, more than $2 million worth of tickets had been sold through mail orders, theatre parties, and group sales. Miss LuPone's opening night performance received an endorsement from Walter Kerr of the New York Times (September 26, 1979), who reported that she "sings the role well and moves with a rattlesnake vitality." Edwin Wilson of the Wall Street Journal (September 26, 1979) also praised Miss LuPone's interpretation. "She captures the complex nature of her heroine," he wrote, and "is a talented singer as well." Yet her performance was criticized by certain reviewers who found it too dispassionate to justify the fervor of Eva Perón's supporters, and some critics attacked the book of the musical for being dramatically deficient. The following spring Miss LuPone received a Tony Award as best featured actress in a musical during the 1979–80 Broadway season. She also won a Drama Desk Award.

Since Evita is a pop opera in which virtually every word is sung and the actress portraying Eva Perón is on stage for all but four minutes, the London producers of the show employed two leading actresses, with one replacing the other periodically. Although she at first feared she might damage her voice, Patti LuPone played all of the shows except matinees. She adhered to a strict diet that forbade sugar, alcohol, and food containing preservatives, took several kinds of vitamins three times daily, went straight home after most performances, and slept for ten to twelve hours a night. In order to rest her voice, she tried not to speak before noon each day and gave few interviews. She began her daily routine of voice warmup exercises each day at 3:00 P.M., followed by a voice lesson at 5:30.

In March 1980, after fears of straining her voice had subsided, Patti LuPone launched a cabaret act, singing at midnight (after performing in Evita earlier in the evening) for five sold-out Saturdays at Les Mouches, a supper club–discothèque on Manhattan's West Side. Her program of fifteen songs included "Latin from Manhattan," "Downtown," "Love for Sale," "Because the Night," and "Don't Cry for Me, Argentina." Although her act was generally well received by the critics, with Rex Reed noting in the New York Daily News (March 5, 1980) that "she hypnotizes even the busboys," a four-night engagement at the Savoy club in Manhattan in May 1981 was far less of a hit with reviewers. Wayne Robins of Newsday (May 9, 1981), for example, called her act "incredibly ill-conceived and poorly executed." When she resurrected her cabaret act again in the fall of 1982, this time at the Bottom Line in Greenwich Village, reviews were mostly negative, with Stephen Holden of the New York Times (October 17, 1982) complaining that her voice was "all brass and no silk."

In September 1980 Patti LuPone extended her contract to play in Evita for another six months, conceding that her main reason for doing so was the lack of other offers. "Casting directors forget what you did in the past," she told an interviewer for the New York Times (September 19, 1980). "They think I'm blond and much older, so unless they need a blond fascist dictator, I won't get a call." Although she had no other work lined up, she left the cast of Evita two months before her contract expired, giving her last performance on January 10, 1981. "I'm physically exhausted and I'm restless as an actor," she explained to Jerry Parker of Newsday (January 10, 1981), after announcing her decision. "It's dangerous to stay with a role too long—a danger of typecasting. I don't know what I'll do, but sometimes an actor has to take that risk." She declined an offer to play Lady Macbeth at Lincoln Center's Vivian Beaumont Theatre, explaining, "I've just been playing her for two years," and she did not work again until the following winter, when she appeared as Rosalind in Shakespeare's As You Like It at the Tyrone Guthrie Theatre in Minneapolis. In the spring of 1982 Miss LuPone made another brief venture into film, playing a harried Philadelphia housewife in Fighting Back, which also featured Michael Sarazin and Tom Skerritt. She then rejected an offer to audition for the lead in the ill-fated Broadway musical A Doll's Life, also directed by Harold Prince, in order to reprise the role of Ruth in The Woods, which ran for eight weeks in the spring of 1982 at the Off-Broadway Second Stage Theatre. In the fall she appeared in David Mamet's Edmond at the Provincetown Playhouse in Greenwich Village.

Patti LuPone's most notable role during the early 1980s was that of the downtrodden prostitute Moll in a revival of Marc Blitzstein's proletarian musical The Cradle Will Rock, which was presented by alumni of the Acting Company at the American Place Theatre. The May 1983 production was staged by John Houseman, who first produced the show with Orson Welles in 1937. In her review for the New Yorker (May 23, 1983), Edith Oliver spoke for other critics in observing that "Patti LuPone sings and acts with simplicity and beauty . . . , and her rendition of 'Nickel Under My Foot' is most lovely."

Patti LuPone also appeared in 1983 as Cleo in America Kicks Up Its Heels, at the Playwrights Horizons Mainstage Theatre in Manhattan, and with Eartha Kitt and Ken Page in Stars of Broadway, at the Colonie Coliseum in Albany, New York. In the spring of 1984 she played Nancy in a revival of the musical Oliver! at the Mark Hellinger Theatre that closed quickly despite positive reviews for her performance from, among others, Clive Barnes of the New York Post (April 30, 1984). "I did some of my best work after Evita," she said during an interview with David Sacks of the New York Times Magazine (January 24, 1988). "But it wasn't in the public eye, and it didn't command a lot of notice, therefore I was nothing."

In November 1984 Miss LuPone played a reporter in the first American production of the Italian playwright Dario Fo's political farce Accidental Death of an Anarchist, which had a brief run on Broadway at the Belasco Theatre. After taking her cabaret act to Resorts International in Atlantic City in February 1985, she went to Washington, D.C., to appear in the American National Theatre's production of Shakespeare's Henry IV, Part I, directed by Peter Sellars and staged at the Kennedy

Center. She then portrayed the hero's lover in Sellars's offbeat follow-up production, *The Count of Monte Cristo*. In films, she had small parts in *Cat's Eye* (1985), *Witness* (1985), and *Wise Guys* (1986).

While appearing in a Houseman revival of *The Cradle Will Rock* at the Old Vic Theatre in London in 1985, Patti LuPone got one of the biggest breaks of her career when she was spotted by the producer Cameron Mackintosh, who cast her to play the part of Fantine in the Royal Shakespeare Company production of *Les Misérables*, which opened at the Barbican Theatre on September 28. Although her character, an unwed mother who becomes a prostitute, dies of tuberculosis in the first act, her performance left an indelible impression. The first American ever to play a principal part in a Royal Shakespeare Company production, she received a Laurence Olivier Award (the British equivalent of the Tony Award) for best actress in a musical. After rejecting for personal reasons an offer from Mackintosh to play Fantine in the Broadway production of *Les Misérables*, she played Lady Bird Johnson in NBC's three-hour television movie *LBJ: The Early Years*, which was telecast in early 1987 and featured Randy Quaid in the title role.

Patti LuPone's most rewarding role since *Evita* was that of Reno Sweeney in a revival of the 1934 Cole Porter musical *Anything Goes*, which opened at the Vivian Beaumont Theatre on October 19, 1987. The resident director of the Vivian Beaumont, Jerry Zaks, chose her for the part of the evangelist turned nightclub-singer who vainly pursues a young stockbroker before falling for an English lord because, as he told David Sacks, "I wanted someone who was appealing, who was vital and sexy and funny and had a great voice." The role was made memorable by the late Ethel Merman in the original, but Miss LuPone said she felt no pressure in delivering the great Cole Porter songs "Anything Goes," "You're the Top," "I Get a Kick Out of You," and "Blow, Gabriel, Blow," all of which had been written expressly for the brassy voice of Miss Merman; in fact, she was confident enough to sing in Miss Merman's own key. In his review for the *New York Times* (October 20, 1987), Frank Rich wrote, "Ms. LuPone's Reno is a mature, uninhibited jazz dame: loose, trashy, funny, sexy. Ethel Merman she's not . . . but who is? Ms. LuPone has her own brash American style and, most of all, a blazing spontaneity: With this Reno, *everything* goes." Miss LuPone earned her third Tony nomination for her performance. She remained in the role until March 1989, when she was succeeded by Leslie Uggams.

In the fall of 1989, Patti LuPone began starring in the critically praised ABC televised drama *Life Goes On*, about a middle-class American family with a teenage son who is afflicted with Down syndrome. Patti LuPone played the boy's mother, a former singer who gave up her successful career to take care of her handicapped son.

Patti LuPone stands five feet, two inches tall, has straight brown hair, an angular face, and what Caroline Moorhead described in the London *Times*

(January 29, 1986) as "an enormous, elastic mouth." She herself admitted to Linda Winer that "this is not an easily castable face. . . . It's kinda unusual." Miss LuPone wears contact lenses onstage ("Otherwise, I'd fall into the orchestra pit") and red horn-rimmed glasses offstage. She takes pride in the fact that, unlike most celebrities, she is a casual dresser. As she related in the interview with David Sacks, "During *Evita* I was constantly harassed—by my dance captain, my wardrobe mistress, and everyone else—to dress up. I was a star. There is an illusion you're expected to present. But I don't feel easy with that." A workaholic with frenetic energy, Miss LuPone requires ten hours of sleep a night even when she is not performing. Meticulously neat, she knows exactly where everything is in both her dressing room and her apartment. She smokes cigarettes but intends to quit. Among her hobbies are cooking, watching such television shows as *The Honeymooners, Star Trek*, and *The Twilight Zone*, and following the fortunes of the New York Rangers hockey team. Patti LuPone has sung the national anthem before several Rangers games at Manhattan's Madison Square Garden, and she has also performed it at Shea Stadium in Queens and at Giants Stadium in East Rutherford, New Jersey.

Between 1971 and 1978 Miss LuPone shared a New York apartment with her Juilliard classmate Kevin Kline. While filming *LBJ: The Early Years* in 1986, she met and fell in love with Matt Johnston, a cameraman who also worked on the production. The couple married on December 12, 1988 at the Vivian Beaumont Theatre. The two live in Miss LuPone's six-room apartment in the Chelsea section of Manhattan while waiting for construction to be completed on their three-bedroom white-cedar log house in northwestern Connecticut.

References: *After Dark* 8:46+ N '75 pors; *Interview* 10:33+ O '80 por; *N Y Daily News* p4 Je 10 '80 por, p8 N 18 '80 pors; *N Y Newsday* II p4+ Ap 18 '76 pors; II p2+ O 21 '79 pors; II p4+ O 18 '87 pors; *N Y Times Mag* p22+ Ja 24 '88 pors; *Who's Who in America*, 1988–89

Mahfouz, Naguib

Dec. 11, 1911(?)- Egyptian writer. Address: 172 Nile St., Cairo, Egypt

Among Western literary critics, the 1988 Nobel laureate Naguib Mahfouz has been variously described as the "Egyptian Balzac," the "Egyptian Dickens," or the "Egyptian Dostoevsky" because of his vivid social frescoes of twentieth-century Cairo. Among his friends, meanwhile, he was for many years known much more modestly as Al-Sabir—"the patient one"—because of the determination with which he pursued his writing in rel-

Naguib Mahfouz

ative obscurity. But following the announcement of his award on October 13, 1988, the wry septuagenarian (who is also known as one of the best joketellers in Cairo) gave himself a new name: from now on, he quipped to reporters gathered outside his apartment, he will not be called Mahfouz, but Mahzouz ("the lucky one").

In awarding the Nobel Prize for literature to Mahfouz, the Swedish Academy of Letters brought belated international recognition to a writer whom the Arab world has long considered its greatest living novelist. A master of observation and expression alike, Mahfouz is credited with Egyptianizing the essentially Western genre of the novel, with shaping classical Arabic into a vehicle of popular speech, and, above all, with giving voice to what the critic Tahar Bekri has aptly described as "the disappointments and dreams of the [Egyptian] man in the street."

In the course of a career spanning five decades and four political regimes, Mahfouz has made his way through a succession of genres and styles. His youthful attempts at historical fiction in the late 1930s were succeeded by the realist novels of the 1940s and 1950s for which he is best known. Those were followed in turn by the symbolist and absurdist short stories and plays of the 1960s and, most recently, by the synthesis of realism and modernism that he has made his own since the 1970s. But whatever the form, whatever the theme, whatever the political and social context, one constant runs through all of Mahfouz's work: his bond with the Egyptian people. An international reputation, he told *Le Monde*'s Alexandre Buccianti in a 1985 interview, was of little interest to him: "Nothing is as valuable as the hours of passionate discussion among friends on the terrace of a cafe alongside the Nile or the Mediterranean."

Naguib Mahfouz was born around 1911 in the Gamaliyya quarter of Old Cairo that has served as the setting for many of his works. The youngest of seven children in the family of a minor civil servant, he was eight years old at the time of Egypt's 1919 Revolution, and his own coming of age in the period between the two world wars coincided with an era of intense nationalist activity against British rule. While he was still quite young, the family moved to the modern neighborhood of al-'Abbasiyya. Although he apparently had a brief bout with epilepsy around the age of ten, he recalls his childhood as a happy one.

As a teenager, Mahfouz was an avid fan of Egyptian detective novels and a compulsive moviegoer. He also enjoyed playing soccer, listening to the music of the legendary songstress Umm Kalthoum, and spending time with friends, often in Old Cairo. The result, he told Salwa Al-Neimi in a March 1988 interview for *Magazine Littéraire*, was that he learned to discipline himself at an early age: "To be able to do all that, I had to divide my time very carefully. . . . I wanted to be brilliant so I had to work hard."

In high school Mahfouz studied philosophy and languages, acquiring a sound knowledge of Arabic literature, both medieval and modern. Among the writers who influenced him were Taha Hussein, the giant of Arabic letters, the journalist and social reformer Salama Musa, and the poet and essayist 'Abbas al-Akkad. From Hussein he learned the meaning of intellectual revolt; from Musa, "to believe in science, socialism, and tolerance"; and from al-Akkad, the value of the arts, democracy, and individual liberty. Through Musa in particular, he began reading translations of Western thinkers such as Darwin, Marx, Freud, and Kant, and at eighteen he underwent the spiritual crisis that he later attributed to the autobiographical figure of Kamal in the first volume of his trilogy.

In 1930 Mahfouz entered the newly established University of Cairo (then King Fuad I University) as a philosophy student. Soon afterward, he published his first article—on the eventual triumph of socialism—and throughout his undergraduate years, he contributed essays on philosophical subjects to various magazines, including Salama Musa's *Al-Majalla al-jadida*. He was less successful with articles and short stories he submitted to the popular press, but he still managed to get his name into print by sending letters to various columnists and often deliberately provoking a published response.

Classes at the University of Cairo were in English and French, and Mahfouz's access to those languages, though limited at first, greatly increased the scope of his reading. To improve his English, he undertook an Arabic translation of James Baikie's *Ancient Egypt*, which he published in 1932. By the time of his graduation two years later, he was able to cultivate his growing literary interests through wide-ranging translations. Among his favorite authors were Tolstoy, Dostoevsky, Chekhov, Proust, Mann, Kafka, Joyce, and the playwrights

O'Neill, Shaw, Ibsen, and Strindberg. He has insisted that he felt no particular attraction to Balzac or Zola, and he has cheerfully admitted that he never managed to finish a story by Dickens.

After completing his undergraduate work, Mahfouz took a secretarial post in the university administration and enrolled in a master's degree program, with the aim of writing a thesis in aesthetics. But that carefully reasoned attempt to bridge his dual interest in philosophy and literature did not work out, and he found himself torn between the two subjects. Opting for literature, he dropped out of graduate school, then decided to limit himself to prose fiction rather than poetry or criticism. A spate of short stories in the manner of de Maupassant, Chekhov, and their Egyptian disciples followed. Those sketches anticipated his later novels in their combination of surface detail and psychological depth, as well as in their critical (and often humorous) stance. Some eighty of them —another fifty were apparently destroyed— made their way into political and cultural magazines, and in 1938 Mahfouz published his first collection, Hams al-junun (A Whisper of Madness).

In 1939 Mahfouz went to work in the Ministry of Religious Affairs, where he was to remain for the next fifteen years. In the same year he had one of his novels accepted for publication by Salama Musa, who had rejected three previous attempts. An historical fiction in the Walter Scott mode, 'Abath al-aqdar (Games of Fate) was set in the Pharaonic period, a subject of increasing interest to members of the nationalist movement. Mahfouz's tale of tyrannical rule and the expulsion of foreign invaders was not without strong contemporary implications in an Egypt governed by the despotic Ismail Sidki under British tutelage, and Mahfouz later acknowledged that he had used ancient history in order to avoid the censors. At the time, he envisioned a series of some forty novels dealing with the period, for which he embarked on an ambitious program of research. Two of those novels, Radubis (Radobis, 1943) and Kifah Tibah (The Struggle of Thebes, 1944), were actually written soon after Games of Fate.

According to Sasson Somekh, whose The Changing Rhythm: A Study of Naguib Mahfouz's Novels (1973) is the most extensive treatment in the English language of Mahfouz's work to date, the optimism of the Pharaonic novels was dimmed by the impact on Egypt of World War II: the military raids and the fear of a German invasion, the economic hardships, and the political chaos, including misguided nationalist support for Hitler. Mahfouz apparently went through a period of retreat, and, when he reemerged, both his subject matter and his style were radically different.

Mahfouz's first new venture was Al-Qahira al-jadida (New Cairo, 1946), which explored the web of personal and political corruption in Egyptian society through the viewpoints of three philosophy students at the University of Cairo in the late 1920s. According to Mahfouz, his sudden decision to abandon the Pharaonic project and move into

contemporary social realism was something he still cannot explain, but, in short order, he wrote two more novels in the same vein: Khan al-Khalili (published in 1945, while New Cairo was held up by the censors), which focuses on a family of petty functionaries struggling to survive in Cairo during World War II, and Zuqaq al-midaqq (1947, translated as Midaq Alley, 1966; 1977), a vivid evocation of how the war affected the inhabitants of a single street in the neighborhood where Mahfouz was born.

Although those two novels drew praise from a few Egyptian critics—the respected scholar Sayyid Qutb, for example, hailed New Cairo and Khan al-Khalili as "the starting point of modern Arabic fiction"—Mahfouz remained largely ignored in official literary circles. That was even more the case with the two following novels in the same social realist vein, Al-Sarab (The Mirage, 1949) and Bidaya wa nihaya (1951, translated as The Beginning and the End, 1987). By that time, he was also working as a screenwriter in the film industry, a parallel career that began when he met the director Salah Abou Seif in 1945 and agreed to write an adaptation of a pre-Islamic romance, Antar wa Abla (1948). Arguing that a scenario was really no different from a novel, Abou Seif persuaded the reluctant screenwriter to continue, and over the next decade their collaboration yielded a series of successful films that captured the flavor of contemporary Egyptian life in much the same way as did Mahfouz's novels. Through those and other films that he scripted for such well-known directors as Youssef Chahine, Atef Salim, Niazi Mustapha, and Tawfiq Salah, he exerted what Claude-Michel Cluny calls "a determining influence on the orientation of Egyptian cinema in the fifties."

For Egypt, that period marked a major political turning point—the Egyptian Revolution of 1952, which ended the monarchy and brought Gamal Abdel Nasser to power. For Mahfouz, who had so meticulously chronicled the demise of the old regime, the Nasser era brought the official recognition that had eluded him. The breakthrough came with the publication of Bayn al-qasrayn (Between the Two Palaces, 1956), the first volume of the 1,500-page trilogy that remains his most beloved work, and is now the most famous novel in the Arabic language. In that elaborate evocation of his own petit-bourgeois milieu, Mahfouz follows three generations of a Cairo family from the end of World War I to 1944. Between the Two Palaces (each volume bears the name of the street or neighborhood where the main characters live) is set in the turbulent period leading up to the nationalist revolt of 1919 and focuses on the patriarchal figure of Ahmad Abd al-Gawwad, whose control over his wife and five children ebbs with the passing of the traditional society he represents. The second volume, Qasr al-shawq (The Palace of Desire, 1957), begins five years later, with its action focused on Abd al-Gawwad's oldest son, Yasin, whose dissolute lifestyle mirrors the larger political and social corruption that followed the failure of the nationalist movement. But when the third volume, *Al-Sukkariyya* (The Sugar Bowl, 1957), resumes in 1935, the generation of Abd al-Gawwad's grandchildren—the Marxists and the Muslim fundamentalists, the homosexuals, and the young women entering the university for the first time—shows a renewed commitment that gives some small hope for the future.

In a 1957 interview, Mahfouz commented that for him, "The hero of *Between the Two Palaces* is time. . . . Everything changes in *Between the Two Palaces, The Palace of Desire,* and *The Sugar Bowl* because of time." Like his earlier novels, the trilogy is less the story of individuals than that of Egyptian society. "The destinies of the individual characters are the microcosm, but the macrocosm is the destiny of modern Egypt," the literary critic M. M. Badawi wrote in the *Times Literary Supplement* (September 25, 1988), explaining that "the struggle of the younger generation to attain their domestic freedom, to shape their own lives, mirrors the nation's struggle to achieve political independence."

For the reading public in Egypt and the rest of the Arab world, the living tapestry of the Cairo trilogy was not only an immediate success but also an enduring one. By 1985 *Between the Two Palaces* had gone through thirteen printings, and a pirated Lebanese version had sold more than one million copies. ("If my books weren't pirated so much," Mahfouz told an interviewer for *Jeune Afrique* at the time, "I'd be very rich today. But thank God anyway.") With the publication of *The Palace of Desire* in 1957, he was awarded the State Prize for Literature, and, in the following year, Taha Hussein, referring to *Between the Two Palaces,* declared, "I do not doubt that this novel can stand comparison with the work of whatever international novelists you want to name, in any language at all."

Altogether, Mahfouz spent eleven years on the trilogy—one year for research, six for the actual writing, and, because of its length, another four to see it into print. His original intention, he later explained, was to continue with seven more novels "of the same realistic and critical tendency," but, following the completion of the trilogy manuscript in 1952, he abandoned his plan and, in fact, considered abandoning writing altogether. According to Mahfouz, the reason for that "halt," as he calls it, was the Egyptian Revolution. When the old society disappeared, he lost all desire to criticize it. At the time, he believed that he was finished as a writer. During the next five years, he prepared the trilogy for publication and worked on a number of major screenplays. He also married, had his first child, and finally transferred out of the Ministry of Religious Affairs to a post in the Arts Administration. But for the one and only time in his adult life, he ceased all literary activity. When he resumed, in 1957, his writing had undergone yet another major metamorphosis.

In contrast to the dense and flowing realism of the Cairo trilogy, *Awlad haritna* (The Children of Our Lane, 1959, translated as *Children of Gebelawi,* 1981) is an allegorical montage of 114 short chapters—the same number as the Koran—tracing the quest for religious knowledge from Adam and Eve to the present day, when the Creator-figure, Gebelawi, is inadvertently killed by a modern-day prophet, the scientist. Serialized in *Al-Ahram* in the autumn of 1959, *Children of Gebelawi* was well received by the general public but immediately condemned as a work of blasphemy by al-Azhar, the seat of Muslim learning. In the face of angry attack at Friday prayer services, street demonstrations, and demands that Mahfouz be brought to trial, *Al-Ahram* had to go through President Nasser in order to complete the serialization, and the novel was never published in Egypt. (A slightly expurgated version was finally brought out in Lebanon eight years later.)

Around the same time, Mahfouz was named head of the State Cinema Organization where, in addition to taking on key responsibilities for funding and censorship, he was involved in the literary adaptations that had become a staple of the Egyptian cinema. From 1960 on, some thirty of his own novels and short stories were also adapted, beginning with Salah Abou Seif's version of *The Beginning and the End,* which won the National Film Prize in 1962.

Resuming his former level of productivity, Mahfouz published six novels and short-story collections between 1961 and 1967. Experimental in form, symbolic in content, and often anguished in mood, these works reflect Mahfouz's growing interest in the conventions of European modernism. *Al-Liss wa'l kilab* (1961, translated as *The Thief and the Dogs,* 1985), for example, offers a stylized, subjective portrait of a victim driven mad by the desire for revenge. With that novel, Mahfouz turned for the first time to the stream-of-consciousness technique to create what the translator Trevor Le Gassick called "a keenly accurate vision of the workings of a sick and embittered mind." With *Al-Samman wa'l-kharif* (1962, translated as *Autumn Quail,* 1986), he returned to a somewhat more realistic mode to tackle the politically sensitive theme of the Nasser government's failure to rehabilitate the intellectuals of the old regime. But in the novels and short-story collections that followed—*Dunya 'Illah* (1964, translated as *God's World,* 1973), *Al-Tariq* (1964, translated as *The Search,* 1987), *Bayt sayyi' al-sum'a* (The House of Ill Repute, 1965), *Al-Shahhat* (1965, translated as *The Beggar,* 1987), *Tharthara fawq al-nil* (Smalltalk on the Nile, 1966)—he moved resolutely toward an inner world of spiritual quests and crises.

For all of its "metaphysical" dimensions, that phase of Mahfouz's literary career was no less a commentary on the Nasser era, detailing, as Trevor Le Gassick wrote in his introduction to *The Thief and the Dogs,* "with delicacy and great courage the crisis of identity and conscience suffered by Egyptian intellectuals" in a period of "pervasive malaise and dissatisfaction." His bitter self-scrutiny reached its extreme with *Miramar* (1967, translated as *Miramar,* 1978), a bleak political parable in which the lone figure of hope in a world of duplicity and corruption is a young peasant girl from the countryside. In contrast to the bustling microcosm of the Cairo trilogy, the claustrophobic *Miramar* is set in a rundown boarding house of that name in Alexandria, and time, Mahfouz's "hero" a decade earlier, is virtually brought to a standstill while each character recounts the same sequence of events from a different perspective.

In the wake of the Six-Day War in June 1967, *Miramar* was seen by Egyptian critics as a prescient forewarning of the disastrous defeat suffered at the hands of Israel. Yet for Mahfouz, like many other Arab intellectuals, the war was a sign, in part at least, of his own ineffectiveness. "Before 1967," he told an interviewer from the Cairo weekly *Rose al-Yusuf* in 1969, "writers were closing their eyes to the weak points." The novel form itself, he argued, was out of touch with the Egyptian reality. "It can only develop in a stable society," he told one interviewer. Following the shock of the war, he turned exclusively to short stories and one-act "plays for reading," which first appeared in the popular press and then in book form. With *Taht al-mizalla* (Under the Awning, 1969), consisting of stories and plays that, as Mahfouz specified in the epigraph, were written between October and December 1967, "thus, after the Six-Day War," the last vestiges of realism give way to the absurd. In stories and plays alike, narrative is replaced by discontinuous tableaux and description by dialogue, as nameless characters in unknown places pursue undefined quests, mainly with tragic results. For frustrated critics, these works posed "riddles" that had to be unraveled. But, as Mahfouz later explained, that hermetic world was "a necesssity" for him: "The Arabs were going through a period of darkness, bewilderment—taking stock. At that time I was not expressing myself. I was grumbling."

With *Al-Mar'aya* (1972, translated as *Mirrors*, 1977), first serialized in a radio and television magazine in 1971, Mahfouz returned to a somewhat more accesible form of fiction, possibly in response to the "riddles" charge. Like *Miramar*, his last novel before the Six-Day War, the work was structured around multiple viewpoints, but the individual units were much shorter, taking the form of fifty-five autobiographical sketches presented without commentary in alphabetical order by the name of the fictitious subject-author. Much closer to his classic novels was *Al-Hubb taht al-matar* (Love in the Rain, 1973), in which Mahfouz profited from the liberalized climate just before the Arab-Israeli War of 1973 to take a look at the 1967 war and its impact on Egypt's younger generation.

Since his retirement in 1972, Mahfouz has produced some fourteen novels and five short-story collections, of which two novels have appeared in English translation: *Hadrat al-muhtaram* (1975, translated as *Respected Sir*, 1987) and *Afrah al-qubba* (1981, translated as *Wedding Song*, 1987). In the mid-1970s he returned to the cinema to collaborate on several adaptations of his novels, including Kamal al-Sheikh's *The Thief and the Dogs* (1974), Hussein Kamal's *Love in the Rain* (1975), and Ali Badrakhan's *The Karnak* (1976), based on a 1974 novel of the same name.

Although critics have been more reserved about Mahfouz's later works, they remain popular with Egyptian readers. Even when Mahfouz wound up on the Arab boycott list in the late 1970s for his support of the Camp David accords, the public criticized his position but continued to read his books, and the bestowal of the Nobel Prize was welcomed throughout the Arab world. In late December 1988 the unauthorized re-serialization of the controversial *Children of Gebelawi* in a Cairo newspaper touched off another protest from al-Azhar and a barrage of attacks from Muslim fundamentalists, who called on Mahfouz to renounce the "cursed" novel, "even if he obtained the Nobel Prize because of it."

Renowned for his simplicity as much as for his discipline, Mahfouz continues to live in a modest Cairo apartment with his wife, Attiyat-Allah, their two daughters, Umm Kalthum and Fatima, and two dogs. Despite chronic health problems, including partial deafness and failing eyesight, he follows an unvarying work routine that begins every morning with a ninety-minute walk that takes him through the streets of Cairo to the Ali Baba cafe, where he reads the newspapers. He then returns home to write for several hours and, after taking a nap, spends the afternoon with friends, except for Thursdays, when he receives visitors at the office reserved for him at *Al-Ahram*. Apart from two government-mandated voyages to Yemen and Yugoslavia, he has never traveled outside of Egypt, and the Nobel Award ceremony in Stockholm proved no exception. Citing health problems, he declined to attend and sent his two daughters to accept the $390,000 prize on his behalf.

References: *N Y Review of Books* 36:19+ F 3 '89; *N Y Times* A p1+ O 14 '88 por, C p22 N 25 '88, C p19 D 8 '88 por; *Times Literary Supplement* p1104 S 25 '81; *Vanity Fair* 52:234+ N '89 pors; *International Who's Who, 1989-90*; Pelded, Mattityahu. *Religion, My Own* (1983); Somekh, Sasson. *The Changing Rhythm: A Study of Naguib Mahfouz's Novels* (1973); *World Authors 1975-1980* (1985)

Mapplethorpe, Robert

(mā´ pəl-thôrp)

Nov. 4, 1946- Photographer. Address: 24 Bond St., New York, N.Y. 10012; c/o Robert Miller Gallery, 724 Fifth Ave., New York, N.Y. 10019

BULLETIN: Robert Mapplethorpe died on March 9, 1989 in Boston, Massachusetts. Obituary: *N Y Times* D p16 Mr 10 '89

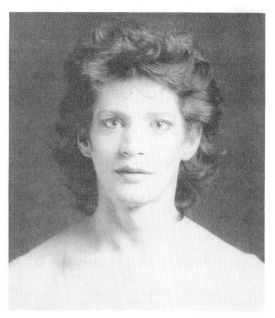

Robert Mapplethorpe

"My work is about seeing—seeing things like they haven't been seen before," Robert Mapplethorpe said in a 1986 interview. When his graphic photographs of the homosexual S&M scene first appeared publicly in 1977 at the art gallery the Kitchen, they turned the art world upside down, destroying previous notions of what subject matter was considered permissible in photography and redefining the traditional concept of beauty. With a slick and sophisticated style, Mapplethorpe juxtaposed underground, subculture subject matter with classical composition, which is also evident in his subsequent photographs of black male nudes and flowers—often with homoerotic overtones—and celebrity portraits. "My work is about order," he has said. "I'm a perfectionist."

Although many critics found his photographs overly slick and outrageous in content, Mapplethorpe's work came to epitomize New York's intellectual climate in the 1970s and early 1980s, combining, as one critic observed, "the appetite for both glamour and decadence, high fashion and subterranean sex. " Calling on his background in sculpture, Mapplethorpe turned the photograph into an art object, and he often devised elaborate frames, played with different matting techniques, and printed photographs on linen and silk between panels of fabrics. "He changed the medium he worked in and he changed the way we see it," one critic has noted. "At his best, his work was a slap in the face."

Robert Mapplethorpe was born on November 4, 1946 to Harry Mapplethorpe, an electrician, and his wife, Joan, in Floral Park, a predominantly middle-class and Roman Catholic neighborhood in the New York City borough of Queens. He was the third of the family's six children. Robert went to

Mass every Sunday, and he has acknowledged that his Roman Catholic upbringing played an important role in his interpretation of reality. "A church has a certain magic mystery for a child," he told Ingrid Sischy, as reported in her essay "A Society Artist," which appeared in the Whitney Museum's 1988 exhibition catalogue *Robert Mapplethorpe.* "It still shows in how I arrange things. It's always been this way—whenever I'd put something together I'd notice it was symmetrical."

His *enfant terrible* temperament surfaced early, and in 1963, at the age of sixteen, Mapplethorpe left home to study art at the Pratt Institute in Brooklyn, New York, where he concentrated on painting, drawing, and sculpture. "I wanted to have the freedom to do what I wanted to do," he explained to Dominick Dunne in an interview for *Vanity Fair* (February 1989). "The only way to do that was to break away. I didn't want to have to worry about what my parents thought." While at Pratt, he found a kindred spirit in the person of Patti Smith, the poet and musician, whom he met when she wandered by mistake into his basement apartment in Brooklyn. The two became such close friends that they lived together in Brooklyn and, later, at the Chelsea Hotel in Manhattan. "Patti and I built on each other's confidence. We were never jealous of each other's work," Mapplethorpe explained to Dunne. "We inspired each other."

After graduating from Pratt in 1970, Mapplethorpe began playing around with the idea of the photograph as an object. He appropriated images of macho stereotypes, such as cowboys and bikers, from gay pornographic magazines that he recut, spray-painted, and assembled into collages. For *Model Parade* (1972), Mapplethorpe lifted two pages from a male physique magazine using synthetic emulsion, then arranged the images on a piece of canvas. For his *Julius of California* (1971), he spray-painted a picture of a cowboy, highlighting the encircled genital area. *Leatherman II* (1970) features two photographs of a man's neck and thigh area superimposed over a photograph of a male torso. Mapplethorpe's use of commercially produced imagery reflected the influence of the artists Man Ray, Marcel Duchamp, and Andy Warhol. In 1970 Patti Smith served as narrator for the underground film *Robert Having His Nipple Pierced*, which Susan Daley made about Mapplethorpe.

Mapplethorpe's interest in photography grew out of his impatience with the amount of time it took to produce a painting or a piece of sculpture. "I was bored by the time I was halfway through something," he told Anne Horton in an interview that appeared in the catalogue *Robert Mapplethorpe 1986,* which was published for a 1987 exhibition at the Galerie Raab in West Berlin and the Galerie Kicken-Pauseback in Cologne, West Germany. "Photography is just like the perfect way to make a sculpture. You can do it in an afternoon, put all this concentration into it and then you're on to something else."

Fearing that he might eventually be sued for using other people's photographs, in the early 1970s Mapplethorpe began taking his own pictures with a Polaroid camera that John McKendry, the curator of photographs and prints at the Metropolitan Museum of Art, gave to him. McKendry and his wife, Maxine de la Falaise, treated Mapplethorpe almost like a son and introduced him to their socially elite set of friends. The Polaroid appealed to Mapplethorpe because of its immediacy and contemporaneity at a time when painting had been termed "dead." In *Self Portrait* (1971), he combined three different Polaroid shots of himself naked, keeping them slightly out of alignment, and framed them behind a screen mesh in a purple paper bag—reinforcing the notion of object. His portraits of Patti Smith and the celebrated transvestite Candy Darling continued the idea of creating an object that includes photographic information: *Patti Smith (Don't Touch Here)* (1973) and *Candy Darling* (1973) both feature a progression of images encased in Polaroid cassettes.

An interest in eroticism and homoeroticism was evident in those early works as well. *Untitled* (1972) features a spray-painted image of two boys kissing, with a highlighted rectangle placed where the censorship bar would normally appear. *Self Portrait* (1973) depicts Mapplethorpe bare-chested in a leather vest and, in an early reference to S&M material, with a clamp attached to his right nipple. What Mapplethorpe was trying to reproduce in those types of photographs was the reaction he experienced when he first looked at male pornographic magazines in Times Square in the late 1960s. "A kid gets a certain kind of reaction, which of course once you've been exposed to everything you don't get," Mapplethorpe told Ingrid Sischy. "I got that feeling in my stomach, it's not a directly sexual one, it's something more potent than that. I thought if could somehow bring that element into art, if I could somehow retain that feeling, I would be doing something that was uniquely my own."

The turning point in Mapplethorpe's artistic development occurred in the early 1970s, when, at the age of twenty-five, he met Sam Wagstaff, a former museum curator and advertising executive, who called up and asked, "Are you the shy pornographer?" At Mapplethorpe's suggestion, Wagstaff began collecting photographs, eventually amassing a collection that served as an education in the history of photography for both of them. "Through him [Wagstaff] I started looking at photographs in a much more serious way," Mapplethorpe recounted to Dominick Dunne. "I got to know dealers. I went with him when he was buying things. It was a great education, although I had my own vision right from the beginning." Wagstaff encouraged Mapplethorpe to concentrate on photography and provided him with a loft on Bond Street in Manhattan, as well as financial support. The two were lovers for a couple of years, and then they became best friends. As one woman friend told Dunne: "Sam made Robert's career. He showed Robert this other way of life. . . . When Robert met Sam, all the doors opened for him."

By the mid-1970s, Mapplethorpe was consistently emphasizing the sculptural quality of photographs. In *Wood on Wood* (1974), he set two black-and-white photographs of the back of a wood frame onto the front of the same frame, so that both sides are visible at the same time. In *Self Portrait* (1974) the viewer's attention is divided between the image of a bare-chested Mapplethorpe hugging a blank wall and the formal aspects of the composition: a green frame resembling the shape of a Polaroid print after it is pulled from the camera, with cut-off edges at one end and a pull-tab at the other. That concern with formalism reappears in *François* (1974–75), in which four head profiles are each cropped within a trapezoidal frame, each shot tinted in a different primary color—reminiscent of the multipanel paintings of Brice Marden and Donald Judd.

It was in 1976 that Mapplethorpe's first solo exhibition, "Polaroids," opened at the Light Gallery in Manhattan, featuring self-portraits and portraits of friends, including the painter Brice Marden and Holly Solomon, the art dealer, as well as photographs of flowers and nudes. Many of the photographs were presented in sequence and in painted cases. "Sometimes to me the structure in which a photograph is presented is as important as the photograph itself," Mapplethorpe told Anne Horton. One series, *Patti Smith (Don't Touch Here)* (1973), features four shots of Miss Smith, framed in plastic Polaroid cassettes, two on each side of a central cassette containing the manufacturer's warning: "Don't touch here handle only by edges." Commenting on his early work, Kay Larson observed in *New York* (August 15, 1988) magazine: "These early pictures are set pieces—promising but self-conscious and labored, like the work of many young artists."

Spurred by invitations to show at two galleries in 1977, Mapplethorpe started using a large-format press camera and then a Hasselblad, which resulted in greater penetration of his subjects because he could slow down the shutter speeds. With his new equipment, he created the works shown in the exhibitions "Flowers" and "Portraits" at the Holly Solomon Gallery, and "Erotic Pictures" at the Kitchen. The latter exhibition, featuring photographs of the homosexual S&M scene, resulted in instant notoriety for Mapplethorpe. "For me S&M means sex and magic, not sadomasochism," he told Dunne. The photographs depicted men in leather, often with their genitals exposed, performing various sexual acts or posing with S&M paraphernalia, such as whips and chains. Mapplethorpe's approach was participatory rather than voyeuristic, and he was more interested in the experience than in the photography. "These were friends of mine, and they weren't hired, or manipulated into doing things they didn't want to do," he explained to Richard Lacayo of *Time* (August 22, 1988) magazine. "The situation had already existed, they weren't people play-acting and doing something they hadn't done before; they had put it together for that photo session," he told Gary Indiana for

Bomb (Winter 1988). "So I had a very large amount of control over the situation."

The shock value of the homoerotic photographs—such as *Mark Stevens (Mr. 10 1/2)* (1976), in which a man in leather pants with the front cut out arches over a ledge so that his genitals lie flat on it, *Brian Ridley and Lyle Heeter* (1979), in which two men decked out in S&M regalia pose in a living room, and *Self Portrait* (1978), depicting Mapplethorpe, with his back to the camera, bending over while inserting a whip in his rectum—was tempered by the symmetry of the compositions, their conventional backdrops, and precise lighting. Mapplethorpe's aim, Richard Marshall pointed out in his essay "Mapplethorpe's Vision," which appeared in the Whitney Museum exhibition catalogue, was to "instill through his photographs dignity and beauty to a subject that was outside the accepted norms of behavior." That preoccupation reflected his Roman Catholic upbringing. As Steven Koch noted in an article for *Art in America* (November 1986), Mapplethorpe's combining aestheticism with "shame-laden concerns" was "an effort at reconciliation—a reconciliation, which, like grace, is an essentially religious concept."

The integration of formal and subjective elements was carried over as well into the other types of photographs that Mapplethorpe produced in the late 1970s: portraits and still lifes of flowers. In the triptych portrait *Brice Marden, New York* (1976), for example, the third panel is a piece of glass that forces the viewer to look through the picture. In *Easter Lilies with Mirror* (1979), four different views of lilies radiate from a central mirror, which engages likewise the spectator. As Richard Marshall observed, the artist's preoccupation with composition and viewer participation indicates that Mapplethorpe wanted his work to be experienced by the same criteria used for painting and sculpture.

In the early 1980s Mapplethorpe moved away from serial compositions and S&M themes to more refined subjects and images: male and female nudes, still lifes of flowers, and portraits of celebrities. In addition to enlarging the size of his work so that it would be more striking in an exhibition setting, he introduced a number of new printing techniques, including platinum prints on linen and paper, Cibachrome color prints, dye transfer, and color Polaroids.

In his flower pictures, such as *Orchid and Leaf in White Vase* and *Baby's Breath*, both from 1982, Mapplethorpe continued to attempt to balance classical presentation with sexual themes. For Mapplethorpe, flowers represented the sexual organs of plants. He also associated them with the phallic, in contrast to the female connotations of flowers as painted by Georgia O'Keeffe. Mapplethorpe also reversed the usual female body stereotypes in his photographs of Lisa Lyon, the female bodybuilder, which were collected in the book *Lady: Lisa Lyon* (1983) and featured Miss Lyon in a variety of postures, including as a bride, a leather-clad S&M queen, and a pin-up girl. Some pictures depict the female body in a manner usually reserved for the male body, with strong lighting emphasizing Miss Lyon's musculature. Those photographs make certain portions of her body almost abstract, a practice that Mapplethorpe was to develop further with his subsequent male nudes. A sense of humor is evident in such photographs as *Lisa Lyon* (1982), in which the bodybuilder tweaks her nipples while staring defiantly into the camera—an image that "coolly aims a shotgun at the cultural prohibition against self-arousal," as Kay Larson noted in her *New York* magazine review.

Mapplethorpe's studies of black male nudes were collected in two books: *Black Males* (1980) and the *Black Book* (1986). Those photographs illustrate his tendency to see people as objects and their bodies as pieces of sculpture. Using "top of the line" models, Cathleen McGuigan noted in *Newsweek* (July 25, 1988), Mapplethorpe captured on film, often using silver gelatin prints, torsos, backs, and buttocks that are "so flawless they look like polished bronze." They also recall the influence of the still lifes of Edward Weston. The figures are often paired with flowers, as in *Ken Moody* (1984) and *Dennis Speight* (1983), suggesting a parallel between the sexual nature of flowers and the models' exposed genitals. In *Ken Moody and Robert Sherman* (1984), another arresting image results from the almost overlapping of two shaven heads—one black and one white—in profile. The 1985 collection *Black Flowers* juxtaposed studies of flowers next to those of male nudes.

In pictures such as *Man in Polyester Suit* (1980) and *Untitled* (1982), Mapplethorpe depersonalized the figures depicted by obscuring their faces and conducted instead an "unabashed exploration of what has always been treated as the body's disgraced member," in the words of Richard Howard in his essay "The Mapplethorpe Effect," which was included in the Whitney exhibition catalogue. In the first, that member is featured prominently while the rest of the torso of a black man is clothed in a cheap suit. In the second, a naked man stands with a Ku Klux Klan–type hood over his head. The photographs of *Thomas* (1986), in which a nude model strains in various poses against the confines of Leonardo da Vinci's circle and square, demonstrate Mapplethorpe's continued preoccupation with geometry. That preoccupation led to a period when Mapplethorpe worked exclusively with geometric designs, resulting in, for example, *White X with Silver Cross* (1983) and *Star with Frosted Glass* (1983).

The slickness that has been attributed to Mapplethorpe's art is perhaps most evident in his celebrity portraits, many of which appeared in Andy Warhol's *Interview* magazine, *Vogue*, and *Gentlemen's Quarterly*. Some of these photographs were collected in the books *Certain People* (1985) and *50 New York Artists* (1986). "*Certain People* are, mostly, people found, coaxed, or arranged into a certainty about themselves," Susan Sontag wrote in her introduction to the book, which features self-portraits of Mapplethorpe on the front and back covers. In one, he is made up like a woman; in the other, he poses as a street tough. In photographing his portrait subjects, Mapplethorpe tried to find the part of them that is self-confident. "I'm only half the act of taking pictures, if we're talking about portraiture, so it's a matter of having somebody just feel right themselves and about how they're relating to you," he explained in an interview published in Chicago's Institute of Contemporary Art exhibition catalogue. "Then you can get a magic moment out of them."

There is a "delightful impishness," in the words of one critic, to Mapplethorpe's portrait in 1982 of Louise Bourgeois, the sculptor, who smiles and holds under her arm her own sculpture of male genitals. Other portraits are more solemn, and Mapplethorpe's customary stark lighting and blank backgrounds create figures who seem "sculpted of marble," as Cathleen McGuigan noted in Newsweek, in portraits of such luminaries as Philip Johnson (1978), Donald Sutherland (1983), Doris Saatchi (1984), Grace Jones (1984), and Willem de Kooning (1986). About his portrait Alice Neel (1985), the painter, whom he photographed right before her death, he once remarked, "She knew she was giving me her death mask." Mapplethorpe was fascinated by high society and had no interest in depicting middle-class people: "I know what that's like and it's not interesting," he told Anne Horton in the interview published in Robert Mapplethorpe 1986.

By the late 1980s Mapplethorpe was playing with different materials, lighting, and color, reflecting a heightened concern with the photograph as object. "I know how to make pictures but sometimes it's too easy," he told Anne Horton. "But I can keep creating problems with changing light. I can do color which is what I'm doing now." He expanded his methods of presenting the photograph, including panels of fabric, printing on linen, and using expensive and elaborate framing. In Tulips (1987), once again an image with sexual overtones, Mapplethorpe inserted a platinum print of tulips between two sheathed curtains of colored silk. The same idea was used in his photograph Michael (1987), in which a print of a male nude is framed by two panels of fabric. Calla Lily (1987) is a platinum print on linen, bordered in burgundy-colored velvet. The closeup color photographs of flowers, including Tulip, Orchid, and Poppy, all from 1988, prompted Ingrid Sischy to rhapsodize: "You can witness the emergence of every last drop of color right up to the surface, where it vibrates as though it could lift right off the picture."

Those linen-transfer and color photographs were among the 110 pictures included in the first major museum retrospective of Mapplethorpe's work, held at the Whitney Museum in New York from July 28 through October 23, 1988. Roberta Smith, writing in the New York Times (September 4, 1988), complained about Mapplethorpe's oeuvre: "There are no troublesome or unintelligible parts left over, and in a way perhaps this is what is missing, and what stops one . . . from embracing . . .

this work completely as art." Cathleen McGuigan, on the other hand, writing in Newsweek, stated that his images are "formal and detached, yet charged with feeling. Despite the precision and calculations of Mapplethorpe's vision, the best of his photographs possess this touch of magic."

A slightly larger exhibition that opened at the Institute of Contemporary Art in Philadelphia on December 9, 1988 traveled later to Chicago, Boston, and Washington, D.C. Another indication of Mapplethorpe's artistic prominence is the $10,000 he charges for a portrait sitting and the $20,000 he receives for his photographs. The starting price for a print from the Robert Miller Gallery in New York, which handles his work, is $5,000. Ironically, at the peak of his success, Mapplethorpe's health visibly deteriorated as a result of AIDS, which he was first diagnosed as having at the end of 1986, and he appeared at the Whitney opening in a wheelchair. Sam Wagstaff died of AIDS in January 1987 and designated Mapplethorpe as the principal beneficiary of his fortune, estimated at around $7 million. In 1988 Mapplethorpe established the Robert Mapplethorpe Foundation, to provide funding for AIDS research and for the visual arts. That same year he asked his friends to pay $100 each to attend a viewing of Wagstaff's silver collection, before its sale at Christie's in January 1989, using the funds to support community experiments with new AIDS drugs.

Mapplethorpe's photographs have appeared in one-person exhibitions at, among other institutions, the Corcoran Gallery of Art in Washington, D.C. (1978), the International Center of Photography in New York (1979), the Musée National d'Art Moderne, Paris (1983), the Stedelijk Museum, Amsterdam (1988), and the National Portrait Gallery, London (1988). His work is included in the permanent collections of the Museum of Fine Arts, Houston; the Hara Museum of Contemporary Art, Tokyo; the Corcoran Gallery in Washington, D.C.; the Boston Museum of Fine Arts; the Centre Georges Pompidou, Paris; the Stedelijk Museum, Amsterdam; the Victoria and Albert Museum, London; and the Australian National Gallery, Canberra.

Robert Mapplethorpe lives in a midtown Manhattan apartment whose stylishly decorated interior was featured in the June 1988 issue of House & Garden magazine. "You create your own world," Mapplethorpe told Dominick Dunne. "The one that I want to live in is very precise, very controlled." That control is evident also in his habit of paying his bills immediately on receiving them. Mapplethorpe collects photographs, furniture, fabric, and art objects, and he has designed furniture pieces, including a coffee table that was produced in a limited edition.

References: Art & Artists p15+ N '83; Art in America 71:145+ N '86 por; ARTnews 82:53+ N '83; Bomb p18+ Winter '88 por; N Y Newsday II p4+ Ag 1 '88 pors; N Y Times II p29+ Jl 31 '88, D p16 Mr 10 '89 por; Vanity Fair 52:124+ F '89 pors; Marshall, Richard. *Robert Mapplethorpe* (1988); Who's Who in America, 1988–89

Marino, Dan

Sept. 15, 1961– Football player. Address: c/o Miami Dolphins, Joe Robbie Stadium, 2269 N.W. 199th St., Miami, Fla. 33056

Dan Marino, the Miami Dolphins' rifle-armed quarterback, has risen to National Football League superstardom faster than any signal caller before him and has played a major role in shifting the emphasis in professional football from the run to the pass. Endowed with an extraordinarily strong arm and a lightning-fast release, Marino, in the words of Jim Finks, the general manager of the New Orleans Saints, "plays the position as well as anybody this league has ever seen." Marino's career passing efficiency rating (a statistical formula developed by the NFL to evaluate quarterbacks by combining their statistics in the major passing categories) is the highest in league history. He holds seventeen NFL and twenty Dolphin team passing records and led the league in completions, passing yards, and touchdown passes in each of his first three full years as a starting quarterback. In 1984, his second year as a pro, Marino had probably the greatest individual season any NFL quarterback has ever had, setting single-season records for TD passes, completions, and passing yards, as he led the Dolphins to the Super Bowl. His quick rise to stardom astonished the football world, since even highly talented young quarterbacks usually take several years to learn how to exploit NFL defenses, which are much more complex than those employed by

college teams. Marino's great natural talent has been complemented by the Dolphins' outstanding offensive line and gifted wide receivers, as well as by several rules changes that have been instituted by the NFL since the early 1980s to aid the passing game.

Born on September 15, 1961 in Pittsburgh, Pennsylvania, Daniel Constantine Marino Jr. is the oldest of the three children, and the only son, of Dan Marino Sr. and Veronica (Kolczynski) Marino. The Marinos lived in a two-story brick walk-up on Parkview Avenue in Pittsburgh's South Oakland area, a middle-class Italian and Irish neighborhood, in which Dan attended St. Regis, a Roman Catholic parochial school located directly across the street from his house. He quarterbacked the school's football team, which his father coached, and developed his arm by tossing footballs around with his dad after school. Dan Marino Sr. worked evenings as a delivery-truck driver for the Pittsburgh *Post-Gazette*, leaving him free in the afternoons to play with his strong-armed son, who now attributes his signature fast release and sidearm throwing motion to those early lessons. "The biggest thing in my early development is that my dad had a job where he could be home in the afternoon, waiting for me to get out of school," Marino explained to Mark Whicker during an interview for *Inside Sports* (September 1982). "Then we would throw to each other the rest of the day. My dad keeps me in perspective. Plus, he's the best coach I ever had."

Dan Marino's athletic prowess was not matched in the classroom. His grades were so poor that his sixth-grade teacher at St. Regis predicted to his parents that he would never graduate from high school. "Danny could recall everything on a bubble-gum card, but couldn't remember when the Civil War started," Dan Marino Sr. recalled to Douglas S. Looney of *Sports Illustrated* (September 1, 1982). He urged his son to study harder, lest he sidetrack his athletic ambitions. The boy's grades improved somewhat, but just barely enough to earn him admission to the high school of his choice, Central Catholic, one of Pittsburgh's top athletic schools, where he became a "B" student. As quarterback, placekicker, and punter on the football team and as a pitcher on the baseball team, he earned a reputation as one of Pennsylvania's outstanding high school athletes. Marino compiled a pitching record of 25-1 and a scout for the Cincinnati Reds clocked his fastball at ninety-two miles-per-hour, exceptional for a high schooler. In his senior year he complemented his pitching feats with a .550 batting average. Meanwhile, Marino's football talents were so considerable that officials from the University of Pittsburgh began scouting him during his sophomore year and, in his junior year, coveted Marino for their football team.

A tough decision confronted Marino when he completed his senior year at Central Catholic, since, in addition to the University of Pittsburgh, he was being pursued by football scouts from dozens of other colleges and was receiving scholarship offers from UCLA, Michigan State, Clemson, and Arizona State. To make matters even more difficult, he also received an offer to play baseball from the Kansas City Royals, who selected him in the fourth round of the free-agent draft in June 1979. For a time, Marino contemplated playing both professional baseball in the Kansas City Royals organization and college football, but he eventually decided to concentrate on football at the University of Pittsburgh, whose campus is a mere four blocks from the house in which he grew up. The opportunity to play with his family and friends as spectators influenced Marino's decision. "I have strong personal and family ties to the city of Pittsburgh," he explained during the press conference at which he announced that he had chosen Pittsburgh.

As a freshman in 1979, Marino was called on to lead the Pitt Panther offense midway through the season, after the starting quarterback, Rick Trocano, suffered a leg injury. Marino's drop-back passing style and strong arm fit perfectly into Pitt's pro-style offense and he led the team to five straight wins, including a 29-14 defeat of archrival Penn State and a 16-10 win over Arizona in the postseason Fiesta Bowl. In all, Marino connected on 130 of 222 passes for 1,680 yards and ten touchdowns, as the Panthers went, 11-1. In the passing efficiency ratings compiled by the National Collegiate Athletic Association, Marino ranked tenth in the country. As a sophomore, he threw for fifteen touchdowns and led the Panthers to another 11-1 record, including a victory in the Gator Bowl, but he enjoyed his best collegiate season as a junior, setting Pitt records for touchdown passes (thirty-seven), passing yards (2,876), and passes completed (226). He threw six touchdown passes in a game against South Carolina and capped his all-American season with a Most Valuable Player performance in the Sugar Bowl against Georgia, tossing three TDs in a 24-20 triumph. One of the touchdowns, which came with only thirty-five seconds left, won the game for the Panthers, and Pitt finished at 11-1 for the third straight season.

By the time Marino began his senior year at the University of Pittsburgh, the school had become the toast of college football, so much so that many experts predicted a perfect season for the Panthers. Regarded (along with Stanford's John Elway) as the best quarterback in college football, Marino was considered a leading prospect to win the Heisman Trophy as the nation's top collegiate player. He had, after all, finished fourth in the voting for that award in the previous season. His superlative arm, quick release, and supreme self-confidence evoked comparisons with legendary college quarterbacks of the past, including Joe Namath and Ken Stabler. Going one step farther, Bobby Bowden, the Florida State coach, called Marino "a pro quarterback in college."

Yet Dan Marino's senior year at the University of Pittsburgh turned out to be the most frustrating of his college career, since both he and the team failed to perform up to expectations. The Panthers went "only" 9-3, and Marino's performance, as reflected in his statistics, caused him to be booed for the first time by Pitt fans. To make matters worse, his stock among pro scouts dipped after rumors circulated that he had a drug problem and an inflated ego. (The rumors about drug use became so pervasive that the university tested Marino, but the results were negative.)

Although Marino passed for 2,432 yards, his total of seventeen touchdown passes represented a dropoff of twenty from the previous year. In the Cotton Bowl, Pitt could score only three points in losing to Southern Methodist University. "We were ranked number one [in the preseason polls], and to this day I think we had the best team in the country," Marino told Bob Rubin for an Inside Sports (February 1985) article. "But to go undefeated, you have to play well all the time, and we didn't. When it didn't happen, everyone wanted to know why." Marino admitted to Peter Alfano of the New York Times (October 16, 1983) that the tribulations of his senior year prepared him to face the challenges that he encountered as a professional quarterback. "I think it helped me on and off the field," Marino explained. "The thing I learned . . . was that you can't get down to the point where you can't perform or get so overconfident that you don't think you can do any wrong."

Despite his less than spectacular senior season, Marino finished his college career as Pittsburgh's all-time total-offense leader, with 8,290 yards. Only the fourth Pitt player ever to have his uniform number retired, he set school records for career touchdown passes (seventy-nine), passing yards (8,597), and passes completed (693). He ranked fourth in touchdown passes, fifth in passing yardage, and fourth in completions in NCAA history. But many NFL teams, convinced that Marino had peaked in his junior year and concerned about his alleged drug and attitude problems, shied away from him in the first round of the league's annual draft of college players. Twenty-six other players, including five quarterbacks, were selected ahead of Marino, who went to the Miami Dolphins as the next-to-last pick of the first round. The failure of twenty-six NFL teams to draft Marino remains a much-discussed topic among players, fans, and the media. "We just never thought Dan would be around when it was our turn to draft," the Dolphins head coach, Don Shula, told Peter Alfano. "I had always liked everything I saw in him, his mannerisms, his mechanics, especially his quick release. He was a heck of a quarterback to be out there on the twenty-seventh pick; a heck of a buy." His selection by the Miami Dolphins gave Marino the opportunity to play for one of the league's top teams and to work with Shula, an extraordinarily successful coach who is especially adept at coaching quarterbacks.

After signing a four-year, $2 million contract with the Dolphins, Marino began his rookie season as a backup to David Woodley, who had quarterbacked Miami to the Super Bowl the previous season. Fortunately for Marino, Woodley played so poorly in the first few games of 1983 that Shula became impatient and replaced him with the rookie in the third week of the season, late in a game against the Los Angeles Raiders. Marino hit on eleven of seventeen passes, two for touchdowns, to provide all of the Dolphins' scoring in a 27-14 loss. Two weeks later, this time against the New Orleans Saints, Marino replaced Woodley just before halftime, completing twelve of twenty-two passes for 150 yards as Miami lost, 17-7. In the following week, Marino got his first starting assignment, playing against the Buffalo Bills. Although the Dolphins lost the game, 38-35, in overtime, Marino had a spectacular day, completing nineteen of twenty-nine passes for 322 yards and three touchdowns. "The thrill is back," a jubilant Don Shula exulted following the game, and he has made sure that Marino has been Miami's starting quarterback ever since. The next week, Marino threw for three more touchdowns in a 32-14 rout of the New York Jets. The Dolphins lost only one more game the rest of the year and captured the American Football Conference's Eastern Division title, before they were eliminated by the Seattle Seahawks in a divisional playoff game, 27-20. Marino was honored with the conference passing championship and the Rookie of the Year Award. He also became the first rookie quarterback to be selected as a starter in the Pro Bowl, the NFL's all-star game.

Marino's close working relationship with Don Shula was considered a vital element in his success. At Pitt, he often threw into heavy coverage, believing that his arm was strong enough to get the ball to receivers even when they were not open. As a result, he threw twenty-three interceptions in both his junior and senior seasons, but under Shula's tutelage, he learned to stop trying to complete passes to well-covered receivers. In 1983 he threw only six interceptions in 296 passing attempts. In preseason games that year, Shula had allowed Marino to call all of his own plays, thus forcing him to learn the Dolphin's playbook, and he also helped Marino by acknowledging his quarterback's exceptional talent and adapting the team's offense to his skills, rather than trying to make him conform to the Dolphins' system. Long a defense-minded coach, Shula had always favored teams that controlled the game's tempo by running the ball extensively, but Marino brought about a change in that strategy because of his passing prowess and predilection for the long bomb and quick score. In fact, he changed strategies throughout the NFL by demonstrating that a team could win by relying largely on the pass for its offensive production.

Marino's superb rookie performance was quickly overshadowed by a spectacular 1984 season that saw him set NFL records for touchdown passes (forty-eight), passing yards (5,084), and completions (362). The Dolphins went 14-2 and scored at least twenty-eight points in fourteen of their sixteen regular-season games. "His feats this season have left NFL coaches and players gasping in amazement," Greg Logan of Newsday (January 21, 1985) mar-

veled. On the same date Newsweek's Pete Axthelm commented: "Marino is not just what some coaches call an impact player, a man who drastically alters the personality of his team. He is a quantum-leap player who is changing the entire nature of his art." Axthelm went on to compare Marino's effect on pro football with the influence that Babe Ruth, Bill Russell, and Bobby Orr had on baseball, basketball, and hockey, respectively, during their careers. Yet Marino's success was not achieved singlehandedly, since he could count on the help of a strong offensive line and two outstanding wide receivers, Mark Clayton and Mark Duper, familiarly known as the "Marks Brothers," who gave him a double threat that befuddled defenses throughout the league.

Following their extraordinary regular season, the Dolphins roared into the playoffs with convincing wins over Seattle and Pittsburgh. In the latter game, Marino completed twenty-one of thirty-two passes for 421 yards and four touchdowns, as Miami crushed the Steelers, 45-28, and advanced to the Super Bowl against the San Francisco 49ers, a much-anticipated contest that pitted Marino against another of the league's top quarterbacks, Joe Montana. In that game, the 49ers played five defensive backs instead of the normal four, in order to guard against the Dolphins' passing attack, used a four-man rush to force Marino to hurry his passes, and blitzed only one man at a time to avoid leaving gaps in the defense that he could exploit. Although he completed twenty-nine of fifty passes for 318 yards, Marino was sacked four times, a high for the season, and was rushed into throwing two interceptions. The 49ers won easily, 38-16.

After his brilliant 1984 season, Marino tried to renegotiate his contract, which still had two years to go. In the week before the Super Bowl, the Dolphins' owner, Joe Robbie, said he was willing to renegotiate the pact, and in April 1985, three months after that game, Marvin Demoff, Marino's lawyer, submitted a proposal to Robbie asking for $1.8 million a year in an effort to bring Marino's salary in line with the six-year, $6.3 million pact that Montana had signed with the 49ers in 1984. On July 25, the first day of training camp, Robbie and Demoff met in the owner's office in Miami, at which time Demoff lowered his proposal to $1.3 million. Robbie listened attentively and then left the office to prepare a counteroffer, but he discovered when he returned that Marino had left camp. Robbie then announced that he would not negotiate further until Marino returned. Staging a thirty-seven-day walkout, Marino did not come back to the team until just before the regular season started, playing it under the terms of the existing contract.

Marino and the Miami Dolphins enjoyed a less rewarding season in 1985. The San Francisco 49ers' successful Super Bowl strategy had shown the rest of the NFL an effective method for stopping the Dolphins' high-powered offense. Marino missed training camp, and his key supporting players, including Mark Duper and the offensive linemen Ed Newman and Jon Giesler, were sidelined by injuries. Although Marino's statistics were understandably less spectacular than those he compiled in 1984, he still led the league in touchdown passes (thirty), passing yards (4,137), and completions (336). As Greg Logan noted in *Newsday* (January 10, 1986), "An 'off' year for Marino means he went from all-time to merely all-Pro." The Dolphins compiled a record of 12-4 and were the only team to beat the Chicago Bears, the eventual Super Bowl champions. In the divisional playoffs, the Miami Dolphins upended the Cleveland Browns, 24-21, but their hopes of going to the Super Bowl for the second consecutive year were dashed when they lost the AFC championship game, 31-14, to the New England Patriots.

The quarterback's contract squabbles with Joe Robbie continued following the 1985 season, mainly because he was seeking a new five-year contract for $7.5 million. When their talks reached a stalemate in August 1986, Marino blasted the owner of the Miami Dolphins in the press. "I guess Joe Robbie never appreciates anything until it's gone," Marino said to J. David Miller during an interview for an article that appeared in *Sport* (October 1986). "Joe Robbie wants a Cadillac but he only wants to pay for a Volkswagen," Marino said. Although most Dolphin fans sided with Robbie, Marino gained the support of his teammates and many former members of the team, one of whom suggested that Robbie was refusing to meet Marino's demands because of the Dolphins' Super Bowl defeat in 1985. In early September, however, the two sides came together and Marino signed a six-year contract worth $9 million and an additional $100,000 a year in incentives, the largest package to that date for an NFL player.

Although because of their porous defense the Dolphins faltered in 1986 and 1987, finishing with records of 8-8 and 8-7, respectively, and failing to make the playoffs either year, Marino continued to shine. In 1986 he led the conference in passing, throwing for 4,746 yards, the third-highest total in NFL history, and tossing forty-four touchdowns, second all-time to his own forty-eight in 1984. On September 21, Marino threw six touchdown passes against the Jets, a high in his career. In the 1987 season, which was shortened by a strike, Marino led the AFC in completions (263) and touchdown passes (twenty-six), finishing second in passing and passing yards.

The Dolphins' woes continued in 1988. They again failed to qualify for the playoffs, and their record of 6-10 was the worst compiled by a Miami team since 1969. Marino's twenty-eight touchdown passes tied for second-best in the league, but he also threw twenty-three interceptions. On October 23, 1988 Marino passed for 521 yards in a game against the New York Jets, the second-highest single-game passing total in NFL history, but the Dolphins nevertheless lost the game, 44-30, since he was intercepted five times.

Dan Marino stands six feet four inches tall and weighs about 222 pounds. Since January 30, 1985 he has been married to the former Claire Veazey.

They have two sons, Daniel Charles and Michael Joseph. The Marinos live in Fort Lauderdale, Florida. His good looks, curly brown hair, and model-like physique have made Marino a matinee idol of sorts, and he once bared his chest for a photo in *Playgirl* magazine. Described by one sportswriter as a man "who swaggers even when he is standing still," Dan Marino is extremely self-assured. According to Larry Dorman of the *Sporting News* (January 9, 1984): "Marino's bearing bespeaks a confidence that borders on cockiness but doesn't cross the line. It is a hairsbreadth this side of arrogance, a trait that every successful quarterback has. He has evoked comparisons to Joe Namath, and he shrugs them off. 'I'm better-looking than Joe,' he says with a wink."

Some reporters and teammates, however, have characterized Marino as a down-to-earth person who remains dedicated to the working-class values he grew up with. The former Dolphin tackle Bob Baumhower told John Rubin for the *Inside Sports* profile: "He's an easygoing guy, the kind of guy you like to sit down and have a beer with and chew the fat. And he hasn't changed from day one. He's a very real person—no front. What you see is what you get." Writing in the *Sporting News* (November 5, 1984), Paul Attner described Marino as "a shot-and-a-beer guy who likes his neighborhood bar, jeans, rock-'n'-roll, *Archie Bunker's Place* on TV, *Ghostbusters* at the movie houses, golf and, of course, Italian food." Marino has donated time to the Leukemia Fund and to posters encouraging reading for the American Library Association. He is also active in the Miami chapter of the National Italian-American Hall of Fame. Marino holds a B.A. degree in communications from the University of Pittsburgh.

References: *Inside Sports* 4:55+ S '82 pors, 7:26+ F '85 pors, 9:26+ O '87 pors; *N Y Times* V p1+ N 4 '84 por; *Newsweek* 105:62+ Ja 21 '85 pors; *Sporting N* p3+ N 5 '84 por; *Sports Illus* 57:28+ S 1 '82 pors, 61:86+ D 24–31 '84 pors

Marshall, Thurgood

July 2, 1908– Associate Justice of the United States Supreme Court. Address: Supreme Court of the United States, 1 First St., N.E., Washington, D.C. 20543

NOTE: This biography supersedes the article that appeared in *Current Biography* in 1954.

In 1939 Thurgood Marshall was at the forefront of the civil rights movement, arguing cases before the United States Supreme Court in his capacity as chief counsel for the National Association for the Advancement of Colored People Legal Defense and Educational Fund. Fifty years later, as the only black member of the Supreme Court since his ap-

Thurgood Marshall

pointment in 1967, he continues to act upon his longstanding commitment to the constitutionally protected rights of the individual by opposing capital punishment, racial discrimination, and the encroachment of the state upon First Amendment freedoms.

Marshall made his best-known contribution to progress in civil rights while he was still a lawyer for the NAACP, when, in 1954, he persuaded the Supreme Court that "separate but equal" public school systems violated the Fourteenth Amendment's guarantee of equal protection of the laws. After hearing Marshall's argument, the Court unanimously declared that segregation was unconstitutional in the landmark decision *Brown v. Board of Education*. Marshall continued to litigate desegregation cases until 1961, when he was appointed a federal appellate judge by President John F. Kennedy. Four years later, he became President Lyndon B. Johnson's solicitor general. He served in that capacity until his appointment to the Supreme Court.

When Marshall joined the Court, then under the leadership of Chief Justice Earl Warren, he replaced a centrist justice whose vote often created a five-to-four conservative majority. Marshall tipped the balance in favor of a liberal, or activist, majority, but before long he found himself increasingly in the minority. The two chief justices since 1969, Warren E. Burger and William H. Rehnquist, were both appointed to the Court by President Richard M. Nixon. Three additional Nixon appointees were joined by one Gerald R. Ford appointee in the 1970s and by three Ronald Reagan appointees (one of whom replaced a Nixon appointee) in the 1980s. The resulting conservative revanchism has placed Marshall in the position of

frequently dissenting—along with the last remaining Dwight D. Eisenhower appointee, William J. Brennan Jr.—from decisions that would, in his view, lead to the erosion of hard-won civil rights gains.

Thurgood Marshall was born on July 2, 1908, the younger of the two sons of William Canfield Marshall and Norma A. (Williams) Marshall in Baltimore, Maryland. His mother was an elementary school teacher, and his father was a Pullman car waiter before becoming a steward at an all-white yacht club on Chesapeake Bay. He was named after his paternal grandfather, who assumed the name Thoroughgood in compliance with Union Army regulations during the Civil War that required every soldier to record both a first and a last name. His great-grandfather was captured in Africa and brought as a slave to Maryland's eastern shore. Speaking of his great-grandfather, Marshall once said: "His more polite descendants like to think he came from the cultured tribes in Sierra Leone. But we all know that he really came from the toughest part of the Congo." His rebellious nature, according to Marshall, won him his freedom. William Marshall carried on the tradition by advising his son to fight his own battles. Marshall has quoted his father as telling him, "Son, if anyone ever calls you a nigger, you not only got my permission to fight him—you got my orders to fight him."

After graduating with honors from Douglas High School in Baltimore, Marshall enrolled at Lincoln University, an all-black college in Oxford, Pennsylvania. His mother pawned her wedding and engagement rings to help pay his expenses, and he worked part-time as, at different times, a busboy, waiter, baker, and grocery clerk during his college years. Marshall had originally intended to study dentistry, according to his mother's wishes, but because he excelled on the debating team he switched his major to pre-law. "My father turned me into a lawyer without ever telling me what he wanted me to be," Marshall once said, as quoted in the *New York Times* (October 22, 1964). "In a way, he was the most insidious of my family rebels. He taught me how to argue, challenged my logic on every point, even if we were discussing the weather." Marshall graduated with honors in 1929.

After his application to the all-white University of Maryland Law School was rejected on the basis of race, Marshall enrolled at Howard University Law School in Washington, D.C. He was awarded an LL.B. degree, magna cum laude, in 1933. Employing his newly attained knowledge of the law as counsel to the Baltimore chapter of the NAACP, he compelled the law school that had rejected him to admit its first black student in 1935. The student, Donald Murray, was also the first black student admitted to any state law school south of the Mason-Dixon line.

In addition to his work with the NAACP, Marshall maintained a private practice in Baltimore from 1933 to 1937. Specializing in civil rights and criminal law, he often represented clients who could not afford to pay him for his services. The

NAACP did not pay well either, and, even after he moved to the organization's headquarters in New York City to become the assistant to Charles H. Houston, the national counsel for the NAACP, in 1936, he was paid only a modest annual salary. When Houston resigned in 1938 to resume private practice, Marshall was elevated to his post. The following year he helped to found the NAACP Legal Defense and Educational Fund (LDF) to mount a legal assault on segregation. (Since the mid-1950s the LDF has functioned independently of the NAACP.)

As director and chief counsel of the LDF, Marshall was the chief strategist in the campaign to desegregate America's school systems. Much of his time was spent traveling throughout the South, creating a network of sympathetic lawyers to handle civil rights cases and instigating local challenges to segregated education. Although segregation was consistently upheld by the lower courts, Marshall coordinated appeals to the higher courts, and he himself argued the cases before the Supreme Court, having been admitted to practice before that body in 1939. Of the thirty-two cases he argued on behalf of the NAACP, he won twenty-nine.

Marshall's most important victory occurred on May 17, 1954, when the Warren Court ruled unanimously in *Brown v. Board of Education* that "separate educational facilities are inherently unequal," overturning the "separate but equal" doctrine laid down in *Plessy v. Ferguson* (1896). Racial segregation was held, in two separate rulings in *Brown*, to deprive blacks of both equal protection of the laws and due process of law, under the Fourteenth and Fifth amendments, respectively. Much of Marshall's remaining work with the LDF consisted of litigating compliance with the decision on a case-by-case basis. He also worked to eliminate racial discrimination in voting, housing, public accommodations, and the disciplining of black American soldiers stationed in Korea and Japan, countries to which Marshall traveled in 1951 in order to gather firsthand information. He eventually obtained reduced sentences for twenty-two of the forty black soldiers who alleged that they had received unfair trials.

On September 23, 1961 President Kennedy appointed Thurgood Marshall to the United States Court of Appeals for the Second Circuit, which comprises New York, Vermont, and Connecticut. Despite an increase in salary that would nearly double his annual income, it was a tough decision for Marshall to leave the civil rights battle. "I had to fight it out with myself," he said, as quoted in the *New York Times* (October 22, 1964), "but by then I had built up a staff—a damned good staff—an excellent board, and the backing that would let them go ahead. And when one has the opportunity to serve his government, he should think twice before passing it up." In a subsequent interview for the *Washington Post* (December 26, 1965), Marshall told Joseph E. Mohbat: "I've always felt the assault troops never occupy the town. I figured after the school decisions, the assault was over for me. It was time to let newer minds take over."

As an indication of the struggles that still lay ahead for the civil rights movement, Marshall's confirmation was stalled for nearly one year by segregationist senators. He was finally confirmed on September 11, 1962 by a vote of fifty-four to sixteen. During his tenure as a federal appellate judge, he wrote more than 150 decisions. According to Fred P. Graham of the *New York Times* (June 14, 1965), Marshall "tended to tackle tough issues, even when they could be avoided on procedural grounds." Among other things, he ruled that the loyalty oaths required of New York teachers were unconstitutional; curbed the power of immigration authorities to expel aliens summarily; and strengthened the protective powers of the Fourth and Fifth amendments in cases dealing with illegal searches and seizures and double jeopardy.

Marshall took a pay cut and gave up lifetime tenure as a federal judge in order to accept the position of solicitor general, the third-highest post in the Justice Department. In contrast to the year-long delay in his confirmation process four years earlier, he was confirmed by voice vote on August 11, 1965—less than one month after President Johnson offered him the job. Since Johnson had indicated his intention to appoint a black person or a woman to the Supreme Court during his tenure, Marshall's appointment to the Justice Department was widely viewed as a steppingstone to the High Court.

When Marshall succeeded Archibald Cox as solicitor general, Attorney General Nicholas deB. Katzenbach described him as "one of the greatest Americans alive today." "It's no exaggeration to say that a good measure of the civil rights progress we've made is built on what this fellow has done over the years," Katzenbach told Joseph Mohbat. That progress included the Voting Rights Act of 1965, which was signed into law just days before Marshall assumed the job of the nation's chief prosecuting attorney. Authorized by the new voting rights legislation to abolish literacy requirements and other voter qualification tests, including poll taxes, Marshall argued the government's case on appeal before the Supreme Court, thereby dismantling such discriminatory obstacles to full voter participation.

Of the nineteen cases he argued before the Supreme Court as solicitor general, Marshall won fourteen. He also argued, in an amicus brief filed with the California Supreme Court, that the court should declare unconstitutional Proposition 14, an anti–fair housing amendment to the state constitution that was passed in 1964. He contended that popular initiatives were unconstitutional if they furthered racial discrimination—not only despite popular support, but also because of it. "Everybody knows minority groups do not have the strength to win a popular statewide vote," he wrote. One of the few cases Marshall lost for the government was one of the confession cases collected under *Miranda v. Arizona* (1966), in which he argued that criminal suspects unable to afford a lawyer did not have the right to court-appointed counsel. As a Supreme Court justice, however, Marshall has consistently supported the *Miranda* doctrine of right to counsel, beginning with his first major opinion as a member of the High Court.

Few political observers were surprised when President Johnson appointed Marshall to the Supreme Court on June 13, 1967, most recognizing not only Marshall's eminent qualifications, but also the political expediency of appointing the first black Supreme Court justice in an era of acute racial tensions. Marshall was confirmed by the Senate on August 30, by a vote of sixty-nine to eleven. The vacancy on the Court that Marshall filled had been created by the retirement of Justice Tom C. Clark, who had stepped down in order to avoid the appearance of conflict of interest after his son, Ramsey Clark, became Johnson's attorney general. Ramsey Clark, in his chapter of a book on Supreme Court justices edited by Leon Friedman, remarked upon the progress in civil rights symbolized by the replacement of Tom Clark, the grandson of a Confederate soldier, by Thurgood Marshall, the grandson of a Union soldier and great-grandson of a slave.

To the syndicated columnist Joseph Kraft, however, Marshall's appointment symbolized only "the outmoded principle of ethnic representation, and for years to come his seat on the Court will probably be a Negro seat." Calling Marshall's appointment "an unhappily fit climax to a term that has shown the Court to be hung up on outworn liberal and moralistic doctrines of the past," Kraft contended, in a column that appeared in the *Washington Post* on June 15, 1967, that, despite Marshall's "generous sympathies, common sense, and . . . feel for the political issues that bulk largely in the work of the Court," he "will not bring to the Court penetrating analysis or distinction of mind."

In his chapter of the book *The Justices of the Supreme Court, 1789-1978* (1980), Ramsey Clark wrote, "Thurgood Marshall adjusted easily, quietly, almost comfortably to the work of the Supreme Court while its majority possessed an expanding vision of justice." As a civil rights lawyer, Marshall had attempted to expand the Court's definition of equality, but as a member of the liberal majority on the Warren Court, he eschewed ringing constitutional declarations, preferring to use his negotiating skills to encourage unanimity among the justices so that their decisions would carry more weight. This strategy was consistent with Marshall's behavior as a lawyer for the NAACP, according to a longtime friend, who told a reporter for *Newsweek* (June 26, 1967): "He always looked at the big picture. He never wanted to win a battle if it would lose him the war."

The impending demise of the liberal majority signaled by Nixon's unsuccessful attempt to impeach Associate Justice William O. Douglas in 1970 prompted Douglas to wonder how the Court would retain what he saw as its independence, and what others saw as its liberal, activist tendencies. "Marshall['s liberal vote] was weak," lamented Douglas, according to the paraphrasing of his thoughts by Bob Woodward and Scott Armstrong in their book *The Brethren* (1979). In Douglas's view, Marshall was "a correct vote, a follower, but no leader, no fighter. He was not one to speak up articulately or forcefully." But as the Court became more conservative, Marshall resumed the role of outspoken advocate, proving that Douglas's fears were unwarranted. In the words of Ramsey Clark, "Adversity challenged Thurgood Marshall. The people needed a champion again. His enormous passion rose, but a strong discipline directed it toward equal justice under law." According to Woodward and Armstrong, Marshall, a "plainspoken and direct" man, "saw his job as casting his vote and urging his colleagues to do what was right. On the Court, he had little interest in perfecting the finer points of the law."

Marshall expounded on his faith that justice could be achieved lawfully—without "violence for violence's sake," without black separatism—in a speech at Dillard University in New Orleans on May 4, 1969. Recalling that he was in Selma, Alabama a generation before the 1965 civil rights demonstrations, he explained: "I did that because I've never had to defend my country by lying about it. I can tell the truth about it and still be proud. [But] I'm not going to be completely satisfied. I'll be dead before I'll be satisfied." Marshall reiterated the need to avoid the complacency that often accompanies progress in a speech on the occasion of the dedication of a bronze statue in his honor in Baltimore on May 16, 1980. "Some Negroes feel we have arrived," he told the assembled crowd. "Others feel there is nothing more to do. I just want to be sure that when you see this statue, you won't think that's the end of it. I won't have it that way. There's too much work to be done."

Putting his philosophy into practice on the Supreme Court, Marshall often found himself dissenting from major decisions, especially in the area of criminal law, in his efforts to uphold the rights of the individual against preventive detention, illegal searches and surveillance, and improper methods of interrogation. Typical of his dissents was the one from the ruling in *United States v. Agurs* (1976): "One of the most basic elements of fairness in a criminal trial is that available evidence tending to show innocence, as well as that tending to show guilt, be fully aired before the jury; more particularly, it is that the State in its zeal to convict a defendant not suppress evidence that might exonerate him."

A staunch opponent of capital punishment, Marshall described it in his concurring opinion in *Furman v. Georgia* (1972) as "an excessive and unnecessary punishment that violates the Eighth Amendment." He continued: "Capital punishment is imposed discriminatorily against identifiable classes of people; there is evidence that innocent people have been executed before their innocence can be proved; and the death penalty wreaks havoc with our entire criminal justice system." In other opinions, Marshall has affirmed that the right of privacy is the basis for prohibiting states from infringing upon a woman's right to safe, legal, and affordable abortion; declared that the possession of obscene material is protected by the First Amendment; and cautioned that the police must work within the law in their apprehension of criminal suspects.

Recent rulings of the Rehnquist Court to limit affirmative action have been accompanied by Marshall's blistering dissents. For example, he wrote that *Richmond v. Croson* (1989), which rendered Richmond, Virginia's affirmative-action program unconstitutional, represented "a full-scale retreat from the Court's longstanding solicitude to race-conscious remedial efforts directed toward deliverance of the century-old promise of equality of economic opportunity." During the late 1970s and 1980s Marshall publicly denounced the conservative trend of the Court at judicial conferences and Bar Association meetings, and in a series of television interviews with the journalist Carl Rowan. Evaluating the records of American presidents on civil rights, Marshall placed Reagan at "the bottom" and gave high marks only to Johnson and Harry S. Truman.

Conservatives have looked longingly at Marshall's seat on the Court, seeing an opportunity to strengthen their judicial majority. According to the *New York Times* (September 20, 1987), Marshall "strikes most observers as the least healthy, most out-of-shape justice on the court." A heavyset 200 pounder even in his prime, Marshall now carries 250 pounds over a six-foot-two frame and, continuing a lifelong pattern, shuns physical exercise. Marshall suffered a heart attack in 1976, and in 1984 he was hospitalized briefly for viral bronchitis. He also wears a hearing aid and suffers from mild glaucoma. "Don't worry," he assured a 1988 gathering of lawyers and judges, "I'm going to outlive those bastards."

Marshall's limited income during his long years with the NAACP resulted in his being the poorest justice on the Court, according to David O'Brien in *Storm Center* (1986). He lives in Falls Church, Virginia with his second wife, the former Cecelia S. Suyat, a former secretary for the NAACP whom he married on December 17, 1955. The couple have two sons: Thurgood Jr. and John William. Marshall's first wife, Vivian G. (Burey) Marshall, died of cancer in February 1955 after twenty-five years of marriage.

References: Friedman, Leon, ed. The Justices of the Supreme Court, 1789–1978, vol. 5 (1980); International Who's Who, 1989–90; O'Brien, David M. Storm Center: The Supreme Court in American Politics (1986); Who's Who among Black Americans, 1988; Who's Who in America, 1988–89; Woodward, Bob and Scott Armstrong. The Brethren (1979)

Martin, Agnes

Mar. 22, 1912– Artist. Address: c/o The Pace Gallery, 32 E. 57th Street, New York, N.Y. 10022

Although the painter Agnes Martin deliberately moved from New York City to a small town in New Mexico more than twenty years ago, she has retained her almost legendary status as one of the important post-painterly abstract expressionists. "I don't believe in the promotion of art," she once declared. "I believe in its discovery." Half a continent away from the reputation-making center of the American art world and in her late seventies, she has continued to arouse critical interest, for she is one of those artists whose work transcends stylistic labeling yet is always somehow in style.

Over the course of her long career, Miss Martin's name has become synonymous with grid paintings, and her infinite variations on a schema consisting of the interplay of horizontal and vertical lines have been recognized as presaging a number of postmodern art movements, including hard-edge painting, op art, conceptualism, and especially minimalism. But as the poet and critic John Ashbery has pointed out, Agnes Martin's "minimalism" is not merely reductive; it is the result of a slow, thoughtful distillation. Never purely mechanical (as the grid form would suggest) or impersonal, it is her form of expressionist painting.

Portrait of Agnes Martin, 1979. Photograph courtesy of the Pace Gallery

Although in her works she has seemed to be seeking the classical ideal of perfection in pure geometry, she has often asserted, in essays and in interviews, that she does not paint "scientific discoveries or philosophies" but what she has called "the holiday state of mind." However it is defined, her paintings give an ineffable pleasure to those who allow themselves the time to absorb the subtle nuances of line and tonalities that make complex networks of seemingly simple geometric patterns. As the *Artforum* critic Lizzie Borden put it, they demand "a higher degree of consciousness as the response of the viewer to almost invisible events."

Agnes Martin was born in Maklin, Saskatchewan, Canada on March 22, 1912. Following the death of her father, a wheat farmer, a few years later, she moved with her mother, sister, and two brothers to Vancouver, British Columbia, where she attended local primary and secondary schools. Mrs. Martin supported her family by renovating and selling old houses, and throughout her youth Agnes Martin took various jobs with mining and logging companies to supplement the family income. Moving to the United States in 1932, she took classes at Western Washington College in Bellingham from 1935 to 1938. Between 1937 and 1953 Miss Martin taught in public schools in Washington, Delaware, and New Mexico. In between teaching assignments, she continued her education, at Teachers College, Columbia University, from which she received a B.S. degree in art education in 1942, and at the University of New Mexico in Albuquerque, which awarded her an M.A. degree in 1952. She was a painting instructor at the University of New Mexico in the late 1940s and at East Oregon College in La Grande in the 1952–53 academic year. At some point during this period— some sources give 1940, others, 1950—Miss Martin became a naturalized American citizen.

By the mid-1950s Agnes Martin was living in the art colony of Taos, New Mexico, where she joined the Ruins Gallery, which had been founded by a group of artists with a distinctly international orientation. In 1957, however, she returned to New York City at the suggestion of Betty Parsons, a gallery owner who had become interested in her work. Miss Martin settled in one of the abandoned waterfront lofts on Coenties Slip in lower Manhattan, which had recently been taken over by artists. A number of works by Agnes Martin and some of her former neighbors, among them the painters Robert Indiana, Ellsworth Kelly, James Rosenquist, and Jack Youngerman, were brought together in the exhibition "Nine Artists/Coenties Slip," held at the downtown branch of the Whitney Museum of American Art in 1974. Although the Coenties Slip painters never constituted a formal group, they represented, in their diverse ways, a break with abstract expressionism. As more than one critic has noted, Miss Martin's work of the time does have certain affinities with Kelly's brightly colored paintings of geometrical shapes. For example, her twelve-inch-square painting *Islands No. 1* (1960), a work in oil and pencil on canvas that was included in the Whitney show, consists of a rectangular grid made up of rows of short horizontal dashes arranged in pairs, the whole shape enclosed by an inch-wide border. The slight changes of spacing

between the columns of dashes give the seemingly static, formal composition vitality and movement.

In the 1940s Miss Martin's work in watercolors and oils had consisted largely of somewhat conventional portraits and still lifes. As she progressed, she began, in the early 1950s, to paint biomorphic abstractions with a line that became progressively lighter and more fluid. Within a few years, however, she abandoned figurative imagery for subjective, abstract landscape forms that gradually became more geometric and discrete— simplified forms in a light-filled space, the effect provided by pale, translucent background washes. As the references to landscape diminished, the effect of impersonal objectivity increased, and the flatness and frontality of the surface plane was emphasized. In 1958 Miss Martin held her first solo exhibition, at the Betty Parsons Gallery in New York. She subsequently exhibited works at the gallery in solo shows in 1959 and 1961.

Sometime after 1958 Miss Martin began to evolve her grid schema. In her first protogrid compositions, the arrangement of the geometrical elements—which might be dots, circles, or tiny triangles as well as dashes and lines—was enclosed within a rectangular field. For example, *Whispering* (1963), a watercolor on paper, is composed of white spindle-shaped objects with blue ends, arranged in rows against a lighter blue ground. The artist also experimented with collages constructed of small pieces of colored canvas or wood or, as in *The Garden* (1958), of various found objects glued to a background canvas in orderly rows. By 1964 she had dispensed with the enclosing rectangle so that the meshing of horizontal and vertical lines, some of them extending out to the edges of the canvas or sheet of drawing paper, became the dominant motif.

The critic Lawrence Alloway included several of Agnes Martin's compositions in the important exhibition called "Systemic Painting," which he organized at New York's Solomon R. Guggenheim Museum in 1966. These works, along with the contributions of her fellow exhibitors, helped to define a kind of painting known as systemic, or modular, art that Alloway perceived as an outgrowth of minimal art. In these paintings, holistic and self-contained images come together by means of the repetition of a single motif, or module, with no visual climaxes or hierarchical order among the modules, and the field, or space, is inseparable from the design elements within it.

Miss Martin's early grid drawings, which were almost always nine inches square, featured ruled lines done in red ink or colored pencil, or black or gray pencilings over a delicately tinged ground. Drawing, in any case, has remained basic to the artist's work, for in her paintings pencil lines of varying weight can often be seen under the acrylic washes, giving, as the *New York Times* critic Hilton Kramer put it, a "curious intimacy" to her work and directing the viewer's attention to every detail of the composition.

Some of Miss Martin's earlier grids, such as *Orange Grove* (1965), in which every fourth line is orange, seem to have obvious references to nature, but, by the late 1960s, such referential touches had disappeared. The works she completed in the last half of the decade were austere and monochromatic, painted mainly in shades of gray and brown and in acrylics rather than oils. The slight changes in the tonalities of a canvas were, in fact, produced by changes in the penciled or painted lines, from sharp to fuzzy, or in the frequency or spacing of the lines.

Although Miss Martin had been awarded a grant by the National Endowment for the Arts in 1966 and had been exhibiting her work at the Robert Elkon Gallery in New York almost annually since 1961, she abruptly gave up painting in 1967 and moved to Cuba, New Mexico. "Every day I suddenly felt I wanted to die and it was connected with painting," she explained, as quoted in *World Artists 1950-1980*. "It took me several years to find out that the cause was an overdeveloped sense of responsibility." In her six years of self-rediscovery, Miss Martin did not paint at all, concentrating instead on building a small adobe house and a succession of studios and on writing and lecturing. One lecture, delivered at the University of Pennsylvania in 1973, was called "On the Perfection Underlying Life."

Over the years Agnes Martin can be seen as striving to open herself to happiness, which she has defined as the experiencing of one's deepest emotions. At least partly because of her occasionally cryptic remarks, some observers have discerned in her works a mystical or spiritual quality, which she has vehemently denied. On the contrary, as she wrote in an autobiographical note for the catalogue of the "Coenties Slip" exhibition: "I paint out of joy of experience. . . . I paint beauty without idealism, the new beauty that needs very much to be defined by modern philosophers. (I consider idealism, mysticism, and conventions interferences in occasions of real beauty.)"

In none of her writings has Miss Martin been able to explain why the grid appeals to her—except to speculate that the human mind enjoys the classical concept of a perfectly straight line, which does not exist in nature. She is clear, however, about the fact that her paintings "have neither objects, nor space, not time, not anything, no forms." "I paint analogies of belonging and sharing with everything," she has said, as quoted in *Artforum* (Summer 1987). Thus, in *Grey Geese Descending* (1985) she tried to express, in her words, "the emotions we have when we feel" the birds' descent. Numerous quotations from the artist's writings were published in the catalogue that accompanied her only American retrospective exhibition to date, held in 1973 at the Institute of Contemporary Art of the University of Pennsylvania in Philadelphia, where a number of her manuscripts are stored. In addition to writing and lecturing, in 1976 Miss Martin made a full-length motion picture, *Gabriel*, about a little boy's day of freedom and happiness,

which was shown at the institute the following year.

The only art Miss Martin created between 1967 and 1974 was a suite of thirty serigraphs, *On a Clear Day*, which was published by Parasol Press in 1971 and exhibited at the Museum of Modern Art in New York two years later. Variants on the grid, the serigraphs are a deliberate attempt to achieve clarity by means of precise, mechanically rendered gray lines, with all traces of the hand effaced. According to Riva Castleman, a curator at the Museum of Modern Art, when viewed as a whole, the spaces between the lines "compound to indicate a sense of the illimitable scale of infinity."

In the simplicity and solitude of rural New Mexico, Agnes Martin eventually found the freedom and serenity essential for her artistic inspiration, and she began to paint again. In her new works, the impersonal linearity of the pre-1967 grids gave way to compositions based on arrangements of parallel stripes of varying breadth. With the introduction of soft washes of pinks, blues, and yellows, her touch became more painterly. She spread the surface layer of acrylic paint so thinly that light seemed to glow through it, even though the canvas—which was, in most cases, six feet square—had often been prepared with up to eight coats of white gesso. The painted stripes were painstakingly integrated with ruled pencil or ink lines, so that soft played against hard, interval against line.

After viewing a selection of these paintings at the Pace Gallery in New York in May 1976, Thomas B. Hess, the art critic for *New York* magazine, reported that Miss Martin's abstractions were "parallels to experiences of the desert air." Another reviewer, Alan G. Artner of the *Chicago Tribune* (October 5, 1980), saw her shift in format from vertical to horizontal lines as being related to "the horizon lines and atmosphere of the American desert." Years earlier, after Miss Martin's first sojourn in New Mexico, the critic Dore Ashton, writing in the *New York Times* (December 29, 1959), had speculated that the abstract shapes and earth tones of her paintings reflected her love of "the great prairies" and suggested that her "deepest feelings are related to nature." But as the artist herself explained to Mark Stevens in an interview for *Vanity Fair* (March 1989): "The landscape doesn't have any relation to my art. The paintings are not abstractions from nature. I was painting this way . . . before I came to New Mexico. They are really abstract—because the abstract allows you to go beyond words and description."

In his critique of a 1978 showing of Miss Martin's watercolors at the Pace Gallery (her dealer since 1975) for *New York* (April 17, 1978), John Ashbery observed that her paintings had "gained a new luminosity and urgency, though the means remained as limited, if not more so, than before." He described the group of fifty-one works, each of them nine inches square, as a "pale rainbow whose minute gradations resonate all the louder for being so faint." Each small square consisted of horizontal lines in graphite or ink and contrasting bands of translucent watercolor, which apparently had been applied very wet so that the tracing-paper ground wrinkled as it dried, giving the surface a visible texture.

Continuing to experiment, in the mid-1980s Miss Martin began to use a palette knife to make stripes of varying thicknesses, and she no longer consistently penciled lines on the canvas. Most recently, as seen in a solo exhibition at the Pace Gallery in February 1989, she abandoned the soft hues of her watercolors and reverted to the monochrome tints of her earlier works, particularly a whitish gray that, in the view of Mark Stevens, is the most suitable tone for this artist's ongoing search for classical perfection. In these paintings the variations come from the fine distinctions between lighter and darker tones of gray, and, once again, from the differing thicknesses and numbers of the lines and stripes. Painted or drawn on the canvas, the lines sometimes extend all the way to the edges of a work, sometimes abruptly stop short, allowing the painting to "breathe," as one observer put it. Commenting on the show for the New York Times (February 10, 1989), Michael Kimmelman found Miss Martin's latest works "austere," yet expressive of "a certain delicacy," visible in the subtle variations from line to line. "But whatever the configuration," Kimmelman wrote, "regularity is everything. It lends these paintings a kind of balance and solidity that is a minimalist's response to classicism, but it also suggests an effort toward making grandiose landscapes that link Ms. Martin's work with the abstract expressionists."

Miss Martin's paintings are in the collections of several major foreign museums, including the Tate Gallery in London, the Stedelijk Museum in Amsterdam, the Israel Museum in Jerusalem, the Australian National Gallery in Canberra, and the Neue Galerie der Stadt in Aachen, West Germany. In North America, her works hang in the Art Gallery of Ontario in Toronto; the Whitney Museum of American Art, the Museum of Modern Art, and the Solomon R. Guggenheim Museum in New York City; the Albright-Knox Art Gallery in Buffalo, New York; the High Museum of Art in Atlanta, Georgia; the Hirshhorn Museum and Sculpture Garden in Washington, D.C.; the Los Angeles County Museum of Art; and the Walker Art Center in Minneapolis, Minnesota, among others.

In addition to the 1973 retrospective, which traveled from the Institute of Contemporary Art in Philadelphia to the Pasadena (California) Museum of Modern Art, there has been one other comprehensive exhibition of Agnes Martin's work, shown at the Hayward Gallery in London and at the Stedelijk Museum in 1977. In 1980 and 1981 a series of twelve paintings completed in 1979 was exhibited at the Pace Gallery and, subsequently, at a number of art museums in the United States and Canada. Since 1961 Miss Martin has been represented in an impressive number of group exhibitions, including the 1961 and 1988–89 Carnegie Institute Internationals in Pittsburgh, Pennsylvania, the 1967 Annual and 1977 Biennial at the Whit-

ney Museum of American Art, the 1972 Kassel Documenta, and the 1976 and 1980 Venice Biennales. Her works were also featured in the Museum of Modern Art's 1976 "Drawing Now" exhibition, which traveled to museums in Edinburgh, Baden, Zurich, and Oslo, and in "The Reductive Object: A Survey of the Minimalist Aesthetic in the 1960s," held in 1979 at the Institute of Contemporary Art in Boston. A key to Miss Martin's feelings vis-à-vis her viewers is the fact that she likes to have her paintings and drawings hung low for the comfort of persons of average height. In her view, neither the painting nor the artist are real; only the response to art is an unchanging reality.

When he interviewed her for the Vanity Fair profile, Mark Stevens found Agnes Martin to be friendly and affable, but firm in her refusal to relate personal anecdotes, which are, to her, digressions from the main concern: art itself. Like her work, Miss Martin registers an inner security. Her strong, weathered face seems to reflect her down-to-earth, unsentimental approach to life. Her intense blue eyes have a direct, level gaze, and her smile is warm. A 1973 photograph in Newsweek showed her splitting logs, a somewhat stocky figure with close-cropped gray hair, dressed in work clothes and a rancher's broad-brimmed hat. Invited to a Harper's Bazaar luncheon honoring "100 Women of Achievement" in 1967, she turned up in moccasins, a rumpled skirt, and an unironed blouse, apparently unfazed by the presence of elegant women in designer dresses. In the early 1980s she lived in Galisteo, New Mexico, in a small house that, like her studio, she built herself. She has since moved to Lamy, south of the Sangre de Cristo Mountains. Although she has claimed that "it's absolutely necessary to be alone to make artwork," Agnes Martin is no hermit. As she explained to one interviewer, "I paint to make friends and hope I will have as many as Mozart."

References: ARTnews 75:91+ S '76 por; Newsweek 82:74 D 24 '72 por; Vanity Fair 52:50+ Mr '80 por; Vogue 161:114 Je '73 pors; Contemporary Artists (1983); Who's Who in America, 1988–89; Who's Who in American Art (1988); World Artists 1950–1980 (1984)

Martin, (Judith) Lynn (Morley)

Dec. 26, 1939- United States Representative from Illinois. Address: 1214 Longworth Bldg., Washington, D.C. 20515

Ever since she was first elected to Congress in 1980, Congresswoman Lynn Martin of Illinois has immersed herself in the intricacies of the budget process, with the result that she has emerged as the most prominent Republican woman in the House. A protégée of Robert H. Michel of Illinois, the mi-

Lynn Martin

nority leader, she was the first freshman member ever named to the powerful House Budget Committee. Congresswoman Martin first attracted national attention during the 1984 presidential election campaign, when Republican leaders brought her forward to serve as a counterweight to the Democratic vice-presidential nominee, Geraldine Ferraro of New York. After the election she was chosen to be vice-chairperson of the House Republican Conference, a policy-making caucus. When, two years later, she took over temporarily for Delbert Latta, the ailing ranking Republican on the Budget Committee, to lead the panel's minority during a time of delicate budget negotiations, she performed so impressively that she was named one of the "Ten Rising Stars of American Politics" by *U.S. News & World Report*. In June 1989 Lynn Martin announced her candidacy for the 1990 Republican nomination for the United States Senate seat now held by Democrat Paul Simon. Her voting record has defied easy categorization, since she is fiscally conservative but liberal on some social and foreign-policy issues.

Although her searing wit and relentless partisanship have made Lynn Martin some enemies, she is widely respected for her intelligence, diligence, and pragmatic, nonideological approach to social and economic problems. "She's a quick study," Jack Davis, a former Republican colleague in the Illinois delegation who also served with her in the state legislature, has said. "She has the ability to grasp complex topics and reduce them to their essentials and to bore through all the shading and the screening material and get right to the heart of it—and drive a sword through your heart. . . . There is a time when the hard line comes through and the laughter stops and she nails you right to a tree."

Lynn Martin was born Judith Lynn Morley in Evanston, Illinois on December 26, 1939, the younger of the two daughters of Lawrence William Morley, an accountant, and Helen Catherine (Hall) Morley. Raised on Chicago's North Side, Lynn was a brilliant but restless child and something of a tomboy, whose ambitions included becoming a nun, a scientist, or a space traveler to Mars. Encouraged by her father to read, she spent her after-school hours at the public library, devouring a book a day while waiting for her mother to get off work from the department store across the street. At Immaculate Conception parochial grade school in Chicago, she so outshone the other students that one teacher asked the Morleys to urge their daughter to let some of the others have a chance to answer questions in class. She learned her first lesson in hardball politics when she ran for president of her eighth-grade class against her boyfriend. "I lost by one vote," she explained to Cheryl Wetzstein of the *Washington Times* (May 8, 1987). "My vote. You see, I voted for my opponent because I thought it was polite. . . . Well, he voted for himself, and I learned my lesson: If you believe in yourself, vote for yourself."

Following her graduation as an honor student at William Howard Taft High School in Chicago in 1957, she enrolled as an English major at the University of Illinois at Urbana-Champaign. Although she often cut classes, she still managed to graduate with Phi Beta Kappa honors in only three years and with enough education credits to qualify for certification as a teacher. It was at about that time that she abandoned the Democratic party of her parents and became a Republican because, as she has since explained, the Democrats were always talking about the rights of groups of people and had seemed to forget about individual rights.

Within a week after graduating from college in 1960, she married John Martin, an engineering student, who went on to establish a successful printing equipment business in Rockford, Illinois. She soon became pregnant, and, because expectant mothers were not then allowed to teach, she postponed her career plans until after the birth of her daughter Julia. She taught English, government, and economics at Wheaton Central and Saint Francis high schools in Du Page County, Illinois and, from 1965, at Muldoon Catholic and Guilford high schools in Rockford. Popular with her students, she earned a reputation for being exacting but fair. Lynn Martin suspended her teaching career, permanently as it turned out, to give birth to her second daughter, Caroline, in 1969. Meanwhile she had become active in the American Association of University Women and the Junior League.

In 1972 Lynn Martin impetuously entered the race for a seat on the Winnebago County Board. "I was with a typical bunch griping about county government," she told Marianne Taylor of the *Chicago Tribune* (November 30, 1980), "and out of pure ignorance and pure luck, I ran." Encouraged to run by Betty Ann Keegan, a Democratic state senator who did not allow partisanship to cloud her advice to a longtime friend, she jumped into the race. Although she had charged the county board with being out of touch with popular concerns, after winning the seat, she came to respect the dedication of her fellow board members. During her four-year term in county government, she served on the finance and public works committees, despite efforts by the county road supervisor to keep her off the latter panel, because he felt that the profanity prevalent at that male bastion made it an unfit place for a lady.

In 1976 Lynn Martin was elected to the Illinois House, having enlisted the aid of her older daughter's junior high school class in an intensive door-to-door campaign to unseat the Democratic incumbent. In supporting the winner for House Republican leader, Martin was rewarded with an assignment to the Appropriations Committee, where she earned a reputation as a reluctant spender of public funds. Her most significant accomplishment during her single term in the House was a bill barring convicted criminals from profiting from their misdeeds through the publication of a book or any other information medium.

In 1978 Lynn Martin announced her intention to run for the Illinois state senate. Two weeks later, the incumbent Democrat decided to retire. She was elected and won a seat on the Appropriations Committee, where for her persistent efforts to hold down spending she was nicknamed "the Axe." Her most enduring legacy, however, was reform of the state's inadequately regulated nursing homes. Haunted by the suffering of her mother, a victim of Alzheimer's disease who had died in 1974, she cosponsored a bill with Richard M. Daley Jr., then a state senator, requiring minimum standards for nursing homes throughout Illinois and setting forth a bill of rights for nursing home residents.

In 1980 Congressman John B. Anderson relinquished his seat from Illinois's Sixteenth Congressional District, comprising the Greater Rockford area, to run for president, first as a Republican and eventually as an independent. Since she was midway into her first term in the state senate, Lynn Martin was reluctant to jump into the race, but she realized that the seat was unlikely to be vacant again soon. Encouraged to run by national Republican leaders, who feared that the Reverend Don Lyon, an ultraconservative evangelical minister who had given Anderson a surprisingly strong primary challenge in 1978, would sweep the primary, she campaigned on a moderate platform of lower taxes and deregulation of business, balanced by support for the Equal Rights Amendment and a pro-choice position on abortion.

With support from national women's organizations, Lynn Martin erased Lyon's early lead in the polls, topped the five-man Republican field with 45 percent of the vote, and went on to bury her Democratic opponent by a ratio of two-to-one. She has been reelected handily ever since. Although it was reasonable to infer from her first campaign that she might follow in Anderson's footsteps, Lynn Martin made it clear from the outset that she was

no clone of the independent presidential candidate. "We're from a different era," she explained during her *Chicago Tribune* interview. "He was elected in 1960, when more and more hope was placed in government to be the arbiter and the solution to all problems. I started in the 1970s through a more political route, with a stronger feeling that government is not the solution and may in fact be part of the problem."

From her first days in Washington, Lynn Martin impressed Robert H. Michel of Illinois with her depth of knowledge and unerring political instincts. He helped her to get on the influential Budget Committee, even though such a plum assignment had never before gone to a freshman. Although she was thrilled by the unprecedented opportunity, she was at first overwhelmed. She later compared the experience to "getting sex education at age six. It's a little too soon to understand—there's a lot of stuff you really shouldn't know until a lot later." Eventually, she was invited to weekly White House budget meetings to help shape the Reagan administration's legislative strategy. She supported the Gramm-Rudman-Hollings deficit reduction package but often sparred with Secretary of Defense Caspar W. Weinberger and others who urged a massive military buildup at the expense of social programs.

During tense budget negotiations in 1986, Congressman Delbert Latta of Ohio, the ranking Republican on the committee, underwent emergency heart surgery, and Lynn Martin was appointed as acting ranking minority member. To many observers she seemed to outperform the prickly Latta, establishing a cordial working relationship with the committee chairman, William H. Gray 3d of Pennsylvania, and other Democrats. At the same time she helped to defeat attempts to revive agreed-upon spending cuts and rallied Republican forces behind an alternative budget proposal, which, though unsuccessful, drew surprisingly strong support. During her six years on the committee, she came to realize just how difficult, if not impossible, it is to craft a budget that will satisfy competing interest groups. "Not only can't you please everybody," she later complained on the floor, "you actually manage to anger everybody in one way or another. Either you are spending too much on defense or too little; and you are always slighting the hundreds of underfunded domestic needs programs. When you are slicing up such a limited pie to begin with, everybody goes home hungry and angry."

Although Lynn Martin consistently receives higher marks from conservative groups than from liberal ones, her voting record reflects a mind unfettered by ideological restraints. She supported the Reagan administration in voting to provide funds for the construction of the MX missile and the early development of the space-based missile defense system known as Star Wars as well as aid to El Salvador and the Contra rebels fighting the Marxist-led Sandinista regime in Nicaragua. But she stood up to White House pressure in voting for a nuclear freeze and against the production of chemical weapons, and she pleased feminists with her support for the Equal Rights Amendment and federal funding of abortions for poor women. Yet she herself eschews the word "feminist" and, by focusing her energies on budget matters, has carefully avoided being identified with women's issues exclusively. "I don't walk into every meeting humming, 'I Am Woman,'" she once joked. Although at first skeptical about the efficacy of imposing economic sanctions against South Africa, a firsthand look at the oppression of apartheid convinced her to vote to override President Reagan's veto of the 1986 sanctions bill. One of her most significant legislative achievements to date was a 1984 law, which she cosponsored with Democratic congressman Rick Boucher of Virginia, that increased the penalties for such white-collar crimes as fraud, income tax evasion, and antitrust law violations.

As a member of the Administration Committee, Lynn Martin nettled the Democratic leadership with a successful campaign to bring the 30,000 congressional staff members under the protection of the 1964 Civil Rights Act, from which they had been specifically exempt. Having compiled data demonstrating that women staffers typically were relegated to the lowest-paying positions on Capitol Hill, she introduced legislation in 1985 that barred job discrimination on the basis of race, color, religion, national origin, sex, age, or physical handicap. "She relentlessly quizzed the chairmen to determine the salary differential between male and female employees on their staffs," Frank Annunzio of Illinois, the Democratic congressman who chaired the subcommittee on which she served, once noted. "She had some of those chairmen really perspiring."

Lynn Martin seems to take pleasure in seeing the opposition sweat. Often described by her fellow Republicans as "one of the boys," she is also known as the "political Joan Rivers," for her stinging attacks on Democrats. "When she combines her wit and her sarcasm and she's on the attack," Illinois state representative Jack Davis, a Republican, was quoted as saying in the *Chicago Tribune Magazine* (April 13, 1986), "you'd better watch out because she'll carve you up and you won't know what happened until you're bleeding."

It was her ability to think on her feet and bore into an opponent that prompted Republican strategists to tap Lynn Martin to portray Democratic vice-presidential nominee Geraldine Ferraro in mock debates with Vice-President George Bush in 1984. In preparing Bush for his televised confrontation with Ms. Ferraro, she adopted an aggressive debating style that caught Bush by surprise and convinced him that he needed more practice. In a strategy designed at least in part to counter the publicity enjoyed by Democrats that year in naming the first woman to a major party ticket, she was chosen to deliver one of the vice-president's nominating speeches at the party's convention in Dallas and was named chairperson of the Reagan-Bush campaign in Illinois. An early supporter of Bush for

president in 1988, she was the only woman named a national cochairperson of his campaign.

After the 1984 campaign Lynn Martin was elected vice-chairperson of the House Republican Conference, making her the first woman ever to make it into the House GOP leadership. Four years later she ran for conference chairperson but lost narrowly (85-82) to Jerry Lewis of California, partly because Illinois already was represented in the senior leadership by the minority leader and partly because she was rumored, falsely as it turned out, to be slated for a cabinet post in the new Bush administration.

With the convening of the 101st Congress in January 1989, Lynn Martin was appointed to the Rules Committee. She proposed converting the Select Committee on Narcotics Abuse and Control into a standing committee that would bring under its purview drug-related matters now scattered among dozens of committees and subcommittees. Congressman Michel supported the proposal, but it ran into significant Democratic opposition, most notably from Charles B. Rangel of New York, the current chairman of the select committee. Although Lynn Martin supported most of President Bush's early initiatives, she did not hesitate to vote for a sharp boost in the minimum wage despite the certainty of a presidential veto. She has encouraged the administration to compromise in its call for a constitutional amendment giving the president a line-item veto, the power to strike down portions of a bill without having to accept or reject it in its entirety. In collaboration with Republican senator Gordon J. Humphrey of New Hampshire, she proposed legislation requiring Congress to vote upon presidential recision requests within ten days. (Under current law, Congress can simply ignore such requests indefinitely.) Amid the controversy over the alleged misconduct of former Speaker Jim Wright of Texas, she was appointed cochairperson, along with Democrat Vic Fazio of California, of the bipartisan ethics task force established to review standards of official conduct.

With encouragement from President Bush and Republican governor James R. Thompson of Illinois, Lynn Martin decided to give up her safe House seat to run for the Senate in 1990. In the wake of the recent Supreme Court decision fostering state curbs on abortion, the Republican primary between Lynn Martin, who supports a woman's right to choose abortion, and Gary MacDougal, a Chicago businessman opposed to it, is expected to be an early test of popular sentiment on that controversial issue in a state that is developing into a battleground between antiabortion and pro-choice forces.

Lynn Martin is a green-eyed blonde who stands five feet, eight inches tall. Her marriage to John Martin ended in divorce in 1978, and in January 1987 she wed Judge Harry Leinenweber of the United States Court for the Northern District of Illinois. She divides her time between a Washington, D.C., townhouse and a century-old English-type country cottage in the Rockford suburb of Loves

Park, which she purchased in rundown condition in 1984 and renovated herself. For recreation she enjoys cooking, gardening, interior design, working crossword puzzles, and watching wildlife specials on television.

References: Chicago Tribune mag p12+ Ap 13 '86 pors; Washington Post A p13 My 19 '86 por; Washington Woman p15+ N '87 pors; Almanac of American Politics, 1988; Politics in America (1988); Who's Who in America, 1988–89; Who's Who in American Politics, 1989–90

Mason, Bobbie Ann

May 1, 1940– Writer. Address: c/o Amanda Urban, International Creative Management, 40 W. 57th St., New York, N.Y. 10019

The author of two short-story collections and two novels, Bobbie Ann Mason occupies a unique position in contemporary American fiction. Her stories are set in her native western Kentucky, a North-South border state whose working-class inhabitants are beset by signs of social and economic dislocation: farm failures and factory layoffs; new chain stores and shopping malls; cable television and multiple-screen movie theatres; a soaring divorce rate and the availability of safe and legal abortion; and the usurpation of pastoral counseling by psychoanalysis and the charlatanism of those who claim to be psychics. The various responses of rural and small-town Kentuckians to those changes make up the subject matter of her two short-story collections: Shiloh and Other Stories, for which she won the Ernest Hemingway Foundation

Award for first fiction in 1983, and Love Life. Her novels, In Country and Spence + Lila, take place in the same locale and include the same underlying theme of the challenges of social and economic change. She has also written two works of literary criticism.

Anatole Broyard, who reviewed Miss Mason's first collection of short stories for the New York Times (November 23, 1982), was struck by the way her characters are mired in transition between the past and the future. "They don't seem to progress from one thing to another," Broyard wrote, "but to fall between one thing and another, to live in an absence bracketed by nostalgia and apprehension. To be restless or rootless in a small American town is to suffer an American anxiety with none of the camouflaging sophistication of the big city." But Bobbie Ann Mason views the angst produced by the replacement of unquestioned traditions with unprecedented options and choices as a positive development in her characters' lives. "I come from a culture that still [believes in] the American dream," she told Wendy Smith for Taxi (March 1989), "and when these new possibilities are opened up, I think my characters are very optimistic. They may be disappointed; a lot of their dreams are quite naïve and can only lead to disappointment and confusion. But I think optimism is important. I admire their hopefulness—I come from it—and I don't want them to become jaded or cynical."

Bobbie Ann Mason was born on May 1, 1940 near Mayfield, Kentucky, the daughter of Wilburn A. and Christie (Lee) Mason. Her parents are retired dairy farmers who still live on the fifty-four-acre farm where she was raised along with her brother and her sisters. She attended a country school through the eighth grade before going on to Mayfield High School. The shift from the country to the city school in Mayfield, a town of some 8,000 inhabitants, was her first experience of what she has called "a special kind of class difference" between town and country, one that engendered feelings of inferiority in her. In interviews, she still refers to herself as a country girl.

None of her family had attended college, but Miss Mason, despite being very shy—("probably pathologically shy," she has said)—was ambitious. She applied for and won a scholarship to the University of Kentucky in Lexington. "[I] wanted to get out and see the world," she explained to Geoffrey Stokes during an interview for the Village Voice Literary Supplement (May 1989). "I'd seen a lot of movies. And it wasn't so strange for kids in my school to go to college." She majored in journalism and wrote for the University of Kentucky Kernel and, in the summer of 1960, for the Mayfield Messenger as a society columnist.

After obtaining her B.A. degree in 1962, Bobbie Ann Mason moved to New York City, though she was somewhat uncertain of what she intended to do there. "I've never felt that I decided much of anything," she revealed to Mervyn Rothstein in an interview for the New York Times Magazine (May 15, 1988). "Like 'decided' to go to New York. I just sort of did what came along, what was available. There weren't all these choices laid out like, do you want to be a nurse, do you want to be a doctor, or do you want to go into marketing? I didn't know about any of those things. All I knew was I could work in a factory, but if I went to a college then I might not have to go to work in a factory, and then maybe I could get work in an office. And work in an office meant being a secretary maybe, or some kind of clerical work. And nothing was very clear. Nobody explained anything."

In New York City, Bobbie Ann Mason worked for Ideal Publishing Company as a writer for fan magazines like *Movie Life* and *TV Star Parade* from 1962 until 1963. She interviewed such celebrities of the day as Fabian, Ann-Margret, and Annette Funicello and wrote articles about the television series *Bonanza.* "It wasn't the writing career I had had in mind when I was an iconoclastic columnist on the University of Kentucky *Kernel,*" she wrote in an essay for *Contemporary Authors* (1975). She also hated living in New York City. After spending fifteen unhappy months there, she quit her job and enrolled in the State University of New York at Binghamton, from which she obtained an M.A. degree in literature in 1966. Six years later she received a Ph.D. degree from the University of Connecticut.

Miss Mason's doctoral dissertation, an analysis of garden symbolism in the novel *Ada* by Vladimir Nabokov, was published by Ardis in 1974 as *Nabokov's Garden: A Nature Guide to Ada.* The following year she wrote *The Girl Sleuth: A Feminist Guide to the Bobbsey Twins, Nancy Drew, and Their Sisters,* a short critical study, published by the Feminist Press, of female stereotyping in the mystery novels of her childhood. Drawing a connection between her two books in her autobiographical piece for *Contemporary Authors,* Miss Mason wrote: "[Nabokov] read Pushkin as a child, whereas I read Nancy Drew. I am interested in that contrast as a literary theme, and in the culture shock one can experience because of geographical and economic isolation." Moving directly from a study of Nabokov's childhood to remembrances of her own was a revelatory experience that led her to the writing of fiction. "I started to realize a lot about where I'd come from," Miss Mason told Rothstein, "and then . . . to realize that that was the source of my experience and my material for my fiction."

Before turning to fiction, however, Bobbie Ann Mason taught journalism at Mansfield State College (now Mansfield University) in Pennsylvania. As an assistant professor of English there from 1972 to 1979, she used Tom Wolfe's "new journalism" anthology in her classes. "There were a lot of great writers in that anthology," she told Stokes, singling out Joan Didion and Lillian Ross for special mention. "They were making breakthroughs in journalism by the same techniques as fiction, so I kind of absorbed that and then went back to fiction."

Although Miss Mason had begun writing a novel in 1967, she didn't finish it until 1978. "I was very sensitive and if somebody said a critical word I'd quit writing for five years," she recalled in an interview with Helen Dudar for the *Wall Street Journal* (August 22, 1985). By 1979 she had left her teaching post in order to write full-time. She submitted the second story she had ever written to the *New Yorker.* Although it was rejected, she was encouraged by a letter from the magazine's fiction editor, Roger Angell (to whom *Love Life* is dedicated). In the following eighteen months she submitted twenty more stories, the twentieth of which was published by the *New Yorker* in 1980.

A mere two years after Bobbie Ann Mason's western Kentuckians made their first appearance in the pages of the *New Yorker,* sixteen of her stories were collected in *Shiloh and Other Stories,* which was published by Harper & Row in 1982. It not only earned its previously unknown author the Hemingway Award in 1983, but also brought her nominations for the National Book Critics Circle Award and the American Book Award in 1982 and the PEN/Faulkner Award for fiction in 1983. In rapid succession, she received a grant from the Pennsylvania Arts Council in 1983, a fellowship from the National Endowment for the Arts and one from the American Academy and Institute of Arts and Letters in 1984, and a Guggenheim Foundation Fellowship in 1984. She was a contributor to *Best American Short Stories* in 1981 and in 1983, and her work appeared in *The Pushcart Prize: Best of the Small Presses,* Vol. VIII (1983).

As might be expected from such an accumulation of honors, the reviews of *Shiloh* were overwhelmingly—though not entirely—enthusiastic. Calling Bobbie Ann Mason "a full-fledged master of the short story" in her review for the *New Republic* (November 1, 1982), the novelist Anne Tyler wrote that the stories "are extraordinarily touching, in the most delicate and apparently effortless way. They explore, usually, the sense of bewilderment and anxious hopefulness that people feel when suddenly confronted with change." Several reviewers noted the differences between Miss Mason's sheltered characters and her more urbane readers and commended her craftsmanship for closing the gap in understanding. "She portrays the disquieted lives of men and women not blessed with much money or education or luck, but cursed with enough sensitivity and imagination to allow them to suffer regrets," David Quammen wrote in his appraisal for the *New York Times Book Review* (November 21, 1982). "Most compellingly, Miss Mason examines in her various truckdrivers and salesclerks the dawning recognition . . . of having missed something, something important, some alternate life more fruitful than the one that's been led."

Many reviewers cited her ability to invest her unglamorous and often inarticulate characters with dignity by portraying them with both humor and respect. Although she conceded that Miss Mason's "appeal is undeniable," Patricia Vigderman expressed one of the few critical reservations in her review for the *Nation* (March 19, 1983): "Every story is rich with surface details, . . . [but her] stories have no emotional gravity. Mason establishes an energetic comic distance, and then ends the stories with a little lurch of the heart, a closeness that seems tacked on." Robert Towers concurred in his evaluation of *Shiloh* for the *New York Review of Books* (December 16, 1982), complaining that Miss Mason's "stories are open-ended with a vengeance. . . . A few resolutions might add some needed variety to an otherwise remarkable achievement."

For two and a half years after the completion of *Shiloh*, Miss Mason worked on her first completed novel, *In Country*, which was published by Harper & Row in 1985 to considerable acclaim. "Making the jump [from short stories] to the current novel was difficult," the author told Wendy Smith in an interview for *Publishers Weekly* (August 30, 1985), "but it seemed like the right time to do it. I had gotten rather comfortable with the form of a short story, and writing one wasn't very risky because it didn't take that much investment of time or energy. So I guess I didn't want to run away from that challenge."

Writing *In Country* was all the more challenging because of its difficult subject matter. Although the novel is set in western Kentucky in 1984, its title is a Vietnam veterans' phrase denoting their experiences in the wartime jungles of Vietnam. The novel's seventeen-year-old protagonist, Samantha (Sam) Hughes, asks everyone she knows—including an uncle who is suffering from what are probably the effects of the chemical defoliant Agent Orange—about the late 1960s in an effort to understand the meaning of the war that killed her father just before she was born, and she is met "with a wall of reticence and inarticulacy," in the words of one reviewer. "The people around Sam," wrote Alice Bloom in her review for *New England Review and Bread Loaf Quarterly* (Summer 1986), "are so anaesthetized, paralyzed, brutalized, so sentimental or flippant or ignorant that they are no help because they don't know what she wants, or why, and they don't want it themselves. They want just to go along, let the past go." Their apathy towards Sam's inquiry was perceived by some readers as a metaphor for "our government's casual attitude toward those who survived an unpopular war but are having difficulty surviving civilian life," in the words of Joel Conarroe, writing for the *New York Times Book Review* (September 15, 1985).

Bobbie Ann Mason did not set out to write about Vietnam. She began the novel as a short story, "Situation Comedy," in which Sam and her boyfriend sold flowers from a van and watched *M*A*S*H* reruns on television. "At some point," the author said in the interview with Helen Dudar, "I decided Sam's uncle Emmett was a Vietnam veteran, and that accounted for his strangeness, but I wasn't willing to explore it. . . . I wanted it to all be oblique and subdued and I wrote two-thirds of a draft that still had those flowers in it," Miss Mason continued. "Then my editor, Ted Solotaroff,

read it and said I wasn't dealing with the issues." Describing the emergence of the war in the novel, Miss Mason told Wendy Smith: "I think it came out of my unconscious the same way it's coming out of America's unconscious. It's just time for this to surface." Most influential of all was a visit to the Vietnam Memorial in Washington, D.C. "When I went to the memorial," Miss Mason told Hilary DeVries for the *Christian Science Monitor* (November 20, 1985), "I realized I had a right to write this story. Seeing the people who were looking for names on the wall, and their emotions that were so evident. They were Americans, just like my characters. I felt I could write about them."

Most reviewers agreed with Bruce Allen of the *Chicago Tribune Book World* (September 1, 1985) that "what makes [*In Country*] so touching and real is Mason's unpretentious closeness to her characters' feelings." Marilyn Gardner, in her review for the *Christian Science Monitor* (September 6, 1985), wrote, "Characters who in less-skilled hands could seem freakish become charming as Mason exposes their foibles with compassion, gentle humor—even love." In her critical essay for the *New Republic* (September 2, 1985), Diane Johnson also found the story charming, but with a twist: "*In Country* seems less a work of fearless realism than one of romantic pastoral charm." Suggesting that the novel was written in a "new mode of combining an almost photorealistic surface with a strongly ameliorative point of view," she pointed out that the "reassuring resolution, in which people who have suffered from Vietnam can sense if not articulate peace and reconciliation—can come to terms"—is as attractive as it is implausible.

But Alice Bloom, for one, was mystified that "reviewers continue to use words like 'charming' and 'deeply respectful' to describe a vision that is so terrifying, stripping, disheartening. . . . The source of deepest terror in this novel is not the plot or the characterization, but the style: and the recurrent, pervasive image of terror is brand-name junk." Complaining that the author gives Sam "no language to talk or think or feel with," she concluded that "a person who sees, talks, connects, and thinks like this [in the terms of popular culture] . . . is not being equipped, by world or novelist, to look deeply into the nature of things."

Alice Bloom's view of popular culture and brand-name clutter, and its prominent role in Miss Mason's fiction, was shared by many reviewers. Conceding, in the interview with Hilary DeVries, that "the educated, literary reader is trained to pick up on references to popular culture as a negative judgment," Bobbie Ann Mason explained her viewpoint: "My characters live in a world in which television and popular music are an intimate part of their lives, and I take that seriously." She has often commented on the impact of rock music upon her characters. "It's what they listen to, and it's what reflects their feelings," she told Rothstein. Her own icons include Elvis Presley, John Lennon, and especially Bruce Springsteen, with whom Sam of *In Country* is obsessed. "Writing is my version of rock-'n'-roll," she explained to Rothstein. "I identify with Bruce Springsteen's songs, and of course I'm not alone in this. I like the way his songs are stories with characters. He writes about the disintegration of lives due to social forces. But his people keep striving, hoping."

That theme is reworked in Miss Mason's short novel Spence + Lila, which was published by Harper & Row in 1988. Spence and Lila Culpepper are Kentucky farmers in their sixties who look back upon their forty-year marriage. Their reminiscences alternate with grimmer scenes of the present: Lila has checked into a hospital for a mastectomy and another operation. According to Richard Locke's review for the Wall Street Journal (June 28, 1988), the novel's themes "are not so far from some of Nabokov's: sexual love that extends into old age; . . . a country home . . . as a microcosm of benign natural order; the spontaneous lyric eruptions of memory; the details that turn a banal moment into a blaze of intense experience. . . . [Miss Mason's] modest virtuosity creates an uncommonly generous short novel." Other reviewers were less enthusiastic, finding Spence + Lila dull, "gently tedious," even melodramatic, despite the novelist's virtuosity.

Bobbie Ann Mason's latest work is Love Life (1989), a collection of fifteen stories that first appeared in the New Yorker, the Atlantic, Harper's, the Paris Review, Mother Jones, and other magazines. With her usual unerring accuracy and unobtrusive sympathy, she once again mines her Kentucky locale for "finely crafted tales that manage to invest inarticulate, small-town lives with dignity and intimations of meaning," in the words of Michiko Kakutani of the New York Times (March 3, 1989).

Describing the characters in Love Life in an interview with Catherine Foster for the Christian Science Monitor (May 2, 1989), Bobbie Ann Mason said: "They're my people, the people I come from. . . . I think marriage is the arena where the big changes in our society are being reflected, and basically I'm always writing about change. Often it seems that the conflict in the marriage is between somebody who wants to hang on to the past and someone who want to stride out into the future. . . . As the writer of these characters, I see a lot of excitement in their rootlessness, because they're being uprooted from a lot of things I find bad. It takes courage to deal with freedom . . . to forge ahead."

Each of Miss Mason's novels became the basis for a movie. In Country, starring Emily Lloyd and Bruce Willis and directed by Norman Jewison, was released by Warner Brothers in the fall of 1989. Much of the movie was filmed on location in Kentucky with members of the local Vietnam Veterans of America chapter acting as extras. Spence + Lila is being adapted for the screen by the author under the auspices of American Playhouse Productions. Miss Mason is also planning a new novel.

Bobbie Ann Mason "is short, slender and, in a lively, wholesome way, attractive—an older version of the prototypical high school cheerleader of almost every teenager's dreams," according to Mervyn Rothstein. She and her husband of twenty years, the writer Roger B. Rawlings, live in a modest wood house in rural Pennsylvania with their five cats: Alice, Bilbo, Lolita, Kiko, and Albert.

References: N Y Times Mag p50+ My 15 '88 pors; Pub W 228:424+ Ag 30 '85 por; Village Voice Literary Supplement p13+ My '89 por; Contemporary Authors new rev vol 11 (1984); Contemporary Literary Criticism vol 43 (1987); Who's Who of American Women, 1989-90

McCain, John S(idney 3d)

Aug. 29, 1936– United States Senator from Arizona. Address: b. Room 111, Russell Senate Office Bldg., Washington, D.C. 20510

In 1982, only one year after he settled in Arizona, John S. McCain rose from relative obscurity to win the first of two terms in the House of Representatives, and in 1986 he was elected to the Senate to succeed the retiring senator Barry M. Goldwater. McCain's sudden popularity grew out of his heroism during the Vietnam War, for McCain holds the unenviable distinction of being the most severely injured pilot ever to withstand the rigors of a North Vietnamese prison camp. The strength of character that he displayed in surviving more than five years as a prisoner of war, often tortured and most of the time in solitary confinement, and his ability to put the remnants of his life back together so quickly after that ordeal, won the admiration of Arizonans.

Although McCain has established a conservative Republican voting record much in the mold of Senator Goldwater, he has also demonstrated a willingness to oppose and at times openly criticize the Reagan administration on such issues as the security of American marines in Lebanon, the imposition of sanctions against South Africa, and the attempt to determine the fate of American casualties of the Vietnam War still listed as missing in action. Although proud of his service in Vietnam and grateful for the impetus it has given his political career, McCain prefers not to dwell on it. "I don't want to be the POW senator," he said recently. "What I've tried to do is position myself so that if opportunities come along, I'm qualified and ready. My job for the next few years is to acquire a reputation as a serious senator who studies the issues and doesn't try to steal the limelight."

John Sidney McCain 3d was born on August 29, 1936 in the Panama Canal Zone to John S. McCain Jr. and Roberta (Wright) McCain. He comes from a long line of military commanders dating back to Captain William Young, an ancestor who served on the staff of General George Washington during the American Revolution. His paternal grandfather, Admiral John S. McCain, was commander of all the aircraft carriers in the Pacific during World War II. His father, also an admiral, was commander in chief of all United States armed forces in the Pacific during the Vietnam War. The two were the first father and son to become full admirals in navy history. McCain has a sister, Mrs. Jean Flather, and a younger brother, John Pinckney McCain.

McCain grew up at various naval bases in the United States and abroad with the assumption that he would follow in the family's military tradition. On graduating from Episcopal High School in Alexandria, Virginia in 1954, he entered the United States Naval Academy at Annapolis. Although his grades as an electrical engineering student there were satisfactory, he drew so many demerits for breaking curfew and other infractions that he graduated fifth from the bottom of the class of 1958. He was commissioned an ensign and, despite his low class standing, was granted his request for a training slot as a navy pilot.

During the Vietnam War, McCain flew carrier-based attack planes on dangerously low-altitude bombing runs against North Vietnamese positions. On July 29, 1967 he was sitting in the cockpit of his A-4 Skyhawk awaiting takeoff from the deck of the carrier Forrestal when his fuel tank was struck by an errant rocket from one of the other bombers. The resulting chain of explosions and fire killed 130 crewmen and disabled the ship. Miraculously, McCain escaped without serious injury and promptly requested transfer to the carrier Oriskany while the Forrestal underwent repairs.

Less than three months later, on October 26, McCain, by then a lieutenant commander, took off from the Oriskany on his twenty-third air mission, his first against the North Vietnamese capital of Hanoi. Directly over the city, the aircraft's right wing was sheared off by a North Vietnamese surface-to-air missile, and McCain was forced to eject. He plunged into a lake, breaking both arms and his right leg. Fished out by Vietnamese onlookers, he was dragged ashore before an angry crowd of thousands that had by now gathered at the crash site. There, he was beaten and stabbed twice before being taken into custody. For five days he was denied medical attention, but when authorities learned that his father was a high-ranking naval officer, he was taken to a hospital and assigned a cellmate to nurse him back to health.

Five months later, when McCain, though weak, was able to get about on crutches, his cellmate was removed, and he spent the next three and a half years in solitary confinement. Meanwhile, the Vietnamese, who tried to exploit McCain, whom they called the "crown prince," and his father's status for propaganda purposes, offered to release him ahead of the other prisoners in a grand ceremony directed at world opinion. When he refused to cooperate he was severely beaten, an incident that he has described as the low point of his captivity. He was similarly mistreated for trying to communicate with other prisoners through an improvised wall tapping code. Severely malnourished from his single daily ration of noodles, some of which was eaten by his guards, he lost more than a third of his weight in prison. Throughout his confinement he was denied all mail and only once was permitted to write a brief postcard home.

In 1971 McCain was transferred from solitary confinement to a cell with fifty other prisoners, but though he was grateful for the company, conditions remained unbearable. Months later the men staged a riot, for which some of them, including McCain, were punished at a harsher facility outside Hanoi. The hardest part of captivity, McCain has said, was not the physical abuse but the psychological strain and the uncertainty of his fate. Because he was deprived of news from the outside, he rode a roller coaster of emotions with each unfounded rumor of imminent release.

At last, on March 17, 1973, two months after the cessation of hostilities, McCain and the other prisoners were turned over to American authorities. When he underwent medical treatment at Clark Air Force Base in the Philippines and later at Jacksonville, Florida, it was obvious to observers that the years of captivity had taken their toll. Although he was only thirty-six years old, his hair had turned white. Once a robust 160 pounds, he then weighed about 100. Racked by arthritis and deformed joints, he could no longer bend his right knee, raise his right arm above a forty-five-degree angle, or elevate his left shoulder. Yet despite the permanent disabilities and the long years of torture and solitary confinement, McCain emerged from the war remarkably sound of mind. "Perhaps it has made me more sensitive to the underdog than I otherwise would have been," he speculated in an interview with Susan F. Rasky of the New York Times (August 9, 1988). "I know what it is like to be humiliated and degraded. But I don't think it made any change in my basic character." Moreover, he claims never to have had a nightmare or a flashback. For his wartime service, he was awarded the Silver Star, the Legion of Merit, the Distinguished Flying Cross, and other decorations.

After spending four months in recuperation, McCain enrolled at the National War College in Washington, D.C., but he longed to fly again. Through sheer grit and determination, he passed the rigorous flight physical and returned to the skies for two years as commander of a training squadron. In 1977 he was promoted to captain and reassigned to the Department of the Navy's Office of Legislative Affairs, where he served as director of the Navy Senate Liaison Office. Over the next four years, he made extensive legislative contacts and struck up lasting friendships with such politically diversified senators as the Republicans John G. Tower of Texas and William S. Cohen of Maine and the Democrat Gary Hart of Colorado. By 1981 it became obvious that his ultimate goal of commanding an aircraft carrier was now out of his reach. No longer able to pass the flight physical, he retired from the United States Navy.

On his discharge, McCain accepted a job offer from his father-in-law, Jim Hensley, a beer distributor in Phoenix, Arizona. In 1982 a vacancy in Arizona's First Congressional District, a solidly Republican region comprising the greater Phoenix area, was created with the retirement of Congressman John J. Rhodes. Although McCain had been living in Arizona for less than a year, he entered the Republican primary against three seasoned contenders. Since early polls revealed that 97 percent of the people in the district had never heard of John S. McCain, he devoted as many as thirty hours a week to knocking on some 16,000 doors in the Phoenix area. His opponents denounced him as a carpetbagger, a new resident unfamiliar with the state. Although that charge has been effective from time to time in other states where most voters are life residents, it counts for considerably less in Arizona, which since World War II has attracted millions of Americans from out-of-state. Quickly silencing his critics, McCain pointed out that having been born into a navy family and having been a career naval officer himself, he never really had a home state. "The longest place I ever lived was Hanoi," he said, pointedly reminding voters of his war record. With fund-raising assistance from his friend Senator John Tower of Texas and the dedication of a hustling corps of volunteers, McCain topped the four-man field with a third of the vote and went on to defeat Democrat William E. Hegarty by a two-to-one margin in the general election. In 1984 he ran for reelection unopposed in the primary and buried his Democratic opponent, Harry W. Braun 3d, taking 78 percent of the vote to Braun's 22 percent.

During his four years in the House, McCain consistently won high marks from conservative groups, earning a perfect 100 rating from the National Security Index of the American Security Council in 1984. He joined Newt Gingrich of Georgia and other young "new Right" Republicans in clashing with Thomas P. ("Tip") O'Neill, the Speaker of the House. On the House floor, he voted in support of prayer in public schools, the 1985 Gramm-Rudman deficit reduction package, the 1986 tax reform act, continued tobacco subsidies, a resumption of certain handgun sales, and the continued use of the polygraph as a condition for employment under certain circumstances. He opposed the Equal Rights Amendment for women, increased funding to implement the Clean Air Act, trade protection for the textile and apparel industries, the 1983 domestic content bill restricting the use of foreign parts in American automobiles, and the 1986 Immigration Reform and Control Act. In foreign affairs, he opposed the 1983 nuclear freeze resolution and approved funding for the research and development of the MX missile and the Strategic Defense Initiative, increased aid to El Salvador, and arms for the Contra rebels fighting in Nicaragua and the pro-Western guerrillas in Angola.

Although on those and most other issues, McCain fell in line with the Reagan administration, he did not hesitate to oppose the administration on certain critical matters. In a major floor speech in 1983, for example, McCain called for the withdrawal of all United States Marines from Lebanon. In 1986 he joined the two-thirds majority in voting to override President Reagan's veto of sanctions against South Africa. Although he supported the Contra rebels, he urged the administration to abandon its effort to overthrow the Marxist-led Sandinista regime in Nicaragua and instead focus its resources on encouraging the democratic process there. In 1987 McCain exposed and thwarted an administration attempt to remove $28 million from a poverty food program to pay for a salary increase for Agriculture Department employees. He criticized the administration's handling of the Iran-Contra affair, though he blamed both Congress and the White House for failing to work more closely on a coordinated foreign policy, and he empathized with his fellow Vietnam veteran Oliver North, a central figure in the scandal. "Some of these people like Ollie North," he explained to Michael Killian of the *Chicago Tribune* (July 29, 1987), "who saw their comrades and friends spill blood and die on the battlefields in a war that they believe the politicians wouldn't let them win—I think that leads to a mind-set which could rationalize deviating from the established rules and regulations."

Because of his own wartime experience, McCain was active in pressing the Hanoi government to provide more information about those American servicemen still reported as missing in action from the Vietnam War era. While condemning the Vietnamese government for cynically using MIA information as a bargaining chip to win United States diplomatic recognition and aid in rebuilding the country, he privately urged the Reagan administration to restore low-level relations between the two nations.

In 1985 McCain accompanied CBS news broadcaster Walter Cronkite to Vietnam for a special program marking the tenth anniversary of the fall of Saigon. While there, he warned authorities in Hanoi that resolution of the MIA issue was a precondition to resumption of diplomatic ties. He came away convinced that the dire state of the Vietnamese economy and the people's longstanding fear of the Chinese were prompting Hanoi to seek improved relations with the West. In one poignant episode, McCain and Cronkite returned to the Hanoi lake where the veteran had crashed eighteen years earlier. To his surprise, the Vietnamese had erected a monument bearing the likeness of a kneeling American soldier with his arms held up in surrender and an inscription marking the spot where "the famous air pirate" John McCain was shot down. Recognizing him instantly, a gathering crowd began chanting his name as though he were a celebrity. Only in Hanoi, McCain joked, was he more famous than Walter Cronkite.

By 1986 McCain had become so popular among Arizona Republicans that he ran unopposed in the Senate primary for the seat long held by Barry Goldwater, who had announced plans to retire. Early polls gave McCain a comfortable lead over his Democratic opponent, Richard Kimball, but the race tightened somewhat after McCain upset the state's large elderly population with an offhand remark referring to the retirement community of Leisure World as "Seizure World." Moreover, McCain became unnerved by Kimball's charge that his votes on national security matters were influenced by campaign contributions from the political action committees of defense-related industries. But McCain, outspending Kimball by three to one, recovered to win handily, by a margin of 60 percent to 40 percent. Senator McCain was assigned to the Senate Armed Services Committee and its subcommittees on manpower, projection forces, and readiness; the Senate Commerce, Science and Transportation Committee and its subcommittees on aviation, communications, and consumer affairs; and the Senate Select Committee on Indian Affairs.

During his first two years in the upper chamber, McCain emerged as a serious senator whose views on defense and foreign policy are broadly respected. He became more outspoken in his criticism of the Reagan administration for failing to work more closely with Vietnam in determining the fate of the MIAs. After meeting the Vietnamese ambassador to the United Nations in 1988, he openly called for the exchange of interest sections, the first step in the resumption of diplomatic relations. In the face of opposition from the State Department as well as the National League of Families of American Prisoners and Missing in Southeast Asia, McCain noted that unofficial contacts between the two countries had been taking place sporadically for some time. His proposal, he asserted, would only formalize and give structure to those contacts. McCain also spoke out against the president's decision to escort Kuwaiti oil tankers through the dangerous waters of the Persian Gulf.

Senator McCain was a featured speaker at the Republican National Convention in New Orleans, Louisiana in 1988 and was reportedly among those considered as a possible running mate with George Bush. Although McCain was not enthusiastic about the eventual vice-presidential nominee, Senator Dan Quayle of Indiana, he defended Quayle's Vietnam War-era service in the National Guard. "I've spent the last ten years of my life trying to foster an atmosphere of reconciliation in this country and to get people to move beyond the hurts and the scars of that time," he told R. W. Apple Jr. of the New York Times (October 25, 1986). "Now we're threatened, because of the Quayle episode, with another round of finger-pointing, veiled accusations, biography-checking. . . . There's nothing to be gained by going back over that ground." McCain was a part of the Republican "truth squad" that trailed Democratic candidate Michael S. Dukakis early in the campaign. Meanwhile, he has criticized his own party for not reaching out more effectively to blacks or to the poor.

John Sidney McCain 3d stands five feet, nine inches tall and is somewhat overweight. He has been described as affable and unassuming, quick to laugh, and possessed of an irreverent sense of humor, but he also grows impatient easily and struggles to check his formidable temper. He married his first wife, Carol, in 1965 and adopted her two sons, Douglas, a navy pilot, and Andrew. They had a daughter, Sidney Ann, before their divorce in 1980. Later in the same year McCain married Cindy Hensley, with whom he has two children, Meghan and Jack.

References: Time 128:45 N 17 '86 por; US News 94:42 Mr 28 '83 pors, 98:33+ Mr 11 '85 pors; Almanac of American Politics, 1988; Who's Who in America, 1988–89; Who's Who in American Politics 1989–90

McClanahan, Rue

Feb. 21, 1934– Actress. Address: c/o International Creative Management, 8899 Beverly Blvd., Los Angeles, Calif. 90048

Now in its fourth season, The Golden Girls, NBC's risqué but "incorrigibly funny" comedy series about the lives of four single women past fifty who share a house in a retirement resort in Miami, continues to rank among the top ten shows in the Nielsen ratings. As the haughty, man-crazed southern belle Blanche Devereaux, Rue McClanahan is an important component of the show's ensemble cast of veteran actresses, which also includes Beatrice Arthur, Estelle Getty, and Betty White. In explaining the durable popularity of The Golden Girls, Miss McClanahan has said, "I think people relate to the basic idea behind the show—that friendship is important at any age, that you never outgrow the need for love."

Rue McClanahan

Rue McClanahan began acting professionally in 1957 and, for nine years, beginning in 1964, appeared regularly on the Broadway and Off-Broadway stage and in regional theatre. From 1973 to 1978 she portrayed Beatrice Arthur's scatter-brained neighbor, Vivian, on the hit CBS sitcom *Maude*. In analyzing Miss McClanahan's appeal, Paul Witt, the executive producer of *The Golden Girls*, has said: "Rue . . . is very much her own woman, in command of her own destiny. At the same time, she's managed to maintain a kind of gracious femininity that I think has disappeared for the most part in contemporary women."

Of Irish and Indian ancestry, Rue McClanahan was born Eddi-Rue McClanahan in Healdton, Oklahoma on February 21, 1934, the older of the two daughters of William Edwin and Dreda Rheua-Nell (Medaris) McClanahan. Her given name is a contraction of her parents' middle names. Her younger sister, Melinda, is now head of the biology department at Northeast Louisiana University. Because William McClanahan's job as a building contractor involved frequent moves from place to place, Eddi-Rue grew up in various small towns in Oklahoma, Texas, and Louisiana. She made her stage debut at the age of four, appearing in a local production of *The Three Little Kittens*—"character work even then," she observed to Jane Hall for *People* (January 6, 1986) magazine—and at twelve, the revelation struck her "like a bolt of lightning" that it was actually possible to make a living as an actress.

As a child, Eddi-Rue was encouraged by her mother, a beautician, to take dance lessons, and mother and daughter sometimes traveled to nearby cities to see road shows. Her dancing became so proficient that, during her high school years in

Ardmore, Oklahoma, she ran her own dance studio and performed at local functions. When Eddi-Rue received a draft notice on her graduation from Ardmore High School in 1952, she promptly dropped the "Eddi" from her name. Turning down offers of dance scholarships, Rue McClanahan instead majored in drama at the University of Tulsa, where she wrote songs and sketches and choreographed and acted in campus musicals. After receiving her B.A. degree, cum laude, in 1956, she headed for New York City to study at the Metropolitan School of Ballet and with Hanya Holm, the noted modern dancer, teacher, and choreographer. She also studied for the stage with Uta Hagen, Perry Mansfield, and Harold Clurman.

Rue McClanahan made her professional debut, as Rachel in *Inherit the Wind*, in October 1957 at the Erie Playhouse in Erie, Pennsylvania and appeared there in several other productions before heading for the West Coast, where she enrolled in a four-week course at the Pasadena Playhouse and also won one of its scholarships. Among her roles was Blanche DuBois in *A Streetcar Named Desire*. After assignments at the Pasadena Playhouse became scarce, she interspersed small roles in movies and television with odd jobs as a waitress, secretary, and clothing saleswoman. She appeared in three forgettable, limited-release movies, *Walk the Angry Beach* (1961), *The Grass Eater* (1961), and *The Rotten Apple* (1963), and made guest appearances on the small screen in *Malibu Run, Route 66, Empire,* and *Burke's Law*. While a member of a drama company called Theatre East, she met a New York theatre director, who, in 1964, summoned her to that city to appear in a musical version of James Thurber's classic short story *The Secret Life of Walter Mitty*, which ran for ninety-six performances at the Off-Broadway Players Theatre.

During the next nine years, Rue McClanahan compiled an impressive list of theatre credits. In *Walter Mitty* she played Hazel, one of two slighted pickups (Lette Rehnolds, as Ruthie, was the other) of Mitty's college pal. Norman Nadel, writing in the *New York World-Telegram and Sun* (October 27, 1964), felt that Rue McClanahan and Lette Rehnolds provoked "the lustiest laughter of the evening" and called their interpretation of "Two Little Pussycats" "a show-stopper." In 1966 Miss McClanahan, in her first Broadway assignment, understudied the female leads in *The Best Laid Plans*, a comedy that ran for only three performances at the Brooks Atkinson Theatre. She then portrayed a psychiatric nurse in *Big Man*, at the Cherry Lane Theatre, and originated the role of Lady MacBird in Barbara Garson's highly controversial *MacBird!*, which opened on February 22, 1967 at the Off-Broadway Village Gate Theatre. *MacBird!* used the assassination of John F. Kennedy and Lyndon B. Johnson's accession to the presidency to parody *Macbeth* and other Shakespearean texts. Writing in *Newsweek* (March 6, 1967), Jack Kroll found Rue McClanahan to be "excellent" as the prating wife who follows

MacBird around, deodorizing him with Airwick. *MacBird!* closed on January 21, 1968 after 386 performances.

Following the closing of *MacBird!*, Rue McClanahan appeared in three plays with the Hartford Stage Company in Hartford, Connecticut: Brendan Behan's *Hostage* (February 1968), *The Firebugs*, by Max Frisch (April 1968), and *The Threepenny Opera*, by Bertolt Brecht and Kurt Weill (May 1968). The actress made her Broadway debut in the supporting role of the prostitute Sally Weber in Murray Schisgal's *Jimmy Shine*, a comedy that starred Dustin Hoffman as an unsuccessful abstract painter. *Jimmy Shine* opened at the Brooks Atkinson Theatre on December 5, 1968 and ran for 161 performances. Rue McClanahan next played Betty in *The Golden Fleece*, one of a pair of one-act plays written by A. R. Gurney Jr. that were presented under the title *Tonight in Living Color*. *The Golden Fleece*, which opened Off-Broadway at the Actors Playhouse to critical praise on June 10, 1969, is a two-character comedy that retells the Greek myth of Jason and Medea through the framework of a modern suburban marriage.

Critics were even more impressed by Rue McClanahan's contribution to *Who's Happy Now?*, Oliver Hailey's offbeat comedy set in a bar in a small Texas town, which opened on November 17, 1969 at the Village South Theatre. "Most of the fun of the evening . . . ," Edith Oliver wrote in the *New Yorker* (November 29, 1969), "is in the role of Faye Precious, the innocent, sunny, friendly waitress. Rue McClanahan gives it a first-rate comedy performance that is always legitimate—no hokum, nothing but the truth." A critic for *Time* (November 28, 1969) magazine acclaimed *Who's Happy Now?* as "a minor treasure" and commended Miss McClanahan for portraying Faye "with giggly glory and flawless timing." Although the play ended its run after only twenty-four performances, Rue McClanahan received an Obie Award (the abbreviated name for the Off-Broadway theatre awards presented by the *Village Voice* newspaper). She reprised the role of Faye when *Who's Happy Now?* was telecast on May 7, 1975 on PBS's *Theatre in America* series.

In the late 1960s and early 1970s, Rue McClanahan made brief forays into movies and soap operas. In 1969 she played Margaret Jardin in the CBS daytime serial *Where the Heart Is*, and, in 1970, she took on the role of Caroline Johnson, a nanny who becomes so enamored of her boss that she tries to poison his wife with a variety of cream soups, on NBC's *Another World*. "Those scripts [for *Another World*] just begged for parody," Miss McClanahan told Michael Logan of *Soap Opera Digest* (November 15, 1988). "It was the most boring job you could imagine." On film, Miss McClanahan appeared with Eli Wallach and Julie Harris in *The People Next Door* (1970), a drama about drug abuse among teenagers in suburbia. Her portrayal of Della, Wallach's business aide and mistress, was labeled the film's "best performance" by a critic for *Variety* (August 5, 1970). She had minor roles in

They Might Be Giants, *Some of My Best Friends Are . . .* , and *The Pursuit of Happiness*, all of them released in 1971.

Rue McClanahan's stage roles in the early 1970s included that of Barbara Allen's mother in a 1970 Off-Broadway revival of *Dark of the Moon*, a drama of mountain witchcraft. In 1971 she served as a standby for Brenda Vaccaro and Marian Seldes in Oliver Hailey's *Father's Day*, which closed after one performance, and in the following year, she appeared in a revival of Sidney Michaels's *Dylan*, a biographical play about Dylan Thomas, at the Mercer O'Casey Theatre. "I admired . . . the flamboyant gusto of Rue McClanahan's tough and spirited Caitlin [Thomas]," Clive Barnes wrote of her performance in the *New York Times* (February 8, 1972). In *God Says There Is No Peter Ott* she was Avis, the owner of a guest house on Cape Cod. Although Clive Barnes panned the play in his *New York Times* (April 18, 1972) review, he reported that "Rue McClanahan was warm and womanly in the conventional agonies of Avis—and yes, she did try harder." She also gave notable accounts of herself in character roles in two award-winning Off-Broadway dramas restaged for PBS. She portrayed Jo Finn in *Hogan's Goat*, William Alfred's tragedy about Irish immigrants in Brooklyn in 1890, which starred Faye Dunaway and Robert Foxworth and aired on October 11, 1971. As Cora Groves, she headed the cast of *The Rimers of Eldritch*, Lanford Wilson's drama dealing with injustice in a small midwestern community, which was broadcast on November 4, 1972.

Just as Rue McClanahan was about to take over the demanding role of Harriet in Joseph Papp's Broadway production of David Rabe's *Sticks and Bones*, she received a call from Norman Lear that proved crucial in her career. Remembering her impressive performance in *The Golden Fleece* three years earlier, the maverick television producer tapped her for a guest spot on an episode of his spectacularly successful CBS situation comedy *All in the Family*. The episode, which was televised on October 26, 1972, featured Rue McClanahan and Vincent Gardenia as a married couple whom Edith Bunker (Jean Stapleton) invites to dinner, only to discover that they are swingers. She remained in Hollywood to play the best friend, Vivian, in an episode of Lear's new situation comedy *Maude*, a spin-off of *All in the Family* starring Beatrice Arthur, before returning to New York to take on the *Sticks and Bones* role. After portraying Crystal, the wife of the self-destructive director of an Irish touring troupe, in Brian Friel's *Crystal and Fox*, which ran at the McAlpin Rooftop Theatre in the spring of 1973, Miss McClanahan moved to the West Coast after Lear decided to make Vivian a regular character of the *Maude* series. She did not return to Broadway until 1977, when she replaced Tammy Grimes for a week in Neil Simon's *California Suite*.

As the first spin-off of *All in the Family*, the message-laden, often controversial *Maude*, which ran on CBS from 1972 to 1978, was part of the new wave of realistic situation comedies that crested on American network television in the early 1970s. Beatrice Arthur starred as Edith Bunker's cousin, the intimidating and crusading Maude Findlay, described by Norman Lear as "the flip side of Archie Bunker." Maude lived with her fourth husband, Walter (Bill Macy), and her divorced daughter, Carol (Adrienne Barbeau), in suburban Tuckahoe, New York. From 1973 to 1978, Rue McClanahan played to the hilt the ever-fluttering, nattering, and dithering Vivian Harmon, Maude's unliberated best friend and next-door neighbor, the wife of the archconservative Dr. Arthur Harmon (Conrad Bain). Among the more memorable episodes were those in which Vivian makes Maude jealous when she has a facelift; her dog, which she had left in Maude's care, dies; and a well-known poet visits her, but declines to see Maude.

After *Maude* was canceled, Rue McClanahan moved to the short-lived ABC sitcom *Apple Pie*, playing the part of Ginger-Nell Hollyhock, a lonely but unquenchably optimistic Depression-era hairdresser who rounds up a "family" by placing classified ads in the newspaper. The show's cast also included Dabney Coleman, as Miss McClanahan's con man "husband," and Jack Gilford, as her tottering "father." In reviewing the series for the *Los Angeles Times* (September 22, 1978), the critic Howard Rosenberg called *Apple Pie* "a crisply written, highly amusing half-hour that exploits the skills of its first-rate cast," but he concluded that "the show just isn't very funny." The viewing public seemed to agree, and *Apple Pie* was axed after only three episodes. Miss McClanahan's next series was NBC's *Mama's Family*, which premiered on January 22, 1983 and ran until 1985. In that offshoot of the mordantly funny sketches on the old *Carol Burnett Show* about the misadventures of a lower-middle-class southern family, Rue McClanahan played Aunt Fran, the unmarried, highstrung sister of Mama (Vicki Lawrence). A reporter for a local newspaper, Aunt Fran was described by the television critic Tom Shales of the *Washington Post* (January 22, 1983) as "an aging study in self-delusion."

"A gift from the gods" was Rue McClanahan's reaction to the script for the opening episode of *The Golden Girls*. The idea for a series about older people came to the NBC programming chief, Brandon Tartikoff, after he read statistics indicating that, as of 1984, about 37 percent of all Americans were at least forty-five years of age. He passed the concept on to the veteran television writer Susan Harris, the creator of such series as *Benson* and *Soap*, who drew some of her inspiration from her grandmother, who remained active until her death, at the age of ninety-three. When *The Golden Girls* had its premiere on September 14, 1985, it ranked number one in the Nielsen ratings for that week and received wide critical praise, with Jeff Jarvis of *People* (September 9, 1985) calling the show "the glorious best of the new season" and a critic for *Variety* (September 25, 1985) observing that "the writing and performances from the characters all seem to work and the laughs keep coming."

Rue McClanahan and Betty White were delighted that the director Jay Sandrich had decided to cast them against type. Betty White, who had played the man-hungry Sue Ann Nivens on the *Mary Tyler Moore Show*, was cast as the scatterbrained Rose; Rue McClanahan, the unworldly Vivian on *Maude*, became the flirtatious Blanche. Characterizing the members of the quartet for David Gritten, whose interview appeared in the *Chicago Tribune TV Week* (July 24, 1988), Miss McClanahan said: "Dorothy (Beatrice Arthur) is the levelheaded one, the intellect of the group. Rose is sweet, innocent, and sometimes inadvertently hurtful. Sophia (Estelle Getty) is probably the best part of all, very funny. But Blanche was written as frivolous and self-centered, and there's not so much you can do with a character like that." The youngest of the four characters, Blanche is a southern belle of a certain age who, at least in her own mind, is irresistible to men. The character, Rue McClanahan believes, may have been inspired by Scarlett O'Hara of *Gone with the Wind* and Blanche DuBois of *A Streetcar Named Desire*. Despite her incessant chatter about love affairs, Blanche, according to Rue McClanahan, "doesn't do anything—she lives in a fantasy world." Although *The Golden Girls* was criticized by some reviewers for its "overemphasis" on sex and its prodigal use of ribald language and innuendo, it received the Emmy Award for best comedy series in both 1986 and 1987. Three of its stars (Betty White in 1986, Rue McClanahan in 1987, and Beatrice Arthur in 1988) have been awarded the Emmy for best leading actress in a comedy series.

During a brief leave from her duties with *The Golden Girls* in the spring of 1986, Rue McClanahan appeared as Flo, a single mother, in a revival of William Inge's Pulitzer Prize–winning play *Picnic*, first for ten days at the Denver (Colorado) Auditorium Theatre, then for eight weeks at the Ahmanson Theatre in Los Angeles. The production was filmed for presentation on Showtime, the pay-cable television network. In the summer of 1985 she was cast as Jessie in a production of Donald Driver's black comedy *In the Sweet Bye and Bye* that was staged at the Back Alley Theatre in Van Nuys, California. For that performance, she received two Drama-Logue Awards and a Los Angeles Drama Critics' Circle Award nomination. She starred in another black comedy, John Guare's *House of Blue Leaves*, at the Pasadena Playhouse in 1987, as Bananas Shaughnessy, a zookeeper's batty wife.

Somehow, Rue McClanahan has managed to find time to star in several made-for-television movies over the past three years. She played a society woman who tries to reconcile her family in *The Little Match Girl*, a free adaptation of the Hans Christian Andersen tale that was shown on NBC-TV in December 1987. The following year, she portrayed Liberace's mother in an ABC movie about the late pianist, and a widow who scouts for husbands for her unmarried daughters in *Take My Daughters, Please*, also on NBC. *The Man in the*

Brown Suit, telecast on CBS in January 1989, was an engaging adaptation of Agatha Christie's 1924 whodunit, featuring Rue McClanahan as the wealthy, much-married Suzy Blair.

While she loves playing the femme fatale on The Golden Girls, Rue McClanahan insists that she and Blanche have little in common. "I'm not a vamp—I grow tomatoes and make quilts," she told Jane Hall. Miss McClanahan has been married and divorced five times. Her husbands have included the actors Tom Bish, Norman Hartweg, and Peter DeMaio, the realtor Gus Fisher, and her high school sweetheart, Tom Keel. From her marriage to Bish, she has a son, Mark, a jazz guitarist. In an interview with Glenn Esterly of TV Guide (June 6, 1987), the actress said her "rash" decisions to wed were prompted largely "by wanting to put together the ideal family unit that those of us who came into adulthood in the 1950s thought you were meant to

achieve." Miss McClanahan now lives alone in a house in California's San Fernando Valley. The owner of five dogs and two cats, she is active in pet-care charities and animal-rights causes. For relaxation, she enjoys hiking, gardening, sewing, beach-combing, and reading. Professionally interested in writing and directing, in 1986 she and Norman Hartweg collaborated on a musical farce entitled Oedipus, Schmedipus, As Long As You Love Your Mother. "What I really want to do is to own my own theatre," she has said. "I'd like to have a showcase, where I can do my own and other people's work."

References: Chicago Tribune TV Week p4 Ag 23 '87 pors, p3+ Jl 24 '88 pors; Los Angeles Herald-Examiner E p2 Mr 30 '86 pors; People 26:139+ N 10 '86 pors; Soap Opera Digest 13:16+ N 15 '88 pors; TV Guide 23:8+ My 10 '75 por, 35:19+ Je 6 '87 pors; Who's Who in America, 1988–89

McFerrin, Bobby

Mar. 11, 1950- Musician; singer; songwriter.
Address: c/o EMI Publishing, 810 Seventh Ave., New York, N.Y. 10019

Bobby McFerrin, whose astonishingly versatile voice and innovative, unaccompanied arrangements had made him a favorite of jazz buffs for nearly a decade, won the attention and affection of the mainstream audience with the release, in 1988, of his charmingly simple calypso-style song "Don't Worry, Be Happy," which earned the singer three more Grammys to add to his already impressive

collection. Although McFerrin is often characterized as a scat and bebop singer, his repertoire ranges from rhythm-and-blues to rock-'n'-roll to Bach. A pianist by training, he brings to his craft an unusual circular breathing technique, a range of nearly four octaves, and an extraordinary vocal flexibility that even allows him to sing counterpoint with himself. In his concerts, he appears onstage alone, equipped only with a microphone and a bottle of mineral water, yet he manages to create such a variety of sounds that one critic dubbed him "a vocal Cuisinart." A genius at improvisation, McFerrin takes obvious pleasure in drawing concert audiences into his performances, as backup singers, choruses, and dancers. "I consider myself a healer, using music as a potent force to bring people joy," he explained to Dianna Waggoner in an interview for People (September 21, 1987). "A happy heart is good medicine, and I feel like I'm a channel for fun."

The older of the two children of Robert and Sara McFerrin, Bobby McFerrin was born on March 11, 1950 in New York City. Both his parents were professional singers. His father, a baritone, sang leading roles with the New York City Opera, the National Negro Opera Company, and the New England Opera Company before becoming, in the mid-1950s, the first black man to be signed to a contract by the Metropolitan Opera, where his credits included Amonasro in Aïda, Valentin in Faust, and Rigoletto. Tapped to dub Porgy's singing voice for the actor Sidney Poitier in the 1959 film version of George Gershwin's opera Porgy and Bess, Robert McFerrin subsequently enjoyed an international career as a recitalist and voice teacher. Sara McFerrin, a classically trained soprano, has been a voice teacher for many years and currently chairs the voice department at Fullerton Community College in Fullerton, California. Bobby's younger sister, Brenda, is also a singer.

At least partly because he was, in his words, "surrounded by singers," Bobby McFerrin early on chose piano as his instrument. When he was just six years old, he began studying piano and music theory at the Juilliard School's preparatory division for musically gifted children. "I wanted to distinguish myself from everyone else in my family," he explained to Richard Harrington in an interview for the Washington Post (May 3, 1987). He did, however, sing in a church choir, and he has acknowledged having learned from his parents such indispensable vocal skills as "how to breathe musically" and "how to sing commas and spaces, not just lyrics." In 1958 McFerrin moved with his family to Los Angeles. Several years later, his parents divorced. A shy, imaginative, and deeply religious boy, he found an outlet for his emotions in playwriting (he had written five plays by the age of fifteen) and in music. During his senior year in high school, he formed the Bobby Mack Jazz Quintet, which performed at local school and civic functions.

Following his graduation from high school, McFerrin enrolled at California State University in Sacramento, where he majored in music. Always interested in writing his own music, he took courses in music theory, composition, and arranging at California State and, later, at Cerritos College in Norwalk, near Los Angeles. For a time he considered a career in the ministry, but in the early 1970s he dropped out of school to try his luck as a musician. He spent most of the next several years on the road, as a journeyman keyboardist with various top-forty lounge bands and with the Ice Follies. "I would think to myself, 'Am I going to survive playing the same stuff every night?'" McFerrin recounted to Susan Katz of Newsweek (October 6, 1986). "I always messed up the show throwing in some funky licks."

In the mid-1970s, after a show at a Springfield, Illinois nightclub, where he was appearing as a pianist and occasional singer with a touring band, McFerrin met Debbie Lynn Green. The two married in 1975 and settled in Springfield, where McFerrin resumed his musical studies. Two years later, with the help of a musician friend, he landed a job as the pianist in a jazz trio at a bar in Salt Lake City, Utah. The job proved to be short-lived, for when the owner learned that McFerrin was black, he fired the group. In the same week the McFerrins were evicted from their apartment for being an interracial couple. Despite this cold welcome, they remained in Salt Lake City for nearly two years, during which time Bobby eked out a living playing piano in local taverns, at the Salt Lake City Hilton, and for modern dance classes at the University of Utah.

It was while he was working as an accompanist for dance improvisation classes that McFerrin's long-suppressed legacy of vocal artistry finally emerged, in scat singing and other vocal acrobatics that seemed to arise naturally in answer to the dancers' improvised movements. One day in 1977, in what he has since described as "a moment's clarity," he suddenly realized that it was time to make a career change. "I was feeling pretty burned out and wondering what my direction in life was going to be, when an inner voice told me I should sing," he recalled to Francis Davis in a conversation for Rolling Stone (March 28, 1985). "It wasn't a voice from heaven or anything like that, with echo and delay. It was just the sound of my own thoughts, like everybody hears from time to time. The difference was, I acted on it immediately."

Over the next two years, McFerrin worked as a singer in a succession of piano bars and, for a few months, as the lead singer of the Astral Project, a New Orleans–based group. In the summer of 1979, he moved to San Francisco, hoping to find more job opportunities. Within weeks of his arrival he met the noted jazz singer Jon Hendricks, whose lightning-fast vocal improvisations with the popular jazz trio Lambert, Hendricks and Ross in the 1960s had been an inspiration to the young McFerrin. The two men hit it off immediately, and, after an impromptu scatting session that was, in effect, an audition, Hendricks asked McFerrin to join his singing group, which also included his wife, Judith, and daughter Michele.

Touring with Jon Hendricks's vocal group gave McFerrin the exposure he needed. Impressed by the singer's range and style, Bill Cosby helped him obtain bookings in Las Vegas nightspots and at the 1980 Playboy Jazz Festival in Los Angeles. When McFerrin left the group to teach improvisational singing and to play clubs closer to his home, the Hendrickses kept his name in circulation in the jazz community. The informal publicity campaign eventually paid off in a well-received 1981 appearance at the New York Kool Jazz Festival. "Newcomer Bobby McFerrin broke up the 95 percent-full house with his fresh and hard-to-describe style of scatting," a reviewer wrote for Variety (July 8, 1981). Singling out for special praise the singer's "uncanny ability to simulate the sounds of instruments with boppish overtones," the reviewer added, "This is clearly an act that has to be seen to be comprehended."

Appearing with such established stars as George Benson, Herbie Hancock, and Dizzy Gillespie, McFerrin traveled around the country on the Kool Jazz circuit for several months. One Kool Jazz concert, in which he performed several numbers with the trumpeter Wynton Marsalis, among others, was recorded live and released on the Elektra label in 1982 under the title The Young Lions. The album received a number of appreciative notices, although most of the critics focused on Marsalis's mesmerizing horn solos. The singer's first full album, Bobby McFerrin (1982), which included only one unaccompanied tune (Bud Powell's song "Hallucinations"), disappointed those listeners who had heard him perform live, among them the music critic Evan Eisenberg. In his retrospective appraisal of McFerrin's career for the Nation (July 20–27, 1985), Eisenberg wrote that the album, "upholstered in pop instrumentals," was "so mellow that one finds oneself turning the volume down for fear of waking McFerrin up."

Frequent live performances saved Bobby Mc-Ferrin from being dismissed as merely another carbon copy of the popular jazz singer Al Jarreau. In his *New York Times* (November 5, 1982) review of McFerrin's show at the Bottom Line, a New York jazz club, Stephen Holden applauded the singer's uncanny ability to "imitate a whole jazz band with the fluency of a great ventriloquist." Perhaps more important, in Holden's view, McFerrin "infused his virtuosity with a warm good humor and an attachment to his material that gave his interpretations a rare organic unity, with the sounds evolving out of one another in structured sequences."

At the Blue Note and at other clubs, McFerrin was backed up by a small group of jazz musicians, but, early in 1983, having concluded that the increasingly unpredictable nature of his performances was unfair to his accompanists, he decided to go it alone. "Oh, man, that was very scary, because I was really putting myself on the line," he recalled to Dianna Waggoner for the *People* magazine profile. Discounting the advice of some of his friends, who warned him that he might be only briefly successful as a novelty act, McFerrin embarked on a solo concert tour, beginning in Ashland, Oregon in mid-1983. During a subsequent European tour, many promoters, on learning that he would be performing alone, canceled their bookings. Nevertheless, McFerrin's performances, occasionally supplemented by such musicians as Bob Dorough, Chico Freeman, and Pharoah Sanders, delighted European audiences, particularly the Germans, who proceeded to christen him "*Stimmwunder*"—"Wonder Voice."

One of McFerrin's shows in West Germany was taped live in March 1984 and released later in the year as *The Voice*. Although the album had been produced on a shoestring budget by a wary Bruce Lundvall, it was the recording McFerrin had been waiting to make. "I never wanted to climb up on that pop merry-go-round in the first place," he told Francis Davis. "All along it was the second album I was looking forward to. I knew that once I made a solo voice album, people would notice me." The readers of *Down Beat* magazine responded by naming McFerrin best male jazz vocalist, an honor he was to be accorded in each of the following three years. He began to win the approval of a wider audience in December 1984, when he made the first of several appearances on Garrison Keillor's variety show *A Prairie Home Companion*, broadcast live to an estimated two million listeners on National Public Radio. According to the program's producer, Margaret Moos, the people in the studio audience "just about jumped out of their seats and onto the stage" during his set, especially when he sang the Air from Bach's Third Orchestral Suite, in an interpretation that Evan Eisenberg described as "limpid, its pungencies and arabesques not stated, only implied, as in an ink painting by Sesshu or a Bach cello suite."

McFerrin's eclectic concert repertoire includes, in addition to works by Bach, original numbers, such as "I'm My Own Walkman," in which he even manages to create the sound of the static between radio frequencies; tunes by a variety of contemporary artists, from the Beatles to Chick Corea to Antonio Carlos Jobim; a whimsical capsule version of the film *The Wizard of Oz*, complete with sound effects, in which he plays all the characters; and such children's songs as "Heads, Shoulders, Knees, and Toes" and "The Itsy, Bitsy Spider," invariably performed with the assistance of the audience. Although his shows follow no set plan, McFerrin always tries to involve the audience in some way, either by recruiting audience members to serve as his backup group or by encouraging them to suggest ideas for improvised songs. "I view the audience as my helpers," he told Laura Van Tuyl of the *Christian Science Monitor* (April 17, 1987). "Some you have to work on a bit, and I think it's because we've grown up to simply sit back and not participate in the creative process of the artist onstage. But in every one of us, there's this little part of us that wants to somehow participate in a performance."

Over the next several years, McFerrin played jazz clubs, theatres, and concert halls around the United States, usually to standing ovations. After taking in one of McFerrin's shows, at the Blue Note in New York City, Stephen Holden observed in his review for the *New York Times* (September 20, 1984) that the singer "rarely lets his virtuosity get the better of his heart or his sense of humor. . . . McFerrin mixes playfulness and soul in his music in a way that gives his extraordinary voice free rein but that also keeps his ideas rooted in one or another jazz or pop tradition." The playful quality of McFerrin's vocalizations was perhaps never more evident than on his third album, *Spontaneous Inventions* (1986), a collection of solo pieces and unrehearsed duets with the saxophonist Wayne Shorter, the pianist Herbie Hancock, and Robin Williams, the actor and comedian.

McFerrin won his first two Grammy Awards, for best male jazz vocalist and best arranger, in 1986, for the track "Another Night in Tunisia" on the Manhattan Transfer's *Vocalese* album. The following year, he captured the Grammy for best jazz vocalist again, this time for his haunting interpretation of the melancholy title theme of the motion picture *'Round Midnight*. "On 'Round Midnight'," he recalled to Richard Harrington, "I actually tried to feel like I was a lone horn player playing in a smoky room, with just the thrill of a smoky melody." His acceptance "speech," sung in his inimitable style, stopped the show at the Grammy Awards ceremony and won him many new fans, who bought 50,000 copies of *Spontaneous Inventions* during the month following the awards telecast, boosting the album onto *Billboard*'s "top 100" pop music chart.

"Because what I do is spontaneous, I've been called a jazz singer, but increasingly I've found the label restricting," McFerrin told the *New York Times*'s Stephen Holden for an article published on April 27, 1988. "I see myself as a performance artist. Although my work includes jazz and pop singing, it also involves mime, dance, storytelling, and creative work with the audience." Although he continued to maintain a hectic performance schedule, giving more than 100 concerts a year, well into the late 1980s, McFerrin found the time to stretch his talents in collaborations with such innovative artists as Tandy Beal and Meredith Monk. He and Miss Beal, an experimental choreographer known for her unique blend of dance, theatre, and mime, joined forces for an evening of improvised duets, theatrical skits, and audience participation at the Herbst Theatre in San Francisco in 1985. Two years later, he shared the stage of the Brooklyn Academy of Music with Meredith Monk, the primitivist composer and multimedia artist, for a performance of *Duet Behavior*, an exploration of various vocal techniques, including hocketing, that they had created for the academy's 1987 Next Wave Festival. He also recorded a new theme for the *Cosby Show*, one of the most highly rated programs in the history of television.

McFerrin fulfilled a long-held dream in April 1987, when he appeared, along with fellow jazz musicians Stanley Jordan and Michael Petrucciani, at New York City's legendary Carnegie Hall. A year later, on May 3, 1988, he returned to Carnegie Hall for a sold-out solo recital before a wildly enthusiastic crowd. "McFerrin's true art—maybe the only one you can nail him to—is his ability to make us all kids for a while . . . ," Stephen Williams wrote in his review of the concert for *New York Newsday* (May 5, 1988). "McFerrin is so ingratiating and effervescent that even if you consider him just a novelty act, he demands attention." Williams, who is admittedly not among the singer's more ardent admirers, was nevertheless taken by his "one-on-one operetta," in which he played both male and female roles, shifting "from bass to falsetto in nanoseconds," and his "captivating" short-form *Wizard of Oz*.

In between public appearances, McFerrin worked on his fourth album, *Simple Pleasures*, a tribute to the popular music he had grown up with. To create the "full-band" sound he wanted, McFerrin "built the songs track by track," as he put it, in the recording studio, overdubbing his own voice singing bass, melody, and harmony as many as nine times. "Most of the album's appeal stems from the ease with which he can set out the heart of a song with a single telling phrase," J. D. Considine wrote in his critique of *Simple Pleasures* for *Rolling Stone* (October 20, 1988). "His version of the Beatles' 'Drive My Car,' for instance, sums up the calculating sass of the aspiring starlet in a lazy, swooping harmony line on the chorus. Sometimes he even does double duty, as with 'Sunshine of Your Love,' where he manages to recapture the spark of both Jack Bruce's vocal and Eric Clapton's guitar. Still, the best thing about *Simple Pleasures* is that it finds McFerrin focusing on the songs, not on vocal agility."

One of the album's five original tunes, "Don't Worry, Be Happy," became McFerrin's first number-one hit single. With its catchy island beat and its simple, reassuring lyrics ("In every life we have some trouble/But when you worry you make it double/Don't worry, be happy"), the song is, as Jay Cocks observed in *Time* (October 17, 1988), "giddy and good-natured enough to turn a forced march into a dance contest." Contributing to the tune's popularity was its inclusion on the soundtrack of the 1988 motion picture *Cocktail*, one of the top box-office attractions of the year. By February 1989 ten million copies of "Don't Worry, Be Happy" had been sold in the United States alone. In the same month Delacorte Press published lyrics to the song, augmented by twenty new verses and wittily illustrated by Bennett Carlson, in book form. A few weeks later, McFerrin swept the major 1989 Grammy Awards, taking the honors for best male pop vocalist, best song, and record of the year. He also received his fourth Grammy for best male jazz vocalist, for the track "Brothers" on the bassist Rob Wasserman's album *Duets*.

The "overnight ubiquity," to use Bill Barol's description, of "Don't Worry, Be Happy" was not without its drawbacks. "We have entered a golden age of oversimplified niceness and the song was its trumpet charge," Barol observed in *Newsweek* (February 27, 1989). "'Don't Worry, Be Happy' was charming the first time, annoying the hundredth time, infuriating the millionth time around." When George Bush, the Republican candidate in the 1988 election campaign, adopted the ditty as his campaign theme, McFerrin, a supporter of Michael S. Dukakis, the Democratic standard-bearer, publicly voiced his displeasure. He later announced that he would no longer perform the song. "I think it was so popular because it went to the spirit," he told reporters following the 1989 Grammy Awards ceremony. "I think, given the mood at the time, it was such that people wanted something uplifting and jovial and funny."

Weary of touring, McFerrin took an indefinite leave of absence from the concert stage in late 1988. In earlier years he had occasionally spoken of abandoning his career as a solo performer to avoid being typecast. "My primary interest is vocal artistry of all kinds, even spoken word," he told Richard Harrington for his *Washington Post* profile. "I've started telling stories, getting into characters, using my voice in as many ways as possible. . . . I'm interested in doing anything that's going to expand me as an artist." To that end, McFerrin composed and performed the musical accompaniment for several selections from Rudyard Kipling's *Just So Stories*, narrated by actor Jack Nicholson, for the cable television service Showtime and Windham Hill Videos and created the score for the short-lived NBC television series *The Bronx Zoo*, about a public high school in a run-down New York City neighborhood. He has also appeared in television commercials for Ocean Spray fruit juices, one of them featuring him as a Jamaican-accented juice vendor hawking his product on a beach crowded with Bobby McFerrin lookalikes, and for Levi's 501 blue jeans.

Slender and lithe, with a lean face, a close-cropped beard, and the "eyes of a nearsighted doe," in Evan Eisenberg's words, Bobby McFerrin dresses casually, usually in blue jeans and running shoes, on stage and off. A daily reader of the Bible, he is devoted to his family and enjoys spending time at home. When he is not on the road, he regularly makes breakfast for his sons, Taylor John and Jevon Chase. His wife, Debbie, helps manage his business affairs from their home in San Francisco. In recent months he has devoted most of his time to transcribing Bach's keyboard pieces for a projected classical album and to composing choral music for his newly formed twelve-person ensemble Voicestra. When queried about his hopes for the future, McFerrin told Jay Cocks, "There's a wonderful Hesse story about a violinist who wishes to be the best in the world. His wish is granted, and as he's playing, he slowly disappears into the music. That's that hope of every artist. It's certainly mine."

References: Down Beat 55:20+ Je '88 por; Essence 17:24 Ap '87 por; Gentlemen's Q 57:129+ D '87 por; Horizon 30:34+ Jl-Ag '87 por; Newsweek 108:76 O 6 '86 por; People 28:109+ S 21 '87 pors; Rolling Stone p31 Mr 28 '85 por; Time 132:79 O 17 '88 pors; Wall St J p28 My 3 '88; Washington Post G p1+ My 3 '87 por; New Grove Dictionary of Jazz (1988)

Menem, Carlos Saúl

July 2, 1930– President of Argentina. Address: Casa Rosada, Buenos Aires, Argentina

The election of Carlos Saúl Menem to the presidency of Argentina on May 14, 1989 represented the nation's first transfer of power from one constitutionally elected party to another since 1928. A lawyer by training and a three-term governor of La Rioja province, Menem is the first Peronist—with the sole exception of the late dictator Juan Perón himself—ever elected to national office. Peronism, formally embodied in the Justicialist party, has been among the country's strongest political movements since World War II. Although Perón was ousted from the presidency in 1955 after spending nine years in office, the loyalty he commanded

from exile during the following eighteen years was enough to return him to power briefly in 1973 until his death in 1974, when he was succeeded by his vice-president and third wife, Isabel Perón. She was deposed in 1976 by a military junta, whose so-called dirty war against leftist guerrillas and suspected sympathizers left an estimated 9,000 people dead in the late 1970s. In 1983 the military regime permitted free elections after having lost its credibility, along with the Falkland Islands (known as the Malvinas in Argentina and most other Latin countries), in a ten-week war with Great Britain the previous year. The new president, Raúl Alfonsín of the Unión Cívica Radical, or Radical party, took office on December 10, 1983, inaugurating the restoration of democracy in Argentina.

Although Alfonsín earned widespread admiration for prosecuting retired military officers for human rights violations committed during the dirty war, he let the nation's economic problems—themselves a legacy of the Peronist government, in the view of many Argentines—overwhelm his administration. By the summer of 1989 Argentina was in the midst of the worst economic crisis in its history. Hyperinflation, which had recently catapulted a fourth of the nation's thirty-two million people into poverty, led to food riots and looting in the wake of May's elections. Power outages, supply shortages, factory closings and layoffs, and increasing impatience with the government's paralysis precipitated Alfonsín's resignation five months before the end of his six-year term. On assuming the presidency on July 8, 1989, Menem acknowledged the gravity of the situation: "The only thing[s] I can offer my people are work, sacrifice, and hope. Work, sacrifice, and hope. There is no other way to put it. Argentina is broken, devastated, destroyed. . . . This is perhaps our last chance."

Carlos Saúl Menem was born on July 2, 1930 in Anillaco in the province of La Rioja in Argentina's hot and arid northwestern interior. Carlos and his three brothers were brought up as Sunni Moslems by their parents, Saúl and Mohiba (or Mohibe) Menem, who had emigrated from Yabrut, a village north of Damascus, Syria. Saúl Menem's rise from peddler to successful merchant enabled him to put all four of his sons through college. Carlos earned a law degree from Córdoba University in 1958, and his youngest brother, Eduardo, became a lawyer and a senator before being elected president of the Senate in May 1989.

At some point in his youth, Menem converted from Islam to Roman Catholicism, a strategic move for an aspiring politician of Syrian descent in a country whose population is 97 percent of European origin and—more important—92 percent Roman Catholic. Moreover, the provincial and national constitutions require whoever is elected governor or president, respectively, to be Roman Catholic. Despite his religious conversion, Menem married a Moslem whose parents, like his own, were Syrian immigrants to La Rioja. Carlos Menem met Zulema Fátimah Yoma not in La Rioja, but on a visit to Damascus in 1964. They were married in 1966 in an Islamic ceremony, separated twice during the 1980s, and formally reconciled in 1988 with the mediation of the papal nuncio. During the separation, Mrs. Menem reportedly charged her husband with political opportunism in converting to Christianity, according to two articles by Shirley Christian for the *New York Times* (January 8, 1989 and May 16, 1989). Mrs. Menem remains a Moslem.

Carlos Menem's political activism began while he was still a student. In 1955, the year of Perón's ouster, he founded the Juventud Peronista, a Peronist youth group. The following year he went to jail briefly for supporting a revolt aimed at restoring Perón to power. After receiving his law degree, Menem opened a practice in La Rioja, the provincial capital city, and continued his work as legal adviser to the Confederación General del Trabajo (CGT), or General Labor Confederation, which he had begun in 1955. Menem's affiliation with the CGT, an organization of trade unionists who are the backbone of Peronism, continued through 1970. During the political instability that characterized that period, Menem established a loyal following in his native province. He was a candidate for provincial deputy in 1962, but national elections were interrupted that year by a military coup. Elected provincial president of the Justicialist party in 1963, Menem made his first run for governor that year. But he was not elected governor until 1973, the year Perón engineered his political comeback. After the military coup that toppled Perón's widow in 1976, Menem was jailed until 1981 without ever being formally charged. His reelection to the governorship, in 1983 and again in 1987, demonstrated the strength of the Peronist movement.

Peronism has endured in Argentina because its appeal is based on sentiment rather than on any specific blueprint for society. Menem described his view of the movement in an interview with George de Lama for the *Chicago Tribune* (April 2, 1989): "Peronism is a very simple philosophy of life that is nationalist, populist, humanist, social, and Christian." Another Peronist officeholder was quoted by the *New York Times* (May 16, 1989) as

saying that Peronism is primarily "an emotional relationship with a candidate by people who don't understand anything about platforms or policy." That is not to say that Perón himself, who defined justicialism as a middle way between capitalism and socialism, had no coherent policy. An ardent admirer of Hitler and Mussolini, Perón modeled his government on Mussolini's concept of the corporative state, in which the state reconciles the competing interests of industry, business, labor, agriculture, and the poor. In practice that philosophy required huge levels of government spending: on direct benefits to the poor and to members of the newly industrialized working class; on subsidies to nationalized and private industries; on keeping wages artificially high and prices artificially low; and on the military, the bureaucracy, and public construction projects. None of the governments, military or civilian, that ruled during and after Perón's exile had been able to dismantle the dictator's ruinous legacy of inefficient, deficit-ridden public services, unprofitable industries, and powerful unions.

As governor of La Rioja during Alfonsín's presidency, Menem administered the province in the mode traditionally favored by Peronists. He doubled the public payroll in order to reduce the unemployment rate from more than 11 percent to less than 3 percent, lured new industries and investment with attractive tax policies, and printed state bonds that circulated as currency when he was unable to pay his public employees, who outnumbered workers in the private sector in 1986, with Argentina's rapidly declining austral (Argentina's monetary unit, which replaced the peso in 1985). The state bonds served a dual purpose: to bolster the economy and to enhance Menem's personal appeal among the electorate by bearing the likeness of the legendary Juan Faundo Quiroga, a popular nineteenth-century caudillo (chieftain). Menem had styled himself after Quiroga so effectively that the picture on the bonds could easily be mistaken for one of himself. Although slightly built (between five foot four and five foot six) and reportedly polite and soft-spoken, Menem cultivated the macho, athletic image of the caudillo by publicizing his avidity for sports ranging from soccer, tennis, and basketball to racing cars, driving motorcycles, and flying planes. His widely photographed jet-set social life with movie stars—especially beautiful young women—enhanced the machismo of his image, as did his collar-length hair, bushy sideburns, and all-white suits. By 1988 his carefully calculated flamboyance had earned him a cult following.

Menem's celebrity status proved to be a major advantage in a nation whose economy was in such desperate straits that people were prone to look for magical solutions from a charismatic leader. Carlos Grosso, a prominent Peronist, was quoted by the *New York Times* (November 14, 1988) as saying, "Menem is a sort of Reagan. He's a great communicator with a dozen basic ideas who has a great instinct for handling people, but [he] has little interest in detailed programmatic ideas." Menem's personal popularity was such that he was able to recover the loyalty of the *renovadores*, or renewalists, the democratically inclined Peronist faction that had abandoned him in the Justicialist party primary of July 9, 1988. Although Menem had been an early and prominent *renovador*, the group backed Justicialist party president Antonio Cafiero, the governor of Buenos Aires province, in the primary. Menem, then the party's vice-president, turned to the old-line union bosses for support and won the election.

Because Alfonsín was constitutionally ineligible for reelection, the Radical party nominated Eduardo Angeloz to run against Menem in the general election. Well-respected but not well-known, Angeloz was the governor of Córdoba province and a former classmate of Menem's at Córdoba University. Angeloz projected an image of stolid, sensible, conservative expertise and earnest competence that many middle- and upper-middle-class voters found reassuring, but to many he represented only a continuation of the feckless Alfonsín regime, which was unable to implement the very austerity measures that Angeloz was proposing to put the economy on the right track.

Campaigning in poor and working-class neighborhoods in a luxury bus dubbed the Menemobile, Menem deftly exploited the contrast between himself and the conventional, middle-class Angeloz. Speaking from an open platform mounted on the top of the Menemobile, he said, "Maybe those who studied in the great universities of the United States and Europe are more capable than I. I think not. I am the son of immigrants like many of you. I worked as a peon with my father. There is the university of the streets, the university of life. . . . There is the university of prison." (Not only had Angeloz and Menem attended the same university, but Angeloz, too, was descended from immigrants, albeit from Switzerland and one generation earlier.) Menem never failed to recall his time in prison in campaign speeches, invoking it as proof that the credit for restoring democracy to Argentina belongs not just to the Radical party, but "to all of us. I spent five years in prison and from there, along with many others, we fought to bring back democracy," he reminded his listeners. Indeed, Menem was the first Peronist leader to endorse the government of Alfonsín publicly in 1983. "But," Menem continued, "the people can't live on civic conquests alone. They need salaries, production, work."

Aside from promising to bring about a "productive revolution"—a nationalist appeal to Argentines' pride in their country's abundance of natural resources and their formerly high standard of living—Menem provided few clues to how he intended to achieve his goal. He characterized the Justicialist party platform, which called for privatization of state-owned enterprises, as "elastic." In order to avoid alienating any of the disparate elements—from the far Left to the far Right—that constitute his party, Menem became increasingly adept at the art of equivocation. "We are neither privatizers nor antiprivatizers. . . . We are pragmatists," he was quoted as saying by the *Washington Post* (April 24, 1989).

Without access to clear policy positions on which to evaluate Menem's candidacy, voters could only weigh the record of his administration of La Rioja against the promises of his vague but hopeful campaign rhetoric. Alfonsín denounced Menem as "the worst governor in the Argentine Republic" and as a "pliable messiah," but Argentines preferred to obey Menem's exhortation "Follow me! For the hunger of the poor children, for the sadness of the rich children, follow me! For the tables without bread, follow me! I'm not going to deceive you! Follow me!" The response was always fervent and adoring, especially in the most impoverished sectors of society.

If the poor and working class were Peronism's most natural constituency, it can be said that Alfonsín's failure to avert economic disaster in the final months of the campaign aided Menem's victory in the national election by expanding that constituency. Eight million people—one quarter of the population—found themselves living below the poverty level, many for the first time. Inflation for the month of April alone was 33 percent; for May, it would rise to 78.5 percent. The austral had plummeted to one-tenth of its value in dollars one year earlier. Argentina's foreign debt, on which no interest had been paid in over a year and on which no principal payments had been made since 1982, was $60 billion. Only 30,000 people had paid their income taxes that year. In view of the circumstances, it was considered remarkable that the voting on May 14, 1989 proceeded in such a calm and orderly manner.

Of the approximately twenty million ballots cast that day (voting in Argentina is compulsory for everyone between the ages of eighteen and seventy), Menem received 47.3 percent to Angeloz's 37 percent. The remainder was divided among six minor parties. Menem also received 310 of 600 electors, a mere nine more than he needed to command a majority. The Peronists, who already held a majority in the forty-six-member Senate, won control of the lower house of Congress, the 245-member Chamber of Deputies. In his speech conceding the election to Menem on behalf of his party, Alfonsín praised his compatriots for achieving a historic, peaceful transition of power: "Today all of us Argentines were winners." Menem's mood was also conciliatory; of Angeloz, he said, "I have defeated a rival but regained a friend." But others were less sanguine, remembering the loss of civil liberties under previous Peronist regimes and the civil breakdown that twice resulted in military coups.

As Menem worked tirelessly to disarm his sharpest critics and most powerful opponents with his good-natured charm and patriotic appeals for their support, the nation's economic crisis deepened. Alfonsín was intent on becoming the first president in sixty-one years to serve out his entire term, but his government rapidly lost credibility as the economy worsened. Few were willing to make a commitment to a government that was scheduled to leave office on December 10. Inflation soared to 114.5 percent for the month of June and would reach a record-breaking monthly rate of 196.6 percent in July. Food riots in Argentina's three largest cities—Buenos Aires, Córdoba, and Rosario—left fourteen people dead in the final week of May, when 329 supermarkets were looted. Alfonsín declared a thirty-day state of siege and, amid everlouder demands for his resignation, announced that he would turn over the reins of government to Menem on July 8, 1989.

Menem moved swiftly to deal with the economic crisis by appointing non-Peronists, who tend to be more fiscally conservative and more market-oriented than members of his own party, to five out of nine cabinet positions as well as to other top economic posts. Peronist orthodoxy was scrapped in favor of a package of pragmatic emergency measures designed to halt inflation and to restructure the economy over the longer term. Menem's government devalued the currency, raised prices for state-run services, and negotiated a ninety-day wage-and-price freeze with business interests. The president's eagerly awaited disbursement to workers, loudly trumpeted during the campaign, amounted to a one-time bonus equivalent to $12.25 per worker. Steps were taken toward privatization of the state-owned telephone company, toward the suspension of subsidies to private industries, and toward reducing losses at the central bank. In late September Menem visited the United States in an effort to repair Argentina's shattered credibility with foreign bankers and investors; that trip resulted in an agreement with the International Monetary Fund for a $1.5 billion loan. Such actions had an immediate impact on the inflation rate, which decreased to 37.9 percent for the month of August and to about 6 percent for September.

The economy was not the only area in which Menem's policies departed from traditional Peronism (as well as from his own campaign rhetoric). During the campaign, Menem had vowed to recover the Malvinas Islands from the British "pirates," but as president he reopened diplomatic talks with Great Britain. Normalization of relations would no longer be contingent, as it was under Alfonsín's government, upon prior resolution of the issue of sovereignty over the islands. To appease the restive military, low- and mid-level elements of which had mutinied three times under Alfonsín since April 1987, Menem appointed Italo A. Luder as defense minister. Luder, who ran against Alfonsín in 1983, was the acting president who signed the notorious 1976 order for the armed forces to "annihilate the capacity for action of the subversive elements," as quoted by the New York Times (July 13, 1989). On October 6, 1989 Menem pardoned almost 280 persons accused of human rights violations, mutiny, or leftist terrorism, including three who had been incarcerated for negligence in the Falklands War. Eight more pardons were reportedly expected to be issued by the end of the year.

The pardons, effective immediately, sparked loud protests by human rights groups in Argentina, especially by the Mothers of the Plaza de Mayo, relatives of los desaparecidos—those who "disappeared" under the military regime during the late 1970s. Menem's stringent economic measures also came in for some criticism, which did not appear to faze him in the least. He was quoted by the Washington Post (July 11, 1989) as having recently told his advisers, "Better that the people insult me for a year and applaud me for a century, rather than the other way around." But the new president was hardly under siege. Polls taken in August 1989 reported Menem's approval rating at 85 percent, nearly twice his electoral vote.

Carlos Menem's caudillo image, which thrives on well-publicized socializing with women, inevitably contributed to his marital difficulties. In an interview with George de Lama for the Chicago Tribune (May 18, 1989), he said, "I am a seducer, not a womanizer. I can't say I'm a saint, because I have no halo. Let's just say I'm an ordinary man." With his wife sitting beside him, he continued, "If with this lifestyle I have gotten to be president, I have no reason to change it." Carlos and Zulema Menem have two college-age children: Juan Carlos and Zulema María Eva.

References: London Observer p13 My 14 '89; N Y Times A p1+ Ja 8 '89 pors, A p3 My 16 '89 por; Vanity Fair 52:196+ N '89 pors; Díaz, José Antonio and Leuco, Alfredo. The Heir to Perón (1989); International Who's Who, 1989-90

Mirvish, Edwin

July 24, 1914– Canadian entrepreneur; theatrical producer. Address: 581 Bloor St. West, Toronto, Ontario, M6G 1K3, Canada

The Canadian merchandising maverick Edwin ("Honest Ed") Mirvish has an undisputed flair for the theatrical. Early in his remarkable career, he turned his tacky cut-rate retail emporium in Toronto into a multimillion-dollar mecca for bargain-hunters. Honest Ed's Famous Bargain House, which opened its doors to the public in 1948 with several truckloads of fire-sale merchandise and a policy of offering absolutely no service, became the first discount house in North America and a national institution in Canada, thanks to Mirvish's genius for generating free publicity through such novel promotional gimmicks as dance marathons and "door-crasher" specials on such items as $1.98 mink stoles. In the ensuing quarter-century, Mirvish augmented his lucrative venture with six kitschy restaurants and a street of artists' studios that was christened Mirvish Village by the city fathers of Toronto.

Impatient to conquer new frontiers, Mirvish trained his sights on the venerable Royal Alexan-

Edwin Mirvish

dra Theatre, rescuing the landmark building from certain demolition in 1962 and transforming it into a commercial success as a subscription theatre. Although Mirvish acknowledged that theatregoers are less predictable than roast-beef eaters or bargain stalkers, he resolved to stay in the theatre business as long as it continued to turn a profit. Mirvish eventually produced or coproduced many of the touring shows he brought to the Royal Alex, as the theatre is affectionately called. In 1982 he purchased London's historic Old Vic Theatre sight unseen. He subsequently restored it, brought in his formulaic mix of drama and musicals, and leavened its staid traditional clientele with controversial working-class subscribers. Mirvish, who now shares the management of his business empire with his son and only "board member," David, has been called the "Toronto Medici" and Canada's "quintessential entrepreneur." His formula is simple: he refuses to stick with any business venture that fails to make a profit.

Edwin Mirvish was born on July 24, 1914 in Colonial Beach, Virginia to Jewish immigrant parents, David Mirvish and Anna (Kornhauser) Mirvish. A resourceful relative is said to have Americanized the baby's original name of Yehuda to Edwin. The boy's father, a native of Lithuania or of Russia, according to different accounts, traveled alone by steerage to Baltimore, Maryland at the age of thirteen and went to work in a relative's saloon. He later moved to Colonial Beach, Virginia to work with an Austrian immigrant named Jake Kornhauser, whose younger sister, Anna, he later married. For a time, the gullible David peddled the *Encyclopedia of Freemasonry* all over the United States in the company of an unscrupulous partner who pocketed most of the profits.

When Edwin was two, his parents moved to Washington, D.C., where David Mirvish opened an unprofitable grocery. The store foundered under his inept management and, though Ed retained pleasant memories of his early childhood, his parents decided to emigrate once more. When Ed was in the fourth grade and his brother, Robert, was two, the family moved to Toronto, where David, a devoted Mason, embarked on a fleeting resumption of his erstwhile career as an encyclopedia salesman. Unable to make a go of selling encyclopedias or Fuller brushes, he settled down in 1925 to operate D. Mirvish Groceries on Dundas Street West in Toronto's Jewish quarter. The Mirvish family, which numbered five since the birth of Ed's sister, Lorraine, in 1923, lived in a cramped apartment behind the store.

"It was pretty crowded," Ed Mirvish recalled in an interview with David Lancashire for *Smithsonian* (April 1988) magazine. "The upstairs was rented out to a Hebrew school. There was only one bathroom for all of us, and I could never get into it." The family's perpetual impoverishment could be attributed directly to David Mirvish's lenient retail practices. "We carried on the business in a chronic state of bankruptcy. We gave credit and nobody paid," Ed Mirvish told Lancashire. He occasionally helped out at the store, stocking shelves and making deliveries, when he was not tinkering with mechanical gadgets with his best friend, Yale Simpson, who later became a lifelong employee of Mirvish's various enterprises.

The two friends enrolled in a high school industrial course at Central Industrial School, which Mirvish attended until his father died in 1929, forcing him to drop out of school at fifteen to run the family store. A few months later he took a few classes at Harbord Collegiate, but he found that the store was unable to spare him. His formal education came to an abrupt end when he was just sixteen.

For the next nine years Mirvish ran the grocery with the help of his mother and his brother Robert, who left school at thirteen to man the counter, but David Mirvish's legacy of revolving credit provided a shaky foundation from which the store was never able to recover. In 1938, on the day Ed Mirvish closed the grocery, he went to work for his childhood acquaintance, Leon Weinstein, in his chain of stores, Power Supermarkets. Mirvish's three-year tenure with the flourishing Power Supermarkets enterprise included moonlighting forays into ventures of his own, among them a dry-cleaning operation he ran with Yale Simpson and a dress shop called the Sport Bar. As Leon Weinstein later wrote in a brief memoir: "Ed was a standout merchandiser even in those days. He pushed for bigger displays. . . . Time meant nothing to him. Ed worked harder than anybody else, setting a pace that was not appreciated by some of the rest of the staff. His [eventual] business success was no surprise to me."

In June 1940 Mirvish married Anne Maklin, an aspiring singer who soon began clerking in the

Sport Bar, a joint venture the couple embarked upon while he was still working for the Power Supermarkets chain. The tiny dress shop did a brisk business, bucking the then-current cash-only trend by extending credit to women employed at munitions plants during the World War II years. Six months after the Sport Bar opened, Mirvish left Power Supermarkets to concentrate his energies on his own thriving business. When his landlord, a local doctor, died in 1944, Mirvish was quick to make an offer for the man's Bloor Street property, closing the deal in early 1945. Mirvish soon expanded his store and renamed it Anne & Eddy's. Although Anne left the store in 1944 to have the couple's only child, David, Ed Mirvish continued making money from Anne & Eddy's until 1947, when he decided it was time for a change. "Dresses," he explained laconically, "weren't exciting."

By then, Mirvish had also come to realize that he did not enjoy carrying what his wife described as "a service item that needed selling to the customers," nor did he enjoy waiting on people. Inspired by a hunch that was one day to make "Honest Ed" into a household name, he bought up an initial stock of odds and ends from a burned-out Woolworth's store in Hamilton, Ontario and augmented it with thousands of household items acquired from fire sales and jobbers at about a quarter of a cent per item. He closed out Anne & Eddy's, evicted another commercial tenant, and renovated his enlarged store with orange crates and attention-grabbing signs. "Our Building is a dump!" read the store's first newspaper ad, composed by Mirvish himself. "Our Service is rotten! Our Fixtures are orange crates! But!!! Our Prices are the lowest in town! Serve yourself and save a lot of money!"

When Mirvish opened the doors in the spring of 1948 for his first day of business, working-class people willing to part with their money pushed into his emporium all day long, and Honest Ed's Famous Bargain House, which is considered by Jack Batten in his Honest Ed's Story (1972) to be the first discount house in North America, was off and running. Completely devoid of customer service, without credit, delivery, exchanges, refunds, convenient business hours, or the solicitous glamour that characterized department stores of the day, Honest Ed's offered nothing more than cheap prices and vaudevillian sales gimmicks. Mirvish ran round-the-clock sales accompanied by twist contests, zoo animals, seventy-nine-cent dates with famous singers, and the inevitable "loss-leading" specials guaranteed to add even more customers to the endless lines of people who ringed the store each morning, drinking the coffee that Mirvish often sent out to them.

In 1958 Mirvish staged a round-the-clock, seventy-two-hour sale accompanied by a dance marathon. Some 80,000 people turned out for the event, which was held during a three-day blizzard. While the police were in the process of charging Mirvish with breaking late-closing laws, the police chief's wife was marching out of the store with a mink

stole she bought for $1.98. In 1959 Mirvish installed a neon sign so immense that when the mayor pressed a button to turn it on, the power went out on two neighboring streets. "I have always liked the exciting, the zestful and the colorful," Mirvish later told Lancashire during the Smithsonian interview. He expanded his floor space frequently over the years. Once inside, customers had to battle their way to the store's third floor—and back down again past table after table of other tempting bargains—to get in on Honest Ed's "door-crasher" opening special, which might be anything from a can of pork and beans for fifteen cents to an island in Georgian Bay for $1.19.

The creative entrepreneur carved out a career from his own instincts for business, making a trademark of what may be his only identifiable business philosophy: going "against the trend." He pioneered in the discount drug field as early as 1959, taking the College of Pharmacy to court to get his cut-rate pharmacy registered and devising creative ploys for obtaining name-brand merchandise when distributors objected to his discounted prices. He made his own signs (for example: "Honest Ed is a nut, walnut take a pecan and see how much cashew save" or "Honest Ed won't spank his kid but his prices sure hit bottom") and wrote newspaper ads and singing radio commercials. From the outset, he made a great deal of money at it. By 1952 the store's annual gross sales volume topped $2 million, ten years later its gross was $14 million, and by 1987 the annual yield was up to $65 million in sales. Ed's brother Robert, who had joined the merchant marine and become the successful author of twelve published novels about maritime life, explained the store's appeal with characteristic verve. Honest Ed's, he noted, "is the modern equivalent of the medieval marketplace. It's not just a place to shop, it is entertainment as well."

Intent on responding to a city alderman's suggestion that he build a parking lot for his multilevel "rabbit warren" of a store, Mirvish sent his boyhood chum and loyal retainer Yale Simpson out to buy up the houses on either side of Toronto's Markham Street during the late 1950s and early 1960s. By the time Simpson carried out his mission, the alderman was no longer in office, and Mirvish's request for zoning for the lot was denied. Instead, he turned one of the houses into a sculpture studio for his wife, another into an art gallery for his son, and, without waiting for approval from the municipal board in a residential area, leased the rest of the buildings to artists and craftspeople and converted the area behind them into a parking lot. The street was eventually renamed Mirvish Village by the city.

Ed Mirvish was soon to apply his wildly successful business formula to a more theatrical arena by taking his flair for showmanship to the legitimate stage. By 1962 Toronto's historic Royal Alexandra Theatre, a magnificent Edwardian edifice built in 1907 by Cawthra Mulock, the city's youngest millionaire, had fallen on hard times. The theatre, whose audiences had seen Sir John Gielgud, Dame Margot Fonteyn, George M. Cohan, the Barrymores, Tallulah Bankhead, and Orson Welles, among many other world-renowned actors and dancers, was on the verge of being razed and replaced by a parking lot. "Edwin Mirvish's response to this challenge is one of modern Toronto's favorite success stories," Herbert Whittaker wrote in an article for the Toronto *Globe and Mail* (August 19, 1967).

Motivated by an instinctive attraction to theatre, Mirvish, who had never had much time to attend plays, paid $215,000 for the deteriorating building and another $480,000 to restore it to its former Edwardian splendor. Opening in September 1963 with a production of *Never Too Late* starring William Bendix, the theatre quickly disabused Mirvish of any naïve suppositions he may have started out with. Criticized for altering the Royal Alex's usual dramatic fare in favor of touring musicals, he also raised eyebrows by attempting a "name-your-own-price" gimmick intended to bring a new class of patrons into the theatre. Mirvish introduced a one-dollar-seat policy for certain sections of the theatre, only to discover that six-dollar tickets had more inherent snob appeal.

He also discovered to his chagrin that theatre-going and bargain-shopping have very little in common. By keeping his theatre open when he could only offer second-rate entertainment because of the unavailability of popular touring shows, he lost money. "My big mistake was my obsession that the theatre should never be dark," he told a reporter for the Toronto *Globe and Mail* (March 7, 1964). "Last night's unsold tickets aren't worth anything. . . . But in another business there's always some merchandise that can be salvaged."

Among his more successful ideas was the introduction of a credit-card, phone-order system that has made tickets easier to purchase, as well as such loss-leading attractions as the Russian Obratsov Puppets, which, although they fail to turn a profit, have increased the prestige of the theatre. And by 1965 a new class of upscale customers was beginning to patronize Honest Ed's. "People used to apologize for shopping at Honest Ed's," he told David Lancashire. "They'd make out they were getting something for their maid. Now they come here and feel they're patrons of the arts."

For twenty years Mirvish managed the Royal Alex the way he ran his store. He brought in hit musicals, such as the long-running celebration of hippiedom, *Hair*, which bolstered attendance at the 1,497-seat theatre throughout 1969 and 1970. He also built up a loyal subscriber base that peaked at 52,000 in 1982 and has since stabilized at 45,000, despite stiff competition from the barnlike O'Keefe Centre and the more recently erected St. Lawrence Centre. Unlike his competitors, Mirvish has never operated on government subsidies or endowments, attributing the decline in the number of his subscribers to the decreasing level of quality of touring shows, because big stars were no longer willing to

go on the road during the 1980s. His early attempts to produce shows slated for eventual Broadway runs were resounding failures, particularly when the product was a native Canadian play such as *Like Father, Like Fun*, a hit in the boondocks but a flop in more sophisticated venues.

Because he was criticized during the 1970s for the commercialism of many of his shows, Mirvish built the Poor Alex, a 215-seat experimental theatre fashioned from a converted garage and rented out for eighteen dollars a night. His conviction that theatre should be part of an entertainment "package" led him to build a row of six restaurants next door to the Royal Alex on King Street. "Ed's World Famous Restaurants," decorated with such antique flotsam as marble statuary, Chinese vases, and a collection of classic chamber pots, have been as commercially successful as all his other ventures.

In 1982 Mirvish heard from John Gielgud and Peter O'Toole that London's renowned Old Vic Theatre was up for sale. Bidding against the British composer Andrew Lloyd Webber, Mirvish won the approval of the theatre's board of directors, bought the property for just under $1 million, and had it tastefully restored for $3.9 million more. The theatre's gala reopening was attended by the Queen Mother. Although his subscription-series formula came up against more formidable obstacles in London, where many theatregoers are tourists from other countries, Mirvish managed to bring in new blood from London's working classes with his mix of hit musicals, straight drama, and novel promotional devices. By 1987 his London subscription list had reached a modest 6,400.

Within the past few years, Mirvish has turned over the management of both the Royal Alex and the Old Vic to his son, David. Together, they have begun to produce their own shows. In 1987 a Stratford Festival version of Gilbert and Sullivan's *Mikado* that they produced on Broadway was nominated for two Tony Awards. Father and son also produced a revival of *Kiss Me Kate* in London.

Mirvish is a slightly built, dapper man with receding dark hair and a wry grin. He collects antique snuff bottles and chamber pots and goes out two evenings a week to take ballroom dancing lessons with a professional partner. An accomplished dancer, he has won a number of trophies. He never samples the late-night life offered by some of his own restaurants, since he is always in bed by 10 P.M., and he keeps equally strict daytime hours. The holder of several honorary university degrees, Mirvish was named Canada's "quintessential entrepreneur" in 1988 by Canadian graduates of the Harvard Business School. Mirvish and his son, David, a noted art collector, prefer to keep their business empire a simple, straightforward proposition, without a board of directors, shareholders, or even a secretary. Favoring hands-on management strategies, Mirvish has refused to "chain out" Honest Ed's for the same reason. "That way I can make mistakes and still come to work in the morning," he jokes. "If we need a directors' meeting, David and I can talk on the way to the parking lot."

References: Batten, Jack. Honest Ed's Story (1972); Who's Who, 1989

Mitchell, George J(ohn)

Aug. 20, 1933– United States Senator from Maine. Address: b. 176 Russell Senate Office Bldg., Washington, D.C. 20510; h. South Portland, Maine 04106

The meteoric rise of George J. Mitchell from his appointment to a United States Senate vacancy in May 1980 to his election to the post of Senate majority leader on November 29, 1988 is unequaled in the history of the upper chamber in this century, except for the career of Lyndon B. Johnson. A protégé of former senator Edmund S. Muskie, Mitchell has been active in Democratic politics for more than a quarter of a century, but few Americans outside Washington or Maine had ever heard of him until, under the spotlight of the Iran-Contra hearings in 1987, he emerged as a reasonable, plain-spoken antidote to the dramatic testimony of Lieutenant Colonel Oliver North. Although Mitchell may lack the parliamentary skill of his predecessor, Senator Robert C. Byrd of West Virginia, and has never chaired a full committee or steered to passage any significant legislation, he is widely respected for his mastery of the technical details of environmental issues and for his vigorous eight-year crusade against acid rain. He is respected, too, by the opposition because of his instinct for compromise and sense of fair play. "George goes out of his way to reach accommodations, if it can be done," observed Maine's other senator, Republican William S. Cohen, who is a close friend of

Mitchell's. He "can be adversarial, but in the best sense of the word; you won't see any low shots from George Mitchell."

George John Mitchell was born in Waterville, Maine on August 20, 1933, one of the five children of George J. and Mary (Saad) Mitchell. His father, an orphan of Irish immigrants, was raised by a Lebanese-American family and worked as a janitor at Colby College in Waterville. His mother, a Lebanese immigrant, worked the midnight shift in woolen mills for nearly thirty years. A brilliant student, Mitchell attended St. Joseph's grammar school in Waterville and Waterville High School, where he made the basketball team but never became a star like his brothers, Johnny, Paul, and Robbie. He also was an altar boy at the Arab-language Maronite Catholic Church in Waterville. On his graduation from high school in 1950, he enrolled at Bowdoin College in Brunswick, Maine, where he played guard on the basketball team. After earning a bachelor of arts degree from Bowdoin in 1954, he served in the United States Army. During the latter half of his two-year hitch, he was stationed with the Counterintelligence Corps in Berlin. Following his discharge with the rank of first lieutenant, Mitchell worked his way through the Georgetown University Law Center and was admitted to the Maine and Washington, D.C., bars in 1960.

Promptly hired as a trial attorney in the Antitrust Division of the United States Justice Department, Mitchell resigned his post in 1962 to become executive assistant to Democratic senator Edmund S. Muskie of Maine—an association that was to culminate in Mitchell's appointment to the Senate eighteen years later. In 1965 Mitchell left Muskie's staff to enter into private practice as a partner in Jensen, Baird, Gardner, Donovan, and Henry in Portland, Maine. Although he remained with that firm for twelve years, he often took time off to work on Democratic party affairs, often as a supporter of Senator Muskie. From 1966 to 1968 he served as chairman of the Maine State Democratic Committee. When, in 1968, the Democratic presidential nominee, Hubert H. Humphrey, chose Muskie as his running mate, Mitchell was named deputy director of the vice-presidential campaign.

Following the Democratic defeat in that year, Mitchell was appointed to the Commission on Party Structure and Delegate Selection, which, under the chairmanship of Senator George S. McGovern of South Dakota, set out to reform party rules to include more women, minorities, and young people at the expense of party veterans. He led the faction that was opposed to a quota system mandating prescribed numbers of women and minority delegates at the next convention. Following a stint as assistant attorney for Cumberland County, Maine in 1971, Mitchell served as deputy director of Muskie's ill-fated campaign for the 1972 Democratic presidential nomination. After the nominee, George S. McGovern, was soundly defeated that fall, Mitchell ran for chairman of the Democratic National Committee but lost out to Robert S. Strauss of Texas.

In 1974 Mitchell defeated Joseph E. Brennan in Maine's Democratic gubernatorial primary and seemed an odds-on favorite to do the same to the Republican candidate, James S. Erwin, in the general election. In a stunning upset, however, James B. Longley, a Lewiston insurance executive and chairman of a study group created to examine ways to make state government more efficient, undermined Mitchell's strength among blue-collar voters and siphoned off enough Republicans from Erwin to become the first independent elected governor of Maine since 1880. Mitchell came in second, with 37 percent of the vote, to Longley's 40 percent. Erwin got 23 percent.

Mitchell resumed his law practice in Portland and, having served on the Democratic National Committee since 1968, was named to its executive committee in 1974. He resigned from the committee in 1977 after President Jimmy Carter, on the recommendation of Senator Muskie, appointed him United States attorney for Maine. Two years later, again at the urging of Senator Muskie, he was appointed judge of the United States District Court for Northern Maine. He had been presiding in Bangor for less than a year when President Carter appointed Muskie secretary of state, freeing up his Senate seat. Once again, Muskie used his influence to further Mitchell's career, this time by prevailing upon Governor Joseph E. Brennan, whom Maine voters had returned to office in 1978, to appoint Mitchell to serve out his unexpired term in the Senate. "I had forty-eight hours to make the decision," Mitchell told Nancy Perry of the *Portland Press Herald* (July 25, 1988). "Being a United States senator is a rare opportunity, but I knew it would be a difficult election."

Mitchell was expected to lose the seat to Republican David F. Emery, a popular four-term congressman, in 1982. On May 7, 1981, a day Mitchell looks back upon as the worst of his career, a Maine newspaper poll revealed that he was running thirty-six points behind his Republican challenger. Emery sent out letters to veterans touting his own 92 percent House rating by the Veterans of Foreign Wars and deriding Mitchell's zero rating, but he failed to mention that Mitchell had been in the Senate only a month when the VFW ratings were compiled and thus had had no chance to vote on a single issue on which the ratings were based. Condemned in all quarters for distorting Mitchell's record, Emery never got his campaign back on track after that. In a major staff realignment, he hired two of Senator William S. Cohen's top aides and described Mitchell as an aloof figure unconcerned about the needs of common people. Mitchell blamed Cohen's former aides for the nastiness and mudslinging of the Emery campaign and hinted that his staff might reciprocate when Cohen came up for reelection in 1984. Nevertheless, Mitchell won handily, 61 percent to 39 percent, reflecting a massive 58 percent shift in voter sentiment in eighteen months. The distrust between Mitchell and Cohen engendered by that campaign evaporated with the passing of time, and the two

men have since become close friends and collaborators.

In the Senate Mitchell established a liberal voting record that often was at odds with the Reagan administration. Having served as a federal judge, albeit briefly, he was alarmed by a 1981 speech by Attorney General William French Smith that warned the federal courts to heed the "ground swell of conservatism" made evident by the 1980 election and to abandon "subjective judicial policymaking." Mitchell joined the American Bar Association, Common Cause, and others in condemning Smith's remarks as a threat to judicial independence. "The federal courts in this country," Mitchell reminded his colleagues, "were created as an independent branch of government that would be immune from the immediate political pressures that properly are brought to bear on the legislative and executive branches. . . . [They] represent our only branch of government with the insulation from political winds essential to protect, when necessary, unpopular views and politically unrepresented minorites." Mitchell also lined up against the Reagan administration in opposing the following: prayer in public schools; curbs on abortion; a constitutional amendment requiring a balanced budget; funding for the Strategic Defense Initiative; deployment of the MX missile; a resumption of chemical weapons production; and aid to the Contra rebels fighting the Sandinistas in Nicaragua. In 1986 he voted against the confirmation of Justice William H. Rehnquist as chief justice of the United States Supreme Court and joined in overriding President Reagan's veto of sanctions against South Africa.

As a member of the Finance Committee, however, Mitchell was more supportive of the administration, and he and Senator Bill Bradley of New Jersey were the two Democrats working most closely with the Republican chairman, Robert W. Packwood of Oregon, to fashion the sweeping tax reform act of 1986, which cut both tax rates and deductions. What emerged from the committee was a two-tiered tax structure that streamlined the tax code and lowered rates but also eroded the progressivity of the income tax, thus benefiting the affluent disproportionately. In order to tip the balance more in favor of the middle class, Mitchell led a floor fight to impose a third top tax rate of 35 percent. Fearful that the whole package would unravel if members began tacking on amendments, Packwood opposed the Mitchell proposal, which was buried by a vote of seventy-one to twenty-nine.

As a member of the Environment and Public Works Committee, Mitchell made his mark on the environment issue early on in his Senate career by introducing in 1981 the first bill to control acid rain. Since that time he has repeatedly tried and failed to persuade senators from coal-producing states that sulfur dioxide, which spews from power plants and factories and falls to the ground as acid rain, is polluting drinking water, destroying aquatic life, and corroding human lungs. Writing in *National*

Parks (July–August 1987) magazine, Mitchell cited testimony before his subcommittee on environmental protection in which health professionals unanimously warned that current levels of air pollution threaten the lives of children, the elderly, asthmatics, and others with respiratory problems. "The price of our continued inaction increases every year," Mitchell wrote. "The American Lung Association estimates we are spending $16 billion per year on health-care costs associated with air pollution. We are spending another $40 billion in decreased worker productivity. Damage to buildings, statuary, often irreplaceable monuments, and other materials is approximately $7 billion per year."

In 1984 Mitchell won committee passage of a bill requiring midwestern coal-burning states to finance the reduction of sulfur dioxide emissions by 42 percent, but it died on the Senate floor. The next year he tried to compensate selected victims of toxic waste with a provisional fund administered by the Environmental Protection Agency, but the measure failed to pass by a narrow forty-nine to forty-six margin, largely because of fears that such a fund, once created, would evolve into a permanent and expensive program. Despite such failures, Mitchell remains committed to environmental issues, particularly the reduction of acid rain.

In late 1984 Mitchell was appointed chairman of the Democratic Senatorial Campaign Committee, which was charged with winning back control of the Senate in 1986. Amid widespread skepticism of his ability to turn around a fifty-three-to-forty-seven Republican advantage, Mitchell raised a war chest of $12.4 million, nurtured a field of strong candidates, and brought fifty-four Democratic senators into the 100th Congress. He was rewarded with an honorific appointment as deputy president *pro tempore* of the Senate, a post created as a tribute to Senator Hubert H. Humphrey in 1977 and vacant since his death. With the Democratic takeover of the Senate, Mitchell was regarded as a strong contender to ultimately succeed Senator Robert C. Byrd of West Virginia as majority leader.

In 1987 Mitchell was named one of the eleven senators on the Select Committee on Secret Military Assistance to Iran and the Nicaraguan Opposition, the so-called Iran-Contra Committee, chaired by Democrat Daniel K. Inouye of Hawaii. Despite his extensive legal and political background, Mitchell later confessed to having been thoroughly bewildered at times by the Byzantine intricacies of the covert arms-for-hostages deal undertaken by the Reagan administration and by the conflicting testimony of White House aides. What disturbed him most, however, was the testimony and personality of Lieutenant Colonel Oliver North, who, while striking an emotional chord in the American people, seemed to confuse patriotism with loyalty to administration policy.

Mitchell was especially irked by North's plea for Contra aid "for love of God and love of country." He brooded for days on how he could best respond without getting bogged down in a tedious exchange with North or his lawyer. Taking the advice of Harold C. Pachios, a Portland attorney and an old friend, Mitchell decided to focus his summation on North's definition of patriotism. "Of all the qualities which the American people find compelling about you," Mitchell said to North before a national television audience, "none is more impressive than your obvious devotion to this country. Please remember that others share that devotion and recognize that it is possible for an American to disagree with you on aid to the Contras and still love God and still love this country just as much as you do. Although He is regularly asked to do so, God does not take sides in American politics. And in America, disagreement with the policies of the government is not evidence of lack of patriotism." As he spoke, the packed hearing room fell silent, and his office phone lines came alive with calls of support. Mitchell was equally impressive in a nationally televised response to President Reagan's address on the Iran-Contra scandal.

With Senator Cohen, who also served on the committee, Mitchell wrote *Men of Zeal: A Candid Inside Story of the Iran-Contra Hearings* (1988), which *Publishers Weekly* (July 22, 1988) recommended as "a clear exposition of the chronology, probable motivations and the broader implications of Iran-Contra." The authors admitted that the committee left many questions unanswered, including the precise roles played by Vice-President George Bush, CIA director William J. Casey, and the Israeli government. They blamed the scandal on "an excess of zeal and contempt for those who held different views."

In April 1988 Senator Byrd announced that he was stepping down as majority leader. Entering the race for the leadership post were Senator Inouye, a solemn, dignified veteran whose image was tarnished a bit by a lackluster performance as chairman of the Iran-Contra Committee; J. Bennett Johnston of Louisiana, a shrewd parliamentarian who, as chairman of the Energy and Natural Resources Committee, controlled legislation important to a diverse group of senators but whose ties to oil and gas interests disturbed some; and Mitchell, a relative newcomer whose liberal voting record seemed somewhat of a liability in the wake of the recent presidential election but who enjoyed the support of the unusually large Democratic class of 1986, all of whom owed their seats at least partly to Mitchell's campaign direction.

On the first ballot in caucus on November 29, Mitchell surprised observers by drawing twenty-seven votes, just one shy of victory, to fourteen apiece for Inouye and Johnston, both of whom promptly withdrew in favor of Mitchell. "They wanted more than a parliamentarian or legislative manager," Democratic senator Thomas A. Daschle of South Dakota observed in explaining Mitchell's victory. "They wanted someone who could work effectively with the diversity in the chamber. But, more than that, they were looking beyond the chamber for an effective, articulate national spokesman, someone who could frame issues and project what the new Senate is and ought to be." Mitchell wasted little time in reaching out to his rivals, appointing Inouye chairman of the Democratic Steering and Policy Committee and naming Senator John Breaux of Louisiana, who had managed Johnston's campaign for the Democratic leadership, chairman of the Democratic Senate Campaign Committee for the 1990 elections. Meanwhile, on November 8, 1988, Mitchell himself was reelected to the Senate by a four-to-one margin over Jaspar S. Wyman.

Although Mitchell does not pretend to have the parliamentary expertise of the legendary Senator Byrd, he is equally well grounded in the issues and is at ease on the television interview programs that his untelegenic predecessor scrupulously avoided. In an interview with Susan F. Rasky of the New York Times (December 3, 1988), Mitchell stressed that he was sensitive to the complaints of the younger members that the long hours and frequent night sessions undermined their family life and that the archaic rules of the upper chamber should be modernized, but he reassured veterans that he had no radical plans in mind. "I like the traditions that make the Senate unique," Mitchell said, "and I did not seek the position of majority leader to change the Senate."

In his maiden speech as majority leader, in January 1989, Mitchell fleshed out his agenda. "The New Deal and the Reagan reaction to it are over," he declared, in calling for a "new social contract" between the government and the people that is fair, pragmatic, and affordable. He called on President Bush (with whom he had become friends when the two shared Air Force Two on weekend trips to Maine during the Reagan years) to fashion a "credible" budget "based on realistic assumptions." Besides acid-rain controls, the majority leader promised Senate action on childcare, an increase in the minimum wage, further restrictions on the lobbying activities of former government officials, campaign finance reform to curb the influence of political action committees, and a new youth corps of domestic volunteers whose work will earn them credit for education aid.

Mitchell met with Canadian prime minister Brian Mulroney in Ottawa on June 28, 1989. Among the topics they discussed was a clean-air plan unveiled by President Bush on June 12, which called for major reductions in smog, acid rain, and toxic industrial emissions. Although he said Bush's plan was not extensive enough, Mitchell nevertheless praised it as a "dramatic and welcome change in administration policy."

Some Democrats are already talking about Mitchell as a presidential contender in 1992. "I live among a nest of Republicans," former senator Muskie was quoted as saying in the Portland Press Herald article, "and they really swear by Mitchell. He is one of the most respected members of the Senate. I see him on a national ticket. He has that charisma."

George J. Mitchell has been described as soft-spoken, scholarly, sincere, keenly competitive, and judicial in temperament. Behind his owlish aspect and serious demeanor is a ready wit and gifted raconteur. He enjoys playing tennis and an occasional game of cribbage with his brothers, and he is an avid fan of the Boston Celtics and the Boston Red Sox. He and the former Sally L. Heath were married on August 29, 1959. Recently divorced, they have a daughter, Andrea, who is a social worker near Boston, Massachusetts.

References: N Y Times A p1+ N 30 '88 pors; Almanac of American Politics, 1988; Politics in America (1988); Who's Who in American Politics, 1989-90

Morris, Edmund

May 27, 1940– Historian; writer. Address: b. c/o Georges Borchardt, Inc., 136 E. 57th St., New York, N.Y. 10022; h. 240 Central Park South, New York, N.Y. 10019

Edmund Morris, the Pulitzer Prize-winning biographer of Theodore Roosevelt, was chosen to be President Ronald W. Reagan's authorized biographer in October 1985, nearly one year into Reagan's second term. In return for promising not to publish the biography until at least two years after the end of Reagan's presidency, Morris was granted a level of access to information, ranging from monthly interviews with Reagan to attendance at high-level staff meetings, that was unprecedented for a person not on the White House staff. A bidding war for the book ensued immediately among at least seven publishers. In November 1985 Random House bought the book for about $3 million, to be paid to Morris over an eleven-year period. Three million dollars was believed to have been "the highest advance ever paid for a single book," according to Edwin McDowell's article for the *New York Times* (November 27, 1985). "It's important," Robert L. Bernstein, the president and chairman of Random House, explained, as quoted by McDowell, "because for the first time a president is allowing not only a historian but a talented writer to see history as it occurs, without imposing restrictions on the manuscript."

The Rise of Theodore Roosevelt, which earned Morris a Pulitzer Prize for biography and an American Book Award in 1980, was the author's first book. Published in 1979, it is the first volume of a projected trilogy. (Volume two, "Theodore Rex," is scheduled to be published by Random House in the fall of 1990, at the earliest.) According to press reports, it was the Roosevelt book, a copy of which was given to Reagan shortly after he was elected in 1980, that led to Morris's selection as Reagan's biographer. In the lives of two of the twentieth century's most popular Republican presidents, Morris has discerned common themes, which he described to Fred Barnes in an interview for the *New Republic* (February 3, 1986): "Here are two men who in the course of their lives traveled from one end of the political spectrum to the other, yet remained the same person in doing so and at the same time retained their own constituency. Each of them has this uncanny ability to sense or at least express the mood of the American people at a given point in time. And, of course, both have superabundant personal charm, which is translated into power. Personality as power fascinates me."

Edmund Morris was born in Nairobi, Kenya on May 27, 1940 to British parents, Eric Edmund Morris, an airline pilot, and his wife, May (Dowling) Morris. In an interview with Jack Newcombe for the *Book-of-the-Month Club News* (April 1979), Morris called the Nairobi of his childhood a "paradisiacal colonial world." He attended the Prince of Wales School, which he described in an essay for the *Washington Post Book World* (January 9, 1983) as resembling "nothing so much as a British public school of the period preceding World War I. Equatorial heat notwithstanding, we wore flannels, ties, and navy-style blazers which glittered at breast and wrist with the insignia of discipline and sportsmanship. (My own was conspicuously drab.)"

His teachers tended to be "boozy bachelors with malodorous pipes talking endlessly about rugby," as he described them in his *Book World* essay. The one exception was W. W. Atkinson, who taught him to appreciate "the literature, art, and manners of England in the eighteenth century." Morris entertained himself by writing novels "behind cover of an atlas at the rearmost possible desk of every class." His heroes included Alexander the Great, Winston Churchill, and Chuck Yeager. Theodore Roosevelt joined their company when Morris became fascinated by a textbook photograph of TR, as he is commonly referred to, "that evoked a passionate identification with America." Before long, however, Morris had forgotten what he called "a real case of American hero-worship," and his initial fascination lay dormant for the following twenty-five years.

After graduating from high school, Morris studied music and history at Rhodes University in Grahamstown, South Africa in 1959-60, which is as far as he went with formal education. In 1964 he moved to London, where he wrote advertising copy until 1968. That year he immigrated to the United States "for the usual immigrant's reason—to explore one's talents and be rewarded for it," as he explained to Fred Barnes. Morris applied his versatile writing skills to a variety of freelance projects in New York City, including poetry, travel articles, science fiction, radio scripts, screenplays, advertising copy, and mail-order catalogs until 1975, when he joined the staff of the *New York Times* as a contributing editor for one year.

One of his projects during that period was a brief biographical study of Josef Lhévinne, the great Russian-born piano virtuoso who lived from 1876 to 1944, for WNCN radio in New York City in December 1971. According to Morris, the three-and-a-half hour broadcast evoked the greatest listener response in the history of that station. Morris's interest in "biography as literature," and in musical biography in particular, had taken hold during his adolescence, when a desire to become a concert pianist led him to Dent's *Master Musicians* series. Its vivid portraits of classical and romantic composers awakened in him what he has called a "quest for *le temps perdu*," but his quest found no further opportunity for expression until three years after the WNCN broadcast.

Just as Morris's portrait of Josef Lhévinne had resulted from the independent research that he pursued in between copywriting assignments, his next venture into biography came about equally fortuitously. While listening to Richard M. Nixon's televised resignation speech in August 1974, Morris was puzzled to hear the president deliver the following eulogy of his mother: "She was beautiful in face and form . . . as a flower she lived, and as a fair young flower she died." The words were so jarringly out of context that the mystery was only partly cleared up when Nixon added, "Well, that was TR."

Describing his reaction to Nixon's speech in an article that he wrote for the *Wilson Quarterly* (Summer 1983), Morris recalled that he was "consumed with curiosity about the circumstances in which Theodore Roosevelt wrote those words." He discovered that the eulogy had been written in memory of Alice Lee, Roosevelt's first wife, who died at the age of twenty-two in 1884. "It occurred to me," Morris added, "that this period in TR's life [1884-1886] would make an excellent screenplay, comprising his cowboy years out West, his conquest of melancholy and ill health, and his discovery that he was destined for the presidency."

Morris spent the winter of 1974–75 in the Bad Lands of the Dakotas researching and writing his screenplay, which he called "Dude from New York." For the *New York Times* he wrote a story about traveling in the Bad Lands in the company of TR's ghost, which led to his screenplay's being optioned by a Hollywood producer. The screenplay was never produced, but Morris was advised by his agent that a short biography might be in order. In June 1975 he obtained a book contract from Coward, McCann & Geoghegan (now Coward, McCann), which is owned by Putnam's Publishing Group.

The manuscript grew far beyond what Morris's contract had originally called for and severely strained his, and his publisher's, financial resources. John J. Geoghegan, who was then the publisher of Coward, McCann & Geoghegan, recalled the circumstances in an interview for the *New York Times* (December 11, 1985). "I had signed up the Roosevelt book and paid [Morris] his advance," Geoghegan said, "but after about two years, when he had finished half of it, I learned that he was broke. When I read what he had finished, though, I was so struck by its energy and scholarship that I arranged to pay him a monthly sum so he could continue writing." Morris, who has attributed the ever-increasing length of the manuscript to Roosevelt's multifaceted personality, has professed to be amazed "that such an interesting man should have so many dull biographies written about him."

The Rise of Theodore Roosevelt was anything but dull, according to reviewers and the book-buying public, whose enthusiasm made the book a bestseller and a Book-of-the-Month Club selection. Morris won both a Pulitzer Prize and an American Book Award for the 886-page biography, which covers the years from TR's birth in 1858 to the assassination of President William McKinley in 1901. The second volume is to deal with TR's presidency, from 1901 to 1909, and the third will be about his remaining years.

Morris was widely admired by reviewers of *The Rise of Theodore Roosevelt* for his scholarship and narrative skill. In his review for the *New York Times Book Review* (March 25, 1979), W. A. Swanberg wrote: "To an intrinsically compelling history [Morris] adds the two ingredients that so seldom join: thorough research and vivid, thoughtful writing. . . . It takes a special poise to write equably of a man so overloaded with abilities, virtues, and flaws." Daniel J. Boorstin, an historian and a friend of Morris's who served as the Librarian of Congress from 1975 to 1987, was quoted by *U.S. News & World Report* (December 9, 1985) as saying that the book "combined a rare feeling for adventure with a feeling for the nuances of political life." In his review for the *New York Times* (May 21, 1979), Christopher Lehmann-Haupt called *The Rise of Theodore Roosevelt* "stirring," "dramatic," and "wonderfully absorbing." "Because Mr. Morris keeps his distances and submerges his picture of Roosevelt in carefully documented fact," Lehmann-Haupt remarked, "his portrait remains alive and believable, and never deteriorates into mere thesis."

Some reviews were less favorable. Noting "the author's lack of professional training in history," a reviewer for *Choice* (September 1979), the book-selection tool for academic libraries published by the American Library Association, criticized Morris for "his inability to adequately relate TR to the larger sociopolitical movements sweeping America in the late nineteenth century." He nonetheless recommended the book for inclusion "in all libraries." Luther Spoehr, writing in the *Saturday Review* (May 26, 1979), observed, "Despite a superb eye for detail, Morris lacks both a sense of society and theory of personality. . . . By failing to heed muffled notes of doubt, fear, and despair . . . Morris lets a master self-publicist reach beyond the grave to dictate the terms of his own biography." But Spoehr tempered his criticism by declaring that it was "a tribute both to Roosevelt's power of self-dramatization and to Morris's considerable skills as a writer that this one-dimensional portrait consistently sustains interest."

In Ronald Reagan, the "Great Communicator," Morris chose another master of self-publicity. Well aware of the potential pitfalls inherent in writing the life of an imperious personality, Morris said in his interview with Fred Barnes, "Whether I can resist [Reagan's] charm or deal with it so it doesn't overpower me is my real challenge." Undaunted, Morris told an interviewer for *Time* (March 24, 1986) magazine, "I want to do a detailed, literary work on personality as power."

Morris's desire to delineate the transmutations of Reagan's personal appeal into political power did not impel him to pursue the role of his official biographer until 1985, some four years after he had first met the president. During Reagan's first term, a series of meetings among historians and prominent White House staffers—sometimes including Morris and Reagan—took place to explore the idea of an historian in residence and a presidential biography. The meetings were initiated by Richard G. Darman, then a presidential assistant whom President George Bush later named director of the Office of Management and Budget, and by Michael K. Deaver, a longtime friend of the Reagans' who was deputy chief of staff from 1981 to 1985 and who was later convicted of perjury concerning his subsequent lobbying activities.

The meetings culminated in a Valentine's Day dinner at the Washington home of Senator Mark O. Hatfield, Republican of Oregon, who had invited Morris and his wife, Sylvia Jukes Morris, the biographer of Roosevelt's second wife, Edith Kermit Roosevelt; Arthur Link, Woodrow Wilson's biographer; George Nash, Herbert Hoover's biographer; Frank Friedel, Franklin Delano Roosevelt's biographer; Daniel J. Boorstin; and Ronald and Nancy Reagan, among others. A dinner for the Morrises, the Reagans, and Michael Deaver was subsequently arranged with the help of Selwa Roosevelt, Reagan's chief of protocol and the wife of Theodore Roosevelt's grandson, Archibald Roosevelt. (It was she who had given the Reagans copies of the Morrises' books on the Roosevelts.)

The Reagans and the Morrises "liked each other," according to Deaver, as quoted by Sidney Blumenthal in the *Washington Post* (November 22, 1985). "The chemistry between the president and Morris is so good," Deaver said. "Nancy liked him very much. They both liked the Teddy Roosevelt book. And the president said he'd be delighted if he'd do a biography." But Morris did not want to be an historian in residence at the White House. "The danger is you immediately become one of the team," Morris told Fred Barnes. "You become partisan. You lose your independence." Another reason for Morris's reluctance was his immersion in the second volume of his Roosevelt biography. "I couldn't contemplate taking on another president," he explained to Barnes.

The many efforts of Deaver and others to interest Morris in writing Reagan's biography may have had some influence on his eventual decision to go ahead with the project, but in the meantime two symbolic events proved more persuasive than any previous meeting. According to Barnes's interview with Morris, the Independence Day celebrations of 1984 brought home to the biographer the historical significance of Reagan's presidency. Witnessing the fireworks display in the nation's capital, Morris was overcome by the "air of positivism." "It was very euphoric," he told Barnes. "I recognized the political strength of the president. I realized he couldn't lose [his reelection bid]."

Even more crucial in stimulating Morris's biographical impulses was Reagan's controversial visit on May 5, 1985 to the German cemetery in Bitburg, where Nazi Waffen SS troops were buried. On the same day, just before the wreath-laying ceremony at Bitburg, Reagan visited the Nazi death camp at Bergen-Belsen, where he also laid a wreath. Reagan made two speeches that day; one at Bergen-Belsen and one at Bitburg Air Base, but none at the military cemetery overlooking Bitburg. One of those televised speeches gave Morris a "sharp pang," as he recalled in an interview with Francis X. Clines for the *New York Times* (November 25, 1985): "I thought, 'Oh, I wish I was there. I want to see his face. I want to hear those birds in the trees in the cemetery and I want to see the effect of the Holocaust memorial on him.'"

That year Morris contacted Nancy Reagan and Michael Deaver and closed the deal in October 1985. According to the agreed-upon conditions, Morris would not begin writing the book until 1989 and would not publish it until at least 1991. The Reagan White House granted Morris the privilege of being the first historian to consult the presidential papers and gave him access to high-level aides and presidential retreats. Morris even accompanied the president to the Geneva summit between Reagan and Mikhail Gorbachev in November 1985 and once reportedly listened through a keyhole to the leaders' conversation before being led away by a KGB agent. Discussing his extraordinary access to Reagan with Edwin McDowell, Morris said, "I'll be able to sit in on anything not forbidden to me by reasons of national security, more or less at the president's discretion."

It was Morris's remarkable access, in addition to the perceived importance of Reagan's presidency, the increasing popularity of biography, and the demonstrated distinction of the author, that escalated the publishers' bidding to the $3 million threshold. On November 26, 1985 Random House bought first serial rights, book-club rights, and the rights to publication in the United States and Canada, while Morris retained foreign rights. Commenting on his first meeting with Morris, which took place on November 11, Robert L. Bernstein of Random House told Sidney Blumenthal of the *Washington Post* (November 27, 1985): "We liked him enormously. He's understated, extremely direct. You get a terrific feeling of confidence that he'll deliver what he said he'd deliver." Random House also purchased publication rights to the second volume of the Roosevelt biography in a separate deal for an amount reported to be less than $300,000.

Perhaps Morris inspires confidence because, among other reasons, he is satisfied with his calling. In his essay for the *Wilson Quarterly*, he wrote: "I count myself lucky to have become a biographer at a time when biography is once again becoming a serious art form, as it was in the late eighteenth and mid-nineteenth centuries. . . . I confess that Boswell remains the master against whom I vainly measure my own efforts. I also shamelessly imitate him, particularly in the dramatization of dialogue, a quite legitimate device that for some reason has seldom been used by other biographers."

Just as James Boswell had constant access to his subject, Dr. Samuel Johnson, while the great lexicographer was still alive, so Morris has been able to observe at firsthand certain aspects of Reagan's life that would be inaccessible to a biographer decades from now. He enumerated some of those aspects in his interview with Francis X. Clines: "The live texture of day-to-day drama. The sound of voices and tensions in the room. That sort of palpable stuff a writer needs which evaporates by the hour. . . . I'm haunted by the effervescence of facts." Regarding the difficulties that biographers encounter when writing about living subjects, Morris told an interviewer for *U.S. News & World Report* (August 3, 1987): "Sources are more guarded. You have always to consider the feelings of the subject as well. I'm not saying that the biographer . . . should be untrue to himself by writing flattering stuff; all biographers should be brutally honest. But it's a lot easier to do that when somebody is not around."

Discussing the relationship of the biographer to his or her subject during the same interview, Morris said: "Because of the need for honesty, it's wise to avoid writing about anybody you don't have some liking for. . . . If you choose a subject you dislike, you end up with a diatribe. . . . It's equally dangerous to write about somebody you adore, because then you just write sycophantic nonsense."

Therefore, "the ideal attitude is mild affection." As for the ideal subject, Morris quoted Henry James in the interview with Clines: "'A jewel bright and hard, twinkling and trembling; what seemed all depth one moment seemed all surface the next.'"

Morris maintains two homes: what he has called a "small but spectacular" Manhattan apartment with a view of Central Park and a house on Capitol Hill overlooking the Supreme Court park. He lives with his wife, Sylvia Jukes Morris, whom he married in England on May 28, 1966. Her biography of Edith Kermit Roosevelt was published in 1980; she is currently at work on a biography of Clare Boothe Luce. In the interview with Jack Newcombe, Morris acknowledged: "Some friends think this [a cou-

ple's writing biographies of each half of another couple] a curious literary relationship. It seems perfectly natural to me. I don't know why more married writers don't work on parallel projects." Morris's favorite leisure pursuits include swimming, playing the piano, collecting wines, and reading, particularly the works of Henry James, P. G. Wodehouse, Evelyn Waugh, and Leo Tolstoy. In September 1979 Morris became a naturalized American citizen.

References: Book-of-the-Month Club N p5 Ap '79; New Repub 194:10+ F 3 '86; Pub W 215:74+ Mr 5 '79; Wilson Quarterly p165+ Summer '83; Contemporary Authors vols 89–92 (1980)

the interest of national security. Challenging the State Department's unilateral authority in approving export licensing of commercial technology with military applications, he has suggested that the Commerce Department handle cases involving "dual use." Mosbacher, who made his fortune, estimated at over $200 million, as an oil and gas prospector, is one of the Republican party's most successful fund-raisers. One of his more conspicuous achievements was the raising of some $75 million as finance director of Bush's 1988 campaign. "Unlike most businessmen, he's very sophisticated politically," one corporation executive has observed. "He knows the people on Capitol Hill." One of the politicos whom he knows best is his old friend George Bush, who has called him "a close confidant."

Robert Adam Mosbacher was born on March 11, 1927 in Mount Vernon, New York, the younger of the two sons of Emil and Gertrude (Schwartz) Mosbacher, who also had a daughter, Barbara. His father began his career as a runner on the New York Curb Agency (which was to become the American Stock Exchange), and he later worked as a trader on the Exchange, becoming a millionaire by 1917, when he was only twenty-one. Emil Mosbacher had cashed in most of his stock holdings before the 1929 Wall Street crash, so that his two sons—Emil Jr. and Robert—enjoyed affluent boyhoods, commuting between a Park Avenue apartment in Manhattan and a suburban home in White Plains in Westchester County, New York. They were educated at the Choate School, the elite prep school in Wallingford, Connecticut, and they became sailing enthusiasts under the tutelage of their father, who wanted to instill in his sons the value of competitiveness and discipline.

Following prep school, Robert Mosbacher attended Washington and Lee University in Lexington, Virginia, where he majored in business administration, graduating in 1947. After spending a year working for his father, he decided to strike out on his own and moved to Texas, choosing that state because his father had investments in petroleum there. "I fell in love with Houston when I first

Mosbacher, Robert A(dam)

Mar. 11, 1927– United States Secretary of Commerce. Address: Dept. of Commerce, 14th St. between Constitution Ave. and E St., N.W., Washington, D.C. 20230

In the eleven months that Robert A. Mosbacher has occupied the post of secretary of commerce in President George Bush's cabinet, he has proved to be a forceful advocate of business interests. Mosbacher pushed for closer cooperation between government and industry to enable American companies to catch up with their global competitors in the high-tech field, and, regarding the proposed Japanese development of the FSX plane with the help of American know-how, he persuaded Bush to place restrictions on the transfer of technology in arrived," he told Linda Charlton of the *New York Times* (December 8, 1975). "I wanted to be a wildcatter. I wanted to live in the West or Southwest." Arriving in Houston with a little less than $500,000 from his father as a grubstake, Mosbacher pored over tract records in county courthouses before buying oil leases and royalties.

It took another two years before Mosbacher drilled his first well—a dry hole—but in 1954 he found his first million-dollar field of natural gas in southern Texas. Later he began striking oil in Texas along the Wilcox Trend, a location that he has considered his "bread and butter." Vermilion Parish in southern Louisiana also became an important site of drilling activity for Mosbacher. By 1967 he had drilled as deep as 18,000 feet in his quest for oil and had drilled wells in three western Canadian provinces, including no fewer than sixty-eight in Alberta's Hamilton Lake area. During these years, he won a reputation as a firm but fair dealer whose handshake was as good as a contract.

In 1978 Mosbacher bought seven tracts in Montana and found oil on six of them. He also developed some operations in the Rocky Mountains, and he acquired interests in ranching, real estate, and banking. Not all of his ventures proved to be lucrative—he explored for oil unsuccessfully in Spain, for example—and, like other oilmen, he was hurt by the sharp drop in prices in the 1980s, but he kept his debt low even in boom times by avoiding risky ventures, enabling him to ride out the bust cycles that have so often marked the oil and gas business. "I learned that you should never wildcat out of capital or borrowed money," he told Toni Mack for *Forbes* (September 12, 1983) magazine. The family-owned Mosbacher Energy Company, based in Houston, is one of the nation's major independent exploration concerns.

Mosbacher's friendship with George Bush began in the early 1960s. The two had much in common, sharing similar political convictions and similar backgrounds: they were brought up and educated in the East, their fathers were both wealthy Wall Street investors, and both Mosbacher and Bush moved to Texas and earned their fortunes in the oil business, with Bush making his in offshore drilling. Mosbacher raised money for Bush's campaigns for the United States Senate, which he lost to Ralph W. Yarborough in 1964 and to Lloyd Bentsen in 1970, and for Bush's successful run for a seat in the House of Representatives in 1966. The relationship grew closer when Bush helped Mosbacher deal with the death of his first wife in 1970. In the late 1970s Mosbacher steered Bush into a lucrative partnership in a tugboat and barge company servicing the oil industry.

Mosbacher's fund-raising efforts were not confined to aiding Bush. In 1968 he served as the county finance chairman for Richard Nixon's presidential campaign, and he acted as the Republican party's national finance chairman for Texas in 1971 and early 1972. He gave $10,000 to Nixon's reelection campaign in 1972 and later worked on "business and industry" for that campaign. In late

1975 he was appointed fund-raiser for President Gerald R. Ford's election campaign, and the following year he was named finance cochairman for the Republican party. Finding the Ford campaign coffers almost bare, he immediately set out to enlist donors from his own list of 1,700 people and eventually raised more than $14 million. As Robert Odell, the finance director under Mosbacher in that campaign, told Toni Mack for *Forbes,* "An ordinary response would have been 5 percent to 10 percent. Something like 50 percent sent money back. It was incredible. And they did it not so much because it was for the president but because Bob asked."

Acting as Bush's finance chairman during his presidential bid in 1980, Mosbacher was credited, along with James A. Baker 3d, with advising Bush to pull out of the race while he still had a chance to become Ronald Reagan's running mate. As chief fund-raiser for the Bush campaign in 1988, Mosbacher was in charge of an effort that raised an estimated $75 million. A month after the Bush victory, on December 6, 1988, the president-elect named Mosbacher as his choice for the secretary of commerce, saying he would "bring his tremendous energies to promoting United States exports abroad," as reported by Clyde H. Farnsworth in the *New York Times* (January 25, 1989).

In order to avoid a conflict of interest between his holdings and his forthcoming public duties, Mosbacher pledged to place his assets in a blind trust. He also said he would not take part in any decisions involving the oil and gas industries or the cosmetics industry, the field in which his third wife works. Some controversy arose over the appointment because of oil investments that Mosbacher made in the Philippines during the mid-1970s. Philippine companies taking part in the offshore drilling venture were alleged to be fronting for President Ferdinand Marcos, and Mosbacher's oil concessions were later withdrawn, though he received partial compensation.

Mosbacher also ran into opposition from the public-interest group Common Cause, which urged the Senate Commerce, Science and Transportation Committee, before approving his nomination, to demand the public disclosure of the "Team 100" list: the 250 donors who, at Mosbacher's urging, had contributed at least $100,000 each to the Bush campaign. An editorial in the *New York Times* (January 11, 1989) backed that demand, calling for full disclosure of the so-called sewer money—funds raised by both the Michael S. Dukakis and George Bush campaigns ostensibly for "state party activities" (federal campaign law prohibits private donations to presidential general elections) but actually used to support the campaigns' field operations. Just before Mosbacher's confirmation hearing, the Republican party released a list of 249 donors who contributed at least $100,000, although it did not reveal the actual sum from each.

The principal role of the Department of Commerce has been to foster the growth of United States exports in international trade, and, in his confirmation hearings on January 24, Mosbacher announced that he would seek closer cooperation between government and industry, perhaps through less stringent antitrust laws, to enable American manufacturers to compete globally in the field of high technology. He said that he wanted to "make certain" that the United States government was "not an impediment." He also noted that he would like the Department of Commerce to play a leading role in determining technology policy, with one of the department's "high priorities" being the discovery of ways in which the Bush administration could help American industry be on a par with Japan and Western Europe in developing high-definition television (or HDTV) technology, an important technology for the future with applications in telecommunications, semiconductors, and military planning. One of his suggestions was to give "seed money" to a consortium of American companies, enabling them to pool their resources in working on HDTV technology without risking antitrust penalties. Mosbacher also indicated that he supported free investment flows between the United States and its trading partners, except when the foreign acquisition of a strategically important United States plant could have an adverse effect on national security. Such transactions should be "carefully examined," he told the Senate panel.

Described as a dedicated free trader, Mosbacher "does not look kindly on protectionist legislation," Arthur Levitt Jr., the chairman of the American Stock Exchange, told a reporter for Business Week (December 12, 1988). "But he's not going to be anybody's patsy." Mosbacher told the Senate panel that foreign access to the United States should be matched with reciprocal privileges for American exporters, and he said that he favored keeping the current trade sanctions against Japan for failing to meet its commitments to buy more United States semiconductors. Mosbacher also said that he would encourage more research and development and that he believed that the Commerce Department should be responsible for promoting research in commercial technologies, and not the Pentagon, as was then the case. He also indicated that he supported a national environmental effort to clean up America's waters and coasts, since the National Oceanic and Atmospheric Administration is under the aegis of the Department of Commerce.

On the question of the Economic Development Administration (EDA), a $200-million-a-year agency within the Department of Commerce that President Reagan tried to dismantle, Mosbacher told the Senate Commerce, Science and Transportation Committee that he viewed the EDA as "a very strong way to help disadvantaged areas and disadvantaged people." The agency provides public-works grants to states and local communities and guarantees loans to private businesses.

Unanimously confirmed as secretary of commerce by the Senate on January 31, 1989, Mosbacher was sworn into office the following day by Secretary of State James A. Baker 3d at a ceremony attended by President Bush and 2,000 Commerce Department employees. In his speech at that ceremony, Mosbacher said that, in addition to promoting economic growth, he would focus on conducting a fair census in 1990 and on developing minority business as a "special assignment."

Far from apologizing for his fund-raising methods during the Bush campaign, soon after his appointment Mosbacher, in an interview with Richard L. Berke of the New York Times (February 20, 1989), complained that "several hundred" fund-raisers who deserved political appointments, such as ambassadorships, subcabinet posts, or lower-level jobs on federal commissions, were being passed over by the Bush administration in favor of political operatives. Declaring that he intended to take the issue to White House personnel officials and that he hoped to speak directly to the president about it, Mosbacher said, "There's this perception in Washington and politics, and some degree in government, that fund-raisers are nice, interesting people to be sort of patted on the head when you need them and ignored the rest of the time because they don't really understand the process."

One of the first issues that Mosbacher addressed as secretary of commerce was a project enabling Japan, with the help of American technology, to develop the FSX warplane, a new version of the United States's F-16 fighter. Under the proposal, General Dynamics Corporation, which makes the F-16, would receive 35 to 40 percent of the $1.2 billion earmarked for the FSX, with Mitsubishi Heavy Industries in Japan receiving the rest. Although the State and Defense departments advocated moving quickly on the project because delay could lead Japan to produce the plane on its own, the Commerce Department worried that sharing technology with Japan would help Japan's aircraft industry compete with the United States. At a meeting with Brent Scowcroft, the national security adviser, and President Bush in the Oval Office, Mosbacher emphasized that a larger issue was at stake: the decline in American competitiveness, indicative of the need for the United States to protect and take advantage of its prowess in technology.

On March 15, 1989 President Bush presided over a meeting of the National Security Council to resolve differences between the Defense and Commerce departments. At that meeting, Mosbacher indicated that he would approve the FSX deal as long as critical design secrets were not given away. He also persuaded the president to include the Commerce Department in negotiations involving the exchange of sensitive military or technological information. Bush decided to put more stringent restrictions on the transfer of technology as part of the FSX deal—a posture that the Commerce Department had advocated. A few days earlier, at a meeting of a subcabinet-level committee in the National Security Council on March 12, the Commerce Department won another victory when the Defense Department agreed to share with Commerce its role of approving deals involving the transfer of American technology to allies for the purpose of building weapons. The Commerce Department's role will be to make sure that American industries and the United States economy are not adversely affected.

Also in March Mosbacher challenged the State Department's authority over exports of commercial technology with military applications. He argued that, unless a product had a "predominantly military application," it should come under the export licensing of his department rather than the State Department's Office of Munitions Controls, which often vetoes licenses after consulting with the Pentagon when the products have potential military use. The Commerce Department drafted a regulation proposing that, if the State Department determines that a product has a "dual use," its licensing should be handled by the Commerce Department. Meanwhile, the House Foreign Affairs Committee drafted legislation that confirmed the State Department's sole authority as the administrator of the Defense Trade and Export Control Act. In response, Mosbacher appealed to Congressman Dante B. Fascell, the committee chairman, in a letter, which said in part: "We believe Commerce should be an equal partner in the interagency process to determine how the line should be drawn."

On the general issues of trade with Japan, Mosbacher and Carla Hills, the United States trade representative, took Japan to task for failing to abide by its agreements to open its markets to American products. Both officials said that they did not think that retaliatory trade sanctions would influence Japan's protectionism. "Part of the genius of the Japanese is subtlety and procrastination," Mosbacher told a House Energy and Commerce subcommittee, as reported by Terry Atlas in the *Chicago Tribune* (March 3, 1989).

Mosbacher took the lead in Bush's interdepartmental effort to develop a policy on the advancement of American expertise in high technology, enabling American companies such as Motorola, AT&T, and IBM to pool their resources through the relaxation of antitrust laws. "There's a pretty good probability of changing the antitrust laws," he told Peter K. Kilborn of the *New York Times* (May 4, 1989). "I think Congress is ready to do it." The Bush administration considered reducing the capital-gains tax for companies involved in HDTV. Mosbacher agreed to submit a plan on HDTV to the House Energy and Commerce Committee's Subcommittee on Telecommunications and Finance.

Testifying before that subcommittee on March 8, Mosbacher said that he opposed bids by the Sony Corporation and the North American Philips Corporation, based in Japan and the Netherlands, respectively, for Defense Department research grants to develop high-definition television systems. "I believe that we should insist that United States firms closely benefit from the effort," he said, as reported by Calvin Sims of the *New York Times* (March 9, 1989). According to Sims, the Pentagon's Defense Advanced Research Projects Agency announced that it had received eighty-two applications for HDTV research grants totaling

$30 million. In September 1989, however, Mosbacher abandoned his advocacy of the stance that HDTV be the sole focus of government efforts to relax antitrust regulations after criticism that singling out HDTV amounted to a government "industrial policy."

Although Mosbacher disqualified himself from participating in decisions involving the oil and gas industry, he feels strongly that the growing level of oil imports, particularly from Organization of Petroleum Exporting Countries members, threatens national security as well as the balance of payments. In 1985 he took part in an unsuccessful attempt by the oil industry to secure tax concessions aimed at increasing domestic oil production. He has spoken out about the domestic steel industry, noting in an interview with Clyde H. Farnsworth for the *New York Times* (February 15, 1989) that the steel industry could count on continued trade protection because an international agreement banning subsidies to steel producers was unlikely in the foreseeable future. Extensions of steel import quotas granted in 1989, however, were not as long as those advocated by Mosbacher.

The commerce secretary's efforts to prevent the European Community from shutting out American competitors from the post-1992 integrated European market resulted in minor progress in May 1989, when he announced that American and European officials had agreed to allow American executives to "comment" on evolving European product standards. But, after the EC demonstrated protectionist tendencies that threatened to exclude American business interests, he expressed the Bush administration's willingness to reexamine its approach to European unity—an approach that, until Mosbacher's announcement in October 1989, had been characterized by approval and encouragement. Meanwhile, Mosbacher encouraged private American investment in Poland and Hungary in September, following liberalization tendencies in each of those Eastern European countries, and persuaded the administration to relax export controls on sales of personal computers to Eastern-bloc nations.

Before assuming public office, Mosbacher was a director of Texas Commerce Bancshares in Houston and the New York Life Insurance Company. He also served as director of the Texas Heart Institute, the Aspen Institute for Humanistic Studies, and the Center for Strategic and International Studies, a conservative research organization based in Washington, D.C., and as a trustee of the Woodrow Wilson International Center for Scholars. His religious affiliation is Presbyterian. Mosbacher is a former chairman of the Mid-Continent Oil and Gas Association, the National Petroleum Council, and the All American Wildcatters Association, and a former president of the American Association of Petroleum Landmen.

As a world-class sailor, Mosbacher won medals in two Olympic classes—dragons and solings—in 1969 and 1971, the 1958 Mallory Cup as the outstanding sailor in North America, and the Scandinavian Gold Cup in Norway in 1987. His brother, Emil ("Bus") Mosbacher Jr., formerly the head of protocol for the State Department in the Nixon administration, is even better known in the sport, having successfully led the defense of the America's Cup in 1962 and 1967.

A handsome man with blue eyes, a full head of gray hair, and a ready, boyish smile that belies his sixty-two years, Robert Mosbacher is described invariably as affable and charming. By his first wife, Jane Pennybacker Mosbacher, who died of leukemia in 1970, Mosbacher is the father of three daughters—Diane, a physician; Kathryn, a freelance food writer and critic; and Lisa Mears, a homemaker whose husband works for Mosbacher Energy Company—and a son, Robert, who is president of Mosbacher Energy Company. Mosbacher's second marriage, to Humble Oil heiress Sandra

Gerry Smith, ended in divorce in 1982. On March 1, 1985 he married Georgette Paulsin, a former model who is twenty years his junior. She is chief executive of La Prairie, a Swiss manufacturer of expensive face creams that she purchased for $31 million in 1988. The Mosbachers have entertained lavishly in Houston and New York City, where they have an apartment on fashionable Sutton Place; despite expectations that the couple would be as much a part of the social circuit in Washington, D.C., as well, Mosbacher's social life has taken a backseat to the high profile he has achieved as a hardworking commerce secretary.

References: Forbes 132:114+ S 12 '83 por; N Y Times p20 D 8 '75 por, B p14 D 7 '88; Oil and Gas J 65:217+ D 25 '67 por; Vanity Fair 52:143+ F '89 por; Wall St J A p1+ S 1 '89; Who's Who in America, 1988–89

Norman, Greg

Feb. 10, 1955– Golfer. Address: c/o International Management Group, Suite 1300, 1 Erieview Plaza, Cleveland, Ohio 44114

With fans, peers, and experts alike, the most popular player on the Professional Golfers' Association (PGA) tour is almost certainly Greg Norman, a gritty but good-natured Australian (who lives in the United States) with prepossessing sun-kissed looks, powerful athletic gifts, a dramatic, risk-taking game, and classy sportsmanship in victory or defeat. Norman has the highest-velocity clout in golf today, and Jack Nicklaus rates him "the longest

straight hitter ever," with "virtually unlimited potential." A professional since 1976, Norman has won fifty-three tournaments worldwide, including one "major," the British Open, in 1986. Since qualifying for the PGA tour in the United States in 1983, he has won six tournaments and come excruciatingly close to winning the major American events—the Masters, the United States Open, and the PGA Championship. Consistently finishing in the money, the resilient Aussie led the PGA in earnings in 1986, and by the end of 1988 he had a career total of $2,260,698 in PGA tour prize money. He also holds the record for single-year worldwide winnings, with $1.3 million. In the Sony world-class performance rankings as of December 31, 1988, Norman was second, behind Severiano Ballesteros of Spain.

Gregory John Norman was born in the copper-mining town of Mount Isa in subtropical Queensland, Australia on February 10, 1955, and he grew up in the seacoast Queensland cities of Townsville and Brisbane. His father, Merv, was a mining engineer who became the general manager of a mining company. Although his mother, Toini, who was of Finnish descent, was a three-handicap golfer, he did not immediately gravitate to golf. As a child who was competitive and, by his own description, "scrawny" and "skinny," "sort of like one of those before-and-after things," he was at first attracted to contact sports and athletic activities that would contribute to his physical development. He became a schoolboy star in rugby, Australian Rules football, cricket, squash, and track, and in high school he began lifting weights and using body-building machines. Above all, he enjoyed swimming and surfing. His first career aspiration was to be a pilot in the Australian air force.

While caddying for his mother, when he was about sixteen, Norman borrowed her clubs and tried teeing off himself. Discovering that he was a natural power hitter, he began practicing for distance, without immediate regard for accuracy—an initial strategy encouraged by Charlie Earp, the pro at the Royal Queensland Golf Club in Brisbane who became his mentor. After achieving drives in excess of 330 yards, he gradually reduced distance (down to a current average of 280 yards) for the sake of control. Within two years of taking up a golf club he had whittled his handicap down from twenty-seven to scratch. At Earp's insistence, he began a diary (which he still keeps) of his practice times and progress. His chief formative guide, aside from Earp, was Jack Nicklaus, by proxy. Long before he met Nicklaus, in 1976, his bibles were Nicklaus's books *Golf My Way* and *My 55 Ways to Lower Your Golf Score*. Norman also received tutoring from the veteran Australian champion Norman Van Nida.

After graduating from high school, Norman worked briefly as a truck loader before becoming a pro trainee in Sydney and then the apprentice-assistant to Charlie Earp in Brisbane. As Earp's assistant, he supplemented his income of $28 a week by playing for $100 stakes against gambling patrons of the Royal Queensland Golf Club. Because, as he has explained, he "couldn't afford to lose" those matches (known in the game as Nassaus), they helped him develop the sangfroid under pressure that he would later bring to international competition. At the same time, he was dominating local amateur play.

In 1976 Norman joined the Australian professional tour, and the following year he began touring internationally, first in Asia, especially Japan, and then, increasingly, in Europe. "I was learning," he later said of that period. "I was changing my swing. It was too upright. It took me about five years, but I still won at least one tournament every season." Among the luxuries he bought with his earnings was a twenty-five-foot boat, from which he fished in Moreton Bay, near Brisbane. Often when he caught a large fish, nothing was left but the head when he reeled it in, the rest having been bitten off by sharks. Whenever Norman saw a shark, he fired at it with his .303 modified Australian army rifle, a practice that contributed to his nickname, "the Great White Shark."

Norman won the Australian Open in 1980 and 1987; the Australian Masters in 1981, 1983, 1984, and 1987; the Queensland Open in 1983; the Victoria Open in 1984; and the New South Wales Open in 1983 and 1986. He was a member of the Australian Nissan Cup team in 1985 and 1986. Among his early conquests outside Australia were the European Martini (1977, 1979, and 1981) and the Hong Kong Open (1979 and 1983). In 1980 he won the French and Scandinavian opens and the first of his three Suntory World Match Play victories. He won the first of his two Dunlop Masters in 1981 and led the European Order of Merit tour in 1982. In 1983 he won the Kapalua International and several of the events making up the Cannes Invitational. On the European tour in 1982 he had an average drive of 280 yards from the tee, while not always using a driver.

While touring Asia and Europe, Norman made sporadic appearances in the United States, where he first created a stir with his fourth-place finish in the 1981 Masters. In 1983 he played in nine Professional Golfers' Association tournaments, won $71,411 in prize money, and qualified for official participation in the 1984 PGA tour. After a poor start in 1984, he won the Kemper Open. Two weeks later he came from behind in the United States Open to force Fuzzy Zoeller into a playoff, which he lost to Zoeller by eight strokes. The cheerful manner in which he accepted that loss, laughing, joking, and waving a white towel, elicited a positive public reaction that "just amazed" Norman. "I may have been burning inside," he said later, "but I don't understand why so many players get keyed up about the bounces a golf ball takes."

Later in 1984 Norman bested Jack Nicklaus to win the Canadian Open, placed second to Tom Watson in the Western Open, and tied for tenth in the Georgia-Pacific Atlanta Classic. By mid-August 1984 he had finished in the top ten in six of fourteen PGA outings and won $286,724, making him the sixth-highest moneymaker on the tour. In July 1984 Norman's swing, at the point of impact with the ball, was scientifically clocked at 130 miles per hour, the fastest time ever registered by those administering the test. (Earlier, before making concessions to control, his speed was several miles per hour faster.) Tom Watson, another long hitter, had a speed of approximately 113 miles per hour with regular clubs and 125 with lightweight drivers. On June 1, 1986 Norman won his second Kemper, the fourth tournament victory of his PGA career. In four other tournaments, including the Masters and the PGA Championship, he finished or tied for second. In the eleven 1986 tournaments beginning with the Masters and culminating with the PGA, his stroke average was an extraordinary 69.60, and his average in final tournament rounds was 69.94, the best on the tour. He finished the season with a 70.22-stroke average. In a total of nineteen United States starts, he had ten top-ten finishes and seventeen in-monies, collecting a record $653,296.

In sixteen PGA tournaments in 1985, Norman had no wins but finished in the money twelve times, accumulating $165,458. On May 4, 1986, after a succession of near-misses, he won the Panasonic Las Vegas Invitational, pocketing $207,000, the richest prize on the PGA tour. His ninety-hole total of 333 tied the record set by Lanny Wadkins over the same number of holes in the Bob Hope Classic in 1985. In addition, his twenty-seven under par matched the largest sub-par total in tour history, established by Ben Hogan over seventy-two holes in 1945 and equaled by Wadkins in the Hope Classic.

Norman's greatest accomplishment in 1986 was to win the British Open, his first "major" and the confirmation of his position in professional golf's front rank. That open was played on the Ailsa Course in Turnberry, Scotland, an unusually treacherous layout that he negotiated with relative ease, shooting an even-par 280 to win by five strokes over his closest rival, Gordon Brand of England—the biggest margin of victory in the British Open in ten years. In his best round he scored sixty-three, a performance equaled by only nine other golfers in major tournament history. Norman's overall performance in 1986 raised the feasibility of a grand slam, the expectation that one golfer in one season might be able to make a sweep of all four of the top events: the British Open, the American Masters, the United States Open, and the PGA Championship. In addition to winning the British Open, Norman was leading in all three of the American events in 1986 before letting victory slip from his grasp in the final round each time, by a total of nine strokes. In the Masters, against Jack Nicklaus, he was done in by a wild four-iron on the last hole; in the PGA Championship, by Bob Tway's twenty-five-foot bunker blast for a near-miraculous birdie on the seventy-second hole. As of 1986, Norman ranked fifth among PGA pros in distance off the tee, with 277.5 yards. His longest measured drive was 483 yards.

Following the 1986 pro tour, Barry McDermott wrote in Sports Illustrated (August 25, 1986): "There are some who think he [Norman] will never again do as well as he has this year . . . who talk of a faint heart, of a choker's psyche." In summing up his view of Norman's game for McDermott, Jack Nicklaus said: "His biggest fault, if he has one, is that he is so aggressive with his game that he can't tone it down at the end when he might need to. . . . But he'll learn. . . . There comes a time when you realize that you can't fly it over every fairway bunker . . . or shoot it out at every pin. You learn to hit it between the bunkers and leave the ball on the percentage side of the hole." The veteran Australian golfer Jack Newton said: "He may learn to play more conservatively with a lead, but I think Greg will always be an aggressive player. At the Masters he hit into the gallery instead of trying to fade it into the pin, which is not his normal shot, but that's why Greg is a great player. He was thinking about birdie, about winning, not about a playoff. That choker stuff is b.s."

In comparison with 1986, Norman's 1987 season was dismal. Although he finished in the money in all the events and in the top ten in half of them, he did not have a single win on the PGA tour. At the Masters in April, he lost in the playoff when Larry Mize chipped in an incredible 140-foot shot from off the green. He again tied for second in the Beatrice Western Open, and he ended the season with a third place in the Nabisco Championship of Golf. A superstitious or fatalistic golfer might have been spooked by such a streak of bad luck—going back, actually, to the 1986 PGA Championship—but Norman, true to himself, remained "unhexed . . . unafraid . . . unsqueamish about saying what he wants and spitting in the eye of predestination," as Rick Reilly observed in Sports Illustrated (June 22, 1987). Reilly quoted Norman: "I don't believe in the gods of golf. The only god is within yourself. . . . I don't consider those losses a waste of time. . . . I haven't really served my ap-

prenticeship in the major leagues. I'm getting there right now. Those losses I'm taking are going to be to my benefit down the line." Nor did the losses have a negative effect on Norman's devoted following. "No golfer has ever lost back-to-back major championships as thrillingly as Norman . . . ," David Granger wrote in Sport (September 1987). "The sympathy stirred up by these defeats only added to Norman's allure."

With a total of $535,450, Norman ranked seventh among PGA moneymakers in 1987, when he was again foiled by a late chip-in in the Masters. His stroke average was 70.67, and his best Epson statistics were in driving distance (278.2, fourth-best) and putting (1.726, tenth). In 1988, despite a wrist injury that sidelined him for seven and a half weeks, he had seven top-ten and thirteen in-money finishes in fourteen tournaments and won $512,854, seventeenth on the prize list. His stroke average was 69.38. Before his injury forced him to withdraw from the United States Open in June 1988, he finished third in the AT&T Pebble Beach National Pan Am, eleventh in the Bay Hill and the Players, fifth in the Masters, and first in the MCI Heritage Classic (the trophy from which he gave to a young leukemia victim he had invited to accompany him on the course). After his recuperation from his injury, he finished ninth in the PGA Championship.

Between 1987 and the beginning of the American 1989 season, Norman won seven tournaments in Australia and Europe. In the United States beginning in April 1989 he again failed to accomplish the first step toward a grand slam; coming to the final hole of the Masters needing only a par to gain a playoff with the ultimate victor, Nick Faldo, he bogeyed. In the Kemper Open the following month, he dropped out of competition after teeing three shots into water on the seventeenth hole and driving the ball 305 yards into a trap on the eighteenth. He tied for twelfth in a field led by Curtis Strange in the United States Open in June 1989.

In the British Open at Royal Toon, Scotland in July, Norman, down seven strokes, shot a course-record sixty-four in the final round to tie for the lead and earn a spot in the three-man, four-hole playoff. Even with Mark Calcavecchia going into the last hole of the playoff, he drove into a fairway bunker, losing the playoff and the tournament to Calcavecchia, who birdied the last hole. Playing in the International in Castle Rock, Colorado the following month, Norman was facing another playoff until he birdied to break a tie with Clarence Rose on the seventeenth hole of the final round. He won the match with thirteen points under the modified Stableford scoring used in the event. In September, Norman watched his four-shot lead disappear in the last round of the Greater Milwaukee Open, but he recovered for a three-stroke victory.

Tom Weiskopf once said that "the longest three-wood [he had] ever seen" was in a game with Norman in which the Australian reached the par-five, 605-yard twelfth hole in two shots, crushing a three-wood that stopped twelve feet from the cup.

Norman is often compared with Weiskopf, who never realized the full potential of his superb swing and ball-striking ability. "Golf was never my top priority . . . ," Weiskopf told Bob Verdi for *Sports Illustrated* (April 24, 1989). "Greg and I have similarities. He's big and strong too, and a so-so putter, like I was, who can get going on occasion. Where he has the edge on me is upstairs. He's not as emotional." Weiskopf described Norman "in life" as "a great guy, a man's man, who cares about friends and spends a lot of quality time with them and with his family. In golf," he said, Norman "is motivated, demanding, and a perfectionist," but he wondered if he were "mean enough to be the best in a cutthroat business." Norman told Verdi: "I do want to be the best golfer in the world. . . . But I don't think I could be meaner if I wanted to. I give 110 percent on the course, but I sleep at night. Where I was brought up, you give it your best and if somebody beats you fair and square, you congratulate him for it and move on . . . keep trying . . . harder." When he loses, he said, he feels "worse for the people who root" for him than he does for himself.

Norman is "wonderful to watch" on a golf course, as his friend, neighbor, and fellow golfer Nick Price has observed. "He can hold back a bit," Price told Greg Logan for *New York Newsday* (April 5, 1987), "but if he did that, he wouldn't be going on natural instinct. He's like a leopard hunting. . . . He plays for what he is, an outspoken Australian. It's what people expect. And he's fearless." Logan noted, "The measure of Norman's growth and work ethic is that his iron play, short game, and putting [now] all measure up to his driving ability."

"Norman's feet move on almost every swing," Dan Jenkins once wrote in *Golf Digest*. "He addresses his putts on the toe of his club head, he sprays his shots woefully to the right or left when he goes bad, and he is always making you wonder about his judgment. Despite these things, his power can be awesome and his touch at times can be likened to that of a brain surgeon." Norman told Gordon S. White Jr. of the *New York Times* (June 9, 1986): "I don't change my swing or anything like that much no matter where I finish. I just try to do the same thing each time out—try to hit tee shots down the middle and try to hit the approach shots on the green." Where most golfers would wield a six-iron to the green, Norman tends to approach with a wedge. When forced to resort to an iron for safety when a fairway is closely tree-lined or has threatening bunkers, he is likely to prefer a four-iron or a five. He refuses to use the novel "square grooves," irons with faces that make the precise stopping of a shot easier, and he eschews long-drive contests, because he thinks that they are unfair to short drivers and that "the money should go into tournament purses."

Greg Norman, more an athlete than most golfers, is a strapping man, six feet one inch tall and weighing between 185 and 190 pounds. His easy smile, framed by a well-tanned face, reveals gleaming teeth. He walks with a self-confident, loping swagger, usually dresses casually, and often wears a broad suede outback hat over his sun-bleached hair. As he walks the course, no matter what the pressure, he is almost nonchalant, sublimating any nervousness into energy and gaining "electricity," as he says, from his cheerful rapport with the enthusiastic gallery.

As much as he appreciates his fans, Norman is jealous of his privacy, especially his home life. He and Laura Andrassy, a former American Airlines flight attendant, were married in 1982. With their daughter, Morgan Leigh, and son, Gregory, they live in their "dream house," a large beachfront home near that of Jack Nicklaus in Lost Tree Village, an elite enclave of Palm Beach, Florida. On the grounds of the property are a swimming pool and practice greens, where Norman often hits hundreds of shots a day to maintain what he calls his "muscle memory" when he is not touring. He thinks of golf as an essentially solitary sport, conducive to the kind of meditation experienced by a sportsman in the midst of nature. Among his recreations are boating, fishing, hunting, snooker, and driving his several expensive sports cars—fast, when possible, to feel his "adrenalin flow," as it does under pressure in golf tournaments. Although he does not pay much attention generally to spectator sports, he is a fan of the Boston Celtics basketball team.

A late starter who thinks of his golf age as twenty-eight rather than thirty-four, Norman sees his best years before him. He plans "to be out here [on the PGA tour] for the next ten to fourteen years," as he told Gordon S. White Jr. of the *New York Times* (June 12, 1989), and to do so with less scattering of his time and energy elsewhere. "I never once was backed by a sponsor. . . . I made it all myself and paid the expenses all myself. That's why I had to do this [play internationally, outside the tour]. Now I am financially set. . . . I will be able to spend more time with the family. . . . I will be playing more at ease and with less hectic travel and such. All that travel did hurt me, I guess." Norman hosts the RMCC Invitational, a tournament benefiting the Ronald McDonald Children's Charities, held at the Sherwood Country Club in Pasadena, California. He has endorsement contracts—which, according to a report in the *Sporting News* (August 14, 1989), earn him an estimated $8 million a year—with, among others, Spalding, Reebok, *Golf* magazine, McDonald's, and Swan Lager beer. While he has permanent resident status in the United States, he maintains his Australian citizenship as obstinately as his accent, despite the extra tax burden it places on him.

References: *Maclean's* 97:32 Jl 16 '84 por; N Y *Newsday* S p16+ Ap 5 '87 pors; N Y *Times* C p1+ Jl 16 '84 pors, C p14 Je 9 '86 por, V p1+ Je 14 '87 pors, C p9 Je 12 '89 por; *People* 22:85+ Ag 20 '84 pors, 27:149+ Ap 13 '87 pors; *Sport* 78:23+ S '87 por; *Sports Illus* 65:72+ Ag 25 '86 pors, 66:32+ Je 22 '87 pors, 70:54+ Ap 24 '89 pors; *Time* 132:118+

N 21 '88 por; Washington Post E p3 Ap 12 '88 por, C p13 Ag 14 '88 por; Hobbs, Michael. Fifty Masters of Golf (1983)

Norris, Chuck

Mar. 10, 1940– Actor. Address: c/o Mike Emery, 2049 Century Park East, Suite 2400, Los Angeles, Calif. 90067

Once called the "blond Bruce Lee" because of his roles in "chopsocky," kick-and-slam martial arts epics, the former world middleweight karate champion Chuck Norris has made a successful transition to the action-adventure genre. Although not as prepossessing physically as such macho men as Arnold Schwarzenegger and Sylvester Stallone, Norris is inheriting the mantle of such screen tough guys as Clint Eastwood, Charles Bronson, and Steve McQueen. He is midway through a seven-year contract that will have earned him $25 million, and his films have grossed over $500 million worldwide.

That handsome remuneration is certainly not for his acting ability. In the words of Time magazine writer Kurt Anderson, "Norris comes across as an expressionless blank. . . . His body is impeccable, but the voice is flat and high-pitched. . . . [Yet] he is . . . the most successful really terrible actor since Audie Murphy." Another film critic, Vincent Canby of the New York Times, offered a clue when he compared the "aggressive impassivity" of Eastwood and Bronson with Chuck Norris's "comparatively unthreatening physical presence . . . rather like a shy but friendly Airedale," and, in another plausible explanation, Dave Kehr

of the Chicago Tribune noted: "He's decent, regular, average—just folks. . . . Norris owes his appeal to his undisguised amateur status." The film producer Raymond J. Wagner has said of Norris, "He's an enormously nice human being, and that can be sensed on the screen."

In film after film, Chuck Norris plays a loner in Clint Eastwood's Dirty Harry tradition—often a cop or a soldier (or, frequently, an ex-cop or ex-soldier) who has not received the backing he deserves from his weak-kneed or corrupt superiors. He may not go out of his way to look for trouble, but trouble always finds him, and when it does, Norris goes into action, mowing down battalions of bad guys. A family man who is devoted to his wife of thirty years and his two sons, Norris is also an unabashed flagwaver and patriot who views himself as a role model for youngsters. He has attributed his rise from a troubled and impoverished childhood to the application of self-improvement techniques from which anyone can benefit. In his recent autobiography, The Secret of Inner Strength: My Story (1988), written in collaboration with Joe Hyams, he explained how positive thinking, preparation, and hard work have enabled him to achieve personal and professional success.

The oldest of the three sons of Ray and Wilma (Scarberry) Norris, Carlos Ray Norris (who was named after his family's minister) was born on March 10, 1940 in the prairie town of Ryan, Oklahoma. Both sides of his family were of mixed Irish and Cherokee Indian ancestry. His childhood was one of hardship because his father, an itinerant auto mechanic and Greyhound bus and truck driver, returned from World War II as an alcoholic who was unable to hold a steady job. Although Norris spent much of his early childhood in Wilson, Oklahoma, where his beloved maternal grandmother, Granny Scarberry, took care of the children while the parents worked, the family settled permanently in California in 1949. His father was often absent, and by the time Norris was fifteen, he had moved thirteen times. Finally, in 1956, his mother obtained a divorce, and a year later she married George Knight, a man who gave her boys the support they never received from their natural father.

At North Torrance High School, in Los Angeles County, Norris was a painfully shy "C" student whose ambition was to become a policeman. Since he was too young for that occupation when he graduated from high school in 1958, he enlisted in the United States Air Force as a way of getting into the military police. In boot camp, at Lackland Air Force Base in Texas, he was dubbed "Chuck"—a nickname that stuck.

Assigned to Osan Air Base in Korea as a military policeman, Norris found, to his chagrin, that he could not handle a belligerent drunk without drawing his gun, because he was not a natural athlete. He started to take judo lessons but broke his shoulder in an awkward fall. When he switched to tang soo do, a Korean style of karate using hands and feet as weapons, he found he was not limber enough and endured agony in doing stretching exercises. Although he broke his hand trying to split a pile of roofing tiles and, soon after the hand was out of a cast, rebroke it, as well as his nose, in a fight, Norris persevered and eventually developed a spinning back kick, which later became one of his trademarks. On his second try, he earned his black belt, the highest student rank in karate.

Discharged in August 1962 and still ineligible to become a policeman, Norris went to work at Northrop Aircraft, a defense contractor in southern California, as a $320-a-month file clerk in the records-management department. To supplement his income, he borrowed $600 from a friend to open a night karate school, starting with ten students who paid $10 a month. After two years, he had thirty students. Encouraged, he quit his job and opened a second school. Needing more students to finance his venture, Norris began entering karate tournaments to gain more publicity. In 1967, while competing at Madison Square Garden in New York City, he met Bruce Lee, a karate master who was at that time an actor in the Green Hornet television series. When they returned to California, the two men trained together. Through Lee's influence, Norris obtained a bit part in the espionage film The Wrecking Crew (1968), in which he played Elke Sommer's bodyguard, sparred briefly with Dean Martin, and delivered one line of dialogue: "May I, Mr. Helm?"

Bruce Lee hired Chuck Norris to appear as his adversary in Return of the Dragon (1973), which was filmed mostly in Hong Kong but included a memorable fight scene that was shot in the Colosseum in Rome. In Yellow Faced Tiger (later renamed Slaughter in San Francisco), which was filmed in 1973 for audiences in the Far East and not released in the United States until 1981, Norris had a supporting role as a Caucasian villain, a gang leader who is thrashed by Don Wong, a master of kung fu. Norris also had a bit part in Game of Death, a Bruce Lee vehicle that was incomplete at the time of Lee's death, in 1973, but was posthumously reedited and released in 1979.

From 1968 to 1974, the year in which he retired, Chuck Norris was world middleweight champion in karate. Although he earned the Triple Crown in 1969 for the highest number of tournament wins and was named Black Belt's "Fighter of the Year," Norris was less successful as a businessman. He sold his schools, which by that time numbered five, to a conglomerate, but he later unwisely reassumed control of the mismanaged enterprise and ended up having to sell his Cadillac as well as the schools to pay off his creditors and back taxes.

Steve McQueen, who was one of Norris's celebrity students, advised him, "If you can't do anything else, there's always acting." There were 16,000 unemployed actors in Hollywood at the time, but with McQueen's encouragement Norris decided to take the plunge, because he felt that there was a shortage of heroes on the screen and that he could fill the void. Applying his lifelong positive philosophy of achieving success by setting a goal and visualizing the results, Norris determined to overcome all obstacles. By instructing his screenwriters to give him as few lines as possible, he heeded McQueen's advice to let the character actors determine the plot. "Movies are visual," McQueen told him, "so don't reiterate something verbally that we have seen visually. . . . Put as much of yourself into the character and make it as real as you can. . . . Always remember that the real star is someone the audience identifies with."

In Breaker! Breaker! (1977), Norris played a truck driver who thwarts a corrupt judge in a speed-trap town. He received a much needed $10,000 for his part in the film, which, although it cost only $240,000 to make, grossed $13 million in box-office receipts. But his ambition was to make a film of his own, playing a character who would become a positive role model for young people, similar to such Western heroes as John Wayne and Gary Cooper, whom he had idolized in his fatherless childhood. After three years of making the rounds with a script written on speculation by a friend who was a writer, Norris found investors willing to put up $1 million to make Good Guys Wear Black (1978).

Good Guys Wear Black ushered in a number of films in which Norris portrayed a Vietnam veteran, perhaps reflecting not only America's national trauma but also a personal loss, since his younger brother Wieland had been killed in 1970 while leading his squad through Vietcong-held territory. Norris played a former commando whose unit, employed to rescue prisoners of war behind enemy lines, is betrayed by a corrupt politician. Among the astonishing feats he performed in the film was karate-kicking an enemy through the windshield of a speeding car. Although Norris says that by the fourth time he saw the film he considered it the worst movie he had ever seen in his life, Good Guys Wear Black grossed $18 million.

A Force of One (1979) featured Norris as a Vietnam Special Forces veteran who was recruited to help teach martial arts to a narcotics squad in a small town in California. In The Octagon (1980), which took its title from the name of a Central American terrorist camp, he pulverized a secret order of hooded Oriental killers. In the course of making those three martial arts epics for American Cinema, Norris's salary rose from $40,000 to $250,000, and his staff grew to 100. The three films eventually grossed more than $100 million.

In An Eye for an Eye (1981), Norris played a former San Francisco undercover cop in pursuit of drug smugglers who had killed his partner. Silent Rage (1982) crossed over into the horror genre, with Norris demolishing a superhumanly strong psychopath as well as an entire gang of bikers. In Forced Vengeance (1982), he appeared as the security chief of a casino on an island off Hong Kong who liquidates the villains attempting to take over the operation. Lone Wolf McQuade (1983) featured Norris as a Texas Ranger pitted against a black-hearted arms dealer, played by David Carradine, the former star of TV's Kung Fu. The film culminated in a karate versus kung fu confrontation, although it also featured plenty of the usual hardware in the form of guns, grenades, helicopters, bulldozers, and the like. Norris himself views *Lone Wolf McQuade* as an important transitional film, in which he crossed over the bridge from kung fu–martial arts to the action-adventure genre, starring heroes who, in his words, "fight only when they have to."

Norris's two tributes to his brother Wieland, *Missing in Action* (1984) and *Missing in Action 2: The Beginning* (1985), were produced by the Cannon Group at a time when some bigger companies were still reluctant to risk their money on Vietnam themes. In *Missing in Action*, which was filmed in the Philippines, Norris, as Colonel James Braddock, returns to Vietnam after the war to rescue remaining American prisoners of war. The top-grossing film of 1984, *Missing in Action* earned more than $6 million during the first weekend of its release. Its sequel is a flashback to Braddock's earlier captivity and escape. In *Braddock: Missing in Action 3* (1987), the colonel learns that the Vietnamese wife he left for dead during the Saigon airlift is still alive and has a son by him. When he returns for them, he also rescues several dozen mistreated Amerasian children from an orphanage.

Code of Silence (1985) called upon Norris to use shotgun, pistol, and more exotic weaponry—including an automated tank—as well as hands and feet in playing a Chicago police sergeant who invades a drug den and single-handedly wipes out an army of hoodlums. There were only two karate sequences (compared to seventeen in *Forced Vengeance*, for example), modifying his "chuck fu" image. *Code of Silence* was the first of Norris's films to win applause from such exigent critics as Vincent Canby of the *New York Times*, who called it "a first-rate action picture" that "put Mr. Norris up there with the two other big guys of Hollywood law and order—Clint Eastwood and Charles Bronson." *Code of Silence* grossed almost $11 million during its first two weekends, ranked number one on the box-office charts for a month, and made Norris a bankable actor for the first time, free to make virtually any film he chose to do.

Invasion U.S.A. (1985) was inspired by an article that Norris had read in *Reader's Digest* contending that hundreds of terrorist agents had been planted underground in the United States by henchmen of the Ayatollah Khomeini. In the film, which he co-scripted, communist mercenaries come ashore on the Florida coast in three landing craft, put on police uniforms, and slaughter the citizenry. Their nemesis is Norris, a CIA antiterrorist specialist who comes out of retirement. One scene alone, in which the terrorists attack a shopping mall, cost $5 million to film and required 350 extras. *Invasion U.S.A.* took in over $6.8 million during its first weekend and turned out to be the box-office hit of the 1985 summer season.

In *The Delta Force* (1986), Norris was given an opportunity to rewrite recent history. The script was based on the 1985 hijacking of a Trans World Airlines jet by Arab terrorists. Among the hostages were passengers who were singled out for "Jewish-sounding names" and a United States Navy serviceman, who was killed. One of the flight attendants, a German woman, interceded to save the lives of others, and the remaining hostages were eventually freed after Israel released Lebanese Shi'ite detainees. The movie, which was almost entirely filmed in Israel, boasted a stellar cast, including Lee Marvin, Martin Balsam, Shelley Winters, George Kennedy, Robert Vaughn, Susan Strasberg, Joey Bishop, Lainie Kazan, and the German actress Hanna Schygulla. But in this revisionist version, which brought to mind elements of disaster films like *Airport* and *The Poseidon Adventure* in a manner that many critics found tasteless, Chuck Norris and Lee Marvin, as members of the elite American Delta Force, rescue the hostages and kill the terrorists. "We just changed the ending, that's all," Norris told Jay Maeder of the New York *Daily News* (October 13, 1985). "If you don't do it in real life, then you do the next best thing and do it in the movies."

In 1986 Norris signed an exclusive contract with the Cannon Group to make fourteen pictures in the following seven years for $25 million. In 1987 he appeared not only in the third *Missing in Action* film but also in *Firewalker*, a departure for him in that the action-adventure elements were played largely for laughs, as in *Raiders of the Lost Ark*. For the first time, in *Hero and the Terror* (1988), Norris showed signs of physical vulnerability, by almost being beaten to death in single combat, and of emotional vulnerability, by fainting when his pregnant girlfriend goes into labor. Films on Norris's future agenda include "America's Red Army," which deals with a Middle East crisis, "Scorpio," about the crack epidemic, and "Death March."

During an interview with Chris Sheridan of the *Chicago Tribune* (August 25, 1988), Norris recalled: "When I first started, I didn't know the first thing about acting, so I was too stupid to know it was supposed to be hard." In a way, acting is for him the direct opposite of karate, a discipline in which students are taught to conceal their emotions, never revealing anger or fear to their opponents. But they are akin, he feels, in that the essence of both drama and competition is conflict. He used to rehearse a match mentally before each tournament; he now rehearses a scene first in his mind, visualizing it in advance.

Because Chuck Norris shuns anything that would impair his image as a positive role model for the young, he refuses to appear in hard-breathing sex scenes. Although most of his films are rated "R" because of their high level of violence, he argues that the characters he plays use their fighting skills only as a last resort. Questioned on that issue by an interviewer for *Parade* (December 29, 1985), he replied: "We're faced with violence every day. I'm not provoking the violence; what I'm trying to project is how to deal with it."

Chuck Norris sees himself as "a conservative, a real flagwaver, a big Ronald Reagan fan." He is an admirer of Jerry Falwell and other standard-bearers of the religious Right, an advocate of prayer in the public schools, and an archfoe of "permissiveness," which he considers pernicious "in our school system, in our family life, and, in the end, in our society as a whole." The marked increase in drug use is, he believes, a KGB-backed Communist conspiracy.

Five feet, ten inches in height, Chuck Norris weighs 170 pounds and has strawberry-blond hair and blue eyes. Since Lone Wolf McQuade, he has generally appeared bearded. To stay in top physical condition, he works out at his well-equipped home gym for three hours a day, six days a week, with a training partner. Although he eats sensibly and in moderation and avoids red meat, he admits to a weakness for chocolate malteds and for Snickers candy bars. He also indulges in iced tea with a little Grand Marnier "for a sweetener." Since 1981 he has competed successfully against other celebrity drivers in his favorite recreation, off-road racing.

After spending almost twenty years in a five-bedroom house in Rolling Hills Estates in southern California, Norris and his wife, the former Dianne Holechek, whom he married in December 1958,

have moved to a more secluded home in the Santa Ana Hills. They have a second home in the Caribbean. Norris recently bought his wife, whom he considers his best friend, an unprofitable restaurant in Newport Beach, explaining, "I'd buy her the moon if she wanted it because she stood by me through the hard years." His two sons, Mike and Eric, are actors who have appeared in his films, and his brother Aaron, formerly a stunt coordinator, directed the third Missing in Action picture and the forthcoming "Scorpio."

"You know, it's funny how things happen," Norris told Bruce Cook of the Chicago Tribune (January 29, 1988). "If I hadn't lost my schools, I wouldn't have tried acting. I thought the worst thing in the world had happened to me, but it was really a blessing in disguise. That's what my book is all about. A catastrophe is only a catastrophe if you can't make something better out of it. One door closes, and a bigger one opens. I really believe that."

References: N Y Times II p15+ My 12 '85 por, II p14 S 1 '85 por; Parade p4+ D 29 '85 pors; People 23:61+ Je 3 '85 pors; Time 125:67 My 20 '85 por; Who's Who in America, 1988–89

Nykvist, Sven (Vilhem)

(nē´ kvist)

Dec. 3, 1922- Swedish cinematographer.
Address: c/o Milton Forman, 10390 Wilshire Blvd., Suite 1709, Los Angeles, Calif. 90024

For thirty years, ever since his work on Ingmar Bergman's 1960 film The Virgin Spring, Sven Nykvist has been one of the most famous and influential cinematographers in the world. Best known for his austere use of contrast, lighting, and color on twenty-two of Bergman's most celebrated movies, Nykvist's eye and camera have also brought the films of such diverse American and European directors as Woody Allen, Paul Mazursky, Norman Jewison, Volker Schlöndorff, and André Tarkovsky to the screen.

Sven Vilhem Nykvist was born in Moheda, in southern Sweden, on December 3, 1922, the son of Gustaf Nathanael and Gerda Emilia (Nilson) Nykvist. Both of his parents were Lutheran missionaries based in the Belgian Congo, where they spent most of their adult lives. Because malaria was rampant in the Congo, the Nykvists considered it too dangerous a place in which to raise their son. Consequently, Sven spent his childhood in the care of relatives in Sweden and saw his parents only every four years, when they were permitted to come home on a leave of absence.

It was during his parents' visits that Nykvist was first introduced to the wonders of photography, by means of the slides that his father had taken of their life in Africa. "The photographs were my only

contact," he told David Denby in an interview for the New York Times (April 25, 1976), "the only way to satisfy my longing for them. I was overpowered by these images of people and animals, and I remember having endless fantasies of living with my parents there. After they would return to Africa we would mail photographs back and forth as a way of keeping together." By the time he was twelve, he had begun taking pictures with his own box camera.

Although Nykvist's parents introduced him to photography, on their return to Sweden in about 1935 they nearly deprived him of his early experience of motion pictures by strictly forbidding him to attend movies. "Like many deeply religious people, they thought children would learn bad habits—drinking, smoking, sexual promiscuity—by watching the adults on screen. Of course, what's forbidden becomes immensely powerful and I would sneak away to a theatre whenever I had the money," Nykvist has recalled.

Nykvist's own introduction to motion picture photography grew out of his interest in high jumping. At fifteen, he became interested in improving his style and technique and bought an 8-mm Keystone camera with slow-motion capability in order to photograph himself in action. "I prepared everything and asked a man to push the button," he recalled during an interview with John Curtin for the New York Times (June 12, 1983).

Because there were no film schools in Sweden, Nykvist was obliged to attend the Stockholm Municipal School for Photographers, a still-photography school, for a year. At nineteen he got a job at the Sandrew movie studio in Stockholm as a camera assistant and "focus puller"—the member of a film crew whose duty it was to move the lens as an actor or actress moved toward or away from the camera. His first assignment was the 1941 film The Poor Millionaire, directed by Sigurd Wallen and photographed by Hilding Bladh. Nykvist worked at Sandrew for two years but left the studio following the completion of the 1943 feature In the Darkest Corner of Småland, directed by Schamyl Bauman, to work at Italy's Cinecittà studio, near Rome. Despite his relative lack of experience, Nykvist found himself in demand as a result of his fluency in several languages. "There were few cinematographers who could speak German and English," he recalled, as quoted in Millimeter (July–August 1976) magazine, "and because I could, I was able to work as an interpreter as well as an assistant." Nykvist remained at Cinecittà for nine months, working under the directors Franco Vigni and Mario Soldati, among others.

Returning to Sweden in 1944, Nykvist resumed his work as a focus puller. In 1945, while he was assigned to a film entitled The Children from Frostmo Mountain, the crew's cameraman became ill, and he volunteered to take over shooting the picture. Nykvist's unexpected opportunity to break into his desired profession resulted in near disaster. "I underexposed the whole first day," he told the interviewer for Millimeter. "The scenes were done in a small cottage with small windows, and the director had said that I had too much light, and he told me to take it down. So I put blinders over all the lights, and then the next day looking at the rushes you couldn't see anything at all. I said to myself, 'This is my first and last day as a cinematographer.'"

Instead, the director, Rolf Husberg, took responsibility for the mistake and allowed Nykvist to finish the picture and to set the lighting himself. Following The Children from Frostmo Mountain, Nykvist worked on Good Morning, Bill and 13 Chairs in 1945, Salt Water Spray and Tough Old Boys in 1946, and Maj from Malo in 1947. Although unexhibited outside of Sweden, those early films provided Nykvist with invaluable experience as a photographer and taught him to avoid a common pitfall among cinematographers. "One of the problems with spending a long time as an assistant is that you learn only the techniques of the people you assist," he explained in the Millimeter interview, "but I got to learn lighting for myself. I learned by my own mistakes."

Despite his unexpectedly early start as a cinematographer, Nykvist found his work increasingly unproductive during the middle 1940s. By 1947, following Maj from Malo, he had reached a crisis point. Feeling that he was not making any progress, he decided not to work for a while. He left Svensk Filmindustri in 1947 for a long-delayed visit with his parents in the Belgian Congo. Having brought along his camera and a tape recorder, Nykvist spent four months shooting footage in the Congo. He later sold the resulting documentary, In the Footsteps of the Witch Doctor, to a distributor in the United States.

His interest in filmmaking restored, on his return to Sweden Nykvist went back to work in the studio. During the late 1940s and early 1950s, an extraordinarily productive time for him, his films included Lazy Lena and Blue-Eyed Per, Spring at Sjösala, Tall Lasse from Delsbo, and The Devil and the Man from Småland (photographed in collaboration with Carl Edlund), all in 1949, and Loffe Becomes a Policeman (1950), The Land of Rye (1951), and When Lilacs Blossom (1952). In addition to his feature films, Nykvist photographed, co-directed, and co-scripted (with Olaf Bergström) the 1952 documentary Under the Southern Cross and filmed a documentary called Reverence for Life (1952), about Dr. Albert Schweitzer's work in Africa.

The turning point in Nykvist's career came in 1953, in the form of a new film—The Naked Night (later renamed Sawdust and Tinsel)—by the celebrated stage and screen director Ingmar Bergman. Bergman and his longtime cinematographer, Gunnar Fischer, had parted company over personality conflicts, and the director's choice for his replacement, Göran Strindberg, was scheduled to go to Hollywood to study the new widescreen filming process known as CinemaScope. Nykvist was selected in Strindberg's place to photograph the interior scenes of The Naked Night, and Hilding Bladh was chosen to film the exteriors.

"Bergman was unhappy at first," Nykvist recalled in Variety (October 5, 1988), "and called me to a morning meeting where for minutes we just exchanged stares. Finally he said, 'If you don't make good shots today . . . ' (there was a good long pause), 'then we reshoot.' He was testing me to see if I was afraid of him, and then tested me again on some very tough shots. Finally he said later on in the filming: 'I think we should work a whole life together.'" Bergman's breakthrough film with British and American audiences when it was released in both countries in 1956, *The Naked Night* was the first film photographed by Nykvist to obtain wide distribution outside Scandinavia.

The early association between Nykvist and Bergman proved to be short-lived, for the director went on to use a succession of photographers before returning to Fischer. Nykvist continued working at Svensk Filmindustri, photographing *Storm over Tjurö* (1954), *Karin Mansdotter* (1954), *Salka Valka* (1954), *The True and the False* (1955), *The Last Form* (1955), and *Darling at Sea* (1955). By 1956 Nykvist was one of the busiest cinematographers working in Sweden, with six of the thirty-nine films issued that year carrying his credit as photographer. He also served as co-director (with Lars Henrik Ottoson and Loren Marmstedt) as well as cinematographer on the documentary *Gorilla*, filmed that year in the Belgian Congo. Nykvist's other projects in 1956 ranged widely, from the crime-drama *Children of the Night* to the musical *Girl in a Dressing Gown* to the rock-'n'-roll-dance film *The Brave Soldier Jonsson*. Nykvist continued with those comparatively routine, local-market assignments, including such thrillers as *Lady in Black* (1958) and such light comedies as *May I Borrow Your Wife?* (1959).

In 1959, however, Nykvist's career took a giant leap forward when he was asked by Ingmar Bergman to photograph his next film, *The Virgin Spring*. A horripilating medieval drama about rape, murder, and revenge, the film took critics around the world by storm with its stark, startling images and visual style and won the Oscar for best foreign film in 1960. Although Bergman returned to Gunnar Fischer for *The Devil's Eye* (1960), Nykvist was back for *Through a Glass Darkly* (1961), which won the Oscar for best foreign film, and the two men have worked together ever since. Ironically, although Nykvist can claim the honors for the distinctive look of each of Bergman's movies from that point on, he has taken great care to give Bergman credit for teaching him more than he thought there was to know about photography. "When I started out, I thought a cinematographer was a man who took very beautiful, well-exposed shots," Nykvist has said. "As a matter of fact, I didn't know very much about lighting when I started with Ingmar Bergman. We didn't talk much about lighting [on *The Naked Night*]. [*The Virgin Spring*] was when he got me interested in lighting."

By the time the two collaborators were working on Bergman's celebrated trilogy of *Through a Glass Darkly* (1961), *Winter Light* (1963), and *The Silence* (1963), they had begun to develop a lasting rapport. In addition to going along with Bergman's standard procedure in working with his entire crew, which involves taking crew members into isolation in the north of Sweden two months before shooting begins in order to discuss the script, Nykvist developed a special give-and-take with the director in working out the lighting of his films. "[*Winter Light* was] a very, very difficult picture," Nykvist has recalled. "It all took place between eleven and two in the evening. It was in a church in winter and there was no sun at all. There was no light coming in except from the cloudy sky, so we couldn't have any shadows at all. And we tried to make it look exactly like that. We spent almost a month in churches in the north of Sweden, where we were shooting, studying the light. We watched it every day between eleven and two. I took snapshots every fifth minute, which I put into the script. I changed my whole photographic style by starting to use reflected light. Now, when I put on direct light, it hurts in my heart."

It was through interaction such as this that Nykvist developed his unique ability to capture the psychological mood of Bergman's scripts in his lighting and composition on the screen, but, in doing so, he had to rediscover simplicity and abandon his established technique of making what he once called "beautiful shots with much backlighting, many effects, absolutely none of which was motivated by anything in the film at all." For *The Silence*, Nykvist used specially coated film stock to create the luminous, hallucinogenic effects needed in the drama about two women's sexual encounters. For Bergman's *Persona* (1966), Nykvist used similar technical tricks in the dream sequences. Both films were marked by an overall restraint new to Nykvist that has since become central to his work. Sometimes that restraint failed to work, as in the case of *All These Women* (1964), Nykvist's first color film with Bergman, which, as he put it, was shot "in the most conservative manner, according to the Kodak rule book." The two men later perfected their work with color on *The Passion of Anna* (1969), a stark drama about the relationship between a man and a woman on a remote island, in which color film stock was used under very low light to startling effect.

Throughout the 1960s Nykvist's career followed a two-tier track as he worked on his internationally famous films with Bergman while continuing to photograph movies targeted for Scandinavian audiences. Among the non-Bergman movies with which he was associated during the early 1960s were *The Judge* (1960), directed by Alf Sjöberg; *A Matter of Morals* (1960), an American-Swedish co-production directed by the veteran American filmmaker John Cromwell; *Trust Me, Darling* (1961); *The Singing Leaves* (1963); *To Love* (1964); *The Dress* (1964); and *Loving Couples* (1964), directed by the Swedish actress turned filmmaker Mai Zetterling. But from 1961 onward, Nykvist's career was inextricably linked with that of Bergman, and, apart from *Loving Couples*, none of those non-Bergman films made any major impact outside of Sweden. Nykvist's 1965 documentary, *The Vine Bridge*, which he directed as well as photographed in Africa, went unnoticed outside of his own country. By 1970, however, even his non-Bergman films were international productions, among them *First Love* (1970), *One Day in* the Life of Ivan Denisovich (1971), and *Siddhartha* (1972).

Nykvist worked with Bergman on *Hour of the Wolf* (1968), *Shame* (1968), *The Ritual* (1969), *The Passion of Anna* (1969), and *The Touch* (1971). All of them were warmly received by Bergman's international audience, though critics were decidedly more enthusiastic about the accomplished and forceful *Hour of the Wolf*, *Shame*, and *The Passion of Anna* than they were about *The Touch*, which suffered from casting and script problems.

It was with *Cries and Whispers* (1972), however, that both Bergman and Nykvist made an indelible impression upon a new generation of filmgoers. That harrowing drama, about a woman dying in agony from cancer, her sisters, and a maidservant, received several Academy Award nominations, including one for best picture. Bergman himself was nominated for best screenplay and best direction, but it was Nykvist who actually won the Oscar, for his cinematography. Nykvist reportedly regards *Cries and Whispers* as his most satisfying achievement to date. A major international success, *Cries and Whispers* gave Nykvist a following unique among cinematographers because of its extraordinary look and its virtuosic use of variations of red. "There were different shades of that color in the different rooms," he has explained. "Every room had a different color. I've told people that and they say, 'Oh, we didn't see it.' Okay, they didn't see it, but they did *feel* it. Ingmar wrote that into the script."

Although Nykvist was gratified by the new wave of recognition, at least one consequence of that success caused him some concern. In 1973 Bergman made a low-budget six-hour program for Swedish television entitled *Scenes from a Marriage*, which was shot on a forty-day schedule. Its production occurred at a time when public interest in Bergman's work in the United States had surged to an all-time high, leading the producer to decide to release *Scenes from a Marriage* as a 168-minute theatrical film. "Bergman promised me it would never be blown up to 35-mm," Nykvist later lamented. "He absolutely promised me that, and we said that this is for television so, remember, we shall always be very close with the camera."

Bergman's two features in the mid-1970s, *The Magic Flute* (1974) and *Face to Face* (1976), were produced with both Swedish television and American theatrical release in mind, forcing Nykvist to make difficult compromises that he disliked as a cinematographer, though he understood the economic benefits. When, after the completion of Bergman's *Serpent's Egg* (1977) and *Autumn Sonata* (1978), the director's career was interrupted by a protracted dispute with Swedish tax officials, Nykvist began working increasingly in Hollywood. His American screen credits included Louis Malle's *Pretty Baby*, Paul Mazursky's *Willie and Phil* (1980), Bob Rafelson's remake of *The Postman Always Rings Twice* (1981), and *Cannery Row* (1982). During that hiatus, Nykvist's only work with Bergman was on *From the Life of the Marionettes*

(1980), a German-produced feature built around two characters from *Scenes from a Marriage*. Nykvist also shared the co-directing and coproducing chores with Erland Josephson and Ingrid Thulin, two veteran performers who appeared in *Cries and Whispers* and other Bergman movies, on *One Plus One*, a drama made in 1977 but not released in the United States until 1980. In 1982 Bergman and Nykvist worked together on what the director announced would be his final feature film, the internationally acclaimed and somewhat autobiographical family drama *Fanny and Alexander*. In 1983 Nykvist received the Los Angeles Film Critics Association's Award for best cinematography for his contribution to that film.

Since *Fanny and Alexander*, Nykvist's cinematography has graced a vast range of films shot around the world, including Volker Schlöndorff's French-made *Swann in Love* (1984); André Tarkovsky's swan song, *The Sacrifice* (1986), which was filmed in Sweden; and the Hollywood production *Agnes of God* (1986). He began collaborating with Woody Allen on *Another Woman* in 1987 and has since shot Allen's portion of the omnibus film *New York Stories* and his *Crimes and Misdemeanors*, both of which were released in 1989. Nykvist was nominated for an Academy Award for his contribution to *The Unbearable Lightness of Being* (1988) and was the recipient of the Eastman Kodak Award for that film. On March 29, 1989 he received the Artistic Award from Local 659 of the International Photographers of the Motion Picture Industry for his work over a forty-five-year career.

Sven Nykvist is a tall, lean, handsome man with a grey beard and blue eyes. He lives in Stockholm when he is not shooting on location or in studios around the world. "This has to be the only business in the world," he remarked in a 1980 studio biography, "where you are paid, and well paid, to visit some of the most famous and beautiful places in the world." Apart from photography, Nykvist enjoys gardening. His favorite still photographers are Henri Cartier-Bresson and Jean-Henri Lartigue, of whom he says: "They have really caught life in their photographs. And I try to do the same thing with film." It is for Ingmar Bergman, however, that he reserves the highest praise. "Ingmar Bergman has meant more to me than almost anyone else in my whole life because of what he taught me. He got me interested in what I think is the most important thing in photography—using light to create the right mood."

References: *Filmmakers Newsletter* p28+ My '76; *Millimeter* p12+ Jl-Ag '76; *N Y Times* II p1+ Ap 25 '76, II p21+ Je 12 '83; *Screen Series-Sweden 1* (1970); *Svensk Filmografi 5* (1950–1959); *Svensk Filmografi 6* (1960–1969); *Who's Who in America*, 1988–89

Parks, Rosa

Feb. 4, 1913– Civil rights activist. Address: 305 Federal Bldg., 231 W. Lafayette, Detroit, Mich. 48226

The modern civil rights movement began with Rosa Parks's refusal to surrender her seat on a bus to a white man on December 1, 1955 in Montgomery, Alabama. Her arrest for violating the city's segregation laws was the catalyst for a mass boycott of the city's buses, whose ridership had been 70 percent black. That boycott brought Martin Luther King Jr. to national prominence as president of the Montgomery Improvement Association, a group of ministers dedicated to the spiritual and organizational leadership of the boycott. The Montgomery Improvement Association filed a federal suit challenging the constitutionality of the segregation law on February 1, 1956, and the boycott continued until December 20, 1956, when a Supreme Court order declaring Montgomery's segregated seating laws unconstitutional was served on city officials. The next day blacks returned to the integrated buses, but not without violent incidents.

Rosa Parks's continuing involvement in the American civil rights movement antedated the Montgomery, Alabama bus boycott by more than two decades. From 1943 to 1956 she was a secretary for the Montgomery branch of the National Association for the Advancement of Colored People. In 1957 she moved to Detroit, Michigan, where she worked for nonviolent social change with Martin Luther King Jr.'s Southern Christian Leadership Conference (SCLC). Mrs. Parks earned her living primarily as a seamstress until 1965, when she went to work for Congressman John Conyers Jr., Democrat from Michigan, and she has been his re-

ceptionist, secretary, and administrative assistant for twenty-five years. In 1987 she founded an institute to provide leadership and career training to black youth. Continuing to speak out on civil rights issues, she makes about twenty-five public appearances each year. In an interview with Marney Rich published verbatim in the *Chicago Tribune* (April 3, 1988), Rosa Parks said that she wants to be remembered "as a person who wanted to be free and wanted others to be free."

Rosa Parks was born Rosa Louise (or Lee) McCauley on February 4, 1913 in Tuskegee, Alabama to James McCauley, a carpenter, and Leona (Edwards) McCauley, a teacher. At the age of two she moved to her grandparents' farm in Pine Level, Alabama with her mother and her younger brother, Sylvester. At the age of eleven she enrolled in the Montgomery Industrial School for Girls, a private school founded by liberal-minded women from the northern United States. The school's philosophy of self-worth was consistent with Leona McCauley's advice to "take advantage of the opportunities, no matter how few they were."

Opportunities were few indeed. "Back then," Mrs. Parks recalled in the *Chicago Tribune* interview, "we didn't have any civil rights. It was just a matter of survival; . . . of existing from one day to the next. I remember going to sleep as a girl hearing the [Ku Klux] Klan ride at night and hearing a lynching and being afraid the house would burn down." In the same interview, she cited her lifelong acquaintance with fear as the reason for her relative fearlessness in deciding to appeal her conviction during the bus boycott. "I didn't have any special fear," she said. "It was more of a relief to know . . . that I wasn't alone. If I was going to be fearful, it would have been as far back as I can remember, not just that separate incident."

Rosa Parks's sensitivity to the injustices committed against black Americans was evident in her selection of a husband and in her work. In 1932 she married Raymond Parks, a barber who was active in black voter registration and other civil rights causes. After attending Alabama State College (now Alabama State University) in Montgomery for a time, Mrs. Parks worked for the Montgomery Voters League, the NAACP Youth Council, and other civic and religious organizations. In 1943 she was elected secretary of the Montgomery branch of the NAACP. She recalled her work with that organization during an interview with Roxanne Brown for *Ebony* (February 14, 1988): "In the early 1940s and 1950s I worked on numerous cases with the NAACP, but we did not get the publicity. There were cases of flogging, peonage, murder, and rape. We didn't seem to have too many successes. It was more a matter of trying to challenge the powers that be, and to let it be known that we did not wish to be continued as second-class citizens."

During the 1940s and 1950s, Mrs. Parks supported herself by taking in sewing at home, working as a housekeeper and as a seamstress, and, for a time, as a life insurance agent. To get to work she was forced to depend on Montgomery City Lines buses, whose patronage was 70 percent black in a city of 50,000 black citizens and 70,000 white citizens. By 1955 seating arrangements in some southern cities, as well as in the northern, eastern, and western United States, had been integrated, but a pernicious system of segregated seating arrangements persisted in Montgomery.

The first ten seats of every bus were reserved for white passengers, regardless of whether there were any white patrons on the bus, so that it was not uncommon for black women to stand over empty seats with their arms full of packages. Occasionally a black passenger would sit in the white section, either from sheer exhaustion or because the person was from out of town, and therefore ignorant of the law. When that happened, the passenger would be ordered, often in obscene language, to move. The orders would sometimes be backed by the threat of physical violence, which was carried out in some cases. If the white section was filled to capacity when white patrons boarded the bus, passengers in the black section were required to relinquish their seats to white passengers. The bus drivers, all of whom were white men, were empowered by law to enforce those practices and to use their own discretion in allocating bus seats according to race.

Thus it happened that on December 1, 1955 Rosa Parks and three other black passengers were asked to vacate an entire row of seats—the first row behind the white section (not in the white section, as is commonly believed)—so that one white man could sit down. Mrs. Parks recognized the bus driver, James F. Blake, as the same one who, in 1943, had evicted her from his bus for boarding through the front door. (Black passengers were often forced to pay their fares at the front of the bus, then get off and reenter through the rear door. Sometimes the driver would drive away before a passenger could board the bus from the rear after having paid up front.)

On December 1, when Blake asked the row of black passengers to get up, none of them moved at first. As recounted by Mrs. Parks in the Chicago Tribune interview, Blake then said, "You all make it light on yourselves and let me have those seats." All of them stood up except Mrs. Parks, who was tired from the day's work at Montgomery Fair department store, where she was employed as a seamstress. Blake asked her if she were going to stand up. "No, I'm not," she replied. When Blake threatened to call the police, she said, "You may go on and do so." Two police officers boarded the bus to arrest Mrs. Parks, who was still seated. When one of them asked her why she did not stand up, she said, "I don't think I should have to. Why do you push us around so?" He answered, "I don't know, but the law is the law, and you are under arrest."

Rosa Parks was taken to jail, booked, fingerprinted, incarcerated, and fined fourteen dollars. That day, three people arrived at the jail to obtain her release on bond: Clifford Durr, a white liberal lawyer; his wife, Virginia Durr, a white civil rights activist who had employed Mrs. Parks as a seamstress; and E. D. Nixon, the former president of the NAACP's state and local branches, for whom Mrs. Parks worked as a secretary. E. D. Nixon was also a Pullman porter, the regional director of the Brotherhood of Sleeping Car Porters, and the president of the Progressive Democratic Association of Montgomery.

Nixon and the Durrs escorted Mrs. Parks to her home. Nixon asked her if she would be willing to appeal the case, but her mother and her husband feared for her safety if she challenged the segregation law she had been charged with violating. Raymond Parks was quoted by Taylor Branch in his book Parting the Waters: America in the King Years 1954–63 (1988) as having warned, "The white folks will kill you, Rosa." But she had no fear above or beyond that with which she had always lived. According to Branch, she replied to Nixon's request with the words, "If you think it will mean something to Montgomery and do some good, I'll be happy to go along with it."

Fred Gray, one of Montgomery's two black lawyers, agreed to represent Mrs. Parks in her appeal to the state courts. On the night of her arrest, Gray informed Jo Ann Robinson, an English professor and the president of the Women's Political Council (WPC), of the incident. Among the city's sixty-eight black organizations, the WPC was the group most involved in planning the ensuing bus boycott. Just four days after the Supreme Court declared school segregation unconstitutional in Brown v. Board of Education of Topeka (May 17, 1954), the WPC had sent a letter to the mayor of Montgomery complaining about the seating practices and requesting alleviation. The letter warned the mayor to act swiftly, "for even now plans are being made to ride [the buses] less, or not at all."

Instead of improving, the conditions for black bus passengers worsened that year and the next. In 1955 two black teenage girls were arrested in separate incidents, the circumstances of which closely resembled those surrounding Rosa Parks's case. The cases of the two teenagers, Claudette Colvin and Mary Louise Smith, heightened dissatisfaction in the black community. The WPC planned a boycott of the buses and drafted instructions that were lacking only in the date the boycott would take place. Rosa Parks convened the NAACP Youth Council to plan a campaign. As it turned out, both teenagers' cases were found unsuitable for the role of catalyst in the mass action, for reasons such as lost momentum, the unwed and pregnant condition of one of the teenagers, and the futility of fighting a charge of disorderly conduct rather than one of violating the segregation laws.

When Jo Ann Robinson heard of Mrs. Parks's arrest from Fred Gray, she saw in her an ideal candidate on whose behalf to launch the boycott, for she was a highly respected member of the community. As described by Mrs. Robinson in her recently published memoir, The Montgomery Bus Boycott and the Women Who Started It, Mrs. Parks was "quiet, unassuming, and pleasant in manner and appearance; dignified and reserved; of high morals and strong character."

On Friday, December 2, Jo Ann Robinson and the WPC produced and distributed throughout Montgomery thousands of leaflets announcing that a one-day bus boycott would take place on Monday, December 5, the day of Rosa Parks's trial. Each leaflet read, in part: "Another Negro woman has been arrested and thrown in jail because she refused to get up out of her seat on the bus for a white person to sit down. . . . If we do not do something to stop these arrests, they will continue. . . . We are, therefore, asking every Negro to stay off the buses Monday in protest of the arrest and trial."

The leaflets blanketed the town, informing nearly every black congregation of the boycott, and on December 2 the congregations decided to support the boycott, even if their ministers failed to take the initiative. Becoming aware of the level of support among their congregations and deciding that their guidance would benefit the movement, the clergymen formed the Interdenominational Ministerial Alliance (IMA). The IMA met that evening at Dexter Avenue Baptist Church, where Martin Luther King Jr., then twenty-six, was pastor, and drafted their own condensed version of the WPC's leaflet. They added a call for a mass meeting on the evening of December 5 at Holt Street Baptist Church, where they planned to determine whether they should continue the boycott.

Only a few white passengers rode the buses on December 5, and virtually no black passengers were on board. Helmeted policemen on motorcycles trailed the buses, ostensibly to protect black passengers from what the police called "Negro 'goon squads.'" Historians have noted that the black citizens of Montgomery had nothing to fear from each other—there were no 'goon squads'—but much to fear from the presence of extra policemen (all of whom were white). Ironically, the police only served to scare away those blacks who might otherwise have ridden the buses that day.

The people gathered in and around the Holt Street Baptist Church that night resolved to continue the boycott until their demands for improved bus service were met. The IMA absorbed many of those present and became the Montgomery Improvement Association (MIA), which elected Martin Luther King Jr. as its president. In the following weeks of the boycott, the MIA and the WPC met repeatedly with the city commissioners (three white men) and the bus company's management to press for three objectives. In the words of Mrs. Robinson, the boycotters wanted "more courtesy from drivers, . . . that Negroes sit from rear toward the front and whites from the front toward the rear until all seats were taken, . . . [and] that Negro bus drivers be employed to operate the buses on predominantly black routes."

The city commissioners refused repeatedly to grant any of the boycotters' demands, despite the mounting monetary losses sustained by the bus company. In January 1956 the city commissioners

joined the White Citizens Council, whose membership included rabid segregationists, and that month a "get-tough" policy was adopted in a fruitless attempt to coerce black citizens into abandoning their aims. Policemen harassed carpool drivers by detaining them for inordinate lengths of time on spurious charges and by issuing tickets for miniscule or imaginary traffic violations. Blacks who walked to work risked being beaten by whites, who also threw bricks, rotten food, and urine-filled balloons from passing cars. Their hostility served only to inspire the boycotters to persevere.

Many boycotters, including Rosa Parks, lost their jobs. On January 30 King's house was bombed while he was away, and on March 22 he was convicted and fined $1,000 for violating the state anti-boycott law. Enjoined from most of its activities by a court order, the Alabama NAACP was unable to function normally for the following eight years.

Nevertheless, the boycott continued. The MIA's demands did not include full-scale integration until February 1, 1956, when Fred Gray filed a federal suit challenging segregated seating per se. According to Mrs. Robinson, Rosa Parks was not one of the plaintiffs named in the suit, but it was filed on behalf of all those affected by substandard treatment on the buses, as well as on behalf of the plaintiffs. On June 5, 1956 three federal judges voted two to one to rule bus segregation unconstitutional. The city of Montgomery appealed to the United States Supreme Court, which upheld the lower court's decision, but the buses were not officially desegregated until the order was served on city officials by United States marshals on December 20, 1956.

The boycott had lasted 382 days. When, on December 21, Rosa Parks was photographed sitting on the integrated buses for the first time, one of the drivers with whom she was photographed was James Blake, the man who had arrested her. "He didn't react at all, and neither did I," she recalled in an interview for the Montgomery *Advertiser* (February 24, 1982). Referring to the desegregation of the buses, she said, "I don't recall that I felt anything great about it. It didn't feel like a victory, actually. There still had to be a great deal to do."

The desegregation of the buses was a costly victory for all concerned. The Parks family was harassed and threatened continually over the telephone, Mrs. Parks lost her job, and her husband was unable to work after suffering a nervous breakdown. In August 1957 Rosa and Raymond Parks, by now both unemployed, moved with Leona McCauley to Detroit, Michigan, where Sylvester McCauley had rented a two-family flat for them.

Mrs. Parks's first few years in Detroit were especially difficult, according to an article by Alex Poinsett for *Jet* (July 14, 1960). She found a job supervising guest rooms at the Hampton Institute in Virginia in 1958 for $3,600 a year, but was forced to quit because she was unable to move her family from Detroit, and when she returned to Detroit with $1,300 in savings, they were quickly depleted. In July 1958 her husband was hospitalized with pneumonia, and in December 1959 she herself was hospitalized with stomach ulcers. Having lost her apartment, she moved her family into two small rooms in the meeting hall of the Progressive Civic League in Detroit, where she took in sewing while her husband worked as caretaker of the building. By 1961 she had earned enough money to move into an apartment. Meanwhile, she had been raising funds at rallies for the NAACP around the country.

Since March 1965, Rosa Parks has been working in the office of Congressman John Conyers Jr., a Democratic member of the United States House of Representatives who, since his election for the first time in 1964, has acquired a reputation in Congress as a leader in civil rights, welfare, opposition to American military involvement in Vietnam, and black voter registration drives. Mrs. Parks runs his office in Detroit, greets visitors, and sometimes gets involved in cases dealing with job guidance and cultural planning. She remains active in the NAACP, the SCLC, and the Women's Public Affairs Committee of 1000. She also serves as deaconess of St. Matthew A.M.E. church in Detroit.

For the past three decades, in speeches at conventions, churches, and official celebrations, Rosa Parks has tried to make her fellow Americans, especially young people, aware of the history of civil rights in the United States. Her services are especially in demand during the anniversaries of civil rights actions that are celebrated in December, the observance of Martin Luther King Jr.'s birthday in January, and the events of Black History Month, in February. In 1987 she founded the Rosa and Raymond Parks Institute for Self-Development, established to offer guidance to black youth in preparation for leadership and choice of careers. In 1988 she gave speeches around the country in celebration of her seventy-fifth birthday, the 125th anniversary of the Emancipation Proclamation, and the twenty-fifth anniversary of the March on Washington. On June 30, 1989 she attended a White House celebration of the twenty-fifth anniversary of the Civil Rights Act, at which President George Bush, in speaking of her momentous refusal to give up her bus seat, mistakenly referred to the town in which the act took place as Birmingham, not Montgomery. After the ceremony, which took place in the wake of several recent Supreme Court decisions that were inimical to civil rights progress, Mrs. Parks told reporters, "We need stronger, better leadership. Instead of having better ceremonies we need better programs."

Among Rosa Parks's awards are the NAACP's Spingarn Medal (1979), the Martin Luther King Jr. Award (1980), Ebony's thirty-fifth Service Award (1980), the Martin Luther King Jr. Nonviolent Peace Prize (1980), and the Martin Luther King Jr. Leadership Award (1987). She holds an honorary degree from Shaw College, and she had a street named after her in Detroit in 1969. In recognition of her service, the SCLC has annually sponsored the Rosa Parks Freedom Award since 1963, and since 1979 the Virginia-based Women in Community Service has sponsored its own Rosa Parks Award.

During her interview for the Chicago Tribune, Rosa Parks articulated her creed: "I do the very best I can to look upon life with optimism and hope and looking forward to a better day, but I don't think there is anything such as complete happiness. It pains me that there is still a lot of Klan activity and racism. . . . I think when you say you're happy, you have everything that you need and everything that you want, and nothing more to wish for. I haven't reached that stage yet."

Rosa Parks's silver hair frames a pleasant face, and when she is recognized on the street or in her office in Detroit, observers are struck by her youthfulness. Although her husband died in 1977, and her brother and mother died within a few years after that, she has thirteen nieces and nephews to keep her from feeling lonely. In March 1988 she had a pacemaker installed to regulate an irregular heartbeat, and in February 1989 she was briefly hospitalized for chest pains. Her most recent recognition was bestowed on her in 1989 by the Neville Brothers, who wrote a song called "Sister Rosa" for their album Yellow Moon. Its reggae chorus is "Thank you, Miss Rosa/You are the spark/You started our freedom movement."

References: Chicago Tribune VI p3 Ap 13 '88 pors; Ebony 26:180+ Ag '71 pors, 32:54+ S '77 por, 43:68+ F '88 pors; Sepia p23+ Je '74 pors; Branch, Taylor. Parting the Waters: America in the King Years 1954–63 (1988); Famous American Women (1980); Giddings, Paula. When and Where I Enter: The Impact of Black Women on Race and Sex in America (1984); In Black and White (1985); Negro Almanac (1976); Robinson, Jo Ann Gibson. The Montgomery Bus Boycott and the Women Who Started It (1987); Who's Who among Black Americans, 1988

Pendleton, Moses

Mar. 28, 1949– Choreographer; dancer. Address: c/o Momix, Box 35, Washington, Conn. 06793

Although he has virtually no formal training in the art, Moses Pendleton has been a creative force in the development of modern dance for nearly two decades. The cofounder of the Pilobolus Dance Theatre and, later, the founder of Momix, he used a startling blend of acrobatics, surrealistic humor, and performance art to create unique works whose daring physicality stretched the boundaries of contemporary choreography. Although collective choreography and a communal spirit were central to the creation and evolution of Pilobolus and, to a lesser degree, of Momix, Pendleton himself is emphatically an individualist, drawing from both the New England tradition of independence and the dadaist practice of thumbing one's nose at conventional standards of aesthetics.

Moses Pendleton

Moses Robert Andrew Pendleton was born at St. Johnsbury, Vermont on March 28, 1949, one of the six children of Nelson Augustus and Mary Elizabeth (Patchel) Pendleton. (He adopted the name Moses in honor of his revered paternal grandfather, a prominent businessman who was the president of the American Woolen Company.) Reared on a dairy farm, he encountered tragedy early in his life. His father, who had been severely burned in a fire, committed suicide when Moses was twelve; his mother suffered a nervous breakdown and died of cancer when he was eighteen. "I watched cows die and I watched my father die and I watched my mother die and I watched life go on," Pendleton told an interviewer for *People* (July 20, 1981). "Shocks make you what you are." According to Phil Holland, a longtime friend quoted in the same *People* profile, the energy and wit of Pendleton's creations grew out of his family's misfortunes. "He definitely made a choice to be positive and cheer people up," Holland said.

Following his graduation from high school, Moses Pendleton enrolled at Dartmouth College in Hanover, New Hampshire, mainly because he hoped to be selected for the United States Olympic Nordic ski team, whose coach was a faculty member at Dartmouth. While he was a student there, he became a champion cross-country skiier, but he was forced to abandon his dream of competing in the Olympics when he broke his leg. As part of his rehabilitation, he began taking a modern dance class taught by Alison Chase. Assigned to create an original dance piece, Pendleton collaborated with two other young athletes, Jonathan Wolken and Steve Johnson, on an eleven-minute gymnastic work called *Pilobolus*, after a light-sensitive fungus commonly found in barns that, in Pendleton's

words, "explodes with unearthly energy." In describing the piece to Anna Kisselgoff in a conversation for the *New York Times* (March 5, 1976), Pendleton explained that the central image—individual dancers "trying to break out of a cluster and then being thrown back into a glob"—was representative of what was "almost a nostalgic college-days feeling of togetherness."

The choreographer Murray Louis saw *Pilobolus* performed at a college dance festival and was sufficiently impressed to invite the three young men to put on the work at the Space in New York City, where he and fellow choreographer Alwin Nikolais rehearsed their own companies. Anna Kisselgoff, the *New York Times*'s dance critic, attended that performance and wrote a favorable review that brought the group to the attention of the dance world. Upon receiving his B.A. degree in English from Dartmouth in 1971, Pendleton joined forces with Wolken and two new recruits, Lee Harris and Robby Barnett, to form a professional troupe, which they named the Pilobolus Dance Theatre. With the encouragement of Louis and Nikolais and Pendleton's enthusiastic promotion, the fledgling dance company was an instant success on the college circuit and at avant-garde festivals. "We had the kind of sensational impact of a rock group—way beyond the dance world," Pendleton recalled years later, as quoted in the *New York Times* (December 11, 1988).

Because they had little formal dance training, the four young men drew on their athletic backgrounds to create acrobatic group designs, such as *Ocellus* (1972) and *Anendrom* (1972). "We'd make interesting shapes and forms because we didn't know how to make arabesques and pirouettes," Pendleton told the interviewer for *People* magazine. As Deborah Jowitt observed in her book *Time and the Dancing Image* (1988), the "image of male bonding" underlay virtually all of Pilobolus's early works. That image was perhaps never clearer, Miss Jowitt wrote, than in Ed Emshwiller's 1973 film *Pilobolus and Joan*, in which Pendleton, Wolken, Barnett, and Harris took on the role of an insect who is trying to make its way in the human world: "Linked, feet on each other's shoulders, they walk down the street like a large pink caterpillar. . . . Tiered, they explore a potter's studio. Sitting on one another's laps, they read a newspaper. Stacked on top of each other, they sleep beside their human sweetheart, folk singer Joan McDermott. Emshwiller's dazzling camera effects turn their dances into the splitting and rejoining of a single organism, into a slow-motion, erotic blossoming of flesh."

In 1973 Alison Chase, the group's teacher, and Martha Clarke, a former member of Anna Sokolow's modern dance company, joined Pilobolus, and Lee Harris, who had objected to the addition of women, left. He was succeeded by Michael Tracy. At first, the presence of the two women seemed to have little impact on the group's repertoire or style. In *Ciona* (1973), for example, they simply became, in Deborah Jowitt's words, "lighter-weight components of Pilobolus's mandalas, whirligigs,

[and] interlocking structures." But gradually the nature of the group's creations changed. Pendleton described the transformation in terms of *Monkshood's Farewell* (1974), a collaborative effort drawn from medieval imagery. "Until *Monkshood's*, we tended to put things together from an abstract point of view, even though the works had always had a basic theatricality," he explained, as quoted in Robert Coe's *Dance in America* (1984). "But this was the first time that we began to organize the material with a dramatic logic."

Untitled (1975), the group's most popular early work, featured Alison Chase and Martha Clarke as nine-foot-tall Victorian women, whose billowing skirts conceal two naked men. This *"fin-de-siècle* Freudian nightmare," as Deborah Jowitt described it, was included, along with *Monkshood's Farewell*, in the mixed bill Pilobolus presented during its successful weekend engagement at the Brooklyn Academy of Music in March 1976. Clive Barnes, who reviewed the company's performances for the *New York Times* (March 14, 1976), was especially taken by *Untitled*. "The images of the dance are quite unusual in their dramatic implications—their suggestion, for example, of the masculinity inherent in women and the customary male fear of it," he wrote. "But the work is also unusual in its choreographic texture, its blend of naturalistic movement, mime, dance, and downright gimmickry." Both *Untitled* and *Monkshood's Farewell* were featured in a *Dance in America* program devoted to the Pilobolus Dance Theatre, which was first broadcast on PBS on May 4, 1977.

Monkshood's Farewell and, to a lesser extent, *Untitled* were choreographed collectively by the six members of Pilobolus at their communal farm near Norwich, Vermont. "From the beginning, we aligned the work and the lifestyle," Pendleton explained to Anna Kisselgoff in the interview for the March 5, 1976 *New York Times* article about the troupe. In his view, the togetherness was responsible for the company's energy and innovative ideas. "It freed us to experiment," he told Miss Kisselgoff. "You know, it's the same when a kid won't break a window by himself, but he will do it if he's with others." Among the other works created by Pendleton and his colleagues during that period were the duet *Alraune* (1975), *Lost in Fauna* (1976), *Shizen* (1977), a sensuous pas de deux for Pendleton and Alison Chase set to Japanese flute music, and *The Eve of Samhain* (1977), in which, for the first time, each dancer played a specific, individualized character. In the last-named work, which tells the story of an archeologist who is visited by an assortment of mythological figures on Halloween, Pendleton took the part of a jabbering, blind soothsayer.

Intrigued by Pilobolus's unique inventions, the French fashion designer Pierre Cardin provided financial assistance to the group for three years in the mid-1970s and helped fund its tours of Europe and South America as well as its Broadway debut, at the St. James Theatre in 1977. In his review for the *New York Times* (September 11, 1977), Clive

Barnes attributed the success of Pilobolus's four-week, nearly sold-out engagement at the St. James to the troupe's "actual, unmistakable, almost incredible, newness." The reason for this, he continued, was that the members of Pilobolus "were never really taught, and they're not really dancers." They seldom used music, he explained, and the relation between movement and any accompanying sounds was often "tenuous to the point of the arbitrary." Moreover, kinetics and balance were never realized in dance terms. "When someone is lifted he or she is lifted as a dead weight," Barnes wrote. "There is no assisting jump as there almost always is in dance—again, there's no real continuum of movement with Pilobolus, no continuity. Dance phrases are not so much fragmented as dislocated, there's no natural flow of the movement, merely an exploratory use of the possibilities of the body."

Success brought Pilobolus international fame, but with it came increased internal stress. The emphasis on group choreography and communal living exacted a commitment that conflicted with individual needs, and the extensive touring posed problems for those who desired a home and family. Martha Clarke left the company in 1979, and, soon afterwards, four other members, although they remained with the group, stopped performing. In 1981 the troupe moved to Washington, Connecticut to be closer to the New York dance scene and yet far enough away to maintain its independence. The company also hired professionals to manage its business affairs. Perhaps most important, the group began to emphasize individualism in choreography and in performance. "Some of us are now interested in pursuing theatrical ideas that won't necessarily require us to be carrying two or three hundred pounds on our backs and doing the multilimbed Pilobolus movements people expect to see," Pendleton told Debra Cash in an interview for *Dial* (October 1981) magazine.

Over the next few years, Pendleton choreographed several works for Pilobolus, including *Day Two* (1981), *Stabat Mater* (1985), and *Carmina Burana Side II* (1985). A re-creation of an actual episode in the company's history, *Day Two* recalls a hot, humid summer day on which the dancers, frustrated and exhausted after toiling for hours on a new piece, rushed gratefully out of their stuffy studio into a thunderstorm, leaping and shouting and rolling in the wet grass. The piece ends with the dancers flinging themselves across the stage in a series of astounding body slides through puddles of water. "The slides are a completely unnecessary folly, yet the minute they start we know how exactly right they are," Arlene Croce observed in her review of a performance of *Day Two* for the *New Yorker* (November 30, 1981). In her view, the work mingled "beauty and absurdity in the intensest degrees, so that we are constantly caught between laughter and pain. . . . Without being a ballet company, without claiming much in the way of a legitimate dance style, Pilobolus does something quite similar: it gives us the logic of fantasy."

In 1985 Pilobolus opened at the Joyce Theater in Manhattan for its first full New York season in three years. After seeing the company's opening-night program, Anna Kisselgoff remarked, in her review for the *New York Times* (February 7, 1985): "Pilobolus has gone adult on us. It was better as a child." She concluded that, in attaining a more polished professional technique, the troupe had lost the communal spirit that had distinguished its earlier efforts. Miss Kisselgoff particularly disliked the group's new dance-drama *Maria La Baja*, which she dismissed as "pretentious," but she found much to admire in Pendleton's *Bonsai* (1979), a "variation on a centaur theme" that he had originally created for the Five by Two Plus Company, and in his "irreverently charming" *Stabat Mater*, in which a nun's prayer for a male figure is answered when a cathedral arch comes to life.

In a subsequent season at the Joyce, Pendleton's theatre piece *Carmina Burana Side II* was hailed by Clive Barnes as "a major breakthrough" for the choreographer and for Pilobolus. "This must be the most exciting work, dramatically and choreographically, that Pilobolus has ever staged," he wrote in *Dance and Dancers* (March–April 1987). "What Pendleton has done is to theatricalize the piece into an unearthly dance of death" reminiscent of the feverishly imaginative paintings of Hieronymous Bosch. Pendleton's most recent work for Pilobolus is *Debut C*, which was given its premiere at the Joyce Theatre in December 1988. Set to music by Debussy, the piece was described by Jennifer Dunning, writing in the *New York Times* (December 17, 1988), as "a typically Pilobolian exploration of play and shape," but, in her view, it wavered "between kitsch and dance of a straightforward, even heroic mold." Miss Dunning saw in the work "irritating" references to other sources, such as Nijinsky's *Afternoon of a Faun* and Thomas Eakins's paintings of bathers, that seemed to have "little apparent function in the dance." Although she admired *Debut C*'s "very beautiful visual imagery," she felt that it was nonetheless "a thing of parts."

Although Pendleton has remained closely involved with Pilobolus as one of its five artistic directors (the others are Jonathan Wolken, Robby Barnett, Alison Chase, and Michael Tracy), he has also energetically pursued other artistic endeavors, perhaps most notably as the director of Momix, the innovative dance company that he founded in 1980. Momix takes its name from a brand of cattle feed. "I almost thought of calling it Meow Mix," Pendleton told Janice Berman of *Newsday* (December 27, 1986). "It's a brand of surrealism we're trying to sell. We're mixing one element that you wouldn't think would mix with another, and giving it a try, and putting our heart and soul into it."

Having originated as a solo dance that Pendleton performed as part of the closing ceremonies of the 1980 Winter Olympics in Lake Placid, New York, Momix, unlike Pilobolus, has emphasized solo performance from its beginning. Initially comprising just two dancers, Alison Chase and Pendleton, the company gradually expanded to include

about a dozen performers. Drawing on the constantly shifting images of film and television, Pendleton has created for Momix a variety of short, fast-paced pieces that depend heavily on props, lighting, and costumes for their effect. *Skiva*, for example, is a duet for a pair of dancers on skis, and *Venus Envy* features two dancers encased in a giant oyster shell. In *Brainwaving*, as Deborah Jowitt pointed out in *Time and the Dancing Image*, "there isn't a dancer in sight. Standing loops travel along a white rope stretched across the stage. . . . Yet you know that only the nuances of timing and effort of two invisible dancers could bring such an effect to life."

To Marilyn Hunt, who commented on a Momix performance at Montclair (New Jersey) State College for *Dancemagazine* (April 1986), the "trappings" seemed "too often Momix's end rather than its means." Other reviewers, however, delighted in the company's imaginative use of props and lighting. When Momix first appeared in London, as part of the International Mime Festival at the Sadler's Wells Theatre in February 1988, Mary Clarke, the *Guardian*'s influential dance critic, enthusiastically applauded the troupe in her review of February 21, 1988, calling it "brilliantly clever and enormously entertaining" as well as "very highly skilled." Momix has been featured on several television specials in Europe, and it performed in David Byrne's film *True Stories* (1986) and in Prince's music video *Batman* (1989).

Since the late 1970s Pendleton has also been commissioned to perform and/or choreograph works for a number of international ballet and opera companies. Among the dances he created are *Intégrale Erik Satie*, for the Paris Opera Ballet in 1979; a revival of Picabia's dadaist ballet *Relâche*, for the Joffrey Ballet in 1980; and *Pulcinella*, for the Ballet National de Nancy in 1985. He also created the dance sequences for La Scala Opera's 1981 production of Mussorgsky's *Khovanshchina* and the Grand Théâtre de Genève's staging of *Parsifal* in 1982. In 1987 Pendleton choreographed a new version of Rameau's *ballet bouffe Platée* for the Spoleto Festival U.S.A., and the following year he mounted a revival of Jean Cocteau's *Les Mariés de la Tour Eiffel* for the inauguration of the Alliance Française's Florence Gould Hall in New York City.

In 1982 Pendleton was the subject of the documentary *Moses Pendleton Presents Moses Pendleton*, which was made for the ARTS cable television service and first broadcast on October 11, 1982. Shot on location at the choreographer's gabled, white Victorian house in Washington, Connecticut on his thirty-second birthday, the film is "a portrait of an artist coming to terms with his demons, channeling the life force into dance," Amanda Smith observed in *Dancemagazine* (January 1985). "It is a work about dance as a life-sustaining activity, and it implies that dance is a metaphor for life itself." The documentary won the CINE Golden Eagle Award from the Council on International Non-Theatrical Events in 1983.

Moses Pendleton has been an instructor of choreography and an artist in residence at various colleges and universities throughout the United States. His numerous honors include the Scotsman Award, for his performance at the Edinburgh Fringe Festival in 1973; a 1975 Berlin Critics' Prize, for his work with Pilobolus; a National Endowment for the Arts grant, in 1975; and a Guggenheim Fellowship in choreography, in 1977. Although he still enjoys performing, Pendleton dislikes touring, preferring to stay at home with his daughter, Quinn Elizabeth, and his wife, Cynthia Quinn, a Momix dancer. His daughter often appears with Momix.

"She's my dance partner," he told Janice Berman. "I do temple dancing with her. I experience the world vicariously through her eyes as she floats like an astronaut through the house." In recent years, Pendleton has increasingly devoted his spare time to photography, with his camera most frequently focused on his daughter. In February 1987 he exhibited a selection of his photographs at a gallery in Milford, Connecticut.

References: N Y Newsday II p5 D 27 '88 por; N Y Times C p24 Ja 2 '87 por; People 11:71 Jl 20 '81 por; Who's Who in America, 1989–90

Pinnock, Trevor

Dec. 16, 1946– British conductor; musician.
Address: c/o Basil Douglas Artists' Management, 8 St. George's Terrace, London NW1 8XJ England

"I feel much of the mystery attached to baroque music should be taken away," the harpsichordist and conductor Trevor Pinnock has said, and he has accomplished that aim with his historically accurate yet vibrant performances of baroque music, both as an acclaimed soloist and as the conductor of the English Concert, one of Great Britain's leading baroque ensembles, which Pinnock founded in 1973. That group's performances, on original instruments, are painstakingly researched, but the result is anything but stilted. "Something of the new-minted, carelessly thrown off (although not at all carelessly prepared), faintly improvisatory air

of a first performance in a seventeenth-century music room comes through these present-day recitals of the English Concert," a critic observed in 1973. "And it entirely takes off the cobwebs—as Trevor Pinnock intends."

Pinnock's seven solo albums and forty-five recordings of the works of Bach, Vivaldi, and Handel with the English Concert—all on the Archiv label—have generated mostly rave reviews, and the English Concert's recording of Vivaldi's Four Seasons has been hailed as the definitive version, with one reviewer exclaiming, "Few will be able to resist the exuberance of this one." About his recordings, Pinnock has commented, "We try to create in the recording studio the intimate and relaxed atmosphere of our public concerts, as far as possible." Pinnock's latest venture is the Classical Band, a forty- to fifty-member original-instrument orchestra that concentrates on the music of Mozart, Haydn, and Beethoven. "We're fascinated by the colors of the old instruments' sounds," Pinnock said in a 1984 interview, "and we find that we can exploit the instruments to their fullest potential in the music that was written for them."

Trevor David Pinnock was born on December 16, 1946 in Canterbury, Kent, England to Kenneth Alfred Thomas and Joyce Edith (Muggleton) Pinnock. His father was a book publisher. Pinnock was the second of four children, two boys and two girls. His interest in music surfaced early, and he became a chorister at Canterbury Cathedral when he was just seven years old. "It was a tremendous musical training," he recalled in an interview with Allan Kozinn for Ovation (October 1984). "As a chorister at Canterbury Cathedral, one has the discipline of an adult professional musician. We felt we were in a very privileged position—as if we were the most important people there."

At about the same time, Pinnock took up the piano, but he eventually turned to the organ because of his work with the cathedral choir. He attended the Wincheap County Primary School in Canterbury from 1951 to 1954, the Canterbury Cathedral Choir School from 1954 to 1960, and Sir Roger Manwood's Grammar School in Sandwich, Kent from 1960 to 1961. By the time he was fourteen, Pinnock had found part-time employment as a church organist, and he distinguished himself on that instrument at the Simon Langton Grammar School in Canterbury, which he attended from 1960 to 1965. Even then, he had reservations about a career as an organist. "I had too much of a performer's temperament," Pinnock told Kozinn, "which is not exactly the most suitable thing if one is doing a church job. So, I wasn't completely happy."

It was at the age of fourteen that Pinnock began to study the harpsichord. At nineteen, he qualified for a foundation scholarship as an organ student at the Royal College of Music, but he continued to cultivate his interest in the harpsichord and founded, in 1966, his first early-music group, the Galliard Harpsichord Trio, with Anthony Pleeth on the cello, Stephen Preston playing the flute, and himself on the harpsichord. In 1967 Pinnock informed his teachers and the administrators at the Royal College of Music that he intended to concentrate on the harpsichord. "They said, 'Oh, you can't possibly make a living as a harpsichordist. You should become a cathedral organist and play harpsichord on the side,'" he explained to Kozinn. Pinnock's insistence resulted in the loss of his scholarship, but he nonetheless spent his final year at the college studying the harpsichord under the tutelage of Millicent Silver, among other teachers.

The Galliard Harpsichord Trio played only a limited number of engagements during its career, from 1966 to 1972. "In truth," Pinnock later admitted to Kozinn, "there *wasn't* much going on in the way of harpsichord concerts then: The Galliard trio would play a London concert, and there would be two or three other groups who might give one or two London concerts a year." Like other baroque chamber ensembles of that period, such as the Boyd Neel Orchestra and the Academy of St. Martin in the Fields, the Galliard trio played modern instruments. Their engagements in 1968 included a broadcast performance on the BBC's Third Programme during June and concerts at the Painswick Music Society, Wells Cathedral, Fenton House, and the Purcell Room, one of London's premier recital halls. In his review for *Musical Opinion* (June 1968) of the group's performance of Rameau's Concert no. 5 in D Minor, Vivaldi's Sonata no. 5 in E Minor, and Handel's Flute Sonata in E Minor at the Painswick Music Society, E. M. Webster called the trio "exceptionally talented, deeply involved in the music of its choice—and yet possessed of a remarkable sense of style." About Pinnock's performance on the harpsichord, Webster noted that he "plays Scarlatti with wit and delicacy, but can equally produce a serious, quiet gravity for Handel and Vivaldi when required. His musicianship is impeccable, and his technique cheerfully effortless."

By the early 1970s the group had become one of the more successful period-music ensembles then in existence, and Pinnock had gained recognition as a leading specialist in his field. In 1971 he was commissioned to coach Glenda Jackson in playing the virginal, a small spinet popular in the sixteenth and seventeenth centuries, for her portrayal of Queen Elizabeth I in the BBC series *Elizabeth R,* which was shown in the United States on PBS's *Masterpiece Theatre* during its 1971–72 season. Pinnock also ghosted the music for Miss Jackson in one installment of the series.

Despite their success, which included a residency at the Purcell Room, the Galliard trio had to deal with the frustrations of a limited repertoire and a dependence on modern instruments. "The more we learned about historical style," Pinnock explained to Kozinn in a *New York Times* (January 30, 1983) interview, "the less willing we were to accept the compromises necessary to make the music effective on modern instruments." When Preston began playing the baroque flute, the group disbanded in 1972.

By early 1973, however, Pinnock, Pleeth, and Preston were back together as the nucleus of the English Concert, a larger ensemble that also included four string players, among them the concertmaster Simon Standage. Reflecting the new group's more fluid makeup, the English Concert brought in such guest soloists as Jordi Savall, the Swiss viola da gamba virtuoso, and the baroque violinist Levon Chilingirian. Unlike the Galliard trio, the English Concert used either original baroque-era instruments or modern replicas, allowing for the re-creation of authentic style and sound. Pinnock was able to secure the loan of original harpsichords from the Victoria and Albert Museum for recitals and recordings, among them a Kirkman harpsichord restored by Derek Adlam of Kent. His own instrument was a modern copy of a 1745 Dulcken, Antwerp instrument by Clayson and Garrett.

The English Concert made its debut on May 4, 1973 at the Purcell Room as part of the English Bach Festival, with a program that included Bach's Triple Concerto in A Minor, BWV 1044, sonatas by Rosenmüller, and Quantz's Flute Concerto in D Major. Commenting in the British publication *Musical Times* (June 1973), Howard Mayer Brown applauded the "exhilarating vitality and energy which so enlivened" the group's performance. "Much of this success," he continued, "can be attributed to the director of the group, Trevor Pinnock, who led from the harpsichord, and whose subtle and commanding sense of rhythm kept the pace lively and the motion moving forward." Brown was less impressed by the English Concert's earlier performance, on April 27, of Bach's *Goldberg* Variations. On that occasion, he noted a general lack of "poise and maturity" but found that Pinnock had again "proved himself a sensitive and intelligent musician."

Shortly thereafter, Pinnock, playing three harpsichords from the Victoria and Albert Museum, including the virginals of Elizabeth I, made his debut recording, for the British CRD label. In November 1973 he gave a major recital at the Horniman Museum, in which he performed on eight different harpsichords. About Pinnock's technique, the critic for *Music and Musicians* (December 1973) observed, "He seems able to produce almost any mood and gradation of tone from surprisingly cantabile lyricism to crystal brilliance." In playing the period instruments, the reviewer continued, Pinnock "customarily uses the early style of fingering (mostly without the thumb) which he finds adds a certain crispness of articulation to the more rapid passages."

By the end of 1973 the English Concert had secured a series of recitals in museums and historic houses in Britain through the National Trust, as well as tours of Spain and the United States. The group's ambitious plans for those concerts included performing unpublished and recently rediscovered works, such as the Buonamente Sinfonia, which the ensemble played in a November 1973 recital, and seventeenth-century Italian string music. Within months, the English Concert had earned the designation "well-established" from Robert Maycock of *Music and Musicians* (February 1974). "Time and again in the English Concert's programs one discovers the real meaning of passages that sound surprisingly coarse on modern instruments," Maycock wrote of their December 5, 1973 concert at Queen Elizabeth Hall, during which portions of Bach's Fourth *Brandenburg* Concerto and Double Violin Concerto were performed. The group was soon appointed baroque ensemble in residence at the Victoria and Albert Museum, and Pinnock's career as a solo harpsichordist flourished as well. His second album, of Rameau harpsichord sonatas, was released on the CRD label early in 1975 to critical applause, the reviewer for *Gramophone* (February 1975) magazine praising especially his "splendid technique" and "thoroughly musical sense of rubato." Another selection of Rameau's works was issued in May 1976. On the recital circuit, too, Pinnock continued to attract appreciative audiences. His interpretation of Bach's *Goldberg* Variations, played on a modern copy of a 1745 Dulcken harpsichord at the Purcell Room on February 17, 1976, was enthusiastically received by laymen and critics alike. Quibbling only with "a few small fluffs and an occasional non-matching of ornaments in canonic parts," the reviewer for *Music and Musicians* (May 1976) found that "Pinnock emerged very creditably from what is a gruelling test even for more mature players."

Signed to the CRD label early in 1975, the English Concert soon cut its debut recording, of harpsichord concertos by C. P. E. Bach and a Mozart adaptation of J. C. Bach harpsichord sonatas. "The performances themselves are stylish and efficient," Stanley Sadie wrote in *Gramophone* (June 1975). "Trevor Pinnock's fingerwork is always neat and crisp in the ornamental writing and passage work." The following year, CRD released the English Concert's recording of Vivaldi's *Four Seasons*, which has since been acclaimed as "the finest recorded performance [of that work] that has ever been made" by a reviewer for the *American Record Guide* (September 1979). Stoddard Lincoln, writing in *Stereo Review* (January 1977), was equally enchanted: "Conductor Trevor Pinnock

has turned in . . . a superb account from every point of view. . . . Not only are they [the English Concert] technically perfect, but they bring out the full *expressive* capability of their instruments as well. They are aided in this by Mr. Pinnock's carefully wrought interpretation: the conductor scrupulously observes all of Vivaldi's original dynamic markings, but he is not afraid to use effective crescendos and diminuendos (as well as the traditionally accepted terrace dynamics of the period) where a more modern sensibility indicates."

The Four Seasons proved to be Pinnock's and the English Concert's breakthrough record, selling extremely well in both England and the United States, where it was imported first by HNH Records and, later, by Qualiton Imports, which still carries the title as a compact disc. The recording was also subsequently licensed by Vanguard Records in America, which issued it in 1979. The latter release established Pinnock and the English Concert in the United States, appearing as it did at a time when fascination with baroque music on authentic period instruments had spread to mainstream classical listeners.

Pinnock's success on the tiny CRD label brought him to the attention of Deutsche Grammophon, and in 1978 he and the English Concert signed an exclusive recording contract with DG's early-music label, Archiv, which specializes in recording period music on authentic instruments. Among the group's first recordings for Archiv was Bach's Concerto in A Minor for flute, violin, and harpsichord. Released in May 1979, the record received a Dutch Edison Award. In 1979 and 1980 the English Concert recorded the Bach Orchestral Suites nos. 1 through 4, which Scott Cantrell, writing in *High Fidelity* (November 1979), praised for the "buoyancy of the phrasing and articulation." "The playing is both impeccable and marvelously effortless, and the interpretations are as rich in elegant detail as they are secure in broader stylistic properties," Cantrell further observed.

In 1980 Pinnock's and the group's fortunes blossomed with the release of a recital disc of English baroque music, which won a Dutch Edison Award, and a recording of symphonies by C. P. E. Bach, which received both a British Gramophone Record Award and the Deutscher Schallplattenpreis. Pinnock's solo harpsichord recordings during those first years at Archiv included Bach's *Goldberg* Variations and Toccatas in C Minor, D Minor, E Minor, G Minor, and G Major. Stoddard Lincoln, writing in *Stereo Review* (July 1981) about Pinnock's recording of the *Goldberg* Variations on a 1646 Andreas Ruckers harpsichord, noted that "virtuoso technique, fine musicianship, and a sense of projection are all characteristics of his playing." Commenting on the toccatas, a reviewer for the *American Record Guide* (September 1979) observed: "Pinnock understands what a Bach toccata is all about. In the strict fugal sections he is precise without ever being dull or less than vibrant." Pinnock also recorded Padre Antonio Soler's sonatas for two keyboards, with Kenneth Gilbert. Much of

Pinnock's work between 1981 and 1985, like that of the English Concert, was devoted to recording for Archiv all of the orchestral music by Bach and Handel, in time for the 1985 tercentenary celebrations of both composers.

A new digital recording of Vivaldi's *Four Seasons*, issued in 1983, became the fourth-best-selling classical release that year, as well as the top-selling compact disc in the Deutsche Grammophon catalogue. In his critique for *High Fidelity* (May 1984), Allan Kozinn described that performance, based on manuscripts at the Henry Watson Music and Arts Library in Manchester that are believed to predate the 1725 version, as "the finest recording of the *Seasons* I've heard." "Beyond the surface brilliance of the performance, though, a considerable part of this disc's appeal lies in the carefully thought-out and sometimes chancy performance decisions Pinnock and company have made," Kozinn observed. During 1983 and 1984 the English Concert gave the first twentieth-century performance of Rameau's opera *Acante et Cephise* as well as a televised performance of Handel's *Music for the Royal Fireworks*.

Making his solo recital debut in the United States on January 31, 1983, at the Metropolitan Museum of Art in New York City, Pinnock played Bach's Partita in D, Handel's "Harmonious Blacksmith" Suite, six Bach preludes, and Scarlatti's Sonata in D. That solo performance was followed by an American tour with an eight-player version of the English Concert, which included a stop at the Metropolitan Museum of Art on May 6, 1983. In his review of that concert for the *New York Times* (May 8, 1983), Bernard Holland remarked, "Accuracy of intonation and technical control were quickly taken for granted—which is not always the case at concerts with original instruments." A second tour of the United States followed in 1984, with eleven performances in New York, Los Angeles, and Boston, among other cities, and in the spring of 1985 the English Concert became the first British baroque ensemble to visit Japan. Pinnock's additional engagements in the United States include acting as artistic adviser to the Boston Early Music Festival Orchestra and as guest conductor of the Detroit Symphony, the San Francisco Symphony, the Boston Symphony, and the St. Paul Chamber Orchestra, and at the Mostly Mozart, Tanglewood, and Pepsico Summerfare festivals.

Pinnock made his conducting debut in the United States in July 1984, as a guest conductor at the Grant Park Festival in Chicago, Illinois. His sensitive treatment of Mozart's First Flute Concerto earned him the admiration of the *Chicago Tribune*'s Alan G. Artner, who pronounced him a "first-rate stylist." When Pinnock appeared as conductor with the Orchestra of St. Luke's at Carnegie Hall in April 1986, however, Peter G. Davis, the music critic for *New York* (April 28, 1986) magazine, lamented, "This unfortunate concert suggested that Pinnock still has quite a bit to learn about the craft of conducting, especially when he is con-

fronted with an unfamiliar orchestra." Davis particularly objected to Pinnock's use of an amplified harpsichord for Bach's D-Minor Concerto and his interpretation of Haydn's Symphony no. 93, which "seemed like a rough first reading" to Davis.

In October 1988 Pinnock became the first early-music specialist to appear as guest conductor at the Metropolitan Opera in New York, where he conducted Handel's rarely performed opera *Julius Caesar*. A reporter for *Newsweek* (October 3, 1988) described Pinnock as "the most important element in the mix," for he managed to coax "a rare—and splendid—sound" from the orchestra's modern instruments. In December 1988 Pinnock played the harpsichord while conducting the New York Chamber Symphony in four concerts devoted to Bach's *Brandenburg* Concertos at the Ninety-second Street Y. Among the English Concert's more ambitious recordings of the late 1980s was a performance of Handel's *Messiah*, which, in addition to authentic instruments and the English Concert choir, included the substitution of an alto for a bass in the aria "For Who May Abide the Day of His Coming." Pinnock also conducted a performance of the *Messiah* at Carnegie Hall on December 15, 1988 with the St. Luke's Orchestra (on modern instruments) and the New York Choral Artists.

Eager to explore the classical repertoire on original instruments as well, in March 1989 Pinnock met with some of New York City's most respected orchestral players to establish the Classical Band. "It grew out of wanting to play classical music, which demands bigger forces," Pinnock told a reporter for *Newsweek* (October 3, 1988). "I wasn't willing to risk ruining the English Concert by suddenly doubling its size. The idea is to have an orchestra for which I can formulate a basic sound and discipline, but also give to other conductors." The Classical Band is the first original-instrument orchestra in the United States that is devoted to the music of Haydn, Mozart, and Beethoven. Its much-heralded debut concert, at Columbia University's Kathryn Bache Miller Theatre on May 10, 1989, disappointed most critics. Tim Page, writing in *New York Newsday* (May 12, 1989) about the group's performance of Haydn's *Military* Symphony, Mozart's A-Major Piano Concerto—which Pinnock conducted while playing the solo part on a reconstructed 1795 Anton Walter fortepiano—and Beethoven's Eighth Symphony, commented that "the group sounded, for the most part, ill-blended and underrehearsed." The group has scheduled a series of Carnegie Hall concerts during the 1989–90 season, and Pinnock signed a new contract with Deutsche Grammophon to record eight compact discs a year from 1990 until 1996—three with the Classical Band and five with the English Concert. The planned recordings with the Classical Band include Haydn's *Paris* and *London* symphonies, Mozart's late symphonies, Requiem, and several piano concertos, and Rossini's overtures.

Trevor Pinnock is of medium height and slender, with dark hair. The reporter for *Newsweek* described him as looking "considerably younger" than his age. His meticulous scholarship is offset by often hilarious comments that he offers onstage to explain his program. Pinnock lives in London with his wife, the former Polly Nobes, who is a violinist and a member of the English Concert.

References: Gramophone 56:1868+ My '79, 59:531+ O '81 por, 64:346+ S '86 por; Music and Musicians 22:18+ D '73 por; Newsweek 112:54+ O 3 '88 por; Ovation 5:14+ O '84; International Who's Who, 1989-90

Powers, J(ames) F(arl)

July 8, 1917- Writer. Address: c/o Alfred A. Knopf, Inc., 201 E. 50th St., New York, N.Y. 10022

Despite his comparatively slim output of just two novels and three short-story collections in more than forty years of writing, J. F. Powers's fiction is imbued with such intelligence, humor, and compassion that, as his biographer, John V. Hagopian, asserts, his work "will surely endure." A lifelong Roman Catholic, Powers writes chiefly about priests in the American Midwest, especially in Minnesota, and develops his stories with brilliant satire and consummate craftsmanship. Some critics have attacked Powers's work for being excessively parochial, but he has also won praise for writing in a Joycean spirit that combines gravity with grace, realism with beauty. As the Boston Globe critic Mark Feeney has written, "No one has ever given a fuller fictional portrait of the culture of American Catholicism, which he presents lovingly and

devastatingly." Powers's first novel, Morte D'Urban, won the 1963 National Book Award, and Wheat That Springeth Green, his second novel, published in August 1988, was also nominated for that award.

James Farl Powers was born in Jacksonville, Illinois on July 8, 1917, one of the three children of James Ansbury Powers, a dairy and poultry manager for Swift & Company, and Zella (Routzong) Powers. Both of Powers's parents were creative: his father played the piano in his spare time, and his mother was an amateur painter. As a boy, Powers played baseball, basketball, and football, sold Liberty magazine and Rosebud salve, and read the Tom Swift novels, Horatio Alger Jr., the Greek myths, the Arthurian legends, Oliver Twist, Pinocchio, and Gulliver's Travels. Although his family was economically comfortable, Powers later recalled that his Catholicism made him feel like an outsider in Jacksonville, a town in the west central part of the state, near Springfield. As he explained to Donald McDonald in an interview for the Critic (October–November 1960), "The town was Protestant. The best people were Protestants and you felt that. That, to some extent, made a philosopher out of me. It made me mad." In 1924 the family moved to Rockford, Illinois, where Powers attended both parochial and public schools. Six years later, the family relocated once more, this time to Quincy, Illinois, where he was taught by Franciscan friars at Quincy College Academy. One of his teachers at the school, Father Edgar Eberle, recalled the youngster as having a wry wit, although he was "inclined to become moody and discouraged."

After graduating from Quincy College Academy in 1935, Powers, unlike several of his classmates, decided against entering the priesthood. As he explained to McDonald: "I just didn't care for the look of the life. The praying would have attracted me. I wouldn't have minded the celibacy, but I wouldn't have liked the social side, the constant footwork. I couldn't see myself standing outside church Sunday morning talking to a bunch of old women." Instead, Powers joined his family in Chicago. "I worked in Marshall Field's department store, selling books, shirts, and even linoleum for a day," Powers recalled to Pete Hamill during an interview for the New York Post Sunday Magazine (March 24, 1963). He also worked for a time as a door-to-door salesman for the Fidelity Insurance Company, and in 1937 he chauffeured a wealthy investor across the South in a new Packard, taking a typewriter along in case he felt inspired to write. "I know now that I was a writer then, for better or worse," Powers was quoted as saying in the anthology Catholic Authors (1981). "It was the only thing I cared about being."

In 1938 Powers became an editor for the Work Projects Administration's Historical Records Survey in Chicago. During the years that he worked on the survey, he took courses in the evenings at Wright Junior College and then at the downtown branch of Northwestern University. When his part of the survey was completed, in 1941, he worked briefly at Brentano's bookshop in Chicago, until he was fired for refusing to buy war bonds. It was around that time that Powers began associating with the laborers, European refugees, and black jazz musicians who would become the subjects of many of his early short stories. Powers was one of only three layman to attend a retreat for priests at St. John's Abbey in Collegeville, Minnesota in early 1943, and later that year he held a solitary retreat at an orphanage in Oakmont, Pennsylvania, where he read and meditated intensively.

Shortly after making that retreat, Powers wrote what became his first significant story, "Lions, Harts, Leaping Does," which dealt with a dying priest, Father Didymus, whose religious convictions remain unshaken despite his onerous sense of being unworthy of God. It appeared first in the literary quarterly Accent (Autumn 1943) and became part of Powers's first collection of short fiction, Prince of Darkness and Other Stories. Selected for the O. Henry Prize Stories of 1944 and for the 1944 edition of Best American Short Stories, "Lions, Harts, Leaping Does" was warmly received by critics and established Powers as a new writer to be reckoned with. Writing in the Catholic weekly Commonweal (August 22, 1947), Henry Rago acclaimed it as "one of the finest stories ever written in this country." Also in 1943 Powers published three essays on his religious views for the publication Catholic Worker, in one of which he stated his conviction that "a saint is not an abnormal person. He is simply a mature Christian. Anyone who is not a saint is spiritually undersized—the world is full of spiritual midgets."

Powers, who had become a pacifist during World War II, resisted induction into the armed forces and was arrested in April 1943. Indicted by a grand jury in May, he began serving a three-year term at Sandstone Prison in Minnesota in November. He served thirteen months and twenty days of the sentence before being paroled, in November 1944. Powers then worked as an orderly at a hospital in St. Paul, Minnesota, while continuing to write and publish stories in magazines and journals.

In his first collection, Prince of Darkness and Other Stories (1947), J. F. Powers dealt principally with two themes: the Roman Catholic clergy and racial conflict in Chicago. The collection contained three stories about racial tension, the most notable of which was "He Don't Plant Cotton," a piece about three black jazz musicians who are fired from a Chicago nightclub following a disagreement with a group of drunken white customers. In Contemporary Novelists (1976) Hayden Carruth noted that "He Don't Plant Cotton" preceded by a decade the start of the civil rights movement, adding, "Nothing since then has surpassed Powers's story in seriousness, integrity, and artistic relevance." Carruth also credited "He Don't Plant Cotton" and "Lions, Harts, Leaping Does" with being "among the best short stories written in America during the years of mid-century."

In the title story of Prince of Darkness, Powers introduced Father Ernest Burner, a character who would reappear in future stories. Father Burner has been in the priesthood for twenty years, but he is still a curate, although he hopes the archbishop will grant him a pastorship. Instead, he is transferred to another parish to continue his curate's duties. Gluttonous and ambitious, Father Burner was viewed by some critics as a satanic figure. In "The Forks," Father Eudex, a liberal young curate who assists a conservative pastor in a middle-class parish, decides to destroy a donation from a local tractor company rather than hand it over to the church, or, as the pastor suggests, use it to buy a new car for himself. Writing in the New York Review of Books (May 27, 1982), Mary Gordon praised the story for its portrayal of "power and authority, youth and age, idealism and Realpolitik . . . , the uneasy cohabitation of God and Mammon." Powers dealt with the priesthood again in "The Valiant Woman," which dramatizes the dilemma of a priest who cannot fire his well-meaning, yet insufferable, housekeeper without violating his sense of Christian charity. Powers told Donald McDonald that while he was writing "The Valiant Woman," a magazine editor asked him to change its main character from a priest to a professor, but he refused. "I might have made the change, but it would have been a different thing then," he explained. "I think the water of irony, the gin of irony maybe, is purer and higher proof in the life of a priest who is committed to both worlds, you might say."

A year before the publication of Prince of Darkness and Other Stories, Powers had married the writer Elizabeth ("Betty") Alice Wahl. In the same year, he accepted a part-time teaching position at Saint John's College (now University) in Collegeville, Minnesota. In 1948 he received fellowships from the Guggenheim Foundation and from the National Institute of Arts and Letters. For two years, beginning in 1949, he taught creative writing at Marquette University in Milwaukee, Wisconsin. Powers and his wife moved to Greystones, Ireland in October 1951, remaining for fourteen months.

In The Presence of Grace (1956), his next collection of short stories, four of which had been published originally in the New Yorker, Powers concentrated on religious themes to a greater extent than he had in Prince of Darkness and Other Stories. All but two of the nine pieces in the collection are about priests, and two of those are narrated by a rectory cat. The critical anthology American Writers Since 1900 (1980) quoted Clarence A. Glasrud as observing: "Wit and subtle irony are still at work on priestly foibles in the . . . stories of The Presence of Grace, but the absurdities seem less vicious and more forgivable." And the critic Frank O'Connor, who was himself an accomplished short-story writer, remarked, as quoted in the National Observer (March 23, 1964), "After the darkness of so much American fiction, this book produces a peculiar shock of delight."

One of the collection's most noteworthy stories, "The Devil Was the Joker," was written by Powers during his sojourn in Ireland. Although it resembles the title story of Prince of Darkness in theme, in this instance the satanic figure is not a priest but a traveling salesman named Mr. McMaster, or "Mac," who makes the rounds of parishes hawking *Clementine,* a publication of the fictional Order of St. Clement. Mac is also a trafficker in rosaries, medals, scapulars, and other religious items. A recovering alcoholic and a non-Catholic, Mac is "fat and fifty or so, with a candy-pink face, sparse orange hair, and pop-eyes." When he offers an ex-seminarian named Myles Flynn an opportunity to work as his companion and driver, Myles takes the job because he wants to avoid military service in the Korean War and hopes to meet a pastor or bishop who can help him to return to a seminary. Mac shamelessly exploits Myles and all the parish priests whom they encounter, but even though Myles succumbs to drinking, he refuses Mac's request to baptize him.

In the autumn of 1957 the Powers family returned to Ireland, settling in Dalkey. Renting an office in Dublin, Powers began work on his first novel, *Morte D'Urban,* which he completed in an office above a shoe store in St. Cloud, Minnesota, three years after his return to the United States in July 1958. A novel of epic form and sweep, *Morte D'Urban* (1962) is the story of Father Urban Roche, a member of the Order of St. Clement, who is assigned to the diocese of the Great Plains in Minnesota. In Mary Gordon's words, Father Roche "has perfected the skills of the successful executive and adapted them to the service of the church." In his cliché-ridden manner of speech, Urban refers to God as "the Good Thief of Time, accosting us wherever we go, along the highways and byways of life." Priests, in Father Urban's world, are "those heroic family doctors of the soul." Motivated by a desire to compensate for the sense of inferiority he has always felt to Protestants, Urban, according to Mary Gordon, "sees the priesthood as the easiest way to stay in the best hotels, to meet the best people, to live like a Protestant."

When he began writing *Morte D'Urban,* Powers intended it to be a short story, but he eventually decided to expand it into a novel. Nonetheless, eight of the fifteen chapters appeared first as short stories in various magazines—a fact that led many critics to attack the novel for its episodic structure and lack of overall unity. For example, William H. Gass, in his review for the *Nation* (September 29, 1962), commented, "The formula . . . which has served Powers's shorter fiction so well does not lend itself as readily to the longer form. His situations tend to close upon themselves, making the novel a trifle episodic." In the same vein, Granville Hicks of the *Saturday Review* (September 15, 1962) wrote that "the novel is not Powers's métier. . . . There are no dramatic incidents and no large issues." Other critics, however, saw in *Morte D'Urban* a unified work of literature, worthy of praise. John P. Sisk of the Catholic journal *Renascence* (1963) wrote that "the novel is not simply a gallery of memorable portraits; characters are revealed in action and interaction," and Marie J. Henault, reviewing the novel in *America* (March 2, 1963), pointed out, "Powers's amusing satire, with its great fun in incidental *reductio ad absurdum* . . . , should not prevent us from seeing the fundamental seriousness of *Morte D'Urban.* Carefully employing the devices of the novelist—plot, character, and symbolism—Powers here presents the great theme of individual salvation."

Although *Morte D'Urban* had a modest sale of 25,000 copies, Powers was honored with the National Book Award in 1963, edging out Katherine Anne Porter's best-selling *Ship of Fools,* and he also received the Thermod Monsen Award for the best book of the year by a midwesterner. In spite of those honors, Powers expressed dismay that *Morte D'Urban* failed to generate larger sales, and he was especially disappointed that the royalties from his novel failed to provide enough money for the purchase of a new house. "I thought when I'd finished it that it was a good book—and I guess it was, because nobody bought it," Powers said in an interview with Paul Hendrickson of the *National Observer* (November 29, 1975). "I guess I was hoping it would drop down into people's laps, become a small, modern classic—the way *Catcher in the Rye* has."

Powers moved his family, which by this time included five children, back to Ireland shortly after winning the National Book Award. They settled in Greystones, where Powers began work on his next novel, tentatively called "Joe and Bill." The novel was eventually published in 1988 under the title *Wheat That Springeth Green.* Although the royalties generated by *Morte D'Urban* lasted only two years, Powers rejected offers from Hollywood to make the novel into a film, because of his concern that the "flicker" merchants would reduce it to a farce. He returned to the United States in 1965 and served for a year as writer in residence at Smith College in Northampton, Massachusetts, then moved back to Ireland, where he remained for most of the next nine years.

Returning to Minnesota in 1975, Powers told Paul Hendrickson that he and his family loved living in Ireland but realized "that chapter is over now." Shortly after his return, Powers's third and most recent collection of short stories, *Look How the Fish Live* (1975), was published. Eagerly anticipated by many critics, *Look How the Fish Live* was the first Powers collection to be released in nineteen years. It received mixed reviews, with Peter Prescott of *Newsweek* (October 13, 1975), for instance, noting that "five of these ten stories are about priestly problems, but of this lot only one, 'Farewell,' is up to Powers's previous standard of wit and design." Writing in the *New York Times Book Review* (November 2, 1975), Tom McHale was equally negative, observing that Powers "seems not to have grown in the last twelve years. . . . The content of the majority of these stories is depressingly familiar." Other critics dissented, however. L. J. Davis of the *New Republic* (November 29, 1975) dismissed the five non-Catholic stories in the collection, but he insisted that the five stories dealing with the church "constitute the real book, and they are pure, unalloyed gold." And Mary Blackwell of *Library Journal* (December 1, 1975) found that *Look How the Fish Live* "takes its place with equal distinction alongside Powers's two earlier collections," adding, "The stories demonstrate anew that Powers has depth, subtlety, richness of style and theme, an accurate ear for dialogue, and a gentle wit all his own."

After receiving the National Book Award for *Morte D'Urban* in 1963, J. F. Powers vowed that his next novel would not have a priest as its main character, but he failed to live up to that promise. His second novel, *Wheat That Springeth Green*, recounts the story of Father Joe Hackett from his childhood in the 1920s to his days as the rector of a suburban parish in the late 1960s. The book garnered mostly positive notices. William Pritchard of the *New Republic* (September 26, 1988) called it "the best book [Powers] has written," pointing out that the novel "makes its appeal through the variety of and charm of its particular performances, to which strong story lines and thematic emphases take a back seat." Indeed, the novel ingratiates itself with the reader, in part, through Joe's mental one-liners, such as "People . . . have a right to be judged by their own standards until these can be raised." Writing in *Time* (August 29, 1988), Christopher Porterfield noted that, as in other Powers works, "the central dilemma is that however much a priest may try to look to the next world, he remains hopelessly, haplessly entangled in this one." In addition to its National Book Award nomination, *Wheat That Springeth Green* was nominated for the 1988 National Book Critics Circle Award.

Since 1976 Powers has taught for one semester a year at St. John's University in Collegeville. Powers and Elizabeth Wahl met on November 10, 1945, became engaged two days later, and married on April 22, 1946. They had five children: Katherine Anne (named for Katherine Anne Porter), Mary, James, Hugh, and Jane. Now a widower, Powers lives in a plain stucco house on the campus of St. John's University. In addition to the National Institute of Arts and Letters grant and the Guggenheim Fellowship he was awarded in 1948, Powers has received a Rockefeller–University of Iowa Writers' Workshop fellowship and a Rockefeller–Kenyon *Review* fellowship.

References: Critic 19:20+ O–N '60 por; N Y R of *Bks* 24:29+ My 7 '82; N Y Times C p19 S 15 '88 por; *National Observer* p23 N 29 '75 por; *American Writers since 1900* (1980); *Contemporary Authors new rev vol* 2 (1981); *Contemporary Literary Criticism vol* 8 (1978); *Contemporary Novelists* (1976); Hagopian, John. V. J. F. Powers (1968)

Puttnam, David

Feb. 25, 1941– British filmmaker. Address: Enigma Productions, 11/15 Queens Gate Place Mews, London SW7 5BG, England

As the producer of twenty-nine films—ranging from harrowing dramas and gentle comedies to documentaries and rock-'n'-roll movies—David Puttnam has tried to impart his values, comprising a strong sense of justice coupled with a belief in the sanctity of the individual, to international audiences. In an interview with David Ansen for *Newsweek* (May 20, 1985), Puttnam said, "I have a precise notion of the world I'd like to live in, and what I try to do is make films which are likely to nudge it in that direction."

Puttnam's attempts to reshape contemporary society have resulted in such critically acclaimed films as *Midnight Express, Chariots of Fire, Local Hero, The Killing Fields,* and *The Mission.* His success in helping to revitalize the flagging British film industry has been attributed not only to his ability to produce high-quality films with relatively modest budgets, but also to his willingness to take chances on untried directors. In 1988 he was honored for his "ongoing contributions to the development of young talent in the movie business" by the Eastman Board of Governors with the Eastman Second Century Award.

Because he is almost as well known for his vociferous criticism of the Hollywood studio establishment as he is for his moralistic films, Puttnam surprised many industry observers by joining that establishment in September 1986, when he became chairman and chief executive officer of Columbia Pictures, a subsidiary of the Coca-Cola Company. As the first Englishman to head a major American studio since Charlie Chaplin founded United Artists with D. W. Griffith, Douglas Fairbanks, and Mary Pickford in 1919, Puttnam continued to speak out against inflated star salaries, uncontrolled film budgets, expensive talent-agency packages, and "cronyism without merit." In so doing, he reportedly alienated some people at the same time that he won the admiration of others. Twelve months into his three-and-a-half-year contract, Puttnam resigned to resume his career as an independent producer.

David Terence Puttnam was born on February 25, 1941 to Marie Beatrix and Leonard Arthur Puttnam in Southgate, in north London. He grew up with his younger sister, Lesley, in an environment he described as one "of almost mythic ordinariness—the middle middle class," in an interview with Aljean Harmetz for the New York Times (May 3, 1983). "My mother was a Mum," he said, "serving pieces of cake and pots of tea." His father, as described by Tina Brown for her article in Vanity Fair (April 1988), was "a star news photographer with strong ideas of what England should stand for, who quit Fleet Street in disgust at the cynicism that took over after the war."

Like his father, David Puttnam grew up to adhere firmly to a set of values, which in his case were shaped by American movies. "My entire ethical base was not put together from home and church, but from American movies of the fifties," he told Kathy Stephen in an interview for the Christian Science Monitor (February 13, 1985). "The awakening of a set of ethical beliefs for life came from the cinema." Puttnam was more specific in the interview with Aljean Harmetz for the New York Times. "Any ethical base in my life was implanted by Robert Rossen, Elia Kazan, Fred Zinnemann, and Stanley Kramer," Puttnam said. His favorite movie was Inherit the Wind. "I loved the fact the issue of evolution was being resolved by force of argument, that centuries of bigotry were being demolished by logic," he explained.

Puttnam apparently enjoyed watching logical debate on the screen more than he liked formal education. At the age of sixteen he dropped out of the Minchenden Grammar School in London, though he had attended it on a scholarship. He worked at an advertising agency for the following eight years, rising through its ranks from messenger to account executive within three years. From 1966 to 1968 he worked as a photographers' agent, handling David Bailey and Richard Avedon, among other celebrated clients.

In 1968 Puttnam formed his own film production company, Enigma Productions, which took its name from a comment scrawled on his final school report: "This boy is a complete enigma." He launched his production company during a prolonged slump in the British film industry that began in the 1950s, when it lost confidence in the face of emerging competition from television and American movies and exacerbated its problems by a failure to invest. In an article that he wrote for the London Observer (March 17, 1985), Puttnam blamed what he called "under-informed and complacent senior management" for being unable "to come to grips with large-scale investment decisions."

During a time of declining theatre attendance in Britain, Puttnam was able to produce quality films without paying huge salaries to actors or directors. One reason he excelled at cost control was the fact that he relied on fledgling directors, at least four of whom he had known since his advertising days: Alan Parker, Ridley Scott, Michael Apted, and Adrian Lyne. Parker wrote the script for Puttnam's first film, Melody (1971), and went on to direct two other films for him: Bugsy Malone (1976) and Midnight Express (1978), each of which won several British Academy Awards. Midnight Express, which catapulted Puttnam into the American market, also received two American Academy Awards.

Explaining his recruitment of former directors of commercials in an interview with Charles Schreger for the Los Angeles Times (April 14, 1979), Puttnam mentioned their willingness to work as part of a team, their inexpensiveness, and his belief that directors' first efforts are often their best work. "Finally," he said, "when you give these people a chance, I think you have a sheer level of enthusiasm and originality and novelty, because what you're plugging into is twenty years of dreams. I don't know a guy who's making commercials who doesn't want to make features."

Puttnam himself has never wanted to direct, though he has acknowledged that it is often assumed that a producer is merely a frustrated film director. In an interview with Bruce Cook for the Chicago Tribune (July 27, 1982), he said: "What I want to do is scream from the rooftops, 'Being a producer is a fantastic job if you do it right!'" Doing it right, according to him, entails "casting" the director and the writer, raising the necessary funds, anticipating audience reaction throughout the production process, and, above all, choosing promising movie material.

Most, if not all, of Puttnam's productions originate in factual material. Midnight Express, one of the producer's first commercial successes in the American market, was inspired by the ordeal suffered by an American hashish smuggler in a Turkish prison. The idea for Chariots of Fire (1981), an uplifting story of two 1924 Olympic gold medalists, was born when Puttnam was confined to bed because of illness with nothing to read but a history of the Olympic Games. Chariots of Fire won four Academy Awards, including an Oscar for best picture of 1982, and by August 1982 it had grossed more than $30 million in the United States—more than any other non-American film up to that time. Local Hero (1983) was based on a newspaper account of the sale of a Scottish coastal property to a powerful American oil company. And an article by Sydney H. Schanberg for the New York Times Magazine in 1980, about his relationship with Dith

Pran, his Cambodian assistant and interpreter during his years as a *Times* war correspondent in Cambodia, resulted in the highly praised *The Killing Fields* (1984), Puttnam's account of Dith Pran's struggle for freedom after the Khmer Rouge takeover in 1975.

Puttnam prefers to work with the factual in order to remind his audiences that there is much more to moviegoing than mere escapism. True stories "give the film a spine and something to fall back on," he explained to Dalya Alberge in an interview for *Films & Filming* (March 1983). "I have a problem and always have had in literature based on pure fiction." Paradoxically, he also believes that global appeal can only be achieved by rooting a film in a specific time or place. Commenting on his talent for spotting the movie potential of factual material, he credited his advertising background. "I'm market-oriented," he told Kathy Stephen. "That's to say I'm good at spotting gaps and the potential of ideas. I've always felt that, in a crunch, I could . . . spend a day walking around London, and invent a business during that day, and earn a living at it."

Apparently Puttnam knew his market better than some people gave him credit for. Even though *Midnight Express* had been a box-office hit in 1978, the script for *Chariots of Fire* was rejected by an executive at Columbia Pictures just one year later, with the comment: "I'm sorry to tell you this has no validity at all in the American marketplace because of the style and tone as well as the subject matter." After *Chariots of Fire* proved its "validity in the marketplace," Puttnam's films were hailed as harbingers of a new era in British filmmaking.

Chariots of Fire appealed to its viewers' sense of justice, but *Midnight Express* drew crowds for reasons that were disturbing to its producer. Puttnam described his reaction to the first public screening of the movie in an interview with Tina Brown, the editor in chief of *Vanity Fair*, whose article about him appeared in its April 1988 issue: "I expected the audience to dive under their seats in the scene where the trusty gets his tongue bitten off, but instead they started to cheer. I was horrified. I realized the extraordinary impact of the medium we don't fully understand." He then sought out a Jesuit priest in London, Father Jack Mahoney, who told him: "You're in control. Do something about it."

Acting on Father Mahoney's advice, with *Chariots of Fire* and *The Killing Fields*, Puttnam consolidated his reputation for consistently displaying an ethical awareness, while avoiding explicit or gratuitous sex and violence in his films. "I find the present situation terrifying," he admitted to Dalya Alberge. "We are effectively desensitizing an entire generation, and every single year that goes by, the acceptance level increases. . . . The notion of violence or damage to property is anathema to me and something I couldn't put on the screen." Four years later, he was quoted by the *Wall Street Journal* (February 20, 1987) as saying, "I'm opposed fundamentally to antisocial films

which damage the social fabric and to people who make films that stir the pot with hostility."

Puttnam has been equally outspoken on the proper strategies for improving his country's film industry. In 1985 he wrote an article for the London *Observer* (March 17) in support of British Film Year, an effort to boost theatre attendance, for the average Briton, according to Puttnam, goes to the movies only once a year, whereas the average American attends six times a year. Tactics to raise the general level of awareness included the physical refurbishment of shabby and uncomfortable movie theatres, an educational program to encourage the use of film in schools, a screenwriting competition, and festivals, tours, seminars, and star premieres. Calling for higher levels of investment and greater recognition of the artistic and social role of the cinema, Puttnam described British cinema as "an unfortunate hybrid of a commercial American system and the state-subsidized Eastern European version, with neither state nor commerce offering sufficient resources." He even suggested that he could make a good case for nationalized cinema.

By 1985 Puttnam had won all of the top movie industry awards except the Cannes Film Festival's highest award, the Golden Palm, and he won that in the following year for *The Mission*. Having reached the zenith of his profession in terms of awards, he felt ready for a change in career. He was considering accepting a fellowship at Harvard University when two executives of Columbia Pictures Industries, a subsidiary of the Coca-Cola Company, went to London in June 1986 to offer him the chairmanship of Columbia Pictures, a company that had been losing money during the previous two years under the stewardship of Guy McElwaine. Contemplating the prospect of becoming a studio head, Puttnam realized that he would be expected to concentrate on both profitability and quality, goals often perceived as being at odds. He believed in the feasibility of accomplishing both goals, since, as a producer, he had often achieved them himself. In his interview with a reporter from the *New York Times* (July 5, 1986), he said he believed that Columbia could be "humanist without being sentimental and entertaining without being condescending."

That philosophy carried over into his negotiations with the Coca-Cola executives before he accepted the position, in September 1986. In a letter to the company that has since been widely quoted, Puttnam wrote: "The medium is too powerful and too important an influence on the way we live—the way we see ourselves, to be left solely to the tyranny of the box office or reduced to the sum of the lowest common denominator of public taste." According to Tina Brown, his contract called for "$3 million a year, autonomy for any picture with a budget of up to $30 million, with control over production and also over marketing and distribution worldwide." The one stipulation Columbia did not like, but agreed to after all, was the length of the contract, which amounted to only three and a half years, as opposed to the usual five. Some people felt that Puttnam was naïve in his insistence on such a short contract, given that it can easily take from one to two years to bring a film from concept to screen. His ambition to change the system in so short a time was also seen as a sign of naïveté, to which Puttnam has pleaded guilty. In an interview with a reporter from *People* (November 16, 1987), he said: "To me the opposite of naïveté is cynicism, and cynicism is just a glamorized version of despair. If being thought of as naïve is the price I have to pay, it's a fair price to me." He also paid that price because of his professed aversion to deal-making based on personal relationships.

Puttnam's acknowledged method of operating was not the only factor that set him apart from his colleagues in Hollywood. By purposefully (and vocally) declining to make blockbusters, such as *Rambo* (Puttnam's example), in favor of quality films that he expected to earn small but regular profits, he earned an undeserved reputation for having a highbrow taste that would not translate into profits. But he nonetheless stressed his interest in the commercial viability of his projects. During an interview with Laura Landro for the *Wall Street Journal* (February 20, 1987), for example, he said, "I want to shrug off this image that I'm some artsy European who makes art films."

Puttnam exacerbated the substantive philosophical differences he had with his counterparts by being outspoken in his defiance of conventional practices, such as paying the inflated salaries demanded by top film stars and accepting talent-agency packages. His outspokenness was what rankled many people in the industry, as well as his being an outsider who would leave Hollywood well before the consequences of his policies had run their course.

Corresponding to his proclivity for speaking his mind was Puttnam's disdain for the lavish lifestyles typical of those in his position. He chose, for example, a home in an area that was less prestigious than Beverly Hills, and although the house, which once belonged to Greta Garbo, was equipped with a swimming pool, he assured reporters that he had searched for a house without one. He rejected a Mercedes or a Rolls-Royce in favor of an Audi, and he avoided Hollywood parties and the traditional "power" restaurants, preferring to go home each night to read books and scripts.

Almost obscured by all the gossip about his lifestyle and candor were the substantial accomplishments of Puttnam at Columbia before his resignation. That announcement came in September 1987, in the wake of the merger of Columbia Pictures and Tri-Star into an entity called Columbia Pictures Entertainment. The net effect of his tenure cannot be measured until all the films that Puttnam either inherited and approved, such as *Old Gringo*, which was released in October 1989, or brought to the studio himself, such as *Housekeeping* (1987), *The Last Emperor* (1987), and *School Daze* (1988), have had their full run in the movie theatres. In 1988 Columbia released fif-

teen of Puttnam's films; some dozen others were either released or sold to other studios (or being offered unsuccessfully for sale) in 1989. Although he reduced Columbia's average cost per film, according to *Vanity Fair*, from $14.4 million to $10.7 million, the discrepancy between 1988's total production cost and the studio's take at American and Canadian theatres represented a $73 million loss, according to the *New York Times* (February 2, 1989).

Reports of Puttnam's compensation upon his resignation, which capped the shortest tenure at the helm of a major studio in recent history, varied from $5 million (*Vanity Fair*) to $7 million (*Variety*). Whatever the amount, it was enough to enable him to visit Kenya and Thailand, where he bought a strip of Thai beach, before returning to England in April 1988. In September 1988 the *New York Times* reported that Puttnam had formed a joint venture with Warner Brothers, Fujisankei Communications, British Satellite Broadcasting, and County Natwest Ventures. According to the *Times*, Puttnam's Enigma Productions was scheduled to make six feature films over four years with a revolving production fund of $50 million.

According to more than one interviewer, David Puttnam looks more like a college professor than a movie tycoon. In 1961, at the age of twenty, he married Patricia ("Patsy") Mary Jones, then seventeen, and the fact that their marriage, which he has called his "single best success story," has lasted for twenty-eight years was often cited by the Los Angeles press as yet another example of Puttnam's maverick lifestyle. The couple has two children, both in their twenties, Sasha and Debbie. As of January 1987, Sasha was a member of a rock band and Debbie was a researcher for the popular CBS television news program *60 Minutes*.

References: Christian Sci Mon p23+ F 13 '85 por; Films & Filming p7+ Mr '83 por; London Observer p19 Mr 17 '85 por, p9 Ag 30 '87 por; N Y Daily News p1+ Ja 11 '87 pors; Vanity Fair 51:96+ Ap '88 pors; Wall St J p1+ F 20 '87; International Who's Who, 1989–90; Kipps, Charles. Out of Focus: Power, Pride, and Prejudice—David Puttnam in Hollywood (1989); Who's Who 1989; Who's Who in America, 1988–89; Yule, Andrew. Fast Fade: David Puttnam, Columbia Pictures, and the Battle for Hollywood (1989)

Quayle, (James) Dan(forth)

Feb. 4, 1947– Vice-President of the United States. Address: b. The White House, 1600 Pennsylvania Ave., Washington, D.C. 20500; h. The Admiral's House, 34th St. & Massachusetts Ave., Washington, D.C. 20501

Vice-President George Bush surprised American voters when he announced that Dan Quayle, a for-

Dan Quayle

ty-one-year-old Republican senator from Indiana, would be his running mate against Governor Michael S. Dukakis of Massachusetts and Senator Lloyd Bentsen of Texas in the general election of November 1988. Quayle was not a familiar figure to most Americans, many of whom heard his name for the first time when Bush announced his choice at the Republican National Convention in New Orleans in August 1988. The final months of the Bush-Quayle campaign were filled with speculation in the media about the logic of Bush's choice and the quality of his judgment as Quayle's qualifications came under intense and sometimes merciless public scrutiny.

A scion of the conservative Pulliam newspaper publishing dynasty, Dan Quayle managed one of the family-owned newspapers and at the same time shared a law practice with his wife for two years before his election to the House of Representatives in 1976. His four years in the House were followed by eight years in the Senate that were characterized less by legislative achievement than by ideological consistency. Quayle's conservative voting record and star-spangled-banner rhetoric, combined with his youth, telegenic good looks, easy charm, and loyalty, were some of the reasons behind Bush's selection of Quayle for the vice-presidency, according to political observers. But some contended that Quayle's lack of intellectual distinction and his gaffe-ridden campaign speeches made him more of an albatross than an asset in the Republican drive to hold on to the White House. Such concerns were heightened by Quayle's inability to quell interest in the circumstances of his admission to the Indiana National Guard during the Vietnam War.

Whether Quayle's presence on the ticket contributed to or detracted from the Republican victory on election day is a matter of contention. Quayle volunteered his own analysis in an interview with B. Drummond Ayres Jr. for the New York Times (November 20, 1988). The Dukakis campaign's focus on the vice-presidential contest, Quayle believes, inadvertently revealed how much the Democrats had depended on Bentsen. "Any time the top of the ticket needs help from the bottom of the ticket," Quayle said, "other than regional balance, other than political interests, I think you're in trouble. The top of the ticket's got to stand on its own two feet. And certainly George Bush didn't need my help."

James Danforth Quayle was born on February 4, 1947 in Indianapolis, Indiana to James C. ("Jim") Quayle and Corinne (Pulliam) Quayle. He was named after James Danforth, a longtime friend of the family who was killed in World War II. Both of Quayle's parents grew up in influential families. His maternal grandfather, Eugene C. Pulliam, was a self-made billionaire whose media conglomerate, Central Newspapers, eventually comprised five newspapers in Indiana and two in Arizona. According to Bruce E. Babbitt, a former governor of Arizona, Pulliam used his newspapers to champion conservative causes and was venerated as "the founding father of the Republican party in Arizona."

Quayle's father's family ran the Chicago Dowel Company, best known for its manufacture of Lincoln Logs, the popular building toy. In 1948 Jim Quayle began working for Pulliam's Huntington (Indiana) Herald-Press, where he sold advertising until his transfer to the Arizona Republic and the Phoenix Gazette in 1955. Growing up with his two younger brothers, Chris and Mike, and his younger sister, Martha, in a house next to a golf course in Phoenix, Dan Quayle acquired an abiding passion for golf, and his precocious interest in politics did not lag far behind. Both enthusiasms were influenced by his maternal grandfather, one of whose close friends was Barry M. Goldwater, the Republican senator from Arizona who ran for president in 1964. Dan Quayle first became involved in politics when he handed out leaflets for Goldwater at the Arizona state fair.

In 1963 the Quayles returned to Indiana, where Jim Quayle became publisher of the Huntington Herald-Press. There, he and his wife, Corinne, joined the local chapter of the rabidly anticommunist John Birch Society, which was founded in 1958 on the premise that the federal government was infiltrated with communists and their agents, one of whom, the founders believed, was President Dwight D. Eisenhower. The extreme right-wing views of the Quayles are said to have strongly influenced their son's developing political consciousness, but, when Dan Quayle was recently asked whether his opinions were shaped by the John Birch Society in particular, he said, "Absolutely not."

Quayle was nonetheless more deeply involved in politics than many American high school students were. He often attended rallies for local Republican candidates and stood on street corners distributing campaign literature. Some of his high school cronies have recalled during interviews that Quayle was nicknamed Eddie Haskell, after the *Leave It to Beaver* sitcom character who was known for his ingratiating manner with adults, but he was equally popular with his peers, with whom he played golf and basketball. He often cruised the town's main drag in a car whose vanity plates read "AuH20," the chemical symbol for Barry Goldwater's surname.

But Quayle's immersion in golf and Republican politics apparently left him so little time for study that his mediocre academic record led the school's guidance counselor to advise him against applying to DePauw University, in Greencastle, Indiana, though it was the alma mater of both of his parents and of his grandfather. He applied anyway and was accepted in 1965. At DePauw he majored in political science, captained the golf team, and became vice-president of Delta Kappa Epsilon, the same social fraternity that had been pledged by his father and grandfather, as well as by George Bush, during his college days at Yale. By all accounts, Quayle never flaunted his family's wealth: he earned spending money by waiting on tables at a sorority house and worked as a pressman and court reporter for his father's newspaper during his summer vacations. During the summer of 1968 he was a driver for aides to Richard M. Nixon at the Republican Convention in Miami Beach, Florida.

Quayle earned his B.A. degree in political science from DePauw in 1969, but not without some difficulty. He failed the comprehensive exam in political science, and his second try at the same test brought him what he later referred to as a "gentleman's C." Although his college records have not been released, his father told the *Washington Post* (August 21, 1988) that Dan's grade-point average was below 2.6. "He was not a serious student," recalled Michael Lawrence, a former political science professor at DePauw who was quoted by the *Chicago Tribune* (September 4, 1988). "He did mediocre work. He was just a charming, nice guy." Lawrence's assessment was less charitable in an interview with *Newsweek* (August 29, 1988): "He was vapid, ordinary, and relied on his personality to cut corners." His low grades were cited by faculty members who opposed awarding Quayle an honorary degree in 1982, but the degree was nevertheless bestowed at the insistence of Richard Rosser, then the president of the university.

On graduating on May 24, Quayle would have been eligible for induction into the armed services, for he had passed his pre-induction physical in April, had he not managed to enlist in the Indiana National Guard five days earlier. He faced a dilemma common to many college-educated, upper-middle-class men of his generation—whether to allow himself to be drafted or to find an alternative. Few of the prevailing options for men of his privileged background were available to him, but his family connections provided him with more freedom of choice.

Quayle's conservative views ruled out protesting the draft, fleeing to Canada, or filing for conscientious-objector status. (If there was anything Quayle objected to concerning the war effort, it was "the no-win policy aspect," as he explained during a press conference on August 19, 1988 in Huntington.) He had no family to support, no medical disability, and no job essential to the national security that would exempt him from the draft. Although he wanted to go to law school (having considered and rejected the idea of becoming a professional golfer), he could not have used that to escape the draft, because deferments for graduate students had been abolished in 1967.

It was common knowledge in 1969 that joining the National Guard substantially lessened one's chances of being sent to Vietnam. President Lyndon B. Johnson had twice rejected the idea of mobilizing the entire guard, though some units were sent overseas. Only ninety-seven out of 58,135 Americans killed in the Vietnam War were National Guardsmen. In 1970 the president of the National Guard Association estimated that 90 percent of those who joined the guard did so to avoid service in Vietnam. During his press conference on August 19, Quayle maintained not only that he was not among that 90 percent majority, but also that he did not consider the lesser likelihood of Vietnam duty to be one of the benefits of guard service. He insisted that the only thing he was trying to avoid by joining the guard was a two-year commitment to active duty, which would have postponed his plans for law school. He added that he would have been proud to go to Vietnam if his unit had been called up.

More disturbing to members of the press than Quayle's motives for joining the guard—which were troublesome only in light of his promilitary views, past and present, and his record of voting against veterans' benefits—were his methods. Skirting the normal application process, Quayle called his parents and Wendell Phillippi, a managing editor at the Pulliam-owned Indianapolis *News* and a retired major general in the Indiana National Guard, and expressed his interest in getting into the guard. Phillippi recommended Quayle to a guard official, who reserved a place for Quayle and personally swore him in, bypassing the unit's commanding officer.

When first questioned in New Orleans on August 17, 1988 about that sequence of events, Quayle displayed what many considered to be remarkable insensitivity with the flippant remark "I did not know in 1969 that I would be in this room today, I'll confess." Two days later at an outdoor press conference in Huntington, where he was surrounded by supporters who heckled the press so loudly that one reporter compared the scene to *The Morton Downey Jr. Show*, Quayle proved to be a master of the fine art of stonewalling. Trying to deflect criticism by repeatedly claiming that the media were impugning the integrity of the National Guard rather than his own, he said that he "got in fairly" and that he resented the implication that guard service was not patriotic.

One reporter tried to clarify the issue by telling Quayle that "the implication is that people were dying in Vietnam and you were writing press releases." After being trained as a welder, Quayle was assigned as a clerk-typist to the public information unit of the headquarters detachment, where he wrote press releases for the twelve-page quarterly *Indiana National Guardsman*. In 1973 he was assigned as a military journalist, which remained his title for the rest of his six-year service, until 1975. While thus occupied for one weekend every month and for two weeks every summer, Quayle held a series of daytime jobs in state government. From July to September 1971 he was an investigator with the Consumer Protection Division of the attorney general's office, and, following that assignment, he became an administrative assistant to Governor Edgar Whitcomb until 1973. From 1973 until 1974 he served as the director of the Inheritance Tax Division of the Indiana Department of Revenue. In 1974 he graduated from Indiana University Law School, where he had enrolled in an evening program designed for students whose academic records were poor enough to preclude admission otherwise. He passed the bar in July 1974.

In the same year, Quayle joined the family business as an associate publisher and general manager of the Huntington *Herald-Press*, where he might have continued to work indefinitely, like his father before him, had he not had two watershed experiences in 1972. The more important one was his marriage to Marilyn Tucker, a fellow law student whose accumulation of Girl Scout honor badges had earned her the nickname "Merit." After passing the bar exam on the same day in 1974, the couple promptly set up the law practice of Quayle & Quayle in the upstairs office of the Huntington *Herald-Press*. Jim Quayle's friends helped the Quayles to establish a client base and coached them on unfamiliar legal procedures. His marriage, Quayle told an interviewer for *USA Today* (August 29, 1988), made him "very serious about life." "I had a far stronger sense of where I wanted to go and what I wanted to do with myself," he said.

The second crucial experience was Quayle's viewing of the 1972 movie *The Candidate*, which starred Robert Redford as a somewhat vapid politician whose qualifications consisted mainly of blond good looks and charm (When he unexpectedly won election to the United States Senate, the Redford character asked his aides, "What do we do now?"). The movie made a tremendous impression on Quayle, according to friends; but when his turn came to run for office in 1976, it was not on his own initiative. Almost as if he were reprising the Redford role, Quayle was asked by his party to enter what seemed to be a hopeless race in Indiana's Fourth Congressional District against an eight-term Democratic incumbent after the Republican candidate unexpectedly dropped out.

When Quayle approached his father about leaving the Huntington *Herald-Press* to run for J. Edward Roush's House seat, his father reportedly said, "Go ahead, you won't win." Marilyn Quayle elaborated on the circumstances of her husband's entry into politics in an interview with *New York Newsday* (October 24, 1988): "We thought it was a joke when he [the Allen County Republican chairman Orvas E. Beers] asked Dan to run." With the help of four prominent local Republicans who called themselves "Quayle's Quartet," the candidate won an upset victory by attacking Roush's liberalism on social issues and his weakness on defense. An effective campaigner, Quayle was reelected in 1978 by the largest margin that the district had ever witnessed.

Although Quayle's nickname in the House, "Wet Head," hinted that he may have spent more time in the shower after playing golf than he did in committee meetings, he nonetheless managed to push through a handful of minor amendments during his four-year tenure. They included a prohibition on chemical or biological weapons testing near population centers unless local officials are given thirty days' notice; a provision that the American hostages in Iran need not pay federal income tax during their captivity; and a ban on funding for President Jimmy Carter's pardon program granting amnesty to draft dodgers (but not to deserters) in 1977.

Despite his modest accomplishments in the House, in 1980 Quayle went on to become, at the age of thirty-three, the youngest senator ever elected in Indiana. After the state's popular Republican governor, Otis Bowen, withdrew from the race against Senator Birch E. Bayh, the three-term Democratic incumbent, Quayle announced his candidacy and won 54 percent of the vote by portraying Bayh as a free-spending liberal whose pro-choice stance on abortion alienated him from mainstream values. The Reagan landslide and the shrill denunciations of Bayh by the National Conservative Political Action Committee (NCPAC) are considered partly responsible for Quayle's victory, even though Quayle said, after the election, that NCPAC's endorsement had been detrimental to his campaign. (Eight years later, Bayh's son, Evan Bayh, was elected the first Democratic governor of Indiana in twenty years.) In 1986 Quayle was reelected with 61 percent of the vote, the largest margin ever achieved to that date in a statewide Indiana race. His opponent, Jill Long, refused to advertise or post mailings even though she was virtually unknown, and she was outspent by Quayle by a ratio of fifteen to one. (In March 1989 she won Quayle's former House seat in the Fourth Congressional District.)

By all accounts Quayle applied himself far more diligently in the Senate than he had in the House. In *The Making of a Senator: Dan Quayle* (1989), an installment of a larger study of the Senate by the political science professor Richard F. Fenno Jr., Quayle is portrayed less as a darling of the New Right than as a pragmatic politician unafraid to deviate occasionally from conservative guidelines. A member of the committees on the budget, armed services, and labor and human resources, Quayle told Fenno that he did not want to serve on the Judiciary Committee because it would be involved with issues like abortion, busing, voting rights, and school prayer. "I'm not interested in those issues," Quayle said, "and I want to stay as far away from them as I can. . . . Some of the New Right people really want to turn the clock back. . . . There's no way they're going to do that. We won't let them."

The legislation on which Quayle plumes himself the most is a case in point. In formulating the Job Training and Partnership Act of 1982, which provides for cooperation between private businesses and state officials in job training, Quayle persuaded Senator Edward M. Kennedy, Democrat of Massachusetts, to cosponsor the bill. Although hindered by his Republican colleagues and Labor Department officials, Quayle also persuaded President Reagan to support the bill. The legislation was intended, in part, to benefit Quayle's farm-belt constituency, which was suffering from an unemployment rate of 12 percent.

Quayle also voted to override Reagan's vetoes of economic sanctions against South Africa and of the Clean Water Act reauthorization bill and supported the creation of a national holiday honoring Martin Luther King Jr., among other departures from hard-line conservatism. But those were exceptions to his overall backing of administration policies. Quayle supported a balanced-budget amendment, increases in defense spending, military aid to the Nicaraguan Contras, capital punishment for drug dealers, and early deployment of a strategic defense system; he opposed gun-control legislation, federal funding for abortion, the Equal Rights Amendment, the Civil Rights Restoration Act, and plant-closing notification.

Quayle even placed himself to the right of the administration on the Intermediate-range Nuclear Forces Treaty, which he initially opposed. He supported the treaty reluctantly only after certain points in the treaty were clarified. He also coauthored a resolution calling for stricter verification procedures in any future strategic arms treaty. Contrary to his stated intention not to get heavily involved in conservative litmus-test issues, he led the successful fight for confirmation of one of Reagan's more controversial judicial appointments in 1986. After a protracted struggle, Vice-President George Bush cast the tie-breaking vote that confirmed the appointment of Daniel A. Manion, the son of a prominent member of the John Birch Society and a classmate of Quayle's from his law-school days, to the United States Court of Appeals for the Seventh Circuit.

Although Quayle has repeatedly said that George Bush did not need his help to win the presidential election of 1988, Bush was obliged to justify his choice of a relatively unknown legislator over arguably more qualified prospects. Of all the ticket-enhancing qualities attributed to Quayle during the campaign, including his good looks, youth, appeal to baby boomers, midwestern origins, and enthusiasm, the characteristic that was touted least often seemed, in retrospect, the most salient: his conservative views.

During Vice-President Quayle's first 100 days in office he often took a more conservative stance than President Bush, indicating that Quayle may have been chosen in part to placate the right wing of the Republican party, for whom Bush seems too moderate. Discussing one of many examples of Quayle's assertiveness, an unnamed senior White House official told the Washington Post (March 28, 1989), "I think Bush not only approves of it, he welcomes it. Quayle is much more comfortable doing it than Bush was as vice-president or is now. He likes others to do it for him." But Richard Viguerie, the right-wing direct-mail specialist, told the New York Times (January 31, 1989): "We're thrilled to have Dan Quayle in the administration. But no one that I'm aware of believes that Dan Quayle is making policy." The vice-president himself has said, in an Associated Press interview on November 30, 1988, that he will not be a "so-called spear carrier for all the so-called conservative issues."

The only job provided for the vice-president in the Constitution is that of president of the Senate. After being dissuaded from making that an activist role—which has never been done because of the impracticality of the idea— Quayle settled into the roles that Bush provided for him: chairman of the National Space Council and head of a task force on competitiveness. During his first year in office he toured Central America, South America, Asia, and Australia and was dispatched to the scene of the oil spill in Alaska in May 1989, as well as to California following the earthquake of October 1989. Disaster preparedness is the project Marilyn Quayle has quietly taken in her role as "second lady."

The telegenic face of the blond, blue-eyed Dan Quayle does not reflect his forty-two years. Lee Eisenberg, the editor of Esquire, has called it "the face of a fraternity party" in explaining his opinion that Quayle does not, as many have contended, resemble Robert Redford. On the Quayles' arrival in Washington in 1977, they sold their house in Huntington and bought a house in McLean, Virginia for $128,950. According to Washingtonian magazine, the value of the Quayle home had appreciated to $425,000 by 1989, when the family moved into the official (since 1974) vice-president's residence—a thirty-three-room house built on the grounds of the United States Naval Observatory in 1893—which the Quayles plan to remodel. The Quayles recently rented out their house in McLean. The Quayles have three children—Tucker Danforth, Benjamin Eugene, and Mary Corinne—and a Labrador puppy, Breezy. According to the accounting firm of Price Waterhouse, Quayle's net worth in September 1988 was $859,700, and the assets of the much-vaunted (by the press, not by Quayle) Pulliam fortune will not be distributed until twenty-one years after the death of Quayle's oldest son, Tucker. In addition to golfing, Quayle, who is five foot ten and weighs 176 pounds, enjoys tennis, basketball, skiing, fly fishing, and reading, according to his official press release. He is a Presbyterian.

References: *Chicago Tribune mag* p8+ S 17 '89 pors; *N Y Times Mag* p18+ Je 25 '89 pors; Fenno, Richard F., Jr. *The Making of a Senator: Dan Quayle* (1989); *International Who's Who, 1988-89*; *Politics in America* (1988); *Who's Who in America, 1988-89*; *Who's Who in American Politics, 1988-89*; *Who's Who in the Midwest, 1988-89*; *Who's Who in the World, 1988-89*

Rafsanjani, (Ali Akbar) Hashemi

1934- President of Iran. Address: Office of the President, Teheran, Iran

The new president of Iran, the ayatollah Hashemi Rafsanjani, is as enigmatic and unpredictable as the Islamic republic that he leads. Rafsanjani is a longtime disciple of the late ayatollah Ruhollah Khomeini and a founding member of the Islamic Republican party that consolidated power in the hands of Shi'ite clerics in the wake of the fall of the Shah Mohammed Riza Pahlevi in 1979. Although he has openly encouraged terrorism and praised those who have taken American hostages in the Middle East, Rafsanjani has at times condemned terrorism and worked behind the scenes to help secure the release of the hostages. Within Iran, he is known as "the shark" or "the survivor" not only because he has withstood several assassination attempts but also because he has shown a marked ability to negotiate the treacherous shoals of Iranian politics.

RAFSANJANI

Rafsanjani's career nearly came to an abrupt end when his enemies exposed his scheme to trade hostages for arms with the "Great Satan," the United States, in the mid-1980s. Among the fanatical Islamic clerics who dominate the theocracy of Iran, he is regarded as the most pragmatic. Although he has given out mixed signals since the death of Ayatollah Khomeini in the late spring of 1989, most observers believe that his ultimate goal is to normalize relations with the West and rebuild his country from the devastation wrought by its disastrous eight-year war with Iraq. "If I had to choose a guy to be president," observed Graham Fuller, a former senior Iranian analyst in the administration of President Ronald Reagan, "Rafsanjani is one of the halfway rational and pragmatic figures, essentially more a political figure than religious."

Ali Akbar Hashemi Rafsanjani was born in 1934 in Rafsanjan, a town in the Iranian province of Kerman, the son of a prosperous pistachio grower. Rafsanjani's younger brother, Mohammad, is the general manager of the state-run television and radio broadcasting system. From his early teens Rafsanjani underwent religious training in local schools, and in the 1950s he studied under Ruhollah Khomeini at the Qom theological seminary. He graduated from Qom late in the decade as a hojatolislam, a Shi'ite clerical rank just below that of ayatollah, which he held until his elevation to the presidency in 1989.

Like many Iranian clerics, Rafsanjani opposed the modernization program of Shah Mohammed Riza Pahlevi. The radicalizing event in his life was the arrest of Khomeini and some of his supporters in 1962, following protests against the shah's "white revolution" reforms. When he was exiled in 1964, Khomeini relied on Rafsanjani to raise funds and organize an underground movement in Iran. Rafsanjani himself was arrested at least three times by the shah's forces: In 1965 he was jailed briefly on charges, which were later dropped, that he took part in the assassination of Prime Minister Hasan Ali Mansur. In 1971 he again was detained and released for lack of evidence, this time for his alleged involvement with the Mujahidin al-Khalq, a leftist guerrilla group, but in 1975 the authorities established his association with the guerrillas, and he served three years of a six-year sentence.

With the overthrow of the shah early in 1979, Rafsanjani helped to found the Islamic Republican party and served on the Revolutionary Council, which oversaw the transition from a monarchy to a theocracy. As the under secretary of the interior in the provisional government, he played a key role in ending a strike by oil workers, thus stabilizing the government and giving Ayatollah Khomeini time to consolidate his power. In May 1979 Rafsanjani was gravely wounded by a pair of gunmen shortly after he spoke out against secular elements in Iran. In the following year he was elected as a representative from Teheran to the *Majlis*, the Iranian parliament, where, because of his close association with Khomeini, he was elected speaker with 146 votes out of 196 cast on July 20. In the struggle between "the neckties and the turbans," he joined in engineering the ouster of President Abolhassan Bani-Sadr in June 1981, and he helped in other ways to ensure the success of the Islamic Revolution in Iran.

Throughout the first decade of the Islamic Republic, Rafsanjani dominated the *Majlis* as speaker and emerged as the country's second-most-powerful official, after Khomeini. Beginning with June 1980 he also served as *Imam Jomeh,* the leader of the Friday prayer service in Teheran, whose weekly sermons are broadcast nationally and monitored abroad. Rafsanjani frequently used that influential pulpit to make policy pronouncements, to convey messages to foreign leaders, or to undermine his opposition at home. It was never clear, especially in the West, exactly where Rafsanjani stood within the narrow radical spectrum of Iranian politics. One week he would rant against the Reagan administration as the Great Satan or call on his Shi'ite followers to terrorize Americans abroad; the next, he might call for conciliation and hold out the prospect of friendlier relations with the West.

To his critics, including an unnamed Iranian journalist who was quoted in the *Christian Science Monitor* (June 8, 1988), Rafsanjani is nothing but an opportunist. "Prior to the revolution," the journalist said of him, "he worked closely with moderates like Mehdi Bazargan. But when he felt Bazargan was persona non grata in the Islamic establishment, Rafsanjani didn't hesistate to insult him in public. Also, he had good relations with Tudeh [the Communist party of Iran] leadership. But when Tudeh members were arrested in 1983, he began attacking them with scathing words."

Others, however, see Rafsanjani as a consummate politician whose delicate maneuvers are largely responsible for holding the fragile Islamic Republic together. "He is the only major politician to have solidly bridged the gap between revolutionary organizations and conventional state institutions," Robin Wright, a senior associate at the Carnegie Endowment for International Peace, has observed, as quoted in the *Christian Science Monitor* (August 27, 1987). "Divisions between the two are at the heart of Iran's current power struggle. Equally important are his skills as a power broker and public speaker. . . . He is also the most engaging of the theocracy's usually severe public figures." Robin Wright also noted that, compared with his colleagues, Rafsanjani seems downright modern, since he upholds the right of women to higher education and to careers of their own and condemns the extreme penalties of Islamic justice.

Rafsanjani was a major architect of the eight-year war with Iraq, which bled Iran of many of its young men and drained an estimated $350 billion from its treasury. As Khomeini's personal representative on the Supreme Defense Council, he helped to plan and direct such successful operations as the occupation of the Faw Peninsula, Iraq's only access to the Persian Gulf, in February 1986 and the capture of territory outside Basra, Iraq in January 1987. Isolated from much of the rest of the world and unable to secure a reliable source for arms and spare parts, Iran failed to capitalize on those victories and could only fight Iraq to a costly stalemate. In June 1988, after Iraq regained the Faw and Basra territories and the United States sank or damaged six Iranian vessels and key gulf oil platforms in retaliation for an Iranian mine explosion that damaged an American frigate, Khomeini named Rafsanjani commander in chief of the Iranian armed forces, a post that Khomeini had heretofore held himself. Rafsanjani, who had no formal military training, integrated the 350,000-man Revolutionary Guard into the regular army, ending a rivalry between the two groups and a duplication of effort that had cost Iran dearly on the battlefield. With victory no longer possible, however, Rafsanjani at length prevailed upon Khomeini to accept a United Nations cease-fire resolution, to be effective on August 20, 1988.

Meanwhile, Rafsanjani led Iran in its first tentative steps to normalize relations with the West by renewing diplomatic ties with France and Canada, in June 1988. By the end of that year, moreover, he had begun to ease import restrictions. In June 1989 he visited Moscow, becoming the highest-ranking Iranian official to call on the Soviet capital since the Islamic Revolution. In several days of talks with Mikhail Gorbachev, who called the visit a "landmark event" in the history of the neighboring countries, the two leaders tried to overcome the animosity generated by the Soviet Union's military support of Iraq and its invasion of Afghanistan. Gorbachev pledged to provide Iran with defensive weapons, and the two leaders agreed to restore rail service across their common border and to complete 100 miles of track between Tedzhen, in the Soviet Union, and Mashhad, Iran, giving the Soviet Union access to the Arabian Sea and the Indian Ocean. They also considered reopening the Iranian natural gas pipeline, closed during the Iran-Iraq war, and even canvassed the possibility of joint Soviet-Iranian space activity. Perhaps most important for Gorbachev was Rafsanjani's agreement not to stir religious passions among Moslems in Azerbaijan and other Soviet republics.

Restoring relations with the United States, however, was impossible as long as American hostages were being held in the Middle East by Islamic groups with close ties to Iran. Rafsanjani has been intimately involved with the fate of Western hostages since the takeover of the American embassy in 1979, an act he once called "one of the most constructive measures in history." As the government's principal negotiator with the militants who had seized the embassy and a close adviser to Khomeini, he helped to prolong the ordeal with maximum advantage for Iran.

With the subsequent taking of other hostages by pro-Iranian terrorists in Lebanon, the Reagan administration desperately sought some voice of reason in Iran and thought they found it in Rafsanjani. In secret meetings and indirect contacts with representatives of the Reagan administration, Rafsanjani agreed to secure the release of some of the hostages in exchange for American arms needed for the war with Iraq. When political enemies of Rafsanjani leaked word of the covert arrangement through a Lebanese periodical in 1986, that disclosure touched off the Iran-Contra scandal in the United States, which in turn revealed that Israel was involved in the arms transfer. Rafsanjani was widely criticized in Iran for dealing with the two most reviled enemies of Islam, and only intervention from Khomeini himself spared him the consequences of a formal parliamentary investigation.

For some time after that, Rafsanjani was compelled to rule out dealing with the United States, but by mid-1988 he once again was talking publicly of facilitating the release of the hostages if the Reagan administration would show good faith by releasing certain frozen Iranian assets. In August 1989, following his election as president, Rafsanjani condemned the murder of one of the American hostages, Lieutenant Colonel William Higgins, a United Nations observer, by the pro-Iranian Organization of the Oppressed on Earth and reportedly intervened to stay the announced execution of another American, Joseph Cicippio.

Once again adopting a conciliatory tone, Rafsanjani addressed President George Bush explicitly in a Friday prayer service, as reported in the *New York Times* (August 5, 1989): "The freedom of the hostages is solvable. They have intelligent and manageable solutions. One cannot solve the issue with such bullying ways, with arrogant confrontations, and tyranny. Come along wisely; we then will help you to solve the problems there so that the people of the region may live in peace and tranquility." The Bush administration pronounced the sermon the opening of a new phase in American-Iranian relations, but hopes for a quick return of the hostages were soon dashed as hard-liners in Iran called on the Hezbollah, the Lebanese Shi'ite group that controls the hostages, to refrain from negotiating a settlement, and Rafsanjani once again adopted an anti-American stance.

Analysts traced the new phase to the long-expected death of Ayatollah Khomeini, on June 3, 1989. In the intense power struggle that ensued among Rafsanjani, Khomeini's son Ahmad, and President Ali Khamenei, an agreement was reached in which Ali Khamenei succeeded Khomeini as *marja*, or grand ayatollah, the spiritual leader of Iran; Rafsanjani was elected president with enhanced powers; and Ahmad Khomeini was relegated to custodian of his father's papers. In late July Rafsanjani was elected president with 95 percent of the vote over the former agriculture minister, Abbas Sheibani, the only one of seventy-eight announced candidates whom the government pronounced sufficiently pious and experienced to challenge him.

Rafsanjani took office as president on August 3, 1989. Forty-five constitutional reforms insisted upon by him, and enacted in referendum, restored substantial executive power to the presidency. Rafsanjani is the first Iranian postrevolution executive with the authority to dismiss a minister or veto a cabinet decision without parliamentary approval. On becoming president, he was elevated to the rank of ayatollah, conferring upon him the authority to interpret Islamic doctrine.

Rafsanjani's first statements in the post-Khomenei era have been characteristically ambiguous. He has vowed to carry on the Islamic Revolution along the course charted by the late religious leader, and he has underscored the point by echoing Khomeini's call for the assassination of Salman Rushdie, the author of the novel *The Satanic Verses*, which Khomeini had condemned as blasphemous. But Rafsanjani has also purged many hard-liners from the government and called for an end to extremism for the sake of economic recovery. "Dams cannot be built by slogans," he declared in his inaugural address on August 17. In what was seen as a major effort to consolidate his power, he won parliamentary approval, after days of debate, for a new cabinet free of some of the most radical hard-liners in the Iranian government. Among those ousted were the interior minister, Ali Akbar Mohtashemi, and the intelligence chief, Hojatoleslam Mohammadi Rey-Shahri. He also placed loyal supporters in the key ministries of defense, finance, and justice. Once again, Rafsanjani succeeded in making reform palatable to key hard-liners, having won over the support of the new parliamentary speaker, Mehdi Karrubi, as well as the new spiritual leader, the ayatollah Khamenei.

President Rafsanjani has announced plans for economic reforms that he promises will reverse the dangerous spiral of stagnation, inflation, and shortages that threaten to destroy the once-prosperous country. At the time he assumed office, one in three Iranians was unemployed, industrial plants were running at about 30 percent of capacity, and estimates of the annual inflation rate ranged from 22 percent to nearly 70 percent. Repairing the damage from the war with Iraq alone was expected to cost $100 billion. Rafsanjani and all but the most fanatical clerics seem to realize that the only road to economic recovery for Iran lies in normalization of relations with the West and the access to foreign capital that would come with it. According to some Iranians and to foreign diplomats with long experience in Iran, Rafsanjani's success in disciplining the Islamic Revolution is likely to hinge on the fate of his economic program. "Rafsanjani has put himself in the front line," observed an unnamed Iranian exile who was quoted in the *Manchester Guardian Weekly* (August 6, 1989). "The people will credit him for the better life he has promised them, or blame him if things continue to get worse."

On October 23, 1989, in his first press conference with foreign reporters since his election, Rafsanjani described the five-year, $112 billion economic plan devised by his government as "realistic" rather than "ambitious." Among other things, the plan called for an increase in involvement by the private sector and about $20 billion in foreign investment in certain key industries. When asked about the fate of the Western hostages, Rafsanjani denounced the taking of hostages as "an inhuman act" and said that Iran was willing to use its influence to secure the hostages' release if the United States would release Iranian assets seized in 1979 and supply information regarding the kidnapping of several Iranian diplomats by right-wing Christian forces in Lebanon in 1982.

Unlike many of the grim-faced mullahs epitomized by the late ayatollah Khomeini, Hashemi Rafsanjani typically displays an inscrutable smirk as he engages members of the foreign press in brisk repartee. In public he usually wears floor-length robes and a white turban, from which he exposes

a shock of brown hair. He has been described as quick-witted, well-informed, and sharp-tongued, and as a gifted orator who knows how to exploit the media to best advantage. Little is known of his private life. He is married to a traditional Islamic woman, who wears the chador and stays out of public view but reportedly exercises considerable private influence over him. They have several children, including a son who has graduated from a Belgian university.

References: Christian Sci Mon p9 S 10 '85 por; International Who's Who, 1989-1990

Rakowski, Mieczyslaw (Franciszek)

(rä-kôf´ skĕ, mye-chi´ släf [frän-tsē´ shek])

Dec. 1, 1926– General Secretary of the Polish United Workers' party; former Polish prime minister. Address: Urzad Rady Ministrów, Al. Ujazdowskie 1/3, 00-583 Warsaw, Poland

As Poland's prime minister from September 27, 1988 to August 2, 1989, Mieczyslaw Rakowski attempted to placate the government's critics and reform the country's troubled economy. During his short tenure he tried to reach an accommodation with the leaders of Solidarity—the independent trade union that had been banned from December 1981 until April 1989—without alienating Communist party hard-liners. Positioned as he was between two strong competing factions, Rakowski did not win reelection to parliament in the elections of June 1989—the first open elections in forty years. The elections gave Solidarity ninety-nine of 100

seats in the newly created Senate (upper chamber) and all 161 open seats in the 460-seat Sejm (lower chamber). Rakowski's defeat, which was doubly humiliating since he ran unopposed, rendered his continuation as prime minister untenable, and he tendered his resignation on July 4. Five days earlier he had succeeded General Wojciech Jaruzelski as Communist party leader. Ten days earlier, Jaruzelski, who had been party leader and chief of state since 1981, was elected president with new executive-style powers. But Solidarity's gains were substantial enough to persuade Jaruzelski to appoint one of their number prime minister in a Solidarity-led coalition government. The coalition began governing with the confirmation of the Solidarity activist Tadeusz Mazowiecki as prime minister on August 24. (The man Rakowski had nominated as his immediate successor, the interior minister General Czeslaw Kisczcak, had lasted in office for only fifteen days in August.) Rakowski, who was not a party to the coalition agreed upon between Jaruzelski and Solidarity leader Lech Walesa on August 17, denounced the trade union's "takeover" of Poland, though he had argued in favor of Solidarity's legalization earlier that year.

Rakowski was always something of an enigma to Western observers. As editor in chief, for a quarter of a century, of *Polityka*, the country's most influential champion of economic and political reform, he was hailed in the West as a fearless "liberal" who more than once defied authorities in order to maintain a measure of journalistic independence from the party line. Although his credibility was so great outside the Communist bloc that he became known as "Mr. Poland for Foreigners," all that changed when he joined the government in 1981 as chief negotiator in talks with Solidarity and then defended the government's decision to impose martial law and outlaw the independent trade union. Rakowski once spoke admiringly of Lech Walesa, but the two subsequently became bitter enemies.

These metamorphoses led many observers to wonder which Rakowski would emerge as the Polish government grappled with worker unrest, product shortages, inflationary pressures, tens of billions of dollars in foreign debt, and the changing character of the Soviet Union. "One cannot be sure what kind of politics he will practice," Bronislaw Geremek, a Solidarity adviser, observed. "He has changed many times. He can be the last prime minister of martial law or the first prime minster of the new period. The question will be what role Rakowski will play. Will he be the promoter of renewal or the fighter against Solidarity as he was?"

Mieczylsaw Franciszek Rakowski was born on December 1, 1926 in Kowalewko, Szubin District, in western Poland. During the 1939 German invasion that touched off World War II, his father was executed by a Nazi firing squad. Rakowski spent part of the German occupation working in a railroad repair shop in Poznan and then studied journalism at the Higher School of Social Sciences at Cracow and the Institute of Social Sciences in Warsaw. Following the end of the war in 1945, he served in the Polish Army as a political officer. The next year he joined the Communist party, and in 1949 he was assigned to the staff of the central committee of the Polish United Workers' party, where he drafted party documents and propaganda material.

In 1952 Rakowski married Wanda Wilkomirska, a Jewish musician who introduced him to the artists and intellectuals resisting Communist authority and who, perhaps more than anyone, shaped his subsequent liberalism. Rakowski's interest in reform was whetted in 1956 with the rise of Wladyslaw Gomulka as party leader, and it was during that decisive year that he helped to found *Polityka,* a reform-oriented newspaper that under his guidance became what one Polish Catholic journalist called "the best weekly in all the socialist camp." From 1958 to 1961 he served as chairman of the general board of the Polish Journalists' Association. As subeditor of *Polityka* in 1957 and as its editor in chief from 1958 to 1982, Rakowski developed a reputation as a tenacious, clear-thinking journalist who was fiercely loyal to his staff. Although he was candid and courageous enough to point out the shortcomings of the Communist government, he was also pragmatic and flexible enough not to go too far in testing the tolerance of authorities. He perfected the delicate art of writing in metaphors to avoid the wrath of government censors while at the same time he drove home critical points to his readers, who easily caught the drift of what he was saying. Although it was officially a party newspaper, staffed by party members, *Polityka* won loyal subscribers among intellectuals and dissidents and attracted the nation's most respected journalists as contributors.

As Gomulka's promises of greater freedom and economic reform gave way in the mid-1960s to renewed repression, Rakowski staunchly defended *Polityka.* He refused to join other official publications in systematically attacking the Catholic church in 1966, and, during the anti-Zionist campaign of 1968, he declined to run anti-Semitic articles and ignored a party directive that all periodicals purge their staffs of Jews. According to the *Wall Street Journal* (April 9, 1982), he declared

at the time, "If I am prepared to give up one tooth, I'll have to give up all of them." When he was denounced by other party journalists as "a low-grade patriot," he appealed directly to Gomulka and won the leader's protection from conservative hard-liners.

With the fall of Gomulka and the rise of Edward Gierek following the food riots of 1970, Rakowski called on the party to invite non-Communists into the political process. "Among the millions of non-party people," he editorialized in *Polityka,* "there are many individuals superior in intelligence and performance to many Party members. . . . A wise cadre policy must strictly observe the principle of equal opportunity for Party and non-Party people alike." Although he supported Gierek's attempts at reform, he discreetly distanced himself from Gierek when violent demonstrations again erupted in the mid-1970s, culminating in the strikes of July 1980 that gave rise to Solidarity.

In January 1981, amid the growing strength of Solidarity, Rakowski wrote an article, "To Respect Your Partner," in which he urged the government to recognize the role of the independent trade union in society, to work with it in overcoming Poland's pressing problems, and to create a joint commission as a forum for a regular dialogue between the government and Solidarity. The article caught the eye of General Wojciech Jaruzelski, who invited Rakowski to test his proposal as deputy prime minister in charge of negotiations with the trade union.

Rakowski's appointment was met with widespread optimism about the chances for a peaceful settlement with the volatile leadership of Solidarity. The government seemed genuinely prepared to recognize the independent trade union as an integral part of Polish society, and Lech Walesa and his followers appeared eager to play a constructive role in social planning. By the end of March 1981, following tense negotiations, Rakowski and Walesa reached a tentative agreement, in which the government admitted its past errors and Solidarity called off its strike. In an interview with John Darnton, the Warsaw bureau chief for the *New York Times* (May 10, 1981), Rakowski called the new cooperation a watershed in Polish socialism, but at the same time he warned of the dangers of failure. "The world will look upon us as idiots if we do not create a cohesive, efficient, and working economic system," he said. "So far, the world admires Polish ideas. But you cannot earn a single dollar from the export of ideas and we have been known as exporters of ideas for a few hundred years. To be an example for other countries, more is needed. We need high productivity, good work organization, and an effectively operating state system." He went on to praise Walesa as "a man of high caliber" committed to "the defense of workers' interests," although he cautioned that some of those around him were unrealistic and seemed to be more interested in leading a political movement than in getting back to work.

At the ninth Extraordinary Congress of the Polish Communist party in July 1981, Rakowski electrified the delegates with a stirring denunciation of extremists on both ends of the political spectrum. He blamed Poland's economic distress and popular unrest on hidebound party conservatives unwilling to experiment with change and on indecision in the Central Committee and the Politburo as well as on radicals, including those in Solidarity, who wanted to abandon Marxism-Leninism for a Western-style democracy. He called on the party to stop interfering with the day-to-day operations of government and urged a measure of autonomy for workers and a greater voice for all nonparty members willing to accept socialism. He closed to such sustained cheering that the speaker was forced to abandon the podium until order could be restored.

That euphoria soon evaporated, however, as negotiations with Solidarity broke down in acrimony and mutual distrust. During four days of talks in early August 1981, Rakowski and Walesa disagreed sharply about Solidarity's proposed role in the distribution of Poland's limited supply of food—so much so that government television news coverage of the meetings frequently featured an angry Rakowski shaking his finger in Walesa's face. He derided Walesa, an electrician by trade, for his lack of formal education, referring to him sarcastically as "Dr. Walesa." A joint communiqué was finally drafted and tentatively agreed to, but at the last minute the government unilaterally introduced different wording that Solidarity refused to accept. At that juncture, Rakowski denounced the union leadership as "arrogant" and stormed out of the conference, never to return. In speeches defending the government's actions, he began referring to Solidarity leaders as "peasants" and "blockheads." He reportedly resented Solidarity for never giving him credit for his years of standing up to party hard-liners and developed during those meetings an enduring personal hatred of Walesa.

The breakdown in the talks subjected Rakowski to a fresh round of criticism from party hard-liners, who had opposed any concessions to Solidarity, and from embittered trade union leaders, who suspected that he had bargained in bad faith in order to give the government time to prepare a direct assault against them. On December 13, 1981 General Jaruzelski imposed martial law and banned Solidarity after only sixteen months of legal existence. Dissidents were rounded up; press censorship was tightened. Rakowski not only actively supported the edict but, as deputy prime minister, oversaw its administration. In one instance, he evicted hundreds of college students from dormitories in Wroclaw for simply protesting the government's action. Ignoring his last-minute plea to remain, one-third of his staff at Polityka resigned in protest against martial law.

Because of his liberal credentials, Rakowski was dispatched abroad to try to persuade the West that martial law was necessary to avert a civil war and a Soviet invasion, but his former admirers were puzzled and disappointed that he had apparently sold out to Polish authorities. Some, however, were not surprised. "He was sincere when he believed in democracy," Richard T. Davies, the United States ambassador to Poland during the 1970s, was quoted as saying in Time (January 25, 1982) magazine. "But you had to know what he meant—as long as democracy was granted from on high, not from below, because that threatened the authorities."

In his book The Poles (1982), the British journalist Stewart Steven detected a similar consistency in Rakowski's career and warned the West of its folly in believing that every Eastern bloc reformer is really a closet democrat. "Rakowski has never changed," Steven wrote. "Rakowski is a committed Marxist-Leninist who went along with Solidarity. He regarded it as an essentially positive force as long as it did not seek to take over what he regarded as the prerogatives of government or change the political system which has existed in Poland since the war. Communism, he will argue passionately, is well able to subsist alongside an independent trade union movement and, indeed, benefit from such an association."

Although martial law was suspended in December 1982, confrontation with the still-banned Solidarity movement continued. When, in 1983, Rakowski lectured shipyard workers in Gdansk that their union leaders were turning them away from their government and leading them down the path to anarchy, he was met with hoots and jeers. Walesa responded by charging that Rakowski had used Solidarity to gratify his own ambition. "You've moved to the top by clambering over our backs," Walesa cried. "The least you can do is acknowledge it." Rakowski was not to remain at the top for long, however, for in 1985 Jaruzelski gave in to conservative demands for his ouster by demoting him to the powerless position of deputy speaker of the Sejm, Poland's unicameral legislature.

With the rise of Mikhail Gorbachev and a gradual thawing of the political climate in the Soviet Union, Rakowski returned to favor in Warsaw. After being away from the center of power for two years, he was elected to the Politburo in December 1987 and named central committee secretary for propaganda. Ironically, he now was in charge of the same press censorship that he had resisted for a quarter of a century. He also directed television coverage of the 1988 general strikes spawned by government-imposed price hikes that drove food costs up by 40 percent and tripled the price of coal. On September 19 Prime Minister Zbigniew Messner was ousted as the scapegoat for the failures of the government's economic policies, and one week later Jaruzelski nominated Rakowski as the new prime minister. The choice was ratified by the Sejm with an unusually large 10 percent abstention rate.

In his brief acceptance speech, Prime Minister Rakowski sent a clear signal that he intended to reach out to his critics. "The new government," he declared, "will deem winning the trust of a significant part of society its primary task. I am aware that this can be done not through words, but deeds." He quickly met with Poland's Roman Catholic primate, Jozef Cardinal Glemp, Catholic lay leaders, intellectuals, and business leaders. The promise of renewed dialogue with Solidarity prompted union leaders to extend a suspension of strike activity. Although Rakowski retained some of Messner's cabinet, he brought in fresh faces to the key posts of finance, industry, and foreign trade, and he seemed prepared to introduce free-market forces into the Polish economy. "Profit must be the fundamental index," he asserted, "production must be profitable and economical, and prices must be shaped by market rigors." Rakowski pledged to avoid the price hikes that brought down the Messner regime, but he warned that Poland would not be immune from harsh economic realities and wondered aloud if the Polish people were prepared to support such reforms. "To be consistent in restructuring our economy," he said, "means, in effect, that enterprises will be bankrupted or liquidated, that thousands of people may face the necessity of changing jobs, retraining for jobs, or even a temporary search for jobs. Will we get public approval for a situation where men seek jobs and jobs don't seek men?"

In the weeks that followed, Rakowski eased travel restrictions, encouraged private and foreign investment, and made it possible for farmers to bring their goods to market without going through the government bureaucracy. But many observers wondered how Rakowski would resolve his conflict with Solidarity, which had set forth as an essential condition of its cooperation with the government the reinstatement of its legal status as a trade union. Although he pledged to renew a dialogue with Solidarity, he kept postponing the date for formal talks, and he again began to refer to independent trade union activity as a threat to state security. In some of his speeches he hinted that reforms could go forward without the cooperation of Solidarity. Then, in a decision fraught with symbolism, he announced that on December 1, 1988 the government would begin the liquidation of the first of some 150 unprofitable state-run businesses around the country. The first to be closed, Rakowski decided, was the Lenin shipyard in Gdansk, the site of the 1980 labor unrest that had given birth to Solidarity.

Critics who viewed the action as a direct slap at Solidarity were quick to point out that other plants on the government's closure list were losing more money and gobbling up more government subsidies than the Lenin yard. Writing in the New York Times (November 12, 1988), Milan Svec, a consultant at the Institute for National Strategic Studies at the National Defense University, concluded that, in closing the Gdansk works, Rakowski believed that he was killing two birds with one stone. "Mr. Rakowski wants to prove that while he is no democrat, he can experiment with the gradual introduction of a free market," Svec observed. "But he also wants to prove that while Solidarity might

be the country's strongest supporter of democracy, it is ill-equipped to accept a free market—in fact, is an enemy of the free market." Krzysztof Sliwinski, a journalist for the Catholic monthly ZNAK, suggested a slightly different motive to William Echikson of the Christian Science Monitor (November 30, 1988): "Rakowski is saying, 'O.K., I'll give you private enterprise and capitalism. Then you won't need political freedom and Solidarity.'"

In January 1989 Rakowski again seemed to be extending the olive branch to Solidarity. Over the bitter opposition of some party leaders, he won central committee approval for a resolution that would re-legalize Solidarity for a two-year trial period if the independent trade union agreed to certain conditions. But that act proved to be the beginning of the end of Rakowski's tenure as prime minister, and crucially decisive events followed in rapid succession. Solidarity was legalized in April, won almost all of the parliamentary seats open to opposition candidates in June, and formed a new government with the Communists in September. Meanwhile, Rakowski resigned after failing to win reelection to parliament in June. Of twenty-three cabinet posts, only four went to the Communist party under Rakowski, who had been elected general secretary on June 29 by the central committee. Those four were the ministries of defense, interior, foreign trade, and transportation.

Mieczyslaw Rakowski's personal life has not endeared him to the Communist party hierarchy. His first wife, the violinist Wanda Wilkomirska, was an active dissident in the radical Committee for Social Self-Defense before their divorce in 1977 and later defected to West Germany. Their two grown sons also have fled Poland. His second wife, Elzbieta Kepińska, an actress, has been a member of Solidarity. Rakowski, who walks with a distinctive swagger, has been described as intelligent, witty, charming, ambitious, and acutely sensitive to criticism. He spurns the drab suits of the Eastern bloc for stylish Western cuts. He speaks fluent German, Russian, and English. His Polish language writings on politics and history include The Federal Republic of Germany from a Short Distance (1958), The West Looks for Ideology (1961), and The Foreign Policy of the Polish People's Republic (1974).

References: N Y Times A p10 S 28 '88 por; International Who's Who, 1989-90

Reed, Lou

1942- Musician; songwriter. Address: c/o Sire Records, 75 Rockefeller Plaza, New York, N.Y. 10019

Although "Walk on the Wild Side" is his only indisputable hit, Lou Reed has been for twenty-five years one of the most important performers in American rock-'n'-roll. As lead singer and chief

Lou Reed

songwriter for the Velvet Underground, the influential band produced by Andy Warhol that attracted only a cult following in the 1960s but became the prototype for later art-rockers like Talking Heads, Reed was the Jack Kerouac of rock. Cultivating the somewhat sinister image of white urban hipster with his black attire and "shades," Reed introduced previously taboo subject matter, such as drugs and aberrant sexuality, into the American pop song and, along with Bob Dylan and Van Morrison, expanded the form of the rock song beyond the repetitious pattern of verse-chorus/verse-chorus/ bridge/chorus. As a solo recording artist in the 1970s and 1980s, Reed took on and then discarded a succession of styles and personas, from "rock-'n'-roll animal" to, finally, the contented, average family man.

In his most compelling songs, Lou Reed was the Louis-Ferdinand Céline of New York nightmare, whose corrosive musical journalism amounted to a tour of hell conducted by one of the damned. Like Céline, he seemed to have embarked on a journey to the end of night. His cool detachment from his subject matter and his dispassionate stage presence seemed the musical equivalent of Warhol's glacial neutrality, but in the mid-1980s he began to take up committed social commentary. In 1989 he released *New York*, a suite of fourteen songs. In *New York* he again confronted social malaise, but this time he pilloried the conditions that have caused institutions to crumble in a metropolis afflicted by an underclass numbed by drugs, an indifferent middle class, and a ruling class mired in greed and corruption.

The older of two children, Lou Reed was born Louis Alan Reed in Brooklyn, New York in 1942. When Lou was young, his father, a successful ac-

countant and businessman, moved the family to Freeport, an affluent town on Long Island's south shore, where Lou studied classical music on the piano and three-chord rock-'n'-roll on the guitar. Lou Reed is reluctant to discuss any aspect of his personal life, but he has acknowledged that as a teenager he was subjected to electroshock therapy, an experience he described in the song "Kill Your Sons." "I was just a little depressed and it was a dumb doctor," he explained to an interviewer from *People* (March 30, 1981) magazine.

From the few guarded comments Reed has made about his adolescence, it appears that he was not especially close to his mother and that the antipathy between Reed and his father has abated very little over the years. "I went to great lengths to escape the whole thing," Reed said of his family when he spoke to an interviewer from the New York *Daily News* (April 9, 1978). "I couldn't relate to it then and I can't now. I keep a distance from my family for my own emotional safety and so I can do the things I want to get done. My mother called me up very proud about a review. But I think it kills my old man to this day. If I had been a failure at [music], if I'd come home with my tail between my legs, I think they would have been a lot happier."

What changed Lou Reed's life was his discovery that mastering just three simple chords enabled him to play elemental rock-'n'-roll on the guitar. Influenced by the "doo-wop" style of rhythm-and-blues vocal groups, the rockabilly of early Elvis Presley and Carl Perkins, and the teen angst ballads of Dion & the Belmonts, Reed played rhythm guitar and sang in a group called the Shades, who changed their name to the Jades for a record they cut in 1957. The "A side" of that single was a run-of-the-mill teen heartache number entitled "So Blue," but the flip side was "Leave Him for Me," a credible doo-wop imitation written by the fourteen-year-old Reed. As David Fricke noted in a profile of Reed for *Rolling Stone* (September 25, 1986), "Though it was hardly indicative of the Velvet Underground's white-noise wail-to-come or the grim, almost conversational tone of junkie confessions like 'Heroin,' that 1957 single had everything to do with Reed's formative experiences as a songwriter and performer. No matter what extremes he went to in later years, Reed always made his strongest, most lasting statements with a simple rock-'n'-roll heartbeat."

In the early 1960s, Reed escaped from suburban family life by attending Syracuse University, where he majored in English, with a minor in modern philosophy, and adopted the stance of the rebellious bohemian. At that time, ROTC was mandatory for all males on college campuses, but he contrived to be kicked out of his campus unit and its two-year commitment to military service by pointing an unloaded gun at his commanding officer's head. Having acquired a passion for progressive jazz, he hosted a jazz program on the campus radio station until he was ousted, allegedly for belching during a public service message for muscular dystrophy. It was, however, the doomed poet and critic Delmore Schwartz who most influenced Reed, providing the aspiring songwriter with a literary model for the role of artist-outsider that he was so assiduously cultivating. In the late 1930s and the 1940s, Schwartz had given promise of becoming a likely successor to T. S. Eliot, but, during the brief time that he taught at Syracuse, he was on the verge of succumbing to the madness that would soon engulf him. Although his "teaching" consisted largely of gossiping with visiting authors and reading to his students from the works of Eliot and Joyce, Schwartz enjoyed classroom give-and-take with students like Reed, who was by then playing guitar in local bar bands. "It was a thrill knowing him," Reed has said of Schwartz, though the poet gave short shrift to Reed's idea of writing pop songs with literate lyrics.

After graduating from Syracuse in 1964, Reed headed for New York City, where he found work as a hack songwriter for Pickwick Records, which released bargain-bin albums made up of tunes that imitated hits of the day and exploited their popularity. "At Pickwick," Reed told David Fricke, "I was like an unsuccessful Ellie Greenwich, a poor man's Carole King." But while he was writing innocuous ditties like "The Ostrich" by day, by night Reed was composing songs like the iconic "Heroin," a harrowing chronicle of drug enslavement. Partly because no one wanted to listen to Reed, whose singing voice is deadpan and far from pretty, in 1965 he joined with fellow guitarist and Syracuse student Sterling Morrison, the avant-garde, Welsh-born viola player John Cale, and drummer Maureen Tucker, the sister of another of Reed's college friends, to form the Velvet Underground, named after the blurb for a pornographic novel. In the mid-1960s, after the emergence of the Beatles, the Rolling Stones, and the electrified Bob Dylan, the most ambitious undertaking in rock music was that of the Velvet Underground. "The music," Gene Santoro wrote in the Nation (February 27, 1989), "was shot through with grungy feedback, Reed's howling-at-the-abyss guitar and John Cale's sawed-to-the-bone electrified viola and droning keyboards; underneath rumbled Maureen Tucker's drums and Sterling Morrison's guitar and bass." In addition to the feathery, understated drumming by Maureen Tucker and the chordal drone achieved by the interplay of Reed's and Morrison's guitars, much of the band's sophistication was inspired by the classically trained Cale, who integrated the avant-garde composer La Monte Young's harmonic repetitive structures into its sound. To the ears of 1960s listeners, the Velvet Underground's lyrics, largely written by Reed, were as abrasive as their music. Trying to voice "adult" concerns, Reed borrowed from such diverse idioms as the Berlin cabaret songs of Bertolt Brecht and Kurt Weill, the narrative expansiveness of Bob Dylan, and the subversively dark literary themes explored by Jean Genet and William Burroughs.

The result was a stark yet often poignant urban realism in songs like "Waiting for the Man," about a white boy's trip to Harlem to meet his drug connection; "Venus in Furs," ostensibly about sadomasochism but also a meditation on the power of sexuality and the sexuality of power; and "Heroin," in which lines like "I'm goin' to nullify my life" took on the force of poetic declamation through Reed's unique vocal delivery, which was flat, half spoken and half sung, yet evocative. "My prime ambition," he explained to David Fricke, "was to knock the door down on what rock-'n'-roll songs were about. . . . I wanted to put adult things in it, real life as it was going on all around us. Drugs, violence, New York, all this stuff. . . . The other idea was that the music matched the words. If the words were scary, the music would get scary." It seemed to one who had studied with Delmore Schwartz that frank discussions of sex and drugs, even when set to music, were common subjects for writers to explore. "I never in a million years thought people would be outraged by what I was doing," Reed told David Fricke. "You could go to your neighborhood bookstore and get any of that."

Andy Warhol discovered the Velvet Underground at the Café Bizarre in 1966. The seminal painter of pop art, Warhol was also the avatar of the "hip" artistic underground in downtown Manhattan, where uptown café society mingled with the trendsetting demimonde of artists, fashion designers, musicians, and their camp followers, who were legion. Officially billed as the band's "producer," Warhol lent them his imprimatur of approval, helped them secure a recording contract with MGM/Verve, and put them on the road as part of his Exploding Plastic Inevitable, a traveling freak-show "happening" reminiscent of the uninhibited scene that transpired nightly at Warhol's studio, the now legendary Factory. When David Fricke interviewed him for Rolling Stone (May 4, 1989), Reed explained how Warhol actually "produced" the Velvets, as the group was popularly known: "By keeping people away from us, because they thought he was producing it. [MGM/Verve] didn't sign us because of us. We were signed because of Andy. And he took all the flak. We said, 'He's the producer,' and he would say 'Oh, that was great.' 'Oh, you should leave it that way.'"

Looking back on the Velvets' first album two decades after its release, a reviewer for Rolling Stone (August 27, 1987) commented, "This . . . monument of lyrical and musical innovation in rock, . . . a record of continuing influence, . . . was banged out, for the most part, in a crumbling four-track studio over two days at a cost of $1,500." The Velvet Underground & Nico (1967), "produced" by Warhol, whose artwork for the jacket cover, a banana painted on a white ground, has made the LP a collectible, featured songs like "Heroin," "There She Goes Again," "The Black Angel's Death Song," and "Venus in Furs," which remain timely almost a generation after their release. Nico was Reed's girlfriend, a German-born model who aspired to be an international chanteuse in the manner of Marlene Dietrich. She sang the lead vocal on the poignant "All Tomorrow's Parties," which, along with "Femme Fatale," "I'll Be Your Mirror," and "Sunday Morning," showcased Reed's ability to compose what one critic called "complexly gorgeous odes to love and life."

Although the Velvet Underground released three more albums that were ahead of their time—*White Light, White Heat* (1968), *The Velvet Underground* (1969), and *Loaded* (1970)—the band gradually fell apart in the years between 1967 and 1970. Reed infuriated Warhol by firing him in 1967, when the band tried to expand its following beyond its cult devotees in New York. After the release, in 1968, of the noise-rock *White Light, White Heat*, John Cale quit the band and was replaced by the bassist Doug Yule. Two years later, while *Loaded* was being recorded, Reed made his departure, exhausting the Velvets as a creative force. It has been said that only 1,000 people heard the first Velvets LP in the 1960s, but each of them went out, got a guitar, and started a band.

The Velvets never sold many albums in the 1960s largely because, as Gene Santoro wrote in the *Nation*, "while the counterculture was painting itself Day-Glo, ingesting consciousness-expanding substances and organizing its politics, Lou Reed . . . was penning lyrics about heroin, sadomasochism, and street violence." But when the punk–New Wave irruption of the late 1970s shook the foundations of the rock establishment, Reed was lionized as the "godfather of punk," and the Velvets were acknowledged to be the spiritual precursors of such incandescent art-rockers as Patti Smith, Television, and Talking Heads in New York and Joy Division, the Cure, and the Psychedelic Furs in Great Britain. "The Velvet Underground was not just some freakish experimental group," Robert Quine, an influential rock guitarist and Reed acolyte, has said. "It was straight from Little Richard and Elvis, getting as experimental as possible but never losing the basic, hypnotic, funky feel of nice simple rock-'n'-roll."

After leaving the Velvets, Reed entered upon a period that he has called one of "exile and pondering." In fact, he was working as a typist for his father's company, but in 1972 he resurfaced with *Transformer*, an album produced by David Bowie, the superstar British glitter-rocker who had cited Reed as one of his principal influences. *Transformer* yielded "Walk on the Wild Side," Reed's homage to the sexually ambiguous debauchees who served as Warhol's gaggle of self-appointed "superstars" in the 1960s, which became his only radio hit despite its fairly explicit lyrics. Just as he was on the edge of pop stardom, Reed released *Berlin* (1973), which he called his "version of *Hamlet*." It is now regarded as one of the rock masterpieces of the 1970s, though it was too morbid and depressing to receive extensive radio airplay. Set in the divided city of the title, the album was not unlike some of the more squalid and lugubrious films of Rainer Werner Fassbinder, but in the form of a song cycle that told the story of a young American expatriate who falls in love with a German woman, Caroline. After a series of mutual betrayals, they become amphetamine junkies, and Caroline eventually kills herself. "If people don't like *Berlin*," Reed said in 1974, "it's because it's too real. It's not like a TV program where all the bad things that happen to people are tolerable. Life isn't that way."

In the early 1970s, Reed's image was that of the dark prince of artistic rock-'n'-roll. With his heavily made-up eyes, black-painted lips and fingernails, hair shaved, for a time, in the shape of an iron cross, emaciated figure, and wan pallor, he looked like a glitter-rocker who took his decadence all too seriously. During performances of "Heroin," Reed would pretend to shoot up on stage, and for much of the decade he shared an apartment in Greenwich Village with his transvestite lover, Rachel. He also had a reputation for being combative with journalists and influential music critics, especially John Rockwell of the *New York Times* and Robert Christgau of the *Village Voice*, both of whom were Reed supporters, and for publicly castigating music-industry executives.

With the 1974 release of the visceral *Rock-'n'-Roll Animal*, which is widely regarded as one of rock's five most powerful recordings, Reed once again became a candidate for pop stardom. But, as if to confound both his critics and his growing audience of listeners, in 1975 he recorded the most inaccessible LP of his career, *Metal Machine Music*—a two-disc set made up of high-decibel noise and guitar feedback that was, Reed said, "unrestrained" by considerations of "tempo or key." As he has explained, his next album, *Coney Island Baby* (1976), was a "continuation of what he was doing with the Velvet Underground." Indeed, the title track is a lovely, almost nostalgic reminiscence about growing up on Long Island, whereas the ominously gripping "Kicks" is about someone who delights in killing people. Reed's follow-up LP, *Sally Can't Dance* (1977), despite its admirable and grimly amusing title track, was thought by many critics to be an unsuccessful self-parody, a cynical attempt to cash in on his "rock-'n'-roll animal" persona. It was, wrote Tom Carson in *Rolling Stone* (April 6, 1978), "his trashiest LP, . . . Lou Reed [turning] his own poetry into graffiti."

"I do me better than anyone else does," Reed boasted in response to emerging rockers like Patti Smith, an avowed Reed cultist, and Richard Hell and the Voidoids, who were inspired by the droning guitar sound the Velvets had pioneered in the 1960s. And in 1978 Reed produced his most compelling musical statement of the decade, *Street Hassle*. In his *Rolling Stone* review, Tom Carson wrote that, in the years since the breakup of the Velvet Underground, "Reed's bizarre and half-baked semistardom became a travesty of his art, as one of the most magical raw nerves of our time coarsened into a crude, death-trip clown. . . . While much of Reed's solo work was far from bad, one has to remember that his admirers expected him to surpass Bob Dylan, and the Velvets' LPs had promised nothing less. . . . *Street Hassle* is . . . a confession of failure that becomes a stunning . . . triumph. . . . Its premise is to accept being damned as an irrevocable condition, and then speak as truthfully as possible about what that may mean." *Street Hassle* produced no hit songs, but the eleven-minute title track, about a junkie whose lover dies from an overdose, was a tour de force. It consisted of three narrative fragments that were marvels of literary compression ("Love has gone away/Took the rings off my fingers/And there's nothing left to say"). Appearing uncredited on the LP, Bruce Springsteen startled Reed fans when he recited the song's concluding verse, which contained lines Reed had written especially for Springsteen ("Tramps like us babe/We were born to pay").

As John Rockwell observed in the *New York Times* (April 16, 1978),"Reed has swung so wildly between the poles of cynical, commercial reductions of his ideas and aggressive experimentation that he has sometimes left his fans completely confused." Accordingly, Reed's follow-up LP to *Street Hassle* departed from his signature style of simple, three-chord, guitar-based songs to explore the densely layered electronic sound of synthesizer-oriented progressive rock and the free-form jazz styles that were being developed by Ornette Coleman and Don Cherry. The result of that experimentation was *The Bells* (1979), which included the cuts "Disco Mystic," a tongue-in-chic "dance" number, "Families," about the pain of parents and children with radically different ways of life, and the title track, which featured the trumpet playing of Don Cherry.

In his *New York Times* (May 13, 1979) review, John Rockwell applauded *The Bells* as one of the artist's "good" efforts, but he went on to say what Reed had created was "not a very commercial sound. . . . It's not even a sound that one would want to listen to over and over again. But as a part of . . . Reed's ongoing attempt to tame and exploit whatever demons lie within him, it's a valuable document." On *Growing Up in Public* (1980), Reed continued to exorcise his demons in songs like "Standing on Ceremony" and "My Old Man," both of which deal with an embattled family's unresolved conflicts, and the title track, an autobiographical number in which Reed addresses the problem of "growing up in public with [your] pants pulled down." Critics felt that his lyrics were among the most astringent of his career, but they also asserted that the LP's music was weakened by Reed's continuing lack of emphasis on the guitar.

The acclaimed *Blue Mask* (1982) was Reed's "goodbye to all that," the summation of his experience as chronicler-participant of New York's urban underworld in the tumultuous 1960s and 1970s. That Reed had survived the New York netherworld of drugs, drink, and sexual excess to make one of the most ambitious albums of the 1980s called to mind Nietzsche's aphorism "What does not kill me makes me stronger." *The Blue Mask* marked a musical turning point for Reed and re-

flected profound changes in his personal life as well. Musically, Reed returned to playing guitar, recording the LP with the classically trained bassist Fernando Saunders and with Robert Quine, one of Reed's own rock-'n'-roll progeny, who had played guitar for Richard Hell and the Voidoids. Reed's personal life gained stability when he married the British-born writer Sylvia Morales on Valentine's Day 1980 and later moved with her to a rustic retreat in New Jersey. "I don't know what I would have done without her," Reed said in 1982. "I've got help for the first time in my life. And I'm surrounded by good, caring, honest business people. In my life, that's a real change."

In the *New York Times* (March 10, 1982), Robert Palmer wrote that *The Blue Mask* was "stark, harrowing, and ultimately uplifting rock-and-roll. It is the most powerful and consistent album . . . Reed has made since 1967." The "harrowing" cuts dealt with alcoholism, rape, and masochism, while the "uplifting" numbers, especially the last song on the LP, "Heavenly Arms," about the redemptive powers of love between man and woman, were inspired by Reed's newfound domestic contentment, and on "Average Guy" Reed announced that the muse of rock-'n'-roll also visited those who led quiet lives and sought ordinary pleasures. Recording again with Quine and Saunders, in 1983 Reed released *Legendary Hearts*, a soulful album with lyrics as deeply personal as those of *The Blue Mask*, and *New Sensation* (1984) was an upbeat celebration of marital bliss and the "average guy" outlook on life. *Mistrial* (1986), however, took a more hard-edged approach to rock than its recent predecessors, and the cuts "Video Violence" and "The Original Wrapper," the latter Reed's synthesis of heavy metal and rap, evinced a burgeoning interest in political issues.

It was apparent that the rock-'n'-roll animal of the 1970s was becoming the political animal of the 1980s. In 1986 Reed sang on "Sun City," the multi-artist condemnation of apartheid, and joined with the British rock artists Peter Gabriel and Sting as a featured performer on the Amnesty International tour, a series of benefit concerts for the organization that exposes human rights abuses throughout the world. "I don't write about political prisoners," Reed told David Fricke. "I write about internal prisoners, people who are going through internal battles in a really small framework, close relationships, betrayed friendships. . . . [But] the days of me being aloof about certain things are over. I couldn't not be vocal about apartheid."

On *New York* (1989), the most commercially successful album of his career to date, Reed addressed himself in scathing terms to the sources of political and moral rot in New York City. Indeed, if the novel *The Bonfire of the Vanities* dramatizes Tom Wolfe's vision of the decline and fall of New York in the 1980s, *New York* is Reed's own raging bonfire of private greed, public corruption, and yuppie complacency. On "Romeo Had Juliette," a story of "love under siege," as one writer put it, Reed sings: "Manhattan's sinking like a rock/Into the filthy Hudson, what a shock/They wrote a book about it/They said it was like ancient Rome." On the wistful "Halloween Parade," Reed, whose "Walk on the Wild Side" was once a hymn for sexual thrill seekers, patrols Christopher Street in the Village, memorializing the many friends he has lost, victims of AIDS ("The past keeps . . . knockin' on my door/And I don't want to hear it anymore"). On the melodic "Dirty Blvd." Reed sings about Pedro, who lives in a $2,000-a-month room in a welfare hotel, where "no one . . . dreams of being a doctor or a lawyer or anything, they dream of dealing on the dirty boulevard." "Hold On" is Reed's unflinching version of the evening news: "There's blacks with knives and whites with guns fighting in Howard Beach/There's no such thing as human rights when you walk the New York streets/ . . . The haves and have-nots are bleeding in the tub/That's New York's future not mine." On *New York*'s most controversial track, the anti–anti-Semitic "Good Evening Mr. Waldheim," Reed does not refrain from naming names as he chides Pope John Paul II for meeting with the Austrian chancellor who was a military servant of the Third Reich during the Holocaust and condemns Jesse Jackson for accepting the political support of the virulently anti-Semitic Nation of Islam sects ("If I ran for president and once was a member of the Klan/Wouldn't you call me on it the way I call you on Farrakhan").

Although many of the songs were not bolstered by distinctive melodies, critics agreed that *New York* was an important signpost on the landscape of 1980s rock-'n'-roll. But Reed did not want strong supporting melodies on *New York*; musically, he said, the album was a celebration of his "favorite guitar sounds" and a homage to the four-piece band he has been recording with since *Mistrial*—Reed and Mike Rathke on guitars, Rob Wasserman on bass, and *New York*'s coproducer, Fred Maher, on drums. The Velvets' Maureen Tucker played drums on two songs, one of which was "Dime Store Mystery," Reed's moving elegy to his mentor, Andy Warhol, who died in 1987.

Reviewing the album in the *New Yorker* (April 24, 1989), Mark Moses praised Reed for having come up with a "talky bull session as full of insight and preposterousness as anything he has done." Moses felt it was surprising that "Reed still feels he has to make a case for his literary reputation, after more than two decades of stunning, though erratic, work." Reed, who has published poems in the *Paris Review* and other journals, insists that his ambition would have been "to write the Great American Novel" had he not loved the sound of drums, guitars, and rock-'n'-roll. His songs, he says, form a coherent thematic whole and constitute the musical equivalent of the novel he might have written. When he tries to write short stories, he suddenly "hears" drum and guitar parts and, inevitably, his literary jottings turn into songs.

In the past, Lou Reed tended to alternate between disdainful taciturnity and hostility in interviews with journalists and critics, members of

professions he once viewed with contempt. He has since mellowed, and interviewers routinely describe him as charming and sharply intelligent but guarded when asked, as invariably he is, about the autobiographical content of songs like "Heroin" and "Sister Ray." "I couldn't still be around if I had done everything I am reputed to have done" is Reed's stock retort to questions about his past drug use. "Lou Reed is my protagonist," he explained to a reporter from *People*. "Sometimes he's 20, sometimes 80 percent me, but never 100. He's a vehicle to go places I wouldn't go or say things I don't go along with." In the early 1980s Reed gave up hard drinking; his only remaining vice is cigarettes, and that, he has said, will be the next to go.

So emblematic of urban hipness and downtown New York "cool" is Lou Reed that in 1986 he appeared in a television commercial as a pitchman for Honda motorcycles. Because he feeds off of the city creatively, he and his wife maintain an apartment in Manhattan, though their farm in New Jersey is their primary residence. His marriage to the former Sylvia Morales is the second for Reed, who was briefly married and then divorced in 1972. He is currently collaborating with John Cale, his former partner in the Velvet Underground, on an eagerly awaited requiem for Andy Warhol. Entitled *Songs for 'Drella*, after "Cinderella," Reed's nickname for his late friend, it is scheduled to close out the Next Wave Festival at the Brooklyn Academy of Music in December 1989.

References: *Chicago Tribune* XIII p8+ Ap 2 '89; *Gentlemen's Q* 56:211+ S '86; *N Y Times* II p17+ Jl 20 '80, C p21 Mr 10 '82 por, C p22 Ja 6 '89 por, V p23+ Ja 22 '89 por; *Washington Post* C p7 Ja 11 '89 por, B p1+ Mr 13 '89 pors

---

Reilly, William K(ane)

Jan. 26, 1940– Administrator of the Environmental Protection Agency. Address: Environmental Protection Agency, 401 M St., S.W., Washington, D.C. 20460

Although some environmentalists have been skeptical of President George Bush's oft-repeated commitment to their cause, nearly all of them were heartened by his decision to appoint William K. Reilly as administrator of the Environmental Protection Agency. The first professional environmentalist to head the agency since its founding in 1970, Reilly brought with him not only an unimpeachable reputation for defending the earth's resources but also an instinct for achieving workable compromises. As president of the Conservation Foundation, an environmental research group, since 1973 and, concurrently, of the World Wildlife Fund since 1985, Reilly reached out to developers and manufacturers in seeking ways to preserve the environment without choking off economic growth

William K. Reilly

and commerce. His efforts earned him "a well-deserved reputation for focusing on solutions to environmental problems, not on polemics," in the opinion of Jeffery C. Van, a spokesman for the Chemical Manufacturers Association. As EPA chief, Reilly, a self-styled conservationist whose distaste for confrontation prompts him to avoid the label of "environmental activist," has vowed to tackle such thorny issues as acid rain pollution, toxic waste disposal, global warming, and wetlands protection.

William Kane Reilly was born in Decatur, Illinois on January 26, 1940 to George and Margaret Reilly. He spent his childhood on a farm in his native state, but when he was fourteen he was sent to live with an aunt in the considerably different environment of Fall River, Massachusetts, where he graduated from B. M. C. Durfee High School in 1958. A model student, he was a member of the National Honor Society and a captain of the school's debating team. In 1962 he received a B.A. degree in history from Yale University, and he graduated from Harvard Law School in 1965. After practicing law briefly with the firm of Ross and Hardies in Chicago, Reilly served in the United States Army from 1966 to 1967, rising to the rank of captain. In 1969 he was appointed associate director of the Urban Policy Center in Washington, and in the following year, he joined the senior staff of President Richard Nixon's Council on Environmental Quality. While serving on the council, he completed requirements for a master's degree in urban planning from Columbia University, which he received in 1971.

In 1972 Reilly was appointed executive director of the Task Force on Land Use and Urban Growth by its chairman, Laurance S. Rockefeller. Having assembled a well-balanced staff of lawyers, architects, journalists, economists, biologists, and urban planners, Reilly pored over all significant reports on land use and urban growth issued since the late 1960s and all relevant state and national bills either recently enacted or under consideration. In its final report in 1973, the task force recommended that Congress use a carrot-and-stick approach to impose a national land-use policy by granting incentives of federal aid to states that cooperated and withholding highway or other funds from states that failed to comply. Reilly edited *The Use of Land: A Citizens' Policy Guide to Urban Growth* (1973), in which contributors detailed the work of the task force.

In 1973 Reilly was named president of the Conservation Foundation, a nonprofit environmental research group based in Washington. Over the next sixteen years, he transformed it from a small think tank into a successful force for environmental protection around the world. In 1985 he oversaw the foundation's merger with and became president of the World Wildlife Fund (WWF), which focuses its resources on international concerns in general and Latin America and the Caribbean in particular. The WWF specializes in the protection of the tropical rain forests, whose rich diversity of animal and plant life has been endangered by pollution and development. Under Reilly's leadership, the combined operation grew to a membership of 600,000 and a staff of 200, which supported hundreds of projects on an annual budget of $35 million.

Throughout the Nixon, Ford, and Carter years, Reilly avoided making any criticism of White House environmental policy, but, beginning in 1982, he cautiously took on the Reagan administration. He criticized the controversial secretary of the interior, James G. Watt, for his hostility to environmental concerns and warned that his successor, William P. Clark, was merely a less obvious advocate of the same policy. In the publication *Environment* (July–August 1985), he described the first half of the 1980s as "a time of retrenchment, of cutbacks in domestic spending, of diminished confidence in federal initiatives as responses to national needs . . . , of reluctance to 'lock up' the nation's resources, of preference for the market as a determinant of resource use rather than the commitment to preservation and public enjoyment."

In its 1985 report "National Parks for a New Generation," the Conservation Foundation faulted the Reagan administration for reversing two decades of park development and warned that existing parks were threatened by a surge in visitor traffic and pollution generated by nearby commercial development. The report called for a ten-year effort to modernize and reinvigorate the National Park Service as the "chief guardian of the nation's most treasured assets." Dubbed "Preservation '95," the program called for an enlarged budget, more staff members skilled in preservation techniques, better planning to identify endangered areas, and career incentives for park specialists in such areas as citizen participation and scientific research. It also called for an expansion of the park system to include the Florida Keys, Big Sur, and Lake Tahoe.

In a broader assessment of the state of the American environment in the mid-1980s that he made for an article in *USA Today* (September 1985) magazine, Reilly warned that the threat to clean air and water had shifted from a few widely used pollutants to a myriad of trace toxic substances whose long-term effects on human development were not clearly understood or even measured adequately. He conceded that, since the 1970s, much progress had been made in ridding the air of conventional pollutants, reclaiming waterways for swimmers and fishermen, and limiting man's exposure to lead and certain other toxic substances, but he noted that, in part because of EPA budget restraints imposed by the Reagan administration, the levels of many toxic substances were no longer monitored properly, enforcement of compliance with EPA directives was spotty, and not much was being done to stay ahead of emerging dangers.

Reilly cited a recent National Academy of Sciences study that revealed that the federal government had tested less than 2 percent of known chemicals sufficiently to establish safe levels for humans. Moreover, he charged that, although the EPA had persuaded industry and local governments to install costly antipollution equipment, the operation and maintenance of such machinery was not inspected regularly. He also warned that, unless sulfur emissions from coal-burning facilities were curbed, the resulting precipitation that falls as acid rain would destroy East Coast and Canadian marine life, stunt forest growth, and endanger human health. To resolve those issues, Reilly urged a new spirit of cooperation among environmentalists, industry, and state and local governments. "Environmental policy at mid-decade," he concluded, "is suspended between old problems and new, between progress and polarization." Without rational compromise, he warned, both the nation's resources and, ultimately, industrial development would fall victim to environmental gridlock.

Reilly stressed the same theme of cooperation regarding conservation efforts in Latin America in his remarks before the twenty-fifth anniversary conference of the WWF in September 1986. After pointing with pride to the organization's recent achievements in helping to discover and classify hundreds of fish species in Brazil, reintroduce the endangered golden lion tamarin into the Brazilian rain forest, and bring the vicuña back from the brink of extinction, he emphasized that industrial and commercial development was not only compatible with but of critical importance to a successful environmental policy in the hemisphere. "To reach the nonconservationist professionals who guide development, who plan roads and dams and hydroelectric facilities," he declared, "requires a more utilitarian message than the ones that draw on fear and sentiment that have worked so well with the press and the public for conservationists in the United States."

Not content to challenge such easy targets as industrial polluters and zealous commercial developers, Reilly also has singled out the more sympathetic figure of the family farmer as a danger to the environment. In a speech before the National Agricultural Forum in Arlington, Virginia in October 1986, delivered on the same day that the Conservation Foundation released its report "Agriculture and the Environment in a Changing World Economy," Reilly warned that agricultural programs in the United States and Europe foster inefficient land use and overproduction, which in turn introduce excessive amounts of chemicals into the soil. Reilly asserted that the message that governments send to farmers through generous crop subsidies and promises to purchase excess yields is "Produce as much as you can—put marginal land and wildlife habitat to the plow, and make heavy use of fertilizer, pesticides, and other inputs. Don't worry about selling your crop at a profit on the market because the government will buy it at a higher price, and either store it or export it; society will absorb the economic and environmental cost." Calling for cooperation, not confrontation, he urged conservationists to recognize that the family farm must be restored to profitability before farmers can be expected to focus their energies on conservation, and he asked farmers to remember that environmentalists who care so deeply about land conservation are "the farmer's strongest potential friend and ally."

Throughout his tenure as president of the Conservation Foundation, Reilly worked closely with other environmental groups, industry, and all levels of government to foster agreement on toxic waste cleanup, protection of water supplies, and conservation in the Third World. In July 1987 he called together a diverse group of competing interests to discuss the alarming loss of wetlands, which have been disappearing in the United States at an annual rate of hundreds of thousands of acres for the past thirty years. Under Reilly's encouragement, the group of environmentalists, developers, industrialists, and federal regulators hammered out over a sixteen-month period an agreement that set a "no net loss" target for wetlands. Similarly, representatives from the WWF sat down with officials from American banks and Third World governments to work out a "debt-for-nature swap," in which officials in developing countries agree to safeguard certain endangered resources in exchange for an assumption of debt by the banks.

The few environmentalists who criticized Reilly's performance as head of the Conservation Foundation pointed to his activities in 1988, when the organization was retained by the Coalition on Superfund, a group representing those responsible for the disposal of hazardous waste, to study the workability of the superfund law requiring producers of such waste to pay all cleanup costs. Although the superfund study, which many thought might lead to regulatory relief for polluters, foundered under criticism from Congress and other environmental groups, some, including Viveca Novak, a senior writer for *Common Cause* magazine, took Reilly to task for trying to ingratiate himself with producers of hazardous waste.

When, on December 21, 1988, President-elect Bush, on the recommendation of former EPA chief William D. Ruckelshaus, named William K. Reilly to succeed Lee M. Thomas as administrator of the EPA, his announcement was greeted with enthusiasm by nearly all environmental groups and with approval by industry representatives. "He is very well respected in the conservation community," Jim Maddy, the executive director of the League of Conservation Voters, said. "If given enough support from the White House and the Office of Management and Budget, he is somebody who will do an outstanding job as administrator of the EPA." Among the few who expressed some doubt that Reilly's accommodative style was suitable for enforcing compliance with EPA directives was Daniel F. Becker, the legislative director of the Environmental Action Foundation. "The challenge for Bill Reilly now," Becker asserted, "is to stop negotiating with polluters and make them obey the law." At a press conference announcing the appointment, Reilly refused to be drawn into criticism of the Reagan administration's environmental policy, but, at his confirmation hearing, he laid out an agenda that marked a clear break with the previous administration. Promising "vigorous and aggressive enforcement of the environmental laws," he vowed to strengthen the Clean Air Act to curb acid rain and to seek international cooperation in reducing the production of chlorofluorocarbons, which are depleting the earth's protective ozone layer. He also pledged to protect the wetlands and clean up toxic waste dumps.

In his first interview as EPA administrator, Reilly informed Philip Shabecoff of the *New York Times* (February 22, 1989) that toxic waste cleanup was his number-one priority. Dismissing suggestions that new laws were necessary, he vowed to "carry a big stick and to be so aggressive in enforcing the [existing] law and pursuing the responsible parties" that the very threat of swift enforcement would prod polluters to clean up sites voluntarily. He also promised action to check urban smog, remove dangerous chemicals from the market more quickly, encourage stricter fuel efficiency standards in the auto industry, step up recycling efforts to ease the strain on solid waste disposal facilities, and seek international cooperation on such issues as global warming and ozone depletion.

In March 1989 the EPA proposed a comprehensive plan for the 1990s to slow the greenhouse effect, in which fossil fuel emissions and chlorofluorocarbons trap solar radiation and warm the earth excessively. Unless checked, the greenhouse effect is expected to raise the planet's temperature by from three to nine degrees by the middle of the next century. Reilly proposed an international agreement requiring all new cars worldwide to get at least forty miles to the gallon, and he urged foreign auto makers to follow the American lead in mandating the installation of catalytic converters to reduce exhaust emissions. He called for fees on coal, oil, and natural gas and increased research into solar power in an effort to wean consumers away from fossil fuels, proposed a major forestation project to absorb carbon dioxide emissions, and recommended a ban on all chlorofluorocarbons.

Later that month, Reilly delighted environmentalists by suspending plans by the United States Army Corps of Engineers and the Denver Water Board to build the Two Forks Dam on the South Platte River, which was expected to service Denver and forty-one outlying water districts. That decision, the first in which an EPA administrator had overruled the recommendation of its regional director, relieved those who were concerned that the dam would disrupt wildlife migration patterns, flood a scenic canyon, and foul a prime trout stream. Although Colorado officials were outraged that their long-range plans to alleviate an expected water shortage were overruled by Washington, Reilly stood his ground, citing the threat of "very heavy, final, and irremediable loss of an environmental treasure of national significance."

Days after revoking the dam permit, Reilly was dispatched to Alaska, together with the secretary of transportation, Samuel K. Skinner, and the Coast Guard commandant, Paul Yost, to inspect the worst oil spill in North American history, caused when the Exxon supertanker *Valdez* ran aground in Prince William Sound. On May 18, 1989 Reilly and Skinner issued a report to the president that sharply criticized the response of the federal government and the oil industry to the spill. Concluding that the response to the accident was "unequal to the task," the report urged the drafting of "realistic worst-case scenarios" to prepare for future accidents.

In mid-June 1989, at Reilly's urging, President Bush proposed a sweeping revision of the Clean Air Act of 1970 that would require public utilities to reduce emissions of sulfur dioxide, a leading component of acid rain, by nearly half. The bill also contained measures that would sharply reduce emissions of toxic chemicals by industry and lower the levels of urban smog. Other presidential aides, most notably Richard G. Darman, the director of the Office of Management and Budget, opposed the plan on the grounds that it was too costly. In July 1989 William K. Reilly announced that the EPA would impose a gradual ban on the production and importation of most products made of asbestos, exposure to which may cause cancer.

Most environmentalists are pleased that, under the leadership of William K. Reilly, morale at the EPA has been restored. Its 15,000 employees seem reinvigorated under an administrator who has direct access to the president and who is committed to returning the agency to the forefront of the environmental struggle. "People need to see the environment as a cause that is positive, hopeful, and attractive," Reilly observed in the interview with Philip Shabecoff. "The costs that we bear to maintain the environment and improve it have to be seen as highly worthwhile investments in our future, as important as investments in education, science, and defense."

William K. Reilly, a tall, handsome, nattily dressed figure, has been described as soft-spoken, brilliant, and endowed with a playful sense of humor. He speaks five languages. Since 1965 he has been married to the former Elizabeth Bennett Buxton, a classical musician and vocalist with whom he sings Mozart duets. They and their two daughters, Katherine and Margaret, divide their time between two Virginia residences—a country home near Leesburg and a townhouse in Alexandria.

References: N Y Times p25 D 23 '88 por;
Washington Post A p4 D 22 '88; Who's Who in
America, 1988–89

Richards, Keith

Dec. 18, 1943– Musician; songwriter. Address:
c/o Raindrop Services, 1776 Broadway, New
York, N.Y. 10019

It has been said that if Mick Jagger is the heart of the Rolling Stones, Keith Richards, its lead guitarist, is the group's musical soul. It is Richards who is responsible for the Stones' signature aggressive, gritty sound, so prominently featured in such classics as "(I Can't Get No) Satisfaction," "Brown Sugar," and "Honky Tonk Women," which Richards also wrote, and one music critic has called him "perhaps the most rhythmically assured guitarist in rock." A decade-long addiction to heroin, which led many to speculate he would become rock's next drug fatality, culminated in a highly publicized

drug bust and rehabilitation in 1977 and contributed to Richards's reputation as the rude boy of the Rolling Stones—an image that has been enhanced by his guitar-playing style. As Jon Pareles commented in the New York Times (October 9, 1988), "Fans always assumed that . . . Mr. Richards was the raunch specialist, with his rhythm guitar chords cross-cutting the beat, his leads and fills slicing nasty curlicues into a song, [and] his tone distorted a dozen ornery ways."

Although he and his fellow Rolling Stones are now middle-aged, Richards remains as committed as ever to playing rock-'n'-roll. "It's a fallacy that rock-'n'-roll is a juvenile, teenage music," he has said. "It ain't like tennis—there's not a certain amount of years." After Mick Jagger refused to tour with the Stones to promote their 1986 album, Dirty Work, Richards produced his own album, Talk Is Cheap, released in 1988, and went on tour with the core musicians from that LP, calling themselves the X-Pensive Winos. "I've learned that if you give me the right bunch of guys, in a week I'll have 'em sounding like they've been together for years," Richards commented recently. "It's probably because I need it so much myself." The Stones regrouped in 1989, and in August of that year they began a thirty-six-city tour of the United States and Canada to promote their album Steel Wheels.

Keith Richards was born in Dartford, a suburb of London, England on December 18, 1943, the only child of Bert and Doris (Dupree) Richards. His parents, he told Robert Greenfield for a 1971 Rolling Stone magazine interview, were "English working class . . . struggling, thinking they were middle class." Bert Richards worked as a foreman in a General Electric factory. "My dad worked his butt off in order to just keep the rent paid and food for the family," Richards has recalled. Richards's maternal grandfather, Theodore Augustus Dupree, played the saxophone, fiddle, and guitar and had a dance band in the 1930s.

When he was fifteen, Richards was expelled for habitual truancy from the Dartford Technical School. A sympathetic counselor sent him to art college in nearby Sidcup, where he was introduced to blues music and where he jammed on the guitar with students in a room next to the principal's office, playing songs by Little Walter and Big Bill Broonzy. At that time, rock-'n'-roll in Britain was "a brand new thing," Richards later explained to Kurt Loder for Rolling Stone (December 10, 1987). "The world was black-and-white, and then suddenly it went into living color."

In about 1960 Richards bumped into Mick Jagger, a childhood friend who also lived in Dartford, on a commuter train. Richards was en route to art school, and Jagger was on his way to the London School of Economics. They found they had a common interest in rhythm-and-blues and a mutual friend in Dick Taylor, who was also a Sidcup art student. Richards began jamming at Taylor's home with Taylor, Jagger, and other members of a group that called itself Little Boy Blue and the Blue Boys. From that point on, Taylor has recalled, "Mick and

Keith were together. Whoever else came into the band or left, there'd always be Mick and Keith."

In March 1962 the group found "the only club in England where they were playing anything funky as far as anybody knew," Richards recalled to Stanley Booth in an interview for Booth's book *Dance with the Devil: The Rolling Stones and Their Times* (1984). That club was a small room under a tea shop in the London borough of Ealing, where they met Brian Jones, a guitarist with whom Richards felt an immediate rapport. Jones and Richards played together not as "lead" and subordinate "rhythm," but in full interaction, along with Taylor on bass guitar, Ian Stewart on piano, and Jagger as the vocalist. Taking the name the Rolling Stones from the song "The Rolling Stone Blues," by bluesman Muddy Waters, the group, with Mick Avory on drums, made its debut on July 12, 1962 at the Marquee, a club in Soho. "Brian was the one who kept us all together then," Richards later recalled. "Mick was still going to school. I'd dropped out. So we decided we got to live in London to get it together. Time to break loose. So everybody left home, upped and got this pad in London. Chelsea."

When the Rolling Stones started, only a few groups were playing rock-'n'-roll in England, and the early dates were few and far between. During the winter of 1962, they dropped Taylor for Bill Wyman, a bass guitarist with better amplifiers, and replaced their drummer with Charlie Watts. "When we got Charlie, that really made it for us," Richards later said. "We started getting a lot of gigs." The Stones' big break came that winter with a gig at the Crawdaddy Club in suburban Richmond. It turned into a regular Sunday-night engagement, drawing what would become known as "swinging London," as well as Andrew Loog Oldham, who became their manager. At the age of nineteen, Oldham got the Stones out of the London clubs and into ballrooms all over Britain ("where the kids were," Richards once explained). Oldham also procured a record contract for the group, on extremely favorable terms, with Decca and dropped Stewart from the group because his looks were "too normal." (Stewart continued to record with the Stones and later acted as band manager.) He also persuaded Richards to drop the "s" from his name (which he later resumed) to capitalize on the popularity of the British pop star Cliff Richard.

The first Rolling Stones single, Chuck Berry's "Come On," was released on June 7, 1963, the date of their first television appearance. Although Oldham at first wanted the band to promote a somewhat tidy image (they wore neat, hound's-tooth jackets and their haircuts were only marginally longer than those of the Beatles), the Stones provoked calls from viewers criticizing them as "scruffy." Soon Oldham realized that the more the band annoyed parents, the more it would delight teenagers, and the image of the Stones as surly, rebellious, and menacing—the antithesis of the cleancut, lovable Beatles—was established.

During the fall of 1963 the Stones toured Britain with Bo Diddley, the Everly Brothers, and Little Richard. Excitement was starting to build, and sustained frenzy erupted during their second domestic concert tour, in early 1964. "There was a period of six months in England we couldn't play ballrooms anymore because we never got through more than three or four songs every night, man," Richards recalled to Greenfield. "Chaos. Police and too many people in the places, fainting. You know that weird sound that thousands of chicks make when they're really lettin' it go. They couldn't hear the music. We couldn't hear ourselves, for years." The band's first album, *The Rolling Stones*, released in May 1964, went straight to the top of the pop charts, breaking the domination held by the Beatles through most of 1963. The Stones also managed to outstrip their rivals in two 1964 popularity polls. Their early music, however, unlike the Beatles', was not their own: instead, they borrowed from other artists, most prominently from Chuck Berry, whose guitar style and voice were imitated by Richards and Jagger, respectively.

The Rolling Stones started creating their own sound when, in 1964, Oldham locked Richards and Jagger into the kitchen of the northern London basement apartment they were sharing and threatened not to let them out until they wrote a song. The first efforts of the "Glimmer Twins," as they came to be called, included "Time Is on My Side," "Get Off of My Cloud," and "Heart of Stone." As Richards told Robert Greenfield, "The first things, usually I wrote the melody and Mick wrote the words. . . . Every song we've got has pieces of each other in it." In 1964 the Stones released a series of singles that rose high on the pop charts, including "Time Is on My Side," "The Last Time," and "Little Red Rooster," which was banned in the United States because of its blatantly sexual lyrics.

The song "(I Can't Get No) Satisfaction," released in the summer of 1965, featured the famous introductory guitar riff that Richards invented. That song became the Stones' first number-one song on the charts, and it propelled the group to international superstardom. "I learned how to write songs just by sitting down and doing it," Richards told Greenfield. "For me it seems inconceivable that any guitar player can't sit down and write songs." A follow-up single, "Get Off of My Cloud," was released and reached the number-one position on the charts by the end of 1965. Following the release of the albums *12 x 5* (1964) and the *Rolling Stones Now* (1965), their fourth album, *Out of Our Heads* (1965), containing the song "Satisfaction," reached the number-one position in England and the number-two spot on the charts in the United States. By the time of that release, the Stones had developed a distinct musical identity, heavily influenced by the blues, which further evolved with *December's Children* in 1965 and *Big Hits (High Tide and Green Grass)* in 1966.

In contrast to the usually upbeat and positive sound of the Beatles, Richards and Jagger created music that was raunchy and aggressive and which often dealt with taboo themes, such as rape, in

"The Midnight Rambler," and sexual domination, in "Under My Thumb." The sexually suggestive gyrations of Mick Jagger in the Stones' performances enhanced their raunchy reputation and their appeal to teenagers, who came to the Stones' concerts to "work it out." The Stones first toured the United States in 1964, and they made two North American visits in 1965. They also toured Europe in that period, and by 1966 the group was traveling to Australia and New Zealand as well.

During those years, the group's wild lifestyles were well documented by the press. "It wasn't a created image, or a phony thing," Richards told an interviewer for New York Newsday (January 25, 1983). "Things did happen to us. We'd go to a restaurant because we wanted some food, and get thrown out because we didn't have a tie." To many, Richards appeared to epitomize the self-destructive behavior for which the Stones were famous. "Keith represents an image of what the public thinks the Stones are like," Bill Wyman, the Stones' bass player, once told an interviewer. "Gypsy, pirate, drinking, smoking, finally heavy drug taking, swearing. People see Keith and they see the Stones."

Both the Beatles and the Rolling Stones were helping Britain make inroads into its chronic payments deficit, but while the former had been honored by Queen Elizabeth II, the Stones were frequently harrassed by the authorities. In February 1967 police raided a party at Redlands, the fifteenth-century moated Sussex cottage that Richards had bought the previous year, and confiscated illegal drugs. It was after that raid, while the Stones were vacationing in Morocco, that Richards became involved with the actress Anita Pallenberg, who was Brian Jones's girlfriend at the time. When Jones and Anita Pallenberg quarreled en route to Morocco, Richards and the actress went off together, beginning a long-term liaison. After another European tour, extending as far east as Warsaw and Athens, Richards returned to England to stand trial for permitting hashish to be smoked on his property. Found guilty, he was sentenced to a year in jail on June 29 and spent a night at the notorious Wormwood Scrubs prison before being released on bail; Jagger and another defendant were convicted on lesser charges. Richards's sentence was overturned on appeal on July 31.

A projected United States tour was endangered by the drug arrests, and the Stones lay low for the rest of 1967 and in 1968, playing no concerts. They released the albums Got Live If You Want It, Between the Buttons, and Flowers in 1967. In May 1968 the band released the single "Jumpin' Jack Flash," which was to become a perennial stage vehicle for Jagger. Towards the end of the year, they issued one of their finest albums, Beggar's Banquet, which included the song "Sympathy for the Devil." The political upheavals of 1968 were reflected in another song on the LP, "Street Fighting Man."

In May 1969 Brian Jones was dropped from the group and replaced by Mick Taylor. Jones had lost creative control to Richards and Jagger and had begun to miss dates and recording sessions because of his increasing addiction to drugs. When Jones was found drowned in the swimming pool of his Sussex estate on July 3, 1969, the Stones' reputation reached a new level of notoriety. Two days later, they performed a free memorial concert—their first public appearance in over two years—in London's Hyde Park. Also in July, the Stones released one of their most popular singles, "Honky Tonk Women," with "You Can't Always Get What You Want" on the flip side of the American release. Late in the year, while on a new American tour, the Stones released the album Let It Bleed, which included the numbers "Gimme Shelter" and "Midnight Rambler." Their American tour ended on December 6, 1969 with a free concert at the Altamont Speedway in Livermore, California, where one member of a contingent of Hell's Angels who had been retained to keep order stabbed a spectator to death during the performance. That scene was recorded on film by Albert and David Maysles and appeared in their 1970 documentary Gimme Shelter.

Heavily in debt for back taxes, the Stones found relief by moving to France in 1971. In the same year, the group also left Decca (London had handled the American releases) to record on its own label, Rolling Stones Records. Atlantic Records was retained to manufacture and distribute the group's discs in North America. The Stones' first album for their own label was Sticky Fingers, which contained a glossary of drug jargon and included the songs "Brown Sugar," "Sister Morphine," and "Can't You Hear Me Knocking," another showcase for Richards's guitar work. At about this time, Richards and Anita Pallenberg, who had previously been sniffing or skin-popping heroin, began mainlining the drug at the villa they had rented on the Riviera.

In April 1972 the Stones released Exile on Main Street, which was recorded at Richards's villa and included the number "Tumbling Dice." In December a warrant was issued for the arrest of Richards and Anita Pallenberg, but they had moved to the West Indies before returning to their home in Chelsea for Christmas. Richards has admitted that both Sticky Fingers and Exile on Main Street were recorded by the Stones when they were high on drugs.

The Stones played North America in 1972 and Australia, New Zealand, Britain, and the European Continent in 1973. The following year there was no tour, but a film, Ladies and Gentlemen, The Rolling Stones, of the Stones in concert, made during their 1972 tour, was released. Mick Taylor, who had become a heroin addict, quit the group near the end of 1974. He was succeeded by Ron Wood the following year, when the band played a forty-two-stop tour of North America.

While Richards was in Toronto in February 1977 for club dates that were to form the basis of a new Stones album, police searched his hotel room and found enough heroin—twenty-two grams—to arrest him not only for possession but also for intent to traffic—a crime with a possible penalty of life imprisonment. With his freedom and the future of the Rolling Stones at stake, Richards, with Anita Pallenberg, underwent drug rehabilitation. As Richards told Jim Jerome for a *People* (November 21, 1977) magazine article, "I had reached the point of no return. I had this realization that I was endangering everything I wanted to do and what people around me wanted to do." The Stones did not play in public in 1977 but performed in the United States in June and July 1978. In October of that year, Richards pleaded guilty to a reduced charge of heroin possession and was put on probation for one year and ordered to stage a charity performance for the Canadian National Institute for the Blind. That concert took place in April 1979 in Oshawa, Ontario.

Jim Jerome reported that Richards, after he was off heroin, looked healthier and more alert and confident than he had in years. Richards spent most of 1977 at a rented house in Salem, New York. At the time, he owned a house in the Chelsea section of London, which he rarely lived in because of his tax status, a flat in Paris, a house in Jamaica, and a seventeenth-century castle overlooking the English Channel in Chichester. By the end of the year, Richards had reached the point where he could analyze how he became addicted to heroin. As he explained to Jim Jerome, he had used drugs to "take the edge off" the disorientation he felt when not on tour or recording. "I'm somebody who's always got to have something to do, who needs continuity rather than these constantly shifting extremes," he told Jerome. Since he gave up drugs, Richards's therapy consisted of playing more music. "The whole idea is just to keep going, keep playing, never stop," he told an interviewer for the *Chicago Tribune* (April 17, 1986). "It doesn't matter if you're doing if for an audience. That's been a great help to me."

Asked by one interviewer late in 1981 how heroin had affected his playing, Richards said, "I don't think it hurt my music. . . . I may have played a little cooler, but not much." But, at about the same time, he told Kurt Loder in a *Rolling Stone* (November 12, 1981) interview, "Thinking about it, I would probably say yeah, I'd probably have been better, played better, off of it."

After performing in public only twice in three years, the Stones made a fifty-concert tour of the United States in the fall of 1981, playing to more than two million people and grossing more than $50 million. Also in that year, the Stones' new album, *Tattoo You*, topped sales in the United States for nine weeks. Robert Palmer of the *New York Times* (February 6, 1983), reviewing a Hal Ashby film made from three of their performances during the 1981 tour, *Let's Spend the Night Together* (1983), described Richards as being in peak form, healthy and "breathing fire onstage."

The Stones wrapped up a tour of England, Ireland, and continental Europe with a concert at Leeds, England on July 25, 1982. In 1983 the Stones signed a contract with CBS Records to supply,

starting in 1985, four Rolling Stones Records albums for distribution, for a reported figure of between $20 million and $25 million. By 1985, when the band began ten months of work on the album *Dirty Work* (1986), the Stones had not played together, except sporadically, for a couple of years.

That album marked the demise—at least temporarily—of the Stones as a group, since Mick Jagger, who had released his first solo album in 1985, refused to go on tour in 1986 to promote *Dirty Work*. With the benefit of hindsight, Richards has said that his relationship with Jagger deteriorated after he gave up heroin and made it known that he wanted to become more actively involved in the business end as well as the musical end of the Stones—a move that he believes Jagger interpreted as some kind of power play. With Jagger involved in making another album and the Stones scattered, Richards signed a long-term record deal with Virgin Records in 1987 and began work on his first solo album, *Talk Is Cheap*. "The whole idea is, I gotta work," Richards told *Rolling Stone* (September 10, 1987). "I can't sit on my ass—I go crazy, you know?" He also acted as musical director for the 1987 film *Chuck Berry Hail! Hail! Rock 'n' Roll* and produced the soundtrack album. Reviewing that album in the *New York Times* (October 21, 1987), Robert Palmer said that it had the "raw guitar textures and an explosive live sound reminiscent of some Rolling Stones concert recordings." Richards also produced and played the guitar on Aretha Franklin's single "Jumpin' Jack Flash."

Talk Is Cheap, released in October 1988, was written and produced by Richards and the drummer Steve Jordan. Other members of the band that Richards put together for the album were the guitarist Waddy Wachtel, the keyboardist Ivan Neville, the saxophonist Bobby Keyes, and the bassist Charley Drayton. The album includes the song "You Don't Move Me," with its clearly implied anger at Jagger over his decision to make two albums, both of which were indifferently received by the public, as evidenced in the lines: "Now you want to throw the dice/you already crapped out twice." Reviewing the album in the *New York Times* (October 9, 1988), Jon Pareles wrote that it "sounds loose, sloppy, thrown-together, unfinished. That's why I like it—it's a relief to hear a musician open the lid on canned music. . . . Songs sprawl as the musicians try out riffs and grooves, and the singer—Mr. Richards, with his bomb-crater of a voice—shouts and growls his lines in any spaces left by the band." Pareles also noted that "albums like *Talk Is Cheap* . . . reclaim music as work in progress, bringing rock listeners as close to the moment of creation as the musicians dare."

In the fall of 1988 the core musicians from the album, calling themselves the X-Pensive Winos, went on a three-week, ten-city tour of the United States. Writing in the *New York Times* (December 1, 1988) about their concert at New York City's Beacon Theater, Jon Pareles described them as "a rowdy bunch, wandering the stage, grinning and cackling at one another's stomps and twangs. Mr.

Richards laughs the hardest, bending to fling a power chord or kicking waist-high at the end of a verse." Commenting on Richards's guitar playing, Pareles added: "Mr. Richards casually displayed guitar techniques from gnarled blues phrases to the terse plunks of dub reggae, from the fast scratching of funk rhythm guitar to linear, melodic lead guitar. Like the great blues guitarists, he doesn't bother with hyperspeed or fancy harmonies; he just makes the instrument sing and snarl and snicker."

Richards and Jagger resolved their differences in late 1988, and in January 1989 they traveled to Barbados to begin writing songs for a new Rolling Stones album. In just two weeks, the pair churned out forty songs, nine of which were selected for their thirty-fourth album, *Steel Wheels*, which was released in August 1989. *Steel Wheels*, in the opinion of Nicholas Jennings of *Maclean's* (September 11, 1989), "bristles with more bravado than the Stones have demonstrated since they released the supercharged, disco-flavored *Some Girls* in 1978. Although the new record lacks the unpredictable, menacing tone of the Stones' best work, it may well become known as a minor classic itself, largely because it captures the creative sparks that fly when the willful Jagger and the more visceral Richards work together." The Stones played before huge crowds in every city they visited, and when it was announced that the band would perform four shows at New York's Shea Stadium in October, some 300,000 tickets were sold in just six hours. On August 31, 1989 the Stones kicked off the tour with a sold-out concert at Veterans Stadium in Philadelphia.

During his years as a heroin addict, Richards was sometimes described as a glassy-eyed walking corpse, and it was widely speculated that he would become the rock world's next drug fatality. His emaciated junkie look has disappeared, although his craggy features are deeply lined. Once described by a journalist as resembling a "rakish highwayman," Richards is a slender, yet muscular, five feet, ten inches tall, with black hair and brown eyes. Interviewers often comment on his intelligence, charm, and maturity. He wears a death's-head ring on his right hand as a *memento mori*, smokes Marlboro cigarettes, and drinks generous quantities of Rebel Yell bourbon. "Drink has never been a problem," he told Jim Jerome. "I've written some of my best things pissed out of my mind."

Keith Richards and Patti Hansen, the actress and model, were married on his fortieth birthday, December 18, 1983, in Cabo San Lucas, Mexico in a civil ceremony, with Mick Jagger standing in as best man. Richards and his wife have two daughters, Theodora and Alexandra. The couple maintain an apartment in Manhattan and a home near Ocho Rios, Jamaica. Richards also has two children from his long-term relationship with Anita Pallenberg, who, until their breakup in 1980, was identified in the press as his common-law wife. Their son, Marlon, who grew up on Long Island, is now a student in England; their daughter, Dandelion, was raised in England by Richards's mother, who

changed the girl's name to Angela. Richards's parents were divorced in 1963, and he and his father, Bert, were reunited in 1982, following a twenty-year separation. Bert Richards, who now lives on Long Island, plays dominoes with his son on Friday nights. In January 1989 the Rolling Stones were inducted into the Rock-'n'-Roll Hall of Fame.

References: N Y Newsday p4+ Ja 25 '83 por, II p3 Ap 13 '86 por, II p4 O 9 '88 pors; Rolling Stone p25+ N 12 '81 pors, p65+ D 10 '87 pors, p53+ O 6 '88 pors; Norman, Philip. Symphony for the Devil: The Rolling Stones Story (1984); The Rolling Stone Interviews: Talking with the Legends of Rock & Roll 1967–1980 (1981); Weiner, Sue and Howard, Lisa. The Rolling Stones A to Z (1983); Who's Who in America, 1988–89

Riopelle, Jean-Paul
(ryō pel´)

Oct. 7, 1923– Canadian artist. Address: 10 rue Frémincourt, 75015 Paris, France

Jean-Paul Riopelle is a Canadian-born painter, sculptor, and lithographer who has lived and worked in France since 1946. In the late 1940s and early 1950s he combined tachism (action painting) with automatism (the spontaneous expression of the unconscious) in the creation of paintings that were sometimes compared to those of the American artist Jackson Pollock, whose drip paintings are most closely identified with abstract expressionism. During his automatist phase, Riopelle was briefly associated with André Breton and the surrealists, but he severed his connections with them in 1950 because, according to *World Artists,* he had "never felt comfortable within the rigid bureaucratic discipline imposed by Breton." International recognition of Riopelle's work reached its zenith in 1962, when he was awarded the Prix UNESCO at the Venice Biennale. During the ensuing decades, retrospectives of his work—which came to include bronze sculptures, drawings, pastels, and assemblages in addition to his "sculptures in oil," as he has referred to his canvases—were exhibited in Europe, Canada, and the United States. His most recent retrospective, "Riopelle: Paintings from the Fifties," was exhibited at the Pierre Matisse Gallery in New York City in April and May of 1989.

Like many artists, Riopelle objects to the labeling of his oeuvre (as abstract expressionist), as well as to the division of his stylistic development into phases. Marci McDonald quoted him in *Maclean's* (November 9, 1981) as saying, "There is no evolution. An artist only makes one step in life." Nevertheless, the critic J. Russell Harper, in his introductory essay to a Riopelle catalogue of 1963, identified five technical stages through which the artist had progressed: tachist brushwork (1947–48); "controlled drip" (1950–51); mosaiclike surfaces impastoed with a palette knife (1953); larger canvases crisscrossed by wandering lines (mid-1950s); and a trend toward figuration (1959–60). Dismissing such neat delineations of his work in an interview with Pearl Sheffy for the Toronto *Globe and Mail Magazine* (May 9, 1964), Riopelle said, "If there is any predominance in my work, say, of any one color, it's instinctive and more apparent to the viewer than to me."

Some aspects of Riopelle's work, however, are less apparent to the (untutored) viewer than to the artist: namely, the Canadian landscape, rendered abstractly through the juxtaposition of colors, which conveys a sense of light and energy. As Marci McDonald wrote, "Riopelle remains a master of landscape—a painter of nature whose subjects are not abstracted from memory but born of a vivid visceral urgency." In the interview with Pearl Sheffy, the artist affirmed, "My paintings are absolutely landscapes," in an effort to dispel the notion that his work is abstract. "Abstraction means to come from," Riopelle explained, "to be abstracted from or extracted from the mind. . . . When I start to paint, I'm going toward an idea, not coming from it. I have no idea how I start, no preconceived notions." And yet, he said, "the mind always has its concrete references. I still regard my work as figurative." On the other hand, only one year earlier he had declared, "There is no figuration, there is only expression—and expression is just someone in front of things."

To further avoid being pigeonholed, Riopelle told Pearl Sheffy that "the imposed division between abstract and figurative art now is the problem of dealers and critics." Even more cryptic—but also one of his most revealing statements—was his remark to Pierre Schneider, as recorded in Schneider's book *Louvre Dialogues* (1971): "For me, the only reference is nature. Freedom exists only there, and at the same time the strongest constraint. A tree can grow in only one way. There is no tragic, elegiac, or joyous way to be a tree. There is only the right way."

The only son of an architect, Jean-Paul Riopelle was born in Montreal, Quebec, Canada on October 7, 1923. He began painting at the age of eight but trained for a career in engineering at the Montreal Polytechnique. "It was while studying engineering," he told Pearl Sheffy, "that a very curious thing happened to me. I used to go into the country on holidays to do landscapes, which I like very much because they are so free. Then I started to do seascapes, of the sea as seen from above, and I painted three or four canvases of drifting shells. Quite unintentionally, they turned out to be purely abstract."

At the age of twenty Riopelle enrolled in the Académie des Beaux-Arts in Montreal, where he studied from 1943 to 1944. After a stint as a fighter pilot during the final months of World War II, he studied painting briefly in 1945 at the Ecole du Meuble in Montreal under Paul-Emile Borduas, the leading artist of the avant-garde in Quebec. Borduas, Riopelle, and other artists became known as the Automatists because they attempted to allow the unconscious to dictate the creation of their art. (The group's manifesto of 1948, entitled *Refus Global,* would later scandalize all of French Canada with its "multiple rejections" of social and artistic conventions.) Since, according to Riopelle, only portraitists were considered true artists in postwar Montreal, his paintings were not easily apprehended by his compatriots, despite titles such as *Ontario* (1945). (One critic later described *Ontario* as "a truly Canadian painting" whose subjects were the future and painting itself.)

Around 1945 Riopelle sailed for France aboard a cargo ship, reportedly paying for the trip "by playing nursemaid to a shipment of horses." After returning briefly to Canada in order to marry Françoise l'Espérance, a ballet dancer from Montreal, in 1946 Riopelle moved with his wife to Paris, where they have lived ever since, though they visit their families in Montreal at least once a year. Riopelle "sold" his first two paintings at the age of twenty-three, to an insurance company, which had to purchase the works because they had been lost en route to an exhibition in Toronto.

The first exhibitions of Riopelle's work in Paris were mounted in 1947. Having been welcomed by André Breton, Riopelle showed his paintings at the international surrealist exhibition at the Galerie Maeght in Paris. His works were also included in two shows at the Galerie du Luxembourg in Paris: "Automatisme" and "L'Imaginaire." Although the latter showcased a style known as *abstraction lyrique,* Riopelle's "vigorous gestural abstractions," such as *Hochelaga* (1947), were instead more closely aligned with *art informel,* according to an article by David Craven and Richard Leslie for *artscanada* (March–April 1981).

Although he had settled in Paris partly in order to escape the restrictions of Canada's conservative artistic climate, Riopelle did not eschew confrontation with that environment. He not only signed Borduas's *Refus Global* manifesto of August 9, 1948, but also painted a watercolor for the document's cover. Whether his watercolor was a political painting—and whether it can be considered as such apart from its employment as cover art for the manifesto—is open to interpretation. The artist himself denied having political views, according to Pearl Sheffy, who quoted him as saying, "I'd like to have some views on separatism—I really would—but I just don't have any." Nevertheless, Craven and Leslie argued that the manifesto's cover painting "does express concretely many of the [Automatists'] ideas."

The manifesto itself states, "Our duty is simple: to break definitively with all conventions of society." In the words of Herbert Marcuse, "The Great Refusal takes a variety of forms. . . . Today's rebels against the established culture also rebel against the beautiful in this culture . . . and give art a desublimated, sensuous form of frightening immediacy." According to Craven and Leslie, Riopelle's cover painting for *Refus Global* "is as free from past conventions as the society for the future envisioned by the Automatists"; his "overall watercolor corresponds in formal equivalence to an egalitarian society without social ladders"; and his automatist works created between 1946 and 1950 were "intended as anti-hierarchical gestures of equality." For that reason, those critics asserted, the manifesto not only "provoked an immediate scandal in French Canada," but its cover art "became seditious in a society [that, to quote from the manifesto, was] 'spellbound by the annihilating prestige of remembered European masterpieces and disdainful of the authentic creations of its own oppressed.'"

Fourteen years would pass between the circulation of Riopelle's "seditious" watercolor among Canadians and the first major touring retrospective of his work in his native country. In the meantime, he remained unknown to most Canadians, despite his growing popularity in Europe and the United States. His first one-man show, held at the Galerie Nina Dausset in Paris in 1949, was an inauspicious beginning: not one painting was sold. One month later a friend asked if she could use his paintings as a decorative backdrop to an exhibit of her sculptures. Riopelle acquiesced, and all his paintings were sold on opening day. Perhaps more important, a complete stranger offered the artist free use of an atelier, where he worked for the following two years. Until then he had been painting at home amid the distractions provided by the presence of his two very young children.

From 1950 to 1953 Riopelle showed his paintings in Paris, Berlin, and São Paulo. At the beginning of that period he abandoned his brushes in favor of squeezing tubes of paint directly onto the canvas to create such works as *Composition* (1950), in which he trailed thin yellow and white lines over a darker background. That "controlled drip" style began to give way, around 1953, to the mosaiclike impastoed surfaces he created with his palette knife—the style for which he became most widely known. In an essay for *Canadian Art* (October 1952), the eminent French critic Georges Duthuit wrote of Riopelle: "This young Canadian painter, with his glories as of stained glass or of high-warped tapestry, brings certain landscapes before us, or rather about us. . . . The surfaces of earth, of nerves, of epidermis, unfold and flower as one. . . . The principal quality of Riopelle's pictures is their combination of extreme opulence with perfect discretion, so that our poverty is not overwhelmed by an excessive and brutal display of riches; they are rather a conflagration which is like a caress, a silky and smiling onrush of spring."

Riopelle's first group exhibition in the United States, "Younger European Painters," which was held at the Solomon R. Guggenheim Museum in New York City in December 1953, was followed by his first one-man show in the United States, which was mounted at the Pierre Matisse Gallery in New York City in 1954. (Pierre Matisse, the son of the artist Henri Matisse, exhibited Riopelle's work frequently until Pierre Matisse's death in 1989.) In 1954 Riopelle was one of three artists representing the Canadian pavilion at the Venice Biennale. (The other two were Paul-Emile Borduas and Bertram Charles Binning.) In the triptych *Pavane* (1954), according to Leslie Judd Ahlander's review of a Riopelle retrospective for the *Washington Post* (May 13, 1963), "the artist's identification with nature is indicated in the effect of flickering light and shade, green trees and brilliant bursts of warm color, resembling flower petals." Mrs. Ahlander called *Pavane* his "crowning achievement" among his mosaic-style works. She described *Autriche* (1954) as "a study in dynamic tension, as the two dark areas at the sides of the canvas pull away from each other. In *Gravity* (1954) the heavy weight of the reds, thickly slashed on with the knife, pulls heavily to the bottom of the canvas, seemingly dragged out from the lighter areas at the top." She concluded, "It is his lyrical interpretation of nature that is most fascinating in his work." Reviewing the show at the Pierre Matisse Gallery for *ARTnews* (January 1954), another critic was less enthusiastic: "The control is that of even pressure on the palette knife, [but] . . . this is only the beginning of control: the modest man's answer to his own assertion that he can't draw even a straight line. A further step would be to convince you that he had created something."

Riopelle's canvases grew larger and his handling of paint became looser and freer in the course of the decade. In the words of J. Russell Harper: "Riopelle introduced meandering or zigzag lines of green, blue, mauve, or black. They are like calligraphy wandering back and forth over the entire surface." Although a critic writing for *artscanada* (January 1961) asserted that the allover approach had led Riopelle to "repetition, mediocrity, and eventually the dulling of the image he established with his earliest mature work," other critics were favorably impressed by his progress. His paintings in gouache and watercolor, on view at the Pierre Matisse Gallery in 1956, were described as displaying "color harmonics of a sumptuous order," and a one-man show there in 1957 prompted a reviewer for the *New York Herald Tribune* (December 14, 1957) to write that the show marked "a clear step forward in his development. . . . The pictures' chief merit lies in their careful organization, for all their seeming spontaneity." By the early 1960s paintings such as *Par Dela* (1961) were interpreted as tending to be more figurative than Riopelle's earlier work—a trend that was considered to be related to his bronze sculptures of the same period.

During the late 1950s and early 1960s, Riopelle exhibited widely and frequently. His one-man shows were held in New York City, Cologne, Hanover, Basel, Stockholm, London, Paris, Milan, and Turin; group shows in which he took part were mounted in Brussels, Kassel, Pittsburgh, and Minneapolis, among other cities. He was Canada's sole representative at the 1962 Venice Biennale, where he was awarded the Prix UNESCO, having been narrowly defeated for first prize. The Prix UNESCO was the highest honor ever bestowed by the international art community on a Canadian artist. Riopelle's stature was recognized by his compatriots somewhat belatedly with a touring retrospective exhibition of sixty-six paintings and sixteen sculptures, which was organized by the National Gallery of Canada in Ottawa in 1963. At thirty-nine, Riopelle was the youngest artist ever honored in that manner in Canada. The exhibit traveled from Ottawa to Montreal, Toronto, and, in abbreviated form, to Washington, D.C.

Reviewing the compressed version of the retrospective—thirty-one paintings on display at the Phillips Collection in Washington, D.C.—a critic for *Newsweek* (May 27, 1963) wrote that Riopelle's early paintings were evidence of the artist's possession of "the kinetic drive of Jackson Pollock, but also the elegance and cordon bleu quality of the School of Paris. . . . [But the] quality of extreme force [in his paintings] without a hint of aggression or anxiety makes Riopelle different from Pollock, [Franz] Kline, and [Willem] de Kooning. The freedom of a healthy organism that revels, not only in its reflexes, but in the instruments it has mastered—this is what Riopelle's paintings proclaim." That same year Riopelle's bronze sculptures were shown in the United States for the first time, at the Pierre Matisse Gallery. One critic described them as "bold, assured, ornamental, and suggestive of flowering life"; another called them "cleverly naïve." In a review for the *New York Times Magazine* (May 12, 1963), Irving Sandler wrote that his bronzes possess "the same kind of robust sensuousness that has always distinguished his painting," whereas "the pigmentation in Riopelle's canvases suggests modeled relief sculpture."

During the rest of the decade and into the 1970s, Riopelle's work met with increasingly divided crit-

ical opinion. Reviewing a show at the Pierre Matisse Gallery for the *New York Herald Tribune* (April 28, 1965), one critic wrote, "Form has been lost. Energy is there, and richness of surface. But both are unharnessed. The result sputters rather than speaks, blinds rather than excites." And a writer for *Art International* (November 1972) remarked that "many of Riopelle's recent paintings have the effect of exercises in a style that can produce only rather thin variations on itself."

In contrast, an exhibition of oils, pastels, and assemblages at the Pierre Matisse Gallery elicited praise from a reviewer for *Arts Magazine* (December 1969–January 1970): "The imaginative color structure, the control inherent in the virile application of paints, and the sense of aesthetic integrity are what constitute Riopelle's individual brilliance." Discussing the painting *Salut Gérard* (1970) in a review for the *New York Times* (October 12, 1974), John Russell wrote that it has "an openness of construction and [is] a strong welcome change after the crisscrossed *horror vacui* that marked so many of Mr. Riopelle's earlier paintings." Analyzing a series of drawings entitled "Le Roi de Thulé" for *Art International* (December 1974), one critic wrote that one sees in them "an explosive spontaneity exquisitely balanced with stylizations guided by a long tradition of fine picture making." Of the same series Martin Ries wrote, in his review for *Arts Magazine* (December 1974), "What looks like deliberate uglification and negation of authority is stylishly fluid—a youthful bravura with enthusiasm for mélanges and confusions."

Reviewing a 1976 exhibition at the Galerie Gilles Corbeil for *artscanada* (July 1976), René Payant wrote, "Riopelle reverts to the method and style which originally earned him his laurels: the colors applied with the palette knife in broken, fragmented touches that produce a mosaiclike effect on the canvas." Payant contended that the earlier work "possessed an authentic power" that the more recent efforts lacked, making "the revival of his earlier mode look like a plain retreat." He also criticized some of the more scaled-down paintings for their resemblance to "some magnified surface details revealed in a zoom-lens photograph; . . . there seems to be little reason for their existence." Payant was nonetheless impressed by seven untitled pastels (1975) included in the same exhibition, calling them "boldly lyrical" works that "convey the same spirit of exploration and inventiveness that characterized . . . the series known as 'Ficelles et autres jeux' (from 1972)." The "ficelles" series of paintings, which were inspired by Eskimo string games (in which a loop of string is woven between the hands to resemble figures such as dogs and turtles), as well as Riopelle's "hibou" series of owls (1968–70) in oils, bronze, and lithography, were often singled out for praise by critics who, like Payant, had previously soured on what they perceived as the exhaustion of Riopelle's style of painting.

In 1977 the Pierre Matisse Gallery held a retrospective exhibition, entitled "Grands Formats," of twelve large oil paintings completed between 1952 and 1975. Most of the paintings, including *Lac du Nord-Est* (1975) and *Vert-de-Gris* (1975), were larger than six feet by nine feet. One critic, reviewing the show for *Arts Magazine* (June 1977), wrote: "It appears that Riopelle's current concerns have been to maintain the sparkling kinetic surface of his earlier paintings while still introducing a kind of figuration. . . . *Vert-de-Gris* could possibly be a reflection of a medieval altarpiece; perhaps the images are totemic, sacred figures. . . . The artist has moved from pure sensations of color movement toward the symbolic."

A much larger retrospective—indeed, the first and only major international exhibition of his work ever held—was shown at the Beaubourg (Centre Georges Pompidou) in Paris in 1981. An augmented form of the exhibition (fifty-five paintings completed between 1946 and 1977) made stops at the Musée du Québec, the Museum of Modern Art in Mexico City, the Contemporary Art Museum in Caracas, and the Musée d'Art Contemporain in Montreal. Both Marci McDonald, in her review for *Maclean's*, and Virgil Hammock, writing for *artmagazine* (May–July 1982), faulted the exhibition for omitting Riopelle's most recent work, his "hibou" and "ficelles" series, and his sculptures, constructions, ceramics, and engravings. Noting that only thirty-nine of the fifty-five canvases cited in the press release "were actually hung at the Beaubourg," Hammock commented that the show was more of "an important sampling" than a retrospective. Praising Riopelle's good taste as well as his craftsmanship, he concluded that Riopelle "is a very good [abstract expressionist] and in some pictures a *great* one." Marci McDonald, who traced the artist's path "from the dense volcanic eruptions of color dating from his rebellious student days . . . to the stark, simmering tension of his uncharacteristic black-and-white iceberg series [1977] which shocked Paris critics," concluded that "Riopelle has evolved dramatically in style and emphasis. . . . If there is one constant, it is the artist's sense of the land. . . . He has forged the essential link between Cézanne's reduction of the mountains of Provence to children's building blocks and the ultimate distillation of a horizon by the abstractionists."

Those who have interviewed Riopelle invariably comment on his frenzied method of painting for hours at a stretch—a method that, for him, is crucial to his endeavor to close the gap between the artist and the present moment, which is ever slipping into the past. "I know no one, in fact," wrote Schneider, "who reacts more keenly and painfully [than Riopelle] to the slightest deviation from that burning point, the instant." Schneider quoted Riopelle as saying, "I have never hesitated at the moment of making a painting. If there is hesitation, I do not make it." He elaborated on that statement in the interview with Pearl Sheffy in 1964: "When a painter does a good painting, he does it in the throes of terror. When he is in its grips, his name doesn't matter, but if he isn't in this state, he just isn't a real painter, in my opinion. I can paint only in this way. I can never force myself to paint."

The artist's hobbies—auto racing, which was replaced by the less dangerous sport of sailing, and attending circus performances—evidence the same passion for speed as do his works of art. According to Catherine Jones, who interviewed the artist for *Maclean's* (August 3, 1957), "Riopelle looks like Chico Marx; he acts rather like him, too. When he is feeling exuberant, his laugh bursts out like an express train exploding from a tunnel." Pearl Sheffy described him as a "robust man who gives an overwhelming impression of health, strength, and relaxed energy." The Riopelles have two daughters, both of whom were born in the late 1940s: Sylvie and Isolde. Before they had reached the age of ten, Sylvie had begun painting, like her father, and Isolde had announced her desire to become a dancer, like her mother. In 1969 Riopelle was awarded the Companion of the Order of Canada.

References: *artscanada* p66+ Ag-S '71, p47+ Mr-Ap '81; *Maclean's* p17+ Ag 3 '57 pors; *Toronto Globe and Mail* mag p6+ My 9 '64 pors; *Canadian Who's Who*, 1988; *Contemporary Artists* (1983); *International Who's Who*, 1988–89; Lucie-Smith, E. *The Visual Arts Since 1945* (1969); Pellegrini, A. *New Tendencies in Art* (1966); Robert, Guy. *Riopelle, ou la poétique du geste* (1970); Schneider, Pierre. *Louvre Dialogues* (1971); *World Artists 1950–1980* (1984)

Robb, Charles S(pittal)

June 26, 1939– United States Senator from Virginia. Address: b. Room 497, Russell Senate Office Bldg., Washington, D.C. 20510; h. 612 Chain Bridge Rd., McLean, Va. 22102

The election of Charles S. Robb to the United States Senate on November 8, 1988 marked the first time in twenty-two years that Virginians elected a Democratic senator. Robb's victory in the election came as no surprise, for he had recently served as one of Virginia's most popular governors. He was frequently mentioned as a potential vice-presidential candidate for 1988, and even the presidency was said to be within his reach if he should decide to run for the nation's highest office in the future. One explanation for Robb's appeal was provided by the columnist David S. Broder, who described him in an article for the *Washington Post* (October 26, 1986) as "everything that Democrats want: he is movie-star handsome, comfortable on TV, middle-road but modern in his thinking, well-connected, southern, and dazzlingly successful as a politician."

Charles S. Robb

Robb came to national attention for the first time in 1967, when he married President Lyndon B. Johnson's daughter, Lynda Bird, in the first White House wedding since 1914. At the time of his marriage he was an officer in the United States Marine Corps, but by 1974 he had become a practicing lawyer. Three years later, he switched careers again when he was elected lieutenant governor of Virginia. Robb was the only Democrat elected to statewide office in Virginia that year, and in 1981 he led Democrats in their first sweep of the statehouse in sixteen years when he was elected governor.

Since Virginia governors are prevented by state law from serving two consecutive terms, Robb joined the law firm of Hunton & Williams in 1986. His legacy to Virginians was another Democratic administration in Richmond, including the unprecedented election of a black lieutenant governor and a female attorney general. He has tried to broaden his potential constituency by speaking out on foreign and domestic policy issues as chairman of the Democratic Leadership Council from 1986 to 1987 and remains active on its board of directors. In the 101st Congress, Robb serves on the Senate Foreign Relations Committee, the Senate Budget Committee, and the Senate Commerce, Science, and Transportation Committee.

The oldest of four children, Charles Spittal ("Chuck") Robb was born in Phoenix, Arizona on June 26, 1939 to James Spittal ("Jim") Robb and Frances Howard (Woolley) Robb. The family was originally from Virginia, where Robb's ancestors can be traced back to the 1640s. His father had left Virginia and a career in the airline industry in order to operate a dude ranch in Arizona. When the ranch failed in 1949, Jim Robb, seeking work once again with the airlines, moved to Cleveland, Ohio

with two of his sons, Chuck and Robert ("Wick"). Frances Robb, who was recovering from a cataract operation, remained in Arizona for a time with the other two children, David and Marguerite Trenholm ("Trenny").

According to his parents, who were quoted in an interview with Donald P. Baker and Glenn Frankel for a two-part article in the *Washington Post* (September 13 and 14, 1981), Chuck Robb was "very private" as a child and "pulled into a shell" as a teenager. His sister Trenny recalled that "he was always number one at this and that and he always set heavy goals." That paradoxical combination of reserve and driving ambition seemed to serve him well, judging by his achievements in high school and college.

After serving as president of his sophomore class in high school, Robb moved to Fairfax County in northern Virginia when his father was transferred to Washington, D.C. He completed his secondary education at Mount Vernon High School, where he was active in its clubs and in athletics. An academic-athletic scholarship, granted him in 1957, enabled Robb to attend Cornell University, where he majored in engineering. There, he chose the navy unit of the Reserve Officer Training Corps (ROTC) because he considered it to be more competitive than the air force or the army. Low grades cost Robb his academic-athletic scholarship, but his performance in what was then compulsory ROTC earned him another one. He transferred to the University of Wisconsin at Madison for his remaining three years of college to be near his family, which had moved to Milwaukee.

At the University of Wisconsin, Robb felt, as he said in the *Washington Post* interview, like "a square on a campus that was a little radical," and it seemed to him "absurd that the students were spending so much time talking about the House Un-American Activities Committee" rather than concentrating on career preparation. Perhaps that feeling of marching to a different drummer was partly responsible for his losing the election for senior class president, an experience he remembers as formative. "I needed a little taking down," he said during the *Washington Post* interview. "Anybody who goes too long without some setback in life tends to lose an important perspective."

Despite that setback and a C+ average, by the time Robb graduated in 1961 with a B.A. degree in business administration he had won a record number of awards for a graduating senior from the university. As a second lieutenant, he ranked at the top of his class in the NROTC, and he earned straight A's in courses on military subjects.

Soon after graduation Robb joined the United States Marine Corps, where he finished at the top of his officer training class of 400 at Quantico, Virginia. As a junior officer aboard the USS *Northampton,* and subsequently as a company commander at Camp Lejeune, North Carolina, Robb so impressed his senior officers that it was not surprising that his third assignment, as a first lieutenant at the marine barracks in southeast

Washington, led to his becoming a social aide at the White House in June 1966. It was there that Robb met Lynda Bird Johnson, who was then concluding a well-publicized romance with the actor George Hamilton.

The marriage ceremony of Chuck Robb and Lynda Bird Johnson on December 9, 1967 was treated like a royal wedding by the national media. Along with the barrage of publicity came suggestions that Robb, by then a captain, would try to avoid service in Vietnam by taking advantage of his high-level connections. But his critics were silenced when he arrived in Vietnam on April 4, 1968, less than two months after the Tet offensive, having volunteered for a yearlong tour of duty. The rifle company under Robb's command saw combat two weeks later, capturing 350 Viet Cong suspects. For that action, Robb earned a Bronze Star with Combat V, a Vietnamese Cross of Gallantry with Silver Star, and the rank of major before returning to the United States on April 22, 1969. He is currently a lieutenant colonel in the Reserves.

For his remaining year of active duty, Robb volunteered to serve as a Marine Corps recruiter on college campuses. In his speeches to students, he defended his father-in-law's military policy in Vietnam in terms that he reportedly still employs. He recapitulated his stance during the *Washington Post* interview: "We could have engaged in a scorched-earth policy. On many occasions, I had men killed or wounded who wouldn't have been if we had simply gone in with air strikes on essentially defenseless villages who were harboring Viet Cong. We didn't do that, and in that sense it was a compassionate policy, although there wasn't much appreciation of that in the antiwar movement."

There was a great deal of dissent with Robb's viewpoint on the college campuses where he was invited to speak, but he managed to overcome the hostility of student antiwar activists with his sense of humor. "Never once did I walk out not having been able to establish a dialogue," Robb recalled in the *Washington Post* interview. His ability, in his words, to "bring people together and develop a sense of personal respect and communications" was recognized by President Richard M. Nixon, who sent him a congratulatory note after one of Robb's speeches.

In 1971 Lyndon B. Johnson presented Chuck and Lynda Bird Robb with a four-bedroom house in Austin, Texas in an attempt to persuade them to settle near his retirement ranch along the Pedernales River, but Robb declined the offer. When he heard of his son-in-law's polite but firm refusal, Johnson reportedly said of him, with grudging admiration, "He's an independent bastard." Having decided to become a lawyer, Robb remained in Virginia. After obtaining his J.D. degree from the University of Virginia at Charlottesville and passing the bar exam in 1973, he clerked for a year for Judge John D. Butzner of the United States Court of Appeals for the Fourth Circuit. From 1974 to 1977 he was an attorney practicing with the firm of Williams, Connolly & Califano, now known as Williams & Connolly.

In 1977 Robb announced that he would run for lieutenant governor, although at the outset of his political career, his chances of winning the November 8 election seemed uncertain at best. His links to Lyndon B. Johnson were not wholly advantageous in conservative Virginia, where the Great Society programs of the 1960s were much maligned by politicians who openly opposed federal desegregation policies. But Robb, who had grown up in a Republican family, was a conservative Democrat. Although he benefited from the name recognition, money, and political contacts afforded by his marriage, he was able to divorce himself from Johnson's liberalism. He defeated state senator A. Joe Canada in all of the state's ten congressional districts. With 54 percent of the vote, Robb was the only Democrat to win a statewide election in Virginia that year.

Despite his victory, many felt that "Chuckie Bird," as he was derisively nicknamed, had only a slight chance for a successful political career. His performance in the largely ceremonial position of lieutenant governor did little at first to increase his stature. To many observers, Robb seemed too cautious, aloof, and indecisive. His fellow Democrats resented his reluctance to criticize Virginia's Republican governor, the late John M. Dalton, whom Robb openly admired. One unnamed party member reportedly labeled Robb "a potential disaster" for Virginia Democrats.

But Robb turned out to have quite the opposite influence on the state's Democratic party, except that halfway through his four-year term, he was criticized for bungling two political situations of symbolic importance to women and blacks. He did not intend to alienate either of those two key Democratic constituencies, as evidenced by his statements at the time and by his later actions as governor, and both cases represented departures from his usual practice of steering clear of controversy. One instance involved a dispute between President Jimmy Carter and Senator Harry F. Byrd Jr. of Virginia, over Carter's nomination of James E. Sheffield, who is black, for one of four vacant federal judgeships in Virginia. Byrd had submitted a list of ten candidates, all of whom were white men. Three of Byrd's choices were nominated by Carter, along with Sheffield, but Byrd charged that Carter was using a quota system to appoint judges and vowed to oppose Sheffield's confirmation. According to an article by Garrett Epps for the *Washington Post Magazine* (January 25, 1981), Robb suggested that all of Carter's nominees had to be chosen from Byrd's list, which infuriated some black groups. (As it turned out, Byrd effectively blocked Sheffield's confirmation.)

Another example of political gaucherie cited by Robb's critics occurred in July 1980. According to Ronald D. White, writing in the *Washington Post* (July 6, 1980), Robb was heckled by 150 protesters during a speech he was giving at the Old Dominion Boat Club in Alexandria. The club did not admit women, blacks, or Jews as members, and protesters interpreted Robb's decision to speak, despite a boycott by local Democrats, as a sign that he endorsed the club's membership policies. (The club has since opened its doors to women and minorities.) Robb defended his action by saying that the club's policies had no bearing on his decision to speak there, but he also acknowledged that he might not have scheduled his speech had he known that his presence would spark such a controversy.

Despite his political gaffes, Robb proved to be more popular than his opponent in the race for governor one year later. On November 3, 1981 Robb defeated Attorney General J. Marshall Coleman, a conservative Republican, taking 54 percent of the vote, as he had done in 1977. It was widely remarked during the campaign how similar were the two candidates' positions. Robb's victory was credited, in part, to his self-presentation during debates with Coleman, in which he reportedly came across as the more decisive and open-minded candidate. Among the issues he said he favored during a May 19 debate were capital punishment, nuclear power, the state's right-to-work (anti-union) law, a balanced budget, a ceiling on state spending and state employment, the Equal Rights Amendment, and limited funding for abortions.

Fiscally conservative yet socially progressive (by southern standards), Robb made an all-Democratic statehouse acceptable to Virginia voters for the first time in sixteen years. Elected by an unprecedented coalition of blacks, suburbanites, rural conservatives, and industrial workers, he pledged in his inaugural address that he would help Virginia to "reclaim the leadership in national affairs [the state] once had." Among his priorities were education and economic development. According to the New York Times (October 24, 1985), he spent $500 million ($1 billion, as reported by the Washington Post [October 28, 1988]) on public education, including higher salaries for teachers and improvements in school facilities. In recognition of his achievement, he was given the Policy Leadership Award by the National Association of State Boards of Education in October 1988. He also increased government spending for highway construction and the Washington area Metro transit system and approved funding for the creation of the Center for Innovative Technology adjoining Dulles International Airport, a quasi-public corporation set up to facilitate cooperation between universities and high-tech firms in research and development. He managed to pay for those outlays without raising income taxes by reducing the number of state employees and by increasing the gasoline tax, among other measures.

One of the most striking features of Robb's tenure was his appointment of large numbers of women and blacks to state boards, commissions, and agencies. He appointed 657 women during his term, more than the number appointed by any previous governor of Virginia. Many of those posts were important, such as a seat on the State Corporation Commission, a powerful regulatory agency to which Robb appointed the agency's first woman,

Elizabeth Lacy. He also appointed the first black judge, John Charles Thomas, to the state supreme court. During his first year alone, Robb named 175 blacks to state jobs, which was also a record for Virginia. Several reporters noted that those appointments reflected Robb's awareness of the extent to which black support was responsible for his election. He won only 46 percent of the white vote in 1981.

Perhaps Robb's most remarkable achievement as governor was restoring unity to the Virginia Democratic party. Under his leadership, the liberal and conservative wings of the party arranged a truce, and the Democrats won big in the state assembly races. One unnamed Democratic strategist was quoted in the New York Times (October 24, 1985) as saying, "Robb has given Democrats something they haven't had in [a] long time in this state—a popular role model."

Yet Robb's administration had its share of difficulties. In early 1982 the governor was embarrassed by his failure to disclose the formation of a political action committee, dubbed "ChuckPac" by his detractors, with $200,000 in leftover campaign funds. In 1984 six death-row inmates escaped from Mecklenberg prison in the largest death-row prison breakout in United States history. Although the prisoners were captured nineteen days later, prison security became what Robb called his "number one problem." In response to the crisis, he raised prison guards' salaries and urged the State Board of Corrections to study the entire prison system in Virginia.

Despite such problems, Robb finished his term with more popularity than he had when elected, and he smoothly converted that public esteem into his party's gain. Unable by law to serve a second consecutive term, he nevertheless had the satisfaction of seeing the Democrats sweep the statehouse elections in 1985. The election of Gerald L. Baliles as governor, L. Douglas Wilder as the state's first black lieutenant governor, and Mary Sue Terry as the state's first female attorney general was widely perceived as a referendum on the Robb administration. Reflecting on this so-called Robb revolution in their syndicated column of November 13, 1985, the conservative political columnists Rowland Evans and Robert Novak conjectured that "insiders will urge the governor to attempt the impossible and do for his party nationally what he has done for Virginia."

Amid widespread speculation that he might be a vice-presidential or even a presidential candidate in 1988, Robb returned to private law practice, joining the 300-member firm of Hunton & Williams in January 1986. For the next two years his administration maintained a high national profile through his chairmanship of the Democratic Leadership Council, which he cofounded in 1985 with Governor Bruce E. Babbitt of Arizona, Senator Sam Nunn of Georgia, Congressman Richard A. Gephardt of Missouri, and others.

Robb articulated the council's views on many occasions for audiences at universities, fund-raising events, and the National Press Club. In a speech to the Coalition for a Democratic Majority on May 6, 1986, Robb advocated combining Contra aid with "tough, persistent diplomacy." He urged Democrats to "unite behind a new foreign policy that vigorously asserts America's ideals and defends our interests abroad." He contrasted that "new" foreign policy with that of President Ronald Reagan, which, he said, "offers no clear moral alternative to the cynical power-politics of the Soviet Union." On the day of that speech he was given the Henry M. Jackson Friend of Freedom Award by his hosts.

In the spring of 1987 Robb's rapid political ascent hit its first serious snag when a federal grand jury investigating reports of drug trafficking in the Tidewater turned up witnesses who said that, while he was governor, Robb had attended parties in Virginia Beach where cocaine was used. No accusation that he himself used drugs was ever made. Robb freely admitted that he had attended parties while staying at the gubernatorial retreat at Camp Pendleton. In an interview with Donald P. Baker for the *Washington Post* (May 17, 1987), Robb described himself as "a normal, healthy, red-blooded, middle-aged American male who enjoys having fun, letting his hair down, being informal." He categorically denied having any knowledge of drug use on the part of anyone at the beach parties. The grand jury never uncovered any evidence to the contrary, and the matter seemed settled.

In September 1987 Republican senator Paul S. Trible Jr. unexpectedly announced that he would not run for reelection. Many observers cited Robb's popularity as the reason for Trible's decision. On November 11, 1987 Robb announced his candidacy for the Senate seat, thereby ending speculation that he might seek his party's nomination for president. On June 11, 1988 a little-known black Baptist minister and former lobbyist, Maurice Dawkins, took on the unenviable task of opposing the popular former governor. Dawkins was the first black Republican nominee for statewide office in Virginia.

The Senate race seemed hopelessly one-sided until the drug scandal erupted again. In late August 1988 Robb filed a complaint with the Federal Election Commission, charging that an unknown person, whose anonymity was protected by law, had hired a private investigator to pursue drug rumors about him in an effort to influence the election. Dawkins and his party denied any knowledge of the detective's work, but jumped on the issue to embarrass the popular Democrat. Both Robb and Dawkins submitted to drug tests, on which they tested negative. Once again, Robb dismissed any link between him and drugs as being based on "untruth, innuendo, and rumor." A poll taken by Mason-Dixon Opinion Research indicated that although two-thirds of the voters surveyed thought that Robb had displayed "poor judgment" in his social life, he was nevertheless running ahead of Dawkins by a three-to-one ratio.

Robb won the November 8, 1988 election handily, capturing 71 percent of the vote. Robb's victory was one of only four instances in which formerly Republican Senate seats were lost to Democrats that year. He is expected to pursue the same blend of fiscal conservatism and moderate social policies that marked his tenure as governor. In addition to the policy positions already mentioned, Robb reportedly favors a restoration of the draft, research on the Strategic Defense Initiative (popularly known as Star Wars), the linkage of a company's performance to its employees' pay, and an end to isolationist thinking in foreign-policy formulation. He has also indicated that Social Security cuts or tax increases are not out of the question.

Charles S. Robb strikes some observers as possessing typical "tall, dark, and handsome" good looks. In the words of one supporter, Hays T. Watkins, the chairman of the CSX rail conglomerate, "Chuck has a charm about him that leaves people feeling very good about him." Since 1975 he has lived in a twenty-room mansion on Chain Bridge Road overlooking the Potomac. He and Lynda Bird Robb have three daughters: Lucinda Desha, Catherine Lewis, and Jennifer Wickliffe. Lady Bird Johnson has often volunteered her babysitting services to enable the Robbs to campaign. Lynda Robb has been a contributing editor to the *Ladies' Home Journal*, a leader of President Carter's Advisory Committee on Women, and a director of the Virginia Women's Cultural History Project. In his spare time, Robb enjoys golf and volleyball. His religious affiliation is Episcopalian.

References: People 8:67+ Ag 1 '77 pors, 16:44+ O 19 '81 por; Washington Post mag p8+ Ja 25 '81 por, A p1+ S 13 '81 por, A p1+ S 14 '81, C p1+ O 28 '88 por; Who's Who in America, 1988-89; Who's Who in American Politics, 1989-90

Roth, Henry

Feb. 8, 1906– Writer. Address: c/o Jewish Publication Society, 1930 Chestnut St., Philadelphia, Pa. 19103

The publication of *Shifting Landscapes: A Composite, 1927–1987* (1987) by Henry Roth marked an unusual event in the literary world. Roth had leapt into prominence in the 1960s, when *Call It Sleep*, his semiautobiographical novel about a Jewish immigrant boy living on New York's Lower East Side, which had first been published in 1934, was reissued and became a critically acclaimed bestseller. The success was ironic because Roth seemed to have long since disappeared from the literary landscape, having failed to publish any more novels. *Shifting Landscapes* reveals just what was going on in those long years during which Roth struggled to overcome what he believed to be a loss of his creative powers. The book is a collection of Roth's

Henry Roth Chester Higgins Jr./NYT Pictures

fragmentary creative efforts over a period of sixty years, including short stories, essays, and political statements, interspersed with interviews conducted with Roth and extracts from his correspondence. It charts the passage of a creative mind through a nightmare of self-doubt and frustration to the eventual recovery, in his senior years, of the urge and ability to write.

Henry Roth was born on February 8, 1906 in the town of Tysmenica, in Galicia, a crownland of the Austro-Hungarian Empire, in what is now part of the Ukraine, to Herman Roth, a waiter, and Leah (Farb) Roth. When he was about a year old, he was brought by his mother to the United States, where his father had gone earlier and where his sister, Rose, was later born. The family lived at first in the Brownsville section of Brooklyn, then moved to Manhattan's largely Jewish Lower East Side. In 1914 the Roths settled in Harlem, in a section that was at the time predominantly Irish and Italian. Henry Roth has recalled that he was at first unpopular with the other boys in the neighborhood, having no aptitude for street games or baseball, and he devoted much of his time to reading, especially fairy tales. But when, at the age of fourteen, he took a job as assistant to a projectionist in a movie theatre, his status was much enhanced. His ability to get inside information on the latest song hits elevated him to a star role in the street life of Harlem. Nevertheless, as he later maintained, his family's move from the homogenous Lower East Side to heterogenous Harlem resulted in an insecurity that inhibited his creative power for a time. The discontinuity was also reflected in his early rejection of the Orthodox Judaism of his parents and his espousal of atheism.

On graduating from Manhattan's intellectually elite De Witt Clinton High School in 1924, Roth immediately entered the City College of New York. During his freshman year in 1925, he wrote his first published piece, entitled "Impressions of a Plumber," as an assignment for an English course. It so impressed Roth's instructor that he arranged to have it published in *Lavender*, the college literary magazine.

Roth's literary talents were also noted by Eda Lou Walton, a professor of English at City College. The two struck up a friendship, and in 1928, the year he graduated with a B.S. degree, she invited him to stay with her in her house in Greenwich Village, which was a kind of literary salon, frequented by intellectuals and writers such as Margaret Mead, Hart Crane, and Mark Van Doren. The young Roth reveled in the company of such literary lights. He became an avid reader of T. S. Eliot, whom he has described as "the major influence" on his life. The works of James Joyce also helped to inspire him. In 1929 he wrote his first—and only—piece of literary criticism, an analysis of the work of the playwright Lynn Riggs, who was also a member of the Walton circle.

Because Eda Lou Walton supported Roth during the four years it took him to write *Call It Sleep*, he dedicated the book to her. It received good reviews when it was first published, in December 1934, by R. O. Ballou. Writing some years later in *Contemporary Novelists*, Richard J. Fein noted that *Call It Sleep* came to be "recognized as one of the finest American novels of this century, perhaps the best novel about childhood ever written by an American, rivaling Dickens's or Dostoevsky's sense of the pathos of childhood." In the words of Bonnie Lyons in the *Dictionary of Literary Biography*: "*Call It Sleep* is a profound psychological study of David Schearl, who is at once a sensitive child and a mystic in search of divine illumination. . . . The central theme, the search for redemption or mystical transfiguration, is universal, and the delicacy and artistry with which Roth develops his material grow ever more apparent the more the novel is studied."

In 1936 Roth began to work on a second novel, tentatively entitled "If We Had Bacon." But although he received an advance from Scribner's and wrote the first section, which was accepted, he never completed the novel. He has traced his failure in part to his involvement with left-wing ideology. Like many intellectuals in the 1930s, when the shadow of the Great Depression hung over capitalist America, he had become a Marxist. He had joined the Communist party in 1933 and had decided that his second book was to be a proletarian novel, its hero inspired by his involvement with Communism. Had it not been for the party, he has said, he might have written a novel centering on his own adolescent years. But the attempt to write in the spirit of socialist realism about the class struggle, in keeping with party directives, went against the grain of his natural instincts. It made him, in his words, "overly conscious" about himself as a writer. He found himself stalled, unable to continue, and for a time he "just fooled around." He tried to turn his attention to his projected novel about adolescence, but the failure of his effort to produce a proletarian novel seemed to have blocked his ability to do any further writing at the time. "My will was gone, broken by this first failure," he has recalled.

Roth parted company with Eda Lou Walton in 1938 and went to live at Yaddo, an artists' colony at Saratoga Springs, New York. There, he met Muriel Parker, a composer, and they were married in 1939. He worked as a laborer on Works Progress Administration projects, laying pipes and repairing and maintaining streets, while he tried to establish himself as a commercial writer. His first short story, "Broker," was published in 1939 in the New Yorker. It was followed shortly afterward by "Somebody Always Grabs the Purple." A third story, "Many Mansions," was published in Coronet magazine in 1940. ("What a bit of fluff," Roth commented when the story was unearthed over forty years later.) But writing for profit did not inspire Roth. It did not come spontaneously, and he commented that "there were easier forms of making a living."

From 1939 to 1941 Roth was a substitute teacher at Theodore Roosevelt High School in the Bronx, and from 1941 to 1946 he helped the war effort as a precision tool grinder in New York, Providence, and Boston. But his creative powers seemed to have completely dried up. When he and his family moved to Center Montville, Maine in 1946, he was convinced that his literary career was over, and he made a living teaching part-time and doing various odd jobs in the community. In 1949 the family moved to a three-acre farm on the outskirts of Augusta, Maine, where Roth worked until 1953 as an attendant at the state hospital. Then, for about ten years he raised ducks and geese on the farm, an episode of his life that he later described in "The Prisoners," which was published in Italian in 1987. During this period he also did some private tutoring in Latin and mathematics, but he wrote little, and he even destroyed his journals and some of his manuscripts, including his partly finished second novel.

In 1954 a trade journal accepted Roth's do-it-yourself article "Equipment for Pennies." He took its publication as an indication that he might be coming out of what he called "this terrible, terrible bog." Two years later, Roth wrote a short story, "Petey and Yotsee and Mario," inspired by his boyhood memories, which was published in the New Yorker. It was followed by "At Times in Flight: A Parable," published in Commentary in 1959. Written in the first person, in the aftermath of Roth's failure to complete his second novel, the story centers upon a horse race he witnessed, which he viewed as a symbol for the loss of his creative inspiration. He still considers the story one of his favorite short pieces. In 1960 Commentary published "The Dun Dakotas," another meditation on the loss of his creative powers that he has described as a

"parable" dramatizing the "loss of a sense of history."

Meanwhile, events had been set in motion that were to rescue Call It Sleep from obscurity. In 1956 editors of American Scholar, the Phi Beta Kappa magazine, asked noted critics and scholars to name "the most undeservedly neglected book" of the previous quarter of a century. Two distinguished critics, Leslie A. Fiedler and Alfred Kazin, named Call It Sleep. Their comments bore fruit four years later, when a small New York publishing house, Pageant Books, reissued Roth's novel. In an introduction to that edition, Harold U. Ribalow declared, "Call It Sleep is so remarkable an artistic achievement that on its basis alone, Roth stands as one of the major creative novelists of the twentieth century."

When Avon Press published a paperback edition of Call It Sleep in 1964, it quickly became a bestseller, and critical appreciation ran high. Irving Howe, writing in the New York Times Book Review (October 25, 1964), described it as "one of the few genuinely distinguished novels written by a twentieth-century American." Noting that the book was "intensely Jewish in tone and setting," Howe maintained that it "rises above all the dangers that beset the usual ghetto novel: it does not deliquesce into nostalgia, nor sentimentalize poverty and parochialism." Howe was particularly impressed by Roth's depiction of the protagonist's mother, Genya Schearl, who in his view "brings radiance and dignity to every page on which she appears" and "should some day be honored as one of the great women of American literature, a fit companion to Hawthorne's Hester Prynne." Commenting on Call It Sleep in his scholarly survey The Modern Novel in Britain and the United States (1964), Walter Allen observed, "Roth plunges us into a child's mind more directly and more intransigently than any other novelist has done."

Suddenly, Roth was in the public eye, but he was wholly unprepared for his newfound celebrity, which caused him some dismay. After interviewing him for the New York Post (November 8, 1964), for example, Martha MacGregor remarked, "You . . . had a feeling he wished the book would go away." But in May 1965, when Roth received a grant from the National Institute of Arts and Letters, he acknowledged his calling as a writer once more. He traveled to Mexico and to Seville, Spain to gather material for a new novel, and during the trip he began to work on the short story "The Surveyor," about the Spanish Inquisition. Although his letters from that period indicate that he doubted his ability to accomplish anything on the scale of his original plan, the story was completed and published in the New Yorker in 1966. "I'm almost amazed that I can still write good publishable stuff," he remarked shortly after its publication.

Looking back on "The Surveyor" later, Roth said that at the time he was "trying to find something related to Judaism." The remark was significant, because it amounted to a shift in his attitude toward

Judaism and toward Israel in 1967 that produced a decisive change in his life. His readjustment was prompted by the Six-Day Arab-Israeli War. Contrary to what was then the Communist party line, Roth found himself embracing the Israeli cause, and when the Israelis raced to a quick victory his "exaltation knew no bounds," as he put it. His Jewish identity had resurfaced, giving him a new sense of belonging and altering his entire outlook. "Suddenly I had a place in the world and an origin," he has said. Simultaneously, he began to write. He later described the moment as a "rebirth," for he was now committed not only to the support of Israel, but also to a kind of, in his word, "continuum" writing style that was different from anything he had done before. Loose in structure and difficult to define in terms of genre, Roth's "continuum" was a continual search for and exploration of the "landscape of the self; to epitomize its meaning" for himself and others. Much of that writing was in journal form. "It's no longer recognizably narrative, although it may include narrative elements," he said in 1977. "I no longer attempt to maintain an inviolate continuity."

In 1968 Roth held a D. H. Lawrence Fellowship at the University of New Mexico. In his writing, he went back to a story he had begun in 1964. Originally entitled "What Kind Journey," it was published as "Final Dwarf" in the Atlantic in 1969. Roth's literary renaissance continued throughout the 1970s, and 1977 was a particularly notable year, since four of his pieces were published in a period of ten months. "Kaddish," an autobiographical essay that describes his early creative life and his later commitment to Israel, appeared in the Jewish journal Midstream. "Itinerant Ithacan," which Roth has described as an "experimental piece," also covers two aspects of his life: the time when he first became aware of his literary ambitions ("the entrance of the young man into consciousness of a literary impulse, a desire to create great art") and the affinity for Israel that he had discovered only a decade before. He wrote "Report from Mishkenot Sha'ananim" and "Vale Atque Ave" in Israel during a two-month visit that the Roths made as the guests of the Israeli government. For a while, Roth contemplated living in Israel, and he made a return trip to Tel Aviv in 1978. But he rejected the idea of a permanent move for a number of reasons, including differences in language and culture and his own uneasiness. As he told one interviewer, he did not quite feel at home in Israel.

For his essay "The Wrong Place," published in New Orleans Review in 1978, Roth drew on his experiences in Seville during 1965 and 1966. Reflecting on his stay there, he concluded that he "had come to Spain to reunite with Judaism—via a side door!" The essay was followed by the four-page booklet Nature's First Green, a reminiscence about his days as an assistant to a movie projectionist that was published in a limited edition in 1979 by Targ Editions. The editor William ("Bill") Targ had wanted "something very special" to begin a series. Roth has often pointed out that it was thanks to Targ that he began to write with a new determination and sense of purpose, producing "an actual stream of serious, continual, regular writing."

Roth's serious writing is still in progress, in the form of four as yet unpublished autobiographical volumes called "Mercy of a Rude Stream," which he has described as a "memoir-form novel." The first draft was completed in 1984, and a section of it was published in Commentary under the title "Weekends in New York—A Memoir." But Roth does not intend the full novel to be released for publication during his lifetime. In an interview in 1981 he described what he was trying to accomplish: "To portray the evolution of the insufferably self-centered, immature, in many ways parasitic and contemptible autodidactic literary youth into approximate adulthood, approximate regeneration, his reconciliation with self and with the necessity of change."

Meanwhile, Roth's friend Mario Materassi, the Italian translator of Call It Sleep, had finally persuaded him to collect his occasional pieces of writing. Reluctant to undertake the task himself, Roth suggested that Materassi oversee the project. The result was Shifting Landscapes, and Roth, who has always preferred to live quietly, even anonymously if possible, has had to cope with the not entirely welcome publicity surrounding the publication of a book that Morris Dickstein described in the New York Times Book Review (November 27, 1987) as "an engrossing meditation on the creative process." Roth himself has remained ruthlessly self-critical, fearing that the book was "a very meager output for fifty-some odd years."

In an interview for the New York Times Book Review article, at the Roths' mobile home in Albuquerque, New Mexico, where they moved in 1968, Morris Dickstein described Roth's appearance as a study in contrasts. "His large, impressive head, crowned by stray tufts of gray hair, rests on a stocky yet fragile-looking frame stiffened by arthritis," Dickstein wrote. "His hands speak of years of hard manual labor, and his quietly modulated voice radiates dignity and reserve." Penny Kaganoff noted in Publishers Weekly (November 27, 1987) that "Roth's . . . smile exudes a boyish charm as he combs his memory." Bob Groves of the Washington Post (October 25, 1987) observed that Roth "used a cane to maneuver slowly to a chair. His hair was a corona of wispy white. He still speaks with a savvy East Side rasp, something like the old Mercury Theater actor Everett Sloane." Among the honors that Roth has received are the Townsend Harris Medal of the City University of New York and the Italian literary award Premio Nonio.

References: Life 58:75+ Ja 8 '65 por; N Y Times Bk R p1+ N 29 '87 por; Pub W 232:67+ N 27 '87 por; Washington Post G p1+ O 25 '87 por; Contemporary Authors Permanent Series vol 1 (1975); Contemporary Literary Criticism vol 6 (1974); Contemporary Novelists (1982); Dictionary of Literary Biography vol 28 (1984); World Authors 1950–1970 (1975)

Rudman, Warren B(ruce)

May 18, 1930– United States Senator from New Hampshire. Address: 530 Hart Senate Office Bldg., Washington, D.C. 20510

Warren B. Rudman, the junior United States senator from New Hampshire, is perhaps best known for his cosponsorship of the Gramm-Rudman-Hollings Balanced Budget and Emergency Deficit Reduction Control Act of 1985, the most aggressive assault on the national debt since the end of World War II. In its latest revision, it promises to balance the federal budget in stages by 1993. The ranking Republican on the Iran-Contra committee in 1987, Rudman also gained national attention for his blunt criticism of President Ronald Reagan's administration, a performance that helped to raise the televised hearings beyond partisanship and aroused the ire of some hard-line conservatives. Rudman generally supported Reagan's foreign-policy and economic program, but at times he broke openly with the White House, most frequently on social issues. Because of his longstanding reputation for independence of thought, his voting record has always defied easy categorization. "The liberals consider me a conservative, and the conservatives consider me a liberal," Rudman said long before his election to the Senate. "I consider myself a moderate Republican." In the 101st Congress, Rudman is the ranking Republican on the Select Ethics Committee; the Appropriations Subcommittee for Commerce, Justice, State, the Judiciary and Related Agencies; and the Government Affairs Subcommittee on Government Information and Regulation.

Warren Bruce Rudman was born on May 18, 1930 in Boston, Massachusetts to Edward G. and Theresa (Levenson) Rudman. He attended public schools in Nashua, New Hampshire and in 1948 graduated from the Valley Forge Military Academy. After obtaining a B.S. degree from Syracuse University in 1952, he received a commission as a second lieutenant in the United States Army. During the Korean War, he served for fifteen months as a combat platoon leader and a company commander in the Second Infantry Division, earning the Bronze Star and the Combat Infantry Badge. He was discharged with the rank of captain in 1954. Six years later he received a law degree from Boston College and was admitted to the New Hampshire bar. From 1960 to 1969 he practiced law as a partner in the firm of Stein, Rudman and Gormley in Nashua, New Hampshire.

In 1970 Warren B. Rudman entered government service as a legal counsel to Governor Walter R. Peterson, a moderate Republican, who later that year appointed him state attorney general. As New Hampshire's chief law officer for the next six years, Rudman created a consumer protection division, fought successfully against the legalization of gambling, and embroiled the state in several controversies. In 1971, for example, he ruled that the voting residence of the state's college students was the same as that of their parents. His move disrupted campus voter registration efforts and made it more difficult for students to take part in the crucial New Hampshire primary in 1972—the first presidential primary election since the voting age had been lowered to eighteen. Rudman turned back challenges from the American Civil Liberties Union and testified persuasively against a state bill that would have overturned his decision. In 1974 he joined Francis X. Bellotti, the attorney general of Massachusetts, in filing suit in federal district court seeking to postpone construction of the Seabrook nuclear power plant in southeastern New Hampshire, near the Massachusetts border, pending completion of an evacuation plan in the event of an accident. In 1975 Rudman was elected president of the National Association of Attorneys General.

As state attorney general, Rudman served ex officio as a member of the New Hampshire Ballot Law Commission. In a controversial ruling that would come back to haunt him, delaying his entry onto the national stage, Rudman joined in declaring Republican congressman Louis C. Wyman the winner by just two votes in a hotly contested race for the United States Senate in 1974. The losing candidate, the Democrat John A. Durkin, secured the right to a second election, which he won. After President Gerald R. Ford nominated Rudman as chairman of the Interstate Commerce Commission in 1976, Senator Durkin, in apparent retaliation, used his influence on the Commerce Committee to delay confirmation of the appointment, and Rudman eventually withdrew his name. From remarks he made at the time, it seems likely that Rudman would have used his position on the ICC to promote deregulation of the surface transportation industries. After his withdrawal he joined the law firm of Sheehan, Phinney, Bass and Green in Manchester, New Hampshire.

In 1980 Rudman topped an eleven-man primary field with just 20 percent of the vote to win the right to challenge his old nemesis, John Durkin, for Durkin's seat in the Senate. In order to ensure party unity in what promised to be a bruising campaign, Rudman named his principal primary opponent, John H. Sununu (who was to become governor of New Hampshire and, later, White House chief of staff), as his campaign manager and enlisted the aid of Ronald Reagan, then a presidential candidate, in dissuading former governor Wesley Powell, who ran third in the primary, from running as an independent. In his first bid for elective office, Rudman turned out to be an aggressive campaigner, portraying Durkin as a tool of organized labor. Thanks in part to Reagan's stunning victory in the November election, Rudman upset the incumbent, taking 52 percent of the vote to Durkin's 48 percent.

During his first few years in the Senate, Rudman maintained a low profile, assiduously mastering the intricacies of the budget process from his seat on the Appropriations Committee. Overwhelmed by his duties at first, he urged the leadership to reduce the number of committee assignments of each member, arguing that the present system forces members to rely too heavily on their staffs. He also urged more orderly floor debate and encouraged his colleagues to spend more time on the floor listening to each other's remarks. Also during his freshman year, he served as vice-chairman of the Permanent Subcommittee on Investigations, and, at the conclusion of six days of hearings on waterfront corruption, he joined the subcommittee's ranking minority member, Democrat Sam Nunn of Georgia, in sponsoring legislation authorizing the president to remove any union official convicted of a crime. In one of his first visible roles, Rudman led the successful fight in 1982 against the American Medical Association in its attempt to exempt doctors from the regulations of the Federal Trade Commission.

Because Rudman usually supported the Reagan administration's foreign-policy initiatives, he earned fairly high marks from conservative rating groups. He spoke out forcefully for the development of the B-1 bomber, voted for more nuclear-powered aircraft carriers, opposed the nuclear freeze movement, and encouraged the production of chemical weapons. Although he had some misgivings about the MX missile, a personal letter from President Reagan led him to reconsider his stand. He consistently approved military aid to the Contra rebels fighting to overthrow the Marxist-led Sandinista regime in Nicaragua.

On social issues, however, Rudman established a more moderate record. He opposed efforts to limit abortion, for example, and to reintroduce prayer into public schools. As the dominant figure on the appropriations subcommittee that provides funds for the Justice Department, he succeeded in reversing a Reagan administration decision to abolish the

Legal Services Corporation, which operates legal offices for the poor, and, after that, he often criticized the administration for trying to undermine the corporation's mission. At a time when the Reagan administration was adopting a laissez-faire attitude toward business, Rudman was pressing for more vigorous enforcement of the antitrust, consumer protection, and federal trade laws.

Despite his general support of the Reagan-era defense buildup, Rudman often challenged Pentagon assumptions from his seat on the Defense Appropriations Subcommittee. He criticized the military's eagerness to acquire the latest in complex high-technology weaponry, which often turned out to perform not as efficiently as less-expensive and easier-to-maintain older models. Over the Pentagon's objections, he urged a significant reduction in military support personnel and led a successful effort to scrap the Viper, a disposable bazooka. In a celebrated indirect exchange with the secretary of defense, Caspar W. Weinberger, in 1983, Rudman denounced as "asinine" Weinberger's statement that the United States must prepare for the possibility of a protracted nuclear war. "Anybody who talks about protracted nuclear war," Rudman declared, as reported in the Washington Post (April 30, 1983), "has never heard a shot fired in anger. There will be no protracted nuclear war. It'll be very short."

In 1985 Rudman learned that the Republican senator Phil Gramm of Texas was considering ways to mandate a balanced budget by a certain time. Rudman and, later, the Democratic senator Ernest F. Hollings of South Carolina joined Gramm in crafting the landmark legislation, which, since its enactment as an amendment to a bill raising the debt ceiling to more than $2 trillion in December 1985, has hung over the budget process like the sword of Damocles. At the heart of the Gramm-Rudman-Hollings law is sequestration, or the spending cuts that automatically take effect across the board (with a few exceptions, such as interest on the national debt and Social Security benefits) if Congress and the president fail to agree on a budget that meets annual deficit reduction targets. As first written, Gramm-Rudman, as the law is popularly known, held out the promise of a balanced budget by fiscal year 1991, but, when that proved too burdensome, lawmakers revised it to 1993.

Few were completely satisfied with the bill. Its critics charged that, instead of forthrightly dealing with the deficit, Congress put in place what the Democratic congressman William H. Gray 3d called a "flawed doomsday machine" of unknown consequences and questionable constitutionality. The Democratic senator J. Bennett Johnston of Louisiana compared Congress to "the person who writes on the bathroom mirror in lipstick, 'Stop me before I kill again.'" The Pentagon and Secretary Weinberger opposed the bill, because House-Senate conferees had ignored White House pressure to exempt the defense budget from sequestration. One Defense Department official went so far as to charge that it delivered "a message of comfort to the Soviet Union," infuriating Rudman. "The Russians ought to be dancing in the street when they see this country spending itself into bankruptcy," Rudman responded angrily, as quoted in the *Washington Post* (January 22, 1986). "They can defeat us without firing a shot." Even President Reagan, who had campaigned on a pledge to balance the budget, was skeptical of the bill because of the prospect of facing the dilemma of cutting the defense budget or raising taxes. He signed it only reluctantly and without any fanfare. Although the bill's authors recognized that using the threat of arbitrary cuts to blackmail lawmakers into fiscal responsibility was an undesirable way to govern, they saw no other alternative to the deficit problem. "It's a bad idea whose time has come," Rudman said of his own bill.

In February 1986 a special three-judge federal court struck down Gramm-Rudman on the grounds that it violated the separation-of-powers doctrine by investing the power to determine how the automatic spending cuts were to be carried out with the comptroller general, who is appointed by the president but who can be fired by Congress. In July of that year the United States Supreme Court upheld, by a vote of seven to two, the decision of the lower court. In a notable dissent, Justice Bryon R. White criticized the majority for overturning what he described as "one of the most novel and far-reaching legislative responses to a national crisis since the New Deal." Rudman helped to fashion a bill that satisfied the court's objections by granting the president and Congress more discretion in determining how sequestration would be implemented. Again reluctantly, Reagan signed the second version into law on September 29, 1987.

Before the debate over the balanced budget propelled Rudman into the national spotlight, he had considered retiring at the end of one term. "There is a certain sense of despair around here that the major problems in the country have not been faced," he was quoted as saying in *U.S. News & World Report* (November 11, 1985). "This place is 99 percent frustration and 1 percent exhilaration. It's hard to live on that 1 percent." But with the passage of Gramm-Rudman-Hollings, he took on a renewed sense of responsibility in the Senate and acquired an aura of invincibility in the eyes of his constituents back home. In 1986 he proved to be so popular in New Hampshire that his two most formidable Democratic challengers, former senator Durkin and former congressman Norman E. D'Amours, declined to challenge him. Rudman was reelected that year by nearly a two-to-one margin over former Massachusetts governor Endicott Peabody, whom Democrats had hastily enlisted as a sacrificial candidate when a follower of the conservative extremist Lyndon H. LaRouche appeared likely to win the Democratic primary by default.

Soon after his reelection Rudman again was thrust into the limelight as the ranking Republican on the Select Committee on Secret Military Assistance to Iran and the Nicaraguan Opposition, the so-called Iran-Contra committee created to investigate the Reagan administration's sale of arms to Iran in exchange for the release of American hostages and the diversion of some of the profits from the sale to the Contra rebels in Nicaragua. As early as January 1987, as the committee prepared for its public hearings, Rudman called on President Reagan to apologize to the American people for the scandal. Throughout the public phase of the hearings, Rudman was the most outspoken Republican critic of the administration's handling of the affair and thus lent the proceedings a sorely needed bipartisan tone. Although he had been a consistent supporter of the Contras, Rudman sternly criticized Lieutenant Colonel Oliver L. North for his secret campaign to arm the rebels despite a congressional ban on such aid. "The American people have the constitutional right to be wrong," he lectured North, as reported in the *New York Times* (July 14, 1987). "And what Ronald Reagan thinks or what Oliver North thinks or what I think or what anybody else thinks makes not a whit if the American people say enough." What bothered Rudman most about the scandal, however, was not that advisers had abused the president's trust or that the United States was duped into trading arms for hostages or that funds were diverted to the Contras. "That didn't concern me," he said in an interview with John DiStasso of the *Manchester* (New Hampshire) *Union Leader* (August 5, 1987). "What did was the implications this had to our presidency and our Constitution: That someone can cook up an intelligence scheme, feed it to the president, brief him incorrectly, then lie to the secretary of state and the attorney general, and then try to cover up what they did."

Although Rudman was widely praised for rising above partisanship to get at the truth of the scandal, he was roundly criticized by hard-line conservatives, particularly the editorial writers of the *Manchester Union Leader*, perhaps the most influential newspaper in his state. But since his mail was overwhelmingly supportive, Rudman dismissed such criticism as hypocritical. "I want someone from the Right politically to stand up and say, 'I think it was good to sell arms to the Iranians,'" he said with characteristic bluntness to Jay Merwyn of the *Concord* (New Hampshire) *Monitor* (July 3, 1987). "Let them stand up and say that. If they don't believe that, they should keep their mouths shut."

Rudman was the New Hampshire chairman of Senator Robert J. Dole's campaign for the Republican presidential nomination in 1988. Since then, he has generally supported the administration of President George Bush. He was a floor leader in the doomed bid to win Senate confirmation of the former senator John G. Tower as secretary of defense, and he helped to fashion a budget agreement between the White House and Capitol Hill that met the Gramm-Rudman target while honoring Bush's campaign pledge not to raise taxes. Rudman has conceded, however, that the more stringent target of fiscal year 1991 will almost certainly require an increase in revenue. "Everybody realizes," he asserted, according to the *Congressional Quarterly Weekly Report* (May 6, 1989), "this is the best that can be done this year. I mean, I think the 'read my lips' pledge expires on New Year's Eve."

Warren B. Rudman, who once was called "the sledgehammer" by a Republican colleague because of his direct manner and bluntness of speech, has also been described, sometimes in contradictory terms, as kinetic, quick-tempered, informal, and reserved. He is the first to admit that he would not win a popularity contest in the nation's capital. "I don't socialize," he told Lois Romano of the *Washington Post* (January 22, 1986). "I'm not particularly interested in spending evenings with a bunch of strangers. Quite frankly this is not a town that cares for Warren Rudman as a person, or for anything I stand for, or anything I value. If the word 'senator' disappeared from in front of my name, my invitations would go from 200 a week to two a year." Since July 9, 1952 he has been married to the former Shirley Wahl. They have three children: Laura, Alan, and Debra. Rudman is a founder of the New England Aeronautical Institute and Daniel Webster Junior College and served as the chairman of the board of trustees from 1965 to 1981.

References: *Almanac of American Politics, 1988; Politics in America (1988); Who's Who in American Politics, 1989–90*

Ruscha, Edward
(rōō shā´)

Dec. 16, 1937– Artist; photographer. Address: c/o Leo Castelli Gallery, 420 W. Broadway, New York, N.Y. 10012

Influenced by Norman Rockwell, Walt Disney, Jasper Johns, and Robert Rauschenberg, the Los Angeles–based pop artist Edward Ruscha produces works that, in the opinion of one critic, "recall the eerie emptiness of America's billboard culture." Sometimes referred to as "the Andy Warhol of the West Coast," Ruscha is, according to Maurice Tuchman, the senior curator of twentieth-century art at the Los Angeles County Museum of Art, "the most interesting interpreter of the new L.A. that came to maturity, if you can call it that, in the 1960s." Ruscha's *Standard Station, Amarillo, Texas* and *The Los Angeles County Museum on Fire*, both done in oil, are considered classics of pop art, but it is his "word paintings," in which he presents a word or a short phrase, sometimes in three dimensions, against various backgrounds that have brought him his greatest notoriety. Intended primarily to be viewed rather than to be read, those paintings, in the words of the critic Eleanor Heartney, "have always offered reminders of the inadequacy of language and the faulty progress of human communication." In some of his word paintings, Ruscha used as his medium such organic substances as fruits, flowers, axle grease, and even blood. Also a skilled photographer, Ruscha has published fourteen books of photographs that express his abiding interest in the banalities of Los Angeles cityscapes and other stark American scenes.

Of German-Bohemian and Irish descent, Edward Joseph Ruscha 4th was born in Omaha, Nebraska on December 16, 1937, the second of the three children of Edward Joseph Ruscha 3d, an insurance auditor, and Dorothy (Driscoll) Ruscha. He has an older sister, Shelby, and a younger brother, Paul. Ruscha has credited his mother, a housewife who had artistic inclinations and who always encouraged his creative tendencies, with being one of the three greatest influences on his work. (The others, he has said, are Norman Rockwell and Walt Disney.) In 1942 the family moved to Oklahoma City, Oklahoma. Edward entered the first grade at a local Roman Catholic elementary school in 1943, but he was so uncomfortable with its rigid disciplinary policies that he transferred after one year to Hawthorne Elementary School, though he continued to attend Mass on a regular basis throughout his childhood.

Ruscha's first experience with art came at the age of nine, when he painted several large murals on butcher's paper for a school project. Around that time a neighbor named Bob Bonaparte, who was a professional cartoonist, introduced Ruscha to Higgins India ink and Speedball pens, and the boy began to create his own comics. At the age of eleven, Ruscha took his first painting class, from a local portrait painter, Richard Goetz. His other childhood pastimes included stamp collecting and going to the movies.

At Classen High School in Oklahoma City, which he entered in 1953, Ruscha took art classes and developed an interest in printing and typography. Following his graduation in 1956, he moved to Los Angeles, hoping to become a commercial artist. (Asked once by an interviewer why he chose Los Angeles as a place to live, he explained, "It's got the right kind of decadence and lack of charm it takes to make an artist.") After failing to gain admission to the Art Center School, Ruscha enrolled at the Chouinard Art Institute, where he studied industrial and graphic design and developed what was to become a lasting interest in the work of the American artists Jasper Johns and Robert Rauschenberg. Then known primarily as a training school for Walt Disney animators, Chouinard numbered among its staff some important California artists, including Robert Irwin, Billy Al Bengston, and John Altoon. During his years at Chouinard, Ruscha executed a number of unconventional collages, one of which consisted of ashes and cigarette butts attached to a square piece of paper. Another, entitled *Dublin*, featured wood, newspaper, and ink on paper.

Following his graduation from Chouinard in 1960, Ruscha joined the staff of a Los Angeles advertising agency, but, finding the layout and graphics work he was assigned there unrewarding, he quit after a year to travel throughout Europe. His journey included a two-month stay in Paris, where he visited galleries and viewed works by Johns and Rauschenberg. He also took many photographs of street life in Paris and completed several small works, done on paper soaked in linseed oil, that incorporated words with street iconography. In September 1962, by which time he had returned to the United States, Ruscha was for the first time included in a major group show, "New Painting of Common Objects," at the Pasadena (California) Art Museum, an exhibition that also featured works by such noted pop artists as Andy Warhol, Roy Lichtenstein, Jim Dine, and Wayne Thiebaud. His first solo exhibition opened at the Ferus Gallery in Los Angeles on May 20, 1963.

In the early 1960s Ruscha painted such commonplace objects as food tins, comic books, and pencils. In 1962 he completed a series of works, including *Honk, Radio,* and *OOF,* that featured single words on flat, neutral backgrounds. Probably the most discussed of the three, *OOF* was painted on a six-foot-high canvas divided horizontally into three equal sections, with the word "OOF" spelled out against the middle section in block letters about two-feet high. In *Damage* (1964) Ruscha sought to objectify the title word by setting it on fire, and in *Jelly* (1964), another word painting, he used italicized black letters on a white background to create what he has called "the purest drawing I've ever done." He employed three-dimensional letters for the first time in *Large Trademark with Eight Spotlights* (1962), spelling out "20th Century Fox" diagonally across the canvas.

Writing in *Art International* (November 20, 1971), David Bourdon noted that, while Jasper Johns customarily "relegates" the words on his paintings "like captions, to the lower part of the canvas," Edward Ruscha "typically centers his words and treats all other elements as subordinates to this primary image." Ruscha claims to have no interest in the dictionary definitions of the words he selects, contending that he is concerned only with the word's appearance, sound, or spelling. He generally prefers short, brusque-sounding words. "A knowledge of the English language is not a prerequisite to the enjoyment of Ruscha's work," Bourdon observed, "because his words are designed primarily to be looked at, rather than read."

From 1965 to 1967 Edward Ruscha, operating under the pseudonym Eddie Russia, worked for *Artforum* magazine, producing layouts for its illustrations. In January and February of 1966, he was included in his first European exhibition, "Los Angeles Now," which was held at London's Robert Fraser Gallery. Around that time, Ruscha changed his drawing medium from charcoal to gunpowder, creating a series of three-dimensional "paper ribbon" drawings that spelled out words, seemingly in strips and pieces of paper. Usually shown from above at angles of thirty-five to forty-five degrees, the compositions featured sharp-edged letters rendered with such precision that some critics at first thought the paintings had been airbrushed. The series, according to David Bourdon, "created something of a small sensation" when displayed for the first time, in December 1967, at the Alexander Lolas Gallery in New York. Ruscha eventually produced over 300 paper ribbon drawings.

In the middle and late 1960s, Edward Ruscha employed yet another method to objectify words—by spelling them out, three-dimensionally, in what appeared to be spilled liquids. *Annie, Poured from Maple Syrup* (1966), one of the earliest works in that series, featured the word "Annie" in thick-faced type, with tiny, bursting bubbles at the edges of the letters. Other paintings in the so-called liquid word series included *Adios* (1967) and *Desire* (1969). Ruscha then went one step farther, abandoning conventional inks and staining his canvas instead with actual organic substances, such as baked beans, raspberries, chocolate syrup, and axle grease. The first works in that series were published in the portfolio *Stains* (1969). Ruscha continued his organic substances series with *News, Mews, Pews, Brews, Stews, Dues* (1970), a portfolio of six screenprints, each displaying a single word in Old English type. In *Pepto-Caviar Hollywood* (1970), Ruscha reproduced the famous "Hollywood" sign that sits in the hills above the movie capital, screening the sky in Pepto-Bismol antacid and the sign itself, along with the hills behind it, in caviar. In 1971 he began work on a series of "vegetable paintings," in which he used organic juices to spell out words—a series that he displayed in a one-man exhibition at New York's Leo Castelli

Gallery in February 1973 and at the Ace Gallery in Los Angeles in September and October of the same year. Between 1962 and 1972, Ruscha executed more than 1,000 single-word paintings, and, while continuing to produce works of that type, he began in the mid-1970s to paint short phrases, usually set against a multicolored, skylike background. Among the best-known works in that series are *Barns and Farms* (1983) and *Wild Cats of the World* (1985).

Ruscha's most celebrated nonverbal painting of the 1960s was probably his eleven-foot *The Los Angeles County Museum on Fire* (1965-68), which depicted the Los Angeles art museum aflame, as viewed from the air. "I had gone over the art museum in a helicopter, kind of by mistake, and took a lot of pictures of it," Ruscha explained to David Bourdon for *ARTnews* (April 1972). "Also, there was an aerial photograph of the museum on the cover of the telephone book and it was really a nice picture, with a beautiful background to it." In Bourdon's interpretation, the painting's "nightmarish quality . . . may be seen as a dire forecast of California culture."

Over a sixteen-year period beginning in 1962, Ruscha produced fourteen books of snapshotlike photographs, each devoted to a single subject and each featuring simple layouts with minimal copy, usually just a one-line caption beneath the photos. Insisting that he did not want to be regarded as a professional photographer and that he was uninterested in the aesthetic qualities of photography, Ruscha shot most of the pictures spontaneously, without thinking about composition. "If there is any facet of my work that I feel was kissed by angels, I'd say it was my books," Ruscha told David Bourdon. "My other work is definitely tied to a tradition, but I've never followed tradition in my books." The first collection in the series, *Twenty-Six Gasoline Stations* (1962), was inspired by Ruscha's frequent car trips between Los Angeles and Oklahoma City on U.S. Route 66, and it featured photos of service stations in California, Arizona, New Mexico, Texas, and Oklahoma. For *Some Los Angeles Apartments* (1965), Ruscha shot photos of the exteriors of thirty-four southern California apartment buildings. The artist eventually used his photographs of apartment buildings and gas stations as the basis for several paintings, drawings, and prints, the most famous of which was *Standard Station, Amarillo, Texas* (1963). With Los Angeles's famed Sunset Strip as the subject of his next collection of photos, *Every Building on the Sunset Strip* (1966), Ruscha took a different tack, printing the photos on a single twenty-seven-foot-long sheet that folded up, accordionlike, into the book. *Nine Swimming Pools* (1968) was the only book in the series to feature color photos; *Real Estate Opportunities* (1970) contained twenty-five photographs of vacant residential and commercial lots, most of them with signs advertising the lots for sale. "Sometimes the ugliest things have the most potential," Ruscha told Bourdon, in reference to his real-estate collection. "I went off in the car and I went down to these little towns, to Santa Ana,

Downey, places like that. I was exalted at the same time that I was repulsed by the whole thing."

By the middle and late 1980s, Ruscha had eliminated words altogether from a number of his paintings, producing instead a series of black-and-white works that, according to the critic Donald Kuspit of *Artforum* (February 1988), depicted "simple, stark, slightly out-of-focus scenes, with the graininess and melodramatic contrast of early Hollywood films." Often those paintings featured horizontal white bars designed to block or "censor" parts of the composition. In *Name, Address, Phone* (1986), for example, Ruscha placed bars below three tract houses, suggesting, in the words of Alfred Jan of *Flash Art* (February-March 1987), "the depressing, computerized condition of suburbanites." "The pictures . . . are a tease, a mockery of our expectations of a picture, even though they appear to satisfy all the demands of a picture," Kuspit observed. Other works in that series included *The Joshua, Shut This Gate,* and *Drugs, Hardware, Barber, Video* (all dating from 1987). Displayed at the Leo Castelli and Robert Miller galleries in early 1988, the series evoked much critical praise. Eleanor Heartney of *Art in America* (February 1988), for example, hailed the collection as "Ruscha's most eloquent paintings to date." His word paintings from the middle and late 1980s most often featured a word or a phrase spelled out in large white letters superimposed against an image. In *Chain and Cable* (1987), for instance, Ruscha spelled out the title phrase against a galleon.

Galleries that have featured Ruscha's work in one-man exhibitions include Galerie Heiner Friedrich, Munich (1970); Nigel Greenwood Gallery, London (1970, 1973, and 1980); Minneapolis Institute of Arts and Janie C. Lee Gallery, Dallas (both 1972); Leo Castelli Gallery, New York (nine shows between 1973 and 1986); Ace Gallery, Los Angeles (five shows between 1973 and 1980); Françoise Lambert, Milan (1974); Albright-Knox Art Gallery, Buffalo and Stedelijk Museum, Amsterdam (both 1976); Fort Worth Art Museum (1977); Auckland City Art Gallery (1978); Richard Hines Gallery, Seattle, Texas Gallery, Houston and InK Halle für Internationale neue Kunst, Zurich (all 1979); Contemporary Arts Museum, Houston (1983); James Corcoran Gallery, Los Angeles (1985); and Tony Shafrazi Gallery, New York (1988). A Ruscha retrospective, covering the first twenty-two years of the artist's career, opened in the spring of 1982 at the San Francisco Museum of Modern Art, later moving to the Whitney Museum of American Art in New York City, the Vancouver Art Gallery, the San Antonio Museum of Contemporary Art, and the Los Angeles County Museum of Art. Ruscha was also included in the Biennial Exhibition of Contemporary American Painting at the Corcoran Gallery in Washington, D.C., in 1971 and in the Whitney Gallery's Biennial Exhibition in 1987.

Ruscha served as a visiting professor of drawing and printmaking at the University of California, Los Angeles in 1969 and 1970. He has produced and directed a pair of offbeat short films, the first of which was *Premium* (1970), based on his 1969 photo collection, *Crackers*, and the second, *Miracle* (1975). Ruscha's work is featured in the permanent collections of the San Francisco Museum of Modern Art, the Los Angeles County Museum of Art, the Whitney Museum of American Art, the Stedelijk Museum, and the Hirshhorn Museum and Sculpture Garden of the Smithsonian Institution, among others. Since 1972 he has been represented by the Leo Castelli Gallery.

Tanned and handsome, with pale blue eyes and graying blond hair, Edward Ruscha, as described by Victoria Lautman of the *Chicago Tribune* (April 26, 1989), "could easily be mistaken for a forty-year-old actor instead of a fifty-two-year-old painter. . . . He's a living advertisement for the hedonism of southern California, a visual testimony that palm trees, sun, and freeways can really agree with a guy." Ruscha and the former Danna Knego were married in 1967 and divorced in 1976. They have a grown son, Edward Joseph Ruscha 5th. Since his divorce Ruscha has been linked romantically to the actresses Lauren Hutton, Samantha Eggar, Michele Phillips, and Candy Clark. Continuing to make Los Angeles his home base, Ruscha has a studio on Western Avenue in that city and another in the Mojave Desert, about fifty miles north of Palm Springs, California.

References: ARTnews 71:32+ Ap '72 pors; Chicago Tribune VII p21 Ap 26 '89 pors; People 19:85+ My 23 '83 pors; Vanity Fair 49:88+ F '86 pors; Baigell, Matthew. Dictionary of American Art (1982); Who's Who in America, 1988–89

Robin Laurence/NYT Pictures

Saatchi, Maurice

June 21, 1946– Advertising executive. Address: 80 Charlotte St., W1, London, England

The financial wizard and administrative mastermind behind the spectacular growth of the Saatchi & Saatchi Company into the world's largest advertising conglomerate is Maurice Saatchi, the more accessible of the two British brothers who have made a career of being strategically reclusive. After vaulting into prominence in the early 1970s with a series of witty, iconoclastic ads, Maurice and his older brother Charles transformed the British political scene in 1979 with their successful campaign to put the Tory candidate Margaret Thatcher in national office as prime minister of Great Britain.

In his ambition to build Saatchi & Saatchi into a multinational agency, Maurice embarked on a global shopping spree, acquiring advertising and business-services firms. In their rise from obscurity to the pinnacle of the international advertising industry, an endeavor that took about sixteen years, the Saatchi brothers challenged conventional wisdom about the very nature of the business. A master at what Myron Magnet of *Fortune* magazine has called "virtuoso self-promotion," Maurice managed to convince investors, with considerable success, that an agency could be huge, stable, profitable, and still remain creative.

Born in Baghdad, Iraq on June 21, 1946, Maurice Saatchi is the third of four sons of Nathan Saatchi, a prosperous textile importer of Iraqi-Jewish descent, and his wife, Daisy. Charles, the Saatchis' second son, had been born there on June 9, 1943. Positioned as they were between their older brother, David, and their younger brother, Philip, Maurice and Charles became exceptionally close siblings.

Foreseeing imminent disaster for the Jewish population of Iraq at the close of World War II, Nathan Saatchi began searching for a way out during his buying forays in Europe. On a 1946 trip to Great Britain, he bought two cotton and wool mills while house-hunting in Hampstead. The following year, he purchased a house there, sold his business in Baghdad, and moved to England. The family thus narrowly escaped a period of severe repression that impelled 120,000 Iraqi Jews to flee the country.

Nathan Saatchi's sons attended a private nursery school in the company of other children of Iraqi immigrants, while their father set about reestablishing himself in the textile business. By 1954 the Saatchis had moved into a larger house in Highgate, and the boys had enrolled in the state school system in north London. Bright but unruly, Charles struggled with school and eventually dropped out at seventeen to enter the work force, but the quieter and more docile Maurice excelled at his studies. While Charles was getting his first big break in advertising as a junior copywriter at the American-owned Benton & Bowles in Knightsbridge, Maurice was earning a degree in sociology from the London School of Economics, where he had begun his studies in 1964.

At Benton & Bowles, Charles Saatchi met Ross Cramer, a senior art director with whom he eventually defected to Collett Dickinson Pearce, a small agency that by the mid-1960s had already established itself as the most creative in London. There he soon earned a name for himself as one of the best copywriters in Britain, winning several awards with Cramer. Meanwhile, in 1967 Maurice Saatchi graduated with a first-class honors degree and a gold medal for academic achievement from the London School of Economics. Spurning a professor's suggestion that he pursue an academic career, Maurice opted for more lucrative employment.

By that time Charles Saatchi, who had formed a partnership with Cramer in a freelance consultancy, had established a profitable working relationship with the British trade press. Already freelancing for top London agencies, he had a marked flair for generating publicity, but Charles, persistently wary of direct contact, often phoned in inside tips about the agency scene to trade magazine contacts, in exchange for coverage of his own activities. The London *Sunday Times*'s deputy editor, Ivan Fallon, has speculated that Maurice may well have been influenced by his brother's trade press connections when he singled out Haymarket Publishing as the object of his postgraduate job search. Controlled by the Conservative member of Parliament Michael Heseltine and his partner, Lindsay Masters, Haymarket Publishing was on the verge of relaunching a revamped weekly formerly titled *World Press News*, which covered Fleet Street and the advertising industry. Masters offered Maurice a job as a junior assistant, meeting his salary request of twice the firm's customary starting wages.

Maurice helped Haymarket Publishing to plan the relaunching of the weekly, which was renamed *Campaign*. An editorial triumph from its inception, the publication created a stir during a period in which British advertising, long a stodgy shadow of its American counterpart, had begun to progress beyond its primitive stage. By 1970 the agency of Cramer Saatchi had established itself as a frontrunner in the creative vanguard with its series of memorable antismoking ads. As with subsequent Saatchi endeavors, the common characteristic of such campaigns was their "single-minded approach. We aim to express a single idea dramatically," Maurice Saatchi has said.

In the spring of 1970 a Cramer Saatchi copywriter named Jeremy Sinclair found himself faced with creating an advertising concept that would promote the Health Education Council's message on contraception to sexually active young Britons. Sinclair envisioned the image of a pregnant young man, accompanied by the caption "Would you be more careful if it was you that got pregnant?" Both

praised and reviled in the national press, the ad quickly went transatlantic in the pages of *Time* magazine, and the Saatchi legend was born.

Because he had dreamed for years about establishing his own agency, Charles took advantage of Cramer's gravitation toward the movie industry to propose a new partnership to Maurice, who asked Lindsay Masters for the £25,000 start-up capital they needed to get their new venture off the ground. Chagrined at Maurice's impending departure, yet fond of him, the Haymarket chief at first declined to invest in a company about which his magazine would be writing. Masters steered Maurice to the fashion designer Mary Quant and her husband, Alexander Plunket-Greene, who agreed to invest if Masters would. Resolving never to mention the company to any of his editors, Masters capitulated, and within two years, according to Ivan Fallon, the Saatchis had bought out their outside partners. Saatchi & Saatchi, so designated to get full mileage out of the brothers' unusual name, was off and running.

Even though the new agency had been given an unprecedented degree of coverage in the trade press, Charles resolved to kick the business off with a grand gesture. As a result, on September 13, 1979 the brothers ran a full-page ad in the *Sunday Times* announcing their plan to revolutionize the advertising industry. Of that prophetic move, which cost the fledgling enterprise nearly a quarter of its capital, Maurice later said, "That ad put us on the map."

With the so-called third brother, Tim Bell, added to the Saatchi team and three steady clients on board, the company set out to expand its client roster. From the outset, the Saatchis worked as diligently to market their own image as they did on the ads that earned them an overnight reputation for dynamic creativity. "Their first tiny office, characteristically for the Saatchis, looked a lot bigger than it was," Ron Leagas, Saatchi's former managing director, has recalled, "and every time a potential client came on the phone, everybody manned the typewriters to make it sound busy."

At the agency's inception, its artistic firebrand, Charles, was reportedly involved in overseeing the execution of every ad and in wooing new accounts, but by the end of the first year he seldom saw clients, although he remained the firm's dominant creative force. The more genial Maurice emerged as the firm's engaging advance man, meeting with clients, handling the business end of the operation, and planning strategy with his brother. "In 1970," Maurice explained in the *New York Times* (February 3, 1980), "agencies were generally perceived as falling into two groups: big and dull or small, creative and superficial. We thought there was a gap for a large agency that was still young, bright, innovative." In his haste to fill that need, Maurice once compared his immodest ambition for the new company with a description he had read of a giant iron flywheel set in perpetual motion.

Maurice made no secret of his goal of expanding into the lucrative American advertising market and thereby reversing what he termed "the one-way traffic" of advertising revenues and rechanneling the flow "from the U.S. to the U.K." In the agency's early years, he earned a reputation for unprecedented audacity by making takeover offers to agencies larger than his own. By the mid-1970s, his strategy began to pay off, for in 1975, Saatchi acquired the London-based Compton Partners, 49 percent of which was owned by Compton Advertising in New York, in a move that gave the brothers an additional $70 million in billings, the lion's share of the firm's equity, and the huge Procter & Gamble account. It also enabled them to go public with a listing on the London Stock Exchange.

The renamed Saatchi & Saatchi Compton holding company soon embarked on an acquisitions strategy that was to alter the advertising business radically. Maurice aggressively marketed the industry itself to potential investors who harbored outmoded attitudes about the effectiveness of product promotion, then thought to be "ungentlemanly" by the financial pundits of the day. "Maurice Saatchi resolved to teach investors that an agency can be a big, stable institution rather than a collection of undependable, unbusinesslike egomaniacs or the lengthened shadow of a couple of young hotshots," Myron Magnet observed in Fortune (March 19, 1984). The celebrated Saatchi tactic of keeping a low public profile resulted from his eagerness to win over the City, London's staid financial district—a strategy now emulated by other firms emboldened by the Saatchis' success. Throughout the latter part of the decade, the Saatchis exemplified the point by unobtrusively buying or opening agencies in regional England, Scotland, and Ireland.

In 1978 the Saatchis won the account that was to make their name a household word in Great Britain when they were hired by the Tory party to orchestrate Margaret Thatcher's 1979 campaign to unseat the Labour prime minister James Callaghan. Accused by a disconcerted opposition party member of "selling Margaret Thatcher as if she were soap powder," the gleeful Tories took advantage of what Gordon Reece, the former party publicity director, called one of the best campaigns in advertising history. Its highlights included slick, punchy television broadcasts and a now famous poster depicting long lines of unemployed workers under a huge caption reading "Labour Isn't Working."

Such tactics so outraged Labour politicians that the Saatchis' role became a campaign issue, and Callaghan decided to put off calling the election until the following spring, a fatal error. Although Margaret Thatcher's victories in 1979 (and 1983 and 1987) can hardly be fully credited to the Saatchis, Edward Booth-Clibborn, her campaign media director, later declared that the brothers had "changed the face of British politics." Maurice Saatchi was praised by political observers for playing a brilliant tactical role in the campaign, which brought to the fore his considerable talent for devising communications strategies.

By 1979 Saatchi & Saatchi had become Great Britain's largest advertising agency. Between the first two Thatcher campaigns, the firm began a period of corporate growth that was described by Myron Magnet as resembling "a marvel of genetic engineering." Their aim was clear: to become one of what Maurice projected would be by 1990 only a handful of multinational mega-agencies. By 1981, the Saatchis' recent acquisitions had made them Europe's top agency. The following year, they made what was to date the largest acquisition in advertising history by paying $55 million for Compton Communications, the fourteenth-largest ad agency in the world and a minority shareholder in Compton Partners.

In 1983 the Saatchis added the agency McCaffrey & McCall, and in the same year their firm, which was by then widely feared for flouting the industry's proscription against "poaching" the clients of competitors, wooed the British Airways account away from Foote Cone & Belding. For the airline's new campaign, Saatchi created a striking ninety-second television spot depicting the island of Manhattan flying in for a landing at London's Heathrow Airport. Dubbed versions of the ad were soon being aired in more than fifty countries. Having come across a 1983 Harvard Business Review article propounding that companies should create a unified market for their products worldwide, Maurice deployed a controversial theory of "globalization" designed to derive economies of scale by using variations on a single theme to promote the same product in different countries.

Derided in the British press as "Snatchi & Snatchi," the Saatchis were nonetheless envied for Maurice's ability to raise equity on the British stock market to finance the company's skyrocketing growth. He soon began to broaden the concept behind the firm's apparently predatory "spending spree." In 1985 Saatchi acquired the Hay Group, a Philadelphia compensation consulting and headhunting company, as well as two market research firms subsequently merged into a single company. Maurice's drive to add business-services concerns to the Saatchi empire reflected his desire to see the brothers become, as he put it, "the only people who are tackling the total market as a total market." The one-stop shopping strategy has run into several notable snags, among them client concerns over knowledgeability and conflict of interest, falling share prices, and a 1987 rebuff by two commercial banks that Maurice approached with takeover proposals.

In 1986 the Saatchis added Dancer Fitzgerald Sample, DFS-Dorland Worldwide, and Backer & Spielvogel to their stable of ad agencies. In May of that year the huge conglomerate finally attained its original goal of becoming the world's largest ad agency. That April, using capital raised in a staggering $600 million stock offering, the Saatchis paid $450 million for Ted Bates Worldwide. Maurice proffered his customary "earn-out" purchase offer, whereby Saatchi would entice the principals of the targeted firm with a large initial payment, allow the acquired company to operate under its own name, and then tie the amount of future payments to the acquisition's profit performances. The much-lauded maneuver failed to work in the case of Robert Jacoby, the chief executive officer of Bates, who insisted on cash up front and was eventually ousted by the shrewd Saatchis.

Their triumph, however, was short-lived. Client defections caused the loss of hundreds of millions of dollars in billings, some 500 employees were fired, and share prices fell even before the October 1987 stock market debacle. Having edged out the ambitious Tim Bell in 1984, the Saatchis were infuriated when Margaret Thatcher brought Bell in secretly to work for the Tories during her 1987 campaign, and, soon after her reelection, Saatchi resigned the account. In April 1988 Saatchi was dropped outright by tobacco and food megaclient RJR Nabisco, losing $84 million in billings because the agency had produced an antismoking commercial for Northwest Airlines. Its operating earnings for the fiscal year that ended September 30, 1989 were expected to fall 45 percent to $108 million, according to a *Business Week* (October 30, 1989) report. Average net debt, according to the same report, was expected to reach $232 million; in the previous year the company had a cash surplus of $108 million. To quell the fears of the financial community, the brothers hired the French millionaire Robert Louis-Dreyfus to turn the company around starting in January 1990.

The Saatchis' profitability was expected to decline somewhat, since Maurice did not anticipate making any major new advertising acquisitions in the near future. Although debate continues among analysts over whether the Saatchis' business-services "supermarket" approach will work in the long run, the brothers' rapid ascent and unorthodox tactics are believed to have transformed the very nature of competition within the industry and altered such essential components as salary structure. Whether or not the Saatchis succeed at creating the world's largest consulting company, Myron Magnet has observed, "they rewrote some of the ad game's most basic rules."

Curly-haired, bespectacled Maurice Saatchi was described as "mild, donnish, disciplined and urbane" in a *Fortune* (January 5, 1987) magazine profile of the year's fifty most fascinating business people. He serves as the Saatchis' public façade, while the "brilliant, undisciplined, mercurial, profane, and hotly competitive" Charles stays out of the public eye. Although both brothers have been described as publicity-shy, the more affable Maurice grants occasional press interviews and meets with clients. Often characterized as the Howard Hughes of advertising because of his reclusiveness, Charles has amassed one of the world's most impressive collections of contemporary art. That collection is so extensive, in fact, that he and his American wife, Doris Lockhart, opened a private museum in St. John's Wood, London in the spring of 1985 to display it. *ARTnews* reported in May 1985 that the Saatchi brothers spent over $2 million

a year on art, for works by, among many others, Andy Warhol, David Salle, Francesco Clemente, and a number of British artists. Maurice drives a Jensen, enjoys gardening, and maintains a vacation home at Cap Ferrat on the French Riviera. Maurice has one son and one stepson; he and his second wife, the former Haymarket executive Josephine Hart, have produced two plays.

The inseparable Saatchi brothers were the subjects of Ivan Fallon's book *The Brothers: The Rise & Rise of Saatchi & Saatchi* (1988), which was excerpted in the *Sunday Times* and dismissed as a lengthy, yet factually informative, "puff piece" by the critic Maureen Freely in the London *Observer*. Maurice and his brother are reputed to quarrel often enough to generate the creative tension that drives them both. Their mutual ambition is believed to link them in a symbiotic relationship rooted in common goals. "They're collectors," said Jeremy Bullmore, the chairman of Saatchi competitor J. Walter Thompson in Britain. "They collect companies, clients, money, pictures, everything. They vastly enjoy growth and acquisition."

References: Art in America 73:23 Jl '85; ARTnews 84:79 My '85; Bsns W p54 Mr 19 '84, p70 N 26 '84, p92 S 28 '87 por, p60 D D 21 '87 por; Economist 299:79+ Ap 19 '86, 299:75+ My 17 '86; Fortune 109:46+ Mr 19 '84 por, 113:37+ Je 23 '86, 115:96 Ja 5 '87; London Observer p38 Ag 28 '88; N Y Times Mag p34 N 8 '87 por; Newsweek 101:62 My 23 '83; Sunday Times C p1+ Ag 21 '88 pors, C p1+ Ag 28 '88 por; Time 127:53 Ap 28 '86 por, 131:68 Ap 18 '88; Who's Who, 1989

Said, Edward W.

(sä ēd´)

Nov. 1, 1935- Literary critic; educator; political activist. Address: 419 Hamilton Hall, Columbia University, New York, N.Y. 10027

"Where do you stand on the question of Palestine?"—the query with which Edward Said began his March 1987 article for *Harper's* magazine entitled "Interpreting Palestine"—is, in his words, "a shamelessly provocative question, but "an interesting one against the wider background of theories of interpretation." That question exemplifies the "secular criticism" advocated and practiced by Said, a Palestinian Arab who since 1977 has been Columbia University's Parr Professor of English and Comparative Literature and is now Old Dominion Foundation Professor in the Humanities. For Said, who is a member of the Palestine National Council and is generally regarded as the most prominent American spokesman for the Arab cause, interpretation is always political, since "the realities of power and authority" in the world, as he once wrote, "make texts possible." "These realities," Said has insisted, "are what should be

Edward W. Said

taken account of by [academic] criticism and the critical consciousness." He has little tolerance for criticism that defends, as he has put it, "the classics, the virtues of a liberal education, and the precious pleasures of literature" but remains "silent (perhaps incompetent) about the historical and social world in which all these things take place." Writing in the *Dictionary of Literary Biography*, John Kucich observed that the chief effect of Said's career has been to create a "unique" and "much-needed link among humanistic values and traditions, theories of textuality, and cultural politics."

Edward W. Said was born in Jerusalem in what was then Palestine on November 1, 1935, the oldest child and only son of Wadie Said, a prosperous businessman who headed a company that made office equipment and published books, and Hilda (Musa) Said. The family lived in an exclusive section of West Jerusalem. Wadie Said had fled to the United States in 1911, joined the American Army, and served in France during World War I. He later attended college in Cleveland, Ohio before returning to Palestine. Baptized as an Episcopalian, Edward Said attended St. George's, an Anglican preparatory school, where his extracurricular activities included riding, boxing, gymnastics, and playing the piano.

Palestine had been a mandated territory of Great Britain since 1920, but in 1947 the British turned over control of the country to the United Nations, which divided it into an Arab state and a Jewish state and placed the city of Jerusalem under international control. At the age of twelve, Edward Said was forced to use a pass when traveling between his home and his school. "The situation was dangerous and inconvenient," he recalled to Dinitia Smith during an interview for *New York* (January 23, 1989) magazine. In December 1947 the Said family left Jerusalem and settled in Cairo, Egypt. Five months later war broke out between Palestinian Arabs and Jews after the Arabs rejected the partition of Palestine into Jewish and Arab sections, an event that Palestinians ever since have referred to as the *nakbah*, or "disaster." "Israel was established; Palestine was destroyed," Said wrote in his book *After the Last Sky; Palestinian Lives* (1986).

Edward Said attended the American School in Cairo, where his classmates were the children of diplomats from the United States. Later, at Cairo's Victoria College, his schoolmates included the future King Hussein of Jordan and the actor Omar Sharif, then known as Michael Shalhoub. In 1951 Said was sent by his parents to Mount Hermon preparatory school in Mount Hermon, Massachusetts, where, because he was away from home for the first time and allowed to see his parents only during the summer, he was unhappy despite the fact that he was an excellent student. He was much more contented after he enrolled at Princeton University. "For the first time in my life, I was able intellectually to flourish," he told Dinitia Smith. After obtaining an A.B. degree from Princeton in 1957, Said became a graduate student at Harvard University, which granted him his M.A. degree in 1960 and his Ph.D. degree (in English literature) in 1964. Said's doctoral dissertation was on Joseph Conrad, the Polish-born writer whose work, particularly his exploration of colonialism, was to have such a profound influence on him. "I felt, first coming across Conrad when I was a teenager, that in a certain sense I was reading, not so much my own story, but a story written out of bits of my life and put together in a haunting and fantastically obsessive way," Said explained to Imre Salusinszky, who interviewed him for his book *Criticism in Society* (1987). "He has a particular kind of vision which increases in intensity every time I read him, so that now it's almost unbearable for me to read him." In 1963 Edward Said became an instructor of English at Columbia University, where he was promoted to assistant professor in 1965, associate professor in 1968, and full professor in 1970. In 1977 he was appointed Parr Professor of English and Comparative Literature, a position that he continues to hold today, and in 1989 he was appointed Old Dominion Foundation Professor in the Humanities.

Edward Said's first book, *Joseph Conrad and the Fiction of Autobiography* (1966), which grew out of his Ph.D. dissertation, examined the connection between Conrad's letters and his short fiction. According to John Kucich, Said, in the process, detailed "the troubling link between Conrad's thought and the forces of colonialism saturating his culture." A critic for *Choice* (March 1967) called the book "an important addition to Conrad criticism," adding, "It is also valuable as a sophisticated and powerful example of psychological criticism."

In his second book, *Beginnings: Intention and Method* (1975), Edward Said explored the role that changing notions of beginning play in "the production of artistic work or knowledge." A beginning takes place, Said wrote, in the "interplay between the new and the customary" in thought and writing. That interplay is extraordinarily complex since, while "we can regard a beginning as the point at which, in a given work, the writer departs from all other works, a beginning immediately establishes relationships with works already existing, relationships of either continuity or antagonism or some mixture of both." In reviewing *Beginnings* for the *Library Journal* (November 15, 1975), Richard Kuczkowski called the book "rich and fascinating despite needless obscurity and graceless jargon" and "an ingenious exploration of the meaning of modernism." A critic for the *New Yorker* (March 8, 1976) commented that *Beginnings* "is in itself a beginning, for it displays a young scholar's mastery of several fields and his suggestions for further criticism." *Beginnings* won Columbia's prestigious Lionel Trilling Award in 1976.

In an interview that appeared in *Diacritics* (Fall 1976), a review of contemporary criticism, Edward Said spoke of the "two quite separate lives" he leads. "On the one hand," he noted, "I'm a literary scholar, critic, and teacher. I lead a pretty uncontroversial life at a big university. . . . Yet I lead another life, which most other literary people know nothing about . . . . My whole background in the Middle East, my frequent and sometimes protracted visits there, my political involvement: all this exists in a totally different box from the one out of which I pop as a literary critic, professor, etc." It was that other, less well known, aspect of his life that provided the impetus for Said's next several books.

Orientalism (1978), Said's best-known and most controversial book, explores the way in which the West views the Islamic world and defines "orientalism" as the tendency of Western scholars to perceive the East in an essentially hostile and stereotypical way. As he summarized the thesis of his book in an essay for *Time* (April 16, 1979) magazine: "For the West, to understand Islam has meant trying to convert its variety into a monolithic undeveloping essence, its originality into a debased copy of Christian culture, its people into fearsome caricatures. . . . The U.S. inherited the Orientalist legacy, and uncritically employed it in its universities, mass media, popular culture, imperial policy. In films and cartoons, Muslim Arabs, for example, are represented either as bloodthirsty mobs, or as hook-nosed, lecherous sadists." In the book's introduction, Said further explained, "Orientalism is the corporate institution for dealing with the Orient— dealing with it by making statements about it, authorizing views of it, describing it, by teaching it, settling it, ruling over it." That "corporate institution," in fact, "manufactures" the Orient for the benefit of the Western "consumer" of Orientalism. Said argued that, like any successful product, that manufactured Orient is not permitted to change, and whatever portions of its history conflict with the findings of Orientalist scholarship are ignored or argued out of existence. For the Orientalist, Said wrote, "history, politics, and economics do not matter. Islam is Islam, the Orient is the Orient." Said traced the history of Orientalist scholarship from the time of Napoleon's occupation of Egypt to current American and Israeli policies with regard to the Arab world. In that "latest phase," Said observed, "the transference of a popular anti-Semitic animus from a Jewish to an Arab target was made smoothly, since the figure was essentially the same. . . . Insofar as the Arab has any history, it is part of the history given him (or taken from him: the difference is slight) by the Orientalist tradition."

Orientalism, which was nominated for the National Book Critics Circle Award, was eventually translated into fifteen languages, and it has been the subject of many symposiums. According to Dinitia Smith, the book "changed the face of scholarship on the Arab world and the Third World in general." Although critics generally praised the book, they also took into account some of its imperfections. The British historian J. H. Plumb, writing in the *New York Times Book Review* (February 18, 1979), found *Orientalism* to be "pretentiously written" and "drenched in jargon" but added, "There is much in this book that is superb as well as intellectually exciting." In her review for *Library Journal* (November 1, 1978), Elizabeth R. Hayford considered Said's main argument only "partially convincing," but she went on to praise *Orientalism* as "a masterful study with valuable insights for a much wider audience than just the Middle Eastern specialist." One of the book's chief critics was Bernard Lewis, a professor of Near Eastern studies at Princeton whose work on Islam is pilloried in *Orientalism*. As quoted by Dinitia Smith, Lewis dismissed the book as "false" and "absurd" and further contended that it "reveals a disquieting lack of knowledge of what scholars do and what scholarship is about."

Edward Said's next two books, *The Question of Palestine* (1979) and *Covering Islam; How the Media and the Experts Determine How We See the Rest of the World* (1981), also dealt with Western misconceptions of the Orient. In the former, Said quoted such American intellectuals as Reinhold Niebuhr and Edmund Wilson to show the way in which Westerners routinely depict Arabs as being "synonymous with trouble—rootless, mindless, gratuitous trouble." Said tried to refute the common Western tendency to associate Arabs, particularly Palestinians, with terrorism. "In sheer numerical terms," he wrote in *The Question of Palestine*, "in brute numbers of bodies and property destroyed, there is absolutely nothing to compare between what Zionism has done to Palestinians and what, in retaliation, Palestinians have done to Zionists. . . . What is much worse . . . is the hypocrisy of Western . . . journalism and intellectual discourse, which have barely anything to say about Zionist terror." Said also discussed Palestine's crucial role in solving the problems of the Middle East and concluded that the solution is to grant the Palestinians the right of self-determination, ideally in the areas along the Gaza Strip and the West Bank, which have been occupied by Israel since the Six-Day War of 1967.

Reviewing *The Question of Palestine* for the *Library Journal* (November 15, 1979), Elizabeth R. Hayford called it a "passionate" book that "should play an important role in shaping American public opinion and moving government policy." Nicholas Bethell, in his evaluation for the *New York Times Book Review* (January 20, 1980), faulted the book for its inconsistent tone, but he added, "Books such as Mr. Said's need to be written and read, in the hope that understanding will provide a better chance of survival."

In his *Covering Islam*, Said took the American media and academic community to task for what he perceived as their inaccurate depictions of Islam, arguing that both institutions fail to understand the political and religious complexities of Islamic societies. John Kucich summarized *Covering Islam* as follows: "Without denying the unpleasant realities of the Islamic world, Said shows how complex Middle East events are reduced to huge generalizations and ignorant clichés by news networks that manage to make Islam the scapegoat for everything Americans dislike about the present world situation." Said used the American media's coverage of the seizing of the United States embassy in Teheran by Iranian students in November 1979 and the subsequent taking of ninety hostages to illustrate his thesis. "So poorly and with such antagonism did the press report Islam and Iran during 1979 that it can be suspected that a number of opportunities for resolving the hostage crisis were lost, and perhaps this is why the Iranian government suggested early in 1980 that fewer reporters in Iran might quiet the tension and produce a peaceful solution." Anthony Howard, who appraised *Covering Islam* for the *New York Times Book Review* (July 26, 1981), condemned the foregoing analysis for displaying "astonishing naivety." "Anyone, as they say, who believes that, will believe anything," he concluded. But writing in the *Library Journal* (May 1, 1981), D. P. Snider praised Said for making "a very scholarly and eloquent plea for restructuring our perceptions and analysis of the 'Islamic world.' [His] credentials are impressive and his coverage is painstakingly complete."

Said's *The World, the Text, and the Critic* (1983) is a collection of twelve essays (six of which had previously appeared in scholarly journals) that he wrote between 1968 and 1983, on topics ranging from Islam to Jonathan Swift and Joseph Conrad. In "Secular Criticism," Said considered the ongoing interplay between inherited order, or "filiation," and invented order, or "affiliation." Intellectual filiation becomes political, Said suggested, as a result of the process of self-perpetuation natural to all cultures. "In the transmission and persistence of a culture," he wrote, "there is a continual process of reinforcement that excludes, disenfranchises, and renders 'homeless' everything it encounters that is not itself." Since it is natural for

the intellectual to be coopted into that sometimes brutal process of cultural transmission, Said suggested that the task of the secular critic is to oppose his culture's movement towards "a dominion that almost always hides its dark side" under a "cloak" of trumpeted values. *The World, the Text, and the Critic* won the René Wellek Prize of the American Comparative Literature Association and prompted a critic for *Choice* (June 1983) to call it "one of the most important contributions to the debate about the nature of the humanities in the past decade."

After the Last Sky; Palestinian Lives (1986) pairs a text by Edward Said and photographs by the Swiss photographer Jean Mohr in an attempt to portray the transient nature of Palestinian existence. "While the photographs rivet the reader's attention, Said puts their pain and dislocation into words," Elizabeth R. Hayford wrote in her review for the *Library Journal* (December 1986). "The interplay of text and photos makes a powerful statement and reflects Said's poetic skills." In his assessment for the *New York Times Book Review* (November 9, 1986), Richard Ben Cramer observed: "As Mr. Said picks through the photos like remnants of a lost civilization, we feel his deep connection with these very present people. Their roots in the world are gone; the society that was nurturing soil cannot be reconstituted." *Blaming the Victims; Spurious Scholarship and the Palestinian Question* (1988) is a collection of essays on Palestinian history, which Said coedited with Christopher Hitchens. Both men also contributed essays to the book, which, according to the *Library Journal*, is an attempt "to show Palestinian Arab history in a favorable light."

Since 1977 Edward Said has been a member of the Palestine National Council (PNC)—the Palestinian parliament-in-exile. At the PNC meeting held in Algiers in November 1988, he helped to draft a resolution proclaiming the establishment of an independent Palestinian state, envisioned by the Palestine Liberation Organization chairman Yasir Arafat to consist of the West Bank and the Gaza Strip. At the same meeting, Arafat renounced terrorism and, for the first time, recognized Israel's right to exist, thereby relinquishing previous Palestinian claims to all of the land that once constituted Palestine. In response to Arafat's statements, the United States, which had earlier refused to negotiate with the PLO, agreed to begin talks with that organization aimed at resolving the Palestinian-Israeli conflict.

Said's activism has made him the target of many phone threats and hate letters. In 1985 his office at Columbia University was ransacked. "Usually when I give a lecture somewhere," Said told Imre Salusinszky, "there's always a question of security. . . . There's always the danger of violence, of somebody rising in the audience and throwing something or firing a gun at me." Yet Said says he would "get paralyzed" if he allowed himself to become too concerned about such possibilities.

In keeping with his distinguished appearance, Said dresses in well-tailored suits. When at home in his apartment near Columbia University, he speaks Arabic; in the world outside, he speaks American-accented English. Fluent in French, he reads with ease in Italian, German, Spanish, and Latin. Among the many universities that have invited him to serve as a visiting professor are Harvard, Yale, Princeton, and Johns Hopkins. The bibliographical section of his résumé listing the books and essays he has written is twelve pages long. He has received fellowships from, among others, the Guggenheim Foundation and the National Endowment for the Humanities. His first

marriage, to Maire Jaanus on July 8, 1962, ended in divorce. Since December 15, 1970, Said has been married to Mariam Cortas, a Lebanese Quaker. The couple have two teenage children, Wadie and Najla. A talented pianist, Said serves as the music critic for the *Nation*. For relaxation, he plays squash and tennis.

References: N Y Times A p2 F 22 '80 por; New York 22:40+ Ja 23 '89 pors; Time 113:54 Ap 16 '79 por; Washington Post D p1+ Je 7 '88 pors; Contemporary Authors vols 21-22 (1969); Who's Who in America, 1988-89

Sajak, Pat

Oct. 26, 1946- Television personality. Address: c/o CBS-TV, 7800 Beverly Blvd., Los Angeles, Calif. 90036

Since 1981 Pat Sajak has presided over *Wheel of Fortune*, the most popular game show in American television history. Thanks to the simplicity of its format and the likability of its two stars, Pat Sajak and hostess Vanna White, *Wheel of Fortune* has become a pop-culture phenomenon, with millions of loyal viewers and Nielsen ratings unheard of for a show of its kind. In January 1989 Sajak took on a new responsibility when he became host of the first new talk show to appear in the 11:30 P.M. to 1 A.M. (EST) time slot on one of the three major commercial networks in twenty years. (Sajak has continued to serve as host of the syndicated nighttime version of *Wheel of Fortune*, but he left the NBC daytime edition in December 1988.) The *Pat Sajak*

Show, on CBS, appears opposite NBC's *Tonight Show*, hosted by the veteran king of late-night television, Johnny Carson.

Sajak, who once described himself during an interview on *Late Night with David Letterman* as "one of those people who always wanted to work in radio and television," did stints as a weatherman, disc jockey, newscaster, staff announcer, and local talk show host before taking over *Wheel of Fortune*. Like Carson and Letterman, he was born and raised in the Midwest, and his understated, quick-witted, and genial style is often compared to theirs. Like them as well, Sajak possesses a certain mischievous unpredictability that belies his outward demeanor. "He is, in short, a very comfortable sort of fellow, holding in reserve the right to be terribly wicked," John J. O'Connor, the television columnist of the *New York Times*, has observed. Diane K. Shah, who did a profile of Sajak for the *New York Times Magazine* (December 11, 1988), has pointed out that his "appeal is that he manages to come across as everybody's favorite son-in-law while looking slightly smart-aleck, like Peck's Bad Boy. . . . The suspicion lingers that beneath the safe all-American good looks and the jocular manner resides a fellow who is smart, savvy, quick—a fellow with, yes, a secret personality."

Pat Sajak was born in Chicago, Illinois on October 26, 1946, the son of a Polish-American trucking foreman who loaded and unloaded cargo. While growing up on the city's Southwest Side, Sajak once accompanied his father to work and decided on the spot that the trucking business was definitely not for him. When he was about eleven, he began sneaking out of bed to watch the *Tonight Show*, then hosted by Jack Paar, thinking to himself, "Boy, that would be fun to do." Hooked on broadcasting, he took to talking into a wooden spoon as if it were a microphone. Sajak told Cheryl Lavin of the *Chicago Tribune* (January 4, 1987) that he was so intensely private during his high school years that his classmates considered him "funny and mysterious." After high school, Sajak enrolled at Columbia College, a local commuter school. During his junior year there, he got his first broadcasting job, as a newscaster at a tiny Chicago foreign-language station, WEDC. Located in a

Cadillac showroom, the station was owned by a local Polish-American congressman, Roman Pucinski. "The DJ played Spanish music, did Spanish commercials, and I would read the news in English," Sajak recalled for Diane K. Shah. "To this day, I do not know why."

Bored with student life, Sajak left Columbia College after his junior year and enlisted in the United States Army, mistakenly believing that by volunteering he would reduce his chances of being sent to Vietnam and hoping to be assigned to armed-forces radio. To his dismay, he wound up as a finance clerk in Long Binh, thirty-five miles from the South Vietnamese capital city of Saigon, and, though he tried repeatedly to transfer to radio duty, he had no success. Finally, he wrote to Congressman Roman Pucinski, his old WEDC employer, and soon afterward he was transferred to armed-forces radio in Saigon. There, he exaggerated the extent of his civilian radio experience ("I think I lied, actually," he has said) and talked his way into a job as a disc jockey. Although he complied with army edicts that certain "objectionable" top forty records not be played, Sajak found ways to circumvent other restrictions. For instance, when his program director, who outranked him, ordered him to begin playing Christmas carols in October, Sajak, not wanting to make the soldiers homesick prematurely, continued to play rock songs but introduced them as Christmas tunes. And to get around an army rule that on-air personnel always give their rank after announcing their names, Sajak did not identify himself for over a year. He also interjected into his disc jockey patter slyly irreverent asides and references that were easily understood by the enlisted men, but were lost on the officers. "He had an amazing ability to get away with things that nobody else could," Tony Lyons, a fellow soldier and longtime friend of Sajak's, recalled to Diane K. Shah. "He got away with murder."

After serving for eighteen months on armed-forces radio, Sajak was transferred back to the United States and assigned to a military base in Texas. Unhappy there, he persuaded a captain to change his orders, and for the next year he worked at the Pentagon, running a slide projector for the benefit of generals being briefed on the war. Sajak remained in the Washington area following his discharge in 1970. Unable to find a job in radio, he supported himself by working as a desk clerk at the Madison Hotel. Then, acting on a tip from a friend, he moved to the small town of Murray, Kentucky, where he got a job as a disc jockey at radio station WNBS.

After spending a year in Murray, Sajak told himself, "I'm twenty-five and I'm not exactly doing well." Hoping to advance his broadcasting career by breaking into a larger market, he moved to the nearest big city—Nashville, Tennessee. There, he again kept himself afloat financially by working as a desk clerk at a hotel (Howard Johnson's) while he made the rounds of the radio and television stations in the vicinity. Eventually, he was hired as a staff announcer by WSM-TV, the local NBC affili-

ate. Sajak's penchant for mischief-making on the air surfaced in Nashville, just as it had in Vietnam. Assigned to the daily early-morning chore of reading job listings supplied by the state labor department, Sajak decided to liven things up. "One day I would start reading, and after each job I'd just sink a little more in my seat until at the end, it was just the top of my head showing," he told Kathy O'Malley of the Chicago Tribune (December 7, 1988). "Or I would scream the whole thing. Or I would read it backward. Or if I found a good job, I wouldn't give out the number, I'd put it in my pocket." Despite occasional reprimands from his superiors, Sajak continued his clowning. Once, during a late-night movie, he had the station's technicians put him in a small circle in the upper right-hand corner of the screen, from which vantage point he talked back to the characters in the film. Pat Sajak also hosted a public-affairs program at WSM, and he eventually became the station's regular weatherman.

It was while serving as a weatherman at WSM-TV that Sajak attracted the attention of the executives of KNBC-TV, the NBC-owned affiliate in Los Angeles, who hired him in 1977 as their weatherman. The fact that he was now working in the nation's second-largest media market did not keep the irrepressible Sajak from continuing his hijinks. He regularly warned viewers that cold fronts from Canada were rapidly bearing down on balmy southern California, and he once did his forecast while wearing a bandage over his right eye, switching it to his left eye during a commercial. In addition to fulfilling his weather-forecasting duties, Sajak served as a host of a live ninety-minute talk show on Sunday afternoons. "It was a weird show," he told Diane K. Shah. "You'd be out on a trout farm interviewing people who had nothing to do with fish, or they'd send us to a Polish kielbasa festival to conduct a debate between opposing factions on gun control. It was good training, in retrospect. You learned how to tap-dance."

While at KNBC, Sajak auditioned, without success, to be the host of several network game shows that were then in the "pilot" stage. His luck changed, however, in 1981, when Merv Griffin, whose company, Merv Griffin Enterprises, produces the NBC game show Wheel of Fortune, began searching for a host to replace the departing Chuck Woolery. After seven years on the air, Wheel of Fortune had sunk to last place in the ratings for its time slot. Seeking to revive the moribund show, Griffin made three major moves over the next two years. The first was the hiring of Pat Sajak, whose offbeat weather reports Griffin admired, to be the show's new host—a decision that displeased network officials, since Sajak was then unknown nationally. "I put the show on the line," Griffin told Diane K. Shah. "I said if you don't approve Sajak I'm stopping the taping right now." The network executives relented, and Sajak took over as host of Wheel of Fortune in December 1981, after signing a seven-year contract. (He later admitted that he expected the show to be off the air within two years.)

Ten months after Sajak became host, Griffin signed a struggling young model and actress named Vanna White to be the show's hostess, replacing Susan Stafford. Then, in September 1983, Griffin and King World Enterprises introduced a syndicated nighttime version of *Wheel of Fortune* that featured bigger prizes than the daytime show. Griffin's strategies worked brilliantly. By 1986 the evening edition had become the highest-rated syndicated show in television history, reaching 208 markets encompassing 99 percent of the country. It was viewed, on an average day, by 30.7 million people, more than twice as many as watched the second-most-popular syndicated show, *M*A*S*H*. The network version, meanwhile, was consistently NBC's top-rated daytime show, attracting about twelve million viewers a day. Along the way, Pat Sajak and Vanna White became national celebrities and, to some extent, cult figures, at least among "Wheelies," as the devotees of the show came to be known.

In published interviews, Sajak has repeatedly expressed his puzzlement over *Wheel of Fortune's* phenomenal success. "I really haven't the foggiest idea why we're so big," he told Clifford Terry of the *Chicago Tribune* (May 14, 1986). "So rather than come up with a theory to fit the facts, I just don't worry about it. Now, I can point to elements that make it successful: It's a good game, easy to play, kind of compelling. If you walk past the television set, you almost have to play along." Sajak also defended the show against critics who charged that it appealed to the lowest common denominator among television viewers, noting, "We're not doing *The Hallmark Hall of Fame* here. . . . For what it is, I think it's a darn good half-hour." Of his own contribution to the show's success, Sajak has said with his usual modesty: "I have absolutely no talent. I don't sing. I don't dance. I don't act. . . . I think it's a tribute that I've been this successful without really being able to do anything."

Wheel of Fortune is based on the children's word game "hangman." Contestants spin a large roulette wheel, accumulating prize money and earning the right to guess the concealed letters on the game board, which spell out a familiar expression, phrase, or name. The player who correctly guesses the hidden words then uses his accumulated money to purchase various prizes on display. Although the intriguing nature of the game and the appeal of Vanna White have most often been cited as the major ingredients in the show's success, Sajak has also earned praise. In particular, many critics and viewers have welcomed his low-key approach as an agreeable change from the strident and frenetic delivery of other game-show hosts. Criticized for lacking "energy" when he first began to audition for game shows, Sajak has noted wryly that producers now instruct their would-be hosts to tone down their acts "like Sajak does." "I feel as though I performed a service for television," he has said.

The Pat Sajak Show is the brainchild of Michael Brockman, the CBS vice-president for daytime,

children's, and late-night programming, who, while holding a similar position at NBC in the late 1970s, was impressed by Sajak's whimsical weather reports on KNBC. In 1986, after taking over his present post, Brockman approached Sajak about the possibility of hosting a talk show for CBS. "I was very taken with his warmth, his wit, his ability to interview, and his grace in handling people," Brockman has explained. "I also liked that his humor didn't come at the expense of other people. I didn't feel the need to look elsewhere." Brockman encountered little opposition when he presented the idea to CBS's top officials, whose members had been searching for a way to improve the network's traditionally dismal late-night ratings.

On February 24, 1988 CBS announced that Sajak would host a new late-night talk show, beginning in early 1989. Scheduled to air from 11:30 P.M. to 1:00 A.M., *The Pat Sajak Show* would, during its first hour, be competing directly with another talk show, NBC's long-running *Tonight Show*, perennially the top-rated show in that time period. The Sajak program would be the first network talk show audacious enough to appear opposite the indestructible Carson since Merv Griffin himself hosted a show, also on CBS, from 1969 to 1972. Some television critics questioned the choice of Sajak to take on the redoubtable Carson, contending that undertaking ninety minutes of entertaining talk each night required far more talent than was needed to host a largely repetitive game show. They also pointed to the long list of entertainers who had unsuccessfully tried to unseat Carson with late-night talk shows of their own. In addition to Griffin, that list included such names as Joey Bishop, Dick Cavett, Joan Rivers, and Alan Thicke.

Other critics, however, envisioned a brighter future for the show, citing the appeal of Sajak's tongue-in-cheek style and noting that he would bring to his new show the enormous viewer recognition gained in five years of hosting *Wheel of Fortune* twice a day in most of the nation's television markets. Speculation also arose that CBS executives, rather than being concerned with short-term success against Carson, who has presided over *Tonight* since 1962, were actually looking toward the day when he retires, in the hope that Sajak will then inherit much of his sizable audience. That theory was, in fact, substantiated by Brockman. "We are not going to kill off the *Tonight Show*," he assured Diane K. Shah. "It's an institution. But there is a point in time when Carson may not want to do the show anymore. I would like to be in place when that happens." In several published interviews, Sajak expressed a similar desire.

Sajak signed a guaranteed two-year contract with CBS worth a reported $60,000 a week, and the network built him a new $4 million set at its sprawling "Television City" complex in Hollywood. In spite of those expenditures, it was reported that *The Pat Sajak Show* would cost CBS less to produce than the mélange of dramas and feature films, collectively called *Late Night*, that the network had been presenting in the same time slot.

The new show's prospects were damaged, however, when several CBS affiliates, including those in such key markets as Detroit, Atlanta, and Cleveland, announced that they would not carry the show, opting instead to air syndicated reruns of such hit series as *Cheers, Taxi,* and *Hill Street Blues* or the new *Arsenio Hall Show,* a syndicated talk program scheduled to make its debut at about the same time as the Sajak show. Other affiliates said they would delay broadcasting the Sajak show until midnight. In an unusual move, CBS attempted to sell the show to independent stations in those cities where the network affiliate had decided not to carry it or to delay it. Nonetheless, as the launching date for *The Pat Sajak Show* neared, 191 of the 199 CBS affiliates had placed it on their schedules, a significant improvement over *Late Night,* which had been carried by only about half of the network's affiliates.

Although Sajak's contract with NBC expired in December 1988, and he stopped appearing in the daytime version of *Wheel of Fortune* at that time, he will continue to host its syndicated edition until his contract with King World Enterprises runs out in the spring of 1990. Since that responsibility requires him to work only one day a week (usually a Saturday), it does not interfere with his talk show duties. The former professional football player Rolf Benirschke was signed to serve as host for the daytime *Wheel of Fortune,* and Vanna White remained with both the daytime and nighttime programs.

The Pat Sajak Show made its bow on CBS on Monday, January 9, 1989, with a guest list that included the actors Chevy Chase and Michael Gross, the actress Joan Van Ark, the stand-up comedian Dennis Wolfberg, the former baseball commissioner Peter Ueberroth, and the country music singing team the Judds. In appearance and format, the show resembled the *Tonight Show.* After doing an opening monologue, Sajak sat down behind a desk with a microphone in front of him and a painted Hollywood panorama behind him. He bantered genially with his announcer and sidekick, Dan Miller, and then interviewed his guests, each of whom took seats on a long couch next to Sajak's desk at the conclusion of the interview.

Reviews for the first few installments of the new show were mixed. John Leonard of *New York* (January 30, 1989) magazine contended that Sajak tried too hard not to offend anyone and sniped, "Compared with Sajak, Johnny Carson is Mark Twain." Tom Shales of the *Washington Post* (January 12, 1989) called the show "so far . . . a chronically underwhelming experience," though he conceded that Sajak was an "engaging" and "amusing" host "who conceivably could wear well over the long run." Reviewing the first installment in the *Chicago Tribune* (January 11, 1989), Rick Kogan found Sajak to be "an adept and witty conversationalist," but he added that, at ninety minutes, the show was too long to be completely enjoyable. And Merrill Panitt of *TV Guide* (March 18, 1989) said Sajak was "both charming and wit-

ty. . . . His appealing, self-deprecating style works beautifully in a talk show." Meanwhile, the host's boyhood icon, Jack Paar, told Tom Shales that Sajak was "the wittiest one of them all" and predicted, "In the long haul, the guy's going to do very well." *The Pat Sajak Show* garnered strong ratings in its first week on the air, easily beating *Tonight's* substitute host, Jay Leno, on Monday and a Carson rerun from 1988 on Tuesday. After that initial triumph, however, the ratings leveled off, and Carson resumed his hegemony in the late-night time period. For the month of February 1989, Carson averaged a 5.6 rating, compared to Sajak's 3.3.

Following the May "sweeps" rating period, however, Sajak's numbers fell off substantially, particularly among viewers in the eighteen-to-thirty-four age group so much sought-after by advertisers. He was hurt by the popularity of *The Arsenio Hall Show* among younger viewers and by the continued hegemony of Johnny Carson among the middle-aged-and-older audience. In an attempt to stop the ratings slide, CBS, in September, announced that the Sajak show would take on a "hipper" look, with Sajak dressing in casual clothes instead of suits and performing his monologue while standing in front of the desk, rather than at the center of the stage. Then, following the lead of the Carson, Letterman, and Hall shows, *The Pat Sajak Show* was reduced in length from ninety minutes to an hour, as of October 30, 1989.

Pat Sajak is of medium height and has sandy hair and blue eyes. Some observers have said that he resembles Vice-President Dan Quayle, and his voice and mannerisms have been compared to those of such former talk show hosts as Jack Paar and Dick Cavett. He was divorced in 1985, following an eight-year marriage. It was reported that Sajak intends to marry Lesly Brown, a fashion model. Describing himself as "moody" and "secretive," Sajak once rejected a chance to appear on the cover of *People* magazine and avoids the Hollywood social scene. His residence is a large two-story stucco-and-glass house, devoid of photographs or mementos of any kind, in the Hollywood hills. To relax, Sajak enjoys traveling, playing tennis and racquetball, and taking swings in a batting cage. His favorite entertainer is Frank Sinatra. A fan of the Chicago Cubs baseball team, he describes his ideal evening as "eating sausage-and-mushroom pizza and watching a Cubs game."

References: Chicago Tribune V p1+ My 14 '86 *por; V* p1+ D 7 '88 *por; N Y Times Mag* p42+ D 11 '88 *pors; Newsweek* 113:63+ Ja 16 '89 *por; Parade* p23 S 25 '88 *por; Rolling Stone* p23 F 23 '89 *por; Washington Post* II p1+ Ja 10 '89 *pors*

Salinas (de Gortari), Carlos

Apr. 3, 1948– President of Mexico. Address:
Palacio Nacional, Mexico 1, D.F., Mexico

With the inauguration of President Carlos Salinas de Gortari to succeed Miguel de la Madrid on December 1, 1988, Mexico experienced its tenth consecutive peaceful transition of power, a modern record for Latin America. Moreover, no country besides the Soviet Union has been ruled longer by a single party, since Mexico's Institutional Revolutionary party (PRI) has won every presidential election since its founding in 1929. But the election on July 6, 1988 that brought Salinas to power was far different from any in the party's history. For the first time antigovernment forces coalesced around strong opposition candidates and nearly succeeded in denying Salinas and the PRI a majority. Part of the reason that Salinas, the former planning and budget minister in the de la Madrid administration, became the first PRI presidential nominee to receive less than two-thirds of the vote was his effort to restrain the old guard from padding his totals, for election fraud had long been the expected climax to any PRI campaign. Although many other incidents of vote fraud were reported and the opposition candidates never officially conceded defeat, Salinas has succeeded in convincing many observers that the election was more honest than those of the past.

Making a virtue of necessity, Salinas, a self-styled progressive centrist, has welcomed Mexico's new pluralism and has pledged himself to work with the minority parties of both the Left and the Right—which for the first time won significant representation in the Mexican legislature—to solve the country's daunting economic and social prob-

lems. He promised a fundamental restructuring of the party, continuation of de la Madrid's policy of privatizing many of the inefficient state-run businesses, a hospitable business environment for foreign investment, and a return to economic growth even if that means reneging on part of the nation's crushing foreign debt. To accomplish all that without scaring away international bankers or without caving in to the more radical demands of an emboldened opposition at a time when the Mexican economy is reeling from a plunge in world oil prices and Mexicans have seen their purchasing power decimated by triple-digit inflation, Salinas must provide innovative, even inspired, leadership. "He'll have to reject the imperious trappings of previous Mexican leaders," observed Henry G. Cisneros, a friend since college and the former mayor of San Antonio, Texas, "and rule on persuasion and consensus, not authority and directive. He's going to have to be less a technocrat and more of a leader. He'll have to become a real politician." Salinas is the youngest president of Mexico in more than half a century.

Carlos Salinas de Gortari was born on April 3, 1948 in Mexico City to Raúl Salinas Lozano, a former cabinet official and diplomat and currently a senator from the state of Nuevo León, and Margarita de Gortari Carvajal, an economist and cofounder of the Mexican Association of Women Economists. He spent much of his childhood in the ancestral home of the Salinas family in Agualeguas, Nuevo León, near the lower Rio Grande. In a tragic accident that was widely whispered about during the 1988 presidential campaign, Salinas, at the age of three, killed the family's maid while playing with his father's loaded shotgun.

In 1966 Salinas enrolled as an economics major at the National Autonomous University of Mexico, in Mexico City, where he was politically active while working part-time for a legislator, and where he became a favorite student of Miguel de la Madrid, who was then a law professor. He graduated in 1969, after submitting as his senior thesis, "Agriculture, Industrialization, and Employment: The Mexican Case," which won favorable notice in an economics competition. The following year he took time off from his duties as an assistant professor of statistics at the National Autonomous University of Mexico to win a silver medal in horseback riding at the Pan American Games in Cali, Colombia. In 1971 Salinas landed his first government post, as assistant director of public finance under the minister of finance, a friend of his father's, and quickly received a series of promotions. Meanwhile, he obtained master's degrees in public administration and political economy at Harvard University, in 1973 and 1976 respectively, and a doctorate in political economy and government from the same institution in 1978. In preparation for his doctoral thesis, "Production and Political Participation in the Mexican Countryside," he lived with a peasant family in the Mexican village of Tetla. "My time in the country," Salinas later recalled for the *Wall Street Journal*

(August 31, 1988), "taught me the vitality of the Mexican people. My time in government would teach me the way an excessively big state can smother that vitality."

In 1978 Salinas was appointed assistant director of financial planning and within that year was promoted to director general. As director general of economic and social policy and as a top aide to de la Madrid, then the planning and budget minister, from 1979 to 1981, he began using his influence to bring supporters into executive and legislative positions. In 1981 he resigned as head of the Institute of Political, Economic, and Social Studies, the party think tank to which he had belonged for a decade, in order to direct de la Madrid's presidential campaign. With de la Madrid's election in 1982, Salinas succeeded him as planning and budget minister.

Over the next six years, Salinas revitalized the ministry by bringing in young staffers and by appointing women as department heads in unprecedented numbers. He took office at a time, however, when Mexico was in the throes of its worst economic turmoil since the Great Depression of the 1930s. On the basis of major oil discoveries in the mid-1970s, Mexico had been borrowing freely from international bankers who were convinced that the ever-rising price of oil would adequately secure such loans, but with the plunge in world oil prices in the 1980s, the Mexican economy entered into a long downward spiral from which it has never fully recovered. As budget minister, Salinas was the principal architect of de la Madrid's austerity program, which compensated for the lost oil revenue, but at a catastrophic social and political cost. The administration fired thousands of federal workers and slashed the pay scale of those remaining. It sold off hundreds of state-run businesses to private interests and cut crop subsidies to farmers. Taking on the powerful labor unions, it reduced their role in setting wages and prices and opened up the economy to greater competition.

Salinas earned the lasting enmity of the oil workers union by awarding the contracts of Pemex, the national oil company, on merit, ending the practice of reserving half such contracts for the union. To boost other exports, Salinas engineered a severe slide in the peso, reducing its value from seventy to the United States dollar in 1982 to 2,600 in 1987. Those and other draconian measures signaled Mexico's serious intent to restore economic stability. By 1987 some foreign investors had returned, a rise in non-oil exports produced a trade surplus, and foreign reserves were approaching $15 billion. On the downside, the stringent austerity program produced a punishing round of stagflation. Hundreds of thousands of Mexicans lost their jobs in a country that has to create 800,000 jobs a year just to keep pace with the birth rate, and the weak peso propelled the annual inflation rate to more than 100 percent, far outstripping the wages of those who managed to hang on to their jobs.

As de la Madrid neared the end of his single six-year term—the maximum tenure permitted under the Mexican constitution—he prepared to name his choice for the 1987 PRI nomination, a process that in Mexico has long been tantamount to the outgoing president's handpicking his successor. In August 1987 the PRI announced that six cabinet officials were under consideration, but three front runners quickly emerged: the energy minister, Alfredo del Mazo González, whom de la Madrid had often referred to as a brother; the interior minister, Manuel Bartlett Díaz, a skilled politician who would oversee the tabulation of the returns and reportedly the favorite of the United States; and Salinas, the dark-horse candidate who, although popular with party reformers and the international business community, was opposed by the labor unions and by 93 percent of the Mexican people, according to a newspaper poll. Party infighting so muddled the process that on October 4, just hours before de la Madrid named Salinas, del Mazo González, the energy minister, announced that the party had settled on the attorney general, Sergio García Ramírez, as a compromise choice. Salinas was formally nominated at a party convention in November.

From the outset, Salinas insisted that he was committed to a free and fair election. "I am not in a situation in which I want to break records," he declared. "I want to have a totally credible electoral result, whatever it is." In order for Salinas to be able to claim a genuine victory, he needed to avoid the spurious landslide that old guard party loyalists wanted to ensure through vote fraud and yet command a clear enough majority to be able to claim a mandate to continue the unpopular but pragmatically effective austerity program. His early target was about 60 percent of the vote, but no one, including Salinas, foresaw the growing strength of the opposition. His principal rival, Cuauhtémoc Cárdenas, the former governor of Michoacán state and the son of General Lázaro Cárdenas (a founder of the PRI and arguably the most beloved Mexican president of the century), was a leader of the reformist Democratic Current faction of the PRI that bolted party ranks when it refused to open the presidential nomination process to a public primary. He formed the Authentic Party of the Mexican Revolution and, with the support of three socialist parties, challenged Salinas on a markedly nationalist platform. His persistent calls for a repudiation of the national debt, conservation of the nation's oil reserves, and a more radical redistribution of wealth struck a responsive chord with intellectuals, some segments of the middle class, and especially the rural poor, who turned out in large numbers at his rallies without the lures of free food and drink that had become staples of PRI campaigns in the countryside.

On the right, Salinas faced opposition from Manuel Clouthier, a wealthy food exporter and the nominee of the National Action party (PAN), whose proposal to break up the farming communes that were created under the land reforms spawned by the Mexican Revolution into more efficient family plots appealed to the more successful growers in the north. Salinas embarked on a strenuous campaign, crisscrossing the country as many as six days a week for nine months. Although he refused to repudiate the foreign debt openly, he pledged to renegotiate it on more favorable terms and to encourage more foreign investment and trade. Describing himself as a progressive centrist, he promised to continue selling off inefficient state-run businesses and to use the proceeds from privatization to deliver more comprehensive social welfare programs. Always skeptical about a PRI candidate's commitment to a fair election, the opposition saw as an ominous sign a government order barring the Gallup organization from conducting exit polls and complained that the media virtually ignored their campaigns.

Soon after the polls closed on July 6, 1988, the PRI proclaimed Salinas the winner, but the Federal Election Commission, dominated by the party, refused to release the voting figures. Although the commission blamed the delay on computer failure, the opposition charged that the party was using the time to doctor the returns. Salinas himself reportedly was up all night trying to restrain his overzealous supporters, mostly members of the old guard who clung to the slogan All of Everything. While the commission mulled over the tally, the opposition conducted massive street demonstrations to protest what they charged were thousands of incidents of vote fraud in the nation's 55,000 polling places. Those incidents included the burning of ballots marked for opposition candidates, handing paid voters pre-marked PRI ballots, ejecting poll watchers from their stations, and deleting names from voter registration rolls.

A full week after the election, the commission released the numbers, making Salinas the winner with the barest majority, 50.4 percent to 31 percent for Cárdenas and 17 percent for Clouthier. Never before had a PRI presidential candidate ever received less than 70 percent of the vote. In the Senate, which had consisted exclusively of PRI members before the election, Cárdenas's party won both seats from the federal district of Mexico City and the two in his home state of Michoacán, leaving the PRI with a still overwhelming sixty-to-four majority. In the 500-seat Chamber of Deputies, however, the PRI saw its three-to-one majority shrink to 260 to 240, far below the two-thirds required under Mexican law for the passage of major legislation.

The opposition parties continued to protest even as the electoral college convened in September to certify Salinas's election. During three days of heated, at times violent debate, one agitated deputy suffered a heart attack, Mexican Socialist party members sailed paper airplanes made, they said, from illegally discarded Cárdenas ballots, and a gang of opposition members seized the podium long enough to tear up the document declaring Salinas the winner.

Ironically, the unprecedented vigor of the political opposition has strengthened Salinas's bargaining position with the United States and the international financial community, both of which are fearful of further destabilizing Mexico. In October 1988 the United States offered Mexico a $3.5 billion bridge loan to compensate for the oil revenue shortfall until it could negotiate longer-term financing with the World Bank and the International Monetary Fund. The Mexican government rejected the American offer in February 1989, citing the improved position of the Bank of Mexico's international reserves. In his inaugural address on December 1, which was marred by opposition protests challenging his legitimacy, President Salinas made it clear that a return to economic growth must take precedence over continued payment of $11 billion in annual interest charges. "I will avoid confrontation," he said, directing his statement at international creditors concerned that a Mexican default might touch off a wave of debt repudiation in the rest of Latin America. "But I declare emphatically and with conviction that the interests of Mexicans are above the interest of creditors."

Even with a reduction in debt service and a return to modest growth, Salinas faces a host of problems. The quality of health care, basic nutrition, and education has suffered during the economic downturn, which was exacerbated by a devastating earthquake in 1985 and the stock market crash of 1987. The strict wage and price controls and limits on government spending imposed under the terms of the Economic Solidarity Pact, which was forged by representatives from government, labor, and business in December 1987, cooled the torrid inflation rate that peaked at 160 percent. That pact, which was revised in December 1988 and retitled the Pact for Economic Growth and Stability, helped to reduce Mexico's inflation rate from 15.5 percent in January 1989 to 1.4 percent in May. On June 18 Salinas announced that the pact's provisions on wage and price controls, due to expire on July 31, would be extended for another eight months, and on May 31, he announced a six-year economic development plan to promote growth and reduce the fiscal deficit.

Despite an increase in non-oil exports, the sale of crude oil still constitutes about 40 percent of Mexico's total foreign income and remains vulnerable to the whims of the Middle East oil cartel. Further complicating Salinas's job is pressure from the United States on three fronts: emigration, drugs, and trade. The Simpson-Rodino immigration law imposing stiff fines on United States employers who knowingly employ illegal aliens is expected to restrict the flow of poor Mexicans northward and thus shut off an important safety valve for popular discontent. Amid charges that Mexico produces one-third of the marijuana and heroin sold in the United States and that some Mexican officials have facilitated drug trafficking, the Bush administration is likely to pressure Salinas to do more to stamp out the lucrative drug trade. Although the United States is an important trading partner, Salinas has rejected a Washington proposal for a North American common market "from the Yukon to

Yucatán," both because he fears that Mexico cannot compete on equal terms with its two more advanced neighbors on the continent and because such cooperation would fan the potentially explosive nationalist sentiment that fueled the campaign of his leftist opposition.

Despite the troubles looming ahead, President Salinas, long an admirer of Japanese culture and discipline, remains confident that a balanced program of improved productivity, lower debt payments, greater foreign investment, a favorable balance of trade, and reforms within the PRI to accommodate a new multiparty political system can one day transform Mexico into another emerging nation success story, like those of the Pacific rim. "He really feels he has an historic mission to modernize Mexico," Henry Cisneros has said.

Between May and July 1989, Mexico signed three agreements aimed at reducing its $106 billion foreign debt. On May 26 Mexico was granted $4.08 billion in loans from the International Monetary Fund, $3.51 billion of which would be used to pay off debts to commercial banks and support the nation's economic adjustment program. Four days later, Mexico and its foreign government creditors reached agreement on a $2.5 billion debt-restructuring plan, under the terms of which Mexico would pay $2.1 billion in principal and $500 million in interest over the next ten years. Finally, on July 23 Salinas announced that Mexico had reached an agreement with its commercial-bank creditors that would reduce the country's $54 billion in medium- and long-term debt by some $3 billion annually over the next four years. Mexico thus became the first developing country to attempt to lower its debt under a plan introduced in March 1989 by the United States treasury secretary, Nicholas F. Brady.

Carlos Salinas de Gortari stands five feet, five inches tall and weighs about 135 pounds. His bushy mustache and rather large ears stand out against his prematurely bald head. His slight appearance and reputation for energy and hard work have earned him the nickname "*Hormiga Atómica*" ("Atomic Ant"), an image that has captured the imagination of political cartoonists. Although Salinas reportedly is acutely sensitive to personal criticism, he seems comfortable with that image and has amassed a collection of 200 such caricatures of himself. Perhaps because of the crisis facing his people, Salinas typically addresses crowds in sober, even somber, tones, but he is said to be quite witty in private. He also has been described as impatient, blunt in speech, and demanding of his staff. An avid sportsman, he jogs several miles a day and follows both Mexican and American baseball with intense interest. From his postgraduate work with the *campesinos*, he developed a lifelong taste for fiery chili peppers. Salinas is married to the former Yolanda Cecilia Occelli González. Their decision to send their three children, Cecilia, Emiliano, and Juan Cristobal, to a Japanese school in Mexico City drew criticism from some Mexican nationalists.

References: *N Y Times A* p8 O 5 '87; *N Y Times Mag* VI p34+ N 20 '88 pors; *Wall St J A* p1+ Ag 31 '88; *International Who's Who*, 1989–90

Sanders, Lawrence

1920– Writer. Address: c/o G. P. Putnam's Sons, 200 Madison Ave., New York, N.Y. 10016

Lawrence Sanders has consistently topped the bestseller lists at home and abroad since the spectacular success of his first novel, *The Anderson Tapes*, which he wrote at the age of fifty after making a career out of editing pulp fiction and men's magazines. His books, most of which are carefully crafted detective thrillers involving corruption, intrigue, governmental "dirty tricks," violence, and sex, have been translated into fifteen languages, ranging from Hungarian to Japanese, and their worldwide sales run to more than twenty-two million copies. Although he has been criticized for overindulgence in sensationalism, and the response of influential reviewers to his work has always been mixed, Sanders has perfected the art of creating memorable, down-to-earth heroes and fast-moving, suspenseful narrative. Since his books continue to entertain a large segment of the reading public, it came as no surprise when, in May 1988, at an auction involving eight publishing houses, G. P. Putnam's Sons—which has published most of Sanders's work—was more than willing to pay $2.85 million to acquire the rights to his latest novel, *The Devil in the White House*. Given Sanders's obvious familiarity with the subterranean world of crime detection, it is surprising that he does not know any police officers or detectives personally.

He has said that his only research tools are newspaper clippings.

Lawrence Sanders was born in Brooklyn, New York in 1920. His father was an accountant for an engineering firm, and Sanders grew up in Michigan and Minnesota. He decided to become a writer at the age of twelve, when one of his teachers published in the school newspaper a book review that he had written. "Once I saw my byline in print I was sunk," he told an interviewer for *People* (September 16, 1985) magazine. Sanders attended the small liberal arts school Wabash College in Crawfordsville, Indiana, from which he graduated in 1940 with a B.A. degree in English literature. Returning to New York City, he became a staff member of Macy's department store, where he remained until 1943. From 1943 to 1946 he served aboard the battleship USS *Iowa* as a sergeant in the United States Marine Corps.

Sanders's first job after leaving the United States Marines was writing captions for the illustrations in a "girlie" magazine. He then worked as an editor for various adventure and men's magazines while spending his evenings writing war stories, adventure stories, and short detective fiction. He looks back on that period as a valuable apprenticeship: "It's marvelous training because you learn to keep the action moving. Forget philosophy of character. Just get on with it," he told the *People* magazine interviewer. He has pointed out that a number of commercially successful writers, including Mario Puzo, Bruce J. Friedman, and Ernest Tidyman, began their careers by contributing to true-adventure magazines. Sanders worked as a feature editor on *Mechanix Illustrated* for nine years, and for four years he was editor of *Science and Mechanics*. He continued to churn out stories for the mass market at night. "I learned how to write fast and grab the reader's attention," he told a *Publishers Weekly* (August 2, 1976) interviewer. "You *had* to write fast, and if you did, it wasn't a bad living. . . . If I was going well I could knock off a story or an article in an evening."

In 1968 Sanders made one of the most important decisions of his life. Realizing that he could write a novel just as good as the bestsellers he spent much of his time reading, he began working on what eventually became *The Anderson Tapes* (1970). It began as a conventional crime novel, but at the time Sanders was also running a lot of articles in *Science and Mechanics*, where he was still editor, about the burgeoning industry of electronic bugging. Letting his imagination roam, he decided to shape his entire novel around the growing practice of electronic surveillance. The plot centers around the plan of a newly released convict to relieve a luxury Manhattan apartment house of every item of value. The scheme is eventually foiled by the ability of a variety of federal agencies, from the CIA and FBI to the State Liquor Authority and the Federal Trade Commission, to tap everything from telephones to conversations held in New York's Central Park. *The Anderson Tapes* is told entirely through documents and reports gathered from such measures of surveillance.

Deciding that the book had a wider appeal than that of the usual detective novel, Marcia Magill, Sanders's editor at G. P. Putnam's Sons, put it in Putnam's general trade division. Her judgment was confirmed when *The Anderson Tapes* quickly became a bestseller. It won the Edgar Allan Poe Award from the Mystery Writers of America, and in 1971 it was made into a movie, starring Sean Connery, Dyan Cannon, and Martin Balsam. Sanders had the skill, the perceptiveness—and the luck—to hit on the right theme at the right time. *The Anderson Tapes* anticipated by several years the Watergate scandal, which demonstrated how threatening the widespread practice of electronic bugging and taping could be to a democratic society.

Although *The Anderson Tapes* was a popular success, critical reaction to the book was mixed. Christopher Lehmann-Haupt, writing in the *New York Times* (February 20, 1970), regretted the novel's "artificial" quality and thought that its many coincidences and contrivances strained credibility. The reader, he thought, could enjoy it only if he was "fashionably paranoic and willing to believe that the whole world is plugged into a tape recorder." But the reviewer for the *Washington Post Book World* (March 15, 1970) felt that Sanders had "raised the wire-tap recording to something like art."

Whether the critics liked the book or not, the publication of *The Anderson Tapes* was a watershed in Sanders's life. It made him financially independent (the paperback and movie rights were sold for a total of nearly $300,000), and he left his job at *Science and Mechanics* to begin writing full time. Two love stories, *The Pleasures of Helen* (1971) and *Love Songs* (1972), followed without making much impact. Sanders has described them as "apprentice novels."

Success returned with *The First Deadly Sin* (1973), the first of Sanders's novels to feature his hero, Captain Edward X. Delaney, a retired New York chief detective whose task in that novel is to track down a mad ice-ax murderer. Sales of the novel were huge, and a rather dismal movie based on it was released in 1980, but as with *The Anderson Tapes*, critics were sharply divided in their opinions. Silvia Tennebaum in *Newsday* (November 28, 1973) found *The First Deadly Sin* "breathtakingly exciting stuff" but nonetheless complained, "There is too much pop psychology and philosophy. Without the amateurish attempts to give the book a Dostoevskian depth, we would have had a shorter, better novel." But J. Justin Gustainis, writing somwehat hyperbolically in *Best Sellers* (October 1, 1973), thought that a comparison with Dostoevsky showed that Sanders "is every bit as good." Sanders "has a masterful talent for both plotting and characterization," Gustainis asserted. "He undertakes one of the most difficult tasks a writer can face, that of stepping inside a madman's head to show how he rationalizes apparently senseless slaughter." Sanders himself felt that *The First Deadly Sin* marked an advance over his previous work. Financial success had given him independence, and with it the opportunity to perfect his craft. Dialogue had always come naturally to him, but he now became equally skilled in narrative.

The Tomorrow File, which is set in the twenty-first century, followed in 1975. Sanders has described it as his most personal book, although he conceded that "it demands a lot of its readers—perhaps too much." After that came *The Tangent Objective* (1976), the first of two novels set in Africa and featuring a charismatic, power-hungry, treacherous, and violent hero named Obiri Anokye. In the first novel, Anokye takes over the fictional West African nation of Asante from a corrupt king. In its sequel, *The Tangent Factor* (1978), Anokye engages in wars of aggression with the aim of uniting the entire continent under his own rule. By the end of the novel, he has taken over two small neighboring countries and stands poised to attack Nigeria. Joseph McLellan of the *Washington Post* (May 5, 1978) compared *The Tangent Factor* favorably with other novels about Africa written by non-Africans: "The African characters have a depth and solidity rare in earlier novels by non-Africans; and if they are not wholly understood, they are treated with human dignity."

In between the two African books came the *The Second Deadly Sin* (1977), which again featured the hero Edward X. Delaney, this time attempting to unmask the murderer of a leading American artist, and *The Marlow Chronicles* (1977), a mainstream novel about a dying actor who tries to live his last days to the full. Sanders's continuous and rapid output of novels—no fewer than six appeared in the period from 1977 to 1980—came easily to him, and he sees no mystery in the craft of writing. He remarked in an interview with Jack Sullivan for the *New York Times Book Review* (October 5, 1980), "If you have something to say and a vocabulary, all you need is a strict routine. . . . Tell the damn story, and get on with it. I knew a guy who kept rewriting and took eighteen years to finish a novel. What a shame! It was probably better in the first version."

Because of his prolific output Sanders agreed, although reluctantly at first, to write some novels under a pseudonym in order to avoid the risk of overexposure. *Caper* (1980) appeared under the name of Lesley Andress, and two other Sanders novels appeared under the pseudonym of Mark Upton. None of those novels, however, sold well, to Sanders's great disappointment.

In *The Sixth Commandment* (1979), the protagonist and narrator is Samuel Todd, a New York detective who is called upon to investigate the activities of a Nobel Prize–winning doctor who heads a research laboratory that also serves as a rest home for the aged. Todd eventually discovers that the doctor is performing dangerous experiments in a quest for immortality. Although the reviewer writing under the pseudonym of Newgate Callendar, in the *New York Times Book Review* (February 11, 1985), had some reservations about the novel's "two-bit philosophy and moralizing"

and excessive length, he conceded that it was otherwise "a competent job, smoothly written."

The Tenth Commandment (1980) featured a diminutive hero ironically called Joshua Bigg, an investigator for a prestigious New York law firm who is asked to look into an apparent suicide and a disappearance. When asked why he created such an unlikely hero, Sanders explained: "I got fed up with the macho man, the James Bond, the big guy who beats everyone up. Besides being little, Joshua Bigg is a mild-mannered, likable fellow." A staff member of *Kirkus Reviews* (July 15, 1980) agreed with Sanders's judgment: "Josh is a breezily likable narrator who takes lots of time-outs for musings on shortness and updates on his hesitant sex life." And in his enthusiastic appraisal for the *New York Times Book Review* (September 28, 1980), Stanley Ellin called *The Tenth Commandment* "outstanding in characterization, straight-faced humor, and mastery of style." Sanders's so-called *Sin* series featuring Captain Edward X. Delaney continued with *The Third Deadly Sin* (1981), about a female homicidal maniac who leaves a trail of male corpses in hotel rooms. Writing in the *New York Times Book Review* (September 6, 1981), Peter Andrews warned prospective readers that the novel was not for the squeamish, but he added that it "keeps roaring along from start to finish in a manner that is logical, arresting and altogether satisfying." He summed up *The Third Deadly Sin* as "both first-rate thriller and a solid contemporary novel."

In the three novels that followed, many reviewers noted a falling off in Sanders's standards. They were *The Case of Lucy Bending* (1982), about sexual corruption in Florida, *The Seduction of Peter S* (1983), dealing with an actor who becomes the owner of a brothel, and *The Passion of Molly T* (1984), in which members of a feminist organization become terrorists. The last-named novel was panned by *Kirkus Reviews* (July 1, 1984) as a continued "descent into sheer dumb vulgarity," but H. J. Kirchhoff, commenting in the Toronto *Globe and Mail* (January 12, 1985), found the book believable in spite of its shallow characterizations. He especially appreciated the "subtle irony" at the end that "gives the readers something to think about." Weathering the drubbing given it by critics, *The Passion of Molly T* climbed high on the bestseller lists.

With *The Fourth Deadly Sin* (1985), in which detective Delaney searches for the killer of an eminent psychiatrist, Sanders won back some lost ground. Praise from *Publishers Weekly* (June 28, 1985) was extravagant. "Sanders . . . has never written a more tense, engrossing or brilliantly plotted mystery," one of its reviewers said. "Delaney displays that combination of computerlike efficiency and human touch that make him such an appealing detective." Sanders himself takes a different view of Captain Delaney. "I don't like him," he admitted in an interview with Michael Kernan that was published in the *Washington Post* (August 11, 1985). "I think he's an . . . opinionated, pontifical SOB. But the readers love him, mostly the women. I don't understand it."

As Sanders entered his mid-sixties, he gave no sign of slackening his pace. He commented in his interview with Michael Kernan that he usually wrote a hardcover novel in eight or nine months and a paperback in only three or four. "I come up here to my office every night about seven and I write until eleven. If I turn out five pages of long-hand, that's great. I aim for three. . . . I make hardly any changes, never rewrite."

Sanders described his next novel, *The Loves of Harry Dancer* (1985), as a "spiritual espionage" story. It was followed by *The Eighth Commandment* (1986), about the theft of an ancient Greek coin from a New York coin collector. Michael Dorman, writing in *Newsday* (September 7, 1986), deplored its "predictable dialogue" and "absence of tension," but such criticism does not bother Sanders, who has said that he never allows himself to be influenced by reviews.

Discontinuing the *Sin* series, since none of the remaining deadly three—gluttony, envy, and sloth—seemed to be promising material for fiction, Sanders wrote *The Timothy Files* (1987), in which he introduced Timothy Cone, a Vietnam veteran who works as an investigator on Wall Street. His description of Cone early in the novel illustrates Sanders's gift for instant characterization: "Few have heard him laugh. He moves through life, shoulders bowed, carrying a burden he cannot define. But morosity is his nature, and he is continually shocked when good things happen. He expects the end of the world at any minute." An advance review in *Publishers Weekly* (June 17, 1988) hailed that "shabbily dressed, tough-talking, razor-witted Wall Street dick" when the three stories in *Timothy's Game* (1988) appeared a year later. In the *Chicago Tribune* (July 10, 1988), Paul Johnson also reviewed the book favorably, observing, "The stories reflect recent headlines, but basically we enjoy them as much as we do because they are really ancient rituals, encapsulating a gratifyingly primitive morality where transgressors are certain to be punished, simply because what they did was *wrong*." But Sanders is astonished when reviewers find any profound meanings in his work. He once explained: "My aim is to entertain people with my books. I've got enough sense to know I'm not writing literature or art. What I'm trying to do is write intelligent entertainment, and if I can do that I have fulfilled my function."

Lawrence Sanders, who stands six feet tall and was once described as looking not unlike a British diplomat, moved from New York to Florida in 1975. He now lives in a luxurious condominium in Pompano Beach with his companion of forty years, Fleurette Ballou. He uses another condominium as a studio. Sanders does not court publicity, and he told Michael Kernan: "I lead a dull life. If my financial success had come at age twenty-five instead of fifty, I'd have bought yachts, everything would be different. But my style of living hasn't changed all that much. I don't travel, except to my

place in New York twice a year. I drink the same vodka, the same cognac I did before. I don't have any hobbies. I read . . . and I write." He does, however, admit to an interest in cooking, which he finds to be as creative as writing.

References: N Y Times Bk R p44 O 9 '77 por, p44 O 5 '80 por; People 8:59+ N 28 '77 pors, 23:90+ S 16 '85 por; Pub W 210:44+ Ag 2 '76 por; Washington Post G p1+ Ag 11 '85 por; Contemporary Authors vols 81–84 (1979); Contemporary Literary Criticism vol 41 (1987); Twentieth-Century Crime and Mystery Writers (1985)

Sarandon, Susan

Oct. 4, 1946– Actress. Address: c/o Martha Luttrell, International Creative Management, 8899 Beverly Blvd., Los Angeles, Calif. 90048

Like her finest performances, the actress Susan Sarandon is a combination of eccentricity and sophistication, of raw passion and intelligence. From the naïve, manipulatable women she played early in her career, as in the cult classic *The Rocky Horror Picture Show* (1975), to the worldly Annie Savoy of *Bull Durham* (1988), her characters have been marked by a smoldering sexuality and by quirks that set them apart from typical heroines. Falling into an acting career by accident, without the benefit of formal training, Susan Sarandon gained her first real critical recognition in Louis Malle's controversial film *Pretty Baby* (1978), in the Off-Broadway play *A Coupla White Chicks Sitting Around Talking*, and in Malle's *Atlantic City*

(1981), for which she received an Academy Award nomination. An outspoken nonconformist, Ms. Sarandon has appeared in lightweight television movies and sacrificed high-paying film roles to work in plays or films of artistic significance. "To me, the whole point of acting is to experiment and learn—it's like living hundreds of lives in one lifetime," she explained in a 1985 interview. "She is one of those chameleonlike actresses, like some of the best British actors and actresses," the director Frank Pierson once said. "That's almost a handicap. Susan adapts to different roles so completely that she may never become a star on whom the public can project its own fantasies."

Susan Sarandon was born Susan Abigail Tomalin on October 4, 1946 in New York City, the oldest of nine children (five girls and four boys). Like the rest of her Welsh-Italian Catholic family, she was raised in Edison, New Jersey. The discontentment of her conventional but unhappy youth has been traced in part to the problems of her parents, both of whom bore scars from their own childhoods. Her father, Philip Leslie Tomalin, a nightclub singer who became a television producer and advertising executive, had been raised by a brother after the death of his father; her mother, Lenora ("Lee") (Criscione) Tomalin, born when her mother was still in her teens, spent her early years in a girls' boarding school.

Although introverted and, in her words, "a very spacey child," young Susan Sarandon expressed herself through "plays that the neighborhood children would rehearse all summer and never put on," she told Patrick Pacheco during an interview for After Dark (June 1978). She began to widen her horizons when she switched from a Roman Catholic elementary school in Metuchen, New Jersey to a public junior high school in Edison.

After her graduation from high school, Ms. Sarandon enrolled at Catholic University in Washington, D.C., because she could live off-campus with her grandparents. She earned her tuition by working as a secretary for the drama department, cleaning apartments, and modeling for a brochure promoting the now infamous Watergate Hotel. Ms. Sarandon majored in drama, not for professional training, but as an academic interest, and she also studied English, philosophy, and military strategy. She "never wanted to be an actor," she told Michael Ver Meulen for Parade (June 21, 1981). "I never studied." Her introduction to acting came about after she met Chris Sarandon, a graduate student and actor, who had seen her in a freshman show. They were married before her senior year. "We'd been living together, and that was frowned upon at a Catholic college, so we decided it would make things easier for everybody if we got married," she explained to Joyce Wadler in a conversation for Rolling Stone (May 28, 1981). "I didn't think that much about it. The way I saw it, we would just renew every year; it was just one of those things you did for other people to make them comfortable."

Completing her studies in 1968, Susan Sarandon pursued opportunities in modeling while her hus-

band worked in regional theatre in Washington, D.C., Virginia, and Connecticut. Although her interest in drama had not yet developed into the ambition to act, she joined Chris Sarandon when he read for an agent in New York "so he'd have a warm body to play against," she explained to Michael Ver Meulen. To her surprise, the agent asked them both to come back in the fall. When the couple moved to New York, the agent sent Susan Sarandon to audition for a role in the film Joe (1970). "They asked me to do an improvisation," she recalled in an interview with Stephen Farber for American Film (May 1983). "I asked them what that was and then did it, and they gave me the job on the spot. I thought, Gee, this seems easy; maybe I'll try acting for a while." Despite her inexperience Susan Sarandon was cast as the female lead, a troubled teenager who is accidentally shot by her father.

In 1970 and 1971 Susan Sarandon portrayed the neurotic Patrice Kahlam, "the girl everything happened to," on ABC's World Apart, eventually earning $1,000 a week. Ms. Sarandon regards her performances on the soap operas A World Apart and Search for Tomorrow as her "B-movies" and as an opportunity to learn acting technique. Between minor roles in such films as Lady Liberty (1972), an Italian-French comedy featuring Sophia Loren, Ms. Sarandon made her Broadway debut, playing Tricia Nixon, among other characters, in An Evening with Richard Nixon and . . . by Gore Vidal, which opened on April 30, 1972 and closed sixteen performances later. She then returned to television for Calucci's Department (1973) on CBS, and the television movies The Haunting of Rosalind (1973), The Satan Murders (1974), and F. Scott Fitzgerald and the Last of the Belles (1974).

On the big screen, Susan Sarandon appeared in Lovin' Molly (1974), starring Blythe Danner, Anthony Perkins, and Beau Bridges; portrayed the fiancée of the journalist Hildy Johnson (Jack Lemmon) in a remake of The Front Page (1974); and worked opposite Robert Redford in The Great Waldo Pepper (1975), playing a small-town girl who joins Redford's daredevil flying team only to lose her life in a wing-walking stunt. Ms. Sarandon landed a role in The Rocky Horror Picture Show (1975), a low-budget spoof of horror movies and musical comedies, when she visited a friend, Tim Curry, who had the starring role in the film. The producers ended up asking her to read for a part and to sing, although Ms. Sarandon told them that she did not know how to. "Everyone thought I was crazy to do it," she told Stephen Farber. "I did it for no money." One reason Susan Sarandon took the part was because of the challenge it represented. As she explained to Eleanor Blau of the New York Times (January 14, 1983): "I had never even hummed out loud. I was terrified. Since I'm basically lazy, I try for parts that frighten me or seem impossible. So to survive, I will have to learn something and overcome it."

The Rocky Horror Picture Show featured Ms. Sarandon as Janet Weiss, a wholesome Ohio bride who is driven by a storm into a strange mansion, where she and her new husband lose their virginity to Frank N. Furter (Tim Curry), a transvestite from the planet Transylvania, and Janet in turn seduces Frank N. Furter's "monster," a musclebound live sex toy named Rocky. *Rocky Horror* developed a cult following among young audiences. "It was the closest thing to [being] a rock star I've ever known," Ms. Sarandon told Jay Scott of the Toronto *Globe and Mail* (December 5, 1978).

Following *Rocky Horror,* Susan Sarandon appeared in a string of critical disasters. In *One Summer Love* (1976), also released as *Dragonfly,* she portrayed a woman who becomes involved with a young man, played by Beau Bridges, who has recently been released from a mental institution. A reviewer for *Variety* (February 18, 1976) regretted that Ms. Sarandon was "saddled with an ill-defined character by the screenwriter" and that the costume and makeup artists "have conspired to make Sarandon sloppy and frumpy-looking, muting her offbeat beauty." In *The Other Side of Midnight* (1977), based on the best-selling novel by Sidney Sheldon, she played the wife of an American pilot who wants a divorce after he rediscovers the French woman he fell in love with during World War II. She also appeared with Larry Hagman in *Checkered Flag or Crash* (1976), a comedy-adventure about a 1,000-mile car race through the jungle, and in *The Great Smokey Roadblock* (1978), also known as *The Last of the Cowboys,* featuring Henry Fonda as an aging truckdriver on his final run.

Determined to set her own course again, Ms. Sarandon chose to appear as Brooke Shields's mother, Hattie, in *Pretty Baby* (1978), rejecting her agents' advice to do a bigger picture that offered more money and a larger part. "If a role isn't fun, if it doesn't teach you anything, then what's the point in doing it just because it may be a big starring role?" she observed to Patrick Pacheco in the *After Dark* interview. "On the other hand, if an opportunity presents itself to work with an exciting director like Louis Malle and a cameraman as talented as Sven Nykvist, then an actor would be foolish to pass it up just because the character doesn't have enough to do." In the film, a controversial depiction of the development of a child prostitute (Brooke Shields) in New Orleans in 1917, Ms. Sarandon earned generally favorable reviews, with Richard Corliss, writing in *New Times* (May 1, 1978), commenting that the supporting performances in the film are flat, "with the exception of Violet's sexy, selfish, almost pre-moral mother, well played by Susan Sarandon."

Cast again as Brooke Shields's mother in *King of the Gypsies* (1978), loosely adapted from Peter Maas's book of the same name, Susan Sarandon was "extraordinarily adroit at capturing the accent and the mannerisms" of a palm reader, according to the film's writer-director, Frank Pierson, as quoted in *American Film* (May 1983). *Something Short of Paradise* (1979) paired her with David Steinberg in a comedy about a journalist who hesi-

tates to commit herself to a serious relationship. In *Loving Couples* (1980), Ms. Sarandon joined Shirley MacLaine, James Coburn, and Stephen Collins in a farcical ménage à quatre.

Returning to the stage in 1980, in an Off-Broadway production of John Ford Noonan's play *A Coupla White Chicks Sitting Around Talking,* Susan Sarandon received what some critics felt was long-overdue recognition for her portrayal of a repressed suburban housewife, opposite the more flamboyant and uninhibited character played by Eileen Brennan. Writing in the *New York Times* (May 2, 1980), Frank Rich observed: "For those of us who associate [Ms. Sarandon] with dreary roles in dreary movies, the actress we see in *White Chicks* comes as a shock. Miss Sarandon, it turns out, is a rubber-faced comedienne with considerable resources of both charm and craft. It is worth seeing *White Chicks* just to watch her explode."

Performing live in *White Chicks* gave Ms. Sarandon her first sense of her ability to move an audience. The difference between acting in movies and acting on stage "is the difference between making love to yourself and making love to someone else," she told Christian Williams of the *Washington Post* (April 20, 1981). Onstage, "you and the audience become completely involved, laughing and crying together, and if when it's over they applaud, there's no way to avoid believing that you contributed to it." Inspired by that experience, Susan Sarandon formed an improvisational theatre group with Richard Dreyfuss, Peter Boyle, André Gregory, and other actors. Ms. Sarandon described her company, which rehearsed at Joseph Papp's Public Theater in New York City, to Christian Williams as "a place to stretch yourself and take risks."

Atlantic City (1981) showcased one of the finest performances of Susan Sarandon's career. In that film, she played Sally, a clam-bar waitress who is studying to be a croupier in a casino. In the film's most memorable scene, she cleans her bare breasts with lemons while the voyeuristic Lou (Burt Lancaster), who used to work for the mob, watches her through a window. Scripted by John Guare and directed by Louis Malle, *Atlantic City* earned Susan Sarandon an Academy Award nomination, and she received the Canadian Cinema Genie Award for best foreign actress. Ms. Sarandon has acknowledged that Louis Malle helped her feel more comfortable about herself as an actress. The critic Pauline Kael noted in the *New Yorker* (April 6, 1981) that "for once, Susan Sarandon's googly-eyed, slightly stupefied look seems perfect. She doesn't rattle off her lines in her usual manner; she seems to respond to the freshness and the lilt of the dialogue."

Tempest (1982), Paul Mazursky's film version of the play by William Shakespeare, featured Susan Sarandon as Aretha, a contemporary Ariel figure who indiscriminately distributes the key to her apartment. Mazursky sensed that Ms. Sarandon would have a special affinity for the role. "I didn't know her that well," he recalled to Stephen Farber, "but I believed that Susan, like Aretha, was mature enough to meet someone and get involved with him very quickly; I knew she wouldn't be afraid." For that role, Susan Sarandon received the award for best actress at the Venice Film Festival in 1982.

In William Mastrosimone's play *Extremities*, which opened Off-Broadway on December 22, 1982, Susan Sarandon played Marjorie, a woman who immobilizes and tortures an attempted rapist. For the most part, reviews of Ms. Sarandon's performance were favorable, with John Beaufort of the *Christian Science Monitor* (January 5, 1983) calling it "intensely powerful" and Frank Rich of the *New York Times* (December 23, 1982) declaring, "Miss Sarandon is a tough and commanding avenging angel." *Variety*'s critic, however, in a January 5, 1983 review, wrote that "Susan Sarandon is suitably scary as the revenge-seeking victim, although she makes no effort to communicate anything under the character's surface or in her past."

Returning to films, Susan Sarandon next appeared in *The Hunger* (1983), a lavishly produced horror film about a bisexual vampire, played by Catherine Deneuve, who chooses Ms. Sarandon to take the place of her rapidly aging lover (David Bowie). "The real shocker," Kathleen Carroll commented in the New York *Daily News* (April 29, 1983), "is that these two talented stars would even agree to appear in such a predictably blood-soaked piece of dreck." *The Buddy System* (1984) teamed Ms. Sarandon with Richard Dreyfuss as two friends tugged into romance by Ms. Sarandon's character's son. "I liked what the movie says about relationships between men and women," Susan Sarandon observed to Stephen Farber. "In *The Buddy System* these two people go to bed together at the beginning of the movie, and it isn't that exciting, so they decide to become 'just friends.' That enables them to get much closer to each other than they've ever been with anyone else." In *Compromising Positions* (1985), based on the novel by Susan Isaacs, Susan Sarandon portrayed a bored Long Island housewife who turns detective when her philandering dentist is murdered. According to Pauline Kael, writing in the *New Yorker* (September 9, 1985), "Susan Sarandon's smile has never been more incredibly lush, and she does some inspired double takes—just letting her beautiful dark eyes pop."

When Susan Sarandon was cast in the role of Alex, the sculptor, in *The Witches of Eastwick* (1987), she was rudely awakened to the crass realities of Hollywood. Warner Brothers decided to give the part of Alex to Cher and put Ms. Sarandon in the role of Jane, the cellist, instead. Bound to the project by contract, Ms. Sarandon was forced to accept the switch, including the chore of learning how to play the cello at the last minute. She also learned, as she explained to Clarke Taylor of the *Chicago Tribune* (June 14, 1987), "that a promise is not a promise, a person's word is not a person's word." In addition to being saddled with casting problems, Ms. Sarandon was nearly electrocuted

in a scene in which her character was supposed to levitate over a swimming pool.

Because she still lacked major star status, Susan Sarandon was forced to "grovel completely," as she put it, by reading for her next part, as Annie Savoy, the part-time literature professor and baseball groupie who becomes involved with one baseball player a season, teaching him all she knows about sex and baseball, in the film *Bull Durham* (1988). "The studio wasn't particularly interested in me, and the director felt he had to have people read," she told Aimee Lee Ball in an interview for *Mother Jones* (February–March 1989). "I really took a chance by going after it, because the minute you start reading for parts, you've cut your own bargaining position." Julie Salamon, writing in the *Wall Street Journal* (June 16, 1988), observed that Ms. Sarandon as Annie Savoy represented "the best she's been onscreen since her bravura performance as the croupier-in-training in Louis Malle's *Atlantic City*."

Over the years, Susan Sarandon has performed in a number of television movies and miniseries, including *Owen Marshall, Counsellor at Law* (1981); *A.D.* (1985), a twelve-hour epic about the Roman empire after the crucifixion of Christ; and *Women of Valor* (1986), the World War II story of the 104 American nurses who were incarcerated by the Japanese for three years. In an adaptation of Kurt Vonnegut's "Who Am I This Time?" shown on the PBS *American Playhouse* in 1982, Susan Sarandon and Christopher Walken portrayed community theatre actors. "That show has given me back more than anything I've ever done," Ms. Sarandon told Stephen Farber. "I've never had such a great audience response. People came up to me on the street and told me it changed their lives."

Most recently, Susan Sarandon has completed three relatively low-profile films. *Sweetheart's Dance* (1988), in which she and Don Johnson portrayed a small-town Vermont couple facing a midlife crisis, fell victim to continual rewrites. Mercifully, as Joe Queenan observed in *Rolling Stone* (February 9, 1989), the film "bombed so quickly no one heard the explosion." *The January Man* (1989), a detective comedy starring Kevin Kline, offered Susan Sarandon the fun of playing a "complete calculating out-and-out bitch," she told Queenan. That film also quickly disappeared from view. *Dry White Season* (1989), on the other hand, is an antiapartheid movie featuring Marlon Brando that Ms. Sarandon chose to do in spite of the minimal salary she was offered. In that film, Ms. Sarandon plays a journalist who has to come to terms with her desire to remain in South Africa.

"Actors are in a privileged position, being able to create something that affects people and challenges their perspectives," Susan Sarandon told Aimee Lee Ball. "Actors are still the keepers of the dreams." Ms. Sarandon uses her celebrity to communicate with the public about issues of concern to her, such as homelessness, the plight of women and children in Central America, and AIDS research. In April 1984 she traveled to Nicaragua with MADRE, a women's group based in New York, to deliver baby food and milk, and she has taught improvisational theatre techniques to mental patients at Mount Sinai Hospital in New York.

Although Ms. Sarandon was divorced in 1979, she remains friends with her former husband. She continues to use his last name in spite of the admonitions of advisers who believe that an actress's ability to secure roles is enhanced if she seems unmarried. During the late 1970s Susan Sarandon had a three-year relationship with the director Louis Malle, and when Malle married Candice Bergen, his breakup with Ms. Sarandon was the subject of intense tabloid gossip. Susan Sarandon has since had two children, a daughter, Eva, with the Italian director Franco Amurri, and a son by Bull Durham's Tim Robbins, but she has not remarried.

Standing five feet, six and a quarter inches tall, Susan Sarandon is a slim 106 pounds but "generously sculpted," according to Guy Flatley of Newsday (December 22, 1978). Audiences have seen her in a bewildering variety of hairstyles and colors, but her hair is naturally auburn and her large eyes are hazel. Candid and assertive, Ms. Sarandon has won the admiration of directors like Paul Mazursky for her intelligent changes in dialogue and characterization, but she is sometimes reputed to be hard to work with. Ms. Sarandon refuses to give up her apartment in New York City to live in Los Angeles. "I would like to have more power, and I would like to have more consistently interesting parts," she told Aimee Lee Ball, "but I don't have the time or inclination to do certain things that are necessary for that. . . . Sometimes it's frustrating, but I have a good life. My career is a means to my life."

References: After Dark 11:34+ Je '78 por; Am Film 8:30+ My '83 pors; Chicago Tribune VI p17+ My 17 '81 por, XIII p22+ Je 14 '87 pors; XIII p4+ Je 12 '88 pors; Mother Jones 14:30+ F-Mr '89 pors; N Y Daily News leisure section p3+ Ap 16 '78 por; N Y Daily News mag p6+ F 20 '83 pors; N Y Newsday p7 D 22 '78 por; Rolling Stone p36+ My 28 '81 por, p39+ F 9 '89 por; Contemporary Theatre, Film, and Television vol 3 (1986)

Scott, Willard

Mar. 7, 1934– Television and radio personality. Address: c/o NBC Today Program, 30 Rockefeller Plaza, Room 304, New York, N.Y. 10112

"I'm the last great cornball in America," Willard Scott, the weatherman on NBC's weekday morning Today show, once said. Both his fans and his critics agree, but his fans apparently far outnumber his detractors, since Scott has often been credited with keeping Today at the top of the ratings with the breakfast-hour crowd. Scott is the first to admit that he is not a professional meteorologist. "People watch who they want on weather because they like their personality," he has explained. "The information isn't any different. Being corny is my strength." His shticks include his birthday greetings to centenarians and his on-location broadcasting from the rural and small-town America that he loves. America is My Neighborhood (1987), his fourth book, mirrors his television persona: a celebrant of the type of Americana once immortalized by Norman Rockwell on the covers of the Saturday Evening Post—cheerleaders, marching bands, and ordinary folks who have beaten the odds. "He's a great touch of humanity in a high-tech world," Steve Friedman, an NBC executive producer, remarked to Paul Colford of Newsday (October 3, 1986). "His act would be corny if it weren't the man. But it is the man."

Willard Herman Scott was born on March 7, 1934 in Alexandria, Virginia, the only child of Herman and Thelma (Phillips) Scott. In his autobiography The Joy of Living (1982), Willard Scott devoted

several chapters to the family background that shaped his character and personality. Since both the Scotts and the Phillipses were farming people from North Carolina, he grew up with a sense of belonging, of being deeply rooted in family and land. He has attributed his straight-talking honesty to the Scott side of the family and his innate cheerfulness to his Phillips kin. In his autobiography, Scott noted that his mother had inscribed in his baby book that at three months of age he used to smile in his sleep.

Herman Scott was an insurance salesman; Thelma Scott quit her job as a telephone company operator to devote herself full-time to homemaking after Willard was born. Alexandria was then still like a small town instead of a bedroom suburb of Washington, D.C., and the Scott household was open twenty-four hours a day, filled with the bustle of people coming and going. Some of Scott's most vivid childhood memories, however, are of his maternal grandparents' farm in Maryland, where, every weekend, he took part in the ritual of the typical farm workday, rising at 4:30 in the morning to milk the cows before feeding the hogs and plowing the fields. At dinnertime, the table would overflow with food and bonhomie. In *The Joy of Living*, Scott conceded that his remembrance of the Phillips family farm might sound "a little unreal, like some kind of quaint Norman Rockwell painting sprung to life," but he insisted that "what links [him] to the farm is more than nostalgia for the past and an abiding love for chickens." "The strongest pull I feel," he wrote, "is the tug of the honest values of simple living that the farm . . . represented."

When he was only eight years old, Scott was inadvertantly introduced to the radio business by his mother, who had taken him to Washington to see a movie. Leaving the boy at the theatre while she went shopping, she had not yet returned when the movie ended. His boyhood curiosity aroused, young Willard began to explore the building, which also housed the offices of WTOP radio. After a receptionist took him on a tour of the station, radio became an obsession with him. He organized a radio club with friends on his block, and, using a phono oscillator and microphone, he began "broadcasting"—with a range of 100 yards—from the basement of his house. He worked at a variety of boyhood jobs, from peddling newspapers to selling *Reader's Digest*, to raise money for his station and even sold commercial air time to neighborhood businesses for a quarter.

Scott's obsession with radio continued into his teenage years. By hanging around radio station WPIK on Friday nights, he got to know Dave Widder, one of the announcers, whom he talked into putting on a high school show called *Lady Make Believe*, for which Scott was the announcer. Featuring one professional actress and a cast of thirteen high school students, *Lady Make Believe* was soon receiving 400 letters a week from its devotees. Within a short time Scott had two other radio shows: one, on station WCFM, was a fifteen-minute high school news program; the other, a four-hour music show called *Saturday Night Dancing Party*. Soon, he and a friend were also presiding over *High School Hit Parade* on radio station WOL.

What Scott regards as his most important break into show business came when he was sixteen. After unrelenting perseverance on his part, he was hired as a page and "gofer" at WRC radio in Washington, an affiliate of NBC. Although the job itself was mundane, consisting of such chores as fetching coffee and doughnuts and sorting the mail, the atmosphere was charged with excitement for Scott, since radio stars and public personalities frequented the station. His goal was to become an NBC radio announcer, and, with that long-term career objective in mind, he sent the first dollar he ever earned as an NBC page to the network chairman, David Sarnoff, who returned it with his signature. Arthur Godfrey also signed it, and that dollar bill has hung on Scott's wall ever since, as a symbol of company loyalty. "I'm an NBC man," Scott says. "If I were Japanese I'd be out there every morning screaming the company song."

After graduating as class president from George Washington High School, Scott entered American University in Washington, D.C. He once considered becoming a minister—his B.A. degree, which he obtained in 1955, was in philosophy and religion—but his love for radio overcame that earlier ambition. At the campus radio station, Scott teamed up with Eddie Walker, a blind fellow student, with whom he could perform with natural ease, and they soon landed a weekly comedy show on radio station WOL, where Scott had earlier served as host for *High School Hit Parade*. He was still working as a page at WRC, where, in the summer of 1953, about a year after he and Eddie Walker started their show on WOL, he was hired as a summer relief announcer. Two months later the regular announcer, Frank Blair, left for New York and a berth on the *Today* show, and Scott, at nineteen, was hired as the second-youngest regular staff announcer ever to work at NBC. The manager of WRC, Carleton Smith, asked the Scott–Walker team to switch from WOL to WRC for a five-nights-a-week comedy program called *The Joy Boys*, for which Scott wrote the comedy routines and Walker performed as a mimic. Their professional association lasted for seventeen years.

Following his college graduation, Scott enlisted in the United States Navy. At the time, military training was still compulsory, and he decided not to wait to be drafted into the army. Leaving his parents' home for the first time, he went to boot camp in Bainbridge, Maryland, where he escaped the rigors of guard duty by hooking up a radio antenna with some coat hangers for a grateful chief petty officer, who wanted to listen to the *Grand Old Opry* program on Saturday nights. After doing a brief two-week stint at Guantánamo Bay in Cuba, Scott received a plum assignment to the eastern hemisphere headquarters of NATO, the Supreme Allied Command Atlantic, in Norfolk, Virginia, where his chief responsibility was producing a five-minute radio program reviewing the activities of NATO for broadcast over some forty stations on Armed Forces Radio. The go-getting Scott soon landed himself another, more lucrative radio job as a disc jockey at WAVY radio, on which, as "Scotty Watty Doo Dah Day," he hosted a hit-parade show called *Nifty Fifty*. When Scott returned to civilian life in 1958, he and Eddie Walker picked up the *Joy Boys* where they had left off, on WRC until 1972 and, for two years after that, on WWDC.

Willard Scott had his baptism in television even before he went into the navy, starring, as "Farmer Willard," in a Saturday-morning children's show called *Barn Party*, which also featured the first appearance of Jim Henson's Muppets, of later *Sesame Street* fame. Wearing a baggy clown suit, a red wig, and a squeaky bulbous nose, he became, in 1959, Bozo the Clown, the host of a syndicated children's program on WRC-TV. Because the show played to a live audience of children, Scott has credited it with helping him to lose his inhibitions in front of the television cameras. "Bozo" soon was in such demand throughout the Washington area, opening shopping malls and appearing at bar mitzvahs, that when the new fast-food chain McDonald's opened a franchise in Alexandria, Scott was asked to appear as Bozo. He was soon doing commercials for McDonald's and making a personal appearance every time a new McDonald's opened in the Washington area.

When Bozo went off the air in 1962, Scott created the character of Ronald McDonald to continue his public relations work as the local McDonald's clown and mascot, in addition to his ongoing duties as staff anouncer at WRC. As the popularity of the McDonald's chain grew nationally, the parent company began buying back the local franchise operations, and, when the owners came to Washington, they bought the rights to the Ronald McDonald character as well. Although Scott was assured that he would be hired as the national Ronald McDonald, when audition time came he was passed over in favor of Coco, a not-so-chubby clown from the Ringling Brothers and Barnum & Bailey circus.

Since Scott had reported the weather for years as part of his staff announcer duties at WRC radio, it was not surprising that, when the regular weatherman at WRC-TV walked off the job suddenly one night in 1967, he was brought in as an emergency replacement. Disarming his viewers by telling them that they knew more about the weather than he did, he made sure that he had his facts straight by consulting the *Washington Post* weather map, the statistical data from the weather bureau wire service, and the telephone forecast of the National Weather Service. From there, he played it as straight Willard Scott: loose, casual, caring, folksy, and sometimes clowning and outrageous. On Groundhog Day, for example, he dressed up like a groundhog and was filmed coming out of a manhole near the Washington Monument. On April 15, the deadline for filing personal income tax returns, he wore an old whiskey barrel. When a school in Bethesda, Maryland sent him a pink carnation and asked him to announce their school carnival, Scott mentioned the carnival and soon found himself besieged with similar requests. As he wrote in *The Joy of Living*: "There were tutus and tights from the Opera Society which I wore on the air, broad-brimmed hats with pink birds from garden clubs, and a live bullfrog from the Fairfax County fair. All of this gave me tremendous viewer identification . . . [and] instantly set me apart from the other weathermen in town."

A huge local success as WRC's weatherman, Scott virtually became a star, but, after more than a decade of those antics, he became restless and bored. A greater challenge presented itself in 1979, when Bill Small, who was then head of NBC News in New York, offered him the opportunity to audition, on-the-air, for the weatherman spot on the *Today* show. *Today*'s ratings had been sliding in comparison with those of its chief competitor, ABC's *Good Morning America*, and NBC network executives were looking for a perky drawing card. Scott's audition pleased them, but they were even more impressed when Rosalynn Carter, then the first lady, walked into the studio one day and threw her arms around Scott. It turned out that she was a longtime fan of his, from his Washington broadcasts.

In March 1980 Willard Scott began working full-time on the *Today* show. Perceived as loud, fat, and unsophisticated, he hardly fitted the average viewer's concept of a national weatherman. "He was an alien being," coanchor Jane Pauley later recalled of his first months. The letters soon started pouring into the network at the rate of 1,000 a week, but a sizable number were negative. To make matters worse, internal struggles within NBC News over the nature and direction of the *Today* show created a crisis atmosphere on the set. Tension ran high, and Scott was often told to cut his air time.

But the tide soon shifted, and it was all in Scott's favor. His former detractors became avid fans. Articles about him in the media were invariably complimentary, with the *Los Angeles Times* calling him "the big friendly man who's become a national folk hero." By the summer of 1980, when Scott was reporting with the rest of the *Today* staff from the Republican National Convention in Detroit, it had become clear that he had a large national following. Fans arrived at the show with placards reading: "Jane is a 10; Tom [Brokaw, then Jane Pauley's coanchor] is a 10; Willard is an 11." That meant everything to Scott, who had insisted on continuing on *Today* his homespun promotions of small-town events, garden clubs, and church bazaars. He also continued what he himself has admitted is outrageous buffoonery, such as his impersonation of Carmen Miranda, complete with dress, earrings, and banana-covered hat. Paul Colford noted in his *Newsday* article: "On *Today*, Scott seems to have effectively reduced the fifty states to a small town. In spirit, he remains a local broadcaster."

One new and wildly popular feature in Scott's repertoire had its start in mid-1981, when a friend asked Scott to wish his 100-year-old uncle, Clarence, happy birthday on the air, and, going against network advice, Scott obliged him. Soon a trickle of requests for 100-year birthday greetings came to the station, and then the trickle turned into a deluge of some 200 requests a week. Although Scott cannot honor them all, he is delighted with his role in creating an unofficial clearinghouse for soon-to-be centenarians. In his travels around the country for the *Today* show, he visits nursing homes and retirement communities, and he has called his work with the elderly the most rewarding experience of his life.

Scott's trips make up an integral part of his work. He has traveled for the *Today* show throughout Europe, aboard the Orient Express; to China; to Australia; to South America when the program originated from Buenos Aires and Rio de Janeiro; and to Rome during Holy Week. But his most important journeys have been across America, into the "heartland," to Houston, New Orleans, Indianapolis, Cincinnati, and many midwestern small towns. "I love it [traveling] like a hog in a mud puddle," he assured one interviewer. "The weather's the pretense for me to be here," he told Paul Colford. "I've sort of evolved into public relations guy and roving reporter for NBC. I go around to the affiliates and stroke them. . . . It's a traveling medicine show. It's a big hype. That's what it is. But it's a good role for me because I like it."

Scott's first contract with *Today*, in 1980, stipulated that he could not perform in commercials, but the new contract that he negotiated in 1984 lacked that restriction, and he has been featured in ads for Diet Coke, Honeysuckle Turkey, and *USA Today*. The Florida Citrus Commission hired him as their first spokesman since the ill-starred Anita Bryant, calculating that his sunny disposition matched their product. He has filmed commercials for the Ford Dealers of New England, Singer Furniture, Howard Johnson Motor Lodges, the American Nursery Council, True Value Hardware, Purolator, Lipton Tea, Maxwell House coffee, Niagara Mohawk Power, and Gilmore Sprinklers. But he refused an offer from an insurance company because he felt their pitch was exploiting the elderly, and, though he himself enjoys an occasional sip of Jack Daniels, he declines all opportunities to advertise alcoholic beverages.

Scott has also delivered talks to clubs and associations across the United States, including the Association of Operating Room Nurses, the American Hardware Company, the Nursery Marketing Association, the American Fishing Tackle Manufacturers Association, and the National Apartment Association. He has written a cookbook, *Willard Scott's All-American Cookbook* (1986), and in 1987 he appeared sporadically in the sitcom *Valerie's Family*. In 1986, the bicentennial of the American Constitution, he broadcast sixty-second spots on Constitutional history over NBC radio. He took on all those commitments despite the fact that in 1983 he suddenly developed a violent and random phobia of public speaking and experienced attacks of panic when it came time to go on the air. Although he visited doctors and psychiatrists, he found little help and took to licking a 5-mg. Valium just before making a public appearance. In January 1985 he wrote in *People* magazine: "Having a phobia has changed me. I am one of the most egotistical asses you're ever going to run into. . . . Now I know I'm human and subject to all the frailties that humans are subject to."

Unabashed about his prayers for guidance and direction and about the Christian faith that remains the source of his cheerful outlook, Scott has a physical, earthy image of Jesus. In *The Joy of Living*, he speculated: "Maybe he was short and kind of balding. . . . If he walked on earth today he'd probably be on the *Today* show because he used every vehicle of his time to reach people." But his faith failed to cushion him against the impact of the blow when, in March 1989, a five-month-old memo from the *Today* show host, Bryant Gumbel, to its executive producer, Marty Ryan, was leaked to the press. In the memo, Gumbel complained that Scott "holds the show hostage to his assortment of whims, wishes, birthdays, and bad taste. This guy is killing us and no one's even trying to rein him in." Scott felt deeply hurt as well as publicly humiliated, and he hinted that he was considering leaving the show, although on the air the two men patched things up and at least acted like the best of friends. A poll taken by *USA Today* provided some vindication: Scott rated 27,300 people in his favor; only 854 supported Gumbel.

Scott dreams of one day having his own talk show on television and worries that the *Today* executives and audience may one day weary of him. He has admitted, however, that his "guilty secret" is that he actually has more knowledge of the weather than he pretends to have. He owns a farm in Virginia, where he has made meteorology into a full-blown hobby and where he also grows fruits and vegetables, cures a dozen hams each year in the smokehouse, and makes homemade wine from the farm's grapes.

On August 7, 1959 Willard Scott married Mary Ellen Dwyer, and they have two grown children, Mary and Sally. His $1-million-a-year salary allows them to divide their time between their Virginia farm and an apartment on Manhattan's Upper East Side. At six feet, three inches tall, Scott weighs some 285 pounds, testifying to his love of food of all kinds, from Southern barbecue to French chocolate. Because his hair is thinning, he wears a toupee when on television. Scott has received many awards for humanitarian service, including the Private Sector Award for Public Service from President Ronald Reagan in 1985.

References: Broadcasting 110:207 Ja 6 '86 por; Harper's Bazaar 115:38+ Ja '82 por; Ladies Home J 104:62+ N '87 pors; N Y Times III p4 Ap 5 '87 pors; Newsweek 113:61 Mr 13 '89 por; People 14:89+ S 1 '80 pors, 31:45+ Mar 20 '89 pors; Who's Who in America, 1988–89

Sendak, Maurice

*June 10, 1928– Writer; illustrator; theatrical set
and costume designer. Address: 200 Chestnut
Hill Rd., Ridgefield, Conn. 06877*

NOTE: This biography supersedes the article that
appeared in *Current Biography* in 1968.

During the course of a long and prolific career as
a writer and illustrator, Maurice Sendak has redefined the notion of American children's literature
by exploring how children deal with their anxieties
and fears through fantasy. A Sendak book presents
an unsentimental view of childhood, creating a
world inhabited by strange and beautiful creatures. It usually elicits the query "Is it safe for
children?" but Sendak has convincingly demonstrated that children are much more aware of the
vicissitudes of life than their parents give them
credit for. "It is my involvement with this inescap-
able fact of childhood—the awful vulnerability of
children and their struggle to make themselves
King of all Wild Things—that gives my work whatever truth and passion it may have," he said on one
occasion. In addition to writing nineteen books of
his own, including the trilogy *Where the Wild
Things Are* (1963), *In the Night Kitchen* (1970), and
Outside over There (1981), Sendak has illustrated
over sixty books by other authors, most recently the
Grimm fairy tale *Dear Mili* (1988).

"My wish is to combine—in words and pictures,
faithfully and fantastically—my weird, Old
Country-New Country childhood; my obsession
with shtetl life, its spirit; and the illuminating visions especially loved artists have shown me," he
commented in 1970. "All this, mixed and beaten
and smoothed into a picture-book form that has

something resembling the lush, immediate beauty
of music and all its deep, unanalyzable mystery.
Most of all, the mystery—that is the cherished
goal." Since 1980, Sendak has devoted his artistic
energy largely to the designing of sets and costumes for opera, "a place where his haunting vision
of childhood could attain a magical, living
dimension," as his biographer Selma G. Lanes observed. The operas he has worked on include Mozart's *Magic Flute*, Prokofiev's *Love for Three
Oranges*, and musical adaptations of his own
Where the Wild Things Are.

Maurice Bernard Sendak was born on June 10,
1928 in Brooklyn, New York, the youngest of the
three children of Philip and Sarah (Schindler) Sendak, Jewish immigrants from Poland. From an early age Maurice's imagination was fueled by the
bedtime stories, inspired by Jewish folklore, that
his father, a dressmaker in New York City's garment district, made up. Because he was a sickly
child, stricken with the measles and pneumonia at
the age of two and scarlet fever at four, Maurice
spent a major portion of his childhood at home
drawing pictures of the life he observed outside his
window. At the age of nine he started writing stories with his older brother, Jack, and the two hand-
lettered and illustrated their work on pieces of shirt
cardboard that they bound together with tape.

It was his older sister, Natalie, who gave him his
first book, Mark Twain's *Prince and the Pauper*, on
his ninth birthday. "A ritual began with that book,
which I recall very clearly," Sendak told Virginia
Haviland in an interview for the *Quarterly Journal
of the Library of Congress* (October 1971). "It was
such a beautiful object . . . [It] smelled good and
it also had a shiny cover. . . . I remember trying
to bite into it, which I don't imagine is what my sister intended when she bought the book for me. But
the last thing I did . . . was to read it. It was all
right. But I think it started then, a passion for books
and bookmaking." Maurice was also drawn to the
comic books and movies of pop culture, and he was
especially fascinated by Mickey Mouse, who was
born in the same year as Sendak. "I now know that
a good deal of my pleasure in Mickey—a rich sensual pleasure—had to do with his bizarre but gratifying proportions," he told a reporter for *TV Guide*
(November 11, 1978).

During his years at Lafayette High School in
Brooklyn, Sendak held a part-time job with All
American Comics, adapting Mutt and Jeff newspaper comic strips to a comic-book format. Except for
his art classes, Sendak hated school. "School is bad
for you if you have any talent," he told Selma G.
Lanes. "You should be cultivating that talent in
your own particular way." Outside the classroom,
Sendak taught himself cross-hatching and other
techniques from such nineteenth-century illustra-
tors as Wilhelm Busch, Boutet de Monvel, and the
Victorian caricaturist George Cruikshank.

After graduating from high school in 1946, Sendak moved to Manhattan, whose bustling elegance
had always attracted him. He found work constructing papier-mâché fairy tale characters for

Timely Service, a window-display house. It was during his employment there that Sendak's illustrations were first published, as an accompaniment to *Atomics for the Millions* (1947), a book written by his high school physics teacher. When a promotion in 1948 removed him from the work he enjoyed, Sendak quit his job and returned home to his parents, where, "out of a job, out of sorts and money," he spent hours at the window, filling sketchbooks with drawings of Rosie, a ten-year-old girl whom he admired for "her ability to imagine herself into being anything she wanted to be, anywhere in or out of the world," he wrote in his essay "Really Rosie," which appeared in *Rolling Stone* (December 30, 1976). "Rosie occupied both hand and head during that long languishing time and filled my notebooks with ideas that later found their way into every one of my children's books," he recalled in that essay. "I loved Rosie. She knew how to get through a day." In the summer of 1948, Sendak also collaborated with his brother, carving and painting six mechanical wooden toys that Jack had engineered. The brothers brought their creations to the famous New York toy store F. A. O. Schwartz, where store executives admired the toys but felt that they would cost too much to mass-produce. Impressed with Sendak's talent, however, they offered him a job as assistant director of the window-display department, a position he held for the next three years.

While working at F. A. O. Schwartz, Sendak enrolled in some night classes at the Art Students League, largely to please his father. During a display of his drawings at the store, F. A. O. Schwartz's book buyer invited Ursula Nordstrom, Harper & Row's children's book editor, to stop by. Captivated by Sendak's sketches, Miss Nordstrom immediately hired him to illustrate Marcel Aymé's *Wonderful Farm* (1951). Thus began a long and fruitful association. Sendak later told Selma G. Lanes: "We had our disagreements, but she treated me like a hothouse flower, watered me for ten years, and handpicked the works that were to become my permanent backlist and bread-and-butter support."

Sendak's reputation as a children's book illustrator was firmly established with his drawings for Ruth Krauss's book *A Hole Is to Dig* (1952), a collection of such word definitions as "A dream is to look at the night and see things." Subsequently deluged with freelance illustrating offers, Sendak left his job at F. A. O. Schwartz to pursue his true calling and moved to an apartment in Manhattan. Also during his twenties, Sendak underwent psychoanalysis, a process, he told Jonathan Cott in an interview published in *Pipers at the Gates of Dawn* (1983), that "enriched and deepened me and gave me confidence to express much that I might not have without it."

The first book that Sendak both wrote and illustrated was *Kenny's Window* (1956), the story of a young boy's search for the answers to seven questions posed by a rooster in a dream, one of the author's many variations on the theme of children embarking on fantasy journeys to deal with problems they encounter in real life. *Very Far Away*, a tale about running away from home, followed a year later. "People used to comment continually on the fact that the children in my books looked homely—Eastern European Jewish as opposed to the flat, oilcloth look considered normal in children's books," Sendak told Jonathan Cott. "They were just Brooklyn kids, old-looking before their time. But a baby *does* look a hundred years old."

Sendak immortalized the spirited subject of his 1948 sketchbooks in *The Sign on Rosie's Door* (1960). Rosie served as the prototype for the four protagonists in the *Nutshell Library* (1962), a set of books that are just the right size for a child's hand. The *Nutshell Library* contains the stories *Chicken Soup with Rice*, *Alligators All Around*, *One Was Johnny*, and *Pierre*, a cautionary tale about a boy who says "I don't care" until a lion swallows him whole. The four *Nutshell Library* stories were made into filmstrips with cassettes in 1976.

Where the Wild Things Are (1963) represented a turning point in Sendak's career, marking, in his words, "the end of a long apprenticeship." "By that I mean all my previous work now seems to have been an elaborate preparation for it," he explained, in accepting the 1964 Caldecott Medal, which he received for the book, from the American Library Association. "I believe it is an immense step forward for me, a critical stage in my work." *Where the Wild Things Are* tells the story of Max, who is sent to bed without his supper by his parents. Max vents his anger by turning his room into a world of wild creatures (inspired by the faces of his Jewish relatives, Sendak has noted). With a fierce glare and a "BE STILL!" Max conquers and tames the beasts, and, after being crowned "king of all wild things," he enjoys a "wild rumpus." His fury released, Max returns home to supper and his family, who "loved him best of all."

Some critics, including the child psychologist Bruno Bettelheim, felt the book was too frightening for young children, and the reviewer for the *Journal of Nursery Education* cautioned, "We should not like to have it left about where a sensitive child might pore over it in the twilight." Sendak responded in his Caldecott Medal acceptance speech: "Certainly we want to protect our children from new and painful experiences that are beyond their emotional comprehension and that intensify anxiety; and to a point we can prevent premature exposure to such experiences. That is obvious. But what is just as obvious . . . is the fact that from their earliest years children live on familiar terms with disrupting emotions, that fear and anxiety are an intrinsic part of their everyday lives, that they continually cope with frustration as best they can. And it is through fantasy that children achieve catharsis. It is the best means they have for taming Wild Things." By 1985 *Where the Wild Things Are* had sold 2.5 million copies.

The popularity of *Where the Wild Things Are* confirmed Sendak's status as an internationally famous author-illustrator, and he received further acclaim for his collaborations with other writers. Else Holmelund Minarik's *Little Bear* books are perhaps the best-known of those collaborations. Others included Sesyle Joslin's humorous *What Do You Say, Dear?* (1958), two of his brother Jack's books, *Happy Rain* (1956) and *Circus Girl* (1957), and Randall Jarrell's *Bat-Poet* (1963).

Stricken by a heart attack at the age of thirty-nine and upset over the death of his beloved Sealyham terrier and the knowledge that his mother had cancer, Sendak produced a book with the misleadingly jolly title *Higglety, Pigglety, Pop! or, There Must Be More to Life* (1967), illustrated with heavily detailed, somewhat somber black-and-white drawings. The book recounts the adventures of Jennie, a dog taking her name and appearance from Sendak's departed companion, who packs a bag and sets out into the world, telling a potted plant, "There must be more to life than having everything!" After she gains experience, she is rewarded with the leading role in the World Mother Goose Theatre's production of "Higglety, Pigglety, Pop!" performed at the Castle Yonder.

Sendak next spent two years writing and illustrating *In the Night Kitchen* (1970), a process he described later as "a difficult birth." The book provoked some controversy because of the child hero's frontal nudity, but few could resist the gleeful protagonist Mickey (named for Mickey Mouse) or his colorful, cartoon-style world (influenced by Winsor McCay) of buildings shaped like enormous food containers arranged to resemble the New York City skyline. In Sendak's words, the story is "a kind of homage to New York City, the city I loved so much and still love." The story was inspired by an advertisement for the Sunshine bakers, which Sendak remembered seeing as a child and which read, "We Bake While You Sleep." "It seemed to me the most sadistic thing in the world," Sendak told Virginia Haviland in the interview for the *Quarterly Journal of the Library of Congress,* "because all I wanted to do was stay up and watch. . . . It seemed so absurdly cruel and arbitrary for them to do it while I slept."

Once again beginning in a child's bedroom, the story tells of a boy who falls into a pan of cake batter being prepared by three Oliver Hardy–faced bakers. Shaping an airplane from dough, Mickey flies up to a huge bottle of milk and, diving in, rejoices, "I'm in the milk and the milk's in me!" Mickey then returns to his bedroom, sleepy and satiated. "Just as *Where the Wild Things Are* offered a safe outlet for feelings of anger (and alarmed many adults)," Sada Fretz observed in the *Library Journal* (December 15, 1970), "*In the Night Kitchen* celebrates childhood sexuality—or at least, with all the kneading and pounding, the naked immersion in milk, dough and cake batter, sensuality." In 1970 Sendak became the first American to receive the Hans Christian Andersen International Medal for the body of his work.

Leaving New York for the calmer environment of a country home and studio in Ridgefield, Connecticut, Sendak filled the gap left by Jennie's death with Erda, a German shepherd, and Io, a golden retriever. A year later, a collection of twenty-seven Grimm fairy tales, with each story illustrated by one black-and-white drawing by Sendak, was published as *The Juniper Tree* (1973). "I waited until I thought I was old enough to do *The Juniper Tree,*" Sendak told Jonathan Cott.

In his first theatrical endeavor, Sendak wrote and directed *Really Rosie, Starring the Nutshell Kids* (1975), a half-hour animated film adaptation of the *Nutshell Library* and *The Sign on Rosie's Door.* The script, with musical numbers by Carole King, was published as a book and was later developed into an Off-Broadway play, which opened in October 1980 and ran for a year. Sendak won a *New York Times* award for best illustrated children's book with his drawings for Randall Jarrell's *Fly by Night* (1976), in which a boy flies naked in a dream. In the same year, Sendak collaborated with Matthew Margolis on the whimsical tale *Some Swell Pup, or, Are You Sure You Want a Dog?* (1976), his frank depictions of the various messes puppies make, eliciting the usual scandalized protests from some readers.

Sendak spent five years working on the third book in his trilogy, *Outside over There* (1981), in Sendak's opinion his "strangest" but most complex and most personally satisfying book. Nine-year-old Ida, entrusted with the care of her baby sister while her mother sits dreaming in the arbor and her father is away at sea, is busy playing her Magic Horn when goblins steal the baby. Furious, the heroine flies backwards out the window into a sudden rainstorm and, after dissolving the goblins into whirling steam with her horn music, brings the baby safely home. As Sendak noted in his essay "An Informal Talk" (1985), the seeds for the story originated in "The Goblins," a Grimm tale included in *The Juniper Tree,* about goblins who replace a baby with a changeling; Sendak's own childhood fears about the Lindbergh baby's kidnapping; and his terror as a child on reading a story about a little girl in an oversized yellow slicker and boots.

The text of 385 words that Sendak said came to him as he listened to Mozart—his "secret god"—is accompanied by some "hauntingly beautiful watercolors," in the words of John Cech of the *Christian Science Monitor* (May 11, 1981), which "reveal deeper levels of concern that are occurring simultaneously with the external story." The *New York Times* reviewer Christopher Lehmann-Haupt wrote, "There is a grandeur and complexity about the pictures that intimidates. . . . They have a quality of nightmare." John Gardner, however, writing in the *New York Times Book Review* (April 26, 1981), praised "the lyricism and gentle irony of his words and pictures." Sendak received the American Book Award in 1982 for *Outside over There.*

"No other work of art has given me this inner peace and happiness," Sendak explained to Joan F. Mercier for *Publishers Weekly* (April 10, 1981). While he was writing *Outside over There,* he told Jonathan Cott: "*Wild Things* now seems to me to be a very simple book—its simplicity is what made it successful, but I could never be that simple again. *Night Kitchen* I much prefer—it reverberates on double levels. But this third book will reverberate on triple levels. It's so dense already."

The wide-ranging influences on Sendak's art extend from family photographs to King Kong (evident in *Wild Things*), comic books, the "graphically precise and unearthly" images of Arthur Hughes, Beatrix Potter, and Jean de Bruhnoff (the author and illustrator of the *Babar* books), and the art of the nineteenth-century illustrator Randolph Caldecott. "Randolph Caldecott gave me my first demonstration of the subtle uses of rhythm and structure in a picture book," Sendak wrote in his essay "Some of My Pictures." In his Caldecott Medal acceptance speech, he attributed Caldecott's greatness to "the truthfulness of his vision of life," which "children recognize as true to their own lives," such as his picture, at the end of *Hey Diddle Diddle*, of a broken dish and the spoon being taken away by her parents. "Lots of styles permit you to walk in and out of books," Sendak told Virginia Haviland. "So my point is to have a fine style, a fat style, a fairly slim style, and a really rough style." In *Higglety*, for example, Sendak employed a finely cross-hatched style for his pen and ink, black-and-white drawings, whereas in *Night Kitchen* he painted in a soft and rounded style in color.

While finishing *Outside over There*, Sendak worked closely with Selma G. Lanes on the lavish coffee-table book *The Art of Maurice Sendak* (1980). In addition, he began to apply his unique vision to another genre: set and costume design for operas. The director Frank Corsaro, impressed with Sendak's illustrations for *The Juniper Tree*, persuaded a "flabbergasted" Sendak that his art was exactly what was needed for the Houston Grand Opera's production of Mozart's *Magic Flute* during its 1980 season. Sendak recalled to George Heymont in an interview for *Opera News* (September 1986) Corsaro's original phone call to him: "It was a wonderful moment. There was no way [Corsaro] could have guessed how I felt about that opera and its composer. I'm sure I sounded like a gibbering idiot on the phone." Reviewers found the resulting designs "sumptuous," with intriguing overtones of foreboding. (Sendak himself described his sets for the opera as "subterranean and bedeviled.") In 1980 Sendak also designed the sets and costumes for the New York City Opera's production of Leoš Janáček's *Cunning Little Vixen*, and his designs appeared in the 1985 book of the same name.

"I'm not going to do and don't want to do most operas, just the ones I know I can do well and love passionately," Sendak told Peter Wynne for the New York City Opera *Playbill* (July 5–November 17, 1985). He created the librettos, as well as the sets and costumes, for adaptations of his own *Where the Wild Things Are*, with music composed by Oliver Knussen, which was performed in Brussels in 1980, at the National Theatre in London in 1983, and by the New York City Opera. Also with Knussen, Sendak composed an opera based on *Higglety, Pigglety, Pop!*, which, with *Wild Things*, opened the Glyndebourne Opera season in October 1984.

For the 1983 Christmas season, Sendak worked with Kent Stowell of the Pacific Northwest Ballet on the story, costumes, and sets for an unconventional *Nutcracker and the Mouse King*, with sugar coating removed. The collaborators' attempt to bring the story back to E. T. A. Hoffman's original tale was an enormous box-office success. "Hoffman's tale, like all the great Grimm *Märchen*, had many subtexts to uncover," Sendak wrote in his essay "Nutcracker" (1986). Sendak's designs also appeared in the book version, published in 1984, which spent nine weeks on the *New York Times* bestseller list, and in the movie adaptation, released in November 1986. Other operas Sendak has worked on include Sergei Prokofiev's *Love for Three Oranges*, Mozart's *Goose of Cairo*, for the Lyric Opera of Kansas City in 1986, and two one-act operas by Maurice Ravel, *L'Heure Espagnole* and *L'Enfant et les Sortilèges*, performed at Glyndebourne, England in 1986. With Frank Corsaro, Sendak prepared the sets and costumes for the Los Angeles Opera's 1989 production of Mozart's *Idomeneo*. When making his designs for opera, Sendak told George Heymont, he always listens to the music "because the answer to the artistic puzzle lies within the music."

In time for his sixtieth birthday, in 1988, Sendak created the illustrations for *Dear Mili* (1988), a recently discovered Grimm fairy tale that Farrar, Straus & Giroux acquired with Sendak in mind. The story of a child's wartime separation from her mother deeply moved Sendak, who lost many relatives in the Holocaust. With illustrations influenced by van Gogh landscapes and the image of Anne Frank, the book reached number five on the *New York Times* bestseller list four weeks after its first printing. Sendak found the story comforting because "it's straight." "It doesn't dawdle and it allowed me to express very direct feelings that I've earned," he explained to William Goldstein for *Publishers Weekly* (May 20, 1988). "If there are shadows in what I do it's because they belong there." Sendak included in the book a drawing of a reclining Mozart conducting a chorus of children resembling Anne Frank. The drawings and color paintings from *Dear Mili* were on display at the Pierpont Morgan Library in New York City in late 1988 and early 1989. Also in 1988, Farrar, Straus & Giroux published Sendak's first collection of critical essays, *Caldecott & Co.: Notes on Books & Pictures*.

Never married, Maurice Sendak lives in a farmhouse on seven acres in Ridgefield, Connecticut with Runge, a purebred German shepherd, and Io, his longtime canine companion. Five feet seven inches tall, with green eyes and a thick graying beard, Sendak is shy and soft-spoken. Although he loves children, he has few regrets about not having any of his own. He listens to music when he draws.

"Sketching to music is a marvelous stimulant to my imagination," he said in his Caldecott Medal acceptance speech, "and often a piece of music will give me the needed clue to the look and color of a picture."

His eleven-room house is "filled with the treasures of a civilized and playful mind," according to John Lahr, in his article for the *New York Times Magazine* (October 12, 1980), including first editions of Herman Melville, Henry James, and Beatrix Potter, original artwork by Winsor McCay and William Blake, and an extensive collection of Mickey Mouse memorabilia. Sendak's stories are enjoyed in thirteen languages, and 3,000 of his drawings are housed in the A. S. W. Rosenbach Museum and Library in Philadelphia. In 1983 Sendak won the Laura Ingalls Wilder Award for his "substantial and lasting contribution to children's literature." In 1988 he became artistic director of the Sundance Children's Theatre, a newly created branch of Robert Redford's Sundance Institute. The first production he will work on is *Peter Pan*, which is slated for 1990. Sendak taught previously at Yale University and the Parsons School of Design.

References: *Chicago Tribune* XIV p38 D 22 '85 por; *N Y Times Mag* p45+ O 12 '80 pors; *Newsweek* 112:50+ D 19 '88 pors; *Opera N* 51:24+ S '86 por; *Wall St J* p1+ D 20 '79; *Contemporary Authors* new rev vol 11 (1984); Cott, Jonathan. *Pipers at the Gates of Dawn* (1983); Lanes, Selma G. *The Art of Maurice Sendak* (1980); Sendak, Maurice. *Caldecott & Co.: Notes on Books & Pictures* (1988); *Something about the Author* vol 27 (1982); *Who's Who in America, 1988–89*

Shandling, Garry

Nov. 29, 1949– Comedian. Address: c/o Our Production Co., 1438 N. Gower St., Los Angeles, Calif. 90028

In 1978 Garry Shandling quit his job as a television comedy writer because he was frustrated at not being able to submit scripts that departed from traditional sitcom formulas. He went on to become a successful stand-up comedian and a frequent guest on and occasional guest host of NBC's *Tonight Show*. He also wrote, produced, and starred in two comedy specials for Showtime, the pay-cable television service.

In September 1986 Showtime began presenting *It's Garry Shandling's Show*, an innovative parody of television comedies that lampoons the familiar plots, characters, and situations that have been staples of prime-time television for more than three decades. The show, which had been rejected by all three commercial television networks, features Shandling in predicaments that range from the mundane (guest star Rob Reiner is asked to wash the dishes because Shandling cannot find anything else for him to do) to the wildly unpredictable (Shandling and a date dodge cameramen, cables, and the studio audience as they drive to the "movies" in a golf cart). The critical and popular response to *It's Garry Shandling's Show* was so enthusiastic that the new Fox television network began airing episodes of the program in March 1988.

Garry Shandling's comic persona, that of a likable, but self-deprecating, angst-ridden single man who is insecure about his appearance, his relationship with his parents, and his social life, reflects the comedian's own experiences. "I use everything that happens to me," he explained to Patricia O'Haire of the New York *Daily News* (September 18, 1984). "I take my personal experiences and exaggerate them, or I take the unusual things in life that happen to us all and work with them." Much of Shandling's humor is "relationship-oriented," that is, it revolves around his confusions about women, his various dating mishaps, and his sexual insecurity. (Typical Shandling lines include: "I'm dating a girl now . . . who's unaware of it, evidently" and "I made love for an hour and fifteen minutes. Well, it was on the day you push the clocks ahead.") "The act is a little more intense than my real life, because the funniest parts of being single are those lonely, painful moments," Shandling told David Rensin during an interview for *Playboy* (July 1987). "The great dates and great relationships aren't funny. So I talk about the bad ones and people assume that I have a horrible dating life—which is, unfortunately, true."

Born in Chicago, Illinois on November 29, 1949, Garry Shandling is the younger of the two sons of Irving Shandling, a print shop owner, and Muriel Shandling, the proprietor of a pet store. In 1952 the family moved to Tucson, Arizona for the benefit of Garry's brother, Barry, who suffered from cystic fibrosis. When Barry died eight years later at the age of thirteen, ten-year-old Garry was deeply affected by the loss. Otherwise, his childhood was, in his words, "very normal." Unlike many successful comedians, he was neither a loner nor a class clown. "I don't think I was maladjusted in any major way," he explained to Merrill Shindler for Los Angeles (April 1987) magazine. "That's why there's no hostility in my humor. I had . . . a lot of love from my parents. If I was maladjusted in any way, it was simply that I had a creative mind and didn't quite fit in with the norm at school." For fun, he played football and baseball and, by his own irreverent estimate, watched "seventeen hours of TV a day," especially The Steve Allen Show, a prime-time comedy-variety hour than ran from 1956 to 1961, first on NBC and later on ABC, and the Tonight Show. He listened to the 2,000-Year-Old Man, the classic album by Mel Brooks and Carl Reiner, so often that he eventually wore it out.

After high school, Shandling entered the University of Arizona to study electrical engineering, but he switched his major to marketing after his junior year because, as he put it, it was not his "nature to sit in a lab all day and figure out how to blow up Russia." He was drawn increasingly toward comedy writing, and, by the time he was twenty, he had "decided comedy was what [he] wanted to do." That decision was influenced by the positive response he had received from the comedian George Carlin, to whom he submitted some jokes following a performance. After obtaining a degree in marketing and doing postgraduate work in creative writing, also at the University of Arizona, Shandling headed for Hollywood in 1973 to pursue a career as a comedy writer. A chance encounter with the story editor for Sanford and Son, the successful NBC comedy series that starred Redd Foxx as a feisty junk dealer, led to a job as a writer for the show. He also wrote scripts for two ABC situation comedies, Welcome Back, Kotter, about a group of offbeat students at an inner-city high school, and Three's Company, a long-running series about the misadventures of two attractive young women and their male roommate.

Although he was earning a comfortable living as a comedy writer, Shandling felt frustrated at not being allowed to break out of the formulas that television comedy writers are expected to follow. His desire to give free rein to his creative impulses fully materialized in 1977, when a near-fatal automobile accident jolted him into rethinking his life. Shandling was inspecting the damage from a two-car accident when one of the cars was struck by a third car, crushing him between the first two vehicles. For two days, he was on the critical list at the

UCLA Medical Center with a severely damaged spleen and other injuries. The accident caused Shandling to adopt a more contemplative approach toward life and convinced him that he should give up his frustrating writing career and become a stand-up comic. "I came to realize I should do what I want to in my life, and I wanted to do stand-up," he told an interviewer for People (July 21, 1986). After working up a routine during a camping trip, Shandling made his debut on amateur night at the Comedy Store, a Los Angeles nightspot that showcases young comics. "I was scared to death," he admitted to Tom Shales of the Washington Post (April 29, 1988). "I wasn't a natural performer at all. I wore a T-shirt under my shirt 'cause I knew I was going to be sweating." In spite of his trepidation, Shandling, unlike most beginning comedians, enjoyed immediate success. "I got laughs my first few times," he told Merrill Shindler. "I didn't bomb until several times later. I was lucky I got laughs my first time, or I never would have continued. The memory of that first time made me want to go back."

For the next two years, Shandling worked wherever he could—nightclubs, discotheques, even a health food restaurant—usually for no pay, a situation that didn't bother him because he had saved enough money from his television-writing days to support himself, and because, as he explained to Shindler, he was "happier not making any money performing in clubs than making lots of money writing television." In early 1981 he was spotted by a talent scout for the Tonight Show and, on March 18 of that year, he made his debut on the program. The Tonight Show audience responded warmly to Shandling's wry, understated humor, and during the next two years he appeared on the show nine times. He also began working in mainline nightclubs as the opening act for such established performers as the comedienne Joan Rivers and the singers Melissa Manchester and Donna Summer. Then, in August 1983, Shandling's career got a major boost when he was tapped to be guest host of the Tonight Show. The actor and director Albert Brooks, who was scheduled to substitute for the program's host, Johnny Carson, became ill at the last minute, and Shandling was asked to step in. Shandling appeared relaxed as he delivered a comedy monologue, bantered with bandleader Doc Severinsen, and chatted with guests, including the actress Ann Jillian and the comedian Pete Barbutti. At the show's conclusion, Shandling looked into the camera and said, "Johnny, thank you. I can't tell you what it meant to me. I took your parking spot."

Over the next three years, Shandling hosted the Tonight Show on two other occasions and also appeared frequently as a guest on the program. Then, in June 1986, he temporarily became the show's permanent substitute host after Joan Rivers, who had filled that role, decided to begin her own late-night talk show on the Fox network. Shandling also made several appearances on Late Night with David Letterman, and he starred in, wrote, and produced a one-hour comedy special, *Garry Shandling Alone in Vegas*, which was shown in August 1984 on the Showtime network (and subsequently rebroadcast on ABC in September 1988). The success of that telecast led to a second Showtime feature, *The Garry Shandling Show—25th Anniversary Special*, a parody of *Tonight Show* retrospectives, in which Shandling's guests included Johnny Carson himself and a scatological Mr. Ed, the talking horse. The well-executed, sharply written show, telecast in January 1986, was nominated for four ACE Awards, the cable television equivalent of the Emmy.

It's Garry Shandling's Show had its genesis in March 1985 on singer-comedian Mike Nesmith's short-lived late-night series, *Television Parts*. "We had decided," Shandling recalled, "to do a video of me going on a date with a beauty queen, with me talking to the camera, like I was narrating the date. . . . So I thought, why not do a series where I talk to the camera? And I had no idea whether it would work, not until we shot the pilot. It worked better that we ever anticipated." Nonetheless, Shandling was unable to interest any of the three commercial television networks in the program, so that it premiered on Showtime, which had agreed to bankroll six episodes, on September 10, 1986. The cable berth represented a trade-off for Shandling and for Alan Zweibel, the former head writer on the original *Saturday Night Live* program who was the producer and co-creator of Shandling's show. Although their audience would be relatively small, they would be free to improvise, experiment, and mock the usual television fare, all of which would have been impossible on the networks. "Networks have a lot of rules about things you cannot do," Allen Sabinson, a senior vice-president at Showtime, told Stephen Farber of the *New York Times* (April 7, 1987). "We don't have those rules, mainly because we don't have to give advertisers their money back if a show does not perform well. We like the idea of doing a show that pokes fun at the conventions of sitcom."

Television critics liked the idea too and gave the show rave reviews. Writing in *Newsweek* (November 3, 1986), Harry F. Waters called the series "the new season's most original comedy enterprise," and Tom Shales of the *Washington Post* (September 10, 1986) wrote, "Shandling has put together a sweetheart of a sitcom tailored deftly to his on-camera semipersonality. . . . He wafts with ease in and out of a narrative built around the character of himself, a shy but eager single guy who craves female companionship and affection in the midst of the cold hard 1980s." In a review for *TV Guide* (May 16, 1987), the writer and producer Larry Gelbart wrote that *It's Garry Shandling's Show* "defies comparison with any other program on the air today. It is audacious, satirical, hip, sophisticated and wonderfully silly, and, often, miraculously, all of the above at the same time."

The unique aspect of *It's Garry Shandling's Show* is its cast's tacit acknowledgment that they are doing a television program. Shandling and

company mock the traditional practice of pretending that what is happening on a television comedy has anything to do with real life. "We're the TV generation," Shandling told Tom Shales. "So come on, we know it's a show, we're not fooling anybody anymore. So why not do one where you just say, 'It's a show, and it's my life.'" The show's irreverence even extends to its opening theme song, which metronomically announces, "This is the theme to Garry's show/ The opening theme to Garry's show/ This is the music that you hear/ As you watch the credits."

The main set of *It's Garry Shandling's Show* is a replica of the living room in Shandling's real-life home in the Los Angeles suburb of Sherman Oaks. Shandling, playing a comedian named Garry Shandling, who is the star of his own television show, appears at the start of each episode to explain the storyline, and as the show progresses he makes frequent asides to the audience and the camera. This technique—known as breaking drama's imaginary "fourth wall" separating the actors from the audience—dates back to the *George Burns and Gracie Allen* and *Jack Benny* shows of the early 1950s, and, in the modern television era, has also been employed by the ABC comedy-drama series *Moonlighting*. Shandling, however, expands the concept by talking to members of the camera crew and the audience, spying on the other characters in the show by looking into a video monitor, and sometimes turning away from the camera to "take a call from a viewer." He began one episode by inviting the audience to use his apartment while he went to a baseball game. The audience responded by coming onstage, raiding Shandling's refrigerator, and using his pool table. When a show is in progress, Shandling may stop the action to ask the home viewers what he should do about a romantic predicament or to chide the studio audience for not responding more enthusiastically to his jokes. "I'm very disappointed in all of you," he announced to the audience during an early episode, before apologetically telling at-home viewers, "Maybe you'd be better off watching Pat Robertson."

Like his comedy monologues, Shandling's show focuses on his limited success with women, his insecurities, and his obsession with his hair. The show also details Shandling's problems with a cast of supporting characters, including his doting mother (Barbara Cason), his female friend Nancy (Molly Cheek), with whom he has a platonic relationship, and his best friend, Pete (Michael Tucci), who is married. The other actors wander in and out, stopping to advance the plot, to chide Shandling for paying too much attention to the camera, or to reassure him that his hair looks good.

In one episode, Shandling's furniture and personal belongings (including his "lucky" underwear and his inflatable female doll) are stolen from his new apartment. Shandling learns that the apartment was previously owned by Vanna White, the hostess of the television game show *Wheel of Fortune*, leading to a dream sequence in which his possessions appear on *Wheel of Fortune's* "showcase" of prizes, and contestants bid on them. His delight at landing a date with a gorgeous cable television installer turns to dismay when the woman reveals a penchant for watching reruns of the 1960s situation comedy *Gilligan's Island* and singing its theme song. In an episode first aired in April 1987, Shandling announces that he is leaving the series to take the lead in a television drama called *Force Boxman*. He is replaced by Red Buttons, who performs some of the routines that made him a television and movie star in the 1950s. When Shandling decides to return—to the disappointment of his show's cast and crew—Buttons bows out graciously, telling Shandling, "You started it all. All I did was come in and make it funny."

Occasionally, *It's Garry Shandling's Show* aims its barbs at movies. An episode that reviewer Don Merrill of *TV Guide* (February 7, 1987) called "beautifully executed" parodied the 1967 film *The Graduate*, in which Anne Bancroft played Mrs. Robinson, a middle-aged woman who seduces an insecure young man (portrayed by Dustin Hoffman) who later dates her daughter. The episode focused on Shandling's attempts to deal with the advances of his girlfriend's mother, whose name was Mrs. *Robertson*. Adding to the zaniness of the situation, actor Norman Fell dropped by to show a tape of his small part in *The Graduate*, and the show concluded with a spoof of the film's climactic church scene. "It was the most engaging, charming, and original comedy we've seen in many seasons," Merrill wrote. Shandling often goes into a "flashback booth" to help him remember the details of events from his past. Entering the booth to learn what happened during his youth to make him loathe fighting, he discovers that he had accidentally poked out a bully's eye during a fight. In another episode, Shandling goes to a cemetery to talk over a knotty problem with his deceased father. Yet another episode was devoted to Shandling's imaginings about what would happen if he died and went to heaven.

In April 1987 Showtime ordered fifty-four new episodes of *It's Garry Shandling's Show*, to be filmed over three years. Nine months later, soon after the show was named best comedy series of 1987 by the Television Critics Association, the Fox Broadcasting Company announced that it would begin airing episodes in March 1988. The deal, which was expected to increase Shandling's audience from 500,000 to about four million, called for Fox to air the twenty-eight episodes of the show that had been completed, then to run new shows a minimum of thirty days after they are broadcast on Showtime. In its initial airing on the Fox network on March 6, 1988, Shandling's show attracted a 7 percent share of the viewing audience, the highest rating yet garnered by a Fox program. Shandling's next project, a movie entitled, appropriately enough, "It's Garry Shandling's Movie," was scheduled to go into production in the spring of 1989. Written by Shandling and Zweibel, the film, according to Shandling, is "not going to be an extension of the television show. But it will be as offbeat."

Garry Shandling neither smokes nor drinks, and he works out and runs daily, whether at home or on the road. He has been a vegetarian since he recovered from his auto accident, and he has shunned sugar since 1978. His typical breakfast, he says, consists of yogurt, fruit juice, and a banana. He dresses casually, usually in pullover sweaters and shirts, slacks, and sneakers. To escape the pressures of show business, he often goes on solitary camping trips, usually to Big Bear Lake, a resort in the San Bernardino Valley about 100 miles from his home in Sherman Oaks. On those outings, Shandling meditates and reads books on Zen and other Eastern philosophies. He has credited spirituality with strongly influencing his work.

Shandling concedes that his show business persona represents about 70 percent of his true self. Success seems to have had little effect on him, in the opinion of his associates. Alan Rafkin, the director of *It's Garry Shandling's Show*, for example, has described him as "the most decent guy I've ever worked with," and the comedian himself has said, "I haven't changed so far. I think that's been the most disappointing thing to people who know me. I'm exactly the same as I was. I had hoped that I'd have a slightly big head, but it hasn't happened. It's been a huge disappointment." Shandling's friend and fellow comic Joan Rivers says he is even more insecure offstage than on. Although Shandling derives most of his comic material from his experiences as a single man, he is not concerned that his act would suffer if he should decide to marry. "I would feel just as awkward about marriage and be just as confused about how to handle it," he said during the *Playboy* interview. "Mostly, I'm confused about women, but I'm also confused about lots of other things in life. I can apply the confusion to anything."

References: *Chicago Tribune TV Week* p3+ O 25–31 '87 por; *Los Angeles* 32:78+ Ap '87 por; *N Y Daily News* p57 S 18 '84, p30 F 28 '88 por; *N Y Times* C p18 Ap 7 '87 por; *People* 26:77+ Jl 21 '86 pors; *Rolling Stone* p41+ F 26 '87 por; *Washington Post* G p1+ Ap 29 '88 pors

---

Sheehan, Neil

Oct. 27, 1936– Journalist; writer. Address: 4505 Klingle St. N.W., Washington, D.C. 20016

Widely acclaimed for his controversial—and truthful—coverage of the Vietnam War during his years in Saigon as the bureau chief for United Press International and, later, as a correspondent for the *New York Times*, the journalist Neil Sheehan has remained obsessed with the paradoxes of the United States' involvement in that war. Sheehan played a major role in the publication by the *New*

Neil Sheehan © Nancy Crampton

York Times of the Pentagon Papers in 1971, since he was the reporter to whom Daniel Ellsberg entrusted the top-secret documents revealing how successive administrations had purposely misled the public about America's involvement in the Vietnam War.

In 1972 Sheehan attended the funeral, in Washington, D.C., of John Vann, a lieutenant colonel who had left the army after becoming disillusioned with American policy in Vietnam only to return there as a civilian adviser wielding the powers of a general. Sheehan was struck by the number of political and military figures with pivotal roles in influencing American policy in Vietnam who were at the funeral to pay their last respects. "I had the very strong feeling that day that we were burying more than John Vann; we were burying what Henry Luce so boastfully called the American century. We were interring the mind-set that had led us into Vietnam," Sheehan told an interviewer in 1988. Intrigued, Sheehan set out to investigate and explain the factors behind Vann's behavior in Vietnam— an endeavor that took sixteen years. The result, *A Bright Shining Lie; John Paul Vann and America in Vietnam* (1988), has been called the most important book ever written about Vietnam, winning the 1988 Pulitzer Prize for nonfiction and the 1988 National Book Award, among other honors.

Cornelius Mahoney Sheehan was born in Holyoke, Massachusetts on October 27, 1936 to Cornelius Joseph and Mary (O'Shea) Sheehan, who were immigrants from Ireland. Sheehan retained a slight brogue, even after his years at Harvard University, which he attended on a scholarship. He majored in Middle Eastern history and graduated cum laude in 1958. During summer vacations, he worked on a highway construction crew. Sheehan was active in the Republican Club during his Harvard years, although he did not affiliate with any political party after that.

After his graduation from Harvard, Sheehan served in the United States Army for three years, from 1959 to 1962, working as a newsman in Korea and Tokyo. During his assignment in Tokyo, where he edited the *Bayonet*, the weekly newspaper of the Seventh Infantry Division, he was able to moonlight for UPI on the condition that he did not receive a byline. In 1962 he left the army and took a full-time job with UPI as its Saigon bureau chief, becoming the third full-time American correspondent stationed in Vietnam. The other two were Malcolm W. Browne of the Associated Press and Homer Bigart, the legendary *New York Times* war correspondent, whom Sheehan worshipped and followed on his assignments. Sheehan learned the hard way that "hot tips" could be erroneous. One such tip—that 200 Viet Cong had died in a skirmish near the town of My Tho—led to Sheehan's filing a story that had to be retracted after it turned out that only twelve guerrillas had been killed there. It also took precedence over a story that Bigart filed on the battle. "I was mortified and certain I would be canned," Sheehan recalled to William Prochnau in an interview for the *Washington Post Magazine* (October 9, 1988). Although Bigart was angry at first, after Sheehan filed an amended version of his story, Bigart told him: "Don't feel so bad about it, kid. Just don't let it happen again while I am here." When Bigart left Vietnam several months later, he left a note for his successor, David Halberstam, about Sheehan, which read, "The kid from UPI is going to be very good." Sheehan and Halberstam, who became close friends, learned to develop their own sources rather than take official statements at face value, and they often accompanied troops into battle to gain firsthand information.

When Sheehan started covering the war from Saigon, he at first shared the American military leaders' optimism that the United States would prevail. As he told William Prochnau: "I thought the war was a glorious adventure. First of all, we believed in the American cause. We believed totally in the American cause. When I went out on my first operation and there were bullets, I was thrilled. Some people got killed around me. Small arms fire. The South Vietnamese got scared. I looked at them and said, 'Look how fearful they are!' I wasn't afraid. We were winners; we were invulnerable; we were right."

Lieutenant Colonel John Paul Vann, the American military adviser who was headquartered in My Tho, became a valuable source of information to the news correspondents covering the war, for he offered outspoken views about the established military policy. Vann thought the war should be fought with knife and rifle rather than with indiscriminate bombings, and he revealed the ineffectiveness of having the South Vietnamese lead their men into exchanges without American strategic know-how. Vann wanted the United States to take over the corrupt South Vietnamese government and carry out social reforms that would win the allegiance of the peasants.

Patriotic optimism gave way to disillusionment after the battle of Ap Bac, on January 2, 1963, which the South Vietnamese Army lost disastrously to a much smaller Viet Cong force, though the top military brass reported a victory to Washington, D.C. The next day, Sheehan drove to the battlefield, where he saw some eighty bodies sprawled in the rice paddies. While he was there, the village was attacked again by the South Vietnamese, who were shelling their own people. "I never saw any glory in war again," Sheehan told Prochnau, "and I never again went into a battle unafraid." Vann took early retirement from the army that July (although he was to return as a civilian adviser in 1965), and Sheehan's articles became increasingly pessimistic about American efforts. By October 1963 UPI had begun killing Sheehan's stories, insisting that he was acting too emotionally. One story that got the axe connected the United States ambassador, Henry Cabot Lodge, with a plot to overthrow the South Vietnamese leader, Ngo Dinh Diem. UPI sent Sheehan on a one-week vacation to Tokyo, during which time the anticipated coup took place.

The Nieman fellows of Harvard University, however, recognized the importance of the American correspondents' controversial and aggressive coverage of the Vietnam War, and in 1964 they presented the first Louis M. Lyons Award to Sheehan, Halberstam, and Browne for conscience and integrity in journalism and for documenting "the truth as they saw it . . . without yielding to unrelenting pressures."

In June 1964 Sheehan moved to the New York Times, where he worked on the city staff until he was assigned to Djakarta, Indonesia in January 1965. Six months later he returned to Saigon, after Charles Mohr, the New York Times's Saigon bureau chief, asked him to cover the escalating war with him. Transferred to Washington in 1966, Sheehan served as Pentagon correspondent for two years before becoming White House correspondent during the final six months of President Lyndon B. Johnson's administration. He subsequently worked as an investigative reporter, covering political and military issues. Neil Sheehan received some media coverage of his own in January 1971, after he wrote a review, at the request of the editor of the New York Times Book Review, of Mark Lane's Conversations with Americans, a collection of tape-recorded interviews with thirty-two American servicemen who claimed to have firsthand knowledge about atrocities committed by American soldiers in Vietnam. In his December 27, 1970 review, Sheehan called the book irresponsible. From the routine reporting that he did on the interviewees' backgrounds, he had discovered that their professed records and some of their allegations did not check out. "Mr. Lane did not bother to cross-check any of the stories his interviewers told him with army or Marine Corps records," Sheehan wrote. "I asked him why in a telephone conversation. 'Because I believe the most unreliable source regarding the verification of atrocities is the Defense Department,' he said."

It was after Sheehan wrote another review for the New York Times (March 28, 1971), on thirty-three books dealing with American war crimes in Indochina, that Daniel Ellsberg, a former Defense Department analyst who had known Sheehan in Vietnam, decided to release to the New York Times reporter the forty-seven-volume history of American involvement in Vietnam from 1945 to 1967 that Ellsberg had helped compile for Secretary of Defense Robert S. McNamara in the late 1960s. In conducting his research for that project, Ellsberg had become convinced that the Vietnam War was essentially an act of aggression by the United States and not a civil war, as it was officially described. When his attempts to change American policy failed, Ellsberg decided to leak the Pentagon study to the press and contacted Sheehan.

Once the Pentagon Papers were in his hands, Sheehan traveled to New York City, where he placed the papers on the desk of the New York Times's managing editor, A. M. Rosenthal. "The decision to publish was made almost the moment it came into our hands," Rosenthal told a reporter for Time (June 28, 1971) magazine. Sheehan and Gerald Gold, the assistant foreign editor at the New York Times, encamped in a hotel room in Washington to organize the information, but they soon realized that more than two people were needed for the job, and on April 22 they moved to the New York Hilton. There, they were joined by eight or nine other reporters, who became known as the "Project X" team. Working seven days a week for seven weeks, virtually sequestered in their hotel suite, the team read, analyzed, and condensed the papers. The first installment appeared on the front page of the New York Times on June 13, 1971.

After the third installment was published, on June 15, the government obtained an injunction preventing further publication of the series, but the Washington Post, the Boston Globe, and other newspapers continued to publish excerpts and articles. On June 30, based on the First Amendment protection against prior restraint, the United States Supreme Court decided in favor of the New York Times and the Washington Post. According to David Halberstam, in his article "Portrait of an Outsider," Sheehan's life was "totally disrupted" for months as he coped with a grand jury investigation, long sessions with his lawyers, and reports that his friends had been visited by the FBI.

Although the New York Times received the Pulitzer Prize in the public service category in 1972 for its publication of the Pentagon Papers, Sheehan did not receive any personal recognition for his role. It was the second time he had been passed over for the prize. (In 1964 he had been nominated for his articles on corruption in South Vietnam.) "I took a lesson from that experience," Sheehan told a reporter for Newsweek (May 15, 1972). "The people on the advisory board act for institutional considerations that have nothing to do with your work." In the same *Newsweek* article, it was reported that the Pulitzer Prize jury had recommended that Sheehan be cited along with the *New York Times*, but that the idea had been overruled by the advisory board, which claimed that the Pentagon Papers had "dropped in Sheehan's lap." "This is really Neil Sheehan's award," A. M. Rosenthal told the *Newsweek* reporter. "It's his, whether it has his name on it or not." In December 1971 Sheehan received the first annual Drew Pearson Prize for excellence in investigative reporting, from the Drew Pearson Foundation.

In *The Arnheiter Affair* (1972), his first book, Sheehan explored the reasons behind the removal of Lieutenant Commander Marcus Aurelius Arnheiter from his post on the USS *Vance* off the coast of South Vietnam, after only ninety-nine days, in early 1966. During that command, as Sheehan demonstrated, Arnheiter exhibited increasingly peculiar behavior, such as requiring his officers to give speeches on the proper etiquette of the finger bowl, among other topics. Writing in the *New York Times Book Review* (February 6, 1972), Gaddis Smith described *The Arnheiter Affair* as "an entertaining account of a hilarious and yet deeply disturbing episode of the Vietnam War." In January 1974 Arnheiter sued Sheehan for libel. The author spent ten months writing a defense, which ended up being longer than his original manuscript and detailed his sources for documents and interviews. Arnheiter's suit failed.

Although the war was winding down, Sheehan remained preoccupied with the Vietnam experience. "Something was unfinished in me," he explained to Prochnau. "It was eating at me. I had to get this thing out of my system. I needed to leave something behind." After attending the funeral of John Paul Vann in Washington, D.C., in June 1972—a funeral that was heavily attended by government officials who had been involved in the Vietnam War, including Major General William C. Westmoreland and William E. Colby, the head of the CIA, who were pallbearers—Sheehan hit upon a way to deal with his obsession. He would write a biography of the man whom he saw as personifying America's irrational optimism about the war. "Vann epitomized the way we like to think of ourselves in his drive to succeed, his unwillingness to admit defeat, his personal fearlessness," Sheehan told Walter Gelles in a conversation for *Publishers Weekly* (September 2, 1988). "He was full of good intentions, many of them misguided. In the end, he was driven by illusions, just as our war in Vietnam was fueled by illusions."

Taking a leave of absence from the *New York Times* to work on his book, Sheehan expected to complete the project within two or three years. His research was aided by several fellowships, including a Guggenheim fellowship in 1973–74, an Adlai Stevenson fellowship, from 1973 to 1975, a Lehrman Institute fellowship in 1975–76, and a Rockefeller Foundation fellowship in the humanities in 1979–80. During this period, Sheehan made two trips back to Vietnam to interview various people, but his schedule was disrupted in November 1974, when he was seriously injured in a head-on collision. Sheehan suffered ten broken bones, and he was hospitalized for two months. His recovery took over a year and a half, during which time he suspended work on the book.

In 1975 Sheehan resigned from the *New York Times* to devote all his time and energy to his project. He had completed his basic research by 1976, but he did not find the right organizing structure until 1977. By 1979 he had written the first three sections of the book but had exhausted his funds. A one-year fellowship from the Woodrow Wilson International Center for Scholars, in Washington, D.C., provided him with $30,000 and the use of an office, so that by the fall of 1981 he had completed two-thirds of the manuscript. Random House gave him a second advance of $200,000 in 1981. When that ran out, William Shawn, then the editor of the *New Yorker*, advanced him $40,000 for the rights to excerpt the book. By August 1986 the manuscript was completed, but it ran to 470,000 words. Working with Robert Loomis, his editor at Random House, Sheehan agreed to trim his book down to about 350,000 words. He bought a personal computer, learned word processing, and spent another year editing the text.

Critics were effusive in their praise of *A Bright Shining Lie; John Paul Vann and America in Vietnam*, citing its immense power and describing it as the best book ever written about the Vietnam War. Reviewing *A Bright Shining Lie* for the *New York Times* (October 10, 1988), David K. Shipler described the work as "one of the few brilliant histories of the American entanglement in Vietnam. . . . Skillful weaving of anecdote and history, of personal memoir and psychological profile give the book the sense of having been written by a novelist, journalist, and scholar all rolled into one." Joseph Nocura of *Newsweek* (October 10, 1988) stated unequivocally, "Thus . . . sixteen years after he began, Neil Sheehan has written not only the best book ever about Vietnam, but the timeliest," and Ronald Steel rhapsodized in the *New York Times Book Review* (September 25, 1988) that the book was "vividly written and deeply felt, with a power that comes from long reflection and strong emotions." In his review for the *Washington Monthly* (October 1988), Taylor Branch wrote: "Sheehan leaves many of the war's most difficult issues exposed but unresolved. This is a book of scalding reportage, not interpretation. By capturing within the life of one small obsessive daredevil the essence of something so vast and benumbing as Vietnam, Sheehan has written by far the best single account of the war."

In 1988 *A Bright Shining Lie; John Paul Vann and America in Vietnam* won the Pulitzer Prize, the National Book Award in nonfiction, and the Robert F. Kennedy Book Award. It was a main selection of the Book-of-the-Month Club and was excerpted in four installments in the *New Yorker*.

The publishing house Jonathan Cape has planned simultaneous cloth and paperback editions in the United Kingdom, and movie rights have been acquired for a joint production by the Guber-Peters Company, Fonda Films, and Warner Brothers.

As Sheehan revealed in *A Bright Shining Lie*, Vann's personal life paralleled his behavior in Vietnam. A painful childhood (an illegitimate child, he had been abandoned by his mother) created rage and insecurities, manifested in part by sexual promiscuity, that "made him constantly try to prove that he was braver and tougher than anyone else." Although Vann was at first outraged by the indiscriminate killing of civilians, by the end he had given in to the temptation to subject the countryside to bombings and artillery raids. "He ended up prolonging the war, but he didn't know that," Sheehan told Alvin P. Sarnoff in an interview for *U.S. News & World Report* (October 24, 1988). For Sheehan, Vann symbolized many of the contradictions in the American character: "We like to think of ourselves as a simple country with simple motives, when that's not the case. The insecurities that drive us can produce a very unrealistic view of a particular situation, as they did in Vietnam."

Although he sees the Vietnam War as a tragic mistake, Sheehan believes that America's involvement might have prevented a greater tragedy later on. Unlike earlier American soldiers, "the Vietnam veteran brought home a different kind of wisdom," Sheehan told Sarnoff. "He learned that you can fight a bad war, that you can get killed for nothing, that it's a complicated world. This wisdom is necessary to a country over the long run. In that sense, Vietnam can be a very good experience for Americans, and to some extent it already has been."

Over the sixteen years he worked on the book, Sheehan became a virtual recluse in his Washington, D.C., home. He worked six nights a week, reserving Sundays for walks in the countryside, and appeared in the daytime only for neighborhood walks and brief breaks in his garden. His work proceeded slowly, as he painstakingly checked facts and conducted some 385 interviews. For documentation, he relied on Vann's papers and classified documents, including the 7,000-page Pentagon Papers. He went through some 640 tape cassettes and 186 notepads. "I concentrate on one thing at a time to get it right—journalism taught me that," Sheehan told a reporter for *Publishers Weekly* (January 6, 1989). Over the years, he lost fifteen pounds, and he suffered from prolonged insomnia. "I got this overwhelming anxiety, the anxiety would just be enormous, and it went on for years and years and I had to find a way to control it," he told Prochnau.

Sheehan received emotional support in his effort from his wife, Susan Sheehan, an accomplished writer in her own right, whom he married in 1965, and from their two children, Maria Gregory and Catherine Fair. Wrestling with Vann's biography was a kind of combat, and, as he told Prochnau, he applied a lesson he had learned in the army: "It may be raining, it may be snowing, the sun may be shining, but you get up and YOU

MARCH." A tall man with graying hair, Neil Sheehan lives in Washington, D.C., in a modest house. His living room is lined with books and is decorated with ancient Thai pottery, Indian paintings, and a golden Burmese Buddha. Sheehan received an honorary doctorate in literature from Columbia College in Chicago in 1972; the Columbia Journalism Award in 1972; the Sidney Hillman Foundation Award in 1972; the Page One Award from the Newspaper Guild of New York in 1972; the Distinguished Service Award and Bronze Medallion from Sigma Delta Chi in 1972; and the citation of excellence from the Overseas Press Club of America, for the Pentagon Papers series, in 1972.

References: *Chicago Tribune* V p1+ O 9 '88 por; *Esquire* 102:49+ Jl '84 por; *Pub W* 234:83+ S 2 '88 por; *Rolling Stone* p117+ My 18 '89; *US News* 105:73 O 24 '88 por; *Washington Mo* 20:39+ O '88; *Washington Post* mag p23+ O 9 '88 por; *Who's Who in America*, 1988–89

Simon, (Marvin) Neil

July 4, 1927– Writer. Address: c/o A. DaSilva, 502 Park Ave., New York, N.Y. 10022

NOTE: This biography supersedes the article that appeared in *Current Biography* in 1968.

"Relentlessly prolific," as one critic has called him, Neil Simon has consistently produced more Broadway hits than any other American playwright, making him the wealthiest dramatist in history. *Barefoot in the Park* (1963), which was Simon's first runaway hit, *The Prisoner of Second Avenue* (1971), and especially the characters Felix Unger and Oscar Madison from *The Odd Couple* (1965) have become part of popular iconography. "Simon evokes a world very much like the viewers' own and entices them into confronting their own feelings," one critic has written, to explain Simon's enduring appeal. In spite of that success, many critics—until recently—have failed to take Simon seriously, pointing out that his background in writing comedy for television resulted in a penchant for one-liners at the expense of character and plot development. That assessment has changed, however, with Simon's recent semiautobiographical trilogy—*Brighton Beach Memoirs* (1983), *Biloxi Blues* (1985), and *Broadway Bound* (1986)—which reveals a new depth and seriousness. "I think I'm more perceptive than I used to be, and I want to get into my characters more deeply," he said in a 1981 interview. That does not preclude his taking on less serious subjects, as evidenced by *Rumors* (1988), his first farce, which he wrote as an antidote to the personal adversity he was experiencing.

Marvin Neil Simon was born on July 4, 1927 in the Bronx, New York, the second of the two sons of Irving Simon, a garment salesman, and Mamie Simon. Growing up in the Bronx and in the Washington Heights area of Manhattan, he received the nickname "Doc," because of his ability to imitate the family doctor. His comic instincts formed early. "I was constantly being dragged out of the movies for laughing too loud," he has said.

Simon's father periodically abandoned the family, forcing Mamie to support the children by working at Gimbel's department store and organizing poker games. When his parents finally divorced, Simon stayed with relatives in Forest Hills, New York and attended Woodside High School, where, as Simon recalled for Samuel G. Freedman of the *New York Times* (March 24, 1985), he and another Jewish student were ostracized until Simon became the centerfielder and star hitter of the baseball team. "Nobody bothered me anymore," he told Freedman. "But the jokes persisted for the other guy, and I did nothing about it. I didn't know what I could do. And I felt terribly guilty." The anguish of that experience served as the basis for Simon's handling of anti-Semitism in his play *Biloxi Blues*. It was Simon's older brother, Danny, who encouraged him to develop his writing talent. During Simon's teenage years, the two sold material to stand-up comics and radio shows.

Graduating from DeWitt Clinton High School at the age of sixteen, in 1944, Simon studied engineering at New York University under the United States Army Air Force Reserve program. He was sent to Biloxi, Mississippi for basic training, then was stationed at Lowry Field, Colorado, where he attended the University of Denver and served as sports editor of the *Rev-Meter*, the base newspaper. Although he never finished college, Simon taught himself how to write comedy by reading and imitating the work of Robert Benchley and Ring Lardner.

Discharged from the army with the rank of corporal in 1946, Simon got a job in the mailroom at Warner Brothers through his brother, Danny, who worked in the publicity department. Shortly thereafter, the Simon brothers applied to write for the noted humor writer Goodman Ace of CBS, who added the pair, for fifty dollars a week, to his stable of young radio and television comedy writers. Over the next decade, the Simons contributed material to the Robert Q. Lewis radio show, Victor Borge, Buddy Hackett, the *Phil Silvers Arrow Show*, and the *Tallulah Bankhead Show* on NBC-TV, and the Jackie Gleason and Red Buttons shows on CBS. With weekly salaries rising to $1,600, the brothers were able to leave home and move into their own apartment. "Mother used to stop in and fluff our pillows on her way downtown," Neil Simon recalled in a *New York Times Magazine* (March 7, 1965) profile. In 1952 and 1953 the Simons wrote sketches for revues at the summer resort Camp Tamiment, in Pennsylvania, later produced on Broadway as *Catch a Star!* (1955) and *New Faces of 1956* (1956).

Although Danny Simon left the team in 1956 to pursue a career in television directing, Neil Simon continued to write for programs such as the *Sid Caesar Show* (NBC, 1956–57), Phil Silvers's *Sergeant Bilko* (CBS, 1958–59), and the *Garry Moore Show* (CBS, 1959–60), receiving Emmy nominations in 1957 and 1959, for the first and second shows, respectively. During those years he also adapted Broadway shows as television specials, including *Best Foot Forward*, *Dearest Enemy*, and *Connecticut Yankee*. In spite of his success, Simon wanted to branch out into a more self-expressive medium. As he told Terrence McNally in a conversation for the book *Broadway Song & Story: Playwrights/Lyricists/Composers Discuss Their Hits* (1985), "Television meant doing the same thing for the rest of my life, writing what other people wanted me to write. . . . I wanted freedom of expression and you're never going to get it in television. . . . Writing for the theatre you have no one but the public and the critics to answer to."

It was while he was writing for the *Garry Moore Show* that Simon began work on his first play, *Come Blow Your Horn*, which he shaped slowly over the next few years, arriving at television jobs two hours early to develop the comedy. "I wrote it ten times, maybe twenty times, from beginning to end," Simon told Terrence McNally. "It had five different titles. I took it to maybe fifteen of the top Broadway producers of the day. . . . They all liked it; all told me to fix this scene, fix that scene."

Taking its inspiration from life in the bachelor apartment that Simon once shared with his brother, *Come Blow Your Horn* was first performed at the Bucks County Playhouse in New Hope, Pennsylvania in August 1960. Substantially rewritten, it opened on Broadway at the Brooks Atkinson Theatre on February 22, 1961 and ran for two seasons. Reviews were mixed. Howard Taubman, writing in the *New York Times* (February 23, 1961), noted that "its subject matter is thin. But it is smoothly plotted and deftly written."

Encouraged by that relative success, Simon started work on another play, *Barefoot in the Park*, pausing to write the book for *Little Me*, a musical adaptation of the novel by Patrick Dennis, with Sid Caesar playing all seven major male characters. That production opened at the Lunt-Fontanne Theatre on November 17, 1962 and ran for 257 performances. *Barefoot in the Park*, which finally opened on October 23, 1963 at the Biltmore Theatre, under the direction of Mike Nichols, turned out to be an enormous hit, and it firmly established Simon's reputation as a playwright. A partially autobiographical comedy, the play depicts the marital difficulties of a newlywed couple living in a fifth-floor walk-up in New York. With Robert Redford starring as the stuffy young lawyer and Elizabeth Ashley as his lovably wacky wife, *Barefoot in the Park* ran for four years and 1,532 performances. Even Simon, who is known for his modesty, commented to Terrence McNally about the critical reception of that play: "I had never read reviews like that. 'Funniest play I've ever seen; funniest play in the last fifty years.' I would sure hate that to be my first play; there's no way that you could live up to that."

Following that smash hit, Simon's work was so much in demand that, as reported by Tom Prideaux in *Life* (April 9, 1965), Paramount bought the rights to *The Odd Couple*, Simon's next play, on the basis of a forty-word synopsis. Simon sold the television rights to the play as well—a move that he has since regretted and that has reportedly cost him over $20 million. Based on a situation that actually happened to Simon's brother, *The Odd Couple* humorously depicts two divorced men who share an apartment only to discover that, in living together, they encounter the same difficulties they had when they were married. Starring Walter Matthau and Art Carney, the play began a two-year run at the Eugene O'Neill Theatre on March 10, 1965 and eventually won Simon his first Tony Award. Henry Hewes, writing in the *Saturday Review* (March 27, 1965), found the play more substantial than Simon's earlier works: "Simon has partially answered those critics who complain that his plays are entertaining but insubstantial by giving them a truer but still reasonably laugh-strewn evening."

Critics were somewhat disappointed with Simon's next endeavor, the book for the musical *Sweet Charity*, which was developed by the director-choreographer Bob Fosse from Federico Fellini's film *Nights of Cabiria*. The musical opened on January 31, 1966. A reviewer for *Variety* (February 2, 1966) complained: "There are a few humorous passages with the Simon trademark, but the tone is fundamentally sentimental."

When *The Star-Spangled Girl* opened on December 21, 1966 at the Plymouth Theatre, Neil Simon gained the almost unheard-of distinction of having four Broadway productions running simultaneously. The "least successful" of his plays, in Simon's own estimation, *The Star-Spangled Girl* concerns two editors of a radical magazine who

compete for the affections of a conservative southern belle. Reviewers appeared to concur with Simon's appraisal. Emory Lewis, for example, writing in *Cue* (December 31, 1966) magazine, said: "Perhaps this one is not quite in the same league with Simon's other efforts," but he called it a "diverting, modest comedy." The play ran for 261 performances.

Simon reestablished his stride with *Plaza Suite*, another Broadway hit, which opened at the Plymouth Theatre on February 14, 1968 and featured three one-act sketches set in the same hotel suite. In the first sketch, a couple celebrates the twenty-fourth anniversary of their faltering marriage; in the second, a successful but lonely Hollywood producer reunites temporarily with his high school sweetheart; and, in the farcical last act, a married couple combines preparations for their daughter's wedding with efforts to coax her out of the bathroom. Walter Kerr was prompted to observe in his book *Thirty Plays Hath November* (1970), "Whenever a playwright manages to be hilariously funny all night long—and Neil Simon managed to be hilariously funny all night long in *Plaza Suite*—he is in immediate danger of being condescended to. . . . What he is doing is precisely *right*—for him and for the form he works in." Simon also earned praise for his book for the musical *Promises, Promises*, a reworking of the Billy Wilder-I. A. Diamond screenplay for the film *The Apartment*, with music by Burt Bacharach and lyrics by Hal David. In his opening-night review for the *New York Post* (December 2, 1968), Richard Watts Jr. termed Simon's effort "witty and sparkling," and several critics praised the book as Simon's best to date.

Seeking a less superficial tone, Simon attempted, in his next few plays, to treat serious issues within a comic framework. "I used to ask, 'What is a funny situation?' Now I ask, 'What is a sad situation and how can I tell it humorously?'" he explained to Paul D. Zimmerman for *Newsweek* (February 2, 1970). Simon's new seriousness was evident in *The Last of the Red Hot Lovers*, about a man who handles a midlife crisis by seeking extramarital affairs, which opened at the Eugene O'Neill Theatre on December 28, 1969. *The Gingerbread Lady*, which premiered on December 13, 1970, at the Plymouth Theatre, portrays the struggle of an alcoholic one-time singer to get back on her feet. It was generally not well received by the critics, and Simon's attempts at tragicomedy were occasionally subjected to harsh criticism as well. Brendan Gill of the *New Yorker* (December 19, 1970) was among those who were unimpressed: "Mr. Simon's clumsy grapplings with Real Life are being saluted as signs of a newfound compassion and a new breadth of vision on the part of the playwright," he wrote. "They are nothing of the sort."

With *The Prisoner of Second Avenue*, which opened on November 11, 1971 at the Eugene O'Neill Theatre, Simon "hit the jackpot" of seriousness, according to one reviewer. In the play, the harshness of New York life drives a recently fired advertising executive to a nervous breakdown. In his review for the *New York Times* (November 21, 1971), Walter Kerr lamented the absence of plot development but praised the overall result: "He has taken the trouble to trouble his people, tease the laughs to see what real woes lie beneath them. He has made a magnificent effort to part company with the mechanical, and his overall success stands as handsome proof that humor and honesty can be got into bed together."

Neil Simon returned to frothier fare with *The Sunshine Boys*, which was written during the period of time when Simon's first wife, Joan, was fighting a losing battle with cancer. The two title characters are estranged vaudeville partners who are reunited for a television show. Witty bickering, endearing characterizations, and a clever vaudeville routine turned that play into yet another Simon hit. "*The Sunshine Boys* won't tell you anything new about old men," Hugh Hebert wrote in the *Guardian* (January 15, 1976), "but it will keep you laughing unashamedly at what you think you know already."

To cope with his wife's death, in 1973, Neil Simon next adapted several of Anton Chekhov's stories for the stage. *The Good Doctor* opened on November 27, 1973 at the Eugene O'Neill Theatre. The constituent scenes are tied together by a character called The Writer, an amalgam of Chekhov, the writer Trigorin in *The Seagull*, and Simon himself. A reviewer for *Variety* (December 5, 1973) called *The Good Doctor* "one of his creditable accomplishments and one of the better shows of recent seasons."

God's Favorite, a recasting of the Biblical Job as a Jewish millionaire with a nerve-wracking family, opened on December 11, 1974. Not well received by the public or critics, the play closed after 119 performances. Confiding that *God's Favorite* is the play he is least objective about, Simon explained its genesis to Lawrence Linderman in an interview for *Playboy* (February 1979) as "an attempt to release or exorcise some of [his] anguish" over his wife's death. "I was in the middle of the ocean, looking for a log to hang onto, and [this] was the log that I grabbed." Simon also entered analysis, a process he has repeated during other critical periods in his life. He told Terrence McNally that he finds the process "invaluable, not only in getting me through those tough periods: it taught me a way to think about plays. . . . The lessons that I learned in analysis—questions I learned to ask myself—I apply to my plays when I get into trouble." For the 1974–75 Broadway season, Neil Simon received a special Tony Award "for his overall contribution to the theatre."

After moving to California in 1975, Simon used the basic format of *Plaza Suite* to create four new sketches set in a hotel suite in Beverly Hills. *California Suite* opened on June 10, 1976 at the Eugene O'Neill Theatre to mixed reviews, with critics generally citing the first and third acts as superior to the farcical second and fourth acts. In the first

act, a divorced woman comes to California to persuade her daughter to return home to New York, and, in the third, a British actress haggles with her bisexual husband. Edwin Wilson, writing in the *Wall Street Journal* (June 14, 1976), observed: "In showing us the pain of his characters Mr. Simon demonstrates once again how well he understands one of the secrets of comedy: that for human beings the funny bone is often found near a raw nerve, and that when we look at life through a comic prism we are likely to laugh hardest when others suffer the most." Another Broadway hit, *California Suite* ran for 445 performances.

Returning to autobiographical material, Simon next wrote *Chapter Two*, which deals with a widower's guilt over marrying again. The play was based on Simon's own experience, after his second marriage, to the actress Marsha Mason. John Simon was one critic who was not favorably impressed by Simon's attempt at seriousness. As he commented in the *Hudson Review* (Spring 1978), "*Chapter Two* is being heralded as a deepening of Neil Simon's art. . . . The characters in Simon are interchangeable because, with minor differences, they are all Neil Simon: accumulations of wisecracks, machines that chop life down to one-liners, and humanoid contraptions, miserable for the sake of being comically miserable."

Simon's most recent book, for the musical *They're Playing Our Song*, grew out of the relationship between Marvin Hamlisch and Carole Bayer Sager, who wrote the music and lyrics, respectively. Jack Kroll, writing in *Newsweek* (February 26, 1979), stated that "this kind of thing is Neil Simon at his best. He's grasped the essential truth about life today—that no matter how serious the details may be, it's a joke, Mac, a series of routines turned out by the Great Gag Writer in the Sky." The musical was nominated for a Tony Award.

I Ought to Be in Pictures opened at the Eugene O'Neill Theatre on April 3, 1980. The story depicts a screenwriter whose self-esteem and capacity for love are enhanced when he gains the friendship of his daughter, whom he has not seen since his divorce many years before. That play was followed by the offbeat *Fools*, about the efforts of a young schoolteacher to educate the inhabitants of a Ukrainian village who are cursed with stupidity. Critics mostly judged that experiment as unsatisfying. Frank Rich of the *New York Times* (April 7, 1981), for example, called *Fools* an "almost total misfire." Simon admitted to Terrence McNally that *Fools* should never have been produced on Broadway. "I never meant for it to be done on Broadway," he said. "It was a diversion, the kind of play I write when I don't feel like writing a play that deals with my own life. I always meant it as a children's fable, and I always wanted to do it in a regional theatre. *Fools*, which opened at the Eugene O'Neill Theatre on April 6, 1981, lasted for only forty performances.

Heralding a new level of sophistication, Simon's *Brighton Beach Memoirs*, which opened at the Alvin Theatre on March 27, 1983, sparked a critical reexamination of Simon's work. Although not strictly autobiographical, the play recreates the adolescence of Eugene Morris Jerome, a character similar to Simon in his youth, who grows up in a troubled Brooklyn household. "There was sort of a breakthrough for me in *Brighton Beach Memoirs*," Simon told Terrence McNally. "I had never tried to write a tapestry play before. Most of my plays were a confrontation between two people, and the other people around them were peripheral. . . . In doing *Brighton Beach Memoirs*, I said, 'This play is about every character, and I will tell each of their stories.'" Frank Rich of the *New York Times* (April 28, 1983) noted that "if the play's undercurrents don't run deep, its surface mostly gleams." And Clive Barnes of the *New York Post* (March 28, 1983) commented, "He is always brooding on the littleness of life and that ugly comic aspect of the domestic mini-tragedy." *Brighton Beach Memoirs* was awarded the New York Drama Critics Circle Prize for best play. On June 29, 1983, the Alvin Theatre was renamed the Neil Simon Theatre, the first theatre to so commemorate a living playwright.

Even more favorably received than its predecessor, *Biloxi Blues*, the second play in Simon's autobiographical trilogy, was praised for its depth of characterization. Critics especially appreciated Simon's willingness to sacrifice a laugh for character development. *Biloxi Blues*, which premiered on March 28, 1985 at the Neil Simon Theatre, traces Eugene Jerome's experiences in army training camp, where he deals with anti-Semitism and sexual coming-of-age. Howard Kissel of *Women's Wear Daily* (March 29, 1985) called *Biloxi Blues* "certainly Simon's best play, to my mind the first in which he has had the courage to suggest there are things that matter more to him than the reassuring sound of the audience's laughter."

Of the three plays that make up the trilogy, Simon has said that the third, *Broadway Bound*, came most from the heart, perhaps accounting for the attack of anxiety he suffered at the play's premiere in Washington, D.C. "I don't know that this was the hardest play for me to write," he told David Richards for the *Washington Post* (October 19, 1986). "But it is the hardest play to watch, because it cuts so much deeper." *Broadway Bound* opened on Broadway on December 4, 1986 at the Broadhurst Theatre. It deals with Simon's years as an aspiring writer, when he and his brother, Danny, attempted to write material for Broadway comics. It also depicts the stormy relationship between his parents. One scene in particular, in which Eugene Jerome asks his mother to tell him about the time she danced with George Raft, and mother and son end up dancing together, was repeatedly cited by critics for its dramatic impact. As Simon confided to William A. Henry 3d for *Time* (December 15, 1986) magazine, "Until I wrote [that scene], I had not fully resolved how I truly felt about my mother. I had no idea I had been so dependent on her. That is an erotic, truly intimate love scene."

Simon's ability to enjoy his new critical acclaim was dampened by personal tragedy, after the breakup of his third marriage and the death of his son-in-law. As was his custom, he found solace in writing and eventually produced the farce *Rumors*, which opened on November 10, 1988 at the Broadhurst Theatre, becoming Simon's twenty-third production in twenty-eight years. Although the play became a box-office hit, critics were generally disappointed by *Rumors*, which concerns the mishaps that occur at a New York City dinner party. Nevertheless, Edwin Wilson of the *Wall Street Journal* (November 23, 1988) observed, "If Simon has not yet completely mastered farce the first time out, not to worry. He has made a good stab at it, and with his ever-present comic inventiveness, it's still the funniest play around." His most recent play, "Jake's Women," has been scheduled to open on Broadway on April 30, 1990.

In addition to the film versions of many of his plays, Simon has written several screenplays, including *After the Fox* (1966); *The Out-of-Towners* (1970); *The Heartbreak Kid* (1972); the roaringly funny Mel Brooks–style parodies *Murder by Death* (1976) and *The Cheap Detective* (1978); *The Goodbye Girl* (1977), a romantic comedy featuring Richard Dreyfuss and Marsha Mason; *Seems Like Old Times* (1980); *Max Dugan Returns* (1983); *The Lonely Guy* (1984); and *The Slugger's Wife* (1984). The screenplays he has adapted from his own plays include *Barefoot in the Park* (1967), *The Odd Couple* (1968), *Plaza Suite* (1971), *Last of the Red Hot Lovers* (1972), *Prisoner of Second Avenue* (1975), *The Sunshine Boys* (1975), *California Suite* (1978), *Chapter Two* (1979), *Only When I Laugh* (1981), which is an adaptation of *The Gingerbread Lady*, *I Ought to Be in Pictures* (1982), *Brighton Beach Memoirs* (1986), and *Biloxi Blues* (1988). Negotiations are reportedly in progress for film rights to *Rumors*. Simon received Writers Guild Screen Awards in 1968, 1970 and 1975.

Whether at his Manhattan apartment or his house in Bel Air, California, the "tall, owlish-faced" Simon writes daily from about 10:00 A.M. to 5:00 P.M., putting aside ten or more plays for each one he finishes. "I really like being alone in a room, writing," he has said. To avoid interrupting his work, he keeps cookies and dry roasted peanuts handy for refreshment. If a play makes it past page thirty-five, Simon usually completes it and then begins a process of meticulous revision that lasts longer than the original period of composition.

Neil Simon married Joan Baim, a dancer, on September 30, 1953. Several months after she died, in 1973, he married Marsha Mason, whom he met when she auditioned for a role in *The Good Doctor*. "I'm a person who must be married," he told John Corry of the *New York Times* (April 5, 1981). Simon and Mason divorced in 1982, largely over the strain of their two careers, but remain close friends. "I think the fact that it ended after almost ten years did not mean that it was not a good marriage," he told Mervyn Rothstein for the *New*

York Times (November 13, 1988). "Some marriages are destined to go for a long time and some are not. . . . But they were ten good years." His third marriage, to Diane Lander in 1987, also ended in divorce, but Simon, who has two grown daughters and a stepdaughter, refuses to "give up" on the institution of marriage. He enjoys playing tennis and has recently started painting watercolors. He reads nonfiction, mostly the biographies of other writers.

References: Chicago Tribune XIII p4+ N 2 '86; N Y Times II p1+ Mr 27 '83 por, II p1+ Mr 24 '85, II p1+ N 13 '88 por; N Y Times Mag p37+ My 26 '85 por; People 23:105+ Je 17 '85 pors; Time 128:72+ D 15 '86 pors; Washington Post G p1+ Mr 23 '75 por, L p3 Jl 29 '79 por, F p1+ O 19 '86 por; Brady, John. The Craft of the Screenwriter (1981); Contemporary Authors vols 21–22 (1969); Dictionary of Literary Biography vol 7 (1981); Guernsey, Otis L., Jr. Broadway Song & Story (1985); Who's Who in America, 1988–89

Skinner, Samuel K(nox)

June 10, 1938– United States Secretary of Transportation; lawyer. Address: Dept. of Transportation, 400 7th St., S.W., Washington, D.C. 20590

When Samuel K. Skinner arrived in Washington, D.C., to take up his duties as secretary of transportation in President George Bush's administration, he seemed an unlikely candidate for media attention in a cabinet that included such familiar figures as James A. Baker 3d, the secretary of state, Elizabeth H. Dole, the secretary of labor, and Jack Kemp, the secretary of housing and urban development. A former federal prosecutor and part-time regional transportation director, Skinner had never held public office outside Illinois, and his appointment seemed like nothing more than a reward for his service as manager of Bush's election campaign in that crucial state. But in the administration's first 100 days, Skinner emerged as a dominant voice on issues that captured the headlines.

When the machinists' union launched its strike against Eastern Airlines, Skinner prevailed upon President Bush not to intervene, and he vowed to head off any attempt by labor to spread disruption through the use of a secondary boycott of other transportation facilities. In the wake of a massive oil spill off Alaska, Skinner coordinated federal support to assist Exxon in its lagging cleanup effort and publicly criticized the oil giant for its failure to plan adequately for such a catastrophe. Perhaps of more significance in the long run, Skinner has announced plans for a comprehensive national transportation policy that will provide a blueprint for the development of highway, rail, maritime, and air travel into the middle of the next century. "He's a visionary," Theodore Weigle Jr., who served under Skinner at the Regional Transportation Authority of Northeastern Illinois, has said. "He thinks big. He's been playing in the big leagues for quite a long time on his own. He's not the least bit intimidated by big issues or big politics."

Samuel Knox Skinner was born in Chicago, Illinois on June 10, 1938 to Vernon Orlo Skinner and Imelda Jane (Curran) Skinner, and he grew up in Wheaton and Springfield, Illinois. After graduating with a bachelor's degree in accounting from the University of Illinois in 1960, he served as a lieutenant in the United States Army. Hired by International Business Machines (IBM) as a sales representative based in Chicago, Skinner was so attentive to his customer base that he followed up each sale to make sure that the equipment was operating properly and that his client was satisfied. When, for example, the Continental Illinois National Bank and Trust Company converted to a new line of IBM computers, Skinner worked for twenty-four hours at a stretch to ensure its performance. "He took servicing his accounts to an extreme," one Continental Illinois officer has recalled. "He didn't just sell equipment." In 1967 Skinner was named IBM's outstanding salesman of the year for the company's seventeen-state Midwest region. In his spare time, Skinner campaigned in Deerfield, Illinois for Senator Barry M. Goldwater, the Republican presidential nominee in 1964, and studied law in the evening program at DePaul University in Chicago.

In 1968, two years after receiving his law degree and gaining admission to the Illinois bar, Skinner gave up his $47,000-a-year position at IBM to accept an appointment as assistant United States attorney for the northern district of Illinois at a salary of $9,500. The watershed event in his career took place in November 1971, when James R. Thompson was named United States attorney for the district. Ambitious, aggressive, and determined to root out the fraud and graft that had made Chicago a byword for political corruption, Thompson felt an instant rapport with Skinner and has promoted his career ever since. With Skinner heading the Special Investigation Division created to amass evidence against the corrupt political machine of Mayor Richard J. Daley, Thompson racked up a conviction rate of 90 percent of the more than 300 indictments returned during his tenure. Among the successfully prosecuted were Edward J. Barrett, the Cook County clerk and a henchman of Daley's; Earl Bush, Daley's former press secretary; several Chicago aldermen; a score of employees in the county assessor's office; and dozens of policemen and sheriff's deputies.

But by far the biggest fish caught in the Thompson-Skinner net was Judge Otto Kerner, a former governor of Illinois who was at the time sitting on the bench of the United States Court of Appeals for the Seventh District. In 1971 Skinner drafted the official prosecution memo that set in motion the indictment and ultimate conviction of Kerner for bribery, conspiracy, and income tax evasion in connection with an Illinois racetrack deal. Over the next fifteen months, Skinner carefully developed the case, taking personal charge to ensure the cooperation and maximum effectiveness of the prosecution's key witness, Marje Everett, known to members of the press as "the Queen of Illinois Racing." During the trial in early 1973, Skinner conducted the supremely important direct examination of Mrs. Everett and delivered a widely praised closing argument that helped the jury decide to convict, for the first time in history, an incumbent appellate judge. For his work as Thompson's deputy, Skinner received the Outstanding Service Award, the Justice Department's highest honor, in 1972 and again in 1974. In the latter year he was named one of the ten outstanding young citizens of Chicago by the city's Junior Chamber of Commerce.

In 1975, after Thompson resigned to go into private practice in preparation for his run for governor of Illinois, President Gerald R. Ford promoted Skinner to the post of United States attorney. As chief federal prosecutor for the Chicago area over the next two years, Skinner became known as "Sam the Hammer" for his relentless crackdown on corruption. Estimating that as much as 10 percent of Illinois' Medicaid budget was being spent fraudulently, he exposed a Medicaid fraud ring involving medical centers, pharmacies, and diagnostic labs, and he prosecuted dozens of public employees who were fraudulently collecting welfare. By creating a special investigative unit that worked with the Internal Revenue Service and the Commodity Futures Trading Commission, Skinner

uncovered market rigging on the Chicago Board of Trade and the Chicago Mercantile Exchange. Meanwhile, he also taught law at the John Marshall Law School in Chicago, from 1974 to 1977. During the 1976 gubernatorial race, he closely monitored the polls in Chicago to guarantee a fair count in the landslide election of his mentor, James R. Thompson.

In 1977 Skinner resigned from the attorney's office to join the prestigious Chicago law firm of Sidley and Austin. Among his corporate clients was Commonwealth Edison, the electric utility, which he successfully defended in 1980 against charges that it had violated federal regulations in connection with a power station at Cordova, Illinois. That year he campaigned for George Bush in the Illinois presidential primary. Following Ronald Reagan's election, Skinner was named vice-chairman of the President's Commission on Organized Crime, and he emerged as a leading critic of the Teamsters union for its alleged association with underworld figures.

In 1984 Governor Thompson appointed Skinner chairman of the Regional Transportation Authority of Northeastern Illinois, a part-time position that enabled him to maintain his practice at Sidley and Austin. Over the next four years he restored the financially troubled transportation system, the nation's second-largest, to solvency by slashing its administrative personnel by 20 percent and by raising its fares. His strategic thirty-year plan was adopted in 1988. In the same year he directed the Bush presidential campaign in Illinois, helping the candidate to turn back a primary challenge by Senator Robert J. Dole of Kansas and carry the state in the general election.

Within twenty-four hours after that election, Governor Thompson was urging Bush to nominate Skinner for secretary of transportation. "He inspires a lot of loyalty in subordinates and has a great ability to bring conflicting viewpoints together," Thompson said of his former deputy at the time the nomination was announced. "He knows enough to go out and get the very best in professionals to work with. He's incredibly good at people strength." Among the very few to criticize the appointment was the Democratic senator Howard M. Metzenbaum of Ohio, who charged that Skinner, as United States attorney in 1977, had ignored a Food and Drug Administration request for a grand-jury investigation into G. D. Searle and Company's allegedly fraudulent testing of the artificial sweetener NutraSweet, and that soon after that, he had joined Sidley and Austin, the law firm that represented Searle. Skinner maintained that he had acted within Justice Department guidelines, an explanation that eventually satisfied Metzenbaum, who joined the rest of the Senate in making the confirmation vote on January 31, 1989 unanimous.

Although Skinner was one of the few members of the Bush cabinet unfamiliar with Washington, he took up his duties with the alacrity of a veteran. Amid concerns about airline safety in the wake of the terrorist bombing of a Pan Am passenger jet over Lockerbie, Scotland in December 1988, Skinner, in a search for effective countermeasures, met with scores of senators and congressmen and testified five times on Capitol Hill during his first eight weeks in office. Among other things, he ordered the installation at international airports of more sophisticated screening devices capable of detecting plastic explosives and the streamlining of procedures to expedite the airlines' response to security bulletins. Such bulletins, issued by the Federal Aviation Administration to warn the airlines of threats or intelligence reports of imminent terrorist attacks, had come under sharp criticism following the Pan Am bombing because the threat was not disclosed to the general public. Skinner steadfastly defended the need for secrecy, despite the obvious dangers to the public. "Publicizing every threat . . . will have the paradoxical result of making us less, rather than more, safe," he declared, because even empty threats could paralyze air transportation and intelligence sources could be compromised. Skinner also called on friendly governments in Europe and the Middle East to allow American antiterrorist agents to operate in their countries.

Skinner found himself in the midst of another air controversy in March 1989, when the machinists' union went out on strike against financially troubled Eastern Airlines. The secretary of labor, Elizabeth H. Dole, seemed the most likely candidate to be the administration's leading spokesperson on the issue because, as transportation secretary in the Reagan administration, she was well grounded in the issues, but she was reluctant to jeopardize her relations with labor so early in her term as labor secretary. The task then fell to Skinner, who, eager for the fray, argued successfully for the administration to let the strike run its course without government intervention and, in a series of television interviews, warned that he would not tolerate a secondary boycott of other airlines or rail transportation, a tactic that the machinists' union had threatened to invoke. On the first day of the strike, he seemed to side with Eastern's management, declaring publicly that he blamed much of the airline's financial troubles on excessively high labor costs. Stung by criticism from the AFL-CIO president, Lane Kirkland, and others, Skinner quickly sought to restore a sense of balance by also blaming Frank Lorenzo, Eastern's president, for failing to establish a decent relationship with his work force.

What troubled Skinner most about the Eastern strike was the threat it posed that another American airline might go out of business at a time when a mere nine carriers controlled more than 90 percent of the nation's air traffic, and he was concerned that the recent consolidation in the airline industry, if continued, might undermine competition. In his first weeks in office, Skinner met with the presidents of all the major airlines to discuss the status of competition in the industry eleven years after deregulation. He subsequently appoint-

ed a task force to examine the effect upon competition of current airline concentration, computer reservation systems, and the hub-and-spoke route systems. Members of the task force will also determine whether the federal government can play a role in the construction of more airports and whether the number of flights can be increased without lowering safety standards. "We need competition," Skinner said in an interview with a reporter from Barron's (April 3, 1989). "We've gone about as far as we can go in deregulation. Now we've got to make sure it works."

Under President Bush's flexible-freeze policy, the top priorities of the Transportation Department are to be the development of the Federal Aviation Administration's air traffic control program and the Coast Guard's drug interdiction efforts. Budgetary restraints leave little funding for the development of mass transit systems. Consequently, in interviews and in his first testimony before the Appropriations Subcommittee of the Senate Transportation Committee, Skinner made it clear that he expects the federal government to reduce its traditional 80 percent share of the funding for local mass transit projects. "We've got to recognize that the state and local governments must do their share," he explained to Thom Shanker of the Chicago Tribune (February 7, 1989). "They've relied too much in the past on the federal government, and they have not done enough on a local basis, primarily as far as their share of funding."

In a reversal of Reagan administration policy, Skinner has called for stricter fuel efficiency standards for automobiles. Under his predecessor, James H. Burnley, the government's corporate automotive fuel economy standards had been relaxed for the first time since the enabling legislation was passed during the oil shortage in 1975, but Skinner proposed requiring auto manufacturers to produce cars averaging 27.5 miles per gallon (up from the present 26.5) for the 1990-model year.

In March 1989 Skinner was dispatched to Alaska, together with the administrator of the Environmental Protection Agency, William K. Reilly, and the Coast Guard commandant, Paul Yost, to inspect the worst oil spill in North American history, caused when the Exxon Valdez supertanker ran aground in Prince William Sound. Acting on their findings, President Bush assigned Skinner the task of coordinating federal assistance in the cleanup effort. Although the administration at first withheld criticism of Exxon, Skinner eventually blasted the oil giant and the Alyeska Pipeline Service Company, the consortium of several oil companies working the Trans-Alaska pipeline, for their failure to plan adequately for such a catastrophe. In testifying before the Environmental Protection Subcommittee of the Senate Environment and Public Works Committee in April 1989, Skinner called the spill "one of the worst environmental and economic disasters this nation has ever faced" and said of Alyeska's contingency planning, "On a scale of one to ten, it was a zero." Conceding that the federal government must bear some of the blame for failing to regulate the transportation of oil adequately, Skinner called for legislation cracking down on alcohol abuse among seamen and a comprehensive oil-spill liability law, spelling out in detail who is responsible for damages and to what extent.

Skinner's most ambitious endeavor by far is his commitment to the development of a comprehensive national transportation policy. The Reagan administration had rejected the idea as anathema to its decentralization policy of leaving such decisions up to local authorities, but Skinner has argued that the nation must devise a coordinated strategy for the efficient development of highways, mass transit facilities, and airports over the next two decades and beyond, into the middle of the next century. Among the matters he hopes to address are the extent to which mass transit will replace the automobile; the feasibility of a high-speed railroad to service the Northeast corridor; the possibility of constructing new airports in remote areas rather than near cities; and ways of paying for repair of the nation's deteriorating infrastructure. He even is prepared to consider allowing private companies

to enter the field of space travel. "I am totally, with a big T, committed to developing a national transportation policy," Skinner told a group of aviation officials in March 1989. "We are going to have a national transportation policy in this country, or there will be a lot of dead bodies all over the department. One of them will be mine."

Samuel K. Skinner, who has a reputation of unquestioned probity, has been described as being singleminded, aggressive, competitive, tenacious, and "tense like a rubber band" but also as being witty in his relaxed moments. He is an instrument-rated pilot licensed to fly in all weather conditions. Since November 26, 1960 he has been married to the former Susan Ann Thomas. They have three children: Thomas, a lawyer and an assistant to Governor James R. Thompson for economic development; Steven, a law student; and Jane, a recent graduate of Northwestern University.

References: Bsns W p126+ Je 26 '89 por; N Y Times A p25 D 23 '88 por; Washington Post A p4 D 22 '88 por; Who's Who in American Law, 1987–88; Who's Who in American Politics, 1989–90

Smith, Patti

Dec. 30, 1946– Writer; songwriter; singer; graphic artist. Address: c/o Arista Records, Inc., Arista Bldg., 6 W. 57th St., New York, N.Y. 10019

Patti Smith is a former free-form poet turned singer and songwriter who in the mid-1970s became a precursor of punk music, as that rebellious and ecstatic form of rock-'n'-roll was then called. Gaunt, intense, and androgynous in appearance, Miss Smith enlivened the downtown Manhattan avant-garde art scene like a possessed urchin two decades ago. As a creator of spoken or chanted stream-of-consciousness verse in the "beat" idiom, she attracted an underground following that included many of the disaffected and desperate young people of that time. After she formed her own band, the Patti Smith Group, in 1974, her cult grew among rock aficionados who found in her work a romantic excess missing in music, in their view, since the heyday of Jim Morrison, Jimi Hendrix, the Velvet Underground, and the early Rolling Stones.

While some of them were fascinated with her idiosyncratic performances, no A & R people with major record companies would touch Patti Smith's anarchistic and defiantly tasteless lyrics—until 1975, when Clive Davis signed her with his Arista Records. On that label the Patti Smith Group cut three albums—*Horses* (1975), *Radio Ethiopia* (1976), and *Easter* (1978)—before achieving a mainstream breakthrough with Miss Smith's sexy love song "Because the Night," written with Bruce Springsteen. After her fourth Arista release, *Wave*

(1979), Miss Smith retreated into married life. She returned to recording with *Dream of Life* (1988), an album projecting a mellowed artist, exorcised of her demons and finally at peace with herself.

Patti Lee Smith was born into an intellectually offbeat blue-collar family in Chicago, Illinois on December 30, 1946. Her father, Grant Smith, a former tap dancer, was a factory hand and freethinking reader of the Bible, Bertrand Russell, H. G.

Wells, and UFO magazines. Alongside that literature in the Smith household were the children's books bought or borrowed by Patti's mother, Beverly Smith, a waitress and professional singer manqué. Among the first books Patty read were William Butler Yeats's anthology *Silver Pennies,* the works of Lewis Carroll, *The Thousand and One Nights,* and *Little Women.* For the entertainment of her younger siblings—Todd, Kimberly, and Linda—Patti acted out retellings of the stories she read, often embellished by her own vivid imagination. She was always a dreamer, and her parents encouraged her flights into her fantasy life. Drawn to religion as a child, she joined the Jehovah's Witnesses, but her interest in formal religion did not last very long.

Early in Patti's childhood the Smiths moved east, first to Philadelphia, briefly, and then to nearby southwestern New Jersey, where she grew up in the towns of Pitman and Mantua. Frail and highstrung, she was throughout childhood and adolescence tormented by what she has described as "cerebral or hallucinogenic pain," which was at least in part caused or exacerbated by physical illnesses, including scarlet fever and tuberculosis. She also had an optic problem, an erratic movement of her left eye that caused double vision and forced her to wear an eye patch. In addition, she was a tomboyish rebel, ashamed and resentful of her femininity.

Self-conscious and feeling unattractive and awkward ("too skinny, with bad posture, bad skin, and duck feet"), Patti Smith the adolescent put her energy into creativity, including the appreciation of jazz and popular music, to which she would dance and harmonize. Her chief formative musical influences were black, notably the recordings of Little Richard, the Ronettes, Smokey Robinson, and John Coltrane. Later, her musical pantheon was expanded to include such white rock-'n'-roll innovators as Mick Jagger and Bob Dylan. Becoming more and more interested in art and poetry, she began trying her own hand at drawing and writing. In high school she spent her noon hours in the school library, where, poring over art books, she discovered Amadeo Modigliani's thin, flat, elongated female figures, which helped in her acquisition of a positive self-image. Another important discovery for her was the hallucinatory symbolist poetry of Arthur Rimbaud, in whom she found a kindred haunted spirit, deranged with surreal visions.

While still in high school and for a short time after her graduation, Patti Smith worked on an assembly line in a factory—an unhappy experience that she recalled in her song "Piss Factory." At nineteen she gave birth out of wedlock to a daughter (the subject of her poem "Jenny"), who was adopted by a married couple in Philadelphia. While studying briefly on a scholarship at Glassboro (New Jersey) State Teachers College, she was encouraged by one of her teachers, Paul Flick, to pursue art therapeutically, as a "transformation of energy." She tried sculpture but soon decided that

it was not her métier, although she enjoyed struggling with the material, just as she would later enjoy doing basic licks on the guitar with her band.

After dropping out of college, Miss Smith sojourned in Manhattan, made a pilgrimage to Paris (an act of homage to those of her cultural idols who lived or had trod there, including Rimbaud, André Breton, Charles Baudelaire, Jean Genet, Antonin Artaud, and Edith Piaf), and then returned to New York to settle and seek her artistic fortune among the city's bohemian elite. In Manhattan she took up residence in the Chelsea Hotel, which was at that time (the late 1960s) a magnet for rock musicians and avant-garde artists and writers, including Sam Shepard, Lou Reed, William Burroughs, Grace Slick, Janis Joplin, Jimi Hendrix, Johnny Winter, and such Andy Warhol "superstars" as Edie Sedgwick—a loose community of which she quickly became a member.

At the Chelsea Hotel Patti Smith lived at first with the artist and photographer Robert Mapplethorpe, whom she had met at Pratt Institute during her earlier sojourn in New York City, in 1967. Under Mapplethorpe's tutelage she drew assiduously, for hours at a time, day after day, month after month, capturing her previously uncontrollable hallucinations on paper and thus, in her words, exorcising her internal "demons" into "good work." "That was my peak period, 1969–70, when I really made the transition from psychotic to serious art student," she recalled in an interview with Stephen Demorest for the New York *Daily News* (April 10, 1977) on the occasion of an exhibition of her drawings at the Gotham Book Mart gallery in Manhattan. (Andreas Brown, the owner of the Gotham Book Mart, was a principal early patron of her work.)

Miss Smith explained to Demorest the stages in her progress from "psychotic" to artist: "I studied Artaud, Jimi Hendrix, all these people who had demons in them, who, instead of releasing them, wrestled with them. Artaud wrote, 'I have a tiger clawing at my brain,' and it manifested itself as a tumor. I used to have the same things—pains in my head, double vision—and I didn't want to wind up like that. But, you know, Crazy Horse used to say, 'If you take my picture, you steal my soul,' so I figured I'd take a picture of these demons, and if I got them down perfectly I'd rob them of their power."

Her breakthrough drawing, she told Demorest, was *All the Hipsters Go to the Movies,* a picture of a Christian angel and a Muslim angel tearing each other apart. "That constant wrestling represents what I go through, and I finally got that on paper. . . . I learned to control it." Her final obsessive drawing was *Devil on Ice (The Death of Sonja Henie).* The line drawings that followed, including portrait and self-portrait sketches, were forms of documentation and celebration of life rather than exorcism. "I like drawing," she said, "but to me it's like singing. It comes natural. Playing the guitar is the same old struggle as sculpture, and that's when I feel happiest these days. But the struggle that caused me to draw is over." Demorest described the "dream abstracts" of Patti Smith's obsessive period as large (approximately eighteen by twenty-four inches), detailed exercises colored with chalk. Her later, smaller pen and pencil drawings share with the earlier works "an unpolished, layered quality that exposes the bones and sinews of the designs." Demorest wrote: "Some drawings are erotic; others are her visions of celebrities like Bob Dylan, Rimbaud, William Burroughs, and Jim Morrison; and many, like the semiautobiographical *Winghead* comic strip, are highlighted by scribblings ranging from poetry to flashes of wit."

Mapplethorpe featured Patti Smith in several of his short experimental films, and her words captioned his photographs in at least one exhibition. After the close phase of her relationship with Mapplethorpe ended, Sam Shepard, the playwright and actor, became her boyfriend and Svengali for a short time. She and Shepard collaborated on the one-act play *Cowboy Mouth*, a dialogue that they improvised in spontaneous sessions based on a premise: the female character, Cavale, who imagines herself to be a crow, has kidnapped at gunpoint a family man, Slim the Coyote, with the intention of making him a rock-'n'-roll star. In their ambivalent, captor-captive relationship, the two love each other, curse each other, and howl and crow until they reach exhaustion. Shepard and Miss Smith performed the play Off Off Broadway in 1971, and Shepard expanded it into *The Tooth of Crime* (1972).

Later Miss Smith lived on and off with Allen Lanier, the keyboardist with the rock group Blue Oyster Cult, for which she wrote some song lyrics. As she became better known, she earned money by writing rock criticism for the magazines *Creem, Rock, Crawdaddy,* and *Rolling Stone,* but her chief source of livelihood during her early years in New York was a clerking job at Scribner's Fifth Avenue bookstore.

In 1971 Patti Smith began declaiming her vulgar and loose, flagrantly ungrammatical verse (example: "have you seen Dylan's dog/it got wings/it can fly") in public readings in small downtown Manhattan venues, principally St. Mark's Church in the Bowery (her first showcase) and the Mercer Arts Center. The quality of her undisciplined and self-indulgent writing was debatable, but her alternately fierce and funny delivery of it, in a quavering voice, with unexpected verbal riffs, was electrifying, and her combination of menace and allure hypnotized many. The elements of her act included a quirkiness in delivery, body language, and facial expression, and a wardrobe calculated to contribute to the look of a boyish waif that reinforced her gender-bending sensibility. She might on occasion wear a black turtleneck sweater and tight jeans, but her standard stage clothes were a schoolboy's dark suit, jacket slung over her shoulder, complemented by a tieless Baudelaire- or Picasso-style shirt or a torn T-shirt. The total effect of all the elements was a combination of sex and innocence, cockiness and vulnerability, lightened by a sense of humor.

Miss Smith's first collection of poetry, full of nightmarish images and far-out and often violent sexual fantasies, was published by Telegraph Press in 1971 under the title *Seventh Heaven*. The title poem was an erotic revision of the story of Eve in the Garden of Eden. Middle Earth Press issued her slim volume *Kodak* in 1972, and the following year the Gotham Book Mart published her collection of self-described "ravings" *Witt* (pronounced "white").

To underline the rock-'n'-roll rhythms of her spoken poetry, with its repetitive rhymes, Miss Smith recruited as accompanist her friend Lenny Kaye, a writer turned electric guitarist who knew only two or three primitive chord progressions at the time. Her readings became chantings, and, in 1974, encouraged by Allen Lanier, Jane Friedman, her manager, and Tom Verlaine, the leader of the New York underground rock group Television, she decided to make "the next acceleration"—to singing. Expanding her accompaniment into a full band—guitarist Kaye, drummer Jay Dee Daugherty, pianist Richard Sohl, and guitarist and bassist Ivan Kral—she was soon performing her poems as songs at the downtown Manhattan clubs Max's Kansas City and CBGB's. The latter was a fetid Bowery bar that became, in her wake, an internationally famous showcase for New Wave musicians.

The *Newsday* critic Wayne Robbins, who in 1973 had found Miss Smith's speaking-chanting voice to be "uncertain," described her in 1975 as singing "with style and confidence." James Wolcott wrote in *New York* (September 15, 1975) magazine: "Because of her loopy good humor, vitality, and ballsiness, her live act embodies all of the virtues of rock-'n'-roll. . . . Patti not only has *sui generis* rock-star looks (emaciated angularity, choppy raven hair, haze-penetrating eyes), but also the passion of a fan." In *Rolling Stone* (August 14, 1975) Stephen Holden wrote: "Onstage . . . her improvised raps [between songs], often very humorous, combine graphic sexual fantasy with surreal, extraterrestrial visions of violence and supernatural redemption." Holden thought that she seemed "destined to be the queen of rock-'n'-roll for the seventies."

The first rock impresario to see Patti Smith's potential as a rock-'n'-roller—early on, when she was still reading and not yet singing—was Steve Paul, who wanted to groom her for recording on his impressive but small Blue Sky label. Because Paul's idea of a female rock star did not accord with her "dreams of extending poetry into rock," she rejected the opportunity. In 1974 the Patti Smith Group made its first recording, for Mer Records, an ad hoc label created and financed by Lenny Kaye, Robert Mapplethorpe, and the Wartoke Concern, a publicity firm in which Jane Friedman, Miss Smith's manager, was a partner. The recording was the single "Piss Factory," which had on its flip side Miss Smith's outrageous version of the Jimi Hendrix classic "Hey Joe."

When RCA Records began courting Patti Smith early in 1975, Clive Davis, the founder and president of Arista Records, beat RCA to the punch and signed her to a six-figure contract. After the signing, Bob Dylan showed up at a Smith gig at the Other End club in Greenwich Village—a promotional boost for her. *Horses* (1975), her first and best Arista album, was a shrewd compromise between her outlaw instincts and commercial demands. Still, it struck many reviewers as the strongest stuff they had heard since the demise of the Velvet Underground, the perverse 1960s group that inspired a rock tradition—minimal, antisentimental, and hot for visceral stimulation, with a hint of drug-culture connections—in which Miss Smith was clearly following. The most outstanding cut on *Horses* was the blasphemous "Gloria" ("Jesus died for somebody's sins, but not for mine"), her version of the Them hit. It was issued as a single, along with "My Generation." After recording *Horses*, the Patti Smith Group moved up to such venues as the Bottom Line in New York City and toured nationally and internationally.

The restraint exercised in *Horses* was abandoned in the crazily raucous *Radio Ethiopia* (1976), the net message of which was apocalyptic anarchism. The reggae-inflected title cut of that album was a jab at the corporate controllers of radio music playlists as well as a reflection of Patti Smith's fascination with Bob Marley and the Rastafarian religious cult. Despite such appealing songs as "Ask the Land," the hard-rocking "Pumping," and "Ask the Angels" (which was released as a single, along with "Time Is on My Side"), *Radio Ethiopia* was a critical and commercial flop.

When performing in Tampa, Florida on January 23, 1977 Patti Smith fell from the stage and landed on the concrete floor fourteen feet below, suffering a concussion and fracturing several vertebrae in her neck. While in traction, she put together, partly through dictation, the aptly titled book *Babel*, which was published in 1978 by G. P. Putnam's Sons, where she had a friend in editor William Targ, to whom she had been introduced by Andreas Brown. *Babel*, an unstructured catchall of prose sketches and lyrical outpourings, illustrated here and there with line drawings and personal snapshots, boggled the minds of most reviewers. In *Publishers Weekly* (November 28, 1977), Albert H. Johnston described the book as "a volcanic spewing of image and metaphor [that] immures the sacred in the obscene and profane." The reviewer for *Kirkus Reviews* (December 1, 1977) suggested that the "opaque, largely unreadable, sado-masochistic ruminations on sex and violence" might have been inspired by "those modern muses: grass, hash, coke, morphine, and a chaser of Calvados."

The Patti Smith Group's 1978 Arista release *Easter*, more controlled and upbeat than *Radio Ethiopia*, was more successful both commercially and critically. Standing out on the recording was "Because the Night," rendered by Miss Smith in a smoky, sensual roar that beguiled even those previously irritated by her "didactic pose" and "ecstatic squeaking." Released as a single, "Because the Night" was the first song by Miss Smith to inundate the AM radio waves and make the Top Forty charts. Contrasting with the sweetness of "Because the Night" on *Easter* was the ranting "Rock-'n'-Roll Nigger," in which she inducted Jesus Christ into a pantheon of outcast artists that included herself.

The most commercially accessible of the Patti Smith Group's Arista albums was the Top Forty release *Wave* (1979), produced with smooth professionalism by Miss Smith's old friend Todd Rundgren. The riskiest song on the album was the title cut, an essentially sympathetic monologue addressed to the late pope John Paul I. Among the other songs were a thumping cover of the Byrds' "So You Want to Be (a Rock-'n'-Roll Star)" and the bright love lyric "Frederick." The latter, released as a single, was dedicated to and written in collaboration with the Detroit guitarist Fred ("Sonic") Smith, a former member of the revolutionary rock group MC5 and Miss Smith's husband-to-be. After hearing *Wave* and watching Miss Smith perform at the Palladium rock palace in New York City, John Rockwell reported in the *New York Times* (May 25, 1979): "Her most recent disk strikes a balance between her rhapsodic mysticism and her populism. [At the Palladium] her interplay with her adoring audience was witty, comfortable, and loving."

Patti Smith began her long professional sabbatical following a triumphant tour of Europe that culminated in a performance before an audience of 85,000 in Florence, Italy in September 1979. Eight years later she, along with her husband, Fred Smith, reunited with Jay Dee Daugherty and Richard Sohl to make her fifth Arista album, *Dream of Life* (1988), cowritten with her husband, who also coproduced it (with Jimmy Iovine). The tightly crafted yet generally rocking songs were lyrical celebrations of conjugal and maternal love, social communion, and planetary solidarity ("People Have the Power"), mixed with religious or quasi-religious dreamscapes ("Paths That Cross"). Some critics found *Dream of Life* "wan" in comparison with the old Patti Smith Group output. Others described it as "incandescent" and as a "seasoned work" that nevertheless "possesses a bite." The recording reached only the sixty-fifth rung on *Billboard*'s album chart.

After marrying in a small church ceremony in March 1980, Patti and Fred Smith settled down to raising a family in Detroit, Michigan. Their devotion to their children, Jackson Frederick and Jesse Paris, kept them from touring to boost the sales of *Dream of Life*. Regarding that album's cut "People Have the Power" (a title completed with the phrase "to redeem the work of fools"), Patti Smith told Lynn Van Matre of the *Chicago Tribune* that she had been trying to write that majestic song for years. "I was always concerned about the planet and about people, but when I was younger I voiced my concerns in a more adolescent way. . . . I certainly don't regret those [youthful] energies. . . . But . . . that kind of energy must be developed and structured into more beneficial energy. . . . I've developed more empathy and become a lot more compassionate."

In recent years Patti Smith has been writing a novel; studying the Bible, sixteenth-century Japanese literature, and such art as Mexican mural painting and the paintings of Jan Vermeer; and following the work of Mother Teresa of Calcutta among the dying poorest of the world. With her changed perspective on life has come a drastic revision and reduction of her litany of heroes. "I think that I have pretty much come into my own in terms of my work," she told Lynn Van Matre. "There are people I admire—Jesus, Diego Rivera,

my father—and I admire other people's work, but I'm not so preoccupied with that sort of thing. It's a lot of fun [identifying with one's artistic heroes or heroines]. . . . I just don't think that one should be like that their whole life, and now, my children count on me to be strong, to have my own identity."

References: Chicago Tribune XIII p6+ S 4 '88 pors; Cue 45:55 Mr 20 '76 por; Mademoiselle 81:124+ S '75 pors; N Y Daily News III p15 Ap 10 '77 pors; N Y Times Mag p84+ D 21 '75 pors; Newsday II p25+ Ap 20 '75 por, A p4+ D 30 '75; People 30:21 Ag 22 '88; Rolling Stone p39+ Ja 1 '76 pors, p5+ Jl 27 '78 pors; Contemporary Authors vols 93-96 (1980)

Spector, (Harvey) Phil(lip)

Dec. 26, 1940– Recording industry executive. Address: c/o Warner-Spector Records, Inc., 686 S. Arroyo Pkwy., Penthouse Suite, Pasadena, Calif. 91105

In a field dominated by the fame of singers, guitarists, and rock groups, Phil Spector has achieved international stardom as a producer, composer, and arranger of pop songs during his thirty-year career. The hits he created in the 1950s and 1960s—among them "To Know Him Is to Love Him" by the Teddy Bears, "He's a Rebel" and "Uptown" by the Crystals, "Be My Baby" by the Ronettes, and "You've Lost That Lovin' Feelin'" by the Righteous Brothers—are known to the trade as Phil Spector records. Spector's "wall of sound" recording style is internationally recognized, virtually eclipsing the

names of the singing groups he produced in the early years of rock-'n'-roll.

Having produced eighteen gold (million-selling) records by 1966, Spector temporarily retired from the music business. He returned in 1970 to produce the Beatles' Let It Be album and then worked on individual projects with George Harrison and John Lennon. In the late 1970s Spector released several collections of his greatest hits. He is currently working on the digital transfer of sixty of his tracks for their long-awaited debut on compact disc from Rhino Records of Santa Monica, California, in a boxed set, to be entitled "Wall of Sound: The Essential Phil Spector." In January 1989 Spector was inducted into the Rock-'n'-Roll Hall of Fame.

Phil Spector was born Harvey Phillip Spector on December 26, 1940 in the New York City borough of the Bronx, the only son and second child of Benjamin and Bertha Spector. His father, an ironworker, committed suicide by carbon monoxide poisoning when the boy was nine. In 1953 Bertha Spector moved with Phil and his older sister, Shirley, to southern California, where she at first supported her family as a seamstress and then worked as a bookkeeper for California Record Distributors.

At the age of thirteen, Spector was given a guitar for his bar mitzvah, and he began playing jazz in local coffeehouses only three years later. Fascinated by the rhythm-and-blues sounds that he heard on radio stations specializing in black music, or "race music," as it was then called, Spector was writing songs and organizing his classmates into singing groups even before he graduated from Fairfax High School in Los Angeles. One such group, made up of Phil Spector, Marshall Leib, and Annette Kleinbard, was the Teddy Bears, whose song "To Know Him Is to Love Him" was Spector's first big hit. The title was inspired by the epitaph on his father's tombstone.

Released on Dore Records in August 1958, "To Know Him Is to Love Him" languished for weeks until a disc jockey in Minneapolis began playing the song, generating 20,000 orders for it and catapulting it to the number-one position on the Billboard Hot 100 singles chart. "To Know Him Is to Love Him" remained on the charts for twenty-three weeks and sold over one million copies in the United States alone, leading to a guest engagement for the Teddy Bears on Dick Clark's nationally broadcast *American Bandstand* television show.

"To Know Him Is to Love Him" was recorded thirty years later by Emmylou Harris, Dolly Parton, and Linda Ronstadt, and in 1988 it earned a BMI Award as the Most Performed Country Song of the year. The Teddy Bears' success as a group proved less enduring. The teenaged performers received only $3,000 of the $20,000 in royalties they were due under their contract with Dore, and, after a follow-up song flopped, the Teddy Bears moved to Imperial Records, where they cut three singles and an album, all of which were unsuccessful. The group folded in the wake of those failures and a serious auto accident suffered by Annette Kleinbard, the lead singer. Miss Kleinbard is better known today as Carol Connors, who collaborated on the theme song for the award-winning film *Rocky* (1977).

Spector's work with the Teddy Bears so impressed Lester Sill, the head of Trey Records, that he hired the precocious eighteen-year-old to produce Kell Osborne's "The Bells of St. Mary's" (1959) and two singles by a new group organized by Spector—the Spectors Three. The singles failed to reach the charts, and the group was relatively short-lived—unlike Spector's relationship with one of its members, Annette Merar (Mirar, according to some sources). The two were married shortly after that.

While under contract to Lester Sill, Spector worked as a court stenographer from 1959 to 1960 to help pay his tuition for one year at the University of California at Los Angeles following his high school graduation. Unable to continue to afford college, he left UCLA and Trey Records in 1960 for New York City, where he hoped to use the fluency in French that his mother had taught him to get a job as an interpreter with the United Nations. But he fell in with a group of musicians shortly after his arrival and never showed up for his scheduled interview.

Within weeks Spector was playing guitar as a session musician with two of his boyhood idols, Jerry Leiber and Mike Stoller, who composed songs for Elvis Presley. Leiber and Stoller also produced the Drifters and the Coasters for Atlantic Records, where Spector soon became head of artists and repertory. He not only collaborated with the ex-Drifter Ben E. King on "Spanish Harlem" in 1960, which reached number ten on the charts, but is also widely believed to have played a role in its production, though it is officially credited only to Leiber and Stoller. Spector was also involved in the making of Ben E. King's number-four hit "Stand by Me" and Nino Tempo and April Stevens's number-one hit "Deep Purple," both for the Atlantic label. Spector's other Atlantic productions of 1960-61 included songs for LaVern Baker, Billy Storm, and Ruth Brown.

Spector worked as a freelance producer for other labels after Leiber and Stoller had accepted as much work as they could handle. For the Dunes label, he produced Ray Peterson's number-nine hit "Corinna, Corinna" in 1960 and Curtis Lee's number-seven hit "Pretty Little Angel Eyes" the following year. For the Musicor label, he made Gene Pitney's "Every Breath I Take," in which the echo and percussion effects presaged Spector's later trademark sound. For Hill and Range Music, the publishing house known for handling most of the original songs written for Elvis Presley, Spector produced demo records with the legendary rhythm-and-blues composer Doc Pomus. Rumors that Spector worked on the demos for the first album Presley made after his discharge from the army have never been confirmed.

In 1961 Spector returned to Los Angeles to produce "Be My Boy" by the Paris Sisters on Lester Sill's Gregmark label. Although the song rose to only number fifty on the charts, his next vehicle for the Paris Sisters, "I Love How You Love Me," turned out to be his biggest hit since 1958. The number-five song sold more than one million copies and prompted Sill to offer him a partnership in a new label, Philles (for Phil and Les) Records, whose slogan was "Tomorrow's Sound Today." Around that time, Spector also established Mother Bertha, a publishing company to be run by its namesake, Bertha Spector.

Consisting of five New York City high school girls, Spector's first group for Philles, the Crystals, established the label with their debut single, "There's No Other (Like My Baby)," which rose to number twenty in 1962. The Crystals' next release, "Uptown," not only climbed to number thirteen on the charts, but also inspired a string of imitations, notably "Up on the Roof" and "Under the Boardwalk," both by the Drifters. Written by Barry Mann and Cynthia Weil, "Uptown" opens with a moody, trilled bass and delicately plucked mandolin and then soars skyward on a densely packed violin arrangement punctuated by woodblock and castanets, as the Crystals sing of the joys and frustrations of urban life.

In late 1962 Spector bought out his partner and assumed sole ownership of Philles Records. Aside from the Crystals' single "He Hit Me (and It Felt like a Kiss)," which was withdrawn during Spector's quest for control of the company, Philles scored a number of successes in 1962 and 1963. The Crystals' "He's a Rebel," written by Gene Pitney, became the label's first chart-topping hit. Although credited to the Crystals, the lyrics were actually sung by Darlene Love, a Los Angeles-based session vocalist with the Blossoms. As a member of Bob B. Soxx and the Blue Jeans, she recorded a version of "Zip-A-Dee-Doo-Dah" for Philles in 1962 and substituted for the Crystals on their 1963 hit "He's Sure the Boy I Love." That year the Crystals were signed to tour England after making "Da Doo Ron Ron" and "Then He Kissed Me," both top ten hits written by Jeff Barry and Ellie Greenwich, with whom Spector often collaborated as a composer.

Spector scored an even bigger hit in 1963 with "Be My Baby" by the Ronettes, three dancers turned singers who were led by Veronica ("Ronnie") Bennett, whom Spector married in 1967 or 1968 after their affair ended his first marriage. "Be My Baby," featuring an impassioned lead vocal backed by an overdubbed, layered chorus, rose to number two on the charts and led to a British tour for the Ronettes with the Rolling Stones in 1964. In England Spector played the organ on the Rolling Stones' song "Now I've Got a Witness" on their debut album and the guitar on the group's 1964 single "Play with Fire." He found his own music popular with many British artists, including the Beatles, the Searchers, Dusty Springfield, and Petula Clark.

Despite those testimonials to Spector's influence in England, he began to experience setbacks in the United States as British groups came to dominate the charts in 1964. The Ronettes' follow-ups to "Be My Baby" failed to make the top ten, and his other artists were becoming restive with the demands placed upon them by their perfectionist producer, who required them to spend long hours recording and re-recording songs that were sometimes withheld indefinitely. By 1965, the Crystals, Darlene Love, and the Blossoms had left Philles.

Nevertheless, in 1965 the Philles label achieved what many critics consider to be, in the words of Michael Aldred writing in Goldmine (June 17, 1988), "Spector's greatest artistic and commercial triumph": "You've Lost That Lovin' Feelin'" by the vocal duo the Righteous Brothers. "Spector's recording of it," to quote Aldred, "was brilliant, spectacular, and dynamic. It remains an unsurpassed masterpiece." Three more top ten hits of 1965 by the Righteous Brothers followed: "Just Once in My Life," "Unchained Melody," and "Ebb Tide."

The following year Spector's musical fortunes were mixed, despite his having amassed a fortune that made him a multimillionaire at the age of twenty-five. (He had just been dubbed "the first tycoon of teen" in a memorable profile by Tom Wolfe.) The Ronettes' "Walkin' in the Rain" earned Spector and his engineer, Larry Levine, a special citation for special effects (thunder)—the only Grammy ever awarded for a Phil Spector record. In the summer of 1966, the Ronettes—minus Ronnie Bennett, whose impending marriage to Spector was reportedly contingent upon her ceasing to perform or record—opened for the Beatles on their final tour of the United States. But Spector had a bewildering failure that year with Ike and Tina Turner's "River Deep—Mountain High," though it is now generally recognized as a minor classic. Written by Spector with Barry and Greenwich, the song represented one of Spector's inspired production jobs, with its multilayered orchestrations, percussion, choruses, and Tina Turner's lung-bursting vocals.

"River Deep—Mountain High" climbed no higher than number eighty-eight on the American charts and vanished from the charts after only three weeks, leading Spector to close down Philles Records. It received poor reviews and very little airplay: pop stations found it too rhythm-and-blues, and rhythm-and-blues stations considered it too pop. Meanwhile, it soared to number three in England, where it was admired by the likes of George Harrison of the Beatles. Four years later, after the belated release of the River Deep—Mountain High album, the song was successfully revived in a combined recording by the Motown trio the Supremes and the quartet the Four Tops. It became a European hit for the Australian rock group the Easybeats, and the song was later recorded by such diverse artists as Deep Purple, the blues band Brian Auger and the Trinity, and the punk group the Flamin' Groovies.

Those transatlantic discrepancies in the reception of "River Deep—Mountain High" perplexed Spector until at least 1969 and led to much searching for explanations. Some people highlighted the role played by strict categorization of the song into either pop or rhythm-and-blues; others simply held that Spector's time had come and gone; still others, disavowing an outright conspiracy theory, hinted that the industry may have turned against him for the mere pleasure of mowing down a giant. To many of the newer breed of disc jockeys, Spector's records seemed gimmicky and out-of-date; the more complex his "wall of sound" productions became, the less airplay they were given on the radio. Another reason for Spector's temporary eclipse in the late 1960s may have been his staunch refusal to imitate the styles characterizing the so-called British invasion at a time when his favored artistic vehicle—"girl groups" (as they were called) of black teenagers who were often discovered singing in the high schools—was increasingly unavailable.

Spector provided a rare explanation of his motives for temporarily withdrawing from the music business in an interview with Peter Bart for the New York Times (July 10, 1966). "Art is a game," said Spector. "If you win that game too regularly it tends to lessen your motivation. That's why I lost interest in the record business. If I stayed at it I would just be playing for public approval, not for what suits me." In an interview with Jann Wenner, the founding editor of Rolling Stone, three years later, Spector asserted that the quality of popular music had deteriorated in his absence, saying, "It bothers me enough to get back in [the recording industry]."

In the meantime, Spector ventured into the motion picture industry. In 1964-65 he financed and served as musical director of a concert film called The Big TNT Show, featuring the Ronettes, the Byrds, the Lovin' Spoonful, and Bo Diddley, among others. The movie became a staple at revival theatres and college screenings in the 1970s and 1980s and was reissued as part of the home-video compilation That Was Rock (1983). In 1965 he produced the television documentary A Giant Stands 5 Ft. 7 In. (Spector's height—his weight was 131 pounds at the time). He had one comic cameo appearance in a 1968 episode of the television series I Dream of Jeannie and a bit part in Dennis Hopper's hit movie *Easy Rider* (1969). He also provided financing for Hopper's ill-fated *The Last Movie* (1970).

After releasing the *River Deep—Mountain High* album in 1969 (through a distribution arrangement with A&M Records that reactivated Philles) and recording a group called the Checkmates, Ltd., Spector returned to the music business. In 1969 he was entreated by the manager of the Beatles to produce their final album, *Let It Be*, from the tapes of their disjointed sessions of January 1969. Spector agreed and produced John Lennon's "Instant Karma" before completing *Let It Be* in 1970. The album rose to the top of the charts and generated three number-one singles: "Get Back," "Let It Be," and "The Long and Winding Road."

John Lennon and George Harrison enlisted the services of Spector for the solo albums that followed *Let It Be*. In 1970 he produced Lennon's *Plastic Ono Band* and Harrison's *All Things Must Pass*, which reached number six and number one on the charts, respectively. He then released Lennon's *Imagine* in 1971 and his *Sometime in New York City* in 1972. In the same year he worked on Harrison's live benefit album *The Concert for Bangla Desh* and, in 1973, on Harrison's *Living in the Material World* before parting company with both former Beatles.

Spector's productions during the remainder of the decade included Cher's *A Woman's Story* (1974), Dion's *Born to Be with You* (1975), and Leonard Cohen's *Death of a Ladies' Man* (1977), all of which were recorded on his new label, Warner-Spector Records. In the mid-1970s he established yet another label, Phil Spector International (PSI), on which he reissued some of his early hits as well as new material that had just been released for Warner-Spector. Much better received than the aforementioned albums were four greatest-hits collections: *The Best of the Spector Sound* (1975 and 1976) by Polygram in England, *Phil Spector's Greatest Hits* (1977) by Warner-Spector, *Phil Spector 74/79* by PSI, and *Wall of Sound* (1981) by PSI's British branch. Aside from those collections and his work on the forthcoming set from Rhino Records, Spector's most recent work was producing the Ramones' *End of the Century* album in 1980 and coproducing Yoko Ono's *Season of Glass* album in 1981.

Phil Spector is a slender, dark-haired man who looks younger than his forty-eight years. His marriage to Ronnie (Bennett) Spector ended in divorce in 1974. With her, he adopted three children: Gary Phillip and Louis Phillip, who are twins, and Donté Phillip, aged nineteen. *Who's Who in America* lists two other children, the twins Nicole and Phillip. From 1965 until recently Spector's home was a heavily guarded twenty-one-room mansion in Beverly Hills. He currently lives in a huge home in Pasadena, California. He is an enthusiastic gun collector and student of karate.

References: *Goldmine* p6+ Je 17 '88 pors, p26+ Jl 1 '88 pors; *People* 31:84+ F 6 '89 pors; Betrock, Alan. *Girl Groups* (1982); Herbst, Peter, ed. The *Rolling Stone Interviews, 1967–1980* (1981); Ribowsky, Mark. *He's a Rebel* (1989); Stambler, Irwin. *Encyclopedia of Pop, Rock, and Soul* (1974); *Who's Who in America, 1988–89*; Wolfe, Tom. *The Kandy-Kolored Tangerine-Flake Streamline Baby* (1965)

Steel, Danielle

Aug. 14, 1947– Writer. Address: c/o Morton L. Janklow Associates, Inc., 598 Madison Ave., New York, N.Y. 10022

Not without some justification, Danielle Steel, the author of twenty-seven bestsellers written over a period of sixteen years, has been proclaimed a publishing phenomenon. Twenty-five of her bestsellers are novels featuring glamorous heroines beset by obstacles over which they invariably prevail. Although the settings may be historical or contemporary, the problems of the heroines center around the concerns of work, love, and family. Ms. Steel offers her readers escape from the nagging problems of daily life through suspenseful melodrama and the catharsis of happy endings. By combining anodyne entertainment with what she has called "an instinctive sense for the feelings of others," she has acquired one of the largest and most devoted readerships in popular fiction.

Danielle Steel's readers encompass all ages and economic backgrounds, according to figures released by her publisher in 1988. Sixty percent of her fans are female; 40 percent are male. Their boundless admiration is reflected in publishing statistics. Ms. Steel can lay claim to eighty-five million copies of her books in print in forty-two countries. In 1986 she entered the *Guinness Book of World Records* for having at least one of her books on the *New York Times* bestseller list for 225 consecutive weeks, a figure that was later reported to have reached 250 weeks.

Danielle Fernande Schuelein-Steel was born in New York City on August 14, 1947, the only child of John and Norma (Stone) Schuelein-Steel. Her German father belonged to Munich's Löwenbräu beer family; her mother, the daughter of a diplomat, was from Portugal. After her parents' divorce when she was seven or eight, Danielle Steel lived with her father, a man she later described as "a gay blade who was fun but not fatherly." Raised by relatives and servants in Paris and New York City, she was a lonely child who wrote poetry and found companionship in books, especially those by the French novelist Colette. She has described her childhood as "jet set in the geographic sense, but not socially."

Danielle Steel attended school in France and New York City, where she graduated from the Lycée Français before her fifteenth birthday. In 1963 she entered Parsons School of Design with the goal of becoming a fashion designer. The intense pressure to succeed contributed to a stomach ulcer, and within a year she transferred to New York University, which she attended from 1963 to 1967. Her studies there, too, were disrupted temporarily by health problems; she underwent surgery for a tumor and hepatitis. At the age of seventeen or eighteen she married a French banker and immediately acquired homes in Paris, San Francisco, and New York City.

In 1968, feeling "very bored and disenchanted" with her comfortable international life, she began working, against her husband's wishes. She was hired as vice-president of public relations and new business for Supergirls, Ltd., a public relations and advertising agency in Manhattan. "It was a fun venture," she told Jean W. Ross in a 1985 interview for *Contemporary Authors.* "We did things like big corporate parties, PR campaigns with either feminine or youth-market aspects in mind." By 1971 the five-person firm was floundering, but Ms. Steel did not intend to stop working.

At the suggestion of one of her clients, John Mack Carter, then the editor of *Ladies' Home Journal*, Ms. Steel set out for her home in San Francisco to write a book. The project took her only three months and resulted in her first novel, *Going Home*, which was published by Dell as a paperback original in 1973. She explained its theme in an interview with Nancy Faber for *People* (February 5, 1979) magazine with the assertion that "every woman falls in love with a bastard at least once in her life." *Going Home* racked up only moderate sales at the time and was dismissed as "not very interesting" in the *Publishers Weekly* (August 20, 1973) forecast.

Undeterred, Danielle Steel continued to write not only novels and poetry, but also advertising copy for the Grey Advertising Agency in San Francisco in 1973 and 1974. Her poems about love and motherhood were published in women's magazines, but she had to weather the rejection of five manuscripts between the publication of *Going Home* and her next novel, *Passion's Promise*, a Dell paperback that was published in 1977. When asked by Jean Ross how she persevered in spite of those rejections, Ms. Steel answered, "Foolishness, I guess. I just enjoyed what I was doing. I kept saying to myself, I'm going to do one more book, and then I'll quit. I never quit!"

Another reason why Danielle Steel devoted as many as ten hours a day to writing during that period was to stave off loneliness. By 1974 she was divorced with a five-year-old daughter to raise—a situation mirrored in the circumstances of the heroine of her first novel. "After my separation," she told Nancy Faber, "I found I am never lonely when I write. You concoct dream men because there are no men in your life." In 1977 she married Bill Toth, an alcohol and drug abuse counselor with whom she had one son, Nicholas, in 1979.

Fortunately for Ms. Steel, loneliness was not a prerequisite for her writing. After *Passion's Promise*, whose heroine is a journalist who temporarily shelves her career to follow a social activist with whom she has fallen in love, Dell published three more of her paperbacks in 1978 and 1979: *Now and Forever, Season of Passion,* and *The Promise*, a novelization of a screenplay by Garry Michael White. A film version of *Now and Forever* was released by Inter Planetary Pictures in 1983. *The Promise* was an immediate bestseller. Its first printing of two million copies had been exhausted by 1979, and Ms. Steel was signed to a six-figure contract for three more books.

Renouncing the glittering social life led by her characters, Danielle Steel not infrequently spent eighteen hours a day in a flannel nightgown, frantically writing away in her bedroom. (She had hired a housekeeper.) "It drives everyone else crazy," she revealed to Nancy Faber. "People bring me food, and I shovel it in five hours later. Once a book is really going I can't get away from it. Sometimes I forget to comb my hair. And if I'm in the bathtub I'll scrawl notes on the mirror or the wall. Writing is just an all-consuming passion."

The relentless pace that Danielle Steel set for herself, along with her fecund imagination, produced a spate of best-selling Dell paperback romances—*Summer's End* (1980); *To Love Again* (1981); *Palomino* (1981); *A Perfect Stranger* (1982); *Once in a Lifetime* (1982); and *Loving* (1981), a young-adult novel and a Doubleday Book Club main selection. Although critics often expressed their displeasure with the shallow characterization of her heroines and with her repetitive use of passionate love affairs and tear-jerking tragedies in plot development, they generally agreed that her novels met some deep need in her readers. "Steel seems to have an insight into human psychology," a reviewer of *Summer's End* wrote in *Publishers Weekly* (July 2, 1979), "as she persuasively poses the issues of self-dignity, habit, fear, and duty."

During that proliferation of paperback romances, Danielle Steel published her first book of poems in a 1981 paperback original called *Love: Poems by Danielle Steel*. A hardcover edition was published in 1984 after incorporating some poems that originally appeared in *McCall's* and *Cosmopolitan*. Reviewing the paperback version, the *Publishers Weekly* (December 5, 1980) forecast called the poems "sweet snippets that sometimes run to sticky. They will undoubtedly hit home with Steel's fans." A reviewer for *Publishers Weekly* (October 5, 1984) was less charitable when commenting on the hardcover edition: "These are not poems, they are adolescent scribblings, filled with simplistic emotions and clichés."

In 1980 Ms. Steel's first hardcover, *The Ring*, was published by Delacorte, Dell's hardcover affiliate. Much longer than any of her previous books, *The Ring* incorporated a more complex plot and a historical setting that involved more background research. "I wanted to appeal to men and I wanted the hardcover market too," she explained during the interview with Jean Ross. Despite its change in format, that tale of melodramatic separations and reunions during and after World War II did little to bring the author out of the romance genre; Felicia Carparelli, writing in *Library Journal* (September 15, 1980), called the book "enjoyable soap opera reading for pure escape."

Remembrance (1981), another multigenerational, international saga, was published with a great deal of fanfare in October 1981. Dell arranged a national tour for Ms. Steel to promote all twelve of her books, and two influential book clubs had chosen *Remembrance* as their alternate selection. The hype paid off in sales and exposure. The novel was a hardcover and paperback bestseller, and a national poll of college students that year voted Danielle Steel one of the most influential women in the world. The top seven books on the paperback romance list were her titles.

The publicity demands made on the shy, domesticated author were unwelcome. In 1981 she and her two children had just settled into housekeeping with her third husband, a shipping executive named John Traina, and his two boys from a previous marriage. "I hate leaving my children," Ms. Steel told Mary-Ann Bendel in an interview for the *Chicago Tribune* (February 21, 1986). "To get me away from them for two days is a major psychotic event. I develop every malady in the world so I don't have to go."

Danielle Steel's third hardcover, *Crossings* (1982), was appraised in the *New York Times Book Review* (October 3, 1982), and all of her subsequent hardcover novels have been reviewed in that publication. Eden Ross Lipson's evaluation for the *Times* dismissed *Crossings* as having "no writing to speak of," and an early assessment in *Publishers Weekly* (July 2, 1982) forecast found it to be "quiet to the point of dullness and conventionally romantic to the point of sentimentality." Her next hardcover, *Changes* (1983), met with a more favorable reception from Judy Bass for the *New York Times*

(September 11, 1983): "The family's crises [including the death of a heart surgeon's wife after she refuses a transplant] will sound painfully familiar to many because they are credibly told."

Thurston House, published by Dell in 1983, was Ms. Steel's last novel to originate in paperback. A reviewer for *Publishers Weekly* (May 27, 1983) hailed it as "top of the genre" and added, "Steel is a masterful plotter who knows exactly how to please her crowd—with breathless cathartic drama, soppy romance, historical ambience, a host of strongly defined minor characters, numerous well-integrated subplots, and, yes, a happy and satisfying ending."

A reviewer for *Library Journal* (June 11, 1984) described Danielle Steel's next Delacorte novel, *Full Circle* (1984), as "the standard modern story of how a beautiful, intelligent woman can overcome psychological-social problems and have it all—career, love, family." Noting the prevalence of that theme in Ms. Steel's novels, Jean Ross asked her in 1985 if she were "consciously trying to say something to female readers about being able to have both career and family." "No," she replied, "except that's what I believe in. . . . I manage to do both." The reviewer of *Full Circle* noted that "in Steel's fantasy world . . . the women, despite their careers, are never complete until they wed."

In 1983 Ms. Steel became pregnant for the third time. She described the pregnancy and difficult birth of Samantha, her first child with John Traina, in a chapter that she contributed to the nonfiction book *Having a Baby* (1984), which included articles by a total of seven women. Danielle Steel's article, which was excerpted in *McCall's* (April 1984), concluded that, despite the pain, "the baby makes it all worthwhile. . . . Childbirth is a brief moment in a lifetime, which may not even be bad, and the rewards are tremendous and last forever." She repeatedly expressed her gratitude to her husband for staying by her side throughout the ordeal.

With *Family Album* (1985), a novel about a movie star who gives up her career to marry a wealthy man, loses her fortune, and becomes an internationally famous film director, Danielle Steel returned to familiar terrain. It also deals with the coming of age of her five children during the 1960s, a plot device that gives "the author a chance to serve up an entire menu of twentieth-century problems: death in Vietnam, drugs and group sex in Haight-Ashbury, homosexuality . . ., financial ruin and infidelity," to quote Susan Dooley, writing in the *Washington Post* (March 3, 1985). "Danielle Steel is a very bad writer," she added. David H. Ball, an art historian who reviewed *Family Album* for the *Wall Street Journal* (March 11, 1985), agreed, though he conceded that Danielle Steel is "one of the high priestesses of escapist fiction." He quoted one line from *Family Album* as typical of her prose: "And with that a sob broke from her, and she turned her back to him again, her shoulders shaking in the exquisite evening dress by Trigère."

Danielle Steel wrote her next novel, *Fine Things* (1987), in memory of a close friend who died of breast cancer. "Working on this book was an intensely draining experience," she told Eric Sherman in an interview for *Ladies' Home Journal* (June 1987). "Seeing someone so much like me with a fatal illness was terrifying. I love everything about my life, and it scares me to think about it coming to an end." Although the novel marked a change of pace for Ms. Steel, it was not perceived as such by Nadia Cowen, who categorized it as a "romantic potboiler" in her review for the *Chicago Tribune* (March 8, 1987): "Written in the usual language of the genre, her women 'purr contentedly' and 'look up adoringly'; her men, relentlessly 'boyish,' attack sex 'hungrily.' If you can weed through that . . . , then *Fine Things*—with a box of bonbons—is a fine way to spend a Sunday afternoon."

After completing *Fine Things*, Danielle Steel was, in her words, "looking around for something light and funny to write." So she visited the sets of three prime-time soap operas—an experience that led to *Secrets* (1985), a romance about the stars of a fictitious evening soap opera called "Manhattan." A reviewer for *Booklist* (September 15, 1985) accurately predicted that it would be "another smash." Some ABC television executives apparently loved that story about their industry, for they snapped it up along with three of her other novels for adaptation as ABC-TV miniseries: *Crossings, Thurston House,* and *Wanderlust.*

Wanderlust (1986), a novel about a poor little rich girl's encounters with the Nazis, Picasso, and Mrs. Sun Yat-sen during the years between the Great Depression and the London Blitz, received a typically tepid review in *Booklist* (June 1, 1986): "There are no real surprises here, but Steel shows again that she knows how to combine glamour and melodrama in a glittering package." The prevalence of such patronizing reviews was explained by Mary Warner Marien in the *Christian Science Monitor* (September 14, 1987): "Contemporary intellectuals revile bestsellers as brain candy, manufactured, rather than written, only to make a fast buck. People who don't read them often contemptuously think bestsellers satisfy a shallow taste for adventure, for the erotic, or for trivialized history. That is occasionally true, but seldom sufficient to explain the appeal of an author like Danielle Steel. *Wanderlust* is in no sense of the phrase 'a good read,' yet it has flown close to the top of the paperback bestseller list in just a few weeks. . . . The novel succeeds precisely because there are no surprises. Plot turns are cushioned and travel is made easier than on a prepaid tour. . . . The pleasure of the text . . . is the pleasure of your mom's tapioca pudding."

The same best-selling but often derided elements were present in the next three Danielle Steel novels: *Kaleidoscope* (1987), *Zoya* (1988), and *Star* (1989). A reviewer for *Time* (January 11, 1988) magazine called *Kaleidoscope* "one of her better tear-stained efforts." *Zoya* was labeled "a white-bread epic—harmless, bland, easily digestible" (its setting before and after the Russian Revolution notwithstanding) by William J. Harding in the *New York Times Book Review* (July 17, 1988). Reviewing *Star* for *People* (April 17, 1989) magazine, Joanne Kaufman explained why she termed Danielle Steel "a Teflon novelist. Critics can carp (justifiably) at her style. They can complain (accurately) about her paper-thin characterizations and laugh at her dumb plots. It doesn't matter. Steel's novels inexorably hit the bestseller list as if directed by lasers."

"I never had it in mind to be successful," Danielle Steel assured Mary-Ann Bendel during their 1986 interview. She compared her skyward trajectory to that of a mountain climber who says, "Well, I'll go back, but I just want to see what's over there." In late 1989 she published *Daddy*, a novel, and several children's books.

Her success has not interfered with Danielle Steel's quiet and home-centered lifestyle. She and her husband, John Traina, have five daughters and four sons. The oldest, Beatrix, is twenty-one; the youngest, Zara, was born in October 1987. In choosing to have a large family, she was trying to avoid repeating the life she shared with her parents, which she described as "very social, very superficially glamorous" in an interview with Glenn Plaskin for *Family Circle* (May 17, 1988). "The most important things my children have are not ballet lessons or nice clothes, but two parents who really care about them, and who are there for them and love them and want to be with them—which I didn't have."

Danielle Steel is five foot one and she weighs around 103 pounds. Her large green eyes and wide smile light up her youthful face, which is framed by thick brown hair. Typing on a 1948 metal-body Olympia, she works at home, alternating between long periods of daily writing and periods during which she writes only intermittently so that she can spend most of her time with her family. She attributes her success in "having it all" to a supportive husband, an elaborate schedule of activities planned well in advance, the help of five servants, and her religious faith as a Christian Scientist. (Until the age of twenty, she was a Roman Catholic.) She lives in a fifteen-bedroom Victorian house in San Francisco and retreats with her family on weekends to an 1856 Victorian farmhouse north of the city.

References: *Chicago Tribune* p6 F 21 '86 por; *Family Circle* 101:14+ My 17 '88 pors; *People* 11:65+ F 5 '79 pors; *Contemporary Authors* new rev vol 19 (1987); *Who's Who in America,* 1988–89

Stern, Isaac

July 21, 1920– Violinist. Address: c/o ICM Artists Ltd., 40 W. 57th St., New York, N.Y. 10019

NOTE: This biography supersedes the article that appeared in *Current Biography* in 1949.

"We do not know how many hours Isaac lives in a day. We only know that it must be more than twenty-four," the conductor Zubin Mehta has said of his friend Isaac Stern, as quoted in *Time* (July 7, 1980). Stern, who emigrated from the Soviet Union as an infant but studied exclusively in the United States, is considered to be the first American violin virtuoso. His taste and facility are said to be unsurpassed, and his energy is legendary. He has played as many as 200 concerts in a year, made some 100 recordings, and performed in virtually every major country in the world, although he has refused to play in Germany.

Stern's record as a talent scout reads like a Who's Who of music. Among his discoveries are Pinchas Zukerman, Itzhak Perlman, Miriam Fried, Shlomo Mintz, Sergiu Luca, Joseph Swensen, and Cho Liang Lin—a coterie of protégés dubbed the "kosher nostra." One music manager, quoted in the *New York Times Magazine* (October 14, 1979), called him "the biggest powerbroker in the music business." In addition, Stern is largely responsible for launching the drive to save Carnegie Hall from the wrecker's ball. He has founded cultural councils in the United States and Israel, and he has campaigned for civil rights. "I've never been able to live in a cocoon," Stern has said, as quoted in *Time*. "I have a long buttinsky nose." The pianist Eugene Istomin believes that Stern's broad spectrum of activity results from "his *total* need to communicate with other people."

Isaac Stern was born in the town of Kreminiecz (or Kremenets), in the Soviet Ukraine, on July 21, 1920 to music-loving parents. His father, Solomon Stern, was a contractor by trade but an artist at heart. His mother, Clara Stern, studied voice with Aleksandr Glazunov at the Imperial Conservatory in St. Petersburg. When Isaac was ten months old, his parents, fleeing the adversities resulting from the Revolution, took him with them to the United States, settling in San Francisco.

When Isaac Stern was six, he began to take piano lessons because his parents considered music essential as a general education, even though he did not demonstrate a special affinity for it. "I didn't go to a concert at the age of two, and I never begged for a tiny violin," he told Joseph Wechsberg, as quoted in the *New Yorker* (June 5, 1965). It was not until he was eight that he began to show an interest in the violin, prompted by the fact that a boy who lived across the street played the instrument. Even after he was provided with a violin, Isaac did not immediately reveal his gift. But when he was ten, after receiving instruction from a succession of mediocre teachers, his talent came to the surface. "Something suddenly seemed to happen under my fingers," he told Wechsberg.

While Stern was studying the violin at the San Francisco Conservatory of Music, his budding talent came to the attention of a wealthy woman who agreed to finance his musical training. Perhaps most significant, Naoum Blinder, a violinist of the Russian school, who was then the concertmaster of the San Francisco Symphony, took him under his wing. Except for a brief interlude with Yehudi Menuhin's teacher, Louis Persinger, Stern studied with Blinder until he was eighteen. His progress was slow but sure. Blinder's unorthodox teaching methods neglected such "necessities" as scales, exercises, and études and focused on cultivating Stern's independence, musical instinct, and natural technique. Blinder enabled Stern to be his own teacher. "He allowed me to learn: he didn't impose," Stern told Edward Greenfield in an interview for the *Guardian* (February 16, 1987). "If something was going in the wrong direction, he'd stop me. Otherwise he'd let things develop. . . . He taught me to teach myself, which is the greatest thing that a teacher can do."

Stern's musical education took place in the audience as well as behind the music stand. He listened to Rachmaninoff playing Beethoven's piano sonatas and to the Budapest Quartet performing the complete cycle of Beethoven quartets. He heard Wagner's "Ring Cycle" performed by Kirsten Flagstad, Lauritz Melchior, and Lotte Lehmann, at the San Francisco Opera, and he attended recitals by Artur Schnabel, Fritz Kreisler, and Bronislaw Huberman.

Sources differ as to when Stern actually made his professional debut. According to some authorities, he made his first appearance, as a guest artist with the San Francisco Symphony Orchestra under Pierre Monteux, at the age of eleven. But the *New Grove Dictionary of Music and Musicians* (1980) indicates that he made his recital debut in 1935 and first appeared with the San Francisco Symphony under Monteux in 1936 and that in the same year he also played with the Los Angeles Philharmonic under Otto Klemperer. Edward Greenfield wrote in the *Guardian*, "By the time he was fourteen, Stern was being brought in to play quartets and quintets once a week with the front-desk players of the San Francisco Symphony." And Joseph Wechsberg noted in the *New Yorker* that Stern made his local debut at fifteen, performing the Bach D-Minor Concerto for two violins with Blinder and the San Francisco Symphony under Monteux.

When, on October 11, 1937, the seventeen-year-old Stern made his New York City debut at Town Hall, he received thoughtful approval rather than raves. A critic for the *New York Herald Tribune* predicted, "An unusually promising young musician whose talent seems to be following a normal and judicious course of development, he should become an artist of exceptional consequence." Irving Kolodin remarked of Stern in the *New York Sun* (October 12, 1937): "He does already possess one indispensable trait of a fine violinist. That is a solid and well-rounded tone." Stern was disappointed with the reactions of the critics. "They admired my tone and carped at my intonation," he recalled, as quoted in *People* (January 31, 1977). "The consensus was that I should go far. I did. I packed up my violin, convinced I didn't know my elbow from A flat, and went back to California."

Stern's manager, the legendary impresario Sol Hurok, whom he considered a father figure, could wangle only a handful of dates a year for him but retained his faith in the young violinist. Remembering the hardships of those early days, Stern told S. E. Rubin, as reported in the *New York Times Magazine* (October 14, 1979): "I played seven concerts the first year, fourteen the next. I traveled in upper berths in trains. I practiced day and night. What did I know from Carnegie Hall, from arts councils, from big interviews? I worked my head off. . . . I had a tough, hardening apprenticeship. It taught me the value of values."

His arduous apprenticeship paid off. Stern's Carnegie Hall debut, on January 8, 1943, was the turning point in his career, for no less an authority than Virgil Thomson, writing in the *New York Herald Tribune* (January 12, 1943), proclaimed him "one of the world's master fiddle players." After his wartime performances for Allied troops in Greenland, Iceland, and the South Pacific, Stern was deluged by tour and recording offers. He made his screen debut in the 1946 film *Humoresque*, in which his hands were shown as those of John Garfield, who portrayed an ambitious young violinist involved with a wealthy patroness, played by Joan Crawford. By 1947 Stern was playing ninety concerts a year. He made his European debut in 1948, at the Lucerne (Switzerland) Festival, under Charles Munch, and went on to perform in nine European countries that summer alone. His 1949 concert tour comprised 120 concerts in seven months throughout the United States, Europe, and South America. By the time Stern reached his mid-thirties, he was recognized as one of the great violinists of his generation, along with Jascha Heifetz, Nathan Milstein, and Yehudi Menuhin. In 1950, at Pablo Casals's Prades Festival, the renowned cellist pronounced Stern a worthy descendant of Eugène Ysaÿe, the Belgian violinist who, along with Paganini, is one of Stern's heroes. Fittingly, in 1953 Stern played the role of Ysaÿe in the film *Tonight We Sing*, a biography of Sol Hurok.

By the 1970s Stern was said to be the world's highest-paid violinist, earning as much as $10,000 a performance and playing as many as 200 concerts a year. He earned the admiration of his peers, including Yehudi Menuhin, who was moved to say of him: "His playing has warmth, musicality, good taste, discipline, and spontaneity. There is no self-consciousness. It's all of one piece." Such unqualified approval is notable in the light of Stern's eclecticism, for his repertoire spans a wide range of musical history, including premiere performances of contemporary works by Leonard Bernstein, Peter Maxwell Davies, Paul Hindemith, Krzysztof Penderecki, George Rochberg, William Schuman, and Henri Dutilleux.

In an article for the *New York Times* (April 8, 1979), Peter G. Davis called attention to Stern's "catholicity of taste that has drawn him to violin music of all periods" and "his stylistic flexibility." He noted that Stern "invariably seems to perceive all music from the inside with an instinctual sense of what is right in terms of tone, gesture and expression—a treasurable gift." Although not a flawless technician, Stern is flexible and in full command of his instrument. He has been known to devise new fingerings of a difficult passage spontaneously during a performance.

In a review for the *New York Times* (January 25, 1964), Harold C. Schonberg described "a typical Stern evening," in which the violinist played a program of Brahms, Bach, Prokofiev, Ernest Chausson, and Joseph Wieniawski. Accompanied by Alexander Zakin, his piano accompanist since 1940, Stern played with "surety and precision . . . , cleanly turned phrasing, strong rhythm and impeccable technique." Another landmark was Stern's 1968 silver anniversary concert at Carnegie Hall, commemorating his first appearance there twenty-five years earlier. For that concert, he and Zakin revived the violin arrangement of Brahms's op. 120, no. 2, for clarinet and piano and also presented Bach's Sonata in E, along with Bartók's Second Sonata, two Mozart movements, and Ravel's *Tzigane*. In the words of Donal Henahan of the *New York Times* (December 2, 1968), "As impressive as anything else in the recital . . . was the ease with which he changed styles in the program's later works. . . . For the Bartók, which is uncongenial to the violin in many ways, Mr. Stern put aside any search for tonal sheen and made music Bartók's way. A moment later, the same violin was singing the sweetest and gentlest Mozart, putting each grace note and turn in place, as the gallant style demanded."

In describing his objective of attaining top musical quality to Flora Lewis, who interviewed him in Paris for the *New York Times* (July 1, 1980), Stern said: "It's when what comes out is as near as possible to an ideal realization of the way music is written, not just the notes, which are dead, but also the music between the notes, without any interference in the ear of a bad sound, a mistake or an ugly sound, one that doesn't belong. It's like a beautiful woman, perfectly dressed in elegant clothes with colors that go well together, moving with special grace through a garden on a lovely day. It's when everything is right."

Commenting on Stern's down-to-earth stage presence, Louise Sweeney wrote in the *Christian Science Monitor* (September 30, 1980): "Perhaps because Stern just lets the music shine through him, there is little of the star bravura or mystique about his appearances on stage. He walks briskly, matter-of-factly on and off stage, his violin held out slightly in front of him like a staff in his left hand, his right hand grasping the bow. When he performs, he plants his feet wide apart, stands sturdy as an oak tree, and goes about the business of making sublime music without any theatrics."

Stern enriched his already extensive performance repertoire by forming a trio with the pianist Eugene Istomin and the cellist Leonard Rose. Inaugurated at the Israel Festival in 1961, the trio remained in existence until 1983 but performed only occasionally, because of the full solo schedules of its members. "We do it for our own satisfaction and that feeling of freshness," Stern explained to Jane Perlez of the *New York Post* (December 12, 1974). "One of the special qualities we enjoy is the sense of spontaneous pleasure. . . . On stage we listen to each other and play to each other. . . . It is a very intimate language—like a glance between close friends who know each other very well." Although star soloists are reputed to have immense egos, incompatible with the cooperation required for chamber performing, Stern denied that he had such problems. "I've no need of being the great 'I am' constantly," he told Alan M. Kriegsman of the *Washington Post* (November 17, 1973). "Each kind of music has its own dynamics, its own form, its own joys. Being able to perform as a soloist, and knowing the power one has as a soloist, makes the chamber music experience that much larger." The trio concentrated on eighteenth- and nineteenth-century works and achieved particular acclaim for the Beethoven programs it performed around the world in 1970 and 1971 in honor of the 200th anniversary of the composer's birth.

In the 1970s and 1980s, Stern became increasingly involved in television, particularly in such series as *Tonight at Carnegie Hall* and *Live from Lincoln Center*. In addition to his frequent appearances as a guest artist, he has generated ideas for programming. "He's a TV natural," the producer Ruth Leon has said. "He understands television, he's fascinated by its possibilities, and he's the sort of person who can come up with an idea and then keep wheedling people until that idea comes to fruition."

The motion picture *From Mao to Mozart: Isaac Stern in China* chronicles the violinist's 1979 tour of the People's Republic of China, during which he gave master classes to young Chinese musicians. The film won the Academy Award for the best full-length documentary of 1981 and special mention at the Cannes Film Festival. Stern's screen presence was described in the *Nation* (April 25, 1981) as being "as inspiriting as a flourish of trumpets." The reviewer went on to say that "the mere sight of a human being causes him to glow with pleasure, as though he were encountering this marvel of nature for the first time."

Ever eager for opportunities to deploy the power of music, Stern devoted May and June of 1980, the year in which he turned sixty, to serving as "doctor" to two ailing French orchestras, the Orchestre National de France and the Nouvel Orchestre Philharmonique. The cure involved an intensive regimen of rehearsals and eighteen concerts comprising twenty-five works, and it helped to persuade the temperamental members of the two orchestras to cooperate. His energy never fading, Stern went on to Washington, D.C., to perform in five concerts under five different conductors, and he was also booked for concert dates in San Francisco and Los Angeles. By December 1980 he had played sixty concerts in four countries.

Stern has also used his violin as an effective cultural and political tool. In 1956, before any official cultural exchanges had been established, he performed in the Soviet Union. Just as Sol Hurok had encouraged Stern during his lean years, Stern became a mentor to many young musicians, and in doing so he served as a talent scout for Hurok. Among Stern's protégés is the violinist Pinchas Zukerman, who was discovered as a child prodigy in Israel. Others include the violinists Itzhak Perlman, Miriam Fried, Shlomo Mintz, Sergiu Luca, Joseph Swensen, and Cho Liang Lin, the cellist Yo-Yo Ma, and the pianist Yefim Bronfman.

Determined to safeguard Carnegie Hall from threatened demolition in 1960, Stern organized the Citizens' Committee to Save Carnegie Hall. When he succeeded and became president of the Carnegie Hall corporation, detractors accused him of having a conflict of interest. There were complaints that Stern ran the hall like a "mom-and-pop" store and that he filled its schedule with concerts by himself and his protégés, including events like "Isaac Stern and His Friends," a chamber music series designed to invoke the informality of a living-room gathering. Defenders maintain that Stern, who was still president as of 1989, has played no part in programming decisions. Stewart Warkow, the corporation's executive director, has said, as quoted in *New York* (March 12, 1979) magazine: "Isaac has never sat me down and said use so-and-so. He's too honest for that." In later years Stern reduced his personal involvement, although he spearheaded a multimillion-dollar project in the late 1980s to renovate the hall and protect it from the vibrations of the subways below.

Stern's political activism has prompted him to campaign for a number of Democratic candidates, including Lyndon B. Johnson and Hubert Humphrey. He also put his causes on presidential agendas. Having introduced the idea of an arts council during John F. Kennedy's presidency, Stern founded and oversaw the creation of the National Council on the Arts, which was the precursor of the National Endowment for the Arts, during the Johnson administration. His support of the arts extended to testifying before Congress in February 1970 to urge the legislature to increase its allocation of federal funds to the arts, warning that the United States was in danger of becoming "an industrial complex without a soul."

Israel has been the object of Stern's consuming passion, so much so that he is, in effect, a one-man diplomatic service to the Jewish state. In addition to performing there frequently, he has been the chairman, since 1964, of the America-Israel Cultural Foundation, which raises funds for Israel's cultural organizations and subsidizes Israeli musicians. In 1973 he founded the Jerusalem Music Center, where musicians from many nations give master classes.

Stern's unyielding commitment to his beliefs has occasionally threatened to disrupt his schedule of musical engagements. In March 1965 he attempted to cancel an appearance with the National Symphony in Washington in order to go to Selma, Alabama to support civil rights demonstrators there, but he was dissuaded by the National Symphony conductor, Howard Mitchell. In 1967 he boycotted the Athens music festival in a protest against the repressive Greek military junta, and he became the first American artist to sever relations with the USSR in outrage over its restrictions on Soviet artists. In 1974, when the United Nations Educational Scientific and Cultural Organization suspended cultural aid to Israel, Stern organized a musicians' boycott of UNESCO events. On other occasions politics served as a context for Stern's music. After the Six-Day War in 1967, Stern performed the Mendelssohn Concerto with the Israel Philharmonic, conducted by Leonard Bernstein, on Mount Scopus. That concert formed the basis of the film A Journey to Israel.

Stern has received wide recognition for his prodigious talent and contribution to cultural life. In 1974 he was made a commandeur of the French Ordre de la Couronne and in 1979 he became an officier of the Ordre de Légion d'Honneur. In December 1984 President Ronald Reagan presented him with the Kennedy Center Honors Award. CBS Masterworks named him its first Artist Laureate in 1985, and in 1986 the editors of the Musical America International Directory of the Performing Arts selected him as Musician of the Year. In 1987 he received the Wolf Prize, one of the most prestigious and lucrative prizes in the arts and sciences, awarded by the Wolf Foundation, which had been established by the Israeli parliament in 1975 on the initiative of Dr. Ricardo Subirana Lobo Wolf and his wife, Francisca. The award, which he shared with the Polish composer Krzysztof Penderecki, was presented in recognition of Stern's "everlasting humanistic contribution as an artist and educator, which transcends the boundaries of musical performance." Other honors that Stern has received include an Emmy Award for the CBS telecast of the post-renovation opening of Carnegie Hall and the Gold Baton Award from the American Symphony Orchestra League.

Wearing horn-rimmed bifocals over hazel eyes, the rotund, five-foot-six violinist is said to resemble a "cuddly teddy bear." His first marriage, in 1948, to the ballerina Nora Kaye, ended in divorce. He lives with his second wife, Vera Lindenblit Stern, whom he met in Israel on August 1, 1951 and married on August 17, after only four meetings over a period of sixteen days. The Sterns have three children: Shira, Michael, and David. They divide their time between a duplex apartment on Central Park West in New York City and a forty-acre estate in western Connecticut. Stern's favorite activities are playing tennis, during which he wears a glove to protect his strong, dimpled hands from blisters and takes care to follow through on his swing to avoid tennis elbow, and watching spectator sports. He has been known to practice his violin playing while watching football on television with the sound turned off. His habits are erratic. He works best under pressure, practicing anywhere from half an hour to fourteen hours a day, preferring to do so at night and in the small hours of the morning. His two most prized instruments are Alard Guarneri "del Gesù" violins.

Isaac Stern explained his artistic creed during his interview with S. E. Rubin for the New York Times Magazine (October 14, 1979). "I would do better if I lived more healthily, exercised more, ate less," he said. "I'm a hog. I love food and drink. I love tastes and textures. I think I could be called a sensualist. But that is the power source of my playing. When I'm caressing music, it is very sensual. I love feelings and I love gratifying the senses. I would find it difficult to be abstemious."

References: Christian Sci Mon B p2+ S 30 '80 por; Newsweek 96:93+ N 17 '80 pors; New Yorker 41:49+ Je 5 '65 por; N Y Times Mag p40+ O 14 '79 pors; People 7:47+ Ja 31 '77 pors, 14:32 S 29 '80 por; Stereo Review 50:45+ F '85 pors; Time 116:64+ Jl 7 '80 pors; Washington Post C p1+ N 17 '73 por, M p1+ O 5 '80 por; International Who's Who, 1989–90; New Grove Dictionary of Music and Musicians (1980); Who's Who, 1989; Who's Who in America, 1988–89

Stoddard, Brandon

Mar. 31, 1937– Broadcasting executive. Address: ABC, 2040 Ave. of Stars, Fifth floor, Los Angeles, Calif. 90067

Brandon Stoddard, the head of ABC's network production unit, first came to public attention in the late 1970s, when, as the network's senior vice-president in charge of dramatic programs, motion pictures, and novels for television, he was largely responsible for the telecast of the highly rated and critically acclaimed miniseries *Roots*. Over the next decade, as senior vice-president and, later, president of ABC Entertainment, he oversaw the production of some of the most popular miniseries in the history of television, including *Roots: The Next Generations*, *The Winds of War*, and *The Thorn Birds*. Recognized throughout the industry for his willingness to take risks, Stoddard also approved the production of made-for-television movies about such controversial subjects as nuclear war, incest, and homosexuality. In the words of a colleague, Stoddard, who has been with the network since 1970, represents "a touch of class in a business not always known for it."

Brandon Stoddard was born on March 31, 1937, in Bridgeport, Connecticut, the son of Johnson Stoddard, a lawyer, and Constance (Brandon) Stoddard. Reared in the affluent, nearby community of Southport, he was educated at Deerfield Academy, a prestigious prep school in Deerfield, Massachusetts, and at Yale University, from which he earned a B.A. degree in American studies in 1958. While he was a student at Yale, Stoddard appeared in a score of campus theatrical productions and, on his graduation, he headed for New York City to try his luck as an actor. After going through

a series of disappointing auditions, he enrolled at Columbia University's School of Law, but as he told Jean Vallely in an interview for *Esquire* (February 13, 1979), he found his legal studies to be "unbelievably boring." "I kept casting all the cases," he recalled. "I would see where the little boy fell into the vat of sulfuric acid, and I would see all the shots, where the closeups would be. I would storyboard all the cases."

Advertising proved to be more to Stoddard's liking, and in 1960 he took a job with Batten, Barton, Durstine & Osborn as a television programming assistant. In the early 1960s advertising agencies played a major role in the development of television programs, and Stoddard spent much of his time at the firm conducting demographic studies to determine "who the audience was," as he put it. He also devised and presented ideas for advertising campaigns and advised clients on which programs to sponsor. In 1962 Stoddard moved to Grey Advertising, where over the course of the next eight years he worked his way up from program operations supervisor to director of daytime programming and, eventually, to vice-president in charge of radio and television programming.

In 1970 Stoddard accepted a job as director of daytime programming for ABC. Working under Michael Eisner, who was later to become the president of Paramount Pictures, he developed new game shows, children's programs, and soap operas while overseeing the operations of ongoing shows. The ABC daytime schedule soon surpassed that of its rival networks, NBC and CBS, in ratings points, and in 1972 Stoddard was promoted to vice-president of daytime programming. In that capacity, he was responsible for the development of several Emmy Award–winning programs, including *ABC Afterschool Special*, a series of one-hour dramatic specials and documentaries aimed at young people that were broadcast occasionally on weekday afternoons, and *ABC Afternoon Playbreak*, irregularly scheduled ninety-minute dramas.

In recognition of his achievements, ABC named Stoddard network vice-president of motion pictures for television in February 1974. Just three months earlier, NBC had broadcast on four successive nights an eight-hour adaptation of Joseph Wambaugh's best-selling novel *The Blue Knight*. Patterned on the British serial dramas that were the mainstay of PBS's *Masterpiece Theatre*, *The Blue Knight* marked the birth of a new form of network programming—the miniseries. Recognizing the potential of the miniseries as a television "event," Stoddard immediately set to work to secure the rights to novels and original properties whose plots and characters were sufficiently interesting to hold the viewing audience's attention over a period of several nights.

The first miniseries to be produced under Stoddard's aegis was *Rich Man, Poor Man*, a nine-part serialization of Irwin Shaw's sprawling novel chronicling the ups and downs of the Jordache family from 1945 to 1965. When the series was first telecast in February and March 1976, each of its nine installments earned a top-ten slot in the weekly Nielsen ratings, and the program itself placed third in the Nielsens for the 1975–76 television season. A smash hit by any measure, *Rich Man, Poor Man* collected twenty-three Emmy nominations. It also spawned a less successful sequel, *Rich Man, Poor Man, Book II*, which featured some of the same actors and ran on ABC from September 1976 until March 1977.

Despite the popularity of *Rich Man, Poor Man*, no one at ABC—least of all Stoddard—anticipated the astonishing public response to *Roots*, the dramatization of Alex Haley's monumental saga tracing his family history from the capture of a young African, Kunta Kinte, by slave traders in the mid-eighteenth century to the emancipation of Kinte's descendants in the post–Civil War American South more than a century later. Involved in the project from the beginning, Stoddard was determined to bring *Roots* to television in spite of the risks. "TV had never really presented a story about slavery from a black point of view," he explained to Lawrence Linderman in an interview for *Panorama* (March 1980), a monthly periodical devoted to television broadcasting. "The real question was whether a miniseries about blacks could be a successful TV venture when most of the viewers are white." Nevertheless, he continued, "I felt it was something we should do. . . . I felt that the essence of *Roots* would go way beyond just black experience, and that it would be able to touch white, green, yellow, orange, red or blue families as well. It was a distinctly American story whose primary theme was the inalienable dignity of man, and based on that—we went ahead."

In an unprecedented move, ABC televised the twelve-hour adaptation of *Roots* on eight successive nights, beginning on January 23, 1977. Stoddard's decision to broadcast the episodes consecutively over one week had the effect of building interest to a crescendo, so that by the final installment more than eighty million Americans were watching. The highest-rated entertainment program in the history of the medium (the concluding installment won a staggering 71 percent share of the viewing audience), *Roots* earned nine Emmy Awards, including that for best limited series of the 1976–77 season. "I was really bewildered by what happened . . . ," Stoddard told Lawrence Linderman. "I think the truth of it is almost mystical. *Roots* was an idea that simply was not going to be denied."

Eight months after *Roots* established the viability of the miniseries as a formidable weapon in the networks' ratings war, Stoddard kicked off ABC's 1977–78 season with *Washington: Behind Closed Doors*. A twelve-hour drama loosely based on *The Company*, John Ehrlichman's fictionalized account of White House intrigues during the Nixon administration, the miniseries placed first in the ratings on four of the six nights on which it was broadcast. Among the regularly scheduled programs Stoddard helped develop for the 1977–78 season were *Eight Is Enough*, a comedy-drama starring Dick

Van Patten as the father of eight children; *The Love Boat*, a potpourri of romantic vignettes set aboard a luxury cruise ship; and *Fantasy Island*, which starred Ricardo Montalban as the mysterious proprietor of a remote tropical resort where guests could realize their wildest dreams. All three shows scored high with the viewers and finished the season on the A. C. Nielsen Company's list of top-rated programs. At the close of that season, in June 1978, Stoddard was named ABC's senior vice-president, motion pictures and movies for television.

During the 1978–79 television season, Stoddard oversaw the development and production of twenty two-hour made-for-television movies, twenty dramatic pilots, eight continuing series, and twenty-six hours of miniseries. His credits included the hit series *Vega$*, a flashy crime drama set in Las Vegas and starring Robert Urich as a macho private investigator, and *Battlestar Galactica*, an expensive and ambitious science fiction series that was canceled at the end of the season. Stoddard was also associated with two Emmy Award-winning made-for-television movies: *The Jericho Mile*, the story of a convict serving a life sentence for murder who hopes to qualify as a runner on the United States Olympic team, and *Friendly Fire*, a fact-based drama starring Carol Burnett and Ned Beatty as middle-aged parents who become antiwar activists after their son is killed in Vietnam by misdirected American artillery fire. Although neither film was expected to be an audience pleaser, both posted high Nielsen ratings. Viewers and critics also responded well to the miniseries *Pearl*, about life at the Pearl Harbor naval base in the days leading up to the Japanese attack, and *Ike*, which followed the World War II career of General Dwight D. Eisenhower.

The highlight of the 1978–79 season, however, was *Roots: the Next Generations*, a fourteen-hour miniseries that picked up the story of Alex Haley's family in 1882, some twelve years after the narrative of *Roots* ended, and traced the family's history to 1967, the year Haley (played by James Earl Jones) found the African village from which his great-great-great-great-great-grandfather had been kidnapped and sold into slavery. "We had real problems this time around," Stoddard admitted to Jean Vallely. "Suddenly we didn't have the hold in the ship, we didn't have the whips and chains and feet getting cut off. We didn't have the swelling bosoms on the plantations. We didn't have any real heavies like the Ku Klux Klan; all the very dramatic elements from which to work were missing in the second hundred years. But we also had a tremendous opportunity. *Roots I* was a splashy production, but in *Roots II* we have more of a human drama." Although not the phenomenon that *Roots I* was, *Roots II* dominated television viewing on the seven nights on which it was broadcast in February 1979.

Stoddard miscalculated in choosing as ABC's next miniseries *The French Atlantic Affair*, a three-part thriller in which a group of religious cultists seize control of an ocean liner and hold its passengers and crew for ransom. Despite the presence of such familiar faces as Telly Savalas, Chad Everett, and John Houseman, the series, broadcast in November 1979, lured only about one in five television viewers. In contrast, two more-modest efforts, *Attica* and *The Shadow Box*, both telecast in 1980, scored with viewers and critics alike. A dramatization of *A Time to Die*, Tom Wicker's acclaimed account of one of the worst prison riots in American history, *Attica* re-created the 1971 uprising by inmates at the Attica (New York) Correctional Facility and its bloody conclusion, in which thirty-eight people lost their lives. *The Shadow Box*, an adaptation of Michael Cristofer's Pulitzer Prize-winning play about three terminally ill patients and their families, starred Joanne Woodward, Christopher Plummer, and Sylvia Sidney and marked the television directing debut of Paul Newman.

Following the failure of *The French Atlantic Affair* on ABC and of other miniseries broadcast by the rival networks, some industry analysts questioned the continued viability of the miniseries form. In Stoddard's view, however, it was not the long form that was at fault, but "the *content*" of the form. "Everyone in television, I think, felt that because the first group of miniseries were hits, there was a certain magic to a six-hour or eight-hour show," he explained to Lawrence Linderman. "The idea was that by having a miniseries you had an event and, therefore, viewers would watch it. . . . [But] audiences now expect and demand more, and those involved in programming these shows have to be aware that audiences don't remain stagnant in terms of their taste. And I think in many cases we programmed on a static level without taking growth into mind."

As if to prove his point, Stoddard continued to include lavishly produced miniseries in ABC's prime-time schedule, perhaps most notably *Masada*, *The Winds of War*, and *The Thorn Birds*. Set in the first century, *Masada* recounted the story of 960 Zealots who withstood a two-year siege of their mountaintop fortress by the Roman army, then committed suicide rather than be captured. When it was first broadcast in four two-hour segments in April 1981, *Masada* drew a 40 percent share of the audience. Impressive as that figure was, it was dwarfed by the 53 percent share garnered by *The Winds of War*, an eighteen-hour serialization, initially broadcast in February 1983, of Herman Wouk's epic novel about the events leading up to World War II and their effect on a fictional navy family. One month later, the ten-hour dramatization of Colleen McCullough's bestselling *The Thorn Birds* attracted a stunning 59 percent of the viewing audience, making it the second-most-watched miniseries in television history, after *Roots*. A panoramic family saga set in the Australian outback, *The Thorn Birds* starred Richard Chamberlain as an ambitious, guilt-ridden Catholic priest torn between his devotion to the church and his passion for Meggie Cleary, the spirited heroine.

During the 1983–84 season, Stoddard shepherded through production two made-for-television movies—*The Day After* and *Something about Amelia*—with sensitive and highly controversial (some would say inflammatory) themes. Never one to avoid controversy, he told Jean Vallely in the interview for *Esquire*: "You have to know all the rules and regulations, and then you have to be able to break them all. Rules and regulations equal a twenty-eight share. . . . Only when you have the courage to try something new, something that hasn't been seen or done before, then you are going to do well." *The Day After*, shown on November 20, 1983, was a graphic depiction of the grim aftermath of a nuclear attack on the American heartland. About 100 million Americans watched the film, which sparked considerable debate about the nation's nuclear-arms policy and the likelihood of a nuclear war. The first television film to deal frankly with incest, *Something about Amelia*, which premiered on January 9, 1984, also attracted a large audience and elicited praise from the critics for its honest look at a previously taboo subject. Both films were multi-Emmy Award winners.

Stoddard also scored with the films *A Streetcar Named Desire* (1984), an Emmy Award–winning remake of the classic Tennessee Williams play that drew rave reviews for Ann-Margret's poignant portrayal of Blanche DuBois; *The Dollmaker* (1984), a powerful adaptation of Harriette Arnow's novel about a gifted Kentucky mountain woman starring, in her television-movie debut, Jane Fonda, who won an Emmy Award for her gritty performance; *Heartsounds* (1984), featuring James Garner and Mary Tyler Moore as a husband and wife whose devotion to each other is tested by the husband's losing, five-year-long battle against heart disease; and *Consenting Adults* (1985), which paired Marlo Thomas and Martin Sheen as parents trying to come to terms with their college-age son's homosexuality. In his review for the *New York Times* (February 3, 1985), John J. O'Connor praised the last-named film as "a small movie that is likely to have enormous reverberations." O'Connor was much less charitable toward the twelve-hour miniseries *North and South*, labeling it "a staggering contraption, as ingenious and silly as any ever devised by Rube Goldberg." Nevertheless, the adaptation of John Jakes's historical novel about the Civil War was a ratings success, attracting more than a third of the television audience.

On November 12, 1985, just two days before the FCC approved the sale of ABC to Capital Cities Communications, Brandon Stoddard was named president of the network's entertainment division, which oversees all of ABC's programming other than news and sports. Although Stoddard had managed to lure large audiences to ABC's made-for-television movies and short series, the viewership for the network's regularly scheduled fare had been declining steadily during the 1980s, and by 1985 the network was mired in third place, behind NBC and CBS. Only two ABC series—*Dynasty* and *Who's the Boss?*—ranked among the top ten prime-time programs, while seven were among the ten lowest-rated. Shortly after assuming his new post, Stoddard acknowledged to reporters that his task would be a difficult one. "We'll concede this season," he said, as quoted in the New York *Daily News* (January 9, 1986). "Our process of rebuilding won't show up until next fall."

The 1986–87 season, however, proved to be frustrating for the network and for Stoddard. The centerpiece of the weekly schedule, a new situation comedy series starring Lucille Ball as a free-spirited grandmother, was canceled after only eight episodes had been aired. The heavily promoted crime dramas *Heart of the City* and *Sidekicks* left viewers cold, and *Starman*, a sci-fi adventure series about an extraterrestrial and his half-alien, half-human teenage son, failed to find its audience. Stoddard also had to negotiate the minefield of controversy surrounding *Amerika*, the network's ballyhooed, seven-part miniseries about life in the United States following a bloodless Soviet takeover. Production of the $40 million project was interrupted several times, primarily because of pressure from the Soviet government, which had warned ABC that its news operations in Moscow could be jeopardized unless the network abandoned the "deliberate act of psychological warfare." When *Amerika* was finally broadcast in February 1987, it was greeted with mixed reviews and general viewer apathy. At the close of the season, ABC was still in third place, but Stoddard could point to a few successes. The new situation comedies *Perfect Strangers* and *Head of the Class* had done well enough to warrant renewal for a second year, as had *Sledge Hammer!*, a spoof of violent detective movies that was extended on the strength of reviewers' favorable reaction to the show and its star, David Rasche.

The 1987–88 season marked the beginning of ABC's prime-time comeback. Although the highly touted variety series *Dolly*, starring Dolly Parton, failed to live up to its advance billing, the schedule included three hit shows: the situation comedy *Full House*; *Hooperman*, a comedy-drama featuring John Ritter as a police detective; and *thirtysomething*, which capped its first season by winning an Emmy Award for best dramatic series. In addition, the Emmy Award for best comedy series went to the ABC midseason replacement *The Wonder Years*, about growing up in the 1960s. By the end of the season, the ABC prime-time schedule was in second place, ahead of CBS, in the network ratings race.

The prime-time schedule remained largely intact for the 1988–89 season, which got off to a late start because of a twenty-two-week-long writers' strike that did not end until mid-August. One new series, *Roseanne*, a situation comedy showcasing the talents of the stand-up comedienne Roseanne Barr, made its debut on October 18 with the best first-time ratings received by an ABC comedy series in six and a half years. The schedule also included a number of miniseries and special programs, perhaps most notably *Roots: The Gift*, a holiday special in which Kunta Kinte leads the escape of a group of slaves, including a mother and her newborn child, from a plantation on Christmas Eve, and *War and Remembrance*, a thirty-hour continuation of *The Winds of War* that was broadcast in two multipart series, in November 1988 and in May 1989. Produced over a five-year period at a cost estimated to be in excess of $110 million, *War and Remembrance* was considered by most critics to be superior to its predecessor, and Tom Shales of the *Washington Post* went so far as to place it "in a class with *Roots*."

Tired of his high-pressure job and eager to return to active producing, Stoddard resigned his post as president of ABC Entertainment in March 1989 to become head of ABC's new in-house production unit. "I'm smiling for the first time in a long time . . . ," he told reporters after his resignation was made public, as quoted in the *Wall Street Journal* (March 22, 1989). "The job has an awful lot of frustration and not a lot of fun. When you have this job you remember each and every day. It's sort of like serving time in a prison." He was succeeded by Robert Iger, a vice-president of the ABC Television Network Group. In his new post, Stoddard is responsible for all network productions, including those of ABC Films, which produced *War and Remembrance* and the hit series *Moonlighting*.

Brandon Stoddard stands five feet, five inches tall and has gray hair and what one interviewer described as "little chipmunk cheeks." He dresses conservatively, preferring jackets and ties to the casual attire favored by many of his West Coast peers. A private man, Stoddard rarely gives interviews, and his circle of friends includes few show-business personalities. Since February 1984 he has been married to Mary Anne Dolan, a journalist. He has two daughters, Alexandra and Brooke, from an earlier marriage that ended in divorce. From May 1979 until he became ABC's programming chief in 1985, Stoddard also served as president of ABC Motion Pictures. In that position, he was responsible for the theatrical releases *Young Doctors in Love* (1982), *National Lampoon's Class Reunion* (1982), *Silkwood* (1983), which earned five Academy Award nominations, *The Flamingo Kid* (1984), the popular and critically acclaimed *Prizzi's Honor* (1985), and *Spacecamp* (1986).

References: Channels of Communication 5:27+ S-O '85 pors; Esquire 91:75+ F 13 '79 pors; N Y Times II p37 D 18 '83 por; Panorama p16+ Mr '80 pors; TV Guide p8+ Ap 25 '87 por; Wall St J p47 N 13 '85 por; Washington Post B p8 N 13 '85 por; Who's Who in America, 1988–89

Stoltenberg, Gerhard

Sept. 28(?) 1928– German politician. Address: b. Graurheindorferstrasse 108, 5300 Bonn, Federal Republic of Germany; h. Düsternbrooker Weg 70, D-3000, Kiel, Federal Republic of Germany

The phrase "always a bridesmaid, never the bride" might be used to describe the career of West Germany's new defense minister, Gerhard Stoltenberg. During his more than three decades of distinguished public service, the name of the imperturbable, silver-haired politician from Schleswig-Holstein has often been mentioned as a potential chancellor, but Stoltenberg has remained a politician's politician rather than a "man of the people."

Stoltenberg entered politics as a young man, becoming head of the Junge Union, or Young Conservatives, at the age of twenty-seven and winning election to the Bundestag, or Federal Assembly, at the age of twenty-nine. In 1966 he became, at thirty-eight, the youngest man in the cabinet of Chancellor Ludwig Erhard, who appointed him federal minister of scientific research. For the next four years, Stoltenberg presided over the rapid expansion of West Germany's computer, nuclear, and space industries. When the Social Democrats came to power in 1969, he returned to his native state and won election as its land prime minister for three successive terms.

After being mentioned as a possible candidate for the post of chancellor, Stoltenberg surprised political observers by agreeing to become finance minister in the government formed by his rival Helmut Kohl in October 1982. As finance minister, he slashed state spending and enacted a series of rigorous tax cuts. The British publication the

Economist (December 7, 1985) observed that, despite his fiscal austerity, Stoltenberg "achieved something rare among tough-minded finance ministers: popularity."

Stoltenberg's reputation as the "strong man" of Kohl's cabinet undoubtedly influenced the beleaguered chancellor's decision to move him to the political "hot seat" in the defense ministry in April 1989. Only a month after Stoltenberg moved into defense, Bonn precipitated a major crisis in NATO by requesting that the United States begin negotiating for the removal of all short-range nuclear weapons in Europe, almost all of which are based on West German soil. Stoltenberg pursued an anxious few weeks of shuttle diplomacy that finally led to a compromise agreement at NATO's fortieth anniversary meeting, in Brussels, Belgium in May 1989. "Wherever intellectual lucidity, hard work, and clear judgment are required, Stoltenberg can be relied on to perform brilliantly," Kurt Becker wrote in *Die Zeit*. "On the other hand, he has no trace of charisma or even talent for moving speeches or fascinating presentation of ideas."

Gerhard Stoltenberg was born on September 28, 1928 in the Baltic port of Kiel. (*International Who's Who* gives September 29 as the day of his birth.) His father, Paul, was a Protestant clergyman; his mother, Christine, was a schoolteacher. Growing up in a modest home, Stoltenberg acquired the characteristic traits of his native region—namely, caution and cool-headedness. "Those who know him well say North German thrift is probably still a homespun root of some of his economic theory," John Tagliabue observed in the *New York Times* (September 25, 1983).

After attending the Grammar School at Bad Oldesloe, Stoltenberg studied history, social sciences, and philosophy at Kiel University, where he completed his work on a Ph.D. degree in history in 1954. While a graduate student, he visited the United States, spending two months in Philadelphia and two months touring the South and Far West. During that trip, he stayed for ten days at Harvard University, where he sat in on classes taught by McGeorge Bundy and Arthur Schlesinger Jr., and he met Henry A. Kissinger, who edited a journal to which the young German had contributed an article.

After completing his doctorate, Stoltenberg became a research assistant at Kiel University and worked on his *Habilitation*, a piece of original research leading to a university post. On its completion, in 1960, he was appointed a lecturer in modern history. From 1955 to 1961 he served as chairman of the Christian Democrats' youth group, the Junge Union, and got to know the circle of politicians around Chancellor Konrad Adenauer. In 1957 he won election to the Bundestag, where he worked on several budget committees and expanded his knowledge of economic policy.

After spending five years as a university lecturer, Stoltenberg left academic life in 1965 to take an executive position with the Krupp steel conglomerate as an adviser on economic trends, but within a few months he left Krupp to become minister of scientific research in the cabinet of Chancellor Ludwig Erhard. During his four years as science minister, Stoltenberg oversaw a massive restructuring of scientific research and industrial capacity in order to make West Germany more competitive economically with the United States.

During his first year as science minister, Stoltenberg was given a budget increase of 20 percent to reduce West German dependence on American computers and to consolidate its strength in the nuclear reactor industry. He negotiated important agreements with the United States to acquire essential nuclear materials and signed an agreement with France to construct jointly a powerful research reactor in Grenoble. The German space program underwent an even more dramatic expansion during Stoltenberg's term as science minister. In 1967 he announced cabinet approval of a five-year program to develop West Germany's capacity to produce reentry and reusable boosters, electronic propulsion devices, and hybrid rocket boosters. To carry out that plan, he supervised the merging of three research institutes and the forging of new partnerships between the research and industrial sectors, particularly in aviation. His ultimate goal, he told the press, was to develop projects "that provide a rapid spinoff of technical knowledge for industry and the economy."

When, in 1969, the Social Democrats, led by Willy Brandt, defeated the CDU, Stoltenberg returned to Schleswig-Holstein, where he made that province into a CDU stronghold over the next decade. In 1971 he won election as its land prime minister and retained that post through two more elections. While prime minister, he developed his credo of the "social market economy," which he has described as "competition, but under clear rules of the game. A free market but one with social balance."

With unemployment rates running at 9 percent, and with strong competition from the Left, Stoltenberg never enjoyed a huge margin of electoral support, and, in the spring of 1975, his chances to become shadow chancellor were dashed by an election he won by only a single vote. Still, Stoltenberg managed to stay in power and to avoid "sinking into comfortable obscurity in high office," according to Kurt Becker of *Die Zeit.*

Throughout his years in Schleswig-Holstein, Stoltenberg maintained a high profile in national politics. In 1969 he became a federal vice-chairman of the CDU and served as a party spokesman on economic, financial, and energy issues. Named finance minister in 1979, he vehemently attacked the reckless state spending of the SDP. In 1980 and 1982 his name frequently surfaced as a possible candidate for chancellor, but it was Helmut Kohl who led the CDU to victory in October 1982 and formed a new coalition government with the Christian Social Union and the Free Democratic party. Much to some observers' surprise, Kohl asked his archrival Stoltenberg to become finance minister. The choice was a shrewd one, given the

serious economic problems that he faced and Kohl's relative lack of economic experience. The economy was stagnant, and both the federal debt and the unemployment rate were skyrocketing.

In responding to the economic crisis, Stoltenberg quickly overshadowed the minister of economics, Otto Lambsdorff, and established himself as the chief architect of Bonn's economic policy. He first brought state spending under control by slashing social programs, industrial subsidies, and defense spending. He also achieved a modest, two-stage reduction in West German income taxes, which are among the highest in Europe, to stimulate the economy. To raise revenues, he proposed to sell off government shares in Volkswagen, Veba (a chemicals conglomerate), and Lufthansa.

Under Stoltenberg's vigilance, the West German economy revived impressively while experiencing a low rate of inflation, about 2 percent. The growth rate, which had posted a 0.2–1 percent decline in the last two years of the Brandt regime, rose to a healthy 2.5 percent in 1985 and an astounding 3.9 percent in 1988. The federal budget deficit declined from 4 percent of the GNP in 1981 to 1.5 percent in 1985. Unfortunately, unemployment in West Germany remained high, at 9 percent.

The economic revival only increased pressure on Stoltenberg to relax the restraints of his austere financial program. When various interest groups urged him to restore social programs and subsidies, his stubborn refusal caused him problems even with his own cabinet colleagues, especially with the employment minister, Norbert Blüm. Stoltenberg's plans to privatize Lufthansa met with stiff resistance from the Bavarian prime minister, Franz Josef Strauss, to whom he seemed to have a "chief clerk's mentality." Despite such criticisms, Stoltenberg maintained such a high level of popular approval that public opinion polls taken in the fall of 1985 showed him to be the most respected leader in the coalition government, even more highly regarded than Chancellor Kohl.

Stoltenberg showed a similar resolve in resisting foreign pressures to compromise his plan for a long-term economic recovery. As the West German economy boomed, the United States put pressure on Bonn to cut taxes even more drastically to stimulate consumer purchasing and redress its unfavorable balance of imports and exports. But Stoltenberg refused to accelerate the tax cuts planned for 1986 and 1988, insisting that his country would not reflate its economy to become the "locomotive" of the international market.

Although firm in his commitment to his economic principles, Stoltenberg also showed that he could compromise and negotiate when necessary. Soon after taking office, he helped to craft an agreement among the five chief creditor nations—the United States, Great Britain, France, Japan, and West Germany—to increase the emergency funds of the International Monetary Fund, thus forestalling loan defaults and economic collapse among many heavily indebted developing nations.

In March 1983 Stoltenberg played a crucial role at a meeting of the eight Common Market finance ministers to negotiate new currency values. Faced with massive government spending programs and a flagging economy, the French refused to devalue the franc to as low a point as Bonn wanted; Jacques Delors, the French minister, threatened to withdraw his country from the European Monetary System unless he got his way. After days of tense negotiation, the ministers reached a compromise: the West Germans agreed to revalue the mark up by 5.5 percent, and the French devalued the franc by 2.5 percent, 2.3 percent less than the Germans had sought. Agreeing that Stoltenberg had played a key role in hammering out the compromise, his fellow ministers accorded a rare standing ovation at the end of the meeting to "the man who had calmly, deftly steered Europe away from a financial debacle," in the words of a *New York Times* (September 25, 1983) reporter.

Because political analysts interpreted the compromise as a major concession by Bonn, Stoltenberg at first faced heavy criticism from politicians and industrialists in his own country. But a few days later, the magnitude of the French concessions became clear when the Mitterrand government announced a radical new austerity program designed to bring its economy in line with West German policy. Stoltenberg, it was clear, had brought about a considerable concession from the French Socialists.

Stoltenberg's tenure as finance minister of West Germany was not without its embarrassments and setbacks, however. He drew sharp criticism, for example, in 1985 for granting a generous subsidy to farmers, a lapse from his usually frugal policies that no doubt reflected his roots in rural Schleswig-Holstein. Anxious to balance tax cuts with additional revenues, he championed a highly controversial withholding tax on capital savings, which proved to be widely unpopular. Stung by continued denunciations from the administrations of Ronald Reagan and Margaret Thatcher for his tight fiscal policy, Stoltenberg finally agreed in 1987 to adopt some mild "pump-priming" measures to stimulate the German economy, among them reductions in the central bank's discount rates, an investment incentive program, and a modest increase in the budget deficit to allow more social spending.

Despite his sometimes unpopular fiscal stands, Stoltenberg held the "unchallenged role of superstar" in the Kohl cabinet. He remained on good terms with the chancellor, who rightly realized how much his own success depended on the finance minister's skillful handling of the economy. Thus, as Kohl's troubles deepened in 1988, public discontent with domestic and foreign-policy issues cut deeply into his popular support, the chancellor made Stoltenberg the centerpiece of a dramatic, desperate cabinet shuffle. He moved the experienced, coolheaded Stoltenberg from a relatively strong sector, the economy, to the troubled defense ministry, replacing the highly unpopular

defense minister, Rupert Scholz. Stoltenberg immediately became embroiled in a major crisis over NATO policy that had been brewing for years. The agreement between the United States and the Soviet Union to remove intermediate-range nuclear weapons from Europe had left only NATO's short-range missiles in place, almost all of them based in West Germany. The United States and Great Britain argued in favor of modernizing the system to preserve the alliance's "flexible response" capabilities, but West Germany resented the fact that it alone had to bear the brunt of the nuclear system. Bonn found itself caught between two conflicting pressures: NATO's demands for loyalty and the growing antinuclear sentiments of West German voters.

Soon after Stoltenberg became defense minister, the Bonn government issued a formal request that the United States begin negotiating immediately to remove the short-range nuclear weapons from West German soil. Both the United States and Great Britain were furious at the request. The United States secretary of defense Richard Cheney denounced it as a "dangerous threat," and another American official characterized the West German move as "grandstanding by a panic-stricken government."

There followed a period of feverish shuttle diplomacy involving both Gerhard Stoltenberg and the West German foreign minister, Hans-Dietrich Genscher. Stoltenberg made two trips to Washington, D.C., in May 1989, in an effort to avert a major rift at the upcoming NATO meeting in Brussels, Belgium. He proposed that the United States link negotiations on the short-range missiles to Soviet reductions in conventional arms and that a high-level policy group be formed to study the issue. Only a week before the Brussels meeting, the two sides still seemed far apart, but President George Bush arrived at the NATO conference with a surprise proposal to reduce conventional arms in Europe, thus paving the way for a compromise. After some twelve hours of intense negotiation, the NATO allies reached a compromise. The United States agreed that, once the conventional arms reduction was agreed upon, it would then negotiate to reduce the short-range nuclear missiles.

Having survived that crisis, West Germany's new defense minister still faced serious problems, for budget-cutting had left the German military weakened and discontented, and the defense establishment seemed hardly likely to approve of the politically motivated appointment of Stoltenberg to oversee their affairs. Stoltenberg also needed to decide what to do about further deferments of an unpopular extension of military service, which had been voted years ago but never enacted. Analysts expected Stoltenberg to approach his difficult new job with the levelheaded style that has been his political trademark. A former aide described him to a reporter from the *New York Times* (September 25, 1983) as "very cool, very disciplined, well-behaved, restrained to the point of monotony. He's like a Gregorian chant."

Gerhard Stoltenberg is a self-effacing man who does not flaunt his ambition. John Tagliabue described him as "a driven worker and voracious reader who devours facts and figures at an extraordinary rate." He begins his day by reading a big stack of newspapers and news magazines. His English is excellent. "Silver-haired, straight-backed, and hardworking, he looks born to rule," according to a writer for the *Economist* (December 7, 1985). Stoltenberg's fair coloring gives him a youthful look. He is noted for his thriftiness. An aide recalls trying to get him to buy a new suit, but, after taking one look at the price tags, he declined. Stoltenberg's "vices" include red wine, French cuisine, and postprandial cigars.

Gerhard Stoltenberg and his wife, the former Margot Rann, whom he married in 1958, have two children, Susanne and Klaus. They have homes in Kiel and in Bonn, in addition to a country place on the Baltic coast. Stoltenberg enjoys skiing in the winter and golfing in the summer, and he also pursues a love of literature, music, and painting in his leisure moments. He has written four scholarly books, including *Wissenschaft-Hochschule-Politik* (1968) and *Staat und Wissenschaft* (1969). His honors include the Grand Federation Cross of Merit and an honorary doctor's degree from the Universidad de Los Andes in Bogotá, Colombia.

References: Economist 297:76+ D 7 '85 por; German Tribune p7 Ja 1 '84 por, p4 Ag 27 '89 por; N Y Times F p6 S 25 '83 por; International Who's Who, 1989-90; Who's Who in Germany (1988)

Straub, Peter

Mar. 2, 1943– Writer. Address: c/o E. P. Dutton, 2 Park Ave., New York, N.Y. 10016

One of the world's most commercially successful writers of horror fiction, Peter Straub has avowed that he has a messianic desire to elevate the standards of the horror novel, and, in the opinion of most critics, he has achieved just that. Straub began writing in the horror genre after his first novel, *Marriages* (1973), a story of romantic entanglements, failed to attract a large readership or win critical acclaim. Searching for a genre in which his chances for popular success would be enhanced, Straub settled on horror fiction. His first bestseller was *Ghost Story* (1979). *The Talisman* (1984), written in collaboration with Stephen King, was a landmark novel that became the fastest-selling book in publishing history and brought its two authors one of the most profitable publishing contracts ever awarded.

Straub's narrative skill and the inspiration he derives from Edgar Allan Poe, Nathaniel Hawthorne, and other masters of the supernatural has been much commented upon by critics. Even when they are repelled, readers admire his graphic and manipulative literary technique. His best work, in the opinion of Patricia L. Skarda, writing in the *Dictionary of Literary Biography: 1984*, "focuses on private experiences on the margin where nature and supernature meet, where reality converges with dream, where writing leaves off and the imagination takes over." Straub's stories, Patricia L. Skarda continues, depict "the horrors of guilt in characters who explore the past to understand the present." Straub himself has summed up his fiction with the following explanation: "I want readers to feel as if they've left the real world behind just a little bit, but are still buoyed up and confident, as if dreaming. I want them left standing in midair with a lot of peculiar visions in their heads. . . . I write these kinds of books because they satisfy something in me—they let me explore personal problems and visions. To me, it's like doing any other kind of art—like playing a jazz solo, or composing a symphony or writing a long poem."

Peter Francis Straub was born in Milwaukee, Wisconsin on March 2, 1943, the son of Gordon Anthony Straub and Elvena (Nilsestuen) Straub. A gifted child, he taught himself to read when he was about five. "As a kid, I read everything under the sun, from adult books to the backs of breakfast cereal boxes," he recalled to Joseph McLellan of the *Washington Post* (February 16, 1981). But except for horror comics, of which his parents disapproved, supernatural fiction held no particular fascination for him. Straub also displayed an early affinity for writing, and in grade school his homework assignments were so well written that his teachers thought his father had done them.

During his teenage years, Straub attended the exclusive Milwaukee Country Day School. There, and later at the University of Wisconsin in Madison, from which he graduated in 1965 with a B.A. degree in English, Straub was interested in both medicine and writing. "I wanted to be a doctor—a literary doctor like William Carlos Williams," Straub told Joseph Barbato during an interview for *Publishers Weekly* (January 28, 1983), referring to the late American poet and physician. "Then reality intervened. I discovered I had no gift for science and became an English major." In 1966 he received a master's degree from Columbia University, after submitting a thesis on Williams. Still feeling a desire to write, but not knowing what he wanted to write about, Straub became a teacher in the English department of his high school alma mater, the Milwaukee Country Day School.

Fearful that he might become a "sodden Mr. Chips," Straub left teaching after three years. "I grew bored," he explained to Joseph Barbato. "If I'd stayed, I'd have become a gravy-stained old teacher with a beat-up car and an alcohol problem. It seemed like a kind of death, and I had to escape." Later that year, 1969, Straub moved to Ireland, hoping to obtain a Ph.D. degree in literature at University College in Dublin, where he studied under Denis Donoghue, the renowned critic of English and American literature. Immersing himself in poetry, he began a thesis on Victorian literature and D. H. Lawrence and published two books of poems from that period, *Ishmael* and *Open Air*, in 1972. During his second year in Dublin, an urge to write fiction also took hold of him. "I had always thought of myself as a novelist, although I had not written a novel," he related to Joseph McLellan. "I could feel fiction growing inside me, characters and situations forming themselves in my mind as I walked down the street." In the summer of 1972, Straub abandoned his doctoral studies and began a novel, *Marriages*, which was published in 1973, first in England and then in the United States.

The story of a midwestern businessman living in London and conducting an adulterous affair with a mysterious, unnamed Englishwoman, *Marriages* owes a literary debt to Henry James, since it describes an American's encounter with British manners. Not a popular success, *Marriages* received mixed, though mostly negative, reviews. P. J. Earl of *Best Sellers* (May 1, 1973) noted that Straub "spices his tale with subtle wit and shows good insight into human nature" but added that since he found the plot "rather boring and ordinary," he could not recommend the novel. In a similar vein, Dorothy Nyren of the *Library Journal* (April 15, 1973) praised Straub for his adroit sentence construction, yet she concluded that "a good deal more is needed to make this novel worth reading." A more positive notice came from a contributor to the *Times Literary Supplement* (March 23, 1973), who commended Straub for having a "fine sense of the weight of words."

Moving to the Crouch End section of London following the publication of *Marriages*, Straub began writing short fiction for British women's magazines, but his stories were often rejected on the grounds of being "too literary" for the popular market. While Straub was rewriting his second novel, *Under Venus*, which was eventually published in 1984, his literary agent noted the flair for tension-fraught narrative he had displayed in *Marriages* and suggested that he write a Gothic novel instead. He began jotting down notes for the projected novel during walks near his home. "I did that for a month. Then my notes began to scare me, and I knew I had something," he recalled to Joseph McLellan. The publication of the novel *Julia* in 1975 not only signaled the beginning of Peter Straub's career as a writer of horror fiction but also enabled him to keep his head above water financially, following the failure of *Marriages*.

Julia begins with a horripilating scene: Julia and her husband, a lawyer named Magnus Lofting, performing an unsuccessful tracheotomy on their daughter, Kate, who is choking to death at the breakfast table. Ridden by guilt, Julia leaves her overbearing husband and moves into an old house, where she is haunted by the evil ghost of nine-year-old Olivia, the late daughter of Magnus and his first wife. Conceding that "there is an audience for this type of novel," M. G. Schulman, writing in *Library Journal* (October 15, 1975), nonetheless found the horror scenes "deliberately nauseating" and the novel's triumphantly evil dénouement "unpleasant." But Valentine Cunningham in the *New Statesman* (February 27, 1976) called *Julia* an "extraordinarily gripping and tantalising read . . . , for almost anything becomes believable under the novelist's stunning gothic manipulations." A film, *The Haunting of Julia*, was adapted from Straub's novel and released in 1977. Since he had had nothing to do with the script, Straub did not share in the responsibility for the film's critical and box-office failure.

In addition to enabling Straub to earn a living as a writer, *Julia* piqued his interest in horror fiction. "The more I thought about it, the more I looked into it, and the more I worked away at it, the more excitement and possibility I saw in it," Straub told Michael Schumacher during an interview for *Writer's Digest* (January 1985). "I began to see it as a sort of strange branch of surrealism, in which dreamlike things mingle with the stuff of ordinary, realistic novels." Straub's next book, *If You Could See Me Now* (1977), merged elements of the author's academic past with his newly found interest in horror fiction. Its protagonist, Miles Teagarden, is an East Coast academic who is greeted with mysterious silence following his return to the Wisconsin farm community in which he grew up and which has been the site of a recent series of murders. Reviewing *If You Could See Me Now* in the *Spectator* (July 9, 1977), the critic Peter Ackroyd noted that it "quite carefully evokes the real world of everyday folk, while at the same time intimating—through dreams, metaphors and analogies—

the existence of a superior reality which can occasionally be understood." "In a place where everyone is either brutally insane or explicitly nasty, Miles preserves a paradoxical equanimity," Jonathan Keates commented in the *New Statesman* (June 24, 1977). "Crisp, classy, bugaboo, this, full of neatly managed understatements and chillingly calculated surprises."

It was a jacket blurb that Stephen King wrote for *Julia* that first made Straub aware of the best-selling author of such horror fiction blockbusters as *Carrie* and *Salem's Lot*. After being "bowled over" by the latter book, Straub began a correspondence with King. When the two writers met for the first time, in London in 1977, they hit it off immediately and eventually became close friends. King's publishing success, as well as his conviction that horror fiction could be unbridled and at the same time acceptable, impressed Straub. "Steve showed me that the rules—the idea that you should hint at something but must break off before you actually present the reader with it—don't apply," Straub told Joseph Barbato. "That you could show the thing itself—the terrifying, awful, perhaps cornball thing itself, and as long as you did it in big, primary colors, and with all the conviction you could summon up, the reader would be so astonished that he would experience delight."

Thus inspired, and moved by a desire "to take the old standards and explode them, to make them more gorgeous, to work from the real to the unreal and still make the narrative exciting," as he explained to Thomas Lask of the *New York Times* (April 27, 1979), Straub wrote *Ghost Story* (1979), his first bestseller. Set in the fictional upstate New York town of Milburn, an isolated, snowbound village, the novel tells the story of five town elders who gather regularly to swap ghost stories until they are murdered, one by one. A novelist then arrives to confront the evil force that is causing all the havoc. According to Patricia L. Skarda, "*Ghost Story* builds on the conventions of horror fiction with ghosts, possessions, demonic bargains, werewolves, vampires, clairvoyance, telepathy, and literally murderous guilt." While some critics found Straub's prose to be excessively empurpled or were put off by the novel's visceral detail, most of them agreed with Gene Lyons of the *New York Times Book Review* (April 8, 1979), who conceded that *Ghost Story* was "a quite sophisticated literary entertainment."

Ghost Story was also, as Lyons put it, "a hit at the checkout counter," and by 1981, more than two million copies of the paperback edition had been sold. Straub received $80,000 as a publisher's advance, $125,000 from the Book-of-the-Month Club, $792,000 for paperback rights, and additional money for film rights. The motion picture adaptation of *Ghost Story*, released in 1981 and starring Fred Astaire and Melvyn Douglas, was, like the film version of *Julia* before it, both a critical and commercial failure, but Straub again was not involved in the project. He returned to the United States following the publication of *Ghost Story*, and, with

earnings from the novel, purchased a ninety-year-old Victorian mansion in Westport, Connecticut.

Straub's next effort, *Shadowland* (1980), is about the friendship between two youths at an Arizona prep school and their battle against one of the boy's uncles, a master magician who tries to kill them both. The novel disappointed those readers and critics who expected Straub's follow-up to *Ghost Story* to be equally ghoulish, but instead, as Patricia L. Skarda observed, Straub had "turned to the mysteries of magic and fairy tales in a land of shadows." Judy Cooke of the *New Statesman* (April 17, 1981) termed *Shadowland* "not an easy read, but a compulsive one."

In *Floating Dragon* (1983), Straub tried to take horror fiction to new heights. As he explained to Joseph Barbato, "I wanted a really gaudy fireworks display—stuff that would make the reader's jaw drop open and make him say, 'I can't believe I'm reading this.'" Set in affluent Hampstead, Connecticut, the novel incorporates a realistic disaster—a leak of poisonous gas from a local chemical plant—into a matrix of supernatural horror. Alan Bold of the *Times Literary Supplement* (March 11, 1983) wrote that reading *Floating Dragon* requires "a strong stomach" because it contains "sickening scenes of violence and hallucination with bodies being mutilated, insects assaulting the dying and the dead, and bats and dragons hovering malevolently in the air." But he also hailed *Floating Dragon* as "a simple moral tale . . . sustained with great skill as the battle between good and evil is impressively, if agonizingly, stretched over the disturbingly supernatural plot."

Straub's next book, *The Talisman* (1984), was written in collaboration with Stephen King. The idea for a joint novel was hatched late one night in 1978 at Straub's house in London, after the two cronies, according to Straub, had consumed "about a million beers." Although contract commitments prevented them from beginning the novel immediately, they continued to discuss the project in subsequent visits to each other's homes. In 1982 they drafted the opening chapters at Straub's house in Westport and then, by using word processors linked by telephones, wrote alternate sections, completing the project in two years. Both writers insisted that the collaboration went smoothly, even when one of them edited out a passage that the other had written.

A fantasy novel full of allusions to other works, including *Alice in Wonderland, The Wizard of Oz,* and *Huckleberry Finn, The Talisman* describes twelve-year-old Jack Sawyer's coast-to-coast quest for a magical cure for his mother's cancer. Along the way, he discovers "The Territories," a medieval, supernatural reflection of society, which he must save from the bloody machinations of the evil pretender to its throne. Although the figures are unavailable, *The Talisman* reportedly netted Straub and King one of the most lucrative contracts in publishing history. With a record-breaking $550,000 advertising budget—most of it for television commercials on MTV, the music-video channel—*The Talisman* became the fastest-selling book in publishing history, selling more than one million copies in its first ten weeks in bookstores. Straub and King made $1.50 each on every $18.95 book sold.

The Talisman was greeted with mixed reviews. In trying to distinguish the contributions of each collaborator, most critics usually concluded that King had written the fast-moving action sequences and Straub, the more literary passages. One such critic, Christopher Lehmann-Haupt of the *New York Times* (November 8, 1984), complained that the book "inherited the worst traits" of each author: from King, an "affinity for pop-cult teen-age junk" and a "penchant for the endless repetition of cryptic, italicized phrases"; and from Straub, "a literary self-consciousness, an almost ink-stained scholarliness, and an over-fascination with complicated magic effects." Straub, who, like King, insisted that determining which author wrote which section was impossible, bridled at that suggestion, telling Michael Small in *People* (January 28, 1985) that he was "fed up with being described as some kind of embalmed mandarin who thinks in polysyllabic orotund sentences." At least two reviewers, however, praised *The Talisman*. Susan L. Smithers of *Student Library Journal* (January 1985) described the book as "a masterful blend of fantasy and horror with fine characterization, a fast pace and an engrossing and suspenseful plot." And a critic for the *Library Journal* (November 1, 1984) credited it with being "a fiery, powerful jewel," in which "King's grasp of the beauty of horror in the commonplace meshes wonderfully with Peter Straub's classic elegance."

The commercial success of *The Talisman* allowed Straub, later in 1984, to publish a three-novel collection entitled *Wild Animals*. The triptych included the previously published novels *Julia* and *If You Could See Me Now* and the never-before-published *Under Venus*, the novel that Straub had foregone early in his career in order to concentrate on horror fiction. *Under Venus* deals with a young American composer who, after living for a time in Europe, returns to his hometown in Wisconsin to conduct a concert and there encounters family and romantic problems. Reviewing the trio of novels in the *New York Times* (March 24, 1985), Janice Eidus pronounced *Under Venus* "an ambitious and admirable effort" but faulted its "one-dimensional" female characters. The collection as a whole, Eidus wrote, suggests "the ideal Peter Straub novel—a lyrical, innovative blend of the realistic and the supernatural."

With the financial success of *The Talisman* behind him, Straub next addressed himself to a more serious subject, the aftermath of the Vietnam War. *Koko* (1988) recounts the efforts of a group of Vietnam veterans to find and "save" a member of their platoon, who, fifteen years after the end of American involvement in the war, is on a murderous rampage through Southeast Asia. A reviewer for *Publishers Weekly* (August 12, 1988) called *Koko* Straub's "most gripping, most hallucinogenic thrill-

er to date," but Douglas Balz, writing in the *Chicago Tribune* (October 2, 1988), found the story "too close to the truth to be make-believe and never well-enough imagined to be true." Balz praised only two chapters near the end of the novel in which the veterans, closing in on the killer, pay a visit to Milwaukee, the author's hometown. "In those sixty pages," Balz wrote, "Straub's writing matches his vision, but in a book of this size, it is too little, too late."

A round-faced, balding man who wears dark-rimmed glasses, Peter Straub likes stylish clothes, gourmet food, and other appurtenances of affluence, but otherwise leads a conventional, exurban life. He and his wife, the former Susan Bitker, were married in 1966 and have two children, Benjamin and Emma. Straub usually begins writing at about ten in the morning, takes a two-hour lunch break, and then continues writing until about six. "I work a lazy businessman's day, about five hours starting when the errands are done and ending with the evening news," he explained to Jennifer Dunning of the *New York Times Book Review* (May 20, 1979). He used to write in pencil in large manuscript books but now employs a word processor.

Straub spends at least six months "brooding" about a topic for a book and entering his ideas into notebooks before he actually begins writing. "When I'm really tired of that, and I can no longer postpone writing the first sentence, I start writing," he told Michael Schumacher. He believes his horror novels express secret fears. "In real life, terror is unnerving, dehumanizing, but it may be therapeutic when you turn it into fiction," he said during his interview with Joseph McLellan. Admittedly superstitious, Straub refuses to walk under ladders or to light three cigarettes on one match. Although he is satisfied with his reputation as a genre writer, his real commitment is still to literature, to the "love of just writing the language. A delight in making sentences." Besides literature, his great passion is jazz. He always listens to jazz while writing, and his collection of albums numbers in the hundreds. Among his favorite artists are Bix Beiderbecke, John Coltrane, Bill Evans, Hank Jones, Phil Woods, and Zoot Sims. Straub's latest work, "Mystery," was scheduled to be published in January 1990.

References: Pub W 223:39+ Ja 28 '83 por; Washington Post B p1+ F 16 '81 por, C p1+ N 27 '84 pors; Contemporary Authors vols 85–88 (1980); Dictionary of Literary Biography Yearbook: 1984; Who's Who in America, 1988–89

Sullivan, Louis W(ade)

Nov. 3, 1933– United States Secretary of Health and Human Services. Address: Dept. of Health and Human Services, 200 Independence Ave., S.W., Washington, D.C. 20201

The highest-ranking black in the administration of President George Bush and the only black in his cabinet, Dr. Louis W. Sullivan presides over the Department of Health and Human Services and its $400 billion annual budget, the largest of any federal agency. Unlike most of Bush's top-level appointees, Sullivan has had no previous government experience. His appointment proved to be highly controversial after he made apparently contradictory statements about his views on abortion. Just before his nomination, Sullivan said in an interview that he supported a woman's right to have an abortion, but he quickly qualified his stance by explaining that he favored the procedure only in cases of rape, incest, or when the mother's life is endangered. Then, after being nominated by Bush, he told several members of Congress that he advocated overturning the Supreme Court's 1973 *Roe v. Wade* decision, which legalized abortion, only to reverse himself again several days later by announcing that he opposed overturning that landmark ruling. A hematologist who specializes in the treatment of blood disorders caused by vitamin deficiencies, Dr. Sullivan was one of the founders and the first dean of the Morehouse School of Medicine in Atlanta, Georgia. Among the pressing problems that he will have to address in his new position are welfare reform, the soaring cost of medical care, and the AIDS epidemic.

Louis Wade Sullivan was born in Atlanta, Georgia on November 3, 1933, the younger of the two sons of Walter Wade Sullivan, an undertaker, and Lubirda Elizabeth (Priester) Sullivan, a teacher. In his early childhood, the family moved to rural Blakely, Georgia, but, because educational opportunities for blacks were limited there, Louis and his brother, Walter, who is now a chemist and an administrator at the Morehouse School of Medicine, were sent back to Atlanta, where they lived with family friends and attended public schools. Louis Sullivan's parents founded the Blakely chapter of the National Association for the Advancement of Colored People, and his father was once shot and wounded for his activism. "They stayed in that little town for twenty more years to prove a point: that whites couldn't run them out," Walter Sullivan recalled to Ronald Smothers of the *New York Times* (December 23, 1988).

Louis Sullivan graduated magna cum laude from Morehouse College in 1954 and then won a scholarship to Boston University Medical School, from which he graduated cum laude in 1958 as the only black member of his class. After completing his internship and residency at New York Hospital–Cornell Medical Center in New York City, Sullivan obtained, in 1960, a fellowship in pathology at Massachusetts General Hospital in Boston. The following year he received a research fellowship at Thorndike Memorial Laboratory, Harvard University Medical School. In 1963 Sullivan was named an instructor of medicine at the Harvard Medical School. A year later he became an assistant professor of medicine at the New Jersey College of Medicine, remaining in that position until 1966, when he returned to Boston University as an assistant professor of medicine at the medical school and co-director of hematology at the university medical center. Sullivan was promoted to associate professor of medicine in 1968 and to professor of medicine and physiology in 1974.

Sullivan had hoped to become a department chairman at an established medical school by the age of forty-five. By 1975, when he was forty-two, he had, together with a group of other Morehouse College alumni, begun plans to create a new Morehouse-affiliated medical school, which would train physicians to serve in the inner cities and in the rural South, where doctors are scarce. The school got its start in 1978 as a two-year program that prepared students to attend accredited medical schools. Sullivan was appointed dean, and he retained that position when, in 1981, the program became the Morehouse School of Medicine, a fully accredited, four-year institution, independent of Morehouse College. The Morehouse School of Medicine is one of only three predominantly black medical schools in the United States, along with Meharry Medical College in Nashville, Tennessee and Howard University Medical School in Washington, D.C.

Much of Sullivan's early work as dean involved soliciting funds for his fledgling school, which, during its first year of operation, held classes in trailers. Among the sources Sullivan appealed to for help were the United States Congress, the Georgia legislature, the Fulton County Commission, the Atlanta City Council, Atlanta business and community leaders, and the rural constituents of conservative white state legislators. As one of the founders of the National Association of Minority Medical Educators, he criticized the Reagan administration's slashes in federal aid to education, but he nevertheless won sizable federal research grants for his school.

Sullivan's peers agreed that his strong persuasive skills were important factors in the success of his fund-raising campaign. "When government agencies deal with black institutions, they have to have confidence in the individuals, because they don't have confidence in the institutions," Prince Rivers, the provost of largely black Atlanta University, told Ronald Smothers. "Lou Sullivan, as a researcher and scholar, is in a class by himself, and he was able to build that confidence." Dr. James Kaufmann, the head of the policymaking committee of the Georgia Medical Association, told Smothers that Dr. Sullivan's ability to "persuade people is uncanny."

During Sullivan's tenure, the Morehouse School of Medicine was especially active in researching health problems that most commonly afflict minorities, such as sickle-cell anemia, hypertension, and certain forms of cancer. Morehouse officials point with pride to the fact that, since the school was established, about 89 percent of its students have passed second-year national examinations and 99 percent have passed fourth-year exams.

Sullivan first met George Bush in 1982, when he invited the then vice-president to dedicate the first building at the Morehouse School of Medicine. Later that year, he accompanied George and Barbara Bush on a state visit to seven African countries. In 1983 Mrs. Bush was appointed to the medical school's board of trustees, and she has spoken in the school's behalf at more than a dozen fund-raising luncheons. Sullivan delivered a speech introducing Mrs. Bush at the Republican National Convention in August 1988, and, after her husband was elected president in November, she became Sullivan's most ardent supporter for the Department of Health and Human Services position.

The controversy over Sullivan's nomination to head the Department of Health and Human Services began around December 15, when the National Right to Life Committee, a leading anti-abortion group, wrote to Bush, expressing strenuous opposition to the expected appointment. According to that letter, "Nomination of a secretary of health and human services who does not have solid pro-life credentials would produce severe and long-lasting disappointment among hundreds of thousands of pro-life activists who worked hard for the Bush-Quayle ticket. Based on our own inquiries into Dr. Sullivan's background . . . it appears that he is, at best, uninterested and uninformed on the issues of concern to us, and, at worst, unsympathetic." The situation was exacerbated by the appearance in the December 18 edition of the *Atlanta Journal and Constitution* of an interview in which Sullivan was paraphrased as saying that he supported a woman's right to have an abortion, although he opposed federal funding for abortions. In a second interview, which appeared in the same paper a day later, Sullivan said that he believed "there should be that right" to an abortion, "and indeed that is the law as it stands now." But he added, "At the same time, I am aware of the fact that the president-elect feels that that should not be the case, and I would have to, as his secretary, should I be appointed, carry out his policies."

Sullivan's comments further inflamed anti-abortion activists, and speculation arose that Bush might not proceed with the nomination as planned. In a letter to the same Atlanta newspaper, dated December 18 and released to the press two days later, Sullivan reversed his position, stating that he opposed abortion except in cases of rape, incest, or protection of the life of the mother. "I am opposed to federal funding for abortion except when the life of the mother is endangered," he added.

Sullivan's standing among antiabortionists improved somewhat following a five-hour meeting on December 21 with two leading congressional opponents of abortion, Senator Orrin G. Hatch of Utah and Congressman Vin Weber of Minnesota. "I have been convinced . . . that his [Sullivan's] position on the pro-life issue is fully consistent with Vice-President Bush's," said Weber after the meeting, as quoted in *Congressional Quarterly* (December 24, 1988). On December 22 Bush officially nominated Sullivan to be secretary of health and human services, telling reporters that the nominee had "great credentials in the black community" and was "an outstanding leader in the health community." Sullivan then restated the position on abortion he had taken in the letter to the *Atlanta Journal and Constitution*. "This position is the same as that of President-elect Bush, with whom I agree completely," he said.

A month later, Sullivan's views on abortion again made him the center of controversy. According to a story in the *New York Times* (January 24, 1989), the secretary-designate, during a visit to Capitol Hill, had told several members of Congress that he, unlike Bush, opposed overturning the Supreme Court's landmark *Roe v. Wade* decision of 1973, which legalized abortion. Fearful that Sullivan's confirmation by the Senate might be jeopardized, the White House quickly arranged for him to meet with several conservative Republican senators, all of whom strongly oppose abortion. At the conclusion of those meetings, the senators told the press that Sullivan had changed his position and now favored reversing *Roe v. Wade*.

Sullivan's confirmation hearing before the Senate Finance Committee was originally scheduled to take place on February 1, 1989, but, at the request of the White House, the hearing was delayed until February 23, in order to give Sullivan more time to prepare and to allow the FBI to complete its background check on the nominee. At the hearing Sullivan again said he was opposed to abortion, except in cases of rape or incest, or when the life of the mother is threatened, and he told the panel that he favored overturning the *Roe v. Wade* decision. The abortion issue came up in another context during the hearing when Senator William L. Armstrong of Colorado asked Sullivan whether he favored medical research employing fetal tissue obtained as a result of abortions. Opponents of abortion contend that such research may encourage women to have the operation in the belief that they would be benefiting science. The Department of Health and Human Services imposed a funding moratorium in 1988 on any research using tissue from aborted fetuses, but, in January 1989, an advisory committee of the National Institutes of Health recommended lifting the moratorium, noting that nonfederal research had shown fetal tissue to be successful in the treatment of various maladies, including juvenile diabetes and Alzheimer's disease. In the *Atlanta Journal and Constitution* interview, Sullivan had said, "We have a number of medical advances that have occurred as a result of research with fetal tissue that have benefited the lives of many people." But when Armstrong asked him if he favored banning all federal funding for fetal research, Sullivan replied that he had not yet scrutinized the advisory committee's report. "Until I've had the opportunity to review and receive the many-faceted advice from that committee, it would be best that I not take any position," Sullivan said. Angered, Senator Armstrong accused the nominee of "stonewalling."

Sullivan also used the hearing to deny reports that he had been required by the Bush administration to name known abortion foes to key positions in his department. That suspicion arose in late January when Sullivan appointed staunch opponents of abortion to four top-level posts, apparently at the urging of the White House. Those appointments prompted Senator John Heinz of Pennsylvania to say, as quoted in the *Christian Science Monitor* (January 27, 1989), that some of Sullivan's aides "apparently are being chosen on their pro-life views, rather than their expertise in handling health and income-maintenance issues," which constitute most of the department's work. But during his hearing, Sullivan said, "I think it's a disservice to me, as well as to the people I've chosen, to suggest that they have been chosen for reasons other than their competence and what they can provide in leadership and help to the department."

In response to questioning from Senator Lloyd Bentsen of Texas, the committee chairman, Sullivan attempted to place a quietus on two other minor controversies that had surfaced following his nomination. In investigating his background, the FBI had discovered that a member of the Fulton County Board of Commissioners, Reginald Eaves, had received $34,000 over the preceding four years from the Morehouse School of Medicine for serving as a part-time lecturer. The payments prompted suspicion that Eaves, who, in the spring of 1988, had been convicted of accepting bribes in an unre-

lated case, was being paid by Morehouse in order to influence his votes on the county board, which provides financial assistance to the medical school. Sullivan placated the committee by admitting that he had made "a serious error" in not monitoring the situation more closely and by adding that the school had taken steps to prevent a similar situation from occurring again.

On another issue, Sullivan said he would forgo about $300,000 worth of sabbatical pay that he had accrued during his thirteen years at Morehouse, in order to avoid charges of conflict of interest. The Morehouse School of Medicine receives $5.8 million a year in grants from the Department of Health and Human Services. (On March 29, following meetings with officials of the Office of Government Ethics, Sullivan announced that he would accept about $215,000 in severance pay from Morehouse.) Despite those controversies, Sullivan's hearing lasted for only two hours, and, at its conclusion, the Finance Committee voted 19-0 to recommend his nomination to the Senate. On March 1, that body, in a 98-1 vote, confirmed Louis W. Sullivan as the new secretary of health and human services, with Senator Jesse A. Helms of North Carolina casting the lone dissenting vote.

Only a week after his confirmation, Sullivan became embroiled in a wrangle with other federal officials when he endorsed community programs that distribute free hypodermic needles to intravenous drug users in exchange for used ones that might be contaminated with the AIDS virus. In expressing his opinion that the federal government could provide encouragement and financing to support such programs, Sullivan said, as quoted in the *New York Times* (March 9, 1989): "I don't subscribe to the view that it [distributing free needles] condones drug abuse. If this is a strategy that shows promise of helping to arrest the spread of AIDS, I think this is something that does deserve a chance for an appropriate trial." Sullivan added that he did not favor a federal needle-exchange program because of the controversy over the issue.

Sullivan's position did not square with that of the Bush administration, since, on March 10, spokesmen for both the president and his antidrug czar, William J. Bennett, expressed their opposition to needle-exchange programs. Congressman Charles B. Rangel of New York, meanwhile, termed Dr. Sullivan's proposal "tragic, ill-advised, and illegal." Sullivan's position was further undermined when a March 15 *New York Times* story revealed that, just two weeks before he endorsed local programs that distribute free needles, one of his subordinates had issued a memorandum warning AIDS programs financed by the National Institute on Drug Abuse that their federal aid could be jeopardized if they distributed clean needles to drug addicts. Speaking before the House Energy and Commerce Committee's subcommittee on health on July 18, 1989, Sullivan reversed his position, saying he no longer favored needle-exchange programs. He said that he changed his mind following discussions with members of Congress and with experts on AIDS and drug abuse.

In April Sullivan again put himself on a collision course with antiabortion conservatives by recommending that Bush appoint Robert Fulton to head the Family Support Administration, which oversees federal welfare programs. Conservative lawmakers, including Senator Jesse A. Helms, Senator Gordon J. Humphrey of New Hampshire, and Congressman Christopher Smith of New Jersey, charged that Fulton, while director of the Oklahoma Department of Human Services, had not acted forcefully enough to stop a former policy at state-run hospitals of denying surgery to newborn infants from poor families who were afflicted with spina bifida. Although Fulton, who became director in May 1983, said he eliminated the policy as soon as he became aware of it, in early 1984, his critics contended that he acted only after the policy was revealed in a television news report. On May 4, 1989 Helms, Humphrey, and four other conservative Republican senators submitted a letter to President Bush in which they said they viewed Fulton's nomination as "unacceptable," and Fulton withdrew his name from consideration four weeks later.

In an interview with Julie Johnson of the *New York Times* (April 25, 1989), Sullivan said that he had made minority health care and preventive medicine two of his top priorities. Concurrently, during a conference of black health professionals in Washington, Sullivan announced that he had written to Richard G. Darman, the director of the Office of Management and Budget, requesting $42.9 million in new spending in fiscal year 1990 for scholarships and research aid to selected medical schools, an area in which spending was eliminated in the final budget package introduced by President Ronald Reagan. In addition, Sullivan asked for $25 million more for occupational health programs designed mainly to benefit minorities. Those programs were cut by 37 percent in the final Reagan budget. And on April 21, Sullivan endorsed a plan calling for elimination of tuberculosis in the United States by the year 2010. About ten million Americans are infected with the bacterium that causes tuberculosis, and a disproportionately high number of tuberculosis cases are found among poor people in the inner cities and those who are institutionalized.

In October 1989 Sullivan condemned an attempt by Congress to repeal the Medicare Catastrophic Coverage Act of 1988, which provides expanded health benefits to Medicare recipients. Congress considered revoking the plan in response to protests from more affluent senior citizens, who resented having to pay a surtax to finance it. After the House of Representatives voted in favor of repeal on October 4, Sullivan endorsed a proposal by Senator David F. Durenberger of Minnesota that would have sharply reduced the surtax while retaining most of the plan's major benefits, but that proposal was rejected by the Senate on October 6.

Louis Sullivan is a member of the Institute of Medicine of the National Academy of Sciences. He also belongs to the American Society of Hematology, American Society for Clinical Investigation, American Federation for Clinical Research, Society for the Exploration of Biology and Medicine, Federation of American Societies for Experimental Biology, American Association for the Advancement of Science, and the Phi Beta Kappa and Alpha Omega Alpha honor societies. Coworkers have described Sullivan as intense and energetic, but with a restrained, diplomatic manner. "I've never seen Lou lose his cool," Charles R. Hatcher Jr., the director of the Robert W. Woodruff Health Sciences Center at Emory University, has said. "He can handle himself in groups when the going gets hot." Since September 30, 1955 Sullivan has been married to the former Eve Williamson. They have three grown children: Paul (a doctor in Atlanta), Shanta, and Halsted. Sullivan is an Episcopalian.

References: *Chronicle of Higher Education* 35:17+ Ja 4 '89 pors; *Cong Q* 46:3578 D 24 '88 por, 47:392+ F 25 '89 por, 47:461 Mr 4 '89; *N Y Times* A p25 D 23 '88 por, B p5 F 2 '89 por; *Washington Post* A p4 D 22 '88 por, A p1 D 23 '88 por, A p5 F 23 '89 por; *American Men and Women of Science* (1986); *Who's Who in America, 1988–89*

Sununu, John H(enry)

(su noō′ noō)

July 2, 1939– White House Chief of Staff.
Address: b. The White House, 1600 Pennsylvania Ave., Washington, D.C. 20500; h. 24 Samoset Dr., Salem, N.H. 03079

When, on November 17, 1988, President-elect George Bush announced the appointment of John

H. Sununu, the former governor of New Hampshire, as his White House chief of staff, he surprised many political observers as well as some of his closest advisers, since Sununu was neither a Washington "insider" nor a career politician. Before he became governor in 1983, he had spent more than twenty years in engineering—as a teacher of the subject at Tufts University, where he was also associate dean of the College of Engineering, and as the founder of several small consulting firms. When Sununu ran for governor for the first time, in 1982, his political experience consisted of a single term in the New Hampshire state legislature, from 1973 to 1974, and an abortive run for the United States Senate in 1980.

During his three two-year terms as governor of New Hampshire, Sununu transformed a budget deficit into a surplus, improved social services, modernized the state's accounting system, and strongly supported the Seabrook nuclear power plant. He refused to shrink from adopting controversial positions and exhibited a marked reluctance to delegate responsibility. "His biggest asset is his biggest liability," observed Ned Helms, who served as commissioner of health and human services under Sununu, as quoted by David Shribman in an article for the *Wall Street Journal* (November 17, 1988). "He's very, very bright, but sometimes he's so taken with his own brilliance that he doesn't pull out the best in people."

During the 1988 presidential campaign, George Bush had every reason to be grateful to Sununu. The Iowa caucus on February 8 had left him in third place, behind Senator Robert Dole of Kansas and the former television evangelist Pat Robertson, but eight days later he scored a victory in the New Hampshire primary, a comeback for which Sununu is given much of the credit. He helped to develop the negative commercials that derailed Dole's bid for the presidency and irrevocably thwarted the aspirations of Governor Michael S. Dukakis of Massachusetts.

John Henry Sununu has referred to himself as a "universal ethnic." His father, John Sununu Sr., a descendant of Lebanese and Greek Orthodox (of Jerusalem) immigrants who settled in the United States around the turn of the century, was born in Boston, where he worked in the export-import business. His mother, the former Victoria Dada, came from a Greek family that settled in Central America, and she was born in El Salvador. John H. Sununu was born on July 2, 1939 in Havana, Cuba, which his parents were visiting on a business trip to distribute French films.

Sununu and his siblings grew up in the borough of Queens, in New York City, where he attended a parochial elementary school. He won a $10,000 scholarship to LaSalle Military Academy in Oakdale, Long Island, where he became the highest-ranking cadet officer in his class. He then entered the Massachusetts Institute of Technology, where he earned his B.S. degree in 1961, his M.S. degree in 1962, and his Ph.D. degree in 1966, all in engineering. Sununu taught himself computer programming to facilitate the completion of his dissertation in fluid mechanics, and he has been a computer enthusiast ever since.

While he was a student, Sununu founded Astro Dynamics, in 1960, and he worked as its chief engineer until 1965. The following year he established the JHS Engineering Company, and in 1968 he founded Thermal Research. Until 1982 he served as president and chief engineer of both companies. Meanwhile, Sununu was appointed an assistant professor of engineering at Tufts University in 1966. He was promoted to associate professor in 1975. From 1968 to 1973 he served as associate dean of the College of Engineering at Tufts, where he taught until 1982. Sununu's research interests lay in heat transference and temperature control, slow viscous fluid dynamics, approximate methods of mathematical analysis of fluid phenomena, and the design and optimization of heat transfer equipment.

Despite his long career at Tufts University in Boston, Sununu lived in Massachusetts only until 1969, when he moved across the state border to Salem, New Hampshire, where he developed an avocational interest in politics. According to Owen Ullmann, who interviewed him for the *Philadelphia Inquirer* (January 23, 1989), politics became a more absorbing enterprise for Sununu when he realized that he could apply scientific techniques and expertise to the solution of political problems. In 1972 he was elected for a two-year term to the 400-member New Hampshire House of Representatives, the largest in the nation. From 1973 to 1978 Sununu was a member of the Governor's Energy Council, and from 1977 to 1978 he served on the Governor's Advisory Committee on Science and Technology and as the chairman of the Governor's Committee on New Hampshire's Future.

In 1980 Sununu ran for the United States Senate, but he lost the Republican primary to Warren Rudman. The day after his defeat, he became Rudman's campaign manager and helped him to win the general election with 52 percent of the vote. A reporter for *Business Week* (November 28, 1988) quoted Rudman as saying, "We're very close. John is very bright, analytic, and impatient."

Having demonstrated his considerable political skill as Rudman's campaign director, Sununu set out to campaign for himself in the gubernatorial election of 1982. Running a "two-fisted conservative campaign," as one reporter put it, he pledged not to sign any bill that would introduce either a state tax on earned income or a tax on retail sales, neither of which exists in New Hampshire; came out in favor of the completion of the nuclear power plant in Seabrook, New Hampshire, which was overrunning original cost estimates and completion schedules; and endorsed the recruitment of new business to the state, especially industries fleeing the high taxes of neighboring Massachusetts. He defeated the Democratic incumbent, Hugh Gallen, taking 52 percent of the vote in an upset victory.

Since New Hampshire is one of the last three states in the union to limit its gubernatorial term to two years, Sununu came up for reelection in 1984. Stressing the familiar themes—nuclear power, new business, and no new taxes—he won handily, with 67 percent of the vote. But in 1986 he captured only 54 percent of the vote, largely because of his support for the increasingly controversial Seabrook reactor. According to opinion polls taken in 1986, 65 percent of New Hampshire voters opposed the plant. Sununu's 54 percent of the vote, down from 67 percent in 1984, reflected the popularity of his opponent's vocal opposition to Seabrook. Nevertheless, he did not withdraw his support for the plant, despite a host of problems that persisted throughout his administration.

Begun in 1976 and completed ten years later, Seabrook was so continually behind schedule and over budget that the utility companies owning the plant had to raise their rates to finance the project. But higher rates did not save the primary owner, the Public Service Company of New Hampshire, from filing for bankruptcy on January 28, 1988. It was the first bankruptcy of a major public utility company since the Great Depression. Sununu is reported to have expressed the hope that the bankruptcy filing would not eliminate all methods of protecting "both the rate payers of New Hampshire and the state's energy supply."

New Hampshire residents had yet to obtain any amount of energy from Seabrook when the Public Service Company declared bankruptcy. Despite the completion of one of its units in 1986 (construction on the other was halted in 1983), Seabrook was repeatedly denied an operating license because of inadequate contingency planning for emergencies. Dukakis refused to consider any emergency evacuation plan for the six communities in Massachusetts within the ten-mile emergency zone surrounding the plant, which was built two miles from the Massachusetts border. In so doing, he antagonized Sununu, whose role in the erosion of Dukakis's presidential prospects during the 1988 campaign has been variously labeled "designated basher," "lead hatchet man," and "one-man hit squad."

Although Sununu's staunch advocacy of nuclear power may have cost him some votes, in the final months of his administration Seabrook seemed to be staging a comeback. In the decade since the accident at Three Mile Island in 1979, federal law mandated that the cooperation of local and state officials must be obtained before a plant can be licensed. But on November 18, 1988, President Reagan signed an executive order transferring control of emergency planning to the federal government, obviating the legal requirement for Dukakis's approval. One month later, Seabrook was granted a low-level operating license on the condition that its owners raise the decommissioning funds that would be needed if a full-power license were rejected. The opening of the plant was brought one step closer on January 3, 1989, when New Hampshire's evacuation plans were approved by the Nuclear Regulatory Commission.

Sununu enjoyed greater, if not unqualified, success in the area of financial management. In 1983 he inherited a deficit of $44 million in the state's $400 million budget, but by 1985 he had transformed it into a $47.8 million surplus, which was reduced to $15 million by 1988, and which decreased to $10 million by January of 1989. A $13 million deficit, in a budget that had grown to $570 million, was projected for the 1988–89 fiscal year by Sununu's Republican successor, Judd Gregg.

The New Hampshire economy thrived under Sununu's leadership. Presiding over a budget surplus for most of his tenure, Sununu allocated funds for the improvement of the state's correctional, educational, and mental institutions. He accomplished this without imposing "new" taxes, but he did increase two existing taxes: business fees and the real-estate transfer tax on property inherited from the estate of a deceased person. He pointed proudly to his record in an interview with Charlotte Saikowski for the *Christian Science Monitor* (December 28, 1988): "I have showed that there are conservative solutions to . . . the social needs that are out there. Conservatism and compassion mix, and I have demonstrated that."

One of the governor's budget-enhancing solutions involved a technological overhaul of the state's accounting procedures. In a prime example of his penchant for applying scientific techniques to political problems, he spent $5 million on an "integrated financial accounting system" that centralized the state government's fiscal data in one IBM mainframe. Accessing the information with a personal computer that he had installed in his office, Sununu often analyzed the data himself, using Lotus 1-2-3 spreadsheets. He also carried a portable Hewlett-Packard computer for work at home or in his chauffeur-driven car. Tracking of revenues and expenditures was immediately improved, and from then on, budgetary shortfalls were more easily predicted and averted. As quoted in *Time* (January 27, 1986) magazine, Sununu expressed—in a language some called "Sununuese"—his view on the benefits of computerization: "[It] can help the state leverage the capacity of employees to function better."

Control over access to the information in the state's computer system became a contentious issue between Sununu and the legislature. The house passed a bill guaranteeing access for legislative leaders, but Sununu halted it in the senate. "They'll get what we think they need," he said, as quoted in the same article for *Time*. Legislators balked until the governor allowed the chief legislative budget assistant to be given restricted access. Sununu, however, retained primary control over budget data—information that had been more readily available when it was documented solely on paper.

The governor's perceived attempt to subvert the traditional balance of power between his office and the legislature earned him the nickname "King John," which was applied by the conservative Manchester *Union Leader*, according to an editorial in the *Nation* (December 12, 1988). Richard Winters, a political science scholar at Dartmouth College, concurred in that assessment, according to the *Wall Street Journal* (November 17, 1988): "He became an extremely powerful figure in a state where the powers of the governor are not great. He knows how to marshall all the fragments and shards of executive authority. He doesn't shy from the hardball politics, but he also masters the details."

Notwithstanding the disgruntled New Hampshire legislature, Sununu's performance as governor has been praised by members of both parties. Mario Cuomo, the Democratic governor of New York, was quoted by Allan R. Gold in an article for the *New York Times* (November 20, 1988) as saying, "I know John, I like John. He's a tough advocate, extremely competent, very hardworking, and loyal. He's a radical conservative." Cuomo's characterization points to the heart of the confusion displayed by many of Sununu's appraisers, who conceive of conservatism and pragmatism as being mutually exclusive. Knowing Sununu's conservative views—pro-nuclear power, antiabortion, anti-Soviet, in favor of school prayer, against tax increases, and in favor of aid to the Nicaraguan Contras—some journalists have labeled Sununu a darling of the right wing. But others have noted that, with the exception of taxation and the Seabrook reactor, the governor failed to pursue his conservative agenda. Jay Smith, a Republican consultant to Sununu who was quoted in the *New York Times* (November 17, 1988), emphasized Sununu's pragmatism: "He is . . . mainly interested in what works. He will not let ideology stand in the way of getting things done his way."

In contrast to highly charged right-wing crusades, Sununu's conservative initiatives have tended to be procedural. As chairman of the National Governors' Association from 1987 to 1988, he advocated a Constitutional amendment that would allow a two-thirds majority of state legislatures to reject, in addition to their current power to ratify, federal laws. While some proponents stressed the ability of such legislation to pave the way for anti-abortion and balanced-budget amendments, Sununu discussed his concern that the states be capable of exercising the checks-and-balances mechanism built into the Constitution. In an interview with Rod Paul for *Governing* (August 1988) he suggested that current law inhibits the states from acting independently: "People are concerned that a constitutional convention [which is required for state-initiated amendments] . . . will go into areas of constitutional change no one planned in calling for the convention"—a concern shared by many liberals. He also urged the loosening of federal regulation of state use of federal funds, citing over-regulation as the main factor inhibiting the funding of home health care for the elderly.

As a leader among governors, Sununu attained national visibility. In addition to tackling federal-state relations, he led task forces on "new technology education" and acid rain legislation. But the de-

cisive circumstance in his transformation from a regional to a national political figure was his role in the New Hampshire primary in February 1988. He advised George Bush to replace vice-presidential pomp with a man-of-the-people image, created a sophisticated computer program to get out the vote, and assisted in developing a series of "attack commercials" to thwart Dole and Dukakis. Ads portraying Dole as secretly favoring a tax hike destroyed his twenty-point lead, and televised commercials that focused on the pollution of Boston Harbor and the prison furlough program in Massachusetts effectively injured the chances of Sununu's longtime rival, Dukakis.

Following the Bush victory in New Hampshire, Sununu became one of the five national cochairmen of the Bush campaign, and in May he announced that he would not run for reelection that fall. He campaigned enthusiastically for Bush across the nation and acted as the candidate's representative to the Republican platform committee. His role in drafting the platform later came in handy in allaying the anxiety of Jewish groups when Bush announced the appointment of an Arab-American as his chief of staff.

American Jewish organizations were wary of Sununu not only because of his Lebanese heritage, but also because of his refusal—alone among the fifty governors—to sign a pro-Israel petition. The petition, which condemned a 1975 United Nations resolution equating Zionism with racism, was sponsored by the World Zionist Organization in 1986 or 1987. Sununu defended his decision on the grounds that he did not believe governors should make foreign-policy pronouncements, but he added that if he had it to do over again, he would make clear that his action did not signify a lack of commitment to Israel.

Sununu reassured Jewish leaders within days after his appointment was announced by drawing their attention to the strong pro-Israel plank in the Republican party platform, to which he had contributed as Bush's surrogate. The plank reads: "The Republican party reaffirms its support for the rescission of U.N. Resolution 3379, which equates Zionism with racism. Failure to repeal that resolution will justify attenuation of our support for the U.N."

Jewish leaders were not the only ones who entertained misgivings about Sununu's suitability for the White House post. Secretary of State James A. Baker advised Bush to appoint Craig Fuller, who was Bush's chief of staff from 1984 to 1988 and codirector of his transition team. Political commentators were of the opinion that, whereas Fuller would have worked compliantly with the strong-willed secretary of state, Sununu would counterbalance Baker's influence. Bush wanted to create an administration, it was said, with several centers of power, each of which would generate its own policy option. That would presumably widen the pool of choices for Bush, whose decisions would thereby be rendered more meaningful than those for which a more uniform staff, with a single voice, would have provided an opportunity.

The logic of Bush's choice was apparent to many only in hindsight. When it was announced, the decision caught most people by surprise, much as had Bush's choice of Senator Dan Quayle as his running mate. Sununu himself was briefly considered for the role of vice-presidential candidate, perhaps because someone else was once considered for chief of staff, but the candidacy of Frederick V. Malek for chief of staff was terminated when he was criticized for writing a memorandum in 1971 that counted the number of top-ranking Jews on the staff of the Bureau of Labor Statistics.

Sununu was chosen, Bush told reporters during a joint news conference with Sununu on November 18, 1988, for his "experience, . . . leadership in the governors association, . . . respect at all levels; and he's a take-charge kind of guy, he's very active, very energetic." When asked if Sununu was chosen to reassure the "conservative faction of the Republican party," Bush replied: "No. I want to be on everybody's side. And I decided to send a signal that I have a strong chief of staff who in my view will be able to work with Congress and the various strong secretaries . . . in the cabinet." Responding to fears of his famed temper, Sununu smiled and said, "I'm a pussycat." And in subsequent interviews, Sununu tried to be reassuring about how much influence he would wield. "My job will be what George Bush wants my job to be," he said on one occasion.

As chief of staff, Sununu is charged with supervising the daily operation of the White House and the entire White House staff apparatus. He is responsible for overseeing policy development, the general counsel's office, presidential scheduling, communications, and relations with the press and with Congress. His broad responsibilities encouraged detractors to blame him for the perception that the Bush administration was floundering in the spring of 1989. At a March 7 news conference, Bush reaffirmed his faith in his chief of staff: "I have total confidence in John Sununu."

John Sununu was described by Rod Paul in Governing as "a relatively short, hefty man who conveys a sense of power and movement even when seated." He is quick to interrupt others and often gestures in conversation. In 1958 he married the former Nancy Hayes, who used to be chairman of the New Hampshire Republican State Committee. They have eight children, ranging in age from nine to twenty-eight: Catherine, Elizabeth, Christina, John, Michael, James, Christopher, and Peter. Sununu belongs to several engineering associations, and he is a member of various Arab-American groups.

References: Chicago Tribune I p5 N 17 '88 por; Governing 1:51+ Ag '88 por; N Y Times A p1+ N 17 '88 por, A p1 N 20 '88 por; Nat R 41:24+ Mr 24 '89 por; Philadelphia Inquirer A p1+ Ja 23 '89 por; Toronto Globe and Mail A p7 N 22 '88 por; Washington Post A p1+ N 16 '88 por; American Men and Women of Science (1986); Who's Who in America, 1988–89; Who's Who in American Politics, 1989–90

Thatcher, Margaret (Hilda)

Oct. 13, 1925– Prime Minister of Great Britain. Address: 10 Downing St., London SW1, England

NOTE: This biography supersedes the article that appeared in *Current Biography* in 1975.

"I am not a consensus politician, I am a conviction politician," Margaret Thatcher announced in February 1975, when she assumed leadership of the Conservative party. To Mrs. Thatcher, a Tory member of Parliament since 1959, the consensus that she rejected stood for the socialist policies pursued by the Labour party and acquiesced to by the Conservatives in postwar Britain. Following the establishment of a comprehensive welfare state, nationalized industries, and strong unions, Britain experienced decades of declining economic competitiveness and a corresponding loss of international stature. Convinced that nothing short of the eradication of socialism could restore economic prosperity and greatness to the nation, Mrs. Thatcher was prepared to ignore key assumptions taken for granted by her predecessors—that unions had to be appeased and that high levels of unemployment were politically intolerable. The strength of the unions vis-à-vis the government had become so formidable during the 1970s that, by the end of the decade, many Britons were receptive to Mrs. Thatcher's message. In May 1979 she became the first woman in British history to serve as prime minister. Reelected in 1983 and again in 1987, she is the twentieth century's longest-serving British prime minister, the senior statesman of the Western alliance, and the most powerful woman in the world.

One of Britain's few prime ministers to lend her name to an era and a political philosophy, Margaret Thatcher has left an indelible mark on virtually all areas of British life. Under her forceful, if sometimes strident, leadership, the Conservatives accomplished what no previous British government in the postwar period had done: they emasculated the unions, denationalized important industries, curbed inflation, and swelled the ranks of the middle class. But under Mrs. Thatcher's regime (as she herself refers to her long tenure), unemployment skyrocketed—especially in the impoverished northern industrial cities. Critics charged that the gap between the haves and the have-nots—what Disraeli once referred to as the "Two Nations"—was widened by Thatcherism to a degree not seen since the mid-Victorian days of Charles Dickens. But for voters in the service industries in London and southern England, Mrs. Thatcher's policies were credited not only with economic recovery, but also with restoring a sense of pride in being British, which reached new heights in the aftermath of her victory over Argentina in the Falklands War of 1982.

Thatcherism denotes the prime minister's style no less than her policies. Her unbending will, self-righteousness, and love of argument earned her the sobriquet Iron Lady, which was applied to her by the Soviet press after she harshly denounced communism in 1976 and which she has worn as a badge of honor ever since. Her extraordinary political vision and self-confidence, as well as her profoundly nationalistic approach to foreign policy, have prompted comparisons with Winston Churchill, Charles de Gaulle, Elizabeth I, and Victoria. Leaders with whom she has been compared less charitably include Genghis Khan and "Attila the Hen," the latter for her tendency to wear out her opponents in Parliament with her "sometimes hectoring, sometimes condescending" style of debating, in the words of one reporter. R. C. Longworth described her in the *Chicago Tribune* (April 30, 1989) as "perhaps the most admired, hated, fascinating, boring, radical, and conservative leader in the Western world."

Mrs. Thatcher's unparalleled trajectory in British politics is all the more remarkable considering her differences from previous Tory leaders. Unlike them, she is a woman and hails from the lower-middle class in a highly class-conscious society. She was born in Grantham, England on October 13, 1925, the second daughter of Alfred Roberts, a lay Methodist minister and local politician, and Beatrice Roberts, a dressmaker. In a flat over Alfred Roberts's grocery store (he eventually owned two of them), Margaret and her sister Muriel, who was born four years earlier, grew up without indoor plumbing or hot water. Beatrice Roberts was a stolid woman who saw to it that her pretty daughters were always well dressed and well groomed. Citizens of Grantham remember Margaret as "a studious, determined little girl with the cherubic looks of a cupid on a Victorian valentine," according to *Time* (May 14, 1979) magazine.

Alfred Roberts was by far the more influential parent in his daughter's life. On the day that Margaret Thatcher ascended to the nation's highest office, she said, "Well, of course I just owe almost everything to my father. He brought me up to believe almost all the things that I do believe. . . . It's passionately interesting for me that the things that I learned in a small town, in a very modest home, are just the things that I believe have won the election." The values thus imparted were summarized by the British journalist Peter Jenkins in his recent book *Mrs. Thatcher's Revolution* (1988): "The individual owed responsibility to self, family, firm, community, country, God." Independence was another value esteemed by her father, who told her, "You *don't follow the crowd*, you make up your own mind," she recalled in an interview with Gail Sheehy for *Vanity Fair* (June 1989).

Growing up in Grantham, Margaret acquired more than a set of moral precepts from her father; she learned invaluable political skills while accompanying him to meetings of the local Rotary Club, which he founded. Successively a councilman, an alderman, and mayor of Grantham, Alfred Roberts took Margaret on many a political outing. His expectations for her were high, but no higher than her own ambitions. He sent her to a reputable local grammar school and paid for coaching in the classics and Latin so that she could meet the admissions requirements of Oxford University. Margaret also took elocution lessons to improve her accent. At the age of seventeen she enrolled in Somerville College, the best women's college at Oxford, where she majored in chemistry with a view toward combining her scientific expertise with legal training in order to practice patent law. The only extracurricular activity in which she indulged was political debating. Barred from the all-male Oxford Union, the debating society, she joined the Oxford University Conservative Association, which in 1946 elected her its first female president. From there she made a smooth transition into local Tory politics, in which she was actively involved from then on.

After graduating with a B.S. degree in 1947, she worked for four years as a research chemist. (She also holds an M.A. degree from Oxford.) In 1950 she stood for a seat considered almost impossible to win in the solidly Labour district of Dartford, Kent; at the age of twenty-four she was the youngest person running for Parliament. Although she lost with 36 percent of the vote, she tried again the following year and increased her support to 40 percent. Meanwhile, in 1949, she met Denis Thatcher, a wealthy divorced businessman ten years her senior. Their marriage in December 1951 afforded her both financial and emotional security but in no way dampened her political ambitions or hindered her upward progress. On the contrary; by all accounts, Denis Thatcher has been his wife's staunchest supporter during their thirty-eight-year partnership. Around the time of her marriage, Mrs. Thatcher switched her allegiance from the Methodist church to the Church of England.

In August 1953 Mrs. Thatcher gave birth to twins, Carol and Mark. Four months later she passed her bar exam, having squeezed part-time legal study into an already overflowing schedule filled with her job, party politics, and motherhood. She practiced as a barrister specializing first in patent law, then in the more elite area of tax law, until 1961. By then she had served for two years as a member of Parliament from Finchley, a wealthy suburb of London. She has represented that district, which became Barnet, Finchley in 1974, ever since.

Lacking the advantages enjoyed by those who had access to the upper-class old-boy network that still pervades the 650-member House of Commons, Mrs. Thatcher excelled by dint of hard work, intelligence, and a forceful personality. In 1961 the Conservative prime minister, Harold Macmillan, appointed her joint parliamentary secretary to the Ministry of Pensions and National Insurance. From 1964 to 1970 the Conservatives, led by Edward Heath, were out of power. In opposition to the Labour government of Harold Wilson, Mrs. Thatcher served in Heath's shadow cabinet as minister for gas, coal, electricity, and nuclear energy, then for transportation, and finally for education and science.

When Edward Heath was elected prime minister in 1970, Mrs. Thatcher became the only woman in his cabinet. As secretary for education and science, she made a name for herself by abolishing the free-milk program for schoolchildren. Labour MPs shouted her down in Parliament with cries of "Thatcher the milk snatcher" and "Ditch the bitch!" That was a turning point for Mrs. Thatcher. "I thought, I'm not going to be beaten by this," she told Gail Sheehy. From that point on, taunts and resistance to Mrs. Thatcher's agenda would only make her more resolute in pursuing her goals.

As the Heath government repeatedly capitulated to the demands of striking miners, confidence eroded in both the Conservative party and its leader. In March 1974 Heath resigned as prime minister; eleven months later he was deposed as leader of the Conservatives. When none of Heath's loyal deputies stepped forward to succeed him, Mrs. Thatcher seized the initiative, declared her candidacy, and in February 1975 became the first woman to assume the party leadership. During the following four years of Labour government—first under Harold Wilson, then under James Callaghan, beginning in 1976—Mrs. Thatcher called for a return to free-market principles and the dismantling of the welfare state. The message that had earlier fallen on deaf ears began to reach an increasing number of voters as it became clear that the policies pursued by both parties in the past were no longer tenable in the face of growing labor unrest.

The public's patience with powerful unions— and with governmental impotence—was tested more severely than ever before during the so-called winter of discontent in early 1979. Six weeks of strikes by everyone from garbage collectors and gravediggers to hospital workers and teachers culminated in a vote of no confidence for the Callaghan government in March 1979. Mrs. Thatcher proclaimed her willingness to confront the unions during the election campaign that followed, promising also to revive the economy, reduce welfare spending, and improve national defense capabilities. In May 1979 she was elected to a five-year term as prime minister with 43.9 percent of the vote and a parliamentary majority of forty-three seats. Her manifesto had not changed since she became party leader four years earlier. At that time, according to Gail Sheehy, her newly hired speechwriter inadvertently incorporated a quotation from the very same speech of Abraham Lincoln's that Mrs. Thatcher had been carrying with her in her wallet: "You cannot strengthen the weak by weakening the strong. . . . You cannot help the poor by destroying the rich. . . . You cannot help men permanently by doing for them what they could and should do for themselves."

One month after taking office, Mrs. Thatcher revealed her first budget. She slashed the top tax rate on earned income from 83 percent to 60 percent and reduced the highest tax rate on unearned income from 90 percent to 75 percent; raised value-added taxes; and removed restrictive foreign-exchange controls. She took steps to do away with wage-and-price guidelines, reduced government subsidies to inefficient industries, and began selling off state-owned enterprises and public housing to encourage more people to become stockholders and homeowners. Many of those who did also became loyal Tories. But there was no paucity of people who found themselves worse off under Mrs. Thatcher. The number of unemployed doubled between 1979 and 1980, when it surpassed two million. A poll taken in late March 1982 revealed that the Tories trailed both Labour and the Alliance of Liberals and Social Democrats with a 22 percent approval rating. Many Britons were convinced that Mrs. Thatcher would go down in history as England's worst prime minister.

Less than one month later, imminent war provided the embattled leader with an opportunity to win the loyalty of those not persuaded by her economic policies by appealing to their redblooded patriotic instincts. The Argentine attack on the British Falkland Islands in April 1982 was repelled by a British naval task force in ten weeks at a cost of 255 British lives. The military campaign's success, against the odds, was widely credited to Mrs. Thatcher's fierce determination to achieve victory, and her approval rating jumped to 59 percent as a result. Proclaiming that "Great Britain is great again," she called for an early election the following spring. In June 1983 she won a second term with 42.7 percent of the vote and a 144-seat majority, despite the plight of three million unemployed. Most of the economic hardship was borne by the North, which experienced a 20 percent reduction in manufacturing from 1979 to 1981 alone. The Tories obtained most of their support from the more prosperous South.

In her second term Mrs. Thatcher forged ahead with the program she called "popular capitalism" by selling off $30 billion worth of shares in British Telecom, British Airways, Rolls-Royce, and other nationalized concerns to private citizens. By 1987 the proportion of the British electorate who owned stock was 20 percent, triple the number in 1979. Similarly, over one million municipally owned council houses were sold to their occupants during the same period, raising the percentage of home-owners from 52 percent to 66 percent (only 63.9 percent of Americans owned homes in 1988). According to *Fortune* (June 8, 1987) magazine, Britain's economic indicators illustrated that declining competitiveness had been halted, if not reversed. For those who had jobs in 1987, real disposable income was up by 15 percent over 1979 levels. Inflation had dropped from 22 percent in 1980 to 3.4 percent in 1986; the budget deficit decreased from 6 percent of gross domestic product in 1981 to 1 percent in 1987; and the economy had maintained an annual growth rate of 3 percent since the recovery began in 1981, ranking second only to Japan among industrialized nations.

The most important achievement of eight years of Thatcherism was indisputably the prime minister's success in curbing the power of the unions. Even David Owen, the leader of the Social Democratic party, said Mrs. Thatcher deserved credit for that, according to John Newhouse, writing in the *New Yorker* (February 10, 1986). New laws required union leaders to poll members before calling a strike, rendered national unions responsible for the actions of members, and banned sympathy strikes and the closed shop. In March 1984 she took on Arthur Scargill, the Marxist leader of the National Union of Mineworkers, in a violent and acrimonious coal strike that lasted nearly a year, and she won. The successful outcome of her refusal to give in to union demands owed as much to the high level of unemployment, which reduced the leverage of union bosses, as to her intransigence. The number of unionized workers fell by 25 percent to nine million by 1987, depriving the Labour party of much of its constituency.

In international affairs no less than in domestic policy, Mrs. Thatcher convinced Britons—despite dramatic swings in her popularity over the course of her second term—that she provided leadership superior to that of any candidate fielded by the opposition. In contrast to Labour's disastrous (for their electoral prospects) policy of unilateral nuclear disarmament, Mrs. Thatcher inspired confidence with her determination to modernize the nation's nuclear weapons. In meetings with Mikhail Gorbachev in Moscow in April 1987, she spoke out forcefully in favor of linking arms control negotiations to Soviet progress in human rights and defended the need to maintain Britain's independent nuclear deterrent. Her relationship with the Soviet leader is a curiously close one that is based on mutual respect for each other's ability to argue at length without being stumped by the facts. She also sees many parallels between his efforts to reform the Soviet economy and her own battle to reverse Britain's economic decline.

Mrs. Thatcher enjoyed a clubby relationship with President Ronald Reagan as well, though their rapport was based more on shared anti-communism than on the quality of intellectual discourse. In April 1986 Mrs. Thatcher reciprocated the logistical support she had received from Reagan during the Falklands War by allowing him the use of British air bases from which to launch his attack on Libya, and in so doing she withstood a storm of criticism. The argument that her decision was taken in a spirit of international solidarity against terrorism did not prevent her popularity from plummeting, nor did it seem consistent with her contining refusal to join the forty-eight other Commonwealth nations in placing sanctions on South Africa's apartheid regime.

Mrs. Thatcher reiterated her concern regarding deterrence of terrorism at European forums on the political and economic unification of Europe that is slated for 1992. She objected to the abolishment of national border controls, fearing that such measures would facilitate the travel of drug traffickers, illegal immigrants, and international terrorists no less than that of tourists. Closer to home, she condemned the terrorist activity of the Irish Republican Army, which placed a bomb in her hotel in Brighton in 1984. The explosion destroyed her bathroom, which she had left just two minutes before the blast occurred. "All attempts to destroy democracy by terrorism will fail," she vowed. In 1985 she showed similar fortitude in overriding Protestant objections to an agreement giving the Irish Republic a role in Northern Ireland's affairs.

The combination of a vigorous foreign policy and ambitious domestic policies created a seemingly impregnable bastion of Tory support in the 1987 election campaign. Mrs. Thatcher had called an early election once again, this time hoping to reap the political dividends of her recent trip to Moscow—the first in twelve years by a British prime minister. The Labour party put up a much stronger fight under Neil Kinnock in 1987 than it had under Michael Foot in 1983. Kinnock hammered away at the prime minister's inflexible and arrogant style of leadership, and he castigated her for lacking compassion for the poor. Mrs. Thatcher rallied with charges that the Labour party was all talk and no action, reminding the electorate that social services could be paid for only in an expanding economy under Conservative direction.

Elected to an unprecedented third term in June 1987 with 42.8 percent of the vote and a 102-seat majority, Mrs. Thatcher planned to apply her free-market principles to previously untouched areas such as health care, education, utilities, and professional services. That latest round of proposals has encountered stiff resistance. Her agenda includes encouraging greater efficiency in the National Health Service, which serves 90 percent of the British public, by introducing competition for government funding; allowing public schools to develop competitive fees; privatizing the water and electrical utilities, which is opposed by environmentalists and consumers; and ending the historic separation of barristers and solicitors in the legal profession.

Mrs. Thatcher has been censured by journalists and intellectuals for invoking the 1911 Official Secrets Act to harass the British Broadcasting Corporation (which presents issues with a leftist slant, in her view). Her unsuccessful attempt to suppress publication of Peter Wright's *Spycatcher; The Candid Autobiography of a Senior Intelligence Officer* (1987) likewise provoked a public outcry over the erosion of freedom of the press and civil liberties in Britain.

Compounding the difficulties faced by the seemingly indefatigable prime minister, who in 1987 had hinted broadly that she planned to run for a fourth and even a fifth term, was bad news on the economic front in the fall of 1989. Inflation had risen to 7.6 percent, the rate of growth had slowed, interest rates had jumped from 7 percent to 15 percent in just sixteen months, and the trade deficit was estimated at $32 billion. Unemployment was down to two million, or 6.9 percent, but that rate was high enough to attract much of the blame for Britain's rising levels of drug and alcohol abuse and violent crime. Public opinion polls showed the Conservative party trailing the Labour party by ten percentage points.

But it was Mrs. Thatcher's attitude toward British participation in the European Monetary System (EMS)—rather than her domestic economic policies—that precipitated the gravest political crisis her government had thus far experienced. In July 1989 she demoted Sir Geoffrey Howe from the post of foreign secretary to that of deputy prime minister following his vocal support for the economic policies of Nigel Lawson, the chancellor of the exchequer. A staunch advocate of sooner-rather-than-later British membership in the ten-year-old EMS, Lawson resigned on October 26, 1989 in protest over the prime minister's refusal to dismiss Sir Alan Walters, her economic adviser, whose anti-EMS views had been recently published. Hours later, Sir Alan also resigned, causing British journalists to call the situation a crisis and the country's ministers to speculate that a challenge to Mrs. Thatcher's leadership was imminent. Although the prime minister remained confident of her staying power, she was reportedly quoted as saying that she would be likely to run for only one more term, in 1991 or 1992, rather than go "on and on," as she had previously indicated.

At the age of sixty-four, Margaret Thatcher is often described as looking younger and prettier than she did when she first took office ten years ago. The French president François Mitterrand once quipped, "She has the eyes of Caligula and the mouth of Marilyn Monroe." She reportedly enjoys male admiration as much as a good argument, and she is always prepared for either. Mrs. Thatcher spends long hours poring over briefing papers, recharging herself with only three to five hours of sleep a night, coffee, and vitamin tablets. Her husband, Denis, who retired from business in 1975, is an avid golfer. Their daughter, Carol, earned a law degree in 1975 and is a freelance journalist in London. Their son, Mark, is a former race-car driver who is currently an auto executive in Dallas, Texas. Mark's wife, Diane, gave birth to Mrs. Thatcher's first grandchild in March 1989, prompting her to use the royal "we" in exclaiming, "We have become a grandmother."

References: N Y Times Mag p16 My 31 '87 por; New Yorker 61:68+ F 10 '86 por; Time 113:30+ My 14 '79 pors; Vanity Fair 52:102+ Je '89 pors; Gardiner, George. Margaret Thatcher (1975); International Who's Who, 1989–90; International Year Book and Statesmen's Who's Who, 1989; Jenkins, Peter. Mrs. Thatcher's Revolution; The Ending of the Socialist Era (1988); Minogue, Kenneth and Biddiss, eds. Thatcherism, Personality and Politics (1987); Riddell, Peter. The Thatcher Government (1983); Thatcher, Margaret. In Defence of Freedom (1986); Young, Hugo. The Iron Lady; A Biography of Margaret Thatcher (1989)

Thomas, Isiah

Apr. 30, 1961– Basketball player. Address: c/o Detroit Pistons, 3777 Lapeer Rd., Auburn Hills, Mich. 48321

By all accounts, the best pure point guard in basketball is Isiah Thomas, the captain of the Detroit Pistons. Indeed, the six-foot one-inch Thomas is the first "little man"—under six feet three—to be able to dominate a big man's game since the Boston

Celtics' Bob Cousy in the 1950s and the Atlanta Hawks' Lenny Wilkins in the 1960s. When he left Indiana University at the age of twenty, having already led the Hoosiers to the NCAA championship, to join the professional ranks, Thomas was basketball's cherub, a boyishly handsome man-child with a beaming smile and a charismatic presence, both on and off the court. During his first few years as a pro, he was noted for his good works in the public domain as well as for his wondrous, crowd-pleasing style of play, even though the Pistons were one of the National Basketball Association's doormats. In 1987, however, Thomas's image suffered when he seemed to agree with one of his teammates, who had asserted that the Celtic superstar Larry Bird was overrated because he is white. Putting controversy behind him, Thomas recovered to become the undisputed leader of the Motor City "Bad Boys," the bruising, defense-oriented Pistons, who in 1989 won that franchise's first-ever NBA crown.

Isiah Lord Thomas 3d was born in Chicago, Illinois on April 30, 1961, the seventh son and the youngest of the nine children of Mary and Isiah Lord Thomas 2d. When Isiah was about three years old, his father left, leaving the Thomas brood in the capable hands of Mary Thomas. Although Isiah's mother has achieved almost legendary status for the tenacity with which she tried to shield her children from the harsher realities of life in the tough, poverty-stricken West Side neighborhood known as "K-Town" (so called because many of the street names begin with the letter K), stories about Isiah's upbringing tend to diminish his father, a proud, highly intelligent man who had moved to Chicago from Mississippi. After serving in the then segregated United States Army during World War II, Isiah Thomas 2d attended a trade school on the G.I. Bill, then went on to become International Harvester's first black foreman. Concerned about his children's future, he saw that they completed their homework and allowed them to watch only educational television. But when the International Harvester plant closed, he was unable to find comparable work and had to settle for a job as a janitor. Frustrated and increasingly prone to near violent bursts of anger, he eventually left home. "My father was taught to be the 'macho man'—go out, work, take care of your family . . . ," Isiah Thomas told David Bradley in an interview for Sport (May 1988). "Yes, he left, but under the circumstances, it was best that he did leave. Because maybe he would have done something crazy to all of us."

A formidable, strong-willed woman, Mary Thomas was determined to help her children resist the siren call of the mean streets of Chicago's West Side. Indeed, when Isiah and his brothers had scrapes with the law, they came to fear their mother's wrath far more than the authority of the police. Once, when members of a K-Town gang known as the Vice Lords appeared on Mary Thomas's porch, revolvers bulging in their waist bands, and informed her that her six oldest sons were the gang's newest recruits, she retreated to her bedroom, picked up a shotgun, returned to the front door, and leveled both barrels at the assembled hoods. "If you don't get off my porch," Mary Thomas threatened, "I'll blow you across the expressway." As she told William Nack of Sports Illustrated (January 19, 1987), "They didn't come back anymore." Nack reported that "for the next few years, . . . the Thomas kids had a sort of privileged run of the neighborhood, free from molestation by the gangs."

Despite Mary Thomas's efforts, several of her sons eventually turned to the streets. One son became a ranking member of the Vice Lords; another, a pimp and drug dealer. (Both have since reformed.) Lord Henry, her eldest son, passed up the chance to play professional basketball when he became addicted to hard drugs. Gregory Thomas, too, was a gifted athlete, but he developed a drinking problem. Larry, the brother who most often looked after Isiah, turned his back on basketball to become a street hustler. "Thus it was," William Nack wrote in Sports Illustrated, "that Isiah Lord Thomas 3d, the last of the Thomas brothers, became by default the Chosen One, the one . . . to lead the family out of the wilderness of poverty and into the ways of wealth. 'I wanted to try to fulfill Lord Henry's dream,' Thomas says."

"He was well behaved, but spoiled," Mary Thomas said of Isiah when she spoke to Nack. "He's still like that, spoiled rotten—by me and his brothers. They try to put the blame on me, and I can't say I didn't treat him special. He was the baby. He got special attention." According to Ira Berkow of the New York Times (April 27, 1981), Thomas was a "prodigy in basketball the way Mozart was in music. At age three, Amadeus was composing on a harpsichord; at three, Isiah could dribble and shoot baskets." In fact, the three-year-old Isiah provided the entertainment during the halftimes of games at the local Catholic Youth Organization. "We gave Isiah an old jersey that fell like a dress on him, and he wore black oxfords and tossed up shots with a high arc," Brother Alexis recalled. "Isiah was amazing." Thomas honed his skills on a court in Gladys Park, just two blocks from the Thomas home. "That's where I really learned to play," he told William Nack. "There were some basketball players there. I mean, some basketball players."

Raised as a Baptist in the Deep South, Mary Thomas converted to Roman Catholicism, and, while Isiah was a pupil at Our Lady of Sorrows grade school, she worked there in the cafeteria and ran the youth center, where her son was a standout basketball player. When Thomas was in the eighth grade, he applied for a basketball scholarship to Weber High School, a power in the city's Catholic basketball league, but the coach turned him down because he was "too small." Seeing the boy's disappointment, Isiah's brothers pleaded his case to Gene Pingatore, the coach at St. Joseph High School in Westchester, a Chicago suburb. Impressed, Pingatore secured financial aid for Thomas, who was, he said, "a winner." "He had that special aura," Pingatore told Ira Berkow. In the meantime, Mary Thomas, by then working for Chicago's Department of Human Services, had fled the inner city, moving her family west, nearer to the city's white suburbs. Consequently, Isiah had to leave home at six in the morning to commute to Westchester, traveling for ninety minutes on the elevated train and bus before reaching his final stop, from which he had to walk a mile and a half to St. Joseph High School. Although his academic career began inauspiciously—he pulled a D average his freshman year—Thomas soon became an honor student. Under Pingatore's guidance, he also learned to control his freewheeling playground style, especially his tendency to dribble full tilt the length of the court and draw charging fouls. Thomas led St. Joseph to a second-place finish in the state championship tournament in his junior year, and as a senior he was one of the nation's most highly sought-after college prospects.

Recruited by more than 100 colleges, Isiah Thomas chose to attend Indiana University and play for the brilliant yet irascible and controversial Hoosiers coach, Bob Knight, one of the few suitors who did not court the Thomas family with under-the-table inducements. "He didn't try to bribe me," Mary Thomas told Ira Berkow. "Other schools offered hundreds of thousands of dollars. . . . All Bobby Knight promised was he'd try to get Isiah a good education and give him a good opportunity to get better in basketball. . . . I liked that." In his first season under Knight, Thomas made the all-Big Ten Squad; in his second, after having been named a consensus all-American, the nineteen-year-old Thomas led Indiana to the Final Four of the NCAA tournament. In the semifinal round, the Hoosiers demolished Louisiana State University by the score of 67-49, setting up a decisive confrontation with the University of North Carolina. Coached by Dean Smith and led by the star forwards James Worthy and Al Wood, the Tar Heels were favored to win, but two steals by Thomas early in the second half keyed an Indiana surge that turned the game into a rout, 63-50, giving Knight and his Hoosiers their second national championship. Finishing with a game-high twenty-three points, Thomas was named the tournament's most valuable player.

Known as the General Patton of collegiate basketball, Knight can be a brutally demanding and abusive coach. Because Thomas was a sensitive young man, his relationship with Knight was full of tumult and pain. As a result, in the spring of 1981, after considerable soul-searching, Thomas decided to leave school and turn pro. "There was a lot to consider," he admitted to Berkow. "I know I'm a role model for a lot of people back in the ghetto. Not too many of us get the chance to get out, to go to college. If I quit school, what effect would that have on them?" He knew, however, that he would be signed to a lucrative contract, and he wanted to lift his family, especially his mother, out of poverty. In the June 5 National Basketball Association draft, Thomas was the second pick overall—after his

friend Mark Aguirre, the DePaul superstar who also hailed from K-Town—and was signed to a four-year, $1.6 million contract by the lowly Detroit Pistons, whose record of twenty-one wins and sixty-one losses was the second-worst in the NBA for the 1980–81 season. One of the first things Thomas did with his newfound wealth was buy his mother a ranch house in the largely white Chicago suburb of Clarendon Hills.

Playing point guard, Thomas established himself as the Pistons' leader in his rookie season, as the team improved its record to thirty-nine and forty-three. At midseason he was named to the Eastern Conference All-Star team, and he finished the 1981–82 season with an average of seventeen points and almost eight assists per game. The following year, the Pistons won thirty-seven of their eighty-two regular season games. Thomas was named a starter in that season's All-Star game, averaged 22.9 points per game for the year, his personal best as a pro, and once again averaged almost eight assists per game. Since the club was formed in 1941, in Fort Wayne, Indiana, the Pistons had never won an NBA championship, and for most of the 1970s they were in the Eastern Conference cellar. In 1983–84, however, the Pistons posted their first winning record in seven seasons, with forty-nine victories and thirty-three losses. Having averaged 21.3 points and over ten assists, Thomas was signed to a new, ten-year contract worth more than $12 million. He had also been named the most valuable player in the All-Star game, where he scored twenty-one points and passed for fifteen assists. During the 1984–85 season, Thomas set the NBA record for assists, 1,123, an average of 13.1 per game, and in 1986 he was once again named the All-Star game's most valuable player, as he led the Eastern Conference to victory with thirty points, ten assists, and five steals.

Throughout this period, Thomas was celebrated as one of the NBA's unofficial ambassadors of goodwill, along with Julius Erving, Earvin "Magic" Johnson, and Larry Bird. He won the NBA's Walter Kennedy Award for civic responsibility, worked with inner-city children in his spare time, campaigned against drug use, and even persuaded Detroit mayor Coleman Young to sponsor an annual No Crime Day. As a player, he was one of the most exciting, creative, and explosive guards in the NBA, applauded for his outside shooting touch, his peerless ball-handling skills, and his ability to penetrate the lane on a drive and to run the length of the court on both defense and offense.

According to Pat Riley, the coach of the Los Angeles Lakers, Thomas's athletic genius was best displayed in the 1986 All-Star game. "It gives you an idea of what the game's all about," Riley told William Nack. "It's a freewheeling, footloose, and fancy-free game. And he's the best at it. In a ninety-four-foot game, he's probably the best, because he can sustain a quick game for six or seven minutes. In the All-Star game, there's no control; there isn't any structure. . . . And he's been dominating in those games." Thomas himself thinks he is at his best at those times when the Pistons, as he puts it, "need Isiah to be Isiah." "I read the rhythm and the flow of the game," he explained in the interview with *Sport's* David Bradley, "and it might be at the seven-minute mark or the three-minute mark where I'm able to do what I can do. A minute may not be much for other players. But for Isiah . . . I can do a lot in a minute." In that "minute" Thomas takes control of a game by doing whatever the situation demands—scoring, hawking the ball on defense, or simply being creative with his passes and drives into the lane.

The Pistons became legitimate playoff contenders when they acquired, in a trade in the 1986 off-season, Adrian Dantley, a veteran forward with an uncanny ability to score points in bunches. In the subsequent regular season, Thomas averaged 20.6 points and ten assists a game, and in round two of the playoffs he led Detroit to victory over the Atlanta Hawks in just five games of the best-of-seven series. That triumph pitted the Pistons against the defending world champions, the Boston Celtics, in the Eastern Conference finals for the right to vie for the NBA crown with the Los Angeles Lakers. Behind the stellar play of forward Larry Bird, the Celtics took the first two games in Boston, but the Pistons bounced back, winning two straight on their home court, the Pontiac Silverdome. Game five was at the Boston Garden, where the Celtics are nearly invincible, but, with just a few seconds remaining, the Pistons had a one-point lead and the ball out of bounds. Thomas, however, threw a careless in-bounds pass that was intercepted by Bird, who passed to teammate Dennis Johnson for the winning basket. The Pistons evened the series with a victory at the Silverdome, but the seventh game, though bitterly contested, belonged to the Celtics, 117-114, in Boston. In the aftermath of the Pistons' near upset of the Celtics, Dennis Rodman, a rookie Piston, told reporters that Bird was "overrated" because he is white. Asked to comment on his teammate's statement, Thomas replied: "I think Larry Bird is a very, very good basketball player. But I have to agree with Rodman. If he were black, he'd be just another good guy."

A media firestorm engulfed Thomas after his remarks were published nationwide, and in some quarters he was accused of being a "black racist." In an interview with Ira Berkow of the New York *Times* (June 2, 1987), however, Thomas claimed that he had been speaking sarcastically and that he had, in fact, been trying to call attention to the perpetuation of racial stereotypes by sports broadcasters. "What I was referring to," he explained to Berkow, "was not so much Larry Bird, but the perpetuation of stereotypes about blacks. When Bird makes a great play, it's due to his thinking, and his work habits. It's all planned out by him. It's not the case for blacks. All we do is run and jump. We never practice or give a thought to how we play. It's like I came dribbling out of my mother's womb. . . . Magic [Johnson] and Michael Jordan and me, for example, we're playing only on God-given talent, like we're animals, lions and tigers,

who run around wild in a jungle, while Larry's success is due to intelligence and hard work."

Having clarified his remarks, Thomas began to receive support from fellow athletes as well as journalists. For example, Dave Winfield of the New York Yankees told the New York *Daily News* (June 4, 1987) columnist Mike Lupica: "Isiah just got tired of hearing the same things, over and over again. Writers can write things without thinking. Fans say things. . . . It goes on without people meaning it. . . . It is all subtle, often unintentional. It is not malicious. It is just there. Magic is an athlete. Larry is smart. Black college football players are described by announcers as being 'well spoken.'"

Nevertheless, it became a sport for some writers to point out the flaws in Thomas's game, to separate his level of achievement from that of acknowledged superstars like Jordan, Johnson, and Bird. The sportswriters' main criticism of Thomas was that he lacked concentration, that he would play a perfect game for long stretches and then, inexplicably, lose his focus and, for example, throw away a game with an errant pass. Ever since his rookie season Thomas had been torn between his preference for an uninhibited, run-and-shoot style—an NBA All-Star type of game—and his recognition of the need to discipline himself, to subordinate his one-on-one genius to the requirements of doing only that which is necessary to win. "I'm not sure that I'd rather just play than win," Thomas once told Scotty Robertson, his first NBA coach, and even an inveterate Thomas booster like Chuck Daly, the Pistons' coach since the 1983–84 season, once remarked that his point guard's "threshold of boredom in the game is very low." "You live and die with what he does on the court," Daly has observed.

For his part, Thomas felt that it was unfair to criticize him for "inconsistent" play. Nevertheless, he admitted that he occasionally resented the game of basketball because of the power it had over his life. Once, he told Johnette Howard of the *Sporting News* (December 16, 1985), he even considered quitting the NBA: "I started to feel that basketball had too much control over how I felt. Whether I'd be happy or not started to depend on whether we'd win or lose." That conflict was resolved when he decided he had "to try to win every day."

Isiah Thomas put an end to the criticism of his basketball abilities during the 1988 championship series, when the Pistons extended the defending champion Lakers the full seven games. During the regular season, in which Thomas averaged 19.5 points and almost 8.4 assists per game, the Pistons for the first time won their division, the Central, and in the playoffs they overcame the "leprechauns" of Boston Garden, beating the Celtics, who had the home-court advantage, in six games. In the championship match against the Lakers, who were attempting to become the first NBA club to repeat as champions in nineteen years, the Pistons held a three-wins-to-two advantage when the series returned to the LA Forum for game six and, if needed, game seven. Early in the second half of the sixth game, with the Lakers holding the lead, 56-48, Isiah became Isiah. As Roland Lazenby described it in the *Sporting News*: "Thomas scored the next fourteen points in trancelike fashion . . . with a little more than four minutes to go in the period. He landed on the foot of the Lakers' Michael Cooper and had to be helped from the floor with a severely sprained ankle. Thirty-five seconds later, he returned to the game and continued the assault. By the end of the quarter, he had hit eleven of thirteen shots from the floor and scored twenty-five points, setting an NBA record for points in a quarter. Better yet, he had driven his team to an 81-79 lead." Although the Lakers eked out a last-second 103-102 win, Thomas finished game six with forty-three points, eight assists, six steals, and what Lazenby called "enough respect to last a lifetime." Thomas also finished the game with a jammed finger, a bruised eye, a facial cut, and an ankle so badly sprained that he was hobbled in the seventh game, which the Lakers won, 108-105.

When Thomas joined the Pistons, Detroit was known around the NBA as a "soft" team that could be intimidated physically. That reputation changed in 1985, when the Pistons acquired Rick Mahorn, a power forward with a Rock-of-Gibraltar physique and a rough-and-tumble style of play that made him one of the most feared defenders in the league. Another fearsome Piston is Bill Laimbeer, a six-foot-eleven 260-pound center with a velvety jump shot and a reputation for using unsportsmanlike tactics. Two additional intimidators are the young forwards Dennis "Worm" Rodman, a spring-legged rebounder who is regarded as perhaps the top defensive specialist in the NBA, and John "Spider" Salley, a premier shot blocker. Because of their rugged front line, the Pistons became known as pro basketball's "Bad Boys." In a *Rolling Stone* (May 4, 1989) profile of the Pistons, Jeff Coplon pointed out that, while the Bad Boys mystique entertained the fans, it offended some league officials and many players. By the end of the season, Coplon wrote, the Bad Boys were beginning to be perceived as "goons, thugs, terrorists. . . . When they took the court, a hockey game broke out. Normally placid opponents . . . blew up bumps into scuffles, scuffles into brawls. In the cultish NBA, if the Celtics were white America's team, and the Lakers were Club Hollywood, the Pistons belonged to Qaddafi. . . . Piston-bashing was suddenly a blood sport—especially among those most threatened by Detroit's rise."

Midway through the 1988–89 season, the Pistons traded Adrian Dantley to the Dallas Mavericks for Mark Aguirre, Thomas's old friend from Chicago. Thomas and Dantley had never gotten along, largely because Thomas felt that Dantley's methodical drives tended to disrupt the rhythm of the Piston offense, whose tempo it was Thomas's job, as point guard, to regulate. Notwithstanding the loss of Dantley, the Pistons won sixty-five of eighty-two games to compile the best regular-season record in the league. Moreover, the Pistons had developed the best backcourt in basketball, with Thomas being joined by the off guard Joe Dumars, an excellent shooter and playmaker and, along with Rodman, one the league's leading ball-hawking defenders. Backing up Thomas and Dumars was Vinnie Johnson, nicknamed the "Microwave" for his ability to melt down opposing defenses with his streak shooting.

With their bruising front line and three-deep backcourt, the Pistons repeated as Eastern Conference champs, besting Michael Jordan and the Chicago Bulls in six games. All that stood between Thomas and his first championship ring was his good friend Magic Johnson, the leader of the Lakers. Thomas and Johnson are openly affectionate, and their ritual pregame kiss when the Lakers and Pistons meet has become a ballyhooed media event. In the spring of 1989, however, it was the Lakers' turn to be jinxed by injuries, when both Byron Scott and Magic Johnson went down with pulled hamstring muscles. Their backcourt depleted, the Lakers were no match for the Pistons, who swept the two-time champions in four games.

In the estimation of Pistons coach Chuck Daly, Isiah Thomas is a "very complex person." On the one hand, he is a thoughtful, sensitive dreamer who likes to write free-verse poetry and is generous of his time with inner-city children, who idolize him. On the other hand, he has been accused of having one of the most obstreperous egos in professional sports. For example, he is said to be envious of Michael Jordan and his almost superhuman athletic skills, and he is rumored to have been the motivating factor behind the deal that shipped Adrian Dantley to Dallas. Thomas has denied both charges and remains generally undistracted by criticism of his personality. His consuming goal, he said in a recent interview, is "to establish in Detroit [what] they've done in Boston since the 1950s and 1960s, in terms of tradition, in terms of pride, in terms of style of play."

In 1988 Isiah Thomas signed a new eight-year contract with the Pistons worth some $16 million. Although his height is officially listed as six feet one inch, he may actually be an inch or two shorter than that. He is married to the former Lynn Kendall, a Chicago native who was his college sweetheart. They and their son, Joshua, live in the affluent Detroit suburb of Bloomfield Hills, where Thomas has installed in his home his own indoor basketball court. Having promised his mother that he would finish his college degree when he dropped out of Indiana to turn pro, Thomas holds a bachelor's degree in criminal justice. With Matt Dobek, Thomas is the author of *Bad Boys* (1989), an inside account of the Pistons' 1988–89 championship season.

References: Gentlemen's Q 58:190+ F '88 pors; Inside Sports 6:64+ Ap '84 por, 9:21+ N '87 pors; Nation 245:4+ Jl 4-11 '87; Newsweek 98:130 D 14 '81 por; Sport 77:59+ F '86 pors, 79:24+ My '88 pors; Sporting N p35 Mr 28 '81 por; Sports Illus

54:15+ *Ap* 6 '81 pors, 66:60+ *Ja* 19 '87 pors; *Who's Who in America, 1988–89*

Thompson, John

Sept. 2, 1941– Basketball coach. Address: c/o Basketball Office, Georgetown University, Washington, D.C. 20057

"I'm not Mr. Nice Guy," admits John Thompson, who is, along with Bob Knight, the most controversial coach in college basketball today. But whereas Knight coaches at Indiana University, a large, state-supported institution, Thompson, who was the head coach of the 1988 men's Olympic basketball team, has risen to the top of his profession at Georgetown University, a small, Roman Catholic, and academically exclusive school in Washington, D.C. Thompson's teams employ a bruising, harassing style of play, applying relentless defensive pressure designed to wear down the opponent and force turnovers. Off the court, Thompson shields his players from the press and rarely gives interviews himself. In keeping with Georgetown's high academic standards, he requires his players to be full-time students as well. Since Thompson began coaching at Georgetown in 1972, fifty-three of the fifty-five basketball players who entered the university as freshmen, and who did not drop out or transfer, have graduated.

Although his methods, particularly his restriction of media access to players, have been criticized by other coaches, both his players (who address him only as "Mr. Thompson" or "Coach") and his peers regard him with the utmost respect. A self-styled educator as well as a coach, Thomp-

son believes that the lessons learned in athletics apply also to other areas of life. Eric Smith, a former Georgetown player, has summed up Thompson's philosophy as follows: "No one gives you anything on the basketball court if they can help it, and if they can help it, no one gives you anything in life."

The youngest of the four children and the only son of John and Anna Thompson, John Thompson was born on September 2, 1941 in Washington, D.C., and was reared in housing projects in the predominantly black Anacostia section of the city. Although illiterate, Thompson's father was a proud, hardworking man who supported his family by working in a tile factory and as a mechanic. Anna Thompson had studied to be a teacher but was unable to get a job in the District of Columbia school system, since her teaching certificate came from a two-year college. Instead, she worked as a maid for five dollars a day in Washington's affluent northwest section. John Thompson told Leonard Shapiro of the *Washington Post Magazine* (January 13, 1980) that he "grew up in a family full of love," and though he and his three sisters sometimes had to wear secondhand clothing, they never felt deprived.

Devout Roman Catholics, Thompson's parents sent their only son to a parochial elementary school, where he was branded a slow learner until it was discovered that it was his poor eyesight, undiagnosed for several years, that made it difficult for Thompson to learn to read. When he was about eleven, a nun advised his mother to enroll him in a school for retarded children, but Anna Thompson refused, entering her son instead in one of Washington's then segregated public elementary schools. By the age of thirteen, Thompson had developed into a good student and talented athlete who had already attained the towering height of six feet, six inches. Recruited by basketball coaches from several local parochial high schools, he decided to attend northeast Washington's Archbishop Carroll High, where an alumnus secretly paid his tuition.

Thompson, who had reached his adult height of six feet, ten inches by his sophomore year, played center on the Archbishop Carroll basketball team, earning high-school all-American honors and leading the team to fifty-five consecutive victories—a Washington-area record that still stands. Although Washington's Catholic schools had been desegregated by that time, many local summer basketball leagues, to Thompson's dismay, continued to exclude blacks. Colleges from the Midwest and Northeast recruited Thompson, who chose Providence College in Providence, Rhode Island, partly in deference to his mother, who felt that its Dominican priests would look after her son.

While leading the Providence Friars' freshman team to a record of twenty wins and two losses, Thompson averaged over thirty-two points per game. Ballyhooed in the press as "the next Bill Russell," after the great Boston Celtics center, the quiet and withdrawn Thompson was expected by

Providence boosters to lead the Friars to the National Collegiate Athletic Association championship. But after joining the varsity in his sophomore year, Thompson disappointed the faithful by averaging "only" twelve points a game, and the Friars, although they won twenty regular season games, were eliminated by Temple University in the first round of the National Invitation Tournament (NIT) in the spring of 1962. In the following year, Thompson led Providence to the NIT championship, and in 1964, his senior year, the Friars appeared in the NCAA tournament, and he was named New England College Player of the Year.

After graduating from Providence College with a degree in economics, Thompson was selected in the third round of the 1964 NBA draft by the Celtics. In two seasons with the Boston team, he played sparingly, entering games only when Russell needed a rest. "Russell was durable," Red Auerbach explained in a discussion with Roland Lazenby of the *Sporting News* (December 31, 1984). "John didn't get much [playing] time, and he didn't like it. But it didn't turn him sour. . . . He was a smart, tough realist. He had a good sense about life, what was important in it." That "good sense about life" enabled Thompson to turn his back on pro basketball after two seasons with the Celtics. Although he was snapped up in the 1966 NBA expansion draft by the new Chicago Bulls franchise and was also wooed by the New Orleans Buccaneers of the recently formed American Basketball Association, he decided he did not want to be a basketball vagabond and rejected both offers. "The money I could have gotten from Chicago for playing didn't matter because I knew I wouldn't have been happy," Thompson explained to Juan Williams of the *Washington Post Magazine* (August 28, 1988). "I wanted to come home."

Returning to Washington, Thompson married his high school sweetheart and took a job as a social worker and teacher at Federal City College. He studied guidance and counseling on a part-time basis at the University of the District of Columbia, which awarded him a master's degree in 1971 and, though not a member of the faculty, coached basketball at St. Anthony's, a small Catholic high school in northeast Washington. During his six years at St. Anthony's, Thompson created one of the nation's most powerful metropolitan basketball programs, sending a dozen scholarship players into the collegiate ranks and compiling an auspicious record of 122 wins and only 26 losses.

In 1972 John Thompson accepted an offer of the position of head basketball coach at Georgetown University, where school officials were trying to reverse the fortunes of the Hoyas, a team that had lost twenty-three out of twenty-six games in the previous season. Seeking advice, Thompson turned to his friend Dean Smith, the highly successful head basketball coach at the University of North Carolina, who deplored the exploitation of student-athletes at so-called basketball factories, colleges that recruit athletes for the primary purpose of winning games but fail to encourage them

to attend classes. Thompson hired as an assistant Mary Fenlon, a former nun and Latin teacher he had known at St. Anthony's who became the keeper of "Mary's book," a log that Georgetown players must sign regularly, recording their weekly progress in the classroom. Morever, Thompson adopted a strict policy that scholarship players must not only maintain passing grades but attend classes regularly in order to be eligible to play. He also persuaded top high school basketball players in the Washington area to attend Georgetown, rather than out-of-town schools. His first team, which included several players he had coached at St. Anthony's, compiled a record of twelve wins and fourteen losses, an improvement of nine wins over the previous year, and, in the following year, the Hoyas split their twenty-six games. Thompson continued to recruit his players primarily from the talent-rich Washington area, but eyebrows were raised in collegiate basketball circles when, year after year, Georgetown's scholarships were awarded almost exclusively to black athletes.

After opening their 1974–75 campaign with seven successive wins, the Hoyas went into a slump, losing six straight. On entering Georgetown's cramped and decrepit McDonough Arena before a home game in early February, Coach Thompson was greeted by a racist banner that read, "Thompson the Nigger Flop Must Go." Motivated by anger and resentment, Thompson's young players won eleven of their next twelve contests, including a 62-61 upset of West Virginia University in the Eastern Collegiate Athletic Conference championship game that earned Georgetown its first invitation in thirty-two years to the NCAA postseason tourney, which determines the national champion. In the 1975-76 season, Georgetown posted a twenty-one and seven record and won a second consecutive berth in the NCAA tournament, though the Hoyas were eliminated in the first round of play, as they had been the year before.

In the summer of 1976 Thompson served as assistant to Dean Smith at the Summer Olympic Games in Montreal. There, the United States basketball team recaptured the gold medal that it had relinquished to the Soviet Union in 1972, marking the first time a country other than the United States had taken the top prize in Olympic basketball. In the 1976-77 season, Thompson's Hoyas won nineteen and lost nine. The following year, Thompson became miffed when his twenty-three-and-eight club was passed over by the NCAA tournament selection committee, and he spurned an offer to take part in the less-prestigious NIT tournament. In 1978-79 his Hoyas won twenty-four of twenty-eight regular season games, but they were again eliminated in the first round of postseason NCAA play.

Led by senior forwards John Duren and Craig Shelton, in the 1979–80 season the Hoyas came within one point of advancing into the final round of four teams in the NCAA tournament. Thompson's team had recorded twenty-six victories against just five losses when it was upended, 81-80, by the University of Iowa. In 1980–81 the Hoyas were led by Eric ("Sleepy") Floyd, a sharpshooting junior guard who went on to become the first of Thompson's players to make the all-American team. That squad won twenty and lost eleven before being eliminated in the first round of the NCAA tournament.

In 1981 Thompson recruited Patrick Ewing, a much-heralded seven-foot center from Boston who was widely considered to be the best high school basketball player in the United States. A powerful rebounder and a lane-clogging, shot-rejecting intimidator, Ewing became, under Thompson's tutelage, a four-time all-American and one of the most dominating players in college basketball history. In his freshman season, "the baby bull," as Ewing was called, led Georgetown to the NCAA championship game, in which the Hoyas suffered a heartbreaking 63-62 loss in the final seconds to Dean Smith's North Carolina Tar Heels. In Ewing's junior year, Georgetown captured its first national championship, defeating the University of Houston in the title game, 84-75. The Hoyas advanced to the national championship game again in Ewing's senior year, but they were defeated by their conference rival, Villanova, 66-64.

It was during the Ewing era that the phrase "Hoya paranoia" was coined to describe Georgetown's physically intimidating style of play, bellicose attitude towards opponents, and hostile relations with the media. Thompson is a private man who shields his family and his players from the press. For example, on each of the three occasions that his Hoyas have made the NCAA's Final Four, Thompson has sequestered his teams in locations some distance away from the host city. Moreover, when Thompson severely restricted press access to Patrick Ewing, the Georgetown coach was sharply criticized for overprotecting his shy star and for inhibiting his personal growth. In a discussion with Wayne Coffey of Sport (January 1985) that took place during Ewing's senior season, Thompson explained: "I definitely do not protect Patrick. What I attempt to do is provide him with an opportunity to get an education."

The most troubling accusation that has been leveled at Thompson's teams is that their seeming "us against them" mentality results in a brutal, menacing style of play. Indeed, the Hoyas have been involved in several bench-clearing free-for-alls in the 1980s, including two brawls with the University of Pittsburgh Panthers, one of their chief Big East antagonists, during the 1987-88 campaign. In the opinion of Sports Illustrated senior editor John Papanek, Georgetown has "been involved in more fights than any other team at that level," and Lou Carnesecca, the basketball coach at St. John's University, has said that a "preposterous military atmosphere" surrounds the Georgetown team. As Papanek told Juan Williams, Georgetown players "seem to have a persecution complex—they believe the officials and the other team are out to get them . . . . Georgetown's attitude precipitates into actual fights little things that wouldn't amount to anything ordinarily. They are unwilling to let it go as part of the game. They are always willing to fight."

Nevertheless, Thompson insists that he has never advocated fighting or taught his teams to hate their opponents. Georgetown teams emphasize defense, and they are renowned for their mastery of a trapping defense that forces turnovers by harassing the ballhandler regardless of where he is on the court. As Thompson told Juan Williams, the Hoya "style of play lends itself to aggressiveness. We cover the full court for forty minutes, and that brings about and creates frustrations in ourselves and in other people at times."

In his book A Season Inside; One Year in College Basketball (1988), John Feinstein pointed out that the fights between Georgetown and Pittsburgh players called attention both to the aggressiveness of the Hoya style of play and to Thompson's acutely adversarial relations with the media. After police officers were forced to help break up one of the Georgetown-Pittsburgh melees, the CBS-TV sports analyst and former Seton Hall basketball coach, Bill Raftery, observed that a Georgetown player had started the fight and that Thompson's teams had been embroiled in a number of such brawls over the years. Thompson's response was an angry denunciation of Raftery, who, he claimed, had no right to criticize Georgetown, since he had been an "unsuccessful" college coach. (Raftery actually had a career coaching record of 154-141.) "This," wrote Feinstein, "was classic Thompson: Deflect the issue. To begin with, Raftery was a good coach. . . . But even if he had been a terrible coach the point was moot. One did not have to be a . . . coach at all . . . to be appalled by Georgetown's on-court behavior. . . . [Thompson] was the only person who had enough sway with his players to say, 'Don't fight or else,' and know they wouldn't fight." Moreover, as John Papanek observed, "Georgetown basketball seems to have become a symbol of belligerence. And because Thompson is black and the players are black, it has been adopted by black youth as a symbol of belligerence, hostility."

Perhaps the most serious charge that has been leveled at Thompson is that he is a former victim of racism who now practices racial discrimination by fielding all-black teams. Detractors have contended that Thompson refuses to recruit white players, but Georgetown administrators, as well as fellow Big East coaches, including Jim Boeheim of Syracuse, have maintained that Thompson does not discriminate against white athletes. Indeed, the talent scout on Thompson's staff who first contacts prospective recruits is white, and, as the Reverend Timothy Healy, the president of Georgetown University, has explained: "What John does is recruit kids who play in his system. Obviously, he is more comfortable with black kids. . . . Professional basketball players are mostly black. Basketball is a city game. Damn few farm kids come [to Georgetown] to play."

The question of Thompson's possible bias against white ball players was raised most controversially by Brent Musburger, the CBS-TV sports commentator, when Thompson was selected to be the coach of the 1988 United States Olympic men's basketball team. During a televised interview, Musburger said that the restriction Thompson places on media access to Georgetown players was "terribly unfortunate because it overshadows some marvelous things that he has done with a lot of . . . underprivileged city black kids that he brings there [to Georgetown], and they get an opportunity to graduate from a great school." Musburger went on to say that the "number-one question" on the New York sports talk shows was, "Is John Thompson going to put a white basketball player on the United States Olympic team?" Thompson, for his part, excoriated Musburger, asking, "Has Brent seen the financial statements of my students? He's saying a lot of socially deprived black kids [play for Georgetown]. That's a generalization and a very biased statement. I've had several kids who happen to be black that haven't been poor and from disadvantaged families." As to the question of the racial composition of the Olympic team, Thompson said, "I think that's a very dangerous statement for anybody in Brent's position to say because I interpret that as saying there should be a quota of blacks on the Olympic team."

Indeed, Thompson did select a white player, forward Dan Majerle of Central Michigan University, for the Olympic squad. "I don't give any more thought to [a player's race] than I give to which school Dan Majerle went to, or which school Bimbo Coles [another Olympic team member] went to," Thompson told a reporter for the *Washington Post* (July 28, 1988). "All I'm trying to identify are people who can fight over screens, people who can run the floor, people who can play defense." For the 1988 Olympic Games in Seoul, South Korea, Thompson assembled a team of fierce defensive specialists, but he suffered a crushing disappointment when the team from the Soviet Union handily defeated his squad early in the basketball tournament and went on to capture the gold medal. Once favored to win the gold, the United States team was forced to settle for the third-place bronze.

Controversy swirled around Thompson again when, in early 1989, he objected to the NCAA's decision to tighten admissions standards for student-athletes. A measure known as Proposition 48, passed by the NCAA in 1983 and effective in 1986, stipulated that, to be awarded an athletic scholarship, entering freshmen must have a high school grade point average of at least 2.0 (on a 4.0 scale) in a college-preparatory core curriculum and achieve a minimum score of 700 (out of a possible 1600) on the Scholastic Aptitude Test or 15 (out of a possible 36) on the American College Testing Program exam. The rule also contained a provision stating that athletes who met only one of these requirements could still receive a scholarship but could not play or practice with the team during their freshman year. They would also lose a year of athletic eligibility.

Then, on January 11, 1989, the NCAA's member schools passed Proposition 42, which eliminated the latter provision and mandated that student-athletes must meet both academic requirements in order to be granted a scholarship. The passage of Proposition 42, which was to take effect in August 1990, touched off a firestorm of controversy, as black coaches, most notably John Thompson, voiced their strong opposition. In explaining his position to reporters, Thompson said that he believes that the rule penalizes minority students, most of whom attend substandard high schools, and he pointed to studies that indicate that standardized tests are culturally biased in favor of white, middle-class students.

On January 13, 1989, the day before the Hoyas were to play Boston College, Thompson announced that he would not coach in another NCAA-sanctioned game until he was satisfied that something had been done to provide those student-athletes "with appropriate opportunity and hope for access to college." When he walked off the court before the start of the following evening's game, he received a standing ovation from the fans and his players. He also boycotted Georgetown's next game, against Providence, on January 18. The following day, Thompson met with Georgetown administrators and top officials of the NCAA. He persuaded NCAA officials to delay implementation of Proposition 42 until 1991 and, a day later, announced that he was resuming his coaching responsibilities immediately.

Led by Alonzo Mourning, a six-foot-ten freshman center who specializes in shot-blocking, rebounding, and all-around intimidation on defense, Thompson's Hoyas came within one game in 1989 of qualifying for the Final Four in the NCAA tournament. Georgetown handily won the Big East championship tournament in early March and then posted three consecutive wins in the Eastern regional tourney before being upset by the Blue Devils of Duke University. The Hoyas won twenty-six of thirty games over the course of the 1988–89 season, giving Thompson an overall record at Georgetown of 399 wins against just 115 losses.

John Thompson is a registered Democrat and a self-described "capitalist" who believes that money is the only true measure of equality in the United States. As Juan Williams observed, Thompson's "ideology is not centered on the differences between Republicans and Democrats, or even between blacks and whites. The great divide in American life, Thompson says, is between rich and poor." In the same interview, Thompson said: "When I don't have money, I am looking for issues that pertain to getting me money. When I have money, I'm looking at it from a standpoint of how much I am going to be taxed." In addition to the substantial salary he earns for coaching Georgetown's basketball team, Thompson endorses Nike products, appears in a television commercial promoting milk, runs a summer basketball camp, has a contract with WTTG-TV in Washington to make regular appearances on sports shows telecast by that station, and is a highly paid speaker.

A physically imposing man, Thompson stands six feet, ten inches tall and weighs 280 pounds. Because he perspires profusely from the opening tip-off to the final buzzer, he sits at courtside with a towel draped around his neck and mops his forehead repeatedly. Thompson and his wife, Gwendolyn, are the parents of two sons and a daughter and live in a large house in the well-to-do northwest section of Washington. It was given to them by grateful alumni of Georgetown University. Their oldest child, John 3d, is a recent graduate of Princeton, where he played guard for the varsity basketball squad. Ronny, their middle child, plays guard for his father at Georgetown. The youngest of their children, thirteen-year-old Tiffany, stands just three inches shorter than her six-foot-four-inch older brothers.

References: N Y Daily News p12+ Ja 9 '81 pors; N Y Post p94+ Ja 25 '85 pors; Sport 70:21+ Ja '85 pors; Sports Illus 70:16+ Ja 23 '89 pors; Washington Post mag p10+ Ja 13 '80 pors, p65+ F 2 '86 por, p18+ Ag 28 '88 pors; Who's Who in America, 1988–89

Thomson, Kenneth (Roy)

Sept. 1, 1923– Canadian publisher. Address: b. Thomson Newspapers Ltd., Thomson Bldg., 65 Queen Street West, Toronto, Ontario M5H 2M8, Canada; h. 8 Castle Frank Rd., Toronto, Ontario M4W 2Z4, Canada

Since assuming control of his family's diversified international business interests after the death of his father, Roy Thomson, in 1976, Kenneth Thomson has proved to be very much his own person, embarking on an aggressive acquisition strategy that has made him the largest foreign investor in the United States publishing industry. His profitable Thomson Newspapers, made up of weeklies and dailies in the United States and Canada, and International Thomson Organization, involved in specialty and informational publishing, recently merged to form the Thomson Organization, based in Toronto, Canada, the world's fourth-largest me-

dia conglomerate, with 27,500 employees. As one of the world's richest men, Thomson controls a fortune worth an estimated $5 billion. Although industry observers feared that the quiet and soft-spoken Thomson would fail to measure up to the achievements of his colorful father, Thomson boldly reversed the latter's strategy of investing profits from the Canadian operations into business in the United Kingdom, using cash from the family's 20 percent ownership in North Sea oilfields to help finance a $1.5 billion acquisition campaign that has included Canada's Hudson's Bay Company in 1979 and FP Publications in 1980 as well as many publishing concerns in the United States —operations that have prospered because of Thomson's bottom-line orientation. As one observer has remarked about Thomson, "He is as effective as he is unknown."

Kenneth Roy Thomson was born on September 1, 1923 in Toronto, Ontario, the youngest of the three children and the only son of Edna (Irvine) and Roy Thomson. According to Susan Goldenberg in her book *The Thomson Empire* (1984), Thomson experienced a lonely childhood. "He was quiet, not athletic, and his mother would select the youngsters to attend his birthday parties," Goldenberg wrote. Kenneth was two when his father's auto parts dealership failed, and in 1928 the family moved to North Bay, a small mining town 225 miles northeast of Toronto. Kenneth Thomson told David MacFarlane in an interview for *Saturday Night* (October 1980) that his parents did not have much money in those days; their lifestyle, he said, was "extremely simple."

All that changed in 1930, when Roy Thomson began selling De Forest Crosley radios. The following year, in an inspired venture to spur demand for his product, he started his own radio station, CFCH. That start-up caused a sensation in northern Ontario, becoming the cornerstone of what was to grow into one of the world's largest media empires. "All I really knew was that something big was going on in town and that Dad was at the middle of it all," Kenneth Thomson recalled to MacFarlane.

It was not long before Roy Thomson started radio stations in the nearby towns of Timmins and Kirkland Lake. They prospered, as did the

Timmins Press, a newspaper he bought in Timmins. Thus by 1937, when the family moved back to Toronto, Roy Thomson was sufficiently well-off to be able to send his son to Upper Canada College (UCC), a prestigious private school. Kenneth was an average student, and he showed little interest in athletics or in any of the usual extracurricular activities. As he later confided to David MacFarlane: "I didn't give it much of a chance. I was a little bit different from the other guys." When he was sixteen, Thomson worked as a disc jockey at CFCH, his father's first radio station. As reported by Susan Goldenberg in her book, Roy Thomson once commented about his son, "He's a fine boy but I'm just a little concerned that maybe he doesn't push enough."

Following his graduation in 1942 from UCC, Thomson enrolled at the University of Toronto, but he dropped out in December to join the Royal Canadian Air Force. For much of the next three years, he was posted in London, where he rewrote news articles for an air force magazine called Wings Abroad. According to Susan Goldenberg, Thomson enrolled as a graduate student at Cambridge University in 1945, even though he did not have an undergraduate degree. Susan Goldenberg explained that he was accepted at Cambridge after Roy Thomson persuaded the university's administration to bend the rules to admit his son.

Thomson returned to Canada in 1947, after earning an M.A. degree in law, to learn the family business from the bottom up. For the next two years, he worked first as a cub reporter at the Timmins Daily Press, where his salary was double that of the editor, and then as an advertising salesman for the Galt Evening Reporter. Colleagues remember him as quiet, competent, and diligent. From 1950 to 1953 Thomson was groomed for his role as heir-apparent of the Thomson empire, serving a three-year apprenticeship as general manager of the Galt newspaper. His record there was undistinguished—"He didn't introduce anything outstanding," one former company executive told Susan Goldenberg—but, when Roy Thomson moved to Scotland in 1953, his son succeeded him as president and chairman of Thomson Newspapers, which controlled twenty-four dailies and eight weekly newspapers in Canada and twenty-two dailies and six weeklies in the United States.

In 1966 Roy Thomson achieved a lifelong aspiration when he bought the influential Times of London and merged that debt-ridden newspaper with the Sunday Times, which he had purchased in 1958. Before the Times purchase, Thomson's empire was worth approximately $300 million. Roy Thomson announced that, while he himself would not join the Times's board of directors, his son would, as chairman. As a result, in late 1967 Kenneth Thomson and his family moved to London, arousing great curiosity among London newspaper reporters and other observers of the local media scene. As Lord Francis-Williams, who served as press adviser to Prime Minister Clement Attlee, told Alan Harvey of the Toronto Globe and Mail

(December 23, 1967), "The younger man is clearly destined to take over fully, and the sooner we in Britain have a chance to size him up the better."

While Kenneth Thomson lived in England for the next three years, his father pursued an aggressive campaign to expand and diversify the family's holdings, so that by 1971 the Thomsons owned 78 percent of their British arm, the Thomson Organization, and 77 percent of their North American company, Thomson Newspapers, with holdings worth $333 million. Ownership was held through the Thomson Equitable Corporation and the Woodbridge Company, two private companies registered in Ontario. "It's done this way so the debts of one will never become the obligations of the other," Thomson explained to Paul Gibson of the Financial Post (June 12, 1971). The Thomson empire earned 50 percent of its income from newspapers, which, by this time, numbered forty-five in Canada and twenty-three in the United States and which operated with a minimum of editorial influence from the Thomsons. One advertisement for the Thomson newspapers read, as reported by Paul Gibson in his Financial Post story, "A few words about our editorial policy: we don't have one." The Thomsons did, however, develop a reputation for sacrificing journalistic quality to profit considerations, and they caused some controversy when Roy Thomson bought the Peterborough Examiner in February 1968, because of fears that the newspaper's high quality would be compromised.

Other investments included ownership of the British tour operator Thomson Travel; Britannia Airways; book and telephone directory publishing; 50 percent ownership of Scottish and York Holdings, an insurance firm; a 20 percent interest in the Piper and Claymore oil fields, which had been developed with Jean Paul Getty and Armand Hammer; and 100 percent ownership of Dominion-Consolidated Truck Lines. Believing that "the Times is only part of the organization" and that it was "just a drag on the profits," as he told Paul Gibson, Kenneth Thomson moved back to Toronto in 1971. Already the chairman of Thomson Newspapers Limited, he was now named cochairman of Thomson Organization Limited, an assignment that reflected Roy Thomson's intention to eventually pass on to his son control of the corporate empire as well as his hereditary British title, Lord Thomson of Fleet (referring to his ownership of newspapers on Fleet Street in London, the traditional home of the British newspaper industry), which he received in 1964.

The transfer came about on August 4, 1976, when Roy Thomson died in London at the age of eighty-two. Although he was survived by two sisters, Roy Thomson stipulated in his will that his son and his son's male heirs would control the family business. Some observers expected the younger Thomson to falter without Roy Thomson's guidance, since he usually came up short in comparisons with his father. Kenneth Thomson was shy and modest; his father had been ebullient and aggressive. Thomson himself admitted to Oliver

Clausen in an interview for the Toronto Globe and Mail (March 11, 1967): "I sometimes feel I'm caught up in a train of events Dad created. I do hold him in a measure of awe. I suppose it's inevitable that he sometimes seems bigger than life to me. But please don't make me out [to be] a carbon copy of Dad."

But the pessimists' predictions proved unfounded. Behind the scenes, Kenneth Thomson and John Tory, his chief adviser and overseer of the family's two principal holding companies, had gradually been assuming control of the Thomson empire, so that the transition following Roy Thomson's death was a smooth one. And it was soon clear that Kenneth Thomson did not intend to be a carbon copy of his father. One of his first major decisions involved a corporate reorganization. In mid-1978 he created the Canada-based International Thomson Organization Limited (ITOL), reducing the London-based Thomson Organization to the status of a subsidiary of the new company and removing $400 million in North Sea oil profits from the United Kingdom and its currency controls.

Although the move was made primarily for tax reasons and to provide Thomson with investment capital, there was considerable speculation in Britain that the Thomson family was planning to sell its business interests there. Thomson watchers noted that "by default or design" Kenneth Thomson was spending more time in Toronto than in London. In 1978 he moved the newspaper headquarters there from London. Also in that year, Gordon Brunton, the chief executive of International Thomson, announced that he had decided to lessen Thomson's dependency on oil and gas revenues, which he expected to run out by 1988, and to invest instead in "infinite resources," such as information and high-tech publishing ventures. In another reorganizational move, Thomson Newpapers in Canada introduced a system of district managers, with twelve to fifteen newspapers in a region managed by an executive located in the regional headquarters.

In another gesture indicating a decreasing British orientation, in May 1978 Thomson made it known that he was not prepared to continue subsidizing the money-losing Times. He said that the resistance of the newspaper's unions to the introduction of computer technology—leading to work stoppages and almost $2 million in lost profits during the first three months of 1978 alone—constituted "an impossible way to run a business." Thomson issued an ultimatum: unless the Times's unions and management could work out a compromise by November 30, 1978, the newspapers would cease publication. Although the announcement caused an uproar, when no agreement materialized, Thomson suspended publication of the Times, the Sunday Times, and the latter's three supplements.

That eleven-month shutdown was a costly and bitter one for both sides. When union leaders criticized Thomson for refusing to negotiate with them face-to-face, Thomson explained that he did not want to interfere with the efforts of the Times management, which demanded staff reductions, revised dispute procedures, new technology, and continuous production. On October 23, 1980 Thomson announced that he would either sell or close the Times and the Sunday Times by March 1981. "I don't want to use the words bitter or resentful, because I don't want to inflame feelings," Thomson told Ross Laver of the Toronto Globe and Mail (October 23, 1980), "but I have to tell you I feel very, very disappointed. . . . What really did the job for us were these unreasonable labor problems—we just couldn't cope with it any more." In late February 1981 Thomson agreed to sell the newspapers to Rupert Murdoch, the Australian press baron.

Meanwhile, in Toronto, Thomson and his advisers were busy designing a new direction for the Thomson empire. Roy Thomson's strategy had involved buying undervalued monopoly newspapers, sending in new managers to eliminate inefficiencies, and not interfering with the news and editorial departments. Kenneth Thomson now intended to use some of his financial muscle to acquire large corporations. In early March 1979 he made a surprise $306 million bid for the Hudson's Bay Company (HBC), Canada's oldest retailer, offering to buy 51 percent of the company shares at $30 each. A second bidder, the wealthy Toronto industrialist Galen Weston, jumped into the fray, offering $40 a share for 51 percent, but Thomson made another offer of $35 a share for 60 percent of the company's stock. Weston raised his bid to $40 a share for 60 percent of the company, but Thomson won out with an offer of $37 for up to 75 percent of the HBC shares for $545 million. "I think it pays to put your money where your heart is," Thomson commented, as quoted by Ian Brown in Maclean's (April 30, 1979).

On January 12, 1980 Thomson paid $140 million to outbid two competitors for control of FP Publications Limited, a leading Canadian newspaper chain comprised of eight newspapers with a combined circulation of 800,000. Thomson immediately streamlined FP operations, leaving him with the Toronto Globe and Mail, the Winnipeg Free Press, the Lethbridge Herald, and the Victoria Times-Colonist. He closed the money-losing Ottawa Journal, the FP News Service, and the Calgary Albertan, merged the production of the morning and afternoon papers in Victoria, British Columbia, and ended a partnership with the Southam chain by selling his interests in both the Montreal Gazette and the Vancouver Sun newspapers.

Because Thomson's purchase meant that only two Canadian companies, Thomson and Southam, owned fifty-seven of Canada's newspapers, Prime Minister Pierre Trudeau instituted antitrust proceedings and established a Royal Commission on Newspapers, chaired by Thomas Kent, to investigate the increasing concentration of media ownership in Canada. Thomson was called before the commission to provide evidence, and during the commission proceedings he was criticized for penny-pinching and for being indifferent to the editorial quality of Thomson newspapers. "We just have to hope that eventually we'll be able to make people realize that we are producing good newspapers," Thomson responded, as reported by Deborah Dowling in the *Financial Post* (April 25, 1981), "and that we have to produce them within the social and economic context of the community in which they are published." Defending the bottom-line orientation of his newspapers, he further stated: "We were one of the first organizations to institute a financial control system. It's the only way to run a business."

In the wake of that buying activity, in 1983 Thomson was forced to decrease his family's share in ITOL from 82 percent to 73 percent and in Thomson Newspapers by 10 percent to reduce the debt incurred in the HBC buyout and to help finance further acquisitions in the United States. The sale of 6.4 million shares of ITOL stock for $76 million left Thomson with 100 million shares, worth $1.2 billion. Following the sale of the *Times*, Thomson was quoted by a reporter for *Forbes* (March 2, 1981) as saying that he still hoped "to add three to five papers a year" to the company's American holdings. True to his word, by 1985 Thomson had quietly become the largest foreign investor in the United States publishing industry. Analysts noted that, between 1978 and 1988, Thomson spent $1.5 billion to buy small daily and weekly newspapers and such specialized trade publications as *Jane's Fighting Ships*, the *American Banker*, *Physicians' Desk Reference*, and the *Journal of Taxation*.

Under the leadership of Michael Brown, who has been ITOL's chief executive since 1984, the acquisition strategy has been to buy market leaders—publications that do well from subscription revenue alone so that they are relatively recession-proof—then to cut costs and leave management alone. ITOL has also sought publications containing the type of information that can be repackaged in another form. *Jane's Fighting Ships*, for example, led to a new weekly, *Jane's Defence Weekly*, and a number of other periodicals with a military theme. In 1986 Thomson paid $203 million for the Los Angeles-based Cordura Corporation, a publisher of auto repair manuals. In 1987 Thomson bought out Britain's leading legal publisher, and in the following year he acquired four major databases in the United States from Capital Cities/ABC. "He hasn't attracted much attention, but Thomson has had one of the most aggressive acquisition campaigns in publishing in the past half-dozen years," J. Kendrick Noble, a media analyst with PaineWebber Incorporated, pointed out to Edith Terry of *Business Week* (June 9, 1986).

That this strategy has paid off is evident from the strong performance of Thomson shares in the international stock markets. John Soganich, the financial columnist for the media industry publication *Marketing*, reported in his December 5, 1988 column that investment counselors at Canada's top brokerage houses were bullish on the stock

of both Thomson Newspapers and ITOL. In addition to their stability, what strongly appealed to the brokers was the companies' "timely" diversification away from energy investments because of depressed oil prices.

In March 1989 ITOL disposed of the last of its British energy holdings. The $630 million that was realized was reinvested two months later to pay most of the $810 million cost of acquiring the Lawyers Cooperative Publishing Company of Rochester, New York. The remaining $200 million was added to Thomson's aggregate debt of $840 million. That deal made Thomson one of the largest legal publishers in North America. On June 2, 1989 ITOL and Thomson Newspapers merged under the name of the Thomson Corporation, becoming, with 27,500 employees and revenues of $4.7 billion, the world's fourth-largest media conglomerate, behind Time/Warner, the Bertelsmann Group of Germany, and Capital Cities. In North America Thomson currently publishes 156 daily newspapers and thirty-six weeklies. Kenneth Thomson retained his position as chairman of the new company, with his son David, at the age of thirty-two the designated heir-apparent, playing an increasingly bigger role in the day-to-day business operations. The Thomson family holds an estimated 68 percent stake in the new company, which will be based in Toronto but will also maintain offices in New York. The North American newspaper group contributed 48 percent of Thomson's operating profits in 1988, the British publishing group contributed 42 percent, and the travel operations represented 10 percent of profits. 1988 revenues totaled $3.65 billion, with an operating income of $350 million.

Kenneth Thomson married his wife, the former Nora Marilyn Lewis, a Toronto fashion model, in 1956. They have three children: David, Lynne, and Peter. The Thomsons live in the Rosedale district of Toronto, in a twenty-three-room red brick Georgian mansion. They also maintain a home in Kensington Palace Gardens in London. Thomson uses the title he inherited from his father when he is in England. He has amassed an extensive collection of paintings and ivory and wooden carvings. During the early 1960s he began buying the work of his favorite artist, the nineteenth-century Dutch-Canadian painter Cornelius Krieghoff, many of whose paintings he houses in a gallery next to his office. Thomson donated $4.5 million to the Roy Thomson Hall, a concert hall in Toronto.

In his *Saturday Night* piece, David MacFarlane described Kenneth Thomson as a neat, stylishly dressed man whose "grey sideburns and dark-framed glasses distinguish an anonymous but pleasant face." Thomson, who is six feet one inch tall and slim, drinks only occasionally and does not smoke. He dislikes public attention and sits on the board of directors of only a few outside companies. He is a Baptist. His close friends say that Thomson is a friendly, unaffected man who sometimes flies coach class on business trips and answers his own telephone. Apart from devoting time to his Krieghoff art collection, which now contains over 150 paintings and is the world's largest, Thomson relaxes by listening to country-and-western music and by watching western movies, which he collects. Neighbors report seeing him walking his dog and shopping with his wife at the local supermarket—the type of unasssuming behavior befitting someone who once told a reporter, "If you get any highfalutin' ideas about how important you are, look at a few skeletons and you'll soon come down to earth."

References: Maclean's 92:30+ Ap 30 '79 pors; Globe Magazine p6+ Mr 11 '67 pors; Toronto Life p212+ My '80 pors; Toronto Star B p1+ O 21 '84; Canadian Who's Who, 1988; Goldenberg, Susan. The Thomson Empire; The First Fifty Years (1984); International Who's Who, 1989–90; Who's Who, 1989; Who's Who in America, 1988–89

Thyssen-Bornemisza de Kaszon, Baron Hans Heinrich

(tĭs´ĕn-bôr´ ne-mē-sa de ka´ son))

Apr. 13, 1921– Art collector; industrialist.
Address: "Villa Favorita," 6976 Castagnola di Lugano, Switzerland

In international art circles, the collection of Baron Hans Heinrich Thyssen-Bornemisza de Kaszon is considered to be the second-finest in the world, surpassed only by that of the Queen of England. One of Europe's richest men (his annual income is estimated to be about $50 million), the Dutch-born baron inherited his title, his extensive industrial holdings, and part of his art collection from his fa-

ther, the late Baron Heinrich Thyssen-Bornemisza, whose wife was a Hungarian baroness. The first baron had invested a large portion of the family fortune in an acclaimed collection of old master paintings, many of them German primitives. Following his death in 1947, the current baron was at first attracted to collecting by his desire to reassemble his father's collection, which had been divided among several heirs.

A Swiss citizen since 1950, Hans Heinrich (known to friends as "Heinie") has combined his vast wealth with a shrewd eye for acquisitions in expanding and improving a collection that now includes about 1,500 paintings, most of which are housed at the family villa on Lake Lugano, in the Swiss canton of Ticino. The baron has augmented his collection with primitive Italian works, paintings from the German expressionist school, nineteenth-century American landscapes, and other modern and contemporary works. The generous art connoisseur, who broke with family tradition by opening the villa's museum to the public after his father's death, frequently lends his paintings for exhibitions abroad. In December 1988 he signed an agreement with the Spanish Ministry of Culture to exhibit 787 of his paintings in Madrid for a ten-year period, starting in June 1991.

Baron Hans Heinrich Thyssen-Bornemisza de Kaszon was born in The Hague, the Netherlands on April 13, 1921, one of the four children of Baron Heinrich Thyssen-Bornemisza and Baroness Margarethe Bornemisza de Kaszon of Hungary. The German grandfather of Hans Heinrich, August Thyssen, had founded a sprawling empire of steel, iron, mining, banking, and manufacturing concerns so vast that he earned the epithet "the Andrew Carnegie of Europe." August Thyssen's factories supplied the German kaiser with arms during World War I, and following his death in 1926, his oldest son, Fritz, inherited August's steel mills, which he soon merged with other companies to form the Vereinigte Stahlwerke, then the largest mining trust in the world. An early supporter of Adolf Hitler, Fritz Thyssen held several important positions under der Führer, including that of supreme state authority for industry in western Germany, but he eventually broke with Hitler and, in 1939, fled to Switzerland, leaving his German industrial empire to be nationalized after World War II as August Thyssen-Huette. On the death of August, Heinrich, his second son, who had immigrated to Hungary in 1906 and married Baroness Margarethe later that same year, inherited his father's shipbuilding and shipping companies, which the family patriarch had established to transport his company's steel down the Rhine River and throughout the world.

August Thyssen had been a friend and patron of the great French sculptor Auguste Rodin, and the first baron inherited his father's budding interest in art. Following his marriage to Margarethe, Heinrich purchased Rohoncz Castle, his wife's ancestral home in Hungary. The couple lived there until 1919, when, as landowners, they were forced to flee the country following the Communist revolution led by Béla Kun. They settled in the Netherlands, where Hans Heinrich was born two years later. By then an avid collector of art, the older baron had embarked on a quest to acquire paintings, particularly those of the Flemish and German old masters. As Alan Levy wrote in *ARTnews* (November 1979), "On a grand scale, he set out to illustrate the entire history of European painting from the fourteenth to the eighteenth centuries."

Throughout the 1920s and early 1930s, the older baron acquired an impressive range of paintings and other art objects. As his son told Alan Levy, "He bought for love of art, and he was able to afford almost anything he wanted, for he was buying at a time when everybody else was selling." The first baron exhibited some of his acquisitions only once, at the New Pinakothek in Munich in 1930, on which occasion the so-called Rohoncz Collection proved to be such a stunning success that the baron, feeling his connoisseurship had been confirmed by both the public and the critics, continued to expand his holdings. In 1933 he purchased the Villa Favorita, a seventeenth-century Venetian-style retreat on the shore of Lake Lugano, in Switzerland, formerly the estate of Prince Leopold of Prussia, and installed his family there. Four years later, he added a wing to the Villa Favorita to house his growing collection, which by the time of his death in 1947 had grown into the largest private assemblage of old masters in Europe.

Hans Heinrich Thyssen-Bornemisza grew up surrounded by great art and became a willing beneficiary of his father's tutelage, since the first baron taught his children, particularly Heinie, everything he believed they should know about art. As the present baron explained to Alan Levy: "When I was a boy staying with him, and later, when I was visiting him from university, every day I was here we would walk through his gallery. . . . We would stand before a painting, and he might say something about the artist's technique or the relationship between master and pupil—in other words, a technical look at things. And if I had anything to contribute, we would discuss it. But mostly I just listened. He would stand and look at one painting for hours." Since his autocratic father brooked no rebellion from his children, young Heinie generally complied with the strict tutorial regimen.

Educated in his youth at the Realgymnasium in The Hague, he later studied art at the University of Fribourg, in Switzerland, from which he graduated in 1945. When his father died two years later, he inherited his title, the bulk of his industrial holdings, and part of his art collection. Chagrined by the dispersal of almost half of the collection of old masters among several heirs, the young baron embarked on what was to become a lifelong passion when he tried to reassemble those works as a memorial to his father. Buying back as many of the paintings as he could from his brother and two sisters, he soon found himself intrigued by the challenge of the hunt. One coveted work by the Flemish painter Petrus Christus belonged to an aunt, who had promised to leave it to him but gave it instead to the West German chancellor, Konrad Adenauer, and in 1965 the baron was able to buy it back in Switzerland. "One acquisition led to another until the collecting virus had entered his bloodstream," John Walker, the director emeritus of the National Gallery in Washington, D.C., related to Alan Levy. "He told me that each New Year's Eve he made a resolution not to collect anymore, and that by the first of January the resolution was always broken."

In 1948 the new baron made his first important departure from his father's markedly reclusive style. Although the first baron had opened the Villa Favorita's "Pinacoteca," or gallery, briefly for private visits during the late 1930s, he decided to close its doors entirely in 1940. The year after his father's death, the present baron opened the gallery to the public, and its works continue to be available for public viewing today. "Unlike the majority of private collectors, who are reluctant to share their treasures," the art critic Barbara Rose wrote in *House & Garden* (July 1983), "Baron Thyssen . . . wants others to share the pleasure he obviously enjoys in viewing the great art he has collected."

Charged with the postwar reorganization of the family's industrial empire during a time when the Thyssen name was still linked with Fritz's erstwhile support of the Nazi party, the young baron also found himself embroiled in a dispute that had begun during the war between his late father and the United States Justice Department. The conflict concerned a Thyssen-owned American-based bank that the United States government had confiscated because the first baron, though a neutral residing in Switzerland, had had interests in several German industries, some of which manufactured supplies for the German military. In 1949 his son brought suit to regain ownership of the bank, and the case dragged on until 1961, when the United States Court of Appeals for the District of Columbia ruled against the baron. In 1950 Hans Heinrich became a Swiss citizen, though he later moved his official headquarters to Monte Carlo, after the Swiss canton of Ticino imposed a transaction tax that he regarded as confiscatory. He aided refugees of the 1956 Hungarian revolution by establishing a home for some of them in Innsbruck and by publishing a Bible in Hungarian.

Throughout the 1950s, 1960s, and 1970s, Baron Thyssen continued to purchase paintings, sculptures, Oriental carpets, and other art objects, many of them from prestigious sources. Spurning the conventional wisdom that held that the best of the old masters already belonged to museums, he stockpiled treasures that included a Fragonard from Baron Maurice de Rothschild in 1956, a Palma Vecchio from Baron Edouard de Rothschild in 1959, a Lucas van Leyden from Lady Dunsany and a Duccio from the collection of John D. Rockefeller 2d in 1971, and a Rembrandt from Lord Margadale in 1976. "The baron singlehandedly competes with wealthy nations and with great museums," Paul Richard wrote in the *Washington Post* (November

18, 1979). "His eye is sharp, his fortune large, his ambition even larger. He buys and buys and buys."

In 1970 the baron restructured his industrial empire into Thyssen-Bornemisza, N.V., a privately owned conglomerate that then had its headquarters on the outskirts of Amsterdam. Three years later, the group added Indian Head, an American industrial conglomerate, to its interests in shipping, stevedoring, shipbuilding, natural gas distribution, farm machinery, and construction materials. Since then, Thyssen-Bornemisza, N.V., has diversified into various other industries, including storage and container leasing companies, glass manufacturing, and information systems firms. The conglomerate nets 40 percent of its $2.8 billion in annual sales in the United States. Although Baron Thyssen remains its titular head, he has left its administration in recent years to his oldest son, Georg-Heinrich, thus reserving most of his own time and energy for the pursuit of his lifelong dream of amassing the world's greatest private art collection.

In 1972 the baron was accused by Italian police of illegally exporting art treasures from Italy to Switzerland. Although the charges were ultimately dropped for lack of evidence, the episode led Baron Thyssen to be more cautious in lending certain works. Nonetheless, in November 1979, fifty-seven of the baron's old master paintings began a two-year tour of the United States at the National Gallery in Washington, D.C. Many of the treasures in the collection, including the two disputed Italian "exports," were not included in the exhibition because, having been painted on fragile wooden panels, they could not be transported for such a distance safely. In spite of that problem, the tour was a success, particularly in distinguishing the baron's contributions from those of his father. About two-thirds of the 900 paintings then in the collection had been acquired by the first baron, but most of the works in the show had been purchased by Hans Heinrich. John Ashbery, writing in *New York* (December 24, 1979) magazine, commented that the younger baron had made "extraordinary additions to the collection, including works by Rubens, Rembrandt, de Hooch, Petrus Christus, Watteau, Fragonard, and Goya which are in the selection now at Washington. . . . The father and son apparently shared a taste for the rare picture—lucid, luminous, and mysterious. . . . This selection . . . isn't just another assortment of accredited old masters but a highly idiosyncratic anthology, reflecting the inclination of both Thyssens for a privileged kind of art." Unlike his father, Baron Heinrich often buys at public auctions, and at a 1977 auction in Geneva, Switzerland, he made a joint purchase with the Cleveland Museum of Art of the Kingston Tureens, two French rococo silver soup tureens designed by Meissonier, a goldsmith to King Louis XV. The $1.1 million price was the highest amount ever paid for silver tureens at an auction.

The younger baron has concentrated on works produced since the eighteenth century, most of them representing such movements as luminism, cubism, German expressionism (which particularly appeals to him because of its antimilitarism), constructivism, vorticism, and abstract expressionism. "My father refused everything to do with modern painting," he told Alan Levy. "The furthest his collecting went was into a few late nineteenth-century German romantic painters—and I've respected his tastes by not putting anything even that recent into the gallery."

"Twentieth-Century Masters: The Thyssen-Bornemisza Collection" toured the United States in 1982 and 1983, including an appearance at New York's Metropolitan Museum of Art in October 1983. Also in 1983, an exhibition of forty paintings from the baron's old masters collection toured Leningrad, Moscow, and Kiev in an unprecedented cultural exchange that gave Thyssen-Bornemisza the opportunity to exhibit works by Soviet impressionists at the Villa Favorita. Two years later, he arranged yet another exchange of paintings, this time with Hungary.

In January 1986 Thyssen-Bornemisza announced plans to add a wing, costing about $20 million, to the Villa Favorita to accommodate his extensive modern art collection, which had been displayed in various locations, including the offices of his companies and the Federal Reserve Bank of Washington, D.C. When cost overruns forced him to reconsider the project, Spanish authorities, apparently at the behest of the baron's fifth wife, Carmen Cervera, a native of Spain, proposed housing the collection in the eighteenth-century Villahermosa Palace, adjacent to the Prado Museum in Madrid. The Swiss government countered with an offer to pay one-third of the construction costs of the new wing and all operating expenses. After receiving additional offers from Japan, West Germany, England, France, the National Gallery in Washington, and the J. Paul Getty Museum in Malibu, California, Thyssen-Bornemisza decided to accept the Spanish offer. In December 1988 he signed an agreement with the government of Spain to display 787 of his collection's paintings at the Villahermosa Palace for a period of ten years, while Spain agreed to renovate the palace by June 1991, at a cost of about $15 million. Not surprisingly, Spain's acquisition of the cream of the Thyssen-Bornemisza collection was called "the greatest art coup of the century." In addition, the Spanish government agreed to refurbish Pedrables, a medieval cloister in Barcelona, to house seventy-five religious paintings from the collection.

The handsome, dapper Baron Thyssen-Bornemisza has been married five times: to a German princess, two fashion models, a Brazilian banker's daughter, and currently to Carmen ("Tita") Cervera, who was Miss Spain of 1961. He has three sons and a daughter from his first four marriages, and an adopted son from his present marriage. Until recently, his primary residence was at Daylesford, an imposing eighteenth-century English manor house that he and his fourth wife, Liane Denise Shorto, purchased in 1977. After selling the house for a reported $16 million, he and

Tita now divide their time between the Villa Favorita and a new residence on the outskirts of Madrid that they purchased so that they can oversee the renovation of the Villahermosa Palace. Baron Thyssen-Bornemisza also owns several other residences, including a terrace house on London's Chester Square, a chalet in St. Moritz, Switzerland, and beach houses in Sardinia and Jamaica. Adorning the walls of all of his houses are paintings that reflect his highly personal tastes. The baron, a Roman Catholic, speaks Dutch, German, English, and French. Once a champion horseman, he abandoned equestrianism because, as he explained to Barbara Rose during the interview for *House & Garden*, "horses are dangerous at both ends, uncomfortable in the middle, and a boring subject besides."

Baron Thyssen-Bornemisza stands just under six feet tall and has thinning brown hair. Although he has often been characterized as witty and charm-

ing, he has also been described by some observers as a man who appears to be more at ease with paintings than he is with people. He has been known to give guided tours of the Villa Favorita without informing unsuspecting visitors that he is the owner. When asked by Barbara Rose during an interview for *Vogue* (December 1984) what drives him to possess the artworks that he so treasures, he replied: "I really don't know. A sense of rarity and conservation. Art tells you something about a period, a time in history, a personality. Art is what remains of history. It's like a human being I can talk with—it's like a relationship with a human being—a conversation."

References: *ARTnews* 78:88+ N '79 pors; *N Y Times* A p45+ Mr 18 '74 pors, C p11+ D 19 '88 pors; *Smithsonian* 10:76+ N '79 pors; *Vanity Fair* 52:62+ Ja '89 pors; *Vogue* 174:340+ D '84 pors; *Washington Post* L p1+ N 18 '79 pors; *International Who's Who, 1987–88*

Towne, Robert

1936 (?)- Writer; filmmaker. Address: c/o Paul Schwartzman, International Creative Management, 8899 Beverly Blvd., Los Angeles, Calif. 90048

"Movies are like wars," the screenwriter and director Robert Towne once said. "The guy who becomes an expert is the guy who doesn't get killed." Having survived debilitating illness, artistic clashes, and the ups and downs of studio politics, Towne is a prime example of his own epigram, but few

would attribute his expertise to mere endurance. The author of one certain masterpiece of screenwriting, *Chinatown* (1974), Towne has contributed to at least two others, *The Godfather* (1972) and *Shampoo* (1975), which he wrote with Warren Beatty, and has rewritten a number of both screen successes and failures in his legendary capacity as "script doctor."

What sets Towne's screenplays apart is his witty, true-to-life dialogue and his understanding that characters' reactions rather than their actions are a more realistic dramatic device. "I think that most people try to be accommodating in life, but in back of their accommodation is suppressed fear or anger or both," he once explained. "What happens in a dramatic situation is that it surfaces. And it shouldn't surface too easily, or it's not realistic." Towne added directing to his credits with *Personal Best* (1982), followed six years later by *Tequila Sunrise*. In between, he lost control of a project he had been working on for eight years, *Greystoke*, a story of Tarzan that would have remained true to the original Edward Rice Burroughs tale.

Robert Burton Towne was born in Los Angeles, California in 1936 (some sources cite his year of birth as 1934). His father, a women's clothier of Russian-Jewish descent, changed the family name of Schwartz to Towne after he purchased the Towne Smart Shop in San Pedro, California, a port city just south of Los Angeles, where Robert and his younger brother grew up.

Early on, Towne harbored aspirations to be a writer, producing his first short story when he was just six years old. The multiethnic neighborhood in which he grew up had a profound influence on Towne's later development as a writer. As he recalled to John Brady in an interview for *The Craft of the Screenwriter* (1981), "I grew up amidst fishermen, Mexicans, chief petty officers in the merchant marine with three-day growths of beard who could come up and *wheeeeze* on you." That atmosphere permeates the setting of Towne's *Chinatown*, a southern California just beginning to decay into suburbia, a Los Angeles where one could still smell eucalyptus, pepper trees, and water coming out of the ground. After high school, Towne studied English and philosophy at Pomona College in Claremont, worked for a time in military intelligence and as a real-estate salesman, and joined a commercial tuna fishing operation.

Towne first became interested in screenwriting in 1958, when he began taking a Hollywood acting class taught by Jeff Corey. Among the students who attended Corey's workshops during the late 1950s were Robert Blake, James Coburn, Richard Chamberlain, the screenwriter Carol Eastman, Sally Kellerman, and Jack Nicholson, who became Towne's roommate. One of Corey's exercises, at which Nicholson excelled, influenced Towne's evolving sense of dramatic structure. "You are given a situation and told that you must talk about everything *but* the situation to advance the action," Towne explained to John Brady. "Take a very banal situation—a guy trying to seduce a girl. He talks about anything *but* seduction, anything from a rubber duck he had as a child to the food on the table. . . . It's inventive, and it teaches you something about writing." Watching such improvisations over a period of several years, Towne learned "the power of dealing obliquely or elliptically with situations, because most people rarely confront things head-on," he told Brady. "They're afraid to." That experience also gave Towne a sense of Nicholson's specific strengths that proved invaluable in their later work together.

Towne received his first break from the low-budget filmmaker Roger Corman, who took Corey's class to develop a better rapport with actors. Towne's first screenplay, written for Corman, was *The Last Woman on Earth* (1960), a science fiction thriller about a love triangle between two men and a woman who survive a nuclear war. One man, a gangster, seeks to revive civilization, while his rival, once his attorney, complacently accepts their position on a depopulated earth. Towne, who was soon to become notorious for his slow pace of writing, had not yet finished the screenplay when shooting was scheduled to begin. Corman's budget did not permit him to have the screenwriter on location, so he cast Towne as the attorney.

Although Towne's slow-paced perfectionism clashed with Corman's quick, low-cost approach, Towne was hired nonetheless to rewrite Charles Griffith's script for the director's *Creature from the Haunted Sea* (1961). In 1963 he reworked *The Long Ride Home*, a western released as *A Time for Killing* (1967), but he took his name off the screenplay when Corman was replaced by another director. Asked to adapt *The Tomb of Ligeia* for Corman's Edgar Allan Poe series, Towne expanded the story to include elements of hypnotism and necrophilia from other examples of Poe's work, creating a bizarre vision of a man (played by Vin-

cent Price) who maintains a relationship with his first wife through the corpse of his second. Completed on a typically spare Corman budget, *The Tomb of Ligeia* (1965) received the best reviews of any of Corman's Poe films, and Towne has said that he spent more effort on that script than on any other.

In 1964 Towne began writing for television, including teleplays for *The Man from U.N.C.L.E.*, *The Lloyd Bridges Show*, and *The Richard Boone Show*; "The Chameleon," for *The Outer Limits*; and "So Many Pretty Girls, So Little Time," an episode of *Breaking Point* featuring a Don Juan figure similar to the central character of his later *Shampoo*. "I think that dramatic writing for television is, if anything, almost harmful to the potential screenwriter," Towne told Brady, adding that the prevalence of censorship and the preference of television executives for ideas that are presented obviously inhibited creativity.

Towne's revision of *The Long Ride Home* caught the eye of Warren Beatty, who hired him to rework the script for the film *Bonnie and Clyde* (1967). Towne tightened the relationship between Clyde (Beatty) and Bonnie (Faye Dunaway), who were originally part of a ménage à trois with their driver, C. W. (Michael J. Pollard), and he rearranged certain scenes to heighten the dramatic tension. His first suggestion was to emphasize more strongly the inevitability of the outcome. "It was obvious that everybody knew the people in the picture were going to get killed, so that was never an element of mystery, but rather one of suspense," Towne explained to John Brady. "*When* was it going to happen? The other element was: Would Bonnie and Clyde resolve some element in their relationship before [they died]?"

Although he was in demand after that, Towne, ironically, was at the time too ill to write a complete script. "Physically I just couldn't sustain it," he told John Brady. "Something was always coming up to hit me physically." Continually exhausted, he slept twelve hours a night, but, until his malady was diagnosed in 1972 as a complex of allergies, Towne regarded his condition as a psychological problem, a "writer's hypochondria." After that diagnosis and subsequent treatment, Towne was sufficiently cured to be able to tackle a complete script.

Towne shared with Sam Peckinpah the screenwriting credit on *Villa Rides* (1968), a fanciful portrayal of the Mexican revolutionary Pancho Villa that Towne has since described as "a textbook on How Not to Make a Movie." Although he was more pleased with the outcome of his rewrite of the screenplay for *Cisco Pike* (1971), a drama about an ex-drug dealer manipulated by a dishonest cop, Towne removed his name from the credits after a dispute with the director. On *The New Centurions* (1970), a police movie based on the best-selling novel by Joseph Wambaugh, Towne originally shared the credit with Stirling Silliphant, "but after seeing twenty minutes of the film," he told Brady, "I disliked it so much I walked out a little bit dizzy and told my agent to take my name off the picture, which they did. The whole purpose of the book was lost in the movie." Appearing as an actor in Jack Nicholson's directorial debut, *Drive, He Said* (1971), Towne also assisted with script revisions.

Although Towne went uncredited for his work on *The Godfather* (1972), its writer and director, Francis Ford Coppola, publicly acknowledged Towne's assistance upon accepting the Academy Award for best screen adaptation. Towne's most famous contribution to that movie was the tomato patch scene, in which Vito Corleone (Marlon Brando) passes on his domain to his son (Al Pacino). "Coppola basically wanted a scene where the two men would say that they loved each other," Towne has explained, as quoted in the *Dictionary of Literary Biography*. "So I wrote a scene about the succession of power, and through that it was obvious that [they] had a great deal of affection for each other," he told Brady.

The screenplay for *The Last Detail* (1973), written at the request of his friend Jack Nicholson, earned Towne his first Oscar nomination. In the story, adapted from the novel by Daryl Ponicsan, two seasoned sailors (Jack Nicholson and Otis Young), charged with transporting a young enlisted man (Randy Quaid) to prison for an eight-year sentence, choose to give him a taste of life before fulfilling their mission. Resisting the temptation to end the film on a happy or an easily judgmental note, Towne had the older men complete their assigment without "feeling overly guilty," instead of letting their prisoner escape. As he observed in his interview with John Brady: "Typical people are usually very decent, and will go out of their way a little bit to help someone as long as too much courage and too much thought aren't required. Without saying it, I wanted to imply that we're *all* lifers in the navy, and everybody hides behind doing a job, whether it's massacring in My Lai, or taking a kid to jail, or chopping down all the trees on a block, making the residents miserable, because that's your job." With *The Last Detail*, Towne became one of Hollywood's hottest writers, commanding up to $150,000 for adaptations and $300,000 for original scripts, plus a percentage of box-office receipts.

Acknowledged as Towne's masterpiece, the screenplay for *Chinatown* (1974) depicts the corruption behind the development of Towne's beloved Los Angeles in the late 1930s. *Chinatown* "is about greed," Towne told Michael Sragow in an interview for *American Film* (January–February 1989). "But *Chinatown* is about greed and its consequences, not just in the present, but to the future." "I wanted to tell a story about a man who raped the land and his daughter in the name of the future," Towne has explained, as quoted in the *Dictionary of Literary Biography*. "Men like Cross [the film's villain] believe that as they keep building and reproducing, they'll live forever." In the film, the private eye J. J. Gittes (Jack Nicholson) is hired by Evelyn Mulray (Faye Dunaway), with whom he falls in love, as he uncovers corruption and incest, involving Miss Mulray and her father, Noah Cross (John Huston).

Although *Chinatown* won both the Golden Globe and the Academy Award for best screenplay, the fact that the script is analyzed and examined in creative-writing courses strikes Towne as "odd." As he explained to Steven Schiff of *Vanity Fair* (January 1989): "I mean that what I hit upon just by a kind of monkey-at-a-typewriter trial and error—that somebody can extrapolate a formula from it astonishes me. Maybe there are rules, and maybe I stumbled across them, but I don't even know what 'story sense' is. I had the same hard time [on later work] that I had on *Chinatown*." In its final form, the film diverges from Towne's script, which originally had John Huston's character die at the end. Instead, the film's director, Roman Polanski, insisted that Faye Dunaway be killed—an ending that Towne has described as "so cynical it works against itself." As a result of the alteration, Towne resolved not to work again with Polanski, but they were eventually reconciled.

Jay Cocks, writing in *Time* (July 1, 1974) magazine, praised the film's effective depiction of another era: "No film has ever succeeded quite so well as *Chinatown* in conveying the ambience of Los Angeles before the war—sun-kissed, seedy, and easy." And Kathleen Carroll, in the New York *Sunday News* (February 16, 1975), called the *Chinatown* script "corrosive" and "brilliant." Towne received joint billing with Paul Schrader for his rewrite of *The Yakuza* (1975), which had been adapted by Schrader from a story by his brother Leonard. A mystery about a retired American detective who becomes embroiled in the Japanese underworld while searching for a friend's missing daughter, *The Yakuza* was revised by Towne to accommodate its star, Robert Mitchum, an action that alienated Paul Schrader.

In a more humorous vein, Towne collaborated with Warren Beatty on *Shampoo* (1975), the story of a Beverly Hills hairdresser for whom energetic heterosexuality is the essence of life. The story is set on election day in 1968. In a famous speech that represents Towne's sense of voice and character at its best, George Roundbee (Beatty) describes his omnivorous desire: "I go into that shop and they're so great-looking you know. And I, I'm doing their hair, and they feel great, and they smell great. Or I could be out on the street, you know, and I could just stop at a stoplight, or go into an elevator, or I . . . there's a beautiful girl. I, I, I don't know. . . . I mean that's it. I, it makes my day. Makes me feel like I'm gonna live forever. And, as far as I'm concerned, with what I'd like to have done at this point in my life, I know I should have accomplished more. But I've got no regrets. . . . Maybe that means I don't love 'em. Maybe it means I don't love you. I don't know. Nobody's going to tell me I don't like 'em very much."

With his health improving and his reputation at its height, Towne sought additional creative control by directing his next film. *Greystoke* was to be faithful to Edward Rice Burroughs's Tarzan novels, a Tarzan story from the perspective of the ape society in Africa in which the character was raised.

The first hour of the film would be without dialogue, presenting the interaction of the apes with the hero, "for whom the life of an ape was no less important than the life of a human being," Towne told Michael Sragow. While researching the film, Towne doctored several other screenplays, including *The Yakuza, Marathon Man (1976), The Missouri Breaks (1976), Orca (1977), Heaven Can Wait (1978),* and *Reds (1981).* In addition, in the late 1970s Towne spent a year negotiating between the San Pedro tuna fishermen and environmentalists to establish safer fishing practices and decrease the number of porpoises and dolphins killed in fishing nets.

Towne finally decided to make *Personal Best* (1982), his directorial debut, as a practice run before tackling the larger *Greystoke* project. A film about a romantic relationship between two female athletes (Mariel Hemingway and Patrice Donnelly) who are competing for a spot on the United States Olympic team, *Personal Best* ran into budget difficulties, which were exacerbated by a Screen Actors Guild strike. When shooting was halted by the executive producer, David Geffen, Towne was required to give up the right to direct *Greystoke* so that he could complete *Personal Best.* As Towne explained to David Thomson for *Vanity Fair* (November 1985), that was the most painful decision he ever had to make. "It meant for me I had to accept the death of one child to preserve another," he said.

Released in 1982 by Geffen's Warner Brothers, *Personal Best* received half-hearted promotion after Towne sued Warner over "final cut" rights, and it failed at the box office. (Towne has since called that lawsuit "intemperate and foolish.") Although reviews were mixed, many critics shared the admiration of *Newsweek's* (February 8, 1982) Jack Kroll, who applauded its presentation of "track and field as a microcosm for the ecstasies and pain of self-striving" and its "dar[ing], with great delicacy and insight, to show a loving sexual relationship between two young women, not as a statement about homosexuality but as a paradigm of authentic human intimacy." As quoted in the *Dictionary of Literary Biography,* Towne has explained that, because of his profession, he has always empathized with women: "You are always the one at home sweating over the hot typewriter while the authority figure is on the set telling people what to do."

Under the direction of British filmmaker Hugh Hudson, *Greystoke: The Legend of Tarzan, Lord of the Apes* (1984) proved to be uneven. The first part, set among the apes, won praise for its originality, but many thought that the film lost its force once Tarzan reached civilization. In his review for the *Washington Post* (April 29, 1984), Gary Arnold speculated that the English director had toned down Towne's "facetious view of Tarzan's entry into civilized society." Towne has never seen the finished film. As he told Kenneth Turan for the *New York Times* (November 27, 1988), "After the first five minutes, I started crying, I couldn't look

at it." Towne insisted on giving screen credit to his recently deceased Hungarian sheepdog, P. H. Vazak, remarking that he "felt badly about that. If he could've written, he would have done it better." Under his dog's name, Towne received an Oscar nomination.

Meanwhile, Towne's marriage fell apart, but he continued to work steadily, scripting *Mermaid* for Warren Beatty and Ray Stark, but that original fantasy was preempted by *Splash;* rewriting Hal Ashby's *8 Million Ways to Die* (1986) and Roman Polanski's *Frantic* (1988); acting as executive producer of *The Bedroom Window* for his friend Curtis Hanson; and acting in and consulting on James Toback's *Pick-Up Artist.* In 1985 *The Two Jakes,* Towne's sequel to *Chinatown,* was shelved after a dispute between Towne and Jack Nicholson over the casting of the producer Robert Evans, a mutual friend, as the second Jake, a role for which he seemed unsuited.

Tequila Sunrise (1988), Towne's second outing as writer-director, is a detective melodrama about a drug dealer, Dale McKussic (Mel Gibson), who is trying to mend his ways; a police detective, Nick Frescia (Kurt Russell), a high school friend who is assigned to see if McKussic attempts another deal; and the beautiful owner of a restaurant, Jo Ann Vallenari (Michelle Pfeiffer), who captures the hearts of both men. In an interview with Desson Howe of the *Washington Post* (December 3, 1988), Towne described *Tequila Sunrise* as a "parable about the use and abuse of friendship, not unrelated to a town or an industry where there's an awful lot of friendship and business." Reviews were mixed, with most critics praising the screenplay but finding the direction confusing at best.

Towne is currently developing several other projects, including the screenplay for *Cast of Killers,* a dramatization of the Sydney Kirkpatrick-King Vidor-Desmond Taylor Hollywood murder scandal. He plans to be executive producer for *The Two Jakes,* finally back in production, with Jack Nicholson starring and directing, and *The Brotherhood of the Grape,* an adaptation of the 1977 John Fante novel, and he is writing the third part of the *Chinatown* trilogy, set in 1959, about Gittes being sued by his own wife.

A "tall, soft-eyed and sexy" man who "shambles a bit," according to *Vanity Fair's* Steven Schiff, Towne has come to resemble a sage, "donning spectacles and removing them, like a professor showboating at the lectern; he becomes visibly tangled in thickets of thought. In the middle of conversations, he tends to leap up and peer into bookshelves, where he'll eventually locate some beloved passage and read to you in a tender, boyish voice so soft that if often threatens to disperse into ether." Towne won joint custody of his daughter, Katherine, after a painful court battle with his former wife, Julie Payne. He is now remarried, to Luisa, who inspired the Michelle Pfeiffer character in *Tequila Sunrise.* They live in Pacific Palisades.

Towne's uncompromising artistic integrity has earned him a reputation for stubbornness, but the director James Toback explained to Michael Sragow of *American Film* that Towne's tendency to be difficult reflects an unusual sense of craftsmanship, what Toback has called "a very un-Hollywood trait." He refused to write the screenplay for *The Great Gatsby*, for instance, because he was in the middle of writing *Chinatown* and did not want to harm a literary classic. He is known as a "director's writer" because of his willingness to make countless revisions. And as Schiff pointed out, unlike most screenwriters, Towne embellishes his scripts with "nuggets of useless, delicious metaphor glinting among the descriptive passages,"

nuggets that will not appear in the filmed versions. "It helps me imagine the movie," Towne explained. "It's sort of like putting gargoyles on the back of Notre Dame—nobody's going to see it, but I'll know that they're there."

References: Am Film 14:40+ Ja–F '89 por; N Y Sunday News III p9 F 16 '75 por; N Y Times II p13 N 27 '88 por; New York 8:73 Ap 21 '75 por; Vanity Fair 48:59+ N '85 por, 52:38+ Ja '89 por; Washington Post C p1+ D 3 '88 pors; Brady, John. The Craft of the Screenwriter (1981); Contemporary Authors vol 108 (1983); Dictionary of Literary Biography vol 44 (1986)

Travis, Randy

May 4, 1959– Musician. Address: c/o Evelyn Shriver Public Relations, 341 West End Ave., New York, N.Y. 10023

Concentrating solely on traditional country music, the singer Randy Travis has won a loyal following among country music fans and the more mainstream pop music listeners with a voice "that can really sidle around a lyric, [and] sound smooth flowing and knowing at the same time," in the words of one critic, and with songs, some of which he writes himself, emphasizing the values of love and fidelity. "That's all I've ever cared to sing," Travis said in a 1986 interview. "In fact, that's all I've ever listened to." Travis's first three albums—*Storms of Life* (1986), *Always & Forever* (1987), and *Old 8 x 10* (1988)—all went platinum (sold more than one million copies), his concerts

are all sold out, and Travis has won more than forty-three awards, including two Grammies and numerous honors from the Country Music Association as well as several American Music Awards. In 1987, at the age of twenty-eight, he became the youngest member ever of Nashville's Grand Ole Opry. "Do what you love, and be what you are," the handsome and unassuming Travis told an interviewer for *Time* (June 22, 1987) magazine. "To me that's country music. With me, what you see is what you get."

Randy Travis was born Randy Traywick on May 4, 1959 in Marshville, North Carolina, some thirty miles outside of Charlotte. His father, Harold Traywick, raised turkeys and horses and ran his own construction company. His mother, Bobbie Traywick, was a textile worker. Randy was the second oldest of six children and one of four boys. Harold Traywick was an ardent country music fan and had an extensive collection of classic country records, including Hank Williams, Merle Haggard, George Jones, Lefty Frizzell, Ernest Tubb, Gene Autry, Roy Rogers, and Tex Ritter. Randy loved that music, appreciating the sound of the voices even before he was old enough to understand the lyrics.

Since Harold Traywick wanted Randy and his brother Ricky to become country musicians, he bought them guitars, drums, and a piano, gave them music lessons, and insisted that they practice. By the time Randy was ten, he and Ricky were performing as the Traywick Brothers, playing at VFW halls, Moose lodges, fiddlers' conventions, private parties, and square dances, in spite of the family's affiliation with the "hard-shell" Baptist church.

Hating school with a passion, Randy Travis quit by the ninth grade, with the intention of making a living as a musician. He worked for his father's construction business and on the family turkey farm, an occupation he disliked almost as intensely as he had disliked school. By that time, he was singing in local honky-tonks as a solo artist, since his brother Ricky had dropped out. At first, his parents chaperoned him in those places, since fights broke out almost every night. As a performer, Travis had to learn how to hold the attention of the hard-drinking and loud-talking crowds. Influenced by that type of environment, Travis himself soon started drinking and taking drugs. "When I was fourteen, fifteen, sixteen, I was taking acid and Quaaludes and speed and just whatever was there," he told Jack Hurst in an interview for the *Chicago Tribune* (November 13, 1988).

A wild and rebellious adolescent period ensued, with Travis frequently running away from home. He was often arrested and jailed on charges that began with public drunkenness and escalated into driving under the influence, trying to outrun police cars, fighting, and breaking and entering. Sometimes his father bailed him out, but on other occasions he left Travis in jail to teach him a lesson. By his own account, Travis went "about as far down as you could get," destroying his health in the process. "I was almost a diabetic and sick most of the time, just from all the drugs and drinking," he told Hurst. Although Travis was put on probation, his offenses continued to mount, and the court finally ordered him to see a psychiatrist, who diagnosed his case as hopeless.

In between his bouts with the law, Travis continued to pursue a career as a musician. When he was seventeen, he entered a $100 talent contest at the Charlotte nightclub Country City, USA, owned by Lib Hatcher, who immediately recognized Travis's potential. As she recalled to Jack Hurst of the *Chicago Tribune* (February 22, 1987), she was standing at a table holding some papers when Travis started singing. "I dropped the papers," she said. "I thought, 'That's something special.'" Travis won the talent contest, and Mrs. Hatcher offered him a job as the club's regular singer. In spite of his wild behavior offstage, as a performer Travis was extremely shy. "He'd sing his song, then hang his head and sort of get down from the stage," Lib Hatcher recounted to Robert Hilburn, as quoted in the *Los Angeles Times* (March 6, 1988). "He wouldn't even say thank you. But he would talk to me and after we closed at night, he'd get the guitar and he'd sing while we were waiting for the girls to clean up the place."

Meanwhile, Travis faced the possibility of a five-year prison term after being convicted of breaking and entering. Lib Hatcher testified in court in his behalf, telling the judge that Travis was gainfully employed by her and that she would assume responsibility for his behavior. As a result, the judge released Travis into her custody, and he moved in with her and her husband. When her husband objected to the arrangement and the large amount of time that Lib Hatcher was spending at Country City, USA, he ordered her to sell the club and send Travis back to Marshville. Lib Hatcher did not hesitate for a moment: she moved out that night and did not talk to her husband again, until she reached the divorce court. "It was a question of human worth," she told Jack Hurst, in the *Chicago Tribune* (February 22, 1987) interview. "I think I saw the good in Randy that everybody else sees now." Explaining Lib Hatcher's influence on him, Travis told Hurst: "I don't remember exactly how she put it, but soon after she hired me at the

club, she asked me if I had ever thought about taking music seriously—and if I had, that she'd like to manage me and see what we could do with it. Nobody had ever really said that to me before. She made more sense to me than anybody else I had ever talked to. . . . She was somebody I could talk to, and just knowing her helped me straighten out a lot." After he moved in with Lib Hatcher, Travis practiced the guitar extensively. "I'm still not a great player, though," he later admitted to a reporter for *Time* (July 25, 1988). "I just mainly play rhythm."

Lib Hatcher eventually sold Country City, USA and bought a bigger nightclub, with a motel attached to it, and began booking high-priced Nashville acts in order to showcase Travis's talent between sets. In 1979 Joe Stampley, a veteran country singer, provided her with a contact at Paula Records, a local label based in Shreveport, Louisiana that released two Travis singles produced by Stampley: "Dreamin'" and "She's My Woman." In spite of a $10,000 promotional campaign financed by Lib Hatcher, the records barely made it to the bottom of the country charts.

By 1981 Lib Hatcher had concluded that Travis needed the exposure that only Nashville could offer. She sold her Charlotte nightclub and moved with Travis to Nashville, where she bought an old house on Sixteenth Avenue, known as Music Row. She landed a job as the manager of the Nashville Palace, a country supper club, and immediately hired Travis as a short-order cook, because the kitchen was always short-staffed. By January 1983 Travis was working as a regular singer at the club, though he continued to work in the kitchen. "The whole three and a half years we were there, he was singing and working in the kitchen," Lib Hatcher explained to Hurst, as quoted in the *Chicago Tribune* of February 22, 1987. "We'd go in at four in the afternoon, and he'd work in the kitchen 'til nine and then go sing." Because the Palace was just down the street from the Grand Ole Opry, it filled up on weekend nights after the Opry concerts were over with Opry fans, a more discriminating audience than Travis's previous listeners. "I remember the first night I sang at the Palace," Travis told Bob Allen of the *Washington Post* (February 15, 1987). "It was the first time I'd ever been in front of an audience that would actually sit and listen to you. The first time I played there, it scared me to death! I thought they hated me!"

Over the next few years, Travis began to make a name for himself in the area, as the Palace's singing cook. (In the Palace today there is a photo of Travis and a plaque that reads: "Randy Travis: Former Palace Cook, Dishwasher, and Now Famous Star. We are proud of his success.") He appeared occasionally on *Nashville Now* and *Nashville after Hours*, two national cable television shows on the Nashville Network, which is owned by the Opryland Corporation. He sent demonstration tapes to every major record label on Music Row, but he was turned down by all of them at least twice. Under the name Randy Ray, Travis recorded one live album, featuring ten songs that he himself had written, that sold well at the Palace but failed to make an impression on the general public.

Finally, in 1985, Travis got his big break, thanks to changing tastes in the country music industry. For several years previously, music industry executives had concentrated on finding talent with crossover pop appeal, believing that traditional country singers like Travis were passé. Martha Sharp, a senior vice-president at Warner Brothers Records, had accepted that line of reasoning until she attended a marketing meeting sponsored by the Country Music Association, at which she learned that country music fans were turned off by the recent pop orientation of country music artists. Miss Sharp decided to look for a singer who was devoted only to traditional country music. When a friend suggested that she listen to Randy Ray at the Palace, she visited the club to hear him sing and immediately decided to offer him a contract. "I loved his voice," she told Robert Hilburn in an interview for the Los Angeles Times Calendar (March 6, 1988). "But I knew I was going to get a lot of guff. The prevailing opinion at that time was that he was too country, nothing that country would work. Still, my gut told me to go ahead."

With the new surname of Travis, which Miss Sharp picked out for him, Randy Travis released his first single, "Prairie Rose," which appeared on the soundtrack of the movie Rustler's Rhapsody (1985). Although his next single, "On the Other Hand," only reached number sixty-seven on the charts, his third song, "1982," reached number six on Billboard's chart and number one on several other charts. After that success, Warner Brothers rereleased "On the Other Hand," and it too reached the top of the charts. In June 1986 Warner Brothers released Travis's first album, Storms of Life, anticipating sales of 20,000. Within the year, over a million copies were sold—it was the first time a debut album by a country artist had gone platinum—and Storms of Life, containing the hit singles "Diggin' up Bones" and "Reasons I Cheat," which Travis wrote, became the number-one country album in the United States.

What accounted for the runaway success of that album was "the remarkable resonance and maturity of Mr. Travis's voice," as James Hunter pointed out in his appraisal for the New York Times (July 13, 1986). Reviewing Travis's Storms of Life in the Wall Street Journal (November 5, 1986), Nat Hentoff observed: "He sings conversationally. There is no straining for dramatic effect. The people in the stories tell of what's going on inside them; and Mr. Travis becomes each of them so convincingly that their natural presence and cadences make for natural drama." "Reasons I Cheat," the story of a middle-aged man who philanders because his wife does not understand him, was singled out for special praise by several reviewers, who expressed surprise that Travis, at the age of twenty-seven, could write so convincingly about such a subject. "I guess you could just say that I've lived a lot in twenty-seven years," Travis explained to Bob Al-

len during an interview for the Washington Post (February 15, 1987). "I guess where I'm from, I kind of grew up fast."

With a hit album under his belt, Travis took his show on the road, performing with a six-man band an average of five times a week for a total of 182 days in 1986. Traveling at first in a converted bread truck, a van, and a horse trailer, the entourage graduated to a rented tour bus by the end of the year. Acting as Travis's manager and exhibiting her astute business sense, Lib Hatcher hired the New York City–based publicist Evelyn Shriver to handle Travis's account, because of her ability to generate publicity in such publications as Vanity Fair and Elle, which normally do not profile country musicians, and on television shows such as the Today show and Late Night with David Letterman. In October 1986 the Country Music Association voted "On the Other Hand" song of the year, and Travis won that association's Horizon Award as rookie musician of the year. In April 1987 he won four awards at the Academy of Country Music Awards Show, for best male vocalist, best song ("On the Other Hand"), best single ("On the Other Hand"), and album of the year (Storms of Life).

Always & Forever, Travis's second album, was released in May 1987 and included the new songs "Good Intentions" and "I Told You So." In its first month and a half on the market, it sold well over half a million copies; in its first year and a half, it sold some three million. It remained number one on the Billboard country charts for an unprecedented forty-three weeks and was named the Country Music Association album of the year. That album's hit single, "Forever and Ever, Amen," garnered six major awards, including the Country Music Association single of the year and the American Music Award favorite country single—both in 1987—and the Academy of Country Music song of the year and single of the year, both in 1988. In addition, the album Always & Forever was named album of the year by the Country Music Association in 1987. Travis appeared to be the only one who was surprised when the Academy of Country Music named him the top male vocalist in 1987. "Boy, when the academy announced male vocalist of the year, you're talking about a shock," he told a reporter for Time (June 22, 1987). "Winning in the same category with George Jones and George Strait!"

Reviewing Always & Forever for the New York Times (June 28, 1987), Stephen Holden commented, "Mr. Travis possesses a once-in-a-generation country twang that seems to quiver perpetually on the edge of an emotional precipice while maintaining a secure technical footing." In her critique of Always & Forever for Stereo Review (September 1987), Alanna Nash unequivocally ranked Travis among the country greats. "After years of industry predictions that this one and that is the new Merle Haggard, or the heir to the throne of George Jones and Lefty Frizzell," she wrote, "twenty-eight-year-old Randy Travis, with only two albums to his credit, has come along to show he has not so much *aimed* for that honor, but that he was born to it." In 1987, when the Grand Ole Opry, that prestigious bastion of country music tradition, invited Travis to sing on its weekly radio and television show, he became the Opry's youngest member ever. Lib Hatcher pointed out to Robert Hilburn about the Opry's invitation: "When they asked us to join, they didn't just say,'We *want* you, Randy.' They said, 'We *need* you, Randy.'"

Critics seem to agree that what accounts for Travis's stunning success is the combination of his rich voice, his distinct country twang, and, as Jay Cocks wrote in *Time* (July 25, 1988), a style that can rescue the corniest, hackneyed country song "from the brink of bathos with some hair-trigger phrasing and a very sly, very worldly tone of voice." Mark Moses, writing in the *New Yorker* (May 9, 1988), remarked, "As in most masterly country singing, Travis's voice is all about the quiet, painful acknowledgement of limits: the constrained ripple he gives to the end of a phrase betrays a struggle to maintain his reserve." As evidenced by the songs "Forever and Ever, Amen," "My House," and "I Won't Need You Anymore," all of which appear on *Always & Forever*, Travis's stock-in-trade remains traditional story material, emphasizing fidelity, commitment, and marriage as a refuge from the storms of life. In a Celebrity Corner column that appeared in *USA Today*, Travis himself wrote: "I think there's a need to get back to something basic, something understandable. People are searching for a sense of family, a sense of morality or purpose beyond just career success or financial rewards."

A third album, *Old 8 x 10*, was released in July 1988 and sold a million copies in less than four months. Its songs include "Honky Tonk Moon," "Deeper Than the Holler," "Is It Still Over," and the Travis originals "It's Out of My Hands" and "Promises." Appraising the album in the *New York Times* (July 27, 1988), Stephen Holden observed, "Its spare, acoustically oriented arrangements of stark country tunes caress a voice that evokes the archetypal honky-tonk loner." Jay Cocks, writing in *Time* (July 25, 1988), described *Old 8 x 10* as a "blend of sweet vocals and straightforward sentiment." In evaluating the album for the *New York Times* (September 4, 1988), Jon Pareles offered one of the few negative observations about *Old 8 x 10* when he commented that "like too many neo-traditionalists in all fields (as well as the character in the title song), Mr. Travis looks to the past as a refuge, where roles are fixed and conflicts are all settled." In 1988 Travis won nineteen musical awards, including a Grammy for the second straight year in a row, for best male country vocal performance. In the same year he appeared briefly in the western film *Young Guns*. At the People's Choice Awards ceremony in March 1989, Travis was named the favorite male performer. That same month the National Association of Recording Merchandisers named *Old 8 x 10* the best-selling country album by a male artist.

Randy Travis's fourth album, *No Holdin' Back*, was released in October 1989. It includes "Singing the Blues," a hit in the 1950s for both Marty Robbins and Guy Mitchell, Brook Benton's "It's Just a Matter of Time," "When Your World Was Turning for Me," which Travis wrote with Dallas Frazier, and his own "Hard Rock Bottom of Your Heart" and "No Stoppin' Us Now." In his review for *Newsweek* (October 16, 1989), David Gates called *No Holdin' Back* Travis's best work since *Storms of Life*.

Interviewers find Travis somewhat reticent, shy, and refreshingly modest for a superstar. On the subject of country music, however, Travis loses his usual reserve. Explaining his dedication to the songs of traditional country singers, Travis said to Al Cohn in an interview for *New York Newsday* (April 26, 1987): "They sing with emotion and soul. They sing songs that people can easily relate to. The songs are good and simple. It's authentic. They live their music. It's in their soul. You could feel it coming from their soul. That's the way I've always wanted to sound." To a reporter for *Time* (July 25, 1988), he elaborated: "People think country music is related to a bunch of rednecks drinking beer and fighting. They think it's all songs about drinking and cheating. But it covers a lot bigger area than that, you know. Covers everything."

Randy Travis stands five feet ten inches tall and weighs 150 pounds. He has a muscular build, the result of workouts in a gym four days a week, brown hair, and, in the words of one interviewer, "soft, seductive" brown eyes. Travis has given up drinking completely. His business affairs are handled by Lib Hatcher Management, the Lib Hatcher Agency, which arranges his bookings, Special Moments Promotions, which arranges Travis's tours and handles promotions, and the Travis Corporation, which takes care of touring and recording income. All of those operations are headquartered in the house on Sixteenth Avenue in Nashville that Lib Hatcher bought in 1981. In addition, there is a 13,000-member fan club, and Travis's songs have been copyrighted by two publishing companies. Travis spent 186 days on the road in 1987 and 150 days in 1988, traveling in a $400,000 bus. When not on the road, Travis lives with Lib Hatcher in a renovated 100-year-old log cabin on a country property in Cheatham County, some twenty miles outside of Nashville. In January 1989 Travis performed during President George Bush's inaugural festivities. He is scheduled to release a fourth album in September 1989, and "Heroes and Friends," a collection of duets with such country artists as Merle Haggard, Dolly Parton, and George Jones, is scheduled for release in 1990.

There have been innumerable rumors over the years linking Travis and Lib Hatcher, who is in her forties, in a romantic relationship, but both have repeatedly denied the stories. When asked about the relationship, Travis has said only that "it is a great partnership," as quoted in *Time* (July 25, 1988). In addition to owning two farms together, the two travel together on the road, and Lib Hatcher picks out the clothes he wears in concert. With his new wealth, Travis has been able to help out his family financially, buying back farmland that the Traywicks were forced to sell and renovating his parents' and grandparents' houses. Travis owns three horses and enjoys riding through his country property. "Out in the country, now that feels like home," Travis told a reporter for *Time* (July 25, 1988). "That is how I was raised, out away from everybody, and that is what I still like."

References: Chicago Tribune XIII p4+ F 22 '87 por, XIII p4+ N 13 '88 pors; Los Angeles Times calendar p60+ Mar 6 '88 pors; N Y Times Je 25 '89 p28+ pors; Newsweek 108:102 O 27 '86 por; Sat Eve Post 260:60+ O '88 pors; Washington Post F p1+ F 15 '87 por; Who's Who in America, 1988-89

Trenet, Charles
(tre nā´)

May 18, 1913– French singer; songwriter; writer. Address: b. c/o Gilbert M. Rozon, 63 E. Prince Arthur St., Montreal H2X 1B4, Canada; 7 rue Marbeuf, 75008 Paris, France; h. 2 rue Anatole-France, 11100 Narbonne, France; 91 quai de la Varenne, 94210 La Varenne, France

For more than forty years the French singer and songwriter Charles Trenet has been no stranger to the United States, and his pop classic "Beyond the Sea," first introduced to Americans by Benny Goodman in 1945, has been performed by several generations of the country's leading entertainers, including Bing Crosby, Stevie Wonder, Louis Arm-

strong, Ella Fitzgerald, Frank Sinatra, and Sarah Vaughan. But in France, Charles Trenet is an institution, who, with a reputed 1,000 songs and more than fifty years of solo performances behind him, has weathered the ups and downs of history and musical fashion alike. Hardly an hour goes by without the sound of his voice being heard on one radio station or another. Moreover, the lyrics of his songs are quoted in novels, and his music is often used as the background for commercials.

Trenet, Lucien Rioux wrote in a 1983 appreciation of the singer, "has pulled poetry out of its elitist ghetto, has offered it to everyone, has given it a presence in the tiniest gestures of the everyday, in the most banal objects, in the most ordinary sensations. He has taught everyone to believe in crazy hopes, in the necessity of madness, the importance of frenzy. His optimism brought glimmers of light to dark years, chased away the usual cares, and even in the worst moments, made it seem that life was worth living." At the end of his fifty-first year as a solo performer, Trenet was still going strong. In October 1988 he released a new double album, recorded live at his jubilee concert in September 1987, and followed up in November 1988 with a thirteen-record compendium of his near-complete works. In mid-December 1988 he was back on the Paris stage for a two-week stand at the Châtelet Musical Theatre.

Louis Charles August Claude Trenet was born in Perpignan, France on May 18, 1913, the second son of the notary Lucian Trenet and the former Marie-Louis Caussat. "Although he was a notary," Trenet has recalled, "my father wasn't all that bourgeois. He was even a little bohemian." Lucian Trenet's great regret was his failure to pursue a musical career, and as a Sunday musician, he not only sang and played the violin but composed his own music and organized regular soirées with other amateurs. His youthful wife was no less adventuresome for the times. While her husband was away in military service in World War I, she fell in love with another man and, at the war's end, divorced, remarried, and set off for Eastern Europe with her new husband, Benno Vigno.

For Trenet, the breakup of his family was an event of lasting consequences. "All my life," he told one interviewer some sixty years later, "I've run after the childhood I never had: it was eclipsed by family problems . . . so I told myself that if, later on, I had the chance for a real childhood, well, I was certainly going to take it." When his mother left, he and his brother, Antoine, were sent to a nearby Roman Catholic institution called the Free School of the Trinity, where, as he once put it, "the school might have been free, but I was shut up inside." Luckily, his father eventually decided to move back to his native Perpignan, and that low point in Charles Trenet's childhood came to an end.

Notwithstanding his private misery, Trenet was an active child. He taught himself to read at the age of three and a half and displayed a precocious aptitude for music, drama, and art. In Perpignan, he found mentors in two of his father's friends, the Catalan painter Fons-Godail and the journalist Albert Bausil, and by the time he was fifteen, he was studying painting with Fons-Godail, publishing poetry and theatre reviews in Bausil's newspaper, *Le Coq catalan*, and performing in plays staged by Bausil. His skill in French composition so impressed school officials that they considered sending him to Paris to continue his studies, but a fight with other students led to his expulsion instead.

In 1928, after making one more attempt at formal education, Trenet went to live with his mother and stepfather in Berlin. There, he enrolled in design school, since by this time, it was assumed he would become an architect like his grandfather and uncle, but he quickly became bored with the academic training. He continued to paint, however, and when he returned to Perpignan ten months later, his work was judged good enough to merit an exhibition in a local bookstore. But what had really captured his attention in Berlin was American jazz, especially the music of George Gershwin, and the new German cinema, which he got to know firsthand through his stepfather, who was a filmmaker and scriptwriter.

In July 1930 Trenet turned up at his mother's latest residence, in Prague, Czechoslovakia, with the manuscript of a completed novel (*Dodo manières*) in his suitcase and announced his plan to move to Paris, where he had been hired to work as a prop man on Jacques de Baroncelli's film *La Rêve*. Three months later, after telling his father he was going there to study decorative arts, he arrived in Paris. "I was seventeen years old," he recalled in a 1966 interview. "I was doing the clapperboard at Joinville studios, but I didn't do it very well. I was kind of absent-minded and wanted to see if I was photogenic. After each clap, I'd make faces at the camera, so I always heard the director shouting, 'Get out of the way, just get out of the way.'" In spite of his less than auspicious debut, Trenet worked his way up to assistant, and when his stepfather, by that time at the peak of his career, came to Paris to film *Bariole*, Trenet collaborated on the musical score, writing the lyrics to five songs.

Throughout that period Trenet continued to supply *Le Coq catalan* with poems and articles, as well as with serialized novels that he signed with the pseudonym Jacques Brevin. Although a manuscript that he submitted to the Paris publisher Denoël was promptly turned down, it got him an introduction to the avant-garde painter and poet Max Jacob, with whom he formed a lasting friendship. Jacob is reported to have told the aspiring poet, "At your age, I was also writing verses like that, but afterwards I destroyed them," but that acerbic comment only inspired Trenet to work all the harder at his literary pursuits. In 1932 one of his poems was accepted by *La mercure de France*, and in January 1933 he became the youngest member ever admitted to the French Society of Music Authors, Composers, and Editors.

In the cafes and cabarets of Montparnasse, Trenet met other stellar figures of the times, including the painters Maurice Utrillo and André Derain, the dramatist Antonin Artaud, and the writer and filmmaker Jean Cocteau, but the decisive encounter turned out to be with a young piano player, Johnny Hess, who became his partner in the singing duo Charles and Johnny. Putting together a four-song repertoire, they made their debut in a revue at the Palace Theatre in December 1933 but quit three days later because they were placed at the beginning of the bill and finished their act before most of the audience arrived. But in short order they became the hit of a cabaret across the street, Le Fiacre, where a two-week engagement turned into an entire year's run.

A record contract, a deal with a music publisher, and a spate of radio appearances soon followed, including appearances on commercials for France's advertising pioneer, Marcel Bleustein-Blanchet. "These are boys who are lacking neither in youthfulness nor in talent," Paul Brach, a reviewer for the Paris newspaper *Marianne*, wrote. "In their red jackets and V-necked shirts, they calmly express the right to live as singers, avoiding the pitfalls by sticking to the paths that are tried and true. The public appreciates their joyful rhythms, their wholesome melodies, the absence of showing off that justifies their presence."

The Charles and Johnny partnership came to an abrupt end when Trenet was drafted and assigned to Istres Air Force Base in October 1936, but it was not long before he started spending his evenings at the piano bar of the Grand Hotel in Marseilles, which was run by his friend Edmond Bory. In reaction to the teasing that he had endured at the air base for his curly hair and baby face, he had shaved his head and taken to wearing a monocle, prompting Bory to bill him as "Charles, the Singing Madman." Trenet acknowledged in a 1978 interview: "It didn't bother me at all. I have to say that [the name] fit my character. . . . I looked like Erich von Stroheim; I was really outrageous."

During that year of alternating between military service and musical activity (with an occasional stint in military prison for taking French leave), Trenet wrote some of his earliest and most perennial hits: "J'ai ta main," "Je chante," and "Y'a d'la joie" (known in its English version as "There's Happiness Everywhere"). Once released from the service, in October 1937, the "Singing Madman" was taken in hand by his music publisher, Raoul Breton, who immediately got him a contract with Columbia Records. Breton had also been responsible for getting the legendary chanteur Maurice Chevalier to perform "Y'a d'la joie" (as an anniversary present for Breton's wife), and, on the basis of the song's success, he persuaded Trenet to embark on a stage career of his own.

Trenet made his Paris debut in March 1938 with a two-week run as the opening act at the ABC Music Hall. Wearing the blue suit and shirt, white tie, red carnation, and floppy felt hat that have remained his trademark ever since, he performed the three songs that were to precede the main act, but the crowd started chanting, "The Madman, the

Madman, the Madman," forcing him to stay on for an encore. The critics went wild over the twenty-five-year-old performer. "A revelation: Charles Trenet," Pierre Varenne wrote in *Paris-Soir*, a leading daily newspaper. "He's full of enthusiasm and youth, he has rhythm, spirit . . . [and] the divine: poetry. His success was triumphant."

His music-hall breakthrough, with Trenet winding up as the star of the show, led to movie offers as well. Within a year, he had scripted and starred in two romantic films, *La Route enchantée* (*The Enchanted Road*) and *Je chante* (*I'm Singing*), both of which were essentially vehicles for the singer and his hit songs, including "La Route enchantée," "Il pleut dans ma chambre," and "Boum," the winner of the French Song Prize for 1938. Much of his success on stage and screen came from his songwriter's craft—a special way with words and music, and, in particular, an innovative turn toward the upbeat and syncopated rhythms of jazz and swing that were making their way across the Atlantic. And in the era of the Popular Front government, there was no better expression of the spirit of the times. As Lucien Rioux, among others, has pointed out, "People loved Trenet because he sang of freedom, adventure, youth, and the Enchanted Road."

With the onset of World War II Trenet found himself back at Istres Air Force Base, but he was soon transferred to Paris where, having been assigned to organize an entertainment program for all of France's air bases, he established the "Theatre of the Wings." By the time of the German occupation in 1940, he had been demobilized. For the rest of World War II Trenet continued to perform and write and also worked on three more films, including *Adieu Léonard* (1943), which turned out to be an uneasy and unsuccessful collaboration with Pierre and Jacques Prévert. Repeatedly accused of having crypto-Jewish origins (it was speculated that the name Trenet was an anagram for Netter and that he was in fact the grandson of a rabbi), he finally presented a family tree to the authorities. He tried, however, to avoid any cooperation with the Germans and, despite official requests, performed only twice across the Rhine. For the French, meanwhile, his high-spirited music, on the surface so devoid of topical content, acquired a patriotic dimension, perhaps most evident with "Douce France" (1943), which begins: "Sweet France/dear country of my childhood/cradled in tender nonchalance/I've kept you in my heart."

With the war's end Charles Trenet became an international star. A contract that had been kept on hold since 1939 brought him to New York in May 1946 for an immediate and unconditional success. Throughout the second half of the 1940s and the early 1950s, the new "ambassador of French song" repeatedly blazed his way through the United States, Canada, Mexico, and Latin America. His first big hit of the postwar period was "La mer" ("Beyond the Sea"), which, he said, he had "left in a drawer" for four years but which quickly rose to the top of the French song charts and went on to become a hit all over the world. Recorded more than 4,000 times, it has continued to be played an average of twelve times a day.

Trenet's foreign tours kept him away from the French circuit in the late 1940s, but in September 1951 he was back at the Etoile with ten new songs and a long and taxing one-man show that ran for two months. "Everybody that was cheering him in the hall got drawn into his act," Christine de Rivoyre reported in *Le Monde*. "They went for it all—the comic, the hair-trigger poetry, calm one minute and wild the next, the zaniness, the pure madness, the rolling lyricism of 'Beyond the Sea,' the silent pantomimes, and joy that he throws by the handful like confetti." Three years later, after doing another round of concerts in the United States and Latin America, he made his first appearance at the famed Olympia Theatre in Paris. He was forty-one; he had sold eight million records, and he had accumulated a fortune, which he spent on cars and houses. According to one reporter's tally at the time, he owned seven cars in Paris, one in Montreal, and another that he had been storing in Hollywood since his last visit. His properties, meanwhile, included an estate near Aix-en-Provence, which he christened "The House of the Spirits," three adjacent villas at La Varenne, outside of Paris, a country home in Corrèze, an all-white, Hollywood-style villa (complete with swimming pool and golf course) at Juan-les-Pins, an apartment in Montreal, and a house in Quebec.

With the rise of rock music in the late 1950s, there were fewer young faces to be found among Trenet's audiences, and his voice was heard less frequently on the radio, but the singer himself remained unperturbed. "I'm much more afraid of being in style than being out of style," he told an interviewer in 1961, and he continued to maintain his following. In 1963, after another successful round of tours in Europe, the United States, and the Soviet Union, his private life came into public view when a former servant accused him of using "The House of the Spirits" for orgies. Arrested on charges of committing "immodest and unnatural acts with persons of his own sex under twenty-one years of age," he refused bail and spent a month in jail awaiting trial, during which time he composed a song for the warden called "This Is Only a Good-bye." On appeal, his suspended sentence was dropped and his fine reduced by half. Soon he was back on stage in a Paris cabaret, where he performed forty-three songs before the management finally turned off the lights to persuade the reluctant audience to go home. Although he looked "a little tired and wrinkled" at the beginning, one reviewer noted, "by the end of this extraordinary marathon, he was twenty years younger. He was in staggering form!"

Following that legendary event, Trenet reemerged as a literary figure with *Un noir éblouissant* (*A Dazzling Black*, 1965). As he explained at the time to an interviewer from the journal *Combat*, "The subject of my novel—if it really is a novel—is the story of a slightly timid black who has the nerve to want to be free." His first published novel, *Dodo manières*, which he wrote at seventeen, was serialized in *Candide* in 1940, and *La Bonne planète* (*The Good Planet*), written in 1933, appeared in 1949—but he dismissed both of them as "youthful works." Critics were generally enthusiastic about *Un noir éblouissant*, which the *Nouvel observateur* called "a story halfway between surrealism and the baroque" that was, in its best sections, "irresistibly funny."

In 1966, after a five-year absence from the music-hall scene, Trenet made another spectacular appearance at Bobino, where his fans showed up with a list of 342 of his published songs and systematically demanded them in alphabetical order. Three years later he made another "return" to the Paris stage, at the Théâtre de la Ville, and in May 1971, after an absence of fifteen years, he was back at the Olympia with yet another batch of new songs, including one of the year's big hits, "Fidèle" ("Faithful"). Once again the fans went wild, and the atmosphere, *Le Monde's* Claude Sarraute wrote, was "insanity, sheer madness: at one in the morning they were still asking for more, even though they had had almost everything."

By the mid-1970s Trenet was talking about retiring, and he announced that a concert at the Olympia, scheduled for 1975, was to mark the beginning of a three-year farewell tour. He assured members of the press that it was to be a "real goodbye, not a publicity coup," but he never really retired. Before the farewells were over, he released a new record album, and by April 1977 he was back onstage for the first spring festival at Bourges, where he was the hit of the show. At that "incredible spectacle," as a reporter from *Libération* described it, an audience of rock fans went wild for Trenet and called him back for no fewer than six encores.

In the wake of his latest success, Trenet's career soared again, with record albums, concert tours, television specials, a live appearance before some thirty thousand spectators at the Communist party's annual festival, and the publication of a joint autobiography, *Mes jeunes années racontées par ma mère et moi-même* (*My Early Years as Recalled by My Mother and Myself*, 1978). But that gathering momentum was cut short by the death of Marie-Louise Trenet at the end of 1978, after which Trenet withdrew entirely from public life for more than a year. In April 1979 he ended his mourning and released a new record album. "I don't want to become a specialist in comebacks, but I felt a real need to take up with the public again," he explained. Two months later he was feted at the opening of the Rond-Point Theatre in Paris, where he brought down the house with such staples of his repertoire as "Je chante," "Beyond the Sea," and "At Last, At Last," prompting the radio commentator José Artur to declare that "it was one of the greatest moments in [his] life as a spectator."

After the Socialists came to power, Charles Trenet was awarded the Legion of Honor, promoted to commandeur of the Ordre des Arts et des Lettres,

and named president of the Ministry of Culture's Commission for Song, though his bid, in 1982, for election to the Académie Française was voted down by a membership opposed to having a "Singing Madman" in its august midst. Undaunted, Trenet declared he would bequeath "The House of the Spirits" to the academy and soon afterwards published yet another novel, *Pierre, Juliette et l'automate* (*Pierre, Juliette, and the Automation*, 1983).

In 1986 Trenet received yet another form of *hommage* when his "Douce France" was recorded by a popular rock group made up of Algerian immigrants, who sought to recast the World War II anthem in the context of contemporary debates on the French nationality code. In support of their position, he not only gave them the rights to the song but also accompanied them to the National Assembly to distribute copies of the record to French deputies. The next year, Trenet celebrated his fiftieth anniversary as a solo performer by taking to the stage once again, with a gala two-hour concert at the Champs Elysées Theatre followed by two appearances at Lincoln Center in New York City and a tour of Japan, Quebec, and the French provinces. He assured an interviewer from the *New Yorker* on the occasion of his New York visit that he will go on singing until he sees people running for the exits.

In his youth, the curly-haired, pop-eyed Trenet bore an uncanny resemblance to Harpo Marx. With the years, his hair has become shorter and straighter, and his figure considerably rounder, but he still looks much younger than his age and keeps in shape by swimming, running, and lifting weights. His hobbies include painting, writing poetry, and book collecting.

References: *New Yorker* 63:40+ N 9 '87; Beauvarlet, Geneviève. *Trenet* (1983); Cannovo, Richard. *La Ballade de Charles Trenet* (1984); Perez, Michel. *Charles Trenet* (1964, 1979); *Who's Who in France* 1987-88

Vranitzky, Franz

Oct. 4, 1937– Federal Chancellor of Austria.
Address: Office of the Chancellor, Ballhausplatz, 2, 1014 Vienna, Austria

The meteoric political rise of Franz Vranitzky, the federal chancellor of Austria, has placed him at the helm of his nation during one of the most troubled periods in its recent history. Austria's economic woes—a growing budget deficit fueled by ailing state-run industries and rising welfare costs—have been compounded by the international controversy surrounding its current president, Kurt Waldheim, who has been accused of participating in Nazi war crimes in the Balkans during World War II. As Austria has become increasingly isolated

Franz Vranitzky

The first post that Vranitzky secured was in the accounting office of the Siemans-Schukert company. He soon left that job to join the Department of National Economics in the Austrian National Bank in 1961, where he eventually rose to the position of first vice-president. In 1970 Vranitzky resigned to become the personal assistant to the Socialist vice-chancellor and finance minister, Hannes Androsch, who became his political mentor.

Vranitzky returned to banking in 1976, this time as deputy chairman of the board for the Creditanstalt Bankverein, Austria's largest bank. Based on his effective performance there, in 1981 he was asked to take over as chief executive officer of the ailing Österreichische Länderbank. Austria's second-largest bank was on the verge of bankruptcy, due to falling oil prices that had led to large loan defaults. Vranitzky took aggressive action, cutting the bank's ties with insolvent companies to stop its downward slide and persuading the government that the bank must be bailed out with state money to preserve the nation's credit rating. Within three years, he had restored the bank to fiscal health.

That dramatic rescue led to Vranitzky's appointment as finance minister in 1984, succeeding Dr. Herbert Salcher. In spite of his political inexperience, he quickly made his mark on economic policy. Austria's rates of economic growth, inflation, and unemployment were favorable compared to other industrial nations, but the country suffered from a rising budget deficit, fed by skyrocketing pension costs and losses from state-owned industries. Vranitzky moved quickly to cut government borrowing and reduce the national debt, and he succeeded in discarding an unpopular tax on personal savings accounts. To improve Austria's economic prospects abroad, he traveled frequently to Europe and the United States to meet with government officials and financial experts.

Vranitzky got along well with his colleagues, and he maintained good relations with the conservative opposition as well. The finance minister also managed to avoid the kind of financial scandal that had forced his mentor, Hannes Androsch, from office in 1981. When Vranitzky was charged with evading an import duty on some Italian furniture, he was able to produce the necessary receipt. As Robert McFadden reported in the *New York Times* (June 19, 1986), Vranitzky gained "a reputation for economic savvy, administrative ability, and the kind of moves that politicians and voters alike recognize as astute."

When Fred Sinowatz, Austria's Socialist chancellor, resigned after the Socialist candidate for president, Kurt Steyrer, lost the presidential election on June 8, 1986 to Kurt Waldheim, who was supported by the opposition's People's party, Vranitzky, with his personal popularity and pragmatic nonideological style, seemed the logical successor. Steyrer's loss represented a humiliating defeat for the Socialist party, which had been in power since 1966, and the choice of the young former banker seemed the best hope for reversing the party's fortunes. The Austrians referred to their

diplomatically, "the chancellor has come to be viewed by many moderate Austrians as the last bulwark against the erosion of Austria's proud image," according to Serge Schmemann of the *New York Times* (February 17, 1988).

In spite of his scant political experience, Vranitzky, a former banker and Austria's finance minister since 1984, seemed to possess the financial acumen necessary to revive Austria's economy, but political troubles soon dominated his agenda. He was forced to dissolve his government in September 1986, when the Socialists' junior coalition partner, the tiny Freedom party, elected a right-wing nationalist, Jörg Haider, as its head. After the Socialist party won a slim majority in the November snap election, President Waldheim asked Vranitzky to form a "grand coalition" with the conservative People's party. That new government, which took office in January 1987, was soon embroiled in fresh controversy when, in April, the United States barred Waldheim from entering the country because of his World War II activities. Contending that the Waldheim controversy was undermining his ability to govern effectively, Vranitzky threatened to resign in February 1988. Waldheim still remains in his largely ceremonial post of president, and Vranitzky continues to struggle with the shadow that Waldheim's past casts over Austria.

Franz Vranitzky was born on October 4, 1937 in Vienna, Austria to Franz and Rosa Vranitzky. He was educated in Vienna, graduating from Vienna XVII High School in June 1955. At the Vienna College of Commerce (now the University of Commerce), he studied economics and received his degree in 1960. Vranitzky continued to take courses at the University of Vienna after he started working, and he received a Ph.D. degree in economics in 1969.

strategy as "the retreat to the pinstripes," although some Socialists objected to Vranitzky because of his conservatism and his association with Androsch.

Once in office, Vranitzky addressed the problem of the beleaguered state-run industries, particularly the Voest-Alpine steel conglomerate. He proposed selling shares in the national industries, a move that the People's party had long advocated. The unions, however, worried that restructuring and privatizing would lead to job layoffs, a prospect that would threaten Austria's harmonious "social partnership" between labor and industry.

Vranitzky had just started to straighten out Austria's economy when political troubles took over his agenda. In September 1986 the Freedom party, the Socialists' junior coalition partner, elected Jörg Haider, a right-wing nationalist, as its head. The previous year Haider had described a convicted Nazi war criminal as "a soldier who had done his duty." Already concerned about the impact of Waldheim's election on Austria's international reputation, Vranitzky immediately dissolved the government, claiming that "the liberal element had been shoved into the background" of the Freedom party and that it was no longer a suitable coalition partner for the Socialists. The chancellor called a snap election for November, reportedly hoping that his personal popularity might revive flagging support for his party.

During what a reporter for the Economist (November 15, 1986) called a "pancake-flat" campaign, the Socialists made the most of Vranitzky's personal appeal, contrasting him with the colorless conservative People's party leader, Alois Mock. Vranitzky's campaign posters read, "Those who want Vranitzky must vote for him." The candidates espoused basically the same conservative measures, with Vranitzky's economic platform calling for reducing the budget deficit, reforming taxes, and privatizing national industries—a platform not unlike that of the People's party. As the reporter for the Economist pointed out, those similarities were intentional, since neither party "has the stomach for governing alone at a time when Austria's economic troubles require deeply painful remedies." Both major parties avoided harsh rhetoric that might imperil future chances of cooperation. With unpopular economic decisions to be made, they saw an advantage in making them together. In the sixteen years that the Socialists had controlled the government, Austria's budget deficit had increased from .6 percent to 5.3 percent of the gross domestic product (GDP) in 1986, and state spending on social welfare had reached 27 percent of the GDP. On November 6, 1986 Vranitzky and Mock engaged in a televised debate—"a tame affair," according to the Economist reporter. Both Mock and Vranitzky avoided the Waldheim issue. The only excitement in the campaign was provided by Haider, who, in seeking to increase the number of Freedom party parliamentary seats, attempted to attract Austrians who were disenchanted with government corruption and fearful of unemployment.

On election day, November 23, 1986, the Socialists barely held on to their parliamentary majority, winning 43 percent of the vote, down from 47 percent in the previous election. They lost support most heavily among the working-class voters of Vienna and Upper Austria, who feared that Vranitzky's reforms would lead to unemployment. The chancellor picked up votes among middle-class Austrians who felt he had made progress in reforming the state-run industries. The People's party stayed about the same, with 41 percent of the vote. Haider doubled the Freedom party's share of seats from 5 percent to 10 percent, by winning over Austrians who were upset over the Waldheim affair. The newly formed Green party took the remaining seats. Thus the new parliamentary breakdown was eighteen seats for the Freedom party (up from a previous twelve); eighty seats for the Socialists (down from ninety); seventy-six seats for the People's party (down from eighty-one); and nine seats for the Greens.

Reflecting the "peculiarly Austrian" political process, Chancellor Vranitzky resigned on November 25, and President Waldheim immediately asked him to stay on to form a new government. Over the next two months, Vranitzky oversaw the creation of a new "grand coalition" between the Socialists and conservatives, reminiscent of the one that ruled Austria from 1945 to 1966. Haider sarcastically referred to it as a "marriage of elephants." In the government that took office on January 21, 1987, Vranitzky remained chancellor, and his conservative opponent Mock became vice-chancellor and foreign minister. The other cabinet posts were split evenly between the Socialists and the conservatives, with an independent minister of justice. As Vranitzky told Robert J. McCartney of the Washington Post (November 24, 1986) after the election, "It is possible that we have entered a phase in which political decisions have to be made that cannot be explained only in terms of the red-black cliché," referring to the traditional colors of the Socialists and conservatives. The former chancellor Bruno Kreisky expressed his displeasure with Vranitzky's strategy by resigning as honorary president of the Socialist party on January 19, accusing Vranitzky of abandoning socialism and supporting the "banks and the bourgeoisie."

In another interview, Chancellor Vranitzky outlined the primary goals of the new coalition government. "If we want to keep our renowned high standard of living and social welfare, we have to adapt the Austrian economy more quickly to structural changes in international markets," he explained to a reporter for the New York Post (November 18, 1987). Vranitzky emphasized the importance of modernizing Austrian industry, improving its research ties with the universities, and reorganizing the state-run industries. "We cannot afford further contributions to our state industry out of the budget," he added. "Therefore, we will restructure them, partly by bringing in new capital and by selling part of them." Vranitzky also stressed the need to reform the nation's tax system.

In the realm of foreign policy, he committed his government to seeking closer ties with the European Economic Community and the United States.

The goal of improving Austria's economic and diplomatic ties suffered a major setback on April 27, 1987, when the United States Department of Justice announced that it was placing Kurt Waldheim on the list of "undesirable aliens" who would not be allowed to enter the country. The American action signaled the virtual isolation of the Austrian president, who was able to meet only with Pope John Paul II and King Hussein of Jordan.

In a speech to World War II veterans and prisoners of war on December 3, 1986, Vranitzky urged his fellow Austrians to take responsibility for their past. "From the viewpoint of our present situation we must accept our measure of guilt and responsibility, and from this we must deduce the standards for our actions in the future," he said, as quoted in the publication *Austrian Information* (November–December 1986). He then proceeded to quote Bertolt Brecht: "Mankind's memory of sorrow suffered is amazingly short. . . . The worldwide horrors of the 1940s seem forgotten. Yesterday's rain doesn't make us wet, many say. It is this insensitivity which we have to fight: its most extreme degree is death."

After the Justice Department ruling was announced, Vranitzky expressed dismay over its foreign-policy implications. "We should not be indifferent to the fact that in the whole of 1987 only two government leaders visited us," he told Serge Schmemann for the *New York Times* (February 17, 1988). In May 1987 he made a highly symbolic visit to Washington, D.C., to try to repair the damage done to Austria's international image by Waldheim's link with Nazi Germany. Vranitzky explained later in the *New York Post* interview, "I consider it as one of my priorities to maintain our relations with the United States on the high and excellent level they have always been, and this was also the objective of my visit to Washington earlier this year." The American ambassador to Austria, Ronald S. Lauder, assured Vranitzky that he would be warmly welcomed. "We want to show the chancellor that this is directed against Kurt Waldheim and not against the Austrian people," Lauder told James M. Markham of the *New York Times* (May 17, 1987). Vranitzky met with Secretary of State George P. Shultz and for thirty minutes with President Ronald Reagan, failing to persuade them to lift the ban on Waldheim before he finished out his six-year term as president. As Markham noted in his *New York Times* piece, "The isolation and political eclipse of Mr. Waldheim, whose presidential post is largely ceremonial, has enhanced Chancellor Vranitzky's position as chief representative abroad."

Meanwhile, at home the United States' action endangered the fragile coalition between the Socialists and the conservatives, and public opinion polls revealed that Waldheim's supporters were wavering. Vranitzky and the former chancellor Bruno Kreisky took pains to distance themselves from the president. In parliamentary debates, the Socialist deputies criticized a motion that condemned the American action. The discussion of Waldheim grew unprecedentedly bitter in a country where heads of state are never criticized publicly.

Despite the growing pressure on him to resign, Waldheim remained adamant in his insistence that the charges against him were false. He appointed an historical commission to review his case and deliver an impartial judgment. Early in February 1988 the commission returned its findings that Waldheim must have been aware of the war crimes being committed in the Balkans while he was a German army officer, that he had done nothing to stop them, and that he had lied about his military career to avoid exposure, but it did not find any evidence of direct involvement in war crimes. Waldheim dismissed the report as "manipulations, lies, and forgeries," and he blamed his problems on an international Jewish conspiracy. He threatened to use his constitutional powers to dissolve the government if it accepted the report that he had commissioned.

On February 14, 1988 Chancellor Vranitzky held a press conference and threatened to resign himself if the Waldheim affair continued to keep his government from addressing other problems. He said that if the controversy continued to take up all of his time, as reported in the *New York Times* (February 15, 1988), "then I will not be able to take my other real duties seriously, and then the question will arise for me if I actually can go on in that way." Vranitzky then proceeded to criticize Waldheim directly. "There is enough criticism at home and enough to be taken seriously," he said. "The president has not been very accurate with the truth in the course of all these events." Amidst talk that impeachment proceedings should be started against Waldheim, Vranitzky refused to ask for the president's resignation, out of fear of jeopardizing his coalition government.

The Waldheim controversy had already polarized the Austrians, uncovering a deep strain of anti-Semitism among some and motivating others to undertake a long-deferred soul-searching. Vranitzky clearly sided with the latter. On the fiftieth anniversary of the Anschluss, when Nazi Germany invaded Austria, Vranitzky made a speech at the site of the Gestapo headquarters in Vienna, where a large part of the persecution of Austria's 190,000 Jews was carried out. He was enthusiastically applauded for his consistently strong stance against anti-Semitism. As reported by Serge Schmemann for the *New York Times* (March 14, 1988), "Even if we can no longer hear them, let the screams of desperation that sounded from the cellars of this site be a constant reminder to us." On May 11, 1988 Vranitzky was elected chairman of the Socialist party by the Federal Congress of the Austrian Socialist party, succeeding Fred Sinowatz.

Franz Vranitzky is tall, handsome, and boyish-looking. He was a basketball star in his youth, playing as a member of the Austrian National Basketball Team. Vranitzky is invariably described as stylish and cosmopolitan. Walter Greiner of the Austrian Embassy told Robert D. McFadden of the *New York Times* (June 10, 1986): "He is a very elegant man—his vocabulary is elegant, his exterior is elegant, he is very impeccable." Vranitzky speaks English, French, and several other languages. He and his wife, the former Christine Kristen, have one son and one daughter.

References: N Y Times A p8 Je 10 '86, I p1+ My '87 por; International Who's Who, 1989–90

Walsh, Bill

Nov. 30, 1931– Sports commentator. Address: c/o NBC Sports, 30 Rockefeller Plaza, New York, N.Y. 10112

When San Francisco won its third Super Bowl in eight seasons on January 22, 1989, the 49ers were hailed as the football team of the decade. Throughout the 1980s the 49ers had won consistently because they possessed the NFL's most imaginative and sophisticated offense, whose inventor was Bill Walsh, the team's head coach from 1979 until his retirement after the Super Bowl in 1989. One of the most innovative coaches in the history of the game, Walsh has been called the Vince Lombardi of the 1980s and a "genius," though Walsh himself denies that a term so hyperbolic can be applied to anyone in the profession of coaching. An unlikely inheritor of the mantle of the gruff Lombardi, Walsh is a distinguished, cultivated, and white-haired man of professorial appearance who toiled as an assistant

coach and developer of quarterbacks for seventeen years before becoming a head coach at the age of forty-five.

William ("Bill") Walsh was born on November 30, 1931 in Los Angeles, California, the son of a manual laborer. As the coach's son Steve told Ben Kinnley of the *Saturday Evening Post* (October 1985): "They were working-class people. Grandfather worked in railroad yards and in a brickyard." An ardent football fan while growing up in southern California, Walsh attended UCLA and University of Southern California games on Saturdays and Los Angeles Rams games on autumn weekends. He played running back for a local high school football team until after his sophomore year, when his father moved the family to Oregon. One year later the Walsh family moved again, to the San Francisco East Bay area, where Bill graduated from Hayward High School.

Although Walsh wanted to attend one of the state's two most prestigious universities, his high school grades failed to meet the University of California at Berkeley's exacting standards, and he could not afford the tuition at Stanford. Moreover, his unexceptional athletic skills did not induce college football recruiters to beat a path to his door. Consequently, he enrolled at San Mateo Junior College, where he played quarterback for two years before moving on to San Jose State University. At San Jose State, he majored in physical education and played football for coach Bob Bronzan, who switched the young left-hander from quarterback to end on the theory that southpaws lacked "touch" in throwing the ball. Playing both offensive and defensive end, Walsh failed to make his mark as a college athlete, largely because he was often injured, but Bronzan, who recognized Walsh's aptitude for the game, hired him as a graduate assistant coach, and he wrote a recommendation in which he predicted that "Bill Walsh will become *the* outstanding football coach in the United States."

Walsh took his first head coaching job in 1957 at Washington Union High School in Fremont, which was situated in the booming East Bay area of San Francisco. When he arrived, Washington Union had an enrollment of 2,100 and a football team that had won just once in its last twenty-seven outings. Because Walsh installed a passing offense that would have been remarkably sophisticated even for a major football team at the collegiate level, Washington Union won nine out of its ten games in 1958. By 1959, Walsh's last season at the school, Washington Union had 4,000 students in attendance, and its football team was the powerhouse of its conference. As Bill Verigan noted in the New York *Daily News* (January 21, 1985), Walsh had already "showed the traits that would later earn him the label 'genius.'" His quarterback, Bob Hidalgo, discussed his coach's innovations with Verigan: "At the time, everyone was running three yards and a cloud of dust. We ran three wide receivers, a lot of motion and sprint-out pass patterns. Most teams we played only had two receivers in the pass patterns. We had three to five in every play. He'd say, 'This is your primary receiver, then I want you to look here, then here.' At that time everybody played a three-deep zone defense. He really attacked that area. He'd flood the zones with two or three receivers."

By 1959 Walsh had received a master's degree in physical education from San Jose State and completed a hitch in the army at Fort Ord. In 1960 he moved up to the college coaching ranks as an assistant on the staff of Marvin Levy at the University of California at Berkeley, where he served as a recruiter and defensive coordinator. In 1963 he joined John Ralston's staff at Stanford as a defensive backs coach and recruiting coordinator. In a lengthy profile of Walsh for *Inside Sports* (September 1982), Tony Kornheiser wrote that Walsh "not only felt proud" to be affiliated with the state's most exclusive schools, but that he also "felt a certain vindication—the concept plays a large part in his life—when he found out he 'was capable of dealing with that group of people.'" According to Kornheiser, "Walsh used the same recruiting pitch at both schools, emphasizing the academic reputation and telling students that by attending Cal (or Stanford) they could be 'better' than they were. On a number of levels, it was a class pitch."

In 1966 Bill Walsh entered the professional ranks by joining the Oakland Raiders of the now defunct American Football League as an offensive backfield coach. Although he worked on coach Al Davis's staff for only one year, Walsh has always credited the Oakland experience with having the greatest impact on his career. In the mid-1960s, before the merger of the American and National Football leagues, the dominant offensive philosophy in the older NFL was that of the run-oriented ball-control offense, as perfected by Vince Lombardi of the Green Bay Packers. The AFL, on the other hand, was considered a wide-open, pass-happy league, and the guru of the passing offense was Sid Gillman of the San Diego Chargers. Walsh learned the throw-anytime-to-any-legal-receiver approach from Al Davis, who successfully applied Gillman's aerial circus maneuvers at Oakland. According to Walsh, Gillman and Davis were "brilliant football minds" whose tactics formed "the most complicated offensive system the game has ever known."

After spending just one season in the pros, Walsh wanted to become a head coach so badly that he experienced a midlife crisis. "I was probably a little overly ambitious about becoming a head coach," he admitted to Tony Kornheiser. "But it didn't seem to be working out. I didn't want my life to slip by. I wasn't that old, but I felt I could do more with my life." In 1967 he enrolled in Stanford's graduate school of business and became head coach of the San Jose Apaches of the short-lived Continental Football League, which served as a kind of refuge for players who failed to make the grade in the NFL or AFL. By 1968, however, the Apaches franchise had folded, and Walsh had gone back to the AFL, as offensive coordinator and quarterback coach for the newly established Cincinnati Bengals.

The coach of the Cincinnati Bengals was Paul Brown, who had been something of a legend in the NFL as coach of the Cleveland Browns and who as recently as 1964 had taken them to the league championship. During his eight seasons with the Bengals, Walsh became recognized as a designer of lethal, intricate passing offenses and as an expert developer of young quarterbacks who had raw talent but were lacking in an understanding of the conceptual side of modern football. First he molded Greg Cook, an exceptional athlete who went on to win a league passing crown before his career was cut short by injuries. Next was Virgil Carter, who stepped in when Cook was injured and who, despite his modest skills, performed commendably. His greatest success at that juncture was his development of Ken Anderson, a graduate of Augustana College in Illinois and a natural quarterback who blossomed under Walsh's tutelage into one of the most efficient passers in NFL history. From 1968 through the 1975 season, the Bengals made the playoffs three times and, with Anderson at the helm, might have played for a Super Bowl title had they not had to compete for the supremacy of their division with the Pittsburgh Steelers, who won a record four world championships in the 1970s.

Despite the team's success, Walsh was often unhappy during his years in Cincinnati, partly because he and his family were homesick for California. His greater dissatisfaction derived from his troubled relations with Paul Brown. In the 1970s the increasingly sophisticated game of football was beginning to pass Brown by, while it was obvious that his innovative assistant was on the cusp of the game's future. Walsh kept his ambitions in check in the belief that he would be the anointed successor when Brown retired, only to be devastated on January 1, 1976, when Brown abruptly announced his retirement and named his longtime offensive line coach, Bill Johnson, the head coach. Walsh later learned that the Houston Oilers had approached Paul Brown some years earlier in an attempt to acquire Walsh for the purpose of grooming him to become their head coach, but, citing Walsh's contractual obligations to the Bengals, Brown denied other teams access to Walsh and reportedly never informed him of their interest in him.

Walsh has hinted that Brown would not let him go because the Bengals head coach could not count on Walsh's ultimate failure, but for the public record he will only say, "I was caught up in a syndrome where you become too valuable to someone and they can't afford to lose you." Walsh told Tony Kornheiser: "I think I might have scared people off. I think my style may have been too penetrating. I wasn't your typical comfort-zone coach. . . . The people who'd hire me couldn't feel comfortable thinking they'd be in full control." John Madden, the popular television football analyst and former Oakland Raiders coach, has explained that "the

Cincinnati thing hurt. The way people saw it was—if he didn't get the head job at the place he worked, then why should anybody hire him?" "I was a totally frustrated man," Walsh has said of his years as an apprentice to coaches like Paul Brown.

In 1976 Walsh installed his celebrated offensive attack at San Diego, where he also developed a young quarterback named Dan Fouts, who went on become one of the most productive passers in NFL history and who credits that one season under Walsh with having turned his career around. If Walsh had stayed at San Diego he might have succeeded Tommy Prothro as the Chargers coach, but in 1977 he accepted the head coaching job at Stanford University. "The college game is very scientific," Walsh explained when he was interviewed by Ben Kinnley. "It presents as much challenge from the technical standpoint as pro football does. There's more involved in college coaching because of the varying stages of development of your players."

Since its victory over powerful Ohio State in the 1971 Rose Bowl, the Stanford football program had been in decline, but under Walsh it experienced a complete turnaround. He installed a pro-style passing offense, and his 1977 team responded with a record of nine wins in twelve games, including a post-season victory in the Sun Bowl. In addition, Walsh's quarterback, Guy Benjamin, was the NCAA's leading passer that season, as was Benjamin's unheralded successor, Steve Dils, in the 1978 season, when he guided the Cardinals to a regular-season record of seven wins and four losses. In the post-season Bluebonnet Bowl game against Georgia, Stanford was trailing by the score of 22-0 before staging a remarkable comeback to win, 25-22. "Once we'd established a track record at Stanford," Walsh told Tony Kornheiser, "I think it became rather apparent that I was a very good football coach. Very few people become head coaches for the first time at forty-five. Major colleges wonder: Why weren't you a head coach before? Can you do the hard work? Stanford proved my vindication."

In early 1979 the young owner of the San Francisco 49ers, Eddie DeBartolo Jr., named Walsh the head coach of his hapless team, whose fourteen losses in sixteen games in 1978 was the worst record in pro football. Because DeBartolo viewed himself as a businessman and not as a football savant, he also made Walsh general manager, a post that placed him in charge of team personnel. Shrewdly taking advantage of recent changes in rules, Walsh set about installing his intricate offensive system. In the NFL, defense had gained the upper hand over offense in the 1970s. For example, the Pittsburgh Steelers had their nearly impenetrable "Steel Curtain," and the Dallas Cowboys used their innovative "flex" defense to win two Super Bowls. To put more points on the scoreboard, the NFL installed rules giving offensive linemen more latitude in pass blocking and granting receivers more room to run pass patterns. Walsh was the first coach to exploit the new rules that opened up the passing game in the 1980s, and he did so by dreaming up what one writer described as a "ball-control, time-consuming offense in the manner of Vince Lombardi," though Walsh relied on short, high-percentage passes to set up runs instead of "running to daylight," as Lombardi was wont to do, to open up the passing game.

In a profile of Bill Walsh for the *New York Times* (September 12, 1982), Lowell Cohn pointed out that Walsh's system simplified football for his quarterbacks. "In other systems," Cohn wrote, "the quarterback dropped back, tried to read the defense, then figured out which receiver was free against that formation. He had to do all this in about three seconds, or he'd be eating turf. . . . Walsh's quarterbacks do not have the burden of figuring out a defense. Walsh gives them three options to one-half of the field on every pass play. If the first receiver . . . is covered, the quarterback looks for the second, and so on. Someone is bound to be open, and the options are so quick that it is harder to sack or intercept a 49er quarterback than most others." Walsh himself has explained that his talent lies in the "artistic end of football. The variation of movement of eleven players and the orchestration of that facet of football is beautiful to me."

In a discussion with Don Pierson of the *Chicago Tribune* (January 24, 1982), one of Walsh's pupils, Virgil Carter, described how Walsh orchestrated playing-field chaos for his quarterbacks: "On a typical pass play . . . the quarterback watches the middle linebacker. If he drops straight back or to his right, you look left. You know that on your first step back. Then you find the strong safety on your third step. If he's deep, you read the cornerback on your fifth step. If he's back, you throw to the fullback in the flat, no questions asked. It is always a quick decision by the quarterback. . . . It's five steps and the ball is gone, or seven steps and it's gone."

In Walsh's first season, in 1979, the 49ers again won two games while losing fourteen, but, with the presence of quarterback Steve DeBerg, the team's offensive performance improved significantly. In the following season the 49ers won six out of sixteen games, and in midseason Joe Montana, a second-year man, replaced DeBerg as the starting quarterback. Walsh is considered an unerring judge of athletic talent, and the Joe Montana story is a case in point. After a somewhat erratic career at Notre Dame, Montana was not selected by the 49ers until the third round of the 1979 NFL draft. Other teams spurned him because he did not have a "cannon" arm for long passes, but Walsh was impressed by his accuracy on medium-range throws as well as by his mobility, poise, and intelligence. And in 1981 the 49ers stunned the satraps of professional football by compiling an NFL-best record of thirteen wins against only three losses, and Montana led the National Football Conference in passing. In the NFC championship game against the Dallas Cowboys, who liked to call themselves "America's team," it was Montana's late touchdown pass to tight end Dwight Clark that secured a 28-27 49er victory. In the Super Bowl the 49ers faced the Cincinnati Bengals, whose general manager was still Paul Brown and who were led by Walsh's student, Ken Anderson. The game proved to be Walsh's ultimate vindication, for the 49ers won their first Super Bowl by a score of 26-21, and Joe Montana was named the game's Most Valuable Player.

Having directed one of the league's doormats to a Super Bowl victory in just three seasons, Walsh was acclaimed in the media as a "genius," though he disdained the label as sportswriters' hyperbole. In the strike-shortened season of 1982, however, the 49ers were distracted by post–Super Bowl hoopla, drug-related problems, and the collapse of their once-sterling pass defense. As a result, they compiled a losing record of three and six. Walsh, who has described himself as a man who is 'haunted' by the specter of losing, intended to resign as coach until Eddie DeBartolo dissuaded him. Instead, he relinquished the post of general manager and assumed the role of team president, an administrative job that was less demanding but left intact his power over the club. In 1983 the 49ers rebounded, winning ten out of sixteen, and in 1984 they posted the best record in the NFL, losing just one of sixteen regular-season games. In the NFC championship game they defeated the Chicago Bears, 23-0, and in the Super Bowl the 49ers demolished the Miami Dolphins, 38-16, with Joe Montana again winning the game's MVP award.

Following the second 49ers championship in four seasons, Mike Lupica of the New York *Daily News* (January 22, 1985) wrote that Walsh "has become the greatest star in the coaching profession since Lombardi. . . . He has become the sort of star that Don Shula did not become in winning two Super Bowls, that Tom Landry did not become with his two, that Chuck Noll did not become with his remarkable run of four. . . . The 49ers belong to Walsh the way the old Packers were Lombardi's." Walsh's mystique derived partly from his cultivated manner and dignified comportment, and partly from his innovative brilliance. For example, Lowell Cohn noted that there are "endless stories about Walsh's fever to invent. In 1962 Marv Levy of the University of California held coaches meetings in a room with three blackboards. Walsh . . . would scribble a play furiously in any available space, but, before he finished, his mind would skip to another play. He would move to the next board and start writing, while he'd still be talking about the first play. Levy used to follow Walsh around the room with an eraser and rub out the plays because the other coaches were getting confused."

The New York Giants once studied films of three 49ers games and discovered that Walsh had called fifty-two different plays on first down and ten. He would pore over an opposing team's defense, looking for a weakness to exploit, and he often went into games with as many as 100 pass plays drawn up. (Most teams use between thirty and fifty for a single game.) "When we go over the game plan during the week," Joe Montana told Dave An-

derson of the *New York Times* (January 26, 1982), "it doesn't look like it will work. But when we get into the game and use it, it seems that the plan always works." "Most coaches think we ask too much of our team," said Sam Wyche, who was a Walsh quarterback in the 1960s and served on Walsh's San Francisco staff in the 1980s. "It's like final-exam week each week."

Walsh, however, was regarded by some of his peers as an egocentric man who "crowns himself like Napoleon," as one source told Tony Kornheiser. Some of his fellow coaches were annoyed because he refused to invoke the standard football bromides to explain away victory or defeat. Instead of saying that the 49ers had not tried hard enough or that someone had missed a key block, Walsh would discuss how his team had prepared for a game, which to some coaches implied that the 49ers won because they outsmarted and outworked other teams. Walsh was also not one to lavish praise on his assistants. He told Tony Kornheiser that he was "cautious about continuous accolades to people, about heaping trumped-up remarks on people in the hopes of pacifying them." But as one of his former players, the wide receiver Bob Trumpy, explained: "He suffered for years with no credit. I don't blame him for not giving any. He's not up for Humanitarian of the Year. He's a football coach." And as Walsh himself told Frank Litsky of the *New York Times* (January 20, 1985): "I'm supposed to be egocentric, maybe because I'm willing to talk instead of saying 'no comment.' . . . I don't know if I have a big ego. . . . I know if I have a big ego, it hasn't affected the ability of this organization to function smoothly and it hasn't kept everyone from taking part. We have great chemistry in this organization."

In 1985 and 1986 the 49ers fielded strongly competitive teams, but they failed to win an NFC championship. In 1987 the 49ers enjoyed a banner year, compiling an NFL-best record of thirteen and two in the strike-shortened regular season. In the first playoff round, however, they were overpowered by the Minnesota Vikings in a game played at Candlestick Park in San Francisco. Consequently, in 1988, Walsh was stripped of his title of club president by DeBartolo, and, when the 49ers had won just six games after the season was eleven weeks old, there was talk that Walsh's effectiveness as a coach was a thing of the past. But when Montana recovered from a series of nagging injuries, the team rallied to win four of its last five games. They overwhelmed the Bears in the NFC title match, setting up yet another Super Bowl confrontation between the 49ers and the Bengals, who were coached by Sam Wyche, the offense-minded innovator who had been schooled by Walsh.

Super Bowl 1989 was expected to be a high-scoring affair, but with thirty-four seconds remaining in the game the Bengals were protecting a 16-13 lead. Montana, however, led the 49ers on an eleven-play, ninety-two-yard drive that probably secured his and Walsh's eventual induction into the NFL Hall of Fame. He culminated that march with a ten-yard touchdown pass, sealing a 20-16 49ers victory in a game that "should be long remembered as the most exciting in Super Bowl history," according to Thomas George of the New York Times (January 23, 1989). Having been stripped of his presidency of the club, Walsh once again had been "vindicated" by winning a world championship.

When Walsh was asked if he planned to try to tie the record set by Chuck Noll, who coached the Pittsburgh Steelers to four Super Bowl wins, he replied: "That's Star Wars. . . . It gets harder and harder to win in the [NFL] because there's more balance than ever." Coaching, he told Ira Berkow of the New York Times (January 24, 1989), had become "a very stressful occupation," and athletes' agents, he explained, had grown "very mercenary." "Then there's the social scene, in particular the drugs," he added. "That's a monster. [And] in some cases, the ownership makes life stressful for the coach, too, because they get frustrated and impatient, so the coach has no one to turn to for support except his family." A few days later Walsh announced his retirement from coaching. He persuaded DeBartolo to appoint his longtime defensive coordinator, George Seifert, head coach, and Walsh himself moved to the 49ers front office, taking a two-thirds cut in pay from his $1.3 million in annual salary to retain his position as the team's vice-president of football operations.

In July 1989 Walsh left the 49ers to become the chief analyst and color announcer of the NBC network's featured weekly pro football game broadcast at a salary of about $750,000 a year. His appointment was the result of a shakeup at NBC Sports engineered by its executive producer, Terry O'Neil, who felt that Walsh's authority and his ability to explain the complexities of modern football would make NBC football telecasts competitive with those broadcast by the CBS network, whose chief analyst is the colorful John Madden. Newspaper reviewers gave Walsh generally goods marks as a television analyst. "He [does not] spare players or coaches in his criticism," wrote Stan Isaacs in New York Newsday (September 11, 1989). "He [is] no rambunctious John Madden—nor is anybody else. Walsh does give indications, though, of being a likable, intelligent TV presence in the long run."

In his ten seasons with the San Francisco 49ers, Bill Walsh compiled an overall regular-season won-lost record of ninety-two wins, fifty-nine losses, and one tie, and his teams won ten out of fourteen postseason playoff games. The New York Daily News columnist Mike Lupica has captured the aura of quiet authority that Walsh projected on the sidelines. "Walsh," he wrote, "in that familiar, pensive pose. Rodin's thinker, only standing. White sweater to match the hair. Headset on. One arm across the belly. The other bent up from the elbow, with hand to headset. Is he listening to his assistants? Or some personal coaching Muse? All we know for certain is he is about three first downs ahead of everybody else. . . . Walsh seems to be meditating." Walsh relaxes by playing tennis, read-

ing historical nonfiction, and making sketches while his wife, Geri, paints. Walsh and his wife, who is a successful interior designer, have a daughter, Elizabeth, and two sons, Steve and Craig.

References: N Y Times C p13+ Ja 26 '82 por; Newsday p4 Ja 20 '85 por, p95 Ja 22 '85 por; Sport 74:15+ Jl '83 pors; Sporting N p23+ Ja 16 '82 por, p2+ Ja 30 '82 pors; Who's Who in America, 1988–89

Wapner, Joseph A(lbert)

Nov. 15, 1919– Television personality; retired judge. Address: c/o Ralph Edwards Productions, 1717 North Highland Ave., Hollywood, Calif. 90028

More than twenty million viewers tune in daily to The People's Court television show, which since its debut in 1981 has become one of the ten most popular syndicated programs in America. Its presiding judge, Joseph A. Wapner, is in real life a veteran of twenty years on the bench of the California municipal and superior courts. The show's success has made Wapner's name a household word and brought him fame, fortune, and the status of a folk hero. Some commentators, speaking only half in jest, have touted him for appointment to the United States Supreme Court. In his profile of Wapner for the New Yorker (March 31, 1986), E. J. Kahn Jr. hailed him as a "familiar, benign, sensible pillar of stability in a world of wobbly room service." One of his ardent fans, the actor Dustin Hoffman, in his Oscar-winning film Rain Man, portrayed the autistic Raymond as a Wapner fan ("Oh, oh. Time for

Judge Wapner"). In his youth Wapner dreamed of becoming an actor but got sidetracked on a legal career. His show business fame quite unexpectedly came to him only late in his life. In June 1989 a *Washington Post* survey announced that many more Americans, by a margin of 54 percent to 9 percent, knew Wapner's name than they did that of William H. Rehnquist, the chief justice of the United States Supreme Court.

Joseph Albert Wapner was born on November 15, 1919 in Los Angeles, California, into an upper-middle-class Jewish family. "My mother was the kind of housewife you used to see in advertisements for refrigerators," Wapner recalled in his 1987 autobiography, entitled *A View from the Bench.* "She really did put a clean house and a hot dinner for her children and her husband above every other consideration." Since his father, Joseph M. Wapner, was a successful lawyer, Joe Jr. and his sister, Irene, grew up comfortably in a quiet and closely knit downtown neighborhood that has since become a part of the campus of Los Angeles City College. The Wapners shared a duplex with Joe's grandparents and an aunt, and after school each day young Joe ran up the stairs to his grandparents' home, where he spent long hours in "spirited discussions" about family life. "From my earliest recollections, they took me seriously, and listened—and talked—to me as if I were an adult," Wapner wrote in his autobiography. "That means a great deal to the self-esteem of a child."

After appearing in a pageant at the Knights of Pythias hall at the age of seven, Wapner wanted to become an actor, and, after his graduation from Virgil Junior High School in 1934, a family friend arranged for him to attend Hollywood High School, which had a reputation for having the best drama curriculum in town and for being the alma mater of such child stars as Marge Champion and Nanette Fabray. During his senior year there, he was assigned a part in a school production of the Broadway stage hit *The Late Christopher Bean,* in which he was to portray a character named Tallant. He told Doris Klein Bacon of *People* (May 3, 1982) magazine during an interview: "Two weeks before the performance, our coach told me, 'Joe, you don't have any talent, spelled T-A-L-E-N-T.' And I was out of the play." His dismissal from the cast ended a brief romance with an auburn-haired classmate named Judy Turner. An aspiring actress, she eventually dyed her hair blond and found fame in the movies under the name of Lana Turner.

Undaunted, Wapner was as determined as ever to succeed as an actor. Following his graduation from Hollywood High School, he wanted to enroll in drama classes at Los Angeles Community College, but his father persuaded him to attend the University of Southern California, where he majored in philosophy. By the time he graduated in 1941 with a B.A. degree, Wapner had abandoned his dream of becoming an actor and had decided to attend law school. Lacking in self-confidence and convinced that at age twenty-one he was still too immature to enter law school, he took a thirty-five-dollar-per-week job as the assistant credit manager of a jewelry store. It was in that post that he made his first appearance in a courtroom, when he took a case to small-claims court on his employer's behalf and lost.

Rejected by the navy because of his poor eyesight, in June 1942 Wapner enlisted in the United States Army. After completing officer candidate school, he received a commission as a first lieutenant in January 1943, and in the following year he was posted to the South Pacific, where he commanded a platoon in the 132d Infantry of the Americal Division. Wapner saw action in bloody fighting on the islands of Bougainville, Leyte, and Cebu in the Philippines, narrowly escaping death on at least two occasions. On April 8, 1945 he was crossing a rice paddy when his unit came under fire. Feeling a thump on his backpack, Wapner raced for cover, and it was only afterwards that he realized just how lucky he had been. A Japanese sniper's bullet that had ripped through his backpack had been stopped by a can of tuna fish that his mother had mailed to him. He was less lucky two days later.

Pinned down by enemy fire in the hills near the town of Cebu, Wapner and one of his men risked their lives to rescue a wounded medic. A few minutes later, while digging a foxhole, Wapner was hit in the foot and spine by phosphorus and shrapnel fragments from a mortar shell. Although sedated by morphine given to him by medics, he was in excruciating pain the rest of the day and all through the night as desperate hand-to-hand combat raged around him. It was not until the battle eased the following day that he was taken to a field hospital. Along with the Purple Heart that he routinely received for being wounded, Wapner was awarded the Bronze Star for heroism.

Back home in 1945, Wapner was still hobbling around on crutches when he entered the law school of the University of Southern California on November 1. Graduating from law school with his LL.B. degree in 1948, Wapner was admitted to the California bar the following January. "My father had already decided, before I passed the bar, that it was going to be Wapner & Wapner," Wapner recalled to Michael Ryan of the New York *Daily News* (July 5, 1987). "He had the stationery printed. I was a very obedient young man, so I did it." Father and son worked together in a general commercial practice for the next three years; then Joe Jr. struck out on his own for a time. Soon, he had formed another partnership and had begun to dabble in state politics. In 1958 Wapner worked in Edmund G. Brown's successful gubernatorial campaign, and in October of the following year Brown rewarded him with an appointment as a judge of the Los Angeles Municipal Court. It was there, over the course of the next two years, that Wapner earned his judicial spurs, presiding over a real life "people's court" in which he had to decide as many as forty cases—such cases of daily life as dry-cleaning disasters, traffic tickets, small claims, and unpredictable dogs and their masters—in a single day.

In 1961 Wapner was promoted to the Los Angeles Superior Court, where he handled a wide range of both civil and criminal cases. Eight years later his peers elected him presiding judge of the court system. (He was reelected to the post in 1970 and 1971.) As a result, it became his job to supervise more than 200 judges, 800 employees, and an annual budget of $30 million. "I was the only Jew who'd ever been elected [to that position], and I don't know when there'll be another," Wapner told Doris Klein Bacon during the *People* magazine interview.

It was in his position as presiding judge that Wapner developed a reputation as a staunch defender of the concept of judicial independence from executive interference by the governor. In 1975 he was elected to a one-year term as president of the California Judges' Association, and he led the fight against a proposal to cut judges' salaries. His public pronouncements on the issue placed him at odds with the then governor, Edmund G. ("Jerry") Brown Jr., and according to Wapner it may have cost him an appellate judgeship. "As it was reported back to me at the time and later," Wapner wrote in *A View from the Bench*, "when my name was brought up to be an appellate judge, Jerry Brown and his aides recalled the basic disagreements I had with the governor. The nomination never took place." Wapner has commented that what saddened him most in his disappointment was the fact that "in America, a man's career can be stymied because he speaks out for the honor and reputation of his colleagues."

Wapner remained on the superior-court bench until 1979, when he retired at the age of sixty and began spending his days playing tennis, a game for which he has long had a passion, and doing private arbitrations, for which his standard salary was $250 per hour. During his superior-court tenure, he had earned a well-deserved reputation for being able to settle large-scale divorces with a minimum of fuss and acrimony. One of his more celebrated arbitrations was the breakup of one of the marriages of Jack Kent Cooke, the multimillionaire industrialist and sportsman. Both parties so much approved of the way in which he had divided the assets that Cooke invited Wapner to a party for his Washington Redskins football team, and Cooke's ex-wife asked him to officiate at her remarriage.

After two years of retirement, Wapner was offered the opportunity to become a television celebrity. Christian Markey, a superior-court judge who was Wapner's friend and tennis partner, recommended him to the veteran television producers Ralph Edwards, the creator of *This Is Your Life* and other programs, and Stu Billett, who had worked on such successful shows as *Let's Make a Deal* and the *$64,000 Question*. The two men were looking for a retired judge to preside over a courtroom television program that they were developing and hoped to market.

The concept of a courtroom show had been first suggested to Billett in 1976, but, after watching a few trials and weighing the possibilities, he decided that anything involving lawyers was dull on the small screen. The obvious solution was to focus on small-claims court, where litigants argue their own cases and the maximum claim in most states is about $1,500 (although Arkansas imposes a ceiling of $300 and Tennessee, $10,000). "To me, it was like Solomon in the days of the Bible, with everybody yelling at everybody else," Billett told E. J. Kahn Jr. "I found myself taking sides."

Over the course of the next three years, Billett and Edwards experimented with variations upon their courtroom idea. Billett told Kitty Bean Yancey of the *Chicago Tribune* (November 7, 1986) that, when they were approached, network programmers at NBC rejected the concept of the show. "They said people can't argue their own cases on television," Billett explained. "They wanted a comedian judge delivering decisions while a real judge made them behind the scenes."

For a time, Billett and Edwards considered casting a law professor as their judge, but when that failed to work out they opted to find a real judge, preferably someone who had recently retired. The instant they met Wapner, they knew that they had found their man. As Billett told E. J. Kahn Jr.: "When Joe walked in the door, I thought I was looking at Tyrone Power, and I said to myself, 'My God, I hope he's good.' He'd come with such aplomb and such credentials, and Ralph and I . . . were almost afraid." Wapner's audition involved a case in which a huge ex-football player was being sued for assault by a much smaller woman. The parties were arguing loudly when Wapner silenced both of them by simply banging his fist on the table. Having passed his audition with flying colors, he was promptly offered the starring role in *The People's Court*, a new half-hour "strip show" (so called by the television industry because, like a newspaper comic strip, it appears five days a week) that Edwards and Billett planned to market.

When the pilot episode of *The People's Court*, with Judge Wapner presiding, was unveiled at a March 1981 convention of the influential National Association of Television Program Executives, the reviews were mixed. On the one hand, a critic for the weekly show business bible, *Variety*, praised the pilot as "a rare combination of information and entertainment which works smoothly." On the other, the influential John J. O'Connor of the *New York Times* quipped that *The People's Court* "could technically run forever. However, like the judge, I think I've already heard enough." (Making the best of that bad review, Telepictures, the show's distributor, took out an advertisement in *Variety* that announced, "The verdict is in. *The People's Court* could technically run forever.'— John J. O'Connor, the *New York Times*.")

Edwards's hunch that the show had "the sweet smell of success" proved correct. *The People's Court* was an instant ratings hit, and after just one season on the air the program had spawned at least three pallid imitators—*Family Court, Police Court,* and *Custody Court*. By mid-1982, as Doris Klein Bacon reported in *People* magazine, the syndicated show had become a hit in more than ninety markets in the United States and a dozen foreign countries. In the eight seasons since its inception, the popularity of *The People's Court* has continued to grow. According to Carlos Sanchez of the *Washington Post* (April 16, 1989), the show regularly attracts an audience of twenty million viewers in the 200 cities around the United States in which it is aired. Among many other honors, *The People's Court* has been nominated for four Emmy Awards.

Television industry watchers have advanced several reasons for the phenomenal success of *The People's Court*. The Los Angeles lawyer and television reporter Harvey Levin, who serves as the show's legal consultant, told Paul Galloway of the *Chicago Tribune* (March 26, 1989) that the combination of Wapner's personality and judicial skills are the real keys to its success. "He makes the very difficult look easy," Levin said. Harry Waters, the television critic of *Newsweek* (June 16, 1986), feels that the show's gritty realism has a lot to do with its popularity. "No soap opera has so engrossingly captured the wondrous banality of the human condition," Waters has explained.

Researchers cull through the records of the thirty-three small-claims courts in Los Angeles in their search for actual civil cases that have dramatic potential. Of the hundreds of possibilities, just twenty-five cases per week are seriously considered, and the ten that are finally chosen are heard by Wapner each Wednesday at a taping session held in the studios of the Production Group, in Hollywood. As in a real court, the cases are tried without rehearsals, and there are no scripts. Unlike a real court, however, once the parties agree to have their dispute heard by Judge Wapner, they sign a legally binding arbitration contract that sets out some rather unusual ground rules.

The big difference between what transpires in *The People's Court* and in a real small-claims court is explained on-screen near the end of each show: "Both the plaintiff and the defendant have been paid from a fund for their appearance. The amount, if any, awarded in the case is deducted from that fund, and the remainder is divided between both litigants. The amount of the fund is dependent upon the size of the judgment."

The overwhelming success of *The People's Court* has earned Wapner an income in the upper six-figure range as well as celebrity status for himself and the show's other on-camera regulars—the bailiff Rusty Burrell (who once maintained order at the Charles Manson trial) and the "reporter" Doug Llewellyn. The *Boston Globe* columnist Diane White has proclaimed Wapner "an international sex symbol," and more than one other commentator has suggested that he would make an ideal candidate for appointment to the United States Supreme Court. One talk-show host in Tampa, Florida went so far as to suggest that Wapner, who is a lifelong Democrat, run for president of the

United States. Wapner has been honored by various legal agencies and has been invited to speak to law students on the campuses of Harvard, Yale, Arizona, Oklahoma, and Idaho universities. And although he has been a guest on Johnny Carson's late-night talk show, Wapner has turned down offers to appear on NBC's irreverent *Saturday Night Live*. "I'm still a judge," he told Kitty Bean Yancey. "For me to go on a show and become a comedian is not in keeping with who I am and what I am."

Wapner has said of his autobiography, *A View from the Bench*: "If there is a theme to the book it would be justice, and I suppose my own brand of justice. It's a book about human relationships, friendships, and loyalties." The book was a commercial success, in spite of its mixed reviews. Abner J. Mikva, a judge on the United States Court of Appeals for the District of Columbia, has criticized *The People's Court* as "a legal never-never land" where the judge's decisions bear little resemblance to actual law, and, writing in the *Washington Monthly* (February 1988), he summed up *A View from the Bench* as Wapner's "auto-vanity."

If such criticisms bother Wapner, he does not let it show. He has defended his role in *The People's Court* in this way: "[The show] educates people in basic law. It shows that in cases where the claim is monetarily small, they have a place to go. And it teaches people how to present a case." After eight seasons, Wapner feels *The People's Court* is even better than when it started, and he told E. J. Kahn Jr. that he still enjoys doing the show and hopes to preside over it until at least 1994, when he will be seventy-five. "I'll go as long as I have my marbles," he said.

Green-eyed, silver-haired Joseph A. Wapner stands slightly over five feet, nine inches tall and weighs about 155 pounds. He and his wife, the former Mickey Nebenzahl, whom he married in 1945, live in a modest three-bedroom home in Bel Air, a Los Angeles suburb. They have three grown children: Frederick, a municipal court judge in Los Angeles; David, an attorney; and Sarah, who works in the field of childcare. Wapner, whom friends say is an informal person off-camera, has a lively sense of humor despite his feisty temperament. Despite the orthopedic shoes he wears as a result of his war wounds, he is an ardent tennis player who has won a number of amateur tournaments. When he is not preoccupied with a court of one type or another, Wapner enjoys playing bridge and reading.

References: *New Yorker* 62:45+ Mar 31 '86; Wapner, Joseph A. *A View from the Bench* (1987); *Who's Who in America,* 1988–89

Wasserstein, Wendy

Oct. 18, 1950– Writer. Address: c/o Luis Sanjurgo, International Creative Management, 40 W. 57th St., New York, N.Y. 10019

In the past five years the playwright Wendy Wasserstein has emerged as the preeminent theatrical chronicler of the momentous changes in the lives of women over the last generation. She writes satirical comedies, full of quick-fire epigrams and one-liners, but her plays have serious and touching undertones, in which the successes and failures of the women's movement are honestly—sometimes painfully—explored. A graduate of Yale University's School of Drama, Miss Wasserstein first came to prominence with her Off-Broadway play *Uncommon Women and Others*, about life at an elite women's college. *Uncommon Women* was followed by the even more successful *Isn't It Romantic*, which also dealt with the hopes and fears of contemporary women and racked up a two-year run Off Broadway. Her greatest success to date came in 1989, with *The Heidi Chronicles*, which one critic described as "a memorable elegy for her own lost generation." Within weeks of its moving from Off Broadway to Broadway, *The Heidi Chronicles* was awarded the Pulitzer Prize for drama and a Tony Award as best new play of the year, among numerous other honors.

Wendy Wasserstein was born on October 18, 1950 in Brooklyn, New York, the youngest of the four children of Lola (Schleifer) and Morris W. Wasserstein, Jewish immigrants from central Europe who had come to the United States as children in the 1920s. Her father was a prosperous textile manufacturer; her mother, a housewife with a passionate interest in dance and theatre. In the

early 1960s, Wendy Wasserstein moved with her family from the Flatbush section of Brooklyn to Manhattan's affluent Upper East Side, where she grew up in what she has since described as "nice middle-class" surroundings. As a child, she took dancing lessons every Saturday morning from the dancer and choreographer June Taylor. After her class, Miss Wasserstein invariably attended a matinée performance of a Broadway show. "I was a show biz baby, born in a trunk," she told Joanne Kaufman of the *Wall Street Journal* (March 1, 1989). "I always loved the theatre."

Miss Wasserstein was especially fond of musicals, and she quickly discovered that she could get excused from gym classes at the Calhoun School, the exclusive Manhattan prep academy for girls that she attended, by volunteering to write the musical revue for the school's annual mother-daughter luncheon. "I was not a particularly good student in girls' school," she admitted to Leslie Bennetts in an interview for the *New York Times* (May 24, 1981). "I would show up every day in the same work shirt and the headmistress would call my mother and tell her that I should get dressed up and wear pink."

Following her graduation from the Calhoun School, Miss Wasserstein attended Mount Holyoke College in South Hadley, Massachusetts, where she majored in history. Undecided about a career, she toyed with the idea of pursuing a law degree and, at one point, studied to be a congressional intern but, by her own account, she "kept falling asleep" over her books. The turning point came midway through her college career when, at the suggestion of a friend, she took a summer playwriting course at Smith College. Emboldened by that, in her words, "confidence-building experience," during her junior year, which she spent at Amherst College, she began auditioning for and performing in campus theatrical productions. "If you're shy, acting is a way of being someone else," she explained to Leslie Bennetts. "And theatre creates a family, an environment that's very nice. What I didn't know at that point was that you could do something in life that you liked, so I thought I had to take the law boards, which I did every year for years."

After earning her B.A. degree from Mount Holyoke in 1971, Wendy Wasserstein moved back to New York City, where she worked at a succession of odd jobs while she studied creative writing at the City College of New York. Under the guidance of such professional writers as Joseph Heller and Israel Horovitz, she progressed rapidly and, in 1973, saw her play *Any Woman Can't*, which she described to Leslie Bennetts as being about "a girl who gives up and gets married after blowing an audition for tap-dancing class," produced Off-Broadway at Playwrights Horizons, a nonprofit theatre with a reputation for nurturing promising young writers. Later in the same year, she received her M.A. degree from City College and, not without some misgivings, enrolled at Yale University's School of Drama, choosing it over the Graduate

School of Business at Columbia University, which had also accepted her application for admission. "I decided to take the risk of trying something I really wanted to do," she told Sylviane Gold, who interviewed her for the *Wall Street Journal* (February 7, 1984).

During her first few months at Yale, Miss Wasserstein was, by her own admission, "frightened to death." "I felt like I was going from platform to platform, trying to catch the train to Moscow," she has recalled, as quoted in *Interviews with Contemporary Women Playwrights* (1987). "I had no idea what I was doing at drama school. Everyone else I knew was going to law school or marrying lawyers, except for my immediate friends, who seemed as cuckoo as me." Her doubts notwithstanding, Miss Wasserstein thrived at Yale. Among her numerous accomplishments were *Montpelier Pa-zazz*, a collegiate musical, written with David Hollister, that was performed at Playwrights Horizons in June 1976, and the musical revue *When Dinah Shore Ruled the Earth*. A collaboration with fellow playwright Christopher Durang, *Dinah Shore* was a major attraction of the Yale Cabaret's 1977–78 season.

In 1976 Wendy Wasserstein graduated from the Yale School of Drama with an M.F.A. degree. For her master's thesis, she submitted a one-act version of what was to become her first successful play, *Uncommon Women and Others*. Expanded into two acts, the play was subsequently accepted for production at the National Playwrights Conference—the prestigious annual summer workshop at the O'Neill Theatre Center in Waterford, Connecticut that has launched scores of new plays. A few months later, on November 21, 1977, the Phoenix Theatre's production of *Uncommon Women and Others* opened Off Broadway at the Marymount Manhattan Theatre.

Uncommon Women and Others is a wry and affectionate portrait of life in an elite women's college in the early 1970s, when the burgeoning feminist movement was challenging many of the longstanding assumptions about a woman's role in society. As they struggle to realize their dreams of becoming "uncommon" in a world of rapidly changing social and sexual mores, the five central characters must come to terms with new choices—and the doubts and fears associated with them—and with the still-powerful pull of more traditional patterns of behavior. During its limited run at the Phoenix, *Uncommon Women* charmed audiences and critics alike with its perceptiveness, sympathetically drawn characters, and mordant wit.

In his opening-night review for the *New York Post*, Edmund Newton applauded Miss Wasserstein for having "created a group of characters who demand not only sympathy but affection." "The laughs are there, many of them genuine thigh smackers," Newton wrote, "but Miss Wasserstein has shown triumphantly that she knows when to stop. . . . The real triumph of *Uncommon Women* is that you leave the theatre caring deeply about its characters." Pronouncing the play "exuberant to

the point of coltishness," Richard Eder, in his review for the *New York Times*, observed, "Miss Wasserstein, who is young, uses her very large gift for being funny and acute with a young virtuosity that is often self-indulgent." But, he added, whenever the humor threatens to degenerate into "gag-writing," she "blunts her cleverness with what, if it is not yet remarkable wisdom, is a remarkable setting-out to look for it."

Some critics, among them *New York* magazine's John Simon, complained that *Uncommon Women* lacked shape and dramatic conflict and was, at bottom, little more than a series of vignettes. Agreeing that it is "not a conventionally structured play," Miss Wasserstein has since explained, as quoted in *Interviews with Contemporary Women Playwrights*, "It's like an odd sort of documentary. I am more interested in content than form. *Uncommon Women* is episodic. I don't know what actually *happens* in that play. . . . They graduate." *Uncommon Women* has been staged at many regional and university theatres across the country and has earned its author several awards, including the Joseph Jefferson Award and the Inner Boston Critics Award. The play has also been televised by the Public Broadcasting Service as part of its *Theatre in America* series.

Miss Wasserstein's growing reputation as one of the most promising young playwrights in the country received another boost in 1980, when she was commissioned by the Phoenix Theatre to write a new play for its upcoming season. *Isn't It Romantic* is, in a sense, a sequel to *Uncommon Women*, for it examines the lives of two longtime friends, former classmates at a women's college, as they wrestle with the demands of professional careers and personal relationships some six years after their graduation. During the course of the play, the friendship between the two women—Janie Blumberg, a plump, rumpled ("I look like an extra in *Potemkin*," Janie says at one point) Jewish freelance writer, and Harriet Cornwall, a svelte, successful WASP account executive—becomes strained when Harriet announces her engagement.

Isn't It Romantic, the concluding presentation in the Phoenix Theatre's 1980–81 season, opened to mixed reviews at the company's uptown Marymount Manhattan Theatre on May 28, 1981. While he conceded that the play was "compulsively funny," Mel Gussow thought that Miss Wasserstein seemed "a bit unsure what she wants." *Isn't It Romantic* "veers from character comedy to caricature, interspersed with throwaway jokes and routines," he wrote in his review for the *New York Times* (June 15, 1981), "but there is no denying the playwright's comic virtuosity and her ear for contemporary jargon." In Clive Barnes's view, the play was "over-diffuse, over-long, and underorganized," but, as he went on to explain in his review for the *New York Post* (June 16, 1981), "its moments of antic poetry and urbane wit are so persuasive that it scarcely matters. . . . Miss Wasserstein has a natural dramatic gift that only needs a little more organization and form to succeed in a most impressive fashion."

Taking those criticisms seriously, over the next year Miss Wasserstein reworked *Isn't It Romantic* under the guidance of André Bishop, the artistic director of Playwrights Horizons, and the director Gerald Gutierrez. To give the play a stronger narrative line, she decided to focus on the emotional growth of Janie (with whom she admittedly shares a number of character traits, including a self-deprecating wit), describing her transition from an insecure, indecisive woman who is constantly badgered by her indulgent mother and her staid, sensible boyfriend into an individual strong enough to make her own decisions and take responsibility for her choices. "The thing is, you have to see the play as separate from yourself," Miss Wasserstein explained to Michiko Kakutani of the *New York Times* (January 3, 1984). "When I first wrote *Isn't It Romantic*, I think I was devastated that Janie didn't marry the doctor. In the first week at the Phoenix, I even had her getting together with him at the end. But I knew this time it was right for her to dance alone at the end. When I watch her up there . . . , I think it's her story, and I can go and write something else." The revised version of *Isn't It Romantic* opened Off Broadway at Playwrights Horizons on December 15, 1983. A box-office hit, it transferred in April 1984 to a larger Off-Broadway theatre, where it ran for a total of 733 performances. The reviews were universally enthusiastic, the critic for *Variety* (February 1, 1984) going so far as to say that Miss Wasserstein deserved a medal of commendation for taking a good play and making it even better.

In the meantime, Wendy Wasserstein had been hard at work on several other projects. Her play *Tender Offer* was among those performed by the Ensemble Studio Theatre in the spring of 1983, during its annual festival of one-act plays. The delicate *pas de deux* between a disappointed little girl and her father, whose dedication to his job has caused him to miss his daughter's dance recital, was warmly applauded by the New York critics. "Miss Wasserstein has used a trivial incident to trigger important emotions," Edith Oliver wrote in a representative review in the *New Yorker* (June 13, 1983), "and she doesn't falter for a moment." At about the same time, and with the aid of an $18,000 Guggenheim Fellowship, Miss Wasserstein collaborated with the composers and lyricists Jack Feldman and Bruce Sussman on the musical *Miami*, about a teenage boy vacationing in Florida in 1959. Commissioned by Playwrights Horizons, *Miami* was presented to the theatre's subscribers (but not to the press or the public) as a "musical-in-progress" in January 1986.

By the mid-1980s Miss Wasserstein's creative achievements had extended beyond theatre to include television and film. For the PBS *Great Performances* series, she adapted John Cheever's story "The Sorrows of Gin," and for its short-lived comedy anthology *Trying Times*, she wrote the segment "Drive She Said," about the relationship between an art history professor and her driving instructor. During the 1984–85 television season,

she was a regular contributor to the CBS series *Comedy Zone*. Her credits also include two as yet unproduced screenplays: "The House of Husbands," which she wrote with Christopher Durang, and an adaptation of Stephen McCauley's novel *The Object of My Affection*.

Continuing her satirical explorations of the successes and failures of the women's movement, Miss Wasserstein began to write *The Heidi Chronicles*, her most ambitious play to date, in 1986. With the financial support of the British-American Arts Association, which awarded her a grant, she spent the best part of the next two years working on the play. *The Heidi Chronicles* opens with a prologue, set in 1988, in which Heidi Holland, an art history professor, delivers a lecture about women artists who have been neglected by art historians, most of whom are men. The play then flashes back to 1964, showing the teenage Heidi and her friends at a Chicago high school sock hop. As the play traces Heidi's life from adolescence to adulthood, it also relates the history of the women's movement from its early days in the 1960s through the consciousness-raising groups of the 1970s to the myth of the "superwoman" who can "have it all" in the 1980s. In the process, the play touches on such quintessential 1960s events as antiwar protests, the "Clean for Gene" campaign rallies in support of the presidential candidacy of Senator Eugene J. McCarthy, and experiments in communal living (Heidi's friend Susan lives for a while in a rural women's collective in Montana) as well as on such current topics as gay rights, yuppies, AIDS, and single parenthood. The play ends with Heidi's decision to adopt a baby girl from Panama. "I wanted to track change, social change, and how all these movements affected people's personal lives . . . ," Miss Wasserstein commented in an interview with Mervyn Rothstein for the *New York Times* (December 11, 1988). "I want to entertain, but I also want to use the theatre to shake things up a little bit. I want to make people think."

The key to *The Heidi Chronicles*, Miss Wasserstein explained to Janice Berman of *New York Newsday* (December 22, 1988), is contradiction. She illustrated her point by quoting a line from the play: "'Have you ever noticed that what makes you a person keeps you from being a person?' I think that's what *Heidi's* about. What makes you strong is what makes you different." As more than one reviewer noted, *Heidi* is also about disillusionment. Towards the end of the play, Heidi delivers a speech to her high school alumnae association. During the course of her talk, "Women, Where Are We Going?," she tells her audience about a recent conversation she had with her exercise instructor in which she had confessed that she was unhappy. "I don't blame any of us," she says. "We're all concerned, intelligent, good women. It's just that I feel stranded. I thought the point was we were all in this together."

First performed in workshop at the Seattle Repertory Theatre in April 1987, *The Heidi Chronicles* received its New York premiere at Playwrights Horizons on December 11, 1988. After a three-month, sold-out run at that tiny 150-seat house, the play transferred to the considerably larger Plymouth Theatre on Broadway, where it opened in late March 1989 to generally positive notices, particularly for Joan Allen's sensitive interpretation of the role of Heidi. John Simon, writing in *New York* (March 27, 1989) magazine, found the play "clever and funny and sometimes even wise," although it was, for his taste, "a mite too much of a survey course in women's studies." Among the other dissenting voices was that of William A. Henry 3d, a drama critic for *Time* magazine. "*The Heidi Chronicles* is more documentary than drama," he commented in his review of March 20, 1989, "evoking fictionally all the right times and places but rarely attaining much thorny particularity about the people who inhabit them." The "saving grace," in his mind, was Miss Allen's performance in the title role. "While Miss Wasserstein has written whiny and self-congratulatory clichés for the surrounding characters," Henry wrote, "she has given Heidi—or Allen has found—a complex, self-aware, and poignant life."

In addition to the Pulitzer Prize and the Tony Award, *The Heidi Chronicles* has earned for its author virtually every major New York theatre award, including the New York Drama Critics Circle, Outer Critics Circle, and Drama Desk "best new play" honors, the Susan Smith Blackburn Prize, given annually to the most outstanding play written by a woman, and the 1988 Hull-Warriner Award, which is presented by the council of the Dramatists Guild to the author of the best play dealing with controversial subjects involving politics, religion, or social mores.

When *Newsday*'s Gaby Rodgers interviewed Wendy Wasserstein in 1984, she described the playwright, with her loose, curly brown hair, round girlish face, and casual dress, as resembling Janie Blumberg, the heroine of *Isn't It Romantic*. Like Janie, she is "sweet, plump, and quick on the draw." Miss Wasserstein lives in a small apartment in New York City's Greenwich Village with her cat, Ginger, but she wrote most of *The Heidi Chronicles* in a studio in East Hampton, Long Island. "I work better in small spaces," she told Janice Berman. "The closer it seems to a college dorm, the better." The playwright, who once described herself as "a perpetual graduate student who just gets older and older," spends much of her spare time reading. She is especially fond of the works of Tolstoy, Ibsen, and Chekhov, whose generosity of spirit and keen powers of observation she greatly admires. She also enjoys talking with her friends, among them the playwrights Christopher Durang, Terrence McNally, and Marsha Norman and the set designer Heidi Landesman, for whom the central character in *The Heidi Chronicles* was named. Miss Wasserstein is a contributing editor of *New York Woman* magazine and the author of a collection of essays, *Bachelor Girls*, which is scheduled to be published by Knopf in January 1990. She is also a member of the artistic board of Playwrights

Horizons. In June 1988 she was one of six American playwrights commissioned to write new plays for the commercial theatre by the American Playwrights Project, a joint venture of Jujamcyn Theatres and three independent theatrical producers.

References: N Y Daily News mag p10+ Ag 19 '84 por; N Y Times II p1+ My 24 '81 pors; Newsday II p3 Mr 4 '84 por; Newsweek 113:76+ Mr 20 '89 por; Time 133:90+ Mr 27 '89 por; Wall St J p30 F 7 '84; Betsko, Kathleen, and Koenig, Rachel. *Interviews with Contemporary Women Playwrights (1987); Contemporary Authors vol 121 (1987); Contemporary Theatre, Film and Television (1986)*

Watkins, James (David)

Mar. 7, 1927– United States Secretary of Energy. Address: b. Dept. of Energy, 1000 Independence Ave. S.W., Washington, D.C. 20585; h. 3225 Grace St. N.W., Apt. 107, Washington, D.C. 20007

The choice of President George Bush to head the Department of Energy in his new cabinet, James Watkins, is a career naval officer who has had extensive experience in nuclear technology. He takes office at a time when the nation's aging nuclear weapons production network is beginning a major program of modernization and repair under the auspices of the Energy Department. Watkins's military career has included stints as commander of the nuclear attack submarine USS *Snook* and of the navy's first nuclear-powered cruiser, the USS *Long Beach*. He later served as commander of the

Sixth Fleet and of the Pacific Fleet and capped his career with a four-year term as chief of naval operations, the navy's highest noncivilian office, which carries with it membership on the Joint Chiefs of Staff.

Watkins retired from the United States Navy in 1986 and, one year later, was named to a thirteen-member commission created by President Ronald Reagan to examine the AIDS crisis and recommend steps to curtail the spread of the HIV virus. Racked by dissension and disorganization from the start, the AIDS commission seemed on the verge of collapse when, in October 1987, both its chairman and vice-chairman resigned. But Reagan, at the urging of the remaining commissioners, appointed Watkins as the panel's new chief, and the former naval officer quickly put the foundering committee back on course. Watkins wrote the commission's final report, which was released in June 1988, and, with characteristic bluntness, sharply criticized the inaction and moralizing with which the Reagan administration had approached the crisis up to that point. The report also recommended bold new steps to curtail the spread of the deadly epidemic. In the words of A. M. Rosenthal of the *New York Times* (June 10, 1988), James Watkins "has done as much as any American to make the country face the results of the AIDS epidemic."

James David Watkins was born in Alhambra, California, near Los Angeles, on March 7, 1927, the sixth of the seven children of Edward Francis Watkins, a successful executive with Southern California Edison, and Louise Whipple (Ward) Watkins, who, in 1938, became the first woman in California history to run for a seat in the United States Senate. The family was Roman Catholic and Republican. "We were like any other good family in that we had examples in our mother and father," Watkins told Holly G. Miller in an interview for the *Saturday Evening Post* (May-June 1988). "Although we weren't wealthy, we had enough money so that my parents were able to pull me out of a useless school and send me to a good one." When Watkins was a child, his mother often took him and his brother George, who eventually became a navy captain, to navy ports in southern California to watch the ships come in, sometimes making arrangements to take her sons aboard to talk to the officers and dine with them. Watkins developed an early interest in the sea, and, following his graduation from high school in 1945, he enrolled at the United States Naval Academy, in Annapolis, Maryland. There, he was one class behind Jimmy Carter, who sometimes hazed him by forcing him to sing while standing on a chair in the mess hall.

Only an indifferent student, Watkins might have dropped out of the Naval Academy had it not been for the intervention of Earl Jorgenson, a wealthy California businessman and family friend who urged him to complete his degree and promised him a job if he did so. "That gave me such motivational drive, that insurance ticket in my back pocket," Watkins explained to Peter Grier during an interview for the *Christian Science Monitor* (June 4, 1986).

Graduating from the Naval Academy in 1949 with a B.S. degree in naval science, Watkins went on active duty as an ensign. Over the next ten years, he rose steadily through the ranks, and, by 1959, when he earned an M.S. degree in mechanical engineering from the Naval Postgraduate School in Monterey, California, he had risen to lieutenant commander. It was at about that time that Watkins volunteered for the navy's new nuclear submarine program, headed by the legendary admiral Hyman G. Rickover. Following a grueling interview with the admiral, Watkins was invited to join the program, and in 1962 he became an administrative assistant to Rickover, helping him to choose candidates for interviews—an experience he has called "a turning point in my life." In 1964 he was promoted to the rank of commander and placed in charge of the nuclear attack submarine USS *Snook*. During Watkins's two-year tenure as commander of the *Snook*, the ship became the first nuclear-powered submarine to visit Japan, and when it arrived at Yokosuka harbor, it was greeted by 5,000 Japanese protestors, an event that thrust Watkins into newspaper headlines for the first time in his career.

In 1967 Watkins became executive officer of the navy's first nuclear-powered cruiser, the USS *Long Beach*. After relinquishing command of the *Long Beach* in 1969, he assumed the first of a series of administrative positions in the Bureau of Naval Personnel, eventually serving as its chief of personnel from 1975 to 1978. He returned to sea in 1973 and spent the next twenty months as commander of the navy's Cruiser-Destroyer Group One. He became a captain in 1968, a rear admiral in 1971, and a vice admiral in 1975. In 1978 he was named commander of the Sixth Fleet. Promoted to admiral a year later, he became vice-chief of naval operations, a position he held until 1981, when he was appointed commander of the United States Pacific Fleet.

On March 18, 1982 President Ronald Reagan rewarded Watkins for his thirty-three years of service by naming him to succeed Admiral Thomas B. Hayward as chief of naval operations, one of the five positions on the Joint Chiefs of Staff, the nation's principal military advisory body. The nomination proved to be such a popular one on Capitol Hill that Watkins breezed through his confirmation hearing before the Senate Armed Services Committee in just over half an hour. "I know of no appointment to a service command that I have cheered more heartily than yours," Senator John G. Tower of Texas, the chairman of the committee, told Watkins during the hearing. The full Senate confirmed Watkins on May 21, 1982, and he assumed office on July 1, becoming the first navy chief with nuclear submarine experience.

During his four-year term as chief of naval operations, James Watkins presided over a major expansion and modernization of the navy as part of the Reagan administration's defense buildup, but he was also forced to devote considerable time and energy to its manpower needs in the face of a critical shortage of trained officers and skilled techni- cians. Testifying before the Senate Armed Services Committee in February 1985, Watkins urged Con- gress to raise the salaries of submarine officers as a means of retaining their services. He also joined the other members of the Joint Chiefs of Staff in ar- guing against a proposal before Congress that would have reduced military pension benefits, and he spoke out on a variety of other issues. Alarmed when a study he authorized revealed that over 20 percent of a large sample of navy recruits in 1983 and 1984 were unable to read at the ninth-grade le- vel, Watkins voiced concern about America's de- clining literacy levels. He also tried to change the navy's policy of promoting officers who have not attended the Naval War College to senior posi- tions. Deploring the poor physical condition of navy recruits, Watkins pointed to statistics showing that only half of the nation's high schools have a formal fitness program. The navy, he pointed out, was being forced to spend $25 million a year for re- medial reading programs, physical fitness, and drug and alcohol abuse prevention and rehabilita- tion.

Unlike other senior military officers, Watkins had no qualms about ventilating his moral views. A devout Roman Catholic, he explained in an in- terview with Richard Halloran of the *New York Times* (May 6, 1983) that he and the other service chiefs often discussed moral issues at semimonthly prayer breakfasts and that he had concluded that Soviet military objectives were "morally flawed," while those of the West were "morally acceptable." Watkins explained: "I have to look at the balance between the evils involved in nuclear exchange, and I pick the lesser of the evils. That may be a neg- ative way of looking at it, but I don't like to be over- ly positive about nuclear weaponry. I happen to believe that we ought to get rid of them."

During his tenure as chief of naval operations, Watkins emerged as one of the chief architects of President Reagan's controversial Strategic Defense Initiative, or "Star Wars," as it is popularly known. The admiral stirred a public debate in early 1986, when the United States Naval Institute published an article he had written entitled "The Maritime Strategy." In it, Watkins outlined the navy's poten- tial for tipping the nuclear balance in favor of the United States by employing preemptive strikes against missile-carrying Soviet submarines during a major nonnuclear conflict between the two su- perpowers. Watkins wrote that such action by the navy could escalate a nonnuclear war, but he add- ed, "Escalation solely as a result of actions at sea seems improbable given the Soviet land orientation." Watkins's term as chief of naval oper- ations was also notable for the stormy relationship he developed with his civilian supervisor, Secre- tary of the Navy John F. Lehman Jr., which grew out of his belief that Lehman interfered in person- nel and operational matters legally falling under the jurisdiction of the chief of naval operations.

In 1985 speculation arose that Watkins might be named to succeed General John W. Vessey Jr. as chairman of the Joint Chiefs of Staff when Vessey's term expired in June 1986, but Vessey retired be- fore his term ended and was succeeded as chair- man by Admiral William Crowe on October 1, 1985. When Watkins's term as chief of naval opera- tions expired on June 30, 1986, he announced his retirement from the navy, revealing that he planned to devote part of his time to a national pro- gram to promote personal excellence among youth. For the next year, he lobbied government and busi- ness in an attempt to implement the program, which emphasized education, health, and motiva- tion.

On July 23, 1987 Reagan named Watkins as one of thirteen appointees to a presidential commission on Acquired Immune Deficiency Syndrome, or AIDS, the fatal illness that cripples the body's im- mune system, leaving its victims susceptible to can- cer, pneumonia, and other diseases. Established to recommend measures that the government can take to stop the spread of AIDS, to assist in research aimed at finding a cure, and to provide better care for those who have AIDS, the commission was to deliver an initial report to the president within ninety days and a final report within a year. Wat- kins was selected because, during his tenure as chief of naval operations, the military services be- came the first organizations in the country to set up programs to test personnel for the AIDS virus and to develop policies to deal with its victims. The navy began testing personnel on the USS *Midway*, an aircraft carrier, in 1985.

It soon became apparent to Watkins that the AIDS panel—officially known as the Presidential Commission on the Human Immunodeficiency Vi- rus Epidemic—lacked the necessary leadership and direction to achieve its goals. As he told Holly G. Miller, "I had complained from day one that we had no structure, we had no objectives, we hadn't laid out a plan, we hadn't pulled together a staff. What were we doing? Why were we holding hear- ings? What information did we need?" Watkins's frustration was crystallized at a get-acquainted re- ception for members of the commission, held in Washington, D.C., on September 8, 1987. When Dr. W. Eugene Mayberry, the chief executive of the Mayo Clinic and chairman of the commission, asked members if they had any questions or com- ments before being sworn in the following day, Watkins's hand shot up. "Gene, I think this has been one of the most unprofessional sessions I have ever attended in my twenty years in Washington," he announced, and his bluntness got the attention of the other commissioners, who dubbed him "Radio-Free Watkins." When May- berry resigned four weeks later because of infight- ing on the committee and his own admitted inexperience in dealing with Washington red tape, Watkins was offered the chairmanship by Presi- dent Reagan. Disturbed by the course the commis- sion had taken to that point, he was, understandably, hesitant to assume its leadership and did so only after receiving a unanimous vote of support from the remaining commissioners and after being granted the authority to choose two new members to replace Mayberry and Vice-Chairman Woodrow A. Myers Jr., who had also resigned.

In a television interview held shortly after he accepted the position, Watkins admitted, "We frankly haven't done the job that we were asked to do." And he told Reagan, "I'm not sure that I can pull this thing out of the ashes of defeat at this point, but I will try." Since, unlike Mayberry, Watkins lived in Washington and had no other full-time job, he could devote a much greater share of his time to the work of the commission.

One of Watkins's first moves was his appointment of Polly Gault as executive director of the commission, replacing Linda Sheaffer, who had been dismissed following the board's first meeting in September. When Watkins took over, the commission's staff consisted entirely of two secretaries, and its office had unopened mail piled in stacks several feet high. Watkins was also forced to answer charges that the commission, which now included only one doctor who had actually treated an AIDS patient, and one scientist, lacked scientific and medical expertise. Watkins promised to try to correct that problem by recommending that a panel of experts be appointed to serve the commission in an advisory capacity.

The commission issued its interim report in December 1987, a week ahead of schedule, and two months later sent its first set of recommendations to President Reagan. Based on testimony from hundreds of witnesses, the sixty-page document included a total of 180 recommendations. Its principal suggestion was that the effort to prevent the spread of the AIDS virus be concentrated on intravenous drug users, who transmit the virus by sharing contaminated needles and through sexual intercourse. That group, while constituting only one-fourth of current AIDS cases, has the greatest potential for spreading the virus into the heterosexual community, via sexual contact. Noting that the estimated 1.2 million intravenous drug users in the United States have been responsible for 70 percent of AIDS cases among heterosexuals and newborn infants, the document urged hiring 32,000 drug treatment specialists and establishing 3,300 drug treatment centers to provide drug-abuse education and "treatment on demand" to drug addicts. The report's other key suggestions included greatly expanding care for those already infected and providing federal funds to train more doctors and nurses to work in poverty-stricken areas, where the virus is most prevalent. The total cost of implementing the recommendations was estimated at $2 billion a year, to be divided among federal, state, and local governments.

The boldness of the report surprised critics who had viewed the AIDS commission as a halfhearted attempt on the part of the Reagan administration to cover up what they believed was a general lack of concern about the AIDS crisis. Abandoning the moralistic stance adopted by the White House, Watkins said simply, "We believe some major changes in course are necessary."

The committee's final report, written by Watkins and released in early June 1988, also earned generally high marks. Compiled on the basis of forty-three days of hearings and testimony by over 570 witnesses, the report was 269 pages in length and included 579 recommendations for dealing with the epidemic. It criticized the federal government for displaying a "distinct lack of leadership and coordination," which has "resulted in a low, halting and uneven response," and urged Reagan to declare AIDS a national health emergency. The report's key recommendation was that federal antidiscrimination laws be extended to include those infected with the AIDS virus, so that such individuals cannot be fired from their jobs or evicted from their homes or apartments. That controversial proposal, which the Reagan administration had previously opposed on the grounds that it would be impossible to enforce, was passed by the entire commission in an eight-to-five vote on June 17, 1988. The report also proposed that new federal laws be enacted to ensure the confidentiality of individuals who are tested and recommended that state health officials be required to notify the sex partners of infected persons in order that they too can be tested for the virus. While many observers roundly applauded Watkins's recommendations, others, especially those on the political Right, opposed extending civil rights to AIDS victims, most of whom are homosexual men and intravenous drug users. The final report also seemed to confirm a fear expressed by some critics that commission members who were more concerned about the civil rights of AIDS carriers outnumbered those whose main interest was in enacting public health measures to control the spread of the virus.

With the committee's work successfully completed, Watkins found himself widely praised in influential quarters. His management style, which involved dividing the panel into three working groups and allowing members to choose which group they wanted to work on, was praised by commissioner William B. Walsh. "He recognized the personalities on the commission," Walsh told Sally Squires of the Washington Post (June 7, 1988). "He gave deference to different commissioners in areas of their expertise so that they could chair hearings in areas where they felt they had more expertise than he did." And in the same article, Congressman Henry A. Waxman of California was quoted as saying of Watkins, "Through the force of his personal leadership, he has brought together a group of people who by and large were not that knowledgeable about AIDS. He has gotten them to focus on the issues, to try to sort through the opinions, and to act in a responsible way in dealing with the epidemic."

In his interview with Holly G. Miller, Watkins said he had no desire to head another health-related commission. "I'm not a health expert, I'm a manager," he told her. "So if you've got a difficult task, like a national energy policy, I'd love it." That remark proved to be prophetic when, on January 12, 1989, George Bush nominated Watkins to head the Department of Energy in his new administration. In announcing his selection, Bush said the admiral would assume responsibility for "not only the development of energy policies—which will ensure an adequate supply of energy for a growing nation, reduce our dependence on foreign oil, and protect and preserve our environment—but also the design and production of nuclear weapons that are vital to our national defense." Watkins's expertise in nuclear technology was expected to be invaluable in overseeing a multibillion-dollar Energy Department program to clean up and modernize the nation's seventeen nuclear arms plants, two of which, the Savannah River plant in South Carolina and the Rocky Flats plant in Colorado, have been partly closed in order to repair equipment and retrain personnel.

At his confirmation hearing before the Senate Energy and Natural Resources Committee on March 1, Watkins described the condition of the nation's nuclear weapons plants as "a mess" and pledged that the Energy Department would repair the plants and clean up the pollution they had generated. The full Senate unanimously approved Watkins's nomination later that same day, and, just three weeks later, the new secretary submitted to members of Congress the outline of a five-year program to clean up the weapons plants.

In late June, Watkins held his first extensive press conference since becoming energy secretary. He said that his department was hampered by a "culture" of mismanagement and ineptitude that would have to be overcome before the cleanup of the nuclear weapons plants could proceed, and that the longstanding policy of emphasizing production over safety at the plants would have to change. His proposed solutions included the establishment of Energy Department "tiger teams" that would visit the plants to ensure their compliance with environmental and safety guidelines.

Although he is a perfectionist who demands the utmost from himself and those who work for him, Watkins approaches his work in an informal, flexible manner. "He's an absolute joy to work with," Polly Gault told Holly G. Miller, and other associates have expressed similar sentiments. Watkins broods carefully before making important decisions. While chief of naval operations, he was referred to by members of his staff as "Hamlet" because of his propensity for contemplating at great length decisions having moral implications. He is also a longtime opponent of government red tape. Among the military commendations Watkins has received are the Distinguished Service Medal, the Legion of Merit, the Bronze Star Medal, and the Navy Commendation Medal. He has also been awarded decorations from many countries and received numerous honorary degrees.

Since 1950, James Watkins has been married to the former Sheila Jo McKinney, the daughter of a navy captain, whom he met on a blind date while he was stationed in San Diego, shortly after his graduation from the Naval Academy. The couple have six adult children, three daughters and three sons. Two of their sons have elected to make a career of the navy. James and Sheila Jo Watkins live in an apartment in northwestern Washington, D.C. To relax, Watkins enjoys puttering around the house and sailing.

References: Christian Sci Mon p1+ Je 4 '86 por; N Y Times B p8 Mr 19 '82 por, B p8 O 1 '84 por, A p7 Je 4 '88 por; Sat Eve Post 260:50+ My–Je '88 pors; Washington Post (Health supplement) p14+ Je 7 '88 pors; International Who's Who, 1989–90; Who's Who in America, 1988–89

Weaver, Sigourney

Oct. 8, 1949– Actress. Address: c/o International Creative Management, 40 W. 57th St., New York, N.Y. 10019

Since she first came to moviegoers' attention ten years ago in the role of the intrepid spaceship warrant officer Ellen Ripley in the hit science fiction film *Alien*, Sigourney Weaver has gone on to play an incongruous assortment of screen personas, including a television news reporter, a demon-possessed musician, a British foreign service officer, a primatologist, and a stockbroker. Critics generally agree that she is most distinctive for three attributes: the intelligence she projects in her roles, her height (about five feet, eleven inches), which lends her a strong physical presence, and her finely chiseled beauty. "She is one of the few women who can light the screen up," Peter Weir, who directed her in his 1983 film *The Year of Living Dangerously*, has said. Often compared, especially early in her career, to Jane Fonda, Miss Weaver has been labeled "the thinking man's sex symbol" and "the perfect contemporary heroine."

Sigourney Weaver was born Susan Alexandra Weaver on October 8, 1949 in New York City, the younger of the two children and the only daughter of Sylvester ("Pat") Weaver, the well-known television executive, and Elizabeth Inglis, a British actress. Her father, who served as president of the NBC television network from 1949 to 1956, created both the *Today* and *Tonight* shows. After leaving NBC, Weaver tried, unsuccessfully, to start a fourth television network and later became a pioneer in the cable television industry. Sigourney Weaver's mother trained at London's Royal Academy of Dramatic Art and later appeared in such film classics as *The Letter* and Alfred Hitchcock's *Thirty-nine Steps*. Winston ("Doodles") Weaver, an uncle of Sigourney's, was a professional comedian who appeared in several of Bob Hope's films. Pat Weaver's income enabled the family to live in luxury apartment buildings on the Upper East Side of Manhattan and Sigourney to attend the exclusive Chapin and Brearley schools and, later, the equally prestigious Ethel Walker School in Simsbury, Connecticut. "I was a privileged, pampered, sheltered child," Miss Weaver admitted to Richard Corliss during an interview for *Time* (July 28, 1986) magazine. "It was as though every day had a happy ending. I thought everyone's father was head of a network." She had reached her adult height of about five feet, eleven inches by the time she was thirteen, a circumstance that caused her to be clumsy and self-conscious. "I was so big, and I was such a klutz that the only way I could get through school was to be the clown," she recalled to Dotson Rader in a conversation for *Parade* (September 25, 1988).

When she was fourteen, Miss Weaver read F. Scott Fitzgerald's classic American novel *The Great Gatsby* and impulsively decided to change her first name to Sigourney, after a minor male character in that novel. "I was so tall and lanky, and Susan was such a short name," she explained to Dotson Rader. "I thought Sigourney was such a musical name. It fit." Unsure as to whether the name change was permanent, her parents called her simply "S" for the next year. As befitted a member of a socially prominent family, Sigourney Weaver had two "coming-out" parties as a teenager. After high school, she enrolled at Stanford University, where she majored in English with the intention of going on for a Ph.D. degree and becoming a teacher of literature, an ambition that got sidetracked when she developed a permanent interest in acting. She joined other Stanford students in a "guerrilla theatre" ensemble that used drama as a means of protesting American involvement in the Vietnam War, and she also became part of a theatre company that toured the San Francisco Bay area, performing Shakespeare. Meanwhile, she had attracted attention on the Stanford campus by wearing such offbeat items of clothing as an elf costume, and, in her final semester at the university, by living with her boyfriend, who also took to

wearing an elf suit, in a treehouse. Bored by her senior thesis on Mark Twain, she impetuously decided to abandon her plan to pursue a Ph.D. degree and to concentrate on acting. Applying for admission to the Yale Drama School, she was accepted as "Mr." Sigourney Weaver.

Sigourney Weaver has often said that the three years she spent at Yale were among the most unhappy of her life. Her unusual style of dress and her casual approach to theatre did not sit well with members of the Yale drama faculty, who regarded theatre with the utmost gravity. "It was joyless and negative," she said of her Yale experience during her interview with Dotson Rader. "I arrived with such self-confidence and enthusiasm. They soon knocked that out of me. They so much as said I practically was without talent. I really hated the atmosphere there. It was pretentious and terribly pseudo-serious. For six months, they wouldn't cast me even in a tiny role. I had to work in a cabaret." Her first year at Yale was salvaged, to a degree, by a prank she pulled on the faculty for her year-end evaluation. As she explained to Jesse Kornbluth for a *Vanity Fair* (August 1988) profile, "I got this piece of muslin from the costume department and painted a huge target on it, and walked in with my little blazer and my little flannel skirt and opened the blazer and exposed the target. And I said 'Hit me.' And they all went 'Heh heh,' and they took back everything they'd said all year."

Miss Weaver's unhappiness at Yale was mitigated somewhat by the close friendship she formed with her classmate Christopher Durang, who went on to become a noted absurdist playwright. She appeared in two of Durang's plays during this time—*Better Dead Than Sorry*, in which she sang the title song while receiving electroshock therapy, and *The Marriage of Bette and Boo*, playing a woman who laughs while her husband beats her. "We have the same wariness about the world," she told Lee Eisenberg of *Esquire* (November 1986), in discussing her friendship with Durang. "We see the blacker things, which our sense of humor—silly and innocent—makes into funny things."

After graduating from Yale Drama School in 1974, Sigourney Weaver moved to New York to begin an acting career, determined to prove wrong her parents' belief that she was too shy and too tall to make it in the theatre. Their contention at first seemed to be correct, for she had difficulty finding an agent because of her height. Renting an apartment on Manhattan's West Side, she began phoning the show business acquaintances of her parents. One of her first calls was to a family friend who suggested that she abandon her theatrical aspirations and go to work instead at Bloomingdale's department store. "All my father's friends were trying to keep each other's kids from going into a business they knew was rotten," Miss Weaver told Jesse Kornbluth. "*No one* was terribly optimistic about my becoming an actress," she further explained to Charles Leerhsen, who interviewed her for *Savvy Woman* (January 1989). "The message was that I wasn't cut out for it. . . . I was too tall, too Bryn Mawr or something, but my potential, I was always told, lay elsewhere." In spite of his reservations about Sigourney Weaver's decision to enter show business, which he always referred to as "the racket," Pat Weaver supported his daughter while she looked for work. After three months, she landed a job as an understudy in the Broadway revival of Somerset Maugham's *Constant Wife*, directed by Sir John Gielgud, and in 1976 she made her professional debut in Durang's Off-Broadway production of *Titanic*, portraying a homicidal schizophrenic. She also supported herself during those early years by appearing in other Off-Broadway shows, including Albert Innaurato's *Gemini*, by performing in television commercials for Pepsi and Lowenbrau beer, and, for three months, by playing a television news reporter in the NBC soap opera *Somerset*.

Sigourney Weaver made her film debut with a bit part in Woody Allen's *Annie Hall* (1977). Her first big break came when she was cast as Ellen Ripley in Ridley Scott's 1979 science fiction thriller *Alien*. Although the film itself received only mixed reviews, her performance as an officer on an intergalactic ore carrier who singlehandedly lays waste to the reptilian monster that has taken over the ship was universally applauded. Jack Kroll of *Newsweek* (May 28, 1979), for instance, wrote that Miss Weaver "takes the classic B-movie woman's role . . . and raises it to a kind of abstract energy and ambushed grace that's like watching a ballet of pure terror."

Other critics, including Gary Arnold of the *Washington Post* (May 25, 1979), were enough impressed by Miss Weaver's performance in *Alien* to predict future stardom for the young actress. Arnold credited her with bringing "an exciting combination of intelligence, bravery, and sex appeal to the portrayal of warrant officer Ripley—the most courageous and resourceful heroine seen on the screen in years." Her performance was made all the more astounding by the fact that the Ripley role was originally written for a man (reportedly Paul Newman). She arrived at the audition dressed in a T-shirt, jeans, and boots, and won the part, although as she later admitted to Lindsy Van Gelder of the New York *Daily News* (October 30, 1983), "a sci-fi movie wasn't what I had in mind. What I was looking for was a supporting role in a Mike Nichols picture, something classy like that. I was a bit of a snob about it. But the day before I tested, I realized I could make the part anything I wanted—and that I didn't want anyone else to have it." A huge commercial success, *Alien* grossed $4.7 million in its first week alone and brought in over $100 million by the end of its run. The movie also landed Sigourney Weaver on the cover of *Newsweek*, illustrating a feature article on horror films.

To Sigourney Weaver's surprise, the success of *Alien* did not result in her being offered choice parts in new films. After rejecting several unchallenging screen roles, in February 1980 she appeared with Christopher Durang at the Chelsea Theater Center in New York in *Das Lusitania Songspiel*, a two-character cabaret act that they had written together. A series of skits performed in full evening dress, *Das Lusitania Songspiel*, which parodied the works of Bertolt Brecht and Kurt Weill, brought Sigourney Weaver and Christopher Durang Drama Desk nominations for acting and writing. In the fall of 1980 Miss Weaver starred in James McLure's comedy *Lone Star* at the Travel Light Theater in Chicago, playing the part of Elizabeth Caulder, a character described by the critic Eric Zorn of the *Chicago Tribune* (November 3, 1980) as "a high school beauty ten-years-after type who struggles against her own dreams to find contentment in a small Texas town." A film version of *Lone Star*, to be directed by Robert Altman, was planned, but three weeks before shooting was to begin, Twentieth Century–Fox, which had agreed to finance the movie, decided to abandon the project. Miss Weaver continued her stage work in 1981, portraying a woman who dates a bisexual man she meets through a personal ad in Durang's Off-Broadway production *Beyond Therapy*.

In Sigourney Weaver's second film, *Eyewitness* (1981), she portrayed an aloof, self-contained television newswoman named Tony Sokolow who becomes the love object of William Hurt's Darryl Deever, a motorcycle-riding night janitor at a large Manhattan office building. Critics generally approved of the performances of Miss Weaver and William Hurt, but few of them had kind words for the film's plot, which revolves around the murder of an Oriental businessman in the building where Hurt works. In her review of *Eyewitness* for the *New Yorker* (March 23, 1981), Pauline Kael observed that Miss Weaver's "training, temperament, and spectacular good looks" make her "a natural for stardom in this era," but she faulted the director, Peter Yates, and the screenwriter, Steve Tesich, for trying to "put an eighties woman into a claptrap forties-movie situation." In her opinion, after Tony quits her job to marry the man of her parents' choice, "the movie dries up and blows away."

The Year of Living Dangerously (1983), Sigourney Weaver's next film, cast her as a British foreign service officer in Jakarta. Set amid the political turmoil in the Indonesian capital in 1965, the film used the looming revolution as the backdrop for a love affair between the officer and an Australian radio reporter, played by Mel Gibson. The two conduct their affair with what Pauline Kael in the *New Yorker* (February 21, 1983) referred to as "a new-style old-time 'dangerous' steaminess." Miss Kael credited the film's director, Peter Weir, with knowing "what's spectacular about Sigourney Weaver: her brainy female-hunk physicality—her wide-awake dark eyes, the protruding lower lip, the strong, rounded, outthrust jaw. . . . She uses her face and her body, and pours on the passion and laughter; she has the kind of capacity for enjoyment that the young Sophia Loren had." Miss Weaver followed *The Year of Living Dangerously* with *Deal of the Century* (1983), a satire about international weapons dealers that costarred her with Chevy Chase. Her first film comedy, it was also her first box-office failure.

In 1984 Sigourney Weaver returned to the theatre, playing the scatterbrained photojournalist, Darlene, in Mike Nichols's Off-Broadway production of David Rabe's *Hurlyburly*. Termed a "study in misogyny" by Edith Oliver of the *New Yorker* (July 2, 1984), *Hurlyburly* focuses on four men in their thirties (portrayed by William Hurt, Christopher Walken, Harvey Keitel, and Jerry Stiller) who work in the entertainment business in Los Angeles. Separated from their wives and children, they lead lives, in the words of a critic for *Variety* (July 4, 1984), that revolve around "drugs, booze, and mercenary sex." Sigourney Weaver was applauded by several critics for making the best of a thinly written role. Richard Schickel of *Time* (July 2, 1984) noted that her "striking physical presence provides a marvelous ironic contrast to her dithering sensibility," while Jack Kroll of *Newsweek* (July 2, 1984) mentioned her "razor-edged beauty and haute-couture vulnerability." Her work in *Hurlyburly* brought Sigourney Weaver a Tony Award nomination.

The comedy-horror hit *Ghostbusters* (1984) put Miss Weaver's film career back on the right track after the disastrous *Deal of the Century*. She won rave notices for her depiction of Dana, a New York woman whose body is possessed by an evil spirit from ancient Babylon that Bill Murray, Dan Aykroyd, Harold Ramis, and Ernie Hudson try to exorcise. Proclaiming Miss Weaver "an alluring delight," Gary Arnold of the *Washington Post* (June 9, 1984) observed: "She's always excelled at reacting to the romantic overtures of the actors playing opposite her, and this flair takes on a fresh comic charm in her fencing with Murray, whose effrontery seems to tickle her to the verge of spontaneous laughter." And Rex Reed in the *New York Post* (June 8, 1984) reported in his column, "As usual, the calm, collected, and always sexy Sigourney Weaver makes the thankless role of female foil something special indeed." *Ghostbusters* became the biggest commercial success of her career to date, grossing a staggering $22.7 million in its first week alone and eventually making more than $128 million, the sixth-highest total in Hollywood history.

In 1986 Sigourney Weaver reprised the role of Ripley, the warrant officer, in *Aliens*, the sequel to the 1979 hit. The sole survivor of the spaceship Nostromo's first encounter with the aliens on the planet Archeron, Ripley has been in a state of hypersleep for fifty-seven years, without having undergone any aging. In the interim, Archeron has been colonized, and, when contact with its inhabitants is broken off, she reluctantly agrees to accompany a troop of United States Marines back to the planet to investigate. The sequel received more enthusiastic reviews than its predecessor, while Miss Weaver's performance once again evoked almost unanimous acclaim and earned her an Academy Award nomination as best actress. According to a reviewer for *Variety* (July 9, 1986), she "does a smashing job here as Ripley, one of the great fe-

male screen roles of recent years." Commending Sigourney Weaver for being "cool, intelligent, yet vulnerable," Richard Schickel of *Time* (July 28, 1986) predicted that *Aliens* "should make her a major star."

In September 1986, just two months after the release of *Aliens*, Miss Weaver appeared on-screen again, this time in the drama *Half Moon Street*, as a scholar at London's Middle East Institute who supplements her income by working as an "escort." All too predictably, she falls in love with one of her clients, an English diplomat played by Michael Caine. Critics panned the film, placing the blame not on its stars but on its screenwriters, Edward Behr and Bob Swaim. A reviewer for *Variety* (October 1, 1986), for example, called the script "nonsensical and incoherent" and dismissed *Half Moon Street* as "a half-baked excuse for a film."

Sigourney Weaver then appeared with the French film star Gérard Depardieu in the would-be madcap French comedy *One Woman or Two* (1987), as a scheming American advertising executive. Like *Half Moon Street*, *One Woman or Two* generated little enthusiasm from audiences or critics. A reviewer for the New York *Daily News* (February 8, 1987) referred to *One Woman or Two* as "a badly fractured French farce," while Janet Maslin of the *New York Times* (February 6, 1987) panned it as "an idiotic comedy." But one of the few dissenters, Mike McGrady of New York *Newsday* (February 6, 1987), pronounced *One Woman or Two* "a raucous, fast-paced lark," adding that Sigourney Weaver's performance "again proves that nothing is sexier than intelligence."

Collaborating for the first time with her husband, Jim Simpson, the theatre director whom she had married in 1984, Sigourney Weaver put her film career on hold in late 1986 to play Portia in the Classic Stage Company of New York's production of Shakespeare's *Merchant of Venice*. The venture generally failed to impress audiences or critics. Mel Gussow of the *New York Times* (December 22, 1986) tactfully called her an "average" Portia, adding that "in all candidness, this is not Ms. Weaver's finest three and one-quarter hours." He felt that "together, the director and star seem disoriented by Shakespeare." Although Howard Kissel of the New York *Daily News* (December 22, 1986) commended her for taking "time out from a high-powered film career to do Shakespeare," he found that she had "less presence" in *The Merchant of Venice* "than she has had in far less interesting work."

With the release of two hit movies, *Gorillas in the Mist* and *Working Girl*, in 1988, Sigourney Weaver's film career rebounded. In the former, she portrayed the primatologist Dian Fossey, who, from 1967 until her death in 1985, studied and tried to protect from extinction the mountain gorillas of the Virungas Mountains of east central Africa. She was praised by critics for the vitality she brought to the role, as well as for her in-depth exploration of Dian Fossey's obsessive struggle to protect the gorillas from poachers and from members of the Batwa tribe of forest pygmies. As in many of her previous film roles, her physical attributes, in the opinion of several reviewers, enhanced her performance significantly. Writing in the *New York Times* (September 23, 1988), Janet Maslin remarked: "Though much of the strength of Miss Weaver's fine performance comes from the intelligent, muscular resilience she projects so fiercely, a lot of it also derives from the wit and abandon with which she mimics the gorillas' behavior to win their confidence." Miss Weaver's monumental performance notwithstanding, *Gorillas in the Mist* drew mixed reviews, with a *New Yorker* (October 17, 1988) critic noting that, in spite of its serious subject matter, "the movie can't be taken seriously. It's a feminist version of *King Kong*—now it's the gorillas who do the screaming."

In the Mike Nichols comedy *Working Girl*, Miss Weaver played a supporting role to Melanie Griffith and Harrison Ford. As Katharine Parker, an upwardly mobile Wall Street stockbroker, she eventually loses both her job and her boyfriend (played by Ford) to Melanie Griffith. "I had turned it down, but Mike (Nichols) called me and said he thought I was making a mistake," she explained to Tom Green of *USA Today* (September 20, 1988). "So I got to be funny being what I am, which is an overeducated East Coast person—all the things I try to hide under the rug." The film received mostly positive notices, thanks mainly to Melanie Griffith's performance, which, in the opinion of a majority of critics, was one of the year's best. On January 28, 1989 Miss Weaver was awarded two Golden Globe Awards by the Hollywood Foreign Press Association—one for best supporting actress in a comedy, for her role in *Working Girl*, and, in a three-way tie with Shirley MacLaine and Jodie Foster, one for best actress in a drama, for her performance in *Gorillas in the Mist*. Sigourney Weaver also received Academy Award nominations for her work in *Gorillas in the Mist* and *Working Girl*, but she failed to win in either category.

In *Ghostbusters II*, Sigourney Weaver's most recent film vehicle, which was released in June 1989, she again played the part of Dana, now recently divorced and entrusted with the custody of an eight-month-old son whom demonic forces are trying to possess. Critical reaction was divided. David Ansen of *Newsweek* (June 26, 1989), for example, found it less funny than its predecessor, and he faulted its director, Ivan Reitman, for failing to exploit Miss Weaver's comedic talents. But the usually exigent Pauline Kael of the *New Yorker* (July 10, 1989) disagreed completely with her colleague. "*Ghostbusters II* has a nice, lazy, unforced rhythm," she observed. "I found it much more enjoyable than the first *Ghostbusters*—the actors seem more convivial and the special effects less labored."

Various sources list Sigourney Weaver's height as being anywhere between five feet, ten inches to six feet. "I think my greatest asset as an actress has been my height because it's forced people to think of me for distinctive roles," she told Jan Hodenfield

of the New York *Daily News* (January 23, 1981). "You can't hide me onstage—I take up a lot of room." She professes to have no serious avocational interests, and, although she is a confirmed theatregoer, she sees few movies. "I read. And I walk around," she said during an interview with Dan Yakir of *USA Weekend* (July 4-6, 1986). "I go to the gym and I end up doing a lot of traveling. I'd just like to stay at home. Maybe that could be my hobby. . . . When I'm not working, I want to be with my friends and be a normal person. My friends are musicians, actors, painters." She met Jim Simpson, also a Yale Drama School alumnus, while appearing in a production of *Old Times* at the Williamstown, Massachusetts summer theatre festival in 1983. That fall, she invited him to a Halloween party, and, just two months later, the pair decided to marry. They live on Manhattan's Upper West Side.

References: *Chicago Tribune* XIII p4+ Jl 13 '86 pors; N Y Daily News M p3 Ja 23 '81 por; N Y Daily News mag p15+ O 30 '83 pors; N Y Newsday II p3+ Ap 8 '81 pors; New York 17:36+ Je 11 '84 por; Parade p4+ S 25 '88 pors; Time 128:60+ Jl 28 '86 pors; Vanity Fair 51:106+ Ag '88 pors; Who's Who in America, 1988-89

Weller, Michael

Sept. 26, 1942- Writer. Address: b. c/o Rosenstone/Wender, 3 E. 48th St., New York, N.Y. 10017; h. 215 E. 5th St., New York, N.Y. 10003

Because of such plays as *Moonchildren* (1970), *Fishing* (1975), *Loose Ends* (1979), and *Ghosts on*

Fire (1986), Michael Weller has forged a reputation as the leading chronicler, in the theatre, of the generation of Americans who came of age in the 1960s, but he is quick to point out that he has often ventured beyond that limited range. The Ballad of Soapy Smith (1983) deals with the Klondike gold rush; More Than You Deserve (1974) is a musical about the Vietnam War; and Dwarfman, Master of a Million Shapes (1981) concerns the experiences of a science fiction cartoonist. His most recent play, the semiautobiographical Spoils of War (1988), about a teenager's efforts to reunite his estranged parents, was one of the three Weller plays presented in a season-long retrospective at the Off-Broadway Second Stage Theatre in New York City. A talented screenwriter as well, Weller has created the scripts for two acclaimed films, Hair (1979) and Ragtime (1981), both of which were directed by Milos Forman.

Michael Weller was born in New York City on September 26, 1942, the only child of Paul Weller, an artist and photographer, and Rosa (Rush) Weller, an artist, who met through their mutual affiliation with the American Communist party. After graduating from high school, Weller attended Windham College, a two-year institution in Putney, Vermont. He then transferred to Brandeis University in Waltham, Massachusetts, where he studied music under the composers Arthur Berger, Harold Shapiro, and Irving Fine, and, in his senior year, he wrote his first play, a musical adaptation of the Nathanael West novel A Cool Million. His interest aroused, Weller enrolled in a playwriting class, won a prize for best play in a local contest, and, late in his final year at Brandeis, wrote Fred, a two-act play adapted from the novel Malcolm by James Purdy.

His early attempts at playwriting convinced Weller that he had a "knack" for it, and after receiving a B.A. degree in music from Brandeis in 1965, he moved to Manchester, England to pursue a career as a dramatist. "I preferred British drama at that time, and, while I was over there, I found out it was a handy way not to get drafted," Weller explained to Richard Christiansen of the Chicago Tribune (May 24, 1981). He took graduate courses in playwriting at the University of Manchester, where he eventually obtained a master's degree. To support himself, he took on various jobs, including teaching and working as a janitor in a school. During an interview with Chris Chase that appeared in the New York Times (March 5, 1972), Weller recalled: "I was the only janitor with a graduate degree. I used to go around listening to the teachers say all this wrong stuff about drama and then, after classes, I'd call all these kids back and tell them what they really ought to be reading." Weller's play How Ho-Ho Rose and Fell in Seven Short Scenes was performed in 1966 at the University of Manchester and, in 1968, at a theatre festival in Exeter, England. In the same year, his Making of Theodore Thomas, Citizen was produced by London's Stepney Institute and, later, by students at the Toynbee School of Drama, where Weller had obtained a post as a teacher of playwriting.

In 1969 Weller's two-act play Happy Valley was staged as a "fringe" presentation at the Edinburgh Festival, and two one-act works, The Body Builders and Now There's Just the Three of Us, were performed, to favorable notices, in a double bill at London's Open Space Theatre. In her review for the London Observer (August 17, 1969), Helen Dawson credited Weller with possessing "a cool wit, a cryptic eye and a refreshingly controlled sense of dramatic passion." Weller was commissioned by the Royal Court Theatre in London to write a play about the assassination of John F. Kennedy, but the resulting eight-hour epic, entitled The Greatest Little Show on Earth, has never been published or produced.

Weller established the first important beachhead in his career with the premiere, in September 1970, of Cancer at the Royal Court Theatre. Set in 1965, Cancer is a comedy-drama about a group of eight American college seniors who share an apartment in an unnamed university town. Embodying the counterculture movement of the 1960s, they oppose the Vietnam War, smoke marijuana, have open attitudes toward sex, and use uninhibited language. They are against everything that the conventional, "straight" world presents them with, and they try to undermine the establishment with clever and irreverent humor. Cancer moved to the Arena Stage in Washington, D.C., in September 1971, under the new title Moonchildren. Later that year, Weller received the Drama Desk Award for most promising playwright. After a three-month run in Washington, Moonchildren progressed to Broadway, opening at the Royale Theatre on February 21, 1972, but despite a rapturous review from the New York Times drama critic Clive Barnes, the production closed after only sixteen performances. "The producer [David Merrick] didn't think it was going to do enough business, and I just sort of gave up on it," Weller explained to Richard Christiansen.

But when Moonchildren was revived at the Off-Broadway Theatre De Lys (now the Lucille Lortel Theatre) in November 1973, it became a hit. As impressed with the Off-Broadway production as he had been with its Broadway forerunner, Clive Barnes, in his New York Times (November 5, 1973) review, acclaimed Moonchildren as "a joyously funny (yes, funny-funny, as funny as the Marx Brothers) and yet unaffectedly profound play." Michael Weller, Barnes added, "writes dialogue that is both believable and yet surprising, which is no easy trick. . . . There are a hundred and one stories in this play, but what is important is that every single character rings totally true." Regarded as Michael Weller's seminal play, as well as the definitive portrait of American college students in the 1960s, Moonchildren has been given more than 1,000 productions worldwide.

Back in the United States by 1973, where he was the recipient of a Rockefeller Fellowship, Weller wrote the lyrics for a musical about the Vietnam War called More Than You Deserve, which was performed at New York's Public Theater in early

1974 to mostly negative reviews. Edith Oliver, the veteran critic from the *New Yorker* (January 14, 1974), for example, commented, "Many of Mr. Weller's characters are playable and a lot of his comedy works. It is his seriousness that is so awful; his stabs at satire, his gleeful, assumed-Brechtian smirk at pain and death, and his contemptuous equating of sexual impotence with military leadership or capability (to pick three examples) are superficial and childish and secondhand."

Fishing, Michael Weller's follow-up to *Moonchildren,* had its premiere at the Public Theater on February 12, 1975. The play explores the lives of five people who came of age in the 1960s and are now approaching thirty: a married couple living in a cabin in the Pacific Northwest, a male friend who is staying with them, and another married couple who come to visit. All are middle-class holdovers from the counterculture who, although disenchanted with the establishment (except for one of the men, an architect), have been unable to carve out a secure and satisfying lifestyle for themselves. One of the characters contemplates suicide, and all regularly get so high on peyote that one critic, Martin Gottfried of the *New York Post* (February 13, 1975), was prompted to dub *Fishing* "a dope opera." Several of his colleagues were similarly unimpressed. Walter Kerr, commenting in the *New York Times* (February 23, 1975), compared *Fishing* unfavorably to *Moonchildren,* arguing that Weller had "taken refuge in spelling out too plainly the ache that was formerly, gaily, implied." Writing in *New York* (March 10, 1975) magazine, John Simon noted that the play "captures accurately . . . the sound and feel of whimsical, aimless, not yet uncontented lives," but he also felt that it yielded little more than that, "as if a tailor showed us an expertly woven and ingeniously patterned piece of cloth, but teasingly refused to comply with our request to cut it into a suit." Other critics, however, were much kinder. Clive Barnes of the *New York Times* (February 13, 1975) found that "Mr. Weller's ear for dialogue is as convincing as ever, and his good-natured wit . . . is always appealing," and Marilyn Stasio of *Cue* (February 24, 1975) magazine termed *Fishing* "tough, jarring, and terrific." In 1981 *Fishing* was revived at the Second Stage Theatre.

Michael Weller next turned his talents to film. Although he had never had a screenplay produced, he was chosen by the noted Czech-born director Milos Forman to write the script for his film version of the 1960s rock musical *Hair,* because of his lack of preconceived ideas about how to attempt the difficult task of transferring the innovative stage show to the screen. Several critics had expressed their reservations about the project, fearing that, because it was so closely identified with the 1960s, *Hair* would seem hopelessly outdated if revived in the late 1970s, but their concern proved to be groundless, and the film turned out to be a major success. "*Hair* succeeds at all levels—as lowdown fun, as affecting drama, as exhilarating spectacle, and as provocative social observation,"

Frank Rich wrote in *Time* (March 19, 1979) magazine. Kathleen Carroll of the New York *Daily News* (March 14, 1979) called it "every bit as exhilarating and exciting as the original play," and a reviewer for *Variety* (March 14, 1979) commented, "There are moments in *Hair* that are vibrant and innovative."

In *Loose Ends* (1979), Michael Weller addressed the problems of the *Moonchildren* generation for the third time. Under the direction of Alan Schneider, who had also directed *Moonchildren, Loose Ends* opened at the Arena Stage, in Washington, D.C., before moving to the Off-Broadway Circle in the Square Theatre in June 1979. The play's leading characters, Paul and Susan, who were married in the 1960s, have, by the late 1970s, achieved a measure of worldly success, he as a film editor, and she as a photographer, but career conflicts and lack of agreement over whether or not to have children drive the couple apart. They later have a brief, but unsuccessful, reunion. *Loose Ends* is generally regarded as one of Weller's more substantial plays, though critical praise for it was usually mixed with some reservations. According to Richard Eder of the *New York Times* (June 7, 1979), *Loose Ends* is "in many respects a well-made play; it is absorbing for a good deal of the time; it is often funny; it is acted with considerable distinction; and yet at its heart it is a statistic. . . . Amid a good deal of graceful and perceptive writing, the problem of *Loose Ends* is that the play comes to share the flatness of its theme." And Douglas Watt of the New York *Daily News* (June 7, 1979) observed that *Loose Ends* "comes perilously close to resembling a slick soap opera. But there is a becoming honesty in the writing and acting, as well as remarkably natural-sounding dialogue, so that the evening is a resonant and haunting one."

Marital discord again provided the theme for Weller's next work, *Split,* which was first produced as a one-act play at New York's Ensemble Theatre Studio in 1978. Expanded by Weller into two short, interrelated plays, it was performed at the Second Stage Theatre in April 1980. *Split* is the story of Carol and Paul, a seemingly ideal couple whose six-year marriage has landed on the rocks. In the first play, entitled *At Home,* the two alternate between agreement and argument while awaiting the arrival of dinner guests. The second play, *Abroad,* takes place after Carol and Paul have separated and shows them attempting to reorganize their lives and find new romantic partnerships. *Split* received a mixed reception from critics. Marilyn Stasio, writing in the *New York Post* (April 5, 1980), diagnosed as "the trouble with the piece" Weller's refusal "to articulate for his characters the intellectual and emotional roots of the feelings they are too disconnected to discover for themselves," but Mel Gussow of the *New York Times* (April 7, 1980) disagreed, hailing *Split* as "a flourishing harvest of insights about the quest for continuity in relationships."

Less than a month into its run, *Split* was closed by order of Actors Equity Association, the union for

American stage actors, after Michael Weller refused to sign its Showcase Code. That controversial provision states that if an Off-Off Broadway play should move to Broadway or be made into a movie or a work for television, its actors must be either hired for the new production or compensated by the producer for the loss of wages. If the producer fails to provide compensation, the playwright is liable, even if the play is revived many years later. Weller and other playwrights, among them, David Mamet and Albert Innaurato, have voiced their strong opposition to the code. In a prepared statement, Weller said: "Fifty years from now some producer may discover my once-showcased script and decide to put it on its feet. In this event, I would be required to have the producer scour the shuffleboard courts of St. Petersburg, Florida in search of the original cast so that they could be offered first crack at the roles they 'created.'" Weller eventually took legal action against Equity to overturn the Showcase Code.

Teaming up again with Milos Forman, Weller next wrote the screenplay for the film adaptation of *Ragtime*, E. L. Doctorow's novel about pre–World War I America. Writing in the *Saturday Review* (December 1981), Judith Crist called the movie "a dazzler" and lavished praise on both Weller and Forman for retaining the spirit of the novel. "Their film honors its source—and honors them," she concluded. Robert Hatch in the *Nation* (December 12, 1981) termed *Ragtime* "a well-constructed, coherent, eventful period drama that embraces a social theme more serious than such entertainments usually attempt."

With *Dwarfman, Master of a Million Shapes*, which opened at the Goodman Theatre in Chicago on May 22, 1981, Weller resumed his playwriting career. The story of a science fiction cartoonist and his superhero cartoon character, the play, according to Weller, is a "comic burlesque" that grew out of his interest in and admiration for the lesser Elizabethan dramas. While the reviewer for *Variety* (June 17, 1981) described *Dwarfman* as "a touching and funny play, inquiring ingratiatingly on such subjects as the nature of the human spirit and life as a work of art in progress," he also faulted it for its excessive length and reliance on some "useless, vapid, and pretentious material."

The Ballad of Soapy Smith, Weller's epic about the Klondike gold rush of 1897 and 1898, was given its first performance at the Bagley Wright Theatre in Seattle, Washington on October 26, 1983 and its New York premiere at the Public Theater on November 12, 1984. Tracing the rise and fall of a real-life confidence man and featuring a cast of forty, *The Ballad of Soapy Smith* was a marked departure from Weller's earlier work. In his review for *New York* (November 26, 1984) magazine, John Simon wrote that the play was "far from a total success," though he doled out some praise for "a historical play with contemporary relevance, social satire with serious overtones, and [the] daring to accost a large canvas rather than doing yet another miniature." But Edith Oliver of the *New Yorker*

(November 26, 1984) dismissed *The Ballad of Soapy Smith* as "unfocused" and "more an overblown pageant . . . than a play."

Weller returned to the "Big Chill" generation in *Ghosts on Fire*, which had its premiere at the La Jolla Playhouse in La Jolla, California in 1986, before moving to Chicago's Goodman Theatre early in 1987. Its two main characters, Neil and Dan, were underground filmmakers in the 1960s, but Neil now makes television movies in Hollywood, and Dan teaches film at a school in Manhattan. While visiting Dan, Neil learns that he has only a few months to live, and in an effort to lift their spirits, the two friends set off on a trip through the rural South, where they meet Nathan, an uneducated black man who teaches them humility and some simple truths about life. In an interview with Sid Smith of the *Chicago Tribune* (January 11, 1987), who considered *Ghosts on Fire* to be "both Weller's saddest and most hopeful play about his generation so far," Weller explained that he was "interested in exploring a reason for going forward in life that isn't based on selfishness. The point is, it's for other people. You live your life, you do your work, but you don't live it apart from society the way the 1970s would have us believe. I've found that when you get away from the urban centers and into towns where people live by more classically American values, they live in a community. They live for one another."

In December 1987 the Second Stage Theatre mounted a season-long Weller retrospective, including productions of *Moonchildren*, *Loose Ends*, and *Spoils of War*, a new play commissioned for the occasion. Set in the 1950s, *Spoils of War* centers on a sixteen-year-old boy's attempt to reconcile his estranged parents, though his efforts do not lead to the hoped-for happy conclusion. In an interview with Jeremy Gerard of the *New York Times* (May 15, 1988), Weller called *Spoils of War* an "emotional autobiography—which is to say that all the people would be people toward whom I have a very strong emotional response, but the actual portrait of them would not be the real people." The play, Weller continued, is about "that teen period where you just don't know what the hell is going on and there's an inner and an outer world constantly at conflict." He added that *Spoils of War* represented a new style of writing for him. "The play demanded a much more emotional kind of writing than I'm used to, where the people are much more direct with each other. They live without the protection of wit; they don't defend themselves in the way my characters usually do, with a wisecrack right at the moment of great tension."

When *Spoils of War* opened at the Second Stage Theatre on May 17, 1988, Frank Rich of the *New York Times* (May 18, 1988) declared it "the most intense and affecting work of [the playwright's] admirable career." A box-office success as well, *Spoils of War* played to a packed house almost every night and, after some rewriting, moved to Broadway's Music Box Theatre on November 11, 1988, where it fared less well with most critics. "It's not a bad production, just not quite strong enough," a reviewer wrote for *Variety* (November 16, 1988). William A. Henry 3d of *Time* (November 28, 1988), however, felt otherwise, hailing *Spoils of War* as "the only work of lasting value to debut on Broadway this season."

Michael Weller's most recent project was the screenplay for the 1989 film *Lost Angels*, about a group of discontented middle-class teenagers who form a street gang. Directed by Hugh Hudson, the film was panned by a reviewer for *New York* (May 22, 1989). "Weller writes astonishingly clumpy dialogue for the teens," the critic wrote, "and Hudson doesn't allow them any grace, any cool; he makes them mostly loud and stupid, which gives us no reason to watch them."

Michael Weller met his first wife while living in England. They were married in 1970 but later divorced. The playwright and his second wife live with their two-year-old son in an apartment in Manhattan's East Village. An intensely private man, Weller gives few interviews. To help work off his nervous energy, he chain-smokes and bites his nails, sometimes to the point of having to bandage his fingers. Chris Chase reported: "He's a nice-looking fellow, long, wavy brown hair, firm, well-modeled kind of movie star chin. His voice is soft, his manner pleasant."

Modest about his work, Weller rejects the notion, proposed by some critics, that he is a "spokesman" for a generation. He feels that such a label is not only misleading but also discourages consideration of his entire body of work. Dismissing the frequent comparisons of his plays with those of Anton Chekhov as an insult to the great Russian dramatist, Weller points out that he had read little of Chekhov's plays until others began linking them together. He especially admires the plays of the Irish dramatist Sean O'Casey. Weller told Richard Christiansen: "A long time from now, when they dig up the ruins of our civilization, some of the plays of our time may be able to show the way we lived, so that the people who are alive then can say, 'Yes, this is the way it was. This is the way it must have happened.' I hope they'll say that about some of my plays."

References: Chicago Tribune VI p8+ My 24 '81 por, XIII p10+ Ja 11 '87 pors; N Y Newsday II p11+ Ja 3 '88 por; N Y Times II p1+ Mr 5 '72 por, II p7+ Jl 8 '79 pors, II p1+ My 15 '88 pors; Contemporary Authors vols 85–88 (1980); Contemporary Literary Criticism vol 10 (1979)

Wilson, Robert R(athbun)

Mar. 4, 1914– Physicist; sculptor. Address: c/o Department of Physics, Cornell University, Ithaca, N.Y. 14853

The physicist Robert Wilson is best known as the designer of the monumental Fermi National Accelerator Laboratory, or Fermilab, near Batavia, Illinois, some thirty-five miles west of Chicago. Wilson is a sculptor as well as a physicist, and Fermilab, whose design was inspired, in part, by that of the great European cathedrals, is the product of his knowledge in both fields. "It seemed to me that the conditions of its being a beautiful laboratory were the same conditions as its being a successful laboratory," Wilson explained to Linda Dackman in an interview for *Arts & Architecture*.

The Fermilab accelerator was the culmination of an era of spectacular experimental and theoretical progress in particle physics, "almost entirely through a single experimental technique," as Wilson once observed. That technique involved bringing electrically charged particles of matter to high speed, then forcing them to strike other particles. From an examination of the debris released in the aftermath of the collision, as Wilson has explained it, "information is gained about the nature of the particle and about the forces that act between them." During Wilson's tenure as director of Fermilab, from 1967 through 1978, the accelerator eventually raised particles to energies of 500 billion electron volts. Among the scientific milestones

made possible by the powerful accelerator, whose four-mile main ring lies hidden beneath a prairie so ecologically undisturbed that it supports buffalo, geese, and other wildlife, was the detection of the so-called bottom quark and measurement of quark charges that helped to establish the theory of nuclear structure known as quantum chromodynamics.

Robert Rathbun Wilson was born in Frontier, Wyoming on March 4, 1914, the son of Platt E. Wilson, a Wyoming politician, and Edith (Rathbun) Wilson. His parents divorced about eight years later, and for the remainder of his childhood Robert Wilson divided his time between his mother's and father's homes and, in the summers, the cattle ranches of his relatives. "Looking back on it," Wilson told Philip J. Hilts in an interview for Hilts's book *Scientific Temperaments: Three Lives in Contemporary Science* (1982), "there were at least a couple of things [in the ranch experience that were] important to my physics. There was the blacksmith's shop. If the mowing machine broke down, we would go in and hammer out a piece that would replace the broken piece. The equipment for stacking hay was all homemade. We'd go up and cut logs and make devices for stacking. We made all the big box rakes for collecting the hay. . . . It was all made from iron and odd parts lying around. The assumption was that we could do anything in the blacksmith shop. And generally we could."

Wilson has traced his interest in physics to his high school science courses and to two books: the novel *Arrowsmith*, Sinclair Lewis's portrait of a dedicated scientific researcher, and a volume on the mathematics of scientific instruments that, in his words, "hit [him] like a bombshell." As he explained to Philip Hilts: "Here was a thick tome on scientific equipment, a professional book, and I could follow the math. I had thought you had to be pretty good to understand this stuff and to use mathematics as a way of understanding. But I looked at this: 'Gee, this is easy!'" Drawing on his steadily increasing knowledge of physics, Wilson designed and constructed a number of scientific devices, including an ingeniously fashioned "vacuum in a bottle" that, according to Hilts, "could have made [Wilson] rich" had he patented it, and a hand-sized particle accelerator, along with the tiny mercury pump needed to make the apparatus work.

Following his graduation from high school in 1932, Wilson enrolled at the University of California at Berkeley with the intention of majoring in philosophy, but he soon switched to electrical engineering, which, at the height of the Great Depression, seemed to him to be a more practical choice. A few months later, after he chanced to look into the window of a physics laboratory while rushing across a rain-soaked campus on his way to a freshman chemistry class, he switched his major yet again—this time to physics. In the interview with Philip Hilts, he recalled the incident with absolute clarity, describing in vivid detail the flashing and whine of the generators and "the fevered activity of men in laboratory coats." "It just seemed like a heaven," he said.

After he received his B.A. degree in 1936, Wilson remained at the University of California for graduate study under the supervision of Ernest O. Lawrence, the inventor of a new type of particle accelerator called the cyclotron and the director of the university's radiation laboratory. Wilson spent most of his waking hours working in the lab, where he soon distinguished himself as an able and resourceful problem solver. Among other things, he worked out the theory of the cyclotron, specifying the manner in which protons were set whirling in a spiral within the machine's magnetic fields, and invented what is now known as the "Wilson seal." The vacuum-tight seal was part of a mechanism that combined an "internal target" for the accelerated protons with the existing external one, thus increasing the efficiency of the cyclotron ninefold. The improvement in efficiency eventually led to the discovery of carbon 14 and plutonium. Wilson also settled the controversy that arose when Dr. Lawrence proposed raising the energy of the particles the cyclotron produced from twenty-five million volts to 100 million volts—an energy level some prominent physicists thought unreachable—by demonstrating that the energy level could be raised simply by focusing the particle beam more intensely.

Upon taking his Ph.D. degree in 1940, Wilson accepted a position as a physics instructor at Princeton University, where he began his investigation of the proton as a means of explicating the "strong force" within the proton that holds atomic nuclei together. Within weeks of his arrival on campus, Wilson received a telegram from Dr. Lawrence inviting him to join other scientists at the Massachusetts Institute of Technology for a discussion of the escalating war in Europe. Wilson, who had previously concluded that the war would benefit only the munitions makers and that he would therefore oppose it, changed his mind after listening to British scientists graphically describe the effects of Germany's aerial bombardment of Britain. At the conclusion of the meeting, Wilson was asked to help develop sophisticated intelligence-gathering equipment for use in the war effort. Convinced that his refusal might increase Germany's chances of winning the conflict, he agreed. "I chose against the purity of my immortal soul and in favor of a livable world worth living in," he explained years later, as quoted by Philip Hilts.

Before he could begin working on the intelligence equipment, however, Wilson became involved in the effort, led by Enrico Fermi, to create and control nuclear fission as a possible power source for use in the war. Realizing that if the fissionable isotope uranium 235 could be separated from uranium 238, the most common and most stable form of the element, it could be used to construct an atomic bomb, Wilson set out to solve the difficult problem of separating U-235 from U-238, which differed from U-235 only in that it had three extra nonreacting neutrons. One day in 1941, as he was on his way home from the laboratory, it suddenly occurred to him that if he accelerated a beam of uranium, the heavier U-238 isotope would fall slightly behind the lighter U-235. This tendency could be exaggerated by electrical means so that the separated U-235 could be deflected and caught in another container. Impressed by the plan, Wilson's superiors assigned a fifty-man team to the development and construction of the isotope separator, or isotron. As Wilson had predicted, the device effectively separated isotopes, but in 1943 the isotron project was scrapped in favor of Ernest Lawrence's better-funded and better-staffed Calutron project at the Universtiy of California.

Shortly thereafter, Wilson and most of his team of Princeton physicists traveled to Los Alamos, New Mexico to work at the government's new, top-secret atomic research facility, where, under the direction of J. Robert Oppenheimer, thousands of scientists, mathematicians, and armaments specialists were gathering to collaborate on the development and construction of atomic weapons. One of the first to arrive at Los Alamos, Wilson formed and served as the leader of the cyclotron group. In 1944 he took over as head of the research division responsible for experimental nuclear physics and, later, for designing the instruments that measured the intensity of the initial flash during the first test explosion of the bomb, on July 16, 1945. In the interview with Philip Hilts, Wilson recalled that, after they had achieved their goal, a number of physicists involved in the project began to question the morality of atomic weapons research. While they were building the bomb, he told Hilts, they had assumed that they would have a say in the use of their invention. "In fact," he remarked, "we were just like the slaves building the pyramids."

After the end of the war, Wilson accepted a teaching position at Harvard University. While there, he designed the 150 million electron volt (MeV) cyclotron that was to be constructed there and resumed his study of the proton. His observations of proton behavior led him to suggest, in 1946, the radiological use of high-energy particles in cancer therapy and to design a small proton accelerator for that purpose. In 1947 Wilson joined the faculty of Cornell University as a full professor and director of the Laboratory of Nuclear Studies. One of his first tasks was to oversee the construction of a 300 million electron volt synchrotron—a new type of particle accelerator in which the particles travel in a circular path, gaining speed with each revolution, and are kept on track by "bending magnets." "As the energy of the particles increases on each revolution, the field strength in the bending magnets must also be smoothly increased," Wilson explained in an article for Scientific American (January 1980). "The accelerator is called a synchrotron because the particles automatically synchronize with the rising magnetic frequency of the accelerating voltage."

The 300 MeV machine was the first in a series of accelerators, each more powerful than its predecessor, that Wilson built at Cornell. During his tenure there, Wilson used the instruments to continue his exploration of the proton. Instead of bombarding protons with protons, however, he decided to bombard the particles with electrons, which produced more legible scattering patterns than those resulting from proton collisions. The proton-electron collisions helped establish the shape of the proton and confirmed certain assumptions about the structure of the electron as well. In other experiments, Wilson measured the scattering of photons by the electric field of the nucleus of the atom and investigated the first three "excited states" of the proton. One of the spinoffs of Wilson's investigations during this period was the Quantameter, an experimental device that made possible the precise measurement of high-energy x-rays.

By the mid-1960s Wilson's contributions to the development of particle physics had begun to decline. Discouraged, he seriously considered taking up his longtime avocation—sculpture—full-time and half-seriously thought about joining a group of storytellers he had once heard in Santa Fe, New Mexico. Instead, after much soul-searching and consultations with his wife and with his friend and colleague Leon Lederman, who advised him to seek a new challenge because his days as a physicist were "over," Wilson accepted an offer to direct the construction of a 200 billion electron volt synchrotron in northern Illinois. It was at that point that his interest in sculpture and his lifework as a physicist met and fused in what was to become the Fermi National Accelerator Laboratory.

As he contemplated the magnitude of the task before him, Wilson recalled insights about the relationship between art and science that had first struck him while he was serving as an exchange professor at the University of Paris in 1954. While he was in France he had visited "a couple dozen" cathedrals. "After a while," he explained to Philip Hilts, "I began looking at these things very much the way I would look at an accelerator. . . . I wondered how they put them up, how did they know enough physics to assemble those things and not have them *fall down?* . . . I am sure that the builders of the cathedrals would have said that they were making beautiful sculptures in stone, and that these things were an expression of their religious faith. And I would say that I am doing physics research, and there is another kind of faith. . . . I was trying to make high energies, and in the cathedrals there was a great energy of height."

After he accepted the appointment as director of Fermilab, Wilson quickly manifested his faith by announcing that the synchrotron would be operational in five years, far less time than that estimated by specialists in accelerator construction. He also declared that the actual construction costs would be so much lower than the $250 million allotted by Congress—a figure that was itself $100 million less than scientists had originally requested—that several experimental facilities could be built with the extra money. In redesigning and building the accelerator, Wilson found ingenious ways to save money without sacrificing quality. He instituted a program of graduated monetary incentives to reward the most industrious work crews, and he otherwise cajoled, humored, and intimidated construction workers to keep the project ahead of schedule. At one point, he even quoted at length from the medieval French epic Chanson de

Roland. "There is no substitute for a 'gung ho' spirit . . . ," Wilson explained in an article outlining the progress on the Batavia accelerator for *Scientific American* (February 1974). "Without drama it is hard to communicate with a large group." As he admitted to Philip Hilts, the "drama" occasionally included temper tantrums. For instance, when one hapless architect delivered some drawings that did not conform exactly to Wilson's specifications, Wilson tore the plans to shreds, threw them on the floor, and jumped on them.

For the design itself, Wilson relied on pure intellect and artistry. "I am sure that both the designers of cathedrals and the designers of accelerators proceeded almost entirely on educated intuition guided by aesthetics . . . ," he told Hilts. "Modern accelerators are exceedingly complex machines characterized by large mechanical and electrical forms which are pierced by vacuum pipes, and immersed in magnetic fields in which atoms are jiggled by electric fields. . . . Informed by and informing this complex is a nervous system that consists of a ganglia of microprocessors that are governed by a large computer. Now to understand each complicated component and its relationship to the whole would go well beyond my own technical knowledge. So how do I go about designing? . . . I find out a little here, by a calculation, and a little there. . . . Then I draw those parts of the design on paper. After that I just freely and intuitively draw in pleasant-appearing, smooth-connecting lines; lines that cover my ignorance of detail. I keep drawing, correcting here and there until the accelerator appears that it might work. When the parts and forms have essentially the same relationship that parts of a sculpture should have to the whole, then I am satisfied by the design."

By 1971, only four years after Wilson had taken charge of the project, a four-stage acceleration system was in place at Fermilab. It consisted of a Cockcroft-Walton generator that accelerated protons to 750,000 volts; a linear accelerator, through which the protons rode "like surfers" on a wave of electricity, reaching the 200 MeV energy level; a circular "booster" accelerator, in which the protons completed 20,000 laps, with a gain of .4 MeV per lap, ending up at 8 gigaelectron volts (GeV); and, lastly, the main ring, in which the protons circled 200,000 times at near-light speed on their way to an energy level of 400 GeV. Once the 400 GeV level is reached the protons can be deflected out of the main ring and aimed at various experimental targets.

When the Fermilab particle beam was turned on for the first time, it worked well for a few revolutions around the main ring. Then, the moisture from the hot, humid summer air began to condense in the tunnel, soaking the magnets, many of which blew like fuses. Initially puzzled by the unexpected breakdown, the scientists eventually discovered that water had seeped through invisible cracks in the insulation of many of the magnets. Over the next several months, they replaced or rebuilt 350 magnets, but the crisis continued until the ground finally dried out in the winter. The following March, while a harried Wilson was in Washington, D.C., trying to explain the setback to the United States Senate, the Fermilab accelerator finally attained the 200 billion electron volt level it had been designed to reach.

During the course of his Senate testimony, Wilson was asked by one legislator if the accelerator could in any way affect national security. His reply has become part of the folklore of physics. Admitting that the machine would have no discernible impact on national security, he told the senators: "[It] has only to do with the respect with which we regard one another, the dignity of men, our love of culture. It has to do with these things. It has do to with, are we good painters, good sculptors, great poets? I mean all the things we really venerate and honor in our country and are patriotic about. It has nothing to do directly with defending our country except to make it worth defending."

In an article appraising Fermilab's discoveries for *Science 80* (January–February 1980), John Wilhelm contended that the accelerator had so far failed to live up to expectations. For example, it had been widely assumed that the machine would be able to blast quarks out of the protons in which they are bound, but, as Wilhelm reported, "the negative result that free-standing quarks cannot be 'seen' at [Fermilab] energy levels remains one of Fermilab's major findings." Among its many positive findings was the discovery, in 1977, of the upsilon particle—thought to be a combination of bottom and anti-bottom quarks—by Leon Lederman, who was to win the 1988 Nobel Prize in physics. Other Fermilab experiments confirmed the existence of the "weak neutral currents" predicted by the reigning "electroweak" theory of two of the forces that control the subatomic world.

Wilson later pointed out, in his January 1980 article for *Scientific American*, that the discovery of the upsilon was a direct result of the accelerator's power. Throughout his tenure at Fermilab, his goal was to increase steadily the power of the installation's synchrotron. As he explained in the *Scientific American* piece, increasing the power of an accelerator is analogous to increasing the resolution of a microscope: it makes the structure of nature more visible. By 1974 Wilson and his colleagues, anticipating competition in the creation of high-energy collisions from the European Center for Nuclear Research in Geneva, Switzerland, had determined that Fermilab needed to attain an energy level of one trillion electron volts in order to maintain its position as the premier experimental facility in particle physics.

Three years later, at the height of the American energy crisis, Wilson appeared before the House Commerce Committee's Subcommittee on Science and Technology to appeal for increased funding for Fermilab. "We have tremendous copper losses in our electro-magnets . . . ," he told the committee members on March 3, 1977. "If we could replace the copper wire by the superconducting wire that is now becoming practical, we should be able to save as much as $5 million per year." More important, he continued, superconductors could "double our proton energy to 1000 GeV." To that end, Wilson proposed building a second ring of superconducting magnets directly below the existing ring of ordinary magnets so that the protons could be transferred from the old ring to the new, boosting the energy level up to 1000 GeV. "Even more exciting," in his view, was "the possibility" of using "negatively charged protons (antiprotons)" in the accelerator. Unmoved by Wilson's arguments, Congress denied the requested $10 million increase. Shortly thereafter, in early 1978, Wilson resigned as director of Fermilab, citing "subminimal funding." As an "independent person I can see to it that physics goes in the right direction," he told one interviewer. "When you are director of a laboratory and you say your lab needs more funds, you're discounted because that's what you're expected to say."

In the years immediately following his resignation from Fermilab, Wilson devoted most of his time to teaching, as the Peter B. Ritzma Professor at the University of Chicago, from 1978 to 1980, and as the Michael Pupin Professor at Columbia University, from 1980 to 1983. He has also been a guest lecturer at Harvard University, the University of Washington, and the Los Alamos Scientific Laboratory. He is currently physics professor emeritus at Cornell University. In June 1989 he was among the guest speakers at the opening of the nation's first proton-beam cancer treatment center—an idea he had advocated since the late 1940s—at the Loma Linda University Medical Center in Loma Linda, California.

Active in professional organizations throughout his adult life, Dr. Wilson is a member of the American Physical Society, the National Academy of Sciences, the American Academy of Arts and Sciences, and the American Philosophical Society. One of the organizers of the Foundation of American Scientists, he acted as its chairman in 1947 and 1963. He has also served on the editorial board of *Daedalus* magazine, and he is the author of many scholarly articles and, with Raphael Littauer, of the book *Accelerators; Machines of Nuclear Physics* (1960). Among his many honors are the Elliot Cresson Medal, the National Medal of Science, and, most recently, the Enrico Fermi Award, which he received in 1984.

The director emeritus of and architectural consultant to Fermilab since 1979, Robert Wilson regularly visits the facility, and he played a significant role in the design of its Richard P. Feynman Computing Center, which was dedicated in 1988. Several of Wilson's sculptures, including the metal constructions *Möbius Strip* and *Broken Symmetry* and a stone obelisk, are on display at Fermilab. The obelisk, which bears the inscription *"acqua alle funi,"* is a daily reminder of a story Wilson related to his discouraged colleagues during an especially trying time in the laboratory's construction. To illustrate a successful solution to a seemingly insolu-

ble problem, he told them about an attempt to raise, with ropes and pulleys, a 240-ton obelisk in St. Peter's Square in Rome in 1586. When the obelisk was at forty-five degrees, the ropes sagged, and the monument could be raised no further. Finally, someone yelled *"acqua alle funi!"* ("water to the ropes!") The watered ropes tightened, and the obelisk was raised.

Wilson's reputation during his career as a "cowboy" physicist was founded on his knowledge of horsemanship and of the West and on his gunslinger's approach to accelerator building. But as Philip Hilts, for one, has observed, behind this reputation is a visionary who views physics as a form of "internationalism" that contributes to the "common culture of humanity." Wilson, who has been married to the former Jane Inez Scheyer since 1940, has three sons, Daniel, Jonathan, and Rand. He and his wife currently make their home in Ithaca, New York.

References: Physics Today 39:65+ F '86 pors; Sci Am 230:72+ F '74 pors; Science 80 1:46+ Ja-F '80 pors; American Men and Women of Science (1986); Hilts, Philip J. Scientific Temperaments (1982); International Who's Who, 1989–90; Who's Who in America, 1986–87

Wise, Robert

Sept. 10, 1914– Filmmaker. Address: Robert Wise Productions, 315 S. Beverly Dr., Suite 214, Beverly Hills, Calif. 90212

One of Hollywood's most versatile film directors, Robert Wise has had a long and distinguished career that began in 1933, when he took a job as a messenger in RKO studio's cutting room. Over the next few years, he worked his way up to become editor of, among other films, Orson Welles's groundbreaking *Citizen Kane* (1941) and *The Magnificent Ambersons* (1942). Since then, he has directed motion pictures in a variety of genres, including the offbeat horror film *The Curse of the Cat People* (1944), the science fiction classic *The Day the Earth Stood Still* (1951), and *I Want to Live* (1958), a psychological study of a woman awaiting execution in a California prison. After directing two blockbuster musicals, *West Side Story* (1961) and *The Sound of Music* (1965), for which he received Academy Awards, Wise took on fewer, and less successful, projects, such as *The Andromeda Strain* (1971) and *Star Trek—The Motion Picture* (1979), although his later films exhibit the same perfectionism and technical virtuosity that characterize his earlier efforts. "Mine is a prepared approach with ample room for improvising as we go along," the director once said in an interview.

Robert Earl Wise was born in Winchester, Indiana on September 10, 1914, the son of Earl W. Wise, a meat packer, and Olive (Longenecker) Wise. Growing up in the small midwestern community, he cultivated an interest in writing, but he also loved movies. From his childhood on, he haunted the dime matinees at his hometown movie theatre, to which he once won—to his delight—a season pass. Following his graduation from high school in 1931, Wise entered Franklin College, in nearby Franklin, Indiana, where he planned to study journalism, but the Great Depression soon forced him to drop out of school to look for work.

With the help of his older brother David, who worked in the accounting department of RKO Studios in Hollywood, Wise secured a job as a messenger, at a salary of twenty-five cents a week, in the studio's editing department in 1933. He spent the next nine months inspecting, splicing, and transporting prints between the studio's projection and cutting rooms. Promoted to assistant sound and music editor in 1934, he was the apprentice sound effects editor on *Of Human Bondage* (1934) and the sound effects editor on *The Gay Divorcee* (1934), the first major film pairing Fred Astaire and Ginger Rogers, John Ford's *Informer* (1935), and Mark Sandrich's *Top Hat* (1935). In 1935 Wise received his first screen credit, for a ten-minute short that he put together, with the veteran editor T. K. Wood during a lull in their regular schedule, from miscellaneous footage of South Sea Islanders. For his effort, he received a substantial bonus. A hard worker, Wise, who had edited the music for George Stevens's *Alice Adams* (1935), spent two and a half days, with only two hours' sleep, preparing the film for a sneak preview.

The most important lesson that Wise learned from T. K. Wood—and one that has influenced his subsequent work as a director—is that raw film is the cheapest part of a movie, and that a director should shoot as much as he feels he needs to attain the desired result. Wise began to put his steadily in-

creasing knowledge of filmmaking into practice when he made his debut as a film editor on the Fred Astaire–Ginger Rogers film *Carefree* (1938). Working under the editors William Hamilton and Henry Berman, Wise also assisted in the editing of Garson Kanin's *Bachelor Mother* (1939), Gregory La Cava's *Fifth Avenue Girl* (1939), William Dieterle's celebrated *Hunchback of Notre Dame* (1939), and Mark Sandrich's *Story of Vernon and Irene Castle* (1939).

Officially promoted to film editor in 1939, Wise took on an assortment of assignments, including Dorothy Arzner's *Dance, Girl, Dance* (1940), Garson Kanin's *My Favorite Wife* (1940), and William Dieterle's *All That Money Can Buy* (1941). His big break came with Orson Welles's *Citizen Kane* (1941), for which he earned an Academy Award nomination as best editor, and *The Magnificent Ambersons* (1942). In addition to editing the last-named film, Wise supervised its revisions, since Welles was then on location in Brazil, shooting a never-completed documentary. *The Magnificent Ambersons* was extensively recut, and scenes from the middle and final sections of the movie were reshot under the direction of Wise and the unit manager, Fred Fleck. Welles called the result a "mutilation," and a number of critics have pointed out that the non-Wellesian scenes are visually flat.

"I think this ought to be aired a bit," Wise explained to Ralph Appelbaum in an interview for *Filmmakers Newsletter* (April 1976), in which he discussed the controversy over *The Magnificent Ambersons*. "Well, we had sneak previews of the film in Los Angeles and it was terribly painful—audiences laughed at it and walked out in droves. They were some of the worst evenings I've ever spent in my life! But RKO had a film that had cost close to a million and a half, and they at least wanted a picture audiences would sit through. So we did the best we could with Orson's material, although we did have to do some serious cutting and bridging to make the thing work. . . . In terms of a work of art," Wise continued, "I grant you Orson's original film was better. But we were faced with the realities of what the studio was demanding."

Wise spent the next two years working on smaller "A-pictures" and bottom-of-the-bill "B-movies," including *Seven Days' Leave* (1942), directed by Tim Whalen, Richard Wallace's *Bombardier* (1943), and Ray Enright's *Iron Major* (1943). In *The Fallen Sparrow* (1943), an anti-Nazi thriller, Wise directed some of the scenes featuring John Garfield and Maureen O'Hara. His appetite whetted, he scouted out the possibilities for directing an entire film. That opportunity materialized during the production of *The Curse of the Cat People* (1944), a low-budget chiller produced by Val Lewton, who had made a string of sophisticated and inexpensive horror films for the studio. Wise was assigned to edit the film, but he took over the direction after the original director, Gunther Von Fritsch, fell way behind schedule. *The Curse of the Cat People* proved to be a startling directorial debut, and the film was a popular hit. In his review for the *New York Times* (March 4, 1944), Bosley Crowther remarked that the film "makes a rare departure from the ordinary run of horror films and emerges as an oddly touching study of the working of a sensitive child's mind."

Continuing to work with Lewton, Wise next directed *Madamoiselle Fifi* (1944), a wartime drama, and *The Body Snatcher* (1945), based on Robert Louis Stevenson's story and starring Boris Karloff, for Lewton's B-movie production unit. Relegated to more routine B-movies during the postwar era, Wise nonetheless managed to elevate them above their producers' expectations. About *A Game of Death* (1946), Wise's remake of the 1932 RKO hit *The Most Dangerous Game*, a reviewer for *Variety* (November 28, 1945) wrote, "Robert Wise has directed in a tempo that sustains suspense and accentuates the chillerdiller motif." Following *Criminal Court* (1946) and *Born to Kill* (1947), Wise directed *Mystery in Mexico* (1948), an elaborate murder mystery filmed on location in Mexico City. Later in the same year, he graduated to "A-pictures" with *Blood on the Moon*, an adult western starring Robert Mitchum, although Wise and his producer spent so much money on the film that RKO considered finding a "name" director instead. Commenting on Wise's direction, a reviewer for the *New York Times* (November 12, 1948) observed, "He has managed to keep the atmosphere of this leisurely paced film charged with impending violence."

Under the terms of his contract with RKO, Wise was scheduled to make one more film for the studio. That film was *The Set-Up* (1949), a graphic, spellbinding drama about an aging but determined fighter (Robert Ryan) at the end of his career that a *New York Times* (March 30, 1949) reviewer called "a real dilly for those who go for muscular entertainment." "Compact and suspenseful," as a critic for *Variety* put it, *The Set-Up* won the Critics Award as the best picture at the 1949 Cannes Film Festival, and it was nominated for best film by the British Film Academy.

When RKO failed to pick up the option on his contract, Wise directed one film for Warner Brothers—*Three Secrets* (1950). A melodrama about the rescue of an airplane crash victim and the three women who wait to find out whose son the victim is, *Three Secrets* was seen by some critics as little more than a variation of Joseph L. Mankiewicz's popular *A Letter to Three Wives* (1949). Wise then moved to Twentieth Century–Fox, which had offered him a contract to make six pictures in three years, beginning with the Civil War western *Two Flags West* (1950), starring Joseph Cotten and Linda Darnell, and the thriller *The House on Telegraph Hill* (1951). His third film for Twentieth Century–Fox, *The Day the Earth Stood Still* (1951), an adaptation of Henry Bates's short story "Farewell to the Master," has become a classic of the science fiction genre. Rooted in the anxiety of the Cold War era, it deals with an extraterrestrial who comes to earth, landing in Washington, D.C., to warn earthlings that their de-

velopment of nuclear weapons is threatening peace in the universe.

In 1951 Wise formed his first film production company, Aspen Productions, with two former RKO editors, Mark Robson and Theron Warth. With Warth serving as producer and United Artists as distributor, Aspen produced two films, Wise's *Captive City* (1952), starring John Forsyth, and Robson's *Return to Paradise* (1953). Inspired by the Kefauver Commission's investigations into organized crime, *The Captive City* was a powerful documentary-style crime drama that Bosley Crowther of the *New York Times* (March 27, 1952) called "genuine and disturbing." Working in yet another genre, Wise made his first comedy, *Something for the Birds* (1952).

Wise's dexterous handling of the dramatic and action scenes in *The Desert Rats* (1953), Twentieth Century–Fox's hastily conceived followup to its 1951 hit *The Desert Fox*, helped lift the film above its modest origins. *Destination Gobi* (1953), Wise's first color film, was another adventure story, this time about a navy weather team posted in the Gobi Desert during World War II. Wise returned to Warner Brothers later in 1953 to direct *So Big*, based on Edna Ferber's novel about a midwestern family and starring Jane Wyman.

Executive Suite (1954) marked both Wise's debut at MGM and the birth of a new film sub-genre, the "boardroom drama," which explored contemporary business ethics. Wise's direction made the subject "as tense as a crime thriller," in the words of John Douglas Eames, the author of *The MGM Story* (1977), and the movie was a major box-office hit. After making the spectacle *Helen of Troy* (1955) for Warners and the western *Tribute to a Bad Man* (1956), starring James Cagney—both genres that the director has described as his "least favorite"—Wise returned to contemporary drama with *Somebody up There Likes Me* (1956), based on the autobiography of the prize fighter Rocky Graziano. Partly filmed on location on New York's Lower East Side, the movie captured the gritty texture of its setting, anticipating Wise's subsequent work on *West Side Story*. The cast included Paul Newman in the lead role, Pier Angeli, Sal Mineo, and Steve McQueen, who was seen briefly in his first screen appearance. "Robert Wise's direction is fast, aggressive, and bright," Bosley Crowther wrote in the *New York Times* (July 6, 1956). "The representation of the big fight of Graziano with Tony Zale is one of the whoppingest slugfests we've ever seen on the screen."

Wise's last two films for MGM, the musical *This Could Be the Night* (1957) and the drama *Until They Sail* (1957), and his first for United Artists, *Run Silent, Run Deep* (1958), an action film, were competent but relatively undistinguished. His next two United Artists releases, however—*I Want to Live* (1958) and *Odds against Tomorrow* (1959)—were among the most searing and troubling movies of the 1950s. *I Want to Live*, which Wise counts as one of his two favorite films, along with *The Set-Up*, is a gripping account, based on an actual case, of the last weeks in the life of Barbara Graham, a prostitute and thief who was executed for allegedly being involved in a murder. Despite pressure from the Los Angeles police department to abandon the project, Wise and his producer, Walter Wanger, went ahead with the film, which, thanks in large part to Susan Hayward's Oscar-winning portrayal of the doomed woman, was one of the year's top moneymakers.

Wise was heavily involved in the development of the script for *I Want to Live*, particularly the scenes leading up to Miss Graham's execution. "I did much of the interviewing of the actual people involved: the nurse who spent the night with Barbara Graham and gave me much of the tenor and feeling of those scenes; the priest who gave me the clues about how to dramatize the last act," Wise explained to Ralph Appelbaum. "And, of course, my going to San Quentin to see the actual procedures of an execution. I knew that if I was going to deal with this subject matter I wanted to do it honestly and show what it was really like." Paul V. Beckley, the film critic of the *New York Herald Tribune*, praised Wise's direction as "tight and clever." Beckley especially liked the way the director managed to create suspense by varying the tempo of the action, starting off with fast-moving scenes, then slowing down toward the end of the film to heighten the tension.

Odds against Tomorrow (1959), starring Harry Belafonte, Robert Ryan, and Ed Begley, was the first film that Wise both directed and produced. A harrowing account of racial hatred set against the background of a bank holdup in an upstate New York town, the film was shot in black-and-white to give it the sharp, hard quality appropriate to its subject. "The sheer dramatic build-up of this contemplation of a crime is of an artistic caliber that is rarely achieved on the screen," Bosley Crowther wrote in his review of the movie for the *New York Times* (October 16, 1959). Crowther also appreciated the "crisp and credible" performances Wise coaxed from his actors.

With a long list of commercial and critical successes behind him, Wise had, by this point in his career, established himself as one of the most bankable directors in Hollywood. In 1960 he was chosen to direct the Mirsch–United Artists production of the hit Broadway musical *West Side Story*, a contemporary retelling of *Romeo and Juliet*, with music by Leonard Bernstein and lyrics by Stephen Sondheim. Working with the screenwriter Ernest Lehman, who had previously scripted *Executive Suite* and *Somebody up There Likes Me*, and the choreographer Jerome Robbins, who had conceived and directed the Broadway show, Wise pulled the disparate elements of the musical together to create one of the most popular and critically acclaimed motion pictures of 1961. Showered with honors, *West Side Story* collected eleven Academy Awards, including those for best picture and best director. The New York Film Critics also voted it the best picture of the year, and the Directors Guild tapped Wise for its top award.

Shortly thereafter, Wise founded his own production company, Argyle, and produced and directed *Two for the Seesaw* (1962), William Gibson's comedy-drama about a precariously balanced love affair starring Shirley MacLaine and Robert Mitchum, for Mirsch and United Artists. In 1963 Wise returned to MGM to make *The Haunting*, based on a novel by Shirley Jackson. *Variety* praised Wise for his "artful cinematic strokes" in bringing the atmospheric ghost story to the screen, and the movie has achieved a high reputation among connoisseurs of the horror film genre.

Wise had made plans to direct and produce *The Sand Pebbles*, based on Richard McKenna's novel about an American gunboat in China during the 1926 revolution, with financing from the Mirsch Company. In 1964, however, Mirsch backed out of the deal, and Wise was forced to seek other financial backing. Meanwhile, the opportunity arose to direct the film version of the Rodgers and Hammerstein musical *The Sound of Music*, after the movie's original director, William Wyler, withdrew. Wise agreed to take on the Twentieth Century–Fox project, which involved six months of shooting, in exchange for a percentage of the film's profits and an agreement from the studio to bankroll *The Sand Pebbles*. *The Sound of Music* (1965), starring Julie Andrews and Christopher Plummer, became the biggest hit in the history of Hollywood to that date, grossing over $100 million in the first two years of its release despite decidedly mixed notices. A number of critics complained that the film was overly sentimental, but most nonetheless appreciated Wise's brisk direction. Al Cohn, for one, in his review for New York *Newsday* (March 3, 1965), maintained that Wise had ably demonstrated his "ability to enlarge a Broadway musical without losing its mood or meaning in the translation, at least through the first two-thirds of the film." Named the year's best picture by the Academy of Motion Picture Arts and Sciences, *The Sound of Music* also won Wise his second Oscar as best director.

The Sand Pebbles, starring Steve McQueen, Richard Crenna, and Candice Bergen, was released in 1966 to generally lukewarm reviews, most of which focused on its length of 193 minutes. Although it fared poorly at the box office, the movie was nominated for eight Academy Awards, including best picture and best actor, for McQueen. At the awards ceremony, Wise received the 1966 Irving Thalberg Award for his consistently high achievement as a producer. Having gained considerable recognition as a specialist in large-scale films, Wise began taking on fewer projects. Two years elapsed between *The Sand Pebbles* and the release of his next picture, the musical *Star!* (1968), based on the life of Gertrude Lawrence. Despite the presence of Julie Andrews in the lead, the film flopped at the box office. It was subsequently cut for re-release from 194 to 120 minutes and reissued under the title *Those Were the Happy Times*, without many of the production numbers that the critics had liked.

In January 1970 Wise formed a new production company called the Filmmakers Group, in partnership with Mark Robson and the former Paramount executive Bernard Donnenfeld, in order to finance films without the assistance of the studios. The first motion picture that Wise produced and directed for the company was an adaptation of Michael Crichton's bestseller *The Andromeda Strain* (1971), about a deadly virus brought back to earth by a space probe. His next feature, *Two People* (1973), a drama about a Vietnam deserter (Peter Fonda) and a photographer (Lindsay Wagner, in her screen debut), was criticized for its somberness. A sensuous love scene that was praised by some reviewers was seen only in a toned-down version after the original release, because of a June 21, 1973 Supreme Court ruling that redefined obscenity.

Elected president of the Directors Guild of America in 1970, Wise became one of the filmmaking community's most visible and outspoken opponents of the Supreme Court's obscenity ruling. Because of his responsibilities as head of the Directors Guild and the illness of his wife, the former Patricia Doyle, who died of cancer in 1975, Wise was relatively inactive during 1974 and 1975. He returned to directing with *The Hindenburg* (1975), a dramatization of the final flight of the famous airship, which exploded just before landing in Lakehurst, New Jersey on May 6, 1937. Starring George C. Scott and Anne Bancroft, *The Hindenburg* had limited appeal in movie theatres, although it won an Oscar for special effects. Following *Audrey Rose* (1977), the story of a little girl caught up in an occult and psychological struggle, Wise directed *Star Trek—The Motion Picture* (1979), which was lambasted by the critics on its initial release, although it did well at the box office. Wise was away from the director's chair for the next eight years. He returned in 1988 to direct *Rooftops*, a story about homeless children in New York City. Another film project is reportedly in the works, with a release scheduled for 1990.

Described by one interviewer as "anything but flashy," Robert Wise is known for his modesty and self-effacing manner. In addition to serving as president of the Academy of Motion Picture Arts and Sciences from 1984 through 1987, following terms as vice-president and first vice-president, Wise sits on the board of trustees of the American Film Institute and chairs its Center for Advanced Film Studies. He is also a member of the National Council on the Arts. Named chairman of the Directors Guild of America's special projects committee in 1980, he organized the organization's fiftieth anniversary celebration in New York in 1986. As part of that celebration, the Metropolitan Museum of Art held a public screening of *The Day the Earth Stood Still* in Wise's honor. The director and his second wife, the former Millicent Franklyn, reside in Century City, California. His son by his first marriage, Robert Allen Wise, is an assistant cameraman.

References: *Filmmakers Newsletter* p20+ Ap '76 pors; *Films in Review* p5+ Ja '63 pors; *Who's Who in America, 1988–89*; *World Film Directors 1890–1945* (1987)

Woiwode, Larry (Alfred)

(wī´ wōōd-ē)

Oct. 30, 1941– Writer. Address: c/o English Dept., State University of New York at Binghamton, Binghamton, N.Y. 13901

In 1969 Larry Woiwode gained immediate critical recognition for his first novel, *What I'm Going to Do, I Think*, most notably because of its poetic language and powerful descriptions, often of nature, which effectively reflect the characters' emotions. On the strength of that novel, the novelist Anne Tyler called Woiwode "a master at portraying life as most of us know it—subtle, complicated, sometimes mystifying, seldom dramatic or conclusive. . . . He held his readers to the end by sheer craftsmanship." Woiwode's next novel, *Beyond the Bedroom Wall* (1975), a multigenerational saga about a North Dakota family, confirmed his status "as one of the finest of the younger talents in American fiction," according to another critic. What makes that novel unique is its albumlike format, in which diaries, descriptions of photographs, and shifting viewpoints are employed to create a composite picture.

Woiwode's subsequent works have included a collection of poems, *Even Tide* (1977), a short novel, *Poppa John* (1981), and his most recent work of fiction, *Born Brothers* (1988), which complements his earlier *Beyond the Bedroom Wall*. Although critics often find his writing obscure, Woiwode has explained that deliberate obfuscation is not his intent. "If I have any overriding philosophy, literary or personal, it is to tell the truth as clearly as I can," he told an interviewer from *Library Journal* (February 1, 1969). "I don't write with the intention to baffle. . . . If I were to pick out one quality to characterize my writing, it would be 'immediacy.' I like to make the reader *feel* tactilely if I can . . . and I write with a great deal of body English."

Larry Alfred Woiwode was born on October 30, 1941 in Carrington, North Dakota to Everett Carl and Audrey Leone (Johnstone) Woiwode. Carrington was the nearest town with a hospital to his parents' home in the western North Dakota plains town of Sykeston, an isolated and predominantly German community of a few hundred people. Five generations of Woiwode's family have lived in the area. Everett Woiwode taught Shakespeare and creative writing to high school students, and he moved his family from North Dakota to Manito, Illinois when Larry was ten. For reasons that have not been explained, Larry Woiwode spent most of his childhood away from his family, and he nurtured his writing talent through letters he sent home. His writing career began in earnest at the age of fifteen, when the poems he submitted to a local newspaper began appearing in print on a weekly basis.

From 1959 to 1964 Woiwode attended the University of Illinois at Urbana-Champaign, leaving school with an associate of arts degree in rhetoric. During college he worked at a local television station and wrote in his spare time. "I was published often and won several writing prizes," he revealed in the interview for *Library Journal*. After leaving college he tried his hand at acting, securing a position with a Miami, Florida repertory company that staged Shakespearean plays. In 1964 he moved to New York, where he acted in Off-Broadway plays and became friends with the actor Robert De Niro. He also was writing and searching for his own literary voice, trying to extricate himself from the "mannered, Gass-inspired postmodernism—for instance, a story where Abraham Lincoln appears out of a cowboy boot," he related to Michele Field in an interview for *Publishers Weekly* (August 5, 1988). A chance meeting with William Maxwell, the novelist who was on the editorial staff of the *New Yorker* from 1936 to 1976, helped to steer Woiwode in a constructive direction, spurring him to embark on a freelance writing career. Maxwell evaluated and advised him on his early work, and Woiwode was soon selling short stories and poetry to such magazines as the *New Yorker*, the *Atlantic*, *Harper's*, *Mademoiselle*, and *Partisan Review*. (Woiwode acknowledged that assistance in 1988 by dedicating his fourth novel, *Born Brothers*, to Maxwell.) "By grace of God," Woiwode told Herbert Mitgang for the *New York Times Book Review* (August 14, 1988), he was "able to work at [Maxwell's] elbow for about ten years." "Maxwell taught me many things," he continued. "Two of his most memorable maxims are: First, you must be aware that your reader is at least as bright as you are. Second, you must remove everything that is extraneous." Since 1965 Woiwode has given the *New Yorker* a first reading of all his work.

Much of Woiwode's first novel, *What I'm Going to Do, I Think* (1969), appeared as four short stories in the *New Yorker*, between 1966 and 1968. Set on an isolated stretch of the northern Lake Michigan shoreline, the story focuses on the rocky relations of a newlywed couple, Chris and Ellen, who jump into marriage when they discover that Ellen is pregnant. During their stay at the remote cabin, the couple's emotional problems come to the surface, as do their misgivings about the marriage. Ellen reverts to her childhood, playing with toys she finds in the attic; Chris buys a gun and spends his time shooting at targets.

What I'm Going to Do, I Think brought Woiwode widespread critical recognition. The novel won a William Faulkner Award as the best first novel of the year and an American Library Association notable book award. A reviewer for *Time* (June 20, 1969) magazine called the novel "the best three-way confrontation between a young man, life and the Michigan woods since Hemingway's Nick Adams stories." And Alan Pryce-Jones, writing in *Newsday* (May 13, 1969), described *What I'm Going to Do, I Think* as "extremely intelligent and perceptive."

The novel's detractors found fault with Woiwode's characterization of Chris. Writing in the *New York Review of Books* (July 10, 1969), Denis Donoghue, for example, observed that "the limitations of the book are severe, mainly because of Chris. . . . Mr. Woiwode does the best he can for him, but Chris is really not worth the bother." But Michael E. Connaughton noted in the *Dictionary of Literary Biography*: "Woiwode compensates for this unfinished, frustrating conception of character with a stylistic polish and total control unusual for a first novel." Commenting on Woiwode's style, William C. Woods wrote in the *Washington Post* (June 19, 1969) that "the author's concerns are profound; his metaphors, unhappily, are often obscuring. . . . But at his best, he paints scenes of considerable authority."

The acclaim that followed the publication of *What I'm Going to Do, I Think* led to a Guggenheim Fellowship in 1971 and 1972 and a National Book Award judgeship in 1972. In the same year, Woiwode served as a member of the executive board of PEN, the international writers organization. In addition, he was writer in residence at the University of Wisconsin in 1973 and 1974. Woiwode's first novel was translated into eight languages.

In his second novel, the monumental, 600-page *Beyond the Bedroom Wall: A Family Album* (1975), Woiwode created an ambitious and panoramic chronicle tracing the history of the Neumiller family over several generations. It begins with the arrival of Otto Neumiller, a German immigrant, in rural North Dakota in 1881 and follows his rise and fall as a farmer there. The story then moves on to Otto's descendants, many of whom leave North Dakota, marry, raise families of their own, and follow widely diverging careers. The novel concentrates particularly on Otto's son Martin, who courts and marries Alpha Jones. They eventually have five children and move to Illinois, where Alpha dies of uremia at the age of thirty-four, shattering the family. Even years later, her relatives remain scarred by her loss.

Beyond the Bedroom Wall is not told in a conventional manner, employing instead various sources such as letters, work records, diaries, and descriptions of family photographs to create a kind of scrapbook. That collage effect is reflected in the book's subtitle, *A Family Album*, which Woiwode added at his wife's suggestion. Anne Tyler noted in her review for the *National Observer* (October 21, 1975) that the novel "does have the quality of one of those old photo albums. . . . It is a series of moments, carefully selected and chronologically arranged." The result found favor with John Gardner who, in his evaluation for the *New York Times Book Review* (September 28, 1975), contended, "It's a wonderful thing, it seems to me, to laugh and weep one's slow way through an enormous intelligent novel tracing out the life of a family." Gardner also cited Woiwode's "richness of detail, keenness of observation, and insight into the interrelationships of time and place and character."

In contrast to *What I'm Going to Do, I Think*, in which Woiwode concentrated on the lives of only two characters, *Beyond the Bedroom Wall* features a host of vividly drawn characters. Despite that variety, members of the Neumiller family, wrote a staff member of *Booklist* (November 1, 1975), "come across as individuals alive to the beauty and tribulations of midwestern life, distinct personalities revealed here in word portraits as if stopped in time." Peter S. Prescott of *Newsweek* (September 29, 1975) also praised Woiwode's handling of characters: "Woiwode can enter the thoughts of his characters—he is equally at ease with a young girl rejoicing in her talent and with an old man cursing God," though he added that the "book as a whole lacks shape and momentum."

Although several critics compared *Beyond the Bedroom Wall* to the traditional novels of the nineteenth century, Peter S. Prescott more accurately described it as "an assemblage of related short stories and sketches," fourteen of which originally appeared in the *New Yorker*. The novel often shifts from first-person to third-person narrative and jumps about in time from one generation to the next.

Once again, Woiwode's descriptive powers and language were praised by critics. A reviewer for the *Atlantic* (October 1975), for instance, noted: "The events of the novel are the very ordinary ones of every family's existence—the births, deaths, marriages, the growing up. Woiwode evokes each moment in language of pure, cleanly wrought beauty until it is made to seem both universal and extraordinary." And Paul Gray observed in *Time* (September 29, 1975) that "even without cohesive drama or great characters, *Beyond the Bedroom Wall* demonstrates a fine talent for description, coupled with a Proustian ability to recreate the past."

Woiwode admitted to Henry Mitchell in the *Washington Post* (November 6, 1975) that *Beyond the Bedroom Wall* is based partly on family lore. There are also many parallels between the novel and Woiwode's own life. The Neumiller family's move from North Dakota to Illinois reflects his own parents' move there when Woiwode was a boy. Charles Neumiller resembles Woiwode in several ways: both are the second oldest of four children, for example. As Roger Sale remarked in the *New York Review of Books* (November 13, 1975), "Woiwode's love for the Neumillers and for North Dakota—which is unashamedly a love for his own family and childhood home—is a matter of memory and reconstruction." Woiwode himself has pointed out the importance of those North Dakota years. "Although my family moved to Illinois when I was rather young," Woiwode related in the *Library Journal* interview, "I feel that I know North Dakota more completely than any other place I've lived, perhaps because I was more unselective and observant as a child, or because the state has become for me a state of mind, as fictional as it is real." *Beyond the Bedroom Wall* won a fiction award from the Friends of American Writers in 1976, and it was nominated for the National Book Award and the National Book Critics Circle Award the same year.

In 1977 Woiwode published *Even Tide*, a collection of untitled free-verse poems arranged into several long sequences. The poems move from a painful uncertainty at the beginning of the book to a final, religious culmination and are written in a condensed, conversational style that is sometimes cryptically personal. A reviewer for *Choice* (September 1978) called many of the poems "puzzling," "but together they produce movement, perhaps progress." A critic for *Publishers Weekly* (October 31, 1977) commented that "the curse of the crypto-confessional hurts communication, but readers who care will want to look in on even the self-lacerations of a genuine new young poet." And a reviewer for *Library Journal* (January 1, 1978) found that the "distractions, cool tone, colloquial usages, and inconsistent voice are overcome only when strong nature imagery sets free Woiwode's latent lyricism: 'The flute, a likelihood of life, and I know/One song with wheat-colored notes will rise above.' An uneven and difficult first collection."

At the suggestion of his publisher, Farrar, Straus & Giroux, Woiwode interrupted work on the novel that was to become *Born Brothers* to write a short novel, set in New York City, about an "entirely new character." *Poppa John* (1981) is the story of an actor, Ned Daley, who has played a popular, Bible-quoting grandfather named Poppa John in a long-running television soap opera. When the network executives decide that Poppa John should die, Daley is out of a job and cannot find any other acting work because he is so closely identified with the character. Daley deteriorates during the Christmas holiday season, drinking too much, developing an ulcer, and depleting his bank account. Obsessed with memories of his murdered father and of his grandfather, he suffers a mental breakdown. His salvation is brought about by his wife's revelation that the Biblical homilies of Poppa John helped her to regain her own lapsed religious faith.

As Woiwode told Contemporary Authors, "Poppa John met all kinds of critical resistance." Anne Tyler, writing in the New Republic (December 9, 1981), pointed out how different that novel was from its predecessors. She found the style "more involved and convoluted, less direct. The book as a whole is shorter and leaner, more confined in its scope." Joyce Carol Oates, in the New York Times Book Review (November 15, 1981), observed that the narrative "keeps us within the consciousness of one person and forbids, as a consequence of the chill, spare, pitilessly chiseled nature of Mr. Woiwode's prose, any deep emotional involvement with him. . . . Why the author chose to draw back from his material, and to substitute what is in essence a soap opera conclusion for a protracted exploration of Ned's predicament, one cannot imagine." Other critics were more charitable. Jill P. Baumgaertner in Christian Century (February 17, 1982) called the book "a sensitive, well-written novel." Similarly, Donald Newlove in the Saturday Review (November 1981) described Poppa John as being "borne into the reader's mind like an oily dream, its hints and shadows too literary by half, yet at times profoundly inspired."

Woiwode has described his next novel, Born Brothers (1988), as "complementary" to Beyond the Bedroom Wall. Born Brothers picks up where the earlier novel left off and continues the saga of the Neumiller family from the 1960s to the present. The story centers on two brothers, Charles and Jerome, and on their changing relationship as they grow into adulthood. At over 600 pages, the book is as long and complex as Beyond the Bedroom Wall. As Jonathan Yardley noted in the Washington Post (July 17, 1988), the novel "is less a sequel . . . than an amplification and variation upon it." In the interview with Michele Field for Publishers Weekly, Woiwode explained that "indeed some of the elements overlap, some of the incidents are told from a different viewpoint, and in this book you get a different picture of both the mother and the father."

The life story of Charles Neumiller, the narrator of the novel, closely resembles that of Woiwode himself. They were born in the same year, attended the same college and had similar careers, and both share a strong religious faith. Their fathers are also similar: both men worked as schoolteachers. "Born Brothers is about as autobiographical as I'd ever care to be," Woiwode told Mervyn Rothstein for the New York Times (September 5, 1988). He further explained to Michele Field that Born Brothers concerned his personal emigration from the Midwest to New York. "I did want this book to define what a New Yorker is," he related.

The idea for Born Brothers started germinating while Woiwode was in college, then grew when he first moved to New York. He explained to an interviewer for Contemporary Authors: "One day I was thinking, in this little rented room where I was working, if I'm going to be absolutely truthful, I must admit that the person who had perhaps the greatest effect on me was my maternal grandmother." He first wrote a short story about her for the New Yorker. "I felt then that the piece fell right at the center of this big novel I had once visualized, and I knew that it could be a part of it."

The novel gives Charles's version of the family history as he remembers it and as it has affected his life. The pivotal event in his life was the death of his mother when he was a boy, leaving him with a lifelong guilt. Accident-prone as a child, he becomes flighty and irresponsible as a young man, rebelling against his family and competing with his older brother, Jerome. While Charles is unreliable and unsure of what he should do with his life, Jerome is steadfast and successful.

Where Beyond the Bedroom Wall and Born Brothers diverge is in their writing style. In Beyond the Bedroom Wall, Woiwode inserted sections of his own poetry into the prose of the story to create a richer and more lyrical texture. Born Brothers is written in a more direct manner. As Michele Field commented, "Born Brothers is almost the same material related in a very much simpler style. The clarity of the writing is remarkable in Born Brothers, given the book's complex theme."

Born Brothers met with a mixed critical reception, with some reviewers finding it less successful than its predecessor, while others felt that the novel was too long or that Woiwode's language was sometimes opaque. And yet even the least satisfied critics found much to praise. Sven Birkerts in the New Republic (September 12–19, 1988) called Born Brothers a "grand failure. A failure because of its excess and its mounting chaos, and because it cannot be fully grasped without the prior narration of Beyond the Bedroom Wall. Grand because for all his lapses Woiwode is a prodigiously gifted stylist." Peter Heinegg in the Los Angeles Times Book Review (August 7, 1988) found that Woiwode's vision possessed "undeniable honesty, humility, and love." But he also faulted the novelist's language for being "clotted and obscure." Several critics also felt that Jerome was not fully developed as a character. Birkerts, for one, commented, "Jerome never emerges as anything but a shadowy alter-ego."

More positive reviews praised his depiction of childhood. According to the critic for Publishers Weekly (June 10, 1988), "Woiwode is adept at evoking the early impressions, misapprehensions and fears of childhood, as well as its tender or exciting moments." The critic predicted that "most readers will be willingly drawn into the narrative as Woiwode explores the mysterious patterns of human existence." Bette Pesetsky in the New York Times Book Review (August 14, 1988) called Born Brothers "a serious novel, written in a strong and lyrical voice." She also singled out for praise Woiwode's ability to create "perfect descriptions, not a detail astray—a car 'with its trunk curved toward the bumper like a turtle's shell' and a time of physical pain when 'your thighs, bunched umbrellas of weakness as wide as the world, [are] supporting the wail going out your eyes.'"

Michele Field has described Larry Woiwode as a man of "medium stature" who is "almost shy." He married Carole Ann Petersen in 1965, and since the early 1980s the couple has lived with their four children in North Dakota on a farm-ranch, where the family raises grains and horses. During the school year Woiwode teaches in New York State; when school is out, he heads home. The move back to North Dakota came after the couple had spent the late 1960s living in New York City. When their oldest daughter was a year old, the couple decided that the city "was not a place to raise children." They embarked on a cross-country search for a suitable home, influenced by a desire, as Woiwode told Michele Field, "for the part of the country that truly reflected the 'real West.'" After living in ten different states over the next few years, they settled in western North Dakota, the area where Woiwode lived as a child and an area "that seemed least affected by either coast, by either New York or California," he told Michele Field. Although raised a Roman Catholic, Woiwode abandoned religion in the 1960s but later found "the essential truth" in Presbyterianism. "Most of life seems to me a religious experience," he told Mervyn Rothstein. "I consider myself a spiritual person."

Woiwode plans to publish a collection of essays, tentatively called "Wheel at the Cistern." Also in the works is a collection of stories about the characters who appear in Born Brothers, called "The Neumiller Stories." Woiwode is writing a book on North Dakota for its centennial year of 1989, and he plans, at some point, to write a biography of Tolstoy. His next novel will be a "campus novel," in all likelihood, he told Michele Field. "As with Born Brothers, which is about New Yorkers, it is set in the wilderness. But this wilderness is where an academic has gone to complete his dissertation."

Teaching has been a major outlet for Woiwode, who spent 1981 and 1984 teaching at Wheaton College. He has led writing workshops and read from his own work at the University of Notre Dame, Dartmouth College, the University of Iowa, and the City College of the City University of New York. In 1983 he became visiting professor at the State University of New York at Binghamton and, in 1985, he was made a full professor and the director of the school's writing program. He taught Shakespeare and travel writing in a London exchange program of SUNY Binghamton during the 1988 school year. "Teaching is indeed having an effect on my writing," Woiwode told Contemporary Authors, "because for whatever reasons, by seeing, say, two dozen other viewpoints of a story or of fiction, my mind is open to greater possibilities in my own fiction." Woiwode received an honorary Doctor of Letters degree from North Dakota State University in 1977 and a fiction award from the National Institute of Arts and Letters in 1980.

References: Pub W 234:67+ Ag 5 '88 por; Contemporary Authors new rev vol 16 (1986); Contemporary Literary Criticism vol 10 (1979); Contemporary Novelists (1986); Dictionary of Literary Biography vol 6 (1980); Directory of American Poets and Fiction Writers 1987–1988 (1987); World Authors 1975–1980 (1985)

Woods, James

Apr. 18, 1947– Actor. Address: c/o International Creative Management, 40 W. 57th St., New York, N.Y. 10019

"When I get out there," the incendiary American film actor James Woods once said, "I want everybody to say, 'Thank God, I didn't play that part, because I couldn't have done it.' I want people to sit back and literally gasp when they watch me, and say, . . . 'I don't ever want to go there.' I want them to be terrified that somebody else is willing to go through that. . . . I want people to think you can't go that far without an explosion, or an implosion. To have them biting their nails for that moment to happen." For more than a decade Woods specialized in searing portrayals of sociopaths and obsessive sleazebags, like the cop killer in The Onion Field and the crafty gangster in Once Upon a Time in America. Because of his off-kilter looks and intense interpretations of sick and blighted souls, Woods was stereotyped by Hollywood producers and denied the opportunity to play leading-man roles, even though his fellow actor James Garner and his studio boss, John Daly, consider him to be the most accomplished actor of his generation. Moreover, Woods's career suffered because none of his films achieved commercial success, and because in "real life" he can seem to be as manic, driven, and neurotic as his darkest celluloid creations. The *New Yorker* film critic Pauline Kael has called Woods the "most hostile actor in America."

Nevertheless, Woods struggled against the studio system, taking only roles that appealed to him, and eventually came to be regarded as a successful actor largely because of what one writer has described as the "videocassette and cable revolution, which has given people a chance to see movies that played in theatres for only a couple of weeks." In addition to receiving an Academy Award nomination in 1987 for best actor for his performance in the highly regarded Oliver Stone film *Salvador*, Woods has won two Emmy Awards for his portrayal of more appealing characters in the made-for-television movies *Promise* (1986) and *My Name Is Bill W.* (1989). Although for much of the past decade he was Hollywood's most outspoken rebel, he now receives major studio backing and is on the verge of becoming the most unlikely leading man in the contemporary cinema.

James Woods was born in Vernal, Utah on April 18, 1947 to Gail and Martha Woods. His father, a decorated combat veteran of World War II, was, in his opinion, affiliated with G-2, the United States Army intelligence corps, and his work took his family from place to place across the country. In the late 1940s Gail Woods, who had received a major's commission from the army, was stationed with his family on Guam when war broke out in Korea, where he served after his wife and children returned to the United States. By 1957, the year in which James's brother, Michael, was born, the entire family had settled in Warwick, Rhode Island. Two years later James Woods was traumatized by the sudden death of his father, whom he idolized, from complications arising from routine blood-clot surgery.

In an interview, entitled "The Poetics of Rage," with Denise Worrell for *Smart* (September–October 1989) magazine, Woods characterized his father as a "John Wayne [or] Gary Cooper kind of guy." "He was just a very manly man," he recalled. "He was a big, strong, country guy, but . . . very soft-spoken, and his hands were very soft. . . . He'd make my mother breakfast in bed every Sunday. And when I was a kid, he'd sit me on his lap and quote Shakespeare to me, chapter and verse." Although Gail Woods left a legacy of love to his close-knit family, he bequeathed little in the way of financial security for his wife, who had never worked outside the home. According to her older son, Martha Woods was as resourceful and resilient as a "frontier mother." He told Denise Worrell that "she started this preschool called Lad 'n' Lassie. She built it gradually. . . . [Eventually] she had a yearly registration of 105 children. . . . The entire twenty-two years my mother had the school, 25 percent of kids [those who were poor] went for free."

Helping to make ends meet, James Woods worked in the summers for $1.25 an hour on an assembly line at the Speidel Watch Company stuffing watch bands into plastic cases. His brother told Diane K. Shah of *Gentlemen's Quarterly* (March 1988) magazine that James "was a quiet kid, always in his room with the door closed, studying. . . . He would wear those thin ties and white socks. My brother was the ultimate high school nerd." His brother was also brilliant. He scored 180, well above the genius level, on the Stanford-Binet IQ test, and he is one of the few actors in Hollywood who can boast of having scored a perfect 800 on the verbal part of his SAT exams and a 779 on the math portion. Between his junior and senior years, he was one of thirty-five students awarded a National Science Foundation grant to study linear algebra at UCLA.

Woods's career goal was to become an eye surgeon, but he accidentally put his right arm through a glass door on the UCLA campus, and, though his arm was saved after ten hours of emergency surgery, he was forced to change his career plans. Senator John O. Pastore of Rhode Island secured him an appointment to the Air Force Academy on the basis of his SAT scores, which were the highest in the state, but Woods instead accepted a full scholarship from the Massachusetts Institute of Technology, where he majored in political science. He discovered his life's calling the first time he stepped on to the stage in a high school production of Lillian Hellman's *Watch on the Rhine*, in which he was cast as Oscar. Woods, who thinks of himself as one blessed with natural talent, has said that he subjected himself to acting lessons only twice in his life. In his freshman year in college, he joined MIT's Drama Workshop, where he received training in the classical manner of the English stage rather than in the fashionable "method" techniques derived from Lee Strasberg's famous Actors Studio.

Although he has contended that his original motivation was to meet women in the theatre, Woods spent his apprenticeship working in offbeat experimental plays at school and in regional summer-stock productions. By his senior year he had appeared in some thirty-six plays. At that time, Woods found himself flying back and forth between Boston and New York, auditioning for Off-Off-Broadway productions and then going back to take exams at MIT, where he was an honor student. With his mother's approval, he dropped out of college just as he was about to complete his B.A. degree. In past interviews he has hinted that he was troubled by MIT's close ties to the military at a time when the United States government was fighting an undeclared war in Vietnam, but the garrulous Woods has cautioned against taking his words as literal truth. His dramatic flair carries over sometimes into his speech, especially his autobiographical monologues, in which he rains words, including a torrent of profanities, on his interlocutors. In fact, it seems that Woods preferred the lure of the stage more than the prospect of serving as a "policy wonk" at the State Department in Washington, D.C., because he was simply too busy arranging a theatrical career for himself in Manhattan to bother with mundane academic tasks.

Unlike most serious actors of his generation, Woods rejected the idea of training in the "method" in New York. "I skipped all this acting-class [twaddle]," he has noted sarcastically; "you know, everybody else was trying to be a radish or something, or play a tree. I knew how to do accents, how to do age, how to do comedy, how to do drama. I'd done it, I'd been out on the front lines." In an interview with Neil Hickey for TV Guide (April 29, 1989), Woods recalled: "I didn't know anybody in New York. . . . When you have absolutely no connections and don't have much money and you're trying to start up in that massive talent pool, just to get a hearing in the court of theatrical justice is a difficult task." Although he "couldn't get auditions to do dog-food commercials," as he put it, Woods used guile and bluff to get his first job on Broadway, in a production of Brendan Behan's Borstal Boy. "I lied . . . ," he told Denise Worrell. "I waited until the stage manager went [to the bathroom] and then just walked out on stage, said, 'I'm next,' and auditioned. They wanted only resident British actors with real British accents. I said I was from Liverpool, and they said, 'Great,' and hired me."

In 1971, three years after moving to New York, Woods won an Obie Award for his performance in a Brooklyn Academy of Music production of Edward Bond's controversial Saved, in which a baby is stoned to death. That same year Woods was critically praised for his work in Michael Weller's Moonchildren, a well-regarded play about the pre-Woodstock counterculture, which enjoyed a brief run on Broadway in 1972. Having promised himself to win a Tony Award before the age of twenty-five, Woods was disappointed when he failed to be nominated for his Moonchildren portrayal of Bob Rettie, the boy-man whose anguish and unhappy personal relationships convey the dark side of alienation and political radicalism in the 1960s. He continued to work steadily on the stage, appearing in The Trial of the Catonsville Nine, Finishing Touches, and Conduct Unbecoming, but suddenly realized that he no longer enjoyed the contemporary theatre, which he disparaged as "bad English imports, revivals, museum Broadway, [bad] Off-Broadway, [the] Actors Studio doing a production of Three Sisters that was embarrassing." "But I realized," he told Don Shewey, the author of Caught in the Act: New York Actors Face to Face (1986), "I was going to movies every afternoon. I thought, well, if I like movies so much, why don't I do them?"

To scale the walls of fortress Hollywood, Woods had to overcome the resistance of casting directors who constantly refused him auditions, not because he lacked talent but because he "wasn't right for the part," which meant that he was not conventionally handsome, though in fact he has offbeat good looks that have been described as "creepy." Thin and with an angular build, he has a prominent nose, dark, piercing, deep-socketed eyes, and a gaunt, acne-scarred face that has been described as being at once "sensitive" and "psychotic." "They don't know what sexy is in Hollywood," Woods complained when he spoke to Lynn Hirschberg of Esquire (April 1984). "At least now we have some women executives who have more humanity. Before we had a bunch of cigar-chomping, fat, disgusting pigs who . . . would think, 'Let's get some guy who looks like Robert Redford for our movies.' . . . They didn't realize that every major star—Humphrey Bogart, Spencer Tracy, Robert Mitchum—had offbeat appeal. Not blond, blue-eyed walking surfboards." "This," Lynn Hirschberg noted, "is Woods's favorite of all his complaints. He feels he's been abused by Hollywood because of his looks, and so he abuses them back, particularly in the press."

Helped along by his agent, Tony Schwartz, who volunteered to pay for Woods's screen tests out of his own pocket, he began getting bit parts in films with increasing regularity in the middle 1970s. His first assignment was in The Visitors (1971), a low-budget film directed by Elia Kazan in which he played a Vietnam veteran who turns against two of his buddies by implicating them in the commission of war atrocities. Critically praised, The Visitors was a grim, unsettling film that, because it was ahead of its time, failed to please audiences. In the Robert Redford and Barbra Streisand vehicle The Way We Were (1972), Woods played Streisand's left-wing boyfriend—the one she drops for Redford. He had a small part as a bank officer in The Gambler (1974), a probing psychological drama directed by Karel Reisz. In 1977 he played Harold Bloomguard in The Choirboys, director Robert Aldrich's unsuccessful adaptation of the best-selling novel by Joseph Wambaugh.

Woods achieved national recognition in 1978, when he played the role of Karl Weiss, a doomed, embittered Jewish artist, opposite Meryl Streep in Holocaust, the acclaimed miniseries that was broadcast by the NBC television network, but his first break on the big screen came when he was cast as the psychotic cop killer Gregory Powell in The Onion Field (1979), closely based on the best-selling nonfiction book by Joseph Wambaugh. In the New Yorker (October 1, 1979), Donald Barthelme wrote, "It's amazing . . . how good the movie is, with a startling performance by . . . Woods as Powell." Powell, he noted, is a self-described "sexual virtuoso" who is also a "top marksman and master criminal and philosopher of family life. What he is, in fact, is a world-class sociopath." Writing in Newsweek (September 24, 1979), Jack Kroll called the "gripping" Onion Field "one of the best films of the year," partly because of the "hellish" realism that Woods brought to his portrayal of Powell, a real-life cop killer whom Wambaugh had interviewed extensively in prison.

By 1980 Woods had moved to Los Angeles and married Kathryn Greko, a model. Divorced three years later, they continued to see each other until 1985, when Woods serendipitously met Sarah

Owen, whom he married in 1989. Pointing out that he was thirty-three when he first married, Woods told Esquire's Lynn Hirschberg he "got married when Christ died. . . . We both suffered." Kathryn Greko has described Woods as a very lovable control freak. "He loved the way I look," she told Hirschberg, "but he never really trusted me. Jim thinks his way is the only way. That drove me crazy."

It was in Hollywood in the 1980s that Woods gave the performances that eventually gained him a following among viewers of cable television movies and video cassettes. He appeared in The Black Marble (1980), another Wambaugh cop film but one that critics disliked, and in 1982 he worked for the first time with the director Ted Kotcheff, who cast Woods in Split Image (1982) as a ruthless religious-cult deprogrammer. "As played by Woods," David Ansen observed in Newsweek (October 25, 1982), "he's a fascinatingly ambiguous figure, . . . a low-life cretin with ferociously effective methods of deprogramming." In the low-budget prison drama Fast Walking, which was made in 1980 but not released until 1982, Woods gave a highly charged performance as "Fast-Walking Miniver," an amoral prison guard. A cynical, downbeat film that seemed to some reviewers to be an anachronistic throwback to the era of Easy Rider in the 1960s, Fast Walking later gained a following among viewers of after-midnight films on television. In 1981 he had had a small part in Eyewitness, a well-paced thriller starring William Hurt. In Videodrome (1983), a cult film directed by David Cronenberg, Woods was memorably cast as a sleazy cable-television programmer.

Woods gained an even larger cult following when he and Robert De Niro costarred in Once Upon a Time in America (1984), the sprawling, operatic gangster epic directed by Sergio Leone. Woods's "Max" and De Niro's "Noodles" were childhood friends who turned to crime on the streets of New York's Jewish Lower East Side in the 1920s and got caught up in a saga of deceit, corruption, and betrayal spanning several decades. When eighty-three minutes were cut from the version released in the United States, Once Upon a Time in America was virtually eviscerated. It failed at the box office, but over the years the film has proved to be popular in the videocassette format. Also in 1984 Woods played a shadowy and dangerous Los Angeles nightclub owner in Against All Odds, director Taylor Hackford's remake of Out of the Past, a film noir classic from the late 1940s.

Showing the full range of his abilities, Woods has from time to time sought out roles in which he has played the leading role as a sympathetic character. Although his most likable characters have been those he played in made-for-television movies, in the theatrical film Joshua Then and Now (1985) he played a successful novelist rather than a kook or a killer. Joshua Then and Now, which was adapted from an autobiographical novel by the Canadian writer Mordecai Richler, brought Woods praise for his portrayal of a self-made man who has to come to terms with his personal failings, but it fared poorly at the box office.

Directed by Oliver Stone, Salvador (1986) was the film that earned James Woods an Oscar nomination for best actor. In that harrowing motion picture, which dealt with the perfidy of United States involvement in Latin America, Woods was brilliant as Richard Boyle, a manipulative American photojournalist who finds personal redemption in the midst of moral and political squalor. As Diane K. Shah has observed, his "confidence in his own ideas [does] not make Woods the easiest actor to deal with," and his on-the-set battles with Oliver Stone were much discussed in Hollywood. Although one critic pointed out that Woods's Boyle was the "perfect vehicle" for Stone's leftist interpretation of American foreign policy, Stone feared that the actor's insistence upon Boyle's eventual moral awakening might whitewash United States intervention in Latin American politics. "We had screaming matches every day and came close to actual punchouts," Oliver Stone admitted to Diane K. Shah. "He's a lunatic. He always knows better, which is very irritating. In the end, it was like a fifteen-round fight. We were both beaten. But we both respected each other. . . . But if he's right for the role and you want to make the best film possible, you've got to go with him."

Woods won his first Emmy Award, for best supporting actor, in the made-for-television movie Promise, which was broadcast by NBC late in 1986. He played D. J., a schizophrenic who is dependent on the care of his mother and who, when she dies, is forced to adjust to living with his hitherto emotionally distant brother, movingly portrayed by James Garner. Woods has explained that he took the part of D. J. because the "quality of writing in the script was so extraordinary." In the 1987 television film In Love and War on NBC, he played a real-life hero, Commander James Stockdale, the highest-ranking American prisoner of war ever detained by the North Vietnamese, who held him captive for seven years while his wife organized other POW wives at home. For his portrayal of the title character in My Name Is Bill W., which was telecast by NBC in 1989, Woods won the Emmy Award for best actor in a miniseries or special. Once again Woods played a heroic figure from real life, the businessman who turned to drink when he was wiped out by the Great Depression but went on to become the founder of Alcoholics Anonymous. Over the years Woods made a living by taking relatively small parts in television movies. His credits include All the Way Home (1971), A Great American Tragedy (1972), The Disappearance of Aimee (1976), Billion Dollar Bubble (1976), Raid on Entebbe (1977), And Your Name Is Jonah (1979), Footsteps (1982), and Badge of the Assassin (1985). While living in New York in the early 1970s, he also appeared in the feature films Distance (1975) and Alex and the Gypsy (1976).

On the screen in the later 1980s, Woods turned in stellar performances in films like *Best Seller* (1987), in which he played a contract assassin for big corporations who engages a cop turned novelist to publish his explosive, names-naming biography. In *Cop* (1987) he played a ruthless, libidinous detective. The first film in which he played a romantic leading man with a comely leading lady (Sean Young) was *The Boost* (1989), a kind of *Days of Wine and Roses* for the cocaine generation. It was a gripping but depressing film in which Woods gave a harrowing performance as a real-estate salesman in Los Angeles who destroys his life and that of his wife because of his addiction to cocaine.

James Woods has admitted that the role of Hollywood outcast and antistudio renegade was one he played to the hilt. More recently, he has benefited from the sponsorship of Dawn Steel, an old friend of his who currently serves as head of Columbia Pictures. He has always insisted that the emergence of women executives would aid actors whose appeal lies in their talent rather than in looking like what he calls the "Van Heusen shirt man." Indeed, in 1989 Dawn Steel helped to finance *True Believer*, a moderately successful thriller in which Woods plays a hero, Eddie Dodd, a disillusioned attorney who had been a brilliant radical lawyer in the 1960s but now sells his considerable talents to drug dealers. Dodd rediscovers his ideals when he is asked to defend a Korean who is falsely accused of murder. It was hoped that *Immediate Family* (1989), a comedy-drama about a happily married couple who experience the trials of adoptive parenthood, would turn out to be the most important picture of Woods's career, since he played opposite the highly bankable actress Glenn Close, and the film was promoted as a major release by a powerful studio. But *Immediate Family* failed to work up much enthusiasm among critics, who found it to be predictable and sentimental. "Close puts herself in an emotional closet," David Denby wrote in *New York* (September 6, 1989). "She hardly even gets angry. And Woods is cast as an even-tempered veterinarian—for God's sake, James *Woods*, the most feral of actors, the great nihilist of the screen, Dr. No himself! How could he do this to us? . . . Close and Woods have nothing to say—nothing, as actors, to do."

The intensity that Woods projects on the screen extends to the way he lives. His friends describe him as a "bundle of kinetic energy" and as a man who at each waking moment is "fully engaged with life." "Watching Woods work is exhausting," Diane K. Shah wrote. "He makes movies the way some people make war. If you haven't left your blood on the screen, you haven't won the battle." In a profile of the actor for the *New York Times Magazine* (August 20, 1989), Richard B. Woodward observed that Woods's "verbal dexterity, apparent in all his films, and especially in person, allows him to argue both sides of any issue without a flicker of irony. He has the aggressive wit and insecurity of a stand-up comic; and he gives you the impression that he would tell you anything if he thought it might give

him the edge." Woods and the former Sarah Owen, who works as a rider for a horse trainer, make their home in Beverly Hills, California.

References: Esquire 101:197+ Ap '84; Gentlemen's Q 58:276+ Mr '88 pors; N Y Times II p33 D 7 '86 por; N Y Times Mag p50+ Ag 20 '89 pors; Newsday II p3 S 22 '85 pors; People 31:73+ Mr 20 '89 pors; Washington Post B p1+ D 13 '86 pors

Wright, Robert C(harles)

Apr. 23, 1943– Corporation executive. Address: National Broadcasting Company, 30 Rockefeller Plaza, New York, N.Y. 10112

When John F. Welch Jr., the chairman of the General Electric Company, announced in August 1986 that Robert C. Wright, then the president of GE Financial Services, would succeed Grant A. Tinker as the head of NBC, following GE's acquisition of the network and RCA, its parent company, NBC employees and industry observers reacted nervously to the news. The immensely popular Tinker had propelled the network to the top of the ratings, ahead of ABC and CBS, by concentrating on quality programming, while Wright, who had no experience in network television, had a reputation for being the consummate bottom-line manager. During his twelve-year career at GE, Wright made a series of astute business decisions. They included selling the housewares division to Black & Decker and turning the GE Credit Corporation into one of the foremost financial institutions in the United States by buying Kidder Peabody & Company, the investment banking firm, and by introducing innovative financial products, such as a credit line for hospital patients. Wright interrupted his career at GE in 1980 to spend three years as president of Cox Cable Communications, a cable broadcasting company, which he successfully expanded into new markets, generating increased revenues.

Since officially becoming president and chief executive officer of NBC on September 1, 1986, Wright has had to balance profit considerations with a sensitivity to the creative demands of the network's writers and producers. He originally confirmed his status as an "outsider," however, by laying off some 300 employees and issuing two memos, which were leaked to the press, that demanded budget reductions and asked employees to contribute to a proposed NBC political action committee—moves that were especially unpopular given NBC's high profitability at the time. The ensuing criticism prompted Wright to soften his approach, but he remains committed to diversification, seeking out new areas of growth for NBC outside of traditional programming, such as cable television. "NBC in the months ahead will be looking for new business opportunities, new alliances and initiatives inside and outside the broadcast industry to make us stronger," Wright has said. And as he told L. J. Davis for *Channels* (November 1986) magazine: "I want to grow the business. My objective is to strengthen us for the future."

Robert Charles Wright was born on April 23, 1943 in Hempstead, New York. His father worked at different times as an engineer, contractor, and stockbroker; his mother was a schoolteacher. An only child, he grew up on Long Island and attended Chaminade High School, a Roman Catholic boys' school. In 1965 he graduated from Holy Cross College in Worcester, Massachusetts with twin majors in history and psychology and entered the University of Virginia Law School. Three years later, he received his law degree and won admission to the Virginia and New York bars.

In 1969, following active service as a lieutenant in the United States Army reserve infantry, Wright joined General Electric as a lawyer in the plastics group, which was then headed by Welch. The next year, he resigned to accept an appointment as law clerk to Lawrence A. Whipple Jr., the chief judge of the United States District Court for New Jersey, at half the salary of his job at General Electric. At the end of his clerkship, he entered private practice in Newark, New Jersey, but he found it dull compared to his memories of General Electric. "I was like the kid in Des Moines, Iowa, who's seen the women in Paris," he later recalled to Marilyn A. Harris for *Business Week* (August 25, 1986). "I wanted to make decisions, not just write position papers," he added. In 1973 he turned down an offer of a law partnership to rejoin the General Electric plastics division in Pittsfield, Massachusetts. Over the next few years, he rose through the ranks to the posts of manager of strategic planning, general manager of the engineering plastics operation in Pittsfield, and by 1976 he had secured the title of

general sales manager for the plastics division nationwide. Under his direction, revenues in that division increased from $325 million in 1977 to $500 million in 1979. By that time, Wright had become a favorite of Welch, who was himself on a fast track to the top of the company.

In 1979 General Electric announced plans to purchase Cox Broadcasting Corporation, based in Atlanta, Georgia, pending approval by the Federal Communications Commission. Wright was named president of Cox Cable Communications, the cable television subsidiary. When the merger deal fell through the following year, Wright decided to stay with Cox, citing family considerations and Atlanta's pleasant environment. Under Wright's leadership, Cox Cable Communications became a major contender in the cable business, with the employee payroll alone increasing from 900 to 5,000. Wright personally won over local public officials to secure important franchises in four major cities, and over the next three years, the number of Cox subscribers tripled while revenues quadrupled. "We hadn't won a major franchise in years, but Bob made it seem like we couldn't lose," Arthur A. Dwyer, a cable industry executive who worked at Cox during Wright's tenure, recalled to Marilyn A. Harris in the *Business Week* story. "He could take a roomful of hostile city councilmen and turn them right around." While at Cox, Wright also launched Indax, a pioneering venture into interactive cable, through which subscribers could bank or shop from their homes. When the Cox family decided to consolidate the firm by merging the cable division into the broadcast group and passed over Wright to name William A. Schwartz as head of the newly consolidated group, Wright accepted an offer from Welch to return to General Electric in May 1983.

In his new assignment, as vice-president in charge of the housewares and electronics division, Wright supervised production of the toaster ovens, can openers, and other small appliances that had become the hallmarks of General Electric in the modern American kitchen. Dissatisfied with the low profit margin of these products, Wright convinced management to sell off the business to Black & Decker Corporation for $300 million. The audio operations were integrated into other units of the company. Although some analysts questioned the wisdom of abandoning a business that had made GE a household word, Black & Decker's subsequent difficulties with the housewares unit vindicated the sale. As Nicholas Heymann, a former GE executive, explained to L. J. Davis in the *Channels* article: "By selling to Black & Decker, Wright got small appliances' money out at book [value], and Black & Decker found that it had to shut down every one of the GE plants they'd bought, which was expensive because they're all unionized. It was a brilliant move."

In March 1984 Wright was promoted to president and chief executive officer of GE Financial Services, a GE affiliate in Stamford, Connecticut. Over the next two years, he strengthened its principal subsidiary, GE Credit Corporation (GECC), and led it into new areas of growth. Created during the 1930s to finance purchases of refrigerators, GECC, by 1984, derived only 2 percent of its revenue from financing GE products. Ninety-eight percent of its revenue stemmed from corporate, consumer, and real-estate lending. Under Wright, the subsidiary grew into the largest diversified finance company in the United States, with assets exceeding $20 billion and a ranking in the top twenty-five banks in the country, as measured by volume of loans. In 1985 GECC's return on equity reached 21.5 percent, and Moody's Investors Service raised its credit rating to AAA, the highest grade, which was unmatched by any other financial institution except J. P. Morgan and Company.

Wright introduced some precedent-setting financial products, including a line of credit of up to $5,000 to cover hospital bills that ran over the amount provided by health insurance, at an annual interest rate of approximately 18 percent. He also undertook an aggressive acquisition program that took GECC into new areas of opportunity. That program included buying Kerr Leasing and Fleet Management Services, which repairs and maintains motor vehicles; Employers Reinsurance Corporation, which reinsures other insurance companies against unexpectedly heavy property and casualty claims; and Kidder Peabody & Company, the fifteenth-largest brokerage firm in the United States and a major player in the merger and acquisition activity of the 1980s. Wright won high marks for completing the Kidder Peabody deal in a record eleven days, in a flurry of bids and counterbids that at one point had him juggling three phone calls simultaneously. Welch, by then the chairman of General Electric, noted that Wright took "a dynamic, rapidly changing business in General Electric and increased its growth rate and broadened its base through acquisitions, partnerships, team building and creative, futuristic thinking."

Wright's "creative, futuristic thinking" served him in good stead after GE agreed to purchase the RCA Corporation, including its subsidiary NBC, in December 1985 for $6.4 billion. (The Federal Communications Commission approved the merger six months later.) When Grant Tinker, the chairman of NBC, announced that he would resign to concentrate on independent television production, Welch turned to Wright as Tinker's successor. Tinker had urged Welch to choose someone already working for NBC, but Welch wanted to name his own man. Wright was named president and chief executive officer of the network, and Welch took on the title of chairman. At a press conference in New York on August 26, 1986 announcing the turnover, Wright sought to reassure those who questioned his experience in running a network and to emphasize that he shared Tinker's commitment to programming excellence. "My job is not to rebuild NBC, or fix it. It doesn't need any of that," Wright said, as quoted in the New York Daily News (August 27, 1986). "My job is to see that the momentum of quality programming and quality performance is maintained

and accelerated." Wright asserted that he had no plans to cut personnel or the network budget, as both CBS and ABC had been forced to do. "I have no resource constraints, no deadlines," Wright further stated at the press conference, as quoted in the New York Daily News story. "Our objectives are not short-term. General Electric simply wants me to take the best in the 1980s and make it better for the 1990s."

After a month on the job, however, Wright revised his position and began talking about cutbacks. He warned that in spite of NBC's lead in the ratings, multiple financial pressures threatened the future of network broadcasting. "The issues that are motivating the actions of CBS and ABC are certainly alive and well here," he told reporters at a press briefing, as quoted in the New York Times (October 2, 1986). Advertising revenues were flat, he noted, and the network continued to lose viewers to cable, movie rentals, and the growing number of independent stations. Moreover, he said, rising production costs were eating into profits. Later in October 1986, Wright asked senior managers to consider how they could trim costs by 5 percent in their departments. The request, coming at a time when the network was enjoying handsome profits from such hits as The Cosby Show and Family Ties, sparked in-house resentment, which became public when Lawrence K. Grossman, the president of NBC News, openly opposed it. In November, Wright issued a sternly worded memo upbraiding managers for showing up at meetings unprepared to defend their budgets and emphasizing the importance of eliminating duplicative operations. "I . . . have been uncomfortable when you arrive at meetings with no data to back up your positions," he said in the memo, as quoted by the New York Times (October 6, 1986). "We will not operate this business with both belt and suspenders," he further said, as reported by the same source.

A second memo from Wright, leaked to the press in December 1986, caused still more resentment among NBC employees. In it, Wright urged that NBC create a political action committee and that NBC employees contribute to it. If they refused to participate, the memo further stated, the employees should "question their own dedication to the company." Again, Lawrence K. Grossman publicly voiced his opposition, noting that "the news division's policies would preclude anybody from NBC News from participating in anything like that." The late-night talk show host David Letterman began taking semiserious swipes at Wright in his monologue, and Ralph Nader, the consumer advocate, said the creation of a network PAC would seriously undermine the credibility of the news division.

Another unpopular action was the laying off of approximately 150 employees and the inducing of another 150 employees to take early retirements. Wright emphasized that NBC's policy in the future would be to "minimize new hires" and to find ways to meet the company's needs with fewer people. Then, in early December 1986, NBC announced that it was canceling the network's only news magazine program, *1986*, because of projected savings of $10 million. Industry observers questioned the necessity for such cost-cutting measures at a time when operating profits reached an all-time high of $400 million in 1986. Wright's response revealed his typical financial prudence: "GE and Bob Wright will have failed if we wait until NBC stumbles and then try to fix it," he told Alex Taylor 3d in an interview for *Fortune* (March 16, 1987).

In just a few months, network morale had plummeted, and Wright found himself the object of sharp public criticism. "Anything I do seems to be the grounds for public complaint," Wright lamented to Tom Shales, the television critic for the *Washington Post* (December 10, 1986). One *New York Post* headline, for example, screamed: "Network Nickel & Dimed by Ex-Appliance Huckster." But Wright's biggest problem was something he had no control over: his succeeding the enormously popular Grant Tinker. "The best act to follow is a bad act," Les Brown, the publisher of *Channels* magazine, told Alex Taylor 3d in the *Fortune* story. "Wright follows a great act." Stung by all the criticism, Wright backed away from the PAC proposal, raised the news division's 1987 budget slightly, and stopped sending memos on potentially sensitive matters.

In spite of Wright's initial problems, NBC has remained on top in the ratings. With the assistance of Brandon Tartikoff, the president of NBC Entertainment, who, along with Grant Tinker, was largely responsible for turning the network around in the early 1980s, NBC aired, in 1988, the four highest-rated shows and garnered 40 percent of all network broadcast revenue and 70 percent of the profits. Still fearful of the future, however, Wright has continued to play the unenviable role of the Cassandra of the television industry. "We're in the eye of a hurricane," he told Patricia Sellers for *Fortune* (March 14, 1988). "It's my job to wear a big black coat and let people know that things are going to get rough."

In the meantime, Wright has set out to diversify the network into new areas of growth, a talent he honed at General Electric Credit Corporation. One such initiative, in 1987, was NBC's bid for the debt-ridden Turner Broadcasting System, the parent of Cable News Network. Although merger talks broke down in January 1988 over editorial control of CNN, they demonstrated Wright's seriousness about entering the cable market. He next went after Tempo Television, a cable network based in Tulsa, Oklahoma, with a reach of less than eight million households, or less than a tenth of the households serviced by NBC. In May 1988 NBC announced that it had reached an agreement to acquire Tempo and convert it into a financial news and sports channel. Because it will carry feed from the NBC news and sports divisions, production costs are expected to be minimal. As Peter Boyer observed in the *New York Times* (June 6, 1988), the Tempo deal "represents NBC's new understanding that the future of television is fragmentation, and that the key is to begin to control some of the frag-

ments, however small." Wright also held talks with the Walt Disney Company about the possibility of producing eighty sitcom episodes for the Disney Channel cable outlet, representing the first instance of a network's producing an original show for a competing broadcaster.

In another cost-cutting move, Wright considered moving the NBC television studios from their facilities at Rockefeller Center in Manhattan to New Jersey, where the company could take advantage of lower taxes. The Manhattan studios, originally designed for radio broadcasting, were adapted for television but no longer met the needs of modern communications. In December 1987 the network agreed to remain in New York and to remodel the existing facilities at Rockefeller Center in exchange for city tax abatements that will save NBC more than $72 million in real-estate taxes over the next thirty-five years, and will free NBC from paying city sales taxes on at least $1.1 billion in new machinery and equipment.

Robert C. Wright is soft-spoken and bookish-looking. He has a receding hairline and wears wire-rimmed glasses. He has been described as bright and quick-witted with a well-developed sense of humor. Business associates say that he assimilates new information quickly and delegates details to subordinates while he focuses on the big picture. GE insiders have conjectured that Wright is being groomed by Welch to one day become GE chairman. An easy manner and deft handling of those around him also characterize his management style. "Bob Wright is the kind of guy who can fire you and make you like him for it," David Van Valkenburg, who worked with Wright at Cox Communications, told L. J. Davis for the *Channels* magazine profile.

Wright enjoys swimming, boating, and playing tennis and takes great pleasure in putting his sports cars, an Austin-Healy 3000 and a Triumph TR 8, through their paces. Ironically, he claims to have no favorite television shows, although he stays abreast of NBC programs by watching tapes during the ninety-minute commute between his waterfront estate in Fairfield County, Connecticut and Manhattan. Wright married the former Suzanne Werner on August 26, 1967. They have three children: Kate, Christopher, and Maggie.

References: *Channels* 6:35+ N '86 por; *Fortune* 115:97+ Mr 16 '87 pors; *N Y Times* III p1+ My 25 '86 por; *Who's Who in America*, 1988–89

Yeltsin, Boris N(ikolayevich)

Feb. 1, 1931– Soviet politician. Address: The Kremlin, Moscow, USSR

Not many years ago, only a handful of Westerners would have displayed any interest in the rise and fall of a first secretary of the Moscow City Commu-

Boris N. Yeltsin

nist Party Committee. The fact that the fate of Boris Yeltsin, an occupant of that post, was followed so intently in the West and debated so heatedly and openly within the Soviet Union itself testifies to the changes wrought by the Communist party leader, Mikhail Gorbachev, and his policy of *glasnost* ("openness"). Yeltsin's case, however, is considered by many observers to be a bitter irony: a supporter of *glasnost* and *perestroika* (economic "restructuring"), he was punished for wanting to take Gorbachev's policies too far and too fast. Although he was demoted and publicly admonished, Yeltsin has continued to enjoy wide popular support, among Muscovites in particular. In March 1989 he was elected to the Congress of People's Deputies as an at-large member for Moscow.

Boris Nikolayevich Yeltsin was born on February 1, 1931 in Sverdlovsk, an industrial city in the Ural Mountain region of European Russia. He was, in his words, a "little bit of a hooligan" as a boy. When he was eleven, he and two friends sneaked into a weapons warehouse and stole two hand grenades. "When we started to disassemble them, one of the grenades exploded," he told David Remnick in an interview for the *Washington Post* (May 21, 1989). Yeltsin lost the thumb and forefinger of his left hand in the accident. Trained as an engineer at the Urals M. Kirov Polytechnic Institute, he worked at various construction projects from 1955 to 1968. He was thirty years old when he joined the Communist party, in 1961, at the height of Nikita S. Khrushchev's anti-Stalinist reforms, and from 1968 on he engaged in work for the party. In 1976 he was appointed first secretary of the Sverdlovsk District Central Committee, and over the next several years, he gained a reputation as an energetic, charismatic reformer. In July 1985 the new general sec-

retary of the Communist party, Mikhail Gorbachev, brought Yeltsin to Moscow, as secretary of the Central Committee for Construction. When Yeltsin was promoted to first secretary of the Moscow City Party Committee in December 1985, he took over a post with responsibilities somewhat akin to those of an American mayor, with a clear mandate to reform the city bureaucracy, still rife with corruption from the previous administration of Viktor Grishin. In March 1986 he gained the status of a candidate (nonvoting) member of the Politburo, the Communist party's inner decision-making body.

Wasting no time in asserting his new authority, Yeltsin clearly aligned himself with Gorbachev's reform wing of the Communist party and against the old guard. At the Twenty-seventh Party Congress, in February 1986, Yeltsin shocked party insiders, long accustomed to fulsome speeches of self-congratulation, when he took himself to task for his inaction and hypocrisy during the Brezhnev years. In a speech that he delivered to the Moscow City Party Committee later in the month, he advocated "pull[ing] out the roots of bureaucracy, social injustice, and abuses." Practicing what he preached, in April 1986 he announced the arrests of hundreds of corrupt trade officials and publicly castigated several city bureaucrats by name. "Moscow TV and radio programs are of no interest to Muscovites," he announced in another speech. "Muscovites—workers in particular—are straightforward folk," he told an interviewer for *Moskovskaya Pravda*, the Moscow party newspaper. "They call a spade a spade. And sometimes I feel ashamed and embarrassed in front of them because we officials could have done more, but we haven't."

Targeting for criticism the party bureaucrats who reveled in perquisites and privileges, such as shopping at special stores and riding around in chauffeur-driven cars, Yeltsin advocated the abolition of such special privileges and stressed that self-sacrifice rather than self-aggrandizement had to become the standard for party workers. He himself took to riding the city's buses and subways, talking to agitated commuters about the problems of the transport system. He began unannounced visits to city factories and stores, appraising their performance and noting what goods were in short supply. He gained great popular support when, early on in his tenure, he ensured that fresh vegetables would reach the capital by cutting through layers of middlemen and bureaucracy that had previously resulted in produce rotting in warehouses.

Yeltsin tried to beautify and personalize the city by encouraging street cafés and colorful fruit stalls. He formed an urban planning council, with a mandate to preserve historical buildings and restore architectural monuments, guided by his vision of a vibrant city, livable in the present and in tune with its past. Like the mayors of great urban centers everywhere, Yeltsin had to confront problems of overpopulation and housing shortages, crime, alcoholism, drug addiction, inferior education, and un-employment. What made his undertaking so different was that it involved a battle with the en-trenched party machinery, the dislodging of self-satisfied bureaucrats, and the unprecedented fir-ing of people who had considered their jobs and privileges an unalterable part of ideology and life.

Not surprisingly, Yeltsin made enemies, just as Gorbachev himself encountered resistance to his *glasnost* and *perestroika*. Nor did it help matters that Yeltsin was impatient and temperamental, pugnacious and undiplomatic. Even as he pressed for greater democratization in Moscow and in the entire Soviet Union, his subordinates considered him authoritarian, undemocratic, and difficult to work with, but even his critics had to concede that he was hard-working and incorruptible.

On October 21, 1987 the Communist Party Cen-tral Committee met to hear Gorbachev outline the speech that he intended to deliver publicly at the seventieth anniversary celebration of the Russian Revolution. The session was held behind closed doors, as was customary, but because of the ex-traordinary happenings, accounts of the meeting leaked, first to the Western press and then to the Soviet public. According to a reconstruction of the session by Seweryn Bialer in *U.S. News & World Report* (March 28, 1988) that was based on inter-views conducted in Moscow, Gorbachev had dis-tributed a fifteen-page outline of his speech in advance of the meeting, and the agreed-upon ground rules of the session stipulated that there would be no comments or questions following Gor-bachev's address. But when Gorbachev had fin-ished speaking, Yeltsin suddenly requested the right to the floor. At first Gorbachev hesitated, but then granted Yeltsin permission to speak.

To a stunned audience, a nervous Yeltsin said that he had submitted a letter of resignation from both his Moscow Committee and Politburo posts. *Perestroika*, he said, was proceeding too slowly; it had given virtually nothing to the people. He criti-cized the lackadaisical party leadership, singling out in particular Yegor Ligachev, the number-two man in the party hierarchy, whom he accused of adhering to old methods of leadership. Yeltsin con-tended that Ligachev was sabotaging his attempts to improve living conditions for the people of Mos-cow.

Bialer's account fails to mention any direct criti-cism by Yeltsin of Gorbachev himself, but early ac-counts in the Western press, in late October, centered on Yeltsin's reported accusation that Gor-bachev was fostering a cult of personality that threatened to undermine the very programs he was striving to achieve. According to Bialer's recon-struction, when Yeltsin had finished speaking, Gorbachev opened the floor for others to respond. After a short period of silence, Ligachev countered, denying Yeltsin's accusations. Emboldened by Lig-achev, twenty-two other party members followed in turn, denouncing Yeltsin and reproaching him for grandstanding. Yeltsin rebutted, standing by his charges against Ligachev but denying that he was

threatening party unity or Gorbachev's integrity. Then Gorbachev reprimanded Yeltsin for his "petty-bourgeois outburst" and disclosed that this was not the first time that Yeltsin's impatience had led to an uncalled-for confrontation. The Politburo had previously cautioned Yeltsin about his head-strong ways. He had submitted a letter of resigna-tion once before, in August, but had agreed to defer the matter until after the anniversary celebrations. Bitterly castigating Yeltsin for not sticking to that agreement, Gorbachev labeled as "political adventurism" Yeltsin's appeal for accelerating the pace of *perestroika*.

Muscovites first learned of the "Yeltsin affair" from foreign journalists and news sources, for the domestic media were muzzled until after the anni-versary observances. Consequently, rumors abounded. On November 11, Soviet television an-nounced that the Moscow Party Committee had met on that day, with Gorbachev in attendance, and stripped Yeltsin of his post as first secretary. On November 13, *Pravda* printed a three-page spread about the November 11 party meeting, in which Gorbachev assessed Yeltsin's October 21 speech as "politically immature, extremely confus-ing, and contradictory" and accused Yeltsin of put-ting his personal ambitions before the interests of the party. Yeltsin, who had been hospitalized on November 8 for heart problems and who was brought directly to the meeting from the hospital, "confessed" to his party comrades that "ambition" had indeed gotten the better of him. "I am guilty before the Moscow city party organization, Mos-cow City Party Committee, before you, and, of course, I am very guilty before Mikhail Ser-geyevich Gorbachev," he was reported to have said.

Yeltsin's abject confession, as widely reported in the Soviet media, had a chilling effect on many staunch supporters of Gorbachev's *glasnost*. The fact that the full proceedings of the November 11 meeting were released, but not Yeltsin's October 21 speech of accusation, led many to question the openness of "openness." Even corrupt party offi-cials had not been subject to the type of humilia-tion meted out to Yeltsin. Many writers and other intellectuals conjured up images of the Stalinist show trials of the 1930s and their similar degrading expressions of contrition. No one expected Yeltsin to be sent to a prison camp or placed before a firing squad, but the parallels were eerie, nonetheless.

Most Western political analysts interpreted Yeltsin's firing as a victory for party conservatives over Gorbachev's reform wing. Although Gorba-chev had joined in the chorus of denunciation, it was *glasnost* itself that seemed to have suffered a harsh blow. After all, as one of Gorbachev's most ardent promoters, Yeltsin had been trying to do for Moscow what Gorbachev had outlined as his goals for the Soviet Union: eliminate corruption, stream-line the bureaucracy, modernize services, and re-organize production and distribution. Gorbachev was forced into the position of disciplining Yelt-sin's hot-headedness, but as he himself said in an exchange with Soviet editors in January 1988, the "party's rebuff [of Yeltsin] was viewed by a certain part of the intelligentsia, especially young people, as a blow to perestroika."

Reports of the November 11 party meeting put a damper on the Soviet public's belief in Gorbachev's commitment to glasnost, and the strong popular support for Yeltsin manifested itself in hitherto unheard-of demonstrations of protest. On November 17, several hundred students rallied at Moscow State University, demanding the publication of the text of Yeltsin's October 21 speech to the Central Committee. Police broke up a meeting of the "Club of Social Initiatives," assembled in a Moscow factory to debate the Yeltsin affair. At the November 15 "Moscow Forum," sponsored by the reform-minded magazine Ogonyok, several thousand people crowded in, asking why Yeltsin's October speech had never been published and "why," in the words of one participant, "Yeltsin, who until an hour ago was a leader of perestroika, turned by some secret accountings of the authorities into an enemy more wicked than those who for years brought shame to the country?"

Writing from Moscow for the New York Times (November 13, 1987), Francis X. Clines reported an atmosphere "close to political mourning" amongst Muscovites. People spoke freely to him, although anonymously, of their heartfelt esteem for Boris Yeltsin. "He would go to the people and listen" was a typical comment. Nor were the expressions of protest confined to Moscow, for demonstrations were held in Leningrad and Sverdlovsk as well. Authorities became so concerned about those manifestations of solidarity that notices were posted at all post offices in Yeltsin's hometown of Sverdlovsk to the effect that "communications of any kind for B. N. Yeltsin will not be delivered." Yeltsin, who returned to the hospital immediately following the November 11 meeting, was dismissed from his Politburo post in early 1988 and received a new assignment as first deputy chairman for state construction—a demotion but not a banishment to the provinces. In a reconciliatory gesture from the party leadership, he was retained on the party's Central Committee.

The fact that Yeltsin's October 21 speech remained unpublished continued to supply grist for the rumor mill. Several purported versions of the speech circulated underground in Moscow and Leningrad. One widely disseminated version, obtained by Le Monde in Paris, had Yeltsin criticizing the privileges of his fellow party bureaucrats as follows: "It's hard for me to explain to the factory worker why, in the seventieth year of his political power, he is obliged to line up for sausages in which there is more starch than meat, while on our tables there is sturgeon, caviar, and all sorts of delicacies." Soviet officials denied that the Le Monde text was accurate, but Lev Timofeyev, a Soviet intellectual and the editor of the unofficial journal Referendum, pointed out that Yeltsin's October 21 speech had already passed into the realm of "folklore." "It doesn't matter so much whether

Yeltsin said these things," Timofeyev was quoted as saying in the Washington Post (February 13, 1988). "What matters is that Soviets want someone to have said them."

The German-language edition of the Russian paper Moscow News published in its inaugural issue of May 1988 an interview with Yeltsin that was conducted by the Soviet journalist Mikhail Poltoranin. The first Soviet report quoting Yeltsin since his ouster, it was remarkably free of the spirit of remorse and contrition that he had expressed in his "confession" of November 11, 1987. "I belong to those who are prepared to take the route with potholes, and have no fear of the risks," Yeltsin was quoted as saying. Yeltsin branded as forgeries some of the versions of his controversial speech of October 21, 1987 that were circulating in Russia and translated and published abroad, but he refused to give a full account of what he had said, explaining, "I don't want to talk about something I said a half-year ago. I could make a mistake." But, emphasizing the consistency of his position, he added, "I spoke out honestly and directly and said what I felt and thought was right."

In early May of 1988 Yeltsin was quoted in a mass-circulation publication within the Soviet Union called Stroitelnaya Gazeta, a daily publication of the construction industry. In it, Yeltsin both appealed to workers to help achieve perestroika and, at the same time, cautioned the party leadership on the importance of fulfilling the hopes and expectations of the people. Interviews that Yeltsin had conducted with the Novosti press agency and the journal Ogonyok were, however, not published, and in frustration Yeltsin took his case to the foreign media. In the midst of the Reagan-Gorbachev summit in Moscow, in late May of 1988, Yeltsin spoke to reporters of the BBC, once more assailing Ligachev as an opponent of reform. Although the translation of Yeltsin's remarks into English had him calling for Ligachev's dismissal, Yeltsin later denied that he had ever suggested Ligachev's resignation. Caught off-guard and in the full glare of the summit spotlight, Gorbachev said he would make no comment until he had read the full text of Yeltsin's remarks, but he denied that there was any problem with Ligachev.

Yeltsin's penchant for dramatic public outbursts expressed itself in full force at the long-anticipated, well-publicized Nineteenth All-Union Conference of the Communist Party of the Soviet Union, which was held in Moscow during the last week of June 1988. Five thousand delegates from all over the Soviet Union attended the conference, which was historic in the openness of its delegate selection, of its conference debate, and of its media coverage. As Mikhail Gorbachev's show, it was virtually a referendum on glasnost and perestroika. On July 1, the last day of the conference proceedings, Yeltsin took the floor and made an emotional speech. Beginning with attacks on party corruption and privilege, he ended by appealing for his own political rehabilitation: "Rehabilitation after fifty years has now become habitual. . . . But I am asking for political rehabilitation while I am still alive."

Unrepentant, Yeltsin stated, in his publicly televised address, that the only mistake he had made in his October 21 Central Committee speech was one of timing, "before the celebration of the seventieth anniversary of the revolution." It soon became clear, however, that Gorbachev did not share Yeltsin's view of the affair, for in his closing address he denounced Yeltsin for both his emotionalism and his political mistakes. Obviously, the request for rehabilitation had been denied.

Early in 1989 neighborhood organizations in Moscow nominated Yeltsin for the city's at-large seat in the upcoming election for the Congress of People's Deputies. Casting himself as a populist candidate, Yeltsin attracted widespread support in the form of large, apparently spontaneous public demonstrations. At campaign rallies, he repeatedly called for greater political pluralism but denied that he was attempting to undermine Gorbachev. Two weeks before the election, in what some observers saw as an effort to discredit Yeltsin, the Communist party released to the press an official transcript of the Central Committee meeting on October 21, 1987 that had led to Yeltsin's dismissal from the Politburo. Repudiating Yevgeny A. Brakow, the candidate backed by the party, voters gave Yeltsin a landslide victory in the election on March 26, 1989, awarding him 89 percent of the votes.

When the Congress of People's Deputies convened, before live television cameras, late in May, Yeltsin was at first excluded from the 542-seat Supreme Soviet, but after two days of demonstrations in the streets of Moscow, he was named to the new legislature after a fellow reformist, Aleksei I. Kazannik, prevented a potential crisis by stepping down in Yeltsin's favor. Two weeks later the Supreme Soviet approved Yeltsin as head of its committee on construction and architecture. In that post, Yeltsin has argued for trimming the country's estimated $170 billion budget deficit by slicing large capital investments, even those proposed by foreign companies. "Any foreign company that plans a big project involving a lot of construction will have to come before our committee," he said, as quoted in *Business Week* (July 17, 1989).

In September 1989, shortly after he was chosen as the leader of the dissident legislators' opposition caucus, Yeltsin toured the United States, giving speeches—at about $25,000 a lecture, according to the *New York Times* (September 9, 1989)—on Soviet democracy in several major cities and meeting with American economic and business leaders, members of Congress, and, briefly, President George Bush, Vice-President Dan Quayle, and Secretary of State James A. Baker 3d. In his speeches and in interviews with the press, Yeltsin described the Soviet Union as being in a crisis and warned, as quoted in *Newsweek* (September 25, 1989), that Gorbachev had "not more than one year and probably about six months" to get his reform program moving. During his eight-day visit to the

United States, *Pravda* reprinted in full an article from the Italian newspaper *La Repubblica* that portrayed Yeltsin as a drunkard who spent most of his lecture fees on liquor, video equipment, and clothing. Following considerable criticism from skeptical readers and from the weekly *Moscow News*, *Pravda* published a formal apology to Yeltsin.

Six feet tall, broad-shouldered, and with a shock of white hair, Yeltsin is an imposing presence who radiates energy and forcefulness. As is so often the case with Soviet functionaries, little is known about his personal life, although he is said to be married. It is also reported that he is a workaholic who manages to get by on four hours of sleep a night. When he arises, usually at 5:00 A.M., he reads for about two hours—most often books by contemporary authors who, in his words, "have public resonance," among them Anatoly Rybakov, Gavril Popov, and even Aleksandr Solzhenitsyn—then does his morning exercises before heading off to work. In expressing his credo, Yeltsin once said: "Above all, I admire honesty, principle, and character. Correspondingly, I hate dishonesty and toadyism."

References: London Observer p13 Mr 26 '89; Maclean's 100:21 N 23 '87 por; Manchester Guardian W p9 F 26 '89; N Y Times A p3 N 23 '87; New Statesman 112:11+ N 7 '86; Time 133:44+ Mr 20 '89 por; U S News 102:29+ Je 29 '87 por, 104:30+ Mr 28 '88 por; Washington Post C p1+ F 18 '89 pors, A p1+ My 20 '89; International Who's Who, 1989–90

Young, Frank E(dward)

Sept. 1, 1931– Physician; microbiologist; health administrator. Address: c/o Dept. of Health and Human Services, 200 Independence Ave., S.W., Washington, D.C. 20201

BULLETIN: On November 13, 1989 Louis W. Sullivan, the secretary of health and human services, announced that Frank E. Young had accepted a new post as deputy assistant secretary of health for health science and environment.

As the commissioner of the United States Food and Drug Administration, Frank E. Young heads the federal agency that regulates not only foods and drugs but also radiological and medical devices, vaccines, and even cosmetics. More than 7,000 employees come under his supervision in administering an agency monitoring a $570 billion industry that accounts for twenty-five cents of every dollar spent in the United States. Under the 1938 Food, Drug, and Cosmetic Act, as amended in 1962, the FDA is responsible for determining the safety and effectiveness of all new drugs.

Frank E. Young

In his five years at the helm of the FDA, a tenure far longer than that of most of his predecessors, Young has had the satisfaction of announcing approval of a number of new drugs and vaccines, including some created by the genetic engineering techniques that he helped to develop as a practicing microbiologist. But his tenure in office has come to be best known for the persistent quest for effective drugs or vaccines to combat AIDS, the invariably fatal disease that destroys the body's immune system, leaving the victim vulnerable to opportunistic cancers and infections. Although his agency does not create drugs, the FDA has been blamed by activist groups like the Gay and Lesbian Health Foundation for the long period of time it takes to test and approve a potentially effective drug. At his request, Congress has given the FDA permission to allow doctors to prescribe certain drugs still being tested, but Young has cautioned that the prospects for an effective AIDS drug or vaccine in the near future are "very slim."

Frank Edward Young was born in Mineola, Long Island, New York on September 1, 1931, the son of Frank Edward and Erma Frances (Holmes) Young. He attended Union College in Schenectady, New York for his undergraduate work and received his medical degree in 1956 from the State University of New York's Upstate Medical Center in Syracuse. After graduation, he interned at the University Hospitals in Cleveland, Ohio, where he eventually became a resident pathologist. At the same time, he undertook graduate studies in microbiology at Western Reserve University (now Case Western Reserve University) in Cleveland. He received his Ph.D. degree in 1962 and joined the faculty at Western Reserve in the same year.

In 1965 Young joined the Scripps Clinic and Research Foundation in La Jolla, California as an associate member of the departments of microbiology and pathology. He also joined the University of California at San Diego faculty in 1967 as an associate professor. In 1970 he became chairman of the microbiology department and professor of microbiology, pathology, and radiation biology and biophysics at the School of Medicine and Dentistry at the University of Rochester in Rochester, New York. He was also director of the clinical microbiology laboratories at the university's Strong Memorial Hospital, where he became microbiologist in chief in 1976, and of the laboratories of Monroe County's health department.

Young's concerns focused on the fundamental genetics of bacteria, including the mechanism of deoxyribonucleic and mediated transformation of bacterial cells, the regulation of bacterial cell surfaces, the pathobiology of *Neisseria gonorrhoeae*, and the genetics of *Bacillus subtilis*. He published more than 150 scientific articles on his research, including development of some of the earliest cloning enzymes, vectors, and vehicles.

In 1979 Young became dean of the School of Medicine and Dentistry at the University of Rochester and director of the Medical Center. Two years later he was appointed vice-president for health affairs, a position that extended his administrative responsibilities to the university hospital and nursing school. Young is credited with having made the deficit-ridden hospital profitable by revamping its billing and computer system, but it was widely rumored that, by the time he was asked to assume the FDA post, a university review committee was about to oust him as dean because of dissatisfaction with his management style. Specifically, he was in trouble for firing too many people, for, according to one of his aides, he had pruned a lot of deadwood at the hospital.

Because he had virtually no Washington experience, Young was not among the initial contenders for the FDA position. It remains a mystery as to just who nominated him, and Young has professed not to know himself, explaining, "It wouldn't have been polite to ask." He was named commissioner on May 9, 1984 and assumed the post on July 15. On taking office, Young divided his time into three main areas: reviewing the management of the agency, establishing ties with various groups in Washington, and developing a policy statement on the agency's role in regulating the products of biotechnology. Making himself as accessible as possible, he addressed fifty outside groups in his first six months in office and prompted one FDA official to comment, "He goes night and day. He's a whirlwind." But others found him uninformed and needlessly combative. Young, who joined the Public Health Service's commissioned corps when he came to Washington, aroused some resentment by wearing his white, military-style uniform every Wednesday and, on one occasion, by flashing his commissioner's badge to make a point.

Soon after taking office, Young indicated that the FDA had been remiss, under his predecessor, in not preventing the marketing of a Vitamin E solution that had been linked to the deaths of thirty-eight infants. He wrote Congressman Ted Weiss, a Democrat from New York, that "in retrospect, we believe that the . . . episode points out that our enforcement policy . . . needs significant revision as it pertains to newly marketed products." But Young declined to bar the sale of unpasteurized milk, though he acknowledged that it presented a public health problem, on the grounds that it was a matter best handled by the states rather than by the federal government—a decision that was criticized by the Health Research Group, a consumer organization associated with Ralph Nader. Young also resisted a proposed ban on sulfites in food, which are widely used by restaurants to keep food looking fresh, though his agency had linked sulfites to at least five deaths from allergic reactions. Once again, he took the position that any action would be best left to the states. In June 1986 the FDA banned the use of sulfite preservatives in fresh fruits and vegetables, excepting potatoes.

In a new interpretation of food safety laws, Young said in June 1985 that the FDA did not have an absolute legal obligation to ban food additives found to cause cancer in animals. He said that his interpretation of the relevant Delaney clause, attached in 1960 to the Food, Drug, and Cosmetic Act, would allow the agency to approve additives if they posed only a small cancer risk, though that amendment had previously been understood as an absolute ban on substances found to cause cancer in test animals. He rejected a petition by the Public Interest Research Group, founded by Ralph Nader, which had urged a ban on ten widely used food, drug, and cosmetic dyes that had been linked to cancer in laboratory animals. It was, by one count, the twenty-seventh time in twenty-five years that a decision to ban those color additives had been postponed. In October 1987 a federal appeals court ruled that under the Delaney clause no cancer risk whatsoever can be permitted.

But those noninterventionist policies were not necessarily in keeping with Young's own inclinations. According to Business Week (June 17, 1985), political appointees at the Department of Health and Human Services (of which the FDA is a constituent agency) and the Office of Management and Budget were calling the shots on FDA policy, and the agency had lost more than 900 career employees because of morale problems. The conservative Heritage Foundation and the pharmaceutical industry would like to eliminate the 1962 amendments to the Food, Drug and Cosmetic Act, repealing the FDA's authority to review drug efficacy.

On June 19, 1986 Young announced approval of a product designed to help patients who have received kidney transplants to overcome problems that often cause those kidneys to fail or to be rejected by the body. It was the first therapeutic use inside the human body approved by the FDA for the monoclonal antibody technique, which employs an antibody of the immune system to manufacture medically useful products. The technique has been described as one of the most important technical advances in modern biology and could, in principle, be used to overcome the rejection of other transplanted organs.

A month later Young announced the approval of the first genetically engineered vaccine cleared for human use, to prevent hepatitis B infections. He told a news briefing on July 23, 1986 that the procedure "opens up a new era of vaccine prevention. . . . The principle, this type of technique, should be able to be extended to any parasite." By contrast, the old vaccine for hepatitis B was derived from blood plasma, with the possibility that the blood donors might be intravenous drug abusers at high risk of carrying the AIDS virus.

Of particular satisfaction to Young was the approval, on November 13, 1987, of a gene-spliced version of the body's natural clot dissolver, tissue plasminogen activator (TPA), which was being marketed under the brand name of Activase. According to Young, by administering that drug to heart-attack victims within three hours of the initial onset of pain, the damage to the heart that normally accompanies a heart attack could be markedly reduced. Young's gratification in the approval of Activase could be attributed to the fact that his father had died of a heart attack at the age of forty-five.

As a microbiologist formerly engaged in gene splicing and other recombinant deoxyribonucleic acid (DNA) techniques that involve the manipulation of an organism's genetic material, Young is a champion of biotechnology and a firm believer that new regulations are not needed in employing those techniques. "The products of biotechnology are fundamentally similar to those produced by conventional techniques, and they are adequately controlled by existing regulations," he wrote in an article for the Saturday Evening Post (October 1988). Referring to earlier alarms sounded over unintended or unanticipated harm from genetic engineering experiments, he declared: "I believe many of these fears have been greatly exaggerated. . . . The precise techniques of biotechnology in many ways ensure that its products are even safer than those produced through conventional methods."

Another of Young's prime objectives has been to reduce the time lag between the initial development of a drug and its approval by the FDA for general use. The agency cleared thirty new drugs in 1985—a record, according to Young—compared to fourteen in 1983 and twenty-two in 1984. Those approvals, he said, "represent therapeutic advances over existing drugs—another record." In 1988 he contended that the average interval between drug development and FDA approval had been reduced from 11.3 years to 7.5 years, with the FDA's review time averaging only about two years. (Disputing that estimate, the drug industry reckons the total time at ten years and the FDA's review time at thirty months.) In either case, of 100 drugs that enter clinical testing, only twenty are approved.

To critics of the FDA, including the drug companies, the expedited process is still far too long. Representatives of the drug industry say that overly stringent review requirements stretch their testing time out to 5.5 or more years, and they hold the FDA's bureaucratic procedures responsible for the fact that an application to the agency for drug approval may carry as many as 100,000 pages of documentation. With the alarming spread of AIDS, the drug companies found new support for their contention that the FDA had been placing too much emphasis on protecting against unsafe new drugs and not enough emphasis on clearing beneficial new drugs for clinical use as soon as possible.

In March 1987 Young announced that, instead of waiting for researchers to come to the FDA with their results and proposals, the agency had begun contacting drug companies and medical centers in order to keep abreast of their plans. He added that, for the first time in the FDA's history, agency scientists were themselves performing laboratory experiments. Young told the press that tests of AIDS vaccines on human subjects might begin by the end of the summer, though he cautioned that the prospects of a licensed AIDS vaccine in the immediate future seemed "very slim." The first such vaccine, cultured from an insect cell, was approved for testing on August 18, 1987, and the second, made from the virus from which smallpox vaccine is manufactured, was approved three months later, on November 25.

Also in the month of March 1987, the FDA approved azidothymidine, or AZT, for prescription sales, marking the first time that a drug to fight AIDS had been licensed for sale in the United States. The approval came as a result of collaboration among the National Institutes of Health, the FDA, and Burroughs Wellcome Company, which had synthesized the drug as far back as 1964 as a potential cancer treatment but had considered its antiviral properties too toxic for human use. The FDA cut short the testing process in order to make it an experimental treatment for patients with a history of pneumocystis carinii pneumonia, the most common AIDS infection and the leading cause of death for AIDS patients, and it granted Burroughs Wellcome a license to manufacture AZT in 107 days, compared to the usual thirty months. From the time that AZT's effectiveness was first demonstrated in a government laboratory, it took only two years for the drug to become available in drugstores, a time frame that Young has called the "irreducible minimum."

Nevertheless, AIDS victims and their supporters blamed the FDA for the delay in reaching the marketplace of other potentially effective drugs. At a demonstration in New York City in the spring of 1987, angry participants carried signs declaring, "Hey Young—We Want to Grow Old," and the crowd hanged him in effigy from a makeshift scaffold on Wall Street. Despite such incidents, the FDA commissioner has remained accessible. While addressing an AIDS forum sponsored by the Gay and Lesbian Health Foundation in 1988, for example, he persevered in making his speech despite being booed by the audience and forced to witness a "die-in" by AIDS patients. In a Saturday Evening Post (January–February 1989) interview, he told Cory SerVass, "I've been through the experience of literally having people dying before my eyes while they're waiting for medicine to be approved that could save them." Responding to widespread demands, he proposed to Congress in March 1987 that the FDA formally receive the discretionary authority it had used to clear AZT. Shortly after that, regulations went into effect that made it easier for the agency to authorize the experimental use of other new drugs for the desperately ill.

By mid-1988 the FDA had released five experimental drugs to fight life-threatening or serious diseases before all trials of their effectiveness had been completed. Only one was AIDS-related— trimetrexate—which, like AZT, is used to treat AIDS patients with pneumocystis carinii pneumonia. Like AZT, trimetrexate does not cure AIDS, but it does prolong survival and reduce suffering. The meager results of the program's first year— and the distribution of trimetrexate under such tight restrictions that only eighty-nine patients received it—induced advocates of AIDS patients to call it a "sham," a "big lie," and a "public relations exercise." Replying to his critics, Young said: "We can't approve something that isn't there. I think we'll see a substantial number of drugs coming through for AIDS in the future."

In order to still the growing clamor for experimental AIDS drugs, Young announced on July 23, 1988 that the FDA would allow Americans to import unapproved drugs from abroad in small quantities and would permit routine mail shipments of such drugs. The FDA is supposed to try to block the sale of unproved remedies in order to protect the public against fraudulent or unsafe products, but it had been looking the other way while thousands of AIDS patients brought back from Mexico unapproved drugs, such as ribavirin and isoprinosine.

After taking so much heat from AIDS patients and caregivers, Young struck out at academic scientific researchers in June 1988, contending that he had repeatedly asked them to give two years to the FDA to help evaluate applications for potential AIDS drugs and vaccines with no loss in pay. Comparing the gravity and urgency of the struggle against AIDS to World War II, he said that the FDA had 162 applications for AIDS drugs and vaccines pending, but, he charged, researchers preferred to get rich on grant money rather than volunteer their services to his agency.

On October 19, 1988 Young announced a plan calling for the FDA to work more closely with drug developers so that the agency could speed the approval process for substances aimed at life-threatening or severely debilitating diseases. He said that the new procedure could reduce the time it takes to clear promising drugs by a third to a half of the normal time needed for approval. For those special drugs, the FDA said it would merge two stages of the traditional three-step human testing process.

Sometimes forgotten by the public in its concern with AIDS is the continuing need to protect the nation's food supply. Although Young has warned of an "explosion" of disease caused by food-borne microorganisms, he believes that an obsessive fear of chemicals has obscured "the low and decreasing risks associated with both natural and manmade pesticides." The FDA must also stand guard against episodes or threats of deliberate poisoning. Three Americans were killed by cyanide-laced capsules of over-the-counter painkillers in 1986, and, in March 1989, the FDA quarantined all fruit from Chile for several days after it discovered two grapes contaminated with nonlethal amounts of cyanide. Dismissing criticism from fruit importers and Chilean farmers who contended that the agency had panicked, Young said: "I don't think we overreacted. I think the American people have a right to know."

Shortly after the Chilean episode, scandal rocked the FDA generic drug division. By the end of July 1989, three of the thirty staff members who review applications for approval to make and sell generic drugs had pleaded guilty to accepting illegal payments of thousands of dollars from drug companies, and two more were said to be under investigation. Agency officials, who ordered special plant inspections of eleven drug manufacturers, were worried that the manufacturers might have compromised the safety and effectiveness of a variety of medicines that are low-cost chemical copies of brand-name pharmaceuticals. Critics of the FDA say it brought those problems on itself by cutting back on enforcement during the Reagan administration, especially after it shifted its resources from policing the industry to approving new drugs. Testifying before a House of Representatives subcommittee on July 11, 1989, Young said he was "embarrassed and ashamed" about the revelations of misconduct and was willing to call a six-month halt to generic drug approvals, if need be, to correct the situation. His characteristically religious response to the current FDA crisis was to seek consolation in the Bible. Quoting from one of St. Paul's Epistles to the Romans, he said, "All have sinned and fallen short of the glory of God." Meanwhile, the Justice Department and Congress were looking into further violations.

On August 18, 1989 Dr. Louis W. Sullivan, the secretary of health and human services, announced that inspections would be expanded and administrative reforms would be instituted in the regulation of generic drugs. He promised that he would ask Congress for the authority to impose severer penalties on companies indulging in fraud and bribery. Although he made it clear that no evidence has been found that "the safety or effectiveness of generic drugs had been compromised," he said that the time had come "to deal decisively with corrupt and fraudulent practices."

On September 28, 1989 the FDA announced that it would allow an experimental AIDS drug, dideoxyinosine, or DDI, to be distributed widely while tests on the drug continued. DDI not only helps to stop the multiplication of the AIDS virus in the body, but its side effects are also less severe than those produced by AZT. The drug was given to 2,600 people in clinical trials and distributed to doctors who have patients unable to tolerate the side effects of AZT.

Frank E. Young is a stocky, bespectacled man with receding, graying hair. His deep religious faith has helped him to cope with medical crises in his own family, including a malignant melanoma removed from behind his ear in 1984 and the temporary paralysis of one of his sons, caused by a wrestling accident. Young met his wife, the former Leanne Hutchinson, a nurse, while serving a clerkship in medical school. They were married on October 26, 1956 and are the parents of five children: Lorrie, Debora, Peggy, Frank, and Jonathan. In his rare moments of leisure, Young does volunteer work for Love in Action, a group that recruits persons who help the victims of AIDS.

The commissioner of the Food and Drug Administration is a member of the Institute of Medicine of the National Academy of Sciences, the American Association for the Advancement of Science, the American Society of Microbiology, the American Academy of Microbiology, the American Society of Biological Chemists, the Infectious Diseases Society, and Sigma Xi. He holds honorary degrees from Roberts Wesleyan College, Houghton College, the State University of New York, and Long Island University.

References: Barron's 64:13+ Je 4 '84 por; Chicago Tribune X p11+ S 25 '88 por; N Y Times C p1+ Jl 5 '88 por; Sat Eve Post 260:14+ O '88 por, 261:50+ Ja-F '89 pors; Science 227:277+ Ja 18 '85 por; U S News 97:40+ D 3 '84 por; American Men and Women of Science (1986); Who's Who in America, 1984-85

Photo Credits

Waring Abbott/© *1989 Sire Records Company,* Lou Reed; *Andrea Jaffe, Inc.,* James Woods; *AP/Wide World Photos,* Moshe Arens, Anita Baker, Roseanne Barr, Princess Caroline of Monaco, Richard G. Darman, Clint Eastwood, Fang Lizhi, Bill Forsyth, Charles Fuller, Tom Hanks, Florence Griffith Joyner, David Lean, Greg LeMond, Patti LuPone, Naguib Mahfouz, John S. McCain, Rue McClanahan, Carlos Saúl Menem, George J. Mitchell, Rosa Parks, Hashemi Rafsanjani, Mieczyslaw Rakowski, Keith Richards, Garry Shandling, Neil Simon, Phil Spector; Isaac Stern, Hans Heinrich Thyssen-Bornemisza de Kaszon, Robert Towne, Charles Trenet, James Watkins, Boris N. Yeltsin; *Arista,* Patti Smith; *Austrian Information Service,* Franz Vranitzky; *Basic Books,* Rita Levi-Montalcini; © *Jerry Bauer,* Harold Brodkey, Anita Brookner; *Janette Beckman/1988,* Tracy Chapman; *Roy Blakey,* Brian Boitano; *Blues Heaven Foundation, Inc.,* Willie Dixon; *British Information Services,* Margaret Thatcher; *Brooks,* Alan Greenspan; *G. Paul Burnett/NYT Pictures,* David Henry Hwang; © *Chris Callis, courtesy of Parenting,* Maurice Sendak; *Campeau Corp.,* Robert Campeau; *Cannon Films, Inc.,* Chuck Norris; © *1987 Capital Cities/ABC, Inc.,* Brandon Stoddard; © *1988 Copyright Capital Cities/ ABC, Inc.,* Joan Lunden; © *1989 Copyright Capital Cities/ABC, Inc.,* Susan Lucci; *CBS Television City,* Pat Sajak; *Center Theatre Group/Mark Taper Forum, Los Angeles Music Center,* Ming Cho Lee; *Liz Claiborne Inc.,* Liz Claiborne; *Coalition for the Homeless,* Robert M. Hayes; *Columbia Artists Management Inc.,* Christoph Eschenbach, Barbara Hendricks; *Columbia University,* Edward W. Said; *Commission of the European Communities,* Jacques Delors; © *1988 Susan Cook,* Michael Weller; *Council of Economic Advisers,* Michael J. Boskin; *Nancy Crampton,* Ward Just; © *Nancy Crampton,* Neil Sheehan; © *1988 Nancy Crampton,* Larry Woiwode; © *Nancy Crampton 1989,* Jane Freilicher; *Chris Cuffaro, 1989,* Jackson Browne; *Peter Cunningham,* Wendy Wasserstein; *Michel Delsol,* Tama Janowitz; *Democratic National Committee,* Ron Brown; *Department of Transportation,* Samuel K. Skinner; *Richard Derk/NYT Pictures,* Gordon Bunshaft; *Detroit Pistons,* Isiah Thomas; *Michael Dorris,* Louise Erdrich; *Environmental Protection Agency,* William K. Reilly; *Stan Fellerman/IMG Artists,* Arleen Augér; *Fermilab Visual Media Services,* Leon M. Lederman, Robert R. Wilson; *A. Blake Gardner,* Thomas Krens; *Jean-François Gaté,* Patrick Kelly; *Georgetown University Office of Sports Information,* John Thompson; *German Information Center,* Steffi Graf; © *Mark Gerson,* John Keegan; © *Susan Gilbert,* Bobby McFerrin; *Chester Higgens Jr./NYT Pictures,* Henry Roth; *A. Hussein/*© *SIPA-PRESS,* Sir Muda Hassanal Bolkiah; *IBM Corp.,* Richard Garwin; *IN-Press/Presse- und Informationsamt der Stadt Kiel,* Gerhard Stoltenberg; *International Management Group,* Andre Agassi, Greg Norman; *Mark Jury,* Frederick Exley; © *Dimitri Kasterine,* Michael Holroyd; *Jeff Katz,* Randy Travis; *Robin Laurence/NYT Pictures,* Maurice Saatchi; *Leo Castelli Gallery,* Edward Ruscha; © *1987 Jonathan Levine,* Lewis H. Lapham; *Library of Congress,* James H. Billington; *Dan Marschka/National Press Representatives,* John Corigliano; *Robert Miller Gallery, New York,* Robert Mapplethorpe; *Momix,* Moses Pendleton; *Monmouth Park,* Julie Krone; © *1983 André Moreaux,* Peter Straub; © *1987 National Broadcasting Company, Inc.,* Robert C. Wright; © *1989 National Broadcasting Company, Inc.,* Connie Chung, Willard Scott; *Steven Navratil,* Lou Holtz; *W. Neumeister,* Trevor Pinnock; *Nichols & Associates,* Barbara Howar; *notimex,* Carlos Salinas; *NYT Pictures,* F. Ross Johnson, Henry R. Kravis; *Jane O'Neal/*©*MCMLXXXVIII Touchstone Pictures. All Rights Reserved.,* Barbara Hershey; *Terry O'Neill,* George Harrison; © *Copyright 1987 Orion Pictures Corporation,* Claude Berri; *The Pace Gallery, 32 E. 57th St., New York, N.Y. 10022,* Agnes Martin; *Paramount Communications Inc.,* Martin S. Davis; *Wayne Partlow,* C. Boyden Gray; *The People's Court,* Joseph A. Wapner; *Lucian Perkins/ The Washington Post,* Edward Kienholz; *Ron Phillips,* Nestor Almendros; *Pierre Matisse Gallery,* Jean-Paul Riopelle; *Playboy,* Richard Condon. © *Hugh Powers,* J. F. Powers; © *Joyce Ravid,* Don DeLillo; *Republican National Committee,* Lee Atwater; © *1988 Roger Ressmeyer,* Danielle Steel; *Reuters/Bettmann Newsphotos,* Spike Lee; *Robert Wise Productions,* Robert Wise; *Russell Roderer,* Richard B. Cheney; *San Francisco 49ers,* Bill Walsh; *Bonnie Schiffman/*© *1988 Paramount Pictures Corporation,* Arsenio Hall; *Andrew Schwartz,* Sigourney Weaver; *Takashi Seida/*© *1988 Metro-Goldwyn-Mayer Pictures, Inc,* Susan Sarandon; © *Stephen Shames/VISIONS, 1985,* Edmund Morris; © *Shinchosha, Kobo Abé;* © *Peter Sibbald/Picture Group, 1987* Kenneth Thomson; *Pamela J. Smith,* Lawrence Sanders; *Christian Steiner,* Bella Davidovich; © *1987 Martha Swope,* Martha Clarke; *Talent Consultants International Ltd.,* Bo Diddley; *William Taylor,* Michael Graves. *U.S. Department of Commerce,* Robert A. Mosbacher; *U.S. Department of Education,* Lauro F. Cavazos; *U.S. Department of Health and Human Services,* Louis W. Sullivan; *U.S. Food and Drug Administration,* Frank E. Young; *U.S. House of Representatives,* Thomas S. Foley, Newt Gingrich, Henry J. Hyde, Lynn Martin; *U.S. Department of the Interior,* Manuel Lujan Jr.; *U.S. Senate,* David L. Boren, Christopher J. Dodd, Robert W. Kasten Jr., Warren B. Rudman; *U.S. Supreme Court,* Thurgood Marshall; *David Valdez/The White House,* Dan Quayle; *Thomas Victor,* Bobbie Ann Mason; © *Thomas Victor,* Alice Adams; *The White House,* Barbara Bush, John H. Sununu; *Susan Wood,* Betty Friedan; *David Zadia,* Barbara Harris.

OBITUARIES

ALLOTT, GORDON (LLEWELLYN) Jan. 2, 1907–Jan. 17, 1989 Republican U.S. senator from Colorado (1955–73); lawyer; a member of Senate Appropriations and Interior committees, sponsored Colorado River Basin Storage Act of 1968, providing for construction of five water projects in Colorado and one in Arizona; began practicing law in Lamar, Colorado in 1930, eventually becoming attorney for Prowers County, city of Lamar, and towns of Wiley and Hartman; served as major in Army Air Corps during World War II; served two terms (1951–55) as lieutenant governor of Colorado before election to Senate; died in Englewood, Colorado. See *Current Biography* (May) 1955.

Obituary *N Y Times* B p16 Ja 19 '89

ALSOP, JOSEPH W(RIGHT), JR. Oct. 11, 1910–Aug. 28, 1989 Journalist; author; syndicated political columnist; began career as reporter for *New York Herald Tribune*; from Washington, wrote syndicated column "The Capital Parade" with Robert E. Kintner from 1937 to 1940; collaborated with his late brother Stewart on column "Matter of Fact" from 1946 to 1958; wrote "Matter of Fact" by himself from 1958 to 1974; although he considered his work to be primarily reportage, had decided opinions, expressed them bluntly and crustily, and enjoyed polemical frays; was New Deal Democrat, staunch anticommunist, and supporter of Cold War and Vietnam War; with Robert E. Kintner, wrote two books on Washington politics; was also interested in archeology and art and wrote on his own *From the Silent Earth: A Report on the Greek Bronze Age* (1964) and *The Rare Art Traditions* (1982), a quirky history of art collecting; died in Washington, D.C. See *Current Biography* (October) 1952.

Obituary *N Y Times* B p6 Ag 29 '89

ANDERSON, R(OBERT) B(ERNERD) June 4, 1910–Aug. 14, 1989 Former U.S. government official; a Democrat turned Republican; in Republican administration of President Dwight D. Eisenhower, was secretary of navy (1953–54), deputy secretary of defense (1954–55), and secretary of treasury (1957–61); earlier, in Texas, had served in state legislature and high appointive posts; in private sector, was attorney for or officer in numerous corporate ranching, oil, investment banking, and international holding enterprises; late in career, was adviser to and lobbyist for the Reverend Sun Myung Moon's Unification church, among other clients; after pleading guilty to federal income tax evasion and illegal operation of offshore bank, was sentenced to one month in prison and five months' house arrest in 1987; in January 1989 was disbarred by Appellate Division of New York State Supreme Court; died in New York City. See *Current Biography* (July) 1953.

Obituary *N Y Times* B p9 Ag 16 '89

ARMOUR, RICHARD (WILLARD) July 15, 1906–Feb. 28, 1989 Writer; educator; prolific author of some sixty volumes of light verse and satirical and humorous prose, including *It All Started with Columbus* (1953), *Twisted Tales from Shakespeare* (1957), *It All Started with Nudes: An Artful History of Art* (1977), and, most recently, *Educated Guesses* (1983); an authority on Chaucer and English Romantic poets, was professor of English at, among other institutions, Wells College (1934–44) and Scripps College (1945–66); began writing humorous variations of historical incidents "to bring lightness as well as enlightenment into the classroom," as he once put it; in later years, lectured at colleges throughout U.S. and abroad; died in Claremont, California. See *Current Biography* (November) 1958.

Obituary *N Y Times* B p16 Mr 2 '89

ATKINSON, ORIANA (TORREY) Sept. 4, 1894–July 31, 1989 Writer; widow of Brooks Atkinson, late *New York Times* drama critic and (briefly) foreign correspondent; wrote bestsellers *Over at Uncle Joe's* (1947), pleasant memoir of her sojourn in Moscow with her husband before and just after end of World War II, and *Manhattan and Me* (1954), brisk account of changes she observed in her native Manhattan over the years; also wrote, among other books, novel *Big Eyes* (1949) and historical romance *Twin Cousins*, both set in and around Catskill, New York; contributed poetry and articles to numerous magazines and newspapers; died in Huntsville, Alabama. See *Current Biography* (Yearbook) 1953.

Obituary *N Y Times* D p23 Ag 2 '89

ATTWOOD, WILLIAM (HOLLINGSWORTH) July 14, 1919–Apr. 15, 1989 Journalist; publisher; diplomat; began career in late 1940s as foreign correspondent and subsequently held succession of editorial posts at *Look* (1951–60) magazine before entering foreign service; gave detailed account of experiences as U. S. ambassador to Guinea (1961–63) and Kenya (1964–66) in book *The Reds and the Blacks: A Personal Adventure* (1967); returned to journalism in 1966 as editor in chief of Cowles Communications, publisher of *Look* and other magazines; joined New York daily *Newsday* as president and publisher in 1970 and became chairman of the board in 1978; after retirement in 1979, wrote autobiography *Making It through Middle Age: Notes While in Transit* (1982) and *The Twilight Struggle: Tales of the Cold War* (1987); died in New Canaan, Connecticut. See *Current Biography* (January) 1968.

Obituary *N Y Times* p38 Ap 16 '89

AYER, A(LFRED) J(ULES) Oct. 29, 1910–June 27, 1989 British philosopher; university professor; an epistemologist who denied value of all comprehensive ideal philosophical systems; chief British promulgator of logical positivism, Austrian-born movement that contributed to demystification of philosophy through linguistic analysis; as postgraduate student in 1932, sat in on meetings of Vienna Circle, group of mathematics-oriented scholars in rebellion against German idealistic philosophies, which they linked to rise of political irrationalism on continent; expounded Vienna Circle's views in *Language, Truth, and Logic* (1936), provocative manifesto in which he dismissed as meaningless (or merely emotive) metaphysical and ethical speculation not verifiable under scientific methodology, reducing philosophy to an empirical logic, the handmaiden of natural science; modified his views in *The Problem of Knowledge* (1956) and *The Concept of a Person* (1957); in varied academic career, taught principally at Oxford University, from 1933 on; after four years at University of London, returned to Oxford as professor of philosophy of mind and logic (1959–78); was knighted in 1970; retired as Oxford fellow in 1983; died in London, England. See *Current Biography* (May) 1964.

Obituary *N Y Times* D p21 Je 29 '89

BALL, LUCILLE Aug. 6, 1911–Apr. 26, 1989 Actress; producer; rubbery-faced comedienne whose impeccable timing, flair for slapstick, and lovable on-screen persona endeared her to several generations of television viewers around the world; with Desi Arnaz, then her husband, created wildly successful battle-of-the-sexes situation comedy *I Love Lucy* (1951–57, and still in syndication), in which she played Lucy Ricardo, the featherbrained, stagestruck wife of Cuban bandleader Ricky Ricardo, portrayed by Arnaz; continued to play variation of wacky "Lucy" character in sitcoms *The Lucy Show* (1962–68), *Here's Lucy* (1968–74), and short-lived *Life with Lucy* (1986); began career as Hollywood contract player in 1930s and made more than fifty films, including *Stage Door* (1937), *DuBarry Was a Lady* (1943), *Fancy Pants* (1950), and *Mame* (1974); was shrewd business executive, managing mammoth Desilu Productions (1962–67), which she had formed with Arnaz, and, beginning in 1968, Lucille Ball Productions; received countless honors, among them four Emmys and, in 1984, induction into Television Academy Hall of Fame; died following heart surgery in Los Angeles, California. See *Current Biography* (January) 1978.

Obituary *N Y Times* A p1+ Ap 27 '89

BARTHÉ, RICHMOND Jan. 28, 1901–Mar. 6, 1989 Sculptor; best known for realistic portrait busts of stage celebrities and of important figures from black history; created monumental statues of liberators Toussaint L'Ouverture and Jean-Jacques Dessalines for government of Haiti, among other public-works commissions; exhibited widely in U.S. and abroad, most recently in 1981, as part of special exhibition "Afro-American Art" at Museum of African American Art in Santa Monica, California; represented in collections of many museums, including Whitney Museum of American Art, Metropolitan Museum, and Smithsonian Institution; died in Pasadena, California. See *Current Biography* (July) 1940.

Obituary *N Y Times* B p16 Mr 16 '89

BARTHELME, DONALD Apr. 7, 1931–July 23, 1989 Writer; innovative, nonlinear fictional stylist; in both the form and content of his collagelike short stories, parodies, satires, and novels, mirrored the dislocation, anomie, and absurdities in twentieth-century life, and did so with wry, resigned understatement; was seen by literary critics as an "antinovelist" and "poet of order gone" whose stories, reflecting his lapsed Catholicism, were "metaphysical rebellions against the petty chaos, the near-madness they report"; resisting the "minimalist" label, identified with "the alleged postmodernists"; first won national attention with novella *Snow White* (1967), originally published, like most of his stories, in *New Yorker* magazine; published eight short-story collections, including *Unspeakable Practices, Unnatural Acts* (1968), and

three novels, not counting "The King," scheduled for publication in 1990; won a National Book Award in juvenile category for *The Slightly Irregular Fire Engine* (1971); died in Houston, Texas. See *Current Biography* (March) 1976.

Obituary *N Y Times* D p11 Jl 24 '89

BEADLE, G(EORGE) W(ELLS) Oct. 22, 1903–June 9, 1989 Biologist; emeritus educator; major figure in advancement of biochemistry of genetic mutations; co-winner of 1958 Nobel Prize in medicine and physiology for demonstrating how particular genes control synthesis of vitamins and amino acids in plant and animal cells and how, in their absence, hereditary transmission of disturbances in metabolic activity ensues—conclusions with practical implications for pharmaceutical industry's production of penicillin and medicine's approach to both metabolic and infectious disease; also specialized in research clarifying genetics and cytology of Indian (domestic) corn; chaired division of biology at California Institute of Technology (1946–60); earlier, had worked and taught at Cornell and Stanford universities; at University of Chicago, was president from 1961 to 1968 and continued teaching there until 1975; cowrote *An Introduction to Genetics* (1939), *Genetics and Modern Biology* (1963), and *The Language of Life* (1966); died in Pomona, California. See *Current Biography* (April) 1956.

Obituary *N Y Times* D p13 Je 12 '89

BECHTEL, STEPHEN D(AVISON) Sept. 24, 1900–Mar. 14, 1989 Corporation executive; construction engineer; as president of family-owned Bechtel Corporation, presided over company's growth into one of world's largest construction and engineering firms, specializing in colossal building projects in energy field; over course of career, beginning as vice-president in 1925, supervised construction, alone or in concert with other companies, of Hoover and Bonneville dams, Trans-Arabian pipeline, San Francisco–Oakland Bay Bridge, Washington, D.C., and San Francisco subway systems, and scores of refineries, mining complexes, and nuclear and hydroelectric power plants; after official retirement in 1960, continued to serve as senior director; died in San Francisco, California. See *Current Biography* (April) 1957.

Obituary *N Y Times* D p18 Mr 15 '89

BELT, GUILLERMO July 14, 1905–July 2, 1989 Former Cuban government official and diplomat; participated in revolution that overthrew dictator Gerardo Machado y Morales in 1933; in governments controlled by Fulgencio Batista y Zaldivar, served in various cabinet posts until 1938, when Batista, accusing him of complicity in new revolutionary plot, forced him into exile; during hiatus in Batista's rule (1944–52), was ambassador to U.S. (1944–49), a signer of United Nations charter (1944), and head of Cuba's UN delegation (1945–49); concurrently, represented Cuba with Organization of American States; taught international law at St. Thomas of Villanova University in Havana from 1956 to 1959; became U.S. resident in 1961, after Fidel Castro took power; died in Arlington, Virginia. See *Current Biography* (November) 1947.

Obituary *N Y Times* A p12 Jl 7 '89

BENDETSEN, KARL R(OBIN) Oct. 11, 1907–June 28, 1989 Former U.S. government official; business executive; as college student in 1920s, belonged to Washington State National Guard; as lawyer for West Coast mining and labor interests in 1930s, was member of Army Reserve Officers Corps; as colonel with general staff of War Department during World War II, directed forcible movement of 110,000 persons of Japanese origin (including 75,000 U.S. citizens) from West Coast to interior detention camps; served as assistant secretary (1950–52) and under secretary (May–September 1952) of army; later headed Champion International Corporation, a plywood and paper manufacturing conglomerate; retired in 1973; died in Washington, D.C. See *Current Biography* (May) 1952.

Obituary *N Y Times* A p16 Je 30 '89

BERLIN, IRVING May 11, 1888–Sept. 22, 1989 Russian-born songwriter; a Tin Pan Alley titan despite his inability to read or write musical notation and hunt-and-peck piano technique confined to the key of F-sharp; in the opinion of Jerome Kern, was "the nearest thing to a native folk singer since Stephen Foster"; composed 1,500 popular songs, including "Marie from Sunny Italy," "Alexander's Ragtime Band," "A Pretty Girl Is Like a Melody," "God Bless America," "Cheek to Cheek," and "Always"; wrote the scores for eighteen films, including *Top Hat, Holiday Inn, Blue Skies, White Christmas, Easter Parade*, and *There's No Business Like Show Business*, nineteen Broadway musicals, including *Watch Your Step, Annie Get Your Gun, Call Me Madam*, and *Mr. President*, and countless revues; in his World War II show *This Is the Army*, personally sang "Oh, How I Hate to Get Up in the Morning," as he had done in *Yip, Yip, Yaphank* in 1918; died at his home in New York City. See *Current Biography* (May) 1963.

Obituary *N Y Times* p1+ S 23 '89

BIRREN, FABER Sept. 21, 1900–Dec. 30, 1988 Color consultant; pioneered in functional application of color to factories, offices, department stores, banks, schools, and hospitals; trained as painter, set up shop as industrial color consultant in 1934 and over course of career advised such clients as General Motors, Westinghouse, Monsanto, and U.S. Navy; in 1940s, was instrumental in development of national safety color code to reduce industrial accidents; wrote dozens of books about color and its applications, including *Functional Color* (1937), *The Story of Color, from Ancient Mysticism to Modern Science* (1941), *Color Psychology and Color Therapy* (1961), and *Color Perception in Art* (1976); died in Stamford, Connecticut. See *Current Biography* (May) 1956.

Obituary *N Y Times* p9 D 31 '88

BLAIK, EARL H(ENRY) Feb. 15, 1897–May 6, 1989 Football coach; corporation executive; as head football coach at U. S. Military Academy (1941–58), compiled enviable record of 121 victories, thirty-three losses, and ten ties, including five undefeated seasons and back-to-back national championships, in 1944 and 1945; began athletic career as assistant coach at Military Academy (1927–34), his alma mater, and head coach at Dartmouth (1934–41); after leaving football, served as chairman of executive committees of Avco

Corporation and of Blaik Oil Company; named to National Football Hall of Fame in 1959; died in Colorado Springs, Colorado. See *Current Biography* (January) 1945.

Obituary *N Y Times* I p44 My 7 '89

BLAISDELL, THOMAS C(HARLES), JR. Dec. 2, 1895–Dec. 27, 1988 U.S. government official; educator; after decade teaching economics at universities in U.S. and abroad, joined Roosevelt's administration in 1933 and held senior administrative posts in succession of New Deal agencies; during and after World War II, was chief of mission of economic affairs in London; as director of Office of International Trade (1947–49), helped draft Marshall Plan to foster European economic recovery; served as assistant secretary of commerce in Truman administration (1949–51); resumed teaching as professor of political science at University of California at Berkeley in 1951 and continued long after attaining emeritus status in 1963; died in Berkeley, California. See *Current Biography* (July) 1949.

Obituary *N Y Times* p9 D 31 '88

BLANC, MEL(VIN JEROME) May 30, 1908–July 10, 1989 Vocal specialist; voice-over actor on screen, radio, and television; versatile mimic; known as "the man of a thousand voices"; under aegis of Leon Schlesinger Productions beginning in 1935, became voice of menagerie of characters in Warner Brothers' Looney Tunes and Merrie Melodies animated motion picture cartoons, including Porky Pig, Bugs Bunny, Tweetie the canary, Sylvester the cat, Road Runner, Wile E. Coyote, Woody Woodpecker, and Daffy Duck; on radio and television shows, including those of Jack Benny, did incredible range of voices and sound effects; on television in 1960s did title voice on *Bugs Bunny Show* and that of Barney Rubble on *The Flintstones* (still in syndication in 1989); died in Los Angeles, California. See *Current Biography* (June) 1976.

Obituary *N Y Times* A p16 Jl 11 '89

BOLGER, WILLIAM F(REDERICK LEONARD) Mar. 13, 1923–Aug. 21, 1989 Former U.S. postmaster general (1978–84); first career postal employee to rise through the ranks to top of U.S. Postal Service; while guiding service through period of change and challenge into electronic age, oversaw improvement in the lot of postal workers and the service's first financial surplus in thirty-four years; after leaving office, founded T-COM Systems, a business mailing system; died in Arlington, Virginia. See *Current Biography* (October) 1979.

Obituary *N Y Times* D p23 Ag 22 '89

BOLTE, CHARLES L(AWRENCE) May 8, 1895–Feb. 11, 1989 U. S. Army officer; capped nearly forty years of military service with appointment, in 1953, as army's vice-chief of staff; a combat veteran of both world wars, commanded Sixty-ninth and Thirty-fourth Infantry Divisions on Mediterranean front during World War II, earning Silver Star and Distinguished Service Medal; held several staff posts at army headquarters before taking over as commander of Seventh Army, in 1952, and commander in chief of

American army in Europe, in 1953; left service in 1955, but came out of retirement in 1961 to chair Pentagon panel that proposed basing promotions on ability rather than seniority; died in Mount Vernon, Virginia. See *Current Biography* (January) 1954.

Obituary *N Y Times* D p13 F 13 '89

BRADSHAW, THORNTON F(REDERICK) Aug. 4, 1917–Dec. 6, 1988 Business executive; educator; after teaching for ten years (1942–52) on faculty of Harvard Graduate School of Business Administration, joined New York management consulting firm, where he articulated philosophy of long-range corporate planning; tested his theories in series of executive positions, culminating in presidency, over twenty-five-year period (1956–81) at Atlantic Richfield (ARCO), which he built into multibillion-dollar natural resources conglomerate; longtime advocate of social responsibility of business, as ARCO executive lobbied for improved mass transit and formulation of national energy policy; named president of RCA in 1981, restored beleaguered corporation to financial health and secured its future by presiding over its sale in 1985 to General Electric; died in New York City. See *Current Biography* (June) 1982.

Obituary *N Y Times* D p24 D 7 '88

BREWSTER, KINGMAN, JR. June 17, 1919–Nov. 8, 1988 Educator; diplomat; served on law faculties of Harvard (1950–60) and Yale (1960–63); as president of Yale University (1963–77), championed civil rights and civil liberties and exercised diplomatic skills in dealing with campus crises of late 1960s; served as U.S. ambassador to Great Britain (1977–81); was chairman of English Speaking Union (1981–84); engaged in private practice of law (from 1981); was elected to five-year term as master of University College at Oxford (1985); wrote *Antitrust and American Business Abroad* (1958); died at Oxford, England. See *Current Biography* (September) 1979.

Obituary *N Y Times* A p1+ N 9 '88

BRICO, ANTONIA June 26, 1902–Aug. 3, 1989 Conductor; pianist; lifelong struggler against sex discrimination in orchestral world; as guest, made international debut conducting Berlin Philharmonic in 1930 and American debut conducting Los Angeles Philharmonic later in same year; unable to secure conducting position with an established U.S. orchestra, led her own ensemble, the Brico Symphony (originally New York Women's Symphony), for several years, beginning in 1935; in early 1940s settled in Denver, Colorado, where she taught music and directed Denver Community Symphony and Denver Opera; was subject of film *Antonia: Portrait of a Conductor* (1974), directed by her former student Judy Collins, the folksinger; returned to New York to conduct Mostly Mozart Festival Orchestra in 1975; retired from conducting in 1985; died in Denver, Colorado. See *Current Biography* (September) 1948.

Obituary *N Y Times* p10 Ag 5 '89

BRODIE, BERNARD B(ERYL) Aug. 7, 1909–Feb. 27, 1989 Pharmacologist; educator; through contributions to biochemical pharmacology, had significant influ-

ence on development of drug therapies for treatment of cancer, gout, cardiovascular diseases, and mental and emotional illnesses; developed concept of using blood drug levels to determine therapeutic dosages; began pioneering work while teaching biochemistry and pharmacology at New York University Medical School (1935–50) and continued research as director of chemical pharmacology laboratory at National Heart Institute of National Institutes of Health (1950–70); after retirement, served as consultant for pharmaceutical manufacturer Hoffman-LaRoche and as visiting professor at various medical schools; received many honors, including Lasker Award for basic medical research, in 1967, and National Medal of Science, in 1968; died in Charlottesville, Virginia. See *Current Biography* (September) 1969.

Obituary *N Y Times* B p16 Mr 2 '89

BROWN, IRVING (JOSEPH) Nov. 20, 1911–Feb. 10, 1989 Labor union official; as European representative of AFL-CIO (1945–61), was instrumental in founding of International Confederation of Free Trade Unions, whose UN office he headed from 1962 to 1965; entered trade union work in 1932 as organizer for automobile workers' union and rose to post of vice-chairman for labor with War Production Board in early 1940s; from 1965 to 1973, provided technical aid to free trade unions in Africa as executive director of African American Labor Center; returning to AFL-CIO's European office in 1973, was named its director of international affairs in 1982; was serving as senior adviser to AFL-CIO president Lane Kirkland at time of death; awarded Presidential Medal of Freedom in 1988; died in Paris, France. See *Current Biography* (July) 1951.

Obituary *N Y Times* p33 F 11 '89

BROWN, STERLING (ALLEN) May 1, 1901–Jan. 13, 1989 Poet; critic; educator; leading figure in Harlem renaissance of 1920s and 1930s; helped to establish Afro-American literary criticism; taught renowned black scholars and writers; edited, with Arthur P. Davis and Ulysses Lee, *The Negro Caravan* (1941), the first major anthology of black literature; wrote several works of criticism, including *The Negro in American Fiction* and *Negro Poetry and Drama*, both published in 1937; published three collections of poetry; taught at Virginia Seminary and College (1923–26), Lincoln University (1926–28), Fisk University (1928–29), and Howard University (1929–69); died in Takoma Park, Maryland. See *Current Biography* (August) 1982.

Obituary *N Y Times* B p11 Ja 17 '89

BRUCE, LOUIS R(OOKS JR.) Dec. 30, 1906–May 20, 1989 Commissioner of U.S. Bureau of Indian Affairs (1969–73); Native American advocate of Indian rights; helped establish National Congress of American Indians; early in career, ran his family's dairy farm in upstate New York, served as education and youth director of Dairymen's League Cooperative Association, and was National Youth Administration's director of Indian projects in New York State; later worked as advertising executive, expert on cooperative housing with Federal Housing Administration, and public relations executive with cooperative supermarket chain; as commissioner of Bureau of Indian Affairs, opened policy-making positions in agency to more Native Americans; after resigning—in wake of siege of bureau by 500 Indians protesting injustices—founded Native American Consultants; died in Arlington, Virginia. See *Current Biography* (May) 1972.

Obituary *N Y Times* D p25 My 24 '89

BUCK, PAUL H(ERMAN) Aug. 25, 1899–Dec. 23, 1978 Historian; university professor; library administrator; served as director of the Harvard University library (1955–64), member of Harvard history department faculty (1926–69), associate dean of the Faculty of Arts and Sciences (1939–42), dean (1942–45), provost of the university and ex officio dean (1945–53); awarded 1938 Pulitzer Prize for *The Road to Reunion: 1865–1900* (1937), a classic study of the Reconstruction period in the South; was chairman of the board of Dunbarton Oaks Research Library and Collection in Washington, D.C. (1952–53); died in Cambridge, Massachusetts. See *Current Biography* (July) 1955.

Obituary *Contemporary Authors* vols 81–84 (1979)

BUSCH, AUGUST A(NHEUSER) Mar. 28, 1899–Sept. 29, 1989 Corporation executive; beer and baseball mogul; went to work at Anheuser-Busch, his family's St. Louis brewery, in 1922; after taking over presidency of the ailing company, in 1946, turned it into world's largest beer producer, best known for its Budweiser and Michelob brands; in 1953, persuaded company's board to buy St. Louis Cardinals baseball team, of which he was president until his death; following his retirement as chief executive officer of Anheuser-Busch in 1953, was honorary chairman of company; died at Grant's Farm, his estate in Affton, Missouri. See *Current Biography* (July) 1973.

Obituary *N Y Times* p29 S 30 '89

CASSAVETES, JOHN Dec. 9, 1929–Feb. 3, 1989 Actor; screenwriter; improvisational director; independent New Wave filmmaker; controversial pioneer in American *cinéma vérité*; won Critics Award at the Venice Film Festival in 1960 for his first film, *Shadows*, a depiction of race relations influenced by the Method school of acting that was shot on the streets of New York; won five prizes at 1968 Venice festival for directing *Faces*, a study of a crumbling marriage; nominated for Academy Award as best supporting actor in *The Dirty Dozen* (1967); costarred in *Edge of the City*, *Rosemary's Baby*, *Two Minute Warning*, and other films; acted in televised live dramas (1953–56); starred in own weekly television detective series, *Johnny Staccato*, in late 1950s; died in Los Angeles, with his actress wife, Gena Rowlands, at bedside. See *Current Biography* (July) 1969.

Obituary *N Y Times* p32 F 4 '89

CASWELL, HOLLIS L(ELAND) Oct. 22, 1901–Nov. 22, 1988 Educator; dean (1949–54), president (1954–62), and Marshall Field Jr. professor of education (1962–67) at Teachers College of Columbia University; criticized efforts to institute national curriculum for public schools, favoring instead greater differentiation of teaching methods; opposed participation of non-educators in curriculum planning; served as principal editorial adviser to World Book Encyclopedia for

some two decades; acted as consultant to state education departments and local school systems; was the author of *Education in the Elementary School* (1942), among other books; died in Santa Barbara, California. See *Current Biography* (July) 1956.

Obituary *N Y Times* D p24 N 24 '88

CHATWIN, BRUCE (CHARLES) May 13, 1940–Jan. 17, 1989 British travel writer and novelist; art expert and connoisseur; noted for his elegantly written accounts of exotic and remote places; established an enviable reputation with his first book, *In Patagonia* (1977), which was honored with the E. M. Forster Award of the American Academy of Arts and Letters; his other books include *The Viceroy of Ouidah* (1980), *On the Black Hill* (1982), *The Songlines* (1987), and *Utz* (1989), published shortly before his death; wrote travel articles for the London *Sunday Times Magazine* (1973–76); headed the impressionism department at the London art auction house Sotheby & Company (1965–66); died in Nice, France of rare bone disease contracted during travels in China. See *Current Biography* (January) 1988.

Obituary *N Y Times* B p16 Ja 19 '89

COTTON, NORRIS May 11, 1900–Feb. 24, 1989 U.S. senator from New Hampshire (1954–75); lawyer; a self-described "stand-pat, conservative, hidebound, mossback Republican," compiled generally conservative voting record in thirty-year career in U.S. House of Representatives (1946–54) and U.S. Senate; played major role in passage of legislation to improve quality of medical care, particularly through federal support for health manpower training; before election to Congress in 1946, served as municipal judge (1939–43) and as member of New Hampshire state legislature (1943–45), where elected majority leader and speaker; died in Lebanon, New Hampshire. See *Current Biography* (February) 1956.

Obituary *N Y Times* I p36 F 26 '89

COWLEY, MALCOLM Aug. 24, 1898–Mar. 27, 1989 Writer; literary critic and historian; one of twentieth century's most influential critics, celebrated so-called Lost Generation in most famous work, *Exile's Return* (1934), and continued incisive critical and social history of American literature between world wars in *A Second Flowering* (1973) and *The Dream of the Golden Mountain* (1980); as literary editor of *New Republic* (1929–44) and editor at Viking Press (1948–85), awakened or revived interest in work of some of the most brilliant writers of his time, including William Faulkner and John Cheever; wrote hundreds of book reviews and literary essays, mainly for *New Republic*, and many books, most notably collection of autobiographical verse *Blue Juniata* (1929), *—And I Worked at the Writer's Trade* (1978), and *The Flower and the Leaf* (1984), about American literature since 1941; died in New Milford, Connecticut. See *Current Biography* (June) 1979.

Obituary *N Y Times* D p25 Mr 29 '89

DALI, SALVADOR May 11, 1904–Jan. 23, 1989 Spanish artist; flamboyant and eccentric painter who became synonymous in the public mind with surrealism;

best known for such hallucinatory paintings as *The Persistence of Memory* (1931), sometimes called *Soft Watches*, but in midlife returned to classical roots with masterfully crafted portraits and large-scale paintings of traditional religious subjects; among most versatile and prolific of twentieth-century artists, designed furniture, jewelry, china, and glassware, created fashions in collaboration with Chanel and Schiaparelli, produced, with Luis Buñuel, surrealist films *Un chien andalou* (1929) and *L'Age d'or* (1931), and designed sets and costumes for ballets, operas, and theatrical productions; wrote poetry, essays, the novel *Hidden Faces* (1944), and three volumes of autobiography, most recently *The Unspeakable Confession of Salvador Dali* (1976); died in Figueras, Spain. See *Current Biography* (April) 1951.

Obituary *N Y Times* A p1+ Ja 24 '89

DART, RAYMOND A(RTHUR) Feb. 4, 1893–Nov. 22, 1988 Australian-born neuroanatomist; anthropologist; professor of anatomy (1923–58) and dean of medical faculty (1926–43) at University of Witwatersrand in Johannesburg, South Africa; revolutionized study of human origins with discovery, near village of Taungs, in South Africa in 1924, of *Australopithecus africanus*, a fossil man-ape believed to be evolutionary "missing link" between apes and humans; excavated and developed Makapansgat fossil site in Transvaal (1945–55); wrote (with Dennis Craig) autobiography, *Adventures with the Missing Link* (1959); died in Johannesburg. See *Current Biography* (September) 1966.

Obituary *N Y Times* B p8 N 23 '88

DAVIDSON, JOHN F(REDERICK) May 3, 1908–Jan. 21, 1989 U.S. naval officer; educator; served as superintendent of the U.S. Naval Academy at Annapolis, Maryland from 1960 to 1962; began naval service as midshipman in 1925, eventually rising to rear admiral in 1956; commanded the submarines USS *Mackerel* and USS *Blackfish* during World War II; chaired the department of English, history, and government at the U.S. Naval Academy (1951–54); commanded a cruiser division and a submarine squadron during the late 1950s; commanded the Pacific Fleet Training Command from 1962 until retirement in 1964; died in Annapolis, Maryland. See *Current Biography* (November) 1960.

Obituary *N Y Times* D p27 Ja 25 '89

DAVIS, BETTE Apr. 5, 1908–Oct. 6, 1989 Actress; a Hollywood legend; the silver screen's original and quintessential "emancipated" woman, haughty, willful, and defiant against odds; won Academy Awards for best actress for portrayals of flamboyant dipsomaniac in *Dangerous* (1935) and tempestuous southern belle in *Jezebel* (1938); despite such touching melodramatic credits as *Dark Victory* (1939), *All This and Heaven Too* (1940), and *Now, Voyager* (1942), is widely remembered as a classy brazen vixen, high-strung but cool and hard-edged, entering a scene with a crisp wisecrack and moving across the screen brandishing a cigarette and sweeping the air with stylized hand gestures; began career in theatre, including Broadway; established motion picture reputation with her interpretation of slatternly Cockney waitress Mildred in *Of Human Bondage* (1934), her twenty-second picture; with tour-de-force performance as Margo Channing, the tough, fading stage prima donna with the soft heart in *All About Eve* (1950), drew one of her ten Oscar nominations; spoofed herself in title role of superannuated movie star in campy horror film *What Ever Happened to Baby Jane?* (1962); in addition to eighty-six feature films made between 1930 and 1986, appeared in fifteen TV movies; won television Emmy Award as costar of *Strangers: The Story of a Mother and a Daughter* (1979); had expressive eyes, inspiration for 1982 hit popular song "Bette Davis Eyes"; wrote autobiography, *The Lonely Life* (1962); died in Neuilly-sur-Seine, on outskirts of Paris, en route home to West Hollywood from San Sebastian Film Festival in Spain, where she had been honored for lifetime achievement. See *Current Biography* (March) 1953.

Obituary *N Y Times* I p1+ O 8 '89

DeGAETANI, JAN July 10, 1933–Sept. 15, 1989 Singer; a two-and-a-half-octave mezzo-soprano, wide-ranging as concert and recording artist but most at home in chamber music; internationally respected for warmth, intelligence, and sensitivity of her interpretations of works ranging from medieval and Renaissance vocal pieces and Bach and Beethoven masses through nineteenth-century lieder and art songs to music of Stephen Foster, Maurice Ravel, Cole Porter, Arnold Schönberg, and contemporary experimental composers; was admired and loved cult figure in "new music," to which she was especially attracted and which she championed; was collaborative interpreter of such contemporary composers as George Crumb, Jacob Druckman, Elliot Carter, Pierre Boulez, William Schuman, Gyorgy Ligeti, Richard Wernick, Mario Davidovsky, and Peter Maxwell Davies, many of whom wrote music with her voice in mind; in her tours, sang with almost every major conductor and orchestra in the world; had close rapport with her career-long piano accompanist, Gilbert Kalish; made well over a score of recordings, including *Songs of America* (1988); taught for many years at University of Rochester's Eastman School of Music; died in Rochester, New York. See *Current Biography* (October) 1977.

Obituary *N Y Times* I p52 S 17 '89

DE KOONING, ELAINE Mar. 12, 1920–Feb. 1, 1989 Artist; art critic; educator; wife of Willem de Kooning; in portraits and in paintings of landscapes, athletes in action, and bullfighting, fused representational style with techniques of abstract expressionism; held first solo exhibition in 1952; was commissioned to paint President John F. Kennedy's portrait in 1962 for the Truman Library in Independence, Missouri; painted a series of animal images inspired by paleolithic cave paintings (1983–88); taught at Yale, Carnegie-Mellon, and the University of Pennsylvania, among other institutions; died in Southampton, Long Island, New York. See *Current Biography* (July) 1982.

Obituary *N Y Times* B p8 F 2 '89

DEMPSEY, JOHN (NOEL) Jan. 3, 1915–July 16, 1989 Former governor of Connecticut (1961–71); liberal Democrat; as governor, presided over substantial increase in social service and environmental protection programs, which helped set a national trend; previously served as councilman and mayor in Putnam, Connecticut, as state assemblyman, and as lieutenant governor; having chosen not to run again for governor in 1970, returned to Putnam in 1971 to work in family textile business; was for brief time consultant to Southern New England Telephone Company; remained active in politics for many years; died at his home in Killingly, Connecticut. See *Current Biography* (June) 1961.

Obituary *N Y Times* B p6 Jl 17 '89

DORATI, ANTAL Apr. 9, 1906–Nov. 13, 1988 Orchestra conductor; composer; made conducting debut with Budapest Royal Opera in 1924; after serving as conductor with Ballet Russe de Monte Carlo (1933–41), was music director of American Ballet Theatre (1941–45), for whom he arranged and orchestrated music for many ballets, including *Graduation Ball* and *Giselle*; subsequently served as music director of Dallas Symphony (1945–49), Minneapolis Symphony (1949–60), BBC Symphony (1963–66), Stockholm Philharmonic (1966–70), National Symphony in Washington, D.C. (1970–77), and Detroit Symphony (1977–81); was senior conductor of Royal Philharmonic in London (1975–78); made many guest appearances as conductor of operas and concerts; championed works of Bartók and other modern composers; recorded complete set of Haydn symphonies; wrote autobiography *Notes of Seven Decades* (1979); died at his home in Gerzensee, Switzerland. See *Current Biography* (July) 1948.

Obituary *N Y Times* D p26 N 15 '88

DU MAURIER, DAPHNE May 13, 1907–Apr. 19, 1989 Writer; best known for internationally popular Gothic romances, most notably *Rebecca* (1938)—which, like most of her novels, is set on rugged Cornish coast that was her home for most of her life—but also wrote short stories, several plays, a history of Cornwall, biographies of Branwell Brontë, Francis Bacon, and her father, the actor-manager Sir Gerald Du Maurier, and autobiography *Myself When Young; The Shaping of a Writer* (1977); saw many of her books turned into successful films, including *Rebecca* (1940), *Frenchman's Creek* (1944), *My Cousin Rachel* (1953), and *The Birds* (1963), which was based on one of her short stories; named Dame Commander of the British Empire in 1969; died in Par, England. See *Current Biography* (May) 1940.

Obituary *N Y Times* B p13 Ap 20 '89

ELDRIDGE, ROY Jan. 30, 1911–Feb. 26, 1989 Musician; conductor; singer; creative and technically virtuosic jazz trumpeter and bandleader considered by most music historians to be bridge between Louis Armstrong and Dizzy Gillespie; perhaps best remembered for soaring trumpet solo on "Rockin' Chair" and raspy duet with Anita O'Day on "Let Me Off Uptown," both recorded in early 1940s; after serving apprenticeship with Teddy Hill and others, came to prominence in late 1930s as soloist with Fletcher Henderson; crossed color line in 1941 to play with swing bands of Gene Krupa and, later, Artie Shaw; toured U.S. and Europe in 1950s and 1960s with own combos and with such artists as Benny Goodman, Count Basie, and Ella Fitzgerald; from 1969 until heart attack in 1980 led

house band at Jimmy Ryan's jazz club in New York City; died in Valley Stream, New York. See *Current Biography* (March) 1987.

Obituary *N Y Times* B p7 F 28 '89

ENTERS, ANGNA Apr. 28, 1907–Feb. 25, 1989 Dancer; painter; writer; beginning in 1920s, won international following with her distinctive style of dance-mime, a term she originated; created more than 300 character vignettes for her touring Theatre of Angna Enters (1928–60), most notably *Moyen Age*, in which she evoked spirit of Gothic Virgin carved in stone; following success of first New York exhibition in 1933, subsequently exhibited paintings and drawings in many art galleries and museums, including Metropolitan Museum of Art, where some of her works are in the permanent collection; a screenwriter under contract to MGM in 1940s, also wrote three volumes of autobiography, the novel *Among the Daughters* (1956), *On Mime* (1966), an analysis of her work, and several plays; died in Tenafly, New Jersey. See *Current Biography* (June) 1952.

Obituary *N Y Times* B p8 Mr 1 '89

EVANS, MAURICE June 3, 1901–Mar. 12, 1989 Actor; producer; British-born actor whose performances on Broadway and on cross-country tours in 1930s and 1940s in variety of Shakespearean parts, ranging from title roles in *Richard II* and uncut *Hamlet* to Falstaff and Malvolio, earned him reputation as country's foremost classical actor; came to U.S. in 1935, after establishing himself on London stage, primarily with Old Vic company; continued stage success into 1950s with Shavian comedies, most notably *Man and Superman*, and with Broadway smash *Dial "M" for Murder*; produced most of own shows and was coproducer of long-running hits *The Teahouse of the August Moon* (1953) and *No Time for Sergeants* (1955); re-created many of stage successes on television but perhaps best known for role of warlock Maurice on popular series *Bewitched* (1962–74); died in Rottingdean, England. See *Current Biography* (June) 1961.

Obituary *N Y Times* D p27 Mr 14 '89

FISH, MARIE POLAND May 22, 1902–Feb. 1, 1989 Oceanographer; marine biologist; bioacoustician; helped U.S. Navy's antisubmarine vessels distinguish between genuine enemy targets and schools of fish through research in underwater sound detection; analyzed recordings of more than 300 species of marine life; awarded the navy's Distinguished Public Service Award (1966) for twenty years of work for the Office of Naval Research, conducted mostly at the Narragansett Marine Laboratory in Kingston, Rhode Island; died in Westport, Connecticut. See *Current Biography* (October) 1941.

Obituary *N Y Times* B p8 F 2 '89

FITZGERALD, PEGEEN 1910–Jan. 30, 1989 Radio talk-show host; animal-rights activist; ailurophile; with husband, Ed, broadcast *The Fitzgeralds: Book Talk, Back Talk, and Small Talk* on WOR to two million daily listeners from their Manhattan apartment for over forty years; began broadcasting career in 1940 with own program, *Here's Looking at You*, then

Pegeen Prefers; known for familial atmosphere, spontaneity, and good humor in radio commentary on everything from fashion to current events and the arts; after husband's death in 1982, continued broadcasting on WOR, and then WNYC, until medical leave in 1988; headed two animal-rights groups and maintained the Last Post, an animal shelter in Falls Village, Connecticut; died in New York City. See *Current Biography* (April) 1947.

Obituary *N Y Times* D p23 Ja 31 '89

FLEMING, BERRY (JILES) Mar. 19, 1899–Sept. 15, 1989 Writer; journalist; painter; began career in 1922 as reporter for Augusta (Georgia) *Chronicle*; later, as weekly columnist for *Chronicle*, crusaded against local political machine's effort to raze an historic landmark; on basis of that experience, wrote his most popular novel, *Colonel Effingham's Raid* (1943), a satire that was made into screen comedy (1945); wrote some dozen other novels, beginning with *The Conquerer's Stone* (1927), about an eighteenth-century Carolinian pirate, and including *The Lightwood Tree* (1947), covering three centuries of life in a Georgia community, and *The Fortune Tellers* (1951), set in a flood-threatened Georgia town in 1929; when his popularity declined, turned from writing to painting, for almost twenty years; resumed writing with *The Make Believers* (1973); when commercial houses rejected his new books, cofounded Cotton Lane Press to publish them; recently found patron in publisher Martin Shepard, president of Second Chance Press, which began reissuing old Fleming novels in 1987, and of Permanent Press, which published Fleming's new novels *Captain Bennett's Folly* and *Who Dwelt by a Churchyard* in 1989; died in Augusta, Georgia. See *Current Biography* (Yearbook) 1953.

Obituary *N Y Times* p12 S 16 '89

FRANCIS, FRANK (CHALTON) Oct. 5, 1901–Sept. 15, 1988 Librarian; museum administrator; director and principal librarian of British Museum (1959–68); joined British Museum staff in 1926, eventually becoming secretary (1946–47) and keeper of printed books (1948–58); played major role in founding of *British National Bibliography* and publication of third edition of *General Catalogue of Printed Books*; lectured in bibliography at University College London (1945–59); wrote widely on bibliographical subjects and served as editor of several professional journals, including *The Library* (1936–53) and *Journal of Documentation* (1947–68); was knighted in 1960. See *Current Biography* (July) 1959.

Obituary *College and Research Libraries News* F '89

GIAMATTI, A(NGELO) BARTLETT Apr. 4, 1938–Sept. 1, 1989 Baseball commissioner; educator; Renaissance scholar; taught English and comparative literature at Yale University for two decades, beginning in 1966; was president of Yale from 1978 to 1986; became president of major league baseball's National League in December 1986; succeeded Peter V. Ueberroth as commissioner of baseball on April 1, 1989; during his brief tenure as commissioner, was chiefly occupied with case of Cincinnati Reds manager Pete Rose, baseball's all-time hit leader, who was accused of betting on baseball games, including those of his own team; on August 24, 1989 announced "the banishment for life of Pete Rose from baseball"; wrote *The Earthly Paradise and the Renaissance Epic* (1966), *The University and the Public Interest* (1981), and *Exile and Change in Renaissance Literature* (1984), among other books; died in Oak Bluffs, Martha's Vineyard, Massachusetts. See *Current Biography* (April) 1978.

Obituary *N Y Times* p1+ S 2 '89

GOLDMAN, ERIC F(REDERICK) June 12, 1915–Feb. 19, 1989 Historian; educator; spent most of teaching career at Princeton University (1942–85), eventually becoming Rollins Professor of History (1962–85); an authority on modern American history, won Bancroft Prize for *Rendezvous with Destiny: A History of Modern American Reform* (1952); also wrote bestsellers *The Crucial Decade, America 1945–55* (1956) and *The Tragedy of Lyndon Johnson* (1969); as special consultant and adviser to President Lyndon B. Johnson (1964–66), served as liaison between White House and intellectuals outside administration; moderated Emmy Award–winning NBC public-affairs program *The Open Mind* (1959–67) and was commentator on *CBS Morning News* (1975–76); died in Princeton, New Jersey. See *Current Biography* (July) 1964.

Obituary *N Y Times* B p24 F 22 '89

GORMAN, MIKE Dec. 7, 1913–Apr. 1, 1989 Organization official; writer; advocate for mentally ill; directed National Mental Health Committee and National Committee against Mental Illness; began career as reporter for *Daily Oklahoma* in mid-1940s; found his life's cause when routine journalistic assignment led him to see "swamp of lethargy and hopelessness" to which mental patients were consigned in many state hospital systems across country; through his books *Oklahoma Attacks Its Snake Pits* (1948) and *Every Other Bed* (1956), his lobbying of state and federal officials, his public-speaking tours, and his organizational work, was instrumental in attracting attention and resources to the prevention and treatment of psychiatric disorders; served on numerous government commissions on mental illness; was associated with Albert D. Lasker Foundation until 1988; died in Washington, D.C. See *Current Biography* (October) 1956.

Obituary *N Y Times* D p17 Ap 14 '89

GOULD, BEATRICE BLACKMAR 1899 (?)–Jan. 30, 1989 Editor; coedited the *Ladies' Home Journal* with husband, Bruce, from 1935 until both retired in 1962, presiding over threefold increase in circulation, to 7.5 million; instituted an editorial policy dedicated to publishing high-quality fiction and in-depth analyses of politics, international relations, education, and other issues previously neglected by women's magazines; began career as a newspaper reporter and news editor of the women's pages of the New York *Sunday World*; died in Hopewell, New Jersey. See *Current Biography* (November) 1947.

Obituary *N Y Times* D p22 Ja 31 '89

GOULD, (CHARLES) BRUCE July 28, 1898–Aug. 27, 1989 Editor; writer; with his wife, Beatrice Blackmar

Gould, coedited *Ladies' Home Journal*, which became world's largest-selling women's magazine during their long tenure (1935–62); earlier in career, worked successively as daily newspaperman in New York City, freelance contributor to major popular magazines, and an editor of *Saturday Evening Post*; wrote two books on aviation and, with his wife, *American Story* (1968), an account of their lives and work; died at his home in Hopewell, New Jersey. See *Current Biography* (November) 1947.

Obituary *N Y Times* B p5 Ag 30 '89

GRAHAM, SHEILAH 1908(?)–Nov. 17, 1988 Journalist; writer; one of "unholy trio" of Hollywood gossip columnists, along with Hedda Hopper and Louella Parsons; wrote syndicated column for North American Newspaper Alliance for more than three decades, beginning in 1935; served as war correspondent in England (1940–45); was author of *Beloved Infidel* (1958), an account of her love affair with F. Scott Fitzgerald, and other books, including *Confessions of a Hollywood Columnist* (1969), *The Garden of Allah* (1970), and *Hollywood Revisited* (1985); died in Palm Beach, Florida. See *Current Biography* (October) 1969.

Obituary *N Y Times* p10 N 19 '88

GREDE, WILLIAM J(OHN) Feb. 24, 1897–June 5, 1989 Industrialist; self-made businessman; free-enterprise activist; fierce foe of collective bargaining and critic of progressive income tax ("the very foundation of all socialistic programs"); beginning with small Wisconsin foundry in 1920, built Grede Foundries, one of largest independent producers of ductile iron and steel, incorporated in 1940; parried union encroachment preemptively, early on, with generous wage policies and pioneering fringe-benefit programs for his workers; in 1953 served as president of National Association of Manufacturers; in 1958 was one of eleven associates of Robert Welch in founding of John Birch Society, dedicated to fighting alleged international collectivist conspiracy to subvert U.S. republic in name of spurious egalitarianism; was chief executive officer of his company for fifty-three years; died in Brookfield, Wisconsin. See *Current Biography* (February) 1952.

Obituary *N Y Times* A p24 Je 7 '89

GROMYKO, ANDREI A(NDREEVICH) July 1909–July 2, 1989 Soviet statesman; diplomat; foreign minister (1957–85); president (1985–88); a brilliant technocrat and flinty negotiator; despite long-term contribution to East-West détente, best remembered in West for dour, inscrutable visage personifying Soviet foreign policy during Cold War; as junior diplomat and then ambassador in Washington, participated in forging of Soviet-American World War II alliance; helped found UN, where he was permanent Soviet representative from 1946 to 1948; later served briefly as ambassador to Great Britain; after surviving all leadership changes in USSR from Joseph Stalin through Konstantin U. Chernenko, was chief promoter of Mikhail Gorbachev for leadership of Soviet Communist party in 1985; retired from Politboro in April 1989. See *Current Biography* (October) 1958.

Obituary *N Y Times* p1+ Jl 4 '89

HAMMON, WILLIAM McDOWELL July 20, 1904–Sept. 19, 1989 Physician; head of department of epidemiology and microbiology in Graduate School of Public Health at University of Pittsburgh (1950–73); renowned for his experiments in early 1950s with gamma globulin as poliomyelitis preventive precursory to discovery of Salk vaccine; earlier, had directed medical dispensary in Belgian Congo, taught at University of California, and traveled widely in Asia studying tropical diseases for U.S. Public Health Service, U.S. Army, and National Institutes of Health; died at his home in Seminole, Florida. See *Current Biography* (September) 1957.

Obituary *N Y Times* p6 S 23 '89

HANSELL, HAYWOOD S(HEPHERD, JR.) Sept. 28, 1903–Nov. 14, 1988 United States Army Air Force officer; as commander of First Bombardment Division in Europe and later as commander of Twenty-first Bomber Group in Pacific, directed strategic bombing of Germany and Japan in World War II; during Korean conflict, returned to active duty as adviser to Joint Chiefs of Staff; after retirement as major general in 1955, headed Netherlands subsidiary of General Electric Company until 1967; died in Hilton Head, South Carolina. See *Current Biography* (January) 1945.

Obituary *N Y Times* D p28 N 16 '88

HARRINGTON, (EDWARD) MICHAEL Feb. 24, 1928–July 31, 1989 Political activist; writer; cochairman of Democratic Socialists of America; a moderate socialist who believed in working with mainstream liberals, especially in Democratic party, for "incremental changes that create a welfare state that modulates and humanizes capitalist society"; began career in Catholic Worker movement; was best known for his first book, *The Other America: Poverty in the United States* (1962), which helped inspire federal government's "war on poverty" in mid-1960s; wrote fourteen subsequent books, including autobiographies *Fragments of the Century* (1973) and *The Long-Distance Runner* (1988), the semiautobiographical *Taking Sides* (1985), and works expounding political theory and outlining an agenda for a leftist coalition, including *Socialism: Past and Present* (1989); since 1972, was professor of political science at Queens College, City University of New York; died in Larchmont, New York. See *Current Biography* (October) 1988.

Obituary *N Y Times* D p23 Ag 2 '89

HAYS, WAYNE L(EVERE) May 13, 1911–Feb. 10, 1989 U. S. representative from Ohio (1948–76); was high school history teacher before beginning government service as mayor of Flushing, Ohio (1939); over course of twenty-seven-year career in Congress, compiled relatively conservative voting record; a skilled practitioner of cloakroom politics, wielded considerable power as chairman of House Administration Committee, beginning in 1971, and of Democratic Congressional Campaign Committee; resigned in 1976 following scandal surrounding affair with female staff member; elected to Ohio House of Representatives in 1978, but failed to win second term; died in Wheeling, West Virginia. See *Current Biography* (November) 1974.

Obituary *N Y Times* p33 F 11 '89

HELLER, JOHN R(ODERICK), JR. Feb. 27, 1905–May 4, 1989 Physician; U. S. government official; associated with U.S. Public Health Service since 1932, became chief of its venereal disease division in 1943; named director of National Cancer Institute in 1948, oversaw expansion in federally funded research and treatment programs; served as president (1960–65) of Memorial Sloan-Kettering Cancer Center in New York City until partially paralyzed by stroke; acted as special consultant on international cooperation in cancer research to American Cancer Society and National Cancer Institute until official retirement in 1976; received first World Peace through World Health Award from Eleanor Roosevelt Cancer Foundation in 1969, among many other honors; died in Bethesda, Maryland. See *Current Biography* (February) 1949.

Obituary *N Y Times* p10 My 6 '89

HICKERSON, JOHN D(EWEY) Jan. 26, 1898–Jan. 18, 1989 U.S. government official; career foreign service officer; one of the architects of the treaty that established the North Atlantic Treaty Organization (NATO); was adviser to the U.S. delegation at the Dumbarton Oaks conference of 1944 and the United Nations organizing conference in San Francisco in 1945; held foreign service assignments in Mexico, Brazil, and Canada (1920–27); joined State Department in 1927 and, in 1930, became assistant chief of the Division of Western European Affairs and of the Division of European Affairs; appointed director of the Office of European Affairs in 1947; served as assistant secretary of state (1949–53), U.S. ambassador to Finland (1955–59), and to the Philippines (1959–62); died in Bethesda, Maryland. See *Current Biography* (May) 1950.

Obituary *N Y Times* B p5 Ja 20 '89

HIROHITO, EMPEROR OF JAPAN Apr. 29, 1901–Jan. 7, 1989 Japan's longest-reigning monarch; invested with supreme authority on assuming Chrysanthemum Throne in 1926, in practice exerted little influence on Japanese politics until 1945, when, in defiance of generals, decided to accept unconditional surrender, ending World War II; after the war, his powers severely curtailed by new constitution, served as symbol of national unity; tried to bring throne closer to people by making public appearances and by permitting publication of stories and photographs about royal family; as recognized authority on Hydrozoa, wrote fifteen monographs, some of which have been published in English translation, on marine biology; died in Tokyo. See *Current Biography* (March) 1976.

Obituary *N Y Times* p1+ Ja 7 '89

HIRSCH, JOHN (STEPHEN) May 1, 1930–Aug. 1, 1989 Canadian director; cofounder of Manitoba Theatre Center; best known for his work at Ontario's Stratford Festival, Canada's principal theatre, a bulwark of Shakespearean and European classical drama; at the festival, was a guest director (beginning in 1965), co-artistic director, with Jean Gascon (1967–69), and artistic director (1981–85); headed television drama department for Canadian Broadcasting Corporation (1974–77); in U.S., worked with Lincoln Center Repertory and directed on Broadway (*We Bombed in New Haven*, 1968), Off-Broadway, and regionally; in sever-

al North American venues, staged his own translation of *The Dybbuk*; died in Toronto, Canada, of AIDS. See *Current Biography* (April) 1984.

Obituary *N Y Times* A p20 Ag 3 '89

HOFFMAN, ABBIE Nov. 30, 1936–Apr. 12, 1989 Social activist; writer; flamboyant self-styled revolutionary and antiwar activist whose antic behavior and politically inspired pranks made him a media celebrity and, for many young people, the leading ideologue of 1960s; a former organizer in civil rights movement and cofounder of Youth International Party, or Yippies; achieved national notoriety in 1969 when, as one of "Chicago Seven," stood trial for conspiring to disrupt 1968 Democratic National Convention; facing life sentence on cocaine charges, spent six years (1974–80) in hiding; after serving time on lesser charges, was frequent lecturer on college campuses on such topics as apartheid and the environment; wrote several books, including *Revolution for the Hell of It* (1968), *Steal This Book* (1971), and autobiography *Soon to Be a Major Motion Picture* (1980); died, an apparent suicide, in New Hope, Pennsylvania. See *Current Biography* (April) 1981.

Obituary *N Y Times* D p17 Ap 14 '89

HOOK, SIDNEY Dec. 20, 1902–July 12, 1989 Political philosopher; educator; a secular humanist and reconstructed Marxist; rejecting absolute systems, political or religious, believed that morals "are relevant [only] to truths about nature and human nature, truths that rest on scientific evidence"; as a protégé of pragmatist John Dewey, the father of "progressive education," held that correct opinions and behavior come through problem solving in the light of reason, without regard for emotion or prescribed answers; taught philosophy of democracy at New York University, where he headed department of philosophy for thirty-five years, until 1969; since 1973 was senior research fellow at Hoover Institution on War, Revolution, and Peace at Stanford University; wrote dozens of books, including *Toward the Understanding of Karl Marx* (1933), *Pragmatism and the Tragic Sense of Life* (1974), and his autobiography, *Out of Step: An Unquiet Life in the Twentieth Century* (1987); in politics, described himself as a "social democrat" and "Cold War liberal," while his critics, especially those Marxists angry at his passionate anticommunism, called him a "neoconservative"; died in Stanford, California. See *Current Biography* (October) 1952.

Obituary *N Y Times* D p15 Jl 14 '89

HOOPES, DARLINGTON Sept. 11, 1896–Sept. 25, 1989 Socialist party leader; lawyer; came from Quaker family; joined Socialist party at eighteen, in 1914; began political career as assistant city solicitor in Reading, Pennsylvania (1928–32); was a Pennsylvania state representative from 1930 to 1936, when he began four-year term as Reading city solicitor; directed Eastern Cooperatives from 1947 to 1951; in Socialist party, served on national executive committee beginning in 1932; ran for vice-president of U.S. on Socialist ticket headed by Norman Thomas in 1932; chaired party from 1946 to 1957 and from 1960 to 1968; was party's candidate for president in 1952 and 1956; died in Sinking Spring, Pennsylvania. See *Current Biography*

(September) 1952.

Obituary N Y Times D p27 S 27 '89

HOUSEMAN, JOHN Sept. 22, 1902–Oct. 31, 1988 Director; actor; writer; educator; after some four decades in the various facets of the performing arts, finally won fame with his Academy Award–winning motion picture performance of a haughty law school professor in *The Paper Chase* (1973), a role that he later recreated in a popular television series; cofounder, with Orson Welles, of Mercury Theatre, which created a sensation with its 1938 *War of the Worlds* radio broadcast; produced eighteen Hollywood films (1945–62); directed a number of theatrical and opera productions; among many other activities, was artistic director of American Shakespeare Festival (1956–59), head of drama division at Juilliard School (1968–76), and founder, in 1972, of Acting Company, a permanent repertory troupe for Juilliard's drama graduates; traced history of his multiple careers in autobiographies *Run-Through* (1972), *Front and Center* (1979), and *Final Dress* (1983); died in Malibu, California. See *Current Biography* (April) 1984.

Obituary N Y Times A p1+ N 1 '88

HU YAOBANG 1915–Apr. 15, 1989 Chinese government official; as general secretary of the Chinese Communist party (1980–87), was staunch advocate of economic and political reform; a veteran of heroic Long March in mid-1930s, rose steadily in hierarchies of Chinese government and of Communist party over years to appointment, in 1956, to party's Central Committee; in disfavor during Cultural Revolution in mid-1960s, was rehabilitated ten years later and played key role in mentor Deng Xiaoping's consolidation of power; severely criticized by hard-liners for "bourgeois liberalization," was forced to resign in January 1987, after publicly admitting "major mistakes"; died in Beijing, China. See *Current Biography* (November) 1983.

Obituary N Y Times I p38 Ap 16 '89

KÁDÁR, JÁNOS 1912–July 6, 1989 Former prime minister of Hungary and general secretary of Hungarian Communist party; from pawn of cutthroat Stalinism, became, for a time, exemplar of independent reform within Soviet bloc; replacing his former friend László Rajk as interior minister in 1948, played key behind-scenes role in trial that led to Rajk's execution; was himself imprisoned for "Titoist" tendencies from 1951 to 1954, when Prime Minister Imre Nagy helped in his release; returned to government as Nagy supporter; turned coat during nationalist uprising of 1956, reluctantly led by Nagy and suppressed by Soviet forces; as Moscow-backed successor to Nagy, oversaw execution of rebel leaders, including Nagy; gradually changed over following two decades, leading Hungary into an openness then unparalleled in Eastern Europe and short-term economic revival; unresponsive to demands for more reform, was ousted from leadership in 1988 and from all party and ceremonial functions in May 1989; died in Budapest, Hungary on very day that Imre Nagy and his associates were legally rehabilitated by Hungarian Supreme Court. See *Current Biography* (May) 1957.

Obituary N Y Times A p12 Jl 7 '89

KAHANE, MELANIE Nov. 26, 1910–Dec. 22, 1988 Interior and industrial designer; best known for inventive and creative use of colors, textures, and materials; began career in early 1930s as fashion illustrator; as president of own design firm from 1936, planned interiors of countless homes, hotels, and offices, but also designed lighting fixtures, furniture, fabrics, home appliances, and airplane interiors; with husband, broadcast announcer Ben Grauer, appeared on NBC Radio program *Decorating Wavelengths* in late 1950s; inducted into Interior Design Hall of Fame in 1985; died in New York City. See *Current Biography* (July) 1959.

Obituary N Y Times p32 D 24 '88

KARAJAN, HERBERT VON Apr. 5, 1908–July 16, 1989 Austrian-born symphonic and operatic conductor; director of Berlin Philharmonic Orchestra; dominant maestro at Salzburg Festival; founder of Salzburg Easter Festival; widely regarded as most influential conductor of his time; at peak of his career, when he was virtual commuter between Berlin, Salzburg, the Vienna State Opera, and La Scala in Milan, was known as "general music director of Europe"; attempting to combine "Toscanini's precision with [Wilhelm] Furtwängler's fantasy," interpreted late Romantic symphonic repertoire and nineteenth-century opera with sonic elegance and power; directed Berlin Philharmonic for thirty-five years, until April 1989; although his autocratic perfectionism eventually contributed to friction with personnel, shaped Berlin into perhaps most commanding orchestra in world; concerned with preserving his repertoire for posterity, made some 800 audio recordings in addition to films, videotapes, and videodiscs; died in Anif, Austria. See *Current Biography* (September) 1986.

Obituary N Y Times A p1+ Jl 17 '89

KEENY, SPURGEON M(ILTON) July 16, 1893–Oct. 20, 1988 Relief organization official; was engaged in humanitarian welfare work in Asia and Europe for over six decades; joined UNICEF as chief supply officer for Europe in 1948 and served as its regional director for Asia (1950–63); was Asian representative of Taiwan-based Population Council (1963–76); served as consultant to World Bank, Population Council, and other organizations after retirement; was author of *Half the World's Children* (1957); died in Washington, D.C. See *Current Biography* (January) 1958.

Obituary N Y Times B p12 O 24 '88

KEYHOE, DONALD E(DWARD) June 20, 1897–Nov. 29, 1988 Writer; a former military pilot, served as chief of information for civil aeronautics branch of U.S. Department of Commerce (1926–28) and as aide to Charles A. Lindbergh during latter's national tour following solo flight to Paris; beginning in 1930s, contributed scores of articles, mostly about flight, to various magazines; in such books as *Flying Saucers from Outer Space* (1953), *The Flying Saucer Conspiracy* (1955), *Flying Saucers: Top Secret* (1960), and *Aliens from Space* (1973), argued in favor of existence of UFOs piloted by extraterrestrial beings; served as director of National Investigations Committee on Aerial Phenomena; died in New Market, Virginia. See *Current Biography* (June) 1956.

Obituary N Y Times p33 D 3 '88

KHOMEINI, AYATOLLAH RUHOLLA (MUSSAVI)
1900(?)–June 3, 1989 Iranian Shi'ite Muslim leader; founder of Islamic republic; a quiet religious zealot who shook the world; fought what he viewed as corrupting Western influences in Iran vengefully and uncompromisingly, with sense of divine mission that inspired militant fundamentalists throughout Islam to risk or even seek martyrdom in "holy" war against intrusive "infidels"; led revolution that toppled U.S.-backed monarchy of Shah Mohammed Riza Pahlevi in 1979; as "ruler for life" in post-Pahlevi theocracy, proceeded to rebuild Iran in strict accordance with Koran and isolation from outside "pagan" world; allowed summary executions of thousands of drug and sex offenders, religious and political dissidents, and other violators of Islamic code he imposed; condoned taking of American hostages; when Iran-Iraq war came to bloody stalemate in 1988, prayed that "the warrior Iranian people will maintain their revolutionary and sacred rancor and anger in their hearts and use their oppressor-burning flames against the criminal Soviet Union and the world-devouring United States and their surrogates"; in February 1989 issued call for execution of British author Salman Rushdie for writing *The Satanic Verses*, novel containing allegedly blasphemous anti-Islamic satire; died in Teheran, Iran. See *Current Biography* (November) 1979.

Obituary *N Y Times* A p1+ Je 5 '89

KIMBROUGH, EMILY Oct. 23, 1899–Feb. 11, 1989 Writer; held several editorial positions on staff of *Ladies' Home Journal* (1926–29) before turning to freelance writing; attained national celebrity with the publication, in 1942, of best-selling *Our Hearts Were Young and Gay*, a lighthearted reminiscence of a European trip in the 1920s that she wrote with her companion on the journey, Cornelia Otis Skinner; subsequently wrote more than a dozen books in the same vein, including *We Followed Our Hearts to Hollywood* (1943), *Forty Plus and Fancy Free* (1954), *Forever Old, Forever New* (1964), and the autobiography *Now and Then* (1972); in early 1950s hosted her own daily radio program on WCBS in New York City; died in New York City. See *Current Biography* (March) 1944.

Obituary *N Y Times* I p44 F 12 '89

KOONTZ, ELIZABETH D(UNCAN) June 3, 1919–Jan. 6, 1989 Teacher of special education; U.S. government official; as first black president of the National Education Association (1968–69), the nation's largest organization of teachers, urged members to organize, agitate, and, if necessary, strike to resolve grievances; resigned to head the U.S. Labor Department's Women's Bureau; during four-year tenure, spoke out for the rights of black women; supervised nutrition programs for the North Carolina Department of Human Resources (1973–75); appointed U.S. delegate to the United Nations Commission on the Status of Women in 1975; served as North Carolina's assistant state school superintendent (1975–82); a former teacher of special education in North Carolina, was appointed to National Advisory Council on the Education of Disadvantaged Children by President Lyndon B. Johnson in 1965; died in Salisbury, North Carolina. See *Current Biography* (January) 1969.

Obituary *N Y Times* I p26 Ja 8 '89

KRAUS, HANS P(ETER) Oct. 12, 1907–Nov. 1, 1988 Rare-book dealer and collector; after coming to New York City as a refugee from his native Vienna in 1939, founded H. P. Kraus, one of world's most distinguished establishments dealing in rare books and manuscripts, which continued to flourish at time of his death; was honored in 1980 by Library of Congress for contributing his extensive collection of manuscripts, maps, portraits, and medals relating to the life and explorations of Sir Francis Drake; died at his home in Ridgefield, Connecticut. See *Current Biography* (July) 1960.

Obituary *N Y Times* B p21 N 3 '88

KRAUSHAAR, OTTO F(REDERICK) Nov. 19, 1901–Sept. 23, 1989 Educator; after teaching philosophy at several other institutions, notably Smith College, for two decades, in 1949 became president of Goucher College, a women's school (now coeducational), then located on two campuses, in Baltimore and Towson, Maryland; supervised Goucher's consolidation in Towson, completed in 1956; improved the school's finances and saw it become a nationally ranked women's college; retired in 1967; died in Baltimore. See *Current Biography* (November) 1949.

Obituary *N Y Times* B p20 S 26 '89

LAING, R(ONALD) D(AVID) Oct. 7, 1927–Aug. 23, 1989 British psychiatrist; rebelling against orthodox psychotherapy, sought new approaches to the understanding and treatment of "madness"; began with the premises that "insanity" might be a relatively sane response to an insane life situation and that "breakdown may be breakthrough"; departing from the view of the schizophrenic personality as diseased or broken in its core, asserted that schizophrenia might be a defensive façade behind which the true self remains intact; believing that conventional mental institutions often only worsened the mental state of their inmates, founded London-based organization promoting therapeutic communes without the usual hierarchical, doctor-patient distinctions; expounded (and progressively amended) his views in such books as *The Divided Self* (1960) and *Knots* (1970); also wrote *The Making of a Psychiatrist* (1985), an autobiography covering the first thirty years of his life; died while on vacation in Saint-Tropez, France. See *Current Biography* (March) 1973.

Obituary *N Y Times* D p17 Ag 25 '89

LATTIMORE, OWEN July 29, 1900–May 31, 1989 Scholar; leading American authority on history, culture, and politics of Chinese-Soviet frontier, where he spent much of his youth; edited journal *Pacific Affairs* (1934–41); taught at Johns Hopkins University (1938–63) and University of Leeds (1963–70); wrote more than a score of books, including *The Desert Road to Turkestan* (1928), *High Tartary* (1930), *Manchuria: Cradle of Conflict* (1932), and *Nationalism and Revolution in Mongolia* (1955); outside of scholarly circles, gained prominence as subject of McCarthyite political witch hunt in early 1950s; died in Providence, Rhode Island. See *Current Biography* (July) 1964.

Obituary *N Y Times* B p8 Je 1 '89

LAWE, JOHN (EDWARD) Feb. 26, 1922–Jan. 5, 1989 Irish-born labor union official; president of the Transport Workers Union of America (TWU) from 1985 until his death; as president of Local 100, the New York City chapter of TWU (1977–85), led eleven-day strike of New York transit workers in 1980 that crippled the city's subway and bus service; was second vice-president of the New York City Central Labor Council and vice-president of the New York State AFL-CIO; emigrated from Ireland in 1949; was active in New York's Irish-American community affairs; died in the Bronx, New York. See *Current Biography* (January) 1984.

Obituary *N Y Times* D p15 Ja 6 '89

LEE, JENNIE Nov. 3, 1904–Nov. 16, 1988 Labour member of the British Parliament (1929–31, 1945–70); served as member of Labour party's national executive (1958–70) and as party chairman (1967–68); was minister of state for the arts (1967–70) in Harold Wilson's cabinet; played an important role in founding of Open University, providing higher education by correspondence and other means; was married to prominent Labour party figure Aneurin ("Nye") Bevan, who died in 1960; was known as Baroness Lee of Asheridge after being made a life peer in 1970; was author of *My Life with Nye* (1980) and other books; died in London. See *Current Biography* (May) 1946.

Obituary *N Y Times* p10 N 19 '88

LEMNITZER, LYMAN L. Aug. 29, 1899–Nov. 12, 1988 U.S. Army officer; noted as skilled diplomat and planner; during World War II, was in charge of secret mission that resulted in Allied invasion of North Africa; served as commanding general of 34th Antiaircraft Brigade in Tunisian and Sicilian campaigns; took part in secret negotiations that led to surrender of German armies in Italy and southern Austria in 1945; commanded Seventh Infantry Division in Korea (1951–52); as commander in chief of U.S. and UN commands in Korea and Japan (1955–57), helped to build up Japanese defenses; served as chairman of Joint Chiefs of Staff (1960–62) and Supreme Allied Commander in Europe (1963–69); died in Washington, D.C. See *Current Biography* (November) 1955.

Obituary *N Y Times* I p44 N 13 '88

LEONIDOFF, LEON Jan. 2, 1895–July 29, 1989 Producer and director of stage spectacles; was producer at Radio City Music Hall in New York City from day that the Art Deco theatrical palace opened in 1932; as senior producer there (1934–74), was chief creator of hundreds of lavish stage pageants—involving the dancing Rockettes, full orchestra, choruses, guest soloists, stunning light and audio effects, dazzling costumes, and such unexpected lagniappes as circus animals—staged in conjunction with feature films; at hall, initiated "Glory of Easter" and "Nativity" productions that became national seasonal institutions: earlier, founded Isba Russe ballet company, directed ballet at Manhattan's Capital Theatre, and staged shows at Roxy Theatre; produced extravaganzas at two New York World fairs (1939–40 and 1964–65), Expo 67, and Jones Beach Marine Theatre; died in North Palm Beach, Florida. See *Current Biography* (July) 1941.

Obituary *N Y Times* A p17 Ag 1 '89

LILLIE, BEATRICE May 29, 1894–Jan. 20, 1989 Inimitable, sophisticated, and supremely witty Canadian-born comedienne; performed in theatres, movie houses, vaudeville, supper clubs, films, radio, and television for more than fifty years, beginning with André Charlot's *Not Likely* in 1914; made New York debut in *Charlot's Revue of 1924*; brandishing a long cigarette holder and flaunting her pearl necklace, devastated audiences with her signature songs "Mad Dogs and Englishmen" and "There Are Fairies in the Bottom of My Garden"; entertained British and American troops in the Mediterranean sector, Africa, the Middle East, and Germany during World War II; died in Henley-on-Thames, England. See *Current Biography* (September) 1964.

Obituary *N Y Times* p34 Ja 21 '89

LORENZ, KONRAD (ZACHARIAS) Nov. 7, 1903–Feb. 27, 1989 Austrian ethologist; author; shared 1973 Nobel Prize for physiology or medicine with fellow ethologists Niko Tinbergen and Karl von Frisch for discoveries in animal behavior; through studies of behavior of variety of birds, especially greylag geese, developed crucial ethological concepts of imprinting and innate releasing mechanism and established existence of genetically inherited behavior patterns; in provocative bestseller *On Aggression* (1966), drew controversial analogies between instinctual aggression in animals and man; wrote many other books, some illustrated with own line drawings, on animal behavior and related topics, including *King Solomon's Ring* (1952), *Behind the Mirror: A Search for a Natural History of Human Knowledge* (1971), and *Civilised Man's Eight Deadly Sins* (1974); was cofounder and director of Institute for Behavioral Physiology in Seewiesen, Austria (1958–73) and, since 1973, director of department of animal sociology at Austrian Academy of Sciences' Institute of Comparative Ethology; died in Altenburg, Austria. See *Current Biography* (October) 1977.

Obituary *N Y Times* B p8 Mr 1 '89

LOVELESS, HERSCHEL C(ELLEL) May 5, 1911–May 3, 1989 Governor of Iowa (1957–60); a former railroad worker, entered public service as superintendent of streets (1947–49) and mayor (1949–53) of Ottumwa, Iowa; owned and operated Municipal Equipment Company in Ottumwa until election, in 1956, as Iowa's first Democratic governor in eighteen years; appointed to federal Renegotiation Board, which reviews defense and space contracts, in 1961; resigned in 1969 to become vice-president for government affairs of Chromalloy Corporation (1969–78); died in Winchester, Virginia. See *Current Biography* (July) 1958.

Obituary *N Y Times* p10 My 6 '89

MAGNUSON, WARREN G(RANT) Apr. 12, 1905–May 20, 1989 Democratic senator from Washington State (1944–81); U.S. representative (1937–44); had earlier served in his home state as county prosecutor, assistant U.S. district attorney, and state representative; entered Congress as progressive New Dealer; became one of most powerful figures on Capitol Hill, especially with his assumption of chairmanship of Senate Appropriations Committee; was influential in channeling billions of federal dollars into projects of special concern to him, such as National Institutes of Health in Bethesda, Maryland and Health Sciences Center at University of Washington in Seattle; died in Seattle, Washington. See *Current Biography* (October) 1945.

Obituary *N Y Times* I p46 My 21 '89

MAPPLETHORPE, ROBERT Nov. 4, 1946–Mar. 9, 1989 Photographer of flowers, celebrities, and homosexual S&M scene; worked and exhibited primarily in New York City in the 1970s and 1980s; fused sexual themes with classical composition and sculptural qualities in his photographs; established Robert Mapplethorpe Foundation for AIDS research and visual arts (1988); included in the permanent collections of the Boston Museum of Fine Arts, the Centre Georges Pompidou (Paris), the Stedelijk Museum (Amsterdam), and the Victoria and Albert Museum (London), among others; ignited firestorm of controversy (posthumously) in July 1989, when Corcoran Gallery of Art (Washington, D.C.) canceled final exhibit, fearing that the pornographic content of Mapplethorpe's photographs would jeopardize gallery's federal funding, which was indeed restricted by Congress in October according to obscenity criteria; published *Some Women*, a collection of black-and-white portraits, October 1989; raised $2.3 million by auction of belongings at Christie's on October 31, donating proceeds to AIDS research and visual arts programs; died of AIDS in Boston, Massachusetts. See *Current Biography* (May) 1989.

Obituary *N Y Times* D p16 Mr 10 '89

MARCOS, FERDINAND (EDRALIN) Sept. 11, 1917–Sept. 28, 1989 Former president of Republic of Philippines; began political career as representative and senator; was elected president in 1965; exploiting America's need for friendly ruler in Southeast Asia, especially during Vietnam War, drew huge financial funding from Washington while making his country his personal fiefdom; on salary of $5,700 a year, amassed fortune in the billions for himself, his wife, Imelda, and his cronies, while Philippines remained impoverished; nearing end of his mandatory two-year-term limit in 1972, declared martial law on ground of domestic insurgent Communist threat; thereafter ruled by decree, with increasing ruthlessness; retained American support until 1986, when popular uprising led by middle and upper classes forced him from power following assassination of Benigno Aquino, his chief political rival, and attempt to defraud Corazon Aquino, Benigno's widow, of election to presidency; died in exile in Honolulu, Hawaii, without facing U.S. charges of looting Philippine treasury and defrauding U.S. banks. See *Current Biography* (February) 1967.

Obituary *N Y Times* A p1+ S 29 '89

McCLOY, JOHN J(AY) Mar. 31, 1895–Mar. 11, 1989 Lawyer; U.S. government official; a master of bureaucratic negotiation and policy implementation, advised every U.S. president from Franklin D. Roosevelt to Ronald Reagan, particularly on arms control and disarmament; began career in 1920s as corporate lawyer and returned to private law practice in 1960; entered public service in 1941 as assistant secretary of war;

named president of World Bank in 1947, helped rebuild wartorn economies and ensured bank's continued success with visionary yet businesslike management; as U.S. high commissioner for Germany (1949–52), guided Germany's transformation from occupied country to sovereign state; after return to private life in early 1950s, earned unofficial title "chairman of the Establishment" for chairmanship of various firms, institutions, and agencies, including Chase Manhattan Bank (1953–60), Ford Foundation (1953–65), and President's General Advisory Committee on Disarmament (1961–74); died in Stamford, Connecticut. See *Current Biography* (November) 1961.

Obituary *N Y Times* p44 Mr 12 '89

McNELLIS, MAGGI June 1, 1917–May 24, 1989 Broadcaster; prominent in 1940s and 1950s as radio and television panelist, commentator, interviewer, and hostess of her own gossipy magazine-format programs covering fields of entertainment, beauty, fashion, home decoration, and general interest; began career as supper-club singer; made radio debut locally, in New York, with *Maggi McNellis Show* (which she later took to television); went network in 1944 with *Maggi's Private Wire*; later presented *Maggi's Magazine* on television and participated in *Leave It to the Girls*, a panel show offering advice to women on romance and marriage, on both radio and television; off air, moderated charity fashion shows, chaired society balls, and promoted numerous charitable and cultural causes; died at her home in New York City. See *Current Biography* (January) 1955.

Obituary *N Y Times* D p22 My 25 '89

MELLON, WILLIAM LARIMER, JR. June 26, 1910–Aug. 3, 1989 Humanitarian; medical missionary; an heir of the Mellon banking and oil fortune; inspired in midlife by the example of Albert Schweitzer, earned medical degree (1954) and used his inheritance to open (1956) and operate Albert Schweitzer Hospital in Deschapelles in Haiti's Artibonite River Valley, one of most impoverished and medically deprived regions in Western Hemisphere; from beginning, was assisted fully by his wife, Gwen Grant Mellon, a medical technician who says she will carry on the work in Deschapelles; died in Deschapelles. See *Current Biography* (June) 1965.

Obituary *N Y Times* p10 Ag 5 '89

MIKI, TAKEO Mar. 17, 1907–Nov. 13, 1988 Prime Minister of Japan (1974–76); as head of Liberal Democratic party (1974–76), was identified with its progressive wing; was member of national parliament, or Diet (from 1937); represented pro-American policy during pre–World War II years; subsequently served as minister of communications (1947–48), minister of transport (1954–55), director of economic planning agency (1958–59), chairman of atomic energy commission (1961–62), minister of internal trade and industry (1965–66), foreign minister (1966–68), deputy prime minister and head of environmental agency (1972–74); died in Tokyo. See *Current Biography* (April) 1975.

Obituary *N Y Times* D p26 N 15 '88

MILANOV, ZINKA May 17, 1906–May 30, 1989 Yugoslavian-born opera singer; a dramatic soprano as imposing in voice and bearing as in physique; sang with Metropolitan Opera Company from 1937 to 1966; specialized in Verdi, especially title role in *Aïda*; outside of Verdi repertoire, was best known as Santuzza in Mascagni's *Cavalleria Rusticana*; became naturalized American citizen in 1946; in retirement, coached Christa Ludwig, Anna Moffo, and other younger singers; died in New York City. See *Current Biography* (July) 1944.

Obituary *N Y Times* A p20 My 31 '89

MITCHELL, JOHN N(EWTON) Sept. 15, 1913–Nov. 9, 1988 U.S. government official; lawyer; municipal bond specialist; as attorney general under President Richard M. Nixon (1969–72), used methods later held unconstitutional against antiwar demonstrators, black militants, and others; was one of key figures in Watergate scandal, involving break-in at Democratic national headquarters and variety of "dirty tricks" against foes of the administration, resulting in Nixon's resignation in 1974; served nineteen months in federal prison (1977–79) for conspiracy, obstruction of justice, and perjury in connection with Watergate affair; died in Washington, D.C. See *Current Biography* (June) 1969.

Obituary *N Y Times* A p1+ N 10 '88

MOATS, ALICE-LEONE Mar. 12, 1908–May 14, 1989 Journalist; writer; socialite; combined personal globe-trotting with breezy, often humorous foreign correspondence; wrote from Japan, China, Soviet Union, and East Africa for *Collier's* (1940–42) magazine, from Spain for *Collier's* and *New York Herald Tribune* (1943–44), and from Italy for *Newsday* (1963–64); was columnist for *Philadelphia Inquirer* and freelance contributor to magazines ranging from *Cosmopolitan* to *National Review*; wrote nine books, including best-selling *No Nice Girl Swears* (1933), a sassy etiquette guide for debutantes, *Roman Folly* (1965), and *Blind Date with Mars* (1943), in which she recounted her difficulties in entering wartime Soviet Union and then in staying, when her brash ways made her persona non grata; died in Philadelphia, Pennsylvania. See *Current Biography* (May) 1943.

Obituary *N Y Times* B p6 My 16 '89

MUCCIO, JOHN J(OSEPH) Mar. 19, 1900–May 19, 1989 U.S. career diplomat; was first American ambassador to Republic of [South] Korea (1949–52); earlier in career, held lesser diplomatic posts in Germany, several Latin American countries, China, and Hong Kong; returned to Far East as foreign service inspector in 1947; later served as delegate to UN trusteeship council and ambassador to Iceland and Guatemala; after forty years in foreign service, retired in 1961; died in Washington, D.C. See *Current Biography* (January) 1951.

Obituary *N Y Times* D p11 My 22 '89

NEWTON, HUEY P(ERCY) Feb. 17, 1942–Aug. 22, 1989 Political activist; erstwhile proud symbol of his generation's anger and courage in face of racism and classism; in the Oakland, California African-American ghetto in 1966, cofounded with Bobby Seale the paramilitary Black Panther party, dedicated to "black self-defense" and achievement of "power to determine the destiny of our black community"; following violent confrontation with Oakland police in which one officer was killed, served more than two years in prison before charges against him were dismissed; in 1970 resumed leadership of Panthers, ruling out former militant posture in favor of such benign "tools of revolution" as ghetto health clinics, food programs, and other free social services; earned Ph.D. degree in 1980, when his personal self-destructive tailspin had already begun; was in and out of court or jail on long series of criminal charges, including murder of a teenaged prostitute, misappropriation of funds intended for a Panther elementary school, and violation of parole by possession of narcotics paraphernalia; was shot to death outside an Oakland "crack" cocaine house, allegedly by a drug dealer whom he had robbed. See *Current Biography* (February) 1973.

Obituary *N Y Times* A p1+ Ag 23 '89

NOGUCHI, ISAMU Nov. 17, 1904–Dec. 30, 1988 Sculptor; one of most inventive and influential creators of twentieth-century art; integrated Eastern and Western artistic traditions in works that are remarkable for sensitivity to materials and purity of form; best known for abstract sculptures designed to enhance architecture, especially massive *Red Cube* (1968) on plaza of Marine Midland Building in New York, and for sculpture gardens, such as "Park of Peace" in Hiroshima (1952) and Billy Rose Sculpture Garden in Jerusalem (1965), but also designed stage sets, most notably for choreographers Martha Graham and George Balanchine and for John Gielgud's boldly stylized 1955 production of *King Lear*; worked with variety of materials, including clay, wood, and stainless steel, but primary medium was stone—"the fundament of the earth," in his words; awarded Edward MacDowell Medal (1982) for outstanding contribution to the arts and National Medal of Arts (1987); died in New York City. See *Current Biography* (September) 1943.

Obituary *N Y Times* p1+ D 31 '88

OLIVIER, LAURENCE May 20, 1907–July 11, 1989 British actor; director; producer; the ranging, artful lion of twentieth-century English theatre; from Old Vic to film and television, dazzled audiences with his craft and versatility in interpreting, among other playwrights, Sophocles, Shakespeare, Ibsen, Chekhov, Strindberg, and such contemporaries as Noel Coward, Tennessee Williams, Eugene Ionesco, and John Osborne; as an actor, undertook an amazing variety of challenging roles, classical and romantic, majestic and vulgar, with a bold authority perhaps unequaled since Edmund Kean and William Charles Macready; following apprenticeship with Birmingham Repertory Company (1925–28), went into West End and Broadway productions and motion pictures (ultimately, a total of almost sixty); joined Old Vic Theatre Company in 1937 and helped revive that Shakespearian bastion in mid-1940s; was first director of Chichester Festival Theatre; directed National Theatre from 1963 to 1973; became film star in such brooding youthful roles as Heathcliff in *Wuthering Heights* (1939) and Maxim de Winter in *Rebecca* (1940); resoundingly, brought

Shakespeare to mass international audience with his screen adaptations of *Henry V* (1946), *Hamlet* (1948), and *Richard III* (1954); felt special affinity for Archie Rice, the seedy, desperate music-hall trouper he played in *The Entertainer* (stage, 1957; screen, 1960); won special Academy Award as producer, director, and star of *Henry V*; was nominated for Oscars for his comic performance as Andrew Wyke in *Sleuth* (1973) and his interpretation of Christian Szell, the unreconstructed, sadistic Nazi in *Marathon Man* (1976); won special Academy Award for lifetime achievement (1978); in his last years, did his major acting on television, where his credits included a valedictory, thundering *King Lear* (1983); wrote books *Confessions of an Actor* (1982), his autobiography, and *On Acting* (1986), an explanation of his craft; died at his home in Steyning, near Ashurst, England. See *Current Biography* (January) 1979.

Obituary *N Y Times* A p1+ Jl 12 '89

O'MEARA, WALTER (ANDREW) Jan. 29, 1897–Sept 29, 1989 Writer; advertising executive; began advertising career as copywriter and idea creator with J. Walter Thompson agency in 1920; became creative director of Benton and Bowles in 1932; returned to J. Walter Thompson as cochairman of its review board in 1945; later was an executive with Lennon & Newell and a consultant at Sullivan, Stauffer, Colwell & Bayles; wrote historical novels *The Trees Went Forth* (1947), set in a logging camp, *The Grand Partage* (1951), based on the journal of a clerk with the North West Co., and *The Spanish Bride* (1954), about Spaniards trying to keep a foothold in Southwest in 1700s, among others; also wrote *We Made It through the Winter* (1974), a memoir of his Minnesota childhood; died in Cohasset, Massachusetts. See *Current Biography* (Yearbook) 1958.

Obituary *N Y Times* D p12 O 2 '89

ONASSIS, CHRISTINA Dec. 11, 1950–Nov. 19, 1988 Business executive; one of world's wealthiest women; inherited multimillion-dollar shipping and real-estate interests from her father, Greek shipping magnate Aristotle S. Onassis, who died in 1975; was president of fourteen-member multinational board of Alexander Onassis Foundation, which has controlled family fortune since 1975; had one child, Athena Onassis, presumably her sole heir, from her fourth marriage, to the French businessman Thierry Roussel; died, apparently as result of heart attack, while visiting friends in Buenos Aires, Argentina. See *Current Biography* (February) 1976.

Obituary *N Y Times* A p12 N 21 '88

PEPPER, CLAUDE (DENSON) Sept. 8, 1900–May 30, 1989 U.S. liberal Democratic representative from Florida since 1963; former U.S. senator (1936–51); fiery fighter for disadvantaged among his constituents; went to Washington on prolabor platform; became foremost congressional advocate for rights of elderly; was promoter of Medicare and Medicaid and vigilante against depredations on Social Security system; cooperated in President Franklin D. Roosevelt's strategies for enacting New Deal legislation and maneuvering isolationist America into World War II; later supported Fair Deal (but not Cold War and concomitant buildup of nuclear arsenal) and Great Society (including civil rights agenda); had most influence as chairman of House Rules Committee, beginning in 1983; in 1986 won passage of law against mandatory retirement on basis of age; died in Washington, D.C. See *Current Biography* (January) 1983.

Obituary *N Y Times* A p1+ My 31 '89

POTTER, W(ILLIAM) E(VERETT) July 17, 1905–Dec. 5, 1988 Engineer; U.S. government official; during twenty-five-year career in U.S. Army Corps of Engineers, rotated between military and civil works assignments, including river-control project in Missouri and construction of military bases in Alaska; served as governor of Canal Zone (1956–60); after retirement from army in 1960 with rank of major general, became executive vice-president of 1964 New York World's Fair; as vice-president for Florida planning for Walt Disney Productions (1965–73), supervised design and construction of infrastructure for Disney World amusement park; died in Orlando, Florida. See *Current Biography* (December) 1957.

Obituary *N Y Times* D p24 D 7 '88

PRIDE, ALFRED M(ELVILLE) Sept. 10, 1897–Dec. 24, 1988 U.S. naval officer; pioneered development of aircraft carrier operations; began naval service as machinist's mate in World War I, eventually rising to rank of admiral; assisted in outfitting of navy's first aircraft carrier in 1921 and made first landing of autogiro aircraft on carrier ten years later; as captain of USS *Belleau Wood*, led major strikes against Japanese in World War II, earning many combat decorations; later served as chief of navy's Bureau of Aeronautics (1947–51) and commander of Seventh Fleet, from 1953 until retirement in 1959; died in Arnold, Maryland. See *Current Biography* (November) 1954.

Obituary *N Y Times* D p19 D 29 '88

RADNER, GILDA June 28, 1946–May 20, 1989 Comedienne; actress; a lively, squawky-voiced mistress of zany parodic improvisation honed in apprenticeship with a Second City comedy troupe; won national fame and Emmy Award (1978) as a charter star (1975–80) of irreverent NBC television weekly comedy-variety series *Saturday Night Live*; on that show, presented a gallery of eccentric characterizations, from a gumcracking Jewish "princess" and sniffling and hyperactive children to scatterbrained and speech-impeded newscasters and a malaprop-confused editorial replier railing indignantly against undue concern over "Soviet jewelry" and "endangered feces"; in mid-1970s wrote for and performed in syndicated *National Lampoon Radio Show* and Off-Broadway revue *National Lampoon Show*; on Broadway, starred in *Gilda Radner—Live from New York* (1979) and *Lunch Hour* (1980); was featured in several films, including *The Woman in Red* (1984), of which Gene Wilder, her future husband, was writer, director, and costar; wrote *It's Always Something* (1989), a book about her fight against ovarian cancer; died in Los Angeles, California. See *Current Biography* (February) 1980.

Obituary *N Y Times* I p46 My 21 '89

REED, PHILIP D(UNHAM) Nov. 16, 1899–Mar. 10, 1989 Corporation executive; lawyer; engineer; worked as patent attorney before joining General Electric in 1926, where used knowledge of law and engineering to rise through ranks to post of chairman of the board (1940–58); in late 1940s and 1950s, oversaw nationwide expansion of GE's plants to meet increased consumer demand; served as chairman of Federal Reserve Bank of New York (1959–65); throughout career, devoted considerable time and effort to preserving world peace and fostering international cooperation as chief executive of several national and international agencies and organizations, including International Chamber of Commerce, Carnegie Endowment for International Peace, and Council on Foreign Relations; died in Rye, New York. See *Current Biography* (January) 1949.

Obituary *N Y Times* p33 Mr 11 '89

ROBINSON, SUGAR RAY May 3, 1921–Apr. 12, 1989 Boxer; a five-time world middleweight champion, considered by many prizefight experts to have been, pound for pound, best fighter in history of sport; won all eighty-nine amateur bouts and 1939 Golden Gloves featherweight title before making professional debut in 1940, as lightweight; during twenty-five-year pro career, recorded 174 victories (110 knockouts) and only nineteen defeats—ten coming after fortieth birthday; following retirement, devoted most of time to Sugar Ray Robinson Youth Foundation, which he set up in 1969; elected to Boxing Hall of Fame in 1967; wrote autobiography *Sugar Ray* (1970); died in Culver City, California. See *Current Biography* (March) 1951.

Obituary *N Y Times* A p1+ Ap 13 '89

RUSSELL, CHARLES H(INTON) Dec. 27, 1903–Sept. 13, 1989 Republican governor of Nevada (1951–58); had previously served as Nevada state assemblyman (1935–40) and senator (1941–46) and U.S. congressman (1947–49); after his defeat for reelection to Congress, was an administrator of U.S. foreign aid programs in Western Europe and Paraguay; published Ely (Nevada) *Record* from 1929 to 1946; died in Carson City, Nevada. See *Current Biography* (December) 1955.

Obituary *N Y Times* B p6 S 15 '89

SCHECHTER, A(BEL) A(LAN) Aug. 10, 1907–May 24, 1989 Broadcasting executive; consultant; organized and directed National Broadcasting Company's radio news and special events department (1932–42); during World War II, worked with U.S. government in supervision of radio and press communications from war correspondents; following executive stints with Mutual Broadcasting Company and Crowell Collier Publishing Company, returned to NBC as first executive producer of *Today* television show (1951–52); founded own public relations company in 1952; died in automobile accident in Southampton, New York. See *Current Biography* (May) 1941.

Obituary *N Y Times* A p18 My 26 '89

SCHIFF, DOROTHY Mar. 11, 1903–Aug. 30, 1989 Former newspaper publisher; heiress; with inheritance, bought controlling interest in *New York Post*, crusading, deficit-ridden liberal daily, in 1939; while maintaining paper's serious political slant, put it into popular tabloid format, featuring scandal, glamour, human interest, comics, and a host of columnists; during difficult financial times for all Manhattan newspapers, including the prolonged strike of 1962–63, kept *Post* afloat and saw it emerge, from behind, as city's only surviving afternoon daily; after managing from periphery, became *Post's* editor in chief as well as publisher, president, and treasurer in early 1960s; in 1976 sold *Post* to Rupert Murdoch, who later sold it to Peter S. Kalikow; died at her home in New York City. See *Current Biography* (January) 1965.

Obituary *N Y Times* B p11 Ag 31 '89

SCHIOTZ, FREDRIK A(XEL) June 15, 1901–Feb. 25, 1989 Lutheran clergyman; first president of American Lutheran church, created by merger of several smaller Lutheran denominations in 1960; began ministerial work as pastor in 1930, but spent most of career in administrative posts, most notably as director of Lutheran World Federation's department of world missions (1952–54); elected president of Evangelical Lutheran church in 1954, helped forge union with American Lutheran church; during tenure (1960–70) as president of American Lutherans, also served as president of Lutheran World Federation (1963–70); following mandatory retirement in 1970, conducted seminars at Lutheran seminaries throughout U.S. and Canada; died in Minneapolis, Minnesota. See *Current Biography* (April) 1972.

Obituary *N Y Times* B p16 F 27 '89

SCOTT, PETER MARKHAM Sept. 14, 1909–Aug. 29, 1989 British naturalist; painter; ornithologist, wildlife advocate; champion yachtsman and glider pilot; son of Robert Falcon Scott, the Antarctic explorer who died near South Pole in 1912; in view of fellow naturalist and broadcaster David Attenborough, was "the patron saint of conservation"; combined painting of ducks and geese with hunting of same before renouncing wildfowling and becoming protectionist; founded Wildlife and Wetlands Trust in Gloucestershire in 1946; later cofounded World Wildlife Fund (now World Wide Fund for Nature); traveled and explored widely in search and defense of wildlife, including whales; wrote autobiography, *The Eye of the Wind* (1961), and three travel diaries in addition to eighteen books on natural history illustrated with his paintings; provided illustrations for twenty books by others; hosted long-running BBC environmental series *Look*; was knighted in 1973; died in Bristol, England. See *Current Biography* (May) 1968.

Obituary *N Y Times* B p12 Ag 31 '89

SCOTT, SHEILA Apr. 27, 1927–Oct. 20, 1988 British aviator; began flying in 1959, after modest acting career; established over 100 flying records and won numerous trophies and awards, including Harmon International Aviation Trophy (1967); was first British pilot to make round-the-world solo flight in light plane (1966); established world records on London-to-Cape Town and Cape Town-to-London flights (1967); was first woman to fly around the world by way of the North Pole in a light aircraft (1971); was named an officer of Order of the British Empire (1968); wrote *I Must Fly* (1968), among other books. See *Current*

Biography (November) 1974.

Obituary *N Y Times* B p5 O 21 '88

SEARS, ROBERT R(ICHARDSON) Aug. 31, 1908–May 22, 1989 Psychologist; educator; nationally known for his work on psychological development of children, especially studies done with view to aggressiveness as affected by varying degrees of parental discipline and permissiveness; carrying on long-range study of children with high IQs begun by Lewis M. Termanand in 1921, followed the subjects through maturity into advanced years; after affiliations with University of Illinois, Yale University, and University of Iowa, joined faculty of Stanford University, where he was head of psychology department (1953–61), dean of School of Humanities and Sciences (1961–70), and David Starr Jordan professor of psychology (1970–73); died in Menlo Park, California. See *Current Biography* (July) 1952.

Obituary *N Y Times* A p18 My 26 '89

SEEFRIED, IRMGARD Oct. 9, 1919–Nov. 24, 1988 German-born Austrian soprano; was noted for her clear voice and her commanding stage presence; won praise for her interpretations of Mozart and Richard Strauss roles and as a recital and concert singer; made her debut with Vienna State Opera, as Eva in *Die Meistersinger* in 1943 and remained with that company until her retirement in 1980; made her first appearance at Metropolitan Opera in 1953, as Susanna in *Marriage of Figaro*, one of her signature roles; died in Vienna. See *Current Biography* (February) 1956.

Obituary *N Y Times* B p16 N 25 '88

SEGRÈ, EMILIO (GINO) Feb. 1, 1905–Apr. 22, 1989 Physicist; university professor; shared 1959 Nobel Prize in physics for discovery of antiproton; began career in 1930 as member of physics faculty at University of Rome, where he collaborated with Enrico Fermi on production of artificial radioactivity; after immigration to U. S. in 1938, joined physics department at University of California at Berkeley; as group leader at Los Alamos (New Mexico) Scientific Laboratory in World War II, conducted experiments in spontaneous fission; an emeritus professor at Berkeley since 1972, continued to lecture and write scientific articles and books, including two volumes on history of quarks: *From X-rays to Quarks* (1980) and *From Falling Bodies to Radio Waves* (1988); died in Lafayette, California. See *Current Biography* (April) 1960.

Obituary *N Y Times* D p11 Ap 24 '89

SERGIO, LISA Mar. 17, 1905–June 22, 1989 Broadcaster; once known as "Golden Voice of Rome"; began career in 1920s as editor of *Italian Mail*, English-language literary weekly, in Florence, Italy, where she had been born to upper-class Italian father and American mother; after working in archaeology, was broadcaster of news and commentary in French and English on Italian shortwave radio from 1933 to 1937, when she was dismissed for lack of Fascist enthusiasm; fled to U.S. with help of radio developer and family friend Guglielmo Marconi; in U.S., announced opera and classical music broadcasts and interviewed international celebrities for NBC radio network (1937–39) and had own daily news commentary program on New York City station WQXR (1939–46); later taught propaganda analysis at Columbia University and lectured at other universities and colleges; wrote several books, including *I Am My Beloved* (1969), a biography of Anita Garibaldi; died in Washington, D.C. See *Current Biography* (June) 1944.

Obituary *N Y Times* B p8 Je 26 '89

SHOCKLEY, WILLIAM (BRADFORD) Feb. 13, 1910–Aug. 12, 1989 Physicist; professor emeritus of electrical engineering at Stanford University; shared 1956 Nobel Prize for his role in invention of the transistor, which outmoded three-element vacuum tube and revolutionized electronics; in 1936 joined technical staff of Bell Laboratories in Murray Hill, New Jersey, where he did his prize-winning work in collaboration with John Bardeen and Walter H. Brattain; in 1954 left Bell Laboratories to found Shockley Semiconductor Laboratories, a short-lived enterprise that helped spawn "Silicon Valley," the industrial phenomenon that ushered in the computer age; began lecturing at Stanford University in Palo Alto, California in 1958 and was professor there from 1963 to 1975; regarded his revolutionary contribution to electronics as less important than his controversial latter-day study of genetic racial differences as evidenced in such data as IQ tests; died in Palo Alto. See *Current Biography* (December) 1953.

Obituary *N Y Times* D p9 Ag 14 '89

SILLCOX, LEWIS K(ETCHAM) Apr. 30, 1886–Mar. 3, 1989 Mechanical engineer; after twenty-five years as mechanical engineer for various railroads in U.S. and Canada, became vice-president of New York Air Brake Company in 1927; during long career with company, culminating in appointment as vice-chairman of board of directors in 1952, was instrumental in development of improved methods of railway-power application; following retirement in 1959, served one-year term as director of newly created New York State Office of Transportation; throughout career, lectured frequently on engineering, applied mechanics, and economics of transportation at many colleges and universities and contributed numerous articles to technical journals; died in Watertown, New York. See *Current Biography* (December) 1954.

Obituary *N Y Times* p34 Mr 4 '89

SIMENON, GEORGES (JOSEPH CHRISTIAN) Feb. 13, 1903–Sept. 4, 1989 Belgian writer; most prolific, widely published author of twentieth century; wrote an average of four books a year, published simultaneously in more than a score of languages; best known as creator of Inspector Maigret, the intuitive, compassionate Parisian detective featured in eighty-four of his *romans policiers*; also wrote more than 1,000 short stories and articles, the best-selling autobiography *Mémoires Intimes* (1981; *Intimate Memoirs*, 1984), and large number of non-Maigret psychological novels; was deft, impressionistic writer with sure insight into human behavior and mastery of suspenseful narration; died in Lausanne, Switzerland. See *Current Biography* (April) 1970.

Obituary *N Y Times* A p1+ S 7 '89

STEEL, JOHANNES Aug. 3, 1906?–Nov. 30, 1988 Journalist known for decidedly left-wing viewpoint and sensational (and occasionally accurate) prognostications; after fleeing his native Germany in 1933, settled in U.S. and landed job with *New York Post*, eventually becoming its foreign-news editor; in late 1930s and 1940s, worked as commentator and news analyst for New York radio stations WMCA and WOR; more recently, wrote syndicated financial column; was author of many books, including *Hitler as Frankenstein* (1933), *The Bloody Record of Nazi Atrocities* (1944), and autobiography *Escape to the Present* (1937); died in Newtown, Connecticut. See *Current Biography* (June) 1941.

Obituary *N Y Times* p33 D 3 '88

STELOFF, (IDA) FRANCES Dec. 31, 1887–Apr. 15, 1989 Bookseller; founder of Gotham Book Mart, a Manhattan haven for bibliophiles and rendezvous for writers, actors, dancers, and other artists since 1920; through encouragement of literary experimentation, promotion of works by promising untried authors, and staunch opposition to censorship, indirectly influenced development of twentieth-century literature; helped organize, in 1947, James Joyce Society and served for many years as its treasurer; sold Gotham in 1967 but remained on staff as consultant until death; presented with distinguished service award by National Institute of Arts and Letters in 1965; died in New York City. See *Current Biography* (November) 1965.

Obituary *N Y Times* p36 Ap 16 '89

STONE, I(SIDOR) F(EINSTEIN) Dec. 24, 1907–June 18, 1989 Journalist; writer; maverick, radical pamphleteer; a self-described "New Lefty before there was a New Left"; best known for his one-man Washington, D.C.-based newsletters *I. F. Stone's Weekly* (1953–68) and *I. F. Stone's Bi-Weekly* (1969–71), in which he promoted civil liberties and international peace and, above all, issued exposés of official chicanery and disinformation, especially in Pentagon, based on his tireless perusal of public documents; in course of career spanning more than six decades, was associated as writer with New York City's *PM* and *Post*, among other newspapers, and periodicals *Nation* and *New York Review of Books*; wrote twelve books, including *This Is Israel* (1948), *The Truman Era* (1953), *The Hidden History of the Korean War* (1969), *The Killings at Kent State; How Murder Went Unpunished* (1971), and *The Trial of Socrates* (1988); died in Boston, Massachusetts. See *Current Biography* (September) 1972.

Obituary *N Y Times* D p13 Je 19 '89

STONE, IRVING July 14, 1903–Aug. 26, 1989 Writer; the pioneering and most successful master of the contemporary biographical novel; with painstaking research and imaginative artistry, made famous figures from past come alive on printed page with ring of historical truth; wrote more than a score of books, including fictionalized biographies of Sigmund Freud, Jack London, Clarence Darrow, and Abraham and Mary Todd Lincoln; was best known for *Lust for Life* (1934), about Vincent van Gogh, *The President's Lady* (1951), about Andrew and Rachel Jackson, and *The Agony and the Ecstasy* (1961), about Michelangelo—each of which was translated to screen with box-office suc-

cess; saw his books sell in excess of thirty million copies; died in Los Angeles, California. See *Current Biography* (December) 1967.

Obituary *N Y Times* B p6 Ag 28 '89

STUDEBAKER, JOHN W(ARD) June 10, 1887–July 26, 1989 Former U.S. commissioner of education; educational-publishing executive; began career as superintendent of schools in Des Moines, Iowa; as superintendent, promoted public forums as extensions of public school system; explained importance to democracy of such community discussion groups in his books *The American Way* (1935) and *Plain Talk* (1936); was appointed commissioner of education in 1934; as commissioner, developed educational programs for functionally illiterate and for military industry training; resigned in 1948, ostensibly for financial reasons but basically, according to his intimates, because he could not tolerate political domination of his office; after leaving government, was vice-president and chairman of editorial board of Scholastic Magazines for twenty years, until 1968; died in Walnut Creek, California. See *Current Biography* (May) 1942.

Obituary *N Y Times* A p10 Jl 28 '89

SYMINGTON, (WILLIAM) STUART June 26, 1901–Dec. 14, 1988 U.S. senator from Missouri (1953–77); industrialist; twice (in 1956 and 1960) sought Democratic nomination for U.S. president; served as executive of several companies before becoming, in 1938, president and board chairman of Emerson Electric Manufacturing Company in St. Louis; entered government service in 1945 as chairman of Surplus Property Board and subsequently served Truman administration as assistant secretary of war for air (1946–47), secretary of air force (1947–50), and chairman of National Security Resources Board (1950–51); as member of Senate's Foreign Relations and Armed Services committees, advocated strong defense but became increasingly critical of military spending, especially during Vietnam War; died in New Canaan, Connecticut. See *Current Biography* (July) 1956.

Obituary *N Y Times* D p26 D 15 '88

TALLAMY, BERTRAM D(ALLEY) Dec. 1, 1901–Sept. 14, 1989 Civil engineer; government official; as federal highway administrator (1957–61), directed first stage of $33 billion interstate highway construction program authorized by Federal Highway Act of 1956; as New York State superintendent of public works (1948–54), supervised construction of New York State thruway; before going to Washington, was chairman of New York State Thruway Authority; was consulting engineer in Washington from 1961 until his retirement in 1970; died in Washington, D.C. See *Current Biography* (March) 1957.

Obituary *N Y Times* D p25 S 19 '89

TALVELA, MARTTI Feb. 4, 1935–July 22, 1989 Finnish opera singer; a basso with a resplendent voice and giant physique that enhanced the majesty or menace of his wonted mythical, often heroic, roles; in his repertoire, encompassed many Wagnerian and some Verdi and Mozart interpretations but was chiefly identified with title part in Moussorgsky's *Boris*

Godunov; began operatic career with Swedish Royal Opera in 1961; the following year, found mentor and patron in Wieland Wagner, director of Beyreuth (Germany) Festival; made debut with Deutsche Oper in West Berlin in 1963; went on to become familiar performer in great opera centers of Europe and U.S., including Metropolitan; concurrently, sang lieder on concert stage—a difficult, rare pursuit for a bass singer; directed Savonlinna (Finland) Opera Festival from 1972 to 1980; was designated to become director of Finnish National Opera in 1992; died on his farm in Juva, Finland. See *Current Biography* (October) 1983.

Obituary *N Y Times* D p11 Jl 24 '89

THOMPSON, FRANK, JR. July 26, 1918–July 22, 1989 Former Democratic U.S. representative from New Jersey; was first elected to Congress in 1954; served thirteen terms, covering twenty-six years; as chair of House Administration Committee and member of Education and Labor Committee, was powerful promoter of liberal legislation, especially laws promoting the arts, funding education, and supporting labor unions; lost election in 1980, when he was under indictment in "Abscam" scandal, in which he, along with several other members of Congress, had been entrapped by federal undercover agents offering bribes for legislative favors; convicted of bribery and conspiracy, served two years of three-year prison term; died in Baltimore, Maryland. See *Current Biography* (July) 1959.

Obituary *N Y Times* D p11 Jl 24 '89

THOMSON, VIRGIL (GARNETT) Nov. 25, 1896–Sept. 30, 1989 Composer; music critic; guest conductor; described by Leonard Bernstein as a "son of the hymnal, yet highly sophisticated," the creator of "witty and simplistic" music "rarely performed" but exerting an "extraordinary influence . . . on his colleagues, especially Aaron Copland"; with somewhat disingenuous but refreshing naïveté, blended American folk themes and homespun melodies into eclectic musical structures reflecting influences ranging from classical to neoromantic and ultramodern; began career as church organist; sang with Harvard Glee Club; was member of American expatriate community in Paris from 1925 to 1940; in addition to symphonies, symphonic "landscapes," liturgical pieces, cantatas, and sonatas, composed some 100 piano and other musical "portraits" of his friends; wrote incidental and background music for a host of stage productions, mostly classical; became best known for his operas *Four Saints in Three Acts* (1934) and *The Mother of Us All* (1947), both written in collaboration with Gertrude Stein; wrote the scores for several documentary motion pictures, including *Louisiana Story* (1948), for which he won a Pulitzer Prize; as lecturer and as music critic for *New York Herald Tribune* (1940–54) and other publications, produced body of essays collected in six books, including award-winning *The Virgil Thomson Reader* (1981) and not counting "Music with Words," scheduled for publication in 1989; also wrote the autobiography *Virgil Thomson* (1966); impressed other musicians with the "unpredictable, provocative prose" (Leonard Bernstein) and "unquenchable panache" (Ned Rorem) of his criticism; died in Chelsea Hotel, his New York City home since 1940. See

Current Biography (October) 1966.

Obituary *N Y Times* I p42 O 1 '89

TINBERGEN, NIKO(LAAS) Apr. 15, 1907–Dec. 21, 1988 Dutch zoologist; shared 1973 Nobel Prize for physiology or medicine with fellow zoologists Konrad Lorenz and Karl von Frisch for discoveries in animal behavior; best known for research into habits of gulls and other sea birds; pioneered application of ethological research to study of human behavior, particularly that of autistic children; wrote many books, some illustrated with own photos, on animal behavior, including *Social Behavior in Animals* (1953), *The Herring Gull's World* (1960), and two-volume *The Animal and Its World* (1972–73), and co-authored, with wife, Elizabeth, *Early Childhood Autism* (1972) and *Autistic Children; New Hope for a Cure* (1983); was member of faculty of animal behavior at Oxford University from 1949 until death; died in Oxford, England. See *Current Biography* (November) 1975.

Obituary *N Y Times* p32 D 24 '88

TISHLER, MAX Oct. 30, 1907–Mar. 18, 1989 Chemist; educator; leader in development of drugs for treatment of arthritis, hypertension, and heart disease; during thirty-three-year association (1937–69) with pharmaceutical manufacturer Merck & Company, rose from research chemist to president, in 1956, of its Merck Sharp and Dohme Research Laboratories; over course of career, developed commercial processes for manufacture of penicillin, cortisone, certain vitamins, and vaccines to control livestock and poultry diseases; joined chemistry faculty at Wesleyan University in 1970 and was emeritus University Professor of the Sciences at time of his death; awarded National Medal of Science in 1987; died in Middletown, Connecticut. See *Current Biography* (March) 1952.

Obituary *N Y Times* B p10 Mr 20 '89

TUCHMAN, BARBARA W(ERTHEIM) Jan. 30, 1912–Feb. 6, 1989 Biographer; historian; won Pulitzer Prizes for *The Guns of August* (1962), a diplomatic and military history of the outbreak of World War I, and *Stilwell and the American Experience in China, 1911–45* (1971), a biography of General Joseph W. Stilwell set in the context of fast-breaking developments in modern China; emphasized narrative drive and graphic presentation of historical characters in her writing; began career in the 1930s as an editor and European correspondent for the *Nation*, for which she reported on the Spanish Civil War from Madrid and Valencia; wrote series of best-selling books of popularized historical scholarship, including *The Zimmerman Telegram* (1958), *The Proud Tower* (1966), *Notes from China* (1972), *A Distant Mirror* (1978), *Practicing History* (1981), *The March of Folly: From Troy to Vietnam* (1984), and *The First Salute* (1988); died in Greenwich, Connecticut. See *Current Biography* (December) 1963.

Obituary *N Y Times* A p1+ F 7 '89

URQUHART, SIR ROBERT E(LLIOTT) Nov. 28, 1901–Dec. 13, 1988 British military officer; commissioned as second lieutenant in Highland Light Infantry, rose to rank of major general (1943) while serving in variety of posts in Britain and India and on battlefields of Europe during World War II; as commander of First Airborne ("Red Devil") Division, led British forces in heroic but ill-fated battle, which was celebrated in book and film *A Bridge Too Far*, to capture bridge over Rhine near Arnhem, the Netherlands, in 1944; after war, served as director general of Territorial Army (1945-46), Britain's reserves, and as commander of British troops in Malaya (1950-52) and Austria (1952-55); following retirement from military in 1955, was director of Davy and United Engineering Company (1957-70); died at Port of Menteith, Scotland. See *Current Biography* (December) 1944.

Obituary *N Y Times* D p16 D 16 '88

VALENTINA May 1, 1900(?)-Sept. 14, 1989 Fashion designer; dressmaker; stage couturière; in her work, followed her dictums "Simplicity survives the changes of fashion" and "Fit the century, forget the year"; opened chic dress shop on Madison Avenue in New York City in 1928; established herself in theatrical couture in 1933 with costumes for Judith Anderson in play *Come of Age*; enhanced her reputation with such creations as those for Lynn Fontanne in *Idiot's Delight*, Katharine Cornell in *Herod and Marianne*, Katharine Hepburn in *The Philadelphia Story*, and Rosa Ponselle and Gladys Swarthout in productions of opera *Carmen*; for three decades designed stage and off-stage clothes for list of actresses and singers including Helen Hayes, Mary Martin, Zorina, Grace Moore, Jarmila Novotna, Lily Pons, Norma Shearer, Rosalind Russell, and Greta Garbo; also custom-created clothes for such society clients as the Astors, the Vanderbilts, the Mellons, and the McCormicks; died at her home in New York City. See *Current Biography* (December) 1946.

Obituary *N Y Times* B p5 S 15 '89

VOORHEES, DONALD July 26, 1903-Jan. 10, 1989 Conductor; musical director; presided over NBC's highly popular *Bell Telephone Hour*, featuring guest artists in a potpourri of classical and popular music, first on radio (1940-59) and then on television (1959-68); also conducted on many other radio shows, including the Maxwell House *Show Boat*, the *General Motors Hour*, the Ed Wynn *Fire Chief* show, and the CBS *Family Hour*; began career at seventeen, conducting the orchestra for Eddie Cantor's musical *Broadway Brevities of 1920*; mounted the podium for other Broadway shows in the 1920s and late 1930s; died in Cape May Court House, New Jersey. See *Current Biography* (February) 1950.

Obituary *N Y Times* B p10 Ja 11 '89

VREELAND, DIANA (DALZIEL) 1903?-Aug. 22, 1989 Fashion journalist; museum consultant; an arbiter of taste for "the beautiful people" (her coinage); began career as offbeat, semifacetious advice-to-snobs columnist for *Harper's Bazaar* in 1936; was fashion editor of that magazine from 1939 to 1962, when she became editor in chief of *Vogue*; turned *Vogue* from what was essentially a haute couture specialty magazine into a lively, wide-ranging society journal and guide to chic living; after leaving *Vogue*, in 1971, became consultant to Costume Institute of Metropolitan Museum of Art, where she staged famous annual fashion and costume exhibitions; wrote *D.V.* (1984), a book of memoirs; died in New York City. See *Current Biography* (February) 1978.

Obituary *N Y Times* A p1+ Ag 23 '89

WARNER, J(OHN) C(HRISTIAN) May 28, 1897-Apr. 12, 1989 Chemist; educator; as president (1950-65) of Carnegie Institute of Technology, now Carnegie-Mellon University, presided over its growth from small technical college into world-renowned research institution; began career at Carnegie Tech as chemistry instructor in 1920s and served as dean of graduate studies (1945-49) and vice-president (1949-50) before assuming presidency; during World War II, coordinated research on plutonium for Manhattan Project; in 1960s served as first president of consortium of universities that designed mammoth particle accelerator at Fermi National Accelerator Laboratory in Batavia, Illinois; at time of death was emeritus president and emeritus professor of physical chemistry at Carnegie-Mellon; died in Gibsonia, Pennsylvania. See *Current Biography* (October) 1950.

Obituary *N Y Times* B p12 Ap 13 '89

WARREN, ROBERT PENN Apr. 24, 1905-Sept. 15, 1989 Writer; literary critic; university professor; first official poet laureate of U.S. (1986-87); a son of the Old South, in which most of his poems, novels, novellas, and short stories are rooted; was a protégé of John Crowe Ransom, a father of Southern Literary Renaissance; cofounded and edited (1935-42) *Southern Review*; was advisory editor of *Kenyon Review* (1938-61); with Cleanth Brooks, wrote *Understanding Poetry* (1938) and *Understanding Fiction* (1943), textbooks that influenced a generation of university students and helped establish postwar dominance of New Criticism in analysis of literature; won Pulitzer Prize for *All the King's Men* (1946), his best-known novel, which was made into equally successful motion picture (1949); also won two Pulitzer Prizes (1958 and 1979) for his poetry; taught at Vanderbilt University, University of Minnesota, and, beginning in 1950, Yale University; died at his summer home in Stratton, Vermont. See *Current Biography* (June) 1970.

Obituary *N Y Times* p1+ S 16 '89

WEEKS, EDWARD (AUGUSTUS), JR. Feb. 19, 1898-Mar. 11, 1989 Writer; editor of Atlantic Monthly Press (1928-38) and *Atlantic Monthly* (1938-66); worked briefly as manuscript reader and book salesman for Horace Liveright publishing company before joining *Atlantic Monthly* staff, in 1924; as editor of Atlantic Monthly Press, developed short but flourishing list of some 200 titles, including best-selling *Drums along the Mohawk* and *Goodbye, Mr. Chips*; during long editorship of *Atlantic Monthly*, managed to increase circulation while maintaining reputation for literary excellence; wrote two handbooks for aspiring writers—*The Trade of Writing* (1935) and *Breaking into Print* (1962)—and memoirs *The Open Heart* (1956) and *Writers and Friends* (1982), among other books; after retirement, served as senior editor and consultant to Atlantic Monthly Press; died in Thompson, Connecticut. See *Current Biography* (December) 1947.

Obituary *N Y Times* D p26 Mr 14 '89

WEISS, PAUL A(LFRED) Mar. 21, 1898–Sept. 8, 1989 Biologist; professor emeritus at Rockefeller University; specialist in study of cellular development, especially embryo growth and regeneration of damaged nerve and muscle tissue; established principle of autonomous cellular organization, in which cells from different organs, randomly mixed, reconstruct themselves into miniature replicas of donor organs without direction from a cellular high command; further, proved that regenerative nutrition flows from cell nuclei through nerve fibers into all parts of body; began his research in his native Austria; in U.S., worked at several universities, including University of Chicago; wrote eleven books, including *The Science of Life* (1973); died in White Plains, New York. See *Current Biography* (October) 1970.

Obituary *N Y Times* B p10 S 12 '89

WOLMAN, ABEL June 10, 1892–Feb. 22, 1989 Engineer; educator; contributed to development of water-chlorination method eventually adopted by most cities in U.S.; worked on stream pollution for U.S. Public Health Service and as chief engineer of Maryland Department of Health before accepting full-time position with sanitary engineering department of Johns Hopkins University, in 1937; throughout remainder of career, also advised scores of government agencies, both in U.S. and abroad, on water supplies, flood protection, and pollution control, including disposal of radioactive waste; received many awards, including National Medal of Science, in 1975, and Tyler Prize for Environmental Achievement, in 1976; died in Baltimore, Maryland. See *Current Biography* (February) 1957.

Obituary *N Y Times* B p4 F 24 '89

BIOGRAPHICAL REFERENCES

Almanac of American Politics, 1988

American Architects Directory, 1970

American Catholic Who's Who, 1978

American Medical Directory, 1988

American Men and Women of Science, 1989-90

Biographical Directory of the American Congress, 1774-1971 (1971)

Biographical Encyclopaedia & Who's Who of the American Theatre (1966)

Biographical Encyclopedia of Pakistan, 1971-72

Biographical Encyclopedia of Scientists (1981)

Blues Who's Who (1978)

Burke's Peerage, Baronetage, and Knightage, 1970

Canadian Almanac & Directory, 1989

Canadian Who's Who, 1989

Celebrity Register (1990)

China Yearbook, 1982

Chujoy, A., and Manchester, P. W., eds. Dance Encyclopedia (1967)

Columbia Dictionary of Modern European Literature (1980)

Concise Biographical Dictionary of Singers (1969)

Concise Oxford Dictionary of Ballet (1982)

Congressional Directory, 1960-1989

Congressional Quarterly Almanac, 1960-1989

Contemporary Artists (1989)

Contemporary Authors (1962-89)

Contemporary Dramatists (1988)

Contemporary Foreign Language Writers (1989)

Contemporary Literary Criticism, 1973-89

Contemporary Literary Critics (1982)

Contemporary Novelists (1986)

Contemporary Poets (1986)

Contemporary Poets of the English Language (1970)

Contemporary Theatre, Film, and Television (1986)

Debrett's Peerage and Baronetage (1985)

Dictionary of Contemporary American Artists (1988)

Dictionary of International Biography (1975-87)

Dictionary of Latin American and Caribbean Biography (1971)

Dictionary of National Biography, 1971-1980 (1986)

Dictionnaire de biographie française (1972)

Dictionnaire des écrivains français (1971)

Directory of American Scholars (1982)

Directory of British Scientists, 1966-67

Directory of Medical Specialists, 1989-1990

Encyclopedia of Pop, Rock and Soul (1977)

Ewen, D., ed, Composers of Today (1936); Living Musicians (1940; First Supplement 1957); Men and Women Who Make Music (1949); European Composers Today (1954); The New Book of Modern Composers (1961); Composers Since 1900 (1969); Musicians Since 1900 (1978); American Composers (1982); American Songwriters (1987)

Far East and Australasia, 1989

Feather, L. Encyclopedia of Jazz in the Sixties (1967); Encyclopedia of Jazz (1984); Encyclopedia of Jazz in the Seventies (1987)

Filmgoer's Companion (1988)

Football Register, 1984

Foremost Women in Communications (1970)

Gilder, E. The Dictionary of Composers and Their Music (1985)

Grove's Dictionary of Music and Musicians (1955)

Hvem er Hvem? 1973

International Authors and Writers Who's Who, 1989

International Motion Picture Almanac, 1989

International Television Almanac, 1989

International Who's Who, 1989-90

International Who's Who in Art and Antiques, 1976

International Who's Who in Education (1986)

International Who's Who in Medicine (1987)

International Who's Who in Music and Musicians Directory (1988)

International Who's Who in Poetry, 1977

International Who's Who of the Arab World (1984)

International Year Book and Statesmen's Who's Who, 1989

Katz, E. Film Encyclopedia (1982)

Kürschners Deutscher Gelehrten-Kalender, 1970

Leaders in Education (1974)

Leaders in Electronics (1979)

Leaders in Profile (1975)

Martindale-Hubbell Law Directory, 1986

McGraw-Hill Encyclopedia of World Biography (1975)

McGraw-Hill Encyclopedia of World Drama (1984)

McGraw-Hill Modern Scientists and Engineers (1980)

Medical Sciences International Who's Who (1987)

Middle East and North Africa, 1984-85

National Cyclopaedia of American Biography (1926-84)

New Grove Dictionary of Music and Musicians (1980)

New Grove Gospel, Blues, and Jazz (1986)

Nobel Prize Winners (1987)

Nordness, L., ed. Art USA Now (1963)

Notable Australians (1978)

Notable Names in American Theatre (1976)

Nouveau Dictionnaire National des Contemporains (1968)

Official Baseball Register, 1984

Official Catholic Directory, 1989

Oxford Companion to American Theatre (1984)

Oxford Companion to Film (1976)

Oxford Companion to the Theatre (1983)

Oxford Companion to Twentieth-Century Art (1988)

Political Profiles (1976-82)

Politics in America (1990)

Poor's Register of Corporations, Directors and Executives, 1985

Prominent Personalities in the USSR (1968)

Quién es Quién en la Argentina, 1968–69

Robinson, D. 100 Most Important People in the World Today (1972)

Slonimsky, N. Baker's Biographical Dictionary of Musicians (1978)

Something About the Author (1971–89)

Thomas, S. Men of Space (1960–68)

Thompson, K. A. Dictionary of Twentieth-Century Composers (1973)

Thompson, O., ed. International Cyclopedia of Music and Musicians, 1985

Thomson, D. Biographical Dictionary of Film (1981)

Twentieth Century Authors (1942; First Supplement, 1955)

Twentieth-Century Children's Writers (1983)

Twentieth-Century Romance and Gothic Writers (1982)

Twentieth-Century Western Writers (1982)

Two Hundred Contemporary Authors (1969)

Webster's Biographical Dictionary (1971)

Wer ist Wer?, 1988–89

Who's Who, 1989

Who's Who among Black Americans, 1988

Who's Who in Advertising, 1990–91

Who's Who in Africa, 1973

Who's Who in America, 1988–89

Who's Who in American Art, 1989–90

Who's Who in American Education, 1988–89

Who's Who in American Film Now (1987)

Who's Who in American Music: Classical (1985)

Who's Who in American Politics, 1989

Who's Who in Art (1988)

Who's Who in Australia, 1988

Who's Who in Austria, 1983

Who's Who in California, 1987

Who's Who in Canada, 1988

Who's Who in Economics (1986)

Who's Who in Engineering, 1988

Who's Who in Finance and Industry, 1989–90

Who's Who in France, 1983–84

Who's Who in Germany (1980)

Who's Who in Hollywood, 1900–1976

Who's Who in Israel, 1985–86

Who's Who in Italy, 1986

Who's Who in Japan, 1987–88

Who's Who in Labor, 1976

Who's Who in Latin America (1971)

Who's Who in Library and Information Services (1982)

Who's Who in Malaysia and Singapore, 1983

Who's Who in Mexico Today (1988)

Who's Who in Music, 1969

Who's Who in New York State, 1982

Who's Who in Opera, 1976

Who's Who in Philosophy (1969)

Who's Who in Professional Baseball (1973)

Who's Who in Publishing (1971)

Who's Who in Rock Music (1982)

Who's Who in Saudi Arabia, 1984

Who's Who in Science in Europe (1987)

Who's Who in Space, 1987

Who's Who in Spain, 1965

Who's Who in Switzerland, 1988–89

Who's Who in the Arab World, 1986–87

Who's Who in the East, 1989–90

Who's Who in the Midwest, 1988–89

Who's Who in the Motion Picture Industry, 1988–89

Who's Who in the People's Republic of China (1987)

Who's Who in the South and Southwest, 1988–89

Who's Who in the Soviet Union (1989)

Who's Who in the Theatre (1981)

Who's Who in TV and Cable (1983)

Who's Who in the United Nations (1975)

Who's Who in the West, 1987–88

Who's Who in U.S. Executives, 1988–89

Who's Who in Western Europe (1981)

Who's Who in the World, 1988

Who's Who in World Jewry (1987)

Who's Who in Writers, Editors, & Poets (1988)

Who's Who of American Women, 1989–90

Who's Who of British Engineers, 1980

Who's Who of British Scientists, 1980–81

Who's Who of Jazz (1985)

Who's Who of Southern Africa, 1988–89

Who's Who on Television (1983)

World Artists 1950–1980 (1984)

World Authors 1950–1970 (1975)

World Authors 1970–75 (1980)

World Authors 1975–80 (1985)

World Film Directors 1890–1945 (1987)

World Film Directors 1945–1985 (1988)

World Who's Who in Science (1968)

World's Who's Who of Women, 1982

Writers Directory (1988–90)

PERIODICALS AND NEWSPAPERS CONSULTED

ALA Bul—American Library Association Bulletin
After Dark (disc.)
Am Artist—American Artist
Am Film—American Film
Am Scholar—American Scholar
Am Sociol R—American Sociological Review
America
Américas
Arch Rec—Architectural Record
Archaeology
Art & Artists
Artforum
ARTnews
Arts
Arts & Arch—Arts & Architecture
Atlan—Atlantic Monthly

Ballet N—Ballet News (disc.)
Barron's
Book World
Broadcasting
Bsns W—Business Week

Cath World—Catholic World
Chicago Tribune
Christian Sci Mon—Christian Science Monitor
Columbia J R—Columbia Journalism Review
Commonweal
Cong Digest—Congressional Digest
Cong Q—Congressional Quarterly Weekly Report
Cosmo—Cosmopolitan
Cue (now incorporated into New York)
Cur Hist—Current History
Cur World Leaders—Current World Leaders

Dance & Dancers
Dance Mag—Dancemagazine
Discover

Ebony
Economist
Ed & Pub—Editor & Publisher
Encounter
Esquire

Films & Filming
For Affairs—Foreign Affairs
For Policy Bul—Foreign Policy Bulletin
Forbes
Fortune

Gentlemen's Q—Gentlemen's Quarterly
German Tribune
Good H—Good Housekeeping
Guardian

Harper's

Hi Fi—High Fidelity
Hi Fi/Stereo R—Hi/Fi Stereo Review
Horizon

Illus Lond N—Illustrated London News
India News
Inside Sports
International Herald Tribune

Keynote

Ladies Home J—Ladies' Home Journal
Lear's
Le Monde
Lib J—Library Journal
Life
London Observer
London R of Bks—London Review of Books
Los Angeles Times

Manchester Guardian W—Manchester Guardian Weekly
McCall's
Maclean's
Mlle—Mademoiselle
Modern Maturity
Mother Jones
Ms—Ms.
Mus Am—Musical America
Mus Mod Art—Museum of Modern Art Bulletin

N Y Daily News
N Y Herald Tribune Bk R—New York Herald Tribune Book Review (disc.)
N Y Newsday—New York Newsday
N Y Post
N Y R of Bks—New York Review of Books
N Y Sunday News
N Y Times
N Y Times Bk R—New York Times Book Review
N Y Times Mag—New York Times Magazine
N Y Woman—New York Woman
N Y World-Telegram—New York World-Telegram and Sun (disc.)
N Y World Journal Tribune (disc.)
Nat Geog Mag—National Geographic Magazine
Nat R—National Review
Nation
Nations Bsns—Nation's Business
Nature
New Leader
New Repub—New Republic

New Statesman
New York
New Yorker
Newsweek

Omni
Opera N—Opera News
Ovation

Parade
Penthouse
People
Philadelphia Inquirer
Playbill
Playboy
Plays & Players
Pub W—Publishers Weekly

Read Digest—Reader's Digest
Redbook
Rolling Stone

Sat Eve Post—Saturday Evening Post
Sat R—Saturday Review
Savvy—Savvy Woman
Scala (English edition)
Sci Am—Scientific American
Sci Mo—Scientific Monthly
Sci N L—Science News Letter
Science
Smithsonian
Spec—Spectator
Spiegel—Der Spiegel
Sport
Sporting N—Sporting News
Sports Illus—Sports Illustrated

Time
Times—London Times
Times Lit Sup—London Times Literary Supplement
Toronto Globe and Mail
TV Guide

U N Rev—United Nations Review
U S News—U.S. News & World Report

Vanity Fair
Variety
Village Voice
Vogue

Wall St J—Wall Street Journal
Washington J R—Washington Journalism Review
Washington M—Washington Monthly
Washington Post
Wilson Lib Bul—Wilson Library Bulletin
World Monitor
World Press R—World Press Review

Yale R—Yale Review

CLASSIFICATION BY PROFESSION—1989

ADVERTISING
Saatchi, Maurice

ARCHITECTURE
Bunshaft, Gordon
Graves, Michael
Jahn, Helmut

ART
Brookner, Anita
Freilicher, Jane
Kienholz, Edward
Krens, Thomas
Mapplethorpe, Robert
Martin, Agnes
Riopelle, Jean-Paul
Ruscha, Edward
Sendak, Maurice
Thyssen-Bornemisza
    de Kaszon, Baron
    Hans Heinrich
Wilson, Robert R.

BUSINESS
Ailes, Roger E.
Bass, Robert M.
Campeau, Robert
Claiborne, Liz
Davis, Martin S.
Delors, Jacques
Greenspan, Alan
Johnson, F. Ross
Kravis, Henry R.
Lujan, Manuel, Jr.
Mirvish, Edwin
Mosbacher, Robert A.
Saatchi, Maurice
Spector, Phil
Stoddard, Brandon
Thomson, Kenneth
Thyssen-Bornemisza
    de Kaszon, Baron
    Hans Heinrich
Wright, Robert C.

DANCE
Clarke, Martha
Pendleton, Moses

EDUCATION
Augér, Arleen
Billington, James H.
Boren, David L.
Boskin, Michael J.
Cavazos, Lauro F.
Corigliano, John
Friedan, Betty
Graves, Michael
Holtz, Lou
Keegan, John
Lee, Ming Cho
Parks, Rosa
Said, Edward W.
Sullivan, Louis W.
Wilson, Robert R.

ENGINEERING
Sununu, John H.

FASHION
Claiborne, Liz
Kelly, Patrick

FILM
Almendros, Nestor
Barr, Roseanne
Berri, Claude
Condon, Richard
Dixon, Willie
Eastwood, Clint
Forsyth, Bill
Hall, Arsenio
Hanks, Tom
Harrison, George
Hershey, Barbara
Janowitz, Tama
Lean, Sir David
Lee, Spike
Lucci, Susan
LuPone, Patti
McClanahan, Rue

Norris, Chuck
Nykvist, Sven
Puttnam, David
Sarandon, Susan
Simon, Neil
Towne, Robert
Weaver, Sigourney
Weller, Michael
Wise, Robert
Woods, James

FINANCE
Bass, Robert M.
Delors, Jacques
Johnson, F. Ross
Kravis, Henry R.
Vranitzky, Franz

GOVERNMENT AND
    POLITICS, FOREIGN
Arens, Moshe
Bolkiah, Sir Muda Hassanal
Caroline, Princess of
    Monaco
Delors, Jacques
Fang Lizhi
Menem, Carlos Saúl
Rafsanjani, Hashemi
Rakowski, Mieczyslaw
Said, Edward W.
Salinas, Carlos
Stoltenberg, Gerhard
Thatcher, Margaret
Vranitzky, Franz
Yeltsin, Boris N.

GOVERNMENT AND
    POLITICS, U.S.
Ailes, Roger E.
Atwater, Lee
Boren, David L.
Boskin, Michael J.
Brown, Ron
Cavazos, Lauro F.
Cheney, Richard B.
Darman, Richard G.

Dodd, Christopher J.
Eastwood, Clint
Foley, Thomas S.
Gingrich, Newt
Gray, C. Boyden
Greenspan, Alan
Hyde, Henry J.
Kasten, Robert W., Jr.
Lujan, Manuel, Jr.
Marshall, Thurgood
Martin, Lynn
McCain, John S.
Mitchell, George J.
Mosbacher, Robert A.
Quayle, Dan
Reilly, William K.
Rudman, Warren B.
Robb, Charles S.
Skinner, Samuel K.
Sullivan, Louis W.
Sununu, John H.
Watkins, James
Young, Frank E.

INDUSTRY
Bass, Robert M.
Delors, Jacques
Johnson, F. Ross
Mosbacher, Robert A.
Thyssen-Bornemisza
    de Kaszon, Baron
    Hans Heinrich

JOURNALISM
Chung, Connie
Friedan, Betty
Guisewite, Cathy
Howar, Barbara
Just, Ward
Keegan, John
Lapham, Lewis H.
Lewis, FLora
Lunden, Joan
Morris, Edmund
Sheehan, Neil
Thomson, Kenneth

LABOR
Delors, Jacques

LAW
Boren, David L.
Brown, Ron
Dodd, Christopher J.

Foley, Thomas S.
Gray, C. Boyden
Hayes, Robert M.
Hyde, Henry J.
Marshall, Thurgood
Menem, Carlos Saúl
Mitchell, George J.
Quayle, Dan
Rudman, Warren B.
Skinner, Samuel K.
Wapner, Joseph A.

LIBRARY SERVICE
Billington, James H.

LITERATURE
Abé, Kobo
Adams, Alice
Brodkey, Harold
Brookner, Anita
Condon, Richard
DeLillo, Don
Erdrich, Louise
Exley, Frederick
Fuller, Charles
Holroyd, Michael
Janowitz, Tama
Just, Ward
Mahfouz, Naguib
Mason, Bobbie Ann
Powers, J. F.
Roth, Henry
Said, Edward W.
Sanders, Lawrence
Sendak, Maurice
Steel, Danielle
Straub, Peter
Trenet, Charles
Woiwode, Larry

MEDICINE
Cavazos, Lauro F.
Joseph, Stephen
Levi-Montalcini, Rita
Sullivan, Louis W.
Young, Frank E.

MILITARY
Keegan, John
Watkins, James

MUSIC
Augér, Arleen
Baker, Anita
Browne, Jackson
Chapman, Tracy
Corigliano, John
Davidovich, Bella
Dearie, Blossom
Diddley, Bo
Dixon, Willie
Eastwood, Clint
Eschenbach, Christoph
Harrison, George
Hendricks, Barbara
LuPone, Patti
McFerrin, Bobby
Pinnock, Trevor
Reed, Lou
Richards, Keith
Sendak, Maurice
Smith, Patti
Spector, Phil
Stern, Isaac
Travis, Randy
Trenet, Charles

NONFICTION
Billington, James H.
Condon, Richard
Friedan, Betty
Fuller, Charles
Holroyd, Michael
Keegan, John
Lapham, Lewis H.
Lewis, Flora
Morris, Edmund
Said, Edward W.
Sheehan, Neil

ORGANIZATIONS
Atwater, Lee
Brown, Ron
Delors, Jacques
Friedan, Betty
Parks, Rosa

OTHER CLASSIFICATIONS
Bush, Barbara

PUBLISHING
Davis, Martin S.
Lapham, Lewis H.
Quayle, Dan
Thomson, Kenneth

RADIO
  Simon, Neil
  Sajak, Pat
  Scott, Willard

RELIGION
  Harris, Barbara

SCIENCE
  Fang Lizhi
  Garwin, Richard L.
  Joseph, Stephen
  Lederman, Leon M.
  Levi-Montalcini, Rita
  Sullivan, Louis W.
  Wilson, Robert R.
  Young, Frank E.

SOCIAL ACTIVISM
  Brown, Ron
  Browne, Jackson
  Fang Lizhi
  Friedan, Betty
  Hayes, Robert M.
  Marshall, Thurgood
  Parks, Rosa
  Said, Edward W.

SOCIAL SCIENCES
  Boskin, Michael J.
  Greenspan, Alan

SPORTS
  Agassi, Andre

Boitano, Brian
Graf, Steffi
Griffith Joyner, Florence
Holtz, Lou
Krone, Julie
Lasorda, Tommy
LeMond, Greg
Marino, Dan
Norman, Greg
Thomas, Isiah.
Thompson, John
Walsh, Bill

TECHNOLOGY
  Garwin, Richard L.
  Mosbacher, Robert A.

TELEVISION
  Ailes, Roger E.
  Barr, Roseanne
  Chung, Connie
  Dixon, Willie
  Eastwood, Clint
  Hall, Arsenio
  Hanks, Tom
  Hershey, Barbara
  Howar, Barbara
  Lucci, Susan
  Lunden, Joan
  LuPone, Patti
  McClanahan, Rue
  Sajak, Pat

Sarandon, Susan
Scott, Willard
Sendak, Maurice
Shandling, Garry
Simon, Neil
Stoddard, Brandon
Towne, Robert
Wapner, Joseph A.
Wasserstein, Wendy
Woods, James
Wright, Robert C.

THEATRE
  Clarke, Martha
  Fuller, Charles
  Hanks, Tom
  Hwang, David Henry
  Lee, Ming Cho
  Lucci, Susan
  LuPone, Patti
  McClanahan, Rue
  Mirvish, Edwin
  Sarandon, Susan
  Sendak, Maurice
  Simon, Neil
  Wasserstein, Wendy
  Weaver, Sigourney
  Weller, Michael

CUMULATED INDEX—1981–1989

For the index to 1940–1985 biographies, see
Current Biography Cumulated Index 1940–1985.

Babbitt, Bruce E(dward) Apr 87
Backman, Jules obit Jun 82
Bacon, Francis Aug 85
Bacon, Peggy obit Mar 87
Bagnold, Enid (Algerine) obit May 81
Bagramian, Ivan C(hristoforovich) obit Jan 83
Bailey, Sir Donald Coleman obit Jul 85
Bainton, Roland H(erbert) obit Jun 84
Baird, Bil obit May 87
Baker, Anita Apr 89
Baker, Howard (Henry, Jr.) Aug 87
Baker, James A(ddison), 3d Feb 82
Balanchine, George obit Jun 83
Balderston, William obit Oct 83
Baldrige, (Howard) Malcolm Aug 82 obit Sep 87
Baldrige, Letitia (Katherine) Feb 88
Baldwin, James (Arthur) obit Jan 88
Baldwin, Raymond E(arl) obit Nov 86
Baldwin, Roger Nash obit Oct 81
Ball, Lucille obit Jun 89
Ballard, J(ames) G(raham) May 88
Ballard, Robert D(uane) Jun 86
Balmain, Pierre (Alexandre) obit Aug 82
Baltimore, David Jul 83
Bani-Sadr, Abolhassan Feb 81
Banning, Margaret Culkin obit Feb 82
Barber, Samuel obit Mar 81
Barnes, Julian (Patrick) Mar 88
Barnes, Wendell B(urton) obit Aug 85
Barnet, Will Jun 85
Barnett, Ross R(obert) obit Jan 88
Barnsley, Alan (Gabriel) See Fielding, G. obit
Barr, Alfred H(amilton), Jr. obit Oct 81
Barr, Roseanne May 89
Barr, (Frank) Stringfellow obit Apr 82
Barrett, William (C.) Aug 82
Barrow, Errol W(alton) obit Jul 87
Barry, Marion S. May 87
Barthé, Richmond obit May 89
Barthelme, Donald obit Sep 89
Bartlett, Jennifer Nov 85
Barzini, Luigi (Giorgio, Jr.) obit May 84
Basie, Count obit Jun 84
Basie, William See Basie, Count obit

Bass, Robert M(use) Jul 89
Battle, Kathleen Nov 84
Baur, John I(reland) H(owe) obit Jul 87
Bausch, Pina Sep 86
Baxter, Anne obit Feb 86
Bayar, (Mahmut) Celal obit Oct 86
Beadle, G(eorge) W(ells) obit Aug 89
Beard, Charles E(dmund) obit Oct 82
Beard, James (Andrews) obit Mar 85
Bearden, Romare (Howard) obit May 88
Beatrix, Queen of the Netherlands May 81
Beattie, Ann Oct 85
Beatty, Warren May 88
Beau, Lucas Victor obit Jan 87
Beauvoir, Simone (Bertrand) de obit Jun 86
Bechtel, Stephen D(avison) obit May 89
Becker, Boris Feb 87
Behrens, Hildegard Jan 85
Bell, Elliott V(allance) obit Mar 83
Bellow, Saul Nov 88
Belt, Guillermo obit Sep 89
Belushi, John obit Apr 82
Benchley, Nathaniel (Goddard) obit Feb 82
Bendetsen, Karl R(obin) obit Sep 89
Benelli, Giovanni Cardinal obit Jan 83
Benn, Anthony (Neil) Wedgwood See Benn, Tony
Benn, Tony Nov 82
Bennett, Michael Mar 81 obit Aug 87
Bennett, Robert Russell obit Oct 81
Bennett, William J(ohn) Sep 85
Bergen, John J(oseph) obit Feb 81
Berger, Peter L(udwig) Mar 83
Berger, Thomas (Louis) Jun 88
Bergman, (Ernst) Ingmar Oct 81
Bergman, Ingrid obit Oct 82
Berlin, Ellin (Mackay) obit Sep 88
Berlin, Irving obit Nov 89
Berlinguer, Enrico obit Aug 84
Berman, Emile Zola obit Aug 81
Bernardin, Joseph L(ouis) Oct 82
Bernbach, William obit Nov 82
Bernier, Rosamond Feb 88
Bernstein, Philip S(idney) obit Feb 86
Bernstein, Robert L(ouis) Jul 87
Berri, Claude Mar 89

Berri, Nabih Nov 85
Berry, Wendell (Erdman) May 86
Bessmertnova, Natalya Jan 88
Betancourt, Rómulo obit Nov 81
Betancur (Cuartas), Belisario Apr 85
Betjeman, Sir John obit Jul 84
Bettis, Valerie obit Nov 82
Beuys, Joseph obit Mar 86
Bhave, Vinoba obit Jan 83
Bhutto, Benazir Jul 86
Biaggi, Mario Jan 86
Bible, Alan obit Oct 88
Bidault, Georges obit Mar 83
Biddle, Katherine Garrison Chapin obit Jan 84
Biden, Joseph (Robinette), Jr. Jan 87
Bieber, Owen F(rederick) Apr 86
Biller, Moe Jun 87
Billington, James H(adley) May 89
Bingham, (George) Barry obit Sep 88
Bingham, Jonathan B(rewster) obit Aug 86
Binns, Joseph Patterson obit Mar 81
Bird, Larry June 82
Bird, Rose E(lizabeth) May 84
Birren, Faber obit Feb 89
Bishop, Isabel obit Apr 88
Bishop, Jim obit Sep 87
Black, William obit May 83
Blackwell, Betsy Talbot obit Apr 85
Blades, Rubén May 86
Blaik, Earl H(enry) obit Jul 89
Blaisdell, Thomas C(harles), Jr. obit Feb 89
Blake, Eubie obit Apr 83
Blake, Eugene Carson obit Oct 85
Blakey, Art Sep 88
Blanc, Mel(vin Jerome) obit Sep 89
Blanding, Sarah Gibson obit Apr 85
Blier, Bertrand Oct 88
Bliss, Ray C(harles) obit Oct 81
Bloch, Felix obit Nov 83
Block, John R(usling) Apr 82
Bloom, Allan (David) Mar 88
Bloom, Harold Apr 87
Blough, Roger M(iles) obit Jan 86
Bluford, Guion S(tewart), Jr. Sep 84
Bly, Robert (Elwood) Mar 84
Bocuse, Paul Jan 88
Boesak, Allan (Aubrey) Nov 86
Boff, Leonardo Jan 88
Bogosian, Eric Sep 87
Böhm, Karl obit Oct 81
Boitano, Brian Nov 89

Boland, Edward P(atrick) Oct 87

Boland, Frederick H(enry) obit Feb 86

Boles, Paul Darcy obit Jun 84

Bolger, Ray(mond Wallace) obit Mar 87

Bolger, William F(rederick Leonard) obit Oct 89

Bolkiah, Sir Muda Hassanal Oct 89

Böll, Heinrich (Theodor) obit Sep 85

Bolotowsky, Ilya obit Jan 82

Bolte, Charles L(awrence) obit May 89

Bolz, Lothar obit Apr 87

Bonner, Elena See Bonner, Yelena

Bonner, Yelena Apr 87

Bonynge, Richard Feb 81

Boone, Richard obit Mar 81

Boorman, John Jun 88

Boorstin, Daniel J(oseph) Jan 84

Boren, David L(yle) Nov 89

Borges, Jorge Luis obit Aug 86

Borofsky, Jonathan Jul 85

Boskin, Michael J(ay) Sep 89

Bossy, Mike Jun 81

Botha, Roelof F(rederik) May 84

Boult, Sir Adrian (Cedric) obit Apr 83

Bourgeois, Louise Oct 83

Bowen, Otis R(ay) Nov 86

Bowles, Chester (Bliss) obit Jul 86

Boyer, Ernest L. Jan 88

Boyer, Ken(ton Lloyd) obit Oct 82

Boyer, M(arion) W(illard) obit Jan 83

Boy George Oct 85

Boyle, W(illiam) A(nthony) obit Jul 85

Boylston, Helen Dore obit Nov 84

Bradbury, Ray Jul 82

Bradford, Robert F(iske) obit May 83

Bradley, Bill Sep 82

Bradley, Ed May 88

Bradley, Omar N(elson) obit May 81

Bradley, William W(arren) See Bradley, Bill

Bradshaw, Thornton F(rederick) Jun 82 obit Feb 89

Brady, Nicholas F(rederick) Nov 88

Brady, William T(homas) obit Jul 84

Brameld, Theodore obit Jan 88

Brandt, Bill Aug 81 obit Feb 84

Brattain, Walter H(ouser) obit Nov 87

Braudel, Fernand (Paul) Apr 85 obit Jan 86

Brenan, (Edward Fitz-)Gerald Jul 86 obit Mar 87

Brenner, David Mar 87

Brett, George Jul 81

Brett, George P(latt), Jr. obit May 84

Breuer, Marcel (Lajos) obit Aug 81

Brewster, Kingman, Jr. obit Jan 89

Breytenbach, Breyten Jun 86

Brezhnev, Leonid I(lyich) obit Jan 83

Bricker, John W(illiam) obit May 86

Brico, Antonia obit Oct 89

Brinkley, David (McClure) Sep 87

Brinton, Howard H(aines) obit Yrbk 84 (died Apr 73)

Bristow, Gwen obit Yrbk 84 (died Aug 80)

Broadbent, John Edward May 88

Broderick, Matthew May 87

Brodie, Bernard B(eryl) obit May 89

Brodkey, Harold (Roy) Apr 89

Brodsky, Joseph (Alexandrovich) Jul 82

Brody, Jane E(llen) Feb 86

Broglie, Louis (Victor Pierre Raymond) de obit May 87

Brokaw, Tom May 81

Bromley, Dorothy Dunbar obit Feb 86

Brookner, Anita Feb 89

Brooks, Louise Apr 84 obit Oct 85

Brower, Charles (Hendrickson) obit Nov 84

Brown, Cecil (B.) obit Jan 88

Brown, Charles L(ee, Jr.) Sep 81

Brown, George obit Jul 85

Brown, Harrison (Scott) obit Feb 87

Brown, Irving (Joseph) obit May 89

Brown, Rita Mae Sep 86

Brown, Ron(ald Harmon) Jul 89

Brown, Sterling (Allen) Aug 82 obit Apr 89

Browne, Jackson Oct 89

Bruce, Louis R(ooks, Jr.) obit Jul 89

Bruhn, Erik (Belton Evers) obit May 86

Brundtland, Gro Harlem Nov 81

Bruner, Jerome (Seymour) Oct 84

Bryant, Paul W(illiam) obit Mar 83

Brynner, Yul obit Nov 85

Burnham, James obit Jan 88

Buchanan, Patrick J(oseph) Aug 85

Buchanan, Wiley T(homas), Jr. obit Mar 86

Buck, Paul H(erman) obit Apr 89

Buckley, William F(rank), Jr. Oct 82

Buckmaster, Henrietta obit Jun 83

Buffett, Warren E(dward) Nov 87

Bugas, John S(tephen) obit Feb 83

Bunker, Ellsworth obit Nov 84

Bunshaft, Gordon Mar 89

Buñuel, Luis obit Sep 83

Burke, Michael obit Mar 87

Burnet, Sir (Frank) Macfarlane obit Oct 85

Burnham, (Linden) Forbes (Sampson) obit Oct 85

Burns, Arthur F(rank) obit Aug 87

Burns, Eveline M(abel) obit Jan 86

Burr, Donald C(alvin) Sep 86

Burrows, Abe obit Jul 85

Burton, Richard obit Sep 84

Buscaglia, (Felice) Leo(nardo) Oct 83

Busch, August A(nheuser) obit Nov 89

Bush, Barbara (Pierce) Oct 89

Bush, George (Herbert Walker) Sep 83

Buthelezi, Mangosuthu G(atsha) Oct 86

Butler, Richard Austen See Butler of Saffron Walden, R.A.B., Baron obit

Butler of Saffron Walden, Richard Austen Butler, Baron obit May 82

Byrne, David Jun 85

Byrne, John Keyes See Leonard, Hugh

Byrnes, John W(illiam) obit Mar 85

Cabot, John M(oors) obit Apr 81

Caetano, Marcello (José) obit Jan 81

Cagney, James obit May 86

Caine, Michael Jan 88

Calder, Nigel (David Ritchie) Jun 86

Calder, (Peter) Ritchie obit May 86

Calderone, Frank A(nthony) obit Apr 87

Caldicott, Helen Oct 83

Caldwell, Erskine obit May 87

Caldwell, Millard F(illmore) obit Feb 85

Caldwell, Taylor obit Oct 85

Calero (Portocarrero), Adolfo
Oct 87

Callahan, Harry M(orey) Nov
84

Calvino, Italo Feb 84 obit Nov
85

Calvo Sotelo (y Bustelo),
Leopoldo Aug 81

Campbell, Earl Apr 83

Campbell, Joseph Jun 84 obit
Jan 88

Campeau, Robert (Joseph) Mar
89

Cámpora, Héctor José obit Feb
81

Canady, John (Edwin) obit Sep
85

Canetti, Elias Jan 83

Canfield, Cass obit May 86

Canham, Erwin D(ain) obit
Feb 82

Caniff, Milton A(rthur) obit
May 88

Capote, Truman obit Oct 84

Caras, Roger A(ndrew) Apr 88

Carlino, Lewis John May 83

Carlisle, Kitty See Hart, Kitty
Carlisle

Carlson, Frank obit Jul 87

Carlsson, Ingvar (Gosta) Feb
88

Carlucci, Frank (Charles 3d)
Oct 81

Carmichael, Hoagy obit Feb
82

Caro, Anthony Nov 81

Caro, Robert A. Jan 84

Caroline, Princess of Monaco
Nov 89

Carroll, John A(lbert) obit Oct
83

Carroll, Madeleine obit Nov
87

Carroll, Vinnette Sep 83

Carson, Johnny Apr 82

Carter, Benny Jul 87

Carter, (Bessie) Lillian obit Jan
84

Carter, Betty Mar 82

Carter, (William) Hodding, 3d
Aug 81

Carver, Raymond Feb 84 obit
Sep 88

Cary, William L(ucius) obit
Apr 83

Case, Clifford P(hilip) obit Apr
82

Casey, William J(oseph) obit
Jun 87

Caspary, Vera obit Aug 87

Cassavetes, John obit Mar 89

Castelli, Leo Aug 84

Caswell, Hollis L(eland) obit
Jan 89

Catledge, Turner obit Jul 83

Caudill, Rebecca obit Jan 86

Cavazos, Lauro F(red, Jr.) Apr
89

Celler, Emanuel obit Mar 81

Cerezo (Arévalo), (Marco)
Vinicio Mar 87

Chagall, Marc obit May 85

Chagla, Mahomed Ali Currim
obit Jan 84

Chaikin, Joseph Jul 81

Chamberlain, Richard Nov 87

Chamoun, Camille N(imer)
obit Sep 87

Chancellor, John Nov 88

Chandrasekhar, Subrahman-
yan Mar 86

Chapin, Katherine Garrison
See Biddle, K. G. C. obit

Chapman, Albert K(inkade)
obit Yrbk 84

Chapman, Charles F(rederic)
obit Yrbk 84 (died Mar 76)

Chapman, Tracy Aug 89

Charles, Prince of Belgium
obit Jul 83

Charles, (Mary) Eugenia Oct
86

Charlot, Jean obit Yrbk 84
(died Mar 79)

Charlotte, Grand Duchess of
Luxembourg obit Aug 85

Chase, Lucia obit Mar 86

Chase, Mary (Coyle) obit Jan
82

Chase, Stuart obit Jan 86

Chasins, Abram obit Aug 87

Chatwin, Bruce (Charles) Jan
88 obit Mar 89

Chayefsky, Paddy obit Sep 81

Cheever, John obit Aug 82

Cheney, Richard B(ruce) Aug
89

Chernenko, Konstantin
U(stinovich) Aug 84 obit
May 85

Chiang Ching-Kuo obit Mar 88

Chicago, Judy Feb 81

Childs, Lucinda Apr 84

Chillida, Eduardo Sep 85

Chodorov, Edward obit Nov
88

Christopher, Warren M(inor)
Jun 81

Chuikov, Vasili (Ivanovitch)
obit May 82

Chun Doo Hwan Mar 81

Chung, Connie Jul 89

Church, Frank (Forrester) obit
May 84

Church, Sam(uel Morgan), Jr.
Oct 81

Churchill, Caryl Jun 85

Churchill, Sarah obit Jan 83

Chute, (Beatrice) Joy obit Oct
87

Ciardi, John (Anthony) obit
May 86

Cimino, Michael Jan 81

Cisneros, Henry G(abriel) Aug
87

Citrine of Wembley, Walter
McLennan Citrine, Ist Baron obit Apr 83

Clague, Ewan obit Jun 87

Claiborne, Liz Jun 89

Clair, René obit May 81

Claire, Ina obit Apr 85

Clancy, Tom Apr 88

Clapton, Eric Jun 87

Clark, Dick Jan 87

Clark, Lord Kenneth (Mackenzie) obit Jul 83

Clark, Mark W(ayne) obit Jun
84

Clark, William P(atrick) Jul 82

Clarke, Martha Jan 89

Clausen, A(lden) W(inship)
Nov 81

Clavell, James Oct 81

Cleese, John Jan 84

Clemens, Roger Nov 88

Clements, Earle C. obit May
85

Cleveland, James Aug 85

Clinchy, Everett R(oss) obit
Mar 86

Clinton, Bill Apr 88

Close, Charles See Close,
Chuck

Close, Chuck Jul 83

Close, Glenn Nov 84

Coco, James obit Apr 87

Cody, John Patrick Cardinal
obit Jun 82

Coetzee, J(ohn) M. Jan 87

Coggeshall, L(owell) T(helwell)
obit Jan 88

Cohen, Arthur A(llen) obit Jan
87

Cohen, Benjamin V(ictor) obit
Oct 83

Cohen, Wilbur J(oseph) obit
Jul 87

Cohen, William S(ebastian)
Apr 82

Cole, Sterling W(illiam) obit
May 87

Coleman, Lonnie (William)
obit Oct 82

Collingwood, Charles (Cum-
mings) obit Nov 85

Collins, Joan Jan 84

Collins, J(oseph) Lawton obit
Oct 87

Collins, Martha Layne Jan 86

Collins, Marva Nov 86

Collins, Phil Nov 86

Colville, Alex Mar 85

Conable, Barber B., Jr. Jul 84

Condon, Richard Feb 89

Conley, Eugene obit Feb 82

Connelly, Marc obit Feb 81

Conner, Dennis Nov 87

Conti, Tom Jun 85

Conway, Tim Apr 81

Cook, Donald C(larence) obit
Feb 82

Cooke, Terence J(ames) Cardinal obit Nov 83

Coon, Carleton S(tevens) obit
Jul 81

Cooper, Irving S(pencer) obit Jan 86
Corcoran, Thomas Gardiner obit Feb 82
Corea, Chick Oct 88
Cori, Carl F(erdinand) obit Feb 85
Corigliano, John (Paul) Jun 89
Corman, Roger Feb 83
Corson, Fred Pierce obit Apr 85
Cortázar, Julio obit Apr 84
Cory, John Mackenzie obit May 88
Cosby, Bill Oct 86
Cossiga, Francesco Jan 81
Costello, Elvis Sep 83
Cotrubas, Ileana Oct 81
Cotton, Norris obit May 89
Cournand, André F(rederic) obit Apr 88
Cousins, Frank obit Jul 86
Cowles, Gardner, Jr. obit Aug 85
Cowles, John obit Apr 83
Cowles, Virginia (Spencer) obit Nov 83
Cowley, Malcolm obit May 89
Cox, Allyn obit Jan 83
Cox, William Trevor See Trevor, William
Craft, Robert Mar 84
Craig, Walter E(arly) obit Sep 86
Crawford, Broderick obit Jun 86
Crawford, Cheryl obit Nov 86
Craxi, Bettino Feb 84
Creeley, Robert (White) Oct 88
Crenshaw, Ben Sep 85
Crick, Francis Mar 83
Crisler, Herbert Orin obit Oct 82
Cronin, A(rchibald) J(oseph) obit Mar 81
Cronin, Joe obit Nov 84
Cronyn, Hume Jun 88
Crosby, John (O'Hea) Nov 81
Cross, Ben Aug 84
Crossley, Archibald M(addock) obit Jul 85
Crowe, William J(ames), Jr. Jul 88
Crowther, (F.) Bosley obit Apr 81
Cruise, Tom Apr 87
Cruyff, Johan Nov 81
Cruz, Celia Jul 83
Crystal, Billy Feb 87
Cukor, George obit Mar 83
Cullberg, Birgit Nov 82
Cunningham, Sir Alan (Gordon) obit Apr 83
Cunningham, Mary (Elizabeth) Nov 84
Cuomo, Mario (Matthew) Aug 83
Curran, Charles E(dward) Jan 87

Curran, Joseph E(dwin) obit Oct 81
Curzon, Clifford obit Oct 82
Cushman, Robert E(verton), Jr. obit Apr 85

Dacre of Glanton, Baron, See Trevor-Roper, H. R.
Dahlberg, Edwin T(heodore) obit Oct 86
Dalai Lama Jun 82
Dale, Jim Jul 81
Dali, Salvador obit Mar 89
Dalton, Timothy May 88
D'Amato, Alfonse Sep 83
Dangerfield, George (Bubb) obit Mar 87
Daniel, (Marion) Price obit Oct 88
Daniels, Jonathan (Worth) obit Jan 82
Danilova, Alexandra Jul 87
Dannay, Frederic obit Oct 82
Danner, Blythe Jan 81
Darman, Richard G(ordon) May 89
Darrell, R(obert) D(onaldson) obit Jun 88
Dart, Justin W(hitlock) obit Mar 84
Dart, Raymond A(rthur) obit Jan 89
Dassault, Marcel (Bloch) obit Jun 86
D'Aubuisson, Roberto Jul 83
Daugherty, Carroll R(oop) obit Jun 88
Dausset, Jean May 81
Davidovich, Bella May 89
Davidson, John F(rederick) obit Apr 89
Davis, Al(len) Jul 85
Davis, Andrew May 83
Davis, Bette obit Nov 89
Davis, James C(urran) obit Feb 82
Davis, Martin S. Nov 89
Davis, Patti Nov 86
Davis, Peter (Frank) Feb 83
Day, Dorothy obit Jan 81
Dayan, Moshe obit Jan 82
Dean, Arthur H(obson) obit Jan 88
Dean, Laura Oct 88
Dean, William F(rishe) obit Oct 81
Dearden, John Cardinal obit Sep 88
Dearie, Blossom Feb 89
Debray, (Jules) Régis Jun 82
Debus, Kurt H(einrich) obit Nov 83
Decker, Mary Oct 83
Decter, Midge Apr 82
Defferre, Gaston obit Jun 86
DeGaetani, Jan obit Nov 89
Deighton, Len Sep 84

de Kiewiet, Cornelis W(illem) obit Apr 86
de Kiewit, Cornelis W(illem) See de Kiewiet, C. W. obit
De Kooning, Elaine (Marie Catharine) Jul 82 obit Mar 89
De Kooning, Willem Sep 84
De La Madrid (Hurtado), Miguel Apr 83
DeLillo, Don Jan 89
Delors, Jacques (Lucien Jean) Jun 89
Del Tredici, David Mar 83
De Mille, Agnes Jan 85
Demme, Jonathan Apr 85
De Montebello, (Guy-)Philippe (Lannes) Apr 81
Dempsey, Jack obit Jul 83
Dempsey, John (Noel) obit Sep 89
Dempsey, William Harrison See Dempsey, Jack obit
Denebrink, Francis C(ompton) obit Jun 87
Densen-Gerber, Judianne Nov 83
Denton, Jeremiah A(ndrew), Jr. May 82
De Palma, Brian Sep 82
Depardieu, Gérard Oct 87
De Rochemont, Richard (Guertis) obit Sept 82
Dershowitz, Alan M(orton) Sep 86
Deukmejian, (Courken) George, Jr. Jun 83
DeVito, Danny Feb 88
DeVries, William C(astle) Jan 85
Dewey, Charles S(chuveldt) obit Feb 81
Dial, Morse G(rant) obit Jan 83
Diamond, Neil May 81
Diana, Princess of Wales Jan 83
Dickinson, Angie Feb 81
Diddley, Bo Jun 89
Dietz, David obit Apr 85
Dietz, Howard obit Sep 83
Dillard, Annie Jan 83
Diller, Barry (Charles) Apr 86
Dillon, Matt May 85
Dingell, John D(avid), Jr. Aug 83
DiSalle, Michael V(incent) obit Nov 81
Ditka, Mike Oct 87
Dixon, Willie May 89
Dodd, Christopher J(ohn) Oct 89
Dodds, Harold W(illis) obit Jan 81
Dodge, Cleveland E(arl) obit Feb 83
Doe, Samuel K(anyon) May 81
Doenitz, Karl obit Feb 81
Dohnányi, Christoph von Oct 85

Doisy, E(dward) A(delbert) obit Jan 87
Dole, Elizabeth Hanford Jun 83
Dole, Robert J(oseph) Oct 87
Dolin, Anton obit Jan 84
Domenici, Pete V(ichi) Jun 82
Donaldson, Sam Sep 87
Donner, Frederic G(arrett) obit Apr 87
Donovan, Raymond J(ames) Jan 82
Dorati, Antal obit Jan 89
Dorticós (Torrado), Osvaldo obit Aug 83
Doubleday, Nelson May 87
Douglas, Donald W(ills) obit Mar 81
Douglas, James H(enderson), Jr. obit Apr 88
Douglas, Melvyn obit Sep 81
Douglas, Michael Apr 87
Douglas, Thomas C(lement) obit Apr 86
Downey, Morton obit Jan 86
Drabble, Margaret May 81
Draper, Charles Stark obit Sep 87
Drees, Willem obit Jul 88
Drew, George A(lexander) obit May 84
Druckman, Jacob May 81
Drummond, (James) Roscoe obit Nov 83
Duarte (Fuentes), José Napoleón Sep 81
Dubinsky, David obit Jan 83
Dubos, René J(ules) obit Apr 82
Dubuffet, Jean obit Jul 85
Du Maurier, Daphne obit Jun 89
Dunne, John Gregory Jun 83
Dunton, A(rnold) Davidson obit Apr 87
Du Pré, Jacqueline obit Nov 87
Durang, Christopher Jun 87
Durant, Will(iam James) obit Jan 82
Duras, Marguerite Nov 85
Durenberger, David F(erdinand) Oct 88
Durrell, Gerald May 85
Dutoit, Charles Feb 87

Eaker, Ira C(larence) obit Sep 87
Eastland, James O(liver) obit Apr 86
Eastwood, Clint Mar 89
Eckstein, Gustav obit Nov 81
Eckstein, Otto obit May 84
Eco, Umberto Apr 85
Edwards, Blake Jan 83
Edwards, Douglas Aug 88
Edwards, James B(urrows) Nov 82

Edwards, Joan obit Oct 81
Edwards, (W.) Don(lon) Mar 83
Egan, William Allen obit Jul 84
Ehricke, Krafft A. obit Feb 85
Eisenhower, Milton S(tover) obit Jul 85
Eisner, Michael D(ammann) Nov 87
Eldridge, Florence obit Sep 88
Eldridge, Roy Mar 87 obit Apr 89
Eliade, Mircea Nov 85 obit Jun 86
Elizabeth, Queen Mother of Great Britain Aug 81
Elkin, Stanley (Lawrence) Jul 87
Ellerbee, Linda Oct 86
Ellis, Perry Jan 86 obit Jul 86
El Mallakh, Kamal obit Jan 88
Emerson, Faye obit May 83
Enders, John F(ranklin) obit Jan 86
Engstrom, E(lmer) W(illiam) obit Feb 85
Enters, Angna obit Apr 89
Erdrich, Louise Apr 89
Erlander, Tage (Fritiof) obit Aug 85
Ernst, Jimmy obit Apr 84
Ershad, Hussain Muhammad Nov 84
Ervin, Sam(uel) J(ames), Jr. obit Jun 85
Eschenbach, Christoph Aug 89
Estes, Eleanor obit Sep 88
Estes, E(lliott) M(arantette) obit May 88
Estes, Simon Aug 86
Ethridge, Mark (Foster) obit Jun 81
Eurich, Alvin C(hristian) obit Aug 87
Evans, Harold (Matthew) Apr 85
Evans, Linda Mar 86
Evans, Luther H(arris) obit Feb 82
Evans, Maurice obit May 89
Evren, Kenan Apr 84
Exley, Frederick Oct 89
Eyskens, Gaston obit Feb 88

Fabius, Laurent Feb 85
Fagerholm, Karl-August obit Jul 84
Fagg, Fred D(ow), Jr. obit Jan 82
Falwell, Jerry Jan 81
Fang Lizhi Nov 89
Farrar, Margaret (Pether-bridge) obit Aug 84
Farrington, (Mary) Elizabeth Pruett obit Sep 84
Fassbinder, Rainer Werner obit Aug 82

Fauci, Anthony S(tephen) Aug 88
Faure, Edgar obit May 88
Feinsinger, Nathan P(aul) obit Jan 84
Feinstein, Michael Apr 88
Feld, Irvin obit Nov 84
Feldstein, Martin (Stuart) May 83
Feltsman, Vladimir Apr 88
Ferguson, Homer obit Mar 83
Ferrari, Enzo obit Sep 88
Ferraro, Geraldine A(nne) Sep 84
Feynman, Richard P(hillips) Nov 86 obit Apr 88
Fichandler, Zelda Jun 87
Field, Henry obit Mar 86
Fielding, Gabriel obit Apr 87
Fielding, Temple (Hornaday) obit Jul 83
Fierstein, Harvey Feb 84
Fingesten, Peter obit Oct 87
Finnbogadóttir, Vigdis May 87
Fischl, Eric Jun 86
Fish, Marie Poland obit Apr 89
Fishback, Margaret obit Nov 85
Fisher, M(ary) F(rances) K(ennedy) Sep 83
Fisher, Welthy (Blakesley Honsinger) obit Feb 81
Fisk, James Brown obit Oct 81
Fitzgerald, Albert J. obit Jul 82
Fitzgerald, Ed obit Jun 82
FitzGerald, Frances Jun 87
FitzGerald, Garret Aug 84
Fitzgerald, Pegeen obit Apr 89
Fitzgerald, Robert (Stuart) obit Mar 85
Fitzsimmons, Frank E(dward) obit Jul 81
Fitzwater, (Max) Marlin May 88
Fleming, Lady Amalia obit Apr 86
Fleming, Berry (Jiles) obit Nov 89
Fleming, Donald M(ethuen) obit Mar 87
Flesch, Rudolf (Franz) obit Nov 86
Florinsky, Michael T(imofe-evich) obit Jan 82
Flory, Paul J(ohn) obit Nov 85
Flutie, Doug Oct 85
Fo, Dario Nov 86
Foley, Thomas S(tephen) Sep 89
Folon, Jean-Michel Feb 81
Folsom, James E(lisha) obit Jan 88
Fonda, Henry obit Sep 82
Fonda, Jane Jun 86
Fontanne, Lynn obit Sep 83
Foot, Michael (Mackintosh) May 81
Foote, Horton Aug 86

Ford, Frederick W(ayne) obit Sep 86
Ford, Harrison Sep 84
Ford, Henry, II obit Nov 87
Foreman, Richard Jul 88
Forsyth, Bill Jan 89
Forsyth, Frederick May 86
Fortas, Abe obit May 82
Fosse, Bob obit Nov 87
Fossey, Dian May 85 obit Feb 86
Foster, Jodie Jun 81
Fowler, Mark S(tapleton) Mar 86
Fox, Carol obit Sep 81
Fox, Michael J. Nov 87
Fox, Robert J(ohn) obit Jun 84
Fox, Virgil (Keel) obit Jan 81
Francis, Clarence obit Mar 86
Francis, Dick Aug 81
Francis, Frank (Chalton) obit Apr 89
Frankel, Max Apr 87
Franken, Rose obit Aug 88
Fraser of North Cape, Bruce Austin Fraser, 1st Baron obit Apr 81
Frayn, Michael Jan 85
Frederika (Louise), Consort of Paul I, King of the Hellenes obit Apr 81
Freehafer, Edward G(eier) obit Feb 86
Frei (Montalva), Eduardo obit Mar 82
Freilicher, Jane Nov 89
Freud, Anna obit Mar 83
Freud, Lucian Jul 88
Friedan, Betty Mar 89
Friedkin, William Jun 87
Friendly, Fred W. Aug 87
Frings, Ketti (Hartley) obit Apr 81
Frisch, Karl von obit Yrbk 83 (died Jun 82)
Frissell, Toni obit Jun 88
Frye, (Herman) Northrop Aug 83
Fujiyama, Aiichiro obit May 85
Fuller, Charles Jun 89
Fuller, R(ichard) Buckminster, (Jr.) obit Aug 83
Futter, Ellen V(ictoria) Oct 85

Gabor, Zsa Zsa Mar 88
Gaddis, William Nov 87
Gajdusek, D(aniel) Carleton Jun 81
Gale, Robert (Peter) Jan 87
Gallo, Robert C(harles) Oct 86
Gallup, George (Horace) obit Sep 84
Galtieri, Leopoldo (Fortunato) Aug 82
Gandhi, Indira (Priyadarshini Nehru) obit Yrbk 84 Jan 85
Gandhi, Rajiv (Ratna) Apr 85

García Pérez, Alan Nov 85
Gardner, John (Champlin, Jr.) obit Nov 82
Garn, Edwin (Jacob) See Garn, J.
Garn, Jake Aug 85
Garroway, Dave obit Sep 82
Garth, David Jan 81
Garwin, Richard L. Mar 89
Gass, William H(oward) Apr 86
Gates, Thomas S(overeign), Jr. obit May 83
Gay, Peter (Jack) Feb 86
Gayle, Crystal Mar 86
Gehry, Frank O(wen) Jun 87
Geldof, Bob Mar 86
Gemayel, Amin Mar 83
Genet, Jean obit Jun 86
George, Boy See Boy George
George-Brown, Baron See Brown, G. obit
Gephardt, Richard (Andrew) Oct 87
Gerbner, George Aug 83
Gerhardsen, Einar obit Nov 87
Gernreich, Rudi obit Jun 85
Gershwin, Ira obit Oct 83
Gerstenmaier, (Karl Albrecht) Eugen obit May 86
Getty, Gordon P(eter) Feb 85
Geyer, Georgie Anne Aug 86
Giamatti, A(ngelo) Bartlett obit Oct 89
Giauque, William F(rancis) obit May 82
Gibb, Barry Sep 81
Gibson, Mel Apr 84
Gibson, William Jul 83
Gideonse, Harry David obit May 85
Gielgud, John Feb 84
Gilder, George Oct 81
Gilder, Rosamond obit Oct 86
Gilels, Emil G(rigoryevich) obit Jan 86
Giles, Barney McKinney obit Aug 84
Gimbel, Peter (Robin) Jan 82 obit Aug 87
Gingold, Hermione (Ferdinanda) obit Jul 87
Gingrich, Newt(on Leroy) Jul 89
Ginsberg, Allen Apr 87
Giroux, Robert Nov 82
Giuliani, Rudolph (William) Apr 88
Glass, Philip Mar 81
Glasser, Ira Jan 86
Gleason, Jackie obit Aug 87
Glemp, Jozef Sep 82
Glubb, Sir John Bagot obit May 86
Gmeiner, Hermann obit Jun 86
Gobbi, Tito obit May 84
Godfrey, Arthur obit May 83
Godunov, Alexander Feb 83

Goldberg, Whoopi Mar 85
Golden, Harry (Lewis) obit Nov 81
Goldman, Eric F(rederick) obit Apr 89
Goldmann, Nahum obit Oct 82
Goldsmith, Sir James (Michael) Feb 88
Goldsmith, Jimmy See Goldsmith, Sir James (Michael)
Goldstein, Israel obit Jun 86
Goldstein, Joseph L(eonard) Jul 87
Golub, Leon (Albert) Aug 84
Gomulka, Wladyslaw obit Oct 82
Goode, Richard Nov 88
Goode, W(illie) Wilson Oct 85
Goodell, Charles E(llsworth, Jr.) obit Mar 87
Gooden, Dwight (Eugene) Apr 86
Goodman, Benny obit Aug 86
Goodrich, Frances obit Apr 84
Goodrich, Lloyd obit May 87
Gorbachev, Mikhail (Sergeyevich) Aug 85
Gorbachev, Raisa May 88
Gordon, Mary (Catherine) Nov 81
Gordon, Ruth obit Oct 85
Gore, Albert, Jr. Jun 87
Gorin, Igor obit Jun 82
Gorman, Mike obit Jul 89
Gorman, Thomas F(rancis) X(avier) See Gorman, Mike obit
Gorsuch, Anne (McGill) Sep 82
Gosden, Freeman F(isher) obit Feb 83
Gossage, Rich Aug 84
Gottlieb, Robert A(dams) Sep 87
Goudge, Elizabeth obit Aug 84
Gould, Beatrice Blackmar obit Apr 89
Gould, (Charles) Bruce obit Oct 89
Gould, Chester obit Jul 85
Gould, Glenn obit Nov 82
Gould, Stephen Jay Sep 82
Grace, Princess of Monaco obit Nov 82
Graf, Steffi Feb 89
Graham, Bob Jul 86
Graham, (Daniel) Robert See Graham, Bob
Graham, Sheilah obit Jan 89
Gramm, Donald obit Jul 83
Gramm, (William) Phil(ip) May 86
Grandi, Dino, Conte obit Jul 88
Grant, Cary obit Jan 87
Grappelli, Stéphane Aug 88
Grass, Günter (Wilhelm) Jul 83
Grasso, Ella T(ambussi) obit Mar 81

Graves, Michael Jan 89

Graves, Nancy (Stevenson) May 81

Graves, Robert (Ranke) obit Feb 86

Gray, C(layland) Boyden Aug 89

Gray, Gordon obit Feb 83

Gray, Simon (James Holliday) Jun 83

Gray, Spalding Sep 86

Gray, William H., 3d Feb 88

Grede, William J(ohn) obit Aug 89

Greeley, Dana McLean obit Aug 86

Green, Edith S(tarrett) obit Jun 87

Green, Mark J(oseph) Feb 88

Greenberg, Hank obit Oct 86

Greene, Harold H(erman) Aug 85

Greene, Hugh Carleton obit Apr 87

Greene, Lorne obit Oct 87

Greenspan, Alan Jan 89

Greenwood, Joan obit Apr 87

Greer, Germaine Oct 88

Gregorian, Vartan Oct 85

Gretzky, Wayne, Feb 82

Grey, J(ames) D(avid) obit Sep 85

Gribble, Harry Wagstaff (Graham-) obit Apr 81

Griffin, (Samuel) Marvin obit Aug 82

Griffith Joyner, Florence Apr 89

Grillo, Frank Raúl See Machito

Gromyko, Andrei A(ndreevich) obit Aug 89

Gross, H(arold) R(oyce) obit Oct 87

Gross, Paul Magnus obit Jun 86

Grosvenor, Melville Bell obit Jun 82

Grosz, Karoly Sep 88

Groth, John (August) obit Aug 88

Gruenther, Alfred M(aximilian) obit Jul 83

Grumman, Leroy R(andle) obit Jan 83

Grzimek, Bernhard obit May 87

Guare, John Aug 82

Guinness, Alec Mar 81

Guisewite, Cathy (Lee) Feb 89

Gumbel, Bryant Jul 86

Gunn, Thom Nov 88

Gurney, A(lbert) R(amsdell), Jr. Jul 86

Guth, Alan H(arvey) Sep 87

Guthrie, Arlo Feb 82

Gwathmey, Charles Jan 88

Gwathmey, Robert obit Nov 88

Haacke, Hans (Christoph) Jul 87

Habash, George Mar 88

Habib, Philip C(harles) Sep 81

Habré, Hissène Aug 87

Haddon, William, Jr. obit Apr 85

Hagegard, Hakan May 85

Hagerty, James C. obit Jun 81

Haig, Alexander Meigs, Jr. Sep 87

Hale, Clara Jul 85

Haley, Sir William John obit Oct 87

Hall, Arsenio Sep 89

Hall, Donald (Andrew) May 84

Hall, Joyce C(lyde) obit Jan 83

Halleck, Charles A(braham) obit Apr 86

Hallstein, Walter obit May 82

Hamilton, Lee H(erbert) Mar 88

Hamilton, Margaret obit Jul 85

Hamilton, Scott Apr 85

Hammon, William McDowell obit Nov 89

Hammond, E(dward) Cuyler obit Jan 87

Hammond, John (Henry, Jr.) obit Aug 87

Hancock, Herbie Apr 88

Hancock, Joy B(right) obit Oct 86

Handler, Philip obit Feb 82

Handy, Thomas T(roy) obit Jun 82

Hanfmann, George M(axim) A(nossov) obit May 86

Hanks, Nancy obit Mar 83

Hanks, Tom Apr 89

Hanna, William Jul 83

Hansell, Haywood S(hepherd, Jr.) obit Jan 89

Hanson, Duane (Elwood) Oct 83

Hanson, Howard obit Apr 81

Harburg, E(dgar) Y(ipsel) obit Apr 81

Harden, Cecil M(urray) obit Feb 85

Hardwick, Elizabeth Feb 81

Hare, David Aug 83

Haring, Keith Aug 86

Harkness, Rebekah (West) obit Sep 82

Harlech, Fifth Baron See Ormsby-Gore, (W.) D. obit

Harrar, J(acob) George obit Jun 82

Harrell, Lynn Feb 83

Harriman, W(illiam) Averill obit Sep 86

Harrington, (Edward) Michael Oct 88 obit Sep 89

Harris, Sir Arthur Travers obit May 84

Harris, Barbara (Clementine) Jun 89

Harris, Patricia Roberts obit May 85

Harrison, George Jan 89

Harrison, William K(elly), Jr. obit Aug 87

Harrison, Rex Feb 86

Harrison, Wallace K(irkman) obit Jan 82

Harry, Debbie Nov 81

Hart, Kitty Carlisle Oct 82

Hartman, David Jun 81

Harvey, Paul Mar 86

Hass, H(enry) B(ohn) obit Apr 87

Hatch, Orrin G(rant) Aug 82

Hatfield, Mark O(dom) Mar 84

Hauge, Gabriel (Sylfest) obit Sep 81

Haughey, Charles J(ames) Feb 81

Haughton, Daniel J(eremiah) obit Aug 87

Hauser, (Benjamin) Gayelord Feb 85

Havel, Václav Mar 85

Hawke, Bob Aug 83

Hawke, Robert James Lee See Hawke, Bob

Hawking, Stephen W(illiam) May 84

Hawkins, Augustus F(reeman) Feb 83

Hawkins, Paula (Fickes) Sep 85

Hayden, Sterling obit Jul 86

Hayes, Robert M(ichael) Apr 89

Hayes, Woody obit May 87

Hays, (Lawrence) Brooks obit Jan 82

Hays, Wayne L(evere) obit Apr 89

Hayter, Stanley William obit Jun 88

Hayworth, Rita obit Jul 87

Head, Edith obit Jan 82

Heaney, Seamus (Justin) Jan 82

Hearns, Thomas Mar 83

Hearst, Patricia (Campbell) Aug 82

Hecht, Anthony May 86

Heckler, Margaret M(ary O'Shaughnessy) Aug 83

Hedden, Worth Tuttle obit Jan 86

Hefner, Christie (Ann) Oct 86

Heifetz, Jascha obit Feb 88

Heimlich, Henry J(ay) Oct 86

Heinlein, Robert A(nson) obit Jun 88

Heinz, H(enry) J(ohn) obit Apr 87

Heinz, (Henry) John, (3d) Apr 81

Held, Al Jan 86

Hélion, Jean obit Jan 88

Heller, John R(oderick), Jr. obit Jul 89

Heller, Walter W(olfgang) obit Aug 87

Hellman, Lillian obit Aug 84

Helmsley, Harry B(rakmann) Jun 85

Helpmann, Robert obit Nov 86

Helstein, Ralph obit May 85

Hemingway, Mary (Welsh) obit Jan 87

Henderson, Leon obit Jan 87

Henderson, Loy W(esley) obit May 86

Hendricks, Barbara Mar 89

Henley, Beth Feb 83

Hentoff, Nat Aug 86

Herbster, Ben M(ohr) obit Mar 85

Herman, Pee-wee Jan 88

Herman, Woody obit Jan 88

Hernandez, Keith Feb 88

Hersh, Seymour (Myron) Mar 84

Hershey, Barbara Aug 89

Herzog, Chaim Apr 88

Herzog, Paul M(ax) obit Jan 87

Hesburgh, Theodore M(artin) Jul 82

Heseltine, Michael (Ray Dibdin) Jun 85

Hess, Rudolf obit Oct 87

Heston, Charlton Jul 86

Hewitt, Don Jun 88

Hickerson, John D(ewey) obit Apr 89

Hicks, Granville obit Aug 82

Hightower, John M(armann) obit Apr 87

Higley, Harvey V(an Zandt) obit Jan 87

Hildebrand, Joel H(enry) obit Jul 83

Hildreth, Horace A(ugustus) obit Jul 88

Hill, Abram obit Nov 86

Hill, Benny Feb 83

Hill, Lister obit Feb 85

Hillenkoetter, Roscoe H(enry) obit Aug 82

Himmelfarb, Gertrude May 85

Hines, Earl (Kenneth) obit Jun 83

Hines, Fatha See Hines, Earl (Kenneth) obit

Hines, Gregory Jul 85

Hirohito, Emperor of Japan obit Feb 89

Hirsch, John (Stephen) Apr 84 obit Oct 89

Hirsch, Judd Mar 84

Hirshhorn, Joseph H(erman) obit Oct 81

Hite, Shere Feb 88

Hoagland, Edward (Morley) Sept 82

Hobson, Laura Z(ametkin) obit Apr 86

Hodel, Donald P(aul) Jun 87

Hoffa, James R(iddle) obit Mar 83

Hoffer, Eric obit Jul 83

Hoffman, Abbie Apr 81 obit Jun 89

Hoffman, Anna M(arie) Rosenberg obit Jul 83

Hogan, Paul Aug 87

Hogben, Lancelot (Thomas) obit Jan 84

Hogwood, Christopher Jul 85

Hoiby, Lee Mar 87

Holden, William obit Jan 82

Holladay, Wilhelmina (Cole) Oct 87

Holliday, Jennifer Jun 83

Holliger, Heinz Jan 87

Hollings, Ernest F(rederick) Jul 82

Hollomon, J(ohn) Herbert obit Aug 85

Holloway, Stanley obit Mar 82

Holmes, Larry Aug 81

Holroyd, Michael (de Courcy Fraser) Mar 89

Holt, A(ndrew) D(avid) obit Sep 87

Holt, John (Caldwell) Jun 81 obit Nov 85

Holtz, Lou Jun 89

Holyoake, Keith J(acka) obit Feb 84

Hook, Sidney Apr 88 obit Sep 89

Hoopes, Darlington obit Nov 89

Hope, Stanley C. obit Oct 82

Hopper, Dennis Aug 87

Horne, John E(lmer) obit Apr 85

Horne, Lena Nov 85

Horner, H(orace) Mansfield obit Jul 83

Horrocks, Sir B(rian) G(wynne) obit Mar 85

Hosmer, (Chester) Craig obit Mar 83

Houghton, Amory obit Apr 81

Houseman, John Apr 84 obit Jan 89

Houston, James A(rchibald) Jul 87

Houston, Whitney Nov 86

Howar, Barbara Aug 89

Howard, Elston (Gene) obit Feb 81

Howard, Trevor (Wallace) obit Feb 88

Hoxha, Enver obit Jun 85

Ho Ying-Chin obit Jan 88

Hu Yaobang Nov 83

Hudson, Rock obit Nov 85

Hughes, Barnard Sep 81

Hughes, Emmet John obit Nov 82

Hughes, Robert (Studley Forrest) May 87

Hughes, Sarah T(ilghman) obit Jul 85

Hunsaker, Jerome C(larke) obit Nov 84

Hunt, Linda Jan 88

Hunter, Alberta obit Jan 85

Hunter-Gault, Charlayne Apr 87

Hunthausen, Raymond G(erhardt) Aug 87

Huppert, Isabelle Nov 81

Hurd, Peter obit Sep 84

Hurt, John Jan 82

Hurt, William May 86

Hussein, Ahmed obit Feb 85

Hussein, King of Jordan Apr 86

Hussein, Saddam (al-Tikriti) Sep 81

Hussein Ibn Talal See Hussein, King of Jordan

Husted, Marjorie Child obit Feb 87

Huston, John Mar 81 obit Oct 87

Hu Yaobang obit Jun 89

Hwang, David Henry May 89

Hyde, Henry J(ohn) Oct 89

Hynek, J(osef) Allen obit Jun 86

Iacocca, Lee (Anthony) Oct 88

Icahn, Carl C. Apr 86

Idris Senussi I, King of Libya obit Jul 83

Idriss Senussi I, King of Libya See Idris Senussi I, King of Libya obit

Iglesias, Julio Jun 84

Ilg, Frances L(illian) obit Sep 81

Illia, Arturo (Umberto) obit Mar 83

Impellitteri, Vincent R(ichard) obit Mar 87

Ingersoll, Ralph (McAllister) obit May 85

Innaurato, Albert Mar 88

Inouye, Daniel K(en) Sep 87

Irons, Jeremy Aug 84

Irwin, Bill Oct 87

Isherwood, Christopher (William) obit Feb 86

Isozaki, Arata Apr 88

Ivory, James Jul 81

Jackson, Henry M(artin) obit Oct 83

Jackson, Jesse (Louis) Jan 86

Jackson, Michael Nov 83

Jacob, John E(dward) Feb 86

Jacobi, Derek May 81

Jagger, Bianca Apr 87

Jahn, Helmut Feb 89

Jakes, John (William) Sep 88

Jakobovits, Immanuel Jun 88

Jakobovits, Lord See Jakobovits, Immanuel

James, Clive (Vivian Leopold) Nov 84

James, Harry obit Aug 83

Janowitz, Tama Aug 89

Jarrett, Keith May 85
Jaruzelski, Wojciech (Witold) Mar 82
Jarvik, Robert K(offler) Jul 85
Jarvis, Howard (Arnold) obit Sep 86
Javits, Jacob K(oppel) obit Apr 86
Jaworski, Leon obit Feb 83
Jayewardene, J(unius) R(ichard) Jan 84
Jenkins, Ray H(oward) obit Feb 81
Jenkins, Roy (Harris) Oct 82
Jenner, William E(zra) obit May 85
Jennings, Paul (Joseph) obit Oct 87
Jennings, Peter (Charles) Nov 83
Jennings, Waylon Apr 82
Jensen, Jackie obit Oct 82
Jessel, George (Albert) obit Jul 81
Jessup, Philip C(aryl) obit Mar 86
Jobs, Steven (Paul) Mar 83
Joffrey, Robert obit May 88
Johanson, Donald C(arl) Feb 84
John, Tommy Oct 81
Johns, Jasper May 87
Johnson, Ben Jun 88
Johnson, Crockett obit Jan 84
Johnson, Don Apr 86
Johnson, Earvin Jan 82
Johnson, F(rederick) Ross May 89
Johnson, Harold K(eith) obit Nov 83
Johnson, Magic See Johnson, Earvin
Johnson, Pamela Hansford obit Aug 81
Johnson, Sonia Feb 85
Johnson, (Thomas) Walter obit Sep 85
Johnson, Virginia May 85
Jones, Carolyn obit Sep 83
Jones, David C(harles) Jul 82
Jones, Grace Sep 87
Jones, James R(obert) Oct 81
Jones, K. C. Feb 87
Jones, Marvin obit Jan 84
Jordan, James Edward obit May 88
Jordan, Michael Sep 87
Joseph, Stephen (Carl) Jan 89
Joyner, Florence Griffith See Griffith Joyner, F.
Joyner-Kersee, Jackie Jul 87
Julia, Raul Sep 82
Just, Ward May 89

Kádár, János obit Aug 89
Kahane, Melanie obit Feb 89
Kahn, Herman obit Aug 83
Kainen, Jacob Feb 87

Kaiser, Edgar F(osburgh) obit Feb 82
Kalb, Marvin Jul 87
Kalikow, Peter S(tephen) Sep 88
Kampelman, Max M. Jul 86
Kane, Harnett T(homas) obit Yrbk 84
Kane, Joseph Nathan Nov 85
Kania, Stanislaw Jun 81
Kapitsa, Pyotr L(eonidovich) obit May 84
Kapitza, Peter L(eonidovich) See Kapitsa, P. L. obit
Karajan, Herbert von Sep 86 obit Sep 89
Karami, Rashid obit Jul 87
Karmal, Babrak Mar 81
Kasparov, Gary Apr 86
Kassebaum, Nancy Landon Feb 82
Kasten, Robert W(alter), Jr. Jun 89
Kastler, Alfred obit Mar 84
Kaufman, Henry Aug 81
Kavanagh, Dan See Barnes, Julian
Kay, Hershy obit Feb 82
Kaye, Danny obit Apr 87
Kaye, Nora obit Apr 87
Kean, Thomas H(oward) Jul 85
Keegan, John Oct 89
Keene, Donald (Lawrence) Jan 88
Keeny, Spurgeon M(ilton) obit Jan 89
Keighley, William obit Aug 84
Keillor, Garrison Aug 85
Kekkonen, Urho K(aleva) obit Oct 86
Kelly, E(verett) Lowell obit Apr 86
Kelly, Grace See Grace, Princess of Monaco obit
Kelly, John B(renden), Jr. obit Apr 85
Kelly, Patrick Sep 89
Kelly, Petra (Karin) Mar 84
Kelman, Charles D(avid) Jun 84
Kemper, James S(cott) obit Nov 81
Keneally, Thomas (Michael) Jun 87
Kennedy, Anthony M(cLeod) Jul 88
Kennedy, Donald Jul 84
Kennedy, Joseph P(atrick), 2d Jun 88
Kennedy, William May 85
Kennon, Robert F(loyd) obit Apr 88
Kent, Corita obit Nov 86
Kerry, John (Forbes) Jun 88
Kertész, André obit Nov 85
Keyhoe, Donald E(dward) obit Feb 89
Keyserling, Leon H. obit Sep 87

Keyworth, George A(lbert), 2d Mar 86
Khalid, King of Saudi Arabia obit Aug 82
Khamenei, Hojatolislam (Sayed) Ali Nov 87
Khomeini, Ayatollah Ruholla (Mussavi) obit Jul 89
Khashoggi, Adnan (Mohamed) Mar 86
Kiefer, Anselm Jun 88
Kienholz, Edward Aug 89
Kieran, John (Francis) obit Feb 82
Kiesinger, Kurt Georg obit Apr 88
Kiewiet, Cornelis W(illem) de See de Kiewiet, C. W. obit
Killian, James R(hyne), Jr. obit Mar 88
Kim Dae Jung Sep 85
Kimball, Spencer W(oolley) obit Jan 86
Kimbrough, Emily obit Apr 89
King, Charles Glen obit Mar 88
King, Don Jun 84
King, Larry May 85
King, Stephen Oct 81
Kingman, Dave Mar 82
Kingsley, Ben Nov 83
Kinnell, Galway Aug 86
Kinnock, Neil (Gordon) Apr 84
Kinski, Nastassja Jun 84
Kintner, Robert E(dmonds) obit Feb 81
Kirk, Paul G(rattan), Jr. Aug 87
Kirkpatrick, Jeane (Duane) J(ordan) Jul 81
Kirkpatrick, Ralph obit Aug 84
Kishi, Nobusuke obit Sep 87
Kistiakowsky, George B(ogdan) obit Feb 83
Kitaj, R(onald) B(rooks) Apr 82
Kitchell, Iva obit Jan 84
Klein, Edward E(lkan) obit Sep 85
Klein, Julius obit May 84
Kline, Kevin Jul 86
Kline, Nathan S(chellenberg) obit May 83
Knight, Bob May 87
Knight, Gladys Feb 87
Knight, John S(hively) obit Aug 81
Knopf, Alfred A. obit Oct 84
Koestler, Arthur obit Apr 83
Kohout, Pavel Feb 88
Koivisto, Mauno (Henrik) Sep 82
Kolar, Jiri Apr 86
Kolff, Willem Johan May 83
Kolodin, Irving obit Jun 88
Kolvenbach, Peter-Hans May 84
Komar, Vitaly, and Melamid, Aleksandr Oct 84
Koo, V(i) K(yuin) Wellington obit Jan 86

Koontz, Elizabeth D(uncan) obit Apr 89

Koop, C(harles) Everett Sep 83

Koppel, Ted Jul 84

Korda, Michael (Vincent) Aug 85

Kosygin, Aleksei N(ikolayevich) obit Feb 81

Kotschnig, Walter M(aria) obit Sep 85

Kozol, Jonathan Jan 86

Krantz, Judith May 82

Krasna, Norman obit Feb 85

Krasner, Lee obit Aug 84

Kraus, Alfredo Jun 87

Kraus, Hans P(eter) obit Jan 89

Kraus, Lili obit Jan 87

Kraushaar, Otto F(rederick) obit Nov 89

Kravis, Henry R. Mar 89

Krebs, Sir Hans obit Feb 82

Kremer, Gidon Mar 85

Krens, Thomas Apr 89

Krim, Mathilde Aug 87

Krishnamurti, Jiddu obit Apr 86

Kroc, Ray(mond) A. obit Mar 84

Krone, Julie Oct 89

Kucuk, Fazil See Kutchuk, (M.) F. obit

Kuekes, Edward D(aniel) obit Mar 87

Kundera, Milan Mar 83

Kunin, Madeleine (May) Jul 87

Kuralt, Charles Jul 81

Kurtz, Swoosie Oct 87

Kutchuk, (Mustafa) Fazil obit Mar 84

Kuznets, Simon obit Sep 85

Kylian, Jiri Sep 82

Kyser, Kay obit Sep 85

LaBelle, Patti Jul 86

Labouisse, Henry R(ichardson) obit May 87

Lacroix, Christian Apr 88

Ladurie, Emmanuel Le Roy See Le Roy Ladurie, E.

Laeri, J(ohn) Howard obit Aug 86

Laffer, Arthur (Betz) Feb 82

Lagerfeld, Karl Jan 82

Laine, Cleo Feb 86

Laing, Hugh obit Jun 88

Laing, R(onald) D(avid) obit Oct 89

LaMarsh, Judy obit Jan 81

Lamm, Richard D(ouglas) May 85

L'Amour, Louis (Dearborn) obit Jul 88

Lancaster, Burt Apr 86

Lancaster, Osbert obit Sep 86

Lanchester, Elsa obit Feb 87

Land, Edwin H(erbert) Mar 81

Landon, Alf(red Mossman) obit Nov 87

Lang, Jack Aug 83

Lange, David Sep 85

Lange, Jessica May 83

Langer, Susanne K(atharina Knauth) obit Sep 85

Lansing, Sherry (Lee) May 81

Lapham, Lewis H(enry) Mar 89

Lardner, Ring, Jr. Jul 87

Laredo, Ruth Oct 87

Larkin, Philip (Arthur) Jan 85 obit Feb 86

Lasch, Christopher Mar 85

Lash, Joseph P. obit Oct 87

Laski, Marghanita obit Apr 88

Lasorda, Tommy Feb 89

Lattimore, Owen obit Jul 89

Lauder, Estée Jul 86

Laughlin, James May 82

Lauper, Cyndi Aug 85

Laurents, Arthur Nov 84

Lavin, Linda Nov 87

Lawe, John (Edward) Jan 84 obit Apr 89

Lawrence, Jacob Sep 88

Lawson, Nigel Mar 87

Lay, James S(elden), Jr. obit Aug 87

Leakey, Mary (Douglas) Apr 85

Lean, David Jun 89

Lebowitz, Fran(ces Ann) Mar 82

Leboyer, Frédérick Jul 82

Lederman, Leon M(ax) Sep 89

Lee, Doris (Emrick) obit Jan 86

Lee, Jennie obit Jan 89

Lee, Ming Cho Jun 89

Lee, Spike Mar 89

Léger, Jules obit Jan 81

Le Guin, Ursula K(roeber) Jan 83

Lehman, John F(rancis), Jr. Nov 85

Lehrer, James (Charles) Jan 87

Lehrer, Tom Jul 82

Lelouch, Claude Nov 82

Lem, Stanislaw Oct 86

Lemieux, Mario Aug 88

Lemmon, Jack Aug 88

Lemnitzer, Lyman L. obit Jan 89

LeMond, Greg Oct 89

Lendl, Ivan Sep 84

Lengyel, Emil obit Apr 85

Lennon, John obit Feb 81

Lennox, Annie May 88

Lennox-Boyd, Lord Alan T(indal) obit May 83

Leno, Jay Jun 88

Lenya, Lotte obit Jan 82

Leonard, Elmore Sep 85

Leonard, Hugh Apr 83

Leonard, Ray See Leonard, Sugar Ray

Leonard, Sugar Ray Feb 81

Leonidoff, Leon obit Oct 89

Leopold III, King of the Belgians obit Nov 83

Le Pen, Jean-Marie Jan 88

Lerner, Alan Jay obit Aug 86

Le Roy Ladurie, Emmanuel (Bernard) Jul 84

Lesage, Jean obit Feb 81

Leser, Tina obit Mar 86

LeSourd, Catherine Marshall See Marshall, S.C.W. obit

Lévesque, René obit Jan 88

Levi, Julian (Edwin) obit Apr 82

Levi, Primo Mar 87 obit May 87

Levi-Montalcini, Rita Nov 89

Levin, Meyer obit Sep 81

Levine, Joseph E(dward) obit Sep 87

Levine, Philip obit Nov 87

Lewis, Carl Nov 84

Lewis, Drew Feb 82

Lewis, Flora Jan 89

Lewis, Roger obit Jan 88

LeWitt, Sol Jul 86

Li, C(hoh) H(ao) obit Jan 88

Liberace Mar 86 obit Mar 87

Liberman, Alexander May 87

Liberman, Evseï (Grigorevich) obit May 83

Lichtenstein, Harvey May 87

Liebman, Max obit Sep 81

Lilienthal, David E(li) obit Mar 81

Lillie, Beatrice obit Mar 89

Liman, Arthur L(awrence) Jan 88

Limann, Hilla Jun 81

Linden, Hal Jan 87

Link, Edwin (Albert) obit Yrbk 83 (died Sep 81)

Li Peng Nov 88

Lipmann, Fritz (Albert) obit Sep 86

Lipton, Seymour obit Feb 87

Littlejohn, Robert McG(owan) obit Jul 82

Little Richard Sep 86

Livingston, M(ilton) Stanley obit Nov 86

Llewellyn, Richard obit Jan 84

Lloyd Webber, Andrew Jun 82

Lockridge, Richard obit Oct 82

Lodge, Henry Cabot, (Jr.) obit Apr 85

Lodge, John Davis obit Jan 86

Loeb, William obit Nov 81

Loewe, Frederick obit Apr 88

Loewy, Raymond (Fernand) obit Sep 86

Logan, Joshua (Lockwood, 3d) obit Aug 88

Lon Nol obit Jan 86

London, George obit Jun 85

Lonergan, Bernard J(oseph) F(rancis) obit Feb 85

Longo, Luigi obit Jan 81

Loos, Anita obit Oct 81

López Bravo, Gregorio obit Apr 85
Loquasto, Santo Jun 81
Lorenz, Konrad (Zacharias) obit Apr 89
Lorenzo, Frank Feb 87
Loring, Eugene obit Oct 82
Lortel, Lucille Feb 85
Losey, Joseph obit Aug 84
Loudon, Dorothy Jun 84
Louganis, Greg Oct 84
Louis, Joe obit Jun 81
Love, Iris (Cornelia) Aug 82
Loveless, Herschel C(ellel) obit Jul 89
Lovett, Robert A(bercrombie) obit Jun 86
Lowery, Joseph E. Nov 82
Lubbers, Ruud (Rudolph Frans Marie) May 88
Lubell, Samuel obit Oct 87
Lucas, Martha B. See Pate, M. B. L. obit
Lucci, Susan Oct 89
Luce, Clare Boothe obit Nov 87
Lucioni, Luigi obit Sep 88
Ludlam, Charles Aug 86 obit Jul 87
Ludlum, Robert Nov 82
Lujan, Manuel, Jr. Sep 89
Lukas, J(ay) Anthony Jan 87
Lunden, Joan May 89
Luns, Joseph M(arie) A(ntoine) H(ubert) Apr 82
LuPone, Patti Apr 89
Lurie, Alison Feb 86
Lustiger, Jean-Marie Feb 84
Lynch, David May 87
Lynch, J(ohn) Joseph obit Aug 87
Lynd, Staughton (Craig) May 83
Lynde, Paul (Edward) obit Feb 82
Lyng, Richard E(dmund) Sep 86
Lyons, Eugene obit Mar 85
Lyubimov, Yuri (Petrovich) Nov 88

Ma, Yo-Yo Jul 82
MacBride, Seán obit Mar 88
MacDermot, Galt Jul 84
Macdonald, Dwight obit Mar 83
MacDonald, John D(ann) Oct 86 obit Feb 87
MacDonald, Malcolm (John) obit Mar 81
Macdonald, Ross obit Sep 83
MacEachen, Allan J(oseph) Apr 83
Machel, Samora Moises Mar 84 obit Jan 87
Machito Feb 83 obit Jun 84
MacInnes, Helen (Clark) obit Nov 85

MacIver, Loren Nov 87
Mackay, John A(lexander) obit Aug 83
Mackerras, Sir Charles Feb 85
Mackie, Bob Oct 88
MacLeish, Archibald obit Jun 82
Macmillan, (Maurice) Harold obit Feb 87
Macy, John W(illiams), Jr. obit Apr 87
Madden, John Aug 85
Madden, Ray J(ohn) obit Nov 87
Madonna May 86
Magnuson, Warren G(rant) obit Jul 89
Mahathir bin Mohamed Aug 88
Mahfouz, Naguib May 89
Mahon, George (Herman) obit Jan 86
Malamud, Bernard obit May 86
Malenkov, Georgi M(aximilianovich) obit Mar 88
Malik, Adam obit Nov 84
Malik, Charles (Habib) obit Feb 88
Malkovich, John May 88
Malone, Moses Jun 86
Maltz, Albert obit Jul 85
Mamoulian, Rouben obit Jan 88
Mandela, Nelson (Rolihlahla) Jan 84
Mandela, (Nomzamo) Winnie Jan 86
Mandelbrot, Benoit Jun 87
Mandlikova, Hana Jan 86
Mandrell, Barbara Aug 82
Mankiller, Wilma P. Nov 88
Mapplethorpe, Robert May 89 obit Yrbk 89
Marcos, Ferdinand (Edralin) obit Nov 89
Marino, Dan Jan 89
Maris, Roger (Eugene) obit Feb 86
Marjolin, Robert (Ernest) obit Jun 86
Markham, Beryl obit Oct 86
Marriott, J. Willard obit Oct 85
Marsalis, Wynton Oct 84
Marshall, (Sarah) Catherine (Wood) obit May 83
Marshall, E. G. Jun 86
Marshall, Thurgood Sep 89
Martens, Wilfried Feb 87
Martin, Agnes Sep 89
Martin, John Bartlow obit Mar 87
Martin, Judith Jun 86
Martin, Lynn Oct 89
Marton, Eva Apr 85
Marvin, Lee obit Oct 87
Mason, Bobbie Ann Sep 89
Mason, Jackie Jul 87

Mason, James obit Sep 84
Mason, Marsha Apr 81
Massey, Raymond obit Sep 83
Masson, André (Aimé René) obit Jan 88
Masursky, Harold Aug 86
Matthews, Burnita Shelton obit Jun 88
Matthews, H(arrison) Freeman obit Jan 87
Mattingly, Don Oct 88
Mauroy, Pierre Jun 82
Maxwell, (Ian) Robert Sep 88
Maynard, Robert C(lyve) Jun 86
Mayr, Ernst Nov 84
Mays, Benjamin E(lijah) obit May 84
Mazey, Emil obit Nov 83
M'Bow, Amadou-Mahtar May 87
McBride, Lloyd obit Jan 84
McCabe, Thomas B(ayard) obit Jul 82
McCain, John S(idney 3d) Feb 89
McCain, John S(idney), Jr. obit Jun 81
McCall, Tom (Lawson) obit Mar 83
McCarthy, Frank obit Feb 87
McCartney, Paul Jan 86
McClanahan, Rue May 89
McClintock, Barbara Mar 84
McCloy, John J(ay) obit May 89
McColough, C(harles) Peter Jan 81
McCormack, John W(illiam) obit Jan 81
McCracken, James (Eugene) obit Jun 88
McCullough, Colleen Apr 82
McEwen, Terence A(lexander) Jul 85
McFadden, Mary Apr 83
McFarland, Ernest W(illiam) obit Aug 84
McFarlane, Robert C(arl) May 84
McFerrin, Bobby Aug 89
McGannon, Donald H(enry) obit Jul 84
McGee, Fibber See Jordan, J. E. obit
McGinniss, Joe Jan 84
McGuane, Thomas Nov 87
McInerney, Jay Nov 87
McKellen, Ian Jan 84
McKenna, Siobhan obit Jan 87
McKinley, Chuck obit Sep 86
McLaughlin, Ann (Dore) Nov 88
McLaughlin, John (Joseph) Jul 87
McLean, Robert obit Feb 81
McLuhan, (Herbert) Marshall obit Feb 81

McMahon, William obit May 88

McMurtry, Larry (Jeff) Jun 84

McNally, Terrence Mar 88

McNamara, Robert S(trange) Mar 87

McNellis, Maggi obit Aug 89

McPhee, John (Angus) Oct 82

McQueen, Steve obit Jan 81

McRae, Carmen Apr 83

Mearns, David C(hambers) obit Jul 81

Medawar, Peter Brian obit Nov 87

Medeiros, Humberto S(ousa) obit Nov 83

Médici, Emílio Garrastazú obit Jan 86

Medvedev, Roy (Aleksandr) Sep 84

Meese, Edwin, 3d Sep 81

Meier, Richard Jan 85

Melamid, Aleksandr See Komar, V.

Mellencamp, John Cougar Mar 88

Mellon, William Larimer, Jr. obit Oct 89

Mendès-France, Pierre obit Jan 83

Menem, Carlos Saúl Nov 89

Meng, John J(oseph) obit Apr 88

Mengistu Haile Mariam Jul 81

Mennin, Peter obit Aug 83

Menon, K(umara) P(admanbha) S(ivasankara) obit Yrbk 83 (died Nov 82)

Mercer, Mabel obit Jun 84

Mercouri, Melina Mar 88

Merman, Ethel obit Apr 84

Merrifield, R(obert) Bruce Mar 85

Merrill, James (Ingram) Aug 81

Merwin, W(illiam) S(tanley) May 88

Michael, George Nov 88

Michals, Duane (Steven) Apr 81

Michel, Robert H(enry) Sep 81

Mifune, Toshiro Jun 81

Miki, Takeo obit Jan 89

Mikulski, Barbara A(nn) Nov 85

Milanov, Zinka obit Jul 89

Milgram, Stanley obit Mar 85

Milland, Ray obit Apr 86

Millar, Kenneth See Macdonald, R. obit

Miller, Arnold (Ray) obit Sep 85

Miller, Irving obit Feb 81

Miller, James C(lifford), 3d May 86

Miller, Jonathan (Wolfe) Nov 86

Miller, Merle obit Jul 86

Miller, Roger Sep 86

Miller, William E(dward) obit Aug 83

Millo, Aprile Apr 88

Milosz, Czeslaw Oct 81

Miner, Worthington (C.) obit Mar 83

Minnelli, Liza Jul 88

Minnelli, Vincente obit Sep 86

Minsky, Marvin (Lee) Sep 88

Mintoff, Dom Mar 84

Miró, Joan obit Feb 84

Mirvish, Edwin Apr 89

Mitchell, George J(ohn) Apr 89

Mitchell, Howard (Bundy) obit Aug 88

Mitchell, Joan Mar 86

Mitchell, John N(ewton) obit Jan 89

Mitterrand, François (Maurice) Oct 82

Moats, Alice-Leone obit Jul 89

Moch, Jules (Salvador) obit Nov 85

Molotov, Viacheslav M(ikhailovich) obit Jan 87

Monaco, Mario del obit Jan 83

Monk, Meredith Feb 85

Monk, Thelonious obit Apr 82

Monroe, Lucy obit Nov 87

Montagnier, Luc Aug 88

Montagu, Ewen (Edward Samuel) obit Sep 85

Montale, Eugenio obit Nov 81

Montana, Joe Sep 83

Montand, Yves Sep 88

Montebello, (Guy-)Philippe (Lannes) de See De Montebello, Philippe

Montgomery, Robert obit Nov 81

Moody, Joseph E(ugene) obit Jul 84

Moon, Sun Myung Mar 83

Moore, Brian Jan 86

Moore, Dudley Jun 82

Moore, Gerald obit May 87

Moore, Henry (Spencer) obit Oct 86

Morano, Albert Paul obit Feb 88

Moreno, Rita Sep 85

Morgan, Joe Sep 84

Morganfield, McKinley See Waters, Muddy

Morgenthau, Robert M(orris) Jan 86

Morley, Malcolm A. Jun 84

Morris, Edmund Jul 89

Morris, James Jul 86

Morris, Jan Jun 86

Morris, Mark Aug 88

Morris, Wright (Marion) May 82

Morrison, Philip Jul 81

Morse, Philip M(cCord) obit Nov 85

Mortimer, John (Clifford) Apr 83

Morton, Thruston B(allard) obit Oct 82

Mosbacher, Robert A(dam) Jun 89

Moses, Edwin Nov 86

Moses, Robert obit Sep 81

Mosley, J(ohn) Brooke obit Apr 88

Mosley, Sir Oswald (Ernald) obit Feb 81

Motley, Arthur H(arrison) obit Jul 84

Mowat, Farley (McGill) Feb 86

Moynihan, Daniel Patrick Feb 86

Mubarak, (Mohamed) Hosni Apr 82

Muccio, John J(oseph) obit Jul 89

Mudd, Roger (Harrison) Jan 81

Mueller, R(euben) H(erbert) obit Sep 82

Mulliken, Robert S(anderson) obit Jan 87

Mulroney, (Martin) Brian Apr 84

Mumford, L(awrence) Quincy obit Jan 83

Murphy, Charles S(prings) obit Oct 83

Murphy, Eddie Nov 83

Murray, Anne Jan 82

Murray, Bill Jan 85

Murray, Charles (Alan) Jul 86

Myer, Dillon S(eymour) obit Jan 83

Myrdal, Mrs. Alva obit Mar 86

Myrdal, Mrs. Gunnar See Myrdal, Mrs. A. obit

Myrdal, (Karl) Gunnar obit Jul 87

Nader, Ralph Apr 86

Naisbitt, John Nov 84

Najib Ahmadzi Jun 88

Nakasone, Yasuhiro Jun 83

Nakian, Reuben Feb 85 obit Feb 87

Namphy, Henri Sep 88

Narayan, R(asipuram) K(rishnaswami) Sep 87

Nash, Philleo obit Jan 88

Navasky, Victor (Saul) May 86

Navon, Yitzhak May 82

Neagle, Anna obit Jul 86

Neagle, Dame Anna See Neagle, Anna obit

Nearing, Scott obit Oct 83

Neel, Alice (Hartley) obit Jan 85

Nelligan, Kate Jul 83

Nesbitt, Cathleen (Mary) obit Sep 82

Nettles, Graig Jul 84

Neuharth, Allen H(arold) Apr 86

Neuhaus, Richard John Jun 88

Neumann, Emanuel obit Jan 81
Nevelson, Louise obit May 88
Newell, Homer E(dward), Jr. obit Sep 83
Newhouse, Maggi See McNellis, M.
Newman, Paul May 85
Newman, Randy Oct 82
Newton, Huey P(ercy) obit Oct 89
Nicholson, Ben obit Apr 82
Nicolson, Marjorie Hope obit Jun 81
Niemöller, (Friedrich Gustav Emil) Martin obit May 84
Niven, David obit Sep 83
Noah, Yannick Aug 87
Noel-Baker, Philip J(ohn) obit Mar 83
Nofziger, Lyn Jan 83
Noguchi, Isamu obit Feb 89
Nolan, Christopher Sep 88
Nolan, Lloyd obit Nov 85
Noriega (Morena), Manuel Antonio Mar 88
Norman, Greg Aug 89
Norman, Marsha May 84
Norris, Chuck Jan 89
Norstad, Lauris obit Oct 88
North, John Ringling obit Jul 85
Northrop, John Howard obit Sep 87
Northrop, John K(nudsen) obit Apr 81
Novak, Michael Feb 85
Nozick, Robert Jun 82
Nykvist, Sven (Vilhem) Jun 89

Obando y Bravo, Miguel Cardinal Mar 88
Oboler, Arch obit May 87
Obote, (Apollo) Milton Apr 81
O'Boyle, Patrick (Aloysius) Cardinal obit Sep 87
Obraztsova, Elena Feb 83
O'Brien, Leo W(illiam) obit Jul 82
O'Brien, Pat obit Jan 84
Ochsner, (Edward William) Alton obit Nov 81
O'Connor, John J(oseph) Jun 84
O'Connor, Sandra Day Jan 82
Odishaw, Hugh obit Jun 84
O'Dowd, George A. See Boy George
O'Hara, Mary obit Jan 81
O'Keeffe, Georgia obit Apr 86
O'Konski, Alvin E(dward) obit Aug 87
Oliver, James A(rthur) obit May 82
Olivier, Laurence obit Sep 89
Olsen, Kenneth H(arry) Mar 87

Olson, Harry F(erdinand) obit Jun 82
O'Meara, Walter (Andrew) obit Nov 89
Onassis, Christina obit Jan 89
O'Neil, James F(rancis) obit Sep 81
O'Neill, William A(tchison) Feb 85
Opel, John R(oberts) Mar 86
Orff, Carl obit May 82
Ormandy, Eugene obit May 85
Ormsby-Gore, (William) David obit Mar 85
Ortega, Daniel Oct 84
Osborn, Frederick (Henry) obit Mar 81
O'Shea, Milo Jun 82
Ovandia Candia, Alfredo obit Mar 82
Owings, Nathaniel A(lexander) obit Aug 84
Oz, Amos Jul 83
Özal, Turgut Jun 85
Ozick, Cynthia Aug 83

Pace, Frank, Jr. obit Feb 88
Packwood, Bob Jan 81
Padover, Saul K(ussiel) obit Apr 81
Page, Geraldine obit Aug 87
Pahlmann, William C(arroll) obit Jan 88
Paige, Leroy (Robert) obit Aug 82
Paik, Nam June Mar 83
Paisley, Ian (Richard Kyle) Jun 86
Paley, Grace Mar 86
Palme, (Sven) Olof (Joachim) obit Apr 86
Palmer, Lilli obit Mar 86
Pantaleoni, Helenka (Tradeusa Adamowski) obit Mar 87
Papandreou, Andreas (George) Apr 83
Parkening, Christopher Apr 87
Parker, Buddy obit Jun 82
Parks, Rosa May 89
Parsons, Harriet (Oettinger) obit Mar 83
Parsons, Rose Peabody obit Jun 85
Parsons, Mrs. William Barclay See Parsons, R. P. obit
Partch, Virgil F(ranklin) obit Oct 84
Passman, Otto, E(rnest) obit Sep 88
Pastora (Gómez), Edén Jul 86
Pate, Martha B. Lucas obit Jul 83
Paterno, Joe Feb 84
Paton, Alan obit May 88
Patterson, Frederick Douglas obit Jun 88
Paul, Les Aug 87

Pauley, Edwin W(endell) obit Sep 81
Paxton, Tom Sep 82
Payne, (Pierre Stephen) Robert obit Apr 83
Payton, Walter Nov 85
Pears, Peter obit May 86
Peckinpah, Sam obit Feb 85
Peerce, Jan obit Feb 85
Pelikan, Jaroslav (Jan, Jr.) Sep 87
Pella, Giuseppe obit Aug 81
Pelletier, Wilfrid obit Jun 82
Pelli, Cesar Apr 83
Peltz, Mary Ellis (Opdycke) obit Jan 82
Pendleton, Clarence M(cLane), Jr. Sep 84 obit Jul 88
Pendleton, Moses Sep 89
Penniman, Richard Wayne See Little Richard
Penzias, Arno A(llan) Sep 85
Pepper, Claude (Denson) Jan 83 obit Jul 89
Perahia, Murray Mar 82
Pereira, William L(eonard) obit Jan 86
Pérez de Cuéllar, Javier Aug 82
Pérez Esquivel, Adolfo Mar 81
Perkins, Carl D(ewey) obit Sep 84
Perkins, Dexter obit Jul 84
Perkins, R(ichard) Marlin obit Aug 86
Perlman, Alfred E(dward) obit Jul 83
Perry, Gaylord Nov 82
Pertschuk, Michael Sep 86
Peters, Bernadette Sep 84
Petersen, Donald E(ugene) Mar 88
Peterson, David (Robert) Feb 88
Peterson, (Frederick) Val(demar Erastus) obit Jan 84
Peterson, Oscar Oct 83
Petit, Philippe Sep 88
Petrillo, James Caesar obit Jan 85
Phillips, William Oct 84
Picasso, Paloma Apr 86
Pickens, T(homas) Boone, (Jr.) Jul 85
Pidgeon, Walter obit Nov 84
Pierce, Samuel Riley, Jr. Nov 82
Piñero, Miguel Nov 83 obit Aug 88
Piniella, Lou Aug 86
Pinnock, Trevor Sep 89
Plaza (Lasso), Galo obit Mar 87
Plummer, Christopher Aug 88
Plunkett, Jim Feb 82
Poage, W(illiam) R(obert) obit Mar 87

Podgorny, Nikolai (Viktorovich) obit Mar 83
Poindexter, John M(arlan) Nov 87
Pogorelich, Ivo Sep 88
Pollack, Jack H(arrison) obit Feb 85
Pollack, Sydney Sep 86
Ponnamperuma, Cyril (Andrew) Apr 84
Ponnelle, Jean-Pierre Mar 83 obit Sep 88
Popkin, Zelda obit Jul 83
Porter, William J(ames) obit May 88
Potok, Chaim May 83
Potter, W(illiam) E(verett) obit Feb 89
Potvin, Denis Oct 86
Powell, Colin L(uther) Jun 88
Powell, Michael Aug 87
Powell, William obit May 84
Powers, J(ames) F(arl) Jan 89
Prebisch, Raúl obit Jul 86
Preminger, Otto (Ludwig) obit Jun 86
Presser, Jackie Sep 83 obit Aug 88
Pressler, Larry Oct 83
Preston, Robert obit May 87
Prestopino, Gregorio obit Apr 85
Price, Byron obit Sep 81
Price, (Edward) Reynolds Apr 87
Price, George (Cadle) Aug 84
Price, Gwilym A(lexander) obit Aug 85
Price, Margaret Aug 86
Pride, Alfred M(elville) obit Feb 89
Priestley, J(ohn) B(oynton) obit Oct 84
Prigogine, Ilya Feb 87
Primrose, William obit July 82
Prince Feb 86
Prinz, Joachim obit Nov 88
Puig, Manuel Jan 88
Pusey, Merlo J(ohn) obit Jan 86
Putnam, Ashley Mar 82
Puttnam, David Feb 89
Pyle, (John) Howard obit Jan 88
Pym, Francis (Leslie) Sep 82
Pynchon, Thomas Oct 87

Quay, Jan Eduard de obit Aug 85
Quayle, (James) Dan(forth) Jun 89
Quennell, Peter (Courtney) May 84
Quimby, Edith H(inkley) obit Mar 83
Quinn, Sally Oct 88

Rabi, I(sidor) I(saac) obit Mar 88
Radner, Gilda obit Jul 89
Rafferty, Max(well Lewis, Jr.) obit Aug 82
Rafsanjani, (Ali Akbar) Hashemi Nov 89
Rahner, Karl obit May 84
Rainey, Homer P(rice) obit Feb 86
Rakowski, Mieczyslaw (Franciszek) Apr 89
Ram, Jagjivan obit Aug 86
Rambert, Marie Feb 81 obit Aug 82
Ramey, Samuel Jul 81
Ramsey, Lord, of Canterbury obit Jun 88
Ramsey, Arthur Michael, Archbishop of York See Ramsey, Lord, of Canterbury obit
Rand, Ayn May 82 obit May 82
Randi, The Amazing See Randi, James
Randi, James May 87
Rangel, Charles B(ernard) Mar 84
Raskin, Judith obit Feb 85
Rattle, Simon Feb 88
Ratushinskaya, Irina Jul 88
Ratzinger, Joseph Cardinal Apr 86
Rau, Dhanvanthi (Handoo) Rama obit Sep 87
Rau, Johannes Mar 87
Rauschenberg, Robert Oct 87
Rauschning, Hermann obit Apr 83
Rawlings, Jerry (John) Jun 82
Rawls, Lou Mar 84
Ray, Gordon N(orton) obit Feb 87
Reagan, Nancy May 82
Reagan, Patricia Ann See Davis, Patti
Reagan, Ronald (Wilson) Nov 82
Reardon, John obit Jun 88
Redding, J(ay) Saunders obit Apr 88
Reddy, N(eelam) Sanjiva Mar 81
Redford, Robert Mar 82
Redgrave, Sir Michael obit May 85
Redpath, Jean Feb 84
Reed, Ishmael Oct 86
Reed, John S(hepard) Jan 85
Reed, Lou Jul 89
Reed, Philip D(unham) obit May 89
Reeve, Christopher May 82
Regan, Donald T(homas) Nov 81
Reich, Steve Apr 86
Reichelderfer, F(rancis) W(ilton) obit Mar 83

Reid, Kate Mar 85
Reilly, William K(ane) Jul 89
Reiner, Rob May 88
Renault, Mary obit Feb 84
Retton, Mary Lou Feb 86
Rexroth, Kenneth Apr 81 obit Aug 82
Reynolds, William Bradford Jul 88
Rich, Buddy obit May 87
Richards, Keith Feb 89
Richards, Lloyd Oct 87
Richardson, Sir Ralph obit Nov 83
Richie, Lionel Jul 84
Richter, Charles Francis obit Nov 85
Rickover, Hyman G(eorge) obit Aug 86
Riddleberger, James W(illiams) obit Jan 83
Ride, Sally K(risten) Oct 83
Riegle, Donald W(ayne), Jr. Oct 86
Rifkin, Jeremy Feb 86
Righter, Carroll obit Jun 88
Riley, Bridget (Louise) Sep 81
Riley, Pat Aug 88
Ringwald, Molly May 87
Riopelle, Jean-Paul Oct 89
Ríos Montt, José Efraín May 83
Ritchie-Calder, Baron of Balmashannar See Calder, (Peter) Ritchie obit
Ritter, Bruce Jun 83
Rivera, Chita Oct 84
Rivers, Joan Mar 87
Rivlin, Alice M(itchell) Oct 82
Roa (y García), Raúl obit Sep 82
Roach, Max Jul 86
Robarts, John P(armenter) obit Jan 83
Robb, Charles S(pittal) Apr 89
Robertson, Marion Gordon See Robertson, Pat
Robertson, Pat Sep 87
Robinson, Eddie Jun 88
Robinson, John (Arthur Thomas) obit Feb 84
Robinson, M(aurice) R(ichard) obit May 82
Robison, Paula May 82
Robinson, Sugar Ray obit Jun 89
Robitzek, Edward H(einrich) obit May 84
Robson, Dame Flora obit Sep 84
Rocard, Michel (Louis Léon) Oct 88
Rochberg, George Sep 85
Rock, John obit Jan 85
Roderick, David M(ilton) Apr 87
Rodgers, Bill Aug 82
Rogers, Bernard W(illiam) Oct 84

Rogers, Carl R(ansom) obit Mar 87
Rogers, Kenny Jan 81
Rogers, Roy Oct 83
Rogge, O(etje) John obit Jun 81
Roh Tae Woo Feb 88
Romano, Emanuel obit Feb 85
Romano, Umberto obit Nov 82
Romulo, Carlos P(ena) obit Feb 86
Rooney, Andy Jul 82
Roosevelt, Franklin D(elano), Jr. obit Sep 88
Root, Waverley (Lewis) obit Jan 83
Rose, George Sep 84 obit Jun 88
Rose, Leonard obit Jan 85
Rose, William C(umming) obit Jan 86
Rosen, Samuel obit Jan 82
Rosenberg, Anna M(arie) See Hoffman, A. M. R. obit
Rosenstock, Joseph obit Jan 86
Ross, Nancy Wilson obit May 86
Rossellini, Isabella Aug 88
Rostenkowski, Dan(iel D.) Jan 82
Rostropovich, Mstislav Nov 88
Roszak, Theodore [artist] obit Oct 81
Roszak, Theodore [historian] Apr 82
Roth, Henry Jan 89
Roth, William V(ictor), Jr. Apr 83
Rotha, Paul obit May 84
Rothenberg, Susan Mar 85
Rothschild, Louis S(amuel) obit Oct 84
Rouse, James W(ilson) Feb 82
Rowan, Dan obit Nov 87
Roy, Maurice obit Jan 86
Rubbia, Carlo Jun 85
Rubik, Erno Feb 87
Rubin, William (Stanley) Nov 86
Rubinstein, Artur obit Mar 83
Ruder, David S(turtevant) Nov 88
Rudman, Warren B(ruce) Nov 89
Ruffing, Charles H(erbert) obit Apr 86
Ruffing, Red See Ruffing, C. H. obit
Rukeyser, Louis Feb 83
Ruscha, Edward Oct 89
Rushdie, (Ahmed) Salman Nov 86
Russell, Charles H(inton) obit Nov 89
Russell, Donald J(oseph) obit Feb 86
Russell, Mark Mar 81
Rustin, Bayard obit Oct 87
Ryan, T(ubal) Claude obit Nov 82

Ryle, Sir Martin obit Jan 85

Saatchi, Maurice Jan 89
Sabato, Ernesto Oct 85
Sabah, Jaber al-Ahmad al-Jaber al-, Sheik Aug 88
Sacks, Oliver (Wolf) Feb 85
Sadat, Anwar (el-) obit Nov 81
Sadat, Jihan Aug 86
Sade Sep 86
Said, Edward W. Nov 89
St. George, Katharine (Delano Price Collier) obit Jul 83
St. Johns, Adela Rogers obit Sep 88
Sajak, Pat Jul 89
Salam, Abdus Apr 88
Salazar, Alberto May 83
Salerno-Sonnenberg, Nadja Nov 87
Salinas (de Gortari), Carlos Mar 89
Salinger, Pierre (Emil George) Mar 87
Salisbury, Harrison E(vans) Jan 82
Salle, David Sep 86
Sananikone, Phoui obit Feb 84
Sanders, Harland obit Feb 81
Sanders, Lawrence Apr 89
Sanders, Marlene Feb 81
Sanger, Frederick Jul 81
Santmyer, Helen Hooven Feb 85 obit Apr 86
Saragat, Giuseppe obit Jul 88
Sarah, Duchess of York Mar 87
Sarandon, Susan Sep 89
Sargeant, Howland H(ill) obit Apr 84
Sarkis, Elias obit Aug 85
Sarney, José Mar 86
Saroyan, William obit Jul 81
Sarton, May May 82
Saunders, Stuart T(homas) obit Mar 87
Sauvé, Jeanne Aug 84
Saville, Curtis (Lloyd) and Kathleen Jan 86
Saville, Kathleen (McNally) See Saville, C. and K.
Savimbi, Jonas (Malheiro) Aug 86
Savitch, Jessica Jan 83 obit Mar 84
Sawyer, Diane Oct 85
Sayles, John Feb 84
Scalia, Antonin Nov 86
Scargill, Arthur Jan 85
Scavullo, Francesco May 85
Schacht, Al(exander) obit Sep 84
Schaefer, William Donald Jul 88
Schaller, George B(eals) Aug 85
Schapiro, Meyer Jul 84
Schaufuss, Peter May 82

Schechter, A(bel) A(lan) obit Aug 89
Schiff, Dorothy obit Oct 89
Schillebeeckx, Edward Jun 83
Schindler, Alexander M(oshe) Sep 87
Schiotz, Fredrik A(xel) obit May 89
Schlamme, Martha obit Jan 86
Schlauch, Margaret obit Sep 86
Schlöndorff, Volker Aug 83
Schmidt, Benno C(harles), Jr. Aug 86
Schnabel, Julian Nov 83
Schneerson, Menachem Mendel Sep 83
Schneider, Alan obit Jun 84
Schneider, Romy obit Jul 82
Schoenbrun, David (Franz) obit Jul 88
Scholder, Fritz Apr 85
Schrader, Paul Aug 81
Schram, Emil obit Nov 87
Schreyer, Edward Richard Feb 81
Schwartz, Arthur obit Oct 84
Schwartz, Tony Jul 85
Schwarz, Gerard Apr 86
Schwarzhaupt, Elisabeth obit Jan 87
Schygulla, Hanna Jul 84
Scott, Hazel (Dorothy) obit Nov 81
Scott, Michael (Guthrie) obit Apr 85
Scott, Peter Markham obit Nov 89
Scott, Sheila obit Jan 89
Scott, Willard Jul 89
Scourby, Alexander obit Apr 85
Scowcroft, Brent Jul 87
Scull, Robert C. obit Feb 86
Sculley, John Aug 88
Seaga, Edward (Phillip George) Apr 81
Sears, Robert R(ichardson) obit Aug 89
Seefried, Irmgard obit Jan 89
Seghers, Anna obit Jul 83
Segovia, Andrés obit Jul 87
Segrè, Emilio (Gino) obit Jul 89
Seifert, Elizabeth obit Oct 83
Sellars, Peter Jan 86
Selleck, Tom Nov 83
Selye, Hans (Hugo Bruno) Jan 81 obit Jan 83
Sendak, Maurice Jun 89
Sergio, Lisa obit Aug 89
Serkin, Peter Jun 86
Serra, Richard (Antony) Jan 85
Sert, José Luis obit May 83
Sert, Josep Lluis See Sert, José Luis obit
Sessions, Roger obit May 85
Sessions, William S(teele) Jul 88

Seymour, Whitney North obit Jul 83
Shaffer, Peter (Levin) Nov 88
Shamir, Yitzhak Feb 83
Shandling, Garry Apr 89
Shannon, William V(incent) obit Nov 88
Sharansky, Natan See Shcharansky, Anatoly
Sharon, Ariel Apr 81
Shatner, William Jul 87
Shaw, Irwin obit Jul 84
Shawn, Wallace Jun 86
Shcharansky, Anatoly Feb 87
Sheed, Frank (Joseph) Sep 81 obit Jan 82
Sheed, Wilfrid Aug 81
Sheehan, Neil Aug 89
Shehan, Lawrence (Joseph), Cardinal obit Oct 84
Shehu, Mehmet obit Feb 82
Shepherd, Cybill Mar 87
Shepherd, Jean (Parker) Apr 84
Shera, Jesse H(auk) obit Jun 82
Shevardnadze, Eduard (Amvrosiyevich) Feb 86
Shevchenko, Arkady N(ikolayevich) Sep 85
Shields, Brooke Oct 82
Shinwell, Baron See Shinwell, E. obit
Shinwell, Emanuel obit Jun 86
Shivers, Allan obit Mar 85
Shockley, William (Bradford) obit Oct 89
Sholokhov, Mikhail A(leksandrovich) obit Apr 84
Shoup, David M(onroe) obit Mar 83
Shulman, Max obit Oct 88
Shultz, George P(ratt) Apr 88
Sidney, Sylvia Oct 81
Signoret, Simone obit Nov 85
Silber, John R(obert) Feb 84
Siles Zuazo, Hernán Jun 85
Sillcox, Lewis K(etcham) obit May 89
Sills, Beverly Feb 82
Silvers, Phil obit Jan 86
Simenon, Georges (Joseph Christian) obit Nov 89
Simmons, Richard May 82
Simon, (Marvin) Neil Mar 89
Simon, Paul M(artin) Jan 88
Simpson, George Gaylord obit Jan 85
Simpson, Howard E(dward) obit Apr 85
Sinclair, Adelaide Helen Grant Macdonald See Sinclair, Mrs. D. B. obit
Sinclair, Mrs. D. B. obit Jan 83
Singh, Giani Zail Sep 87
Six, Robert F(orman) obit Nov 86
Skinner, Samuel K(nox) Aug 89

Slade, Roy Jun 85
Slatkin, Leonard Feb 86
Slezak, Walter obit Jun 83
Slick, Grace Apr 82
Sliwa, Curtis Feb 83
Sloane, Eric obit May 85
Smith, Carleton obit Jul 84
Smith, James H(opkins), Jr. obit Feb 83
Smith, Kate obit Aug 86
Smith, Liz May 87
Smith, Mary Elizabeth See Smith, Liz
Smith, Patti Apr 89
Smith, Red obit Feb 82
Smith, Roger B(onham) May 86
Smith, William French Jan 82
Smuin, Michael Oct 84
Smyth, H(enry) D(eWolf) obit Nov 86
Sneider, Vern obit Jun 81
Snell, George D(avis) May 86
Snyder, John W(esley) obit Jan 86
Soames, (Arthur) Christopher (John), Baron of Fletching Aug 81 obit Oct 87
Sobhuza II, King of Swaziland Mar 82 obit Oct 82
Söderström, Elisabeth Nov 85
Solarz, Stephen J(oshua) Nov 86
Solzhenitsyn, Aleksandr I(sayevich) Jul 88
Soong Ching-ling. See Sun Yat-sen, Mme. obit
Soss, Wilma (Porter) obit Jan 87
Souvanna Phouma, Prince of Laos obit Mar 84
Sovern, Michael I(ra) Feb 81
Sowell, Thomas Jul 81
Soyer, Isaac obit Sep 81
Soyer, Raphael obit Jan 88
Sparkman, John J(ackson) obit Jan 86
Speakes, Larry Mar 85
Specter, Arlen Aug 88
Spector, (Harvey) Phil(lip) Jul 89
Speer, Albert obit Oct 81
Speidel, Hans obit Feb 85
Spelling, Aaron May 86
Sperry, Roger W(olcott) Jan 86
Spiegelman, Sol(omon) obit Mar 83
Spillane, Mickey Sep 81
Springer, Axel (Caesar) obit Nov 85
Sprinkel, Beryl (Wayne) Jul 87
Staley, Oren Lee obit Nov 88
Stankiewicz, Richard (Peter) obit May 83
Starr, Mark obit Jul 85
Stavropoulos, George (Peter) Mar 85
Steel, Danielle Jul 89
Steel, Johannes obit Feb 89

Stein, Jules (Caesar) obit Jun 81
Steinem, Gloria Mar 88
Steiner, (Francis) George Oct 83
Stella, Frank (Philip) Apr 88
Steloff, (Ida) Frances obit Jun 89
Stenmark, Ingemar Apr 82
Stephanie, Princess of Monaco Aug 86
Steptoe, Patrick C(hristopher) obit Jun 88
Sterling, J(ohn) E(wart) Wallace obit Aug 85
Stern, Isaac Feb 89
Stevens, Robert T(en Broeck) obit Mar 83
Stevenson, William E(dwards) obit May 85
Stever, H(orton) Guyford Jan 81
Stewart, Potter obit Feb 86
Stigler, George J(oseph) Jul 83
Stilwell, Richard Feb 86
Sting Jul 85
Stockman, David (Alan) Aug 81
Stoddard, Brandon Feb 89
Stoddard, George D(insmore) obit Feb 82
Stoessel, Walter J(ohn), Jr. obit Feb 87
Stokes, Anson Phelps, Jr. obit Jan 87
Stoltenberg, Gerhard Sep 89
Stoltzman, Richard Mar 86
Stone, I(sidor) F(einstein) obit Aug 89
Stone, Irving obit Oct 89
Stone, Oliver Jun 87
Stone, Robert (Anthony) Jan 87
Strasberg, Lee obit Apr 82
Straub, Peter Feb 89
Straus, Jack I(sidor) obit Nov 85
Strauss, Franz Josef Feb 87 obit Nov 88
Strawberry, Darryl Jun 84
Streibert, Theodore C(uyler) obit Mar 87
Streit, Clarence K(irshman) obit Sep 86
Stritch, Elaine Jun 88
Stroessner, Alfredo Mar 81
Struble, Arthur D(ewey) obit Jul 83
Stuart, Jesse obit Apr 84
Studebaker, John W(ard) obit Oct 89
Stutz, Geraldine (Veronica) May 83
Styne, Jule May 83
Styron, William (Clark, Jr.) Jun 86
Suesse, Dana obit Jan 88
Sullivan, John L(awrence) obit Oct 82

Sullivan, Leonor (Alice) K(retzer) obit Oct 88
Sullivan, Louis W(ade) Jul 89
Sumner, Gordon See Sting
Sunay, Cevdet obit Aug 82
Sun Myung Moon See Moon, S. M.
Sununu, John H(enry) May 89
Sun Yat-sen, Mme. obit Jul 81
Suslov, Mikhail A(ndreye-vich) obit Mar 82
Susskind, David obit Apr 87
Sutherland, Donald Feb 81
Suzuki, Zenko Jan 81
Swaggart, Jimmy (Lee) Oct 87
Swanson, Gloria obit May 83
Sweeney, James Johnson obit Jul 86
Swigert, Ernest G(oodnough) obit Feb 87
Swing, Joseph M(ay) obit Feb 85
Syberberg, Hans Jürgen Apr 83
Symington, (William) Stuart obit Feb 89
Szent-Györgyi, Albert (von Nagyrapolt) obit Jan 87
Szeryng, Henryk obit Apr 88

Tabb, Mary Decker See Decker, Mary
Taft, Charles P(helps, 2d) obit Aug 83
Takeshita, Noboru May 88
Tallamy, Bertram D(alley) obit Nov 89
Talvela, Martti Oct 83 obit Sep 89
Tambo, Oliver Apr 87
Tandy, Jessica Aug 84
Tange, Kenzo Sep 87
Tavernier, Bertrand Jun 88
Tartikoff, Brandon Apr 87
Tati, Jacques obit Jan 83
Taussig, Helen B(rooke) obit Jul 86
Taylor, A(lan) J(ohn) P(ercivale) Nov 83
Taylor, Cecil Mar 86
Taylor, Elizabeth Oct 85
Taylor, Glen H(earst) obit Jul 84
Taylor, Maxwell D(avenport) obit Jun 87
Taylor, Peter (Hillsman) Apr 87
Tcherkassky, Marianna Nov 85
Teague, Olin E(arl) obit Apr 81
Teale, Edwin Way obit Jan 81
Tebbit, Norman (Beresford) Nov 87
Teller, Edward Nov 83
Tennstedt, Klaus Sep 83
Tenzing Norkey obit Jul 86
Terra, Daniel J(ames) Nov 87

Terry, Luther L(eonidas) obit May 85
Thatcher, Margaret (Hilda) Nov 89
Theorell, (Axel) Hugo (Teodor) obit Oct 82
Thicke, Alan Jun 87
Thiebaud, Wayne Mar 87
Thomas, Charles Allen obit May 82
Thomas, Charles S(parks) obit Jan 84
Thomas, D(onald) M(ichael) Nov 83
Thomas, Franklin A(ugustine) Oct 81
Thomas, Isiah Aug 89
Thomas, Lowell (Jackson) obit Oct 81
Thompson, Daley Nov 86
Thompson, Frank, Jr. obit Sep 89
Thompson, Hunter S(tockton) Mar 81
Thompson, John May 89
Thompson, Paul See Rotha, Paul obit
Thomson, Kenneth (Roy) Jul 89
Thomson, Vernon W(allace) obit Jun 88
Thomson, Virgil (Garnett) obit Nov 89
Thornburgh, Richard L(ewis) Oct 88
Thornton, Charles B(ates) obit Jan 82
Thurman, Howard obit Jun 81
Thyssen-Bornemisza de Kaszon, Baron Hans Heinrich Feb 89
Tiegs, Cheryl Nov 82
Tiger, Lionel Jan 81
Tillstrom, Burr obit Feb 86
Timerman, Jacobo Nov 81
Tinbergen, Niko(laas) obit Feb 89
Tinker, Grant A. Mar 82
Tisch, Laurence A(lan) Feb 87
Tishler, Max obit May 89
Tobin, James Oct 84
Todd, Richard May 82
Tomás, Américo (Deus Rodrigues) obit Nov 87
Tomasson, Helgi Apr 82
Tormé, Mel Mar 83
Torrijos Herrera, Omar obit Sep 81
Tors, Ivan (Lawrence) obit Aug 83
Touré, (Ahmed) Sekou obit May 84
Towle, Katherine A(melia) obit May 86
Towne, Robert Jun 89
Townshend, Peter Aug 83
Trapp, Maria Augusta obit Jun 87
Travis, Randy Sep 89

Trenet, Charles Feb 89
Trevor, William Sep 84
Trevor-Roper, H(ugh) R(edwald) Sep 83
Tribe, Laurence H(enry) Jul 88
Trintignant, Jean-Louis Jul 88
Trippe, Juan T(erry) obit May 81
Trotta, Margarethe von Nov 88
Trottier, Bryan Jun 85
Truffaut, François obit Jan 85
Truman, Bess (Wallace) See Truman, Mrs. Harry S obit
Truman, Mrs. Harry S obit Jan 83
Truman, (Mary) Margaret Jun 87
Trumka, Richard L(ouis) Apr 86
Trump, Donald J(ohn) Feb 84
Tsarapkin, Semyon K(onstantinovich) obit Nov 84
Tsongas, Paul E(fthemios) Jul 81
Tubb, Ernest Oct 83 obit Oct 84
Tuchman, Barbara W(ertheim) obit Mar 89
Tuck, William M(unford) obit Aug 83
Tudor, Anthony obit Jun 87
Tully, Alice Jan 84
Tune, Tommy Jan 83
Turner, John (Napier) Nov 84
Turner, Kathleen Jun 86
Turner, Tina Nov 84
Tutu, Desmond (Mpilo) Jan 85
Twining, Nathan F(arragut) obit May 82
Twombly, Cy Apr 88
Tworkov, Jack obit Oct 82
Tyler, Anne Jun 81
Tyson, Mike Apr 88

Ueberroth, Peter V(ictor) Apr 85
Ullman, Al(bert Conrad) obit Jan 87
Ullman, Tracey Oct 88
Umberto II, King of Italy obit May 83
Underhill, Ruth M(urray) obit Oct 84
Unruh, Jesse M(arvin) obit Sep 87
Updike, John (Hoyer) Oct 84
Urey, Harold C(layton) obit Mar 81
Urquhart, Brian E(dward) Jun 86
Urquhart, Sir Robert E(lliott) obit Feb 89
Urrutia Lleo, Manuel obit Aug 81

Vadim, Roger Jan 84

Vagnozzi, Egidio Cardinal obit Feb 81
Valente, Benita Mar 88
Valentina obit Nov 89
Valenzuela, Fernando Oct 82
Vallee, Rudy obit Aug 86
Van Arsdale, Harry obit Apr 86
Van den Haag, Ernest Oct 83
Vane, John R(obert) May 86
Vaness, Carol Sep 86
Van Wagoner, Murray D(elos) obit Aug 86
Van Zandt, James E(dward) obit Mar 86
Vaughan, Harry H(awkins) obit Jul 81
Veeck, Bill obit Feb 86
Velde, Harold H(immel) obit Jan 86
Vendler, Helen May 86
Vera-Ellen obit Oct 81
Verity, C(alvin) William, Jr. May 88
Vidal, Gore Jun 83
Vidor, King obit Jan 83
Viguerie, Richard A(rt) Jan 83
Vila, George R(aymond) obit Aug 87
Vinson, Carl obit Jul 81
Visser 't Hooft, Willem A(dolf) obit Aug 85
Vogel, Hans-Jochen Jan 84
Vollenweider, Andreas May 87
Von Zell, Harry obit Jan 82
Voorhees, Donald obit Apr 89
Voorhis, (Horace) Jerry obit Nov 84
Vorster, Balthazar Johannes obit Nov 83
Vranitzky, Franz Aug 89
Vreeland, Diana (Dalziel) obit Oct 89

Wadsworth, James J(eremiah) obit May 84
Wagner, Robert Jun 84
Waite, Terence (Hardy) Sep 86
Waitz, Grete Apr 81
Wajda, Andrzej Jul 82
Walcott, Derek (Alton) Apr 84
Waldheim, Kurt Jan 87
Waldron, Hicks B(enjamin) Mar 88
Walesa, Lech Apr 81
Walker, Alice Mar 84
Walker, Herschel Mar 85
Wallace, DeWitt obit May 81
Wallace, Lila (Bell) Acheson obit Jul 84
Wallenstein, Alfred obit Mar 83
Wallop, (John) Douglass obit Jun 85
Walsh, Bill Nov 89
Walters, Vernon (Anthony) Feb 88

Walton, Sir William Turner obit May 83
Wang, An Jan 87
Wang Shih-chieh obit Jun 81
Wapner, Joseph A(lbert) Sep 89
Ward, Barbara (Mary) obit Jul 81
Ward, Benjamin Aug 88
Warhol, Andy Jul 86 obit Apr 87
Waring, Fred obit Sep 84
Warner, J(ohn) C(hristian) obit Jul 89
Warren, Harry obit Nov 81
Warren, Robert Penn obit Nov 89
Washington, Harold Feb 84 obit Jan 88
Wasserburg, Gerald J(oseph) Mar 86
Wasserstein, Wendy Jul 89
Waters, Muddy May 81 obit Jun 83
Waterston, Sam Sep 85
Watkins, James (David) Mar 89
Watt, James G(aius) Jan 82
Wattenberg, Ben J. Jun 85
Watts, Heather May 83
Weaver, Earl Feb 83
Weaver, Sigourney Mar 89
Webb, Jack obit Mar 83
Webb, James H(enry), Jr. Aug 87
Webber, Andrew Lloyd See Lloyd Webber, A.
Wechsberg, Joseph obit Jun 83
Wedel, Cynthia Clark obit Oct 86
Weeks, Edward (Augustus), Jr. obit May 89
Weidenbaum, Murray L(ew) Mar 82
Weidlein, Edward R(ay) obit Nov 83
Wein, George (Theodore) Oct 85
Weinberg, Robert A(llan) Jun 83
Weir, Peter Aug 84
Weiss, Paul A(lfred) obit Nov 89
Weiss, Peter obit Jul 82
Weiss, Ted Oct 85
Weizsäcker, Carl Friedrich von Jan 85
Weizsäcker, Richard von Mar 85
Welch, John F(rancis), Jr. Jan 88
Welch, Robert (Henry Winborne, Jr.) obit Mar 85
Weller, Michael May 89
Welles, (George) Orson obit Nov 85
Wenders, Wim Jul 84
Werner, Oskar obit Jan 85
Wertham, Fredric obit Jan 82

Wesley, Charles H(arris) obit Oct 87
West, Jessamyn obit Apr 84
West, Mae obit Jan 81
West, Dame Rebecca obit May 83
Westheimer, (Karola) Ruth Jan 87
Weston, (Theodore) Brett Feb 82
Wharton, Clifton R(eginald), Jr. Feb 87
White, Betty Jun 87
White, E(lwyn) B(rooks) obit Nov 85
White, Katharine Elkus obit Jun 85
White, Mark (Wells) Aug 86
White, Robert E(dward) May 84
White, Theodore H(arold) obit Jul 86
White, Vanna Jan 88
Whitehead, Don(ald Ford) obit Mar 81
Whitmire, Kathryn (Jean) Mar 88
Whitney, John Hay obit Apr 82
Whittemore, Arthur obit Feb 85
Wick, Charles Z. Mar 85
Wicker, Ireene obit Jan 88
Wiesel, Elie Feb 86
Wilcox, Francis O(rlando) obit Apr 85
Wild, Earl Jul 88
Wilde, Frazar B(ullard) obit Aug 85
Wilder, Alec obit Feb 81
Wilder, Billy Oct 84
Wilkins, Roy obit Oct 81
Will, George F(rederick) Sep 81
Williams, Billy Dee Apr 84
Williams, Edward Bennett obit Sep 88
Williams, Emlyn obit Nov 87
Williams, Eric (Eustace) obit May 81
Williams, G(erhard) Mennen obit Mar 88
Williams, Gluyas obit Apr 82
Williams, Joe Apr 85
Williams, John Jul 83
Williams, John Bell obit May 83
Williams, John J(ames) obit Apr 88
Williams, Mary Lou obit Jul 81
Williams, Paul Jun 83
Williams, Roger J(ohn) obit Apr 88
Williams, Tennessee obit Apr 83
Williams, Vanessa May 84
Willis, Bruce Feb 87
Willis, Paul S. obit Aug 87
Wills, Garry Jun 82

Willson, Meredith obit Aug 84
Wilson, August Aug 87
Wilson, Brian Jul 88
Wilson, Carroll Louis obit Mar 83
Wilson, Kenneth G(eddes) Sep 83
Wilson, Peter (Cecil) obit Aug 84
Wilson, Robert R(athbun) Aug 89
Winchell, Constance M(abel) obit Sep 84
Windsor, Wallis (Warfield), Duchess of obit Jun 86
Winfield, Dave Jan 84
Winfrey, Oprah Mar 87
Winger, Debra Jul 84
Winter, Paul Oct 87
Wise, James DeCamp obit Apr 84
Wise, Robert Sep 89
Witt, Katarina Jul 88
Woiwode, Larry (Alfred) Mar 89
Wolfenden, Lord See Wolfenden, Sir John obit
Wolfenden, Sir John (Frederick) obit Mar 85
Wolman, Abel obit May 89
Wolper, David L(loyd) Oct 86
Wood, John Apr 83
Wood, Louise A(letha) obit Jul 88
Wood, Natalie obit Jan 82
Wood, Robert D(ennis) obit Jul 86

Woodhouse, Barbara (Blackburn) Feb 85 obit Aug 88
Woodhouse, (Margaret) Chase Going obit Apr 85
Woodruff, Judy Sep 86
Woods, Donald Feb 82
Woods, George D(avid) obit Oct 82
Woods, James Nov 89
Woodson, Carter G(odwin) obit Yrbk 84 (died Apr 50)
Woodward, C(omer) Vann May 86
Wörner, Manfred Oct 88
Wright, Louis B(ooker) obit Jun 84
Wright, Peter (Maurice) Feb 88
Wright, Robert C(harles) Jan 89
Wu, K(uo) C(heng) obit Aug 84
Wurf, Jerry obit Feb 82
Wu Yifang obit Jan 86
Wyeth, Andrew (Newell) Nov 81
Wyler, William obit Sep 81
Wyman, Thomas H(unt) Jun 83
Wyszynski, Stefan Cardinal obit Jul 81

Yadin, Yigael obit Aug 84
Yamasaki, Minoru obit Apr 86
Yankelovich, Daniel Mar 82
Yarborough, Cale Jan 87
Yard, Molly Nov 88
Yeager, Jeana May 87
Yeh, George K(ung-)C(hao) obit Jan 82

Yeltsin, Boris N(ikolayevich) Jan 89
Yeutter, Clayton K(eith) Jul 88
Yost, Charles W(oodruff) obit Jul 81
Young, Frank E(dward) Oct 89
Young, John A(lan) Oct 86
Young, Milton R(uben) obit Jul 83
Young, Philip obit Mar 87
Young, Stephen M(arvin) obit Feb 85
Youngerman, Jack Nov 86
Youngman, Henny Oct 86
Yourcenar, Marguerite Nov 82 obit Feb 88
Yukawa, Hideki obit Nov 81

Zablocki, Clement J(ohn) Jun 83 obit Jan 84
Zacharias, Jerrold (Reinach) obit Sep 86
Zevin, B(enjamin) D(avid) obit Feb 85
Zhao Ziyang Jun 84
Zia ul-Haq, Mohammad obit Sep 88
Ziaur Rahman Jun 81 obit Jul 81
Zimbalist, Efrem obit Apr 85
Zorin, Valerian A(lexandrovich) obit Mar 86
Zulli, Floyd, Jr. obit Jan 81
Zwilich, Ellen (Taaffe) Jan 86
Zworykin, Vladimir K(osma) obit Sep 82